September 7-11, 2014
Maui, Hawaii, USA

Association for
Computing Machinery

Advancing Computing as a Science & Profession

MobiCom'14

Proceedings of the 20th Annual International Conference on Mobile Computing and Networking

Sponsored by:

ACM SIGMOBILE

Supported by:

NSF, Cisco, Meraki, Microsoft, Facebook, Google, IBM Research, Inria, Qualcomm Research, Hewlett Packard, and NEC Laboratories America

Association for
Computing Machinery

Advancing Computing as a Science & Profession

The Association for Computing Machinery
2 Penn Plaza, Suite 701
New York, New York 10121-0701

Notice to Past Authors of ACM-Published Articles
ACM intends to create a complete electronic archive of all articles and/or other material previously published by ACM. If you have written a work that has been previously published by ACM in any journal or conference proceedings prior to 1978, or any SIG Newsletter at any time, and you do NOT want this work to appear in the ACM Digital Library, please inform permissions@acm.org, stating the title of the work, the author(s), and where and when published.

ISBN: 978-1-4503-2783-1 (Digital)

ISBN: 978-1-4503-3362-4 (Print)

Additional copies may be ordered prepaid from:

ACM Order Department
PO Box 30777
New York, NY 10087-0777, USA

Phone: 1-800-342-6626 (USA and Canada)
+1-212-626-0500 (Global)
Fax: +1-212-944-1318
E-mail: acmhelp@acm.org
Hours of Operation: 8:30 am – 4:30 pm ET

Printed in the USA

Welcome from the General Chair

Aloha! It is great pleasure and honor to welcome you to the *ACM Annual International Conference on Mobile Computing and Networking (MobiCom 2014).* This is the 20th edition of MobiCom, and what better place to celebrate the 20th anniversary than in Maui! This is the first time MobiCom is hosted on an island. Let's take advantage of the beautiful scenery and ocean view while celebrating the technical advancement and impact we made over the last 20 years and discussing future research directions.

We have an exciting program full of innovative ideas and thought leadership. I am looking forward to four keynotes. Sanjit Biswas (CEO of Meraki, VP/GM of Cisco Cloud Computing Group), who was a best student paper award winner in MobiCom 2005, returns to give a keynote. He will share his journey from his graduate student days to founding a start-up and a high profile acquisition in 2012. Our second keynote will be given by Jeff Gelhlaar (VP of Technology for Qualcomm Technologies) on his vision of future mobile computing. The third keynote is given by this year's Outstanding Contributions Award winner, Leonard Kleinrock (Distinguished Professor of Computer Science Department at UCLA). He is a father of the Internet and won this award for "pioneering contributions to the first multi-hop packet switched radio network which formed the foundation for modern wireless networks." Our last keynote speaker is Kit Colbert (CTO of End User Computing at VMWare) who will present an industry perspective on challenges in mobility.

Ashutosh Sabharwal and Prasun Sinha put together a strong technical program with 36 top rate papers. Chiara Petrioli and Igancio Solis selected seven workshops with emerging topics and worked with each workshop organizers to continue the MobiCom tradition of premium workshops. Shyamnath Gollakota, Ilias Leontiadis, and Ramya Raghavendra are responsible for recruiting 20 very exciting demos. Souvik Sen and Xinyu Zhang are chairing the poster session with 28 posters that showcase promising preliminary research. Saumitra Das is taking care of the Student Research Competition. Continuing the success of the first mobile app competition last year, Eduardo Cuervo and Emiliano Miluzzo will oversee the competition. Thyaga Nandagopal organized two panels that promise to engage the audience. The first panel will discuss the societal challenges of mobile computing, and will be moderated by Lakshminarayanan Subramanian. The second panel welcomes back pioneers and early contributors to MobiCom who will share their vision of the future; this panel will be moderated by Victor Bahl.

In addition, I am grateful for the excellent services from the following organizing committee members. Joseph Camp worked with me on finances. Eugene Chai, Aline Carneiro Viana, and Yung Yi handled publicity. Konstantinos Pelechrinis was the master of the conference website. Aakanksha Chowdhery and Wenjun Hu prepared the publications, including the proceedings you are looking at. Katia Obraczka and Patrick Tague are the registration chairs. Dimitrios Koutsonikolas awarded student travel grant. Marco Levorato and Rui Zhang provided local arrangements. Aaron Schulman assisted me in corporate sponsorships. This year we are blogging for the first time in MobiCom history. I encourage everyone to read, comment, and participate in our blog. Riccardo Crepaldi and Lara Deek are your bloggers and social media chairs.

A conference like MobiCom cannot be successful without the generosity and participation from the sponsors. Our sponsors enable more student participation as well as high quality facility and service. National Science Foundation is our Platinum Sponsor. Cisco/Meraki and Microsoft are the Gold Sponsors. Facebook, Google, IBM, Inria, and Qualcomm are Silver Sponsors. HP and NEC are Bronze Sponsors. Thank you sponsors!

Being a General Chair of MobiCom is an amazing honor and it comes with great responsibility. I have received incredible help not only from the organizing committee, but also from Victor Bahl, the steering committee chair, Suman Banerjee, the SIGMOBILE chair, and April Mosqus and rest of the ACM staff. I thank them sincerely.

Enjoy the conference and location! I hope your MobiCom 2014 experience is technically stimulating while reconnecting with old friends and making new friends. Mahalo.

Sung-Ju Lee
MobiCom 2014 General Chair

Technical Program Committee Chairs' Message

Welcome to the 20th Edition of MobiCom, the Annual International Conference on Mobile Computing and Networking. Now past its teens, MobiCom continues to grow as the powerhouse conference with a vibrant, dedicated and growing community of researchers and practitioners in mobile systems and wireless networks.

36 Accepted Papers: Any research community is judged by the quality of its work and the impact of that work on actual practice. On both those counts, MobiCom 2014 is set to build on the fantastic tradition of previous years. This year's program has 36 high-quality papers, which is the highest number ever accepted. The increase in final number of papers accepted is a sign of widening of the program scope and growth of the research community. The papers range from traditional topics which continue to be of critical interest - like Wireless LANs, cellular networks and others and new emerging areas of wireless charging, visual communications and wireless data-centers among many others. The acceptance rate was 16.4% (36/220).

TPC Composition: MobiCom is "notoriously" famous for its brutally rigorous review process, which is perhaps the key reason why authors tend to submit their best work to MobiCom. The "guardians of quality" have always been the Technical Program Committee (TPC). To ensure we have topical experts in all major categories, we expanded the TPC to 51 members, again the biggest TPC in MobiCom history. The TPC included 13 members from industry - Microsoft Research, Facebook, Google, Narus, NEC Labs, HP Labs, Alcatel Lucent and Intel Labs, a member from National Science Foundation and a member from IMDEA. Furthermore, 6 members are from Europe, 4 from Asia-Pacific, 1 from Africa and rest from North Americas.

Review Process: This year, we also added two new elements to the review process - conditional accepts and anonymous shepherding. The call for papers attracted 220 papers (after rejecting non-conforming papers) from five continents: Asia, Europe, Africa, North America and South America. The review process was conducted in 4 phases using the HotCRP system, where the first three phases were identical to previous years'. In the first phase, each paper was reviewed by at least 3 TPC members. After the first round of review, the reviewers discussed the papers online and the consensus decision was marked for each paper. After the first phase, 76 papers were moved to the second phase of reviews. In the second phase, at least 2 more TPC members provided additional reviews. In the second round, we asked the first round reviewers to provide suggestions for most suitable TPC member for second round reviews. In addition, we also sought their suggestion for external reviewers if there was a need for additional expert opinion. After the second round review and online discussions, 68 papers were selected to be the part of third phase – the TPC meeting discussion. The TPC meeting was held at Rice University on May 29-30, 2014. The one and a half day meeting was attended by 46 members in person and 5 members joined via conference call.

To ensure fairness and preserve the anonymity of all authors and reviewers, papers authored by PC chairs were mixed with a random selection of other papers and were handled out of band by Raghupathy Sivakumar and Nitin Vaidya. The reviews were handled using the HotCRP system using "tokens," a mechanism designed to keep the reviewers anonymous even from the chairs. The related discussions were handled out-of-band over emails between the reviewers. A total of 10 such papers were handled out-of-band of which 5 were discussed at the TPC meeting. Note that these numbers are included in the above paragraph.

The chairs did not participate in any awards committees.

New Elements in the Review Process: At the start of the TPC meeting, the TPC Chairs informed all TPC members that there is no preset target for the number of accepted papers. That allowed the TPC members to focus only on the paper under discussion and whether they consider it as MobiCom quality or not. In addition, the TPC members were informed that all papers will only be *conditionally accepted*, till the authors adequately address all reviewers' concerns. The conditional accept was the first new element in the review process, unlike prior years in which the final decision was made in the TPC meeting itself. At the end of the two-day meeting, 38 papers were conditionally accepted. Two conditionally accepted papers were appealed within 24 hours of the meeting, as the TPC members found additional support to reject those papers. An online discussion followed and a consensus decision was reached to reject the two appealed papers. Thus, the TPC members continued to work *even after the TPC meeting was over!*

The second new element was that of double-blind shepherding, which was a departure from previous years where the double-blind barrier was removed between shepherds and authors after the TPC meeting. The two new elements, conditional accept and double-blind shepherding, were added to address the general feeling in the community that the authors tend to make only minimal changes after they get their accept notification. Further, in the old method, the shepherds had no power to enforce necessary changes, since the authors know their identities *and* authors know that their papers are accepted. The new process, while very cumbersome to implement due to lack of adequate support in HotCRP, was appreciated by many members. The authors, knowing that their paper can be rejected, worked wonders in revising and addressing all concerns. And shepherds felt empowered to conduct their job without any fear of retribution. A very small number of papers were in fact very close to being rejected during the shepherding process, but were ultimately kept in the program after much discussion among TPC members. Some papers underwent significant revisions and within a course of three weeks, they were revised several times to address all concerns. For the first time, we got written comments like "Wow, the authors put in some serious work to revise the paper." As TPC Chairs, we could not be more elated with the result of the new changes.

Sincere Thanks Goes To: We would like to thank all authors who submitted papers to the conference. We would like to thank the entire TPC for their extremely hard work in reviewing a large number of papers and then providing timely and detailed reviews for each of them. In addition an extra thanks goes to the TPC members for being the guinea pigs for a number of important changes made to the review process. The external reviewers also did an excellent job in providing additional reviews for some papers and we are very thankful to them..

We sincerely thank Raghupathy Sivakumar and Nitin Vaidya for handling the out-of-band papers. During the entire process Dong Li provided very timely support for the HotCRP system as it had to be patched several times. Ms. Caroline at Rice took extreme care of impeccably handling all the logistics of the TPC meeting including the delicious food that we enjoyed while at Houston.

Ashutosh Sabharwal and Prasun Sinha
TPC Co-Chairs

Table of Contents

Keynote Address 3

Paper Session 4: Rethinking WLANs

Paper Session 5: The Wide-Area Experience

Paper Session 6: Location Matters

Demonstrations

Posters

Panel Session 2

Paper Session 7: Positioning and Navigating Behind the Doors

Paper Session 8: Smart Devices

Keynote Address 4

Paper Session 9: Advanced Techniques

Paper Session 10: WiFi: Beyond the Traditional

MobiCom 2014 Conference Organization

General Chair: Sung-Ju Lee *(Narus Inc., USA)*

Technical Program Co-Chairs: Ashutosh Sabharwal *(Rice University, USA)*
Prasun Sinha *(Ohio State University, USA)*

Panel Chair: Thyaga Nandagopal *(National Science Foundation, USA)*

Workshops Co-Chairs: Chiara Petrioli *(University of Rome "La Sapienza", Italy)*
Ignacio Solis *(PARC, USA)*

Demo Co-Chairs: Shyamnath Gollakota *(University of Washington, USA)*
Ilias Leontiadis *(Telefonica Research, Spain)*
Ramya Raghavendra *(IBM TJ Watson Research Center, USA)*

Posters Co-Chairs: Souvik Sen *(HP Labs, USA)*
Xinyu Zhang *(University of Wisconsin, USA)*

SRC Chair: Saumitra Das *(Qualcomm Research Center, USA)*

Finance Chair: Joseph Camp *(Southern Methodist University, USA)*

Publicity Co-Chairs: Eugene Chai *(NEC Labs, USA)*
Aline Carneiro Viana *(INRIA, France)*
Yung Yi *(KAIST, Korea)*

Web Chair: Konstantinos Pelechrinis *(University of Pittsburgh, USA)*

Social Media/Blog Co-Chairs: Riccardo Crepaldi *(Google, USA)*
Lara Deek *(University of California, Santa Barbara, USA)*

Publication Co-Chairs: Aakanksha Chowdhery *(Microsoft Research, USA)*
Wenjun Hu *(Yale University, USA)*

Local Arrangements Co-Chairs: Marco Levorato *(University of California, Irvine, USA)*
Rui Zhang *(University of Hawaii, USA)*

Mobile App Competition Co-Chairs: Eduardo Cuervo *(Microsoft Research, USA)*
Emiliano Miluzzo *(AT&T Research, USA)*

Registration Co-Chairs: Katia Obraczka *(UC Santa Cruz, USA)*
Patrick Tague *(Carnegie Mellon University, USA)*

Program Committee (continued):

Srihari Nelakuditi *(University of South Carolina, USA)*
Jason Nieh *(Columbia University, USA)*
Chunyi Peng *(Ohio State University, USA)*
Chiara Petriolli *(Universita' degli Studi di Roma, Italy)*
Lili Qiu *(University of Texas Austin, USA)*
Souvik Sen *(HP Labs, USA)*
Srinivasan Seshan *(Carnegie Mellon University, USA)*
Raghupathy Sivakumar *(Georgia Institute of Technology, USA)*
Alex Snoeren *(University of California San Diego, USA)*
Kannan Srinivasan *(Ohio State University, USA)*
Lakshmi Subramanian *(New York University, USA)*
Karthikeyan Sundaresan *(NEC Labs, USA)*
Nitin Vaidya *(University of Illinois Urbana-Champaign, USA)*
Arun Venkataramani *(University of Massachusetts Amherst, USA)*
Xinbing Wang *(Shanghai Jiao Tong University, China)*
Matt Welsh *(Google, USA)*
Joerg Widmer *(IMDEA, USA)*
Ho Yin Starsky Wong *(Facebook, USA)*
Guoliang Xing *(Michigan State University, USA)*
Moustafa Youssef *(Egypt-Japan University of Science and Technology, Egypt)*
Lin Zhong *(Rice University, USA)*

Additional Reviewers:

Aydin Babakhani
Anirudh Badam
Randall Berry
Bill Bolosky
William Enck
Jeremy Gummeson
Zhu Han
Vikram Jandhyala
Srikanth Kandula
Thanh T. Nguyen
Stefan Saroiu
Jinwoo Shin
Joshua R. Smith
Vijay Subramanian
Wotao Yin
Xia Zhou

MobiCom 2014 Sponsor & Supporters

Sponsor: sigmobile

Platinum Supporter: NSF

Gold Supporters: Cisco Meraki; Microsoft

Silver Supporters: facebook; Google; IBM Research; Inria (informatics mathematics); Qualcomm Research

Bronze Sponsors: hp; NEC Laboratories America — Relentless passion for innovation

From Grad School, to Startup to Acquisition

Sanjit Biswas
CEO Meraki, VP/GM Cisco Cloud Networking Group
San Francisco, CA, USA
sanjit.biswas@cisco.com

ABSTRACT

In 2006, John Bicket and Sanjit Biswas took a leave from their graduate research at MIT to start a networking company called Meraki, which eventually grew to a fast-growing, profitable company acquired by Cisco in 2012 for $1.2 billion.

In this talk, Sanjit will recount the history of Meraki, from the Roofnet project at MIT CSAIL, to bootstrapping the business from the sales of their first product, to scaling up to over 500 employees. He will also share some of the lessons learned along the way, and will discuss some similarities between building computer systems as Ph.D. students and building a company.

Author Keywords

Startup, computer networking, personal experience

MobiCom'14, September 7-11, 2014, Maui, Hawaii, USA.
ACM 978-1-4503-2783-1/14/09.
http://dx.doi.org/10.1145/2639108.2639416

ACM Classification Keywords

K.7.1 [The Computing Profession]

BIO

Sanjit is the former CEO and a co-founder of Meraki, where he managed day-to-day operations from inception through the $1.2 billion acquisition by Cisco in 2012. He now serves as the Vice President and General Manager of the Cisco Cloud Networking Group, headquartered in San Francisco. Sanjit has been recognized as a TR35 honoree by MIT Technology Review, Technology Pioneer by the World Economic Forum, and has received awards for academic research in computer networking.

Sanjit holds a B.S. in Computer Systems Engineering from Stanford and an S.M. in Electrical Engineering and Computer Science from MIT.

MobiCom'14 Panel Overview

Tackling Societal Grand Challenges using Mobile Computing

Lakshminarayanan Subramanian
Moderator
New York University
lakshmi@cs.nyu.edu

Panelists

Sanjit Biswas
Meraki/Cisco
biswas@gmail.com

Gaetano Borriello
Univ of Washington
gaetano@cs.washington.edu

Prabal Dutta
Univ of Michigan
prabal@eecs.umich.edu

Dina Katabi
MIT
dk@mit.edu

Randy H. Katz
UC Berkeley
randy@cs.berkeley.edu

ABSTRACT

Mobile computing has deeply influenced the lives of almost every human in the world on a daily basis. In celebration of the 20th anniversary of Mobicom, Mobicom 2014 features an exciting panel on the topic of tackling societal grand challenges using mobile computing. The panel features five excellent researchers who have had a tremendous impact on the field of mobile computing over the years and whose research work has directly addressed pressing societal problems.

The panel discussion will feature an in-depth discussion of the grand challenges that we face in society today and the role of mobile computing as a frontier platform for addressing these challenges. The panel will cover both a retrospective and futuristic perspective where the retrospective aspects highlight the diverse contributions of the panelists and the futuristic aspects will feature a discussion of their individual views of what are the next big societal problems that Mobicom as a community should tackle.

MobiCom'14, September 7-11, 2014, Maui, Hawaii, USA.

http://dx.doi.org/10.1145/2639108.2641729

Demystifying 60GHz Outdoor Picocells

Yibo Zhu, Zengbin Zhang, Zhinus Marzi, Chris Nelson,
Upamanyu Madhow, Ben Y. Zhao and Haitao Zheng
University of California, Santa Barbara, CA 93106, USA
{yibo,zengbin,ravenben,htzheng}@cs.ucsb.edu, {zh.marzi,sciencectn}@gmail.com, madhow@ece.ucsb.edu

ABSTRACT

Mobile network traffic is set to explode in our near future, driven by the growth of bandwidth-hungry media applications. Current capacity solutions, including buying spectrum, WiFi offloading, and LTE picocells, are unlikely to supply the orders-of-magnitude bandwidth increase we need. In this paper, we explore a dramatically different alternative in the form of 60GHz mmwave picocells with highly directional links. While industry is investigating other mmwave bands (*e.g.* 28GHz to avoid oxygen absorption), we prefer the unlicensed 60GHz band with highly directional, short-range links (~100m). 60GHz links truly reap the spatial reuse benefits of small cells while delivering high per-user data rates and leveraging efforts on indoor 60GHz PHY technology and standards. Using extensive measurements on off-the-shelf 60GHz radios and system-level simulations, we explore the feasibility of 60GHz picocells by characterizing range, attenuation due to reflections, sensitivity to movement and blockage, and interference in typical urban environments. Our results dispel some common myths, and show that there are no fundamental physical barriers to high-capacity 60GHz outdoor picocells. We conclude by identifying open challenges and associated research opportunities.

Categories and Subject Descriptors

C.2.1 [**Network Architecture and Design**]: Wireless communication

Keywords

60 GHz wireless, wireless beamforming, picocells

1. INTRODUCTION

We are all witness today to an explosion in mobile broadband usage. Thanks to bandwidth-hungry HD/3D video applications, industry research predicts that aggregate bandwidth requirements will increase by 1000-fold by 2020 [1]. This staggering growth is taxing mobile cellular networks past their limits and creating a capacity crisis [2]. Existing methods to increase capacity have reached their limits: spectral efficiency is slowly approaching the Shannon limit [15]; and acquiring more spectrum provides limited capacity gains, while facing regulatory hurdles and high monetary costs [2].

To deliver the three orders of magnitude bandwidth growth required by mobile applications, we need to consider dramatically different approaches for delivering wireless content. A viable approach must meet several key requirements. *First*, it must provide total capacity that scales with the number of base stations in a given region. This means base stations must support dense deployments with minimal mutual interference. *Second*, it must increase capacity per base station by increasing amount of spectrum used and minimizing intra-cell interference between nearby mobile users. *Finally*, per-user data rates must be at least an order of magnitude higher than currently available rates, while providing robustness and reliability that match or exceed current standards in mobile and static scenarios.

Going Small. To minimize incremental deployment costs, cellular operators are exploring techniques to deploy smaller, denser cells for higher capacity, *e.g.* LTE picocells on lampposts or WiFi hotspots [3, 13], which augment existing LTE macrocells. Shrinking cell radii from several kilometers down to 100s (or even 10s) of meters is necessary to improve link quality and increase cell capacity. However, this approach is *fundamentally limited* by interference constraints for the carrier frequencies employed in today's cellular systems [30]. Specifically, at carrier frequencies of 1-5 GHz, physical form factor constraints put a hard limit on the number of antennas that can be accommodated on a picocellular basestation and a mobile device. Thus, even MIMO technologies can only mitigate interference to a limited degree, and picocell systems based on low carrier frequencies (LTE, WiFi, TV whitespaces) are unlikely to ever deliver the capacity increase we need [30].

The Promise of mmWave. But there is hope. Higher carrier frequencies, particularly millimeter-wave (mmWave) bands (30-300GHz), offer an attractive alternative. Using highly directional beams that drastically reduce interference, they enable small cells to truly deliver on their promise. Take 60GHz for example. First, the 60GHz band provides 7GHz of unlicensed spectrum for bandwidth hungry mobile applications, and is supported by the IEEE 802.11ad standard [9] (currently targeting indoor multiGigabit wireless networks) that defines multiple data rates between 385Mbps and 6.76Gbps. Second, since 60GHz has a much shorter carrier wavelength, *i.e.* 5mm, it is possible to pack large antenna arrays into relatively small form factors. A 100-element 60GHz array easily fits in no more than a square inch[1], which can be easily integrated into today's mobile devices. Third, the high density of ele-

[1]In theory, this is hundreds of times smaller than arrays with the same number of elements for frequencies at or below 5GHz.

MobiCom'14, September 7-11, 2014, Maui, Hawaii, USA.
Copyright 2014 ACM 978-1-4503-2783-1/14/09 ...$15.00.
http://dx.doi.org/10.1145/2639108.2639121.

ments allows very high aggregate bandwidth, while the narrow directional beams limit interference and provide potentially "unlimited" levels of spatial reuse. Finally, low-cost 60GHz radio chips are already available on the mass market [4, 5], *e.g.* Dell Latitude 6430u laptops can be ordered with multi-Gbps WiloCity 60GHz chips for an additional $37.5.

Clearly, 60GHz links offer an attractive and practical solution that satisfies many of the requirements we mentioned. The goal of this paper is to show that, while most of the attention in academia and industry focuses on 60 GHz for *indoor* applications, it is also a strong candidate for delivering the 1000-fold capacity increase demanded for outdoor cellular networks in dense urban environments.

A 60GHz Picocell Architecture. We propose a picocell architecture using 60GHz links, as depicted in Figure 1. We envision picocellular base stations densely deployed on lampposts or building ledges, with each station mounting multiple antenna arrays on each of its "faces." Properly tuned, each array can transmit independently to a different mobile user. To see the potential of this approach, consider a face which is 6x6 square-inches to a side. This can accommodate up to 36 60GHz 100-element arrays. If each array transmits at 2Gbps, the maximum data rate per face is 72 Gbps. Thus a single base station with 4 faces could support up to 288 Gbps downlink! Augmenting existing LTE cells with such a high-capacity picocell deployment provides a path to future-proofing our cellular networks.

Despite the immense potential of 60GHz outdoor picocells, so far, both industry and academia have *explicitly* precluded 60GHz from outdoor cellular designs [28, 34]. For example, Samsung's recent outdoor mmWave attempts demonstrated a device prototype for transmission at 28GHz (a licensed band) [28]. Key concerns include propagation loss due to oxygen absorption, which peaks at 60GHz, and increase in propagation loss at higher carrier frequencies (unless highly directional antennas are correctly aligned at both endpoints). Another concern is blockage (diffraction around obstacles is more difficult at higher frequencies). These worries led to the limited use of outdoor 60GHz links in static backhauls, where manually adjusted high-gain antennas are positioned high above to avoid potential blockages.

Our Contributions. Our first contribution is to dispel common myths about 60GHz via extensive measurements and simulations, showing that the potential for 60GHz outdoor picocells can be realized without bending the laws of physics. Unlike prior efforts that focus on propagation models [22, 14, 25, 33], we experiment with off-the-shelf 60GHz radios, and study key questions such as transmission range, robustness to blockage and user motion, and spatial reuse. We explore how these issues are affected by future hardware upgrades (especially in terms of increasing the number of antenna elements). Unlike proposals for cellular systems in other mmWave bands [28], design and evaluation of our *outdoor* network can leverage extensive efforts already put into 60GHz PHY hardware and standards for *indoor* networks. Our second contribution is to point out the cross-layer architectural innovations required to truly deliver on this potential, and identifying an interdisciplinary research area spanning the PHY, MAC and networking layers.

We now provide a quick preview of the myths we dispel.

- **Myth #1: 60GHz's range is too small for outdoor picocells.** Within FCC's power regulations, and *taking into account oxygen absorption and heavy rain,* 60GHz offers coverage area that exceeds 130m for 385Mbps and 79m for 2+Gbps. A propagation loss of 36 dB/km due to oxygen absorption and heavy rain makes it difficult to achieve kilometer-long links. But these factors only produce a 3.6 dB loss in signal strength at 100 m.

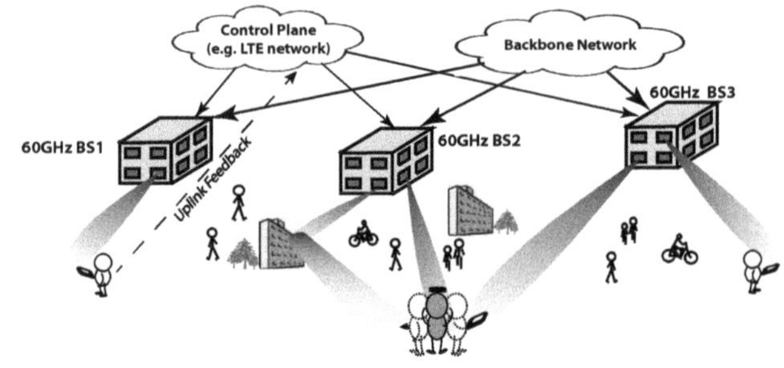

Figure 1: A potential 60GHz picocell architecture for outdoor mobile broadband augmenting existing LTE networks for significant increase in capacity. Each basestation contains many antenna arrays, each containing a large number of elements. Leveraging an LTE uplink as the feedback loop, each basestation can track and form highly directional beams simultaneously to multiple users. The beams follow users through direct or reflected paths, creating high-bandwidth downlink transmissions. Users can form beams in the reverse direction to build 60GHz uplinks, or use existing LTE uplinks.

- **Myth #2: 60GHz is highly sensitive to blockage, hence robust outdoor connectivity is not feasible.** Indeed, 60 GHz links can be blocked easily by a human body (20-50 dB of loss), and we do not have enough transmit power to burn through obstacles. However, an electronically steerable antenna array can point its beam towards one of several reflected paths available off of outdoor surfaces. The additional reflection loss of 5-7 dB can be handled within our desired link budget. We show that this, together with the concept of "picoclouds" (multiple base stations serving a given mobile user), can provide robust connectivity even in obstacle-rich urban environments.
- **Myth #3: User motion will easily break 60GHz links.** Detailed measurements show that electronically steerable antennas in off-the-shelf radios can easily keep up with outdoor pedestrian motion, and only need to realign once every few seconds to maintain high rate connections. In essence, the time constant of electronic adaptation is small compared to the time constants of human mobility.
- **Myth #4: Interference will significantly limit network capacity for small cells.** While this is indeed true at lower carrier frequencies [30], 60GHz's small interference footprint means that 60GHz picocells can be densely deployed with significant overlap but minimal interference, leading to a significant boost in spatial reuse. The reduced interference results from two factors: highly directional links that reduce interference between nearby users, and oxygen absorption and blockage from buildings that severely attenuate interference from distant cells.

In the rest of the paper, we elaborate on these results, and show that 60GHz outdoor picocells are indeed a feasible approach for delivering orders of magnitude increase in network capacity.

Limitations and Future Work. As an exploratory study, our work has several limitations that need to be addressed in future work. *First*, the preceding myths correspond to *physical* properties of 60GHz communication. Thus, dispelling them amounts to saying that, while the characteristics of 60 GHz are very different from those at lower carrier frequencies, there are no fundamental barriers in realizing its immense potential. However, as we discuss in §6, there are significant design challenges (and hence research opportunities) across a range of research disciplines, including hardware, signal processing and cross-layer protocol design. *Second*, our measurement experiments are constrained by limitations of available 60GHz hardware, hence these results are supplemented by projections and simulation-based predictions (see §6 for a discussion on the role of such techniques for future research). *Third*, while picocellular deployments may be used to add capacity in a number of environments, our focus here for 60GHz picocells is restricted to dense urban environments with high availability of reflecting surfaces such as walls. These are also locations likely to first experience full utilization of LTE capacity. Some of our conclusions may not apply, for example, to picocells covering large open spaces, where lower carrier frequencies may be a better choice.

2. BACKGROUND AND METHODOLOGY

In this section we introduce background on 60GHz communications and describe our experimental methodology.

2.1 60GHz Background

Directional Transmissions. To overcome attenuation and reduce interference, 60GHz links use beamforming to concentrate transmission energy in a desired direction. Today, 60GHz beamforming radios are readily available and affordable, either using horn antennas or antenna arrays. Radios with horn antennas use a flaring metal horn to direct radio waves, but require mechanical rotators to achieve fine-grained directional control [42]. On the other hand, radios with antenna arrays implement directional transmissions using electronic beamsteering [26, 4], employing signal processing at RF and baseband to adjust beam directions with minimal delay (*e.g.* a few ns). Such instantaneous beam adaptation makes antenna arrays an ideal fit for picocells.

The performance of antenna arrays scales with the number of antenna elements. The more the elements, the stronger the beam and the less the signal leakage. Today's low-cost 60GHz consumer products use 2×8 arrays (16 elements), while researchers have demonstrated 60GHz 16×16 array prototypes (total of 256 elements) [27]. Furthermore, recent breakthroughs make it computationally feasible to adapt even larger arrays (1000+ elements, but still fitting in palm-sized form factors!) [31], which puts us in a position to take advantage of future hardware advances to synthesize even narrower beams to further increase spatial reuse.

Oxygen Absorption and Rain Loss. At longer ranges, the advantages of directionality are offset by signal strength losses from oxygen absorption, which peaks at 60GHz, causing a loss of about 16 dB/km [6, 40]. While this makes realizing long-range (kilometers) 60 GHz link very difficult, it is actually an advantage for picocellular networks because it significantly enhances spatial reuse while having relatively small impact on the link budget at the link ranges of interest to us, as also confirmed by our testbed experiments in §3. For example, the net loss due to oxygen absorption and very heavy rain of 2 inches/hour is 36 dB/km, which works out to a modest 3.6 dB for a typical link range of 100m.

Impact of FCC Regulations. The emitted power at 60GHz is constrained by the Federal Communications Commission (FCC) as follows: the transmit power plus beamforming gain, termed Effective Isotropic Radiated Power (EIRP), is limited to 40 dBm. For antennas that are extremely directional (e.g., using parabolic dishes), the FCC has relaxed its specifications to permit further increase of EIRP [8], but we are unable to take advantage of this in the operating regime of interest to us: our architecture is based on highly directional, electronically steerable beams, but the beamwidth is still too large for the new FCC regulations to permit an EIRP higher than 40 dBm. Thus, increasing the number of elements in the transmit array does not improve link range if we already at an EIRP of 40 dBm, hence enhancements in link range must come from the receiver, by decreasing the receiver's noise figure or by increasing its antenna directivity. Of course, increasing the number of transmit elements has a big impact on *network* performance, narrower transmit beams reduce interference and enhance spatial reuse.

Leveraging IEEE 802.11ad. The IEEE 802.11ad standard for 60GHz [9] defines a number of modulation and coding schemes to adapt to different range-rate tradeoffs. In our envisioned picocellular architecture, we leverage this 802.11ad *physical layer* on the downlink, and show that link ranges of the order of 100m are attainable (see Table 1). Of course, *our MAC and network layers will be different from that of 802.11ad*, given the need to adapt to a far more dynamic outdoor environment than the indoor networks the 802.11ad standard was currently intended for.

Data rate	RX sensitivity	4 × 4 RX	8 × 8 RX	10 × 10 RX
385 Mbps	-68 dBm	63m	114m	138m
1.155 Gbps	-64 dBm	41m	77m	94m
2.31 Gbps	-61 dBm	30m	57m	70m

Table 1: Outdoor range/rate tradeoffs with 802.11ad PHY

The link budget calculations resulting in these ranges use conservative assumptions (measurements from our testbed lead to more optimistic predictions). The receiver sensitivity for each data rate (*i.e.*, minimum received power required to sustain that data rate), obtained from the 802.11ad standard, already accounts for large values of implementation loss (5 dB) and noise figure (10 dB). The link budget accounts for the FCC EIRP restriction of 40 dBm and loss due to free space propagation and oxygen absorption. On top of that, we add a link margin of 15 dB, which is more than enough to account for reflection loss (in case we are using a bounce rather than a LoS path, which typically leads to at most 5-7 dB loss) and for for rain (even for heavy rain, the additional loss on top of oxygen absorption is about 20 dB/km, hence the rain loss over 100m is 2 dB). That is, the receiver sensitivity as a function of range R (in meters) is computed as

$$P_{RX}(dBm) = EIRP(dBm) + G_{RX}(dBi) - L_{ploss}(R) - L_{margin} \quad (1)$$

where $G_{RX}(dBi) = 10\log_{10} N_{RX}$ is the receiver antenna directivity as a function of the number of receive elements N_{RX} (we consider $N_{RX} = 16, 64, 100$ for the 4×4, 8×8 and 10×10 arrays). The path loss L_{ploss} in dB is

$$L_{ploss}(R) = 10\log_{10} \frac{16\pi^2 R^2}{\lambda^2} + \alpha R \quad (2)$$

with $\alpha = 0.016$ dB/m (16 dB/km) accounting for oxygen absorption, and $\lambda = 0.005$m at 60 GHz.

2.2 Measurement Methodology

Unlike prior efforts that focus on propagation models using custom equipment [14, 22, 25, 33], we experiment with commercial off-the-shelf 60GHz radios. We study key issues regarding the feasibility of 60GHz picocells, including range, sensitivity to motion and blockage, and interference footprint.

Measurement Environments. We perform experiments in two types of environments.

- *Controlled Environments.* These are environments without any uncontrolled pedestrian. We use these measurements to evaluate the impact of individual factors in isolation. To emulate a picocell, we place a radio on a second floor balcony (6m high), representing a basestation fixed on a lamppost (Figure 2). A second radio represents the end user.

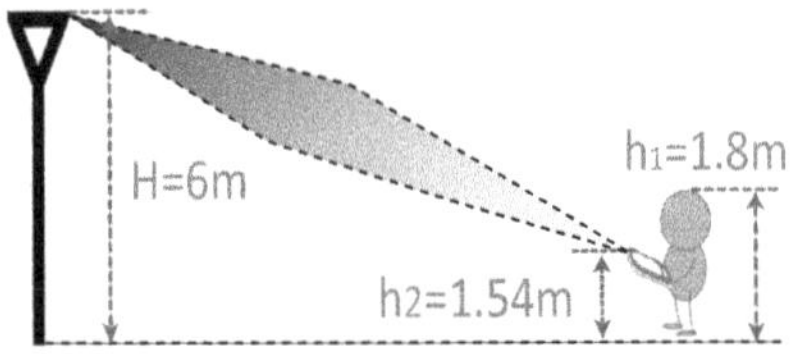

Figure 2: Controlled environment: a picocell system with 60GHz radios at both basestations and mobiles.

Figure 3: Real-life environment: a downtown street area with random pedestrians.

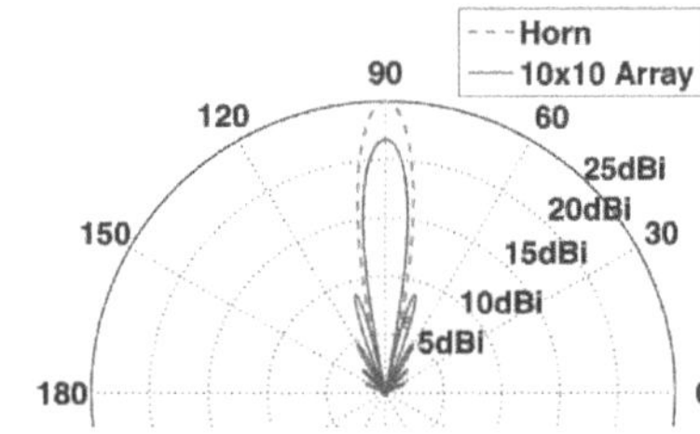

Figure 4: Radiation patterns of our testbed's horn antenna and a 10x10 rectangular array.

- *Real-Life Environments.* We also performed experiments in a downtown street walkway (Figure 3) and a campus plaza during busy hours with uncontrolled pedestrian. The basestation is placed on a second floor balcony (6m high).

60GHz Radio Platforms. We consider two types of 60GHz radios with antenna arrays, representing today's off-the-shelf hardware and high-performance radios for future deployments. By comparing their results, we also seek to identify issues that can be addressed by reasonable hardware upgrades, and those that are fundamental to 60GHz picocells and hence require careful network design. For both platforms, each radio operates on a single 60GHz channel of width 2.16GHz.

- *Wilocity 2×8 Antenna Arrays.* We use pairs of Dell 6430u laptops (as users) and D5000 docks (as basestations), designed for indoor usage. Each has a Wilocity 60GHz radio chipset with a 2×8 rectangular antenna array, operating according to IEEE 802.11ad. Because Wilocity does not provide any information on the beamwidth, we apply the antenna array theory [18] to compute the lower bound on the beamwidth: the horizonal 3dB beamwidth is 13° and the vertical 3dB beamwidth is 60°. Each radio adapts link rate between 385Mbps and 3.85Gbps, and maintains directional connectivity over time (e.g., if the LoS path is blocked, it seeks a reflected path and beamforms along it). Currently, the radio does not provide external control of link directions, hence we rely on its built-in algorithm to manage link directionality. The radio does not report signal strength values but link rates, so we monitor link performance using fine-grained reports on TCP/UDP throughput and link rate.
- *Emulating 10×10 Antenna Arrays.* There are no suitable 60GHz radios with large antenna arrays on the market. Instead, we emulate the performance of a large antenna array using a horn antenna. For experiments that do not consider interference, this can provide accurate results. This is because 60GHz link performance is largely determined by directionality and signal patterns of the main beam lobe[2]. In this regard, large antenna arrays and horn antennas are very close except for differences in antenna gain.

  Specifically, we use two HXI Gigalink 6451 radios with 0dBm transmit power and 1Gbps link rate, operating on a proprietary (non-802.11ad) configuration. Each radio has a horn antenna of 10° 3dB beamwidth and 25dBi gain. Its main lobe pattern closely align with that of a 10x10 array with 1dBi elements with 21dBi gain (Figure 4). We set each radio on a mechanical rotator and adjust its beam direction in units of 0.5^o. Each measurement records the received signal power level (RSS), repeated once every 50ms. The measured noise level is -80dBm.

[2]Antenna arrays produce side lobes (*i.e.* unwanted transmissions in undirected directions) aside from the main lobe. The side lobes are at least 13.26dB weaker than the main lobe and thus not responsible for data communication [20].

Since HXI radios use a proprietary physical layer and only support a single data rate, they cannot fully capture the performance of a picocell operating based on 802.11ad. However, we can extrapolate the attainable range to 802.11ad settings: increasing the EIRP to 40 dBm from the 25 dBm in our testbed leads to a 15-4=11dB increase in RSS (counting the 4dB gain difference of horn antenna and 10×10 arrays). This provides us with a practical means of using our testbed to verify link budget calculations as in eq. (1), and also to predict the supported data rate for each RSS measurement following the 802.11ad receiver sensitivity table. Specifically, we use the 802.11ad receiver sensitivity table to derive the required SNR for each data rate, and use it to derive the data rate supported by each RSS measured by our testbed. A similar methodology has been used in prior work on 60GHz systems [42].

3. SINGLE-USER FEASIBILITY STUDY

Using testbed measurements, we perform initial evaluation on the feasibility of 60GHz picocell systems, focusing on dispelling the four myths discussed in §1.

Assumptions. Due to hardware limitations, our measurement study makes a few assumptions. *First*, our experiments emulate a single array forming a beam to serve a single user, using either 2×8 WiloCity arrays at both ends or 10×10 arrays at both the base station and the user. Our envisioned picocellular base stations would have multiple such arrays, one for each user, as discussed in §1. *Second*, we assume the target user is stationary (sitting or standing), although her body may rotate or move a short distance due to natural posture changes. *Finally*, basestations do not coordinate in these measurements. We study the benefits of coordination via simulations in §4.

3.1 Measurements in Controlled Environments

We begin by verifying the framework for the link budget calculations in §2.1. Our measurements use the HXI radios since they report detailed receiver RSS values. Figure 5(a) plots the RSS values at different link distances under clear weather, along with the well-known Friis model [16] on 60GHz free space propagation with and without oxygen absorption (16dB loss per km). The results show that 60GHz outdoor LoS propagation does follow the classical Friis model with oxygen absorption loss, *i.e.* eq. (2).

3.1.1 Range & Throughput

Our first task is to evaluate the range and throughput of 60GHz transmissions in the context of outdoor picocells.

Picocell LoS Range. Figure 5(b) lists the measured LoS range of the Wilocity 2×8 array under different link rate targets. On a clear day, it can reach 23m at 385Mbps, and 9m at 2.31Gbps. While this is clearly insufficient for 60GHz outdoor picocells, we can easily extrapolate beyond the hardware limitations of the Wilocity platform, which is designed for indoor short-range usage and has an

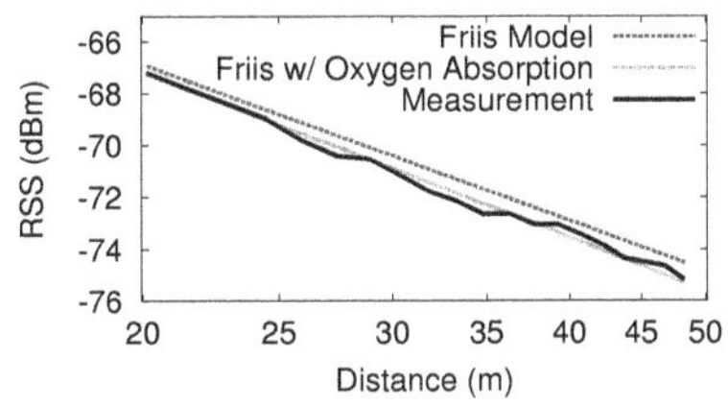

(a) 60GHz Outdoor Propagation

Radio Type	Weather	Minimum Link Rate (Mbps)		
		385	1155	2310
Wilocity 2x8	clear	23m	15m	10m
EIRP=23dBm	heavy rain	22m	-	-
HXI 10x10	clear	178m	124m	93m
EIRP=40dBm	heavy rain	139m	102m	79m

(b) Ranges of 60GHz Arrays

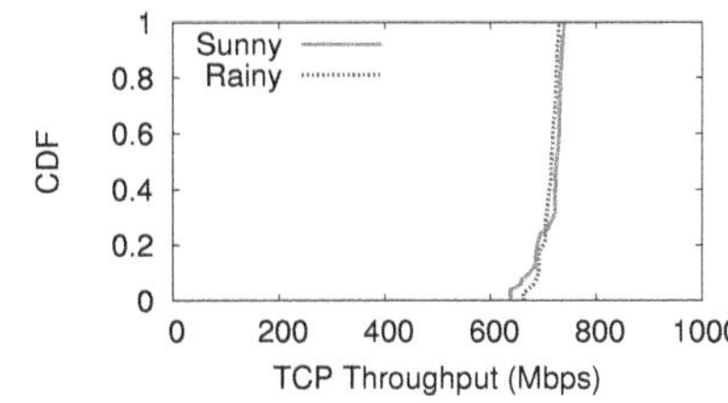

(c) TCP Throughput over Time

Figure 5: Measurements on 60GHz range and throughput. (a) The RSS results collected by HXI radios show that 60GHz outdoor propagation follows the Free-Space Friis meodel with 16dB/km oxygen absorption loss. (b) Downlink LoS ranges when 60GHz radios operate in the 802.11ad single carrier modulation (SC) setting, with 2×8 and 10×10 antenna arrays. The Wilocity 2×8 results are based on actual measurements, while the HXI 10×10 results are projected by increasing EIRP to 40dBm and mapping a data rate to each measured RSS value based on the 802.11ad specification. (c) CDF of per-minute TCP throughput measured over 10 days using the Wilocity radios.

EIRP of 23dBm. When we increase the EIRP from 23dBm to 40dBm, the path loss formula in (2) can be used to translate the 17 dB increase in signal strength to a corresponding increase in range. Because of the mixture of free space loss of $1/R^2$ and exponential decay of $e^{-\alpha R}$, the actual range increase depends on the initial value of range. While this is easy enough to calculate numerically, it is instructive to separately address these two effects via an example. Specifically, can we get a data rate of 385 Mbps at 100 m using 2×8 arrays as in the Wilocity radios in heavy rain (e.g., 2 in/hr, where the loss due to rain and oxygen absorption is about 36 dB/km)? The exponential loss is 3.6 dB at 100 m, and ignoring the baseline loss under the clear conditions for our measurements at the starting range of 23 m, we still have 17-3.6=13.4 dB signal strength increase to compensate for free space loss, leading to 13.4/2=6.7 dB, or 4.67X, increase in range relative to the baseline of 23 m. This yields a range of 100+ m. The point of this calculation is to show that, for the moderate ranges of interest, oxygen absorption and rain have a relatively small effect on the link budget.

In order to quantify the effect of using larger arrays, we project the measurements using our HXI radios, which we using as a proxy for 10×10 arrays, by adding 15 dB to the EIRP (going from 25 dBm to 40 dBm), and subtracting 4 dB in receiver directivity (25dBi horn replaced by 10×10 receive array with 1 dBi elements). If we keep the EIRP fixed, then increasing the number of transmit elements does not help the link budget (it only decreases the emitted power per element), hence the source of performance gain is the increase in receiver directivity. Based on this projection, the range in clear weather is as high as 178 m at 385 Mbps.

Figure 5(b) also lists transmission ranges under heavy rain (0.38in/h). The measured range of Wilocity radios remains the same while that of 10×10 arrays, projected from our HXI measurements, drops to 139m at 385Mbps and 102m at 1.15Gbps. This is as expected, since the additional loss due to rain impacts longer links. However, the range (100+m) is still sufficient to support picocell operations.

Link Throughput over Time. We also measured 60GHz link throughput over 10 days (February 2014) to examine its long-term performance in outdoor environments. The weather condition for the first 9 days was clear and the last day we had heavy rain (0.38in/h). We used the Wilocity radios, set the link distance to 20m, close to its maximum range of 23m, and recorded per-minute TCP throughput using Iperf. Figure 5(c) plots the CDF of the per-minute TCP throughput of the first 9 days and that of the last 1 day. We see that the Wilocity 60GHz link offers 638+Mbps TCP throughput continuously over time (and 700 Mbps 80% of the time). The minor rate fluctuations (638-700 Mbps) are randomly distributed across the measurement period, and may be the result of occasional structure vibrations caused by wind and/or pedestrians walking on the balcony. We see no difference in throughput between clear weather and heavy rain, which confirms that, at short distances, 60GHz is highly robust to weather conditions. We also confirm this observation using the HXI radio measurements. At $50m$, heavy rain (0.38in/h) only introduces 0.86dB RSS loss, which did not introduce any degradation to the link.

3.1.2 Robustness to Blockage

Outdoor 60GHz transmissions experience blockage from various obstacles including buildings, trees, pedestrians and vehicles. Our experiments focus on pedestrians, because they are moving obstacles commonly seen in outdoor settings. We also examine the effectiveness of switching to reflected paths on addressing blockage.

Impact of Pedestrian Blockage. Our experiments show that when holding a 60GHz radio and facing away from a basestation, the user herself will block the LoS signal. This observation triggers another important question: "will the connection to a user, either LoS or via reflection, be constantly blocked by nearby pedestrians?" To answer this question, we measure for both radios the LoS peer impact region, *i.e.* the area around a user where a peer of similar height blocks the LoS path between the basestation and the user. For Wilocity radios, we placed RF absorber around the radio to prevent it from switching path. We also derive the impact region of reflection paths following the same method. Figure 6 shows the LoS impact regions for the HXI radio at different link distances (the Wilocity radio result is similar and thus omitted for brevity).

We see that the observed impact regions are all small areas with a narrow cone shape, and the width (y-axis) is significantly smaller than its length (x-axis). The region also enlarges linearly with the link distance. This is because the basestation is placed in a high location (6m in our experiments, representing a lamppost placement) and the peer must be quite close to the user to block the signal.

Overall, our results imply that in outdoor environments, surrounding static peers can potentially block paths to a user. The impact, however, is limited because the peer has to be in a small region near the user. On the other hand, our measurements in busy walkways (§3.2) show that groups of moving pedestrians have a heavier impact on connectivity. However, such blockage can be effectively addressed by either switching to another reflection path (discussed next) or connecting to another basestation (see §3.2).

Handling Blockage via Reflection. 60GHz signals are reflected by most surfaces with losses of the order of 5-7 dB [21]. Thus, when the LoS path (or an existing path) to a user is blocked, the

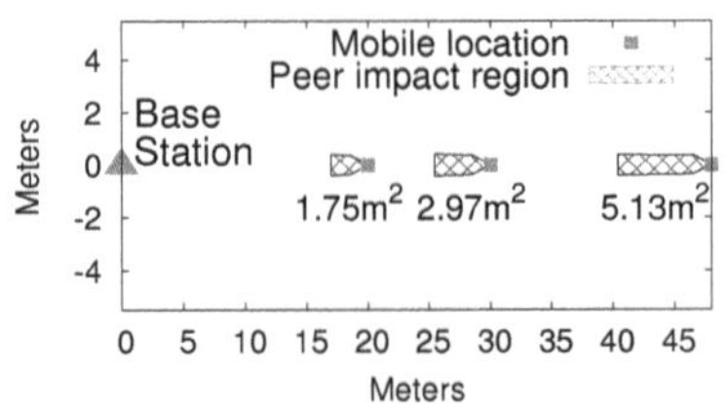

Figure 6: Impact of human blockage in terms of peer impact region for HXI radio. The base station is positioned at (0,0), and receiver is at 20m, 30m and 48m away.

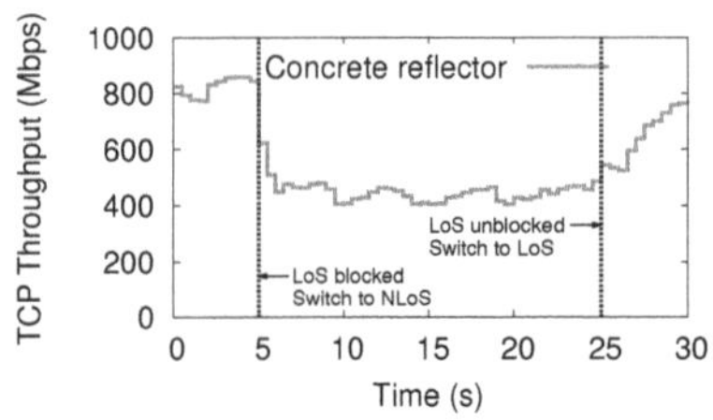

Figure 7: Measured TCP throughput as a Wilocity 60GHz link switches between different paths.

Radio	Path Length	Flat steel, Aluminum, Plastic board	Exterior Building Walls		
			Brick, Paint, Whitewash	Coarse paint	Coarse concrete
Wilocity (2x8)	10m	0%	0%	16%	16%
	15m	0%	17%	33%	33%
HXI (10x10)	30m	0%	17%	33%	46%
	50m	0%	19%	25%	25%
RSS Loss		0dB	3dB	4.5dB	5dB

Table 2: The reflection loss of eight different materials measured using both Wilocity and HXI radios.

basestation can adjust link directionality to create another reflection path. In fact, our measurements show that Wilocity radios can already switch to reflected paths in real time upon LoS blockage (see Figure 7).

Next, we study the impact of reflection on link performance. We experimented with eight surfaces, commonly seen in outdoor street environments. These include three flat surfaces and five exterior building surfaces. We repeated our experiments with different incident angles (10°-80°), and found that the angle has a very minor impact on the result[3]. For brevity we only show the results of 45°. Table 2 shows the normalized throughput loss (compared to a LoS path of the same length) for both 2×8 and 10×10 arrays at different path lengths. The HXI radio experiments also report the amount of RSS loss due to reflection. For both radios, the first three flat (and smooth) materials are perfect reflectors with negligible signal loss. The five building surfaces introduce 3-5dB signal loss and up to 46% throughput loss. The throughput loss varies with the link distance while the signal loss (in dB) remains constant. We noticed that in our results with the HXI radios the measured reflection losses were slightly smaller (*i.e.* better) that those reported in [21]. This might be due to the subtle difference in the reflection materials. Overall, these results show that reflection paths are good alternatives to LoS paths, offering ample opportunities for picocell coverage.

3.1.3 Robustness to User Motion

In practice even a "stationary" user will naturally make local movements, such as change her posture, or move a small distance (*e.g.* up to a few meters). These minor movements could change 60GHz link directionality and thus performance. We now present some initial results on their impact on link performance and implication on picocell design.

Specifically, we seek to examine whether 60GHz radios can realign their arrays to maintain a LoS connection. To do so, we place absorber around the transmitter radio to prevent the use of any reflection path, and measure TCP (or UDP) throughput continuously during the motion to study its impact. We consider four types of user motion: rotating the body, moving closer/further to the basestation[4], moving perpendicularly to the basestation, and moving in a circular motion. Each experiment starts with the basestation and user radio directly facing each other and separated by $10m$ (Wilocity) or $40m$ (HXI). While the absolute results depend on factors like link distance and user body shape, our goal is to understand the general trend and its implication, as well as how the two 60GHz radios react to these motions.

[3]Our results align with existing results: for thick materials ($\geq$3cm), the reflection loss decreases as the incident angle increases [21].

[4]Since the basestation is placed higher than the user radio, moving further/closer to the basestation does change link directionality.

Wilocity 2×8 Array Results. Since 802.11ad already enables radio realignment via beam tracking, we expect that the Wilocity radios can realign with each other to a certain degree. Thus the goal of our measurements is to understand the speed of realignment and the robustness against user motion.

Because Wilocity radios do not expose any information on beam directionality, we first performed a set of UDP experiments to understand their array alignment behaviors. In each experiment, we first let the basestation and user radios face each other and record UDP throughput, and then move/rotate the user radio locally for 1-3s and stop for 15s (to allow re-alignment).

From both UDP and link rate reports, we see that the low-cost Wilocity radios already adapt beam direction on-the-fly to cope with changes in link directionality. But the adaptation has two limitations. *First*, the adaptation is not instantaneous: in our experiments, it takes 2-7s for UDP/link rate to fully recover. Such delay can come from the time for adjusting the array and that for coordinating both ends. *Second*, the amount of beam adjustment is limited, *i.e.* the array cannot tune to all the directions, possibly due to the hardware enclosure and/or low-cost array design.

With these observations in mind, we now study the impact of user motion on TCP performance. Each experiment starts from the two radios being perfectly aligned with TCP throughput at 900Mbps. *First*, we experimented on user rotation at different rotation speeds (40°/s - 100°/s). We found that until the rotation angle reaches 85°, the TCP throughput remains at 600Mbps. After that, the link breaks down.

Next, for the other three patterns, Figure 8 shows the TCP throughput during motion, as a function of the receiver's deviation distance from the original position. We make two observations. *First*, a user moving further/closer or in a small circle at moderate speeds (Figure 8(a)-(b)) lead to a minor degradation in TCP throughput. *Second*, moving perpendicular to the LoS has more impact since it introduces larger/faster directionality changes. During the movement, TCP throughput fluctuates and gradually degrades to 400Mbps as the deviation reaches $8m$. Specifically, when the user moves at 1.5m/h, the throughput first drops due to array misalignment, then rises as both radios align their arrays, and repeats the same pattern. By examining the patterns of peak/valley across all the speeds tested (1.5-5mph), we see that the radio alignment frequency aligns with the above UDP results, *e.g.* once every 2-7s.

In summary, our experiments on Wilocity radios show that today's low-cost 60GHz radios already offer online array alignment to handle moderate user motions. However, these radios are designed for quasi-static indoor environments, and the speed and amount

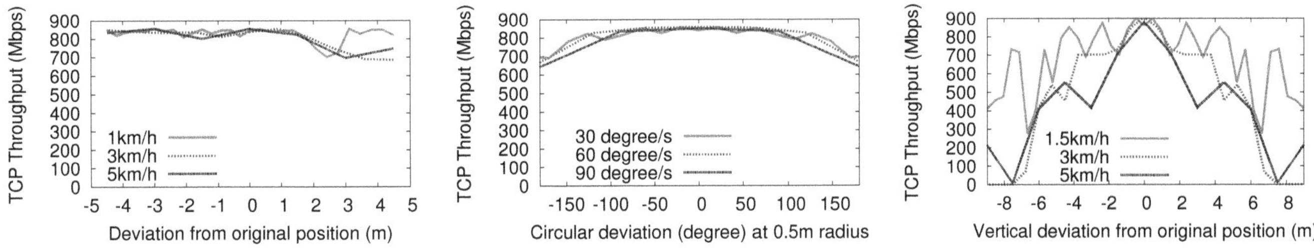

(a) Moving closer/further (b) Moving circularly (c) Moving perpendicularly

Figure 8: Measured throughput using our Wilocity testbed (2x8) when the receiver moves in three different motion patterns.

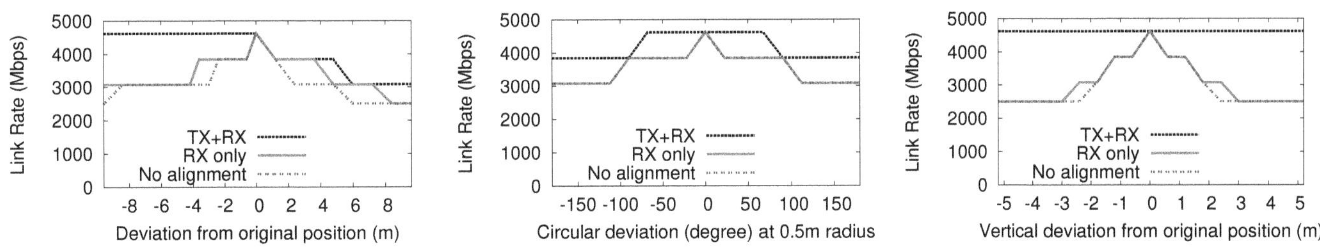

(a) Moving closer/further (b) Moving circularly (c) Moving perpendicularly

Figure 9: Measured RSS values using our HXI testbed (10x10) when the receiver moves in three different motion patterns. We consider three types of alignment methods: no alignment, partial alignment (RX only) and full alignment involving both TX and RX (TX+RX).

of their beam adjustments are not enough to handle certain motion patterns that introduce fast/large changes in link directionality.

Alignment Requirements for 10×10 Arrays. The above discussion triggers another question: *"As the link becomes more directional by using larger arrays, how fast should array alignment take place to handle user motion?"* As already discussed, the horn antennas on the HXI radios serve as a good proxy for 10×10 arrays. Hence, to answer this question, we mount the HXI radios on mechanical rotators (with a precision of 0.5^o) and manually adjust beam directions as the user moves. Each experiment starts with the two radios perfectly aligned. As the user moves, we measure the RSS values of three scenarios: adjusting both TX and RX arrays (full alignment), only adjusting RX array (partial alignment), and no alignment. From these results we estimate the alignment speed required to support typical user motion. Figure 9 plots the link rate projected from the RSS values measured during motion. We make two key observations.

- *Full alignment is required to handle user motion*, which is particularly true for movements towards and perpendicularly to the basestation. It involves both ends and requires a coordination channel between the basestation and the user.
- *Re-alignment once every second is sufficient for local movements.* Again perpendicular movements lead to the fastest signal degradation. Without alignment, the transmitter and receiver beams deviate from each other gradually, *e.g.* 3.6^o when the user moves 2.5m. The RSS drops by 2.47dB and the link throughput to half. At a moderate motion speed of 3-5mph, moving 2.5m takes 1.8s-3s. Thus at a link distance of 40m, re-aligning once every second should maintain quality connections during local movements. We also study the re-alignment frequency at other link distance values, and obtain similar findings.

3.1.4 Interference and Spatial Reuse

We now study the spatial reuse provided by 60GHz links. While averaged performance over large-scale deployments is required to accurately quantify spatial reuse, we use testbed measurements to explore several worst-case interference scenarios when 60GHz picocells are deployed in a street environment. We also examine how the choice of arrays affects the degree of spatial reuse.

Interference Scenarios. Intuitively, two directional links interfere when their directions are too similar to each other. Hence, in the context of 60GHz picocells, we consider in our experiments three example "worst-case" downlink interference scenarios, shown in Figure 10. All three scenarios involve 2 basestations (BS_a, BS_b) deployed on lampposts at the edge of the side walk next to the street, each serving a user (a and b) on the sidewalk, using the same 60GHz channel. In each scenario, the interference condition depends heavily on the angular separation between the two links, which is defined by the distance between the two basestations (D), user a's horizontal distance to BS_a (d) in scenario 1, and the sidewalk depth (l) in scenario 2 and 3. In our experiments, we consider $l = 7m$, modeling major urban streets like those in Manhattan.

Since these interference measurements require at least two links, we used Wilocity radios in our measurements (we only have two HXI radios or one link due to cost constraints). To estimate the performance of larger arrays (thus narrower beams), we mount a metal horn-shaped case on the Wilocity device to reduce its beamwidth to roughly approximate a 10×10 array. However this also eliminates side-beams so our larger-array results are rather optimistic. Later in §4 we use network simulations to further study this issue. Finally, for all the experiments, we place radio absorbers to ensure that both links do not change their path directions.

Findings. We plot in Figure 10(d-f) the normalized TCP throughput loss due to interference. We make two key observations. *First*, the low-cost 2×8 arrays have wide beams that result in large interference. The two basestations must be widely separated to avoid inter-basestation interference: 20-22m for scenario 1 and 2, and >>22m for scenario 3. But upgrading to a larger array can potentially reduce basestation separation to 12-14m for scenario 1 and 2, and 22m for scenario 3, enabling dense basestation deployment.

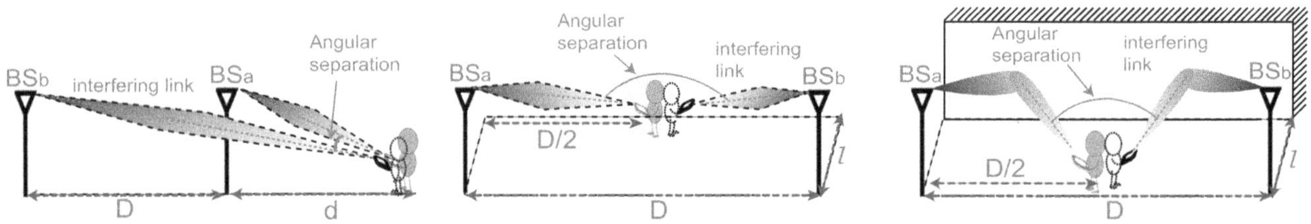

(a) Scenario 1 (b) Scenario 2 (c) Scenario 3

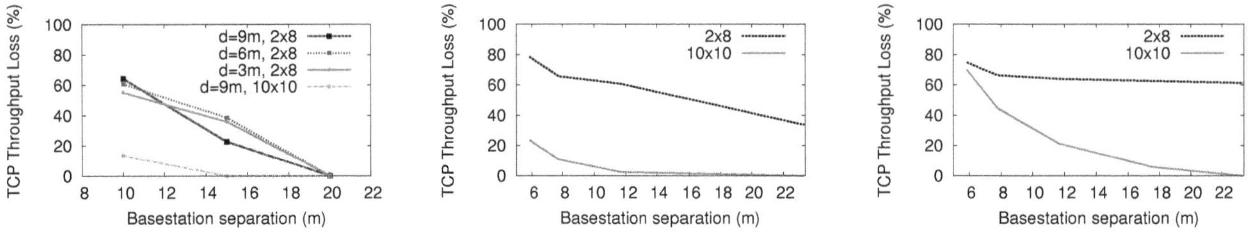

(d) Scenario 1: TCP thpt loss (e) Scenario 2: TCP thpt loss (f) Scenario 3: TCP thpt loss

Figure 10: Three sample "worst-case" interference scenarios for a sidewalk environment and the TCP throughput loss due to interference. Two 60GHz basestations are deployed on lampposts (6m in height) on the edge of the side walk, each serving a user on the sidewalk.

Second, the use of reflected paths (for overcoming blockage) creates diverse interference conditions beyond those of LoS. In certain scenarios, even using a narrow beam array may not eliminate interference. This calls for *coordinated scheduling*, where basestations coordinate user scheduling to proactively avoid heavy interference.

3.2 Measurements in Real-life Environments

Our experiments took place in two sites: a downtown street walkway area and a campus plaza area, both during busy hours with many moving pedestrians. These "in the wild" experiments differ from the "controlled" experiments as follows. *First*, the user is surrounded by *random moving pedestrians* that create unpredictable blockage. *Second*, we use Wilocity radios and leverage its built-in array adaptation mechanisms to maintain link connectivity. *Third*, we deploy multiple basestations around the area to study whether switching between basestations can effectively improve connectivity. At both sites, we placed basestations on a 2nd floor balcony of 6 meters in height, and experimented at 10 user locations (6 at downtown, 4 at campus) and 2 basestation locations. At each location, we let the user face the basestation(s), thus her own body did not block the LoS path. We then recorded TCP throughput and link layer rate (reported by the radio driver) for 1 hour per location.

Single user, single basestation. We first consider the scenario where a single user is being served by a single basestation. To illustrate the impact of pedestrian blockage on link connectivity, we plot in Figure 11(a)-(b) the TCP and link rate traces at two sample user locations at the edge of the walkway, with a roughly 12m link distance. In Figure 11(a), the connection experienced outage (both link rate and TCP rate drop to 0) several times during the first 250s. During this time period, we observed a continuous crowd of pedestrians passing by, creating prolonged blockage to the user. After that, the link rate fluctuates (due to transient pedestrian blockage and subsequent rate adaptation), but the TCP throughput remains stable[5]. In fact, when a small group of 2-3 pedestrians pass by the user, they only create transient blockage. The link rate drops largely but quickly recovers.

In Figure 11(b), between minute 13 and 23, there is a 2-minute outage followed by a period of rate fluctuations. This 10-minute period was in between two class sessions, thus large groups of students passed by our user location. Different from the last example, the link was able to recover and sustain high TCP throughput after the two-minute outage, despite the prolonged blockage. This is because the radios switched to a reflected path (via a nearby building wall) to avoid blockage, and the frequent fluctuation was the result of rate adaptation to mitigate reflection loss. As a result, the link didn't fail repeatedly like in the previous example. In the rest of the hour, the pedestrian density was moderate and only caused transient blockage thus zero outage.

Figure 11(c) shows the link availability, *i.e.* (1-outage), over the busiest 300s across all the measured user locations (thus the period with the lowest availability), for the two basestation locations. The availability varies largely across user locations, and can be as low as 50%. The low availability scenarios are those where the user was on a crowded walkway and blocked by many moving pedestrians.

Single user, multiple basestations. We then examine scenarios where two basestations coordinate to serve a single user. To do so, we place the second basestation 10m-20m away from the first basestation[6]. Because Wilocity radios do not allow clients to switch between basestations on-the-fly, we emulate real-time switching by connecting a second receiver (co-located with the first receiver) to the second basestation on a different 60GHz channel. This allows us to simultaneously measure for each location its link availability to each basestation, and calculate the link availability when enabling real-time switching. Results in Figure 11(c) confirm that serving a user with a picocloud consisting of multiple basestation can effectively boost link availability.

3.3 Summary of Observations

Our detailed measurements dispel the four common myths about 60GHz outdoor picocells listed in §1. We now summarize our findings and their implications on picocell design.

- **Range:** While today's low-cost radios have limited outdoor range due to its low EIRP and small array size (designed for indoor sce-

[5]The Wilocity TCP throughput is capped to 1Gbps, due to the 1Gbps Ethernet interface that connects the radio to the laptop.

[6]We did not observe any notable impact of the separation distance.

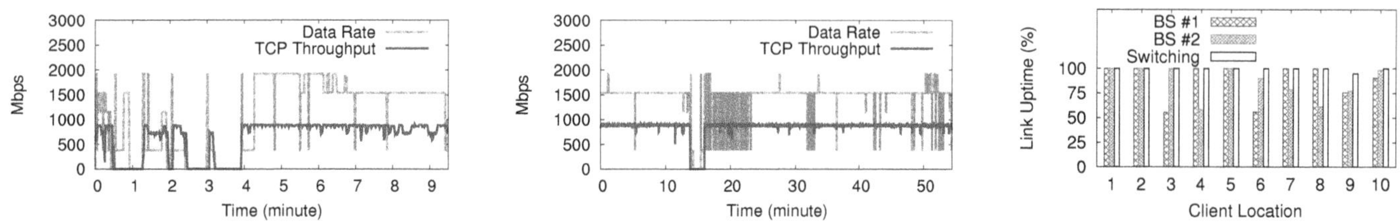

(a) TCP/link trace, a downtown sidewalk point (b) TCP/link trace, a campus plaza point (c) Link Availability

Figure 11: The impact of pedestrian blockage in real-life environments. (a) A 10-minute segment of TCP/ link rate traces at a downtown sidewalk location. (b) A full 1-hour trace at a campus plaza location. (c) Link availability at 10 locations w/ and w/o basestation switching.

narios), larger antenna arrays, *e.g.* 10×10, can support a range up to 100+m at 385Mbps even in heavy rain conditions.

- **Blockage:** The user body, other pedestrians, and other obstacles can all block connections to a user. Hence it is critical to maintain a rich path inventory for each user by continuously tracking both LoS and various reflection paths. When necessary, users can be served using a picocloud comprising of multiple basestations (supported by results in §4).
- **User Motion:** Local user motion changes 60GHz link directionality and degrades performance, unless both endpoints realign their arrays in real time. Since they were designed for quasi-static indoor settings, realignment on Wilocity radios can take up to 7 seconds, making them less robust against certain motion patterns. For larger arrays (10×10) with narrower bandwidth, re-alignment frequency needs to be at least once per second.
- **Spatial Reuse:** Today's low-cost 2×8 arrays have wide beams that limits the degree of spatial reuse. Using larger arrays up to 10×10 can significantly reduce interference footprints, but the large variety of path directions can still lead to considerable interference in certain scenarios. Handling these requires intelligent user scheduling and basestation coordination. While we will provide initial insights on these issues in §4, far more research is needed in this area.

4. SIMULATION RESULTS

In this section, we perform detailed simulations to further examine 60GHz picocells in terms of blockage and interference.

Simulation Setup. We consider a street in a typical urban environment: two basestations are deployed on opposite sides of the street (at lamppost height of $6m$), forming a picocloud to serve users on both sidewalks. Figure 12 plots the geometry of a typical Manhattan street observed from the Google map. Our simulation considers pedestrians, cars and trees as obstacles that can potentially block or attenuate 60GHz links. We model each pedestrian as a cylinder of radius $0.3m$ with height uniformly distributed between $1.5m$ and $2m$, and trees as cyclinders with radius $0.4m$ and height $3m$. We model cars as rectangular cuboids of size $2m \times 4.5m \times 1.5m$. We consider a moderate pedestrian density of $0.08 person/m^2$ [23].

The link budget in our simulations is as in eq. (1)-(2) defined in §2.1, also consistent with the measurement-based feasibility analysis in §3. We consider regular square arrays with standard radiation patterns [18], varying the size of the transmit and receive arrays around default settings of 10 × 10 at each end. We fix the EIRP to 40dBm. Thus, the size of the transmit array does not impact the link budget, but can have a significant effect on interference. The receive array size impacts both link budget and interference. The 60 GHz channel is well characterized by a small number of dominant rays (see [41] and references therein), with path strengths decaying rapidly with multiple bounces. Hence, in our model, we consider the LoS ray and one-bounce paths.

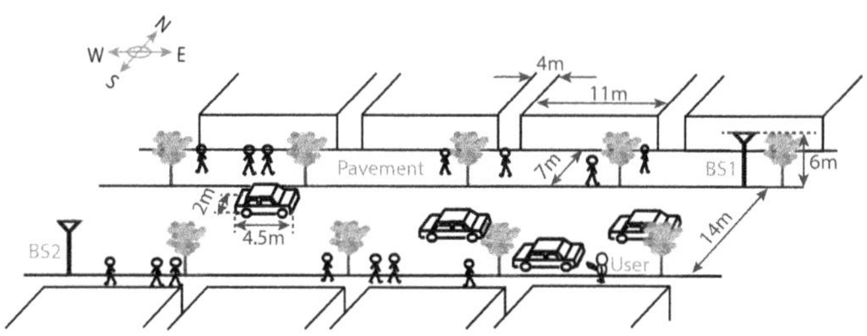

Figure 12: Simulation environment: a typical street in New York City (observed from the Google Map), where two basestations serve users on both sidewalks along the street.

4.1 Link Availability

We consider several factors that may affect link availability. The first is user orientation, *e.g.* when facing basestation 1, the user's body blocks the LoS path from basestation 2. We study its impact by comparing link availability among four possible orientations: north (facing far wall), south (facing near wall), east (facing basestation 1), and west (facing basestation 2). In general, the wall-facing orientations do not have LoS blockage, and the LoS availability is impaired mainly for the east-west orientations. We omit orientation-specific results for brevity; our later results are averaged over these four orientations. The second factor affecting link availability is blockage by other obstacles, *e.g.* other pedestrians, trees, and cars. We consider a moderate pedestrian density of 0.08 per square meter[7]. We find that, in general, cars are not tall enough to block LoS and wall reflections to users on sidewalks, but may disrupt ground reflections. Hence our simulations do not utilize any ground reflections from the street or sidewalk. Finally, the third factor is the presence of gaps between buildings (see Figure 12), which may eliminate possible reflected paths.

Taking into account these factors, we run simulations to estimate the distribution of RSS at different receiver locations, accounting for different receiver orientations and locations of other pedestrians and cars. We use this to compute the *availability rate* for three 802.11ad data rates listed in Table 1 (a data rate is "available" if the RSS exceeds its required receiver sensitivity).

Benefits of Picoclouds and Reflected Paths. Table 3 summarizes the availability rates for four scenarios: a mobile is served by (i) only the LoS path from basestation 1, (ii) a path among the

[7]We obtain similar results for much higher densities since it turns out that blockage of user body is the key source of link impairment.

Data rate (Mbps)	385	1155	2310
LoS (BS1)	66.0%	66.0%	66.0%
LoS + 2 NLoS (BS1)	94.2%	93.8%	93.5%
LoS (BS1& BS2)	94.5%	94.5%	94.5%
6 paths (BS1&BS2)	100%	99.95%	99.95%

Table 3: Effect of picocloud and reflection paths on availability, 10×10 RX array, $100m$ separation between the two basestations.

RX array	BS spacing	Clear			Rainy		
		Data rate (Mbps)					
		385	1155	2310	385	1155	2310
4×4	100m	99.9%	99.5%	99%	99.8%	99.4%	98%
	200m	99.4%	94.6%	85%	98.3%	89.2%	75.7%
8×8	100m	99.9%	99.75%	99.6%	100%	99.75%	99.7%
	200m	99.5%	99.45%	98.9%	99.5%	99%	97.2%
10×10	100m	100%	99.95%	99.95%	99.9%	99.9%	99.8%
	200m	99.5%	99.5%	99.3%	99.5%	99.5%	98.8%

Table 4: Availability rates (blockage scenario).

RX array	Mode	TX array 10×10			TX array 32×32		
		Data rate (Mbps)					
		385	1155	2310	385	1155	2310
4×4	WoC	70%	60%	55%	89.5%	79.5%	72%
	WC	75%	68%	62%	89.8%	82.6%	76%
10×10	WoC	94.3%	91%	81%	98%	96.8%	93%
	WC	94.7%	91%	84%	98%	96.8%	94.8%

Table 5: Availability rates with blockage and interference, where the user pair are co-located in between the two basestations.

RX array	Mode	TX array 10×10			TX array 32×32		
		Data rate (Mbps)					
		385	1155	2310	385	1155	2310
4×4	WoC	59%	48%	46%	73%	58%	52%
	WC	66%	59%	56%	77%	66%	61%
10×10	WoC	90%	81%	75%	92.5%	90%	85%
	WC	91%	85%	81%	93%	91%	88%

Table 6: Availability rates in the offset geometry.

LoS and 2 wall-reflected paths (if feasible) from basestation 1, (iii) only the LoS paths from basestation 1 and 2, and (iv) a path among the total 6 possible paths from basestation 1 and 2. This result assumes a basestation spacing of 100m, but we observe similar conclusions for 150m and 200m. This result shows that using LoS path from a single basestation cannot provide robust connectivity. But when both basestations are involved, the link availability jumps from 66% to 94.5% at 385Mbps. Adding just two wall-reflected paths further increases the availability rate to 99.95-100%.

Basestation Spacing and RX Array Size. Assuming a picocloud of two basestations and the use of both LoS and reflected paths, Table 4 reports the availability rate for different basestation spacing and RX array size. We see that even heavy rain (50mm/hr) barely has any impact. For the 10×10 RX array and a BS spacing of 200m, we have high availability even at 2 Gbps (99.3% in clear, and 98.8% in rainy conditions). This implies that even with a sparse deployment, the network offers robust connectivity and coverage.

4.2 Interference and Spatial Reuse

We report on some preliminary results that indicate the massive spatial reuse achievable in our architecture. To this end, we lower the basestation spacing to 20m, and consider mutual interference between two users, each served by one of two basestations forming a picocloud. In addition to using different receive arrays, we also consider 10×10 and 32×32 transmit arrays. The EIRP is fixed, hence the transmit array size does not impact the link budget, but can have a significant effect on interference.

We first consider a scenario with "multiuser diversity": there are five users, out of which two are picked at any time. We consider two strategies (neither of these is optimal, but they suffice to illustrate the impact of interference). In the first, termed without coordination (WoC), the basestations do not account for interference in scheduling: the first basestation serves the user to which it has the best path, and the second chooses the user to which it has the best path among the remaining 4 users. In the second strategy, termed With Coordination (WC), the first basestation chooses the user for which it has the best path (as before), but the second basestation chooses a user to maximize the minimum SINR among the two chosen users. Our simulations of availability are as before, except that we now also account for the presence of interference in determining receiver sensitivities. We find that the availability is 100% for all antenna combinations, with or without coordination! Basically, noise is not a limiting factor at this shorter range, and a user configuration that is "bad enough" (to produce large interference despite beamforming at both ends) is a rare event. We plan to develop an analytical framework for understanding the probabilities of such rare events in future work.

Next, we consider a "worst-case" scenario where two users next to each other are being served by the two base stations. Table 5 shows availability rates, averaging over the location of the user pair between the basestations, and their individual orientations. Here the transmit array size has a large effect. Using the larger array drops the outage rate from 30% to 10.5% for the smallest 4×4 receive array. For the 10×10 receive array, the main effect of using a larger transmit array is to increase the availability rate for the 2 Gbps rate.

The performance gets slightly worse in the "offset" geometry depicted in Figure 10(a), where the user pair is no longer between the two basestations. The availability in Table 6 drops to 93% even for the largest transmit and receive arrays considered. Of course, these worst-case settings are unlikely for randomly placed users, and can be avoided if we have multiuser diversity (so the picocloud does not have to simultaneously transmit to pairs of nearby users).

These results, despite their preliminary nature, indicate the promise of massive spatial reuse provided by the use of narrow beams at both transmit and receiver, and motivate more detailed analysis and simulations for characterizing the nature of interference in both average and worst cases.

5. RELATED WORK

mmWave Cellular Networks. Picocellular networks in the mm wave bands have attracted significant attention recently. Much recent effort has focused on trying to attain ranges of the order of 200m or even more, thus considered bands such as 28GHz, 38GHz and 73GHz to avoid oxygen absorption that peaks at 60GHz (see [29] and a recent survey [32]). Recent work also proposed to increase range by combining signals from many NLoS paths incoherently [12].

Our proposed 60GHz picocell design differs from existing efforts by taking a different perspective. Aiming for short links (50-100m)[8], the oxygen absorption at 60GHz barely dents the link budget while still cutting down on interference from far-away basestations and hence significantly increasing spatial reuse. Together, the

[8]Mobility management becomes difficult at short ranges. This can be potentially addressed by the picocloud architecture, but still remains an open challenge that demands further research study.

large per-user data rate and large spatial reuse can potentially enable the 1000-fold increase in network capacity. Furthermore, our proposal leverages current and ongoing 60GHz hardware technologies and the IEEE 802.11ad standard developed for indoor applications, while the unlicensed nature of 60GHz bands lowers the entry barrier and promotes innovation.

Outdoor 60GHz Systems. The outdoor use of 60GHz is not new: there are point-to-point Gigabit links on the market today (e.g., [7]), attaining link ranges of kilometers using carefully installed parabolic dishes. These fixed beam antennas have significantly higher directivities than the electronically steerable antenna arrays envisioned in our architecture. Recent work has examined 60GHz mesh networks with electronically steerable links for backhaul [35, 36]. Finally, the impact of blockage on short-range outdoor 60 GHz links has been explored independently in [10, 11] using ray-tracing simulations. Unlike our work, this study is not grounded in measurements, and does not consider the detailed tradeoffs in the picocloud architecture.

60GHz Measurements. There have been significant efforts in 60 GHz channel measurement and modeling both for indoor [24, 17] and outdoor settings [37, 39, 21, 33], confirming the accuracy of quasi-optical propagation models on 60GHz propagation. Most measurements used channel sounding and probing hardware, while others have cleverly adapted commercial radios to indoor measurements [38, 42].

While prior measurement campaigns focus on link level characterization and propagation modeling, to the best of our knowledge, our work is the first measurement-centric study aimed specifically at design and validation of outdoor 60GHz picocell architectures.

6. CONCLUSION

Our measurements and simulations dispel some common myths on 60 GHz outdoor mobile communication, and show that outdoor 60 GHz picocells augmenting existing cellular networks indeed have the potential to deliver orders of magnitude increase in network capacity. Our findings lead us to identify the need for new, novel architectures and system designs such as "picoclouds," as part of a new research area on 60GHz outdoor networks. We conclude by discussing some of the significant challenges that remain.

Cross-layer Modeling. In our experiments, off-the-shelf hardware provides insight into propagation, blockage and interference in simple scenarios. However, today's hardware limitations imply that future research involving more complex scenarios must rely on simulations until more capable platforms (*e.g.,* with externally programmable beamsteering) become available. Therefore, significant effort is necessary to develop models at different layers accurate enough to capture the cross-layer interactions unique to 60 GHz communication.

Specifically, the lowest layer involves tying the physics of propagation and diffraction to link-level models. This includes link availability and data rate as a function of pedestrian configurations, for group motion as well as independent individual motion. Another layer involves signal processing models and algorithms that account for hardware constraints, *e.g.*, RF beamforming with a large number of antenna elements. We can then build to higher layers, including abstractions for user tracking and basestation coordination, and network-level resource management for seamless support of TCP flows.

User Tracking. To establish/maintain links, basestations must track users continuously and build a rich path inventory. GPS location works only for LoS paths, but its localization error is too large to enable highly directive beams. Brute-force beam scans incur large overhead, which prevent online adaptation. A potential solution is compressive adaptation [31], where basestations periodically send 60GHz beacons in random beam directions, and then leverage user feedback to estimate directions of available paths to each user. However, significant effort is required to translate such ideas to practical system designs.

Control Plane. A robust control plane is needed for coordination between basestations and users during bootstrapping, handoff and array (re)alignment. A potential candidate is to use existing LTE services (Figure 1) for this purpose. The resulting control channel is reliable, but the design must be robust to latencies as high as 80ms [19], especially if LTE bands are congested.

Picocloud Architecture & Protocol Design. In the picocloud architecture, basestations must coordinate to maintain user connectivity and minimize interference. This requires new, cross-layer design spanning the PHY, MAC and network layers. Frequent switching between basestations to handle blockage and mobility, together with rate adaptation switching between different paths, requires careful coordination to support applications such as TCP. Given the high frequency of blockages, it is particularly important to avoid naive handoff strategies that could lead to ping-pong effects and race conditions. Such considerations, together with the large per-user rate, call for careful designs that account for backhaul and storage constraints.

Hardware Design. Advances in system-on-chip design enable packing multiple radios into mobile devices. The integration of 60GHz radios poses little difficulty in terms of interference with existing radios, since the frequency band is so far from current WiFi and cellular frequencies. However, another consideration is the integration of (possibly multiple) antenna arrays to receive signals effectively regardless of the device orientation. Limiting radio energy cost for mobile devices is another. While signal processing and RF design for high-speed mmwave links are challenging, our advantage lies in leveraging existing and ongoing hardware development for IEEE 802.11ad.

7. ACKNOWLEDGMENTS

The authors thank the anonymous reviewers for their insightful feedback. This work is supported in part by NSF grant CNS-1317153. Any opinions, findings, and conclusions or recommendations expressed in this material are those of the authors and do not necessarily reflect the views of the NSF.

8. REFERENCES

[1] http://www.techjournal.org/2011/09/mobile-broadband-useage-is-set-to-explode-infographic.

[2] http://money.cnn.com/2012/02/24/technology/spectrum_crunch_solutions/index.htm.

[3] http://www.dailywireless.org/2011/05/06/att-moves-to-hotzones-and-picocells.

[4] http://www.siliconimage.com/news/releasedetails.aspx?id=649.

[5] http://news.cnet.com/8301-30685_3-57326718-264/wilocity-60ghz-wireless-revolution-begins-at-ces/.

[6] http://transition.fcc.gov/Bureaus/Engineering_Technology/Documents/bulletins/oet70/oet70a.pdf.

[7] Cisco Small Cell Wireless Backhaul Ecosystem: A Flexible and Proven Deployment Toolkit. http://www.cisco.com/c/en/us/solutions/collateral/service-provider/small-cell-solutions/brochure_c02-728436.html.

[8] Fcc 13-112. http://hraunfoss.fcc.gov/edocs_public/attachmatch/FCC-13-112A1.pdf.

[9] IEEE 802.11 Task Group AD. http://www.ieee802.org/11/Reports/tgad_update.htm.

[10] Abouelseoud, M., and Charlton, G. The effect of human blockage on the performance of millimeter-wave access link for outdoor coverage. In *Proc. of VTC* (2013).

[11] Abouelseoud, M., and Charlton, G. System level performance of millimeter-wave access link for outdoor coverage. In *Proc. of WCNC* (2013).

[12] Akdeniz, M. R., Liu, Y., Rangan, S., and Erkip, E. Millimeter wave picocellular system evaluation for urban deployments. *arXiv:1304.3963* (2013).

[13] Balasubramanian, A., Mahajan, R., and Venkataramani, A. Augmenting mobile 3G using WiFi. In *Proc. of MobiSys* (2010).

[14] Correia, L., and Reis, J. Wideband characterisation of the propagation channel for outdoors at 60 ghz. In *Proc. of PIMRC* (1996).

[15] Costello, D., and Forney, G.D., J. Channel coding: The road to channel capacity. *Proc. of the IEEE 95*, 6 (2007), 1150–1177.

[16] Friis, H. T. A note on a simple transmission formula. *Proc. of IRE* (1946).

[17] Geng, S., Kivinen, J., Zhao, X., and Vainikainen, P. Millimeter-wave propagation channel characterization for short-range wireless communications. *IEEE TVT 58*, 1 (2009), 3–13.

[18] Hansen, R. C. *Phased array antennas*, 2nd ed. John Wiley & Sons, 2009.

[19] Huang, J., Qian, F., Gerber, A., Mao, Z. M., Sen, S., and Spatscheck, O. A close examination of performance and power characteristics of 4G LTE networks. In *Proc. of MobiSys* (2012).

[20] Kelleher, K. *The Microwave Engineers' Handbook and Buyers' Guide*, 5th ed. New York: Horizon Press, 1964.

[21] Langen, B., Lober, G., and Herzig, W. Reflection and transmission behavior of building materials at 60ghz. In *Proc. of PIMRC* (1994).

[22] Lovnes, G., Reis, J., and Raekken, R. Channel sounding measurements at 59 ghz in city streets. In *Proc. of PIMRC* (1994).

[23] Maeda, K., et al. Urban pedestrian mobility for mobile wireless network simulation. *Ad Hoc Networks 7*, 1 (2009), 153–170.

[24] Maltsev, A., Maslennikov, R., Sevastyanov, A., Khoryaev, A., and Lomayev, A. Experimental investigations of 60 GHz WLAN systems in office environment. *IEEE JSAC 27*, 8 (2009).

[25] Matic, D., Harada, H., and Prasad, R. Indoor and outdoor frequency measurements for mm-waves in the range of 60 ghz. In *Proc. of VTC* (1998).

[26] Natarajan, A., Reynolds, S. K., Tsai, M.-D., Nicolson, S. T., Zhan, J.-H., Kam, D. G., Liu, D., Huang, Y.-L., Valdes-Garcia, A., and Floyd, B. A. A fully-integrated 16-element phased-array receiver in sige bicmos for 60-ghz communications. *IEEE JSSC 46*, 5 (2011), 1059–1075.

[27] Nishi, S., and Tokuda, K. Development of mm-wave video transmission system-development of antenna. In *Proc. of APMC* (2001).

[28] Pi, Z., and Khan, F. An introduction to millimeter-wave mobile broadband systems. *IEEE Comm. Magazine 49* (2009), 101–107.

[29] Pi, Z., and Khan, F. System design and network architecture for a millimeter-wave mobile broadband (mmb) system. In *Proc. of Sarnoff Symposium* (2011).

[30] Ramasamy, D., Ganti, R., and Madhow, U. On the capacity of picocellular networks. In *Proc. of ISIT* (2013).

[31] Ramasamy, D., Venkateswaran, S., and Madhow, U. Compressive tracking with 1000-element arrays: A framework for multi-Gbps mm wave cellular downlinks. In *Proc. of Allerton* (2012).

[32] Rangan, S., Rappaport, T., and Erkip, E. Millimeter-wave cellular wireless networks: Potentials and challenges. *Proc. of the IEEE 102*, 3 (March 2014), 366–385.

[33] Rappaport, T. S., Ben-Dor, E., Murdock, J. N., and Qiao, Y. 38GHz and 60 GHz angle-dependent propagation for cellular & peer-to-peer wireless communications. In *Proc. of ICC* (2012).

[34] Rappaport, T. S., Gutierrez, F., Ben-Dor, E., Murdock, J. N., Qiao, Y., and Tamir, J. I. Broadband millimeter-wave propagation measurements and models using adaptive-beam antennas for outdoor urban cellular communications. *IEEE TAP 61*, 4 (2013), 1850–1859.

[35] Singh, S., Mudumbai, R., and Madhow, U. Distributed coordination with deaf neighbors: efficient medium access for 60 GHz mesh networks. In *Proc. of Infocom* (2010).

[36] Singh, S., Mudumbai, R., and Madhow, U. Interference analysis for highly directional 60-ghz mesh networks: The case for rethinking medium access control. *IEEE/ACM ToN 19*, 5 (oct. 2011).

[37] Smulders, P., and Correia, L. Characterisation of propagation in 60 ghz radio channels. *Electronics & communication engineering journal 9*, 2 (1997), 73–80.

[38] Tie, X., Ramachandran, K., and Mahindra, R. On 60 ghz wireless link performance in indoor environments. In *Proc. of PAM* (2012).

[39] Violette, E., Espeland, R., and Hand, G. R. Millimeter-wave urban and suburban propagation measurements using narrow and wide bandwidth channel probes. *NASA STI/Recon Technical Report 86* (1985), 25683.

[40] Wiltse, J. Corrections to published curves for atmospheric attenuation in the 10 to 1000 ghz region. In *Proc. of ISAP* (1997).

[41] Zhang, H., Venkateswaran, S., and Madhow, U. Channel modeling and mimo capacity for outdoor millimeter wave links. In *Proc. of WCNC* (2010).

[42] Zhou, X., Zhang, Z., Zhu, Y., Li, Y., Kumar, S., Vahdat, A., Zhao, B. Y., and Zheng, H. Mirror mirror on the ceiling: Flexible wireless links for data centers. In *Proc. of SIGCOMM* (2012).

A Vehicle-based Measurement Framework for Enhancing Whitespace Spectrum Databases

Tan Zhang#, Ning Leng$, Suman Banerjee#
University of Wisconsin-Madison
{tzhang, suman}@cs.wisc.edu#, leng@stat.wisc.edu$

ABSTRACT

The present TV whitespace networks rely on spectrum occupancy databases to determine their operating channels. In this paper, we show that such databases cause non-negligible wastage of whitespace spectrum. We also report that whitespace channels can have very different quality due to interference from secondary devices and the leakage from TV broadcasts. Such disparity in channel quality is not captured by existing databases. We propose the use of spectrum measurements to overcome the above limitations of databases. In particular, we describe a system called V-Scope that leverages spectrum sensors on public vehicles to collect and report measurements from the road. These measurements are used as "anchor points" to construct various models to better determine whitespace spectrum, estimate its channel quality, and validate locations of primary and secondary devices.

We have deployed our system on a single metro bus traveling across a mid-sized US city. Based on measurements collected at above 1 million locations over 120 square-km area, we find that a commercial database causes under-utilization of certain whitespace channels over a large area (up to 71% measured locations). Our system can reclaim this spectrum wastage at up to 59% locations, correctly selecting all the suitable whitespace channels at 72 – 83% locations, and achieving a localization accuracy between 16 – 27m.

Categories and Subject Descriptors

C.4 [**Performance of Systems**]: Design studies, Measurement techniques

Keywords

TV Whitespaces; Spectrum Database; Vehicular Sensing; Propagation Model; Channel Quality; Localization

1. INTRODUCTION

Through recent rulings, various spectrum regulatory agencies across the world have opened up a wide swath of spectrum in the UHF television band (512 MHz - 698 MHz), commonly referred to as TV whitespaces, for unlicensed use. As demand for mobile and wireless connectivity continues to grow, such spectrum is going to be particularly attractive to address continued spectrum crunch. One of the fundamental issues in utilizing TV whitespace spectrum is to accurately determine vacant and high-quality channels. As per FCC's ruling [5], the secondary, whitespace devices must not interfere with licensed transmissions from primary spectrum incumbents, i.e., TV broadcasts and licensed wireless microphones. A current FCC-preferred mechanism for determining vacant channels is to have secondary devices to query *spectrum occupancy databases*. These databases are operated by some third-party companies following the FCC's guideline. They rely on a *same*, widely-used propagation model (R6602 [3]) to predict the coverage contour of TV broadcasts. In addition, they set up a fixed (2km) protection contour around licensed microphones and reserve two channels nationwide for their exclusive usage. A channel is concluded to be whitespace if a secondary device is outside the predicted contours of all the primary devices.

Being based solely on a propagation model, such databases are likely to have errors in predicting the availability of whitespace spectrum. Further, the databases have no attempt to distinguish the quality of whitespace channels, nor are they responsible for validating the operating locations of primary and secondary devices. In this work, we explore the use of spectrum measurements combined with propagation models for augmenting databases to i) better determine whitespace spectrum, ii) estimate the quality of whitespace channels, and iii) localize primary and secondary devices.

In particular, we present *V-Scope* (Vehicular Spectrum Scope), a measurement system that leverages public transit buses to carry spectrum sensors and collect measurements opportunistically as they travel [1]. The unique advantage of this approach is that each mobile sensor can add a proportional volume of useful measurements over a relatively *large* area. In addition, these measurements are likely to remain useful for some time, especially for TV broadcasts with a stable signal strength (e.g., < 5dB variation across a 6-week period). We therefore utilize these opportunistic measurements to refine various signal strength models, which can be used by existing databases to efficiently manage outdoor whitespaces.

Whitespace database limitations and V-Scope approach: Existing databases have inevitable inaccuracy in predicting the signal strength of primary devices. This is because the underlying propagation model is unable to capture the environment-induced variation, e.g., shadowing and multipath fading of specific contours, objects, and topologies. Since protecting primary users is at the top

[1]Of course, public transit buses are just one of many possibilities for vehicles that can carry spectrum sensors; other potential examples are mail delivery trucks, taxicabs, and many other third party services that scour different city roads.

MobiCom'14, September 7-11, 2014, Maui, HI, USA.

http://dx.doi.org/10.1145/2639108.2639114.

priority, the databases have to use a very *conservative* model configuration for predicting the coverage of primary devices, which causes under-utilization of some whitespace channels over large area (up to 71%). V-Scope uses two related techniques to improve the accuracy of databases with spectrum measurements. (i) It uses an enhanced version of feature detection to accurately detect primary signals while measuring their power up to the FCC-mandated sensing threshold (-114dBm [5]). (ii) Based on the measured power of primary devices, V-Scope refines the parameters of a propagation model, which can be used by databases to better predict the signal strength of primary devices. In our design, we have developed a *region specific model fitting* procedure to construct a fine-tuned propagation model for each local environment, and adopted a weighted regression algorithm to tolerate the non-uniform distribution of vehicular measurements in model fitting.

Additional enhancements to databases: V-Scope can provide databases with two additional functions enabled by these measurements. First, it allows databases to estimate the quality of whitespace channels. Our measurements show that the noise power in whitespace channels can differ by 40dB at a given location, which can significantly affect the performance of a whitespace link. The large variation in channel quality is contributed by the *co-channel interference* from unlicensed devices (whitespace devices and unlicensed microphones), and *adjacent-channel* leakage from TV broadcasts. Existing databases can not predict this co-channel interference because the precise power information of unlicensed devices is not available. Similarly, they are not able to estimate the leakage of TV broadcasts that depends on specific hardware attributes of a TV transmitter, e.g., sharpness of the front-end filter. To predict co-channel interference, V-Scope uses the same model fitting procedure described above to construct signal strength models for each unlicensed device. For adjacent-channel leakage, V-Scope constructs a leakage model based on an inherent power relationship between a TV signal and its leakage, which is identified by measurements. This model takes the predicted power of a TV broadcast to accurately estimate its leakage power at a same location.

The second function offered by V-Scope is to localize primary and secondary devices. This location information is necessary for constructing propagation models to predict the availability and quality of whitespace channels. However, existing databases do not store such information for most of unlicensed devices [2]. It may also have inaccurate information for primary devices due to various reasons such as incorrect entries to databases and transmitter reallocation. V-Scope utilizes the measured signal strength of these devices to pinpoint their location, thereby providing database operators additional means to obtain and validate such information. We leverage a RSSI modeling technique commonly used in indoor localization systems [1, 16]. An unique challenge in applying this technique to our outdoor scenario is to correctly capture the *large-scale path loss* in front of environment-induced variation, e.g., terrain elevation, shadowing (§ 3.4). Existing model based techniques use all the measurements *indiscriminately* to construct a propagation model. This model is consequently biased by a noisy propagation trend leading to large error (up to 100m). We have enhanced the standard approach by carefully selecting measurements from *certain radiation sectors* and constructing a *sector-specific* model based on the chosen sectors to improve localization accuracy.

While our opportunistic wardriving approach has some unique advantages in collecting wide area measurements, a similar goal can certainly be achieved by other approaches such as local spectrum sensing and crowd-sourcing mobile whitespace devices. Regardless of how measurements are collected, most of our proposed techniques remain useful for enhancing databases based on these measurements. In addition, our techniques can be beneficial to indoor whitespace determination systems like WISER [23].

Key contributions: We have deployed V-Scope on a single public transit bus traveling in a mid-sized US city for a 6-week period. Since our bus operator tends to rotate their buses through multiple routes in the course of each day, we have been able to collect spectrum measurements at more than one million distinct locations (with different pairs of latitude and longitude reported by a GPS device) over a 120 sq. km. area in and around our city.

Based on these measurements and the combination of our proposed techniques, we make the following contributions: (i) we show that commercial databases that are based solely on propagation models cause under-utilization of whitespace spectrum over a wide area (up to 71% measured locations for protecting TV and 70% locations for protecting microphones); (ii) V-Scope can reduce spectrum waste in protecting TV broadcasts by up to 59% locations; (iii) It can identify all the suitable whitespace channels at 72 – 83% locations under different channel quality constraints; and (iv) V-Scope can pinpoint TV-band devices at various locations with low error (16 – 27m), improving state-of-the-art localization techniques by 1.2 – 3.5× in outdoor scenario.

2. LIMITATION OF EXISTING SPECTRUM OCCUPANCY DATABASES

In this section, we motivate the design of V-Scope by demonstrating the two major limitations in existing spectrum databases. First, to tolerate the inaccuracy of propagation models, the databases assign very conservative protection contours for primary devices, which cause non-negligible wastage in whitespace utilization. Second, they are agnostic to the quality of whitespace channels, which can differ significantly at a given location, and thus can have a large impact on the performance of a whitespace network. We start by describing our measurement setup and datasets.

2.1 Measurement setup

Our current deployment consists of a server and a client as shown in Figure 1. The client has been deployed on a metro bus traveling in and around a mid-sized US city for a 6-week period. It uses a laptop to configure a portable spectrum analyzer (WSA4000 [20]) for collecting spectrum samples (FFTs) in all the UHF channels. An omni-directional TV antenna with 0dB gain is used to capture signals from all the directions. Based on these spectrum samples of a channel, the laptop performs some real-time analysis (§ 3.1), i.e., primary detection and power estimation, while obtaining the measured location from a GPS module. It uploads the GPS reading and measurement results to our server over cellular networks. The server is situated in our laboratory, with an Ethernet to receive the measurement results. It queries a commercial database [19] at measured locations to evaluate the database's accuracy.

Datasets: Using this measurement setup, we have collected three datasets from different vehicles. Table 1 summarizes their salient features. *Dataset A* is our main dataset collected from the metro bus, and covers about one million distinct locations over a 120 sq. km. area. The data consists of signal type, power and the database's prediction for all (30) UHF channels at each measured location. We will use this dataset to evaluate the performance of the database and V-Scope as well as studying whitespace channel quality. *Dataset B* contains measurements in a whitespace channel where our whitespace radio was transmitting 12Mbps UDP packets using the 802.11 baseband technology. This whitespace device

[2]Only those fixed, high-power whitespace devices can register their operating locations in the databases [5].

Dataset	Measured Locations	Coverage (sq. km.)	Channels	Vehicle	Target Device
A	1 million	120	30 UHF channels	A metro bus	All TV-band devices
B	3.5K	3	Channel 42	A personal vehicle	A 3.8W whitespace transmitter atop a 8-floor building
C	2.5K	2	Channel 28	A personal vehicle	A 100mW microphone in 5 buildings

Table 1: Summary of datasets.

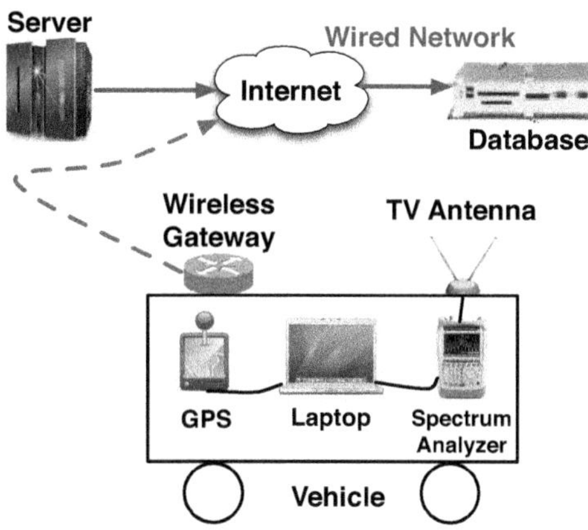

Figure 1: System architecture of V-Scope.

was mounted atop a 8-floor building with a transmit power of 3.8W. *Dataset C* contains measurements in a whitespace channel for a microphone device transmitting at 100mW in 5 different buildings at a downtown area. Dataset B and C were collected from a personal vehicle driving along multiple road stretches, and comprise the signal type and channel power at each measured location. We will use them to benchmark our measurement clustering algorithm (§ 3.2) and localization technique (§ 3.4).

2.2 Inefficiency in protecting primary users

We study the performance of a commercial database (SpectrumBridge [19]) in predicting TV and licensed microphones respectively. Note that other FCC-approved databases would produce the same prediction results. Our focus is to understand its performance tradeoff between the safety in primary protection and efficiency in whitespace utilization. All the evaluation in this section is based on dataset A unless otherwise mentioned.

Performance in protecting TV broadcasts: Borrowing the definition from prior work [10], we divide the errors in whitespace determination into two types, i.e., *false positive* and *false negative* as summarized in Table 2. A false positive is a location where the database mis-predicts an occupied channel (with measured power $\geq$ -114dBm) as whitespaces, whereas the opposite being a false negative. We find negligible false positives (<0.29%) of database in predicting all the TV broadcasts, which is similar to a prior report [10]. Thus, existing databases can reliably protect TV broadcasts. However, Figure 2(a) shows a 13–71% false negative rate in half of these channels, indicating these channels being unnecessarily blocked for unlicensed usage over a wide area. Figure 2(b) shows a typical spatial distribution of false negatives in one such channel, along with those locations with this channel correctly predicted to be whitespace (true negatives). We note most of these false negatives are at the north-east side, which is at the *closer* side to the TV tower. Thus, we believe these false negatives are caused by over-provisioning the protection contour of TV broadcasts.

Performance in protecting licensed microphones: To quantify false negatives in protecting licensed microphones, we calculate the power of about 200k measurements collected in their reserved channels. Figure 2(c) shows that about 70% measurements have very low power, suggesting that microphone signals are unlikely to be present in many reserved locations. While these wardriving measurements might not capture every instance of microphone transmissions, they are statistically sufficient to suggest that licensed microphones are not making efficient use of their reserved channel, possibly due to coarse-grained reservation periods (24 hours) and over-sized protection contours (2km). On the other hand, we find no other type of signals in these channels, suggesting the database to be sufficient in protecting licensed microphones.

	Ground truth	Prediction
False Positive	Occupied	Vacant
False Negative	Vacant	Occupied

Table 2: Two types of errors in whitespace determination.

2.3 Variation in whitespace channel quality

We now study the variation in whitespace channel quality, which are caused by *co-channel interference* from secondary devices and *adjacent-channel leakage* from TV broadcasts.

Magnitude of quality variation: Figure 3 shows the CDF of absolute differences in noise power between the best channel and the worst channel at each measured location. *Overall*, *TV-adjacent*, and *Non-adjacent* choose the worst channel from all the whitespace channels, adjacent channels to TV broadcasts, and non-adjacent channels, respectively. All of them pick the best channel from all the whitespace channels. We observe that the worst channel in *Overall* has a 8dB higher power in median and 17dB higher power in 90-quartile compared to the best channel. Such variation is currently contributed by unlicensed microphone transmission and TV broadcast leakage. We also note the non-adjacent channels generally have better quality than adjacent channels due to the absence of broadcast leakage. However, its worst channel still has 8dB higher power than the best channel at 10% locations due to unlicensed microphones. We envision this quality variation to become more prominent with the future proliferation of whitespace devices.

Prevalence of quality variation: Figure 4 shows the CDF of the amount of whitespace spectrum below different channel power based on our measurements and the database. We observe that for about 80% locations, the amount of whitespace spectrum identified by measurements is similar across different power thresholds, which is about 18 – 24MHz more than that predicted by the database [3]. For the rest 20% locations, this measured amount differs by 12 – 48MHz (2 – 8 channels) between the highest and the lowest power threshold (-65dBm and -80dBm). Thus, whitespace devices are likely to operate in a low-quality channel at these locations, if they randomly pick a channel suggested by the database.

[3]Here we did not consider spectrum wastage in protecting licensed microphones.

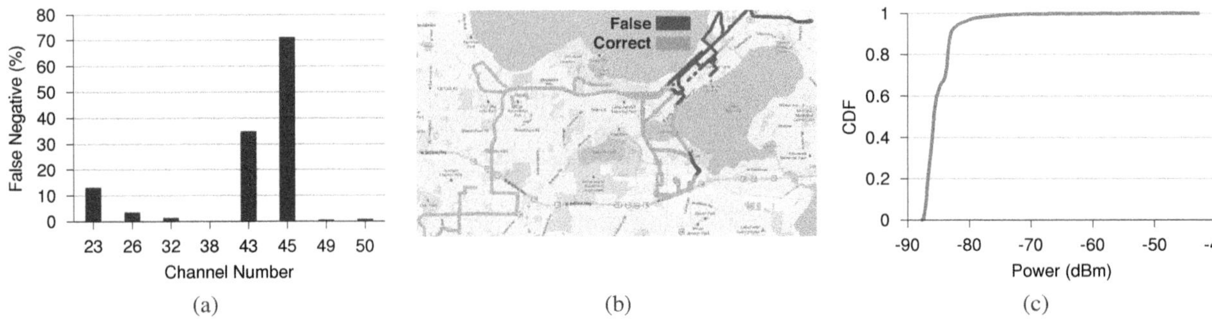

Figure 2: Wastage of whitespace spectrum by existing databases for protecting primary incumbents. (a) False negative rates in predicting TV broadcasts. (b) Spatial distribution of false negatives and true negatives in channel 43. (c) CDF of power measurements collected in reserved channels for licensed microphones.

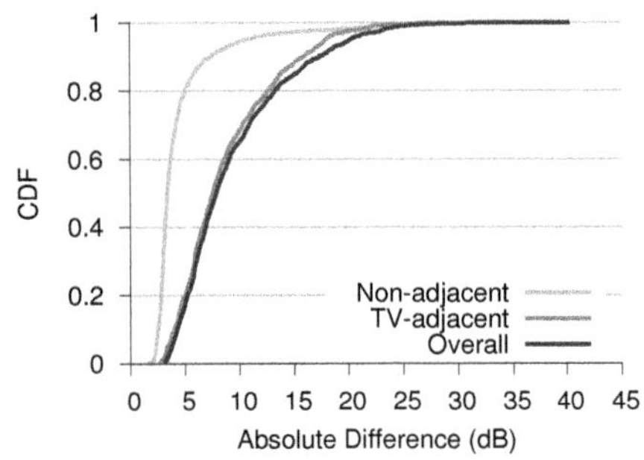

Figure 3: CDF of the maximum power differences of whitespace channels at different measured locations.

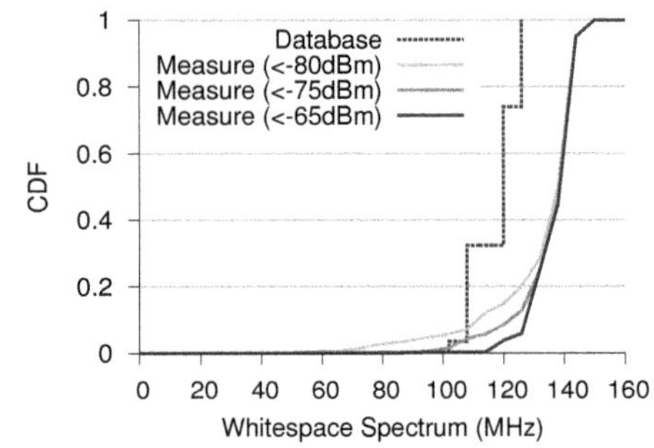

Figure 4: CDF of the available whitespace spectrum at different locations based on measurements and database prediction.

3. V-SCOPE DESIGN

V-Scope is based on our measurement architecture described in § 2.1, and consists of following components to augment databases with measurements — i) primary detection, ii) measurement clustering, iii) propagation model refinement, iv) localization, and v) leakage model construction. Figure 5 shows its operation flow.

Overview: Our proposed system leverages a few clients mounted on public vehicles to detect primary and secondary devices based on spectrum samples collected in different UHF channels (§ 3.1). The detection results that include the device type and and power of each channel are forwarded to our server. The server groups these measurements according to different device types in each UHF channel, and segregates each group for individual devices (§ 3.2). It then localizes those (secondary) devices if their location is not available in databases (§ 3.4). Using each device's location and its associated measurements, the server constructs a propagation model that is tailored to local environment to predict its signal strength (§ 3.3). It also builds a model to predict the power of adjacent-channel leakage from TV broadcasts (§ 3.5). To predict whitespace channels in the vicinity of measurements, the databases can use our refined propagation models to better estimate the coverage of TV broadcasts. Similarly, the databases may use our models constructed for secondary users to predict their in-band interference, while leveraging the leakage model to estimate the adjacent-channel leakage from TV broadcasts. The sum of the predicted power of these interference signals is the quality of a whitespace channel. To predict for those locations far from measurements, the databases may switch back to use its default model (R6602). Finally, we envision the databases to use its current mechanism for protecting licensed microphones due to the limitations of our wardriving approach as will be discussed in § 3.1. We now explain each of these components in detail.

3.1 Zoom-in pilot tracking algorithm for primary detection

Our measurement module aims to utilize spectrum samples for detecting different types of primary transmitters and unlicensed devices (i.e., whitespace devices and unlicensed microphones). We accomplish this task by leveraging feature detection algorithms [8, 11] that identify different signals based on their spectral features. While such a technique performs well for detecting unlicensed signals, we find non-trivial challenges in satisfying the FCC's requirement for detecting primary signals at up to -114dBm in our measurement setup. Such a stringent detection threshold is to tolerate the sensing inaccuracy caused by fading and shadowing, and to take account the transmission range of a whitespace device. We use TV detection to illustrate this challenge and our specific solution.

Existing algorithms detect a TV signal by tracking its pilot in the spectral domain. A pilot is a set of preambles in a TV packet, which produces a predominant peak at a fixed frequency. Unfortunately, for a TV signal close to the detection threshold, even this peak can be overwhelmed by noise and thus unable to be captured. To illustrate this, we attenuated a TV signal to be about -114dBm, while collecting its spectrum over a 6MHz TV channel with the largest number of FFTs (32768) available in our high-end spectrum analyzer [20]. As shown in Figure 6(a), the pilot of this TV spectrum is hard to be distinguished from the noise floor. This is because the noise spectral density is -159dBm/Hz in our spectrum analyzer. When using 32768 FFTs to represent a 6MHz band, the bandwidth per FFT bin is 183Hz (6MHz/32768) and thus the noise power per bin is about -135dBm. As will be discussed later, the pilot power is usually about 10 - 15dB lower than the total power of a TV signal, and thus can be as low as -129dBm. Comparing to the -135dBm noise floor, the 6dB stronger pilot is not robust enough for toler-

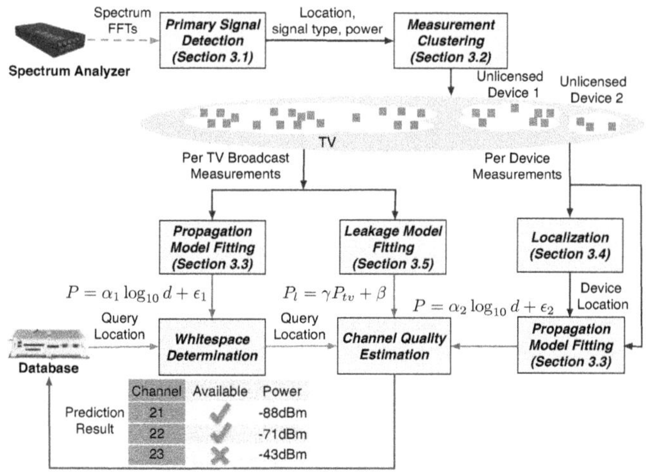

Figure 5: Flow of operations in V-Scope.

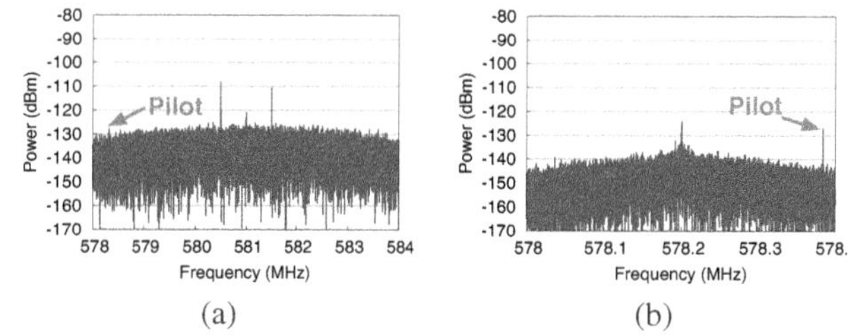

Figure 6: Different spectrum captures of a -114dBm digital TV signal. (a) Full-channel capture; (b) Zoom-in capture at the first 488KHz band. Both captures consist of 32768 FFTs.

Detected / Ground truth	Digital TV	Analog TV	Microphone
Digital TV	94.9%	0.7%	4.4%
Analog TV	0.5%	97.4%	2.1%
Microphone	1.2%	0.7%	98.1%

Table 3: Accuracy of primary detection algorithm.

ating the signal strength fluctuation due to fading and shadowing. Prior systems [11] have overcome this challenge by leveraging low-noise amplifiers to amplify a weak signal by a fixed amount (e.g., 20dB). But such an approach is observed to cause *saturation* of a spectrum analyzer when capturing strong signals (>-35dBm), leading to distorted spectrum that can significantly degrade detection performance. The alternative solution of using tunable amplifiers would largely increase design complexity and hardware cost.

Zoom-in pilot tracking algorithm: Instead of resorting to signal amplification, V-Scope improves the sensitivity of feature detection by capturing the most prominent portion of spectrum with the available FFTs. To detect a TV signal, for example, we configure a spectrum analyzer to capture at a narrow band (488KHz) around its pilot frequency. This can effectively improve spectral resolution while reducing the noise floor, thereby producing a clear pilot peak as shown in Figure 6(b). Since this peak is well distinguishable at the detection threshold after zoom-in, V-Scope uses it as an unique feature to detect TV signals.

The detected pilot is, however, insufficient to determine whether the power of a TV signal to be above or below the -114dBm threshold. We also need the precise power information of a primary signal for constructing its signal strength models (§ 3.3). To achieve this goal, V-Scope leverages the power of a TV pilot to estimate its total power. According to the digital and analog TV standards [2], there is a fixed power offset between a TV signal and its pilot. For example, the pilot of a digital TV is required to be 11.3dB lower than its total power. Figure 7 shows this relationship indeed holds for a DTV signal at a wide range of power, albeit with some variation (10 – 15dB). Thus, V-Scope computes the total power of a TV signal by adding to its pilot power a constant offset η (20dB in our implementation). The estimated power is then compared with the -114dBm detection threshold to determine TV whitespaces.

Our proposed technique can be applied to microphone detection in a similar way. Briefly, we start by examining the 6MHz wide spectrum of each TV channel for detecting potential microphone tones that are narrow spikes carrying audio signals. Since these spikes can also be a result of noise fluctuation, we perform a narrow-band capture around each spike, extracting various features from its zoom-in spectrum for further validation. Once a microphone signal is confirmed, we use the power of its tones in the zoom-in spectrum as its total power because these tones contain most of the power ($> 95\%$) of a microphone signal. Despite the effectiveness of this detection technique, V-Scope might not be able to sense all the intermittent microphone transmissions because a client visits each location only for a short amount of time. To guarantee sufficient protection, we envision the databases to protect licensed microphones as is. As our future work, we intend to enhance our system with static sensors deployed in the proximity of microphone devices to reliably capture their transmission.

To benchmark the accuracy of our detection algorithms, we collected spectrum data from 30 UHF channels at multiple locations. We established the ground truth results by using a TV receiver and our microphone transmitters. The identified primary signals were further attenuated for constructing spectrum traces at a wide range of power (-40dBm to -114dBm). A standard cross validation was then performed by randomly choosing 90% spectrum traces to detect the rest 10%. Table 3 shows the accuracy of our detection algorithm. We observe reasonably low error rates ($<5\%$) in detecting different types of signals.

Summarizing, our measurement procedure works as follows. (a) A client captures spectrum fragments around pilot frequencies in each UHF channel. (b) It extracts a potential pilot by searching for the maximum FFT bin and including all the surrounding bins with power above a threshold. (c) From the obtained FFT bins, several features (e.g., power, center frequency) are extracted and fed to a classifier for detecting TV pilots and broadcast type (analog or digital). (d) If a pilot is detected, the client estimates its total power by adding a specific power offset η to the pilot power. (e) The estimated power is then compared with -114dBm threshold to determine the presence of TV signals. (f) If no TV signal is detected in a given channel, the client further captures a full-channel spectrum to detect microphones and unlicensed devices while measuring their in-band power. g) If the full-channel spectrum contain potential microphone tones, a narrow-band capture is performed around each spike for validation. The entire procedure takes less than 1 second for processing all 30 UHF channels at a location, and produces results of *signal type* and *power* in each channel.

3.2 Measurement clustering

Since a V-Scope client has classified measurements to different device types (i.e., TV, microphone, whitespace devices), our clustering module further segregates measurements among devices of a

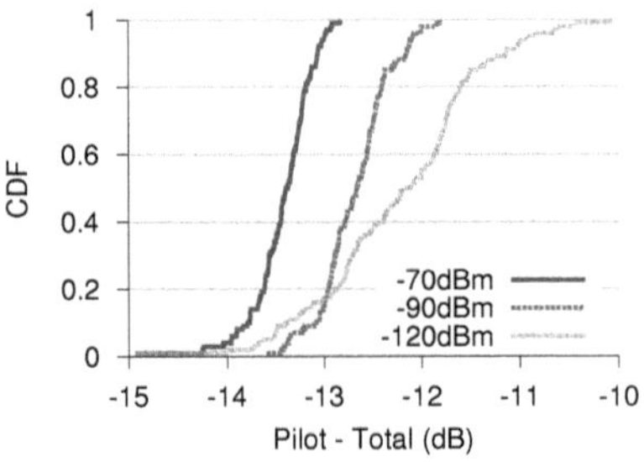

Figure 7: CDF of differences between the power of a digital TV signal and that of its pilot.

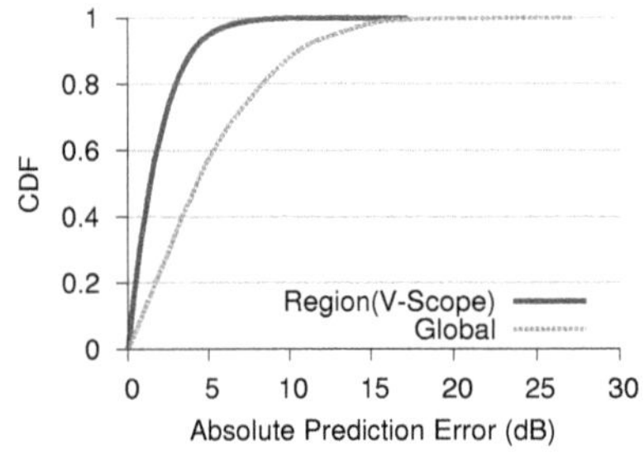

Figure 8: Accuracy of a fitted region model and a global model in predicting the power of TV signals.

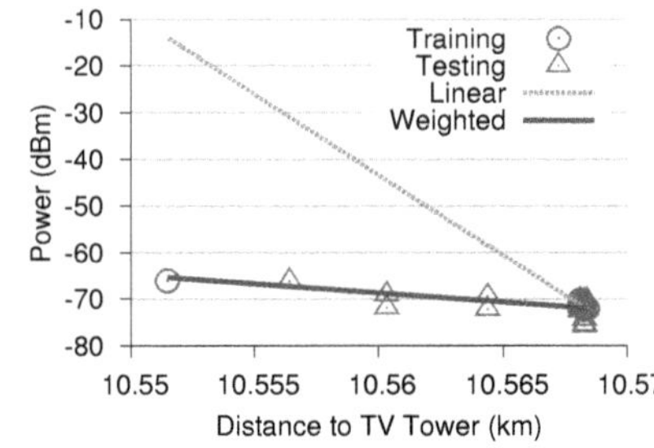

Figure 9: Region models fitted by linear regression and weighted regression in predicting a TV broadcast.

same type. We developed a preliminary algorithm that leverages k-medoids clustering based on the *power* and *inter-distance* of measurements. k-medoids clustering aims to minimize the sum of pairwise dissimilarities of measurements in each cluster. We define the dissimilarity metric between pair of measurements using gower dissimilarity score [6]. An unique feature of gower dissimilarity score is its capability of assigning different weights to observations. By assigning higher weights to stronger measurements, our algorithm is robust to noise and outliers in choosing the center of clusters. Specially, we take only measurements with power $P_n >$ -90 dB to reduce computational overhead. With N selected measurements, we first calculate distance between each pair of measures. This gives us a N-by-N symmetric matrix, in which the (i, n)th entry d_{in} indicates physical distance between measure i and n. We call columns of this matrix as variables, gower dissimilarity score between the ith and jth measure (row) is defined as a weighted sum of dissimilarities for each variable $\frac{\sum_{n=1,\ldots,N} w_n D_{ij}^n}{\sum_{n=1,\ldots,N} w_n}$, in which D_{ij}^n is defined as $|d_{in} - d_{jn}|$ and the weight of variable n is defined as $w_n = log(P_n + 90)$. We iteratively apply this algorithm with different number of clusters k between 1 – k_{max}, and determine the optimal k that can maximize the *silhouette* distance [17]. k_{max} is set to be 100 in our implementation and a R package [9] is used to perform clustering. To evaluate this algorithm, we merged groups of measurements corresponding to different transmission locations of our microphone device in dataset C. We applied our algorithm on the aggregated measurements, and found only 6% measurements mis-classified to a different location. One limitation of our current approach is that mis-classification may happen when devices are close to each other. However, the mis-classified measurements are generally far from a device location and have relatively lower power, thus imposing limited impact on the overall prediction accuracy of V-Scope.

3.3 Region model for predicting signal strength of different devices

Using the clustered measurements of each device, V-Scope refines the parameters of a propagation model that can be used to better predict its signal strength in the vicinity of measurements. To choose an appropriate model, we note that most of the UHF-band models can be generalized in a form of $P = \alpha \log_{10}(d) + \epsilon$, where P is the power of a device at a reception location, d is the distance between this location to the device, α is the rate at which the signal power attenuates over an increasing distance, and ϵ captures both the transmission power of a device and the fixed attenuation of environmental shadowing. The difference of these models lies in how the parameters α, ϵ are determined, e.g., based on antenna height (in Egli, Hata) and various environmental factors (in Longley-Rice, R6602). Since the measured signal strength can best reflect a propagation environment, V-Scope uses this general model and calculates α, ϵ based on measurements.

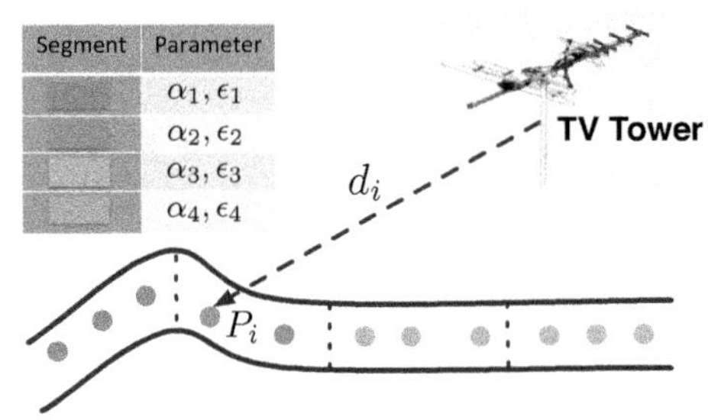

Figure 10: Illustration of region models in V-Scope.

A standard model fitting procedure [13] solves α, ϵ by plugging measurements P_i, d_i into a given propagation model. This forms a set of linear equations $P_i = \alpha \log_{10} d_i + \epsilon$. It uses least-squares linear regression to calculate α, ϵ, with the objective of minimizing the squared sum of fitting errors $\sum_i (P_i - \alpha \log_{10} d_i - \epsilon)^2$. V-Scope improves this approach by (i) fitting an individual set of parameters for each local area to better model its propagation environment, and (ii) performing a weighted regression to avoid fitting bias caused by non-uniform distribution of vehicular measurements.

Region-specific model: V-Scope groups measurements into road segments and fits a different set of parameters for each segment as shown in Figure 10. The motivation is that these regions are likely to have different propagation characteristics, especially in an urban environment. This region-specific variation can hardly be captured by a global propagation model using a single set of parameters. To demonstrate this, we fit different α and ϵ based on measured signal strength of TV broadcasts in each 100m road segment. We compare this model with a global model fitted with all the measurements in predicting the strength of TV signals. Figure 8 shows that our region model achieves a median error of 1.4dB and 75 quartile error of 2.6dB, which are $3\times$ and $2.9\times$ lower than a global model. Thus, V-Scope fits a different set of model parameters (α, ϵ) to better capture each local propagation environment.

Weighted regression fitting: In fitting a region model, we note the non-evenly spaced vehicular measurements can degrade the performance of linear regression. Since a public vehicle drives at a varying speed and stops quite often, V-Scope collects measurements at non-uniform density. This causes linear regression to produce a biased model that favors *densely* measured area, and has

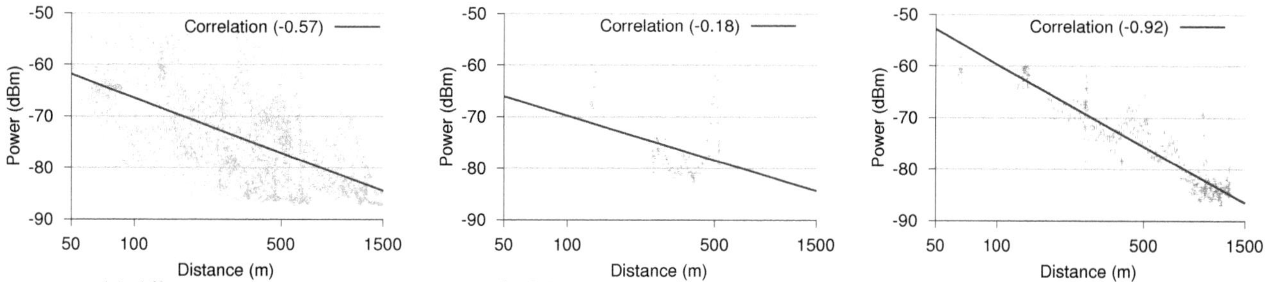

(a) All measurements. (b) Measurements in Sector 1. (c) Measurements in Sector 2.

Figure 11: Measured signal strength vs. propagation range (in log scale) of a whitespace transmitter.

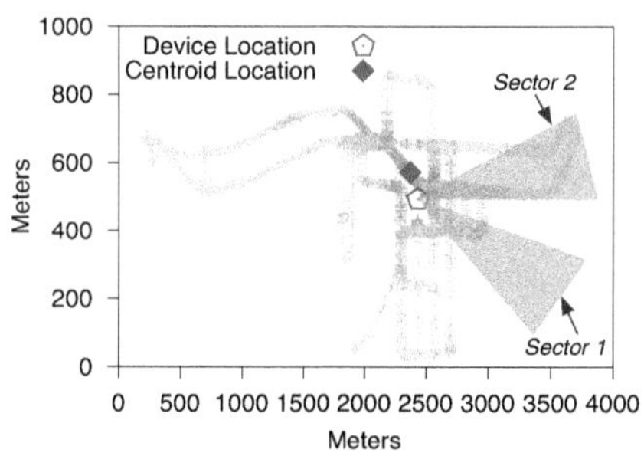

Figure 12: Measurement locations for the whitespace transmitter. A darker color indicates higher power. Two radiation sectors in Figure 11 are also marked.

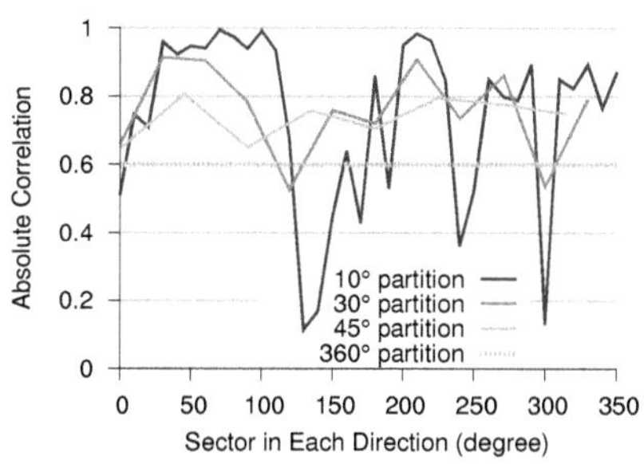

Figure 13: Absolute correlation of all the sectors partitioned from the centroid location with different angles.

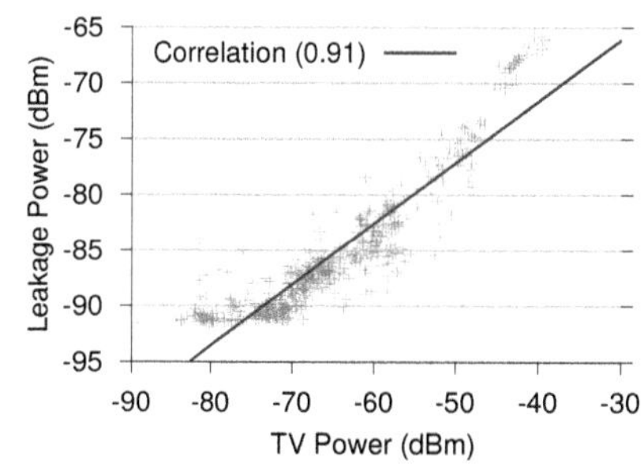

Figure 14: Power of a TV broadcast vs. power of its adjacent-channel leakage at different locations.

large errors at *sparsely* measured area. The underlying reason is that linear regression aims to minimize the squared sum of fitting error; the area with sparse measurements contribute less to this squared sum, thus being under-fitted. Figure 9 shows an example where we fit a model for a 100m region with most of training measurements collocated at a bus top. We observe that the model fitted by linear regression has up to 36dB error in predicting TV signal strength at the testing locations.

V-Scope uses weighted regression to compensate the effect of non-uniform measurement density in model fitting. The algorithm assigns a weight W_i to each measurement i, with the objective of minimizing the weighted squared sum of fitting errors $\sum_i W_i(P_i - \alpha \log_{10} d_i - \epsilon)$. A higher weight can indicate greater importance in fitting a measurement. Therefore, we assign *higher* weights to *sparse* measurements to compensate for the difference in measurement density in model fitting. To accurately capture this measurement sparsity, we calculate the weight of a measurement based on its total distance to other measurements $W_i = \sum_j dist(i,j)$. Figure 9 shows our model fitted by weighted regression achieves high prediction accuracy at all the testing locations.

To recapitulate, our model fitting procedure first bins measurements of each device into road segments. For each segment, it computes a weight for each measurement based on its distance to other measurements. It then takes these measurements and their weights as the input to weighted least-squares regression for constructing region models.

The fitted model will then be used to predict for a m-by-m square-shape region centered around the measured road segment. The region size m is the length of the road segment. We will explore the performance tradeoff between the prediction accuracy and storage overhead of different region sizes in § 4.1. Finally, beyond the coverage of these regions, the database may use its default model (R6602) for predicting TV whitespaces.

3.4 Sector based localization

The above model fitting procedure requires the location of a transmitting device to calculate the distance d_i for each measurement. V-Scope leverages popular *RSSI modeling* techniques [1,16] to localize a device if its location is unknown or awaits validation. Our motivation of using this technique comes from its flexibility in localizing a device from arbitrarily measured locations, and the simplicity of using signal strength (RSSI) information that is readily available from spectrum measurements. Such an approach works similarly to model fitting. It uses signal strength measurements and a propagation model to form a set of equations $P_i = \alpha \log_{10} d_i + \epsilon$. Here d_i is replaced with $\sqrt[2]{(x_t - x_i)^2 + (y_t - y_i)^2}$, where (x_t, y_t) is the transmitter location and (x_i, y_i) is the location of each measurement. The algorithm solves $\alpha, \epsilon, x_t, y_t$ to estimate a device's location. V-Scope adapts this approach to outdoor scenario by (i) carefully selecting measurements in certain radiation sectors of a device and (ii) constructing a *sector-specific* model based on the chosen sectors.

While a RSSI modeling approach is reported to achieve a high accuracy within few meters in an indoor scenario, directly applying this technique to our outdoor area leads to large localization error (up to 100m in § 4.2.2). The reason is that its underlying propagation model matches poorly with the signal strength pattern of a transmitting device in an outdoor scenario. We use the wardriving measurements collected for our whitespace device in dataset B to demonstrate this. Figure 11(a) shows the received signal strength over different transmission ranges for all the measurements. A propagation model expects a *linear* trend of the measured signal strength P_i over an increasing distance $log_{10}d_i$, but we observe many measurements deviate from this trend (the fitted line). We use Pearson correlation coefficient to quantify the linearity of these measurements, with 1 and -1 being an extract positive and negative linear trend and 0 implying no correlation. We find the correlation value to be merely -0.57.

Such a poor linear trend is caused by surrounding environment, e.g., terrain elevation, obstacles, etc. To illustrate this, we decompose measurements according to different radiation sectors of the device with 10-degree angle as shown in Figure 12. Figure 11(b) is a scatter plot for measurements from one such sector. We observe a sharp drop of signal strength at a distance between 350 – 500m due to a building blocking the transmission, but a drastic increase in signal strength beyond 500m due to the rising terrain elevation coupled with diminishing blocking effect of the building at faraway locations. This environmental-induced variation can largely *perturb* a propagation model in capturing the large-scale path loss, leading to large localization error. Fortunately, we find measurements in some other radiation sectors present a less noisy propagation trend as show in Figure 11(c). This is owing to the environmental shadowing being unlikely to affect the signal along all the directions. Thus, V-Scope only uses measurements in a few sectors that present a good propagation trend for localization.

Localization procedure: Our proposed algorithm proceeds in five steps. (a) We use the *centroid* location of the *strongest* measurements (top 5dB) as the partitioning center, while grouping measurements into radiation sectors at a narrow angle (10 degree). The intuition behind this heuristic approach is that the centroid location is usually not far from a device's actual location (e.g., 100m in Figure 12); and by using a narrow angle, some radiation sectors are likely to "fall through" the gaps of a blocking environment, thus having measurements following a good propagation trend. To validate this intuition, Figure 13 shows the *absolute* correlation of measurements in different sectors partitioned at various angles for the whitespace device. We observe that the narrowest angle used in our implementation indeed leads to best correlation (>0.9) for some sectors. (c) Post partitioning, we calculate the Pearson correlation value between the measured signal strength and the transmission range for those sectors that have at least some measurements present. We then select the sectors with a high correlation value (top 0.1 bin) for localization. (d) Given these candidate sectors, we use a *sector-specific* model with different α_j, ϵ_j for each sector j. This is because these chosen sectors can still have a different propagation trend in slope and intercept due to environmental variation. We omit this result for the sake of brevity. (e) We construct linear equations based on measurements from all the chosen sectors, and solve x_t, y_t and all α_j, ϵ_j to estimate a device's location using an optimization function from a statistics package [15].

3.5 Adjacent-channel model for predicting TV broadcast leakage

V-Scope builds a model to predict the leakage power of a TV broadcast into its adjacent channels based on its in-band power [4]. It first identifies those locations with adjacent-channel measurements classified to be noise because the leakage is simply high-power noise. It then leverages a *linear* relationship between the measured power of this TV broadcast and that of its adjacent channel to construct the model. To demonstrate this power relationship, Figure 14 shows the power of a TV broadcast in channel 26 and that of its leakage in channel 27 at each chosen location. We observe that the leakage power increases approximately along a 45-degree line with TV power, and can be as high as -65dBm. The Pearson correlation between these datasets is 0.91. This prominent linear relationship comes from both a TV signal and its leakage being transmitted from a *same* location and at a power of *constant* difference. After traversing along similar paths to any location, their power still differ approximately by this amount leading to a linear trend between the in-band power and adjacent-channel power.

Since the specific leakage trend is different among TV transmitters, V-Scope constructs an individual model for each TV broadcast. The model takes the form $P_l = \gamma P_{tv} + \beta$, where P_{tv} and P_l are the power of a TV signal and its leakage at a given location, and γ, β are tunable parameters to capture the power relationship between these signals. V-Scope calculates γ, β by applying linear regression on the power measurements. To estimate the leakage of a TV broadcast at a given location, the databases can first use our region model to predict its in-band power P_{tv}, then leveraging the leakage model to predict P_l.

[4]Different TV broadcasts are usually allocated in far apart channels, and their adjacent channels therefore do not overlap.

4. EVALUATION

In this section, we evaluate the performance of V-Scope based on three datasets collected over a 120 square-km area in and around a US city as described in § 2.1. We start by evaluating the overall performance of V-Scope in § 4.1. We then benchmark the performance of individual components in § 4.2. Overall, we find V-Scope can reduce false negative rates for protecting TV broadcasts by up to 59%, identify all the suitable whitespace channels at 72 – 83% locations under different channel quality constraints, and localize unlicensed devices at various locations with an error of 16 – 27m.

Implementation: We have implemented the measurement collection module and all the data processing modules in 7500 lines of Python, and built a database query utility in 650 lines of C++.

Methodology: We apply a standard five-fold cross-validation by using 80% randomly selected measurements to construct V-Scope models. The fitted models are used to predict the power of TV broadcasts, unlicensed devices and adjacent-channel leakage at remaining measured (testing) locations. We compare the predicted power of TV broadcasts with the -114dBm threshold to determine TV whitespace, while combining the predicted power of unlicensed devices and adjacent-channel leakage to estimate the noise power of whitespace channels. We compared our predictions with ground truth results based on measurements at these testing locations. To evaluate localization, we use measurements for our whitespace device and microphones operating at various locations, with ground truth locations determined by a GPS device.

Evaluation metrics: We use a variety of metrics to evaluate the performance of V-Scope such as false positive and false negative rates in predicting the availability of TV whitespaces, number of inappropriate whitespace channels selected under different channel quality constraints, absolute error in predicted signal strength, localization error between the actual location and predicted location of different TV-band devices, etc.

4.1 Overall performance of V-Scope

We use dataset A to evaluate overall performance of V-Scope in predicting whitespace channels and estimating their quality. We quantify the gain of V-Scope over a FCC-approved database [19] that predicts whitespace channels based solely on a propagation model without distinguishing their quality. We also evaluate the performance of V-Scope models fitted under different region sizes. This can provide database operators with insights about the tradeoff between prediction accuracy and storage overhead in choosing an appropriate region size for different spectrum management tasks.

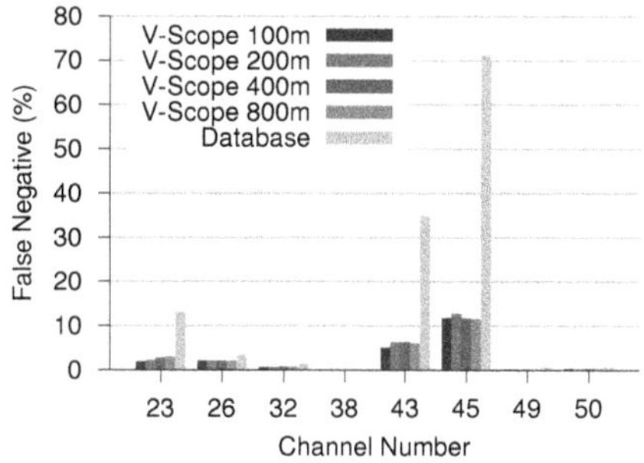

Figure 15: Fraction of locations under-utilized by V-Scope and the database for predicting different TV broadcasts.

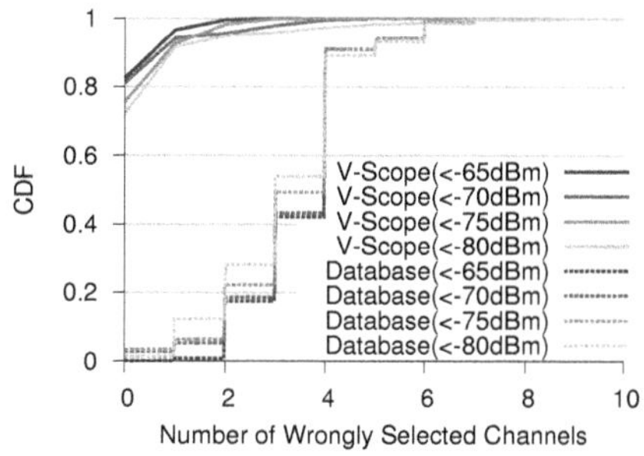

Figure 16: CDF of number of whitespace channels wrongly selected at different locations under various quality constraints.

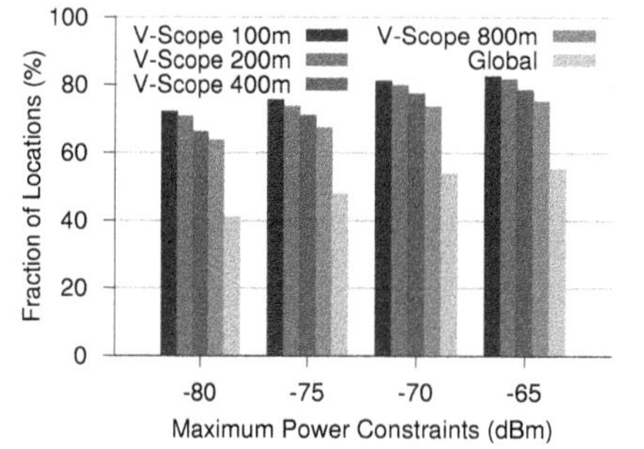

Figure 17: Fraction of locations where all the suitable channels are correctly selected by different V-Scope models.

Approach	Database	VS-100m	VS-200m	VS-400m	VS-800m
False Positive Rate	0.29%	0.29%	0.22%	0.17%	0.17%

Table 4: False positive rates of the database and V-Scope models fitted at different region sizes in predicting TV broadcasts.

4.1.1 Predicting TV whitespace spectrum

We start by quantifying the false negative rates of the database and V-Scope models fitted at different region sizes for predicting TV broadcast channels that are accessible at least in part of our measured area. Figure 15 shows that different V-Scope models can reclaim the spectrum wastage of the databases by up to 59% locations. We then present the false positive rates averaged across different broadcast channels for these approaches in Table 4. Compared to the conservative database, we find the V-Scope models are able to offer same or even better protection to primary users. One important observation is that the V-Scope models fitted under different region sizes present little difference in the accuracy of whitespace determination, e.g., $\leq$2% in false negative rate and $\leq$0.1% in false positive rate. This is because most of their differences in predicted signal strengths are masked when comparing them with the detection threshold. We may therefore use a large region size (e.g., 800m) to fit V-Scope models for TV broadcasts, thereby reducing the overhead of storing model parameters.

4.1.2 Selecting suitable whitespace channels

Using the predicted whitespace channels, we evaluate V-Scope and the database in selecting appropriate channels under different power constraints. A whitespace channel is deemed to be suitable if its interference power is below a given constraint. Such a quality constraint can be estimated by network operators based on parameters such as the distance of wireless links, transmission power, and the minimum signal-to-noise ratio (SNR) for decoding a received signal (under desired modulations).

Figure 16 shows the CDF of the number of wrongly selected channels at different locations for a 100m V-Scope model and the database under different quality constraints. Note that a 5dB increase in two consecutive power constraints can lead to a 15 – 30Mbps drop in the achievable PHY rates for the 802.11n technology [21]. Without attempting to distinguish channel quality, the database can select all the appropriate channels at less than 2% of the locations, and have 3 – 4 channels wrongly selected for 50% of the locations. In contrast, V-Scope correctly selects all the qualified whitespace channels at 72% – 83% locations, and mis-predicts at most 1 channel for 92% – 97% locations. The much higher accuracy suggests that V-Scope can help avoid most of the performance penalty on a whitespace network due to channel mis-selection.

Signal Type	25th	Median	75th	95th	99th
TV broadcast	0.2dB	0.5dB	1.1dB	3.2dB	7.7dB
Unlicensed signal	0.2dB	0.6dB	1.3dB	3.4dB	6.9dB
TV leakage	0.3dB	0.7dB	1.4dB	3.6dB	6.9dB

Table 5: Absolute error in predicting the power of different types of signals by a 100m V-Scope model.

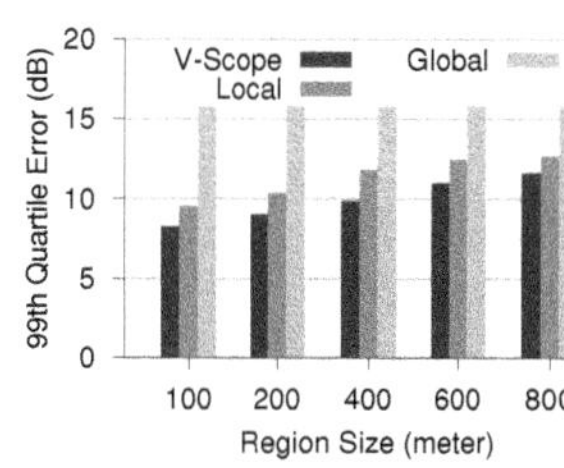

(a) 1-week dataset.

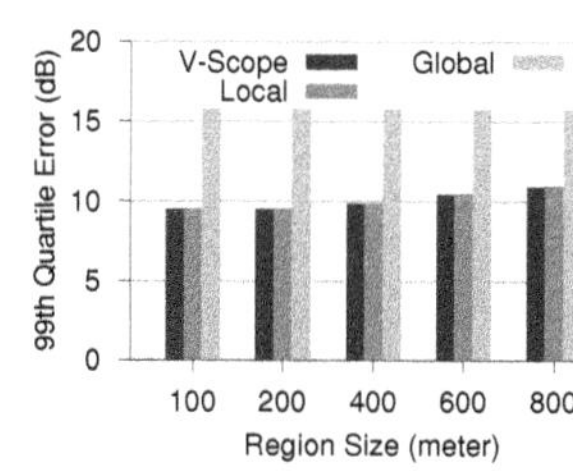

(b) 6-week dataset.

Figure 18: Accuracy in predicting the power of TV signals.

We break down the accuracy of V-Scope in predicting the power of different types of signals in Table 5. We note for all the signal types, the median error is below 0.7dB and a 95 quartile error below 3.6dB, thus explaining its high accuracy in channel selection.

We now study the impact of region sizes on the accuracy of V-Scope models for selecting suitable whitespace channels. Figure 17 shows the fraction of locations where all the appropriate channels are correctly identified by these models. We observe that the accuracy degrades at a larger region size. For example, a 800m region model correctly selects all the suitable channels at 8% – 11% fewer locations than a 100m region model, and a global model has 27% – 31% fewer such locations than a 100m model. This is because a model fitted for a larger region is not fine-tuned enough to capture local environment. The database operators may use this information to choose an appropriate region size for channel quality estimation based on *available storage* and *desired accuracy*.

4.2 Microbenchmarks of V-Scope

We now benchmark the performance of individual components in V-Scope, which are region-specific model in predicting TV broadcasts, sector-based localization algorithm, region-specific model in predicting unlicensed signals, and adjacent-channel models in predicting the leakage of TV broadcasts.

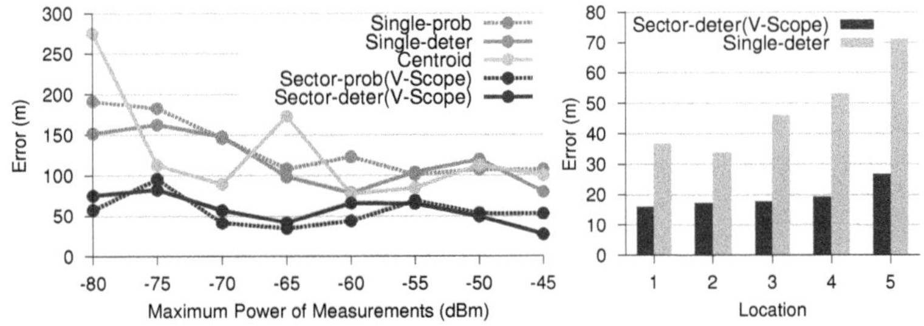

Figure 19: Accuracy in localizing a whitespace device (left) and microphone device (right).

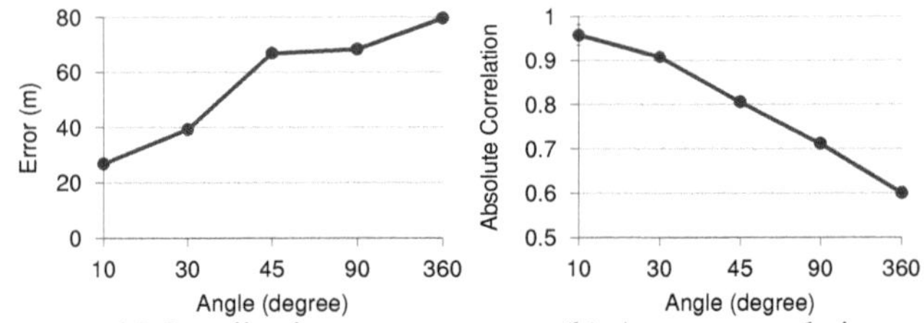

(a) Localization error. (b) Average correlation.

Figure 20: Performance of different partitioning angles used by our approach for localizing the whitespace device.

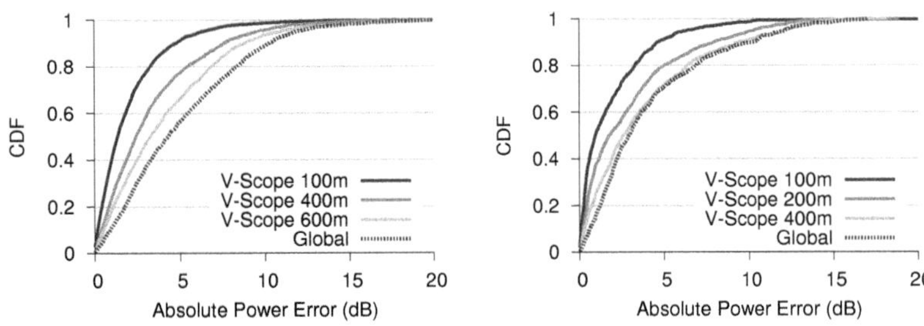

(a) Whitespace transmitter. (b) Unlicensed microphones.

Figure 21: Accuracy in predicting the power of unlicensed devices.

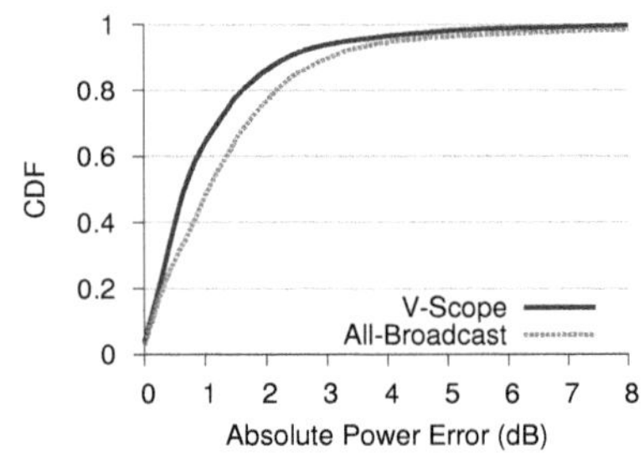

Figure 22: Accuracy in predicting the leakage power from TV broadcasts.

4.2.1 Accuracy in predicting TV broadcasts

We compare the V-Scope model with those models fitted by two alternative approaches. *Global* is a single model fitted for the entire measured area. *Local* is a region model fitted by linear regression instead of weighted regression. We quantify the gain of V-Scope models based on two datasets — dataset A collected during a 6-week period and a subset of it collected in an initial week.

Figure 18(a) shows the 99th quartile error of different models fitted based on the 1-week dataset. We first observe that *Global* has the highest prediction error since a global model can hardly be tailored to different local propagation environments. We then note a 19% – 40% reduction in prediction error achieved by *Local* over *Global* because *Local* tunes an individual model to each small region. V-Scope outperforms *Local* by 8% – 13% due to the use of weighted regression to compensate the non-uniform measurement density in model fitting.

As more measurements were subsequently collected, the measurement density tends to become uniform in each road segment. As a result, Figure 18(b) shows *Local* achieves a similar accuracy to V-Scope based on the 6-week data. This suggests that both versions of regression apply well on uniformly distributed measurements, but our weighted regression has its unique advantage in dealing with *non-uniform* measurements collected during a *short* wardriving period. Finally, we observe the accuracy in predicting the TV power improves at a smaller region size from both datasets.

4.2.2 Accuracy in localizing unlicensed devices

We use measurements collected for our whitespace transmitter and a microphone device in dataset B and C for evaluating our localization technique. The ground truth locations of these devices were obtained by a GPS device as mentioned before.

Overall accuracy: We compare following localization techniques. *Single-deter* and *Single-prob* are two popular RSSI modeling techniques used in EZ system [1] and WiFiNet system [16] respectively. *Single-deter* uses a deterministic propagation model as described in § 3.4, whereas *Single-prob* uses a probability model based on the same propagation trend. *Sector-deter* and *Sector-prob* are our sector based versions of these common techniques. *Centroid* is the center location used by our technique to partition sectors, which is the geometric center of the strongest measurements (top 5dB).

Figure 19(left) shows the error of different algorithms for localizing our whitespace device. The measurements were selected based on different maximum power thresholds to emulate a variety of localization environment. We first observe that *Single-deter* achieves a low error of 26.9m using all the measurements (-45dBm threshold). Under different power thresholds, our sector based techniques improve *Single-deter* and *Single-prob* by 1.2 – 3× and 1.5 – 3.5×, because they carefully choose a few sectors and develop an individual propagation model for them. *Sector-deter* also refines the partitioning center *Centroid* by 1.2 – 4.1×. The error of *Sector-deter* and *Sector-prob* increases by up to 2.8× and 1.8× when using measurements at a lower power (e.g., -80dBm threshold). This is because the low-power measurements present a less distinct path loss trend and the partitioning center (*Centroid*) deviates more from the device's actual location.

Figure 19(right) shows the accuracy of *Sector-deter* and *Single-deter* for localizing our microphone device in 5 different buildings based on clustered measurements as described in § 3.2. The maximum measured power ranges from -70dBm to -60dBm for different operating locations of the device. We observe that our technique *Sector-deter* achieves a low error between 16 – 27m, which are 2 – 2.8× lower than *Single-deter*.

Accuracy over different partitioning angles: Figure 20(a) shows the accuracy of *Sector-deter* with different partitioning angles for localizing the whitespace device. We observe that a larger angle leads to worse performance, e.g., the error increases by 1.5× from the 10-degree angle to the 30-degree angle, and by 2.06× to a 360-degree angle that is the baseline algorithm – *Single-deter*. To explain this performance degradation, we present the absolute correlation ratio averaged over the selected sectors for localization. Note that these sectors have a correlation ratio within the top 0.1 bin of all the sectors (§ 3.4). Figure 20(b) shows the absolute correlation decreases over an increasing angle, with a 360-degree sector having 0.36 lower correlation than a 10-degree. The highest correlation of 10-degree sectors indicates a best match of the selected measurements to the linear path loss trend, which in turn leads to highest accuracy. This justifies our use of the narrowest partitioning angle in the final algorithm.

4.2.3 *Accuracy in predicting unlicensed signals*

Using the device locations predicted by *Sector-deter*, we construct region-specific models for predicting the signal strength of the whitespace device and all (5) the microphone instances. Figure 21 shows the CDF of absolute errors in predicting the signal strength of different types of devices. We observe a 100m V-Scope model can achieve a median error of 1.3dB and 0.9dB, and a 75-quartile error of 2.8dB and 2.7dB for predicting the whitespace and microphone devices respectively. The prediction error increases at a larger region size, with a global model having about 3× higher median error than a 100m region model for both types of devices.

4.2.4 *Accuracy in predicting TV broadcast leakage*

We compare our leakage model tuned to individual TV broadcasts with an alternative model (*All-Broadcast*) comprising a single set of parameters fitted for all the TV broadcasts. Figure 22 shows the CDF of absolute error for predicting the TV leakage power in all the adjacent channels based on dataset A. We observe that V-Scope achieves a 0.7dB median error and a 1.4dB 75-quartile error. *All-Broadcast*, albeit with slightly lower storage overhead, has a 1.6× higher error in median and 1.4× higher error at 75-quartile. The worse performance in *All-Broadcast* is because a single model fitted for all the TV broadcasts cannot accurately capture the specific leakage characteristics of each TV transmitter. Since the overhead of storing a separate set of model parameters for a few TV broadcasts is low, we choose this *broadcast-specific* model in our final design to improve accuracy.

5. DISCUSSION

Impact on FCC ruling: To harvest the benefits of V-Scope, we envision several changes to be made to the current FCC ruling. To ensure the validity of spectrum measurements, the measurement hardware needs to be rigorously tested to ensure the required detection accuracy, perhaps following the same testing procedure for the sensing-based whitespace devices. To utilize the opportunistic measurements, the database may choose an appropriate region size to fit the V-Scope models based on the desired accuracy. It may fall back to use its default model (R6602) when predicting those areas beyond the regions covered by measurements. Finally, while we find non-negligible temporal and spatial under-utilization of whitespace spectrum in microphone protection, our system has *inherent limitations* in reliably protecting licensed microphones with the use of vehicular measurements. To achieve this goal, perhaps some static sensors can be deployed in the proximity of microphone reserved locations for continuously monitoring their activity, or a proactive protocol can be adopted by microphones to alert interference from whitespace devices as suggested in prior work [12].

Coping with deployment cost: Our opportunistic wardriving approach has costs and overheads in deploying and managing whitespace sensors. Perhaps this measurement infrastructure is most useful in urban areas where seizing additional spectrum of good quality can be particularly beneficial to users. In such scenarios, spectrum database providers may contract with public vehicle operators to deploy this infrastructure, and recoup their costs by charging additional fees to use the services enabled by them. In this paper, we do not explore the economic aspects of opportunistic wardriving, but focus on the technical aspects in collecting and utilizing spectrum measurements to augment databases.

Addressing temporal variations and storage overhead: The collected measurements can become invalid with the change of environment and transmission behavior of (secondary) devices. While such temporal variation is observed to be small (<5dB) at most of our measured locations, it can increase with the future proliferation of whitespace devices. We envision to use time-based filtering, backed up by statistical algorithms such as Dixon's test [4], to identify up-to-date measurements. To mitigate storage overhead, the databases may only store the fitted model parameters and device locations while discarding the measurements after using them.

Impact of measurement volume and coverage: Since our measurements are collected on a public transit bus opportunistically, the number of measurements in each region vary to a large extent. For example, different 100m regions can have measurements ranging from two to hundreds. We do not observe any clear trend between the number of measurements and the accuracy of the fitted model. Instead, the location of these measurements can play a more significant role. For example, using densely distributed measurements to fit a model can have lower accuracy than using a few measurements collected on sparse locations, which is the very motivation for our weighted regression model. Finally, the evaluation of our region model is not applicable to those locations beyond road segments. However, for those neighborhoods surrounded by the roads, we expect similar fading and shadowing effects introduced by the same environment, hence rendering our models to be relatively useful in predicting these areas.

6. RELATED WORK

Whitespace spectrum database: In its recent ruling, the FCC mandates commercial databases to use a well-known set of R6602 propagation curves [3] to estimate the coverage of TV broadcasts. We have found non-negligible spectrum wastage in these databases, possibly due to their inability to capture shadowing and fading in an urban environment.

Senseless [10] proposes an improved database design that is based on the Longley-Rice model incorporating terrain data and reported to incur low loss of whitespace spectrum. While V-Scope and Senseless share the same essence of using additional environmental information to calibrate a propagation model, their difference lies in the trade-off between the richness of the environmental data and the associated overhead in collecting such information. Senseless has the apparent advantage of obviating any measurement overhead. But the terrain information alone is somewhat insufficient to thoroughly reveal a propagation environment, e.g., the shadowing effect of buildings. In addition, Senseless is not designed to predict the quality of whitespace channels due to the lack of knowledge about the transmission power of secondary devices and the leakage characteristics of TV broadcasts. In contrast, V-Scope directly uses spectrum measurements in a local environment to tune a propagation model, which can therefore take account most of the environmental effects along with the transmission characteristics of TV-band devices. Hence V-Scope is likely to not only achieve better performance in predicting whitespace channels, but also estimate their quality. As the downside, V-Scope incurs the measurement and storage overhead and is only able to predict confined regions where measurements are available. Given these pros and cons, we believe the selection of either technique depends on the desired functionality and the availability of training information, i.e., terrain data and spectrum measurements.

The design of V-Scope is also motivated by a recent indoor whitespace database (WISER [23]) that is purely based on measurements from sensors placed at strategic indoor locations. Targeting at a different scenario, V-Scope leverages opportunistic spectrum measurements to refine a propagation model for the vast outdoor area.

Propagation model enhancement: Some recent work [13, 14] aims to improve propagation models using a few measurements. Caleb et.al [13] proposes an adaptive path loss model for a 2.5GHz WiMax network based on linear regression. A geo-statistical approach has been subsequently proposed in [14], which interpolates systematically sampled measurements to build radio environment maps. Most of these approaches require measurement locations to be carefully chosen, which can hardly be guaranteed in vehicular sensing. V-Scope leverages weighted regression to remove fitting bias caused by the non-uniform distribution of measurements.

Localization: Existing RSSI modeling systems [1, 16] build a propagation model based on a few indoor measurements to pinpoint a device with an error of few meters. V-Scope adapts the RSSI modeling approach to outdoor scenario by carefully selecting measurements in certain radiation sectors and constructing a sector-specific model. Recent AoA based localization systems [7, 18, 22] are reported to achieve even higher accuracy within a meter, by measuring the arriving angle of a signal with an antenna array. Our current implementation leverages SISO based commercial spectrum analyzers, and thus cannot implement these techniques. We intend to explore their advantage in our future deployment when MIMO based spectrum analyzers become available.

Primary detection: Energy detection is the most straightforward algorithm for primary detection. However, it fails to detect a primary signal below a certain SNR threshold [8]. Subsequent work in feature detection [8, 11] proposes to leverage spectral features of a primary signals to improve detection sensitivity. V-Scope enhances the sensitivity of this technique with zoom-in capturing, while leveraging the detected features to estimate the strength of weak primary signals.

Finally, the concept of opportunistic wardriving on public vehicles was first reported in a position paper [24] that explored the accuracy of existing databases and the potential of a measurement-enhanced propagation model. In this paper, we significantly extend this prior concept by presenting a complete measurement framework that can enhance databases to accurately determine whitespace spectrum, predict its channel quality, and validate device location, backed up by extensive evaluation based on a large volume of measurement data.

7. CONCLUSION

We have presented V-Scope, a measurement framework for TV whitespaces. Our system leverages spectrum sensors mounted on public vehicles to collect spectrum measurements during the drive. These measurements are aggregated to refine various propagation models, which can augment spectrum databases to better identify whitespace spectrum, predict its channel quality, and validate the location of primary and secondary devices. We believe the concept of opportunistic wardriving and our techniques developed to utilize such measurements, can have broader applications in dynamic spectrum access beyond TV whitespaces.

Acknowledgments

We would like to thank the Madison Metro Transit for letting us collect measurements on the bus. We are also grateful to the anonymous reviewers whose feedback helped bring the paper to its final form. Tan Zhang and Suman Banerjee are supported in part by the US National Science Foundation through awards CNS-1040648, CNS-0916955, CNS-0855201, CNS-0747177, CNS-1064944, CNS-1059306, CNS-1345293, CNS-1343363, and CNS-1258290.

8. REFERENCES

[1] K. Chintalapudi, A. Padmanabha Iyer, and V. N. Padmanabhan. Indoor localization without the pain. In *MobiCom*, 2010.

[2] A. T. S. Committee. Atsc digital television standard - part 2: Rf transmission system characteristics, December 2011.

[3] J. Damelin, W. Daniel, H. Fine, and G. Waldo. Development of VHF and UHF propagation curves for TV and FM broadcasting, 1966.

[4] R. Dean and W. Dixon. Simplified statistics for small numbers of observations. *Analytical Chemistry*, 1951.

[5] FCC. Unlicensed operation in the tv broadcast bands, second memorandum opinion and order, 2010.

[6] J. C. Gower. A general coefficient of similarity and some of its properties. *Biometrics*, 1971.

[7] K. Joshi, S. Hong, and S. Katti. Pinpoint: Localizing interfering radios. In *NSDI*, 2013.

[8] H. Kim and K. G. Shin. In-band spectrum sensing in cognitive radio networks: energy detection or feature detection? In *MobiCom*, 2008.

[9] M. Maechler, P. Rousseeuw, A. Struyf, M. Hubert, H. Kurt, M. Studer, and P. Roudier. cluster: Cluster analysis extended rousseeuw et al, 2014.

[10] R. Murty, R. Chandra, T. Moscibroda, and P. V. Bahl. Senseless: A database-driven white spaces network. *IEEE Transactions on Mobile Computing*, 2012.

[11] S. Narlanka, R. Chandra, P. Bahl, and J. Ferrell. A hardware platform for utilizing tv bands with a wi-fi radio. In *LANMAN*, 2007.

[12] G. Nychis, R. Chandra, T. Moscibroda, I. Tashev, and P. Steenkiste. Reclaiming the white spaces: Spectrum efficient coexistence with primary users. In *CoNEXT*, 2011.

[13] C. Phillips, D. Sicker, and D. Grunwald. Bounding the error of path loss models. In *DySPAN*, 2011.

[14] C. Phillips, M. Ton, D. Sicker, and D. Grunwald. Practical radio environment mapping with geostatistics. In *DySpan*, 2012.

[15] R Core Team. The R Stats Package. http://stat.ethz.ch/R-manual/R-devel/library/stats/html/optim.html.

[16] S. Rayanchu, A. Patro, and S. Banerjee. Catching whales and minnows using wifinet: Deconstructing non-wifi interference using wifi hardware. In *NSDI*, 2012.

[17] P. J. Rousseeuw. Silhouettes: a graphical aid to the interpretation and validation of cluster analysis. *Journal of computational and applied mathematics*, 1987.

[18] S. Sen, J. Lee, K.-H. Kim, and P. Congdon. Avoiding multipath to revive inbuilding wifi localization. In *MobiSys*, 2013.

[19] Spectrum Bridge Inc. Spectrum bridge database. http://www.spectrumbridge.com/Home.aspx.

[20] ThinkRf. The thinkrf wireless signals intelligence platform. http://www.thinkrf.com/.

[21] Ubiquiti Inc. Datasheet of ubiquiti sr71-a mimo cards. http://dl.ubnt.com/sr71a_datasheet.pdf.

[22] J. Xiong and K. Jamieson. Arraytrack: A fine-grained indoor location system. In *NSDI*, 2013.

[23] X. Ying, J. Zhang, L. Yan, G. Zhang, M. Chen, and R. Chandra. Exploring indoor white spaces in metropolises. In *MobiCom*, 2013.

[24] T. Zhang and S. Banerjee. Inaccurate spectrum databases?: Public transit to its rescue! In *HotNets*, 2013.

The Case for UHF-Band MU-MIMO

Narendra Anand, Ryan E. Guerra, and Edward W. Knightly
Rice University, Houston, TX, USA
{nanand,war,knightly}@rice.edu

ABSTRACT

While the UHF band exhibits superior propagation characteristics compared to other frequency bands used for broadband communications, limited spectral availability in time and space necessitates high spectral efficiency techniques such as Multi-user MIMO (MU-MIMO). In this paper we design and implement the first open MU-MIMO Software-Defined Radio (SDR) platform that operates on an order of magnitude frequency range, from 300 MHz to 5.8 GHz. We perform a comprehensive set of over-the-air experiments to evaluate the potential of UHF-band MU-MIMO in comparison to 2.4 and 5.8 GHz WiFi bands encompassing a range of operating environments. We evaluate MU-MIMO performance in both outdoor, indoor, line-of-sight (LOS), and non-line-of-sight (NLOS) environments, and demonstrate that while the temporal correlation of the measured UHF environment is increased, it does not come at the cost of increased spatial correlation as measured by the Demmel condition number, thus proving highly attractive for MU-MIMO. This evaluation demonstrates the effectiveness of MU-MIMO transmission techniques in UHF bands for high spectral efficiency and low-overhead wireless access.

Categories and Subject Descriptors

C.2.1 [**Computer-Communication Networks**]: Network Architecture and Design—*Wireless Communication*

General Terms

Measurement, Performance, Reliability, Experimentation, Design

Keywords

Multi-user MIMO, Beamforming, UHF, Channel State Information, Channel Measurement, Channel Correlation, Demmel Condition Number

ACM 978-1-4503-2783-1/14/09 ...$15.00.
http://dx.doi.org/10.1145/2639108.2639144.

1. INTRODUCTION

Multi-user MIMO (MU-MIMO) is a transmission technique that enables a multi-antenna transmitter to transmit multiple, parallel data streams to distinct user nodes. By pre-coding the data streams concurrently through a coherent antenna array, a transmitter can increase its spectral efficiency and overall downlink system capacity. Closed-loop MU-MIMO transmissions first require a transmitter to measure the channel between itself and its receivers (a process known as channel sounding) before transmitting concurrent data streams to the receivers. This direct measurement of Channel State Information (CSI) adds considerable protocol overhead and must occur more often in time-varying channel environments since the beam-formed transmission is sensitive to channel variation. A more temporally-correlated channel would allow a MU-MIMO system to reduce CSI-estimation frequency and improve the accuracy of this estimate for longer lag times.

State-of-the-art MU-MIMO channel models based on empirical measurements have been developed that predict increased channel correlation in lower frequency bands, but are inconclusive with respect to the effect on receiver separability simply because a direct comparison of diverse frequency bands in the same environment has not been attempted [27, 36]. For instance, one might assume that increased propagation through building materials might reduce the amount of multi-path for an indoor environment compared to an 802.11n WLAN [16]. This would have the effect of reducing the ability of a MU-MIMO base station to beam-form separate spatial streams to simultaneous users. Without a comparative study of different frequency bands, it is hard to draw conclusions for UHF

Figure 1: The WURC-enabled MU-MIMO array.

MU-MIMO performance from existing work in 802.11n WLANs [9].

While the recent switch to digital television has released hundreds of megahertz of spectrum in the VHF/UHF frequency band for reassignment (54 MHz to 698 MHz in the United States and 470 MHz to 790 MHz in Europe [8, 12]), only a limited number of channels are available in some locations and in many cases those channels are non-contiguous.

Although both 5 GHz and UHF bands have roughly 600 MHz of available spectrum, many sections of the sub-gigahertz range are already assigned to different licensed technologies (e.g., broadcast television, cellular networks). While the propagation characteristics of the UHF band are more desirable, limited spectrum availability at these frequencies necessitates high spectral efficiency in order to achieve high throughput performance. The expected increased channel temporal correlation may compensate for diminished spectrum in the UHF band by enabling robust, low-overhead MU-MIMO operation, so long at it does not come at the cost of increased spatial correlation between users' wireless channels.

In this paper, we evaluate the efficacy of UHF MU-MIMO in comparison to 2.4 and 5 GHz WiFi bands and make the case for its adoption in a wide variety of transmission scenarios. To accomplish this goal, we design and implement the first open MU-MIMO Software-Defined Radio (SDR) platform that operates on an order of magnitude frequency range, from 300 MHz to 5.8 GHz, shown in Fig. 1. As a key enabling technology, we design and implement WURC, a wideband, high-power SDR front-end for this Wireless Open-access Research Platform (WARP)-based MU-MIMO array (the red daughtercards shown in Fig. 1). WURC is a high-power RF front end that attaches to Xilinx and Altera-based SDR platforms which supplements WARP with a transmitter capable of operation from 300 MHz to 3.8 GHz and optimized for high transmit power for outdoor, long-range links.

We make the following contributions:

- We develop a UHF MU-MIMO testbed using the WARPv3 SDR combined with custom designed UHF daughtercards, allowing for MU-MIMO transmissions in spectrum with an order of magnitude difference (300 MHz to 5.8 GHz) and high UHF transmit power in a small form factor.
- We characterize the UHF MU-MIMO channel in various transmission environments and perform side-by-side comparisons using WARPLab with the 2.4 GHz and 5 GHz WiFi band to verify the theoretical characteristics of each.
- For longer-range topologies that are beyond the capabilities of WARPLab and for fine grain channel characterization, we implement a high speed channel sounding framework that allows for the collection of 4x transmit antenna, wideband channel matrices every 800 μs to an arbitrary number of receivers.
- We find that while the UHF environment demonstrates a relatively similar degree of spatial correlation measured by channel condition number, when compared to other WLAN technologies, it demonstrates superior temporal correlation, thus proving attractive for MU-MIMO techniques.

In the rest of this paper, we first provide the necessary background for MU-MIMO transmissions in § 2; discuss the design, implementation, and verification of the open-source UHF MU-MIMO testbed in § 3; present a model-based analysis of indoor and outdoor MU-MIMO environments in § 4 which is compared to over-the-air experiments utilizing the developed MU-MIMO testbed in § 5; and present related work in § 6 with closing remarks in § 7.

2. BACKGROUND

In this section we briefly discuss MU-MIMO transmission techniques and how the inherent spectrum differences between UHF and 2.4/5 GHz frequency bands affect MU-MIMO transmission performance.

2.1 Multi-user Beamforming

Multi-user beamforming is a multi-antenna transmission technique that allows a transmitter to spatially reuse a wireless channel by transmitting multiple concurrent streams. This is achieved in two steps: First, each data stream is multiplied by a length M vector of complex steering weights (where M is the number of transmit antennas) resulting in M phase twisted copies of each data stream. Second, each receiver's set of M copies are summed together at each antenna to construct K parallel data streams (where K is the number of concurrent receivers) emanating from M antennas.

Weight Selection. Weights are chosen such that the interference between the parallel streams is minimal. To compute these weights, the transmitter must first measure the channel state matrix (H) where each element corresponds to the magnitude and phase difference between each transmit and receive antenna. The optimal method of constructing the steering matrix is Dirty Paper Coding (DPC) [14]; however, its complexity makes it unfeasible to implement. Instead, a method known as Zero-forcing Beamforming (ZFBF) is shown to approach the optimal performance of DPC while employing a computationally feasible weight matrix calculation method, the pseudo-inverse [34] given by

$$W = H^{\dagger} = H^{*} \cdot (H \cdot H^{*}). \tag{1}$$

A key element of ZFBF is the zero-interference condition which is a direct result of the pseudo-inverse. Because $W = H^{\dagger}, h_i w_j = 0$ for $i \neq j$ meaning that the interference from user i's stream on user j is nulled and vice versa. ZFBF precodes the transmitted data streams such that the combined wireless channel between the transmitter and the receivers (H) is separated. If ZFBF works perfectly, we can express the precoded transmission $(W \cdot \text{Tx})$ as:

$$\begin{aligned} W \cdot \text{Tx} \xrightarrow[H]{\text{Transmit}} & H \cdot (W \cdot \text{Tx}) \\ = & \cancel{H} \cdot (\cancel{W} \cdot \text{Tx}) = \text{Tx} \end{aligned} \tag{2}$$

In our work, we focus on the zero-forcing beamforming technique for MU-MIMO.

2.2 MU-MIMO Performance Limitations

The key to the success of this precoding operation is that $H \cdot W$ is the identity matrix so the transmitted streams are received separately at each receiver. We focus on two characteristics of H that can degrade the performance of this precoding operation: an ill-conditioned H [35] or an out-dated H [23].

An ill-conditioned H matrix renders matrix inversion inaccurate [18] and thus $H \cdot W$ is far less likely to equal I. This results in inter-stream interference degrading the received signal strength of a data stream to its intended receiver [23]. Ill-conditioned H matrices are a result of receiver channel correlation, an environment and frequency dependent characteristic that will be discussed in § 4.1.

Out-dated H matrices are a direct result of the latency between the measurement of the H matrix and the transmission of the W precoded data streams. Increased time between the measurement of H and the transmission of $W \cdot$ Tx, results in a higher probability of incorrect transmit precoding. Essentially, the transmitter measures H_t and then calculates $W_t = H_t^{\dagger}$. However, the subsequent precoded transmission is $H_{t+\Delta} \cdot W_t$, which may not equal

I. Whether or not $H_t = H_{t+\Delta}$ is based on environmental variability and user mobility; and, like channel conditioning, is also an environment and frequency dependent characteristic that will be discussed in the following section.

While a large number of studies in § 6 have characterized the indoor and outdoor propagation environment for the purpose of network planning and algorithm design, few are applicable to evaluating MU-MIMO performance and most have focused on a single frequency band. This makes measurement studies of different frequencies and radio technologies difficult to compare.

At the same time, the implementation complexity and computation required for real-time implementation of multi-carrier MU-MIMO is prohibitive for today's software-defined radio platforms [9], thus providing a challenge to empirical measurement of MU-MIMO performance.

3. WURC ARRAY IMPLEMENTATION

In this section, we describe the hardware platforms and software frameworks that we designed and deployed in order to enable an experimental evaluation of UHF MU-MIMO. First, we design and implement a new SDR analog front-end designed for high-power, wideband Single-Input Single-Output (SISO) UHF operation. Using the newly-developed radio and the WARPv3 SDR hardware platform, we then develop an integrated frequency-diverse MU-MIMO system. Finally, we describe our extensive modifications to existing experimental software frameworks that allow us to rapidly gather channel state information and perform over-the-air MU-MIMO evaluations.

3.1 Wideband UHF Radio Card (WURC)

WURC is a new SDR analog front-end designed to enable high-power, long-range experiments and hardware prototypes in the UHF frequency band. It is designed for modularity and compactness, with the goal of enabling prototyping of new MAC and PHY enhancements for UHF and Industrial, Scientific, and Medical (ISM)-band applications [7].

It connects to the host FPGA board via an HSMC or FMC (with custom adapter board) daughtercard slot, and provides a 12-bit digital baseband quadrature interface to the host system, while permitting in-field reconfiguration of RF analog parameters such as channel bandwidth and center frequency between 300-3800 MHz, though it is currently optimized and calibrated for transmissions between 470-798 MHz, and 2400-2500 MHz.

3.1.1 WURC High-Level System Design

MU-MIMO systems generally require a large number of independent transmit and receive RF chains on the base station to generate multiple spatial streams. In addition, a large number of distributed client nodes are required to serve as the mobile user stations. In order to simplify the manufacturing and management of a large number of radios, WURC is designed to be modular, with calibration/control libraries and board-dependent calibration tables stored locally on each daughter-card on a micro-controller. This eases the requirements for integration with a host platform and makes the radios completely interchangeable.

3.1.2 Power Amplifier Design and Verification

In order to operate as an opportunistic transmitter in the UHF band and adapt to various channel bandwidths, spectrum availability, and regulatory domains across the world, WURC is designed to operate at arbitrary channel bandwidths from 1.5 to 28 MHz and carrier frequencies ranging from 300-3800 MHz. This presents a challenge for a high-power RF design since power amplifiers and

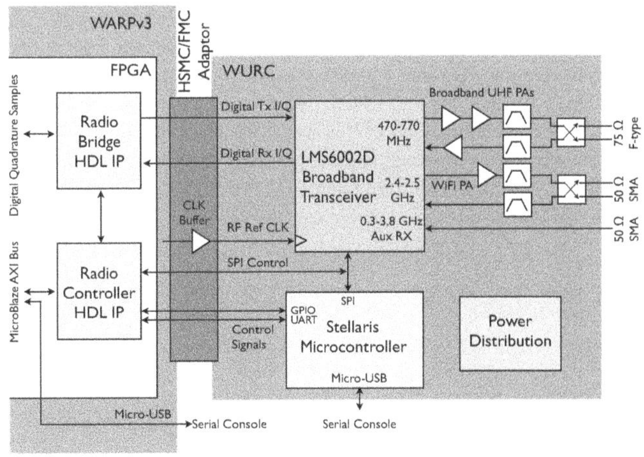

Figure 2: Block diagram of WURC module on a host WARPv3 board.

their associated impedance matching networks are generally optimized for a narrow frequency band.

A common technique for designing high-power analog front-ends is to build multiple switched amplification and filtering chains, each optimized for a narrow band. However, when the system operating frequency range spans multiple octaves, space and cost constraints require that each chain support a wide range of frequencies. In the design of WURC, we target two optimized transmit and receive chains for 470-698 MHz and 2400-2500 MHz, chosen because these two bands allow unlicensed operation and are invaluable for research and testing. In addition, a wide-band balun transformer enables a 300-3800 MHz receiver port that can serve as a wideband spectrum sensor, if required.

Since the bandwidth of an RF chain is generally proportional to $\Delta f/f$, common techniques for designing and implementing discrete power transfer networks (e.g., multi-section Chebyshev transformers [17]) either cannot meet design requirements for passband flatness or result in non-realizable circuits when applied to bandpass designs spanning a large frequency range like 470-698 MHz.

In order to address this problem, we implemented a wideband linear power-transfer network utilizing real-frequency techniques [32] for the UHF front end. We target a design goal of transmit powers up to 30 dBm from 300 to 750 MHz, the maximum power currently allowed by the Federal Communications Commission (FCC) in the United States for unlicensed operation [16]. The 2.4 GHz ISM transmit chain provides up to 27 dBm between 2400-2500 MHz. The RF chain of WURC provides up to 30 dB of dynamic transmit gain, and up to 61 dB of dynamic receive gain, which when combined with its on-board Low-Noise Amplifier (LNA) can provide up to 83 dB of receive gain for improved sensitivity, although noise figure considerations generally limit this application to 72 dBm.

While this design was confirmed at the early design stage with SPICE simulation models, early prototypes demonstrated that package parasitics in the lumped-element broadband power transfer chain were not modeled by the ideal SPICE simulator. These parasitics severely impaired the implemented high-frequency gain response and required a more advanced model and simulation technique to correctly predict their effect. Re-modeling the RF chain in the SpectreRF circuit simulator utilizing empirical S-parameter models resulted in a more accurate simulation, allowing package parasitics to be compensated for in the lumped-element design.

In order to verify the correctness of the implemented design and understand how manufacturing process variation might effect the output frequency response of multiple RF chains in a MU-MIMO system, we built a Python-based batch interface to the WURC's serial UART in order to sweep transmit frequencies while simultaneously controlling a bench-top vector signal analyzer to measure the output power. We implemented a digital frequency synthesizer within the digital baseband reference design in order to generate a constant-power complex sinusoid for ease of measurement.

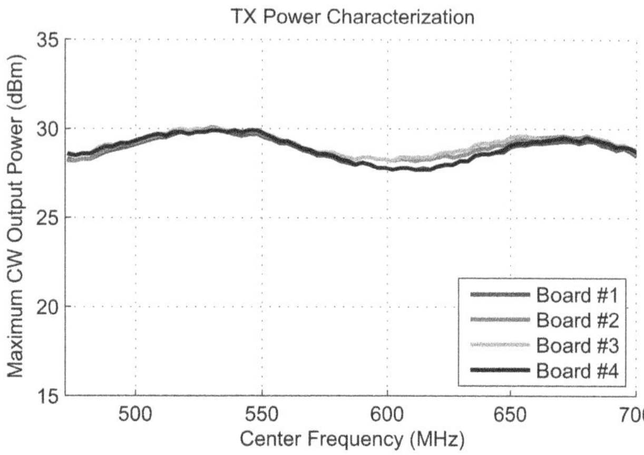

Figure 3: Process variation across multiple fabricated WURC boards has a small effect on output power.

The process variation plot in Fig. 3 was generated by increasing the output transmit gain of each WURC at each center frequency until its output PA began to saturate. This is the delivered output power of WURC near the 1dB compression point of the RF chain. Notably, the process variation across different boards is less than 1 dB, with passband ripple on the order of 2.5 dB. This means that multiple RF chains will maintain similar output power across the entire UHF frequency range.

3.1.3 Radio Architecture

WURC uses a *direct-conversion* quadrature transceiver architecture based around the LMS6002D "field-programmable" transceiver IC in order to minimize size, implementation complexity, and energy-consumption [2]. Because of this, we are able to power the high-power RF chain from the FMC/HSMC-compliant daughtercard slot, further decreasing size and complexity.

All 12-bit DACs/ADCs, programmable analog anti-aliasing channel filters, frequency synthesizers, and direct-conversion mixers are integrated on a single chip while the rest of the board contains power amplifiers and filters, antenna diversity DPDT switch, power distribution, and a microcontroller (Fig. 2). We designed and tested fast-switching control circuits on the discrete amplification stages that allow the system to operate as a TDD transceiver with a switching time of less than 7 μs, or an FDD system with independent transmit and receive fractional-N frequency synthesizers.

Clocking. Since the transmit and receive chains in a MU-MIMO base station require precise phase synchronization, WURC was designed to draw RF reference clocks from the host digital baseband board as in Fig. 4. We placed an additional RF reference and sampling clock buffer on the FMC/HSMC adaptor rather than on the daughtercard itself so that the designed system can scale up to four WURCs driven from a single host FPGA with synchronized clocks; however, we only implement a single-radio adapter at this time.

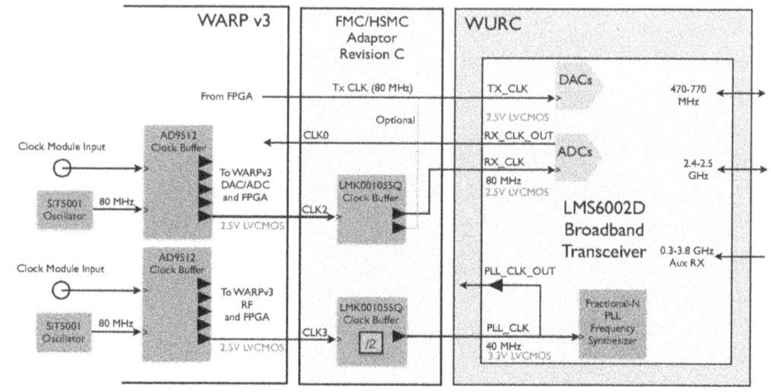

Figure 4: Source-synchronous sampling clocks and RF reference clocks are buffered in stages, permitting daisy-chaining and future fanout to multiple radios.

Control and Calibration. An on-board micro-controller provides a simple, scriptable, two-wire UART or USB UART interface to a host system for command and control of analog parameters such as center frequency, transmit power, and analog channel bandwidth, while providing full read/write configuration register access to the transceiver.

We designed embedded libraries complete with calibration macros that offload complex computation from the host system and handle the loading of stored factory calibration values for transmit and receive baseband IQ-imbalance and local oscillator feedthrough compensation. In addition, we developed automated "factory" calibration procedures that allow us to rapidly calibrate a large number of WURCs for field deployment with minimal setup time.

Each WURC is a highly-integrated SDR front-end module that provides unprecedented capabilities in a small form factor, enabling a wide range of experimental trials and system implementations with excellent RF flexibility.

3.2 WURC Array

In order to evaluate MU-MIMO transmissions at various carrier frequencies and node topologies, we integrate WURC and four WARPv3 modules into a coherent 4-radio array.

Clock Sharing. The MU-MIMO WURC array combines four WARPv3 boards and 4 WURC daughtercards into a single prototype base station providing combined sample and RF-reference clock synchronization, power, and structural support. Synchronization of reference clocks for ADC sampling and RF frequency synthesizers is required for coherent beamforming and is accomplished by forwarding a daisy-chained reference clock from one master WARPv3 baseband board to the others in the array. All radios derive their sampling and RF reference clocks from this forwarded clock and thus remain phase-synchronized.

Antennas. Most studies of UHF propagation involve large, directional antennas intended for signal reception over many kilometers. This is because optimal signal reception and transmission requires antennas of at least 1/2 wavelength to generate a resonating standing wave. On the other hand, a Wireless LAN (WLAN) deployment utilizing UHF frequencies may wish to keep the size of the base station somewhat limited, particularly for indoor deployments. For our experiments, we utilize off-the-shelf passive, omnidirectional 3 dBi DTV antennas (August DTA240) that would provide the largest range of coverage with minimal dependance on direction. In our experimental platform (Fig. 5), it is actually the dual-band 2.4/5.8 GHz band antennas (L-com HG2458-5RD-RSP with 3 dBi and 5 dBi gain, respectively) that are larger in size.

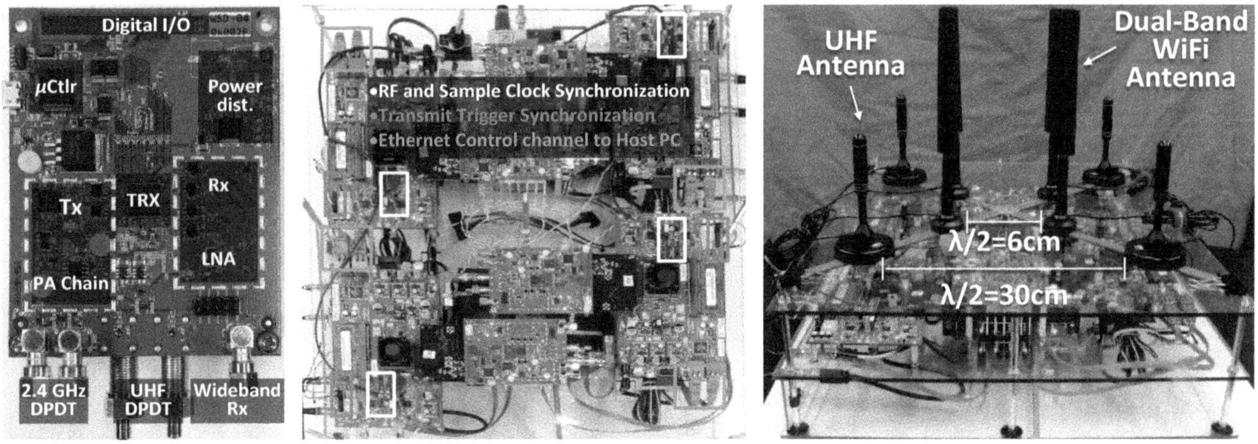

(a) WURC. (b) WURC Array Internals. (c) WURC Array Antennas.

Figure 5: Wideband UHF Radio Card (WURC) hardware platform.

This type of omni-directional antenna array is ideal for indoor MU-MIMO as it provides many opportunities for multipath reflections [9]. In order to guarantee the required channel diversity, each antenna was spaced at least 1/2 wavelength for its respective transmit frequency.

3.3 Software Framework

In addition to the development of custom hardware to meet our design requirements, we build upon or modify a number of existing applications in order to develop an experimental framework for the WURC MU-MIMO array.

3.3.1 WARPLab

The WARPLab 7 framework for WARP hardware provides a means to pre-compute baseband signals in MATLAB, load transmit sample buffers into an array of WARP boards, and then trigger a simultaneous RF transmission of all buffered signals via a back-end ethernet network or a GPIO trigger [6]. Similarly, an arbitrary number of radios can be configured to perform automatic gain control (AGC) and store their received RF samples in buffers for off-line retrieval and processing.

We extend WARPLab's object-oriented framework with additional classes and methods to support the WURC's interfaces. This system provides a powerful workflow for UHF PHY prototyping and measurement studies for multi-antenna systems.

Measurement Speed. WARPLab 7 contains a number of transport improvements that result in the ability to perform near-real-time experiments by rapidly performing cycles of: precompute, load, transmit/receive, fetch, and process on the order of 2.5 ms. A fast central coordinator using jumbo ethernet frames for transporting IQ buffers and a compiled MATLAB-mex transport layer can operate at per-packet time intervals. We observed that extra switches between WARPLab nodes produce measurable switching delay and recommend the use of long ethernet cables and minimization of the number of ethernet hops for backhaul.

While powerful, the primary drawbacks of WARPLab is that it requires a central coordinator connected via gigabit ethernet switches, and real-time protocol implementations generally require processing at sub-packet timescales. These two factors hinder long-distance or mobile experiments.

SINR Measurement Technique. In order to overcome these limitations yet still accurately measure the MU-MIMO channel, we employ a WARPLab-based MU-MIMO transmission framework that is based on measuring received SINR and then computing the Shannon capacity to estimate the achievable rate of a transmission system. This is accomplished by a measurement technique adapted from [9] and shown in Fig. 6. Here, the transmitter beamforms sections of the transmission packet independently to accurately measure the SINR.

In the depicted 4x2 transmission example, the transmitter first sends an LTS preamble for timing synchronization (blue) and then performs a MU-MIMO transmission to both users (red). In the following two sections (green, purple), the transmitter sequentially zeroes out the steering vector to each receiver in order to measure noise and interference at each receiver during a MU-MIMO transmission. In the example 4x2 case, this becomes a single-user beamformed transmission, however in the 4x3 or 4x4 case, two or three receivers would be beamformed to during this measurement.

Thus, the difference between the full MU-MIMO transmission containing both signal, noise, and interference at each receiver (red) and the transmission containing just interference and noise at the zeroed-out receiver (green or purple) is each transmitter's SINR. From there, we can compute aggregate Shannon Capacity as $C = log_2(1 + \text{SINR})$.

3.3.2 Real-Time 802.11a/g-Like Reference Design

We realize a real-time 802.11a/g-interoperable design utilizing the WARPv3 802.11 Reference Design and WURC to transmit over UHF frequencies, with modifications to provide 10 and 5 MHz channels [3]. We develop custom HDL for the radio interface, AGC, and digital filtering necessary for a real-time broadband system, and integrate the hardware and software design with the WARPv3 802.11 Reference Design. This system implements a real-time layer-2 wireless bridge utilizing an 802.11a/g AP and STA design with a completely open network stack.

In particular, the real-time capabilities of the 802.11 reference design are leveraged to provide fine-grained continuous channel estimates from multiple transmitting antennas in order to directly measure the MU-MIMO channel capacity instantaneously and over a long period of time.

3.3.3 Framework Enhancements

In order to enable long-range MIMO channel sounding by a large number of mobile nodes, we make the following enhancements and

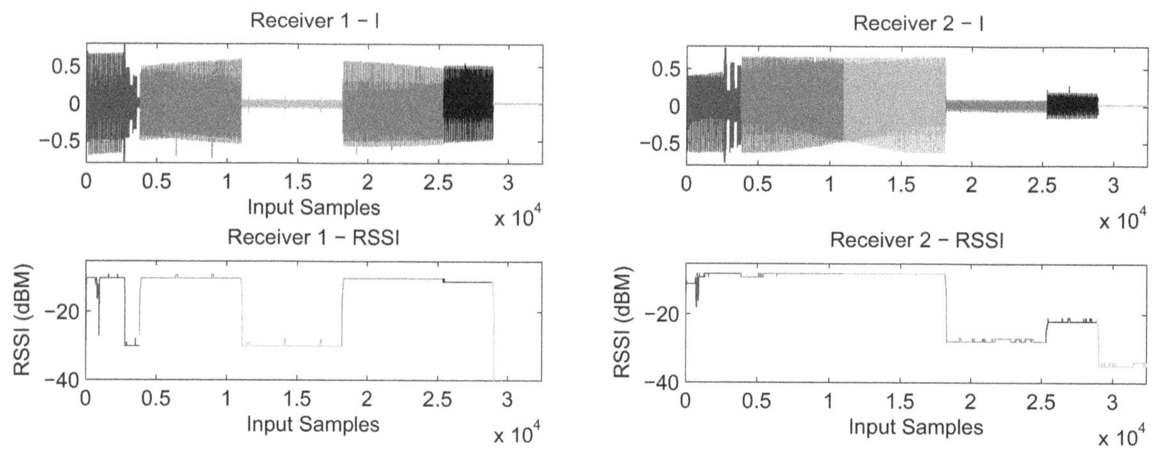

Figure 6: Example RSSI Measurement used in achievable capacity calculation.

modifications to the WARP frameworks described in § 3.3.2 and 3.3.1.

Hardware Integration. We adapt both the WARPLab and 802.11 reference design to work seamlessly with the WURC hardware in place of normal WARP daughter cards. From the perspective of the digital baseband, the analog front-end is transparent, which allows interchangeable analog PHYs to be used with the same digital PHY/MAC for fair comparison. This is especially useful for the MU-MIMO comparison study as it controls for a large number of variables in the radio MAC and PHY chain.

Channel Bandwidth. The 802.11 reference design operates in a 20 MHz channel bandwidth. In order to enable a UHF transmission to fit within one or two contiguous UHF channels of 6 MHz, we modify the 802.11 reference design to operate at 10 and 5 MHz channel bandwidths in compliance with the 802.11 standard. This is accomplished by halving the data sampling rate with added programmable decimation filters and adjusting MAC parameters and receiver DSP blocks to match.

Automatic Gain Control. The range of received power in realistic deployments is sufficiently large that an AGC subsystem is required to guarantee the robust and accurate reception of wideband channel sounding packets, particular when wireless nodes are mobile. Reference designs from the WARP project rely on external power detectors and autocorrelation to detect incoming packets and estimate a target receive gain setting, whereas an external power detector would require additional external circuitry on WURC.

Instead, we design a custom real-time digital loop in hardware to provide AGC convergence within 5.6 μs as required by the 20 MHz 802.11 PLCP and utilizing only the ADC output for packet detection and power estimation. AGC is an enabling technique required to ensure that channel measurement samples have the proper resolution. This is guaranteed when the received signal strength at the ADC input falls within the dynamic range of the ADC (the ADC's ENOB is 10 [2]).

Fig. 7 depicts the performance of the implemented power estimator and AGC subsystem design by reporting a series of experiments over a cable between two WURC nodes with a variable attenuator. The transmit gain is fixed to 25 dB and a 802.11g-like packet with random data payload and 16-QAM OFDM modulation is constructed in MATLAB and transmitted over the cable using the WARPLab framework developed in § 3.3.1. The received packet without Forward Error Correction (FEC) is decoded and its received EVM is calculated as the mean across subcarriers and

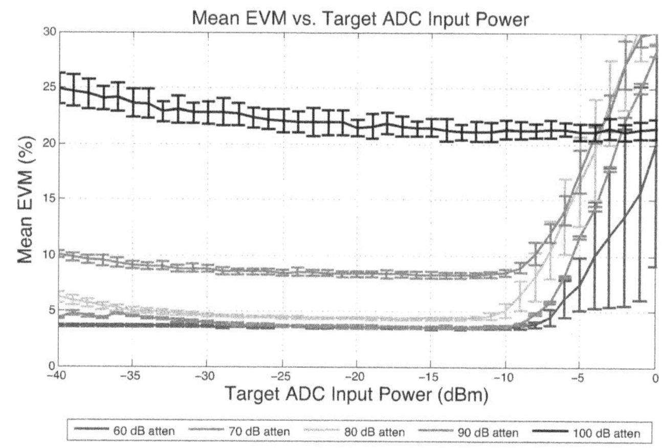

Figure 7: Verification of the implemented received power estimator and AGC operation. Measured with Tx gain at 25 dB, with 16-QAM OFDM modulation.

OFDM symbols of the normalized distance between the received decoded symbol and the intended decoded symbol.

Both the RF path attenuation and target ADC input power are varied under these conditions, resulting in the plot shown in Fig. 7, where the error bars represent one standard deviation across 50 trials. The top plot shows that the ADC operating target of -26 to -13 dBm is optimal for received EVM under a wide range of input powers. For each attenuation value, the bowl of the EVM curve represents the lower bound on the system's 16-QAM receive EVM, with the right-most bound of this range limited by saturation at the ADC and the left-most bound is determined by the system noise floor and quantization error. As expected, high signal attenuation of 100 dB results in a decrease in SINR and thus, minimum achievable EVM. We therefore fix our target ADC input power to -18 dBm in order to ensure that channel measurement packets are detected and received without quantization error and with maximum precision.

Channel Sounding. While the legacy 802.11 design calculates and stores channel state information as required by its OFDM channel equalizers, this information is generally discarded after packet reception. The channel estimation extracted from each received 802.11 PLCP header [21] provides a complete CSI estimation matrix that can be used as a single-antenna sounding event. We modify the physical layer of the 802.11 reference design to treat each of a series of transmitted PLCP headers as separate "packets" for the purpose of CSI measurement from multiple transmitting antennas.

Our custom sounding "packet" is a brief 802.11g-like signal containing PLCP header for packet detection, AGC convergence, and symbol timing extraction. The payload is just long enough to provide error detection bits and identifying information about the transmitter so that the transmitting antenna can be identified. Due to the small size of this sounding packet, it is not compliant with the requirement that 802.11 packets contain an 802.11 and link-layer header. Therefore, we modify the MAC software to pass all packets regardless of valid header or fields to the Ethernet interface for processing.

We construct this special sounding packet in MATLAB and preconfigure the WURC array, running our WARPLab modification, to transmit these packets continuously staggered in time as shown in Figure 8. Tests show that WARPLab continuous-transmit mode remains synchronous over long periods of time if the boards are clock synchronized. We provide sufficient spacing between sounding packets to allow the 802.11 PHY to process the previous packet and reset, and we find that the WARPLab buffer size of 32768 samples over 819.2 μs is sufficient to capture channel variation even at higher frequencies.

We combine this structure with a set of multiple listening nodes that process these channel sounding packets and can then store them for later retrieval. A ten-minute packet trace for a single antenna can run over 1 GB in size, so substantial buffering and disk I/O speed is required for the recording nodes.

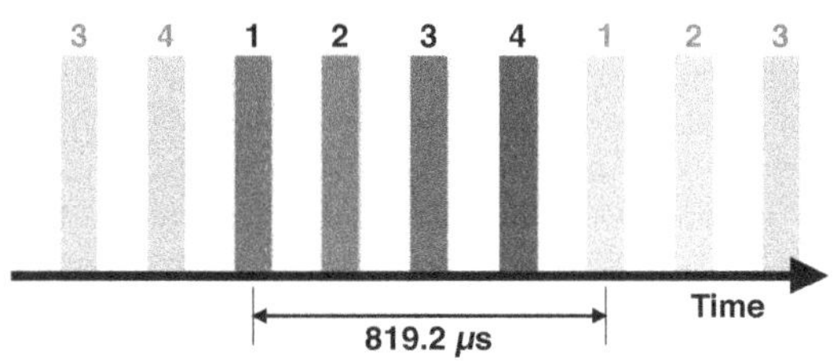

Figure 8: Short timing packets are sent from each of the WURC array antennas in rapid succession consisting of an 802.11 PLCP preamble and a short, 14-byte payload.

4. MODEL-DRIVEN EVALUATION

In order to understand how different environments and operational frequencies will effect the performance of a MU-MIMO system, we first turn to modern statistical MIMO channel models [24]. Since this statistical model requires tuning for different environments and frequencies, we compare the results using two published parametrizations for 300 MHz [36] and 5.8 GHz[27]. These results provide the theoretical motivation for over-the-air experiments to explore common application scenarios for UHF and 2.4/5.8 GHz WiFi.

4.1 UHF vs. 2.4/5 GHz: Channel Models

Spectrum differences between 2.4/5 GHz WiFi and sub-gigahertz frequencies are essentially due to the different manifestations of Doppler effects given each band's wavelength. Doppler effects are a result of transmitter, receiver, and client movement with respect to a transmission's wavelength. Because sub-gigahertz wavelengths are 2-4 times longer than 2.4/5 GHz, environmental variation will affect sub-gigahertz transmissions 2-4 times less (without considering multi-path effects).

Fig. 9 shows the theoretical, freespace 50% coherence time for various sub-gigahertz and 2.4/5 GHz frequencies [28]. The 50% coherence time is expected length of time that the channel characteristics will vary at most 50% given some velocity (effectively channel variation).

The coherence time difference between 2.4/5 GHz WiFi and sub-gigahertz frequencies is between 1-2 *orders of magnitude*. This channel characterization does not consider many real world effects such as multi-path or fading but provides a coarse characterization of the key differences in the two bands.

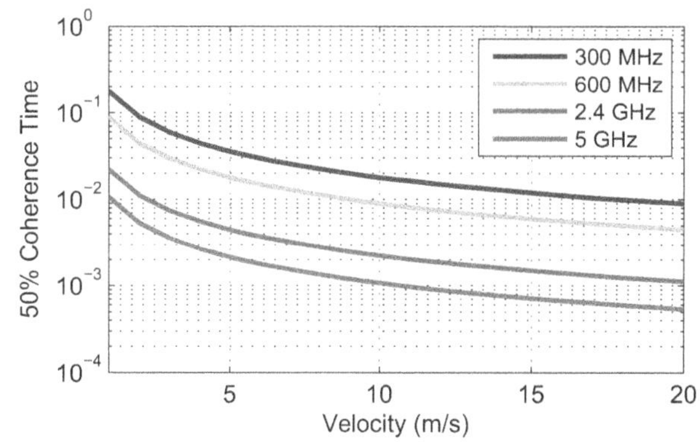

Figure 9: 50% coherence time for various sub-gigahertz and 2.4/5 GHz WiFi frequencies.

For a more realistic characterization of the spectrum differences, we employ the COST 2100 MIMO channel model, a flexible channel model that is well suited for MU-MIMO scenarios [24]. This channel model is tuned with parameters that are extracted from empirical measurements and thus does consider real-world channel effects such as fading, multi-path, and non-line-of-sight (NLOS) transmissions. Parametrized realizations of the COST 2100 model have been created for 300 MHz [36] and 5 GHz [27] bands. Using these models, we generate 15,000 channel snapshots at a simulated rate of 100 snapshots per second to characterize the variation of channel state over time and the separability of individual users. Specifically we explore the temporal correlation and receiver separability (shown in Fig. 10) of the generated matrices.

Temporal correlation is the average autocorrelation between channel snapshots at varying intervals of time calculated as described in [31]. The correlation coefficient at time ρ at time interval ℓ is defined as:

$$\rho_\ell = \frac{\mathbb{E}\left[H_{mn}[k]H^*_{mn}[k+\ell]\right]}{\mathbb{E}\left[H_{mn}[k]H^*_{mn}[k]\right]} \quad (3)$$

where expectation is calculated for all combinations of transmit antenna m, receive antenna n and starting time sample k.

We show the magnitude of the temporal correlation coefficient in Fig. 10(a) for our generated channels. Lower temporal correlation results in less robust MU-MIMO transmissions because the measured channel state has a high probability of being stale. As seen in Fig. 10(a), the temporal correlation of 5 GHz WiFi almost immediately drops to below 0.9 ($T_{0.9}$) a point when when re-sounding the channel is strongly suggested [11].

According to the channel models, the approximate re-sounding time for 5 GHz is 50 ms and 300 MHz is approximately 4.5 s (almost two orders of magnitude longer). This result is similar to what

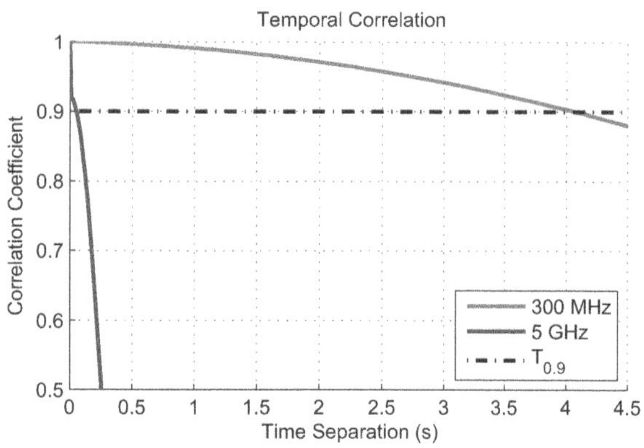

(a) Temporal correlation between channel snapshots from 0 to 10 seconds apart. Higher time correlation allows for more robust MU-MIMO performance. $T_{0.9}$ is 50 ms and 4 s for 5 GHz and 300 MHz respectively.

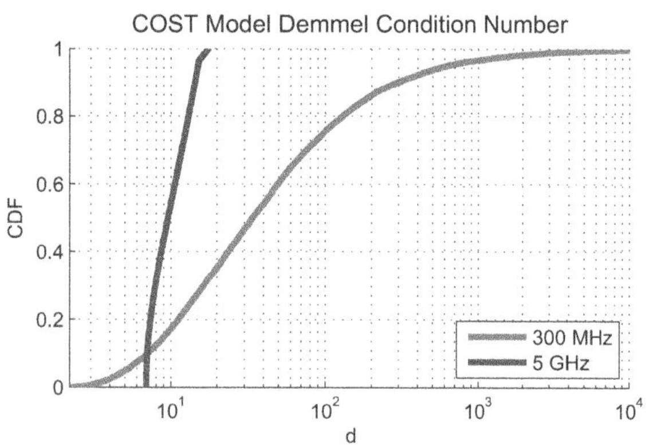

(b) CDF of model-generated Demmel condition number. Left is better for MU-MIMO

Figure 10: Temporal correlation and channel condition of 300 MHz and 5 GHz 2x2 MU-MIMO channels generated by COST 2100 MIMO channel model.

we expect from Doppler effects of the different frequency bands (Fig. 9) and is similar to our indoor temporal characterization in § 5.1.

User separability refers to how well a multi-antenna transmitter can serve a set of users in parallel. The Demmel condition number is a modified matrix condition number that directly predicts the efficacy of an adaptive MIMO or MU-MIMO transmission for a particular channel realization [35].

The Demmel condition number is computed using the eigenvalues λ_k of $HH^\dagger$ as:

$$d \triangleq \frac{\sum_{k=1}^{n} \lambda_k}{\lambda_n} \tag{4}$$

where $\lambda_1 > \lambda_2 > \ldots > \lambda_n$. This ratio represents how well a matrix can be inverted, a key component of many adaptive MU-MIMO techniques such as Zero-Forcing Beamforming [34] and MMSE [30]. Specifically, the higher the condition number, the more numerically unstable the inverse and thus the more inter-user interference during MU-MIMO transmissions reducing received SINR. The condition number ranges from 1 to infinity for well to ill-conditioned matrices, respectively.

This method of calculating the condition number is less forgiving than the traditional singular value ratio. The singular values of H are the square root of the eigenvalues of $HH^\dagger$. Thus, instead of σ_k/σ_n, the Demmel condition number is equivalent to $\sum \sigma^2/\sigma_n^2$ meaning that channel matrices with low singular values (resulting in inaccurate inversion) are even further "penalized." This modification to the condition number better predicts MU-MIMO performance, in fact, it is consistent and accurate enough to be used for determining parameters such as supported modulation rate and user selection [35].

The COST channel models show a significant difference between the 5 GHz WiFi and UHF bands. The CDF shown in Fig. 10(b) depicts how almost all of the generated 5 GHz channel matrices have a Demmel condition number less than 10 while UHF's channel condition varies far more and is significantly worse. This results in an increased ability for a MU-MIMO transmitter to invert the channel matrix and send orthogonal streams to each intended user.

Thus, existing MIMO channel models show that while the UHF channel is more temporally stable over time, its ill-conditioned channel matrices can result in lower served SINR due to inter-user interference. However, the available parametrizations of the COST model are for indoor 5 GHz and outdoor UHF scenarios. We show in § 5 how restricting these bands to these transmission environments does not tell the full story.

5. EXPERIMENT-DRIVEN EVALUATION

The models analyzed in § 4 are parametrized for particular environments, frequency bands, and topologies. While they suggest that the performance of MU-MIMO beamforming in UHF bands may be advantageous, it it difficult to directly predict or simulate UHF performance using these models as they were not validated for application scenarios such as indoor or urban outdoor, nor the UHF frequency band.

In order to address uncertainty in these models for our target application (indoor and outdoor WLAN), we perform a set of experiments utilizing our custom SDR radio platform that allows us to measure the performance of a MU-MIMO transmission over a diverse set of carrier frequencies and characterize the wireless MU-MIMO channel for important temporal and spatial correlation properties.

We perform over-the-air beam-forming transmissions in a densely packed, challenging office scenario with multiple subscriber nodes and demonstrate not only the ability to simultaneously beamform to distinct users in relatively close proximity, but also the relative improvement that shifting to UHF frequencies provides.

Finally, we perform two sets of experiments with a customized MAC and PHY designed to gather dense, wideband, over-the-air channel estimates in realistic indoor and outdoor WLAN scenarios with multiple subscriber nodes. Using this data, we then demonstrate that the spatial correlation for outdoor users remains similar to that of 2.4 GHz WiFi, thus incurring no beamforming "penalty" for utilizing a frequency band with superior propagation and temporal correlation.

5.1 Indoor MU-MIMO Transmissions

Experimental Setup. First, we evaluate the performance of UHF MU-MIMO in an indoor, NLOS, office environment. Experiments were conducted during the work day with people walking through the halls in the environment depicted in Fig. 12.

The transmitting array was placed on a third floor walkway bridge and 6 separate receivers in two adjacent offices within the adjoining hallway. Note that the to-scale depiction in Fig. 12 shows the relative co-location of all receiving nodes with respect to the distance from the transmitter to simulate a densely packed

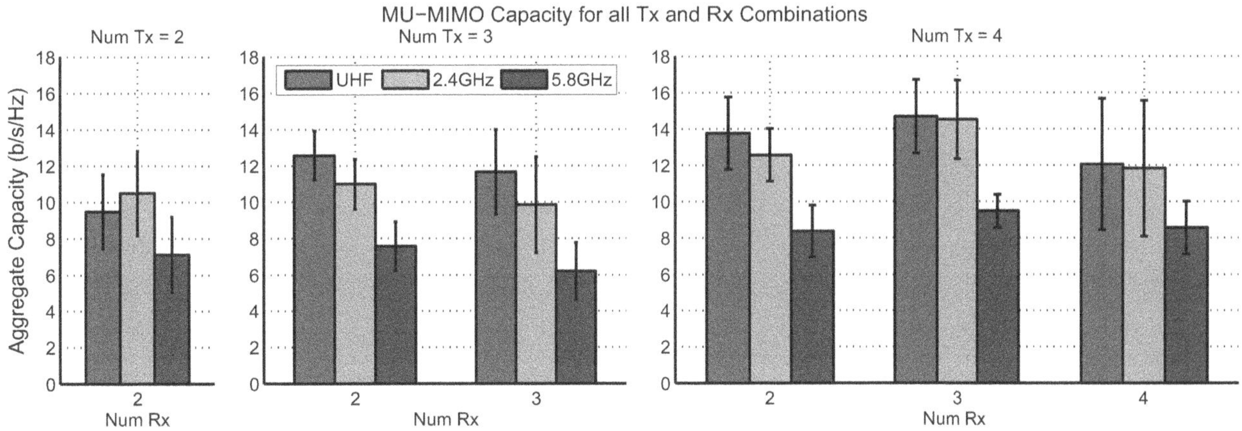

Figure 11: Received MU-MIMO Capacity.

office environment. This represents a realistic, challenging case for indoor stationary MU-MIMO transmissions due to the co-located receivers.

To encompass a wide range of user grouping conditions, every possible combination of transmit and receive antennas are considered. Sixty transmissions are performed for each topology. The center frequencies for each frequency band (*i.e.* channel) were chosen so that transmissions did not encounter interference from other equipment. Specifically, the UHF channel was first directly scanned for existing DTV or microphone transmissions and an experimental license was obtained to operate equipment on that channel. The channels selected for 2.4 and 5.8 GHz are not currently supported by the regulatory domain where these experiments were performed, thus ensuring minimal ISM-band interference. Using the measurement technique specified in § 3.3.1, every possible topology's MU-MIMO capacity is measured for each frequency band and shown in Fig. 11.

MU-MIMO Achievable Sum-Rate Capacity. Based on the channel models and accompanying analysis presented in § 4.1, we expect that the increased spatial correlation of UHF channels will not allow for MU-MIMO transmissions to accurately separate nearby users. However, we find that UHF MU-MIMO transmissions can actually achieve a sum capacity similar to that of 2.4 GHz WiFi transmissions (always between 1-2 b/s/Hz above of below the 2.4 GHz band).

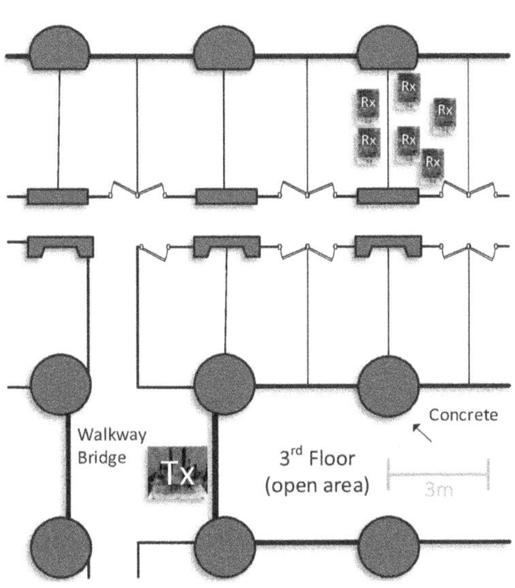

Figure 12: Indoor Experimental Test Setup.

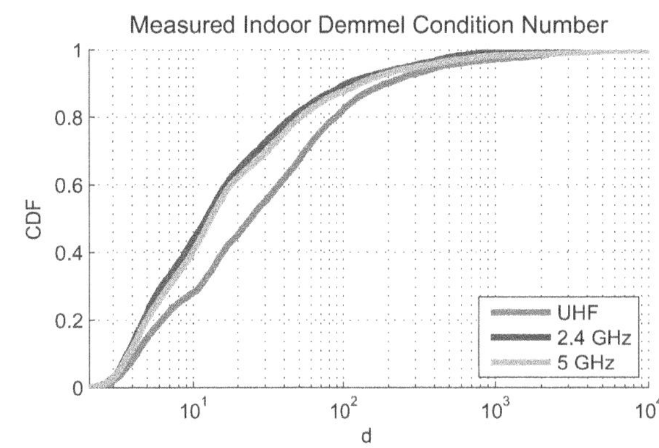

Figure 13: Demmel condition number measured for the indoor environment. Left is better for MU-MIMO.

In fact, we find that majority of the intuition and channel models surrounding UHF MU-MIMO are not specific to the frequency band itself but rather generalized characteristics of MU-MIMO transmissions. For example, the available MU-MIMO channel models characterize *indoor* WiFi and *outdoor* UHF channel environments where, regardless of frequency band, we expect increased difficulty in user separability in outdoor environments. Note the channel condition of the different transmission bands in the NLOS environment in Fig. 13 are similar in contrast to Fig. 10(b). Even though the wavelength of UHF is longer resulting in better propagation through materials, the UHF-band transmission still experiences enough multi-path to successfully beamform to multiple users in parallel.

Additionally, the results shown in Fig. 11 show a known trend of achievable capacity for MU-MIMO transmissions where the MU-MIMO gain plateaus as the available Degrees of Freedom (DoF)[1] are reached. The consistently worse performance of 5.8 GHz is explained by the high attenuation experienced by that frequency band in NLOS conditions combined with its sensitivity to environmental variation.

[1]DoF here refers to how many more transmit antennas there are than receive antennas in a MIMO transmission.

Note that UHF MU-MIMO consistently outperforms 2.4 GHz transmissions except for in the 2x2 transmission scenario. Because the sum transmit power emanating from the array is held constant regardless of the number of transmit antennas in use, the performance differential is solely a result of channel state, specifically it is an indicator of temporal channel correlation due to the WARPLab measurement platform.

As discussed on § 3.3.1, the latency in the WARPLab platform is due to the rate at which the host PC can download and upload samples to each of the WARP boards over Ethernet. In our system, we benchmark a read/write rate of approximately 2.5 ms per buffer and the closed loop beamforming method employed requires between 10 to 20 ms to complete depending on the number of transmit and receive antennas (the difference between a 2x2 and 4x4 transmission scenario).

Measured Temporal Correlation. To gain additional insight into the measured capacity results and to infer real world performance from our MU-MIMO transmissions, we also consider the channel correlation measured during each experiment.

For each topology, we consider each of the 60 MU-MIMO transmissions and their channel matrices. We calculate channel correlation between varying times during the experiment to measure the rate of change of the channel information with respect to time. These calculations are an average over all topologies (all combinations of transmit and receive antennas).

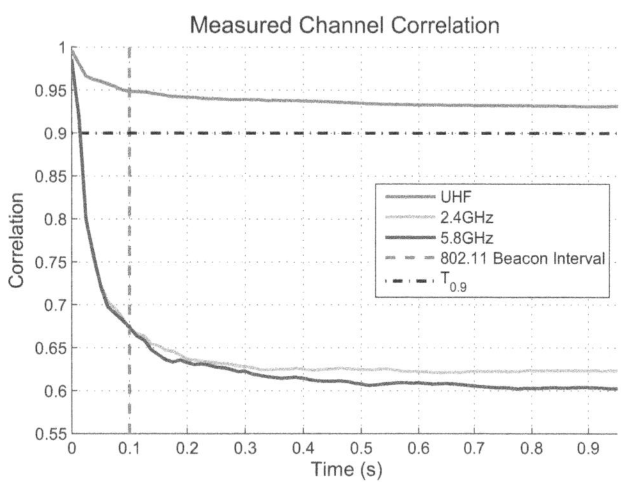

Figure 14: Measured Temporal Channel Correlation, depicting Beacon Interval, and $T_{0.9}$. WARPLab latency is 10-20 ms depending number of transmit and receive antennas.

Fig. 14 shows how the channels decorrelate over the course of one measured second in time. This is effectively an indicator of how long a transmitter has after measuring the channel matrix and before actually transmitting parallel streams using that measurement. A coherence time of $T_{0.9}$ represents when the probability of the channel being too stale to successfully beamform over is high.

First, note that the WARPLab latency range of 10 to 20 ms is approximately $T_{0.9}$ for the the two WiFi frequency bands. This indicates why only the 2x2 transmission scenario has the 2.4 GHz transmitter outperform UHF MU-MIMO; the latency between the sounding and transmission phase was the lowest and just at the $T_{0.9}$ limit.

While the 2.4/5 GHz frequencies both drop significantly within 100 ms, UHF remains above the $T_{0.9}$ threshold for the maximum one measured second difference between channel matrices. While these correlation values are not asymptotic and will eventually degrade, the performance of 2.4 and 5.8 GHz is sufficently low for stationary devices [11].

Also note that the 802.11 beacon packet rate (100 ms) is greater than the interval that 2.4/5 GHz MU-MIMO channels decorrelate. However, the stability of the UHF channel implies that a UHF MU-MIMO system could use periodic protocol packets for exchanging channel state information.

Finally, the channel correlation result shown in Fig. 14 effectively scales the MU-MIMO achievable rate shown in Fig. 12. The rate at which the 2.4/5 GHz channel decorrelates necessitates channel sounding on a per packet basis adding considerable overhead to MU-MIMO transmissions. However, the temporal stability of the UHF MU-MIMO channel allows a transmitter to significantly reduce this overhead intensive sounding process and thus significantly increase the potential MU-MIMO gains.

5.2 Outdoor Channel Characterization

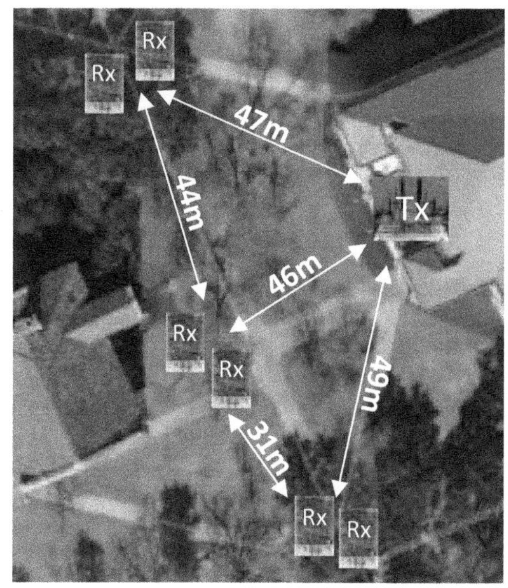

Figure 15: Experimental setup for outdoor channel sounding experiments. Distances between transmitter (on third floor balcony) and receivers shown. Note building and tree locations.

Finally, using the experimental framework developed in § 3, we perform outdoor channel sounding experiments to directly compare the performance and stability of UHF MU-MIMO channels. To that end, we setup an experimental network of a collection of nodes located outdoors being served by our array from a third floor balcony. Although the UHF transmitter is capable of transmitting much further distances, we limited the scale of the topology as shown in Fig. 15 to ensure a fair comparison between UHF and 2.4/5 GHz bands. The locations of the nodes were chosen such that the transmissions from the UHF and 2.4/5 GHz bands would reach the receivers (the UHF band transmitters can easily transmit further than 50 m). However, even by reducing the receiver distance to what is shown in Fig. 15, the 5 GHz band transmissions did not reliably reach the receiving nodes severely limiting the number of measured channel matrices. Thus, we restrict our outdoor comparison to the UHF and 2.4 GHz bands.

Just as we evaluated temporal correlation in the multi-path rich, indoor transmission environment, we seek to similarly characterize the most detrimental aspect of the outdoor MU-MIMO channel: receiver separability. Ill-conditioned channel matrices, as discussed in § 4.1, have a detrimental effect on an MU-MIMO enabled transmitter's ability to separate multiple users.

In the previous section, we found that while temporal stability of UHF was greater than that of 2.4/5 GHz, spatial correlation did not suffer as the UHF MU-MIMO transmissions were able to separate the co-located receivers. However, in an open, outdoor line-of-sight (LOS) environment, we find that both the UHF and 2.4 GHz bands exhibit the same Demmel condition number. Additionally, the CDF of the Demmel condition number closely matches the COST UHF channel condition shown in Fig. 10(b). This suggests that the comparison shown in Fig. 10(b) is not a result of the frequency band itself, but rather the wholly different channel environments in which the model was parametrized.

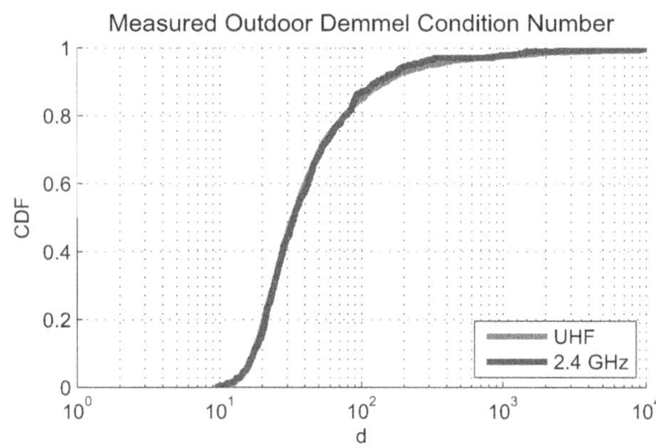

Figure 16: Measured Demmel Condition Number of the outdoor MU-MIMO channel.

6. RELATED WORK

We separate the discussion of related work into platforms and testbeds and UHF band characterization.

6.1 SDR Platforms

A number of common development platforms are capable of some degree of frequency-agility and programmability, e.g., [1, 4, 5]. However, these platforms are generally limited to either narrow-bandwidth applications when used for real-time applications or lack the open hardware and software stack required for research. None of them contain high-power amplifiers for long-range experiments. The form-factor currently required for real-time operation of platforms performing DSP operations on a CPU [1, 4] becomes a limitation when measuring wideband channel statistics for long periods of time with high temporal granularity, as such experiments often require many mobile user nodes.

Furthermore, existing systems do not integrate all components (specifically, a high-power analog front-end or highly dynamic AGC subsystem) necessary for high-bandwidth, long-range experiments. Off-the-shelf UHF amplifiers often are not designed for frequency-flat, wideband operation between 470-698 MHz and their size and external power requirements further hinder the mobility of multiple radio nodes.

WURC is designed to work interchangeably with any digital baseband and only draws power from the expansion card slot available on most FPGA development boards while integrating the remaining components necessary for a high-powered wideband transceiver. In combination with WURC, the WARP digital baseband platform contains a complete real-time layer 2 network stack and large experimental log storage capabilities (2 GB DDR3 RAM) within a small form-factor board, making it feasible to build and deploy a large number of wireless, mobile nodes for UHF MU-MIMO experiments.

6.2 UHF Band Characterization

MU-MIMO 2.4/5 GHz Characterization. While previous work emphasizes the importance of channel coherence time for MU-MIMO systems [9] and theoretical results suggest that center frequency is directly related to channel coherence time [28], these works do not provide the information necessary to perform a comparison based on center frequency. Such an investigation is necessary as MU-MIMO theoretical models for UHF and 2.4/5 GHz WiFi bands are parametrized for different environments (outdoor and indoor respectively). Models suggest that UHF band MU-MIMO exhibits increased temporal correlation at the cost of *increased* spatial correlation compared to 2.4/5 GHz WiFi (which would be detrimental to MU-MIMO due to the difficulty in providing orthogonal streams to the user [9]). However, we show that this tradeoff is not a result of the frequency band; instead, it is a result of the transmission environment. Thus, this discrepancy is not an inherent flaw to existing MU-MIMO channel models; rather, it is a result of incomplete parametrization and comparison of the MU-MIMO channel for all band/environment combinations.

SISO UHF Characterization. Several works explore the propagation characteristics of UHF transmissions in a variety of environments and topologies, e.g., [13, 20, 26, 33]. These works exhaustively analyze the performance of packetized UHF transmissions through different materials and in various environments. However, they focus on single-antenna, single-user transmissions and thus the characterization is restricted to metrics such as path loss, delay profile, and attenuation through materials. In contrast, our work focuses on the aggregate effects of these metrics with respect to MU-MIMO transmissions, namely temporal and spatial correlation in outdoor and indoor environments. Additionally, our work focuses on comparing these characteristics to 2.4/5 GHz bands where MU-MIMO techniques are used prevalently.

MIMO UHF Characterization. Other works exhaustively characterize MIMO transmissions in the UHF band [10, 15, 19, 22, 25]. However, they focus on outdoor, Single-user MIMO transmissions and thus focus on point to point transmissions with a single transmitter/receiver pair, each equipped with multiple antennas. While single-user and multi-user MIMO transmissions can have an equivalent number of transmit/receive antenna paths, the co-located receive antennas in the single-user case drastically reduces the variability in the temporal and spatial correlation with respect to environmental factors. Thus, the usage scenario of distinct MU-MIMO user nodes separated by some distance is not represented in the existing work. Instead, our work focuses on *multi-user* MIMO transmissions and specifically characterizes the effects of separated receivers.

Lastly, uplink MU-MIMO channels were studied in the UHF-band in a rural outdoor environment [29]. In contrast, we focus on downlink transmissions, consider both indoor and urban outdoor environments and provide channel characterization and spatial correlation of groups of users. Additionally, we evaluate *both* UHF and 2.4/5 GHz band MU-MIMO performance to comparatively characterize the performance of a UHF-band MU-MIMO system and provide an open-source platform.

7. CONCLUSION

We design and implement a wideband UHF SDR front-end with the ability to transmit on a diverse set of frequencies. We then utilize this new hardware capability and design an open MU-MIMO testbed, which we use to perform over-the-air experiments to empirically demonstrate that the UHF band is advantageous for MU-MIMO technologies.

8. ACKNOWLEDGMENTS

The authors would like to thank the following people for their assistance in performing experiments included in this work: Rachel J. Gray (Rice University), Yuqiang Mu (Rice University), and Pablo Salvador (IMDEA Networks Institute). This research was supported by NSF grants CNS-1314822, CNS-1126478, CNS-1012831, and a grant from Cisco Systems, Inc.

9. REFERENCES

[1] Ettus USRP. Available at: `https://www.ettus.com`.

[2] Lime Microsystems LMS6002D. Available at: `http://www.limemicro.com/products/LMS6002D.php`.

[3] Mango Communications 802.11 Reference Design. Available at: `http://mangocomm.com/802.11`.

[4] Microsoft SORA. Available at: `http://research.microsoft.com/en-us/projects/sora/`.

[5] Nutaq. Available at: `http://nutaq.com/en`.

[6] Rice University WARP project. Available at: `http://warp.rice.edu`.

[7] Wurc documentation. Available at: `http://http://www.volowireless.com/products/WURC`.

[8] Ofcom . Regulatory requirements for white space devices in the UHF TV band, Jul. 2012. Available at: `www.cept.org/Documents/se-43/6161/`.

[9] E. Aryafar, N. Anand, T. Salonidis, and E. Knightly. Design and experimental evaluation of multi-user beamforming in Wireless LANs. In *Proc. ACM MobiCom*, Chicago, IL, Sept. 2010.

[10] J. Boyer, P. Brown, K. Hayler, M. Garcia, J. Mitchell, P. Moss, and M. Thorp. MIMO for Broadcast–results from a high-power UK trial. In *Proc. IBC*, Amsterdam, The Netherlands, Sept. 2007.

[11] G. Breit. Coherence Time Measurement for TGac Channel Model. In *IEEE 802.11-09/1173r1*, Nov. 2009.

[12] Code of Federal Regulations. Title 47, part 15, subpart H - Television Band Devices, Feb. 2009.

[13] I. Collings, H. Suzuki, and D. Robertson. Ngara broadband access system for rural and regional areas. *Telecommunications Journal of Australia*, 62(1), 2012.

[14] M. Costa. Writing on dirty paper. *IEEE Transactions on Information Theory*, 29(3):439–441, May 1983.

[15] G. Eriksson, S. Linder, K. Wiklundh, P. Holm, P. Johansson, F. Tufvesson, and A. Molisch. Urban peer-to-peer MIMO channel measurements and analysis at 300 MHz. In *Proc. IEEE MILCOM*, San Diego, CA, Nov. 2008.

[16] A. Flores, R. Guerra, E. Knightly, P. Ecclesine, and S. Pandey. IEEE 802.11af: A standard for TV white space spectrum sharing. *IEEE Communications Magazine*, 51(10):92–100, Oct. 2013.

[17] A. Grebennikov. *RF and Microwave Power Amplifier Design*. McGraw-Hill, 2004.

[18] A. Greenbaum and T. Chartier. *Numerical Methods: Design, analysis, and computer implementation of algorithms*. Princeton University Press, 2012.

[19] A. Hammons, J. Hampton, N. Merheb, and M. Cruz. Cooperative MIMO field measurements for military UHF band in low-rise urban environments. In *Proc. IEEE SAM*, Darmstadt, Germany, Jul. 2008.

[20] J. Hampton, N. Merheb, W. Lain, D. Paunil, R. Shuford, J. Abrahamson, and W. Kasch. Propagation characteristics of ground based urban communications in the military UHF band. In *Proc. IEEE MILCOM*, Atlantic City, NJ, Oct. 2005.

[21] IEEE P802.11ac/D4.1. Specification framework for TGac, Nov. 2012.

[22] M. Jung, J.-H. Kim, Y.-K. Yoon, and H.-J. Hong. Multipath characteristics of MIMO channel at the UHF band for wireless systems in the urban area. In *Proc. IEEE ICACT*, Phoenix Park, South Korea, Feb. 2011.

[23] F. Kaltenberger, D. Gesbert, R. Knopp, and M. Kountouris. Correlation and capacity of measured multi-user MIMO channels. In *Proc. IEEE PIMRC*, Cannes, France, Sept. 2008.

[24] L. Liu, C. Oestges, J. Poutanen, K. Haneda, P. Vainikainen, F. Quitin, F. Tufvesson, and P. Doncker. The COST 2100 MIMO channel model. *IEEE Wireless Communications Magazine*, 19(6):92–99, Dec. 2012.

[25] R. Parviainen, J. Ylitalo, J-P.Nuutinen, P. Talmola, J. Henriksson, H. Himmanen, R. Ekman, and E. Huuhka. Experimental investigations on MIMO radio channel characteristics on UHF band. In *Proc. IEEE ICC*, Dresden, Germany, Jun. 2009.

[26] V. Pham and J.-Y. Chouinard. A study on the channel and signal cross correlation of UHF DTV channels. In *Proc. IEEE ISSSE*, Montreal, Canada, Jul. 2007.

[27] J. Poutanen, K. Haneda, L. Lingfeng, C. Oestges, F. Tufvesson, and P. Vainikainen. Parameterization of the COST 2100 MIMO channel model in indoor scenarios. In *Proc. EurAAP EuCAP*, Rome, Italy, Apr. 2011.

[28] T. Rappaport. *Wireless Communications: Principles and Practice*. Prentice Hall, 2001.

[29] H. Suzuki, D. Robertson, N. Ratnayake, and K. Ziri-Castro. Prediction and measurement of multiuser MIMO-OFDM channel in rural Australia. In *Proc. IEEE VTC*, Yokohama, Japan, May 2012.

[30] D. Tse and P. Viswanath. *Fundamentals of wireless communication*. Cambridge University Press, 2005.

[31] J. Wallace, M. Jensen, L. Swindlehurst, and B. Jeffs. Experimental characterization of the MIMO wireless channel: Data acquisition and analysis. *IEEE Transactions on Wireless Communications*, 2(2):335–343, Mar. 2003.

[32] B. Yarman. *Design of ultra wideband power transfer networks*. John Wiley & Sons, 2010.

[33] X. Ying, J. Zhang, L. Yan, G. Zhang, M. Chen, and R. Chandra. Exploring indoor white spaces in metropolises. In *Proc. ACM MobiCom*, Miami, FL, Sept. 2013.

[34] T. Yoo and A. Goldsmith. On the optimality of multiantenna broadcast scheduling using zero-forcing beamforming. *IEEE Journal on Selected Areas in Communications*, 24(3):528–541, Mar. 2006.

[35] C. Zhong, M. McKay, T. Ratnarajah, and K. Wong. Distribution of the Demmel condition number of Wishart matrices. *IEEE Transactions on Communications*, 59(5):1309–1320, May 2011.

[36] M. Zhu, G. Eriksson, and F. Tufvesson. The COST 2100 channel model: Parametrization and validation based on outdoor MIMO measurements at 300 MHz. *IEEE Transactions on Wireless Communications*, 12(2):888–897, Feb. 2013.

Enhancing Reliability to Boost the Throughput over Screen-Camera Links

Anran Wang[1] Shuai Ma[1] Chunming Hu[1] Jinpeng Huai[1] Chunyi Peng[2] Guobin Shen[3]
[1]SKLSDE Lab, Beihang University, China [2]The Ohio State University, USA [3]Microsoft Research, China
{wangar@act., mashuai@, hucm@, huaijp@}buaa.edu.cn chunyi@cse.ohio-state.edu jackysh@microsoft.com

ABSTRACT

With the rapid proliferation of camera-equipped smart devices (*e.g.,* smartphones, pads, tablets), visible light communication (VLC) over screen-camera links emerges as a novel form of near-field communication. Such communication via smart devices is highly competitive for its user-friendliness, security, and infrastructure-less (*i.e.,* no dependency on WiFi or cellular infrastructure). However, existing approaches mostly focus on improving the transmission speed and ignore the transmission reliability. Considering the interplay between the transmission speed and reliability towards effective end-to-end communication, in this paper, we aim to boost the throughput over screen-camera links by enhancing the transmission reliability. To this end, we propose RDCode, a robust dynamic barcode which enables a novel packet-frame-block structure. Based on the layered structure, we design different error correction schemes at three levels: intra-blocks, inter-blocks and inter-frames, in order to verify and recover the lost blocks and frames. Finally, we implement RDCode and experimentally show that RDCode reaches a high level of transmission reliability (*e.g.,* reducing the error rate to 10%) and yields at least two-fold improvement of transmission rate, compared with the existing state-of-the-art approach COBRA.

Categories and Subject Descriptors

C.2.1 [**Network Architecture and Design**]: Wireless communication

Keywords

Dynamic barcodes; transmission; reliability; smartphones

1. INTRODUCTION

Visible light communication (VLC) over screen-camera links has become an attractive short-range wireless communication solution due to the high availability of camera-equipped smartphones over the past years [12, 20, 25, 27, 33]. When data is encoded as a stream of images and displayed in screens, a smartphone can receive the data by capturing the images with its camera and decoding the image stream. Compared with the radio frequency (RF) techniques such as Bluetooth and Wi-Fi, VLC enables direct and secure communications, *e.g.,* by controlling the direction and distance of screen-cameras such that the visible range of a phone's screen content is limited to a few inches. Hence VLC simplifies the complicated authentication process for setting up link connections [12]. In addition, VLC is user-friendly and does not count on the Internet infrastructure. These make VLC over screen-camera links highly competitive for short-range wireless communications, *e.g.,* for applications such as file transfer between smartphones when either no wireless connections are available or security is much concerned. As pointed out by [33], VLC is well suited for one-time transfer as it incurs no charge and no overhead in link setup and management, compared with traditional RF techniques.

QR-Code [17] is commonly adopted for advertisement in the market for retail and tourism for easier information acquisition via smartphones with built-in barcode scanners [33]. By Mary Meeker's latest predictions on mobile Internet trends, four times more QR-Codes were scanned in March 2013 than a year before [1]. However, the capacity limitation makes such static 2D barcodes not appropriate for high-speed VLC.

While [25] and [3] achieve high-speed communications between large LCD monitors and high-speed digital cameras, they are not designed for smartphone platforms with limited capabilities such as small screens and low-quality cameras [12]. Recently, COBRA [12] and LightSync [33] are proposed to solve this problem.

However, data transmission over screen-camera links requires continuous image capturing, and a slight tremble may lead to parts of a frame unrecognizable or loss of a sequence of frames. Different smartphones also have different camera performance, which leads to different error rates by existing works. Further, the asymmetry nature of one-way transmission makes no feedbacks available. Reliable transimission is rather difficult to be obtained.

The absence of reliability also limits the throughput. For example, to keep the bit-error-rate below 10%, we have to restrict the frame of COBRA with less than 8000 symbols in our tests, much smaller than its maximum frame capacity, because distortions and trembles make the error rate increase seriously with the increase of the frame capacity. Another example is that even when we introduce an error correction code (Reed-Solomon [34]) to COBRA, it still has to transmit 2.03 times of the encoded data on average when

MobiCom'14, September 7 - 11, 2014, Maui, Hawaii, USA.
Copyright 2014 ACM 978-1-4503-2783-1/14/09 ...$15.00.
http://dx.doi.org/10.1145/2639108.2639135.

receiving a 128KB file intactly in our tests. This essentially reduces the transmission speed to 3.0KB per second.

Transmission reliability. Reliability is an important concern in short-range wireless communications, including VLC over screen-camera links, for ensuring dependable and effective data transmissions. Different applications have different requirements, and have different definitions of reliability [10]. Here we focus on one-time file transmissions that need fast and/or secure data delivery, and hence, we define *reliability* in terms of three aspects as follows:

(1) *Correctness* ensures that a receiver is able to check whether a received packet is exactly the one sent by the sender. Only correct packets are accepted.

(2) *Integrity* measures the ability that a receiver could obtain and assemble the data sent by the sender, which indicates the percentage of correctly delivered data.

(3) *Ordering* indicates the ability that a receiver is able to know the ordering of packets.

We argue that to achieve high-speed data transmissions, the *transmission rate* is only one side of the coin. The *transmission reliability*, the other side of the coin, is equally important since failed packets in general need to be retransmitted. This motivates us to develop new techniques towards reliable transmissions for applications such as file transfer.

Limitations and uncertainty. To achieve fast and reliable transimissions over screen-camera links, we face substantial challenges, primarily caused by:

Smartphone limitations. It is common that (a) senders with different types of screens may display colors differently and in different luminance levels, and (b) receivers with different lens and sensors may have different color processing mechanisms. This could lead to a common scenario such that the image captured by a receiver may be highly different from the original one from a sender. We summarize these problems as follows.

(1) *Lens distortions*[1]. Commonly found lens distortions of smartphone cameras are radial distortions that straight lines in a captured image become distorted.

(2) *Low border performance.* Due to the physical structure of lens, most digital cameras essentially have poor border performance, *e.g.*, low luminance, more noises and worse sharpness in the border area.

(3) *Color inaccuracies.* Different luminance brightness distribution within a screen and different view angles of a camera often cause colors displayed differently in different areas of shooting ranges.

(4) *Rolling shutter*[2]. Most smartphone cameras use CMOS sensors that adopt roll shutter for image acquisition, in which each frame is recorded not as a single snapshot, but rather by scanning across the frame either vertically or horizontally. As a result, different parts of a captured frame may belong to distinct frames when capturing image streams.

User behavior uncertainty. Different users may behave differently when shooting pictures. The user behavior uncertainty includes but not limited to:

(1) *Different positions.* It is common that users may capture

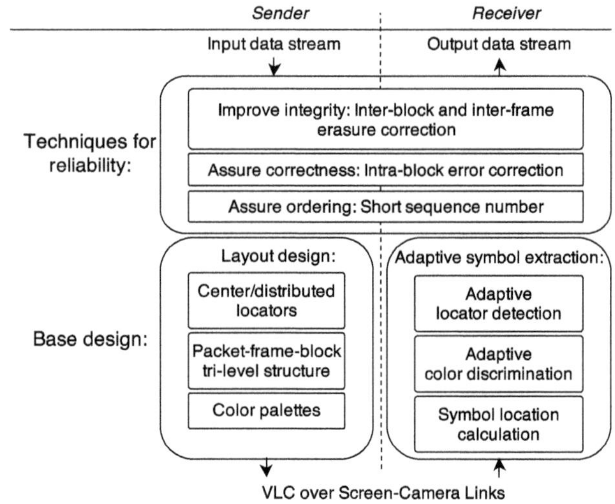

Figure 1: RDCode architecture

only a part of the barcode on the screen because of the restriction of shooting positions.

(2) *Unexpected behaviors*, including mostly trembles of the hands, could interrupt the transmission for a short period.

The two challenges typically introduce two issues: (a) the *locality problem* that for an image with uniform features, the close places in its captured image have similar features, while places far from each other present different features, and (b) the *partial unavailability problem* that leads to either unrecognizable parts of a frame caused by *e.g.,* unsuitable shooting positions or temporally sequential frames loss caused by *e.g.,* trembles.

Other restrictions include the limited computing ability such that standard image processing techniques are not appropriate for continuous image decoding with smartphones. These make it even challenging to build high-speed reliable VLC over screen-camera links using smartphones, as only light-weight techniques could be employed to address the above mentioned problems.

Contributions&Roadmap. We propose a robust dynamic barcode (RDCode) by encoding and decoding a stream of barcode images, which boosts the throughput over screen-camera links by improving the reliability. RDCode reaches a high level of transmission reliability and doubles the transmission rate compared with the existing state-of-the-art approach COBRA, by addressing the aforementioned limitations and uncertainty. To our knowledge, this is the first call for high-speed VLC over screen-camera links using smartphones by enhancing the transmission reliability.

(1) We design a novel packet-frame-block barcode layout (Section 2), such that a packet comprises a sequence of frames, each of which further consists of a set of independent blocks. This design not only enhances the transmission reliability by addressing the smartphone limitations and user behavior uncertainty, but also improves the transmission rate.

(2) We develop a tri-level data correction and ordering approach to enhancing reliability (Section 3), based on the observation that error distributions follow a certain spatial and temporal regularity. Error corrections at intra-blocks, inter-blocks and inter-frames are for the verification of blocks, recovery of lost blocks and recovery of lost frames, respectively. A short sequence number is also attached with each block for

[1]http://en.wikipedia.org/wiki/Lens_Distortion
[2]http://en.wikipedia.org/wiki/Rolling_shutter

Figure 2: A center locator pattern with 7×7 pixels

synchronization. These together enhance the transmission reliability of RDCode with a reasonable overhead.

(3) We implement RDCode on top of an Android platform for file transmissions (Section 4), and its architecture is shown in Fig. 1. We also conduct an extensive experiment study (Section 5), which shows that RDCode reaches a high level of transmission reliability (*e.g.*, reducing the error rate to 10%) and yields at least two-fold improvement of transmission rate, compared with the existing state-of-the-art approach COBRA.

2. BASIC DESIGN

In this section, we introduce the basic design of RDCode, including layout design and adaptive symbol extraction that lay down the base towards high-speed reliable VLC over screen-camera links via smartphones.

2.1 Design Principles

We have done extensive tests, and found that failures of recognizing barcodes are typically due to locality and partial unavailability problems. For example, when capturing a barcode with four corner locators such as COBRA [12], the failed detection of one or two corner locators leads to the complete failure of the entire barcode. Another example is the light reflection or bad border performance that makes a certain region of the captured barcode unreadable. This situation is even serious for dynamic barcodes since continuous locating and decoding frames needs more robustness. This implies that to obtain high transmission reliability, a barcode layout should address the locality and partial unavailability problems (Section 1).

In order to address them, the ideal method is to make each frame and each symbol independent and recoverable, *e.g.*, each frame or symbol has independent locators, sequence number and decoding methods. But it is impossible because massive overhead will be introduced, and a rather high computational complexity is required. A practical solution is to build intermediate layers above the symbols and frames.

This leads to a new design of dynamic barcodes: (a) a packet-frame-block tri-level structure to address the two aforementioned problems, in which each frame is associated with a single center locator and multiple distributed locators, and (b) a sequence of frames are aggregated into a packet as a logical transmission unit.

2.2 Layout Design

Symbols, blocks, frames, packets, center locators, distributed locators and color palettes form the basic structure of RDCode, and we first introduce them in detail.

Symbols. A symbol is a $p \times p$ square of pixels with the same color. Symbols are the basic units for data transmission.

Data symbols. A data symbol is a special class of symbols that is not in a black or white color.

There are in total $c \geq 4$ colors for data symbols, and hence a data symbol indeed encodes a $log_2 c$-bit data. Here black and white colors are reserved for the center and distributed locators to be introduced immediately.

Blocks. A block is a $h \times h$ square of symbols.

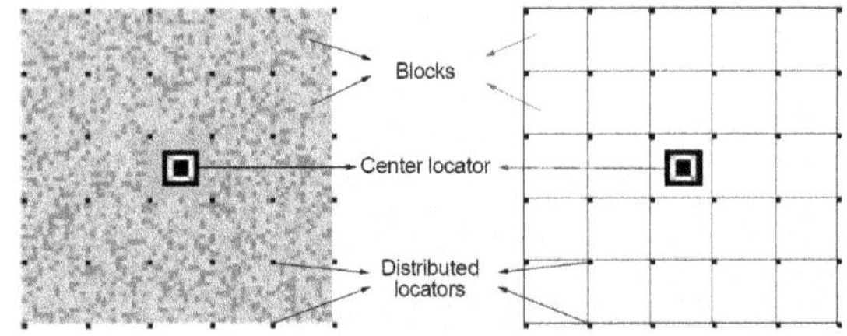

Figure 3: RDCode frame layout

Frames. A frame is a $m \times n$ rectangle of blocks, in which both m and n are odd.

Packets. A packet is a sequence of a fixed number of continuous frames.

Moreover, each block within a frame has a unique index, and each frame has a unique index (i.e., its order in the sequence) within a packet.

We next introduce the center and distributed locators on which symbol extraction heavily relies.

Center locators. There is a unique symbol pattern, referred to as a *center locator*, embedded in the center block of an RDCode frame. The detailed design of center locator is orthogonal to our work. As illustrated in Fig. 2, a center locator of RDCode is a square of symbols, in which (a) the center is a square of black symbols, (b) the borders are all black symbols, (c) there is a symbol inside each border corner with a distinct color of the c colors for data symbols; and finally (d) the rest are filled with white symbols.

Center locators allow fast detection of frames, and the four colorful symbols are used to estimate the shooting angle and image rotation.

Distributed locators. For the ease of explanation, we append a frame with $m \times n$ blocks to $(m+1) \times (n+1)$ blocks with dummy blocks. The top left most *black* symbol inside a block is referred to as a *distributed locator* of the original frame. Here (a) a frame with $m \times n$ blocks has $(m+1) \times (n+1)$ distributed locators, (b) there are four distributed locators around a block, which are used to locate the data symbols of the block, and (c) a frame is further attached with $m+n+1$ extra symbols after distributed locators are introduced, as illustrated by the example frame in Fig. 3.

Distributed locators allow simple and efficient locating and tracking of RDCode, as will be seen immediately.

Color palettes. As most data transmission systems do, a receiver needs to turn the raw channel signals into discrete bits. For barcode based systems, raw channel signals are the pixel colors. To design effective methods to distinguish different colors, we embed another pattern into each block at a fixed position, referred to as a *color palette* which is a square of c symbols, each in a distinct color of the c colors for data symbols.

As a block often has more than 100 symbols, the color palettes and distributed locators in a frame typically incur a reasonable overhead, the price that we have to pay for enhancing transmission reliability. For example, for a RDCode frame containing 11*7 blocks, each of which has 12*12 symbols, only 563 out of all 14,275 of its symbols are dedicated to its center locator, distributed locators and color palettes. In contrast, for a COBRA frame with $132 * 108 = 14,256$ symbols (roughly the same number of symbols as the previous RDCode frame), 1,404 out of its symbols are dedicated to those frame markers, around 2.5 times of RDCode.

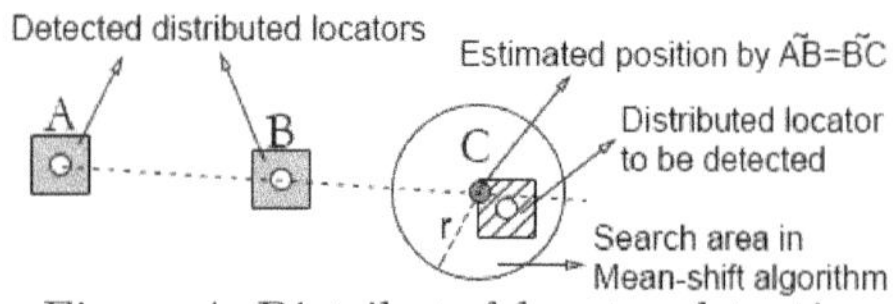

Figure 4: Distributed locator detection

2.3 Adaptive Symbol Extraction

We will next introduce the techniques to achieve adaptive symbol extraction when receiving frames. *Adaptive* means a receiver could adjust its parameters with the changing of its captured frames. This is essential to transmission reliability since the transmission performance should not be affected by different situations. Moreover, in order to address the partially unavailability problem, blocks and locators are treated independently in RDCode .

(1) Adaptive locator detection. We first introduce the adaptive method to detect locators within a frame such that even if some locators fail to be located, those blocks whose locators are correctly detected remain readable.

A receiver will first locate the center locator at the first captured frame, and we adopt the Mean-shift algorithm [6] to detect it in our implementation. Then the receiver analyzes the four colorful symbols in the center locator to detect the rough direction and distance of these symbols, and the perspective distortion of the frame. The receiver could also know the rough side length of symbols using the black symbols inside the center locator.

After that, the receiver recursively detects the distributed locators starting from the four distributed locators around the center block. (a) The positions of the four distributed locators around the center block can be easily computed based on the position of the center locator, the direction and the symbols' side length. The precise positions of the locators are obtained by the Mean-Shift algorithm or fast adjusting algorithm. (b) Then, as long as three out of the four distributed locators around the center block are successfully located, the receiver can recursively locate the rest distributed locators. We define locator A is *adjacent* to locator B if and only if they are around the same block. Then, for any three distinct locators A, B and C in a straight line in the sender frame where A is adjacent to B and B is adjacent to C, if the receiver knows the precise positions of any two of them in the captured frame, it can estimate the position of the third one based on their geometry relationship. For example, if the precise positions of locators A and B are known, the position of locator C can be estimated by assuming vectors $\tilde{\mathbf{AB}} = \tilde{\mathbf{BC}}$, as shown in Fig.4. The Mean-Shift algorithm or fast adjusting algorithm is then processed to get its precise position. This above process repeats until no more distributed locators can be successfully located.

Fast adjusting algorithm. We next introduce the main idea of the fast adjusting algorithm. In our work, Mean-Shift algorithm [5] is used to get the center position of the black area in a center or distributed locator, given an estimated initial search position. The essential step of Mean-Shift algorithm is to calculate the mean position of all the black pixels in a circular search area with radius r in each iteration, which needs to identify the colors of $O(r^2)$ pixels.

Observe that in a captured distributed locator, the black pixels are clustered as a rectangle, and when locating a distributed locator, its precise position is very close to the initial search position that is well estimated by the positions of other distributed locators or the corresponding locator's precise position in the last captured frame. Hence we can use linear search instead of quadratic search (with respect to the search radius r), when the initial search position is already in the distributed locator to be located. We describe this optimization in detail as follows.

Given the pixel at the initial search position, if it is black, it has a high probability that it is right in the distributed locator. As a result, we use *fast adjusting algorithm*: instead of searching the large circle area, it simply searches the left most, right most, top most and bottom most continuous black pixels from the initial search position. Let these four black pixels' positions be p_l, p_r, p_t and p_b, respectively. We denote the precise position of the distributed locator as $((p_l + p_r)/2,\ (p_t + p_b)/2)$ if the color of the pixel at this position is black. Otherwise, the Mean-shift algorithm is used. Gaussian filter [31] is adopted to reduce the interferences from the noises in the process. The above method works well in our implementation.

Note that (a) once a locator is located, it is independently tracked while dealing with the successive frames, and the failed detection of one distributed locator has no effects on other distributed locators. The locators are autonomous, but also co-related. Failed distributed locators still have a chance to be relocated later when two of its adjacent distributed locators are detected. Even if it fails again, the receiver could still use the estimated position instead. (b) Because locators split one frame to several small-sized blocks, this method also addresses radial distortions and increases the accuracy of decoding. (c) Except for detecting the center locator, our approach doesn't need to search the entire frame, and the center locator only needs to be located for the first captured frame. In most cases, the receiver only needs to visit several thousand pixels to locate one frame.

(2) Adaptive color discrimination. We then introduce the adaptive methods to discriminate different colors.

To decode data symbols, a receiver needs to correctly identify their colors. The color palette in a block is firstly identified as its position is fixed. Then the c colors in the color palette are detected using Gaussian filter [31]. Then, for each located data symbol, the Euclidean distances of its color and the c colors in the color palette are computed, and the color with the closest distance is chosen as the color of the data symbol.

The color palette must be identified accurately, or the entire block could be affected. Temporally changing environments and location errors may lead to the failure of the color palette's correct detection. In order to solve this, we adopt a smoothing method. Assume that we have the old color palette of a block represented as a vector $Color_{old}$ and the block at the same position of the next coming frame with a new color palette P. If the block is decoded successfully, we let $Color_{new} = (1 - \mu)Color_{old} + \mu P$ where μ is a parameter set to 0.3 in practice, and keep $Color_{new} = Color_{old}$, otherwise. To prevent incorrectly recognized color palette from affecting subsequent blocks, if the following error correction method cannot correct the block, the color palette of its subsequent block will not adopt the smoothing method.

Black and non-black colors also need to be discriminated when locating distributed locators. The process is similar. The initial color behavior may be known by analyzing the pixels in the central part of a frame. A histogram of their brightness can be built, where the x-axis is the brightness of pixels, and the y-axis is the number of pixels that fall into a brightness bin. Typically, there exist a maximal bin, a minimal bin and another maximal bin in order. The first bin is for black pixels, the third one is for colorful pixels, and hence the mid brightness of the second bin can be used as a brightness threshold, referred to as m, to distinguish black from non-black colors.

Each distributed locator has a different threshold. When detecting a locator, all visited pixels recognized as black or non-black are used to revise the threshold for that locator, and they are split into two groups: (a) one with brightness less than the old brightness threshold m_{old}, and (b) another one with brightness equal or greater than m_{old}, where b and n are the average brightness of the two groups, respectively. Then we adjust the brightness threshold as follows: $m_{new} = (1-\mu)m_{old} + \mu(b+n)/2$. After several frames, each locator has its own adaptive brightness threshold.

(3) Symbol location calculation. After all distributed locators around a block are located, it is easier to locate the symbols of the block. Previous barcode designs such as COBRA and DataMatrix [16] use *timing symbols* at the borders of a frame as references to locate all other symbols, and this incurs high overhead. For RDCode, a block contains much less symbols than a frame, and hence the perspective distortion is not serious. As a result, the location accuracy is high, and there is no need to introduce timing symbols around each block. We simply compute the position P_{xy} of the symbol at coordinate (x, y) as follows.

$$P_t = \begin{pmatrix} \frac{h-x}{h} & \frac{x}{h} \end{pmatrix} \begin{pmatrix} P_1 \\ P_2 \end{pmatrix}$$
$$P_b = \begin{pmatrix} \frac{h-x}{h} & \frac{x}{h} \end{pmatrix} \begin{pmatrix} P_3 \\ P_4 \end{pmatrix}$$
$$P_{xy} = \begin{pmatrix} \frac{h-y}{h} & \frac{y}{h} \end{pmatrix} \begin{pmatrix} P_t \\ P_b \end{pmatrix},$$

where P_1, P_2, P_3 and P_4 denote the four positions of the left top most, right top most, left bottom most and right bottom most distributed locators around a block with $h \times h$ symbols, respectively.

Remarks. RDCode is in nature to address the locality and partial unavailability problems caused by smartphone limitations and user behavior uncertainty.

(1) Blocks and distributed locators in a frame are autonomous. For instance, distributed locators are tracked independently, each of which has its own black color threshold and own color palette. Blocks could also be decoded asynchronously by a receiver, so the rolling shutter limitation could be alleviated. Block autonomy also enables the flexibility to design effective and efficient reliability techniques (to be seen in Section 3).

(2) The adaptive techniques for symbol extraction improve the locating and decoding accuracy, by using successive frames in a dynamic barcode system.

(3) Compared with the design of four corner locators in a frame like COBRA and LightSync, our design of center locators has less failure possibility and less locating time. The incorporation of the center and distributed locators further improves the locating success rate, as distributed locators help the locating of their adjacent distributed locators. As a result, the block locating success rate is significantly improved as shown by our experiments.

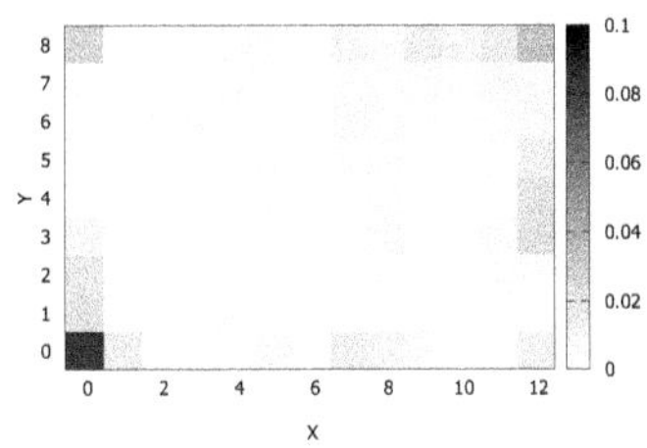

Figure 5: The average bit-error rate in the blocks displayed on an Asus Nexus 7 tablet and captured by smartphones LG Nexus 4 and Samsung Galaxy S3.

(4) It is worth mentioning that there exist more advanced algorithms to improve the success rate of locating frame corners, such as Hough transform [4] and local binarization [35]. However, in a barcode stream decoding scenario using smartphones, the computational overhead should be small in the first place. It is this reason why COBRA adopts a simple heuristic localization algorithm, but not those advanced algorithms. Our localization algorithm is effective and incurs only a small overhead, and it is specifically designed for RDCode, which cannot be directly adopted by COBRA.

3. TECHNIQUES FOR RELIABILITY

In this section, we first analyze the characteristics of error distributions. We then introduce the error correction technique for data correctness and data integrity, followed by the data ordering technique.

3.1 Analyses of Data Errors

We utilize a tablet as the sender and two smartphones with different cameras as receivers to experimentally analyze the error characteristics of the RDCode frames.

Uneven error distribution. We give an analysis of the RDCode frames with 9×13 blocks displayed on a tablet, captured by two different smartphones, and find that in barcode systems, errors are not randomly distributed. We count the average bit-error rates of blocks, *i.e.*, the ratio of error bits among all bits in a block. As shown by Fig. 5, errors are unevenly distributed in a frame and have certain regularity: (a) blocks close to the border area have higher error rates, due to the limitations of smartphones, and (b) other blocks may have a rare amount of errors on average.

Wide range of error rates. Basically the data errors of a dynamic barcode system can be classified into three types with different range of error rates:

(1) *Caused by noises.* Noises are inevitable and the border area has more noises due to the low border performance and the physical structure of image sensors. Typically the error rate is less than 10% due to the data errors caused by noises, depending on the environments and devices.

(2) *Caused by block decoding failures.* When (a) errors occur at some locators due to noises or at data symbols due to partial unavailability, or (b) dirty marks that cause their shelter symbols unreadable, the corresponding blocks often fail to be correctly decoded. This often results in an error rate around 10% to 100% for those affected blocks. Also, border areas has high possibility of block decoding failures since unsuitable shooting positions could easily make border areas out of the capture scope.

(3) *Caused by frame decoding failures.* When trembles happen, the affected frames are likely to be streaking due to motion blur. Almost an entire frame are unable to be decoded. Another reason to cause frame decoding failures is

the fast refresh rate with low brightness, so that receivers could capture overlapped frames. The colors of data symbols within adjacent frames may overlap with each other to make them unreadable. Although LightSync [33] focuses on the overlapped frames, it is for data symbols with black and white colors only, and cannot be used in our work for free.

Limitations of error correction techniques. In one-way communication, the standard approach to protecting data correctness is to use Forward Error Correction (FEC) to correct errors by adding redundant data [32]. When burst errors happen frequently, FEC often cuts no ice. Interleaved codes ameliorate FEC by shuffling the data symbols to several messages to create a uniform error distribution [32]. However, FEC and interleaved FEC cannot be easily incorporated into RDCode, as analyzed below.

(1) FEC is designed to correct random errors, but when the error distribution has regularity, it is not very efficient. A small amount of redundant codes cannot correct all errors, but a large amount of redundant codes lead to small throughput. Hence, messages at different areas should have different error correction ability.

(2) The error rate fluctuates widely and distributes unevenly. To design a good interleaved FEC is extremely difficult, since the intense burst errors may have impacts on other good areas with low-error rates. As data symbols in good areas may not be correctly decoded due to the interleaving, which in turn involves more data to be re-transmitted.

3.2 Tri-level Error Correction

Due to the above error characteristics and the restrictions of traditional error correction techinques, we develop an error correction method of RDCode for: (a) nonuniformity that different areas within a frame should have different error correction abilities, (b) autonomy that partial unavailability should not spread to other locality, and (c) effectiveness that only reasonable overhead should be attached.

The error correction method involves with three levels for the errors within blocks, frames and packets, respectively, among which the first is for data correctness and the last two are for data integrity.

Block level. *Intra-block error correction* is for blocks. Inside the blocks we focus on the errors caused by noises. It's more important to detect errors rather than correct slight errors in this level, since the transmission is not reliable if erroneous data are detected as correct. In our implementation, we use the Reed-Solomon (RS) code [34] for its strong error correction and detection ability. Based on a finite field with 256 elements (1 element represents 1 byte), an $RS(n,k)$ code has the ability to correct up to $\lfloor (n-k)/2 \rfloor$ error bytes and to detect any combinations of up to $n-k$ error bytes, and all the encoded bytes in a block are called an RS message. In order to improve the error detection ability, before encoding into an RS code, the last byte of the original message is set to the XOR of all other bytes in it. A receiver calculates their XORs to verify the correctness after the RS code has been successfully decoded.

Blocks in different areas are encoded with different parameters. For example, blocks in the border and corner areas have more correction ability than the other areas.

Frame level. *Inter-block erasure correction* is for frames. If a block fails to be located, or the intra-block error correction method can detect but cannot correct the errors, it is marked as a missing block. Since we know their indexes, we can apply any erasure code across the blocks. As the error distribution has regularity, RDCode uses a simple parity-check code to recover erased blocks because of its computational efficiency. Other erasure codes (*e.g.*, Reed-Solomon erasure code) could also be used for stronger correction guarantee, but with more computation.

We treat each block as a code element. Some blocks are parity-check blocks, which are also protected by intra-block error correction, but their contents are generated by other blocks. Suppose we have N blocks with indexes $1...N$ in a frame. The statistical missing probabilities of each block [3] are expressed by $P(1..N)$. We sort this array in decreasing order and generate another array $P_{sorted}(1..N)$ in which $P_{sorted}(i)$ is the index of the block with the ith largest missing probability. There are in total p parity-check blocks where p is a parameter set manually. The indexes of those blocks are expressed by $Check(1..p)$, and are determined by:

$$Check(i) = P_{sorted}(\lceil N/2^{p-i} \rceil)$$

Suppose that $Block(i)$ denotes the original message of the block with index i, and for each $i \in [1,p]$, $start = i, end = Check(i) - 1$, then

$$Block(Check(i)) = \bigoplus_{j=start}^{end} Block(P_{sorted}(j)),$$

where $\bigoplus$ is the direct sum operator. When decoding, the parity-check blocks are used to recover the missing blocks. Each parity-check block can recover one missing block that it covers. Since a block with a higher rank in P_{sorted} is involved to a parity-check block that covers fewer blocks, blocks with a high missing possibility are more possible to be recovered. A situation may happen that two blocks may have different original message lengthes due to intra-block error correction. When computing XOR, we let the result have the longest length of all the involved original messages, so that all the content of these messages can be covered.

The code design makes encoding and decoding procedures take linear time regardless of p. This code could recover at most p blocks by using p parity-check blocks.

Packet level. *Inter-frame erasure correction* is for packets. The blocks with the same block index i in a packet are denote as $subpacket(i)$, and $subpacket(i)(j)$ denotes the content of jth block in $subpacket(i)$.

Entire frame loss happens mostly sequentially since trembles last a period of time, typically 0.1 to 0.5 second. Our idea is that it is guaranteed to tolerate q consecutive frames loss within a packet containing n frames by using the last q frames as parity-check frames. We set $start = 1$, $end = \lceil (n-j)/q \rceil - 1$ ($j \in [0,q)$), and for each $i \in [1, block\_number\_per\_frame]$,

$$subpacket(i)(n-j) = \bigoplus_{k=start}^{end} subpacket(i)(n-j-kq)$$

While receiving a packet, after the first two corrections, each valid or missing block is marked in a table. When the next packet is arriving, the receiver will check if there exist some missing but recoverable blocks within each subpacket, and then recover them.

[3] In our implementation, corner blocks have higher missing probability than border blocks, and border blocks have higher missing probability than the remaining blocks.

3.3 Data Ordering

Due to the rolling shutter problem, blocks are asynchronously decoded, *i.e.,* blocks belonging to the same frame of a sender may be captured in different frames by a receiver. A straightforward method to keep the ordering of blocks is to add a full sequence number (including the frame index and packet sequence number) to each block, but this brings too much redundancy. Observe that at most two partial frames from a sender can overlap in a captured frame of a receiver, so the difference of any two blocks' sequence number within a captured frame is equal or less than 1.

The block containing the center locator is different from other blocks since it is always being first located and recognized in RDCode. We simply put the full sequence number of a frame in the center block. Note that this method remains protecting all the data in a block. The data within a block, including the sequence number, has few chances to be wrong if it is correctly decoded by the intra-block error correction method.

Inside each block, there exists a short relative sequence number containing the last 2 bits of the frame index. When dealing with a corrected block, RDCode compares its 2-bit frame index with the last 2 bits of the frame index in the center block, and checks the following.

(1) If they are equal, the full sequence number of this block is the full sequence number in the center block.

(2) If its 2-bit frame index is one smaller/bigger than the last 2 bits of the frame index in the center block (3 is one smaller than 0, and 0 is one bigger than 3), the full sequence number of this block is one smaller/bigger than the full sequence number in the center block.

(3) The case that the 2-bit frame index is two smaller/bigger than the last 2 bits of the frame index in the center block happens rarely. If it happens, the block is simply dropped.

With these, the accurate sequence number of each block is obtained with only 2-bit overhead in each non-center block that contains more than 200 bits data.

Remarks. (1) The novelty of our techniques to enhance the reliability lies in that instead of simply applying a single Reed-Solomon code like most barcode systems, we analyze the characteristics of data errors, utilize our tri-level barcode layout and design a tri-level error correction method to decode the decodable parts of data as much as possible to increase the data integrity. (a) The block level is designed for detecting errors and correcting slight errors caused by noises. (b) The frame level is designed for recovering undecodable blocks caused by partial unavailability problems such as dirty marks or unsuitable shooting positions. And (c) the packet level is designed for tolerating typical trembles by temporally recovering undecodable frames. We adopt Reed-Solomon codes at the block level because of its strong error detection and correction ability, and we also design own parity check codes, a light-weight solution, at the frame and packet levels for the high efficiency.

(2) Although the tri-level scheme used in RDCode works well in our implementation and evaluation, our scheme is not optimal given that many FEC codes exist. However, for communications over screen-camera links, we are the first to analyze some characteristics of the data errors, and explore a multi-level scheme which works much better than using Reed-Solomon codes alone in our tests.

(3) Based on the multi-layer design of RDCode, a more suitable error correction scheme for VLC over screen-camera links is worth further study. For example, we expect to associate each symbol with the confidence of color discrimination, then LDPC codes [7] are feasible for RDCode. In addition, our tri-level scheme belongs to block codes, which enables almost any transmission application including file transmission and data stream transmission. If only targeted on file transmissions with fixed lengths, suboptimal rateless (fountain) codes such as Raptor codes [29] are capable to replace the erasure correction codes in RDCode. It should be pointed out that the visual cryptograhy [22,23] proposed some interesting ideas, *e.g.,* by dividing a pixel to subpixels, to increase the transmission robustness and security, which provides more insights for a further study on coding.

4. IMPLEMENTATION

We have implemented RDCode on an Android 4.2 platform using Scala with the Android SDK and Scala compiler. Our experiments involve with three devices: one tablet (Asus Nexus 7) and two smartphones (LG Nexus 4 and Samsung Galaxy S3). During all the tests, our system runs on all these smart devices smoothly.

We have also developed an online encoder and an online decoder for file transmissions. Since Fountain codes [29] require high time complexity on solving linear systems as pointed out by [33], we make the file repeating in the data stream plus a simple coding scheme. Note that the effectiveness of RDCode design significantly reduces the chances of packet retransmissions. In order to reduce the time used for retransmission waiting, for even loops, we add the first half packets to the second half packets using XOR operations, and for odd loops, we add the second half packets to the first half packets. Using such a coding technique, it significantly reduces the waiting time up to 0.5 loop since if a packet in the second half is missing, receivers can recover it by decoding the corresponding packet in the first half with a constant computation complexity.

How to choose the c colors of symbols is important and complementary to the design of RDCode, which itself deserves a further study. In our tests, the error rate of using 2 colors are almost the same of using 4 colors, while using 8 colors introduces tripled error rate on average. Since 8 colors can present 3 bits data which is only 3/2 times of what 4 colors can present, we choose to use 4 colors. Since the raw data from the camera of Android phones are in the YUV format, we choose to use the most distinct four colors, orange, green, pink and blue in YUV color space for efficiency.

The sender of RDCode has an option to let a user initiate a file transmission, after which the file is encoded to RDCode packets. When forming frames, the sender changes the symbol size to fill in different number of symbols on the screen. Once a frame is produced, it is drawn on the screen.

The drawing procedure itself takes much more time than the encoding procedure since thousands of color squares need to be rendered. To address this problem for the real-time encoding, we use four additional threads, which is equal to the number of CPU cores of Nexus 4 and Galaxy S3. They're all for rendering the squares to a bitmap buffer. Each thread takes charge of rendering one-fourth distinct symbols of a frame. The four threads and the encoder thread form a pipeline that produces and draws frames efficiently. When all packets of a file are transmitted, the sender repeats the above process and resends the packets until the entire file is correctly received.

When a frame contains about 10,000 symbols, our online encoder can produce ten RDCode frames per second, and display the RDCode frames at a 10FPS refresh rate on the screen. The rendered frames are also saved to the flash storage of smartphones to further speed up the process offline and reach a faster refresh rate.

We also use the multi-thread technique to reduce the processing time of a receiver. Since the blocks and distributed locators are autonomous, it is easy to make the decoding procedure in parallel. We further insert a flag to each of the blocks that indicates the frame parity. If a block to be decoded has a flag that is the same as the block in the same place of the last processed frame, and the block is successfully decoded, then there is no need to re-decode the block again since it is identical to the last decoded block. This optimization improves the efficiency of real-time decoding. When the bit rate reaches 300Kbps, it is still able to decode RDCode in real time using our tested smartphones. We have also implemented an offline decoder by further adding a layer to save or load the raw captured data to or from a file stored in an SD card.

The Android platform also provides a few parameters to customize a camera's performance. In our implementation, the camera's ISO is set to 400, its *RecordingHint* is set to true, and the others are using the default. The captured frame rate of our smartphones is kept above 24FPS with this setting in our tests.

5. EVALUATION

In this section, we report the experimental results of RDCode on the various factors of transmission reliability and throughput, compared with the existing state-of-the-art approach COBRA [12]. We test RDCode from four aspects. (a) Base design: to evaluate the RDCode layout and symbol extraction methods to see how it improves the decoding accuracy as well as the reliability under different environments. (b) Error correction: to know how the parameters of our error correction method would affect the result of data correctness and integrity; (c) Benchmark: to measure and compare the system performance of our work and previous works by transmitting files; (d) Decoding efficiency: to know whether our implementation could support real-time decoding on off-the-shelf smartphones.

Experimental settings. Our experimental receiver devices are LG Nexus 4 and Samsung Galaxy S3. They are the off-the-shelf normal Android smartphones equipped with standard screens or cameras, and they both have a camera of 8M pixel resolution and 1280*720@30FPS video capturing rate. Besides the two smartphones, we additionally use an Asus Nexus 7 tablet as the sender device.

Unless otherwise stated, our experiments are tested under an indoor environment with normal light condition (1 to 100 *lx*). (a) Except those tests for trembles and capture positions, the sender and receiver devices are kept still without any relative movement, and the capture scope of the receiver just fits the complete screen of the sender[4]. (b) Except those tests about display brightness and ambient luminance, the brightness of the screen is set to 50% of its maximum brightness. The workload is evaluated by a binary file containing integers produced by the Scala Class Random. In the tests, we use the offline encoder and offline decoder of RDCode, and the source code of COBRA comes from its authors, including an online encoder and an offline decoder written in Java and Matlab, respectively.

5.1 Base Design Comparison

We first evaluate whether our base design could lay down the possibility to reliability. As a most recent approach to establishing screen-camera links between smartphones, the major contribution of COBRA [12] is its base design for fast and adaptive transmissions. The following LightSync [33] adopts COBRA's design so we only compare our work with COBRA. The comparison focuses on two aspects: code extraction accuracy and frame capacity. We disable the error correction method of RDCode in this test.

Accuracy of extracted symbols using different receivers and senders. We measure the bit-error-rate of RDCode and COBRA under different receivers and senders. Note that in COBRA [12] the metric *decoding rate* denotes the percentage of correctly decoded data in the total amount of data contained in a barcode. Since COBRA does not utilize error correction or detection codes, this metric is equal to one minus the *bit-error-rate* if COBRA takes *bits* as the transmission unit. Our experimental results coincide with the results in COBRA.

Since the frame capacity directly determines the performance of barcodes. For RDCode, we set blocks with $12 * 12$ symbols per block and change the number of blocks per frame. For COBRA, we vary the symbol size from 5 to 15, *i.e.*, $5 * 5$ to $15 * 15$ pixels. We only take the successfully located frames into account. We first use Asus Nexus 7 as the sender and the two smartphones as receivers, and report the result in Fig. 6(a). Because of the distortion caused location error and inaccuracy of color matching, the error rates of COBRA differ obviously and increase quickly with the increment of data capacity. Moreover, the original COBRA does not have error detection and correction ability so that COBRA cannot support much reliability. In contrast, the error rate of RDCode keeps low because of its adaptive methods. RDCode improves the maximum available data capacity to about 30000 bits per frame, more than two times of COBRA, with only less than 10% bit errors using two smartphones as receivers. Since the two results of RDCode are very similar, we will only show the average result of the two receivers in the following experiments for simplicity.

Since different senders have different color accuracies and luminance, which may affect the noises on the barcodes, we keep one smartphone as the receiver and use different senders to do the same experiments as above. Results reported in Fig. 6(b) and Fig. 6(c) show that both COBRA and RDCode are not sensitive to senders, while RDCode has a slightly better performance on the uniformity.

Accuracy of extracted symbols under different display brightness and ambient light intensity. Two key parameters of screen to camera communication are the brightness of the display and the ambient light intensity of the capturing environment. The brightness of the display affects the captured noises and color accuracy, and the ambient light intensity affects the visibility of the display. We

[4]It is tested that when the captured image just fits for the entire screen of the sender, their distance is about 21cm.

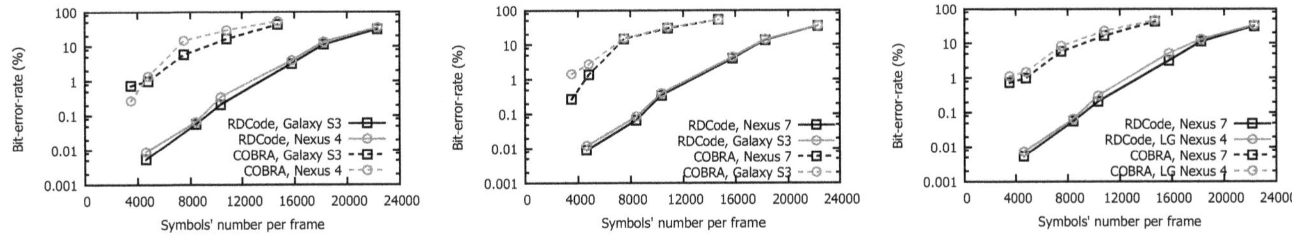

(a) Nexus 7 as the sender (b) Nexus 4 as the receiver (c) Galaxy S3 as the receiver

Figure 6: The bit-error-rates of RDCode and COBRA under different senders and receivers.

Settings	Illuminance (lx)	Brightness of display (%)	Located block ratio (%)	Bit error rate (%)
outdoor (sunlight)	6000-9000	50	0	-
		100	39	15
outdoor (shadow)	100-1000	50	76	9
		100	98	5
indoor (normal)	2-100	50	99	1
		100	100	1
indoor (dark)	0	50	100	1
		100	100	1

Table 1: The located blocks ratio and bit-error-rate under different display brightness and ambient illuminance.

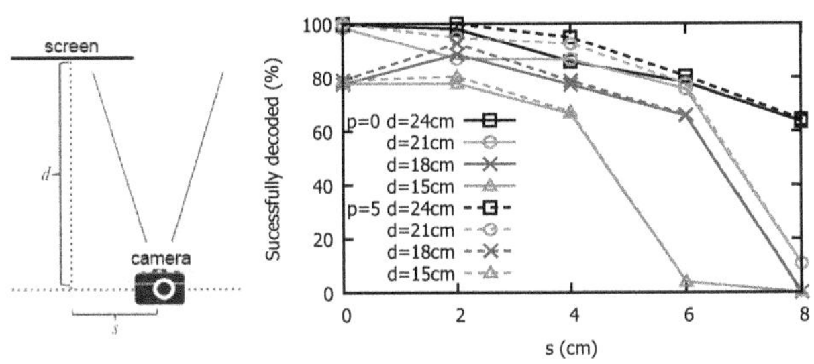

Figure 7: Left figure illustrated the settings of testing partial unavailability. Right figure shows the successfully decoded block ratio *w.r.t.* different distance and shifting.

test two different display brightness, 50% and 100%, under different environments including outdoor under sunlight, outdoor in a shadow, indoor with normal light condition, totally dark indoor, by recording the ambient illuminance using the front ambient light sensor equipped in the sender. In this test we use LG Nexus 4 as the sender and Galaxy S3 as the receiver, respectively. We fix a RDCode frame to contain 11*9 blocks each of which contains 12*12 symbols in the tests.

The result is shown in Table 1 by measuring two metrics: (a) the *located blocks ratio*, which is defined as the ratio of the successfully located blocks by the receiver in all the displayed blocks by the sender, and (b) the *bit-error-rate*, the ratio of bit errors in successfully located blocks. Results show that RDCode does not work well under intense sunlight. This is a common problem for VLC over screen-camera links due to the limitations of current LCDs, as the luminance of LCDs is much smaller than the strong sunlight. However, with the emerging of new technologies such as e-ink display[5], this problem could be alleviated.

5.2 Data Correction

In this experiment, we fix in a frame the block number to 13*9 and each block contains 12*12 symbols, so that a frame contains 156*108 symbols (exclude the leftmost and bottommost distributed locators).

Comparison with standalone error correction codes. We first compare the decoding performance of our tri-level error correction scheme with a standalone error correction code applied to our design. We have tested two candidates: (1) RS code over GF(256) and each block contains one message. (2) Interleaved RS code over GF(256), those bytes of the same index within each block form a message. We change the code rate by varying the parameter $n-k$. For our tri-level error correction scheme, we change the code rate by varying the parameters $n-k$ and p . As Fig. 10 shows, our method is more efficient than the two standalone error correction codes on the screen-camera transmission channel, by obtaining more corrected blocks with the same code rate. Although there exists a rather small possibility that a wrong message is determined right by RS code in theory, during all of our experiments, no such cases happen.

Data integrity: successfully decoded block ratio within a frame. By combining intra-block error correction with inter-block erasure correction, we may change their parameters p and $n-k$, capture and decode one static barcode frame, and evaluate the average *successfully decoded block ratio* (Fig. 8) that denotes the percentage of successfully decoded blocks in all sent blocks. Note that border blocks have worse error rates so we double the $n-k$ parameter of those blocks. From the figures we know that the setting of $n-k=6$ and $p=4$ is enough for the balance of per-frame data integrity and data capacity.

When partial unavailability problems happen, some blocks may be unavailable. We do a simple test that measures the data integrity under this case. Fig. 7 (left) illustrates that the receiver is placed at different distance d and different shifting s. It is clear that the more s or less d is, the smaller part of a frame can be captured. The right chart of Fig. 7 shows RDCode has the ability to decode available blocks as much as possible. Oppositely, as we tested, previous works such as COBRA have no such ability and a whole frame is undecodable as soon as a corner tracker is lost tracking, which reduces the data integrity seriously.

Data integrity: successfully decoded block ratio among multiple frames. When displaying barcode sequence, the aim of inter-frame erasure correction is to tolerate temporal partial unavailability problems mainly caused by trembles. Figure 11 plots the decoding ratio and transmission speed with regards to the changing acceleration caused by trembles. In this experiment, we put the sender at a fixed position, and held the receiver with a hand by a real

[5]http://en.wikipedia.org/wiki/E_Ink

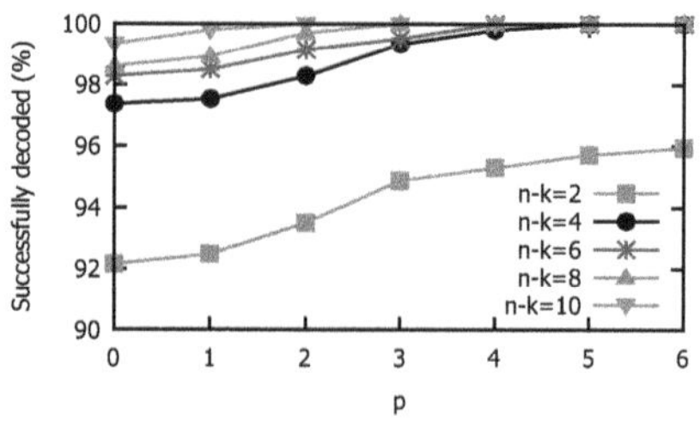

Figure 8: The successfully decoded blocks ratio within a single frame *w.r.t.* error correction parameters.

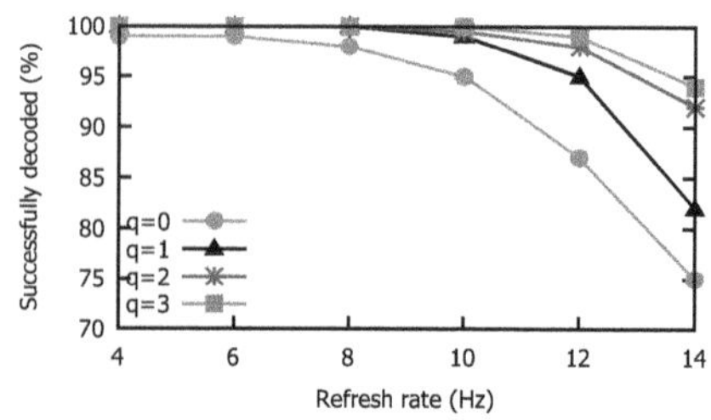

Figure 9: The successfully decoded blocks ratio *w.r.t.* sender's refresh rate and inter-frame erasure correction parameters.

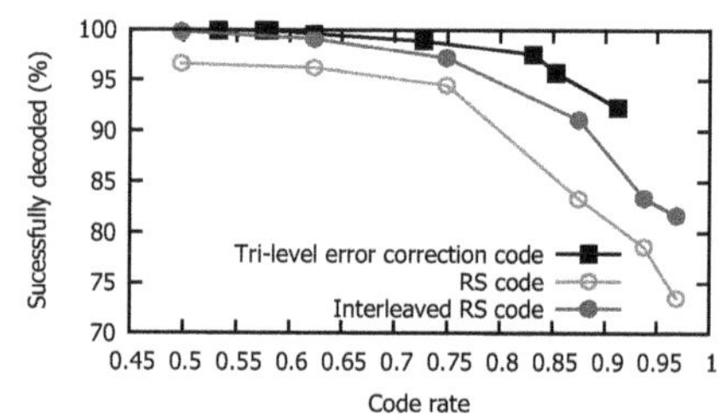

Figure 10: The correcting ability of tri-level error correction code, Reed-Solomon (RS) code and interleaved RS code.

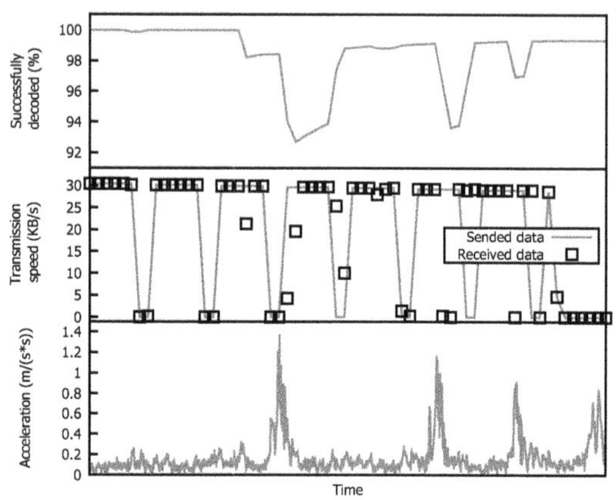

Figure 11: The relationship among successfully decoded blocks ratio, instant transmission speed and changing acceleration caused by trembles.

user to capture RDCode. We fix the sender's refresh rate to 8FPS and $q = 2$. We then capture an RDCode containing 8 packets by hand and record the changing acceleration of the receiver, and in the meanwhile we record the instant data sent rate, received rate and successfully decoded block ratio. As shown in Fig. 11, the inter-frame erasure correction can recover most blocks in lost frames caused by unexpected trembles. As a result, more than 99% data is obtained. Although not all data are received, inter-frame erasure correction plays an important role by recovering most lost blocks.

When no trembles happen, since inter-frame erasure correction is based on block operations, it could also significantly improve the packet integrity. For example, in order to solve *aliasing*, the refresh rate of senders should be at most half of the capture rate of receivers, which is at least 24FPS. As Fig. 9 shows, when $q = 0$, the successfully decoded block ratio drops suddenly when the refresh rate is beyond 10FPS. But when $q = 2$, inter-frame error correction increases the maximum tolerable refresh rate to 12FPS by recovering overlapped frames.

5.3 Benchmarks

We now set $n - k = 6$, $p = 4$ and $q = 2$ as the error correction parameters, and focus on the whole system to find out the best trade-off between transmission speed and reliability. We do experiments under three common block numbers (11*7, 13*9, 15*9), and each block contains 12*12 symbols. We also set different refresh rates for senders.

Throughput and packet error rates. *Throughput* means successfully decoded bytes per unit time excluding the redundant error correction codes. Packet is the transmission unit of the system. If a packet is not completely received, we say that it is a packet error since the packet cannot be recovered unless re-transmission. The packet error rate is the metric for packet-level data integrity. We measure the throughput and packet error rate by processing 100 packets under different settings. The result is reported in Fig. 12, which shows that the packet error rate is tolerable, about 5%, under 10FPS refresh rate and 156*108 symbols per frame. In this case, the maximum throughput is about 21.8KB/s.

Comparison on goodput. The final measurement of transmission performance is to transmit a real file and test the goodput. *Goodput* measures the application layer performance. In RDCode, goodput means the transmitted file size divided by total transmission time. We use a 128,000 byte file containing pseudo-random data. Figure 13 shows the maximum, minimum and average goodput. The entire transmission process finished within 1.5 loops in most cases.

We also want to show how COBRA performs at the application layer. Since COBRA does not focus on reliability, we first encode the original data by Reed-Solomon code over $GF(256)$, and then add a header to indicate the full sequence number to each frame. The online encoder of COBRA cannot be used under refresh rates larger than 5FPS due to its low drawing performance. Hence, we use the generated image files to make a video to play offline.

The experiments of COBRA cannot be successfully done when the symbol number per frame is more than about 110*70 since location errors happen frequently. Also, when the refresh rate reaches 10, *i.e.,* the same as RDCode, a number of frames are lost due to the rolling shutter problem. As a result, we set 100*60 symbols per frame, and test two refresh rate: 10FPS and 7FPS.

We test the average loops and goodput by transmitting a single 128KB file. Meanwhile, we also record the bit-error-rate and successfully decoded block ratio of both COBRA and RDCode. We use *bandwidth* to measure the raw bit rate sent by the receiver. Table 2 shows that RDCode provides a big advantage for both transmission speed and reliability. First, keeping error rates at a low level, the base design of RDCode supports a higher bandwidth by increasing the data capacity within each frame. Second, our goodput is even much better than the throughput of COBRA, because our error correction methods increase the data integrity and reduce the retransmission loops. The big difference between the throughput and goodput of COBRA indicates COBRA is not designed for reliable transmissions and frequent re-transmissions are typically needed.

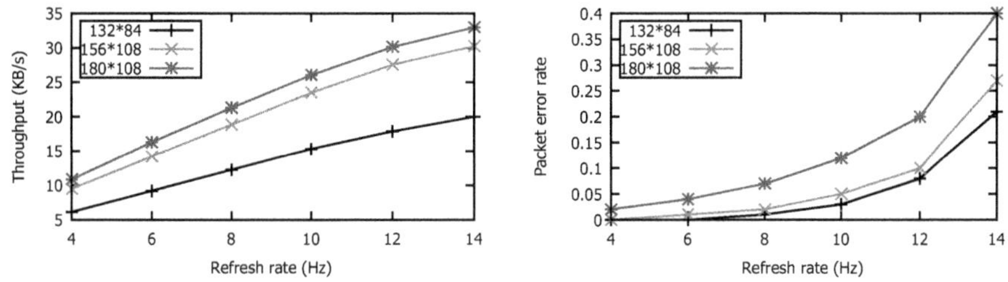

(a) Throughput (b) Packet loss rate

Figure 12: The relationship between the throughput and packet error rate under different refresh rates and symbol counts.

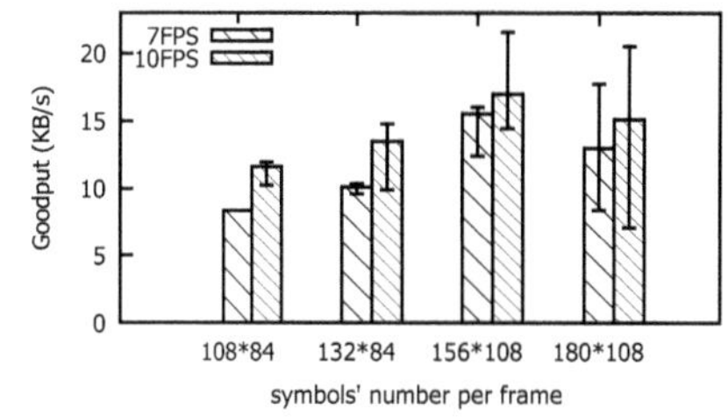

Figure 13: The maximum, minimum and average transmission speed when receiving a 128KB file under different barcode sizes and refresh rates.

Setting		Base design		After error correction		File transmission	
		Bandwidth	Bit-error-rate	Maximum Throughput	Successfully decoded blocks	Goodput	Average loops
RDCode	156*108@10FPS, $p=4, n-k=6, q=2$	$324kbps$	1.1%	21.8KB/s	99.2%	17.0KB/s	1.28
COBRA	100*60@10FPS, $RS(255,191)$	$120kbps$	4.5%	8.8KB/s	89.4%	2.1KB/s	4.13
	100*60@7FPS, $RS(255,191)$	$84kbps$	2.1%	6.1KB/s	94.6%	3.0KB/s	2.03
	100*60@7FPS, $RS(255,127)$			4.1KB/s	98.8%	2.6KB/s	1.60

Table 2: Comparison of the goodput of file transmit application between RDCode and COBRA.

We did not compare RDCode with LightSync. One reason is that LightSync is based on the design of COBRA, and limits its symbol to only represent one bit as LightSync only uses two colors. Hence its available data capacity per frame is the half of COBRA. Its inter-frame erasure code also halves the throughput. Another reason is that we could not get its source code and its binary executable file cannot run properly under Android 4.x. However, LightSync [33] stated its maximum throughput is about 11KB/s, much less than the one of RDCode.

5.4 Decoding Efficiency

We finally show that the decode processing time is the requirement of online real-time decoding. In order to decode the frames in real time with smartphones, in our implementation, the processing time of decoding each frame at smartphone must be smaller than the frame interval of the sender. If the sender's refresh rate is 10FPS, then the processing time must be less than 100ms. We keep $12 * 12$ symbols per block, vary the frame size, and use LG Nexus 4 to capture and decode about 5 seconds, and then we test the average processing time per frame. Error correction parameters are set to $p = 4, n - k = 6, q = 2$. The center locator is only needed to be located at the first captured frame, and the decoder tracks the distributed locators during the following frames. As shown in Table 3, the experiments demonstrate that locating does not take much time. The main drawback is that the pixel sampling depends on the operating system. Overall, the decoder can process the received data in real time under the limited computing ability of smartphones.

6. RELATED WORK

Visible Light Communication. Visible Light Communication(VLC) [13] is a kind of data communications that uses the visible light as a medium. Many works [2, 8] are dedicated to gain a fast transmission channel using visible light. However, extra equipments are needed, which are not available by ordinary people.

Symbols count	84*60		156*108	
Thread count	1	4	1	4
Center locator	63ms		68ms	
Distributed locator	13ms		14ms	
Data extraction	44ms	13ms	150ms	43ms
Error correction	7ms	4ms	27ms	9ms
Total	64ms	30ms	191ms	66ms

Table 3: The average processing time per frame by decoder.

Barcodes. Various barcodes are usable nowadays including one dimensional barcodes [15] and two dimensional barcodes [16, 17]. Some new barcode designs such as High Capacity Color Barcode (HCCB) [24] use multiple colors to multiply the data capacity. With the help of various decoding techniques to improve the decoding quality [19], popular barcodes have a high first-read rate (FRR) [18] during the scanning process.

Screen-camera links. Due to the high availability of smartphones, VLC over screen-camera links are widely studied recently. Approaches like [25] modulate data using OFDM technology and achieve a high throughput using high definition LCDs and high quality cameras. 4D Barcode [21] is the first attempt to decode sequential barcode streams using phones to the best of our knowledge. It uses sequential Data Matrix barcodes [16] to multiply the throughput, and uses different color channels with redundant data to reduce errors. Because its design is based on traditional barcodes, decoding takes lots of time and the throughput is low. COBRA [12] contributes a novel barcode design for real-time phone to phone transmission, and optimizations for alleviating decoding errors caused by motion blur. COBRA makes the link more adaptive to smartphones, but the locality and partial availability problems discussed in Section 1 are not in their consideration.

These works use at most half of the capture frame rate as the sender's refresh rate since the continuous frames may overlap. LightSync [33] contributes to solve the frame synchronization problem based on COBRA. However, it limits the colors to black and white which reduces the throughput. Further, although both LightSync and RDCode address the rolling shutter problem, they are orthogonal to each other.

Data transmissions. In duplex unicast transmission, many network protocols such as TCP [26] support reliable transmissions. However, it is difficult to apply their techniques for one-way communications.

[11] discussed some schemes to obtain a reliable multicast channel, and their methods use feedbacks to ensure the data integrity [30]. If no feedbacks are available, FEC codes [32], such as Reed-Solomon [34] and LDPC [7], are used to keep the correctness [28], and to control the errors on one-way channels, which has been widely studied to obtain better correction ability and more efficient encoding and decoding algorithms. Most standard barcodes such as QR-Code use Reed-Solomon code as their FEC codes. If error positions are known, *erasure codes* can be used to fix errors with less redundancy [9]. Fountain codes such as Raptor codes [29] are a class of erasure codes that do not have a fixed code rate. Different codes can be combined to improve the correction ability for various channels [14].

7. CONCLUSION

We have proposed RDCode, a robust dynamic barcode, which boosts the throughput over screen-camera links via smartphones by enhancing transmission reliability. (a) We design a packet-frame-block barcode layout and symbol extraction techniques to address the locality and partial unavailability problems, caused by smartphone limitations and user behavior uncertainty. (b) We develop a tri-level error correction approach to enhancing reliability. (c) We implement RDCode on top of an Android platform for file transmissions, and our experimental results show that RDCode both improves the transmission reliability and speed, compared with the existing state-of-the-art approach COBRA.

Several topics are targeted for future work. First, our design brings the possibility to customize colors, but how to choose colors effectively and efficiently worths a further study. Second, we are to investigate the impacts of different FEC codes on RDCode. In addition, we are exploring other possibilities to boost reliability over screen-camera links. Finally, customized frame shapes may be incorporated to improve the aesthetical effect.

Acknowledgments. This work is supported in part by 973 program (No. 2014CB340304), NSFC (No. 61322207) and SKLSDE grant (No. SKLSDE-2014ZX-20).

8. REFERENCES

[1] Mary Meeker's Internet trends report, 2013.

[2] M. Z. Afgani, H. Haas, H. Elgala, and D. Knipp. Visible light communication using OFDM. In *TRIDENTCOM*, 2006.

[3] A. Ashok, M. Gruteser, N. B. Mandayam, J. Silva, M. Varga, and K. J. Dana. Challenge: mobile optical networks through visual mimo. In *MOBICOM*, 2010.

[4] D. H. Ballard. Generalizing the hough transform to detect arbitrary shapes. *Pattern recognition*, 13(2):111–122, 1981.

[5] Y. Cheng. Mean shift, mode seeking, and clustering. *Pattern Analysis and Machine Intelligence, IEEE Transactions on*, 17(8):790–799, 1995.

[6] D. Comaniciu, V. Ramesh, and P. Meer. Real-time tracking of non-rigid objects using mean shift. In *CVPR*, 2000.

[7] M. C. Davey and D. J. MacKay. Low density parity check codes over GF (q). In *Information Theory Workshop*, 1998.

[8] H. Elgala, R. Mesleh, and H. Haas. Indoor broadcasting via white LEDs and OFDM. *TCE*, 55(3):1127–1134, 2009.

[9] G. Forney Jr. On decoding bch codes. *IEEE Transactions on Information Theory*, 11(4):549–557, 1965.

[10] I. Guvenc, S. Gezici, Z. Sahinoglu, and U. C. Kozat. *Reliable Communications for Short-Range Wireless Systems*. Cambridge University Press, 2011.

[11] M. Handley, S. Floyd, B. Whetten, R. Kermode, L. Vicisano, and M. Luby. rfc 2887. *IETF Request For Comments*, 2000.

[12] T. Hao, R. Zhou, and G. Xing. Cobra: color barcode streaming for smartphone systems. In *MobiSys*, 2012.

[13] S. Haruyama. Visible light communication. *Journal of JSME*, 107(1030):710–711, 2004.

[14] H. Imai and S. Hirakawa. A new multilevel coding method using error-correcting codes. *TIT*, 23(3):371–377, 1977.

[15] I15420:2009. Information Technology - Automatic identification and data capture techniques - EAN/UPC bar code symbology specification.

[16] I16022:2006. Automatic identification and data capture techniques - Data Matrix bar code symbology specification.

[17] I18004:2000. Automatic identification and data capture techniques - Bar code symbology - QR Code.

[18] H. Kato and K. T. Tan. First read rate analysis of 2d-barcodes for camera phone applications as a ubiquitous computing tool. In *TENCON*, 2007.

[19] H. Kato, K. T. Tan, and D. Chai. Development of a novel finder pattern for effective color 2d-barcode detection. In *ISPA*, 2008.

[20] R. Kraemer and M. Katz. *Short-Range Wireless Communications: Emerging Technologies and Applications*. Wiley, 2009.

[21] T. Langlotz and O. Bimber. Unsynchronized 4d barcodes. In *Advances in Visual Computing*, pages 363–374. Springer, 2007.

[22] M. Naor and A. Shamir. Visual cryptography. In *Advances in Cryptology-EUROCRYPT'94*, pages 1–12. Springer, 1995.

[23] M. Naor and A. Shamir. Visual cryptography ii: Improving the contrast via the cover base. In *Security Protocols*, pages 197–202. Springer, 1997.

[24] D. Parikh and G. Jancke. Localization and segmentation of a 2d high capacity color barcode. In *WACV*, 2008.

[25] S. D. Perli, N. Ahmed, and D. Katabi. Pixnet: interference-free wireless links using lcd-camera pairs. In *MobiCom*, 2010.

[26] J. Postel. Transmission control protocol. 1981.

[27] Q. Pu and W. Hu. Smooth transmission over unsychronized vlc links. In *CoNEXT student workshop*, 2012.

[28] L. Rizzo. Effective erasure codes for reliable computer communication protocols. *Computer Communication Review (ACM SIGCOMM)*, 27(2):24–36, 1997.

[29] A. Shokrollahi. Raptor codes. *IEEE Transactions on Information Theory*, 52(6):2551–2567, 2006.

[30] P. R. T. P. Specification. Rfc 3208, 2001.

[31] S. E. Umbaugh. *Computer Vision and Image Processing: A Practical Approach Using Cviptools with Cdrom*. Prentice Hall PTR, 1997.

[32] C. Wang, D. Sklar, and D. Johnson. Forward error-correction coding. *Crosslink*, 3(1):26–29, 2001.

[33] Q. P. Wenjun Hu, Hao Gu. Lightsync: Unsynchronized visual communication over screen-camera links. In *MobiCom*, 2013.

[34] S. B. Wicker and V. K. Bhargava. *Reed-Solomon Codes and Their Applications*. Wiley, 1999.

[35] H. Yang, A. C. Kot, and X. Jiang. Binarization of low-quality barcode images captured by mobile phones using local window of adaptive location and size. *TIP*, 21(1):418–425, 2012.

The Future of Mobile Computing

Jeff Gehlhaar
VP of Technology for Qualcomm Technologies, Inc.
San Diego, CA USA
www.qualcomm.com/research

ABSTRACT

Jeff Gehlhaar, VP of Technology for Qualcomm Technologies, Inc. will discuss the future of mobile computing which will entail a much more personalized user experience.

As the world continues to shift towards a more connected world, people are using their mobile devices in new ways and having higher expectations of what they can do with those devices. This is leading to the next frontier of mobile being much more personalized with mobile devices becoming extensions of the user, understanding where you are, where you've been and what you want to do or act on next. This is also resulting in services and applications that have traditionally been delivered via the cloud, migrating to mobile which present unique challenges and opportunities in mobile.

In this talk we will explore the new and exciting technologies that Qualcomm Research is working on to advance the frontier in personalized devices and help solve some of these challenges. Starting with always on sensor processing that make basic predictions about where you are and what actions you are performing, to research in brain inspired computing and embedded cognition, Qualcomm is working to make devices which are always with you, smarter and truly personal.

To further this vision of transforming the future of mobile computing, Qualcomm Research has also been working in the area of brain inspired computation and neural networks for a number of years. Early work has focused on biologically inspired approaches, involving spiking neural networks and understanding the complex behaviors of the brain. Recent advances in the industry around deep neural networks have resulted in state-of-the-art performance in machine learning pattern matching tasks. As mobile SOCs continue to gain significant computational power, bringing applications powered by deep learning to mobile devices is becoming possible. We will explore the near term opportunities like object recognition, scene classification, applications for smarter mobile cameras, automotive, and robotics. We will also look at other aspects of brain inspired computing including the potential of a new kind of low power hardware.

Join Jeff as he shares his insight on how Qualcomm Research has been spearheading research to make future mobile devices smarter with the ability to "sense" and "see" their environment as humans do in a power efficient manner.

Author Keywords

Artifical intelligence, sensor future, mobile computing, brain inspired computing, machine learning, neural networks, power efficient, embedded computing.

ACM Classification Keywords

I.2.6 Artificial Intelligence: Learning.

MobiCom'14, September 7-11, 2014, Maui, Hawaii, USA.
ACM 978-1-4503-2783-1/14/09.
http://dx.doi.org/10.1145/2639108.2639417

BIO

Jeff Gehlhaar is Vice President of Technology for Qualcomm Research and currently leads the engineering team developing Qualcomm's Zeroth processor for brain inspired computing, persuing fundamental research into machine learning, spiking neural networks, spiking sensors and novel hardware and software architectures to support this next advance in computing.

During his 23 years at Qualcomm, Jeff led a variety of projects encompassing software for networking and embedded system, hardware bring up, and software engineering. Jeff lead the software research team developing LTE and LTE-Advanced networking protocols, and has worked across a broad range of technologies and programs: from the integration of an on-board microprocessor into Qualcomm's first fully integrated CDMA mobile modem (early SoC), to large-scale network management software for cellular systems.

From 1999-2003 he was Vice President of Engineering and COO for Mohomine, an In-Q-Tel backed knowledge mining startup applying machine learning algorithms to text classification and information extraction applications for both government and commercial customers.

He is a graduate of the Jacobs School of Engineering, UC San Diego.

Full-Duplex without Strings: Enabling Full-Duplex with Half-Duplex Clients

Karthikeyan Sundaresan, Mohammad Khojastepour,
Eugene Chai, Sampath Rangarajan
Mobile Communications and Networking Research
NEC Laboratories America, Princeton, NJ
{karthiks,amir,eugene,sampath}@nec-labs.com

ABSTRACT

Enabling wireless full-duplex (from an AP) with multiple half-duplex (HD) clients is key to widespread adoption of full-duplex (FD) in commercial networks. However, enabling FD in such networks is fundamentally challenged by a new form of uplink-downlink interference (UDI), arising between HD clients operating simultaneously in the uplink and downlink directions. In this context, we first show that spatial interference alignment (IA) between clients is an effective and scalable technique to address UDI and hence enable FD in these networks, especially in the presence of MIMO.

We then present our solution and system *FDoS*: *Full-Duplex without Strings* that incorporates this notion. We build the theory of applying spatial IA to full-duplex networks in general and present elegant, implementation-friendly constructions for generating IA solutions, by leveraging the structure of interference specific to these networks. In the process, *FDoS* shows that only four HD clients are sufficient to eliminate UDI through IA and enable $2N$ streams at an N transceiver AP. *FDoS* also includes an efficient MAC design at the AP to handle clients with heterogeneous antenna capabilities, maximize the throughput of the enabled streams in the FD session as well as reduce the overhead incurred in *FDoS* by *half* by facilitating a distributed implementation. A prototype of *FDoS* on WARP radios showcases its ability to address UDI effectively, and hence enable $2N$ streams (for $N = 2, 4$) in varied settings with just four HD clients, and sustain rate gains of 1.75-2x over HD MU-MIMO systems.

Categories and Subject Descriptors

C.2.1 [**Network Architecture and Design**]: Wireless communication

Keywords

Full-duplex; half-duplex clients; uplink-downlink interference; spatial interference alignment

MobiCom'14, September 7-11, 2014, Maui, Hawaii, USA.

http://dx.doi.org/10.1145/2639108.2639127.

1. INTRODUCTION

Wireless full-duplex (FD) allows a device to transmit and receive at the same time in the same frequency band, thereby potentially doubling the link capacity. Although promising, one of the key challenges in realizing full-duplex is the Self-Interference (SI) generated by the Tx antenna at the Rx antenna on the device, which can be several orders of magnitude stronger than the received signal from a desired node. Several research works have looked at addressing this SI problem in the analog domain through antenna [7, 10, 1] and RF cancellation [16, 12, 8, 4] techniques, as well as through digital cancellation [12, 8] schemes.

With the focus being on addressing the SI problem, current works have primarily looked at FD from a peer-peer standpoint, with both nodes of the link being FD enabled. However, to allow for widespread adoption of FD, it is important to enable FD in commercial networks. In such networks, while the AP can be envisoned to be burdened with additional processing for FD, it is hard to embed FD functionality in client devices that are energy constrained to begin with. Hence, the key to widespread adoption of FD lies in enabling it with half-duplex (HD) clients.

Enabling FD with half-duplex clients requires at least two clients - one for transmitting to the AP, while the other for receiving from the AP simultaneously. However, this introduces a new form of interference between the uplink and downlink clients of the FD session as shown in Fig. 1(a)(i). We refer to this interference that is specific to FD communication as the *uplink-downlink interference* (UDI, also called inter-node interference [3, 17]). There are two simple, but practical approaches to addressing UDI with HD clients. (1) *Leverage Client Separation*: Separating the UL and DL clients of the FD session as far away as possible is one option to alleviate UDI. However, [1] showed that this significantly reduces the opportunities for FD in a cell and reduces the gains from FD to as low as 20-30% even in the presence of ideal SI cancellation. (2) *Use of Side-channel*: With most client devices being equipped with both 3G/4G and WiFi interfaces, it is possible to send a coded version of the interfering packet from the UL client to the DL client through a side (orthogonal) channel (eg. WiFi interface), while the primary channel (eg. 3G/4G) is being used for FD communication (eg. [3]). This would allow the DL client to partially or completely remove the UDI on its primary channel as shown in Fig. 1(a)(ii). However, such a solution comes at the expense of additional bandwidth, which when accounted for, diminishes the gains from FD. Further, both these approaches do not address multi-stream FD (i.e. FD with MIMO). Hence, the focus of this work is to adddress the UDI problem arising in full-duplex communication with half-duplex clients efficiently using the same bandwidth and allowing it to scale to multi-stream FD transmissions.

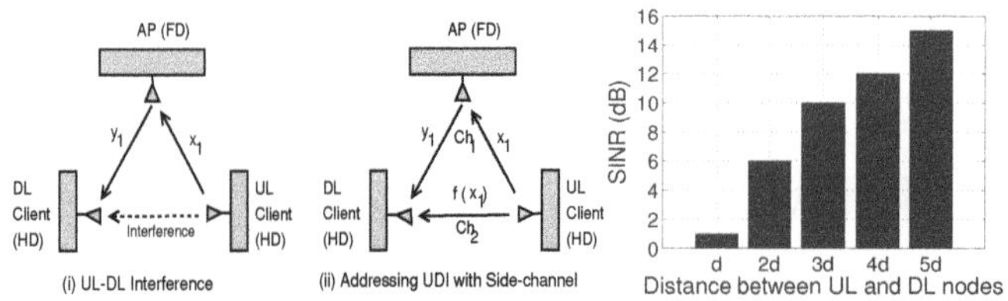

(a) UDI Illustration (b) UDI Impact

Figure 1: Uplink-Downlink Interference in FD

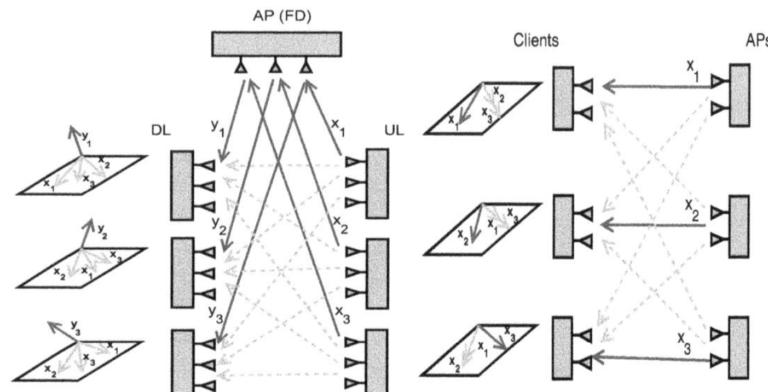

(a) IA to address UDI in FD (b) IA Illustration in HD

Figure 2: Spatial Interference Alignment.

Towards this challenge, one of our main contributions in this work is in showing that *spatial interference alignment is a practical and effective approach to addressing the UDI problem in full-duplex both efficiently and scalably*. In other words, with multiple antennas being available at the HD clients, UL clients can align their transmissions (interference) towards the DL clients in a FD session to eliminate the UDI as shown in Fig. 2(a). To put our proposal in perspective, note that for an AP and client (half-duplex) devices with N transceivers in a cell, while conventional FD systems enable $2N$ streams only in restricted settings (where UL and DL clients do not interfere or employ side channels) and interference alignment solutions (for HD systems) are limited to N streams, *employing spatial interference alignment intelligently with full-duplex will enable $2N$ streams without any restriction on the client topologies or sacrifice of bandwidth*, thereby enabling FD in realistic network settings.

We present our solution and system, *FDoS- Full Duplex without Strings*, that addresses several challenges arising in the process of translating this notion into reality.

(1) Specifically, although carried out in the same bandwidth, spatial interference alignment (IA) requires the estimation of channels between the UL and DL clients. This is an overhead specific to *FDoS* and scales with the number of DL and UL clients involved in the IA process during the FD session. Our key result here is in showing that irrespective of the number of antennas at the AP and clients (say N), exactly *four* clients - two in the DL and two in the UL, are necessary and sufficient to enable $2N$ streams with FD in any topology. This is an interesting result in that the additional overhead from IA is fixed (constant), restricted to *four* additional channel estimations and does not depend on N. This is in contrast to the results for HD systems [5, 11], where $2(N-1)$ streams are possible with IA alone, but the overhead scales with N^2 (N if clients can receive from multiple transmitters [11]).

(2) While the analytical result only indicates the existence of a solution, constructing a feasible IA solution is a hard problem in itself. Here, we present a low-complexity construction in *FDoS*, that proposes the notion of an *interference alignment network* and leverages its structure to generate a feasible IA solution supporting $2N$ streams for any given topology.

(3) In translating our solution from data streams to actual throughput, *FDoS* incorporates a MAC design at the AP that helps maximize the aggregate throughput from the FD session. The role of the MAC is two-fold: (i) compute the IA solution and MIMO precoders at the clients and AP in an efficient manner to not only handle the UDI problem and enable $2N$ streams but to also maximize the throughput of those enabled streams, and (ii) handle clients with heterogeneous antenna capabilities ($1 \leq M \leq N$) by determining when FD must be enabled and how *FDoS* must be adapted to use the antenna resources effectively.

(4) Finally, our solution lends itself naturally to a distributed implementation across clients. This is leveraged by *FDoS* through intelligent feedback mechanisms to further reduce the overhead incurred in executing our solution by *half*.

We prototype *FDoS* using the WARP software-defined radio platform. While the AP is enabled with full-duplex, the clients are half-duplex. Results from our extensive experiments for a single cell are promising and reveal that *FDoS* can (i) provide an UDI suppression of 10-20 dB, (ii) enable $2N$ streams (for $N = 2, 4$) in various settings, and (iii) deliver rate gains of 1.75x-2x over HD MU-MIMO systems, and 1.5x-2x over FD systems that do not address UDI. Our contributions in this work are multi-fold:

- We show that spatial interference alignment is an effective approach to address the UDI problem in FD communication and build the theory and design behind its application.
- We propose our solution and system *FDoS*, which shows that four clients are both necessary and sufficient to enable $2N$ streams in FD with the help of IA and present an elegant construction to realize such a solution in reality.
- We design an efficient MAC to handle clients with heterogeneous antenna capabilities, maximize the throughput of the enabled streams in the FD session and reduce the additional (albeit constant) overhead incurred in *FDoS* by half through a distributed implementation.
- We build a prototype of *FDoS* with WARP radios and showcase its ability to enable $2N$ streams with high throughput in various practical settings with just four clients.

2. BACKGROUND AND MOTIVATION

2.1 UDI in Distributed FD Networks

2.1.1 *Distributed Full-duplex*

Full-duplex networks can be of two types: peer-peer and distributed. In peer-peer, both the nodes of a FD link are FD enabled and is characteristic of relay and backhaul networks. On the other hand, in distributed FD networks, only the AP is FD enabled, while the client devices are half-duplex. This is characteristic of practical wireless networks (eg. WLANs), where one can expect to burden the AP with additional (FD) processing, while the clients are legacy half-duplex devices that are energy constrained. The focus of this work is on distributed FD networks, which unlike its peer-peer counterpart, require at least two clients to enable a FD session - one that transmits to the AP, while the other simultaneously receives from the AP as shown in Fig. 1(a)(i). Such a configuration results in a new form of interference created by the uplink client on the downlink client during the FD session. We refer to this interference that is unique to distributed FD networks, as the *uplink-downlink interference* (UDI), which forms a critical challenge towards realizing FD in practical networks.

2.1.2 Significance of UDI

We conduct experiments on our WARP testbed (details in Section 6) of a simple 3 node distributed FD network as shown in Fig. 1(a)(i). In reality, the impact of UDI depends on the specific clients chosen on the UL and DL directions for the FD session, which in turn depends on a variety of MAC related factors such as the set of active clients available in the UL and DL, their local channel status (busy/idle), queue occupancy, scheduling policies, etc. To account for these variations, we vary the position of the UL and DL clients to create several topologies and measure the SINR at the DL client in the presence of the UL client's transmission. Fig. 1b presents the DL SINR as a function of the distance between UL and DL clients, relative to the distance (d) between AP and the DL client. It can be seen that UDI can reduce SINR by more than 10 dB even for relatively large distances between the UL and DL clients, leaving little room for leveraging client separation. This significantly diminishes the opportunities and hence gains from full-duplex. Further, such restriction on topology would only be increased when multi-user MIMO is enabled from different clients in both the UL and DL directions - one has to now remove UDI between multiple pairs of UL and DL clients simultaneously (as seen in Fig. 2).

2.2 Role of IA in Addressing UDI

We first provide a quick primer on the general notion of interference alignment.

2.2.1 Interference Alignment

IA allows more interfering streams to be accommodated in lesser resource dimensions, thereby leaving room to accommodate more desired streams. While the resource dimensions can correspond to those in time, frequency (called frequency or symbol extension) or space (antennas), our focus in this work is on spatial IA. The latter allows for a practical realization in MIMO systems, unlike the former approaches that by relying on certain hard-to-realize channel assumptions (eg. non-causal CSI), serve mainly as theoretical constructs. The example in Fig. 2(b) illustrates spatial IA. Three APs with two antennas each, desire to send a single data stream to their respective clients, each with two antennas. Being limited to two antennas (two spatial dimensions) at the clients and assuming no transmitter cooperation, only two of the streams can be delivered in this network without IA. However, with IA all three streams can be delivered. The two interfering streams at each of the clients can be aligned to consume a single spatial dimension (*degree of freedom*, DoF), thereby allowing the other dimension for its desired stream. The alignment is realized through a process known as *precoding*, whereby the data stream at the transmitter is multiplied by a precoding vector ($\vec{v}$) before being transmitted through the antennas onto the channel such that

$$\mathbf{H}_{ji}\vec{v}_i \overset{s}{=} \mathbf{H}_{jk}\vec{v}_k, \quad \forall j, \text{s.t. } j \neq i \neq k \tag{1}$$

where H_{ji} is the channel matrix between transmitter i and receiver j, and $\overset{s}{=}$ indicates that the span of the vector spaces defined by matrices on either sides of the operator are the same. The precoders at the different transmitters are chosen based on the above constraints to realize the desired alignment, while the receive filters at the receivers are chosen orthogonal to the space of the interference to receive the desired streams.

2.2.2 Spatial IA: A Promising Candidate

We propose to leverage *spatial interference alignment* (IA)[1] towards addressing the UDI problem in distributed FD networks. Specifically, with multiple antennas being available at clients, (half-duplex) UL clients can use their spatial dimensions effectively to align their interference (i.e. transmissions to full-duplex AP) towards the (half-duplex) DL clients in a FD session as shown in Fig. 2(a). Using the channel state information (CSI) between the UL and DL clients, appropriate precoders (at UL clients) and receive filters (at DL clients) can be designed to enable such alignment. Thus, IA can potentially eliminate the UDI and hence enable N streams each on both the DL and UL simultaneously (for N antenna devices).

Benefits: Such an approach has all the desired attributes of a good solution. (i) *Efficient*: It operates in the same bandwidth does not require an additional channel. (ii) *Topology-agnostic:* It does not depend on the separation between the UL and DL clients or their topology since UDI is addressed explicitly. (iii) *Scalable:* Working with multiple antennas, it can potentially secure FD's multiplexing gain even in the presence of MIMO and plurality of clients. (iv) *Deployable:* IA, being a form of precoding, is only as challenging as multi-user MIMO systems and can be realized in practice with the AP serving as the FD session coordinator.

Challenges: However, translating this vision into a practical system requires addressing several challenges at both the PHY and MAC.

■ *At the PHY*, the key challenge is to design a closed-form IA solution that (a) can eliminate UDI to enable $2N$ streams with the smallest number of HD clients, thereby taming the CSI overhead (in IA) that scales with the latter; and (b) is easy and efficient to realize in practice.

■ *At the MAC*, the key challenge is to translate and adapt the PHY layer IA solution from one that simply enables $2N$ streams to one that (a) maximizes the throughput of the enabled streams through the design of efficient MIMO precoders and receive filters at AP and clients; and (b) effectively leverages the heterogeneous antenna capabilities at clients (eg. smartphones/tablets with two antennas, smart TVs/laptops with more antennas) to maximize FD performance.

Towards addressing these challenges, we now present our solution and system, *FDoS- Full-Duplex without Strings.* We first develop the theory of applying IA to distributed FD networks and present our analytical results in Section 3. This is followed by the design components of *FDoS* that handle all the practical MAC challenges in Section 4.

3. IA IN DISTRIBUTED FD NETWORKS

3.1 Primer on IA Theory

Consider the conventional HD interference channel as shown in Fig. 3(a), where there are K links, each consisting of an M antenna transmitter communicating with an N antenna receiver. The DoF on each of the HD communication links (d_i, Fig. 3(b)) essentially correspond to the rank of the precoding matrices $\mathbf{V}_i$ and receive filters $\mathbf{U}_j$ such that [20]

$$\mathbf{U}_j\mathbf{H}_{ji}\mathbf{V}_i = 0, \quad \forall i \neq j \tag{2}$$
$$Rank(\mathbf{U}_i\mathbf{H}_{ii}\mathbf{V}_i) = d_i, \quad \forall i = j$$

[1] In the rest of this paper, IA refers to spatial IA.

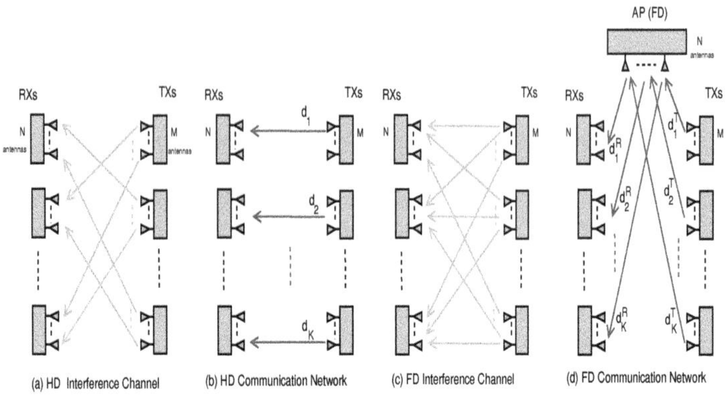

Figure 3: Interference Network: HD vs. FD.

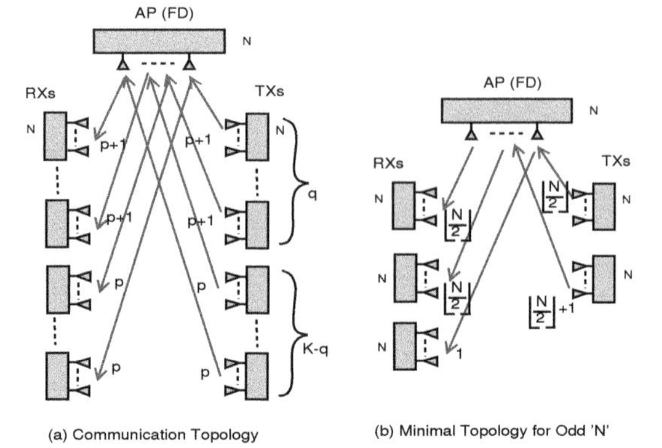

Figure 4: Symmetric FDIC.

where $\mathbf{U}_j$ and $\mathbf{V}_i$ are of size $d_j \times N$ and $M \times d_i$ respectively, while $\mathbf{H}_{ji}$ is the channel between receiver j and transmitter i and is of size $N \times M$. While the first constraint ensures that interfering streams are aligned in the null space of the receivers, the second constraint ensures that d_i DoFs are available for the *desired* (communication) streams at the receiver of link i. For generic channel matrices $\mathbf{H}$, it is sufficient to satisfy the first set of constraints (i.e IA), which automatically leads to the second set being satisfied [20].

Necessary Conditions: Based on the above constraints, one can easily obtain the following necessary conditions [20] for a given network to support the desired DoFs ($d_i, \forall i$).

$$d_i \leq \min\{M, N\} \tag{3}$$
$$\sum_{i:(i,j)\in\mathcal{S}} d_i(M-d_i) + \sum_{j:(i,j)\in\mathcal{S}} d_j(N-d_j) \geq \sum_{i,j:(i,j)\in\mathcal{S}} d_i d_j$$

where $\mathcal{S} \subseteq \mathcal{E} = \{(i,j); i,j \in [1,K]\}$. The first condition indicates that the DoF on a link is limited by the minimum of the number of antennas on either ends of the communication link. The second condition indicates that to have a feasible IA solution, the system defined on any subset ($\mathcal{E}$) of the interference constraints (i.e. $\mathcal{S}$) must not be over-constrained. Note that matrices $\mathbf{V}_i$ and $\mathbf{U}_j$ are composed of d_i and d_j vectors respectively. Hence, a single interference constraint in Eqn. 2 between transmitter i and receiver j is comprised of $d_i d_j$ equations, while each transmitter and receiver give rise to $d_i(M-d_i)$ and $d_j(N-d_j)$ variables respectively [20]. We refer to this condition as the *dimension counting* argument.

3.2 Distributed FD Interference Channel

In the HD interference channel (Fig. 3(a)), the DoF (used synonymously with number of data streams) are defined on a per-link basis, with every receiver (receiving desired streams) being subject to interference from the transmitters of the *other* links. Such an interference network (graph) captures even FD networks in the peer-peer mode. However, the case of distributed FD networks (i.e. in a single cell) is quite different for two reasons. **(1)** Here, all the desired streams either originate or terminate at a single common node, namely the AP (see Fig. 3(d)), which does not receive interference from any other node in the network (other than self-interference during FD, for which we assume ideal suppression in analysis). This results in an interference network (called full-duplex interference channel, FDIC) that is fully bipartite and decoupled from the desired/communication stream network as shown in Figs. 3(c),(d). **(2)** Further, with no desired streams exchanged between the nodes in the interference network (i.e. clients), this allows for the DoF notion to be applied on a per-node basis, with the uplink and downlink clients potentially operating on different DoF. Thus, the IA constraints for FDIC are as follows.

$$\begin{aligned} \mathbf{U}_j\mathbf{H}_{ji}\mathbf{V}_i &= 0,\ \forall i,j \\ Rank(\mathbf{U}_j\mathbf{H}_{j0}\mathbf{V}_0) &= d_j^R,\ \forall j \in \{\text{DL clients}\} \\ Rank(\mathbf{U}_0\mathbf{H}_{0i}\mathbf{V}_i) &= d_i^T,\ \forall i \in \{\text{UL clients}\} \end{aligned} \tag{4}$$

where, index 0 represents the AP. While the first constraint ensures elimination of interference between "all" pairs of UL and DL clients, the last two constraints allow for varied DoF at each node, with d_j^R and d_i^T being the DoF for the downlink client (receiver) j and uplink client (transmitter) i respectively. As we will show subsequently (Section 3.6), the unique nature of interference in distributed FD networks, makes IA much more valuable in these networks than in HD networks.

3.3 Necessary Conditions for FDIC

With IA in HD and peer-peer FD networks, the goal is to typically determine the maximum DoF that can be achieved over the interference network. In contrast, with the AP controlling (originating/terminating) all the desired streams in distributed FD networks, the maximum number of streams that can be enabled in a single cell by an N transceiver AP is $2N$ streams[2]. Hence, we are interested in the alternate question: *how many clients are needed for the IA solution to help address the UDI problem and help realize the $2N$ streams in FD?* Answering this question will help us understand how to control the overhead incurred from IA (due to additional CSI estimation) in our solution. Further, given N antenna HD clients and a limit of N streams in either direction in FD, we are primarily interested in enabling $2N$ streams in *symmetric* FDIC. Here, the number of antennas at each client is the same (N) and the aggregate $2N$ streams (DoF) are uniformly distributed across the K clients in either direction as shown in Fig. 4(a) (i.e. p or $p+1$ streams at each client, where $p = \lfloor \frac{N}{K} \rfloor$; i.e. $N = pK + q$; $p, q \in \mathcal{Z}^+; q < K$). Clients with asymmetric antennas and DoF on DL and UL are considered in Section 4.4. We now have the following encouraging result.

LEMMA 1. *For N antenna HD clients, only four clients are necessary for IA to enable $2N$ streams in symmetric FDIC, if N is even. If N is odd, six clients are necessary, which reduces to five (Fig. 4(b)) in an asymmetric FDIC.*

[2] We assume N antennas are sufficient to generate $2N$ streams in FD [4]. However, our results and solution apply even if additional antennas (eg. $2N$ [7]) are needed.

PROOF. We first consider the case of N being even. With an upper bound of N DoF in either direction of FD, we consider K clients each on the DL and UL such that the N DoF are divided uniformly among the K clients with q clients obtaining $p+1$ DoF and the remaining $K-q$ clients obtaining p DoF (where $N = pK+q$, $p, q \in \mathcal{Z}; p = \lfloor \frac{N}{K} \rfloor; q < K$). With two types of clients (requiring p or $p+1$ DoF) in either direction, we have four types of interference pairs between clients, resulting in the following number of interference constraints (equation).

$$\begin{aligned} |\mathcal{E}| &= p(p+1)(K-q)q + (p=1)^2 q^2 \\ &+ p^2(K-q)^2 + p(p+1)(K-q)q \\ &= ((p+1)q + p(K-1)) = N^2 \end{aligned} \quad (5)$$

Counting the number of variables per client, we obtain the aggregate number of variables (A) as,

$$\begin{aligned} A &= (p+1)(N-p-1)2q + p(N-p)2(K-q) \\ &= 2N^2 - 2Np - 2q(p+1) \quad \text{\% on simplification} \end{aligned}$$

Now, for the dimension counting argument to hold, we need $A \geq |\mathcal{E}|$, i.e.

$$2N^2 - 2Np - 2q(p+1) \geq N^2$$

Applying $N = pK + q$ and simplifying, the constraint reduces to,

$$K(K-2)p^2 + 2(K-2)pq + q(q-2) \geq 0 \quad (6)$$

When N is even, the above constraint holds for $K \geq 2$ (where $q = 0$ when $K = 2$). However, when N is odd, $K = 2$ results in $q = 1$, which does not satisfy the constraint. However, with $K \geq 3$, the constraint is satisfied for N being odd.

Thus, when N is even, we need at least two clients on both DL and UL (four in total) to remove UDI through IA and hence enable $2N$ streams. One might wonder if assuming an asymmetric number of clients on DL and UL can help realize $2N$ streams with lesser clients. Note that with three clients, one of the directions has a single client that must send/receive N streams, thereby becoming the bottleneck for IA. Hence $2N$ streams is not possible with three clients. Further, there is no notion of IA for two clients.

When N is odd, we need at least three clients in either direction (six in total) for the symmetric FDIC. However, with an asymmetric set-up, five clients may be sufficient with three clients in only one of the directions as shown in Fig. 4(b). Specifically, we have the number of variables ($4\lfloor \frac{N}{2} \rfloor^2 + 6\lfloor \frac{N}{2} \rfloor$) to be greater than the number of equations ($4\lfloor \frac{N}{2} \rfloor^2 + 4\lfloor \frac{N}{2} \rfloor + 1$) in this case. □

We now show that indeed such a solution can be constructed in practice with a small number of HD clients.

3.4 Constructing a Feasible Solution

Note that the condition on the minimum number of clients is only a necessary condition and hence does not guarantee that a feasible IA solution can be found with four clients. Indeed the problem of constructing feasible IA solutions for maximizing the number of streams is a challenging one even in HD networks, where algebraic solutions are available only for small scale networks [5]. In contrast, for our desired objective of eliminating UDI to enable $2N$ streams, we show that the *structure of interference in symmetric FDIC can be intelligently leveraged to construct a generic IA solution. Further, the solution is implementation-friendly, applies to general topologies and can be realized with a small number of clients.* First, we introduce the following definition.

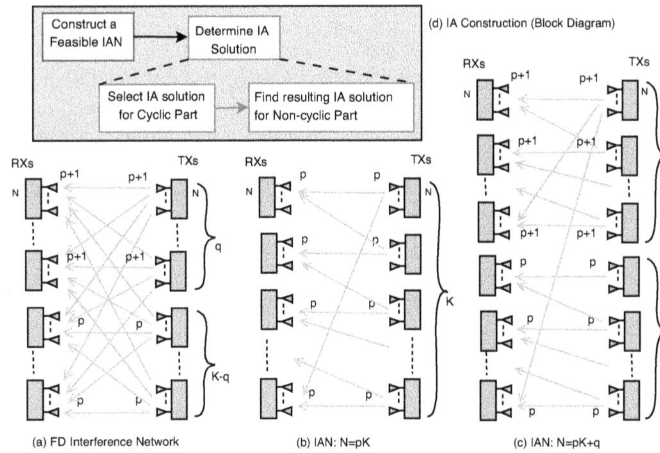

Figure 5: Interference Alignment Network.

DEFINITION 1. *An interference alignment network (IAN) is a subset of the original interference network that captures interference only due to transmit streams that need IA at the receivers.*

In other words, IAN discounts those interfering streams that can be suppressed by allocating an equivalent number of DoF at the receivers (i.e. interference suppression), thereby not requiring IA for handling those streams. In the example in Fig. 5(a) (with $q = 0$), say, we have four clients ($K = 4$) each on the DL and UL in FDIC, each equipped with $N = 4$ antennas (AP has 4 antennas as well) and transmits/receives only a single stream ($p = 1$) to generate a total of 8 streams through FD. Note that all interfering streams do not need to be aligned in this example given the requirement of a single stream with four available dimensions (4 DoF) at each client. Hence, while the interference network is a fully bipartite graph as shown in Fig. 5(a), the resulting IAN is as shown in Fig. 5(b) (with $K = 4$). Here, the IAN requires only two of the UL clients' streams to be *aligned* (using one DoF) at a DL client, while the other two UL streams are handled directly through interference suppression (using two DoF), thereby leaving behind one DoF for receiving the desired DL stream.

LEMMA 2. *For N antenna HD clients, if the necessary conditions are satisfied, there exists a feasible IAN with at most one (un-directed) cycle that can enable $2N$ streams in symmetric FDIC.*

The proof is by means of providing a construction for a feasible IA solution. This is achieved as a two-step process (see Fig. 5(d)), where the part of the interference network that needs IA (i.e IAN) is first determined, and then leveraged to construct the actual IA solution.

Step 1 - IAN Construction: In symmetric FDIC, q clients require to send or receive $p+1$ streams, while the remaining $K-q$ clients require p streams. The necessary conditions have been shown to be satisfied for this interference network earlier. We now construct the following IAN with a *single un-directed cycle* involving $2K$ clients as shown in Fig. 5(c). This IAN has three types of DL clients: (i) q of them receiving $p+1$ desired streams and interference from $2(p+1)$ streams from two UL clients; (ii) $K-q-1$ of them receiving p streams and interference from $2p$ streams from two UL clients; and (iii) one DL client receiving p streams and interference from $2p+1$ streams from two UL clients. Now the key question is whether applying IA for streams in this IAN is sufficient to support $2N$ streams in the original interference network (Fig. 5(a)), i.e. *is this IAN feasible?*

Feasibility: Consider a DL client receiving $p+1$ desired streams. $d_{IA} = p+1$ dimensions are used to align interference from a net $2(p+1)$ streams from the two UL clients (two edges in IAN). Further, $(K-2)$ edges, i.e. $(K-q)$ edges with p streams each and $(q-2)$ edges with $p+1$ streams each, are removed at the DL client (compared to original interference network). This requires that $d_{IS} = (K-q)p + (q-2)(p+1)$ dimensions are set aside at the client to handle these streams through interference suppression. This eventually leaves $N - d_{IA} - d_{IS} = p+1$ remaining dimensions, which is sufficient to receive the desired $(p+1)$ streams at the client. Similarly, the desired streams at the other types of DL clients can also be shown to be supported by this IAN. Hence, *the IAN in Fig. 5(c) is indeed feasible and can support $2N$ streams through FD.*

Step 2 - IA Solution: The individual IA conditions for this IAN can be given separately for the cyclic (top $2q$ nodes) and the non-cyclic (bottom $2(K-q)$ nodes) part as,

$$\mathbf{H}_{ii}\mathbf{V}_i \stackrel{s}{=} \mathbf{H}_{ik}\mathbf{V}_k, \quad \forall i \in [1,q], k = (i+1)(mod)q \qquad (7)$$

$$\mathbf{H}_{ii}\mathbf{V}_i \stackrel{s}{=} \mathbf{H}_{ik}\mathbf{V}_k, \quad \forall i \in [q+1,K], k = (i+1)(mod)K$$

The crucial *single cycle* property of the IAN ensures that a feasible IA solution, satisfying the above system of IA constraints exists, and can be generated as follows. Substituting variables back in the cyclic part, we get,

$$\mathbf{V}_1 \stackrel{s}{=} \left(\prod_{i=q}^{1} \mathbf{H}_{ik_i}^{-1}\mathbf{H}_{ii}\right)\mathbf{V}_1, \quad k_i = (i+1)(mod)q \qquad (8)$$

(*i*) Thus, $\mathbf{V}_1$ can be composed of any $p+1$ Eigen vectors of the matrix $\prod_{i=q}^{1} \mathbf{H}_{ik_i}^{-1}\mathbf{H}_{ii}$ to provide the required $N \times (p+1)$ matrix. The rest of the precoding matrices in the cycle ($\mathbf{V}_i$, $i \in [2,q]$) can then be computed sequentially from the first set of constraints in Eqns. 7.

(*ii*) Since, the second set of constraints couple the rest of the precoding matrices ($\mathbf{V}_i, i \in [q+1,K]$) to $\mathbf{V}_1$ through DL client K (i.e. $\mathbf{V}_K$), once $\mathbf{V}_1$ is computed, they can be determined as well. However, these $K-q$ precoding matrices are $N \times p$ in size compared to $\mathbf{V}_1$ that is $N \times (p+1)$ in size. Hence, we first obtain $\mathbf{V}_K$ as an $N \times (p+1)$ precoding matrix from $\mathbf{V}_K = \mathbf{H}_{K1}^{-1}\mathbf{H}_{KK}\mathbf{V}_1$. Since only p streams are transmitted by the UL client K, we then pick p out of the $p+1$ vectors in $\mathbf{V}_K$ to make it $N \times p$ in size.

(*iii*) Thereafter, the remaining precoding matrices $\mathbf{V}_i, i \in [q+1, K-1]$ of size $N \times p$ can be sequentially obtained from $\mathbf{V}_K$ from the second set of constraints in Eqns. 7.

(*iv*) The corresponding receive filters ($\mathbf{U}_i$) of dimensions $N \times (p+1)$ or $N \times p$ are obtained orthogonal to the sub-space spanned by $\mathbf{H}_{ii}\mathbf{V}_i$.

Remarks: (1) In the special case, when $N = Kp$, i.e. $q = 0$, the IAN consists of a single Hamiltonian cycle, with all clients requiring the same p streams as shown in Fig. 5(b). This simplifies the solution to only the cyclic part of the generic $N = Kp+q$ case, and would require only the first step of the construction, albeit applied over all the clients.

(2) Since IANs with at most a single cycle can be constructed for symmetric FDICs, this indicates that a feasible IA solution (based on our construction) always exists for these networks. Hence, the necessary conditions for IA in Eqns. 3 also serve as sufficient conditions in symmetric FDIC.

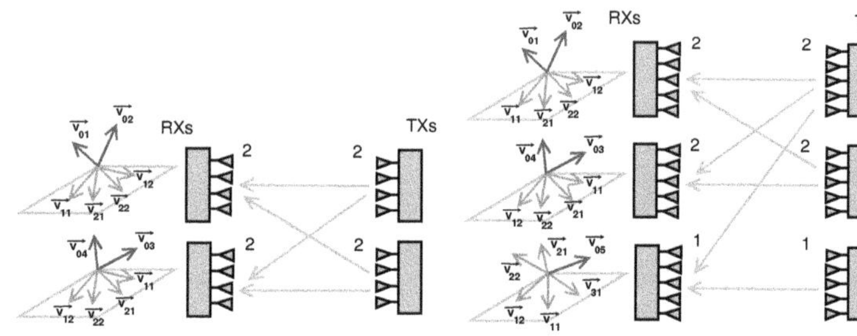

(a) 8 streams with N=4 (b) 10 streams with N=5

Figure 6: Examples of IA Construction.

3.5 *FDoS* Solution

While we can construct a feasible IA solution for any symmetric FDIC with $2K$ clients, to minimize the overhead of CSI from IA, our solution enables FD with exactly four clients (two DL and two UL clients) with $\frac{N}{2}$ streams each. Recall that this is the smallest number of clients needed to realize $2N$ streams when N is even (here $q = 0$). The IA construction is as follows.

(*i*) $\mathbf{V}_1$ is composed of $\frac{N}{2}$ Eigen vectors of the $N \times N$ matrix $\mathbf{H}_{21}^{-1}\mathbf{H}_{22}\mathbf{H}_{12}^{-1}\mathbf{H}_{11}$ to result in $N \times \frac{N}{2}$ precoding matrix for UL client 1.

(*ii*) $\mathbf{V}_2$ is again a $N \times \frac{N}{2}$ precoding matrix for UL client 2 that is given by $\mathbf{V}_2 \stackrel{s}{=} \mathbf{H}_{12}^{-1}\mathbf{H}_{11}\mathbf{V}_1$.

(*iii*) From $\mathbf{V}_1$ and $\mathbf{V}_2$, the $\frac{N}{2}$ dimensional receive filters for the two DL clients, namely $\mathbf{U}_1$ and $\mathbf{U}_2$ (matrices of size $\frac{N}{2} \times N$) are obtained orthogonal to the sub-space spanned by $\mathbf{H}_{11}\mathbf{V}_1$ and $\mathbf{H}_{22}\mathbf{V}_2$ respectively.

Similarly, when N is odd, our construction would require six clients ($K = 3$) and would follow the appropriate procedure in Section 3.4 depending on whether N is a multiple of 3 or not. Figure 6 illustrates the IAN and IA construction pictorially for $N = 4$ and $N = 5$ respectively.

3.6 The Result in Perspective

To put our result in perspective, we consider two relevant and recent results from IA in the spatial (MIMO) domain for HD systems [5, 11]. Recently, [5] showed that in a HD MIMO interference channel with K communication links containing N antenna nodes, one can potentially achieve $\frac{2NK}{K+1}$ streams, i.e. $2(N-1)$ streams (when $K = N-1$) with IA alone, while requiring $O(N^2)$ transceivers and $O(N^2)$ CSI estimations of $N \times N$ links. When clients are allowed to receive from multiple APs, [11] showed that $2(N-1)$ streams are possible with IA alone, but with $N-1$ APs and two clients, thereby requiring $O(N)$ CSI estimations and $O(N^2)$ transceivers. In contrast, we have shown that IA in FD systems can help generate $2N$ streams with $O(N)$ transceivers and just four HD clients (and one FD AP), restricting the CSI estimations to just 8 links (4 with respect to AP, and 4 between clients) that is independent of N. One can attribute this interesting result specifically to the structure of FDIC, wherein half the interfering streams are those that are generated by the AP (intended for DL clients), which are automatically available for self-interference cancellation during its reception of half the desired streams (from UL clients). Hence, IA is needed only for the other half of the interference streams that are generated by the UL clients on the DL clients.

Another interesting point to note is that in HD systems, one can scale the number of concurrent streams (with number of APs) or equivalently achieve $2N$ streams with lesser number of APs by allowing for AP cooperation (i.e sharing data streams between APs, eg. network MIMO). However, the role of IA vanishes in such scenarios, where AP cooperation/processing handles all the interference between APs. In contrast, even if APs are allowed to cooperate, the UDI problem (being specific to clients) will continue to pose a challenge for FD systems. Hence, we believe that IA plays a key role in handling the UDI problem in FD networks. Further, the nature of FDIC, makes IA an ideal solution to address UDI and enable $2N$ streams in an efficient manner (with low, fixed overhead) with just four HD clients.

4. *FDoS*: DESIGN COMPONENTS

We now present the various MAC layer design components that aim to leverage our results from the previous section to build a practical solution for FD with half-duplex clients in a single cell.

4.1 Client Selection

In any closed-loop MIMO transmission from/to an AP (eg. multi-user MIMO), the net rate (throughput) depends on the channels of the set of clients (and their mutual interference) involved in the transmission. If the CSI is available for all clients, then the best subset of clients can be selected for the transmission. However, collecting the CSI estimates not only constitutes overhead but also incurs latency, which could render the CSI estimates invalid/stale (depending on the channel coherence time) during operation. For this reason, 802.11ac decouples client selection from the MU-MIMO transmission process - clients are first chosen based on QoS/scheduling policies, CSI is estimated only for the chosen clients, and then MU-MIMO transmission is optimized (through precoding) for the chosen clients. In the case of FD with IA, the rate of the FD session not only depends on individual client channels with respect to the AP but also on the channels between the clients. The latter amplifies the CSI estimation problem in FD systems with IA, thereby prompting us to decouple client selection from precoder optimization in a manner similar to 802.11ac systems.

4.2 Maximizing Throughput

While our solution from Section 3 eliminates the UDI between the chosen clients through IA, it does not directly contribute to improving the throughput of the desired streams. Hence, once the four clients (two on DL and two on UL) are chosen by the AP scheduler based on priorities/weights, queue occupancy, etc. (we pick proportional fairness), *FDoS* focuses on optimizing the rate of the FD session for the chosen set of clients.

Recall that in addition to the precoders and receive filters at the clients, we also need to design a precoder and receive filter for the AP $(\mathbf{V}_0, \mathbf{U}_0)$. The core problem to address is as follows: we need to construct precoders $(\mathbf{V}_i)$ at the UL clients and the receive filter at the AP $(\mathbf{U}_0)$ for the UL streams, while also constructing the precoder $(\mathbf{V}_0)$ at the AP and the receive filters $(\mathbf{U}_j)$ at the DL clients for the DL streams in FD. These two MU-MIMO problems in either directions are coupled through the interference between the UL and DL streams at the AP as well as the DL clients. While the former is addressed through self-interference cancellation, the latter is addressed through IA.

FDoS adopts a modular approach to determining the precoders and receiver filters for the AP and clients through a two-step procedure as follows. Since the UDI problem is responsible for coupling the two MU-MIMO problems, *FDoS* first determines the IA solution for UDI (Section 3). Then, leveraging the flexibility of the precoders and receive filters already designed at the clients from the IA process, *FDoS* optimizes the receive filter and precoder at the AP in the UL and DL directions to maximize the rate of the UL and DL streams respectively. The key steps are as follows.

---

(1) Optimize the precoders ($\mathbf{V}_1$ and $\mathbf{V}_2$) at the UL clients and receive filter ($\mathbf{U}_0$) at the AP to maximize the rate of the UL streams. Note that, the design of $\mathbf{V}_1$ (to remove UDI) allows the flexibility of picking $\frac{N}{2}$ eigen vectors (out of N) of the matrix $\mathbf{H}_{21}^{-1}\mathbf{H}_{22}\mathbf{H}_{12}^{-1}\mathbf{H}_{11}$. These $\frac{N}{2}$ vectors that form $\mathbf{V}_1$ are chosen appropriately to maximize the rate of the N UL streams to the AP as follows.

- Let $\mathbf{V}_1' = [\vec{v}_{11}\vec{v}_{12}\cdots\vec{v}_{1N}]$. For every $\vec{v}_{1i}$, the corresponding vector in $\mathbf{V}_2'$ is given as $\vec{v}_{2i} = \mathbf{H}_{12}^{-1}\mathbf{H}_{11}\vec{v}_{1i}$. Pair the eigen vectors from $\mathbf{V}_1'$ and $\mathbf{V}_2'$ as $\{(\vec{v}_{1i}, \vec{v}_{2i})\}, \forall i \in [1, N]$.
- Compute the rate metric for the UL streams corresponding to every pair of their eigen vectors as,
$$R_{i,UL} = \text{Rate}(\vec{u}_{0i}^{1}\mathbf{H}_{01}^{U}\vec{v}_{1i}) + \text{Rate}(\vec{u}_{0i}^{2}\mathbf{H}_{02}^{U}\vec{v}_{2i}) \quad (9)$$
where $\vec{u}_{0i}^{1}$ and $\vec{u}_{0i}^{2}$ are the receive filter vectors (eg. LMMSE filters) at the AP (total of N vectors) corresponding to the precoding vectors at UL clients 1 and 2 respectively. Given $\vec{v}_{1i}$ and $\vec{v}_{2i}$, $\vec{u}_{0i}^{1}$ and $\vec{u}_{0i}^{2}$ can be easily computed to maximize the individual rate terms in the above equation. We employ the Shannon formula for the rate function [19].
- Arrange the pair of eigen vectors in descending order of their uplink rate metric. Then, pick the top $\frac{N}{2}$ pairs to construct the corresponding precoding matrices $\mathbf{V}_1$ and $\mathbf{V}_2$ of size $N \times \frac{N}{2}$ for the two UL clients. Similarly, use the corresponding $\frac{N}{2}$ receive filter vectors $(\vec{u}_{0i}^{1}, \vec{u}_{0i}^{2})$ (computed above) for the AP to construct the $\frac{N}{2} \times N$ receive filter matrices $\mathbf{U}_0^1$ and $\mathbf{U}_0^2$, and hence its final $N \times N$ receive filter matrix $\mathbf{U}_0 = [\mathbf{U}_0^{1^T}\mathbf{U}_0^{1^T}]^T$.

(2) Compute receive filters ($\mathbf{U}_1$ and $\mathbf{U}_2$) for DL clients to remove UDI. Given $\mathbf{V}_1$ and $\mathbf{V}_2$, the receive filters $\mathbf{U}_1$ and $\mathbf{U}_2$ of size $\frac{N}{2} \times N$ at DL clients 1 and 2 are obtained orthogonal to the sub-space spanned by $\mathbf{H}_{11}\mathbf{V}_1$ and $\mathbf{H}_{22}\mathbf{V}_2$ respectively, wherein the interference from both UL clients have been aligned.

(3) Determine the precoding matrix ($\mathbf{V}_0$) for the AP to maximize the rate of the DL streams. Having computed the receive filters $\mathbf{U}_1$ and $\mathbf{U}_2$ based on IA, the precoding matrix for the AP $\mathbf{V}_0$ is computed to maximize the rate of the N downlink streams,

$$R_{DL} = \text{Rate}(\mathbf{U}_1\mathbf{H}_{10}^{D}\mathbf{V}_0^1) + \text{Rate}(\mathbf{U}_2\mathbf{H}_{20}^{D}\mathbf{V}_0^2) \quad (10)$$

where $\mathbf{V}_0^1$ and $\mathbf{V}_0^2$ are the two $N \times \frac{N}{2}$ precoding matrices with respect to the two DL clients, that together form the $N \times N$ precoding matrix $\mathbf{V}_0$ at the AP, i.e. $\mathbf{V}_0 = [\mathbf{V}_0^1\mathbf{V}_0^2]$.

Note that *FDoS* optimizes the UL precoders first. However, one could also start by optimizing the DL precoders. While one can envision to jointly address the UL and DL MU-MIMO problems (along with IA) through a very complex optimization problem, this will not favor implementation. In contrast, we will now show how our modular approach allows for a distributed implementation, thereby reducing overhead.

4.3 Reducing Overhead

A straight-forward implementation of the above solution will consist of the following steps.

(*i*) AP sends pilots for channel estimation at DL clients, followed by UL clients 1 and 2 for channel estimation at the AP $(\mathbf{H}_{01}^{U}, \mathbf{H}_{02}^{U})$ as well as at the DL clients.

(*ii*) DL clients 1 and 2 estimate and feedback DL CSI $\mathbf{H}_{10}^{D}$ and $\mathbf{H}_{20}^{D}$ respectively to the AP.

(*iii*) In addition, DL client 1 estimates and feeds back UL-DL CSI $\mathbf{H}_{11}$ and $\mathbf{H}_{12}$ to the AP for IA. Similarly, DL client 2 feeds back $\mathbf{H}_{21}$ and $\mathbf{H}_{22}$ to the AP.

(*iv*) With all the required CSI, the AP computes all the desired precoders and receive filters, $\mathbf{V}_0, \mathbf{V}_1, \mathbf{V}_2, \mathbf{U}_0, \mathbf{U}_1, \mathbf{U}_2$. AP then transmits $\mathbf{V}_1, \mathbf{V}_2$ to the UL clients, which the DL clients overhear and use to compute their own receive filters $\mathbf{U}_1$ and $\mathbf{U}_2$.

Note that the transmission of pilots from the AP (step 1) and feedback of CSI from the DL clients (step 2) are common to a HD MU-MIMO (downlink) system. However, the pilots from the UL clients (step 1), feedback of inter-client CSI (step 3) and precoders for the UL clients (step 4) are specific to our FD system, thereby constituting additional (albeit fixed) overhead. With the pilots constituting negligible overhead relative to the CSI and precoder feedback, the bulk of the overhead is incurred in steps 3 and 4.

We propose an alternate approach that leverages the distributed nature of our solution to reduce the overhead incurred by *half*. While steps 1 and 2 are the same, the remaining steps are as follows (also refer to Fig. 7).

(*iii*) DL client 1 feeds back only $\mathbf{H}_{12}^{-1}\mathbf{H}_{11}$ to AP for IA. Similarly, DL client 2 feeds back only $\mathbf{H}_{21}^{-1}\mathbf{H}_{22}$ to AP.

(*iv*) AP then transmits only $\mathbf{V}_1$ to the UL clients, which UL client 2 and DL clients use to compute their precoder $\mathbf{V}_2$ and receiver filters $\mathbf{U}_1$, $\mathbf{U}_2$ respectively.

Thus, the overhead of four $N \times N$ CSI matrices and two $N \times \frac{N}{2}$ precoder matrices is reduced to two $N \times N$ CSI matrices and a single $N \times \frac{N}{2}$ precoder matrix, brining about an overhead reduction of **half**.

Distributed Realization: The above approach with reduced feedback information is sufficient to execute our entire solution. Note that the aggregated CSI information provided by the DL clients is sufficient for the AP to execute Step 1 of our Algorithm in Section 4.2 and hence obtain $\mathbf{V}_1, \mathbf{V}_2, \mathbf{U}_0$. The AP then provides only $\mathbf{V}_1$ as feedback to the UL and DL clients. UL client 2 uses this information along with $\mathbf{H}_{12}^{-1}\mathbf{H}_{11}$ (overhead during feed back from DL client 1) to compute its own precoder $\mathbf{V}_2$ locally as in Step 1, i.e. $\mathbf{V}_2 = \mathbf{H}_{12}^{-1}\mathbf{H}_{11}\mathbf{V}_1$. Similarly, DL clients 1 and 2 also locally compute $\mathbf{V}_2$. Now, with access to both $\mathbf{V}_1$ and $\mathbf{V}_2$ and their local CSI, i.e. $(\mathbf{H}_{11}, \mathbf{H}_{12})$ for DL client 1 and $(\mathbf{H}_{21}, \mathbf{H}_{22})$ for DL client 2, both the DL clients can compute their respective receive filters $\mathbf{U}_1$ and $\mathbf{U}_2$ locally as in Step 2. The AP also has all the necessary information to compute the same receive filters $\mathbf{U}_1$ and $\mathbf{U}_2$ that will be used at the DL clients and hence its corresponding precoder V_0 as in Step 3.

4.4 Handling Heterogeneity

In reality, one might encounter scenarios, where clients have varied number of antennas. We consider such cases to understand when and how *FDoS* and more generally full-duplex can be applied.

Case 1: All clients have $M = 1$ *antenna* - Although the AP has N antennas, if the HD clients are all restricted to a single antenna, no spatial IA is possible. Hence, UDI will have to be addressed by relying on client separation, side channels [3], etc. However, it is hard to scale such approaches from single stream (in either direction) to MIMO FD systems. Consequently, it might be beneficial to operate the system in half-duplex in such cases (especially for large N), where MU-MIMO can be applied to generate N streams in a single direction.

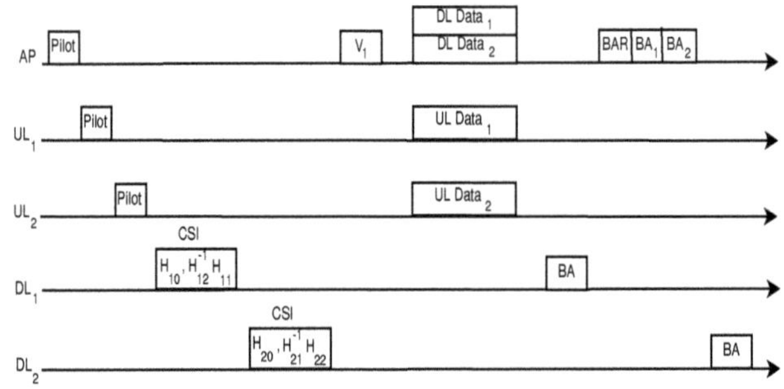

Figure 7: *FDoS* Operation Timeline.

Case 2: All clients have M $(1 < M \leq N)$ *antennas* - Here IA is possible and *FDoS* can be applied to deliver $2M$ streams in FD. However, depending on how $2M$ compares to N, one still needs to decide whether to operate the system in FD or HD.

Case 3: Some clients have M $(1 < M \leq N)$ *antennas and others have* N *antennas* - This is a practical scenario that can arise often. For eg. smartphones/tablets with two antennas and laptops, smart TVs with more antennas. We show that the performance of *FDoS* is not restricted by clients with lesser antennas (i.e. $2M$ streams), but provides a graceful performance ($M + N$ streams) utilizing all the available antennas in the system effectively.

THEOREM 1. FDoS *delivers* $M + N$ *streams with four HD clients, two each with* M *and* N *antennas respectively* (M, N *being even).*

The proof (construction) is deferred to a technical report [18] in the interest of space. We provide a brief sketch of our construction here. With UDI channel matrices being non-square, the problem is particularly challenging in asymmetric FDIC compared to symmetric FDIC. Our construction involves decomposing the IAN into (i) a *symmetric* part that employs IA and hence our solution from symmetric FDIC, and (ii) an *asymmetric* part employing interference suppression (1 DoF for every interfering stream). The symmetric part consists of x antennas and admits $\frac{x}{2}$ streams at each of the UL and DL clients, where $x = \min\{2M - N, M\}$. The asymmetric part consists of the remaining $M - x$ antennas at each UL client, which admits $\frac{M-x}{2}$ transmit streams, and $N - x$ antennas at each DL client, which admits $\frac{N-x}{2}$ receive streams. This results in a net $\frac{M}{2}$ and $\frac{N}{2}$ streams at each UL and DL client respectively.

Note that the above result holds irrespective of whether the UL clients have M antennas and DL clients have N antennas or vice versa as the scenarios are reciprocal. Hence, the IA construction for one scenario can be obtained in a manner reciprocal to that of the other.

4.5 Summary of Operations in *FDoS*

We now outline the complete sequence of steps in executing an FD session in *FDoS* (see Fig. 7 for illustration).

(1) *Decide FD vs. HD*: Based on desired scheduling/QoS policies (proportional fairness in our case), the four clients for a FD session in *FDoS* are chosen by the AP. Given the number of antennas available at the clients[3], the total number of streams possible through

[3]Scheduling decisions can also incorporate information on number of client antennas.

FD is determined (Section 4.4). FD is then enabled only if it can generate more streams (than N in HD). Decoupling CSI from the decision process, avoids incurring FD-related CSI overhead even before FD mode is chosen.

(2) *Channel Estimation and Feedback*: Once FD is chosen, the clients in the session are notified. The channels between AP and the four clients as well as between the clients themselves are estimated, followed by the intelligent (reduced) feedback procedure as outlined in Section 4.3.

(3) *Distributed Computation of Solution:* In addition to determining its own precoder and receive filter, the AP disseminates the precoder for one of the UL clients. Using this, the rest of the precoder and receive filters are computed locally at each of the clients (Sections 4.2,4.3).

(4) *Executing FD Session:* The FD session is then enabled by the AP between the four clients in the symmetric ($2M$ or $2N$ streams) or asymmetric ($M + N$ streams) mode as appropriate. The AP serves as the point coordinator (eg. cellular BS, PCF mode in 802.11) for the FD session.

(5) *ACK Delivery:* The delivery of ACKs follows a procedure similar to downlink MU-MIMO operation in 802.11ac, wherein the AP solicits block ACKs (BA) from each of the MU-MIMO clients (except the first client) sequentially. In our case, in addition to a block ACK request (BAR) for the second DL client, the AP also needs to send back two ACKs to the two UL clients. This is achieved by piggybacking the two ACKs for the UL clients onto the ACK-request for the second DL client as shown in Fig. 7, thereby not having to incur additional transmissions.

5. IMPLEMENTATION

We prototype *FDoS* using WARPLab in a 6-node WARP testbed that uses a combination of v2 and v3 WARP boards. We use a 802.11-compatible OFDM PHY with 64 sub-carriers for UL and DL transmissions. The key implementation details are as follows.

Full Duplex. We implement a simple MIMO full-duplex platform employing a mix of analog and digital cancellation techniques (similar to [7, 10, 1]) for the FD AP. We employ two WARP nodes to construct the AP, one for transmission and other for reception simultaneously, and synchronize their clocks (only within the AP). Due to the effort needed to realize self-interference (SI) suppression over a wide-band channel, our platform currently achieves around 28 dB of analog SI signal cancellation over a 1 MHz OFDM channel. Note that the impact of UDI is independent of the amount of SI canceled at the FD node. Hence, even though our FD implementation may not sufficiently cancel all self-interference, it suffices to illustrate the benefits that can be achieved by eliminating UDI, the latter being the focus in *FDoS*. One can also employ more sophisticated techniques for SI cancellation (eg. [4]) to achieve SI suppression over a wide-band channel in *FDoS*. As for *FDoS*'s IA solution itself, it works even over a 10 MHz wide-band channel.

Antenna configuration. We evaluate *FDoS* under homogeneous and heterogeneous antenna configurations. Under the homogeneous setting, each HD (UL, DL) and FD (AP) node has the same number of antennas (2 or 4). Under the heterogeneous configuration, UL and FD nodes have 4 antennas while DL nodes have only 2 antennas. These configurations are representative of real-world wireless networks: mobile devices (e.g. tablets and cellphones) can be expected to have up to 2 antennas while larger devices (e.g. laptops, desktops) can easily hold 4 or more.

Clock synchronization. While it is convenient to maintain clock and phase synchronization between all nodes in a testbed via a wired back-channel, such an approach may not be realistic in all scenarios. Current wireless devices cannot be expected to have such fine-grained clock synchronization. Hence, we do not maintain clock synchronization between the clients and also between AP and clients. As we show later, *FDoS* is still able to eliminate UDI under such conditions.

CSI measurement. We measure all UL and DL CSI using separate probe packets. The precoders and receiver filters computed from these CSIs based on *FDoS*'s design are then used in subsequent data frames. Due to the high latency involved in WARPLab, the delay between the CSI measurements and data transmissions is larger than that found in typical WiFi transmissions. While it is reasonable to allow for CSI estimation and application within the coherence time of the channel for a single scheme, it cannot accommodate the comparison of multiple schemes over a single fixed channel.

6. PERFORMANCE EVALUATION

6.1 Set-up

Test-bed: The experiments are conducted in an indoor office environment. Two WARP nodes jointly serve as the FD AP, while the remaining four nodes serve as four HD clients that are distributed around the AP. The WARP nodes are distributed in a lab area with rich multipath. We have observed several multipath components to be equally strong in our lab space based on our experiments. The transmit power and spatial distance between the clients as well as that between the clients and AP are varied to create numerous topologies.

More than the specific topology, the key factor that impacts UDI is the "relative" strength of the UL-DL interference channel compared to the desired AP-DL channel during the FD session. Hence, we have categorized various topologies into bins based on the relative strengths (power) between these two channels, which is in turn used as a metric to benchmark the performance of various schemes under varying levels of UDI.

Our results are averaged over several topologies as well as over multiple runs.

Baselines and Metrics: We evaluate *FDoS* against two baselines: (i) *FDoS* without the IA component, i.e. DL and UL operate independently without alleviating their mutual interference (No-Align), and (ii) a half-duplex MU-MIMO system employing conventional ZFBF for its DL and UL (MU-MIMO). CSI are estimated on each of the 64 sub-carriers and precoding is carried out on a sub-carrier basis in our experiments. Since the channels and their CSI cannot be ensured to be static across different schemes, it was not possible to compare the different schemes point-to-point for a given fixed channel. The CSI was estimated and applied before the application of each scheme. Hence, we resorted to the CDF of the SINR distribution resulting from the application of different schemes. Each of our experiment involves sending about 500-1000 frames back-back to generate enough samples for a confident comparison.

We use SINR measured from the experiments as our primary metric and translate it to rate using the Shannon capacity formula wherever appropriate. While the rate for an FD system is computed as the sum of the DL and UL rates, that for the corresponding HD system is computed as the average.

6.2 Benchmarking IA

We first evaluate the performance of the IA delivered by *FDoS* in practice. We consider a homogeneous N ($N = 2, 4$) antenna set-up, wherein the AP and client nodes are all equipped with N antennas, and generate N streams on the UL and DL simultaneously. The impact of *FDoS* in suppressing UDI (called alignment

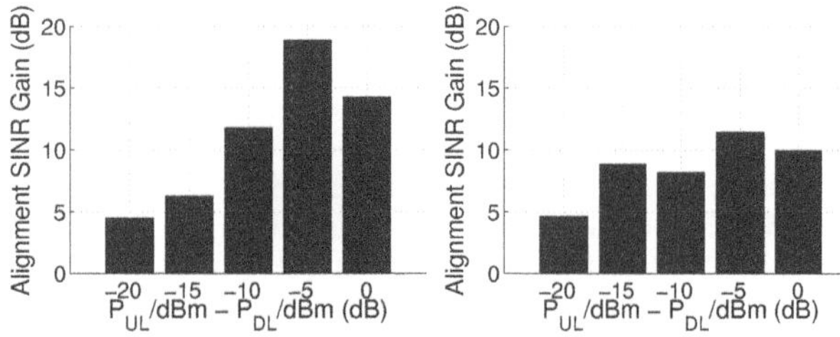

(a) 2-antennas (b) 4-antennas

Figure 8: Substantial UDI Suppression from IA

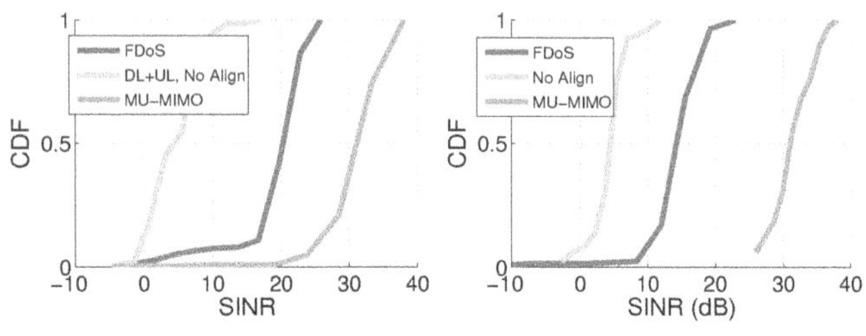

(a) 2-antennas (b) 4-antennas

Figure 9: Improvement in DL SINR from *FDoS*

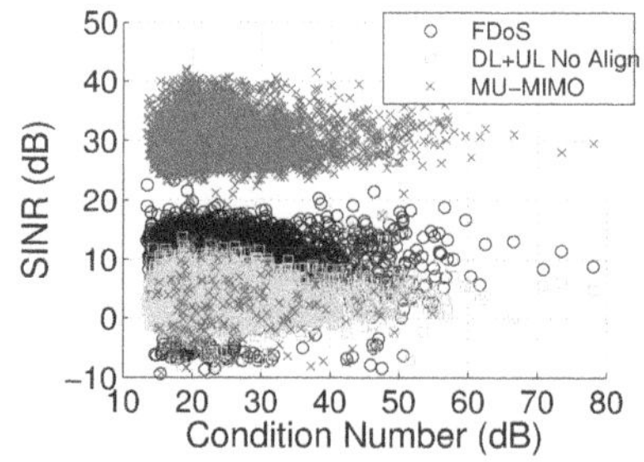

Figure 10: Impact of CSI quality on *FDoS*

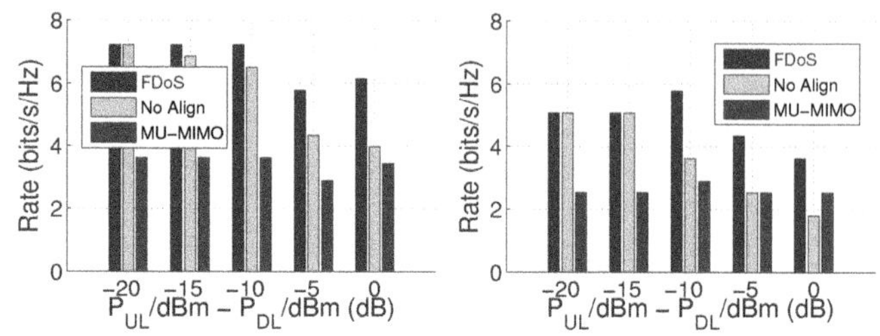

(a) 2-antennas (b) 4-antennas

Figure 11: *FDoS* achieves close to 2x under strong UDI

gain) per DL stream during FD is captured in Fig. 8 as a function of increasing UL transmit power. Since transmit powers cannot be directly measured, we vary the transmit gain of the UL nodes relative to that of the AP and capture the resulting transmit power difference between them ($P_{UL} - P_{DL}$). It can be seen that UDI and the room needed for its suppression is less at lower transmit powers. However, at higher transmit powers, *FDoS* provides a large UDI suppression of up to 20 dB per DL stream in the 2 antenna case even without any clock sync between the nodes. In the 4 antenna case, the lack of clock sync has a larger impact and limits the UDI suppression in *FDoS* to 12 dB per stream, which is still promising to enable appreciable rate gains on the DL. This clearly indicates *FDoS*'s ability to handle UDI effectively, and hence enable $2N$ streams (4 and 8 streams in our experiments) in a distributed FD network.

6.3 *FDoS* Performance

SINR Performance: We now evaluate *FDoS* by measuring the performance delivered to the DL streams in the presence of UDI (Fig. 9) and the resulting net rate (Figs. 11a, 11b). The UL clients operate at 5 dB lower power than the FD AP node. Fig. 9 presents the CDF (over topologies and runs) of the DL SINR (averaged over the streams). Fig. 9(a) shows that UDI can significantly hurt performance in the 2 antenna case, bringing down the median HD SINR (i.e without any UDI) by about 30 dB. It is very promising that *FDoS* can suppress almost 20 dB of the UDI to suffer only a 10 dB median loss in SINR, which is more than compensated for by the additional streams that it enables on the DL.

In the 4 antenna case in Fig. 9(b), lack of clock sync limits median UDI suppression to 12 dB, and hence suffers a slightly larger loss of 15 dB compared to HD. However, the UDI suppression is still significant to provide an appreciable FD gain over HD as we show subsequently. Note that there are two factors that can affect IA performance: (i) change in CSI between estimation and IA execution, and (ii) clock drifts between nodes. The impact of these will be more for larger number of antennas. With experiments, we have verified that the impact of the former is more significant than the latter. Hence, if the first factor can be addressed through implementation on a faster SDR platform, we believe it could boost IA performance even for larger number of antennas.

Impact of CSI Quality: For the 2 antenna case, we present the DL SINR (averaged over the two streams) as a function of the DL CSI quality in Fig. 10. Here, the condition number of the CSI matrix (ratio of largest to smallest eigen values of matrix) is used as a measure of the CSI quality for MU-MIMO. The clustering of the SINR values along a horizontal band indicates that *FDoS*'s ability to suppress UDI is fairly robust to the nature of CSI.

Rate Performance: We present the aggregate rate results in Figs. 11a and 11b. We can see that *FDoS* provides a rate gain of 1.75x - 2x over HD MU-MIMO, thereby helping to achieve most of the multiplexing gain offered by FD under strong UDI. Further, its gain over No-Align is about 1.5x - 2x and increases with increasing number of antennas (streams), owing to the rate gain from 10-20 dB UDI suppression *per stream*. Further, No-Align performs even worse than the HD MU-MIMO system in the 4 antenna case, owing to a larger impact from UDI that goes un-addressed.

6.4 Handling Heterogeneity

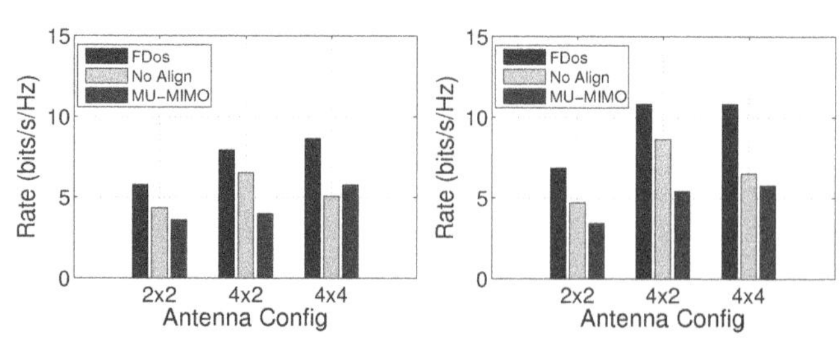

(a) 0 dB (b) -5 dB

Figure 12: *FDoS* handles heterogeneity gracefully

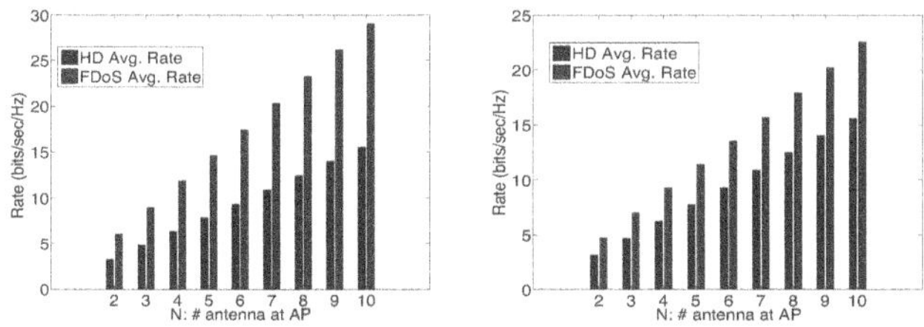

(a) *FDoS* w rate optimization (b) *FDoS* w/o rate optimization

Figure 13: Scalability and Rate Optimization in *FDoS*

In addition to the homogeneous 2 and 4 antenna cases, we now consider a heterogeneous case. Here, the AP has 4 antennas, but the two DL clients have only 2 antennas each while the two UL clients have four antennas each. Hence, the UL clients transmit 2 streams each, while the DL clients receive one stream each. We did not consider the reciprocal case, where the UL clients have 2 antennas each, while the DL clients have 4 antennas each, since interference suppression is sufficient (IA is not required) to enable 6 streams in this scenario. On the other hand, the considered scenario, where the UL clients have more antennas and send 4 streams is interesting, since IA is now required to enable the 6 streams simultaneously in FD. Although the UL streams might appear to overwhelm the resources at the DL clients, this scenario is indeed possible and requires a slightly different construction (reciprocal of the construction for the case, where DL clients have more antennas than UL clients) as we discussed in Section 4.4. We present the average rate results comparing this heterogeneous case with the 2 and 4 antenna homogeneous cases in Fig. 12. *FDoS*'s ability to leverage clients with heterogeneous antenna capabilities effectively allows it to support six streams (without being restricted to four). This helps bridge the performance gap in rate between the homogeneous 2 and 4 antenna cases gracefully.

6.5 Scalability and SI Suppression

We now employ simulations to evaluate *FDoS*'s ability to optimize the rate of the FD streams in scenarios with (i) large number of antennas, and (ii) odd number of antennas; aspects that we could not accomplish with our testbed. Recall, that the odd N case, involves a different construction compared to the even N case and also requires six HD clients. Our simulations are conducted in Matlab and employ standard 3GPP channel models. We present the aggregate rate results as a function of N in Fig. 13(a). It can be seen that the performance gains of *FDoS* are similar to those observed in the experiments and scale well as a function of N. More importantly, it also verifies our solution for the odd N case. When the precoders are not optimized to maximize rate (i.e. only addressing UDI), the FD gains are less enhanced as seen from comparing Figs. 13(a) and (b). This emphasizes the importance of not just addressing UDI but also maximizing the rate of the FD streams in *FDoS*.

In Fig. 14, we evaluate *FDoS* as a function of the SI suppression capability at the FD (AP) node (for $N = 4$). It can be seen that while the aggregate rate (specifically UL rate) decreases with smaller SI suppression, the FD gains from *FDoS* are appreciable even for 20-30 dB SI suppression. This is largely due to *FDoS*'s ability to eliminate the other critical component of interference, namely UDI.

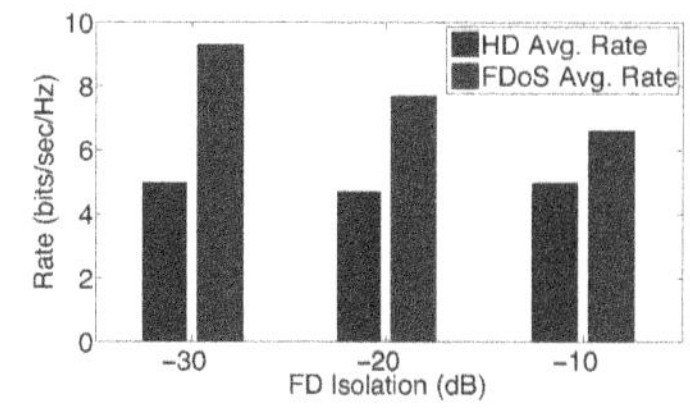

Figure 14: Impact of SI suppression on *FDoS*

7. RELATED WORK AND DISCUSSIONS

7.1 Related Work

Interference Alignment (IA): The notion of interference alignment was introduced in [6]. In general, characterizing the maximum number of streams that can be supported and realized through IA in interference channels has been an elusive problem and has been considered under various network settings in the communications literature (see [13, 2] and references therein). Recently, [5] showed that in an interference channel with K links, with each node of the link having N antennas each, one can potentially achieve $2N$ streams asymptotically (as $K \to \infty$) with IA alone. In the networking space, IA has been leveraged along with transmitter cooperation (packet sharing) to generate $2N$ streams on the uplink and $2N - 2$ streams on the downlink. A distributed version of the scheme was later proposed in [14]. Further, [15] considered the realization of blind IA in practice. Note that the above results are for half-duplex systems. As we will show later, interestingly, the interference channel generated by the distributed FD network is different from that in the HD network and hence warrants a fresh understanding of the applicability of IA in FD.

Full Duplex (FD): The bulk of the system works on FD have focused on addressing self-interference through antenna [7, 10, 1], RF [16, 9, 12, 8, 4] and digital [9, 12, 8, 4] cancellation. Recently, [21] tried to effectively leverage exposed terminals along with FD transmissions in a network. The focus of these works has been on the peer-peer FD model. The importance of distributed FD with HD clients and hence the need to address UDI was only recently considered in [3]. The focus of [3] has been to theoretically characterize the benefits of having a side-channel in a three-node distributed FD network. However, the cost of the side-channel as well as scalability to multiple streams in FD (i.e. MIMO in either direction of FD) was not considered.

FD+IA: Recently, [17] proposed the use of IA in the time domain (through symbol extension) for addressing UDI in FD networks, albeit with FD capability at both the AP and (single-antenna) clients. The focus of [17] is characterizing DoF for such an all-FD network from an information-theoretic perspective. Being based on time alignment, it requires the interference channel (CSI) to repeat itself in the future, when it can be leveraged to eliminate UDI in the past and is hence not conducive for a practical realization.

Our focus in this work has been to address the UDI problem through a *practical, bandwidth-efficient and scalable* solution, and hence enable full-duplex with *HD* clients.

7.2 Discussions

We now discuss various aspects that can impose practical limitations on *FDoS*.

Sensitivity to CSI and Mobility: By relying on CSI, *FDoS* is applicable to clients whose channels have coherence times reasonable enough to amortize the overhead of CSI estimation. However, with MU-MIMO becoming mainstream (802.11ac), such limitation would be imposed on any FD or HD system that employs closed-loop MIMO (even in the absence of IA). By a similar token, applicability to mobile clients (potentially pedestrian mobility) is also realistic only if the coherence time of the mobile client's channel can accommodate the CSI estimation latency.

FD Gains at Higher Layers: In addition to addressing UDI, another factor that impacts the higher layer FD gains is the opportunity for FD in the first place. The latter is in turn dependent on the relative volume of UL and DL traffic. However, it is a factor common to FD systems in general. *FDoS*'s focus has been on maximizing the FD gains during the FD opportunities created by the MAC. However, optimizing for FD opportunities requires a careful design of the MAC traffic scheduler and forms an interesting problem in itself.

In *FDoS*, the AP/BS coordinates the FD session similar to a synchronous, cellular set-up. In an asynchronous system like WiFi, there could be other inefficiencies in leveraging the FD gains such as contention overhead to coordinate the UL and DL clients to operate simultaneously in a FD session.

Energy Implications: The additional spatial dimensions (antennas) at clients are essentially the price to pay for addressing UDI. While this may not be a significant energy concern for the receiving DL clients, *FDoS* solution employs one additional client employing N antennas (and the corresponding additional energy) on the UL transmission compared to a baseline FD scheme that does not address UDI and hence requires only one client each on the UL and DL.

Multi-cell Networks: Extending *FDoS* to multi-cell networks is a very challenging problem since UDI now has to be addressed both within and across cells and forms an interesting avenue for future research.

8. CONCLUSIONS

We consider and address the challenging problem of uplink-downlink interference (UDI) in distributed FD networks by leveraging spatial interference alignment in an efficient, practical and scalable manner. We build the theory and design of applying IA to distributed FD networks and show that four HD clients are sufficient to enable the multiplexing gain of two possible with FD. We present our system *FDoS* that leverages the structure of interference in these networks to construct elegant IA solutions, while incorporating several MAC layer design elements to translate our solution into reality. A prototype evaluation of *FDoS* using WARP radios shows significant promise for *FDoS* in addressing UDI and truly enabling FD with HD clients.

9. REFERENCES

[1] E. Aryafar, A. Khojastepour, K. Sundaresan, S. Rangarajan, and M. Chiang. MIDU: Enabling mimo full-duplex. In *Proceedings of ACM MobiCom*, Sept 2012.

[2] O. E. Ayach, S. W. Peters, and R. W. Heath. The practical challenges of interference alignment. In *IEEE Wireless Communications Magazine*, Feb 2013.

[3] J. Bai and A. Sabharwal. Distributed full-duplex via wireless side channels: Bounds and protocols. *Arxiv*, abs/1212.5300, 2012.

[4] D. Bharadia, E. McMilin, and S. Katti. Full-duplex radios. In *Proceedings of ACM SIGCOMM*, Aug 2013.

[5] G. Bresler, D. Cartwright, and D. Tse. Interference alignment for the mimo interference channel. *arxiv*, arXiv:1303.5678, 2013.

[6] V. Cadambe and S. A. Jafar. Interference alignment and degrees of freedom of the k user interference channel. *Transactions on Information Theory*, 54(8):3425–3441, Aug 2008.

[7] J. Choi, M. Jain, K. Srinivasan, P. Levis, and S. Katti. Achieving single channel, full duplex wireless communication. In *Proceedings of ACM MobiCom*, Sep 2010.

[8] M. Duarte, C. Dick, and A. Sabharwal. Experiment-driven characterization of full-duplex wireless systems. *IEEE Transactions on Wireless Communications*, Sept 2012.

[9] M. Duarte and A. Sabharwal. Full-duplex wireless communications using off-the-shelf radios: Feasibility and first results. In *Asilomar Conference*, Nov 2010.

[10] E. Everett, M. Duarte, C. Dick, and A. Sabharwal. Empowering full-duplex wireless communication by exploiting directional diversity. In *Asilomar Conference*, Nov 2011.

[11] S. Gollakota, S. Perli, and D. Katabi. Interference alignment and cancellation. In *Proceedings of ACM SIGCOMM*, Aug 2009.

[12] M. Jain, T.M. Kim, D. Bharadia, S. Seth, K. Srinivasan, P. Levis, S. Katti, and P. Sinha. Practical, real-time, full duplex wireless. In *Proceedings of ACM MobiCom*, Sep 2011.

[13] S. W. Jeon and M. Gatspar. A survey on interference networks: Interference alignment and neutralization. *Journal of Entropy*, 14(10):1842–1863, 2012.

[14] K. Lin, S. Gollakota, and D. Katabi. Random access heterogeneous mimo networks. In *Proceedings of ACM SIGCOMM*, Aug 2011.

[15] K. Miller, A. Sanne, K. Srinivasan, and S. Vishwanath. Enabling real-time interference alignment: Promises and challenges. In *ACM MobiHoc*, June 2012.

[16] B. Radunovic, D. Gunawardena, P. Key, A. Proutiere, N. Singh, V. Balan, and G. Dejean. Rethinking indoor wireless mesh design: Low power low frequency, full-duplex. MSR-TR-2009-27.

[17] A. Sahai, S. Diggavi, and A. Sabharwal. On degrees of freedom of full-duplex uplink-downlink channel. In *IEEE ITW*, 2013.

[18] K. Sundaresan, M. Khojastepour, E. Chai, and S. Rangarajan. Full-duplex without strings: Enabling full-duplex with half-duplex clients. In *NEC Labs Technical Report, 2014-TR027*, Mar 2014.

[19] D. Tse and P. Viswanath. *Fundamentals of Wireless Communication*. Cambridge University Press, 2005.

[20] C. M. Yetis, T. Guo, S. A. Jafar, and A. H. Kayran. Feasibility conditions for interference alignment. In *IEEE Globecom*, 2009.

[21] W Zhou, K. Srinivasan, and P. Sinha. Rctc: Rapid transmission coordination in full-duplex wireless networks. In *IEEE ICNP*, 2013.

Enabling Instantaneous Feedback with Full-duplex Backscatter

Vincent Liu†, Vamsi Talla†, Shyamnath Gollakota
University of Washington
{liuv, vamsit, gshyam}@uw.edu
†Co-primary Student Authors

Abstract– This paper introduces the first design that enables full-duplex communication on battery-free backscatter devices. Specifically, it gives receivers a way to provide low-rate feedback to the transmitter on the same frequency as that of the backscatter transmissions, using neither multiple antennas nor power-consuming cancellation hardware. Our design achieves this goal using only fully-passive analog components that consume near-zero power. We integrate our design with the backscatter network stack and demonstrate that it can minimize energy wastes that occur due to collisions and also correct for errors and changes in channel conditions at a granularity smaller than that of a packet. To show the feasibility of our design, we build a hardware prototype using off-the-shelf analog components. Our evaluation shows that our design cancels the self-interference down to the noise floor, while consuming only 0.25 μW and 0.54 μW of transmit and receive power, respectively.

Categories and Subject Descriptors

C.2.1 [**Network Architecture and Design**]: Wireless communication

Keywords

Backscatter; Full-duplex wireless; Wireless

1. Introduction

Backscatter communication is a promising technique for low-power computing devices. RFID, for instance, has enabled a multitude of useful applications [27, 34] that take advantage of the fact that one side of the link can be completely battery-free. More recently, researchers have shown the feasibility of using backscatter to communicate directly between two low-power devices [18]. The power draw of this technique is such that both devices can operate solely off of harvested energy. By creating a network of battery-free devices that can communicate with each other, this can enable the types of applications envisioned by the Internet-of-Things (e.g., smart homes).

Unfortunately, existing link- and network-layer protocols are ill suited for such communication networks. Extreme power constraints not only magnify the effects of collisions and failed transmissions, they also make it difficult for these devices to use multi-

MobiCom'14, September 7-11, 2014, Maui, Hawaii, USA.

http://dx.doi.org/10.1145/2639108.2639136.

Figure 1: **Full-duplex Backscatter Prototype:** A photo of our Full-duplex Backscatter prototype. This side contains the transmitter switch, while the receiver is implemented on the other side.

round protocols like RTS-CTS—storing increasing amounts of energy becomes exponentially hard. In this paper, we explore the feasibility of an instantaneous feedback channel where a receiver can simultaneously send feedback information while still receiving the original transmission. Such a feedback channel could address many of the problems facing these devices:

- *Packet Collisions:* Instantaneous feedback could be used to terminate transmission as soon as a collision is detected. Because recharge time dominates transmission time [28], enabling early termination increases throughput by orders of magnitude.
- *Rate Adaptation:* Instead of waiting for packet drops to adjust rate, a feedback channel allows us to gather bit error rate statistics and use them to change rate at the level of bits rather than packets. This is particularly important for backscatter devices, as their transmission rates are orders of magnitude lower than traditional radio communication (e.g., Wi-Fi). Thus, they take significantly longer to transmit the same amount of data—long enough that the channel may change within the span of a single packet.
- *Retransmissions:* In the same way, we can use a feedback channel to inform transmitters of bit-level errors. Thus, the transmitter only needs to retransmit the subset of bits that were incorrect, rather than throwing away the packet entirely and trying again.

Traditional radio communication designs have explored the idea of adding a feedback channel, but none of those existing approaches are applicable to backscatter systems. They mainly fall into two categories: frequency-division duplexing and full-duplex communication. Frequency division is not practical because battery-free backscattering tags use simple analog envelope detectors for reception and switches for transmissions. They therefore cannot be designed to be frequency selective while maintaining low power consumption [28].[1] Similarly, recent work on full-duplex communication [9, 5] does not apply because these devices do not have

[1] RFID tags can not decode in the presence of concurrent transmissions in non-overlapping frequency bands.

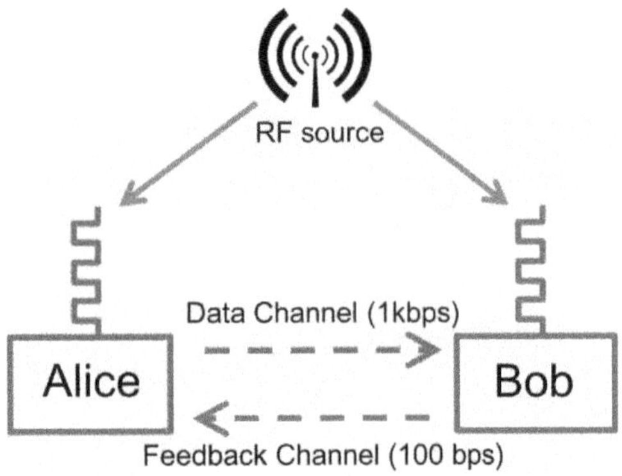

Figure 2: **Full-duplex Backscatter:** Two battery-free devices, Alice and Bob, communicate by backscattering signals from the RF source. Alice transmits to Bob at a high rate on the data channel and receives instantaneous feedback from Bob on the feedback channel.

the computational or energy resources to implement complex interference cancellation techniques or include space-consuming arrays of antennas. In fact, existing full-duplex designs are prototyped on software radios, each of which consumes more than 1-2 Watts of power [11, 2]. More importantly, these designs use components such as ADCs and oscillators that are power-consuming and hence are not applicable for backscattering devices [6].

We introduce a novel technique called Full-duplex Backscatter with which backscatter devices can obtain instantaneous feedback on the same frequency as that of the transmission, without multiple antennas or power-consuming cancellation hardware. Our technique uses fully-passive analog components in order to enable devices to simultaneously maintain a data channel and a low-rate feedback channel in the opposite direction. Because everything is done using simple analog components such as diodes and resistors, we incur near-zero power cost. Finally, we go on to show that the resulting feedback channel can be used to address each of the above problems in the network stack design.

To understand Full-duplex Backscatter, consider the ambient backscatter [18] setup in Fig. 2 with two battery-free devices, Alice and Bob. Alice communicates with Bob by backscattering the transmissions from the RF source; she does so by reflecting or absorbing the incident signals to convey a '0' bit and '1' bit, respectively. Bob receives these bits by tracking the changes in the average amplitude of its received signal.

The challenge in creating a simultaneous feedback channel from Bob to Alice is that the act of backscattering at Bob creates large changes in Bob's received signal amplitude that greatly degrades his decoding capabilities. Conceptually, since Bob uses the same antenna to receive and transmit, the amplitude of his received signal will change significantly based on whether he is reflecting (sending a '0') or absorbing (sending a '1') on the feedback channel.

Our intuition is as follows: *Since Bob's receiver decodes by tracking the amplitude of the received signal, if Bob can backscatter information without changing the amplitude, he will not create any self-interference.*[2] Our approach is therefore to reflect and absorb a *fixed* amount of signal, such that the amplitude of the received signal is constant. To achieve this, Full-duplex Backscatter changes the impedance of the antenna to create phase shifts to the received signal while maintaining the same amplitude. Two reflections with different phases will interfere with the ambient signal at Alice to create two different amplitude levels that Alice can decode using a standard, amplitude-tracking backscatter receiver. We note, however, that while in theory one can pick the impedance values to create equal-amplitude signals with different phase shifts, practical circuits have small impedance mismatches that result in residual interference. In §4, we describe how Full-duplex Backscatter leverages the low rate of the feedback channel to eliminate the effect of this residual interference.

To demonstrate the feasibility of our techniques, we built the prototype in Fig. 1 using off-the-shelf components. Our prototypes communicate with each other by backscattering continuous wave transmissions from an RF source in the 920 MHz range. We configure the devices to transmit at 100 bps on the feedback channel and 1 kbps on the data channel; the latter is the state-of-the-art for device-to-device backscatter communication [18]. Our evaluation shows that our hardware reduces the self-interference close to the noise floor across the frequency range and for a range of receiver power levels, while consuming only 0.25 μW and 0.54 μW of transmit and receive power respectively.

We also integrate the feedback channel provided on our prototype into the backscatter network stack in order to perform collision detection, implement rate adaptation at sub-packet granularities, and reduce retransmissions by performing in-frame error correction. Our results are as follows:

- By terminating colliding transmissions early, we reduce transmitter recharge time by two orders of magnitude for small 64-byte packets across the operational range of receive power levels. The reduction is higher for longer packet sizes.
- By performing in-frame error correction, we reduce the number of retransmitted bits by an order of magnitude, for a range of bit error rates on the data channel.
- Performing in-frame rate adaptation can increase the throughput of a backscatter communication system by about 33% compared to an idealized, SNR-based, packet-level adaptation algorithm. We note that existing backscatter systems do not have access to SNR and thus the benefits of our system are likely greater.

Contributions. In this paper, we:

- Introduce the first design that enables an instantaneous feedback channel on battery-free backscatter devices. We do so leveraging the properties of backscatter communication to perform self-interference cancellation using only passive analog components.
- Develop and integrate the feedback channel with the network stack to address collisions, fine-grained rate adaptation, and error-correction on battery-free devices.
- Design and build an hardware prototype that demonstrates the feasibility of our techniques and protocols in practice.

Network designers have traditionally believed that a full-duplex feedback channel is difficult to achieve on battery-free devices. In this paper, we not only demonstrate the feasibility of such a channel but also show that it can enable link-layer and network-layer mechanisms that can significantly benefit backscatter communication. We believe that this is an important step towards creating a network of backscatter devices that can communicate with each other.

2. THE CASE FOR FEEDBACK IN BACKSCATTER SYSTEMS

A feedback channel has multiple benefits for both traditional backscatter (between a battery-free device and a powered reader) as well as ambient backscatter communication (between two battery-free devices). The key operational challenge for these devices is that they may not have enough energy to transmit multiple pack-

[2]Decoding both amplitude and phase information requires power-consuming oscillators [13] that are avoided in backscatter devices. Thus, phase is a free-parameter that is available for our purposes.

ets back-to-back due to the fact that they largely rely on harvested power—a resource that is both limited and unpredictable.[3]

Below, we provide three illustrative examples of core issues in backscatter communication, and discuss how an instantaneous feedback channel can help address these issues.

Wireless Collisions. Collisions in power-constrained scenarios are problematic because the power used to transmit the packet is essentially wasted. This problem is aggravated when backscatter communication is used in general scenarios beyond traditional RFID/NFC systems that read/write small bits of information. As the packet sizes increase in general backscatter communication, the amount of power wasted in transmitting an undecodable packet increases proportionally. The problem is even worse in scenarios like ambient backscatter communication [18] where a network of battery-free devices communicate with each other without a central coordinator. In such networks, the presence of hidden terminals can aggravate the collision problem.

Multi-round protocols such as RTS-CTS are not attractive in this domain because the devices may not have enough power to transmit and receive multiple packets in succession.

An instantaneous feedback channel can help alleviate the problem of collisions and hidden terminals. Specifically, the receiver can send a message back to the transmitter informing it of the presence of a collision. Since the feedback arrives at the transmitter while it still is transmitting, it can terminate transmission immediately and avoid power waste.

Rate Adaptation. Rate adaptation enables devices to adapt to changing channel conditions to achieve good throughput. The problem here is that backscatter devices generally have low transmission rates. So low, in fact, that traditional rate adaptation reacts too slowly to be effective—channel quality can change significantly within the span of a single packet. This is important because, whereas maximum transmission time for an 802.11g packet is 542 μs [16], backscatter devices such as those proposed in [18] can take twice as much time to transmit a single bit. These devices can take up to 2s to transmit a 256 byte packet. Even an environment that changes at a modest rate (e.g., a person walking) can create changes within that time frame. Note that reducing the packet size is not a desirable solution since it increases the overhead of the preambles and the headers significantly.

An instantaneous feedback channel can address this problem by delivering feedback about channel conditions within the duration of a single packet transmission. This is beneficial in scenarios like that of wearable devices [24], which can experience channel changes as the person moves in the environment.

Retransmissions. Finally, we consider the issue of retransmission. While forward error correction, which may include rate adaptation, can effectively decrease the frequency of failures, there are inevitably cases where certain bits are unrecoverable. This traditionally requires retransmission of the entire packet.

The challenge in backscatter communication is that retransmissions are very undesirable—more than in traditional communication. Not only is the penalty of failed/wasted transmissions much higher in these types of devices, so is the probability of errors. As an example, consider the problem presented in the preceding case. In dynamic channels, packets take so long to transmit that it is likely that the channel will change or interference will occur during the course of a single transmission. Even if only a single bit is unrecoverable, retransmitting an entire packet means that the energy spent in the transmission of the original packet was wasted.

An instantaneous feedback channel can be used to address the above issue by allowing the transmitter to only retransmit the set of bits that are incorrectly received. Specifically, the receiver can use the feedback channel to transmit checksums of small subsets of bits [37] during the packet transmission. The transmitter can use these checksums to identify subsets of bits that are incorrectly received. Note that since these checksums are transmitted on the feedback channel at the same time as the packet transmissions, they do not add additional transmission overhead to the system.

Road Map for the Rest of the Paper. We first provide a background of how backscatter communication works. We then describe in detail our design for achieving the instantaneous feedback channel. Finally, we describe how we can integrate the feedback channel with the backscatter network stack to address the above issues.

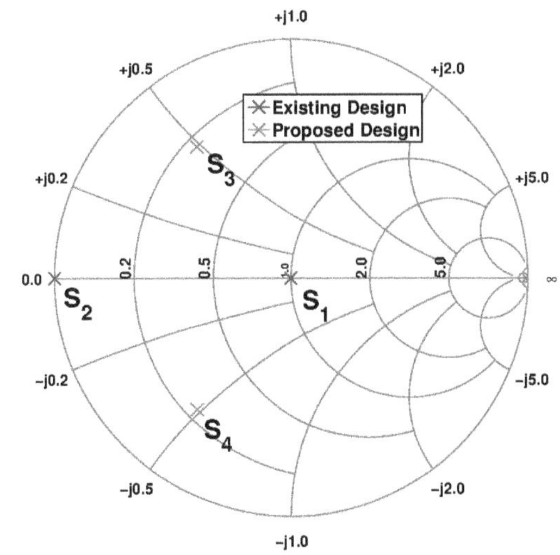

Figure 3: **Smith Chart:** A Smith chart is used to represent impedances and their effect on reflection of incident signals. Each point on the Smith chart corresponds to an input impedance state Z, whose distance to the center of the Smith chart represents the absolute value of the coefficient of reflection, $|\Gamma|$. The center of the Smith chart S_1 corresponds to the matched impedance state, while impedance state S_2 corresponds to the short state. A conventional backscatter transmitter switches between S_1 and S_2. In our design, transmitters switch between the S_3 and S_4 impedance states instead.

3. BACKGROUND ON BACKSCATTER

Backscatter communication is markedly different from traditional radio communication. Rather than generating radio signals—a process that requires orders of magnitude more power than is harvestable—many battery-free device designs [23, 18] have adopted the strategy of re-purposing existing signals in order to communicate. These systems leverage existing RF waves, either from a nearby reader or from ambient signal sources [18]. By backscattering RF waves rather than generating their own (as in traditional communication), these devices can decrease the power required to communicate by several orders of magnitude. While the reduction in the power consumption is enough to make charging delays practical, since these systems still work in energy-constrained environments, problems of collisions, rate adaptation, and retransmissions stress the system. In the rest of this section, we provide a general overview of the design of backscatter devices that applies for both RFID as well as ambient backscatter [18] systems.

To illustrate how backscatter works, consider two devices, Alice and Bob, and say Alice wishes to send a packet to Bob. At a

[3]One might think that a solution to this problem would be to simply gather enough energy for multiple packets; in §5.1, we explain why storing more energy is not straightforward due to leakage issues.

high level, she does so by switching between two states: reflecting and non-reflecting. In the reflecting state, Bob will see a superposition of the original ambient wave as well as Alice's reflected wave. In the non-reflecting state, Bob will simply see the original wave alone. These two states can be used as two bits, which Bob can distinguish between so as to decode a string of '0's and '1's. We describe in detail how current backscatter systems achieve such transmission and reception capabilities in hardware.

Backscatter Transmitter Designs. The job of a backscattering transmitter is to create two distinct superpositions of waves at the receiver. As mentioned above, it does so by switching between two states, which we call reflecting and non-reflecting. Intuitively, RF signals get reflected when they cross two materials that have different impedance values. Since the impedance of an antenna is different from the air around it, a fraction of the incident RF signals get reflected off the antenna. Backscatter works by creating an *additional* impedance boundary between the antenna and the circuitry of the backscattering device.

To be more formal, let's consider the Smith chart shown in Fig. 3. Existing backscatter transmitters switch the impedance presented to the antenna between state S_1 (corresponding to an impedance matched to the antenna) and state S_2 (corresponding to an impedance that is shorted). The difference in reflected power between the two states increases with the square of the conjugate match reflection coefficient:

$$\Gamma^* = \frac{Z_a^* - Z_L}{Z_a + Z_L}$$

where Z_a is the resonant antenna impedance, and Z_L is the complex load impedance. In the matched state S_1, $Z_L = Z_a^*$, $\Gamma^* = 0$, and there is no reflection due to load impedance. In contrast, in the shorted state S_2, $Z_L = 0$, $\Gamma^* = \frac{Z_a^*}{Z_a}$, and some fraction of the wave is reflected. By switching between these two impedances, a transmitter can change the amplitude of the reflected signals and convey information to the receiver.[4]

Backscatter Receiver Designs. The reflecting and non-reflecting states at the transmitter create two different resulting signals, which the receiver hardware should differentiate to decode the transmitted bits. The challenge is that the ultra-low-power devices that use backscatter communication typically do not have enough power to perform complex demodulation on the signal. In fact, they often do not have enough power to operate conventional radio components such as Analog-to-Digital Converters (ADCs) and oscillators (that generate the carrier frequency).

Current receiver designs address this problem by relying on the fact that the received signal has two different amplitudes that can be extracted in hardware using a simple envelope detector circuit with passive components (i.e., a diode combined with an RC circuit). A naive approach to decode the bits from the output of such an envelope detector is to use a full-range ADC. However to reduce the power consumption, backscattering devices instead use a low-power comparator circuit. Specifically, the comparator takes as inputs the signal envelope and its long-term average. In the absence of a backscattering transmitter, the envelope does not vary and the output of the comparator is steady. In presence of a transmitter, the signal envelope varies with respect to the long-term average and the comparator uses this difference to decode the bits.

[4]As in any backscatter system (including RFID), it is possible that the two impedance states result in little or no difference in the amplitude of the signals at the receiver. However, the probability of such an event is very low since it requires the channel phase to match exactly to cancel the effect of the two impedance states.

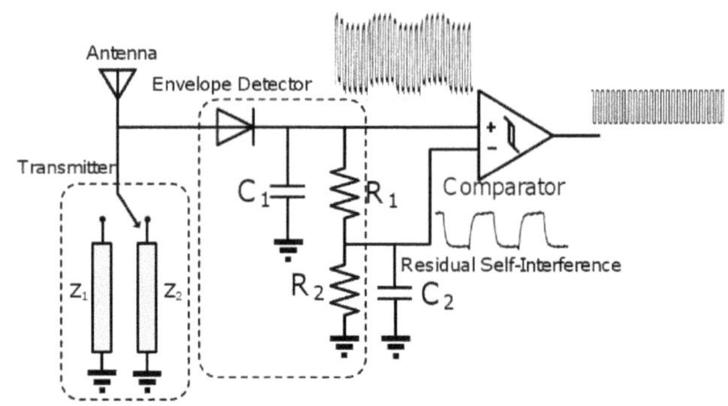

Figure 4: **Bob's Transmitter and Receiver:** Bob switches between Z_1 and Z_2 at a low rate to transmit data to Alice. Bob's receiver consists of three main components: an envelope detector to remove the carrier frequency, a low pass filter to isolate the low frequency residual self-interference and a comparator to cancel the residual self-interference from the output of the envelope detector and decode the received bits. In effect by doing so, Bob is implementing a high pass filter by using a low pass filter to track the residual interference and subtracting it from the enevelop signal using a low power comparator. The high pass operation cancels the low rate self-inteference from the desired high rate signal.

4. FULL-DUPLEX BACKSCATTER DESIGN

We introduce Full-duplex Backscatter, a novel communication technique that creates a low-rate, instantaneous feedback channel for backscatter devices. Our goal is to design a feedback channel that uses a single antenna for transmit and receive and consumes a negligible amount of power.

Creating such a feedback channel is challenging for at least three reasons. First, conventional backscatter transmitters actively change the amplitude of reflected signal to encode data. This is bad for the receiver, which relies on changes in the amplitude of the received signal to decode transmissions. Because the transmitter and receiver share a single antenna, a device's transmitter will create a great deal of interference for it's own receiver. Second, backscatter transmitters and receivers must share the same signal. Conservation of energy means that there is a fundamental tradeoff between the strength of the signal scattered by the transmitter and the strength of the signal received by the receiver. Finally, backscatter devices have severe power, area, and cost constraints that rule out traditional interference-cancellation techniques including multiple antennas and complex adaptive cancellation techniques.

4.1 Overview

Our approach hinges on two ideas. (1) The design of a transmitter that can backscatter information with minimal changes in the amplitude of its reflections. We show that such a design provides significant cancellation in practice. (2) To deal with the residual interference we exploit the rate difference between the data and feedback channels to design custom receiver circuits for the data and feedback channel receivers respectively. At a high level, the receiver of the feedback channel sees high-frequency residual interference, whereas the data channel receiver sees low-frequency residual interference. We use low-pass and high-pass filters designed using passive components to eliminate this interference. We describe these two ideas in more detail below.

4.2 Full-duplex Backscatter Transmitter Design

Rather than modulating the amplitude of its reflections, a Full-duplex Backscatter transmitter reflects/absorbs a fixed amount of signal, such that the amplitude of the received signal is constant. At a high level, the devices transmits information by switching be-

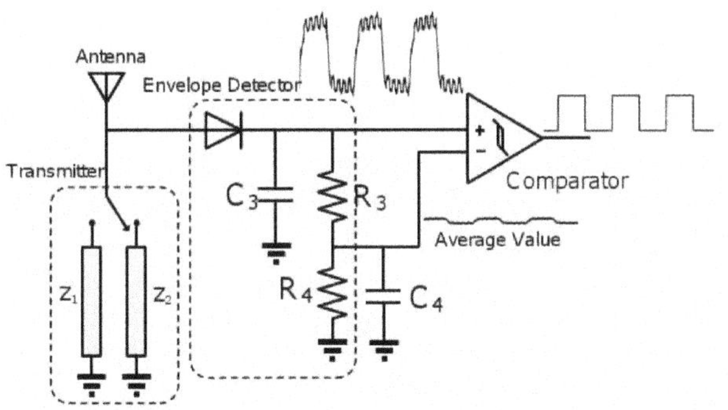

Figure 5: **Alice's Transmitter and Receiver:** Alice switches between Z_1 and Z_2 impedances at a high rate to transmit data to Bob. The receiver on Alice consists of two main components: an envelope detector/low pass filter to remove the carrier frequency and self-interference and another low pass filter to track the average value. These two signals are fed to a comparator to threshold the received signal and decode the digital bits sent by Bob.

tween two impedances that modulate the *phase* of the reflected signal instead of the amplitude.

More formally, we can understand our design using a Smith chart shown in Fig. 3. The transmitter switches between two conjugately-matched impedance states corresponding to S_3 and S_4. The two impedance states S_3 and S_4 are chosen such that the magnitude of the reflection coefficient $|\Gamma^*|$ and hence the magnitude of the signal reflected in the two states is equal. However, because the Γ in the two states are complex conjugates of each other, the reflected signals are out of phase. The two reflections with different phases from the transmitter will interfere with the ambient signal at the corresponding receiver to create waves with two different amplitude levels. We can thus, in principle, decode the bits on the receiver using a standard, amplitude-tracking backscatter receiver.

Note that using complex impedances to change the phase does not necessarily degrade the quality of transmissions. In particular, the quality of the transmitted signal is a function of the distance between the two impedance states on the Smith chart. Said differently, the greater the distance between the two impedance states, the greater the difference between the two received bit values. Thus, the above approach can achieve equal or greater signal quality than traditional backscatter transmitters.

In theory, the above technique should result in perfect cancellation; however, in practice, impedance mismatches occur due to component variations and other effects. These mismatches result in residual interference. We describe how our receiver addresses such residual interference in the next section.

4.3 Full-duplex Backscatter Receiver Design

A Full-duplex Backscatter receiver has two main components: an envelope detector and a threshold computation stage that either performs a low-pass filter or a high-pass filter operation. The envelope detector is used to remove the RF carrier frequency and extract amplitude information. This operation is similar to that used in traditional backscatter receivers.

The threshold computation stage on the other hand takes the amplitude information from the output of the envelope detector and looks at how the amplitude changes over time. The goal here is to remove the effect of the residual interference. We do so by leveraging the fact that the two devices are transmitting at different rates. As an example, consider Bob from Fig. 2 whose received signal is illustrated in Fig. 4.

We can use a low-pass filter consisting of resistors R_1, R_2, capacitors C_1 and C_2 and a comparator to track the slowly-varying self-interference and compute a time-varying threshold as shown in the figure. We feed the received signal to the positive terminal and the computed slowly varying threshold to the negative terminal of the comparator. This is essentially performing a high pass filter operation that subtracts the low rate interference from the received signal and enables Bob to efficiently decode Alice's transmissions.

The operations at Alice, as shown in Fig. 5, are analogous but different. Specifically, we implement an envelope detector using different C_3, C_4, R_3, and R_4 that suppresses both the RF carrier and the high-frequency self-interference. We then use a low pass filter consisting of R_4 and C_4 to compute the long-term average of the envelope and subtract this average from the output of the envelope detector to decode the low-rate feedback transmissions from Bob.

We note that in principle, it is possible to use a conventional amplitude modulating transmitter in combination with the presented residual interference cancellation techniques to enable a simultaneous feedback channel. However, in practice, use of such conventional transmitters results in a residual interference of about 100 dB (relative to the noise floor). In order to eliminate such residual interference, we need to implement high-order filters. Given the losses associated with passive components such as capacitors and resistors and loading effects of cascaded passive filters, a practical implementation of such filters using only passive components is not a feasible in practice. Hence, we believe that our proposed phase modulating transmitter architecture followed by the residual cancellation technique is essential to the design of an instantaneous backscatter feedback system.

4.4 Putting Things Together

For simplicity, we have thus far described the Alice and Bob's designs separately. In reality, every device must take on multiple roles depending on whether it has a packet to send, wants to receive a packet, or is simply stay idle. We must therefore answer two questions. First, how do we consolidate the two design illustrated in Fig. 5 and Fig. 4? And second, how do we engineer the system to maximize receive and harvesting efficiency?

A simple way to consolidate the above designs is to include hardware for both the forward and feedback channels between which the device can opportunistically switch based on it's operating state. In particular, devices need to have four impedance values—two for the forward channel and two for the feedback channel. Devices also need two receive chains for each target transmission rate in order to implement the low-pass and high-pass filters. We note that in an ASIC implementation, tunable resistors and capacitors can be used to eliminate hardware redundancy between the different states.

For both reception and harvesting, efficiency is highest when the matched impedance is close to S_1 in Fig. 3 (where it reflects the least amount of energy back on the antenna). Since the transmitter design on the feedback channel picks impedance values S_3 and S_4 that are necessarily distinct from S_1, the receiver efficiency of the data channel is lower than existing backscatter receivers. To address this issue, we jointly optimize the impedance values at the transmitters of both the data channel (Alice) and feedback channel (Bob) to ensure that the efficiency (receive BER) of the data channel remains the same. This translates into impedances values that are closer to the origin for Bob's feedback transmissions and those that are further from the origin for Alice's data transmissions. In our prototype implementation this results in a feedback rate that is one-tenth of the data rate.

Our design has an additional impedance value for the case when there are no ongoing transmissions. During this state, the device does not need to transmit any signals and therefore can fully optimize for receive/harvesting efficiency by staying in the S_1 state. This is important because during transmission, the forward channel has a harvesting efficiency of 44.83% compared to 50% in a traditional backscatter system. Because communication periods are typically very short in energy-constrained systems, staying in a matched state during idle periods makes these losses negligible.

5. A LINK-LAYER DESIGN FOR FULL-DUPLEX BACKSCATTER

The hardware design in the preceding section enables an entirely new set of protocols for general-purpose backscatter devices. In this paper, we explore one example instantiation of a link-layer protocol for backscatter communication. In particular, our protocol tackles the three problems described in §2: wireless collisions, error correction, and rate adaptation.

In this section, we first explain how RF power harvesting can affect protocol design. We then describe our link-layer protocol that uses the feedback channel to address the above problems.

5.1 Design Principle

Our protocols strive to minimize the amount of energy required to transmit a single packet successfully. To see why this is desirable, we need to look at the workings of an RF energy harvester.

The purpose of a device's harvesting circuitry is to charge up a capacitor that can be discharged whenever the device needs to perform computation, sensing, or communication. At a high level, harvesting happens in two stages: rectification and energy storage. When a signal arrives through the antenna, it translates into a voltage value, say, $V(t)$. The rectification stage in addition to converting the time-varying AC signal to a DC voltage, also acts as a voltage multiplier i.e., it raises the voltage of the signal by trading off current. The resulting DC voltage is applied to the storage capacitor in order to charge it up.

In an ideal world, one could convert arbitrarily weak voltage signals into arbitrary amounts of energy in two ways:

- *Increasing the voltage value.* Adding more stages to the rectification stage will increase the voltage multiplication effect [36]. This can potentially be used to increase the voltage applied to the capacitor and therefore the total energy stored by the capacitor.
- *Increasing the capacitor size.* Increasing the capacitance of the capacitor increases the amount of charge it can hold for a given voltage according to $Q_{max} = CV$.

Unfortunately, in practice, both of the above approaches come with significant tradeoffs that limit their applicability. First, adding more stages to the voltage multiplier decreases harvesting efficiency and also significantly increases power losses due to parasitic capacitances and leakage effects [17]. Second, increasing the size of the capacitor increases the charge time disproportionately. For instance, doubling the size of the capacitor would increase the time to fully charge by more than 8*x*. Furthermore, larger capacitors generally have greater leakage currents, decreasing the sensitivity of the harvester and charge time even further.

The above discussion implies that we need to leverage our feedback channel to minimize the need for multiple packet transmissions that requires significant amounts of energy.

5.2 Link-layer Protocol

An instantaneous feedback channel allows us to design a MAC protocol that minimizes the amount of energy required to send a packet. Our protocol reduces the penalty associated with collisions and aids in detection of hidden terminals, all with minimal energy requirements. It is inspired by a variety of related work including CSMA/CD [20], busy tones [12], μACKs [37], and others [21], but the underlying mechanism is simple: use the feedback channel to acknowledge data transmissions at a fine granularity.

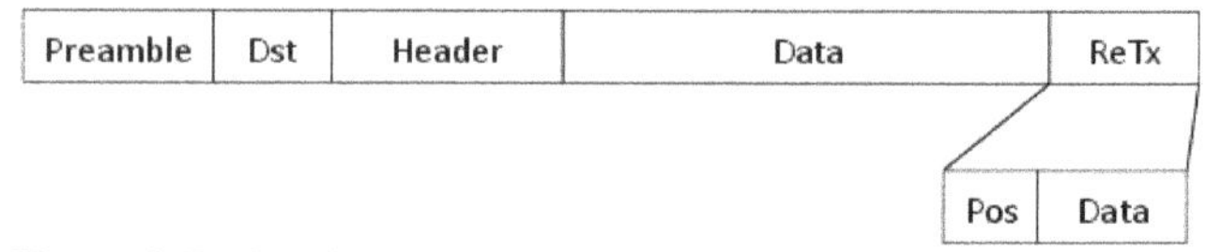

Figure 6: **Packet format:** The packet format used on the data channel. At the end of every packet, the transmitter can optionally append retransmissions of bit chunks and their positions.

For ease of exposition, we describe the feedback and data channels separately. We begin by describing the feedback channel operation in the common case; we later describe how the data channel takes advantage of feedback.

5.2.1 *Feedback Channel*

Our system uses the feedback channel to acknowledge ongoing data transmissions. We consider a source sending a packet using the format shown in Fig. 6. The destination uses the feedback channel to perform the following operations:

1. The destination first decodes the transmitted preamble and the first field of the header (i.e., the destination address). As soon as the destination realizes that it is the intended recipient, it begins transmitting a preamble on the feedback channel.
2. The destination will then divide the packet (including header) into chunks of b bits. For each group of b bits, it computes a c-bit checksum. The destination transmits the checksum back to the source on the feedback channel.

The ratio of b to c is determined by the difference in transmission rate between the data and the feedback channels. For instance, a 1 kbps data channel with a 100 bps feedback channel, must satisfy the following condition: $\frac{b}{c} = 10$. The time for both the data and feedback transmissions are therefore approximately equal, with the feedback channel lagging behind the data channel slightly. Our prototype implementation uses 40 and 4 bits for b and c respectively.

5.2.2 *Data Channel*

The source uses the above feedback channel to adapt its own transmissions to errors and collisions. In particular, it performs the following protocol:

1. The source first listens on the medium to ensure there are no existing transmissions.[5] If the channel is empty, it begins to transmit the preamble, header, and payload. Otherwise, it exponentially backs off before retrying. See §5.3 for details.
2. While transmitting, the source continues to listen on the feedback channel for errors. It uses the incoming checksums to change rates at the level of bits rather than entire packets. If it detects a collision, it will terminate the transmission and back off accordingly. See §5.4 and §5.3 for details.
3. At the end of the packet, any failed groups of bits are retransmitted along with a short header denoting their position in the original stream. See §5.5 for details.

5.3 Dealing With Collisions

There are two places where collisions can occur: (*a*) at the beginning of the packet, during the preamble or destination address

[5]In backscatter-style communication, this can be effectively implemented by simply checking the output of the receive chain for bit transitions [18].

and (b) in the middle of the packet. Collisions at the beginning of the packet can occur when two nodes start to transmit simultaneously or when the new transmitter cannot hear the existing connection. These collisions can either interfere with the forward channel or the feedback channel, but in both cases, no feedback will return and the data channel transmitter will assume a collision has happened. If the collision happens in the middle of a packet, we leverage our bit-level rate adaptation to account for the resulting bit errors. Further, devices assume that a collision has occurred after multiple (more than one) consecutive drops happen in the data rate during our bit-level rate adaptation.

Backoff is implemented similarly to existing protocols: the detecting transmitter will wait for a random number of time slots between 0 and 2^r, where r is the number of retries attempted by the device. Our link-layer protocol detects collisions, even from hidden terminals, and minimizes their effects. We note the following about the effect of collisions in our system.

Firstly, by terminating the packet as soon as a collision is detected, our design can minimize the energy penalty associated with collisions. Specifically, recharging the energy spent during the short amount of time before collision detection at the transmitter takes significantly less time than recovering the energy required for an entire packet.

Secondly, the transmitter that detects the collision does not need to jam/inform the any other transmitters because bit-level error correction can correct from any collision-related errors. As long as the preamble and header are decoded correctly, any subsequent bit errors can be corrected as long as the network ends up with a single active transmitter-receiver pair.

Thirdly, the feedback channel is compatible with our collision detection technique because transmitters should see a checksum of their own transmissions. Any competing transmission will cause the bits on the feedback channel to differ from the expected bits significantly, allowing the transmitter to detect a collision.

Finally, we note that false positives in detecting collisions can occur due to bit errors; however a conservative collision detection estimate is preferable to retransmission of the entire packet.

5.4 Adapting Rate at a Fine Granularity

Rate adaptation proceeds in a fashion similar to existing techniques, except at the level of b-bit chunks rather than entire packets. The exact algorithm used is orthogonal to our work, but we take [30] as a baseline. At a high level, the goal of the rate control algorithm in [30] is to maximize throughput while occasionally testing alternative rates ($\sim$10% of the time). Throughput for a particular rate is defined by $(\textit{Probability of success} * \textit{Transmission rate})$, where the probability of success is based upon an exponentially-weighted, moving average of chunk-level success rates. If through the occasional probes, we find an alternative rate with a higher throughput, we will switch to that rate. If the line code is self-clocking, the receiver will adjust to rate changes automatically.

The above protocol allows us to adjust rates at the level of chunks of b bits, rather than entire packets. Adjusting the rate at a fine granularity gives devices the ability to react very quickly to changes in channel state. More importantly, we can react within the span of a single packet—a useful benefit since bit rates are often very low in backscatter systems. It also allows us to react after fewer packet drops, as looking at small chunks of bits gives us a much greater sample size for rate adaptation rather than just coarse packet drops.

5.5 In-Packet Error Correction

Finally, the source can use the feedback channel to decrease the energy penalty of bit errors. Specifically, error correction in our system proceeds in a manner similar to that of [37]: the transmitter resends failed bit sequences at the end of each packet along with their position in the original stream.

This type of error correction is necessary to make the above bit-level rate adaption useful—without it, errors in the packet would make the entire packet useless. The additional benefit to being able to tolerate bit errors in this fashion is (as mentioned above) that collisions no longer necessarily cause all transmissions to be wasted.

6. PROTOTYPE IMPLEMENTATION

We implement a Full-duplex Backscatter prototype shown in Fig. 1 on four-layer printed circuit boards (PCB) using off the shelf components. The PCBs were designed in Altium software and were fabricated by Sunstone circuits. Our prototype uses a dipole antenna consisting of two sections of 3-inch long 16 AWG magnetic copper wire. We implemented prototypes capable of 1 kbps transmission on the data channel and 100 bps on the feedback channel. The hardware is tuned to operate at frequencies in the 3 MHz band centered at 920 MHz. Since the bit rates used by backscatter data communication are significantly lower than traditional radio communication (e.g., Wi-Fi), a 3 MHz data bandwidth does not limit the underlying RF source bandwidth. Specifically, as long as the data bandwidth is less than 3 MHz, the system would work even with an underlying RF source with higher bandwidth (e.g., TV signals). This is because the circuit would low-pass filter out the higher frequency components. Evaluating feedback hardware for the TV band is however not in the scope of this paper.

The transmitter is implemented using the ADG919 RF switch [1] connected directly to the antenna terminals. On the data channel, the transmitter's S_3 impedance states are implemented using a series combination of a 10 Ω resistor and a 1 nH inductor, while the S_4 state is implemented using a 1.8 pF capacitor. For the feedback channel, the transmitter's S_3 impedance states are implemented using a parallel combination of a 6.8 nH inductor and a 50 Ω resistor, while the S_4 state is implemented using a series combination of a 15 Ω resistor and a 0.8 pF capacitor. Note that these impedance values are specific to the choice of the switch and impedance network on the PCB. The power consumption of our analog transmitter design (including the switch) is about 0.25 μW.

On the receiver we use a TS881 [3] as the ultra-low power comparator. On the data channel's receiver, the capacitor and resistor values R_1, R_2, C_1, and C_2 shown in Fig. 4 are set to 100 $k\Omega$, 10 $M\Omega$, 4.7 nF and 1.47 nF, respectively. On the feedback channel's receiver, the capacitor and resistor values R_3, R_4, C_3, and C_4 are set to 100 $k\Omega$, 10 $M\Omega$, 27 nF, and 220 nF respectively. The analog prototype receiver (including the comparator) consumes 0.54 μW.

7. EVALUATION

Next, we evaluate various practical aspects of our Full-duplex Backscatter prototype. In particular, we first measure the effect of our low-power backscatter cancellation technique described in §4.2 as a function of the input power level. Next, we evaluate the effect of the feedback channel on the bit error rate (BER) of the data channel at the receiver. We also evaluate the bit error rate (BER) achieved on the feedback channel as a function of the distance between the backscatter devices. Finally, we evaluate the feedback channel with collisions, retransmissions, and rate adaptation.

7.1 Full-duplex Backscatter Cancellation Effectiveness

In this section, we evaluate how well our design in §4.2 reduces the self-interference from the feedback channel.

Experiments: To do this, we examine the degree to which we decrease self-interference at the destination (i.e., the device sending

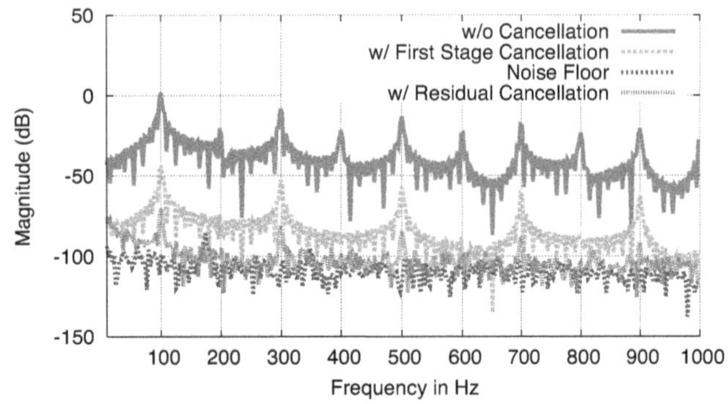

(a) Power level at receiver: -1.7 dBm

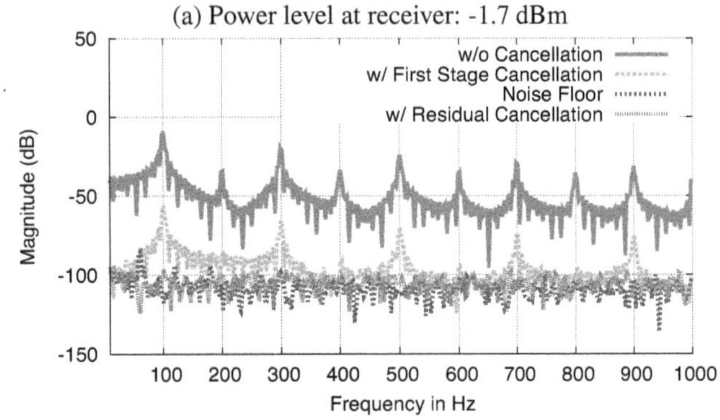

(b) Power level at receiver: -20 dBm

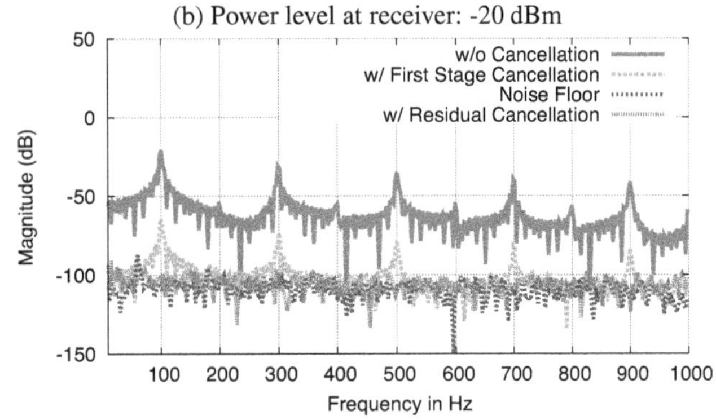

(c) Power level at receiver: -30 dBm

Figure 7: **Self-interference Cancellation in Full-duplex Backscatter:** The graphs show the strength of the voltage signal received over a frequency spectrum due to the device's own 100 bps transmissions. Our technique reduces the self-interference from the feedback channel down to the noise floor of the device across the frequency range. We note that the typical power level at the receiver is less than -15 dBm.

the feedback) using the transmitter cancellation (described in §4.2) and the residual cancellation techniques (described in §4.3). We place the Full-duplex Backscatter prototype device in the presence of a continuous wave transmission from an RFID reader at 920 MHz and configure it to continually transmit an alternating sequence of bits at 100 bps. Note that this is one feedback bit for every 10 data bits on an ambient backscatter communication system, which as we show later is sufficient to address the networking issues described in §2. We then tap into the outputs of the envelope detector and the low pass filter on our prototype board and connect it to an ADC to get direct access to the voltage values.

Results: Fig. 7 shows the magnitude of the voltage values (in dB) across the frequency spectrum. Each plot shows the frequency-domain representation of the received voltage values with just the transmitter cancellation technique, with both transmitter and receiver cancellation techniques (to cancel the residual interference as described in §4.3) and without our cancellation technique. They also depict noise values when there is no transmission on the feedback channel. We plot the results for three different received power levels of the RFID continuous wave signals at the receiver. The graphs show the following:

- In the absence of our cancellation circuit, the plots show spikes at frequencies corresponding to the odd multiples of 100 Hz. This is expected because the bit rate on the feedback channel is 100 bps which results in a spike at 100 Hz. Further since the transmitted signal on the feedback channel is approximately a square wave, we also see spikes at frequencies that are odd multiples of 100 Hz.
- Our technique reduces the interference from the feedback channel to the noise floor of our device across the frequency range. This is very significant and is impressive since this approach requires near-zero power compared to a conventional device.
- The reduction in self-interference is similar for different power levels of the received signal. This results in higher power levels having higher residual interference (in comparison to noise). In the next section, we will demonstrate how this cancellation technique results in comparable receive bit error rates for systems with and without the feedback channel.
- The self-interference reduction varies by about 5-8 dB across time and also the 3 MHz operational bandwidth. This variation is expected because the conjugate impedance network used for the cancellation is implemented using off the shelf resistors, capacitors and inductors that have tolerances and variations that change with environmental conditions.

7.2 Effect on Data Channel BER

Experiments: We place two prototype devices at different distances from each other. The devices are both configured to transmit an alternating sequence of bits at the same time—the sender transmits data bits at a rate of 1 kbps, and the receiver of the data packet transmits bits at a rate of 100 bps on the feedback channel. We place the two devices in the presence of an RF signal source that broadcasts continuous wave RFID signals centered at 920 MHz. The source has a dipole antenna and is placed equidistant from both the tags. To analyze the BER, we connect an NI myDAQ to the output of the receiver's receive chain. We capture 100 seconds of data at each distance value, which corresponds to a total of 10^5 bits; when no bit errors occur we set the BER to 10^{-5}. We consider distance values of up to 1.5 meters, which spans the communication range of the ambient backscatter devices in [18]. We also vary the RF power to span the receive power levels from -18 dBm to -4 dBm; the lower value is the minimum power level at which the harvester [25] works.

Results: Fig. 8 shows BER versus the average received power at our prototype devices for three different tag-to-tag distances. We also plot as a baseline the bit error rate results for the ambient backscatter prototype that we replicate from [18] that does not have a feedback channel. The results show the following:

- For both Full-duplex Backscatter and existing backscatter systems, as the distance between the devices increases the BER increases. Similarly, BER reduces as the RF power level at the prototype devices increases.
- We do not observe any bit errors for both the systems when the distance between the tags is less than or equal to 1 m. As the distance increases to 1.5 m, we start observing bit errors for lower power values. We note that in these cases, the observed bit error

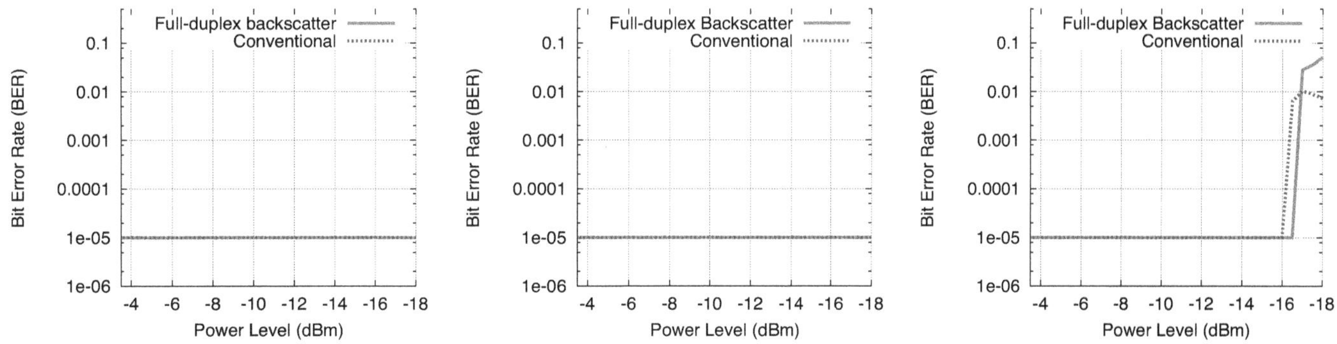

(a) Distance: 0.75 meters (b) Distance: 1 meters (c) Distance: 1.5 meters

Figure 8: **Data BER versus power:** BER as observed by the receiver of the forward data channel. We show the variation in BER versus power at the tag for three different tag-to-tag distances. The plots show that the feedback channel does not significantly affect the data BER.

rate for our system across all three distances is comparable to conventional backscatter.

- In some cases, the bit error rate for our system is worse than existing backscatter systems and is better in other scenarios. This is because existing backscatter systems modulate information by changing the amplitude of the transmission (i.e., using ASK modulation). In contrast, we encode information in phase values (i.e., effectively use PSK modulation). Thus, the signals in our design interfere differently than those of a traditional backscatter system and hence exhibit the above noted behavior. The key point however is that, the feedback channel in our results does not significantly affect the performance of the forward data channel.

7.3 BER of the Feedback Channel versus Distance

Next, we evaluate the performance of the feedback channel. Specifically, we measure the bit error rate on the feedback channel by measuring its BER.

Experiments: As before, we place two prototype devices in the presence of an RF source broadcasting an RFID continuous wave transmission at 920 MHz. The data rate and feedback rate are set to 1 kbps and 100 bps respectively. We vary the distance between the two devices and measure the bit error rate on the feedback channel. We again measure the BER with the assistance of an NI myDAQ and compare the received feedback bits with those transmitted. We transmit a total of 10^{-4} bits in each experiment. Note that this value is less than that of the previous set of experiments since the feedback channel has a lower bit rate than the data channel. We set the bit error rate to 10^{-4} in experiments which do not see any bit errors. We run the experiments at a fixed transmit power of 7.5 dBm at the RF source. The BER trends are similar at other power levels.

Results: Fig. 9 shows the BER of our feedback channel at different distances between the two prototype devices. The figure shows that the feedback channel sees bit errors as we approach 2 meters between the transmitter and receiver. However, we do not see any bit errors even at distances greater than 1.7 meters. Further, the observed feedback BERs match very well with the observed BERs on the data channel. This implies that the feedback channel is reliable enough to not be a limiting factor.

8. EVALUATING FULL-DUPLEX BACKSCATTER'S NETWORK STACK

Finally, we evaluate how our feedback-channel-enabled network protocol addresses collisions, retransmissions, and rate adaptation.

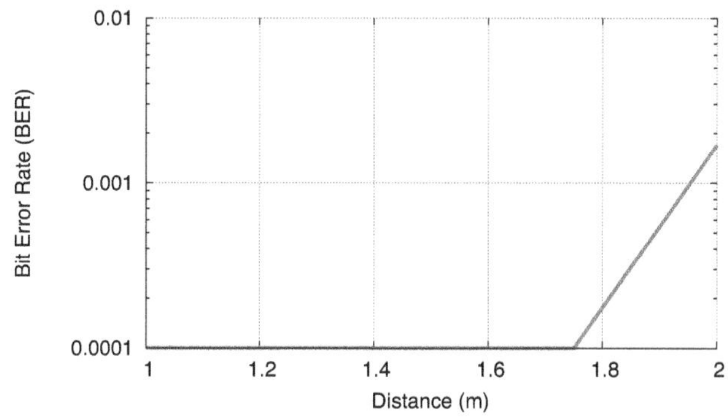

Figure 9: **Feedback BER versus distance:** BER observed on the feedback channel. We show the variation in BER versus distance between the two devices.

8.1 Recharge-time Reduction during Collisions

As described in §5.3, a feedback channel allows our prototype device to terminate its transmission when it detects a collision. We use the metric of recharge time to evaluate the benefit of this feature. Terminating wasteful transmissions can result in a reduction in the recharge time at the transmitter since it can conserve power that is otherwise wasted in transmitting a undecodable packet. This metric is very useful because recharging and duty cycling tend to be the bottleneck in virtually all energy-constrained systems.

Experiments: To evaluate the benefits of Full-duplex Backscatter in this context, we measure the time it takes to recover from a collision. Our prototype devices use a preamble length of eight bits and transmit at a rate of 1 kbps on the data channel (similar to the design in [18]). The feedback channel also uses a preamble length of eight bits and has a bit rate of 100 bps. We measure the time it takes for the transmitter to detect an existing transmission and then terminate its own. We then calculate the total delay from the beginning of the canceled transmission to the time at which the device has enough power to retry transmitting the packet, given a packet size of 64 bytes. We repeat the measurements for both scenarios, with and without the feedback channel. In the absence of the feedback channel the transmitter continues transmitting the whole packet even in the presence of the collision.

Results: Fig. 10 shows results for the above experiments. We plot the recharge time it takes to collect enough power to retransmit the collided packet as a function of the power level received at the prototype device. The figure shows the graphs for both conventional and our systems. The results show the following:

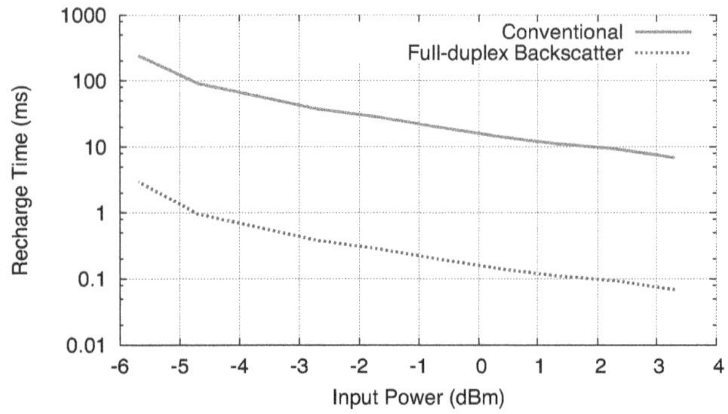

Figure 10: **Recharge time reduction:** The time needed to recover from a packet collision in Full-duplex Backscatter versus conventional transmitters. The x-axis plots the available power at the device. Our system reduces the recharge time by two orders of magnitude.

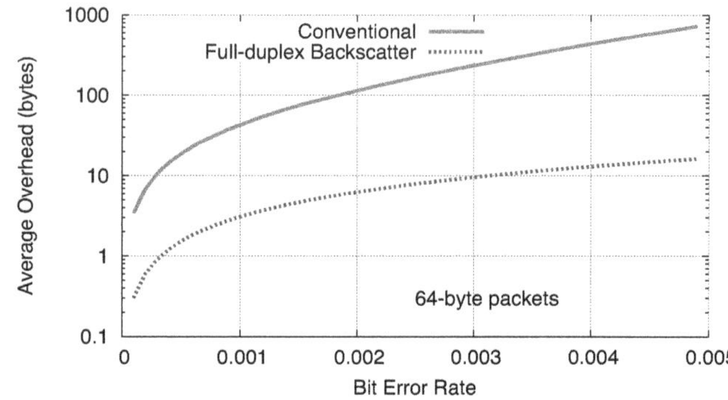

Figure 11: **Overhead of transmitting a single packet:** This graph shows the average number of extra bits transmitted for a given error rate. The extra bits are either in the form of a retransmitted packet in the case of conventional receivers or retransmitted bit sequences in the case of Full-duplex Backscatter. Our system reduces the overhead by at least an order of magnitude.

- Our system decreases the time between retries by two orders of magnitude. The savings are expected to be higher for packet sizes longer than 64 bytes. This is because recharge times are nonlinear—as the number of wasted bits grows, the recharge time non-linearly increases. Thus terminating the transmission earlier minimizes the recharge time it takes to collect enough energy for packet retransmissions.
- The recharge time is higher at lower power levels. This is expected because in power-constrained scenarios, the capacitor takes longer to collect the required energy. This is further complicated by leakage issues as explained in §5.1. We note that Full-duplex Backscatter can provide orders of magnitude reduction across all power levels, specifically in power-constrained scenarios.

8.2 In-frame Error Correction

We next look at the effectiveness of our feedback channel in achieving in-frame error correction. The error correction mechanism described in §5.5 decreases latency and increases throughput. This is because it allows us to recover from bit errors by sending a few extra bits at the end of a packet, rather than re-sending the entire packet. We evaluate these benefits in practice.

Experiments: The backscatter transmitter sends bits at a bit rate of 1 kbps using a packet size of 64 bytes. The receiver computes a 4-bit checksum for every chunk of 40 received bits. It then transmits these checksum bits on the feedback channel to the transmitter. The transmitter uses the checksum to detect when chunks of bits are incorrectly decoded at the receiver. The transmitter then retransmits these chunks at the end of the packet as described in §5.5. We change the distance between the transmitter and the receiver to span a range of bit error rates. We calculate the additional bytes of data that are necessary to deliver a fully correct packet using our prototype. We also repeat the experiments for existing backscatter systems that have to retransmit complete packets until at least one is successfully decoded.

Results: Fig. 11 shows the results of our experiments. The figure plots the overhead, i.e., the number of extra bytes necessary to deliver a single, correct packet as a function of the bit error rate observed on the data channel. The average overhead is plotted in log-scale. The figure shows the following:

- The average overhead incurred by our system is at least an order of magnitude less than in conventional systems, even for low error rates. This is because, for a single error, our system would need to transmit an additional 47 bits. On the other hand, a conventional system would need to retransmit the entire packet (i.e., 64 bytes) assuming the second packet arrives error-free.
- Further, as the average bit error rate on the data channel increases, the overhead for existing backscatter systems increases much faster than the overhead incurred on our system. In Fig. 11, the Full-duplex Backscatter system has an order of magnitude less overhead for low error rates, but as the BER increases to 0.005, the overhead increases to two orders of magnitude. This is due to the fact that the probability that a 64-byte packet is correctly decoded becomes increasingly small at higher BERs. On the other hand, the probability that a chunk of 40 bits is decoded without error grows at a much slower rate.
- We note that Full-duplex Backscatter's advantage over conventional backscatter systems in both of the above points increases with larger packet size. We also note that the actual cost of this overhead in terms of time, energy, and throughput is much higher than shown here. The underlying issue is recharge time. As we saw in the previous section, charge time magnifies the penalty associated with retransmission of extra bits. Full-duplex Backscatter can reduce this charge time and hence alleviate these issues.

8.3 Rate Adaptation

Finally, we evaluate our intra-packet rate adaptation.

Experiments: We place a transmitter and a receiver in the presence of our 920 MHz signal source. We adapt the rate of the transmitter between three rates of 100 bps, 1 kbps, and 10 kbps. We compare three rate adaptation strategies: "slowest", which always chooses 100 bps; "packet-level", which models an idealized algorithm that chooses the best rate for the SNR at the beginning of the packet; and "bit-level", which implements the algorithm described in §5.4. Since we would like to compare the three algorithms in the same scenarios, we connect our receiver to a myDAQ that continually takes measurements of the received voltage values. The transmitter is set to continuously transmit bits as we move the receiver in the area around the transmitter at an average speed of about 3 m/s. From the captured traces, we compute the SNR at every time instance. Since the SNR determines the achievable bit rate, we use it to compute the achievable throughput of the three algorithms given the captured voltage traces.

Results: In Fig. 12, we plot the throughput of each rate adaptation strategy. Our results show the following:

- Bit-level rate adaptation increases performance by $\sim$33% compared to an idealized SNR-based packet-level algorithm. Further, when compared to the slowest-rate strategy, the speedup is almost 3x. This is because devices can take advantage of and protect against channel changes. We also note that since backscatter

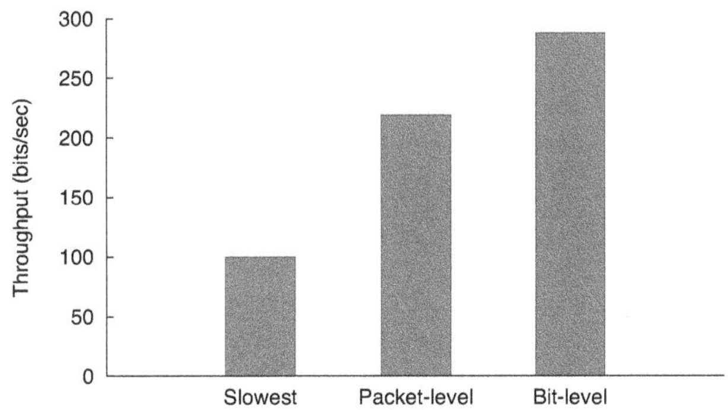

Figure 12: **Effect of Rate Adaptation:** A graph of the throughput for different rate adaptation algorithms. The throughput is calculated using real channel traces with an average mobility of 3 m/s.

devices do not have ADCs, they do not have SNR information. Thus, we can expect higher throughput gains in practice.

- We note that about 30% of packets in the packet-level strategy failed due to changes in the channel within the span of a single packet. This is due to the fact that transmission rates are extremely low in these types of systems.

9. RELATED WORK

There has been recent interest in improving the performance of backscatter systems [7, 26, 15]. Prior work has also proposed coding techniques to address the problem of collisions and increase the efficiency of RFID networks [6, 22, 35]. More recently, work on ambient backscatter [18] enabled two battery-free devices to communicate by backscattering signals from an RF source. Our work builds on these foundational works and achieves the first instantaneous feedback channel for backscatter communication systems.

Our work is also related to recent research on full-duplex communication that uses passive cancellation techniques [12], active cancellation (both in the analog and digital domain) [5, 29], or a combination of the above [9, 8]. While these approaches are effective for traditional radio communication, their reliance on space-consuming antenna arrays and/or power-hungry cancellation techniques are not applicable to ultra-low power backscatter communication, that has a power budget which is orders of magnitude lower. We also note that our goal is not to design a full-duplex radio. Instead we set out to create a low-rate feedback channel for backscatter devices that can address many of the higher-layer issues facing these devices.

Similarly, there has also been previous work on implementing full-duplex communication through clever combinations of signal processing, modulation and coding techniques [19, 10, 4]. Like the above approaches, these assume that at least one of the participants are powered and can therefore perform relatively complex synchronization and decoding that are not applicable to the types of devices that we investigate in this paper.

Full-duplex Backscatter is also related to prior work that implements QAM transmissions on RFID tags by using complex impedances [33]. Our work is similar in that we also use complex impedances to adjust the phase of the reflected signal; however, the purpose of our system is complementary and is to enable a feedback channel between the backscatter devices and demonstrate the benefits of such a channel for the link- and the network-layers.

Finally, there is a large body of work related to network-layer protocols for wireless sensor network or other types of mesh networks. Some of these works deal with half-duplex mesh networks and how to implement MAC protocols [32], rate adaptation [14], and hidden terminal detection [31]. Others are designed for duplexed communication [12]. In contrast, the focus of this paper is to enable a instantaneous feedback channel for battery-free backscatter devices, which is a goal that is complementary to prior efforts.

10. CONCLUSION

Energy, and specifically the energy required for communication, is a key bottleneck in the design of computing devices. Recent developments in backscatter communication promise to remove this bottleneck. Specifically, they promise to provide a way for devices to send bits to one another using orders of magnitude less power than is required today. However, an essential question remains: how do we design link- and network-layer protocols for these networks. Existing protocols are ill-suited to these devices where even the transmission of a single packet can exhaust all available energy.

In this paper, we introduce a novel technique called Full-duplex Backscatter that enables almost-zero-power, instantaneous feedback and use it to implement a network stack tailored for battery-free devices. Our technique uses passive, analog circuitry in order to allow for a low-rate feedback channel that operates alongside any data transfer. In addition, we presented a network stack that uses Full-duplex Backscatter to minimize the energy wastes associated with MAC, rate adaptation, and error correction. We believe that our technique improves the practicality of battery-free devices and brings us closer to having a practical, generalized backscatter communication system.

Acknowledgements: We would like to thank Matt Reynolds for helpful discussions during the design of Full-duplex Backscatter's hardware and the anonymous MOBICOM reviewers for their helpful comments. This research is funded in part by Qualcomm Innovation Fellowship, Washington Research Foundation gift, NSF, and University of Washington.

11. REFERENCES

[1] Adg919 rf switch datasheet, analog devices.

[2] Software defined radio hardware survey, scott johnston.

[3] Ts 881 datasheet, stmicroelectronics, july 2012.

[4] D. Bharadia, K. R. Joshi, and S. Katti. Full duplex backscatter. In Proceedings of the Twelfth ACM Workshop on Hot Topics in Networks, 2013.

[5] D. Bharadia, E. McMilin, and S. Katti. Full duplex radios. In Proceedings of the ACM SIGCOMM, pages 375–386. ACM, 2013.

[6] M. Buettner. Backscatter Protocols and Energy-Efficient Computing for RF-Powered Devices. PhD thesis, University of Washington, Seattle, WA, 2012.

[7] M. Buettner, B. Greenstein, and D. Wetherall. Dewdrop: An energy-aware runtime for computational rfid. In Proceedings of NSDI'11, 2011.

[8] M. Duarte. Full-duplex Wireless: Design, Implementation and Characterization. PhD thesis, Rice University, May 2012.

[9] M. Duarte and A. Sabharwal. Full-duplex wireless communications using off-the-shelf radios: Feasibility and first results. In 2010 ASILOMAR, pages 1558–1562, Nov 2010.

[10] D. Guo and L. Zhang. Virtual full-duplex wireless communication via rapid on-off-division duplex. CoRR, abs/1010.2667, 2010.

[11] E. Inc. Universal software radio peripheral. http://ettus.com.

[12] M. Jain, J. I. Choi, T. Kim, D. Bharadia, S. Seth, K. Srinivasan, P. Levis, S. Katti, and P. Sinha. Practical, real-time, full duplex wireless. In Proceedings of the 17th

annual international conference on Mobile computing and networking, pages 301–312. ACM, 2011.

[13] B. Kellogg, V. Talla, and S. Gollakota. Bringing gesture recognition to all devices. In NSDI, 2014.

[14] S. Kim, R. Fonseca, P. Dutta, A. Tavakoli, D. Culler, P. Levis, S. Shenker, and I. Stoica. Flush: a reliable bulk transport protocol for multihop wireless networks. In Proceedings of the 5th international conference on Embedded networked sensor systems, pages 351–365. ACM, 2007.

[15] M. Kodialam and T. Nandagopal. Fast and reliable estimation schemes in rfid systems. In Proceedings of Mobicom 2006.

[16] C.-J. M. Liang, N. B. Priyantha, J. Liu, and A. Terzis. Surviving wi-fi interference in low power zigbee networks. In Proceedings of the 8th ACM Conference on Embedded Networked Sensor Systems, pages 309–322. ACM, 2010.

[17] M. M. Liu. Demystifying switched capacitor circuits. Newnes, 2006.

[18] V. Liu, A. Parks, V. Talla, S. Gollakota, D. Wetherall, and J. R. Smith. Ambient backscatter: Wireless communication out of thin air. In Proceedings of the ACM SIGCOMM, 2013.

[19] J. MacLellan, R. Shober, G. Vannucci, and G. Wright. Tag for use in a radio communication system, July 15 1997. US Patent 5,649,296.

[20] R. M. Metcalfe and D. R. Boggs. Ethernet: Distributed packet switching for local computer networks. Commun. ACM, 19(7):395–404, July 1976.

[21] A. Mishra, S. Rayanchu, D. Agrawal, and S. Banerjee. Supporting continuous mobility through multi-rate wireless packetization. In HotMobile, 2008.

[22] C. Mutti and C. Floerkemeier. Cdma-based rfid systems in dense scenarios: Concepts and challenges. In RFID, 2008.

[23] P. V. Nikitin, S. Ramamurthy, R. Martinez, and K. Rao. Passive tag-to-tag communication. In RFID, 2012.

[24] C. Occhiuzzi, S. Cippitelli, and G. Marrocco. Modeling, design and experimentation of wearable rfid sensor tag. Antennas and Propagation, IEEE Transactions on, 58(8):2490–2498, 2010.

[25] A. N. Parks, A. P. Sample, Y. Zhao, and J. R. Smith. A wireless sensing platform utilizing ambient rf energy. In BioWireleSS, 2013 IEEE Topical Conference on, pages 154–156. IEEE, 2013.

[26] B. Ransford, J. Sorber, and K. Fu. Mementos: system support for long-running computation on RFID-scale devices. SIGPLAN Not., 46(3):159–170, Mar. 2011.

[27] S. Roy, V. Jandhyala, J. Smith, D. Wetherall, B. Otis, R. Chakraborty, M. Buettner, D. Yeager, Y.-C. Ko, and A. Sample. Rfid: From supply chains to sensor nets. Proceedings of the IEEE, 98(9):1583 –1592, sept. 2010.

[28] A. Sample, D. Yeager, P. Powledge, A. Mamishev, and J. Smith. Design of an rfid-based battery-free programmable sensing platform. IEEE Transactions on Instrumentation and Measurement, 57.

[29] S. Sen, R. Roy Choudhury, and S. Nelakuditi. CSMA/CN: Carrier sense multiple access with collision notification. In MobiCom, 2010.

[30] D. Smithies and F. Fietkau. minstrel: MadWiFi and Linux kernel rate selection algorithm. 2005.

[31] J. So and N. H. Vaidya. Multi-channel mac for ad hoc networks: handling multi-channel hidden terminals using a single transceiver. In Proceedings of the 5th ACM international symposium on Mobile ad hoc networking and computing, pages 222–233. ACM, 2004.

[32] K. Srinivasan, P. Dutta, A. Tavakoli, and P. Levis. An empirical study of low-power wireless. ACM Transactions on Sensor Networks (TOSN), 6(2):16, 2010.

[33] S. Thomas and M. Reynolds. A 96 mbit/sec, 15.5 pj/bit 16-qam modulator for uhf backscatter communication. In RFID,, 2012 IEEE International Conference on, pages 185 –190, april 2012.

[34] E. Welbourne, L. Battle, G. Cole, K. Gould, K. Rector, S. Raymer, M. Balazinska, and G. Borriello. Building the internet of things using rfid: The rfid ecosystem experience. Internet Computing, IEEE, 13(3):48 –55, may-june 2009.

[35] L.-C. Wuu, Y.-J. Chen, C.-H. Hung, and W.-C. Kuo. Zero-collision rfid tags identification based on cdma. In International Conference on Information Assurance and Security, 2009.

[36] J. Yi, W.-H. Ki, and C.-Y. Tsui. Analysis and design strategy of uhf micro-power cmos rectifiers for micro-sensor and rfid applications. Circuits and Systems I: Regular Papers, IEEE Transactions on, 54(1):153–166, 2007.

[37] J. Zhang, H. Shen, K. Tan, R. Chandra, Y. Zhang, and Q. Zhang. Frame retransmissions considered harmful: improving spectrum efficiency using micro-acks. In Proceedings of MOBICOM 2012.

Strata: Layered Coding for Scalable Visual Communication

Wenjun Hu*, Jingshu Mao†, Zihui Huang†, Yiqing Xue†,
Junfeng She†, Kaigui Bian†, and Guobin Shen‡

*Yale University †Peking University ‡Microsoft Research

wenjun.hu@yale.edu {scenetree, rogerhzh, alfalfa.xue, plutoshe}@gmail.com
bkg@pku.edu.cn jacky.shen@microsoft.com

ABSTRACT

Existing code designs for display-camera based visual communication all have an all-or-nothing behavior, i.e., they assume the entire code must be decoded. However, diverse operational conditions due to device hardware diversity (in camera resolution and frame rate) and distance range motivate more scalable designs. In this paper, we borrow the notion of hierarchical modulation from traditional RF communication, and design Strata, a layered coding scheme for visual communication. Strata can support a range of frame capture resolutions and rates, and deliver information rates correspondingly. Strata embeds information at multiple granularity into the same code area spatially or the same frame interval temporally. It ensures all layers are decodable independently, by controlling the amount of interference between adjacent layers. Further, our design is recursive and extends readily to generate more layers. Compared with existing codes, it significantly extends the operational range, though at the expense of less capacity than a single-layer code.

Categories and Subject Descriptors

C.2.1 [**Network Architecture and Design**]: Wireless Communication

Keywords

Display-camera links; layered coding; scalable visual communication

1. INTRODUCTION

Displays and phone cameras are widely available, and the quality of both is improving at a fast pace. They offer communication opportunities over the optical channel, where information can be transmitted over the spatial-temporal domains. Even without the temporal domain, a single image can still convey much information. Indeed, 2D barcodes such as QR codes are simple examples that use such a channel. With scanner apps easily available, we can potentially turn any surface into a transmitter. A Google search suggests QR codes are now used widely in advertising (Figure 1), and we expect more innovative usage of similar codes in future. More generally, videos of barcodes can leverage the full spatial-temporal channel.

MobiCom'14, September 7-11, 2014, Maui, Hawaii, USA.
Copyright 2014 ACM 978-1-4503-2783-1/14/09 ...$15.00.
http://dx.doi.org/10.1145/2639108.2639132 .

(a) (b) (c) (d)

Figure 1: QR codes are used in a variety of contexts.

From a communication point of view, however, existing 2D barcodes offer limited flexibility. For example, they only work for a small distance range, and the captured image quality (in terms of size, completeness, clarity) must be sufficiently high to ensure successful decoding, even with forward error correction. They have an all-or-nothing behavior.

In contrast, there are many situations where more flexibility is desirable. At an abstract level, we often see information layered and expressed at multiple granularity. Figure 2 shows a simple example. When viewed at a distance, we only see a big M. When zooming in, however, there is more detailed information about MobiCom within the big M. Many advertisements around us actually follow a similar spirit, often achieved by adopting fonts of different sizes to highlight information of varying importance. We may also acquire only partial information and gather the complete information only when further needs arise, e.g., the name and the phone number in a contact card, the name of a tourist attraction (and the first paragraph of its general description) on an information board, and the name and the manufacturer of some merchandise, as opposed to the full details.

Considering the barcode scanning operation, there are also many justifications for scalable support. The display itself could take a variety of forms (Figure 1), from a sheet of paper

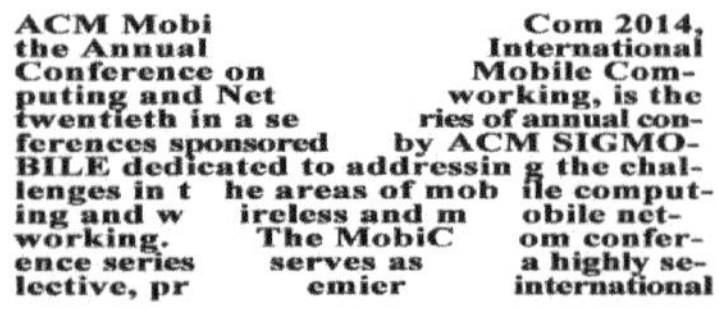

Figure 2: An example sign with information at multiple granularity.

or a wall, both reflecting light and potentially offering low resolutions, to a display, typically LCD or LED, which emits light and can also show dynamic content. The receiving end, the phone cameras, boasts of more diverse capability in terms of the captured image size, resolution, and video recording frame rate. The operational environment is no less simple. A barcode might be indoors or outdoors, under various lighting conditions, and is hardly viewed at a fixed distance away. When a single displayed code is expected to work under diverse conditions, we need a scalable coding mechanism to mimic a one-size-fits-all effect.

There are several challenges to support scalable coding. First, we need to understand the optical channel behavior under different conditions. All the effects can be modeled with some channel distortion. Specifically, pixel colors may mix together spatially (when viewed at a distance) or temporally (when captured at a low frame rate), and we need to handle undersampled signals. Second, we need to design a layered coding scheme that scale with capture conditions and device capability. Third, we need to handle the large dynamic range of color variation and lighting effects as a result of diverse operational conditions.

A previous proposal for hierarchical coding on an LED array of traffic lights [1] is the closest to meeting our requirements. It suggested the potential of accommodating several viewing distances by following a process analogous to multi-resolution image compression. However, it only addresses a subset of the issues we discussed, and involves a computationally intensive wavelet transform.

More generally, we can borrow the notion of multi-resolution coding from traditional RF wireless communication and scalable video coding (SVC) for *channel* and *source* coding respectively. In particular, hierarchical modulation (HM) is a technique that overlays symbols from two or more layers, intended to be decodable at different channel SNRs.

Following a similar spirit to HM, we design Strata, which achieves spatial-temporal layered coding for any input information. Strata embeds information at multiple granularity into the same code area spatially or the same frame interval temporally. It ensures all layers are decodable by controlling the amount of interference between adjacent layers. Spatially, Strata essentially uses code blocks of non-uniform resolutions while bounding the effect of the finer layers on the more coarse layers. Across frames, Strata adopts non-uniform frame intervals, such that a high-rate camera can decode more frames, while a low-rate camera simply treats the extra frames as noise. Furthermore, our design is recursive and can be readily extended to generate more layers. Our experiment results confirm that Strata can indeed scale with a range of capture distances and device capabilities, i.e., resolutions and frame rates. We do trade some amount of per-layer capacity for scaling over a large operational range.

In summary, we make several contributions in this paper:

First, we realize the vision of general multi-resolution visual communication with concrete layered coding schemes, by translating different axes of scalability all into scaling with the captured resolutions. Although there are many existing barcode designs, we are not aware of one that supports scalable coding as outlined in the paper.

Second, we propose Strata, which adopts non-uniform spatial resolutions and frame rates. Further, the design can be readily extended following a recursive construction.

Third, we explore the design space and show the performance of Strata under various conditions.

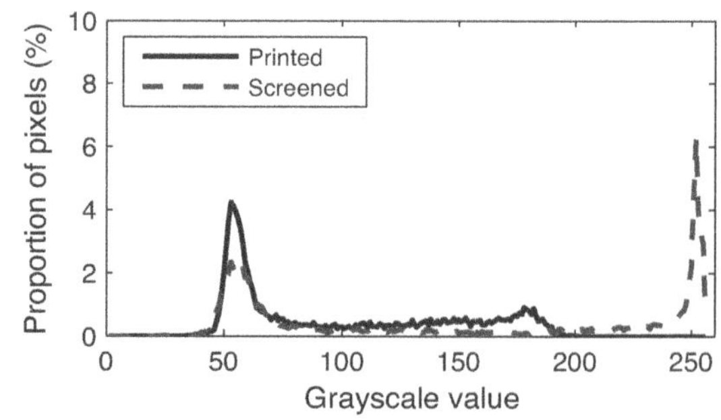

Figure 3: The grayscale value distributions in captured images of printed vs screened codes.

2. MOTIVATION FOR SCALABLE CODING

Conventional coding schemes require the code to be received in its entirety, which implies a fixed supported range of spatial resolutions or frame rates. This is the case for each code instance, even if error correction is employed to ease the requirements. However, we face wide-ranging operational conditions in practice, which impose several challenges on the code and related system design.

2.1 Multi-resolution information sources

Examples abound of information expressed or acquired in multiple resolutions. For example, it is common for an advertisement to use various font sizes to highlight different information. When one visits a Wikipedia page, quite often only the synopsis at the top of the page is of interest, rather than the full page. Therefore, papers start with abstracts and news articles start with headlines to highlight the key information. It would be nice to provide a coding primitive to cater to the requirements from the information sources for transmission.

2.2 Diverse operational conditions

Diverse transmitters. As Figure 1 suggests, barcodes are now shown on a wide variety of surfaces. For a printed code, its resolution is constrained by the printing quality, and typical laser printers support 600×600 dpi. The material, especially its smoothness property also affects the amount of light reflected and the perceived resolution of the displayed image. Similarly, LCDs and LEDs also vary in performance. For simplicity, we consider the most common cases, where barcodes are printed on paper or displayed on computer screens. As long as the display resolution is sufficiently high, the captured images will mainly differ in brightness. Figure 3 shows the grayscale value distributions for images captured on a Nexus 5, 5 m from either the printed code or the screened code. The screened code is noticeably brighter, showing a high peak of white blocks.

Table 1: Device specifications.

Device name	Image	Video	CPU	Sensor Aperture
Nokia Lumia 1020	38 MP effective 7152×5368 px	1080p@30fps	Dual-core 1.5 GHz Krait	2/3-in F/2.2
Samsung Note 3	13 MP 4128×3096 px	1080p@60fps 2160p@30fps	Quad-core 2.3 GHz	1/3.2-in F/2.2
iPhone 5s	8 MP 3264×2448 px	1080p@30fps 720p@120fps	Dual-core 1.3 GHz	1/3-in F/2.2
LG Nexus 5	8 MP 3264×2448 px	1080p@30fps	Quad-core 2.3 GHz	1/3.2-in F/2.4
Samsung S2	8 MP 3264×2448 px	1080p@30fps	Dual-core 1.2GHz	1/3-in F/2.0
Samsung Note 2	8 MP 3264×2448 px	1080p@30fps	Quad-core 1.6 GHz	1/3.2-in F/2.6
HTC Incredible	8 MP, 3264×2448 px	720p@30fps	Scorpion 1GHz	1/3.2-in F/2.4
iPhone 4	5 MP 2592×1936 px	720p@30fps	1 GHz	1/3-in F/2.0
HTC Desire	5 MP 2592×1944 px	480p@15fps 720p@30fps	Quad-core 1.2 GHz	1/4-in F/2.8

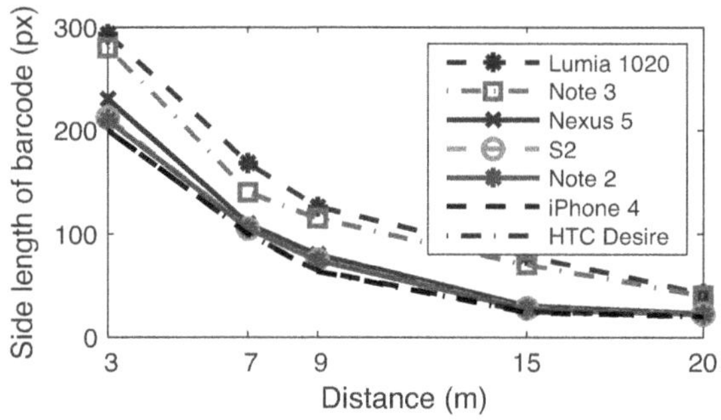

Figure 4: The captured code area size on a phone camera varies with hardware quality and the capture distance.

Diverse receivers. Phone cameras exhibit notable differences in terms of hardware capability, in particular, the image resolution and video frame capture rate. Table 1 lists the specifications for several recent models.

Transmission range. Given a 20×20 (cm^2) barcode displayed on a laptop screen outdoors, Figure 4 shows the sizes of the captured barcode at various distances by the devices. The captured area size drops by almost a factor of 8 from 3 m to 20 m.

The captured image has to be small enough to fit inside the overall captured scene, while large enough to show a sufficient resolution to permit decoding. As a result, a typical QR code image can only support a certain distance range, and cannot be successfully decoded either too close to or too far from it. With a Note 3 to capture a version 13 QR code with 65×65 blocks, Table 2 shows the range determined by the overall displayed code image size. Table 3 further shows the longest distance at which a single-bit monochrome code block of a given size is still decodable using the Note 3.

2.3 Challenges

The above measurements suggest three main challenges to designing a system to cater to diverse conditions.

Understanding the optical channel. All the diverse conditions discussed can be captured by the channel quality, and we need to analyze the channel. In particular, we are dealing with spatial or temporal undersampling, i.e., when the received resolution might be smaller than the displayed, or when the receive frame rate might be lower than needed.

Multi-resolution code design for scalability. Barcode display is a broadcast scenario, where the same display is expected to work for all receiving cameras. Ideally, the higher the resolution of the captured code image, the more information we expect to decode. A high resolution may be achieved with a high-end camera or by capturing the code image at a short distance. We can similarly define *rate scalability*, i.e., the throughput should scale with the frame capture rate of a barcode video over the same time period, the higher the frame rate, the more decoded bits. This is another view of temporal scalability. Therefore, we need a multi-resolution coding mechanism that scales spatially and temporally.

Table 2: QR code sizes and supported ranges.

Image side length (cm)	6.4	15	22	33
Range (m)	0.2–2	0.45–3	0.55–4	0.8–5

Table 3: Capture limit of a single-bit code block.

Block side length (cm, px)	0.31 26 px	0.625 52 px	1.25 104 px	2.5 208 px
Limit (m)	3	5	9	> 20

Handling large dynamic ranges. A side effect from the wide-ranging operational conditions is a large dynamic range of the raw color input. The receiver needs to be able to adapt to the color ranges to ensure correct decoding.

2.4 A leaf from a traditional RF wireless book

For traditional RF wireless, there are also similar issues of designing scalable codes to suit diverse channel conditions. Hierarchical modulation (HM), also called layered modulation, is a technique for multiplexing and modulating multiple data streams into a single symbol stream and transmitted concurrently. Only the base layer can be decoded at a low channel SNR, while the enhancement layer, typically carrying more information, can be further decoded at a sufficiently high SNR. This way, HM offers some scalability at a range of channel SNRs.

Power allocation between layers in HM potentially poses a large dynamic range requirement, which is handled by gain control for the amplifiers for traditional radio transceivers. We face a similar issue.

Therefore, we can borrow similar concepts and techniques from traditional RF wireless for the scalable visual communications scenarios.

3. UNDERSTANDING THE CHANNEL

We start with a simplified view of the channel model, and use that to analyze the capacity. This builds an intuition for the code design. We then empirically measure the channel to understand some system design considerations.

3.1 Channel formulation

Channel unit. Our channel unit is composed of two corresponding square blocks in the displayed and captured images respectively, each containing some number of pixels. This is analogous to the notion of a narrowband single-antenna channel for traditional RF wireless. Symbols are represented by different colors for the displayed code block. For simplicity, we will only consider grayscale color values.

Undersampling. When the captured frame resolution or rate is too low compared to the displayed, we observe undersampled signals. Handling these cases is the key to achieving scalable code design.

The colors of the original blocks mix together when undersampled, either spatially or temporally. Assuming no other distortions, the mixed color is simply a linear average of the original colors [5]. Therefore, the observed signal on our undersampled channel unit is produced by combining the colors of the corresponding displayed blocks adjacent either in time or space. This is analogous to directly adding the channel coefficients of the original channels to obtain that for the composite channel.

The overall channel. Each frame supports many spatial channel units, analogous to MIMO [2], except that the *visual* MIMO channel units are orthogonal, since light propagation is directional. Temporally, each frame corresponds to a time slot, so the code blocks at the same position in different frames simply indicate orthogonal temporal channels.

3.2 Capacity analysis

Since there is no multipath for our optical channels, the total spatial and temporal code capacity is just the per-block capacity summed over all blocks in time and space. We therefore focus on the single-block capacity analysis.

Code block color and miscolor errors. In either the displayed or the received image, we use (u, v) to denote a code block at the u-th row and v-th column.

Each pixel uses k colors to represent log k bits of information (e.g., two colors can represent a single bit, 0 or 1). Color $\kappa \in [0, k-1]$ is assigned to a pixel if the pixel's grayscale value falls within the range of color κ.

Given $b \times b$ pixels in code block (u, v), we determine the color of a code block (u, v) as color κ if this color is assigned to the maximum number of pixels in this code block. In other words, color κ is the *dominant color* among the pixels of this code block.

Incorrectly recognizing a code block color will cause bit errors in the decoding process. We refer to this as a *miscolor error*. Miscolor errors may occur for three reasons. First, the colors of the individual pixels may be determined incorrectly due to hardware-induced pixel noise or ambient lighting effects such as reflections. Second, each pixel in a captured image may be a mixture of multiple displayed pixels in the raw image due to spatial or temporal undersampling. Third, the dominant color of a code block may be incorrectly determined due to the proportion of the pixels showing the expected color.

SNR and capacity. We consider the pixels showing the intended color of the block as *signal*, and any pixel exhibiting a miscolor error for whatever reason (hardware artifacts, ambient lighting effects, or image distortion due to imperfect capture) as *noise*. Let $SNR(u, v)$ denote the signal-to-noise ratio detected in the block of the received image. We can define it as

$$SNR(u, v) = \frac{\alpha(u, v)}{\beta(u, v)}$$

where $\alpha(u, v)$ denotes the number of pixels with the *right* color, i.e., the color of the corresponding block of the displayed image, and $\beta(u, v)$ denotes the number of pixels with the *wrong* color(s) or 1, when no such pixels exist.

Let $c(u, v)$ denote the channel capacity of a code block (u, v). Following the classical RF channel capacity definition per single-antenna channel per time slot for narrowband,

$$c(u, v) = \log(1 + SNR(u, v))$$

This applies generically to the channel regardless of the specific modulation choices. For example, we can use black and white to represent a single bit, 0 or 1, which requires an

Figure 5: Spatial mixing of blocks.

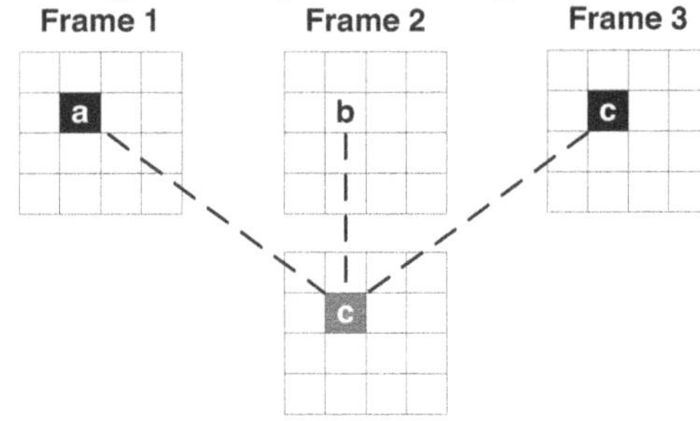

Figure 6: Temporal mixing of blocks.

SNR of at least 1. We can also use four colors to represent 2 bits each, which requires an SNR of at least 3.

Multi-layer code capacity. The same capacity argument applies to a multi-layer code with a slight modification to the SNR definition. If our modulation consists of a coarse layer and a fine layer, then the latter is interference when decoding the former. Therefore, the noise term for the coarse layer can count in the contribution from the fine layer.

3.3 Intuition for code design

Based on the capacity expression, we need the SNR$\geq$1 to guarantee 1 bit in the coarse layer. In other words, at least half of the pixels in the coarse layer code block should take the dominant color. Since the input bit distribution for the fine layer is unpredictable, the only way to ensure this color dominance is to always set some of those pixels to the intended dominant color. Hence, we need some notion of a *reserved block*.

Figures 5 and 6 illustrate how blocks mix spatially and temporally to produce a block at the more coarse resolution.

Spatially, we need to reserve some pixels in the fine layer, i.e., we can only use a portion of the fine blocks as effective information blocks. For example, a and b in Figure 5 should both be white to ensure the mixed block is perceived as white.

Temporally, we need to reserve some number of frames, or control the frame rate in effect. For example, a and c in Figure 6 should both be black to ensure black dominates in the mixed block.

3.4 Empirical measurements

Practical conditions are more complex than the formulation above, so we next measure the channel empirically and study relevant system effects, mainly the exposure control.

Color mixing. The color mixing behavior is more complicated in practice than simply averaging the colors of the raw pixels. First, light from the raw displayed pixels diffuses over distance, and so the displayed images appear darker (*grayer*) when viewed further away. Second, the average phone camera automatically adjusts focus, contrast, and exposure, whose effects also vary with distance. As it is neither easy nor necessary to separate the individual contributions of these factors, we simply investigate their combined effects on the color mixing behavior.

We display five patterns on the screen for the color mixing test, all black, all white, and the three mixed black and

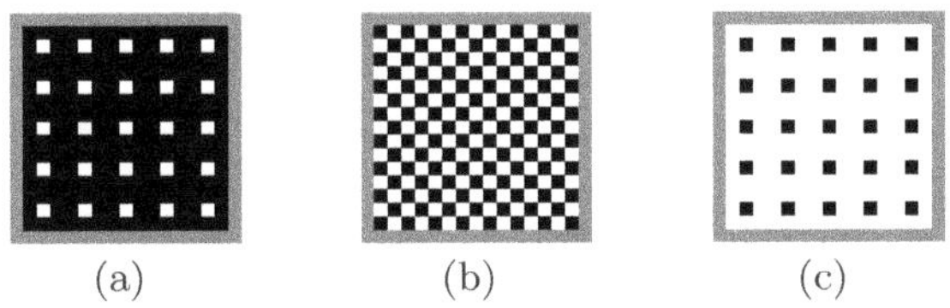

(a) (b) (c)

Figure 7: Three mixed-color patterns for testing: (a) Units of 1 white block surrounded by 8 black blocks; (b) alternating white and black blocks; and (c) Units of 1 black block surrounded by 8 white blocks.

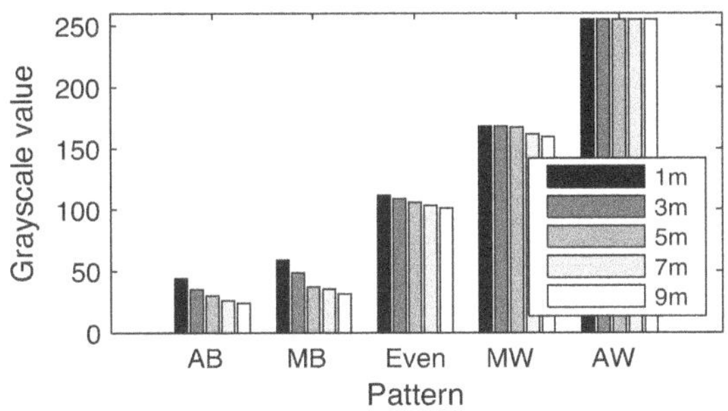

Figure 8: Grayscale values of captured images with different proportions of white displayed. Left to right: all black, mostly black, even split of white and black, mostly white, and all white.

white frames shown in Figure 7. These are captured on the Nexus 5 at several distances. Figure 8 shows the average colors of the individual captured frames, sorted by the display pattern and the distance. For the same distance, we see an approximately linear color mixing behavior as earlier assumed, although the grayscale values for longer distances are smaller (closer to the black end). White is better preserved over distance. For mixed-color frames, the more white blocks, the less the difference across distances.

Exposure control. We make a specially arranged block pattern (Figure 9(a)) on screen to assess the effects of exposure control. Figure 9(b) shows the captured image at 28 m, enlarged to the same size as that of the original image. The captured image becomes noticeably grayer with distance, due to light diffusion. Pixel colors are noisier near color change boundaries than inside the blocks. Further, isolated black blocks can be overridden by the surrounding white blocks at a distance. Therefore, we should avoid isolated black blocks in our encoding and avoid sampling colors at block boundaries for decoding.

4. Strata ENCODING

Strata builds on the intuition and system considerations developed previously, and works for either a single barcode image or a video of barcodes.. It is essentially a hierarchical modulation achieved by adjusting the number of code blocks for different layers. This is analogous to adjusting the power allocation between layers in classical HM.

4.1 Assumptions and scope

Strata aims to achieve spatial and temporal scalability as defined in Section 2.3. The latter is translated to *rate scalability*, although we will discuss the relevant operations in the time domain, as they apply across frames. Specifically, Strata is built on three assumptions:

(a) (b)

Figure 9: (a) Original screened image of white and black blocks. (b) Captured image at 28 m, enlarged to the same size as the original image.

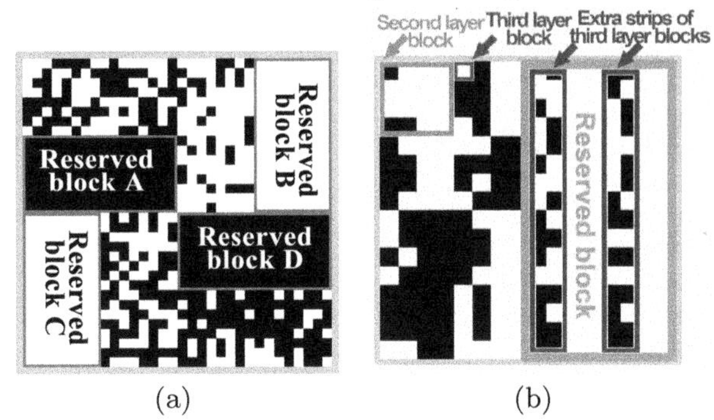

(a) (b)

Figure 10: Examples of layered spatial coding. (a) A two-layer code with 4 base layer blocks and 256 enhancement layer blocks within each base layer block. The reserved block can take up different positions and orientations within the base layer block. (b) A three-layer code with bits from the third layer in the reserved block of the first layer.

First, spatially we still capture the entire code image, only that the sizes of the captured images differ, hence the resolutions. In future, we could also consider the case of capturing only a fraction of the overall barcode.

Second, it is fine to receive and decode only *partial* information. This is especially the case for the temporal domain to support streaming. A previous work, LightSync [6], already provides a mechanism for recovering *all* information from a high-rate looping display, where a low-rate camera needs more time.

Third, Strata guarantees the performance of the layer with the most coarse granularity, while opportunistically packing and recovering bits in the finer-grained layers.

As with most barcode designs, we only use black and white for now to represent single-bit symbols. This also means the code design could tolerate more noise than if more colors are adopted to represent multi-bit symbols.

Terminology. Since most discussion centers on how to manage encoding and decoding for two adjacent layers, we will refer to the more coarse layer of the two, layer n, as the *base layer* and the finer layer, layer $n+1$, the *enhancement layer*. Where multiple layers are mentioned, the layer with the finest granularity takes the largest index number.

4.2 Spatial code

The spatial component of Strata is simply a per-frame base code. Therefore, it works regardless of whether the transmitter is a static poster or a display with dynamic content.

Basic recursive code construction. The spatial code is constructed by recursively increasing code block resolutions at successive layers. Figure 10(a) shows an example two-layer code image.

A block in layer n (the *base layer*) is divided into k smaller blocks for the next finer layer, layer $n+1$ (the *enhancement layer*). We refer to k as the scaling factor. A fraction, p, of the enhancement layer blocks form a large *reserved block* carrying the same color as the base layer. The remaining smaller blocks carry data for the enhancement layer. We find that $k = 16$ and $p = \frac{1}{2}$ provide good tradeoffs in terms of the overall performance (Figure 14).

The block division approach aligns pixel boundaries of the blocks of adjacent layers and minimizes the effects of noise at the block edge (noted at the end of Section 3.4), so this simplifies code block detection. Furthermore, this makes it easier to control the color proportion of the composite enhancement layer blocks. Reserving half of the enhancement layer blocks limits the effect of the colors of the remaining enhancement layer blocks on the base layer block regardless. Adopting a contiguous reserved block mitigates the effects of over-exposure (Figure 9) and lets us harness extra bits.

Taken as a whole, Strata produces a barcode with non-uniform spatial resolutions. The reserved block effectively reduces the local resolution to address undersampling.

Additional bits from the reserved block orientation. By using the positions and orientations of the reserved blocks, we can accommodate 2 more bits per group of multi-layer code, as shown by the blocks A-D in Figure 10(a). This requires that there are no contiguous chunks of white or black code blocks in the enhancement layer. To ensure we recognize the reserved block unambiguously, we also apply a *block mask* to the data blocks, such as the one for QR code, to randomize the locations of the white and black blocks. This minimizes the probability of data blocks in the same color accidentally forming the shape of the reserved block. The mask is equivalent to a scrambler for conventional wireless communication systems to avoid long runs of 1 or 0.

Although it might be possible to use other shapes and orientations as well, it would take exponentially more combinations for us to gain each additional bit, and the return for such efforts diminishes very quickly.

Harnessing extra capacity. Furthermore, code blocks for layer $n+2$ (or $n+3$) can be inserted to the reserved block of layer n. Figure 10(b) shows how two more strips of layer $n+2$ blocks can be added. The capacity of layer $n+2$ (or $n+3$) doubles with these two additional strips.

This process is possible due to the base layer capacity being slightly larger than 1 with high probability, and so we could tolerate more noise in the reserved block for layer n. If we allocate more bits to the immediate next layer, layer $n+1$, the granularity might be too coarse. After another layer, however, the granularity is fine enough that we have more control in how much noise is added to layer n.

It is difficult to fully use the extra capacity, however, because the information bits could be completely random. We need to be conservative when not knowing the bit distribution of the original message, though this could be relaxed with the addition of error correction bits.

The spatial code parameters, the reserved block size (p) and the scaling factor (k), can be tuned based on the bit value distribution of the information bits and whether error correction is used. We will discuss this more in Section 6.3.

Encoding in the pixel domain vs frequency domain. We follow pixel domain encoding with code blocks for several reasons. First, frequency domain encoding requires high-precision pixels, whereas code blocks are more robust when the display or printing resolution is lower than ideal. Further, our preliminary experiments suggest that code blocks can tolerate slightly blurry captured images caused by hand motion, whereas frequency domain encoding is more sensitive to motion-induced blur. Second, spatial undersampling causes inter-pixel interference in the captured images, which cannot be resolved in the frequency domain. Third, frequency domain processing is computationally more intensive, as shown in previous work [4].

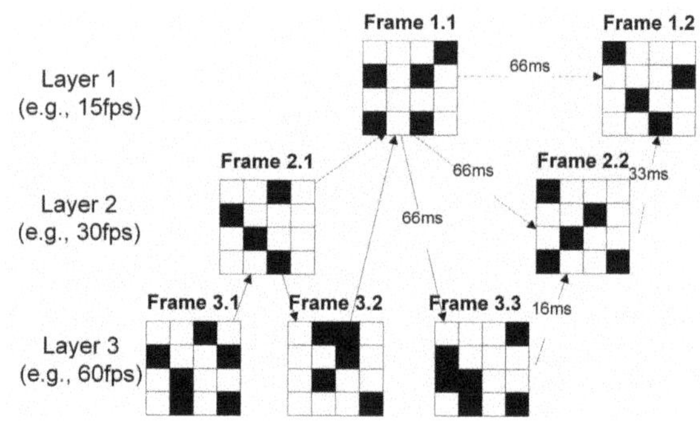

(a) Interleaved temporal layers.

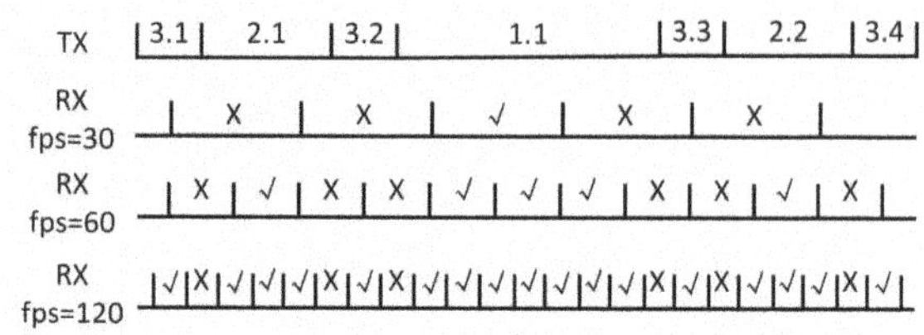

(b) Received frame components.

Figure 11: Example of temporal Strata encoding.

4.3 Temporal code

The temporal component of Strata mainly applies to barcode videos. The base layers are the frames received at the low(est) frame rates.

As shown in previous work [6], such frames are often mixtures of the original frames. If we could control the proportion of the original frames in such a mixed frame, we could follow a similar approach to the spatial code construction. Unfortunately, this is not the case due to typical phone cameras employing a rolling shutter [6]. We therefore construct the temporal code differently, while still following the notion of the *reserved block*.

When the frame capture rate is twice the display rate, we receive a single, decodable frame, alternating with a mixed frame of two consecutive original displayed frames. Since the mixed frame is normally to be discarded, it would not matter even if it is a mixture of more frames. Therefore, we sandwich each base layer frame between two immediate enhancement layer frames. Further layers can be added recursively. Figure 11 illustrates how frames are interleaved at the display and mixed at the receiver. The times on the arrows in Figure 11(a) indicate the perceived intervals between consecutive frames in the layered code. Frame durations are shown schematically in Figure 11(b) following the interleaving. A tick indicates a decodable, single frame, whereas a cross is a mixed frame to be discarded. While Layer 1 frames can be decoded by all receivers, Layer 3 frames can only be decoded by the 120-fps receiver.

Overall, the barcode video essentially adopts non-uniform frame rates. Given that the common frame rate capability varies from 15 to 120 fps (Table 1 and [6]), our target rate for different layers ranges from 7.5 fps to 60 fps.

It is also possible to adopt non-uniform rates within each frame, i.e., a regular frame can be divided into a few parts, with each part following a different uniform frame rate. However, this approach performs worse (Section 6.5) and does not compose easily with the spatial code.

4.4 Spatial-temporal code

By design, our spatial code is an intra-frame code, whereas the temporal code is inter-frame, and the coding mechanisms are orthogonal. Therefore, we can concatenate both to form a layered spatial-temporal code. In other words, each frame of the barcode video can follow the design of the spatial code, with the frames arranged at non-uniform intervals according to the temporal code.

Given the layer correspondence, when using such a code, information for the same layer should be filled across frames.

It is possible to have a more sophisticated design, including more interleaving both intra-frame and inter-frame for error protection. We leave this to future work.

4.5 Frame format

Spatial. As with typical barcodes, we need some mechanisms to locate the barcode image per frame and to identify the code block sizes.

In theory, we could just treat the overall image as a single bit as the first layer and decode from there. In practice, we need a minimum number of bits to transmit useful messages, so we still add some *timing blocks* to indicate the number of first layer blocks present.

Since our code design applies to the data area only, we can simply follow existing corner and timing block designs such as those for QR code or Data Matrix for the most coarse layer. This way, we also inherit any built-in mechanisms for correcting perspective distortion and rotation when capturing the image[1]. There is no need for more dedicated blocks for the finer layers, since we follow the block division rule to encode and detect successive layers. For the spatial part, we could add recursively defined localization blocks to better combat perspective distortion, although we omit these in the current version.

Temporal. For the temporal code, a frame sequence number field is added to each frame to identify individual frames. The block size for this field is the same as that of the most coarse layer in each frame.

5. Strata DECODING

5.1 Exposure control

As mentioned earlier, we need to avoid over-exposure especially when capturing the barcode from afar. Phone cameras are usually set to normal exposure for natural scenes in daylight, but generally support a few additional settings. For the Android camera app, these are -2, -1, 1, and 2. Our measurements show that the optimal exposure settings need to be lower than for natural scenes, hence, typically -2 for screened barcodes and -1 for printed barcodes (Figure 12).

Therefore, we first estimate the average intensity of the first captured barcode image. If the average is too close to the white end, we adopt -2; -1 otherwise.

5.2 Detecting and decoding spatial layers

For each frame, we first detect the image area and the code block size of the most coarse layer following the same procedure as for QR code or Data Matrix. The decoder then determines the color of each pixel within the image area in preparation for the decoding. We also divide the image area into the first layer blocks.

Decoding then proceeds layer by layer. For each block of layer i, the decoder skips the outermost $1/3$ of pixels from each side to avoid inaccurate edges. It examines the colors of the remaining pixels of the block, counts the numbers of the black and white pixels respectively, and determines the dominant color. This is considered the color of the block. All blocks of layer i can then be decoded as 0 or 1, which completes decoding for this layer. Each block is then divided in 16 to obtain the blocks for layer $i+1$, and their colors are similarly determined by the majority rule.

The reserved block. We identify the location and orientation of the largest contiguous color chunk to decode the extra bits for the immediate next layer. For the enhancement layer blocks within each base layer block, we assign indices to each block row-wise and column-wise, starting from the top left corner, and calculate the grayscale value of each enhancement layer block.

Say the reserved block is white, containing half of the enhancement blocks. It can take one of the four position and orientation combinations, left, right, top, or bottom. In the row-wise index assignment, the reserved block is at the top (or bottom) if the low-indexed (or high-indexed) blocks show very high grayscale values. Similarly, in the column-wise index assignment, high grayscale values for the low-indexed (or high-indexed) blocks indicate the reserved block is on the left (or right).

The strips for layer $i+2$. The decoding of the added data bits in these inserted strips is the same as that of the original data bits for layer $i+2$.

Stopping rule. If there is error correction, decoding stops if the number of bit errors in the current layer exceeds a threshold, which is set based on the error correction code rate. Otherwise, decoding stops once we reach the pixel layer, i.e., when the code block cannot be divided further.

Note that the information in each layer is independently decodable. In other words, bit errors in layer n have no direct effect on layer $n+1$. Due to the code construction, however, the bit error rate increases with reduced resolution, and therefore we follow a layer decoding order to avoid decoding mostly corrupt enhancement layers. This also has the benefit of simplifying data block localization, or we would need nested timing blocks to indicate the size of data block at each layer.

5.3 Temporal

There is no specific decoder for the temporal part. We simply try to decode any frame captured using the spatial

[1]While the color mixing behavior in different parts of the frame might differ due to perspective distortion, in practice the difference is negligible. When the camera is close to the display and perspective distortion is most noticeable, there is little undersampling. Conversely, when the effect of undersampling is noticeable further away, the effect of perspective distortion is negligible.

decoder. In addition, we decode the frame sequence number of the frame. A frame is discarded if the error rate exceeds a threshold, which indicates unrecoverable frame mixing. If multiple frames with the same sequence number are decoded, we keep results for the best one.

Compared with the spatial decoding process, the temporal process tries to recover all layers as they are received in an interleaved fashion, and then collates frames for the corresponding layers after all frames are decoded.

Note that the temporal process can only decode frames without mixing, and therefore, the color mixing spatially will not be affected further across frames, and we do not need to adjust the reserved block size.

6. PERFORMANCE

6.1 General setup

We follow the setups below unless otherwise stated.

Strata instance. The Strata instance for experiments is composed of four spatial layers per frame, with 1, 10, 160, and 2560 bits respectively. Extra strips of fourth-layer bits were inserted to both of the first two layers. No error correction was included. This can be added easily using an existing algorithm.

The per-frame barcode measures 20×20 (cm^2) when displayed on screen, with the smallest code blocks measuring 26×26 pixels. The printed version measures 21×21 (cm^2).

For the video version, the Strata instance also includes four layers, corresponding to 7.5, 15, 30, and 60 fps respectively, interleaved as described earlier.

Decoder. We implement both an online, real-time decoder as an Android app and an offline version run on a desktop. The latter takes a captured barcode image (in `.jpg`) or video (in `.mp4`) and decodes it using the same algorithm as the app. The offline decoder offers a fairer comparison for the experiments involving the iPhone 5s and the Lumia 1020, and also makes it easier to log and analyze intermediate results[2]. Therefore, we mainly report results from the offline decoder, but uses the online Android decoder to measure timing. We also perform simulations to show the effects of certain spatial parameters without additional channel distortion.

Default experimental conditions. The default receiving phone is the Nexus 5, which has the average camera among all phones that are common on the market. The Lumia 1020 and the iPhone 4 have the best and worst cameras respectively among our devices.

Experiments were mostly run outdoors to capture the barcodes over a large distance range, from 1 m to 28 m. At each distance point, the camera was held as steadily as possible[3]. Each data point is averaged over 5 measurements. As the performance degraded to showing almost random bit errors after 20 m, we omit results for longer distances.

As the spatial and temporal components of Strata are orthogonal, there is little extra to show for the combined version. We will mainly note whether a spatial frame can be

[2]Logging intermediate results in the app version often makes it too slow to achieve real-time processing for barcode videos.
[3]While slight hand shake does not pose an issue as mentioned in Section 4.2, images captured on a moving camera requires deblurring before they can be decoded, which is beyond the scope of this paper.

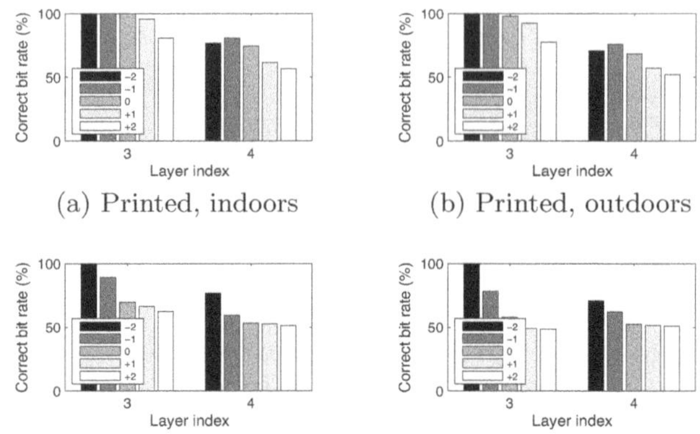

(a) Printed, indoors (b) Printed, outdoors

(c) Screened, indoors (d) Screened, outdoors

Figure 12: Decoding performance at various exposure settings for printed barcode vs screened, indoors and outdoors.

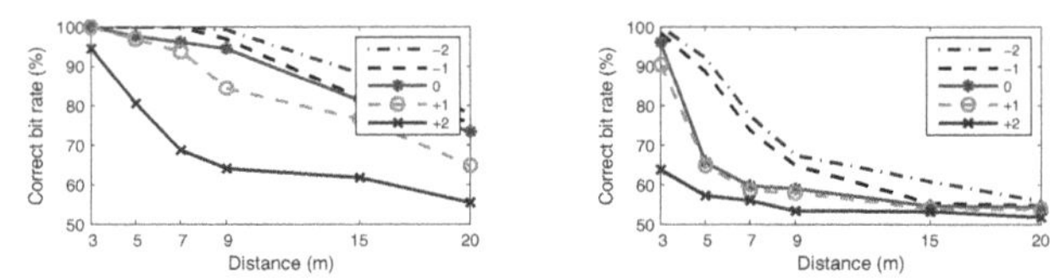

(a) Decoding performance of the third layer (b) Decoding performance of the fourth layer

Figure 13: Decoding performance for various exposure settings and distances.

decoded fast enough, such that the temporal results would be equivalent to spatial-temporal results.

6.2 Exposure setting and environment

We start by verifying the exposure settings and any effect from the ambient lighting conditions.

Using the Nexus 5 to capture a barcode 5 m away from where it is displayed, we evaluate the decoding performance at various exposure settings, for a printed barcode or a screened barcode, both indoors and outdoors. Figure 12 suggests that the difference between indoors and outdoors is minor once the exposure setting is adjusted properly. A low exposure setting is better for barcode capture, with printed code favoring -1 and screened code favoring -2. This is further seen in Figure 13 for screened code over a large distance.

Therefore, we only run experiments for screened code outdoors in the following, so that we can manage a large distance range more easily.

6.3 Spatial microbenchmarks

Choice of spatial parameters. There are two main parameters in the spatial code design: *the reserved block size* and *the scaling factor for block division* to proceed to the next layer.

We consider three cases, where the scaling factors between adjacent layers are 1:4, 1:16, and 1:64, i.e., whether there are 4, 16, or 64 enhancement blocks in each base layer block. We set the reserved block to a fixed color (say black), and randomly assign black or white to the remaining enhancement blocks. We then compute the miscolor error rate for the base layer block as the reserved block varies in size. This set of the experiments are done in simulations to show the inherent tradeoff in the code design even without any hardware

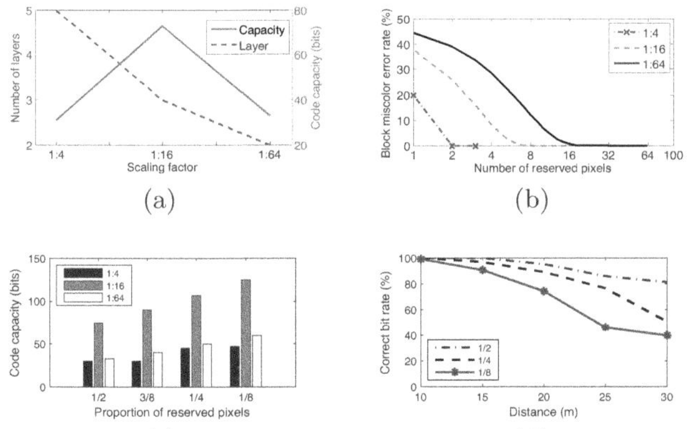

(a) (b) (c) (d)

Figure 14: (a) Capacity and layer count tradeoff with scaling factors. (b) Base layer block miscolor rate vs reserved block size for different scaling factors. (c) Capacity vs reserved block sizes for different scaling factors. (d) For 1:16, *measured* miscolor rate at different distances.

distortion in practice. Phone-based experiments confirm the simulation results, so we only present the simulation results unless otherwise stated.

Figure 14 shows several tradeoffs between the scaling factor, the reserved block size, and the total capacity.

We can accommodate more layers with a small scaling factor like 1:4 (Figure 14(a)). However, the reserved block size must also be larger proportionally (Figure 14(b)), and there is more wasted capacity due to the reserved block with each additional layer. Between 1:16 and 1:64, 1:64 needs a smaller reserved block size, while 1:16 supports more layers, and hence a higher capacity overall (Figure 14(a)). This is confirmed by Figure 14(c), which shows that 1:16 achieves the fastest increase in capacity with more layers.

As a byproduct of the scaling factor, we can harness additional bits from the reserved block shape. Assuming a rectangular contiguous reserved block shape, using the current position-and-orientation approach, we get 0 bit for 1:4, slightly over 2 bits for 1:16, and slightly over 3 bits for 1:64. Hence, 1:16 is again a good tradeoff point.

Figure 14(d) shows how the *measured* miscolor error rate of the base layer block varies with the reserved block size for 1:16. This shows that the reserved block needs to be about half unless the enhancement layer blocks are very fine. Since this works per pair of adjacent layers, we do not need to worry about the effect of even finer layers (layers $n+2$, $n+3$, ...) on the base layer.

If we know the data bit distribution or use an error correction code, we could also reduce the reserved block size. In subsequent experiments, we use a conservative reserved block size to guarantee correct decoding.

Extra strips. Given we have decided to use 1:16 and half as the reserved block size, previous figures show that the reserved block is actually larger than necessary. However, the block resolution of the immediate enhancement layer, layer $n+1$, does not permit efficient use of the redundancy in the reserved block. Therefore, we could carve out extra areas for layer $n+2$, where its blocks are 1/64 of the layer n blocks. We can use the results for 1:64 previously to understand how much effect the layer $n+2$ blocks have on the layer n block. Figure 14(b) shows that, for 1:64, a reserved block size of 1/4 is probably sufficient. This means we could repurpose half of the reserved block for layer $n+2$ blocks for extra capacity, hence the justification for the extra strips.

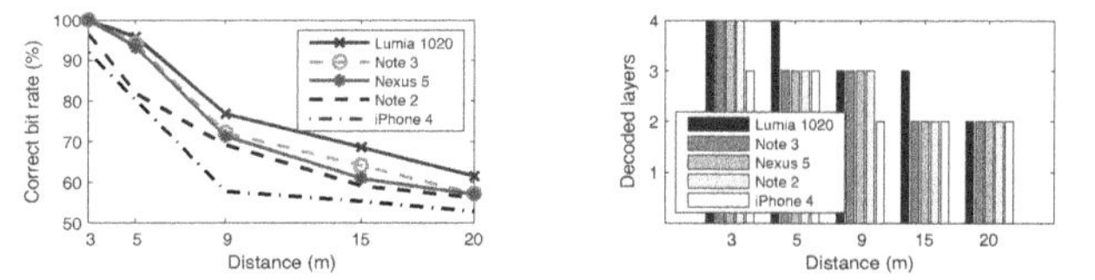

(a) Correctly decoded bits across layers (b) Completely decodable layers

Figure 15: Decoding performance across distances.

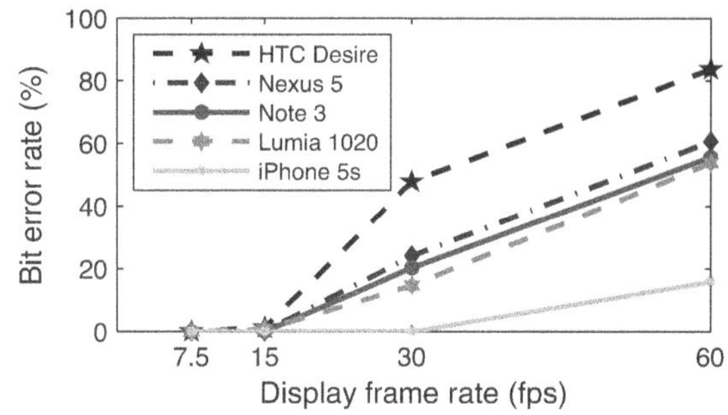

Figure 16: Decoding performance per temporal layer across phones.

Single-image decoding times. Using the slowest phones, we measure the decoding time of a single frame using the online Android app. For a Strata image captured at 4 m, decoding all four layers after barcode localization takes around 5 ms on the Note 2, and 7 to 8 ms on the S2. The localization step currently takes 52 ms, though could be reduced by adopting a COBRA[4] like corner design.

6.4 Scalability of Strata

Strata is designed to scale with the frame capture resolution and rate, so we assess how its performance scales with the capture distances and hardware capability.

Spatial. Figure 15 shows the performance of a single captured Strata image across devices over various distances. The performance degrades with increasing distance and scales with increasing camera resolution as expected. The Lumia 1020 and the iPhone 4, carrying the best and worst phone cameras, can decode the most and fewest bits correctly. If we consider a layer fully decoded with a BER$\leq$ 3%, the Lumia 1020 can decode more layers at 5 m and 15 m.

Temporal. Figure 16 shows the decoding performance of the Strata video on different phones, measured in bit error rate for each layer. Counting the distinctive frames only, the effective average frame rate is 22.03 fps for the iPhone 5s, 14.30 fps for the Nexus 5, and 7.23 fps for the HTC Desire.

6.5 Comparison with alternatives

We next assess how Strata compares with existing single-layer designs and potential alternative multi-layer designs.

Strata vs existing, single-layer codes. For the temporal component, the conventional approach is to adopt a uniform, low frame display rate that is half of the lowest frame capture rate supported across devices. For the phones used in the last experiments, this would be 7.5 fps, and the effective frame rates on all phones would also be in

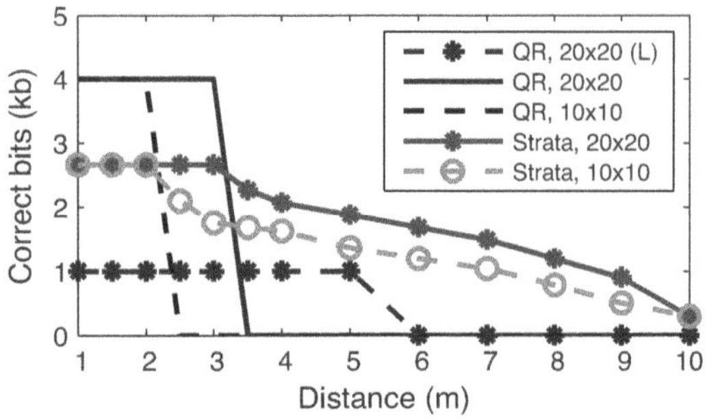

Figure 17: Performance of Strata vs QR code.

the vicinity. Clearly, Strata offers better performance for a high-rate phone. LightSync [6] takes a different approach to frame synchronization and could achieve a higher average rate for a high-rate phone. However, the mechanism does not exactly compare with that in Strata. We will discuss this more in Section 7.

Spatially, it is natural to compare Strata with an existing barcode, such as QR code. We generate a QR code image and a single-image Strata instance with four layers, such that the code area sizes for both are the same[4]. The code block resolution of the QR code is the same as that of the finest, fourth layer of the Strata instance. Therefore, the capacities of the QR code and Strata images are 4096 and 2731 bits respectively. Given the capacity difference, we plot the number of decodable bits at various distances for each in Figure 17, indicated by the suffix "20×20" in the legend. Further, since there is no error protection in the Strata instance, we skip error correction for the QR code as well and count the raw decodable bits. To highlight the tradeoff between the code image size and the decodable distance, we also include comparison of the same images but a quarter of the size (the "10×10" lines) as well as a 1024-bit, 20×20 QR code with bigger blocks, of the same size as the third layer blocks of the 20×20 Strata image (the "QR, 20×20 (L)" line).

As expected, QR code can only support *either* a high capacity *or* a long distance, but not both at the same time. It carries a high capacity at a short distance, but is then completely undecodable. Merely enlarging the overall code image size only increases the farthest distance in small increments. A longer distance can be supported by adopting a larger code block, but sacrificing capacity significantly. Adding further error protection achieves the same qualitative effect as adjusting the code block size, as the latter can be viewed as repetition coding over a block of pixels, the simplest form of protection.

In contrast, a Strata code strikes a balance between capacity and range. Compared with the high-capacity QR code, it offers a much longer range, though at the expense of a lower overall capacity in exchange for guaranteed performance for the more coarse layers. Compared with the larger, low-capacity QR code, Strata still achieves an extended range while offering more than twice the capacity.

Spatial *dithering* vs multi-level grayscales. Using the proportions of black and white enhancement layer blocks to control the overall base layer block color is analogous to *dithering*. A natural alternative is to use pairs of different grayscale values directly to indicate different layers. However, it is very difficult to distinguish more than black and white in practice. Assuming we choose two other grayscale color values in addition to black and white, use them in pairs, and generate a 2-layer code, we can then plot the grayscale value distribution of the received pixel colors. If we could see four distinctive, narrow peaks, then we would be able to calibrate block colors unambiguously to decode the two layers separately. Unfortunately, Figure 18 shows this is not the case for several different choices of grayscale values. In fact, Figure 8 earlier showed that the perceived grayscale values would decrease with distance and cluster near the darker end. Therefore, a multi-level grayscale design would not work[5].

[4]This QR code does not follow standard versions as a result.

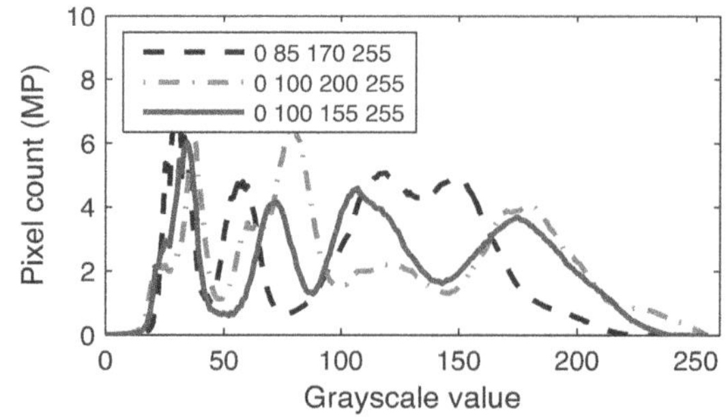

Figure 18: Pixel color distribution of the images of multi-level grayscale designs, captured 1 m away.

Table 4: Pixel and frequency domain coding.

Error rate (%)	1 m	3 m	5 m	7 m	9 m
Screened (Strata)	0	0	0	0	0
Printed (Strata)	0	0	0	0	1.9
Screened (Haar)	5.4	9.7	12	25.4	47
Printed (Haar)	14.4	26.1	39	41	47.6
Screened (OFDM)	6.2	21	27.7	30.5	48.2
Printed (OFDM)	30.1	32.4	44.9	47	49

Spatial Strata vs frequency-domain coding. Previous work PixNet [12] can achieve a high capacity per frame by encoding in the frequency domain using 2D OFDM. The hierarchical LED array coding [1] also transmits in the frequency domain with a Haar wavelet transform. It divides a 16×16 matrix into four 8×8 regions for information of three priority levels, and then transforms the matrix with Haar wavelets before displaying the result on the LED array. In contrast, single-image Strata encodes in the spatial domain following the reasons outlined at the end of Section 4.2.

We generate a 16×16 Haar wavelet encoding as prescribed, and a three-layer Strata image of the same size. To mimic PixNet, we generate a code image of the same size using 2D OFDM, using only the lowest 20 frequency bands as in PixNet, but without any error correction.

Table 4 shows that frequency-domain encoding suffers much higher decoding error rates than Strata even at small distances. The error rates roughly reflect the decoding performance of the medium-priority layers. The higher the frequency bands, the more sensitive their performance to the spatial undersampling. Figure 19 shows that the high-frequency components very quickly drop below 0.5, the thresh-

[5]We find that it is possible to layer two decodable single-layer barcodes using more different colors, but this is equivalent to using four colors per symbol to modulate two bits and cannot be easily extended to more layers.

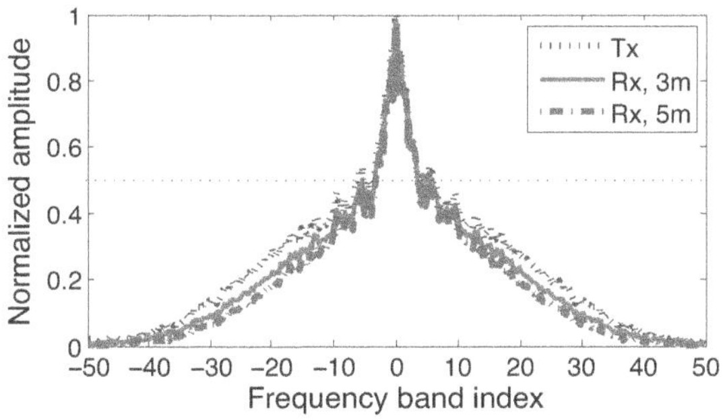

Figure 19: Frequency responses of a printed image encoded with 2D OFDM and captured images.

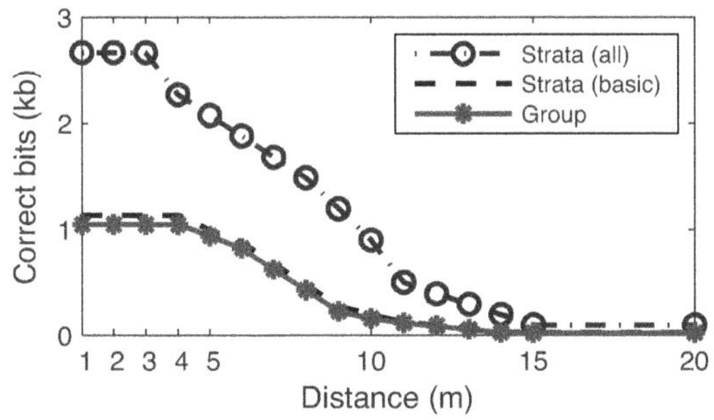

Figure 20: Performance of Strata vs Group of single-layer spatial code.

old for being recognized as the correct color. The results for other distances and for screened code images are similar.

Strata vs group of codes. Another simple alternative design is to have a group of single-layer barcodes of different code block resolutions, such that different parts of the group code will be visible at different distances. We generate such a code example by dividing the total 20×20 (cm^2) code area into four quarters, fitting a single-layer code in each, with 2×2, 4×4, 8×8, and 32×32 blocks respectively, 1108 bits total. The block resolutions for the latter two quarters correspond to those of the third and fourth layers in Strata. We also include a version of Strata without the extra fourth-layer strips or the bits harnessed from the reserved block placement. Its capacity is 1161 bits, compared to 2731 bits for the regular Strata with all the capacity-enhancing features.

Figure 20 shows that all three designs can scale with the distance, with the regular Strata able to carry more than twice as many bits as the group version at all distances. In fact, another main advantage of Strata is its extensibility and faster capacity growth with each additional layer. We can easily devise Strata code instances with five or more layers following the recursive construction. In contrast, it is difficult to similarly pack a group of five or more single-layer codes neatly in one area without tailoring the design to each new layer configuration. Hence, we do not show further comparison results for codes with five or more layers.

We also generate a similar group of barcode videos, essentially dividing a single frame in four, with the four quarters employing different frame rates. Figure 21 shows similar trends to the plots in Figure 16 with slightly different error rates. Therefore, the performance of the two approaches are comparable. However, having the whole frame following the same frame rate makes it readily composable with the spatial layers, and therefore offers more flexibility. Furthermore, it is also harder to extend the quarterly frame design to accommodate more layers.

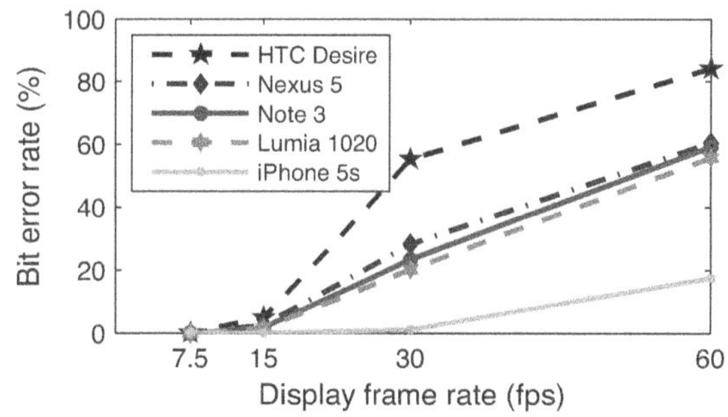

Figure 21: Performance of quarterly frame design for temporal scalability.

7. RELATED WORK

Visible Light Communication (VLC) techniques have been explored over communication links between LEDs (transmitters) and photodiodes (receivers) [10, 11, 2], or between off-the-shelf LCD screens and cameras [5, 12, 4, 6]. Our scheme is also a type of VLC, but works for both static (e.g., a sheet of paper) and dynamic displays.

In particular, hierarchical VLC coding on LED arrays [1] encodes three-level information with Haar wavelets to be captured by cameras at several distances. We have explained the disadvantages of frequency-domain encoding. A further issue due to the Haar wavelet transform is that decoding errors in the lower priority layers will propagate to the higher priority layers. In comparison, Strata also aims to deliver information at different resolutions, but more generally covering spatial and temporal domains with a simple, recursive design and independent layers.

Screen-camera based VLC systems. Several screen-camera based systems employ one-way video streaming for information transmission.

PixNet [12] is a high-capacity code optimized for high-resolution displays and cameras. Given the high decoding complexity, it is not suited to real-time streaming on phones. COBRA [4] adopts a special code layout supporting fast corner detection and code scan to achieve real-time decoding of barcode streams and some blur-resilience. LightSync [6] addresses imperfect frame synchronization as a result of the frame rate mismatch between the display and the camera. Through in-frame color tracking and an inter-frame linear erasure code, LightSync supports a much higher frame display rate than permitted with conventional sampling approaches. 4D barcode [8] also targets synchronization by repeating 2D frames on multiple, orthogonal color channels, which effectively reduces the display frame rate. VRCodes [15] encode over all dimensions of color, time, and space while remaining unobtrusive to the human eye. Decoding is possible with a rolling-shutter camera.

In contrast, Strata follows a different goal of scalable code design, by adopting layered coding structures both spatially and temporally. For the temporal part, we share with LightSync in achieving effective frame rates that scale with the camera's hardware capability. However, the two systems follow different philosophies. LightSync tries to recover undersampled signals over time, but Strata aims to remove undersampling locally. LightSync relies on a looping display to effectively slow down the display rate, whereas Strata works in a streaming mode to decode potentially partial information at all times. LightSync achieves a higher rate per unit time, but only after a minimum amount of capture time.

Barcode design and detection. A vast majority of existing work focuses on better detecting the barcode or redesigning the barcode for higher throughput, better user experience, or more robustness. All are intra-frame codes. We mainly focus on multi-layer designs.

PiCode (or ViCode) [7] takes a watermarking like approach to embed pictures (or videos) into the code. DualCodes [14] superpose a color barcode onto a black-and-white barcode to achieve a higher spatial information density. These approaches typically accommodate at most two layers of information, and do not exhibit the same scalability properties we aim for. In contrast, Strata supports more layers and allow information to be extracted at different granularity.

Recursive 2D barcode [13] is designed for transmission in the near infrared band to be hidden in a map. It recursively encodes simple map location indicators viewable at several distances, but with low information densities. Strata follows a more general goal and employs tightly packed code blocks spatially to achieve a much higher capacity.

Related concepts in source coding and traditional wireless. As we mentioned earlier, the notion of scalable, layered coding is borrowed from traditional wireless communications, especially hierarchical modulation as an example of scalable *channel* coding. SVC is among the best known examples of scalable *source* coding, and more recent proposals include [9, 3] on 3D camera sensing and [16] on image coding, to name a few.

Although SVC is also a type of multi-resolution coding, it follows a fundamentally different mechanism. The cause of distortion is lossy compression via the quantization of analog signals to digital representations, which can be controlled at the encoder by analyzing source information distribution. In contrast, HM and Strata are subject to channel distortions that are unknown at the encoder. Therefore, the encoder can only estimate the channel condition and needs to be sufficiently conservative to account for a range of possible channel distortions to ensure decodability.

Note further that the layers in HM or SVC are dependent, i.e., the enhancement layer would be useless if the base layer is not correctly decoded. In contrast, the layers in Strata are independent for more robustness.

8. CONCLUSION

As cameras become widely available along with mobile devices, increasingly they are capable of acting as the receiving end of communication over surface-camera or display-camera links. There are diverse operational conditions due to device diversity and distance ranges. However, existing coding schemes do not cater to these.

In this paper, we propose Strata, a layered coding scheme to achieve scalable performance, spatially with the frame capture resolutions and temporally with the frame capture rates. Strata borrows the notion of hierarchical modulation from traditional wireless communications. Our scheme embeds information at multiple granularity into the same code area spatially or into the same frame interval temporally. It ensures all layers are decodable by controlling the amount of interference between adjacent layers. Furthermore, our design is recursive and extends easily to add layers. Our experiment results confirm that Strata can indeed scale with a range of capture distances and frame rates. We do trade some amount of per-layer capacity for scaling over a large operational range.

The current capacity increase behavior still follows a few discrete steps. There is certainly room for improvement to achieve more graceful increases.

Furthermore, we essentially focus on scalable *channel* coding and provide a primitive for degradable communication. To better utilize such codes, we also need scalable *source* coding. This is analogous to layering scalable video coding over hierarchical modulation. We leave it to the application to partition the raw information to the effect of hierarchical or scalable source coding.

9. REFERENCES

[1] S. Arai, S. Mase, T. Yamazato, T. Endo, T. Fujii, M. Tanimoto, K. Kidono, Y. Kimura, and Y. Ninomiya. Experimental on hierarchical transmission scheme for visible light communication using LED traffic light and high-speed camera. In *Proceedings of VTC Fall*. IEEE, 2007.

[2] A. Ashok, M. Gruteser, N. Mandayam, J. Silva, M. Varga, and K. Dana. Challenge: Mobile optical networks through visual MIMO. In *Proceedings of MobiCom*, 2010.

[3] I. Daribo. Hierarchical requantization of depth data for 3D visual communications. In *Proceedings of International Conference on Digital Information and Communication Technology and its Applications (DICTAP)*, pages 104–109. IEEE, 2012.

[4] T. Hao, R. Zhou, and G. Xing. COBRA: Color Barcode Streaming for Smartphone Systems. In *Proceedings of MobiSys*, 2012.

[5] S. Hranilovic and F. R. Kschischang. A Pixelated MIMO Wireless Optical Communication System. *IEEE Journal of Selected Topics in Quantum Electronics*, 2006.

[6] W. Hu, H. Gu, and Q. Pu. LightSync: Unsynchronized visual communication over screen-camera links. In *Proceedings of MobiCom*, pages 15–26. ACM, 2013.

[7] W. Huang and W. H. Mow. PiCode: 2D barcode with embedded picture and ViCode: 3D barcode with embedded video. In *Proceedings of MobiCom*, pages 139–142. ACM, 2013.

[8] T. Langlotz and O. Bimber. Unsynchronized 4D Barcodes Coding and Decoding Time-Multiplexed 2D Colorcodes. In *Proceedings of the International Symposium on Visual Computing*, 2007.

[9] S. Lee, J. Choi, S. Oh, J. Ryu, and J. Park. A real-time 3D IR camera based on hierarchical orthogonal coding. In *Proceedings of IEEE ICRA*. IEEE, 2006.

[10] M. Nakagawa. The world of visible optical communication - It opens with LED — Light Communications. *Kogyo Chosakai Publishing, Inc.*

[11] G. Pang, T. Kwan, H. Liu, and C. Chan. LED Wireless. *IEEE Industry Applications Magazine*, 2002.

[12] S. D. Perli, N. Ahmed, and D. Katabi. PixNet: LCD-camera pairs as communication links. In *Proceedings of MobiCom*, 2010.

[13] D. Reilly, H. Chen, and G. Smolyn. Toward fluid, mobile and ubiquitous interaction with paper using recursive 2D barcodes. In *Proceedings of Workshop on Pervasive Mobile Interaction Devices*, 2007.

[14] M. Werner and M. Schönfeld. DualCodes: Backward Compatible Multi-layer 2D-Barcodes. In *Mobile and Ubiquitous Systems: Computing, Networking, and Services*, pages 25–36. Springer, 2013.

[15] G. Woo, A. Lippman, and R. Raskar. VRCodes: Unobtrusive and Active Visual Codes for Interaction by Exploiting Rolling Shutter. In *IEEE International Symposium on Mixed and Augmented Reality*, 2012.

[16] S. Zhu and B. Zeng. A novel enhancement for hierarchical image coding. *Journal of Visual Communication and Image Representation*, 24(1):12–22, 2013.

It Starts with iGaze: Visual Attention Driven Networking with Smart Glasses

Lan Zhang[1], Xiang-Yang Li[1,2], Wenchao Huang[3], Kebin Liu[1], Shuwei Zong[4]
Xuesi Jian[2], Puchun Feng[1], Taeho Jung[2], Yunhao Liu[1]
[1]School of Software and TNLIST, Tsinghua University, China
[2]Department of Computer Science, Illinois Institute of Technology, USA
[3]Department of Computer Science, University of Science and Technology of China
[4]Department of Computer Science, Suzhou Institute for Advanced Study, China
lan@greenorbs.com, xli@cs.iit.edu, yunhao@greenorbs.com

ABSTRACT

In this work, we explore a new networking mechanism with smart glasses, through which users can express their interest and connect to a target simply by a gaze. Doing this, we attempt to let wearable devices understand human attention and intention, and pair devices carried by users according to such attention and intention. To achieve this ambitious goal, we propose a proof-of-concept system **iGaze**, a visual attention driven networking suite: an **iGaze** glass (hardware), and a networking protocol **VAN** (software). Our glass, **iGaze** glass, is a low-cost head-mounted glass with a camera, orientation sensors, microphone and speakers, which are embedded with our software for visual attention capture and networking. A visual attention driven networking protocol (**VAN**) is carefully designed and implemented. In **VAN**, we design an energy efficient and highly accurate visual attention determination scheme using single camera to capture user's communication interest and a double-matching scheme based on visual direction detection and Doppler effect of acoustic signal to lock the target devices. Using our system, we conduct a series of trials for various application scenarios to demonstrate the effectiveness of our system.

Categories and Subject Descriptors

C.3 [**Special-purpose and application-based systems**]: Real-time and embedded systems

General Terms

Design, Experimentation, Performance

Keywords

Smart Glasses; Attention Driven Networking; Device Paring; Gaze Tracking

1. INTRODUCTION

Emerging wearable computing devices attract extensive attention worldwide. Smart glasses, *e.g.*, Google Glass and Vuzix Smart Glasses, are computerized eyeglasses. They not only are miniature video monitors, but also possess enhanced data processing functionalities. Besides, modern smart glasses are equipped with various sensors, such as gyroscope, accelerometer and GPS, to enrich their capabilities.

Many efforts have been devoted to improve human interfaces on or using smart glasses, *e.g.* controlling smart glasses using relatively simple voice commands, gesture control with a tilt of your head, photo and video capture, viewing and posting social status updates, and navigation. Some smart glasses also include features like augmented reality overlays. However smart glasses are still in the early stage and looking for revolutionary applications.

In this work, we explore a new networking mode with smart glasses that may enable a whole new set of applications. That is, smart glasses are supposed to provide users a novel way to communicate with surrounding physical and cyber world which is driven by their visual attention. We have a vision of the future world which has already been imagined in science fiction films, where people wearing smart glasses can establish network connections with their interest targets simply by a gaze. People can directly send messages to others without exchanging contact information explicitly, retrieve rich information about an object in the field of view[1] freely using their eye gazes. For example, in an academic conference, researchers can exchange information such as research interests by simply looking at each other. In a museum, visitors can obtain the detailed descriptions of an artwork by staring at it. Also, many new features can be brought to the game design, *e.g.*, real-scene role-playing games and interactive games with users in your sight. Moreover, the advertisements can also be significantly enhanced with such augmented reality. When people look at a signboard or product, relevant promotion information can be sent to the potential customers' smart glasses immediately. As a result, the store can provide more precise targeted ads and take advantage of the big impulse buying market [27].

These requirements can hardly be fulfilled by existing network solutions, such as using pre-exchanged identifiers, interest-based methods, gesture-based methods and image recognition. Most traditional networking systems rely on pre-exchanged network identifiers, *e.g.*, email, IP and web account, to start communications. Some interest based systems provide customized information services using the user's profile and mining results of his/her historical behaviors, *e.g.*, [13]. A few gesture-based device pairing approaches [22, 28] attempt to pair devices in proximity. However, those efforts are targeting handhold smart devices, *e.g.*, smart phones. Their requirements for phone displacement (> 20cm) [22]

[1]Using only proximity to retrieve information of an object may overwhelm a user with objects that are not in her vision focus.

MobiCom'14, September 7-11, 2014, Maui, Hawaii, USA.
Copyright 2014 ACM 978-1-4503-2783-1/14/09 ...$15.00.
http://dx.doi.org/10.1145/2639108.2639119.

and movement speed ($2 \sim 6m/s$) [28] are hard to achieve using head-mounted glasses. Besides, certain augmented reality could also be enabled with a world camera in a visual fashion, *e.g.*, using QR codes or object recognition techniques. But, to utilize the QR code, there are restrictions for scanning distances and angles to the target. For example, with a high quality camera (as the one of iPhone 5s) and a big QR code ($10cm \times 10cm$), the code is only scannable within a distance less than 3m and a view angle less than 30°. Worse cameras make the restrictions much stricter. Object recognition usually requires extensive training and is vulnerable to environment noise. It cannot distinguish two objects with the same appearance. More importantly, there could be multiple objects in the user's field of view. Without understanding the true interested target of the user, it is hard to determine which object to connect.

To achieve this future vision, we propose a new way to establish network connections using smart glasses, by which the user can connect to a target simply by a gaze. To this end, we address the following challenges.

1) How to accurately capture the vision plane attention of a user in realtime? Eye gaze is a good clue to represent people's interest and intention [4,5,14,24,25], and smart glasses with the eye camera (*i.e.*, camera capturing images of the user's eye) enable realtime eye movement tracking. In this work we propose to address this problem by inferring the gaze direction of a user from his/her eye movements. The challenges in achieving efficient eye gaze detection lie in three aspects: the bulky hardware and power hungry tracker, the user experience issue and the scalability. Existing state-of-the-art eye gaze determination solutions [11, 18, 20] usually leverage two cameras to conduct 3D reconstruction, which incur high hardware, energy and computation cost for resource limited wearable glasses. A few work need only one camera [7, 9, 12], but they require personalized training or calibration. Instead, our approach is designed to achieve high accuracy with only one low-resolution camera. For better user experience, our solution should put no restriction on the user's movement, and the set up (*e.g.*, calibration) difficulty should be minimum. Besides, we need to reduce power consumption of continuous image capturing and processing. To support these, we develop a low-cost glasses hardware, with an eye camera, a microphone and speakers, which are embedded with our software for visual attention capture.

2) *How to match the target on device plane according to user's visual attention?* In our visual attention driven network, we face the issue of addressing a network device without any pre-exchanged contact information, and match a user's visual target with the target's device. At a high level, we address this problem based on the observation that the direction of user's visual attention (indicated by sightline direction) is consistent with the direction from the user to his/her target, and is also consistent with the direction between smart the glasses worn by them. Technically, we capture the direction of a user's sightline with the onboard sensors and camera. We also capture the direction from user's smart glasses to the target smart glasses by tracking the subtle relative displacement of two head-mounted speakers during arbitrary head movements. It is also a challenge to reduce the negative impact of inaccuracy of earth coordinate and device coordinate system on matching the device directions and eye gaze directions.

In summary, the **contributions** of this work are as follows:

1) painting the vision of a new networking mode in which connections are established following users' visual attention and introducing the first system that enables the user communicate and information exchange with surrounding world simply by a gaze.

2) presenting a novel scheme to capture a user's visual attention and then the visual target. We also propose a Phase Locked

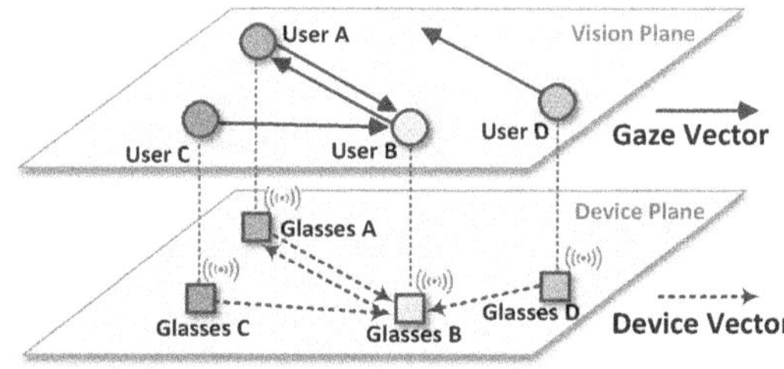

Figure 1: Gaze vectors and device vectors of a visual attention based networking system.

Loop (PLL) based solution to estimate the direction from the user to his/her target leveraging the Doppler effect caused by mild arbitrary head movements. Then we correlate the user's visual target to target smart glasses with a double-matching strategy.

3) designing and implementing a platform, **iGaze**, for the visual attention driven networking, consisting of a set of hardware and software. Our system can accurately capture the user's vision direction and successfully connect the user's device to a target.

4) using the proposed system to conduct a series of trials for various application scenarios to demonstrate the performance of our system. Our extensive user studies show that our system works robustly across individuals. Our lab testing shows that 95% of users attentions are captured correctly by setting the fixation duration window to $0.6s$. The mean error of relative gaze direction computed is less than 5°, and the error in the relative device direction is less than 5° when two users are separated by 4 meters.

2. SYSTEM OVERVIEW

2.1 iGaze Design Space

iGaze is designed to enable a new communication mode for smart glasses users. We focus on making the networking devices smarter that can understand the user's attention and automatically connect to the target of interest.

• **iGaze** has separated and modularized hardware and software design. It can run on top of existing networking protocols, *e.g.*, Wi-Fi.

• **iGaze** applies to scenarios where networking participators do not need to exchange contact information such as IP, email, web account before connecting to each other.

• **iGaze** assumes the initiator is equipped with camera to capture her visual attention at realtime and all participating devices possess computing, networking functionalities and some common sensors, *e.g.*, gyroscope and microphone.

• **iGaze** applies to scenarios where the visual target for communication is relatively static during the connection initialization to achieve high matching accuracy. One of our future works is to enable **iGaze** to locate and connect to mobile targets at a reasonably high moving speed.

Each user is associated with a *co-located* smart device. That is, the device is regarded as being at the same location with its user. In the world through a user' eyes (*vision plane* shown in Fig. 1), there are objects in the field of view and he/she usually gazes at visual targets of interest to him/her, *e.g.*, another user or an artwork. In the cyber world (*device plane* in Fig. 1), a device only "sees" the network identifiers of other devices in proximity, without knowing which one is corresponding to which target in vision plane. The gap between these two planes raises a challenge for our system.

Two types of scenarios are considered in this work: social networking and object-oriented augmented reality. In the first one, the user wears smart glasses and looks around while the glasses are tracking his/her gaze direction. When two users have an eye

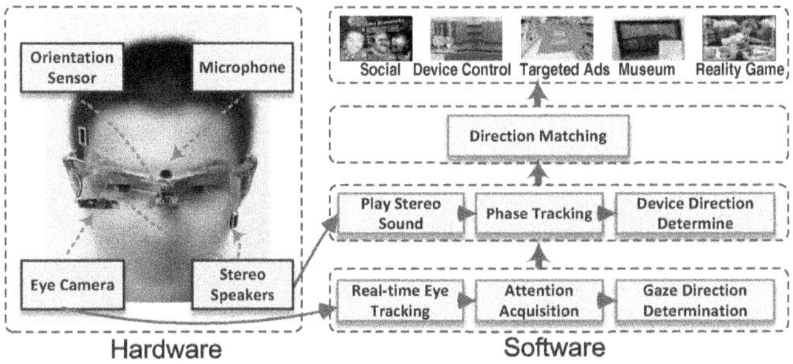

Figure 2: Our smart glasses iGaze prototype.

contact, a network connection is built between their glasses. This scenario is fitted into many social applications. This type of applications require all participating devices to possess eye cameras, and we refer to this mode as *bidirectional* application mode. In the second case, the user wearing smart glasses wants to obtain certain information about the visual target object by gazing it. For example, visitors can obtain the description of an artwork when they gaze at it for a certain time period. In these applications, the target objects need to have devices (without cameras) to respond to the 'gaze query', and we refer to this mode as *unidirectional* application mode.

2.2 Principal of Gaze Based Networking

What we look for is a bond between the vision plane and device plane, which are dissociated currently. Note that finding the gaze direction and finding the direction of pairing devices are themselves challenging tasks. To address this association issue, we raise our idea based on the following observations. As shown in Fig. 1, when a user A is looking at a visual target B, we define the observer A's **gaze vector** as $\mathcal{V}_A$, whose direction is the direction of A's sightline and magnitude is the distance from A to B. In the device plane, we define the **device vector** $\mathcal{U}_{AB}$ as the vector from A's glasses to B's glasses. Both types of vectors can be denoted as a 2-tuple (α, ℓ), where α is the direction and ℓ is the magnitude. We define the concept of *consistency* between a gaze vector and a device vector.

DEFINITION 1. *A gaze vector (α_g, ℓ_g) is said to be* consistent *with a device (or another gaze) vector (α_d, ℓ_d) if their directions and magnitudes hold the following conditions: $|\alpha_g - \alpha_d| < \theta$ and $|\ell_g - \ell_d| < \eta$. Here θ and η are predetermined constants that will impact the false positive and false negative ratios of* ***iGaze*** *in building gaze based connections. We will use θ as the direction consistency threshold in the rest of the paper.*

Two observations help us to design our visual attention driven networking protocol.

OBSERVATION 1. *Given an observer and his/her gaze vector, among all device vectors started from the observer's device, only the device vector to the correct visual target's device is consistent with the gaze vector.*

As an example in Fig. 1, for the observer A, only the device vector $\mathcal{U}_{AB}$ is consistent with the gaze vector $\mathcal{V}_A$. Then in the unidirectional mode, our system learns that device B is the correct match to A's visual target. In the bidirectional mode, establishing a connection requires a pair of users to look at each other. Our system should also confirm that device A is the correct match to B's visual target, *i.e.* $\mathcal{U}_{BA}$ is also consistent with $\mathcal{V}_B$. Note that, $\mathcal{U}_{BA}$ and $\mathcal{U}_{AB}$ have same magnitude and opposite directions. For a practical bidirectional system, since smart glasses continuously capture the direction of the user's sightline, it is not necessary to determine all device vectors from device A to all its neighbors.

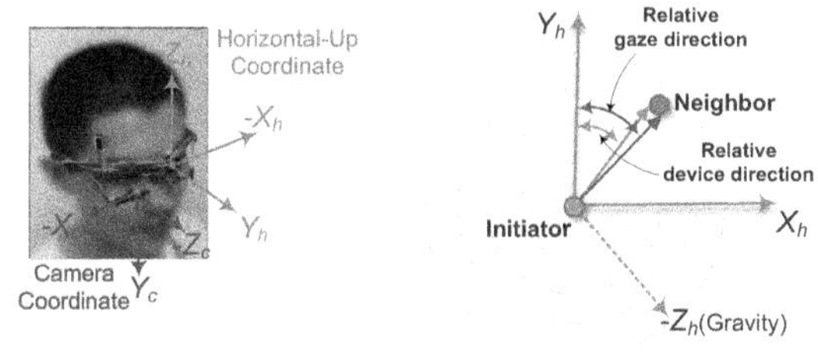

(a) The HU coordinate of our glasses.
(b) Relative gaze/device direction in the HU coordinate.

Figure 3: Direction representation in the HU coordinate system of our glasses.

OBSERVATION 2. *Given a pair of users who are looking at each other, their gaze vectors have opposite directions.*

Taking the scenario in Fig. 1 as an example, both gaze vectors $\mathcal{V}_B$ and $\mathcal{V}_D$ have opposite direction to $\mathcal{V}_A$. Thus user A can firstly exclude user C by the direction of gaze vectors and only compute vectors $\mathcal{U}_{AB}$ and $\mathcal{U}_{AD}$ in the device plane. For bidirectional applications with many users, the first round of sightline direction matching can greatly reduce the overhead in determining pair-wise device vectors.

2.3 System Architecture

Our system includes both software components for visual attention driven networking and the smart glasses hardware.

Software: There are three major building blocks:

• **Gaze vector acquisition**: This component includes three modules. The real-time eye tracking module captures the movement of a user's eye using the eye camera at real-time. Attention acquisition component takes the eye movement data as input to detect a visual attention when the gaze lasts for a reasonable time. The threshold is predetermined and can be dynamically adjusted by users. After a visual attention has been captured, the gaze vector determination calculates the corresponding gaze vector to the visual target. To avoid unwanted paring when eyes happen to be fixed on a certain object, we ask the users to make a mild head gesture (*e.g.*, head nod) as the postfix of the attention.

• **Device vector estimation**: When the user makes a head gesture, his/her smart glasses emit inaudible acoustic signal to adjacent devices. Candidate devices invoke the phase tracking and device direction determination modules to estimate the device vector by exploiting Doppler effect.

• **Visual attention driven networking (VAN)**: It defines the message format and communication process in our visual attention driven networks. **VAN** constructs a connection from initiator to the visual target's device based on the matching results of the gaze vector and device vectors.

Hardware: In this work, we design our own hardware to support the system functionalities as shown in Fig. 2. Limited smart glasses are available on the market with high prices, and their software platforms are diverse. To explore the feasibility and efficiency of our proof-of-concept prototype and conduct multi-user networking experiments, we instrument **iGaze** glass, which is a low-cost head-mounted smart glass. It has an eye camera, an orientation sensor (including a gyroscope and a magnetic sensor), a microphone and two speakers. Using the gyroscope sensor, we can determine the pose of our glasses. The direction of gaze vector is captured by eye camera and the device vector is determined using two speakers, one microphone and the gyroscope.

In order to evaluate the consistency between the gaze vector and device vectors and reduce the negative impact of coordinate conversion, we introduce a temporary coordinate system, named *horizontal-up coordinate* (HU coordinate), which can be determined using only gyroscope. For each round of connection construction, the gaze and device vectors are calculated in the same HU coordinate system. When an initiator's attention is captured, our system uses the pose of the initiator's glasses at this very moment to determine the HU coordinate, whose origin is the origin of his/her gyroscope. Its Z axis always points to the up direction (opposite to the gravity direction) and its X and Y axes lie on the horizontal plane. The X axis is the projection of the line passing through two speakers. Our system also records the current pose of initiator's gyroscope as its initial state. Using the eye camera, we can obtain the gaze direction in *camera coordinate* as shown in Fig. 3(a). As the frame of the glasses is rigid and the relative position between the gyroscope and eye camera is fixed, the gaze vector can be simply transformed from camera coordinate to HU coordinate with known fixed system parameters. The details will be discussed in Section 3. Also, the device vector is determined in HU coordinate using two speakers, one microphone and the gyroscope sensor (Section 4).

As shown in Fig. 3(b), based on Observation 1, we use the HU coordinate instead of the earth coordinate for accurate direction matching. The reasons are two-fold: (1) **iGaze** only needs the relative directions with respect to initiator to match gaze vector and device vector. (2) A gyroscope is enough to determine the device pose in HU coordinate. For the earth coordinate, a magnetic sensor is used to understand north and east, but the accuracy of the magnetic sensor is much lower than the gyroscope. Converting directions in HU coordinate into earth coordinate could cause an accuracy loss.

Note that in the bidirectional mode, based on Observation 2, a coarse matching between the initiator and neighbors is conducted using their gaze directions in the earth coordinate. For this purpose, the gaze directions in the earth coordinate are obtained using the magnetic sensor, and low accuracy (*e.g.*, $\pm 20°$) gaze directions can sufficiently filter a large portion of unlikely candidates. But we still use direction in the HU coordinate for the final match decision.

2.4 Networking Protocol

While a user A is using our glasses, once he/she pays attention to a target, his/her gaze vector pointing to the visual target is obtained. Then the system runs the **VAN** protocol to build a network connection between A and his/her target. Here the user A plays the role of the *initiator* of this protocol. As illustrated in Fig. 4, in a *bidirectional mode*, a connection establishment requires two users to pay attention to each other, and the **VAN** protocol works as the following steps. (1) The initiating **iGaze** glass issues a connection request by broadcasting the direction α_r of his/her gaze vector to all neighbors. Neighboring devices can connect each other using Wi-Fi direct in an Ad Hoc mode, or communicate in the same subnet by joining the same access point (*e.g.*, "Starbucks" or "MobiCom 2014"). In other cases, devices can connect to a server. With a basic location service (*e.g.*, GPS), the server can determine the initiator's neighbors efficiently and transmit messages among them. (2) Every neighbor **iGaze** glass caches this request. Within a gaze direction matching time window, each **iGaze** glass waits for a local visual attention event (*i.e.*, the user is paying attention to an object). If there isn't any event before the expiration time, **VAN** just drops this request, otherwise it compares the direction α_r of the request gaze vector and direction α_l of local gaze vector. Based on the Observation 2, if $\pi - \Theta < |\alpha_r - \alpha_l| < \pi + \Theta$, **VAN** replies the initiator as a *candidate* of the target device and starts to capture acoustic signal using the microphone. Here Θ is larger than the direction consistency threshold θ, since the gaze direction matching uses inaccurate directions in the earth coordinate, and it only aims to filter out noncandidates. (3) The initiator waits for replies until the expiration time. If there are any replies within the time window, the initiator makes a head gesture as an acknowledgement, and meanwhile, his/her **iGaze** glass emits a stereo acoustic signal. (4) Each candidate device receives the signal and calculates the direction β of the device vector from the initiator to itself. Based on the Observation 1, if $|\alpha_r - \beta| < \theta$, then it is the target device and replies an acknowledgement to the initiator. (5) Based on the acknowledgement, the initiator maps his/her gaze vector to the network ID of the target. Then the initiator can obtain information from the target or start a communication between them.

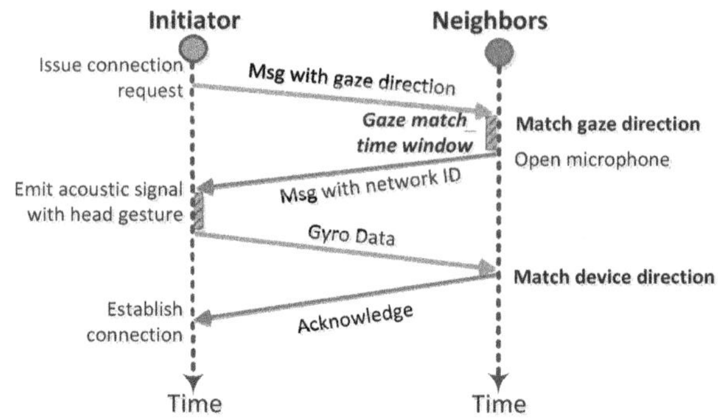

Figure 4: Networking protocol (VAN) after a gaze.

In the unidirectional mode, **VAN** runs similarly as in the bidirectional mode, except the Step (2). In Step (2), each neighbor doesn't wait for a local visual attention event or compare the gaze directions. As soon as it receives the request, it directly replies the initiator as a *candidate* of the target device and starts to capture the acoustic signal.

3. GAZE DIRECTION ACQUISITION

With the eye camera, **iGaze** tracks the iris of the eye and determines the gaze vector. Many sophisticated eye gaze determination solutions, *e.g.* [11, 18, 20], use two cameras for 3D reconstruction to achieve high accuracy. But those methods incur high hardware, energy and computation cost for resource limited wearable glasses. There are a few works that need only one camera [7, 9, 12, 29], but they require personalized training or calibration. To overcome those limitations which may hinder the adoption of gaze tracking techniques for wearable glasses, we design our head-mounted hardware to possess a gyroscope which has fixed relative position to the eye camera. With the hardware, our gaze tracking approach has the following advantages:

- Our glasses achieve sufficient gaze direction accuracy for applications using only one low-resolution camera. Simple geometry model and carefully designed methods are applied to remove the ambiguities caused by single eye image, also to reduce the computation complexity.
- For good user experience, our solution has no restriction on the user's movement. The paring protocol only needs relative gaze direction in the temporary HU coordinate of the glasses, which can be obtained using eye camera and gyroscope. As a result, little manual set up (e.g., calibration) is required for user's convenience.
- Instead of tracking eye movement continuously, we use the gyroscope to detect a head fixation before invoking the camera to capture and process the eye image, which greatly reduces the energy and computation cost. We also detect eye fixation before gaze direction calculation, which saves computation too.

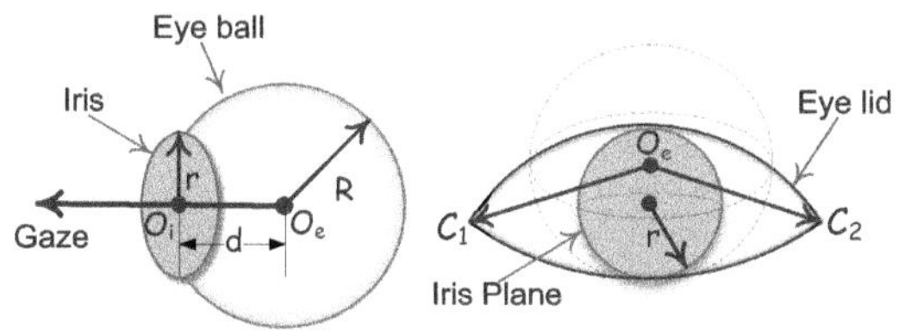

Figure 5: A simplified geometry model of eye.

3.1 Geometry Model for Gaze Detection

Eye model. The structure of eye can be closely approximated using a simple geometry model as presented in Fig. 5. The eyeball is a sphere whose radius is R. The contour of the iris plane is a circle of radius r. The gaze direction can be determined by the optical axis of the eye, which passes through the center of the eye ball O_e and the center of the iris O_i. While the user is looking around, the eyeball rotates around its center O_e and the gaze direction changes.

Projection model. By detecting the iris in the image captured by the eye camera, we get the projection of the iris on the image plane. The projection model is presented in Fig. 6. There are three coordinate systems involved. The origin of the *eye coordinate* is the center of the eye ball O_e. Its X and Y axes lie on the iris plane and the X axis is the intersection line of the iris plane and the horizontal plane. Its Z axis is from the eye ball center O_e to the iris center O_i, *i.e.* the gaze direction. The *camera coordinate* has the principal optical axis as its Z axis. Its X and Y axes are aligned with the axes of the camera's image plane. As presented in Section 2.3, the gaze vector is firstly obtained in camera coordinate and then converted into HU coordinate for comparing with device vectors.

Basic idea. The iris contour is a circle, but its projection on the image plane is elliptical. Intuitively, when the eye looks straight ahead, the projection of iris looks more like a circle; when the eye looks off to one side, it looks more and more close to an ellipse. When the relative position between the eye and camera is fixed, the ellipse parameters are determined by the norm direction or the iris plane, *i.e.* the gaze direction. Based on this idea, we can estimate the pose of the iris circle by back-projecting the ellipse onto a circle in 3D space. The challenge is that with only a single elliptical image, there are many circles satisfying the projection cone. In this work, we remove ambiguities using anthropometric property of eyeball, the hardware position and the principal in [29]. Based on our design, the system requires little manual calibration. Moreover, to reduce computation, we acquire the user's attention before calculating his/her gaze direction. And we further reduce the cost for continuous image capturing and processing greatly by detecting head fixation using gyroscope before opening the camera module.

3.2 Visual Attention Detection

Before calculating the gaze direction, we first detect the user's attention. Many results in the cognitive and neural areas show that attentional and oculomotor processes are tightly integrated at neural level and there is a close relationship between visual attention and eye fixation [4,5,14,24,25]. There are two basic statuses of eye-movement: fixations and saccades. Considering the *fixation* status as the sign of visual attention, we use an eye-movement velocity-threshold method to detect the fixation for its better efficiency over other similar methods [5,24,25]. First, we binarize the image captured by the eye camera with a threshold, and detect the iris area based on its contour. Note that the threshold is calculated by an adaptive algorithm which provides proper thresholds for different eye colors and light conditions. Then, we fit the iris area into an ellipse eye model as in Fig. 6. By detecting the real-time position (I_x, I_y) (Fig. 6) of the iris ellipse, our method calculates the point-to-point eye-movement velocity of two continuous iris images. Within a time window, if the mean of velocities is lower than a given threshold, then it is a fixation, otherwise it is a saccade. Unlike gestures who typically have a prefix (e.g., "OK Glass" of Google Glass) to avoid false alarm rate, gaze lacks such prefix. To avoid false positive detection of the attention, we introduce the head gesture as the user's postfix of his attention, which is also used to detect the device direction (in Section 4).

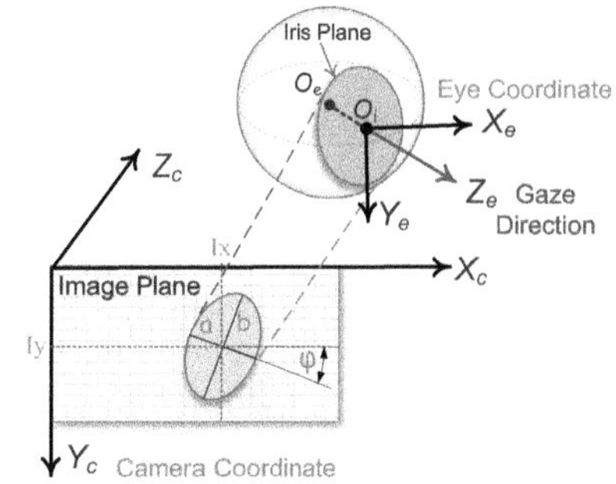

Figure 6: Iris projection on the image plane.

3.3 Direction of Gaze Vector

As soon as a fixation is detected, **VAN** is started to connect the target. At this moment, the HU coordinate system for this round is determined according to the head pose, and the pose of the gyroscope in this HU coordinate is also obtained. Then the iris ellipse of the fixation is used to compute the gaze direction. Let the transformation of the gaze vector from the HU coordinates $\mathcal{V}_h = (x_h, y_h, z_h)$ to the camera coordinates $\mathcal{V}_c = (x_c, y_c, z_c)$ by $\mathcal{V}_c = R_{hc} \cdot \mathcal{V}_h$. In our **iGaze** glass, the relative position between eye camera and the gyroscope is fixed (which is known as a system internal parameter), and the pose of the gyroscope in HU coordinate is known. Hence it is easy to determine R_{hc}.

Now the core issue is to determine gaze direction, *i.e.* the normal direction of the iris plane, in the camera coordinate system from a single elliptical image of the iris. We solve this problem in the following steps. Referring to the projection model in Fig. 6, the projected ellipse in the camera coordinate system is defined by the conic: $\mathbf{v}_c^T A \mathbf{v}_c = 0$. Here A is the conic matrix obtained by applying an affine transformation S to a conic H in the form $A = S^T H S$. Here S and H are determined by the ellipse parameters (Fig. 5) as

$$S = \begin{pmatrix} \cos\phi & -\sin\phi & -I_x\cos\phi + I_y\sin\phi \\ \sin\phi & \cos\phi & -I_x\sin\phi - I_y\cos\phi \\ 0 & 0 & 1 \end{pmatrix},$$

$$H = \begin{pmatrix} \frac{1}{a^2} & 0 & 0 \\ 0 & \frac{1}{b^2} & 0 \\ 0 & 0 & 1 \end{pmatrix}$$

We define the transformation between the eye coordinates and camera coordinates as $\mathbf{v}_c = R_{ec}\mathbf{v}_e + \mathbf{t}$. Here $R_{ec} = (\mathbf{r}_1, \mathbf{r}_2, \mathbf{r}_3)$ is a 3×3 matrix. Given a point in the iris plane $\mathbf{v}_e = (x_e, y_e, 0)^T$, let $\mathbf{u}_e = (x_e, y_e, 1)^T$ be the homogenous coordinate of $\mathbf{v}_e$. With $\mathbf{u}_c = \mathbf{v}_c/z_c = (x_c/z_c, y_c/z_c, 1)^T$ and $G = (\mathbf{r}_1\ \mathbf{r}_2\ \mathbf{t})$, we have

$$z_c\mathbf{u}_c = G\mathbf{u}_e. \tag{1}$$

Using the eyeball model, the back-projected circle in the iris plane is defined by

$$\mathbf{u}_e^T Q \mathbf{u}_e = 0, \text{where } Q = \begin{pmatrix} \frac{1}{r^2} & 0 & 0 \\ 0 & \frac{1}{r^2} & 0 \\ 0 & 0 & 1 \end{pmatrix}. \tag{2}$$

And its projection in image plane should be

$$\mathbf{u}_c^T A \mathbf{u}_c = 0. \quad (3)$$

Combing (1) and (3) yields

$$\mathbf{u}_e^T G^T A G \mathbf{u}_e = 0. \quad (4)$$

Because Eq. (2) and (4) define the same conic, we obtain

$$G^T A G = kQ, \quad (5)$$

here k is an unknown scale factor. Until now, we get the Eq. (5) providing 6 constraints. But there are 8 independent unknowns, three in R_{ec}, three in $\mathbf{t}$, k and r. We are interested in R_{ec} which determines the relation between gaze direction and camera orientation. Since the radius of the iris and eyeball are very close to an anatomical constants (7mm and 13mm) [18], we set $r = 7$ mm to reduce one unknown. Then by solving Eq. (5), we get eight solutions. We impose that, the gaze direction always pointing the front of the head and the iris must lie in front of the image plane, So, six solutions can be eliminated, leaving two solutions that cannot be disambiguated. Call the two solutions as $(\mathcal{V}_1, O_{i1})$ and $(\mathcal{V}_2, O_{i2})$, each solution consists of the gaze vector and the center of the iris. To eliminate the other incorrect solutions, we apply the principal in [29], that the distance between the two corners of an eye and the center of the eyeball O_e should be equal. Hence, as shown in Fig. 5, $O_eC_1 = O_eC_2$ must be satisfied. Also we have $d = \sqrt{(R^2 - r^2)} = 11mm$. With each solution, we get the center of the eye ball O_e in 3D space, and compute a pair of O_eC_1 and O_eC_2. If $|O_{e1}C_1 - O_{e1}C_2| < |O_{e2}C_1 - O_{e2}C_2|$, then $(\mathcal{V}_1, O_{i1})$ is chosen as the solution, otherwise $(\mathcal{V}_2, O_{i2})$ is the solution.

With this technique, we achieve sufficient gaze direction accuracy using one eye camera with low computation cost. In our system implementation, we further reduce the computation and energy overhead by detecting a head fixation using gyroscope before image capturing and processing, and we will discuss the detail in Section 5.

4. DEVICES DIRECTION ACQUISITION

In **VAN**, as shown in Fig. 4, after the gaze direction matching phase, the initiator needs to determine the direction of the device. There are a few methods proposed to estimate device direction by measuring relative displacements [22, 28]. However, those efforts target handhold smart devices, *e.g.*, smart phones. The ranging based methods usually require large phone displacement, *e.g.*, larger than 20cm [22], and the Doppler effect based methods require high movement speed, *e.g.*, $2 \sim 6m/s$ [28], both of which are hard to achieve by head-mounted glasses. For smart glasses, the new challenge is to precisely estimate device direction with arbitrary mild (small amplitude and speed) head movements which make the Doppler effect very subtle to measure.

Facing this challenge, we propose to track the subtle relative displacement of two head-mounted speakers, *i.e.*, variants of distance between the speakers and the receiver, based on the Phase Locked Loop (PLL) technique. Specifically, when the initiator makes a head gesture, *e.g.*, head nod, two speakers of our glasses broadcast a binaural signal with two sine waves at different frequencies, which are at high-frequency channels and inaudible to human. When a target device receives these signals, the frequency of each signal is shifted due to the Doppler effects. By PLL, the receiver can track the precise phase of the received signal, where the phase shift is in proportion to relative displacement. In this way, the measuring accuracy of the relative displacement is less than $1mm$, with a small distance between the two speakers, *i.e.*, $18cm$. Finally, we obtain the relative direction of the receiver to the initiator by studying its relation with the relative displacement. With our method, any form of head gestures are supported. Considering that too complicated gestures may impose inconvenience for users, our system provides two simple gestures, head nod and shake, as the default setting.

In the rest of this section, we present details of our techniques for relative displacement tracking and direction measuring.

4.1 Tracking Relative Displacement

Assume the source broadcasts non-audible sine wave at frequency f_a. Meanwhile, the source is moving towards the receiver at velocity v while the receiver is static. Then, the frequency f_r of received sine wave is shifted due to Doppler effects. Specifically, $f_r = \frac{v_a}{v_a - v} f_a$, where v_a is traveling speed of sound. Hence, the frequency shift $f = f_r - f_a = \frac{v}{v_a - v} f_a$. In our case, since $v \ll v_a$, $f \approx \frac{f_a}{v_a} v$.

We then deduce the relationship between phase shift and relative displacement (from the acoustic source to the receiver). Assume the emitted signal is $s(t) = \sin(2\pi f_a t)$. Due to Doppler effects, we model the received signal as

$$r(t) = \sin(2\pi f_a t + \phi_t) \quad (6)$$

Here, ϕ_t is the phase of the received signal with $\frac{d\phi_t}{dt} = 2\pi f(t) = 2\pi \frac{f_a}{v_a} v(t)$. Hence, when the source moves from place A_1 to place A_2 (with $\|A_1A_2\| \leq$ half of wavelength) and the receiver is at place R, the relative displacement is

$$d = \|RA_1\| - \|RA_2\| = \frac{v_a}{2\pi f_a}(\phi_{t_1} - \phi_{t_2}) \quad (7)$$

where ϕ_{t_1} and ϕ_{t_2} denote the phase of the received signal when the source is at place A_1 and A_2 respectively. Therefore, the relative displacement can be inferred from the calculated phase which is further detailed in the next subsection.

4.2 Tracking the Phase of Received Signal

We calculate the real-time phase ϕ_t from the received signal. To track the phase from $r(t)$, the received signal needs to be preprocessed. More specifically, the actual received signal before preprocessing is denoted as $r_0(t) = A_t \sin(2\pi f_a t + \phi_t) + \sigma_t$, where σ_t is the noise and A_t is the changing amplitude. The original signal $r_0(t)$ first passes through the Band Pass Filter (BPF) to remove the noise σ_t. Then, the filtered signal reshapes its wave by using Automatic Gain Control (AGC) [23]. After that, the changing amplitude A_t becomes approximately constant 1, which means A_t is also eliminated and the processed signal is then close to $r(t)$. Finally, we use Phase Locked Loop (PLL) [1] to calculate the real-time phase ϕ_t from $r(t)$ in Eq. (6). To get the precise ϕ_t, we update an adaptive estimation of ϕ_t in real time, denoted as $\theta[k]$, to achieve that $\theta[k] \approx \phi_t$, where $t = kT_s$ and T_s is the sampling period of audio recording. To make θ converge to ϕ after enough iterations, we define the corresponding function $J_{PLL}(\theta)$ such that J_{PLL} converges to its maximum at the same time when θ converges to ϕ. We update $\theta[k]$ in the iterations as $\theta[k+1] = \theta[k] + \mu \frac{dJ_{PLL}}{d\theta}$, where μ is a small positive constant that determines the speed of convergence in the iteration. According to [1], we choose $J_{PLL}(\theta) = \text{LPF}\{r(t)\cos(2\pi f_a t + \theta(t))\}$. Here, LPF is the Low Pass Filter which excludes high frequency component. The estimation of $\theta[k]$ is $\theta[k+1] = \theta[k] - \mu\text{LPF}\{r[k]\sin(2\pi f_a k T_s + \theta[k])\}$.

4.3 Measuring Device Direction

We then show how to measure direction in HU coordinate from initiator S to receiver R using relative displacement.

Notice that an **iGaze** glass S has two speakers, denoted as S_l and S_r. Denote the distance from R to S_l and S_r as l_l and l_r respectively. Hence, l_l and l_r change continually when the device

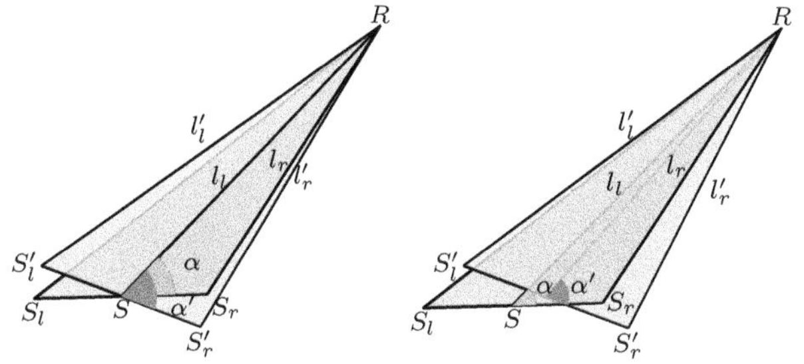

(a) Case 1. (b) Case 2.

Figure 7: Computing direction from device S to device R

S is moving. In other words, there are relative displacements $d_l = l_l - l_l'$ and $d_r = l_r - l_r'$ and they can be tracked in real time. Furthermore, the relative displacements are then used to calculate the direction by combining the tracked relative displacement and the real-time direction of S_lS_r. The other input is the distance of the two speakers $\varpi = |S_lS_r|$. Therefore, $|S_lS| = |SS_r| = \frac{\varpi}{2}$. We also let S be the midpoint of line segment S_lS_r. Assume that the direction of S_lS_r and SR at the projection of horizontal plane in WCS is β and γ. Then γ is the target angle we calculate. Assume $\hat{\alpha}$ is the projection of α at the horizontal plane. Since $\gamma = \beta + \hat{\alpha}$ and β can be obtained from inertial sensors of the mobile device (*i.e.*, gyroscope, accelerometer), we can calculate the angle α from which γ is indirectly obtained. To illustrate our method in detail, we first consider a simple case (case 1) and then a more general case (case 2) as follows.

Case 1: Two speakers rotate around the midpoint S of two speakers in 3D space, shown in Fig. 7(a).

Hence, the distance $l = |SR|$ does not change when rotating. Actually in this case, only one speaker is needed for calculating α. For instance, we use the relative displacement of speaker at S_2. According to the law of cosines,

$$\begin{cases} l_r^2 = l^2 + \frac{\varpi^2}{4} - \varpi l \cos\alpha \\ l_r'^2 = l^2 + \frac{\varpi^2}{4} - \varpi l \cos\alpha' \end{cases} \tag{8}$$

In our case, l is from 2m to 8m and $|S_lS_r|/2 < 0.09m$ that l is much larger than $|S_lS_r|/2$. Moreover, in our experiment, we use the calculated displacement d_r at the time interval of 0.01s that $|d_r| = |l_r - l_r'| < 0.01s * 1m/s = 0.01m$. Hence, it can be inferred that $l_r \approx l_r' \approx l$.

From Eq. (8), we have $\varpi \cos\alpha' - \varpi \cos\alpha - 2d_r \approx 0$. Note that α' can be calculated by gyroscope if α is given. Hence, for the series of tracked d_r and gyroscope data, α can be estimated from this equation by Maximum Likelihood Estimation.

Case 2: Two speakers rotate arbitrarily around any point in 3D space, as in Fig. 7(b). The point it rotates around may change arbitrarily when moving.

A key observation here is that the movement of **iGaze** glass can be decomposed into two movements: rotation around midpoint and translational movement, and the relative displacement caused by rotating component is very small (*i.e.*, less than $\frac{18}{2}$cm). Consequently, the displacement component caused by translational movement becomes relatively high. To address the challenge raised by possible arbitrary head movement, we utilize the relative displacements of two speakers (*i.e.*, d_l, d_r), and $d_l - d_r$ eliminates the displacement resulting from translational movement. Hence, we can infer an equation

$$\varpi \cos\alpha' - \varpi \cos\alpha + d_l - d_r \approx 0 \tag{9}$$

As a result, similar to Case 1, we estimate the angle α using this equation and finally obtain the device direction γ.

Component	Description
Raspberry Pi II	700MHz CPU, 512MB RAM, Linux
Eye Camera	Maximum Resolution 640x480 @ 30fps
Gyroscope	MPU6050, 6-axis, Accuracy - 0.01°
Magnetic Sensor	3-axis, Accuracy - $512c/G$
Wi-Fi	OURLINK, 300Mbps, USB port
Microphone	Sample rate 44100Hz
Stereo Speakers	Frequency range 180Hz-20KHz

Table 1: Specifications of iGaze glass

5. PROTOTYPE IMPLEMENTATION

Establishing network connection based on visual attention is an unexplored mode of communication. We design and implement a proof-of-concept smart glasses prototype system, named **iGaze**, to start network connection with the visual target. **iGaze** consists of a low-cost smart glasses hardware and a set of software. The system architecture is illustrated in Fig. 2. After we address the challenges of determining gaze direction in Section 3 and device direction in Section 4, here we present the hardware and software design issues and the implementation specifications.

5.1 Hardware Prototype

Fig. 2 illustrates our prototype hardware. To obtain gaze direction, **iGaze** glass has a fixed eye camera tracking the eye movement. It is 3cm away from the eye. A fixed gyroscope is embedded in the front-head position of the glasses to determine device pose in the HU coordinate and simplify the coordinate transformation. A magnetic sensor is co-located with the gyroscope, which is only used in the bidirectional mode to exclude unlikely neighbors with gaze direction. For the devices direction, **iGaze** glass has a central microphone and two separated speakers with a fixed distance (18cm).

A platform is required for the data processing, which should be light-weight and convenient for various **iGaze** applications development. In our implementation, we use Raspberry Pi with a Wi-Fi module. It is a credit-card-sized single-board computer with Linux operating system. All head-mounted sensors are connected to its hardware data interfaces. It supports a wide range of programming languages, *e.g.* Python, C++, Java and Perl. Our prototype system is mainly designed to explore the feasibility of visual attention based network connection establishment. And the current version of our glasses doesn't have a head-mounted screen. The data received and processed by Raspberry Pi can be accessed by any smart device with a screen (*e.g.*, smart phone, pad and laptop) via wireless channel in real time. The specifications of **iGaze** glass is presented in Table 1.

5.2 Software Prototype and Key Parameters

We implement all software blocks of **iGaze** for Linux using C++. It supports both unidirectional and bidirectional application modes. In the unidirectional mode, the target could also be a device without an eye camera. So we also implement the device direction estimation and **VAN** for Android system using Java, which enables our glasses to connect an android device in unidirectional applications. The visual attention acquisition components are developed based on the OpenCV library.

Specifically, the eye camera captures images at the frequency of 30fps with a low resolution 320×240. To identify visual attention, the eye movement velocity threshold is set to 20pixes/s in the scale of the eye image and the detection time window is set to 0.6s. We will further analyze these two parameters in Section 6. In the unidirectional mode, the initiator nods head after he/she pay attention to a target as a postfix of attention. But for the bidirectional mode, there is a gaze direction matching phase. Once there are replies from coarsely matched users, our system uses a beep to inform the initiator to nod his/her head. While the initiator nods head, the speakers play a binaural acoustic signal consisting of two inaudible high frequency sine waves. In the default setting, the left track is 19KHz and the right track is 19.5KHz. For the wireless communication of **VAN**, both AP and Ad Hoc modes are implemented.

In our implementation, we improve our software to address the challenge that, the smart glasses are resource limited, while image processing could be computation-intensive and power-hungry. We use a trick to reduce the overhead in real-time eye-tracking, while keeping the attention acquisition accuracy. We observe the data of orientation sensor of 30 volunteers and notice that, when a user is paying attention to a visual target, his/her head is usually in a fixation status. Specifically, the orientation changes around three axes (especially the Z axis) show plateaus during the staring. Analyzing orientation data (sample rate is 50Hz) is much more efficient than processing the video. So, in our system, eye tracking only starts when the variance of three orientations are within a threshold for a small time window. In our experiments, the time window is 10 samples (0.2s). With this improvement, significant computation and energy cost for image processing can be saved.

There is also another implementation issue that needs to be addressed: when a receiver computes his/her direction to the initiator, the acoustic wave is recorded by the receiver while the corresponding glasses orientation samples are from the initiator's **iGaze** glass. Before calculating the direction, the acoustic wave and orientation samples need fine-grained synchronization. As **iGaze** glass records orientation sensor samples exactly when it is broadcasting the acoustic signal, so the challenge is to locate the start time of the initiator's sine signal in the recorded noisy wave. We observe the sequence of relative displacements of two speakers changes smoothly if they are calculated using the expected sine signal, otherwise, it jitters severely. To achieve coarse-grained synchronization, we divide the displacement sequence into segments and calculate the standard deviation (std) of each segment and find the segment from which the std falls below a threshold, *i.e.*, the start time of the initiator's sine signal. Specifically, each segment contains 500 consecutive calculated displacements (about 0.01s), and the threshold is set to 0.2cm. Then we refine the synchronization by adding the synchronization error as an unknown to the Maximum likelihood Estimation of the device direction. That is, we make Maximum likelihood Estimation according to Eq. (9) with 2 unknowns: the synchronization error and the pair-wise direction. In our experiment, we find that the coarse-grained synchronization achieves a very small error (within 0.15s). And the refinement further reduces the error with little overhead due to small searching space.

We develop two applications for system evaluation: (1) a social application in bidirectional mode, by which people gaze at each other to express their intention for friending. Once a pair of users are matched successfully, they follow each other on Twitter automatically. (2) a smart device application in unidirectional mode, by which a user looks at a sensor among various sensors placed on desks, a connection between them is built and the real-time sensing data is sent to the user.

6. EXPERIMENTS AND EVALUATION

We evaluate **iGaze** by measuring the micro-benchmark performance and studying two typical applications.

6.1 Micro Benchmark

We investigate the following metrics: accuracy of gaze direction and device direction, and power consumption.

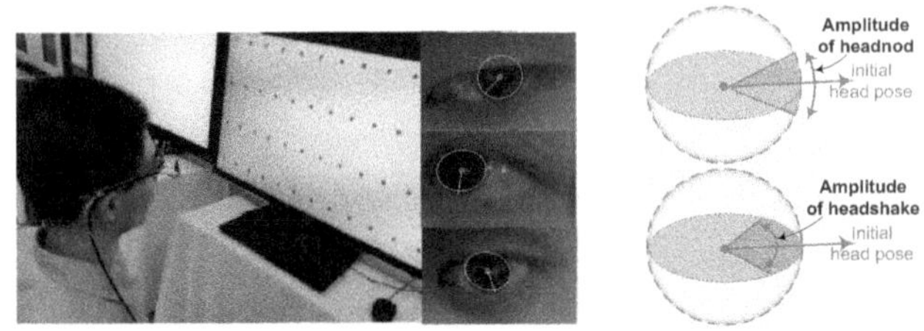

(a) Gaze capture. (b) Head gestures amplitude.

Figure 8: Experiment and samples of gaze capture, and amplitude of two basic head gestures.

6.1.1 Gaze Direction Accuracy

In this part, we evaluate the accuracy of our attention acquisition and relative gaze direction (as shown in Fig. 3(b)) estimation methods with the help of a large screen (47-inch). The screen displays marks which are separated from each other with a fixed distance. We have 30 volunteers (12 female and 18 male) wearing **iGaze** to pay attention to these marks in sequence, while **iGaze** is capturing their eye movements. Fig. 8(a) shows the experiments scenario and samples of our eye tracking results. Note that, the gaze direction accuracy is equivalent to the angle resolution of **iGaze**. So the distance to the screen won't effect the accuracy measurement. Before each run, the relative position between **iGaze** and the screen is recorded and the volunteer changes his/her attention by rotating eye ball. For each volunteer, about 100 gaze data are collected.

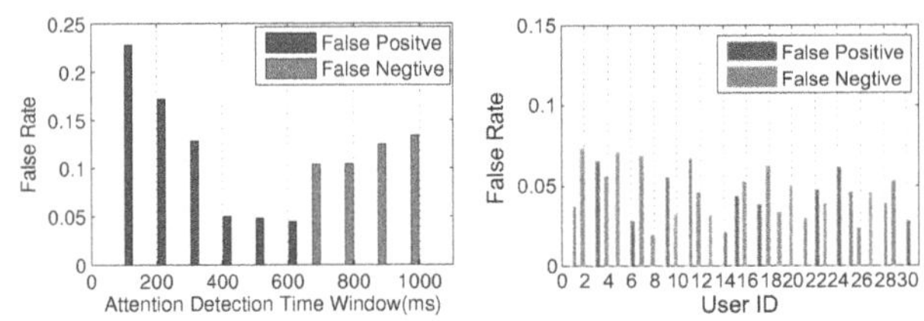

(a) False rate vs time window. (b) False rate vs users.

Figure 9: False positive and negative of attention detection against different time windows and users.

To get the true attention, we manually label their eye tracking data by asking volunteers to hit the blank key when they are paying attention to a marker. Two factors determine the accuracy of attention detection: attention detection time window and the eye movement velocity threshold. Fig. 9(a) presents the relationship between the time window and false rate. As the time window is getting larger, the false positive reduces while false negative increases. In the following experiments, we choose the window size when the two false metrics are equal (0.6s in our experiments). Obviously, larger threshold will cause higher false positive. However, the threshold setting could be tricky due to anatomical diversity. As shown in Fig.9(b), when we set the threshold to 20 pixels/second for our glasses, the accuracy varies among users. In the worst case, the false negative is 7% for the user No.2. But overall the correct attention detection ratio is $\simeq 95\%$.

It is difficult to obtain the true gaze direction of people. As a result, we test the equivalent angle resolution of **iGaze** by adjusting the density of markers on the screen, and estimating the marker the volunteer is paying attention to. We get the error range of calculated gaze direction by comparing the estimated markers with the true sequence. The highest resolution we test is 5°, *i.e.*, from the volunteer's view these markers are 5° separated from each other. And in this case, the ratio of correctly estimated markers are about 91%. About 8% estimated markers are incorrect, but they are ad-

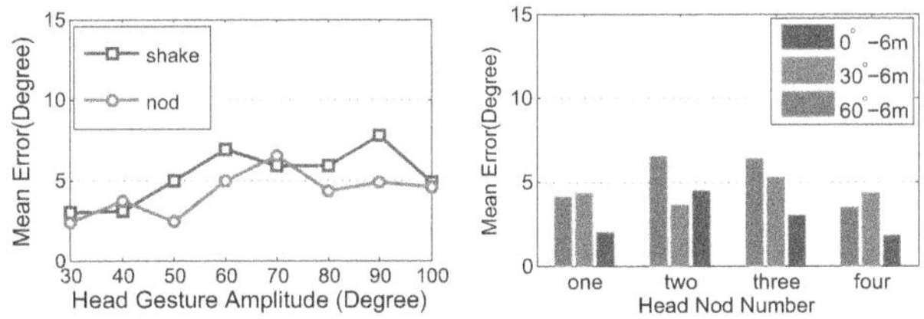

(a) Gesture amplitude. (b) Gesture number.

Figure 10: Device direction error v.s. head gesture patterns.

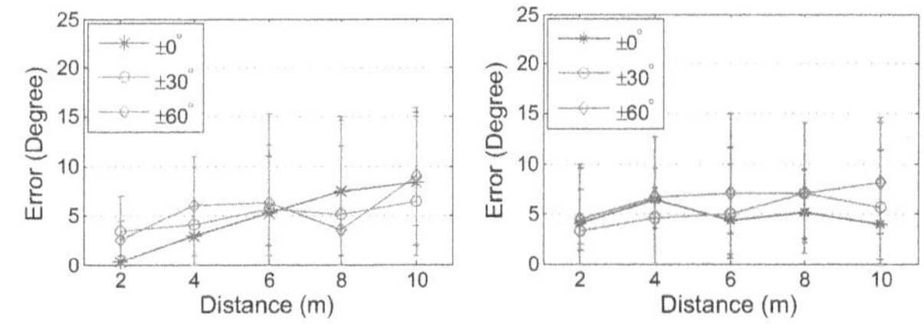

(a) Head nod. (b) Head shake.

Figure 11: Device direction error v.s. distance.

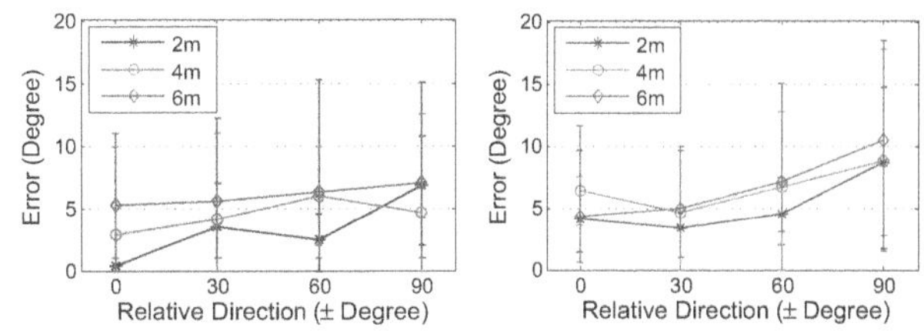

(a) Head nod. (b) Head shake.

Figure 12: Device direction error v.s. relative angle.

jacent to the correct markers. It means that, the error of the gaze direction is within $5°$ for 91% cases, and less than $10°$ for other 8% cases. For the rest 1% cases, the largest deviation is $15°$. The current version of **iGaze** has a lower accuracy than some sophisticated solutions [11, 18, 20]. For example, a recent work use two camera for 3D reconstruction [11] to achieve $1°$ accuracy. But energy, computation cost and user experience are crucial factors for practical wearable devices, and image capturing and processing are especially power-hungry and computation-intensive. As a tradeoff, **iGaze** achieves sufficient accuracy for most social and augment reality applications with only one camera and requiring little manual calibration. With our modularization design, any future advance in gaze direction estimation can be adopted as the building block of iGaze.

6.1.2 Device Direction Accuracy

The speaker from the initiator emits a stereo acoustic signal while he/she makes a head gesture for a receiver to estimate their relative direction. Our system provides two default simple head gestures for users, head nod and shake. As illustrated in Fig. 8(b), the *amplitude of head gesture* defines the maximum angle to what extent the user nods/shakes his/her head. The *relative direction* defines the angle between the direction from *sender* to *receiver* and the orientation that the sender is facing in the HU coordinate, as shown in Fig. 3(b). We conduct a set of experiments in a $200m^2$ hall in an office building to measure the estimation accuracy. We have 30 volunteers to act as the initiator and nod/shake his/her head freely. One receiver records the signal at different distances and relative directions to the initiator. For each relative position, the experiment is repeated for 10 runs and these positions are manually marked as ground truth. First we investigate an interesting and important question that how sensitive is the estimation to the head gesture pattern of the initiator. Here, for the pattern, we refer to the gesture's amplitude and number. These factors affect the initiator's user experience since it is uncomfortable for user to move head drastically.

Pattern of head gesture. We test the impact of different head gesture patterns on the device direction accuracy under several fixed combinations of the device distance and relative direction. In the first test, the head gesture number for one round is fixed to two, and each volunteer runs the test with 20 times free head nod and 20 times free head shake. The amplitudes are calculated by head mounted gyroscope. We find diverse amplitudes among different users. Fig. 10(a) presents the mean direction error against different amplitudes for both nod and shake. The result shows that, fixing other variables, the direction estimation is not sensitive to the amplitude, and high accuracy (error $\leq 4°$) can be achieved with only a mild nod/shake ($\leq 30°$). In the second test, volunteers are asked to nod/shake their heads for different number of times. Due to user experience, we only evaluate the head nod/shake number up to 4. The results are depicted in Fig. 10(b). The estimation accuracy does not show an accuracy improvement with increasing head nod number and it is the same case for the head shake gesture. The reasons are two-fold: first, one head nod/shake has provided sufficient information to achieve high direction accuracy; second, the gyro data has a drift increasing with time which could cancel the benefit of more samples or even reduce the accuracy. In conclusion, our device direction estimation is robust against different head gestures and patterns and only one mild head gesture is sufficient for highly accurate estimation.

With free head gesture patterns, two factors affect the accuracy: distance and relative direction between devices. We evaluate one factor at a time while fixing the other.

Distance between devices:

Experiments are conducted to evaluate the impact of device distance on the direction accuracy with fixed relative device direction. At each distance, experiments are repeated 20 times for each head gesture. The results are plotted in Fig. 11 and show that for both head nod and shake gestures, our method achieves less than $5°$ error within 4 meters and achieves less than $9°$ error within 10 meters. It outperforms [22] whose accuracy is $10°$ with a 1m distance and [28] whose accuracy is $30°$ with a 4m distance. It implies that we can distinguish two targets ($4m$ away from initiator) whom are separated by $30cm$. As expected, when the distance gets larger, the accuracy decreases. But the error is still less than $15°$ in the worst case when the relative direction is less than $\pm 90°$. The increasing error is caused by the multi-path effect for indoor environment and signal energy reduction.

Relative direction between devices: Then we fix the device distance to evaluate the relationship between direction accuracy and the receiver's relative direction to the sender. The results are plotted in Fig. 12. We find that, as the relative direction increases, there is higher chance that the receiver suffers a Non-Line of Sight (NLoS) acoustic signal. The NLoS effect reduces accuracy of measured relative displacement and the latter device direction. For the head shake gesture, the mean error increases from $6°$ to $10°$ when the relative direction changes from $0°$ to $\pm 90°$. Head nodding suffers less from the NLoS effect, and its mean error remains less than $7°$ within the $\pm 90°$ range. However, when the receiver moves to the back of the initiator, the accuracy declines sharply and the estimation tends to look like random since no emitted acoustic signal can directly arrive at the receiver. To remove potential mismatches caused by this effect, we notice that, when the minimum

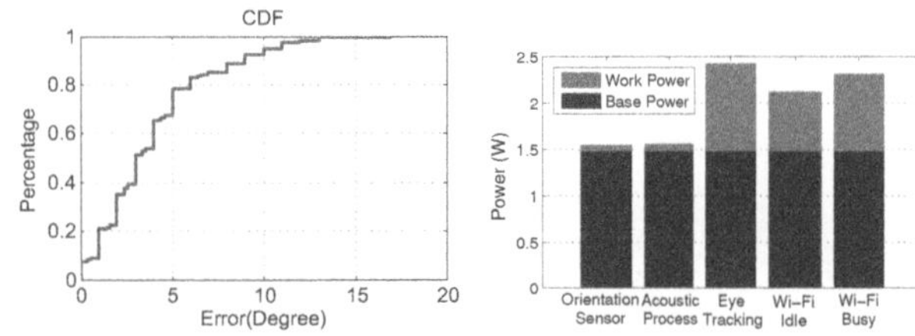

(a) device direction error (b) Energy consumption

Figure 13: Device direction error and energy consumption of each module.

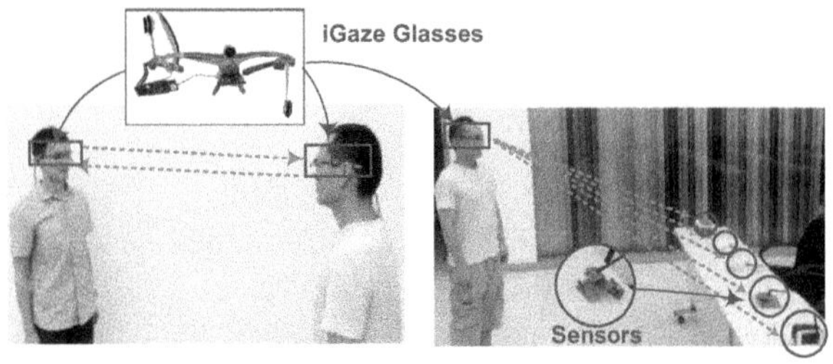

Figure 14: Experiment scenarios of two cases: social application (left), smart device application (right).

value, which is the result of Maximum Likelihood Estimation using Eq. (9), is higher than a threshold, it infers that the calculated device displacement is noisy and the estimated direction is not accurate. So **iGaze** sets a threshold on the minimum value and a receiver can find that his/her position is at the back of the initiator.

By placing the receivers uniformly in the initiator's field of view within range of 10m, we measure the overall accuracy of the device direction estimation. The initiator can nod or shake head as he/she likes. With 30 volunteers, there are 300 runs in total, and Fig. 13(a) plots the result. For 80% cases, the device direction error is less than 5° and for 95% cases, the device direction error is less than 10°.

6.1.3 Computing Cost and Energy Consumption

We evaluate the computation cost (delay) by measuring the runtime of each component. It takes the Raspberry Pi about 30 ms to process one eye image to obtain the gaze direction, including iris ellipse fitting and gaze vector calculation. To process the one-second acoustic signal and gyro data to get the device direction, the Raspberry Pi needs about 200 ms. Other computations (*e.g.*, coordinate conversion and direction matching) are negligible. As a conclusion, all computing of our system are completed in realtime.

We evaluate the energy cost of **iGaze** by measuring the current and voltage using oscilloscope. To test the power consumption of each component, firstly we test the base power of our glasses when all sensors and communication modules are off and no software component is running. Then, we run a single component each time while other components are off and test its power consumption. Fig. 13(b) plots measurement results. As expected, the orientation sensor (including a gyroscope and a magnetic sensor) and our device direction estimation component are quite power-saving, and the eye tracking component costs much more energy than them. Hence, as presented in Section 5, we improve the implementation of **iGaze** to greatly reduce the energy waste for unwanted image processing by filtering out saccade periods according to the real-time gyroscope status. With a normal 2600mAh lithium battery, iGaze can work continuously for about 5 hours when Wi-Fi module is always on, and eye camera is on for half the time (*i.e.*, the user's head is fixed for half the time).

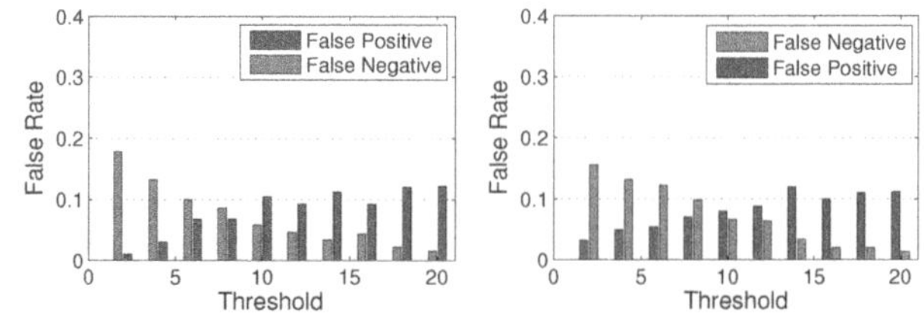

(a) Social case. (b) Smart device case.

Figure 15: False positive and false negative changes with consistency threshold for two cases.

6.2 Case Based System Evaluation

Understanding the performance of each component, we then evaluate the integrated system by case studies. Two cases are considered: *social case* and *smart device case*. In the social case, we have 4 volunteers wearing **iGaze**, two of them pay attention to each other to build a networking. They change their relative position freely in a $100m^2$ room to evaluate the system performance. In the smart device case, 8 environment sensors are placed 50 cm apart from each other. 30 volunteers wearing **iGaze** pay attention to a sensor to "read" its real-time sensing data in the unidirectional mode. Fig.14 shows the experiment scenarios of two cases.

We are interested in the following metrics: communication cost, delay and connection correctness. For the social networking establishment, communication cost is mainly caused by transmitting the gyroscope data during emitting the acoustic signal to potential targets. One-second gyro data is 600B. The other data packets only contain gaze direction, network ID and acknowledge respectively. As presented in Section 6.1.3, the delay caused by computation is only about 230ms. In real applications, the wait time is mainly caused by human factors, including the time for paying attention and head nodding. For example, for our social application it is reasonable to require mutual 1s long attention before starting friending. In our smart device case, the attention detection time window is set to 600ms. The time window for attention acquisition can be adjusted for different applications and users. For the social case, before playing acoustic signal, because there is a mutual gaze matching phase, the initiator will be informed to nod his/her head by a beep if there is any coarsely matched users, *i.e.*, someone is looking back at him/her. The reaction time varies between individuals, and in our experiments it is less than 1s for 90% cases. For the smart device case, the initiator just nods head after he/she pays attention to a device. A 1s acoustic signal is sufficient for one head nod. Considering the human factors, in most cases a connection can be built within about 3 seconds from the initiator starts to pay attention to a target.

The connection correctness is determined by the accuracy of the gaze direction and device directions inherently. But the consistency threshold θ determines the false rate of the system output. Fig. 15 shows the false positive and false negative of two cases by changing the setting of the consistency threshold. Here the false positive is the case that a connection is established with a wrong target; and false negative is the case that a small threshold makes the correct target fail to match and no connection is built. We see that, in our two cases, with a proper threshold, false positive is less than 3% while the false negative is about 15%.

7. DISCUSSION AND OPEN ISSUES

The design and instrumentation of a computational smart eyeglasses platform, such as **iGaze**, is extremely complex due to the challenges incurred by noisy sensor data, the mounting and wearing positions of the frame, and uncontrollable user movement. Visual attention driven based networking, interaction, and control is a barely explored area. While our evaluations demonstrate that **iGaze** is promising, there are a few steps to take before such kind of platforms is ready to practical use with scalability.

Intention Capture and Understanding: In this work, a key component is to capture and understand the user visual intention. This is clearly a daunting task even for human being. Our initial implementation takes advantage of some simplified assumptions such as that user will not move her/his head much when he/she is interested in networking or an object. However, in practice, the head might move around during conversation while the eye might continue to track the interested object. Sometimes, in the gaze direction there may exist multiple objects (*e.g.*, side by side, or one being in front of another). In contrary, multiple users may be interested in a same object, thus, some sort of collision avoidance protocol need to be designed in **VAN**. Furthermore, a user may be interested in a moving object, *e.g.*, moving vehicles and running people. Our platform needs to develop new methods that can successfully address these dynamics. Possible solutions are to incorporate a distance estimation module to estimate the distance between two devices, *e.g.*, the method in [32], incorporate a light-weighted efficient gaze tracking using eye-camera only.

Privacy and Security Considerations: A key factor that may impact the adoption of smart glasses is their privacy and security implications. In this work, our main focus is on the functionality and feasibility of our prototype, so we apply some simple strategies to protect various aspects of privacies. For example, when the gazed target is an object, users may turn off the unidirectional mode to avoid unwanted contact (such as SPAM). However, advanced privacy-preserving protocols can be integrated into our system to achieve the following security-related properties. (1)our system can provide a "do-not-track" setting for users who do not want to be connected by others; (2) various profile matching protocols (*e.g.*, [31]) can be introduced to verify the identity of the users to prevent Man-In-The-Middle attack or impersonate attack; (3) some proof/verification protocols can be leveraged to allow users to verify the correctness of the information provided by other users so that no malicious users can fake their directions. Other device-based key extraction protocols can also be adopted, *e.g.*, [30]. Clearly, security implications that will emerge when smart glasses become popular are not limited to above three, and many of them are very challenging. We leave them as our future works to pursue due to the space limit.

Others: While our current proof-of-concept platform operates at low power with COTS devices, considerable performance improvements are possible by using a hardware-only instrumentation. We note that an equally important design issue is the aesthetic perspective of the **iGaze** design, while aesthetic design aspects are beyond the scope of this work. In future platforms, we have to consider where to place these sensors, speakers, and cameras. We need a graceful tradeoff between functionality and the aesthetic design.

8. RELATED WORK

iGaze is related to existing works in the following areas:

Vision-based augment reality systems. Vision related techniques have been widely applied in augment reality systems. Abe et al. [2] propose a methodology to retrieve real-time information from the web. Ha et al. [8] present a scalable vision-based object tracking method for mobile augmented reality systems. Malik et al. [15] study the problem of vision-based pattern tracking with real-time video feeds. [21] uses a head mounted world camera to model the gaze cone and focuses on finding people looking at the same target using image processing techniques. Without eye tracking, it cannot understand the connection intention of people. It works poorly when people are looking at each other and cannot establish a connection to the visual target either.

Gaze tracking. Gaze-tracking technique is an important part of those vision-based systems. Most of those works use multiple cameras. For example, Newman et al. [18] propose to use two cameras and a face model of the user. Ohno and Mukawa [20] use one camera to track the pose of the head and another infra-red camera to capture the pupil location. In those work, a personalized calibration is needed by seeing some markers on the screen. Shih et al. [26] propose a gaze tracking technique without calibration. At least two cameras and at least two point light sources are needed for this solution. Methods requiring multiple cameras incur high hardware, energy and computation cost for wearable glasses. There are a few single camera based gaze tracking techniques. Nishino and Narya [19] use ellipse models for gaze estimation. Wang et al. [29] determine the gaze direction with an iris geometrical model. Starburst [12] only needs a single infra-red camera, it uses RANSAC fit and the model-based optimization to make higher accurate. Hennessey et al. [9] propose a single-camera eye-tracking system with free head motion. Personalized calibration is also required in all the above methods. For the ease of use, we need to minimize manual calibration, and the computation cost must be further reduced for resource limited wearable glasses.

Devices pairing. In our system, we gather the gaze direction information in order to make it as an evidence for pairing two devices together. Although so many devices pairing methods have been proposed, but our solution is tailored for smart glasses and convenient with the well-collected vision information. In general, pairing methods can be classified into three groups: key sharing, measuring the same local environment data and out-of-band(OOB) authentication. OOB is currently the most promising and practical way. For example, Balfanz et al. [3] use "Pre-Authentication" on location-limited channel to do identity authentication. McCune et al. [17] leverage camera-screen as the OOB channel and the QR code as the evidence to make pairing. There are methods based on audio [6] or accelerometers [16] as the OOB channel. Those approaches require a face-to-face communication between people before initiating a pairing procedure. Some "throw and share" applications have been raised recently. Point&Connect [22] offers a device pairing solution when a user points his/her phone towards the intended target. It understands the target selection by measuring maximum distance change based on acoustic signals. Due to that it is range based and has limited raging accuracy (about 7mm), it requires a larger than 20cm displacement towards the target to achieve 90% correctness. Spartacus [28] uses Doppler effect to start an interaction with a neighboring device through a gesture. It uses FFT to calculate speed which suffers time-frequency resolution problem. Hence, it requires a high speed of phone movement ($2 \sim 6$ m/s). Both the large displacement and speed can hardly be achieved by head-mounted devices. Swadloon [10] also uses Doppler effect to find accurate device direction, but it requires phone movement in a horizontal plane. **iGaze** uses Phase Locked Loop (PLL) to track the relative displacement of two head-mounted speakers at high resolution (far less than 1mm) and it outperforms related work for arbitrary mild head movement.

9. CONCLUSION

In this work, we present **iGaze**, a first-of-its-kind low power smart glass that is designed to support vision driven networking by tracking the gaze in realtime and correctly pairing users' devices when mutual gazes happen. This paper presents a soup-to-nuts instrumentation of such a system, including a complete hardware prototype, a full implementation of a suite of software for gaze detection, device pairing and networking. We extensively evaluate our system on several subjects. Our results show that **iGaze** supports accurate real time networking by a gaze. Our design is highly significant as it paves a way for more exciting ubiquitous vision driven applications, including interest-targeted mobile advertising, reality-augmented interactive gaming, and behavior-based cyber-physical systems.

10. ACKNOWLEDGMENTS

This research is partially supported by NSFC under Grant No. 61125020, NSFC CERG-61361166009. The research of Li is partially supported by NSF CNS-1035894, NSF ECCS-1247944, NSF ECCS-1343306, NSFC under Grants No. 61170216, No. 61228202. We thank all the reviewers for their valuable comments and helpful suggestions.

11. REFERENCES

[1] *Telecommunication Breakdown; Concepts of communication Transmitted via Software-Defined Radio.*

[2] ABE, N., OOGAMI, W., SHIMADA, A., NAGAHARA, H., AND TANIGUCHI, R. Clickable real world: Interaction with real-world landmarks using mobile phone camera. In *IEEE TENCON* (2010).

[3] BALFANZ, D., SMETTERS, D. K., STEWART, P., AND WONG, H. C. Talking to strangers: Authentication in ad-hoc wireless networks. In *NDSS* (2002).

[4] CORBETTA, M., AKBUDAK, E., CONTURO, T. E., SNYDER, A. Z., OLLINGER, J. M., DRURY, H. A., LINENWEBER, M. R., PETERSEN, S. E., RAICHLE, M. E., VAN ESSEN, D. C., ET AL. A common network of functional areas for attention and eye movements. *Neuron 21*, 4 (1998), 761–773.

[5] ERKELENS, C. J., AND VOGELS, I. M. The initial direction and landing position of saccades. *Studies in Visual Information Processing 6* (1995), 133–144.

[6] GOODRICH, M. T., SIRIVIANOS, M., SOLIS, J., TSUDIK, G., AND UZUN, E. Loud and clear: Human-verifiable authentication based on audio. In *ICDCS* (2006), IEEE.

[7] GOSS, D. A., AND WEST, R. W. *Introduction to the Optics of the Eye*. Butterworth-Heinemann Medical, 2001.

[8] HA, J., CHO, K., AND YANG, H. S. Scalable recognition and tracking for mobile augmented reality. In *SIGGRAPH* (2010), ACM, pp. 155–160.

[9] HENNESSEY, C., NOUREDDIN, B., AND LAWRENCE, P. A single camera eye-gaze tracking system with free head motion. In *ETRA* (2006), ACM.

[10] HUANG, W., XIONG, Y., LI, X., LIN, H., MAO, X., YANG, P., AND LIU, Y. Shake and walk: Acoustic direction finding and fine-grained indoor localization using smartphones. In *Infocom* (2014), IEEE.

[11] KOHLBECHER, S., BARDINST, S., BARTL, K., SCHNEIDER, E., POITSCHKE, T., AND ABLASSMEIER, M. Calibration-free eye tracking by reconstruction of the pupil ellipse in 3d space. In *ETRA* (2008), ACM.

[12] LI, D., WINFIELD, D., AND PARKHURST, D. J. Starburst: A hybrid algorithm for video-based eye tracking combining feature-based and model-based approaches. In *CVPR Workshops* (2005), IEEE, pp. 79–79.

[13] LI, Z., WANG, C., JIANG, C., AND LI, X.-Y. Lass: Local-activity and social-similarity based data forwarding in mobile social networks. *TPDS* (2013).

[14] LIVERSEDGE, S. P., AND FINDLAY, J. M. Saccadic eye movements and cognition. *Trends in cognitive sciences 4*, 1 (2000), 6–14.

[15] MALIK, S., MCDONALD, C., AND ROTH, G. Hand tracking for interactive pattern-based augmented reality.

[16] MAYRHOFER, R., AND GELLERSEN, H. Shake well before use: Authentication based on accelerometer data. In *Pervasive computing*. Springer, 2007, pp. 144–161.

[17] MCCUNE, J. M., PERRIG, A., AND REITER, M. K. Seeing-is-believing: Using camera phones for human-verifiable authentication. In *S&Privacy* (2005), IEEE.

[18] NEWMAN, R., MATSUMOTO, Y., ROUGEAUX, S., AND ZELINSKY, A. Real-time stereo tracking for head pose and gaze estimation. In *International Conference on Automatic Face and Gesture Recognition* (2000), IEEE, pp. 122–128.

[19] NISHINO, K., AND NAYAR, S. K. Eyes for relighting. In *ACM Transactions on Graphics* (2004), vol. 23, pp. 704–711.

[20] OHNO, T., AND MUKAWA, N. A free-head, simple calibration, gaze tracking system that enables gaze-based interaction. In *ETRA* (2004), ACM.

[21] PARK, H. S., JAIN, E., AND SHEIKH, Y. 3d social saliency from head-mounted cameras. In *Advances in Neural Information Processing Systems* (2012), pp. 431–439.

[22] PENG, C., SHEN, G., ZHANG, Y., AND LU, S. Point&connect: intention-based device pairing for mobile phone users. In *MobiSys* (2009), ACM, pp. 137–150.

[23] RICE, M. *Digital Communications: A Discrete-Time Approach*. Prentice Hall, 2008.

[24] SALVUCCI, D. D., AND GOLDBERG, J. H. Identifying fixations and saccades in eye-tracking protocols. In *ETRA* (2000).

[25] SEN, T., AND MEGAW, T. The effects of task variables and prolonged performance on saccadic eye movement parameters. *Advances in Psychology 22* (1984), 103–111.

[26] SHIH, S.-W., WU, Y.-T., AND LIU, J. A calibration-free gaze tracking technique. In *International Conference on Pattern Recognition* (2000), vol. 4, IEEE, pp. 201–204.

[27] STERN, H. The significance of impulse buying today. *The Journal of Marketing* (1962), 59–62.

[28] SUN, Z., PUROHIT, A., BOSE, R., AND ZHANG, P. Spartacus: spatially-aware interaction for mobile devices through energy-efficient audio sensing. In *MobiSys* (2013).

[29] WANG, J., SUNG, E., AND VENKATESWARLU, R. Eye gaze estimation from a single image of one eye. In *International Conference on Computer Vision* (2003), IEEE, pp. 136–143.

[30] XI, W., LI, X.-Y., QIAN, C., HAN, J., TANG, S., ZHAO, J., AND ZHAO, K. Keep: Fast secret key extraction protocol for d2d communication. In *IWQoS* (2014), IEEE.

[31] ZHANG, L., LI, X.-Y., AND LIU, Y. Message in a sealed bottle: Privacy preserving friending in social networks. In *ICDCS* (2013), IEEE.

[32] ZHANG, L., LIU, K., JIANG, Y., LI, X.-Y., LIU, Y., AND YANG, P. Montage: Combine frames with movement continuity for realtime multi-user tracking. In *Infocom* (2014), IEEE.

Wireless Barcodes for Tagging Infrastructure

Farnoosh Moshir
Department of Computer Science
Portland State University
Portland, OR 97207
moshir2@pdx.edu

Suresh Singh
Department of Computer Science
Portland State University
Portland, OR 97207
singh@cs.pdx.edu

ABSTRACT

There are numerous scenarios where embedding static information into objects would prove to be very useful. For example, by embedding navigation information into the road surface we could enable driverless cars, similarly embedding information into major infrastructure such as building walls would enable easier classification of debris, and so forth. The key requirement is that the embedded information should survive as long as the infrastructure itself. We discuss the concept of wireless barcodes that allow us to achieve exactly this goal of tagging infrastructure. The barcodes are designed to be read at terahertz frequencies that allows good packing of information (bits/m). We use a TDoA (Time Difference of Arrival) technique to read the barcodes which provides robustness to wear and tear of the surface. This paper reports on the results of an experimental study that examines the challenges in building such barcodes and demonstrates the idea by constructing such a barcode.

Categories and Subject Descriptors

H.4 [**Information Systems Applications**]: Miscellaneous; C.2.1 [**Computer Communication Networks**]: Network Architecture and Design—*Wireless communication*

Keywords

Barcodes; Propagation; Terahertz

1. INTRODUCTION

Imagine a scenario where Alice is traveling in her driverless car and encounters thick fog on the isolated mountain road. Her car comes to a stop because there are no visual cues and the GPS signal is blocked by the high valley walls. In another scenario, Bob is driving along and comes to an old interesting bridge. He would like to know more about it but there are no plaques. In both these examples incorporating information into the road or the bridge would help with navigation in Alice's case and allow Bob to learn more about the bridge's history. This paper develops the concept of embedding information into infrastructure with the property that the information is as long lived as the infrastructure itself and the information can be read wirelessly. Thus, in the case of the driverless car, if we can embed *static* navigation information such as speed, steering angle, road gradient etc. into the road at periodic intervals, the car could continue driving in bad conditions. Similarly, by embedding information about the bridge into its structure, we could ensure future generations could directly read information about the bridge.

Our approach for embedding information is based on the concept of optical barcodes. However, our wireless barcodes are different in that they are read using RF and information is encoded in the accurate estimation of relative distance as opposed to intensity, as in optical barcodes. Our wireless barcodes are also entirely different from RFID tags since we use no electronic component in the wireless barcode. It is instructive to see why optical barcodes or RFID tags would be unsuitable in the two examples given previously. Optical barcodes cannot work in the presence of any form of visual impairment and they are not long lived in outdoor environments since information is stored in difference in light intensity (and possibly color). RFID tags are electronic and as such have limited life that is drastically reduced due to exposure to weather (for instance capacitors have limited life due to deterioration of the dielectric see http://www.illinoiscapacitor.com/ tech-center/life-calculators.aspx).

1.1 Wireless Barcodes

The idea behind wireless barcodes is explained in Figure 1 where we see a signal hitting a surface which is in the shape of a step of depth d. Assuming normal incidence, the path travelled by the two reflections differ by $2d$. We can use the difference in arrival times of the two signals to embed information. If the bandwidth of the signal is large then time difference of arrival (TDoA) between the two signals will provide a reliable way of encoding information allowing us to create a barcode by using different values of d. For example, Figure 2 illustrates a barcode consisting of four *symbols* s_i each of which corresponds to a different d. In the figure we have indicated a reference surface and the information surfaces. The symbol s_i is determined based on the TDoA of the signal reflected off the *information surface* with respect to the signal reflected off the *reference surface*. If D different depths d can be reliably identified using TDoA then, in the above example, we have embedded $4 \times \log_2 D$

MobiCom'14, September 7-11, 2014, Maui, Hawaii, USA.
Copyright 2014 ACM 978-1-4503-2783-1/14/09 ...$15.00.
http://dx.doi.org/10.1145/2639108.2639125.

bits of information. *Note that we need to use a reference surface because the distance between the barcode reader and the barcode can vary as a car drives or due to hand shake.*

Let us return to the driverless car scenario from earlier. Imagine that we embed small plastic tags in the center of the lane of a road at some spacing. The material used can be similar to the plastic reflectors that are embedded at lane boundaries in many of the roads today. The tag contains a thin strip of reflective material (reflective to the frequency band being used) in a pattern that embeds information as in Figure 2. As the car drives along, a reader at the bottom of the car reads the embedded *static* information and passes it up to the navigation hardware. Thus, even in zero visibility conditions the car will be able to travel safely. In the bridge example, we could construct the barcode in the cement surface as a series of dips at a corner of the structure. A hand held reader, perhaps using a radio built into the smartphone, would be able to read the coded information.

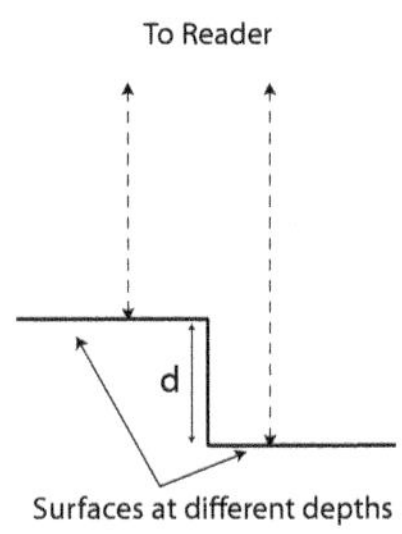

Figure 1: Encoding data using physical deformations.

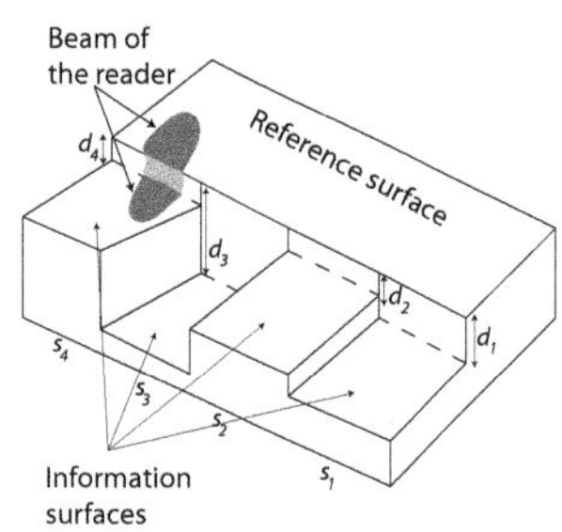

Figure 2: Example of a tag embedded in the road for navigation hints.

The size of the barcodes, specifically values of d, will affect the usability of wireless barcodes in general. For instance, it is unrealistic to use barcodes with d values in the range of several centimeters for car navigation or even labeling bridges because of the large size of the barcodes. In this paper we develop barcodes with d values measured in millimeters using terahertz radio frequencies where the large bandwidth gives us the needed precision for measuring TDoA.

1.2 Contributions and Paper Organization

In the next section we study the challenges in building barcodes based on the idea of TDoA and use Matlab simulations to illustrate the key points. Specifically, we discuss the impact of bandwidth, surface roughness and radio power on the key design parameters of barcodes. Section 3 presents the barcode design and barcode reader algorithm. Section 4 provides experimental measurements of barcode symbols built out of cement and copper. In section 4.3 we describe a prototype barcode built using copper and demonstrate the entire concept developed in this paper. We summarize optical barcodes, RFIDs, passive RF tags, chipless RF tags and terahertz tags in section 5. We conclude in section 6.

2. CHALLENGES

There are many possible designs for barcodes that use the idea of encoding data using TDoA including 2D barcodes. However, all these designs are conceptually similar and therefore we focus only on linear barcodes. We assume

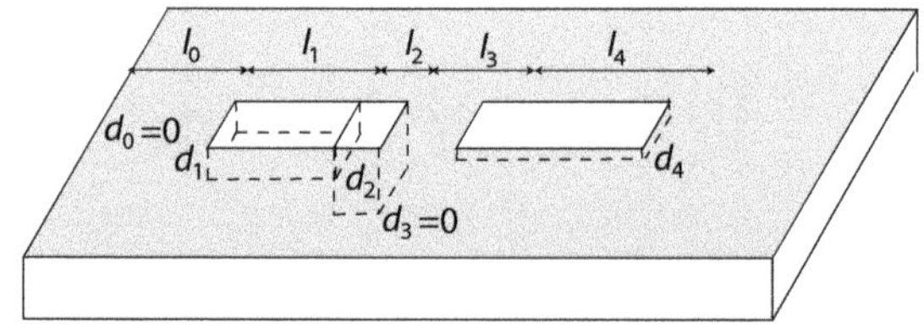

Figure 3: Example of a linear wireless barcode.

that the barcode reader emits a narrow *collimated beam*[1] and the beam is moved over the barcode to read the symbols. This is similar to pen-type optical barcode readers and *for this section we assume that the beam is very narrow.* Figure 3 illustrates a linear barcode where five symbols have been encoded: $< d_0, l_0 >, < d_1, l_1 >, < d_2, l_2 >, < d_3, l_3 >, < d_4, l_4 >$. In this example we use the length as well as depth to encode a symbol. If a barcode reader can distinguish between D different depths$\Delta\ d, 2\Delta d, \cdots, D\Delta d$ and between K different lengths$\Delta\ l, 2\Delta l, \cdots, K\Delta l$ then we have a total of DK possible symbols each of which can encode $\log_2 DK$ bits.

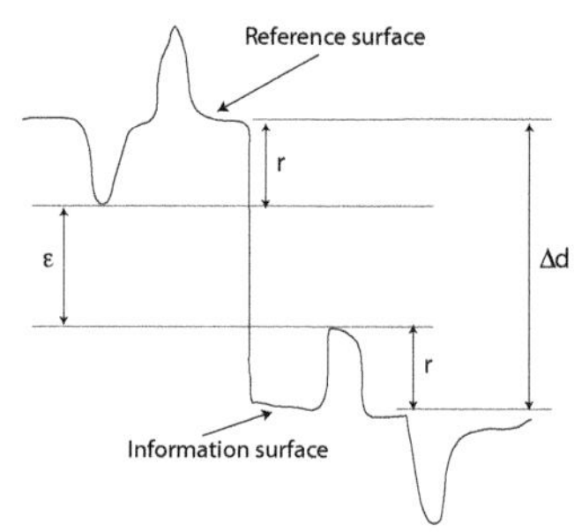

Figure 4: Relation of roughness to Δd.

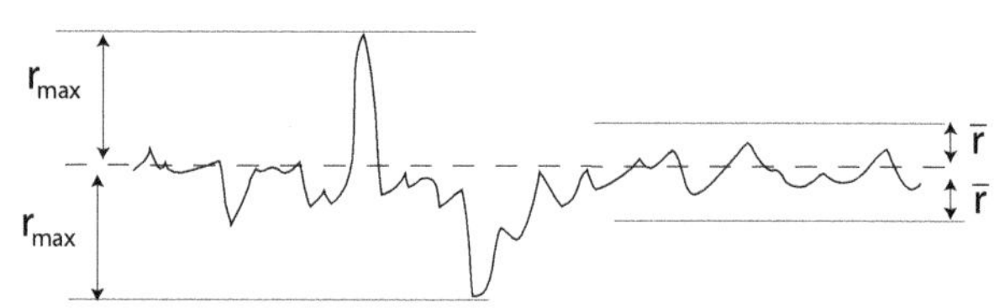

Figure 5: A 1D rough surface.

There are several factors that affect the selection of minimum depth$\Delta\ d$ and minimum length$\Delta\ l$. The signal transmitted by the barcode reader may suffer from frequency-specific attenuation in the atmosphere as well as absorption and scattering in the material that forms the barcode. Indeed, the effective bandwidth used to read the barcode may well be smaller than the bandwidth of the transmitted signal. Given a reflected bandwidth of B Hz, the problem of ranging using radio echos in radar systems provides us with a lower bound on the minimum measurable$\Delta\ d$ using TDoA techniques. If the bandwidth of the signal is B Hz then the minimal distance ϵ between two targets that can be

[1] A collimated beam is one where the focus of the beam is at infinity and the diameter of the beam is the diameter of the collimating lens. Collimating beams at optical or terahertz frequencies have minimal divergence at small distances.

measured is roughly $\epsilon \propto c/2B$ meters where c is the speed of propagation [5]. For instance, if the signal reflected off the barcode has a bandwidth of 1 GHz we get $\epsilon > 15$ cm whereas, if the bandwidth is 300 GHz, then we get a more practical value $\epsilon > 0.5$ mm.

Unfortunately, we cannot expect wireless barcodes to be etched on perfectly reflective surfaces. Indeed, given the environments that motivate this research, we should expect the surfaces to be rough. Figure 4 illustrates a worst case scenario where the reference surface as well as the information surface are rough. In the figure we quantify the roughness by the maximum size of a peak or valley on the surface by r. Based on this figure, we can thus develop an estimate for Δd as the inequality:$\Delta\ d > \epsilon + 2r$. However, this estimate may be very pessimistic if the surface has mostly smaller bumps and valleys. A more useful model is to use the mean of r [2, 17]. For sake of explanation let us consider a one dimensional surface shown in Figure 5. Given a 90° angle of incidence of the reader signal, the time difference of arrival of various reflections off this surface will differ by up to $4r_{\max}/c$ where c is the propagation speed (this is because the maximum depth difference is $2r_{\max}$ that is doubled for round-trip time). However, an overwhelming majority of the reflected signal will arrive in a smaller time window $4\bar{r}/c$. In this case, a smaller value$\Delta\ d > 2\bar{r} + \epsilon$ is sufficient.

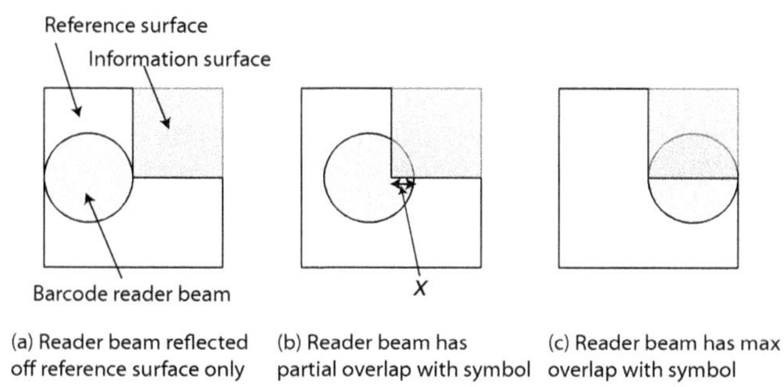

Figure 6: Detecting the start of a symbol.

The ability of the reader to detect the start and end of a symbol provides a lower bound on$\Delta\ l$. Consider Figure 6 where we illustrate a top view of the barcode and reader beam. The symbol is shown by the shaded box (assume it is at depth d). In Figure 6(a) the barcode reader will detect only one reflected signal of intensity P_0. In position Figure 6(b) there are two reflected signals – one from the reference surface at intensity P_r and another from the information surface P_i. As the barcode reader beam moves to the right, P_r decreases while P_i increases as shown in Figure 6(c) when the two intensities are the same. In order to detect the start of the symbol as early as possible (to minimize error in estimating l) we need to consider three factors:

- $d > \Delta d$ to detect the symbol. Indeed if d is large then the start of the symbol can be detected earlier (for a smaller P_i) because the reflection from the information surface will be well-separated in time from the reflection from the reference surface allowing even a weak signal to be detected.

- The relative intensity $P_i/P_r > \tau(d)$ (for some threshold $\tau(d)$) in order to detect the start of the signal. As noted above, this threshold could well be dependent on d with a smaller threshold being sufficient for larger values of d.

- The total signal intensity P_0 should exceed some minimal threshold as well so that P_i/P_r is not obfuscated by noise.

- Surface roughness (denoted as σ) will diffuse the reflected signals causing two effects – a smaller value of P_i and P_r as well as spreading in time of the received signal due to variable path lengths followed by different components.

2.1 Simulation Study

In order to examine the inter-dependence between signal intensity P_0, bandwidth B, depth d, roughness σ and detecting the start of a symbol we conducted a simulation study in which we used two bandwidths of 10 GHz and 300 GHz. We generate a pulse and then filter it using a raised cosine filter with a roll off factor of 1 to obtain the necessary bandwidth. We consider two cases for the reflected signals – one in which the reflective surface is perfect (only noise is added) and another in which the surface is rough. We examine the perfect reflective case first to study the relationship between P_0, B, d and$\Delta\ l$. Subsequently we add in a rough surface and study how this impacts the earlier analysis.

For the perfect reflective surface case, the signal received by the barcode reader $s(t)$ from a symbol at depth d can be written as,

$$\begin{aligned}
&s(t) = s_r(t) + s_i(t - t_i), \text{ where } t_i = \tfrac{2d}{c} \\
&s_r(t) = \sqrt{\tfrac{P_r}{P_0}}\, s_0(t) \\
&s_i(t - t_i) = \sqrt{\tfrac{P_i}{P_0}}\, s_0(t - t_i) \\
&|s_0(t)|^2 = P_0
\end{aligned}$$

where P_r, P_i denotes the intensity of the signal from the reference surface and information surface respectively.

In order to identify the location of the reflections from the reference and from the information surface, we cross-correlate the received signal $s(t)$ with $s_0(t)$. Note that all barcodes indicate the start of the barcode with special symbols. In our case, we can start the barcode with just the reference surface which gives us $s_0(t)$. We compute,

$$\begin{aligned}
s_0(t) \star s(t) &= s_0(t) \star \sqrt{\tfrac{P_r}{P_0}}\, s_0(t) + s_0(t) \star \sqrt{\tfrac{P_i}{P_0}}\, s_0(t - t_i) \\
&= \sqrt{\tfrac{P_r}{P_0}} \int_{-\infty}^{\infty} s_0(\tau) s(t + \tau) d\tau + \\
&\quad \sqrt{\tfrac{P_i}{P_0}} \int_{-\infty}^{\infty} s_0(\tau) s(t + \tau - t_i) d\tau
\end{aligned}$$

This results in the time reversed correlation plot with two peaks corresponding to the information symbol and the reference. We apply a linear scan to the correlation data to identify these peaks (via thresholding), compute the time difference between these peaks and infer the value of d (Figures 16 and 17 show the time domain and cross-correlation plots for reading a symbol made from cement).

Relationship between$\Delta\ d, P_0, B$:

As a first step in our analysis, we illuminated the symbol with half the reader beam as shown in Figure 6(c). Using this setting we then determine the minimum depth$\Delta\ d$ that can be reliably read for different values of P_0 and bandwidth. Figure 7 plots the minimum value of$\Delta\ d$ versus P_0. The first observation is that in all cases, the power of the reader has a significant impact onΔ d. This is to be expected since at small values ofΔ d the time separation of the two reflections is small and can be easily overwhelmed by noise. The second observation is that a larger bandwidth results in smallerΔ d for all power values which is due to the inverse relationship between TDoA estimation and bandwidth. For a 300 GHz bandwidth, we can detect depths of as little as 0.4mm while with a 10 GHz bandwidth we can go no smaller than 8.1 mm.

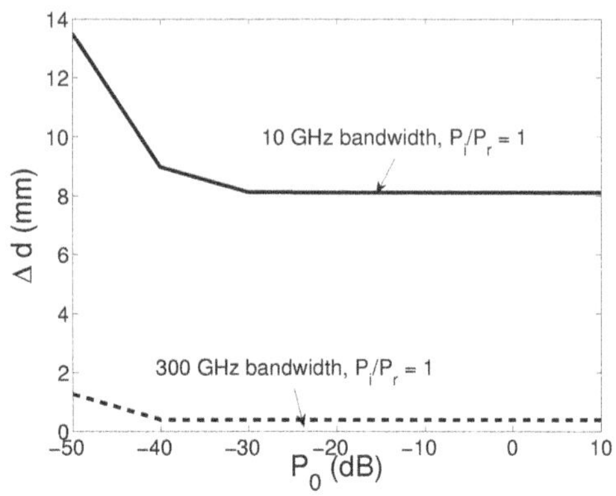

Figure 7: Min Δd versus power P_0 when $P_i/P_r = 1$.

Relationship betweenΔ $l, P_0, P_i/P_r$:

Let us use $d = 1, 2$ mm for $B = 300$ GHz andΔ $d = 15$ mm for $B = 10$ GHz in order to determine lower bounds forΔ l. Referring to Figure 6(b) we note a small overlap of the reader beam with the symbol. The value ofΔ l is the smallest x in the figure at which the reader can detect the symbol. As is evident, detecting the symbol is dependent on P_0 as well as the ratio P_i/P_r. This relationship is plotted in Figure 8 where we plot the *minimum* value of P_i/P_r needed to detect the symbol for different P_0. When P_0 is small, we need almost 50% coverage of the symbol as shown in Figure 6(c) to be able to detect the symbol. Clearly in this case, the error in determining the actual start of the symbol is of the order of the beam radius. As P_0 increases past -30 dB, however, the symbols can be reliably detected when the ratio is quite small. For the 10 GHz case, the symbol can be detected when $P_i/P_r > -23$ dB while for 300 GHz, $P_i/P_r > -33$ dB is sufficient when $d = 1$ mm and $P_i/P_r > -36$ dB is sufficient when $d = 2$ mm. Note that the greater the depth d the lower the relative signal intensity needed. This makes sense since the time separation between the reference and information symbols is better allowing detection even at low power values.

If we assume a circular reader beam of radius 1 cm then we can use the minimum P_i/P_r values from above to determine the minimum value ofΔ l at which point we can detect the start of a symbol. This is done simply by relating the signal intensity ratio to the ratio of the area of the symbol covered by the reader beam to the area of the covered reference surface. Figure 9 plotsΔ l versus P_0. As we can see for 10 GHz,Δ $l > 0.6$ mm while for 300 GHz the values are either 0.2 mm for $d =$ 1mm or 0.1 mm for $d = 2$ mm.

Relationship of roughness σ onΔ l:

Finally, we study the impact of a non-smooth surface on Δl assuming that $P_0 = 0$ dB and $B = 300$ GHz. The rough-

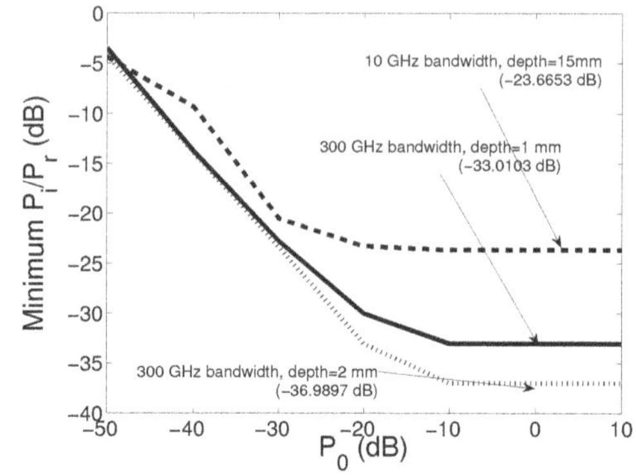

Figure 8: Minimum P_i/P_r to detect the symbol.

ness of the surface at terahertz frequencies is well modeled by a truncated zero-mean Gaussian distribution [8]. Let us assume that the random variable r from Figure 4 takes equally spaced discrete values in some range $r \in R = [-r', +r']$. For a given σ we obtain a truncated zero-mean Gaussian distribution and generate probabilities $p_r, r \in R$. We can then write $s_r(t)$ as,

$$s_r(t) = \sqrt{\frac{P_r}{P_0}} \sum_{r \in R} p_r s_0(t - t_r), \text{ where } t_r = \frac{2r}{c}$$

For our simulation shown in Figure 10 we vary $\sigma = 0$ to 0.2 for seven roughness values varying from $r = -0.3$ mm to $r = 0.3$ mm. [8] reports values of $\sigma = 0.15$ for plaster. Note that $\sigma = 0$ corresponds to the perfectly smooth case studied above. We note thatΔ l increases with σ as expected. Further,Δ l increases faster for $d = 1$ mm. This is simply because the rough surface causes the reflected signal to spread in time and with a small d the reference signal and the information signal begin to overlap.

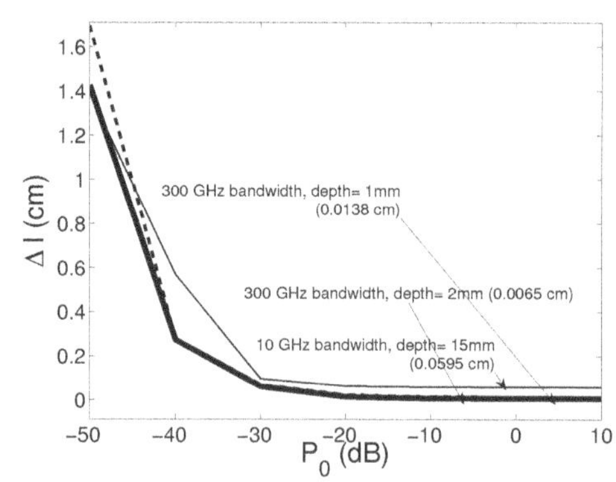

Figure 9: Minimum Δl versus power.

2.2 Summary

Our simulations clearly illustrate the relationship between B, d, Δl, σ and P_0. For the remainder of this paper, we will focus our attention on the terahertz frequency band only due to the large available bandwidth. We will also limit ourselves to d values measured in whole millimeters because

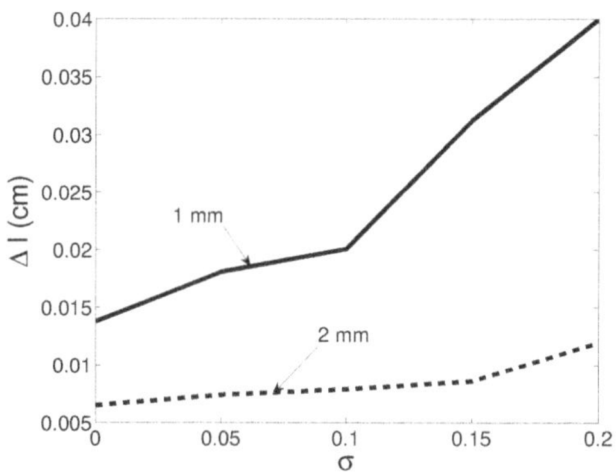

Figure 10: Minimum Δl versus variance of roughness.

surface roughness negatively affectsΔ l and hence it affects the length of barcode symbols.

3. BARCODE DESIGN AND READER ALGORITHM

The discussion above assumes a very narrow reader beam. While this may well be feasible in the future, the hardware we use produces a beam with a diameter of $\sim$2 cm. As we see below, the diameter of the beam has a significant impact on the design of the barcode by limiting the minimum size of symbols.

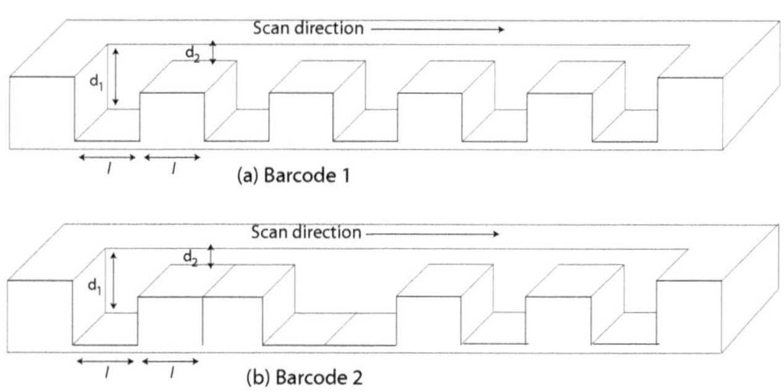

Figure 11: Example of two barcodes.

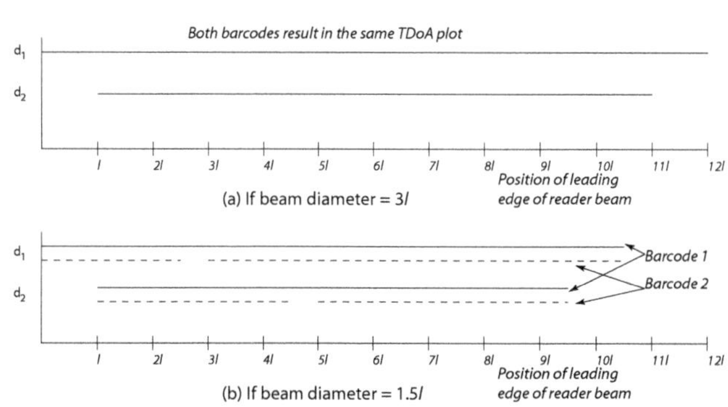

Figure 12: Reading barcodes from Figure 11 using two different beam diameters (we call it TDoA signatures).

Consider the two barcodes illustrated in Figure 11. Assume that we use the same length l for all symbols. In Barcode 1 the data encoded is: $< d_1, l >, < d_2, l >, < d_1, l >, < d_2, l >, < d_1, l >, < d_2, l >, < d_1, l >, < d_2, l >, < d_1, l >$ while Barcode 2 encodes: $< d_1, l >, < d_2, l >, < d_2, l >, < d_1, l >, < d_1, l >, < d_2, l >, < d_1, l >, < d_2, l >, < d_1, l >$. If we assume that the barcode reader has a diameter of $3l$ we obtain TDoA values as illustrated in Figure 12(a). In this plot the x-axis denotes the position of the leading edge of the reader beam. Since the reader beam is $3l$ it cannot distinguish between Barcode 1 and Barcode 2 producing exactly the same TDoA plots. If, however, we use a beam diameter of $1.5l$ we obtain the TDoA plot in Figure 12(b). The solid line in the plot corresponds to Barocde 1 while the dashed line corresponds to Barcode 2. It is easy to see that in this case we can correctly distinguish between the two barcodes. This result can be formalized as a theorem.

Theorem 1: If we assume that all the symbol lengths l are the the same, then we can uniquely read a barcode if Barcode reader Diameter $< 2l$.

Proof: Let us assume four consecutive depths (symbols) of the barcode are a, b, c, d (they do not need to be distinct). Figure 13 shows the position of the *right edge* of the reader beam over which the reader will read each of the symbols. Thus, a contributes to the TDoA measurement from the left edge of symbol a for length l + Diameter (assuming Diameter $> l$). In the figure, we show the TDoA components contributed when the reader starts reading c. For segment $[3l, 2l + \text{Diameter}]$ TDoA components of a, b, c are present. For segment $[2l + \text{Diameter}, 4l]$ only components from b, c are present and from $[4l, 3l + \text{Diameter}]$ components from b, c, d are present.

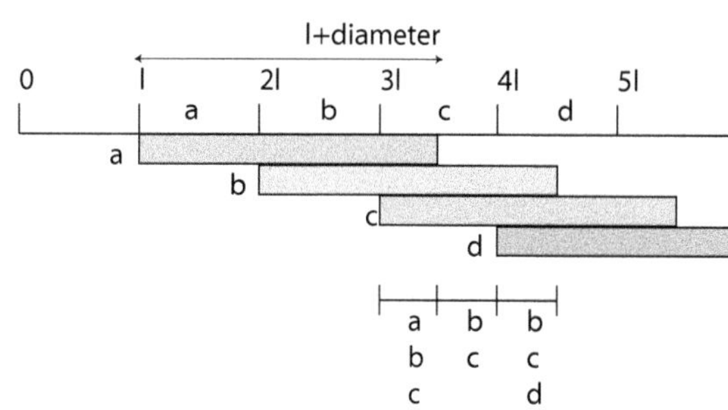

Figure 13: Illustration for Theorem 1.

Let us assume that a different barcode gives the same TDoA signature and the first symbol where these two barcodes differ is at symbol c. Let us write the TDoA signature of the two barcodes from $[3l, 3l + \text{Diameter}]$ as,

$$\begin{array}{ccc|ccc} a & b & b & a & b & b \\ b & c & c & b & e & e \\ c & & d & e & & f \end{array}$$

If we assume the two barcodes have the same signature, we need to come up with an assignment of a, b, c to a, b, e such that the two signatures are the same. Consider the different cases. If $a \neq b \neq c$ then c must equal e to make $a, b, c = a, b, e$. Similarly, if $a = b = c$ then c must again equal e to make the signatures the same. Indeed, to make $a, b, c = a, b, e$ we have no choice but to equate c and e. This means that it is impossible to construct different barcodes that yield the same TDoA signature if Diameter $< 2l$. $\square$

The theorem can be simply extended to the case when symbols of different length are used, but with one caveat.

Observation: The reader cannot distinguish between $< d, kl >$ and two consecutive symbols $< d, ml >, < d, (k-m)l >$ for $m \geq 1$ since we do not use any kind of separator between consecutive symbols.

With the above theorem and observation in hand, we can now develop an algorithm that enables the reading of linear barcodes given a left-to-right scan direction. For ease of explanation we will assume all symbols are of the same length l. Symbols of longer lengths such as kl can be treated as k consecutive symbols of length l.

Algorithm: Assume that the barcode has been scanned and a representation of the TDoA data, as illustrated in Figure 12, is maintained. For each of the symbols d_i that appears in the barcode, we will see one or more segments as shown in the figure.

1. As a first step we delete the right hand (Diameter $- l$) portion of each segment. Thus, in Figure 12(b) if we consider the dotted line for Barcode 2, we will trim the segments $[0, 2.5l], [3l, 10.5l]$ for d_1 to $[0, 2l), [3l, 10l)$[2].

2. Since we scan left to right, at location 0 we will see a single symbol (the first symbol of the barcode). There will not be more than one symbol at position 0 since the barcode reader beam has just started overlapping the first symbol at this point. Let this symbol be d_i.

   - *Location* $\leftarrow 0$,
   - *Output symbol* d_i,
   - *Current symbols* $\leftarrow \{d_i\}$

3. *Location* $\leftarrow$ *Location* $+ l$

4. *Current symbols* $\leftarrow$ all symbols that are seen at this location

5. If *Current symbols - previous Output symbol* $= \{d_j\}$

   then *Output symbol* d_j,

   else *Output symbol* is *previous Output symbol*

6. Go to 3.

7. Let nl be the total length of the barcode. There will be only one symbol whose TDoA signature extends from $[nl, (n+1)l]$. The above algorithm will output this last symbol twice. Therefore, we delete the last symbol output by the above steps and the remaining sequence of symbols denotes the complete barcode. In Figure 12(b), the TDoA signature of d_1 extends up to $10l$ (after trimming in step 1 above) since this last symbol is read by the trailing edge of the reader beam (while the leading edge is already on the right reference surface).

To see the algorithm in operation let us consider Barcode 2 in Figure 12(b). We first trim the segments for d_1 to $[0, 2l), [3l, 10l)$ and for d_2 to $[l, 4l), [5l, 9l)$. At location 0 symbol d_1 is output. Location is updated to l and *Current symbols* $= \{d_1, d_2\}$. We compute *Current symbols - previous Output symbol* $= \{d_2\}$ and therefore *Output symbol* d_2. Location is incremented to $2l$. Here *Current symbols* $= \{d_2\}$ only because we have trimmed d_1's first segment down to $[0, 2l)$. In this case *Current symbols - previous Output symbol* is the null set and so *Output symbol* d_2. When location is $3l$ we have *Current symbols* $= \{d_1, d_2\}$ and thus we output d_1. And so on. Observe that since Diameter $< 2l$ and since we trim the right Diameter $- l$ portion of each segment, we will never see 3 symbols at once.

[2]The notation $[a, b)$ denotes an interval that is open to the right. Therefore $b \notin [a, b)$.

4. PROTOTYPE COPPER AND CEMENT BARCODE SYMBOLS

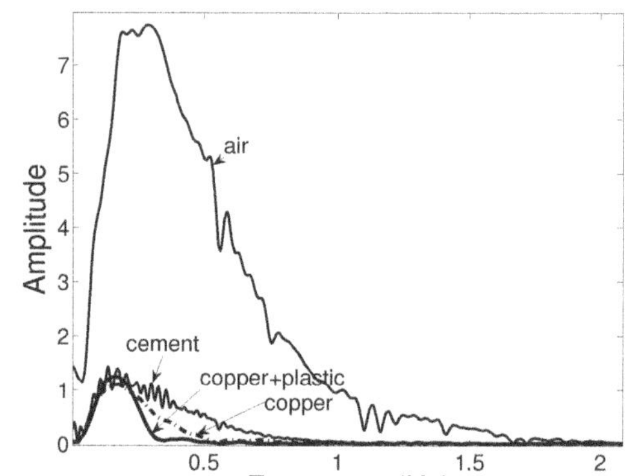

Figure 14: Spectrum of reflected signals.

Given the goal of tagging infrastructure, we construct barcode symbols from two different types of materials – copper and cement. We select copper because it provides a good reflective surface that is representative of other metallic surfaces that might be used for building such barcodes. We select cement because it is a very common building material with more roughness.

As a prelude to designing and constructing barcodes with these materials, we first measure the reflected bandwidth B of the signal. For this, we use a Picometrix 4000 Time-Domain Terahertz system that generates picosecond pulses covering up to 2 THz. In Figure 14 we plot the frequency domain of the signals reflected off cement, copper and copper covered with 0.5 cm thick plastic (this last can be used to enclose the barcode when embedded in the road). We also show the spectrum of the received pulse when traveling through free space. The dips we see in the free space plot correspond to water absorption lines (the relative humidity of the lab is set to 42%). It is interesting to note that cement has a much greater bandwidth (70-800 GHz) as compared with copper (70-500 GHz). Copper covered with thick plastic shows the smallest bandwidth (70-340 GHz). The lower end is filtered at 70 GHz to avoid interference with electronics that operate upto 70 GHz such as Wifi and 60 GHz systems.

We also conducted propagation measurements of terahertz signals as a function of distance. Figure 15 plots the received intensity as a function of distance for the case when the air is dry and when it has 42% relative humidity (RH). If we assume that the barcodes need to be read up to distances of half a meter (i.e., 1m round trip distance), the received

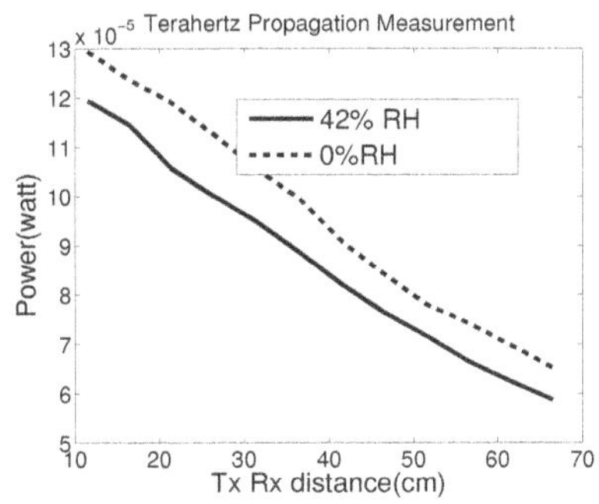

Figure 15: Measured intensity versus distance plot.

intensity will be -17.45 dBm[3] which is quite sufficient for our purposes in the car and bridge examples.

4.1 Symbol Design

The Picometrix system we use has a beam diameter of about 2cm. Therefore, given the constraint from Theorem 1, the symbols have to be at least 1cm long. The minimum symbol depth depends on the bandwidth of the signal as well as noise and other factors like roughness. Given that copper plus plastic has the smallest bandwidth of 270 GHz, we obtain a minimumΔ $d = 0.55$ mm. For our prototypes we decided to useΔ $d = 1$ mm since it would be more robust to noise, misalignment of the barcode with respect to the reader and increased roughness.

As we noted in section 2, given D depths and K lengths there are DK possible symbols each of which can represent $\log_2 DK$ bits. We selected $D = 4$ (1 mm to 4 mm depths) because using more depths would make the barcode too bulky and thick. To select K we performed a simple optimization where the goal is to *minimize the length of the barcode.* The following theorem shows that using $K = 1$ is optimal.

Theorem 2: Given N random bits to encode, using $K = 1$ gives the minimum barcode length.
Proof: To encode N bits, we require $\lceil N/b \rceil$ symbols where $b = \log_2 DK$ bits/symbol. Since the bit stream is random, the average length of each barcode symbol will be $(K+1)l/2$ where the lengths are $l, 2l, \cdots, Kl$. Therefore the total length of the barcode is:

$$\frac{(K+1)l}{2}\left\lceil \frac{N}{\log_2 DK} \right\rceil$$

Given that N, D, l are constant, this value is minimized at the smallest K which is 1. □.

Therefore, for our prototype barcodes we consider $D = 4$, $l = 1$ cm and $K = 1$.

4.2 Individual Symbols

We constructed individual barcode symbols using quick-dry cement purchased from a hardware store. Using a simple mold (in the form of a step) we constructed symbols for the four values of d. Figure 16 plots the time-domain signal received from the symbol with $d = 1$ mm. The two peaks we see between 0.5 and 1 correspond to the reference and the information surfaces. The first peak is the reference surface (closer to the reader hence the ToA is smaller). The small peaks we see around 1.5e-10 and 2.5e-10 correspond to small surface deformations in the cement. Figure 17 plots the cross-correlation of the signal with a reference signal $s_0(t)$. Note that time is reversed in the correlation plot with the y-axis being the square of the correlation coefficient. Each of the indices corresponds to 78 femtoseconds. The symbol and the reference signals are clearly visible in the plot.

We also constructed a sample barcode in copper consisting of two symbols $d = 2, 4$ mm. Figure 18 plots the time domain signal of two symbol reflections plus the reference and Figure 19 plots the cross-correlation with a reference signal. It is trivial to identify the two symbols by using a simple linear-time thresholding algorithm. Symbol A corresponds to $d = 2$ mm and B corresponds to $d = 4$ mm.

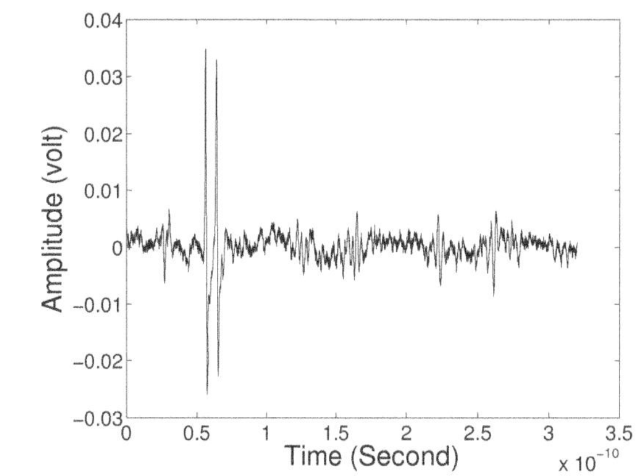

Figure 16: Reading one symbol made of cement.

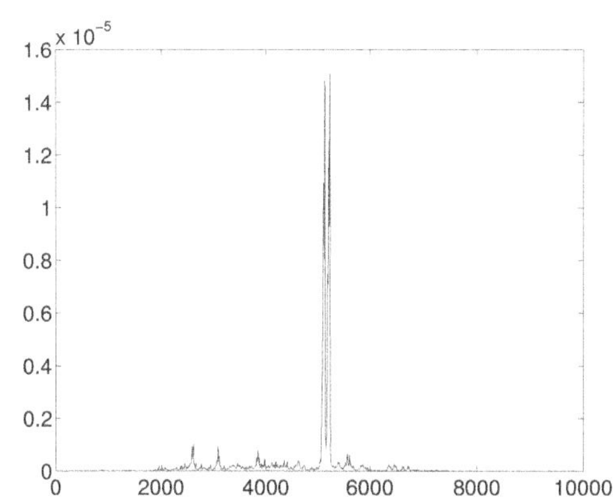

Figure 17: Cross-correlation of the time domain signals from Figure 16.

4.3 "Maui" Barcode in Copper

To demonstrate the entire concept of wireless barcodes we built a barcode in copper for the word *Maui.* We used the standard ASCII encoding for these four letters giving us 32 bits. We assigned two bits per symbol as follows: 00 − 1 mm, 01 − 2 mm, 11 − 3 mm and 10 − 4 mm. Thus, we get 16 symbols for the barcode. Since the length of each symbol was 1 cm, the total length of the barcode is 16 cm. Of course, a smaller barcode would be possible if the reader beam was narrower.

[3]We use a simple linear fit to obtain this value where the received power (watts) = -1.1279e-6 × *distance* + 0.00013075.

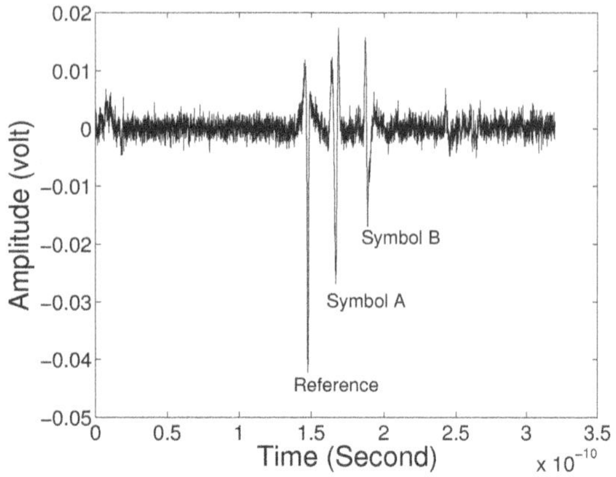

Figure 18: Reading two symbols made of copper.

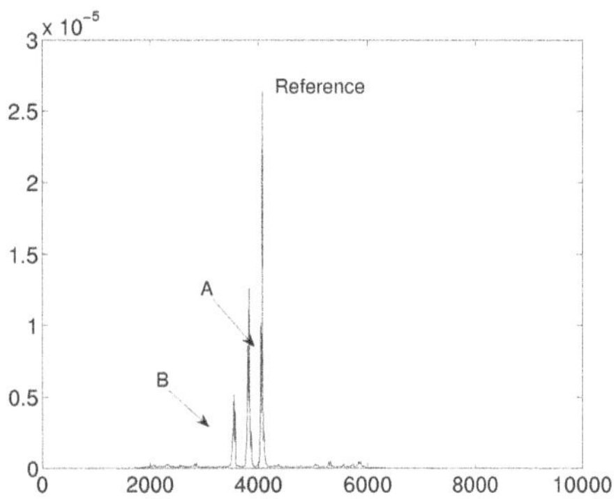

Figure 19: Cross-correlation of the time domain signals from Figure 18.

Figure 20 shows a photograph of the barcode we constructed along with the 0.5 cm thick plastic covering that we used in our measurements. This structure could potentially be embedded into a surface such as a roadway and be resistant to damage for long periods of time. The figure shows the reference surface also appears on the left and right of the barcode. this is required so we know when the barcode starts and ends. The length of the barcode in the figure is somewhat longer than 16 cm. This is because we cut and glued together the pieces to make the barcode by hand. This is also why there is a small irregularity in the reference surface around the middle point.

We read the barcode using the Picometrix system. The system moves the head in 1 mm increments. We used a single lengthwise scan of the barcode (which yields 165 individual measurements) to run our algorithm. The data produced in each scan resembles Figure 18. This is used to construct the cross-correlation plot which is then used to determine the symbols being seen. The algorithm to find the symbols is quite simple – we use a threshold to filter out all the values of the correlation plot to obtain only the maximum values of the peaks (three in the case of Figure 19). The rightmost peak is taken to be the reference surface and any peaks to the left of it are information symbols whose value is computed by using the TDoA values that can be read off from the x-axis. The 165 individual images of the barcode produced by the barcode reader when put together produce a plot like

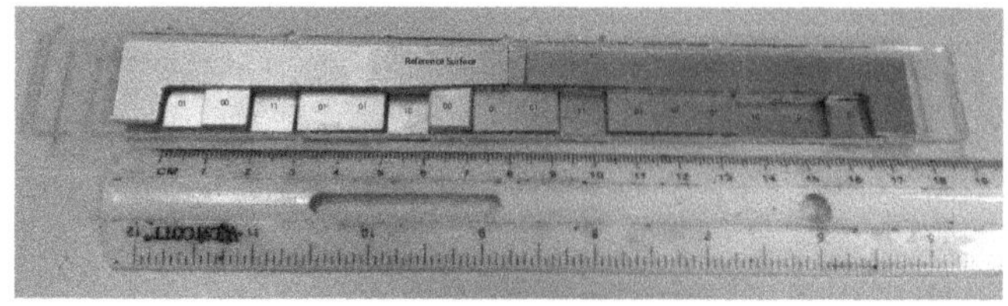

Figure 20: Photograph of the "Maui" barcode in copper.

Figure 12. We ran the algorithm described earlier on the data thus produced and the results are shown in Figure 21. Observe that symbols overlap in the plot which is because as the reader beam moves left to right it will overlap more than one symbol.

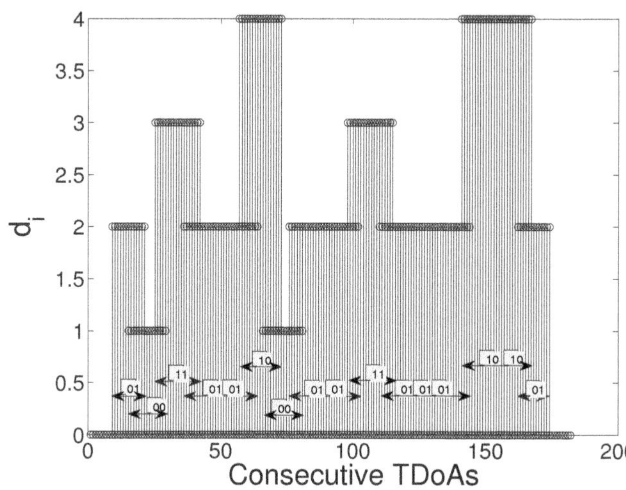

Figure 21: Reading the "Maui" barcode.

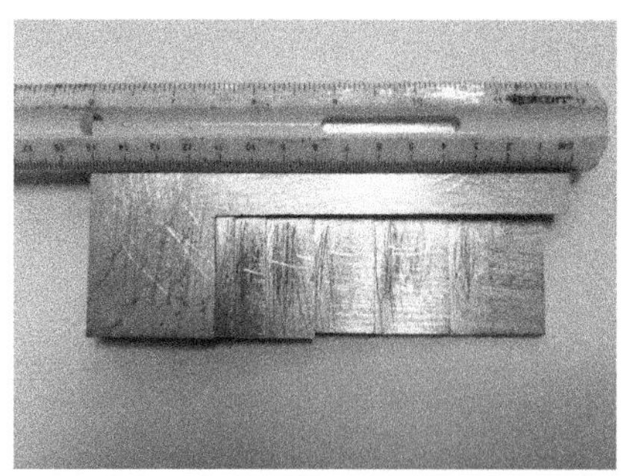

Figure 22: Barcode that was read under 1mm of water.

We also conducted an experiment to study the impact of surface roughness and water on the ability to read barcodes. For this, we built a different barcode with consecutive symbol lengths of 0.5 cm, 1cm, 1.5cm, 2cm, 2.5cm, 3cm and increasing depths from 1mm to 6mm (see Figure 22). We first scratched the surface with No. 40 sandpaper and then we stabbed it repeatedly with a screwdriver. Next we covered the barcode with 1mm layer of water. Figure 23 shows that we are able to read this barcode correctly as well. This

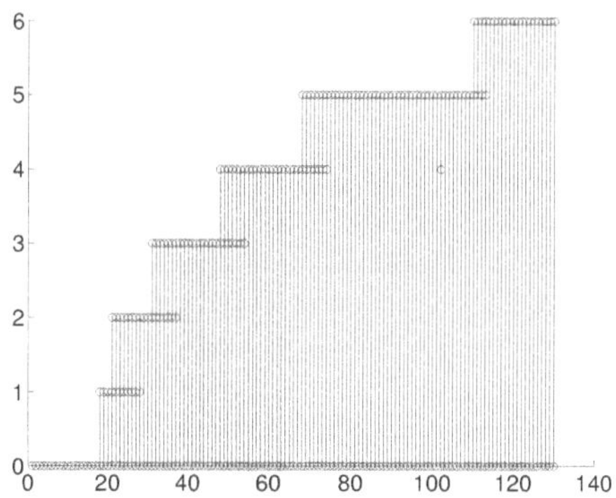

Figure 23: TDoA signature of Figure 22.

is not surprising because, as is evident from Figure 14 the bandwidth reflected by copper excludes the bands that are absorbed by water. In summary, the design we have provided appears able to meet our goals of providing a robust way to tag infrastructure.

4.4 Discussion

The results in Figures 21 and 23 were based on a single scan of the barcode. In reality, we could do multiple simultaneous scans (as is done in optical barcodes) in order to reduce reader error that will occur due to barcode degradation over time. We also note that in our design the barcodes were relatively long because the reader beam is quite wide. Given a narrow reader beam, the symbols can be made very short, of the order of 0.5mm, based on the discussion in section 2. In that case, the *Maui* barcode would shrink to less than 1cm in total length.

Readers may question the practicality of our overall barcode design concept, particularly given the fact that we used relatively sophisticated equipment for our measurements. In this context, we note that recent work on single chip design of terahertz transmitters [7],[4] and receivers [6] indicates that in the near future, handheld terahertz readers will be feasible and could also be incorporated into mobile devices. Indeed other work on small size (1 cm) high-gain antennas with 5^0 beams [21] for terahertz will allow incorporating highly directional terahertz beams into portable readers as well.

One of our primary motivations in this work was to enable navigation for driverless cars. Therefore an important question is whether our tags can be read at vehicular speeds v m/s. Assuming a round-trip distance of 1m between the barcode and the reader, the car will travel $\frac{v}{3}10^{-8}$ m in the time it takes the reflected pulse to return, a very small distance, even at highway speeds, given a beam radius of 0.5 mm or larger. Also note that since we use reference surfaces, the fact that the car bounces on its springs as it travels will not affect the readability of our symbols.

Finally, we note that CDs and DVDs encode single bits of information in a series of pits which appears similar to our idea, but is not. To read a CD, a beam of light is sent to the surface of the disc and depending on the presence or absence of a pit, the beam is reflected at two different angles. The receiver decodes a 1 if it receives the beam and a 0 if no beam is received. This technique can clearly not be used for tagging infrastructure because wear over time will create random reflections. Fundamentally, our technique is different because we use TDoA to encode information while CDs use angles of reflection (and require very strict distances between the disc and the reader).

5. RELATED WORK

5.1 Optical Barcodes

The original barcodes, which are called one-dimensional barcodes, encode data by alternating the intensity of reflection along one dimension. These intervals usually are parallel black and white strips with different widths on a smooth surface. Information is encoded by varying the width of these black and white strips. Optical readers typically found in grocery stores perform multiple parallel reads of the whole barcode all at once. This allows robust error correction. Universal product code (UPC), International Article Number (EAN-13), and code 39 are some examples of the most widely used one-dimensional barcodes, [1, 11].

Two-dimensional (matrix) barcodes represent data in a two-dimensional matrix of pixels. Therefore, in comparison with one-dimensional barcodes, two-dimensional barcodes can represent more data per unit area. DataMatrix, MaxiCode, PDF417, and QR code are some examples of this barcode category. Here, image processing methods are used to extract data from patterns presented in both horizontal and vertical components of the barcode.

5.2 RFID (Radio Frequency Identification)

RFID is a technique for identifying objects with RF signals. The tag stores information electronically. A reader sends an RF signal to the tag and reads the tag's response. The reader maintains the electromagnetic field to power the tag during the half duplex transmission and reception. Because RF signals are used, the information can be read in a non-line-of-sight (NLOS) channel between reader and tag unlike optical barcodes. RFID operation frequencies are in the UHF band around 900 MHz and 2.4 GHz, and in SHF band at 5.8 GHz [19]. Recently, [13] demonstrated an entirely novel approach for battery-free communication between both the devices. The communicating devices use ambient radio signals (e.g., broadcast TV signals) for power as well as for carrying information. They have demonstrated data rates as high as 1 kbps at distance of under 2.5 feet.

5.3 Chipless RFID tags (RF Barcodes)

Encoding data in RF barcodes is different from classical RFID tags. In the RF technique, the reader transmits a RF signal to the tag. The reflected signal from the tag has a specific shape depending on the tag structure. These different electromagnetic footprints are used to encode data on RF tags. Here, there are no transmission protocols between reader and the tag. Therefore, chipless RF tags are much simpler than RFID tags.

In 2002, Hartmann [10] introduced the first chipless RF tags. These tags had antennas that receive and guide the RF signal into a Surface Acoustic Wave (SAW) substrate. Then several reflectors on the SAW substrate reflect the received signal at specific times, in what is called a time domain approach (TDA). These differences in time of the reflections are used to encode data.

In 2005, Jalaly and Robertson [12] introduced chipless RF tags without antennas. These tags have arrays of metallic strips that behave as resonant bandpass or band stop

	[10]	[16]	[12]	[19]
No. bits	2	23	5	22.9
Tag size (mm)	1	10.8×6.4	18×2.5	20×40
Info. density (bits/meter)	1,000	1,797	1,000	572

Table 1: Encoding density of chipless tags.

filters tuned to predetermined frequencies. In this technique, which is called frequency-domain approach (FDA), resonators resonant some specific frequencies. Therefore, presence or absence of resonance at a known frequency is used to encode data.

Later, in 2009, Preradovic et al. [16] used spiral resonators and were able to encode 35 bits of data. However, In the technique that Jalaly and Robertson, and Preradovic et al. have used, each bit requires one resonator. Therefore, the the size of the RF is relatively big. Mukherjee [14] and Balbin and Karmakr [3] used phase differences to encode data on the RF tag.

In 2011, Vena et al. [19] increased the RF tag data capacity by proposing a hybrid method that uses both phase and frequency to encode data. The authors have designed their RF tag with multiple metallic "C-shape" resonator elements. The structure specification of each of these resonators create a specific electromagnetic footprint when the tag is illuminated by an RF signal.

We can compare our barcodes against RFID tags in term of cost of the tag, reader cost, usability in infrastructure applications and scalability. It is easy to see that our barcodes are inexpensive though the reader cost is higher. Let us now consider scalability and use in infrastructure (we ignore the obvious frailty of RFID tags for the moment). A key limitation we note is that RFID tags cannot be placed too close to one another because these tags do not run any form of MAC protocol and thus illuminating more than one such tag will cause corrupted data at the reader. The simplest design would require tags of length l to be separated by a distance l so that the reader is only seeing one tag at once as it moves. Using the information from the first two rows of Table 1 we can obtain an information encoding density shown on the last row of the table ($0.5\times$ number of bits/smallest dimension of tag – we multiply by 0.5 since tags of length l are separated by distance l). In the computation we used the smaller dimension to get an upper bound. In comparison, the information coding density of our wireless barcodes from Theorem 1 is $\frac{\log_2 D}{r}$ where r is the reader beam radius and D is the number of depths used. For example, if $r = 1$ mm and $D = 4$ then we have a density of 2 kbits/meter. Of course, the equipment we use currently has a much greater radius but that will change in the future. It is interesting to observe that given a vehicular speed of v m/s, the data rate can be written as *Information density* $\times v$ bits/sec. For a car driving at 100 kmph, our 2 bit design above yields a data rate of 54 kbps.

5.4 Ultrasound Identification (USID) Tags

These tags transmit ultrasonic signals to advertise their location to readers. Unlike RFID tags, these tags are more resistant to multi-path, though they do require use of directional microphones for detection. It is interesting to consider whether ultrasonic waves could be used to read our barcodes instead of terahertz or whether we could simply replace our barcodes with USID entirely. Using USID in outdoor environments suffers from the same longevity problem of RFID and other electronic technology. On the other hand, using ultrasonics to read our barcodes is an interesting question. Ultrasonic waves are significantly attenuated in air and the degree of attenuation depends on temperature, pressure, humidity and frequency. In order to be able to read our barcodes, we require a resolution of 1 mm which gives us a bandwidth of 170 kHz (we use the formula $c/2B$ from [5] where $c = 340$ m/s). The attenuation of ultrasound at this frequency is 15 dB/m at 20^0C [20]. However, a more serious problem is that this frequency propagates well through cement [23] and is in fact used for detecting faults inside cement structures. Therefore, the reflected signal back at the reader will likely be extremely weak. If we use higher frequencies, we do not need to be concerned by the problem of transmission through cement but the attenuation factor increases to 80 dB/m for 500 kHz and 250 dB/m for 1 MHz. Another challenge in using ultrasonics to read our barcodes is car speed. Assuming a speed of 100 km/h and a round trip distance of 1 m between the reader and barcode, the car will have traveled 8 cm in the time it takes an ultrasonic pulse to return. Given that cars drive at variable speeds, the reader design and placement is challenging.

5.5 Terahertz Tags

Tedjini et al. [18] for the first time extended the concept of RF tags to the THz domain. In THz tags, data is encoded in the volume of the tag. Therefore, the security of the THz tags is greater than RF tags. In THz tags a periodic structure of two dielectric layers with different refractive indexes will exhibit ranges of forbidden frequencies when the electromagnetic signal propagates through the tag. Breaking the periodicity of the structure will create narrow defect modes in the forbidden bands. Tedjini et al. have encoded data by using the presence or absence of these defect modes at different frequency positions. The authors used high resistive silicon wafers that are separated by layers of air. Changing the thickness of the air layer in the center of the structure breaks the periodicity of the structure and causes defects in the forbidden band gap (FBG) around 150 GHz frequency. This THz tag creates four different FBGs. However, because of the thickness dispersion of the silicon wafer, the last three FBGs are damaged and only the first FBG is useable. The authors were able to encode 2 bits of data on each THz tag.

Hamdi et al. [9] also used the same idea but they create the dialectic layers from cheaper materials and they were able to encode 10 bits of data on the frequency range of the first FBG (150–600 GHz). In another work, Perret et al. [15] believe that with an FBG-width of 254 GHz and the resolution of 1 GHz, 20 effective bits can be encoded in THz tags. The forbidden bands that are created by breaking the periodicity of dielectric layers are extremely narrow and noise can degrade their performance. The thickness of dielectric layers is in the order of μm and even a small error in their depth could cause errors.

5.6 Barcodes for Digitally Fabricated Objects

Recently there has been significant interest in embedding information into objects constructed using 3D printing technology. Of particular relevance to the present paper is an approach called Infrastructs [22] that uses terahertz radios for reading information embedded into printed objects. The key idea is to use plastics with different refractive indices (to the terahertz frequencies) arranged in layers to encode information. When such a three dimensional structure is illuminated by a perpendicular terahertz beam, portions of the beam are reflected back from each of the boundaries between different materials. *By noting the ToA of different reflections as well as if the returned pulse has a positive peak followed by negative peak (for '0') or vice versa (for '1'), the encoded information can be decoded.*

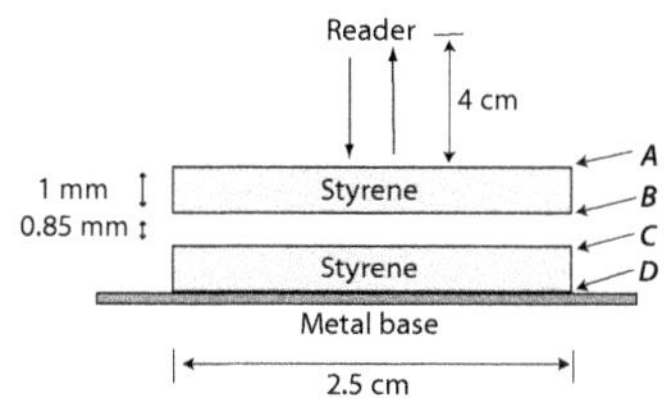

Figure 24: Infrastruct symbol.

Since Infrastructs require *transmission through layers of plastic media*, this approach is unsuitable for tagging infrastructure and severely limits what materials can be used. To illustrate this, we conducted an experiment. We constructed a simple symbol by separating two 2.5 cm square pieces of 1 mm thick Styrene sheets by an air gap of 0.85 mm and placing it on a metal plate to ensure good reflectivity. The symbol size as well as the idea of air gaps and using a metal coating are all based on the description in [22]. We use the Picometrix 4000 system to illuminate this tag and capture the reflected pulses. Figure 24 shows the symbol and as indicated the distance between the reader and the symbol is 4 cm. We expect to see 4 reflected pulses at the four surface boundaries marked by *A, B, C, D*. Figure 25(a) illustrates the four reflected pulses as well as secondary reflections where the pulse bounces between various boundaries before making it back to the reader. To examine how readable this simple symbol is in the presence of normal wear, we next scratch the top surface with No. 40 sandpaper. Figure 25(b) illustrates the significant attenuation in the reflected pulses and the fact that due to the roughness, each of the reflected pulses spreads in time causing *B* and *C* to overlap. If we look carefully we see that the reflections from *B, C* in Figure 25(a) are − peak followed by + for *B* and then + peak followed by − for *C*. In Figure 25(b) we see two consecutive pulses with − peak followed by + peak. In other words, here we cannot distinguish *C* from *B*+*C*. Indeed, we see no transition similar to the one in Figure 25(a) for *C* indicating that the data encoded in *C* is lost. Finally, we used a damp cloth to lightly wet the surface of the symbol. As Figure 25(c) shows, we now only get reflections from *A* and *D*. The reflection from *D* is severely attenuated (as are the reflections from *B* and *C*) due to transmission through water. The reflection from *A* is however strong.

There are two important conclusions we can derive from this experiment. First, embedding Infrastructs into infrastructure is not beneficial because these tags will quickly become unreadable. Second, this experiment illustrates why our barcodes work well even in presence of roughness and moisture. Observe that in presence of dampness, we get a strong reflected pulse in Figure 25(c). This reflection occurs between the air/water boundary on the top surface. In our approach, since we encode symbols using different depths with respect to a reference surface, we will continue to be able to read the symbols because this reflection is always present. Indeed, this is the point also illustrated in Figures 22 and 23. In Figure 26 we show the detail of one signal received when reading Figure 22 where it is easy to pick out the two symbols at depths 1 and 2mm with respect to the reference signal despite a rough wet surface. We also note that the cement symbols we read in Figure 16 also had a rough surface but we could read them because we only rely on the reflection from the top surfaces.

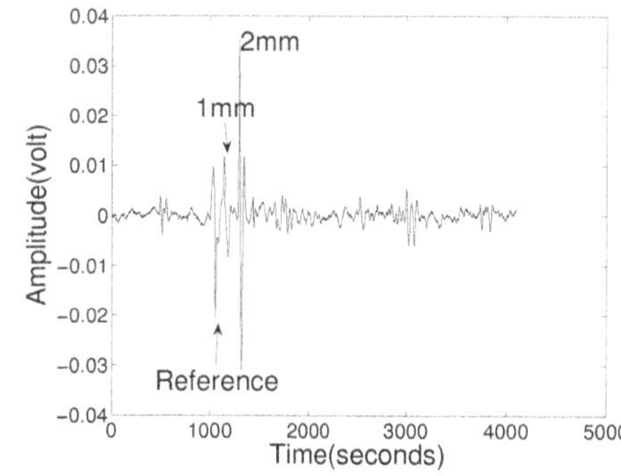

Figure 26: Detail of one signal from Figure 22.

5.7 Discussion

The barcodes we discuss in this paper are quite different from the various types of barcodes discussed above. Unlike the optical barcodes, our barcodes can be read even after significant degradation since we use TDoA rather than intensity. Unlike the chipless barcodes and the terahertz tags, our barcodes contain no electronic components or dielectric materials. Finally, unlike Infrastructs, our barcodes do not rely on transmission through material and thus can easily be built into building materials and can continue to be read despite scratches and dampness.

6. CONCLUSIONS

We present the concept of building barcodes into hard surfaces such as those used in constructing roads and bridges. The goal of these barcodes is to survive as long as the infrastructure they are built upon. In order to read the barcodes we use terahertz frequencies that enable us to have relatively small barcode symbols. We develop the underlying theory behind such barcodes and illustrate the concept using a homemade copper barcode.

Acknowledgement

This work was funded by award NSF 1217994.

7. REFERENCES

[1] http://en.wikipedia.org/wiki/barcode.

[2] R. F. Anastasi and E. I. Madaras. Terahertz nde for metallic surface roughness evaluation. In *The 4th International Workshop on Ultrasonic and Advanced Methods for Nondestructive Testing and Material Characterization*, Dartmouth, MA, 19 June 2006.

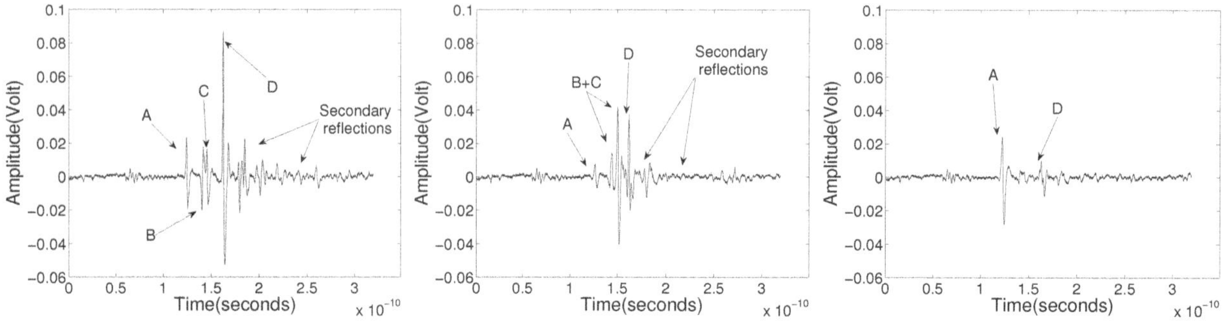

(a) Smooth surface (b) Rough surface (c) Damp surface

Figure 25: Measurements of a single Infrastruct symbol.

[3] Isaac Balbin and Nemai Chandra Karmakar. Phase-encoded chipless rfid transponder for large-scale low-cost applications. *IEEE Microwave and Wireless Components Letters*, 19(8):509–511, 2009.

[4] D. Huang et al. Terahertz cmos frequency generator using linear superposition technique. *IEEE J. Solid-State Circuits*, 43(12):2730 – 2738, 2008.

[5] Gang Li et al. Bandwidth dependence of cw ranging to uhf rfid tags in severe multipath environments. In *IEEE International Conference on RFID*, pages 19–25, 12-14 April 2011.

[6] H. Sherry et al. A 1kpixel cmos camera chip for 25fps real-time terahertz imaging applications. In *Proceedings IEEE ISSCC*, pages 252 – 254, 2012.

[7] M. Feiginov et al. Resonant-tunnelling-diode oscillators operating at frequencies above 1.1 thz. *Applied Physics Letters*, 99(23), 2011.

[8] R. Piesiewicz et al. Scattering analysis for the modeling of thz communication systems. *IEEE Transactions on Antennas and Propagation*, 55(11):3002 – 3009, November 2007.

[9] M. Hamdi, F. Garet, L. Duvillaret, Ph Martinez, and G. Eymin-Petot-Tourtollet. New approach for chipless and low cost identification tag in the THz frequency domain. In *2012 IEEE International Conference on RFID-Technologies and Applications (RFID-TA)*, pages 24–28. IEEE, 2012.

[10] Clinton S Hartmann. A global SAW ID tag with large data capacity. In *Ultrasonics Symposium, 2002. Proceedings. 2002 IEEE*, volume 1, pages 65–69. IEEE, 2002.

[11] Karim Houni, Wadih Sawaya, and Yves Delignon. One-dimensional barcode reading: an information theoretic approach. *Applied optics*, 47(8):1025–1036, 2008.

[12] I. Jalaly and I. D. Robertson. Rf barcodes using multiple frequency bands. In *2005 IEEE MTT-S International Microwave Symposium Diges*, pages 4–pp. IEEE, 2005.

[13] V. Liu, A. Parks, V. Talla, S. Gollakota, D. Wetherall, and J. R. Smith. Ambient backscatter: wireless communication out of thin air. In *Proceedings ACM Sigcomm*, Hong Kong, August 13 – 17 2013.

[14] S. Mukherjee. Chipless radio frequency identification by remote measurement of complex impedance. In *2007 European Conference on Wireless Technologies*, pages 249–252. IEEE, 2007.

[15] Etienne Perret, Maher Hamdi, Guy Eymin Petot Tourtollet, Raji Nair, Frederic Garet, Anastasia Delattre, Arnaud Vena, Lionel Duvillaret, Philippe Martinez, Smail Tedjini, and Yann Boutnant. THID, the next step of chipless RFID. In *2013 IEEE International Conference on RFID (RFID)*, pages 261–268. IEEE, 2013.

[16] Stevan Preradovic, Sushim Roy, and Nemai Karmakar. Fully printable multi-bit chipless rfid transponder on flexible laminate. In *Microwave Conference, 2009. APMC 2009. Asia Pacific*, pages 2371–2374. IEEE, 2009.

[17] G. Sundberg, L. M. Zurk, S. Schecklman, and S. Henry. Modeling rough-surface and granular scattering at terahertz frequencies using the finite-difference time-domain method. *IEEE transactions on Geoscience and Remote Sensing*, 48(10):3709–3719, October 2010.

[18] S. Tedjini, E. Perret, V. Deepu, M. Bernier, F. Garet, and L. Duvillaret. Chipless tags for RF and THz identification. In *2010 Proceedings of the Fourth European Conference on Antennas and Propagation (EuCAP)*, pages 1–5. IEEE, 2010.

[19] Arnaud Vena, Etienne Perret, and Smail Tedjinil. Chipless RFID tag using hybrid coding technique. *IEEE Transactions on Microwave Theory and Techniques*, 59(12):3356–3364, 2011.

[20] A Vladišauskas and L Jakevičius. Absorption of ultrasonic waves in air. *Ultragarsas*, 1:50, 2004.

[21] Y. Wang, M. Ke, M. J. Lancaster, and J. Chen. Micromachined 300-ghz su-8-based slotted waveguide antenna. *IEEE Antennas and Wireless Propahation Letters*, 10:573 – 576, 2011.

[22] Karl D. D. Willis and Andrew D. Wilson. Infrastructs: Fabricating information inside physical objects for imaging in the terahertz region. *ACM Transactions on Graphics*, 32(4):138:1 – 138:10, July 2013.

[23] I. Q. Yaman, G. Inci, N. Yesiller, and Aktan H, M. Ultrasonic pulse velocity in concrete using direct and indirect transmission. *ACI Materials Journal*, pages 450 – 457, Nov – Dec 2001.

Enabling Physical Analytics in Retail Stores Using Smart Glasses

Swati Rallapalli
UT Austin
swati@cs.utexas.edu

Aishwarya Ganesan
Microsoft Research India
t-aigane@microsoft.com

Krishna Kant Chintalapudi
Microsoft Research India
krchinta@microsoft.com

Venkata N. Padmanabhan
Microsoft Research India
padmanab@microsoft.com

Lili Qiu
UT Austin
lili@cs.utexas.edu

ABSTRACT

We consider the problem of tracking physical browsing by users in indoor spaces such as retail stores. Analogous to online browsing, where users choose to go to certain webpages, dwell on a subset of pages of interest to them, and click on links of interest while ignoring others, we can draw parallels in the physical setting, where a user might *walk* purposefully to a section of interest, *dwell* there for a while, *gaze* at specific items, and *reach out* for the ones that they wish to examine more closely.

As our first contribution, we design techniques to track each of these elements of physical browsing using a combination of a first-person vision enabled by smart glasses, and inertial sensing using both the glasses and a smartphone. We address key challenges, including energy efficiency by using the less expensive inertial sensors to trigger the more expensive vision processing.

Second, during gazing, we present a method for identifying the item(s) within view that the user is likely to focus on based on measuring the orientation of the user's head.

Finally, unlike in the online context, where every webpage is just a click away, proximity is important in the physical browsing setting. To enable the tracking of nearby items, even if outside the field of view, we use data gathered from smart-glasses-enabled users to infer the *product layout* using a novel technique called *AutoLayout*. Further, we show how such inferences made from a small population of smart-glasses-enabled users could aid in tracking the physical browsing by the many smartphone-only users.

Categories and Subject Descriptors

C.2.m [**Computer Systems Organization**]: COMPUTER - COMMUNICATION NETWORKS - Miscellaneous

Keywords

Physical Analytics; Wearables; Smart Glasses; Retail Spaces; Localization; WiFi

MobiCom'14, September 7–11, 2014, Maui, HI, USA.

http://dx.doi.org/10.1145/2639108.2639126.

1. INTRODUCTION

Web analytics is a multi-billion dollar business today, providing tools that measure and analyze users' online browsing behavior to help companies assess the effectiveness of their websites. A typical tool will track webpage-related events, such as page views, clicks, and the degree to which different landing pages are associated with online purchases.

Most purchases today, however, occur in the physical realm, *e.g.*, at retail stores and shopping malls. While many retailers track shoppers' purchases (*e.g.*, as part of customer loyalty programs) in order to perform analytics, these systems do not provide insight into shoppers' behavior *during* the shopping process, which we refer to as *physical browsing* in this paper. For example, which sections of the store did the shopper spend most of his or her time in? Which products did the shopper express interest in by gazing at them or reaching out for them? How many shoppers reached out for competing products A and B, say to compare these?

We believe that access to physical browsing information of shoppers in retail stores can not only provide crucial insights into shoppers' needs and interests but also reveal the effectiveness of the store layout itself. Furthermore, such *physical analytics* that track in-store shopping behavior could also be combined with online information such as web browsing history or a shopping list to generate automatic alerts, say when there is a match between the physical browsing context and the online information.

One approach would be for the retail stores themselves to use their in-store surveillance videos to mine this information. However, many retail stores today neither possess the expertise nor the resources to gather and analyze tons of surveillance data for this purpose. Furthermore, this approach would *not* allow aggregating data across a user's online and physical browsing or indeed even just physical browsing across different stores that a user may visit since an individual store is unlikely to be willing to share information with potential competitors. On the other hand, the advent of smart glasses such as Google Glass [23], equipped with a camera, inertial sensors and WiFi, enables user-driven data gathering, both (privately) tracking an individual user's visits across stores and crowd-sourcing store layout information based on the visits by a community of users. Furthermore, from the viewpoint of an individual user, there would be an incentive to participate since their physical browsing information could be used directly for their own benefit (*e.g.*, for receiving personalized alerts from a digital personal assistant) rather than being shared for the stores' business purposes. For it to scale to a wide footprint, such a user-driven approach should ideally *not* depend on any support from the disparate stores that the user may visit. Therefore, in this paper we ask the question, *"How can we develop a system that leverages* *smart glasses to track physical browsing, without depending on the store itself for any a priori information (*e.g.*, store layout or product information) or infrastructure support, and without requiring any explicit input from the shopper?"*

Further, while smart glasses seem poised for rapid growth and could even supplant smartphones down the road, for the foreseeable future it is likely that most shoppers will only be carrying smartphones. Thus, an important question is *"How can we use the data from the few smart glasses enabled users to track physical browsing by the large number of shoppers only carrying smartphones?"*

The ThirdEye system: In this paper, we present a system called ThirdEye to address the above questions. ThirdEye only uses image, inertial sensor, and WiFi data crowd-sourced from shoppers wearing smart glasses to track the physical browsing of shoppers, without requiring any input from either the store owners or from the shoppers themselves. ThirdEye includes three main components: *shopping behavior classification*, *user attention identification*, and *product layout inferencing*. We discuss them briefly in turn.

Shopping behavior classification: By analyzing over 50 video streams from 7 shoppers wearing the Google Glass, shadowing them as they were shopping and interviewing them, we have identified four distinct behaviors that shoppers exhibit at retail stores: *purposeful walking*, *dwelling*, *gazing*, and *reaching out*.

A shopper who knows what they wish to purchase or is in a hurry would likely walk purposefully to the relevant section. They might then dwell in a specific area (*e.g.*, an aisle) for a length of time. Such dwelling is characterized by slow, unpurposeful movement, say with the shopper ambling around nearby locations. Thereafter, having further narrowed down the products of interest, the shopper might gaze for a little time, looking steadily at a product or a set of closely-placed products, perhaps to search for or make up their mind about the products. Finally, the shopper might reach out for a product of interest with his or her hands, either to examine it more closely or to purchase it.

ThirdEye uses video and inertial sensing from smart glasses to determine whether the shopper is walking, dwelling, gazing, or reaching out. A key challenge is in tracking all of these activities accurately and in an energy-efficient manner. Since continuous video is extremely expensive in terms of energy consumption, our general strategy is to rely on inertial sensors as much as possible and to trigger vision only when necessary.

Purposeful walking: To detect purposeful walking, we simply leverage prior work [40] based on inertial sensing alone.

Dwelling: We develop a novel dwell detection scheme that uses inertial sensors to distinguish between walking and dwelling, with an accuracy of over 95% (Section 3.4). The scheme is based on the observation that while dwelling, the net physical displacement would be small even though the user may be moving continuously.

Gazing: While gaze is characterized by almost zero head movement, as described in Section 3.3, our experiments indicate that detecting gaze solely based on inertial sensing, even from head-mounted devices like smart glasses, leads to a large number of false positives (as high as 33%), with dwelling often being confused for gazing. Thus, we use inertial sensing based detection to turn on the video and then propose a scheme where vision based techniques can be used to complement inertial sensing, to achieve both energy efficiency and a gaze detection accuracy of 88% at a very low false positive rate of 1.2%.

Reaching out: Our scheme for detecting reaching out relies on the observation that hands are almost always seen within the field of view of the shopper (and hence of the Glass) whenever the shopper reaches out. The reason is simply that shoppers are typically looking at an item while reaching out for it. So we first detect hands, and then also examine the neighborhood of the detected hand to minimize false positives (Section 3.6), thereby achieving an accuracy of 86% with tests run on several shoppers.

User Attention Identification: Once we establish that the shopper is gazing, the video feed can be used to identify the products within the shopper's field of view using existing techniques such as Google reverse image search. However, as we discuss in Section 4.2, our experiments reveal the presence of as many as 16 products in the shopper's field of view. An important task then is to accurately identify the shopper's item of focus among the many products within view, *i.e.*, which item the shopper is looking at.

A naive approach would be to use the distance between an item and the center of the field of view as an (inverse) measure of the likelihood of it being the object of the shopper's focus. However, as we discuss in Section 4.2, the item of interest may not lie at the center of the field of view, depending on the orientation of the shopper's head. By analyzing ground truth data from several real shoppers, we develop a model for the likelihood of an item being at the shopper's focus, depending both on its position within the field of view and the orientation of the shopper's head, obtained from the Glass.

Layout Inferencing: Thus far, we have focused on identifying items within the shopper's field of view. However, limiting ourselves to such items would not be sufficient from the viewpoint of our goal of tracking physical browsing. For instance, an application might wish to generate a proximity-based alert for an item that is quite close yet out of view (*e.g.*, it might be right behind the shopper). Also, there would be no vision-based sensing for shoppers who only have a smartphone and no Glass. Thus, inferring the layout of the products becomes an important goal for ThirdEye.

Since we do not rely on the store to provide us with a map, we design a novel scheme called *AutoLayout* that fuses video, WiFi, and inertial sensor data from the Glass devices worn by various shoppers, to simultaneously track them while also constructing and updating the *product layout* in a virtual coordinate space (Section 5). The advantage of this scheme is that we can localize not only Glass-enabled shoppers but also shoppers who carry only smartphones using WiFi and inertial sensor data, albeit with reduced accuracy.

Contributions: Our key contributions are:

- A first-of-its-kind system, ThirdEye, to track physical browsing in retail stores using data from smart glasses, and without relying on input from either the store or the shoppers.
- Techniques to identify shopper behavior such as dwelling and gazing using video and inertial sensors.
- A scheme to determine the shopper's focus while gazing.
- A scheme to simultaneously track shoppers and infer the product layout using video, WiFi and inertial sensing data from smart glass users, and using this to also track physical browsing of the smartphone-only users albeit at a reduced accuracy.
- An implementation of ThirdEye and its evaluation in two retail stores, with the participation of 7 shoppers.

2. RELATED WORK

Prior work of relevance to ThirdEye spans a wide range: localization, vision-based sensing, robotics, human activity sensing, and physical analytics in retail (including the work in start-ups).

Indoor Localization and Sensing: There has been extensive work in indoor localization and sensing [49, 50, 39, 24, 27, 5] that cover spaces both big (*e.g.*, buildings) [48, 42] and small (*e.g.*, retail stores) [14, 12, 45], both using infrastructure (*e.g.*, WiFi, RFID) [10, 29, 37, 51] and not (*e.g.*, purely-phone based, crowd-sourcing) [9,

34, 16], sensing both the environment [41, 53] and the users [44, 13]. Despite much work on WiFi localization, existing work can achieve high accuracy only at the expense of a high calibration cost or requiring additional information or modifications to WiFi Access Points (APs) (*e.g.*, Horus [53] requires detailed profiling of the indoor space ahead of time, Zee [40] requires maps and ArrayTrack [51] requires modified APs). In comparison, our system achieves semantically meaningful information, such as item or category labels without requiring external input (*e.g.*, a map) or other human input (*e.g.*, manually-assigned labels from crowd-sourcing).

SurroundSense [9] proposes an interesting approach that fingerprints locations based on visual, acoustic, and motion signals. The goal is to determine which store the user is located in. In comparison, ThirdEye seeks to identify the user's context in a more fine-grained manner than just the identity of the store that they are in (*e.g.*, whether the user is gazing and if so at which item) and do so without requiring any fingerprinting in advance.

CrowdInside [8] presents a method for constructing indoor floor plans by leveraging the movement of users carrying smartphones. It uses dead-reckoning together with anchor points to prevent error accumulation. The anchor points are defined by the unique inertial sensor signatures corresponding to elevators, escalators, and stairs. However, such inertial-based anchor points might be few in number or even non-existent within a store. In contrast, by leveraging vision, ThirdEye is able to identify more accurate, item-level landmarks. Furthermore, by combining this with both inertial tracking and WiFi information, ThirdEye provides a unified framework that caters to both smart glass users and smartphone-only users.

Vision: There is a vast body of research on vision-based place recognition and pose estimation. For example, [7] construct a 3D model of a city based on a large number of photos collected online, which can then be used to estimate the pose (*i.e.*, position and orientation) of an observer with a given view. [33] determines the location where a photograph was taken by matching it with photographs of popular landmarks. [38] develops an approach that retrieves similar images from a visual database on a mobile device with a small memory footprint.

Vision-based approaches are generally expensive, especially if it involves building a 3D model, hence these have generally only been applied to well-known landmarks. The insides of stores are typically lacking in such distinctive landmarks and are often crowded with people, posing challenges. In ThirdEye, we make limited use of image information to recognize items rather than scenes, thereby sidestepping these challenges.

Robotics: There is a vast body of work on robot navigation, specifically on the classical problem of simultaneous localization and mapping (SLAM) [32]. While the robots typically have access to precise wheel odometry, ThirdEye uses only human walking and does not use specialized sensors, such as laser range-finders.

There have also been prior SLAM-like efforts in the context of human motion. FootSLAM [42] uses foot-mounted inertial sensors to track a user's walk, while FeetSLAM [43] extends this to combine the trajectories of multiple users, assuming each walk is sufficiently long. Neither uses WiFi or visual information. WiFiSLAM [19] only uses WiFi information, not inertial sensing. Only visual information is used in MonoSLAM [18]. Zee [40] combines smartphone-based inertial and WiFi sensing but requires an a priori map. To our knowledge, ThirdEye is the first system that combines inertial and WiFi sensing with visual information to construct a map from walks by multiple humans, even when the individual walks are short.

Human-activity sensing: There has been much work on fine-grained human-activity sensing using wearable devices such as pedometers, heart-rate monitors, microphones, etc. [15, 20, 17]. ThirdEye focuses on a small subset of activities of relevance in the physical browsing context and enables these using smart glasses. As more wearable devices become prevalent, we could leverage those too; regardless, ThirdEye's ability to combine inertial, WiFi, and visual information would help provide physical context to the sensed information (*e.g.*, associating a jump in the user's heart rate with them gazing at particular object on display).

Shopping behavior: [28] places sensors on people to track their trajectories, and uses a clustering scheme to predict users' future behaviors (*e.g.*, fast walking, idle walking, or stopping). [31] studies 701 hours of sensor data collected from 195 in-situ customers to understand customer behavior in shopping malls. [52] monitors customers' shopping time. In comparison to these specific studies, ThirdEye provides a broad and systematic framework for combining multiple sensing modalities to track physical browsing by users.

Retail analytics start-ups: Nearby Systems [36] requires retail stores to deploy a customized WiFi localization infrastructure to analyze in-store customers (dwell times, visit frequency, window conversions, etc.) Euclid Analytics [21] leverages existing in-store WiFi infrastructure to provide similar analytics to retail stores. Neither approach provides fine-grained, item-level information. Apple's iBeacon [26] transmits location-specific messages in a store to nearby smartphones via Bluetooth Low Energy (BLE). Mondelez [46] requires retail stores to deploy cameras in shelves that use facial-recognition to provide insights into demographics of customers that browse a given product. In comparison to these systems, which require extensive infrastructure roll-out or support and hence are meant to be deployed by store owners, ThirdEye does not require any special infrastructure and hence is amenable to crowdsourcing. Moreover, ThirdEye provides more fine-grained analysis including user behaviors.

3. BEHAVIOR CLASSIFICATION

As discussed in Section 1, there are four modes exhibited by a typical shopper: purposeful walking, dwelling, gazing, and reaching out. We now describe these in greater detail and present the detection techniques used by ThirdEye.

3.1 Understanding the behaviors

Upon entering a store, a shopper might walk purposefully towards a certain section of the store that they have in mind or in a certain direction. Upon reaching the section or aisle of interest, the shopper would typically slow down and dwell, i.e., amble around, say looking within an aisle for their product of interest. Occasionally, the shopper might stand at a spot and gaze at products on the shelf, visually scanning these to find the one of interest and perhaps making up their mind to reach out to it. Finally, the shoppers might reach out to the item of interest, either to pick it up or just to read the information on it.

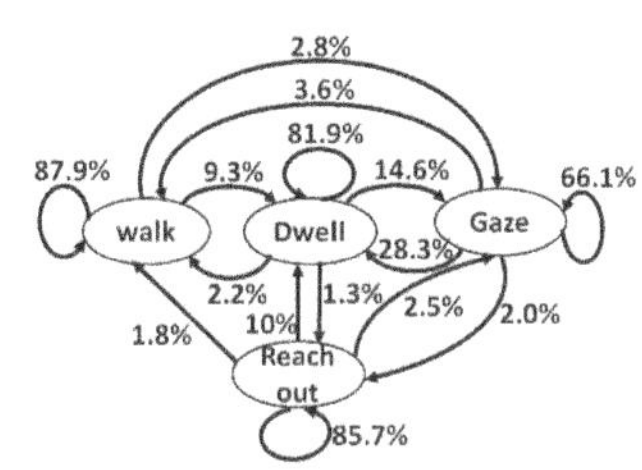

Figure 1: An example model for shopping behavior

The amount of time spent by the shoppers in each of the four modes would reflect their shopping intent. For example, shoppers who have time to kill or are unsure of what they intend to buy might spend a considerable length of time dwelling. Shoppers trying to compare and select among different brands/options of a specific item might be gazing. Finally, the act of reaching out indicates the greatest intent where the shoppers either intend to purchase the item or read information written on the item such as calorie contents or net weight. These behaviors may be exhibited in various sections of the store and may even be repeated by a shopper as (s)he comes back for a second look.

		To				P(State)
	State	Walk	Dwell	Gaze	Reach Out	
From	Walk	87.9%	9.3%	2.8%	0%	17.3%
	Dwell	2.2%	81.9%	14.6%	1.3%	50.7%
	Gaze	3.6%	28.3%	66.1%	2.0%	23.8%
	Reach Out	1.8%	10%	2.5%	85.7%	8.2%

Table 1: State transition probabilities

Figure 1 models the various behaviors as a finite state machine quantifying the probabilities of transitioning from one state to another at a granularity of one second. Table 1 reports the state transition probabilities estimated by studying the behavior of 7 shoppers who shopped in two large stores in the United States, a grocery store and a department store, while wearing Google Glass. We shadowed the shoppers, taking notes as they shopped, interviewed them in the end, and finally studied the video obtained from their Google Glass. Thus, we manually classified the time spent by the shoppers in the store as walking, dwelling, gazing, or reaching out. We make the following observations:

- Shoppers tend to spend a majority of their time dwelling (50.7%) (as indicated by the P(State) column in Table 1), followed by gazing (23.7%) and walking (17.3%).
- Most frequent inter-state transitions are between dwell and gaze.
- For all four states, the high probability of remaining in the same state indicates that shoppers tend to continue in their current mode for several seconds before transitioning to another.

3.2 Behavior Classification Overview

ThirdEye automatically classifies shopper behavior into one of the four categories: walking, dwelling, gazing, and reaching out — using the inertial sensor data (*i.e.*, accelerometer and 3-axis compass) and the video feed from the camera of the Google Glass. ThirdEye also makes use of the inertial sensor data on shoppers' smartphones, where available, as discussed later in this section.

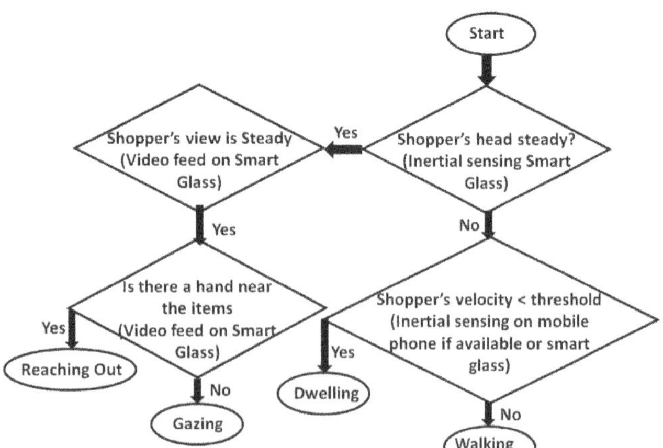

Figure 2: Overview of Behavior Classification Algorithm

Turning on the video on Google Glass causes a high power drain on the device (as discussed in detail in Section 6), while inertial sensing results in much less power drain. Consequently, in our behavior classification scheme, we try to minimize the duration for which the video is turned on. Figure 2 depicts the high-level flow of our behavior classification scheme. We ran our scheme once every second, thus shopper behavior was classified at the granularity of each second.

Gaze detection: The first step in our scheme is to detect whether or not the person is gazing. Since shoppers typically hold their head steady while gazing and are also not walking, this can be detected by measuring the standard deviation in inertial sensor measurements on the smart glass. However, as will be discussed in Section 3.3, just relying on inertial sensors leads to a large number of false positives. Consequently, we use a preliminary detection based on a low standard deviation in the inertial sensor measurements on the smart glass as a trigger to turn on the video and analyze the scene to confirm that the person is indeed gazing (Section 3.3).

Dwelling and Walking: If there is a high standard deviation in the inertial sensors, this could mean that the person is either dwelling or walking. We use the step counter in Zee [40] to detect steps from the accelerometer. As discussed in Section 3.4, the accuracy of the step counter is higher when the accelerometer readings from the shopper's smartphone are used compared to when measurements from the smart glasses are used. This is because of spurious step detections caused by head movement. The step count is combined with compass data from the smart glasses to estimate the average velocity of the shopper. If the magnitude of average velocity is less than a certain threshold, the behavior is classified as dwelling, otherwise it is classified as walking.

Reaching out: In order to detect reaching out, we rely on detecting the shopper's hand in the field of view. As described in Section 3.6, we train an existing classifier [2] to detect hands in the video feed.

3.3 Gaze Detection

Gaze is an important signal since, when a shopper gazes at one or more products, it reflects his or her interest in those products. We expect the person's head to be relatively steady while they are gazing. This can be detected using the inertial sensors on the smart glasses, in particular the accelerometer and the 3-axis compass. We use the rule $std(a_i) < th_a$ and $std(\theta_i) < th_\theta$ for $i \in \{x, y, z\}$, *i.e.*, the standard deviation in the acceleration values along all three axes must be lower than the threshold th_a, and the standard deviation along all three axes of compass must be lower than the threshold th_θ. Figure 3 depicts the dependence of false negatives (*i.e.*, missing gaze detection) and false positives (*i.e.*, mistaking other behavior as gazing) as a function of various combinations of threshold values. As seen from Figure 3, reducing th_a and th_{theta} decreases the false positives but increases the false negatives. While false negatives lead to missing actual gazing events, false positives will lead to turning on the video too frequently leading to higher power consumption. In our implementation, we chose thresholds at th_{theta} = 4.4 degrees and th_a = 0.7g m/s^2, to limit false negatives to 10% while minimizing false positives (at 33%).

Using optical flow to confirm gaze: However, 33% false positives is still too high. Since video has already been turned on now, one way to reduce this is to analyze the video feed to determine whether the person is indeed gazing. In order to achieve this, we rely on the property that when the shopper is gazing (s)he will intentionally make sure that there is very little change in what (s)he is seeing, from one moment to the next. Therefore, we used a vision based technique — *optical flow* [25] — applied to the video captured by the Glass. Optical flow measures the movement of pixels between consecutive images. We perform the optical flow computation on frames captured at 10 frames per second and calculate the average magnitude of the optical flow vectors over a one-second window. We then apply a threshold to this average optical flow value to de-

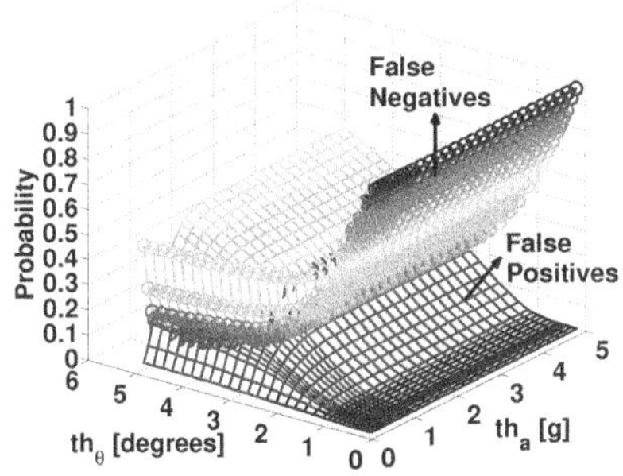

Figure 3: Choosing thresholds for gaze detection using inertial sensors

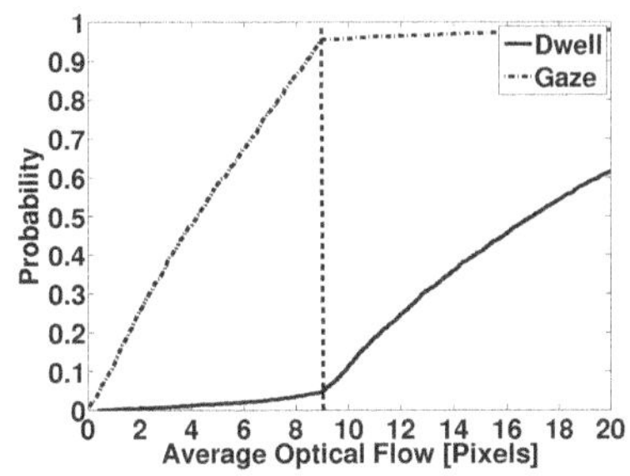

Figure 4: Choosing threshold for Optical flow based gaze detection

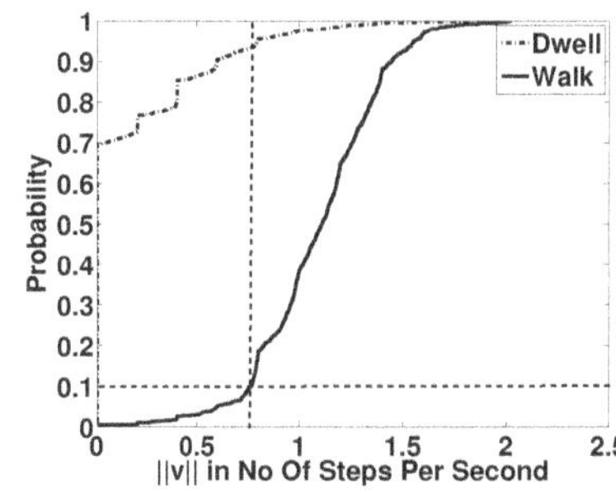

Figure 5: Choosing the threshold for Dwell Detection

cide whether the shopper is, in fact, gazing. Figure 4 depicts the cumulative distribution function of the optical flow for dwell and gaze behaviors obtained from the labeled videos (from experiments where the camera was turned on all the time, to understand the difference between the optical flow values during dwell and gaze). As seen from Figure 4, a threshold of 9 pixels, achieves a high detection rate (97%) while keeping the false detections low (2%) if video is on all the time. We achieve a detection rate of 88% with 1.2% false detections for our energy efficient scheme where the video is turned on only after gaze is detected by the inertial sensors.

Finally, we shed some light on why gaze detection based just on the inertial sensors leads to a high false positive rate of 33%. We rule out the movement of a shopper's eyes while their head is held steady as a significant cause since the optical flow method, which also does no eye tracking, yields a low false positive rate of 2%. Based on a closer examination, we identify three reasons for the significant difference in the detection rate in the two cases: (1) the shopper stands at a spot and leans forward, *i.e.*, zooms in, while holding their head steady to examine a product closely, (2) the shopper is looking at an object that they are holding and turning around from side to side (*e.g.*, to examine the front and back of a product), and (3) the shopper is looking steadily at a distant scene, which is a more common reason. In each case, inertial sensors based detection concludes that the shopper is gazing while the optical flow based approach concludes the opposite. One could argue that at least cases (1) and (2) correspond to the shopper, in fact, showing attention in a manner that the notion of gazing is intended to capture. However, we have taken the conservative position of restricting gazing to only cases where the visual image seen by the user is steady.

3.4 Dwell Detection

Dwelling refers to the shopper lingering around the same location. While the shopper could be taking steps during dwelling, they would tend to be ambling around, but roughly remaining in the vicinity, *i.e.*, having a small net displacement. Consequently, there could be significant movement during dwelling, so dwell detection based on simple approaches such as measuring the accelerometer magnitude or even looking for a reduction in the step rate, may not work correctly. Therefore, to build an effective detector, we rely on the intuition that unlike purposeful walking, in dwelling, the net displacement of the shopper will be very small, even though he/she may be walking around. In other words, dwelling is detected by a sharp drop in the magnitude of the average velocity vector of the shopper.

Device	Step Count Error [%]
Phone	2.6%
Glass	10.2%

Table 2: Step detection accuracy in mobile phone vs smart glasses

As discussed in Section 1, we use the step counter in Zee [40] to detect walking. Since most shoppers are likely to be carrying a smartphone with them, even if they are wearing smart glasses, measurements from either the smartphone or the smart glasses (or both) can be used to detect and count steps reliably. In our experiments, we found detection to be superior when done in the mobile phone as compared to smart glasses, as indicated in Table 2. This is because a shopper's head movements during shopping are mistaken for steps. Consequently, in ThirdEye we use inertial sensors from the phone for step counting, whenever possible.

In order to detect dwelling, we continuously compute the net displacement over a window of the past τ seconds by using the compass in the Google Glass to provide the instantaneous direction of the shopper's motion. Suppose that the shopper takes K steps during a τ-second window. Further, suppose that at the ith step, his/her orientation was θ_i. Then, we compute the magnitude of the net velocity vector as,

$$\|v\| = \sqrt{\left(\sum_{i=1}^{i=K} \cos\theta_i\right)^2 + \left(\sum_{i=1}^{i=K} \sin\theta_i\right)^2} \quad (1)$$

When $\|v\|$ drops below a certain threshold $\|v\|_{dwell}$ steps/sec, we conclude that the user is dwelling. In our implementation we set $\tau = 5$ seconds, under the assumption that any period shorter than 5 seconds cannot be considered as dwelling.

In order to choose the threshold $\|v\|_{dwell}$, we considered the distributions of velocities seen during walking and during dwelling, namely $\phi_{walk}(\|v\|)$ and $\phi_{dwell}(\|v\|)$ (depicted in Figure 5), as derived from the ground truth obtained from the videos collected from the shoppers. As seen from Figure 5, the threshold of 0.71 was chosen to allow 10% false errors (*i.e.*, walking is mistaken as dwelling) while providing a detection rate of about 95% (*i.e.*, dwelling is mistaken as walking 5% of the time).

3.5 Summary of Dwell, Walk, Gaze Detection

Overall, using inertial sensing based dwell detection and inertial sensing plus optical flow based gaze detection, ThirdEye is able to effectively classify the shopper's traversal into walking, dwelling, and gazing. Table 3 shows the confusion matrix for this classification based on 3 hours of store visit data from 7 shoppers. The large values along the diagonal (in bold) show that the classification is correct in the overwhelming majority of cases. It is also worth

Predicted⇒ Actual⇓	Walk	Dwell	Gaze
Walk	**90.4%**	9.1%	0.5%
Dwell	3.4%	**95.8%**	0.8%
Gaze	1.4%	10.7%	**87.9%**

Table 3: The confusion matrix for classification of walk vs. dwell vs. gaze

remembering that there is an element of subjectivity in the ground truth, and that might account for some of the misclassifications.

3.6 Reaching Out Detection

When the shopper eventually reaches out for a product, it indicates a very high degree of interest in that product. How can we detect such reaching out events? Unsurprisingly, we find that measurements from smart glasses or smartphone based inertial sensors are inadequate for distinguishing reaching out from gazing, since these sensors do not detect movement of the shopper's arm or hand.

Our detection scheme relies on the observation that in most cases of reaching out, the user's hand becomes visible in the image, whereas it tends not to be seen in the image when the shopper is walking, dwelling, or gazing. This is because users tend to look at whatever they are reaching out for and moreover the camera in the smart glasses typically sees what the user sees.

To detect hands, we trained a TextonBoost classifier [2] on 100 hand images from various shoppers. The classifier identifies the areas covered by a hand and marks them as depicted in Figure 6 and Figure 7. These figures also show two typical causes of error that arise from using the classifier, namely *hand fragmentation* and *spurious detections*. As seen in Figure 6, the presence of a watch on the hand fragments the hand into two separate parts. On the other hand, in Figure 7 the presence of items with similar texture and color as the hand results in spurious detections. To deal with fragmentation, we cluster together all fragments that either have overlapping bounding boxes or bounding boxes that are within 50 pixels of each other at their closest points. To deal with spurious detections, we rely on the observation that most spurious fragments tend to be much smaller in area compared to a real hand. Consequently we eliminated all fragments that occupied fewer than 1500 pixels (0.16% of the image). Overall, our reaching out detection scheme has a success rate of 86%, and a false detection rate of about 15%, based on testing over several videos from the training set. Further, we may miss detections when shoppers are reaching out for items in the lower shelves, as their hands may not appear within the field of view. Our reaching-out detection is currently offline since it involves more expensive vision processing and is an analytics step to understand the user's interests. Perhaps tapping sensor data from other devices such as smart watches would improve the reliability and computation cost of reaching out detection in such cases. Also, the use of more advanced pattern recognition techniques such as deep learning [30] could increase the success rate while reducing the false detections. We defer an exploration of these directions to future work.

4. ATTENTION IDENTIFICATION

Once it is established that the shopper is either gazing or reaching out, the next step is to identify the item(s) that the shopper is bestowing their attention on. Here, visual input plays a key role.

4.1 Reverse Image Search

ThirdEye captures images and invokes a cloud service to perform reverse image search, *i.e.*, identify the objects contained within the image. In our current implementation, we use Google's service [3], although ThirdEye is not tied to it and could also invoke alternative services, such as Bing Vision [1] and Nokia Point & Find [4].

Reverse image search involves object recognition, which in turn involves extracting image features (*e.g.*, using an algorithm such as SIFT [35]), comparing these with precomputed features from a large corpus of existing images to find a match, and retrieving meta-data associated with the matching image(s) in the corpus (*e.g.*, product name). The scale and complexity of this computation necessitates running it on the cloud (*e.g.*, the corpus of product images could run into the tens of millions). In turn, this calls for being selective in how frequently reverse image search requests are sent.

Therefore, only when gazing or reaching out are detected, does ThirdEye capture images and invoke the cloud service. During each period of gazing, ThirdEye captures all the images during the gazing period. Each image is then divided into 25 overlapping parts (in order to avoid images being broken at the borders) and each part is sent up to the cloud separately to minimize the chances of object recognition failing because of image-complexity issues. An example is depicted in Figure 8 with the overlapping parts that are sent for look up. In the example in Figure 8, 2 out of 5 brands were detected by Google reverse image search. Our evaluation based on manually studying the frames indicates that this scheme detects 53% of the products in the frame correctly. 7% are false positives, in other words, products are recognized incorrectly when they are absent. Finally, almost 40% of the products are never recognized. Further analysis indicated that almost all these 40% were not popular brand names but local brand names or items without labels like fruits and vegetables. Note that human computation (*e.g.*, through Amazon Mechanical Turk) could be used for brands that are not listed as a part of Google reverse image search and thus improve the database.

Figure 9 depicts the distribution of reverse image look up times over all our look ups. As seen from Figure 9, the look up times vary between 250 ms and 1 sec. with a mean of 650 ms.

4.2 Focus Within Field of View

In general, the number of items within the field of view of the Glass could be large. Figure 10 depicts the cumulative distribution function of the number of items recognized in any given frame. As seen from the figure, in some cases the number of items seen can be as large as 16. It is likely, however, that the shopper is only focused on one or perhaps a small number out of these items in his/her field of view. Our goal, therefore, is to identify the shopper's focus within the field of view.

It might be tempting to assume that the shopper's focus lies at the center of the field of view of their Glass. Figure 11 depicts the distribution of center of attention from the videos from several shoppers as they gazed. To learn the center of attention, we shadowed each shopper (*i.e.*, walked with them) as they shopped and also interviewed them afterwards while playing back the video recording from their Glass. As seen from the figure, the center of attention of the shopper is not necessarily at the center of the screen but is distributed over various pixels in the view. The dotted rectangle ABCD in Figure 11 depicts the area that includes 90% of the centers of attention as indicated by the shoppers. Based on Figure 11, the region of the video that might include the center of attention with 90% probability is only about 27% ($\frac{575\times426}{1280\times720}$) of the frame.

Further, as seen from the figure, there is a clear bias towards the left of the field of view. In fact, the mean x value in Figure 11 is $x_o = 511$. This is simply a consequence of the fact that the front-facing camera in Glass is mounted to one side (to the top-right of the right eye), so the center of the shopper's field of view lies to the left of that of the Glass.

Dependence of Attention on Head-Tilt: At a first glance, Figure 11 seems to indicate that the variation along y-axis of the center of attention is random and has a spread across the entire view (580 out of 720 pixels). However, deeper analysis revealed an interesting fact – *the center of attention in fact depends on the tilt of the head of the person.* Figure 12 depicts the dependence of the y-coordinate of the center of attention as a function of tilt of the head δ, as measured by the compass on the Google Glass. As seen from Figure 12,

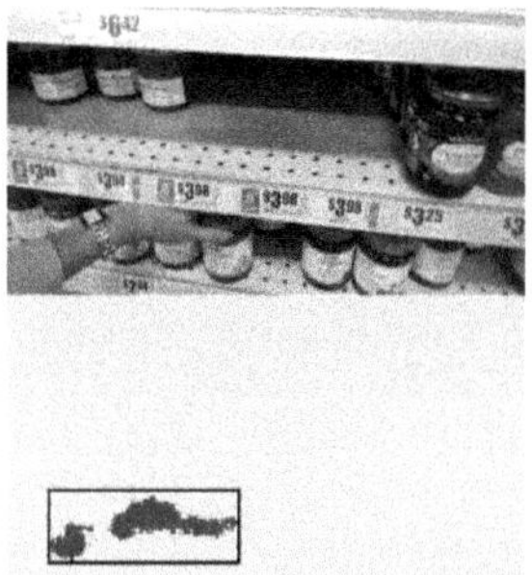

Figure 6: Two pieces of same hand

Figure 7: Spurious hand

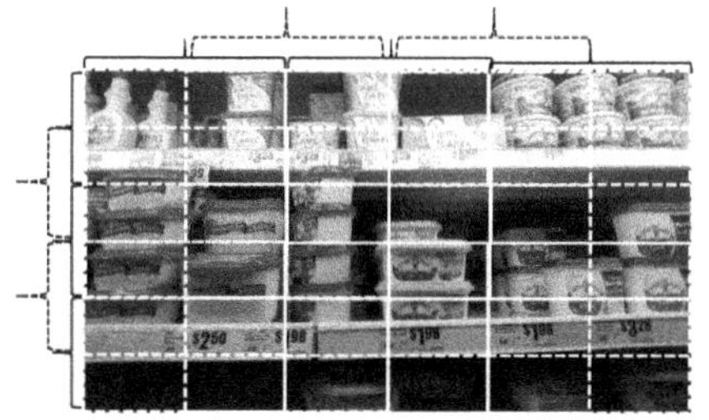

Figure 8: Reverse image search example. Brands found: Lands o lakes butter, Earth Balance. Brands missed: Spreadable butter, Olivio, Smart Balance

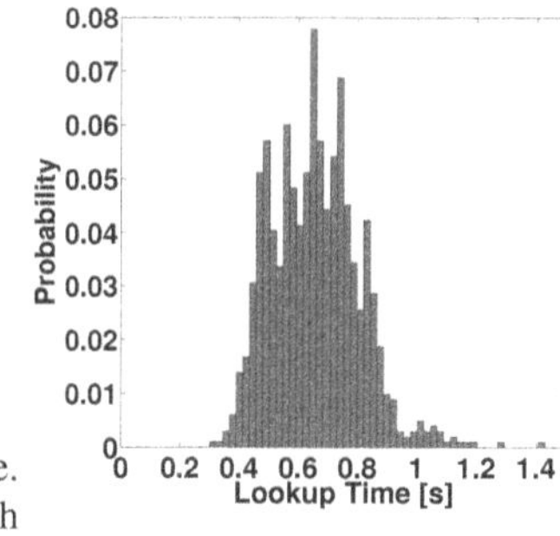

Figure 9: Distribution of reverse search times

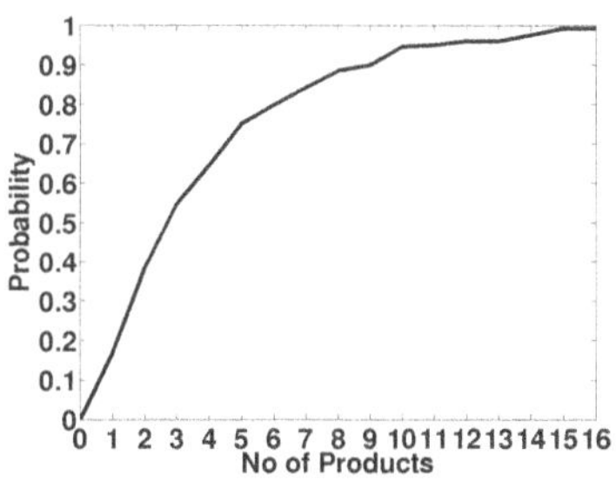

Figure 10: CDF of number of items seen in the field of view

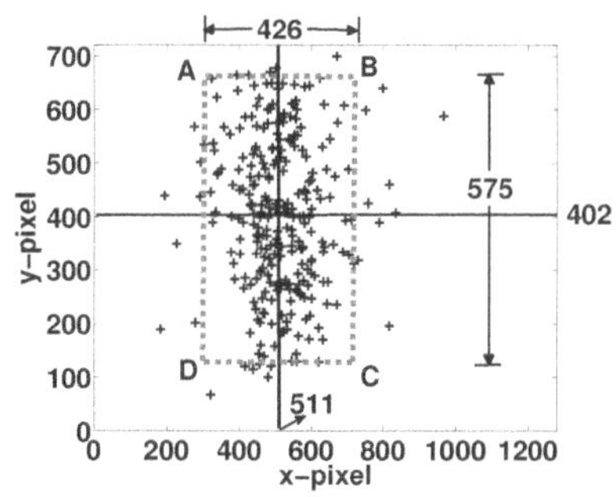

Figure 11: Distribution of center of attention

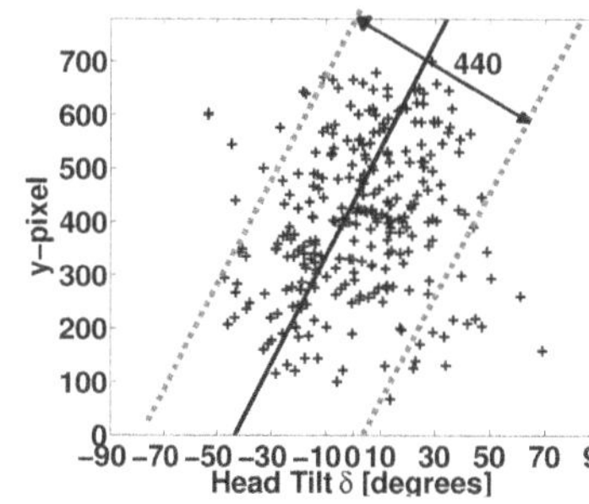

Figure 12: Dependence of center of attention on tilt

there is a mild linear dependence of the center of attention on the head tilt. We used RANSAC [22] (a popular scheme used in computer vision that is robust to outliers) to find the equation of the line to be $y = m\delta + c$, where $m = 10.05$ and $c = 436.38$ (depicted in Figure 12).

In hindsight, this makes sense, since when a shopper looks up or down towards a product, he/she accomplishes this by partly turning head up/down and partly by rolling their eye-balls. Consequently, the shopper's focus within their field of view would tend to shift in the same direction as their head is tilting. The region that includes the 90% of the centers of attention is also indicated by the dotted lines in Figure 12. As seen from the figure, the spread around the line now has reduced to 440 (60% of 720) instead of 575 (80% of 720) pixels (in Figure 11).

Probability Distributions for center of attention: Since it is in principle impossible to determine exactly which item the shopper is focused on, we resort to assigning a probability value $P(x, y|\delta)$ to an item in his field of view at the x and y pixel position, given the head-tilt, δ, as obtained from the compass:

$$P(x, y|\delta) = \Phi_X(x - x_o)\Phi_Y(y - m\delta - c) \tag{2}$$

The distributions $\Phi_X(z)$ and $\Phi_Y(z)$ are obtained using histograms from actual data. Figure 13 depicts the function $P(x, y|\delta)$ as a function of $x - x_o$, and $y - m\delta - c$.

Evaluation of Focus of Attention: We now ask the question how accurately we can identify the item that the person is looking at during gaze? We consider two schemes to measure the relative importance of various items in view. Our first scheme, deemed Naive in Table 4, naively uses distance from the center of the video (*i.e.*, pixel 640, 360) while our second scheme, deemed Max-Likelihood in Table 4, uses $P(x, y|\delta)$. In Table 4 we measure the fraction of times the top ranked item corresponded to the correct item the shopper was gazing at and also the fraction of times where the correct item was among the top three ranked item.

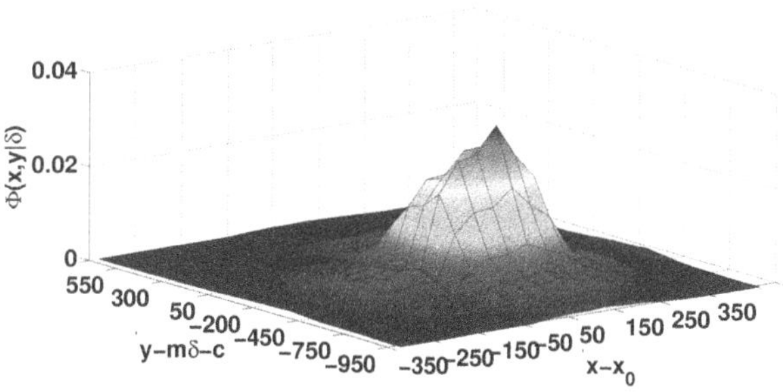

Figure 13: $\Phi(x, y|\delta)$

As seen from Table 4 the Max-likelihood approach is 76% accurate in terms of pin-pointing the correct item being gazed at, while the Naive approach only succeeds 66% of the time. Further, about 90% of the time, the correct item is among the top three prospective candidate items.

Scheme	Top 1	Top 2	Top 3
Naive	66%	80%	86%
Max-Likelihood	76%	86%	90%

Table 4: Determination of focus of attention

Devices such as the Tobii glasses [6] perform eye tracking, which can enable more accurate user attention identification than we present in this paper, but these are sophisticated devices which include multiple eye cameras in addition to a front-facing scene camera.

5. AUTOLAYOUT DESIGN

As discussed in Section 1, another important requirement to enable physical browsing analytics is information regarding the layout of products within a store. However, given the immense number of stores in the world, including the many that a single shopper could visit over time, and the likely reluctance of store owners to share information with their competitors, a crowd-sourcing based solution that can organically build layout maps without any help from the stores is attractive. Further, since we do not wish to discomfort the shoppers during their shopping, we also do not wish to seek any inputs from the shoppers. Therefore, we propose *AutoLayout*, which automatically infers layout based on video feed, inertial sensing data, and WiFi measurements obtained from the shoppers equipped with smart glasses. If individual store owners make partial or complete layout information available to us (*e.g.*, distance between certain products), we can incorporate it into our AutoLayout framework to further enhance accuracy.

Inferring layout from crowd-sourced data is challenging:

- We have no control over shopper behavior, *i.e.*, no control over how they walk or where they dwell.
- There is no ground truth available from the shoppers since we do not seek any input from them.
- While there is much existing work on building 3-D layouts from image or video data, these assume availability of well-known landmarks, which are usually not available in stores. Moreover, they also require extensive imagery with overlapping coverage, which is problematic in our context because we have no control over where the shoppers go or which way they look and recording the video continuously incurs prohibitive energy cost.

The key idea in AutoLayout is that while different shoppers walk in different ways within the store, WiFi APs and positions of products in the store can serve as anchors to align these different walks. The anchors can be identified using both WiFi RSS and images from the videos. AutoLayout simultaneously estimates the product locations and tracks the shoppers in a virtual 2-D coordinate system. Further, AutoLayout constructs a WiFi propagation model (based on EZ [16]) so that it can track both smart glass users and smartphone users, albeit with reduced accuracy for smartphone users.

5.1 Data Collected by AutoLayout

AutoLayout continuously collects inertial sensor data, WiFi data and opportunistically collects video feeds (whenever the shopper is gazing at products).

Inertial Data: As shoppers enter a store, in the background AutoLayout constantly keeps collecting inertial sensing data (accelerometer, compass), and continuously counts steps and tracks the direction θ, as obtained from the Google Glass, as the shopper walks around the store. Thus, for the ith step that the kth shopper takes, a direction value θ_k^i is recorded.

Video Data: Suppose that after the mth step, the kth shopper stops to gaze at or reach out for a product within the store, then as discussed in Section 4, the camera on the Google Glass is turned on and various products within view are identified by processing the images. Let I denote the set of all products in the store. Each product I_j is also associated with a list L_j of $< m, k >$ pairs indicating that the kth shopper was in the immediate vicinity of the product at this m^{th} step. Note that the same shopper may approach the same product repeatedly.

WiFi Data: The glasses perform periodic WiFi scans to record the WiFi signal strengths. Suppose that, the lth WiFi access point AP_l was seen by the kth shopper at the nth step and the measured signal strength was $r^{l,k,n}$. For each WiFi access point, a list W_l is maintained that stores the values, $r^{l,k,n}$.

5.2 Joint Layout Construction and Tracking

The unknowns that AutoLayout needs to estimate are:

- x_k^i, 2-D location vector of the kth shopper after his i^{th} step
- z^j, 2-D location vector of jth product within the store, and,
- $< P_l, y^l, \gamma_l >$, P_l is the transmit power of the WiFi AP_l, y^l is its location, and γ_l is the path loss constant for the Log Distance Path Loss (LDPL) propagation model [16]. This is because, AutoLayout uses the LDPL model to predict the received signal strength at various locations from the APs.

The approach taken by AutoLayout is to minimize the objective function, which quantifies various errors, as shown below:

$$\begin{aligned}
J &= J_X + J_Y + J_{AP} \\
J_X &= \tfrac{1}{\sigma_X^2} \textstyle\sum_i \sum_k \|x_k^{i+1} - x_k^i - \hat{e}_k^i\|^2 \\
\hat{e}_k^i &= [\ \cos\theta_k^i \quad \sin\theta_k^i\ ]^T \\
J_Y &= \tfrac{1}{\sigma_Y^2} \textstyle\sum_{j, I_j \in I} \sum_{<m,k> \in L_j} \|x_k^m - z^j\|^2 \\
J_{AP} &= \tfrac{1}{\sigma_{AP}^2} \textstyle\sum_l \sum_{r^{l,k,n} \in W_l} \left\| \begin{matrix} r^{l,k,n} - \\ rss(P_l, \gamma_l, y^l, x_k^n) \end{matrix} \right\| \\
rss(P, \gamma, y, x) &= P - 10\gamma \log(\|y - x\|)
\end{aligned} \tag{3}$$

In Eqn 3, the overall error objective function J comprises of three parts. First, J_X captures the constraint that shopper locations x_k^{i+1} and x_k^i coming from two consecutive steps of the same shopper must be separated by a single step and may be subject to σ_X (0.1 in our implementation) standard deviation of error. Second, J_Y captures the fact that all shopper locations from where a particular product was gazed at by the shopper must be very close to each other (we use a variance σ_Y, 1 step in our implementation, to account for the fact that the shoppers may not be exactly at the same place). This term essentially ties all the tracks from all the shopper together into the same coordinate system. Third, J_{AP} minimizes the difference between measured RSS and estimated RSS based on the parameters describing the LDPL model for all APs across all observations made by all shoppers. Since no global reference frame can be established, AutoLayout arbitrarily fixes any one position of a shopper as the origin. Our implementation simply chooses $x_0^0 = \mathbf{0}$.

5.3 The Optimization

Optimizing Eqn 3 is no easy task since the search involves a large number of unknowns and the objective is non-linear with multiple local minima. Consequently, we take a four-step approach to solve the optimization problem.

1. Obtain an initial estimate for shopper locations x_k^i and product locations z^j using the *BFSLoc* algorithm described shortly.
2. Optimize the partial objective function $J_{part} = J_X + J_Y$ to refine x_k^i and z^j using gradient descent method.
3. Obtain an initial guess for all the AP parameters $< P_l, y^l, \gamma_l >$ by minimizing J_{AP} using gradient descent method based on the existing values for x_k^i and z^j.
4. Starting with current values of the unknowns as the initial values, we iteratively optimize the overall objective function J as follows: first search x_k^i and z^j's that optimize J while fixing APs' parameters, and then search APs' parameters that optimize J while fixing x_k^i's and z^j's, and iterate. We iterate until the objective function improvement is within 10^{-5}.

In the interest of brevity, we do not describe gradient descent, since it is a well known optimization method. We describe BFSLoc, the first step in the AutoLayout procedure outlined above.

BFSLoc: The key idea in BFSLoc is to estimate locations (either product location or shopper location) using the shortest possible explanation. BFSLoc starts by constructing a graph where each shopper's location or product's location is associated with a node as depicted in Figure 14. Edges exists between nodes that represent consecutive steps from the same shopper (*i.e.*, x_k^i and x_k^{i+1}).

Edges also exist between nodes that represent a product location z^j and a shopper location x_k^m when the product has been seen at that shopper location ($< m, k > \in L_j$).

The BFSLoc algorithm involves performing a breath first traversal on this graph starting from x_0^0 until all the nodes are traversed. Upon visiting any node a from a parent/previous node b, the value of the unknown corresponding to the node is computed:

- if $a = x_k^{i+1}$ and $b = x_k^i$, compute $x_k^{i+1} = x_k^i + \hat{e}_k^i$.
- if $a = x_k^{i-1}$ and $b = x_k^i$, compute $x_k^{i-1} = x_k^i - \hat{e}_k^i$.
- if $a = x_k^i$ and $b = z^j$, compute $x_k^i = R(z^j, \rho)$, where $R(z, \rho)$ generates a random location in a disc of radius ρ with its center as the 2-D location z.
- if $a = z^j$ and $b = x_k^i$, compute $z^j = R(x_k^i, \rho)$

The intuition here is that, starting from x_0^0 (which by definition is a certain location in our virtual coordinate space), we wish to estimate the location of all entities, whether a shopper at a particular step in their walk or a particular product, by following the fewest "links in the chain", with a view to minimize the accumulated error. We emphasize that BFSLoc is only the first step in AutoLayout procedure, so our goal in this first step is to obtain a good initial guess, not the correct estimates.

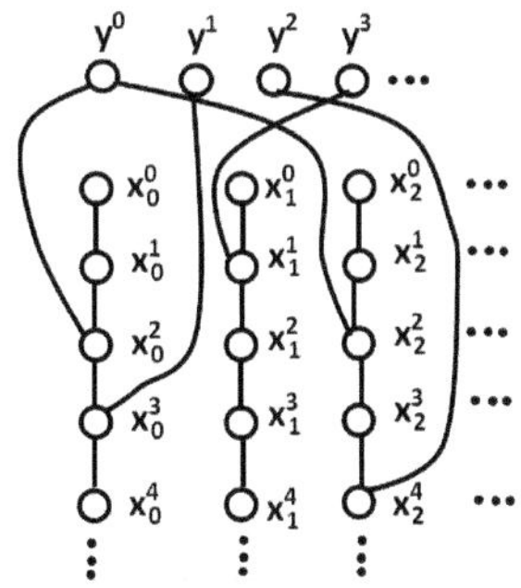

Figure 14: BFSLoc graph

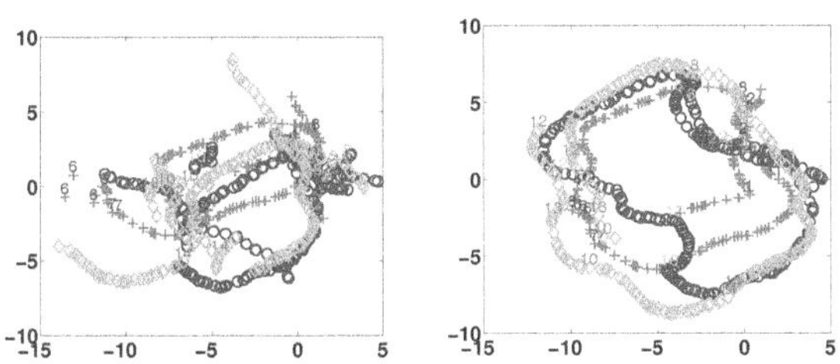

(a) After BFSLoc (b) After Optimization

Figure 15: Function example of AutoLayout

5.4 An example of AutoLayout Functioning

In order to provide an intuition to the reader about the functioning of AutoLayout, we now show an example. In this example, three different shoppers were asked to take a rectangular route through the aisles in a retail store. The entire route was about 80m long. During the measurement, they occasionally walked, gazed and dwelled. Using the video, inertial and WiFi data from the three shoppers, we used AutoLayout to construct the product locations and the tracks of the shoppers. Figure 15 shows the layouts obtained after applying BFSLoc and after the entire optimization process. As seen from Figure 15 at the end of BFSLoc, the tracks of the three shoppers are very fragmented and do not overlap very well. This is due to the following reasons. First, there are errors in the compass measurements and in counting steps. Second, shopper stride lengths are different. However, after the optimization, AutoLayout not only determines the relative product locations but also identifies the entire path taken by the various shoppers. As a result in Figure 15 (b) the tracks after optimization look closer to the rectangular paths that the shoppers took. Moreover we also see AutoLayout inferred two large overlapping rectangles (where the two shoppers walked around the same set of aisles) and one smaller rectangle where the user turned around in the previous aisle.

5.5 Tracking Users in real Time

For tracking shoppers in real-time, we use the same scheme as above except that we only consider the shopper's locations as unknown. Thus, the moment the shopper sees a product while gazing, a WiFi scan is performed and his/her location is initialized. Thereafter, the subsequent locations are estimated by performing a gradient decent on J over only the shopper's locations. The optimization converges very rapidly in real-time since the initial location estimate is already quite close to the shopper's real location.

5.6 Dealing with shopper's head movements

An important measurement in AutoLayout is the shopper's direction of motion. Since smart glasses are located on the top of the head and face the direction of the user, they typically are aligned in the direction of motion of the shopper. However, shoppers often turn their heads to look around and sometimes they walk with their heads oriented obliquely while watching something interesting or talking. Thus, a key challenge in using smart glasses is detecting the fact that the shopper has turned his head and not updating the direction of his/her path.

One obvious approach is to see if head movements can be detected and distinguished from actual change in direction of shopper's path. However, after studying several shoppers, we realized that it is often not possible to distinguish this based on accelerometer, compass or gyroscope measurements. Consequently, we take a very different approach based on the fact that most Google Glass users also carry their mobile phone along with them (usually in hand or pocket). The key idea is that when the shopper turns his/her head, the Google Glass compass orientation changes, but there is no change in the orientation seen by the mobile phone. Below we describe our scheme to correct for head movements.

1. We estimate the median offset between Google Glass and phone. As most of the time people walk while looking straight ahead, this accurately provides an estimate of the mobile phone's orientation with respect to straight ahead as α.
2. Direction of user's heading is then, $\theta = \theta_{mob} + \alpha$ where θ_{mob} is orientation given by the mobile phone.

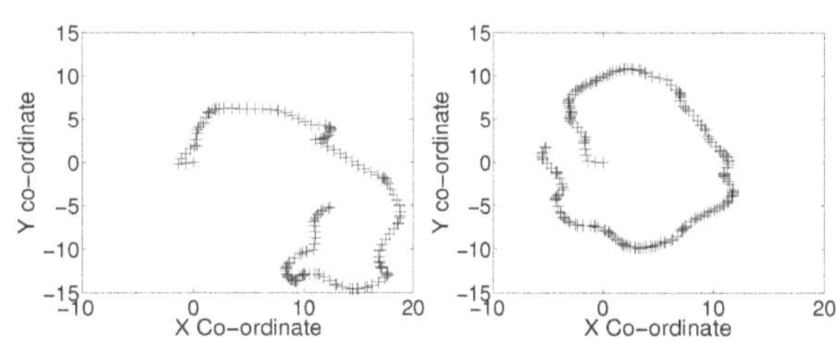

(a) Uncorrected (b) Corrected

Figure 16: Shopper tracks before and after compass correction

Figure 16 depicts the benefits of using the above scheme on a real shopper's track who started and came back to the entrance of the shop after taking about 100 steps (about 70m). This track was computed by simply adding $\hat{e}_k^i$ (the direction vectors). As seen from Figure 16, correction significantly improves the track quality.

Detecting when phone is taken out of pocket: One problem with relying on the shoppers' mobile phones for correcting the direction is that the shoppers might occasionally take their phone out to use it. However such events can be detected very reliably since they

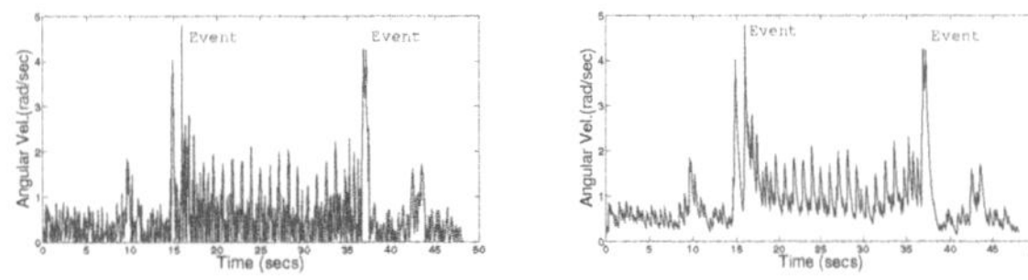

(a) Raw Signal (b) Onset Signal

Figure 17: Absolute value of angular velocity about Z axis

involve sudden motion. Once having detected such an event, we simply re-estimate the median offset from the Google Glass.

We show the events in the Figure 17 (a). We detect the onset of such events based on the absolute value of the signal as shown in Figure 17 (b). We examine 20 traces from 2 users, with each user taking the smartphone out of the pocket and putting it in the pocket for 5 of 10 of their walks. In the other 5 walks, no such event occurs. We compute the CDF of the onset signal over all the walks and vary the detection threshold from top 0.2% to 5% of the signal values. We apply this threshold to quantify true detection accuracy and false alarms. We quantify fraction of the times the event was detected versus the fraction of total seconds that we wrongly detected as pick up events. As shown in Table 5, we can detect up to 85% of phone putting in/pulling out of pocket events without any false alarms and up to 95% of the events with only false alarms during 0.33% of the total time of the walk.

We also tested other cases like holding phone in hand and swaying hands while walking. We find that this action does not change the orientation significantly. For example, we found that the standard deviation of compass heading when user is walking with phone held still in hands is 5.98 over 6 walks by 2 users where each walk was a straight line of about 25 m. It was 8.4 when the users were swaying their hands.

True detection [%]	False Alarm [%]
85	0
90	0.11
95	0.33
100	19

Table 5: Detecting change in phone position

6. ENERGY MEASUREMENTS

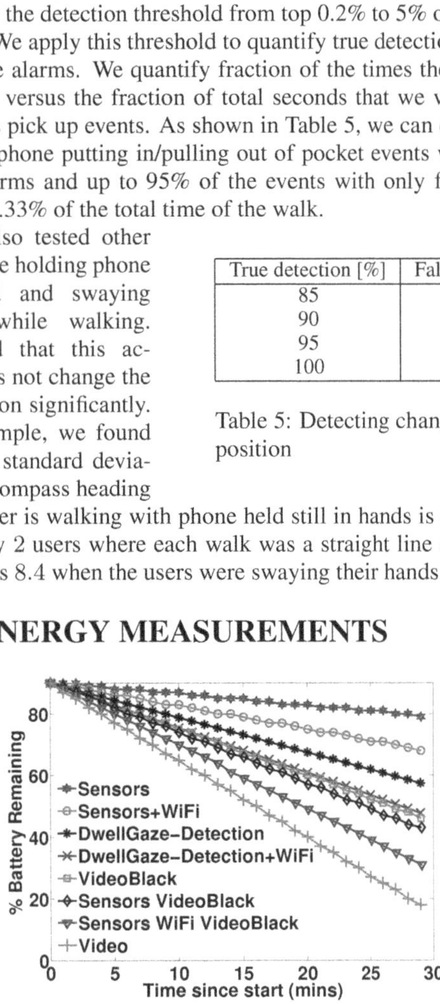

Figure 18: Power measurement on the Google Glass

In this section, we evaluate the power consumption of running the inertial sensors (accelerometer and compass), WiFi, Video capture and our dwell and gaze algorithms on the Google Glass. Since we can not remove the battery and bypass it using a power monitor, we use the android API to monitor battery level [11] and log the remaining battery level every minute. We plot the result for various combinations as shown in Figure 18. We plot the battery level starting from 90% for the next 30 minutes. The legend and the description below are arranged in an increasing rate of power consumption for ease of reading.

Sensors: Here accelerometer and compass were sampled at the fastest allowed rate, *i.e.*, 200 Hz samples were received.

Sensors+WiFi: Since AutoLayout uses WiFi (to enable ThirdEye for non-smart glass users), here we measure the impact of performing back-to-back WiFi scans while simultaneously sensing from accelerometer and compass at 200Hz.

DwellGaze: Here we evaluate the power consumption as the shoppers go shopping during their due course without scanning WiFi. Note that, here VideoBack is turned on only when the glasses detect that the person is gazing (this includes the effect of 33% false positives and 10% false negatives).

DwellGaze+WiFi: Here we compute the same as DwellGaze except with back-to-back WiFi scans for AutoLayout.

VideoBlack: VideoBlack [47] is an application that takes video without displaying on screen so it is energy efficient compared to Video. This is also the default method of taking a video in Google Glass. Video is simply stored, no other computation is performed during the measurement.

Sensors+VideoBlack: During gaze, once video is turned on, we measure the impact of storing video while simultaneously sensing accelerometer and compass at 200Hz.

Sensors+VideoBlack+WiFi: Here we measure the impact of running WiFi scans back-to-back simultaneously with sensing at 200Hz and storing video using VideoBlack.

Video: Here the video on the smart glasses is turned on and stored.

Table 6 depicts the predicted lifetime of various schemes based on our measurements. As seen from Table 6, VideoBlack provides almost 60% higher energy savings than using Video. Further, even VideoBlack is more than 3× expensive compared to using inertial sensors indicating the need for judiciously turning on Video. Continuous WiFi also has a significant impact and typically cuts lifetime significantly. Optimized schemes can be designed to use WiFi sparingly for AutoLayout, however we defer it to future. Thus, the lifetime of ThirdEye is approximately between 70 min (for WiFi turned on continuously) and 90 min (with WiFi scanning turned off).

Scheme	Predicted Lifetime [m]
Sensors	265
Sensors+WiFi	134
DwellGaze	89
DwellGaze+WiFi	69
VideoBlack	75
Sensors+VideoBlack	70
Sensors+VideoBlack+WiFi	49
Video	47

Table 6: Predicted Lifetime

7. EXPERIMENTAL EVALUATION

In this section, we evaluate two aspects of ThirdEye: the performance of AutoLayout and the performance of a shopping list reminder application for shoppers without smart glasses.

Experimental Methodology: We tested AutoLayout on 7 shoppers comprising three males and four females of different heights who shopped at a large grocery store (over 2 Km^2 in area) in the US. First, we performed a survey of the store, and measured the relative locations of about 67 different products for obtaining the ground truth. Each shopper was provided with a Google Glass and a smart phone that they would place in their pocket. The smart phone and the Google Glass communicated using Bluetooth. We shadowed each shopper as they went about their due course of shopping without interfering. Each shopper turned on Google

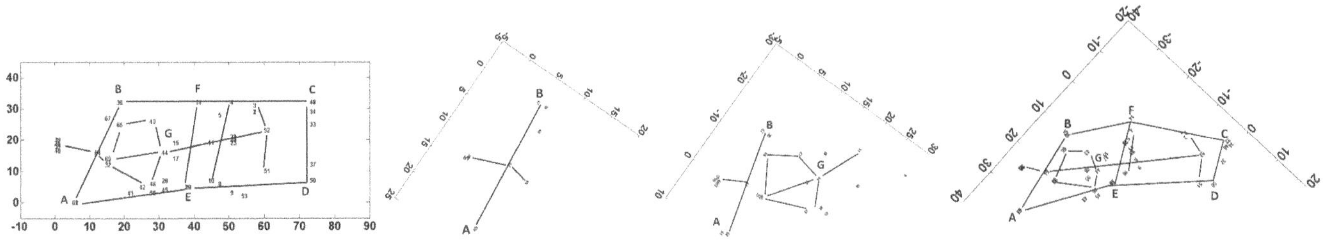

(a) Actual layout (scale in m) (b) Inferred layout after 2 shoppers (c) Inferred layout after 4 shoppers (d) Inferred layout after 7 shoppers

Figure 19: How ThirdEye inferred layout of the shop improves with more shoppers

K	$\eta_{true}(K)$	$\eta_{false}(K)$
1	60%	40%
3	62%	29%
5	67%	26%
10	80%	18%

Table 7: Product layout proximity in AutoLayout

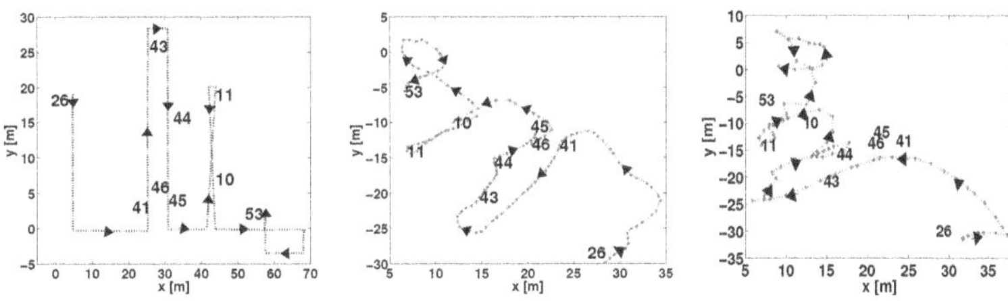

(a) Original Path (b) Path inferred by glass users (c) Path inferred by smartphone users

Figure 20: How ThirdEye tracks shoppers' paths

K	$\eta_{true}(K)$	$\eta_{false}(K)$
1	17%	85%
3	29%	64%
5	38%	59%
10	60%	40%

Table 8: Performance for Non-Smart Glass Users

Glass and smart phone at different locations within the shop (hence the start locations were different), visited different parts of the shop while taking different paths. While shadowing we noted the path that each shopper took and the locations where they gazed, for obtaining the ground truth.

Product Layout Generated by ThirdEye: AutoLayout generates a product layout of the store in a virtual 2-D coordinate system by merging the measurements from various shoppers with possibly different stride lengths. Consequently, the virtual coordinate will typically be a scaled, rotated (and possibly reflected), and sometimes distorted version of the original layout. However, one important property that it preserves is proximity relationships *i.e.*, products that are close physically will also be close in the virtual map.

First, to provide intuition into how the original layout compares to that inferred by AutoLayout, in Figure 19 we depict the original and inferred layouts containing 67 different products within a large grocery store (a unique number is assigned to each brand in the Figure). To aid the readers in comparing the original and inferred layouts, we have connected lines between the locations of a few brands (labeled as A,B,C,D,E,F) that are located far away. Figure 19 depicts the evolution of the layouts inferred by ThirdEye as data from more and more shoppers is obtained. The evolution naturally depends on the exact areas where the shoppers visited. As seen from the Figure, after 7 shoppers visited the shop, the inferred layout approximately matches the original layout and proximity relationships are preserved in most cases (albeit rotation and scaling).

How well does AutoLayout Preserve Proximity Relationships? In order to answer this question, for each ith product we create the set $\mathbf{\Psi}_i(K)$ containing its K closest neighboring products using the ground truth data and the $\mathbf{\Omega}_i(K)$ containing its K closest neighbors based on the layout inferred from AutoLayout. We then evaluate average true detections $\eta_{true}(K)$ and average false detections η_{false} as

$$\eta_{true}(K) = \frac{\sum |\mathbf{\Psi}_i(K) \cap \mathbf{\Omega}_i(K)|}{\sum |\mathbf{\Psi}_i(K)|} \quad (4)$$

$$\eta_{false}(K) = \frac{\sum |\mathbf{\Omega}_i(K) - (\mathbf{\Psi}_i(K) \cap \mathbf{\Omega}_i(K))|}{\sum |\mathbf{\Psi}_i(K)|} \quad (5)$$

Here $|\bullet|$ represents cardinality of the set.

As seen from Table 7, AutoLayout predicts the closest product correctly about 60% of the time and reports incorrectly about 40% of the time. Note that predicting the closest product is particularly challenging given the close proximity of the products within the layout. The correct prediction ratio increases as the value of K increases and is about 80% for the set of closest 10 products. This can be very useful for a reminder application that can remind the shopper of a product they intended to buy when they are purchasing another product nearby or help provide a timely discount offer and convince them into purchasing another product that is close by.

How well does AutoLayout Track Shoppers With and Without Glasses? ThirdEye tracks shoppers in a rotated, scaled and potentially reflected coordinate system. Since it also constructs the product layout in this coordinate system, it can place the shopper relative to the products in the shop. Figure 20 (a) depicts the true path (ground truth) and Figure 20 (b) depicts the path inferred by ThirdEye in its coordinate system for one of the shoppers. In this case, the coordinate system is rotated, scaled and reflected. The products that the shopper passes by are marked by unique numbers assigned to them. In the example, the shopper starts at product 26 and walks to product 53, passing through a total of 9 products locations. As seen in Figure 20 (b), ThirdEye successfully tracks the shopper in its own corresponding rotated, scaled and reflected coordinate system. Figure 20 (c) depicts the same path inferred by ThirdEye without using smart glass data, *i.e.*, using mobile-phone inertial and WiFi data. As shown in Figure 20 (c), the inferred path is similar to the actual path though at a reduced accuracy.

How well does the reminder application work for shoppers without Glasses? We consider an application, where the shopper has a shopping list and is reminded to purchase as soon as he comes near one of the products in his shopping list. In order to evaluate how well the inferred map helps this application, we tested AutoLayout on shoppers without using their video from the Glass. We used AutoLayout to locate the person at each location (s)he dwelled (using only WiFi and inertial data from his mobile phone) and then used the inferred map to determine all the top K nearest products and then compared with the ground truth layout map.

Table 8 depicts the true and false detection rates as we vary the number of items K. As seen from Table 8, errors are higher than the case of Glass users due to lower localization accuracy. Nevertheless with an increasing K, we are able to cover the top K nearest items more accurately, indicating not only that AutoLayout preserves proximity but even shoppers without smart glasses can benefit from the proximity information.

8. CONCLUSION

In this paper, we have presented ThirdEye, a system for tracking physical browsing by users in retail stores using data gleaned from vision, WiFi, and inertial sensors. Through our evaluation in two large retail stores in US, we show the effectiveness of ThirdEye, despite not requiring any input from the store or the users themselves. In future work, we plan to conduct a more in-depth physical analytics of shoppers based on ThirdEye's ability to track user browsing.

Acknowledgements

This work is supported in part by NSF Grants CCF-1117009 and CNS-1343383. We are grateful to our anonymous shepherd and reviewers for their valuable comments to help improve our work. We thank our friends and lab-mates for their shopping data.

9. REFERENCES

[1] Bing vision. http://en.wikipedia.org/wiki/Bing_Vision.

[2] Code for textonboost. http://jamie.shotton.org/work/code/TextonBoost.zip.

[3] Google search by image. http://www.google.com/insidesearch/features/images/searchbyimage.html.

[4] Nokia point and find. https://betalabs.nokia.com/trials/nokia-point-and-find.

[5] Time Domain. http://www.timedomain.com/.

[6] Tobii. http://www.tobii.com/.

[7] S. Agarwal, N. Snavely, I. Simon, S. M. Seitz, and R. Szeliski. Building rome in a day. In *Proc. of ICCV*, 2009.

[8] M. Alzantot and M. Youssef. Crowdinside: automatic construction of indoor floorplans. In *Proc. of the 20th International Conference on Advances in Geographic Information Systems*, 2012.

[9] M. Azizyan, I. Constandache, and R. R. Choudhury. SurroundSense: Mobile Phone Localization via Ambience Fingerprinting. In *Proc. of Mobicom*, 2009.

[10] P. Bahl and V. N. Padmanabhan. RADAR: An Inbuilding RF-based User Location and Tracking System. In *Proc. of INFOCOM*, 2000.

[11] Battery level api. http://developer.android.com/training/monitoring-device-state/battery-monitoring.html.

[12] K. Bauer, D. Mccoy, B. Greenstein, D. Grunwald, and D. Sicker. Using Wireless Physical Layer Information to Construct Implicit Identifiers. In *Proc. of HotPETs*, 2008.

[13] S. Beauregard and H. Haas. Pedestrian Dead Reckoning: A Basis for Personal Positioning. In *Proc. of WPNC*, 2006.

[14] V. Brik, S. Banerjee, M. Gruteser, and S. Oh. Wireless Device Identification with Radiometric Signatures. In *Proc. of MobiCom*, 2008.

[15] A. Campbell et al. The Rise of People-Centric Sensing. *IEEE Internet Computing*, Jul/Aug 2008.

[16] K. Chintalapudi, A. P. Iyer, and V. N. Padmanabhan. Indoor Localization Without the Pain. In *Proc. of MobiCom*, 2010.

[17] T. Choudhury, S. Consolvo, B. Harrison, and J. Hightower. The Mobile Sensing Platform: An Embedded Activity Recognition System. *IEEE Pervasive Computing*, Apr-Jun 2008.

[18] A. J. Davidson, I. D. Reid, N. D. Molton, and O. Stasse. MonoSLAM: Real-Time Single Camera SLAM. *IEEE PAMI*, 29(6), Jun 2007.

[19] B. F. Dieter and F. N. Lawrence. Wifi-slam using gaussian process latent variable models. In *Proc. of the International Joint Conference on Artificial Intelligence (IJCAI)*, 2007.

[20] S. B. Eisenman, E. Miluzzo, N. D. Lane, R. A. Peterson, G.-S. Ahn, and A. T. Campbell. The BikeNet Mobile Sensing System for Cyclist Experience Mapping. In *Proc. of SenSys*, 2007.

[21] Euclid Analytics. Answers and insights for qsr, coffee, specialty retail, and large format stores, October 2013. http://euclidanalytics.com/.

[22] M. A. Fischler and R. C. Bolles. Random Sample Consensus: A Paradigm for Model Fitting with Applications to Image Analysis and Automated Cartography. *Communication of the ACM*, 24(6):381–395, 1981.

[23] Google glasses. http://www.google.com/glass/start/.

[24] A. Haeberlen, E. Flannery, A. M. Ladd, A. Rudys, D. S. Wallach, and L. E. Kavraki. Practical Robust Localization over Large-Scale 802.11 Wireless Networks. In *Proc. of MobiCom*, 2004.

[25] B. Horn and B. Schunck. Determining Optical Flow. *Artifical Intelligence*, 17, 1981.

[26] ibeacon. http://tech.fortune.cnn.com/2014/02/28/apples-ibeacon-signals-turning-point-for-mobile-engagement/.

[27] N. B. John, J. Heidemann, and D. Estrin. GPS-Less Low Cost Outdoor Localization For Very Small Devices. *IEEE Personal Communications Magazine*, 7:28–34, 2000.

[28] T. Kanda, D. F. Glas, M. Shiomi, H. Ishiguro, and N. Hagita. Who will be the customer?: A social robot that anticipates people's behavior from their trajectories. In *Proc. of UbiComp*, 2008.

[29] P. Krishnan, A. S. Krishnakumar, W. H. Ju, C. Mallows, and S. Ganu. A System for LEASE: Location Estimation Assisted by Stationery Emitters for Indoor RF Wireless Networks. In *Proc. of INFOCOM*, 2004.

[30] A. Krizhevsky, I. Sutskever, and G. E. Hinton. ImageNet Classification with Deep Convolutional Neural Networks. In *Proc. of NIPS*, 2012.

[31] S. Lee, C. Yoo, C. Min, and J. Song. Understanding customer malling behavior in an urban shopping mall using smartphones. In *Proc. of ACM Workshop on Mobile Systems for Computional Social Science (co-located with UbiComp)*, 2013.

[32] J. Leonard and H. F. Durrant-whyte. Simultanoues Map Building and Localization for an Autonomous Mobile Robot. In *IROS*, pages 1442–1447, 1991.

[33] Y. Li, N. Snavely, D. Huttenlocher, and P. Fua. Worldwide pose estimation using 3d point clouds. In *Proc. of ECCV*, 2012.

[34] H. Lim, L. Kung, J. Hou, and H. Luo. Zero-Configuration, Robust Indoor Localization: Theory and Experimentation. In *Proc. of INFOCOM*, 2006.

[35] D. Lowe. Object Recognition from Local Scale-Invariant Features. In *Proc. of ICCV*, 1999.

[36] Nearbuy Systems. In-store mobile commerce, October 2013. http://www.nearbuysystems.com/.

[37] L. Ni, Y. Liu, C. Yiu, and A. Patil. LANDMARC: Indoor Location Sensing Using Active RFID. *Wireless Network*, 2004.

[38] J. Panda, M. S. Brown, and C. V. Jawahar. Offline mobile instance retrieval with a small memory footprint. In *Proc. of ICCV*, 2013.

[39] N. B. Priyantha, A. Chakraborty, and H. Balakrishnan. The Cricket Location-Support System. In *Proc. of MobiCom*, 2000.

[40] A. Rai, K. Chintalapudi, V. N. Padmanabhan, and R. Sen. Zee: Zero-Effort Crowdsourcing for Indoor Localization. In *Proc. of MobiCom*, 2012.

[41] T. Rappaport. *Wireless Communications Principles and Practice*. Prentice Hall, 2001.

[42] P. Robertson, M. Angermann, and B. Krach. Simultaneous Localization and Mapping for Pedestrians using only Foot-Mounted Inertial Sensors. In *Proc. of UbiComp*, 2009.

[43] P. Robertson, M. G. Puyol, and M. Angermann. Collaborative Pedestrian Mapping of Buildings: Using Inertial Sensors and FootSLAM. In *Proc. of ION GNSS*, Sep 2011.

[44] S. Sen, R. R. Choudhury, and S. Nelakuditi. SpinLoc: Spin once to know your location. In *Proc. of HotMobile*, 2012.

[45] S. Sen, B. Radunovic, R. R. Choudhury, and T. Minka. Precise Indoor Localization using PHY Layer Information. In *Proc. of HotNets*, 2011.

[46] L. Stampler. That chocolate chip cookie in the checkout aisle is watching you. *Time NewsFeed*, October 2013. http://newsfeed.time.com/2013/10/16/that-chocolate-chip-cookie-in-the-checkout-aisle-is-watching-you/.

[47] Videoblack. http://glass-apps.org/videoblack-google-glass-app.

[48] H. Wang, S. Sen, A. Elgohary, M. Farid, M. Youssef, and R. R. Choudhury. No Need to War-Drive: Unsupervised Indoor Localization. In *Proc. of MobiSys*, 2012.

[49] R. Want and et al. The Active Badge Location System. *ACM Transactions on Information Systems*, Jan 1992.

[50] A. Ward, A. Jones, and A. Hopper. A New Location Technique for the Active Office. *IEEE Per. Comm.*, 4(5):42–47, 1997.

[51] J. Xiong and K. Jamieson. ArrayTrack: A Fine-Grained Indoor Location System. In *Proc. of HotMobile*, 2012.

[52] C. You, C. Wei, Y. Chen, H. Chu, and M. Chen. Using mobile phones to monitor shopping time at physical stores. *IEEE Pervasive Computing*, 2011.

[53] M. Youssef and A. Agrawala. The Horus WLAN Location Determination System. In *Proc. of MobiSys*, 2005.

Some of My Simple Results

Leonard Kleinrock
Computer Science Department
University of California, Los Angeles
lk@cs.ucla.edu

ABSTRACT
A number of interesting problems that I have addressed over the years which yielded surprisingly simple results will be presented. Many of these had intuitively pleasing interpretations or especially simple proofs and/or insights.

Author Keywords
Internet; packet switching networks; packet radio networks; local area networks; broadband networks; intelligent software agents; performance evaluation

ACM Classification Keywords
C.2.0 [GENERAL]: DATA COMMUNICATION

BIO
Dr. Leonard Kleinrock is considered a father of the Internet, having developed the mathematical theory of packet networks, the technology underpinning the Internet, while an MIT graduate student. This was in 1962, many years before the birth of the Internet which occurred in his laboratory when his UCLA Host computer became the first Internet node in September 1969. A month later, he directed the transmission of the first message ever to pass over the Internet. He wrote the first paper and published the first book on the subject.

Dr. Kleinrock received his Ph.D. from MIT in 1963. He currently serves as a Distinguished Professor of Computer Science at UCLA. He has published over 250 papers and authored six books on a wide array of subjects including packet switching networks, packet radio networks, local area networks, broadband networks, nomadic computing, peer-to-peer networks, and intelligent software agents.

Dr. Kleinrock is a member of the National Academy of Engineering, the American Academy of Arts and Sciences, an IEEE fellow, an ACM fellow, an INFORMS Fellow, and an IEC fellow. Among his many honors, he is the recipient of the Ericsson Prize, the NAE Draper Prize, the Marconi Prize, the Okawa Prize, the Dan David Prize, and was further recognized when he received the 2007 National Medal of Science, the highest honor for achievement in science bestowed by the President of the United States.

MobiCom'14, September 7-11, 2014, Maui, Hawaii, USA.
ACM 978-1-4503-2783-1/14/09.
http://dx.doi.org/10.1145/2639108.2655084

Enfold: Downclocking OFDM in WiFi

Feng Lu, Patrick Ling, Geoffrey M. Voelker and Alex C. Snoeren
University of California, San Diego

Abstract

Dynamic voltage and frequency scaling (DVFS) has long been used as a technique to save power in a variety of computing domains but typically not in communications devices. A fundamental limit that prevents decreasing the clock frequency is the Nyquist(-Shannon) sampling theorem, which states that the sampling rate must be twice the signal bandwidth. Recently, researchers have leveraged compressive sensing to demonstrate the possibility of decoding a sparse signal below Nyquist rate. In this work, we dramatically extend the state of the art by showing how to decode non-sparse signals, in particular, OFDM systems at sub-Nyquist rates. We exploit the aliasing that results from under-sampling and observe that there exists well-defined structure in terms of how OFDM signals are "folded up" under aliasing. Based on our observations, we present Enfold, which allows existing WiFi chipsets to decode standards-compliant WiFi frames while operating at 50% and 25% of their rated clock rate. Our design is able to attain greater than 96% and 83% raw packet reception rates for moderate SNR while reducing the clock rate by 2× and 4×, respectively. Moreover, our approach can be easily applied to other communication systems based on OFDM modulation. When evaluated on popular smartphone app traces, Enfold reduces energy consumption by up to 34%.

Categories and Subject Descriptors

C.2.1 [**Computer Communication Networks**]: Network Architecture and Design—*Wireless Communication*

General Terms

Algorithms, Design, Experimentation, Measurement, Performance

Keywords

Downclocking; OFDM; Energy Efficiency; WiFi; DVFS

1. INTRODUCTION

The link rate of popular wireless technologies, such as 802.11, has increased markedly over the past two decades: 802.11ac promises near-gigabit speeds in handset form factors. Yet only a small fraction of the devices outfitted with such radios actually make use of the full channel capacity, and, even if they do, only do so sporadically. Hence many existing wireless devices frequently under-utilize the channel, yet reap no particular benefits for doing so. In particular, neither transmission nor reception is power proportional in typical devices, even when the channel quality is sufficiently high to support far more energy-efficient modulations and encodings. While devices aggressively try to move their radios into low-power states whenever possible, studies show [13, 23] that many common applications for both smartphones and laptops keep radios in full-power mode a large fraction of the time.

Given the importance of energy efficiency in power-constrained environments like battery-powered laptops, smartphones, and the like, a number of recent research efforts have focused on bringing a widely used technique for energy savings in CMOS, namely dynamic voltage and frequency scaling (DVFS), to standards-compliant radios. In particular, researchers have demonstrated that it is possible to downclock a radio when channel quality is sufficiently high, yet still detect [23], receive, and even transmit [13] WiFi frames. Modern WiFi chipsets typically have a single clock driving both RF and baseband. The potential power savings are significant—over 40% in some cases—yet the existing systems have limited application. Specifically, they either require modifying the 802.11 standard [23], or limit communication to 1 or 2 Mbps (DSSS) encodings [13].

In this work, we demonstrate that it is feasible to successfully receive and decode OFDM modulation while sampling below the Nyquist frequency. In particular, we show that a standards-compliant 802.11a/g frame transmitted at 6 or 9 Mbps can be detected, received, and decoded by a receiver running at a 50% or even 25% clock rate given sufficient channel quality. While our implementation focuses specifically on WiFi to demonstrate that we are able to overcome the various challenges in addition to decoding, such as synchronization, frequency offset and phase recovery, our basic approach can be applied to any communications system based upon OFDM modulation, significantly broadening the applicability of downclocking when compared to the state of the art.

Technically, our approach is based on exploiting the aliasing that is inherent in under-sampling an OFDM signal. Unlike previous work, which assumed the signal was sparse, OFDM signals are extremely dense and, therefore, downclocking yields significant interference across subcarriers. We show, however, that the particular structure of this interference can be used to convert the modulation into a more complicated, but still decodable, form. In particular, by folding the subcarriers on top of each other, we decode frames transmitted with a form of QAM as if they were encoded with a more dense QAM modulation.

This paper makes three main contributions:

- We explore the fundamental structure of downsampled OFDM encodings, and demonstrate that it can be leveraged to decode QAM-based modulations at both half and quarter clock rates.
- We design and implement a standards-compliant WiFi receiver based on the Microsoft Sora software radio platform

MobiCom'14, September 7-11, 2014, Maui, Hawaii, USA.

ACM 978-1-4503-2783-1/14/09 ...$15.00.
http://dx.doi.org/10.1145/2639108.2639123.

that is able to inter-operate with commercial WiFi chipsets while using downclocked reception.

- Through experimentation with our prototype, we quantify the effectiveness of our design, and explore the limitations of our prototype implementation.

The remainder of this paper is structured as follows. We begin in Section 2 with a brief survey of related work. Section 3 describes the fundamental underpinnings of our approach, while Section 4 surveys the practical challenges to implementing a real downclocked WiFi receiver. We describe how our design addresses each of these challenges in Section 5. We then introduce our implementation and the modifications needed to support Enfold on existing infrastructure in Section 6. Section 7 evaluates our approach, both in simulation and in practice with real WiFi devices. Finally, in Section 8 we evaluate the energy saving benefits of Enfold based on network traces of popular smartphone apps.

2. RELATED WORK

Our work follows on the heels of several recent efforts to bring DVFS to radios. In particular, in order to reduce power consumption, researchers have applied compressive sensing or sparse recovery to bring the sampling rate under Nyquist. As a result, the clock frequency and hardware complexity can be reduced substantially. For example, compressive sensing has been widely used in the field of spectrum sensing, which could potentially lower the ADC sampling rate by orders of magnitude [19]. Recently, Hassanieh *et al.* [10] showed how to reduce the runtime of GPS synchronization by exploiting the sparse nature of synchronization.

Our own previous work on the SloMo system [13] leverages the inherent sparsity in Direct Sequence Spread Spectrum (DSSS) modulation used by 802.11b at 1 and 2 Mbps to allow WiFi transceivers to operate their radios at lower clock rates. The approach taken by SloMo, however, is limited to these rates and cannot be applied to OFDM. Enfold fundamentally differs both from SloMo and from all previous approaches we are aware of because there is no sparsity anywhere in the system. Instead, we exploit the fact that there exists well-defined structure within the signal spectrum when aliasing occurs.

3. HARNESSING ALIASING

Nyquist sampling theory dictates that to successfully receive a signal, the receiver must sample the channel at twice the bandwidth of that signal. When the sampling rate is below Nyquist rate, aliasing occurs, where the signal spectrum folds up and the transmitted signal is no longer recoverable. Clearly, aliasing is an undesirable effect in any communication system. Consequently, modern wireless transceivers are fundamentally gated by the Nyquist sampling theory and must operate with a minimal clock frequency of Nyquist rate. However, we observe that there exists well-defined structure in terms of how the signal spectrum folds up under aliasing. Based on the design of OFDM communication systems, we show how the structure can be exploited to enable downclocked operation.

3.1 Downclocked OFDM modulation

At a high level, an OFDM communication system is defined by the inverse FFT and FFT operations. In the context of 802.11, this implies the following: a) data bits are modulated and coded on a number of subcarriers and inverse FFTs are taken over these coded values to produce the time domain signal at the transmitter; b) the time domain signal is sampled at the receiver and FFTs are performed over the data samples to recover the encoded values. To focus on the essence of our idea, we defer details related to timing, frequency synchronization, channel estimation, etc., to later sections, and focus for the moment entirely on modulation.

Here, we consider a single OFDM symbol and denote the data encoded on each subcarrier as C_i, and channel impulse response for each subcarrier as H_i, where $0 \le i \le 63$ in the case of 802.11g. Thus, the sampled signal at the receiver, when expressed in the frequency domain, will be $C_i H_i$ for subcarrier i. Correspondingly, the 64 time domain data samples at the receiver can be written as:

$$D_k = \frac{1}{64}\sum_{i=0}^{63} C_i H_i e^{j2\pi ki/64} + W_k, \quad k = 0, \ldots, 63 \tag{1}$$

where W_k is the channel noise. To recover the transmitted data, FFT is performed on the 64 data samples, D_k, and the resulting frequency response is expressed as:

$$F_l = \sum_{k=0}^{63} D_k e^{-j2\pi kl/64}, \quad l = 0, \ldots, 63 \tag{2}$$

Now let us substitute Eq. (1) to Eq. (2):

$$\begin{aligned} F_l &= \sum_{k=0}^{63}\Big(\frac{1}{64}\sum_{i=0}^{63} C_i H_i e^{j2\pi ki/64} + W_k\Big)e^{-j2\pi kl/64} \\ &= \frac{1}{64}\sum_{i=0}^{63}\sum_{k=0}^{63} C_i H_i e^{j2\pi k(i-l)/64} + N_l \\ &= C_l H_l + N_l \end{aligned}$$

where $N_l = \sum_{k=0}^{63} W_k e^{-j2\pi kl/64}$ is the channel noise expressed in the frequency domain at subcarrier l, which results in a non-zero decoding error. Subsequently, the transmitted data is estimated as F_l/H_l.

Now let us suppose the incoming data is sampled at a 50% clock rate. 32 samples will be produced, i.e., $D_{2k}(k = 0, \ldots, 31)$. Correspondingly we perform a 32-point FFT operation on these data samples to yield the following frequency response:

$$\begin{aligned} \tilde{F}_l &= \sum_{k=0}^{31} D_{2k} e^{-j2\pi kl/32} \\ &= \sum_{k=0}^{31}\Big(\frac{1}{64}\sum_{i=0}^{63} C_i H_i e^{j2\pi 2ki/64} + W_{2k}\Big)e^{-j2\pi kl/32} \\ &= \frac{1}{64}\sum_{i=0}^{63}\sum_{k=0}^{31} C_i H_i e^{j2\pi k(i-l)/32} + \tilde{N}_l \\ &= 0.5 * (C_l H_l + C_{l+32} H_{l+32}) + \tilde{N}_l \end{aligned} \tag{3}$$

Notice that $\sum_{k=0}^{31} C_i H_i e^{j2\pi k(i-l)/32}$ equals to 0 if $(i-l)/32$ is not an integer. We refer to 0.5 in Eq. (3) as the downclocking scaling coefficient. One way to interpret the aliasing effect given Eq. (3) is that the frequency response for subcarrier l is the average of the responses for subcarrier l and $l + 32$ (if they were sampled at full rate), for $l = 0, \ldots, 31$. Similarly, the frequency response for subcarrier l at a 25% clock rate would be the sum of the responses for subcarrier l, $l+16$, $l+32$, and $l+48$ (should the full sampling rate have been applied), scaled by the downclocking coefficient, 0.25 under 25% downclocking.

Hence, aliasing effectively transforms the original n-QAM (quadrature amplitude modulation) system to n^2-QAM at the receiver side for a 50% clock rate. For example, if BPSK (binary phase shift keying) is used at the sender, the resulting modulation due to aliasing would be 4-QAM. Similarly when downsampling

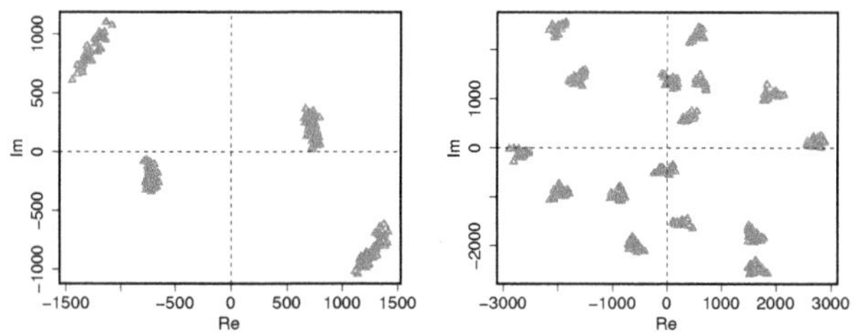

(a) 50% downclocking. (b) 25% downclocking.

Figure 1: Frequency response (constellation diagrams) on subcarrier 6 for two real WiFi packets under downclocking.

at 25% clock rate, n-QAM transmissions will be transformed into n^4-QAM. Figure 1 shows the constellation diagram for a subcarrier of two real WiFi packets when received at 50% and 25% clock rates, respectively, which serves as a concrete example of how the modulation scheme is transformed.

In sum, when aliasing happens the signal spectrum folds up and superimposes on itself in a well-defined manner, thereby enabling a systematic decoding of the compounded frequency responses.

3.2 Decoding aliasing induced modulation

We now explain how to decode the original data bits. We choose 802.11g 6-Mbps transmissions and a 50% reception clock rate as an example to illustrate our idea with an understanding that the approach holds for other rates and downclocking options. At 6 Mbps, a group of 48 bits are mapped into 48 complex numbers during the modulation mapping step, where each bit is mapped to either $1 + 0j$ or $-1 + 0j$ using BPSK modulation. These 48 complex numbers are then encoded on 48 out of the 64 subcarriers. Recall from Eq. (3) that the frequency response is the sum of $C_l H_l$ and $C_{l+32} H_{l+32}$ for subcarrier l at the receiver side. Given the values of C_l the frequency response F_l takes one of the four values, $\frac{1}{2}(\pm H_l \pm H_{l+32})$, depending on the bits mapped to subcarrier l and $l + 32$ on the sender side (e.g., 00, 01, 10, and 11). This encoding functions identically to 4-QAM: two bits are mapped to one of four possible complex numbers.

Therefore, similar to how a QAM system is decoded, we employ minimum distance decoding to recover the original bits. However, since the modulation transformation is induced by aliasing, and the channel response for subcarriers is random,[1] the resulting 4-QAM modulation differs from a standard one. In the standard 4-QAM scheme, two bits are mapped to one of the four complex numbers (also known as constellation points) equispaced around a circle. On the other hand, with aliasing induced modulation, the four code points could be anywhere in the constellation diagram depending on the channel response. Their separation depends on the relationship between the channel responses. In the absolute worse case where $H_l = H_{l+32}$, two constellation points collapse into one, which leads to at least a 25% bit error rate (BER). We observe, however, that this devastating scenario is unlikely in practice (Section 7.2.1).

Similarly, when a 25% clock rate is used, the original BPSK modulation becomes 16-QAM modulation. Aliasing induced modulation can be extended to other rates (e.g., 12 Mbps and higher) as well; the resulting modulation scheme would simply yield more densely packed constellation points compared to the original scheme.

[1]Subcarrier response is not entirely independent, but we defer a careful study of the impact of this phenomena to future work.

4. WIFI RECEPTION

Previous work has demonstrated that common smartphone apps would benefit greatly from dynamic voltage and frequency scaling (DVFS) by reducing the clock frequency. The only existing downclocked receiver design [13], however, is limited to 802.11b. Recent WiFi generations (e.g., 802.11a/g/n/ac) are all OFDM-based communication systems. We showed in the previous section that it is entirely possible to decode OFDM signals by exploiting the frequency spectrum structure under aliasing. However, real communication systems are much more complex than what we have discussed so far and there are many other components that need to be in place before a receiver is in a position to decode the actual OFDM symbol.

The designers of WiFi obviously never anticipated it would be used by downclocked radios, so existing approaches to any or all of clock synchronization, frequency compensation, pilot tracking, etc., might not function when downclocked. We start in this section with a brief overview of the 802.11 frame structure and the typical decoding pipeline of a standard, full clock rate WiFi receiver, and then address the challenges imposed by downclocked operation in the following section.

4.1 Frame structure

Two key tasks for any OFDM communication system are timing synchronization and frequency offset compensation. To meet these requirements, a WiFi frame is prepended by a preamble, which serves the purpose of preparing the receiver to decode the actual data part. The top portion of Figure 3 shows the detailed structure of an 802.11g WiFi frame. The preamble consists of 10 identical "short" OFDM symbols and 2 identical "long" OFDM symbols, with durations $0.8\mu s$ and $4\mu s$, and sequence lengths 16 and 64 (80 including the cyclic prefix), respectively. We explain below how a receiver uses the repetitive structure of the preamble to perform both time and frequency synchronization.

Immediately following the preamble is the physical layer (PHY) header, which contains information such as the data encoding rate, payload length, service field, etc. The first 24 bits of the PHY header are encoded at 6 Mbps while the remaining 16 bits are encoded at the same rate as the actual data; depending on the current channel condition, the data may be transmitted at different modulation rates. In most WiFi devices, the PHY header (first 24 bits) is added by the hardware without the driver's intervention.

4.2 Reception pipeline

In addition to decoding, a receiver performs five important steps to correctly recover the transmitted signal.

Timing synchronization. A WiFi receiver will continuously sample the channel to look for a preamble. The 10 short OFDM symbols in the preamble help the receiver to lock onto the data stream and define the OFDM symbol boundary. Once the symbol boundary is determined, FFT can be performed on the time domain samples to obtain their corresponding frequency-domain values.

Frequency compensation. Before computing the FFT, however, since the clock oscillator frequency is never exactly the same at the sender and receiver, the frequency offset needs to be estimated and compensated. Otherwise, orthogonality among subcarriers will be compromised and data transmitted on one subcarrier would interfere with another. Hence, receivers also use both the short and long OFDM symbols in the preamble to perform frequency offset estimation (or frequency synchronization).

Channel estimation. Once both timing and frequency are synchronized, the next decoding stage estimates the wireless channel response, i.e., channel estimation. With the estimated channel response, the results of computing the FFT on the time domain samples can be mapped to the actual data bits transmitted.

Viterbi decoding. To compensate and correct for bit errors, the raw decoded bits are fed into a Viterbi decoder, whose output is de-scrambled and subsequently passed on. (Obviously, symmetric operations are performed at the sender before transmission.)

Phase compensation. There is one additional step that is performed throughout the entire data decoding process: phase compensation. Since the sampling clock could drift slowly as time goes by, FFT results would vary even when the same OFDM symbol is transmitted repeatedly. Therefore, phase compensation is used to correct the variation of FFT results across OFDM symbols.

Viterbi decoding, scrambling, and subsequent stages work on the decoded data bits and are therefore entirely agnostic to the underlying clock and sampling rate. The remaining stages of the pipeline—timing synchronization, frequency compensation, channel estimation, and phase compensation—operate on the time domain data samples, and are impacted by operating at lower clock rates.

5. DOWNCLOCKING WIFI

In this section, we systematically examine the impact of downclocking in detail and propose a series of techniques to address these challenges.

5.1 Timing synchronization

The purpose of timing synchronization is to enable the receiver to first detect the presence of a valid WiFi packet and then correctly locate the boundary between adjacent OFDM symbols. Timing synchronization uses the short preamble only, i.e., the 10 repetitive short OFDM symbols. The IEEE 802.11 specification [11] does not mandate any particular timing synchronization algorithm. Although there are many timing synchronization algorithms for OFDM, we, like many others [17, 20, 22], use the auto(cross)-correlation approach.

The short OFDM symbol has a sequence length of 16 and exhibits very good cross-correlation properties. Let us denote the incoming time domain data samples as $r(.)$. Then the cross-correlation is computed as:

$$cros(i) = \frac{\sum_{j=0}^{15} r(i+j)S^*(j)}{\sum_{j=0}^{15} |S(j)|^2} \quad (4)$$

where $S^*(.)$ is the complex conjugate of the short OFDM sequence expressed in the time domain. If sampling at full clock rate, there will be 16 time domain samples corresponding to one short OFDM symbol, and $S(.)$ has the same length. The correlation output, $cros(i)$, produces a peak only when the incoming signal $r(.)$ fully aligns with $S(.)$, i.e., $r(i+j) \approx S(j)$ (the approximation is due to the presence of noise). Otherwise, the magnitude of the correlation output is much smaller compared to the peak value. Thus, the cross-correlation peak enables accurate OFDM symbol boundary detection (i.e., fine timing synchronization).

Due to the repetitive structure of the short preamble, a receiver can correlate the received data samples with themselves at one short OFDM symbol delay. Specifically, the receiver tracks of the following auto-correlation output:

$$auto(i) = \sum_{j=0}^{15} r(i+j)r^*(i+j+16). \quad (5)$$

The rational is that, when a valid WiFi frame is present, $r(i) = r(i+16)$ as 16 samples corresponds to one short OFDM symbol duration. When the auto-correlation index i is within the range of

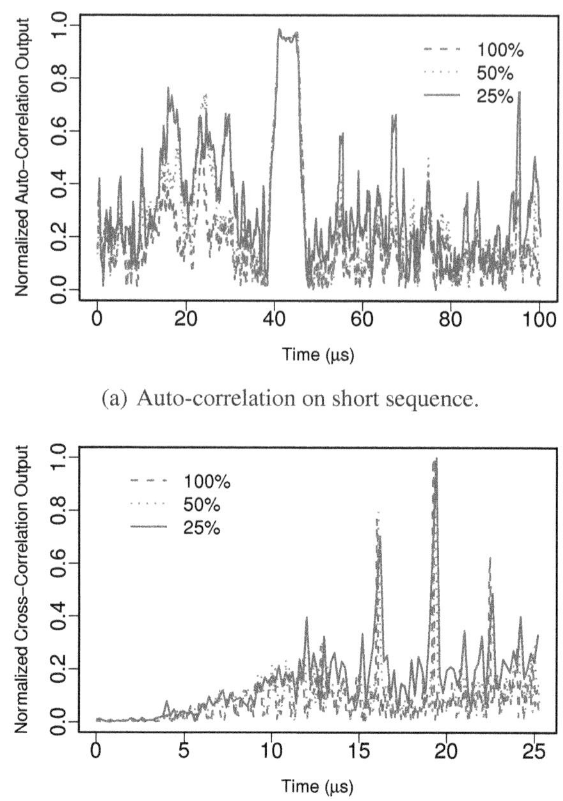

(a) Auto-correlation on short sequence.

(b) Cross-correlation on long sequence.

Figure 2: Correlation responses at variout clock rates for raw data samples of a real WiFi packet captured by USRP.

the short preamble, the output from Eq. (5) spikes and stays high. This auto-correlation result produces a plateau over time, which is known as coarse timing synchronization. Clearly, the cross-correlation peak defined in Eq. (4) must happen within the plateau to be meaningful. Thus, by combining the outputs of both results, we can safely detect the presence of a WiFi frame and correctly identify symbol boundaries.

Downclocking will reduce the number of time domain samples by half (or a quarter) depending on the clock rate. First we note that, regardless of the sampling rate, Eq. (5) will hold when $r(i) = (i+8)$ or $r(i) = (i+4)$ if sampling at 50% or 25% clock rates, although the noise floor (when the auto-correlation is failing within the short preamble) approaches the plateau. Nevertheless, the plateau could still have separation and, perhaps more importantly, its width roughly equals the duration of the short preamble, which is invariant among different clock rates (see Figure 2(a)).

Unfortunately for cross-correlation, the downsampled subsequences no longer exhibit convenient correlation properties: there could be multiple comparable peaks within one short OFDM symbol. So we turn to the long OFDM symbols and evaluate its cross-correlation properties. It turns out that the long preamble sequence (consisting of 128 samples across two symbols) also exhibits excellent cross-correlation properties, in part because its time domain samples are generated similarly to the short preamble.

Figure 2(b) illustrates the effect of using the 128 sample long OFDM symbols for timing synchronization on an actual WiFi packet. The cross-correlation output produces three peaks. The middle peak corresponds to full alignment, while the first corresponds to a partial alignment with the first OFDM symbol and the third corresponds to a partial alignment with the second OFDM symbol. These correlation peaks make it straightforward to identify the starting sample index for the remaining OFDM symbols. We also note that the peaks for different clock rates are superimposed on each other, confirming that the approach works for all clock rates. In Section 7.1, we show in practice that timing synchronization works quite well even for a 25% clock rate at low SNR values.

5.2 Frequency compensation

Standard frequency compensation algorithms explore the following relationship between two transmitted back-to-back identical OFDM symbols. Let $r(1), \ldots, r(n)$ and $r(n+1), \ldots, r(2n)$ correspond to the time domain samples at the receiver for two identical OFDM symbols, respectively. Then the following property always holds for any $1 \leq i \leq n$:

$$r(n+i) = e^{j2\pi\Delta f_c T} r(i), \tag{6}$$

where Δf_c is the frequency offset and T is the OFDM symbol duration. Hence the frequency offset is estimated as the ratio between $r(n+i)$ and $r(i)$, taking the average for all possible values of i.

With downclocking, the relationship described by Eq. (6) still holds for data samples spaced by one symbol duration, although the average is now taken over fewer samples. Since downclocking will only use half or a quarter of the samples compared to the full clock rate, the frequency offset estimation accuracy is reduced by 3 dB and 6 dB, respectively. As discussed in the previous section, the preamble consists of 10 repetitive short OFDM symbols and 2 repetitive long OFDM symbols. When downclocking, we use both for frequency offset estimation (i.e., coarse and fine frequency synchronization), taking the average over fewer data samples.

As with timing synchronization, in Section 7.1 we show that our frequency compensation technique also works well in practice.

5.3 Channel estimation

Once the timing and frequency synchronization is achieved, the next step is to understand the channel response. In a WiFi frame, the long preamble supports channel estimation because the data bits encoded on each subcarrier are known *a priori*. Let us assume that the FFT results for the long OFDM symbol are $F_0, F_1, \ldots, F_{63}$; the wireless channel response is estimated as

$$H_i = F_i / C_i, \quad 0 \leq i \leq 63 \tag{7}$$

where H_i is the channel response for subcarrier i and C_i is the data encoded on subcarrier i (known to both sender and receiver). However, when downclocking, the channel response will fold up and estimating individual subcarrier channel responses is no longer feasible. While there are approaches in the literature that determine channel responses under such conditions [15, 21] using compressive sensing, they make certain assumptions regarding the channel. Unfortunately, these assumptions are not necessarily true in general for the WiFi environment. Hence, we develop an alternative method to find the per-subcarrier channel response (coefficients).

The aliasing effect, when translated into the frequency domain, is equivalent to summing the channel coefficients at indices spaced by 32 or 16, depending on downclocking rate. More specifically, when sampling at full clock rate, FFT is taken over 64 time domain samples and produces 64 subcarrier responses, which are used to estimate channel response as defined by Eq. (7). Now when sampled at 50(25)% clock rate, we obtain 32(16) equations after performing FFT, where each equation consists of 2(4) unknowns (see Eq. (3)). We leverage the fact that the WiFi channel response remains invariant over the course of a single packet. Therefore, if we transmit multiple known OFDM symbols (e.g., training symbols), we could potentially recover all the unknowns by collecting equations from multiple symbols. One caveat is that all the training OFDM symbols must be phase compensated.

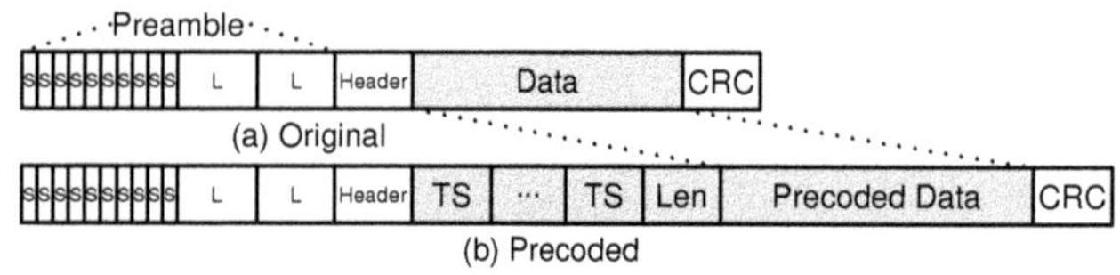

Figure 3: WiFi packet structure for both original and precoded versions. Note that our modifications are restricted to the data payload only (gray area).

5.4 Phase compensation

To compensate for any possible phase shift across OFDM symbols, the WiFi standard inserts known data in certain subcarriers (pilots) for every OFDM symbol. By comparing the pilot subcarrier responses between symbols, the phase shift is estimated and the data subcarrier values are compensated accordingly. Unfortunately, due to the particular set of subcarriers selected to be pilots, when downclocking the pilot subcarriers fold on top of data subcarriers (which contain unknown data). Hence, downclocking cannot use the pilots to compensate the phase difference. We could re-define the pilot subcarriers such that their indices are spaced by 16 so that one pilot subcarrier will always add up with another pilot under downsampling rate of 50% or 25%. However, doing so would violate our goal of being entirely 802.11 standard compliant.

5.5 Data precoding

Rather than change the WiFi frame structure or how the subcarriers are mapped, we elect to transmit additional symbols in the payload of the frame. At a high level, we re-encode the original data bits such that: 1) additional channel training symbols are introduced; 2) pilot structure is restored. It is non-trivial to realize both (1) and (2) for a number of reasons, however.

5.5.1 From bits to subcarriers

Up to now, our discussion has primarily centered around coded values on subcarriers. However, there are multiple stages such as scrambling, convolutional encoding, interleaving, and subcarrier mapping sitting between raw data bits and the values encoded on the subcarriers. In particular, the raw data bits are XOR-ed first with scrambler bits, which then pass through a convolutional encoder. The output of the convolutional encoder not only depends on the current bit but also the past bit history, where the history length depends on the size of the convolutional encoder register. In the context of 6-Mbps WiFi, every 24 scrambled input bits generate a block of 48 bits, i.e., input bit k will produce output bits $2k$ and $2k+1$, where $0 \leq k \leq 23$. These 48 bits, after interleaving, modulation mapping and subcarrier assignments, generate a single OFDM symbol. In addition, there is a fixed one-to-one correspondence between the 48 bits and the 48 (out of 64) subcarriers. For example, bit 16 maps to subcarrier 39: the coded values on subcarrier 39 will be $1+0j(-1+0j)$ if bit 16 is 1(0).

Conversely, if we want to set the coded value on subcarrier 39 to be $1+0j$ (i.e., for use as a pilot), we need to ensure that bit 16 is 1. Since the convolutional output bit is produced by taking XOR operations among the current input bit and some past input bits, there always exists some input bit value (i.e., could be 0 or 1) such that the output bit has the desired value. Therefore, we try both values for input bit 8 and check which one produces a value 1 on output bit 16.

5.5.2 Pilot restoration

For 802.11g, the four pilots are inserted at the following subcarriers: 7, 21, 43 and 57. Under downclocking, these pilots will fold up with various data subcarriers, which we coin *pilot images*. For example, the pilot-image for subcarrier 7 is subcarrier 39 under 50% sampling rate. To restore these pilots with downclocking, the pilot-images have to be encoded with known values. To simplify our design, we set the data encoded on a pilot-image subcarrier to be the same as its corresponding pilot. To enforce the same data encoded on both pilot and pilot-image, we modify the input bit stream to the convolutional encoder in the following way.

Let us denote the original raw input data bits (excluding the additional training symbols) as $b_0, b_1, \ldots, b_n$ and the scrambler sequence output as $x_0, x_1, x_2, \ldots$. At 6 Mbps, each group of 48 convolutional encoder output bits is mapped to a single OFDM symbol (48 out of 64 subcarriers). We run the convolutional encoder as normal while the input bits are coming through. For each incoming data bit b_i, it first gets scrambled with some scrambler output x_j. The scrambled bit is then fed into the convolutional encoder and two output bits are generated. Whenever we are about to produce an output bit that is going to be mapped onto a pilot-image subcarrier, we "pause" the input bit stream to the convolutional encoder and instead insert a new bit c such that the value encoded on the pilot-image subcarrier is the same as the corresponding pilot value.

For example, if output bit 16 is about to be produced (which will be mapped to subcarrier 39), we check the current value of pilot subcarrier 7. If subcarrier 7 has value $1 + 0j$, we need to ensure that output bit 16 is 1, and 0 otherwise. The newly inserted bit c is selected such that bit 16 yields the desired value. The two convolutional encoder output bits (generated by the same input bit) are never mapped onto pilot-image subcarriers at the same time, thus there always exists a bit c such that the pilot-image subcarrier possesses the same value as its respective pilot. We update the convolutional encoder with bit c.

Next, given the desired input bit c, we then XOR it with the current scrambler bit, say x_k, to produce the raw data bit $\tilde{c}$. Afterwards, x_k is discarded and the next raw data bit b_i is scrambled with x_{k+1} to produce the new input bit for the convolutional encoder, which resumes normal operation. Correspondingly, the precoded data will be: $\ldots, b_{i-1}, \tilde{c}, b_i, \ldots$. This process is repeated until all input bits are exhausted and $\tilde{c}$ is inserted for every pilot-image subcarrier encountered. Since the positions of the convolutional output bits that are mapped to pilot-images are fixed, the bit indices for inserted bits $\tilde{c}$ are known as well. Hence, the receiver can simply discard the inserted pilot bits $\tilde{c}$ to recover the original data.

5.5.3 Training symbols

We describe how we generate the additional training symbols with reference to 50% clock rate; the same strategy applies for a 25% clock rate. With 50% downclocking, the FFT is performed over 32 data samples for one OFDM symbol. Let us denote the data encoded on subcarrier i as C_i at the sender side and the channel response for subcarrier i as H_i $(0 \le i \le 63)$; the frequency responses after FFT can be written as:

$$\tilde{F}_j = \frac{H_j}{2}C_j + \frac{H_{j+32}}{2}C_{j+32}, 0 \le j \le 31.$$

To recover the channel coefficients H_js, we need at least two such equations and thus two OFDM training symbols. Furthermore, the two equations must be independent from each other, i.e., (C_j, C_{j+32}) from symbol 1 and (C_j, C_{j+32}) from symbol 2 must form a full rank 2×2 matrix.

We first generate a random binary string of 48 bits (sufficient for two OFDM symbols) and precode these bits so that the pilots are restored. We then compute the rank of the resulting matrix (e.g., $[C_j, C_{j+32}]^{S_1}$, $[C_j, C_{j+32}]^{S_2}$) for each subcarrier, where S_i is the ith OFDM symbol. If all the matrices have a rank 2, we use S_1 and S_2 as the training symbols. If not, we repeat until they do. This offline process only needs to be executed once and the resulting training symbols are used for every precoded packet.

5.6 Additional considerations

So far we have covered the main components in enabling downclocked OFDM frame reception. Here, we mention a few additional details that are important for a standards-compliant design.

Transmission. While our approach allows downclocked reception of OFDM symbols, we cannot transmit OFDM symbols while downclocked. There are two options. First, some WiFi chipsets (e.g., MAXIM 2831 [13]) are able to switch their clocks within 9 μs (i.e., less than SIFS), which would allow the WiFi chipset to spend most of the time in downclocked mode and only switch back to full clock rate for transmission. Alternatively, we could transmit using 802.11b encodings while remaining downclocked as proposed by Lu *et. al.* [13]. We experimentally verified that a WiFi device will accept 802.11b (DSSS) frames, e.g., layer-2 ACKs, when sending 802.11g (OFDM) frames. We used a commercial WiFi NIC (Intel 6200) to send OFDM frames to our prototype while the latter replies with DSSS frames. Both nodes are able to communicate with each other without any problem.

Scrambler Seed. Our design assumes that the scrambling sequence is known, which can be derived deterministically from the scrambler seed. Commercial NICs often use an internal LFSR to generate the scrambler seeds. If the LFSR design and its initial seed are exposed, we could potentially determine the current scrambler seed at any moment. Unfortunately, we are unable to find a specific NIC that currently does so. The closest that we have found is the Atheros 93xx series chipset, where the scrambler seed can be temporarily disabled by configuring the *MAC_PCU_DIAG_SW* register. When scrambling is disabled, we could implement a soft scrambler in the driver to avoid long runs of 1s and 0s. We believe there is no reason the NIC could not expose either the scrambler seed or the LFSR directly to the driver.

Extension to 802.11n/ac. Although our discussion focuses on 802.11g, our approach is generic to other OFDM communication systems. The newer WiFi specs such as .11n and .11ac are based on OFDM as well. A direct way of applying our solution to .11n/ac is to configure these systems to operate in Single-Input-Single-Output (SISO) mode [8], which is similar to the setup of .11g we described here. In fact, 802.11n/ac include a channel sounding process to estimate channel response and could apply channel precoding for transmitted frames, both leading to simplified downclocked decoding at the receiver and better performance. We leave combining MIMO and downclocking for future study.

Added Complexity. Both Enfold transmitters and receivers have additional tasks to perform when compared to regular nodes. However, most of these tasks employ standard communication algorithms such as minimum distance decoding, correlation and etc. Therefore, the additional computation power incurred is negligible compared to the communication cost. Although downclocking does convert the modulation scheme into a denser one, the power required to decode does not depend significantly on constellation density in existing chipsets [8].

6. IMPLEMENTATION

We implement Enfold on the Microsoft Sora software defined radio platform [20]. The modifications are standards compatible and do not require any sender hardware changes.

6.1 Sender

Since Sora uses a fixed scrambler sequence for all packets, i.e., a constant scrambler seed, we take advantage of this fixed sequence to precode data before it is transmitted by the NIC. Depending on the downclocked clock rate at the receiver (50% or 25%), we add 2 or 8 channel training symbols as part of the encoded data payload.[2] The pilot restoration logic described in Section 5.5.2 consists of about 300 LoC.

Since our modifications are restricted to the data portion only, the NIC generates a standard physical layer packet header and CRC. As a result, the OFDM symbols corresponding to the header and CRC cannot be phase compensated by a downclocked device. Therefore, on the sender side we also include the original CRC (computed based on the uncoded data) as part of the precoded data. To ensure that the precoded data is an integral number of OFDM symbols—so that the entire coded data portion can be phase compensated—we add trailing zero bits at the end. As a result, we also include an additional OFDM symbol to encode the length of original data so that the receiver knows when to stop decoding.

Figure 3 (bottom half) shows the structure of a precoded WiFi packet. At a 50% downclock rate, the new pilots are subcarriers 7 and 21, and the pilot-image subcarriers 39 and 53 are used to code pilot values. Similarly for 25% downclocking, the new pilots are 7 and 11, and the pilot-image subcarriers are 23, 39, 55, 11 and 59. As a result, the effective throughput for 50% and 25% downclocking are 91.6% and 79.1% of the original data rate (6 Mbps). In our experiments, two pilot subcarriers are sufficient to bound the phase estimation error within 0.12 radians (6.8 degrees).

Any non-Enfold node can receive and decode a Enfold-precoded WiFi packet; the data content would simply not be recognizable, similar to encrypted data.

6.2 Receiver

Due to hardware limitations with our Sora receiver, we cannot change the clock rate of the hardware. Instead, we emulate downclocking by decimating every other raw channel sample at for a 50% rate, and three of every four samples for a 25% rate. We modify and reimplement the timing and frequency synchronization modules to accommodate downclocked rates. We postpone decoding the physical layer header (one OFDM symbol), which contains the packet length and payload modulation scheme, until after the channel has been estimated.[3]

As the header symbol is not phase compensated, we exploit the fact that there are limited possibilities (4 and 16 possibilities for 50% and 25% downclocking, respectively) that a data subcarrier could be. Therefore, we use a data subcarrier as the pilot by enumerating all 4(16) possibilities (obtained from the training symbols) when decoding the header symbol. The header symbol contains sufficient information (e.g., parity and modulation) to enable Enfold to determine the correct output among all possibilities.

Once the header is decoded, the number of data OFDM symbols is known. For each incoming OFDM symbol, we first apply phase compensation and then use a minimum distance decoder to determine the data bits. These data bits go to the Viterbi decoding chain and are subsequently descrambled. Once all symbols are decoded, we start to decode the precoded data payload by essentially discarding the inserted pilot bits. Finally, we compare the computed CRC with the CRC included as part of the precoded data payload; we ignore the default MAC layer CRC.

One subtlety not discussed earlier is the service field, which consists of 16 bits with the first 8 bits set to zero so that the receiver can determine the scrambler seed. In our implementation, we include the service field as part of the training symbol since the receiver knows the scrambler seed. In the general case where the scrambler seed is not known at the receiver, we can place a known bit pattern on the 8 reserved bits and use the same approach for decoding the service field as the header symbol.

6.3 Network interactions

In this section, we discuss how Enfold nodes interact with Access Point (AP) and share the network with regular nodes, in particular, the modifications needed to support Enfold in existing deployed infrastructure.

Precoding at AP. Given the current pilot subcarrier placement, an Enfold-capable AP has to precode the data to restore pilot structure at downclocked receivers. To remain 802.11-standard compliant, we implement the precoding step in Sora's link-adaptation layer, leaving the lower MAC/PHY layer untouched. To verify that our implementation is truly standard compliant, we transmit a stream of UDP packets with our prototype Enfold AP and use Wireshark on a Macbook Pro to capture (in promiscuous mode) the precoded WiFi packets and apply a corresponding decoding process on the dumped packet trace. All packets sent by the Enfold transmitter are correctly decoded, thus confirming the standard (or at least Apple) compatibility of Enfold.

Beacon and Scanning. Although Enfold-precoded packets can be correctly received by non-Enfold nodes, they would need to apply the corresponding decoding process to recover the original data. Therefore, broadcast packets, such as beacon frames, are unlikely to be understood by both Enfold and non-Enfold nodes simultaneously. Hence, to support Enfold-enabled nodes, an AP would need to broadcast two types of beacon frames, original and precoded. To reduce the network overhead due to two beacon frames, the AP could broadcast Enfold beacons at larger time interval (e.g., every a few hundred milliseconds). The reduced beacon time is unlikely to impact the scanning and association process, given these happen on the order of several seconds. For traffic indication purposes during PSM, since Enfold nodes choose to operate in downclocked mode, it is very unlikely that the incoming network traffic is frequent. Waking up on a larger interval would not impact app-level performance such as user perceived response time.

Managing Downclocked Mode. Depending on the current network traffic and SNR conditions, an Enfold node may choose to switch from downclocked to normal mode and vice versa. Since the AP must precode data for downclocked operation, it needs to be notified of such mode transitions. We envision two ways of realizing this process. Clearly, one could design customized packets and protocol for such a purpose. Alternatively, realizing that most deployed WiFi networks have good SNR [6], lower data rates such as 6/9 Mbps may never be picked by the rate selection algorithm of non-Enfold nodes.. Thus, and AP could dedicate 6 and 9 Mbps for downclocked operation, and the AP would by default send precoded frame for 6 and 9 Mbps. As a consequence, Enfold nodes could leverage the existing re-association request frame to inform the AP that it only supports 6/9 Mbps and enter downclocked mode. An obvious concern is the potential loss of energy savings by not

[2] We tried other numbers of channel training symbols as well; 2 and 8 yield a good balance between overhead and estimation accuracy.

[3] Since our implementation currently assumes that the data payload is fixed at 6 Mbps, we do not rely on the packet header to determine the payload modulation scheme.

Clock Rate	P_d(9 dB)	P_d(14 dB)	P_d(24 dB)	P_d(34 dB)
50%	0.993	1.0	1.0	1.0
25%	0.958	1.0	1.0	1.0

Table 1: Probability of detection P_d with different SNRs at 50% and 25% downclock rates.

using higher data rates while in downclocked mode. However, as demonstrated in Section 8, the majority of the energy saving benefits can be attained with 6 and 9 Mbps for most smartphone apps.

7. EVALUATION

In this section we evaluate downclocked OFDM reception in practice. We first evaluate specific steps of frame decoding on raw channel samples captured on the GNU Radio Universal Software Radio Peripheral (USRP) [7], which allows us to control SNR over a wider range. We then evaluate the Enfold prototype system implementation on Sora [20], a fully programmable software defined radio platform.

7.1 Microbenchmark results

For our microbenchmarks we use the GNU Radio USRP platform to capture raw channel samples of 802.11g packets sent by a Sora node. We use the USRP board for packet capture because, unlike Sora, it has a hardware automatic gain control (AGC) on-board whose gain is adjustable. By varying the hardware AGC gain from 0 to 50, we can experimentally sweep the SRN range from 9 dB to 35 dB (a gain above 50 leads to saturation in our experiments).

For each gain setting we capture 10 seconds of raw channel samples, containing approximately 3000 WiFi packets. With the raw channel samples, we can emulate the effect of downclocking on various aspects of frame reception on the same data at all clock rates. At the full 100% clock rate, we use all the samples. At 50%, we use every other sample, and at 25% we use every fourth sample. In an actual implementation, unlike reduced bandwidth operations where the number of digital samples remains unchanged [5], the baseband logic needs to be similarly adjusted to take a correspondingly lower number of samples.

7.1.1 Packet detection

First, we show that packet detection is not a constraint for OFDM decoding at downclocked rates. We employ a simple energy-based detector which tracks the average energy for a fixed duration and compares the output with a pre-defined threshold. Table 1 shows the detection probability for a range of SNR values. We treat the detection results at the normal clock rate of 100% as ground truth. If using the detection algorithm at full clock rate signals a packet, but using it at a lower clock rate does not, then we count the detection as having failed at the lower clock rate.

When SNR is extremely poor (9 dB), Enfold operating at 50% and 25% clock rates can still detect over 99% and 95% of the packets, respectively. For SNRs of 14 dB (which is still very poor) and above, both clock rates yield a 100% detection rate. These results indicate that packet detection is invariant with respect to clock rate for much of the SNR range, and certainly for SNR regimes expected of 802.11 communication.[4] Conversely, we find only 10–20 falsely detected packets (out of the roughly 3000 packets captured in 10 seconds) when downclocked.

[4]To place these values in context, many vendors (e.g., AT&T [1], Blackberry [2] and Cisco [3]) recommend coverage with a minimum of 25 dB when planning WiFi deployments.

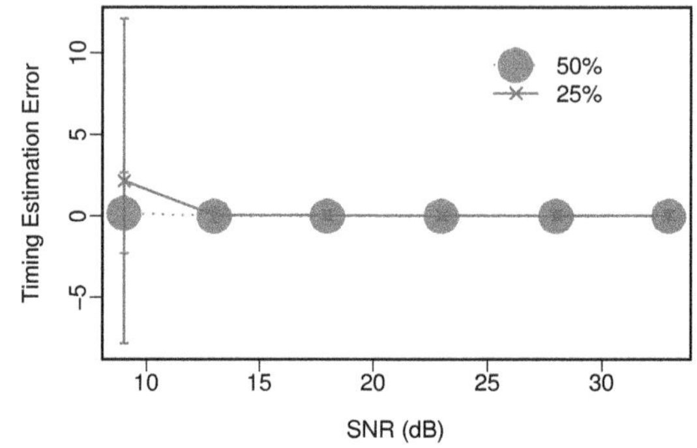

Figure 4: Timing synchronization offset error with downclocking at 50% and 25%.

7.1.2 Timing synchronization

Next, we confirm that we can make timing synchronization also perform well for downclocked OFDM decoding. Recall from Section 5.1 that, since the sub-sampled short preamble sequence no longer exhibits excellent cross-correlation properties at downclocked rates, we instead perform cross-correlation on the long preamble sequence. Figure 4 shows the timing estimation error (measured in number of samples) for both 50% and 25% downclock rates relative to the timing estimation error at the full 100% clock rate. In effect, it measures the additional error of downclocking relative to the baseline error at 100%. Error bars show the standard deviation among the packets captured at each SNR.

When the SNR is extremely poor (9 dB), the synchronization error is substantial for downclocking at 25%. However, the synchronization error quickly converges to zero at 13 dB and above, and certainly for the expected SNR operating regime for 802.11. These results confirm our initial hypothesis that auto-correlation, which looks for repetitively transmitted symbols, will likely perform poorly when the noise level is very high. At such high noise levels, interference adds together rather than canceling out as in the cross-correlation case. Since we rely on the output of auto-correlation to begin the search for cross-correlation peak, at 9 dB SNR, the 25% auto-correlation output already differs significantly from the 100% output. However, even with just slightly lower noise levels (at 13 dB in our case), our method can accurately determine symbol boundaries.

7.1.3 Frequency offset estimation

In Section 5.2, we showed theoretically that frequency offset estimation is oblivious to clock rate. As a final microbenchmark, we confirm that it is also not a constraint for downclocked OFDM decoding in practice. As above, we consider the frequency offset estimation obtained from decoding at the 100% clock rate as the ground truth for comparing estimations performed at the 50% and 25% clock rates. For the SNR range we could measure across (9–35dB), the estimation error at 50% and 25% clock rates are within 2.2% and 6.8% of the 100% rates on average. Previous work [12] has characterized that a frequency estimation error of 10% leads to $\leq 2dB$ reduction in SNR, which is almost negligible for the SNR regime we consider.

7.2 Prototype system evaluation

Our second set of experiments evaluates the Enfold implementation on the Sora platform at 6 Mbps data rates.[5] In particular, we

[5]9 Mbps shares the same BPSK modulation scheme per-subcarrier as 6 Mbps while the coding rate changes to 3/4.

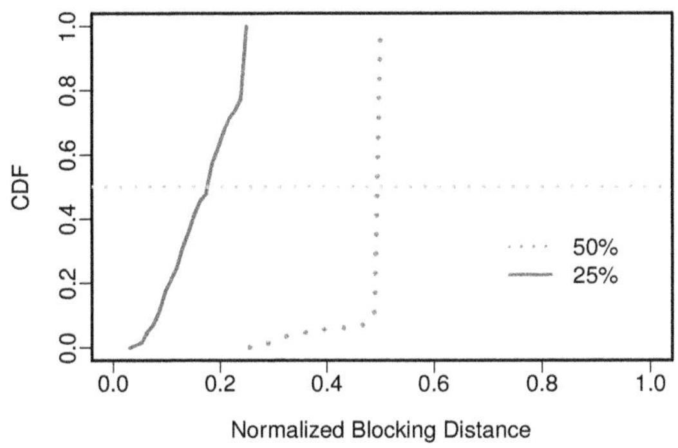

Figure 5: CDF of normalized blocking distance (relative to 100%) for 2000 WiFi packets.

explore the decoding performance of individual subcarriers, the decoding performance of entire packets across a range of SNR values, and the ability to trade off decoding performance with raw data rate at very fine subcarrier granularities. Note that, since the Sora radio board does not have hardware AGC, in these experiments we use their provided HWVeri tool [4] to calibrate the SNR of two Enfold nodes at the start of each experiment.

7.2.1 Aliasing induced modulation

As discussed in Section 3.2, aliasing induced modulation introduces additional constellation points that could lead to decoding errors. Our first experiment with the prototype explores the effect of aliasing on the constellations in practice. Lacking a precise metric to quantify this impact, we calculate what we term the blocking distance in constellations.

Each subcarrier at the original 100% clock rate will have a BPSK constellation diagram. At a 50% clock rate, two subcarriers will be aliased into a single 4-QAM constellation (twice the number of points). And at 25%, four subcarriers will be aliased into a single 16-QAM constellation (eight times the number of points). Since decoding performance fundamentally depends upon a distance threshold in the constellation, we calculate a minimum distance among constellations to capture the effect of aliasing. If aliasing multiple subcarriers introduces many bit errors, the constellation points would have poor separation as represented by a too small minimum distance.

As an example, consider the set of four subcarriers {10, 26, 42, 58} which would be aliased together when downclocking at 25%. At a 100% clock rate, these subcarriers would each have their own BPSK constellation diagram. At 50%, though, there will be just two 4-QAM constellations for the subcarrier pairs {10, 42} and {26, 58}, and at 25% there will be just one 16-QAM constellation for all four.

For each packet, we calculate the minimal of minimum distances for all constellation diagrams for a particular clock setting. At 100%, we calculate the minimum distance among constellation points for each subcarrier and record the minimal among the four subcarriers; at 50% it is the minimal among two constellations, and at 25% it is the minimum of the one resulting constellation. For each clock rate, we term this minimal distance the blocking distance. In an ideal decoding situation for downclocking, the blocking distance at 50% would be exactly half the blocking distance at 100%, and similarly the blocking distance at 25% would be one quarter of 100%.

Figure 5 shows the CDF of the blocking distance for constellation diagrams for the 50% and 25% clock rates normalized to the blocking distance at 100%. Each curve is a distribution over 2000 packets received by our Sora implementation. We focus on just the four subcarriers {10, 26, 42, 58}, which are representative of the other subcarrier sets.[6] The distribution of blocking distances at the 50% clock rate is close to ideal: nearly 90% of the packets have a blocking distance that is half of the 100% distance. Performance at 25%, though, is notably worse: the blocking distances range from 0.03 to 0.25, with a median of 0.16; only 20% of the packets have a blocking distance close to a quarter of the 100% distance. This large variation at a 25% clock rate is not surprising. With four subcarrier responses added together, there will be more randomness in the aliasing induced constellation diagram.

Translating these blocking distances into SNR for per-subcarrier signal quality degradation, the penalty due to downclocking is 3 dB and 7.9 dB for 50% and 25% on average, respectively. In our next experiment we show how this degradation impacts overall packet reception, which of course requires all subcarriers to be successfully decoded.

7.2.2 Packet reception rate vs SNR

With a sense of decoding performance per-subcarrier at downclocked rates, we now measure the overall packet reception ratio (PRR) of our prototype implementation under a range of SNR conditions. We measure packet decoding in two rounds of different packet sizes, one with small packets (100 bytes) and another with large packets (1000 bytes). Each round of packet sizes consists of 50 runs, where each run has 100 back-to-back packet transmissions and attempted decodings. We disable retransmissions. We transmit the two rounds back-to-back at a 100% clock rate, and then repeat the transmissions at 50% downclocked decoding rates and again at 25%. Altogether, the experiment transmits 30,000 packets.

We also vary the distance between the two Enfold nodes to induce different SNRs. Unfortunately, as noted above, due to the lack of hardware AGC on the Sora platform our SNR dynamic range is rather limited (20–30 dB as reported by Sora). As discussed above, this SNR range is at the very low end for recommended 802.11 operation, with 25 dB the recommended minimum when planning coverage. We could not receive any packet below 20 dB, i.e., it represents a sharp cut off in terms of PRR.

Figure 6 shows the results of these experiments. When SNR is at least 25 dB (the recommended minimum SNR for enterprise WiFi networks [1, 2, 3]), decoding at both 100% and 50% clock rates achieve $\geq$ 95% PRR for both packet sizes. For these operating regimes, the performance difference between the two clock rates is negligible. Below the 25 dB threshold, downclocking at 50% has a 67–75% PRR. Although lower than decoding at the full 100% rate, it is quite reasonable at such a low SNR.

For the challenging 25% clock rate, when SNR is 30 dB (5 dB above the recommended minimum), Enfold achieved 83% and 52% PRR for small and large packet sizes, respectively. For small packets, such a PRR translates to reasonable application performance with retransmissions, but the PRR for large packets will have a noticeable impact. At the edge SNR (25 dB), downclocking at 25% had poor performance, achieving 46% (small) and 20% (large) PRRs, respectively. Below 25 dB, downclocking at 25% is unusable for both packet sizes.

In sum, we find these results very promising. Note that the highest SNR we could achieve with the Sora platform was 30 dB, which is below typical operating conditions. A recent measurement study [6] of deployed university WiFi networks indicates that

[6]Standard 802.11 uses only 52 subcarriers (including 4 pilot subcarriers) out of 64. The unused 12 subcarriers are set to zero, which makes downclocked decoding involving these subcarriers easier. In this experiment, we avoid these 12 subcarriers in the set we chose.

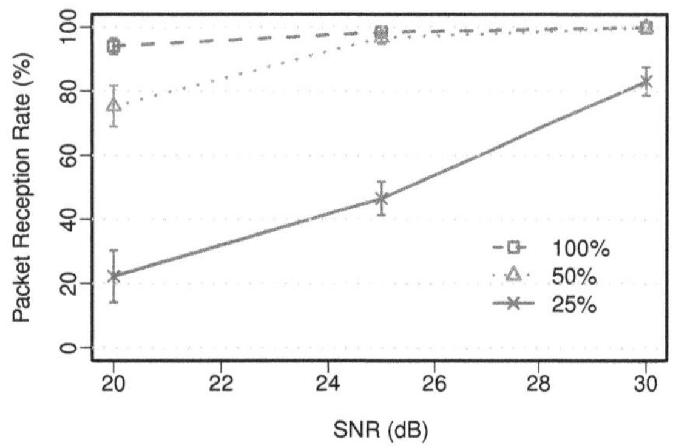

(a) Small packet (100 bytes)

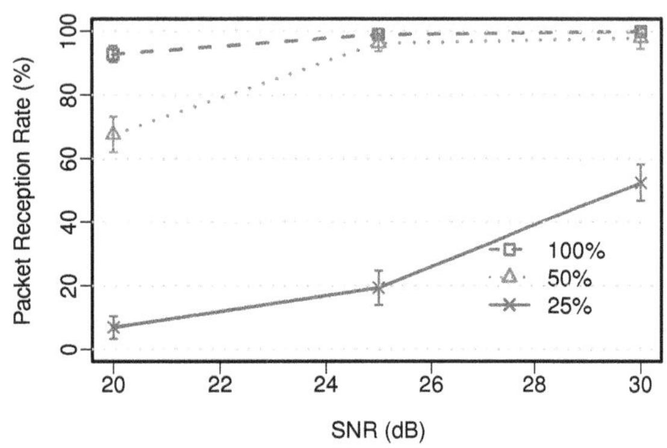

(b) Large packet (1000 bytes)

Figure 6: Packet reception rate as a function of SNR.

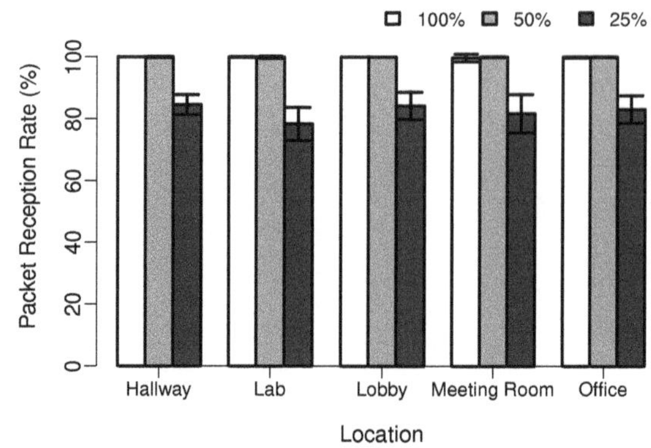

(a) Small packet (100 bytes)

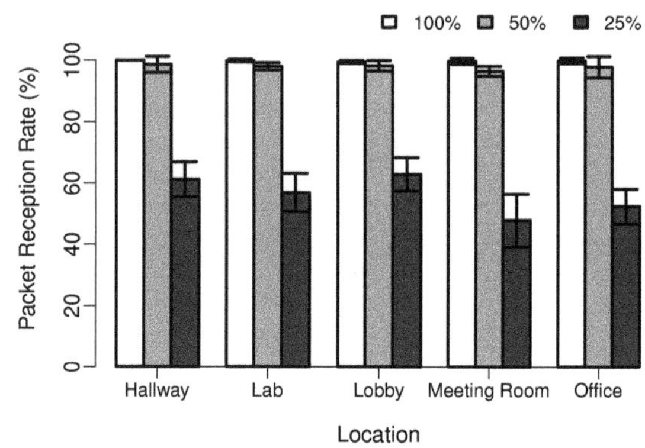

(b) Large packet (1000 bytes)

Figure 7: Raw packet reception ratio for different clock rates at five different locations.

only 3% of WiFi frames experience retransmission (PRR is roughly 97%). According to a WiFi hotspot study conducted by Pang *et al.* [18], a near 100% PRR corresponds to an SNR regime around 40 dB or more. On the other hand, when SNR goes below 20 dB, nodes struggle to even obtain IP addresses after association (9 out of 181 successful DHCP attempts) [9]. Although we could not measure at higher SNRs, our results show that downclocking at 50% already achieves excellent results even at low SNRs, nearly matching the performance of decoding at 100% at 25 dB. When downclocking at 25%, the situation is more complex. Our results up to 30 dB show that PRR is increasingly close to maximum performance for small packets. However, there is still substantial headroom for large packets and we cannot yet estimate at what SNR both curves will approach 100%. Thus, for poor or moderate SNRs with 25% downclocking, it remains an open question as to whether and when it is worthwhile trading off PRR for energy savings.

7.2.3 Impact of wireless environment

As measured in Section 7.2.1, the performance of aliasing induced modulation entirely depends on the surrounding wireless environment, reflected in the blocking distance. In the extreme case where the channel response is flat for the entire spectrum, given how bits are mapped under BPSK, multiple constellation points would collapse onto each other under aliasing. In our previous experiments, all nodes were in the same room (a seven-person office). In this experiment, we vary locations to evaluate the performance of downclocking under a much wider range of wireless conditions.

We repeat the experiments in Section 7.2.2 at four additional locations in the same building but with significantly different propagation environments. These locations are a meeting room (smaller than the office), a long hallway, a floor lobby of mixed open space and furniture, and a lab (much larger than the office). In all locations we use a fixed SNR of 30 dB.

Figure 7 shows the packet reception ratios for all locations and both packet sizes. Error bars show the standard deviation across 50 runs. For both the 100% and 50% clock rates, the PRRs are indistinguishable for all locations regardless of the packet size. For the 25% downclock rate, though, the PRR does vary across locations. The PRR varies moderately for small packets (78% to 85%), but has a larger variation for larger packets (48% to 63%). These results confirm that the downclocking performance Enfold achieves is stable across different wireless environments, and not tied the opportune conditions of just one environment.

7.2.4 Trading throughput for PRR

In the last set of experiments, we explore one of the design freedoms offered by Enfold. Recall from Section 5.3 that we restore the pilot subcarriers by placing known values on selected subcarriers. We explore this design parameter further by putting known values on other data subcarriers. The benefits are twofold: these known values (bits) improve the performance of the Viterbi decoder and they help to reduce the size of constellation diagram. For instance, for the subcarrier set from the experiment in Section 7.2.1, if we put a known data value on subcarrier 10, the resulting constellation diagram under 25% clock rate will degenerate to 8-QAM instead of 16-QAM. However, using more subcarriers will reduce the effective data throughput. In situations where both power and interference are challenging, such as sensors, applications might want to trade off reliability for throughput at lower power. To explore this trade-off, we repeat the experiment in Section 7.2.2 at a 25% clock rate while adding known bits to subcarriers.

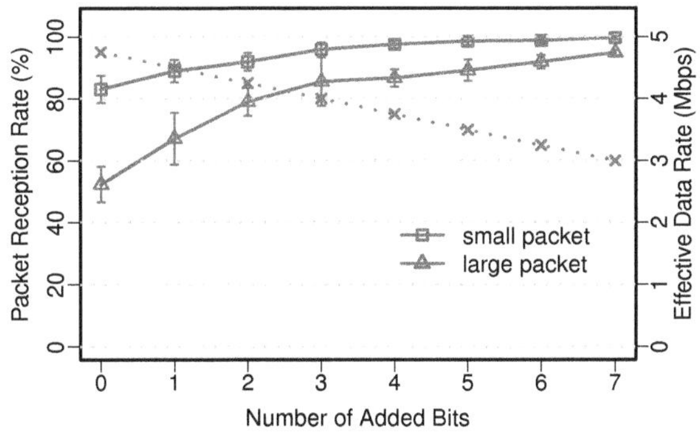

Figure 8: PRR with additional known bits on subcarriers for a 25% downclock rate (SNR = 30dB). The right y-axis shows the corresponding effective throughput.

Figure 8 shows the PRR performance and effective data rate with respect to the number of known bits sent (0 additional bit corresponds to the results for 25% at 30 dB in Section 7.2.2). As discussed above, standard 802.11 only uses 52 out of 64 subcarriers for data. As a result, only 3 out of the 16 subcarriers are 16-QAM modulated when downclocked to 25%.

Therefore, we put the known bits on these three subcarriers first, which helps PRR by reducing the original 16-QAM modulation to 8-QAM. Consequently, PRR improves substantially for both small and large packet sizes. For example, with 3 known bits added, PRR jumps to 96% and 85% for small and large packet, respectively. After adding 3 bits, all constellation diagrams on the 16 subcarriers are 8-QAM modulation (except subcarrier 0 which is 4-QAM). Each additional bit then transforms one of the 8-QAM constellation diagrams to 4-QAM. As expected PRR continues to improve, but with a smaller delta than when transforming 16-QAM to 8-QAM.

The trade-off in improved PRR is a reduction in data throughput in proportion to the number of additional known bits used for pilots. The PRR eventually reaches excellent PRRs of 99.6% (small) and 94.7% (large) when adding 7 bits, but at that point the effective data rate drops to 3 Mbps (half of the raw PHY layer data rate). In summary, Enfold provides the flexibility to trade off effective data rate for PRR performance, improving Enfold's applicability in poor SNR regimes where applications favor such a trade-off.

8. ENERGY CONSUMPTION

Finally, we evaluate the benefits of downclocking OFDM by estimating the energy consumption of Enfold compared to related techniques on traces of smartphone app usage. We start with the SloMo data set used by Lu *et al.* [13], which contains high fidelity WiFi packet traces from nine popular smartphone apps (each with >5 million downloads) including familiar Internet services like Facebook and Gmail as well as smartphone-specific services such as Pocket Legends (an online massively multiplayer game) and TuneIn Radio (a streaming audio service). Considering that the majority of the SloMo traces focus on low data rate apps, we add three traces of higher bandwidth apps: Wyslink (live TV streaming, 479 kbps), FaceTime (1499 kbps), and YouTube (588 kbps).

Given the lack of a real downclocked WiFi chipset with which to measure power consumption, we use a device power model to estimate the network energy consumption of each app given its network behavior in the traces. We use the WiFi power model from [13, 16], which is based on measurements of a Nexus One reported by Manweiler *et al.* [14]. When a WiFi chipset is actively transmitting or receiving, it stays in the high power state. Once network transfers complete, it transitions to the idle state (note that the power consumption in idle is still comparable to the active state). When there is no network activity for a while (the tail time), it transitions to the light sleep state. Note that the light sleep state also consumes a significant amount of power in anticipation of immediate wake-up. When the chipset is not woken up for about 500 ms, it finally moves to the deep sleep state where the power consumption is nearly negligible. The detailed parameters associated with each state and clock rate are given in [13]. Furthermore, the power model used is deliberately conservative.[7] For example, the idle power consumption for the 25% clock rate is only 65% of the idle power at full rate.

We compare energy consumption among OFDM downclocking with Enfold, DSSS downclocking with SloMo, and the default power save mode (PSM) in 802.11g as a baseline. While our Enfold prototype employs a 6-Mbps rate, we also introduce a hypothetical case where the downclocked reception data rate is set to 54 Mbps (the highest rate in 11g) with 100% PRR to estimate how much potential energy savings remain unrealized because Enfold does not operate at higher rates. We also conservatively assume the chipset does not have a fast-switching clock. Therefore, although an Enfold node can receive at a 6 Mbps OFDM data rate, it would have to transition to a 2-Mbps DSSS data rate for transmission (including ACKs). On the other hand, the data rates used for PSM are the actual ones reported by the packet capture software in the trace.

Enfold consistently outperforms PSM for all the app traces, and matches or exceeds SloMo depending on the app workload. Figure 9 compares the normalized energy consumption of PSM, SloMo (2-Mbps DSSS rate with 100% PRR) and Enfold (4.75-Mbps with 63% PRR in Section 7.2.3). We focus on six representative apps out of the twelve; the remaining apps have low data rates with performance similar to Skype voice (i.e., both SloMo and Enfold improve upon PSM, but behave similarly to each other).

Apps like Skype voice frequently require network access but the amount of data transferred is low (data rates range from 10s to 100s kbps). As a consequence, the WiFi card either stays in constant awake mode (CAM) or is woken up intermittently every few seconds, and therefore the network energy consumption is largely dominated by idle listening for the network tail time. Given their small app data rates, the extra energy spent on transmission and reception due to slower data rate or retransmissions is more than compensated for by the energy saved during the idle state, and to a certain extent, sleep state. Even the 2-Mbps DSSS rate in SloMo are sufficient for these apps. As a result, both SloMo and Enfold save significant energy (up to 34%) for these apps compared to PSM.

However, as the app data rate increases (e.g., Skype Video, Wyslink) or interactivity reduces (e.g., Pandora, which prefetches the entire song before playing out) or both (YouTube, which downloads chunks of data every 10–20 seconds), SloMo has small or negative benefits. The energy saved in the idle listening and sleep states is matched or exceeded by the energy expended for transmission and reception at the slower data rate; for some apps, SloMo consumes over 20% more energy than PSM. In contrast, given the increased data rates supported (~2.4x SloMo rate for the current implementation), Enfold is able to save appreciable energy for these apps: from Skype Video (9%) to Pandora (19%). YouTube sees little benefit (3%) because it already uses the network efficiently, particularly in the face of retransmissions with Enfold's 63% PRR.

In the best case of a network with good SNR conditions and an improved PRR of 100%, energy savings are correspondingly better: from Skype Video (10%) to Pandora (21%) (with YouTube at 8%, showing the effects of PRR). In sum, Enfold significantly extends

[7] The maximum possible energy savings in this model is 35%.

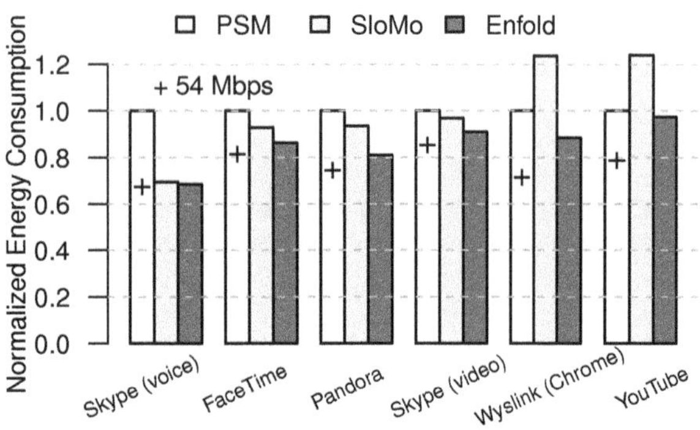

Figure 9: Energy comparison among PSM, SloMo, and Enfold. We also include a hypothetical case where the downclocked reception data rate is 54 Mbps and PRR is 100%. Results are normalized with respect to PSM.

the range of apps that benefit from downclocking. Compared to the hypothetical 54-Mbps case at 100% PRR, the additional energy gain over 6 Mbps in Enfold is small compared to the substantial difference in data rate: Pandora (4.5%), FaceTime (3.6%), Skype Video (3.9%), Wyslink (8.4%) and YouTube (12%). As a result, for these popular apps Enfold at 6 Mbps already captures much of the energy savings.

As a final note, we also evaluated energy consumption with Enfold for other data rates and PRRs (the throughput-PRR trade-off enabled in Section 7.2.4). The results among these Enfold variants are roughly the same with a 2–3% variation. Although the difference in energy consumption is small, higher PRR leads to fewer retransmissions and reduced network contention.

9. CONCLUSION

In this paper we present an approach for successfully receiving and decoding OFDM modulation while sampling below the Nyquist frequency. We exploit the aliasing that results from undersampling and observe that there exists well-defined structure in terms of how OFDM signals are "folded up" under aliasing. In particular, we show that a standards-compliant 802.11a/g frame can be detected, received, and decoded by a receiver running at a 50% or even 25% clock rate given sufficient channel quality. We design and implement a standards-compliant 802.11 receiver on the Sora platform and experimentally show that our aliasing induced modulation can attain greater than 96% and 83% raw packet reception rates while reducing the clock rate by 2× and 4×, respectively. Enfold explicitly trades throughput (SNR) for energy savings by moving to downclocked states with potentially reduced data rates in proportion to downclocking ratio. Based on published WiFi traces, we show such trade-off is worthwhile; Enfold could reduce network energy consumption by up to 34% for many popular smartphone apps. Even when nodes are in sleep mode, the energy saving benefit still persists for downclocked beacon listening and AP scanning.

Acknowledgments

We would like to thank the anonymous reviewers and our shepherd for their detailed feedback. This work was supported by generous research, operational and in-kind support from the UCSD Center for Networked Systems (CNS).

10. REFERENCES

[1] AT&T Enhanced Push-To-Talk Deployment Guide. http://www.business.att.com/content/other/wi-fi-for-website.pdf.

[2] Best practice: Planning your organization's Wi-Fi infrastructure. http://docs.blackberry.com/en/admin/deliverables/20034/BBMVS_BP_WiFi_infrastructure_1177026_11.jsp.

[3] Cisco 7920 Wireless IP Phone Design and Deployment Guide. http://www.mwtn.net/ASSETS/MANUALS/cisco_7920.pdf.

[4] Sora SDK manual. http://research.microsoft.com/apps/pubs/default.aspx?id=160799.

[5] CHANDRA, R., MAHAJAN, R., MOSCIBRODA, T., RAGHAVENDRA, R., AND BAHL, P. A Case for Adapting Channel Width in Wireless Networks. In *Proceedings of ACM SIGCOMM* (Aug. 2008).

[6] CHEN, X., JIN, R., SUH, K., WANG, B., AND WEI, W. Network Performance of Smart Mobile Handhelds in a University Campus WiFi Network. In *Proceedings of ACM IMC* (Nov. 2012).

[7] ETTUS RESEARCH LLC. Universal Software Radio Peripheral (USRP). http://www.ettus.com/.

[8] HALPERIN, D., GREENSTEIN, B., SETH, A., AND WETHERALL, D. Demystifying 802.11n Power Consumption. In *Proceedings of USENIX HotPower* (Oct. 2010).

[9] HAN, D., AGARWALA, A., ANDERSEN, D. G., KAMINSKY, M., PAPAGIANNAKI, K., AND SESHAN, S. Mark-and-Sweep: Getting the "Inside" Scoop on Neighborhood Networks. In *Proceedings of ACM IMC* (Oct. 2008).

[10] HASSANIEH, H., ADIB, F., KATABI, D., AND INDYK, P. Faster GPS via the Sparse Fourier Transform. In *Proceedings of ACM MobiCom* (Aug. 2012).

[11] IEEE. IEEE 802.11g-2003: Further Higher Data Rate Extension in the 2.4 GHz Band, 2003.

[12] LEE, J., LOU, H.-L., TOUMPAKARIS, D., AND CIOFFI, J. M. Effect of Carrier Frequency Offset on OFDM Systems for Multipath Fading Channels. In *Proceedings of IEEE GLOBECOM* (Dec. 2004).

[13] LU, F., VOELKER, G. M., AND SNOEREN, A. C. SloMo: Downclocking WiFi Communication. In *Proceedings of USENIX NSDI* (Apr. 2013).

[14] MANWEILER, J., AND CHOUDHURY, R. R. Avoiding the Rush Hours: WiFi Energy Management via Traffic Isolation. In *Proceedings of ACM MobiSys* (June 2011).

[15] MENG, J., YIN, W., LI, Y., NGUYEN, N., AND HAN, Z. Compressive Sensing Based High-Resolution Channel Estimation for OFDM System. *IEEE Journal of Selected Topics in Signal Processing 6*, 1 (2012), 15–25.

[16] MITTAL, R., KANSAL, A., AND CHANDRA, R. Empowering Developers to Estimate App Energy Consumption. In *Proceedings of ACM MobiCom* (Aug. 2012).

[17] MODY, A. N., AND STUBER, G. L. Synchronization for MIMO OFDM systems. In *Proceedings of IEEE GLOBECOM* (Nov. 2001).

[18] PANG, J., GREENSTEIN, B., KAMINSKY, M., MCCOY, D., AND SESHAN, S. Wifi-Reports: Improving Wireless Network Selection with Collaboration. In *Proceedings of ACM MobiSys* (June 2009).

[19] POLO, Y. L., WANG, Y., PANDHARIPANDE, A., AND LEUS, G. Compressive Wide-Band Spectrum Sensing. In *Proceedings of IEEE ICASSP* (Apr. 2009).

[20] TAN, K., ZHANG, J., WU, H., JI, F., LIU, H., YE, Y., WANG, S., ZHANG, Y., WANG, W., AND VOELKER, G. M. Sora: High Performance Software Radio Using General Purpose Multi-core Processors. In *Proceedings of USENIX NSDI* (Apr. 2009).

[21] TAUBOCK, G., AND HLAWATSCH, F. A Compressed Sensing Technique for OFDM Channel Estimation in Mobile Environments: Exploiting Channel Sparsity for Reducing Pilots. In *Proceedings of IEEE ICASSP* (Apr. 2008).

[22] YIP, K.-W., WU, Y.-C., AND NG, T.-S. Timing-Synchronization Analysis for IEEE 802.11a Wireless LANs in Frequency-Nonselective Rician Fading Environments. *IEEE Transactions on Wireless Communications 3*, 2 (2004), 387–394.

[23] ZHANG, X., AND SHIN, K. G. E-MiLi: Energy-Minimizing Idle Listening in Wireless Networks. In *Proceedings of ACM MobiCom* (Sept. 2011).

Combating Inter-cell Interference in 802.11ac-based Multi-user MIMO Networks

Hang Yu, Oscar Bejarano, and Lin Zhong
Department of Electrical and Computer Engineering, Rice University, Houston, TX
{Hang.Yu, obejarano, lzhong}@rice.edu

Abstract

In an 802.11ac-based MU-MIMO network comprised of multiple cells[1], inter-cell interference allows only a single AP to serve its clients at the same time, significantly limiting the network capacity. In this work, we overcome this limitation by letting the APs and clients in interfering cells coordinately cancel the inter-cell interference using their antennas for beamforming. To achieve such coordinated interference cancellation in a practical way, we propose a novel two-step optimization. First, without requiring any channel knowledge, each AP and client optimizes the use of its antennas for either data communication or inter-cell interference cancellation, in order to maximize the total number of deliverable streams in the MU-MIMO network. Second, with only partial channel knowledge, each AP and client optimizes their beamforming weights after the optimal antenna usage has been identified in the first step. Our solution, CoaCa, integrates this two-step optimization into 802.11ac with small modifications and negligible overhead, allowing each AP and client to locally perform the two-step optimization. Our experimental evaluation indicates that for a MU-MIMO network with two cells, by cancelling the inter-cell interference CoaCa can convert the majority of the expected number of streams increase (50%-67%) into network capacity improvement (41%-52%).

Categories and Subject Descriptors

C.2.1 [**COMPUTER-COMMUNICATION NETWORKS**]: Network Architecture and Design - Wireless Communication

Keywords

Inter-cell interference; multi-user MIMO; 802.11ac; CoaCa

1. INTRODUCTION

For 802.11 networks comprised of multiple cells, inter-cell interference has become a key factor that limits the network capacity because it prevents the APs in neighboring cells from serving their clients concurrently. To cancel inter-cell interference with *beamforming*, the interfering AP and client are required to (*i*) be aware of the channel between them, and (*ii*) coordinate to determine their duty of cancellation. Yet, neither of the two requirements is directly supported by existing 802.11 protocols. There have been efforts in supporting them in 802.11n that features single-user MIMO (SU-MIMO). 802.11n+ proposed in [10] seeks to enable concurrent links across multiple cells. n+ cancels the inter-cell interference by (*i*) letting nodes in one cell overhear the transmissions from nodes in the other cell to acquire necessary channel knowledge, and (*ii*) coordinating nodes in the two cells by opportunistically starting the concurrent link in the overhearing cell afterwards. Notably, the interference cancellation coordination in n+ is one-way: nodes in the overhearing cell must use their spare antennas to cancel the inter-cell interference. The number of spare antennas should be no smaller than that of the ongoing streams in the overheard cell. Since an 802.11n link with SU-MIMO usually includes one or two streams, only one or two spare antennas are needed for each node in the overhearing cell.

For the newer 802.11ac supporting multi-user MIMO (MU-MIMO), an AP can transmit to multiple, say K (e.g., K=4) clients simultaneously. When a cell is congested with more clients than antennas on the AP, the AP delivers a single stream to each served client so that the number of streams is equal to the number of clients, denoted as the *multiplexing gain* of MU-MIMO. To increase the multiplexing gain by starting concurrent streams in the overhearing cell, n+ would require each AP and client in it to have at least K spare antennas to cancel the inter-cell interference, which is usually infeasible in practice. The fundamental reason why n+ does not effectively extend to 802.11ac is its one-way coordination for inter-cell interference cancellation, where nodes in the overhearing cell have to contribute all the required antennas to solely carry the burden of cancellation. Our key insight in this work is that when two congested MU-MIMO cells "jointly coordinate," the number of required antennas on their nodes can be reduced and more streams can be delivered concurrently.

Let us consider the example in Figure 1. With three antennas on each AP and three clients in each cell, n+ only allows a single AP (AP1 or AP2) to serve its clients at a time, therefore activating only up to three streams in the network. Instead of solely relying on the nodes in one cell to cancel the inter-cell interference like in n+, we do it in the following alternative way. First, each AP uses two antennas to serve two clients (Client 1 and Client 3 in Cell 1, Client4 and Client6 in Cell 2), and the third antenna to cancel the inter-cell interference to one client in the other cell (Client1 in Cell 1, Client4 in Cell 2). Then, the other client in each cell (Client3 in Cell 1, Client6 in Cell 2) uses its three

[1]We use *cell* to denote the domain of an access point (AP) and its associated clients.

MobiCom'14, September 7-11, 2014, Maui, Hawaii, USA.

http://dx.doi.org/10.1145/2639108.2639122.

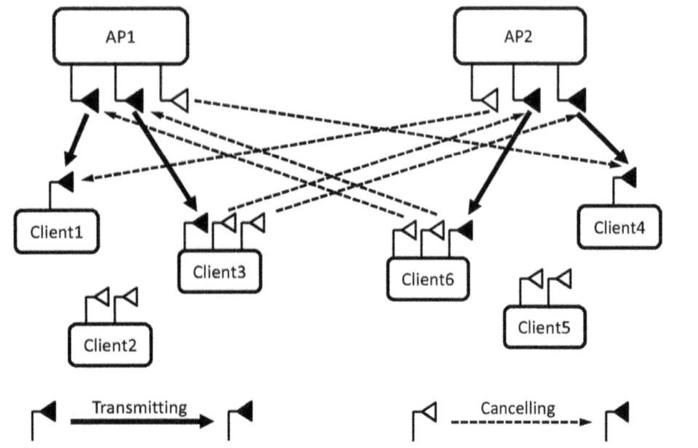

Figure 1: An example with two APs each serving up to three clients. Jointly coordinating the two cells to cancel the inter-cell interference delivers the maximum number of (four) streams.

antennas to cancel the inter-cell interference from the two streams sent by each AP. Consequently, we can activate four simultaneous streams in the network. Observe that both APs and clients have properly shared the responsibility of canceling the interference between them. Therefore, compared to n+ this is a more effective way to use the antennas on each AP and client. In fact, such joint cell coordination maximizes the number of streams or clients. The central question we seek to answer is: *how to practically achieve this cell coordination in a MU-MIMO network composed of multiple interfering cells?*

Determining the beamforming weights for each AP and client that cancel inter-cell interference with joint coordination is a non-trivial process. The theoretically optimal solution that maximizes network capacity can be empirically found by jointly optimizing the beamforming weights for all APs and clients. The optimal solution may not completely eliminate inter-cell interference since interference below the noise power is often no longer considered the capacity-limiting factor. However, identifying the optimal solution is neither practical nor compatible with 802.11ac because (*i*) it is computationally intractable due to the lack of an analytical solution, and (*ii*) it has to be done in a centralized way with full channel knowledge of the entire MU-MIMO network.

In this work, we present a novel solution that allows distributed cell coordination for inter-cell interference cancellation, and can be practically integrated into 802.11ac. The key idea in our solution is that the process of identifying the beamforming weights can be broken into two separate steps, namely *antenna usage optimization* and *beamforming weight optimization*. The first step determines how each AP and client antenna should be used: data communication or inter-cell interference cancellation. The optimal antenna usage of each AP and client collectively maximizes the number of streams in the MU-MIMO network. The second step determines the beamforming weights of each AP and client based on its optimized antenna usage. Given the use of antennas, it is possible to adopt practical beamforming techniques with a closed-form solution such as zero-forcing beamforming. The feasibility of such two-step optimization is based on an important heuristic we use to simplify the problem: we strive to completely eliminate inter-cell interference and maximize the multiplexing gain of MU-MIMO. Only with this heuristic the antenna usage can be reduced into a binary form including data communication and inter-cell interference cancellation, and optimized in a separate step prior to the optimization of beamforming weights.

The separation of the antenna usage optimization and beamforming weight optimization greatly simplifies the cell coordination effort, allowing us to practically integrate such two-step optimization into 802.11ac. Our proposed protocol, called CoaCa (Coordinated optimization of the AP and Client antennas), leverages the channel sounding process in 802.11ac to let each AP and client locally perform the two-step optimization in a distributed way. CoaCa includes two key designs. First, by interleaving the channel sounding process from all the APs, each node can easily acquire the necessary global information to optimize the use of their antennas. Such information including the number of antennas on each node only needs a few bits to be represented and can be explicitly shared by each AP. Second, by reporting and overhearing the beamformed channels in the interleaved channel sounding, each node can obtain just enough channel knowledge to optimize its beamforming weights. CoaCa incurs negligible overhead over 802.11ac and compatibly works with unmodified 802.11ac clients. While the current design of CoaCa only allows downlink MU-MIMO which is consistent to 802.11ac, the optimized beamforming weights for the APs and clients can be also used for uplink MU-MIMO leveraging channel reciprocity. However, realizing uplink MU-MIMO faces a new set of challenges such as misaligned symbol timing and clock frequency offset between clients, which are studied by other prior work, e.g., [17] and outside the scope of this work.

We realize a prototype of CoaCa on the WARP platform [14], and evaluate its performance in realistic indoor wireless environments. Our experimental results show that on average CoaCa is able to improve the capacity of a two-cell MU-MIMO network by 41% to 52%, with no more than four antennas on each AP and client. Even though the capacity gain is lower than the multiplexing gain increase (50% to 67%), CoaCa considerably outperforms existing solutions that often only allow a single cell to operate. While our evaluation does not include a large-scale MU-MIMO network, a *cell clustering* technique can be adopted to transform a large-scale network into several small clusters where each of them includes only two to three cells. In fact, the distributed nature of CoaCa makes it hard to gracefully scale with the number of cells. Unlike centralized solutions such as Network-MIMO [2,12] that can convert interference into signals, CoaCa must cancel the interference, requiring a much larger number of antennas on the interfering AP and clients. By transferring a large-scale MU-MIMO network into small clusters, we can apply CoaCa to each cluster independently, requiring only a small thus practical number of antennas on the APs and clients.

In summary, this work makes the following contributions:

- A novel solution that allows the APs and clients in multiple interfering MU-MIMO cells to coordinately cancel the inter-cell interference in two separate steps, including antenna usage optimization and beamforming weight optimization.
- An algorithm that efficiently identifies the optimal antenna usage for each AP and client in the MU-MIMO network to maximize the multiplexing gain.
- An analytical study of the channel knowledge requirement for each AP and client to locally optimize the beamforming weights based on its optimal antenna usage.
- A protocol that integrates antenna usage optimization and beamforming weight optimization into 802.11ac with small modifications and negligible overhead.

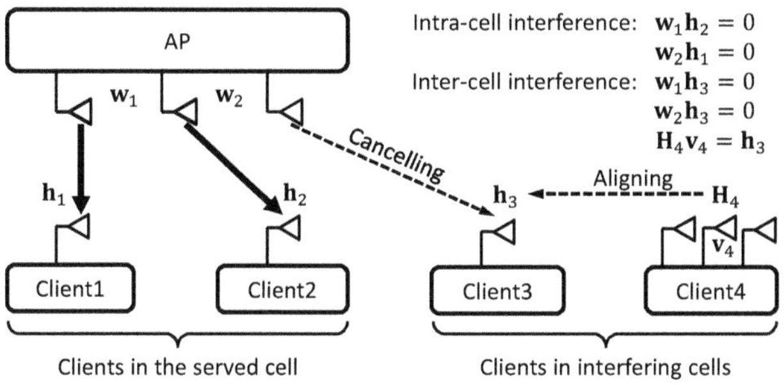

Figure 2: Intra-cell and inter-cell interference cancellation in a MU-MIMO network. The AP uses three antennas to cancel the intra-cell interference between Client1 and Client2, and the inter-cell interference to Client3. Given two additional antennas Client3 could cancel the inter-cell interference from the AP, saving one antenna for the latter. Client4 employs interference alignment to align its channel to that of Client3, so that the inter-cell interference from the AP is naturally eliminated when the AP cancels the interference to Client3.

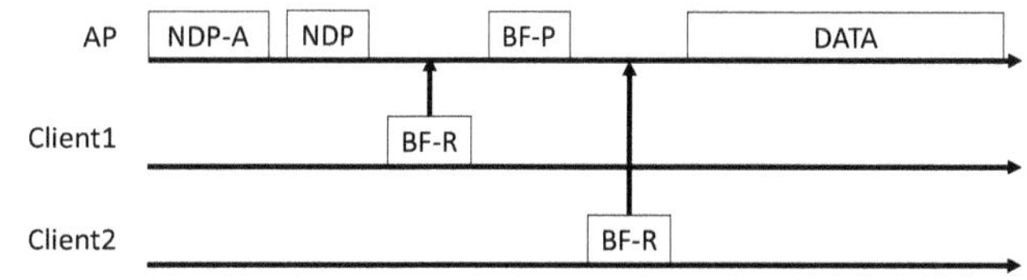

Figure 3: The channel sounding process in 802.11ac. First the AP sends a NDP-A frame and a NDP frame for all specified clients to estimate their downlink channels, and then each client sequentially replies with a BF-R frame containing the estimated channels.

2. BACKGROUND

In this section first we discuss relevant MU-MIMO techniques for interference cancellation. Then we present an overview of the supported MU-MIMO feature in the IEEE 802.11ac protocol.

2.1 Interference Cancellation in MU-MIMO

MU-MIMO improves network capacity by achieving a *multiplexing gain*, defined as the number of concurrent streams or simultaneously served clients. To appreciate the multiplexing gain in a MU-MIMO network composed of multiple interfering cells, both intra-cell and inter-cell interference must be sufficiently suppressed with the *beamforming* technique which we introduce below.

Intra-cell interference cancellation. To cancel the intra-cell interference, a MU-MIMO AP uses transmit beamforming to *precode* the data stream to each client. The downlink channels of the simultaneously served clients must be orthogonalized such that each client only receives its own stream without interference. The precoding strategy of the AP that achieves such orthogonality is known as *zero-forcing beamforming* (ZFBF). In zero-forcing beamforming, the transmit beamforming weight vectors, a.k.a. the precoding vectors of the AP, $\mathbf{w}_j$, are chosen to orthogonalize the channel vectors from the AP to the clients, $\mathbf{h}_k$, i.e., $\mathbf{w}_j\mathbf{h}_k$=0 $(j \neq k)$. To satisfy the orthogonality constraints, the dimension of $\mathbf{w}_j$, which is the number of antennas on the AP, must be no smaller than the number of served clients. This is the maximum multiplexing gain that can be achieved in a single MU-MIMO cell.

Inter-cell interference cancellation. The zero-forcing beamforming technique can be extended to cancel the inter-cell interference. That is, if there are any spare antennas on the AP after cancelling the intra-cell interference, they can be used to orthogonalize the channel vectors of the clients in other cells in the same way. Note that in the proper context without introducing ambiguity, we use *antenna* to refer to the *Degree of Freedom* (DoF) provided by a physical antenna on an AP or a client. In Figure 2, since there are three antennas, the AP uses two of them to cancel the intra-cell interference between Client1 and Client2, and the third (spare) one to cancel the inter-cell interference to Client3 in the interfering cell.

Inter-cell interference can be alternatively cancelled by a client if the client features multiple antennas for receive beamforming, a.k.a., post-combining [23]. Note that receive beamforming actually allows a client to separate and recover both the intended and interference streams. For ease of explanation we simply use the term *interference cancellation* to denote such capability of a receive beamforming client. To cancel the inter-cell interference, the client j chooses its receive beamforming weight vector, a.k.a. the post-combining vector, $\mathbf{v}_j$, such that $\mathbf{w}_k\mathbf{H}_j\mathbf{v}_j$=0 for all served clients k by the AP, where $\mathbf{H}_j$ is the channel matrix from the AP to client j. For example, in Figure 2 if Client3 had two spare antennas they could be used to cancel the two streams from the AP to Client1 and Client2, saving the third antenna on the AP. This would provide the AP with the flexibility to use its third antenna to potentially serve another client. Without inter-cell interference, multiple client antennas can be used to increase the SNR of the received stream via maximum ratio combining (MRC) [18].

Another technique for dealing with inter-cell interference is *interference alignment* [6, 8, 10, 11]. The key idea in interference alignment is to align the channel vectors of multiple clients, i.e., $\mathbf{H}_j\mathbf{v}_j$=$\mathbf{H}_k\mathbf{v}_k$, so that the interference between the AP and these clients traverses a single aligned channel and requires fewer AP antennas to be cancelled. Such alignment can be conceptually understood as if the client used its own antennas to cancel the interference saving the antennas on the AP. Note that interference alignment is more commonly assumed for uplink transmission, e.g., multiple clients transmit to an AP they interfere with on an aligned channel. In this work we leverage channel reciprocity to apply interference alignment to downlink MU-MIMO in which the AP transmits to multiple clients it interferes with on the same aligned channel. In Figure 2, without interference alignment, the AP would need two spare antennas to cancel the inter-cell interference to both Client3 and Client4. When Client4 aligns its channel to that of Client3 by setting $\mathbf{H}_4\mathbf{v}_4$=$\mathbf{h}_3$, the AP only needs one antenna to cancel the inter-cell interference.

2.2 MU-MIMO in 802.11ac

Now we briefly introduce the MU-MIMO feature supported by 802.11ac [4], the latest amendment to the 802.11 protocol family. 802.11ac allows the AP to use MU-MIMO techniques to simultaneously transmit downlink streams to up to four of its served clients. For APs in the interference range of each other, 802.11ac does not allow them to transmit at the same time; instead, the APs contend to access the medium using CSMA/CA.

Channel knowledge is necessary for the AP to calculate the transmit beamforming weights that cancel the intra-cell interference. To acquire channel knowledge, 802.11ac mandates an explicit channel sounding process, which we show in Figure 3. To sound the channel, the AP first broadcasts a *Null Data Packet Announcement* (NDP-A) frame. The purpose of the NDP-A frame is to specify the set of clients the AP is about to serve, and notify them to prepare for estimating and reporting their downlink channels. After the NDP-A frame, the AP sends a *Null Data Packet* (NDP) frame that allows the clients to estimate their downlink channels leveraging the training symbols in the frame. Then, the

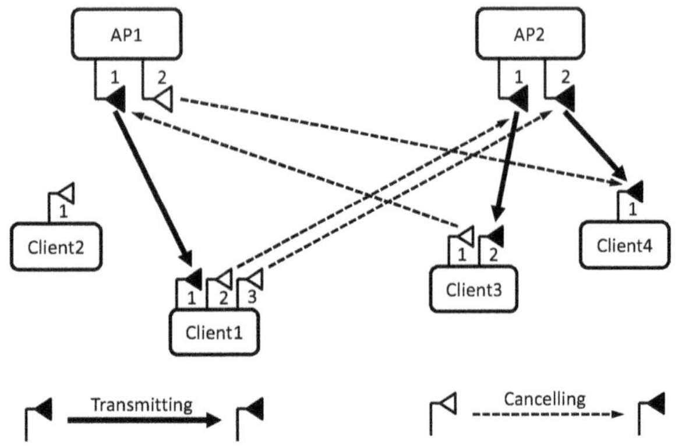

Figure 4: The optimal use of the AP and client antennas in our illustrative example. The interference from AP2 to Client1 is cancelled by Client1, while the interference from AP1 to Client3 and Client4 are cancelled by Client3 and AP1, respectively.

specified clients sequentially report their estimated channels to the AP with a *Beamforming Report* (BF-R) frame. The NDP-A frame designates a client that must immediately reply with the BF-R frame after the NDP frame, while other clients must wait for the *Beamforming Report Poll* (BF-P) frame from the AP to respond. The explicit channel sounding process in 802.11ac does not require channel reciprocity which is needed by implicit channel estimation [16]. The inter-frame interval in the channel sounding process is *SIFS* (16 μs), which is shorter than *DIFS* (34 μs) and thereby provides the APs and clients guaranteed medium access without being intervened by other 802.11 nodes.

3. OVERVIEW

To improve the capacity of an 802.11ac-based MU-MIMO network by allowing more streams in its cells, we propose a novel solution that practically achieves coordinated inter-cell interference cancellation with AP and client beamforming. The key idea in our solution is that the process of determining the beamforming weights for each AP and client can be broken into two steps, namely *antenna usage optimization* and *beamforming weight optimization*. We are motivated by the following important observation: when we strive to completely eliminate interference, the two optimizations can be executed sequentially. This is because the constraint of completely eliminating inter-cell interference reduces the antenna usage into a binary form. That is, one antenna can be used for either transmitting or receiving streams, or cancelling inter-cell interference. It is therefore plausible to optimize the beamforming weights solely based on the given optimized antenna usage.

Such two-step optimization significantly reduces the cell coordination effort for cancelling the inter-cell interference. First, coordinately optimizing the antenna usage by each AP and client merely requires the information of the number of antennas on all nodes in the network. Without needing any channel knowledge, cell coordination in this step is simplified since the required information can be represented with only a few bits and explicitly shared by each AP with negligible overhead. Second, given the optimized antenna usage, an AP or a client is fully aware of its duty toward cancelling the inter-cell interference. To determine the optimal beamforming weights that fulfill this duty, the AP or client only needs a subset of channel knowledge in the network. Such reduction of the required channel knowledge further makes cell coordination easier. With much simplified cell coordination, the two-step optimization can be integrated into 802.11ac retaining the distributed nature of the protocol. Our proposed solution, called CoaCa, leverages *interleaved channel sounding* and *channel reporting and overhearing* to let each AP and client optimize their antenna usage and beamforming weights in a local but coordinated way.

Table 1: The optimal use of the AP and client antennas in our illustrative example, where "→" and "--→" indicate data communication and inter-cell interference cancellation, respectively.

	Antenna 1	Antenna 2	Antenna 3
AP1	→ Client1	--→ Client4	×
AP2	→ Client3	→ Client4	×
Client1	← AP1	←-- AP2	←-- AP2
Client3	←-- AP1	← AP2	×
Client4	← AP2	×	×

4. ANTENNA USAGE OPTIMIZATION

In this section, we provide an algorithm that identifies the best antenna usage for each AP and client to maximize the multiplexing gain of the MU-MIMO network. Recall that an AP or a client antenna is used for either delivering streams or cancelling inter-cell interference. Therefore, our algorithm finds the optimal allocation of the AP and client antennas for such two uses. In the following, we first use a simple but illustrative example with two APs and four clients to demonstrate the process of finding the optimal antenna usage, and then provide the algorithm that applies to MU-MIMO networks with arbitrary number of cells.

4.1 Illustrative Example

Our example shown in Figure 4 includes two MU-MIMO cells where each AP is equipped with two antennas and serves up to two clients simultaneously. To find the optimal antenna usage, our algorithm needs to identify the best set of clients in each cell that can be simultaneously served by their corresponding AP. In other words, the selected clients must be capable of coordinately cancelling the inter-cell interference with their interfering AP.

Our algorithm starts by letting a single AP, say AP1, serve both of its clients, and tries to add concurrently served clients in the other cell similarly to n+. Clearly, with only two antennas, AP2 cannot cancel the interference to both clients in Cell 1 while serving either of its own clients. Then, unlike n+ which simply stops and lets AP1 serve its two clients, our algorithm asks AP1 to serve only a single client, say Client1, and again seeks to add concurrently served clients in Cell 2. Noticeably, now AP2 can serve both of its clients if the inter-cell interference is cancelled in the following way. First, Client1 uses its three antennas to cancel the two interfering streams from AP2. Second, Client3 uses its two antennas to cancel the interfering stream from AP1. Last, while Client4 with a single antenna cannot cancel the interfering stream from AP1, observe that AP1 has a spare antenna that can be just leveraged to cancel the interference to Client4. This way, we have found the best set of clients to serve in each cell that collectively achieves a multiplexing gain of three. We illustrate the optimal use of each AP and client antenna in Table 1.

4.2 Network of Two Cells

We next present our algorithm that identifies the best antenna usage for a two-cell MU-MIMO network with arbitrary number of clients and arbitrary number of antennas on each AP and client.

Our algorithm is motivated by the optimization process for the illustrative example in Section 4.1.

Since we are only interested in congested MU-MIMO networks where the number of associated clients is no smaller than that of the AP antennas, we assume in Cell 1 AP1 has N antennas and the N clients have P_n $(n = 1, 2, \cdots, N)$ antennas, and in Cell 2 AP2 has M antennas and the M clients have Q_m $(m = 1, 2, \cdots, M)$ antennas. We further assume the clients in each cell are sorted based on their number of equipped antennas:

$$P_1 \leq P_2 \leq \cdots \leq P_N,$$
$$Q_1 \leq Q_2 \leq \cdots \leq Q_M.$$

Algorithm for optimizing the antenna usage. Similar to the example in Section 4.1, to obtain the optimal antenna usage, our algorithm needs to determine the optimal set of served clients in both cells given that the inter-cell interference can be coordinately cancelled. Initially, our algorithm allows only Cell 1 to operate, by letting AP1 serve all its N clients. Then, it seeks to add clients in Cell 2 that can be concurrently served by AP2. The maximum number of added clients in Cell 2, denoted as L, is constrained by the inter-cell interference from AP2 to clients in Cell 1 and that from AP1 to clients in Cell 2. First, AP2 may use up to L' antennas to transmit L' streams to L' clients in Cell 2. While these L' data streams as inter-cell interference may be cancelled by a few clients in Cell 1 with enough ($\geq L'$+1) antennas, the remaining clients in Cell 1 that do not have enough ($\leq L'$) antennas must rely on the spare M-L' antennas on AP2 to cancel the inter-cell interference. We can keep increasing L' until those clients in Cell 1 that must cancel their inter-cell interference do not have enough antennas:

$$L' = \max(n : P_{M-n+1} \geq n + 1). \tag{1}$$

Second, up to L'' clients in Cell 2 can be served by AP2 where these clients must have enough ($\geq N$+1) antennas to cancel the interference from AP1. We can keep increasing L'' until these clients do not have enough antennas:

$$L'' = M - \min(m : Q_m \geq N + 1) + 1. \tag{2}$$

Note, we define $P_{N+1} = Q_{M+1} = +\infty$ to ensure the correctness of Equation (1) and (2) in cases where L'=0 and L''=0. The maximum number of added clients in Cell 2 is then given by

$$L = \min(L', L''). \tag{3}$$

In the next step, we let AP1 remove clients from its served set. When AP1 removes K $(K = 1, 2, \cdots, N)$ clients, these clients must have the fewest $(P_1, P_2, \cdots, P_K)$ antennas. Afterwards, AP1 has K spare antennas that can be exploited to cancel the interference to clients in Cell 2. Naturally, up to K clients in Cell 2 can be served by AP2 not subject to the interference from AP1. Since such interference cancellation is performed by AP1, clients in Cell 2 with the fewest $(Q_1, Q_2, \cdots, Q_K)$ antennas can be picked to enjoy such benefit. Therefore, Cell 2 is left with M-K clients with $Q_{K+1}, \cdots, Q_M$ antennas, and Cell 1 is left with N-K clients with $P_{K+1}, \cdots, P_N$ antennas. Similar to the previous step where K=0, we have

$$L'(K) = \max(n : P_{K+M-n+1} \geq n + 1), \tag{4}$$

$$L''(K) = M - \min(m : Q_{K+m} \geq N - K + 1) + 1, \tag{5}$$

and

$$L(K) = \min(L'(K), L''(K)). \tag{6}$$

It is easy to verify that $L(N)$=M where only a single cell (Cell 2) is operating similar to 802.11ac.

Finally, for each K=0, 1, $\cdots$, N our algorithm calculates $L(K)$, and finds the optimal set of clients (N-K in Cell 1, L in Cell 2) that maximizes the number of streams N-K+$L(K)$. Given the optimal set of clients in each cell and their duty in cancelling the inter-cell interference, the optimal use of the AP and client antennas is meanwhile determined.

We must note that our algorithm is orchestrated to maximize the number of streams or clients without (*i*) considering fairness between clients, and (*ii*) avoiding channel hardening that may reduce network capacity when serving more clients [18, 22]. That is, our algorithm preferably selects clients with more antennas over those with fewer antennas, and lets each AP simultaneously serve all selected clients. To consider these two issues, client selection schemes can be combined with our algorithm without modification to the latter. First, to take client fairness into account, an AP can remove clients with lower priority from the selected set even though they have more antennas, and sort clients with the same number of antennas based on their relative priority. Second, to avoid channel hardening to occur, an AP can select clients further based on the historical observations of their channel orthogonality, which is the key to determine the capacity scaling toward the number of served clients. Additionally, even among the selected clients, an AP has the freedom to serve only a subset of them, after receiving their reported channels and more accurately evaluating their channel orthogonality. Clearly, such client selection schemes can be executed separately, before or after our algorithm outputs the best set of clients and their antenna usage.

4.3 Network of More than Two Cells

We next extend our algorithm to T (T>2) cells. With T cells, we need to rewrite N and K as vectors, meaning that the T-1 APs serve (N_1-K_1, $\cdots$, N_{T-1}-K_{T-1}) clients respectively. Then, the maximum number of clients that can be added in the last cell is given by

$$L'(K_1, \cdots, K_{T-1}) = \max(n : P'_{M-n+1} \geq n + 1), \tag{7}$$

$$L''(K_1, \cdots, K_{T-1}) = |\{Q'_m : Q'_m \geq \sum_{t=1}^{T-1}(N_t - K_t) + 1\}|, \tag{8}$$

and

$$L(K_1, \cdots, K_{T-1}) = \min(L', L''), \tag{9}$$

where "$|\cdot|$" represents the cardinality of a set, P'_n the number of spare antennas on client n, and Q'_m the equivalent number of antennas on client m, determined by K'_t, the number of spare antennas on AP t. The spare antennas on an AP or a client are defined as the remaining antennas after a few of them are used to cancel the inter-cell interference within the first T-1 cells. The equivalent number of antennas Q'_m is defined in the following way. For a given client in the last cell, if an AP in the previous T-1 cells uses one spare antenna to cancel the interference to the client, the client can be considered to equivalently have N_t-K_t additional antennas for canceling this AP's interference. In other words, one can "transfer" the interference cancellation capability from an AP to a client it interferes with by providing the client such equivalent antennas. Given Q'_m, the best allocation of the spare antennas on the T-1 APs is given by successively assigning those of each AP to the K'_t clients in the last cell that have the smallest Q'_m.

Given the definitions of P'_n, Q'_m and K'_t, we next explain how Equation (7) and (8) are derived. For Equation (7), notice that the last AP can only cancel the interference to M-L' clients in all previous T-1 cells. These clients who may belong to more than one cell must have the fewest spare antennas. The remaining clients must have enough spare antennas to cancel the L' streams from the last AP. For Equation (8), the served clients in the last cell should not be subject to the interference from all previous T-1 APs. Since we have considered the interference cancellation from the T-1 APs with their spare antennas, we just need to find the maximum number of clients in the last cell with enough antennas, i.e., $Q'_m \geq \sum_{t=1}^{T-1}(N_t - K_t) + 1$. After calculating L for each $(K_1, \cdots, K_{T-1})$, we can find the optimal set of clients in each cell with the maximum multiplexing gain.

It is noticed that the above algorithm works in a recursive manner. Therefore, the complexity exponentially increases with the number of cells, T. To deal with this scalability issue, a cell clustering technique can be leveraged to convert a large-scale MU-MIMO network into a few small clusters, each of which includes up to three cells. We elaborate the cell clustering technique in Section 7.

4.4 Practical Implications

It is observed that our proposed algorithm only requires the information about the number of antennas on each AP and client to identify the optimal antenna usage. Such information is global in the MU-MIMO network, but can be compactly represented with only a few bits. Therefore, explicitly sharing such information in the network does not incur noticeable overhead, significantly simplifying the cell coordination. Given such information, each AP and client can execute the same algorithm in a synchronized way to achieve coordination. In section 6.1, we discuss how CoaCa leverages interleaved channel sounding to easily provide each AP and client such information with standard 802.11ac control frames.

5. CHANNEL ANALYSIS FOR BEAMFORMING WEIGHT OPTIMIZATION

In this section, we analyze the channel knowledge requirement for an AP or a client to optimize its transmit or receive beamforming weights. To calculate the beamforming weights that enable the optimal antenna usage, an AP or client must have certain channel knowledge based on which it cancels the intra-cell and inter-cell interference using the beamforming techniques presented in Section 2. In the following, we first study the two-cell example in Section 4.1 in order to simplify the analysis and obtain insightful findings, and then extend our analysis to a MU-MIMO network with arbitrary number of cells.

5.1 Illustrative Example

We reuse the example in Figure 4 to study the channel knowledge each AP and client needs to compute its optimal beamforming weights. We use $\mathbf{H}_{i\to j}$ ($\mathbf{h}_{i\to j}$) to denote the channel matrix (vector) from AP i to client j, and $\mathbf{w}_j$, $\mathbf{v}_j$ to denote the AP's transmit beamforming weight vector for client j, and the receive beamforming weight vector of client j, respectively.

Channel knowledge for AP1. AP1 uses its two antennas to send a data stream to Client1 and cancel the inter-cell interference to Client4. To do this, $\mathbf{w}_1$ must be orthogonal to $\mathbf{h}_{1\to 4}$, i.e., $\mathbf{w}_1 = \mathbf{h}_{1\to 4}^{\perp}$ where "$\perp$" represents the null space of a vector. As a result, AP1 only needs the knowledge of $\mathbf{h}_{1\to 4}$.

Channel knowledge for AP2. AP2 performs zero-forcing beamforming to simultaneously send streams to Client3 and Client4 without cancelling inter-cell interference. To do this, AP2 only needs the knowledge of $\mathbf{H}_{2\to 3}\mathbf{v}_3$ and $\mathbf{h}_{2\to 4}$. Note that $\mathbf{H}_{2\to 3}\mathbf{v}_3$ is the beamformed channel of Client3: it combines the physical channel matrix from AP2 to Client3 ($\mathbf{H}_{2\to 3}$) and the determined beamforming weight vector of Client3 ($\mathbf{v}_3$) as a single channel vector ($\mathbf{H}_{2\to 3}\mathbf{v}_3$). Compared to a physical channel matrix, a beamformed channel vector is much more efficient for a client to report since it needs fewer bits to be represented [18]. To cancel the intra-cell interference with zero-forcing beamforming, the knowledge of such beamformed channels is enough for AP2 by setting $\mathbf{w}_4 = (\mathbf{H}_{2\to 3}\mathbf{v}_3)^{\perp}$ and $\mathbf{w}_3 = \mathbf{h}_{2\to 4}^{\perp}$.

Channel knowledge for Client1. Client1 uses its three antennas to receive its stream from AP1 and cancel the inter-cell interference from AP2. Since AP2 sends two streams to Client3 and Client4, Client1 needs to cancel both of them. To do this, Client1 simply cancels the signals sent from the two physical antennas at AP2. In other words, $\mathbf{v}_1$ is chosen as $\mathbf{v}_1 = \mathbf{H}_{2\to 1}^{\perp}$ where "$\perp$" here refers to the joint null space of all rows of the matrix. Consequently, the required channel knowledge for Client1 is restricted to its own channels from AP2, $\mathbf{H}_{2\to 1}$.

Channel knowledge for Client3. Unlike Client4 who has a single antenna and needs not cancel the inter-cell interference, Client3 uses its two antennas to receive its stream from AP2 and cancel the inter-cell interference from AP1. Therefore, $\mathbf{v}_3$ must be orthogonal to the signal vector from AP1, i.e., $\mathbf{v}_3 = (\mathbf{w}_1\mathbf{H}_{1\to 3})^{\perp}$, which suggests $\mathbf{w}_1$ is needed for Client3 to calculate $\mathbf{v}_3$. However, observe that $\mathbf{w}_1 = \mathbf{h}_{1\to 4}^{\perp}$ so that the required channel knowledge for Client3 actually becomes $\mathbf{h}_{1\to 4}$ and its own channel from AP1, $\mathbf{H}_{1\to 3}$.

5.2 Network of Two Cells

Motivated by the findings from the illustrate example, we next analyze the channel knowledge requirement of the beamforming weight optimization for a two-cell MU-MIMO network with arbitrary configuration. In particular, we prove three key theorems regarding such requirement that can be summarized as follows: to calculate the optimal beamforming weights based on the optimal antenna usage, an AP or a client only needs the channel knowledge owned by a particular set of clients in the network. With this requirement, we can not only reduce the cell coordination effort, but also guarantee the optimality of the computed beamforming weights. We next elaborate the three theorems:

THEOREM 1. *To calculate the optimal beamforming weights, an AP only needs the channel knowledge owned by the clients it serves, and the clinets it interferes with holding the interference cancellation responsibility.*

THEOREM 2. *To calculate the optimal beamforming weights, a client only needs the channel knowledge owned by certain clients in the same cell.*

THEOREM 3. *For clients in the same cell, there exists a proper order of them with which each client can calculate the optimal beamforming weights solely based on the channel knowledge owned by clients ranked before it.*

To prove these theorems, let us consider a two-cell network after antenna usage optimization, where AP1 having N antennas serves N-K clients and AP2 having M antennas serves M-J clients (see Section 4.2). Recall that the optimal use of an AP antenna is to either deliver a stream to a served client, or cancel the inter-cell interference to a client the AP interferes with. As a result, we can partition the antennas on AP1 into two sets: N-K antennas used to serve N-K clients in Cell 1, and K antennas used to cancel the interference to K clients in Cell 2. Similar antenna partitioning can be applied to AP2. Afterwards, clients in each cell can be also partitioned according to their responsibility of cancelling the inter-cell interference. In Cell 1 and Cell 2, J and K clients rely on

AP2 and AP1 to cancel the inter-cell interference, while the rest N-K-J and M-J-K clients use their own antennas to cancel the interference, respectively.

Proof of Theorem 1. We use AP1 for the proof of Theorem 1. To serve the N-K clients in Cell 1 and cancel the interference to the K clients in Cell 2, AP1 only needs to know the channels from itself to these clients. The channels from AP2 to theses clients are not needed since AP1 is not involved in the inter-cell interference from AP2. The channels from AP1 to the M-J-K clients in Cell 2 are also unnecessary, since these clients use their own antennas to cancel the interference.

Proof of Theorem 2 and Theorem 3. We use clients in Cell 1 for the proof of Theorem 2 and 3. First, the J clients do not need any channel knowledge owned by other clients to optimize its beamforming weights. This is because their antennas do not contribute to inter-cell interference cancellation. Instead, they can be used to improve the client SNR by employing MRC based on their own channels $\mathbf{H}_{1\to j}$. We call these J clients the *MRC clients*. Second, the N-K-J clients need certain channel knowledge owned by other clients to cancel the interference from AP2. To do this, they perform interference alignment toward the channels of the other J clients, so that

$$\text{span}(\mathbf{H}_{2\to 1}\mathbf{v}_1, \cdots, \mathbf{H}_{2\to J}\mathbf{v}_J) =$$

$$\text{span}(\mathbf{H}_{2\to J+1}\mathbf{v}_{J+1}, \cdots, \mathbf{H}_{2\to N-K}\mathbf{v}_{N-K}). \quad (10)$$

Through interference alignment, the beamformed channels of the N-K-J clients, which we call the *IA clients*, are aligned to the channels of the MRC clients. When there are no MRC clients, the IA clients simply cancel the interference from the M physical antennas on AP2. When AP2 cancels the interference to the J MRC clients, the signal vector must be perpendicular to span($\mathbf{H}_{2\to 1}\mathbf{v}_1, \cdots, \mathbf{H}_{2\to J}\mathbf{v}_J$), which meanwhile creates no interference to the N-K-J IA clients. Clearly, the IA clients only need the knowledge of the beamformed channels, $\mathbf{H}_{2\to j}\mathbf{v}_j$, from the MRC clients, and the optimal client order is given by ranking the MRC clients before the IA clients. The relative order between the MRC clients or between the IA clients does not have an impact.

5.3 Network of More than Two Cells

The above three theorems hold true for a MU-MIMO network with more than two cells, which we briefly explain as follows. First, Theorem 1 is self-explanatory given its proof for the two-cell network. Second, for Theorem 2, observe that for a given interfering AP, the process of partitioning the clients into MRC clients and IA clients is still feasible. Then, a client only needs the channel knowledge from those that are identified as MRC clients while the client itself is identified as an IA client. Apparently such channel knowledge is restricted to the client's own cell. For Theorem 3, the best client order is decided by the number of antennas the client carries in an increasing manner. This is because an IA client always has more antennas than a MRC client does. Then, after sorting all clients in a cell based on their number of antennas, a client only needs the channel knowledge from clients that are ranked before it.

5.4 Practical Implications

The analysis on the channel knowledge requirement tells us that the beamforming weight optimization for an AP or a client can be potentially performed in a distributed way due to reduced cell coordination. Theorem 1 indicates that an AP does not need the channel knowledge owned by all clients, and does not need to share its channel knowledge with other APs. Theorem 2 suggests that a client does not need to acquire any channel knowledge from clients in other cells. Theorem 3 implies that even in a single cell, a client only needs the channel knowledge from a particular set of clients. In Section 6.2, we elaborate how CoaCa leverages channel reporting and overhearing to provide each AP and client the necessary channel knowledge for its beamforming weight optimization, without incurring any coordination overhead.

6. INTEGRATION WITH 802.11ac

We next present CoaCa, a protocol that integrates both antenna usage optimization and beamforming weight optimization into 802.11ac. CoaCa includes two key designs to achieve coordinated inter-cell interference cancellation, namely *interleaved channel sounding* and *channel reporting and overhearing*. With these two designs, each AP and client can locally perform the two-step optimization in a distributed but coordinated way.

6.1 Interleaved Channel Sounding

To provide the APs and clients with necessary information to optimize their antenna usage, CoaCa proposes *interleaved channel sounding*, in which the key idea is to let the APs in all cells send their NDP-A and NDP frame sequentially one after another, before each AP polls its served clients. The NDP-A frame can contain the information about the number of antennas on the AP and that on the clients the AP plans to serve. With interleaved channel sounding, such information can be timely broadcast to the entire MU-MIMO network, and used by all APs and clients to optimize their antenna usage with the same algorithm provided in Section 4 in a coordinated way. Moreover, the NDP frames allow the IA clients to estimate their channel matrix from the interfering APs, which is necessary to optimize their beamforming weights together with the overheard channel vectors from the MRC clients (see Section 6.2).

We illustrate the timeline of interleaved channel sounding in Figure 5 using the example in Figure 4. In the channel sounding process of 802.11ac, after an AP, say AP1, sends the NDP-A and NDP frame, the first served client, say Client1, will immediately respond with the BF-R frame after SIFS time. Unlike 802.11ac, in CoaCa no clients in Cell 1 is allowed to immediately respond; instead, AP2 sends its NDP-A and NDP frame SIFS time after AP1 sends its NDP frame. Only after both AP1 and AP2 send their NDP-A and NDP frame, each of them sequentially polls their clients with a BF-P frame and their clients respond with their BF-R frames in the same order.

Viability. The interleaved channel sounding ensures correct behaviour of the involved APs and their served clients. To interleave the channel sounding from multiple APs, an AP must be able to send its NDP-A and BF-P frame at the proper time with guaranteed medium access. In addition, the APs must sound their channels in a pre-determined order without introducing collision. For example, according to Figure 5, AP2 must (*i*) send its NDP-A frame immediately after AP1 sends its NDP frame, and (*ii*) poll its clients only after Client1 has sent its BF-R frame. CoaCa uses two techniques to ensure this coordinated behaviour, which we discuss based on Figure 5. First, CoaCa adopts CHAIN, a technique proposed in [24]. The key idea in CHAIN is that AP2 piggybacks its NDP-A or BF-P frame SIFS time after the ongoing frame from AP1 or Client1 finishes; this gives AP2 prioritized medium access since other 802.11 nodes must wait for at least DIFS time to contend for the medium. To determine their relative channel sounding order, AP1 and AP2 only need to coordinate once to initiate the transmissions in CHAIN. Second, to avoid collision between AP2 and Client1 who might also send its BF-R frame after

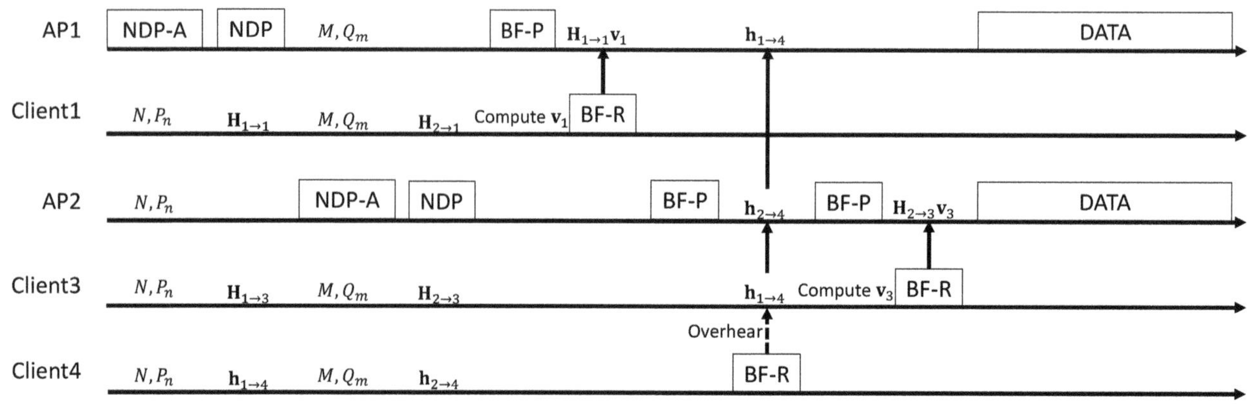

Figure 5: Timeline of CoaCa where two APs concurrently serve their clients. To provide each AP and client the necessary information to optimize its antenna usage, the first AP starts polling its clients with the optimal order only after all the APs have transmitted their NDP-A and NDP frames. To optimize its beamforming weights based on the optimal antenna usage, a client overhears the reported beamformed channels from other clients in the same cell that report before it.

SIFS time, CoaCa refrains Client1 from immediately responding. This is achieved by having AP1 specify a "fake" client with an invalid MAC address as the first responding client in the NDP-A frame. This way, all clients in Cell 1 yield to AP2.

Interoperability. CoaCa APs and clients can interoperate with unmodified 802.11ac clients. The key reason is that in the proposed interleaved channel sounding a CoaCa client still passively responds to the BF-P frame from its AP, similar to an unmodified 802.11ac client. In addition, CoaCa concatenates the number of antennas information (2 bytes) to the NDP-A frame and modifies the duration field, to ensure it can be decoded even by an unmodified 802.11ac client.

Overhead. The interleaved channel sounding introduces negligible overhead compared to 802.11ac. First, observe that in the interleaved channel sounding an extra BF-P frame from each AP is required to poll the first served client. Such overhead is not only negligible but also justified since *(i)* the BF-P frame is much shorter than the NDP-A and BF-R frame that constitute the major portion of channel sounding, and *(ii)* the extra BF-P frame eliminates the necessity for the first client to initiate the transmissions in CHAIN, which would otherwise require the client to overhear clients in other cells and negate the reduction of cell coordination in CoaCa˙Second, the BF-R frame may have to contain the estimated channels from not only the associated AP but also the interfering APs. Such extra channel information seemingly increases the size of the BF-R frame in a proportional manner. However, due to the use of beamformed channels (see Section 6.2), such extra channel information can be more than compensated by the proportionally reduced information in each estimated channel, once the client is equipped with multiple antennas.

6.2 Channel Reporting and Overhearing

To provide the APs and clients with required channel knowledge to optimize their beamforming weights, similarly to the technique adopted by [18], in CoaCa *a client reports the necessary beamformed channels in the BF-R frame and overhears other clients' BF-R frames for their beamformed channels*, as illustrated in Figure 5. First, reporting the beamformed channel $\mathbf{H}_{i\to j}\mathbf{v}_j$ instead of the physical channel $\mathbf{H}_{i\to j}$ can proportionally reduce the size of the BF-R frame which is known to incur substantial overhead [5,21] to the channel sounding process of 802.11ac. This is because the beamformed channel is a vector while the physical channel is a matrix that needs many more bits to encode when the client has multiple antennas. Reducing the size of the BF-R frame is especially beneficial for the MRC clients who must report the channels to not only its associated AP but also the interfering APs holding the interference cancellation responsibility (see Theorem 1). Such extra channel information as additional overhead can be more than compensated by the reduced size of the BF-R frame when the client has multiple antennas. Second, since the beamformed channels are explicitly contained in the BF-R frame, a client that overhears the BF-R frame can easily acquire such knowledge by decoding the frame. The channel knowledge is guaranteed accurate once the BF-R frame is successfully decoded.

Decodability. An AP or a client is able to decode the overheard BF-R frames with high probability, given the following two observations. First, Theorem 1 and Theorem 2 indicate that an AP only needs to overhear the BF-R frames from the MRC clients it interferes with, and a client only needs to overhear the BF-R frames from the MRC clients in the same cell. This significantly reduces the likelihood that an AP or a client is too distant from the client it seeks to overhear. Second, the BF-R frame is considered a control frame and commonly sent at base rate (6 Mbps) in order to improve its reliability [4]. This in turn extends its transmission range and reduces the possibility of frame decoding failure.

Sufficiency. Reporting and overhearing the beamformed channels can provide the APs and clients just enough channel knowledge. First, according to Section 5.2, the beamformed channel is sufficient for the APs to perform interference cancellation, and for the IA clients to perform interference alignment. Second, the AP can poll its clients in the optimal order to make sure a client has acquired enough beamformed channels before it determines the optimal beamforming weights and reports its own beamformed channel. This is because Theorem 3 indicates that if the clients in each cell send their BF-R frames following the optimal order, each client only needs the channel knowledge owned by clients ranked before it.

7. CELL CLUSTERING

In this section, we address the scalability issue of CoaCa toward the number of cells in the MU-MIMO network. In particular, the following reasons make it hard to apply CoaCa to a large-scale network with more than a few cells. First and most importantly, the number of required antennas on the APs and clients to appreciate the multiplexing gain improvement from

CoaCa significantly increases with more cells. Given that each AP and each client usually cannot afford more than eight and more than four antennas respectively, we find that CoaCa cannot provide obvious capacity improvement when the network includes more than three cells. Second, as revealed in Section 4.3, the complexity of the recursive algorithm to identify the optimal antenna usage exponentially increases with the number of cells. Third, the duration of the interleaved channel sounding scales up proportionally to the number of cells, which may lead to having outdated estimated channels. Finally, to receive the NDP-A frames and enable CHAIN, an AP must be in the overhearing range of all other APs, which becomes much more challenging with more cells.

We rely on a *cell clustering* technique to tackle the scalability issue of CoaCa. That is, we group all cells in the MU-MIMO network into clusters such that *within each cluster there are up to three cells*. Then, we apply CoaCa to each cluster, and employ standard CSMA/CA for the medium access between clusters. There are two important motivations for us to allow up to three cells in each cluster. First, cell clustering with such scale does not reduce the effectiveness of CoaCa. As mentioned earlier, when an AP has no more than eight antennas and a client has no more than four antennas, to maximize the number of streams CoaCa usually does not need to allow more than three APs to concurrently serve their clients. Therefore, even if the MU-MIMO network included more than three cells, they would not lead to a multiplexing gain increase. Notably, CoaCa seeks to most effectively leverage the available antennas from each AP and client in the network, by letting them coordinately cancel the inter-cell interference in a distributed way. Yet, it is incapable of going beyond such number of antenna constraint. To further increase the number of streams in the network, one must employ centralized solutions such as Network-MIMO [2, 12, 19] to convert interference into signals. Second, cell clustering with up to three APs can greatly simplify the operation of CHAIN in situations where only a subset of APs in a cluster intend to serve their clients. That is, in CHAIN, to ensure correct medium access the AP without packets to its clients may have to send an intermediate frame that triggers the NDP-A frame from the AP following it. With up to three APs in a cluster, this can be replaced by a much simpler design where the second and third AP use SIFS (16 μs) and PIFS (25 μs) in CHAIN to guarantee their relative priority, without the need of sending the triggering frame by the second AP.

Determining the included cells in a cluster can be accomplished by a cluster formation algorithm, which is outside of the scope of this work. We believe existing approaches based on assigning a master AP for managing each cluster, e.g., the one proposed by [25], can be adopted with appropriate adaptation.

8. EXPERIMENTAL EVALUATION

Finally we experimentally evaluate the performance of CoaCa in real-world indoor environments.

8.1 WARP-based Implementation

We implement CoaCa on WARP [14], a flexible software defined radio (SDR) platform. We choose the WARPLab framework [13] for our implementation and evaluation but have extensively modified it to improve its real-time capability. In WARPLab, through gigabytes Ethernet cables, multiple WARP boards configured as APs or clients are interconnected to and controlled by a central computer that runs MATLAB. By implementing part of the baseband processing in MATLAB, one can achieve great flexibility to develop and evaluate physical layer techniques such as beamforming; this feature of WARPLab makes it a desirable framework for our implementation and evaluation of CoaCa.

Since the baseband processing occurs in MATLAB, we cannot implement the 802.11ac MAC satisfying the timing constraint. Therefore, our evaluation of CoaCa is focused on its PHY, i.e., the network capacity improvement from the increased multiplexing gain achieved by antenna usage optimization and beamforming weight optimization. We move the process of client polling, beamformed channel reporting and overhearing in the interleaved channel sounding into emulation. That is, after each AP sequentially sends its NDP-A and NDP frame that allows the clients to estimate their channels, we emulate the BF-P and BF-R frames on the central computer. To do this, we assume each AP and client possesses the same knowledge of the reported and overheard beamformed channels, as if they were obtained from actual BF-R frames over the air. Note that such emulation is close-to-reality since the BF-R frame delivers the channel knowledge in an explicit and reliable way. Then, based on the channel knowledge, the APs and clients calculate their optimal beamforming weights, with which they coordinately cancel the inter-cell interference, and transmit and receive the data frames. We calculate the network capacity based on the measured signal-to-noise-and-interference ratio (SINR) at each served client. While the actual throughput gain by MU-MIMO is known to be reduced by the channel sounding overhead [5, 21], we do not incorporate such overhead into our evaluation since it equally exists in 802.11ac according to Section 6.1.

8.2 Experimental Setup

In our experiments we construct a MU-MIMO network with two cells. We use each WARP board to serve as either an 802.11ac AP or an 802.11ac client so that the number of AP and client antennas can be up to four. To evaluate the capability of CoaCa to eliminate inter-cell interference, we deploy the APs and clients within a single interference domain so that the capacity of each served client is interference instead of noise limited. Our experiments are conducted in a three-floor campus building that is representative of indoor environments. To make sure the interleaved channel sounding does not exceed the channel coherence time, we run the experiments at nighttime when we observe the wireless environment is static. To limit the interference within our MU-MIMO network, we select a clean Wi-Fi channel (# 14) that does not have any ongoing traffic.

8.3 Accuracy of Interference Cancellation and Interference Alignment

Since CoaCa relies on interference cancellation and interference alignment to eliminate inter-cell interference, we first evaluate their accuracy on WARP under realistic indoor wireless channels. Note that interference cancellation and alignment can be inaccurate due to (*i*) errors in the estimated and overheard channels used to compute the beamforming weights, and (*ii*) channel noise and hardware imperfection that distort the received signals. Toward this, we use three micro-benchmarks with two or three nodes to study how much inter-cell interference between an AP and a client can be eliminated. To evaluate interference cancellation by the AP, we assume an AP having two to four antennas cancels the interference to a client via transmit beamforming; to evaluate interference cancellation by the client, we assume a client having two to four antennas cancels the interference from an interfering AP with receive beamforming; to evaluate interference alignment by the client, we assume an AP cancels the interference to one client via transmit beamforming, and another client aligns its

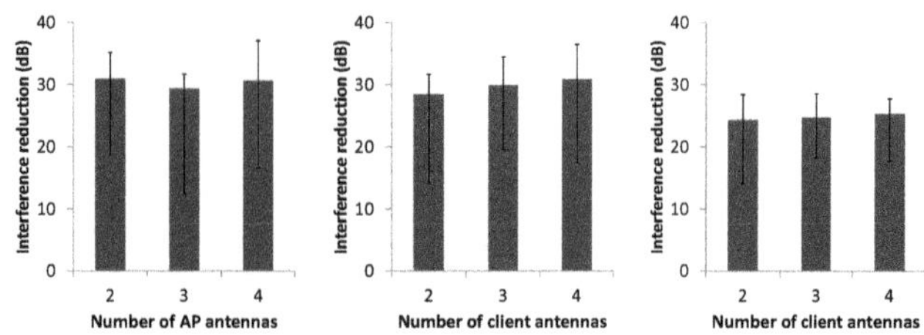

Figure 6: Interference reduction from interference cancellation by the AP (Left), interference cancellation by the client (Middle), and interference alignment by the client (Right). On average interference cancellation and interference alignment achieve 30 dB and 25 dB interference reduction, respectively. The number of AP or client antennas does not have an obvious impact on the cancellation or alignment accuracy.

channel to that of the first client via receive beamforming. In each micro-benchmark we assume the beamforming AP or client owns the necessary channel knowledge, which is obtained right before the node transmits or receives. For all the experiments, we measure the original interference power and residual interference power after cancellation or alignment to compute the interference reduction. Note that we have properly scaled the transmit power from the AP to make sure the interference power is always above the noise floor of the client even after cancellation. This is to avoid underestimation of the effectiveness of interference cancellation and alignment when the client becomes noise limited.

Figure 6 shows the interference reduction (dB) achieved by interference cancellation and interference alignment performed by the AP or client, with different number of antennas. We highlight the following findings from Figure 6. First, on average interference cancellation and alignment are able to reduce the interference by 30 dB and 25 dB, respectively. This is often sufficient to reduce the interference to below the noise floor in 802.11ac networks. Second, interference cancellation by the AP via transmit beamforming, and by the client via receive beamforming have similar accuracy. This is because with explicit channel estimation the AP and client own the same channel knowledge, and therefore the accuracy of interference cancellation is not subject to channel calibration errors that only exist in systems with implicit channel estimation such as [16]. Third, the number of antennas for interference cancellation and alignment does not have a clear impact on the accuracy. While somewhat counter-intuitive, this finding can be explained by the observation that additional antennas cannot reduce channel estimation error or hardware nonlinearity. Last, the accuracy of interference alignment is lower than that of interference cancellation. This is because interference alignment suffers more from channel estimation errors by leveraging the channel knowledge from more than one clients. Consistent findings regarding the effectiveness of interference cancellation and alignment are also reported in [10].

8.4 Network Capacity Improvement

We next evaluate the effectiveness of CoaCa on improving the capacity of a MU-MIMO network by achieving a higher multiplexing gain. We compare CoaCa with two existing schemes: (*i*) MACCO [18] which does not cancel inter-cell interference by allowing a single AP to transmit and using the client antennas to improve the channel orthogonality and capacity scalability; (*ii*) n+ [10] which allows an AP in one cell to serve its clients first and the AP in the other cell to opportunistically transmit at the same time. Note, given that each cell is congested, n+ cannot

Table 2: Number of antennas on the APs and clients for Case 1-4.

	AP1	AP2	Cell 1 clients	Cell 2 clients
Case 1	2	2	2/2	2/2
Case 2	2	2	1/2	1/3
Case 3	2	3	4/4	3/3/4
Case 4	4	4	1/2/4/4	1/2/4/4

increase the multiplexing gain and may only provide a diversity gain as explored in [7]. Therefore, for a given channel condition we compare CoaCa with either MACCO or n+, whichever achieves better network capacity. For simplicity we use "MACCO/n+" to denote the better scheme among the two of them. We select four representative cases with different numbers of antennas on the APs and clients, summarized in Table 2. For each case, we run multiple instances of the experiment by deploying the APs and clients in different locations. It is important to mention that CoaCa improves the network capacity by aiming to deliver more streams in the MU-MIMO network, which is known to be a suboptimal approach. Therefore, the actual capacity improvement of CoaCa is dependent on the channel condition, i.e., the orthogonality between the channels of multiple served clients. Conducting the experiment under various channel conditions allows us to observe not only the average but also the wort-case performance of CoaCa. To randomize the channel conditions, we arbitrate the AP and client locations in each experiment instance, since previous work has observed that in an indoor environment with rich multipath the channel condition does not have a clear dependence on the node locations [1, 18]. This way, our experiments cover channel conditions that are either beneficial or adverse to CoaCa.

Figure 7 shows our results. In each plot, one data point corresponds to the measured capacity for CoaCa (X axis) and MACCO/n+ (Y axis) under a single experiment instance. The expected multiplexing gain increase from CoaCa defined as the increase of the number of streams in the two MU-MIMO cells, is also plotted for comparison. We report the following important findings from Figure 7. First, when CoaCa delivers more streams it considerably improves the network capacity, i.e., on average by 40%, 52% and 41% for Case 2, 3 and 4, respectively. When CoaCa cannot deliver more streams due to insufficient antennas on the APs or clients, e.g., in Case 1, on average it achieves similar network capacity to MACCO/n+. Second, the network capacity improvement from CoaCa is lower than the expected multiplexing gain increase (50%, 67%, and 50% for case 2, 3, and 4, respectively). This is because CoaCa is theoretically suboptimal and cannot proportionally increase the network capacity due to its two-step optimization. The per-client capacity can be reduced when the antennas are used to cancel the inter-cell interference instead of enhancing the client SNR. Finally, even in Case 2, 3 and 4 where CoaCa allows more streams, there is a small probability that CoaCa does not increase the network capacity. This happens when the antenna usage optimization yields few spare AP and client antennas to enhance the SNR, and the channel orthogonality between clients are far from being orthogonal, such that the capacity of each cell suffers from serious channel hardening. Such worst-case performance confirms that due to the use of two-step optimization as a key heuristic CoaCa does not necessarily maximize the network capacity. However, given its considerable capacity gain on average, we believe the heuristic that makes CoaCa practical outweighs its worst-case performance.

Dependency on the client SNR. We next evaluate how the client SNR impacts the network capacity gain from CoaCa. We need to

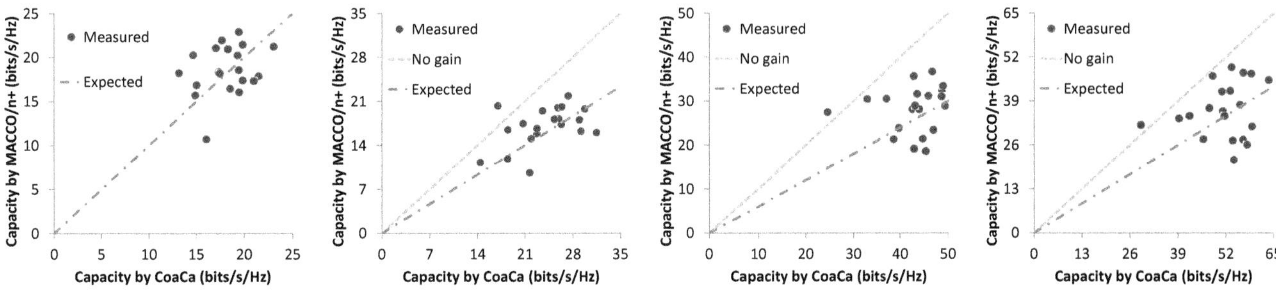

(a) Case 1 (b) Case 2 (c) Case 3 (d) Case 4

Figure 7: Network capacity achieved by MACCO/n+ and CoaCa for four cases with different numbers of antennas on APs and clients. CoaCa outperforms MACCO/n+ when it delivers more streams. However the capacity improvement from CoaCa is lower than the expected multiplexing gain increase due to imperfect channel orthogonality.

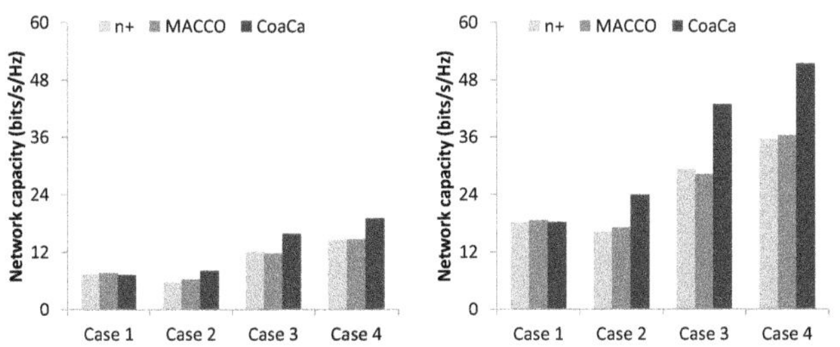

(a) Low SNR (b) High SNR

Figure 8: Network capacity achieved by n+, MACCO, and CoaCa with high (measured) and low (emulated) client SNR. CoaCa achieves more capacity improvement with higher client SNR, due to the logarithmic relationship between capacity and SNR.

mention that when the client capacity is interference-limited, the client often has a moderate or high SNR (about 15-25 dB according to our measurements). Therefore we emulate a low SNR regime for each case above, by reducing the transmit power on the two APs by approximately 15 dB. We demonstrate the results in Figure 8 where the average network capacity for n+, MACCO, and CoaCa are compared for both high (measured) SNR and low (emulated) SNR regimes. Clearly, when the client SNR is reduced, CoaCa achieves less network capacity gain: for Case 2-4 the improvement decreases to 28%, 35%, and 30%, respectively. This is because with lower SNR, the logarithmic relationship between capacity and SNR becomes closer to linear, and cancelling the inter-cell interference reduces more capacity with a diminished SNR.

9. RELATED WORK

MU-MIMO techniques such as zero-forcing beamforming have been demonstrated practical in real-world wireless environments using software-defined radio (SDR) platforms e.g., [1, 15–17, 22]. The authors in [1] investigated the feasibility of zero-forcing beamforming in real indoor environments, with a small number of antennas on the AP ($\leq$4) and a few clients. The authors in [17] proposed a solution that allows uncoordinated, unsynchronized spatial multiple access from multiple clients. The authors in [16] and [22] study the base station (AP) architecture that features a large number of antennas ($\geq$8) and serves many clients. All these work is restricted to a single cell including one AP and multiple associated clients. Inter-cell interference as an important capacity limiting factor for MU-MIMO networks remains experimentally under-explored.

An effective but practically expensive way to tackle inter-cell interference in MU-MIMO networks is to let neighbouring APs collaborate with each other via a high-speed, low-latency connection, e.g., [2, 3, 8, 9, 12]. There are different ways of exploiting such AP connection. Network-MIMO [2, 12] allows multiple neighbouring APs to behave as a single massive AP, by synchronizing their time and frequency, and sharing their transmitted and received samples. IAC proposed in [8] only needs the APs to share the samples for joint encoding and decoding without synchronization. Robinhood proposed in [3] requires a set of APs to retransmit the received packets from the clients to the rest of APs, while cancelling the interference between the packets. OpenRF proposed in [9] uses a central controller to coordinate neighbouring APs to cancel inter-cell interference. Due to the requirement of AP connection and a centralized solution, the applicability of these approaches is restricted to carefully planned and centrally controlled networks such as an enterprise network. By leveraging multi-antenna clients to assist the interfering AP to coordinately cancel inter-cell interference, our solution is distributed and can be applied to any 802.11ac networks.

802.11n+ presented in [10] leverages beamforming to enable concurrent streams in 802.11n networks with SU-MIMO. It allows nodes in one cell to transmit and receive first, and nodes in other cells to opportunistically transmit and receive by cancelling the interference to and from the first cell. Due to the lack of joint coordination between multiple cells, n+ cannot work effectively in 802.11ac networks with MU-MIMO as we demonstrated in Section 1 using the example in Figure 1. By achieving better coordination, our solution can enable more streams than n+ does in 802.11ac networks, only requiring small protocol modifications and incurring negligible overhead. NEMOx proposed in [25] seeks to enable efficient spatial reuse in distributed MIMO networks, by proposing a scalable architecture that connects a smaller number of neighbouring APs for clustered Network-MIMO. Each cluster including multiple connected APs that form a giant virtual AP contends with each other via asynchronous CSMA. Within the interference range, no more than one virtual AP is allowed to operate at the same time. Our solution similarly clusters the APs and assumes CSMA between clusters, but employs a fundamentally different approach to address the interference inside a cluster. Instead of connecting the APs to employ Network-MIMO, our solution relies on the AP and clients to coordinately cancel the inter-cell interference.

In this work, we exploit the multiple antennas on clients to combat the inter-cell interference in multiple MU-MIMO cells and to achieve a higher multiplexing gain. Alternatively, MACCO proposed in [18] seeks to use the client antennas to improve the channel orthogonality between the clients, in order to make the capacity of a single MU-MIMO cell better scale with the number of clients. Our work and [18] actually represent two different ways of leveraging the client antennas to achieve either a SNR gain or a multiplexing gain, and therefore need to address completely different technical challenges. More importantly, the applicability of [18] is restricted to a single cell or multiple cells where inter-cell interference is insignificant; in this work we focus on situations where inter-cell interference stands as the bottleneck of the MU-MIMO network capacity and proposes a solution to overcome it.

10. CONCLUSION

In this work, we tackle the inter-cell interference problem in 802.11ac-based MU-MIMO networks by seeking to enable coordinated interference cancellation in a practical way. To achieve this, we propose a solution consisting of two separate optimizations: antenna usage optimization and beamforming weight optimization. With the separation, both optimizations can be integrated into 802.11ac with small modifications and negligible overhead. The experimental evaluation of our protocol, CoaCa, demonstrates its effectiveness to eliminate inter-cell interference and improve the network capacity in realistic indoor wireless environments.

ACKNOWLEDGEMENTS

This work was funded in part by NSF grants MRI 0923479, NetSE 101283, MRI 1126478, CNS 1218700 and CNS 1314822. The authors would like to thank Ashutosh Sabharwal for many insightful suggestions. The authors also thank the anonymous reviewers and the paper shepherd for their constructive comments that have considerably improved the paper.

11. REFERENCES

[1] E. Aryafar, N. Anand, T. Salonidis, and E. W. Knightly. Design and Experimental Evaluation of Multi-User Beamforming in Wireless LANs. In *Proc. ACM Int. Conf. Mobile Computing and Networking (MobiCom)*, 2010.

[2] H. V. Balan, R. Rogalin, A. Michaloliakos, and K. Psounis. Achieving High Data Rates in a Distributed MIMO System. In *Proc. ACM Int. Conf. Mobile Computing and Networking (MobiCom)*, 2012.

[3] T. Bansal, B. Chen, K. Srinivasan, and P. Sinha. RobinHood: Sharing the Happiness in a Wireless Jungle. In *Proc. ACM Int. Workshop Mobile Computing Systems and Applications (HotMobile)*, 2014.

[4] O. Bejarano, E. W. Knightly, and M. Park. IEEE 802.11ac: From Channelization to Multi-User MIMO. *IEEE Communication Magazine*, 2013.

[5] O. Bejarano, E. Magistretti, O. Gurewitz, and E. W. Knightly. MUTE: Sounding Inhibition for MU-MIMO WLANs. In *Proc. IEEE Int. Conf. Sensing, Communication and Networking (SECON)*, 2014.

[6] V. R. Cadambe and S. A. Jafar. Interference Alignment and Degrees of Freedom of the K-User Interference Channel. *IEEE Trans. on Information Theory*, 2008.

[7] B. Chen, K. C. Lin, and H. Wei. Harnessing Receive Diversity in Distributed Multi-User MIMO Networks. In *Proc. ACM SIGCOMM (Poster)*, 2013.

[8] S. Gollakota, S. D. Perli, and D. Katabi. Interference Alignment and Cancellation. In *Proc. ACM SIGCOMM*, 2009.

[9] S. Kumar, D. Cifuentes, S. Gollakota, and D. Katabi. Bringing Cross-Layer MIMO to TodayâĂŹs Wireless LANs. In *Proc. ACM SIGCOMM*, 2013.

[10] K. C. Lin, S. Gollakota, and D. Katabi. Random Access Heterogeneous MIMO networks. In *Proc. ACM SIGCOMM*, 2011.

[11] M. A. Maddah-Ali, A. S. Motahari, and A. K. Khandani. Communication Over MIMO X Channels: Interference Alignment, Decomposition, and Performance Analysis. *IEEE Trans. on Information Theory*, 2008.

[12] H. Rahul, S. Kumar, and D. Katabi. JMB: Scaling Wireless Capacity with User Demands. In *Proc. ACM SIGCOMM*, 2012.

[13] Rice University. WARPLab. `http://warp.rice.edu/trac/wiki/WARPLab`.

[14] Rice University. Wireless Open Access Research Platform (WARP). `http://warp.rice.edu/trac`.

[15] W. Shen, Y. Tung, K. Lee, K. C. Lin, S. Gollakota, D. Katabi, and M. Chen. Rate Adaptation for 802.11 Multiuser MIMO Networks. In *Proc. ACM Int. Conf. Mobile Computing and Networking (MobiCom)*, 2012.

[16] C. Shepard, H. Yu, N. Anand, E. Li, T. Marzetta, R. Yang, and L. Zhong. Argos: Practical Many-antenna Base Stations. In *Proc. ACM Int. Conf. Mobile Computing and Networking (MobiCom)*, 2012.

[17] K. Tan, H. Liu, J. Fang, W. Wang, J. Zhang, M. Chen, and G. M. Voelker. SAM: Enabling Practical Spatial Multiple Access in Wireless LAN. In *Proc. ACM Int. Conf. Mobile Computing and Networking (MobiCom)*, 2009.

[18] *Withheld for blind review*. Achieving Better Channel Orthogonality for Improved User Scaling of Multi-user MIMO. In *submission to MobiCom (submission ID: 107)*, 2014.

[19] S. Venkatesan, A. Lozano, and R. Valenzuela. Network MIMO: Overcoming Intercell Interference in Indoor Wireless Systems. In *Proc. IEEE Asilomar Conf. on Signals, Systems and Computers (ACSSC)*, 2007.

[20] X. Xie and X. Zhang. Scalable User Selection for MU-MIMO Networks. In *Proc. IEEE Conf. Computer Communications (INFOCOM)*, 2014.

[21] X. Xie, X. Zhang, and K. Sundaresan. Adaptive Feedback Compression for MIMO Networks. In *Proc. ACM Int. Conf. Mobile Computing and Networking (MobiCom)*, 2013.

[22] Q. Yang, X. Li, H. Yao, J. Fang, K. Tan, W. Hu, J. Zhang, and Y. Zhang. BigStation: Enabling Scalable Real-time Signal Processing in Large MU-MIMO Systems. In *Proc. ACM SIGCOMM*, 2013.

[23] H. Yu, L. Zhong, A. Sabharwal, and D. Kao. Beamforming on Mobile Devices: A First Study. In *Proc. ACM Int. Conf. Mobile Computing and Networking (MobiCom)*, 2011.

[24] Z. Zeng, Y. Gao, K. Tan, and P. R. Kumar. CHAIN: Introducing Minimum Controlled Coordination into Random Access MAC. In *Proc. IEEE Conf. Computer Communications (INFOCOM)*, 2011.

[25] X. Zhang, K. Sundaresan, M. A. Khojastepour, S. Rangarajan, and K. G. Shin. NEMOx: Scalable Network MIMO for Wireless Networks. In *Proc. ACM Int. Conf. Mobile Computing and Networking (MobiCom)*, 2013.

Phaser: Enabling Phased Array Signal Processing on Commodity WiFi Access Points

Jon Gjengset, Jie Xiong, Graeme McPhillips, Kyle Jamieson
Department of Computer Science, University College London
{j.gjengset, j.xiong, g.mcphillips, k.jamieson}@cs.ucl.ac.uk

ABSTRACT

Signal processing on antenna arrays has received much recent attention in the mobile and wireless networking research communities, with array signal processing approaches addressing the problems of human movement detection, indoor mobile device localization, and wireless network security. However, there are two important challenges inherent in the design of these systems that must be overcome if they are to be of practical use on commodity hardware. First, phase differences between the radio oscillators behind each antenna can make readings unusable, and so must be corrected in order for most techniques to yield high-fidelity results. Second, while the number of antennas on commodity access points is usually limited, most array processing increases in fidelity with more antennas. These issues work in synergistic opposition to array processing: without phase offset correction, no phase-difference array processing is possible, and with fewer antennas, automatic correction of these phase offsets becomes even more challenging. We present Phaser, a system that solves these intertwined problems to make phased array signal processing truly practical on the many WiFi access points deployed in the real world. Our experimental results on three- and five-antenna 802.11-based hardware show that 802.11 NICs can be calibrated and synchronized to a 20° median phase error, enabling inexpensive deployment of numerous phase-difference based spectral analysis techniques previously only available on costly, special-purpose hardware.

Categories and Subject Descriptors

C.3 [**Special-purpose and application-based systems**]: Signal processing systems

Keywords

Phased-array; Signal processing; NICs synchronization; Phase calibration; Angle-of-arrival; Location tracking

1. INTRODUCTION

In recent years, there has been renewed interest within the mobile and wireless networking communities in addressing problems related to the sensing of signals using multi-antenna (MIMO) access points. Recent examples include systems that localize RFID tags [27] and WiFi devices [22, 30], enhance WiFi security [31], and passive radar systems that pinpoint human movements [1, 2, 17].

These systems, and others, share an important common thread: they all rely on phased array signal processing; a set of techniques that makes various comparisons between the radio signals received from each of the antennas of the access point (AP). Phased array processing has been applied in weather and military radar, seismology, and astronomy to great benefit, but its application to indoor and outdoor wireless and mobile communications presents new challenges and dictates novel system designs, as the above work demonstrates.

While the aforementioned work makes phased array signal processing practical in mobile wireless local-area network designs, two important challenges remain that must be overcome if it is to be widely deployed on off-the-shelf hardware:

1. On a single commodity wireless NIC, the RF oscillators are frequency locked, preventing their relative phases from drifting over time. However, these oscillators still have an unknown, absolute phase offset relative to one another. This offset must be compensated for in order to obtain readings from an AP that have meaning in physical space.
2. Today's cutting-edge APs are equipped with multiple unsynchronized network interface cards (NICs), each with multiple antennas [32], but phased-array signal processing benefits most from phase difference readings between all pairs of antennas, whether they share a radio card or not. The complete lack of synchronization across NICs in both time and radio frequency stymies attempts to run the above systems across multiple NICs at the same AP.

In this paper, we present *Phaser*; a system that enables phased array signal processing for commodity WiFi APs. We also propose minor, cost-effective hardware modifications that can further improve the phase-data fidelity on such APs. WiFi today is ubiquitous, with APs deployed everywhere people congregate. Phaser's vision is to convert every one of these APs into a miniature phased array receiver, so that when integrated with Phaser, the above systems can truly run pervasively—everywhere WiFi APs are deployed.

To realize this vision, Phaser addresses these challenges with three corresponding wireless system components that we implement at a backend server connected to the APs over Ethernet backhaul:

First, novel software-based digital signal processing on the general-purpose CPU of the backend server works alongside an inexpensive custom antenna design at the AP to enable multiple commodity NICs to be synchronized in time and frequency, and form a larger and more useful phased array.

Second, Phaser introduces a novel phase *autocalibration* algorithm that corrects the phase offsets between the different radio

MobiCom'14, September 7-11, 2014, Maui, Hawaii, USA.
ACM 978-1-4503-2783-1/14/09.
http://dx.doi.org/10.1145/2639108.2639139.

oscillators at an AP. Our autocalibration algorithm operates without the need for human interaction, and works in the presence of noise and indoor multipath reflections.[1]

Finally, Phaser leverages signal onset detection to reduce the effects of multipath reflections, yielding significantly improved end-to-end performance.

We observe that the system's components require only the addition of software-based digital signal processing on a general-purpose CPU, and for multicard operation, the addition of custom-designed, yet simple and inexpensive hardware: RF switches, splitters and antennas with known geometries. Most of the computational load is performed by a server connected to the Ethernet backhaul, further reducing the changes needed on the APs. We therefore position Phaser as a likely design pattern for future 802.11 AP hardware designs that is compatible with the MIMO designs in 802.11n and upcoming MU-MIMO designs in 802.11ac.

Contributions. To summarize, this paper makes the following three research contributions:

1. We introduce a multicard synchronization algorithm and design that allows multiple NICs to take phase-difference readings as if they were one large antenna array.
2. We propose an autocalibration algorithm so APs may calibrate their antennas automatically—even across multiple NICs—based on transmissions from other clients or APs.
3. We further integrate the above two ideas with a multipath suppression algorithm, which significantly reduces the impact of multipath on Phaser's performance.

Non-goals. Phaser aims to enable phased signal processing on commodity hardware, and does so by correcting for a number of factors that introduce phase errors into the readings reported by an AP's NICs. While there are many other digital communication techniques in use in the wireless community that are also based on wireless phase data, the particularities of Phaser make it unsuitable for use with some of these. Specifically, Phaser is not meant to be used to synchronize MIMO transmissions, nor does it enable improved packet reception or decoding. The attentive reader will realize that Phaser's phase difference accuracy and multi-card synchronization are simply not of sufficiently high fidelity for these applications.

Paper roadmap. The rest of this paper is organized as follows: we begin with a detailed description of Phaser's design (§2), followed by details of our implementation on commodity Intel 5300 NIC hardware, combined with a custom, low-cost antenna hardware circuit design (§3). Our experimental evaluation (§4) measures the quality of the Phaser AP improvements both in isolation in an anechoic chamber and in end-to-end operation in an office environment. Results show that Phaser can resolve multipath reflections using multiple NICs to a $\pm 2^{\circ}$ accuracy, and automatically calibrate APs in a busy office environment to an average accuracy of 20° phase error, yielding qualitatively similar angle-of-arrival information to that of expensive, specialized hardware built for phased array processing. We also report improvements in calibration, and a significant (35%) improvement in median accuracy for a location system running on top of Phaser due to multipath suppression alone. We cover related work in §5 and conclude in §6.

2. DESIGN

In this section, we discuss the main components of Phaser that allow accurate phase-difference readings to be extracted from commodity RF hardware. We first describe the theory of multicard operation in §2.1. In §2.2, we tackle the problem of automatic detection of radio-chain phase offsets, and in §2.3, we describe an optimization that reduces the detrimental effects of multipath signals.

[1] N.B.: this phase calibration is conceptually distinct from the "calibration" or "war-driving" that some indoor location systems require, involving a human taking readings within an indoor space.

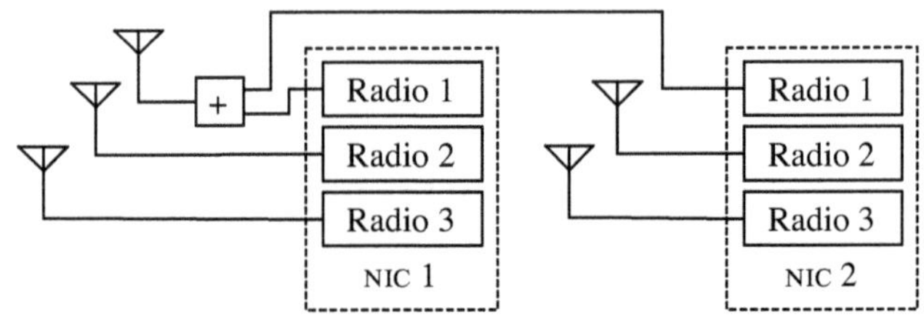

Figure 1: Phaser's multi-radio hardware design for the case of two NICs. The design generalizes to any number of NICs, each sharing one antenna from their first radio.

2.1 Multicard operation

On a single NIC, phase data from each antenna can be compared after compensating for the phase offsets introduced by each of the radio chain oscillators as described in §2.2. However, across radios, many other factors distort the OFDM signal, and each of these varies slightly between the two NICs:

1. The sampling frequency f_s, with which the RF front end samples the incoming signal in the time domain.
2. The carrier frequency f_c to which the RF front end is tuned.
3. The RF sample clock time offset τ, measured in time samples relative to the beginning of an OFDM symbol. This varies because the two NICs detect and acquire the incoming frame at slightly different points in time.
4. RF oscillator phase offset ϕ. As noted above, this varies between antennas on one NIC because it is locked to a random but constant value at power-up. It varies between antennas on different NICs because the two NICs' RF oscillators are not frequency-locked.

To further complicate matters, all the above quantities vary on a frame-by-frame basis, so any correction algorithm must be able to work at line rate as frames arrive from the NIC. In this section, we present a hardware design and a synchronization algorithm that lets us compensate for these differences, and thereby enable phase-difference signal processing across antennas on multiple NICs as if they were phase-locked.

2.1.1 *Hardware design*

To achieve higher antenna counts, Phaser augments an AP's NIC with one or more receive-only NICs, operating on the same channel. Phaser splits the incoming signal from one antenna and routes it to one radio chain on both NICs, as shown in Figure 1. This allows one radio chain on each NIC to receive a signal that we know is equal (as viewed at the antenna) to that which a radio chain on the primary NIC received, but sacrifices one antenna that may otherwise be used for spatial multiplexing. While this is unfortunate, we believe this is a reasonable trade-off for deployments where the opportunities provided by phased signal processing outweigh the need for increased throughput. The result is a five-antenna AP, but the raw CSI[2] readings from the two unsynchronized NICs cannot be combined for phased array processing without compensating for the aforementioned inter-NIC irregularities.

[2] The WiFi standards refer to the channel readings that arrive with each received frame as *channel state information* or CSI. CSI readings are primarily used for channel estimation, but also contain the phase information that phased-array signal processing techniques require. We refer to phase information and CSI interchangeably throughout this paper.

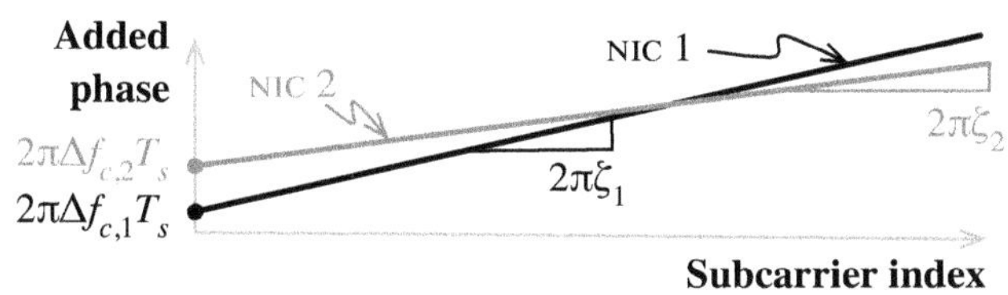

Figure 2: Phase added to a CSI measurement of an OFDM reception due to transmitter-receiver carrier frequency differences $\Delta f_{c,1}$, $\Delta f_{c,2}$ and the respective sampling frequency differences ζ_1, ζ_2 between the transmitter and each of the receiving NICs.

2.1.2 *Software synchronization algorithm*

Upon receiving CSI from each NIC, we first isolate the readings from the shared antenna introduced above. We then arbitrarily, but consistently across packets, select one NIC as the *primary*. For the purposes of discussion, we refer to the frequency-domain CSI of the primary and secondary NIC as $H_1[k]$ and $H_2[k]$, respectively. We now seek a transformation of $H_2[k]$ so that readings for the shared antenna on that NIC matches the readings taken by the primary. We know such a transformation must exist since the two NICs have observed the same signal at the same antenna.

Synchronizing carrier and sampling frequency. We first reconcile f_c and f_s between the two NICs. A difference in f_c between an OFDM sender and receiver manifests as an added phase in H_2 whose magnitude is constant across subcarriers [25]. Suppose the difference in f_c between the sender and NIC 1 is $\Delta f_{c,1}$, and the difference in f_c between sender and NIC 2 is $\Delta f_{c,2}$. The two NICs will experience added phases whose y-intercepts are as shown in Figure 2.

Furthermore, if the sender transmits with a sampling frequency of f_s', then the fractional difference in sampling frequency between sender and NIC 1 is $\zeta_1 = \frac{f_{s,1}}{f_s'} - 1$, with an analogous definition for NIC 2. This manifests as an added phase whose magnitude varies linearly across subcarriers [25] with slopes $2\pi\zeta_1$ and $2\pi\zeta_2$ for NICs 1 and 2, respectively, as shown in Figure 2.

We correct for both carrier and sampling frequency differences by setting the angle of each complex sample from the second card to the angle of the corresponding sample from the primary card while leaving the magnitudes untouched. In the frequency domain, this rotates $H_2[k]$ by the difference between the two curves shown in Figure 2, creating a new CSI for NIC 2 with a constant phase shift of $\gamma = 2\pi\left(\Delta f_{c,2} - \Delta f_{c,1}\right)T_s$ and a phase shift linear in frequency of slope $\alpha = 2\pi\left(\zeta_2 - \zeta_1\right)$:

$$H_2'[k] = H_2[k]e^{j(\gamma+\alpha k)}. \tag{1}$$

This transformation is valid since we know that the received signals for both NICs were equal at the shared antenna.

Synchronizing sample clocks. Due to multipath effects, two NICs also acquire an incoming transmission at slightly different points in time, causing a shift τ in the time-domain samples. To see the effect this has on the CSI, let us examine the Discrete Fourier Transform of NIC 2's CSI:

$$H_2[k] = \sum_{n=0}^{N-1} h_2[n]e^{-j2\pi kn/N}. \tag{2}$$

If we circularly shift $h_2[n]$ in time by a whole number of samples, it can be shown that the effect in the frequency domain is again a phase shift linear in frequency:

$$H_2[k]e^{2\pi j\tau_0 k/N} = \sum_{n=0}^{N-1} h_2\left[(n-\tau_0)_N\right]e^{-j2\pi kn/N}. \tag{3}$$

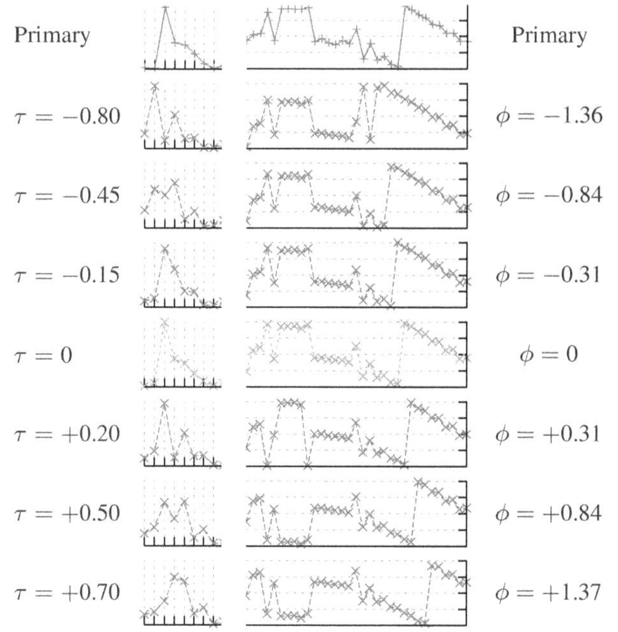

(a) Clock delay **(b)** Oscillator phase offset

Figure 3: Magnitude (a) and phase (b) for consecutive time-domain samples from NIC 1 and NIC 2 with different Phaser search parameters after compensating for f_c and f_s.

Comparing the right-hand-side of Equation 1 with the left-hand-side of Equation 3 we see that the carrier and sampling frequency synchronization step also corrects such time shifts.

This shift will in practice be *less* than one sample period in magnitude. Nonetheless, it can also be shown that a linear phase shift in frequency whose slope is fractional approximates a filter that shifts the sampled signal $h_2[n]$ by reconstructing the underlying continuous signal and resampling that fractional number of samples later in time [13]. The upshot of this is that our carrier and sampling frequency synchronization step also synchronizes the two NICs in time even down to a fraction of a time sample.

Figure 3(a) shows the shared antenna signal from the primary NIC (uppermost plot) and from another NIC, with varying fractional delays applied (remaining plots) after f_c and f_s have been compensated for. We see that the frequency-domain transformation has temporally aligned the two signals. Note that for the longer fractional delay, the peak falls between two samples, and thus becomes obscured.

Correcting oscillator phase offset. The absolute phase measured by the radio chains connected to the shared antenna on each card varies, as their oscillators have different phases. More importantly, the two vary continuously and independently of each other, and can thus not simply be measured once like the inter-antenna phase offsets on a single NIC with frequency-locked oscillators discussed in §2.2. In order to give the appearance that the oscillators from the two NICs are all phase-locked[3], our synchronization algorithm must therefore also cancel out this unpredictable phase offset.

This phase offset manifests as a phase rotation of every time-domain sample. Again, however, consider the right-hand-side of Equation 1. By adjusting γ to equalize phase in the frequency domain, we do the same in the time domain, and so align the phase

[3] If two oscillators are phase-locked, their absolute phase difference is constant over time.

of the primary NIC's signal with the secondary's, as shown in Figure 3(b).

To complete the synchronization, we apply the correction $e^{j(\gamma+\alpha k)}$ from Equation 1 to the samples from all the other antennas on the non-primary NIC. We also multiply the magnitude of the time-domain samples taken from the shared antenna by the number of cards present in order to counter loss introduced by the splitter. This gives us a set of readings that can be treated as phase-locked, despite being from different cards. We note that this synchronization algorithm also compensates for any differences in phase caused by slightly different cable lengths to the shared antenna for the two cards, or by phase unbalance in the splitter, as these are subsumed by the constant phase shift γ of Equation 1.

2.1.3 Interchannel interference

The astute reader will observe that the carrier frequency offset (CFO) and the sampling frequency offset (SFO) both introduce intercarrier interference (ICI), which contributes additional noise to the received signal. If this noise is too large, it would break Phaser's assumption that the phase offset between the shared antenna on two cards is the same for any other pair of antennas, causing multicard synchronization to fail.

The relationship between ICI and SFO, CFO and other factors such as transmitter movement is well understood [9], and both theoretical and experimental results show that the power of ICI caused by SFO is usually several orders of magnitude smaller than the power of the received signal. The 802.11 specification requires conforming sampling clocks to be accurate to 20 ppm, giving an ICI that is 80 dB weaker than the power of the original signal. For Phaser, this means that SFO-induced ICI can safely be considered negligible noise.

CFO on the other hand can introduce ICI that greatly distorts the received signal, and could thus introduce a significant error term in Phaser. However, given the short timescale of the 802.11 preamble over which the CSI is computed, the coarse and fine Schmidl-Cox synchronization performed by 802.11 OFDM receivers effectively eliminates the CFO between the sender and the receiver. The near-zero remaining CFO causes no noteworthy ICI, and thus can also be safely ignored.

2.2 Autocalibration

Since each radio chain connects to a different RF oscillator, their absolute phases differ despite being frequency-locked. In order to obtain useful phase-difference data, array processing systems must eliminate these constant phase differences. While these could be measured by splitting a reference signal along carefully-measured cables [30], or by transmitting a known signal from one antenna to the other antennas on the same AP [24], these approaches interrupt normal communication, and become disruptive if multiple devices have to be calibrated, or if devices restart and require recalibration.

In this section, we propose a technique for automatically calibrating an AP $\mathcal{A}$ that has just been powered up. We present our method in three stages: first, at the lower level, we present a metric, *η-scoring*, for evaluating the degree of correspondence between a pseudospectrum and a given bearing (§2.2.1). Then we present a technique for determining likely candidate phase offsets from a single transmission (§2.2.2. Finally, we give the full algorithm, which uses η-scoring, cross-packet calibration and a "reset" mechanism to achieve resilience against multipath RF propagation (§2.2.3).

Requirements. The only information autocalibration needs is the locations of the APs and potentially other transmitters in the system; for APs, these are assumed to be entered by the sysadmin who installs the AP into Phaser's database, but Phaser can also use transmissions from clients whose position is determined by a localization system.

Metric (η-score):

1. Find a normalizing constant k such that $\int k\mathcal{P}(\theta)\,\mathrm{d}\theta$ is one, and set $\mathcal{P}' = k\mathcal{P}$.
2. Construct a Gaussian *mask* $g_\alpha(\theta)$ with an expected value α and a variance according to the desired level of error tolerance. Set $\bar{g}_\alpha(\theta) = 1 - g_\alpha(\theta)$.
3. Calculate $\eta(\mathcal{P}, \alpha) = \dfrac{\int g_\alpha(\theta)\mathcal{P}'(\theta)\,\mathrm{d}\theta}{\int \bar{g}_\alpha(\theta)\mathcal{P}'(\theta)\,\mathrm{d}\theta}$.

Figure 4: Scoring a pseudospectrum $\mathcal{P}$ arising from a trial combination of phase offsets against a bearing to the AP α. The output of this calculation, the η-score, feeds into the overall autocalibration algorithm.

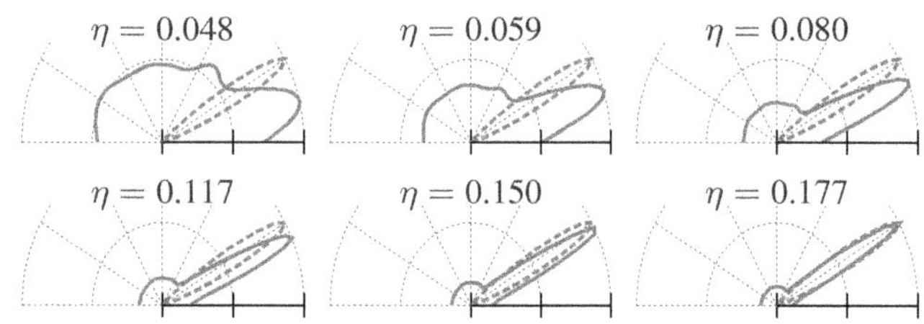

Figure 5: η-scoring different phase combinations that yield various pseudospectra (solid red curves) with energy directed towards and away from the true bearing (broken blue curve).

2.2.1 Scoring individual frames

When CSI for a frame arrives at the autocalibrating AP $\mathcal{A}$, we use spectral techniques on phase-difference readings from the CSI to construct an angle-of-arrival *pseudospectrum* [20]; an estimate of the power of the incoming signal versus bearing to the AP. Since we know the location of the transmitter and the receiver, we have a relatively accurate estimate of the direct-path bearing $\hat{\alpha}$, and thus we know in which direction we are likely to sense energy. As the phase difference, and hence the pseudospectrum, changes with different oscillator phase offsets, we are able to use Phaser's η-scoring metric to find a set of phase offsets that produce a pseudospectrum with energy directed toward $\hat{\alpha}$. The careful reader will note that when an obstruction blocks the direct path to $\mathcal{A}$, this approach in isolation will miss the direct path and score a reflected path highly. We rely on the "outer loop" of the autocalibration algorithm (§2.2.3) to overcome this challenge.

To determine the extent to which a pseudospectrum $\mathcal{P}$ matches $\hat{\alpha}$, we seek a metric that increases in the presence of peaks towards bearing $\hat{\alpha}$, and decreases in the presence of peaks at bearings away from $\hat{\alpha}$. Since $\hat{\alpha}$ is an estimate, we also want the metric to be continuous with respect to bearing, so that $\mathcal{P}$'s peak does not have to *exactly* coincide with $\hat{\alpha}$.

By comparing the area under $\mathcal{P}$ in the vicinity of AP bearing α with the area under $\mathcal{P}$ toward all other bearings, the *η-score* $\eta(\mathcal{P}, \alpha)$ shown in Figure 4 fulfills the above goals. Peaks in directions away from α, or a high noise floor, increase the denominator in Step 3, thus decreasing $\eta(\mathcal{P}, \alpha)$. Figure 5 shows η for six different combinations of phase offsets for a linear three-antenna array. As desired, the η-score is highest when a peak is present in the direction of $\hat{\alpha}$, and lower when there are peaks elsewhere.

The Gaussian ensures that pseudospectra with peaks close to α also get high η-scores, thus tolerating inaccuracies in the estimation of α. The width of the Gaussian should be chosen such that it matches the width of a peak in a pseudospectrum with most power directed toward the signal's true bearing. With increasing number of antennas, peaks get sharper, and thus the variance of the smoothing function should be decreased. For arrays with relatively few antennas, an experimental sensitivity analysis (§4.2.2) shows that a Gaussian with variance $\sigma^2 = 0.1$ works well.

2.2.2 *Autocalibration algorithm*

Upon receiving CSI from a frame[4] at $\mathcal{A}$, an N-antenna AP, we need to explore the $N-1$-dimensional phase offset space, but an exhaustive search of all phase offset combinations on each received transmission would be very expensive for large N. To make this operation tractable, we observe that an N-antenna array can be viewed as a number of smaller and overlapping L-antenna sub-arrays.

We begin with the algorithm for each L-antenna subarray $\mathcal{A}_i$. This maintains a *current best set* of phase offsets $\mathcal{B}_i$, which starts out empty. Each candidate E in $\mathcal{B}_i$ consists of a set of $L-1$ phase offsets $\phi_1^E, \ldots, \phi_{L-1}^E$ along with the η-score of the pseudospectrum resulting from applying those phase offsets to the frame's received CSI. We now consider every combination of the $L-1$ possible phase offsets with a *phase granularity* $\Delta\phi$ a candidate for insertion into $\mathcal{B}_i$. Given a candidate C, we now need to decide whether C should be inserted into $\mathcal{B}_i$, and if so, which element to evict from $\mathcal{B}_i$ once it grows beyond a certain *candidate population size* S. We explore the effect of varying S and $\Delta\phi$ in §4.2.

We aim for each $\mathcal{B}_i$ to contain phase offset combinations that yield good η-scores, while still maintaining diversity so that if the ground-truth correct phase offset has a lower η-score, it will not be completely disappear from $\mathcal{B}$. To achieve this, we compare C with a randomly-selected $E \in \mathcal{B}$ and probabilistically replace E by C based on two ratios. The first, $\Delta\eta = \eta_C/\eta_E$, measures how much better C's η-score is than E's. The second ratio captures the impact of replacing E by C on diversity. We compute

$$\sigma^2_{\mathcal{B}_i} = \sum_{k=1}^{L-1} \sum_{E \in \mathcal{B}_i} \left(\phi_k^E - \bar{\phi}_k\right)^2 \tag{4}$$

where $\bar{\phi}_k$ is the average phase offset for antenna pair k in $\mathcal{B}_i$. Then we compare $\sigma^2_{\mathcal{B}_i}$ with $\sigma^2_{\mathcal{B}_i \setminus \{E\} \cup \{C\}}$ by the ratio

$$\Delta\sigma^2_{CE} = \sigma^2_{\mathcal{B}_i \setminus \{E\} \cup \{C\}} / \sigma^2_{\mathcal{B}_i}. \tag{5}$$

The two ratios $\Delta\eta$ and $\Delta\sigma^2_{CE}$ give us information about how much better or worse C is than E. To determine the probability of replacement, $p_r(C,E)$, we first observe that, as the population stabilizes, $\Delta\eta$ and $\Delta\sigma^2_{CE}$ will generally be very close to one. We therefore want to increase $p_r(C,E)$'s sensitivity when the ratios are close to one, and cap it such that we discard obviously poor ratios and keep obviously good ratios. This can be achieved by applying a shifted exponential function to each ratio as shown in Equation 6:

$$p_r(C,E) = a\left(b^{\Delta\eta-1}/2 + b^{\Delta\sigma^2_{CE}-1}/2 - c\right) + 1/2. \tag{6}$$

By choosing a and b, we can adjust the sensitivity of the probability to small changes in $\Delta\eta$ or $\Delta\sigma^2$ when the ratios are close to one. We pick c to center the distribution at zero, meaning c is uniquely determined by the choice of a and b. By adding $1/2$ to p_r, we normalize $p_r(C,E) = 0.5$ when C and E are equally good candidates.

The choice of a and b will depend upon the expected variation in $\Delta\eta$ and $\Delta\sigma^2$. While the expected variation in $\Delta\sigma^2$ is unpredictable across transmissions, and thus cannot be tuned for specifically, the variation in $\Delta\eta$ will vary depending on the array geometry, because different antenna geometries may produce different distributions of η scores as combinations of ϕ are searched. We have found that for a five-antenna uniformly linear array, $a = 10$, $b = 2.718$ and $c = 1$ yields good diversity in the population while still maintaining high η-scores across several deployments.

After this selection, we have $N/(L-1)$ populations, each containing the best candidates for one sub-array. We can now generate candidates for $\mathcal{B}$, the final population, by picking one candidate from each population, $c_i \in \mathcal{B}_i$, and subtracting the phase offset of the overlapping antenna in c_0 from all phase offsets in each c_i. The resulting candidate is probabilistically inserted into $\mathcal{B}$ in the same way as for each $\mathcal{B}_i$.

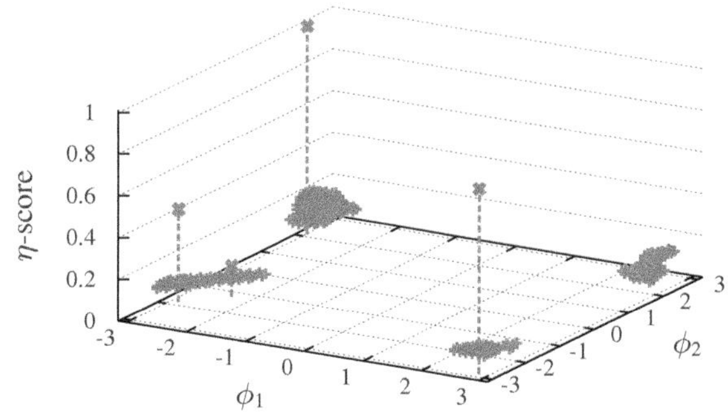

Figure 6: Phaser's cross-packet calibration clustering algorithm operating with packets from four different APs.

2.2.3 *Multi-packet operation*

After this process completes, $\mathcal{B}$ contains a diverse set of phase offset combinations[5] that all yield high η-scores. We reduce this to a single combination with the observation that across frames from different transmitters, combinations close to the ground-truth phase offsets E^* appear in almost every population $\mathcal{B}$, and phase offsets due to multipath reflections vary randomly across populations from different transmitters. To exploit this, we introduce a *cross-packet population*, Ψ, into which all elements of each $\mathcal{B}^k$ (the final candidate phase offset set for received frame k) are placed such that $\Psi = \mathcal{B}^1 \cup \ldots \cup \mathcal{B}^K$ across K received packets. Then we apply standard clustering algorithms to Ψ, where the distance between two samples is determined by the unwrapped Euclidean distance of the phase offsets and the sample's η-score. Figure 6 shows the result of performing this clustering on a three-antenna array across 50 packets received from three transmitters.

To estimate the correct phase offset combination, we now find the cluster with the highest product of number of samples and average η-score, and the parameters of its centroid are used as the true phase offset combination. This metric dictates the height of the dotted line going through each identified centroid in the figure. This ordering rewards phase combinations that consistently give pseudospectra that have good correlation with the true angle of arrival (AoA).

2.2.4 *Practical considerations for autocalibration*

AP placement estimation error. Autocalibration only has an estimate of the bearings of incoming signals. Because of this, the η-score will not reach a maximum for the true combination of phase

[4]Possibly from multiple cards and combined as explained in §2.1.

[5]Several phase combinations can yield peaks toward a given bearing depending on the multipath environment and the antenna geometry.

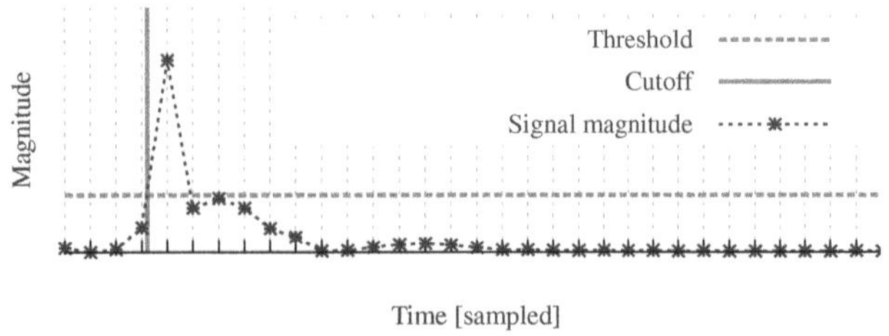

Figure 7: Magnitude of sampled time-domain signal showing line-of-sight arrival and multipath arrivals. Horizontal line indicates onset threshold, vertical line indicates cutoff point after upsampling.

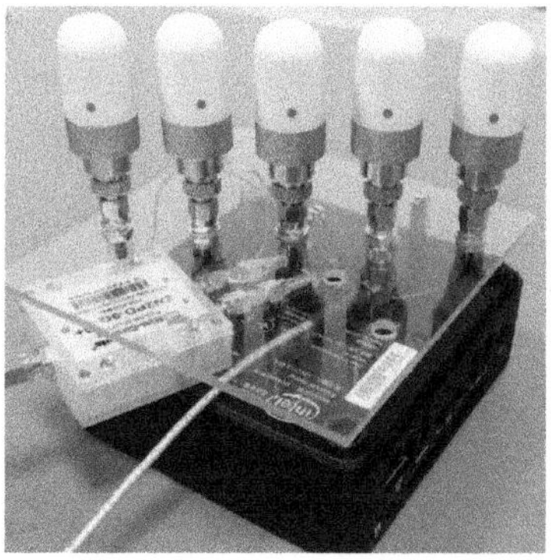

Figure 8: The 5-antenna Phaser AP with one antenna shared by both NICs. The signal from this shared antenna is split and fed into one RF front end on each NICs.

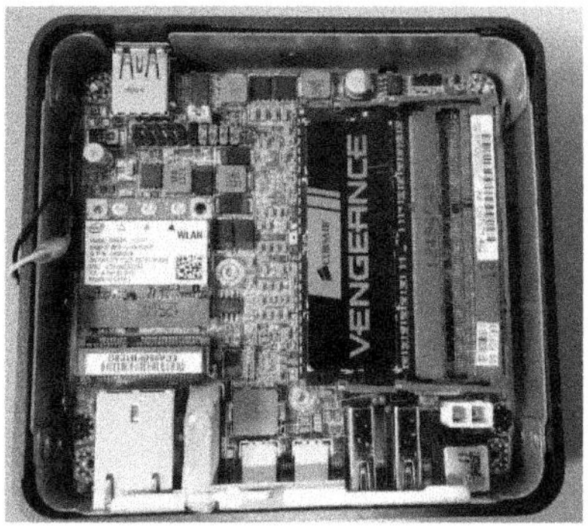

Figure 9: The inside of Phaser AP with one Intel 5300 card shown. Two NICs are employed to have a total of six available RF chains.

offsets as the peak of the pseudospectrum for the true phase offsets will no longer align with the bearing that autocalibration is attempting to maximize against.

To counter this problem, we add another dimension to the search in each L-antenna sub-array. For each phase offset combination, we calculate the η-score for several smaller rotations of the normalized pseudospectrum $\mathcal{P}'$. Since we assume that the system knows the rotation and location fairly accurately, only a very narrow range of rotations ($\pm 5°$) need to be searched. Due to the Gaussian smoothing, we can also search quite coarsely, as even an approximate match will receive a higher η-score. When performing probabilistic insertion, we now also consider the rotation that was used in conjunction with the phase offsets we are iterating on top of. Since a rotation of $\mathcal{P}'$ is computationally trivial, recalculating the η-score for a small number of rotations is a sufficiently inexpensive operation that it does not significantly impact the running time of the autocalibration algorithm.

Calibration reset. Occasionally, this algorithm may yield incorrect phase offsets, causing an AP to be miscalibrated. Once autocalibration has terminated, the AP participates in a larger, multi-AP system along with other nearby APs. Suppose this system is a location tracking system and estimates a client's location as $\mathbf{x}$. The calibrated AP $\mathcal{A}$ measures the degree to which it agrees with that location by evaluating its pseudospectrum at the bearing corresponding to $\mathbf{x}$, $\theta_{\mathbf{x}}$. If $\mathcal{A}$ consistently disagrees with the location system's estimate across many clients, it is likely that $\mathcal{A}$ has been miscalibrated. Phaser thus resets the calibration and reruns autocalibration. This alleviates the event that a burst of packets from a far-away AP or client miscalibrates $\mathcal{A}$.

2.3 Onset detection

Real-world wireless environments are replete with walls and other objects that reflect wireless signals, causing multipath reflections that complicate angle-of-arrival computations significantly. These additional signals can significantly reduce the fidelity of the pseudospectra, particularly for antenna-constrained arrays.

To address this, Phaser uses a simple, yet effective optimization that allows it to suppress a large portion of the multipath power in an incoming signal. Consider the magnitude of an incoming signal over time shown in Figure 7. There is typically a clear peak for the line-of-sight (LOS) arrival, and then later peaks and bumps for the arriving reflected signals. This observation matches what we know of the fundamentals of physics; reflected signals must necessarily arrive at a strictly later point in time than the LOS signals.

We use this insight to suppress the multipath arrivals: we apply a peak detection algorithm to the received signal's magnitude, identify the first peak, and eliminate any samples appearing after that peak when doing spectral analysis of the signal. Since we are looking at a sampled signal, this technique cannot eliminate multipath signals that arrive within the same sampling period as the LOS arrival. However, as we show experimentally in §4.3, the effect of removing even some of the multipath signals is substantial.

We also observe that the incoming signal can be upsampled by using a higher number of samples in the inverse Fourier Transform applied to the frequency-domain in the CSI. This increased resolution allows us to further improve multipath suppression; instead of removing any samples after the LOS peak, we eliminate all samples after the *onset* of this peak. While this will reduce the gain of the LOS signal, it will also significantly reduce the impact of multipath transmissions that fall within the same sample period. Figure 7 shows the cutoff point for a received signal using a third of the signal's min-max span as the onset detection threshold. This optimization is further evaluated in §4.3.

3. IMPLEMENTATION

We have implemented Phaser on *Intel Next Unit of Computing* devices with *Intel Wireless Link 5300* 802.11n MIMO NICs as shown in Figure 8 and 9. Using this commodity hardware, we have access to 802.11 CSI readings [10], which enables us to extract per-subcarrier phase information. Because of firmware limitations, we were only able to get reliable phase readings at 5 GHz. Antennas are spaced at a half-wavelength distance (2.68 cm) in a linear form to yield maximum AoA spectrum resolution which is also the arrangement preferred in commodity APs. As shown in Figure 8, a splitter is employed to feed the signal received from the shared antenna to both of the NICs for synchronization purpose.

System data flow. The APs are set up in promiscuous wireless monitoring mode, and forward all 802.11 headers and CSI readings

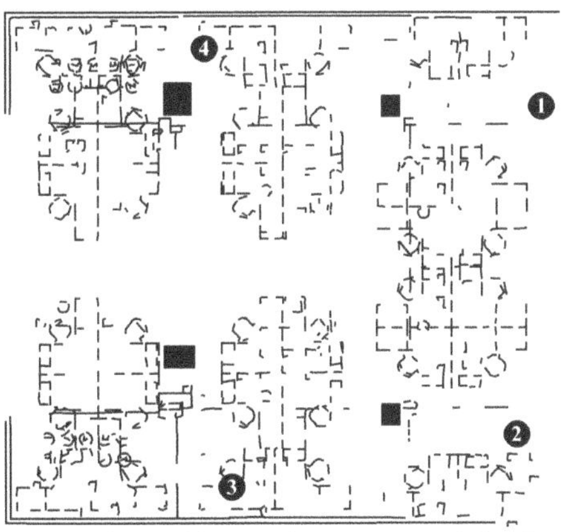

Figure 10: Map of the office environment used for the following experimental evaluation. The office measures 2,055 square feet and is populated with numerous partition walls and concrete pillars (denoted by black rectangles). For localization experiments, 25 sample locations throughout the office were used. AP locations are denoted by circled numbers.

Figure 11: AP (far) and client (near) setup in anechoic chamber with multipath reflector.

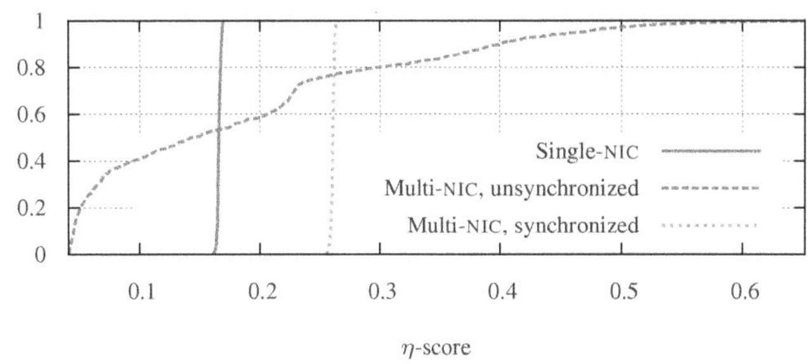

Figure 12: η-scores of a transmitter at 210° with and without multi-NIC operation in an anechoic chamber.

back to a central server over an Ethernet backhaul. The server then arranges these into groups based on timing and header information to determine which readings belong to the same original transmission. If the server detects that it has received multiple CSI readings from different cards on the same AP, it performs multicard merging as described in §2.1 and replaces them with the merged reading. Upon receiving a CSI reading from an uncalibrated AP, the server initiates the single-packet autocalibration algorithm from §2.2.2, while applying the multipath suppression algorithm (§2.3). After a sufficient number of such packets have been processed for an AP, the system performs the multipacket clustering described in §2.2.3, after which the AP becomes operational.

Replay function. A particular challenge that arises in the evaluation of wireless systems that operate in real-time is the constantly-changing wireless channel. This makes comparisons between two different experimental runs invalid. To combat this issue, we implement a *replay* function which we believe is beneficial not only to Phaser but also to other real-time systems. To accomplish this, Phaser records detailed information about each experiment including packet arrival times, signal amplitude and phase, packet content, and the AP's calibration data in a log file for replaying purposes. For 30 minutes of real-time experiments with Phaser, the size of the log file is reasonably small: around 100 MB. With this replay function employed, we are able to evaluate different schemes and different parameter settings while keeping the experimental setup and environmental factors unchanged.

4. EVALUATION

Methodology. We experiment in both a busy, uncontrolled 2,055-square foot open-plan office shown in Figure 10 and the controlled anechoic chamber environment of Figure 11. The office is populated with concrete pillars as indicated, as well as numerous wooden partition walls throughout. Co-channel interference and overlapping channel interference are also present in the office. Our APs are mounted near the ceiling, and so the environment is a partial line-of-sight environment: non-line-of-sight when a partition or concrete pillar blocks the mobile's path to an AP. Because of the firmware limitations mentioned in §3, Phaser on the Intel 5300 NICs can only operate at 5 GHz. As higher-frequency signals are subject to worse multipath reflections from walls and nearby objects, this carrier frequency is in the most challenging band of the WiFi spectrum.

Evaluation roadmap. We begin with measurements of the accuracy of multicard operation (§4.1) in an anechoic chamber. We then evaluate autocalibration (§4.2) and multipath suppression (§4.3), and report end-to-end results from a localization system built atop Phaser (§4.4), all in the office.

4.1 Multicard operation

In order to test multicard operation in isolation, we perform manual cable calibration on an AP, and place the AP with a client in an interference-free anechoic chamber where the multipath environment can be completely controlled. Our test setup is shown in Figure 11: the metal plate is used to introduce a multipath reflection in later experiments. We average across 1,000 frame transmissions in each experiment.

Line-of-sight. We present data from a single, three-antenna NIC, two three-antenna unsynchronized NICs, and two three-antenna NICs with Phaser's inter-NIC synchronization (§2.1). Figure 12 shows η-score distributions across frames from each of these three experiments with the client at 210° to the AP's broadside. Since the experiment took place in a controlled environment, we expect very little variation in the score over time. While this holds for both single-NIC and synchronized multi-NIC operation, we see that for unsynchronized multi-NIC operation, the η-score varies widely across frames as the oscillators of the two cards drift relative to each other. This shows that the multi-NIC synchronization is working correctly; the resulting pseudospectra are stable over time, and more importantly, are of greater fidelity than for a single NIC. We also note that the η-score is higher for multi-NIC operation than single-NIC. This is due to sharper pseudospectra produced as number of antennas increases.

Multipath. Another advantage of a larger array is the ability to resolve multiple arriving signals. Figure 13 shows a similar experi-

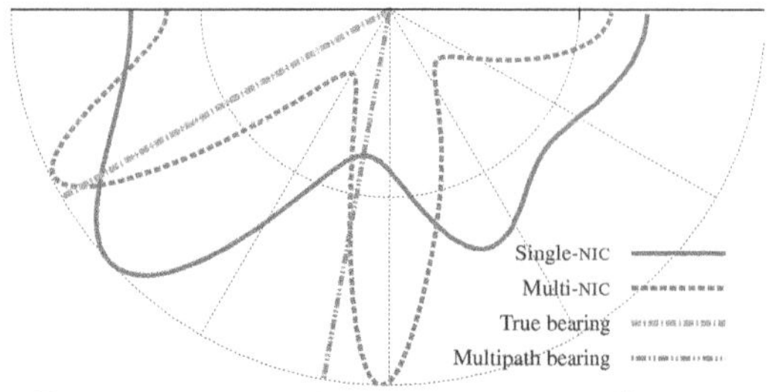

Figure 13: Pseudospectra with a transmitter at 210° and a multipath reflector at 100° from a single-NIC, three-antenna array and a multi-NIC, five-antenna array.

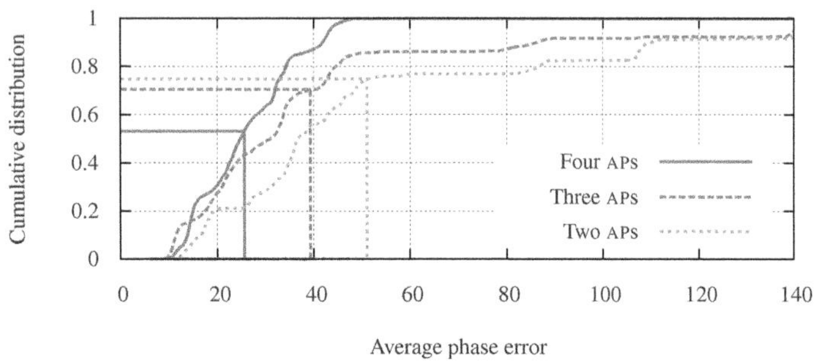

Figure 14: Average single-NIC phase error as the number of calibration transmitters varies. Vertical and horizontal lines denote the mean and the order statistic of the mean respectively.

ment, but with an additional signal arriving at 100° to the array's broadside. This skews the three-antenna pseudospectrum, whereas the five-antenna pseudospectrum clearly distinguishes the two incoming signals.

4.2 Autocalibration

To evaluate how well autocalibration functions in a real office environment, we place four multi-NIC Phaser APs in the ceiling of our open lab. The true phase offsets were determined by applying manual calibration using an RF signal splitter as described in §2.2.

4.2.1 Number of APs

One of the most important factors for autocalibration is the number of distinct signal sources, as increased path diversity helps eliminate incorrect phase offset combinations caused by persistent multipath fading or interference. In Figure 14, we use this four-AP setup, running autocalibration with differently-sized subsets of APs enabled. Accuracy decreases with transmitter diversity because the clustering at the end of the autocalibration process only works if the true phase offset combination is the only one with samples present in every population. As the number of distinct transmitters decreases, incorrect phase offset combinations are more likely to be present in a sufficient number of populations that they are considered to be more likely candidates than the true phase offset combination. We obtain good calibration accuracy with four, and acceptable accuracy with three active APs.

4.2.2 Sensitivity analysis: Search parameters

In §2.2, we mention a number of parameters that can affect the performance of autocalibration; principally the number of transmitters K, the number of transmissions, and the population size S. In addition, the granularity at which the phase offsets are searched when generating candidate phase combinations, $\Delta\phi$, clearly affects the accuracy achievable through calibration. Figure 15 shows how modifying each parameter affects the accuracy of autocalibration.

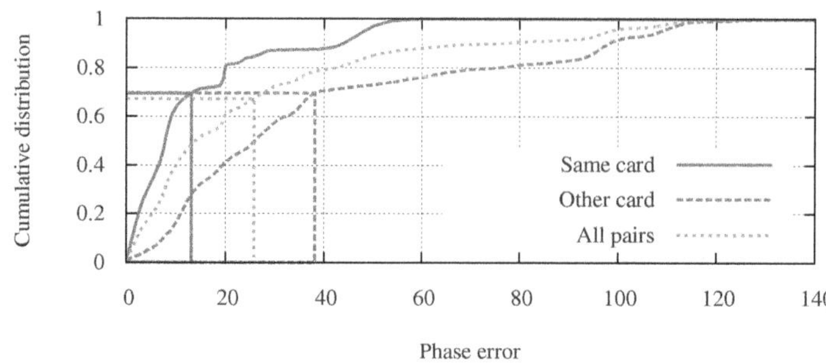

Figure 16: Phase error distribution across antenna pairs for antennas pairs on the same card versus different cards

Population size. Recall from §2.2 that population size S determines the number of phase combinations that "survive" each iteration. As S increases, we retain more combinations from each packet, giving the final step of autocalibration and clustering more samples to work with. Results show that increasing the population size S increases the number of samples for the true combination. When we then cluster at the end of the autocalibration process, the cluster near the true combination will have more points, and the end result becomes more accurate.

Step size. The choice of $\Delta\phi$ presents a trade-off between computational cost versus calibration accuracy; as the steps become coarser, the phase difference between the true offsets and their closest step will increase, and so will the overall error. A smaller step size will reduce this quantization error, but will also increase the number of combinations needed for calibration, making it slower. Below a step size of 6°, noise in the calibration process will surpass the step error and we will reach a point of diminishing returns, for both single-NIC and multi-NIC measurements. This correlates well with the lowest observed phase errors across all runs.

Number of frames. We measure the effect of changing the number of frames K that the autocalibration algorithm waits for before performing clustering and picking the final phase offset combination. As this number is lowered, we would expect to see a similar degradation to what is observed as the number of transmitters decreases; fewer samples means incorrect phase offset combinations have a greater chance of creating winning clusters. We observe this trend in Figure 15—as we sample more transmissions, the true phase combinations become more numerous in the final population, and their cluster is more likely to dominate.

Gaussian variance of η-score. Finally, we measure the effect of changing the width of the Gaussian curve that the η-score metric correlates against, as described in §2.2.1. We observe low sensitivity to the width of the Gaussian and good performance at our chosen value ($\sigma^2 = 0.1$).

4.2.3 Phase error and spatial resolution

It is important to make a distinction between phase error and the spatial resolution of the resulting pseudospectra. Though they are both measured in degrees, and a higher phase error will generally cause the resulting pseudospectrum to degrade in quality, there is not a one-to-one correspondence between the two.

To illustrate the impact of phase error on a pseudospectrum, consider Figure 17 where we show a pseudospectrum produced with the correct phase offsets, as well as pseudospectra where each phase offset is perturbed by a random error of $\pm 20 \pm 5$ or $\pm 30 \pm 5$. While

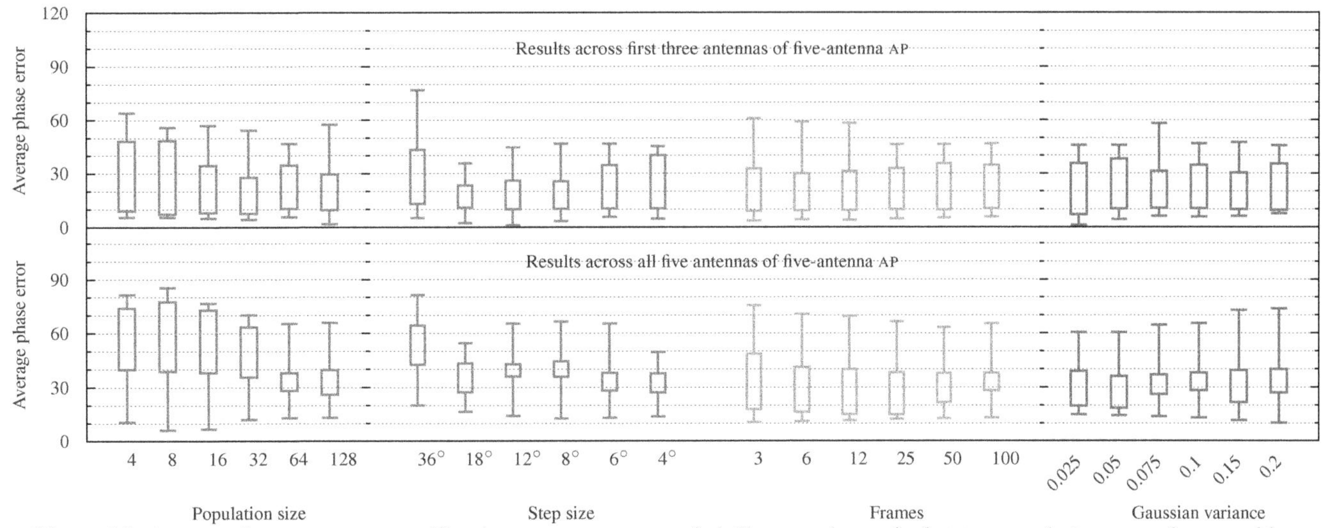

Figure 15: Average phase error as autocalibration parameters are varied. Top row shows single-NIC error, bottom row shows multi-NIC error. The non-variable parameters are held at 64 survivors, 100 packets, 6° step size, and $\sigma^2 = 0.1$. Boxes denote the 25th and 75th order statistics, while whiskers denote the 5th and 95th percentile order statistics. Results are without multipath suppression.

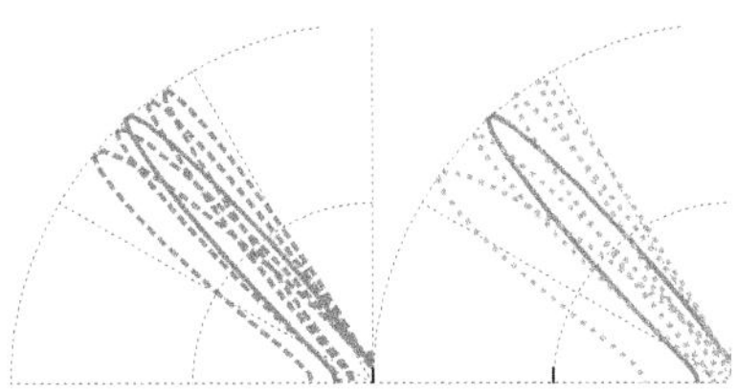

Figure 17: Pseudospectra for varying average phase errors. Solid red line indicates AoA spectrum with perfect calibration. Dashed blue lines (left) show 20° error, dotted green lines (right) show 30° error.

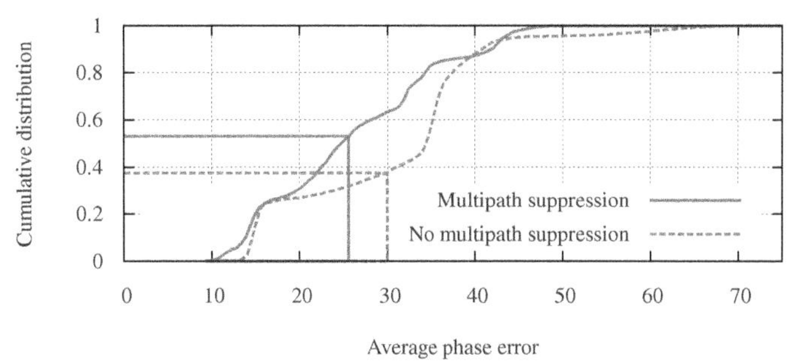

Figure 18: Autocalibration phase error distribution with/without multipath suppression.

the error is noticeable, the overall shape of the pseudospectrum is maintained even for an average phase error of 30°.

4.2.4 Impact of synchronization on autocalibration

From the lower half of Figure 15, autocalibration accuracy lessens for antennas on a non-primary NIC. By plotting the distribution of absolute phase error for the phase offsets for antennas on the primary NIC and on the secondary NIC separately for a five-antenna, dual-NIC array, we explore the error multi-NIC synchronization introduces.

Figure 16 shows the distribution of phase errors across 700 calibration runs on the four APs in our testbed. The mean phase error increases by almost 20° for the antennas on the secondary NIC. While this is a noticeable error, the fidelity gain from more antennas often outweighs the noise synchronization introduces.

4.3 Multipath suppression

To demonstrate the efficacy of our multipath suppression algorithm, we run the autocalibration algorithm on the same dataset with multipath suppression enabled and disabled. Since the algorithm is non-deterministic, we also run a number of iterations for each configuration. The dataset is the same used for the autocalibration evaluation in §4.2.

Figure 18 shows the calibration error distribution for both versions across all antennas on each AP. Multipath suppression alone reduces the median calibration error from 34° to 24° for multicard operation, and from 12° to 6° for the primary NIC (not shown). We explore the impact of this in the end-to-end evaluation in §4.4.

4.4 Application: Localization

In order to determine whether Phaser truly enables practical phased-array signal processing on commodity hardware, we implement an angle-of-arrival based location tracking system [30] on top of Phaser. In this context, the server constructs pseudospectra from phase-difference information obtained from each AP's reading in a transmission group and uses this information to triangulate the transmitter's location. This is done by finding the location on the map that maximizes $\prod P_i(\theta_i)$; the combined pseudospectrum probability across APs for the candidate location's bearing to each AP. All APs in the deployment are first calibrated using autocalibration. Figure 19 shows the end-to-end localization error of this system when deployed on Phaser with four five-antenna APs in our office environment. We also replay the same trace without multipath suppression enabled to evaluate the effect onset detection has on localization accuracy. Results show that Phaser enables practical indoor location estimation on off-the-shelf hardware with little configuration and no training. Multipath suppression further improves mean accuracy by almost a meter, and the 95th-percentile by over two meters. The median accuracy improves by over 50 cm, representing a 35% improvement due to onset detection alone.

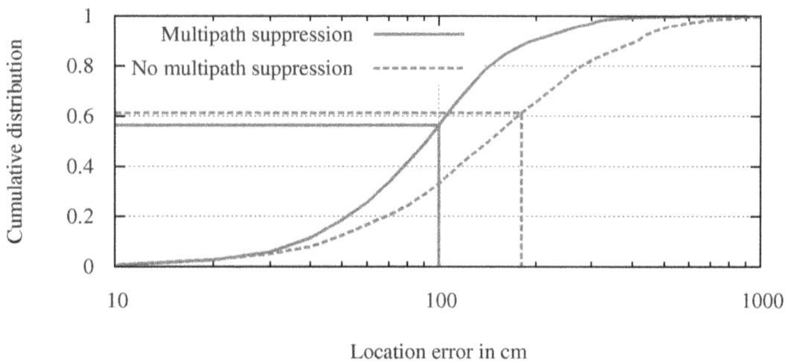

Figure 19: End-to-end localization system error with four multi-NIC five-antenna APs, with and without multipath suppression.

5. RELATED WORK

In this section we survey prior work in location estimation (§5.1), radio imaging (§5.2), and phase calibration (§5.3), and describe how these systems relate to Phaser.

5.1 Indoor location systems

Phaser's functionality is most directly applicable to indoor location systems, and there are many different such systems.

Ultrasound and light-based methods. Active Badge [28], Bat [29, 11], and Cricket [16] systems are among the pioneers in the ultrasound and ultrasound/RF area, but require specialized hardware and per-room infrastructure. In contrast, localization systems built on top of Phaser are much cheaper and easier to deploy thanks to the ubiquity of wireless APs.

RF-based methods. The RADAR system [3, 4] pioneered this popular approach based on AP radio signal strength maps, with further work refining the approach probabilistically [35], through perturbation [34], and by exploring the use of cross-technology interference [8]. To build the radio map without human involvement, follow-on work uses crowdsourcing, step counting, smartphone inertial sensors [18, 26, 33], and GPS [6]. Other approaches leverage ray tracing [7] or human intervention (either by manual location input [15], or a user's spinning movement [21]) to obviate the need for manual radio map construction. These RF-based methods, however, often suffer from poor spatial resolution compared to angle-of-arrival based methods.

RF angle-of-arrival based methods. These measure the two-dimensional bearing at which a transmission arrives at the AP [14, 30]. Further work refines these methods to use a smartphone's inertial sensors to estimate the line-of-sight path to the AP [22], or attempt to isolate the line-of-sight signal in order to decrease the complexity of angle-of-arrival estimation [12]. Phaser's autocalibration can augment these systems to make them even more practical, and Phaser's multipath suppression and multicard operation components make them even more functional.

Spot localization. PinLoc [23] places the mobile in one of several pre-defined, geographically separated spots by statistical clustering and classification of 802.11n CSI information. Phaser's multicard operation can offer these systems the ability to classify based on five or more antennas instead of three, potentially improving system performance.

5.2 Radio imaging

Also known as device-free localization and passive radar, this work uses RF measurements to localize humans and objects moving about in space, without the need for them to be carrying RF transmitters. WiSee [17] uses Doppler shift analysis combined with MIMO spatial signatures to analyze human motion, and so Phaser's multi-antenna processing design can complement it. Wi-Vi [2] uses inverse synthetic aperture radar combined with angle-of-arrival measurements using the MUSIC algorithm [20] to track users through walls, and so all three parts of Phaser can add direct benefit.

Other such systems use signal strength and/or Doppler shift measurements only. Ichnaea [19] uses statistical processing on received signal strength (RSS) measurements, and MonoStream uses image processing on the magnitude information of 802.11n CSI data to recognize trained patterns when users stand at various locations. Chetty *et al.* [5] describe a single-antenna passive bistatic radar system that can track targets through a wall. Here Phaser is of no immediate benefit, but in general, coherent combination of data from multiple antennas boosts fidelity, and so with this addition, Phaser can offer complementary benefits to these systems.

5.3 Phase calibration

Muti-user MIMO transmit beamforming systems like Argos [24] also need to perform phase calibration. To do so, Argos sends from one antenna on the WARP FPGA-based AP while receiving on the others. But this approach is not directly applicable to current commodity NICs, as they usually do not support transmitting on one antenna while receiving on the other antennas simultaneously. Nevertheless, a similar calibration technique can be applied on APs with multiple NICs; the cards can take turns transmitting and receiving for a brief period after the AP first comes online in order to gather information similar to that obtained in Argos' calibration phase. However, this calibration technique has a number of drawbacks that make it problematic to use in practice. First, it requires multiple NICs to be present for it to work. As the current trend is for the number of antennas per NIC to increase, the need for multiple NICs is declining, and having a hard requirement on additional hardware for the sole purpose of calibration is undesirable. Second, using an APs own transmissions for calibration means additional shielding is required between the antennas and the antenna ports on the NICs, as any signal leaking between the two will severely skew calibration results. Finally, with dense antenna geometries, and particularly for linear arrays, the antennas themselves will add multipath reflections and obstruct line-of-sight signal propagation, introducing additional errors into the calibration results. Phaser's autocalibration mechanism is not subject to these problems, but does require cooperation with other APs or mobile clients to function, which is not the case for Argos-like calibration.

6. CONCLUSION

We have described Phaser, a system that allows commodity WiFi APs with or without minor cost-effective hardware modifications to become phased array signal processing platforms capable of high-fidelity array signal processing. Phaser contributes novel design techniques for multi-NIC operation and automatic calibration, and introduces an effective technique for multipath suppression. We have experimentally measured the fidelity of Phaser's phase measurements, and in an application study we have demonstrated good end-to-end indoor location accuracy. Finally, we have outlined three distinct kinds of wireless systems that benefit from Phaser (§5).

Acknowledgements

The research leading to these results has received funding from the European Research Council under the European Union's Seventh Framework Programme (FP/2007-2013), ERC Grant Agreement n° 279976. We thank the anonymous reviewers and shepherd for their useful feedback.

7. REFERENCES

[1] H. Abdel-Nasser, R. Samir, I. Sabek, and M. Youssef. MonoStream: A minimal-hardware high accuracy device-free WLAN localization system. In WCNC, 2013.

[2] F. Adib and D. Katabi. See through walls with WiFi! In SIGCOMM, 2013.

[3] P. Bahl and V. Padmanabhan. RADAR: An in-building RF-based user location and tracking system. In INFOCOM, 2000.

[4] P. Bahl, V. Padmanabhan, and A. Balachandran. Enhancements to the RADAR user location and tracking system. Technical Report MSR-TR-2000-12, 2000.

[5] K. Chetty, G. Smith, and K. Woodbridge. Through-the-wall sensing of personnel using passive bistatic radar at standoff distances. IEEE *Trans. on Geo. and Remote Sensing*, 50(4):1218–26.

[6] K. Chintalapudi, A. Iyer, and V. Padmanabhan. Indoor localization without the pain. In *MobiCom*, 2010.

[7] A. Eleryan, M. Elsabagh, and M. Youssef. AROMA: Automatic generation of radio maps for localization systems. In WINTECH, 2011.

[8] Y. Gao, J. Niu, R. Zhou, and G. Xing. ZiFind: Exploiting cross-technology interference signatures for energy-efficient indoor localization. In INFOCOM, 2013.

[9] M. García and C. Oberli. Intercarrier interference in OFDM: A general model for transmissions in mobile environments with imperfect synchronization. *EURASIP Journal on Wireless Communications and Networking*, June 2009.

[10] D. Halperin, W. Hu, A. Sheth, and D. Wetherall. Tool release: Gathering 802.11n traces with channel state information. SIGCOMM CCR, 41(1), 2011.

[11] R. Harle and A. Hopper. Deploying and evaluating a location-aware system. In *MobiSys*, 2005.

[12] D. Inserra and A. Tonello. A frequency-domain los angle-of-arrival estimation approach in multipath channels. *Vehicular Technology, IEEE Transactions on*, 62(6):2812–2818, July 2013.

[13] T. Laakso, V. Valimaki, M. Karjalainen, and U. Laine. Splitting the unit delay. IEEE *Sig. Proc. Mag.*, 13(1):30–60, 1996.

[14] D. Niculescu and B. Nath. VOR base stations for indoor 802.11 positioning. In ACM *MobiCom*, 2004.

[15] J. Park, B. Charrow, D. Curtis, J. Battat, E. Minkov, J. Hicks, S. Teller, and J. Ledlie. Growing an organic indoor location system. In *MobiSys*, 2010.

[16] N. Priyantha, A. Chakraborty, and H. Balakrishnan. The Cricket location-support system. In *MobiCom*, 2000.

[17] Q. Pu, S. Gupta, S. Gollakota, and S. Patel. Whole-home gesture recognition using wireless signals. In *MobiCom*, 2013.

[18] A. Rai, K. Chintalapudi, V. Padmanabhan, and R. Sen. Zee: Zero-effort crowdsourcing for indoor localization. In *MobiCom*, 2012.

[19] A. Saeed, A. Kosba, and M. Youssef. Ichnaea: A low-overhead robust WLAN device-free passive localization system. IEEE *J. on Sel. Topics in Sig. Proc.*, 8(1), 2014.

[20] R. Schmidt. Multiple emitter location and signal parameter estimation. IEEE *Trans. on Antennas and Propagation*, AP-34(3):276–80, 1986.

[21] S. Sen, R. Choudhury, and S. Nelakuditi. SpinLoc: Spin once to know your location. In *HotMobile*, 2012.

[22] S. Sen, J. Lee, K. Kim, and P. Congdon. Avoiding multipath to revive inbuilding WiFi localization. In *MobiSys*, 2013.

[23] S. Sen, B. Radunovic, R. Choudhury, and T. Minka. Spot localization using PHY layer information. In *MobiSys*, 2012.

[24] C. Shepard, H. Yu, N. Anand, L. Li, T. Marzetta, R. Yang, and L. Zhong. Argos: Practical many-antenna base stations. In *MobiCom*, 2012.

[25] J. K. Tan. An adaptive orthogonal frequency division multiplexing baseband modem for wideband wireless channels. Master's thesis, Massachusetts Institute of Technology, June 2006. pp. 43-47.

[26] H. Wang, S. Sen, A. Elgohary, M. Farid, M. Youssef, and R. Choudhury. No need to war drive: Unsupervised indoor localization. In *MobiSys*, 2012.

[27] J. Wang and D. Katabi. Dude, where's my card? RFID positioning that works with multipath and non-line of sight. In SIGCOMM, 2013.

[28] R. Want, A. Hopper, V. Falcao, and J. Gibbons. The active badge location system. *ACM Trans. on Information Systems*, 10(1):91–102, Jan. 1992.

[29] A. Ward, A. Jones, and A. Hopper. A new location technique for the active office. *IEEE Personal Communications*, 4(5):42–47, Oct. 1997.

[30] J. Xiong and K. Jamieson. ArrayTrack: A fine-grained indoor location system. In NSDI, 2013.

[31] J. Xiong and K. Jamieson. Securearray: improving wifi security with fine-grained physical-layer information. In *MobiCom*, 2013.

[32] Y. Yang, B. Chen, K. Srinivasan, and N. Shroff. Characterizing the achievable throughput in wireless networks with two active rf chains. In INFOCOM, 2014.

[33] Z. Yang, C. Wu, and Y. Liu. Locating in fingerprint space: Wireless indoor localization with little human intervention. In *MobiCom*, 2012.

[34] M. Youssef and A. Agrawala. Small-scale compensation for WLAN location determination systems. In WCNC, 2003.

[35] M. Youssef and A. Agrawala. The Horus WLAN location determination system. In *MobiSys*, 2005.

BBN: Throughput Scaling in Dense Enterprise WLANs with Blind Beamforming and Nulling

Wenjie Zhou†, Tarun Bansal†, Prasun Sinha and Kannan Srinivasan
Department of Computer Science and Engineering, The Ohio State University
2015 Neil Avenue, Columbus, OH 43210
{zhouwe, bansal, prasun, kannan}@cse.ohio-state.edu
†Co-primary Authors

ABSTRACT

Today's Enterprise Wireless LANs are comprised of densely deployed access points. This paper proposes BBN, an interference nulling scheme that leverages the high density of access points to enable multiple mobile devices to transmit simultaneously to multiple access points (APs), all within a single collision domain. BBN also leverages the capability of the APs to communicate with each other on the wired backbone to migrate most of the decoding complexity to the APs, while keeping the design at the mobile clients simple. Finally, we leverage the static nature of the access points to make BBN more practical in networks where the mobility of clients inhibit the use of traditional interference alignment schemes. We implement a prototype of BBN on USRP testbed showing its feasibility. The experiment results show that BBN provides a throughput gain of 1.48× over omniscient TDMA. Results from our trace-driven simulations show that BBN obtains a throughput of up to 5.6× over omniscient TDMA.

Categories and Subject Descriptors

C.2.1 [**Network Architecture and Design**]: Wireless communication, Network communications

Keywords

Enterprise Networks; Blind Beamforming and Nulling;

1. INTRODUCTION

The recent explosive growth in the number of mobile devices and the data generated by these devices has led to a decrease in the channel resources available to each individual device. Network administrators have tried to tackle this problem by densely deploying access points so that users can almost always find a closeby AP with good signal strength. However, dense deployment of APs does not scale well with the throughput demands. In the existing network protocols [18, 24], when one mobile client is transmitting uplink packets to an access point, the nearby clients have to remain silent to avoid interference to the ongoing transmission.

Recently, multiple algorithms have been proposed that help in scaling the throughput with number of wireless devices. **Interference Alignment (IA)** [7] is one of such techniques that requires clients to participate in a schedule with exponential number of slots. However, mobile clients are really mobile. They may not stay at the same place for a long time. **Multi-User MIMO (MU-MIMO) [9]** enables scaling of throughput with number of devices, but it requires APs to exchange samples over the backbone. Although, the wired backbone in Enterprise Wireless LANs (EWLANs) is underutilized [11, 6], exchanging samples requires significantly higher bandwidth compared to exchanging packets which cannot be supported by current wired networks [11, 12]. **Joint beamforming** based algorithms such as [15, 21] work only for the downlink traffic. To perform joint beamforming, these algorithms require all transmitters to share the contents of all packets to be transmitted. However, mobile devices are not connected through a wired backbone, and are unable to share the packets amongst each others.

This paper proposes BBN, the first implementation of Blind Beamforming and Nulling scheme that enables multiple nearby access points to concurrently receive uplink packets from multiple mobile clients, all within a single collision domain without overwhelming the backbone. BBN does not increase energy consumption on the clients compared to 802.11 and executes exactly over two time slots. BBN leverages three properties that are unique to EWLANs: (i) *Dense deployment of APs (See Fig. 3 and [18])*; (ii) *Capability of these APs to exchange packets with each other over the underutilized wired backbone*; and, (iii) *Immobility of APs resulting in relatively stationary channels* (See Fig. 2). When an AP is receiving uplink data, existing algorithms [18] including IEEE 802.11 WiFi, suppress nearby APs to transmit or receive data. In contrast, BBN makes use of the energy-rich access points to assist their clients (mobile devices) in decoding their packets at their respective access points. In BBN, the clients only participate in the first slot and the access points participate for the clients in the second slot.

Consider the example enterprise WLAN shown in Fig. 1(a) where all the APs and the three clients are in a single collision domain. Assume that the three users want to upload one packet each to the backbone. An omniscient TDMA scheduling algorithm with global knowledge would require three time slots to complete this upload. In BBN, in the first slot as shown in Fig. 1(a), all users will transmit at

MobiCom'14, September 7-11, 2014, Maui, Hawaii, USA.

http://dx.doi.org/10.1145/2639108.2639113 .

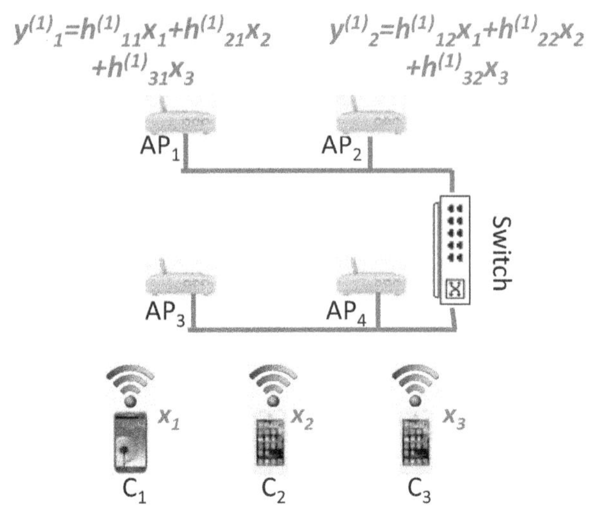

(a) First slot. x_1, x_2 and x_3 are the three packets transmitted by C_1, C_2 and C_3, respectively. $y_i^{(1)}$ are the received samples at AP_i in the first slot. $h_{ij}^{(1)}$ is the channel from client i to AP_j during time slot 1.

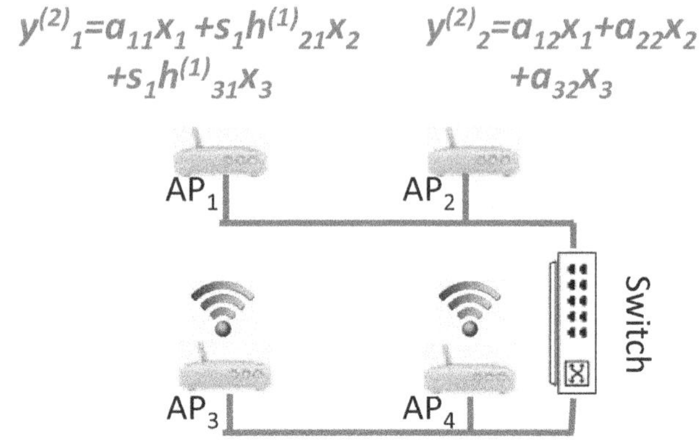

(b) Second slot. A subset of APs (AP_3 and AP_4) transmit in the second slot while the rest of the APs receive. $y_i^{(2)}$ are the received samples at AP_i in the second slot. a_{ij} are the combined channel coefficients of client i at AP_j after the transmissions of the second slot. s_i is the scaling coefficient at AP_i compared with first slot.

Figure 1: Illustration of BBN over a topology of 3 clients and 4 APs. All devices belong to the same collision domain and can hear each other. More details about the expressions are discussed in Section 2.

the same time. All the 4 APs will receive a combination of three transmitted packets. In the second slot, AP_3 and AP_4 will retransmit the received signals by first precoding [13] them such that the following condition is satisfied as shown in Fig. 1(b): At AP_1, samples corresponding to x_2 and x_3 in the second slot align with the samples corresponding to x_2 and x_3 in the first slot. Decoding happens in multiple steps as follows:

1. At the end of the second slot, AP_1 scales the samples received by AP_1 in the second slot and subtracts them from the samples received in the first slot. This scaling is done such that samples corresponding to x_2 and x_3 are *nulled*. Afterwards, it is left with only the samples corresponding to x_1. AP_1 decodes the samples to obtain the packet transmitted by C_1. Next, it transmits the decoded packet over the backbone to AP_2.

2. AP_2 recreates the samples corresponding to x_1 and subtracts them from the samples received in the first slot and the second slot.

3. After subtraction, AP_2 is left with two equations (one from each slot), and two variables (x_2 and x_3). AP_2 solves the two equations to obtain x_2 and x_3.

4. Afterwards, AP_1 and AP_2 forward x_1, x_2 and x_3 towards their destinations.

BBN enables the three transmitters with single antenna to upload three packets in two slots, improving the throughput by 50% compared to omniscient TDMA. In Section 2, we show that in networks with high enough density of APs, BBN enables N mobile clients to transmit N uplink packets in exactly two slots resulting in unbounded throughput. Also, note that BBN requires the APs to exchange only the decoded packets instead of the raw samples. Compared with our previous work RobinHood [5], which works only in a single collision domain, BBN supports multiple collision domain and is more robust to decoding failures.

The focus of BBN is to increase throughput of the uplink traffic for clients with a single antenna. This is in contrast with [21, 15] that focus on downlink traffic. Recently, uplink traffic [12, 6] has been growing at a fast rate due to the emergence of a wide-range of applications, such as cloud computing, video conferencing, online gaming, VoIP, and traffic generated from mobile devices (e.g., location information or sensor readings). BBN makes extensive use of the wired backbone. Besides transmitting the decoded packets, the channel state information, which are required to do nulling in the second slot, are also exchanged over the backbone. Since BBN migrates most of the complexity from the mobile devices to the APs, it allows BBN to work even when the channel from clients to APs is rapidly changing due to client mobility. BBN works as long as the APs are time-synchronized with each other and it places very few requirements on the clients. This paper makes the following contributions:

1. We propose a blind beamforming and nulling scheme, BBN, that scales uplink throughput with the number of access points. BBN also works over multiple collision domains.

2. This paper shows the first implementation of blind beamforming and nulling on USRP radios. Experiments performed on our testbed show that BBN achieves 1.48× throughput compared to omniscient TDMA.

3. Trace-driven simulation results show that in a large Enterprise WLAN, BBN can leverage the density of

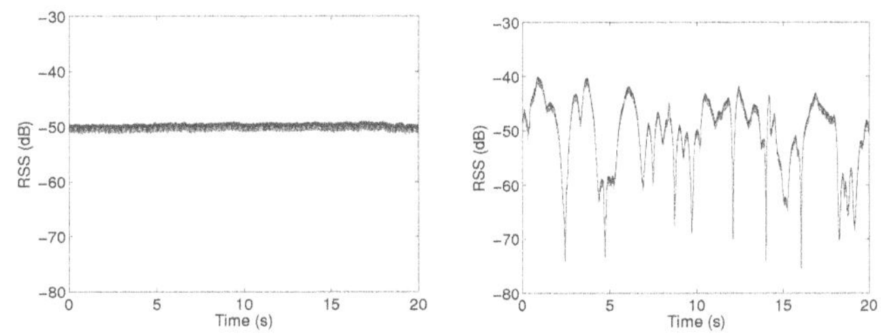

(a) Channel between a pair of APs (b) Channel between a mobile client and an AP

Figure 2: Received Signal Strength (RSS) in an office environment. The channel between APs is relatively stationary compared to channel between AP and mobile client.

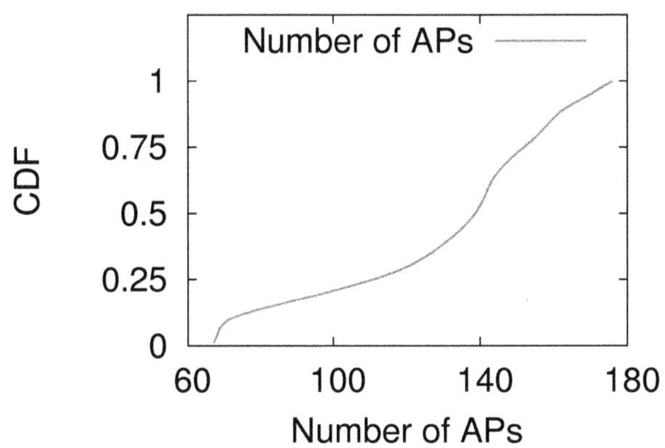

Figure 3: CDF of number of APs observed across different locations. The data was collected at multiple places including a hospital, a large university library and an apartment complex.

the access points. In EWLANs with high density of APs, BBN provides a throughput of 5.6× compared to omniscient TDMA and 52.4× compared to IEEE 802.11.

2. ILLUSTRATION

Before discussing BBN in detail, we define a few notations. All of the clients and APs in BBN are assumed to have only one antenna. The network consists of clients C_1, C_2 and C_3 and four APs from AP_1 to AP_4 that are connected through a wired backbone. Let $h_{ij}^{(1)}$ be the channel coefficient between C_i and AP_j in slot 1. In the second slot, a subset of APs are selected to transmit. For this example, this set consists of AP_3 and AP_4. Let $h_{kj}^{(2)}$ be the channel coefficient between AP_k and AP_j in slot 2. In this section, we assume that all the wireless devices are in single collision domain (*i.e.*, they can all hear each other). In Section 5, we extend BBN to networks with multiple collision domains. Let x_i be the packet sent by C_i in slot 1. In the following discussion, we ignore the presence of noise since it is not possible to null the noise. However, we do take noise into account in our analysis (See Section 4.4) and then later in our simulations (Section 7). Let $y_{ik}^{(t)}$ be the component of x_i received by AP_k in slot t. We have:

$$y_{ik}^{(1)} = h_{ik}^{(1)} x_i \tag{1}$$

Let v_k be the precoding vector for AP_k in the second slot and M be the total number of APs (In this example, we have $M = 4$). Let $y_{ij}^{(2)}$ be the component of x_i received by AP_j in slot 2. We have:

$$y_{ij}^{(2)} = \sum_{k=3}^{M} h_{kj}^{(2)} v_k y_{ik}^{(1)} = \sum_{k=3}^{M} h_{kj}^{(2)} v_k h_{ik}^{(1)} x_i \tag{2}$$

We want to ensure that components of x_2 and x_3 at AP_1 are a linear combination of their components in the first slot. Let s_i be the scaling coefficient at AP_i. Thus,

$$y_{21}^{(2)} = \sum_{k=3}^{M} h_{k1}^{(2)} v_k h_{2k}^{(1)} x_2 = s_1 y_{21}^{(1)} = s_1 h_{21}^{(1)} x_2 \tag{3}$$

$$y_{31}^{(2)} = \sum_{k=3}^{M} h_{k1}^{(2)} v_k h_{3k}^{(1)} x_3 = s_1 y_{31}^{(1)} = s_1 h_{31}^{(1)} x_3 \tag{4}$$

Simplifying these equations, we get

$$\sum_{k=3}^{M} h_{k1}^{(2)} v_k h_{2k}^{(1)} - s_1 h_{21}^{(1)} = 0 \tag{5}$$

$$\sum_{k=3}^{M} h_{k1}^{(2)} v_k h_{3k}^{(1)} - s_1 h_{31}^{(1)} = 0 \tag{6}$$

Since, the right sides of Eqs. 5 and 6 are all 0, instead of 2, at least 3 variables are required to obtain non-zero solutions. One of these variables is the scaling coefficient (s_1). Thus, a total of 2 transmitting APs are required to supply these variables. Further, two receiving APs are also required such that the first AP decodes x_1 while the second AP decodes x_2 and x_3. Thus, in total $M = 2 + 2 = 4$ APs are required to support 3 clients as in Fig. 1.

In BBN, for the network shown in Fig. 1, at the end of slot 1, AP 3 and AP 4 solve Eqs. 5 and 6 to obtain precoding vectors which are then used during slot 2 (See Eq. 2). This computation may take time (due to communication among APs over the backbone). In general wireless networks, this creates inaccuracies since the channel between APs and the mobile clients may change from the time the channel state information (CSI) was measured to the time when the APs retransmit the data in the second slot. Thus, the precoding vectors that were computed based on old CSI may not be suitable for the channel's current state. This may lead to inaccurate beamforming and nulling. However, in BBN, the mobile clients do not participate in the second slot. Only the APs transmit and receive data in the second slot. Due to the immobile nature of the APs, the channel (or CSI) between APs changes very slowly (See Fig. 2(a)). Thus, the CSI computed among APs is valid for longer duration compared to CSI between mobile clients and APs. *By requiring only the APs to transmit in the second slot, BBN ensures higher accuracy of joint beamforming and joint nulling.*

Number of APs required: In general, if there are N clients in the network, then BBN needs to align $(N-1)$ packets at the first AP, $(N-2)$ packets at the second AP and so on. Thus, a total of at least $(N-1)+(N-2)+\cdots+2 = \frac{N^2-N-2}{2}$ variables are required to satisfy all the constraints. However, to obtain a non-zero solution, we need to include one extra AP, *i.e.* a total of $\frac{N^2-N}{2}$ APs. However, $N-2$ of the variables are supplied by the scaling coefficients at the receiving APs. Thus, a total of $\frac{N^2-N}{2}-(N-2)=\frac{N^2-3N+4}{2}$ transmitting APs are required. Finally, $N-1$ receiving APs are also required in slot 2, where the first $N-2$ receiving APs decode one unique packet while the last AP decodes 2 packets. Therefore, with $\frac{N^2-3N+4}{2}+N-1=\frac{N^2-N+2}{2}$ APs, BBN can leverage this high density of APs to decode N uplink packets in exactly two slots. Further, in contrast to [5], BBN requires N fewer APs.

3. CHALLENGES

Note that when the APs (*i.e.*, AP_3 and AP_4) in slot 2 transmit, they have to align the samples of x_2 and x_3 at AP_1. To achieve this, they precode the signals that they received in the first slot and transmit. However, in contrast to the existing solutions [21], in BBN, the transmitting APs are not aware of what they are transmitting (since they are unable to decode the samples received in the first slot). We call this *Blind Beamforming and Nulling*. Although the idea behind BBN is simple, there are multiple challenges that need to be handled to make it practical.

1. **Oblivious to the contents of the transmitted signal:** The APs transmitting in slot 2 are not aware of the contents of the signals transmitted in slot 2. Despite this, they need to cancel out (or align) the different contents of the signal at different receiving APs.

2. **Synchronization**: In order for the APs transmitting in slot 2 to align their signals at the receiving APs, these transmitting APs are required to be synchronized at the sample level. This requirement is similar to the requirements of the other existing algorithms that focus on downlink traffic [21, 15, 20]. Observe that BBN does not impose synchronization requirement on the mobile clients.

3. **Multi-collision domain:** The previous discussion assumes that all clients and all APs can hear each other directly. However, this may not be true for large scale EWLANs. Thus, we need a mechanism to extend BBN to such networks.

4. **Inconsistency in the AP density:** To decode N packets, BBN requires $\frac{N^2-N+2}{2}$ access points nearby. However, the actual number of APs present may be higher or lower than this number. If the number of available APs is higher, then BBN can make use of all of them. On the other hand, if the number of available APs is smaller, than a mechanism is required to select a subset of the clients.

5. **Robustness:** Unlike downlink [21], where each client individually decodes its own packet, in BBN, decoding happens in a cascading fashion. Decoding of a packet depends on the successful decoding of the previous packets. Clearly, in such a design, failure in decoding of one packet, makes all future decodings unsuccessful. We need a new mechanism to increase the robustness of the decoding.

How we handle these challenges are explained in the next two sections.

4. PHYSICAL LAYER DESIGN

In this section, we explain the physical layer working of BBN using three different phases. First, we explain how multiple clients transmit simultaneously to the APs and how the channel state information between clients and APs is estimated. Then, we show how the APs conduct blind-beamforming and nulling without knowing the contents of the transmitted signals. Finally, the decoding process is explained. In BBN, the clients participate in only the first phase while the APs participate in all the three phases.

4.1 Phase I: Client transmission

As explained in Section 2, the transmissions in BBN are divided into two slots. In the first slot, the clients transmit concurrently to the APs. Besides the received combined samples from the clients to APs, the channel state information (CSI) between all the clients and APs is also computed in this phase. To obtain the CSIs, each client sends an access code (or unique PN sequences [17] assigned to each client) that is free of interference.

The transmission timeline of Phase I is shown in Fig. 4. First, the APs broadcast an *approve* message. This message contains the IDs of the clients that are allowed to transmit in this slot (For more details on how the APs select the subset of clients, refer to Section 5 that describes the MAC design of BBN). The relative order of the IDs determines the time when a client should transmit its access code. Since the clients are not synchronized, the transmission of access codes may partially overlap with each other due to wireless propagation delay. To avoid this overlap, a small time gap, called inter-access-code-space (IACS), is inserted between the transmissions. Finally, after the transmission of access codes, the clients transmit their packets simultaneously. All the APs compute the CSI from different clients using the interference-free access codes and also store the received samples corresponding to the data packets. In our experiments and simulations, we set the duration of IACS to $2\mu s$, which is enough to compensate for the propagation delay if the maximum distance between the clients and APs is no more than 300 meters.

To conduct blind-beamforming, besides the CSIs between the clients and APs, the CSIs between the transmitting APs and receiving APs are also required. As shown in Fig. 4, all of the APs broadcast their access codes one after the other. When one AP broadcasts, all other APs can estimate the CSI from that AP. The estimated CSIs along with the CSIs between clients and APs are forwarded to a *group-head AP* through the wired backbone network. The head AP, uses these CSIs to compute the best sets of transmitting APs, the set of receiving APs, the decoding order, and the precoding vector to be used by each of the transmitting AP. This information is then sent back by the group-head AP to every AP in the group. In Fig. 5, AP_3 and AP_4 are selected as the transmitting APs.

This computation at the group-head AP and the distribution of result back to APs may take some time due to delays over the wired backbone. To ensure that all APs have received the computed results back from the group-head AP, BBN requires all APs to wait for Backbone-Inter-Frame-Space (BIFS) duration.

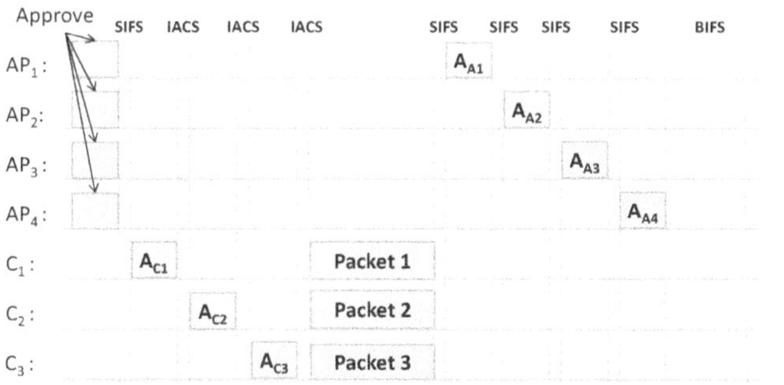

Figure 4: Phase I time-line: A_{Ci} and A_{Aj} represent the access codes for C_i and AP_j, respectively.

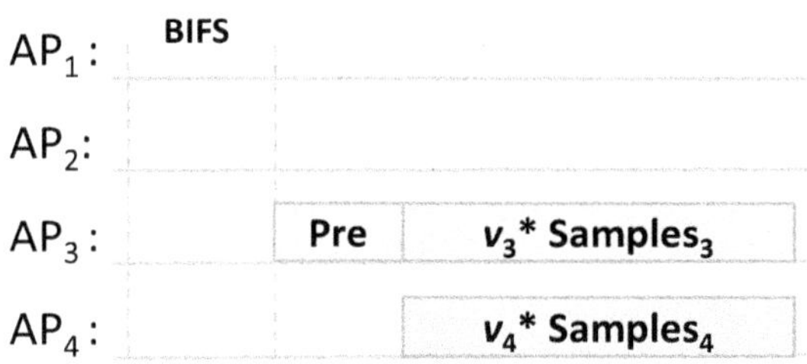

Figure 5: Phase II time-line: v_i denotes the precoding vector of AP_i.

4.2 Phase II: Blind-beamforming

After waiting for BIFS time, all APs multiply the samples received in the first slot with their precoding vectors and retransmit them (See Fig. 5). The value of BIFS can be selected on the basis of the speed of the Ethernet and the expected delays involved. To avoid wastage of wireless channel during BIFS, APs in BBN participate in another set of communication (*e.g.*, downlink traffic) while waiting to hear back from the group-head AP. Observe that since the APs are relatively stationary, the precoding vectors computed by group-head AP are valid for a long duration as described in Section 2. Further, due to the relatively stationary channel among APs, we do not need to frequently measure the channel among APs which further reduces the overhead incurred during Phase I. The short packet **Pre** sent by AP_3 is a sequence known to all of the APs. The purpose of sending this sequence is two fold: 1.) it can be viewed as a preamble for the receiving APs to detect the correct start point of the retransmission; 2.) it can be used to estimate the sampling offset between the transmitting APs and receiving APs using the same techniques as in packet subtraction [6, 10].

4.3 Phase III: Decoding Packets

In BBN, the packets are decoded in a sequential order. The first AP decodes one packet and sends it to the next AP which, upon receiving the packet, recreates the received samples, and then subtracts those samples from the received samples. The remaining samples are decoded to obtain the second packet. This process is continued until all packets have been decoded. Performing a successful subtraction requires estimating various offsets such as frequency offset, sampling offset, and phase offset. Once the offsets have been estimated, the AP needs to recreate the received samples. This sequential decoding and packet subtraction have been well-studied in the literature [6, 10]. We refer the reader to the existing literature.

Another practical issue to note is that there is sampling offset between the transmitting APs and the receiving APs in the second slot. This offset makes it difficult to align the components of x_2 and x_3 received by AP_1 in the second slot with the corresponding components received in the first slot. To that end, the packet **Pre** as explained in the previous section can be used to estimate the offset.

4.4 Computing the Packet Decoding Order

In the previous discussion (Sec. 2), we assumed that x_1 is decoded first, followed by x_2 and x_3. We also assumed that joint precoding leaves no residual noise. However, in practice, joint precoding and packet subtraction are not perfect and leave some residual noise. Thus, in this section, we compute the optimal order in which packets should be decoded such that the decoding accuracy is maximized in the presence of the residual noise. To determine the optimal decoding order, we need to compute the expected received signal strength (RSS) of each packet (say x_i) at each AP (say AP_j). The exact value of RSS depends on the precoding vectors which in turn depend on the rest of the matching. This makes the problem combinatorial in nature.

We compute the expected RSS of client i at AP_j using a heuristic. In the second slot, let AP_N to AP_M be the set of transmitting APs and AP_1 to AP_{N-1} be the set of receiving APs. Observe that in the second slot, AP_j receives components of x_i that have been retransmitted by all APs in the range AP_N to AP_M. Thus, components of x_i arrive at AP_j through $M - N + 1$ different paths. Each of these $M - N + 1$ paths start at client i, pass through some transmitting AP (say AP_k) and end at AP_j. Further, each of these paths consist of two links: First from C_i to AP_k and, second from AP_k to AP_j. We say that RSS_{ij} is expected to be high only if there is at least one path on which x_i has high signal strength on both the links. If P_0 is the transmission power level, then, we can estimate the RSS of x_i at AP_j as follows:

$$RSS_{ij} \approx P_0 \times \max_{k=N...M} \left(\min \left(||h_{ik}^{(1)}||^2, ||h_{kj}^{(2)}||^2 \right) \right) \quad (7)$$

Consider client C_i that transmits packet x_i at data-rate R_i. Let AP_j be the receiving AP that decodes x_i. If τ_i is the minimum SNR required to decode x_i where τ_i depends on the physical layer data rate, then the residual noise that can be tolerated at AP_j during the decoding is given by [6]: $\frac{RSS_{ij}}{\tau_i}$. Using this, BBN computes the maximum residual noise that each packet can tolerate. Let us say AP_j decodes the ith packet in the decoding sequence.

Observe that in BBN the packets are decoded sequentially. So, if a packet is not decoded correctly, then all other packets that depend on it can't be decoded either. So, in order to improve the decoding probability of all the packets, the decoding order is chosen by arranging the packets in non-increasing order of the maximum residual noise that they can tolerate.

5. MAC DESIGN

In this section, we first explain how BBN works in large scale networks. Next, we explain how BBN leverages the variation in the density of access points to improve the throughput of the uplink traffic. Finally, we explain how BBN co-exists with ongoing downlink traffic in the network.

5.1 Multi-Collision Domain

The previous sections describe how BBN works in a single collision domain. To work in a practical multi-collision domain, BBN needs to solve multiple challenges:

1. In a multi-collision domain network, an AP may not be able to hear all other APs. This makes it difficult to synchronize them since one of the best performning algorithms with high synchronization accuracy [20] works only within a single collision domain.
2. The traffic distribution may be different across different parts of the network. For example, some parts of network may experience higher downlink traffic compared to others.
3. The MAC algorithm should ensure fairness across different clients.
4. Previous discussion of BBN requires that all cooperating APs and all clients are able to hear each other. Satisfying this requirement is challenging since frequent mobility of clients requires frequent re-computations.

BBN as described in Section 2 requires that: (i) **All cooperating APs should be able to hear each other**; and, (ii) **All APs should be able to hear all clients**. So, one naive way of extending BBN to multi-collision networks would be to arrange both the APs and clients in groups such that within each group all APs and all clients can hear each other. However, this naive approach would require frequent re-computation of groups due to client mobility.

To ensure that BBN works with mobile networks without requiring frequent re-computations, we divide the EWLAN into cliques of APs while only satisfying the first requirement. Satisfying that requirement implies decomposing the graph into as few cliques of APs as possible. Since, decomposing graphs into fewest cliques is an NP-Hard problem, BBN uses a greedy polynomial-time algorithm to compute such cliques. Our polynomial-time algorithm repeatedly finds a maximal clique among all APs. Then, it removes the vertices (and the edges incident on them) that are part of the maximal clique. The algorithm then runs on the remaining graph to find the maximal clique. This process is repeated until every AP is a part of some clique. All the APs that are in the same maximal clique, form a single *group*. This decomposition algorithm can be run by a central server similar to [24, 15]. *Ensuring that all APs in the same group can hear each other allows BBN to leverage the existing synchronization algorithms (such as SourceSync [20]) to synchronize all the APs that are part of the same group.*

Observe that since the APs are immobile, once the membership of different groups has been computed, it can be used for long periods of time. It is possible that an AP may not be able to hear a client that belongs to the same group. Thus, grouping based on APs only satisfies the first requirement specified above while the second requirement may be violated. We handle this in Subsection 5.2.1.

Computing neighbor relationship among groups: To prevent interference from neighboring groups and to keep groups independent, BBN ensures that at any time if the APs belonging to group G are communicating, then the APs belonging to neighboring groups should not communicate. Two groups (say G_i and G_j) are said to be neighbors of each other if (i) There exists a wireless device (an AP or a client) in G_i that is in the interference range of a wireless device in G_j; or, (ii) There exists a wireless device (an AP or a client) in G_j that is in the interference range of a wireless device in G_i. To decouple the dependence of neighbor-relation from the location of mobile clients, BBN takes a conservative approach such that G_i and G_j are called neighbors even if there could potentially exist a client that can be in the transmission range of some AP in G_i while being in the interference range of some AP in G_j. *By decoupling the neighbor relationship from the location of mobile clients, BBN significantly reduces the overhead that may otherwise arise due to frequent re-computations.*

Scheduling different groups: To ensure that two neighboring groups are not transmitting simultaneously, BBN uses a central server [21, 15, 24] that manages the interference among neighboring groups. Since the schedule length in BBN is always two slots across all the groups, it makes it convenient for the server to schedule the active groups. In BBN, at any time t, the server computes the set of groups that will communicate for the next two slots (t and $t+1$). This set is computed using maximum independent set techniques such that two groups are allowed to transmit/receive simultaneously only if they do not interfere with each other. However, due to unexpected delays on the wired backbone, the latency from the central server to the APs may result in APs unnecessarily waiting for the control messages from the server while the wireless channel is idle. To avoid this waiting, the server in BBN proactively computes the schedule and transmits it to the APs over the backbone.

Client-AP association: In BBN, clients do not permanently associate with any specific AP or a group. The clients simply wait for the *poll* packet from any neighboring AP and transmit uplink data as soon as they receive the corresponding *approve* packet as shown in Fig. 6. The *poll* packet is a special control packet that is broadcast by the APs, requesting the clients to reply if they have any uplink packet. *By keeping the clients stateless, BBN reduces the control messages exchanged between APs and clients.*

ACK transmission: In BBN, the APs decode the packets during Phase 3. After decoding, the APs send ACK over the wireless to the clients as shown in Fig. 6.

Downlink traffic: Uplink transmissions in BBN can co-exist with downlink traffic. Each group in BBN can either perform downlink transmissions or uplink transmissions, independently of the other groups. For downlink communication, existing algorithms [21, 15, 24] can be used. The central server used in BBN can also be used for managing downlink interference as in the existing algorithms [15, 24].

5.2 Computing the set of transmitting clients

In a system with N clients and $\frac{N^2-N+2}{2}$ APs, BBN guarantees that each client can transmit 1 packet every two slots. Within a single group, it is possible that the number of APs may not be high enough to support all the clients. In that case, the group-head AP selects a subset of clients that would transmit in the first time slot. To ensure fairness among clients, BBN uses a weighted credit based system [15] such that the credit of a client is high if it has not been scheduled for a long period of time. Thus, the clients with the highest credit are given priority to transmit. This is further described in Section 5.2.1.

Fig. 6 explains the complete working of BBN. Initially, the APs in a group (if allowed by the central server) poll the network for uplink traffic. To make sure that all of the clients are able to receive the poll message, the APs broadcast the same poll message simultaneously. This is followed by a contention period in which different clients transmit short packets conveying their credit balance to contend for the uplink transmission. At the same time, all APs in the group hear for such packets and forward them to the "group-head AP". The group-head AP upon receiving the forwarded packets from all APs computes the set of clients that are allowed to transmit their data packets. This information is conveyed by the group-head AP back to the other APs. Next, all the APs simultaneously broadcast the *Approve* message that contains the list of clients that are allowed to transmit in this slot. Finally, the approved clients transmit their data packets which are decoded by the APs in three phases as described in Section 4. Broadcasting simultaneously requires the APs to be synchronized with each other. However, since all APs can hear each other, we achieve this synchronization using SourceSync as discussed before. This information exchange among APs may take some time due to non-zero latency over the wired backbone. During this time, the APs may utilize the wireless channel for other transmissions.

On the other hand, it is also possible that the number of clients are low while there are more APs available (*e.g.*, in highly dense networks such as in Fig. 3). In that case, BBN can leverage the extra APs to further improve the robustness of decoding as discussed in Section 5.3.

5.2.1 Approve *algorithm*

In each group, a single AP is elected as the *group-head AP* that executes the *Approve* algorithm to compute the set of clients that are allowed to transmit. *Approve* (Algorithm 1) greedily computes the schedule. In each iteration, it adds the client with the highest credit value to the schedule (Line 8), thereby improving fairness. For such a client, it picks the best AP (say AP_j) that has not yet been paired with some other client (Lines 11-15). Next, Approve tries to add this client-AP pair to the schedule S and checks if S is still satisfiable (Lines 16-18). This check is done by Algorithm *Satisfiable*. If this pair makes S unsatisfiable (Lines 19-21), then the pair is removed from S. Also, C_i is marked as ineligible since it cannot be paired with any AP. This process is repeated until no more client-AP pairs can be added to S (Lines 9-10).

Algorithm *Satisfiable* determines if a given schedule is satisfiable or not. When doing this computation, *Satisfiable* takes into account the set of clients that each AP can hear. Without loss of generality, let S be the schedule such that $S = \{(C_i, AP_i) : AP_i$ is the receiving AP for packet x_i and x_i is the ith packet to be decoded$\}$. *Satisfiable* should return true if for every client-AP pair, say (C_i, AP_i), it can find a subset of $i-1$ unique APs in the same group that can align x_i at the receiving APs (AP_1 to AP_{i-1}). In other words, for every client-AP pair, say (C_i, AP_i), *Satisfiable* needs to find $i-1$ other APs that are in the transmission range of C_i. This computation can be done by reducing this problem to a Max Flow problem. We refer the reader to the technical report [1] for detailed discussion.

Algorithm 1: *Approve*: Computes the set of clients that will be approved in this slot

1 **Input:** For every eligible packet P_i, its transmitter C_i. Also, information on which AP can hear which client.
2 **Output:** (i) Set of clients that will be approved in this slot. (ii) The matching from the approved clients to the APs indicating which AP decodes which packet. (iii) The decoding order.
`// Set eligibility of all clients to true`
3 $E_i \leftarrow true\ \forall i : 1 \le i \le N$
4 $\mathcal{A} \leftarrow$ All APs in the current group
`// S is an ordered schedule that tells us which AP decodes which packet. The client-AP pairs are arranged in the order in which they are decoded.`
5 $S \leftarrow \{\}$
6 **while** *true* **do**
7 $\quad CSet \leftarrow \{C_x : E_x = true$ and $C_x \notin S\}$
8 $\quad C_i \leftarrow C_i \in CSet$ and C_i has the highest credit balance
9 $\quad$ **if** $C_i = null$ **then**
10 $\quad\quad$ **return** S
11 $\quad Set \leftarrow \{(C_i, AP_j) : AP_j \notin S\}$
12 $\quad (C_i, AP_j) \leftarrow (C_i, AP_j) \in Set$ and RSS_{ij} is maximum
13 $\quad$ **if** $AP_j = null$ **then**
14 $\quad\quad E_i \leftarrow false$
15 $\quad\quad$ **continue**
16 $\quad S \leftarrow S \cup \{(C_i, AP_j)\}$
17 $\quad$ Compute the decoding order in S based on the residual noise tolerance.
18 $\quad isSatisfiable \leftarrow Satisfiable(S, \mathcal{A})$
19 $\quad$ **if** $isSatisfiable = false$ **then**
20 $\quad\quad E_i \leftarrow false$
21 $\quad\quad S \leftarrow S \backslash \{(C_i, AP_j)\}$
22 **return** S

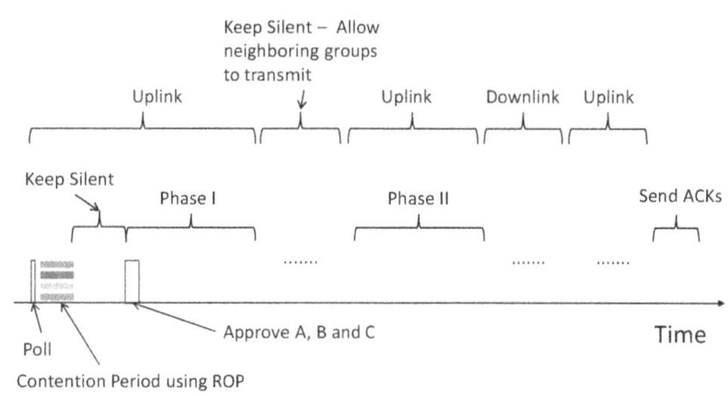

Figure 6: Timeline of data transmission in a large network. The data sent by clients during contention phase are transmitted using the Rapid OFDM Polling (ROP) [30] scheme to decrease overhead. All nodes keep silent after ROP and wait for the group-head AP to calculate and distribute the *Approve* message through the backbone network. Phase III is executed in the background over the wired backbone allowing wireless channel to be used for other purposes.

5.3 Robustness

In BBN, the first AP decodes one packet while $N-1$ packets are nulled using blind beamforming. The second AP decodes the second packet (while the other $N-2$ packets are nulled using blind beamforming) and so on. Thus, if an AP cannot decode a packet due to inaccuracies in blind beamforming or packet subtraction, then all the following packets that depend on it can also not be decoded. Therefore, to ensure that the first few packets in the decoding order can be decoded with high probability, BBN leverages the high density of APs. Specifically, BBN increases the decoding robustness of the packets if the number of APs present in a group are more than the minimum required (See Sec. 2).

Let $C_1, C_2, C_i, \cdots, C_N$ be the order in which the clients are decoded (See Section 4.4). Let the number of APs in the group be M and E be the number of extra APs that are present such that $E = M - \frac{N^2-N+2}{2}$. Recall that exactly $N-i$ packets are nulled (or aligned) at the AP that decodes the packet from client C_i. If we require one of the extra APs to independently decode the packet from C_i, then we will need another $N-i$ extra transmitting APs to ensure that packets from $C_{i+1}, C_{i+2}, \cdots, C_N$ are nulled at this extra AP. Thus, to decode the packet from C_i at two different APs, we need an additional $N-i+1$ APs (including one extra AP for receiving).

BBN increases the decoding robustness as follows: The APs in BBN find the *first* client C_i in the decoding sequence that satisfies the two requirements: (i) The packet from C_i is decoded at only one AP; and, (ii) $E \geq N-i+1$. Let C_i be the first client in the decoding sequence that satisfies the two constraints. Then, BBN ensures that the packet transmitted by C_i can be independently decoded by two different APs. BBN decreases E by $N-i+1$ since this is the number of APs required to achieve independent decoding of C_i. Finally, this process is repeated as long as possible to achieve independent decodings of some packets. Thus, in highly dense networks, BBN leverages the extra APs present in the network to further increase the decoding probability of each packet. Even if extra APs are not available, BBN can restrict the number of clients that transmit simultaneously. This frees up some APs that can be used for increasing the robustness of decoding. Currently, we leave the problem of proactively reducing the number of transmitters to increase the decoding robustness as our future work.

6. EXPERIMENTS

6.1 Setup

We evaluate BBN in a testbed with 7 USRP N210 nodes. The setup is as follows:

1. **Hardware and software setup:** Each USRP is equipped with a WBX daughterboard and operates in the 400 MHz band. All nodes are within single collision domain. At the receiver side, we use the GNURadio for signal processing. The decoding is done offline in Matlab. All of the AP nodes are synchronized with an external clock source generated by OctoClock-G [2]. In practice, SourceSync [20] can be used to synchronize the transmitting APs to a nanosecond level accuracy.

2. **OFDM and modulation setup:** We use a 512 FFT system, with 200 subcarriers used for data transmitting. The cyclic prefix length is set to 128. Unless otherwise mentioned, Binary Phase Shift Keying (BPSK) is used as the modulation scheme. The sampling rate is set to 1MHz.

Apart from implementing BBN, we also implemented **Omniscient TDMA** that utilizes a central server. This server is aware of (i) packet queue at different clients; and, (ii) the channel between all clients and all APs. Omni-TDMA schedules the three different clients in a round-robin fashion with each client transmitting to the AP to which it has the best channel.

6.2 Micro-Benchmarks

Many works have shown the effectiveness of beamforming [21, 11]. Since our blind-beamforming and nulling involves transmitting unknown samples, its effectiveness and accuracy is unclear. In this section, we evaluate the performance of blind-beamforming and nulling using the signal to interference and noise ratio (SINR). In the following experiments, 3 clients and 4 APs were deployed in our testbed as shown in Fig. 1.

6.2.1 *Blind-beamforming and Nulling Effects*

First of all, we study the blind-beamforming and nulling effect as described in Section 4. Since there are a total of 12 links between all APs and clients, it is difficult to control the SNR of every link. Instead, we place the clients and APs randomly in our testbed and record the actual SNRs. We repeat the experiment 20 times for each of the 50 randomly chosen topologies. Over various topologies, the SNR between clients and APs varied from 6 dB to 35 dB. We compute the final interference to noise ratio (INR) of packet x_1 when it is decoded by AP_1. The INR distribution is shown in Fig. 7(a). The median of the INR is 0.7 dB, which is just slightly above the noise floor, and the 90th percentile INR is 3.7 dB. This indicates that residual interference from blind-beamforming and nulling is relatively small and demonstrates the practicality of BBN.

The INR distribution in Fig. 7(a) shows that it could be as high as 10 dB, which is a large value compared with typical SNR values, *e.g.*, 20 dB. We look deeper into the INR results and present it in an another way in Fig. 7(b). The y-axis is the final INR of packet x_1 at AP_1. The x-axis is the range of signal to interference ratio (SIR) in dB that x_1 experiences in the first slot across all of the APs. The smaller the value on the x-axis, the higher the amount of interference to be cancelled in the second slot. This figure shows that as the SIR increases, the final INR decreases. When the first slot SIR is larger than -12 dB, the median of the that is 0.6 dB and the 90th percentile is 2.7 dB (Fig. 7(b)). Based on this result, we can enable BBN when the SIR value is larger than a threshold and fall back to the default IEEE 802.11 scheme when the SIR value is small. We leave the study of computing the exact threshold value as future work.

6.2.2 *Sampling Offset*

As discussed in Section 4.3, there is sampling offset between the samples received by AP_1 from phase I and phase II. To study the effect of the sampling offset, we turn off the sampling offset correction in BBN and compute the residual interference to noise ratio for x_1. The result shown in Fig. 7(a) shows that without sampling offset correction, the median INR increases by 1.1 dB and the 90th percentile increases by 2.2 dB. This demonstrates that the sampling offset correction done in BBN reduces the residual interference.

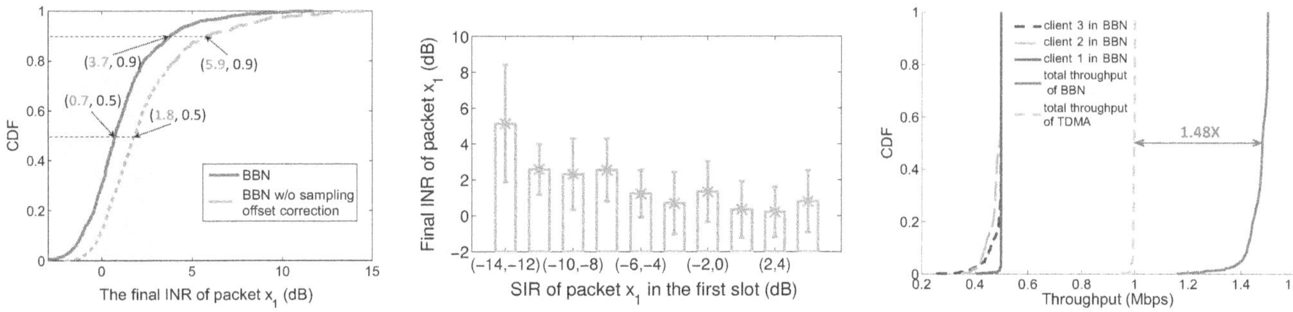

(a) Final INR distribution of x_1 at the first decoding AP. The median of the INR is 0.7 dB and the 90th percentile INR is 3.7 dB.

(b) Final INR of the packet x_1 at the first decoding AP.

(c) Throughput of BBN compared to Omniscient TDMA.

Figure 7: Experiment results collected over USRP testbed.

6.3 Throughput

In this section, we study the throughput performance of BBN. The throughput of each client in BBN is recorded and compared with that of omniscient TDMA. A total of 20000 packets are transmitted by each client across different topologies. Fig. 7(c) shows that on an average, BBN provides a throughput gain of 1.48× compared with omniscient TDMA. The figure also shows the throughput of client 1 is higher than that of clients 2 and 3. This is because x_2 and x_3 are decoded only if x_1 is decoded. Further, even if x_1 is decoded, x_2 and x_3 may not be decoded due to the residual interference from subtraction.

7. TRACE-DRIVEN SIMULATION

This section explains the setup and the results from the trace-driven simulations.

7.1 Simulation Setup

Apart from implementing BBN, we also implemented two other algorithms: (i) **Omniscient TDMA algorithm:** Described before in Section 6. However, this time similar to BBN, Omniscient TDMA also uses a credit-based system where a client has high credit value if it has not transmitted for a long time. In each slot, it schedules a maximum independent set of "client to AP" links (where weight of link = credit of the client × throughput of the client when using that link). The physical layer rate of a link is chosen by picking the highest data rate that can be decoded by the AP; and, (ii) **IEEE 802.11g (without RTS/CTS).** To evaluate the gain provided by BBN irrespective of the downlink algorithm used, only the uplink traffic from clients to APs was generated. Various traces were incorporated into the simulation: (i) **Noise due to Blind Beamforming and Nulling:** The simulator incorporated noise arising due to imperfect nulling. For this, we used the traces collected from our experiments (See Fig. 7(a)). (ii) **Noise due to subtraction:** When an AP subtracts a packet, it has to recreate its samples and correct for various offsets such as sampling offset and frequency offset. An imperfect correction leads to imperfect subtraction resulting in residual noise. The simulator incorporated this residual noise using the traces collected by us in experiments. (iii) **Path Loss between clients and APs:** Incorporated from the traces [25]. (iv) **Path Loss between APs:** Incorporated from the traces [25]. For simplicity, the packets were assumed to be of constant length (1500 bytes). In practice, one may use packet aggregation to avoid the overhead induced by small sized packets. In this section, we study the behavior of BBN in a large EWLAN that spans over multiple collision domains (*e.g.*, the campus of a university). Our simulator first randomly deploys 1000 clients in a field of size 500m × 500m. APs are also deployed randomly and the number of APs is varied. In this setup, different devices may belong to different groups as described in Section 5. The overhead of different protocols was taken into account during the simulation. For BBN, this includes the overhead of all the control packets in both wired and wireless domains. As discussed in previous sections, when the APs are exchanging control packets over the backbone for the purpose of computing the set of approved clients or for computing the precoding vectors, at that time the wireless channel can be utilized for other transmissions. In the simulation also, during these periods, the central server allows the neighboring groups to use the wireless channel for their transmissions. Also, APs in BBN used extra APs to further increase the decoding robustness as described in Section 5.3. Finally, clients in BBN and IEEE 802.11 used the Auto Rate Fallback (ARF) algorithm to determine the physical layer data rate.

7.2 Results

Next, we describe the results from our trace-driven simulations.

1. **Total Throughput across all clients:** Throughput increases for all algorithms as they leverage the increase in the physical layer data rate (See Fig. 8(a)). For 802.11, the increase is not substantial since a large number of collisions (due to hidden terminals) reduces the number of successful transmissions. With increase in number of APs, the throughput in BBN increases because of two reasons: (i) Higher AP density implies more APs are present in each group, resulting in higher throughput since more clients can be supported at the same time; and, (ii) Higher data rate at clients due to

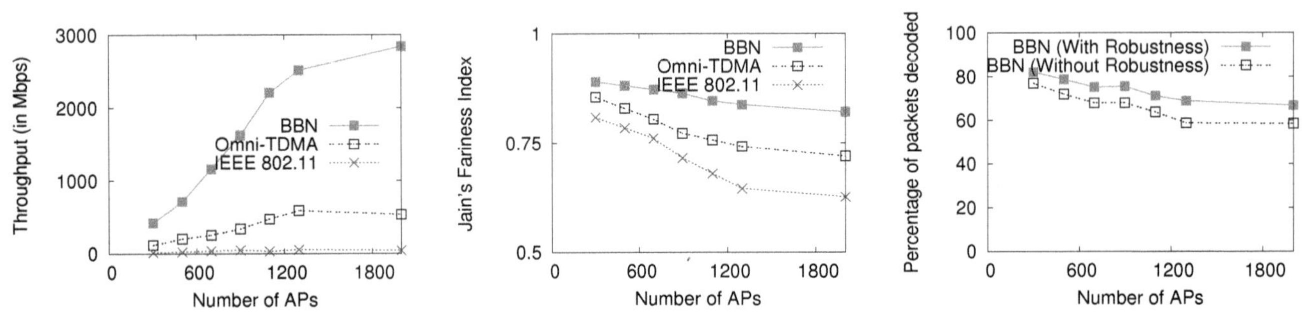

(a) Total Throughput (b) Jain's Fairness Index (c) Percentage of packets decoded

Figure 8: Trace-Driven Simulation Results for Multi-Collision Domain

higher AP density. As the density of the APs increase, throughput in BBN increases substantially compared to TDMA. When the number of APs is 2000, each client is in the range of an average of 76 APs. At that density, BBN throughput is 5.6× compared to TDMA, and 52.4× compared to IEEE 802.11. This is lower than the expected gain since in BBN, clients use ARF to adjust their physical layer data rate while clients in Omniscient TDMA transmit at the best possible data rate.

2. **Fairness:** Fig. 8(b) shows the variation in Jain's fairness index with variation in number of APs. IEEE 802.11 has very low fairness since a client may get starved if it is in the range of multiple APs. The fairness index of BBN is higher than other algorithms since BBN allows all clients to transmit. BBN has higher fairness than TDMA since BBN performs precoding over transmissions from all clients. Thus, even the clients that are far away from all APs may experience high throughput due to beamforming from multiple helper APs.

3. **Decoding probability:** As the density of the network becomes higher, the length of the decoding chain increases. Thus, a decoding failure on one packet implies a decoding failure on all the other packets that depend on it. Fig. 8(c) shows the percentage of packets decoded successfully decreases with increase in density. However, still the throughput in BBN increases (See Fig. 8(a)) since higher density enables multiple clients in APs to transmit successfully. Further, with high density of APs, BBN can use robustness techniques discussed in Section 5.3 to increase the decoding probability. Fig. 8(c) also shows the decoding probability when BBN does not use robustness techniques described before. With the increase in number of APs, there is a higher chance that BBN can leverage those APs to improve robustness. Thus, with increasing density, the improvement provided by robustness further increase.

8. DISCUSSION

In this section, we discuss some further modifications that make BBN more practical.

Reducing overhead of channel estimation: To compute the precoding vectors, the APs in BBN require the knowledge of channel between all clients and APs as well as the channel between all APs. The problem of computing the channel from clients to APs has been well studied in the context of MIMO networks [11, 29]. To compute the channel values, we plan to use PN sequences to estimate the channel from multiple transmitters simultaneously [16].

Overhead on the backbone: In BBN when decoding N uplink packets, the APs need to exchange $\frac{(N-1)\times(N-2)}{2}$ data packets. This is in contrast with [21] that requires exchange of $(N-1)\times(N)$ data packets when performing joint beamforming for the downlink traffic. In a MU-MIMO system where APs exchange sample information through the backbone, the overhead on the backbone is almost $23N$ packets if the data rate is 24 Mbps (16 QAM, 1/2 coding rate) and the 802.11a standard is used. BBN introduces less overhead on the backbone compared to MU-MIMO if the number of clients is no more than **24**, while achieving the same throughput gain of $N/2$. In addition, APs in BBN also need to exchange relatively smaller control packets related to channel state information, scheduling etc. The number of participating clients can be adjusted based on how much overhead can be tolerated on the wired backbone.

APs with multiple antennas: If the APs are equipped with multiple antennas, BBN can leverage them to reduce the number of required APs. Specifically, if each AP is equipped with K antennas, then to receive N uplink packets simultaneously, BBN would require only $\frac{N'^2-N'+2}{2K}$ APs where $N' = N-(K-1)$, a reduction by a factor of more than K. On the other hand, with M APs each with K antennas, BBN can support around $\sqrt{2MK}+K$ clients instead of $\sqrt{2M}$ clients with one antenna per AP.

Packet Aggregation: In practice, packet sizes can be different and clients may pick different data rates, resulting in different uplink transmission durations. However, the transmissions in BBN are scheduled slot by slot. This slot based scheduling may result in a waste of channel resources since the transmission of some clients may not take the whole slot duration. To solve this problem, we use the same technique, packet aggregation, as in 802.11n standard. More specifically, we aggregate and split packets based on the data rates to create virtual packets that take exactly one slot to transmit.

9. RELATED WORK

Although BBN builds on several prior work, it differs from them in various ways.

Backbone usage: The idea of using the wired backbone to increase wireless throughput is not new. In MegaMIMO[21], multiple APs cooperatively precode the transmissions such that each client receives only the packets intended for it while the other transmissions are canceled out. However, MegaMIMO requires that transmitters exchange packets among themselves and thus, it works only for the downlink transmissions. On the other hand, BBN improves the throughput for the uplink traffic. Also, in contrast to MegaMIMO and OpenRF [15], transmitters in BBN jointly perform nulling without knowing the actual contents of the packets.

A recently proposed protocol Symphony [6] also focuses on uplink traffic. However, in contrast to BBN, Symphony improves the network throughput only when the APs are in different collision domains. In Epicenter [12], authors propose that APs should exchange coarse representations of symbols to decode corrupted bits. Similarly, authors in [28] also propose that APs exchange bits or raw samples on the backbone to facilitate packet decoding. In all these algorithms, the APs cooperate to decode the same packet whereas in BBN, APs encourage transmitters to collide and then cooperate to decode multiple packets simultaneously without exchanging the raw samples.

The idea of using the backbone for improving the uplink throughput was also proposed in our earlier work called RobinHood [5]. There are several differences between RobinHood and BBN. First, RobinHood was designed for a single collision domain, whereas BBN works for multiple collision domains. Second, BBN includes several techniques to increase the decoding probability. And third, it requires N fewer APs as compared to RobinHood since BBN utilizes the samples from the first slot at the receiving APs.

Interference Alignment: Previously, researchers (see [13] and references therein) have used interference alignment to improve the capacity of wireless networks. However, unlike BBN, they either require APs to exchange samples over the backbone [4], work only for the downlink traffic [26], assume presence of significant number of clients [19], require multiple antennas at transmitters or receivers [11], require the antennas to be physically moved [3] to a certain point, require the channel to change from one slot to another [7], precode over exponential number of time slots [7], or provide limited throughput gain [3], or do not scale with number of APs [11]. These assumptions are not practical in mobile networks since if the client is stationary, the channel may not change [27] from one packet to another. In contrast to the previous works, BBN works even if the channel stays stationary. The concept of interactive interference alignment [8] is similar to our work. However, it requires three slots to finish the transmissions. Also it requires the clients to be synchronized and transmit in two of the slots. TurboRate [23] introduces a client rate adaptation scheme for multiuser MIMO networks. Each client learns the direction of its signal received at the AP and uses SNR after projection on the direction of other clients to pick the best uplink data rate. The idea of SNR projection could help us design a better data rate selection algorithm for BBN.

Wireless Relays: Researchers [22, 14] have also looked at the problem of using special relay nodes to assist in high speed communication between specific pairs of source and destination nodes. In contrast, the focus of BBN is to leverage the high density of APs and the wired backbone to carefully select the set of destination APs, determine which AP decodes which packet, and to use the wired backbone to migrate all the complexity away from the clients. Further, with previous works, it is possible that the destination AP is unable to decode a packet due to low SNR. However, in BBN, APs leverage the high density of APs to increase robustness (See Sec. 5.3).

10. CONCLUSIONS AND FUTURE WORK

In the previous sections, we discussed BBN, a blind beamforming and nulling scheme that leverages the high density of access points to enable multiple mobile devices to transmit simultaneously. Feasibility of BBN was verified on a USRP testbed. Measurements show that BBN achieves a throughput gain of 1.48× over omniscient TDMA. Using trace-driven simulations, we showed that in dense wireless LANs, BBN provides a throughput of up to 5.6× compared to omniscient TDMA. Currently, traffic to BBN may interfere significantly with the packet exchange in BBN. One way to avoid this is for wireless devices in BBN to send RTS/CTS at the beginning so as to block the wireless channel for a certain duration.

Acknowledgements

This material is based upon work partially supported by the National Science Foundation under Grants CNS-1161490 and CNS-1302620.

11. REFERENCES

[1] BBN. Tech. rep. `http://sites.google.com/site/anontechrep765/`.

[2] OctoClock-G, accessed Jan. 2014. `https://www.ettus.com/product/details/OctoClock-G`.

[3] Adib, F., Kumar, S., Aryan, O., Gollakota, S., and Katabi, D. Interference Alignment by Motion. In *Proc. of ACM MobiCom 2013*.

[4] Annapureddy, V. S., El Gamal, A., and Veeravalli, V. V. Degrees of Freedom of Interference Channels with CoMP Transmission and Reception. *IEEE Transactions on Information Theory 58*, 9 (2012), 5740–5760.

[5] Bansal, T., and *et al.* RobinHood: Sharing the Happiness in a Wireless Jungle. In *Proc. of ACM HotMobile 2014*.

[6] Bansal, T., and *et al.* Symphony: Cooperative Packet Recovery over the Wired Backbone in Enterprise WLANs. In *ACM MobiCom 2013*.

[7] Cadambe, V. R., and Jafar, S. A. Interference Alignment and the Degrees of Freedom for the K User Interference Channel. *IEEE Transactions on Information Theory* (2007).

[8] Geng, Q., Kannan, S., and Viswanath, P. Interactive Interference Alignment. *CoRR* (2013).

[9] Gesbert, D., Kountouris, M., Heath, R., Chae, C.-B., and Salzer, T. Shifting the MIMO Paradigm. *Signal Processing Magazine, IEEE 24*, 5 (Sept 2007), 36–46.

[10] Gollakota, S., and Katabi, D. Zigzag Decoding: Combating Hidden Terminals in Wireless Networks. In *ACM SIGCOMM 2008.*

[11] Gollakota, S., Perli, S. D., and Katabi, D. Interference Alignment and Cancellation. In *Proc. of ACM SIGCOMM 2009.*

[12] Gowda, M., Sen, S., Roy Choudhury, R., and S., L. Cooperative Packet Recovery in Enterprise WLANs. In *IEEE INFOCOM 2013.*

[13] Jafar, S. A. *Interference Alignment: A New Look at Signal Dimensions in a Communication Network.* Now Publishers, 2011.

[14] Kuhn, M., Berger, S., Hammerstrom, I., and Wittneben, A. Power Line Enhanced Cooperative Wireless Communications. *IEEE JSAC 24*, 7 (2006), 1401–1410.

[15] Kumar, S., Cifuentes, D., Gollakota, S., and Katabi, D. Bringing Cross-Layer MIMO to Today's Wireless LANs. In *Proc. of ACM SIGCOMM 2013.*

[16] Li, T., and *et al.* CRMA: Collision-Resistant Multiple Access. In *Proc. of ACM MobiCom 2011.*

[17] Magistretti, E., Gurewitz, O., and Knightly, E. 802.11 ec: Collision Avoidance Without Control Messages. In *Proc. of ACM MobiCom* (2012).

[18] Murty, R., Padhye, J., Chandra, R., Wolman, A., and Zill, B. Designing High Performance Enterprise Wi-Fi Networks. In *Proc. of USENIX NSDI 2008.*

[19] Nazer, B., and *et al.* Ergodic Interference Alignment. In *Proc. of IEEE ISIT 2009.*

[20] Rahul, H., Hassanieh, H., and Katabi, D. SourceSync: A Distributed Wireless Architecture for Exploiting Sender Diversity. In *Proc. of ACM SIGCOMM 2010.*

[21] Rahul, H., Kumar, S., and Katabi, D. MegaMIMO: Scaling Wireless Capacity with User Demand. In *Proc. of ACM SIGCOMM 2012.*

[22] Rankov, B., and Wittneben, A. Spectral Efficient Protocols for Half-Duplex Fading Relay Channels. *IEEE Journal on Selected Areas in Communications 25*, 2 (2007), 379–389.

[23] Shen, W.-L., Tung, Y.-C., Lee, K.-C., Lin, K. C.-J., Gollakota, S., Katabi, D., and Chen, M.-S. Rate Adaptation for 802.11 Multiuser Mimo Networks. In *Proc. of ACM Mobicom 2012*, pp. 29–40.

[24] Shrivastava, V., and *et al.* CENTAUR: Realizing the Full Potential of Centralized WLANs Through a Hybrid Data Path. In *Proc. of ACM MobiCom 2009.*

[25] Stanford Information Networking Group (SING). SING Datasets. `http://sing.stanford.edu/srikank/datasets.html`.

[26] Suh, C., Ho, M., and Tse, D. N. Downlink Interference Alignment. *IEEE Transactions on Communications 59*, 9 (2011), 2616–2626.

[27] Vutukuru, M., Balakrishnan, H., and Jamieson, K. Cross-Layer Wireless Bit Rate Adaptation. In *Proc. of ACM SIGCOMM* (2009).

[28] Woo, G. R., Kheradpour, P., Shen, D., and Katabi, D. Beyond the Bits: Cooperative Packet Recovery Using Physical Layer Information. In *Proc. of ACM MobiCom 2007.*

[29] Xie, X., Zhang, X., and Sundaresan, K. Adaptive Feedback Compression for MIMO Networks. In *Proc. of ACM MobiCom 2013.*

[30] Zhou, W., Li, D., Srinivasan, K., and Sinha, P. DOMINO: Relative Scheduling in Enterprise Wireless LANs. In *Proc. of ACM CoNEXT 2013.*

Discovering Fine-grained RRC State Dynamics and Performance Impacts in Cellular Networks

Sanae Rosen, Haokun Luo,
Qi Alfred Chen, Z. Morley Mao
University of Michigan
{sanae, haokun, alfchen, zmao} @umich.edu

Jie Hui, Aaron Drake, Kevin Lau
T-Mobile USA Inc.*
{Jie.Hui, Aaron.Drake, Kevin.Lau}
@t-mobile.com

ABSTRACT

To conserve power while ensuring good performance on resource-constrained mobile devices, devices transition between different *Radio Resource Control* (RRC) states in response to network traffic and according to parameters specific to network operators. As RRC states significantly affect application power consumption and performance, it is important to understand how RRC state timers interact with network traffic patterns. In this paper, we show that the impact of RRC states on performance is significantly more complex and diverse than found in previous work. To do so, we introduce an open-source tool that allows the impact of RRC states on network and application performance to be measured in a robust and accurate manner on unmodified user devices, and deploy the tool in 23 countries around the world to test a broad range of cellular network technologies. We detect previously unknown performance problems which increase network latencies by up to several seconds and for LTE, can increase packet losses by an order of magnitude. Through an in-depth cross-layer analysis of several carriers, we examine the lower-layer causes of these problems. We determine that the highly complex state transitions of certain carriers, and in particular poor interactions between state demotions and network traffic, can lead to substantial, unexpected latencies.

Categories and Subject Descriptors

C.2.1 [**Network Architecture and Design**]: wireless communication; C.4 [**Performance of Systems**]: measurement techniques, performance attributes

Keywords

4G LTE; 3G; smartphones; RRC state machine; application QoE; cellular network performance

[1]The views presented here are as individuals and do not necessarily reflect any position of T-Mobile.

MobiCom'14, September 7-11, 2014, Maui, Hawaii, USA.
Copyright 2014 ACM 978-1-4503-2783-1/14/09 ...$15.00.
http://dx.doi.org/10.1145/2639108.2639115.

1. INTRODUCTION

Mobile clients' network traffic patterns cause cellular networks (such as 3G and 4G LTE) to transition between network states, known as *RRC (Radio Resource Control)* states. These states have different performance and energy consumption characteristics, and transitioning to a high-power state adds additional latencies. By using high-power RRC states only when necessary, and leveraging the temporal locality of network transmissions to avoid state promotion latencies, users can experience good network performance on resource-constrained mobile devices. Although the RRC states are largely defined by a set of specifications [7, 8], many aspects of the RRC state machine, such as timers for transitioning between states, are configured by the carrier.

Previous work [16, 22, 24, 23, 37] has measured RRC state configurations, either in controlled, in-lab experiments, or on specific device models which support logging RRC state transitions directly. They focus on measuring and inferring RRC state timers as they are implemented by the carrier, assuming that performance in those states fits a particular, consistent, ideal model. In this paper, we present a collection of measurement techniques and datasets that greatly improve our understanding of the impact of RRC state transitions, especially on application performance.

First, we present a tool that improves upon previous RRC inference approaches to make RRC measurements on real user devices *practical*, *scalable* and *robust*. This allows us to collect data on user-experienced performance directly, allowing us to capture non-ideal RRC state performance behavior, and uncover previous unknown performance problems.

To do so, we improve previous RRC measurement techniques to allow them to work effectively outside the lab and to run with no active user input needed. We account for interfering traffic and unrelated network congestion, and also measure the impact on application protocols such as HTTP and DNS requests directly. We present a snapshot of the data collected to date, covering 23 countries, and we are able to collect RRC state performance data on an ongoing, continuous basis. We make the tool available for carriers, researchers and other interested parties to use and adapt. Our method makes the ongoing monitoring of worldwide RRC state performance characteristics practical and eliminates the need for manual measurements or device-specific features.

Motivating the need for our global, systematic approach to measuring RRC state performance from a user perspective, we discovered a previously unknown cause of performance problems: *RRC state demotion delays*, not to be confused with the well-known *promotion* delays that occur when sending packets when the device is in a low-power state. The overhead of promotions has been explored in prior work, but the impact of the demotion process itself has been assumed to be non-critical. During state demotions, when no data has been transmitted for several seconds, devices enter a lower power state. For some carriers, we discovered there can be a delay of up to several seconds when a packet is sent around the time the demotion process occurs (in addition to the delay incurred by the subsequent state promotion. For many carriers these demotion delays are often be the determining factor in the latency experienced by the user.

Next, to understand and verify the existence of the performance problems discovered, we perform an in-depth, cross-layer examination of the causes and application impact of state transitions. We examine the impact of RRC and RLC (Radio Link Control) messages on RRC state transition latencies for several carriers, using a tool called QxDM that logs these low-layer control and data plane messages on mobile devices [6]. We discover major differences between carriers in the implementation of RRC state changes and cell tower communication. In particular, the use of the optional FACH state for 3G networks as a performance optimization in many implementations actually leads to significant performance problems.

Additionally, we examine the impact of RRC states on higher-layer network protocols and Android applications. In addition to gathering the impact of RRC states on HTTP requests, DNS lookups and TCP connections, we also develop an application for in-lab testing of Android applications in order to systematically measure the impact of RRC states on user-perceived performance in major applications. In doing so, we demonstrate that RRC transition latencies — including the previously unknown demotion latencies — can have a substantial impact on user-perceived performance.

Maintaining up-to-date information on RRC state implementations and their impact on performance is especially valuable to carriers and app developers, such as those using tools like ARO [17] to allow them to optimize application performance and battery consumption. Furthermore, there has been interest recently by "power users" in understanding how issues such as RRC state implementations, as they differ among carriers, can affect performance [35, 18]. In this paper, we present a first dataset collected from this app over several months, and as this dataset continues to grow, we expect it to continue to be a useful resource for collecting data on RRC state performance.

We summarize our contributions as follows:

- We provide an open-source RRC inference framework that measures the impact of RRC state transitions on user performance. Unlike previous approaches, it can be run on any unmodified Android device and network type, allowing RRC state characterization to be easily crowdsourced.
- We survey how RRC states impact performance in carriers in 23 countries and provide an open data set of the results.
- We uncover previously unknown, severe latency problems that exist in many cellular network technologies and carriers around the world.
- Using cross-layer analysis, we investigate how unrelated RRC and other low-layer control plane messages and delays cause higher-layer state transition latencies.
- We measure the impact of RRC states on application latencies as a whole, demonstrating that RRC states, especially transitions, have a significant impact on application-level latency as well as individual packets.

We start by giving an overview of RRC state machines (§2) and related work in RRC state measurement and mobile measurements (§3). We then describe our measurement methodology (§4), including our inference approach for the global deployment and the approach used for cross-layer local experiments. We then discuss our global results (§5) followed by an in-depth examination and confirmation of results from several carriers (§6). Finally, we examine the impact on application performance (§7) and discuss the implications of our finding and future work (§8).

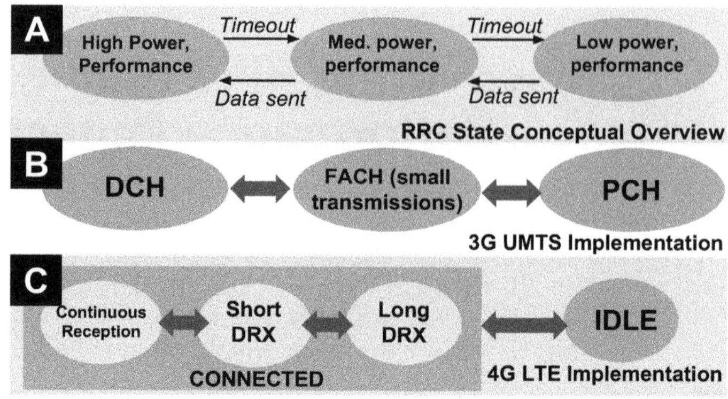

Figure 1: A: Overview of RRC state machine design. B-C: possible 3G and 4G state machines.

2. BACKGROUND

For cellular network protocols, there is a tradeoff between latency and battery consumption. Figure 1A gives a conceptual overview of how this tradeoff is managed. Mobile devices do not maintain a constant, active network connection due to their limited battery life, and switch to a high-power, active state to send data. Because this transition incurs additional latencies, the device remains in this state for several seconds, since network traffic often comes in bursts. There may also be an intermediate state where small amounts of data can be transmitted without the high power consumption of the fully active state.

These are known as *RRC States*, and are defined by 3GPP specifications [7, 8]. Carriers may configure their RRC state machine timers differently, subject to the constraints of the protocol specification. For 3G network technologies [7], there are two to three main states: DCH, which is high-power and high-bandwidth, FACH, an optional state which is low power and can only transmit a small amount of data before entering FACH, and PCH, where no transmission is possible. An example of a 3G state machine is shown in Figure 1B. For 4G LTE, as shown in Figure 1C, there are two main states: CONNECTED, a higher-power state, and IDLE, a lower-power state where no data is transmitted. CONNECTED often has sub-states where the device is active only at intervals of tens or hundreds of milliseconds after a few hundreds of milliseconds of idle time. This is known as *Discontinuous reception*, or DRX.

It is known that RRC timers can have a substantial impact on application performance and power consumption. In particular, periodic messages may be affected by long promotion latencies and lead to the device being in a high-power state longer than needed. The latter problem can be addressed in part through *fast dormancy* [19], where the device transitions to a low-power state early when no additional data transmissions are expected. We show in §5 that fast dormancy is rarely enabled in practice, perhaps due to the added complexity of implementing such a system and problems with certain implementations [29, 19].

In this paper, we explore how RRC timers impact performance in depth. It is known that state *promotions*—moving from a lower-power state to a higher-power state—involve additional latencies. We refer to these latencies as *promotion latencies*. We

Table 1: **Summary of results in figures and tables**

Section	Name	Key finding	Dataset
§4 (Methodology)	Table 2, Fig. 3	Validation of inferred RRC timers	CONTROLLED
§5 (Results)	Fig 5, 6, 7, 8	State transition delays for all network types can be substantial.	GLOBAL
§6 (Root causes)	Fig 9, 10	Causes of LTE transition delays.	COTNROLLED
§6 (Root causes)	Fig 11	Causes of 3G transition delays.	CONTROLLED
§7 (App impact)	Fig 12, 14, 13,	RRC states affect a variety of application and transport protocols.	GLOBAL (12), CONTROLLED

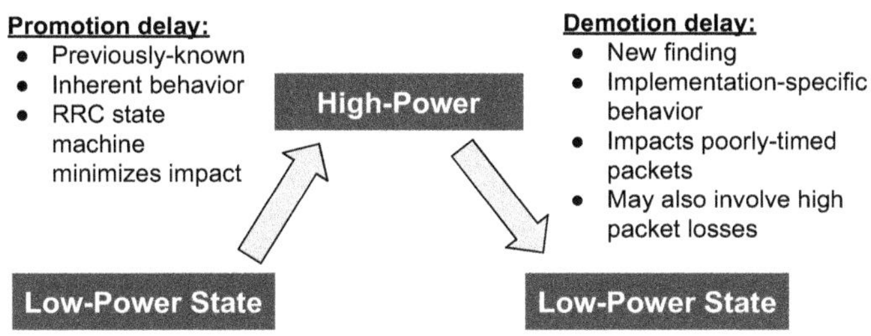

Figure 2: Comparison of promotion delays with newly-discovered demotion delays. Demotion delays occur when packets are delayed or lost when sent during the RRC state demotion process.

perform a cross-layer, experimental examination of variations in these latencies across carriers, and how implementation differences among carriers lead to these variations. We also discover that the impact of *demotions* on latency can also be quite substantial, which have previously been disregarded. Moving from a high-power to a low-power state in some cases takes several seconds, and for LTE may significantly increase the packet loss rate. We summarize the differences between these two delays in Figure 2.

3. RELATED WORK

Previous work examined power and performance characteristics of RRC state machines in both 3G [16] and 4G LTE networks [22, 24] in controlled environments, as well as specific features of those networks such as DRX [23]. Work by Souders [35] estimates RRC state machine performance through a web app, at a coarser granularity and without accounting for background network activity on phones. Recently, RILAnalyzer [37] leveraged chipset-specific functionality to monitor 3G RRC state transition events directly and measure how often applications cause excessive RRC state promotions. Unlike previous work, we focus on measuring and understanding how dynamic, non-ideal RRC state transition behavior varies and cause different performance trends on different carriers around the world.

Examining lower-layer control messages specifically, a Qualcomm whitepaper [27] explains how control plane messages in different network technologies are expected to lead to different promotion latencies. We also examine the demotion delays and take an experimental approach to determining the performance impact of RRC state transitions on different devices, uncovering new sources of delay. Work by Li *et al.* [33] examines the overhead of 3G transitions for one carrier, focusing on the number of signaling messages and on state promotions, rather than state demotions. Work by He *et al.* [21] investigates the impact of device type on low-layer control and data plane overhead. These papers demonstrate the importance of examining the impact of RRC control plane messages on performance.

Motivating our work, there has been a great deal of interest in understanding how applications can improve performance by accounting for RRC state timers, especially by temporally clustering network traffic. ARO [17] presents a tool for optimizing application performance, which accounts for poor interactions between applications and RRC state machines. TailTheft [20] prefetches or delays traffic to reduce the amount of traffic sent in high-latency states. Work by Lagar-Cavilla *et al.* [25] also proposes transmitting delay-tolerant traffic immediately after other data transmissions. Work by Evensen *et al.* [15] predicts when state promotions happen and schedules data accordingly to decrease latency. Work by Aucinas *et al.* [10] demonstrates the high costs of intermittent application transmissions. RadioJockey [31] investigates how to effectively trigger fast dormancy based on network traffic patterns, and TailEnder [28] and work by Deng *et al.* [34] propose a method of scheduling data transfers to minimize energy consumption without impacting user-perceived performance.

Our more accurate, per-carrier RRC state performance model would allow these tools to better determine the impact of RRC states on application traffic patterns and suggest performance improvements. In particular, we find that sending packets around state demotions should be avoided.

More generally, our work is related to efforts on measuring performance characteristics of cellular networks from the perspective of mobile devices. The Livelab project [12] also makes use of users running a measurement app on their phones. A wide range of findings on how users interact with mobile devices have been published, including measuring web usage in the wild [11]. Work by Halepovic *et al.* [14] presents a method of passively measuring HTTP transaction latency. Work by Gember *et al.* [9] determines how to accurately measure user-perceived performance on user devices. JamLogger [5] is an ongoing project to collect general performance and user activity on mobile devices. Unlike these projects, the mobile device measurement component of our work focuses on RRC performance.

4. MEASUREMENT METHODOLOGY

To understand RRC state performance, particularly the impact of RRC state transitions, we use three complementary approaches to develop a cross-layer understanding of RRC performance problems, their causes, and their impacts on application performance. First, we collect data on the impact of RRC state transitions on performance from carriers worldwide using an open-source cellular network testing tool for Android (§4.1). We then use local, controlled experiments to investigate the performance impact of RRC states. Starting at the RLC (Radio Link Control) layer, we examine control and data messages directly using a tool called QxDM (Qualcomm eXtensible diagnostic monitor) [6], in order to understand the causes of the observed transition delays (§4.2). Finally, we built an application controller tool in order to test the impact of RRC states on user-perceived performance at the application layer (§4.3). We describe approach in turn below.

We produce two datasets to analyze RRC state transitions. One, which we call GLOBAL, is gathered from user devices worldwide. The other consists of data from various global experiments, which we call CONTROLLED.

4.1 Automated RRC Performance Measurement

Previous work has inferred RRC state timers by observing how packet latencies change as the time between packets increases [16, 22], and other work has looked at directly monitoring RRC state timers on certain chipsets [37]. Unlike previous work, we focus on *user-perceived performance* in addition to inferring the timers set by carriers. Measuring RRC state timers directly does not capture the performance impact of RRC transitions, and inferring RRC timers in a controlled environment does not allow RRC states to be measured on a large scale. We overcome these challenges, allowing us to deploy a RRC inference tool worldwide.

In a controlled environment, the standard technique used is as follows [16, 22]: first, a UDP packet is sent to ensure the device is in a high power state. Next, the device is left idle for a period of time before another UDP packet is sent and echoed back by the target server. The latency of the second packet can then be compared to the latency of the first packet; if there is a substantial increase, it implies that a state promotion has occurred between them, adding latency. By examining a range of inter-packet intervals, the time at which a state transition occurs after a packet is sent can be determined. To distinguish between PCH and FACH, where a transition only occurs for sufficiently large packets, we perform this test with empty packets and 1 KB packets.

We modify this technique so it can be automated and so we can crowdsource the measurement of RRC state parameters and performance globally, as several tools already do with latency and throughput [4, 1]. This allows us to detect global carrier-dependent effects, to capture probabilistically occurring problems (whose presence we then confirm through controlled experiments), and to detect any differences over time, among different device types, or different geographic regions.

There are two main challenges in supporting crowdsourced measurements: dealing with interfering traffic on the device, and dealing with unrelated network congestion and variable latencies in different geographic locations. First, knowledge of all network traffic on the device is needed. A Linux utility (*/proc/net/dev*) can be used to monitor the total traffic on the device. Tests were discarded and rescheduled when more traffic than expected was observed. Second, data collected on user devices is not as "clean" as that collected in the lab. Changing network congestion and highly lossy networks can lead to variations in performance that are unrelated to RRC states. We consider only networks that have at least 5 complete measurement results, and before identifying RRC state transitions, we eliminate outliers and consider the average latency for each inter-packet interval. Furthermore, all data shown in the paper is normalized by subtracting the baseline latency where no RRC state change occurs. The application also monitors how much data and power it consumes to avoid exceeding limits placed by the user, and can pause tests when the network type changes (such as when switching to WiFi).

To measure RRC states on a large scale, we added this method to MobiPerf [4], an open-source network measurement tool for Android devices, and released it to the public. This RRC test runs automatically in the background to allow ongoing monitoring with no user involvement, and sends results back to a server, along with information such as the carrier and signal strength at the time the measurements were taken. User identifiable data is anonymized. To observe the impact of RRC states on HTTP requests, DNS lookups, and TCP handshakes, we sent the request in question after a large UDP packet followed by a varying time interval, and measured the latency of that request. Furthermore, as we measure RRC states repeatedly over time, we are able to observe dynamically configured timer values varying from test to test, such as those resulting from fast dormancy. We refer to the dataset we produce using these experiments as GLOBAL throughout the paper.

	Demotion type	App	QxDM
3G	C1 DCH⇒FACH	3 ± 0.5 s	3.1 ± 0.1 s
3G	C1 FACH⇒PCH	6.5 ± 0.5 s	6.2 ± 0.8 s
3G	C2 DCH⇒Disconn.	10 ± 0.5 s	10.3 ± 0.1 s
	— fast dormancy	3 ± 0.5 s	3.2 ± 0.1 s
LTE	C1 Conn.⇒Idle	10 ± 0.5 s	10.5 ± 0.1 s
LTE	C2 Conn.⇒Idle	10 ± 0.5 s	10.2 ± 0.1 s

Table 2: Comparison of ground truth demotion timers from QxDM with values measured through the application.

4.2 Layer 2 Root Cause Analysis with QxDM

QxDM [6] is a debugging tool that can view all network data and signaling messages in the form of a pcap-like trace. Using this tool, we can map IP packets to RLC PDUs (Packet Data Units), which are layer 2 data-plane messages. QxDM produces detailed logs of all these events and the corresponding timestamps. We parse these logs and map lower layer messages to the UDP packets sent. By performing the test repeatedly we can eliminate messages that do not occur for each transition and calculate the average times between key events. We confirm this mapping by comparing bytes in the RLC PDUs and the packets sent.

Using these logs, we determine how RLC PDU delays and low-layer control-plane messages affect user-visible performance around RRC state transitions. We combine pcap traces with QxDM logs to determine what RLC events surround IP packet transmissions, using timestamps to match events at both layers. For 3G, we are able to map individual PDUs to IP packets as the contents of PDUs are logged.

To perform this analysis, we use a modified RRC state testing application which repeatedly cycles through inter-packet intervals in order to induce RRC state transitions. By analyzing the resulting trace, we can determine which of the control messages related to each RRC state transition result in substantial delays. We also determine if any non-RRC state transition related processes are interrupting state transitions. We analyzed traces from two different carriers with different RRC state implementations and different transition delay behavior, and performed some of the analysis on a third carrier. In §6, we break down the causes of various RRC state delays, and compare carriers with differing delay behavior in order to both validate the presence of the observed differences and previously unknown delays, in addition to understanding their causes.

A limitation of this approach, unlike the app-based approach, is that it cannot be performed on actively-used devices in the wild, as proprietary software, specially configured devices, and some external equipment is needed. It is complementary to the app-based approach, which allows for a broad survey of RRC state performance to be performed, covering many carriers, locations, and device types. This approach is more suitable for in-depth examination of specific performance problems, and is likely of

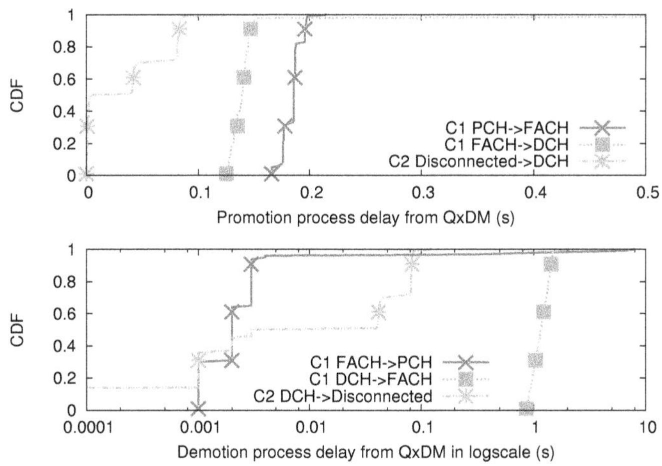

Figure 3: Measurement of demotion and promotion delays for two carriers in QxDM.

most use to carriers who, having detected a performance problem, are interested in understanding how best to address it.

Finally, in order to validate the application-based RRC state measurement methodology, we use QxDM to determine a ground truth for RRC state timers. After determining timers from two carriers for RRC states, we then verify the values by comparing the inferred RRC timers with the ground truth values from QxDM, shown in Table 2. As we infer the RRC timers set by the carriers from changes in the measured performance, RRC demotion delays — which result in elevated and variable latencies during RRC demotions — often obscure the precise timer configured by the carrier, so these values can only be inferred to within about a second. This limitation applies only to inferring the *demotion timers*, not to be confused with the *demotion or promotion latency*, which we measure at the millisecond granularity. In this paper, our goal is primarily to measure how RRC states affect performance in practice, and since we found that RRC state demotions are not an instantaneous process, the impact of RRC states on packet latencies does not appear at the precise moment of the underlying state transition.

We also confirm the presence of the long demotion delays observed in our application measurements. We focus on two major carriers with over a hundred million subscribers each, which we refer to as C1 and C2. For some of our analysis, we also examined a third major carrier, C3. In Figure 3, we show C1 has a substantially longer RRC demotion process delay than C2, which prevents packets from being sent during that time and results in significantly longer transmission delays at the application layer. We evaluate this in §7. We refer to the dataset produced by these local, controlled experiments as CONTROLLED throughout the paper.

4.3 Application Controller

We developed an application controller which simulates user behavior on major Android applications such as Facebook. This controller enables us to systematically evaluate the impact of RRC state transition delays on user-perceived application performance in §7 through a cross-layer analysis framework. Built upon the Android Test Case framework [2], this controller programmatically triggers Android UI events such as clicking buttons and entering text. To measure user-perceived UI latency, the controller also logs UI events, such as the start and end time of the news feed loading. As measured by Android DDMS [3], an application performance profiling tool, our controller incurs a computational overhead

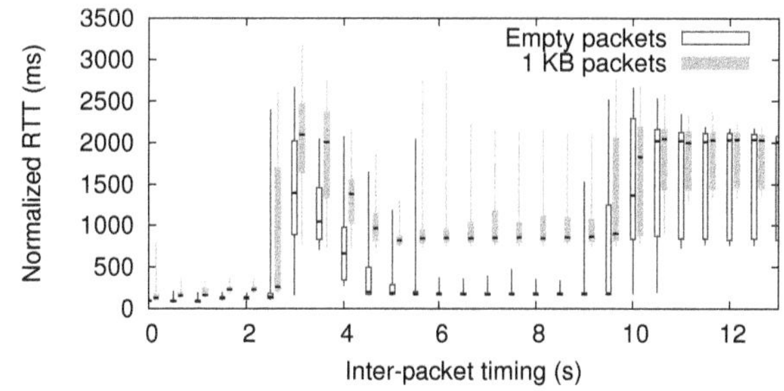

Figure 4: Example of observed round-trip times while transitioning through RRC states. Median, quartile and 5%/95% values shown. Data normalized by subtracting the baseline RTT in the highest power state.

of less than 2% and thus has minimal impact on the latency measurements. This also contributes to the CONTROLLED dataset.

5. GLOBAL PERFORMANCE MEASUREMENTS

Our RRC state measurement approach allows any Android device on any cellular network to measure the impact of RRC state and state transitions on user-perceived performance. In §4.1, we describe how our improved RRC inference methodology allows the tool to be deployed on uncontrolled user devices worldwide, and in this section we make use of data collected by that tool (the aforementioned GLOBAL dataset.) This tool measures network performance automatically and in the background on Android devices, allowing users to effortlessly monitor performance trends. Users can limit the amount of data consumed, and all data sent to the server is anonymized to protect the user's privacy. Promotion delay trends are roughly consistent with those in previous work [16, 22], although we have confirmed with the authors of the work that many of the timers for the carriers have changed. Our results are also consistent with more recent work that measures some RRC state changes directly, although we could not directly compare the anonymized carriers [37]. Our inference tool allows our knowledge of RRC timers to easily be kept up to date, and allows us to investigate a much larger dataset of carriers. In doing so, we uncover previously unknown demotion delays.

In Figure 4, we give an example of measurements from one device type and carrier (packet sizes do not include headers). The round-trip time for large packets is higher for inter-packet frequencies between 4–9 seconds, which is a characteristic of FACH. The round-trip time for both packets increases substantially for intervals greater than 10 seconds, which is characteristic of PCH. We also found that even in PCH, large packets still have a larger round-trip time than small packets, due to network delays. In this graph, as in all graphs of this type, we average values over several tests and then subtract the median latency in the highest power state in order to eliminate the effects of network latency.

We observe behavior inconsistent with the ideal model of RRC state transitions that has been discussed in the past. In Figure 4, there is a period of several seconds after a packet is sent, from about 2.5 to 4 seconds, when the next packet experiences unexpectedly high round-trip times. We refer to this delay as the *demotion delay*, and the period of time where it occurs as the *demotion period*. Where there are no demotion delays, we instead identify the interpacket interval at which the demotion occurs to be the promotion period. For example, in Figure 4, a demotion also occurs between 9.5 and 10 seconds.

Dataset Overview: Our dataset consists of 650 000 sets of RRC tests in total at the time of writing, and we continue to collect more data. Each measurement set includes the results of a set of measurements with interpacket intervals from 0 to 15 s, increasing by half-second increments. We repeat this test with both empty and one kilobyte packets, and we collect the round-trip time, the number of lost packets, the signal strength, and metadata about each measurement, including the carrier, manufacturer, OS, and a coarse-grained location. We also measure the impact of RRC states on HTTP, DNS and TCP requests in a separate set of tests that occurs less frequently, as it is more data and power intensive. In this set of tests we also examine the effect of varying packet sizes on RRC state performance.

Due to lost packets, interrupted measurements and unrelated network delays, a single set of tests was usually insufficient. For our final results, we consider carriers with more than 5 complete tests only, so that transient network delays, unrelated to RRC, will not affect our results. We also excluded six carriers where network noise was so high that all RRC states were indistinguishable. After filtering out carriers with insufficient data for our analysis, we analyzed 44 carriers in 23 countries covering every continent. Data on 69 distinct device model types and seven distinct network types was collected, including 2G, 3G and 4G technologies. In this paper we focus on 3G and 4G, which have been adopted by most carriers. 7 carriers use LTE, 23 use HSPA+, 16 use HSPA, 25 use HSPDA, and 6 use EVDO_A, with many carriers supporting more than one technology. In particular, most carriers with LTE also provide 3G.

Carrier and device characteristics: Almost all carriers with LTE have a demotion timer to CONNECTED of 10 seconds, but with 3G technologies, the timers vary greatly, from 2 to 10 seconds. Carriers providing multiple 3G technologies generally use the same timers for each. About 2/3 of carriers with HSPA, HSPDA or HSPA+ have no FACH state, or at least no FACH state with a measurable performance impact. We only saw definitive evidence of fast dormancy — a demotion timer varying substantially from test to test — with one carrier. Two more carriers exhibited variations of about a second. As fast dormancy and other dynamic RRC state timer approaches become more prevalent, the ability to measure these variations will become increasingly valuable.

For 3G, we also examined the impact of packet sizes on RRC state transitions, by varying the packet payload size from 0 to 1000 bytes by increments of 200 bytes. Dramatic increases in latency, indicating the size threshold for a promotion from FACH, all occurred between 0 and 200 bytes. Given the small threshold for a promotion from FACH and the high associated demotion overheads, FACH may not provide much benefit. We also observed that RTTs increase steadily with packet size by as much as a few hundred milliseconds in all states.

Transition delays: Ideally, the overhead of acquiring radio resources to use the radio channel should be fairly constant, independent of the idle time of the device. We observed that when network transmissions are sent when the demotion timer expires and the device undergoes a state demotion, there is an unexpected and undesirable increase in the delay to promote back to a high power state. This problem occurs for a large number of carriers.

We start by describing detailed results from three major carriers, illustrative of three different observed behavior patterns, and then summarize results globally. Values are normalized by the average latency in the absence of any RRC state change. Round-trip times during state transitions are shown separately.

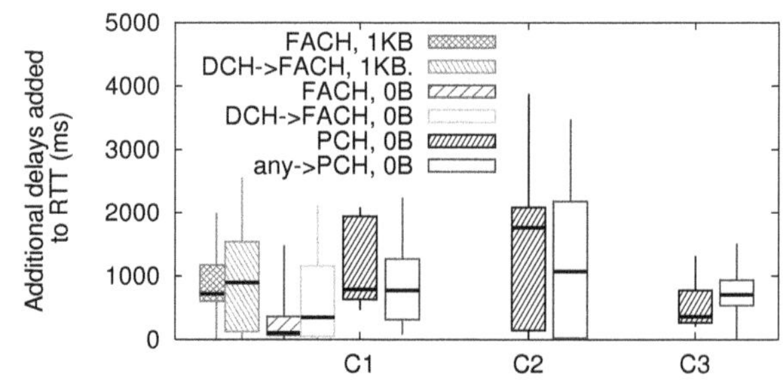

Figure 5: Variations in delays due to 3G states and state transitions, normalized against the DCH RTT. Median, quartile and 5th/95th% values shown.

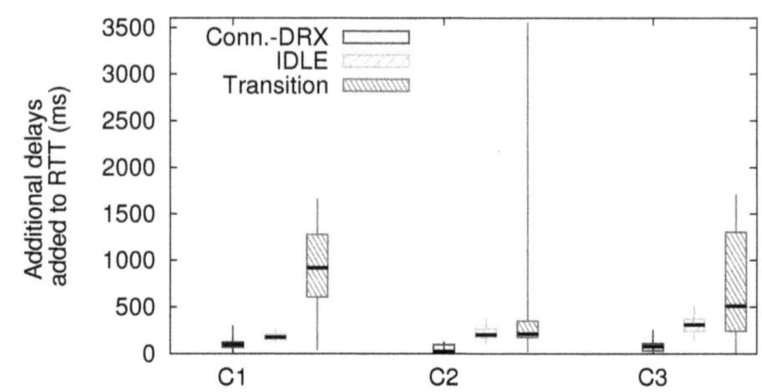

Figure 6: Delays due to LTE states and state demotions, normalized against the RTT of an empty packet sent in CONNECTED with no DRX.

In Figure 5 we show results from all 3G technologies for each carrier. As described above, we separate measurements into categories of RRC states and transitions based on observed, consistent changes in RRC states, such as those in Figure 4.

C1 makes use of FACH. When sending packets in FACH, latency becomes higher for larger packets, as expected. However, when sending packets during the transition from DCH to FACH, round-trip times are both higher and more variable. This is especially noticeable for small packets. Performance in PCH is also worse, but the demotion to PCH does not lead to additional latencies.

C2 does not implement FACH and does not always experience observable demotion delays, although when network performance is otherwise poor (including in some local experiments), demotion delays for this carrier appear. Network performance when sending data from low-power states is worse for this carrier than for others, although network performance for this carrier was generally poor. Finally, C3 is a CDMA network and thus does not implement FACH, but still experiences noticeable demotion delays.

In Figure 6, we compare LTE performance for the three carriers, comparing CONNECTED against IDLE and against the demotion period from CONNECTED to IDLE. LTE is supposed to perform better than 3G, but this is not necessarily true during demotions. For all three carriers the tail latency is substantially higher during state transitions, lasting potentially up to several seconds. For C1 and C3, the median values are substantially higher as well. In §6, we discover this difference is due to differences in how state transitions in these carriers are affected by control-plane activity. Different state change implementations, in this case, have both lead to performance problems.

For LTE, we also found packet loss rates during state transitions are higher than average, by up to an order of magnitude. To measure loss rates, we sent out ten empty packets simultaneously

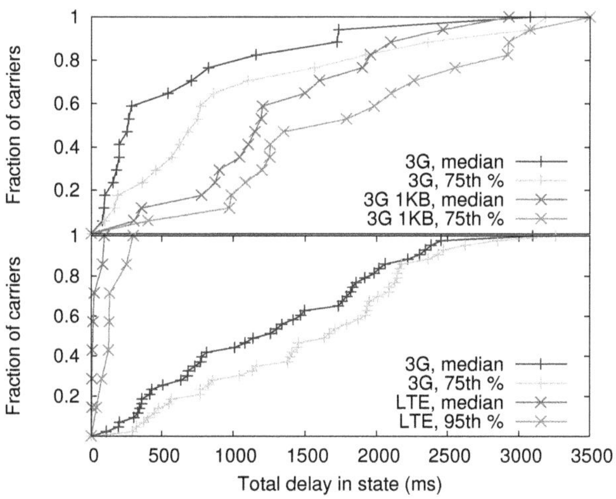

Figure 7: CDFs of promotion delays in each RRC state over all carriers, when promoting from FACH (upper graph) and from IDLE/PCH (lower graph).

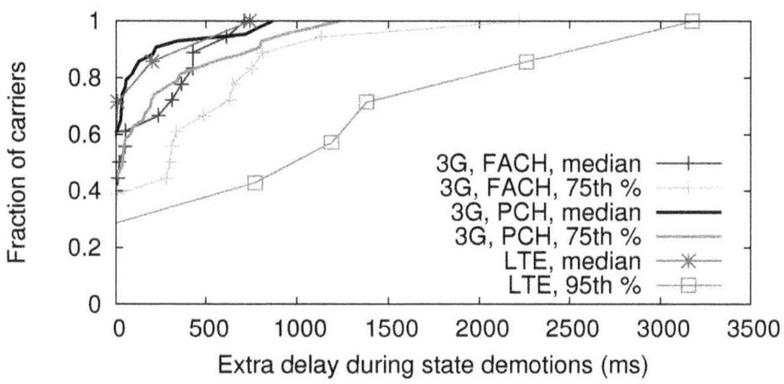

Figure 8: CDF over all carriers of additional latencies caused by transmissions during state demotions (minus promotion transition times in the new RRC state).

and counted how many were echoed back. C1, C2 and C3 experienced packet loss rates of 26%, 63% and 68% respectively. Normal loss rates were 1–3% depending on the network state (aside from C3 which experienced loss rates of up to 30% of packets).

We next examine trends across all carriers, starting by examining the impact of state *promotions* in Figure 7, which have been examined in previous work only for a small number of carriers. Promotions from FACH generally take several seconds, and are often triggered even when an empty packet is sent, meaning users get no performance benefit from FACH in these cases. Promotion times from PCH can also be long, and vary greatly from carrier to carrier. LTE promotion delays are generally no more than a few hundred milliseconds.

In Figure 8, we show the additional latencies added by attempting to send data near a state demotion, on top of the state promotion delays. We compare median values during state demotions with median values for state promotions only, and likewise for 75th and 95th percentile values. Ideally, no additional latency should be incurred, if the demotion is aborted, allowing the device to simply remain in the high-power state. This is not the case, especially for demotions to FACH. Eliminating FACH (as many carriers have) would likely reduce, though not completely eliminate, the prevalence of this demotion delay problem.

For LTE, median latencies are generally not affected by state promotions. It seems our local carriers explored above have somewhat atypical behavior, underscoring the need for a broad

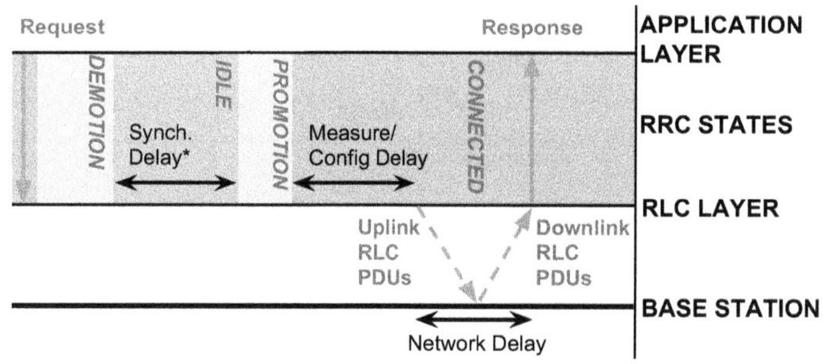

Figure 9: A cross-layer overview of RRC-related sources of transition delays for LTE. * indicates a delay present in only some carriers. The situation for 3G is similar, with longer demotions and promotions, and longer measurement delays.

survey of network performance. However, tail latencies are frequently affected. Note that we show 95th percentile latencies and not 75th percentile latencies. As we saw earlier, these tail latencies are substantially higher during demotions than any other time. Given the low network delays in LTE generally, these delays can have a major relative impact on user-perceived performance. As major web services go to great lengths to reduce tail latencies for 0.01% of users due to the potential revenue impacts [13], these latencies can be quite significant.

Finally, we investigated whether other factors lead to differences in RRC state timers among different carriers. We did not observe differences in RRC state configuration for the same carrier in different locations within a single country. In most cases, timer configurations were the same in different countries for international carriers, with the exception of two cases where subsidiaries of the same company operating in different countries had different timers in those countries. We did not detect differences in RRC state machines by device type, either. Unfortunately, using client measurements we could not directly confirm differences between different carrier equipment vendors.

Summary: State demotion delays are common worldwide, though not experienced by every carrier, and occur in both 3G and LTE. They can have a critical effect on performance, in some cases causing delays of several seconds; state demotion delays (and to a lesser extent, state promotion delays) can add additional latencies of up to several seconds on top of the normal state promotion latency. Additionally, in LTE, state demotions are associated with high packet loss rates. More generally, we have shown that running RRC state performance tests on user devices is an effective way of monitoring global RRC state performance trends.

6. BREAKDOWN OF RRC TRANSITION DELAY CAUSES

Through controlled, in-lab testing of RRC latencies, we examine the events that contribute to RRC state delays, using the methodology described in §4.2 to produce some of the CONTROLLED dataset. We collect measurements through QxDM, which provides detailed visibility of control messages related to RRC state transitions and RLC data messages. Consistent with previous work in this area [33, 21] we find promotion delays can be quite significant, although we focus on user-perceived latency rather than signaling overhead. We also determine that the overhead of state demotions can be significant, which has been overlooked. Although delays during state transitions occur in nearly all cellular network technologies, the causes of these delays (as well as their magnitudes) differ as shown in §5.

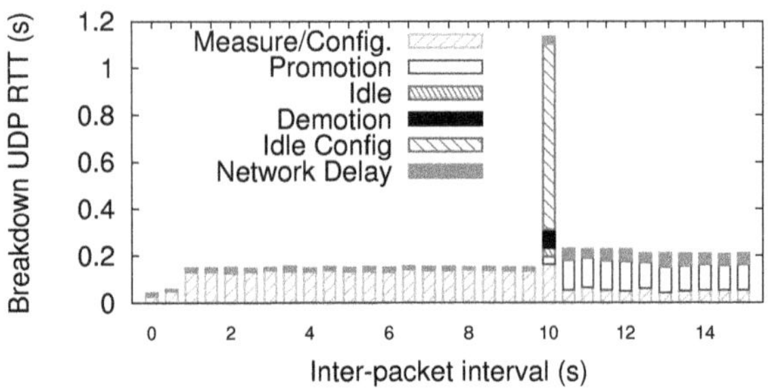

Figure 10: Median values of sources of LTE transmission delays for C1, using QxDM logs to determine the timing of layer 2 events. C2 is similar but lacks "Idle Config." The state demotion delay can be seen at 10 seconds.

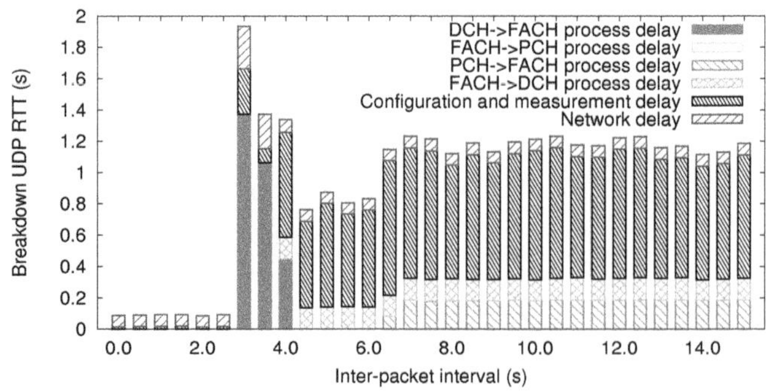

Figure 11: Breakdown of RTTs for varying inter-packet intervals, including a demotion to FACH at 3s and a demotion to PCH at 6.5s, based on QxDM logs. The demotion to FACH from DCH results in higher delays.

Breakdown of promotion delays in LTE: First, we examine state promotions that do not occur in the vicinity of state demotions. Although previous work has identified that state promotions cause delays [16, 22], the root causes of these delays and variations in these delays have yet to be examined. We summarize the median delays for different inter-packet intervals in Figure 10, and give an overview of the events involved in RRC state demotions and promotions in Figure 9. These include all delays that appear when sending a UDP packet, both delays in the network and lower-layer processing delays on the device.

We found that for LTE, state promotions from IDLE add a highly varying delay to the overall latency. This delay includes the effects of Discontinuous Reception (DRX), where devices will only send data during a small window of time, with a period of a few hundred milliseconds. In the messages logged by QxDM, the promotion process begins with a request to switch to a higher-bandwidth, more reliable channel. This message is sent on an unreliable network channel, so delays during this process due to poor network conditions can substantially increase the overall time to process a packet. This contributes significantly to the high variation in worst-case or tail network latency seen in Figure 6. A detailed description of some of the messages involved in state promotions (though not demotions) for LTE and 3G can be found in a white paper by Mohan et al. [27].

Breakdown of demotion delays in LTE: In Figure 10, it can be seen that packets sent during state demotions are accompanied by a large number of measurement and configuration messages before they occur, leading to higher latencies, although the state transition itself is a short process. Although there is a subsequent promotion after the demotion occurs, we found that it is generally quite short, since the promotion occurs immediately, without going through a DRX cycle.

We have isolated one set of message delays in particular that can add several seconds of delays, labeled "Idle config." These messages appear to be related to transmission synchronizations with the base station, although they are not well-documented. If, during a demotion, an IP packet is sent before this message appears, then the entire configuration process completes before the state transition process begins, leading to long delays. However, if an IP packet is sent after it appears, then this process is aborted and a state transition begins right away, so this delay only appears for a narrow window of inter-packet timings. This illustrates the dependencies of control messages on the data packet timing.

This problem appears to be implementation specific and not due to any problem with the LTE specification. These messages do not appear for C2, which explains the lower median latencies during demotions seen in Figure 6. Additionally, for all carriers, the device occasionally momentarily disconnects from the network before selecting a new cell tower, causing long delays. This appears to be responsible for the long 95th percentile latencies seen in Figure 6. This is likely unavoidable as user movement or poor network performance may necessitate this switch.

Breakdown of promotion delays in 3G: We summarize the breakdown of latency causes in Figure 11 as they vary by inter-packet interval. For 3G, promotion times are often longer — roughly 1200 ms on average where they occur. After a state promotion, additional control plane messages are sent, such as messages to measure channel conditions. These messages take up significantly more time than the state promotions themselves, and the messages seen can vary. One series of system information messages adds additional delays of hundreds of milliseconds where it occurs, leading to high latency variations. This set of messages occurs periodically, every few hundred milliseconds, not just during state transitions. Overall, state promotions in 3G are more complex and involve more messages being exchanged. 3G state promotions are already known to be slow for this reason [27, 33].

Breakdown of demotion delays in 3G: In Figure 11, it can be seen that state demotions have a substantial impact when the inter-packet interval is between 3 and 4 seconds. Unlike with LTE, it is simply the demotion process itself which can be slow, rather than other control plane messages which cause unexpected delays. This makes promotion latencies more common as well as affect a larger range of inter-packet intervals. It is also interesting to note that when a state demotion is interrupted by a packet being sent, there is often no subsequent promotion delay.

Interestingly, several carriers appear to lack these demotion delays altogether. We were able to examine one such carrier in depth using QxDM. This carrier's demotion process is substantially simpler, consisting of sending one message to the base station followed by a small amount of additional delay due to device configuration operations. As this adds a median time delay of 175 ms, it did not have a statistically significant effect on the user-experienced latency. This suggests that this carrier, and likely the others which lack demotion delays, are using a different RRC state transition implementation. This carrier also omits the FACH state, although we found in our global study of 36 carriers that not all carriers which omit FACH lack significant transition delays.

Summary: We have determined that, for both LTE and 3G, carrier-specific, RRC state related messaging and configuration delays can interact poorly with certain network state patterns. At least one carrier has been able to reduce these delays greatly. In general, LTE's state transition procedure ensures much better

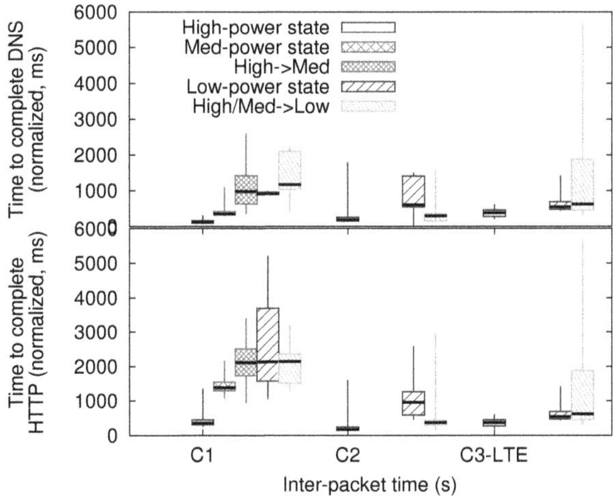

Figure 12: Performance of different carriers with different inter-packet timings, for DNS lookups and HTTP connections to a small website.

average performance than 3G's, largely due to a lower amount of control-plane signaling needed in order to transmit data or change RRC states. Delays in LTE are primarily due to poor interactions between certain control-plane messages and the state demotion process, affecting only a subset of requests (although it can add delays of several seconds). Delays in 3G, however, are generally due to issues with state demotion implementations. Additionally, while it was already known that state promotions can cause network delays, we experimentally quantify which components of the state promotion process lead to promotion delays. The overall observation is that RRC state transitions contribute significantly to tail latencies on mobile devices.

7. APPLICATION IMPACT

In this section, we explore how upper-layer protocols are affected by RRC state transitions, using both our globally deployed RRC state measurement tool and in-lab controlled experiments. We find that HTTP connections, DNS lookups, and mobile applications can all be significantly impacted by RRC state transitions.

7.1 HTTP and DNS Results from Global Deployment

In our public deployment (*i.e.*, the GLOBAL dataset), we measured the impact of RRC states on DNS and HTTP requests, which are more representative of real network traffic than individual UDP packets. Testing with UDP packets allows us to understand the impact of RRC states without being affected by network protocol features, but UDP is not representative of most network traffic. In Figure 12, we show the impact of RRC state on a DNS lookup and on the loading of a small web page in our global study, focusing on the carriers discussed in-depth before.

The behavior we observed for these tests was consistent with that we observed for UDP packets, exhibiting the same performance patterns. The completion times for DNS lookups and HTTP requests for C1 were strongly affected by state demotion delays in 3G, whereas C2 was less affected. For C1, FACH unsurprisingly performs worse than DCH. Data sent during the demotion to FACH performs comparably to the performance in PCH. Performance during the demotion to PCH is not significantly worse than in PCH proper. Also consistent with our UDP results, we found that for C2 there were no state demotion delays. For LTE, the tail results during state demotions are substantial, in one case lasting more than five seconds for a DNS lookup.

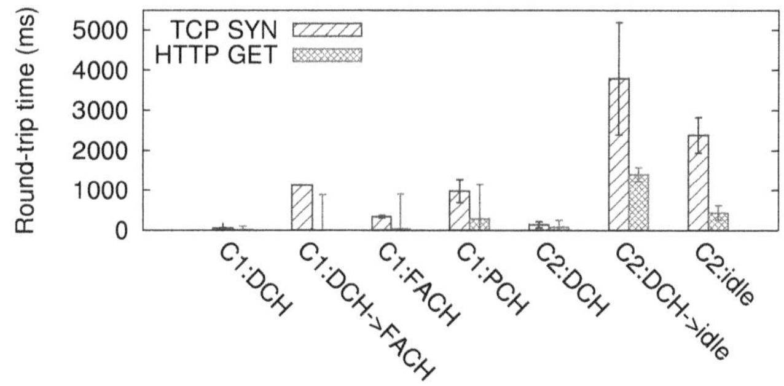

Figure 13: Effect of RRC states on TCP SYN RTTs and HTTP GET latencies.

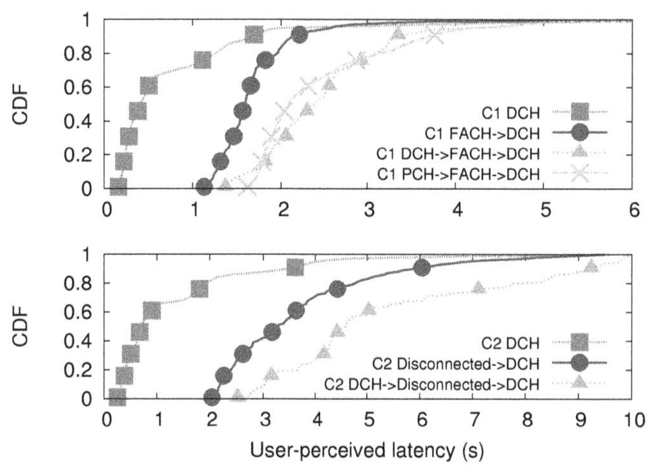

Figure 14: Effect of RRC states and transitions on user-perceived latency in web browsing experiments.

7.2 Controlled Web Browsing Experiments

To verify our findings, we also examined RRC state delays in different circumstances in controlled, in-lab experiments, contributing to our CONTROLLED dataset. We evaluated the page loading time in a browser for 10 major websites, including search, social networking, e-commerce, news, sports and finance websites. We varied the inter-request time from 1s to 11s, with a granularity of 0.1s. In total, we generated 3000 HTTP requests for both C1 and C2 over an entire day. In Figure 13, we show the TCP SYN RTTs and the HTTP GET request RTTs from TCP flows. RRC state demotion delays increase the SYN RTT substantially. As the HTTP GET request starts with a SYN request, it suffers from the same demotion delays.

We also evaluated the user-experienced network latency overall for these requests. We measured the latency from the first SYN packet until the last packet related to the HTTP request was received, which excludes Android UI and other system latencies. In Figure 14, we show the distribution of user-experienced latencies when browsing in various RRC states as well as during state transitions. Starting in a low-power state has a substantial performance impact, adding 0.5–3s to the user-perceived latency. C2's throughput is significantly worse than C1's at our location, so the overall network performance differs from that in our global study.

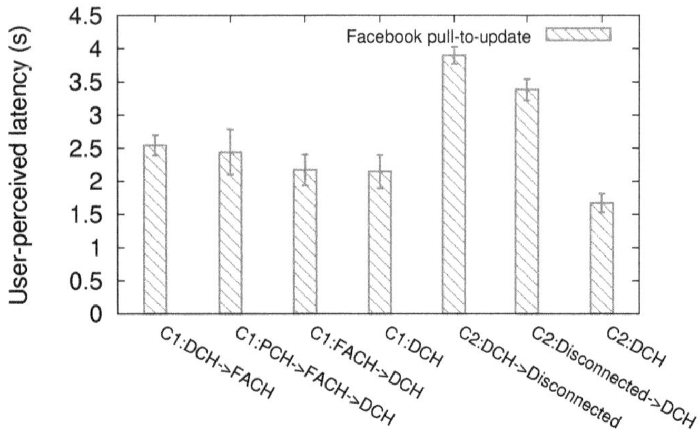

Figure 15: Impact of additional RRC state transition delays on Facebook's pull-to-update action.

Unlike C2, C1 has an intermediate FACH state and thus two demotions. As a result, there is a higher chance that users of C1 transmit data during a state demotion. In our controlled experiments, we found that for C2, 2.4% of HTTP GET requests experienced demotion delays, and for C1, 4.25% of requests were affected.

We also examined a 9 month user study trace of browsing traffic we collected, and we simulated the RRC state transitions for that carrier, counting how many packets would have fallen into the demotion period. For C1, which has relatively short timers and long transition periods, 3.2% of requests would have been affected. For C2, only 0.2% would have been affected. Since this carrier's timers are much longer, the chance of a packet being sent during the demotion period is much lower. However, this comes at the cost of higher energy consumption.

We briefly examined the impact of these RRC states on a major video streaming service as well, and found that packets are sent continuously, causing the device to remain in DCH and thus avoiding all transition problems (at the cost of high energy consumption). It has been proposed that streaming apps could save a substantial amount of energy by batching data [36, 17]. These sorts of optimizations would mean that streaming apps would then need to account for RRC state dynamics. In particular, interruptions in streaming video are highly undesirable, and so avoiding unexpected network delays is critical.

7.3 Case Study: Facebook Application

Through controlled experiments, we also examined the Facebook application, one of the most popular social networking apps [32]. A major Facebook feature is its news feed [30]. We examined the time to fetch new news feed content over the network in response to the user pulling down on the list (the "pull-to-update" action). As described in §4.3, to systematically and repeatedly measure the latency associated with app operations, we created a controller application that repeatedly performs this action, logging the timestamp when the action is initiated and when the news feed finishes loading.

We performed the experiment on two Android 4.2.2 Samsung Galaxy S3 devices. We created two Facebook accounts, A and B, which are friends with one another. One device with account A repeatedly uploaded two photos to generate news feed data. The other account performed a pull-to-update operation, varying the time intervals between each action. As shown in Figure 15, the DCH⇒FACH demotion process increases the user perceived latency by 398 ms for C1, and the DCH⇒Disconnected process introduces an additional 2.225s delay for C2. The results are consistent with the web browsing experiments. As with those experiments, the RRC state transition delay is worse for C2 due to exceptionally poor network performance where we performed the experiment.

Summary: We show that the problems we observed are not just limited to affecting individual packet latencies. RRC state transitions, especially RRC state demotions, can greatly impact the performance of network and application layer protocols, as well as the performance of web browsing and network applications directly, adding delays of up to five seconds in the worst case. The degree to which transitions impact application performance varies significantly by carrier, but can often add delays of over a second.

8. DISCUSSION

It is well known that there is a tradeoff between performance and battery consumption when setting RRC state timers. Our findings suggest that these tradeoff decisions have been made with an incomplete understanding of the impact on performance, as RRC state performance is more complex than previously believed. These findings have implications both for carriers and for developers.

Recommendations for carriers: In general, we have shown that the impact of RRC states on user-perceived performance is complex, unpredictable, and highly dependent on implementation details not defined in an official specification. Given these challenges, the tools we have introduced are valuable in helping carriers ensure their performance requirements are met. We next describe concretely how carriers can benefit from the measurement tools we discuss in this paper.

Given some power and performance goals a carrier wants to achieve with its RRC state configuration, the carrier can then use our RRC performance measurement tool to ensure that their state transition performance is as expected, and if not, make adjustments to their timers. For many carriers, our dataset of RRC state performance measurements already contains this information. If the carrier is not in our dataset it is easy to use our open-source application to collect this data. In addition to determining the performance impact of RRC states in practice, there are two major pitfalls they should watch out for in their RRC state implementation.

The first is the presence of RRC demotion delays or packet losses. These can be detected by our application, and a tool such as QxDM can confirm the existence of this problem, as well as pinpoint some possible causes. Then, the carrier can determine if this is a configuration or implementation bug that can be addressed. In general, we found that longer timers make these demotion problems less likely, as then traffic is less likely to be sent during a state demotion. For carriers with long RRC timers, the probability of traffic being impacted by bad RRC state demotions is low. However, carriers who value preserving battery life more should pay close attention to their RRC state implementations. Furthermore, at least one carrier appears to have simplified its RRC state demotion process, reducing demotion delays. LTE also has lower demotion delays due to a simpler demotion process.

The second potential problem is that often users do not in practice gain any performance benefit from FACH. For many carriers, demotions to FACH are particularly impacted by long demotion delays. FACH is supposed to provide a level of performance between DCH and IDLE, but in many cases, high state demotion delays mean that sending packets in FACH is worse than sending packets in IDLE for some traffic patterns. While we do not suggest eliminating FACH in every case — some carriers which use FACH do achieve performance benefits — carriers which use FACH should investigate, through measurements on real user devices, whether FACH is beneficial in practice. Given the frequently marginal benefits gained by FACH, it seems that LTE's approach of eliminating the intermediate power state makes sense.

Finally, the carrier is likely also interested in the impact of the RRC state configuration on real, major applications. Our app can crowdsource small-scale HTTP and DNS performance measurements, that can then be confirmed using in-lab testing, as in § 7. Using these methods, carriers can be confident that their RRC state configuration has the performance properties they expect.

Recommendations for developers: Our findings also have implications on how application developers should design applications. We have found that the impact of certain inter-packet interval patterns can have an even worse performance impact than previously believed. This underscores the importance of batching data to ensure both good performance and power consumption.

Furthermore, our techniques for measuring the impact of RRC states on application QoE, both in-lab and through application deployments, would be valuable to developers. It is known that long inter-packet intervals lead to performance and power issues, but recent work [26] has argued that excessive batching and prefetching has a significant negative effect on data usage. An understanding of when application performance is and is not significantly impacted by RRC state transitions, which is carrier dependent, would assist developers in deciding whether or not batching data is necessary to achieve good performance. For instance, if the app developer is not overly concerned about battery life, but wants to conserve data and ensure good performance, it might not make sense to batch downloads too aggressively on carriers with long RRC state timers. Conversely, on carriers with high state transition delays, batching downloads might be more critical. It would even be possible for developers to use our RRC performance measurement method in their own apps, to determine if specific network requests of concern are substantially impacted by RRC state, and thus whether batching network traffic would reduce RRC state transition delays.

Furthermore, recent work has examined allowing applications to account for RRC state in order to reduce latency and save power during network transmissions [17, 20, 25, 15]. By using the dataset of RRC state performance gathered through our tool, these tools can update their model of RRC state implementations as they change over time and account for differences between carriers worldwide. Further development of libraries and frameworks to allow app developers to easily account for complex, varying network performance and power consumption behavior would be highly valuable.

Impact of battery consumption: In this paper, we have focused on measuring the impact of RRC state on application performance. However, RRC states also have a significant impact on battery consumption as well. Accurately measuring power consumption at a fine-grained level on unmodified user devices is inherently challenging. Latency can be measured directly, but accurately inferring power consumption on arbitrary user devices with no specialized equipment remains an open area of research. However, once a model of battery consumption in different power states has been developed for a specific model of device, battery consumption from cellular network usage could be estimated. Assuming that power in each state is constant or linear with time for a given signal strength, as in previous work [17] the power consumption of an application could be calculated from the inferred RRC state timers for each carrier, making network power consumption estimates more accurate.

9. CONCLUSION

In this paper, we examined the impact of RRC states on user-perceived performance in depth. We uncovered several previously unknown implementation artifacts that can lead to delays of up to several seconds, and have demonstrated the impact of RRC states on latency and packet loss for various network protocols and applications. We have investigated the root causes of these performance problems by examining RLC-layer messages in order to determine what configuration events and messages cause the delays observed. In doing so, we confirm the presence of these unexpected delays, and determine that, while they are partially unavoidable, they are exacerbated by complex, multi-stage state transitions and unexpected negative interactions with other control-plane configuration events. Furthermore, we discovered that some carriers have configured their RRC state machines to avoid many of these pitfalls, suggesting these problems are fixable.

In addition to identifying specific, previously unknown performance problems in networks around the world, this paper also motivates the need for continuous, long-term and global monitoring of cellular network configurations and the impact on performance, with a emphasis on uncovering unexpected and non-ideal behavior. As applications increasingly account for underlying cellular network implementation details to avoid excessive power consumption, data usage or latency, properly understanding how the underlying cellular network affects application performance in practice is crucial.

10. ACKNOWLEDGEMENTS

We would like to thank our anonymous reviewers and shepherd for their valuable comments. We would also like to thank Kranthi Sontineni, Randy Meyerson, Warren McNeel, and the Product Experience and QoE Lab team at T-Mobile for their assistance. This research was supported in part by the National Science Foundation under grants CNS-1059372, CNS-1039657, CNS-1345226, and CNS-0964545, as well as by an NSERC Canada PGS M scholarship.

11. REFERENCES

[1] 4GTest. `http://mobiperf.com/4g.html`.

[2] Android Activity Testing. `http://developer.android.com/tools/testing/activity_testing.html`.

[3] Android DDMS. `http://developer.android.com/tools/debugging/ddms.html`.

[4] MobiPerf. `http://mobiperf.com`.

[5] NU JamLogger: A Study of User Activity and System Performance on Mobile Architectures. `http://www.ece.northwestern.edu/microarchitecture/jamlogger/`, 2009.

[6] QxDM Professional Proven Diagnostic Tool for Evaluating Handset and Network Performance. `http://www.qualcomm.com/media/documents/files/qxdm-professional-qualcomm-extensible-diagnostic-monitor.pdf`, 2012.

[7] 3GPP TS 35.331: Radio Resource Control (RRC) - UMTS, 2013.

[8] 3GPP TS 36.331: Radio Resource Control (RRC) - LTE, 2013.

[9] A. Gember, A. Akella, J. Pang, A. Varshavsky, and R. Caceres. Obtaining Representative Measurements of Cellular Network Performance. In *Proc. ACM IMC*, 2012.

[10] A. Aucinas, N. Vallina-Rodriguez, Y. Grunenberger, V. Erramili, K. Papagiannaki, J. Crowcroft, and D. Whetheral. Staying Online While Mobile: The Hidden Costs. In *Proc. ACM CoNEXT*, 2013.

[11] C. C. Tossell, P. Kortum, A. Rahmati, C. Shepard, and L. Zhong. Characterizing web use on smartphones. In *ACM CHI*, 2012.

[12] C. Shepard, A. Rahmati, C. Tossell, L. Zhong, and P. Kortum. LiveLab: Measuring Wireless Networks and Smartphone Users in the Field. In *Proc. Hotmetrics*, 2010.

[13] G. DeCandia, D. Hastorun, M. Jampani, G. Kakulapati, A. Lakshman, A. Pilchin, S. Sivasubramanian, P. Vosshall, and W. Vogels. Dynamo: Amazon's highly available key-value store. In *Proc. ACM SOSP*, 2007.

[14] E. Halepovic, J. Pang, and O. Spatscheck. Can you GET Me Now? Estimating the Time-to-First-Byte of HTTP Transactions with Passive Measurements. In *Proc. ACM IMC*, 2012.

[15] K. R. Evensen, D. Baltrünas, S. Ferlin-Oliveira, and A. Kvalbein. Preempting State Promotions to Improve Application Performance in Mobile broadband Networks. In *Proc. ACM MobiArch*, 2013.

[16] F. Qian, Z. Wang, A. Gerber, Z. M. Mao, S. Sen, and O. Spatscheck. Characterizing Radio Resource Allocation for 3G Networks. In *Proc. ACM IMC*, 2010.

[17] F. Qian, Z. Wang, A. Gerber,Z. M. Mao, S. Sen, and O. Spatscheck. Profiling Resource Usage for Mobile Applications: A Cross-layer Approach. In *Proc. ACM MobiSys*, 2011.

[18] E. Griffin. Fast dormancy - save your battery from 3g drainage. `https://www.youtube.com/watch?v=O8L50sCY7CI`, 2012.

[19] GSMA. Fast dormancy best practices. `http://www.gsma.com/newsroom/wp-content/uploads/2013/08/TS18v1-0.pdf`, 2011.

[20] Y. Z. Hao Liu, Yaoxue Zhang. TailTheft: leveraging the wasted time for saving energy in cellular communications. In *Proc. ACM MobiArch*, 2011.

[21] X. He, P. P. C. Lee, L. Pan, C. He, and J. C. S. Lui. A panoramic view of 3g data/control-plane traffic: Mobile device perspective. In *IFIP*, 2012.

[22] J. Huang, F. Qian, A. Gerber, Z. M. Mao, S. Sen, and O. Spatscheck. A Close Examination of Perfomance and Power Characteristics of 4G LTE Networks. In *Proc. ACM MobiSys*, 2012.

[23] J. Wigard, T. Kolding, L. Dalsgaard, and C. Coletti. On the User Performance of LTE UE Power Savings Schemes with Discontinuous Reception in LTE. In *Proc. International Conference on Communications*, 2009.

[24] L. Zhou, H. Xu, H. Tian, Y. Gao, L. Du, and L. Chen. Performance Analysis of Power Saving Mechanism with Adjustable DRX Cycles in 3GPP LTE. In *IEEE VTC*, 2008.

[25] H. A. Lagar-Cavilla, K. Joshi, A. Varshavsky, J. Bickford, and D. Parra. Traffic backfilling: subsidizing lunch for delay-tolerant applications in UMTS networks. In *Proc. ACM MobiHeld*, 2011.

[26] Lenin Ravindranath, Sharad Agarwal, Jitendra Padhye, Christopher Riederer. Procrastinator: pacing mobile apps' usage of the network. In *Proc. ACM MobiSys*, 2014.

[27] S. Mohan, R. Kapoor, and B. Mohanty. Latency in hspa data networks. Technical report, Qualcomm, 2011.

[28] N. Balasubramanian, A. Balasubramanian, and A. Venkataramani. Energy Consumption in Mobile Phones: A Measurement Study and Implications for Network Applications. In *Proc. ACM IMC*, 2009.

[29] Nokia Siemens Networks. Understanding smartphone behavior in the network, 2011.

[30] J. Osofsky. More ways to drive traffic to news and publishing sites. `https://www.facebook.com/notes/facebook-media/more-ways-to-drive-traffic-to-news-and-publishing-sites/585971984771628`, 2013.

[31] P. K. Athivarapu, R. Bhagwan, S. Guha, V. Navda, R. Ramjee, D. Arora, V. N. Padmanabhan, and G. Varghese. RadioJockey: Mining Program Execution to Optimize Cellular Radio Usage. In *Proc. ACM MobiCom*, 2012.

[32] E. Protalinski. Facebook passes 1.23 billion monthly active users, 945 million mobile users, and 757 million daily users. `http://thenextweb.com/facebook/2014/01/29/facebook-passes-1-23-billion-monthly-active-users-945-million-mobile-users-757-million-daily-users`, 2014.

[33] L. Qian, E. W. Chan, P. P. Lee, and C. He. Characterization of 3G Control-Plane Signaling Overhead from a Data-Plane Perspective. In *MSWiM*, 2012.

[34] S. Deng, and H. Balakrishnan. Traffic-Aware Techniques to Reduce 3G/LTE Wireless Energy Consumption. In *Proc. ACM CoNEXT*, 2012.

[35] S. Souders. Making a mobile connection. `http://www.stevesouders.com/blog/2011/09/21/making-a-mobile-connection/`, 2011.

[36] A. Schulman, V. Navda, R. Ramjee, N. Spring, P. Deshpande, C. Grunewald, K. Jain, and V. N. Padmanabhan. Bartendr: A practical approach to energy-aware cellular data scheduling. In *Proc. ACM MobiCom*, 2013.

[37] N. Vallina-Rodriguez, A. Auçinas, M. Almeida, Y. Grunenberger, K. Papagiannaki, and J. Crowcroft. Rilanalyzer: A comprehensive 3g monitor on your phone. In *Proc. ACM IMC*, 2013.

A Practical Traffic Management System for Integrated LTE-WiFi Networks

Rajesh Mahindra
NEC Laboratories America, Inc.
rajesh@nec-labs.com

Hari Viswanathan
Rutgers University
vhariharasudhan@gmail.com

Karthik Sundaresan
NEC Laboratories America, Inc.
karthiks@nec-labs.com

Mustafa Y. Arslan
NEC Laboratories America, Inc.
marslan@nec-labs.com

Sampath Rangarajan
NEC Laboratories America, Inc.
sampath@nec-labs.com

Abstract

Mobile operators are leveraging WiFi to relieve the pressure posed on their networks by the surging bandwidth demand of applications. However, operators often lack intelligent mechanisms to control the way users access their WiFi networks. This lack of sophisticated control creates poor network utilization, which in turn degrades the quality of experience (QoE). To meet user traffic demands, it is evident that operators need solutions that optimally balance user traffic across cellular and WiFi networks. Motivated by the lack of practical solutions in this space, we design and implement `ATOM`- an end-to-end system for adaptive traffic offloading for WiFi-LTE deployments. `ATOM` has two novel components: (i) A network interface selection algorithm that maps user traffic across WiFi and LTE to optimize user QoE and (ii) an interface switching service that seamlessly re-directs ongoing user sessions in a cost-effective and standards-compatible manner. Our evaluations on a real LTE-WiFi testbed using YouTube traffic reveals that `ATOM` reduces video stalls by 3-4 times compared to naive solutions.

Categories and Subject Descriptors

C.2.1 [**Computer-Communication Networks**]: Network Architecture and Design—*Wireless Communication*

Keywords

Cellular Networks; WiFi offload; Traffic Management

1. INTRODUCTION

Cellular networks are facing an unprecedented increase in data traffic due to the popularity of bandwidth-intensive mobile services. Although operators are continuously upgrading their networks to cope with such increase, the growth in network capacity is still considerably behind the bandwidth demand [1]. Hence, most operators around the world (e.g., China Mobile, AT&T) are aggressively deploying WLANs for additional capacity since WiFi is cheap and easy to deploy at scale [2, 3, 4]. However, sustaining good QoE in such heterogeneous deployments requires a much more sophisticated solution than simply deploying unmanaged WLANs. For next-generation mobile networks, a solution that carefully manages the network interface (e.g., WiFi vs. LTE) of user flows forms a critical component of network optimization. Although such solutions exist today, they suffer from the following limitations:

Drawbacks of Current Solutions: (i) *Naive, static and coarse-grained policies*: Operators rely on connection managers on user devices that are generally configured to select WiFi as the default interface when available [5]. Since WiFi APs are usually deployed in hot-spot areas to begin with, one can expect a large number of users to receive a strong signal from WiFi APs during peak periods. Hence such naive policies do not translate to higher user throughput, since the load of the WiFi AP is not accounted for in interface selection. In addition, most operators do not have the capability to switch the interface of a flow seamlessly (i.e., without breaking) across WiFi and cellular; the interface selection is thus decided only when initiating the connection. Hence, the selection is not adaptive to the dynamic conditions of wireless networks. Finally, the same level of throughput translates to different levels of QoE for a user depending on the application. Hence, loading all the application flows [6, 7] of a user on to the same interface does not translate to improved QoE for all the flows as the capacity of that interface has to be shared by multiple such flows from other users as well. (ii) *Lack of practical solutions:* While some studies [7, 8, 9, 10] have focused on interface selection, they only solve a part of the problem by simply providing algorithms for interface assignment assuming that a framework for seamless switching exists. In addition to the theoretical complexity of the problem, designing such a framework alone has several practical constraints and challenges that it must account for to deliver a readily deployable solution. While there exist some systems efforts that schedule user data across WiFi and cellular interfaces [11, 12], they are limited to delay-tolerant traffic and cannot support real-time applications such as video.

Challenges: (i) *Practicality:* The framework must be light-weight, scalable and designed as an overlay solution over current LTE networks without requiring additional standards support. (ii) *Adaptiveness:* To sustain high QoE, the system must dynamically choose interfaces in order to adapt to flow arrivals, departures and changing wireless link conditions. (iii) *Seamlessness:* In the event of an interface (and thus IP address) change during an ongoing user session, the framework should not break the existing connections and should seamlessly migrate user flows between WiFi and LTE. (iv) *Business interests:* Seamless flow migration currently requires that all WiFi traffic gets backhauled to the LTE core network for proper IP anchoring, thereby significantly increasing the operational costs. Thus, it is challenging to provide a dynamic solution given the lack

MobiCom'14, September 7-11, 2014, Maui, Hawaii, USA.

http://dx.doi.org/10.1145/2639108.2639120.

of incentive for operators to invest heavily on user QoE for OTT (over-the-top) traffic. Thus, *the key challenge is to not just design a scalable, dynamic and seamless traffic management solution, but to also build an end-end system that can be easily deployed in any operator's core network (i.e. being operator agnostic) without requiring tight data plane integration between WiFi and LTE.*

To address these challenges, we design ATOM- a system that adaptively maps user flows to the appropriate network interface to improve user QoE. ATOM has two key components: (i) A fine-grained traffic management solution that uses a practical algorithm for interface selection to maximize the network-wide utility. (ii) A switching service that seamlessly changes the interface for certain user flows *without the need for data plane integration*, thereby reducing backhaul costs for the operators. We observe that certain characteristics of HTTP video streaming and browsing can be exploited to enable seamless re-direction of such flows, via HTTP proxies, to avoid backhauling these traffic types from WiFi to the LTE network. However, ATOM's formulation is not limited to HTTP and also supports non-HTTP flows (although such flows would not benefit from the backhaul reduction). Nevertheless, we believe that ATOM offers important backhaul cost savings since most of the traffic in mobile networks is video streaming over HTTP [13].

We have prototyped and evaluated ATOM on a heterogeneous LTE-WiFi testbed using real Web traffic. Our evaluations show that ATOM effectively reduces the video buffering periods for a user from an average of 8 to 2 per minute. We also evaluated the seamless interface switching functionality of ATOM with several Web video services. To the best of our knowledge, this is the first detailed design and implementation of a practical system that manages user traffic across LTE and WiFi networks. A noteworthy aspect of ATOM is that it is operator-agnostic and standards-compatible, and can hence be readily deployed for any operator looking to manage its LTE and WiFi networks efficiently. Our contributions are multi-fold: (i) We establish the hardness of the interface assignment problem and propose a greedy algorithm with performance guarantees under certain conditions. Our algorithm is scalable and practical to implement. (ii) We design and build an end-to-end dynamic traffic management system that seamlessly switches the interface for user flows and (iii) we conduct extensive evaluations using both prototype experiments and large-scale simulations.

2. BACKGROUND AND MOTIVATION

In this section, we give a brief overview of the LTE network architecture, then expand on the evolution of the integration of WiFi with LTE and motivate the need for an effective traffic management solution for LTE and WiFi networks.

2.1 LTE Networks

The top-half of Figure 1 shows a simplified 4G LTE network architecture, mainly consisting of two parts: the Evolved Packet Core (EPC) Network and the Radio Access Network (RAN). The EPC or the mobile core network consists of both the control and data plane functions. The control plane functionality is provided by the MME (Mobility Management Entity), HSS (Home Subscriber Server) and the PCRF (Policy and charging rules function). The MME handles session and subscriber management including user authentication, mobility management and idle terminal location management. The HSS includes a database that stores the user profile information while the PCRF manages the service policy and configures the QoS parameters for each user traffic flow. The data plane functionality in the EPC is split between the S-GW (Serving gateway) and the PDN-GW (Packet Data Network gateway). The S-GW acts as a local mobility anchor for user sessions as clients

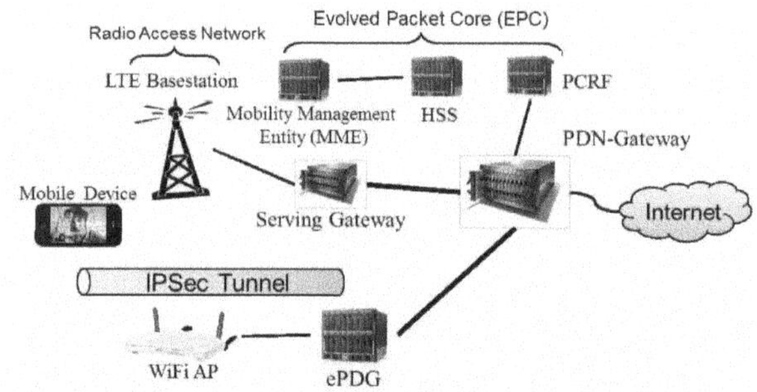

Figure 1: LTE Network Architecture.

move across base stations. The PDN-GW is connected to multiple S-GWs and routes user traffic towards external networks, while also performing policy enforcement for resource management, packet filtering and charging functions. The RAN includes basestations (or eNodeBs) that perform radio resource management and interference mitigation.

2.2 WiFi Integration in Operator Networks

Several standard bodies such as 3GPP and WiFi Alliance (WFA) have defined solutions for the network integration of LTE and WiFi. These solutions are mainly classified into two types: (i) *Access control*: To enable subscriber validation, seamless authentication and billing across LTE and WiFi networks is an important step to ensure WiFi integration. However, the method of authentication varies across operators. Most of the operators provide SIM-based authentication [14] enabling them to maintain a unified subscriber database for both their LTE and WiFi networks, while other operators have adopted the traditional web-based authentication which requires the users to enter their credentials in the browser. (ii) *Data-plane integration*: To enable offloading capabilities and seamless mobility between LTE and WiFi networks, a tight data-plane integration is required across the networks. Such integration involves the backhauling of WiFi traffic to the LTE core network. Specifically, 3GPP has standardized the I-WLAN architecture [15] to integrate WiFi traffic into LTE's mobile core network. The architecture as shown in Figure 1 enables the integration using the ePDG (evolved Packet Data Gateway), which serves as a gateway connecting the WiFi access points with the PDN gateway. IPsec tunnels are established between each mobile device and the ePDG, and the IP address is anchored at the PDN gateway. Since the IP address is maintained across the WiFi and LTE networks, flows can be seamlessly migrated across the networks. The PMIPv6 protocol is employed and the ePDG updates the IP address binding at the PDN gateway after authentication and tunnel establishment with the mobile device. Although tight integration will enable operators to ensure policy control, better QoE management and seamless mobility over their networks, it has been resisted by most operators due to the significant increase in backhauling costs.

2.3 Current Deployments

In the near future, it is expected that operators will transition to using their WiFi networks for new services and revenue generation and provide better QoE for their users rather than just offloading for coverage or during congestion. Moreover, operators are quickly upgrading their network to LTE that offer superior rates than 3G networks and are deploying WiFi APs in areas of high network access. However, current deployments are not designed to use the LTE and WiFi network optimally to ensure good QoE for applications and users. Although most devices are pre-configured with connection managers, they mainly implement functions for network discovery, selection and authentication.

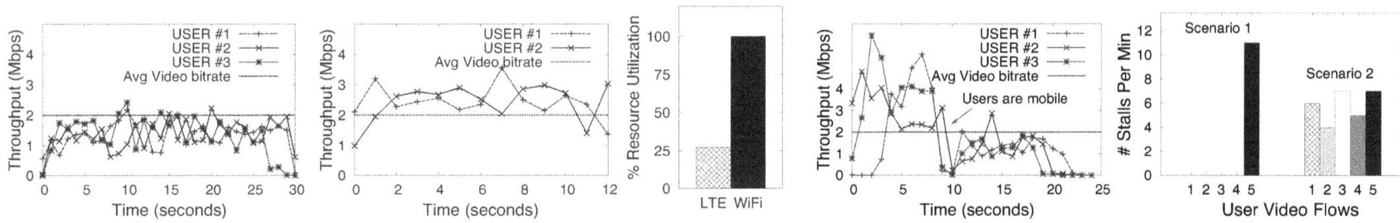

(a)WiFi (Static) (b) LTE (c) Resource Util (d) WiFi (Dynamic) (e) Course-grained Policies

Figure 2: Limitations of Current deployments.

Short-comings: We bring to light a few key issues with current deployments through experiments on our LTE testbed and address them in the design of ATOM. The experiments are conducted using a network of a single LTE basestation and a WiFi AP.

(i) Naive policies: Most connection managers [5] are configured with simple policies that ensure the device connects to a WiFi AP in case a connection is made. A few connection managers use the WiFi interface only if the signal strength is above some threshold. However since they do not take the current load on the AP into account, the QoE of the users could suffer during congestion. To drive our point, we setup an experiment such that 6 users are randomly distributed and are within the coverage of the WiFi AP, while 2 users are outside the coverage of the WiFi AP. All the 8 users stream videos from YouTube with an average bit-rate of about 2 Mbps. We plot the throughput obtained by 3 out of the 6 WiFi users and the 2 LTE users in Figures 2(a) and (b) respectively. We see that the throughput of WiFi users is less than the average bit-rate (2Mbps) of the video resulting in stalls in the video stream while the throughput of LTE users is above the average bit-rate resulting in a smooth stream. Figure 2(c) depicts the resource utilization: while the WiFi AP is over-utilized, the utilization of the LTE basestation is only 25%.

(ii) Static decisions: Moreover, it is not sufficient to make interface selection decision at the initiation of a user flow as wireless conditions change significantly due to user arrival/departure and mobility. To drive our point, we use a similar setup with 4 users on the WiFi AP. As shown in Figure 2(d), initially all the WiFi users receive throughput in excess of the video bit-rate. At around 10 seconds, we move a couple of the WiFi users away from the AP at walking speeds. As a result of the user mobility, the WiFi AP is unable to support the video rates of its users as shown in Figure 2(d) affecting the video of the users mid-stream. However, to enable dynamic traffic management, operators are required to poses the capability to switch the interface of user flows seamlessly across their LTE and WiFi networks. Such a capability needs tight dataplace integration of the WiFi network with the LTE network. While the integration of access control (authentication) methods for WiFi have been widely adopted by operators [4], tighter integration of data or bearer plane to the LTE network has been resisted by most operators, mainly due to: (1) Backhauling large amounts of WiFi traffic through their LTE core network significantly increases both Operational costs (OP-EX) in terms of backhaul costs and Capital costs (CAP-EX) in order to scale their LTE core gateways. (2) Most of the traffic and services on mobile networks is OTT (Over-the-top) that does not generate direct revenue for the operators. Hence there is little incentive for operators to invest significantly in order to provide QoE for such services. (3) In most scenarios, we discovered that the WiFi business units of operators are managed independently from the LTE business.

(iii) Coarse-grained policies[6, 7]: Operators will desire the ability to perform interface selection on a per-application level rather than a per-user or per-device level. This capability ensures (a) operators can provide QoE depending upon the application requirements and (b) content providers may be willing to pay mobile operators for better QoE for users accessing their applications in the future. Operators will need to differentiate the performance of such flows over other OTT traffic. We conduct an experiment to show the disadvantage of the inability to perform fine-grained traffic management. The experiment is setup with 8 LTE users within the coverage of the WiFi AP and 4 LTE users outside the WiFi coverage. All the 8 users download a large file from the WiFi AP. One of the WiFi users (User#5) also streams a YouTube video of average rate 2Mbps. All the 4 LTE users stream the same YouTube video from the LTE basestation. Figure 2(e) plots the average number of stalls in the video session of the 4 LTE users and User#5. Scenario 1 represents the case where all the traffic of User#5 is mapped to the WiFi AP since the user is within the coverage of the AP. Clearly, the video flow of User#5 suffers significantly as the WiFi AP is congested. Scenario 2 represents the case with user-level traffic management where both the flows of User#5 (video and file-download) are moved to the LTE network. This results in the LTE network getting congested and the video of all the 5 users suffer. A fine-grained traffic management solution would move the video flow of User#5 to LTE while keeping the file-download flow on the WiFi AP, resulting in good performance for the video of all the 5 users.

3. ATOM DESIGN

To address the afore-mentioned drawbacks, we propose ATOM, an end-to-end traffic management system that enables operators to flexibly and efficiently manage user traffic flows across a heterogeneous network of LTE and WiFi APs. Before describing ATOM in detail, we explain our key design considerations:

(i) *Network-centric*: ATOM is designed as a centralized solution that leverages a complete network view (of cell load, user QoE etc.) to determine the optimal interface selection. This gives ATOM an important advantage over client-based distributed solutions (e.g., [8]), which require proprietary signaling from the network (creating wireless link overhead and requiring change in standards) to obtain load information easily accessible by ATOM. ATOM is a gateway-level solution that can be deployed within the LTE mobile core network as opposed to being deployed within each LTE eNodeB. This design has the following benefits: (a) Deep packet inspection (DPI) modules, policy engines etc. are already present within the LTE EPC and ATOM interfaces with these gateways to acquire appropriate information. Hence it is better to co-locate ATOM with them. (b) Deploying ATOM in each basestation hinders deployability as it increases the basestations computational requirement.

(ii) *Scalability*: While maintaining a centralized view of the network, ATOM is carefully designed to scale to large deployments by treating each LTE cell (and the WiFi APs in its coverage) in isolation when deciding the network interface for users.Since traffic from an LTE cell is offloaded to the WiFi APs that are within its

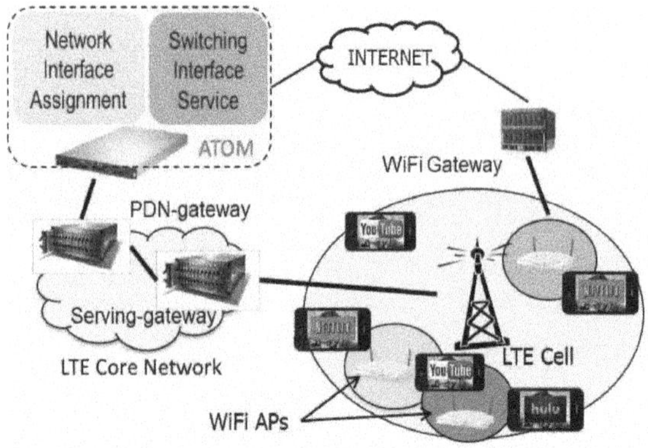

Figure 3: ATOM's Architecture.

coverage, multiple ATOM instances run in parallel where each instance independently manages the user flows in a given LTE cell. This design choice ensures that ATOM can be scaled-up as the operator deploys more LTE basestations and/or WiFi access points as opposed to traditional middle boxes that need to be scaled-out. This design also ensures further performance optimizations, wherein ATOM instances are instantiated only for congested cells.

(iii) *Seamless Switching*: ATOM incorporates a mechanism to seamlessly switch user traffic flows across LTE and WiFi interfaces. This mechanism is designed such that (1) it is cost effective (2) it enables adaptive or dynamic traffic management given that wireless conditions change over time. Moreover, it is hard to estimate or define application requirements on the onset of a TCP connection from a mobile device. Hence, ATOM sets simple static policies on the mobile device, for instance all connections are initiated over the WiFi interface. With seamless switching, the appropriate decision for an application flow can be taken while the session is ongoing. This ensures operators can define more sophisticated policies, for instance based on resolution of video selected by the user.

(iv) *Pricing*: Users are generally charged based on two plans: (i) Price per byte: This is a fixed amount per KB of data (ii) Tiered data-caps: Users have a data limit (e.g., 3GB per month) paying a fixed monthly price. Moreover, operators offer WiFi free of cost to their current customers. However, such a model may change as operators offer similar carrier-grade service on their WiFi networks as they do on their LTE networks. With this in mind, we design ATOM to incorporate general pricing mechanisms to ensure that its design is applicable to either of the above pricing scenarios.

Considering the above, ATOM is instantiated as a gateway-level solution in the operator's access network external to the basestations as shown in Figure 3. Since the gateway will typically handle traffic for multiple basestations, it hosts multiple ATOM instances, each handling traffic for one LTE basestation. ATOM's design has two components: (i) Network Interface Assignment (NIA) component and (ii) the Interface Switching Service (ISS).

4. NETWORK INTERFACE ASSIGNMENT

This is the component that manages all user flows that belong to a given LTE cell. Specifically, it takes as input the signal strength of every user to its potential set of WiFi APs and the LTE basestation, relative QoS priority (or weights) and the current network interface of each user flow. It then computes the appropriate network interface (i.e., a specific WiFi AP or the LTE basestation) for each user flow. In this section, we formulate the network assignment as a utility optimization problem with a per-flow utility function to ensure differentiated QoS across applications.

Network Model: ATOM operates at the level of a LTE cell where one or more WiFi APs are deployed within the coverage of that cell as in Figure 3. ATOM also handles scenarios where the coverage of several WiFi APs overlap resulting in certain users having the option to connect to multiple WiFi APs. Hence, NIA computes the specific WiFi AP or LTE basestation that is used by each user flow. Since NIA operates at coarse time-scales (T is in orders of seconds), it leaves the fine-grained packet scheduling function to be performed by the LTE basestation and the WiFi APs locally. To allow this decoupling, the throughput is modeled as the average throughput of the client over the time T based on the scheduling policy. The problem can be formulated as:

$$x^* = \arg\max_x \sum_{j=0}^{B}\sum_{i=1}^{N} x_{ji} U(t_{ji}) \quad (1)$$
$$\text{subject to} \quad \sum_{j=0}^{B} x_{ji} = 1$$

where B is the total number of WiFi APs within the coverage of the LTE basestation (represented by $j = 0$). The indicator variable $x = \{x_{ji}, \forall j\}$ denotes the association vector for user flows i.e., $x_{ji} = 1$ if flow i is assigned AP j. t_{ji} is the average throughput estimated for flow i when associated with the AP j. The constraint ensures that exactly one WiFi AP or LTE basestation is chosen for a user flow. Different flows of a user are allowed to pick potentially different WiFi APs. In practice, this can be realized using the virtualization capability found in most WiFi cards to create virtual WiFi networks that can run on a single WiFi physical interface [16]. The challenge in solving the above optimization lies in the utility (and throughput) function that couples the decisions of user flows assigned to the same interface.

Throughput and Fairness Models: LTE and WiFi have different MAC protocols with potentially distinct fairness (bandwidth sharing) policies that directly affects the throughput of the user flows.

LTE eNodeBs typically employ proportional fair scheduling. They also schedule the resources to the user flows in proportion to a weight that defines the relative priorities of the flows. In this case, the throughput of a user can be shown to depend on the total number of the other users and their relative weights as follows.

$$t_{ji} = \frac{w_i \times r_{ij}}{\sum_{i \in N_j} w_i} \quad \forall i \in N_j \quad (2)$$

where w_i is the weight for user flow i; r_{ij} is the average link-layer rate (or the PHY rate) of user i on AP j (the eNodeB in this case) depending on the average signal-to-noise ratio (SNR) of the user on that AP and N_j is the total number of active users on AP j.

On the other hand, WLANs when operated distributively, typically use a throughput-based fairness model. Here, all the users served by the same AP get the same throughput at steady state. This is because the APs implement a round-robin scheduling scheme for the downlink packets. In this case, the average downlink throughput of a WiFi user can be expressed as:

$$t_{ji} = \frac{L}{\sum_{i \in N_j} \frac{w_i L}{r_{ij}}} \quad \forall i \in N_j \quad (3)$$

where L is the average size of a packet in bits.

However, when the operator controls both the LTE and WiFi networks, then it is possible to instrument a uniform fairness policy (say proportional fairness) across both these networks. In this case, the throughput of WiFi users would follow a throughput model similar to that for LTE. Also, we assume that interference between neighboring LTE cells and WiFi APs is taken care of through their respective interference management algorithms (frequency reuse in

LTE and channel selection in WiFi), so as to not affect the throughput models.

Choice of Utility Function: While the design of NIA would work with concave utility functions in general, we incorporate the logarithm function as the utility function for all user flows. Although applications might have diverse requirements for QoE and operators will want to provide differentiated services to different application flows, NIA employs the log utility function generally to all application flows since: (a) It ensures a simple system design (b) recent advancements in end-to-end adaptation by application flows (for instance adaptive video streaming [17]) allows modeling most application traffic as elastic. Such a function ensures that the marginal utility of a flow decreases as the throughput increases. (c) log functions are extensively used as the utility function for resource management in wireless networks [18, 19]. Hence, NIA defines the utility function for every user flow as the product of the weight of the flow and the log of the average throughput obtained by the flow. Operators can set the weights of the flows accordingly to differentiate among applications and/or users.

$$U(t_i) = w_i \times \log(t_i) \tag{4}$$

Pricing Model: The notion of pricing the different interfaces based on their consumption can be easily incorporated in our utility framework. The utility of an interface assignment for a user flow i can be updated as $(U(t_{ij}) - E_{ij})$, where E_{ij} is the associated cost for flow i using the interface j and is defined based on the pricing model of the operator: (i) *Pricing per byte*: E_{ij} can be made to capture consumption in the current epoch as $E_{ij} = C_j w_i$ [8], where C_j is the cost per unit weight of the flow. Since the actual flow throughput in an epoch depends on multiple factors, the cost is typically based on the weights [8], which influences how throughput is shared. (ii) *Tiered Data-caps*: On the other hand, E_{ij} can capture data usage till the previous epoch as $E_{ij} = C_j \frac{D_{kj}}{n_k}$. C_j would now be the cost per unit KB of data (given by dividing the data cap of the user by the monthly cost of the plan), D_k is the total data usage till the previous epoch by user k on network j, and n_k is the total number of flows at user k, thereby splitting the cost of a user equally across all its flows. Hence, the associated cost of an interface E_{ij} is higher for the flows of the users with higher data usage in the past on that interface. Instead of a linear function, one could also consider other functions of data usage. Note that the pricing is mainly used to serve as a deterrent in picking an interface. By appearing as a constant in a given epoch, it does not directly influence the per-epoch optimization problem.

4.1 Problem Hardness

Considering even the simplest topology with one LTE eNodeB and one WiFi AP, the complexity for solving the problem grows exponentially with the number of user flows. Intuitively, the problem is hard because the correct choice of a network interface for a given user flow depends on the exact combination of other user flows assigned to the APs. Specifically for WiFi, the throughput of a user flow depends on the PHY rates of the other users attached to the AP (throughput fairness) and in the case of LTE, the throughput of a user flow depends on the weights of the other users attached to the eNodeB (see Equations (2) and (3)). The proof that Problem 1 is NP-Hard for a network of an LTE basestation and a WiFi AP is deferred to the Appendix. The complexity of the problem further increases when considering multiple WiFi APs within a LTE cell, especially the case where some of the APs may have overlapping coverage. Note that Problem 1 is NP Hard even for the case where the WiFi APs employ Proportional Fair scheduling. However, for a certain case when the user weights are unity and both LTE and WiFi perform proportional fairness scheduling, the problem is optimally solvable (proof similar to the load balancing problem in [20]). But this case is not applicable to ATOM, since ATOM is designed to provide differentiated QoS to applications and users.

Algorithm 1 NIA Algorithm

1: INPUT: $\forall i \in \mathcal{N}$: # of Active user flows, $\forall j \in \mathcal{B}$: # of WiFi APs,
   $\mathcal{S}_0$: Set of Active flows not within the coverage of WiFi,
   $\mathcal{S}_j$ Set of Active flows within the coverage of AP j.
2: OUTPUT: User flow Association $\mathcal{A}_j, \forall j \in \mathcal{B}$
3: $\pi \leftarrow \{B\}, \mathcal{A}_0 \leftarrow \{\mathcal{S}_0\}$
4: $\mathcal{L}_j \leftarrow \{\mathcal{S}_j\}, \forall j \in \mathcal{B}$
5: % Outer Loop
6: **for** $x \in [1 : |\mathcal{B}|]$ **do**
7:     % Inner Loop
8:     **for** $j \in \pi$ **do**
9:         $\mathcal{A}_j = \emptyset$
10:         $\mathcal{A}_{0j} = \mathcal{A}_0 \cup \mathcal{L}_j$
11:         **for** $i \in \mathcal{L}_j$ **do**
12:             $i^* = \arg\max_{(i) s.t.\ i \notin \mathcal{A}_j} \{\sum_{k \in \mathcal{A}_j \cup i} U(t_{jk}) + \sum_{k \in \mathcal{A}_{0j} - i} U(t_{0k}) - \sum_{k \in \mathcal{A}_j} U(t_{jk}) - \sum_{k \in \mathcal{A}_{0j}} U(t_{0k})\}$
13:             $\mathcal{A}_j \leftarrow \mathcal{A}_j \cup i^*$
14:             $\mathcal{A}_{0j} \leftarrow \mathcal{A}_{0j} - i^*$
15:         **end for**
16:         $U_j = \sum_{i \in \mathcal{A}_j} U(t_{ji}) + \sum_{i \in \mathcal{A}_0} U(t_{0i})$
17:     **end for**
18:     $b \leftarrow \arg\max_j U_j$
19:     $\pi \leftarrow \pi - b$
20:     $\mathcal{L}_j \leftarrow \mathcal{S}_j - \mathcal{A}_b, \forall j \in \mathcal{B}, j \neq b$
21:     $\mathcal{A}_0 \leftarrow \mathcal{A}_{0b}$
22: **end for**

4.2 Algorithm

NIA employs a practical yet efficient greedy algorithm. The algorithm executes in two steps as shown in Algorithm 1. It takes as input the number of active user flows N, the number of WiFi APs B within the coverage of the LTE cell, the subset of active user flows S_j that are within the coverage of the WiFi AP j and the subset S_0 that includes flows which are not in the coverage of any WiFi AP. Note that the sets S_j may not be independent since some users may be covered by more than one WiFi AP. Initially all active user flows that are not within the coverage of a WiFi AP are assigned to the LTE eNodeB (i.e., $A_0 \leftarrow S_0$). π represents the set of all the WiFi APs whose users have not been assigned an interface yet and L_j represents the set of user flows that belong to a WiFi AP's coverage but have not been assigned an interface yet (i.e., $L_j \subseteq S_j$). The final solution is given by the subsets $\mathcal{A}_0$ and $\mathcal{A}_j$ that consist of the flows that are assigned to the LTE cell and WiFi AP j respectively.

In the outer loop at every step, NIA considers each WiFi AP $\in \pi$ in isolation. It finds the best combination of user flows across the LTE cell and a particular WiFi AP. It then finalizes the interface assignment for all the user flows of that WiFi AP, which yields the highest utility among all the WiFi APs that are part of the set π (step 18). Having fixed the interface assignment for user flows of a WiFi AP in a single round, the initial condition is reset with this assignment. Specifically, the WiFi AP for which the interface assignment is finalized is removed from the set π (Step 19). The user flows that are assigned to an interface are removed from the set L_j of the other WiFi APs (Step 20) that also cover these flows so that they are not considered in the following rounds. The user flows assigned to the LTE basestation are added to the set A_0 (Step 21). The steps are repeated for each of the remaining WiFi APs until the user flows of all WiFi APs have been assigned an interface. As discussed above, since the assignment of user flows to a LTE basestation and a single WiFi AP is also computationally complex,

NIA employs a greedy algorithm to compute the assignment in the inner loop (steps 8-17).

The inner loop performs the assignment of user flows for each pair of WiFi AP (whose flows have not been assigned an interface yet) and the LTE basestation. Initially, no user flows are assigned to the WiFi AP (Step 9). The assignment for the LTE basestation (Step 10) is initialized with the user flows that are already assigned to LTE (A_0) and the unassigned user flows that are within the coverage of the WiFi AP j (L_j). Starting with these initial assignments, NIA moves user flows one by one from the LTE basestation to the WiFi AP such that the incremental utility is maximized. For each user flow, the incremental utility is the difference in utility with the current assignment (i.e. LTE) and the interface assignment with the user flow moved to the WiFi AP (Step 12). NIA stops moving flows from the basestation to the WiFi AP when none of the remaining flows result in a positive increase in the marginal utility. After this step, NIA commits the utility for the particular WiFi AP as shown in step 16.

Performance Guarantee: Given the complexity of the problem in the general case, it is hard to claim a worst-case guarantee for our algorithm. However, extensive evaluations show that average-case performance is convincing. The algorithm runs in $\mathcal{O}(B^2N)$ where B is the number of WiFi APs and N is the number of flows.

5. INTERFACE SWITCHING SERVICE

The goal of the ISS framework is to provide a service to the NIA to enable dynamically switching the interface of user flows to ensure effective traffic management. Every T seconds, based on the decisions made by the NIA, the ISS switches the network for the appropriate user flows. The fundamental problem in providing seamless connectivity across networks is maintaining the end-to-end TCP connection since the IP address of the user changes. While standards bodies such as 3GPP adopt the approach of maintaining the same IP address by anchoring all the traffic through a common gateway, ISS takes a different, yet seamless and low-overhead approach for HTTP-based traffic flows based on two key observations: (i) Mobile operators are resisting tight integration of the data planes of their LTE and WiFi networks to avoid significant increase in backhauling costs for the WiFi traffic (as discussed in Section 2). (ii) HTTP is the dominant mobile protocol (over 90% traffic carried over HTTP [21]). More importantly, HTTP-based video traffic accounts for more than 60% of the total bytes carried on mobile networks and is expected to increase to more than 75% [22, 13]. Although UDP protocol is more suited for video streaming, HTTP/TCP protocol has been employed widely to leverage existing benefits of HTTP, namely caching, CDNs, traversal through NAT, content naming etc. Keeping the above mentioned observations in mind, ISS intelligently leverages certain characteristics of HTTP-based video streaming and web-browsing (discussed below) to design a switching service that switches network interface of flows without anchoring the connection through a single gateway, thereby avoiding backhauling of WiFi traffic through the LTE core network. Please note that although ISS takes a different approach from the 3GPP standard based approaches like I-WLAN, it is a complementary solution and can be deployed as an overlay over existing I-WLAN deployments. This ensures that backhauling can be avoided for atleast HTTP-based flows using ISS, while remaining flows are backhauled using I-WLAN to ensure dynamic interface switching. Given that bulk of the internet traffic is HTTP based including video flows, ISS provides significant cost savings for the operators by avoiding backhauling HTTP flows.

Quick Primer on HTTP: Traditionally HTTP-based videos used to be treated as file downloads. However, with recent advancements, two popular schemes have emerged: (i) HTTP progressive download (PD): In this scheme, video players typically request the video in byte ranges instead of downloading the whole file. HTTP-PD was introduced for video pacing i.e., the client requests chunks of videos at a download rate that matches the playing rate and avoids wasting bandwidth in case the user quits the player before the video ends. HTTP-PD also allows users to seek to a later point in the video. (ii) Dynamically adaptive streaming over HTTP (DASH): The design of DASH [17] is aligned with HTTP-PD, however it allows the player to request different encoded versions of the video ensuring adaptability to network conditions. The original video is encoded into multiple bit-rates and divided into segments or chunks that typically contain 4-10 seconds of video. First, the player downloads a file containing the URL for each chunk for every encoded version of the video. The player sends HTTP-GET requests to the server to download the chunk of the appropriate bit-rate according to measured TCP throughput. Similarly, browsing traffic typically consists of several relatively small sized objects (e.g., html, images etc.) and each object is requested by an individual HTTP-GET request.

Leveraging HTTP: The ISS framework leverages the above characteristics of HTTP-based video streaming and browsing wherein the content within a session is downloaded using multiple HTTP GET requests over time. Specifically, when the interface or network of these flows have to be switched, subsequent HTTP-GET requests of these flows can be performed over the new interface. Although, typically HTTP-GET requests are multiplexed over existing TCP connections, sending HTTP requests over multiple TCP connections in parallel is supported by HTTP. Hence, the subsequent HTTP-GET requests are made over one or more TCP connections that are set up over the new interface or network. Although this applies only to HTTP-based video streaming and browsing flows, these traffic flows do not need to be backhauled to the LTE network, thereby saving significant costs for the operator. This is especially important, given that video traffic accounts for a sizeable portion of the total bytes carried by mobile networks and web traffic is the most popular traffic type.

5.1 Design of ISS

ISS is designed using HTTP proxies in the LTE network and a HTTP proxy at the mobile device to enable seamless interface switching on existing mobile networks as shown in Figure 4. The applications and the browser on the mobile device are configured to use the *HTTP proxy* on the device, which ensures that the HTTP requests are sent over the appropriate interface. In other words, all HTTP traffic generated from the device is routed through the HTTP proxy on the device. The HTTP proxy is a light-weight user-space program that is capable of proxying the HTTP request from the application or the browser to either the network proxy or directly to the content servers. The HTTP proxy listens for commands to switch interfaces from the *Control Logic* on the device. Similarly, on the LTE network-side the ISS framework consists of a HTTP Proxy and a Control Logic. The Control Logic exposes an interface for the NIA to send commands for switching the network interfaces of user flows based on the output of the algorithm. The network-side Control Logic maintains a persistent TCP connection with the Control Logic on every device through the LTE network to relay the commands from the NIA to the appropriate devices as shown in Figure 4. The HTTP Proxy within the LTE network is employed for HTTP traffic that excludes video streaming and browsing to ensure seamless switching for other types of traffic. Most mobile operators already deploy HTTP proxies for optimizations and caching purposes. ISS switches the user flows based on the traffic type:

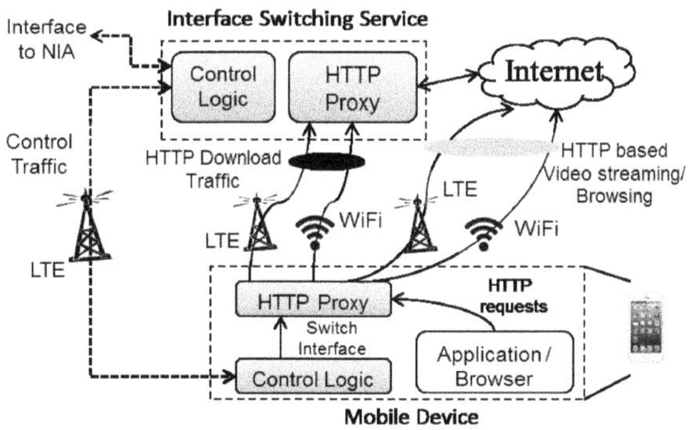

Figure 4: Interface Switching Service.

1. HTTP-based downloads: These flows include downloading of medium to large files (e.g., Dropbox), software updates etc. To ensure that such flows are seamlessly switched between LTE and WiFi, they are always routed through the in-network HTTP proxy as shown in Figure 4. Routing HTTP traffic through the same proxy for both LTE and WiFi ensures that the flow is anchored at a single server and hence the interface switching at the device is transparent to the content servers. Specifically upon instruction to switch interfaces from the ISS, the HTTP proxy on the device sets up a TCP connection with the in-network proxy using the new interface. The in-network proxy tears down the TCP connection over the current interface before sending data over the new TCP connection to keep the HTTP session alive.

2. HTTP-based video streaming and browsing: Unlike the previous traffic type, these flows are not routed through the in-network HTTP proxy as shown in Figure 4. After receiving a command from the control logic to switch the network interface for a specific web session, the HTTP proxy on the device simply requests the subsequent objects from the new interface, while continuing to receive existing objects from the current interface. In a similar fashion, for video flows, the HTTP proxy on the device simply requests the subsequent video chunks from the new interface.

By leveraging HTTP proxies, ATOM realizes a seamless interface switching service that can be readily deployed. Further, with video traffic not requiring an in-network HTTP proxy, ATOM avoids backhauling the bulk of the traffic (being video) from the core network. Although, we can avoid backhauling of HTTP-based download flows using HTTP byte-range manipulation at the proxy on the device, we avoid HTTP header modifications to ensure a simple design and proper operation across different platforms and applications.

3. Non HTTP-traffic: ATOM resorts to using standards-based approaches such as I-WLAN to support seamless switching for non-HTTP traffic. Hence, these flows will need to be backhauled through the mobile core network.

6. PROTOTYPE

Our test-bed consists of a LTE basestation (or eNodeB), openEPC software EPC [23], Madwifi-based WiFi APs and Linux laptops as clients with both Verizon Pantech LTE dongles [24] and Broadcom WiFi cards (see Figure 5). The eNodeB is a 3GPP Release 9 compliant LTE small cell on the 700 MHz band. Considerable effort, involving code modifications to the openEPC components, was spent to integrate the eNodeB (closed-source) with the EPC to ensure interoperability with commercially available LTE clients (closed-source). Our EPC network [23] consists of MME, HSS, PCRF for control plane and S-GW and PDN-GW for data plane functions. In addition, the Internet gateway provides connectivity to the Internet and includes key functions such as NAT and DNS.

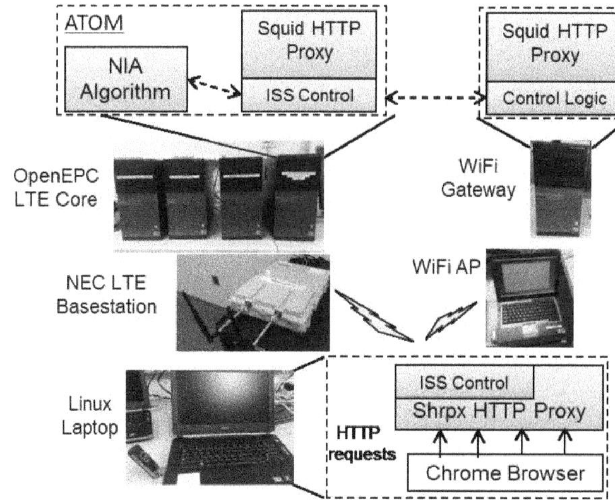

Figure 5: ATOM Prototype.

The LTE clients are Pantech USB dongles with USIM cards programmed with the appropriate identification name and secret code to connect with the eNodeB. Since the eNodeB and the clients communicate on Verizon's licensed band, we use custom built frequency converters. These convert the frequency in both downlink and uplink from 700 MHz to 2.6 GHz, where we have an experimental license to conduct over the air experiments.

Network: We implemented ATOM on the Internet gateway that connects directly to the PDN-gateway. NIA is implemented within the Click modular router using C++, while the ISS-control is a standalone C++ application. NIA periodically gathers the following information from ISS (a) number of user flows active on LTE basestation and WiFi APs, (b) current interface used by each flow (c) weights of application flows and (d) link-layer or PHY rate of each flow. A control logic component is also implemented within the WiFi gateway that provides information about active user flows over the WiFi APs and the link-layer rate of each WiFi user (collected from the APs) to the ISS-control. Once NIA has all the information in an epoch, it executes the algorithm to assign the network interface to each flow and sends a message to the ISS-control with information about all user flows that need to be switched to a new interface. The prototype also includes two Squid [25] HTTP proxies in the network side for both LTE and WiFi networks.

Client Device: We implement ISS-control within the Shrpx based HTTP proxy module [26] that runs as a user-space process. The Chrome browser is configured using the PAC (Proxy Auto Configuration) file to use the Shrpx proxy as the default proxy for all applications. Hence, all HTTP requests from Chrome are made to the Shrpx proxy. Initially when the device comes online, the ISS-control establishes a persistent TCP connection and registers using a unique ID with the ISS-control on the network side. When a new application flow is initiated, the Shrpx proxy always connects using the WiFi network if available. We now explain the steps involved when the interface of a particular flow is moved from WiFi to LTE.

In the case of *HTTP-based download* flows, the following steps are involved: (a) Upon the initiation of a new connection from the browser, the shrpx proxy initiates a TCP connection to the Squid proxy on the LTE network through the WiFi interface.(b) Upon receiving a command from the ISS-control to switch the network interface from WiFi to LTE, the Shrpx proxy establishes a new TCP connection with the same Squid Proxy through the LTE network. (c) The Squid proxy then terminates the previous TCP connections over WiFi, before sending HTTP data over the LTE network to ensure seamless continuity of the HTTP session.

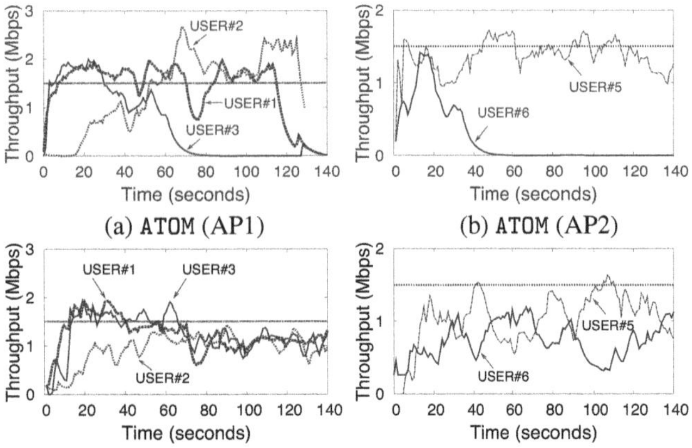

(a) ATOM (AP1) (b) ATOM (AP2)

(c) NO-ATOM (AP1) (d) NO-ATOM (AP2)

Figure 6: ATOM ensures good throughput.

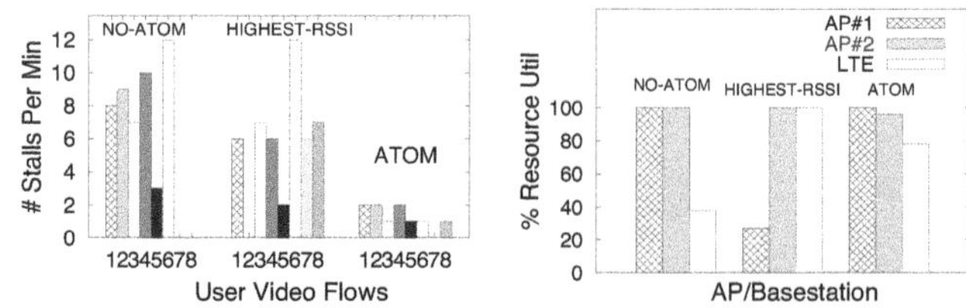

(a) Stalls (b) Utilization

Figure 7: ATOM ensures high QoE and network util.

In the case of *HTTP-based video streaming or browsing* flows, the following steps are involved: (a) Upon the initiation of a new connection from the browser, the shrpx proxy initiates a TCP connection to the Squid proxy on the WiFi network through the WiFi interface avoiding backhauling traffic through the LTE network. (b) Upon receiving a command from the ISS-control to switch the network interface from WiFi to LTE, the Shrpx proxy establishes a new TCP connection with a Squid Proxy on the LTE network through the LTE interface. (c) The Shrpx proxy then forwards all HTTP requests for subsequent objects from the browser to the Squid prpxy through the LTE network. (d) The Shrpx proxy breaks the TCP connections with the Squid proxy over the WiFi network after all the pending HTTP requests have been downloaded. For both traffic types, the same procedure is repeated when a connection has to be switched to WiFi from LTE.

Currently, we employ SPDY [27] as the protocol between Shrpx and the Squid proxies. Although the network (both LTE and WiFi) proxies are not required for HTTP-based video streaming or Web browsing traffic types, they are employed in our prototype since Shrpx is currently not designed to connect to multiple servers. Since most Web servers require multiple simultaneous TCP connections, Shrpx is configured to relay the HTTP requests to the respective Squid proxy based on the current network interface used by the device. An important aspect of our implementation is that it can be readily deployed by instrumenting existing mobile protocols and is completely standards compatible.

In summary, ATOM executes as follows: (i) User flows always initiate the connection from WiFi if available and register with the ISS in the network; (ii) NIA executes periodically to select interfaces for all active user flows and (iii) NIA sends a command to the ISS including user flows with new interface information.

7. PERFORMANCE EVALUATION

In this section, we demonstrate the efficacy of ATOM using experiments on our prototype and large-scale simulations.

7.1 Prototype Evaluation

We consider two types of workloads including video streaming from YouTube and HTTP based file downloads. We evaluate ATOM using metrics such as throughput and number of stalls due to buffering in the video streams (interested readers can see our prototype demo in [28]). NO-ATOM represents the baseline that maps user flows to WiFi APs if the user is within the coverage of a WiFi AP.

1) Static Experiment: We setup a network of one LTE eNodeB and two WiFi APs with a total of 11 users; 5 users are within the coverage of WiFi AP1, 4 users are within the coverage of WiFi AP2 and 2 users can only access the eNodeB. AP1 is placed close to the eNodeB while AP2 is placed further from the eNodeB and all the users are distributed randomly. In WiFi AP1, 4 users steam YouTube videos of average bit-rate 1.5 Mbps while 1 user downloads a large-file. In WiFi AP2, 2 users stream YouTube videos of average bit-rate 1.5 Mbps while 2 users download large-files. Both the LTE users stream YouTube videos of average bit-rate 1.5 Mbps. We compare the throughput of WiFi users for the case with and without ATOM (NO-ATOM).

Figure 6(c) and (d) plot the throughput for 3 video streaming flows on WiFi AP1 and 2 video streaming flows on WiFi AP2. Clearly, the throughput cannot be sustained to meet the average bit-rate of the video since both the APs are congested. On the other hand, ATOM ensures that flows of Users#3 and 4 from WiFi AP1 and User#6 from WiFi AP2 are moved to the eNodeB to ensure that the throughput received by all users meets their requirement of 1.5 Mbps. Figures 6(a) and (b) plot the throughput received by the users on the WiFi AP1 and 2 respectively. Hence, by effectively distributing user flows across LTE and WiFi APs, ATOM decreases the number of stalls from an average of $8 - 10$ stalls per minute with NO-ATOM to at most $1 - 2$ stalls per minute (Figure 7(a)). ATOM also improves the resource utilization of the eNodeB from 40% to almost 80% as seen in Figure 7(b).

We repeated the same experiment by selecting the interface based on the strongest signal, labeled as Highest-RSSI. In this case, most of the users of WiFi AP1 (Users#1,3 and 4) select the eNodeB while users of WiFi AP2 chose WiFi since users of WiFi AP2 are placed further from the eNodeB than those of WiFi AP1. Hence, the eNodeB gets congested resulting in high number of stalls for all users including Users#7 and 8 that can only connect to the eNodeB (see Figure 7(a)). Although this scenario improves the utilization of the eNodeB (Figure 7(b)), the overall network utilization is lower than ATOM as WiFi AP1 is largely under-utilized. Hence, even in static conditions, current solutions cause severe degradation in user QoE and network under-utilization.

2) Network Dynamics: (i) *User Flows Arrival/Departure*: In this experiment, we have a network of one eNodeB and one WiFi AP. There are 4 users streaming YouTube videos of average bit-rate of 1.5 Mbps. Users#1, 2 and 3 are within WiFi coverage while User#4 can only access the eNodeB. We introduce 2 WiFi users with background traffic at around 30 seconds into the experiment such that the flows are active for about 40 seconds. Figure 8(c) plots the throughput for the 3 WiFi users with NO-ATOM. Initially, the users receive throughput above their requirement of 1.5 Mpbs. However, during the time period from 30 to 70 seconds, the throughput of all the 3 users falls below 1.5 Mbps due to the presence of the 2 background flows on the WiFi AP. On the other hand, ATOM moves the video flow of User#1 to the eNodeB at around 30 seconds as shown in Figure 8(a), (b). ATOM is aware that the eNodeB has sufficient capacity to support the video flow of User#1 without affecting the video of User#4. The throughput achieved by Users#1 and 4 on the eNodeB is shown in Figure 8(b); traffic from the video

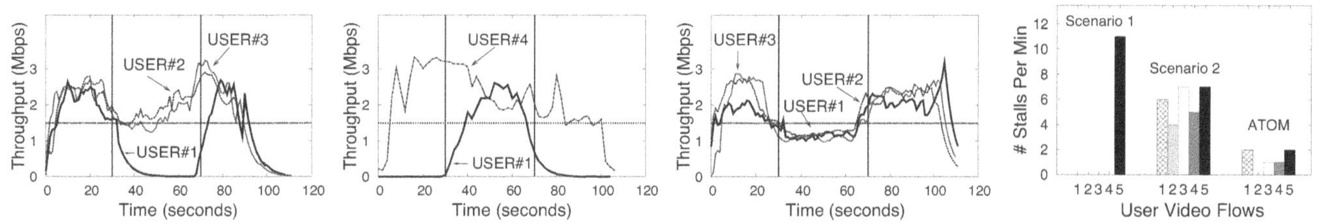

(a) ATOM(AP) (b) ATOM (LTE BS) (c) NO-ATOM(AP) (d) Fine-grained traffic management

Figure 8: Efficacy of ATOM with network dynamics.

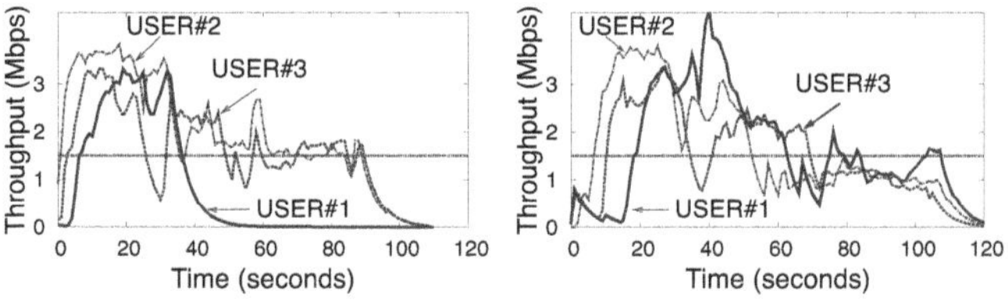

(a) ATOM (AP) (b) NO-ATOM (AP)

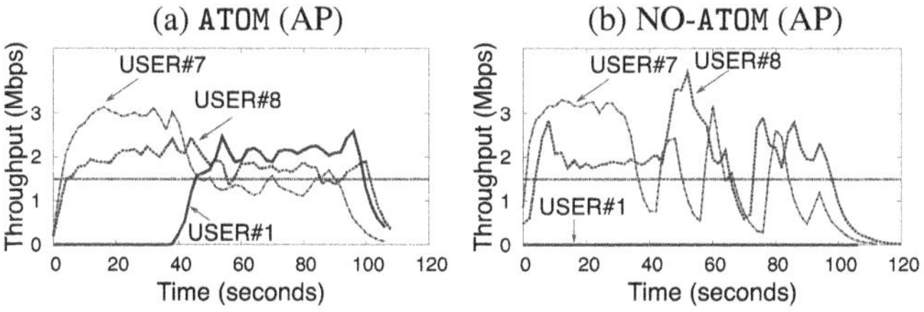

(c) ATOM (LTE BS) (b) NO-ATOM (LTE BS)

Figure 9: Efficacy of ATOM with user mobility.

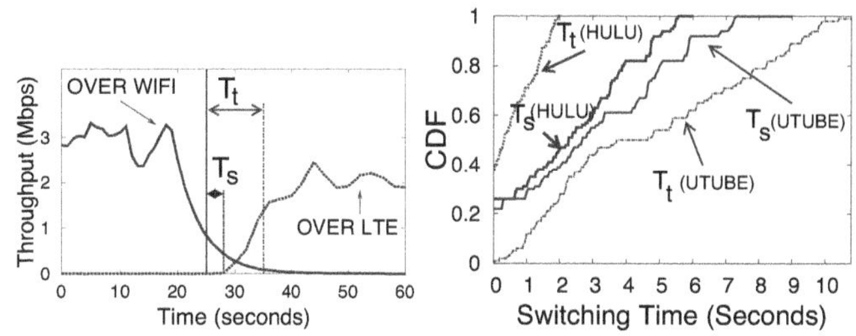

(a) Throughput (YouTube) (b) Switching Time

Figure 10: Benchmarking the ISS.

flow of User#1 starts around 30 seconds on the eNodeB. Around 70 seconds, ATOM moves the video flow of User#1 back to the WiFi AP since the 2 background flows ended during that time releasing resources of the WiFi AP. After 70 seconds, the video flows of Users#1,2 and 3 receive throughput above 1.5 Mbps as clear from Figure 8(a) resulting in a smooth video for all the 3 users.

(ii) *User Mobility*: We set up a network with one eNodeB and one WiFi AP. There are 8 users and 6 of them are within the coverage of the WiFi AP. All users stream YouTube videos of average bitrate 1.5 Mbps. Initially, all 6 users are placed close to the WiFi AP such that they receive good throughput and hence a smooth video. At about 30 seconds, 2 users are moved away from the WiFi AP at walking speeds such that they are still in the coverage of the WiFi AP. We plot the throughput obtained by 3 (Users#1, 2 and 3) out of the 6 users over WiFi in Figure 9(b). Clearly, as the users move away from the WiFi AP, more resources are needed to meet the throughput requirement of the users causing network congestion. This in turn causes stalls in the WiFi users' video streams. However the 2 LTE users, specifically Users#7 and 8 get sufficient throughput as shown in Figure 9(d) to stream the video smoothly as the eNodeB has enough resources. On the other hand, ATOM moves Users#1 and 4 to the eNodeB relieving the congestion in the WiFi AP. As seen from Figure 9(a), Users#2 and 3 receive throughput above their requirement of 1.5 Mpbs sustaining good video quality. Although User#1 is moved to the eNodeB at around 40 seconds into the experiment as shown in Figure 9(c), the eNodeB has sufficient capacity to support the video rates of Users#1, 7 and 8. Hence, ATOM adapts to link quality fluctuations due to user mobility.

3) Fine-grained Adaptation: In this experiment, we show the ability of ATOM to perform fine-grained traffic management. There are 8 LTE users within the coverage of the WiFi AP and 4 LTE users outside the WiFi coverage. All 8 users download a large file from the WiFi AP. One of the WiFi users (User#5) also streams a YouTube video of average rate 2 Mbps. All 4 LTE users stream the same YouTube video from the eNodeB. Figure 8(d) plots the average number of video stalls for 4 LTE users and User#5. Scenario 1 represents the case where all the traffic of User#5 is mapped to the WiFi AP since the user is within the coverage of the AP. Clearly, the video flow of User#5 suffers significantly as the WiFi AP is congested. Scenario 2 represents the case with user-level traffic management where both the flows of User#5 (video and file-download) are moved to the LTE network. This results in the LTE network getting congested and the video of all the 5 users suffer. With ATOM's flow-level interface management, the video flow of User#5 is moved to LTE while the file-download flow is kept on WiFi. Since ATOM operates at the granularity of user flows, the increased flexibility allows ATOM to ensure good QoE by reducing the average stalls per user from 6-8 with NO-ATOM to 1-2.

4) Benchmarking the ISS: We investigate the switching time taken by the ISS specifically for HTTP-based video streaming since video traffic accounts for significant percentage of the total traffic. We measure the switching time using two metrics defined as: (i) Start Time (T_s): It is the time taken for downlink traffic to start on the new interface. (ii) Termination Time (T_t): It is the time taken for traffic to completely stop on the current interface. Both the metrics are measured relative to the time that the command to switch the interface is received by the client. Figure 10(a) shows how we measure T_s and T_t by plotting the throughput of a video flow that is moved from WiFi AP to LTE basestation at around 25 seconds. T_s is the time taken for traffic of the flow to start over LTE and T_t is the time taken for traffic to completely stop over WiFi. We setup the experiment by streaming a single video over WiFi initially and configure the ISS to switch the interface of the flow every 30 seconds between WiFi and LTE. We repeat the experiment for several different videos from YouTube (represents HTTP-PD) and Hulu (represents adaptive video streaming). Figure 10(b) plots the CDF of the two metrics T_s and T_t for the different video streams. Clearly, the median switching times are within a couple of seconds and hence, within the expected time-scale for the execution of ATOM. Notice that the times are larger for HTTP-PD streams (YouTube) than the adaptive video streams (Hulu). On further investigation, we noticed that players supporting adaptive video streaming typically request video chunks of lower size (typically 2-4 secs of video) than those requested by regular video streams like YouTube. Also, adaptive video players request the chunks at a rate that closely

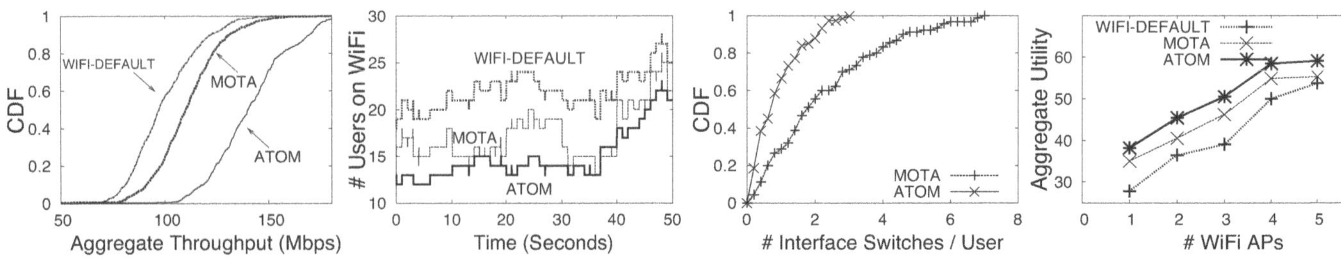

(a) Throughput (b) # Assigned WiFi Users (c) Avg Interface Switches (d) Aggr Utility

Figure 11: Large-scale evaluation of `ATOM`.

matches the play-out rate to ensure adaptiveness to changing network conditions. This behavior results in Hulu streams having a lower T_s and T_t than those shown by YouTube streams. Given the growing popularity of adaptive video streaming, we expect most video services to show results similar to those shown with Hulu (we did see similar results with CBS, Netflix). Moreover, note that although YouTube streams have a relatively higher value of T_t, as seen in Figure 10(a), the amount of traffic downloaded during that time (25 to 35 seconds) is significantly less than the average rate of the video (2 Mbps) since the traffic consists of the residual bytes for video chunks that were requested before receiving the interface switching command and all subsequent chunks are requested from the new interface.

7.2 Simulations

Set-up: We developed MATLAB® code simulating a network of one eNodeB and multiple WiFi APs (randomly distributed within the eNodeB coverage) and used 3GPP path-loss models to generate user SNRs. We use different rate tables for LTE and WiFi to choose the best link-layer rate for a user based on its SNR. We distribute the users in a uniformly random fashion within the cell such that there is a non-zero probability of a user not falling in the range of any WiFi APs. The inter-access times of flows for each user are exponentially distributed and each user flow is active for 120 seconds. When active, each flow has backlogged downlink traffic. The SNRs vary across different flows over time. The number of users and the parameter of the exponential distribution are jointly chosen such that the number of active user flows in the system varies from 20 to 40 in steady state. The MAC scheduler executes every 10 milliseconds and uses a PF-based policy for the eNodeB and a RR-based policy for the WiFi APs. `ATOM` is executed every second and it is assumed that interface switching occurs instantaneously.

Reference schemes: We compare `ATOM` with the following schemes for interface selection: (i) WiFi-Default: This is the case where the users always connect to an available WiFi AP. (ii) MOTA: MOTA [8] is a client-side solution that asynchronously executes the interface selection decision at the client to maximize the utility of a user. MOTA requires additional signaling about the load of each WiFi AP and eNodeB to each client. Similar to `ATOM`, we employ a log utility function of the throughput for each user in MOTA. MOTA is executed every second on each client and the eNodeB and WiFi APs broadcast the required information every 10 seconds. Each client computes the expected throughput on every interface based on the update received from the APs and the eNodeB every 10 seconds. However, clients always have accurate information about the throughput on the current interface, i.e., the interface on which they have an active flow. Although MOTA may be hard to deploy as it requires additional signaling overhead and standards support, it represents the ideal client-level solution for interface selection.

1) Performance: We setup a network of a single LTE basestation with 3 WiFi APs in its coverage and vary the number of user flows.

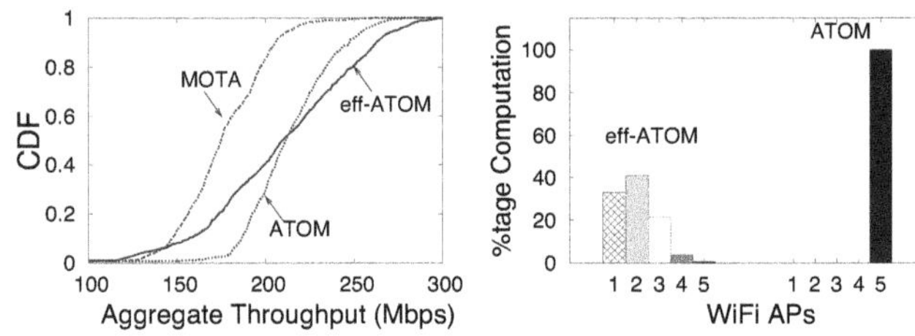

(a)Performance (b) Computation

Figure 12: Performance vs Computational efficiency.

The aggregate throughput obtained by all the clients for the 3 scenarios is shown in Figure 11(a). Figure 11(b) depicts the aggregate number of user flows that are mapped to the WiFi APs over time for a small period in the simulation. As a centralized technique, `ATOM` maps the appropriate number of user flows to WiFi APs and LTE resulting in better resource utilization and load balancing than MOTA. Although MOTA accounts for the load conditions of the eNodeB and the APs, it is not as efficient resulting in significantly lower throughput than `ATOM`. In this particular case, `ATOM` achieves an average aggregate throughput of almost 140 Mbps with a 5 percentile throughput in excess of 100 Mbps. On the other hand, WiFi-Default and MOTA achieve an average aggregate throughput of 90 and 110 Mbps respectively, with a 5th percentile throughput of about 70 and 80 Mbps respectively. A by-product of dynamic traffic management is that it leads to interface switching for user flows. As seen in Figure 11(c), `ATOM` is effective in achieving a higher throughput while keeping the average number of switches per user per session below 0.5, while MOTA causes an average of 2 switches per user per session. Switching the interface of a user flow causes additional signaling in the mobile network and hence, excessive switching may be undesirable for an operator. To investigate the fairness and QoE of user flows, we plot the aggregate utility obtained by each scheme. As seen in Figure 11(d), `ATOM` achieves better aggregate utility than MOTA with increasing number of WiFi APs. `ATOM` thus achieves significant gains not only over naive schemes such as WiFi-Default but is more efficient than distributed schemes such as MOTA.

2) Computational Efficiency: While `ATOM` is scalable operating at the granularity of a single LTE cell, we also investigate an approach to trade-off performance of `ATOM` for reducing its computational requirements further. At each epoch, the modified algorithm, namely eff-`ATOM` is executed only for the WiFi APs that have a change in state and the assignment of the user flows of the other WiFi APs is kept unchanged. Change of state for a WiFi AP occurs if there was at least a user flow that arrived or departed from the WiFi AP or there was a change in the average link layer rate of a user belonging to that WiFi AP in the previous epoch. We use a similar setup for this experiment as the previous one, with 5 WiFi APs. Figure 12(a) compares the performance of eff-`ATOM` with both `ATOM` and MOTA. Clearly, although there is a slight degradation in the

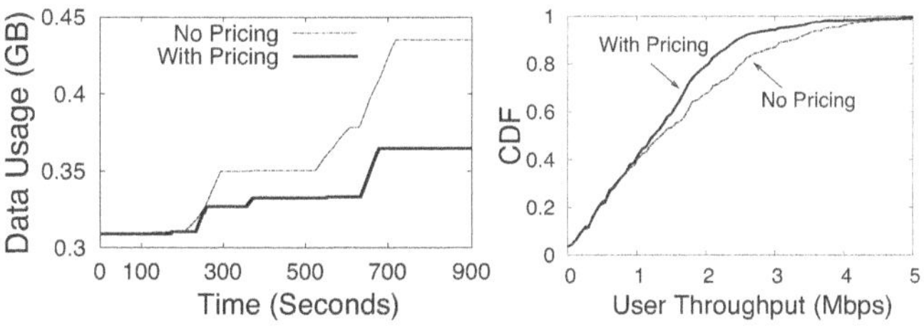

(a) Data Usage over LTE (b) User Throughput

Figure 13: Considering interface cost

aggregate throughput for eff-ATOM compared to ATOM, it still performs better than MOTA. Figure 12(b) depicts the percentage of cycles spent on computing the interface assignment for the number of WiFi APs. Specifically, eff-ATOM only computes the interface assignment for 1,2 and 3 WiFi APs 30, 40 and 20% of the times, while ATOM always computes the interface assignment for all the 5 WiFi APs. Hence, if we consider the computation expense of a WiFi AP as a single unit, eff-ATOM is 65% more efficient than ATOM.

3) Pricing: To study the effect of different pricing models, we conducted simulations with a similar setup but added a cost to the LTE interface. The scenario mimics the case in today's networks, where the users have a data cap and pay for usage on the LTE network, while the usage on WiFi networks is free. We plot the CDF of the throughput obtained by one of the users in Figure 13(b) with and without incorporating pricing. With pricing, there is a deterrence for ATOM to move the user flow to the LTE network due to the associated cost. This results in a slightly lower throughput for the user. However, the data usage of the user over LTE is lower over time as shown in Figure 13(a) with the pricing function since the flows of the user are kept over WiFi more often than the case with no pricing. Hence, ATOM allows an operator to balance the utility for additional throughput (QoE) in an interface with its associated cost or data usage on a per user and/or flow basis.

8. RELATED WORK

Commercial Solutions: Technologies from Qualcomm [29] and Interdigital [30] provide WiFi offloading with intelligence mainly at the mobile devices. They claim to manage user flows across WiFi and 3G/LTE networks based on throughput and delay measurements. They rely on integration with the I-WLAN architecture to provide seamless connectivity. Although not widely deployed, the existence of such solutions indicates the importance of managed WiFi offloading. Since these technologies incorporate context in their solution and provide management across 3rd party WLANs that are not managed by the operator, they can be used as complementary solutions to ATOM.

Client-side Optimizations: Recent studies [7, 8, 9, 10, 31] have proposed distributed algorithms for interface selection. Most of these solutions either require additional signaling from the network or leverage P2P to disseminate the current network. As shown in our evaluations, even with network load information, such solutions are not as efficient as a centralized solution such as ATOM. Some studies also argued the feasibility of using public WiFi for offloading 3G traffic [11, 12]. However, the scope is limited to delay tolerant traffic and may require changes to the applications to support the framework. There is also a recent study [32] that proposes seamless switching of user traffic but it does not provide any intelligence for optimal interface selection.

Network Solutions: Several studies have proposed network-driven algorithms for interface selection or user association to optimally balance the load across heterogeneous networks. A few of these works [6, 33, 34, 35] use utility-based optimization to maximize the throughput obtained by the users. However, these works (i) assume idealized settings with little or no consideration of practical constraints (ii) are tightly integrated with the basestation schedulers hindering their deployability and (iii) do not provide an end-to-end solution that dynamically selects interfaces adapting to changes in the mobile network. ATOM on the other hand is a comprehensive solution for traffic management for heterogeneous WiFi-LTE networks that is adaptive, light-weight, scalable and deployable in today's mobile networks.

9. DISCUSSIONS

Mobility: While ATOM works well for static and mobile clients at moderate speeds, clients with vehicular mobility may require additional support to use context information (e.g., speed) to ensure that such users are treated as LTE-only users to avoid unnecessary switching due to limited WiFi coverage.

Scalability: Since ATOM is designed to execute for every LTE cell independently, it can be scaled-up easily as LTE cells are added to the network. Typically in current LTE deployments, the coverage of macro, metro and small cells is greater than that of WiFi APs. Hence, considering each LTE cell in isolation ensures scalability without much compromise in performance. However, we envision that future cellular networks may be significantly more denser with smaller cell sizes resulting in overlapping coverage across several cells. It is an interesting avenue for future work to design a scalable system for such dense deployments to manages flows belonging to several LTE cells and WiFi APs.

Cellular networks have large number of cells and user flows, provisioning both CPU and storage (for state information) resources for ATOM instances to manage each LTE cell can be expensive. In practical deployments, operators could execute ATOM instances to manage only the subset of LTE cells that are loaded beyond a threshold. Moreover, the epoch time T can be increased to reduce processing overhead (say 1 minute) and ATOM can be executed as and when user flows arrive and/or depart.

Signaling Overhead: ATOM relies on feedback messages from the basestations and WiFi access points which introduces extra overhead on the network. In order to provide quantitative insights into the traffic overhead introduced by ATOM, we performed back of the envelope calculations. The feedback message contains the flows current IP address/port numbers, average transmission rate for that user on the LTE basestation and on the WiFi AP(s). Assuming two WiFi APs on average, these values can be composed in 10 bytes and an average of 50 active flows per LTE basestation, the feedback packet would be about 500 bytes per basestation. If we assume that a particular data center manages a network of about 1000 basestations and also an epoch time (T) of 10 seconds, the total data rate for feedback messages is around 400 Kbps. In the same network assuming an average user data traffic rate of 10 Mbps per basestation (typically peak rate of LTE basestations is about 60 Mbps), the total average user data traffic would be around 10 Gbps. Thus, the network overhead for ATOM under the above assumptions would amount to less than 0.05% of aggregate user data traffic.

Excessive Switching: Although the execution time for ATOM will be in the order of several seconds in practice to ensure stability of the system, in certain highly dynamic scenarios, ATOM may cause certain flows to switch frequently between interfaces. However, excessive interface switching for a flow can be avoided by using a deterrence for flows based on the history of switches performed for that flow in the recent past.

Energy Consumption: Although we do not explicitly consider interface energy consumption in ATOM, the energy consumption could be easily incorporated in the utility framework. Depending on the interface, the energy cost can be added as a deterrent for using a particular interface. This can capture scenarios where clients with critical battery levels are assigned to a more energy-efficient interface even though that may not be the best interface in terms of throughput. However, since energy models are complex and depend on the energy consumption of other system components, we exclude it in the design of ATOM to ensure simplicity.

10. CONCLUSION

To summarize, we designed and implemented a standards compatible framework, ATOM that enables an operator to effectively manage traffic flows across a heterogeneous network of LTE and WiFi APs. ATOM consists of two novel components: (i) NIA dynamically assigns interfaces to user flows and (ii) ISS provides seamless interface switching for HTTP-based flows to enable dynamic traffic management, while saving significant backhaul costs for the operators for HTTP-based video streaming and Web browsing, making it an attractive solution for current networks.

Acknowledgments: This paper benefited significantly from MobiCom 2014 reviewer comments, for which we are very thankful. We would also like to thank Narayan Prasad, NEC Labs for various inputs related to the theoretical aspects of the algorithm.

11. REFERENCES

[1] Cisco visual networking index: Global mobile data traffic forecast update, 2009-2014. http://tinyurl.com/klotw6g.

[2] China Mobile WiFi services. http://tinyurl.com/m7lj366.

[3] KDDI WiFi services. http://tinyurl.com/mzpelfv.

[4] AT&T WiFi services. http://www.att.com/gen/general?pid=5949.

[5] AT&T connection manager. *http://tinyurl.com/msgo4ou.*

[6] Ye et. al. User Association for Load Balancing in Heterogeneous Cellular Networks. *arXiv:1205.2833v2*, 2012.

[7] Aryafar et. al. RAT Selection Games in HetNets. *IEEE Infocom*, 2012.

[8] Deb et. al. MOTA: Engineering an Operator Agnostic Mobile Service. ACM Mobicom, 2011.

[9] Coucheney et. al. Fair and Efficient User-Network Association Algorithm for Multi-Technology Wireless Networks. *IEEE Infocom*, 2009.

[10] Zhu et. al. Network Selection in Heterogeneous Wireless Networks: Evolution with Incomplete Information. *IEEE WCNC*, 2010.

[11] Lee et. al. Mobile data offloading: How much can wifi deliver? *IEEE/ACM Transactions on Networking*, 21(2), 2013.

[12] Balasubramanian et. al. Augmenting Mobile 3G Using WiFi. ACM MobiSys '10, 2010.

[13] Ericsson Traffic Report. http://tinyurl.com/l4sg5td.

[14] Aptilo SIM-based auth. sols. http://tinyurl.com/o5pqqvb.

[15] 3GPP Spec for I-WLAN. http://www.3gpp.org/DynaReport/24327.htm.

[16] Chandra et. al. MultiNet: Connecting to Multiple IEEE 802.11 Networks Using a Single Wireless Card. In *IEEE Infocom*, 2004.

[17] Mpeg dash standard. http://dashif.org/mpeg-dash.

[18] F. Kelly. Charging and rate control for elastic traffic. In *European Transactions on Telecommunications*, 1997.

[19] Andrews et. al. Optimal Utility Based Multi-User Throughput Allocation subject to Throughput Contraints. In *IEEE Infocom*, 2005.

[20] Prasad et. al. Exploiting Cell dormancy and Load Balancing in LTE HetNets: Optimizing the proportional fairness utility. In *ICC*, 2014.

[21] Sandvine traffic report. http://tinyurl.com/ntaddrh.

[22] Erman et. al. To Cache or not to Cache: The 3G case. In *IEEE Internet Computing*, 2011.

[23] OpenEPC. http://www.openepc.net.

[24] Pantech LTE dongle. http://www.pantechusa.com/modems.

[25] Squid HTTP Proxy. http://www.squid-cache.org/.

[26] shrpx HTTP/SPDY Proxy. https://github.com/tatsuhiro-t/spdylay.

[27] SPDY web protocol. http://www.chromium.org/spdy.

[28] Atom project page. http://tinyurl.com/pousloq.

[29] Qualcomm CnE solution. http://tinyurl.com/ky29ogc.

[30] Interdigital SAM solution. http://tinyurl.com/q94s674.

[31] Pedrasa et. al. Information Exchange for Enhanced Network Selection. In *WCNC*, 2010.

[32] Rahmati et. al. Seamless TCP Migration on Smartphones without Network Support. In *Transactions on Mobile Computing*, 2014.

[33] Wang et. al. Mathematical Modeling for Network Selection in Heterogeneous Wireless Networks. *IEEE Comm. Survey and Tutorial*, 2012.

[34] Shen et. al. Cost-Function-based Network Selection Strategy in Integrated Wireless and Mobile Networks. *IEEE AINAW*, 2007.

[35] Chan et. al. A Utility-Based Network Selection Scheme for Multiple Services in Heterogeneous Networks. *IEEE WNCMC*, 2005.

Appendix: To prove that Problem 1 is NP-Hard, we consider a simple instance of the problem: Given a set of $\mathcal{S}$ user flows, find a solution to split the flows among a LTE basestation L and a WiFi AP W so as to maximize the overall utility (given by equation 4). Each flow belongs to a user whose PHY rates for LTE basestation L are $r_{Wi} = 1$ and WiFi AP W are $r_{Li} = \frac{1}{w_i}$ resp.

Proof: The throughput for a particular user on WiFi AP with $\mathcal{S}_W$ user flows is given by (Equation 3):

$$t_{Wi} = \frac{1}{\sum_{i \in \mathcal{S}_W} \frac{w_i}{r_{Wi}}} \implies t_{Wi} = \frac{1}{\sum_{i \in \mathcal{S}_W} w_i} \qquad \forall i \in \mathcal{S}_W$$

Hence the utility U_W for all the flows assigned to WiFi is given as:

$$U_W = \sum_{i \in \mathcal{S}_W} w_i \times \log(t_{Wi})$$

$$U_W = \sum_{i \in \mathcal{S}_W} w_i \times \log(\frac{1}{\sum_{i \in \mathcal{S}_W} w_i}) \tag{5}$$

Similarly, the throughput for a particular user on the LTE basestation with $\mathcal{S}_L$ user flows is given by (Equation 2):

$$t_{Li} = \frac{w_i \times r_{Li}}{\sum_{i \in \mathcal{S}_L} w_i} \implies t_{Li} = \frac{1}{\sum_{i \in \mathcal{S}_L} w_i} \qquad \forall i \in \mathcal{S}_L$$

Hence the utility U_L for all the flows assigned to LTE is given as:

$$U_L = \sum_{i \in \mathcal{S}_L} w_i \times \log(t_{Li})$$

$$U_L = \sum_{i \in \mathcal{S}_L} w_i \times \log(\frac{1}{\sum_{i \in \mathcal{S}_L} w_i}) \tag{6}$$

Let $X = \sum_{i \in \mathcal{S}_L} w_i$. Applying normalized weights, without loss of generality: $1 - X = \sum_{i \in \mathcal{S}_W} w_i$

Hence, the overall utility of the system U is given by

$$U = U_W + U_L$$

$$U = X \log(\frac{1}{X}) + (1 - X) \log(\frac{1}{1 - X}) \tag{7}$$

The solution that maximizes the above utility function is $X = \frac{1}{2}$. Hence, Problem 1 can be defined as: Given a set of flows $\mathcal{S}$, the solution should return a set of flows $\mathcal{S}_W$ and a set of flows $\mathcal{S}_L$ such that the sum of the weights of the flows belonging to the two sets are equal. This is an instance of the subset sum problem (partition problem): Given a set of k integers, the solution should return two subsets such that the sum of the integers of the first set is equal to that of the second set. Our problem can be mapped to a subset sum problem where the input is the set S with elements that have a weight w_i, and the output will be two sets such that the sum of the weights of the elements of each set are equal. Since, subset sum problem is proven to be NP Complete, the proof is sufficient to show that Problem 1 is NP Hard.

Exploring Human Mobility with Multi-Source Data at Extremely Large Metropolitan Scales *

Desheng Zhang† zhang@cs.umn.edu
Jun Huang‡ jun.huang@siat.ac.cn
Ye Li ‡ li.ye@siat.ac.cn
Fan Zhang‡ zhangfan@siat.ac.cn
Chengzhong Xu‡ cz.xu@siat.ac.cn
Tian He† tianhe@cs.umn.edu

†Department of Computer Science and Engineering, University of Minnesota, USA
‡Shenzhen Institute of Advanced Technology, Chinese Academy of Sciences, China

ABSTRACT

Expanding our knowledge about human mobility is essential for building efficient wireless protocols and mobile applications. Previous human mobility studies have typically been built upon empirical single-source data (e.g., cellphone or transit data), which inevitably introduces a bias against residents not contributing this type of data, e.g., call detail records cannot be obtained from the residents without cellphone activities, and transit data cannot cover the residents who walk or ride private vehicles. To address this issue, we propose and implement a novel architecture mPat to explore human mobility using multi-source data. A reference implementation of mPat was developed at an unprecedented scale upon the urban infrastructures of Shenzhen, China. The novelty and uniqueness of mPat lie in its three layers: (i) a data feed layer consisting of real-time data feeds from 24 thousand vehicles, 16 million smart cards and 10 million cellphones; (ii) a mobility abstraction layer exploring the correlation and divergence among the multi-source data to analyze and infer human mobility; and (iii) an application layer to improve urban efficiency based on the human mobility findings of the study. The evaluation shows that mPat achieves a 75% inference accuracy, and that its real-world application reduces passenger travel time by 36%.

1. INTRODUCTION

Human mobility patterns are of great importance for both the design and evaluation of wireless network protocols and mobile applications [4]. Recently, the study of human mobility has gained significant attention, thanks to the ubiquity of human location tracking devices, e.g., onboard GPS devices [8], cellphones [11], and Automatic Fare Collection (AFC) devices deployed by urban transit (e.g., subways [12], buses [3], and taxicabs [16]). A large collection of data from these devices can serve as a powerful macroscope to observe large-scale mobility patterns with high accuracy over long periods, which holds the potential to revolutionize the research on wireless networks and mobile services, such as optimization on Wi-Fi AP or cell tower deployment, mobile network pricing, and traffic-based advertising.

Based on various empirical datasets, several human mobility models have been proposed [7] [9] [10] [11] [15] [17] that capture human mobility to a certain degree yet all share the common drawback of biased sampling:

- The research based on cellphone data assumes that a high penetration of cellphones implies that cellphone users' mobility can serve as a general proxy for all residents' mobility. But based on our empirical results in Section 3, the mobility (at cell tower levels) captured by cellphone data depends crucially on how often residents have cellphone activities, and thus has a bias against residents who are not engaged in cellphone activities during their movements.
- The research based on urban transit data assumes that residents of large urban cities usually employ urban transit (i.e., taxicabs [7], buses [3] or subway [12]) for travel. But based on our empirical results in Section 3, an approach based on data from one type of transit has a bias against residents using other types of transit. To our knowledge, there has been no research based on data from all forms of urban transit (taxicabs, buses, subways and private vehicles).

In short, we argue that almost all state-of-the-art theory and practice on human mobility have focused on single-source empirical data in isolation from one another. Essentially, they all utilize just one portion of urban residents who are involved with a specific empirical dataset as a sample for the entire urban population, which inevitably introduces a sampling bias against the uninvolved residents. The key reason for these single-source approaches is that previous researchers have been severely constrained by the capability of urban infrastructures to collect and consolidate large-scale data in a timely and low-cost fashion.

Now, however, the rapid expansion of urban infrastructure in recent years has offered new research opportunities to exploit real-time multi-source data to rectify sampling

*Prof. Tian He is the corresponding author of this paper.

MobiCom'14, September 7-11, 2014, Maui, HI, USA.

ACM 978-1-4503-2783-1/14/09 ...$15.00.
http://dx.doi.org/10.1145/2639108.2639116 .

bias. In particular, data from cellular networks can be consolidated with data from urban transit networks that integrate various sensors, communication devices and automatic fare collection devices. Therefore, such urban infrastructures are capable of capturing almost all residents traveling within an urban scale (e.g., taxicab users, bus users, subway users and cellphone users) under well-structured incentive and privacy-preserving mechanisms. Although these comprehensive multi-source data have the potential to revolutionize human mobility research, until now our knowledge of the correlation, divergence and integration among these multi-source data has been extremely limited.

To deepen our understanding on how these data can be used for the study of human mobility, we propose an architecture called mPat, which improves the urban efficiency by uniquely analyzing and inferring real-time Mobility PATterns based on the correlation and divergence among multi-source data provided by urban infrastructures, including cellular networks and transit networks. While cellphone and transit data have been studied in previous human mobility research, they have been exploited in isolation by separate researchers for different cities. In contrast, mPat incorporates data from transit networks and cellphone networks, allowing fellow researchers to examine human mobility within detailed transit contexts and to gain deeper insight. Specifically, our contributions are as follows:

- To our knowledge, we conduct the first work to design a generic architecture mPat to analyze and infer human mobility, instead of sampling a particular group of residents. In mPat, we uniquely establish multi-source data feeds through urban infrastructures to obtain mobility abstraction for application designs. The mobility abstraction essentially is the narrow waist of mPat, allowing a separation between the data feeds and the applications for fellow researchers to add more feeds or applications without redesigning the whole infrastructure. We provide a reference implementation of mPat in Shenzhen, the most crowded city in China (17,150 people per KM^2).
- We establish a feeding mechanism for multi-source data feeds and collect the data as follows: (i) 1 billion calling records for a 10.4 million user cellular network, (ii) 22 billion GPS and fare records for a 14,000 taxicab network, (iii) 1 billion GPS records for a 10,000 bus network, and (iv) 6 billion transaction records for 16 million smart cards used to pay subway and bus fares. To our knowledge, the feeds and datasets established for this study provide the highest quality of any previous human mobility research for the human mobility study in three aspects: the most detailed data including call detail records, fare records, and GPS records; the largest resident coverage, i.e., 10.4 million residents; the most complete urban data including cellular, taxicab, bus and subway networks for the same city. These datasets are available at [1].
- We make several key attempts to explore spatio-temporal correlations and divergence between multi-source data. We transparentize the heterogenous features of these data to abstract the high-level human mobility knowledge by which we are able to infer human mobility patterns. Based on our 91-day evaluation, mPat infers urban mobility with an average accuracy of 75%, and outperforms a statistical model by 57% and a single-source model by 39%. The ground truth of the urban mobility is based on a dataset about cellphone location updates.
- Based on the mobility patterns estimated by mPat, we select urban region pairs with high human mobility yet low transit mobility to optimize the effectiveness of Inter Region Transit (IRT) services. Based on our 31-day experiment, IRT reduces resident travel times by 36% on average, indicating mPat's real-world value.

The rest of the paper is organized as follows. Sections 2 and 3 give the related work and motivations. Section 4 presents an overview. Section 5 introduces the data feeds. Section 6 describes the mobility abstraction. Section 7 evaluates mPat. Section 8 presents our application, followed by a discussion and conclusion in Sections 9 and 10.

2. RELATED WORK

Recently, analyzing human mobility based on empirical data has received significant attention, due to the ubiquity of GPS devices and urban infrastructure upgrades. We summarize the related work by the utilized empirical data.

Cellphone Data: Numerous methods have been proposed for the study of human mobility based on call detail records (CDR), e.g., modeling how cellphone users move [11]; predicting where cellphone users will travel next [6]; and identifying cellphone users' important locations, e.g., work or home [10]. To our knowledge, we are the first to correlate cellphone data with transit data to address the bias issue in order to increase analysis accuracy.

Transit Data: Transit GPS data are another important source for research in human mobility, e.g., identifying human mobility based on data from taxicabs [7], buses [3], subways [12], and private cars [8]. In contrast, our method is based on data from the entire set of urban transit networks correlated with data from cellular networks, instead of sampling residents using a specific transit mode.

Other Data: Recently, human mobility has also been investigated by examining social networks or mobile ad hoc networks, e.g., with check-in data [5] and proximity data [2]. While these data provide additional details, the number of involved residents is usually small compared to transit and cellphone users, which leads to a potential bias toward not only the residents who choose to reveal their locations but the places they choose to reveal.

In short, despite the recent explosion in human mobility research, the bulk of work has focused on biased single-source datasets. This drawback points out a need for the integration and utilization of multi-source data. To meet this need, we aim to provide a novel architecture mPat, which is uniquely built upon real-time multi-source feeds to abstract human mobility for real-world applications. Thus, for the first time, mPat is able to provide insights on not only where and when but also how (e.g., by bus) almost all urban residents move. As a result, we believe mPat will substantially assist the mobile computing community in designing better applications.

3. MOTIVATIONS

In this section, we introduce two design motivations based on the empirical data we collected in Shenzhen.

3.1 Drawback of Using Single-Source Data

The previous research on human mobility has relied on individual data generated from single-source feeds, e.g., cellphone or transit networks, which typically leads to biased sampling with inaccurate results. To provide such evidence, in Figure 1, we give the number of residents going to the Shenzhen airport during a 24 hour period based on four empirical single-source datasets, i.e., cellphone, taxicab, bus, and subway. We aggregate the residents using taxicabs, buses and subways as the urban transit residents for a clear comparison with the cellphone users.

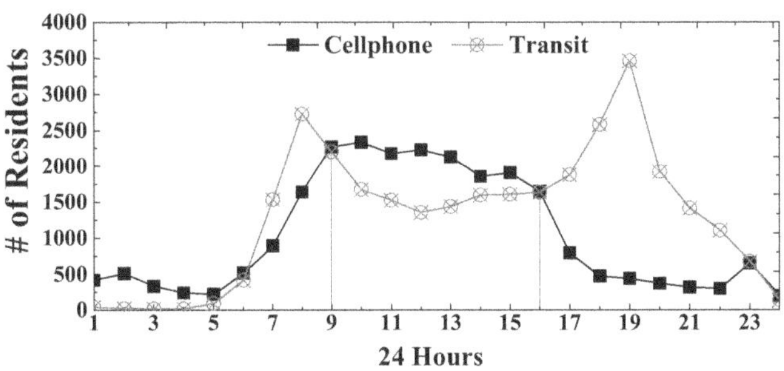

Fig 1: Tracked Residents to Airport in 24 Hours

As shown in Figure 1, we can use only cellphone activities to track most residents between 12AM and 5AM, during which the transit systems are not in service, except taxicabs. During non-rush hours, i.e., from 9AM to 4PM, the cellphone data track more residents than the transit data, because residents travel by private vehicles as well as by public transit during this period. Interestingly, we note that during the morning and evening rush hours, the transit data track more residents than cellphone data because it is difficult to make phone calls in the extremely crowded subway and buses in Shenzhen. Further, neither cellphone nor transit data can track a total resident count close to the daily departure passenger count of 51,000 provided by the Shenzhen airport. This is because neither of two datasets can track the residents using private vehicles and lacking cellphone activities. In short, Figure 1 indicates that both the cellphone and transit data are the single-source data that result in biased samples, a key drawback if used alone to infer residents' mobility, motivating us to explore multi-source data as follows.

3.2 Potential of Using Multi-Source Data

To investigate the potential of multi-source data, we render the daily mobility patterns obtained from cellphone and transit data in Shenzhen in Figures 2 and 3. The size of a vertex indicates the number of residents in an urban region, and the thickness of an edge indicates the volume of mobility. We found both similarities (e.g., travel to the downtown area) and differences (e.g., travel to the commercial area) in these two figures. Both the similarity and difference suggested to us to utilize the Pearson coefficients to explore their correlation in Figure 4. The correlation between the cellphone and transit data in the early morning is higher than at other time periods, which is because most residents use taxicabs to reach the airport in the early

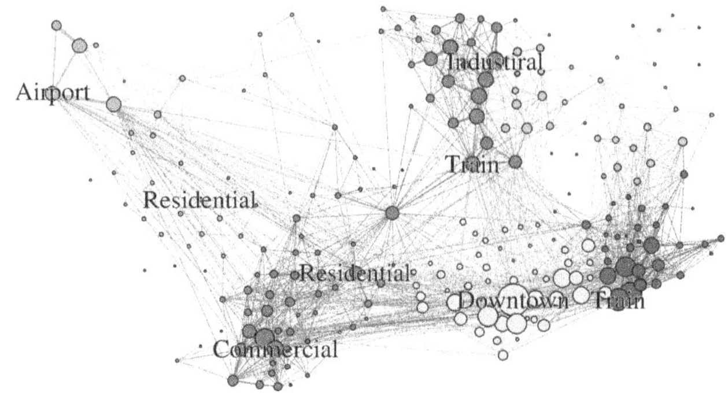

Fig 2: Human Mobility from Cellphone Data

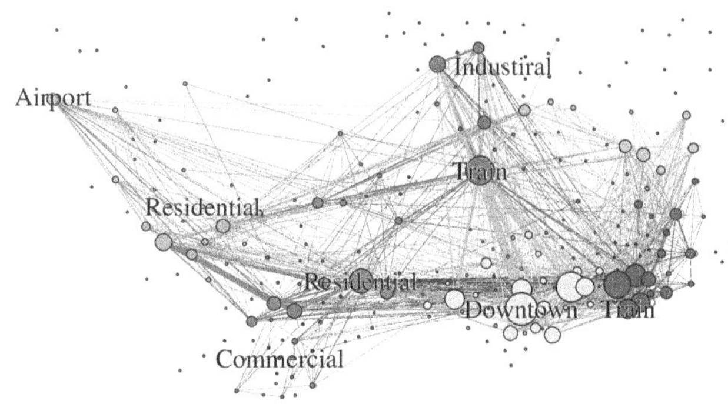

Fig 3: Human Mobility from Transit Data

morning, when public transit systems are not in service. Those residents are more likely to use their cellphones during such trips, leading to relatively high correlation. In contrast, during the rest of the day, the correlation is low because most residents reach the airport through public transit such as subway and buses. It is inconvenient to make phone calls in crowded environments, especially in the rush hour. The average Pearson coefficient value during the period is 0.22, indicating that cellphone and transit data are not highly correlated and have individual diversities.

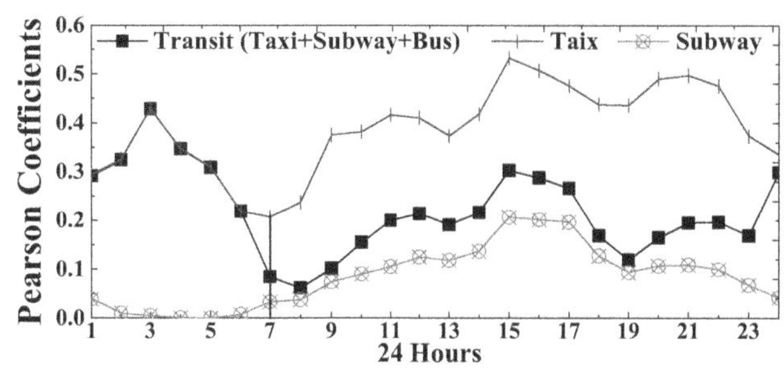

Fig 4: Correlation of Cellphone and Other Data

3.3 Summary

Our observation of our empirical data leads us to conclude that (i) the mobility obtained from cellular infrastructure or transit systems alone cannot unveil overall human mobility, and (ii) the correlation between these multi-source data suggests that they can be exploited together to compensate for the individual limitations thanks to their inherent diversities. These conclusions motivated us to investigate a novel approach using multi-source data. In the rest of this paper, we present our mPat architecture as well as a reference implementation in Shenzhen.

4. MPAT ARCHITECTURE

In this section, we present mPat's architecture, which consists of three layers, as shown in Figure 5.

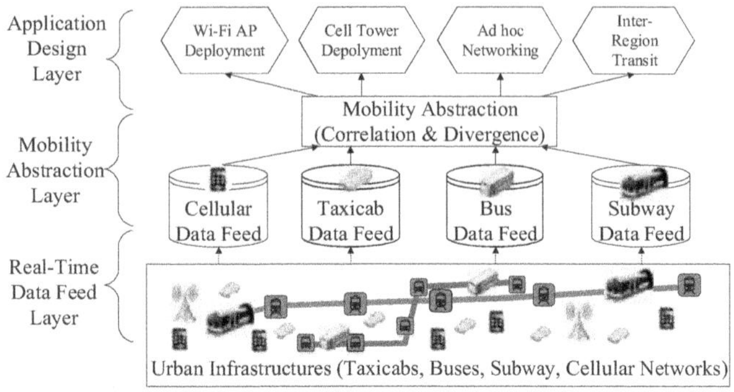

Fig 5: mPat Architecture

Real-Time Data Feed Layer ensures a secure and reliable feeding mechanism to establish multi-source data feeds through urban infrastructures. At the macro level, mPat establishes the data feed for anonymous cellphones in the cellular networks; at the micro level, mPat establishes the data feeds in the transit networks including taxicabs, buses and subways. The details are given in Section 5.

Mobility Abstraction Layer transparentizes heterogeneous features in the multi-source data to enable an effective mobility abstraction in an urban partition with extracted trips. As a result, mPat provides novel mobility analyses to unveil both the correlation and divergence between residents using cellphones and those using urban transit, which are exploited for a real-time mobility inference. The details are given in Sections 6 and 7.

Application Design Layer bridges our mobility abstraction to real-world applications to improve urban efficiency, such as increasing urban transit ridership and reducing travel time for urban residents by uncovering urban region pairs with high human mobility yet low transit mobility. The details are given in Section 8.

Similar to the IP layer, i.e., the narrow waist of the Internet, the mobility abstraction layer essentially serves as the narrow waist of mPat, allowing a separation between the data feeds and applications. Based on the real-time input from the data feeds, the mobility abstraction provides appropriate service interfaces for accurate rendering of human mobility, which are then utilized by the applications to improve performance. mPat's three-level architecture suggests a horizontal view of building high-performance applications, but traditional stand-alone closed systems (e.g., cellular networks) do not have such capacities. The narrow waist allows fellow researchers to add more transit modes (e.g., bicycles) or applications without redesigning the whole architecture.

Since cross-cutting design issues are better exposed when examined under a real-world implementation, we implement mPat based on urban infrastructures in Shenzhen as follows.

5. REAL-TIME DATA FEED LAYER

In this section, we first introduce the data feeds and then present our data storage and management.

We have been collaborating with several Shenzhen government agencies and service providers, and establishing a reliable feeding mechanism that feeds mPat various data collected within Shenzhen infrastructures. This mechanism enables continuous capture and delivery of data from the service providers to mPat's data feed layer with end-to-end sub-second latency. We briefly introduce the established feeds in the layer as follows.

- Cellphone Data Feed is established for 10.4 million users in Shenzhen. The total records of data (including call detail records [CDR] among 17859 cell towers) are more than 5 million per day.
- Taxicab Data Feed is established through Shenzhen Transport Committee, to which all taxicab companies upload their taxicab status (GPS and occupancy) in real time by a cellular network used by all taxicabs in Shenzhen. The temporal granularity for this feed is extremely high, i.e., the uploading period is less than 30s. The daily size of all taxicab status data is 2 GB.
- Subway Data Feed is established by streaming entering and exiting records in smart card transactions. Such a feed accounts for more than 16 million smart cards, leading to 10 million daily transactions.
- Bus Data Feed consists of two parts: a GPS feed for all buses in real time (2 GB per day), and a transaction record feed from 16 million smart cards, generating 10,000 records per minute during the rush hour.

Our endeavor to consolidate the above feeds enables an extremely fine-grained mobility tracking that is unprecedented in terms of both quantity and quality. To facilitate mobility analyses based on real-time and historical data, we have stored the data from these feeds as in Figure 6.

Cellphone Dataset		Taxicab GPS Dataset	
Collection Period	10/01/13-Now	Collection Period	01/01/12-Now
Number of Users	10,432,246	Number of Taxis	14,453
Data Size	680 GB	Data Size	1.7 TB
Record Number	434,546,754	Record Number	22,439,795,235
Format		Format	
SIM ID	Date and Time	Plate Mumber	Date and Time
Cell Tower ID	Activities	Status	GPS Coordinates
Bus GPS Dataset		**Smart Card for Subway & Bus**	
Collection Period	01/01/13-Now	Collection Period	07/01/11-Now
Number of Vehicles	10,000	Number of Cards	16,000,000
Data Size	720 GB	Data Size	600 GB
Record Number	9,195,565,798	Record Number	6,212,660,742
Format		Format	
Plate Number	Date and Time	Card ID	Date and Time
Velocity	GPS Coordinates	Device ID	Station Name

Fig 6: Datasets from Real-Time Feeds

Such big amounts of mobility data require significant efforts for the efficient storage and management. We utilize a 34 TB Hadoop Distributed File System (HDFS) on a cluster consisting of 11 nodes, each of which is equipped with 32 cores and 32 GB RAM. For daily management, we use the MapReduce based Pig and Hive. Pig is a high-level data-flow execution framework for parallel computation and Hive is a data warehouse infrastructure for data summarization and ad hoc querying.

Due to the extremely large size of our data, we found three main kinds of errant data. (i) Missing Data: e.g., a taxicab's GPS data were not uploaded within a given time period. Such missing data are detected by monitoring the temporal consistence of incoming data for every data source, e.g., a taxicab. (ii) Duplicated Data: e.g., the smart card datasets show two identical records for the same smart card. Such duplicated data are detected by comparing the timestamp of every record belonging to the same data source, e.g., the same smart card. (iii) Data with Logical Errors: e.g., GPS coordinates show that a vehicle is off the road. Such data with logical errors are detected later when we analyze the data. The above errors may result from various reasons, e.g., hardware malfunctions, software issues, and communications.

To address the above errors, for all incoming data, we first filter out the duplicated records and the records with missing or errant attributes. Then we correct the obvious numerical errors by various known contexts. We next store the data by dates and categories. Finally we compare the temporal consistence of the data to detect the missing records. Admittedly, the missing or filtered out data (which accounted for 11% of the total data) may impact the performance of our later analyses, but given the long time period, we believe we are still be able to provide insightful analyses in Section 6 as follows.

6. MOBILITY ABSTRACTION LAYER

We first describe two building blocks of our study, then study the correlation and divergence between the individual mobility, and finally provide the online mobility inference.

6.1 Building Blocks

Trip Extraction. We extract our basic mobility unit, i.e., trip, from the cellphone and transit data. For transit users, the trip extraction is straightforward because (i) for taxicab users, the origins and destinations (indicated as OD) are given by taxicab status records with GPS coordinates; (ii) for subway and bus users, the origins and destinations are given by the transaction records of smart cards and bus status records with GPS coordinates. But for cellphone users, it is more complicated because the cellphone data describe the mobile trace of a user by a sequence of cell towers with GPS coordinates, without the specific OD to define trips. Various methods have been proposed to divide a continuous trace into different trips based on the geometric feature of the trace. In this work, we focus on the mobility pattern inference, instead of dividing mobile traces. Therefore, we utilize one of the state-of-the-art methods [7] to obtain the trips based on the trace. In short, this method utilizes a graph theory concept called stretch factor to find several anchor points on a continuous trace as alternative origins and destinations, thus identifying the trips on the trace. Although our dataset includes records from several million cellphone users, the average number of cellphone records for every user is fewer than 10 per day. Our experiment indicates this method is scalable in cellphone record processing. With the obtained trips, we map all mobility into a spatial partition as follows.

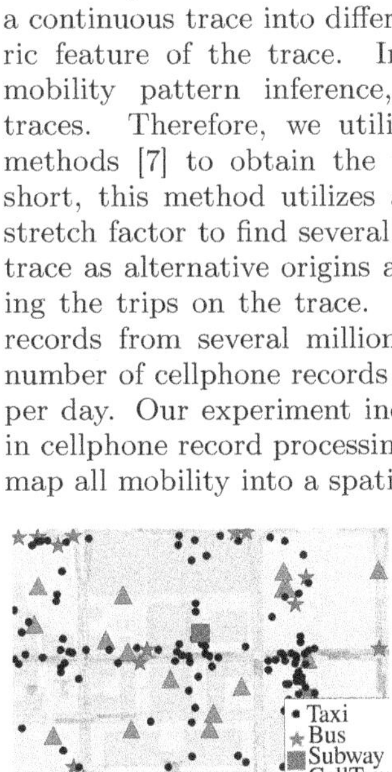

Fig 7: Granularity

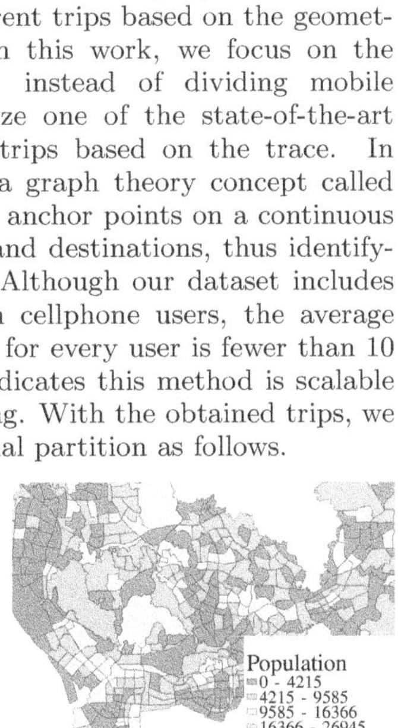

Fig 8: Spatial Partition

Spatial Partition: The spatial partition is dependent on the spatial granularity of the collected data, which is shown in Figure 7. The ability to accommodate various levels of granularity means that mPat is not tied to a specific spatial partition. In other words, mPat works under a various range of spatial partitions with different granularity, as later indicated by our evaluation in Section 7. In our reference implementation, we aim to use a logical spatial partition on the Shenzhen urban area to study the spatial and temporal features of extracted trips in region levels. Some previous models use data driven methods to perform clustering algorithms (e.g., K-means) on digitally logged locations of interest for a particular group of residents, e.g., taxicab passengers [17]. But it is not suitable for our analysis of all urban residents. Further, some fixed grid based partitions are also popular, but such physical partitions lack real-world logical meaning. We argue that most urban areas have their own logical spatial partitions, e.g., Zip+4 area partition, and they typically have a sophisticated logical meaning. Thus, we utilize an administrative region partition that divides Shenzhen urban area of 1,991 KM^2 into 496 administrative regions, based on geographical, residential and traffic features, as shown in Figure 8 in which the color of regions indicates the population density.

6.2 Offline Human Mobility Analysis

We explore spatio-temporal correlation and divergence between the mobility (in terms of trips) obtained by cellphone and transit data. Such correlation and divergence serve as the empirical guidelines for our later inference.

6.2.1 *Spatial Correlation*

We systemically study the mobility based on cellphone and transit data in terms of two key spatial components of a trip: the length and the OD.

To investigate the lengths of trips, we plot their distribution based on cellphone and transit data in Figure 9. We observed that the proportion of the cellphone trips shorter than 1KM or larger than 35KM is much higher than that of the transit trips. Further, the proportion of the cellphone trips with lengths from 1KM to 35KM is slightly lower than that of the transit trips. These observations make sense in the real world. This is because residents typically (i) walk for a trip shorter than 1KM, (ii) take personal vehicles or long-distance transit services for a trip longer than 35KM, and (iii) use either urban transit or other transportation for a trip between 1KM and 35KM. It suggests that cellphone data track more residents with short or long trips, while the transit data track more residents with medium-length trips.

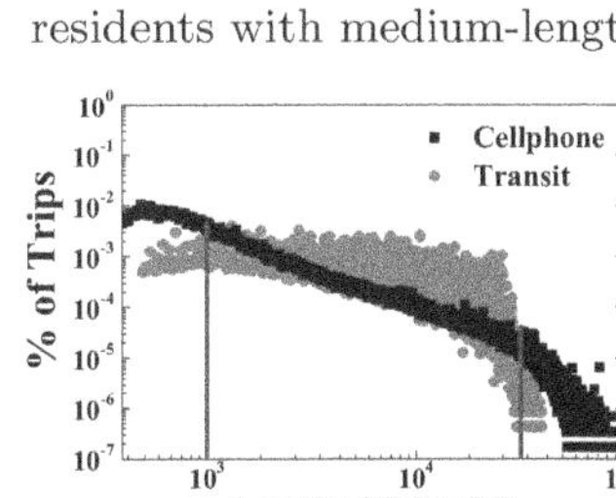

Fig 9: Length Distribution

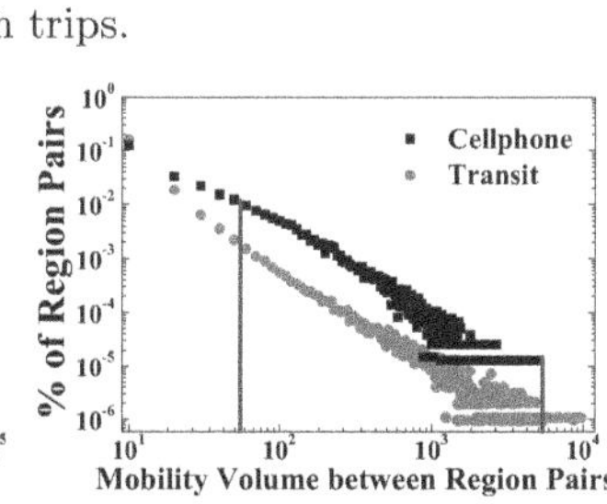

Fig 10: OD Distribution

To investigate the origins and destinations (OD) of trips, we study the volume distribution of the trips among 496 × 496 region pairs (i.e., OD combinations) based on their ODs, shown in Figure 10. For the most region pairs, the number of cellphone trips is fewer than 50 in a day, while among certain region pairs, the number of trips is much higher, e.g., 5,000. In terms of power-law distributions, the exponent of cellphone trips is smaller than the exponent of transit trips. It indicates that the cellphone trips are spatially distributed more evenly than the transit trips. This is because the cellphone data track residents between almost all region pairs, but the transit data only track residents between the region pairs with public transit. It suggests that cellphone data are more effective when used to track the residents in terms of the OD diversity.

6.2.2 *Temporal Correlation*

We explore the temporal correlation between cellphone and transit trips to validate whether the cellphone data temporally outweigh the transit data for human mobility analyses. We plot the probability of mobility (i.e., a trip occurs for a resident) during 24 hours in Figure 11. This probability is obtained by dividing the number of trips by the total Shenzhen population. We compare the probability based on the transit and cellphone data online (by one-hour slots). We found that in every hour, the probability of transit trips is higher than the probability of cellphone trips. This is because a cellphone resident is considered as being on a trip, only if this resident has cellphone activities involving different cellphone towers. As a result, this suggests that the transit data can track more trips than cellphone data online.

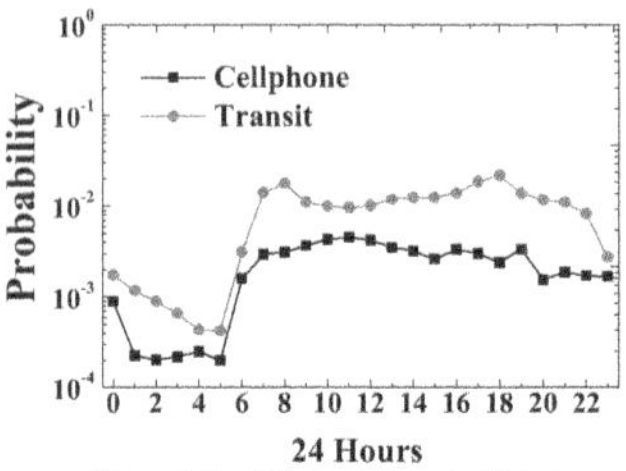

Fig 11: Temporal Dist.

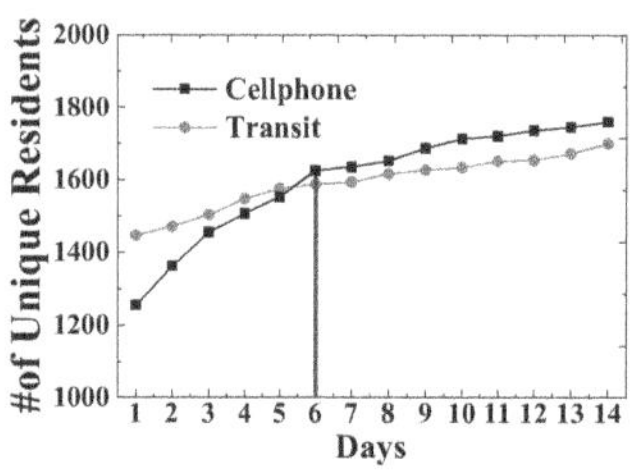

Fig 12: Cumulative Tracking

The ineffectiveness of the cellphone data for online analyses is because many cellphone users did not have cellphone activities involving different cell towers during trips, i.e., the temporal sparseness. But we wonder if we cumulatively use both the historical and real-time data from cellphone users, can we track more trips or residents using the cellphone data, and if so, how many days of historical data we have to use. In fact, certain particular trips for the same resident have a highly repeatable temporal pattern, e.g., daily commutes. Thus, if a resident did not have cellphone activities for a trip on one day, s/he may have cellphone activities for the same trip on other days. In Figure 12, we track the cumulative number of unique residents in trips by both cellphone and transit data between two representative regions from a residential region to an industrial park (e.g., daily commutes) during a one-hour slot 7:30AM-8:30AM. We found that increasing the use of the historical data leads to an increase in the number of residents on trips tracked by the cellphone or transit data. But when the historical data period used is longer than 6 days, the cellphone data track more residents than the transit data. This suggests that the cellphone data can be used for the online analyses, but they have to be used together with the historical data due to the temporal sparseness of cellphone activities.

6.2.3 *Divergence*

In addition to the spatio-temporal correlation, we also study another important metric: divergence which is defined as the difference between the numbers of residents tracked by the online cellphone and transit data. This difference offers insight about how much historical cellphone data we have to use together with the online cellphone data to track the actual number of residents. Theoretically, we can use all historical data, but that involves prolonged processing time, and may not be suitable for the applications requiring real-time inference.

To obtain such a divergence, we first individually obtain cellphone and transit trips based on the online data. Then, we deduct the transit trips from the cellphone trips to obtain the average divergence in region-pair levels. After the deduction, the trip volume for any region pairs could be positive or negative: the positive volume indicates the partial cellphone trips of the residents having cellphone activities but not using urban transit, whereas the negative volume indicates the partial transit trips of the residents lacking cellphone activities but using urban transit. We study the effectiveness of the cellphone or transit data to track residents on these two kinds of region pairs by two divergences in Figures 13 and 14.

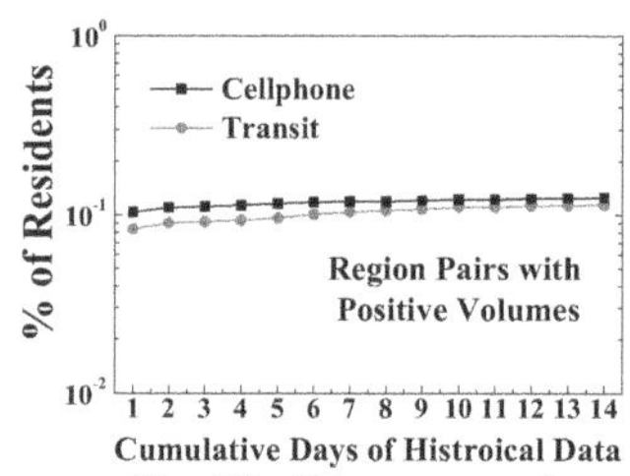

Fig 13: Divergence 1

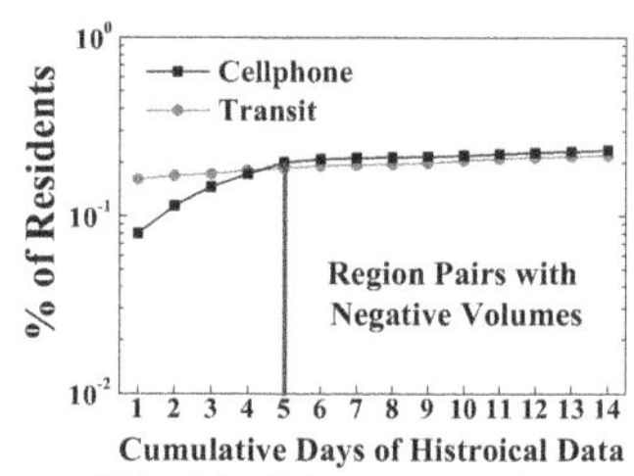

Fig 14: Divergence 2

For the region pairs with positive volumes (accounting for 31% of all region pairs), Figure 13 gives the percentage of residents in trips cumulatively tracked in 14 days among all the residents in Shenzhen. We found that for these region pairs, the effectiveness of cumulative tracking for both transit and cellphone data are fairly stable. After the first day among 14 days, the cumulative tracking for both the cellphone and transit data cannot find many new residents among these region pairs. This is because among these region pairs (usually far away from each other with the stable transit demand), the daily cellphone activities are intensive, so only few days of cellphone data may capture the majority of the cellphone users. This suggests that for region pairs with positive volumes, the mobility inference based on a short period of historical data may be sufficient, because a long period of the historical data can provide only few additional residents.

Figure 14 shows a similar plot to that in Figure 13, except that Figure 14 is for the region pairs with negative volumes (accounting for 69% of all region pairs). We found that the cumulative tracking based on the cellphone data seems to be more effective on a few earlier days (i.e., fewer than 5 days), whereas the cumulative tracking based on the transit data is not so effective, i.e., a 14-day historical dataset can track only a limited number of new residents. An important phenomenon we found is that the cellphone data-based cumulative tracking became less effective (as shown by the slope of the curve) after the total residents tracked by the cellphone data are close to or more than the total residents tracked by the transit data. One explanation for such an empirical result is that all transit residents may use the cellphone at least once during the five days of the transit, so the cumulative cellphone data can track almost all the transit residents within a few days along with additional private car users. This phenomenon serves as a key design guideline for our later mobility inference to balance the inference accuracy and the utilization of the historical data.

6.2.4 *Remark*

In this subsection, we empirically analyze both the correlation and divergence between the trips obtained by cellphone and transit data, leading to a few insights for our mobility inference design. In particular, (i) the historical cellphone data are more effective than the transit data in various spatial metrics as in Section 6.2.1; (ii) the online cellphone data, due to their temporal spareness, have to be used together with the historical cellphone data to outweigh the transit data, as in Section 6.2.2; and (iii) the effectiveness of the historical cellphone data is different for various region pairs, and such effectiveness can be indicated by the mobility divergence between the cellphone and transit data as in Section 6.2.3.

6.3 Online Human Mobility Inference

In this subsection, we infer real-time online human mobility patterns based on the insights obtained in the last subsection. Such real-time mobility indicates how many residents are traveling between urban regions in a spatial partition. To this end, we propose a concept called a mobility graph. For a time slot τ, the mobility graph G is a directed graph where (i) a vertex indicates one region in a given spatial partition; (ii) an edge between two vertices indicates the mobility between two associated regions; (iii) a weight on an edge indicates the real-time mobility volume during the slot τ. As follows, we introduce how to infer such a mobility graph G for all the residents, based on the correlation and divergency between (i) the mobility graph G^c for the residents with cellphone activities in the previous slot, and (ii) the mobility graph G^t for the residents in the transit systems at the end of the previous slot.

6.3.1 *Inferring Overview*

There are two methods to infer G to cover all residents' mobility. First, G can be obtained by combining G^c and $G^{\bar{c}}$, i.e., combining the mobility patterns for the resident groups with and without cellphone activities at the end of the previous slot. Second, G can be obtained by combining G^t and $G^{\bar{t}}$, i.e., combining the mobility patterns for the resident groups using urban transit or private vehicles, respectively, in the previous slot. But in reality, neither of two methods works since the current infrastructures can track neither the residents lacking cellphone activities nor the residents using private vehicles.

Accordingly, in this work, we uniquely combine the above two methods together, based on our previous analyses. In particular, we first obtain G^c for the residents with cellphone activities based on the real-time online cellphone data. We then estimate $G^{\bar{c}}$ for the residents without cellphone activities based on the historical cellphone data. This is built upon the observation that the residents who were not captured by the cellphone data today may be captured by the historical data before due to repeatable daily travel patterns as shown in Figure 12. But due to the big size (several TBs) of our historical data and the real-time requirement for the online inference, we iteratively use partial historical data by batches as the retrospective data to estimate $G^{\bar{c}}$ in cumulation, instead of using all historical data at once. Such iterative estimation is challenging, because we could easily overestimate or underestimate $G^{\bar{c}}$ due to lack of knowledge on when to stop the iterative estimation.

To address this challenge, we use mobility graph G^t for the residents using urban transit as a threshold to stop the iteration if the cumulated $G^{\bar{c}}$ plus G^c completely covers G^t. The rationale behind this condition is based on our observation of the mobility divergence in Figures 13 and 14 in Section 6.2.3. For the region pairs with negative divergence volumes (i.e., the region pairs where the real-time cellphone mobility is more than the real-time transit mobility), the historical cellphone data based inference can only find few new residents compared to the residents they already found as in Figure 13. However, for the region pairs with negative divergence volumes (i.e., region pairs where the real-time cellphone mobility is less than the real-time transit mobility), the historical cellphone data based inference can find many new residents in recent few days, but they become much less effective after the obtained cellphone mobility $G^{\bar{c}}$ plus G^c covers the mobility G^t captured by the current transit data, as in Figure 14. Consequently, if $G^{\bar{c}} + G^c$ covers G^t, we stop continuing to iteratively train the historical cellphone data. Based on previous our analyses, if we stop the iteration earlier, we may underestimate the number of new residents; but if we stop the iteration later, we may obtain the limited new residents yet require much longer processing time. Such a balance is evaluated in Section 7.4.

Note that we use the transit data to assist in the utilization of the cellphone data instead of the other way around, which is because by our analyses in Sections 6.2.1 and 6.2.2, if combined with the historical data, the cellphone data are more effective than the transit data for tracking residents online.

6.3.2 *Inferring Algorithm*

The prerequisite for the inferring algorithm is to obtain G^c and G^t based on historical and real-time data, which is introduced in Section 6.3.3. Another input is the historical cellphone dataset $D[1, ..., K]$ of K days of the data related to the cellphone users without activities in the latest slot, which are used to infer the repeatable trips that were not captured by today's data due to lack of cellphone activities. Given them, our inferring algorithm is described as follows.

Algorithm 1 Inference of Mobility Graph G

Require: (i) G^c; (ii) G^t; (iii) $D[1, ..., K]$;
Ensure: Inferred G;
$k \leftarrow 0$;
repeat
  Estimate $G^{\bar{c}}$ based on $D[K-k, ..., K]$;
  $k \leftarrow k+1$;
until $G^c + G^{\bar{c}}$ covers G^t or $k = K$
$G \leftarrow G^c + G^{\bar{c}}$;

The rationale behind our algorithm is as follows. We first infer $G^{\bar{c}}$ for the cellphone users without activities by the Kth related day of data in $D[K]$ as the retrospective data, e.g., the same day of the week in the previous week. On one hand, if $G^c + G^{\bar{c}}$ completely covers G^t, then it suggests that the mobility pattern of the cellphone users (shown by $G^c + G^{\bar{c}}$) has covered the mobility pattern of the residents using urban transit (shown by G^t). It suggests that the inferring process after this stage will track limited residents, so we use $G^c + G^{\bar{c}}$ to infer G and stop the algorithm. On the other hand, if $G^c + G^{\bar{c}}$ does not cover G^t, then it suggests that the training process after this stage will continue to track more residents, so the current $G^c + G^{\bar{c}}$ cannot be used to infer G. Thus, we continue to cumulatively estimate $G^{\bar{c}}$ based on one more previous related day of data as the increased retrospective data about these uncaptured cellphone users (i.e., the retrospective data increase to the data $D[K-1, K]$ including both $(K-1)$th and Kth related day), which is to compensate for the situation where a resident who still has no cellphone activities in the Kth related day. At the worst-case scenario, we go through the historical datasets of all related days to cumulatively estimate $G^{\bar{c}}$. Note that we increase the retrospective data from the latest to the earliest due to the freshness of the latest data.

These are three unresolved issues in the algorithm: (i) how to infer G^c and G^t, (ii) how to determine if $G^c + G^{\bar{c}}$ covers G^t, and (iii) how to iteratively estimate $G^{\bar{c}}$. These issues are discussed in the following three subsections.

6.3.3 G^c and G^t Inference

The inference about G^c and G^t is a classic topic for many data mining applications [7]. To focus on our key novelty, we maintain and update the conditional probability distributions over the set of destinations that a particular cellphone or transit user can go to, given the previous trip history and three real-time contexts, i.e., the current location, the time of day and the day of week. With these distributions, we obtain G^c and G^t with a straightforward probabilistic method. Note that this probabilistic method has a high accuracy because the majority of residents are regular commuters traveling between home and workplace. For example, Figure 16 gives the CDF of distinct exiting stations for residents taking subways in a week, and we found that 67% of all these residents only exit at two distinct stations or fewer, e.g., home and workplace. As a result, it allows us to provide very accurate inference on which station a resident will exit, given the real-time contexts. In addition to the exiting station, we are also able to infer the exiting time. We notice that public transit systems have relatively stable travel time between stations in different time periods. Figure 15 gives the average subway travel time in a week between Shenzhen train station and Shenzhen airport, and we found that the travel time is stable about 74 minutes with a 2 minute variance. This nice feature allows us to use the timing information from smartcard transactions when residents enter the transit systems to infer the mobility.

6.3.4 G^t Coverage

In this work, $G^c + G^{\bar{c}}$ covers G^t, if the mobility in $G^c + G^{\bar{c}}$ spatially and temporally covers the mobility in G^t. This special spatio-temporal correlation can be validated by an edge-based weight comparison, i.e., $G^c + G^{\bar{c}}$ covers G^t, if the weight of every edge in $G^c + G^{\bar{c}}$ is larger than or equal to the weight of the corresponding edge in G^t. This edge-based weight comparison is possible because the two involved graphs (i.e., $G^c + G^{\bar{c}}$ and G^t) have the same vertices (due to self loops for every vertex associated to an urban region) and edges, and the differences are weights on edges (if no mobility exists between two vertices, the corresponding weight is 0). As a result, the fact that a graph $G^c + G^{\bar{c}}$ covers G^t can be validated by a condition: the weight (i.e., the volume) of every edge in $G^c + G^{\bar{c}}$ is higher than the weight of the corresponding edge in G^t. Such a validation is scalable and can be completed in the polynomial time due to the limited number of edges.

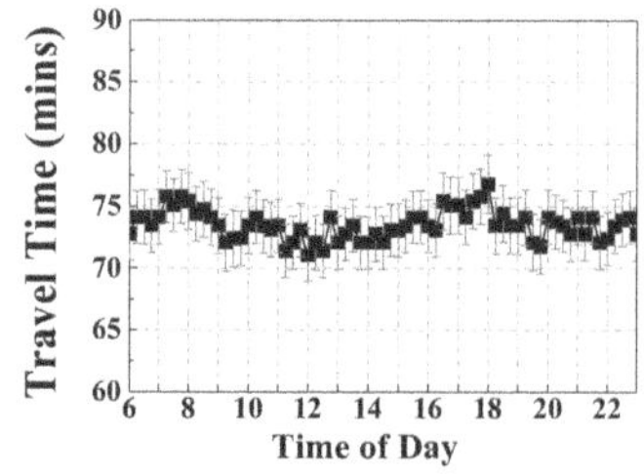

Fig 15: Travel Time

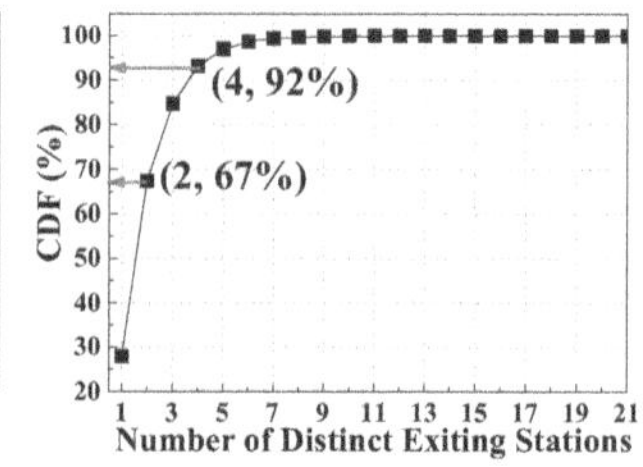

Fig 16: Distinct Stations

6.3.5 $G^{\bar{c}}$ Estimation

Iteratively estimating $G^{\bar{c}}$ by the cumulatively increasing retrospective data is equal to iteratively increasing the weights on edges of $G^{\bar{c}}$. As in Algorithm 1, we increase weights on edges of $G^{\bar{c}}$ by the retrospective data on a daily basis, which is based on the observation that most residents move among regions in regular daily patterns [17], e.g., daily commutes. So if they were not captured by the cellphone data today, they may be captured during a time with the similar contexts, e.g., the time of the day and the day of the week. As a result, for every uncaptured cellphone user due to lack of cellphone activities in the latest slot, we validate if this user was captured by the data of the previous related days in the retrospective data. If this user was indeed captured, we increase the weight on the corresponding edge of $G^{\bar{c}}$ to reflect this new captured mobility.

The key step for our estimation is to find the related historical data $D[1, ..., K]$. In this work, we categorize the cellphone data by two contexts, the time of the day and the day of the week. Then, for a particular time slot of a day, the related historical data are the historical data with the same contexts. For example, if we have the latest 14 weeks of the cellphone data as the total historical data, then for the slot from 7AM to 8AM on the next Monday, the related historical data are the historical data belonging to the 14 time slots from 7AM to 8AM, one for each of 14 previous Mondays. These related historical data $D[1, ..., K]$ would become the retrospective data $D[K-i, ..., K]$ during the ith iteration in Algorithm 1.

7. MPAT EVALUATION

7.1 Evaluation Methodology

We compare mPat with two state-of-the-art models. The Radiation model [14] infers the mobility based on the population density of an origin region and a destination region and that of the surrounding regions. To estimate the

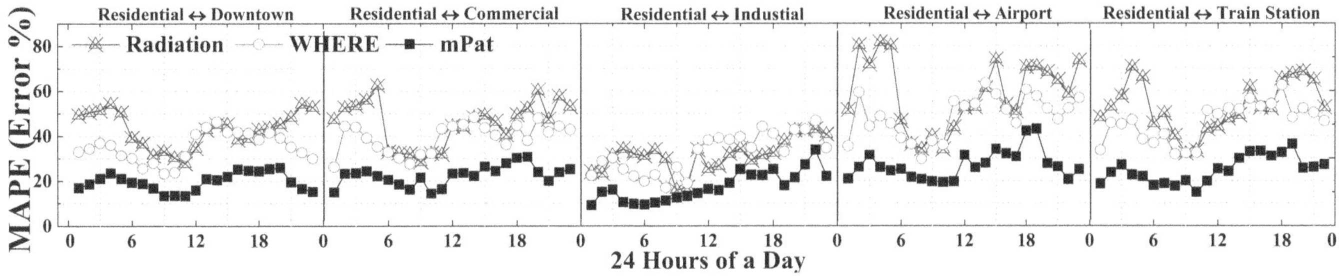

Fig 17: MAPE under One Hour Slot for 24 Hours of a day

region population, we allocate every cellphone user to a region where he/she stays the most at a particular slot based on three months of the cellphone data. Radiation serves as a statistical model suitable for the situation where the real-time data are not available. The WHERE model [11] takes the spatial and temporal probability distributions drawn from the cellphone data and produces synthetic cellphone data to indicate the inferred mobility. WHERE serves as a single-source approach for the situation where only the cellphone data are available. Further, we study the effect of the multi-source data correlation by comparing mPat to one of its variants called mPat-S, which uses all historical data as the retrospective data for the inference.

We utilize three months (91 days) of datasets from all feeds in Figure 6 on a rolling basis. We divide the data into two subsets: the testing set including the data for one particular day as the real-time streaming data; and the historical set including the data for the remaining of 90 days as the historical data. For a particular day, if we use one hour slots, at the end of the first slot, i.e., 1AM, we use mPat to infer the mobility for the slot from 12AM to 1AM, based on both the "real-time" data from 12AM to 1AM in the testing set, and all the data in the historical set. We test the models with Mean Average Percent Error (MAPE) in a time slot as MAPE $= \frac{100}{n}\sum_{i=1}^{n}\frac{|\bar{\mathbf{T}}_i - \mathbf{T}_i|}{\bar{\mathbf{T}}_i}$, where $n = 496 \times 496 = 246016$ is the total number of region pairs; $\mathbf{T}_i$ is the inferred mobility between a region pair i; $\bar{\mathbf{T}}_i$ is the ground truth of the mobility between a region pair i. We move the data in the testing set forward for 90 days, leading to 90 experiments. The average results were reported.

Note that it is almost impossible to accurately obtain the ground truth $\bar{\mathbf{T}}$ of urban mobility, unless we put a GPS tracker on every resident in a city for 24 hours a day. In order to infer the ground truth, we introduce another novel cellphone related dataset for the evaluation purpose. It contains regular location updates of 7.6 million active cellphone users in Shenzhen with 200 million records per day. The unique feature about this new dataset is that it was obtained by sampling locations of all the cellphone users every 15 minutes on average at the cell tower levels, whether the users have cellphone activities or not. The only requirement is that the users have to turn on the cellphones. We use the mobility obtained from this dataset as the ground truth for the evaluation. We believe the mobility based on this new dataset is much closer to the actual ground truth than the previous methods.

Note that unlike call detail records (CDRs) which are stored for billing purposes during regular cellular operations, this "ground truth" dataset is obtained through extensive instrumentation of cellular infrastructures. It requires significant extra support in terms of software, hardware, and regulation policies. For example, this "ground truth" dataset grows more than 100GB per day and consolidating such a large dataset also requires a significant investment on computing infrastructure. Consequently, without immediate benefits, the cellphone service providers have no incentive to store this large-scale streaming dataset in regular operations, and hence it cannot be used as a regular input of mPat. In our particular case, this "ground truth" dataset was obtained during peak performance testing. Thus, unlike the generic datasets we introduced as the input of mPat, we obtained this new dataset from the providers offline and did not have regular real-time access to it.

With the "ground truth" dataset available, we first compare the inference models on two different spatial partitions, i.e., urban region level and road segment level, to show their accuracy under different granularity. Further, we investigate the impact of the historical data size on the accuracy and the running time of mPat to show its feasibility and robustness for the real-time inferences, justifying the mPat design. Finally, we present a summary.

7.2 Accuracy on Region Levels

We compare three models' inferring accuracy in terms of MAPE values in different lengths of slots with a low-level comparison on five representative region pairs and a high-level comparison of all 246016 region pairs.

Figure 17 plots the MAPE under one hour slots with the two-way mobility between a residential region and a downtown region, commercial region, industrial region, airport region, and train station region. In general, mPat outperforms WHERE, which outperforms Radiation. This is because Radiation considers only the population to infer the mobility instead of the historical trips, and WHERE uses only the cellphone data and does not correlate them to the transit data. In particular, the performance gain between mPat and others is lower during the rush hour. This is because the repeatable mobility patterns are higher in the rush hour, so all models have a better performance. Comparing the five region pairs, we found that for the region pairs on which the residents go for commutes (e.g., between the residential region and the industrial region), all models perform better than the region pairs between which residents go for traveling (i.e., between the residential region and the airport region). This is because the repeatable mobility pattern of such traveling is limited.

Figure 18 gives the MAPE on all region pairs under one hour slots during 24 hours. The MAPE of all three models are higher than the MAPE we observed in Figure 17. This is because urban mobility may change dramatically between different region pairs, and some remote region pairs with few transit services lead to higher MAPE. But the relative performance between the three models is similar to Figure 17. WHERE outperforms Radiation by 19% on average, but in the morning rush hour Radiation outperforms WHERE by 9%. mPat outperforms Radiation by 57% and WHERE by 39%, resulting from its utilization of the correlation between the cellphone and transit data.

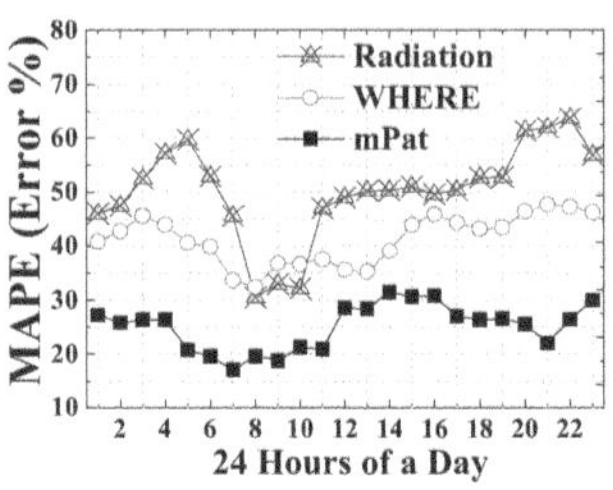

Fig 18: Hourly MAPE

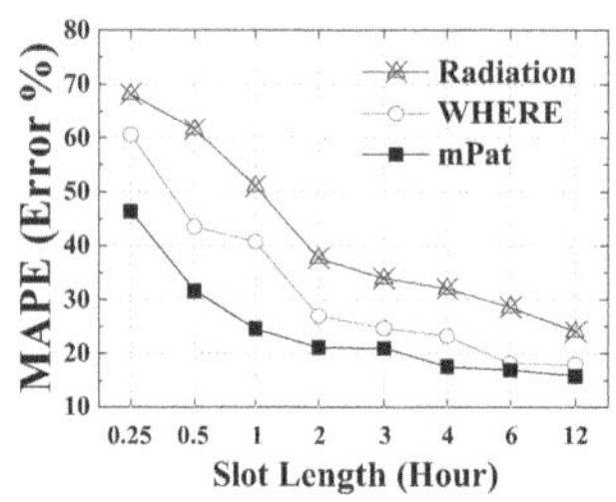

Fig 19: Effects of Lengths

Figure 19 plots the MAPE of all models with different slot lengths. The MAPE of all models reduces with an increase in the lengths of the time slots, because the urban mobility in a longer slot becomes more stable. mPat outperforms WHERE and Radiation significantly if the slot is shorter than 2 hours. But when the slot becomes longer than 6 hours, mPat and WHERE have a similar performance, because in such a long time slot, the cellphone data alone have a satisfactory performance to infer the mobility.

7.3 Accuracy on Street Levels

We study mPat at a different spatial granularity by showing the MAPE on the road segment level. Based on a digital map of Shenzhen, we assign the transit stations, taxicab locations, and cell towers to the closest road segments based on the Euclidean distance between them.

Figure 20 plots the MAPE of the inferred mobility from one of the busiest streets in the downtown Fu Hua Road to the busiest street in a residential area Le Yuan Road. mPat performs better than WHERE and Radiation, especially at night when residents do not have many phone activities but still use urban transit. WHERE significantly outperforms Radiation during in the early morning and the regular day time, but Radiation has good accuracy during the morning rush hour. This is because during the rush hour, passenger demand is relative stable compared to other times.

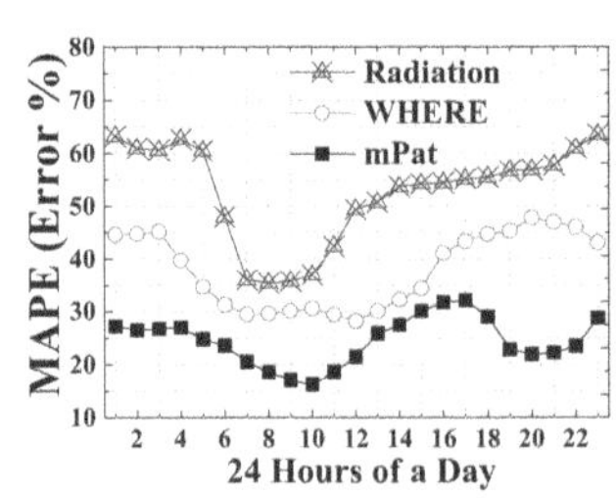

Fig 20: MAPE in One Pair

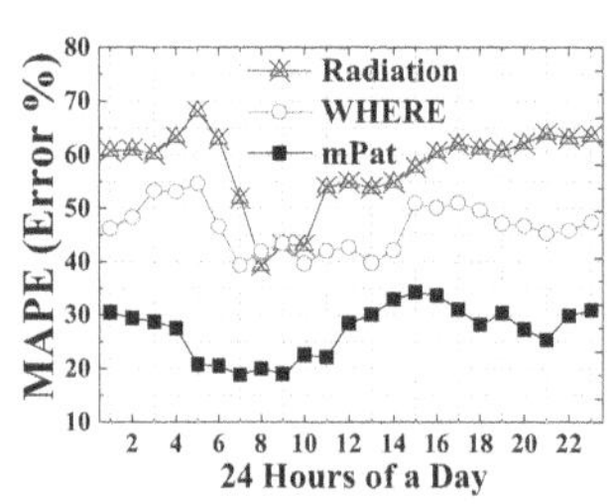

Fig 21: MAPE in 1000 Pairs

Figure 21 shows the average MAPE between 1,000 randomly selected segment pairs. The MAPE of all three models are higher than the MAPE in Figure 20 although their relative performance is similar to that in Figure 20. mPat is better than WHERE, but WHERE is normally better than Radiation. Compared to Figure 18, we found an 11% accuracy loss in mPat due to the finer granularity.

7.4 Justification of mPat's Iterative Design

We justify the design of mPat by comparing it to mPat-S, which does not use the transit data as a stop condition to iteratively utilize the historical data. Figures 22 and 23 plot the MAPE and running times on different data sizes. The more historical data, the lower the MAPE error and the longer the running time. mPat-S has a 9% accuracy gain over mPat, but mPat saves 71% of the running time. This is because with the same historical data, although mPat has the same historical data as mPat-S, mPat only uses a part of the historical data if the inferred mobility covers the transit mobility. This key feature of mPat leads to slightly higher MAPE but significantly shorter running times, which justifies the design of mPat.

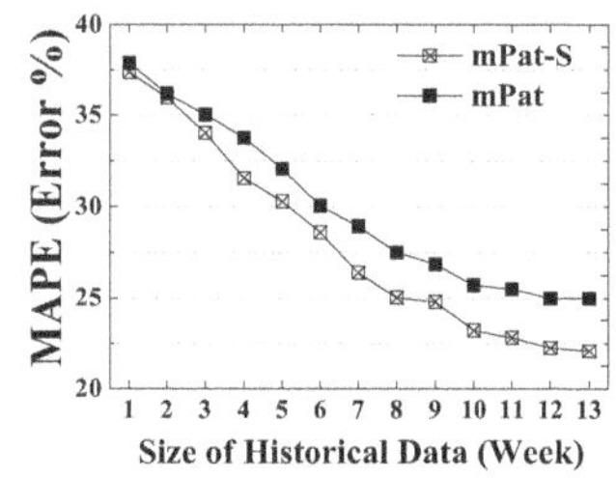

Fig 22: Data vs. MAPE

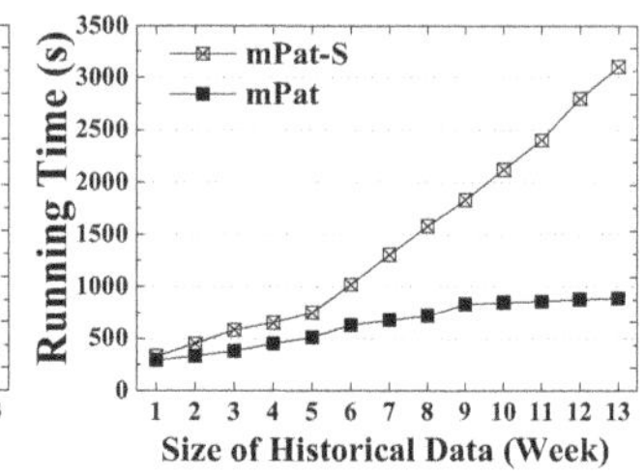

Fig 23: Data vs. Time

7.5 mPat Evaluation Summary

We make the following observations: (i) The inference accuracy is highly dependent on both locations and times as in Figures 17 and 18. On average, all models have better performance in the morning rush hour, due to the predictability of the morning commutes. (ii) The length of slots has a significant impact on the performance of all models as in Figure 19. It is intuitive that a longer slot has lower error rates, yet it also leads to low usability for real-time applications. (iii) The spatial granularity also has an impact on performance as seen by comparing Figures 20 and 21 to Figures 17 and 18, but the accuracy loss due to increasing granularity is not significant. (iv) Running time can be reduced by 71% with a 9% accuracy loss by using the correlation between cellphone and transit data as in Figures 22 and 23.

8. INTER REGION TRANSIT SERVICE

Recently, the Shenzhen transport committee launched a pilot program to provide non-stop express transit services between several fixed location pairs with high passenger transit demand, but the passengers have concerns that the routes (i.e., the provided location pairs) are limited [13]. In this section, we facilitate this pilot program by proposing and evaluating a novel transit service called Inter Region Transit IRT based on our human mobility pattern analysis and inference. IRT is designed to identify the urban region pairs between which there is high human mobility yet low public transit mobility (i.e., the portion of human mobility supported by public transit) and then to provide non-stop transit services among these identified pairs. IRT is potentially capable of reducing the travel time between these undersupplied regional pairs.

8.1 IRT Design Overview

The design of IRT is described in terms of coverage, capacity, and schedule. Based on the inferred human and transit mobility, (i) Coverage: we find the undersupplied region pairs with high human mobility yet low transit mobility according to a given undersupply ratio ρ as a threshold, i.e., a region pair has IRT services only if its $\frac{\text{Human Mobility}}{\text{Transit Mobility}} > \rho$; (ii) Capacity: we individually decide the number of IRT vehicles for every region pair based on (a) the difference between human mobility and transit mobility among this region pair (i.e., potential passengers), (b) the vehicle capacity (e.g., 20-seat bus), (c) the schedule period (e.g., one hour) and (d) the travel time between this region pair; (iii) Schedule: we compute the departure times of vehicles leaving the service stop of a region (e.g., a logical centroid of a region) based on the number of vehicles and the schedule periods. Figure 24 gives an IRT example.

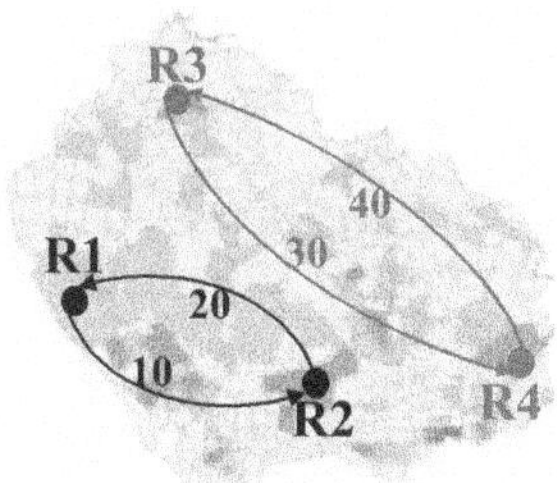

Fig 24: IRT Example

Fig 25: IRT Implementation

Based on a given ratio ρ, we find two undersupplied region pairs (R_1, R_2) and (R_3, R_4) by the historical human and transit mobility patterns. Then, based on the historical mobility inference for the next service period, there are 10, 20, 30 and 40 residents unaccounted for, i.e., the difference between human and transit mobility. Finally, we set the number of vehicles and the departure time based on the schedule period, the travel time, and the vehicle capacity.

8.2 Real World Experiment

We implemented IRT in one pair of undersupplied regions as a real-world effort. Since it requires a permit to deliver passengers in Shenzhen, we invited 12 volunteers who daily commute between these two regions for the evaluation. As shown in Figure 25, based on the number of volunteers, we rented 3 regular taxicabs to deliver them from a subway station as a service stop in one region to their workplace as another service stop in another region. At the subway station, 12 volunteers were picked up, and then were directly driven to their work. We calculated the departure times for every vehicle, but since these volunteers had to be driven to their work eventually, we only logged these departure times, instead having vehicles leave based on the calculated times. Then, we calculated what these passengers' travel times would be if the vehicles left based on departure times and went back to pick them up. But in reality, the vehicles waited and picked up them in one round at the subway station as one service stop and then dropped them off at their workplace as another service stop. We videotaped the service using three smart phones with which the travel time between two service stops was calculated. In Figure 26, we compare the travel time in IRT to the time of walking or taking a regular bus between the two service stops for a 31-day evaluation. We found that IRT reduces the travel time, compared to 43 mins of taking a bus or 57 mins of walking. But since the taxicabs are faster than the buses in terms of speed, we use a factor ν to account for the speed difference. In the experiment, ν is obtained based on our historical bus and taxicab GPS datasets. We found that IRT with ν still saves significant travel time for passengers.

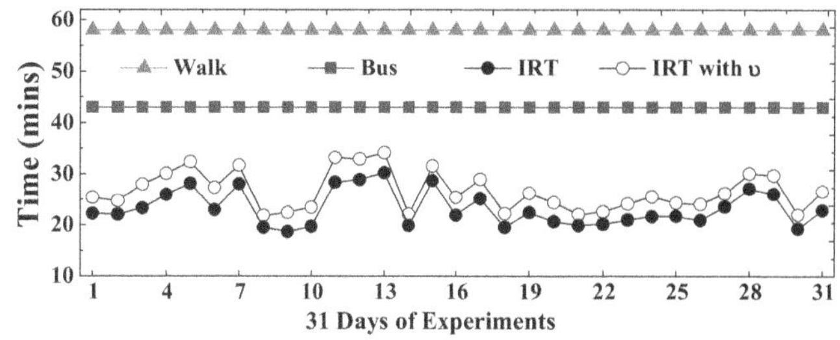

Fig 26: Average Travel Time in 31 days

8.3 Trace Driven Evaluation

We evaluate the performance of IRT by investigating the impact of the time of the day and the undersupply ratio ρ (default setting $\rho = 2$) on the percentage of reduced travel time. The original travel time between a pair of regions is given by the average travel time of three public transit modes, taxicab, bus, and subway; the new travel time in IRT is calculated based on the average travel time of taxicabs, since IRT is an express transit service without intermediate stops between regions, and thus IRT passengers' travel time is similar to that of taxicab passengers. But we still account for the speed difference with ν, which is obtained by the historical GPS data.

Impact of Time of Day. Figure 27 plots the percentages of the reduced travel time in 24 hours. During the 24 hours of a day, there is a high percentage of reduced travel time during the morning and evening rush hour, but in the non-rush hour period, e.g., during the early morning, the percentage of reduced travel time is low. This is because in the rush hour, many passengers use bus and subway services, leading to prolonged travel time due to intermediate stops between regions, whereas in the early morning, most travel passengers use taxicab services without intermediate stops, leading to a similar travel time as IRT.

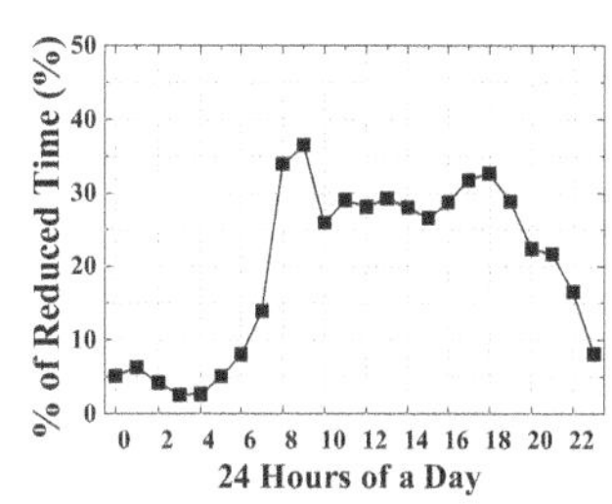

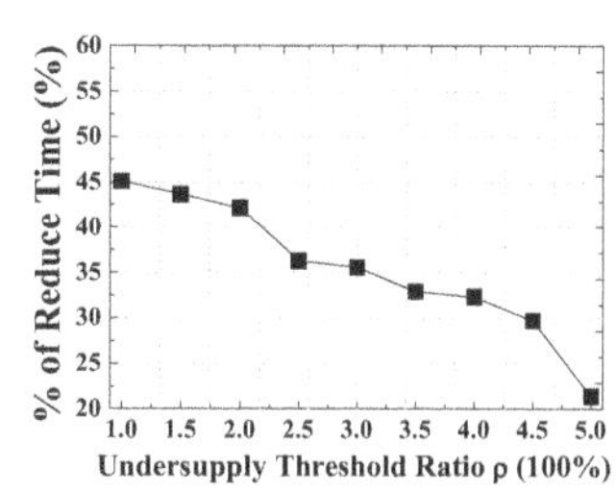

Fig 27: Reduced Time in 24H Fig 28: Reduced Time vs. ρ

Impact of Undersupply Ratio. IRT services are deployed between a region pair only if between this pair, $\frac{\text{Human Mobility}}{\text{Transit Mobility}} > \rho$. Figure 28 plots the impact of ρ on the reduced travel time. With the increase of ρ, the average travel time decreases. This is because the larger the ρ, the fewer the region pairs that have IRT services. Further, the region pairs without IRT typically do not have an undersupply of urban transit services between them, so the residents traveling between these pairs typically use private or urban transit with a shorter travel time. Thus, the percentage of the reduced time decreases when ρ is larger.

9. DISCUSSION

We discuss some issues about our architecture as follows.

Value of mPat Mobility Study: In this work, we use transportation as an example to show the benefit of human mobility models that serve as a key supporting layer for numerous applications. Basically, since most personal mobile devices are carried by users, the mobility patterns of the users are also the mobility patterns of these devices. Built upon the mobile devices' future locations and associated dwell time obtained from these mobility patterns, some typical mobile and wireless applications with great social or commercial benefits include Wi-Fi AP or cell tower deployments, ad hoc networking, infrastructureless message disseminations, and mobile network pricing.

Privacy Protections: Although data that can be used for the study of human mobility study are extremely valuable, privacy concerns regarding their utilization have inhibited their release and wider applications. We briefly discuss the active steps we took to protect privacy. (i) Anonymization: All data from feeds are anonymized by the employees of the service providers who are not involved in our project, and each identifiable ID (e.g., SIM card IDs) is replaced by a serial identifier. (ii) Minimal Exposure: We only store and process information that is useful for our mobility analysis, and delete other information for minimal exposure, e.g., we store the cell tower IDs to infer locations in the cellphone data, but not durations of calls. (iii) Aggregation: Our mobility patterns are given in aggregated results in a temporal-spatial partition and are not focused on individual cellphone or transit users.

Higher Dimension Multi-Source Traces: In the current Shenzhen implementation, we focus only on transit and cellphone activity datasets. As to future work, other urban trace data will be included in our mPat architecture to increase the accuracy of analyses and inferences. These datasets include (i) data of a growing bicycle network with 8,000 bicycles in Shenzhen for rental using smart cards; and (ii) data of the private vehicles that are tracked by onboard GPS installed by themselves or the manufacturers for location-based services. We envision combining these trace data about private transit with public transit data and then study their relationship with the cellphone data for a more accurate inference. To realize such a vision, we must provide incentives and privacy-preserving mechanisms to encourage residents to opt in.

10. CONCLUSION

In this work, we design, implement and evaluate an architecture for the analysis and inference of the human mobility with a 75% inference accuracy. Our endeavors offer a few valuable insights are that (i) the studies based on single-source data introduce biases into human mobility research, and the correlation as well as the divergence among multi-source data have the potential to address such biases; (ii) multi-source data can be used for cross-referencing in the real-time inferences to reduce the data needed to be processed for a shorter running time yet still maintain performance; and (iii) while it is challenging to integrate heterogenous large-scale feeds, it is more challenging to negotiate with service providers for real-time access and to protect the privacy of studied residents.

11. ACKNOWLEDGEMENTS

The authors thank the anonymous reviewers for their valuable feedback. This work was supported in part by the US NSF Grants CNS-0845994, CNS-1239226 and China NSFC Grant 61100220, as well as the UMN Thesis Travel Grant and the visiting support by Cloud Computing Center in SIAT.

12. REFERENCES

[1] Sample Datasets. In `http://www-users.cs.umn.edu/~zhang/`.

[2] Backstrom, L., Sun, E., and Marlow, C. Find me if you can: Improving geographical prediction with social and spatial proximity. In WWW '10.

[3] Bhattacharya, S., Phithakkitnukoon, S., Nurmi, P., Klami, A., Veloso, M., and Bento, C. Gaussian process-based predictive modeling for bus ridership. UbiComp '13.

[4] Bogo, F., and Peserico, E. Optimal throughput and delay in delay-tolerant networks with ballistic mobility. MobiCom '13.

[5] Cho, E., Myers, S. A., and Leskovec, J. Friendship and mobility: User movement in location-based social networks. KDD '11.

[6] Dufková, K., Le Boudec, J.-Y., Kencl, L., and Bjelica, M. Predicting user-cell association in cellular networks. MELT'09.

[7] Ganti, R., Srivatsa, M., Ranganathan, A., and Han, J. Inferring human mobility patterns from taxicab traces. UbiComp '13.

[8] Giannotti, F., Nanni, M., Pedreschi, D., Pinelli, F., Renso, C., Rinzivillo, S., and Trasarti, R. Unveiling the complexity of human mobility by querying and mining massive trajectory data. The VLDB Journal.

[9] Gonzalez, M. C., Hidalgo, C. A., and Barabasi, A.-L. Understanding individual human mobility patterns. Nature.

[10] Isaacman, S., Becker, R., Cáceres, R., Kobourov, S., Rowland, J., and Varshavsky, A. A tale of two cities. In HotMobile '10.

[11] Isaacman, S., Becker, R., Cáceres, R., Martonosi, M., Rowland, J., Varshavsky, A., and Willinger, W. Human mobility modeling at metropolitan scales. MobiSys '12.

[12] Lathia, N., and Capra, L. How smart is your smartcard?: Measuring travel behaviours, perceptions, and incentives. UbiComp '11.

[13] Shenzhen Customized Public Transit . In http://house.people.com.cn/n/2014/0411/c164220-24882370.html.

[14] Simini, F., Gonzĺćlez, M. C., Maritan, A., and Barabĺćsi, A.-L. A universal model for mobility and migration patterns. Nature.

[15] Song, C., Qu, Z., Blumm, N., and Barabasi, A.-L. Limits of predictability in human mobility. Science.

[16] Zhang, D., Li, Y., Zhang, F., Lu, M., Liu, Y., and He, T. coRide: Carpool Service with a Win-win Fare Model for Large-scale Taxicab Networks. SenSys '13.

[17] Zheng, Y., Liu, Y., Yuan, J., and Xie, X. Urban computing with taxicabs. UbiComp '11.

Modeling Web Quality-of-Experience on Cellular Networks

Athula Balachandran†, Vaneet Aggarwal‡, Emir Halepovic‡, Jeffrey Pang‡,
Srinivasan Seshan†, Shobha Venkataraman‡, He Yan‡
†Computer Science Department, Carnegie Mellon University, Pittsburgh, PA, USA
‡AT&T Labs – Research, Bedminster, NJ, USA
{abalacha,srini}@cs.cmu.edu, {vaneet,emir,jeffpang,shvenk,yanhe}@research.att.com

ABSTRACT

Recent studies have shown that web browsing is one of the most prominent cellular applications. It is therefore important for cellular network operators to understand how radio network characteristics (such as signal strength, handovers, load, etc.) influence users' web browsing Quality-of-Experience (web QoE). Understanding the relationship between web QoE and network characteristics is a pre-requisite for cellular network operators to detect when and where degraded network conditions actually impact web QoE. Unfortunately, cellular network operators do not have access to detailed server-side or client-side logs to directly measure web QoE metrics, such as abandonment rate and session length. In this paper, we first devise a machine-learning-based mechanism to infer web QoE metrics from network traces accurately. We then present a large-scale study characterizing the impact of network characteristics on web QoE using a month-long anonymized dataset collected from a major cellular network provider. Our results show that improving signal-to-noise ratio, decreasing load and reducing handovers can improve user experience. We find that web QoE is very sensitive to inter-radio-access-technology (IRAT) handovers. We further find that higher radio data link rate does not necessarily lead to better web QoE. Since many network characteristics are interrelated, we also use machine learning to accurately model the influence of radio network characteristics on user experience metrics. This model can be used by cellular network operators to prioritize the improvement of network factors that most influence web QoE.

Categories and Subject Descriptors

C.4 [**Performance and Systems**]: measurement techniques, performance attributes; C.2.3 [**Computer System Organization**]: computer communication system—network operations

Keywords

Cellular Network; Quality of Experience (QoE), Web Browsing, Performance

MobiCom'14, September 7-11, 2014, Maui, Hawaii, USA.
Copyright 2014 ACM 978-1-4503-2783-1/14/09 ...$15.00.
http://dx.doi.org/10.1145/2639108.2639137.

1. INTRODUCTION

Mobile web data usage is predicted to increase eleven-fold between 2013 and 2018 [1], and web browsing is already one of the most dominant applications on cellular networks [33]. Therefore, it is important for cellular operators to ensure that web browsing sessions provide a better Quality-of-Experience (QoE), i.e., a set of web user experience metrics, such as session length (the number of pages a user clicks through) and abandonment (whether a user leaves a website after visiting the landing page), which we hereafter refer to as *web QoE*. The ability to monitor web QoE is essential to determining when and where degraded network conditions actually impair user experience. Moreover, understanding the relationship between web QoE and radio factors can help troubleshoot such conditions and help operators evaluate the inherent trade-offs in potential solutions. For example, an operator may want to decide whether to increase a cell's transmit power to improve signal strength, or decrease it to reduce handovers from overlapping cells.

Prior work on monitoring web QoE relies heavily on client-side or server-side instrumentation such as browser plugins and server logs. Past work has studied the impact of web page complexity on user experience [18, 24], developing better browsers [28], detecting inefficiencies in HTTP [30] etc. These works have led to best practices that have helped improve website designs, browsers and network protocols. However, the network between the website and the user also plays a critical role in the user experience, particularly in wireless mobile networks. To complement these studies, we take a "cellular operator view" of web QoE. Understanding web QoE from an operator's perspective is more challenging because, unlike other stakeholders, network operators do not have access to detailed client-side or server-side logs, any feedback from the end hosts, or any a priori domain knowledge about website structure. Hence, it is imperative for network operators to accurately estimate QoE metrics using only network measurements.

To complicate matters, websites have evolved from serving relatively static objects, such as hypertext and images, to hosting rich mobile media applications. These sites typically deliver dynamic and personalized content that often includes third-party content such as advertising [18]. Such design typically involves fetching large number of objects from multiple domains and servers. This significant change in web page structure and content over the last decade makes accurate estimation of web QoE metrics from mobile network traces even more challenging. A key challenge is that there is not yet a scalable and accurate method to distinguish between different mobile browsing sessions or to associate each HTTP transaction with a browsing session, by only observing flow-level network traffic. Previous approaches (e.g., [24]) were designed for the "desktop" web and fare poorly when applied to mobile websites.

To the best of our knowledge, this paper presents the first large-scale measurement-driven study that characterizes and models mobile web QoE and relates it to the measurable radio network characteristics, such as radio signal strength, handovers, data rate, etc. To this end, we use a month-long anonymized data set collected from a Tier-1 US-based cellular network and analyze web browsing sessions of 3 leading mobile websites that consistently appear in the top 100 [6]. For this analysis, we design mechanisms to measure and evaluate the two key web QoE metrics that quantify user experience using only network data: session length (number of pages a user clicks through) and abandonment rate (if a user leaves the website after visting the landing page). Moreover, we show that partial download ratio (fraction of page objects that download incomplete) is a measure that likely captures user disatisfaction even for single-click sessions (the majority for some websites), as it correlates well with the other two metrics.

We make the following contributions:

- We design and evaluate a novel technique to reconstruct mobile web sessions and detect user clicks[1] from HTTP traces, and demonstrate that it significantly outperforms current state-of-the-art method. Our approach is based on bag-of-words and Naive Bayes, an approach borrowed from text classification, and extracts features from HTTP headers. It detects clicks on mobile websites with about 20% higher recall and higher precision compared to the previous state-of-the-art [24].
- We quantify the individual impact of various network characteristics on mobile web QoE in the wild, and derive actionable findings for cellular operators. For example, we find that web QoE is very sensitive to inter-radio-access-technology (IRAT) handovers: most sessions with IRAT handovers were abandoned. Somewhat surprisingly, we find that web QoE is not noticeably influenced by the mean radio download or uplink rate (in contrast to mobile video QoE [32]). Moreover, higher radio signal strength (RSSI) does not correlate with higher web QoE, suggesting that web QoE is not power limited. Further, we establish which radio-level metrics are strong indicators of QoE, and which should not be relied upon.
- We capture the complex relationships between the various network parameters and user experience using *intuitive* and *accurate* machine-learning models. Given only radio network characteristics, which are available to network operators even without traffic monitoring, our model can predict the web QoE with accuracy as high as 84%, improving accuracy by 20% compared to the obvious baseline. Network operators can use this model to continuously monitor and improve web QoE by adjusting network parameters.

The rest of the paper is organized as follows. In Section 2, we present the background and details of our data collection process. In Section 3, we discuss related work. In Section 4 we describe and evaluate our approach for estimating user experience metrics from network traces. In Section 5 we present a characterization of how different network parameters affect web browsing experience. We develop a unified web QoE model for web browsing experience and present our findings in Section 6. We conclude in Section 8.

2. BACKGROUND

Mobile network users care about the web experience rather than individual network metrics such as throughput and latency. Thus, cellular carriers have a significant interest in using their infrastructure to measure and improve web QoE rather than traditional network metrics, especially when there are trade-offs. To better understand the challenges in measuring web QoE, this section first provides a brief overview of the cellular network architecture, focusing on most relevant aspects for our study, the datasets we use, and the applications of web QoE.

2.1 Cellular Network Architecture

A Universal Mobile Telecommunication System (UMTS) is a 3rd Generation (3G) mobile data network, consisting of two major components: a Radio Access Network (RAN) and a Core Network (CN). The RAN includes user equipment (UE), base transceiver stations (i.e., NodeBs), and Radio Network Controllers (RNCs). The CN consists of Serving GPRS Support Nodes (SGSNs) and Gateway GPRS Support Nodes (GGSNs). A UE is a mobile device (smartphone, 3G card, etc.) that connects to the NodeB over the radio channel.

Each base station has multiple antennas (typically 3-6), each of which provides radio coverage for an area called a cell sector, which has a particular frequency and other channel characteristics. The primary cell sector is periodically selected based on the signal strength information, while the UE maintains connections to a set of sectors in range called the active set. The traffic to and from the UE is sent to the corresponding NodeB, via RNC, which controls multiple NodeBs, schedules transmissions, and performs all Radio Resource Control (RRC), such as signaling, handovers, and assignment of Radio Access Bearers (RABs).

Within the CN, an SGSN transfers data between RNC and GGSN on behalf of the UE. A GGSN acts as a packet gateway and router between the cellular network and external networks such as the Internet. A GGSN also maintains IP connectivity between UEs and external IP networks.

2.2 Data Collection Apparatus

Mobile operators often collect metrics derived from the traffic that passes through network elements in order to manage the network. For example, radio statistics such as RSSI and handovers are often collected from RNCs and end-to-end throughput and latency metrics are often derived from measurements in the GGSN. This paper is interested in whether such low-level network measurements can be used to measure and understand mobile web QoE.

Thus, for the purposes of this study, we simultaneously collect two anonymized data sets, HTTP transaction records from the interfaces between GGSNs and SGSNs, and radio data from a set of RNCs. The datasets cover a major metropolitan area in the western United States over the duration of one month in 2012.

The HTTP records contain IP flow-level information for web-browsing sessions, and it includes items like client and server IP addresses and TCP ports, flow duration, anonymized device identifier (IMEI), bytes transfered, and TCP flags. Also included are relevant HTTP headers, which include information on URL, user agent, content type, content length, etc. The query parameters in URLs are anonymized via hashing.The radio data contains event-level information for each anonymized user. For example, this data includes RRC measurement reports that periodically report the RSSI, signal to noise ratio, etc. of each UE to the RNC, handover events, RRC throughput utilization, etc. The signal strength and throughput measurements are reported every 2 seconds. Other measurements are reported based on discrete event level data (e.g., when a handover happens, when user connects, disconnects etc.). A full list of events that we use is in Section 5.

Throughout this paper, our analysis focuses on three leading mobile websites (*News*, *Social*, *Wiki*) that consistently appear in the top 100 [6]. Our one month long HTTP trace contains informa-

[1]We use the term *clicks* to refer to mobile "taps" as well as traditional mouse "clicks."

tion on 2 million web sessions to these 3 websites comprising 70 million HTTP requests and around 1 million different UEs. Our radio dataset contains complete information about 100,000 of these sessions.

We emphasize that all the device and user identifiers are anonymized before any analysis is conducted in order to protect privacy. In addition, the outputs of models in this paper are aggregated (e.g., per region and/or network element), so it does not permit the reversal of anonymization or re-identification of users.

2.3 Web QoE Applications

Mobile operators monitor network metrics for several purposes, and the ability to monitor web QoE would complement the same applications. First, continuous measurement of metrics permits early detection of network problems. Monitoring web QoE would permit operators to prioritize problems that have the most impact on actual user experience and the understanding of how network factors influence web QoE would help troubleshooting. Second, trending network metrics is invaluable for capacity planning, as they provide objective benchmarks to measure the relationship between investment in infrastructure, such as base stations, and user experience. Third, cellular networks are extremely complex to manage and optimize, involving a huge amount of parameter tuning in the RAN and CN. The adjustment of these parameters often involve implicit trade-offs between different aspects of network performance, such as average capacity vs. peak latency. Monitoring web QoE and understanding how various network factors influence it provide an objective way for operators to perform such parameter optimizations.

3. RELATED WORK

Web traffic modeling: The most widely used technique to model web traffic and identify web pages from network traces is based on idle time [27]. It has been used extensively for characterizing web traffic in several works [16, 34]. This approach works well for simple static web pages. However, it does not work well for most web pages today since they include dynamic content (shown in Section 4). To overcome this limitation, a page detection algorithm that works for dynamic content was proposed [24]. However, it only identifies clicks resulting in new web pages and does not identify clicks within a page. We propose and evaluate a text classification-based mechanism that has high accuracy in identifying user clicks in Section 4.

Web Performance Studies: There have been several efforts made in previous works towards improving web performance. These include developing better browsers specifically for mobile devices [28], techniques to optimize webpages [3, 4], and detecting inefficiencies in HTTP [15, 30]. More recent work has characterized how web site complexity can affect user experience [18]. Unlike these past works, the focus of our work is on understanding the impact of cellular radio characteristics on mobile web browsing sessions with the aim of helping network operators make informed choices on improving web QoE.

Performance of network protocols over cellular networks: Past work has also looked at the performance of TCP and HTTP on LTE network highlighting the need to develop more LTE-friendly transport and application protocols [12], characterized the physical and MAC layers in CDMA and its impact on TCP performance [10], studied how large buffers in cellular networks cause TCP queing delays [11]. These efforts have helped understand and improve transport layer and application performance over cellular network, and hence user experience indirectly. In this work understanding the impact of transport layer protocols on user experience is not our immediate focus—the goal of this paper is on understanding how radio network parameters impact user experience.

Measures of web browsing user experience: User experience studies in the past have shown that a complete page load time has an impact on user satisfaction [17, 20, 21]. These works are primarily based on controlled studies with few users, and they involve logging page load times and user feedback using client-side instrumentation techniques. However, since network operators do not have access to client-side logs, it is challenging to exactly measure the page load time. However, in our traces we observe that large fraction of the pages are only partially downloaded and we define the partial download ratio metric to capture user experience. Similarly, past work has also extensively used several metrics related to user browsing behavior to quantify user satisfaction including user clicks, dwell time and scrolling [23, 26]. We also use metrics related to user click behavior. However, since we do not have client-side instrumentation, we are unable to capture other behavior such as dwell time and scrolling and incorporate them in our study. Moreover, our work takes a step forward by analyzing the impact of radio network factors on these different user experience metrics.

QoE in other domains: Several past efforts study the impact of network factors on user experience and user satisfaction in other applications. Measured impact of bitrate, jitter, and delay on VoIP call duration is used with a machine-learning approach to derive a user satisfaction metric [13]. Past works have employed machine-learning algorithms to develop predictive models for Internet video user engagement [14, 32]. Radio network factors, such as signal strength and handovers, are used to quantify their impact on video viewing experience [32]. Our work focuses on performing a similar analysis for mobile web browsing experience.

4. EXTRACTING USER EXPERIENCE METRICS

Network operators cannot access detailed server-side or client-side logs of user browsing patterns. Hence they need to reconstruct web browsing sessions and estimate user experience metrics from network traces. However, over the years, webpages have evolved from serving relatively simple static objects such as hypertext to serving dynamic and even personalized content. This makes it even more challenging to reconstruct mobile web sessions and extract user activities from network traces alone.

Previous work identified *engagement* as a key measure of user experience because more satisfied users tend to stay around longer and use an application more [13, 14, 25, 36]. For web browsing, two central engagement metrics recognized in the web analytics industry are *session length* (i.e., the number of pages a user clicks through) and *abandonment* or bounce rate (i.e., if a user leaves the website after only visiting the landing page) [19]. Unfortunately, both of these metrics necessitate the identification of user *clicks*, which is non-trivial from the perspective of an operator. The difficulty comes from lack of access to client-side or server-slide logs and HTTP records do not readily distinguish requests that are initiated automatically by the browser (e.g., embedded objects) and those that are initiated by user activity.

In Section 4.1, we present and evaluate a novel click detection algorithm based on machine learning, which achieves higher accuracy than the best known approach. Then, in Section 4.1.2, we extract different user experience metrics from the dataset using our algorithm. Based on our findings, we propose *partial download ratio* as a more fine-grain metric that more precisely captures user

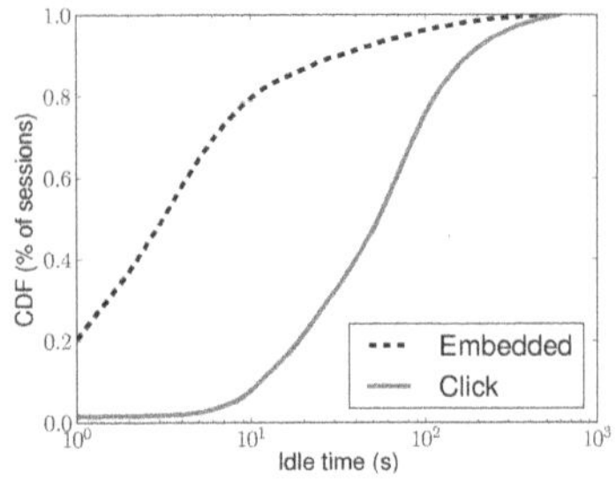

Figure 1: CDF of arrival time for clicks vs embedded objects

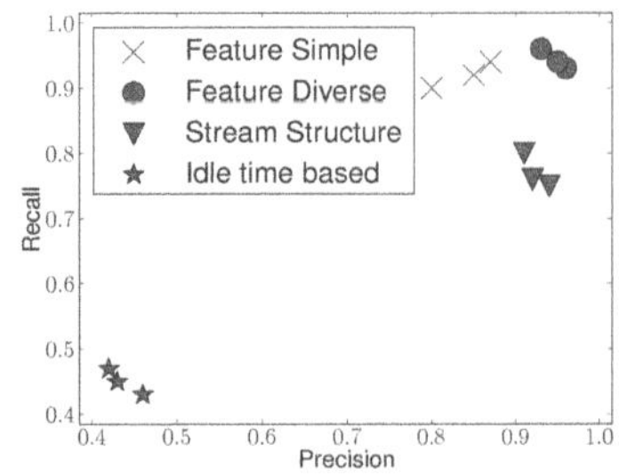

Figure 2: Our approaches have higher precision and recall compared to previous approaches

experience impairments due to network conditions, as opposed to user interest.

4.1 Detecting Clicks

4.1.1 Limitations of Previous Techniques

The most common approach for differentiating between clicks and embedded objects using network traces is to use the idle time between requests [16, 27, 34]. This approach is based on the assumption that the idle time for requests for embedded objects will be extremely short since they are automatically generated by the browser, whereas requests generated by clicks would typically have higher idle time since they require manual intervention. Therefore, these techniques use a pre-defined threshold and classify a request as embedded object if and only if the idle time is shorter than the threshold. However, we find that in modern mobile web pages, a non-trival fraction of embedded objects have idle times as long as many user clicks (e.g., requests generated by periodic beacons from third-party analytic services [24]). For example, Figure 1 shows the distribution of arrival times for next click and next embedded objects. This figure is based on web requests from around 50,000 web sessions on the three websites. We labeled each of the web requests in these sessions as clicks or embedded objects manually. An idle time threshold approach would select a point on the x-axis and classify all objects to the left as embedded and those to the right as clicks. We see that there is no idle time threshold that we can select that achieves lower than 20% error on at least one of the two classes.

To improve on this approach, StreamStructure [24] exploits the structure of "desktop" web pages to detect requests for new webpages. However, we show in the next section that it is not as adept at identifying clicks in mobile web pages. Moreover, it is a page detection algorithm that is used to identify clicks resulting in new pages. Other client-side interaction (e.g., clicking to play a video within a page) are not identified by this algorithm.

4.1.2 Our Approach

Our approach to differentiate between clicks and embedded objects is based on our observation that most of the embedded objects are hosted by third party services such as advertising agencies, Content Distribution Networks (CDNs) and analytics services [18]. This opens up an opportunity to distinguish embedded objects from clicks by inspecting request URLs. For example, a request to google-analytics.com is *very likely* to be an embedded object, while a request to news.google.com is *very likely* to be a click. Hence we can employ text based classification algorithms that have been extensively used in other domains (such as spam filtering [31] and sentiment analysis [22]) to classify requests. We would need to learn the classification model separately for each website/domain. In the remainder of the section, we explain four steps in our approach.

Step 1: Grouping Sessions: We first filter our sessions to a specific website. We only study traffic originating from web browsers, and hence filter out traffic of native mobile apps using User Agent HTTP header. Similar to the approach in StreamStructure [24], we group requests into different sessions using the anonymized IMEI and Referer header information. The IMEI information helps us separate sessions from different devices. The Referer field identifies the address of an object from which the new request came from. The first request in a session has an empty Referer field. The Referer field is further used to build the request chain within a session. It also helps us separate simultaneous requests from multiple browser instances from the same user equipment.

Step 2: Extracting Features: In order to perform text classification, we extract features from the requested URLs. We extract two sets of features to represent the URLs:

- Feature simple: We extract a bag of words [29] from the domain name. For example, the feature set for the URL www.blog.xyz.com/my/blog/abc.html is <blog, xyz, com>.
- Feature diverse: In addition to domain name features, we include features from the URN and type of content. Hence, the feature set for the above URL would be domain = <blog, xyz, com>, urn = <my, blog, abc.html> and type = html.

Step 3: Automatic Labeling to Obtain Training Set: In order to create a classification model to label the URLs as clicks and embedded objects, we need a training set labeled with the ground truth. To obtain the training set, we inspect only the very first 10 seconds of every web session. We assume that only the first request during this time frame was a click and the remaining requests are for embedded objects and collect both feature simple and feature diverse along with the ground truth based on the assumption. We pick 10 seconds because based on the ground truth in Figure 1, almost all user clicks have an idle time of more than 10 seconds and almost 80% of the embedded objects are requested with this time frame. This automatic labeling technique enables our approach to be applied to any website without any manual labeling or ground truth.

Step 4: Running Classification Algorithm: We first learn the classifier model using the training set, and then input the entire dataset and classify each request as the click or embedded object. After testing with multiple machine learning algorithms (such as decision trees, logistic regression, Support Vector Machines [29]), we found that Naive Bayes performs the best compared to other approaches. This is not surprising given that Naive Bayes has been found to perform the best in other text classification problems as well [7].

4.1.3 Validation

To validate our approach, we apply it to the three web sites we study. For each web site, we manually inspect its structure in detail

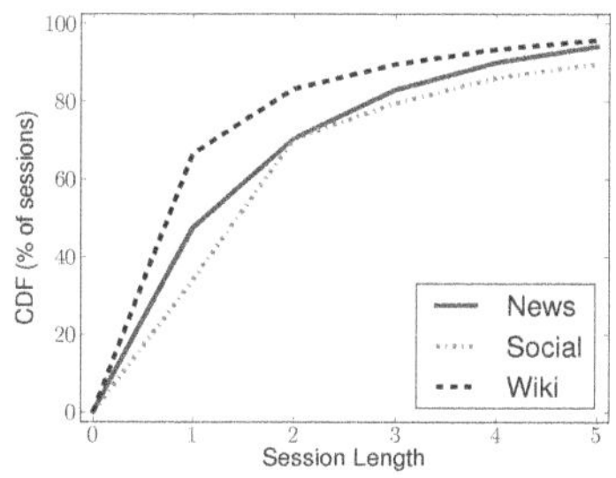

(a) Session Length

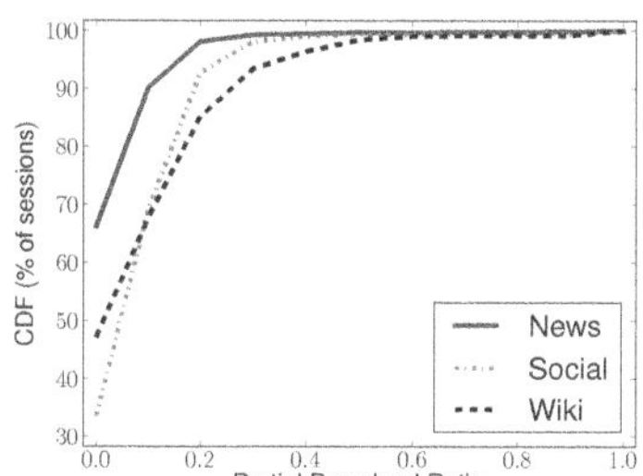

(b) Partial Download Ratio

Figure 3: CDF of user experience metrics

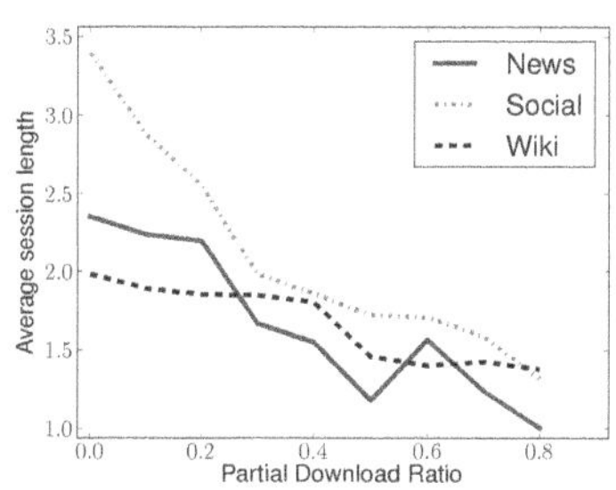

Figure 4: Session length decreases with increasing partial download ratio

in order to label each HTTP request as either a click or a as an embedded object. We manually label one day of trace data with roughly 50,000 sessions.

We then compare the idle-time threshold based approach, StreamStructure and our approach (both using Feature simple and Feature diverse) and then estimate the performance in terms of both precision and recall. Precision is defined as the number of correct clicks identified by the total number of clicks identified, and recall is defined as the number of correct clicks identified by the total number of clicks. Figure 2 shows the precision and recall using each the three websites. Our Feature simple and Feature diverse have higher recall than the previous baselines. Feature diverse has higher precision than Feature simple because some embedded objects are hosted on the main domain. Feature simple will incorrectly classify this object as a click since it just uses features from the domain name. In the remainder of this paper, we hence use the Feature diverse approach to identify clicks.

4.2 Measuring User Experience

As described earlier, session length and abandonment rate are two important metrics that the web industry recognizes as representative of user engagement. Our click detection algorithm presented above enables operators to estimate session length and abandonment rate using only HTTP traces collected from the network. However, session length and abandonment rate are relatively coarse engagement metrics because they are also influenced by user interest, which is a confounding factor that is difficult to measure for both network and website operators. Indeed, we find that many web sessions are only one click (and thus, by definition, abandoned). These metrics do little to distinguish satisfied and dissatisfied users of these single-click sessions. In this section, we show that *partial download ratio*, i.e., the fraction of HTTP objects that are not completely downloaded in a session, is strongly correlated with session length and abandonment rate, so we can use it as a proxy to estimate user experience, even for sessions lasting a single click.

To better understand the session length, abandonment rate, and partial download ratio metrics, we extract web sessions and estimate number of clicks for each session for the three different websites from the entire 1 month HTTP record trace. Figure 3(a) shows the distribution of session lengths. We observe that all sessions have length less than 10 on all the three websites. A significant fraction the sessions on all the three websites have a length of 1 (47% for News, 33% for Social, 67% for Wiki). The overall abandonment rate is 35% for the three websites. These observations highlight the need for a user engagement metric that can highlight network problems in sessions of length one.

One such candidate measure in common use is the web page load time (i.e., the time it takes to load a page). However, it is known that web page load time is difficult to measure from HTTP traces because the traces do not capture the browser's rendering pipeline [35]. Moreover, without a priori knowledge of web page structure, operators can not easily distinguish complete vs. incomplete page loads. Therefore, naïvely using download time to approximate page load time would incorrectly suggest that abandoned pages have low load time.

Instead, we propose that partial download ratio is a useful proxy metric for user engagement. Figure 4 shows the average session length as a function of the partial download ratio. We see that there is roughly a negative linear relationship between the partial download ratio and session length, supporting our hypothesis that users are less engaged when more objects on the page fail to load completely (or do not load completely before the user moves on). The linear coefficient is different for each website, as website design likely influences how much partially downloaded content effects the user experience, but the coefficient can be easily learned using regression. For example, using a linear fit to determine session length in terms of partial download ratio, the partial download ratio co-effieceints for the News, Social, and Wiki websites are -1.6, -2.36, -0.85 respectively. Figure 3(b) shows the distribution of partial download ratios for each session. We also observe that over 60% of the sessions have objects that are partially downloaded on each website.

Figure 5 shows the average session length, abandonment rate, and partial download ratio by time of day. We observe strong temporal patterns in the user engagement metrics. Lower session lengths, higher abandonment and higher partial download ratio occur during peak hours (10 am - 6pm) compared to the rest of the day.

Corresponding to the different linear coefficients we see in Figure 4, we observe that the web QoE metrics are different across different websites. This is likely because, as previous work has showed [18], user experience is dependent on factors other than network quality, such as how mobile-friendly the website is, the number of objects, type of objects etc.

5. ANALYZING NETWORK FACTORS

Our first goal is to understand the relationships between individual network factors and web QoE, with the end goal of building

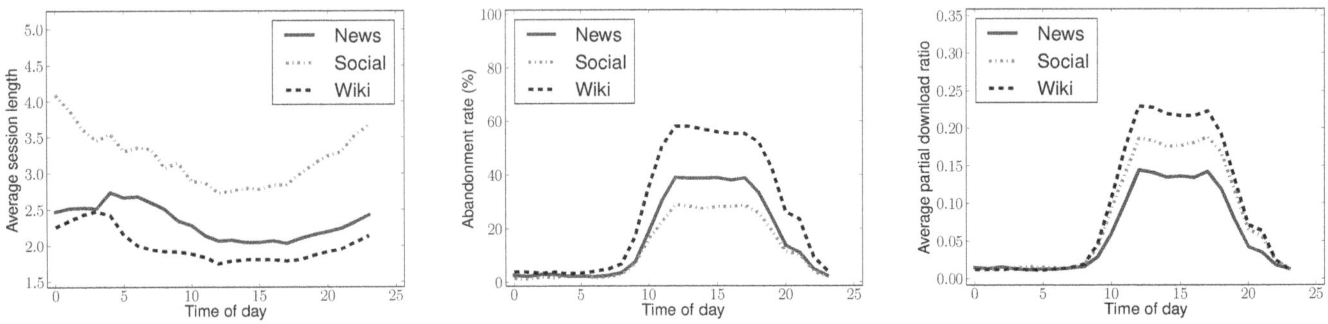

(a) Session Length (b) Abandonment Rate (c) Partial Download Ratio

Figure 5: Time of day effects on the experience metrics

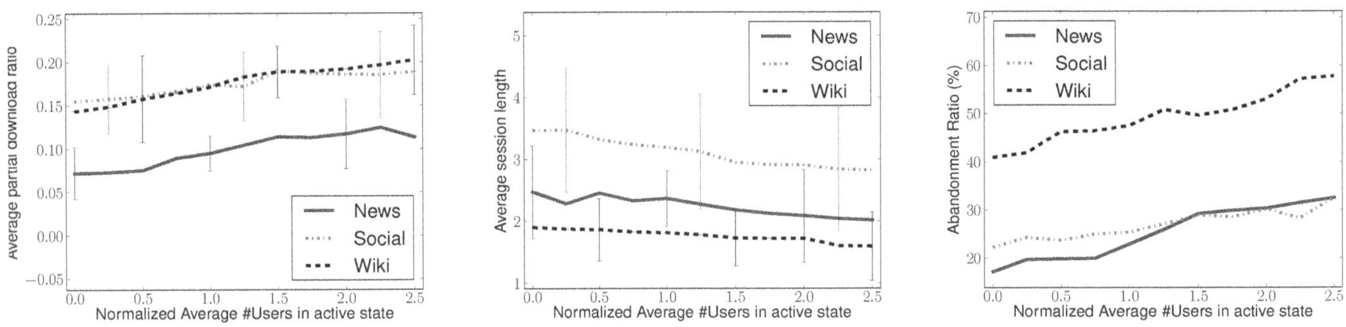

(a) Partial Download Ratio (b) Session Length (c) Abandonment Rate

Figure 6: Higher load in the cell (measured in terms of number of active users) leads to worse web QoE. Session length has higher variance since it is a more "noisier" metric as explained in Section 4.2

models that can be used to improve web QoE by tuning various network parameters. We first itemize all radio network factors that we study, which may effect web QoE:

- *Number of soft handovers (SOHO):* A soft handover occurs when a cell sector is added or removed from the set of cell sectors that a UE is connected to. A SOHO is a "make-before-break" handover in that the link to the new sector is established before an old link is removed. From radio network data that we collected from the RNCs, we count the total number of soft handovers during a session.
- *Number of inter-frequency handovers (IFHO):* An IFHO occurs when the UE switches to a cell sector that is operating on a different frequency. An IFHO is a "break-before-make" handover because a device can only listen on one frequency at a time; thus, it must break the link with all old sectors before establishing the link with the new one. We count the number of inter-frequency handovers during a web session.
- *Number of inter-radio access technology (IRAT) handovers:* An IRAT handover happens when a UE switches between different radio access technologies (e.g., UMTS to GPRS or EDGE). These do not include handovers to and from WiFi since our data collection apparatus does not capture such handovers. An IRAT handover is also a "break-before-make" handover because the device must disconnect entirely from the current radio network before connecting to the new one. This process involves a significant amount of network signaling and can take several seconds.
- *Number of admission control failures (ACF):* We count the number of times the UE fails to complete the admission control procedure during the web browsing session. These events mostly occur when the radio network is overloaded.
- *Number of RRC failures (RRC):* An RRC failure occurs if the RNC is overloaded and it cannot allocate a request from the UE for more radio resources. We count the number of RRC failures within a web session.
- *Average Received Signal Code Power (RSCP):* This is the downlink power received by the UE receiver on the pilot channel. It is measured in dBm.
- *Average received energy per chip of the pilot channel over the noise power density (ECNO):* It is expressed in dB and it measures how well a signal can be distinguished from the noise in a cell. It is measured in dB. Note that ECNO is measured on the pilot channel and thus may be different from the SINR of the traffic channel.
- *Average received Signal Strength Indicator (RSSI):* Expressed in dBm, it is the wide-band received power within the relevant channel bandwidth. It is related to RSCP and ECNO as follows: RSSI = RSCP - ECNO. Note that RSSI is measured on the pilot channel and thus may be different from the received power of the signal on the traffic channel.
- *Average uplink and downlink radio data throughput:* We compute the average uplink and downlink data rates for the UE when it is in active state during the web session in Kbps. Note that the radio data rate is not equivalent to the long-term through-

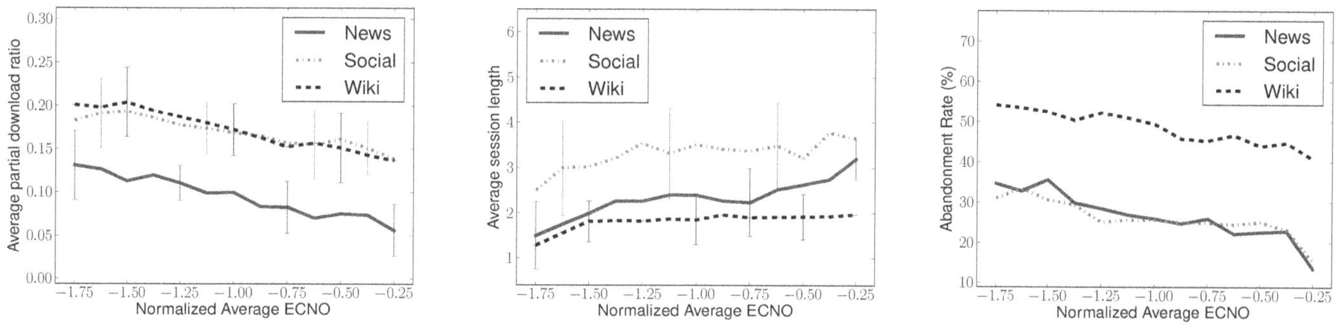

(a) Partial Download Ratio *(b)* Session Length *(c)* Abandonment Rate

Figure 7: Higher signal energy to interference (ECNO) leads to better web QoE

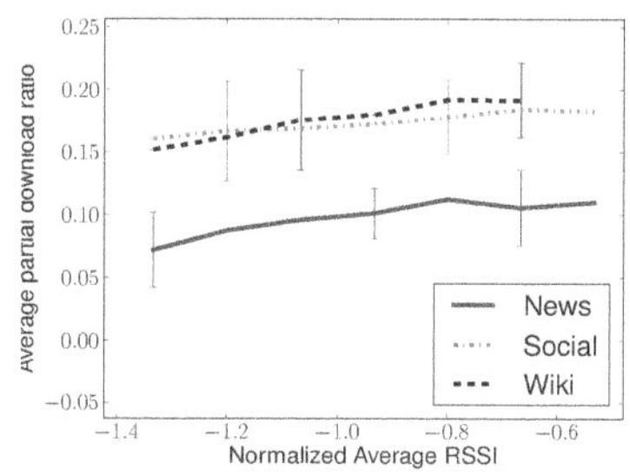

Figure 8: Surprisingly, higher received signal strength leads to higher partial download ratio

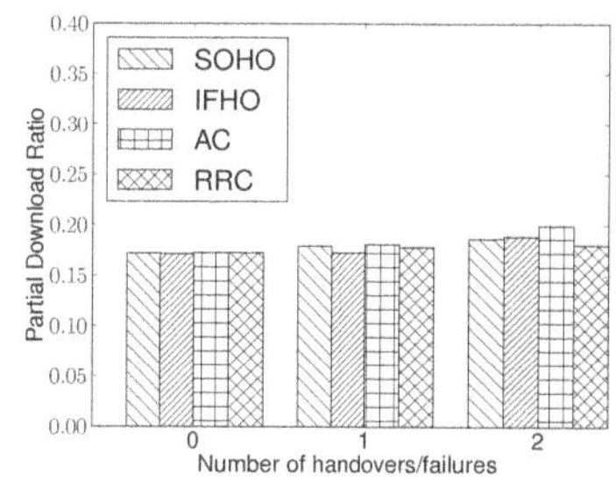

Figure 10: The impact of soft handovers, inter-frequency handovers, access control failures and RRC failures on web QoE is minimal

put because it is only measured when the device is scheduled to send/receive data (the radio link is time and code division multiplexed). The radio data rate does not count the non-scheduled time slots in the denominator of the throughput calculation. The number of users in active state (see below) serves as an estimate of the number of competing flows, as a sector schedules each user in a proportionally fair manner.

- *Average number of users in active state:* We measure the number of active users served by each cell at a minute-level granularity. Using this information we compute the average number of users that are served by the cell that the UE is connected to during the web session. This is an indication of the load in the cell.

We report the normalized the value of RSCP, ECNO, RSSI, average uplink and downlink throughput and number of users in active state as a fraction of the mean of the metric. For example, instead of reporting the absolute value of RSSI, we report RSSI/mean(RSSI) and hence the plots can be read as x% above or below the average.

5.1 How network factors impact web QoE

To understand how each network factor individually affects web QoE metrics, we plot web QoE metrics against measured values of network factors from our radio data. The main takeaways are as follows:

1. Higher network load results in worse web QoE. Number of users in active state in a cell is an indication of load in the network. As Figure 6 shows, there is a linear relationship between the load and various web QoE metrics. For instance, adding 25% more users than the average can increase abandonment by 2 full percentage points. Increasing cell load also leads to lower session lengths and higher number of partially downloaded objects on average. This relationship between load and web QoE metrics holds even when conditioned by time-of-day, though cell load is significantly higher during peak hours (not shown due to space constraints). The results suggest that cellular network operators can improve web QoE by decreasing cell load by deploying more radio cells or re-distributing users across cells.

2. Higher signal strength (RSSI) does not necessarily correlate with better user experience, but higher signal energy to interference (ECNO) does. As Figure 7 shows, increasing the signal energy to interference (ECNO) by 10% above average reduces abandonment rate by about 2 percentage points, increases average session length between 2.6% and 9.4% and improves partial download ratio by 0.7 percentage points. In contrast, Figure 8 shows that sessions with higher RSSI have higher partial download ratio on average.

These results confirm that, similar to recent WiFi findings, ECNO (an analogous measure to the SINR of WiFi beacons) is a better indicator of channel quality than RSSI because RSSI does not exclude the power of noise and interference. This finding suggests that web QoE is interference and noise limited, not power (i.e., coverage) limited. We did not observe any impact of RSCP on user experience metrics (not shown).

3. IRAT handovers lead to worse web QoE. IRAT handovers had the strongest impact on user experience, as seen in Figure 9. Sessions with IRAT handovers are much shorter than those without IRAT handovers. Also, all sessions with more than 1 IRAT handover were abandoned. The impact of other handovers (soft handovers, inter-frequency handovers) and failure events (access control failure, RRC failure) on web QoE were negligible. Figure 10 shows that increasing number of such handovers and failures leads to minimal increase in partial download ratio. This indicates high

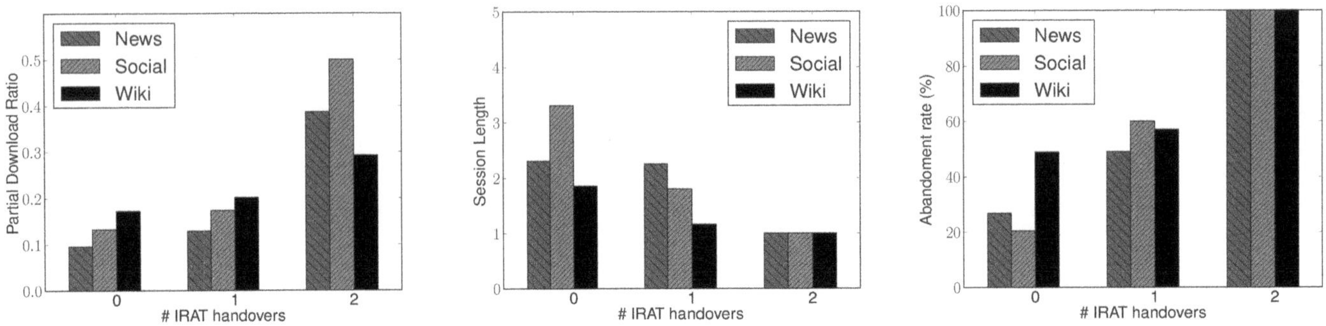

(a) Partial Download Ratio *(b)* Session Length *(c)* Abandonment Rate

Figure 9: IRAT handovers have a strong impact on web QoE—all sessions with 2 handovers are abandoned.

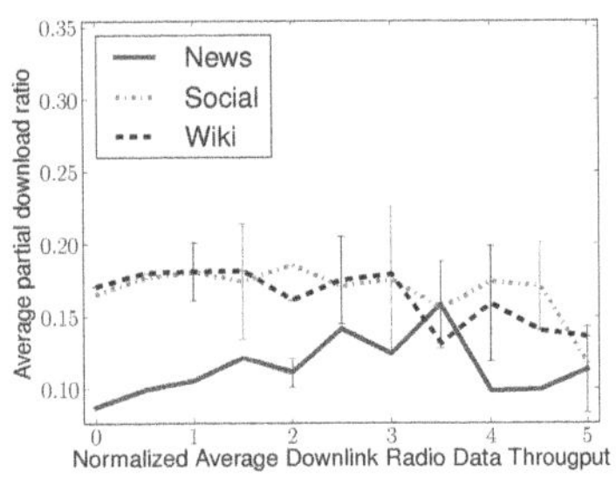

(a) Downlink

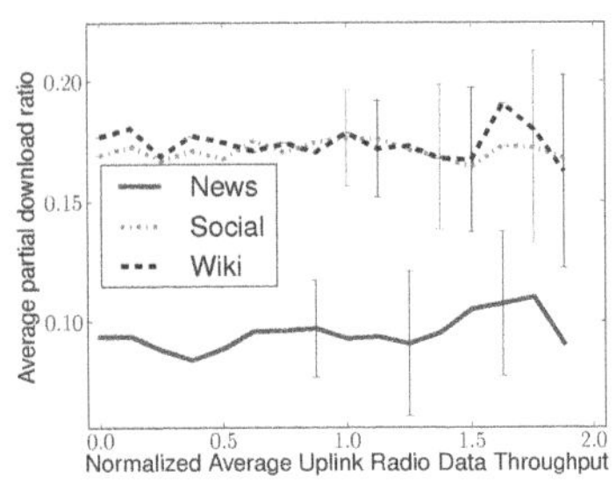

(b) Uplink

Figure 11: Radio data link rate does not impact partial download ratio

robustness against these types of events, hence they should not be used to assess web QoE and their management would likely yield insignificant improvement.

4. Higher radio data rate does not necessarily lead to better web QoE. Figure 11 shows the impact of radio data rate on partial download ratio. As web objects are primarily downloaded onto the mobile device, we start by looking at the downlink direction and find that higher data rates do not improve partial download ratio (Figure 11a). As expected, uplink data rate shows no impact (Figure 11b). We find similar relationship between data link rates and other web QoE metrics (not shown). While it may not be intuitive that data rate and web QoE metrics have weak relationship, it has been shown that web browsing traffic is more latency-limited than throughput-limited [5,9].

5.2 Analysis on Other Websites

To test whether the observations we made above hold for other websites, we analyze one day's worth of HTTP records and radio data for five other leading mobile websites (*Shopping*, *Marketplace*, *News2*, *Social News* and *Blog*) that consistently appear in the top 100 [6].

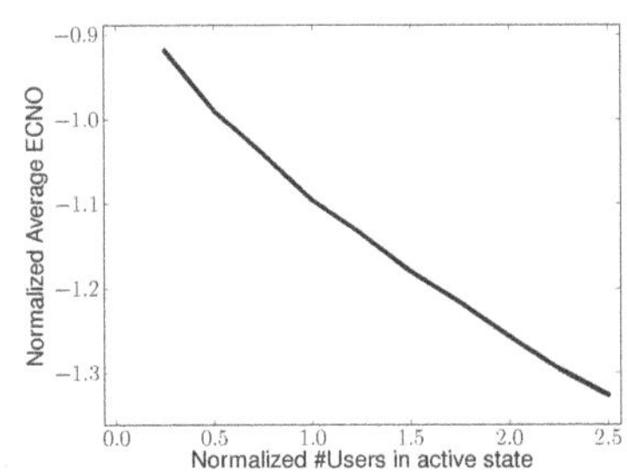

Figure 12: Number of users vs ECNO

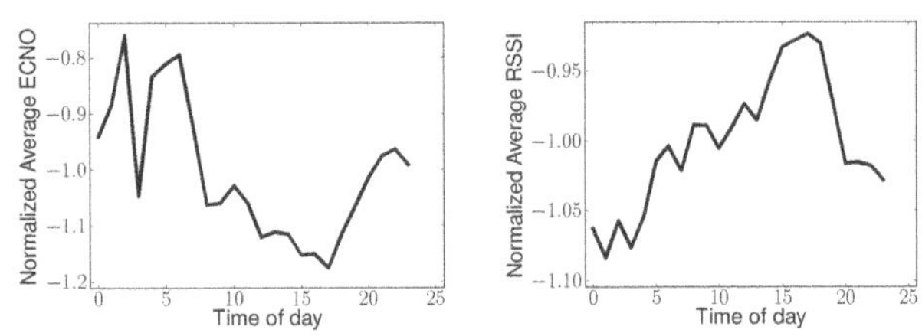

(a) ECNO *(b)* RSSI

Figure 13: Time of day effect on signal strength parameters

In Table 2, we characterize these websites based on two key metrics of website complexity that past work has identified [18]—namely, (1) the average number of objects requested per click and (2) the average number of domains from which requests are served. We found that these websites represent a varied range both for complexity and for user behavior. For example, *News*, *News2*, *Social* and *Blog* have the highest complexity these metrics, whereas

# IRAT handovers	Normalized ECNO	Normalized RSSI
0	-1.09	-0.97
1	-1.53	-1.15
2	-1.84	-1.21

Table 1: We observed lower average ECNO and RSSI for sessions with IRAT handovers

Shopping and *Marketplace* are less complex. Moreover, users tend to have different browsing behavior on these websites: *Shopping*, *Marketplace*, and *Social News* sites understandably tend to have higher session lengths, while *Wiki* and *Blog* tend to have low session lengths.

Table 2 shows that our result hold for this varied set by correlating the impact of increasing each of the radio network factors on partial download ratio. For each radio network factor (e.g., RSSI, ECNO, etc.), we tabulate the slope of the partial download ratio vs. the network factor. For each of RSSI, ECNO, # IRAT handovers and # Users, the partial download ratio graphs exhibit the same trend on increasing the radio network factor even across the varied set of websites. For example, increasing ECNO decreases partial download ratio (i.e., negative slope across all sites).

5.3 Comparison with Other Mobile Applications

Our findings that higher load (in number of users) and lower signal to noise ratio (ECNO) correlate with lower web QoE is not entirely surprising and confirms previous findings on the relationship between these network factors and QoE of mobile video streaming [32]. Interestingly, as in the case of video streaming, the relationship between these two network factors and abandonment rate are both linear and have roughly the same slope.

In contrast to findings on video streaming, however, we observed that only IRAT handovers were disruptive to web QoE and that web QoE metrics were uncorrelated with SOHOs and IFHOs. This finding suggests that web browsing is more tolerant to minor handover disruptions than video streaming. IRAT handovers are much more disruptive because changing radio technologies can take several seconds to complete, which is long enough to influence user perceived latency. Moreover, we find that, unlike mobile video streaming, the radio data rate is uncorrelated with web QoE metrics. This may be because video streaming is a more bandwidth intensive application, whereas web browsing is more sensitive to latency.

In summary, our findings complement previous work on cellular mobile video [32], demonstrating that reducing load and improving ECNO are equally important for both applications. However, carriers need not optimize handovers (except IRAT) or radio throughput rates if they only want to improve web QoE.

5.4 Dependencies and Other Factors

We found that many network factors under study are not independent of each other. An obvious example is that RSSI is related to ECNO and RSCP (as we mentioned earlier). We also found several other dependencies between the radio network factors. Some examples are:

- The number of users in active state in a cell and ECNO are dependent on each other [8]. As shown in Figure 12, there is a linear relationship between the two—adding more users into the cell steadily decreases ECNO.
- Table 1 shows that sessions that experience IRAT handovers also experience lower signal strength (RSSI) and lower signal energy to interference (ECNO).

Further analyzing the radio network factors, we also observed significant time of day effects. Figure 13 shows the average value of RSSI and ECNO observed per hour of the day over the entire one month dataset. We observe that average signal strength to interference (ECNO) is lower during peak hours compared to non-peak hours. On the other hand, average signal strength (RSSI) is higher during peak hours compared to non-peak hours. In Section 4, we also observed strong temporal effects on the various user experience metrics (Figure 5). These could also be caused by external factors/reasons—for example, users are less likely to engage in long browsing sessions during working hours pointing to the need for including external factors such as time of day into the analysis.

Model	Avg. Accuracy (%)
Radio factors alone	73.02
Radio factors + time of day	79.25
Radio factors + time of day + website	83.95

Table 3: Adding time of day and learning a separate decision tree for each website improves accuracy.

In summary, complex interdependencies between network factors as well as external factors (e.g. time of day) make it very challenging to understand and quantify the true impact of each network factor using correlation analysis. This points to the need to use more systematic techniques, including machine learning algorithms, to capture the complex relationships in order to quantify the impact of network factors.

6. MODELING WEB QOE

Our end goal is to develop models that can be used by cellular network operators to improve web QoE by tuning network parameters. For example, our model should help answer the question "how much can we improve the partial download ratio if we increase ECNO by 1 dB?". The model should also help network operators monitor web QoE metrics using only radio network characteristics. To achieve this goal, the QoE models that we build should be *intuitive*, *accurate*, and must be able to *predict web QoE from network factors alone*.

Building an accurate QoE model is challenging because of the complex relationships between network factors and web QoE metrics, interdependencies between various network factors, and also due to external factors (e.g., differences between websites, time of day effects). To tackle these challenges, we use machine learning to capture the dependencies and relationships, and develop and evaluate models that can predict web QoE metrics. The model we derive will express web QoE metrics as a function of radio parameters; specifically, we wish to capture the relationship:

$$WebQoE = f(RadioNetworkParameter_{1..n})$$

where $WebQoE$ denotes one of the user experience metrics (partial download ratio, abandonment, or session length), and $RadioNetworkParameter_i$ denotes the ith observed radio network parameter listed in Section 5.

6.1 Evaluation

We predict: (1) partial download ratio, (2) session length, (3) if the session includes partially downloaded pages or not (*part* or *full*), and (4) if the user will abandon a session or not (*abandoned* or *not-abandoned*). The choice of the machine learning algorithm is important because the model it learns should be expressive enough to capture all the complex relationships and dependencies. After experimenting with different regression, tree and bayes algorithms (such as linear and logistic regression, variations of decision trees and naive Bayes) we found that linear regression worked best for (1) and (2), and C4.5 decision tree algorithm was able to predict the binary classification most accurately for tasks (3) and (4). We use 10-fold cross-validation to evaluate all our models [29].

Evaluating Linear Regression Models: Since most network factors have a linear relationship with web QoE metrics (session length and partial download ratio) and since they are linearly dependent on

	Website complexity		Average webQoE			Impact of increasing radio factor on Partial Download Ratio (P.D.R.)			
Website	# Domains	# Objects	Average P.D.R	Average Session Length	Abandon Rate (%)	RSSI	ECNO	# IRAT	# Users
News	13.4	23.1	0.1	2.2	21	0.0006	-0.007	0.15	0.0004
Social	13.1	20.2	0.15	3.1	23	0.0004	-0.004	0.06	0.0003
Wiki	3.69	13.31	0.16	1.8	41	0.0011	-0.005	0.18	0.0003
Shopping	4.6	7.5	0.12	8.5	10	0.0015	-0.004	0.07	0.0003
Marketplace	3.2	3.6	0.04	12.3	5	0.0007	-0.001	0.06	0.0002
News2	15.7	29.9	0.09	3.4	15	0.0010	-0.008	0.17	0.0004
Social News	11.65	7.38	0.03	10.9	8	0.002	-0.005	0.12	0.0003
Blog	11.89	20.40	0.17	2.65	30	0.0003	-0.009	0.19	0.0005

Table 2: Observations made in Section 5.1 hold for a varied set of websites

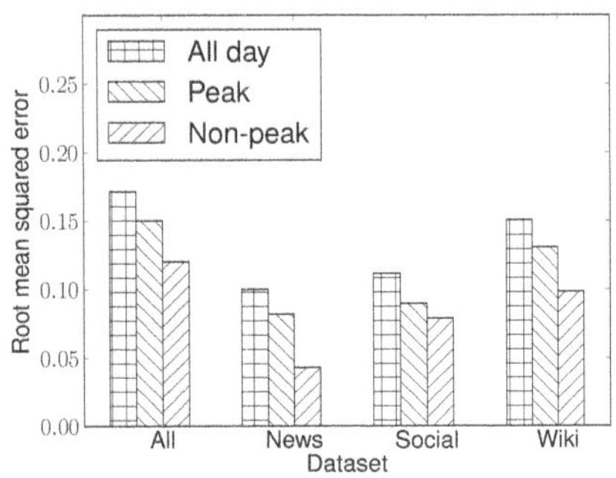

Figure 14: Learning a separate regression models for each website and time of day (peak/non-peak) improves accuracy.

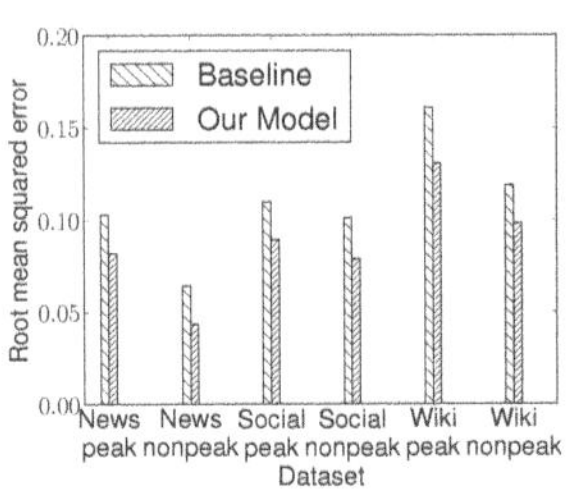

(a) Partial Download Ratio

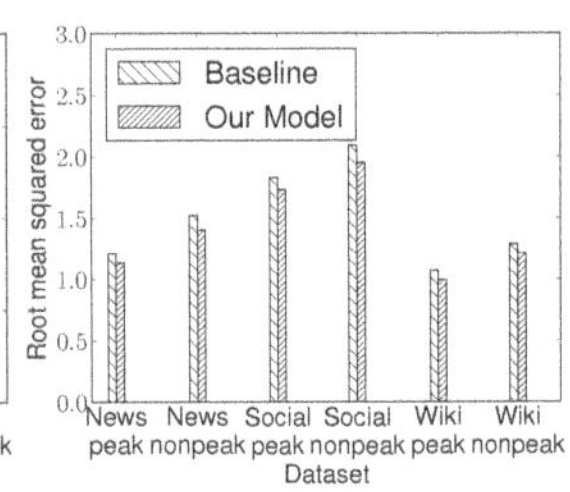

(b) Session Length

Figure 15: Our models are more accurate than the baseline in predicting partial download ratio.

each other (Section 4), linear regression is well-suited for capturing these relationships. To measure the "goodness-of-fit" of linear regression, we use the standard measure of root mean squared error (RMSE), where lower RMSE values indicate better prediction. Figure 14 shows RMSE when using linear regression to predict partial download ratio. We show the results for each website separately on the x-axis, as well as the results for data from all web sites taken together ("*All*"). The three bars in each cluster represent RMSE for the entire day, for peak hours only, and for non-peak hours only—each of these have separately learned models due to significant time of day effects. We see that separate models for time of day and individual web sites results in significant prediction improvement, as indicated by lower RMSE values.

	Partial		Abandonment	
Dataset	Model	Baseline	Model	Baseline
News	80.4	59.7	78.6	75.6
Social	87.7	72.5	82.0	78.6
Wiki	80.6	70.3	62.3	53.3

Table 4: Our models are more accurate than the baseline in predicting partial downloads and abandonment.

We repeated these experiments for session length and found similar improvements from splitting data and learning models for each split (not shown). Hence, our final linear regression models for both partial download ratio and session length are *each* a collection of six linear regression models: one each for each combination of web site (*News*, *Social*, *Wiki*) and time of day (*Peak*, *Non-peak*).

We compare the performance of our models with a baseline model that always predicts the mean (using the ZeroR classifier [2]) for the particular dataset in Figure 15. In the case of partial download ratio, our model has around 20% lower RMSE compared to the baseline. For session length, our model has up to 10% lower RMSE. Predicting session length is not as accurate as predicting partial download ratio because session length is more affected by external confounding factors (e.g. user interest), which are very difficult to capture from network traces.

Evaluating Decision Tree Models: We also develop models that make binary predictions for users' web sessions, such as "will this session have partially downloaded pages?" and "will the user abandon this session?". The C4.5 decision tree algorithm performed the best in predicting both these classifications. Table 3 shows the accuracy for predicting partial downloads. Refining the model by inputting the time of day (in terms of hour of day (0-23)) along with learning a separate model for each website led to around 11% improvement in accuracy. We observed this for the decision tree that predicts abandonment as well. Essentially, our models for predicting abandonment and partial downloads are both a collection of 3 decision trees, one for each website. They take both the radio factors as well as time of day as input.

Further, we compared our model against a baseline model that predicts the majority class using the ZeroR classifier [2] for each dataset in Table 4. Our partial download model achieves up to 20% higher accuracy compared to the baseline while our abandonment model achieves up to 10% more accuracy. Again, smaller improvement for abandonment is due to confounding factors like user interest that we cannot measure, but can significantly influence user abandonment.

6.2 Insights and Discussion

Fortunately, both linear regression and decision tree algorithms that gave the highest accuracy also generate very intuitive models. They can hence provide insights to network operators towards tuning network factors to improve web QoE. For example, Table 5 shows the regression co-efficients for our partial download ratio model. We observe that the features that the models learnt (number

Dataset	# active users	RSSI (dBm)	ECNO (dB)	# SOHO	# IRAT	Constant
News Nonpeak	0.0002	0.0005	-0.0043	0	0	0.0411
News Peak	0.0002	0	-0.0032	0	0	0.0976
Social Nonpeak	0.0002	0.0005	-0.0037	-0.0007	0.0639	0.0485
Social Peak	0.0002	0.0005	-0.0047	-0.0005	0.0627	0.1367
Wiki Nonpeak	0.0002	0.0003	-0.0042	-0.0005	0.0871	0.0848
Wiki Peak	0.0002	0.0004	-0.0037	-0.0004	0.0799	0.2022

Table 5: Linear regression coefficients of the model that predicts partial download ratio.

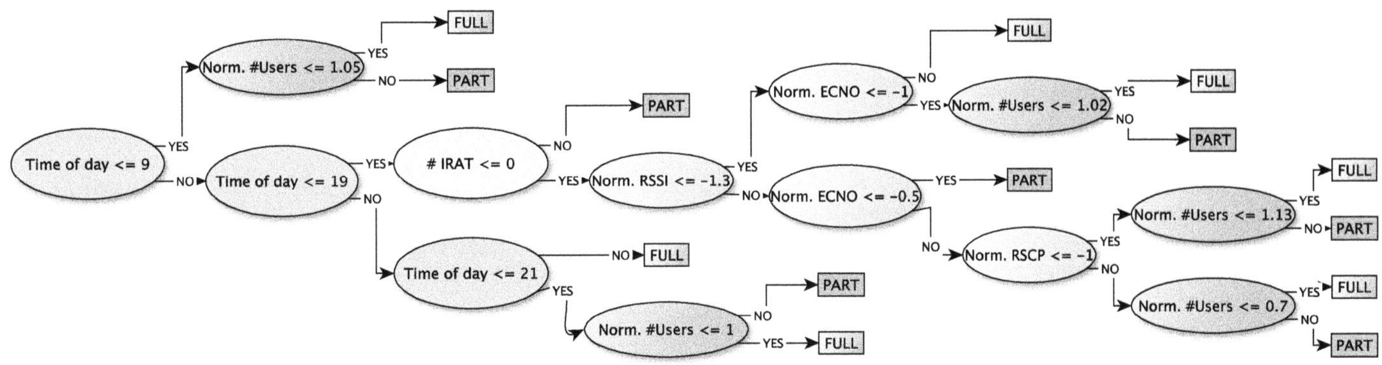

Figure 16: Pruned decision tree that predicts partial downloads

of users, ECNO, RSSI etc.) are the same as those that we found to be impactful in Section 5. Moreover, the model also ignores factors such as downlink and uplink throughput that we found to not have an impact on web QoE metrics.

Interestingly, the value of the regression co-efficients are similar across the different datasets. This implies that irrespective of the time of day and the website, tuning a particular network parameter has the same impact on partial download ratio. For example, improving ECNO by 1 dB decreases partial download ratio by roughly 0.004 across all times of day and websites. Network operators can hence use this model to understand the true impact of a parameter. For example, comparing the co-efficients, decreasing IRAT handovers and improving ECNO has the highest impact on improving partial download ratio. We also found similar conclusions from analyzing the regression co-efficients for session length (not shown due to space constraints).

Figure 16 shows the pruned decision tree that we learnt for predicting partial download for the *Wiki* website. Again, consistent with our analysis in Section 5, the model picks parameters such as Number of users, ECNO, IRAT etc. to branch on, reconfirming the impact of these factors. Further, the decision tree rules separate the data based on time of day into a similar classification that we made for peak vs. non-peak (e.g., Time of day $<= 9$, Time of day > 9 and Time of day $<= 19$, Time of day > 19). We also observe that the feature splits conform with several of our observations. For example, during non-peak hours the partial downloads are lower (if Time of day > 21, predict *full*). Also if load is higher partial downloads are higher (if Normalized Num User $<= 1.05$, predict *full* otherwise *part*).

7. DISCUSSION

Other websites and native apps: In this paper, we developed and analyzed QoE models primarily for three different websites. However, preliminary analysis in Section 5.2 indicates that the general observations also hold for other websites with different complexities. We also found that (1) the same machine learning algorithms (decision trees and linear regression) performed the best across different websites, (2) the model parameters are similar across websites, and (3) the *ordering* of the importance of network parameters is the same across different websites. Furthermore, our methodology is completely automated and can be easily applied to other websites. In this paper we focused on traffic from web browsers by filtering based on the User Agent string; this analysis does not include traffic from native mobile apps, and applying our techniques to this type of traffic is an interesting direction for future work.

New technologies: Our study is based on traffic collected from a UMTS network. However, we expect our methodology and results to generally apply to newer technologies such as 4G Long Term Evolution (LTE). Radio network parameters in UMTS have analogous parameters in LTE. For example, the number of users in active state in UMTS is related to the number of users in CONNECTED state in LTE. Similarly, number of RRC failures in LTE is related to the number of RRC failures in UMTS. We observed that the number of IRAT handovers has the highest impact on user experience. This for instance might have a lesser impact when switching between UMTS and LTE since the handovers are expected to complete faster. Similarly since web browsing is more latency-limited than throughput-limited, higher throughput offered by LTE may not have a significant impact on web QoE.

Encrypted traffic: Our click detection algorithm uses URL to classify if a web request is a click or an embedded object. With SSL/TLS traffic, the entire user payload including HTTP URL is encrypted and hence we cannot apply the current methodology. However, a network operator can still identify the domain to which an encrypted web request is sent by correlating the IP address of the web request from DNS server logs—the IP address will likely correspond to a prior DNS request/reply pair. Our click detection technique can be tailored to use this information in the future. Also, encryption would not affect our QoE prediction methodology, since it is based on radio statistics and completely independent of traffic encryption.

Limitations: One of the main constraints faced by a network operator is the lack of client-side instrumentation. This makes it difficult to differentiate between the abandonment caused by the lack of user interest from the ones caused by network issues. For example, a user could potentially have abandoned the session due to lack of interest, and yet the network would have delivered all the data. It is impossible to identify such a situation from network logs alone. Similarly, network operators cannot identify cellular-to-WiFi handovers from cellular network traces alone, and would mistakingly mark such handovers as abandonments. Nonetheless, operators are typically interested in aggregate performance trends and changes that signify network issues or improvements. A few false positives or negatives introduced by these limitations are unlikely to significantly alter the behavior of aggregate metrics.

8. CONCLUSION

In this paper, we presented a large-scale study that analyzed web QoE, such as session length, abandonment rate and partial download ratio, from a "cellular network operator" point of view. Understanding web QoE from a network operator perspective is challenging due to lack of visibility or instrumentation at clients and servers and a priori knowledge of web site structure. We developed and evaluated text-classification-based mechanisms to extract mobile web browsing sessions and accurately estimate various web QoE metrics from network traces. Our classification approach has 20% higher precision than previous state-of-the-art. Further, we analyzed the impact of various radio network factors on web QoE. We observed that web QoE is particularly sensitive to IRAT handovers, ECNO and load in the cell. Moreover, we identified radio metrics that are often considered important, but show negligible impact on web QoE, such as average radio link data rate, soft handovers, and inter-frequency handovers. Finally, we developed *accurate* and *intuitive* machine learning models that can predict various web QoE metrics from *network factors alone*. Our models can be used by network operators to monitor web QoE using standard radio network metrics alone and prioritize improvement of network factors that have the highest impact.

Acknowledgments

We thank our anonymous shepherd and reviewers for their feedback that helped improve our paper. This work is supported in part by NSF FIA Grant CNS-1040801.

9. REFERENCES

[1] Cisco visual networking index: Global mobile data forecast update 2013-2018. `http://goo.gl/fjHsga`.

[2] Data mining with weka. `http://goo.gl/YD9Awt`.

[3] Firebug. `getfirebug.com`.

[4] Google page speed. `http://goo.gl/p1biC0`.

[5] Impatient Web Users. `http://goo.gl/4jPDkv`.

[6] Quantcast website ranking. `http://goo.gl/QH7te2`.

[7] Text classification. `http://goo.gl/iN6syK`.

[8] Wcdma - network planning and optimization. `http://goo.gl/Alivjh`.

[9] Using Predictive Prefetching to Improve W.W.W. Latency. In *SIGCOMM Computer Communivation Review*, 1996.

[10] Experiences in a 3G Network: Interplay between the Wireless Channel and Applications. In *MOBICOM*, 2008.

[11] Tackling bufferbloat in 3G/4G networks. In *IMC*, 2012.

[12] An In-depth Study of LTE: Effect of Network Protocol and Application Behavior on Performance. In *SIGCOMM*, 2013.

[13] K. Chen, C. Huang, P. Huang, C. Lei. Quantifying Skype User Satisfaction. In *Proc. SIGCOMM*, 2006.

[14] A. Balachandran, V. Sekar, A. Akella, S. Seshan, I. Stoica, and H. Zhang. Developing a Predictive Model of Quality of Experience for Internet Video. In *SIGCOMM*, 2013.

[15] H. Balakrishnan, V. N. Padmanabhan, S. Seshan, M. Stemm, and R. H. Katz. TCP Behavior of a Busy Internet Server: Analysis and Improvements. In *INFOCOM*, 1998.

[16] P. Barford and M. Crovella. Generating Representative Web Workloads for Network and Server Performance Evaluation. In *SIGMETRICS*, 1998.

[17] A. Bouch, A. Kuchinsky, and N. Bhatti. Quality is in the Eye of the Beholder: Meeting UsersâĂŹ Requirements for Internet Quality of Service. In *CHI*, 2000.

[18] M. Butkiewicz, H. V. Madhyastha, and V. Sekar. Understanding Website Complexity: Measurements, Metrics and Implications. In *IMC*, 2011.

[19] B. Clifton. *Advanced Web Metrics with Google Analytics*. John Wiley and Sons, 2012.

[20] H. Cui and E. Biersack. On the Relationship between QoE and QoS for Web Sessions. In *Eurecom Research Report*, 2012.

[21] D. F. Galletta, R. Henry, S. McCoy, and P. Polak. Web Site Delays: How Tolerant are Users? In *Journal of the Association of Information Systems*, 2004.

[22] N. Godbole, M. Srinivasaiah, and S. Skiena. Large-Scale Sentiment Analysis for News and Blogs. In *ICWSM*, 2007.

[23] A. Hassan, Y. Song, and L. wei He. A Task Level Metric for Measuring Web Search Satisfaction and its Application on Improving Relevance Estimation. In *CIKM*, 2011.

[24] S. Ihm and V. S. Pai. Towards Understanding Modern Web Traffic. In *IMC*, 2011.

[25] S. S. Krishnan and R. K. Sitaraman. Video stream quality impacts viewer behavior: Inferring causality using quasi-experimental designs. In *IMC*, 2012.

[26] C. Liu, R. W. White, and S. Dumais. Understanding Web Browsing Behaviors through Weibull Analysis of Dwell Time. In *SIGIR*, 2010.

[27] B. A. Mah. An Empirical Model of HTTP Network TrafïňĄc. In *INFOCOM*, 1997.

[28] L. A. Meyerovich and R. Bodik. Fast and Parallel Webpage Layout. In *WWW*, 2010.

[29] T. Mitchell. *Machine Learning*. McGraw-Hill.

[30] J. C. Mogul. The Case for Persistent-Connection HTTP. In *SIGCOMM*, 1995.

[31] M. Sahami, S. Dumais, D. Heckerman, and E. Horvitz. A Bayesian Approach to Filtering Junk E-Mail. In *AAAI*, 1998.

[32] M. Z. Shafiq, J. Erman, L. Ji, A. X. Liu, J. Pang, and J. Wang. Understanding the Impact of Network Dynamics on Mobile Video User Engagement. In *SIGMETRICS*, 2014.

[33] M. Z. Shafiq, L. Ji, A. X. Liu, J. Pang, and J. Wang. Characterizing Geospatial Dynamics of Application Usage in a 3G Cellular Data Network . In *INFOCOM*, 2012.

[34] F. D. Smith, F. H. Campos, K. Jeffay, and D. Ott. What TCP/IP Protocol Headers Can Tell Us About the Web. In *SIGMETRICS*, 2001.

[35] S. Sundaresan, N. Feamster, R. Teixeira, and N. Magharei. Measuring and Mitigating Web Performance Bottlenecks in Broadband Access Networks. In *IMC*, 2013.

[36] T. Tullis and W. Albert. *Measuring the User Experience: Collecting, Analyzing, and Presenting Usability Metrics.* Morgan Kaufmann Publishers Inc., San Francisco, CA, USA, 2008.

Where Are You From? Confusing Location Distinction Using Virtual Multipath Camouflage

Song Fang, Yao Liu
University of South Florida
{songf@mail, yliu@cse}.usf.edu

Wenbo Shen
North Carolina State University
wshen3@ncsu.edu

Haojin Zhu
Shanghai Jiaotong University
zhu-hj@cs.sjtu.edu.cn

ABSTRACT

In wireless networks, location distinction aims to detect location changes or facilitate authentication of wireless users. To achieve location distinction, recent research has been focused on investigating the spatial uncorrelation property of wireless channels. Specifically, the differences of wireless channel characteristics are used to distinguish locations or identify location changes.

However, we discover a new attack against all existing location distinction approaches that are built on the spatial uncorrelation property of wireless channels. In such an attack, the adversary can easily hide her location changes or impersonate movements by injecting fake wireless channel characteristics into a target receiver. Experimental results on our USRP-based prototype show that the discovered attack can craft any desired channel characteristic with a successful probability of 95.0% to defeat spatial uncorrelation based location distinction schemes. To defend against this attack, we propose a detection technique that utilizes an auxiliary receiver or antenna to identify these fake channel characteristics. Experiments demonstrate that our novel detection method achieves a detection rate higher than 91.2% while maintaining a very low false alarm rate.

Categories and Subject Descriptors

C.2.3 [**Computer-Communication Networks**]: Network Operations—*Network Monitoring*

Keywords

Channel impulse response, Multipath, Security, MIMO

1. INTRODUCTION

Location distinction in wireless networks aims to detect a wireless user's location change, movement or facilitate location-based authentication. Enforcing location distinction is important for many wireless applications [1, 2]. For example,

MobiCom'14, September 07 - 11 2014, Maui, HI, USA.

http://dx.doi.org/10.1145/2639108.2639117 .

- Wireless sensor networks are usually utilized to monitor a target area by sensing the physical or environmental conditions (e.g., temperature, sound, and pressure). Administrators of the sensor networks would like to enforce location distinction to prevent an unauthorized person from moving the sensors away from the area of interest.
- Wireless networks are vulnerable to the sybil attack due to the broadcast nature of the wireless medium [3]. In a sybil attack, an adversary forges a significant amount of fake user identities to fool a networked system. By enforcing location distinction, the administrator can tell whether or not all identities are originated from the same location, and thus detect such attacks.
- Active radio frequency identification (RFID) tags are often used in warehouses for tracking inventory and maintaining the physical security. It has been assumed that "location distinction is critical to provide a warning and to be able to focus resources (e.g., security, cameras, and personnel) on moving objects" [1].

Location distinction using wireless physical layer information has been extensively studied during the past several years (e.g., [1–6]). Scientists discovered that wireless channels normally exhibit the spatial uncorrelation property; i.e., the characteristics of the wireless channel become uncorrelated every a half carrier wavelength over distance [7].

The spatial uncorrelation property of wireless channels has been widely explored and adopted to enforce location distinction of wireless devices (e.g., [1–6]). Specifically, the changes of wireless channel characteristics have been utilized to identify the location changes of a wireless transmitter.

In our study, however, we discover a new attack against all existing location distinction approaches that are built on the spatial uncorrelation property of wireless channels. By launching such an attack, the adversary can generate any wireless channel characteristics chosen by herself at a target receiver to deteriorate the location distinction capability of the receiver. The key idea of the discovered attack is to create a *virtual multipath channel* as undetectable camouflage to make the receiver believe a specified channel characteristic chosen by the attacker.

To understand the virtual multipath channel, we first explain the multipath effect, which is the fundamental reason for the spatial uncorrelation property. Wireless signals normally propagate in the air through multiple paths due to obstacle reflection, diffraction, and scattering. Therefore, for wireless signals sent from different locations, the destination receiver can observe different channel characteristics from these signals, because they experience different multi-

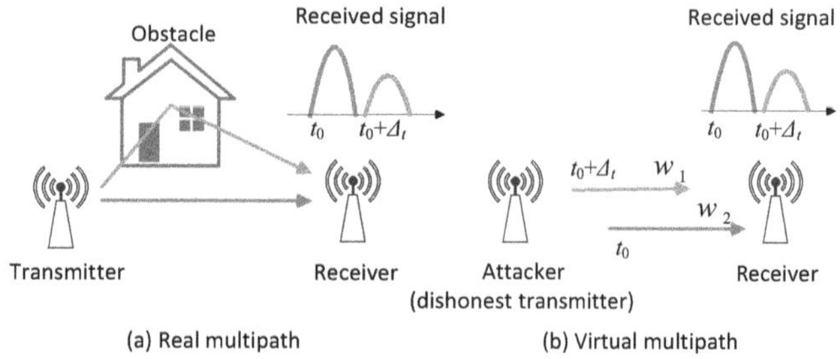

Figure 1: Creating a virtual multipath similar to the real multipath propagation.

paths and accordingly undergo different channel effects (e.g, power attenuation, phase shifting, and delay). To fool a receiver, the attacker needs to create an "artificial channel" that can exhibit a multipath propagation feature similar to the real-world multipath.

We give an example to illustrate how the attacker can create such a channel. Figure 1(a) shows a simple real multipath scenario, where a signal sent by the transmitter travels on two paths, i.e., the reflection path and the direct path. At time t_0, the receiver starts to receive the signal copy that travels on the direct path. The reflection path is longer than the direct path, and thus at a later time $t_0+\Delta_t$, the receivers receives the aggregation of the signal copy from the direct path and the one from the reflection path.

Now consider the scenario in Figure 1(b): there is only one direct path between the attacker (i.e., a dishonest transmitter) and the receiver, but the attacker wants to make the receiver believe that there are two paths existing similar to the real multipath propagation shown in Figure 1(a). To this end, the attacker sends the signal alone first. After duration Δ_t, she superimposes a fresh signal copy into the one already in transmission. For both the original signal and the time-delayed copy, the attacker multiplies them with attenuation factors w_1 and w_2 to mimic the signal amplitude attenuation caused by real paths. Consequently, the receiver observes an aggregation of one signal plus a time-delayed copy, with each undergoing a certain amplitude attenuation, and thus thinks that they are caused by the multipath effect.

The example in Figure 1(b) assumes that there exists only one direct path between the attacker and the receiver (i.e., no multipath effect is considered). In practice, the attacker's crafted multipath signal is affected by the real multipath effect as well, and she should have a way to deal with the impact caused by the real multipath between herself and the receiver. Our research reveals that the attacker can easily achieve this goal by reverse-engineering existing wireless channel estimation algorithms and performing linear transformations to the original signal.

To defend against this attack, we propose a detection technique utilizing an auxiliary receiver (or antenna) at a different location to identify the virtual multipath channels and the fake channel characteristics. Specifically, the attacker must craft its transmitting signal to make the target receiver believe a particular channel characteristic. However, we show that the crafted signal exhibits inconsistent channel characteristics to the auxiliary receiver. Based on this result, we create a defense scheme that does not require the receivers to have any prior knowledge about the real channel characteristics between themselves and the transmitter.

We perform real-world experimental evaluation on the Universal Software Radio Peripherals (USRPs). The experimental results show that an attacker, by using the virtual multipath channel as camouflage, can fool a target to believe any desired channel characteristic with successful probability of 95.0%. However, when the defense approach is enforced, the attack can be discovered with probability more than 91.2% and the false alarm rate can be reduced to 0 with a carefully chosen detection threshold. The experimental results suggest that the discovered attack is a real threat to existing location distinction schemes using the spatial uncorrelation property, and demonstrate the success of the defense approach. Our contributions are summarized as follows.

- We discovered the multipath propagation can be artificially made in a lab environment, and created a technique that can successfully generate virtual multipath channels.
- Based on the virtual multipath channel, we identified a new type of attacks that can defeat all existing location distinction algorithms using the spatial uncorrelated property of wireless channels.
- We created a defense technique to detect such attacks and protect location distinction systems.
- We implemented real-world prototypes of both the attack and the defense technique. We experimented on top of the prototype implementations to examine the practical impact of the attacks and the effectiveness of the proposed defense method.

2. PRELIMINARIES

In this section, we show how location distinction is usually enforced and introduce the prevalent algorithms that are used to estimate wireless channel characteristics.

2.1 Channel Impulse Response and Location Distinction

As mentioned earlier, a wireless signal usually propagates in the air along multiple paths due to reflection, diffraction, and scattering [1]. As a result, a receiver receives multiple copies of the signal from different paths, each of which has a different delay due to the path it traverses on. The received signal is the sum of these time delayed signal copies. Each path imposes a *response* (e.g., delay and attenuation) on the signal traveling along it [1], and the superposition of all responses between two nodes is referred to as a *channel impulse response* [8]. Wireless channels can be characterized by channel impulse responses.

The multipath effects of different wireless links are different, and so are the channel impulse responses [1]. Due to this reason, a channel impulse response has been utilized to provide location distinction [1,2]. Specifically, to determine if the transmitter has changed its location, the receiver estimates the channel impulse response of a newly received signal and compares it with the previous estimation result. The location change is detected if the difference between the newly estimated channel impulse response and the previous one exceeds a certain threshold.

2.2 Estimating Channel Impulse Responses

Estimating channel impulse responses is a must-have function for most modern wireless systems [8,9]. With the correct channel estimation result, the communicators are able to adapt transmissions to current channel conditions, which is critical for achieving reliable communication with high data rates [8].

Note that the signal propagation paths are unresolvable if the differences between the arrival times of the signals traveling on these paths are much smaller than the symbol duration, which is the transmission time of a wireless physical-layer unit [8]. Hence, existing channel estimation algorithms assume a resolvable multipath, i.e., the arrival times of signal copies traveling on different paths are larger than the symbol duration.

Channel impulse responses are usually estimated using training sequences [10]. Specifically, the transmitter sends a training sequence (i.e., a sequence of bits) over the wireless channel, while the receiver uses the same training sequence and the corresponding received signal samples to estimate the channel impulse response. The training sequence can be pre-shared [10] or reconstructed from the received signal [1].

The physical layer channel estimation can be processed in either frequency (e.g. [1, 2]) or time domain (e.g., [10]), which are inter-convertible due to the linear relation between the two domains. In the following, we describe the channel estimation method in the time domain.

Mathematical Formulation: The estimation of channel impulse responses exploits the (known) training sequence and the corresponding received samples. The transmitter converts the training sequence into M physical layer symbols (i.e., complex numbers that are transmission units at the physical layer [8]). The transmitter then sends the M symbols to the wireless channel.

Let $\mathbf{x} = [x_1, x_2, ..., x_M]$ denote the transmitted symbols in the training sequence. Assume that there exist at most L resolvable paths (L can be computed based on practice wireless system configurations [8]). Thus, the receiver can receive L copies of $\mathbf{x}$, each traveling on one path and undergoing a response caused by the corresponding path. The vector $\mathbf{y}$ of received symbols is the convolution sum of the L copies of $\mathbf{x}$. Let $\mathbf{h} = [h_1, h_2, ..., h_L]^T$ be the channel impulse response, where h_i is the response of the i-th path. The received symbols $\mathbf{y}$ can be represented by [10]

$$\mathbf{y} = \mathbf{h} * \mathbf{x} + \mathbf{n}, \tag{1}$$

where $\mathbf{n}$ is the noise and $*$ is the convolution operator. The matrix form of Equation (1) is

$$\mathbf{y} = \begin{bmatrix} x_1 & 0 & \cdot & 0 \\ x_2 & x_1 & \cdot & \cdot \\ \cdot & x_2 & \cdot & 0 \\ \cdot & \cdot & \cdot & \cdot \\ x_L & \cdot & \cdot & x_1 \\ \cdot & \cdot & \cdot & \cdot \\ x_M & \cdot & \cdot & x_{M-L+1} \\ 0 & x_M & \cdot & \cdot \\ \cdot & \cdot & \cdot & \cdot \\ 0 & 0 & \cdot & x_M \end{bmatrix} \begin{bmatrix} h_1 \\ h_2 \\ \cdot \\ \cdot \\ h_L \end{bmatrix} + \mathbf{n} \tag{2}$$

Rewriting Equation (2) in a compact matrix form yields

$$\mathbf{y} = \mathbf{X}\mathbf{h} + \mathbf{n}, \tag{3}$$

where $\mathbf{X}$ is a $(L + M - 1) \times L$ Toeplitz matrix, containing L delayed versions of the transmitted symbols $\mathbf{x}$, and $\mathbf{y}$ is a vector consisting of $(L + M - 1)$ received symbols.

Estimation: Two types of estimators are generally used to estimate $\mathbf{h}$ from Equation (3): least-square (LS) estimator and linear minimum mean squared error (LMMSE) estimator [11].

The LS estimator is given by $\hat{\mathbf{h}}_{\text{LS}} = (\mathbf{X}^H\mathbf{X})^{-1}\mathbf{X}^H\mathbf{y}$, where $(\cdot)^H$ and $(\cdot)^{-1}$ are the conjugate transpose and matrix inverse operators [12]. The LMMSE estimator is written as $\hat{\mathbf{h}}_{\text{LMMSE}} = \mathbf{R}_h(\mathbf{R}_h + \sigma_n^2(\mathbf{X}\mathbf{X}^H)^{-1})^{-1}\mathbf{X}^H\mathbf{y}$, where $\mathbf{R}_h$ is the multipath channel correlation matrix (i.e., the statistical expectation of $\mathbf{h}\mathbf{h}^H$) and σ_n^2 is the variance of the noise [13], which are both assumed to be known as prior knowledge.

If the correlation matrix $\mathbf{R}_h$ and noise variance σ_n^2 are both known, the LMMSE estimator is used; otherwise, the LS estimator is used. In this paper, we focus on the LS estimator, because for location distinction schemes in a realistic environment, the precise channel correlation statistics and noise knowledge are difficult to obtain due to the time-vary property of wireless channels and potential movements of wireless nodes.

3. SYSTEM ASSUMPTIONS AND ADVERSARY MODEL

The location distinction system consists of a transmitter and a receiver. Both are equipped with radio interfaces that can transmit and receive wireless signals. The receiver aims to verify whether or not the transmitter has changed location. Towards this goal, the receiver estimates the channel impulse response from a wireless signal received from the transmitter, and then compares it with the previous estimation results to generate a decision. To constantly enforce the location distinction, the receiver periodically sends an inquiry to the transmitter, and the transmitter responds the inquiry by sending wireless signals back to the receiver.

We assume that the transmitter is malicious and aims to hide her location change or impersonate movements while she is actually static. To achieve this objective, the transmitter attempts to mislead the receiver through creating a virtual multipath channel, which can fool the receiver to estimate a fake wireless channel impulse response chosen by the transmitter. We assume that the malicious transmitter knows the training sequence used for the channel estimation. Note that in many commercial wireless communication systems, the channel estimation training sequences are made available to the public. For example, the training sequences in WiFi systems consist of short (64-bit) and long (128-bit) preambles specified in the 802.11 standard [14].

We further assume that the malicious transmitter knows the actual channel impulse response between herself and the receiver. This can be achieved by estimating the channel impulse response from the wireless signals (e.g., location distinction inquiries) emitted by the receiver.

4. VIRTUAL MULTIPATH ATTACK

In this section, we describe how to create a virtual multipath channel to defeat location distinction algorithms. The attacker can launch two types of attacks. In a basic attack, the attacker can use any weights to craft a virtual multipath signal. This will fool the receiver to obtain random, incorrect estimates of the channel impulse response. In an advanced attack, with the knowledge of the real channel impulse response between herself and the receiver, the attacker is able to compute exact weights that make the receiver to estimate the chosen channel impulse responses specified by the attacker. In the following discussion, we focus on the

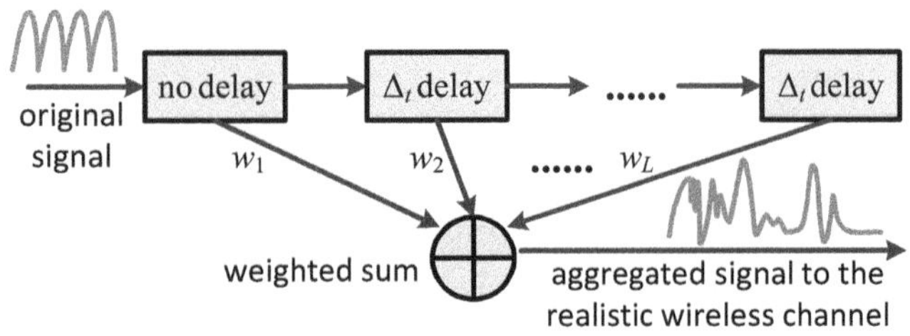

Figure 2: Inside the attacker: she first sums (with weights) all delayed copies of the original signal, then transmits the aggregated signal out.

advanced attack due to the more misleading nature of such attacks.

4.1 Overview of The Attack

As we mentioned earlier, the attacker can generate an aggregated signal with time-delayed copies to emulate the real multipath effect.

To launch the attack, the attacker needs to know when she should add a delayed copy into the transmitting signal. According to Equation 2, the channel estimator models each path by delaying it for one symbol duration. Specifically, the i-th arrived signal copy arrives at time $t_0 + (i-1) \cdot 1/R$, where t_0 is the arrival time of the first arrived signal copy and R is the transmission symbol rate. Thus, the attacker can superimpose a copy into the transmitting signal at time t_0', $t_0'+1/R$, $\cdots$, $t_0'+(L-1)\cdot 1/R$ to emulate L paths, where t_0' is the start time of the attacker's first transmission. Accordingly, the time delay for a signal copy is $\Delta_t = 1/R$. Figure 2 illustrates the attacker's signal manipulation and transmission process. For the i-th delayed signal copy $\mathbf{s}_i$, she multiplies it with a weight of w_i. Hence, the attacker's transmitting signal $\mathbf{x}_a$ can be represented as $\sum_{i=1}^{L} w_i \mathbf{s}_i$. The purpose of using weights w_1, w_2, ... , w_L is to make sure that when the transmitting signal $\mathbf{x}_a$ propagates to the receiver through the real multipath environment, it can result in the attacker's desired channel impulse response observed at the receiver. In the following, we give a high-level overview regarding how to obtain these weights.

Let $\mathbf{h}$ denote the channel impulse response between the attacker and the receiver. The signal $\mathbf{y}_a$ received from the attacker can be represented as $\mathbf{y}_a = \mathbf{h} * \mathbf{x}_a + \mathbf{n}$, where $\mathbf{x}_a$ and $\mathbf{n}$ are the transmitting signal and the channel noise, respectively. The receiver uses $\mathbf{y}_a$ to estimate the channel impulse response, and the estimation result is given by $(\mathbf{X}^H\mathbf{X})^{-1}\mathbf{X}^H\mathbf{y}_a$, where $\mathbf{X}$ is a Toeplitz matrix constructed from the training sequence. Let $\mathbf{h}_a$ denote the channel impulse response chosen by the attacker. The attacker aims to make this estimation result equal to $\mathbf{h}_a$, i.e., $(\mathbf{X}^H\mathbf{X})^{-1}\mathbf{X}^H\mathbf{y}_a = \mathbf{h}_a$. By substituting $\mathbf{y}_a = \mathbf{h} * \mathbf{x}_a + \mathbf{n}$ and $\mathbf{x}_a = \Sigma_{i=1}^{L} w_i \mathbf{s}_i$ into this equation, the attacker can solve the weights and we show the detailed calculation process in Section 4.2.

4.2 Obtaining the Weights

A technical challenge for the attacker is that she needs to obtain the weights used in the virtual multipath channel to make the receiver believe a particular channel impulse response. In the following, we show how the attacker can obtain such weights. When training sequence $[x_1, x_2, \cdots, x_M]$ first goes through the virtual channel with weights w_1, w_2, $\cdots$, w_L, the resulting transmitting signal $\mathbf{x}_a$ can be represented in the following matrix form.

$$\mathbf{x}_a = \begin{bmatrix} x_1 & 0 & \cdot & 0 \\ x_2 & x_1 & \cdot & \cdot \\ \cdot & x_2 & \cdot & 0 \\ \cdot & \cdot & \cdot & \cdot \\ x_L & \cdot & \cdot & x_1 \\ \cdot & \cdot & \cdot & \cdot \\ x_M & \cdot & \cdot & x_{M-L+1} \\ 0 & x_M & \cdot & \cdot \\ \cdot & \cdot & \cdot & \cdot \\ 0 & 0 & \cdot & x_M \end{bmatrix} \begin{bmatrix} w_1 \\ w_2 \\ \cdot \\ \cdot \\ w_L \end{bmatrix} = \mathbf{X}\mathbf{w}.$$

The length of $\mathbf{x}_a$ is $L+M-1$, and we let $\mathbf{x}_a = [x_{a_1}, x_{a_2}, ..., x_{a_{L+M-1}}]$. The transmitting symbols x_a will go through the real multipath channel and the corresponding received symbols $\mathbf{y}_a$ is (we omit the noise term for the sake of simplicity)

$$\mathbf{y}_a = \mathbf{h} * \mathbf{x}_a = \mathbf{X}_a\mathbf{h}$$
$$= \begin{bmatrix} x_{a_1} & 0 & \cdot & 0 \\ x_{a_2} & x_{a_1} & \cdot & \cdot \\ \cdot & x_{a_2} & \cdot & 0 \\ x_{a_L} & \cdot & \cdot & x_{a_1} \\ \cdot & \cdot & \cdot & \cdot \\ x_{a_{M+L-1}} & \cdot & \cdot & x_{a_{M-L+1}} \\ \cdot & \cdot & \cdot & \cdot \\ 0 & x_{a_{M+L-1}} & \cdot & \cdot \\ \cdot & \cdot & \cdot & \cdot \\ 0 & 0 & \cdot & x_{a_{M+L-1}} \end{bmatrix} \begin{bmatrix} h_1 \\ h_2 \\ \cdot \\ \cdot \\ h_L \end{bmatrix}.$$

The length of $\mathbf{y}_a$ is $L + (L+M-1) - 1 = 2L + M - 2$. Assume that the receiver is not aware that the original training sequence has been manipulated by the attacker. He thinks that the length of the training sequence is M, the number of paths is L, and hence the number of corresponding received symbols should be $M + L - 1$. The receiver then uses the first received $M + L - 1$ symbols to calculate the channel impulse response. Let $\mathbf{y}_a'$ denote the vector formed by these symbols and we can represent $\mathbf{y}_a'$ as

$$\mathbf{y}_\mathbf{a}' = \mathbf{I}\mathbf{y}_a = \mathbf{I}(\mathbf{X}_\mathbf{a}\mathbf{h}),$$

where $\mathbf{I}_{L+M-1}$ is an $(L+M-1)\times(2L+M-2)$ matrix whose diagonal elements are all 1's. The receiver estimates the channel impulse response based on the following equation

$$\mathbf{y}_a' = \mathbf{X}\hat{\mathbf{h}}.$$

The attacker must make $\hat{\mathbf{h}} = \mathbf{h}_a$ hold. Thus, using matrix operations, we have

$$\mathbf{y}_a' = \mathbf{X}\hat{\mathbf{h}} = \mathbf{X}\mathbf{h}_a = \mathbf{I}(\mathbf{X}_\mathbf{a}\mathbf{h})$$
$$= \begin{bmatrix} h_1 & 0 & \cdot & 0 & 0 & \cdot & 0 \\ h_2 & h_1 & \cdot & \cdot & 0 & \cdot & 0 \\ \cdot & h_2 & \cdot & \cdot & 0 & \cdot & 0 \\ \cdot & \cdot & \cdot & h_1 & 0 & \cdot & 0 \\ h_L & \cdot & \cdot & h_2 & h_1 & \cdot & 0 \\ 0 & h_L & \cdot & \cdot & h_2 & \cdot & 0 \\ \cdot & \cdot & \cdot & \cdot & \cdot & \cdot & \cdot \\ 0 & 0 & \cdot & h_L & h_{L-1} & \cdot & h_1 \end{bmatrix} \begin{bmatrix} x_{a_1} \\ x_{a_2} \\ \cdot \\ \cdot \\ x_{a_M} \\ x_{a_{M+1}} \\ \cdot \\ x_{a_{M+L-1}} \end{bmatrix}$$
$$= \mathbf{H}\mathbf{x}_\mathbf{a},$$

where $\mathbf{H}$ is a Toeplitz matrix of $\mathbf{h}$. We can then solve $\mathbf{x}_a$ from the above equation, and

$$\mathbf{x}_a = (\mathbf{H}^\mathbf{H}\mathbf{H})^{-1}\mathbf{H}^H\mathbf{y}_a' = (\mathbf{H}^\mathbf{H}\mathbf{H})^{-1}\mathbf{H}^H(\mathbf{X}\mathbf{h}_\mathbf{a}).$$

Note that $\mathbf{x}_a = \mathbf{X}\mathbf{w}$. Thus, we can solve the weights $\mathbf{w}$ from the above equations, and that gives us

$$\mathbf{w} = (\mathbf{X^H X})^{-1}\mathbf{X}^H[(\mathbf{H^H H})^{-1}\mathbf{H}^H(\mathbf{X h_a})].$$

4.3 Attacks against OFDM Systems

Orthogonal frequency-division multiplexing (OFDM) is a popular wireless communication scheme that encodes the digital signal using multiple sub-carrier frequencies. These sub-carriers are normally narrow-band (e.g., 802.11 a/g physical layer advocates an OFDM sub-carrier bandwidth less than 0.5MHZ). Thus, OFDM systems are robust against channel fading caused by the multipath effect. For an OFDM system, the channel estimation is accomplished by estimating the channel impulse response of each sub-carrier. Due to the lack of the multipath fading, the channel estimation result of each sub-carrier is a complex number rather than a vector, and the final channel estimation output of an OFDM system is formed by these complex numbers.

The virtual channel attacks can be easily extended to OFDM systems, because the mapping from the time-domain to frequency-domain is linear. The delay-and-sum process can be replaced by a much simpler procedure, in which the attacker multiplies chosen weights to sub-carriers. Specifically, let $[h_1, h_2, ..., h_n]$ denote the actual channel characteristic between the attacker and the receiver, where h_i is the channel characteristic of the i-th sub-carrier and n is the number of sub-carriers. Further let $[x_1, x_2, ..., x_n]$ denote the training sequence encoded by the OFDM modulator, where x_i is the i-th element of the encoded training sequence. The symbol received at the i-th carrier can be represented by $y_i = h_i x_i$. To fool the receiver to obtain a fake channel estimation result of $[h_{a_1}, h_{a_2}, ..., h_{a_n}]$, the attacker needs to make the equation $h_i x_{a_i} = h_{a_i} x_i$ hold, where x_{a_i} is the symbol to be transmitted by the attacker at the i-th sub-carrier. Thus, $x_{a_i} = \frac{h_{a_i} x_i}{h_i}$, and the weights that the attacker needs to multiply to sub-carriers are $\frac{h_{a_1}}{h_1}, \frac{h_{a_2}}{h_2}, ..., \frac{h_{a_n}}{h_n}$.

4.3.1 *Impact of Oversampling*

In this paper, we follow the same way to formulate the problem as in the wireless communication literature: sampling at the baseband rate (Nyquist rate) is sufficient to represent any signal. Thus, in theory, oversampling does not affect the results of channel estimation or the virtual channel manipulation. In practice, oversampling can surely provide better signal representation. Thus, the output symbols generated by the virtual multipath processing will be then oversampled at the subsequent intermediate frequency (IF) and radio-frequency (RF) modules to generate better digital signal representations. Oversampling in OFDM is padding zeros in null subcarriers and then taking a longer IFFT at the transmitter. A corresponding FFT with the same size is performed at the receiver, then data is recovered at the data subcarrier (not at the null subcarriers). Thus, oversampling does not affect the virtual channel manipulation for OFDM either.

4.4 Initial Simulation

As an initial validation, we simulate the virtual multipath attack using the CRAWDAD data set [15], which contains over 9300 real channel impulse responses measured in an indoor environment with obstacles (e.g., offices and furniture) and scatters (e.g., windows and doors).

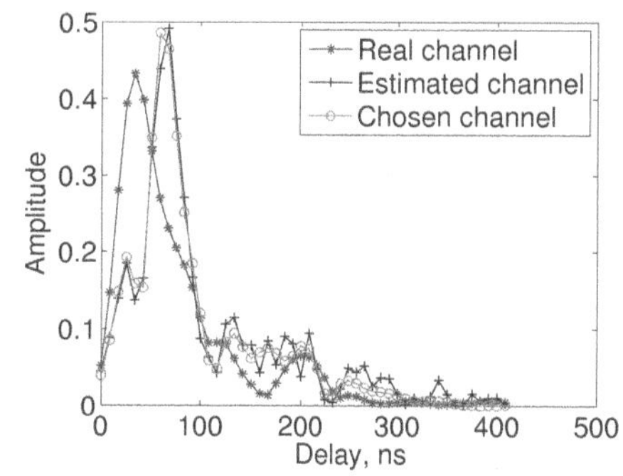

Figure 3: The channel impulse response $\mathbf{h}_r$ estimated at the receiver.

4.4.1 *Simulation Process*

We pick two nodes (i.e., nodes 31 and 40) from the data set as the attacker and the receiver, and obtain the channel impulse response $\mathbf{h}$ between them. We randomly choose another channel impulse response $\mathbf{h}_a$ (i.e., the one between nodes 34 and 40) from the data set, and the attacker aims to fool the receiver to get a channel estimation result of $\mathbf{h}_a$ rather than $\mathbf{h}$.

We generate a training sequence $\mathbf{x}$ of 64 bits using a pseudorandom number generator. The attacker computes the weights based on $\mathbf{h}$, $\mathbf{h}_a$, and $\mathbf{x}$, and then creates a virtual multipath channel by aggregating the weighted delayed copies of the training sequence $\mathbf{x}$ as shown in Figure 2. Thus, the corresponding received symbols $\mathbf{y}'_a$ can be computed via $\mathbf{y}'_a = \mathbf{I}(\mathbf{X_a h})) + \mathbf{n}$, where $\mathbf{n}$ is the gaussian noise and we set the signal-to-noise (SNR) 20dB in the simulation. Finally, the receiver estimates the corresponding channel impulse response from the virtual channel.

4.4.2 *Simulation Result*

Figure 3 plots the real channel impulse response $\mathbf{h}$ between the attacker and the receiver, the chosen channel impulse response $\mathbf{h}_a$ that the attacker wants to emulate, and the channel impulse response $\mathbf{h}_r$ estimated by the receiver. We can observe that $\mathbf{h}_a$ is very close to $\mathbf{h}_r$ under the virtual multipath attack.

The CRAWDAD data set stores five measurements of the channel impulse response for every pair of nodes. In the simulation, for the real channel impulse response $\mathbf{h}$, we randomly pick one as the comparison base. The Euclidean distance between the other four real channel impulse responses and $\mathbf{h}$ ranges between 0.0490 and 0.2297. The Euclidean distance between the estimated channel impulse response $\mathbf{h}_r$ and $\mathbf{h}$ is 0.5782, which is out of the above range. However, the Euclidean distance between $\mathbf{h}_r$ and $\mathbf{h}_a$ is 0.1054, which falls into the normal range of variation of the channel impulse responses. This means that once the attacker establishes a virtual multipath channel, the attacker can hide her real locations since $\mathbf{h}_r \neq \mathbf{h}$, or impersonate a node at a different location since $\mathbf{h}_r \approx \mathbf{h}_a$.

We repeated the simulation using all data in the CRAWDAD data set. Figure 4 plots the empirical empirical cumulative distribution functions (CDFs) of the Euclidean distance d_{real} between the the chosen channel and the real channel response, as well as that of the Euclidean distance d_{est} between the chosen one and the channel impulse response estimated under the attack. We can see that the probability that d_{est} is smaller than d_{est} is high. In particular, 95.13% of d_{est} is less than 0.2295, whereas only 1.59% of d_{real} is less than this value. Thus, if the receiver uses 0.2295 as the detection threshold to verify channel impulse responses, the receiver will get a mis-detection rate of 0.9513 and a false alarm rate of 0.9841 (i.e., 1 - 0.0159).

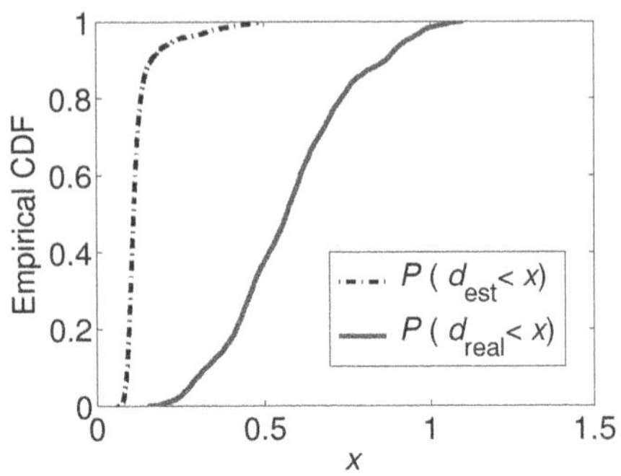

Figure 4: The empirical cumulative distribution functions of d_{real} and d_{est} using the CRAWDAD data set

The simulation result demonstrates the theoretical feasibility of the virtual multipath attack. In Section 6, we reveal the practical impact of such attacks with real world experiments.

4.5 Discussion

4.5.1 *Complexity at the Attacker*

To launch virtual multipath attacks, the attacker requires to sum all delayed signal components with weights, as shown in Figure 2. This delay-and-sum process can be easily implemented using software (e.g. designing a delay-and-sum C++ module in GNU radio for USRP) or hardware (e.g. using flip-flop components to delay signals and using accumulators to sum all signal components in FPGA). Such an architecture does not significantly incur software or hardware complexity.

4.5.2 *Message Demodulation at the Receiver*

By adding delayed signals together, a virtual multipath attacker introduces inter-symbol interference to its transmission signals. We note that such signals are decodable at the receiver. It is common for a receiver to receive signals with inter-symbol interference due to the wireless multipath effect. A receiver normally uses channel estimation results to learn multipath channel conditions [8]. The estimated channel impulse response is then used in the demodulation process to compensate the multipath effect and convert the self-interference signal into a meaningful message.

As long as the attacker passes the training and the information payload through the same virtual channel as shown in Figure 2, the received signal at the receiver will go through the same combined channel effect of virtual and realistic channels. In this regard, although the receiver obtains the estimation of a fake channel impulse response, such an estimation result still represents the combined channel effect that the data goes through. Therefore, the receiver will successfully decode the original message using this estimation result. The only impact of virtual multipath attacks is that the receiver is fooled by fake channel impulse responses.

4.5.3 *Attacks against Blind Channel Estimation*

Although most common wireless networks (e.g., WiFi, ZigBee, 3G/4G) use training based channel estimation, some advanced communication systems may also use blind channel estimation algorithms (e.g., [16, 17]) to obtain channel impulse responses. Such algorithms use all the information of a packet including the header and the data payload to estimate the channel. Therefore, the attacker should always keep attacking during the period of data transmission to fool both training-based and blind methods; i.e., all the training and data signals must go through the same delay-and-sum process shown in Figure 2.

4.5.4 *Impact of the Time Delay*

Theoretically, the attacker can set an arbitrarily small delay (e.g, 1 nanosecond) to create a much richer virtual multipath effect at the receiver. However, modern channel estimation algorithms estimate only resolvable paths whose inter-arrival durations are no less than one symbol duration, and it has been shown that using the estimation of resolvable paths is sufficient to compensate the channel effect for signal demodulation. Thus, at the receiver's point of view, the channel consists of multiple resolvable paths. This means that it is sufficient to set the delay in virtual channel generation to be one symbol duration (e.g., just generate resolvable paths) to fool the receiver's view on the channel. Even if the attacker reduces the delay to generate a more fine-grained virtual multipath channel, the receiver can still observe the resolvable paths and the corresponding channel impulse response. Thus, decreasing the delay can only add implementation complexity to the attacker, but will not cause more impact of the attack at the receiver. On the other hand, if attacker utilize a larger delay (e.g., larger than the symbol duration), the receiver may not observe enough multipath effect under the virtual multipath attacks and thus the attack impact is limited. Therefore, it is reasonable to set the delay to be one symbol duration to balance the attack effect and complexity.

4.5.5 *Feasibility of the Attack*

To generate chosen channel impulse response at the receiver, the attacker needs to know the actual channel impulse response between herself and the receiver. In many cases, the attacker can obtain this information from the wireless signals emitted by the receiver, because wireless communication is normally built upon certain protocols like 802.11 and TCP/IP and thus it is two-way, e.g., WiFi networks, Bluetooth, wireless sensor networks, and GSM networks. For one-way communications (transmitter $\rightarrow$ receiver), the attacker cannot hear the wireless signals from the receiver, and thus it may not be able to generate specified channel impulse responses at the receiver. However, in this case, the attack impact still exists. Although the attacker cannot control the channel impulse responses estimated at the receiver, she can always use random weights to generate random channel impulse responses at the receiver. As a result, the receiver can still be fooled to make wrong decisions. For example, sybil attacks can still be successful when the attacker sets different weights in the virtual channel even without the real channel information.

4.5.6 *Example Attack Scenarios*

The example scenarios where virtual multipath attacks may exist include: (1) movement detection: an attacker may hide its movement by creating a static virtual channel impulse response at the receiver, e.g., a wireless sensor can be moved from the monitoring area but the movement is not detected; (2) detection of sybil attacks: an attacker may bypass the detection of sybil attack by pretending identities that are originated from different locations; (3) authentication: the attacker may impersonate another wireless transmitter. This attack scenario requires the attacker to know the channel impulse response between the target transmitter and the receiver, and thus imposes some limitations to the attacker. However, since the virtual multipath channel attacks can produce any channel estimation results at the receiver, such attacks are still a threat to existing channel fingerprinting based authentication schemes; (4) In addition to the attack scenarios, on the other hand, the attacks can be further utilized to enhance the wireless security. For example, the virtual channels can be used to provide a rich set of shared keys between two wireless devices, or enable anonymous communications by protecting location privacy of wireless users via virtual channel camouflage.

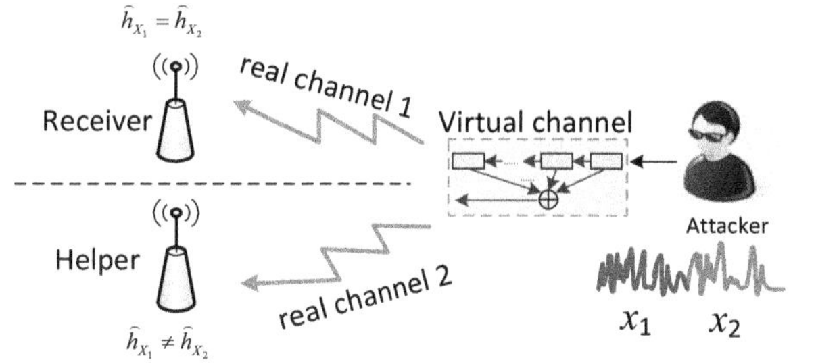

Figure 5: The receiver uses two different training sequences $\mathbf{x}_1$ and $\mathbf{x}_2$ to estimate the channel impulse response from two successive transmissions, respectively. For both transmissions, a malicious transmitter (i.e., the attacker) must solve the corresponding weights $\mathbf{w}_1$ and $\mathbf{w}_2$, so that the receiver will observe the fake channel impulse response chosen by herself. However, such $\mathbf{w}_1$ and $\mathbf{w}_2$ do not necessarily enable the helper to obtain the same channel estimation results. Thus, a dramatic change of estimated channel impulse responses at the helper can indicate the potential existence of virtual multipath attacks.

5. DEFENDING AGAINST THE VIRTUAL MULTIPATH ATTACK

Virtual multipath attackers are able to make the receiver believe any channel characteristic the attacker chooses. At the receiver, it seems that there is no way to tell whether the signal goes through real or virtual multipath scenario. Hence, existing location distinction methods built upon distinguishing locations from channel characteristics (e.g., [1–3,6]) will be easily defeated by virtual multipath attacks.

The intuition behind our defense strategy is that *nobody can craft one key to open two different doors*. In other words, if a receiver cannot tell whether there is an attack or not, maybe a second receiver can. As a result, the proposed approach makes use of an auxiliary receiver or antenna, which we refer to as a *helper*. The helper is placed more than half a wavelength away from the receiver to ensure a distinct channel characteristic. We let the receiver use two different training sequences $\mathbf{x}_1$ and $\mathbf{x}_2$ to estimate the channel impulse response alternatively. Without loss of generality, we assume that the receiver uses $\mathbf{x}_1$ to estimate the channel from the first transmission, and uses $\mathbf{x}_2$ to estimate the channel from the second transmission.

We discover that for both transmissions, at the receiver, the virtual channel created by a malicious transmitter (i.e., the attacker) can result in the same estimated channel impulse responses (equal to the one chosen by the attacker). However, at the helper, the virtual channel leads to different estimated channel impulse responses. We summarize the defense approach in Figure 5. The reason that the attacker cannot fool both the receiver and the helper is detailed next.

5.1 Defense Analysis

Let $\mathbf{h}$ denote the real channel impulse response between the attacker and the receiver. For the first transmission, the attacker must solve the weights, so that the equation $\mathbf{h} * \mathbf{x}_{a1} = \mathbf{h}_a * \mathbf{x}_1$ hold and the receiver will obtain $\mathbf{h}_a$ as the channel impulse response, where $\mathbf{x}_{a1}$ is the aggregated signal with weighted time-delayed copies of the training sequence $\mathbf{x}_1$. Let $\mathbf{h}_{\text{help}}$ denote the real channel impulse response between the attacker and the helper. The corresponding signal received by the helper can be represented as $\mathbf{h}_{\text{help}} * \mathbf{x}_{a1}$. Thus, the channel impulse response $\hat{\mathbf{h}}_{\text{help}_1}$ estimated by the helper can be solved from the equation that $\hat{\mathbf{h}}_{\text{help}_1} * \mathbf{x}_1 = \mathbf{h}_{\text{help}} * \mathbf{x}_{a1}$, and we have

$$\hat{\mathbf{h}}_{\text{help}_1} = (\mathbf{X_1}^H \mathbf{X_1})^{-1} \mathbf{X_1}^H (\mathbf{h}_{\text{help}} * \mathbf{x}_{a1}), \quad (4)$$

where $\mathbf{X}_1$ is a Toeplitz matrix of $\mathbf{x}_1$.

For the second transmission, both the receiver and the helper use the training sequence $\mathbf{x}_2$ to estimate the channel. Similarly, to fool the receiver, the attacker must generate another weights $\mathbf{w}_2$, so that the corresponding aggregated signal $\mathbf{x}_{a2}$ makes the equation $\mathbf{h} * \mathbf{x}_{a2} = \mathbf{h}_a * \mathbf{x}_2$ hold. The corresponding channel impulse response $\hat{\mathbf{h}}_{\text{help}_2}$ estimated by the helper is

$$\hat{\mathbf{h}}_{\text{help}_2} = (\mathbf{X_2}^H \mathbf{X_2})^{-1} \mathbf{X_2}^H (\mathbf{h}_{\text{help}} * \mathbf{x}_{a2}), \quad (5)$$

where $\mathbf{X}_2$ is a Toeplitz matrix of $\mathbf{x}_2$.

Note that for both transmissions, the channel impulse response estimated by the receiver are always the same, because the weights are "customized" so that the receiver will obtain the attacker's chosen channel impulse response after the channel estimation. However, from Equations 4 and 5, we can see that the first estimated channel impulse response $\hat{\mathbf{h}}_{\text{help}_1}$ is not necessarily equal to the second estimated channel impulse response $\hat{\mathbf{h}}_{\text{help}_2}$, because $\mathbf{X}_1 \neq \mathbf{X}_2$. This means the attacker cannot fool the receiver and the helper at the same time.

Thus, if the successive estimated channel impulse responses show dramatic changes in a short time at the helper, the helper then triggers an alert at the receiver regarding the existence of potential virtual multipath attacks. In practice, the helper may use a threshold to enforce the detection. If $||\hat{\mathbf{h}}_{\text{help}_1} - \hat{\mathbf{h}}_{\text{help}_2}||$ is larger than the threshold, then the attack is assumed. The threshold can be selected based on the empirical studies to achieve an optimized detection accuracy. In Section 6.4, we show an example of the threshold selection. Note that in the defense system, the helper and the receiver can switch their roles, i.e., if the attacker attempts to fool the helper instead of the receiver, the receiver will estimate two different channel impulse responses and therefore detect such a attack.

5.1.1 Attackers with Helper

The attacker may also bring a second transmitter to confuse the receiver. Figure 6 shows such a scenario. We refer to the attacker's second transmitter as the *attacker's helper*. Let $\mathbf{h}_{11}$, $\mathbf{h}_{12}$, $\mathbf{h}_{21}$, $\mathbf{h}_{22}$ denote the channel impulse responses between the attacker and the receiver, the attacker and the receiver's helper, the attacker's helper and the receiver, and the attacker's helper and the receiver's helper, respectively. To successfully launch the virtual channel attacks without being detected, the attacker must generate the same channel impulse response at the receiver's helper for both transmissions. Let $\mathbf{h}_{\text{help}}$ denote such a channel impulse response. Further let $\mathbf{h}_a$ denote the one that the attacker expects to generate at the receiver for both transmissions. The attacker needs to make the following equation hold:

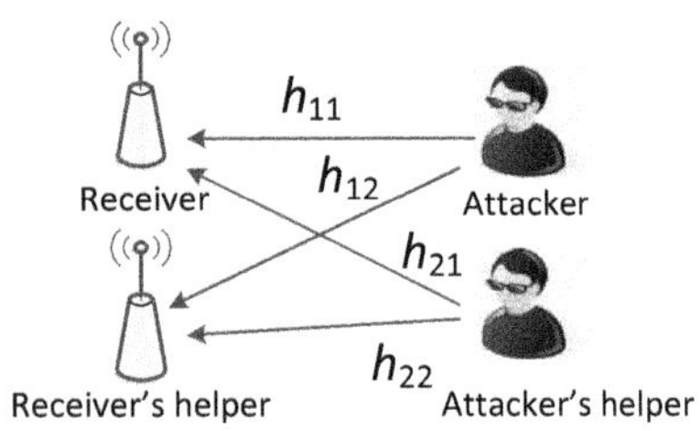

Figure 6: The attacker also brings a second transmitter to confuse the receiver.

$$\begin{cases} \mathbf{h}_{11} * \mathbf{x}_{a1} + \mathbf{h}_{21} * \mathbf{x}_{h1} = \mathbf{h}_a * \mathbf{x}_1 \\ \mathbf{h}_{12} * \mathbf{x}_{a1} + \mathbf{h}_{22} * \mathbf{x}_{h1} = \mathbf{h}_{\text{help}} * \mathbf{x}_1 \\ \mathbf{h}_{11} * \mathbf{x}_{a2} + \mathbf{h}_{21} * \mathbf{x}_{h2} = \mathbf{h}_a * \mathbf{x}_2 \\ \mathbf{h}_{12} * \mathbf{x}_{a2} + \mathbf{h}_{22} * \mathbf{x}_{h2} = \mathbf{h}_{\text{help}} * \mathbf{x}_2 \end{cases}, \tag{6}$$

where $\mathbf{x}_{a1}$, $\mathbf{x}_{h1}$, $\mathbf{x}_{a2}$, and $\mathbf{x}_{h2}$ are the actual signals to be transmitted by the attacker and her helper for the first and second transmissions. To break the proposed defense, the attacker must solve them from Equation 6. This implies that $\mathbf{h}_{11}$, $\mathbf{h}_{12}$, $\mathbf{h}_{21}$, $\mathbf{h}_{22}$ should be all available to the attacker. Otherwise, the linear system lacks necessary coefficients to generate solutions. However, the acquisition of $\mathbf{h}_{12}$ and $\mathbf{h}_{22}$ will impose difficulty for the attacker, because the receiver's helper can be designed passive, i.e., it receives wireless signals but doesn't actively send out wireless signals to the channel. Due to the close proximity, the receiver can communicate with its helper through the cable connection or internal circuit. A passive helper of the receiver eliminates the chance for the attacker to extract the channel impulse responses based on heard wireless signals.

5.1.2 Extending to MIMO systems

In case of a very powerful attacker, who is able to set up a collaborator transmitter that is co-located with the receiver's helper (i.e., at the exact physical location of the receiver's helper), $\mathbf{h}_{12}$ and $\mathbf{h}_{22}$ may be obtained from the wireless signals sent by the collaborator transmitter. Nevertheless, the defense methods can be easily extended to deal with these attacks by increasing the number of helpers at the receiver.

To facilitate the reader's understanding, we consider a multiple-input and multiple-output (MIMO) scenario, where the receiver and the attacker have M and N antennas respectively. Assume the fake channel impulse responses that the attacker aims to generate at the receiver's antennas are $\mathbf{h}_1, \mathbf{h}_2, ..., \mathbf{h}_M$, and the real channel impulse responses between each of the attacker's antenna and each of the receiver's antennas is denote as $\mathbf{h}_{ij}$, where $i = 1, 2, ..., N$ and $j = 1, 2, ..., M$. We assume $\mathbf{h}_{ij}$ are all available to the attacker due to the existence of the collaborator transmitters placed at the same locations as the receiver's antennas. Let $\mathbf{x}_{a1_i}$ and $\mathbf{x}_{a2_i} (i = 1, 2, \cdots, N)$ denote the signals to be transmitted by the attacker's i-th antenna for the first and second transmissions. Similar to the previous discussion, the attacker must solve them from $\sum_{i=1}^{N} \mathbf{h}_{ij} * \mathbf{x}_{a1_i} = \mathbf{h}_j * \mathbf{x}_1$ and $\sum_{i=1}^{N} \mathbf{h}_{ij} * \mathbf{x}_{a2_i} = \mathbf{h}_j * \mathbf{x}_2$ for $\forall j \in \{1, 2, ..., M\}$.

If $N \geq M$, the attacker can find a unique solution or infinite solutions of $\mathbf{x}_{a1_i}$ and $\mathbf{x}_{a2_i}$. However, if $N < M$, this linear system is overdetermined, which yields no feasible solution. This means that the attacker cannot find appropriate values of transmitted signals (or weights), so that the receiver will observe the same channel impulse responses at all antennas for two transmissions. Therefore, if the number of the receiver's helper nodes is greater than that of the attacker's helper nodes, the virtual multipath channel attacks can be detected.

5.1.3 Defense Discussion

The receiver can normally use one passive helper, i.e., a secret wireless tap, to detect the attacks. The exception happens when the attacker knows all channel information from her and her helpers to the receiver's passive helper (by placing a spy node that is co-located with or extremely close to the receiver's helper), which is in fact a very harsh requirement for the attacker.

We point out that under this circumstance it is still feasible to detect virtual multipath attacks as long as the receiver has more helpers than the attacker. A significant advantage of the receiver over the attacker is that the receiver just needs to find contradiction to detect the attack; while the attacker has to know all channel information for signal manipulation to make sure no contradiction is found. In particular, when the receiver adds one more passive helper, it actually reduces the attack situation to the normal case. In order to beat the defense, the attacker must meet all the following requirements at the same time to beat the receiver: (1) add one helper, (2) add one spy node at the exact location of the receiver's new helper to know the channel information, (3) synchronize herself and all her helpers to transmit the manipulated signal at the physical-layer symbol level. Hence, the attacker has much more costs to beat the receiver with more passive helpers.

5.2 A Case Study

We show an example of the defense approach using the real measured channel data from the CRAWDAD data set. We randomly pick three nodes from the data set, and they are used as the attacker (node 14), the receiver (node 3), and the helper (node 32), respectively. We also randomly pick one channel impulse response (between nodes 4 and 9) from the data set, and it is used as the fake channel impulse response that the attacker would like to fool the receiver. Let $\mathbf{h}$, $\mathbf{h}_{\text{help}}$, and $\mathbf{h}_a$ denote the channel impulse responses between the attacker and the receiver, the attacker and the helper, and the fake one chosen by the attacker.

We generate two 64-bit training sequences $\mathbf{x}_1$ and $\mathbf{x}_2$. For the first and the second transmissions, we compute the weight vectors $\mathbf{w}_1$ and $\mathbf{w}_2$, so that the corresponding virtual channels will result in estimated channel impulse responses that are equal to $\mathbf{h}_a$ at the receiver. As discussed earlier, these weight vectors should be computed based on $\mathbf{h}$, $\mathbf{h}_a$, $\mathbf{x}_1$, and $\mathbf{x}_2$.

Figure 7 shows the channel estimation outcomes at the receiver for the first and the second transmissions, respectively. We can see that both estimated channel impulse responses are consistent with each other. The Euclidean distance between them is 0.1127. We also calculate the channel estimation results at the helper. As shown in Figure 8, these channel estimates significantly differ from each other. The Euclidean distance between them is as high as 0.5701, which is out of the normal range of variation of the channel impulse responses. Thus, the virtual multipath attack is detected.

6. EXPERIMENTAL EVALUATION

We build a prototype channel measurement system to demonstrate the impact of the virtual multipath attack and the effectiveness of the proposed defense technique. Our prototype is implemented on top of USRPs [18], which are equipped with AD and DA converters as the RF front ends, and XCVR2400 daughter boards operating in the 2.4 GHz range as transceivers. The software toolkit is GNURadio [19].

6.1 Evaluation Setup

We perform the experiment in a campus building with small offices, wooden doors, windows, metal and wooden furniture, and computers. Our prototype system consists of a malicious transmitter and a receiver. Each node is a USRP connected to a commodity PC. The receiver estimates the channel impulse responses from received signals, and verifies whether or not there is a location change by comparing a newly estimated channel impulse response with an old one. The transmitter runs the attacker program, which computes the weight vector to form the virtual channel, passes the original signal through the virtual channel, and then feeds the virtual channel output to the real wireless channel. Note that the maximum number of resolvable multipaths L is usually configured to an empirical constant value depending on wireless system setups [8]. In this experiment, we set $L = 5$ for our proof-of-concept implementation.

Figure 9 shows the positions of the receiver and the transmitter. We place the transmitter at 10 different locations to launch the attack, and the receiver periodically estimates the channel impulse responses.

6.2 Example Attacks

We examine two example attacks. The first one injects a randomly chosen channel impulse response into the receiver. The second one reproduces a same channel impulse response in the CRAWDAD data set. For both attacks, we place the transmitter at location 2 shown in Figure 9.

6.2.1 *First example: Generating A Random Channel Response*

The first example is a virtual multipath attack with intent to generate a random channel impulse response. Figure 10 plots the real channel impulse response between the transmitter and the receiver, the channel impulse response chosen by the attacker, and the estimated channel impulse response at the receiver. The y-axis and the x-axis indicate the power gain and the relevant path respectively. We can see that the chosen channel impulse response and the estimated one are very similar to each other, but both of them significantly deviate from the real channel. The Euclidean distance between the chosen channel and the real channel is 0.3025, whereas that between the chosen channel and the estimated channel is as small as 0.0686.

6.2.2 *Second Example: Replicating A Same Channel Response in A Different Building*

In the second example, an attacker aims to generate a channel impulse response in our office building such that the generate channel impulse response is exactly the same as one in the CRAWDAD data set, which was collected in an office building in the University of Utah. We note our USRP system is different from the CRAWDAD measurement system, Sigtek model ST-515, which has a much higher bandwidth (40MHz) than the USRP (10MHz). Therefore, the CRAWDAD measurement system can observe richer multipaths. Nevertheless, even with a relatively low-end USRP, we can still duplicate the resolvable paths in a channel impulse response measured in the CRAWDAD data set.

Specifically, we select one channel impulse response (between nodes 14 and 43) from the CRAWDAD data set and we plot it as "CRAWDAD channel" in Figure 11. We can see that this channel impulse response carries three peaks and thus exhibits three resolvable multipaths. We launch the virtual multipath attack to make a replica of the same three resolvable multipaths observed at the receiver in our experiment, which is shown as "Crafted channel" in Figure 11. The attack's crafted channel impulse response of the resolvable multipaths closely matches the CRAWDAD channel response and their Euclidean distance is as small as 0.0036.

6.3 Overall Attack Impact

To examine the overall impact of the virtual multipath attacks, we perform the following experiment. For each location in Figure 9, we estimate the channel impulse responses during a short time window (around 10 – 30 seconds). For each estimates, we perform 100 trials, and in each trial we randomly generate a length-5 vector whose elements range between 0 and 1. This vector is used as the attacker's chosen channel impulse response. We then launch the virtual multipath attack and record the Euclidean distance d_{real} between the chosen channel impulse response and the pervious channel impulse response estimated in the absence of the attacks (i.e., the real channel response), and also record the Euclidean distance d_{est} between the chosen one and the channel impulse response estimated under the attacks. We repeat the same experiment for the other 9 locations.

Ideally, a successful attacker should have a large value of d_{real} (indicating that the attacker's chosen channel significantly differs from the real channel) and a small value of d_{est} (indicating that the attacker's chosen channel is close to the receiver's estimated channel).

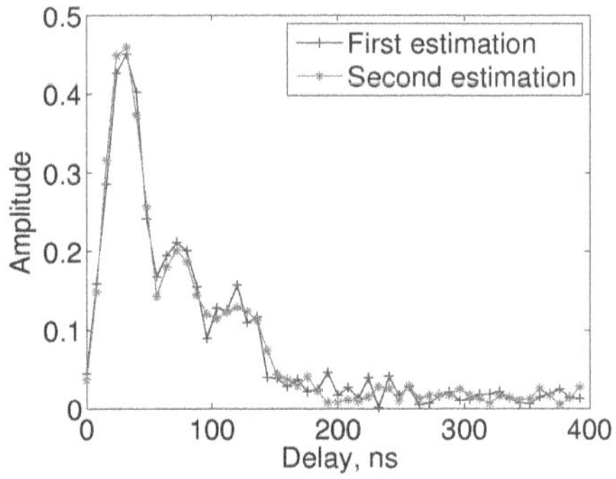

Figure 7: Both estimates are consistent with each other.

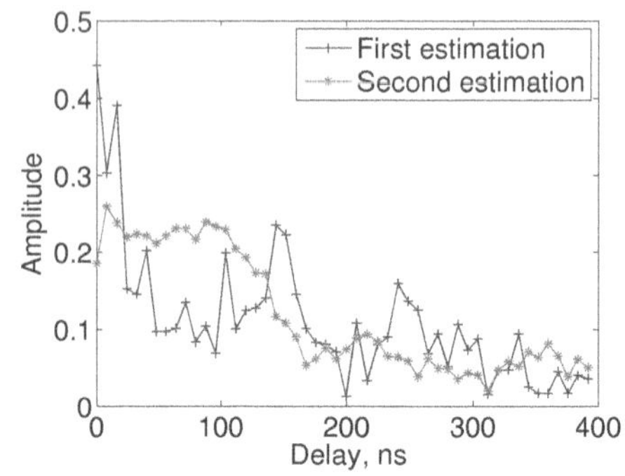

Figure 8: Both estimates significantly differ from each other.

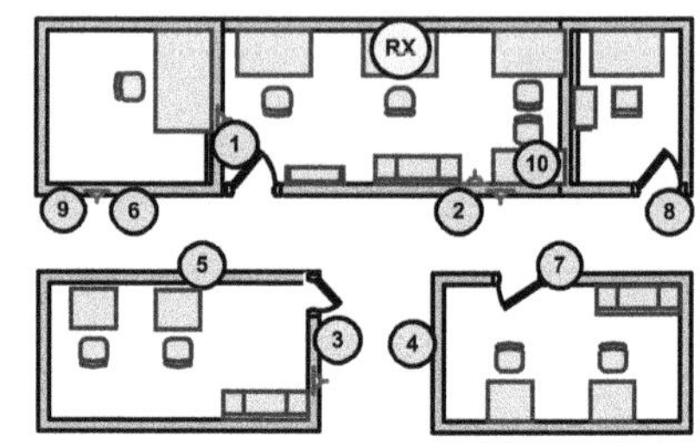

Figure 9: Floorplan of the building where the experiment is conducted.

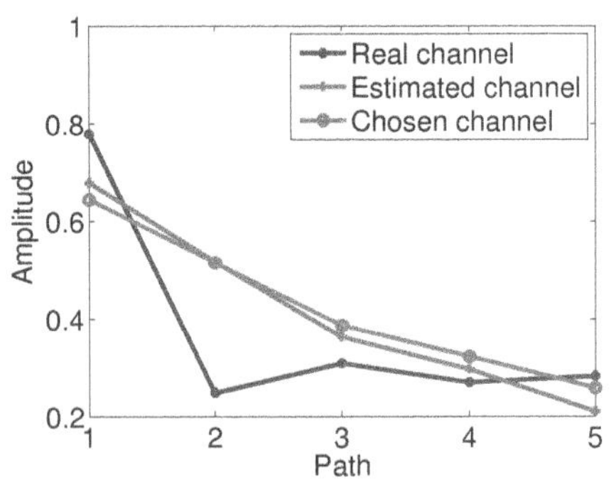

Figure 10: The Euclidean distance of the real and estimated channels.

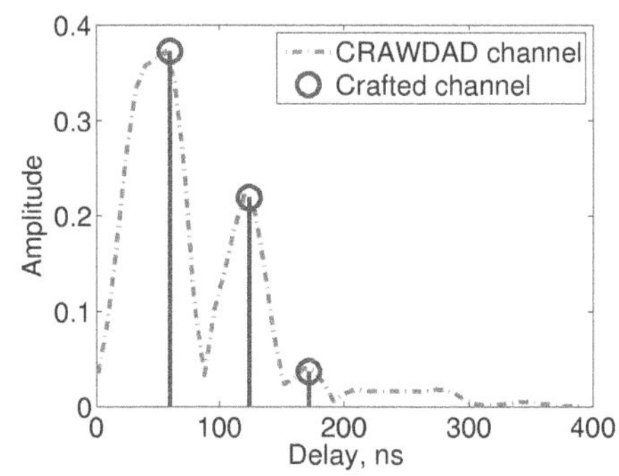

Figure 11: A replica of the CRAWDAD channel impulse response.

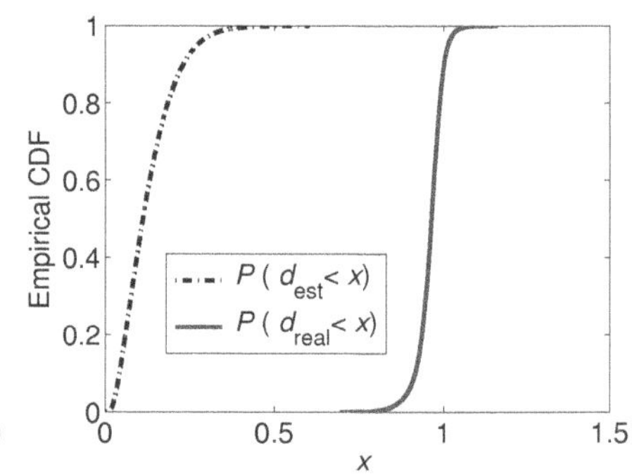

Figure 12: The empirical CDFs of d_{real} and d_{est}.

Denoted by $P(d_{\text{real}} < x)$ and $P(d_{\text{est}} < x)$ the empirical CDFs of d_{real} and d_{est}, respectively. Figure 12 shows $P(d_{\text{real}} < x)$ and $P(d_{\text{est}} < x)$ for $0 \leq x \leq 1.5$. We can see that d_{est} is less than 0.25 with probability 95.0%, d_{real} is larger than 0.9 with probability 95.0%. This means that d_{real} is much larger than d_{est} with high probability, therefore the attacker can drag the estimated value of channel impulse response far away from its true value, and make it very close to her specified one.

Existing schemes in general compare the difference between the receiver's current estimated channel and previous reference channel with a threshold to check a location change [1, 2]. Since our attacker can inject any random channel impulse response into the receiver with a very high accuracy, the performance of existing location distinction schemes can be significantly degraded by the virtual multipath attack. For example, given a threshold set less than 0.5 for location change detection in our system, when the attack is launched, the receiver will think that the transmitter moves because all the differences between the estimated channel in the presence of the attack and the reference channel (attack-free channel) exceed the threshold of 0.5. However, the estimated channel and the real channel are actually measured at the same location, and thus the location distinction false alarm rate is raised to 100% under the virtual multipath attack.

Similarly, the virtual multipath attack can also easily defeat any method verifying that nodes are from different locations based on examining the difference of their channel impulse responses (e.g., [3,6]).

6.4 Evaluation of the Defense Method

We first show the practical feasibility of our defense method, then evaluate the performance.

6.4.1 Feasibility Evaluation

The defense approach functions based on a critical observation that the attacker cannot fool both the receiver and the helper at the same time. Thus, in our feasibility evaluation, we would like to examine how the channel estimation results of the receiver and the helper differ from each other, so that such an inconsistency can reveal the existence of the virtual multipath attack. Towards this goal, we perform the following experiment.

We place the attacker and the helper at each pair of the 10 locations, and we have $10 \times 9 = 90$ pairs of locations in total. Throughout the experiment, the receiver maintains its original position as marked in Figure 9. The attacker launches the virtual multipath attack, and both the receiver and the helper continuously do the channel estimation. Two 16-bit training sequences $\mathbf{x}_1$ (0xacdd) and $\mathbf{x}_2$ (0xa4e2) are alternatively used for estimating the channel impulse responses.

The helper and the receiver estimate the channel impulse responses from two successive transmissions, then calculate the Euclidean distance between both estimates. Let d_{helper} and d_{rec} denote the distances computed by the helper and the receiver, respectively. As analyzed in Section 5.1, d_{helper} should be much larger than d_{rec}.

Figures 13 and 14 show the channel impulse responses estimated using $\mathbf{x}_1$ and $\mathbf{x}_2$ at the receiver and the helper, when the attacker and the helper are placed at locations 2 and 8, respectively. We can see that the virtual multipath attack leads to a much larger distance at the helper than the receiver, i.e., $d_{\text{helper}} \gg d_{\text{rec}}$. Specifically, $d_{\text{rec}} = 0.0093$ and $d_{\text{helper}} = 0.1199$.

6.4.2 Performance Evaluation

As mentioned earlier, the helper may use a threshold to enforce the detection. If d_{helper} is larger than the threshold, then the attack is assumed. In general, detection and false positive rate are two performance metrics associated with a detection method. The detection rate is the probability that d_{helper} is larger than the threshold when there is indeed an attack. The false positive rate is the probability that d_{helper} is larger than the threshold when there is no attack.

In this experiment, we evaluate the performance of the proposed defense approach in terms of detection and false positive rates. We have 90 pairs of locations to place the attacker and the helper. From each pair of the locations, we can obtain the corresponding distances d_{helper} and d_{rec}.

We show the empirical CDFs $P(d_{\text{helper}} < x)$ and $P(d_{\text{rec}} < x)$ in Figure 15. We can see that in all experiments, d_{rec} is always less than 0.0151 (i.e., $P(d_{\text{rec}} < 0.0151)$=1), whereas d_{helper} is always greater than 0.0156. This means that if the helper uses 0.0151 as the detection threshold, the defense system can achieve a detection rate of 1 as well as a false positive rate of 0. In general, any threshold ranging between 0.0151 and 0.0156 can lead to the detection of all attacks, and meanwhile maintain the usability of the receiver.

The helper may select imperfect thresholds that do not fall in this range. However, it is still possible to achieve a high detection accuracy. For example, if the threshold is set to 0.02, the detection rate is as high as 91.2%, the false positive rate is still 0, which are obtained from Figure 15.

7. RELATED WORK

Existing location distinction approaches have been focused on exploiting the spatial uncorrelation property of wireless channels (e.g., [1–3, 5, 6]). These approaches demonstrated their success in various wireless scenarios, especially for the high-frequency systems (e.g., WiFi networks) that feature a very short electromagnetic wavelength. However, two recent studies identified a vulnerability of these approaches [7, 20], and they discovered that the wireless spatial uncorrelation property may be violated in a poor multipath environment (e.g., strong line-of-sight path). The work in [4, 21] made a further attempt to attack location distinction systems using channel impulse responses. The authors found that a third-party attacker may impersonate Alice to Bob by mimicking the channel impulse response of the wireless link between them, and the authors named such attacks as *mimicry attacks*. Although both mimicry attacks and the virtual multipath attacks are against the security measures based on the wireless channel characteristics, they differ from each other in the following aspects:

First, a pre-condition to launch mimicry attacks is the knowledge of the real channel impulse response between Alice and Bob (thus they assume the existence of a spy node). However, a virtual multipath attacker can still launch attacks without this knowledge. Moreover, if the attacker knows the real channel impulse response, she can make the receiver believe a specific channel impulse response. Therefore, virtual multipath attacks have a broader attack impact and less prerequisites. In addition, we extend the virtual multipath attacks and the defense to MIMO and OFDM systems. It should be possible to extend mimicry attacks to these systems as well, because the attacker can directly manipulate the training signals for OFDM and MIMO systems with the knowledge of all channel information. However, mimicry attacks require to place a spy node close to the receiver. Thus, it becomes much more difficult to launch mimicry attacks when the receiver is equipped with a MIMO system, because the attacker has to place one spy node for each antenna to know the channel.

Second, both attacks differ in technical design methodology. The essential way of mimicry attacks is to manipulate the training signal such that the receiver believes an impersonated channel impulse response. Such a manipulation at the training signal level fools the receiver to accept an incorrect channel estimate, but the data payload after the training signal still goes through the real channel. As a result, the receiver will use an incorrect channel estimate to compensate the real channel effect, leading to incorrect packet decoding. In contrast, the virtual multipath attack uses a delay-and-sum process (with chosen weights) to create a virtual channel and pass all the data (e.g., training sequence and data payload) to be transmitted through this virtual channel. The receiver then not only gets a faked channel impulse response, but also uses it to successfully decode the entire data payload. Hence, the design methodology of virtual channel attacks ensures more stealthiness and consistency to fool the receiver.

Third, the proposed defense against the virtual multipath attack does not require any shared secret key between the transmitter and the receiver, whereas the defense proposed in [4] requires that the communicators to share a secret key. Such a requirement indicates that a key distribution and management system should be deployed prior to the enforcement of the defense, which reduces the scalability and feasibility of the relevant approach.

Finally, because of the simplicity of the delay-and-sum process, as discussed earlier, the virtual multipath attacks can be interestingly extended to enhance the wireless security. For example, researchers have proposed to establish a key between two wireless devices using the channel impulse responses between them. Such a key is totally determined by the wireless physical layer feature and cannot be easily manipulated by the users. The idea of virtual channel attacks can be utilized here to enable the transmitter to control and update the shared key periodically and provide a rich set of shared keys among wireless users. Such attacks can also enable anonymous communications by protecting location privacy of wireless users via virtual channel camouflage.

Another recent work that is closely relevant with the proposed defense approach is SecureArray [22]. This work utilizes the physical angle-of-arrive (AOA) of a multi-antenna access point to enforce user authentication. Our proposed defense technique uses channel impulse responses observed by multiple antennas to protect location distinction systems and their security extensions. Both methods employ multiple antennas for the security purpose. However, our defense targets attacks against location distinction systems that are

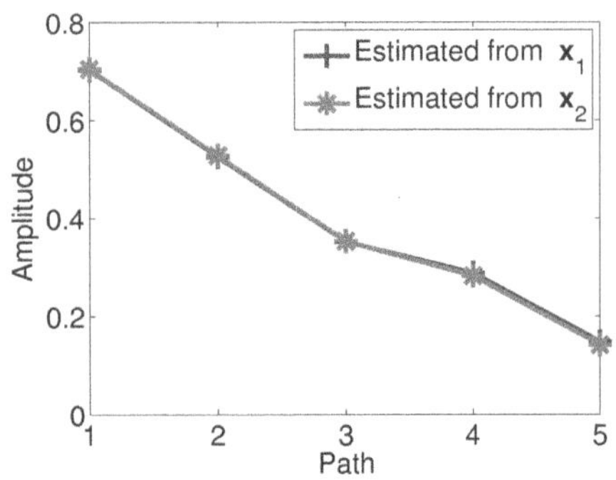

Figure 13: The channel impulse responses estimated at the receiver.

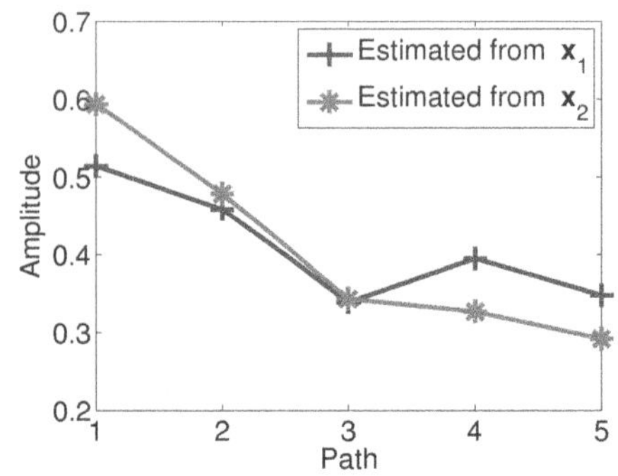

Figure 14: The channel impulse responses estimated at the helper.

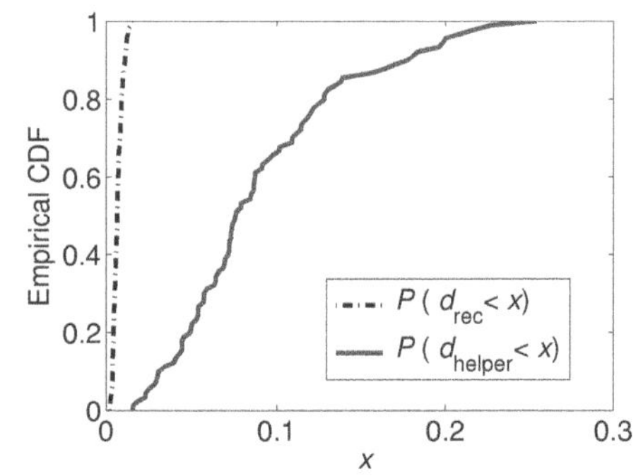

Figure 15: The empirical CDFs of d_{helper} and d_{rec}.

built on the spatial uncorrelation property of wireless channels, whereas SecureArray is designed to combat spoofing attacks that attempt to impersonate legitimate WiFi clients. Both approaches apply to different application domains.

We point out that the virtual multipath attack discovered in this paper doesn't target traditional localization systems using AOA, TOA, RSS, etc. Thus, complementary analysis and measures are necessary to protect these systems.

8. CONCLUSION

We identified a new attack against existing location distinction approaches that built on the spatial uncorrelation property of wireless channels. By launching such attacks, the attacker can create virtual multipath channels to deteriorate the location distinction capability of a target receiver. To defend against this attack, we proposed a detection technique that utilizes a helper receiver to identify the existence of virtual channels. We performed real-world evaluation on the USRP platform running GNURadio. The experimental results demonstrated both the feasibility of the virtual multipath attack and the effectiveness of the defense approach.

9. REFERENCES

[1] N. Patwari and S. K. Kasera, "Robust location distinction using temporal link signatures," in *Proc. of ACM MobiCom '07*, September 2007, pp. 111–122.

[2] J. Zhang, M. H. Firooz, N. Patwari, and S. K. Kasera, "Advancing wireless link signatures for location distinction," in *Proc. of ACM MobiCom '08*, September 2008, pp. 26–37.

[3] L. Xiao, L. J. Greenstein, N. B. Mandayam, and W. Trappe, "Channel-based detection of sybil attacks in wireless networks," *IEEE Trans. Information Forensics and Security*, vol. 4, pp. 492 – 503, 2009.

[4] Y. Liu and P. Ning, "Enhanced wireless channel authentication using time-synched link signature," in *Proc. of IEEE INFOCOM '12*, March 2012.

[5] Z. Li, W. Xu, R. Miller, and W. Trappe, "Securing wireless systems via lower layer enforcements," in *Proc. of ACM WiSe '06*, September 2006, pp. 33–42.

[6] Y. Liu, P. Ning, and H. Dai, "Authenticating primary users' signals in cognitive radio networks via integrated cryptographic and wireless link signatures," in *Proc. of IEEE S&P '10*, May 2010, pp. 286–301.

[7] X. He, H. Dai, W. Shen, and P. Ning, "Is link signature dependable for wireless security?" in *Proc. of IEEE INFOCOM '13*, April 2013.

[8] A. Goldsmith, *Wireless Communications*. Cambridge University Press, 2005.

[9] A. F. Molisch, *Wireless Communications, 2nd Edition*. Wiley India Pvt. Limited, 2007.

[10] R. Safaya, "A multipath channel estimation algorithm using a kalman filter," Thesis, University of Kansas, 2000.

[11] M. Biguesh and A. B. Gershman, "Training-based mimo channel estimation: A study of estimator tradeoffs and optimal training signals," *IEEE Trans. Signal Processing*, vol. 54, no. 3, pp. 884–893, 2006.

[12] K. S. Shanmugan and A. M. Breipohl, *Random signals: detection, estimation, and data analysis*. Wiley, May 1988.

[13] O. Edfors, M. Sandell, J. J. V. de Beek, S. K. Wilson, and P. O. Borjesson, "OFDM channel estimation by singular value decomposition," *IEEE Trans. Communications*, vol. 46, no. 7, pp. 931 – 939, 1998.

[14] IEEE, "IEEE 802.11: Wireless LANs," 2007.

[15] SPAN, "Measured channel impulse response data set," `http://span.ece.utah.edu/pmwiki/pmwiki.php?n=Main.MeasuredCIRDataSet`.

[16] M. K. Tsatsanis and G. B. Giannakis, "Blind estimation of direct sequence spread spectrum signals in multipath," *IEEE Trans. Signal Processing*, vol. 5, no. 45, pp. 1241 – 1252, 1997.

[17] G. T. Zhou, M. Viberg, and T. McKelvey, "A first-order statistical method for channel estimation," *IEEE Signal Processing Letters*, vol. 10, no. 3, pp. 57 – 60, 2003.

[18] ETTUS, "USRP-Universal Software Radio Peripheral," `http://www.ettus.com`.

[19] "GNU Radio Software," `http://gnuradio.org/trac`.

[20] M. Edman, A. Kiayias, and B. Yener, "On passive inference attacks against physical-layer key extraction," in *Proceedings of the Fourth European Workshop on System Security*, 2011.

[21] Y. Liu and P. Ning, "Poster: Mimicry attacks against wireless link signature," in *Proc. of ACM CCS*, 2011.

[22] J. Xiong and K. Jamieson, "Securearray: Improving wifi security with fine-grained physical-layer information," in *Proc. of ACM MobiCom '13*, 2013.

Tagoram: Real-Time Tracking of Mobile RFID Tags to High Precision Using COTS Devices

Lei Yang*, Yekui Chen*, Xiang-Yang Li*,†, Chaowei Xiao*, Mo Li‡, Yunhao Liu*

*School of Software and TNLIST, Tsinghua University, China
†Department of Computer Science, Illinois Institute of Technology, USA
‡School of Computer Engineering, Nanyang Technological University, Singapore

young@tagsys.org, yekui@tagsys.org, xli@cs.iit.edu,
xiaocw11@mails.tsinghua.edu.cn, limo@ntu.edu.sg, yunhao@greenorbs.com

ABSTRACT

In many applications, we have to identify an object and then locate the object to within high precision (centimeter- or millimeter-level). Legacy systems that can provide such accuracy are either expensive or suffering from performance degradation resulting from various impacts, *e.g.*, occlusion for computer vision based approaches.

In this work, we present an RFID-based system, Tagoram, for object localization and tracking using COTS RFID tags and readers. Tracking *mobile* RFID tags in *real time* has been a daunting task, especially challenging for achieving *high precision*. Our system achieves these three goals by leveraging the phase value of the backscattered signal, provided by the COTS RFID readers, to estimate the location of the object. In Tagoram, we exploit the tag's mobility to build a virtual antenna array by using readings from a few physical antennas over a time window. To illustrate the basic idea of our system, we firstly focus on a simple scenario where the tag is moving along a fixed track known to the system. We propose Differential Augmented Hologram (DAH) which will facilitate the instant tracking of the mobile RFID tag to a high precision. We then devise a comprehensive solution to accurately recover the tag's moving trajectories and its locations, relaxing the assumption of knowing tag's track function in advance.

We have implemented the Tagoram system using COTS RFID tags and readers. The system has been tested extensively in the lab environment and used for more than a year in real airline applications. For lab environment, we can track the mobile tags in real time with a millimeter accuracy to a median of $5mm$ and $7.29mm$ using linear and circular track respectively. In our year-long large scale baggage sortation systems deployed in two airports, our results from real deployments show that Tagoram can achieve a centimeter-level accuracy to a median of $6.35cm$ in these real deployments.

Categories and Subject Descriptors

C.2 [**Computer Systems Organization**]: Computer Communications Networks

MobiCom'14, September 07-11, 2014, Maui, Hawaii, USA.

ACM 978-1-4503-2783-1/14/09 ...$15.00.
http://dx.doi.org/10.1145/2639108.2639111 .

Keywords

RFID; Tracking; Localization; DAH; Tagoram

1. INTRODUCTION

Radio Frequency IDentification (RFID) is a rapidly developing technology which uses RF signals for automatic identification of objects. One of its most promising applications is to track the mobile objects accurately. Many applications would benefit from higher tracking accuracy. For example, supermarkets can deeply mine the consumers' shopping habits by monitoring the items' trajectories. Similarly, it is useful to conduct automatic recognition of complex multi-player behaviors through the tagged football in a world-wide game. Plenty of new battery-free human-machine interactive device can be developed using the tags, like writing letters in the air by attaching a tag on a finger. Exact tracking information is also indispensable for some emerging RFID applications like automated customer checkout. Today's robots routinely replace human labor in assembly tasks. It has been of a great interest in both the robotics academic community and industry to enable robot search for a desired object, pick it up, fetch and delivery it from a assembly lines. These tasks require tracking the object to cm-level and even mm-level accuracy [1]. Another typical application is the object sortation. Slightest tracking error may result in incorrect baggage sortation and delivery in airport. According to the report of our partner airline operator, Hainan Airline, over 90% of its baggage losses are due to the tracking and sorting error on the airport conveyors. In this paper, we target at the problem of tracking mobile RFID tags at high precision (cm- and mm- level), in order to meet the needs of challenging applications.

Existing RFID localization techniques cannot be directly applied due to the following reasons. First, to the best of our knowledge there are seldom reported approaches that can achieve high precision of localization accuracy, especially for mobile tags. Second, many RFID localization approaches (*e.g.*, [2–10]) rely on pre-deployed reference tags for accurate calibration, which is infeasible for a tracking system spanning a long pipeline (*e.g.*, the sortation line in the airport). Third, the mobile tag experiences fast-changing environment with non-ideal communication conditions such as multipath reflections of RF signals, varied orientation of tags, *etc.*, which fail most existing localization techniques for their assumption on static communication environment.

In this paper, we design Tagoram, which exploits the phase value of received signal for *real-time* tracking of *mobile* tags with a *high precision*. We observe that the COTS RFID products support fine-grained resolution in detecting the phase of received RF signals, *i.e.*, with accuracy ≈ 0.0015 radians. This accuracy offers an opportunity to locate the object with accuracy of millimeter-level displacement. Developing a practical system out of the basic principle, however, entails substantial challenges. First, the RF phase measurement is affected by the basic thermal noise at the receiver side, which results in the practically measured RF phase a random variable following Gaussian distribution. How to derive a definite and accurate tracking result from the indefinite phase measurement remains challenging. Second, the device diversity in phase measurement introduces extra phase shifts we call "*diversity term*". Different RFID tags or readers have different diversity terms. Prior calibration of all tags and readers is impractical and computationally infeasible and we need to carefully sidestep the problem. Third, the fast changing environment makes the phase measurement a complex result mixing RF propagation through the line-of-sight (LOS) with the None LOS. It is hard to separate them and thus non-trivial to accurately derive the tag position. We propose a hologram based approach, called *Tagoram*, to tackle above challenges using COTS RFID tags and readers with a few physical antennas. We build an RF phase hologram with observations from different reader antennas and at different time of scan. To tackle the challenges of mobile tags, we assume the antennas moving to the opposite direction relative to the mobile tag. Such fictitious reader "mobility" offers individual RF phase observations from different positions relative to the tag, and they form an RF hologram as if they were obtained from a virtual antenna array. If the tag movement velocity and its moving track is known in advance, the positions of the antenna array relative to the tag can be determined. We can thus rely on the instant hologram to derive the initial position of the tag and thus precisely track the tag movement. In order to tackle previously identified challenges we further develop Differential Augmented Hologram (DAH) approach from the naive one. The details will be elaborated in §4. In §5, we then relax the assumption that we know the tag moving track in advance and devise a technique to accurately recover the tag movement from antenna observations. We first identify a series of candidate tag moving paths using the continuously estimated tag velocity from the antenna array. Then DAH is extended to identify the one with the highest likelihood of generating the observed RF phases. To enable real-time localization and tracking, we propose several techniques to speedup the computation of hologram.

Summary of results: We implement Tagoram using a COTS reader equipped with 4 antennas (see §6). We first conduct extensive testbed experiments in indoor environment with all communication irregularities and compare with RSS [2], OTrak [3], PinIt [6] and BackPos [9] in §7. The tags are attached to objects moving on different tracks. In our result, Tagoram achieves mm-level accuracy to a median of $5mm$ and $7.29mm$ under linear and circular track respectively using DAH, offering about $82\times$, $21\times$, $16\times$ and $55\times$ improvement compared to above four methods, in a controllable case where the track is known and without need of reference tags. Even in an uncontrollable case with 4 antennas, Tagoram can still achieve centimeter accuracy to a median error distance of $12.3cm$. In addition, Tagoram adopts a strategy of incremental computation to generate the final hologram. Our experiment shows that it only takes about 2.5 seconds to get a high accuracy. For most of real time application, especially for the control of mechanical system like sorting or assembly system, it is within an acceptable level.

We then perform large scale trial studies in tracking RFID tagged baggages with real airport baggage sortation systems, presented in §8. We develop a customized device with multi-antenna equiped RFID reader, called *TrackPoint*. Ten TrackPoints are deployed for automatic baggage sortation in two of the busiest airports in China, Beijing Capital International Airport (BCIA T1) and Sanya Phoenix International Airport (SPIA). Long term pilot studies have been launched since January 2013. The trial studies have by far consumed 110,000 RFID tags. 12 billion traced records were collected during the study. In this practical application environment millions of baggages were conveyed and there exist various metal transport vehicles that create rich multipath signal reflections. The practical tracking results show that Tagoram achieves a centimeter-level accuracy to a median error distance of $6.35cm$.

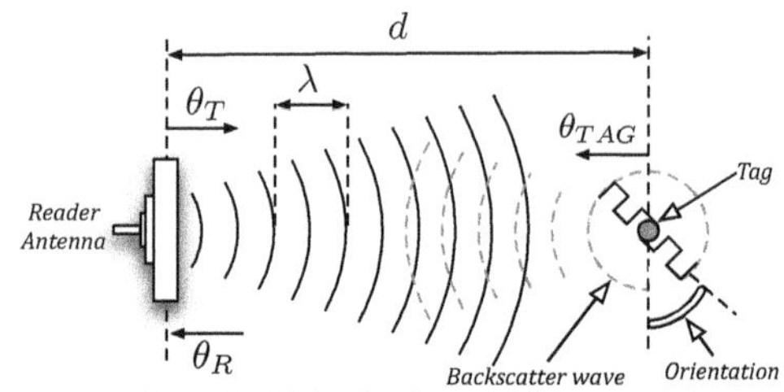

$$\theta = (\frac{2\pi}{\lambda} \times 2d + \underbrace{\theta_T + \theta_R + \theta_{TAG}}_{\text{diversity term}}) \bmod 2\pi$$

Figure 1: Backscatter communication

Contribution: To summarize, we made the following contributions: First, to best of our knowledge, Tagoram is the first system that can successfully limit the negative impact of the multipath phenomena and the phase measurement error (caused by thermal noise and tag diversity). Second, we design and implement the Tagoram system, purely based on COTS RFID products which makes the fast adoption and deployment possible. Third, we systematically evaluate the system under indoor environment and two sorting environment at two airports. As a result, Tagoram can provide *real-time* tracking of *mobile* tags with a high precision.

The rest of the paper is organized as follows. We present the background and preliminary studies in §2. The main design of Tagoram is overviewed in §3. We present the details of Tagoram for controlled moving trajectory using DAH in §4 and uncontrolled trajectory in §5. The implementation of Tagoram is described in §6 and evaluated in §7 and §8. We review the related work in §9 and conclude our work in §10.

2. BACKGROUND

Passive RFID system communicates using a backscatter radio link. The tags, no battery equipped, purely harvest energy from the reader's signal. Fig. 1 illustrates a conceptual diagram of the backscatter communication between a reader and a passive tag. The wireless signal from the reader's antenna induces a voltage on the tag's antenna and the radiated wave makes its way back to the reader's antenna, induces a voltage, and therefore produces a signal that can be detected: a backscatter signal. The tag modulates its data on the backscatter signals using ON-OFF keying through changing the impedance on its antenna. A COTS reader is usually connected to 4 directional antennas. These antennas transmit signals alternatively in exclusive time-slots to avoid the reader collision. The tag *orientation* is defined as the angle between the reader antenna's polarization direction and the tag's antenna.

RF phase: The RF phase is a common parameter supported by COTS readers. Suppose d is the distance between the reader antenna and the tag, the signal traverses a total distance of $2d$ back and forth in backscatter communication. Besides the RF phase rotation over distance, the reader's transmitter, the tag's reflection characteristic, and the reader's receiver circuits will all introduce some additional phase rotations, denoted as θ_T, θ_{TAG} and θ_R respectively. The total phase rotation [11] output by the reader can be expressed as

$$\begin{cases} \theta = \left(\frac{2\pi}{\lambda} \times 2d + c\right) \bmod 2\pi \\ c = \theta_T + \theta_R + \theta_{TAG} \end{cases} \tag{1}$$

where λ is the wavelength. The term c is called *diversity term*, which is related to the hardware characteristics. The phase is a periodic function with period 2π radians which repeats every $\lambda/2$ in the distance of backscatter communication. Most modern COTS RFID readers, *e.g.* ImpinJ R420 [12], are able to report the θ as a phase difference of transmitted and received signal. One RF phase estimate is output each time a tag that is successfully interrogated, depending on the individual antenna and channel. A typical UHF reader has 16 channels working at 920 $\sim$ 926 MHz ISM band. Thus, the resolution can be achieved 0.0015 radians in theory, thereby offering $\approx 320mm * 0.0015/(4 \times 3.14) = 0.038mm$ ranging resolution [1]. Such ultra-high resolution makes the RF phase an attractive indicator for mm-level localization and tracking.

Challenges and empirical studies: (*i*) The phase estimate is derived from the received signal where the thermal noise from reader receiver is always present, leading to measurement errors. We conduct an empirical studies over 100 tags with environment temperature from 0° to 40°C, various frequencies (920 $\sim$ 926MHz) including 16 channels, and RSS from -70 to -30dbm (different orientations). One set of the results measured at the 5th channel is depicted in Fig. 2(a). These experiments suggest that the phase measurement results contain random errors, following a typical Gaussian distribution with a standard deviation of 0.1 radians. In the following sections, we will consider the phase measurement as a Gaussian random variable instead of an accurate value. (*ii*) To validate the existence of tag's diversity on RF phase. We place 70 tags at a same position in turn. Each tag is interrogated for 100 times and the average value is reported in Fig. 2(b). We observe that the measured phase values are distributed among 0.3007 $\sim$ 5.8438 radians. Such an observation suggests that the tag's diversity takes impact on phase measurement and cannot be ignored in practice. We also perform the Kolmogorov-Smirnov test (KS-test) to study their predictability. These values pass the test to be verified over a uniform distribution with 0.5 significant level, which means that the tag diversity is hard to infer. In summary, both the thermal noise and tag diversity challenge the phase measurement and further affect the tracking accuracy, which were not fully studied previously.

3. TAGORAM OVERVIEW

Tagoram is an RFID-based practical tracking system towards mobile objects. As a running example, we mainly present the system in the context of conveyor or assembly task. Tagoram's technique applies to a variety of tracking applications, including robot manipulation.

3.1 Scope

Ultra-low cost of UHF tags (5-10 cents each) become the preferred choice of many industry applications. Following the common practices, we concentrate on the tracking of UHF tags in this paper. Today's COTS readers have an operating range of around $10m$ [12]. In this work, we focus on locating and tracking mobile tags that are not moving at a high speed. As presented in [13]

[1] $320mm$ is the average wavelength among 16 channels.

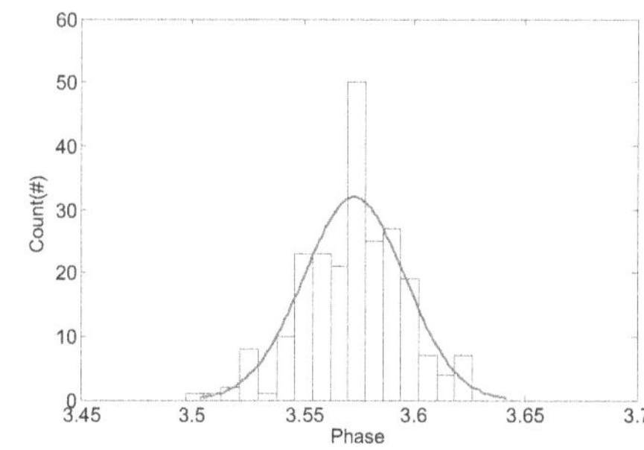

(a) Phase distribution

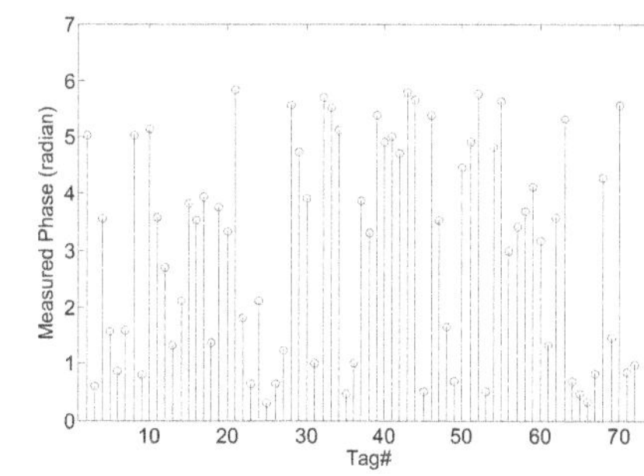

(b) Tag diversity

Figure 2: Empirical studies on measured RF phase. (a) The phase obeys a Gaussian distribution. (b) The diversity takes an impact on measured phase.

(we had similar observations in our experiments) the system suffers from serious packet loss when the tag moves with a high speed, resulting that the tag even cannot be interrogated. Thus, our system considers the case where tags move with a relative low speed.

3.2 Problem Definition

We consider the mobile RFID tag tracking applications, where the tags move within a surveillance region monitored by M RF antennas, denoted as $\mathcal{A} = \{A_1, A_2, \cdots, A_M\}$, with known locations. These antennas are connected to the same reader and scheduled at different time slots in a round robin approach [14]. For brevity, we use A_m to indicate the mth antenna as well as its coordinate. Our approach is mainly presented in 2D surveillance region, but it can be easily extended to 3D space (discussed later in §4.3). The surveillance plane is divided into grids, with W rows and L columns. Suppose the reader has taken N rounds of antennas schedule, there are total $M \times N$ phase measurements so far. Formally, we use a matrix Θ to denote these measurements.

$$\Theta = \begin{pmatrix} \theta_{1,1} & \cdots & \theta_{1,N} \\ \vdots & \vdots & \vdots \\ \theta_{M,1} & \cdots & \theta_{M,N} \end{pmatrix} \tag{2}$$

The element $\theta_{m,n}$ denotes the nth phase value measured by the mth antenna. Besides the measured values, we also record the time stamps when the phases are measured:

$$\mathbf{T} = \begin{pmatrix} t_{1,1} & \cdots & t_{1,N} \\ \vdots & \vdots & \vdots \\ t_{M,1} & \cdots & t_{M,N} \end{pmatrix} = t_0 + \begin{pmatrix} \Delta_{1,1} & \cdots & \Delta_{1,N} \\ \vdots & \vdots & \vdots \\ \Delta_{M,1} & \cdots & \Delta_{M,N} \end{pmatrix} \tag{3}$$

The element $t_{m,n}$ is the time that the tag is interrogated for n^{th} time by the mth antenna. The time matrix $\mathbf{T}$ is normalized based on the time t_0. No constraint is put on choice of t_0 and we always

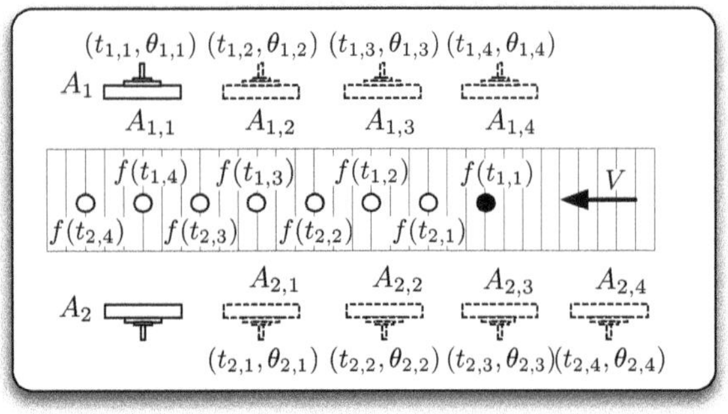

Figure 3: Virtual antenna matrix. The target tag moves from right to left. Total 8 virtual antennas are constructed.

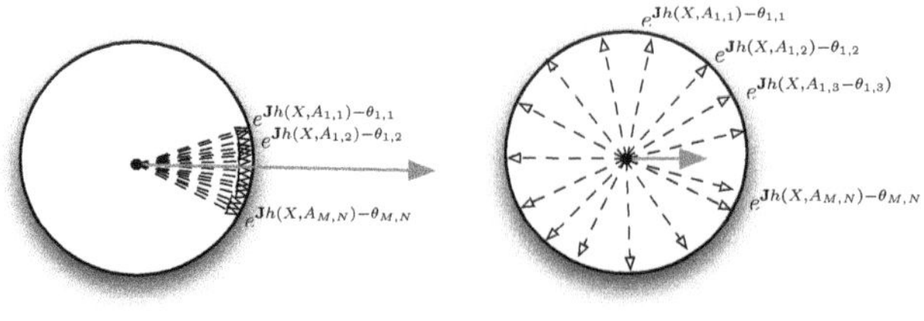

(a) Waves reinforced (b) Waves canceled out

Figure 4: Superimposing the observations from different antennas.

choose the time when the tag is firstly interrogated as the base time, *i.e.* $t_0 = \min\{t_{m,n}\}$, throughout this paper. The $\Delta_{m,n}$ is the time difference, *i.e.* $\Delta_{m,n} = (t_{m,n} - t_0)$. We formally define the tracking problem as follows:

PROBLEM 1. *Given* Θ, $\mathbf{T}$ *and* $\mathcal{A}$, *how to find the tag's trajectory coordinates, i.e.* $\{f(t_{1,1}), f(t_{1,2}), \cdots, f(t_{M,N})\}$, *at an arbitrary interrogated time? Here* $f(t)$ *is the time-dependent trajectory function outputting the tag's coordinate at time t.*

The trajectory is a function of time series indicating the trace that a moving object follows through space, which emphasizes the time-space relationship. To avoid the confusion of relevant concept, we define another term, *track*, indicating the path along which the tag might move. The track is a geometric function, which may formulate a close-loop conveyor belt, a passageway through the building, or a highway based on the road. The track function may be composed by a complex piecewise function but irrelevant to time.

3.3 Solution

In this paper, we propose a holistic system, Tagoram, to address the instant tag tracking problem. Tagoram decomposes it into two stages.

• **Controllable Case**: First, we consider a simplified case where the tags move along a known track with a constant speed. This case mostly occurs at a conveyor belt or assembly line where the objects are conveyed by a predefined track. Then the trajectory function can be expressed as:

$$f(t) = f(t_0) + \int_{t_0}^{t} \vec{V}(t)dt \tag{4}$$

where $\vec{V}(t)$ is the speed function. Note the trajectory function may follow a more complex model but it can be always abstracted as the above equation. The $f(t_0)$ is termed as the *initial position* where the tag is interrogated at time t_0. As long as the tag's position at time t_0 is estimated, its location at an arbitrary time t can be inferred using Equation 4 in combination with the track function. Thus, the main task in this case is to locate the tag's initial position $f(t_0)$. We present our solution in §4.

• **Uncontrollable Case**: We then consider a general case where no prior knowledge about the tag's moving track is known by our system. Thanks to the highly efficient anti-collision capability, the tag can be observed at a high frequency. We approximate its irregular and unpredictable trajectory at run time by exploiting the differentials between consecutive phase values. Then we use the approach introduced in §5 to identify a set of potential trajectories and converting the problem of selecting the optimal trajectory into a task in first stage.

4. MOVEMENT WITH KNOWN TRACK

In this section, we discuss the first case in context of conveyor or assembly with known track function and constant speed $\vec{V}(t)$ to find out the mobile tag's trajectory.

4.1 Using Virtual Antenna Matrix

As the tag is moving along a trajectory, M physical antennas will interrogate the tag at n different time slots $\{t_{m,1}, t_{m,2}, \cdots, t_{m,n}\}$. Instead of viewing the tag moves along the known track function, we view each antenna moves in the opposite direction, while the tag stays at a fixed position $f(t_0)$ without any motion. Thus the collected phase values Θ is assumed to be collected by a *virtual antenna matrix* $\mathbf{A}$, denoted as:

$$\mathbf{A} = \begin{pmatrix} A_{1,1} & \cdots & A_{1,N} \\ \vdots & \vdots & \vdots \\ A_{M,1} & \cdots & A_{M,N} \end{pmatrix} \tag{5}$$

where the virtual antenna $A_{m,n}$ is derived from real antenna A_m and its relative coordinate to the tag is calculated by:

$$A_{m,n} = A_m - \vec{V} \times \Delta_{m,n} \tag{6}$$

All of virtual antennas in $\{A_{m,1}, \cdots, A_{m,n}\}$ have the same diversity term c. Fig. 3 illustrates an example where the moving tag is interrogated 4 times by two antennas. The tag is firstly interrogated in position $f(t_0)$ at time $t_{1,1}$ where $t_0 = t_{1,1}$. Total 8 virtual antennas are constructed. The virtual antenna $A_{1,1}$ coincides with the real antenna A_1.

4.2 RF Hologram

The tag's mobility offers individual RF phase observations from these different directions using antenna matrix. The surveillance plane is partitioned into $W \times L$ grids at mm level (less than $1cm$). For each grid, we use its centroid as its coordinate. We build an RF hologram with observations from these antennas with different time of scan to derive the $f(t_0)$. The RF hologram is a likelihood exhibition using an image to display the likelihood that how a partitioned grid in tag's motion plane is likely to be the initial position. We start our technique by presenting a naive straightforward hologram solution and then present techniques that can address the negative impacts of thermal noise and device diversity.

Naive Hologram: Let $h(X, A)$ be the theoretical phase value emitted from antenna A and reflected at grid X. Ignoring the diversity term, $h(X, A)$ can be defined as follows:

$$h(X, A) = \frac{4\pi}{\lambda}|XA| \bmod 2\pi \tag{7}$$

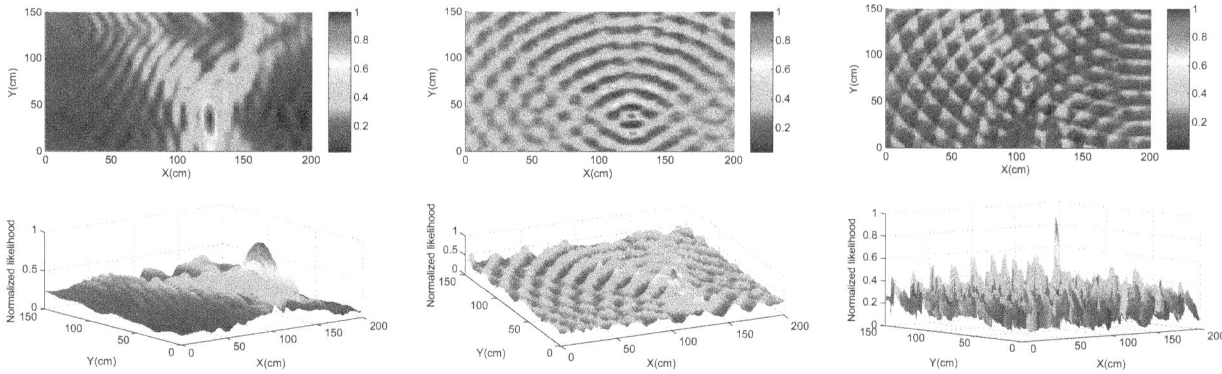

(a) Naive Hologram (b) Augmented Hologram (c) Differential Augmented Hologram

Figure 5: RF Hologram. The RF hologram is an image exhibiting the likelihood that how a partitioned grid is likely to be the initial position. The ground truth is highlighted with plus notation. Three columns shows the three kinds of holograms using both 2D image and 3D mesh.

where $|\cdot|$ measures the Euclidean distance between position A and X. An RF Hologram $\mathbf{I}$ is expressed as following image:

$$\mathbf{I} = \begin{pmatrix} x_{1,1} & \cdots & x_{1,L} \\ \vdots & \vdots & \vdots \\ x_{1,W} & \cdots & x_{W,L} \end{pmatrix} \quad (8)$$

The image has a resolution of $W \times L$, in which each pixel $x_{w,l} \in \mathbf{I}$ is mapped to a partitioned grid $X_{w,l}$. The naive hologram is defined as follows.

DEFINITION 1 (NAIVE HOLOGRAM). *The naive hologram is an image in which the pixel value $x_{w,l}$, indicating the likelihood that the corresponding grid $X_{w,i}$ is the initial position, is calculated by*

$$x_{w,l} = \left| \sum_{m=1}^{M} \sum_{n=1}^{N} S(X_{w,l}, A_{m,n}, \theta_{m,n}) \right| \quad (9)$$

where $S(X, A, \theta) = e^{\mathbf{J}(h(X,A)-\theta)}$. The term $\mathbf{J}$ denotes the imaginary number and the term $e^{\mathbf{J}\theta}$ represents a complex exponential signal with unit amplitude.

The pixel value is the amplitude of the summed waves. A key point here is that all measured phase values are viewed to originate from the same initial position as we use a virtual antenna matrix. If the grid X is the initial position, the theoretical phase value equals to the measured one. The vector of the signal $e^{\mathbf{J}(h(X,A)-\theta)}$ will be close to the real axis at positive direction as $h(X, A)-\theta$ approaches 0. All observations from different antennas add up for each other, as shown in Fig. 4(a). Otherwise, when X is not the initial position, $h(X, A) - \theta$ will take a value in $[0, 2\pi]$. Different $S(X, A, \theta)$ will cancel each other, resulting the final superimposing of these values $\sum_{m,n} S(X, A_{m,n}, \theta_{m,n})$ at a low level, as shown in Fig. 4(b).

To illustrate RF hologram in details, an experimental study is performed where two antennas are placed aside the belt and one tag moves through the surveillance plane (detailed methodology is described in §7). In our experiment, a tag is interrogated 220 times by 2 antennas when the tag is moving within the range of the reader, and therefore a virtual antenna matrix with size of 2×220 are built. The ground truth of initial position is $f(t_0) = (108, 68)$. The naive hologram and its corresponding 3D-mesh structure are shown in Fig. 5(a). Here light colors denote lower amplitude values. Note that the likelihood is normalized in all figures. From the figure, we can see that at the positions close to the target location $f(t_0)$, the sum grows as the signals constructively add up to each other. On the other hand, at the positions away from to the $f(t_0)$ the signals superimpose at random phase angles and the sum is significantly lower. The hologram I suggests a likelihood function of tag being at every possible grid. An RF hologram leverages the statistical correlation to find the optimal solution instead of pursuing accurate analytical solution that might not exist in practice.

Augmented Hologram: We define Peek-Signal-to-Noise-Ratio (PSNR) for a pixel in the hologram:

$$PSNR(x_{w,l}) = \frac{x_{w,l}}{\sum_{i=1}^{W} \sum_{j=1}^{L} x_{i,j}}$$

Obviously, a pixel with higher PSNR suggests a higher probability that the initial position is at the corresponding grid. In practice, due to the thermal noise, it is hard to catch the exact initial position with the maximum PSNR. As shown in Fig. 5(a), the pixel $(122, 35)$ with maximum PSNR deviates from the ground truth about $358mm$ away. We have to consider all pixels whose PSNRs are greater than a predefined threshold as possible candidate locations. The size of the candidate group determines the tracking error. As Fig. 5(a) depicts, the hologram cannot give distinctive result about the initial position. There exists a large continuous region with relatively high PSNRs.

In naive RF hologram, the amplitudes of signal $e^{\mathbf{J}(h(X,A)-\theta)}$ are uniformly set to one because the measured amplitude, *i.e.* RSS, is notably distorted as a result of the severe multipath environment. As aforementioned, the measured phase $\theta_{m,n}$, affected by the thermal noise, is a random variable that follows a typical Gaussian distribution *i.e.* $\theta_{m,n} \sim \mathcal{N}(\mu, \sigma)$. Suppose the tag is at $X_{w,l}$, its phase expectation measured by antenna $A_{m,n}$ is $h(X_{w,l}, A_{m,n})$, thereby, $h(X_{w,l}, A_{m,n}) - \theta_{m,n} \sim \mathcal{N}(0, \sigma)$. The standard deviation σ is caused by the receiver's thermal noise being irrelevant to the distance. Based on the experiments presented in § 2, we adopt $\sigma = 0.1$ in following sections. To reduce the impact of receiver's thermal noise, we propose *Augmented Hologram* (AH) by assigning a *virtual amplitude* $\|S\|$.

DEFINITION 2 (AH). *The augmented hologram is an image in which the pixel value $x_{w,l}$ is calculated by*

$$x_{w,l} = \left| \sum_{m=1}^{M} \sum_{n=1}^{N} \|S(X_{w,l}, A_{m,n}, \theta_{m,n})\| S(X_{w,l}, A_{m,n}, \theta_{m,n}) \right| \quad (10)$$

$$\text{where} \begin{cases} \|S(X,A,\theta)\| = 2 \times F(|h(X,A) - \theta|; 0, 0.1) \\ F(x;\mu,\sigma) = \dfrac{1}{\sigma\sqrt{2\pi}} \displaystyle\int_x^{\infty} \exp\left(-\dfrac{(t-\mu)^2}{2\sigma^2}\right) dt \end{cases}$$

and $F(x;\mu,\sigma)$ *is the cumulative probability function of Gaussian distribution* $\mathcal{N}(\mu,\sigma)$.

The assigned amplitude $\|S(X_{w,l}, A_{m,n}, \theta_{m,n})\|$ is the cumulative probability that the measured phase is emitted from $A_{m,n}$ and backscattered at grid $X_{w,l}$. Doing so enhances the amplitude of these waves with higher probability and weakens others. In effect, those pixels whose measured phase values are very close to theoretical values, are augmented in the hologram. Fig. 5(b) depicts the augmented hologram using the same observed data as those in Fig. 5(a). We see that AH breaks up the large continuous region that has higher PSNRs into several points and reinforces the initial position.

Differential Augmented Hologram: From the augmented hologram, we find that there still exist some candidate positions with higher PSNR, distributed around the ground truth. These few spots make the tracking error around $200mm$. We believe these ambiguities are caused by the device diversity across different antennas. The measured phase θ equals to $h(X,A) + c$. Assume tag's initial position is at grid T, then

$$S(X,A,\theta) = e^{\mathbf{J}(h(X,A)-(h(T,A)+c))}$$

In theory, the maximum amplitude should happen when $X = T$. In practice, the energy is spread across grids X that $h(X,A) = h(T,A) + c$. As each antenna takes a different impact on the c, the uncalibrated θ violates our basic assumption that the phase measured by each virtual antenna would originate from the initial position. To eliminate such influence caused by the diversity term, we further propose *Differential Augmented Hologram* (DAH) redefining a new virtual signal $\mathbb{S}$.

DEFINITION 3 (DAH). *The differential augmented hologram is an image in which the pixel value is calculated by*

$$x_{w,l} = \left| \sum_{m=1}^{M} \sum_{n=1}^{N} \|\mathbb{S}(X_{w,l}, A_{m,n}, \theta_{m,n})\| \mathbb{S}(X_{w,l}, A_{m,n}, \theta_{m,n}) \right| \tag{11}$$

where

$$\begin{cases} \mathbb{S}(X_{w,l}, A_{m,n}, \theta_{m,n}) = e^{\mathbf{J}\theta_{dif}} \\ \|\mathbb{S}(X_{w,l}, A_{m,n}, \theta_{m,n})\| = 2 \times F(|\theta_{dif}|; 0, 0.1 \times \sqrt{2}) \\ \theta_{dif} = (h(X_{w,l}, A_{m,n}) - \theta_{m,n}) - (h(X_{w,l}, A_{m,1}) - \theta_{m,1}) \end{cases}$$

The virtual signal $e^{\mathbf{J}\theta_{\text{dif}}}$ is constructed using the difference of phase difference. We reconstruct the virtual signal $\mathbb{S}$. Note that $(h(X_{w,l}, A_{m,n}) - \theta_{m,n}) - (h(X_{w,l}, A_{m,1}) - \theta_{m,1})$ $= (h(X_{w,l}, A_{m,n}) - (h(T, A_{m,n}) + c)) - (h(X_{w,l}, A_{m,1}) - (h(T, A_{m,1}) + c)) = h(X_{w,l}, A_{m,n}) - h(T, A_{m,n}) + h(T, A_{m,1}) - h(X_{w,l}, A_{m,1})$. A key observation here is that the diversity term c is eliminated through subtracting the measured phase difference from the theoretical difference between the $A_{m,n}$ and $A_{m,1}$. Since each row of virtual antennas $A_{m,n}$ is derived from a same physical antenna A_m and each row of phase measurements $\theta_{m,n}$ are taken by the same antenna A_m, so the subtraction is treated differently for different rows. For each row, we choose the first virtual antenna as the calibration base. In addition, the θ_{dif} introduces subtraction of two random variables, $\theta_{m,n}$ and $\theta_{m,1}$. Notice that $(h(X_{w,l}, A_{m,n}) - \theta_{m,n}) \sim \mathcal{N}(0,\sigma)$ and $(h(X_{w,l}, A_{m,1}) - \theta_{m,1}) \sim \mathcal{N}(0,\sigma)$, then $\theta_{dif} \sim \mathcal{N}(0, \sqrt{2} \times \sigma)$, so we set the σ of cumulative probability function to $0.1 \times \sqrt{2}$ instead of 0.1. In addition, another benefit from phase difference is able to eliminate the impact of doppler effect, because $\theta_{m,1} \sim \theta_{m,n}$ almost contains the equal phase deviation caused by the doppler effect, during a small sampling interval. Fig. 5(c) shows that the correct initial position has an extremely intensive PSNR that approximately exceeds $2\times$ than those in other pixels. The error can be reduced to within $10mm$.

4.3 Achieving Realtime Tracking

The computations involved in deriving DAH may introduce much overhead, thus jeopardize the real time tracking capability. The problem will be more severe for applications where the tracking in the 3D space rather than a 2D plane. Suppose the reader's read zone is approximately considered as a cuboid with a size of $W \times L \times H$, the reader's read zone is partitioned into H planes, each of which has a size of $W \times L$. The extracted initial position located in the grid which related pixel has the higher PSNR among H holograms. Compared with 2D scenario, the computations required are increased thousands of times for 3D scenario.

4.3.1 Hashtable on Phase

Reviewing the 2D-hologram in Fig. 5(c), we find that the majority of pixels have low PSNR values (blue) in hologram, where the related computations are not necessary. It can reduce computation time if these pixels are ignored. In fact, given a measured phase $\theta_{m,n}$, we can find out a group of arcs originated from antenna $A_{m,n}$, across which the grid X meets $h(X, A_{m,n}) = \theta_{m,n}$, called as candidate grid. Obviously, the initial position definitely do not locate in non-candidate grids. This inspires us to find a way of quickly releasing these candidate grids and ignoring others for saving computations. We implement the idea using a hashtable.

Hashtable construction: Assume the antennas locate at origin first and address this issue later, we traverse each grid X within the read zone, calculate the phase θ emitting from origin and backscattered at X, and hash the grid to the phase table. A COTS reader supports 0.00015 radians phase resolution where the reported phase is encoded with 12 bits, so each phase table contains $2^{12} = 4096$ entries.

Applying: When applying, the antenna's coordinate $A_{m,n}$ as well as its measured phase $\theta_{m,n}$ are input. Using $\lambda_{m,n}$ and $\theta_{m,n}$ can obtain a set of candidate grids from the hashtable, *i.e.* $C_{m,n} = \{X | h(X,0) = \theta_{m,n}\}$. However, due to the thermal noise, the measured phase vibrates with a standard deviation of σ radians. To tolerate the vibration, all grids whose calculated phase within $[\theta_{m,n} - \sigma, \theta_{m,n} + \sigma]$ should be all fetched and merged, *i.e.* $C_{m,n} = \{X \| h(X,0) - \theta_{m,n}| \le \sigma\}$. The hashtable is built on the assumption that the antenna locates at origin while the antenna is at $A_{m,n}$ in practice. We must translate the origin to $A_{m,n}$. It is equivalent to translating the selected grids by a vector of $A_{m,n}$, *i.e.* $X + \vec{A}_{m,n}$, *i.e.* $C_{m,n} = \{X + \vec{A}_{m,n} \| h(X,0) - \theta_{m,n}| \le \sigma\}$. In theory, the initial position must be inside the common intersected grid of these candidate sets. However, there might not exist a common intersection among them at all because of multipath effect, *i.e.* $\bigcap_{i=1,j=1}^{M,N} C_{m,n} = \emptyset$. Hence, all candidate grids which are included at least three candidate sets should be involved in the hologram generation.

The hashtable reduces the computations from two aspects: First, the majority of grids are non-candidate and can be ignored. Second, our experiments show that 70% of computation time are consumed to resolve Euclidean distance in $h(X,A)$. The hashtable makes this part of computation not needed any more. Our evaluations show that the hashtable reduces 60% of computations.

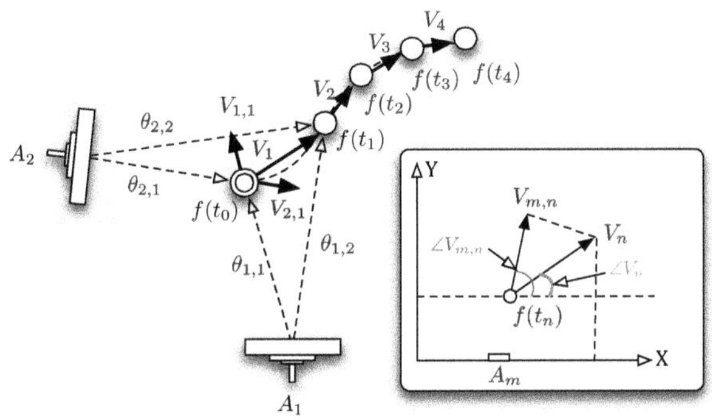

Figure 6: Modeling tag's movement. Each antenna estimates a tag's radial velocity component along the direction between them.

4.3.2 *Incremental Generation*

It appears that the entire hologram is generated once enough phase measurements are collected. Actually, the generation is an incremental process. The sum in Eqn. (12) can be decomposed into a superimpose of $M \times N$ sub-holograms. Correspondingly, the computation can be decomposed into many time windows every time a read is collected. Usually, the tag is interrogated about 30 times per second so that the time window equals $0.03s$, which is long enough to generate a sub-hologram. Therefore, our approach is able to guarantee the realtime object tracking at second level.

5. MOVEMENT WITH UNKNOWN TRACK

In this section, we relax the assumption that tag's track function is known in prior. Tagarom deals with the unpredictable movement with the following two steps:

- *Fitting tag's trajectory*: Tagoram acquires the phase measured by M antennas from different directions to fit tag's trajectory every round of antenna scheduled.
- *Selecting the optimal trajectory*: Tagoram utilizes the DAH to evaluate all fitted trajectories and selects the optimal one corresponding to the pixel with maximum PSNR.

Below we describe these two steps in detail.

5.1 Fitting Tag's Trajectory

A tag can be interrogated for about 30 times per second in COTS RFID system [12] while the most advanced automatic sorting system [15] supports a maximum conveyor velocity of $274.8mm/s$. On average, the tag moves about $274.8 * \frac{1}{30} = 9.16mm$, which is far less than half a wavelength of available channel ($\approx 160mm$). This feature motivates us to estimate the tag's radical speed through the phase difference of two adjacent reads. As illustrated in Fig. 6, the tag's displacement Δd during two adjacent reads $\theta_{m,n}$ and $\theta_{m,n+1}$ for antenna A_m can be approximated using Eq. (1):

$$\Delta d = \begin{cases} \frac{\theta_{m,n+1}-\theta_{m,n}}{4\pi} \times \lambda, & |\theta_{m,n} - \theta_{m,n+1}| < \pi \\ \frac{(2\pi-\theta_{m,n}+\theta_{m,n+1})}{4\pi} \times \lambda, & \theta_{m,n} - \theta_{m,n+1} \geq \pi \\ \frac{\theta_{m,n+1}-\theta_{m,n}-2\pi}{4\pi} \times \lambda, & \theta_{m,n} - \theta_{m,n+1} \leq -\pi \end{cases} \quad (12)$$

Note that since above equation has taken a phase difference for given m^{th} antenna, the antenna dependent diversity term has been naturally eliminated. On the other hand, $\Delta d \ll |f(t_{m,n}) - A_m|$, then it is reasonable to approximate tag's displacement along the radical direction *i.e.* $A_m \rightarrow f(t_{m,n})$, equal to Δd. Further, the radical instant speed $\widetilde{V}_{m,n}$ can be estimated as follows:

$$\begin{cases} \widetilde{V}_{m,n} \approx \frac{\Delta d}{t_{m,n+1}-t_{m,n}} \\ \angle\widetilde{V}_{m,n} \approx \angle(f(t_n) - A_m) \end{cases} \quad (13)$$

$\angle X$ is the vector X's direction, defined as the angle with x-axis. For completeness, we give an applicable upper band on the tag's speed, $160mm/0.033s = 484.9mm/s$.

Speed chain: There are m real antennas monitoring the surveillance region, so we can estimate m instant radical speeds every round of antenna schedule. The displacement between any two adjacent reads is so small that we simply model the tag's movement during a round as a uniform linear motion. The entire trajectory can be well approximated by a piecewise linear curve. As shown in Fig. 6, let $\vec{V}_n$ denote the tag's real speed during the nth round, and $\vec{V}_{m,n}$ be the radical speed measured by the mth antenna during the nth round. Actually, $\vec{V}_{m,n}$ is the instant projection of $\vec{V}_n$ at direction of $A_m \rightarrow f(t_{m,n})$, namely:

$$|\vec{V}_{m,n}| = |\vec{V}_n| \cos(\angle\vec{V}_n - \angle\vec{V}_{m,n}) \quad (14)$$

Above equation has two unknown parameters, the tag's speed magnitude $|\vec{V}_n|$ and direction $\angle\vec{V}_n$. In theory, given two arbitrary estimated radical speeds in different directions, both parameters can be solved. Usually, a typical COTS RFID system supplies $M \geq 3$ antennas in practice, which yields $\binom{M}{2}$ resolutions. So we adopt fitting method to estimate the two parameters. The problem is formalized as follows:

$$\begin{aligned} &\min |V_{m,n} - \widetilde{V}_{m,n}| \\ &\text{subject to: } \{(\widetilde{V}_{1,n}, \angle\widetilde{V}_{1,n}), \cdots, (\widetilde{V}_{M,n}, \angle\widetilde{V}_{M,n})\} \end{aligned} \quad (15)$$

We adopt the nonlinear least squares to estimate the tag's instant speed $\vec{V}_n$ in n^{th} schedule, and use the GaussNewton method which is based on a linear approximation of the objective function in the neighborhood of parameter vector. We start with an initial approximation of the parameter vector and iteratively update this parameter vector until it converges to a local minimum of an objective function. When every round of antenna scheduling ends, a group of measurements are obtained and the tag's speed during this schedule can be fitted. Since we have N schedules for now, the output is actually a chain of tag's speeds:

$$\mathcal{V} = \{\vec{V}_1, \cdots, \vec{V}_N\}$$

Trajectory function: We segment tag's trajectory into a serials of uniform linear movements in each round. The trajectory can be obtained using following recursive equation:

$$f(t_n) = f(t_{n-1}) + (t_n - t_{n-1}) \cdot \vec{V}_n = f(t_0) + \sum_{k=1}^{n}(t_k - t_{k-1}) \cdot \vec{V}_k \quad (16)$$

where $\vec{V}_k \in \mathcal{V}$. As long as we know the initial position $f(t_0)$, the tag's trajectory can be recursively inferred. Note that the optimized method, such as Kalman filter [10], can be utilized to address the measurement noise, which is not discussed in this paper due to the space limit.

5.2 Selecting the Optimal Trajectory

Although the trajectory can be approximately calculated through Eqn. (16), there still exists an unknown parameter $f(t_0)$, namely the initial position. Given an arbitrate $f(t_0)$, either way Tagoram can fit a trajectory. Choosing different grid as initial position may result in a different speed chain and further produce different trajectory. Which is the optimal one that most approaches the ground truth? We leverage the DAH to answer this question. Being similar to track the initial position in §4, we assume $f(t_0) = X_{w,l}$ and fit a trajectory $f_{w,l}$. There are total $W \times L$ candidate trajectories. We superimpose all phase measurements along $f_{w,l}$ to $f_{w,l}(t_0)$ as the same process as tracking initial position using DAH. Our rational

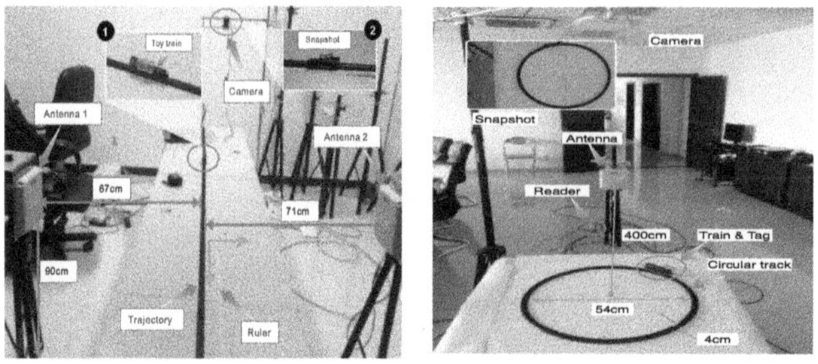

(a) Linear Track (b) Circular Track

Figure 7: Experiment setups

behind is that if the fitted trajectory approaches the ground truth, the superimposed amplitude at initial position should reach the maximum among $W \times L$ trajectories. Eventually, the trajectory with high maximum PSNR is selected as the optimal one.

6. IMPLEMENTATION

We build Tagoram using ImpinJ [12] reader and Alien EPC Gen-2 UHF RFIDs [16]. The system is evaluated both in our lab and a long-term pilot study.

Hardware: We adopt an ImpinJ Speedway modeled R420 reader without any hardware or firmware modification. The reader supports four directional antennas at most, being compatible with EPC Gen2 standard. The whole RFID system operates in the 920 $\sim$ 926 MHz band with frequency hopping. The size of antenna is $225mm \times 225mm \times 40mm$.The reader is connected to host through the wireless network (TCP/IP). It has local clock and attaches a timestamp for each tag read. We adopt the timestamp provided by the reader instead of the received time as the timing measurement to calculate the phase values, in order to eliminate the influence of network latency. Four reader antennas with circular polarization manufactured by Yeon technology [17] are employed to provide $\geq 8dBic$ gain in two directions. Two types of tags from Alien Corp [16], modeled 2×2 *Inlay* and *Squiggle Inlay*, are employed. Both of them are employed in our lab experiment and pilot study.

Software: We adopt LLRP protocol [18] to communicate with the reader. ImpinJ reader extends this protocol for supporting the phase report. We adjust the configuration of reader to immediately report reading whenever tag is detected. The software is implemented using Java. In lab experiment, we run the software at a Lenovo PC, which equips Intel(R) Celeron CPU G530 at 2.4 GHz and 2G memory. In our pilot study, it runs at an industrial computers with Atom 1.66GHz, 2G memory, and 16G SSD.

7. MICROBENCHMARK

We start with microbenchmark experiments in a testbed environment at our lab with regard to two cases, controllable and uncontrollable case, compared with other methods.

7.1 Evaluation in controllable case

We emulate a mobile object via a toy train on which a tag is attached, moving at a constant speed of $0.176m/s$ on a track. Because an arbitrate track can be decomposed into pieces of linear and arc-shaped tracks in practice, we mainly focus on two basic tracks here.

Linear Track: Two antennas are separated in both sides of the track, as shown in Fig. 7(a). Their distances to the track are $670mm$ and $710mm$ respectively. The width of belt is $1300mm$. Both the tag's x-axis and y-axis are going to be calculated. Observe that in this testing scenario, the accuracy along x-axis (*i.e.*, track direction) is more important.

Circular Track: We employ a circular track and an RF antenna to measure the accuracy for nonlinear track, as shown in Fig. 7(b). The track's internal diameter is $540mm$. The distance, from the track's center to the antenna, equals $4000mm$ for accuracy comparison and varies from $1000mm$ to $15000mm$ when discussing its impact on accuracy.

To capture the ground truth with high-accuracy, we install a camera above the track. When the tag is firstly interrogated, the system immediately trigger the camera to take a snapshot on the train, from which the initial position can be identified. When calculating, both tag and antennas are treated as points located in their centroids.

7.1.1 *Accuracy among different methods*

First, we present the accuracy compared with other four localization methods under a controllable environment. We repeat the experiments using five methods over 100 measurements. Fig. 8 plots the final results in which the accuracy is exhibited in x-axis, y-axis and the combination of them. This figure shows the accuracy achieved by RSS, OTrack, PinIt, BackPos and DAH.

RSS: The difference between the RSSs of a pair of tags is used as an indicator for their spatial distance as in past work [2]. Based on the RSS distance, the nearest neighbors of the target tag are identified. The reference tags are deployed aside the track. The RSS scheme has a combined error distance of $600mm$, suffering from the high variation in behavior across tags, like the antenna gain and tag's orientation.

OTrack: [3] designed a method to determine baggage order via the changes of RSS and read rate. This method focuses on the object sequence conveyed, so there is no result along y-axis. OTrack has a median error distance of $150mm$, 75% reduction as compared to the RSS-based scheme.

PinIt: PinIt [6] uses synthetic aperture radar (SAR) created via antenna motion to extract the multipath profiles for each tag, and leverages the reference tags to locate the target tag as same way as RSS based methods. PinIt achieves a mean error distance of $120mm$, agreed with the report in [6], using 10 reference tags separated $130mm$ apart. PinIt is not appropriate in mobile context, because the fast-changing environment violates the tag's multipath profile at every moment, even the movement is very small. In addition, it is not practical to deploy a large number of reference tags on conveyor or assembly line. Even so, their locations become unknown when moving.

BackPos: BackPos [9] is a phase based method, which introduces the technique of hyperbolic positioning in RFID localization. It obtains a mean combined error distance of $400mm$ and a standard deviation of $200mm$. BackPos is anchor-free but sacrifices the area of feasible region.

DAH: Using linear track, our method DAH has a median error distance of $5mm$, $13mm$ and $14mm$ in x-axis, y-axis and combined dimension, outperforming RSS, OTrack,PinIt and BackPos by $43\times$, $11\times$, $8.5\times$ and $28\times$ respectively. This significant improvement is due to the careful consideration of thermal noise and device diversity. The accuracies along the x-axis always are better than y-axis among all methods except OTrack. This is because the tag moves along x-axis providing a relatively larger displacement than y-axis. This verifies that the tag's mobility can improve the tracking accuracy. Since the DAH leverages the statistical results from different directions, its track accuracy is rather stable as well, *i.e.* standard deviation $\approx 2mm$. Fig. 9 plots the CDFs of error measured using the circular track. DAH has a mean error distance of $4.14mm$, $4.98mm$ and $7.29mm$ in x-axis, y-axis

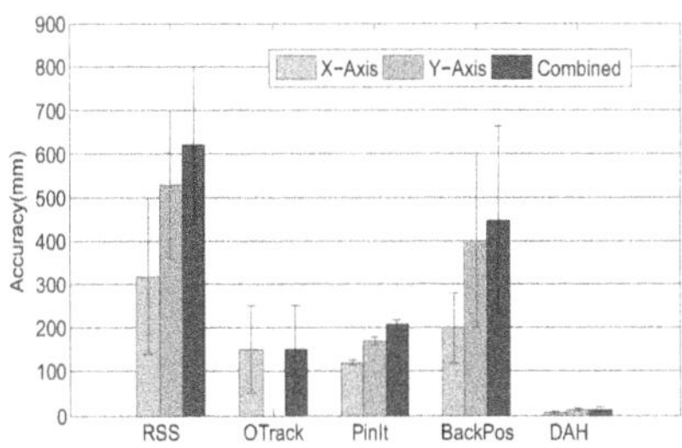

Figure 8: Accuracy comparison

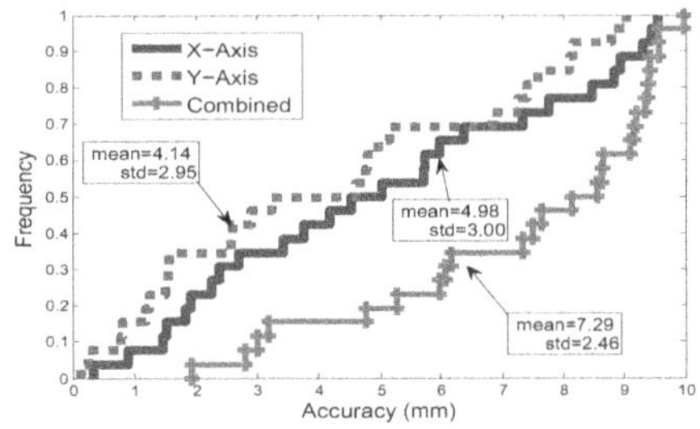

Figure 9: Tracking in circular track

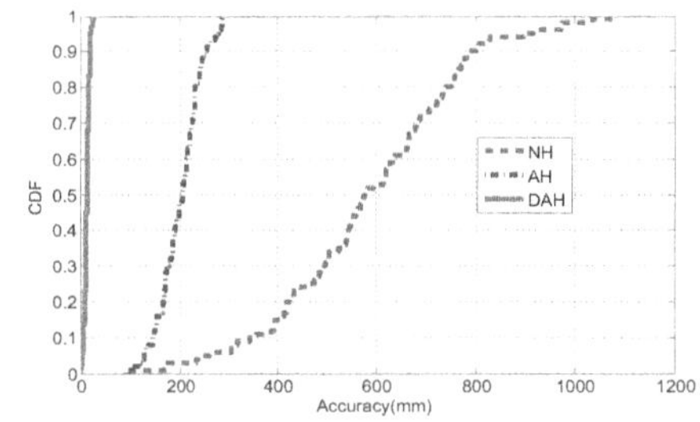

Figure 10: Different holograms

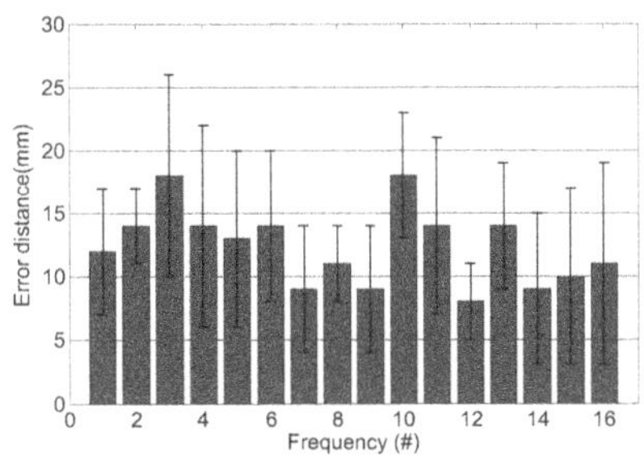

Figure 11: Impact of frequency

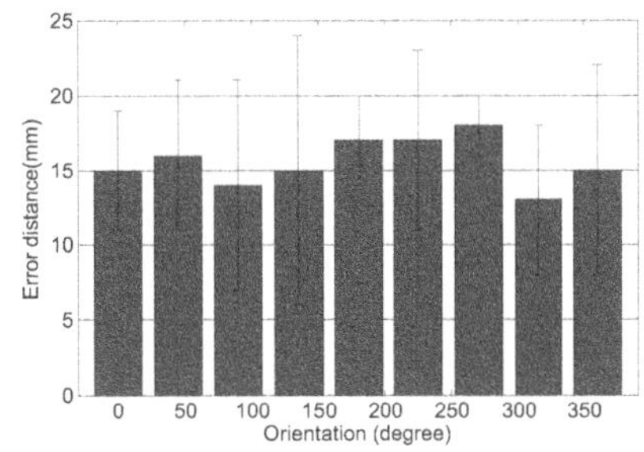

Figure 12: Impact of orientation

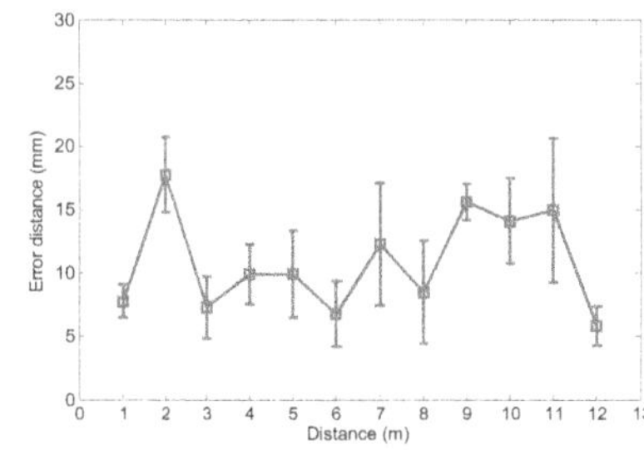

Figure 13: Impact of distance

and combined dimension, outperforming others by $82\times$, $21\times$, $16\times$ and $55\times$ respectively. Apparently, the accuracy of DAH in circular track is better than that of linear track. In this situation, the accuracies along the x-axis and y-axis perform equally well, because the tag takes almost the same displacement along two dimensions.

Summary: DAH is able to achieve mm-level accuracy and reliable performance using COTS RFID products under a controllable environment. Our method DAH outputs a significant improvement on the accuracy from three aspects. First, DAH carefully deals with the influences caused by the thermal noise and device diversity. To best of our knowledge, we are the first to address these two issues. Other phase based methods, like PinIt and BackPos, have to perform a set of calibration experiments firstly to eliminate the diversity. However, it is infeasible to do calibrations in practice, especially when confronting thousands of tags, like the baggage sortation in airport. Second, we observe the opportunity that the tag's mobility can help the reader measure its phase from various directions. Most of preview schemes focus on stationary instead of mobile tags, ignoring this important observation. Lots of measurements from different directions can statistically reduce the influence of multipath effect, because the unexpected and unordered wave propagation through NLOS will canceled out for each other, while even a small number of LOS propagations can reinforce amplitudes at initial position. Third, the DAH has ability to eliminate the influences from the Doppler effect, because the similar impacts taken by the Doppler effect during a short interval ($t_{m,1} \sim t_{m,n}$) are subtracted by the difference operations of DAH, *i.e.* $(\theta_{m,n} - \theta_{m,1})$.

7.1.2 Accuracy among different holograms

Next we compare the tacking results among NH, AH and DAH using linear track. Fig. 10 shows their error distances. As we can see, NH has a mean accuracy of $600mm$ and a standard deviation of $100mm$. AH overcomes the deviation coming from the thermal noise and reduces 60% deviation. DAH further removes the influence of device diversity. Its 90th percentile is $18mm$, and 99th is $25mm$. These experiments fully demonstrates the effectiveness of DAH.

7.1.3 Realtime performance

The realtime is an important metric in tracking applications. Next, we investigate Tagoram's delay performance in finding the tag's localization.

Read time. Tagoram takes an incremental process to generate hologram. Once receiving a read from the reader, Tagoram produces an intermediate hologram and superimposes it to the last one. The final hologram is released after enough reads received. So we firstly measure the time taken for generating an intermediate hologram. The results are shown in Fig. 17(a). The read time is the interval during which the reader interrogates two consecutive reads. It is an upper bound which should be taken for producing an intermediate result. The median read time is $33ms$. Any computation exceeds this bound might affect the realtime feature.

We can see that the time consumed for a hologram of $10^3 \times 10^3$ resolution without optimization, has a median of $118ms$, which far exceeds than $3\times$ readtime bound. More worse, the time rises several fold as the resolution increases. The generation with optimization using hashtable always keeps a low time cost compared with read time, achieving a median of $25ms$ even the resolution is up to $10^5 \times 10^5$. In fact, the main overhead for optimized method is to load the hash table from disk and perform the operation of set intersection, both of which are weakly relevant to the hologram resolution.

Accuracy vs. Realtime. Tagoram outputs the initial position after collecting enough reads. The question here is how many reads are needed to obtain an accurate result? Fig. 17(b) plots the relationship between accuracy and realtime. The result shows that the accuracy tends towards stability when more than 120 reads are collected. Thus, it is reasonable to output a position result after received 120 reads.

Summary: With regard of the time taken for incremental generation, Tagoram needs $120 \times 25ms = 2500ms$ in total for hologram calculation. We believe 2.5 seconds of delay is within an acceptable level for major realtime applications, especially for the control of mechanical system, like conveyor or robot arm. It is worth to note that the real-time partially depends on the efficiency of RFID's anti-collision algorithm.

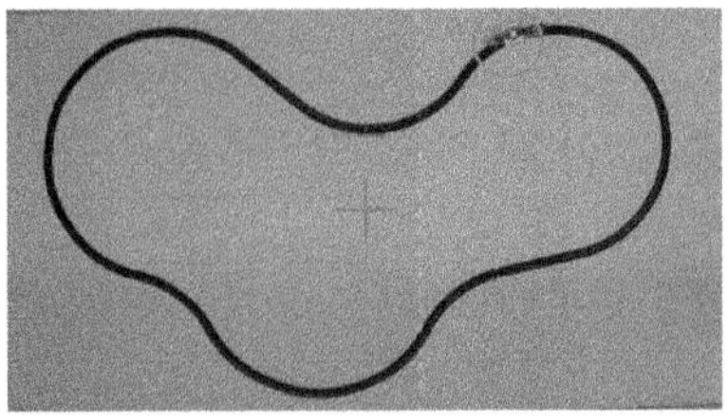

Figure 14: Top view of the track

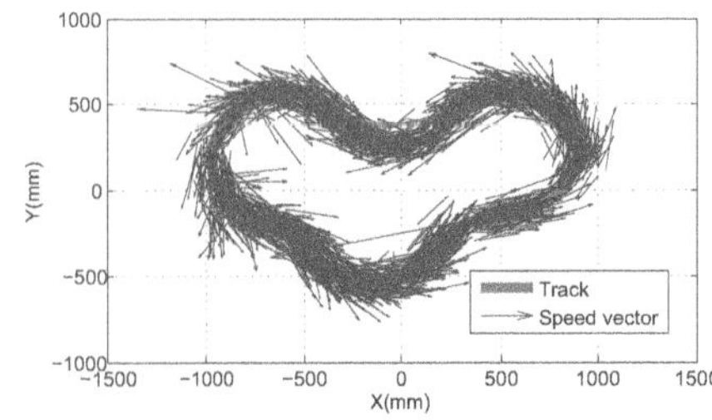

Figure 15: Estimated speed

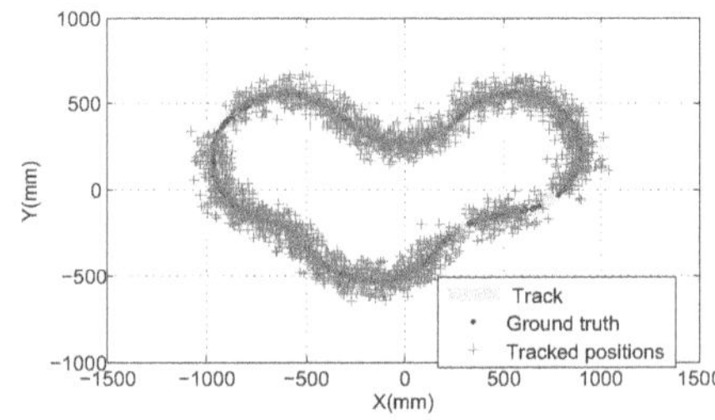

Figure 16: Fitted trajectory

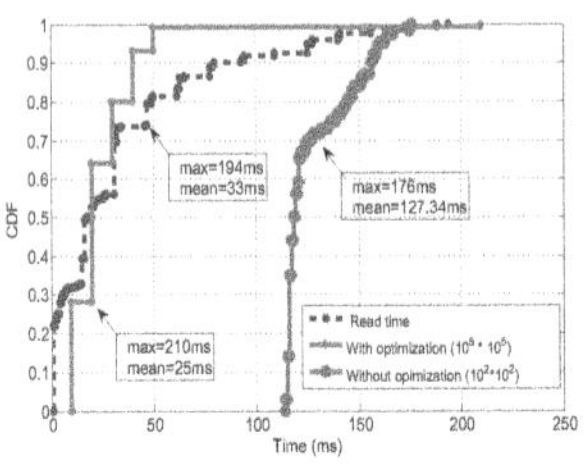

(a) Read time

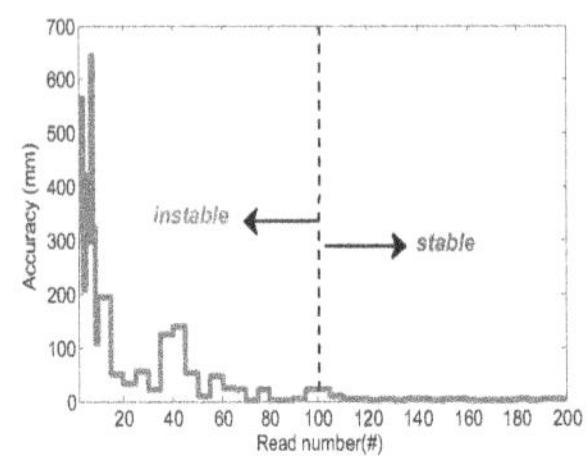

(b) Stability

Figure 17: Incremental generation

7.1.4 Impacts of Parameters

Impact of frequency: A UHF reader hops between 16 channels in the 920 $\sim$ 926 MHz ISM band in China. We look at whether the frequency has impacts on the accuracy of DAH. Fig. 11 plots the accuracy for 16 channels. The results show that DAH is irrelevant to frequency. In fact, it is well known that there exists frequency selective fading in wireless communication. Frequency hopping can help improve the connectivity between reader and tag. **Impact of orientation:** The tag orientation is defined as the angle between the reader antenna's polarization direction and the tag's antenna as shown in Fig. 1. To measure its influence on our tracking accuracy, we adjust the orientation from $0°$ to $360°$ and plot the accuracy in Fig. 12. As expected, the result almost remains a same level. **Impact of distance:** Fig. 13 shows the accuracy with varying distance from $1m$ to $12m$ using circular track. As we can see, its 50th percentile is $9mm$, and 90th percentile is $17mm$. DAH does not exhibit clear correlation with the distance. Thus, the distance is not a crucial factor affecting DAH's accuracy. Especially, a mean error distance of $5mm$ can be obtained, when placing the antenna at distance of $12m$ ($22\times$ than displacement the tag takes). In fact, it is more reasonable to model the antenna as a point locating at is centroid when it keeps far away from tag. **Summary**: These extensive experiment results verify that Tagoram's accuracy is preserved over frequency, orientation and distance changes.

7.2 Evaluation in uncontrollable case

We then study the tacking accuracy in a uncontrollable case where the track function is not known in advance. In the experiment, the tag moves along an irregular track, as shown in Fig. 14. Four antennas are deployed around the surveillance region and their coordinates are $(\pm 2000mm, \pm 2000mm)$. Fig. 14 shows a snapshot of the track and the moving toy train. We collect 5 minutes data in total during which the tag moves about 10 laps anticlockwise.

The first step is to estimate the speed chain using the tag's phase values measured by the four antennas. The estimated speed results are shown in Fig. 15. To display the vector clearly in the figure, the speed is magnified by $1000\times$, so the speed unit is mm/s. We can see that the estimation has a better effect in the smooth part than the curve part, because we assume the tag takes a linear uniform motion during a schedule window. The estimated speed has a mean of $210.2mm/s$ while the ground truth speed is $212mm/s$. The result is extremely accurate, which demonstrates the effectiveness of Tagoram. Fig. 16 illustrates the final fitted trajectory. In our experiment, the tag's position is produced when every 200 reads are collected. Tagoram achieves a median of $12.3cm$ accuracy with a standard deviation of $5cm$.

8. PILOT STUDY

We are collaborating with the Hainan Airline to conduct a RFID-Assisted Sortation System, called *TagAssist*. The ultimate goal of TagAssist is to pursue a guarantee for the passengers, "Never lose your baggage!" To achieve this goal, TagAssist introduces the RFID technology to conduct automatic baggage tracking and checking services for the goal of eliminating baggage losses. Our design and implementation address many practical issues, while in this discussion, we mainly focus on one key issue that how to accurately track tag on a conveyor system?

We have instrumented our system in two airports, BCIA T1 and SPIA, both of which employ the manual sortation. When the passenger checks in, the agent pulls up the the passenger's itinerary on the computer and prints out one or more RFID tags to attach to each pieces of passenger's baggages. To reduce the cost, tens of thousands of baggages enter conveyor system to be transported by a shared conveyor system every day in an airport, resulting that the baggages from different check-in counters are mixed together. It needs human power to separate these baggages according to their flight numbers. The sorting task is finished in the sortation carousel. The sortation carousel is composed of a circularly conveyor used to buffer the baggage, like the baggage claim in arrival hall (see Fig. 18(a)). The baggages are buffered in the carousel until being sorted. It is common to see that the baggages are "thrown" on top of each other in practice.

The sorters, each of who is in charge of sorting a flight of baggages, stand by the carousel along the conveyor. His mission is to find out and carry the target baggages from the carousel to the carriage (see Fig. 18(b)). It is an error-prone step for the sorter to pick an expected one out of packs of baggages. To help improve the sorting accuracy and efficiency, we built four large screens (see Fig. 18(e)), to show the tracked baggages' trajectories, assisting the sorters to find out their baggages. In the screen, the baggage carousel is proportionally displayed, where there are lots of small squares in representation of baggages. The baggages from different flights are filled with different colors. With the help of baggage visualization and accurately tracking, the sorter can quickly and clearly catch sight of the bags which he is responsible for, and fast position the baggages when searching them. Therefore, the real-time tracking with high accuracy is necessary, especially in rush hours.

The conveyor system comprises a huge mechanical network and could be hundreds of meters long. It is impossible to deploy hun-

(a) Carousel (b) Sorting behavior (c) TrackPoint (d) Components (e) Visualization

Figure 18: Pictures taken from airport. (a) The baggages are conveyed from the check-in counters to the sortation carousel. (b) The sorting behavior is to find and pick the baggages from the carousel to carriages. (c) A TrackPoint is deployed across the conveyor belt. (d) The main components inside the TrackPoint. (e) A screen to show each tag's trajectory assisting the sorters to find their targets.

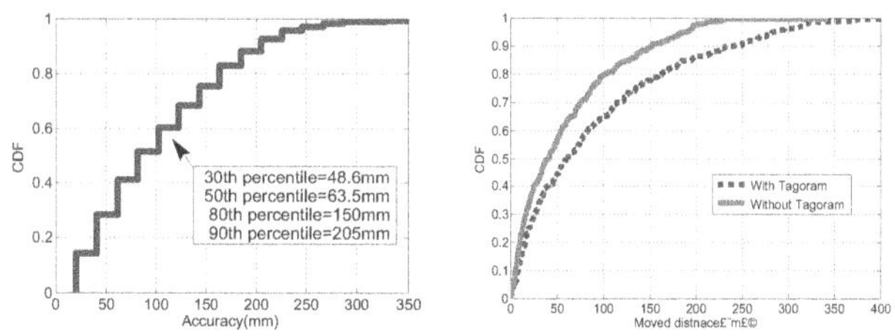

(a) Accuracy (b) Efficiency

Figure 19: Tracking effectiveness

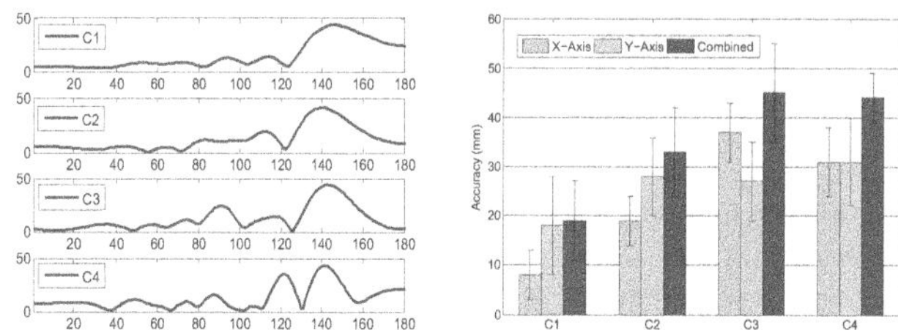

(a) Multipath (b) Accuracy

Figure 20: Tracking robustness to multipath

dreds of readers along the conveyor belt for full coverage. So we design and customize a tracking device, called as *TrackPoint* (see Fig. 18(c)). It composes of one RFID reader and three RF antennas (see Fig. 18(d)), placed across the conveyor. When a tag is passing through the TrackPoint, it is interrogated repeatedly by the reader and tracked using Tagoram with DAH. These devices has been deployed both in BCIA T1 and SPIA, the real industry environment since January 2013. The system has been running for over a year. Each deployment contains 5 TrackPoints (across the conveyor belts), 4 visualization screens (aside the carousels), and 22 RFID Printers (on check-in counters). So far, the study totally consumed $110,000$ RFID tags involving 53 destination airports, 93 air lines, and $1,094$ flights. We collected 12 billions of RFID reads from TrackPoints. Each read including EPC, RSS, phase and timestamp information.

8.1 Tracking Accuracy

Tracking baggages on the conveyor system is a controllable case where the DAH algorithm is adopted. Since the positions of TrackPoints and conveyor velocity are fixed and known in advance, we exactly know how long should the baggage is conveyed from one TrackPoint to another. If the tracking accuracy is precise, this inferred distance should concentrate on the ground truth. So we measure the tracking accuracy by comparing two consecutive tracked distances between two consecutive TrackPoints for a same baggage with the theoretical values. The accuracy is shown in Fig. 19(a) We find Tagoram achieves a median accuracy of $63.5mm$. Its 80th percentile is $150mm$ and 90th percentile is $200mm$. Compared with the results in microbenchmark, the main source affecting the tracking accuracy comes from the versatile environment.

8.2 Tracking Efficiency

The sortation workspace contains a circularly conveyor for buffering baggages. The baggages will continue to be transported circularly until being sorted. The accurate tracking can help the sorters quickly and correctly find out the target baggages and reduces the unavailing movements. So we employ movement distance of baggage taken on the carousel as a metric to indirectly evaluate the tracking efficiency. Fig. 19(b) shows the moved distance before the baggage is sorted, which decreases about 30% after using Tagoram. This indicates our system indeed enable sorting activities much more efficient.

8.3 Tracking Robustness

In practical wireless communication conditions, especially the indoor environments, the signal propagation along NLOS introduces multipath effects which challenges the accuracy in accurate phase measurements. In NLOS, the signals bounce off walls and other objects and arrive at the reader's receivers from multiple directions. We project the received signals into different directions ($0^\circ \sim 180^\circ$) using the method in [6] to visually display the interference situation. The top four cases occurred are plotted in Fig. 20(a) and their corresponding tracking accuracies are illustrated in Fig. 20(b). In the first case $C1$, there exist three obvious propagation paths from 140°, 115° and 90°. The localization accuracy is $19mm$ without much affect. But the accuracy is indeed influenced a little as the number of paths increase. $C4$ has the most complex environment where there are more than 7 propagation paths and the direction of 20° and 140° almost has the same amplitude as ground truth. Even under such serious situation, the accuracy still holds under $60mm$. This shows that Tagoram has strong tolerance to multipath effect.

9. RELATED WORK

Fine-grained RFID localization has been well studied. These approaches can be classified into three categories.

RSS based methods: Early work on RFID localization is based on RSS. The RSS of reference tags deployed at known positions are recorded and used to locate the target tags [2–5,19]. However, RSS is not a reliable location indicator, especially for UHF tags, which is highly relevant to the tag's orientation and antenna gain [4]. In mobile environment, the orientation cannot be known.

Phase based methods: There is a growing interest in using phase information to locate tags. These methods can be divided into two categories, AoA (Angle of Arrival) and SAR (synthetic aperture). AoA locates the tag by measuring the phase difference between the received signals at different antennas, [5, 7, 8]. The major challenges for these methods are to deal with NLOS. SAR methods are firstly used in Radar system for both object localization and terrain imaging with help of antenna array [1, 6, 20, 21]. PinIt [6] employs a moved antenna to measure the multipath profiles of reference tags at known positions and locates the target tag. The technique of PinIt is further applied in robot object manipulation [1]. The merit of PinIt is able to locate tag in NLOS environment. However, it needs to deploy dense reference tags in advance. Miesen *et al.* [20] also employ the moving antenna to construct SAR and find out tag's location with naive hologram. Parr [21] extends the technique proposed in [20] in mobile context to determine whether a tag moves along a supposed trajectory. While Tagoram employs tag's mobility to generate Inverse SAR-style antenna array, it significantly differs from previous work in that it focuses on tracking mobile tag in mm-level while dealing with both thermal noise and device diversity. Besides, Tagoram is able to track the mobile tag under uncontrollable case in which the trajectory function is unknown.

Proximity based methods: The last type of localization technique is based on proximity [22–27]. This approach relies on dense deployment of antenna. When the target tag enters in the radio range of an antenna, its location is assumed to be the same as this receiver. Liu *et al.* present a new communication system that enables two battery-free devices to communicate using ambient RF as the only source of power. which might open a new tracking technique among tags within few centimeter [25].

10. CONCLUSION

In this work we present Tagoram for real-time tracking of mobile RFID tags using Commercial Off-The-Shelf (COTS) RFID tags and readers, to a high precision (cm- and mm-level). A key innovation is to build a differential augmented hologram using the phase values collected from physical antennas, and to leverage the tag mobility to construct a virtual antenna array. Tagoram can pinpoint the tag position to an accuracy of a few centimeter, providing the necessary precision for many novel applications, such as object grasping by robot. The system Tagoram not only has been tested and used in practical applications, but also will open up a wide range of exciting opportunities due to its instant tracking and extremely high accuracy.

11. ACKNOWLEDGMENT

This research is partially supported by NSFC under Grant No. 61190110 and NSFC CERG-61361166009. The research of Xiang-Yang Li is partially supported by NSF CNS-1035894, NSF ECCS-1247944, NSF ECCS-1343306, National Natural Science Foundation of China under Grants No. 61170216, No. 61228202. The research of Mo Li is supported from Singapore MOE AcRF Tier 1 grant RG17/13, and Nanyang Assistant Professorship (NAP) grant M4080738.020 of NTU. We thank all the reviewers and shepherds for their valuable comments and helpful suggestions.

12. REFERENCES

[1] J. Wang, F. Adib, R. Knepper, D. Katabi, and D. Rus, "Rf-compass: robot object manipulation using rfids," in *Proc. of ACM MobiCom*, 2013.

[2] L. Ni, Y. Liu, Y. Lau, and A. Patil, "Landmarc: Indoor location sensing using active rfid," *Wireless networks*, 2004.

[3] L. Shangguan, Z. Li, Z. Yang, M. Li, and Y. Liu, "Otrack: Order tracking for luggage in mobile rfid systems," in *Proc. of IEEE INFOCOM*, 2013.

[4] J. D. Griffin and G. D. Durgin, "Complete link budgets for backscatter-radio and rfid systems," *IEEE Antennas and Propagation Magazine*, vol. 51, no. 2, pp. 11–25, 2009.

[5] C. Hekimian-Williams, B. Grant, X. Liu, Z. Zhang, and P. Kumar, "Accurate localization of rfid tags using phase difference," in *Proc. of IEEE RFID*, 2010.

[6] J. Wang and D. Katabi, "Dude, where's my card?: Rfid positioning that works with multipath and non-line of sight," in *Proc. of ACM SIGCOMM*, 2013.

[7] S. Azzouzi, M. Cremer, U. Dettmar, R. Kronberger, and T. Knie, "New measurement results for the localization of uhf rfid transponders using an angle of arrival (aoa) approach," in *Proc. of IEEE RFID*, 2011.

[8] P. V. Nikitin, R. Martinez, S. Ramamurthy, H. Leland, G. Spiess, and K. Rao, "Phase based spatial identification of uhf rfid tags," in *Proc. of IEEE RFID*, 2010.

[9] T. Liu, L. Yang, Q. Lin, Y. Guo, and Y. Liu, "Anchor-free backscatter positioning for rfid tagswith high accuracy," in *Proc. of IEEE INFOCOM*, 2014.

[10] S. Sarkka, V. V. Viikari, M. Huusko, and K. Jaakkola, "Phase-based uhf rfid tracking with nonlinear kalman filtering and smoothing," *IEEE Sensors Journal*, vol. 12, no. 5, pp. 904–910, 2012.

[11] ImpinJ, "Speedway revolution reader application note: Low level user data support," in *Speedway Revolution Reader Application Note*, 2010.

[12] "Impinj, Inc," http://www.impinj.com/.

[13] P. Zhang, J. Gummeson, and D. Ganesan, "Blink: A high throughput link layer for backscatter communication," in *Proc. of ACM MobiSys*, 2012.

[14] L. Yang, J. Han, Y. Qi, C. Wang, T. Gu, and Y. Liu, "Season: Shelving interference and joint identification in large-scale rfid systems," in *Proc. of IEEE INFOCOM*, 2011.

[15] "Dematic," http://www.dematic.com/linear-sorters.

[16] "Alien," http://www.alientechnology.com/tags.

[17] "Yeon," http://www.yeon.com.tw/.

[18] EPCglobal, "Low level reader protocol (llrp)," 2010.

[19] G. Li, D. Arnitz, R. Ebelt, U. Muehlmann, K. Witrisal, and M. Vossiek, "Bandwidth dependence of cw ranging to uhf rfid tags in severe multipath environments," in *Proc. of IEEE RFID*.

[20] R. Miesen, F. Kirsch, and M. Vossiek, "Holographic localization of passive uhf rfid transponders," in *Proc. of IEEE RFID*, 2011.

[21] A. Parr, R. Miesen, and M. Vossiek, "Inverse sar approach for localization of moving rfid tags," in *Proc. of IEEE RFID*, 2013.

[22] W. Zhu, J. Cao, Y. Xu, L. Yang, and J. Kong, "Fault-tolerant rfid reader localization based on passive rfid tags," in *Proc. of IEEE INFOCOM*, 2012.

[23] Y. Liu, L. Chen, J. Pei, Q. Chen, and Y. Zhao, "Mining frequent trajectory patterns for activity monitoring using radio frequency tag arrays," in *Proc. of IEEE PerCom*, 2007.

[24] Y. Guo, L. Yang, B. Li, T. Liu, and Y. Liu, "Rollcaller: User-friendly indoor navigation system using human-item spatial relation," 2014.

[25] V. Liu, A. Parks, V. Talla, S. Gollakota, D. Wetherall, and J. R. Smith, "Ambient backscatter: Wireless communication out of thin air," in *Proc. of ACM SIGCOMM*, 2013.

[26] Y. Zheng and M. Li, "P-mti: Physical-layer missing tag identification via compressive sensing," in *Proc. of IEEE INFOCOM*, 2013.

[27] L. Yang, Y. Qi, J. Fang, and *et al.*, "Frogeye: Perception of the slightest tag motion," in *Proc. of IEEE INFOCOM*, 2014.

Jigsaw: Indoor Floor Plan Reconstruction via Mobile Crowdsensing *

Ruipeng Gao[1], Mingmin Zhao[1], Tao Ye[1], Fan Ye[1,2], Yizhou Wang[1],
Kaigui Bian[1], Tao Wang[1], Xiaoming Li[1]
EECS School, Peking University, Beijing 100871, China[1]
ECE Department, Stony Brook University, Stony Brook, NY 11794, USA[2]
{gaoruipeng, zhaomingmin, pkuleonye, yefan[1], yizhou.wang, bkg, wangtao, lxm}@pku.edu.cn,
fan.ye@stonybrook.edu[2]

ABSTRACT

The lack of floor plans is a critical reason behind the current sporadic availability of indoor localization service. Service providers have to go through effort-intensive and time-consuming business negotiations with building operators, or hire dedicated personnel to gather such data. In this paper, we propose Jigsaw, a floor plan reconstruction system that leverages crowdsensed data from mobile users. It extracts the position, size and orientation information of individual landmark objects from images taken by users. It also obtains the spatial relation between adjacent landmark objects from inertial sensor data, then computes the coordinates and orientations of these objects on an initial floor plan. By combining user mobility traces and locations where images are taken, it produces complete floor plans with hallway connectivity, room sizes and shapes. Our experiments on 3 stories of 2 large shopping malls show that the 90-percentile errors of positions and orientations of landmark objects are about $1 \sim 2m$ and $5 \sim 9°$, while the hallway connectivity is 100% correct.

Categories and Subject Descriptors

H.3.4 [**Information Storage and Retrieval**]: Systems and Software; C.2.4 [**Computer-Communication Networks**]: Distributed Systems

Keywords

indoor floor plan reconstruction; mobile crowdsensing

1. INTRODUCTION

In contrast to the almost ubiquitous coverage outdoors, localization service is at best sporadic indoors. The industry state-of-the-art, Google Indoor Maps [2], covers 10,000 locations worldwide, which is only a small fraction of millions of indoor environments (e.g., airports, train stations, shopping malls, museums and hospitals) on the Earth. One major obstacle to ubiquitous coverage is the lack of indoor floor plans. Service providers have to conduct effort-intensive and time-consuming business negotiations with building owners or operators to collect the floor plans, or wait for them to voluntarily upload such data. Neither is conducive to large scale coverage in short time.

In this paper, we propose *Jigsaw*, which leverages crowdsensed data from mobile users to construct the floor plans of complex indoor environments. It avoids the intensive effort and time overhead in the business negotiation process for service providers. They do not need to talk to building owners/operators one by one, or hire dedicated personnel to measure indoor environments inch by inch. This opens up the possibility of fast and scalable floor plan reconstruction.

The concept of mobile crowdsensing [12] is more and more popular. Recent work has used crowdsensed data to localize users [34] and reduce the calibration efforts of WiFi signatures [23, 38]. Among others [14, 22, 26, 27], CrowdInside [3] pioneers the efforts of constructing hallway/room shape and connectivity of floor plans. It uses inertial data to build and combine user mobility traces to derive the approximate shape of accessible areas of floor plans.

Nevertheless, there exists much space for improvements. Inertial data do not give the accurate coordinates and orientations of indoor POIs (e.g., store entrances in shopping malls, henceforth called *landmarks*), which are critical to guide users. Due to error accumulation in dead reckoning, "anchor points" (e.g., entrances/exits of elevators/escalators/ stairs and locations with GPS reception) with unique sensing data signatures are needed to correct the drift in mobile traces. But in many large indoor environments such anchor points can be too sparse to provide sufficient correction. Thus both over- and under-estimation of accessible areas can easily happen, e.g., when a trace drifts into walls, or there exist corners users seldom walk into.

Jigsaw combines computer vision and mobile techniques, and uses optimization and probabilistic formulations to build relatively complete and accurate floor plans. We use computer vision techniques to extract geometric features (e.g., widths of store entrances, lengths and orientations of adjoining walls) of individual landmarks from images. We then design several types of data-gathering *micro-tasks*, each a series of actions that users can take to collect data

*This work is done at Peking University and supported in part by China NSFC Grants 61370056, 61231010, 61121002, 61201245, 61272340 and 973 Grant 2014CB340400.

MobiCom'14, September 7-11, 2014, Maui, Hawaii, USA.

http://dx.doi.org/10.1145/2639108.2639134.

specifically useful for building floor plans. We derive the relative spatial relationship between adjacent landmarks from inertial data of some types of micro-tasks, and compute the optimal coordinates and orientations of landmarks in a common floor plane. Then user mobility traces from another type of micro-task are used to obtain the hallway connectivity, orientation and room shapes/sizes, using combinatorial optimization and probabilistic occupancy techniques.

Jigsaw design is based on the realization that computer vision and mobile techniques have complementary strengths. Vision ones can produce accurate geometric information when the area has stable and distinct visual features. This is suitable for landmarks where logos, decorations constitute rich features, and detailed information about their positions/orientations is desired. Mobile techniques give only rough sketches of accessible areas with much lower computing overhead, which is suitable for in-between sections such as textureless or glass walls where much fewer stable features exist, while less detailed information is required. Thus we leverage "expensive" vision techniques to obtain more accurate and detailed information about individual landmarks, and use "cheap" inertial data to obtain the placement of landmarks on a large, common floor plane, and derive the less critical hallway and room information at lower fidelity. The optimization and probabilistic formulations give us more solid foundations and better robustness to combat errors from data.

We make the following contributions in this work:

- We identify suitable computer vision techniques and design a *landmark modeling* algorithm that takes their output from landmark images to derive the coordinates of major geometry features (e.g., store entrances and adjoining wall segments) and camera poses in their local coordinate systems.

- We design micro-tasks to measure the spatial relationship between landmarks, and devise a *landmark placement* algorithm that uses a Maximum Likelihood Estimation (MLE) formulation to compute the optimal coordinates, orientations of landmarks in a common floor plane.

- We devise several *augmentation algorithms* that reconstruct wall boundaries using a combinatorial optimization formulation, and obtain hallway connectivity and orientation, room size/shape using probabilistic occupancy maps that are robust to noises in mobile user traces.

- We develop a prototype and conduct extensive experiments in three stories of two large complex indoor environments. The results show that the position and orientation errors of landmarks are about $1 \sim 2m$ and $5^\circ \sim 9^\circ$ at 90-percentile, with 100% correct isle topology connectivity, which demonstrate the effectiveness of our design.

Note that we do not claim novelty in developing new computer vision techniques. Our main contribution is the identification and combination of appropriate vision and mobile techniques in new ways suitable for floor plan construction, and accompanying mathematical formulations and solutions that yield much improved accuracy despite errors and noises from image and inertial data sources.

The rest of the paper is organized as follows: We given an overview (Section 2), then present the design of the landmark modeling, placement and augmentation algorithms (Section 3, 4 and 5). We conduct experimental evaluation of our design and demonstrate its effectiveness in Section 6. After a discussion (Section 7) of limitations, comparison to related work (Section 8), we conclude the paper (Section 9).

2. DESIGN OVERVIEW

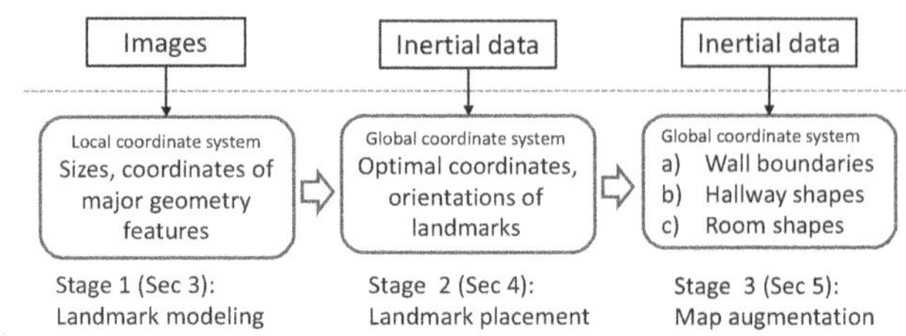

Figure 1: Jigsaw contains 3 stages: landmark modeling, landmark placement and map augmentation. Each stages uses image or inertial data and output from the previous stage.

Jigsaw utilizes images, acceleration and gyroscope data. The reconstruction consists of three stages: landmark modeling, placement and augmentation (Figure 1). First, two computer vision techniques, Structure from Motion (SfM) [29] and vanishing line detection [18], are used to obtain the sizes and coordinates of major geometry measurements of each landmark in its local coordinate system (Section 3). SfM also produces the location and orientation of the camera for each image, effectively localizing the user who took the picture. Next, two types of micro-tasks, Click-Rotate-Click (CRC) and Click-Walk-Click (CWC), are used to gather gyroscope and acceleration data to measure the distances and orientation differences between landmarks. The measurements are used as constraints in an MLE formulation to compute the most likely coordinates and orientations of landmarks in a global coordinate system (Section 4). Finally, a combinatorial optimization is used to connect landmarks' adjoining wall segments into continuous boundaries, and probabilistic occupancy maps are used to obtain hallway connectivity, orientation and room sizes/shapes from inertial user traces (Section 5).

Different from opportunistic data gathering adopted in most existing work [3, 23, 34, 38], we assume the users pro-actively take a bit effort to conduct different data-gathering *micro-tasks*. Each micro-task defines one or a few actions to gather different data in certain spatial areas and temporal durations. Examples include: taking a single photo of a store entrance; taking a photo of one store and then spinning the body to take a photo of another store; walking a certain trajectory while taking a photo immediately before/after the walk. Such micro-tasks allow us to gather data useful in specific stages. We assume service providers have certain incentive mechanisms [37] to reward users of their efforts, and we do not consider intentional spam in this work.

3. LANDMARK MODELING

In this section, we describe how we extract sizes and coordinates of major geometry features (e.g., widths of store entrances, lengths/orientations of adjoining walls) of landmarks from their images.

3.1 The Landmark Model

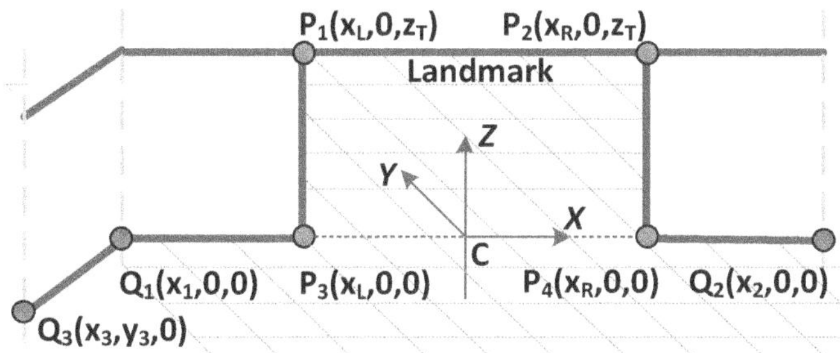

Figure 2: The model of this exemplary store entrance has 4 geometric vertices $P_1 \sim P_4$ and 3 connecting points of wall segments $Q_1 \sim Q_3$ in its local coordinate system.

We use a very simple model to describe the major geometry features of a landmark. As illustrated in Figure 2, a landmark is denoted by $L = (P, Q)$, where P are the main geometric vertices of the landmark (e.g., the four corners $P_1 \sim P_4$ of a store entrance), and Q are connecting points of adjoining wall segments on the floor (e.g., $Q_1 \sim Q_3$ for two wall segments). Each landmark has a local coordinate system, and we place its origin C at the center of the store's entrance line $\overline{P_3P_4}$. The X-axis is co-linear with $\overrightarrow{CP_4}$, the X-Y plane is the ground floor, and the three axes follow the right-hand rule.

We leverage the output of two computer vision techniques, Structure from Motion(SfM) [29] and vanishing line detection [18], to obtain the coordinates of P, Q from landmark images.

Structure from Motion is a mature computer vision technique commonly used to construct the 3D models of an object. Given a set of images of the same object (e.g., a building) from different viewpoints, it produces: 1) a "point cloud" consisting of many points in a local 3D coordinate system. Each point represents a physical point on the object [1]; and 2) the pose (i.e., 3D coordinates and orientations) of the camera for each image, which effectively localizes the camera/user taking that image.

Using SfM only and as-is, however, may not be the best match for indoor floor plan reconstruction. First, SfM relies on large numbers of evenly distributed stable and distinctive image features for detailed and accurate 3D model reconstruction. Although landmarks themselves usually enjoy rich features due to logos, decorations, many in-between sections have too few (e.g., textureless walls), interior (e.g., transparent glass walls) or dynamic (e.g., moving customers) features, which SfM may not handle well. Second, the "point cloud" produced by SfM is not what we need for constructing floor maps. We still have to derive the coordinates of those geometric features in our model, e.g., the corners of an entrance.

3.2 Coordinates of Geometric Vertices

To obtain the coordinates of major geometry vertices needed in the model, we explore a two-phase algorithm. First, we use an existing vanishing line detection algorithm [18] to produce line segments for each image of the same landmark (Figure 3b). We merge co-linear and parallel segments close to each other into long line segments (Figure 3b). This is done using an intersection angle threshold and a distance threshold between two line segments, and both thresholds are set empirically. The merging is repeated for all line segment pairs until no further merging is possible. We filter out the remaining short segments and leave only the long ones.

(a) (b) (c)

Figure 3: Geometric vertices detection work flow: (a) original image. (b) detect line segments parallel to the three orthogonal axes. (c) merged long line segments corresponding to the landmark's major contour lines. Different colors represent different dimensions.

Next, we project merged 2D long lines from each image back into the 3D coordinate system using transformation matrices produced by SfM [29]. We then use an adapted k-means algorithm to cluster the projected 3D lines into groups according to their distance in 3D, and merge each cluster into a 3D line segment. This gives the likely 3D contour lines of the landmark. The intersection points of them are computed for major geometry vertices.

One practical issue that the above algorithm addresses is images taken from relatively extreme angles. Long contour lines (e.g., $\overline{P_1P_2}$ in Figure 2) may become a short segment on such pictures. Because the majority of images are taken more or less front and center, real contour lines will have sufficient numbers of long line segments after the merging and projection. Thus the second phase clustering can identify them while removing "noises" from images of extreme angles.

Due to the same reason, we find that the coordinates of wall segment connecting points farther from the center are not as accurate. This is simply because most images would cover the center of the landmark (e.g., store entrance) but may miss some peripheral areas farther away. Next we use a more reliable method to derive coordinates of wall connecting points.

3.3 Connecting Points of Wall Segments

We project the 3D point cloud of the landmark onto the floor plane, and search for densely distributed points in line shape to find wall segments and their connecting points. This is because the projection of feature points on the same vertical plane/wall would fall onto the joining line to the floor (e.g., $\overline{P_3Q_1}$ of the wall segment adjoining the entrance on left).

We start from some geometry vertices computed previously (e.g., $\overline{P_3P_4}$ gives the projected line of the entrance wall in Figure 2, marked as two diamonds in Figure 4), then find the two ends (e.g., marked as two crosses in Figure 4) of this wall. From each end the search for the next connecting point continues, until no lines consisting of densely distributed points can be found. Figure 4 shows three wall connecting points discovered.

3.4 Example

Figure 4 shows the point cloud of one store entrance projected onto the floor plane and SfM produced camera

[1] To be more exact, each point represents a "feature point" as detected by certain feature extractor algorithms (e.g., [4, 20]).

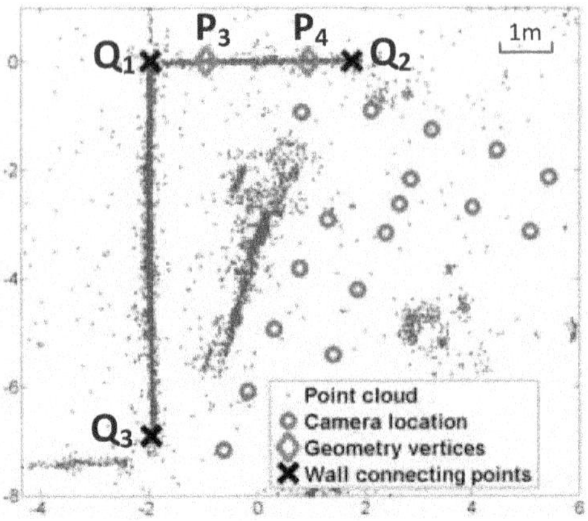

Figure 4: A landmark's point cloud projected to the floor plan, with camera locations, critical contour line (P_3 and P_4) and connecting points of wall segments (Q_1 , Q_2 and Q_3).

locations. We mark the geometry vertices (diamonds) and wall connecting points (crosses). In this example, the width of the entrance has an error of 0.086m (4.78% of the true width 1.8m). We also detect two external wall segments along the hallway, and their intersection angle error is 0.08° out of 90° (0.09%). We find that the 176 camera locations produced by SfM (only some of them are shown) are quite accurate. The localization error is within $1.2m$ at 90% percentile, and maximum error is $1.5m$. We also test how the number of images impacts SfM's localization performance. As we vary the number of photos from 20 to 160, we find that about 80 images are sufficient for camera localization: 75 (94%) images are localized, with 90% error of $1.8m$ and maximum error of $5.2m$. We will present more systematic evaluation results in Section 6.

4. LANDMARK PLACEMENT

In this section, we estimate the *configuration* of landmarks, which is defined as the coordinates and orientations of landmarks in the global 2d coordinate system. We also derive the global coordinates of locations where photos are taken. To this end, we first obtain the spatial relationship between adjacent landmarks from inertial and image data. The determination of the configuration is formulated as an optimization problem that finds the most likely coordinates and orientations of landmarks that achieve the maximal consistency with those pairwise relationship observations.

Once the landmarks' global coordinates are known, the global positions where photos are taken is a simple coordination transformation of the camera location in each landmark's local coordinate system (described in Section 3) to the global one. Such camera positions play an important role in the *augumentation algorithm* for the occupancy map in Section 5.

4.1 Notations

Suppose there are n local coordinate systems corresponding to n landmarks $l_1, l_2, ..., l_n$. $X_i = (x_i, y_i) \in \mathbb{R}^2$ and $\phi_i \in [-\pi, \pi)$ are the x-y coordinates and orientation of landmark l_i in the global coordinate system, respectively. $\boldsymbol{\theta} = (\boldsymbol{X}, \boldsymbol{\phi})$ is the configuration of landmarks to be determined, where $\boldsymbol{X} = (X_1, ..., X_n)$, $\boldsymbol{\phi} = (\phi_1, ..., \phi_n)$.

$R_i = R(\phi_i) = \begin{bmatrix} cos\phi_i & -sin\phi_i \\ sin\phi_i & cos\phi_i \end{bmatrix}$ is the rotation matrix used in coordinate transformation between the global and local coordinate systems of landmark l_i. $X_j^i = (x_j^i, y_j^i) = R(\phi_i)^T(X_j - X_i)$ and $\phi_j^i = \phi_j - \phi_i$ are the x-y coordinates and orientation of landmark l_j in the local coordinate system of landmark l_i, respectively.

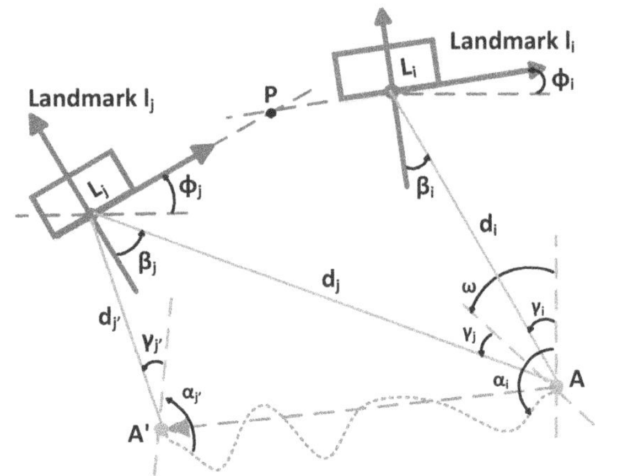

Figure 5: Click-Rotate-Click and Click-Walk-Click: A is where two photos of landmark l_i and l_j are taken in CRC. (d_i, β_i, γ_i) are the length of AL_i, angle formed by line AL_i and normal direction of L_i, angle formed by line AL_i and direction of camera, respectively. P is the intersection point of the two x-axes of the two local coordinate systems. A' is where the walk ends in CWC.

4.2 Spatial Relation Acquisition

The spatial relationship between two adjacent landmarks l_i, l_j are X_j^i and ϕ_j^i, the coordinates and orientation of landmark l_j in the local coordinate system of landmark l_i (or vice versa, illustrated in Figure 5). It is difficult to obtain such measurements directly from users because they do not carry tools such as tapes. We design two data-gathering micro-tasks where the user takes a few actions to gather inertial and image data, from which we compute the pairwise relationship observations.

Click-Rotate-Click (CRC): In this micro-task, a user clicks to take a photo of a landmark l_i from position A (shown in Figure 5), then spins the body and camera for a certain angle (e.g., ω degrees) to take another photo of a second landmark l_j. The angle ω can be obtained quite accurately from the gyroscope [23, 34].

(d_i, β_i, γ_i) represents the distance between camera A and landmark l_i, angle formed by line L_iA and the normal line of landmark l_i, angle formed by line L_iA and the direction of camera A, respectively. They can be derived from the camera pose (i.e., coordinates and orientation in $l_i's$ location coordinate system) as produced by SfM (Section 3). Similar is (d_j, β_j, γ_j). P represents the intersection point of the two x-axes in the two landmarks' local coordinate systems.

From plane geometry, quadrangle AL_iPL_j is uniquely determined given $(d_i, \beta_i, \gamma_i), (d_j, \beta_j, \gamma_j)$ and ω . Thus we can calculate an observation of one landmark's coordinates and orientation in the other's local coordinate system (and vice versa), namely, observations of (ϕ_j^i, X_j^i), (ϕ_i^j, X_i^j) denoted as (O_j^i, Z_j^i) and (O_i^j, Z_i^j).

Click-Walk-Click (CWC): In this micro-task, a user clicks to take a photo of landmark l_i, then walks to another location A' to take another photo of a second landmark l_j. This is useful when two landmarks are farther away and finding one location to take proper photos for both is difficult. The distance $|AA'|$ could be calculated from step counting method [23], and the angle between the direction when user takes a photo and his/her walking direction, i.e. (α_i, α_j') at two locations A and A', could be obtained from placement offset estimation method [24] and gyroscope readings. Measurements calculation here is similar to that of Click-Rotate-Click except that the quadrangle is replaced by a pentagon as illustrated in figure 5.

The two camera locations in CWC can be used as "anchor points" to calibrate the trace. Due to well-known error accumulation [3] in inertial tracking, many methods use anchor points (places of known locations such as entrances/exits of escalators, elevators, stairs) to pinpoint the trace on the floor. In environments with large open space, such anchor points may be sparse. CWC addresses the sparsity issue because users can take photos almost anywhere.

Nevertheless, we use CWC between two landmarks only when CRC is difficult to conduct, because the accuracy of step counting based inertial tracking is limited compared to that of the gyroscope in CRC. Jigsaw utilizes both types of measurements while considering their varying qualities, by assigning different confidences to each type in a common optimization problem (described next in Section 4.3).

4.3 Problem Formulation

We use Maximum Likelihood Estimation (MLE) to formulate the optimal configuration problem. Our problem is represented as a Bayesian belief network(Figure 6) describing the conditional dependence structure among variables (denoted as nodes), where each variable only directly depends on its predecessors.

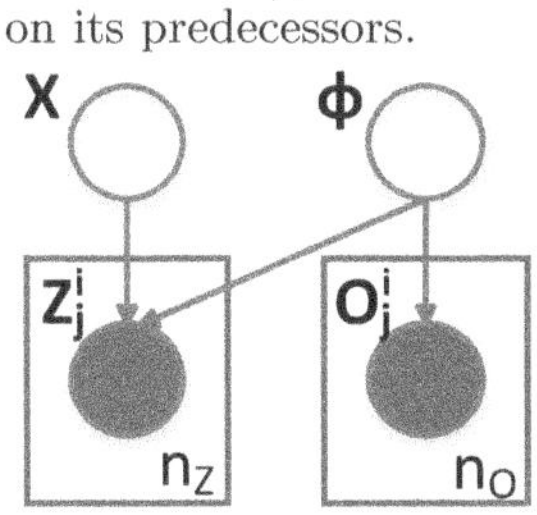

Figure 6: Bayesian belief network representation of our problem. X is the coordinates while ϕ is the orientations of all the landmarks. $\boldsymbol{\theta} = (\boldsymbol{X}, \boldsymbol{\phi})$ is the hidden variable we need to estimate based on measurements. Z_j^i, O_j^i measures the coordinates and orientation of landmark j in the coordinates system of landmark i. Measurements of each kind are aggregated together with the total number of that kind denoted by n_Z, n_O.

We denote the maximum likelihood estimation of $\boldsymbol{\theta}$ as $\boldsymbol{\theta}^*$. The intuition for maximizing $P(\boldsymbol{Z}, \boldsymbol{O}|\boldsymbol{X}, \boldsymbol{\phi})$ is that we try to find a configuration of landmarks $\boldsymbol{\theta}^* = (\boldsymbol{X}^*, \boldsymbol{\phi}^*)$ under which those measurements $\boldsymbol{Z}, \boldsymbol{O}$ (i.e., observations of $\boldsymbol{X}, \boldsymbol{\phi}$) are most likely to be observed.

We have the following equations based on the conditional dependence in the graphical model:

$$\begin{aligned}\boldsymbol{\theta}^* &= \arg\max_{\boldsymbol{\theta}} P(\boldsymbol{Z}, \boldsymbol{O}|\boldsymbol{X}, \boldsymbol{\phi}) = \arg\max_{\boldsymbol{\theta}} P(\boldsymbol{O}|\boldsymbol{\phi})P(\boldsymbol{Z}|\boldsymbol{\phi}, \boldsymbol{X}) \\ &= \arg\min_{\boldsymbol{\theta}} -\sum_{O_j^i} \log P(O_j^i|\boldsymbol{\phi}) - \sum_{Z_j^i} \log P(Z_j^i|\boldsymbol{\phi}, \boldsymbol{X})\end{aligned}$$

As is standard in probabilistic mapping literature [7], we assume Gaussian measurement models that give further transformation into:

$$\boldsymbol{\theta}^* = \arg\min_{\boldsymbol{\theta}} \sum_{O_j^i} \frac{\|\phi_j^i - O_j^i\|^2}{\sigma_O^2} + \sum_{Z_j^i} \frac{\|X_j^i - Z_j^i\|^2}{\lambda_Z^2} \tag{1}$$

where σ_O, λ_Z are covariances of normally distributed zero-mean measurement noises for different kinds of measurements. As noted in Section 4.2, we assign small σ_O, λ_Z for CRC measurements to give them predominance over those of CWC.

Without losing generality, we can simply use variable substitution to yield an equivalent nonlinear least squares formulation:

$$\underset{\boldsymbol{\phi}, \boldsymbol{X}}{\text{minimize}} \quad \sum_{O_j^i} \|\phi_j^i - O_j^i\|^2 + \sum_{Z_j^i} \|X_j^i - Z_j^i\|^2 \tag{2}$$

The intuition is that we try to find a configuration of landmarks $\boldsymbol{\theta}^* = (\boldsymbol{X}^*, \boldsymbol{\phi}^*)$ such that the aggregate difference between ϕ_j^i, X_j^i derived from $(\boldsymbol{X}^*, \boldsymbol{\phi}^*)$ and their measurements O_j^i, Z_j^i is minimized.

4.4 Optimization Algorithm

Let's denote problem (2) as:

$$\underset{\boldsymbol{\phi}, \boldsymbol{X}}{\text{minimize}} \quad f(\boldsymbol{\phi}) + g(\boldsymbol{\phi}, \boldsymbol{X}) \tag{3}$$

since the two terms in (2) are functions of $\boldsymbol{\phi}$ and $(\boldsymbol{\phi}, \boldsymbol{X})$.

Careful examination [13] shows that each term in $g(\boldsymbol{\phi}, \boldsymbol{X})$ is linear square of $\boldsymbol{X}$, thus $g(\boldsymbol{\phi}, \boldsymbol{X})$ is a typical linear least squares of $\boldsymbol{X}$ with a closed form solution. We denote the the minimum as $h(\boldsymbol{\phi})$. Thus problem (3) is equivalent to:

$$\underset{\boldsymbol{\phi}}{\text{minimize}} \quad f(\boldsymbol{\phi}) + h(\boldsymbol{\phi}) \tag{4}$$

We solve this problem based on an observation: minimizing $f(\boldsymbol{\phi})$ gives the most likely orientation $\boldsymbol{\phi}'$ of landmarks with orientation relationship observations only. Due to relatively accurate gyroscope data, $\boldsymbol{\phi}'$ would be very close to the global optimal $\boldsymbol{\phi}^*$ that minimizes $f(\boldsymbol{\phi}) + h(\boldsymbol{\phi})$. Thus we find the optimum of $f(\boldsymbol{\phi})$ as the initial value, then use stochastic gradient descent (SGD) to find the global minimum $\boldsymbol{\phi}^*$.

STEP 1: Find $\boldsymbol{\phi}'$ given measurements $\boldsymbol{O}$.

$$\underset{\boldsymbol{\phi}}{\text{minimize}} \quad f(\boldsymbol{\phi}) = \sum_{O_j^i} \|\phi_j^i - O_j^i\|^2 \tag{5}$$

Note that this is not a linear least squares problem since the result of the subtraction on angles is periodic with a period of 2π. What adds to the difficulty is the loop dependence of the orientations of different landmarks. The effect of adjusting the orientation of one landmark would propagate along pairwise relationship observations, eventually back to itself.

We solve this problem as follows: First we find the maximum spanning tree in the orientation dependence graph where edges are relationship observations between landmarks. This problem $f_{MST}(\boldsymbol{\phi})$ can be easily solved because adjusting the orientation of one landmark has a one-way effects on its decedents only. Again, due to the accuracy of gyroscope and relatively small number of removed edges (i.e., relationship observations), the resulting $\boldsymbol{\phi}'_{MST}$ would

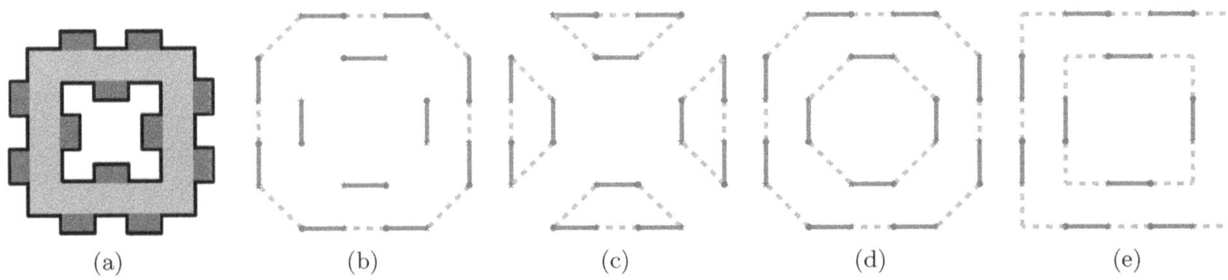

Figure 7: Comparison between different algorithms: (a) Example scenario (b) convex hull of all wall segments (c) one possible output of the greedy method (d) minimal weight matching using distance as weight (e) our minimal weight matching method.

be in near neighborhood of the true optimum ϕ'. Then we perform gradient descent from ϕ'_{MST} find a minimum likely to be ϕ'. In reality we do find them are usually in close neighborhood.

STEP 2: perform stochastic gradient descent (SGD) from ϕ' to find ϕ^*. Based on the intuition explained earlier that ϕ' is close to ϕ^*, we perform SGD which is known to be able to climb out of "local minima" to find the global minimum with higher probability.

5. MAP AUGMENTATION

After obtaining the optimal coordinates and orientations of the landmarks, we need more details for a relatively complete floor plan: 1) wall reconstruction for external boundaries of the hallway; 2) hallway structure; and 3) rough shapes of rooms. Next we describe how to construct such details.

5.1 Wall Reconstruction

Connecting wall segments between adjacent landmarks in manners "most consistent" with the likely architectural structure of buildings is not trivial. Naive methods such as using a convex hull to cover all segments produces an external boundary but may not connect those segments "inside" the hull (Figure 7(b)).

To formally define the problem, we represent a wall segment as a line segment with its normal direction pointing to the hallway, and denote the endpoints on its left/right side as L and R (shown in Figure 8). Thus k wall segments have two sets of endpoints $\boldsymbol{L} = \{L_1, L_2, ..., L_k\}$ and $\boldsymbol{R} = \{R_1, R_2, ..., R_k\}$. We need to add new wall segments connecting each endpoint in $\boldsymbol{L}$ to one in $\boldsymbol{R}$ (shown in Figure 8).

Every possible solution corresponds to a perfect matching π, where π is a permutation of $(1, 2, ..., k)$, indicating $L(i)$ and $R(\pi(i))$ are linked for $i = 1, 2, ..., k$. Thus the problem becomes a combinatorial optimization problem that finds the perfect matching with the minimal weight (i.e., most likely connection manner) in a bipartite graph.

A simple greedy algorithm uses distance as weight and connects every endpoint in set $\boldsymbol{L}$ to the closest (i.e., least distance) one in set $\boldsymbol{R}$ directly. The drawback is that the result depends on the order of connecting endpoints, and 90° corners commonly seen in buildings may be missing. E.g., Figure 7(c) and 7(d) show two possible results, where one is incorrect while the other does not have 90° corners.

To address the above issues, we consider the two following options of linking two adjacent wall segments. Each option carries a weight, which can be computed given two endpoints

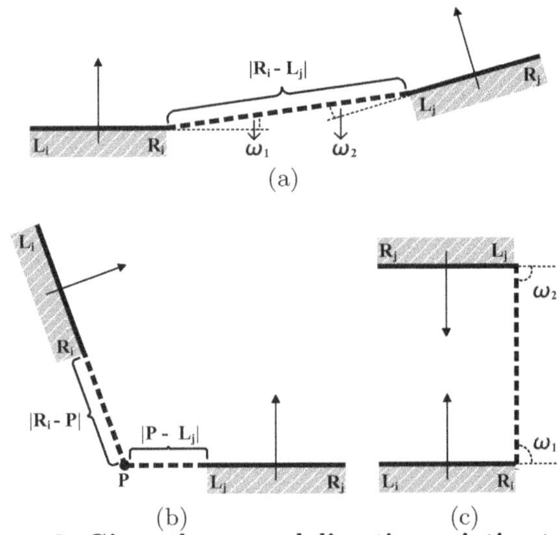

Figure 8: Given the normal direction pointing to the hallway, two endpoints of a wall segment are labeled L and R. New wall segments must link endpoints with different labels. Three cases of connection are shown: (a) two nearly collinear segments; (b) two nearly perpendicular segments; and (c) two nearly opposite segments.

in $\boldsymbol{L}$ and $\boldsymbol{R}$. The weight represents the likelihood of the option: a smaller one indicates a more likely linking manner.

Linking with another segment directly. Two segments (L_i, R_i) and (L_j, R_j) are linked by another segment between L_i and R_j directly. The weight is defined as:

$$w_{ij}^{(1)} = |R_i - L_j|(\omega_1 + \omega_2) \tag{6}$$

where $|R_i - L_j|$ is the distance between two endpoints R_i and L_j and ω_1, ω_2 are the turning angles from segments (L_i, R_i), (L_j, R_j) to the newly added segment (illustrated in Figure 8(a) and 8(c)). Such direct linking is more likely when two adjacent segments are collinear or facing each other.

Extending to an intersection. If the two segments are not parallel, extending them from endpoints R_i and L_j reaches a point of intersection. This is another possibility and its weight is defined as:

$$w_{ij}^{(2)} = \frac{|R_i - P| + |P - L_j|}{2} \tag{7}$$

where P is the point of intersection and $|R_i - P|$ and $|P - L_j|$ are the distances among them (illustrated in Figure 8(b)). For two (close to) perpendicular segments, the

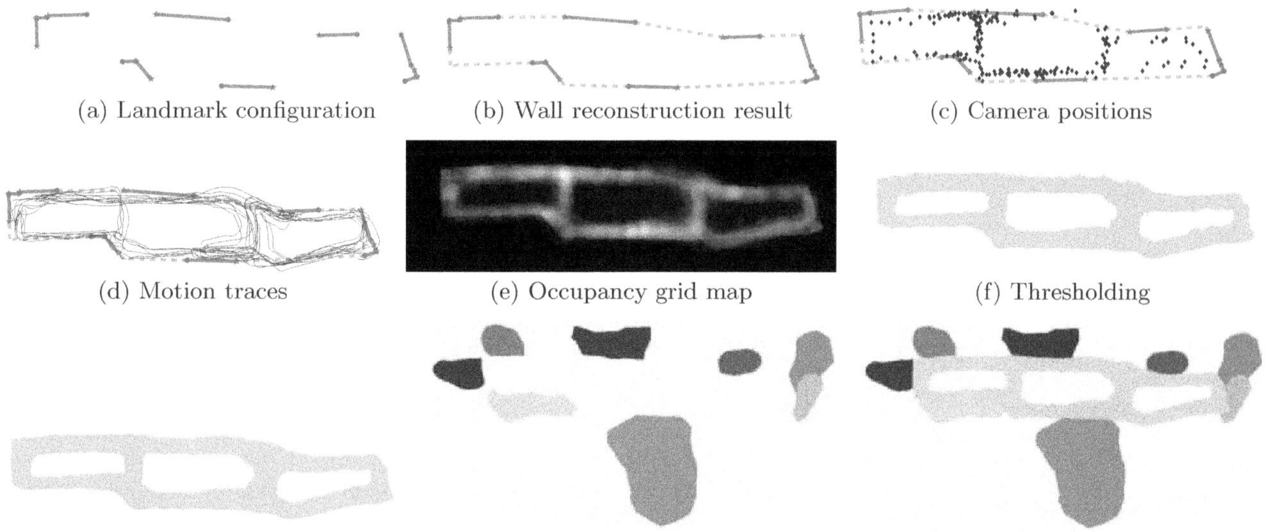

(a) Landmark configuration (b) Wall reconstruction result (c) Camera positions

(d) Motion traces (e) Occupancy grid map (f) Thresholding

(g) Smoothing (h) Room reconstruction result (i) Final floor plan

Figure 9: Augmentation process: (a) shows landmark configuration results. (b) depicts hallway external boundary after wall reconstruction. (c) and (d) show camera positions and motion traces. Combining the above, occupancy grid map is shown in (e), followed by thresholding (f), and smoothing (g). (h) depicts room reconstruction results and the final floor plan is shown in (i).

above equation produces a smaller weight, ensuring proper connection for 90° corners.

Given the configuration of landmarks estimated in Section 4, we calculate $w_{ij}^{(1)}$ and $w_{ij}^{(2)}$ for each pair of wall segments based on (6) and (7). We define the weight w_{ij} of linking L_i and R_j as the smaller of the two:

$$w_{ij} = \begin{cases} \min(w_{ij}^{(1)}, w_{ij}^{(2)}), & i \neq j; \\ \infty, & i = j. \end{cases} \quad (8)$$

the weight is ∞ if $i = j$ since the two endpoints of the same segment is already connected.

Given all the weights, we can find the perfect matching π^* to minimize the total weight as follows:

$$\underset{\pi}{\text{minimize}} \quad \sum_{i=1}^{k} w_{i\pi(i)}. \quad (9)$$

While a naive exhaustive search needs factorial time, we recognize that finding the perfect matching with minimal weight in a bipartite graph can be solved effectively by Kuhn-Munkres algorithm [16] in polynomial time ($O(n^3)$) where n is the number of landmarks, which is usually a small number (e.g., tens of stores for one floor of a mall). Figure 7(e) shows the correct result produced by our algorithm and Figure 9(b) illustrates the outcome in a real environment.

5.2 Hallway Reconstruction

To reconstruct the structure of the whole hallway, we first build the occupancy grid map [30], which is a dominant paradigm for environment modeling in mobile robotics. Occupancy grid map represents environments by fine-grained grid cells each with a variable representing the probability that the cell is accessible.

In Jigsaw, it can be regarded as a confidence map that reflects the positions accessible to people. This confidence map is initialized as a matrix full of zeros. We add confidence to a cell if there is evidence that it is accessible and the scale of the confidence we add depends on how much we trust the evidence. We fuse three kinds of cues to reconstruct the occupancy grid map.

External boundary of the hallway: This is reconstructed in Section 5.1. Due to obstacles (e.g., indoor plants placed next to the wall), the accessible positions are not equivalent to the region bounded by the external boundary. Since the area in front of landmarks are often the entrance, it is always accessible and we assign higher confidence. Places in front of a newly added wall is usually accessible but obstacles may exist. Thus we assign less confidence to such places.

Positions of cameras: Positions of cameras can be computed given the configuration of landmarks and relative position between cameras and landmarks. Such positions are obviously accessible. So we add confidence to places around every camera's position. Figure 9(c) depicts positions of cameras with the result of wall reconstruction.

Motion traces in the hallway: The shape of motion traces can be computed using methods such as [23,24]. The traces can be calibrated by taking photos and using their locations as anchor points. Given such information, we can correct the step length, which is one main source of error in step-counting based tracking. Such traces in the hallway add confidence to positions along them. Because motion traces usually carry higher errors, we assign less confidence along motion traces comparing to positions of cameras. Figure 9(d) depicts motion traces in the hallway with the result of wall reconstruction.

The final occupancy grid map is shown in Figure 9(e). We use an automatic threshold based binaryzation technique [21] to determine whether each cell is accessible, thus creating a binary map indicating which cells are accessible. The accumulation of evidences makes our method robust to noises and outliers in crowdsensed input: a cell is considered accessibly only when there is enough evidence. The result of thresholding is depicted in Figure 9(f). To further improve the result, we implement a smoothing algorithm based on

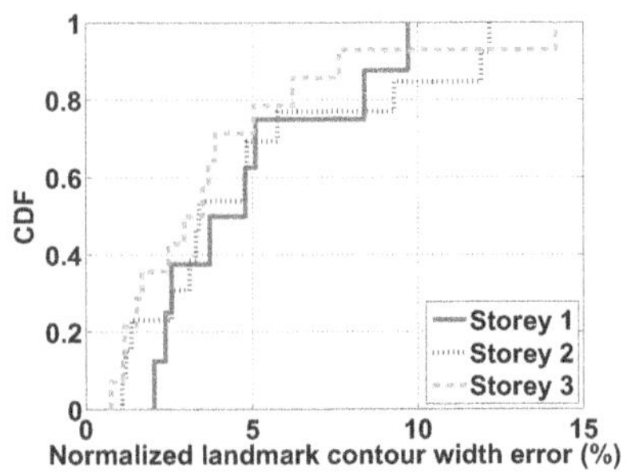

Figure 10: Normalized store entrance width error.

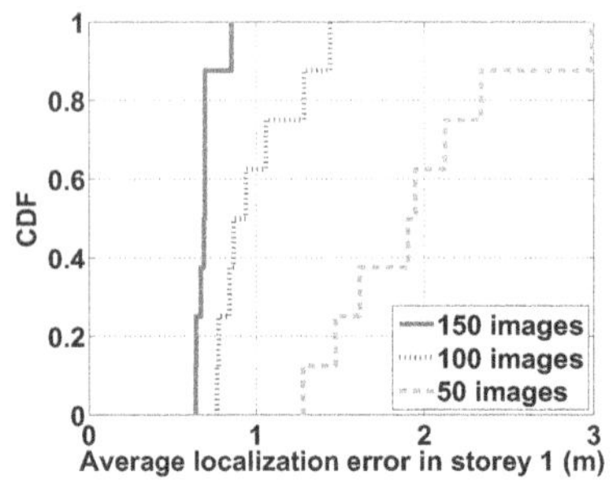

Figure 11: Impact of image quantities

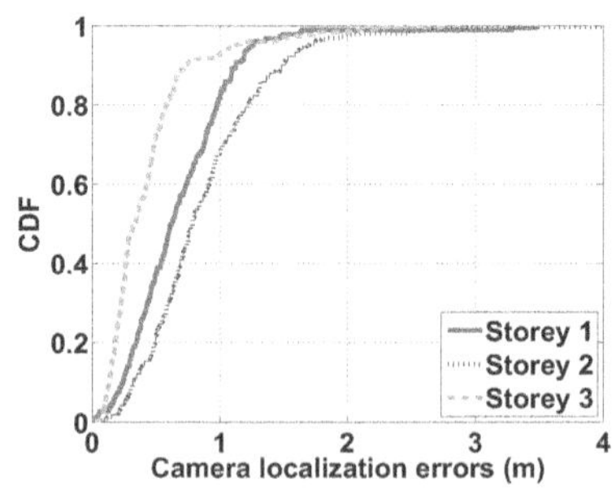

Figure 12: Image localization errors.

alpha-shape [3], which is a generalization of the concept of convex hull. Figure 9(g) shows the final result of hallway reconstruction after smoothing.

5.3 Room Reconstruction

We use the same confidence map technique to fuse two kinds of cues for robust estimation of the shape of rooms.

Wall segments in landmark models: These wall segments are not only part of the external boundary of the hallway, but also the boundary of the room. Thus the places inside the detected wall segments are part of the room with a high confidence.

Motion traces inside the room: We have a data-gathering micro-task similar to CWC to collect data for rooms. A user takes a photo of a landmark, then walks into this room. After walking for a while, the user exits and takes another photo. The photos are used to determine the initial/final locations of the trace, and the area along the trace receives confidence. We perform similar thresholding of the cumulated confidence to determine the accessibility of each cell, producing room reconstruction results similar to that shown in Figure 9(h). The final floor plan at the end of map augmentation is in Figure 9(i).

6. PERFORMANCE EVALUATION

6.1 Methodology

We use iPhone 4s to collect images and motion sensor data in three environments: two storeys of a $150 \times 75m$ shopping mall (labeled storey 1 and 2) of irregular shape, and one storey of a $140 \times 40m$ long and narrow mall comprised of two parts connected by two long corridors (labeled part I and II of storey 3). In these environments, we select 8, 13 and 14 store entrances as landmarks and collect about 150 photos at different distances and angles for each landmark. In each environment, we have 182, 184 and 151 locations where users conduct "Click-Rotate-Click" to take two images of two nearby landmarks, and 24 "Click-Walk-Click" to take two images of two far away landmarks in different parts in storey 3. We also collect 96, 106 and 73 user traces along the hallway of each environment, and about 7 traces inside each store.

6.2 Landmark Modeling

First we examine the accuracy of estimated widths of store entrances using normalized error (error divided by the true width). As Figure 10 shows, 90-percentile error is about 10%, which indicates that the inferred parameters of major geometry vertices are quite accurate. We also find that large errors are caused by obstructions such as pillars or hanging scrolls.

We evaluate wall segment detection accuracy, and observe that the recall (i.e., detected wall segments in all existing segments) is 91.7%, 88.2% and 100% in three indoor environments, respectively; while the precision (i.e., fraction of detected ones that are correct) are all 100%. This shows that the wall connecting point detection is quite accurate as well. Those segments not detected are due to extreme angles (e.g., less than 15° difference) to the entrance wall, which are considered part of the same segment by the algorithm.

We measure how the quantity of images impact localization accuracy to understand its impact on SfM performance. For each environment, we randomly select 50, 100 and 150 images for each landmark. We can see that the fraction of localized images increase steadily from 74.5%, 95% to 99.3%. When there are sufficient images (e.g., 100 $\sim$ 150), nearly all of them are localized.

We also observe similar trend in the average localization error for each landmark in storey 1 (shown in Figure 11; the other two are similar). When there are sufficient images, the average error is less than 2m. Thus 100 $\sim$ 150 images for each landmark would be an appropriate amount.

Finally we examine image localization accuracy (shown in Figure 12). We observe that localization errors are about $1 \sim 1.5m$ at 90-percentile. The large errors are due to "isolated" images taken from extreme distances (e.g., too faraway) or angles (e.g., almost parallel to the entrance wall), which cannot find enough matching feature points with the majority of images taken more front and center. We observe that storey 3 has the least error, due to its smaller size so images are distributed more densely and thus appear similar to each other.

6.3 Landmark Placement

Measurements accuracy. We first evaluate the relative position and orientation errors as derived from pairwise measurements (Section 4.2) between adjacent landmarks. Relative position error is the distance between a landmark's derived position and its true position, both in the other landmark's coordinate system. Relative orientation error quantifies how close the derived orientation difference is to ground truth.

We use 182, 184, 151 CRC measurements in three environments, and 24 CWC measurements in storey 3 between its two parts. Figure 13(a) and 13(b) show the cumulative distribution functions (CDF) of relative position and orientation errors in three environments. We can see that for CRC measurements, the 80-percentile relative position errors are about 2 $\sim$ 7m, while that of relative orientation about 10 $\sim$ 20°, both of which have quite some inaccuracies. CWC measurements have worse position errors (80-percentile around 10m) but comparable

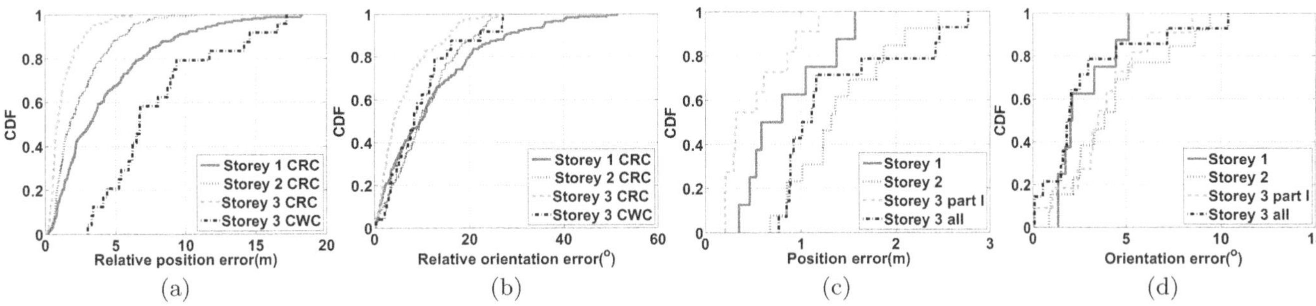

Figure 13: CDFs of landmark placement evaluation: (a) relative position error extracted from crowdsourced data; (b) relative orientation error extracted from crowdsourced data; (c) position error of proposed algorithm for landmark level mapping; (d) orientation error of proposed algorithm for landmark level mapping.

orientation errors (80-percentile at 15°). This is because of errors in stride length estimation, but the gyroscope remains accurate.

Landmark configuration. We compare the computed landmark positions and orientations to respective ground truth to examine errors in the derived configuration. Figure 13(c) and 13(d) show the CDFs of position and orientation errors. Since CRC measurements alone cannot join the two parts of storey 3, we give CRC accuracy for part I (containing most stores). Compared with respective errors in measurements (shown in Figure 13(a) and 13(b)), both position and orientation errors improve (e.g., $1 \sim 2m$ and $5 \sim 9°$ at 90-percentile). This is because errors in measurements are statistically symmetric, thus the impacts tend to cancel out each other.

After CWC measurements are combined, there is not much change in orientation but slight degradation in positions (e.g., 2.5m at 90-percentile) due to relatively lower accuracy of CWC position measurements. This shows that CWC may impact the accuracy. Thus we use them only when CRC alone cannot establish the spatial relationship between faraway landmarks. The relative positions in each part do not change much, due to different weights assigned to CRC and CWC measurements. In summary, the landmark placement algorithm successfully combines all measurements for better estimation of the most likely configuration.

6.4 Floor plan performance

The reconstructed floor plans and their respective ground truths are shown in Figure 14(a), 14(b), 14(c) and Figure 14(d), 14(e), 14(f).

Positions of feature points. We evaluate the quality of floor plans using the root mean square error (RMSE). Given n feature positions on a floor plan with 2D coordinates $X_i^{map} = (x_i^{map}, y_i^{map})$, and their corresponding ground truth coordinates $X_i^{test} = (x_i^{test}, y_i^{test})$, $i = 1, 2, ..., n$, the RMSE is calculated by

$$e_{RMS} = \sqrt{\frac{\sum_{i=1}^{n} (X_i^{map} - X_i^{test})^2}{n}} \tag{10}$$

For each environment, we select two sets of feature positions, one for landmarks, the other for center points of hallway intersections. We can see that RMSEs of landmarks are small (e.g., $< 1.5m$) while those for intersections are slightly larger (Table 1). Note that for storey 3, we calculate the RMSEs for the left and the right part separately since each part was reconstructed using relatively accurate CRC data while the connecting hallway between them uses less accurate CWC data.

Table 1: RMSE of floor plans (m)

	Landmarks	Intersections
Storey 1	0.94	1.25
Storey 2	1.49	1.80
Storey 3	0.61/0.15	0.91/0.49

Hallway shape. We also evaluate how close the shapes of constructed hallways resemble respective ground truth. We overlay the reconstructed hallway onto its ground truth to achieve maximum overlap by aligning both the center point and the orientation. Precision is the ratio of the size of the overlap area to the whole reconstructed hallway, and recall is that to the ground truth hallway. F-score is the harmonic average of precision and recall. The results are shown in Table 2. We can see that Jigsaw achieves a precision around 80%, a recall around 90% and a F-score around 84% for the first two storeys. This shows the effect of the calibration of traces by camera locations, and probabilistic occupancy maps that are more robust to errors and outliers. The reason that recalls are higher than precisions (as shown in Figure 14) is that reconstructed hallway is a little thicker than the ground truth due to errors in traces. Storey 3 has a relative lower performance because only CWC data can be used to connect the left and right parts.

Table 2: Evaluation of hallway shape

	Precision	Recall	F-score
Storey 1	77.8%	92.0%	84.3%
Storey 2	81.2%	93.3%	86.9%
Storey 3	74.5%	86.0%	79.8%

Room size. We use the error of reconstructed room size as the metric. Jigsaw achieves an average error of 25.6%, 28.3% and 28.9% respectively for 3 storeys. Given the fact that some part of room is not accessible, the errors are relatively small since camera localization provides accurate anchor points to calibrate the errors of inertial traces and the probabilistic occupancy map provides robustness to outliers.

6.5 Comparison with CrowdInside

We compare the reconstruction performance of Jigsaw to that of CrowdInside [3]. Jigsaw utilizes vision techniques and incurs more overhead in collecting and processing images, producing detailed positions and orientations of individual landmarks. CrowdInside is much lighter weight and uses mostly mobile traces. Its design is based on several assumptions: 1) sufficient numbers of anchor points (e.g., locations with GPS reception or special inertial data

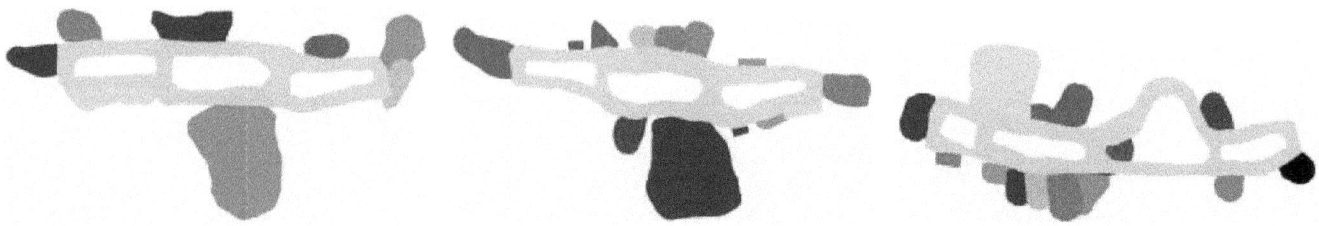

(a) Reconstructed floor plan 1 (b) Reconstructed floor plan 2 (c) Reconstructed floor plan 3

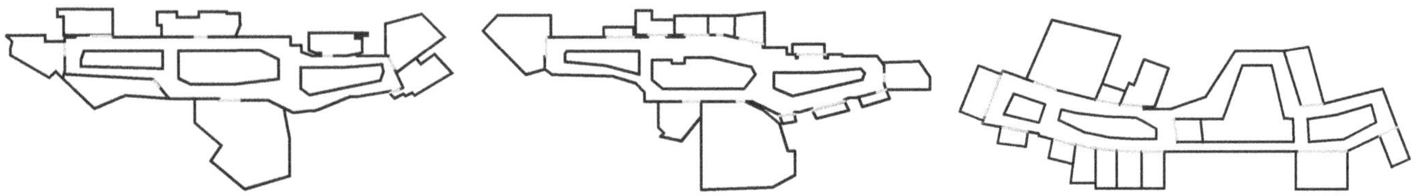

(d) Ground truth floor plan 1 (e) Ground truth floor plan 2 (f) Ground truth floor plan 3

Figure 14: Reconstructed floor plans and ground truth floor plans

signature such as escalators/elevators/stairs) for calibrating traces; 2) sufficient amount of traces that pass through these anchor points; 3) distinctive WiFi signatures in different rooms.

In reality we find that they may not always hold in all environments. For example, in storey 2 there are only 3 inertial anchor points and no GPS reception; traces that do not pass through (e.g., start/end at) these 3 anchor points cannot be placed relative to other traces on the common ground plane; variations in WiFi signatures may cause incorrect room classification. As a result, the direct application of CrowdInside where these requirements do not hold may generate "unusable" floor plans that is hard to recognize.

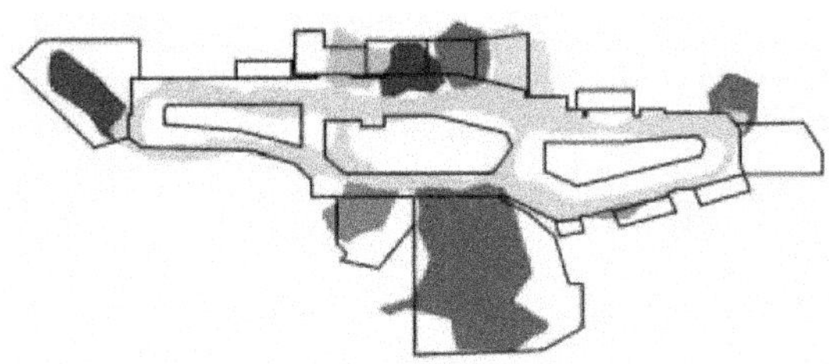

Figure 15: Constructed floor plan of storey 2 by CrowdInside++, which has several artificial improvements that are not always possible in reality.

To deal with these conditions, we make several artificial improvements to CrowdInside: 1) We double the number of anchor points and assume they are all GPS-based, thus more accurate global coordinates can be used to calibrate traces; 2) we make all traces pass through adjacent anchor points so they can be placed on the common floor plane; 3) we manually classify room traces so that their labeling is 100% correct. We call such an artificially improved version CrowdInside++.

The landmark positions of CrowdInside++ have an RMSE of $6.26m$, and the maximum error $8.92m$; the RMSE of intersections is $7.36m$ and maximum error is $9.84m$. All of these are four times larger than those of Jigsaw. We also notice that CrowdInside++ does not detect a few small-sized stores due to the ambiguity differentiating hallway and store traces. While Jigsaw uses images and can always detect such stores. The hallway shape of CrowdInside++ has a 48.2% recall, a 64.0% precision and a 55.0% F-score, which are much worse than those of Jigsaw shown in Table 2. The average error for room sizes is 42.7%, also much larger than that of Jigsaw. Note such performance is achieved after several artificial improvements which may not always be possible in reality.

The above shows that inertial-only approach cannot handle error accumulation well when there are not sufficient anchor points, while Jigsaw can use any camera location to calibrate traces. The landmark placement optimization and the probabilistic occupancy map also make Jigsaw much more robust to errors and outliers, whereas the deterministic alpha-shape in CrowdInside cannot tolerate outliers.

7. DISCUSSION

In practise, the performance of SfM may be affected by multiple factors, some of which have been studied in literature. When the number of images is insufficient, the point cloud may not be accurate enough. There has been work [8] that guides the selection of images such that a small quantity can still produce reasonably good output. Such technique may help improve the performance on camera localization. The scale-invariant features extracted by SIFT [20] gives SfM robustness against differences in resolution, orientation, and certain illumination conditions (e.g., noon vs. morning sunlight). Random variations such as moving customer flows, obstructions such as pillars constitute disturbances to the appearances of landmarks. Thus more images of stable features would be needed to offset the impact of such disturbances.

Our landmark model needs image classification so that images of the same landmark are used as input. With proper and sufficient incentives, users may be willing to tag photos to help ease the classification. There also has been study [35] on automated classification that can achieve high accuracy. Our landmark model is quite simple and most suitable for store or room entrances on a frontal wall. Although this captures a great portion of indoor landmarks, there are others (e.g., a Christmas tree) that do not fit this model, and more advanced model would be needed.

Accurate user trajectories are shown quite a challenge [23, 24] because inertial data is impacted by many factors such as the make/model, position of the device (e.g., in hand/pocket), relative movement to the human body (e.g., holding still vs. swinging arms). Some of these may change during the user movements. In light of that, we assign a relatively lower confidence to such trajectories and use a probabilistic model when using them to build hallway and room occupancy maps.

The collection of image and inertial data takes some energy. The power consumption for accelerometer and gyroscope sampling is pretty low (e.g., about 30mW [1]), while people customarily take tens of or more photos during a trip. Jigsaw uses downsized images of 800×600 resolution, each about 100kB. Based on WiFi radio transmission power around 700mW [5] and practical speed of 2MB/s, uploading 20 photos would cost about 0.7 Joule. Compared to the battery capacity of 20k Joules, we believe the capturing and uploading of a few tens images, and collecting a few traces, do not constitute any signification power consumption for an user. The photos may contain customer faces, which may need to be blurred (e.g., like Google street view) for privacy. On the other hand, we find that store owners welcome such exposure because they view the appearance of their logos on maps as a form of advertisement.

8. RELATED WORK

Floor plan construction. Indoor floor plan construction is a relatively new problem in mobile computing. A few pieces of work has conducted very valuable initial investigation, using mostly inertial and WiFi data. CrowdInside [3] leverages inertial data from accelerometer, gyroscope and compass to reconstruct users' mobile trajectories, and use "anchor points" with unique sensing data such as elevators, stairs, escalators and locations with GPS reception to correct accumulated errors. The trajectories serve as hints about accessible areas, from which hallways, rooms can be identified. Such "anchor" points are also used for user localization (e.g., Unloc [34]).

Jiang et. al. [14] propose a series of algorithms to detect similarities in WiFi signatures between different rooms and hallway segments to find their adjacency, and combine inertial data to obtain hallway lengths and orientations to construct floor plans. Walkie-Markie [26] also leverages WiFi signals, but it uses locations where the trend of WiFi signal strength reverses direction as anchor points, which are found to be more stable than signatures themselves. MapGenie [22] uses mobile trajectories as well. But instead of the sensors in smartphones, it leverages foot-mounted IMU (Inertail Measurement Unit) which is less affected by different positions of the phone.

Compared to the above, we combine vision and mobile techniques of complementary strengths, extracting detailed geometry information about individual landmarks from images, while inferring the structure and shapes of the hallway and rooms from inertial data. We also use optimization and probabilistic techniques so that the results are robust to errors and outliers in crowdsensed data.

SLAM. Learning maps in an unexplored environment is the famous SLAM (Simultaneous Localization And Mapping) problem in robotics [10, 11]. One has to estimate the poses (2D/3D locations and orientations) of the robot, and locations of landmarks from robot control and environment measurement parameters. Various sensors such as odometry, gyroscope, depth/stereo cameras and laser rangers are used.

We share similar goals with SLAM, but our input and problem have significant differences. First, crowdsensed data is not just noisy, but also piece-wise, collected from mostly uncoordinated users. While in SLAM a robot usually has special high precision sensors (e.g., laser ranges, depth/stearo cameras) and systematically explores all accessible areas. We use commodity mobile devices which do not have such sensors; the mobile trajectories are also highly noisy due to error accumulation. Second, we estimate landmarks' orientations as well, while SLAM does only their locations. The existence of loops in the dependence relationship of measurements also adds to the complexity of our problem.

3D construction. There has been significant amount of literature for reconstructing the 3D model of buildings in computer vision. They take different approaches and require different kinds and amount of data. Some of them are interactive [6,28] and need continuous user intervention; some are automatic [9,36] and exploit prior knowledge about the relations among building primitives (e.g., walls, doors and windows); some take advantage of laser ranger data to produce very detailed and accurate exterior models [33].

Indoor floor plan is essentially a 2D model and we realize that indiscriminate and uniform details are not necessary. This insight enables us to use vision techniques for individual landmarks only while using much lighter weight mobile techniques for landmark placement, hallway and rooms. This approach greatly reduces the effort and overhead for capturing and processing large amount of data (some of which may require special hardware such as laser rangers not available on commodity mobile devices), yet still generate reasonably complete and accurate floor plans.

Vision-based localization. Computer vision techniques have been used for localization as well. Some work [15,17,32] compares a test image against a database of pre-captured benchmark images, finds the "closest" match and uses its location. Sextant [31] leverages photos and gyroscope on smartphones to measure users' relative positions to physical objects, thus localizing users. Some first reconstruct 3D model of the scene using depth information (e.g., from laser rangers) or by crawling large numbers of Internet images, and then computes the most likely location of an image against the 3D scene model [19, 25]. We simply leverage the ability of SfM to compute the pose, thus the location of the camera taking the image.

9. CONCLUSION

In this paper, we propose Jigsaw, which combines vision and mobile techniques that take crowdsensed image and inertial data to produce floor plans for complex indoor environments. It addresses one key obstacle to the ubiquitous coverage of indoor localization service: lack of floor plans at service providers. Jigsaw enables service providers to reconstruct floor plans at scale from mobile users' data, thus avoiding the intensive efforts and time needed in business negotiations or environment surveys. We have presented the detailed design, and conducted extensive experiments in three storeys (two with irregular shapes) of two large shopping malls. The results demonstrate that Jigsaw can produce reasonably complete and accurate locations/orientations of landmarks, and structures/shapes of hallways and rooms.

10. REFERENCES

[1] Accelerometer, Gyro and IMU Buying Guide. `https://www.sparkfun.com/pages/accel_gyro_guide`.

[2] Google indoor maps availability. `http://support.google.com/gmm/bin/answer.py?hl=en\&answer=1685827`.

[3] M. Alzantot and M. Youssef. Crowdinside: Automatic construction of indoor floorplans. In *SIGSPATIAL*, 2012.
[4] H. Bay, A. Ess, T. Tuytelaars, and L. V. Gool. Surf: Speeded up robust features. In *Computer Vision and Image Understanding*, 2008.
[5] A. Carroll and G. Heiser. An analysis of power consumption in a smartphone. In *Proceedings of USENIX Annual Technical Conference*, 2010.
[6] P. E. Debevec, C. J. Taylor, and J. Malik. Modeling and rendering architecture from photographs. In *SIGGRAPH*, 1996.
[7] F. Dellaert and M. Kaess. Square root sam: Simultaneous localization and mapping via square root information smoothing. *The International Journal of Robotics Research*, 25(12):1181–1203, 2006.
[8] J. Delon and B. Rouge. Small baseline stereovision. *Journal of Mathematical Imaging and Vision*, 2007.
[9] A. Dick, P. Torr, and R. Cipolla. Modelling and interpretation of architecture from several images. *International Journal of Computer Vision*, pages 111–134, November 2004.
[10] H. Durrant-Whyte and T. Bailey. Simultaneous localisation and mapping (slam): Part I the essential algorithms. *Robotics and Automation Magazine*, 2006.
[11] H. Durrant-Whyte and T. Bailey. Simultaneous localisation and mapping (slam): Part II state of the art. *Robotics and Automation Magazine*, 2006.
[12] R. Ganti, F. Ye, and H. Lei. Mobile crowdsensing: Current state and future challenges. *IEEE Communication Magzine*, 2011.
[13] S. Huang, Y. Lai, U. Frese, and G. Dissanayake. How far is slam from a linear least squares problem? In *Intelligent Robots and Systems (IROS), 2010 IEEE/RSJ International Conference on*, pages 3011–3016. IEEE, 2010.
[14] Y. Jiang, Y. Xiang, X. Pan, K. Li, Q. Lv, R. P. Dick, L. Shang, and M. Hannigan. Hallway based automatic indoor floorplan construction using room fingerprints. In *Ubicomp*, 2013.
[15] J. Kosecka, L. Zhou, P. Barber, and Z. Duric. Qualitative image based localization in indoors environments. In *IEEE CVPR*, 2003.
[16] H. W. Kuhn. The hungarian method for the assignment problem. *Naval research logistics quarterly*, 2(1-2):83–97, 1955.
[17] P. Lamon, I. R. Nourbakhsh, B. Jensen, and R. Siegwart. Deriving and matching image fingerprint sequences for mobile robot localization. In *IEEE International Conference on Robotics and Automation*, 2001.
[18] D. C. Lee, M. Hebert, and T. Kanade. Geometric reasoning for single image structure recovery. In *IEEE CVPR*, 2009.
[19] J. Z. Liang, N. Corso, E. Turner, and A. Zakhor. Image based localization in indoor environments. In *IEEE COM.Geo*, 2013.
[20] D. G. Lowe. Object recognition from local scale-invariant features. In *ICCV*, 1999.
[21] N. Otsu. A threshold selection method from gray-level histograms. *IEEE Transactions on Systems, Man, and Cybernetics*, 9(1):62–66, 1979.
[22] D. Philipp, P. Baier, C. Dibak, F. DÍźrr, K. Rothermel, S. Becker, M. Peter, and D. Fritsch. Mapgenie: Grammar-enhanced indoor map construction from crowd-sourced data. In *Percom*, 2014.
[23] A. Rai, K. K. Chintalapudi, V. N. Padmanabhan, and R. Sen. Zee: Zero-effort crowdsourcing for indoor localization. In *Mobicom*, pages 293–304, 2012.
[24] N. Roy, H. Wang, and R. R. Choudhury. I am a smartphone and i can tell my users walking direction. In *Mobisys*, 2014.
[25] T. Sattler, B. Leibe, and L. Kobbelt. Fast image-based localization using direct 2d-to-3d matching. In *13th IEEE International Conference on Computer Vision(ICCV)*, 2011.
[26] G. Shen, Z. Chen, P. Zhang, T. Moscibroda, and Y. Zhang. Walkie-markie: Indoor pathway mapping made easy. In *NSDI*, 2013.
[27] H. Shin, Y. Chon, and H. Cha. Unsupervised construction of an indoor floor plan using a smartphone. *IEEE Transactions on Systems, Man, and Cybernetics*, 2012.
[28] S. Sinha, D. Steedly, R. Szeliski, M. Agrawala, and M. Polle-Feys. Interactive 3d architectural modeling from unordered photo collections. *ACM Transactions on Graphics*, 2008.
[29] N. Snavely, I. Simon, M. Goesele, R. Szeliski, and M. Seitzs. Scene reconstruction and visualization from community photo collections. *Proceedings of the IEEE*, 1998.
[30] S. Thrun. Learning occupancy grid maps with forward sensor models. *Autonomous robots*, 15(2):111–127, 2003.
[31] Y. Tian, R. Gao, K. Bian, F. Ye, T. Wang, Y. Wang, and X. Li. Towards ubiquitous indoor localization service leveraging environmental physical features. In *IEEE INFOCOM*, 2014.
[32] I. Ulrich and I. Nourbakhsh. Appearance-based place recognition for topological localization. In *IEEE International Conference on Robotics and Automation*, 2000.
[33] C. A. Vanegas, D. Aliaga, and B. Benes. Automatic extraction of manhattan-world building masses from 3d laser range scans. *IEEE Transactions on Visualization and Computer Graphics*, 2012.
[34] H. Wang, S. Sen, A. Elgohary, M. Farid, M. Youssef, and R. R. Choudhury. No need to war-drive: Unsupervised indoor localization. In *MobiSys*, 2012.
[35] S. Wang, J. Joo, Y. Wang, and S. C. Zhu. Weakly supervised learning for attribute localization in outdoor scenes. In *CVPR*, 2013.
[36] J. Xiao, T. Fang, P. Zhao, M. Lhuillier, and L. Quan. Image-based street-side city modeling. *ACM Transactions on Graphics*, pages 273–289, 2009.
[37] D. Yang, G. Xue, X. Fang, and J. Tang. Crowdsourcing to smartphones: incentive mechanism design for mobile phone sensing. In *MobiCom*, 2012.
[38] Z. Yang, C. Wu, and Y. Liu. Locating in fingerprint space: Wireless indoor localization with little human intervention. In *Mobicom*, pages 269–280, 2012.

Demo: Real-time Breath Monitoring Using Wireless Signals

Fadel Adib Zachary Kabelac Hongzi Mao Dina Katabi Robert C. Miller
Massachusetts Institute of Technology
{fadel,zek,hongzi,dk,rcm}@csail.mit.edu

ABSTRACT

This demo presents Vital-Radio, a wireless sensing technology that monitors breathing remotely, without requiring any body contact. Vital-Radio operates by transmitting a low-power wireless signal and monitoring its reflections off the human body. It uses these reflections to track motion associated with breathing, i.e., the chest movements caused by inhaling and exhaling. The demo will enable any person to sit in front of the device and check that it tracks their inhale and exhale process. The person may hold his/her breath and check that the device detects the breath holding event in real-time.

Categories and Subject Descriptors C.2.2 [**Network Architecture and Design**]: Wireless Communication. H.5.2 [**Information Interfaces and Presentation**]: User Interfaces - Input devices and strategies.

Keywords Wireless; Vital Signs; Breathing; Smart Homes; Seeing Through Walls

1. INTRODUCTION

The past few years have witnessed a surge of interest in ubiquitous health-monitoring [4, 5]. Today, we see smart homes that continuously monitor temperature and air quality and use this information to improve the health and comfort of their inhabitants. As health-monitoring technologies advance further, one would imagine that future smart homes would not only monitor the environment, but also monitor our vital signs, such as breathing. They may use this information to track our activity level, e.g., "did the user exercise today?" or alert us to subtle health issues: "does the user breathe regularly during sleep?" If non-intrusive in-home continuous monitoring of breathing existed, it would enable healthcare professionals to study how these signals correlate with our sleep quality and our overall health, which can have a significant impact on our healthcare system.

Unfortunately, existing technologies for tracking breathing typically require body contact. In particular, they require the user to wear a chest band [6] or nasal probe [3], or to lie on a special mattress [1], and hence are inconvenient for continuous monitoring. Some recent advances can extract breathing from a video by tracking subtle chest motion [7]. While these technologies operate without body contact, they require the users to continuously face a video camera, which would interfere with their daily activities. Ideally, one would like a smart home to monitor its inhabitants' vital signs the same way it monitors air quality, i.e., without requiring the user to wear or carry a device or interrupt her natural activities.

MobiCom'14, September 7-11, 2014, Maui, Hawaii, USA.
ACM 978-1-4503-2783-1/14/09.
http://dx.doi.org/10.1145/2639108.2641756 .

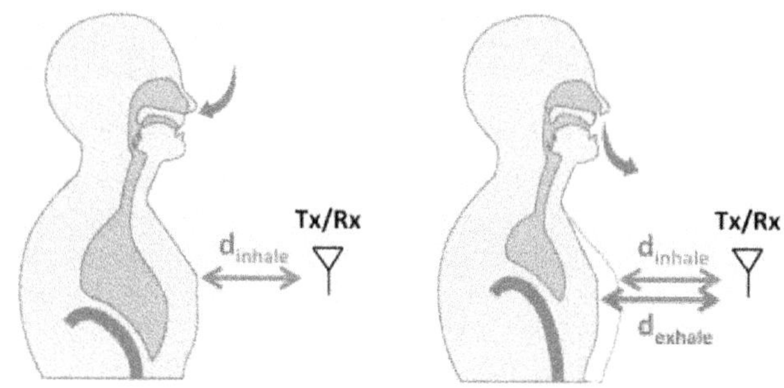

(a) **Inhale Motion** (b) **Exhale Motion**

Figure 1: Chest Motion due to Breathing. (a) shows how when the person inhales, his chest expands and becomes closer to the antenna (the distance between the chest and the antenna is d_{inhale}). (b) shows how when the person exhales, his chest contracts and becomes further away from the antenna, and the distance between the chest and the antenna d_{exhale} is larger than d_{inhale}.

In this demo, we take the first step toward smart homes that monitor people's vital signs without body instrumentation, and actively contribute to their inhabitants' well-being. The demo presents Vital-Radio a technology that tracks breathing remotely without physical contact with the body. It does so by monitoring the minute chest motion due to the inhale and exhale process as shown in Fig. 1. It works in non-controlled settings with no prior training. Further, since Vital-Radio uses wireless signals that can traverse walls and obstacles, it operates correctly even if the user is in an adjacent room or occluded by a piece of furniture.

2. OVERVIEW OF VITAL-RADIO

Vital-Radio transmits a low-power wireless signal and monitors its reflections off the human body. It processes these reflections to identify subtle periodic motions like breathing, and distinguish them from large or non-periodic movements due to a person walking or moving a limb.

To develop Vital-Radio, we built on WiTrack [2], which provides accurate motion tracking using radio reflections off a human body. WiTrack uses a frequency sweeping technique called FMCW to separate reflected signals according to the distance of the reflector from the device. WiTrack then eliminates signals reflected off static objects like furniture and walls by leveraging that such static reflections do not change over time and hence can be canceled by subtracting consecutive versions of the received signal. This leaves the system with signals reflected off moving objects and the locations of such reflectors. WiTrack processes these signals to localize a moving person and track his location over time. The accuracy of WiTrack's localization however is 10cm to 15cm. Hence, the system is too coarse to detect changes in the chest position due to breathing.

Vital-Radio builds on WiTrack and operates in three steps. In the first step, Vital-Radio uses WiTrack to eliminate reflections from

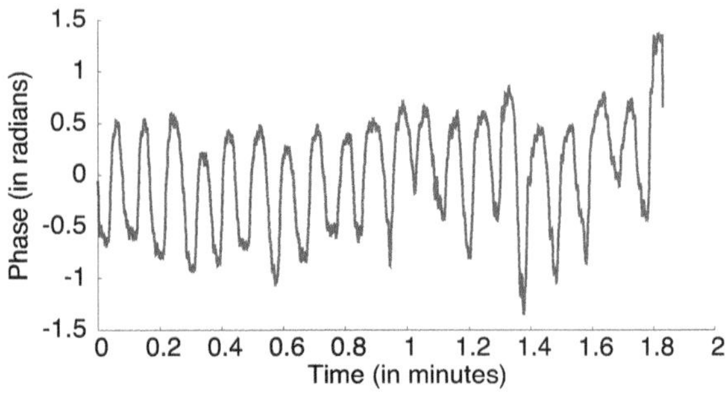

Figure 2: Breathing Motion. The figure shows the breathing motion of a person in terms of the phase.

static objects (e.g., walls and furniture) and sort reflections from moving objects (i.e., people) into bins based on their distances from the device. Thus, at the output of this step, we have the time signal reflected off the human body, $s(t)$, and we will have eliminated interference and noise due to reflections off other objects.

In the second step, Vital-Radio identifies changes in the signal due to body motion as opposed to breathing motion. Specifically, when a person moves his arm or walks around, the motion of his body parts would be much larger than his chest movements, and would mask breathing. Vital-Radio needs to identify limb motion from breathing motion to prevent such movements from causing errors in breath monitoring and being detected as breathing irregularities. To do that, Vital-Radio leverages that the breathing motion is slow in comparison to human body motion. For example, a person walks at about one meter per second; however, when breathing, the chest moves less than a millimeter per second. Hence, in comparison to breathing, a leg or arm movement would cause very rapid variations. Vital-Radio embeds this observation in an algorithm for detecting body motion. Once it detects large motion intervals, it eliminates them and focuses on the time intervals which have no major limb motion.

In the third step, Vital-Radio analyzes the signal to track the breathing motion. In contrast to WiTrack, however, which looks only at the signal's power to detect the presence of a moving reflector, Vital-Radio focuses on the phase of the reflected signal. It uses the phase variations to track subtle sub-centimeter oscillations in a reflector (e.g., chest breathing motion) even when the reflector itself does not change its overall distance from the device. Fig. 2 shows the phase variations due to the breathing of a person sitting 3 meters away from the device. The increase and decrease in the phase correspond to the inhale and exhale process. This person's breathing rate is 11 breaths per minute.

3. Demo Setup

Our demo setup is shown in Fig. 3. It includes the WiTrack [2] hardware connected to a transmit-receive antenna pair at the front-end and to a machine via the USRP software radio at the back-end. Processing is performed in real-time in the UHD driver of the USRP and the phase of the FMCW bin that corresponds to the chest location is output on the screen in real-time. The proposed demo at MobiCom will be set up in a $3m \times 2.5m$ space in a corner of a room.[1] The demo will monitor the breathing of a user who sits on a chair within that region. The user can move his chair as desired within the region.

[1]Placing the setup in the corner of the room, i.e., near 2 walls, will allow us to minimize interference due to reflections of other people in the vicinity.

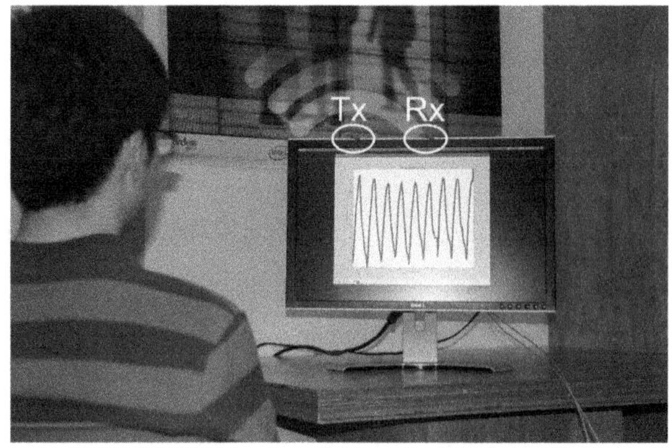

Figure 3: Demo Setup. The figure shows a person sitting on a chair in front of a screen that outputs the exhale and inhale motion due to his breathing as demonstrated by the crests and valleys respectively. The transmit and receive antennas of Vital-Radio are placed on top of the screen.

4. References

[1] Baby Sleep Monitor. `http://www.ibabyguard.com/`. iBabyGuard.

[2] F. Adib, Z. Kabelac, D. Katabi, and R. C. Miller. 3D Tracking via Body Radio Reflections. In *Usenix NSDI*, 2014.

[3] GigaOm. Could a breath-monitoring headset improve your health? http://gigaom.com/2013/09/20/could-a-breath-monitoring-headset-improve-your-health/.

[4] F. M. Healthcare. Market for embedded health monitoring-gadgets to hit 170M devices by 2017. http://www.fiercemobilehealthcare.com/story/market-embedded-health-monitoring-gadgets-hit-170m-devices-2017/2012-08-03.

[5] InformationWeek. Health-Monitoring Devices Market Outpaces Telehealth. http://www.informationweek.com/mobile/health-monitoring-devices-market-outpaces-telehealth/d/d-id/1104636.

[6] Vivonoetics. Respiration: Single or Dual-Band. http://vivonoetics.com/products/vivosense/analyzing/respiration-single-or-dual-band/.

[7] H.-Y. Wu, M. Rubinstein, E. Shih, J. Guttag, F. Durand, and W. Freeman. Eulerian video magnification for revealing subtle changes in the world. *ACM SIGGRAPH*, 2012.

Demo: PhoneLets – Offloading the Phone off your Phone for Energy, Cost and Network Load Optimization

Andrius Aucinas
Computer Laboratory
University of Cambridge
andrius.aucinas@cl.cam.ac.uk

Jon Crowcroft
Computer Laboratory
University of Cambridge
jon.crowcroft@cl.cam.ac.uk

ABSTRACT

This demo presents how phone functionality can be offloaded from a smartphone over wireless link to a *PhoneLet* by sharing one SIM card across multiple devices. This can lead to significant cost and network load reductions by decreasing the number of simultaneously connected mobile clients. Furthermore, it can save energy for the mobile user when connected to a powered *PhoneLet* by offloading phone functionality. It absorbs the energy cost of online presence and inefficient mobile applications' communication patterns, instead providing connectivity for the user over a WiFi link.

Categories and Subject Descriptors

C.2.3 [**Computer-communication networks**]: Network OperationsNetwork Management

Keywords

Mobile; Energy; Cellular; Networks; SIM; Subscriber Management

1. WHAT PHONELETS ARE

A modern smartphone has more in common with a computer than a phone, and connectivity to the Internet and surrounding devices (the *Internet of Things*) is tipping the balance even further. Importance of cellular networks, however, remains as they provide almost ubiquitous Internet connectivity around the world. Cellular connectivity has its own problems. This demo shows how *PhoneLets* allow one SIM (Subscriber Identity Module) to be shared between nearby devices. This addresses the following problems with cellular connectivity:

Firstly, connectivity is relatively expensive for users [4], typically requiring a separate subscription for each device connected to the cellular network, e.g. smartphone and tablet as well as broadband connectivity at home and at work. Using *PhoneLets* to share a single SIM across devices solves this issue.

MobiCom'14, September 7-11, 2014, Maui, Hawaii, USA.
ACM 978-1-4503-2783-1/14/09.
http://dx.doi.org/10.1145/2639108.2641744.

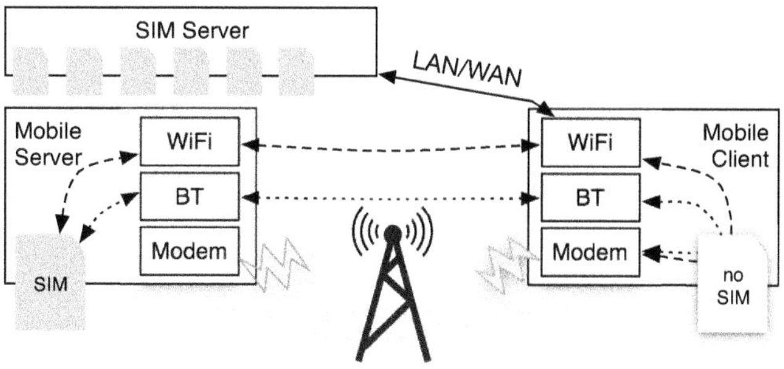

Figure 1: Architecture of PhoneLets and interaction with different types of servers

Secondly, the increasing number of connected, periodically communicating clients increases infrastructure costs and also increases cellular network load, in extreme cases causing *signaling storms* [9] that can bring down an entire network. *PhoneLets* reduce the number of simultaneously connected clients by sharing the same cellular link across multiple clients.

Finally, energy consumption of always connected clients is high compared to short-range radio technologies. Sharing a cellular link also helps reduce it for mobile devices.

PhoneLets enable phone offloading by exploiting remote SIM functionality of existing hardware. A cellular module exchange commands with a SIM/UICC module over a wireless communication link rather than direct, physical connection. Uses of such technology have included automotive as well as electronic currency [8]. *PhoneLets* infrastructure establishes and manages secure communication channels between participating entities and allows a device to connect to a cellular network without a physical SIM card.

2. PHONELETS DESIGN

Figure 1 shows the overall concept and system architecture. There are three types of entities: 1) mobile server, a mobile device which can share its SIM with other clients, 2) SIM server which may host and provide more sets of credentials over local or wide-area networks and 3) a mobile client which can use either of the methods.

The SIM card is a special I/O device in a mobile platform: due to its security requirements it is not exposed to the platform's operating system. Instead, it is managed by the modem's firmware which routes all communication between the network and the subscriber module. Standard remote IO approaches are similar in their nature (*e.g.*, RIO [6] enables

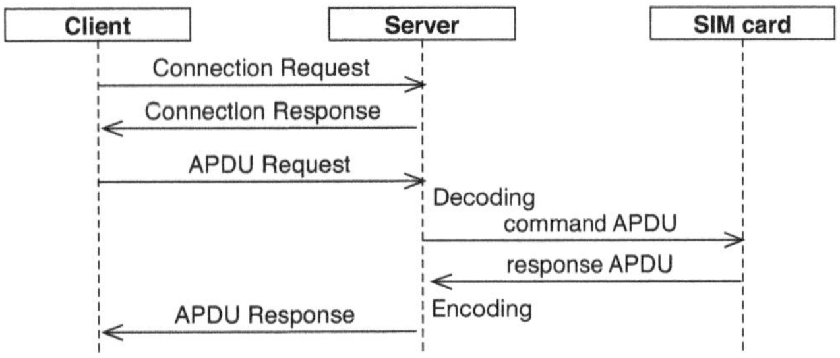

Figure 2: Communication sequence between client, server and remote SIM card

transparently accessing I/O devices of a remote mobile system) but are not applicable in this setting as they require OS support.

Interaction with the subscriber module requires lower level protocols understood by the modem firmware. Our design extends the standard RSAP (Remote SIM Access Protocol) [1] by using a SIM server which is not capable of mobile connectivity itself and by using arbitrary communication links to access a remote SIM card (*no SIM* in the mobile client). Our work for this demo focused primarily on the client and SIM server design. We use off-the-shelf hardware as the mobile server for backwards-compatibility.

The mobile client can obtain network credentials from any server – a user's mobile phone, a co-located or a remote SIM server – as long as it can reach it. The key observation is that there are few operations that require access to the SIM card due to its interface speed (it would be infeasible to use it on the data path) and instead it is used to generate encryption keys. The generating keys, however, can never be accessed directly. Part of the network's security however comes from the network authenticating the subscriber for any major operation (e.g. placing or receiving calls, establishing PDP context). The cellular module therefore must always be able to access the remote card using standard Application Protocol Data Unit (APDU) messages (Fig. 2).

Importantly, we do not clone the SIM card and by design the system disables connectivity for one device before enabling it for another one to prevent multiple devices sharing the same credentials simultaneously. Only one device is connected to the cellular network and may share (*tether*) the connectivity to other devices over another channel. One cellular module is also only capable of being registered with one network, enforcing a strict one-to-one mapping.

2.1 Prototype

Our demo mobile client (Fig. 3), the *PhoneLet*, consists of a Telit UC864 cellular module connected to a raspberryPI as a controller, which also uses WiFi and BlueTooth (BT) dongles for local wireless connectivity. The controller runs a modified version of the Ofono open telephony stack and manages communication between the cellular module and multiple backends.

The two example servers are an off-the-shelf Samsung Galaxy S4 and our custom server that only interfaces with SIM cards through a smartcard reader, also running on a raspberryPI. In our prototype, the server is connected to a WiFi AP to be reachable by the mobile client. We replace the BT communication channel with a more secure option - TCP link with certificate-based authentication of

Figure 3: Client prototype

Use case	Energy consumption (mA)
Idle - airplane mode	5
Ifle - BlueTooth	6
Idle - WiFi	8
Idle - 3G	10
Apps background - WiFi	27
BlueTooth SIM access	28
Apps background - 3G	40
WiFi tethering (idle)	80

Table 1: Energy consumption of an idle device with different radios enabled. (Apps background = Google apps and Facebook)

both client and server, and strong encryption for all data exchange. Once the client establishes a connection to either backend, it registers with the network and takes on the role of a phone.

3. ENERGY SAVING OPPORTUNITIES

Reduced mobile client energy consumption is an important motivation for *PhoneLets*. We analyze energy consumption of the client in a few example scenarios using our early prototype. The *PhoneLet* itself is not yet energy-optimized, i.e. the controlling RaspberryPI is not meant for mobile uses, so we focused on energy comparison of the mobile SIM server - a phone carried by the user from which we offload phone functionality.

We measured energy consumption of a Samsung Galaxy S4[1] in a number of scenarios. Table. 1[2] presents energy consumption of the different device radios, depending on their use, ranging from an idle device with only a particular radio enabled, to different methods of sharing connectivity and simple application usage patterns.

The absolute values will vary with different devices and network configuration or conditions and application use, but the overall results remain. In particular, energy consumption of the different idle radios is similar, but cellular networks are significantly less efficient for current applications' network usage patterns [5]. Therefore, replacing the cellular link with a WiFi one to another, powered device can bring significant savings - 32.5% in our example case.

[1]Using Monsoon Power Monitor `http://www.msoon.com/LabEquipment/PowerMonitor/`

[2]Current drain (mA) is chosen over power (mW) as power depends on voltage that decays with the battery discharge

The default BT implementation of RSAP is not efficient enough - maintaining access alone consumes almost three times the amount of energy of an idle device connected to a 3G network. Instead, we have implemented SIM sharing over WiFi using our custom client and verified that the BT version is unnecessarily wasteful - once the PhoneLet has registered to the network, there is no communication with the SIM server for as long as the device is idle. For example, a phone call is successfully received after 30 minutes of no activity. The current Android platform does not allow RSAP to run over WiFi, but based on our measurements we expect energy consumption of an optimized implementation to be close to that of an idle WiFi channel - 3.5x less than BT.

Finally, we measured energy consumption of WiFi tethering. With just one idle client it is almost 3x higher than the BT case. RSAP is effectively an alternative to WiFi tethering when the mobile client provides connectivity to other devices. Therefore we expect energy consumption of an optimized WiFi mobile client to be close to 10x less than WiFi tethering.

These are early results, but they point to a potential use-case where a powered *PhoneLet* is registered to the network on behalf of a WiFi-connected client at a considerable energy benefit. The benefit would be further improved when network access is shared across multiple such devices and SIM access load is balanced across them as the savings for each individual device would add up. This use-case is outside the scope of the current demo.

4. DEMO: WIRELESS SIM SHARING

To demonstrate the working prototype of the system, we show our client *PhoneLet* (Fig. 3), communicating with an off-the shelf mobile device or our SIM server to share their credentials for network registration in the following steps:

1. Make a phone call to the mobile server (phone) and show that it is ringing
2. Start sharing its SIM card with the client and show that the client is registered to the network with the same ID by making a phone call to it
3. Start using SIM card in the SIM server over WiFi and show that the client is registered to the network with a different ID by making a call to the other number.

In the three steps we show our prototype's ability to offload phone functionality from a phone - share subscriber credentials between multiple clients and select which one will be connected to the network.

5. DISCUSSION

In addition to connectivity, *PhoneLets* offers management of an individual's ID - the phone number. There have been multiple offerings with such function: multiple SIM cards associated with a number or VoIP-based solutions (*e.g.,* Google Voice), however they do not solve the problem of an increasing number of cellular clients and billing depends on service provider.

One cellular network in UK has offered a service to make phonecalls from tablets and laptops over WiFi to its users using a special application[3], blurring the line between mobile and the Internet. If WiFi Internet connectivity is available, the approach could help reduce energy consumption by disabling cellular radio.

[3]O2 TU Go `http://www.o2.co.uk/apps/tu-go`

It is well known that WiFi tethering consumes a lot of energy. Cool-Tether [7] proposed to reverse the roles of a mobile gateway and client and turn the client into WiFi AP. Our proposal also reduces energy consumption of the mobile gateway by completely changing the roles of the entities. Instead, the client (*PhoneLet*) uses the cellular network directly, avoiding additional wireless communication with the gateway.

Reprogrammable SIM cards [2] such as embedded SIM [3] have been proposed for provisioning in M2M communication. They maintain a physical secure element to store credentials, but provide mechanisms to manage them over the air. The architecture allows operators to retain full control over the credentials, including when new ones can be installed or old ones removed through centralized management and subsequently reduced flexibility on the client side.

Finally, questions that remain to be answered in future work include not only optimizations of the management and control protocols, but also the development of usage policies in multi-user environments and guaranteed isolation properties as well as adaptation of energy-aware routing protocols for distributed nodes.

6. SUMMARY

Increasingly, smartphones are replicating computer use, with phone now a very secondary function to email, social media and entertainment. However mobile network connections remain expensive both financially and in terms of the energy they use. *PhoneLets* is a system that allows a single mobile subscription to be shared between multiple devices, allowing much of the mobile functionality of a cellular device to be offloaded. This allows the financial and energy costs of a cellular connection to be shared between multiple devices.

More information and demonstration video is available via `phonelets.smart-e.org`.

7. REFERENCES

[1] SIM Access Profile. Technical Report SAP_SPEC, Bluetooth SIG, 2008. V11r00.

[2] Reprogrammable SIMs: Technology, Evolution and Implications. Technical report, CSMG, OFcom, 2012.

[3] Embedded SIM Remote Provisioning Architecture. Technical Report 2FAST.13, GSM Association, 2013.

[4] EU27 mobile data cost competitiveness report. Technical report, Rewheel Consulting, 2013.

[5] A. Aucinas, N. Vallina-Rodriguez, Y. Grunenberger, V. Erramilli, K. Papagiannaki, J. Crowcroft, and D. Wetherall. Staying online while mobile: the hidden costs. In *CoNEXT '13*, 2013.

[6] A. A. Sani, K. Boos, M. H. Yun, and L. Zhong. Rio: a system solution for sharing i/o between mobile systems. In *MobiSys '14*, 2014.

[7] A. Sharma, V. Navda, R. Ramjee, V. N. Padmanabhan, and E. M. Belding. Cool-Tether: energy efficient on-the-fly wifi hot-spots using mobile phones. In *CoNEXT '09*, 2009.

[8] H. C. Subramanian. Sim access profile: Electronic currency using sim access profile. 2003.

[9] C. Yang. Weather the signaling storm. Technical report, Huawei, 2011.

Demo: Mobile Opportunistic System for Experience Sharing (MOSES) in Indoor Exhibitions

Fehmi Ben Abdesslem
SICS Swedish ICT
Stockholm, Sweden
fehmi@sics.se

Anders Lindgren
SICS Swedish ICT
Stockholm, Sweden
andersl@sics.se

ABSTRACT

Information-Centric Networking (ICN) is an alternative architecture for computer networks, where the communication is focused on the data being transferred instead of the communicating hosts. This paper describes a demo of an experience sharing application for mobile phones built on an ICN platform designed for devices with intermittent connectivity. In particular, we detail how this application will be showcased in an indoor exhibition where experience is shared with media content that is geo-tagged using Bluetooth beacons and spread opportunistically to other users.

1. INTRODUCTION

Information-Centric Networking (ICN) is an alternative communication architecture focusing on the content rather than the hosts. It emerged from the observation that the Internet nowadays is mainly used as a content distribution network, where users share and consume content instead of explicitely requesting an end-to-end communication with a remote host.

This architecture is particularly interesting for the most popular applications on the Internet, such as web browsing [6], file sharing [3], or even video streaming [5]. Experimental platforms have been implemented over IP such as DONA [4], CCN [2], or NetInf [1] for applications to directly request named content instead of specifying host destination. A convergence layer is typically used to map the requested content to an IP destination hosting that content.

Modifying and revisiting the core architecture supporting these traditional applications is a challenging task, as despite its benefits, any proposed ICN implementation would still compete with mature original host-centric implementations. The emergence of less mature network paradigms such as the Internet of Things (IoT) or Delay-Tolerant Networks (DTN) is a timely opportunity to explore how they can benefit from an ICN architecture and include such architecture in their design. A growing interest is observed in the research community, leading to international research projects and standardisation efforts[1]. In the MOSES project, work has been carried out to develop platforms for opportunistic experience sharing in large events and remote areas.

This paper describes a scenario involving a mobile application built with an ICN architecture over a DTN within the MOSES project. The application is an indoor instantiation of the experience sharing platform to be deployed over a set of users particpating in an exhibition or conference, and used to share their experience with other fellow participants.

[1]http://irtf.org/icnrg

MobiCom'14, September 7-11, 2014, Maui, Hawaii, USA.
ACM 978-1-4503-2783-1/14/09.
http://dx.doi.org/10.1145/2639108.2641750.

2. SCENARIO

When participating in an exhibition, sharing experience and communicating with other participants is useful to spread information and make new contacts. However, most exhibitions not only lack the appropriate mobile software, but also lack the infrastructure to support such application. Especially in international venues where roaming charges apply for many participants, access to the internet cannot be assumed and relied on by any application.

In this scenario, most participants of an exhibition or conference do not have internet access. However, they do have smartphones featuring communication technologies such as Bluetooth and WiFi, and an embedded camera to take pictures. When the participants are in the exhibition or conference venue, they would like to share their thoughts or comments on products and ideas being presented to fellow participants. Their experience can be shared with multimedia content, but also with simple text messages about related works or products, tips, or even warnings about scams and plagiarism. All shared content is geo-tagged when created so that the content can be made available to fellow participants who are currently in the same location, or will be visiting the area later on.

At any time, users can see the content previously shared by other users within a custom range of their location. When approaching a stall, or entering a room, the relevant information shared by other participants can be read, and photos of demonstrations can be at the location at which they were spotted.

Accessing local information with a limited connectivity to the Internet is made possible using a DTN. When content is created, it is shared with other users in range, using a device-to-device communication link (eg, Bluetooth). Content is then spread in an epidemic fashion, each user sharing their own content and the content collected so far from other users. Only local information is interesting to the users, but their cache might contain content that was created in remote locations, that was epidemically spread to them after several hops. To limit the size of their cache and/or to limit the transfers and save battery, users can choose to only receive, store, and forward, content that are within a custom range of their own location.

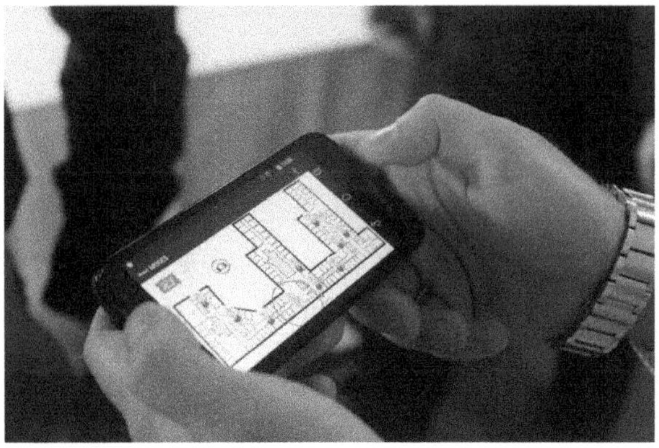

Figure 1: The application running on an Android smartphone, and displaying a map of the area with markers indicating where media content were shared by other participants.

This scenario is prone to benefit from an ICN architecture: users are not interested in communicating with a particular device, but are rather interested in getting content, wherever it comes from.

3. IMPLEMENTATION AND DEMONSTRATION

The application is currently implemented on the Android operating system, and has been tested on smartphones. Content is created using the smartphone itself, using the built-in camera and the virtual keyboard on the touch screen for the text messages. The content is then geo-tagged using the either (i) the built-in positioning systems such as GPS, Wi-Fi or cellular-based positioning system, or (ii) for indoor locations, a custom Bluetooth-based position system, that was built by deploying Bluetooth Low Energy devices.

A NetInf implementation for Android is used by the application to communicate with other devices in Bluetooth range. The application regularly sends Search requests that are sent by NetInf to all devices in range. A Search-Response is then returned to the application, with a list of content IDs available, along with the corresponding meta-data. The application then sends a request to all devices in range to get the content it does not already have in-cache. By only requesting the content without specifying hosts, the architecture is information-centric.

Controlled experiments are being conducted in laboratory to study how content is spread and how efficient the system is in different conditions. In parallel, experiments in the wild with real users is important to observe the behaviour of the system in a real environment. The system will be demonstrated during the demo sessions of the ACM Mobicom'14 conference. Five pref-configured smartphones will be distributed to voluntary participants of the workshop and other participants will be invited to download and run the application on their own smartphones, including an implementation of NetInf. Participants will then be invited to run and use the application (as shown in Figure 1) by sharing their experience with media content.

3.1 Customisability

Each exhibition is different, and it is important that the system is easily customisable to new deployments. Therefore, our prototype supports rapid customisation for new events. It allows a new map to be loaded into the system and an edit mode allows an administrator to specify on the map where the Bluetooth beacons are located to make the system ready for use. This will allow us to quickly adapt the prototype to the floor plan of the Mobicom demo session and deploy a system that is customised to this particular event.

Figure 2: Estimote devices, using the Bluetooth Low Energy technology, will be deployed to allow geo-tagging of the content created by smartphones.

4. SETUP

The demonstration involves both equipment deployment and participants. A table with a laptop and paper versions of this article will be disposed on a table to provide more information to the participants.

4.1 Equipment

Three types of equipment will be deployed: Smartphones, Bluetooth devices, and Raspberry Pis.

Five pre-configured smartphones, with the last version of the application and an adapted version of NetInf pre-installed will be made available for participants to use.

To allow indoor localisation of the content created by the smartphones, 5 devices broadcasting regular Bluetooth signals, called Estimotes [2], will be deployed around the demonstration area, as shown in Figure 2.

Finally, a Raspberry Pi will be deployed to collect all content created by the participants and emulate an intermittent internet connectivity. The device will act as a simple Wi-Fi access point.

4.2 Participants

While participants will be able to download and install the application on their own device, the current communication technology being Bluetooth, it would require from them to pair their device with a few existing devices. We expect most participants to just use one of the smartphones made available to them (already paired with other smartphones), walk around for a few minutes sharing and consuming content, and come back to us to give back the smartphone.

5. EXPECTED OUTCOME AND ONGOING WORK

The demonstration will allow to collect important logs to understand how the content is created and spread to the other participants. Such deployment will also provide valuable feedback from the participants to improve the application. Our ongoing work includes optimising the application to use less battery and spread the content more efficiently. We are also designing and deploying this application in other contexts to shape it as a generic experience sharing application.

[2] `http://www.estimote.com`

6. ACKNOWLEDGMENTS

This work was carried out during the tenure of an ERCIM "Alain Bensoussan" Fellowship Programme. The research leading to these results has received funding from the EU Seventh Framework Programme (FP7/2007-2013) under grant agreement No. 246016.

This work was partially funded by the Future Networking Solutions action line of the European Institute of Innovation and Technology ICT Labs, and by the FP7 Marie Curie IRSES project MobileCloud under grant agreement No. 612212.

7. REFERENCES

[1] C. Dannewitz, D. Kutscher, B. Ohlman, S. Farrell, B. Ahlgren, and H. Karl. Network of information (netinf)–an information-centric networking architecture. *Computer Communications*, 36(7):721–735, 2013.

[2] V. Jacobson, D. K. Smetters, J. D. Thornton, M. F. Plass, N. H. Briggs, and R. L. Braynard. Networking named content. In *Proceedings of the 5th international conference on Emerging networking experiments and technologies*, pages 1–12. ACM, 2009.

[3] K. Katsaros, G. Xylomenos, and G. C. Polyzos. Multicache: An overlay architecture for information-centric networking. *Computer Networks*, 55(4):936–947, 2011.

[4] T. Koponen, M. Chawla, B.-G. Chun, A. Ermolinskiy, K. H. Kim, S. Shenker, and I. Stoica. A data-oriented (and beyond) network architecture. *ACM SIGCOMM Computer Communication Review*, 37(4):181–192, 2007.

[5] J. P. Papanis, S. I. Papapanagiotou, A. S. Mousas, G. V. Lioudakis, D. I. Kaklamani, and I. S. Venieris. On the use of attribute-based encryption for multimedia content protection over information-centric networks. *Transactions on Emerging Telecommunications Technologies*, 25(4):422–435, 2014.

[6] L. Rosenfeld and P. Morville. *Information architecture for the world wide web*. O'Reilly Media, Inc., 2002.

Demo: Tracking User Browsing on a Demo Floor

Aishwarya Ganesan
Microsoft Research India
t-aigane@microsoft.com

Swati Rallapalli
The University of Texas at Austin
swati@cs.utexas.edu

Krishna Kant Chintalapudi
Microsoft Research India
krchinta@microsoft.com

Venkata N. Padmanabhan
Microsoft Research India
padmanab@microsoft.com

Lili Qiu
The University of Texas at Austin
lili@cs.utexas.edu

Categories and Subject Descriptors

C.2.m [**Computer Systems Organization**]: COMPUTER - COMMUNICATION NETWORKS - Miscellaneous

Keywords

Physical Analytics, User Browsing, Wearables, Smart Glasses

1. TECHNICAL OVERVIEW

Our demo tracks physical browsing by users in indoor spaces. Analogous to online browsing, where users choose to go to certain webpages, dwell on a subset of pages of interest to them, and click on links of interest while ignoring others, we can draw parallels in the physical setting, where a user might *walk* purposefully to a section of interest, *dwell* there for a while, and *gaze* at specific items that they wish to know more about.

We have a developed a system called ThirdEye to track physical browsing by users in indoor spaces, such as retail stores. ThirdEye classifies the user's browsing into different modes, such as walking, dwelling, and gazing, analogous to the various modes of online (web) browsing. It further identifies which object and what type of object the user is gazing.

The design of ThirdEye centers on leveraging smart glasses worn by users as they browse, together with the smartphone carried by them. The front-facing camera on the smart glasses is in a position to capture the scene being viewed by a user. However, turning on the camera imposes a very significant drain on the battery, so ThirdEye uses the less expensive inertial sensors to the extent possible and triggers the camera only when the user is likely to be gazing. Once it is extablished that the user is gazing, images captured by the camera are passed to a cloud service to identify the objects in the scene. Below we briefly describe our approach. For more details on ThirdEye, including evaluation in actual retail stores, please see our paper [6] from Mobicom 2014.

1.1 Behavior Classification

ThirdEye automatically classifies shopper behavior into walking, dwelling, and gazing — using sensor data obtained from the shopper's smart glasses: inertial data obtained from the accelerometer, 3-axis compass, gyroscope sensors, and the video feed obtained from the camera sensor. ThirdEye also makes use of data from the inertial sensors on shoppers' smartphones, where available, as discussed later in this section.

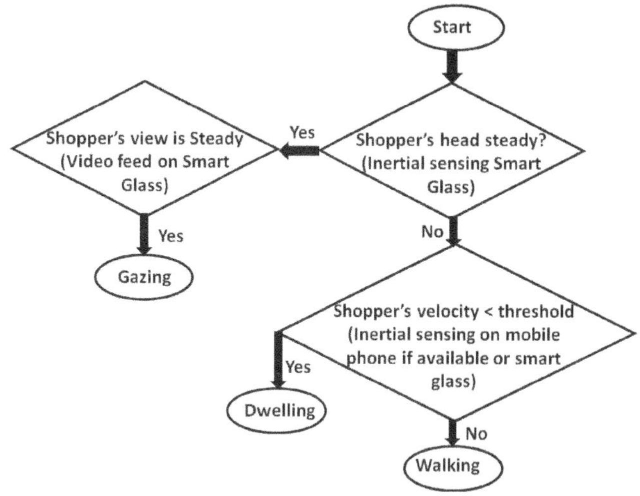

Figure 1: Overview of Behavior Classification Algorithm

Turning on the video on smart glasses causes a high power drain on the device, while inertial sensing results in much less power drain. Consequently, in our behavior classification scheme, we try to minimize the duration for which the video is turned on. Figure 1 depicts the high-level flow of our behavior classification scheme.

Gaze detection: The first step in our scheme is to detect whether or not the person is gazing. Since shoppers typically hold their head steady while gazing and are also not walking, this can be detected by measuring the standard deviation in inertial sensor measurements on the smart glass. However, just relying on inertial sensors leads to a large number of false positives. Consequently, we use a preliminary detection based on a low standard deviation in the inertial sensor measurements on the smart glass as a trigger to turn on the video and analyze the scene to confirm that the person is indeed gazing.

Dwelling and Walking: If there is a high standard deviation in the inertial sensors, this could mean that the person is either dwelling or walking. We use the step counter in Zee [5] to detect steps from the accelerometer. The accuracy of the step counter is higher when the accelerometer readings from the shopper's smartphone are used compared to when measurements from the smart glasses are used.

MobiCom'14, September 7–11, 2014, Maui, HI, USA.
ACM 978-1-4503-2783-1/14/09 ...$15.00.
http://dx.doi.org/10.1145/2639108.2641754.

This is because of spurious step detections caused by head movement. The step count is combined with compass data from the smart glasses to estimate the average velocity of the shopper. If the magnitude of average velocity is less than a certain threshold, the behavior is classified as dwelling, otherwise it is classified as walking.

1.2 Attention Identification

Once a user is identified as gazing, ThirdEye further determines which object in the field of view the user is gazing at and what is the object.

In general, the number of items within the field of view of the Glass could be large. In some cases, the number of items seen can be as large as 16. It is likely, however, that the shopper is only focused on one or perhaps a small number out of these items in his/her field of view. So our goal is to identify the shopper's focus within the field of view.

Our evaluation shows that a user's focus often does not lie at the center of the field of view of his/her smart glasses. So we develop the following scheme based on users' head-tilt.

Dependence of Attention on Head-Tilt: Our analysis revealed an interesting fact – *the center of attention in fact depends on the tilt of the head of the person.* In hindsight, this makes sense, since when a shopper looks up or down towards a product, he/she accomplishes this by partly turning head up/down and partly by rolling their eyeballs. Consequently, the shopper's focus within their field of view would tend to shift in the same direction as their head is tilting.

Probability Distributions for center of attention: Since it is in principle impossible to determine exactly which item the shopper is focused on, we resort to assigning a probability value $P(x, y|\delta)$ to an item in his field of view at the x and y pixel position, given the head-tilt, δ, as obtained from the compass:

$$P(x, y|\delta) = \Phi_X(x - x_o)\Phi_Y(y - m\delta - c) \quad (1)$$

The distributions $\Phi_X(z)$ and $\Phi_Y(z)$ are obtained using histograms from actual data. Figure 2 depicts the function $P(x, y|\delta)$ as a function of $x - x_o$, and $y - m\delta - c$.

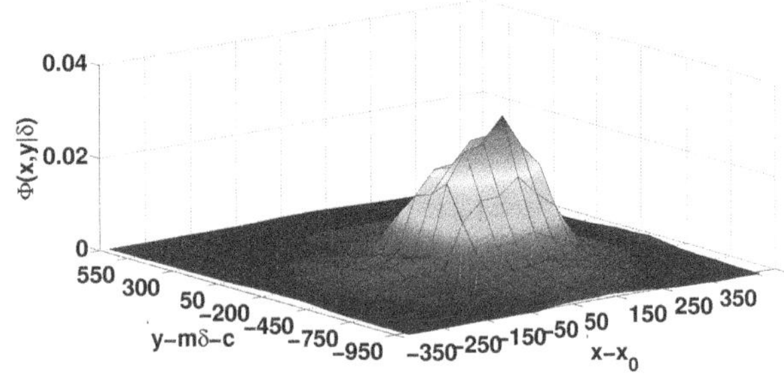

Figure 2: $\Phi(x, y|\delta)$

1.3 Object Recognition

ThirdEye captures images and invokes a cloud service to perform either reverse image search or image matching to identify the objects contained within the image. In our current implementation, we use Google's service [2], although ThirdEye is not tied to it and could also invoke alternative services, such as Bing Vision [1] and Nokia Point & Find [3].

Reverse image search involves object recognition, which in turn involves extracting image features (*e.g.*, using an algorithm such as SIFT [4]), comparing these with precomputed features from a large corpus of existing images to find a match, and retrieving meta-data associated with the matching image(s) in the corpus (*e.g.*, product name). The scale and complexity of this computation necessitates running it on the cloud (*e.g.*, the corpus of product images could run into the tens of millions). In turn, this calls for being selective in how frequently reverse image search requests are sent.

Therefore, only when gazing is detected, does ThirdEye capture images and invoke the cloud service. During each period of gazing, ThirdEye captures all the images during the gazing period.

2. PROPOSED DEMO

The proposed demo includes (i) behavior classification to identify if a user is dwelling, walking, and gazing, (ii) attention identification to detect which object the user is gazing at, and (iii) using reverse image search or image matching to recognize the type of the object. We have a few smart glasses, which can be given to visitors to wear. As a user walks around a demo floor wearing smart glasses, ThirdEye will track their mode of browsing: walking around the floor, dwelling in a particular area, or gazing. This output will be displayed on a monitor at the demo booth, so that it can be viewed by the visitors to the booth. We will also show the energy-saving techniques employed by ThirdEye in action, reporting when the camera is turned on or off.

3. EQUIPMENT NEEDS AND LOGISTICS

We will bring the laptops, smartphones, and smart glasses needed for the demo. We will need the conference to provide a large display to be placed in the demo booth to show the results of tracking visitors.

4. REFERENCES

[1] Bing vision. http://en.wikipedia.org/wiki/Bing_Vision.

[2] Google search by image. http://www.google.com/insidesearch/features/images/searchbyimage.html.

[3] Nokia point and find. https://betalabs.nokia.com/trials/nokia-point-and-find.

[4] D. Lowe. Object Recognition from Local Scale-Invariant Features. In *Proc. of ICCV*, 1999.

[5] A. Rai, K. Chintalapudi, V. N. Padmanabhan, and R. Sen. Zee: Zero-Effort Crowdsourcing for Indoor Localization. In *Proc. of MobiCom*, 2012.

[6] S. Rallapalli, A. Ganesan, K. Chintalapudi, V. N. Padmanabhan, and L. Qiu. Enabling Physical Analytics in Retail Stores Using Smart Glasses. In *Proc. of MobiCom*, 2014.

Demo: An Open-Source Development Platform for Long-Range UHF-Connected WiFi Hotspots

Ryan E. Guerra, Narendra Anand, and Edward W. Knightly
Rice University, Houston, TX, USA
{war,nanand,knightly}@rice.edu

ABSTRACT

We present a real-time software-defined radio (SDR) platform for prototyping and measuring the performance of broadband UHF radio networks operating over long distances with point-to-multipoint (PTMP) non-line-of-sight (NLOS) networks. Enabled by the Wideband UHF Radio Card (WURC), a custom high-power and frequency-flexible radio transceiver daughter-card for FPGA-based digital basebands, the 802.11 DCF-like MAC and PHY implementation is completely open source. We demonstrate a long-range PTMP NLOS network bonding several of the white space television channels available in Maui, Hawaii. Off-the-shelf client devices can use this network via 802.11a/g links implemented with the same SDR framework. The multi-carrier channel estimates and real-time MAC statistics of connected nodes in UHF and 2.4 GHz are recorded and displayed in real-time, demonstrating an unprecedented amount of flexibility in unlicensed frequency bands, enabling real-time TV-band cognitive networks and small-cell research deployments.

A demonstration video is available at the following link: `http://youtu.be/dTOJHRICklQ`.

Categories and Subject Descriptors

C.2.1 [**Computer-Communication Networks**]: Network Architecture and Design—*Wireless Communication*

Keywords

Last-Mile; UHF; Software-Defined Radio; MAC; Channel Measurement; WiFi Hotspot; Small Cell

MobiCom'14, September 7-11, 2014, Maui, Hawaii, USA.
ACM 978-1-4503-2783-1/14/09.
http://dx.doi.org/10.1145/2639108.2641753.

Figure 1: Mobile network node with WARPv3 digital baseband and attached WURC daughtercard with small UHF antenna.

1. INTRODUCTION

The applications and capabilities of cognitive radio networks have increased greatly now that unlicensed devices may operate on unoccupied UHF channels (50-800 MHz) in many countries around the world [6]. The excellent propagation characteristics of the UHF band enable new applications for unlicensed networks in promising areas like machine-to-machine communications (M2M), rural last-mile broadband, and smart-utility backhaul [6].

Efficient design, deployment, and operation of these networks depend on the development of new technologies and techniques for increasing spectral efficiency [5], enabling co-existence with other unlicensed devices, and aggressively detecting and utilizing spectrum-sharing opportunities.

While the integration and flexibility of wireless components has been increasing to the point that highly-configurable radio front-ends are available, to date there has been no highly-configurable real-time reference design available for researchers interested in development and prototyping MAC and higher-layer systems in the UHF band, particularly with respect to high-power, high-bandwidth applications.

With that in mind, we designed WURC as a complete high-power analog front-end for state-of-the-art Software-Define Radio (SDR) that can enable experimental wireless development at long-range with a completely open MAC and PHY implementation. In Figure 1, we show a single network node consisting of a digital baseband build on the WARPv3 platform [2] and the WURC analog daughtercard with a small UHF antenna. This forms the basic building-block of our demonstration network.

2. REAL-TIME UHF BACKHAUL

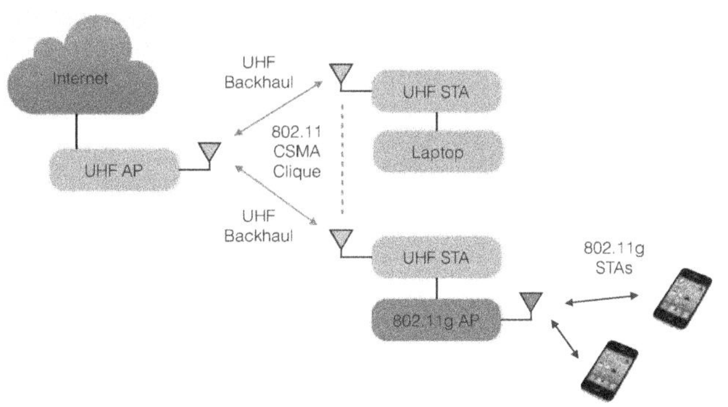

Figure 2: Diagram of the demo network topology.

A previous system utilizing the WURC platform [4] focused on physical-layer research and development, relying on off-line processing of captured RF samples [3] to enable rapid testing and iteration on different waveforms and complex MIMO precoding or decoding schemes. Cognitive radio is getting its first large-scale test case in the UHF bands The integration of the WURC platform with the WARP 802.11a/g [1] reference design enables long-range, non-line-of-sight (NLOS) UHF links with high bandwidth.

A number of enabling contributions were developed for the WURC platform:

- a broadband power-transfer network for the UHF power amplification chain to create a relatively flat frequency response from 470-698 MHz;
- a new automatic gain control (AGC) loop developed in HDL that can meet 802.11g timing requirements for packet detection and receive gain convergence without an external power detector like the native WARPv3 RF chains;
- modifications to the 802.11a/g reference design [1] to enable variable-rate channel bandwidths of 5, 10 and 20 MHz as specified in the 802.11-2012 standard and to allow transmissions to fit within a single North American UHF channel of 6 MHz, or multiple channels with wider channel bandwidth;
- an automated calibration and characterization framework to correct analog impairments and process variation across many fabricated modules;
- integration, driver development, and physical layer tuning to support the new hardware with simple APIs that let the researcher rapidly prototype their system.

Additional details about the component implementation and an example of physical-later applications of the WURC platform are available in [5].

In this demo, we present a real-time network composed of at least three WURC-enabled SDR nodes operating on free broadcast television channels available in the Maui, Hawaii area. An experimental license has been obtained to operate on these unused UHF channels.

In the demonstration topology, a wired internet connection is shared from the UHF AP to STA nodes (green nodes) via a Layer 2 wireless bridge following the 802.11 Distributed Coordination Function (DCF). Wireless client devices owned by conference attendees can share this connection further by connecting to an open 802.11a/g network hosted by another WARP board connected via a layer 2 ethernet bridge. The broadcast SSID of this hotspot is "Rice-SuperWiFi."

This demonstration network is open source and programable at all layers, allowing the researcher to modify a system of interest and test on an operational, large-scale network if desired. The UHF reference design has been verified to operate at distances up to 1 kilometer in an outdoor, point-to-multipoint, NLOS network, as well as in an indoor, NLOS, multi-floor infrastructure deployment spanning the coverage areas of tens of WiFi access points.

In addition, the power of the open platform is demonstrated by measuring the channel state information and real-time MAC parameters of connected clients at both the UHF and WiFi nodes in real-time. Users of the network are able to browse the internet at broadband speeds while the monitoring system shows their network actions and channel statistics.

3. FUTURE WORK FOR UHF NETWORKS

The development and release of the WURC analog front-end enables a number of different research tracks:

Small-Cell Research. The presented reference design has been verified to operate at broadband speeds up to 1 kilometer NLOS in a point-to-multipoint outdoor deployment as well as indoors with multi-floor NLOS coverage from a single access point. While 2.4 GHz WiFi networks have been deployed in outdoor scenarios, they are severely limited by path loss and shadowing, whereas unlicensed devices in the UHF band benefit from an extended practical range that is realized by WURC. This enables at-scale deployments of open small-cell networks without the expense of LTE or WiMAX equipment and a completely open network stack. Interoperability with commodity equipment and access to queuing and scheduling at each point in the wireless network enables a host of possible quality-of-service applications.

UHF-Band MAC. Network topologies and channel availability in the UHF bands will be significantly different than the short-range WLANs envisioned by 802.11ac and 802.11af, while proposed solutions like 802.22 or LTE in UHF-bands represent significant investment in infrastructure and network coordination. The design of efficient MAC protocols that adapt to the different network topologies in UHF, coordinate spectrum sensing to identify spectrum reuse opportunities, or coordinate spectral usage through spectrum databases is currently a hot topic in the wireless research community. The demonstrated reference design allows rapid testing of new protocols by providing an out-of-the-box solution that can serve as a building-block.

Interference Mitigation and Coexistence. Cognitive radio networks in the UHF band will be operating in an environment with many interferers, both primary spectrum users (DTV transmitter and microphones) and secondary spectrum users (unlicensed UHF-band devices). MIMO beamforming and interference cancellation techniques can be used to mitigate both primary-to-secondary user interferences as well as secondary-to-primary user interference. WURC enables operational network topologies and environmental measurements at large scale and in true, outdoor environments, allowing researchers to prototype and test their systems.

Acknowledgments

This research was supported by NSF grants CNS-1314822, CNS-1126478, CNS-1012831, and a grant from Cisco Systems, Inc.

4. REFERENCES

[1] Mango 802.11 reference design. [online]. Available at: `http://mangocomm.com/802.11`.

[2] Rice University WARP project. Available at: `http://warp.rice.edu`.

[3] MobiCom demonstration video preview, June 2014. Available at: `http://youtu.be/dTOJHRICklQ`.

[4] WURC documentation, June 2014. Available at: `http://www.volowireless.com/products/WURC`.

[5] N. Anand, R. Guerra, and E. Knightly. The Case for UHF-Band MU-MIMO. In *Proc. ACM MobiCom*, Maui, HI, Aug. 2014.

[6] A. Flores, R. Guerra, E. Knightly, P. Ecclesine, and S. Pandey. IEEE 802.11af: A Standard for TV White Space Spectrum Sharing. *IEEE Communications Magazine*, 2013. 51(10):92-100.

Demo: Real-Time MU-MIMO Channel Analysis with a Custom 802.11 Implementation

Chris Hunter, Patrick Murphy, and Erik Welsh
Mango Communications, Inc.
Houston, TX USA
[chunter, murphpo, welsh]@mangocomm.com

ABSTRACT

We present a demonstration of the real-time capture and analysis of multi-user MIMO (MU-MIMO) channel state information from commercial Wi-Fi devices. Our system is built with an array of WARP v3 nodes running the Mango Communications 802.11 Reference Design, an open-source, real-time FPGA implementation of the 802.11a/g MAC and PHY. One WARP v3 node acts as an 802.11 access point (AP), which serves Internet access to client devices. The other nodes implement an array of multi-antenna 802.11 monitors. Every monitor node simultaneously receives packets transmitted by the Wi-Fi clients associated with the AP. The nodes extract MAC headers and channel estimates from each packet and offload these to a PC for analysis. All MAC, PHY, and channel analysis processes run in real time.

Categories and Subject Descriptors

C.2.1 [**Computer-Communication Networks**]: Network Architecture and Design—*Wireless communication*; C.4.3 [**Performance of Systems**]: [Measurement Techniques]

Keywords

IEEE 802.11; OFDM PHY; DCF MAC; MU-MIMO

1. INTRODUCTION

Multi-user MIMO (MU-MIMO) techniques play a key role in upcoming wireless standards. One of the core requirements of MU-MIMO systems is accurate and recent knowledge of the wireless propagation environment. Stale or inaccurate channel state information can collapse the performance gains enabled by MU-MIMO processing. Building systems that can gather and analyze MU-MIMO channel data in real time is a key research challenge.

In this demonstration, we present a system for MU-MIMO channel characterization that allows the study of channel dynamics in real time. This system is built on the Mango 802.11 Reference Design [1], an open-source, real-time implementation of the 802.11a/g Medium Access Control (MAC) layer and physical (PHY) layer [2] that runs on WARP v3 hardware. Basing our channel measurement system on a custom 802.11 stack allows characterization of channels between our array and standard Wi-Fi devices. During the demo conference attendees can associate their personal Wi-Fi devices with our array and observe how position and movement impact the real-time channel state information gathered by the array.

In Section 2, we first describe the 802.11 Reference Design that forms the foundation of our MU-MIMO channel characterization demo. In Section 3, we then present the specific details of the MU-MIMO demonstration. Finally, in Section 4, we list the requirements for our demonstration.

MobiCom'14, September 7-11, 2014, Maui, Hawaii, USA.
ACM 978-1-4503-2783-1/14/09.
http://dx.doi.org/10.1145/2639108.2641746.

2. 802.11 REFERENCE DESIGN

Our system is an extension of the Mango 802.11 Reference Design. This design interoperates with commercial Wi-Fi devices and implements both access point (AP) and station (STA) roles. All MAC and PHY processing is implemented in the FPGA of the WARP v3 hardware. The MAC and PHY source code is open, allowing researchers to study and extend the design to explore variations to the standard. This combination of real-time operation, interoperability with standard devices, and extensibility at all layers enables a wide range of wireless communications and networking research.

In addition to implementing a standards-compliant MAC and PHY, the Mango 802.11 Reference Design provides the WARPnet framework for conducting wireless experiments with many nodes. This framework provides deep visibility and control of the MAC and PHY in hardware. WARPnet records all transmit and receive events in a log stored in on-board RAM. The receive log entries include the MAC header, packet payload, received power, antenna selection, and per-subcarrier channel estimates from the PHY. The transmit log entries include low-level DCF transmissions and retransmissions with the current contention window value and the instantaneous per-transmission backoff slot count selections. The WARPnet framework is designed to be modified and extended by researchers to accommodate new experiments. A few example extensions are presented in [3].

In addition to these low-level capture capabilities of the framework, we have developed high-level analysis and visualization tools:

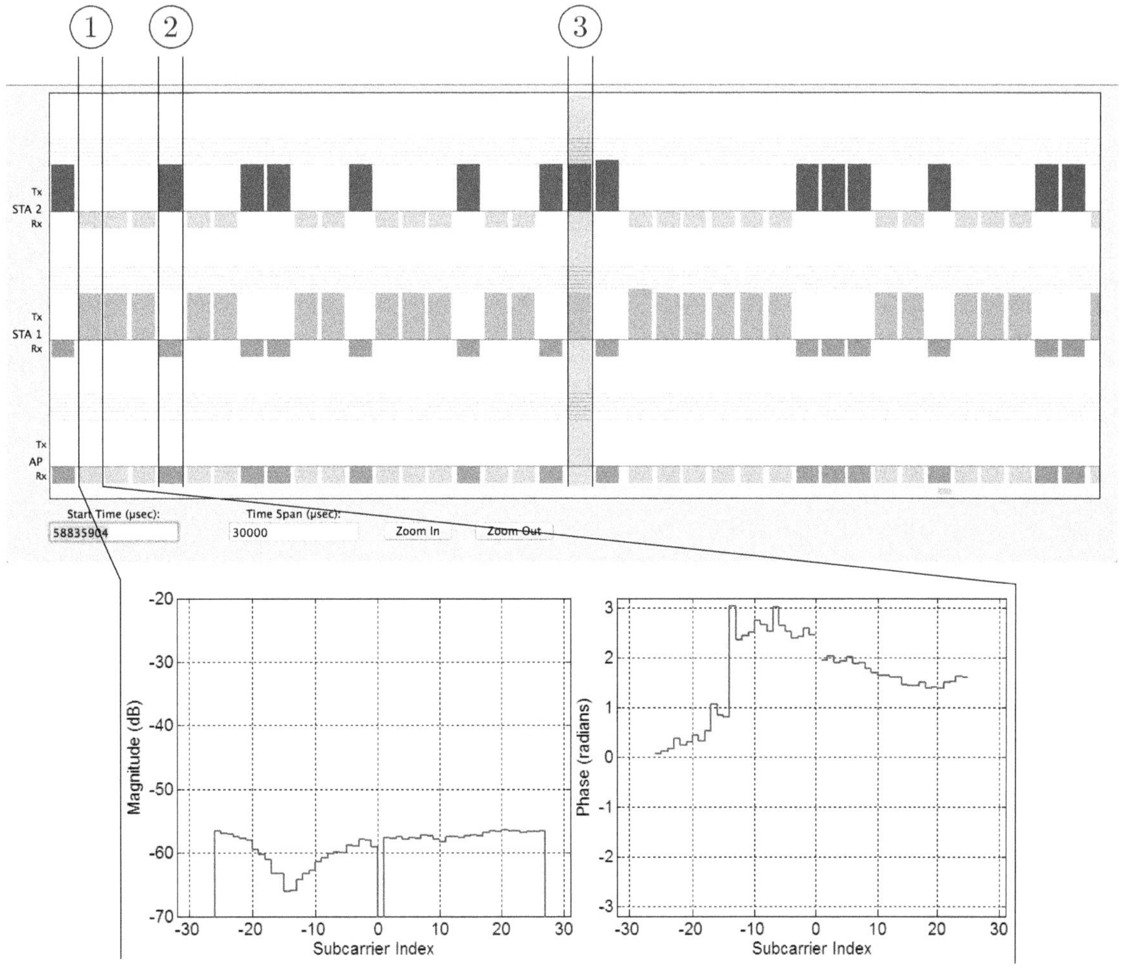

Figure 1: Screenshot of interactive event visualizer.

Real-time Channel Visualizer: Every received frame is logged alongside that reception's view of the wireless channel. The channel visualizer displays the wireless channel for any selected packet, making it easy to see frequency-selective fading.

Collision Analyzer: By analyzing the transmission logs of every node on the network, the collision analyzer utility can identify instances of multiple nodes transmitting simultaneously. The utility also analyzes the receive events at non-transmitting nodes to discern whether any packet was received. The utility highlights these "captured" transmissions in its timeline display.

Interactive Event Visualizer: The log data from multiple nodes are jointly analyzed, with the results displayed in an interactive application. This application allows panning through timelines of wireless events and enables spotting interesting or unexpected behaviors on both short and long time scales.

Figure 1 shows an example screenshot of the interactive event visualizer. In the experiment that generated the data in this figure, two station nodes (STA 1 and STA 2) are both transmitting backlogged flows to a common AP. Three events are annotated in the figure that warrant discussion:

(1): This event shows a transmission from STA 1 to the AP as an "up" orange bar in the STA 1 timeline. The "down" light orange bar in the AP's timeline denotes the successful reception at the AP. Also shown for this event is the AP's channel estimates for the actual packet reception. We can see that the packet underwent a moderate amount of multipath fading, manifesting as frequency selectivity in the channel response. This physical layer channel data is available for every packet in the timeline but it is only shown for one event here for clarity.

(2): This event shows a transmission from STA 2 to the AP as a blue bar in the STA 2 timeline. The light blue bar in the AP's timeline denotes the successful reception of the packet at the AP.

(3): This event shows a collision between transmissions by STA 1 and STA 2, resulting in no reception at the AP. This collision region, highlighted in grey, is identified automatically by the collision analyzer utility, allowing rapid panning through large datasets to find examples of contention.

Together, these events showcase a very powerful analysis tool for understanding MAC and PHY behaviors across multiple nodes. These tools will be available during our demonstration for use by visitors.

3. DEMONSTRATION

Our demonstration uses the Mango 802.11 Reference Design and WARPnet experiments framework to gather, analyze, and visualize channel data gathered from a 16-antenna array. The array gathers channel data from transmissions by Wi-Fi devices provided by conference attendees. A custom application analyzes the channel data to calculate instantaneous achievable multi-user channel capacity. Users can interact with the demonstration in real time and witness how the instantaneous channels between their devices and the array can affect MU-MIMO performance.

The demo hardware consists of five WARP v3 kits. One WARP v3 kit uses the Mango 802.11 Reference Design in AP mode, allowing conference attendees to associate with their phones. This AP provides Internet access to the attendees as well as generating regular traffic to each phone to probe the wireless channel. The other four WARP v3 kits are equipped with 4 radio interfaces each and run the 802.11 Reference Design in a receive-only monitor mode. Together these kits form a 16-antenna array. The array nodes stream received packets and channel observations via WARPnet to a PC that runs a custom analysis application.

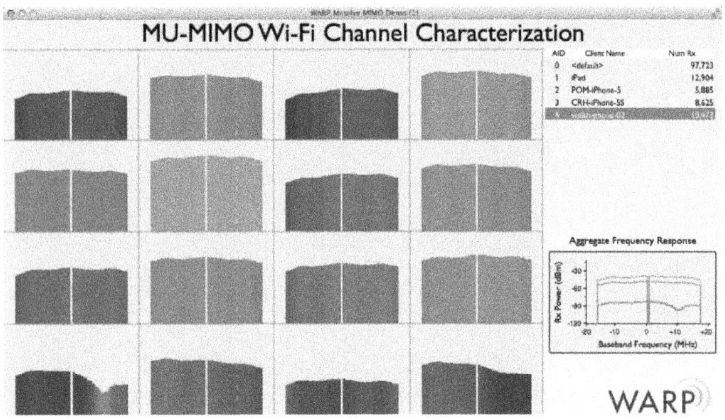

(a) Per-subcarrier channel magnitudes

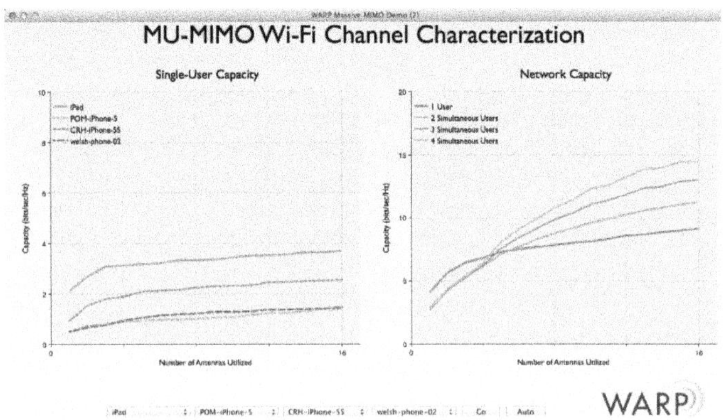

(b) Capacities calculated from real channel estimates

Figure 2: The real-time analysis application provides a detailed view of the MU-MIMO channel characterization as well as the potential performance of multi-user schemes that are subjected to those same channels.

The analysis application consumes and analyzes the channel data from the 16-antenna WARP array. Two visualizations are displayed in real time. The first display, illustrated in Figure 2(a), shows the magnitude of each complex channel coefficient for each subcarrier from every array antenna. This display updates live, allowing users to see the direct impact of moving their devices on the measured channel responses.

The second display, illustrated in Figure 2(b), shows the instantaneous capacity of a multi-user network with access to the same channel estimates. Users are able to observe the tradeoffs exposed by multi-user techniques and explore the channel conditions where multiple users can be supported as well as the conditions where they cannot. On this display, the left graph shows the per-user capacity of a traditional single-user system. Here, each of the four users has its own dedicated timeslot, and increasing the number of antennas only increases SNR through single-user beamforming gains – a strategy that is well known to have diminishing returns in terms of rate and throughput. On the right side of the same figure we see the sum network capacity across all the users. The red line shows the network capacity of a traditional single-user system. This line is the sum of the four lines in the left plot. On the other extreme, the green line shows the capacity of the network if all four users could be served simultaneously. Specifically, the analysis behind this plot assumes the well-known conjugate beamforming approach to MU-MIMO. With this strategy, there is an unavoidable increase in interference between users when all are served simultaneously. Under certain channel conditions and numbers of antennas employed, this tradeoff prevents MU-MIMO from providing gains.

A video of the full demonstration is available [4].

4. DEMO REQUIREMENTS

We will bring the necessary WARP v3 kits, PCs and accessories. The venue resources required for our demo are:

- $\approx$ 6 ft $\times$ 3 ft table space (additional space would be welcome);
- Electrical power, at least 2 A @ 120 V;
- If available, a power strip with 8 free outlets (we can supply this otherwise);
- If available, a wired Internet connection which does not require authentication;
- Approximately 1 hour of setup time.

5. REFERENCES

[1] "Mango 802.11 Reference Design." [Online]. Available: http://mangocomm.com/802.11

[2] "IEEE Standard for Information technology–Telecommunications and information exchange between systems Local and metropolitan area networks–Specific requirements Part 11: Wireless LAN Medium Access Control (MAC) and Physical Layer (PHY) Specifications," *IEEE Std 802.11-2012*, pp. 1–2793, March 2012.

[3] "WARPnet." [Online]. Available: http://warpproject.org/trac/wiki/WARPnet

[4] "Demo Video." [Online]. Available: http://mangocomm.com/mobicom2014-demo

Demo: ShadowMaps, The Urban Phone Tracking System

Andrew Irish
Dept. of Electrical and Computer Engineering
UC Santa Barbara
Santa Barbara, CA 93106
andrewirish@ece.ucsb.edu

Jason Isaacs
Dept. of Electrical and Computer Engineering
UC Santa Barbara
Santa Barbara, CA 93106
jtisaacs@ece.ucsb.edu

Daniel Iland
Dept. of Computer Science
UC Santa Barbara
Santa Barbara, CA 93106
iland@cs.ucsb.edu

João Hespanha
Dept. of Electrical and Computer Engineering
UC Santa Barbara
Santa Barbara, CA 93106
hespanha@ece.ucsb.edu

Elizabeth Belding
Dept. of Computer Science
UC Santa Barbara
Santa Barbara, CA 93106
ebelding@cs.ucsb.edu

Upamanyu Madhow
Dept. of Electrical and Computer Engineering
UC Santa Barbara
Santa Barbara, CA 93106
madhow@ece.ucsb.edu

ABSTRACT

Due to frequent non-line-of-sight (NLOS) signal reception, geopositioning using Global Navigation Satellite Systems (GNSS), such as GPS, is unreliable in urban environments, with errors on the order of tens of meters. This poses a major problem for mobile services that benefit from accurate urban localization, such as navigation, geofencing, and hyperlocal advertising applications. Mobile network operators also seek improvements in localization, as government regulators increase handset location accuracy requirements of enhanced 991 service (e911). In our demonstration, we will present the most recent prototype of our urban location improvement technology, called ShadowMaps, which will be shown to accurately track a mobile device in an urban environment, with up to an order of magnitude reduction in GNSS positioning error.

Categories and Subject Descriptors

H.4 [**Information Systems Applications**]: Miscellaneous

Keywords

System Demonstration; GNSS; GPS; Localization Improvement; Crowdsourcing; 3D Mapping

1. INTRODUCTION

Many mobile services, including location-based advertising, navigation, and emergency response applications, benefit from or require accurate geolocalization outdoors. Another, more specific example is a so called "phone finder" app that allows a user to remotely track their device if it is lost or stolen via a web interface. Unfortunately, however, in dense urban environments accuracy of the often relied upon Global Positioning System (GPS) degrades significantly, with errors on the order of tens of meters [5].

MobiCom'14, September 7-11, 2014, Maui, Hawaii, USA.
ACM 978-1-4503-2783-1/14/09.
http://dx.doi.org/10.1145/2639108.2641755.

The main culprit for this performance bottleneck is that in large cities the line-of-sight (LOS) to various satellites becomes occluded by buildings, leading to non-light-of-sight (NLOS) and multipath signal reception. As a result, the only satellites useful for accurate trilateration come from a narrow region in the sky, yielding poor satellite geometries and positioning accuracy, particularly in the cross street direction. The underlying geometry problem is not solved even as additional constellations of Global Navigation Satellite Systems (GNSS) – such as the Russian GLONASS – become supported by mobile devices. Fortunately, though, this urban "Shadowing Problem" can be exploited in two steps, as we have shown in previous research [1, 2, 4]. In our demonstration, we will showcase an end-to-end application of our previous research, the real-time phone tracking system called *ShadowMaps.*

1.1 Probabilistic 3D Mapping

The first step to exploiting the Shadowing Problem is to use crowdsourced satellite signal-to-noise ratio (SNR) measurements to create 3D maps of the environment. Intuitively, this is made feasible by the simple observation that, for example, the SNR of signals obstructed by buildings is lower on average than that of LOS signals. Reality, however, is more complicated: multipath fading can be severe in urban environments, leading to low SNR values even for LOS satellites. As a consequence, in cities single SNR measurements are generally unreliable indicators of whether a satellite is LOS or NLOS. To address this, in [1, 2] we proposed to use large amounts of GNSS data and to assign likelihoods of blockage to satellite-to-receiver "rays" in accordance with a wireless channel model. Afterwards, one can then "probabilistically stitch" many such rays together into 3D maps using machine learning techniques. If the necessary GNSS data is crowdsourced from many devices and cloud-based computation is leveraged, building such 3D maps can be done cheaply and scalably.

1.2 Real-time Positioning

The second step is to use a sort of reverse process to mapping, called Shadow Matching (SM). As illustrated in Figure 1, in SM 3D map databases and real-time satellite coordinates can be used to compute the shadows of buildings with respect to various satellites. Then, lower (or higher) satellite signal-to-noise ratio (SNR) measurements can be used to probabilistically match the device's location to areas inside (or outside) various shadows, reducing positioning uncertainty.

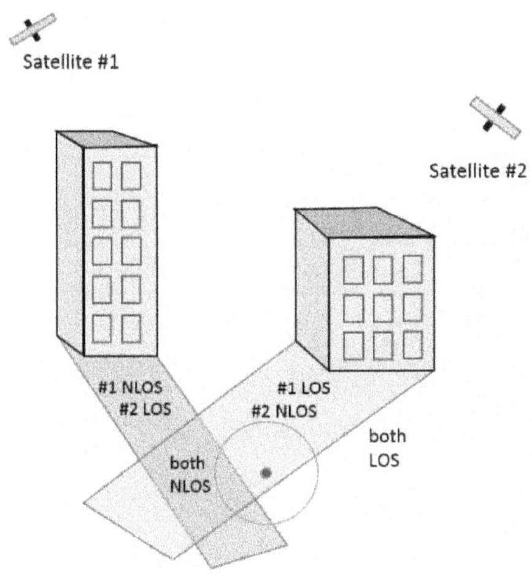

Figure 1: Illustration of positioning improvement using Shadow Matching.

Figure 2: Google Maps aerial view of the portion of UCSB campus that was mapped in [1], with 2 out of a total of 34 input datasets shown for reference.

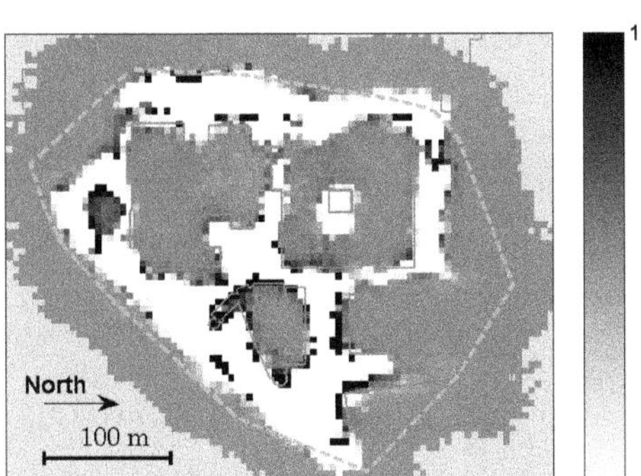

Figure 3: Example horizontal slice (5-10 m. above ground) of the resulting map. White/black areas correspond to low/high probability of occupancy, and building contours obtained from OpenStreetMap are shown in red.

Of course, in practice any useful SM algorithm must also enforce motion continuity for the device whose location is being tracked. In [4], we describe a simple particle filter that performs SM in addition to considering such kinematic constraints, and which is also fully implementable in application level software. Showing how such a software-based SM filter functions in a real system will be the focus of our demonstration.

2. EXAMPLE EXPERIMENTAL RESULTS

At the time of the writing of this document, we have prototyped our mapping and positioning algorithms in downtown Santa Barbara and on the University of California, Santa Barbara (UCSB) campus. Although our offline mapping algorithms will not be the focus of our demonstration, some results of our UCSB mapping experiments are shown in Figures 2 and 3, which were created from about 7 hours of GPS data collected outdoors over several days using an Android tablet. The results from a separate downtown Santa Barbara experiment, where over 25 hours of data was logged using 4 Android devices, can be seen in Figures 4 and 5; in this experiment, 2D OpenStreetMap mapping data was used as a-priori information on the bottom two layers of the map.

Figure 4: Aerial view of downtown Santa Barbara, with GNSS traces in red and mapped region outlined in yellow.

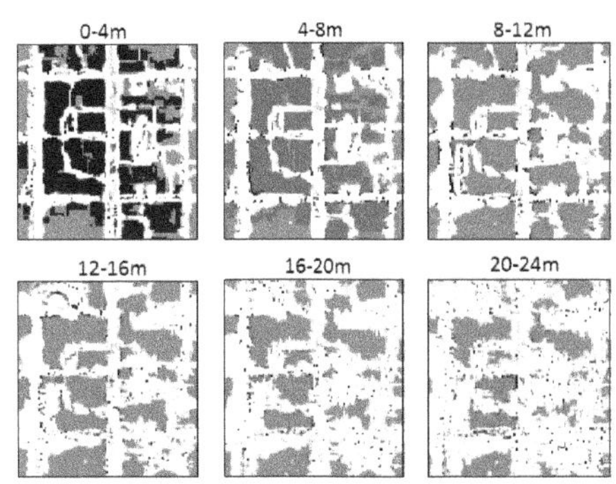

Figure 5: Horizontal layers of the generated occupancy map of downtown Santa Barbara.

Since having published [4], we have made significant progress with our localization algorithms. Specifically, we have improved the performance of our particle filter, which we have successfully prototyped both on campus at UCSB (as shown in Figure 6) and in downtown Santa Barbara (see Figure 7 and our YouTube video [3]).

3. SYSTEM DEMONSTRATION DETAILS

In our demonstration we will remotely and accurately track an Android device traversing an urban environment that we will have previously mapped (for example Santa Barbara – an area we have already mapped – or alternatively San Francisco, a portion of which we plan to map this summer). Our Android phone finder app,

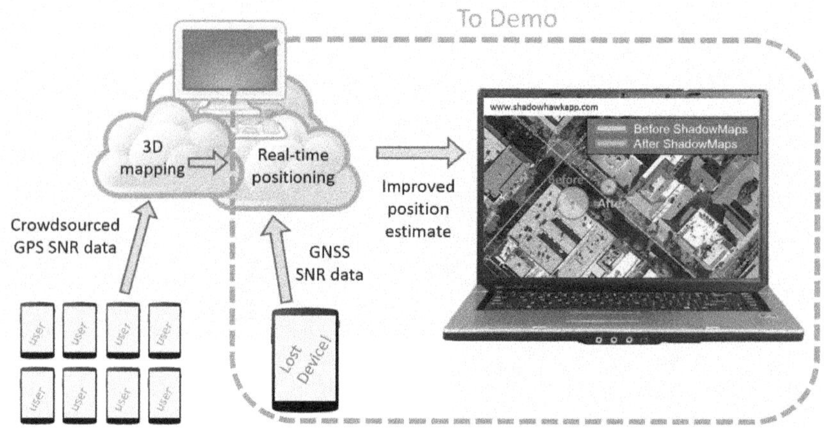

Figure 8: ShadowMaps system architecture and the components comprising the demonstration.

Figure 6: Positioning improvement at UCSB: true path in yellow, standalone GNSS output in red, and corrected (post-SM) path in light blue.

Figure 7: Positioning improvement in downtown Santa Barbara: true path in yellow, a-GNSS output in red, and corrected (post-SM) path in light blue.

called ShadowHawk, runs as a background service on the device, passively providing satellite SNR data to our servers, as well as some ancillary information (GNSS latitude-longitude fix, uncertainty, etc.). There, our real-time positioning routines compute and store revised position fixes. These improved position estimates can be viewed through a map-based web interface, which displays the current location and past locations of the tracked device. The web interface will be displayed on a laptop on site at MobiCom. This is the main user interface (UI) for ShadowHawk. As a means of verifying ground truth, our demo will also include a live video feed of the user who is being tracked (one of the authors) walking in the area of interest. A schematic of the ShadowMaps system which highlights the portions we will demonstrate is shown in Figure 8.

3.1 Facilities and equipment needed

We will need power plugs for a laptop and a TV monitor to display our tracking results. Additionally, we will need a table large enough to fit these items and a reliable internet connection (preferably wired) for the real-time demonstration. Setup time should be at most half an hour.

4. REFERENCES

[1] A. T. Irish, J. T. Isaacs, F. Quitin, J. P. Hespanha, and U. Madhow. Belief propagation based localization and mapping using sparsely sampled GNSS SNR measurements. In *Proc. of the International Conference on Robotics and Automation*, 2014.

[2] A. T. Irish, J. T. Isaacs, F. Quitin, J. P. Hespanha, and U. Madhow. Probabilistic 3D mapping based on GNSS SNR measurements. In *Proc. of 2014 IEEE International Conference on Acoustics and Signal Processing*, 2014.

[3] J. T. Isaacs, D. Iland, and A. T. Irish. MobiCom 14 demonstration proposal video. `http://youtu.be/c8R5FXF8Aso`. Accessed: 2014-07-15.

[4] J. T. Isaacs, A. T. Irish, F. Quitin, U. Madhow, and J. P. Hespanha. Bayesian localization and mapping using GNSS SNR measurements. In *Proc. of 2014 IEEE Position Location and Navigation Symposium*, 2014.

[5] M. Park, H. Kim, S. Lee, and K. Bae. Performance evaluation of Android location service at the urban canyon. In *16th International Conference on Advanced Communication Technology*, pages 662–665. IEEE, 2014.

Demo: Simulating the Impact of Communication Performance on Road Traffic Safety at Intersections

Stefan Joerer[*‡], Bastian Bloessl[†], Matthaeus Huber[*], Abbas Jamalipour[‡] and Falko Dressler[†]

[*]Institute of Computer Science, University of Innsbruck, Austria
[†]Distributed Embedded Systems, Institute of Computer Science, University of Paderborn, Germany
[‡]School of Electrical & Information Engineering, University of Sydney, Australia

{joerer,bloessl,matthaeus.huber,dressler}@ccs-labs.org, a.jamalipour@ieee.org

ABSTRACT

Performance evaluation of communication protocols is usually carried out using typical network metrics as delay, jitter, or goodput. However, recent studies in the context of Inter-Vehicle Communication (IVC) have shown that using these metrics is not sufficient for evaluating vehicular safety applications. To highlight the importance of safety metrics and their applicability, we extended our existing simulation framework Veins to visualize these metrics live while the road traffic and network simulation are running in parallel. In particular, we demonstrate the impact of communication on intersection assistance applications. To simulate different intersection approaches, we implemented a simulation model that resembles different kinds of driver behavior and enables crashes at intersections. The resulting situations are displayed in the road traffic simulator and give the visitor insights on the current state of endangered vehicles. Furthermore, an autonomous controller has been implemented which tries to avoid accidents and hence shows the real-world impact, i.e., accidents can be avoided using advanced beaconing techniques. To increase interactivity of the demo, visitors will have the possibility to interact with and take control over endangered vehicles.

1. INTRODUCTION

Inter-Vehicle Communications (IVCs) will enable future vehicles to run diverse applications ranging from entertainment to vehicular safety applications. Current research is focusing on vehicular safety applications, since they are regarded as the main driver to deploy Dedicated Short-Range Communication (DSRC) radios [4]. Envisioned safety applications are manifold. One particularly challenging application regarding the communications point of view are so-called intersection assistance applications, as they require reliable real-time communication mostly under demanding Non Line of Sight (NLOS) conditions.

MobiCom'14, September 7-11, 2014, Maui, Hawaii, USA.
ACM 978-1-4503-2783-1/14/09
http://dx.doi.org/10.1145/2639108.2641737.

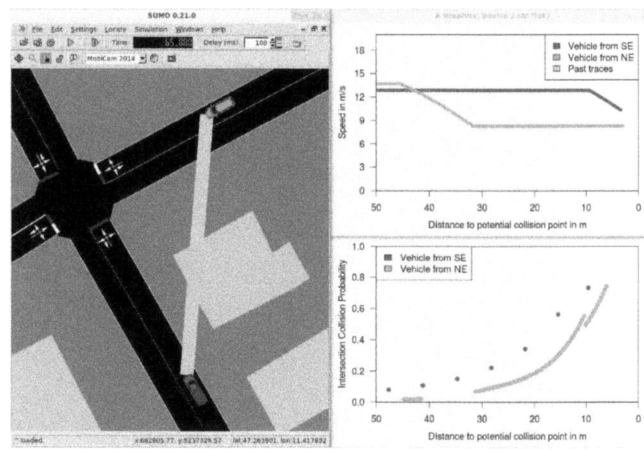

Figure 1: Overview of the demo GUI.

In the past decade, several standards for IVC have been developed (e.g., [7]). Although first Field Operational Tests (FOTs) have been conducted it is still unclear to which extent IVC will be able to support safety applications. Moreover, FOTs are not the primary method to develop and investigate new communication protocols or strategies. Therefore, current research on vehicular safety applications is relying on extensive simulation studies to investigate the effects of communication on vehicular safety applications [1, 8].

Usually communication protocols are evaluated with typical network metrics as goodput, latency, jitter, and in case of wireless networks, channel load and collisions. However, these metrics are not adequate to assess the impact of communication on life saving applications, i.e., a high throughput might not be an indicator that a lot of accidents can be avoided. Thus more adequate safety metrics for IVC have been proposed [5]. We made a first step towards safety metrics by introducing the *intersection collision probability*, which is a measure for crash likelihood at intersections [9]. The evolution of the intersection collision probability is depicted in the lower right part in Figure 1.

Our work follows a line of research that was started earlier. In 2005 a complete simulation architecture for IVC based intersection assistance applications has been presented in [2]. Interestingly, the authors showed the impact of their Time Division Multiple Access (TDMA) based communication strategy already by proofing the reduction of crashes and by showing the average speed of colliding vehicles. Meanwhile the IEEE 802.11p standard using CSMA/CA has been released and beacon-based solutions with congestion control mechanisms [7] are proposed instead of TDMA approaches. Therefore, an up-to-date simulation environment for intersection assistance applications will help to study and design communication strategies.

This demo highlights how *Communication Performance* and safety metrics have an impact on *Road Traffic Safety*. To demonstrate the impact of different communication strategies this demo is based on the following contributions:

- We integrated the calculation of the intersection collision probability into the Veins simulation framework.
- We developed an intersection approach model that allows to simulate arbitrary driver behaviors which lead to CRASH situations (Section 2.1).
- We implemented a simple autonomous reaction controller as well as an interaction interface which both allow to omit crashes (Section 2.2).

More specifically, this demo points out that, in certain situations, current standards (e.g., ETSI Transmit Rate Control (TRC)) are not able to provide sufficient communication opportunities. Furthermore, we show how this limitation can be overcome with the help of so called *situation-based rate adaptation* proposed in [8].

2. INTEGRATION WITH VEINS

As a basis we use the Veins simulation framework[1] which couples the road traffic simulator SUMO and the network simulator OMNeT++ bidirectionally. We extended this framework to simulate arbitrary collision situations at intersections, to detect crash situations, and to perform autonomously reactions of endangered vehicles when the communication-based intersection assistance application triggers them.

Our simulation includes several vehicles in vicinity of the intersection. For being able to demonstrate the effect of communication, we consider always only two dangerously approaching vehicles at a time. As depicted in Figure 1 the monitored vehicles are coloured blue and red as long as they have not been communicating with each other. When the monitored vehicles receive a Cooperative Awareness Message (CAM), they can calculate their intersection collision probability as defined in [9] and change their color according to the estimated crash likelihood (starting from green over yellow to red). In addition the evolution of the intersection collision probability is plotted live for both monitored vehicles (cf. Figure 1 lower plot on the right) dependent on the distance whenever they receive a CAM. Moreover, the upper plot in Figure 1 depicts the vehicle dynamics of both vehicles, i.e., the driven speed at distances of less than 50 m to the intersection.

Other vehicles are yellow for visibility reasons and do not influence the colliding vehicles from a road traffic point of view. Nevertheless, all vehicles are exchanging CAMs and hence, the communication of the two potential collision vehicles is influenced by all present vehicles in the simulation. Communication is simulated in OMNeT++ using detailed models for radio propagation, physical layer, Medium Access Control (MAC), and the ETSI TRC. The simulation models and parameters are listed in Table 1.

[1]`http://veins.car2x.org/`

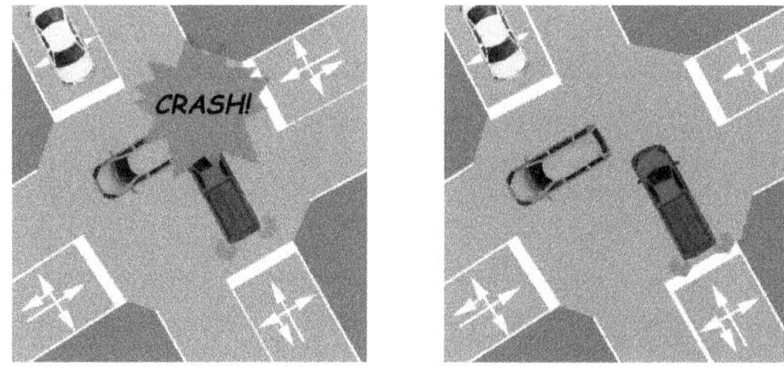

(a) CRASH Situation (b) NO CRASH Situation

Figure 2: Detailed view of intersection area.

2.1 Simulating Crashes at Intersections

For being able to simulate and analyse arbitrary intersection approaches we implemented a simulation model which is parameterized by the *aggressiveness* and *discipline* of the driver as proposed in [6]. The aggressiveness parameter accounts for the fact that not all drivers are pushing the brake pedal equally. The second parameter simulates driver's braking reaction (i.e., drivers do no always brake in time) and hence called discipline. In particular this allows to simulate crashes with different speeds, acceleration/deceleration behaviors; where right-of-way rules or traffic lights are ignored by the drivers. More precisely, the vehicles in the road traffic simulator SUMO ignore traffic rules and their speed as well as acceleration or deceleration are completely controlled via a so-called `CollisionScenario` implemented in OMNeT++. To ensure that the demo is easy to follow the simulation model always executes only one `CollisionScenario` at a time.

Basically, the `CollisionScenario` determines the simulated driver behavior by randomly choosing aggressiveness and discipline (D_{agg} and D_{dis}, respectively) as well as a crossing speed (v_{cross}). Based on this information, the crossing times (t_{c1} and t_{c2}) of both vehicles to the potential collision position can be computed. Moreover, the time delta t_δ can be calculated by $t_\delta = |t_{c1} - t_{c2}|$. The value of this time delta t_δ is used by the intersection approach model and affects the outcome of the corresponding `CollisionScenario`, i.e., CRASH or NO CRASH. Depending on the speed and outline of the vehicles very small deltas (less than 1 s) typically result in CRASH (cf. Figure 2a). Whereas, larger deltas (more than 1.0 s) usually still imitate dangerous driving behavior, but result in NO CRASH (cf. Figure 2b). The parameters used for the intersection approach model are listed in Table 1.

Even though the autonomous controller or the people interacting with the demo try to avoid crashes, they can still occur. Therefore, a collision detection algorithm is executed every simulation time step, which checks whether the outlines of any two vehicles at the intersection are overlapping. The collision detection is parameterized with the values listed in the lower part of Table 1.

2.2 Crash Avoidance

Our demo has two modes that can be executed: One makes use of a simple autonomous reaction controller to demonstrate the real-world impact of different communication strategies. The other one allows visitors of the demo trying to avoid a crash by taking control over one of the two endangered vehicles.

	Parameter	Value
PHY & MAC	Path loss model	Free space ($\alpha = 2.0$)
	Shadowing model	Building Shadowing [11]
	Attenuation per wall [11]	$\beta = 9.0$ dB
	Attenuation per m [11]	$\gamma = 0.4$ dB
	PHY model	IEEE 802.11p
	MAC model	IEEE 1609.4
	Frequency	5.89 GHz
	Bitrate	6 Mbit/s
	Access category	AC_VO
	MSDU size	193 B
	Transmit power	30 dBm
TRC	I_{min}, I_{def}, I_{max}	0.04 s, 0.5 s, 1 s
	b_{min}, b_{max}	0.15, 0.40
	T_{M}, T_{DCC}, T_{up}, T_{down}	1 s, 1 s, 1 s, 5 s
Road traffic simulation	Max. speed [3, Tab. IV]	$\sim \mathcal{N}(13.89, 2.92)$ m/s
	Max. acceleration	2.1 m/s^2
	Max. deceleration [10]	9.55 m/s^2
	Driver aggression D_{agg}	$\sim \mathcal{U}(10, 90)$ %
	Driver discipline D_{dis}	$\sim \mathcal{U}(10, 90)$ %
	Crossing speed v_{cross}	$\sim \mathcal{U}(3, 12)$ m/s
	Time Delta t_δ	$\sim \mathcal{U}(0.1, 1.0)$ s
	Simulation time step	10 ms
	Vehicle length	5.0 m
	Vehicle width	1.75 m

Table 1: Simulation parameters for the demo.

The autonomous reaction controller monitors the intersection collision probability for both endangered vehicles individually. When the collision probability exceeds a threshold of 50 %, the vehicles are reacting as follows:

1. The vehicle closer to the potential collision point is continuing with the same speed.

2. The vehicle further away is going to perform a full stop immediately with the maximum deceleration rate.

Obviously, this is not sufficient for all possible crash situations and thus more effort is needed to develop more advanced reactions controllers, but by using this approach we can already observe a major impact of communication on road traffic safety.

3. POSSIBLE FUTURE SAFETY METRICS

In [8] we have used *intersection approach model* described in Section 2.1 to investigate the impact of communication fairness on road traffic safety. One safety metric in that paper was the *unsafe time* that a vehicle experienced during the last three seconds before a crash.

In future the presented simulation framework can be used in conjunction with any realistic autonomous controller or a driver reaction model to evaluate communication protocols and strategies for intersection assistance applications. We suggest future simulation the use of the following more comprehensive safety metrics:

- *Percentage of avoided crashes*

- The *reduced collision speed* and the *reduced maximum percentage of possible overlap*, might serve together as impact reduction metric, for the remaining crashes.

4. ACKNOWLEDGMENTS AND VIDEO

Stefan Joerer acknowledges support from the Endeavour Research Fellowship which made a collaboration with the University of Sydney possible. We would like to thank Mariam Joerer for providing hand-drawn vehicles for the road traffic simulation visualization.

A one minute video clip that shows the demo is available at `www.youtube.com/watch?v=FwQxbcOmfB8&hd=1`.

5. REFERENCES

[1] N. An, M. Maile, D. Jiang, J. Mittag, and H. Hartenstein. Balancing the Requirements for a Zero False Positive/Negative Forward Collision Warnings. In *IEEE/IFIP WONS 2013*, pages 191–195, Banff, Canada, March 2013. IEEE.

[2] A. Avila, G. Korkmaz, Y. Liu, H. Teh, E. Ekici, F. Özgüner, Ü. Özgüner, K. Redmill, O. Takeshita, K. Tokuda, M. Hamaguchi, S. Nakabayashi, and H. Tsutsui. A Complete Simulator Architecture for Inter-vehicle Communication Based Intersection Warning Systems. In *IEEE ITSC 2005*, pages 461–466, Vienna, Austria, September 2005. IEEE.

[3] H. Chen, L. Cao, and D. B. Logan. Investigation Into the Effect of an Intersection Crash Warning System on Driving Performance in a Simulator. *Traffic Injury Prevention*, 12(5):529–537, 2011.

[4] F. Dressler, H. Hartenstein, O. Altintas, and O. K. Tonguz. Inter-Vehicle Communication - Quo Vadis. *IEEE Communications Magazine*, 52(6):170–177, June 2014.

[5] F. Dressler, F. Kargl, J. Ott, O. K. Tonguz, and L. Wischhof. Research Challenges in Inter-Vehicular Communication - Lessons of the 2010 Dagstuhl Seminar. *IEEE Communications Magazine*, 49(5):158–164, May 2011.

[6] J. Edelmann and M. Plöchl. A driver model for vehicle dynamics simulation. In *EAEC 11*, pages 1–14, Budapest, Hungary, May 2012. GTE.

[7] European Telecommunications Standards Institute. Intelligent Transport Systems (ITS); Decentralized Congestion Control Mechanisms for Intelligent Transport Systems operating in the 5 GHz range; Access layer part. TS 102 687 V1.1.1, ETSI, July 2011.

[8] S. Joerer, B. Bloessl, M. Segata, C. Sommer, R. Lo Cigno, and F. Dressler. Fairness Kills Safety: A Comparative Study for Intersection Assistance Applications. In *IEEE PIMRC 2014*, Washington, D.C., September 2014. IEEE. to appear.

[9] S. Joerer, M. Segata, B. Bloessl, R. Lo Cigno, C. Sommer, and F. Dressler. A Vehicular Networking Perspective on Estimating Vehicle Collision Probability at Intersections. *IEEE Transactions on Vehicular Technology*, 63(4):1802–1812, May 2014.

[10] D. Schrauben and J. Flegel. Police Vehicle Evaluation Model Year 2013. Technical report, Michigan State Police, Precision Driving Unit, December 2012.

[11] C. Sommer, D. Eckhoff, R. German, and F. Dressler. A Computationally Inexpensive Empirical Model of IEEE 802.11p Radio Shadowing in Urban Environments. In *8th IEEE/IFIP Conference on Wireless On demand Network Systems and Services (WONS 2011)*, pages 84–90, Bardonecchia, Italy, January 2011. IEEE.

Demo: Co-primary Spectrum Sharing with Inter-Operator D2D Trial

Markku Jokinen
Centre for Wireless Communications
P.O.Box 4500
FI-90014, University of Oulu
markku.jokinen@ee.oulu.fi

Marko Mäkeläinen
Centre for Wireless Communications
P.O.Box 4500
FI-90014, University of Oulu
marko.makelainen@ee.oulu.fi

Tuomo Hänninen
Centre for Wireless Communications
P.O.Box 4500
FI-90014, University of Oulu
tuomo.hanninen@ee.oulu.fi

ABSTRACT

A co-primary spectrum sharing trial is presented in this paper. It is presenting a flexible way to share resources between multiple operators in order to increase spectral efficiency. In this trial the differences in traffic patterns of the mobile network operators are exploited to ease up the peak traffic demands of particular operator. This shared recourse is also usable for inter-operator D2D communication, when two users of different operators want to communicate and operators need to negotiate resource allocation for this communication link. We will also introduce Wireless Open Access Research Platform as our choice for the implementation of this trial.

Categories and Subject Descriptors

B.4.1 [**Input/Output and Data Communications**]: Data Communications Devices—*receivers, transmitters*; C.2.3 [**Network Operations**]: Network management, Network monitoring

Keywords

inter-operator; sharing; WARP

1. INTRODUCTION

Current spectrum allocation policy in use is known as fixed spectrum access (FSA), where the access is either licensed or unlicensed. Licensed spectrum results in a predictable quality of service (QoS) [1]. Small part of the spectrum is unlicensed. As anyone can use the spectrum, the QoS is unpredictable [1]. More efficient spectrum utilization can be achieved through spectrum sharing and dynamic spectrum access (DSA) techniques [2].

Sharing between operators have been shown to increase overall performance of the network [3]. This allows network to exploit differences in traffic patterns of different mobile network operators (MNOs) and to even out peaks in traffic demand. Hence, orthogonal traffic patterns will give the best performance gain to the network.

We will introduce a novel design for sharing resources between MNOs, the method is called co-primary spectrum sharing (CoPSS). This method is intended to pico cell applications where multiple MNOs are present at the same geological area or indoors. Suitability of these resources for inter-operator D2D communication is also shown. Wireless Open Access Research Platform (WARP) is our choice as the platform, and more precisely Linux Enriched design for WARP (LE-WARP), as it offers good basics of building experimental networks.

MobiCom'14, September 7-11, 2014, Maui, Hawaii, USA.
ACM 978-1-4503-2783-1/14/09.
http://dx.doi.org/10.1145/2639108.2641749.

2. WIRELESS OPEN ACCESS RESEARCH PLATFORM

Heart of the WARP is field-programmable gate array (FPGA) chip, which enables flexible designs to be implemented on the board [4]. WARP design can be divided into three different layers. Physical (PH) layer algorithms are running on the FPGA, taking care of the real time signal processing requirements. FPGA is also housing general purpose processor cores, taking care of running medium access control (MAC) and network (NET) layer control code. For WARP open source orthogonal frequency-division multiplexing (OFDM) reference design is provided by Rice University.

2.1 Linux Enriched design for WARP

LE-WARP design extends functionality of OFDM reference design [4] with a fully functional operating system on the board. Linux operation system allows user to run applications on the platform e.g. routing and traffic generation programs, making it more independent part of the research network. [5]

LE-WARP design enables building a self-contained real time network out of WARP nodes. Recently our studies have been focusing on centralized networks emulating real-life mobile networks which contain base stations (BSs) and user equipments (UEs). Building a network requires routing. The LE-WARP design offers an easy way for implementing this. [6]

LE-WARP design enables the illustration of the network with a graphical user interface (GUI). The example view of CWC GUI is presented in Fig 1. It also enables control of the network and individual node with control panel, and traffic generation to see how the network will respond in different load scenarios.

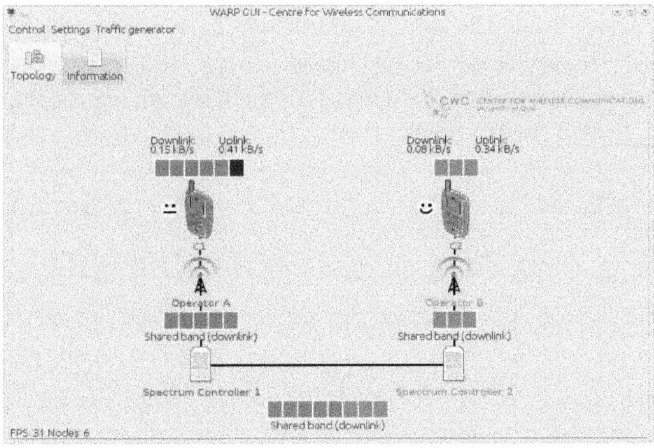

Figure 1: An example view of CWC UI.

3. CO-PRIMARY SPECTRUM SHARING

Co-primary spectrum sharing (CoPSS) concept enables multiple MNOs to simultaneously share the spectrum, i.e., the band will have multiple licensees instead of just one. Even though the spectrum is shared, the access is still controlled via license. CoPSS is not intended to replace the guaranteed exclusive band, that the MNOs have, but to provide additional band through sharing. For the MNO, the benefit of CoPSS is the additional resources it can use, e.g., to cope with temporary peaks in demand.

Although, MNO's base stations are able to gather extensive information of their networks and hardware, MNOs are not willing to exchange that information with each other. Therefore, an information sharing model where only the minimum amount of information is exchanged among MNOs has to be considered. The exchanged parameters have to be selected or defined so that only the parameters essential for co-operation are sent.

The control for the co-operative spectrum usage is distributed to spectrum controllers (SC) which each MNO is using. These are the key elements for information exchange and making decisions. Because the distributed SC of each MNO is similar, it puts all the MNOs as equal partners to access the shared band. The identical distributed SCs will always end up at the same outcome how the spectrum is shared. It is assumed that assigning a master MNO for controlling the resource allocation is not desirable. In this trial, the co-primary spectrum is shared among two operators and D2D usage.

4. TRIAL SETUP

In the Trial setup, a mobile network with two BSs of different MNOs and two user connected to each BS is used. Both BSs and user nodes are implemented with LE-WARP design. In Fig. 2 an architecture of the co-primary spectrum sharing environment is illustrated. The trial network can dynamically allocate shared spectrum according to traffic demand of each BSs and presence of D2D communication in the network. Distributed SCs are used for decision making. Both BSs are assumed to belong to different MNOs and to operate on common coverage area. GUI will be used to illustrate the operation of the trial network.

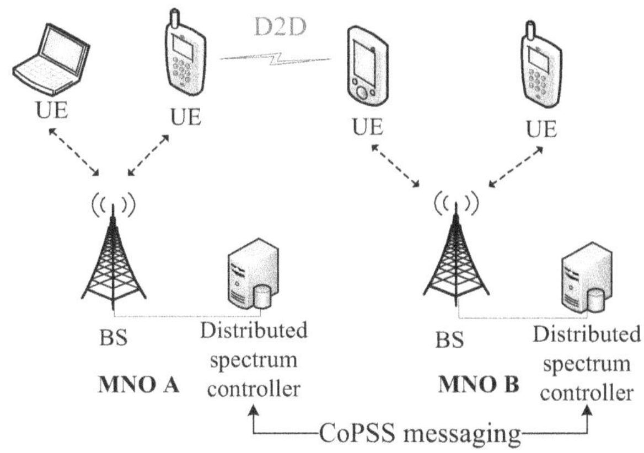

Figure 2: An architecture of the co-primary spectrum sharing trial.

Acknowledgment

This research was done in the CORE+ project which was supported by VTT Technical Research Centre of Finland, University of Oulu, Centria University of Applied Sciences, Nokia, PehuTec, EXFO, Elektrobit, Anite, Rugged Tooling, Finnish Defence Forces, Finnish Communications Regulatory Authority, and Tekes the Finnish Funding Agency for Innovation.

5. REFERENCES

[1] M. Fitch and R. Raulefs. Radio access and spectrum, a white paper on spectrum sharing. Technical report, QoSMOS, October 2012. URL: `http://www.ict-qosmos.eu/fileadmin/documents/Dissemination/White_Papers/RAS_Cluster_white_paper.pdf`.

[2] H. Kamal, M. Coupechoux, and P. Godlewski. Inter-operator spectrum sharing for cellular networks using game theory. In *Personal, Indoor and Mobile Radio Communications, 2009 IEEE 20th International Symposium on*, pages 425–429, 2009.

[3] G. Middleton, K. Hooli, A. Tolli, and J. Lilleberg. Inter-operator spectrum sharing in a broadband cellular network. In *Spread Spectrum Techniques and Applications, 2006 IEEE Ninth International Symposium on*, pages 376–380, 2006.

[4] Warp project. URL: `http://warpproject.org`.

[5] M. Jokinen and H. Tuomivaara. LE-WARP: Linux enriched design for wireless open-access research platform. In *Proceedings of the 4th International Conference on Cognitive Radio and Advanced Spectrum Management*, CogART '11, pages 16:1–16:5, New ork, N , USA, 2011. ACM.

[6] J. Niemelä. *Linux enriched design in second generation WARP*. 2013. Master's thesis : University of Oulu, Department of Electrical Engineering.

6. DEMO REQUIREMENTS

- Table of at least 2m x 1m
- Power supply
- Demo setup is using 5GHz band with band width of 10MHz, center frequency is tunable, but usage of the band should be known in advance.
- Demonstration setup includes six WARP nodes, tree laptops and Ethernet router. These equipment will be brought by us to the venue.
- Display of at least 24" (optional)
- Poster stands for two posters.
- One hour time for setting up the demo equipments before demo session.

Demo: Enabling AGILE Spectrum Adaptation in Commercial 802.11 WLAN Deployments

Stratos Keranidis⊕, Kostas Chounos⊕, Thanasis Korakis⊕,
Iordanis Koutsopoulos⊎ and Leandros Tassiulas⊕
○Department of Computer and Communication Engineering, University of Thessaly, Greece
+Centre for Research and Technology Hellas, CERTH, Greece
∪Department of Computer Science, Athens University of Economics and Business, Greece
{efkerani, hounos, korakis, leandros}@uth.gr, jordan@aueb.gr

ABSTRACT

In this work, we present the AGILE Spectrum Adaptation system that is able to dynamically tune the channel central frequency and bandwidth of wireless links in an adaptive to the interference and traffic conditions way. The developed system is able to detect under-utilised spectrum fragments and optimally adjust the occupied spectrum. Through the online execution of 3 specifically designed experimental scenarios, we demonstrate the ability to implement distributed spectrum adaptation in commercial WLAN deployments, along with the obtained performance benefits.

1. INTRODUCTION

The unlicensed part of the wireless spectrum is currently experiencing unprecedented levels of congestion, especially in densely populated urban areas. The resulting spectrum scarcity mainly results due to the tremendous growth of IEEE 802.11 WLAN deployments. Towards avoiding heavily utilised spectrum fragments and improving throughput performance, a large body of work [1, 2, 3, 4] has proposed approaches that dynamically tune the operating channel, by considering the prevailing interference and traffic conditions. Moreover, due to the fact that the ISM band is also home for other wireless protocols and a large range of RF devices, cross-technology interference is considered as a major performance degradation factor for 802.11 networks as well. Towards identifying non-802.11 devices, the work of [5] implemented a signal classification framework on top of commercial 802.11 hardware that makes use of detailed spectral scanning information. While identification of the unique type of RF device that generates performance anomalies was enabled, interference mitigation through proper spectrum adaptation was not addressed in this work.

The lack of interference-free channels has recently led researchers to the development of more sophisticated spectrum adaptation mechanisms that use channels of arbitrarily configured central frequency and bandwidth. Such mechanisms are to able to provide for versatile spectrum adaptation and hence improve spectrum efficiency, which is considered as a major goal in the field of dynamic spectrum access. In this context, several innovative schemes [6, 7] have been proposed and implemented on custom built research prototypes, clearly showcasing the benefits that agile spectrum adaptation is able to offer. The limitation of the aforementioned approaches is that they are not compatible with the 802.11 protocol, hence not offering for direct performance comparison with the standard. On the other hand, the work in [8] was the first to implement flexible channellisation on enterprise 802.11 networks, through the introduction of a central controller entity that is used to adapt spectrum configurations per link and resolve potential conflicts, which exacerbate due to the use of varying channel widths. However, the adopted centralised architecture that is not consistent with the distributed operation of the 802.11 protocol consisted the proposed approach non-applicable to common uncoordinated WLAN deployments.

In this work, we present AGILE - an approach to adapt the occupied spectrum based on distributed decisions that are taken locally at the AP. Efficient detection of transmissions that utilise different bandwidth configurations and identification of potential link conflicts is based on the collection of spectral occupancy information that is derived from the commercial 802.11n compatible Atheros AR9380 wireless chipset. Following this generic approach, we are able to characterise the Power Spectral Density (PSD) and Duty Cycle (DC) of active transmissions per frequency and thus efficiently identify heavily-utilised spectrum fragments that are occupied by any type of RF transmissions (even non-802.11). The developed scheme is not restricted by the standard channellisation and is able to appropriately configure the central frequency of operation at the granularity of 1 MHz. Towards increasing spectrum efficiency, channel bandwidth is also adapted among the 4 supported by the standard channel widths (40 MHz, 20 MHz, 10 MHz and 5 MHz), in order to constantly utilise the minimum required bandwidth that is able to meet the application-layer traffic requirements. Associated stations are informed about updated spectrum parameters through information that is embedded in *Beacon* frames and reconfiguration is able to take place per each *Beacon* interval. As collection of spectral information and subsequent spectrum adaptation induce only minimal overhead, the entire procedure runs in parallel with normal network operation and is totally transparent to higher protocol layers. To the best of our knowl-

MobiCom'14, September 7-11, 2014, Maui, Hawaii, USA.
ACM 978-1-4503-2783-1/14/09.
http://dx.doi.org/10.1145/2639108.2641752 .

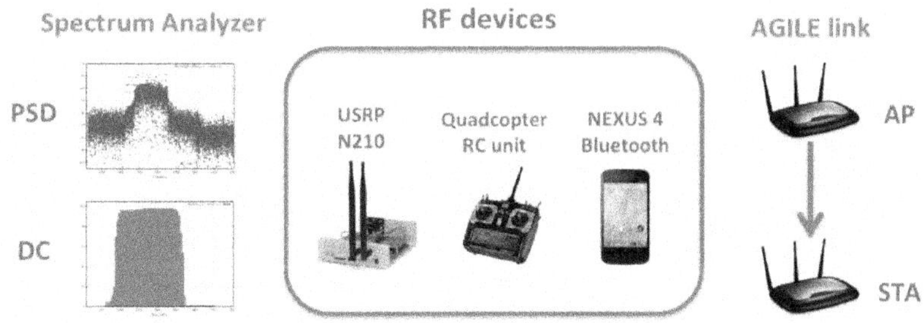

Figure 1: Experimental Topology in Scenario 1.

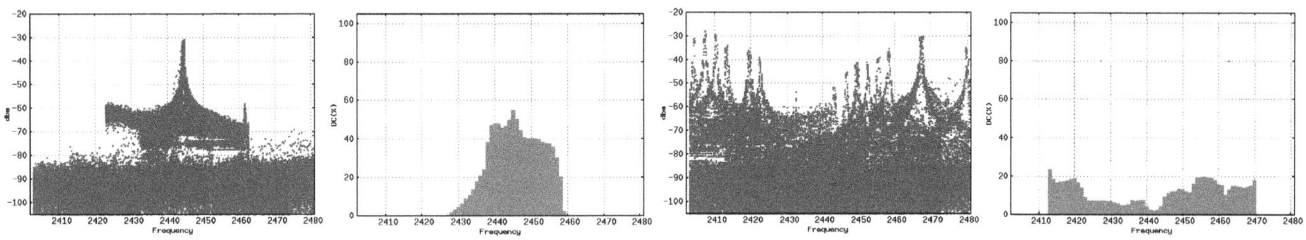

(a) Microwave oven PSD (b) Microwave oven DC (c) Quadcopter R/C PSD (d) Quadcopter R/C DC

Figure 2: Power Spectral Density and Duty Cycle characterization of varying type RF transmissions.

edge, AGILE is the first driver level implementation of fully distributed spectrum adaptation in commercial WLAN deployments that is also built on top of the high-throughput 802.11n protocol version.

In this demonstration, we will showcase three different experimental scenarios that clearly demonstrate the advantages of AGILE spectrum adaptation in commercial 802.11 WLAN deployments.

2. EXPERIMENTAL DEMONSTRATION

In Scenario 1, we demonstrate the ability of AGILE to detect non-802.11 RF devices, while Scenario 2 is designed to showcase the increased throughput performance that bandwidth reduction is able to offer under high-interference conditions. Finally, in Scenario 3 we show how AGILE is able to tune the operational bandwidth in order to meet the application-layer traffic requirements. In all experiments, we will use one PC as a Spectrum Analyzer that is built on top of the commercial AR9380 chipset to represent the PSD and DC evaluation of the entire band under consideration every 500 ms. Moreover, the AGILE mechanisms will be running on commercial TP-Link routers that feature the AR9380 chipset, in order to demonstrate the straightforward applicability of the developed framework in commercial off-the-self devices.

2.1 Scenario 1

In this scenario, we use several RF devices that operate in the 2.4 GHz band and show how AGILE is able to detect ongoing non-802.11 transmissions and appropriately tune the central frequency to operate on the least utilised part of the spectrum. The experimental topology is depicted in Fig. 1. More specifically, we use the Software-defined Radio USRP N210 to emulate the operation of a microwave oven that occupies several channels of the 2.4 GHz band with the duty cycle of 50% and a wireless camera that uses a bandwidth of 18 MHz and duty cycle of 100%. In addition, we will also employ two frequency hopping devices, a Quadcopter R/C unit that transmits at the high power of 27 dBm and a Bluetooth 4.0 transceiver of LG Nexus 4 that transmits at 10 mW. Indicative PSD plots that will be showcased during the demonstration are presented in Fig. 2(a) and Fig. 2(c), while the detected DC is depicted in Fig. 2(b) and Fig 2(d) accordingly.

2.2 Scenario 2

In Scenario 2, we aim at demonstrating the ability of AGILE to adapt under rich in interference environments and configure the experimental topology that is depicted in Fig. 3(a). To this end, we establish two wireless links on the 5 GHz band that occupy 20 MHz of bandwidth and use them as potential interferers for a third link that implements the proposed mechanism. In the first phase, the two interfering links operate on frequencies 5221 MHz and 5251 MHz accordingly, leaving a part of 10 MHz spectrum space unoccupied. In the second phase, we switch the central frequency of the second interfering link by 10 MHz and assign the central frequency of 5261 MHz, resulting in 20 MHz of unoccupied spectrum. The AGILE-enabled link will be dynamically configuring the optimal frequency and bandwidth parameters, towards improving throughput performance that will also be depicted in parallel with the experiment execution.

2.3 Scenario 3

Finally, in Scenario 3 we will establish a link that features varying application-layer traffic requirements and showcase how AGILE is able to tune the operational bandwidth in order to successfully meet the traffic demands that vary over time, as illustrated in Fig. 3(b). In this scenario, demo spectators will also have the ability to interact with the system by tuning the central frequency and bandwidth of an interfering link through a user friendly interface and observe how AGILE adapts to the resulting environment. The experimental topology of this scenario is presented in Fig. 3(c).

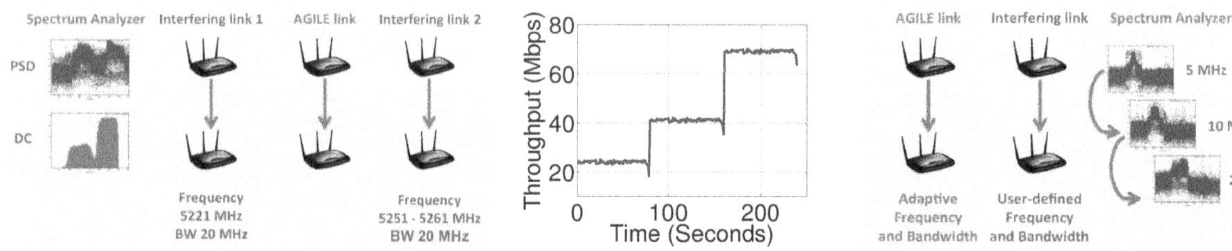

(a) Scenario 2 - Topology (b) Scenario 3 - Traffic demand (c) Scenario 3 - Topology

Figure 3: Experimental configuration in Scenarios 2 and 3.

3. DEMO REQUIREMENTS

For the purposes of this demonstration, we will bring:

- our projector and laptops
- 6 wireless Routers, 1 wireless node to operate as the Spectrum Analyzer and the 3 RF devices that will be used in Scenario 2,

while we will also require:

- a desk of 2 meters length to place the equipment,
- power supply for all the devices.
- 30 minutes for setup and testing.

4. CONCLUSIONS

In this demo paper we showcase the AGILE system that implements Spectrum Adaptation in commercial 802.11 devices. The implemented approach operates as a spectrum occupancy detector that appropriately configures the link to operate on the spectrum fragment that features the lowest Duty Cycle. As revealed through the three different demonstrated scenarios, the implemented mechanism is able to dynamically adapt to the prevailing channel and traffic conditions and offer significant improvement in comparison with conventional 802.11 systems.

5. ACKNOWLEDGEMENTS

The authors acknowledge the support of the European Commission through IP project CREW (FP7-258301).

6. REFERENCES

[1] A. Mishra, V. Shrivastava, D. Agrawal, S. Banerjee, and S. Ganguly. Distributed Channel Management in Uncoordinated Wireless Environments. In *Proceedings of MOBICOM*, 2006.

[2] B. Kauffmann, F. Baccelli, A. Chaintreau, V. Mhatre, K. Papagiannaki, and C. Diot. Measurement-Based Self Organization of Interfering 802.11 Wireless Access Networks. In *Proceedings of INFOCOM*, 2007.

[3] S. Chieochan, E. Hossain, and J. Diamond. Channel assignment schemes for infrastructure-based 802.11 WLANs: A survey. *Communications Surveys Tutorials, IEEE*, 2010.

[4] G. Kazdaridis, S. Keranidis, A. Fiamegkos, T. Korakis, I. Koutsopoulos, and L. Tassiulas. Novel Metrics and Experimentation Insights for Dynamic Frequency Selection in Wireless LANs. In *Proceedings of ACM WiNTECH*, 2011.

[5] Shravan Rayanchu, Ashish Patro, and Suman Banerjee. Airshark: Detecting non-WiFi RF Devices Using Commodity WiFi Hardware. In *Proceedings of IMC*, 2011.

[6] Krishna C., Bozidar R., Vlad B., Michael B., Srinivas Yerramalli, Vishnu Navda, and Ramachandran Ramjee. WiFi-NC : WiFi Over Narrow Channels. In *Proceedings of NSDI*, 2012.

[7] S. Yun, D. Kim, and L. Qiu. Fine-grained Spectrum Adaptation in WiFi Networks. In *Proceedings of MOBICOM*, 2013.

[8] S. Rayanchu, V. Shrivastava, S. Banerjee, and R. Chandra. FLUID: Improving Throughputs in Enterprise Wireless Lans Through Flexible Channelization. In *Proceedings of MOBICOM*, 2011.

Demo — Luxapose: Indoor Positioning with Mobile Phones and Visible Light

Ye-Sheng Kuo, Pat Pannuto, and Prabal Dutta
Electrical Engineering and Computer Science Department
University of Michigan
Ann Arbor, MI 48109
{samkuo,ppannuto,prabal}@umich.edu

ABSTRACT

We explore the indoor positioning problem with unmodified smartphones and slightly-modified commercial LED luminaires. The luminaires—modified to allow rapid, on-off keying—transmit their identifiers and/or locations encoded in human-imperceptible optical pulses. A camera-equipped smartphone, using just a single image frame capture, can detect the presence of the luminaires in the image, decode their transmitted identifiers and/or locations, and determine the smartphone's location and orientation relative to the luminaires. Continuous image capture and processing enables continuous position updates. The key insights underlying this work are (i) the driver circuits of emerging LED lighting systems can be easily modified to transmit data through on-off keying; (ii) the rolling shutter effect of CMOS imagers can be leveraged to receive many bits of data encoded in the optical transmissions with just a single frame capture, (iii) a camera is intrinsically an angle-of-arrival sensor, so the projection of multiple nearby light sources with known positions onto a camera's image plane can be framed as an instance of a sufficiently-constrained angle-of-arrival localization problem, and (iv) this problem can be solved with optimization techniques.

Categories and Subject Descriptors

B.4.2 [**HARDWARE**]: Input/Output and Data Communications—*Input/Output Devices*; C.3 [**COMPUTER-COMMUNICATION NETWORKS**]: Special-Purpose and Application-Based Systems

General Terms

Design, Experimentation, Measurement, Performance

Keywords

Indoor localization; Mobile phones; Angle-of-arrival; Image processing

MobiCom'14, Sep 07–11, 2014, Maui, HI, USA.
ACM 978-1-4503-2783-1/14/09.
http://dx.doi.org/10.1145/2639108.2641747

1. INTRODUCTION

Accurate indoor positioning can enable a wide range of location-based services across many sectors. Retailers, supermarkets, and shopping malls, for example, are interested in indoor positioning because it can provide improved navigation which helps avoid unrealized sales when customers cannot find items they seek, and it increases revenues from incremental sales from targeted advertising [4]. Indeed, the desire to deploy indoor location-based services is one reason that the overall demand for mobile indoor positioning in the retail sector is projected to grow to $5 billion by 2018 [3]. However, despite the strong demand forecast, indoor positioning remains a "grand challenge," and no existing system offers accurate location and orientation using unmodified smartphones [5].

WiFi and other RF-based approaches deliver accuracies measured in meters and no orientation information, making them a poor fit for many applications like retail navigation and shelf-level advertising [1, 2, 10]. Visible light-based approaches have shown some promise for indoor positioning, but recent systems offer landmarks with approximate room-level semantic localization [8], depend on custom hardware and received signal strength (RSS) techniques that are difficult to calibrate, or require phone attachments and user-in-the-loop gestures [5].

We propose a new approach to accurate indoor positioning that leverages trends in solid-state lighting, camera-enabled smartphones, and retailer-specific mobile applications. Our design consists of visible light beacons, smartphones, and a cloud/cloudlet server that work together to determine a phone's location and orientation, and support location-based services. Each beacon consists of a programmable oscillator or microcontroller that controls one or more LEDs in a luminaire. A beacon's identity is encoded in the modulation frequency and optically broadcast by the luminaire. The smartphone's camera takes pictures periodically and these pictures are processed to determine the beacon location and identity. Once beacon identities and coordinates are determined, an angle-of-arrival localization algorithm determines the phone's absolute position and orientation in the local coordinate system. Our angle-of-arrival positioning principle assumes that three or more beacons with known 3-D coordinates have been detected and located in an image captured by a smartphone. When an OOK-modulated light source illuminates the camera, distinct light and dark bands appear in images. The width of the bands depend on the frequency of the light. We employ an image processing pipeline to determine the extent of the beacons, estimate their centroids, and extract their embedded frequencies, which yields the inputs needed for positioning. Assuming that the camera geometry is known and the pixels onto which the beacons are projected is determined, we estimate the position and orientation of the smartphone with respect to the beacons' coordinate system through the geometry of similar triangles.

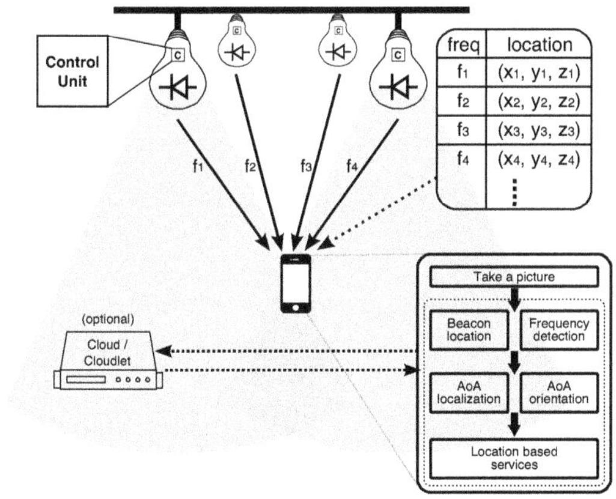

Figure 1: Luxapose indoor positioning system architecture. The system consists of visible light beacons, mobile phones, and a cloud/-cloudlet server. Beacons transmit their identities or coordinates using human-imperceptible visible light. A phone receives these transmissions using its camera and recruits a combination of local and cloud resources to determine its precise location and orientation relative to the beacons' coordinate system using an angle-of-arrival localization algorithm, thereby enabling location-based services.

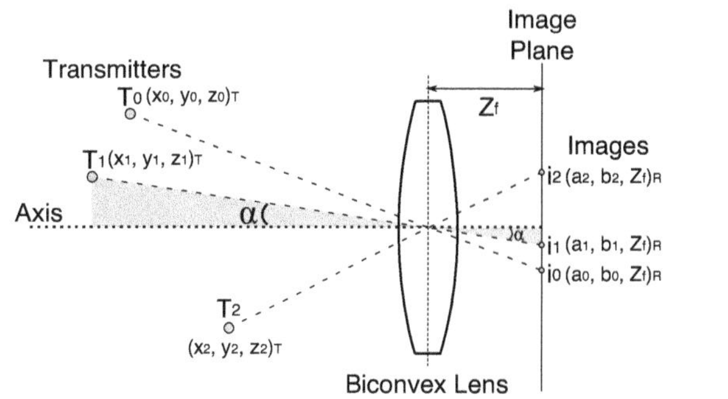

Figure 2: Optical AoA localization. When the scene is in focus, transmitters are distinctly projected onto the image plane. Knowing the transmitters' locations $T_j(x_j, y_j, z_j)_T$ in a global reference frame, and their image $i_j(a_j, b_j, Z_f)_R$ in the receiver's reference frame, allows us to estimate the receiver's global location and orientation.

2. SYSTEM OVERVIEW

The Luxapose indoor positioning system consists of visible light beacons, smartphones, and a cloud/cloudlet server, as Figure 1 shows. These elements work together to determine a smartphone's location and orientation, and support location-based services. An oscillator or microcontroller modulates LED lights to broadcast luminaire identities and/or coordinates. The camera in a smartphone takes pictures of these luminaires periodically. These pictures are sent to a cloudlet server to decode and to determine the beacon locations and extract identities. A lookup table may be consulted to convert identities into corresponding coordinates. With beacon identities and coordinates, an angle-of-arrival localization algorithm determines the phone's position and orientation in the venue's coordinate system.

2.1 Optical Angle-of-Arrival Localization

Luxapose uses optical angle-of-arrival (AoA) localization principles based on an ideal camera with a biconvex lens. An important property of a simple biconvex lens is that a ray of light that passes through the center of the lens is not refracted, as shown in Figure 2. Thus, a transmitter, the center of the lens, and the projection of transmitter onto the camera imager plane form a straight line.

2.2 Estimating Position and Orientation

To begin, we assume transmitters' locations are known. For example, transmitters $T_0, T_1, \cdots T_{N-1}$ are at locations $(x_n, y_n, z_n)_T$, $n = 0, 1, \cdots N-1$. From the receiver's frame of reference ($(0,0,0)_R$ is center of lens), their projection on the imager can be extracted and expressed as $(a_n, b_n, Z_f)_R$, where Z_f is the distance from lens to imager and the unit of a_n, b_n, Z_f is pixels. By the geometry of similar triangles, we can find transmitter locations in receiver's frame of reference to be $(u_n, v_n, w_n)_R$. The relationship between two domains can be expressed as follows:

$$\begin{bmatrix} x_0 & x_1 & \dots & x_{N-1} \\ y_0 & y_1 & \dots & y_{N-1} \\ z_0 & y_1 & \dots & z_{N-1} \end{bmatrix} = \mathbf{R} \times \begin{bmatrix} u_0 & u_1 & \dots & u_{N-1} \\ v_0 & v_1 & \dots & v_{N-1} \\ w_0 & w_1 & \dots & w_{N-1} \end{bmatrix} + \mathbf{T},$$

where **R** is a 3-by-3 rotation matrix and **T** is a 3-by-1 translation matrix. The three elements of **T** (T_x, T_y, T_z) represent the receiver's location in the transmitters' frame of reference. The 3-by-3 rotation matrix **R** is represented using three column vectors, $\overrightarrow{r_1}$, $\overrightarrow{r_2}$, and $\overrightarrow{r_3}$, as follows:

$$\mathbf{R} = \begin{bmatrix} \overrightarrow{r_1} & \overrightarrow{r_2} & \overrightarrow{r_3} \end{bmatrix},$$

where the column vectors $\overrightarrow{r_1}$, $\overrightarrow{r_2}$ and $\overrightarrow{r_3}$ are the components of the unit vectors $\hat{x}'$, $\hat{y}'$, and $\hat{z}'$, respectively, projected onto the x, y, and z axes in the transmitters' frame of reference.

2.3 Luxapose Photogrammetry

Our positioning scheme requires: i) identifying the location of the transmitter projections on the captured image (a_i, b_i, Z_f), and ii) labeling each of the transmitters, that is determining which (x_j, y_j, z_j) map to which (a_i, b_i, Z_f).

i) We convert the image to grayscale, blur it, and pass it through a binary OTSU filter [6] to find the minimum enclosing circle of the contours for each blob [9]. (a_i, b_i, Z_f) can be found and we examine the corresponding subregions to decode data.

ii) We label transmitters by assigning each an unique frequency. CMOS imagers expose one column of pixels at a time, sweeping across the image creating a "rolling shutter". When capturing an image of an LED that is rapidly turning on and off, the result is a banding effect where some columns capture the LED when it is on and others when it is off, as seen Figure 3. One approach to decode the frequency is taking FFT on the subregions from (i).

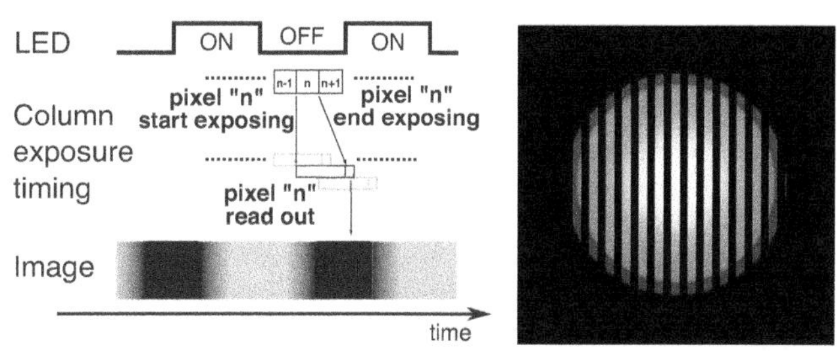

(a) Distinctive banding pattern resulting from the rolling shutter effect of a CMOS camera capturing a rapidly flashing LED.

(b) 1 kHz pure tone with 50% duty cycle taken with a short exposure.

Figure 3: The effect of the CMOS rolling shutter and the image is taken by a Nokia Lumia 1020 of a modified Commercial Electric T66 10 cm ceiling LED with short exposure time ($^1/_{16667}$ s).

(a) Demo Setup. (b) Real-time Localization Results.

Figure 4: VLC Localization Demo. The demo setup as shown in (a) requires a reasonable floor area (minimum ~2×2 m). A position grid is laid out using tape as a ground truth guide for demo participants. LED beacons are placed at periodic points throughout the grid. This simulates traditional ceiling-mounted lighting infrastructure in a much more portable form. Participants are given mobile phones pre-loaded with our localization app and allowed to wander the demo area. On a display as in (b), real-time location and orientation estimates for each user are shown. Users will be able to use both the front and rear-facing camera of the phone to see the impact of imager quality on localization estimates. A live video of this demo is available at http://youtu.be/HSNY0XVXM1w.

3. DEMONSTRATION

Our demo, as seen in Figure 4 and online at http://youtu.be/HSNY0XVXM1w, will perform real-time localization of multiple, independent users. Each demo participant will be given a Nokia Lumia 1020 smartphone pre-loaded with our localization application. The application features both single-frame mode, allowing participants to take carefully posed photos to see the results, and continuous mode, allowing participants to wander the space while the system tracks their location. Location estimates will be shown in real-time on a nearby display. As camera quality is important to Luxapose, participants will be able to use both the front- and rear-facing cameras, comparing the usuability, performance, and accuracy of each.

The hardware (LEDs, control boards) and software (phone application, cloud service, image processing, localization solver) for our demo are available at https://github.com/lab11/vlc-localization. Location estimates are uploaded into our cloud data aggregation and streaming service, GATD [7] (available: https://github.com/lab11/gatd). Our visualization front-end runs as a browser application and is available at https://github.com/lab11/gatd-lab11/blob/master/web/work-in-progress/VLC-demo.jinja.

Since the location estimates run through GATD, users will be able to record their sessions and replay their traversal through the grid both during and after the demo (much like the "Replay Train Experiment" on http://inductor.eecs.umich.edu/VLC-localization.html). We will make an effort to provide a custom replay for each user, however we anticipate that this may prove challenging at scale.

4. MATERIALS AND SETUP

Our demo setup requires a resonable amount of open space for participants to walk around in. The smallest viable open space is about 7'×7' (~2×2 m). The demo also requires a screen to display real-time localization results. A larger screen is better, however something as small as a laptop will work if necessary. The demo will require access to AC power and WiFi.

The demo is relatively simple to setup and should only require a half an hour of preparation time at the most. The demo uses the grid as a frame of reference and should not require any local calibration, speeding and easing deployment. The demo is quick to tear down, requiring no more than 5 minutes.

5. RELATED PAPER

This work is a demonstration of the system proposed and presented in our paper *Luxapose: Indoor Positioning with Mobile Phones and Visible Light*, presented at MobiCom '14.

6. REFERENCES

[1] P. Bahl and V. N. Padmanabhan. RADAR: An in-building RF-based user location and tracking system. In *Proc. 19th Annual Joint Conference of the IEEE Computer and Communications Societies. (INFOCOM '00)*, volume 2, 2000.

[2] K. Chintalapudi, A. Padmanabha Iyer, and V. N. Padmanabhan. Indoor localization without the pain. In *Proc. of the 16th ACM Annual International Conference on Mobile Computing and Networking (MobiCom '10)*, 2010.

[3] P. Connolly and D. Boone. Indoor location in retail: Where is the money? ABI Research Report, 2013.

[4] A. Jovicic, J. Li, and T. Richardson. Visible light communication: Opportunities, challenges and the path to market. *IEEE Communications Magazine*, 51(12), 2013.

[5] L. Li, P. Hu, C. Peng, G. Shen, and F. Zhao. Epsilon: A visible light based positioning system. In *Proc. of the 11th USENIX Symposium on Networked Systems Design and Implementation (NSDI '14)*, 2014.

[6] N. Otsu. A Threshold Selection Method from Gray-level Histograms. *IEEE Transactions on Systems, Man and Cybernetics*, 9(1), 1979.

[7] P. Pannuto, B. Campbell, and P. Dutta. GATD: A robust, extensible, versatile swarm dataplane. In *The First International Workshop on the Swarm at the Edge of the Cloud*, SEC '13, 2013.

[8] N. Rajagopal, P. Lazik, and A. Rowe. Visual light landmarks for mobile devices. In *Proc. of the 13th ACM/IEEE International Conference on Information Processing in Sensor Networks (IPSN '14)*, 2014.

[9] S. Suzuki et al. Topological structural analysis of digitized binary images by border following. *Computer Vision, Graphics, and Image Processing*, 30(1), 1985.

[10] M. A. Youssef et al. The Horus WLAN location determination system. In *Proc. of the 3rd International Conference on Mobile Systems, Applications, and Services*, 2005.

Demo: A Cognitive Solution for Commercial Wireless Conferencing System

Wei Liu, Eli De Poorter
Pieter Becue, Bart Jooris, Vincent Sercu
Ingrid Moerman
University Ghent - iMinds
Gaston Crommenlaan 8 Ghent, Belgium
{lwei, eldpoort, pbecue, bjooris, vsercu,imoerman}@intec.ugent.be

Jeroen Vanhaverbeke
Carl Lylon, John Gesquiere
Televic
Leo Bekaertlaan 1
Izegem, Belgium
{J.Vanhaverbeke, C.Lylon, J.Gesquiere}@televic.com

ABSTRACT

In a modern conference room, various of video and audio devices are provided to ensure efficient communications. This is commonly referred to as a conferencing system. Compared to wired conferencing systems, wireless systems require less deployment effort, but may become unreliable when the selected radio spectrum is highly occupied. This demo focuses on improving the quality of service of a commercial wireless conferencing system using dynamic channel selection based on real-time spectrum sensing. The proposed solution is verified in a large-scale wireless testbed, and the result shows that the link of the conferencing system is indeed more robust against interference when cognitive solution is applied.

Keywords

Wireless conferencing system; Cognitive Radio

1. INTRODUCTION

In a modern conference room, audio infrastructures (eg, micro phones and loudspeakers) are provided to ensure clear and efficient communications. In addition, video devices and real-time interpretation units are also widely used for remote and international conferences. In general, the infrastructures deployed in a conference room to facilitate communication is called a conferencing system. Most existing conferencing systems rely on wired connections, which usually require heavy deployment efforts. In addition, it is difficulty to reorganize the layout of the conference room once the deployment is finished.

To overcome the limitations of wired conferencing system, Televic [1] proposes the Confidea wireless conferencing system [2]. It contains two types of devices: the wireless centralized access point (WCAP) and the wireless delegate unit, as shown in Figure 1. A conference room equipped with the Confidea system is shown in Figure 2. The WCAP and delegate units operate in the unlicensed Industrial, Scientific, Medical (ISM) frequency band, which allows the conferencing system to be used without extra licensing cost. However, the existing wireless technologies in the ISM bands (eg, Bluetooth, Zibee, Wi-Fi) may cause severe interference to the connection between the WCAP and the delegate units.

MobiCom'14, September 7-11, 2014, Maui, Hawaii, USA.
ACM 978-1-4503-2783-1/14/09.
http://dx.doi.org/10.1145/2639108.2641751.

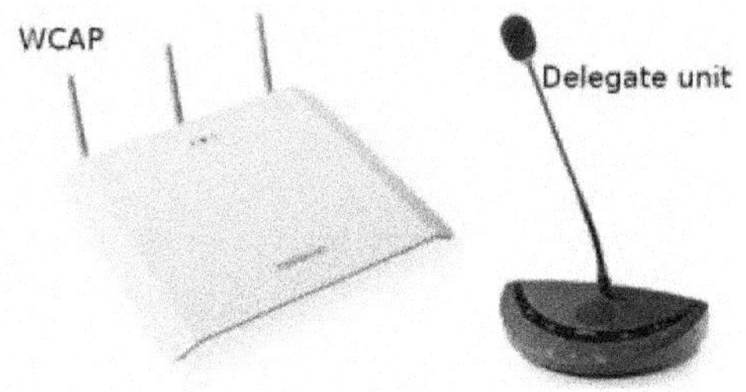

Figure 1: The Confidea WCAP and delegate unit

Figure 2: A conference room equipped with Confidea system

To this end, Cognitive Radio (CR) techniques are used to improve the connection quality. More specifically, the WCAP's operating channel is updated in real-time according to the radio spectrum utilization. In this demo, the spectrum sensing is performed by a dedicated application together with the Software-Defined Radio (SDR) — USRP[3] . The complete solution is tested and verified in a large scale wireless testbed — w-iLab.t[4].

The rest of the paper is organized as follows: Section 2 briefly introduces the implementation of the demo setup; Section 3 describes the demo scenario as well as the expected result; Finally Section 4 concludes this demo and points out the direction for future work.

2. DEMO IMPLEMENTATION

The w-iLab.t testbed is a generic and heterogeneous wireless testbed. It is located at a utility room where no regular human activity is present. The majority of devices in the w-iLab.t testbed are embedded PCs equipped with Wi-Fi, Bluetooth interfaces and sensor devices. Each embedded PC are attached to a poll, and can be remotely configured via a backbone Ethernet interface. For simplicity, an embedded PC together with the attached wireless devices is referred to as a "node". The overall testbed topology forms a grid.

Two Confidea delegate units and one WCAP are deployed in w-iLab.t testbed. The two delegate units are mounted on two adjacent nodes respectively. On one node, the audio output of the embedded PC is connected to the audio input of the delegate unit via the audio jack cable, which forms the "speaker" node. On the other node, the audio output of the delegate is connected to the microphone input on the embedded PC via an audio jack cable, which can act as the "listener". During testing, the audio signal is transferred via the WCAP from the delegate at the "speaker" to the delegate at the "listener". The "listener" node records the audio into an "mp3" file, which can be used for audio quality analysis. The complete setup is illustrated in Figure 3.

The WCAP updates its channel in real-time, based on the spectrum information collected by a dedicated sensing application. This application uses the raw samples from USRP to perform Fast Fourier Transfer (FFT) based energy detection. Parallelism and multi-threading are used to increase the processing speed of the sensing application [5]. The sensing application together with USRP hardware forms a USRP sensing engine. Each USRP sensing engine has an instantaneous bandwidth of 20 MHz, we use sweeping in frequency domain and cooperation of multiple USRP's to cover a wider frequency range. The sensing result is stored into a database at run time, which can be queried by the WCAP periodically.

3. DEMO SCENARIO

The demo consists of three stages. In all the stages, a piece of music is played at the "speaker" node and recorded at the "listener" node. At the same time, spectrum information is provided by USRP sensing engines and plotted in spectrogram in real-time.

In the first stage, the WCAP is configured to stay on a static channel and no background interference is introduced. The audience can hear that the recorded audio has a similar quality with the original audio file. In the second stage, the WCAP is still using a static channel, in addition, background interference is generated on the same channel. The audience can hear that the recorded audio quality has dropped compared to the first recording. In the third stage, the WCAP is configured to use dynamic channel configuration based on the spectrum information from USRP sensing engines. We can see on the spectrogram that the WCAP becomes "aware" of the interferer, and is able to actively avoid the interference. Audiences are encouraged to catch the channel of the WCAP by configuring the interferer in real-time. The recorded audio in this stage may contain short interruptions, but the we observe that the overall audio quality is much better than the recording from the second stage.

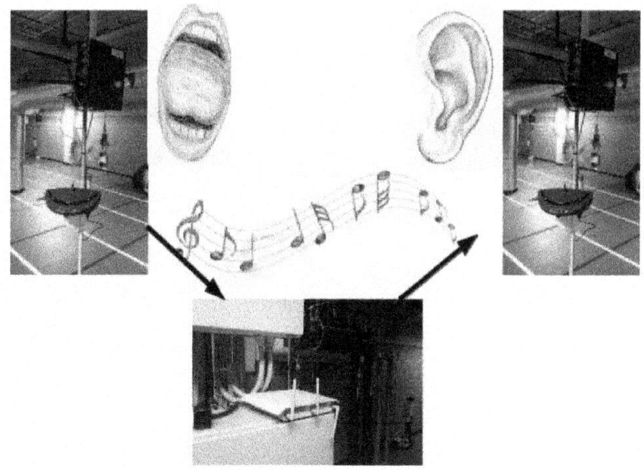

Figure 3: Demo scenario

4. CONCLUSIONS

This demo proves that dynamic channel selection can greatly improve the quality of service for the wireless conferencing system. In addition, it is shown that the custom-developed sensing application based on SDR can cooperate with commercial devices to achieve better performance. Finally, this demo also illustrates how to test a real-life application on a remote infrastructure in a convenient approach.

5. ACKNOWLEDGMENTS

The research leading to this demo has received funding from the European Union's Seventh Framework Programme FP7/2007-2013 under grant agreements n 258301 (CREW project) and Belgium national project QoCON.

6. REFERENCES

[1] Televic Portal: `http://www.televic.com/en/`, last accessed in March 2014.

[2] Confidea wireless conferencing system: `http://www.televic-conference.com/en/confidea-wireless-conference-system`, last accessed in March 2014

[3] Universal Software Radio Platform (USRP): `https://www.ettus.com/product`, last accessed in March 2014

[4] S. Bouckaert et al. "Federating wired and wireless test facilities through Emulab and OMF: the iLab.t use case" in the proceedings of TridentCom 2012

[5] Wei Liu, Daan Pareit, Eli De Poorter, Ingrid Modrman: "Advanced spectrum sensing with parallel processing based on software-defined radio" in EURASIP Journal on Wireless Communications and Networking, 2013

Demo – OpenAirInterface: An Open LTE Network in a PC

Navid Nikaein, Raymond Knopp, Florian Kaltenberger, Lionel Gauthier,
Christian Bonnet, Dominique Nussbaum, and Riadh Ghaddab
Eurecom
06410 Biot Sophia-Antipolis, France
nikaeinn,knopp,bonnet,kaltenberger,gauthier,nussbaum,ghaddab@eurecom.fr

ABSTRACT

LTE 4G cellular networks are gradually being adopted by all major operators in the world and are expected to rule the cellular landscape at least for the current decade. They will also form the starting point for further progress beyond the current generation of mobile cellular networks to chalk a path towards fifth generation mobile networks. The lack of open cellular ecosystem has limited applied research in this field within the boundaries of vendor and operator R&D groups. Furthermore, several new approaches and technologies are being considered as potential elements making up such a future mobile network, including cloudification of radio network, radio network programability and APIs following SDN principles, native support of machine-type communication, and massive MIMO. Research on these technologies requires realistic and flexible experimentation platforms that offer a wide range of experimentation modes from real-world experimentation to controlled and scalable evaluations while at the same time retaining backward compatibility with current generation systems.

In this work, we present OpenAirInterface (OAI) as a suitably flexible platform towards open LTE ecosystem and playground [1]. We will demonstrate an example of the use of OAI to deploy a low-cost open LTE network using commodity hardware with standard LTE-compatible devices. We also show the reconfigurability features of the platform.

Categories and Subject Descriptors

C.2.1 [**Computer-Communication Networks**]: Network Architecture and Design - Wireless Communication System

Keywords

OpenAirInterface, LTE, Open Cellular Ecosystem

1. INTRODUCTION

Cellular systems are among one of the last industries expected to converge from a slow-moving proprietary and expensive HW/SW platforms towards an open SW platforms leveraging commodity hardware. This is required to build an open cellular ecosystem and foster innovations in the wireless world as already produced in OpenStack for cloud services and Android for mobile OS. Currently, the only open cellular ecosystem is that of OpenBTS, which provides an open development kit for 2G systems [2].

In this work, we present OpenAirInterface (OAI) wireless technology platform as a first opensource software-based implementation of the LTE system spanning the full protocol stack of 3GPP standard both in E-UTRAN and EPC [1]. It can be used to build and customized an LTE base station and core network on a PC and connect a commercial UEs to test different configurations and network setups and monitor the network and mobile device in realtime. OAI is based on a PC hosted software radio frontend architecture. With OAI, the transceiver functionality is realized via a software radio front end connected to a host computer for processing. This approach is similar to other software-defined radio (SDR) prototyping platforms in the wireless networking research community such as SORA [3]. Other similar approaches combining PCs and FPGA-based processing make use of NI LabVIEW software [4] or using the WARP [5] architecture. To our best knowledge, OpenAirInterface is the only fully x86-based SDR solution in open-source, providing both UE, eNB, and core-network functionality. A similar closed-source development commercialized by Amarisoft (LTE 100) which targets several USRP platforms provides eNB and core-network functionality on standard Linux-based PCs [6]. OAI is written in standard C for several realtime Linux variants optimized for x86 and released as free software under the terms of version 3 of the GNU General Public License (GPLv3). OAI provides a rich development environment with a rang of build-in tools such as highly realistic emulation modes, soft monitoring and debugging tools, protocol analyzer, performance profiler, and configurable logging system for all layers and channels.

Towards building an open cellular ecosystem for flexible and low-cost 4G deployment and experimentations, OAI aims at the following objectives:

- Open and integrated development environment under the control of the experimenters;
- Fully software-based network functions offering flexibility to architect, instantiate, and reconfigure the network components (at the edge, core, or cloud using the same or different addressing space);
- Playground for commercial handsets as well as application, service, and content providers;
- Rapid prototyping of 3GPP compliant and non-compliant use-cases as well as new concepts towards 5G systems ranging from M2M/IoT and software-defined networking to cloud-RAN and massive MIMO.

MobiCom'14, September 7-11, 2014, Maui, Hawaii, USA.
ACM 978-1-4503-2783-1/14/09.
http://dx.doi.org/10.1145/2639108.2641745.

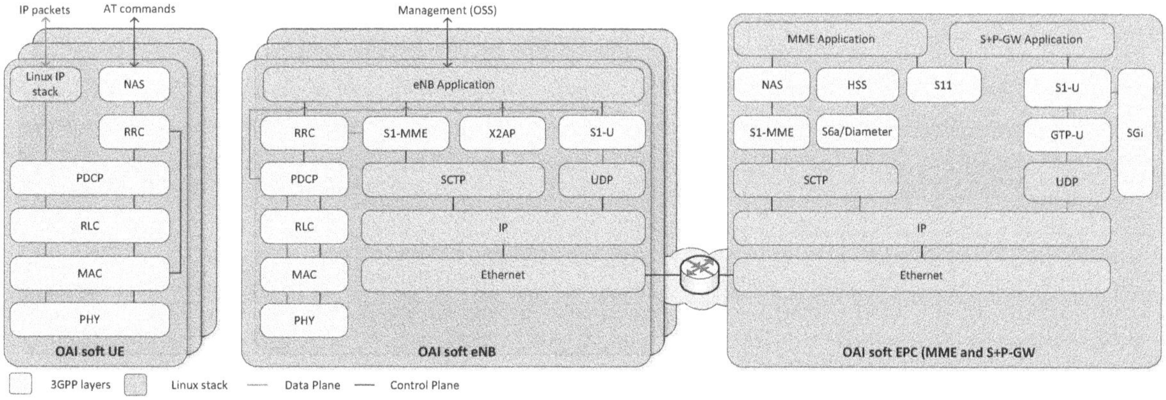

Figure 1: OpenAirInterface LTE software stack.

2. OPENAIRINTERFACE (OAI)

2.1 Software

Currently, the OAI platform includes a full software implementation of 4th generation mobile cellular systems compliant with 3GPP LTE standards in C under realtime Linux optimized for x86. At the Physical layer, it provides the following features:

- LTE release 8.6 compliant, with a subset of release 10;
- FDD and TDD configurations in 5, 10, and 20 MHz bandwidth;
- Transmission mode: 1 (SISO), and 2, 4, 5, and 6 (MIMO 2x2);
- CQI/PMI reporting;
- All DL channels are supported: PSS, SSS, PBCH, PCFICH, PHICH, PDCCH, PDSCH, PMCH;
- All UL channels are supported: PRACH, PUSCH, PUCCH, SRS, DRS;
- HARQ support (UL and DL);
- Highly optimized base band processing (including turbo decoder). With AVX2 optimization, a full software solution would fit with an average of 1x86 core per eNB instance (64QAM in downlink, 16QAM in uplink, 20MHz, SISO).

For the E-UTRAN protocol stack, it provides:

- LTE release 8.6 compliant and a subset of release 10 features;
- Implements the MAC, RLC, PDCP and RRC layers;
- protocol service for Rel10 eMBMS (MCH, MCCH, MTCH)
- Priority-based MAC scheduler with dynamic MCS selection;
- Fully reconfigurable protocol stack;
- Integrity check and encryption using the AES and Sonw3G algorithms;
- Support of RRC measurement with measurement gap;
- Standard S1AP and GTP-U interfaces to the Core Network;
- IPv4 and IPv6 support.

Evolved packet core network features:

- MME, SGW, PGW and HSS implementations. OAI reuses standards compliant stacks of GTPv1u and GTPv2c application protocols from the open-source software implementation of EPC called nwEPC [7];
- NAS integrity and encryption using the AES and Snow3G algorithms;
- UE procedures handling: attach, authentication, service access, radio bearer establishment;
- Transparent access to the IP network (no external Serving Gateway nor PDN Gateway are necessary). Configurable access point name, IP range, DNS and E-RAB QoS;
- IPv4 and IPv6 support.

Figure 1 shows a schematic of the implemented LTE protocol stack in OAI. OAI can be used in the context of a rich software development environment including Aeroflex-Geisler LEON / GRLIB, RTOS either RTAI or RT-PREEMPT, Linux, GNU, Wireshark, control and monitoring tools, message and time analyser, low level loggin system, traffic generator, profiling tools and soft scope. It also provide tools for protocol validation, performance evaluation and pre-deployment system test. Several interoperability tests have been successfully performed with the commercial LTE-enabled mobile devices, namely Huawei E392, E398u-1, Bandrich 500 as well as with commercial 3rd party EPC prototypes. OAI platform can be used in several different configurations involving commercial components to varying degrees:

- OAI UE ↔ OAI eNB + OAI EPC
- OAI UE ↔ OAI eNB + Commercial EPC
- OAI UE ↔ Commercial eNB + OAI EPC
- OAI UE ↔ Commercial eNB + Commercial EPC
- Commercial UE ↔ Commercial eNB + OAI EPC
- Commercial UE ↔ OAI eNB + Commercial EPC
- Commercial UE ↔ OAI eNB + OAI EPC

2.2 Hardware

For real-world experimentation and validation, the default software radio frontend for OAI is ExpressMIMO2 PCI Express (PCIe) board. This board features a LEON3 embedded system based on Spartan 6 LX150T FPGA as well as 4 high-quality RF chipsets from Lime Micro Systems (LMS6002), which are LTE-grade MIMO RF front-ends for small cell eNBs. It supports stand-alone operation at low-power levels (maximum 0 dBm transmit power per channel) simply by connecting an antenna to the board. External RF for high-power and TDD/FDD duplexing can be connected to ExpressMIMO2 depending on the deployment scenario. RF equipment can be configured for both TDD or FDD operation with channel bandwidths up to 20 MHz covering a very large part of the available RF spectrum (250 MHz-3.8 GHz) and a subset of LTE MIMO transmission modes. ExpressMIMO2 boards are reasonably-priced and completely open (GNU GPL), both at the hardware and software level. Figure 2 shows the ExpressMIMO2 hardware platform.

The embedded software for the FPGA is booted via the PC or can reside entirely in the boot ROM which is part of the FPGA design. In the current design, the embedded software is booted by

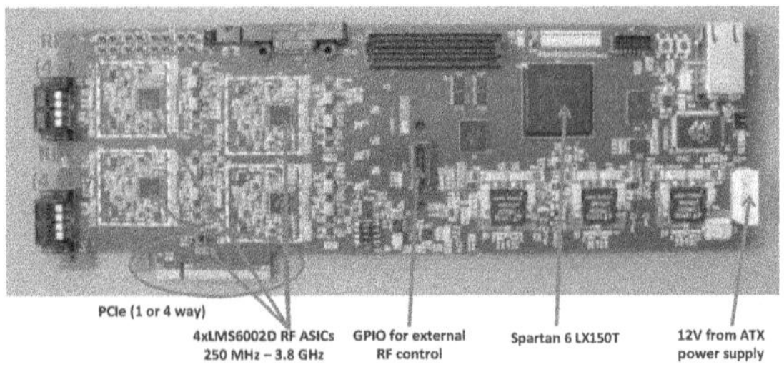

Figure 2: OAI ExpressMIMO2 hardware platform.

PCIexpress dynamically under control of the PC device driver. The basic design does not include any on-FPGA signal processing and consumes approximately 10-15% of the FPGA resources. There is significant room left for additional processing on the FPGA, for instance Xilinx FFT processors to offload some processing from the host PC if required.

Besides ExpressMIMO2, OAI now supports the UHD interface on recent USRP PC-hosted software radio platforms which are widely used in the research community. Specifically, Agilent China has recently succeeded in interconnecting the OpenAirInterface softmodem software with a USRP B210 platform [8]. This development is now delivered as part of the publicly-available software package from the OAI website and SVN server [1]. EURECOM will continue to maintain this development and extend to X300 (USRP-Rio) family products. This achievement illustrates the validity of the standard PC plus generic SDR frontend approach taken in OAI since the code has been independently ported successfully on a totally different hardware target.

3. DEMO DESCRIPTION

The considered demonstration scenario are depicted in Figure 3 and 4, and consists of 1 commercial LTE-enabled smartphone or Dongle (Huawei ascend P7 or E398u-1) and a laptop equipped with a USB LTE dongle (Huawei E398u-1 or Bandrich C500), 1 OAI soft eNB and 1 OAI soft EPC running on the top of Intel-based PC(s). Different setups are possible ranging from an all-in-one PC to all in a physically separated entities, which are deployment-specific. For the demo, we plan to demonstrate an all-in-one setup, where OAI soft eNB and EPC functions are performed inside the same PC. In such a configuration, eNB is running on the host PC under realtime Linux, MME and S+P-GW running on the top of a VM, and HSS in another VM.

The demonstration will be deployed in FDD SISO mode. Two target frequencies will be used: band 13 (USA) and band 7 (Europe) in a controlled indoor radio environment. In the proposed demonstration, we will assess the following objectives

- Successful attach procedure (control-plane), and video streaming in downlink (data-plane);
- High-level of reconfigurability and programmability spanning all the layers allowing all kind of setups from protocols to radio frequency;
- demonstrate the mobile device behaviour in realtime;
- Usage of commodity hardware to run LTE network in a PC.

The aforementioned experimental scenario will be demonstrated in live and the obtained results will be presented in parallel with the experiment execution. We will discuss the network programmability/reconfigurability through open APIs as well as the usage of OAI in both small-cell and cloud-RAN centralized processing.

4. DEMO REQUIREMENTS

The following equipments will be used for the demonstration:

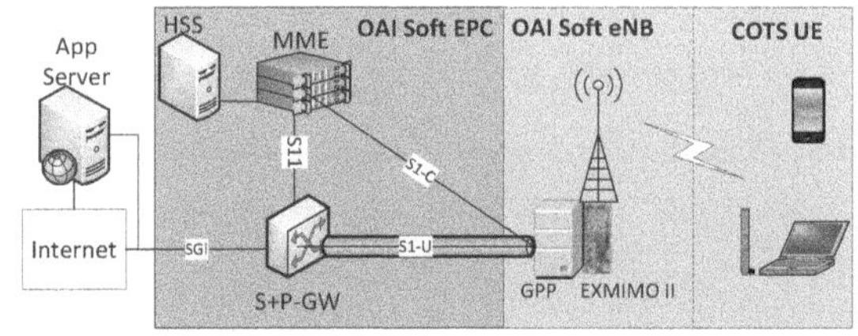

Figure 3: Demo setup and involved entities.

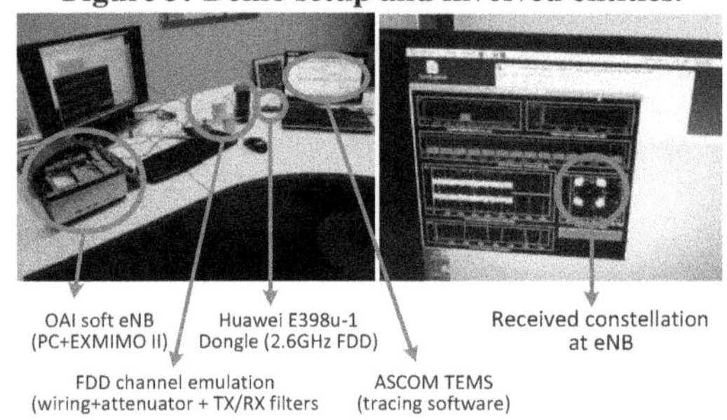

Figure 4: Hardware components of the demo.

- a PC running OAI EPC and OAI eNB with EXMIMOII card;
- one LTE UE dongle and one LTE smartphone;
- cables, filters, small antenna and attenuators.

In addition, we also require:

- a desk of 3 meters length to place the equipment;
- power supply plugs for all the devices and Internet access;
- 5 to 10 minutes to show and explain the demo.

5. CONCLUSION

We present the OpenAirInterface as a suitably flexible platform for an open cellular ecosystem both for 4G experimentation as well as for 5G research. It offers an open-source reference software implementation of 3GPP-compliant LTE system and a subset of LTE-A features for real-time indoor/outdoor experimentation and demonstration.

In the demo, we present an all-in-one LTE network deployment in a PC based on OpenAirInterface platform. We show the interoperability with commercial LTE enabled USB dongle and smartphones highlighting the complete attach procedure, establishment of default data radio bearer, and a live video transmission in downlink. We also show the reconfigurability features of the platform.

Acknowledgement

The research and development leading to these results has received funding from the European Research Council under the European Community Seventh Framework Programme (FP7/2014- 2017) grant agreement 612050 FLEX project and 318306 NEWCOM# project.

6. REFERENCES

[1] The OpenAirInterface Platform. www.openairinterface.org/, Repository: svn.eurecom.fr/openair4G/trunk.

[2] OpenBTS Project. www.openbts.org/.

[3] K. Tan and al. Sora: High-Performance Software Radio Using General Purpose Multi-Core Processors. *Communications of the ACM*, 2011.

[4] S. Shearman and al. Software Defined Radio Prototyping Platforms Enable a Flexible Approach to Design. *IEEE Microwave Magazine*, 2012.

[5] K. Amiri and al. Warp, a unified wireless network testbed for education and research. In *Proceedings of IEEE MSE*, 2007.

[6] Amarisoft. www.amarisoft.com/.

[7] nwEPC - EPC SAE Gateway. http://sourceforge.net/projects/nwepc/.

[8] Ettus USRP B210. www.ettus.com/product/details/UN210-KIT.

Demo: TV White Space Networking Capabilities and Potential with an Embedded & Open-API Platform

George Nychis
Adaptrum
george@adaptrum.com

Bruce DeBruhl
Carnegie Mellon University
debruhl@cmu.edu

Haiyun Tang
Adaptrum
haiyun@adaptrum.com

ABSTRACT

Over the past decade, white space networking has garnered significant effort and attention from media, industry, regulators, and academics world-wide. Together, these entities have helped push white space in to a unique position of potentially changing how we access the spectrum forever. Now, building white space networks with full-featured and fully certified equipment is critical in moving forward and retaining the spectrum and position that we have put ourselves in.

In our demonstration, we will exhibit a fully embedded and FCC-certified white space networking platform that is available and capable of building out TV white space networks. Additionally, we provide an interactive display with data taken from our commercial deployments that further show its capabilities of supporting various applications. Using the many available channels at the conference location, we will demonstrate some of these capabilities (e.g., ability to penetrate in-door environments), as well as future capabilities (e.g., novel functionality built on the platform). With an open-API (across all layers), the platform is conducive to studying current capabilities and novel research.

1. INTRODUCTION

White space networking has significant potential to improve efficiency of the wireless spectrum by opening idle portions of licensed spectrum for unlicensed access. The basic notion of white space is: at a given geographical location if no primary user is active in a "white space" band, then a secondary unlicensed user is allowed to access it. While seemingly basic in principle, many complexities arise in this form of spectrum access to guarantee interference-free access for primary users [2, 4], as well as effective and efficient use of idle spectrum by secondary users (e.g., through varying bandwidth [6] or discontiguous spectrum access [9, 8]).

TV white space has played a critical "initial role" in paving the way for this new paradigm of spectrum access. With idle UHF spectrum being left over from the transition of analog to digital TV, the FCC made a historic ruling in 2008 that allowed white space spectrum access for the first time in history [3]. This access, currently limited within the TV bands (470 - 700 MHz), can provide up to 200 MHz of additional spectrum in the US with significantly better propagation and penetration as compared to 2.4 and 5 GHz due to the greater wavelengths at the lower frequencies [5, 7]. Given this potential, similar rulings are being made world-wide by regulatory bodies (e.g., in Singapore, India, Africa, the UK, and Canada).

In addition to TV white space being able to provide connectivity in many emerging markets, new applications are enabled through TV white space. The most widely discussed has been campus-wide and city-wide networks, now possible due to its propagation characteristics allowing greater areas to be covered with fewer radios and less infrastructure. Many new emergency response networks can be built leveraging TV white space for backhaul communication such as in marine applications (coastal communication with ships), power grid applications (during outages and failure), as well as providing preparedness across sparse areas such as national parks like Yosemite (which spans more than 3 thousand square kilometers).

The success of TV white space through real deployments of these applications (and others) is critical to its adoption and the potential of white space spectrum access in other bands. Along with the significant effort and attention white space has gained from media, industry, regulators, and academics world-wide, more TV white space deployments and demonstrations of their capabilities are needed. With half a decade passed since the initial ruling, it is time critical for the future of white space spectrum access that such networks begin being built out and demonstrated. Additionally, flexible fully certified platforms are needed to allow continued technological development.

Towards these goals, we will present and demonstrate the *Adaptrum Cognitive Radio System* (ACRS) 2.0. It is a ruggedized, embedded, and fully FCC certified radio that can create point-to-point and point-to-multipoint white space networks. With an open-API of over 100 controls to modify and monitor many aspects of the radio in real-time (across all layers), one can develop novel functionality and study the capabilities of white space networking.

To demonstrate the capabilities of our radio system and white space networks in general, we will 1) Create over-the-air white space links at the conference location using the over 20 free TV white space channels at the geographic location, and 2) Provide an interactive display of data collected from

MobiCom'14, September 7-11, 2014, Maui, Hawaii, USA.
ACM 978-1-4503-2783-1/14/09.
http://dx.doi.org/10.1145/2639108.2641740 .

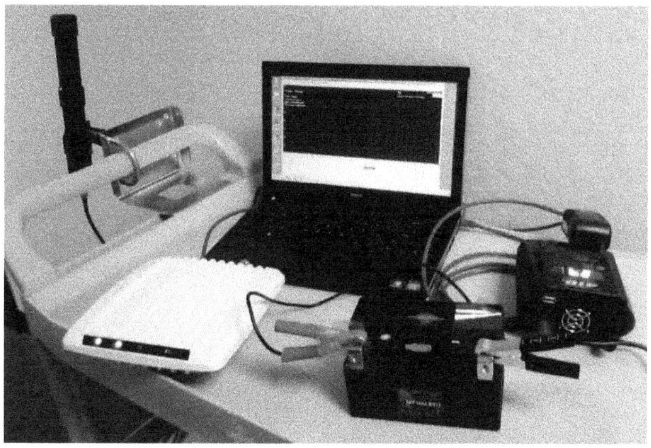

Figure 1: In this figure, we show a mobile unit which uses a battery and power-inverter to run an ACRS2.

our live and commercial white space deployments. The latter provides deeper insight in to white space capability that exceeds the limitations of what we can demonstrate at the venue. We will allow for live experimentation of the network with mobile clients that participants can move around the conference area to better understand its propagation. Below, we provide a background on the radio system and then provide more specifics of our demonstration.

2. ADAPTRUM COGNITIVE RADIO SYSTEM (ACRS) 2.0

To demonstrate and test the capabilities of white space networks we use the Adaptrum Cognitive Radio System 2.0 (ACRS2) platform. The ACRS2 is an off-the-shelf white space networking solution that is fully FCC compliant and currently undergoing compliance tests in other countries worldwide. The device is designed and constructed for rugged conditions allowing for outdoor usage and mobile testing. Below, we provide several details of the system.

PHY & MAC Layer: ACRS2 implements an adaptive OFDMA PHY layer with a TDD MAC layer (similar to the IEEE 802.22 [1]) with 94 percent channel bandwidth efficiency. 7 and 8 MHz channel sizes are supported for use in international countries. The PHY layer is implemented on FPGA / ASIC and the MAC layer mainly runs on a co-located ARM processor.

Emission: The transmit power of ACRS2 is max 23 dBm conducted with up to 1 W max power with an enhanced PA option. Adjacent channel emission is less than -55 dBc. The device supports omni-directional and directional antennas.

Data Rates: Given our physical layer, combined upload and download data rates of up to 12 Mbps per 6 MHz channel are supported. The uplink and downlink ratio can be configured in any way (e.g., 1:1, 1:3:, 4:1).

Database Access: The ACRS2 is fully functional and certified for use with the Telcordia iconectiv database, Microsoft TV white space database, and is currently the only radio certified for use with the Google spectrum database.

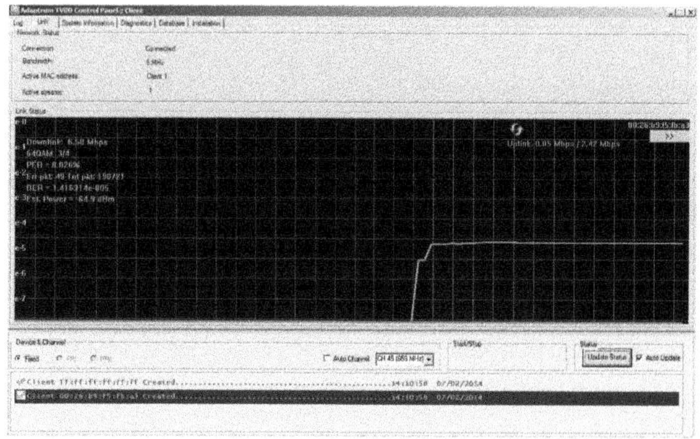

Figure 2: Screenshot of the GUI participants will see with link quality, BER, PER, throughput, etc.

Open-API: A key feature of our radio system is our open API of over 100 controls to modify and monitor aspects of the radio in real-time. To the best of our knowledge, our white space radio system is the only certifiable radio with such control. For example, the API opens up control over the physical layer (e.g., to disable certain subcarriers), rate adaptation, the MAC layer, and allows reading of real-time signal and environmental information from the radio.

3. DEMONSTRATION

For our demonstration, we provide 2 ways participants can interact with our white space networks to learn more about current capabilities and potential. First, we provide demonstration of live white space links and networks using the ACRS2 system at the conference location. Second, we provide an interactive display with details of some of our deployments and trials world-wide so that participants can better understand capabilities beyond the confines of the conference location. We describe these in detail below.

3.1 Live White Space Links

We will demonstrate multiple links to show the potential of white space radio in a multi-user scenario. This will include a link between two units in a room, a link across an indoor environment, and a link from an indoor to outdoor environment. The link between two distant indoor locations will provide a view of the resiliency of white space communications in multi-path environments while the outdoor link will demonstrate the potential of white space communications over long distance.

Additionally, at the end of these links we wish to provide a Wi-Fi connection so conference attendees can browse the Internet and test how the system performs in a real world scenario. This will require a backhaul Internet connection at the in-door conference location.

One of the key points of our system and recent work is also mobility. We will provide 2 mobile units on separate carts that conference participants can wheel around the building to see how white space penetrates in-door environments. As shown in Figure 1, we will power the unit from a battery system to provide full mobility and even allow participants to experiment on different floors (and even outdoors). The users will be able to use our desktop application to monitor signal strength, BER, packet error rates, throughput (uplink

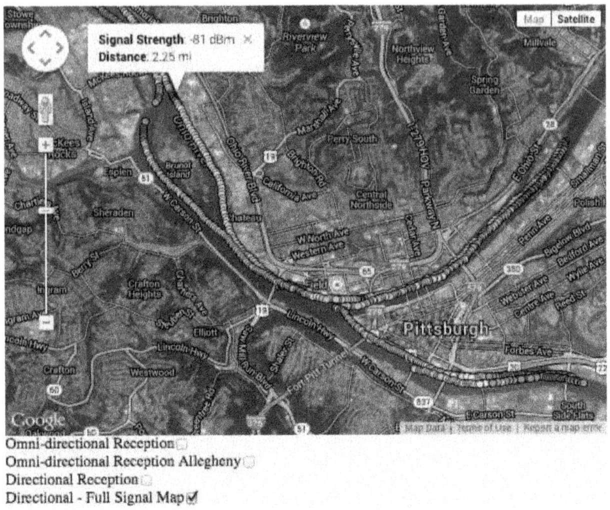

Figure 3: Example interactive overlay of real data captured from a marine deployment in Pittsburgh.

and downlink), as well as noise in the environment (shown in Figure 2).

While what we have discussed above demonstrates current white space capabilities, we will also demonstrate white space potential by showing some of the more advanced features that can be built on top of the platform with our open API. As the final part of our live demonstration, we will demonstrate an application of discontiguous spectrum access where the radio by suppressing subcarriers around a wireless microphone (primary user) that avoids all audible interference with the device.

3.2 Interactive Display of Current Networks

To allow participants to better understand white space networking capabilities beyond the confines of demonstration area, we will provide a workstation that has a map of our current commercial deployments and interactive functionality to view data collected from them. This provides insight in to propagation of white space networks through terrain and cities.

In particular, we will highlight a marine application in Pittsburgh, PA to provide connectivity to boats and barges through its rivers. As shown in Figure 3, users will be able to click on various data points to see signal strength, SNR, throughput, latency, and noise. By selecting various checkboxes (that vary by deployment), users will be able to see different propagation characteristics and coverage given different antennas.

We will also provide data from deployments at West Virginia University (campus), Namibia (emerging), and Butano State Park (heavily wooded). Time permitting, we may be able to provide additional data sets. To the best of our knowledge, this is some of the first publicly available data of live and commercial white space networks. This data provide significant insight in to white space capabilities of penetrating various types of terrain, foliage, and city-scapes.

4. NEEDS FOR DEMONSTRATION

The venue fortunately has availability of white space spectrum on over 20 channels allowing for a robust demonstration of white space capabilities. The exact demonstration can be tailored to available space and setup constraints at the venue. As a bare minimum we need at least two power outlets, a place to set up laptops, monitors, and posters, as well as space to set-up 2 tripods for our antennas. We also need Internet backhaul, preferably with 12 Mbps data rate. We are willing to pay the conference hotel for the Internet backhaul capability.

We can provide a demonstration of the use of white space networking in an indoor environment if a location across the hotel where we can setup a unit and a second antenna. We are also currently considering options to demonstrate the range of white space communications in outdoor environments. We can show historic data mapping this, and can provide a live demonstration if access to the roof of the hotel or a high balcony on the hotel is provided.

We also can provide a demonstration of mobility in white space if we can use a cart to setup a battery powered unit and portable antenna. This can be moved around in the demo-area or in an external area and provide an interactive experience for conference participants.

5. CONCLUSIONS

In conclusion, TV white space networks play a critical role in demonstrating the potential of white space spectrum bands and connectivity. Our demonstration is focused on exactly this: showing current capabilities of white space networks with fully certified equipment, as well as future potential. The live component of our demonstration will allow participants to gain insight in to these current capabilities in in-door environments as well as outdoor with our mobile unit setup. The interactive data component of our demo will provide a unique view in to some of the first commercial white space networks, their performance, and their operation. Finally, we hope to demonstrate that platform's potential to the academic community as a viable platform for novel research and studies in the white space.

6. REFERENCES

[1] IEEE 802.22 Working Group on WRANs, http://www.ieee802.org/22/.

[2] Unlicensed Operation in the TV Broadcast Bands. `http://hraunfoss.fcc.gov/edocs_public/attachmatch/FCC-04-113A1.pdf`, May 2004.

[3] FCC press release, FCC Adopts Rules for Unlicensed Use of Television White Spaces. `http://hraunfoss.fcc.gov/edocs_public/attachmatch/FCC-08-260A1.pdf`, 2008.

[4] FCC press release, FCC Frees Up Vacant TV Airwaves For "Super Wi-Fi" Technologies and Other Technologies. `http://www.fcc.gov/Daily_Releases/Daily_Business/2010/db0923/DOC-301650A1.pdf`, September 2010.

[5] P. Bahl, R. Chandra, T. Moscibroda, R. Murty, and M. Welsh. White space networking with wi-fi like connectivity. SIGCOMM '09.

[6] R. Chandra, R. Mahajan, T. Moscibroda, R. Raghavendra, and P. Bahl. A case for adapting channel width in wireless networks. SIGCOMM '08.

[7] R. Chandra, T. Moscibroda, P. Bahl, R. Murty, G. Nychis, and X. Wang. A campus-wide testbed over the tv white spaces. *SIGMOBILE Mob. Comput. Commun. Rev.*, 15(3):2–9, Nov. 2011.

[8] G. Nychis, R. Chandra, T. Moscibroda, I. Tashev, and P. Steenkiste. Reclaiming the white spaces: spectrum efficient coexistence with primary users. CoNEXT '11.

[9] H. Rahul, N. Kushman, D. Katabi, C. Sodini, and F. Edalat. Learning to share: narrowband-friendly wideband networks. SIGCOMM '08.

Demo: Software Defined Radio – on a Smartphone, as an App!

Yongtae Park
Korea University
ytpark@korea.ac.kr

JeongGil Ko
ETRI
jeonggil.ko@etri.re.kr

Hyogon Kim
Korea University
hyogon@korea.ac.kr

1. INTRODUCTION

In this demo, we showcase the first software defined radio (SDR) implementation that runs on today's smartphones. Using the SDR, the smartphones are shown to talk to real IEEE 802.15.4 devices such as sensor motes or Phillips Hue (TM) lightbulbs that otherwise they cannot natively communicate with. Furthermore, we make the SDR available as downloadable software ("app") on Google app store, so that anyone may freely download, use, and purge on his or her smartphone, independently of OS upgrades. Detaching SDR from OS allows almost immediate deployment of wireless protocols, and only on the phones that do need them. By enabling smartphones to speak non-native protocols in this manner, smartphone vendors will be able to support a wide range of wireless protocols without investing separate hardware and real estate in their devices. A promising application area for this concept could be Internet of Things (IoT), where protocols are diverse, typically low-speed, and not well supported by today's smartphones. Therefore, we believe that the smartphones with SDR will become a strong enabler or facilitator of many interesting applications in the IoT environment. We also believe that the concept of *wireless protocol as a smartphone app* will accelerate wireless protocol design–test–deployment cycle, catalyzing wireless protocol evolutions on smartphones.

2. IMPLEMENTATION

2.1 Hardware

Today's smartphone architectures delegate the physical (PHY) and medium access control (MAC) layer computations to the baseband processor (BP), which is interfaced to the radio front end. They do not offer a direct path from the application processor (AP) to the radio front, which would be required for software radios on smartphones. Therefore, we bypass the smartphones' native baseband and protocol processing chips through their USB interface. Namely, we connect an external radio front to the application processor via the USB2.0 I/O (Figure 1). It is never intended to be a recommended configuration, but just a practical workaround that is used to prove the real-time operability of smartphone SDR, under the current smartphone architecture limitations. For the external radio, we use USRP1 [1]. Note that it does *not* perform digital signal processing, but only serves as a rudimentary radio front that performs analog processing (*e.g.* sampling) and analog-to-digital conversion and *vice versa*. All digital signal processing is performed at the smartphone.

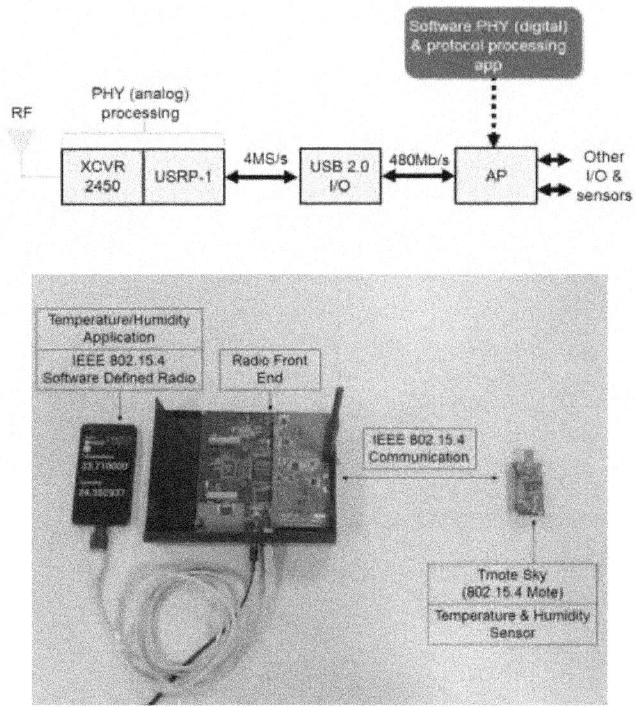

Figure 1: Schematic and implementation (shown to talk to a IEEE 802.15.4-based sensor mote to get humidity and temperature readings)

We use three smartphone platforms in our instrumentation: Samsung Galaxy S2, Google Nexus, and Samsung Galaxy S4 LTE-A (Table 1). They were introduced to the market on February of 2011, November of 2011, and October of 2013, respectively.

MobiCom'14, September 7-11, 2014, Maui, Hawaii, USA.
ACM 978-1-4503-2783-1/14/09.
http://dx.doi.org/10.1145/2639108.2641742.

Platform	Google Nexus	Galaxy S2	Galaxy S4
AP	OMAP 4460	Exynos 4210	Snapdragon 800
Cores	2		4
Clock	1.2GHz	1.2GHz 1.5GHz	2.265GHz
OS	Android 4.0 (Ice Cream Sandwich)	Android 2.3 (Gingerbread)	Android 4.3 (Jellybean)
L0 Cache	–		8KB
L1 Cache	32KB (instr.) 32KB (data)		16KB (instr.) 16KB (data)
L2 Cache	1MB		2MB

Table 1: Specifications of the employed smartphones

2.2 Software radio

For the IEEE 802.15.4 SDR, we ported the UCLA extension to the GNU Radio [2] on the smartphones that employ ARM cores. For real-time MAC/PHY processing, we must meet the timing requirements in encoding, decoding, response generation (e.g. ACK and CTS), and event trigger timing (e.g. CCA) [3]. The encoding and the decoding parts should be done in real-time in order to get the full transmission rate. The IEEE 802.15.4 Physical-layer Protocol Data Unit (PPDU) has 11 to 31 bytes of overhead, plus the payload data bytes. For our measurements, we use two payload lengths: 9 for short packets and 100 for long packets. With 100 bytes payload, the deadline for encoding and decoding steps is 3.84ms. For 9 bytes of data payload, it is 0.896ms. The acknowledgement time t_{ack} in the IEEE 802.15.4 has the following requirement: $t_{TA} \leq t_{ack} \leq t_{TA} + t_{BO}$. Here, t_{TA} is the turnaround time that is 12 symbols long (0.192ms). The t_{BO} is a unit backoff period that is 20 symbols long, so the acknowledgement time is between 0.192ms and 0.512ms.

Figure 2 shows the software architecture of our implementation. The two shaded blobs comprise the "SDR app." To put them into perspective, we also show the standard Android software framework as backdrop.

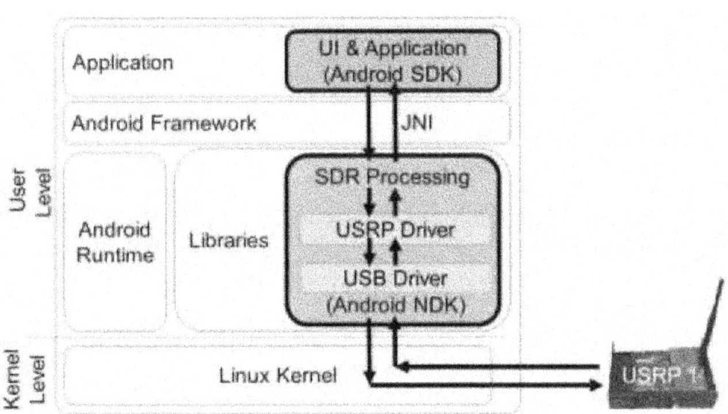

Figure 2: Software architecture of the SDR app on an Android smartphone

The "SDR Processing" logic is implemented as an embedded library in the app. This module performs the baseband processing, packetization, and CRC computation among others. In addition, it has two drivers that let the app use the USRP1 radio through the kernel. The SDR processing logic calls the USRP Driver, which in turn calls the USB Driver to talk to the external USRP1 radio front. This entire module is implemented using Android NDK. Note that most of the USRP and USB driver routines would not be included if the radio front is natively supported for the SDR.

The second module of the SDR app, "UI & Application," wraps the SDR Processing logic and presents an application that uses the 802.15.4 software radio to the user. Note that it is also possible to implement the SDR Processing as a separate "app," so that another app that implements the application may talk to the SDR Processing through an app-to-app communication to use it. The two modules are internally connected by JAVA Native Interface (JNI). Since SSR is self-contained with necessary libraries, it does not require any additional support from Android or the Linux kernel to run on smartphones, except that we must manually give the SDR app the root privilege when prompted by the app. Other than that, copying the firmware and image of USRP1 to smartphone to upload these files to USRP1 when the application opens USB connection, and setting up the path of image and firmware file to use USRP1 are all automatically done when the SDR app is downloded from Google Playstore and installed on the smartphone. These apps can be searched on the app store using the keywords "Softbee," which is Software Zigbee in short. They are for communication with Zigbee sensor motes, communication with Phillips Hue lightbulbs, and communication with radio-controlled (RC) cars.

3. PERFORMANCE

Fig. 3 shows the breakdown of the average decoding times for per-block, 9B-payload, and 100B-payload packets. We can see that Galaxy S2 violates the deadline, whereas S4 makes it. The result shows that the most recent smartphones can readily process low-speed protocols in real-time, thanks to the increased application processor speed. For encoding, we use five transmission intervals of 0ms (back-to-back), 50ms and higher in order to measure the effects of cache sizes and USB access times since packet transmission activity can be less continuous than that of reception. Fig. 4 shows the breakdown of the average encoding times for three types of packets on S2 and S4. For data packets, we notice S4 can meet the deadline in all gaps tested. For ACK, only back-to-back case on S4 can barely meet the deadline.

For SDRs, power consumption is generally a critical problem. When the SDR app is running continuously, the measured battery consumption is 209.44 μAh [4]. With slightly under 3,000mAh battery pack considered for the most recent smartphones such as Galaxy S5, therefore, the continuous SSR operation will completely drain the battery in four hours. Note that this number does not include the USRP1 radio front that uses a separate power source, so the estimate is a liberal one. However, if the smartphone SDR is used for IoT environment, most interactions with IoT devices are sporadic and short-lived; they are not like cellular or Wi-Fi usage. Therefore, we expect that the power issue will be less critical in the smartphone SDR for IoT applications. More details of the implemented SDR and the performance evaluation that includes not only IEEE 802.15.4 software radio but also IEEE 802.11a and b can be found in our unabridged technical report version [4].

4. APPLICATIONS

In order to demonstrate that the SDR app is a working prototype, we let it talk to several ZigBee devices available

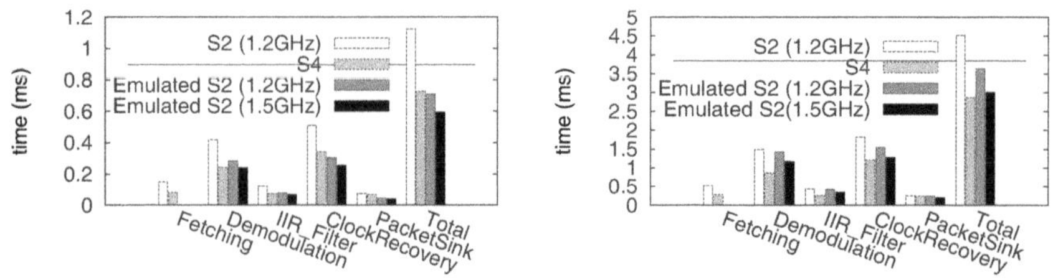

Figure 3: Breakdown of 802.15.4 decoding times on Galaxy S2 and S4: 9B (left) and 100B (right) packets

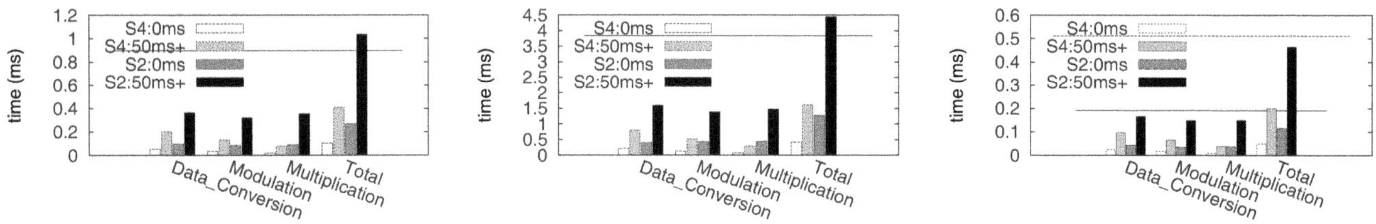

Figure 4: Breakdown of encoding times: 9B (left), and 100B (center); and ACK generation (right)

on the market. They are TMote Sky sensor motes, IoT lighting system, and radio-controlled mobile robots *etc.*, all providing a ZigBee interface. Although Galaxy smartphones do not have native ZigBee chips in it, they can communicate with these devices using the implemented 802.15.4 software radio. The Phillips Hue (TM) light control directly using Zigbee can be seen at YouTube [5]. Internet of Things (IoT) products have finally begun to arrive at the mass market. One of the recent products is Phillips Hue lightbulbs, which change color and luminance at user's command. It is composed of LED lightbulbs and a bridge. Users' smartphones connect to the bridge through Wi-Fi, and the bridge connects to the lighbulbs through ZigBee. Using the SDR app, we can capture the 802.15.4 packets exchanged between the bridge and lightbulbs, with very few losses. We can take one step further, and let the SDR app mimic the bridge by sending 802.15.4 packets to control the lightbulbs. We first let the app record the packets generated from the Hue bridge to the lights, which the app uses to turn them on and off.

Fig. 1 shows another example application, where a Galaxy S2 reads in sensing data from a TMote Sky mote through its software ZigBee radio. The SDR app that displays the room temperature and humidity obtains the data from the mote through the 802.15.4 communication. The application can also command the mote to blink lights of different colors. ZigBee sensor networks are used in industry (*e.g.* for factory automation) and home (*e.g.* for HVAC), and using smartphones to talk to sensor motes in the environments without specialized devices would be able to reduce cost and improve user experience. With open and shared radio fronts, it can happen immediately.

5. ARRANGEMENTS FOR DEMO

We will use our own Galaxy smartphones and USRP1 radio front, sensor motes, Phillips Hue lighbulbs along with a laptop to show the video clips of the SDR operation. A regular desktop size space will be enough for the demo. Internet connectivity is required to download the SDR app from the Google Playstore. No other facilities are required.

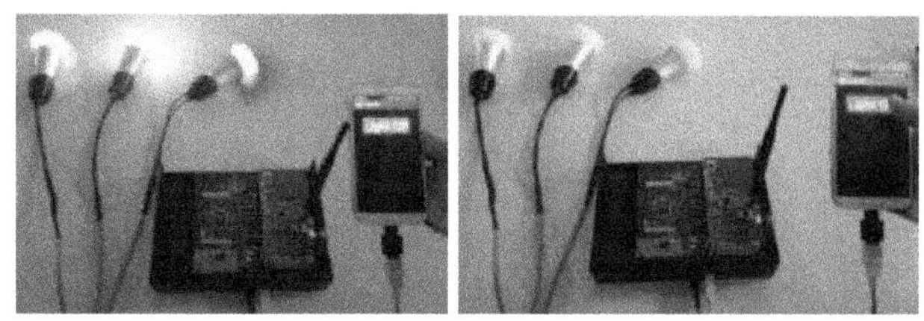

Figure 5: Light control using Softbee/Lightcontrol

Acknowledgements

This work was supported by the Mid-career Researcher Program through NRF grant funded by the MEST (2011-0028892) and the MSIP, Korea and Microsoft Research, under IT/SW Creative research program supervised by the NIPA (NIPA-2013-H0503-13-1022).

6. REFERENCES

[1] LLC Ettus Research. USRP.

[2] T. Schmid. GNU Radio 802.15.4 En- and Decoding, 2006.

[3] K. Tan et al. Sora: High-Performance Software Radio Using General-Purpose Multi-Core Processors. *CACM*, 54(1), January 2011.

[4] Y. Park and H. Kim. http://widen.korea.ac.kr/spsdr.pdf, 2014.

[5] Y. Park. Softbee, http://www.youtube.com/watch?v=tb3uuDw-1VE&feature=youtu.be, 2014.

Demo: RollingLight - Universal Camera Communications for Single LED

Hsin-Mu Tsai, Hao-Min Lin, and Hui-Yu Lee
Department of Computer Science and Information Engineering
National Taiwan University, Taipei, Taiwan
{hsinmu,d00922003,r01922028} @csie.ntu.edu.tw

Categories and Subject Descriptors

C.2.1 [**Network Architecture and Design**]: Wireless Communication

Keywords

Visible Light Communications; Camera Communications; Rolling Shutter; Frequency Shift Keying

1. INTRODUCTION

Camera communication (CamCom) is a form of visible light communication (VLC) that makes use of a camera as the receiver. One very important advantage of CamCom is that the acquired images during the receiving process provide a means to *visually associate* the physical object with the transmitted information, since the receiver has the knowledge of which pixels in the images are transmitting. Figure 1 shows a simple example. A user points her smartphone camera at multiple lights, touches the screen to select one, and uses the virtual switch that appears on the screen to adjust the lighting level. In this scenario, the lights simply periodically transmit simple identifiers, such as IP addresses, to the smartphone. The system is able to directly associate what the user sees (the image pixels corresponding to the light selected by the user) to the transmitted information (the identifier of the light). An out-of-band channel, such as WiFi, can then be used to send the actual command to the selected light to adjust the setting. Compared to the conventional approach of identifying a particular set of visual features unique to the object with computer vision techniques, this approach is simpler, more intuitive, and more accurate.

The biggest limitation of CamCom is that the data rate is severely limited by the frame rate of the camera. A modern consumer-grade camera usually has a frame rate of 30 frames per second (fps), which translates to a sampling rate of 30 Hz and an undesirable data rate of 15 bits per second (bps) [5] per transmitting LED. Several existing works [1, 4] exploit rolling shutter, which exists in most modern CMOS cameras, to increase the data rate. Cameras with rolling shutter have each row of pixels exposed and read out at slightly different points in time, which are separated by a constant read-out time. Although this creates undesirable effects in images such as wobble or skew, this however creates a new opportunity to improve the sampling rate to tens of KHz, which in turn improves the data rate.

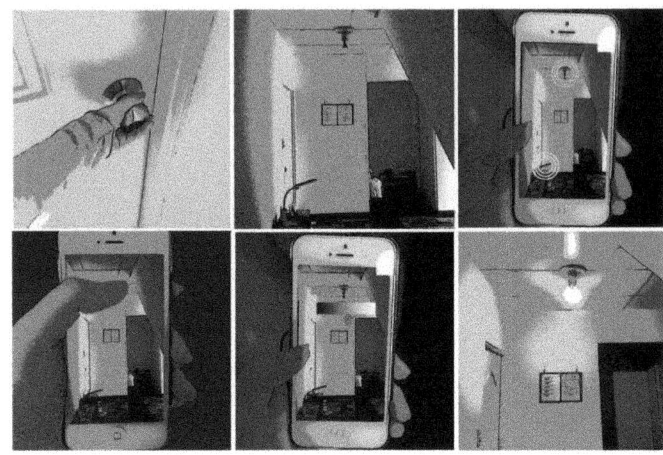

Figure 1: An example of utilizing CamCom for visual association.

To create a system that works for every CMOS camera, many challenges are not yet addressed by existing works. Those include:

1. **Different sampling rate used by different cameras.** For the system to be useful, it is apparent that the transmitted optical signal needs to be compatible with a range of different cameras with different hardware specifications. One of the biggest challenges is that the sampling rates, which is the inverse of the readout time, is drastically different among cameras (see Table 1), creating difficulties in designing the modulation format.

2. **Significant time gaps between received signal segments.** Different from conventional communication channel, the rolling shutter sampling process is not continuous in time and time gaps are present between segments of consecutive signal samples. This is due to two reasons: (1) significant time difference between the end of exposure for the last row of pixels in the current frame and the start of exposure for

MobiCom'14, September 7-11, 2014, Maui, Hawaii, USA.
ACM ACM 978-1-4503-2783-1/14/09.
http://dx.doi.org/10.1145/2639108.2641748.

Table 1: Summary of Camera Parameters

	Image Resolution ($X_{\max}$ x $Y_{\max}$)	Frame Rate (fps)	Measured Read-out Time / Sampling Rate	Time Gap (ms) (Percentage of Frame Duration)
Point Grey Flea3	2048×1080	30	14.75 μs / 67.80 KHz	17.40 (52.23%)
Apple iPhone 5S	1920×1080	29.98	19.15 μs / 52.22 KHz	12.67 (37.99%)
Apple iPhone 4S	1920×1080	29.87	24.48 μs / 40.85 KHz	7.04 (21.03%)
HTC New One	1920×1080	30	18.79 μs / 53.22 KHz	13.04 (39.11%)
Apple iPhone 4	1280×720	29.97	44.88 μs / 22.28 KHz	1.05 (3.15%)
HTC Desire HD	800×480	29.08	55.18 μs / 18.12 KHz	7.90 (22.97%)
Google Nexus One	720×480	30.57	59.66 μs / 16.76 KHz	4.07 (12.45%)

the first row of pixels in the next frame. According to our measurement results, this could be up to 50% of the frame duration (the inverse of the frame rate) for some cameras (see Table 1); and (2) the transmitting light does not necessarily occupy all rows of pixels in the image. As a result, depending on the size of the transmitting light in the image, an additional percentage of signal samples are lost. This creates difficulty in designing a modulation format for the receiver to operate at different distances.

3. **The long exposure (shutter) time required by imaging distorts high frequency components of the signal.** To acquire an image, the camera sensor needs to expose the array of photodiodes to incoming photons for a period of time. The exposure operation of the camera sensor essentially integrates the received signal over the period of exposure time, and thus acts as a low-pass filter. This distorts the high frequency components of the signal, and in most cases the symbol rate of the system cannot go beyond the inverse of the exposure time. In most mobile devices, the exposure time of the camera is not configurable by the user. For example, the achievable throughput of the system proposed in [1] is severely limited due to these reasons.

4. **The transmitting LED and the receiving camera are not synchronized.** For almost all cameras, time synchronization with the transmitting LED is not possible since the user has no control over the timing of the exposure operation. This means that the symbol durations (i.e., frame durations) of the transmitter and the receiver are not aligned and are different, creating difficulty in decoding the transmission.

In this demonstration, we present RollingLight, a CamCom system that works for a wide range of CMOS cameras, including those in smartphones, tablets, and laptops. To address the first three of the four previously mentioned challenges, we propose and utilize a novel **Rolling Shutter Frequency Shift Keying (RS-FSK)** modulation format, while we leave the last one for future work. Utilizing only a single LED as the transmitter, our system can achieve a data rate of 15 byte/s per transmitting LED with a 30 fps camera.

2. RS-FSK MODULATION

Transmission. The fundamental idea of RS-FSK is to use to square waves of a number of different *frequencies* as different symbols, mapped to different bit patterns of the same length. The signal of the i-th symbol is represented by the fundamental frequency f_i of the square wave:

$$s_i(t) = I_{\max} \left\lceil \frac{\cos(2\pi f_i t)}{2} \right\rceil \quad (1)$$

where $I_{\max}$ is the maximum output intensity of the transmitting light.

A frequency modulation is advantageous in the following aspects: (1) The transmitted frequency can be demodulated by receivers with different sampling rates, as long as the sampling rate satisfies the Nyquist rate requirement. This implies that cameras with different read-out time, i.e., different sampling rate, are all compatible to a single transmission signal format. (2) Demodulation is still possible when some segments of signal samples are lost in a symbol period, as long as the longest remaining signal segment has a length larger than the transmitted signal period. This addresses the time gap challenge previously described. (3) The average intensity stays the same for all symbols, implying that the transmission is not observable by human eyes as long as the frequency is higher than 100 Hz.

Reception. The transmitted signal period is the inverse of the transmitted signal frequency f_i. As rows of pixels are sequentially obtained with sampling period T_r (i.e., read-out time), one cycle of square wave transmission results in a pair of bright strip and dark strip in the image, the sum of whose widths is given by

$$W = \frac{1}{f_i T_r} \quad . \quad (2)$$

Note that the width of the bright strip could be larger than the width of the dark strip in the image. This is due to blooming, the overflow of charge from a saturated pixel into its neighboring pixel [3]. We thus consider the widths of the bright strip and the dark strip together in the calculation, to average out the effect. Since W might not be an integer, averaging the observed widths over a large image area would help to improve the accuracy. Then, the transmitted symbol can be determined with the estimated value of W and eq.(2).

To have a more robust method to accurately determine the period of the signal, i.e., the average width of a pair of bright and dark strips in the image, we modified a well-known pitch detection algorithm (PDA), YIN [2], which is originally designed to determine the fundamental frequency of a segment of audio signal in speech or music. We chose to use a method that operates in time domain, so that computationally expensive Fourier Transform operation can be avoided.

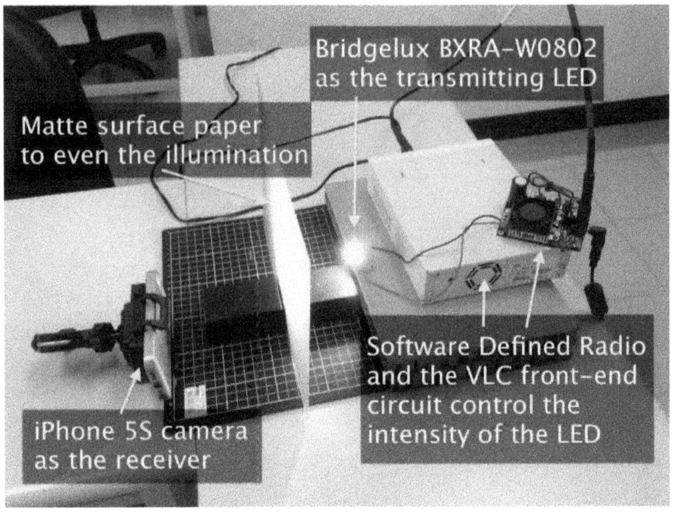

Figure 2: System components of the prototype

3. PROTOTYPE

To allow flexibility in system development, the transmitter is implemented with a software defined radio platform. Digital signal samples of RS-FSK are generated by a computer, then passed to a Ettus Universal Software Radio Peripheral (USRP) N200. USRP then converts the samples to analog voltage-varying signal, which in turn is converted to current-varying signal by a custom-made VLC front-end circuit board to control the output intensity of the connected LED component (see Fig. 2). A high brightness LED array suitable for indoor illumination purposes, Bridgelux BXRA-W0802, is chosen as the transmitting LED, with a maximum output power of 26 Watt. In the demonstration, the user can specify a text message to be repeatedly transmitted by the LED. The dimension of the transmitting LED is also included as part of the transmitted packet, to allow accurate calculation of the distance between the two devices using photogrammetry.

Two cameras are used in the demonstration as the receiver. Point Grey Flea 3 (FL3-U3-88S2C-C) is a high-speed USB camera built for experimental purposes. The images are captured with 2048×1080 resolution at 30 fps and processed in real-time on the laptop. The decoded text message and the estimated transmitter-receiver distance are displayed on the screen.

To show that our system also works for cameras on mobile devices and the decoding process can be executed in real-time with their processors, we also implement an iOS RS-FSK decoding app, running on an iPhone 5S. The images are captured with 1920×1080 resolution at 30 fps and processed in real-time by the app. Similarly, the decoded text message is displayed on the screen of the phone.

Our demonstration video can be found at the following URL: `http://goo.gl/o53dsU`.

4. DEMONSTRATION LOGISTICS

We need a 3×1 meter space and half an hour to set up our demonstration. In terms of equipment, two power strips and a large LCD monitor (which helps the audience see the received message clearly) are needed for our demonstration.

5. ACKNOWLEDGMENTS

This work is supported in part by National Science Council, National Taiwan University, and Intel Corporation under grants NSC-102-2911-I-002-001, NSC-102-2221-E-002-093-MY2, and NTU-103R7501.

6. REFERENCES

[1] C. Danakis, M. Afgani, G. Povey, I. Underwood, and H. Haas. Using a CMOS camera sensor for visible light communication. In *Proc. Optical Wireless Communications Workshop, IEEE Global Communications Conference (GLOBECOM)*, pages 1244–1248, December 2012.

[2] A. De Cheveigné and H. Kawahara. YIN, a fundamental frequency estimator for speech and music. *The Journal of the Acoustical Society of America*, 111(4):1917–1930, 2002.

[3] A. El Gamal and H. Eltoukhy. CMOS image sensors. *Circuits and Devices Magazine*, 21(3):6–20, 2005.

[4] N. Rajagopal, P. Lazik, and A. Rowe. Visual light landmarks for mobile devices. In *Proc. ACM/IEEE International Symposium on Information Processing in Sensor Networks (IPSN)*, pages 249–260, 2014.

[5] R. D. Roberts. Undersampled Frequency Shift ON-OFF Keying (UFSOOK) for Camera Communications (CamCom). In *Proc. Wireless and Optical Communication Conference (WOCC)*, pages 645–648, May 2013.

Demo: A Robust Barcode System for Data Transmissions over Screen-Camera Links

Anran Wang[1] Shuai Ma[1] Chunming Hu[1] Jinpeng Huai[1] Chunyi Peng[2] Guobin Shen[3]
[1]SKLSDE Lab, Beihang University, China [2]The Ohio State University, USA [3]Microsoft Research, China
{wangar@act., mashuai@, hucm@, huaijp@}buaa.edu.cn chunyi@cse.ohio-state.edu jackysh@microsoft.com

ABSTRACT

Visible light communication (VLC) over screen-camera links emerges as a novel form of near-field communication, and it offers a user-friendly, infrastructure-less and secure communication, which is highly competitive for one-time file transfer [1–4]. However, the limitations of smart devices and the uncertainty of user behaviors seriously impair the transmission reliability and hinder its applicability. Worse still, existing approaches [1, 2, 4] mostly focus on improving the transmission speed and ignore the transmission reliability. Hence, RDCode is proposed to boost the throughput over screen-camera links, by making use of a novel barcode design and several effective techniques to enhance the transmission reliability [3]. In this demo, we show that our RDCode prototype system addresses many practical challenges.

A short video on our prototype system is accessible from http://mashuai.buaa.edu.cn/demo/RDCode.mp4.

Categories and Subject Descriptors

C.2.1 [**Network Architecture and Design**]: Wireless communication

Keywords

Dynamic barcodes; transmission; reliability; smartphones

1. INTRODUCTION

As the rapid proliferation of camera-equipped smart devices, visible light communication (VLC) over screen-camera links, as a novel form of near-field communication, has provided an attractive solution for its user-friendliness, security and infrastructure-less. Compared with the traditional radio frequency (RF) techniques such as Bluetooth and WiFi, VLC does not depend on the Internet infrastructure and enables direct and secure communications, which simplifies the complicated authentication process for setting up link connections. Hence, VLC is well suited for one-time transfer as it incurs no charge and no overhead in link setup and management, compared with traditional RF techniques [3, 4].

MobiCom'14, September 7 - 11, 2014, Maui, Hawaii, USA.
ACM 978-1-4503-2783-1/14/09.
http://dx.doi.org/10.1145/2639108.2641741.

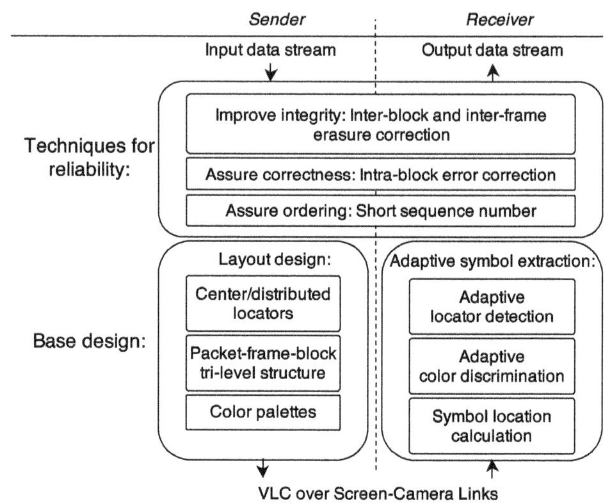

Figure 1: RDCode architecture

To achieve high-speed data transmissions, the *transmission rate* is only one side of the coin. The *transmission reliability* is equally important for many applications such as file transmission. However, previous works [1,2,4] mostly spend their efforts on improving the transmission speed, while ignore the transmission reliability. We give an analysis of the typical problems that impair the transmission reliability and summarize these into two categories: smartphone limitations and user behavior uncertainty [3], which introduce two challenging issues: (a) the *locality problem* that for an image with uniform features, the close places in its captured image have similar features, while places far from each other present different features, and (b) the *partial unavailability problem* that leads to either unrecognizable parts of a frame caused by *e.g.,* unsuitable shooting positions or temporally sequential frames loss caused by *e.g.,* trembles [3].

As a first step towards solving all these problems, we have proposed RDCode [3], a robust barcode system for high-speed data transmissions over screen-camera links. The architecture of RDCode is shown in Fig. 1. Finally, we implement the RDCode prototype system as a file transmission App on an Android platform.

2. RDCode DESIGN

In this section, we briefly introduce our RDCode design. RDCode is a VLC system designed for high-speed data trans-

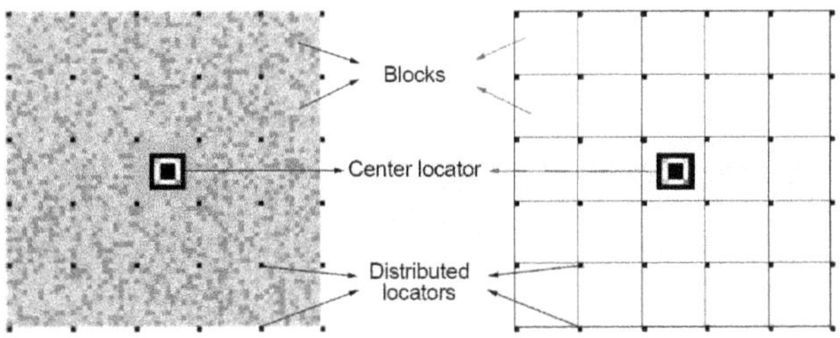

Figure 2: The frame layout of RDCode design

missions over screen-camera links, and it consists of three layers. (a) The first layer is the barcode layout and its corresponding locating and data extraction methods, which lay a foundation for reliable transmissions; (b) The second layer is the error correction and data ordering methods to enhance the reliability; And (c) the last layer is for a specific application, *i.e.*, file transmissions in our implementation. These together enable RDCode to reach a high transmission speed by enhancing the transmission reliability.

2.1 Barcode Layout

RDCode has a novel tri-level barcode layout such that (a) a packet comprises a sequence of frames, (b) each frame consists of a set of independent blocks, and (c) each block is a square of symbols, shown in Fig. 2.

To increase the locating success rate for receivers, a frame of RDCode contains a single specifically designed locator at the center block, referred to as the *center locator*, and each block in a frame also contains another pattern (*i.e.*, a single black symbol) at the left-top corner of the block, referred to as the *distributed locator*.

We incorporate an adaptive locator detection method into RDCode to recognize the barcode sequence. It first searches and identifies the center locator, then makes use of a best-effort approach to identifying all the distributed locators, by taking advantage of the positions of the located neighboring locators of a distributed locator to speed up the detection process. It is easy to know that the four distributed locators around a block can determine the positions of the symbols in the block. The adaptive techniques for symbol extraction improve the locating and decoding accuracy, by using successive frames in our dynamic barcode system.

The barcode layout of RDCode along with the adaptive locating methods lay a foundation for reaching high-speed reliable data transmissions.

2.2 Data Protection Techniques

Based on an analysis of the spatial and temporal distributions of errors, we apply (a) the Reed-Solomon (RS) code for block level error corrections, and (b) two kinds of parity-check codes for frames and packets, respectively. Our experiments show that the error correcting method behaves much better than using the Reed-Solomon code alone. In order to keep the block and frame ordering, we further put a short header denoting the relative sequence number in each block, and the full sequence number can be calculated by looking up a certain kind of meta data in the center block.

2.3 File Transmission Techniques

We finally build a layer on the top of RDCode for file transmissions. A file is treated as binary data, and read into a bit array that keeps repeating in the source data stream. During the transmission process, we need to keep the data intact and complete within a short time. Hence, we propose an efficient optimization to encode the packets into a combination of these packets in certain order. This significantly reduces the extra transmissions when the file is not completely received in the first transfer.

Remarks. RDCode significantly improves the transmission speed by enhancing the transmission reliability.
(1) The barcode layout and adaptive symbol extraction methods are in nature to address locality problems and partial unavailability problems, since different blocks are autonomous. They are located, recognized and decoded independently and asynchronously. As a result, the data reliability is improved. Moreover, our adaptive techniques improve the locating and decoding accuracy, and hence increase the data capacity per frame as well as transmission speed.
(2) The novelty of the data protection techniques lies in that instead of simply applying a single Reed-Solomon code like most barcode systems, we analyze the characteristics of data errors, utilize our tri-level barcode layout and design a tri-level error correction method to decode the decodable parts of data as much as possible to increase the data integrity.

3. RDCODE DEMONSTRATIONS

In this section, we describe two demonstrations to show that RDCode achieves a high transmission performance, and that our work has a potential to be adopted by commercial products. The file transmission using our RDCode prototype system is illustrated in Fig. 3.
(1) In the first demonstration, we show how to transmit a file from a laptop to a smartphone. We use our laptop as the sender, and an Android smartphone Samsung Galaxy S3 as the receiver. The file can be in any format such as JPEG image files and plain text files. We allow a user to choose a file to transmit.

There exist a number of files in various types in a specific directory of our laptop. As long as the source file is chosen, the online encoder of RDCode immediately starts generating frames and simultaneously play the barcode stream. At the other side, the receiver, held by hands, captures the screen of the sender, and simultaneously decodes the image frames. During the demonstration, we (a) change the distance between the sender and receiver, (b) adjust the shooting angle, and (c) even block some area of the sender display. Users can see that the transmission process eventually terminates and the received file is intact and complete.

After the transmission is done, we then plug the receiver into the laptop and show some statistics such as transmission rates and successfully decoded block ratios during the transmission. These statistics are shown with another application running on our laptop.
(2) In the second demonstration, we show how to transmit a file from a tablet to a smartphone. Here we use a tablet Asus Nexus 7 as the sender, and an Android phone Samsung Galaxy S3 as the receiver. An image file is chosen to be transmitted from the sender, and an RDCode frame with a customized shape is generated in the tablet, by disabling some blocks within a frame. The receiver is able to successfully capture and decode RDCode frames, and finally the entire received image is presented on its screen.

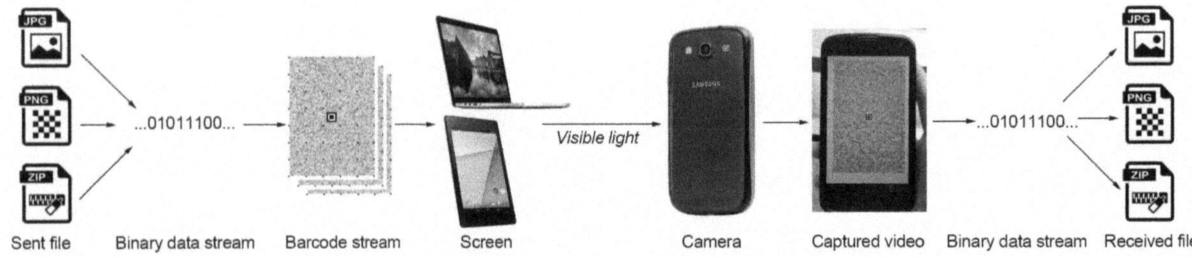

Figure 3: File transmissions using the RDCode prototype system

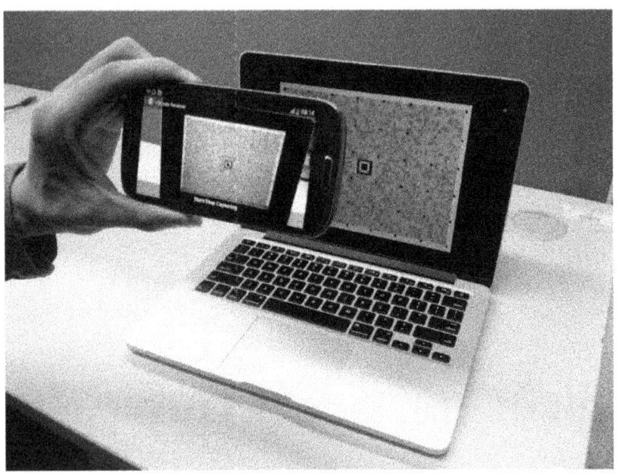

Figure 4: RDCode setup

4. DEMO SETUP

We need to port our RDCode App to an Android smartphone and an Android tablet with the Android 4.2 operating system. The RDCode App contains both an online encoder and an online decoder, which are developed using Scala with the Android SDK and Scala compiler. For the convenience of demonstration, we migrate the sender to a laptop with Mac OS X 10.9.

Our prototype system is easy to set up. As shown by Fig. 4, we initiate an application to encode a file into RDCode frames, and trigger the RDCode App on our Samsung Galaxy S3 smartphone to receive the file. The tablet is put on its holder to keep still, and is placed beside the laptop when not needed.

5. DEMO REQUIREMENTS

Our demonstration requires a laptop, a tablet and a smartphone. To put on our devices, a desk larger than 80cm*50cm is needed, and we also need an AC power supply with more than 4 plugs. There are two extra requirements. First, a large LCD display connected to our laptop would make people easier to see our prototype system. Second, it would be nice if we could pin a poster around our demonstration desk.

Acknowledgments. This work is supported in part by 973 program (No. 2014CB340304), NSFC (No. 61322207) and SKLSDE grant (No. SKLSDE-2014ZX-20).

6. REFERENCES

[1] T. Hao, R. Zhou, and G. Xing. Cobra: color barcode streaming for smartphone systems. In *MobiSys*, 2012.

[2] T. Hao, R. Zhou, and G. Xing. Demo: a barcode streaming system for smartphones. In *MobiSys*, 2012.

[3] A. Wang, S. Ma, C. Hu, J. Huai, C. Peng, and G. Shen. Enhancing reliability to boost the throughput over screen-camera links. In *MobiCom*, 2014.

[4] Q. P. Wenjun Hu, Hao Gu. Lightsync: Unsynchronized visual communication over screen-camera links. In *MobiCom*, 2013.

Demo: High-Precision RFID Tracking Using COTS Devices

Lei Yang*, Yekui Chen*, Chen Chen*,
Xiang-Yang Li*,†, Xuan Ding*, Yi Guo‡, Yunhao Liu*

*School of Software and TNLIST, Tsinghua University, China
†Department of Computer Science, Illinois Institute of Technology, USA

{young, yekui, chenchen}@tagsys.org, xli@cs.iit.edu, {xuan,yi}@tagsys.org,
yunhao@greenorbs.com

ABSTRACT

In many applications, we have to identify an object and then locate the object to within high precision (centimeter- or millimeter-level). Tracking *mobile* RFID tags in *real time* has been a daunting task, especially challenging for achieving *high precision*. We achieve these three goals by leveraging the phase value of the backscattered signal, provided by the COTS RFID readers, to estimate the location of the object. To illustrate the basic idea of our system, we firstly focus on a simple scenario where the tag is moving along a fixed track known to the system. We propose Differential Augmented Hologram (DAH) which will facilitate the instant tracking of the mobile RFID tag to a high precision. We then devise a comprehensive solution to accurately recover the tag's moving trajectory and its locations, relaxing the assumption of knowing tag's track function in advance.

Categories and Subject Descriptors

C.2 [**Computer Systems Organization**]: Computer Communications Networks

Keywords

RFID; Tracking; Localization

1. INTRODUCTION

Radio Frequency IDentification (RFID) is a rapidly developing technology which uses RF signals for automatic identification of objects. One of its most promising applications is to track the mobile objects accurately. Many applications would benefit from higher tracking accuracy. For example, supermarkets can deeply mine the consumers' shopping habits by monitoring the items' trajectories. Similarly, it is useful to conduct automatic recognition of complex multi-player behaviors through the tagged football in a world-wide game. Plenty of new battery-free human-machine interactive device can be developed using the tags, like writing letters in the air by attaching a tag on a finger. Today's robots routinely replace human labor in assembly tasks. It has been of a great interest in both the robotics academic community and industry to enable robot search for a desired object, pick it up, fetch and delivery it from a assembly lines. These tasks require tracking the object to cm-level and even mm-level accuracy.

We observe that the COTS RFID products support fine-grained resolution in detecting the phase of received RF signals, *i.e.*, with accuracy ≈ 0.0015 radians. This accuracy offers an opportunity to locate the object with accuracy of millimeter-level displacement. Developing a practical system out of the basic principle, however, entails substantial challenges. First, the RF phase measurement is affected by the basic thermal noise at the receiver side, which results in the practically measured RF phase a random variable following Gaussian distribution. How to derive a definite and accurate tracking result from the indefinite phase measurement remains challenging. Second, the device diversity in phase measurement introduces extra phase shifts we call "*diversity term*". Different RFID tags or readers have different diversity terms. Prior calibration of all tags and readers is impractical and computationally infeasible and we need to carefully sidestep the problem. Third, the fast changing environment makes the phase measurement a complex result mixing RF propagation through the line-of-sight (LOS) with the None LOS. It is hard to separate them and thus non-trivial to accurately derive the tag position.

In this study, we design Tagoram, which exploits the phase value of received signal for *real-time* tracking of *mobile* tags with a *high precision*. We propose a hologram based approach, called *Tagoram*, to tackle above challenges using COTS RFID tags and readers with a few physical antennas. We build an RF phase hologram with observations from different reader antennas and at different time of scan. To tackle the challenges of mobile tags, we assume the antennas moving to the opposite direction relative to the mobile tag. Such fictitious reader "mobility" offers individual RF phase observations from different positions relative to the tag, and they form an RF hologram as if they were obtained from a virtual antenna array. If the tag movement velocity and its moving track is known in advance, the positions of the antenna array relative to the tag can be determined. We can thus rely on the instant hologram to derive the initial position of the tag and thus precisely track the tag movement. In order to tackle previously identified challenges we further develop Differential Augmented Hologram (DAH) approach from the naive one. We then relax the assumption that we know the tag moving track in advance and devise a technique to accurately recover the tag movement from antenna observations. We first identify a series of candidate tag moving paths using the continuously estimated tag velocity from the antenna array. Then DAH is extended to identify the one with the highest likelihood of generating the observed RF phases. To enable real-time localization and tracking, we propose several techniques to speedup the computation of hologram.

MobiCom'14, September 7-11, 2014, Maui, Hawaii, USA.
ACM 978-1-4503-2783-1/14/09.
http://dx.doi.org/10.1145/2639108.2641743 .

2. TAGORAM DESIGN

2.1 Background

Passive RFID system communicates using a backscatter radio link. The tags, no battery equipped, purely harvest energy from the reader's signal. The RF phase is a common parameter supported by COTS readers. The signal traverses a total distance of $2d$ back and forth in backscatter communication where d is the distance between the reader antenna and the tag. Besides the RF phase rotation over distance, the reader's transmitter, the tag's reflection characteristic, and the reader's receiver circuits will all introduce some additional phase rotations, denoted as θ_T, θ_{TAG} and θ_R respectively. The total phase rotation output by the reader can be expressed as

$$\begin{cases} \theta = \left(\frac{2\pi}{\lambda} \times 2d + c\right) \bmod 2\pi \\ c = \theta_T + \theta_R + \theta_{TAG} \end{cases} \tag{1}$$

where λ is the wavelength. The term c is called *diversity term*, which is related to the hardware characteristics. The phase is a periodic function with period 2π radians which repeats every $\lambda/2$ in the distance of backscatter communication.

2.2 Challenges

(*i*) The phase estimate is derived from the received signal where the thermal noise from reader receiver is always present, leading to measurement errors. We conduct an empirical studies over 100 tags with environment temperature from 0° to 40°C, various frequencies ($920 \sim 926$MHz) including 16 channels, and RSS from -70 to -30dbm (different orientations). One set of the results measured at the 5th channel is depicted in Fig. 1(a). These experiments suggest that trehe phase measurement results contain random errors, following a typical Gaussian distribution with a standard deviation of 0.1 radians. In the following sections, we will consider the phase measurement as a Gaussian random variable instead of an accurate value. (*ii*) To validate the existence of tag's diversity on RF phase. We place 70 tags at a same position in turn. Each tag is interrogated for 100 times and the average value is reported in Fig. 1(b). We observe that the measured phase values are distributed among $0.3007 \sim 5.8438$ radians. Such an observation suggests that the tag's diversity takes impact on phase measurement and cannot be ignored in practice. We also perform the Kolmogorov-Smirnov test (KS-test) to study their predictability. These values pass the test to be verified over a uniform distribution with 0.5 significant level, which means that the tag diversity is hard to infer. In summary, both the thermal noise and tag diversity challenge the phase measurement and further affect the tracking accuracy, which were not fully studied previously.

2.3 Solution

In this paper, we propose a holistic system, Tagoram, to address the instant tag tracking problem. Tagoram decomposes it into two stages.

• **Controllable Case**: First, we consider a simplified case where the tags move along a known track with a constant speed. This case mostly occurs at a conveyor belt or assembly line where the objects are conveyed by a predefined track. Then the trajectory function can be expressed as:

$$f(t) = f(t_0) + \int_{t_0}^{t} \vec{V}(t)dt \tag{2}$$

where $\vec{V}(t)$ is the speed function. Note the trajectory function may follow a more complex model but it can be always abstracted as

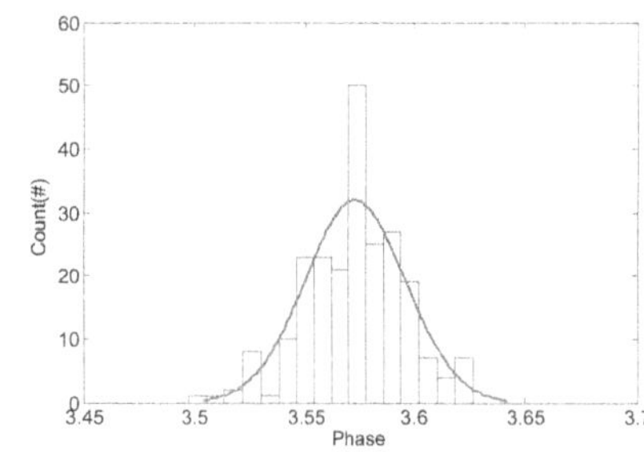

(a) Phase distribution

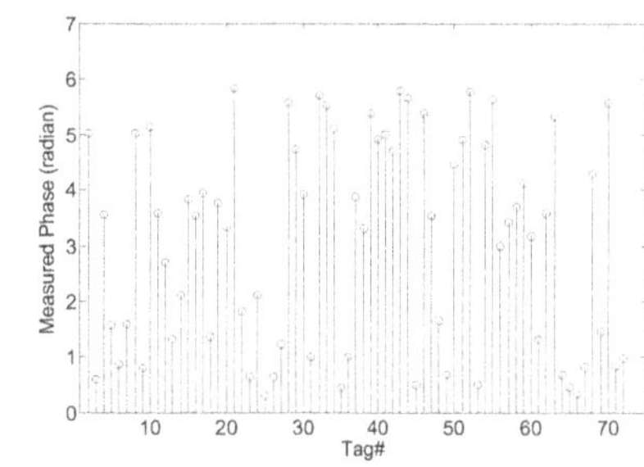

(b) Tag diversity

Figure 1: Empirical studies on measured RF phase. (a) The phase obeys a Gaussian distribution. (b) The diversity takes an impact on measured phase.

the above equation. The $f(t_0)$ is termed as the *initial position* where the tag is interrogated at time t_0. As long as the tag's position at time t_0 is estimated, its location at an arbitrary time t can be inferred using Eqn. 2 in combination with the track function. Thus, the main task in this case is to locate the tag's initial position $f(t_0)$. We build an RF hologram with observations from these antennas with different time of scan to derive the $f(t_0)$. The RF hologram is a likelihood exhibition using an image to display the likelihood that how a partitioned grid in tag's motion plane is likely to be the initial position. We start our technique by presenting a naive straightforward hologram solution (Naive Hologram , AH) and then present techniques that can address the negative impacts of thermal noise (Augmented Hologram, AH) and device diversity (Differential Augmented Hologram, DAH). The detailed information can be referred to our recent work [1].

To illustrate RF hologram, an experimental study using a linear track. The naive hologram and its corresponding 3D-mesh structure are shown in Fig. 2(a). Here light colors denote lower amplitude values. From the figure, we can see that at the positions close to the target location $f(t_0)$, the sum grows as the signals constructively add up to each other. On the other hand, at the positions away from to the $f(t_0)$ the signals superimpose at random phase angles and the sum is significantly lower. However, naive hologram cannot give distinctive result about the initial position. There exists a large continuous region with relatively high values. Fig. 2(b) depicts the augmented hologram using the same observed data as those in Fig. 2(a). We see that AH breaks up the large continuous region that has higher values. into several points and reinforces the initial position. Fig. 2(c) shows that the correct initial position has an extremely intensive value that approximately exceeds $2\times$ than those in other pixels. The error can be reduced to within $10mm$.

• **Uncontrollable Case**: We then consider a general case where no prior knowledge about the tag's moving track is known by our system. Thanks to the highly efficient anti-collision capability, the tag can be observed at a high frequency. We approximate its ir-

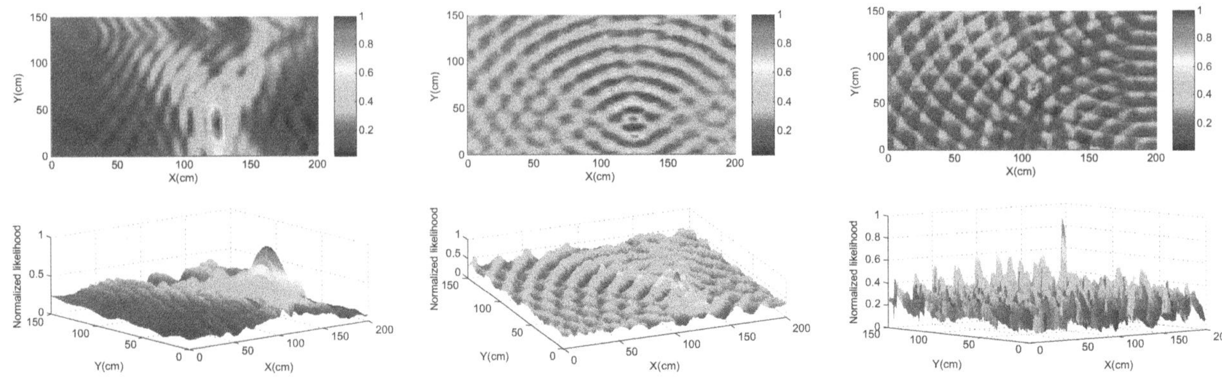

(a) Naive Hologram (b) Augmented Hologram (c) Differential Augmented Hologram

Figure 2: RF Hologram. The RF hologram is an image exhibiting the likelihood that how a partitioned grid is likely to be the initial position. The ground truth is highlighted with plus notation. Three columns shows the three kinds of holograms using both 2D image and 3D mesh.

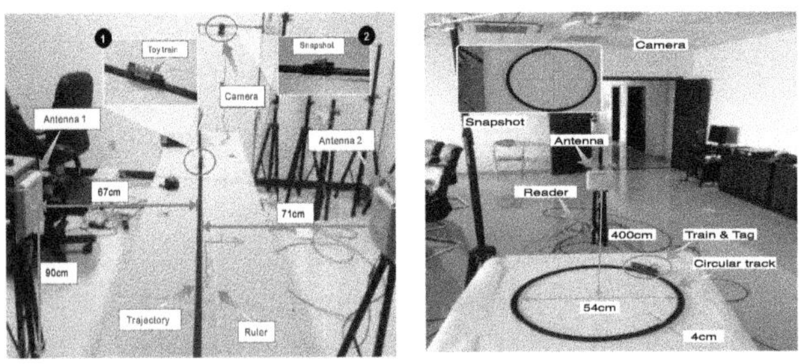

(a) Linear Track (b) Circular Track

Figure 3: Experiment setups

regular and unpredictable trajectory at run time by exploiting the differentials between consecutive phase values. Then we use the DAH to identify a set of potential trajectories and converting the problem of selecting the optimal trajectory into a task in first stage. Tagarom deals with the unpredictable movement with the following two steps. First, Tagoram acquires the phase measured by M antennas from different directions to recover tag's trajectory every round of antenna scheduled. Second, Tagoram utilizes the DAH to evaluate all fitted trajectories and selects the optimal one corresponding to the pixel with maximum value.

3. IMPLEMENTATION

We build Tagoram using ImpinJ [2] reader and Alien EPC Gen-2 UHF RFIDs [3].

Hardware: We adopt an ImpinJ Speedway modeled R420 reader without any hardware or firmware modification. The reader supports four directional antennas at most, being compatible with EPC Gen2 standard. The whole RFID system operates in the 920 $\sim$ 926 MHz band with frequency hopping. The size of antenna is $225mm \times 225mm \times 40mm$.The reader is connected to host through the wireless network (TCP/IP). Four reader antennas with circular polarization are employed to provide $\geq 8dBic$ gain in two directions. Two types of tags from Alien Corp [3], modeled 2×2 *Inlay* and *Squiggle Inlay*, are employed. Both of them are employed in our lab experiment and pilot study.

Software: We adopt LLRP protocol [4] to communicate with the reader. ImpinJ reader extends this protocol for supporting the phase report. We adjust the configuration of reader to immediately report reading whenever tag is detected. The software is implemented using C# and WPF. We run the software at a Lenovo PC, which equips Intel(R) Celeron CPU G530 at 2.4 GHz and 2G memory.

Track: We emulate a mobile object via a toy train on which a tag is attached, moving at a constant speed of $0.176m/s$ on a track. Because an arbitrate track can be decomposed into pieces of linear and arc-shaped tracks in practice, we mainly focus on two basic tracks, linear track and circular track, as shown in Fig. 3. To capture the ground truth with high-accuracy, we install a camera above the track. When the tag is firstly interrogated, the system immediately trigger the camera to take a snapshot on the train, from which the initial position can be identified.

4. FACILITY REQUIREMENTS

For convenience, we are going to employ a circular track when demonstration. Our facility requirements can be listed as follows.

• **Equipment requirement**: First, one ImpinJ Reader modeled R420 and four antennas are needed, which is used to collect the phase values. Second, a toy train attached a RFID tag and a circular track are employed to automatically generate the movement with known track. Third, a camera is installed on the top for capturing the ground truth. Last, one or two notebook computers will also be used to calculate and display the train's trajectory.

• **Space requirement**: We need an exhibition space with an area of $2m \times 2m$ at least. A desk or table will be better. On the desk or table, notebooks and the track will be placed.

• **Power and Internet requirement:** The power plugins needed for the notebooks and reader. In the demo, the Wi-Fi connection might be required.

5. ACKNOWLEDGMENT

This research is partially supported by NSFC under Grant No. 61190110 and NSFC CERG-61361166009. The research of Xiang-Yang Li is partially supported by NSF CNS-1035894, NSF ECCS-1247944, NSF ECCS-1343306, National Natural Science Foundation of China under Grants No. 61170216, No. 61228202.

6. REFERENCES

[1] L. Yang, Y. Chen, X.-Y. Li, C. Xiao, M. Li, and Y. Liu, "Tagoram: Real-time tracking of mobile rfid tags to high precision using cots devices," in *Proc. of ACM MobiCom*, 2014.

[2] "Impinj, Inc," http://www.impinj.com/.

[3] "Alien," http://www.alientechnology.com/tags.

[4] EPCglobal, "Low level reader protocol (llrp)," 2010.

Demo: Visual Attention Driven Networking with Smart Glasses

Lan Zhang[1], Xiang-Yang Li[1,2], Wenchao Huang[3], Kebin Liu[1], Shuwei Zong[4], Xuesi Jian[2], Puchun Feng[1], Taeho Jung[2], Yunhao Liu[1]
[1]School of Software and TNLIST, Tsinghua University, China
[2]Department of Computer Science, Illinois Institute of Technology, USA
[3]Department of Computer Science, University of Science and Technology of China
[4]Department of Computer Science, Suzhou Institute for Advanced Study, China
lan@greenorbs.com, xli@cs.iit.edu, yunhao@greenorbs.com

ABSTRACT

In this demo, we propose a proof-of-concept networking system for smart glasses, through which users can express their interest and connect to a target simply by a gaze. Our system **iGaze** is a visual attention driven networking suite: an **iGaze** glass (hardware) and a networking protocol **VAN** (software). Our glass is a low-cost head-mounted glass with a camera, orientation sensors, microphone and speakers, which are embedded with our software for visual attention capture and networking. A visual attention driven networking protocol (**VAN**) is carefully designed and implemented. In **VAN**, we design an energy efficient and highly accurate visual attention determination scheme using single camera to capture user's communication interest and a double-matching scheme based on visual direction detection and Doppler effect of acoustic signal to lock the target devices. **iGaze** has separated and modularized hardware and software design. It can run on top of existing networking protocols, *e.g.*, Wi-Fi.

Categories and Subject Descriptors

C.3 [**Special-purpose and application-based systems**]: Real-time and embedded systems

General Terms

Design, Experimentation, Performance

Keywords

Smart Glasses; Attention Driven Networking; Device Paring; Gaze Tracking

1. INTRODUCTION

Emerging wearable computing devices attract extensive attention worldwide. Smart glasses, *e.g.*, Google Glass and Vuzix Smart Glasses, are computerized eyeglasses, which are usually equipped with various sensors, such as cameras, gyroscope, accelerometer and GPS, to enrich their capabilities. Many efforts have been devoted to improve human interfaces on or using smart glasses, *e.g.* controlling smart glasses using simple voice commands and head gestures, photo and video capture, and navigation. Some smart glasses also include features like augmented reality overlays. However smart glasses are still in the early stage and looking for revolutionary applications.

In this demo, we explore a novel networking mode with smart glasses that may enable a whole new set of applications. That is, smart glasses users can communicate with surrounding physical and cyber world by their visual attention. People can directly send messages to others without exchanging contact information explicitly or retrieve rich information about an object in the field of view freely using their eye gazes. Eye gaze based networking will bring much convenience to people in a conference and visitors in a museum; also bring many new features to the real-scene game and interactive game design. Moreover, the advertisements can also be significantly enhanced with such visual attention based augmented reality.

These requirements can hardly be fulfilled by existing network solutions. Some interest based systems provide customized information services using the user's profile and mining results of his/her historical behaviors, *e.g.*, [1]. A few gesture-based device pairing approaches [2,3] attempt to pair devices in proximity. However, those efforts are targeting handhold smart devices, *e.g.*, smart phones. Their requirements for phone displacement ($\geq$ 20cm) [2] and movement speed ($2 \sim 6m/s$) [3] are hard to achieve using head-mounted glasses. Besides, certain augmented reality could also be enabled with a world camera in a visual fashion, *e.g.*, using QR codes or object recognition techniques. But, to utilize the QR code, there are restrictions for scanning distances ($\leq$ 3m) and angles ($\geq 30°$) to the target. Object recognition usually requires extensive training and computing, and is vulnerable to environment noise. It cannot distinguish two objects with the same appearance or determine the user's interested target when there are multiple objects in the field of view.

To achieve this future vision, we propose a new smart glasses system by which a user can connect to a target simply by a gaze. The goals and contributions of this demo can be summarized as follows:

• Our approach is designed to capture a user's visual attention and then the visual target with high accuracy using only one low-resolution eye camera (*i.e.*, camera capturing images of the user's eye). We introduce a simplified geometry model to reduce the computation complexity. For better user experience, our solution puts no restriction on the user's movement, and minimums the set up

MobiCom'14, September 7-11, 2014, Maui, Hawaii, USA.
ACM 978-1-4503-2783-1/14/09.
http://dx.doi.org/10.1145/2639108.2641739.

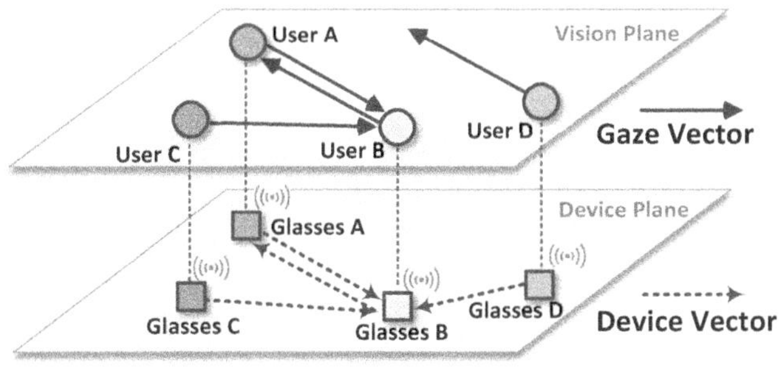

Figure 1: Gaze vectors and device vectors of a visual attention based networking system.

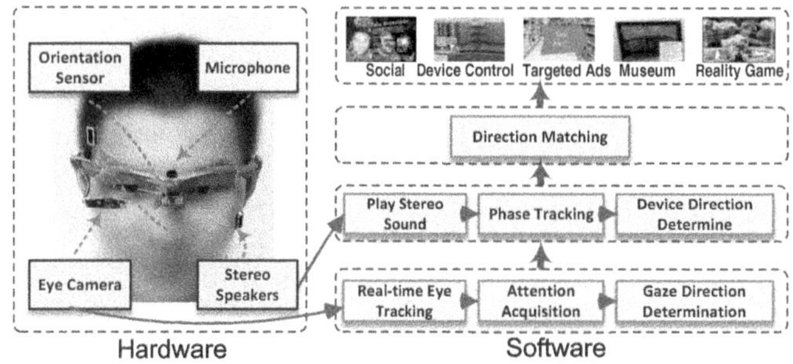

Figure 2: Our smart glasses iGaze prototype.

(*e.g.*, calibration) difficulty. Besides, we use gyroscope to reduce power consumption of continuous image capturing and processing. To support these, we develop a low-cost glasses hardware, with an eye camera, orientation sensors, a microphone and speakers, which are embedded with our software for visual attention capture.

• Our system establishes a network connection by matching a user's visual target with the target's device. At a high level, we address this problem based on the observation that the user's sightline direction is consistent with the direction between smart glasses worn by them. Technically, we capture the direction of a user's sightline with the onboard sensors and camera. We also propose a Phase Locked Loop (PLL) based method to estimate the direction from user's smart glasses to the target smart glasses by tracking the subtle relative displacement of two head-mounted speakers during arbitrary head movements.

• Our system works robustly across individuals and achieves high accuracy for users' attentions capturing, gaze direction and device direction estimation.

2. SYSTEM OVERVIEW

2.1 iGaze Design Space

iGaze is designed to enable a new communication mode for smart glasses users. We focus on making the networking devices smarter that can understand the user's attention and automatically connect to the target of interest. Our demo assumes that the initiator is equipped with our glasses to capture her visual attention at realtime and all participating devices possess computing, networking functionalities and some common sensors, *e.g.*, gyroscope and microphone. **iGaze** has separated and modularized hardware and software design. It can run on top of existing networking protocols, *e.g.*, Wi-Fi. It applies to scenarios where networking participators do not need to exchange contact information such as IP, email, web account before connecting to each other.

As shown in Fig. 1, each user in the vision plane is associated with a *co-located* smart device in the device plane. The challenge is how to match the target on device plane according to user's visual attention? Two types of scenarios are considered in this work: social networking and object-oriented augmented reality. In the first one (*bidirectional* application mode), the user wears smart glasses and looks around while the glasses are tracking his/her gaze direction. When two users have an eye contact, a network connection is built between their glasses. This scenario is fitted into many social applications. This type of applications require all participating devices to possess eye cameras. In the second case (*unidirectional* application mode), the user wearing smart glasses wants to obtain certain information about the visual target object by gazing it. For example, visitors can obtain the description of an artwork when they gaze at it for a certain time period. In these applications, the target objects need to have devices (without cameras) to respond to the 'gaze query'.

2.2 Principal of Gaze Based Networking

What we look for is a bond between the vision plane and device plane, which are dissociated currently. Note that finding the gaze direction and finding the direction of pairing devices are themselves challenging tasks. To address this association issue, we raise our idea based on the following observations. As shown in Fig. 1, when a user A is looking at a visual target B, we define the observer A's **gaze vector** as $\mathcal{V}_A$, whose direction is the direction of A's sightline and magnitude is the distance from A to B. In the device plane, we define the **device vector** $\mathcal{U}_{AB}$ as the vector from A's glasses to B's glasses. We say two vectors are consistent if the differences between their directions and magnitudes are both less than given thresholds.

Our first observation is that given an observer and his/her gaze vector, among all device vectors started from the observer's device, only the device vector to the correct visual target's device is consistent with the gaze vector. As an example in Fig. 1, for the observer A, only the device vector $\mathcal{U}_{AB}$ is consistent with the gaze vector $\mathcal{V}_A$. Then our system learns that device B is the correct match to A's visual target.

Our second observation is that given a pair of users who are looking at each other, their gaze vectors have opposite directions. Taking the scenario in Fig. 1 as an example, both gaze vectors $\mathcal{V}_B$ and $\mathcal{V}_D$ have opposite direction to $\mathcal{V}_A$. Thus user A can firstly exclude user C by the direction of gaze vectors and only compute vectors $\mathcal{U}_{AB}$ and $\mathcal{U}_{AD}$ in the device plane. For bidirectional applications with many users, the first round of sightline direction matching can greatly reduce the overhead in determining pair-wise device vectors.

2.3 System Design and Implementation

Based on our observations, our system is designed to consist of software components for visual attention driven networking and the smart glasses hardware.

Software: There are three major building blocks:

- **Gaze vector acquisition**: This component includes three modules. The real-time eye tracking module captures the movement of a user's eye using the eye camera at real-time. Attention acquisition component takes the eye movement data as input to detect a visual attention when the gaze lasts for a reasonable time. The threshold is predetermined and can be dynamically adjusted by users. After a visual attention has been captured, the gaze vector determination calculates

Component	Description
Raspberry Pi II	700MHz CPU, 512MB RAM, Linux
Eye Camera	Maximum Resolution 640x480 @ 30fps
Gyroscope	MPU6050, 6-axis, Accuracy - 0.01°
Magnetic Sensor	3-axis, Accuracy - $512c/G$
Wi-Fi	OURLINK, 300Mbps, USB port
Microphone	Sample rate 44100Hz
Stereo Speakers	Frequency range 180Hz-20KHz

Table 1: Specifications of iGaze glass

the corresponding gaze vector to the visual target. The basic idea is that, the iris contour is a circle, but its projection on the camera image plane is elliptical, and the ellipse parameters are determined by the gaze direction. The gaze direction is estimated by determining the pose of the iris circle by back-projecting the ellipse onto a circle in 3D space. The challenge is that with only a single elliptical image, there are many circles satisfying the projection cone. In this demo, we remove ambiguities of back-projecting using a anthropometric model of eyeball, the hardware position and the principal in [4]. Based on our design, the system requires little manual calibration. Moreover, we reduce the cost for continuous image capturing and processing greatly by detecting head fixation using gyroscope before opening the camera module. To avoid unwanted paring when eyes happen to be fixed on a certain object, we ask the users to make a mild head gesture (*e.g.*, head nod) as the postfix of the attention.

- **Device vector estimation**: When the user makes a head gesture, *e.g.*, head nod, two speakers of his/her glasses emit a binaural inaudible acoustic signal with two sine waves at different frequencies (19kHz and 19.5kHz). At receivers, the frequency of each signal is shifted due to the Doppler effects. Candidate devices invoke the phase tracking and device direction determination modules to estimate the device vector as follows. By PLL, a receiver tracks the precise phase of the received signal, where the phase shift is in proportion to relative displacement of two speakers. In this way, the measuring accuracy of the relative displacement is less than $1mm$, with a small distance between the two speakers, *i.e.*, $18cm$. Then the receiver estimates its relative direction to the initiator by the relative displacement. With our method, different types of head gestures are supported.

- **Visual attention driven networking (VAN)**: It defines the message format and communication process in our visual attention driven networks. **VAN** constructs a connection from initiator to the visual target's device based on the matching results of the gaze vector and device vectors.

We implement all software blocks of iGaze using C++. It supports both unidirectional and bidirectional application modes. In the unidirectional mode, the target could also be a device without an eye camera. So we also implement the device direction estimation and VAN for Android system using Java, which enables our glasses to connect an android device in unidirectional applications. The visual attention acquisition components are developed based on the OpenCV library. For the wireless communication of VAN, both AP and Ad Hoc modes are implemented.

Hardware: Fig. 2 illustrates our prototype hardware. To obtain gaze direction, **iGaze** glass has a fixed eye camera tracking the eye movement. It is 3cm away from the eye. A fixed gyroscope is embedded in the front-head position of the glasses to determine the device coordinate and simplify the coordinate transformation. A magnetic sensor is co-located with the gyroscope, which is only used in the bidirectional mode to exclude unlikely neighbors with gaze direction. For the devices direction, **iGaze** glass has a central microphone and two separated speakers with a fixed distance (18cm). For the data processing and data transmission, we use Raspberry Pi with a Wi-Fi module. It is a credit-card-sized single-board computer with Linux operating system. All head-mounted sensors are connected to its hardware data interfaces. It supports a wide range of programming languages, *e.g.* Python, C++, Java and Perl. The specifications of **iGaze** glass is presented in Table 1.

3. FACILITY REQUIREMENTS

Our facility requirements can be listed as follows:

- Equipment requirement: Several iGaze Glasses (more than 3) together with Raspberry Pi platforms are needed in the demo. One WiFi AP is required to build a local area network. Besides, a display is needed to show the results.

- Space requirement: The requirements for exhibition space is 10 square meters or more to simulate a social scenario.

- Power and Internet requirement: The power plug is needed for battery charging. The smart glasses is powered by rechargeable batteries. It would be better if there is Internet connection.

4. OTHER INFORMATION

This research is partially supported by NSFC under Grant No. 61125020, NSFC CERG-61361166009. The research of Li is partially supported by NSF CNS-1035894, NSF ECCS-1247944, NSF ECCS-1343306, NSFC under Grants No. 61170216, No. 61228202. This work is related to our recent work [5].

5. REFERENCES

[1] LI, Z., WANG, C., JIANG, C., AND LI, X.-Y. Lass: Local-activity and social-similarity based data forwarding in mobile social networks. *TPDS* (2013).

[2] PENG, C., SHEN, G., ZHANG, Y., AND LU, S. Point&connect: intention-based device pairing for mobile phone users. In *MobiSys* (2009), ACM, pp. 137–150.

[3] SUN, Z., PUROHIT, A., BOSE, R., AND ZHANG, P. Spartacus: spatially-aware interaction for mobile devices through energy-efficient audio sensing. In *MobiSys* (2013).

[4] WANG, J., SUNG, E., AND VENKATESWARLU, R. Eye gaze estimation from a single image of one eye. In *International Conference on Computer Vision* (2003), IEEE, pp. 136–143.

[5] ZHANG, L., LI, X.-Y., HUANG, W., LIU, K., ZONG, S., JIAN, X., FENG, P., JUNG, T., AND LIU, Y. It starts with igaze: Visual attention driven networking with smart glasses. In *Mobicom* (2014), ACM.

Demo: Instant Phone Attitude Estimation and Its Applications

Pengfei Zhou, Weiming Chan, Shiqi Jiang, Jiajue Ou, Mo Li
Nanyang Technological University, Singapore
{pfzhou, wchan3, sjiang004, jou1, limo}@ntu.edu.sg

Guobin Shen
Microsoft Research, China
jackysh@microsoft.com

ABSTRACT

The phone attitude is an essential input to many smartphone applications. Based on in-depth understanding of the nature of the MEMS gyroscope and other IMU sensors, we propose A^3 – an accurate and automatic attitude detector for commodity smartphones. In the demo, we show the performance of our attitude tracking algorithm and its usability in attitude-based mobile applications.

Categories and Subject Descriptors

C.4 [**Performance of Systems**]: Modeling techniques, Performance attributes; C.5.3 [**Computer System Implementation**]: Portable devices

Keywords

Mobile Phone Attitude, Gyroscope, IMU Sensors, Attitude-based Applications

1. INTRODUCTION

Smartphones are becoming more and more powerful and provide a good platform for mobile applications [9, 4, 3, 2]. The phone attitude [8] gives the 3D orientation of the phone with respect to the earth coordinate system. It is an essential input to many mobile applications such as mobile gaming, gesture and activity recognition [5], 3D photography, dead reckoning based localization and navigation [7, 6, 1], etc.

In this demo, we show the performance of our attitude tracking algorithm and the attitude-based mobile applications. The design details of our algorithm are presented in our MobiCom paper [8] and we briefly introduce the design principles here. The phone attitude can be estimated based on the readings of three IMU (Inertial Measurement Unit) sensors, i.e., gyroscope, compass and accelerometer. We follow the device specification and conduct controlled experiments to investigate how different environmental factors impact on the gyroscope performance and how the best accuracy can be achieved in an appropriate condition range. We also characterize the nature of the accelerometer and compass sensor to understand their performance in various conditions. Based on the comprehensive study, we propose to estimate the phone attitude primarily based on the gyroscope output, i.e., the 3-axis angular velocities, but also incorporate the compass and the accelerometer for opportunistic calibration. The three types of IMU sensors are of different natures and their accuracy varies in different condition ranges. In particular, the gyroscope provides a cumulative estimation of the attitude through continuous integration on angular velocities that is accurate in general but suffers from error accumulation. On the other hand, the compass sensor and accelerometer provide instant attitude estimation which is independent of previous states but the accuracy highly depends on the instant environment dynamics and phone motions. We develop a practical approach that calibrates the cumulative gyroscope estimation when we have higher confidence in compass and accelerometer readings. In this work we propose a "opportunistic calibration" technique that looks at the concordance of the three types of sensors in estimating short period attitude changes. High consistency indicates high instant confidence of the compass and gravity outputs and thus a positive calibration opportunity. Sufficient calibration opportunities can be identified using this approach.

MobiCom'14, September 7-11, 2014, Maui, Hawaii, USA.
ACM 978-1-4503-2783-1/14/09.
http://dx.doi.org/10.1145/2639108.2641738.

2. PHONE ATTITUDE FROM IMU SENSORS

In this section, we introduce the basic operations performed on the readings of the IMU sensors to derive the accurate phone attitude. Two independent methods of estimating the phone attitude are introduced.

2.1 Gyroscope

The MEMS gyroscope used in smartphones detects the 3-axis angular velocities of the phone motion. To derive the instant phone attitude, we need to perform continuous integration on the angular velocities. We deal with two coordinate systems in deriving the phone attitude. One is the earth coordinate system (we call "geo-frame") and the other one is the phone body coordinate system (we call "body-frame").

The goal is to get the phone attitude in the geo-frame, i.e., to calculate the relative difference between the body-frame and geo-frame. Figure 1 depicts the output of the MEMS gyroscope, which are the real-time 3-axis angular velocities (ω_x, ω_y, and ω_z) around the *Roll*, *Yaw*, and *Pitch* axis in the phone body-frame. X_e (pointing to the Earth east), Y_e (pointing to the earth north) and Z_e (parallel with the

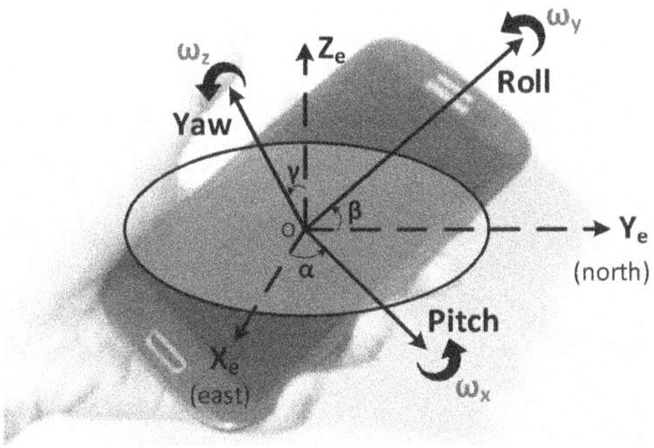

Figure 1: The output of the MEMS gyroscope is 3 angular velocities around the *Roll*, *Yaw*, and *Pitch* axis in the phone body-frame.

gravity) are the three reference axes in the geo-frame. With continuous integration, the phone attitude can be calculated and represented as the relative difference of the two coordinate systems, which can be described by a rotation matrix, or the angles between the three supporting axes in the two frames, i.e., α, β, and γ (shown in Figure 1).

In order to accurately integrate the angular velocities, we apply the Euler Axis/Angle method to do the integration and tackle the problem from the perspective of the geo-frame, which is fixed during the phone motion. The method finds an equation of the rotation speed in the geo-frame based on differential. During the integration, the total phone motion time is divided into multiple time slots and the phone rotation is a sequential combination of the rotation within each slot.

Performance Summary. According to our experimental studies, the impact of different factors on MEMS gyroscope performance is summarized as follows.

- The tracking error accumulates as the time increases. If the phone motion is within the dynamic range and sensor bandwidth, the gyroscope tracking result is accurate in a short time period. But the error can be big after a long time period (e.g., 10 mins) even when the motion frequency is low.
- The tracking error is highly related to the motions, i.e., the angular velocity and linear acceleration, and can be approximately estimated according to them. At the same time, the high frequency motion (i.e., the phone motion is out of the dynamic range) significantly pollutes the consequent attitude tracking result.

2.2 Gravity and Compass

The phone attitude also can be estimated using the gravity and compass sensor readings. As depicted in Figure 2, given the direction of gravity on the phone body-frame, the phone attitude is constrained on a conical surface in the geo-frame. On the other hand, the compass outputs the angle δ between Y' and Y_e axis (pointing to the earth north) in the geo-frame, where Y' is the projection of Y axis of the body-frame on the X_e-Y_e plane of the geo-frame. Considering the angle δ between Y' and Y_e, we can thus uniquely fix the phone attitude on the conical surface. This provides us an alternative way to determine the phone attitude.

Compared with gyroscope. The attitude estimation from the compass and accelerometer is independent and of

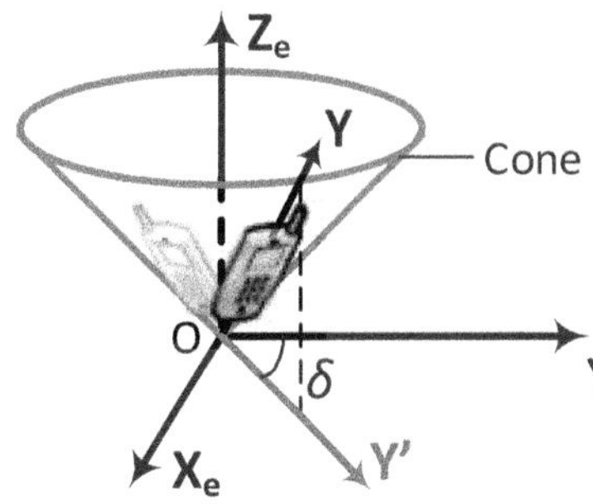

Figure 2: Attitude from the compass and gravity.

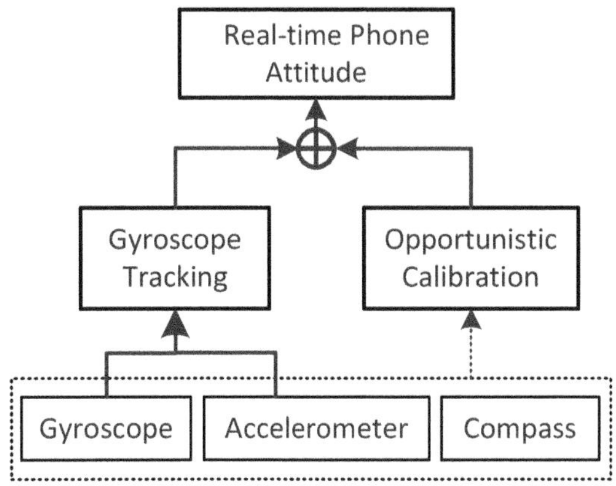

Figure 3: A^3 architecture.

different nature compared with the result from the gyroscope. The compass and accelerometer give instant status estimation which is unrelated to any previous estimations, while the gyroscope gives a cumulative estimation of the attitude through continuous integration on angular velocities. Such different natures in their performance provide us the opportunity to complement the gyroscope estimation with calibration from the compass and accelerometer at "good" moments.

3. OPPORTUNISTIC CALIBRATION

We use an opportunistic calibration technique to identify "good" opportunities to calibrate the phone attitude. The basic idea is to leverage the gyroscope estimation to capture phone attitude dynamics. As our experiments reveal in §2.1, the gyroscope can provide very accurate attitude tracking in short time periods (e.g., within 10s). Although the instant attitude estimation of gyroscope may not be accurate due to base errors from previous states, the estimated attitude change is accurate for most of the time (when phone motion is within the safe range of the gyroscope), which sets a very good reference. We compare with the attitude change derived from the compass and gravity, and if both estimations derive the same change of phone attitude we believe the compass and gravity make an accurate attitude estimation. As the output of the compass and gravity is the instant attitude estimation, which is independent of previous states of the phone, we can then use it to reset the current attitude estimation and continue the gyroscope estimation from the new attitude base.

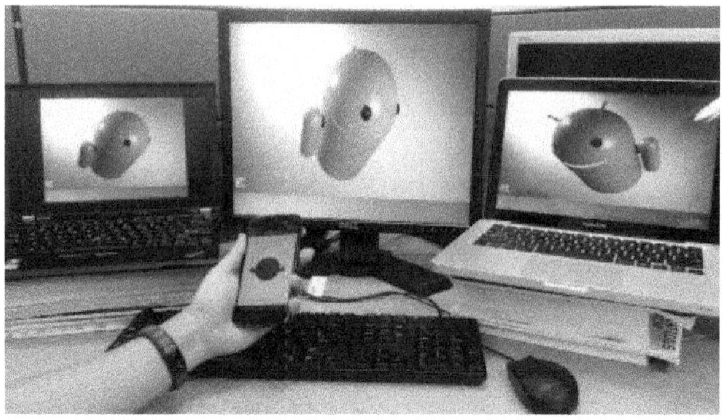

Figure 4: The phone attitude estimation result comparison from different algorithms.

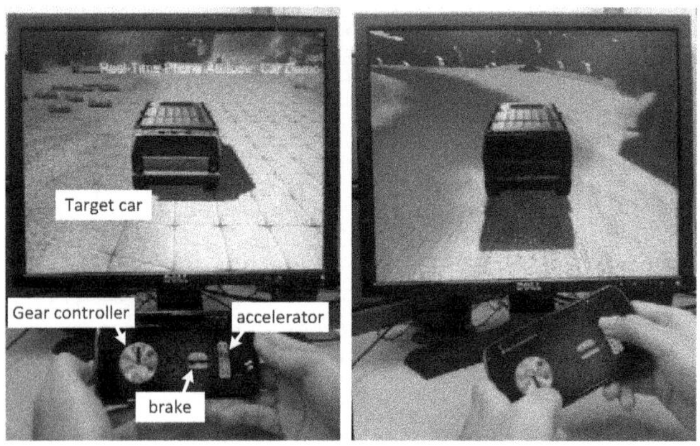

(a) Driving a car using the phone as a controller

(b) The car is turning and accelerating

Figure 5: Car driving demo setting.

We incorporate the three IMU sensors and propose A^3, an accurate and automatic attitude detector to continuously estimate the phone attitude. Figure 3 illustrates the A^3 system architecture. There are two major components: gyroscope tracking and opportunistic calibration. As depicted in Figure 3 (left), A^3 tracks the phone attitude using the gyroscope. The angular velocities are adaptively integrated to calculate the phone attitude (the rotation matrix $\mathbf{R}$). The tracking error of the gyroscope is carefully estimated based on the real time monitoring of the phone motion.

4. THE DEMONSTRATION

In this demo, we will show the basic performance of our algorithm under two experiment settings. We will show the performance comparison of different algorithms under various conditions, and introduce a mobile application that can benefit from accurate attitude estimation.

Performance comparison. In the demo, we will compare the performance of different algorithms for phone attitude estimation. As depicted in Figure 4, the user can use the phone in arbitrary ways. Different algorithms estimate the real-time phone attitude independently and their tracking results are displayed on 3 different screens. Users can examine the estimation result of individual axis, i.e., *Roll*, *Yaw*, and *Pitch* axis, separately, and also the overall phone attitude along the 3 axes. In the demo, we will also introduce some influences from the magnet and high frequency phone motion, etc., which may pollute the sensor output and may be harmful for the algorithms. Users can see the impact of the influences on different algorithms and compare their performance in tough environments.

Attitude-based applications. In the demo, we will also show the potential attitude based applications. Users can play a car driving game using smartphones. Two snapshots are shown in Figure 5. Figure 5(a) introduces the game settings. The smartphone is used as a controller, with which the player can change the gear, accelerate the car or make a brake. The target car and the driving environment are displayed on a PC or laptop screen. The phone attitude is used to make turns. As depicted in Figure 5(b), the player is using the phone attitude to make a left turn and accelerate the car at the same time.

Equipments and settings. In the demo, we will bring 3 laptops and 2 mobile phones by ourselves. Additionally, we need a table (around 1m×0.5m size), a board for the introduction poster (A0 size), and an electronic screen (around 25∼30inch) for the attitude-based games. Mobile phones use the WiFi network to transmit data to laptops. The setup time is about 10 minutes.

5. REFERENCES

[1] M. Li, Y. Liu, J. Wang, and Z. Yang. Sensor network navigation without locations. In *IEEE INFOCOM 2009*, pages 2419–2427, 2009.

[2] Z. Li, M. Li, J. Wang, and Z. Cao. Ubiquitous data collection for mobile users in wireless sensor networks. In *IEEE INFOCOM 2011*, pages 2246–2254, 2011.

[3] S. Liu, Y. Liu, L. M. Ni, J. Fan, and M. Li. Towards mobility-based clustering. In *KDD'10*, pages 919–928, 2010.

[4] S. Liu, Y. Yue, and R. Krishnan. Adaptive collective routing using gaussian process dynamic congestion models. In *KDD'13*, pages 704–712, 2013.

[5] M. Shahzad, A. X. Liu, and A. Samuel. Secure unlocking of mobile touch screen devices by simple gestures: You can see it but you can not do it. In *ACM MobiCom 2013*, pages 39–50, 2013.

[6] Z. Yang, C. Wu, and Y. Liu. Locating in fingerprint space: Wireless indoor localization with little human intervention. In *ACM Mobicom 2012*, pages 269–280, 2012.

[7] Y. Zheng, G. Shen, L. Li, C. Zhao, M. Li, and F. Zhao. Travi-navi: Self-deployable indoor navigation system. In *ACM MobiCom 2014*, 2014.

[8] P. Zhou, M. Li, and G. Shen. Use it free: Instantly knowing your phone attitude. In *ACM MobiCom 2014*, 2014.

[9] P. Zhou, Y. Zheng, Z. Li, M. Li, and G. Shen. Iodetector: a generic service for indoor outdoor detection. In *ACM SenSys 2012*, pages 361–362, 2012.

Poster: Clock Synchronization for Distributed Wireless Protocols at the Physical Layer

Omid Abari, Hariharan Rahul, and Dina Katabi
Massachusetts Institute of Technology
Cambridge, MA, USA
abari@csail.mit.edu, rahul@csail.mit.edu, dina@csail.mit.edu

SUMMARY- Implementing distributed wireless protocols at the physical layer today is challenging because different nodes have different clocks, each of which has slightly different frequencies. This causes the nodes to have frequency offset relative to each other. As a result, transmitted signals from these nodes do not combine in a predictable manner over time. Past work tackles this challenge and builds distributed PHY layer systems by attempting to address the effects of the frequency offset and compensating for it in the transmitted signals. In this poster, we address this challenge by addressing the root cause - the different clocks with different frequencies on the different nodes. We present AirClock, a new wireless coordination primitive that enables multiple nodes to act as if they are driven by a single clock that they receive wirelessly over the air. AirClock presents a synchronized abstraction to the physical layer, and hence enables direct implementation of diverse kinds of distributed PHY protocols. We illustrate AirClock's versatility by using it to build two systems: (1) distributed MIMO, and (2) distributed rate adaptation for wireless sensors, and show that they can provide significant performance benefits over today's systems.

Categories and Subject Descriptors

C.2.1 [**Computer-Communication Networks**]: Network Architecture and Design

Keywords

Clock Synchronization; Distributed MIMO; Wireless; Wireless Sensors

1. Introduction

Distributed processing is common at higher layers of the network stack. Yet, at the physical layer, each node typically performs its signal processing independently of other nodes in the network. This architecture is despite the benefits from distributed computation. In fact, the ability to coordinate nodes at the physical layer brings dramatic benefits. Consider, for *e.g.*, distributed MIMO, where multiple wireless nodes coordinate their transmissions to emulate one MIMO transmitter with the sum of antennas on all nodes. Such a design scales wireless throughput with the number of transmitters [10, 1]. In fact, information theory presents many theoretical distributed physical layer designs that could bring significant gains if transformed into practical systems, such as distributed lattice coding [8], noisy network coding [6], transmitter cooperation for cognitive networks [7], etc.

The difficulty in building practical distributed PHY systems is fundamental. Theoretical schemes typically require that the different wireless nodes operate in lockstep with each other, so that the combined output of the wireless system generated from the computations and actions of individual wireless nodes follows a predictable pattern. However, independent wireless nodes have different clocks with different oscillator frequencies. As a result, different nodes will always have an offset in their carrier frequencies (CFO); the CFO causes two signals to rotate with respect to each other. The output signals formed by the distributed wireless system, therefore, no longer follows the desired pattern; for example, signals that are coordinated to be in-phase and combine constructively could become completely out-of-phase over time, and cancel each other. While having a consistent notion of time is important for distributed protocols both at higher and lower layers, the problem becomes significantly harder at the physical layer, where tiny timing errors of few nanoseconds or even less can cause large errors in the distributed protocol [10].

So, why do different nodes have different clock and oscillator frequencies? Today, each node has a local crystal that generates a low frequency sine wave, which is used as a reference clock. A special circuit called a Phase Locked Loop (PLL) uses the reference to generate the desired carrier frequency. For example, if the node is a Wi-Fi radio, the crystal might generate a 10 MHz sine wave, which the PLL then upconverts to a center frequency in the 2.4 GHz or 5 GHz bands. The key problem is that reference clocks on different nodes have slightly different frequencies due to different crystals and temperature changes. Since the PLLs on different nodes lock to reference clocks with different frequencies, their output signals have different frequencies, and this leads to frequency offsets between nodes.

2. Our Solution: AirClock

This abstract explores a solution that addresses the *root cause* of the problem, *i.e.*, the different reference clocks. It does so by replacing these different clocks with a single reference clock that is shared across all the nodes. If wireless nodes were driven by the same reference clock, they would have the same oscillator frequencies, and it would eliminate much of the complexity in building distributed PHY protocols.

One could of course share the reference among multiple wireless nodes by using wires from a single external clock. However, such a system defeats the notion of a wireless network since all nodes are now wired to a central device!

MobiCom'14, September 7-11, 2014, Maui, Hawaii, USA.
ACM 978-1-4503-2783-1/14/09.
http://dx.doi.org/10.1145/2639108.2642894 .

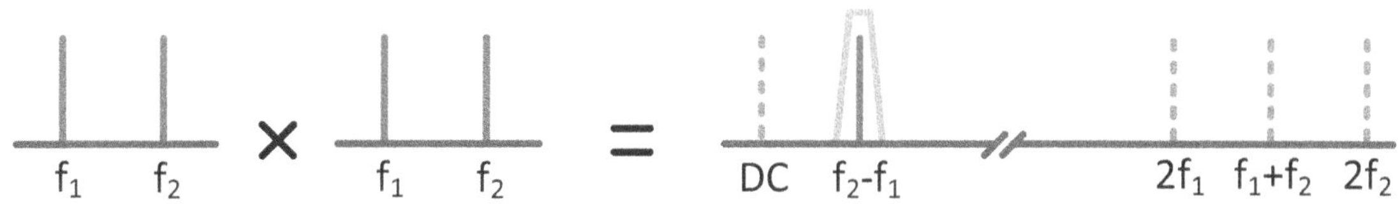

Figure 1—AirClock's Design. Nodes multiply received signal by itself and extract the clock by applying a bandpass filter centered at f_{ref}.

We therefore focus on a design that feeds the shared reference clock to multiple nodes across the wireless medium. At first blush, it might seem that we can simply wirelessly transmit the low frequency wave previously generated by the local crystal on each node, and use it as a shared reference. However, such a system is not feasible for two reasons. First, transmitting at such low frequencies (typical crystal generated frequencies are in the range of 10-40 MHz) does not comply with FCC regulations [4]. Second, efficient antennas to capture low frequency signals can be large [2] and, therefore, impractical for many wireless nodes.

We introduce AirClock, a practical system that enables distributed wireless nodes to share a reference clock using the wireless medium. AirClock leverages the recently opened white spaces to transmit two single tones separated by the desired clock frequency (*e.g.*, for a clock of 10 MHz, AirClock can send tones at 175 MHz and 185 MHz). To obtain the shared clock, each wireless node multiplies the received signal by itself and applies a band pass filter to extract the desired clock frequency. To see why this system works, recall that the multiplication of two sine waves at different frequencies produces sine waves whose frequencies are the sum and difference of the original frequencies. Specifically, if the two transmitted tones are at frequencies f_1 and f_2, and the desired clock has a frequency of $f_{ref} = f_1 - f_2$, we have:

$$(\cos(2\pi f_1 t) + \cos(2\pi f_2 t)) \cdot (\cos(2\pi f_1 t) + \cos(2\pi f_2 t)) =$$
$$1 + \mathbf{\cos(2\pi f_{ref} t)} + \cos(2\pi(f_1 + f_2)t)$$
$$+\frac{1}{2}\cos(2\pi(f_1 + f_1)t) + \frac{1}{2}\cos(2\pi(f_2 + f_2)t)$$

Then, by applying a band pass filter centered at f_{ref}, a node can extract the desired clock signal (the term highlighted in bold) and eliminate the undesired frequencies in the signal. [1] Fig. 1 illustrates this concept.

Since all nodes extract the reference clock only from the received signal without using any other external signals, they all extract the same reference frequency, thereby eliminating frequency offsets between nodes.

AirClock has several key features. (a) It is **versatile**. Since AirClock transparently provides a synchronized clock abstraction across multiple independent nodes, it enables straightforward implementation of very different kinds of distributed PHY schemes without application or protocol specific mechanisms. (b) Its design is **simple**. Since AirClock only needs to generate a sine wave as a reference clock, it only needs an amplifier, mixer, and filter, and avoids most of the complexity of a typical receiver, such as ADCs, baseband processing such as demodulation, equalization, decoding *etc.* (c) It easily **integrates with standard transceiver architectures**. Specifically, it can be deployed as a standalone module whose output can be plugged in as an input to the PLL, replacing the output of the local crystal.

[1] Note that one cannot share the reference clock by simply upconverting the 10 MHz to a higher frequency at the transmitter and downconverting at the receiver to retrieve the reference clock. This is because downconversion would require the receiver to have a local oscillator to generate the carrier frequency, which would lead to a frequency offset in the retrieved clock signal.

3. APPLICATIONS OF AIRCLOCK

AirClock is versatile and can be used as a synchronization primitive underlying various distributed PHY systems. Below, we describe two examples:

(a) Distributed MIMO without phase coordination: Distributed MIMO is a powerful concept that allows multiple wireless transmitters to behave like one huge MIMO transmitter with the number of antennas equal to the sum of antennas on all the cooperating nodes. These distributed transmitters can use AirClock as a primitive to synchronize their oscillators, and ensure coherent phase transmission. Such a system eliminates the need for a coherent phase transmission protocol in baseband [10, 1].

(b) Distributed Rate Adaptation for Sensors: Traditional sensor systems such as Zigbee [3] are typically capable of using only a single low rate, and hence cannot exploit good channel conditions to improve throughput. Distributed rate adaptation schemes that allow multiple nodes to transmit simultaneously and thereby exploit good channel conditions, have been designed and implemented for backscatter networks such as RFIDs [11]. However, such schemes do not work for wireless sensors since, unlike RFIDs, sensors have independent local oscillators, and hence suffer from frequency offsets. By using AirClock, sensor networks can eliminate frequency offsets between nodes, enabling them to leverage backscatter distributed rate adaptation algorithms. We design and implement the first practical distributed rate adaptation system for sensor networks.

4. RESULTS SUMMARY

We built a prototype of AirClock using off the shelf components and integrated it with USRPs to demonstrate distributed PHY applications. We evaluated AirClock and its applications in an indoor testbed with line-of-sight and non line-of-sight scenarios. Our results show the following:

- AirClock can provide tight synchronization across multiple nodes. In particular, in our testbed, the median and 95th percentile CFO between two AirClock nodes operating at 2.45 GHz are 0.38Hz (0.16 parts per billion) and 1.24Hz (0.5 parts per billion) respectively. AirClock can thus achieve orders of magnitude tighter synchronization than the traditional situation of free running oscillators on independent nodes.
- To investigate the impact of AirClock's synchronization on the received signal, we transmit OFDM packets using 64-QAM modulation. We then estimate the received signal after channel equalization on the receiver. We repeat the experiment with three different synchronization modes between transmitter and receiver nodes: (a) independent clocks (*i.e.*, local crystals), (b) single external clock shared over a wire between the nodes, and (c) AirClock synchronization at both nodes. Fig. 2 plots the received constellation. We see that the transmit and receive oscillators have significant CFO with each other when using their local

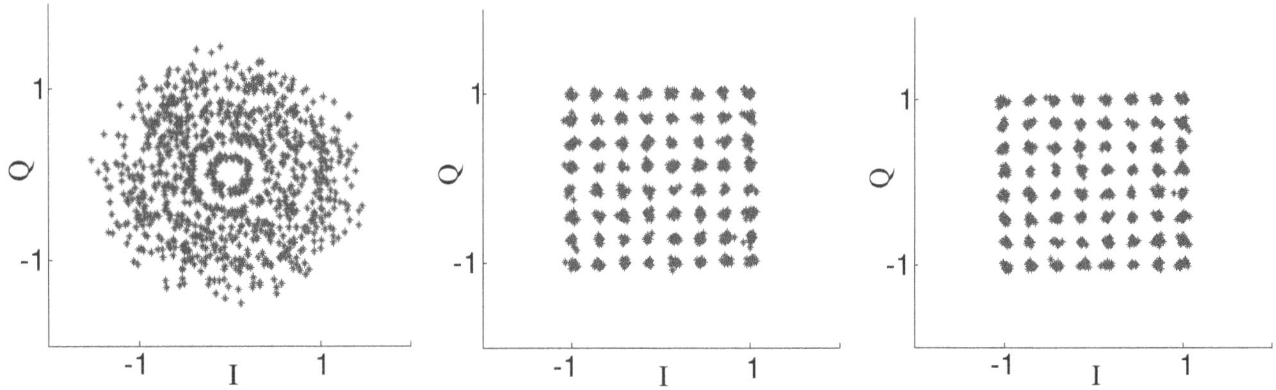

(a) Independent clocks (b) Over-the-wire synchronization (c) AirClock

Figure 2—Received constellation points for 64-QAM in different synchronization scenarios. With different crystals, the transmitter and receiver are not synchronized, leading to rotation of the constellation points. In contrast, while using over-the-wire synchronization, the received constellation points after equalization do not rotate relative to each other, showing that the transmitter and receiver oscillators are synchronized. AirClock provides performance similar to over-the-wire synchronization by using a wireless reference signal.

crystals. As a result, the observed constellation rotates over time. In contrast, the observed constellation points with AirClock are tightly clustered around the expected points, similar to the case when both nodes are connected to a single external clock over the wire. This provides visual evidence that AirClock provides tight synchronization comparable to a shared wired reference.

- AirClock delivers a distributed MIMO system whose throughput scales linearly with the number of transmitters. Specifically, with 5 transmitters, AirClock's distributed MIMO delivers a median throughput gain of 4.4× over traditional 802.11 style unicast, across the operational range of Wi-Fi SNRs (5-20 dB).
- An AirClock based Zigbee system achieves throughput gains over traditional Zigbee by using distributed rate adaptation. Specifically, with 6 Zigbee nodes transmitting jointly to a central node, AirClock provides throughput gains of $1.64 - 3\times$ across a range of SNRs (5-20 dB).

5. RELATED WORK

(a) Shared clocks: One traditional solution to synchronize clocks in a wireless network is to use global positioning system (GPS)-disciplined oscillator to generate the reference signal [5]. Due to their complexity, these clock generators cost thousands of dollars which makes them infeasible for use in each wireless node. In addition, GPS only works outdoors. In contrast, AirClock does not require expensive hardware and can work in indoor applications.

Also, terrestrial time signals such as WWV [9], transmitted by NIST, can synchronize receivers on the order of seconds. Similarly, traditional clock synchronization schemes like NTP can synchronize nodes to within 10s of msecs. However, unlike AirClock, these schemes are too coarse grained for PHY systems, which require synchronization on the order of nanoseconds.

(b) Phase tracking and compensation: The typical approach for dealing with frequency offset in wireless nodes is to estimate the resulting phase rotation and compensate for it. For distributed MIMO, schemes such as MegaMIMO and AirSync [1, 10] incorporate sophisticated schemes to track transmitter phase drift and correct signals prior to transmission. These schemes are necessary to ensure that the signals from different transmitters combine coherently at each receiver. In contrast, with AirClock, wireless nodes synchronizes their clocks over the air eliminating the need for phase tracking and compensation either at the receiver or other transmitters and can achieve both diversity and multiplexing gain. Further, AirClock's system is independent of the protocol,and modulation schemes, and applies to various wireless technology (WiFi, Bluetooth, Zigbee, etc.).

6. CONCLUSION

This extended abstract presents AirClock, a system that can synchronize multiple nodes using a reference signal that they receive over the wireless medium, and describes distributed PHY applications that can be built using AirClock's synchronization primitive. We believe that AirClock's synchronization primitive can serve as a building block that brings a large body of distributed information theoretic schemes closer to practice.

REFERENCES

[1] H. V. Balan, R. Rogalin, A. Michaloliakos, K. Psounis, and G. Caire. Airsync: Enabling distributed multiuser mimo with full spatial multiplexing. 2012.

[2] C. A. Balanis. *Antenna theory: analysis and design.* John Wiley & Sons, 2012.

[3] P. Baronti, P. Pillai, V. W. Chook, S. Chessa, A. Gotta, and Y. F. Hu. Wireless sensor networks: A survey on the state of the art and the 802.15. 4 and ZigBee standards. *Computer communications*, 30(7):1655–1695, 2007.

[4] FCC, "FCC online table of frequency allocation, April 16, 2013".

[5] Jackson Labs, Fury GPSDO. `http://jackson-labs.com/`.

[6] S. H. Lim, Y.-H. Kim, A. El Gamal, and S.-Y. Chung. Noisy network coding. *IEEE Transactions on Information Theory*, 57(5):3132–3152, 2011.

[7] I. Maric, N. Liu, and A. Goldsmith. Encoding against an interferer's codebook. In *46th Annual Allerton Conference on Communication, Control, and Computing, 2008*, pages 523–530. IEEE, 2008.

[8] B. Nazer and M. Gastpar. The case for structured random codes in network capacity theorems. *Eur. Trans. on Telecommunications*, 19(4):455–474, 2008.

[9] NIST. Radio Station WWV. `http://www.nist.gov/pml/div688/grp40/wwv.cfm/`.

[10] H. Rahul, S. S. Kumar, and D. Katabi. MegaMIMO: Scaling wireless capacity with user demand. In *SIGCOMM*, 2012.

[11] J. Wang, H. Hassanieh, D. Katabi, and P. Indyk. Efficient and reliable low-power backscatter networks. *ACM SIGCOMM Computer Communication Review*, 42(4):61–72, 2012.

Poster: Geometrical Distance Distribution for Modeling Performance Metrics in Wireless Communication Networks

Fei Tong, Maryam Ahmadi, Jianping Pan
Computer Science
University of Victoria, BC, Canada
{tongfei, mahmadi, pan}@uvic.ca

Lei Zheng, Lin Cai
Electrical and Computer Engineering
University of Victoria, BC, Canada
{zhengl, cai}@ece.uvic.ca

ABSTRACT

Geometrical distance distribution (GDD) between nodes in wireless communication networks plays a significant role in modeling network performance metrics. Existing work on obtaining GDD assumes the network geometry to be a regular one, such as circle and square. Due to the various complex effects of wireless signals, however, the network geometry usually is quite irregular. Therefore, this paper proposes a novel systematic and unified approach to obtain the GDD between two random nodes associated with arbitrary network geometries. To the best of our knowledge, this is the first work that will fill the gap in the literature of this field.

Categories and Subject Descriptors

C.2.1 [**Computer-Communication Networks**]: Wireless communication; C.4 [**Performance of Systems**]: Modeling techniques

Keywords

Geometrical distance distribution, Wireless communication networks, Line kinematic measure, Arbitrary geometries

1. INTRODUCTION

Communicating nodes in a wireless network, such as ad-hoc or cellular network, are typically distributed in the network area following a certain distribution. Geometrical distance distribution (GDD) between nodes plays an important role in determining several fundamental performance metrics of the networks, which can be further utilized in network protocol design, modeling, analysis, performance evaluation, and optimization. For example, in [3], the GDD between the mobile collector and its nearest node requesting data collection is employed to evaluate the system service disciplines; in [5] and [12], GDD was applied to the localization problem and the minimization of energy consumption, respectively, in wireless sensor networks; in [10], a model based on GDD was utilized for capacity analysis and interference estimation in mobile cellular systems; other metrics such as node degree, outage probability, connectivity, path loss, and SINR in wireless networks are all related to GDD [2, 8, 11].

In general, there are two types of GDD significantly useful in wireless communication networks: *1)* between a reference node and a random one, and *2)* between two random nodes. For the former, in our recent work [1], there is a breakthrough in obtaining the GDD from an arbitrary reference node to a random node in an arbitrary polygon, which breaks the unrealistic limitations and assumptions that the network area has to be regular and the reference node has to be inside. For the latter, however, to the best of our knowledge, similar limitations and assumptions are still there. Existing approaches can only be applied to the regular network geometry, such as circle [2, 5], square [3, 12] and regular hexagon [2, 11], while in realistic scenarios, the network geometry usually is quite irregular due to the effects from complex environment factors and network topology control.

In this paper, a novel systematic and unified approach based on line kinematic measure (LKM) [4, 6] is proposed to obtain the second-type GDD associated with arbitrary network geometries, which will fill the gap in the literature of this field. Specifically, the GDD either within a geometry or between two separate, adjacent and overlapped geometries can be obtained. As a case study, we present the GDD associated with arbitrary triangles, based on which the GDD associated with arbitrary n-gons ($n \geq 4$) can be obtained through a decomposition and recursion (D&R) approach with polygon triangulation, avoiding the complexity of directly applying LKM as n becomes large. All results are verified through simulations.

2. UNDERLYING APPROACH: LKM

As in most existing work [11], we consider uniformly-distributed networks with two cases of the shape shown below. The approach can be extended to nonuniform networks.

2.1 GDD within a convex geometry

As shown in Fig. 1(a), a random line $\mathcal{G}$ with orientation θ (without loss of generality, with regard to x-axis) intersects with a convex geometry $\mathcal{K}$ of area S, producing a chord with length $|AB| = l$. There are two points, say P_1 and P_2, independently and uniformly distributed on the chord, with $|AP_1| = d_1$ and $|AP_2| = d_2$ ($0 \leq d_1, d_2 \leq l$). Given that $|d_1 - d_2| \leq d$ ($0 \leq d \leq l$) with the domain of integration shown as in Fig. 1(b), the *kinematic measure* of a set of line segments $\{P_1P_2\}$ of length at most d on the chord is [4]

$$F_{\mathcal{G}}(d) = \iint_{|d_1-d_2|\leq d} |d_1 - d_2| \, \mathrm{d}d_1 \mathrm{d}d_2 = d^2 l - \tfrac{2}{3}d^3 . \quad (1)$$

MobiCom'14, September 7-11, 2014, Maui, Hawaii, USA.
ACM 978-1-4503-2783-1/14/09.
http://dx.doi.org/10.1145/2639108.2642905.

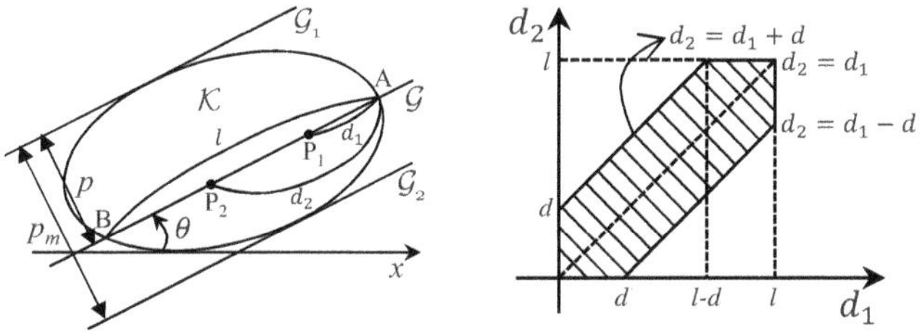

(a) LKM (b) Domain of $|d_1 - d_2| \le d$

Figure 1: Two random points in a convex geometry.

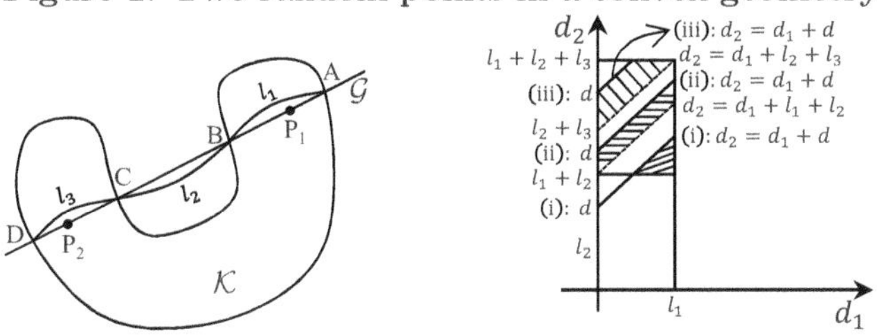

(a) Two random points respectively on two separate segments produced by a line intersecting with a concave $\mathcal{K}$

(b) Domain of $d_2 - d_1 \le d$, with three cases: (i) $l_2 \le d \le l_1 + l_2$; (ii) $l_1 + l_2 \le d \le l_2 + l_3$; (iii) $l_2 + l_3 \le d \le l_1 + l_2 + l_3$

Figure 2: Two random points in a concave geometry.

The derivative of $F_{\mathcal{G}}(d)$, referred to as the *kinematic measure* of a set of line segments $\{P_1P_2\}$ of length d is

$$f_{\mathcal{G}}(d) = \frac{\mathrm{d}F_{\mathcal{G}}(d)}{\mathrm{d}d} = 2d(l-d) \ . \tag{2}$$

There are two tangents known as *support lines* with the same orientation θ that completely encompass $\mathcal{K}$, *i.e.*, $\mathcal{G}_1$ and $\mathcal{G}_2$ in Fig. 1(a). Therefore, a line $\mathcal{G}$ intersecting with $\mathcal{K}$ is determined by θ ($0 \le \theta \le \pi$) and its distance p to, without loss of generality, $\mathcal{G}_1$ ($0 \le p \le p_m$, where p_m known as *width* is the distance between the two tangents). According to [6], the kinematic measure of a set of lines $\mathcal{G}(p,\theta)$ is defined as the integral over the set of a differential form $\mathrm{d}\mathcal{G} = \mathrm{d}p \wedge \mathrm{d}\theta$. Since the probability density of a randomly selected point in $\mathcal{K}$ is $\frac{1}{S}$, by considering the kinematic measure of all lines intersecting with $\mathcal{K}$, the PDF of the GDD within $\mathcal{K}$ is

$$f_D(d) = \frac{1}{S^2}\int_0^{\pi}\int_0^{p_m} f_{\mathcal{G}}(d)\,\mathrm{d}\mathcal{G} \ . \tag{3}$$

2.2 GDD between two separate regions

For the GDD within a concave geometry and that between two geometries with or without connection, it is necessary to consider the random distance between two separate regions, where LKM still applies [4]. As shown in Fig. 2(a), a line $\mathcal{G}$ intersecting with a concave geometry $\mathcal{K}$ produces two segments, $AB = l_1$ and $CD = l_3$ inside $\mathcal{K}$, and another segment $|BC| = l_2$ outside. Point P_1 and P_2 are independently and uniformly distributed on AB and CD, respectively, with $|AP_1| = d_1$ and $|AP_2| = d_2$. Obviously, $0 \le d_1 \le l_1$ and $l_1 + l_2 \le d_2 \le l_1 + l_2 + l_3$. Given that $|P_1P_2| = d_2 - d_1 \le d$, and assuming $l_1 \le l_3$ (thus $l_1 + l_2 \le l_2 + l_3$), there are three cases of the range of d to obtain the kinematic measure of a set of line segments $\{P_1P_2\}$ of length at most d, with the corresponding domain of integration as shown in Fig. 2(b) (for $l_3 \le l_1$, $l_2 + l_3 \le l_1 + l_2$, and the analysis is the same):

(i) $l_2 \le d \le l_1 + l_2$:

$$\begin{aligned} F^{\mathrm{i}}_{\mathcal{G}}(d) &= \iint_{d_2 - d_1 \le d} (d_2 - d_1)\,\mathrm{d}d_1\mathrm{d}d_2 = \tfrac{1}{6}(l_2 - d)^2(l_2 + 2d) \ . \\ f^{\mathrm{i}}_{\mathcal{G}}(d) &= (d - l_2)d \ . \end{aligned}$$

(ii) $l_1 + l_2 \le d \le l_2 + l_3$:

$$\begin{aligned} F^{\mathrm{ii}}_{\mathcal{G}}(d) &= \tfrac{l_1}{2}(d + l_1 + l_2)(d - l_1 - l_2) \ , \\ f^{\mathrm{ii}}_{\mathcal{G}}(d) &= l_1 d \ . \end{aligned}$$

(iii) $l_2 + l_3 \le d \le l_1 + l_2 + l_3$:

$$\begin{aligned} F^{\mathrm{iii}}_{\mathcal{G}}(d) &= \tfrac{1}{6}(2l_2 + 2l_3 + d)(l_2 + l_3 - d)^2 \\ &\quad - \tfrac{1}{2}\left((l_2 + l_3)^2 - d^2\right)(l_1 + l_2 + l_3 - d) \ , \\ f^{\mathrm{iii}}_{\mathcal{G}}(d) &= (l_1 + l_2 + l_3 - d)d \ . \end{aligned}$$

Combining the other case that P_1 is on CD and P_2 on AB, which leads to the same results, the kinematic measure of a set of line segments $\{P_1P_2\}$ of length d is

$$f_{\mathcal{G}}(d) = \begin{cases} 2f^{\mathrm{i}}_{\mathcal{G}}(d), & l_2 \le d \le l_1 + l_2 \\ 2f^{\mathrm{ii}}_{\mathcal{G}}(d), & l_1 + l_2 \le d \le l_2 + l_3 \\ 2f^{\mathrm{iii}}_{\mathcal{G}}(d), & l_2 + l_3 \le d \le l_1 + l_2 + l_3 \end{cases} \ . \tag{4}$$

By generalizing (3) to consider the kinematic measure of all lines intersecting with $\mathcal{K}$, the GDD within $\mathcal{K}$ can be obtained based on (2) and (4).

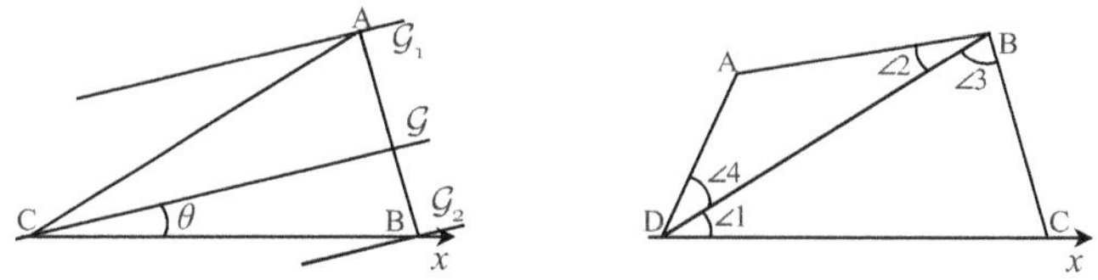

(a) one triangle (b) two triangles form a convex quadrangle

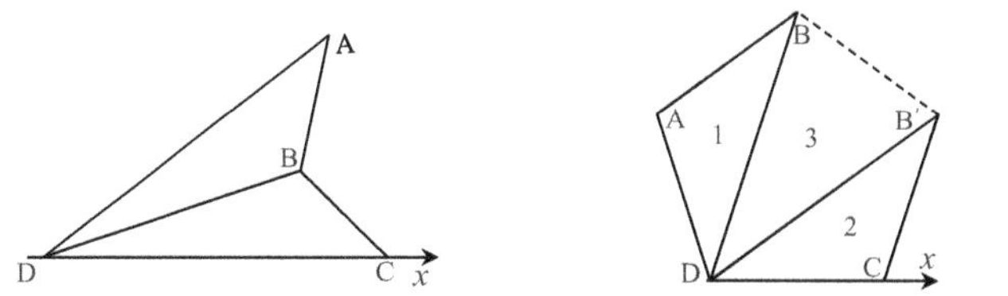

(c) two triangles form a concave quadrangle (d) two triangles form a regular pentagon

Figure 3: GDD associated with triangles.

3. CASE STUDIES

Based on the LKM-based approach, we first show the GDDs associated with triangles (triangle-GDDs), including the GDD within a triangle, and that between two triangles sharing either a common side or a common vertex. The results are then further utilized to obtain the GDD associated with arbitrary n-gons ($n \ge 4$) based on D&R, since any polygon can be triangulated. The triangle-GDDs can also be utilized for the performance modeling in triangle-based sensor networks [7] and triangle cellular systems [9].

3.1 GDD within a Triangle

An arbitrary triangle $\triangle ABC$ of area S is shown in Fig. 3(a), with CB on x-axis. For the GDD within $\triangle ABC$, we design a systematic algorithm for the numerical integration of (3), based on which the closed-form expression can be obtained. Specifically, let θ increase from 0 to π with a fixed small step of $\delta\theta$ (*e.g.*, $\delta\theta = \frac{\pi}{180}$). The distance between the two tangents parallel with $\mathcal{G}$, *i.e.*, $\mathcal{G}_1$ and $\mathcal{G}_2$ which completely encompass the whole triangle, is p_m. The distances between $\mathcal{G}_1$ and $\mathcal{G}$ and between $\mathcal{G}_2$ and $\mathcal{G}$ are p_1 and p_2, respectively. Obviously, $p_m = p_1 + p_2$. With a fixed small δp (*e.g.*,

Algorithm 1 Systematic algorithm for numerical integration to obtain the PDF of GDD within an arbitrary triangle

```
Input: Parameters related to △ABC; distance d; δθ; δp; f_D(d) = 0.
Output: PDF: f_D(d);
for (θ = 0; θ ≤ π; θ = θ + δθ) do
    for (p = 0; p ≤ p_m; p = p + δp) do
        Based on trigonometry to calculate l, the length of chord
        produced by G(θ, p) intersecting the triangle;
        if l ≥ d then
            f_D(d) = f_D(d) + 2d(l−d)/S^2; /* based on (3) */
        end if
    end for
end for
```

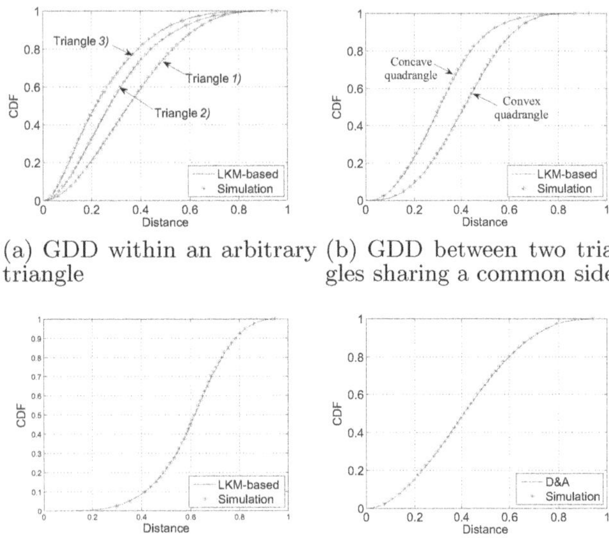

(a) GDD within an arbitrary triangle

(b) GDD between two triangles sharing a common side

(c) GDD between two triangles in a regular pentagon

(d) GDD within a regual pentagon

Figure 4: GDD verification through simulation.

$\delta p = \frac{1}{1{,}000}$), let p increase from 0 to p_m with step δp (corresponding to the line translation from $\mathcal{G}_1$ to $\mathcal{G}_2$), we can obtain $\frac{p_m}{\delta p}$ chords. For each chord of length l (calculated based on trigonometry), we can obtain $f_{\mathcal{G}}(d)$ according to (2), based on which the PDF of the GDD can be obtained according to (3). The systematic algorithm is summarized in Alg. 1, with regularity helping obtain the PDF symbolically.

Three triangles are selected for verification, all of which have the longest side length of 1: *1)* $(\frac{60\pi}{180}, \frac{60\pi}{180}, \frac{60\pi}{180})$, *2)* $(\frac{80\pi}{180}, \frac{70\pi}{180}, \frac{30\pi}{180})$, *3)* $(\frac{130\pi}{180}, \frac{30\pi}{180}, \frac{20\pi}{180})$. For simplicity, only CDFs obtained by integrating corresponding PDFs, are shown here and hereafter. As shown in Fig. 4(a), the close match with simulation demonstrates the correctness of our approach, which is, however, much faster than simulation.

3.2 GDD between Two Triangles

According to (4), the LKM-based approach can also be utilized to obtain the GDD between two triangles sharing either a common side or a common vertex. For the former, the two triangles can form either a convex or concave quadrangle. Due to the page limit, only the comparison results with simulation are shown here.

For two triangles forming a convex quadrangle (Fig. 3(b)): $(\angle A = \frac{120\pi}{180}, \angle 4 = \frac{35\pi}{180}, \angle 2 = \frac{25\pi}{180})$ and $(\angle C = \frac{80\pi}{180}, \angle 1 = \angle 3 = \frac{50\pi}{180})$ and those forming a concave quadrangle (Fig. 3(c)): $(\angle ABD = \frac{110\pi}{180}, \angle A = \frac{40\pi}{180}, \angle ADB = \frac{30\pi}{180})$ and $(\angle CBD = \frac{160\pi}{180}, \angle C = \frac{15\pi}{180}, \angle CDB = \frac{5\pi}{180})$, and those forming a regular pentagon (Fig. 3(d)), the results in close match with simulation are shown in Fig. 4(b) and 4(c), respectively.

3.3 GDD associated with n-gons ($n \geq 4$)

With the triangle-GDDs obtained above, the GDD associated with arbitrary n-gons ($n \geq 4$) can be obtained based on D&R to avoid the complexity of applying LKM as n becomes large, since any polygon can be triangulated. Hence, the GDD-related performance metrics of a wireless network in an arbitrary polygon can be quantified. Take the regular pentagon in Fig. 3(d) for example. $\triangle ABD$, $\triangle B'CD$ and $\triangle BB'D$ are labeled by 1, 2 and 3, respectively. The GDD within the pentagon can be given by a probabilistic sum,

$$F = \tfrac{2S_1}{S}\left(\tfrac{S_1}{S}F_{11} + \tfrac{S_3}{S}F_{13} + \tfrac{S_2}{S}F_{12}\right) + \tfrac{S_3}{S}\left(\tfrac{S_3}{S}F_{33} + \tfrac{2S_1}{S}F_{13}\right),$$

where S is the area of the pentagon, S_x is the area of x, and F_{xy} is the CDF of the GDD between x and y. The comparison with simulation in close match is shown in Fig. 4(d).

4. REFERENCES

[1] M. Ahmadi and J. Pan. Random distances associated with arbitrary triangles: a recursive approach with an arbitrary reference point. *UVicSpace*, http://hdl.handle.net/1828/5134, 2014.

[2] P. Fan, G. Li, K. Cai, and K. Letaief. On the geometrical characteristic of wireless ad-hoc networks and its application in network performance analysis. *IEEE TWC*, 6(4):1256–1265, 2007.

[3] L. He, Z. Yang, J. Pan, L. Cai, J. Xu, and Y. Gu. Evaluating service disciplines for on-demand mobile data collection in sensor networks. *IEEE TMC*, 13(4):797–810, 2014.

[4] T. Koshizuka and S. Ohtsu. Distance distribution in an arbitrary region and its application to the daily trip in tokyo. *Urban Planning Society of Japanese*, 36:871–876, 2001.

[5] R. S. Leão and V. C. Barbosa. Exploiting the distribution of distances between nodes to efficiently solve the localization problem in wireless sensor networks. In *ACM PM^{2}HW^{2}N*, 2010.

[6] L. A. Santaló. *Integral Geometry and Geometric Probability.* Cambridge University Press, 2004.

[7] L.-C. Shiu, C.-Y. Lee, and C. S. Yang. The divide-and-conquer deployment algorithm based on triangles for wireless sensor networks. *Sensors Journal, IEEE*, 11(3):781–790, 2011.

[8] S. Srinivasa and M. Haenggi. Distance distributions in finite uniformly random networks: Theory and applications. *IEEE TVT*, 59(2):940–949, 2010.

[9] Z. Wang, X. Lv, and J. Zhu. Information-theoretic capacity analysis in triangle cellular communication system. In *IEEE VTC*, 2006.

[10] Y. Zhuang, Y. Luo, L. Cai, and J. Pan. A geometric probability model for capacity analysis and interference estimation in wireless mobile cellular systems. In *IEEE GLOBECOM*, 2011.

[11] Y. Zhuang and J. Pan. A geometrical probability approach to location-critical network performance metrics. In *IEEE INFOCOM*, 2012.

[12] Y. Zhuang, J. Pan, and L. Cai. Minimizing energy consumption with probabilistic distance models in wireless sensor networks. In *IEEE INFOCOM*, 2010.

Poster: Overheard ACK With Token Passing: An Optimization to 802.11 MAC Protocol *

Shegufta Bakht Ahsan
Department of Computer Science
University of Illinois at Urbana-Champaign
sbahsan2@illinois.edu

Nitin Vaidya
Department of Computer Science
University of Illinois at Urbana-Champaign
nhv@illinois.edu

ABSTRACT

Distributed Coordination Function (DCF) is defined in IEEE 802.11 standard, which is widely used in practice. Despite of its wide use, it has several limitations. Because of the idle and collision times, it suffers from poor channel utilization. Besides, the control packets, particularly, *Acknowledgement (ACK)*, consume non-trivial amount of bandwidth. Though the number of control bits in an ACK frame is small, the added overheads like the *preamble*, *packet header* etc. make the situation worse. In this paper, we propose a scheme called *Overheard ACK* where the *explicit* ACK frame has been eliminated by using the leverage of *packet overhearing*. Also, by incorporating *explicit* and *implicit* token-passing, this protocol attempts to schedule transmissions without having to use random access, dramatically reducing the idle time and collision time. Simulation results using *NS2* confirm that this protocol significantly outperforms the conventional 802.11 DCF.

Categories and Subject Descriptors

C.2.2 [**Network Protocols**]: Protocol architecture (OSI model)

Keywords

Packet Overhearing; Token Passing

1. INTRODUCTION

IEEE 802.11 is a standardized protocol for wireless networks. This protocol uses the Distributed Coordination Function (DCF) as its primary Medium Access Control (MAC) method [1]. To resolve channel contention, DCF employs Carrier Sense Multiple Access with Collision Avoidance (CSMA/CA) scheme with binary exponential backoff algorithm. DCF imposes two kinds of overheads; one is the channel idle time and the other is the collision overhead. Also, in DCF, a node transmits an ACK packet in reply to a received DATA packet, which also adds to the overhead (each MAC frame also has the overhead of the *preamble* and *frame header*).

This paper presents a solution that incorporates *Overheard ACK* and *token-passing* to significantly reduce the overhead due to *backoff time*, *packet collision* and *explicit ACK frame*. The two key features of our solution are as follows:

- Acknoledgements are piggybacked on data frames when possible (similar to transport layer TCP protocol). Using the leverage of packet overhearing, this approach significantly reduces the overhead of sending explicit ACK packets.
- Each ongoing transmission passes a *token* to another host who will then have a higher priority to transmit after the ongoing transmission completes.

2. RELATED WORK

The protocol presented in this paper is build on our prior work [4], in which we developed *Token-DCF*, an opportunistic MAC protocol for wireless networks, which reduces idle time and collision time by implementing an opportunistic token passing mechanism. In this scheme, with a certain probability p, a transmitting node might select one of its neighbours as a privileged node by mentioning that neighbour's ID in a token. By overhearing, all neighbours receive the token. Only the *privileged* neighbour mentioned in the token starts transmitting after SIFS interval of time. All other *non-privileged* neighbours have to wait for *DIFS+backoff* time to access the channel. Thus whenever a privileged node transmits on the channel, the idle time of the channel is reduced to SIFS.

In other related work, Choudhury et al. propose an "implicit MAC acknowledgement" scheme [3] where the explicit ACK frame has been eliminated by piggybacking ACK information in RTS/CTS frame.

3. PROTOCOL DESCRIPTION

Overheard ACK is implemented in the MAC layer of the protocol stack. In this protocol, each STA embeds its latest network layer packet queue length in the MAC header of

*This research is supported in part by National Science Foundation awards CNS-11-17539 and Futurewei Technologies. Any opinions, findings, and conclusions or recommendations expressed here are those of the authors and do not necessarily reflect the views of the funding agencies or the U.S. government.

MobiCom'14, September 7-11, 2014, Maui, Hawaii, USA.
ACM 978-1-4503-2783-1/14/09.
http://dx.doi.org/10.1145/2639108.2642903 .

the transmitted packet. AP maintains a database where queue length of each neighbour is stored, based on which AP *explicitly* or *implicitly* selects a privileged STA. Instead of waiting for *DIFS+backoff* time, a privileged STA can access the channel just after *SIFS* time. We describe our protocol as a sequence of events at the MAC layer.

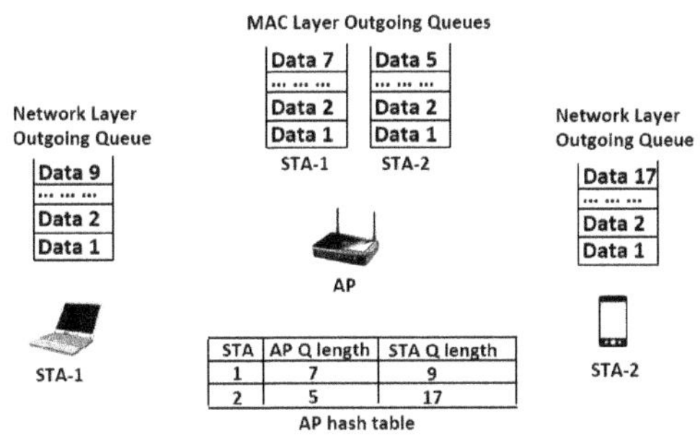

Figure 1: Queue design of Overheard ACK

Figure 1 presents a simple scenario with an AP and two station STA_1 and STA_2 with queue length 9 and 17 respectively. First we will describe the case where *implicit scheduling* is used. Let's assume that for all STAs, AP has always at least one data packet to send. When AP receives a DATA from STA_1, it schedules an ACK after SIFS interval. The larger queue size of STA_2 implies that it has more data to send to AP. Our simple scheduling algorithm, which selects the neighbour with the maximum queue length as a privileged node, selects STA_2 as privileged. Therefore AP selects a DATA packet destined for STA_2 and merges it with ACK. The combined packet now contains *ACK*, ACK_{dest}, *DATA* and $DATA_{dest}$. After SIFS interval, instead of sending the ACK to STA_1, AP sends the merged packet to STA_2. STA_1 receives the combined packet by overhearing and parses the desired ACK. STA_2 receives the packet directly and parses the DATA. At this point, after SIFS interval STA_2 schedules an ACK. But it has at least one DATA packet destined to AP, waiting in the network layer queue. Therefore it merges the ACK with the DATA packet. After SIFS interval, it sends the combined packet to AP. Now AP receives the desired ACK and another new DATA from STA_2. As like before, its scheduler module selects a new privileged STA, merges the ACK and DATA packet, and sends the merged packet to the privileged STA. In this way AP can *implicitly* select a privileged STA. This scheme avoids sending explicit ACK by merging it with the DATA packet. Most of the time the *merged packet* is the only type of packet transmitted in the channel. In this approach, backoff stage does not occur before each packet transmission, rather there is only SIFS interval between two consecutive transmissions, which results in better throughput than the *Token-DCF* scheme.

Now we will consider the second case, where AP *explicitly* schedules a STA. It can be further divided into two situations where the traffic patterns are mainly: *a*) *up-stream* data and *b*) *down-stream* data. In the first situation, AP has the knowledge about each STA's queue size, based on which it can select a privileged STA. As most of the time AP has no data to send, it returns *explicit ACK frame* in response to the incoming DATA from STAs. But this time the *ID* of the privileged station is explicitly embedded with the transmitted ACK frame. As all the STAs overhears the ACK frame, only the privileged STA schedules the next transmission after SIFS interval. In the second situation, AP plays the role as a transmitter and receives only ACK packets. Hence it announces itself as the privileged node and after receiving an ACK packet, it waits for SIFS interval to transmit the next DATA packet. Though both of these schemes cannot eliminate explicit ACK, but here packets are transferred just after SIFS interval. Hence its throughput is similar to the *Token-DCF* scheme, which is still better than the conventional IEEE 802.11 DCF scheme.

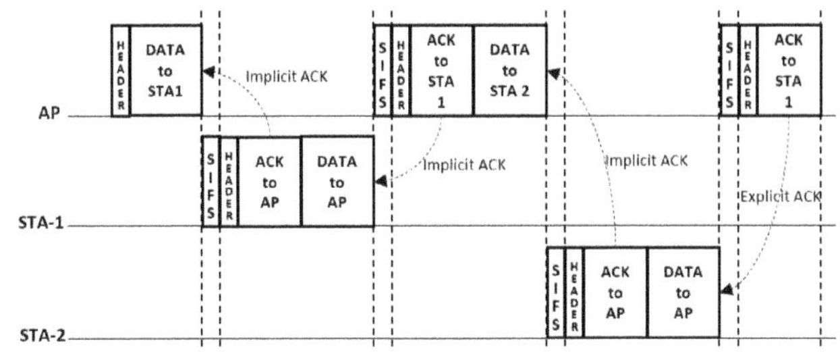

Figure 2: Channel access method of Overheard ACK

In this protocol, network layer queue of the AP has been replaced by a number of dedicated MAC layer queues for each STA. Each queue associated with a STA, holds outgoing packets destined to that STA. AP maintains a hash table (Figure 1) where against each STA, the number of outgoing packet inside AP's dedicated queue and the number of outgoing packets inside that STA's network layer queue are stored. AP uses this information for scheduling the next transmitting station. The channel access mechanism of *Overheard ACK* is shown in Figure 2. For more details of the protocol, readers are encouraged to refer to Reference [2].

4. CONCLUSION

In this paper we present *Overheard ACK*, a MAC protocol which by employing packet overhearing and eliminating explicit ACK frames, improves the channel utilization. Primarily we are using a simple scheduling algorithm, which selects each station with equal probability. Our simulation results show that this protocol outperforms the *Token-DCF* protocol. The encouraging results lead us to extend this research for making it more robust and efficient.

5. REFERENCES

[1] *IEEE Std. 802.11-2077, Part 11: Wireless LAN Medium Access Control (MAC) and Physical Layer (PHY) Specifications*, June 2007.

[2] S. B. Ahsan and N. Vaidya. Overheard ack with token passing: an optimization to 802.11 mac protocol. ACM S3 Workshop, September 2014.

[3] R. R. Choudhury, A. Chakravarty, and T. Ueda. Implicit mac acknowledgment: An improvement to 802.11. IEEE/ACM Wireless Telecommunications Symposium (WTS), April 2005.

[4] G. Hosseinabadi and N. H. Vaidya. Token-dcf: An opportunistic mac protocol for wireless networks. In *COMSNETS*, pages 1–9, 2013.

Poster: In-Lane Communication Framework Using Smartphone's Inertial Sensors

Abdulla Alasaadi
Department of Computer Science
Old Dominion University
aalasaad@cs.odu.edu

Tamer Nadeem
Department of Computer Science
Old Dominion University
nadeem@cs.odu.edu

ABSTRACT
In this paper, we describe the in-lane communication framework that enables the communication between vehicles on the same lane. The system creates a unique signature for each lane using smartphone inertial sensors. The calculated lane signature will be attached with each broadcasted message, where other vehicles on the street compare it with their own lane signature to decide if the received message came from a vehicle on the same lane or not. The paper concentrates on finding the right features that can be used to identify a lane in a road. To identify a lane with a unique signature, the paper proposes a combination of driving features and road features. The paper uses the inertial sensors because the current GPS systems are not accurate enough to locate vehicles with a lane level accuracy. The ability to establish a communication channel between vehicles on the same lane can enhance the road safety and enable several interesting navigation applications.

Categories and Subject Descriptors
C.3 [**Special-Purpose and Application-Based Systems**]: Signal processing systems.

General Terms
Design, Reliability, Experimentation.

Keywords
Traffic, mobile computing, lane detection, communication.

1. INTRODUCTION
Identifying the vehicle's lane and establishing a communication channel between vehicles on the same lane can enhance road safety by exchanging alerts between drivers or between the infrastructure and drivers. The system uses the driver's smartphone to identify his lane because most drivers are attached with smartphones that come with different types of motion sensors such as accelerometer and gyroscope. In addition to that, Current GPS systems are not accurate enough to locate cars with lane level accuracy [1].

MobiCom'14, September 07-11, 2014, Maui, HI, USA.
ACM 978-1-4503-2783-1/14/09.
http://dx.doi.org/10.1145/2639108.2642912

Such system can be used by police cars or in traffic lights to deliver customized messages and alerts to vehicles in specific lane. A driver can inform cars in the back about a bump, a pothole, accident or a stopped car.

The in-lane communication system has two main steps, creating a lane signature, and recognizing the lane signature. Using an android application created for such purpose, the system collects and analyzes the readings from the smartphones' motion sensors. At any point, the driver can send a specific message to vehicles driving on the same lane. Other vehicles should decide if the message belongs to them or not by comparing their own lane signature with the lane signature attached to the original message.

2. METHODOLOGY
2.1 Data Collection and processing
An Android application has been created to collect and process the readings of the inertial sensors. At any point when the driver decides to share an alert message with vehicles in the same lane, the application sends the message attached with a lane signature created by the signature module.

2.2 Calculating Lane Signature and Sending the Message
Creating the lane signature is the most important part because it specifies the message recipients. To create the lane signature, first the system has to find the right features that can help in distinguishing between two or more lanes. Lane detection existing technologies [2][3][4][5] are based on vision and image processing; but their accuracy is affected by many external factors. The proposed system uses the smartphone inertial sensors to extract multiple features from the sensors; these features can be divided into two types:

1- Physical features.

2- Driving based features

Physical features are the mean, standard deviation, energy, correlation, and median extracted from the raw readings from gyroscope and accelerometer for predefined number of seconds.

Driving based features are the features extracted from the driving behavior and the environment of each lane such as average speed, maximum speed, minimum speed, number of stops, waiting time, time between stops, and number of bumps.

When the driver chooses to send a message, the signature is attached to the message and got broadcasted to the neighbor vehicles.

2.3 Receiving the message

When neighbor vehicles receive a message, they fetch the lane signature that comes with the message and compare it with their own lane signature, and if they match, then the receiver vehicle considers that message as a message sent from a vehicle on the same lane.

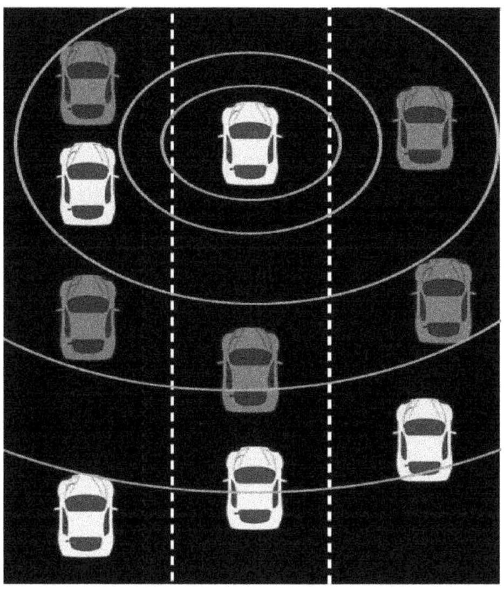

Figure 1. Vehicle sends messages to nearby cars.

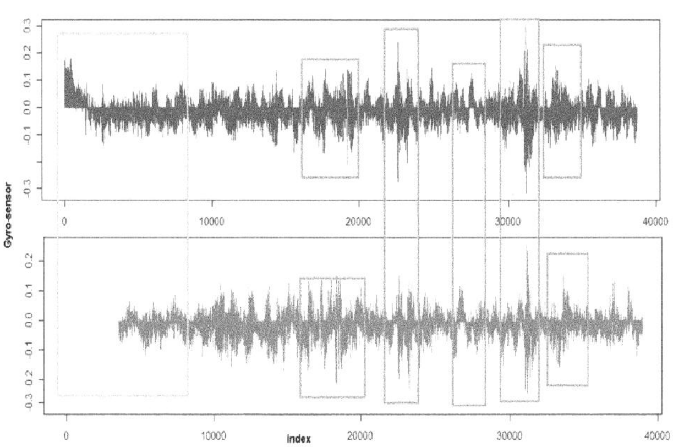

Figure 2. Gyroscope readings for one lane in two different runs.

3. EXPERIMENT AND RESULTS

3.1 Experiments

Different types of experiments used to test the modules of the system. First, experiments were conducted to test the lane identification module, where we used single car with multiple runs, then we used multiple cars driving at the same time.

The system has been tested in different types of roads and environments and the results showed good performance near intersections, exits, ramps, low speed roads and the HOV lanes. The average speed and number of stops can differentiate between an exit lane and other lanes in a highway, especially when the traffic is high. In some cases when the speed, number of stops and other driving features are not good enough to identify a lane, we found the physical features performing better in identifying lanes.

3.2 Results

Physical and driving features were able to classify vehicles based on their lanes. In some regions, the system was able to identify vehicles' lanes with 90% accuracy.

Figure 2 shows the similarity in the gyroscope sensor readings for two different cars running in the same lane. These similarities represent the physical features in the two runs. Road bumps and potholes make a good physical feature that can be easily identified

Figure 3 shows the results of driving in three-lane low speed road for 20 times. The green numbers are the vehicles considered to be in lane 1, red numbers are the vehicles in lane 2, and the blue numbers are the vehicles in the third lane. All lanes were identified successfully except the vehicles represented by numbers surrounded by circles which gives 80% total accuracy. The table in the corner of figure 3 represents the accuracy of identifying the lanes using some physical features individually.

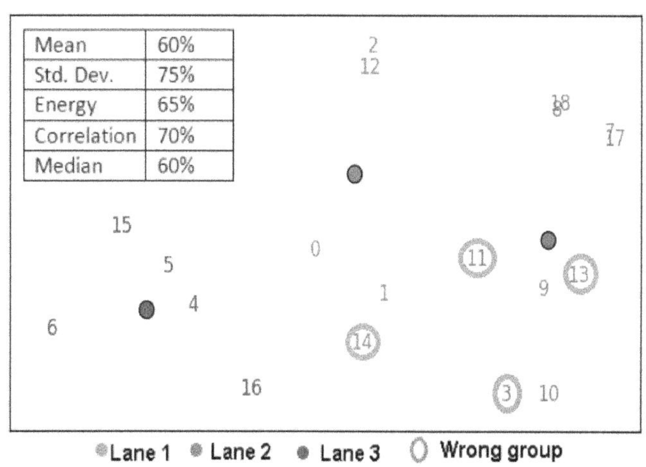

Mean	60%
Std. Dev.	75%
Energy	65%
Correlation	70%
Median	60%

Figure 3. Classifying vehicles based on their lanes using Gyroscope only.

Table 1 shows the accuracy of identifying lanes in different environments using different driving features. Average speed gave a very high accuracy in identifying busy exit ramps but lower accuracy in identifying inner city streets, while average waiting time per stop can identify the city streets with better accuracy.

Table 1. The accuracy of identifying lanes in different environments using different features

Feature	Correct est. city street	Busy exit ramp	Intersection
Average speed	76.32	94.82	82.64
No. of Stops	84.97	76.34	81.08
Waiting Time	88.20	76.34	86.32
Physical Features	78.47	83.84	84.61
All	86.64	91.47	84..74

4. CONCLUSION

The extracted features give a good accuracy in identifying vehicle's lane. The system extracts physical features and driving features. Physical features are based on the physical characteristics of the road, and the driving features are extracted from the readings of the sensors. Combining these features generate the lane signature. The signature will be attached with the broadcasted messages to identify the targeted vehicles. The in lane communication systems can be used in many applications related to safety and navigation.

5. REFERENCES

[1] Wing, M. G., Eklund, A., & Kellogg, L. D. (2005). Consumer-grade global positioning system (GPS) accuracy and reliability. Journal of Forestry, 103(4), 169-173.

[2] Kim, Z. (2008). Robust lane detection and tracking in challenging scenarios. Intelligent Transportation Systems, IEEE Transactions on, 9(1), 16-26.

[3] McCall, J. C., & Trivedi, M. M. (2004, June). An integrated, robust approach to lane marking detection and lane tracking. In Intelligent Vehicles Symposium, 2004 IEEE (pp. 533-537). IEEE.

[4] Kluge, K., & Lakshmanan, S. (1995, September). A deformable-template approach to lane detection. In Intelligent Vehicles' 95 Symposium., Proceedings of the (pp. 54-59). IEEE.

[5] Sparbert, J., Dietmayer, K., & Streller, D. (2001). Lane detection and street type classification using laser range images. In Intelligent Transportation Systems, 2001. Proceedings. 2001 IEEE (pp. 454-459). IEEE.

POSTER: A Coarse-Fine Corner Detection Approach for Two-Dimensional Barcode Decoding*

Changsheng Chen and Wai Ho Mow
HKUST BARCODE GROUP
Hong Kong University of Science and Technology (HKUST), Hong Kong
{eecschen, eewhmow}@ust.hk

ABSTRACT

Two-dimensional barcodes are widely used in mobile advertisement business, while their decoding performance is not always satisfactory under uncontrolled environments. The corner detection accuracy has been identified as a critical factor affecting the overall system performance. The standard barcode detector performs a candidate search in the binarized barcode image based on the rectangular shape of the barcode. Its performance is not very accurate due to the limited accuracy of the binarized image. In this work, we proposed a coarse-fine corner detection approach for locating the barcode region. It performs far more accurately than the standard barcode detection scheme while keeps the computational complexity affordable. Experimental results for high capacity barcodes show that the proposed detection scheme can extend the range of operation parameters, such as wider angles, and much lower the detection bit error rate, relative to the standard barcode decoder.

Categories and Subject Descriptors

B.4 [INPUT/OUTPUT AND DATA COMMUNICATIONS]

Keywords

2D Barcode; Corner Detection; Matched Filtering

1. INTRODUCTION

The performance of two-dimensional (2D) barcode decoding is often unreliable due to the difficulties in barcode detection process [1, 2]. The challenges are from various factors, e.g., uneven lighting condition, complex background, limited image quality, etc. Current barcode decoding systems require to recapture the barcode image if the detection is not successful. Insufficient barcode detection accuracy may result in slow and unreliable decoding systems. The objective of our work is to increase the barcode detection accuracy and, subsequently, improve the speed and reliability of the overall system.

A standard barcode detection algorithm has been implemented in a popular open source barcode decoding library, named ZXing ("Zebra Crossing") [3]. This algorithm detects the candidate barcode region in the binarized barcode image by a rectangular searching window. The window starts from the image center and searches for the smallest candidate rectangle that fits the non-white region in the center. However, this approach relies on the accuracy of the input binarized barcode image which is sensitive to aforementioned distortions.

In this work, we propose a coarse-fine corner detection approach which refines the output corner locations from the coarse corner detection stage. For initial insight, we directly employ ZXing's detection scheme as the coarse corner detection stage. In the fine detection stage, the rough barcode corners are analyzed to obtain the module[1] size, and the accurate corner positions are then detected by four customized matched filters.

The organization of this paper is as follows. Section 2 reviews a new picture embedding barcode, called PiCode, recently introduced from our research group and describes how it motivates this work. PiCode is also used as the example barcode pattern throughout this work. Section 3 describes the proposed coarse-fine corner detection approach and shows some experimental results. Section 5 concludes this paper.

2. PICTURE BARCODE: PICODE

The common binary 2D barcode patterns as shown in Fig. 1 (a) and (b) are originally designed for industrial applications, e.g., object tracking, item labelling, etc. On the other hand, the multimedia nature of the mobile advertisement business motivates the introduction of PiCode [4][2](shown in Fig. 1 (c)) to integrate a 2D barcode pattern with a color picture, e.g., a company logo or product picture. It provides visual hints of the barcode content even before the customers scan the barcode pattern. However, the logo cannot be eas-

*This work was supported by the Hong Kong Research Grants Council (Project Number 616512).
The authors would like to acknowledge the other members of the HKUST Barcode Group for making various contributions on which this work is based.

MobiCom'14, September 7-11, 2014, Maui, Hawaii, USA.
ACM 978-1-4503-2783-1/14/09.
http://dx.doi.org/10.1145/2639108.2642915.

[1]As illustrated in Fig. 2, a module is the smallest element in a barcode which encodes bit '0' or '1'.
[2]PiCode is the winner of the MobiCom'2013 Best Mobile App Award; c.f. `http://www.sigmobile.org/mobicom/2013/app_winners.html`

Figure 1: A comparison between binary 2D barcodes with embedded HKUST logo and PiCode: (a)(d) QR code; (b)(e) Data Matrix code; (c)(f) PiCode.

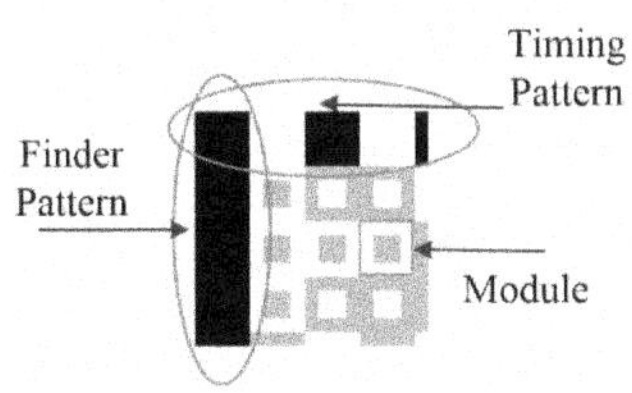

Figure 2: The top-left corner of a PiCode.

ily embedded into traditional 2D barcodes, especially, when their high capacity versions are needed. This is because some reference patterns are located at the center region of high capacity barcodes as shown in Fig. 1 (d) and (e). To improve the aesthetic appearance of PiCode, no such pattern is included in its central barcode area. Moreover, to achieve better visual effect, a single module in the PiCode is further divided into multiple bi-level pixels as illustrated in Fig. 2. With less reference pattern and a more customized module structure, PiCode requires the corner detection step to be much more accurate than that in the standard decoders for conventional 2D barcodes. This motivates us to propose a better corner detection algorithm for PiCode. In general, achieving higher corner detection accuracy is very important for extending the range of operation scenarios for all barcode patterns, especially for those practical applications in which the required barcode capacity increases (or module size decreases).

3. COARSE-FINE CORNER DETECTION & EXPERIMENTAL RESULTS

The proposed coarse-fine corner detection approach first receives the coarse corner locations from a standard barcode detector. Here, we employ the detector implemented in ZXing [3] since it is very widely used in commercial mobile software applications which incorporate a barcode decoder. A module size estimation step is then followed to calculate the module size of the PiCode with the information from the neighbouring pixels. Next, four matched filter templates for the four corners, respectively, are designed with prior knowledge on the structure of finder and timing patterns. Finally, matched filtering operations are performed over the four corner regions with the corresponding templates. Note that the accuracy of module size estimation is the key to the performance of the fine corner detection.

Table 1: Decoding performance comparisons.

Scheme	Angle	BER 29×29	BER 45×45
ZXing's [3]	$-20°$	1.25%	47%
	$0°$	0.57%	48%
	$20°$	1.18%	50%
Proposed	$-20°$	~0%	0.61%
	$0°$	~0%	0.84%
	$20°$	~0%	0.17%

In the following, large scale experiments are conducted to show the advantages of the proposed corner detection scheme. To collect the barcode images, a mobile phone camera is used to capture the displayed PiCode images with different dimensions from different angles. Five hundred images are collected for each barcode dimension and each capture angle. The experimental settings are as follows:

- Display: Dell E2313H 23" LED-Lit monitor;
- Camera: Nexus 5 with VGA *preview* resolution;
- Barcode size: 15×15 cm^2 on display;
- Barcode dimension: 29×29 or 45×45 module^2;
- Embedded logo: a *blank* image;
- Distance: 30 cm from camera to PiCode center;
- Capture angles: -20, 0, and 20 degree(s).

It should be noted that the camera is set to work at the preview mode which is the normal working condition in most barcode mobile apps. The two barcode dimensions represent PiCodes with low and high capacities which are illustrated in Fig. 1 (c) and (f), respectively. A blank picture is used as the logo image to isolate the distortions from the embedding operation. For comparison, the captured images are fed into the decoders with the proposed coarse-fine corner detection algorithm and ZXing's algorithm. Here, the detection bit error rate (BER), i.e., without channel decoding, is used as a primary performance metric (partly because it allows the Shannon capacity limit of the barcode channel to be estimated).

As shown in Table 1, all the PiCode images with dimension 29×29 modules can be decoded at a BER below 1.25% using ZXing's algorithm, and at ~0% BER (i.e., 0 error out of the 500 samples) with the proposed algorithm. On the other hand, for high capacity PiCode with 45×45 modules, the BERs of ZXing's approach are near 50%. This is because the corners are not detected with high enough accuracy. Small errors in corner detection deteriorates the overall performance of the decoder. However, the proposed coarse-fine corner detections scheme offers much higher accuracy and the BERs are decreased to below 1%. It is worth mentioning that the decoding time cost is about 1.6 second per image with unoptimized Matlab implementation. It is therefore claimed that the complexity of the proposed corner detection algorithm is very affordable in a practical implementation platform with highly optimized code.

4. CONCLUSIONS

This work has introduced a novel and efficient way to detect the corners of 2D barcodes with customized matched filtering. Experimental results for high capacity PiCode show that the proposed detection scheme can improve the barcode decoding performance significantly at very affordable complexity. Our coarse-fine corner detection approach can be easily adapted to detect general barcode patterns and can extend their range of operation in practical scenarios. It has successfully addressed the problem of achieving high corner detection accuracy, which will become more and more critical as the barcode capacity increases to meet the need of future applications.

5. REFERENCES

[1] D. Parikh and G. Jancke. Localization and segmentation of a 2D high capacity color barcode. In *IEEE Workshop on Applications of Computer Vision*, pages 1–6, Jan 2008.

[2] H. Yang, A.C. Kot, and X. Jiang. Binarization of low-quality barcode images captured by mobile phones using local window of adaptive location and size. *IEEE Transactions on Image Processing*, 21(1):418–425, Jan 2012.

[3] ZXing, Multi-format 1D/2D barcode image processing library. Available at https://github.com/zxing/zxing/.

[4] W. Huang and W.H. Mow. PiCode: 2D barcode with embedded picture and ViCode: 3D barcode with embedded video. In *MobiCom.*, 2013.

Poster: Detection of Transportation Mode Based on Smartphones for Reducing Distracted Driving

Xin Gao, Jie Tian, Guiling Wang
Department of Computer Science
New Jersey Institute of Technology
Newark, NJ 07102, USA
{xg54, jt66, gwang}@njit.edu

ABSTRACT

Nowadays, distracted driving is becoming a very dangerous epidemic on the roadways. A lot of activities may lead to distracted driving, such as texting, making phone calls, using GPS or road maps, eating, using in-car entertainment systems, etc. As the number of smartphones is rapidly growing year by year, using smartphone is by far the most dangerous and alarming driver distraction. In this paper, we design an app on iPhone for reducing the smartphone-related distracted driving, which can run in the background and can lock the smartphone screen with no passwords required when it detects that the user is driving. After the user finishes driving, the lock will be removed immediately. We also describe a DTM algorithm to detect the transportation mode and give the performance analysis of our system. The results show that our system can save more energy than other related applications.

Categories and Subject Descriptors

H.4 [**Information Systems Applications**]: Miscellaneous; C.2 [**Computer Communication Networks**]: Miscellaneous

Keywords

Distracted driving; GPS; Transportation mode; Smartphone; DTM

1. INTRODUCTION

Distracted driving is dangerous to the safety of driver, passenger and even pedestrian, which diverts driver's attention away from the roads. At any time in a day across America, nearly 660,000 drivers are using smartphones or manipulating electronic devices while driving since 2010[1]. According to the U.S. Department of Transportation's National Highway Transportation Safety Administration (NHTSA) Report, 3328 people were killed and 421,000 were injured in distraction-affected crashes in 2012. Despite the increasing accident statistics, however, only a small amount of cars on the roads today have driver alert systems in cars. And it will takes a long time for the new techniques to be common in most cars. Therefore, an effective app on smartphones is useful and easy to be implemented at the moment.

A lot of apps [2, 3, 4, 5, 6] have been developed for detecting dangerous and protecting drivers in recent years. For example, CarSafe [6] is an app designed to prevent drivers' drowsy for Android phones. It needs to be on all the time and costs plenty of phone energy. The app in [3] is also designed on Android platform. It uses context-awareness to block phone calls when the user is driving. A good method TEXIVE is designed in [2], which can distinguish between drivers and passengers and detect the texting operations during driving. But it cannot distinguish between them if the smartphones are put besides them. Since the smartphones become bigger, drivers often put them in the middle of the two front seats. In [4], the app can only determine if an individual is stationary, walking, running, biking, or in motorized transport. It cannot distinguish between driving and taking a public transit.

In our work, we propose DTM (Detection of Transportation Mode) algorithm to distinguish whether the driver is static, walking, running, on a bus, in a train, in a light rail, or driving a car. We design an app on iPhone with embedded sensors, i.e. accelerometer, GPS, magnetometer and gyroscope. The app can run in the background and can lock the smartphone screen when driving detected. When driving finished, the lock will be removed immediately. No passwords are required here, which means the user cannot unlock the phone while driving until he slows down or parks the car on the roadside.

The remainder of this paper is structured as follows: In Section 2, we design a system for reducing distracted driving based on iOS platform and describe a DTM algorithm using embedded sensors in the smartphone to detect the transportation mode. We give the analysis and system performance in Section 3. Section 4 is the conclusion including a discussion of our future direction.

MobiCom'14, Sep 07-11, 2014, Maui, HI, USA.
ACM 978-1-4503-2783-1/14/09.
http://dx.doi.org/10.1145/2639108.2642911.

2. SYSTEM DESIGN

The design of our system is based on obtaining embedded sensor data from smartphones, and determining the transportation mode for reducing distracted driving with a locked smartphone screen when driving detected. The application collects location and speed information from the Global Positioning System receiver, using Google Maps Ap-

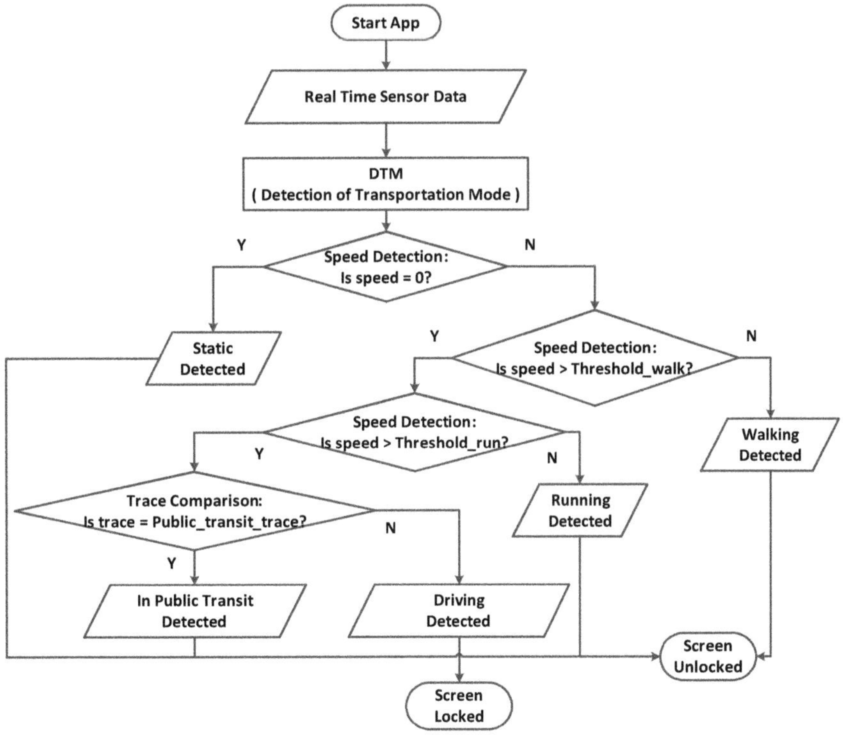

Figure 1: Flow of DTM Algorithm

plication Programming Interface (API) to determine the location. With the API, we can compare the route of the user with Google Maps and get the exact location. Since the driver may drive at the same way as the bus or other public transit, we add a "delay" time to the system. During this period of time, if the routes are same, the user is detected as on a public transit; if not, we need to lock the smartphone screen. We use plugins in iOS to lock the screen, which can easily activate screen or deactivate screen at the status we determine.

Figure 1 shows the flow of our proposed DTM algorithm. The real time sensor data are accelerometer, GPS, magnetometer and gyroscope data. We first do a pre-processing of these input data, then follow the steps of DTM algorithm to get the final detection result and give a response. We can determine whether the user is static, walking, running, on a public transit or driving in a car. We also make our app better by using a customized function. With the function, users can customize their own speeds. For example, older people can set speed at a very low value, since they may run at a very slow speed even slower than the walking speed of the teenagers. The users need to click the setting button and then walk or run for a period of time, e.g. 5 minutes. When they finish, they click ok. The system will select the middle part data of this period and calculate the average speed, which can show the normal speed of the person. We need this function to make our app suitable and comfortable to all users.

3. DATA ANALYSIS AND RESULTS

We do a data analysis on accelerometer sensor data and magnetometer sensor data when the user is on a light rail or driving respectively, as shown in Figure 2 and Figure 3.

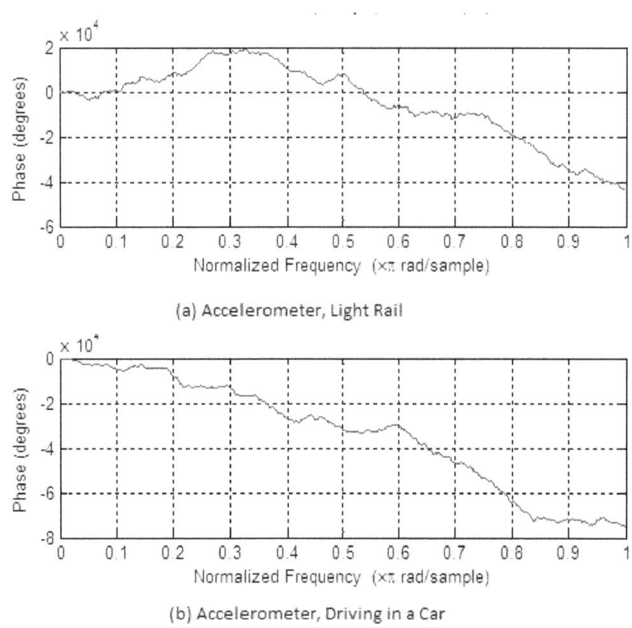

Figure 2: Data extracted from accelerometer when user is driving or on a light rail

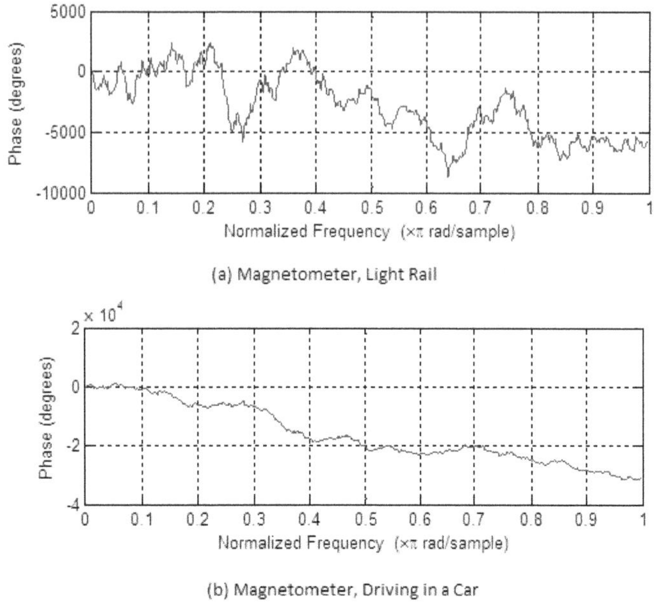

Figure 3: Data extracted from magnetometer when user is driving or on a light rail

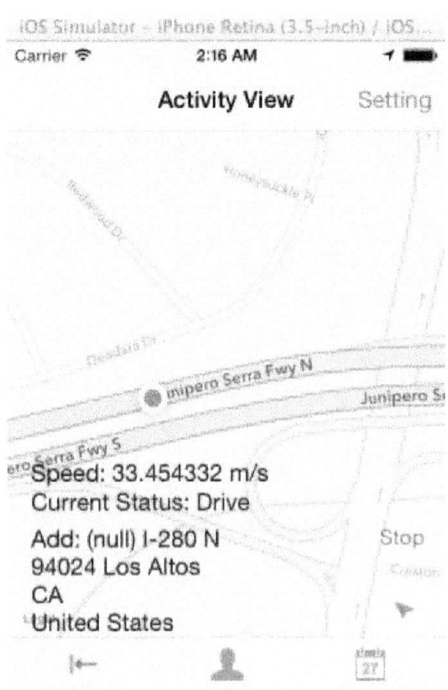

Figure 4: A Screenshot of App

Figure 4 shows the screenshot of our app running on iOS simulator. It can determine the current status and give the address of current location. We click the start button to run the app and collect GPS data. After we click the stop button, we stop receving GPS data and close our app. The app can run in the background, which saves a lot of energy. But using GPS still needs some energy. We need to improve this later. Compared to other related apps, our app can save more energy.

4. CONCLUSION AND FUTURE WORK

This paper describes a DTM algorithm to do the detection of transportation mode for reducing distracted driving on iOS platform. It compares the routes with the public transit routes and determines whether the user is in a public transit or driving. It also gives the data analysis on real world data acquired using different smartphones. Since the public transit can stop at each station, we will add the algorithm of stop detection as a module in our future app.

The future work may also include the experiments of the combination of the DTM algorithm and an algorithm determining whether the user is a driver or just a passenger by putting a specific tag in the car.

5. ACKNOWLEDGMENTS

Many thanks to Zhe Yu for his help with data collection in the experiment. Besides, we would like to thank anonymous reviewers for valuable comments on our work.

6. REFERENCES

[1] What is distracted driving? `http://www.distraction.gov/content/get-the-facts/facts-and-statistics.html`.

[2] C. Bo, X. Jian, X.-Y. Li, X. Mao, Y. Wang, and F. Li. You're driving and texting: detecting drivers using personal smart phones by leveraging inertial sensors. In *Proceedings of the 19th annual international conference on Mobile computing & networking*, pages 199–202. ACM, 2013.

[3] J. Lindqvist and J. Hong. Undistracted driving: a mobile phone that doesn't distract. In *Proceedings of the 12th Workshop on Mobile Computing Systems and Applications*, pages 70–75. ACM, 2011.

[4] S. Reddy, J. Burke, D. Estrin, M. Hansen, and M. Srivastava. Determining transportation mode on mobile phones. In *Wearable Computers, 2008. ISWC 2008. 12th IEEE International Symposium on*, pages 25–28. IEEE, 2008.

[5] J. Yang, S. Sidhom, G. Chandrasekaran, T. Vu, H. Liu, N. Cecan, Y. Chen, M. Gruteser, and R. P. Martin. Detecting driver phone use leveraging car speakers. In *Proceedings of the 17th annual international conference on Mobile computing and networking*, pages 97–108. ACM, 2011.

[6] C.-W. You, M. Montes-de Oca, T. J. Bao, N. D. Lane, H. Lu, G. Cardone, L. Torresani, and A. T. Campbell. Carsafe: a driver safety app that detects dangerous driving behavior using dual-cameras on smartphones. In *Proceedings of the 2012 ACM Conference on Ubiquitous Computing*, pages 671–672. ACM, 2012.

Ziria: Language for Rapid Prototyping of Wireless PHY

Mahanth Gowda[1] UIUC
gowda2@illinois.edu

Gordon Stewart[1] Princeton
jsseven@cs.princeton.edu

Geoffrey Mainland[2] Drexel
mainland@cs.drexel.edu

Božidar Radunović
Microsoft Research
bozidar@microsoft.com

Dimitrios Vytiniotis
Microsoft Research
dimitris@microsoft.com

Doug Patterson
Microsoft
dougpatt@microsoft.com

ABSTRACT

Software-defined radio (SDR) brings the flexibility of software to the domain of wireless protocol design, promising an ideal platform both for research and innovation and rapid deployment of new protocols on existing hardware. However, existing SDR programming platforms require either careful hand-tuning of low-level code, negating many of the advantages of software, or are too slow to be useful practically.

We present Ziria, the first software-defined radio programming platform that is both easily programmable and performant. Ziria introduces a novel programming model tailored to wireless physical layer tasks and captures the inherent and important distinction between data and control paths in this domain. Ziria provides the capability of implementing a real-time WiFi PHY running at 20 MHz.

Categories and Subject Descriptors

C.3 [**Computer Systems Organization**]: Special Purpose and Application Based Systems—*Signal processing systems*

Keywords

Languages; Signal Processing; Wireless; Compilers

1. INTRODUCTION

The past few years have witnessed tremendous innovation in the design and implementation of wireless protocols, both in industry and academia ([1, 2]). Much of the work has occurred at the physical (PHY) layer of the protocol stack, which manages the translation between radio hardware signals and protocol packets. The numerous new signal processing algorithms and novel coding schemes that have resulted—many of which were first implemented using software-defined radio (SDR) platforms—have greatly increased the efficiency of radio communication channels.

However, SDRs have not yet reached the mainstream of wireless research. The main impediment is implementation complexity. Wireless PHY algorithms have to be very fast and efficient to meet line rate requirements. Software has to process tens of millions of complex samples per second, which is equivalent to a processing rate of close to a gigabit per second. To cope with these speeds a programmer has to have a good understanding of the underlying SDR hardware architecture and the effects of her design choices on performance.

In order to design wireless algorithms, an SDR programmer has to have a profound understanding of signal processing and wireless networking, and in order to efficiently implement them she has to be an expert in computer architecture and system design. An average student finds it quite hard to master all these areas. Only very few research groups have found enough resources to pursue this line of research.

To illustrate this complexity we consider two popular SDR designs. The first example is FPGA-based platforms, such as Warp [3] and Lyrtech [4]. A typical state-of-the-art SDR programming tool for FPGA platforms is based on Matlab, Simulink and an FPGA compiler. One of the main benefits of this environment is a rich set of DSP building blocks (such as basic fixed-point arithmetics, FFT, encoders, decoders, etc.). Further, being integrated in Matlab, this environment provides a programmer with powerful tools for debugging input and output signals, and for simulating different real-world effects using readily available libraries. However, the programming model is essentially the same as hardware design in VHDL or Verilog. A programmer has to have a fundamental understanding of how FPGAs operate. She has to be aware of different propagation delays and their effects on the system performance. One misplaced delay element can easily lead to a week of debugging!

Recently, several SDR platforms, such as GnuRadio [5] and Sora [6], allow programmers to design SDR code on general-purpose CPU processors. The hardware part of the platform performs analog-to-digital and digital-to-analog conversion of the baseband signals and supplies these signals to a CPU, where a programmer can further process it as desired.

Signal processing on a CPU provides great flexibility and permits rapid experimentation, but often at the price of decreased performance. Writing fast, real-time PHY code on a CPU can be equally, if not more complex than programming FPGAs. In fact, most of the recent academic works on SDR do not even attempt to process signals in real-time. They

[1]This work was done during an internship with Microsoft Research.

[2]Part of the work was done while the author was with Microsoft Research.

MobiCom'14, Sep 07-11 2014, Maui, HI, USA.
ACM 978-1-4503-2783-1/14/09
http://dx.doi.org/10.1145/2639108.2642893.

only use SDR platforms to capture signals. Post-processing is later done offline at much smaller processing rates than required by PHY. This approach clearly precludes any real-world networking experiments on SDR platforms.

One of the first CPU-based SDR platforms that has managed to process wireless baseband signals at a line rate is Sora [6]. It has demonstrated interoperability with commodity WiFi cards. But this performance comes with increased complexity. The code for Sora has to be written in C/C++ and a programmer needs to manually optimize the code to achieve the required speeds. Sora has put substantial effort into designing a C++ template library that eases the programming pain. However, use of templates imposes several limitations, in particular on state sharing and dynamic reconfigurability of the dataflow graphs. It is worth noting that GnuRadio has a similar architecture based on C++ templates and similar limitations. We next overview the architecture of Ziria and explain how it addresses these issues.

2. ZIRIA

We give a high-level overview of main components of Ziria.

2.1 Language Overview

Expressions.

The Ziria language consists of two main parts. The first is an expression language used to encode basic imperative calculations. This language is a mix of Matlab and C designed to make the right trade-off between programmability and efficiency. It is a strongly typed language, which allows us to simplify memory management. It also supports array operations, like Matlab, which allows for efficient mapping to SSE vector instructions. An example of a code in the expression language is given inside the *execute* keyword in Listing 1.

Computations.

Ziria's computation language is designed to capture the control flow of a PHY program and map it to an efficient execution model. It consists of *stream transformers*, which map values from input to output streams and which never terminate, and *stream computers*, which can halt with a return value. Composition of stream transformers and computers is depicted in Figure 1. Many of the standard wireless PHY blocks are stream transformers. For example, a scrambler reads an input bit, XORs it with internal state, writes the result to the output, and updates its internal state. FFT is also a stream transformer. In the case of WiFi, it reads 64 complex numbers, performs FFT on them and writes 64 complex numbers to the output stream.

Stream computers also map stream inputs to stream outputs, but additionally may *halt* with a control value. In the right-hand side of Figure 1, this control value is depicted as the fat "Control" arrow connecting the computer to the transformer. In Ziria, the control value is used to *dynamically reconfigure* the rest of the processing pipeline; in the figure, this corresponds to switching from the "Computer" to the "Transformer" in the lower right corner. After reconfiguration, the inputs that originally flowed to the computer are routed to the next component in the pipeline—in this case, the "Transformer." Both components output to the same stream. This dynamic reconfiguration is called *binding* and it directly

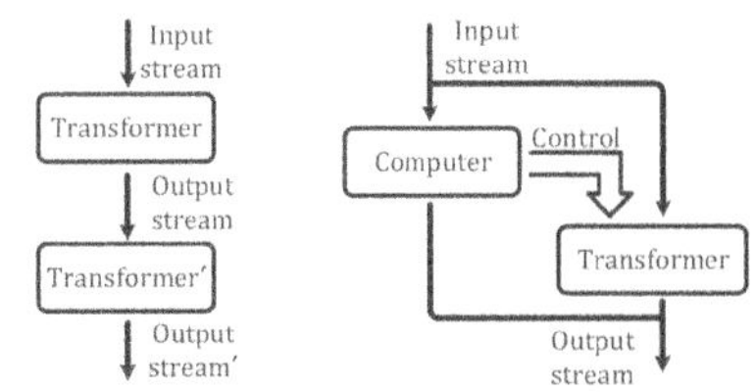

Figure 1: Transformer-transformer composition (left); computer-transformer composition (right).

reflects the control flow of many PHY-layer protocols, which read a preamble or packet header from the input stream and then reconfigure computation of the rest of the stream based on data in the preamble.

2.2 Optimizing Compiler

The Ziria optimizing compiler consists of two parts. It has a front-end which parses a Ziria program and stores it in an abstract representation, and then performs several optimization passes on it. It also has a back-end which compiles the optimized abstract representation into a low-level execution model optimized for a target architecture. Our current back-end targets a low-level execution model in C for the Sora SDR platform, but it can easily be extended to other platforms, such as GnuRadio.

There are several benefits of this approach when compared to the existing approaches:

Dynamic staging of the control graph: Ziria language for staging data flows allows for a dynamic reconfiguration of the control graph. This reconfiguration is very flexible, so for example a downstream component can reconfigure an upstream component or any other part of the graphs (for example using parameter passing and the repeat construct). This is in contrast with Sora and GnuRadio C++ templates that allow limited downstream reconfigurability using the multiplexing block.

No need for shared state: Ziria dynamic reconfigurability and parameter passing between blocks eliminate the need for share states. Instead, a state is passed explicitly between components and all the dependencies are checked at the compile time. This is in contrast with Sora and GnuRadio which heavily rely on shared states. One example of a negative consequence is that an unitialized state cannot be detected by the compiler and causes program misbehaviour.

Code optimization: Ziria compiler's optimization phase can optimize jointly the imperative part of the language and the data-flow graph. It can merge data-flow blocks, change input and output widths, inline expressions and unroll loops. One example of a useful code optimization are look-up tables. Ziria compiler can automatically identify blocks of code that operate on small bit inputs (e.g. scrambler and encoder) and convert them into lookup tables, which execute much faster on a CPU than bit operations. All this is in contrast to Sora and GnuRadio C++ template libraries where C compiler does not have an explicit understanding of the control flow graph and can perform far fewer optimizations. Lookup tables have to be implemented and tuned manually.

Overall, Ziria code is much more concise. For example, an implementation of a WiFi scrambler in Sora takes 90 lines of C++ code. The same code can be implemented in Ziria in 13 lines. It is easier to understand and has very similar performance to the hand-tuned Sora code.

3. EXAMPLES: TX SCRAMBLER

This section walks through an example code of a signal processing block (Scrambler) in Ziria.

Scrambler.

In signal processing domains, the purpose of a scrambler is to XOR input data with a pseudorandom sequence. This reduces the probability of sending data sequences that have undesirable signal properties, such as all 1's or all 0's, over the air (cf. Section 17.3.5.4 of [7]).

```
1  let comp scrambler() =
2    var scrmbl_st: arr[7] bit := {1,1,1,1,1,1,1};
3        tmp: bit; y: bit;
4    repeat seq{
5      x ← take;
6      do {
7        tmp := (scrmbl_st[3] ^ scrmbl_st[0]);
8        scrmbl_st[0:5] := scrmbl_st[1:6];
9        scrmbl_st[6] := tmp;
10       y := x ^ tmp};
11     emit (y)}
```

Listing 1: Scrambler function of WiFi 802.11a/g transmitter in Ziria

Scrambler is a let-bound Ziria computation taking no arguments, is an example of a feedback shift register. The scrambler's body declares three local variables (lines 2 through 3): `scrmbl_st`, an array of 7 bits that gives the current state of the shift register, and two one-bit references: `tmp` and `y`. Scrambler **take**s a value from the input stream (line 5), then performs an imperative computation that assigns `tmp` the XOR of taps 3 and 0 in the shift register, shifts the register state left by one, feeds `tmp` into position 6 of the register, and finally returns the XOR of `tmp` and the input bit `x`.

There are two interesting aspects. First, because both the WiFi standard and the code in the listing operate on bit arrays, one can easily verify by inspection that the listing code matches the definitions found in the WiFi standard. This would be more difficult if we implemented the scrambler directly in a more efficient fashion, say by using an integer rather than a bitvector to store the scrambler state, and by shifting instead of indexing into the array. Second, we remark that, when compiled with the Ziria compiler, the scrambler in Listing 1 compiles to quite efficient code. In the context of our WiFi pipeline, the Ziria compiler first automatically generates a lookup table for the scrambler and then vectorizes the code to operate on multiple inputs at a time. This gives a $14.8x$ speedup over the same code compiled without optimizations. As comparison, in the current Sora implementation, the same scrambler is defined as a hand-written lookup table, an excerpt of which is shown in Listing 1.

```
const unsigned char
SCRAMBLE_11A_LUT[SCRAMBLE_11A_LUT_SIZE] = {
    0x00, 0x91, 0x22, 0xb3, 0x44, 0xd5, 0x66, 0xf7,
    0x19, 0x88, 0x3b, 0xaa, 0x5d, 0xcc, 0x7f, 0xee,
    //... 13 lines elided ...
    0x87, 0x16, 0xa5, 0x34, 0xc3, 0x52, 0xe1, 0x70,};
```

Listing 2: Sora lookup table corresponding to the Ziria scrambler implementation in Listing 1

The lookup table implementation may be efficient, but it gives the reader no insight into the computation being performed. Nor is it easy to verify by inspection that this implementation meets the scrambler specification given in the WiFi standard.

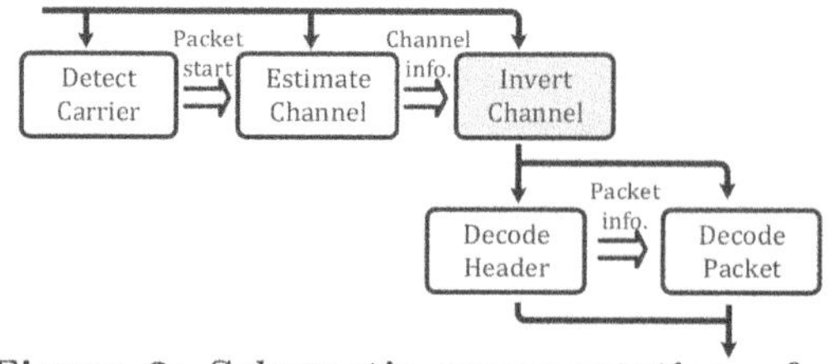

Figure 2: Schematic representation of a WiFi receiver. The shaded box is a transformer; the white boxes are computers.

4. WIFI IMPLEMENTATION

In the previous section, we saw an example of the design of a signal processing block in Ziria. Using many such building blocks, Figure 2 illustrates the high level block diagram of an 802.11a/g receiver in Ziria.

The first block, "Detect Carrier," determines whether a WiFi transmitter is operating on the radio channel by looking for a known constant preamble sequence. Once carrier detection observes the preamble of a valid packet transmission, the pipeline enters a channel estimation phase, operating over the subsequent 160 input samples, in which it attempts to quantify physical effects such as multipath fading on the transmitted signal. The channel information is then used in the channel inversion block of the steady state of the pipeline (in gray) to nullify these effects. This block feeds input data first to a block that decodes the packet header, then to a block that decodes the packet payload. Information from the header decoding phase such as the data rate is used to configure the packet decoding stage.

Both the transmitter and the receiver of a 20MHz WiFi are fully implemented in Ziria, apart from specialized implementations of IFFT, FFT, and the Viterbi decoder. Currently, the code compiles to Sora SDR platforms. The transmitter/receiver are fully integrated in the Windows networking stack, by exposing an Ethernet interface. We are able to run a few real-world network applications on the top of our PHY. Our compiler optimizations (such as auto-vectorization, LUT-ing, etc) achieve over $5x$ improvement over a naive compilation strategy. The entire Ziria compiler toolchain has been open-sourced [8], with the hope that the entire MOBICOM community may benefit from it.

5. REFERENCES

[1] S. Sen *et al.*, "No time to countdown: Migrating backoff to the frequency domain," in *MOBICOM*, 2011.

[2] T. Li *et al.*, "CRMA: Collision-resistant multiple access," in *MOBICOM*, 2011.

[3] P. Murphy, A. Sabharwal, and B. Aazhang, "Design of WARP: a wireless open-access research platform," in *ESPC*, 2006.

[4] Nutaq, "Zeptosdr." `http://nutaq.com/en/products/zeptosdr`.

[5] E. Blossom, "GNURadio: tools for exploring the radio frequency spectrum," *Linux Journal*, vol. 2004, no. 122, p. 4, 2004.

[6] K. Tan *et al.*, "Sora: High performance software radio using general purpose multi-core processors," 2009.

[7] IEEE, "Part 11: Wireless LAN MAC and PHY specifications high-speed physical layer in the 5 GHz band," 1999.

[8] "Ziria." `http://research.microsoft.com/en-us/projects/ziria/`.

SAfeDJ Community: Situation-Aware In-Car Music Delivery for Safe Driving

Xiping Hu[1], Jun-qi Deng[2], Wenyan Hu[3], Georgios Fotopoulos[4], Edith C.-H. Ngai[4], Zhengguo Sheng[1], Min Liang[5], Xitong Li[6], Victor C. M. Leung[1], Sidney Fels[1]
[1] The University of British Columbia, Canada | [2] The University of Hong Kong, Hong Kong | [3] Nankai University, China | [4] Uppsala University, Sweden | [5] IBM, China | [6] Massachusetts Institute of Technology, USA
{xipingh,zhengguo,vleung,ssfels}@ece.ubc.ca, jqdeng@eee.hku.hk, edith.ngai@it.uu.se, gzliangm@cn.ibm.com, xitongli@mit.edu

ABSTRACT
Driving is an integral part of our everyday lives, but it is also a time when people are uniquely vulnerable. Poor road condition, traffic congestion and long driving time may bring negative emotion to drivers and increase the chance of traffic accidents. We propose SAfeDJ, a situation-aware in-car music delivery application, which turns people's trips into pleasant journeys and driving into a safe and enjoyable activity. SAfeDJ aims at helping drivers to diminish fatigue and negative emotion. It is built on a vehicular healthcare platform that enables communications among drivers and integrates with multiple types of sensors to promote safe driving. Prototype implementation and initial results of SAfeDJ have demonstrated its desired functionality in drivers' daily lives and feasibility for real-world deployment.

Categories and Subject Descriptors
C.2.4 [**Computer Systems Organization**]: COMPUTER COMMUNICATION NETWORKS - Distributed Systems - Distributed applications.

General Terms
Design, Human Factors, Algorithms.

Keywords
Vehicular sensor application, situation-aware, cloud.

1. INTRODUCTION
According to the statistics published by the World Health Organization (WHO), 1.2 million people die and 50 million people are injured or disabled on roads every year [1]. Statistics in Europe shows that approximately 10-20% of all traffic accidents are due to diminished vigilance of drivers due to, e.g., fatigue or negative emotion. Previous research has demonstrated that not only does listening to suitable music while driving not impair driving performance, but it could lead to an improved mood and a more relaxed body state, which could improve driving performance and promote safe driving significantly [2]. Thus, we propose SAfeDJ, a novel situation-aware music delivery application for drivers, to help drivers to diminish fatigue and negative emotion during driving.

MobiCom'14, September 7-11, 2014, Maui, Hawaii, USA.
Copyright 2014 ACM 978-1-4503-2783-1/14/09.
http://dx.doi.org/10.1145/2639108.2642902.

SAfeDJ integrates multiple sensors with drivers' social contexts, leverages the advantages of cloud computing and information retrieval, and incorporates a novel cognitive music recommendation mechanism that can intelligently deliver suitable music to drivers according to each driver's specific situations. SAfeDJ provides a seamless and economic solution with a user-friendly (tab-based) mobile application to drivers, enables them to conveniently enjoy favorable music suitable for their situations (traffic conditions, environmental conditions, mood, etc.) through smartphones while driving. For example, this mechanism may deliver lounge music to drivers when they feel tired, and intelligently switch to light music when the traffic congestion is intensive and the driver's blood pressure is high. Furthermore, SAfeDJ enables the drivers to manually or automatically share enjoyable music with friends over social networks while driving. This feature could help to stimulate and improve their driving experience together with friends towards safe driving in a social context.

Currently, a variety of mobile application based solutions have been proposed for safety improvement in vehicular application scenarios, such as V-Cloud [3], CrashHelp [4], and LCCA system [5]. Most of them focus on the long-term health monitoring of vehicular users, or only consider the real-time traffic situations to avoid traffic accidents. However, there is no music-oriented mobile application specifically designed for vehicular users yet. Some music recommendation systems available in the market, like Last.fm and Xiami, recommend music to users only based on their listening behavior and history. Different from them, SAfeDJ orchestrates multiple sources of sensing data and recommends music not only based on drivers' listening behaviors, but also their current situations while driving.

2. SYSTEM ARCHITECTURE DESIGN
Figure 1 shows the system architecture of SAfeDJ with three tiers: network tier, mobile device tier, and cloud tier.

Network tier: It makes use of any available wireless network connectivity within vehicular ad hoc networks (VANETs) and between mobile devices, vehicle onboard systems, and the Internet, employing technologies such as WiFi direct, Bluetooth, Dedicated Short Range Communications (DSRC), and wide area cellular networks. The network tier enables fast communications between the drivers and the cloud servers. This is crucial to support mobile applications for safe driving, which requires real-time collection and dissemination of health and traffic data efficiently and reliably over the heterogeneous vehicular networks.

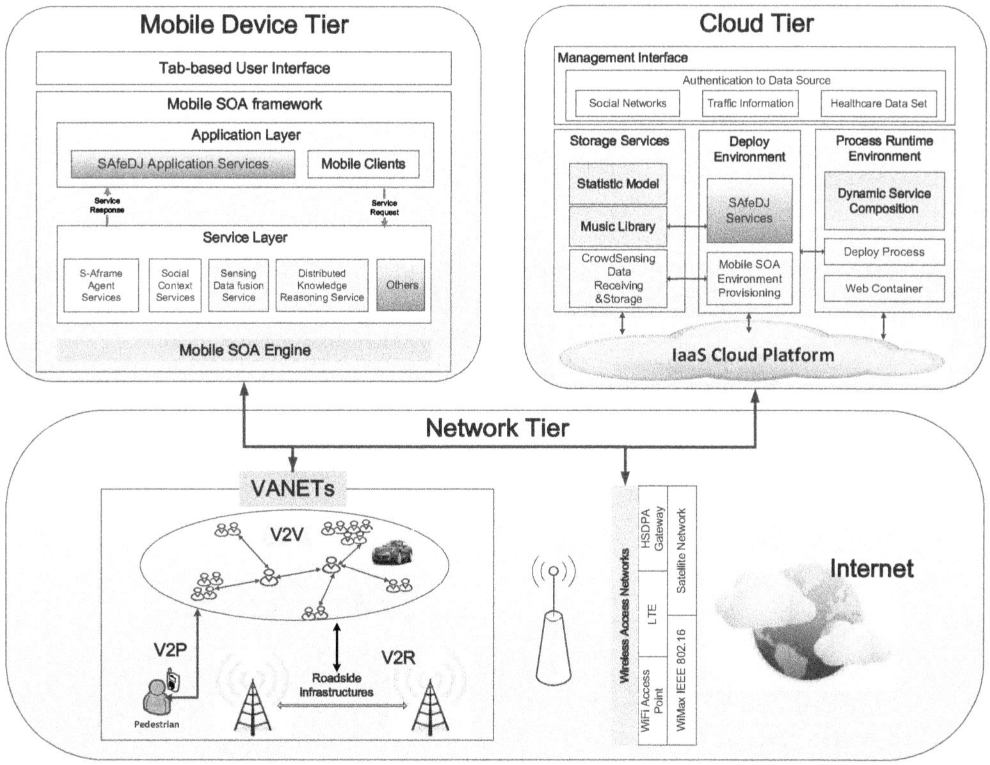

Figure 1. System architecture design

Mobile device tier: Based on the mobile Service Oriented Architecture (SOA) framework [6] developed in our former work, the SAfeDJ in-car music delivery application could be deployed on different mobile devices and work self-adaptively across VANETs and via cloud platforms over the Internet. Moreover, in order to store and interpret the health-related sensing data (e.g., from wearable sensors, mobile devices, and sensors on board vehicles), music preferences, and dynamic traffic data efficiently, we provide two novel services for sensing data storage and distributed knowledge reasoning. They enable real-time state analysis and music matching by aggregating multi-dimensional sensing data.

Cloud tier: The cloud tier works in parallel with the mobile device tier. The cloud tier could be built based on the Vita cloud platform [7] introduced in our earlier work. The cloud tier works as a central coordinating platform to: i) aggregate the health-related sensing data (e.g., the medical history of the driver), traffic data (e.g., road traffic monitoring through crowdsensing [8]), and Internet services (e.g., weather and geographic information, social activities) from multiple sources; ii) interpret the data, perform matching and deliver appropriate music to the drivers according to their situations dynamically. The text should be in two 8.45 cm (3.33") columns with a .83 cm (.33") gutter.

3. SAFEDJ MOBILE APPLICATION

Based on the cloud-based system architecture, we develop and deploy a prototype of SAfeDJ to demonstrate the functionalities of situation-aware in-car music delivery for safe driving. As shown in Figure 2, SAfeDJ consists of three major components: (i) Sensing data fusion service, (ii) Music library and matching service, and (iii) Music sharing and social networks. The sensing data fusion service provides real-time state analysis of the current driving situation by integrating the driver's health data, the car sensors, and the road information. The health data (e.g., heart rate) of drivers can be collected by wearable sensors such as wristbands, while the car data (e.g., speed, temperature, fuel consumption) can be read by advanced onboard diagnostic port scanners. The outside environment can be deduced with the roadside and in-car sensors, news summary, and updates from other drivers. All the input data will be fed into the real-time state analysis module to infer the mood of the driver and the current driving condition.

Then, the state analysis module will perform music matching based on the road situation and mood of driver. For example, if the driver is under stress as he is late for work in a traffic jam, then some relaxing music will be played to relieve his stress. The music library will be updated from time to time, and be connected to the music sharing service via social networks. This enables drivers to share enjoyable music with their friends who have similar music preferences or experience similar traffic conditions.

In addition, to implement the prototype of SAfeDJ, a number of techniques are adopted. For example, to store and interpret the integrated sensing data on mobile devices, we implement a SQLite database and lightweight ontology-based similarity computation methods [8]. To set up the cloud platform to communicate with mobile devices efficiently, *RESTful Web service*, *Apache ODE*, *JBoss jBPM* [7] and a series of open source packages are adopted.

As shown in the bottom of Figure 2, under these experimental settings, the cloud platform of SAfeDJ can finish the information retrieval tasks and return the results to a mobile device efficiently in real driving scenarios (less than 7s even in quite intensive computing situations when the size of data set is 36000). It shows

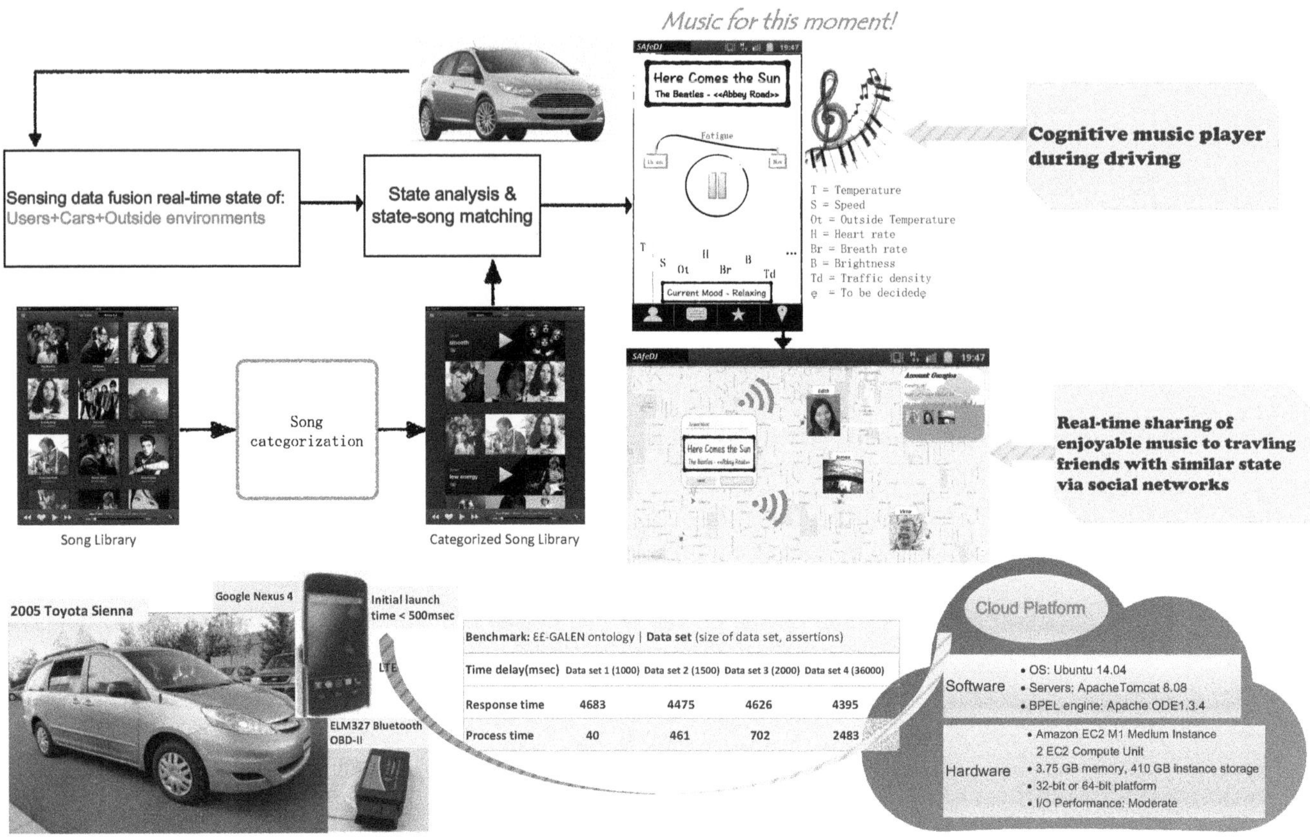

Figure 2. SAfeDJ mobile application for situation-aware in-car music delivery

that our solution can deliver favorable music to drivers' mobile devices on board vehicles efficiently in practice.

4. CONCLUSIONS AND FUTURE WORK

In this paper, we have proposed SAfeDJ, a novel situation-aware in-car music delivery application for promoting safe driving. It is designed based on a cloud-based network architecture, which supports the deployment of multi-dimensional sensing devices, intelligent data aggregation and state analysis, and music matching for drivers according to their mood, music preference, and driving situation. SAfeDJ also connects drivers with their driving friends via social networks for sharing enjoyable music. We have implemented a prototype version of SAfeDJ and performed initial experiments to verify its functionality and practicability in real driving situations. In the future, we shall conduct comprehensive experiments to evaluate the system performance of SAfeDJ under different geographic (e.g., urban vs. rural) and traffic situations (e.g., traffic jams). We shall also explore the relations between traffic conditions, health data and music preferences.

5. ACKNOWLEDGMENTS

This work is supported in part by the NSERC DIVA Strategic Research Network, by TELUS and other industry partners, and by STINT initial grant for international collaboration and SSF Profun, Vinnova Innovation Grant 2014-00655.

6. REFERENCES

[1] World Health Organization, 2014, World report on road traffic injury prevention, available: http://www.who.int/violence_injury_prevention/publications/road_traffic/world_report/en/

[2] M. Zwaag et al. The influence of music on mood and performance while driving. *Ergonomics*, vol. 55, no.1 pp. 12-22, 2012.

[3] H. Abid, L. Phuong, J. Wang, S. Lee, and S. Qaisar. V-Cloud: vehicular cyber-physical systems and cloud computing. In *Proc. ACM ISBEALL,* 2011.

[4] B. Schooley, et al. CrashHelp: A GIS tool for managing emergency medical responses to motor vehicle crashes. In *Proc. ISCRAM,* 2010.

[5] L. Chan, and P. Chong. A lane-level cooperative collision avoidance system based on vehicular sensor networks. In *Proc. ACM MobiCom*, pp. 131-134, 2013.

[6] X. Hu, V. C. M. Leung, W. Du, B. C. Seet, and P. Nasiopoulos. A Service-oriented Mobile Social Networking Platform for Disaster Situations. In *Proc. HICSS*, pp.136-145, 2013.

[7] X. Hu, T.H.S. Chu, H.C.B. Chan, and V.C.M. Leung. Vita: A Crowdsensing-oriented Mobile Cyber Physical System. *IEEE Trans. Emerging Topics in Computing*, vol.1, no. 1, pp. 148-165, 2013.

[8] X. Hu, X. Li, E.C.-H. Ngai, V.C.M. Leung, and P. Kruchten. Multi-dimensional context-aware social network architecture for mobile crowdsensing, *IEEE Commun. Mag.*, vol. 52, no. 6, pp. 78-87, 2014.

Poster: A Framework for Instant Mobile Web Browsing with Smart Prefetching and Caching

Huan Huang, Hailong Sun, Guoqing Ma, Xu Wang, Xudong Liu
School of Computer Science and Engineering, Beihang University
Beijing, China 100191
{huangh,sunhl,magq,wangxu,liuxd}@act.buaa.edu.cn

ABSTRACT

Mobile users often suffer from a slow page loading time due to intermittently connected wireless networks and increasing size of mobile Web pages. Although existing approaches of prefetching and caching are widely used to reduce the browsing latency, they may fail to work effectively because most Web page visits are singletons and the cache hit ratio is unsatisfying. In this work, we design and implement a framework to reduce Web browsing latency for mobile users with a smart prefetching strategy and caching mechanism. The prefetching strategy leverages the skSLRU model, which predicts and prefetches Web pages based on their contents with consideration of user contexts and the devices' status such as power consuming and cellular data usage. And our caching mechanism mainly consider the resources like CSS and JavaScript files shared among Web pages in a website. Moreover, instead of using RAM, we use ROM, the internal flash memory of devices to store cached resources with proper lifecycle so as to avoid the useful resources to be untimely evicted or expired and thus improve the hit ratio. Our evaluations show that 90% of the homepages and 60% of other pages are fetched before users' visiting, and the page loading time is no more than one second.

Categories and Subject Descriptors

C.2.4 [**Computer-Communication Networks**]: Distributed Systems[Distributed Application, Client/Server]

Keywords

Mobile Web browsing; Prefetching; Caching

1. INTRODUCTION

Web browser is one of the most important applications on mobile devices, but it turns out to be slow in the page loading process [5] due to mobile wireless networks with relatively low bandwidth and intermittent connectivity. Furthermore, currently the size of mobile Web pages is getting larger because of the increasing usage of component resources like images, JavaScript and CSS. Therefore end-users suffer a 7-second loading time for mobile Web pages averagely [1], which leads to the unsatisfying Web browsing experiences.

In order to reduce page loading time, prefetching [2, 3] and caching [4] have been widely used to avoid real-time resource loading from network. Unfortunately, they may not work effectively for mobile Web browsing. For *prefetching*, most existing methods are based on the historical URL records but 75% of the Web page visits are singletons [6]; As for *caching*, only 30% of the requested resources can be fetched from local storage directly even with unlimited size of cache [6], and current caching mechanisms usually invalidate cached resources very soon for data freshness and evict them quickly as the cache size is limited. However, we observe that (1) most Web browsing falls into specific sections of a few websites and (2) the Web pages in the same website usually share a large portion of page component resources and these resources may still be used in the following Web page visits, which is also pointed out in [3, 6].

Basing on these observations, we design and implement a framework for instant mobile Web browsing with smart prefetching and caching. First, our prefetching strategy is able to predict and prefetch Web pages by computing the relevance between the contents of the new Web pages with the visited pages of each user. Moreover, this strategy takes the limited battery, system resources and network connections of mobile devices into consideration in determining when and how many resources to prefetch. Second, our caching mechanism avoids the useful resources to be untimely evicted or expired by localizing them in the ROM rather than RAM with a suitable lifecycle. We also provide interfaces for users and developers to achieve their personalized caching mechanisms. Finally, the experimental results show that, with our framework, more than 90% of the homepages and 60% of other Web pages can be prefetched before users' visiting, and the time to render out them is below one second.

MobiCom'14, September 7-11, 2014, Maui, Hawaii, USA.
ACM 978-1-4503-2783-1/14/09.
http://dx.doi.org/10.1145/2639108.2642899 .

2. FRAMEWORK OVERVIEW

2.1 Architecture of the Framework

Fig. 1 depicts the architecture of our framework, which consists of a Web browser and a server for accelerating computing of prefetching. Our prefetching strategy relies on the cooperation of both the statistics in the browser and the prefetching model on the server side. And the caching mechanism is implemented in the Web browser.

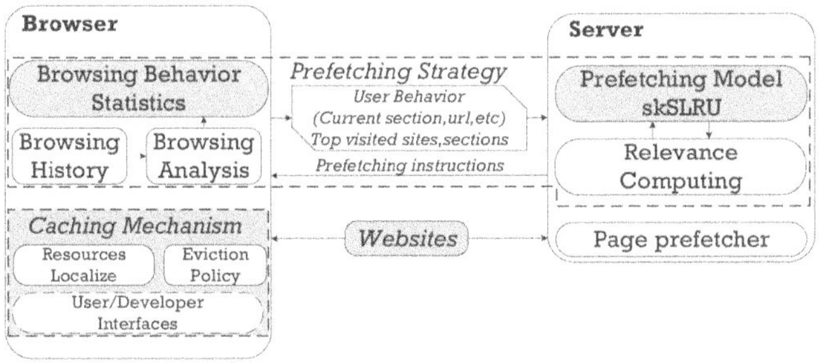

Figure 1: Architecture of the framework

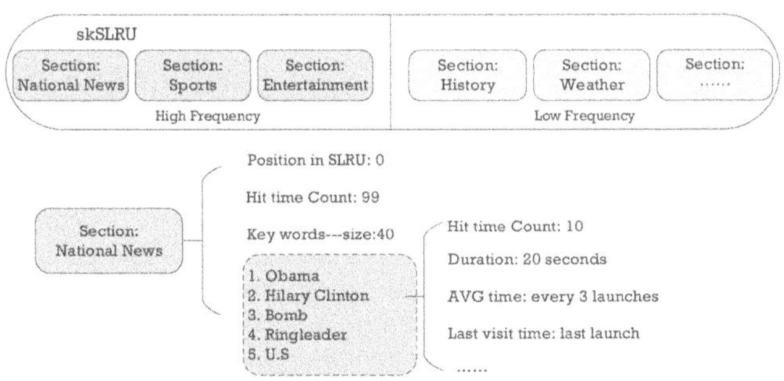

Figure 2: The skSLRU model

2.2 Prefetching Strategy

The prefetching strategy solves the problems of what to prefetch, when to prefetch and how many resources to fetch with corresponding solutions. In terms of what to prefetch, the solution is a combination of the local browsing behavior statistics and a prefetching model on the server, as shown in Fig. 1. As most websites are organized in a tree structure, starting from the homepage to a few sections like *sports* and *news*. Pages are updated all the time while the URL addresses of homepages and the index pages of sections remain unchanged. As a result, we compute the statistics in five time periods each day, i.e. 0:00-3:00, 6:00-10:00, 10:00-14:00, 14:00-18:00 and 18:00-0:00. And the visited websites in each period are ranked based on the visiting frequency. At the same time, via analysing the URL traces, we also get the top visited sections in each website. With the computed browser behavior statistics, the browser will inform the prefetching model on the server of which sites and sections are most likely to be visited at a specific time.

During the web browsing, the browser requests content prefetching instructions from skSLRU (section and keyword-based SLRU). As depicted in Fig. 2, this model is built on the basis of SLRU and each rectangle represents a frequently visited section. Sections in the "High Frequency" part are visited more recently and frequently, and less in "Low Frequency" part. This model receives a user's browsing behaviors from the browser including the sites and sections that a user is visiting or is likely to visit. In the example shown in Fig. 2, keywords like "Obama" and "Bomb" appear repeatedly in the visited pages, so we assume a user is interested in pages containing these words or other semantically related words. As shown in Fig. 3, these keywords can help us find the most relevant pages in the same section through the executing process of skSLRU. As a result, the browser gets the prefetching instructions from our server about which pages to fetch.

As for when and how many page resources to prefetch, we perform prefetching in parallel with user browsing and fetch resources with the consideration of user contexts and devices' status such as remaining power and network conditions. Existing mobile browsers do not make use of the time when people are reading or searching for interesting pages. According to our traces, people usually stay in a Web page for 20 seconds averagely, which is long enough to prefetch pages possibly to be visited later. In addition, the number of pages to prefetch depends not only on the network condition (e.g. WIFI or 3G/4G), but also on the battery status. In this work, resources are fetched when a WIFI connection is available or when a device is charged for power.

2.3 Caching Mechanism

Caching may not work well for mobile devices. As people tend to use the applications randomly, the memory space may already be recycled by "Garbage Collection" before a future visit. Even if the requested resources are in cache, 60% of them still send requests to the server for data freshness [6], and these requests cause extra latency. More importantly, it is known that mobile users are more sensitive to long Web page loading time than to data freshness. Hence we build a new caching mechanism relying on the following factors:

- 76% of the resources in a Web page are shared by at least another page in the same site [6].
- Homepages and section pages do not change too much during a day.
- JavaScript/CSS files which belong to the website remain unchanged for a long period of time. For example, in our experimental results, most files are not updated even for two months.

In our caching mechanism, resources fetched each time are cached separately. For example, resources like JavaScript and CSS which are unlikely to change and shared by most pages in the same website are stored in the ROM with a long lifecycle. And images belong to the CSS files which we find to be relatively large are fetched in a WIFI network gradually to save the data usage. Localizing these files is important to eliminate latency. Because when the html is being parsed, the requests of JavaScript/CSS files block the following processes and the Web page cannot be rendered out quickly. Resources like jpeg/png/html have a shorter lifecycle. For instance, as most pictures related to news in

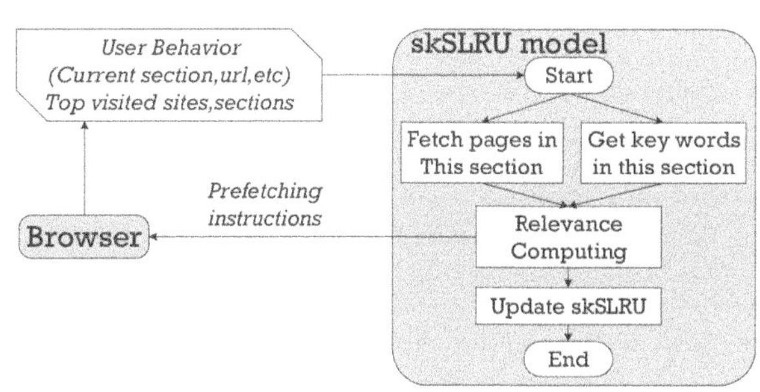

Figure 3: The executing process of skSLRU

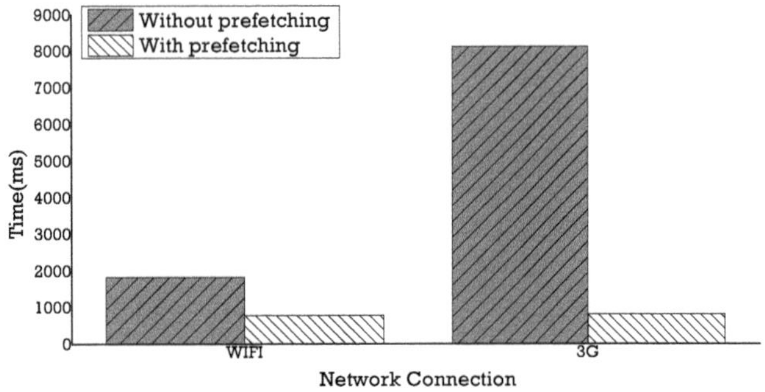

Figure 4: Processing time of rendering Web pages

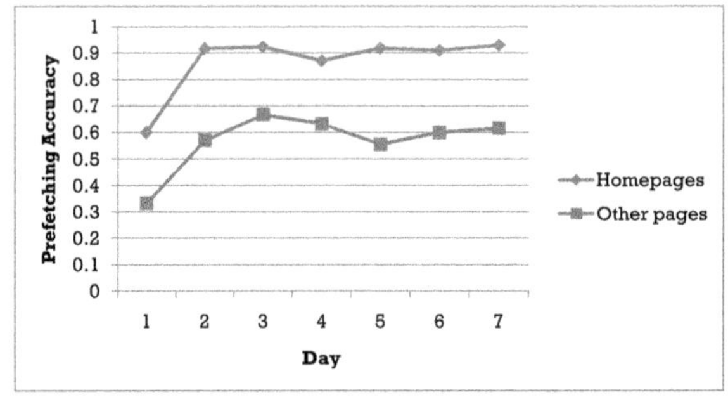

Figure 5: Accuracy of page prefetching during one week

the homepage stay the same through a day, these pictures will be evicted next day if they do not appear again. In fact, those pictures will hardly be visited later, thus evicting these useless images from memory is important. What's more, there are no revalidation requests for localized resources. As this caching mechanism bypasses the HTTP/1.1 protocol.

The mechanism also offers interfaces for website developers and mobile users. As most Web pages do not change too much, we allow users to set their own tolerance levels of Web page freshness for instant browsing. As for the developers, they can customize their own caching strategies to reduce latency on the browser side with a simple configuration file linked to their pages.

2.4 Implementation of the Framework

Our browser is developed based on Android WebView, but the framework we have implemented can be used not only for this browser, but also for a large portion of mobile applications which use WebView to display contents as well. The browser communicates with the skSLRU model on the server through a Web service.

3. EVALUATION RESULTS

We ask 15 students at Beihang University to use the implemented browser to browse Web contents with both WIFI or 3G Internet connections. And we collect the user browsing data for a month, starting from May 20 to June 20 in 2014. In this section, we present the obtained data to show the effectiveness of our framework. Fig. 4 shows the improvements of Web page loading time. It is satisfying to see the main contents of prefetched pages to be rendered out in less than one second. Users can use this framework whether online or offline. And even in the case of slow and unstable network conditions, our browser can load the requested Web pages in a surprisingly short period of time thanks to our smart prefetching strategy.

Fig. 5 depicts the prefetching accuracy of homepages and other pages with skSLRU, which shows 90% of the homepages and 60% of other pages are fetched before users' visiting. We also provide an interesting function in the prototype: the browser can highlight the prefetched pages' titles in the index pages. As a result, users can know which pages are already prefetched and stored locally, and they can read them online or offline. Users can also open the browser under a WIFI condition to get more offline Web contents they want to read.

4. CONCLUSIONS

Mobile users always expect instant Web browsing experience. In this work, we propose a framework for reducing Web page browsing latency, in which two techniques are involved. First, Web pages are prefetched based on the analysis of Web page content and user browsing behavior. Second, common resources of Web pages in a website are cached and reused in page loading. Besides, with the interfaces offered by this framework, the browsing experience can be personalized to better serve various mobile user requirements. A prototype of this framework has been implemented with Android WebView.

5. ACKNOWLEDGMENTS

This work was supported by National Natural Science Foundation of China (No.61370057), China 863 program (No. 2012AA011203), Beijing Nova Program(No. 2011022), A Foundation for the Author of National Excellent Doctoral Dissertation of PR China (No.201159) and the Program for New Century Excellent Talents in University.

6. REFERENCES

[1] Is the web getting faster? http://analytics.blogspot.com/2013/04/is-web-getting-faster.html.

[2] B. D. Higgins, J. Flinn, T. J. Giuli, B. Noble, C. Peplin, and D. Watson. Informed mobile prefetching. In *Proceedings of the 10th international conference on Mobile systems, applications, and services*, pages 155–168. ACM, 2012.

[3] D. Lymberopoulos, O. Riva, K. Strauss, A. Mittal, and A. Ntoulas. Pocketweb: instant web browsing for mobile devices. In *ACM SIGARCH Computer Architecture News*, volume 40, pages 1–12. ACM, 2012.

[4] H. Wang, M. Liu, Y. Guo, and X. Chen. Similarity-based web browser optimization. In *Proceedings of the 23rd international conference on World wide web*, pages 575–584. International World Wide Web Conferences Steering Committee, 2014.

[5] Z. Wang, F. X. Lin, L. Zhong, and M. Chishtie. Why are web browsers slow on smartphones? In *Proceedings of the 12th Workshop on Mobile Computing Systems and Applications*, pages 91–96. ACM, 2011.

[6] Z. Wang, F. X. Lin, L. Zhong, and M. Chishtie. How far can client-only solutions go for mobile browser speed? In *Proceedings of the 21st international conference on World Wide Web*, pages 31–40. ACM, 2012.

Poster: Adaptive Flow Control for Wireless Serial Bus using Wi-Fi Transmission Opportunity

Woo-Sung Jung, Keun-Woo Lim, Young-Bae Ko
Department of Computer Engineering, Ajou University
Suwon, Republic of Korea
woosung@uns.ajou.ac.kr, kwlim27@uns.ajou.ac.kr, youngko@ajou.ac.kr

ABSTRACT
This poster proposes an adaptive flow control scheme for reliable packet delivery of Universal Serial Bus (USB) services when they are transmitted through wireless medium. In the future, USB can be utilized with the Wi-Fi technology to provide Wi-Fi USB (WSB). However, the data transmission of Wi-Fi and USB are asynchronous due to their different Medium Access Control (MAC) characteristics, which may result in buffer overflow. To prevent buffer overflow, we propose an adaptive flow control scheme that can select between the various transmission speeds of USB to match with the bandwidth provided by the Wi-Fi layer. Preliminary results of the proposed scheme evaluated via the NS-3 shows that the packet delivery ratio of USB data can be substantially increased, thus providing better USB reliability.

Categories and Subject Descriptors
C.2.1 [**Computer Systems Organization**]: Network Architecture and Design – *Wireless Communication*

Keywords
Wireless Serial Bus; Wi-Fi P2P; Flow Control

1. INTRODUCTION
The technology of WSB, where the wired transmission medium of USB adapter is replaced using Wi-Fi MAC, is becoming a prominent future technology for various wireless multimedia and file transfer services. Through WSB, many existing USB applications can be easily utilized in handheld devices without any significant modifications to the existing standards. Furthermore, unlike the existing Wireless USB standard that was designed to utilize the defunct Ultra Wide Band (UWB) bandwidth for wireless support of USB data transmission, the WSB can utilize the globally used IEEE 802.11 [1] to provide high transmission rates and reliable data forwarding.

The biggest issue that WSB currently faces is the asynchronous-ness between the IEEE 802.11 MAC and USB. Conventional Wi-Fi implementations on current embedded devices utilize a contention-based medium access approach, where data are transmitted only when the wireless medium is thought to be vacant. Therefore, wireless medium cannot always be guaranteed for exclusive usage. On the other hand, USB transmission protocol guarantees and allocates specific bandwidth to different types of service applications, and transmits them in a time-division approach. Therefore, due to the differences, buffer overflow may occur, especially when the transmission rate of USB exceeds that of Wi-Fi. This is because the USB protocol controls its data transmission rate only according to the status of other device's USB layer, regardless of the conditions of Wi-Fi MAC. Standards such as Wireless Serial Extension (WSE) [2] present the concept of temporary buffer storage between the Wi-Fi and USB to alleviate this problem, but cannot be the ultimate solution. Furthermore, due to device constraints and design complexity, some embedded devices may not be able to utilize the WSE.

In this work, we propose a lightweight WSB architecture where the USB transmission protocol and Wi-Fi MAC are directly cooperative with each other to match the transmission behavior and prevent buffer overflow in the network. In particular, we utilize the Transmission Opportunity (TxOP) parameter in the Wi-Fi, which is utilized to temporarily guarantee the wireless medium for more bandwidth. When the TxOP is enabled, the transmission rate of USB is increased to quickly transmit its data. On the other hand, when it becomes disabled, USB transmission rate is decreased to prevent buffer overflow. To adjust the USB transmission rate, different standards of USB can be utilized in between data transmission. Preliminary analysis of our proposed scheme is done using NS-3 simulator, and shows that it can greatly outperform conventional USB data transmission methods.

2. BACKGROUND
From a USB device, data such as asynchronous, bulk, and interrupt data can be generated [3]. According to the data type, USB data transmission protocol can allocate different bandwidth and priority, and transmit them according to the allocation. However, as conventional USB utilizes wired medium, these data are almost always

MobiCom'14, September 7-11, 2014, Maui, Hawaii, USA.
ACM 978-1-4503-2783-1/14/09.
http://dx.doi.org/10.1145/2639108.2642900

guaranteed of the bandwidth, and even transmitted without contention. Depending on the USB standard, the transmission rate of USB can differ. For instance in USB 1.1, full-speed of 12 Mbps can be supported, whereas in USB 2.0 high-speed can be added, which can provide up to 480 Mbps. USB 3.0 [4] can further increase to super-speed, with speed up to 5 Gbps. In the traditional USB, if a speed is configured upon enumeration of two devices, the rate does not change afterwards. Full-speed and High-speed utilize the same port for data transmission, while USB 3.0 super-speed requires another exclusive port for its connection. Note that, in the wireless case, full-speed and high-speed can be toggled as it does not require configuration as in the wired settings.

The Wi-Fi, on the other hand, can guarantee a certain amount of bandwidth by using TxOP. TxOP, as defined in the 802.11 standard, can guarantee exclusive usage of the bandwidth for high-priority data. In the case of data with Video access category (AC_VI), 3.008 ms of TxOP is guaranteed, while Voice access category (AC_VO) guarantees 1.504 ms. The TxOP time is gained when a data frame with the corresponding access category wins the contention for the wireless medium and transmitted.

3. THE PROPOSED SCHEME

The overall architecture of the proposed scheme can be seen in Figure 1, where USB device and its transmission protocol is directly linked with the Wi-Fi MAC without utilizing any middle layer or adaptation layer such as WSE. Through this architecture, the implementation of such environment can be less complex and ideal for hardware-constraint devices. We assume that the device is a mobile device with single Wi-Fi 802.11n without MIMO capabilities, with speed up to 65 Mbps. The initial USB speed is Full-speed, as static High-speed will easily congest the Wi-Fi MAC and cause buffer overflow.

As shown in the figure, two modules are newly implemented in the USB device: *Wi-Fi TxOP handler module* and *Flow Control Toggle module*. The Wi-Fi TxOP handler module will constantly check the Wi-Fi MAC to sense whether the TxOP time becomes enabled from an AC_VO or AC_VI data frame transmission. When TxOP time becomes enabled, the following equation is used to calculate t_{remt} which is the possible remaining time of TxOP after all data in the AC_VO or AC_VI queue is transmitted:

$$t_{remt} = t_{txop} - \frac{d_q}{x/t_x} \quad (1)$$

,where x is the amount of bytes transmitted in the last TxOP time, t_x is the amount of time consumed to transmit data in the last TxOP time, t_{txop} is the default TxOP time for specific access category, and d_q is the current amount of bytes remaining in the Wi-Fi queue of either AC_VO or AC_VI. Therefore, the equation (1) can estimate the time

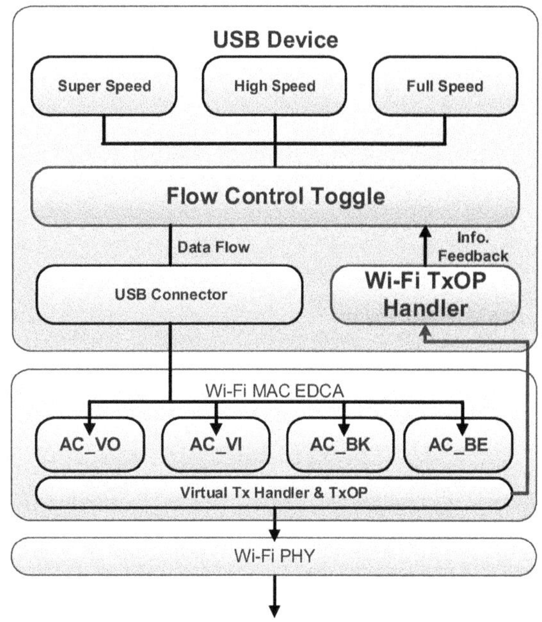

Figure 1. Architecture of the Proposed Scheme

that will be required to transmit all the data in the current queue, and also the time that will be remaining after all data are transmitted. If $t_{remt} < 0$, this indicates that the current TxOP time is not enough to transmit all the data in the queue. However, if $t_{remt} > 0$, then the remaining TxOP time can be utilized to transmit the data with bandwidth guarantee. Therefore, in this case, the Wi-Fi TxOP handler module notifies the Flow Control Toggle module to speed up its data transmission. Upon receiving the notification, the Flow Control Toggle module switches the initial data transmission rate of Full-speed to High-speed. This will enable the USB data transmission to speed up and instantly transmit more data towards the Wi-Fi MAC. The High-speed is maintained until Wi-Fi TxOP Handler indicates that the TxOP time is ended, in which case the speed is reverted back to Full-speed.

In the switching process, maintaining the maximum 480 Mbps of High-speed may become too fast for Wi-Fi MAC to handle. Therefore, the speed-up process must be done in a more passive manner. This can be achieved through the different speed rates of USB 2.0. As noted in [3], the speed of data transmission in High-speed can be controlled upon modifying the data payload of each USB frame. Whereas data payload of 512 bytes can guarantee about 400 Mbps, payload of 1 byte does 8 Mbps, with middle levels of 2, 4, 8, 16, 32, 64, 128, and 256 bytes. To toggle these data payload levels, the current d_q and d_{q-1}, the remaining bytes of last TxOP can be compared. If $d_q > d_{q-1}$, then this indicates that the queue level has increased and congestion may occur. Therefore, USB data payload level is decreased by one. On the other hand, only when $d_q = 0$, the USB data payload level is increased by one to speed up the data transmission.

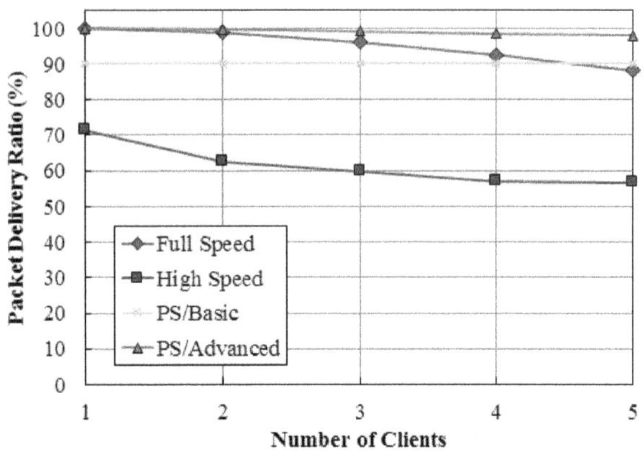

(a) Packet delivery ratio

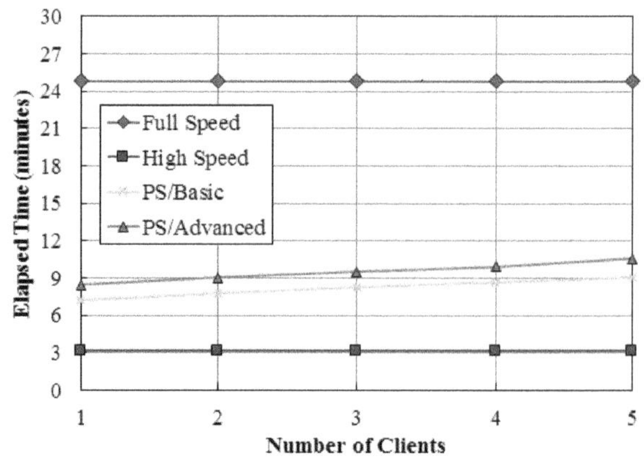

(b) Elapsed time for 1 GB bulk transmission

Figure 2. Performance evaluation of the proposed scheme

In the case when better MAC protocols are used, for instance 802.11n with MIMO capabilities or 802.11ac [5], the Full-speed does not need to be used as 802.11n MIMO can support up to 600 Mbps and 802.11ac more than 1 Gbps. In this case, Super-speed of USB 3.0 (5 Gbps) can be used instead. However, as stated above, Super-speed of USB 3.0 cannot be toggled with USB 1.0 or USB 2.0 due to different connector/port usage. Instead, Super-speed can toggle its speed using a parameter defined in the USB 3.0 standard called *NumP*, which is a value between 1 and 15 to indicate how many data frames can be transmitted in a burst manner. Therefore, adjusting between values from 1 to 15 can allow Super-speed to control its transmission rate depending on the TxOP status and prevent buffer overflow.

4. EVALUATION AND FUTURE WORKS

The preliminary analysis of our scheme is conducted using NS-3. In the simulation environment, one wireless USB dock is considered with increasing number of USB devices with each transmitting one 1 GB bulk data. Each USB device is equipped with one 802.11n interface having no MIMO, therefore providing up to 65 Mbps. The base QoS used is AC_VI, which can provide 3.008 ms TxOP every time it wins medium contention. For the USB standard, USB 2.0 is used and measured. For higher-speed Wi-Fi technologies, USB 3.0 can also be used, but here we omit these results due to space constraints. For performance comparison, packet delivery ratio and elapsed time for data transmission is measured. The elapsed time for data transmission denotes the average time taken to transmit 1 GB bulk data by each device. Four methods of USB data transmission are compared; static Full-speed, static High-speed, basic proposed scheme, and advanced proposed scheme. In the basic proposed scheme, the speed adjusting in High-speed is statically configured to maximum speed. In the advanced proposed scheme, the High-speed toggle is passively controlled depending on the status of Wi-Fi queue level. The simulation results are shown in Figure 2.

As seen from Figure 2 (a), static High-speed causes much buffer overflow, resulting in high data loss. The basic proposed scheme can alleviate this problem by adjusting between High-speed and Full-speed. However, as High-speed is always configured to maximum speed, overflow may still occur. The advanced proposed scheme can guarantee the highest performance as it can monitor the level of Wi-Fi MAC queue and prevent buffer overflow. In Figure 2 (b), High-Speed transmission actually guarantees the lowest elapsed time. However, as the packet delivery ratio is low, the transmitted data is mostly broken, making the short elapsed time meaningless. Even though the proposed schemes consume little more time than High-speed, this is at a cost of preventing buffer overflow and is acceptable as it is much faster than Full-speed.

Through the control of WSB data transmission when used in conjunction with Wi-Fi, we could solve the buffer overflow problem and guarantee higher reliability of WSB services. For future work, we will design detailed mechanisms for USB 3.0 in conjunction with advanced Wi-Fi protocols such as 802.11ac and 802.11 ad. Furthermore, we will design our protocol using actual smartphone testbeds and conduct more realistic experiments.

5. ACKNOWLEDGMENTS

This work is supported by the National Research Foundation of Korea (NRF) grant funded by the Korea government (MEST) (2012-003573)

6. REFERENCES

[1] IEEE P802.11™-2012, Part 11: Wireless LAN medium access control (MAC) and physical layer (PHY) specifications, IEEE, 2012.

[2] WGA Specification, WiGig Serial Extension (WSE) Specification version 1.0, Dec. 2011.

[3] Universal Serial Bus Specification, Rev. 2.0 Apr. 2000.

[4] Universal Serial Bus Specification, Rev. 3.0 Aug. 2008

Poster: SensingKit – A Multi-Platform Mobile Sensing Framework for Large-Scale Experiments

Kleomenis Katevas†, Hamed Haddadi†◇, Laurissa Tokarchuk†
†Queen Mary University of London, ◇Qatar Computing Research Institute
{k.katevas, hamed.haddadi, laurissa.tokarchuk}@qmul.ac.uk

ABSTRACT

With the rapid rise in variety of available smartphones today and their rich sensing capabilities, there is an increasing interest in using mobile sensing in large-scale experiments and commercial applications. Motivated by the lack of a universal, multi-platform library, in this paper we present *SensingKit*, an efficient, open-source, client-server system that supports both iOS and Android mobile devices. SensingKit is capable of continuous sensing the device's motion (Accelerometer, Gyroscope, Magnetometer), location (GPS) and proximity to other smartphones (Bluetooth Smart). The data are temporarily saved to the device's memory and transmitted to a server for further analysis over any Internet connection. We believe that this platform will be beneficial to all researchers and developers who need to perform mobile sensing in their applications and experiments.

Categories and Subject Descriptors

C.4 [**Performance of Systems**]: Measurement techniques; D.2.13 [**Software Engineering**]: Reusable Software—*Reusable libraries*

General Terms

Experimentation, Measurement, Performance

Keywords

Mobile sensing, Spatio-temporal data, Motion data, iOS, Android

1. INTRODUCTION

The ubiquity of smartphones as well as the variety of their onboard sensors have enabled the automated acquisition of large scale data, inspiring a wealth of research opportunities. Mobile operating systems such as Android and iOS provide application programming interfaces (APIs) to access these sensors. Lane et al. [2] in a recent survey paper discussed the importance of continuous sensing among different mobile platforms. Various mobile sensing frameworks have been designed that provide continuous sensing, like MobiSens [4], EmotionSense [3] and Funf [1]. However, these platforms are currently limited to work on Android or Nokia Maemo phones, limiting the sampling space of users participating in different studies. Since Android and iOS are the two main players in the mobile ecosystem, there is a clear need for supporting continuous sensing in these two mobile environments.

In this work, we present an early prototype of SensingKit, a new mobile sensing framework compatible with iOS and Android devices. SensingKit enables capturing motion (Accelerometer, Gyroscope and Magnetometer), location (GPS) and proximity (Bluetooth Smart) data and transmitting them to a server over any Internet connection. Since the two operating systems are equipped with sensor fusion techniques, both the raw measurements, and fussed data like Linear Acceleration, Gravity and Rotation are supported. Furthermore, SensingKit can also be configured to capture user's natively-labelled activity in supported devices, classified as *standing*, *walking*, *running*, *driving* in iOS, with the addition of *cycling* in Android.

To achieve this, we have developed two open-source libraries, *SensingKit-iOS* and *SensingKit-Android*, that researchers can include into their custom made applications with only a few lines of code. In addition, a server framework has been developed, referred to as the *SensingServer*, which is responsible for receiving the data, synchronising them and finally exporting them into CSV or JSON format.

Beside the multi-platform characteristic, SensingKit has some unique features that are not available in other sensing libraries. It supports the Bluetooth Smart (4.0) specification for capturing the proximity between devices, a feature that has significantly reduced power consumption and highest sampling rate compared to the classic Bluetooth. Furthermore, in order to avoid timing issues when the user, or even when the device itself changes the system time, the timing in the sensor measurements depends on the device's CPU time base register rather than the system's clock. In some modern devices like the iPhone 5S and Nexus S5 that are equipped with a motion co-processor, the library is capable of using the processor's activity recognition, having only a minimum affect on the device's battery life. Finally, the server framework is equipped with a plug-in architecture that can automate some of the usual data processing before the extraction (e.g., perform data interpolation, produce magnitude vector, etc).

MobiCom'14, MobiCom'14, Sep 07-11 2014, Maui, HI, USA
ACM 978-1-4503-2783-1/14/09.
http://dx.doi.org/10.1145/2639108.2642910.

Our objective in this work is to provide an easy-to-use sensing framework that developers and researchers can use to provide continuous sensing in iOS and Android applications. In Section 2, we present the System Architecture and technical details of the framework. The system was evaluated, as reported in Section 3, by measuring the battery consumption of SensingKit running on three mobile phones. In Section 4 we present the conclusions and discuss the future research in this space.

2. PLATFORM ARCHITECTURE

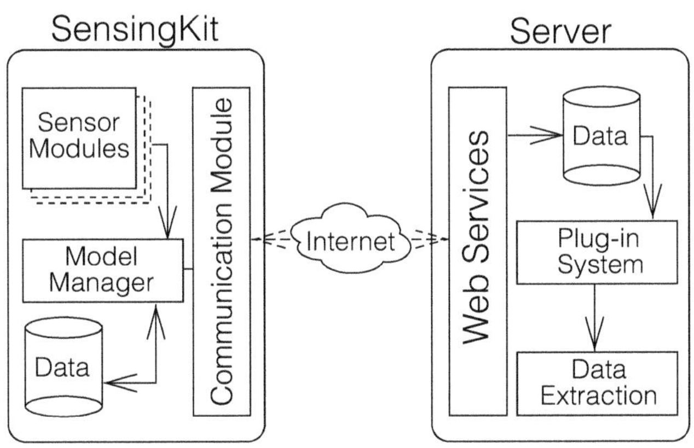

Figure 1: SensingKit System Architecture

SensingKit is a client/server system, consisting of two separate software frameworks: the *client library*, located in the users mobile devices and the *server framework*. Figure 1 gives an overview of the system architecture.

Client libraries for Android and iOS

SensingKit is a modular mobile framework developed in the native programming language of each platform (Java for the Android and Objective-C for the iOS version). It supports mobile devices running iOS v7.0 and Android v2.3.3[1] and above.

For every sensing category, a sensing module exists in SensingKit. Table 1 presents the available sensing modules of the framework. It is important to mention that due to the modular design of this library, it is easy to develop a new module and extend its sensing capabilities.

Table 1: Modules of SensingKit

Module	Information sensed
Motion	Linear Acceleration, Gravity, Rotation, Activity Classification.*
Location	Outdoor location using GPS sensor.
Proximity	Proximity sensing using Bluetooth Smart (4.0).
Battery	Power consumption of the device.

*Raw data from the 3-axis Accelerometer, Gyroscope and Magnetometer sensors are also provided.

For proximity sensing, SensingKit uses the new Bluetooth Smart (4.0) proximity profile. This profile allows to broadcast a device's presence, scan for other devices and estimate the distance between them. Bluetooth Smart is only fully supported in the latest Android *L* mobile operating system. Android 4.3 devices are only limited to scan and connect to other devices (*Observer and Central mode*) and not to advertise its presence to the nearby devices (*Peripheral mode*).

The library collects the data from the sensing modules and saves them to the device's memory using ModelManager module. When a Wi-Fi connection is available it submits them on the server through CommunicationManager. If the data remain to the memory for longer than 24 hours, it will try to submit them over a Cellular network.

Server platform

The server platform is built using the Python programming language. It is responsible for collecting the data captured from a client app, over an Internet connection. It consists of three main components: the *web-services*, the *plug-in system* and the *data extraction module*.

The web-services component is responsible for providing the appropriate communication methods to the client libraries. It provides methods for assigning a unique identification to each client, for sending the server's time so that the data can easily be synchronised later, and finally, for receiving the collected data.

The plug-in system provides a Python interface for writing custom plug-ins that pre-process the data before extraction. This is useful for the researcher as it can perform some initial automated data processing. The mandatory data-sync plug-in is pre-installed and processes the data so that they have the same timing with minimum delay between devices. Further optional plug-ins such as the *interpolation* and *magnitude* are also available.

Finally, the data extraction module is used to extract the data in various formats such as JSON and CSV.

3. USE-CASE DEMONSTRATION

In order to demonstrate a sample use of our sensing platform, we measured the battery life performance while using SensingKit in three mobile devices: an iPhone 5S running iOS 7.1.2, a Google Nexus 4 running Android KitKat 4.4.4 and a Samsung Galaxy S2 running Android Jelly Bean 4.1.2. All devices were set into Flight Mode, having Wi-Fi and Cellular connectivity disabled. No application or process rather than SensingKit was running in the background. Since Galaxy S2 devices are not equipped with a Bluetooth Smart (4.0) radio, proximity sensing was not possible with that device. Finally, due to limitations of the current Android platform (Android KitKat 4.4.4) the Nexus 4 device was only able to scan for other devices and not to broadcast its presence. Table 2 shows the specifications of each device, including the highest sampling rate that is supported.

Figure 2 shows the energy consumption of SensingKit running for 24 hours on the three mobile devices described above. For each device, we show the consumption of the library while sensing motion, proximity and battery levels. In addition, we visualise the library running in "idle" mode, when it only senses the battery levels. Due to limitations in the iOS platform, it is only possible to read the iPhone's battery level with a 5% resolution whereas in Android the resolution is 1%.

The results show that the Galaxy S2 lasted for 13.1 hours while capturing motion in 100Hz but not proximity. The

[1]Android *L*/iOS 7 and Bluetooth 4.0 radio is required to use Bluetooth Smart proximity sensing.

Table 2: Device Specification

Device	Op. System	Processor	Memory	Battery	Bluetooth	Max Sampling
iPhone 5S	iOS 7.1.2	1.3 Ghz Dual-core	1GB	1560 mAh	4.0	100Hz
Nexus 4	KitKat 4.4.4	1.5 Ghz Quad-core	2GB	2100 mAh	4.0	200Hz
Galaxy S2	Jelly Bean 4.1.2	1.2 Ghz Dual-core	1GB	1650 mAh	3.0+HS	100Hz

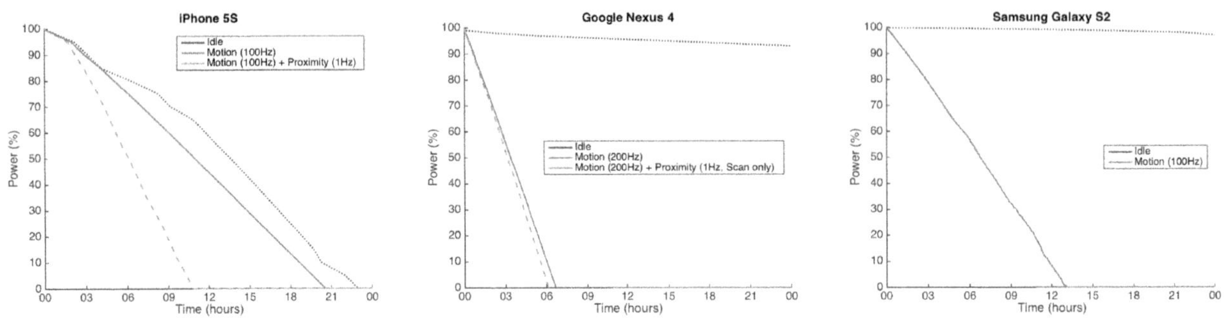

(a) (b) (c)

Figure 2: Battery consumption of SensingKit running on an iPhone 5S, Google Nexus 4 and Samsung Galaxy S2 smartphone.

iPhone 5S was capturing motion in the same sampling rate (100Hz), and lasted 11.5 hours with proximity sensing enabled (1Hz) and 20.3 hours with proximity sensing disabled. Finally, the Nexus 4 device was measuring motion with double the sampling rate of the other two devices (200Hz), and lasted 6.1 hours with proximity sensing enabled (1Hz) and 6.4 hours with proximity sensing disabled.

The effect of SensingKit in the iPhone's battery life is quite noticeable when it runs in "idle" mode, as the library keeps the device's CPU usage to 6-7%, just for monitoring the battery in the background. In addition, proximity sensing also has an impact on the battery life, showing a 43.3% decrease on the iPhone 5S whereas in the case of Nexus 4, the device only works in *Observer mode* and the battery slightly decreases by 4.7%.

It is important to mention that Figure 2 only represents the battery consumption of the specific mobile devices listed in Table 2 and should not be viewed as a comparison between the three devices.

4. CONCLUSIONS AND FUTURE WORK

In this work, we have presented an early implementation of a continuous sensing system that works in both Android and iOS environments. A first prototype of this system has already been developed and is being used in related crowdsensing experiments. We plan to continue the development of this framework, extend its sensing capabilities, evaluate it and release it to the public in open-source in the near future. We believe that this work will be beneficial for researchers willing to conduct large-scale experiments using mobile sensing.

More information about SensingKit as well as the complete source-code will be made available on www.sensingkit.org.

5. ACKNOWLEDGEMENTS

This work is supported by funding from the UK Defence Science and Technology Laboratory.

6. REFERENCES

[1] N. Aharony, W. Pan, C. Ip, I. Khayal, and A. Pentland. Social fMRI: Investigating and shaping social mechanisms in the real world. *Pervasive and Mobile Computing*, 7(6):643–659, 2011.

[2] N. D. Lane, E. Miluzzo, H. Lu, D. Peebles, T. Choudhury, and A. T. Campbell. A survey of mobile phone sensing. *Communications Magazine, IEEE*, 48(9):140–150, 2010.

[3] K. K. Rachuri, M. Musolesi, C. Mascolo, P. J. Rentfrow, C. Longworth, and A. Aucinas. EmotionSense: a mobile phones based adaptive platform for experimental social psychology research. In *Ubicomp '10: Proceedings of the 12th ACM international conference on Ubiquitous computing*, page 281, New York, USA, Sept. 2010.

[4] P. Wu, J. Zhu, and J. Y. Zhang. MobiSens: A Versatile Mobile Sensing Platform for Real-World Applications. *Mobile Networks and Applications*, 18(1):60–80, Nov. 2012.

Poster: Locating RFID Tags by Rotation

Tao Li†, Wei Xi†, Shaojie Tang‡, Jinsong Han†, Jizhong Zhao†, Xiang-Yang Li§, Zhi Wang†, Zhiping Jiang†
†Department of Computer Science and Technology, Xi'an Jiaotong University, China
‡School of Management, The University of Texas at Dallas, USA
§Department of Computer Science, Illinois Institute of Technology, USA
{taolitx, weixi.cs}@gmail.com, shaojie.tang@utdallas.edu, {hanjinsong, zjz}@mail.xjtu.edu.cn, xli@cs.iit.edu, {wangzhi.xjtu, jiangzp.cs}@gmail.com

ABSTRACT

Locating objects labeled with RFID tags is an important issue which should be addressed in many applications, such as warehouse management, goods management in supermarket and finding of lost objects. Some existing works use large numbers of reference tags which involve lots of manpower to deploy them. Others achieve high accuracy, but rely on sophisticated equipments which are hardly available in large scale to the industry. This work exploits the radiation pattern of existing directional panel antenna which is steerable and derives angle-of-arrival(AoA) information from the energy reflected by the target tag when the antenna is rotating. We use Commercial Off-The-Shelf (COTS) equipments and get median position accuracy of 29cm in our preliminary experiment.

Categories and Subject Descriptors

C2.2 [**Computer Systems Organization**]: Computer-Communications Networks

Keywords

RFID; Tag; Localization; Antenna; Radiation pattern

1. INTRODUCTION

Radio Frequency IDentification (RFID) technology has attracted much attention from both the industry and research communities due to its low cost and ease of deployment. With RFID tags, large numbers of objects, such as goods in the supermarket, different kinds of cards and car keys, can be identified. In addition to identifying, locating these identified objects becomes an important issue, which can be applied in warehouse management, finding lost mails in the sortation centre and etc.

Many works have been done to locate RFID tags. Fingerprint-based approaches[5] suffer from multipath and non-line-of sight effect. Differences in orientation and antenna gain also affect the accuracy [2]. PinIt[6] uses a moving antenna to collect multipath profiles of target tags and compare them with references. Backloc[3] derives distance difference from the phase difference and get high accuracy, but this method cannot work in multipath environment and the feasible region is limited. Sherlock[4] rotates antennas as us, but relies on accurate estimation of the edge of radiation pattern which is impractical in multipath environment. Also, it takes tens minutes to finish the localization.

MobiCom'14, September 7-11, 2014, Maui, Hawaii, USA

ACM 978-1-4503-2783-1/14/09.
http://dx.doi.org/10.1145/2639108.2642907

This work makes attempts to exploit the radiation pattern of existing directional panel antennas which are commercially available and most commonly used. As illustrated in Figure 1(b), the directional panel antenna radiates different amounts of energy to different directions. That is, the energy harvested by tags is related to their relative direction (not just distance) to the antenna, so the energy reflected(sensed by antenna). We rotate the antenna around a fixed axis to steer its beam across 360° and collect RSS values reflected by the target tag at the same time. We do not care the exact RSS values sensed by the antenna and just pay attention to the variation trend of the values when the antenna is rotating. As a result, we can concentrate on the influence of directions instead of distance relative to the antenna. We then derive angle-of-arrival(AoA) information of reflected signal from the series of RSS values. In previous works, AoA information tends to be computed with sophisticated antenna array which is only available in laboratory[7]. This work intends to use COTS equipment and get median angle estimation accuracy of $3.x°$.

2. PRELIMINARY

To reduce power waste and focus radiation on the intended direction, RFID reader system tends to adopt directional antenna. As an example, Figure 1(a) shows the radiation pattern of a directional panel antenna. For any direction d relative to the centre of the antenna, the distance L to the pattern surface indicates the power density in that direction[1]. To show more clearly the power gain diversity of different directions, we can extract slices of the radiation pattern above in planes that pass through symmetry axes of the antenna. Figure 1(b) shows such 2-D pattern. We can observe that the gain reaches the maximum in the direction vertical to the antenna plane(the center of the beam) and decrease gradually to the two sides. Also, the 2-D radiation pattern is almost symmetric in the front side of the antenna. Finally, the gain changes little with angle in the centre of the beam and we call it the stability of the gain.

Experiments have verified the above observations. Figure 1(c) illustrates the RSS values sampled every 15 degrees when the antenna is rotating in a ideal environment. The RSS values show a pattern similar to the 2-D radiation pattern of antenna in Figure 1(b). Originally, the tag is 0° relative to antenna plane. First, we can see that the received RSS gets maximum at 90° when the tag is in the center of the beam. That is, when the antenna plane is directly facing the tag, the tag harvests more energy and then reflects more. Second, the pattern is almost symmetric as Figure 1(b). Third, the RSS values show the stability as the gain in the radiation pattern when the tag is near the centre of the beam. The paper adopts these observations as basic ideas to estimate tags' direction relative to the antenna.

3. ANTENNAROTATION SYSTEM

Our AntennaRotation System adopts AoA-based positioning methods and use two *steerable antennas* connected to one reader. The two antennas estimate the angles separately and then combine the information to calculate the locations of target tags. We steer the antenna beam across 360° with a user defined original

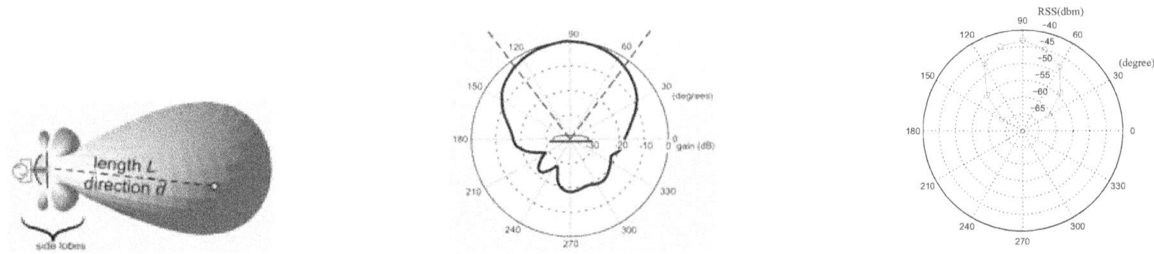

(a) (b) (c)

Figure 1: (a) is a pseudo-3D radiation pattern for a directional antenna. (b) is an example of radiation pattern in the horizontal plane for a commercial directional panel antenna. (c) is the sensed RSS from a single tag by a steerable antenna.

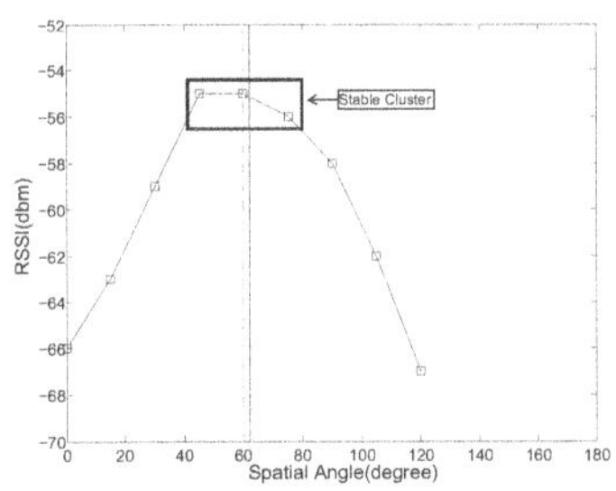

Figure 2: The RSSI trend of a tag. The red dashed line is the estimated direction and the black line is the actual direction of the tag

state(0 degree) and note down the sensed RSS every 15°. In the first subsection, we discuss how to acquire the tag's direction relative to the antenna in normal environment where multipath is rich, but the line-of-sight exists. In second subsection, we put attention to non-line-of-sight scenario where the multipath signal is stronger than line-of-sight signal.

3.1 Angle-of-Arrival Acquisition

Because of the multipath effect and the RSS fluctuation, the reflected RSSI sensed by the antenna may not reach the maximum when the tag is in the center of the beam. Also, the received RSS pattern may not show perfect symmetry. However, the *stability* remains in most of the scenarios and can be used to decide tag's direction relative to the antenna. To measure the stability of the RSS reflected by a tag when the antenna steers its beam to a particular direction, we define the Two-side RSS Difference(TRD) as follows:

$$TRD_d = |RSSI_d - RSSI_{d-1}| + |RSSI_d - RSSI_{d+1}|$$

where d is the direction to which the antenna steers the beam. We compute the TRDs of all the steering directions and then choose the most stable one(with minimum TRD). To reduce error, we construct a *stable cluster* consisting of consecutive directions with $TRD < M$(M is a user defined threshold). We first add the most stable direction to the cluster and search for directions within the threshold along the two sides of new added direction. We iteratively add new directions until meeting a direction out of the threshold. We then compute the average of these direction angles as a estimation of the target tag's direction(angle-of-arrival). Algorithm 1 describes the process in detail. Figure 2 shows the estimated direction in red dashed line.

3.2 Mitigating Non-Line of Sight

Method discussed above works well in the environment where multipath is not heavy. However, when the line-of-sight between the target tag and antenna is blocked, signals reflected from ambient objects such as walls may be stronger than the line-of-sight

Algorithm 1 Accurate Angle Acquisition

Input:
The 24 RSS samples sensed every 15° in 0 – 360°: $RSSI_0, RSSI_1, ..., RSSI_{23}$;

Output:
The target tag's direction relative to the antenna, D;

1: Calculate the TRD for every direction and then we get $TRD_0, TRD_1, ..., TRD_{23}$;
2: Find the direction D_{min} with minimum TRD;
3: Add D_{min} to the stable cluster S ;
4: Search for the two adjacent directions of D_{min} : D_{min-1} and D_{min+1}. If they exist and the $TRDs < M$, then add the direction to S, or stop searching in that side;
5: Iteratively search and add the newly added direction's adjacent directions to S until their $ARDs \nless M$;
6: Calculate the average angle D_{ave} of the directions in S
7: **return** D_{ave};

ones causing large error. Figure 4 illustrates this scenario and Figure 3(a) shows the collected RSS data from the desired tag. The estimated angle from the data shows a large shift to the wall and the error is up to 26° which is unacceptable to the application. In such scenario, we introduce a small number of reference tags to help the target tag to find its correct direction.

When the antenna steers its beam across 360°, energy the tag can harvests changes dramatically. Now we explain that the variation of RSSI sensed by the rotating antenna can largely reflects the tag's position relative to the antenna. First, when the tag is in the beam of the antenna, it can harvest energy or it can harvest little. Also, the tag can harvest different amount of energy in different regions of the beam. The tag tends to harvest more energy when it is near the center of the beam and less when it is far away. Furthermore, the signal between tags in different position and the antenna undergoes different reflection and obstruction when the antenna is rotating. Adjacent tags tends to be located in adjacent parts of the beam and undergo similar multipath interference and obstruction. For example, Figure 3(b) shows the RSS sensed from a reference tag 15cm apart from the target tag in Figure 4. We can see that the RSS sensed from the two tags undergoes similar fluctuation and the estimated directions shift to wall side together.

How to measure the similarity between RSS trends of signal responded by tags is the central issue. Note that the measurement should not be affected by the differences of tags' antenna gain which cause large matching error as the traditional fingerprint-based method. Given the vector **RSSI** of RSS sensed by the rotating antenna, we calculate Forward RSS Difference(FRD)

$$FRD_d = RSSI_{d+1} - RSSI_d$$

where d is the direction to which the antenna steers the beam. Figure 3(c) illustrates the RSS differences of the two adjacent tags in Figure 4. We can see that the two differences are similar except that target tag fluctuates more drastically than the refer-

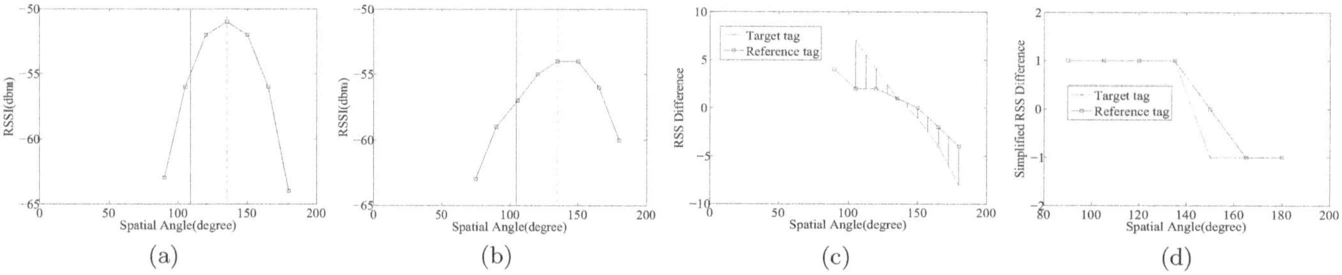

Figure 3: (a)(b) is the data collected from the target and reference tags respectively in Figure 4. (c) is the difference of RSS trend sensed from the two tags in Figure 4. (d) is the simplified RSS difference of the two tags.

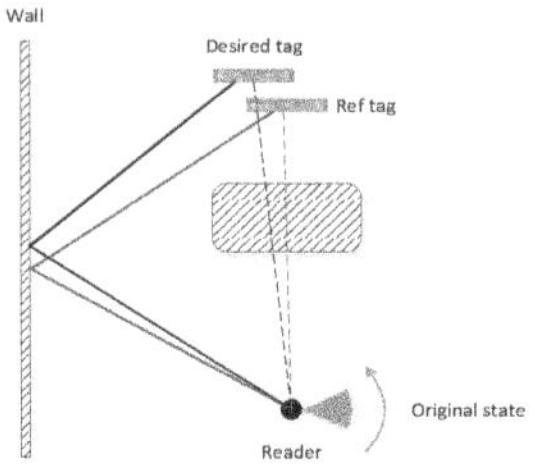

Figure 4

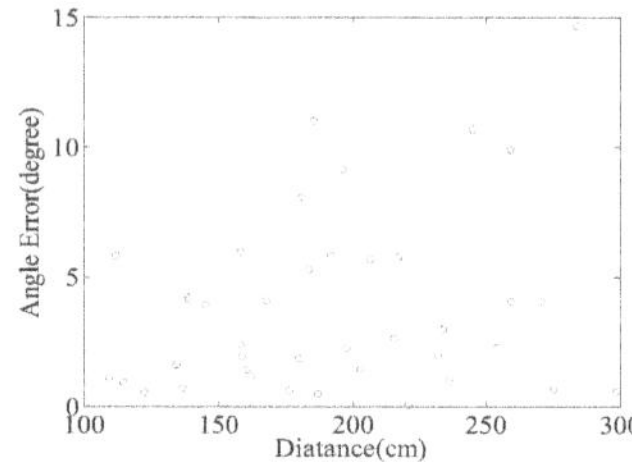

Figure 5

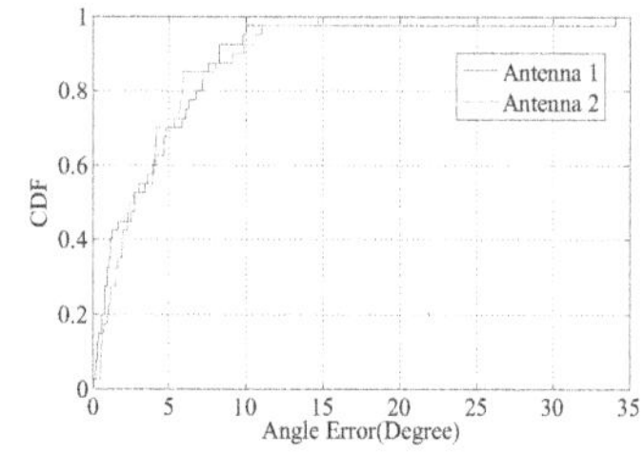

Figure 6

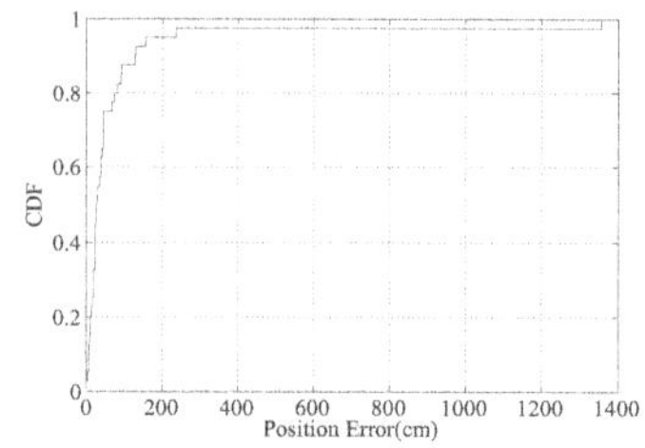

Figure 7

ence tag. From our experiment, we speculate that the difference of fluctuation intensity results from difference of tags' hardware(e.g. antenna sensitivity). To avoid such difference, we do not measure the exact difference of adjacent RSS, but just determine if the RSS is higher, equal or lower than former one. We simplify Forward RSS Difference as follows

$$SFRD_d = \begin{cases} 1 & RSSI_d > RSSI_{d-1} \\ 0 & RSSI_d = RSSI_{d-1} \\ -1 & RSSI_d < RSSI_{d-1} \end{cases}$$

Note that sometimes the antenna senses nothing(RSS value is NaN), we say NaN is lowest RSS value. We get Figure 3(d) after the simple comparison which shows a high level of similarity. Then we define the Distance between RSS trends of two tags as

$$Distance = \sum_{d=0}^{n} |tag1's \quad SFRD_d - tag2's \quad SFRD_d|.$$

Based on the distance to reference tags, we can calculate the target tags' position.

4. PRELIMINARY RESULTS

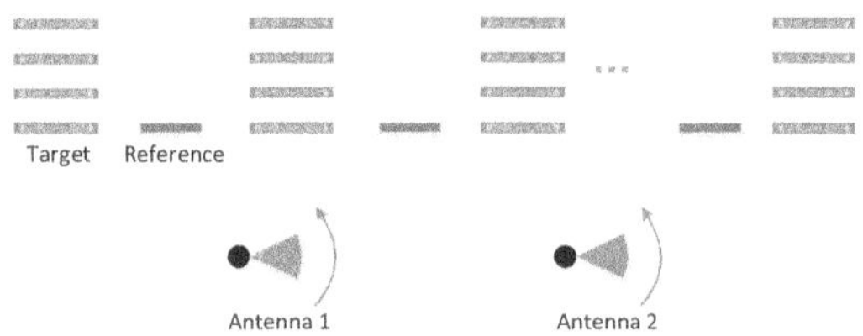

Figure 8: Preliminary experiment scenario

Our preliminary experiment was conducted in a multipath rich room of $50m^2$. We use two directional panel antennas which are connected to one reader and deploy 4×10 target tags(blue) and 9 reference tags(red) in the room, as illustrated in Figure 8. We investigate the 40 tags and show the influence of distance between tags and antenna on the angle estimation error in Figure 5. Figure 6 shows the angle estimation error CDF and we get median error of 3.1° and 3.4° from the two antennas respectively. The result median position accuracy is 29cm and Figure 7 shows the position error CDF. Our preliminary experiment shows failure to a very few tags, because they are not read well by both antennas for a couple of reasons(e.g., location, hardware flaw). We will add more antennas to solve some large estimation errors and devise applicable decision-making algorithm based on the data.

5. ACKNOWLEDGEMENT

This work is partially supported by the National Natural Science Foundation of China (NSFC) under Grant No. 61325013, 61033015 and 61373175, Specialized Research Fund for the Doctoral Program of Higher Education under Grant No. 20130201120016, and the Fundamental Research Funds for the Central Universities of China under Project No. 2012jdgz02 (Xi'an Jiaotong University).

6. REFERENCES

[1] D. M. Dobkin. *The RF in RFID: UHF RFID in Practice.* Newnes, 2012.

[2] J. D. Griffin and G. D. Durgin. Complete link budgets for backscatter-radio and rfid systems. *Antennas and Propagation Magazine, IEEE*, 51(2):11–25, 2009.

[3] T. Liu, L. Yang, Q. Lin, Y. Guo, and Y. Liu. Anchor-free backscatter positioning for rfid tags with high accuracy. In *Proceedings of IEEE INFOCOM*, 2014.

[4] A. Nemmaluri, M. D. Corner, and P. Shenoy. Sherlock: automatically locating objects for humans. In *Proceedings of ACM Mobisys*, pages 187–198. ACM, 2008.

[5] L. M. Ni, Y. Liu, Y. C. Lau, and A. P. Patil. Landmarc: indoor location sensing using active rfid. *Wireless networks*, 10(6):701–710, 2004.

[6] J. Wang and D. Katabi. Dude, where's my card?: Rfid positioning that works with multipath and non-line of sight. In *Proceedings of the ACM SIGCOMM*, pages 51–62. ACM, 2013.

[7] J. Xiong and K. Jamieson. Arraytrack: A fine-grained indoor location system. In *NSDI*, pages 71–84, 2013.

Poster: HiLight – Hiding Bits in Pixel Translucency Changes

Tianxing Li, Chuankai An, Andrew Campbell, and Xia Zhou
Department of Computer Science, Dartmouth College, Hanover, NH
{tianxing, chuankai, campbell, xia@cs.dartmouth.edu}

ABSTRACT

We present HiLight, a new form of screen-camera communication without the need of any coded images (*e.g.* barcodes) for off-the-shelf smart devices. HiLight hides information underlying any images shown on a LED or an OLED screen, so that camera-equipped smart devices can fetch the information by turning their cameras to the screen. HiLight achieves this by leveraging the orthogonal transparency (alpha) channel, a well-known concept in computer graphics, to embed bits into pixel translucency changes without the need of modifying pixel color values. We demonstrated HiLight's feasibility using smartphones. By offering an unobtrusive, flexible, and lightweight communication channel between screens and cameras, HiLight opens up opportunities for new HCI and context-aware applications to emerge, *e.g.* smart glass communicates with screens for additional personalized information to realize augmented reality.

Categories and Subject Descriptors

C.2.1 [**Network Architecture and Design**]: Wireless communication

Keywords

Screen-camera link, visible light communication

1. INTRODUCTION

Screens and cameras are ubiquitous, not only in laptops, but also in today's smart devices such as smartphones, smart watches, and smart glass. Communication between screens and cameras has been attracting growing interest, where information is encoded into visual frames on the screen and cameras-equipped devices extract the information from the captured frames. Operating on the visible light spectrum, screen-camera links are highly directional and interference-free, offering a promising out-of-band communication approach for short-range information acquiring.

While exciting, most existing screen-camera proposals rely on specialized coded images on the screen to transmit data. These coded images (*e.g.* barcodes) are typically visible to users. They either occupy the whole screen, or interfere with the content currently shown on the screen, creating an unpleasant viewing experience.

To overcome the above limitations, we propose HiLight, a flexible and robust form of screen-camera communication channel that hides information underlying any image currently shown on the screen. The key idea of HiLight is to embed information into pixel translucency changes on the LED or OLED screen, so that camera-equipped devices can decode the information based on the perceived color intensity changes. HiLight utilizes an orthogonal transparency channel (alpha channel) to change pixel translucency and opacity. The level of pixel translucency change is configured so that it is perceivable to only cameras but not human eyes. Furthermore, by controlling the translucency changes of each pixel independently, HiLight enables multiple transmitter elements on the screen to transmit data simultaneously. This creates a MIMO communication channel between screen and cameras [2], which can be used to boost data rate or to improve transmission reliability.

Operating on a separate transparency (alpha) channel, HiLight provides three key benefits. *First*, without adding any specialized coded images, HiLight enables unobtrusive, on-demand data transmissions while preserving the user's viewing experience. *Second*, HiLight does not require any modifications to pixel color (RGB) values of the existing image on the screen. Hence HiLight entails low overhead to encode information and is applicable to transmit data in real time for off-the-shelf smart devices. *Third*, HiLight leverages the *relative changes*, rather than the absolute values, of perceived color values to decode information. This makes the system less susceptible to problems such as image distortion, image blur, and frame synchronization.

By offering an unobtrusive, flexible, and lightweight hidden communication channel between screens and cameras, HiLight presents opportunities for new HCI and context-aware applications for smart devices. For example, a user wearing smart glasses can acquire additional personalized information from the screen (*e.g.* TV screen, smartphone or tablet screen) without affecting the content he/she and other users are currently viewing.

2. HiLight DESIGN

We design HiLight to achieve two goals: 1) unobtrusive data transmissions between screen and cameras without using any coded images; and 2) low encoding overhead to enable on-demand, real-time data transmission for off-the-shelf smart devices.

2.1 Background and Design Rationale

Alpha Channel. As a standard technique in computer graphics, the alpha channel has been widely used to form a composite image with partial or full transparency [4]. The alpha channel stores ad-

MobiCom'14, September 7-11, 2014, Maui, Hawaii, USA.
ACM 978-1-4503-2783-1/14/09.
http://dx.doi.org/10.1145/2639108.2642895 .

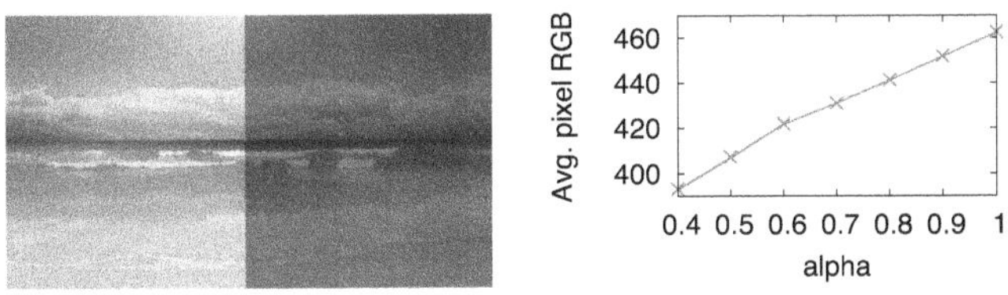

(a) Changing α values of the right half screen from 1 to 0.5

(b) Perceived RGB value at receiver's camera

Figure 1: The impact of changing pixels' α values. (a) shows the dimming effect resulting from tuning α from 1 to 0.5, using Samsung Note 3; (b) shows the average RGB value of the frame captured by Samsung S5 when varying the alpha values of the transmitter's screen.

ditional data with a value (α) between 0 and 1 to indicate the pixel translucency. An alpha value of 0 means that the foreground image pixel is fully transparent, and 1 means that the pixel is fully opaque. Therefore, decreasing the alpha value of a pixel essentially dims the pixel. As an example, Figure 1(a) shows the screen of a Samsung Note 3 Android phone, where we uniformly set the α values of the right half of the screen to 0.5, resulting into a darker appearance.

This dimming effect is perceived as color intensity changes (summation of RGB channel values) by the camera (receiver). As shown in Figure 1(b), increasing α value leads to a linear increase in the RGB value perceived by the receiver's camera. Most importantly, even for the α value change of 0.01 ($\alpha = 0.99$), which is not perceivable by human eyes, the camera of S5 is able to detect the RGB value change. This is because α value is used to multiply the RGB color values. Most importantly, even for the α value change of 0.01 ($\alpha = 0.99$), which is not perceivable by human eyes, the camera of S5 is able to detect the RGB value change. The results demonstrate the potential for off-the-shelf, camera-equipped smart devices to decode information embedded in pixel translucency changes.

Design Rationale of HiLight. HiLight encodes information into pixel's translucency (α) changes on transmitter's LED or OLED screen. To decode the information, camera-equipped smart devices utilize the perceived RGB value changes in captured frames. To make the translucency changes unperceivable by T, HiLight changes the α value by 0.01 ($\alpha = 0.99$) to dim a pixel, and the translucency changes as the screen refreshes. The screens in today's smartphones support 60Hz refresh rate, which is sufficient to avoid the direct flicker effect when a user views a static image [3]. Furthermore, we can divide the screen into grids, and change the α values of all pixels in each grid independently. *Hence each grid functions as an independent transmitter element, resulting into a MIMO channel between screen and cameras.* Overall, operating on the alpha channel, HiLight provides a communication channel unobtrusive to users with low encoding overhead.

2.2 Design Challenges

The efficacy of HiLight depends on its ability of detecting small changes in pixel translucency and reliably decoding information under various practical settings. This is non-trivial even for a static image because of three challenges. *First*, illumination changes from ambient light and noises of camera sensors can interfere with the coded translucency changes. *Second*, detecting translucency changes is harder for darker images with lower RGB values. This is because the pixel's RGB value is multiplied by an α value. Hence for a given α change, the larger the pixel's RGB value, the larger the absolute RGB value change, and hence the more easily the camera can detect the changes. *Third*, to support on-demand data transmission, the receiver needs to synchronize with the transmitter and

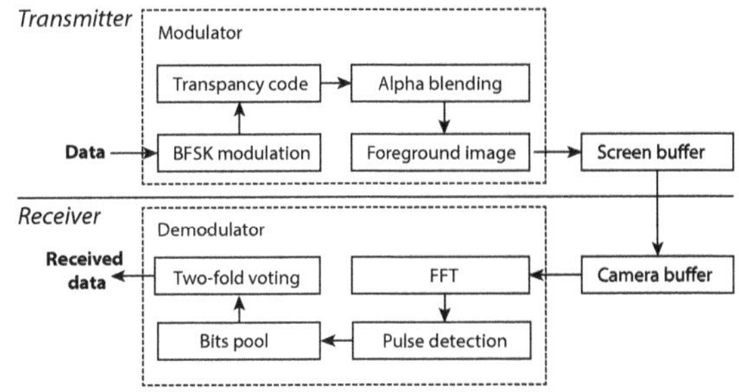

Figure 2: HiLight system overview.

detect the starting point of a data stream. This is challenging given that screen-camera communication is a one-way channel.

2.3 Initial Solution

We now briefly describe our initial solution to tackling the above challenges. Overall, HiLight encodes data using Frequency Shift Keys (FSK). We carefully design the modulation keys to avoid low frequency components close to environmental noise. To detect the start and end of a data stream, HiLight aggregates the perceived bits of all pixels on both the time and spatial domain to reduce the impact of frame synchronization and environmental noise. Figure 2 shows the flowchart of HiLight. We introduce each step in detail, assuming that the receiver records video at 60fps.

Modulating Data. For a given bit stream and pre-defined grids on the screen, the transmitter modulates bits using BFSK. Here bit 0 and 1 are represented by different frequency (20Hz and 30Hz, respectively) of translucency changes over a certain number of frames (24 frames in our implementation). HiLight adjusts the duty cycle to remove the low frequency components (< 20Hz), thus reducing the impact of environmental noise on the frequency power of the data bit.

To transmit a bit, the transmitter generates a sequence of α values of each pixel for 24 frames. Pixels within a grid have the same α value. It then applies alpha blending method [5], a standard technique in computer graphics, using OpenGL API to combine the foreground image with background image (black matte), and outputs the frames into the screen buffer.

Demodulating Data. Once the receiver captures frames in its camera buffer, it applies Fast Fourier Transform (FFT) to project the translucency changes in a decoding window (24 frames) into the frequency domain. The receiver checks the power of 20Hz and 30Hz frequency components, which represent $'0'$ and $'1'$ in frequency domain. The receiver then outputs the corresponding bit into a candidate pool. The receiver slides the decoding window by one frame and repeats the above procedure.

Given all candidate bits in the bit pool, HiLight determines the received bit for every 24 frames as the bit with the most appearances. To detect the first frame of a data transmission, HiLight checks the number of detected bits for a given frame. If more than 60% of grids detect a bit, HiLight treats this frame as the first frame. We observe that a decoding window of 24 frames can remove most errors caused by frame synchronization and environmental noise (*e.g.*, ambient light and camera sensor noise).

3. HiLight EXPERIMENTS

We now examine the feasibility of HiLight using off-the-shelf smart phones. We implemented HiLight's modulation and demodulation in a MATLAB emulator. The modulator takes the random bits we generated and a static image as input, and outputs a video where the data bits are embedded into pixel translucency changes.

Figure 3: Experimental setup with Samsung Note 3 (right) as the transmitter and Samsung S5 as the receiver (left).

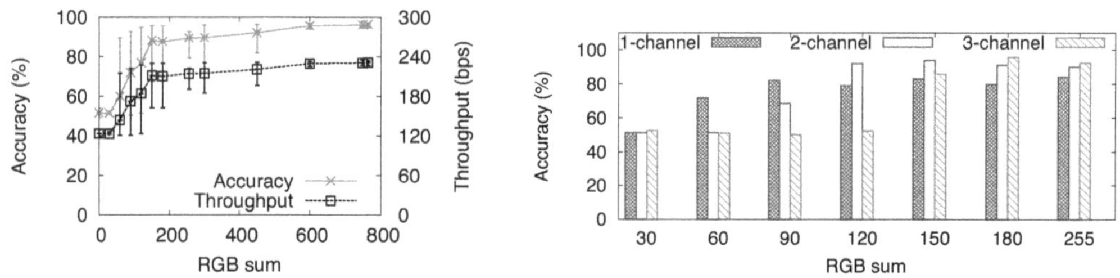

(a) Impact of RGB sum

(b) Impact of RGB value distribution

Figure 4: Impact of foreground image color on HiLight accuracy and throughput, using HiLight basic design without erasure coding, grid size of 94.5mm^2, and 61 single-color foreground images.

We play the video on a Samsung Note 3 Android phone as the transmitter, and use a Samsung S5 phone to capture the frames. These captured frames are the input for the demodulator to decode transmitted bits. As the next step, we plan to implement the modulation and demodulation on existing smart device for real-time encoding and decoding (Section 4).

Experimental Setup. As shown in Figure 3, we fix the receiver (left) and the transmitter (right) on two phone holders. This avoids the problems of image alignment and image blur (we plan it for a ongoing work), and allows us to focus on examining HiLight feasibility. Specifically, the transmitter is a Samsung Note 3 with 5.7-inch OLED display (1920 x 1080 pixels). The display is 12.6cm x 7.2cm in size and its refreshing rate is 60Hz. The receiver is a Samsung S5 with a rear camera that has a resolution of 16 megapixels and supports 120fps video recording. To match the refreshing rate of the display, we used 60fps at the receiver side. For all experiments, we used the default auto-focus function on S5's camera to record videos. We ignore the first 2 seconds of the video because of the high noise during initializing the auto-focus function.

We evaluate HiLight in terms of its accuracy and throughput. The accuracy is the ratio of correct received bits over all transmitted bits, and the throughput is the number of bits the receiver successfully receives per second.

Preliminary Results. As we discussed in Section 2.2, the color of screen's foreground image affects camera's ability of detecting color intensity changes. To understand the impact of image color on HiLight system, we tested 61 single-color images with colors varying from black (0, 0, 0) to white (255, 255, 255). The transmitter and receiver is 15cm away, which maximizes the area of the transmitter's screen in the viewfinder of the receiver's camera and prevents the out-of-focus problem. We divided the transmitter's screen into grids, where each grid is 94.5mm^2 in size and has 160x135 pixels. Using the basic HiLight design without erasure coding, we encoded bits using each single-color image as the foreground image, played the video on Note 3 phone's screen, and decoded bits using the frames captured by S5's camera. We repeated the experiment for 5 rounds for each image. All experiments were performed under fluorescent lamp with illuminance ≈14lux.

Figure 4(a) shows the accuracy and throughput of HiLight as a function of each image color's RGB sum. A larger RGB sum indicates a brighter color. As expected, as the color becomes brighter, HiLight's performance gradually stabilizes. This is because the pixel translucency changes for brighter colors lead to larger absolute color intensity changes, and hence are easier for the camera to detect. Overall we observe that once the RGB sum is above 200, HiLight achieves 90%+ accuracy and 230-240bps throughput.

We further examine the impact of RGB value distribution in three RGB channels (red, green, and blue), by testing colors with the same RGB sum. Taking an RGB sum of 30 as an example, we examined 1-channel colors such as (30, 0, 0), 2-channel colors such as (15, 15, 0), and 3-channel colors such as (10, 10, 10). Figure 4(b) shows the resulting accuracy for different RGB distributions for each given RGB sum. We observe that for 2-channel and 3-channel colors, HiLight requires a higher RGB sum (120 - 150) to achieve 80%+ accuracy and stabilize. Compared to 1-channel colors, 2-channel and 3-channel colors spread the RGB value across more channels and each color channel has a lower value. Hence HiLight performs better when the RGB value at non-zero color channel is above a threshold (50 - 60).

4. CONCLUSION AND FUTURE WORK

We presented HiLight, a new form of screen-camera communication that hides information underlying any image on the screen. We introduced our initial HiLight system design, and demonstrated its feasibility using off-the-shelf smartphones.

Moving forward, we plan to address four challenges. *First*, HiLight currently supports only static foreground images. Supporting video brings new challenges, because a video naturally contains image changes and the resulting color intensity changes interfere with decoding HiLight data. We are studying modulation schemes to extract color intensity changes associated with the transmitted data. *Second*, HiLight's throughput is limited by the speed of pixel translucency changes on an OLED screen, which is bounded by the screen's refreshing rate (60Hz in most existing smart devices). Theoretically each pixel on an OLED screen has a response time of 0.01ms - 0.1ms [1], and thus physically supports a changing frequency between 10KHz and 100KHz. We are investigating techniques to approach this physical limit and further boost the data rate. *Third*, we are exploring schemes to adapt transmitter's configuration (*e.g.* coding redundancy, the level of pixel translucency changes, grid size), based on the current link condition (*e.g.* ambient light level, image darkness) and receiver-side feedback (*e.g.* link distance). Such adaptation is essential for HiLight to support mobile receivers and diverse environmental settings. *Fourth*, we plan to implement modulation and demodulation on existing smart devices to support real-time data transmissions between OLED screens and smart devices (*e.g.* smartphones, smart glass).

5. REFERENCES

[1] `http://en.wikipedia.org/wiki/OLED`.

[2] Ashok, A., et al. Challenge: Mobile optical networks through visual MIMO. In *Proc. of MobiCom* (2010).

[3] Bullough, J., et al. Effects of flicker characteristics from solid-state lighting on detection, acceptability and comfort. *Lighting Research and Technology 43*, 3 (2011), 337–348.

[4] Porter, T., and Duff, T. Compositing digital images. In *ACM Siggraph Computer Graphics* (1984).

[5] Tan, K. W., et al. FOCUS: a usable & effective approach to OLED display power management. In *UbiComp* (2013).

Poster: Retrofitting Computer Vision Libraries for Concurrent Support on Mobile Devices

Robert LiKamWa, Eddie Reyes, and Lin Zhong

Department of Electrical and Computer Engineering
Rice University, Houston, TX 77005

roblkw@rice.edu, jer3@rice.edu, lzhong@rice.edu

ABSTRACT

While computer vision algorithms and libraries have enabled and accelerated the adoption of vision processing into mobile and wearable applications, vision is a resource-hungry operation, and is thus not efficient enough to run on multiple applications simultaneously. However, we observe that many vision algorithms share identical sets of frames and features to perform their analyses, computed from the same library calls. Leveraging this observation, we design a split-process architecture to retrofit existing vision libraries to allow applications to transparently share the computational, memory, and energy overhead of vision processing.

Categories and Subject Descriptors

D.4.1 [**Operating Systems**]: Process Management—*Multiprocessing/multiprogramming/multitasking; Concurrency*; I.4 [**Image Processing and Computer Vision**]: Miscellaneous

Keywords

Split-process; Remote execution; Shared Memory Management

1. INTRODUCTION

Mobile devices use computer vision for a variety of tasks, including object detection, text recognition, eye-gaze tracking, and barcode scanning. We envision a future in which many apps continuously and concurrently run on mobile and wearable devices, analyzing camera frames to understand a user's environment.

Unfortunately, because of system constraints, a device can run only one computer vision application at a time. On all mobile platforms, only one app may access the camera stream at any given time, hindering multiple vision apps from running simultaneously. But even if multiple apps read the camera stream, the vision algorithms are barely computationally efficient enough to be run in real time in one application, much less in multiple apps. Fortunately, many computer vision apps use identical sets of features to perform their analyses. Furthermore, many apps are powered by the same standard computer vision library, OpenCV. Thus, by intercepting library calls to cache previously captured frames and previously computed features and share these objects between applications, we can enable multiple apps to run simultaneously, yet efficiently.

To this end, we design the Starfish system, a split-process architecture which retrofits existing shared libraries to allow multiple apps to take advantage of previously computed vision operations from other apps. Using Starfish, apps offload vision computations to a central process, which transparently executes and shares computation results among multiple apps. In doing so, the Starfish system provides many system benefits, especially reduced CPU utilization, reduced memory allocation, and reduced energy consumption.

1.1 Vision Observations

From our background understanding of vision apps, we observe the following:

Observation 1: Vision libraries are common-case utilities. Over 100,000 Android apps use OpenCV to perform vision processing. Thus, optimizing vision library performance improves a widely-used developer tool.

Observation 2: Vision is memory-expensive and compute-intensive. Vision requires heavy resource utilization to process frames and features. Processing 1920x1080 frames at 30 fps operates on 186 MB/s of data. There is much need to alleviate memory pressure and computation pressure.

Observation 3: Function use is repetitive *within* apps. Vision apps run iteratively, capturing new camera frames, computing features, and performing other complex tasks. Intuitively, the same library functions are called many times in a single app as each new frame is processed.

Observation 4: Function use is repetitive *across* apps. Multiple apps request the same processed elements as the basis for their algorithms, e.g., grayscale frames, blurred images, Harris corners, integral image, SIFT-like features. This provides great opportunity for computation reuse and memory reuse.

These observations motivate and guide our Starfish design, which concurrently services a multitude of concurrently running apps through memory and computation reuse across a split-process architecture.

MobiCom'14, September 7-11, 2014, Maui, Hawaii, USA.
ACM 978-1-4503-2783-1/14/09.
http://dx.doi.org/10.1145/2639108.2642891 .

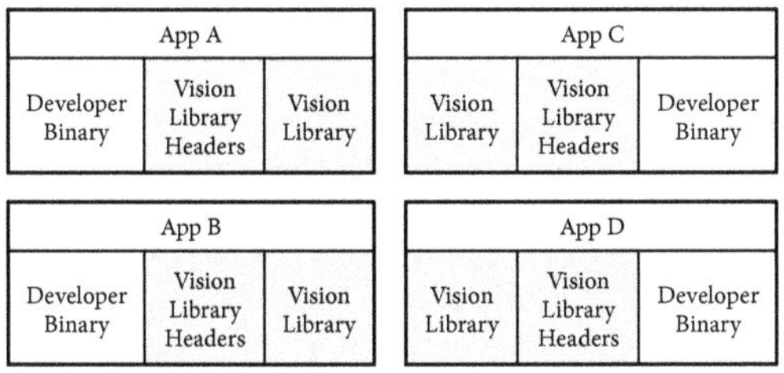

Figure 1: Legacy applications linked to a computer vision library. Each application computes independently. In mobile systems, only one application can run at a time.

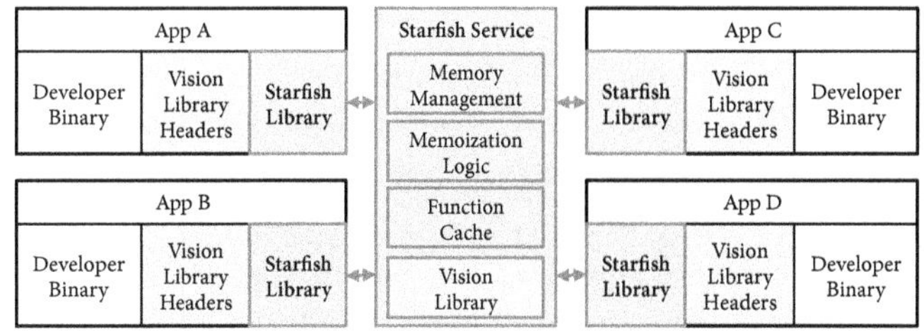

Figure 2: Applications linked to Starfish Library. Starfish exports the same vision library headers, but uses a Service Process to execute and cache library tasks.

2. STARFISH DESIGN

This section describes the general system architecture of Starfish and the decisions guiding its design.

2.1 Objectives and Constraints

We design Starfish to achieve three major objectives:

- **Isolate library function execution.** Starfish executes library function calls on a separate process which may optionally run on a different processor. This creates new opportunities for processing optimization and security control.
- **Reduce redundant computation calls.** Starfish memoizes and shares recently computed operations with all applications requesting the same computation. This decreases computational workload, memory pressure, and energy consumption.
- **Multiplex access from multiple applications to the same resources.** If multiple applications request computation on a camera frame service, many systems only allow one application to use the camera resource at a time. Starfish allows multiple processes to access the same camera frames, which also increases the potential for memoization opportunities. The Starfish design also naturally multiplexes access to heterogeneous computing resources, such as the GPGPU, specialized vision hardware, or cloud services, all of which would typically be tied to a single process.

The function isolation goal is shared by those of offloading systems, such as Odessa [4], COMET [3], MAUI [2], or CloneCloud [1]. However, Starfish is constrained by the following:

- **Starfish is transparent to the application developer.** The application source code will not be altered. This requires that Starfish library functions should return and modify objects exactly as done by the original library.
- **Starfish cannot modify library function execution.** Although OpenCV is open-source, maintaining forked code would be difficult to support. Thus, we call library functions as-is to perform the vision computations.
- **Starfish should behave consistently.** Regardless of whether or not a computation has been cached, Starfish should appear to have the same computational performance for a consistent user experience.
- **The app developer cannot be trusted.** We must prevent attacks and faults from affecting other Starfish apps. Hence, we protect against malicious app developers. We do, however, trust the kernel and the central Starfish Service, which we introduce later.

2.2 Design Choices

The design of Starfish incorporates important decisions into its system architecture to achieve the objectives within our constraints.

2.2.1 Library Function Indirection

We intercept library calls to introduce Starfish functionality, as shown in Figure 2. By operating through library function calls, interfaced with the library headers, we leave the app developer's source code untouched. This allows the developer the convenience of developing the app outside of the Starfish environment. Furthermore, if an app is deployed on a device without access to the Starfish system, it can use the original library in its place, as shown in Figure 1.

Because Starfish replaces the original library, Starfish functions must follow the library's API, taking the expected library input and returning the expected library output. This also requires that object structures as defined by the original library are not altered, especially as they are typically defined in the library headers themselves. For example, we cannot introduce shared pointers, smart references, or other constructs into the library objects.

With library function indirection, Starfish maintains the illusion that all calls execute through the original library.

2.2.2 Centralized Computation and Memory

To handle library computation requests, Starfish introduces a central service process that runs in userspace. The central service schedules library function executions and maintains a record of previously computed functions, returning previously cached results where possible.

Central computing avoids security flaws introduced by computing amongst multiple untrusted applications. A distributed computation and storage scenario could introduce accidentally or maliciously generated errors, which could then be propagated to future library function calls as putatively valid results. Instead, by performing the computation and storage in the central process, Starfish provides tight security and control over the function result memoization mechanisms.

2.3 Starfish Architecture

Based on the above decisions, we design the Starfish Architecture, illustrated in Figure 2, as a split-process system to efficiently perform library computations. To centrally execute and cache computations, we introduce a Starfish *Service* process. We call the multiple computer vision applications the *Legs* of Starfish. Our execution model assumes the Service and Leg processes share physical memory, although the processes may be hosted on different processor cores.

2.3.1 *Starfish Leg*

At runtime, the developer's application binary is dynamically linked with the Starfish Library in place of the original computer vision library. Together, they form the Starfish Leg application. This keeps the application source code unaltered. All header files of the original library are used, but to implement the functions, the Leg's Starfish Library makes a request to the Service process to service library requests. In the case of any unsupported functions and failure conditions, the Leg's Starfish Library passes the function parameters to the original library and returns the resulting values. This fully preserves the original functionality of the library.

2.3.2 *Starfish Central Service*

The Service is a central process whose main responsibility is to memoize function calls for future use by the Starfish Legs. Thus, it is important to remember recently performed function call arguments and outputs. As it acts as the library function server for procedure calls from the Legs, the Service must efficiently route input and output objects from the Legs who request function calls.

Starfish Legs communicate with an already-running Service. If the Service is not running, the Leg asks the operating system to launch a new Service to initiate the Starfish System.

3. CHALLENGES AND OPPORTUNITIES

The Starfish architecture introduces systems challenges and opportunities we intend to address.

Efficient resource passing across processes: While maintaining secure sharing of computed results, the system must operate with minimized overhead, passing resources over shared memory to and from the central process. The goal will be to reduce the marshalling bottleneck of transmitting large objects, such as image frames.

Caching and retrieving function results across multiple apps: Starfish must efficiently search for previously computed results, maximizing vision function reuse. While cach-ing or retrieving function calls, Starfish must avoid concurrency conflicts due to requests from multiple apps. Furthermore, Starfish must enforce consistent code behavior, whether a function call is a cached result or computed for the first time.

Multiplexing mobile OS camera mechanisms: Mobile operating systems are designed for single application usage, delivering camera frames only to the foreground application. For deployment on current frameworks, Starfish must work around the existing mobile OS camera infrastructure, capturing foreground frames and delivering them across multiple applications upon request. We also intend to provide an alternative mechanism that redesigns the operating system's camera service to optimize the multiplexed frame delivery.

4. CONCLUSION

Mobile and wearable systems limit computer vision capabilities to single apps due to their slow computational power, limited memory availability, and restricted frame delivery structures. In this abstract, we have described Starfish, a split-process solution that retrofits existing vision libraries to share computational and memory resources to decrease the footprint of concurrently running multiple computer vision applications. In future work, we hope to address the systems challenges and evaluate the Starfish architecture on multiple concurrent vision applications.

5. REFERENCES

[1] Byung-Gon Chun, Sunghwan Ihm, Petros Maniatis, Mayur Naik, and Ashwin Patti. Clonecloud: elastic execution between mobile device and cloud. In *Proceedings of the sixth conference on Computer systems*, pages 301–314. ACM, 2011.

[2] Eduardo Cuervo, Aruna Balasubramanian, Dae-ki Cho, Alec Wolman, Stefan Saroiu, Ranveer Chandra, and Paramvir Bahl. Maui: making smartphones last longer with code offload. In *Proceedings of the 8th international conference on Mobile systems, applications, and services*, pages 49–62. ACM, 2010.

[3] Mark S Gordon, Davoud Anoushe Jamshidi, Scott A Mahlke, Zhuoqing Morley Mao, and Xu Chen. Comet: Code offload by migrating execution transparently. In *Proceedings of OSDI*, pages 93–106, 2012.

[4] Moo-Ryong Ra, Anmol Sheth, Lily Mummert, Padmanabhan Pillai, David Wetherall, and Ramesh Govindan. Odessa: enabling interactive perception applications on mobile devices. In *Proceedings of the 9th international conference on Mobile systems, applications, and services*, pages 43–56. ACM, 2011.

Poster: AirEye-Blind Monitor the ISM Band Using Narrowband Radio

Meng Meng*
Microsoft Research, Beijing, China
Xi'an Jiaotong University, Xi'an, China
v-memeng@microsoft.com

Kun Tan
Microsoft Research, Beijing, China
kuntan@microsoft.com

Wenjie Wang
Xi'an Jiaotong University, Xi'an, China
wjwang@xjtu.edu.cn

ABSTRACT

In this poster, we present a novel spectrum monitor, named AirEye, that monitors a wide spectrum band using only a narrowband radio. Unlike previous work, AirEye *blindly* extracts cyclic features from received waveform and performs classification without any prior knowledge on the transmitted signals. Although AirEye uses only a narrowband radio, it can still identify any signal that is wider than the radio bandwidth. Finally, AirEye exploits the signal sparsity in both radio and cyclic frequency dimensions to significantly speedup the feature extraction.

Categories and Subject Descriptors

C.2.1 [**COMPUTER-COMMUNICATION NETWORKS**]: Network Architecture and Design–Wireless communication

Keywords

Cyclic feature; Blind classify; Scanning

1. INTRODUCTION

Unlicensed wireless spectrum, like Industrial Scientific Medical (ISM) band, is becoming increasingly crowded with the proliferation of various wireless technologies. As a consequence, the mutual electromagnetic interference among these wireless devices may cause significant performance degradation on one another. For example, Wi-Fi networks may suffer severe throughput loss and unacceptable latency due to interference from other radio devices [1]. Therefore, there is a strong need for a powerful monitoring tool that precisely identifies the diverse radio activities in real-time, over a wide spectrum band, *e.g.*, 200 MHz bandwidth. Ideally, this monitoring tool should be able to extract features from radio waveforms and classify them without any prior knowledge, so that it can easily accommodate any emerging new wireless technologies. In other words, the monitor should be able to extract features and perform classification in a *blind* manner.

To identify a wireless transmission, the first step is to extract certain features from received radio signals. The features utilized in previous work can be grouped into two broad categories: mac-layer based and physical-layer based.

Airshark [4] utilizes typical mac-layer features to identify transmissions. For instance, it measures the time spacing between two consecutive transmissions and if this spacing is roughly equal to $625\mu s$, it determines the transmissions are from Bluetooth devices since the spacing time is very close to that specified in Bluetooth standard. However, while the mac-layer features are very useful, they have the following issues: First, not all wireless protocols are publicly accessible. Many wireless devices simply use proprietary MAC protocol, like Microsoft XBox game controller. Even for these open protocols, not all transmission patterns have distinct mac-layer features. For example, while the Short Inter-Frame Spacing (SIFS) can be used to identify Wi-Fi unicast packets, broadcast traffic cannot be identified using this feature – in fact, it seems hard to find any mac-layer features to identify the broadcast transmissions.

On the other hand, physical-layer features are extracted directly from signal waveforms. Airshark demonstrates that a simple physical-layer feature, the spectral shape of a radio signal, can be used to identify some radio transmissions. However, spectral shapes are not robust. They may change rapidly with different multipath fading environment. A much better feature, however, is the *cyclostationary* of radio signals. Signal's cyclostationary is used extensively in spectrum sensing for cognitive radio, and according to Gardner [2], almost all communication signals contain *underlying periodicities* due to sampling, modulating, coding, and other periodic operations. These underlying periodicities, namely cyclic features, can be observed in the cyclic spectrum, which is a bi-frequency plane obtained by Spectral Correlation Function (SCF). Compared with spectrum shape, the cyclic spectrum of a signal is much more robust to noise and multipath fading. Recent work, DOF [3], has built a wireless signal analysis system based on the cyclo-

*This work was performed while Meng Meng was research intern at Microsoft Research Asia.

MobiCom'14, September 7-11, 2014, Maui, Hawaii, USA.
ACM 978-1-4503-2783-1/14/09.
http://dx.doi.org/10.1145/2639108.2642890.

stationary theory. DOF estimates the cyclic spectrum of a few typical wireless technologies, like WiFi, Zigbee and Bluetooth in advance, and searches the nonzero points in the bi-frequency plane for each wireless type. The positions of these nonzero points are stored as a prior model for each wireless technology. Then, at the runtime, DOF computes SCF values of an input signal based on the stored positions for all known wireless types. These computed SCF values are further constructed into feature vectors for classification. Since DOF needs prior models for wireless signals, it cannot work blindly. Further, to work properly, DOF requires a radio that is as wide as the spectrum band it is monitoring. Indeed, to monitor the full 2.4GHz ISM band, it uses a modified channel sounder with a bandwidth 100MHz. Clearly, such a wideband radio is very expensive and consumes a lot of power.

In this paper, we seek to build a wideband spectrum monitor using only a narrowband radio, which can blindly extract signal's cyclic feature and identify different transmissions. The core challenges of our system are two-folds: First, since the system relies on narrowband radio, there could be wireless signals whose bandwidth is wider than our radio's bandwidth. This means we cannot completely sample these wideband signals. It is a challenging task for us to construct the cyclic spectrum of a signal without a full knowledge. Second, since we assume no prior knowledge on wireless signals, we may need to compute the entire the cyclic spectrum and search for signal features. However, the cyclic spectrum is a two-dimension bi-frequency plane, and the frequency ranges of its two axises are both proportional to the monitoring bandwidth. As a consequence, the computation would grow huge when monitoring bandwidth is wide.

We address the aforementioned two challenges by following two techniques:

1. In AirEye, the monitoring radio keeps on sweeping the entire band. Therefore, we can sense a wideband signal several times at different frequency bands. All these received samples, also incomplete by their own, can be combined together to generate the entire cyclic spectrum of the wideband signal. The key observation is that the cyclic spectrum actually measures the cross-correlations of a set of narrow spectra components at different frequencies.

2. While the spectrum band is heavily used over the time, we observe at any particular instance, *i.e.*, during a scanning period, signals transmitted over the entire spectrum band are still sparse. Moreover, we observe that the cyclic features over the cyclic frequency axis are also sparse. By exploiting the signal sparsity on both dimensions, we can significantly reduce the computation and search space.

2. AIREYE DESIGN

2.1 Understanding Cyclic Spectrum

Almost all signals created in communication systems exhibit periodicities of their second order statistics, due to sampling, modulating, etc. In order to analyze these periodicities of received wideband signal $x(t)$, a key function SCF is typically utilized, which can be expressed as

$$S_x(\alpha, f) = \iint_{-\infty}^{\infty} x(t+\frac{\tau}{2})x^*(t-\frac{\tau}{2})e^{-j2\pi\alpha t}e^{-j2\pi f\tau}dtd\tau \quad (1)$$

The SCF, also termed cyclic spectrum, is a bi-frequency plane with respect to *cyclic frequency* α and *spectral frequency* f. For communication signals, nonzero value appears only at some specific cyclic frequencies, which is related to their symbol rate, chip rate, etc. In other words, signal with different modulation schemes will exhibit distinct cyclic frequencies. Moreover, cyclic frequencies of each signal are *sparse* and *discrete* on the α-axis. Therefore, these cyclic frequencies could be a perfect benchmark for signal type classification.

2.2 Wideband Scanning and Cyclic Spectrum Estimation

Assuming the entire ISM band locates in the frequency range $[f_0 - f_{max}, f_0 + f_{max}]$, where f_0 represents for center frequency and $2f_{max}$ stands for the bandwidth ,then its cyclic spectrum plane supports for $|f| + \frac{|\alpha|}{2} < f_{max}$. The whole band can be split into N sub-bands, and a narrowband radio with tunable RF frequency is scanning each band orderly. For more reliable results, we adopt sub-band overlap scanning scheme. Figure 1 illustrates our scanning procedure clearly, the radio switches its center frequency to receive signal on different sub-band as time t goes on. The received data are numbered starting from 1.

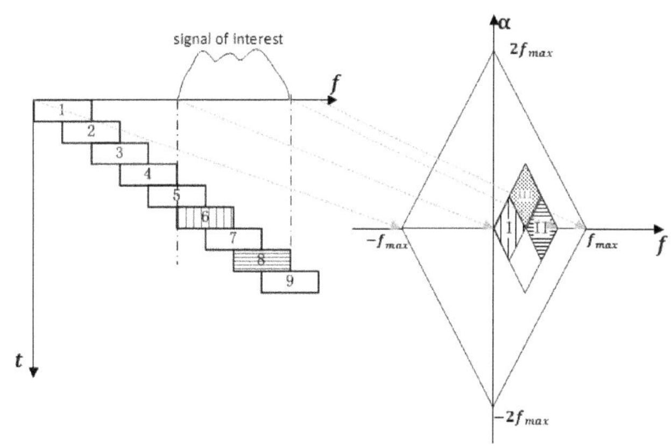

Figure 1: Reconstruct cyclic spectrum using narrowband radio

Taken another interpretation discussed in [2], equation 1 can be rewritten as

$$S_x(\alpha, f) = X(f + \frac{\alpha}{2})X^*(f - \frac{\alpha}{2}) \quad (2)$$

where $X(f)$ is the Fourier transform of signal $x(t)$. Equation 2 actually implies that the value of SCF at spectral frequency f and cyclic frequency α is the cross correlation of two spectral components of $x(t)$ at frequencies $f + \frac{1}{2}\alpha$ and $f - \frac{1}{2}\alpha$. That is to say, although the received signal $x(t)$ is wideband, to estimate the SCF at specific (α_0, f_0) only needs two narrowband spectral components.

On this basis, FFT transformation can be used to extract every spectral components of received signal, which makes the reconstruction of wideband spectrum with single narrowband radio possibly. If the signal of interest is bandlimited within the received radio, this signal will surely be captured completely. However we inevitably encounter some cases where the bandwidth of signal is larger than the received radio. As shown in Figure 1, a signal of interest is beyond our radio's bandwidth, but received data labeled from 5 to 9 all contain this signal. The spectral components gained from received data 6 can be used to estimate part I of cyclic spectrum, and similarly, part II can be estimated using received data 8. While for part III, which can not be estimated directly, is actually measured based on the correlation between the spectral components from received data 6 and 8.

To extract the cyclic features blindly, we need to search for the nonzero points on the entire cyclic spectrum $|f| + \frac{|\alpha|}{2} < f_{max}$. As f_{max} could be more than 100MHz, the total search space is quite huge. When we transform the received signal to frequency domain by N-FFT, where we extract N spectral components denoted as $X(f_1), X(f_2), ..., X(f_N)$. According to Equation 2, to estimate the cyclic spectrum we need to compute the cross correlation of spectral components pairwise. Thus, the number of total points needed to search on cyclic spectrum is N^2. Note that, N also determines the cyclic frequency resolution. Thus, there is a tradeoff between the search space and precision, and we can tune N to find a balance between them. Moreover, inspired by compressive sensing, we can take advantage of signal's sparseness in frequency domain and cyclic frequency domain to reduce the search space. If a signal is bandlimited with B, then the cyclic spectrum $S_x(\alpha, f)$ can be nonzero only for a diamond-shaped region around the origin of the bi-frequency plane, as shown in Figure 2. In other words, the potential cyclic spectrum support for a bandpass waveform is directly related to its center frequency and bandwidth, and the ISM band during one round scanning can be reasonable seen as non-busy which implies signal sparseness. Therefore, the center frequency and bandwidth of a signal of interest can be an important key which guides us to reconstruct specific region of cyclic spectrum smartly.

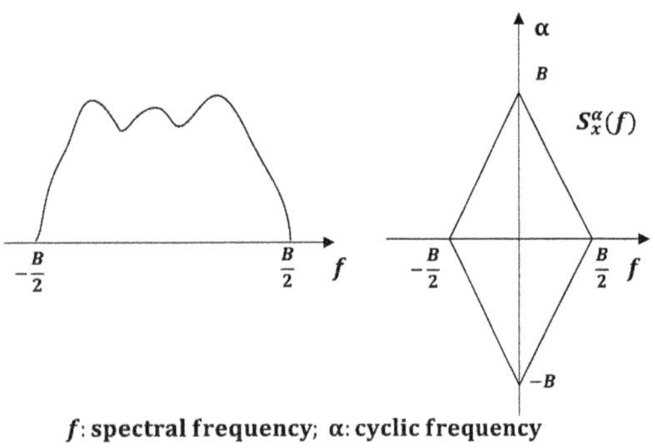

Figure 2: Bifrequency support for cyclic spectrum of bandlimited signal

2.3 Feature Extraction

According to cyclostationary theory, if a signal exhibits nonzero SCF components at a cyclic frequency α_0, then it would also be nonzero components at integer multiples of α_0. In practice, most communication signals we may meet are almost cyclostationary, which means their cyclic spectrum contains not only one fundamental cyclic frequency. We choose the set of a signal's fundamental cyclic frequencies as its features for identification. More specifically, for one signal of interest with center frequency f_0 and bandwidth B, its *α-profile* on the basis of estimated cyclic spectrum can be computed as:

$$I(\alpha, f_0) = \max_{f \in [f_0 - \frac{B}{2}, f_0 + \frac{B}{2}]} |S_x(\alpha, f)| \quad (3)$$

Find all fundamental cyclic frequencies of $I(\alpha, f_0)$, denoted as $F(f_0)$, which is the extracted feature:

$$F(f_0) = \{\alpha : I(\alpha, f_0) \geq Th \wedge \forall \alpha_i, \alpha_j, gcd(\alpha_i, \alpha_j) = 1\} \quad (4)$$

where Th is the threshold used to prune cyclic frequencies with low *α-profile*, and *gcd* stands for greatest common divisor, which is used to eliminate non-fundamental cyclic frequency. As a result, different $\{\alpha_i\}$ can distinguish different communication types, f_0 can tell different transmissions for same communication type.

3. EXPERIMENT

We implement the idea above on sora [5]. We mainly test the transmissions from three typical wireless devices: wireless mouse, wifi(802.11a) and Bluetooth of smartphone. One single radio with bandwidth 20MHz keeps scanning the ISM band, and we can blindly classify different transmissions correctly. To illustrate the distinct cyclic features of different transmissions, we plot the *α-profile* of cyclic spectrum in Figure 3. As shown, Bluetooth signal has fundamental cyclic frequency 0.1, 11a wifi signal exhibits feature at cyclic frequency 0.43, and wireless mouse has cyclic frequency 0.23. By extracting this primary cyclic frequencies, different signals can be identified.

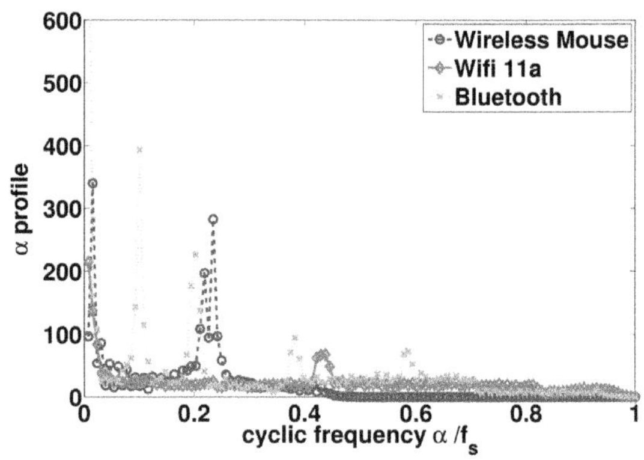

Figure 3: The α profile of cyclic spectrum of three different transmissions

4. REFERENCES

[1] BANDSPEED. Understanding the Effects of Radio Frequency (RF) Interference on WLAN Performance and Security. Tech. rep., 2010.

[2] GARDNER, W. A. The spectral correlation theory of cyclostationary time-series. *Signal processing 11*, 1 (1986), 13–36.

[3] HONG, S. S., AND KATTI, S. R. Dof: a local wireless information plane. In *ACM SIGCOMM 2011* (2011), vol. 41, ACM, pp. 230–241.

[4] RAYANCHU, S., PATRO, A., AND BANERJEE, S. Airshark: Detecting non-wifi rf devices using commodity wifi hardware. In *ACM SIGCOMM 2011* (2011), ACM, pp. 137–154.

[5] TAN, K., LIU, H., ZHANG, J., ZHANG, Y., FANG, J., AND VOELKER, G. M. Sora: high-performance software radio using general-purpose multi-core processors. *Communications of the ACM 54*, 1 (2011), 99–107.

Poster: Promoting the Spatial Reuse of Millimeter Wave Networks Via Software-Defined Cross-Layer Design

Yong Niu
Electronic Engineering Dept.
Tsinghua University
Beijing 100084, China

Yong Li
Electronic Engineering Dept.
Tsinghua University
Beijing 100084, China
liyong07@tsinghua.edu.cn

Depeng Jin
Electronic Engineering Dept.
Tsinghua University
Beijing 100084, China

ABSTRACT

Recently, millimeter wave communications in 60 GHz band have attracted considerable attention from academia, industry, and standards bodies. To overcome huge propagation loss, high gain directional antennas are used. Consequently, concurrent transmissions (spatial reuse) are enabled within a basic service set (BSS) and even among BSSs, which provides huge potential to improve the network capacity. In this paper, we propose a software-defined mmWave network architecture, where a centralized controller is introduced by abstracting the cross-layer control functions from the network layer to physical layer. Efficient coordination is achieved in this architecture to maximize the spatial reuse.

Categories and Subject Descriptors

C.2.0 [**Computer-Communication Networks**]: General

Keywords

Millimeter wave communications; SDN; spatial reuse.

1. INTRODUCTION

Recently, millimeter wave (mmWave) communications in 60 GHz band appear as a promising candidate to enable multi-gigabit wireless services [1]. However, due to its high carrier frequency, mmWave communications suffer from high propagation loss. Consequently, high gain directional antennas are synthesized at both the transmitter and receiver, and beamforming (BF) has been adopted as an essential technique. On the other hand, directional transmission enable less interference, and concurrent transmission (spatial reuse) can be exploited to greatly increase the network capacity. However, interference between links cannot be neglected due to the limited distance. In the network layer, packets forwarding should be optimized to promote the spatial reuse. In the MAC layer, concurrent transmission scheduling and interference management are needed to accommodate traffic demand of flows. In the physical layer, beamforming between the transmitter and receiver should be coordinated to avoid collision and the deafness problem. Thus, efficient coordination from the network layer to physical layer is needed to promote the spatial reuse within a basic service set (BSS) and among BSSs.

Architecturally borrowing the idea of Software-Defined Network (SDN) [2], which advocates separating the control plane and data plane, and abstracting the control functions of the network into a logically centralized controller, we propose a software-defined mmWave network architecture via cross-layer design. In this architecture, a logically centralized programmable controller is introduced by abstracting the control functions from the network layer to the physical layer. In this way, optimized routing path selection, efficient concurrent transmission scheduling and interference management, and coordinated beamforming for each link can be achieved through the software-defined and cross-layer controlling, and the spatial reuse within a BSS and among BSSs is fully exploited to improve network performance. After illustrating the overall architecture, we qualitatively analyze a typical scenario in our software-defined mmWave network architecture, where the spatial reuse among BSSs is exploited to improve flow throughput and overcome blockage.

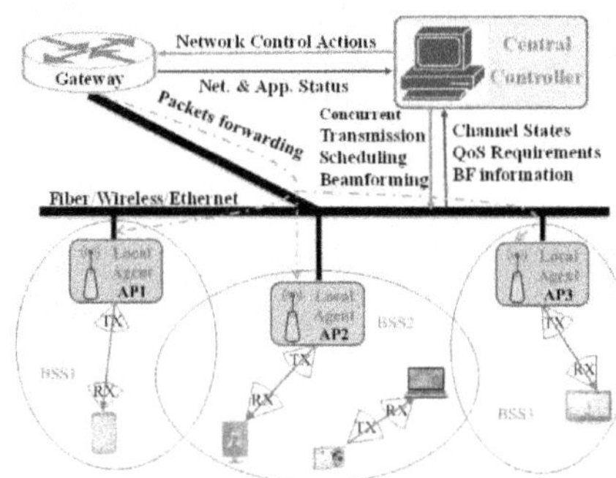

Figure 1: Overview of our proposed software-defined mmWave network architecture.

2. ARCHITECTURE OVERVIEW

Our software-defined mmWave network is illustrated in Fig. 1. The control plane consists of central controller and

MobiCom'14, September 7-11, 2014, Maui, Hawaii, USA.
ACM 978-1-4503-2783-1/14/09.
http://dx.doi.org/10.1145/2639108.2642917.

local agents, while the data plane consists of forwarding and wireless communication devices, such as gateway and access points (APs). The central controller usually resides on the gateway, makes the rules, and controls the behaviors of the gateway and APs from the global perspective. The central controller and APs can be connected via wireless, fibre, or Ethernet. Due to the inherent delay between the central controller and APs, there are local agents residing on APs to adapt to the rapidly varying network states. Between the control plane and the data plane, the measurement interface and control interface are defined. Through the measurement interface, network and application statuses, channel states, QoS requirements, and BF information are collected and reported to the control plane periodically. Based on these measurement results, control flows of packets forwarding, concurrent transmission scheduling, and beamforming for cross-layer optimization are resolved and translated to the actions of APs and the gateway through the control interface. As the example illustrated in Fig. 1, different applications are supported within each BSS. Concurrent transmissions are enabled among BSSs as well as within each BSS with beamforming at both transmitter and receiver. In the BSS of AP2, AP2 is providing low-latency audio services to the music player, and the camera is transmitting a large number of photos to the laptop. Meanwhile, AP1 is providing reliable services to the mobile phone; AP3 is transmitting bandwidth-hungry video stream to the HDTV.

In our software-defined mmWave network, the measurements of network states should be accurate and timely to ensure real controlling of the central controller. Besides, cross-layer optimization algorithms with packets forwarding, concurrent transmission scheduling, and beamforming combined together for the central controller are are also open problems which warrant further investigations.

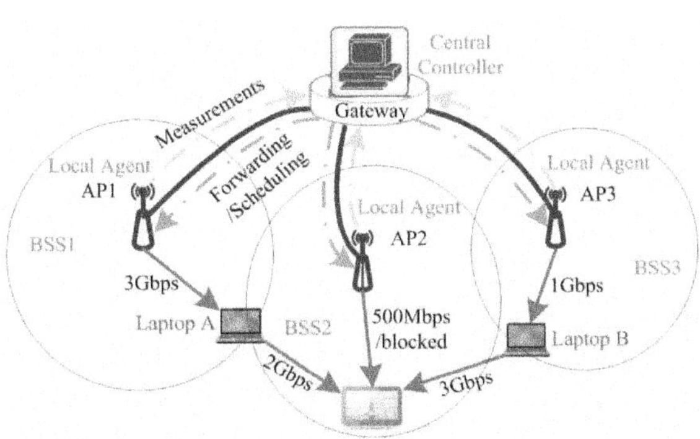

Figure 2: An example of exploiting spatial reuse among BSSs to improve down link throughput.

3. APPLICATION SCENARIOS

In this section, we qualitatively analyze that the spatial reuse among BSSs can be fully exploited in our software-defined mmWave network to improve down link throughput and overcome blockage. As shown in Fig. 2, if the down link from AP2 to the HDTV has a transmission rate of 500 Mbps, or is blocked by obstacles, due to the limited time slots scheduled to this flow under heavy load, its throughput requirement, e.g., 1.5 Gbps, cannot be satisfied.

In our software-defined mmWave network, the central controller will exploit the spatial reuse among BSSs to address this problem. Based on the network states obtained through the measurement interface, the central controller finds out two paths from the gateway to the HDTV. The first path is Gateway → AP1 → Laptop A → HDTV; the second path is Gateway → AP3 → Laptop B → HDTV. The hops in each path should have higher transmission rates to ensure transmission efficiency. Then the central controller instructs the gateway to distribute the traffic of this down link to AP1, AP2 (if the direct link from AP2 to the HDTV is not blocked), and AP3 respectively. Afterwards, the link from AP1 to the laptop A, the link from AP2 to the HDTV, and the link from AP3 to the Laptop B will be scheduled to transmit the distributed traffic concurrently with beamforming at both the transmitter and receiver. Finally, the laptop A and the laptop B will transmit the distributed traffic to the HDTV respectively at a high transmission rate. The direct transmissions between devices within different BSSs are supported in the network. In this way, throughput of the flow to the HDTV will be improved due to the concurrent transmissions among BSSs, and it also overcomes blockage if the direct link from AP2 to the HDTV is blocked. To ensure the efficacy of mechanisms as above, relay stations may be specially deployed to replace the laptop A and laptop B.

4. CONCLUSIONS AND FUTURE WORK

In this paper, we proposed the software-defined mmWave network architecture, which achieves efficient and cross-layer controlling by a centralized controller, to promote the spatial reuse within a BSS and among BSSs.

To deploy such a software-defined mmWave communication system in practice, we are designing the interface between the control plane and data plane (e.g., OpenFlow) to facilitate efficient and centralized controlling. Besides, we are specifying the control mechanisms and measurement techniques in our design. Then we will implement the system and evaluate its performance in real indoor environment.

Acknowledgment

This work is supported by National Basic Research Program of China (973 Program) (No. 2013CB329001), National Nature Science Foundation of China (No. 61301080, No. 91338102, No. 91338203, and No. 61273214), National High Technology Research and Development Program (No. 2013AA013501 and No. 2013AA013505), and Chinaï£¡ï£¡s Next Generation Internet (No. CNGI-12-03-007).

5. REFERENCES

[1] Part 11: wireless LAN medium access control (MAC) and physical layer (PHY) specifications–amendment 3: enhancements for very high throughput in the 60 GHz band, IEEE P802.11adTM/D9.0, July 2012.

[2] H. Kim and N. Feamster, "Improving network management with software defined networking," *IEEE Communications Magazine*, vol. 51, no. 2, pp. 114–119, Feb. 2013.

[3] I. K. Son, S. Mao, M. X. Gong, and Y. Li, "On frame-based scheduling for directional mmWave WPANs," in *Proc. IEEE INFOCOM* (Orlando, FL), Mar. 25-30, 2012, pp. 2149–2157.

Are You Driving? Non-intrusive Driver Detection using Built-in Smartphone Sensors

Homin Park, DaeHan Ahn, Myounggyu Won, Sang H. Son, Taejoon Park
Daegu Gyeongbuk Institute of Science and Technology
Daegu, South Korea
{andrewpark, daehan, mgwon, son, tjpark}@dgist.ac.kr

ABSTRACT

In this work, we address a fundamental problem of distinguishing the driver from passengers using a fusion of embedded sensors (accelerometers, gyroscopes, microphones, and magnetic sensors) in a smart phone. Compared with the state-of-the-art solutions, a key property of our solution is non-intrusiveness, i.e., enabling accurate driver phone detection without relying on any particular situations, events, and dedicated hardware devices. Our system only utilizes naturally arising driver motions, i.e., sitting down sideways, closing the vehicle door, and starting the vehicle, to determine whether the user enters the vehicle from left or right and whether the user is seated in the front or rear seats.

Categories and Subject Descriptors

H.4 [**Information Systems Applications**]: Miscellaneous; D.2.8 [**Software Engineering**]: Metrics—*complexity measures, performance measures*

Keywords

Driver Phone Detection; Driving Safety; Smartphone

1. INTRODUCTION

Any activities that could divert driver's attention away from the road endanger safety of the driver and others. Among various activities known to cause distractions, smartphone usage is by far the most alarming distraction since it requires visual, manual, and cognitive attentions from the driver. Based on the studies carried out in Virginia Tech Transportation Institute, sending or receiving a text takes driver's eyes off from the road for an average of 4.6 seconds. Assuming the vehicle is travelling at 55 mph, this leads to the equivalent of driving the length of an entire football field, blind [3]. As a result, statistics indicate that 15 to 25 percent of crashes at all levels are caused by distracted drivers [2] (mostly due to cell phone use), which leads to approximately 400,000 injuries per year. Efforts to prohibit drivers from using the phone while driving are already quite active. Forty-three states from U.S. have accepted the laws to ban texting while driving according to the National Highway Traffic Safety Administration [1], and such legislation is becoming critical world-wide. In the research domain, a variety of techniques have been developed to detect the driver's phone usage [10][4][5]. However, the state-of-the-art solutions often rely on particular situations (e.g., a phone in a pocket [4]) and events (e.g., driving over a bump [4], making a number of turns [10]). Some solutions are activated only when the driver is about to use the phone [5], which is not suitable for many driving safety applications.

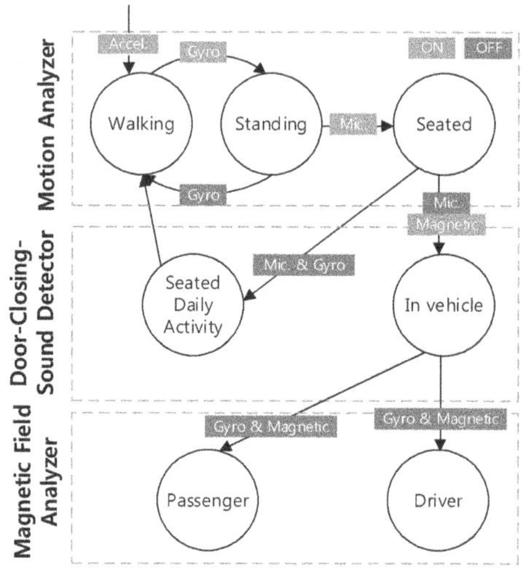

Figure 1: An overview of proposed system

In this work, a *non-intrusive solution* is proposed to distinguish the driver phone from passenger phones. A salient aspect of our proposed solution is that it requires neither additional dedicated hardware devices, nor any particular events and actions. Multiple built-in sensors, i.e. accelerometer, gyroscope, microphone, and magnetic sensors are effectively fused together to enable the detection leveraging only natural and indispensable driver actions – approaching the vehicle, standing still while opening the door, sitting down sideways, closing the vehicle door, and starting the vehicle, thus allowing for seamless system operations. Our proposed solution can be used with various driving safety applications which might suppress incoming and outgoing messages of the driver's phone, or activate voice recognition systems such as Siri or S-Voice.

MobiCom'14, September 7-11, 2014, Maui, Hawaii, USA.
ACM 978-1-4503-2783-1/14/09.
http://dx.doi.org/10.1145/2639108.2642896.

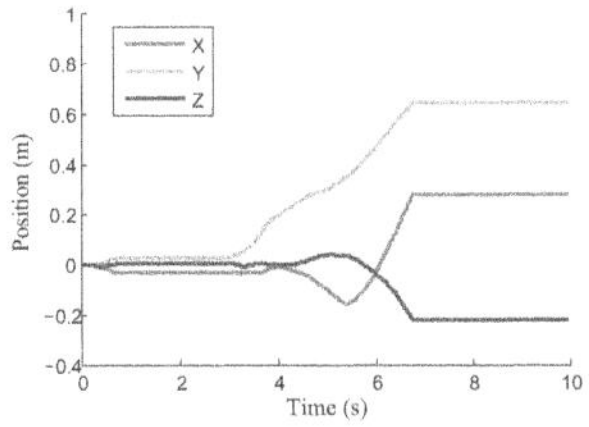

Figure 2: Relative Position

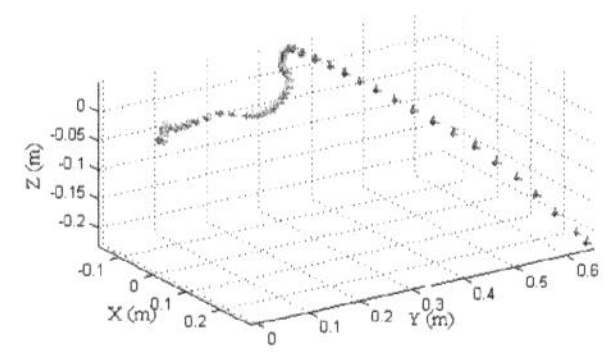

Figure 3: 3D Representation

2. SYSTEM DESIGN

The proposed system consists of three main components: Motion Analyzer (MA), Door-closing-sound Detector (DD), and Magnetic Field Analyzer (MFA). A component diagram of our system is shown in Figure 1 in which the components have states; and the state transitions are made when key events are captured using the sensors that are turned on at the given state. As illustrated, MA uses accelerometer and gyroscope sensors to classify walking, standing, and sitting down states. When the user is sitting down, the trajectory of given motion is captured, and will be used to identify the direction of vehicle entrance. Once the system concludes a user have been seated in the vehicle, microphones will be turned on to detect the vehicle-door-closing sound, which distinguishes daily sitting motions from entering a vehicle. After vehicle entrance is confirmed with vehicle-door-closing sound, the proposed system determines whether the user has entered the vehicle from the left or right by analyzing the direction of vehicle movements and the sitting down motion trajectories. MFA then comes into play to determine whether the user is seated in the front or back using magnetic sensors. With classified direction of vehicle entrance and seated location, our system determines whether the user is a driver or not. The details of each component are presented in the following subsections.

2.1 Motion Analyzer

MA uses the accelerometer and gyroscope to detect the sitting motion. An immediately faced challenge is that the gyroscope consumes too much energy, which makes it difficult to keep this sensor turned on. Thus, it is important to activate the gyroscope only when necessary. A key idea to address such challenge is that the gyroscope is activated only when a standing motion is detected (i.e., using the accelerometer) leveraging the fact that a standing motion is momentarily accompanied before the sitting motion. Once the gyroscope is turned on, the accelerometer readings are converted into absolute coordinates to capture the motion trajectories as shown Figures 2 and 3. As illustrated in Figure 2, a user was sitting down shortly after one second, which resulted in significant sensor reading changes in all 3 axes. Such accelerometer readings can be interpreted as a trajectory shown in Figure 3. The trajectory information is then fed to a classifier to determine whether given motion is sitting down or not. When the sitting motion is detected and the vehicle starts to move forward, the trajectory information is used to determine whether the user has entered a vehicle from left or right. Assuming the positive x-axis is the direction of vehicle movement, trajectory illustrated in Figure 3 leads us to conclude that the user have entered a vehicle from the right.

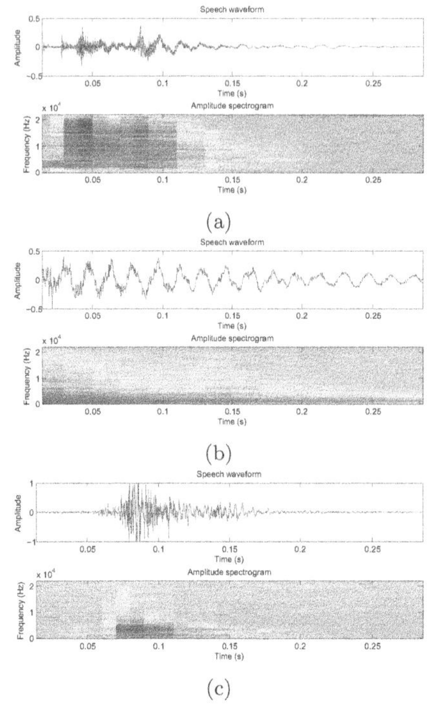

Figure 4: Sound analysis for (a) lab door (b) bathroom door (c) vehicle door

2.2 Door-closing-sound Detector

When the driver is seated, the next natural activity that the driver typically performs is closing the vehicle door. To detect the sound, DD turns on the microphone and starts to capture the sounds frame by frame. We leverage the fact that vehicle-door-closing sound has distinctive characteristics allowing for relatively easy sound classification. Vehicle doors are carefully designed to provide profound and reliable door-closing sound because it is one of the important factors affecting consumer's first impression [7]. Figure 4 illustrates distinctive acoustic signal characteristics of various types of door closing sounds. While other sounds consist of a wide range of frequencies that are strong enough to be audible, the frequency contents of vehicle-door-closing sound are concentrated in the low frequency range. In addition, vehicle-door-closing-sound signals tend to decay much quicker than the others. With such distinctive characteristics, we adopt the one-class classifier [9] to detect and differentiate the vehicle-door-closing sound from all kinds of other sounds that can be monitored during daily activities involving sitting motion. For the classification processes, each sound frame is analyzed to create a feature vector that contains chosen acoustic characteristics including – Short Time Energy, Fast Fourier Transform, Filterbank Energy, and Mel-frequency [6]. Such feature vector is used to generate aforementioned classifier, and to detect the vehicle-door-closing sound.

2.3 Magnetic Field Analyzer

Once the user is concluded to be in a vehicle with a specific direction of entrance, MFA now determines whether the phone is in the front or rear seats. Figure 5 and 6 illustrate that the rate of MF change (ROMFC) from the front

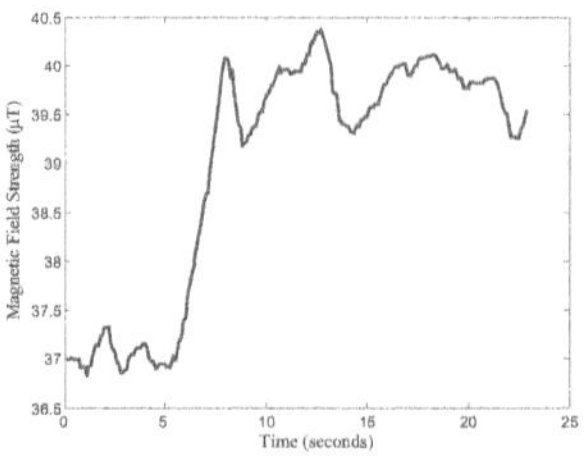

Figure 5: MF of front seat

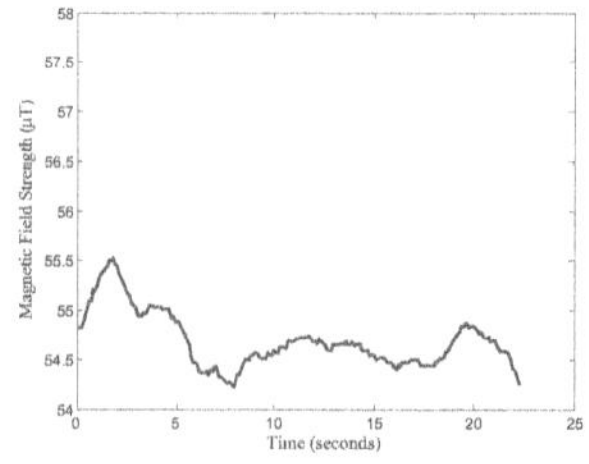

Figure 6: MF of rear seat

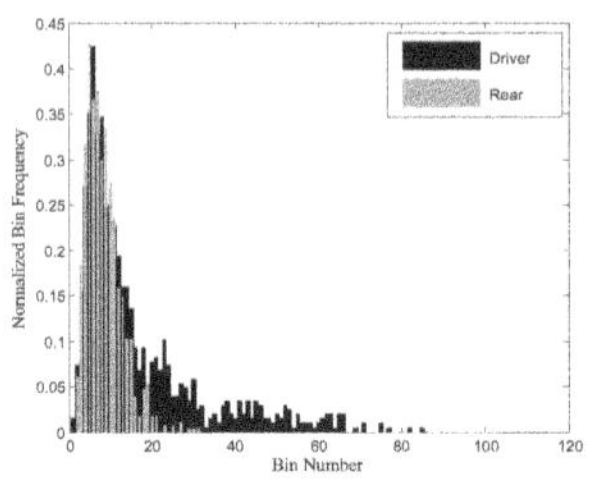

Figure 7: Normalized bin frequency graph for front and rear seats

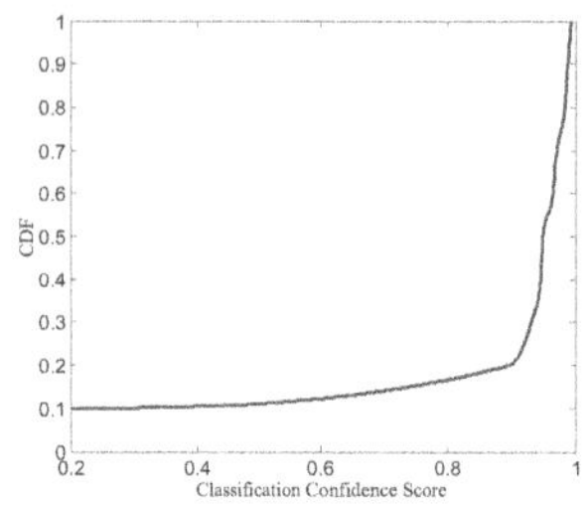

Figure 8: CDF of sound classification confidence scores

seat is much greater than that of rear, while overall MF strength from the front might be weaker. Such phenomenon is well expected since electronic and mechanical devices are installed and used around the front than the rear. In addition, we found that such overall MF reading difference between front and rear is attributed to the environmental factors, including orientation of the phone, location of the vehicle, and individual vehicle characteristics. Although the MF strength value itself does not distinguish the front from the rear, the ROMFC can be used to yield meaningful information.

To determine whether the user has been seated in the front or not, we compute the ROMFC for each time window, and generate a bin-based frequency histogram. Such histogram is generated by dividing the range of ROMFC values into n bins where each bin consists of dedicated sub-range of ROMFC values. For our work, we divided the range into 100 bins. With every ROMFC value computed, we identify the matching bin and increment the frequencies. Once frequency histogram is generated, given values are normalized as shown in Figure 7. Histogram from the driver (front) seat shows a long-tailed distribution while the rear seat shows a bell-shaped distribution concentrated on the left corner. With incoming data that needs to be classified, we create a corresponding bin-based frequency histogram, and apply the Earth Mover's Distance [8] to identify the similarity with reference histograms. The similarity indicate whether the incoming MF readings are from the driver (front) or rear seats of the vehicle.

3. PRELIMINARY RESULTS

Some preliminary experimental results are presented. Results for the fully integrated system are left as our future work. We first measured the accuracy of detecting sitting in vehicle which involves MA and DD. As Table 1 shows, sitting motions from daily activities were detected with accuracy of 100%, while the accuracy for detecting the event

Table 1: Accuracy of Detecting the Sitting Motion

	Sitting Event	
Detected	In Vehicle	From Daily Activity
In Vehicle	97%	3%
From Daily Activity	-	100%

Table 2: Accuracy of MFA

	Phone Location	
Detected	Front	Rear
Front	98%	2%
Rear	-	100%

of sitting in the vehicle had some small errors of ~3%, which is possibly attributed to some inaccuracy for detecting the door-closing sound. Figure 8 depicts the Cumulative Distributed Function (CDF) of sound classification confidence scores. It shows that DD has an average of 95.83% classification confidence. Finally, Table 2 displays the detection accuracy for MFA, i.e., determining whether the phone is in the front or in the back of the vehicle. The accuracy was measured with VW Jetta, and as shown, it has an accuracy of about 98%. We leave the measurements with various kinds of vehicle models as future work.

Acknowledgment

This research was supported in part by the DGIST R&D Program of MSIP of Korea (CPS Global Center) and the Global Research Laboratory Program through NRF funded by MSIP of Korea (2013K1A1A2A02078326).

4. REFERENCES

[1] Distracted driving laws. `http://www.ghsa.org/html/stateinfo/laws/cellphone_laws.html`.

[2] Governors highway safety association. `http://www.ghsa.org/html/issues/distraction/index.html`.

[3] Official website for distracted driving. `http://www.distraction.gov/content/get-the-facts/facts-and-statistics.html`.

[4] C. Bo, X. Jian, X.-Y. Li, X. Mao, Y. Wang, and F. Li. You're driving and texting: detecting drivers using personal smart phones by leveraging inertial sensors. In *Proc. of MobiCom*, 2013.

[5] J. G. Elias. Driver handheld computing device lock-out, Apr. 22 2014. US Patent 8,706,143.

[6] Y. Guo and M. Hazas. Localising speech, footsteps and other sounds using resource-constrained devices. In *Proc. of IPSN*, 2011.

[7] E. Parizet, E. Guyader, and V. Nosulenko. Analysis of car door closing sound quality. *Applied Acoustics*, 69(1):12–22, 2008.

[8] Y. Rubner, C. Tomasi, and L. J. Guibas. The earth mover's distance as a metric for image retrieval. *International Journal of Computer Vision*, 40(2):99–121, 2000.

[9] D. M. Tax and R. P. Duin. Support vector data description. *Machine learning*, 54(1):45–66, 2004.

[10] Y. Wang, J. Yang, H. Liu, Y. Chen, M. Gruteser, and R. P. Martin. Sensing vehicle dynamics for determining driver phone use. In *Proc. of MobiSys*, 2013.

Poster: Am I Indoor or Outdoor?

Valentin Radu
valentin.radu@ed.ac.uk

Panagiota Katsikouli
p.katsikouli@sms.ed.ac.uk

Rik Sarkar
rsarkar@inf.ed.ac.uk

Mahesh K. Marina
mahesh@ed.ac.uk

The University of Edinburgh, UK

ABSTRACT

The environmental context of a mobile device determines where/how it is used, which can be exploited for efficient operation and better usability. In this work we describe a general method using only the lightweight sensors on a smartphone to detect if a device is indoor or outdoor. Using semi-supervised machine learning techniques, our method automatically learns characteristics of new environments and devices, thereby achieves detection accuracy of over 90% even in unfamiliar circumstances. Therefore, it easily outperforms existing indoor-outdoor detection techniques based on static algorithms, or relying on energy hungry and unreliable GPS.

Categories and Subject Descriptors

C.3 [**Special-Purpose and Application-Based Systems**]: Signal processing systems; D.4.8 [**Performance**]: Modeling and prediction

General Terms

Design, Experimentation, Performance

Keywords

context detection; indoor-outdoor; smartphone sensing; machine learning

1. INTRODUCTION

With rapid adoption of smartphones, context sensing/detection is becoming increasingly important to enable new and sophisticated context-aware mobile apps. There are various forms of context concerning a mobile user including location, environment, time and activity. While time is straightforward to identify with a smartphone, other aspects of context are harder to determine and require more advanced integration of several inbuilt sensors on modern smartphones.

The focus of this work is on detecting whether a user is indoor or outdoor, an aspect of environmental context, which we refer to as the *Indoor-Outdoor (IO) Detection* problem. This user context information is important for a variety of applications including personalization applications (change volume, screen brightness, application shortcuts), power saving (turn off GPS indoors, turn off WiFi radio outdoors) and reminders. Currently, there are two existing techniques for IO detection. One is based on GPS and uses the drop in confidence or inability to obtain a fix as a cue to infer that the user is indoors (e.g., [3, 4]). The other called IODetector [5] combines estimations from cell signal, light and magnetic intensity based features.

In this work, we first experimentally examine the effectiveness of these two techniques in different real-world settings in detail, and find that neither of them provides satisfactory results. GPS is unreliable because it is sometimes possible to get GPS fix while indoors and not get it in some outdoor locations. More crucially, GPS is among the most energy hungry smartphone sensors. On the other hand, the accuracy with IODetector is quite poor because it does IO detection using fixed thresholds for sensor features that are not appropriate across different environments.

Motivated by the above observations, we propose a new approach to IO detection that is based on *semi-supervised learning*. Underlying our proposal is a model that continuously adapts as the user visits new environments, with characteristics distinct from those seen previously, by obtaining new training data on the fly without user involvement. Like IODetector, it still relies only on low power sensors and can be fully implemented on the phone. As a result, it overcomes the limitations of existing techniques. Specifically, our method can achieve very high accuracy (greater than 90%) across diverse and unseen environments while being energy-efficient.

2. PREVIOUS SOLUTIONS

2.1 GPS based Indoor-Outdoor detection

GPS signals are usually available outdoors where the sky is directly visible, and are often weak or unavailable indoors when the sky is obscured by ceiling and walls. Thus, the estimated accuracy of GPS localization can be used to detect if a user is indoors [3].

The primary drawback of GPS is that it is among the most energy hungry sensors on the phone. We observed that with a power consumption of 370mW, the GPS uses one order of magnitude more power than the microphone, the magnetic and the light sensors, and up to two orders of magnitude more power than the accelerometer and the battery thermometer, for continuous sensing.

Moreover, GPS can sometimes get a satellite fix indoors (e.g., when the user is close to a door or window), which reduces its reliability as an indoor-outdoor classifier. In our experiments we found that indoor/outdoor state can be correctly determined with an accuracy around 70-80%, even with a carefully chosen threshold on GPS localization accuracy as shown later.

MobiCom'14, September 7-11, 2014, Maui, Hawaii, USA.
ACM 978-1-4503-2783-1/14/09.
http://dx.doi.org/10.1145/2639108.2642916.

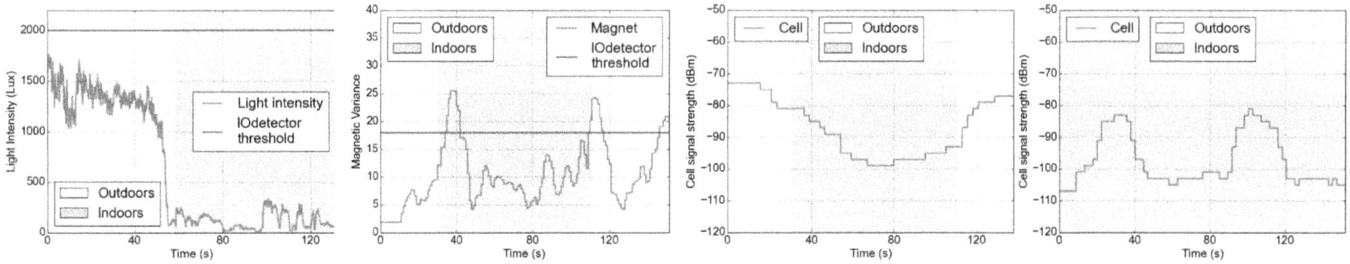

(a) Light detector (b) Magnetic detector (c) Cell signal at transition (d) Cell signal indoor

Figure 1: Illustration of cases where IODetector components (light, magnetic and cell) fail to correctly distinguish between indoors and outdoors. (a) The light intensity is always below the threshold. (b) The magnetic variance is low indoors. (c) The cell signal strength decreases slowly for cell component to detect transition. (d) The cell component detects transitions indoors while moving between rooms due to rapid signal variations. Background shaded (non-shaded) portions in the figures indicate actual ground truth, indoor (outdoor).

2.2 IODetector

IODetector [5] is a recent work that uses low power sensors available on smartphones (light, cell radio and magnetic field sensors) to determine indoor, outdoor and semi-outdoor states. Each of these three sensors works independently to estimate a state and a confidence value. The final state is determined after adding all the confidence values.

Fundamentally, IODetector is built based on some experimental observations: (1) In daytime, in outdoors, light intensity is typically above 2000 Lux; (2) When the user's context changes from outdoors to indoors, the cell signal strength drops rapidly due to attenuation from walls and ceilings; and (3) Magnetic field sensed by the phone tends to change rapidly when the user is moving indoors where there are possibly many appliances, electric currents and metallic objects nearby, compared to outdoors.

These observations may hold in some cases, but we find that they do not hold always and across different environments. Because IODetector has hard-coded thresholds for all the three components (light, cell and magnetic), the system is invariant to changes in relevant factors like environments, weather conditions, seasons, latitude and devices, which ultimately hurts the accuracy of the IO detection.

Figure 1 presents some cases where the IODetector components fail to detect the right IO state because of the non-adaptive nature of their respective thresholds. In figure 1(a), even though the light intensity changes drastically at the transition from outdoor to indoor, the component fails to distinguish between the two states because the light level is always below the threshold, even outdoors. In figure 1(b), the magnetic variance is below the threshold for most of the time, both indoors and outdoors. The cell signal decreases when moving from outdoor to indoors in figure 1(c), but the speed with which this happens is too slow for the component to detect the transition. On the other hand, in figure 1(d) the cell component erroneously detects IO transitions when moving between the rooms of the same building.

3. ROBUST INDOOR-OUTDOOR DETECTION WITH SEMI-SUPERVISED LEARNING

In this section, we present a novel, adaptive IO detection approach that overcomes the problems due to static thresholds as with IODetector, while at the same time avoids the use of energy-hungry sensors like GPS and Wi-Fi. Moreover, unlike IODetector, we are interested mainly in the basic states, which are indoor and outdoor, since these are the ones most relevant to context-aware applications. A semi-outdoor state considered in IODetector system is difficult for many applications to interpret since the environment characteristics for this state are unpredictable. Indoor/outdoor transitions are objectively defined, by crossing a threshold such as a door, but the determination of a state to be semi-outdoor is fairly subjective. This makes it difficult to obtain meaningful ground truths from users to evaluate the reliability of a method using semi-outdoor state.

Specifically, we employ a semi-supervised learning approach, which targets situations where obtaining annotated information with the ground-truth is impractical or expensive to obtain [6]. An additional advantage of semi-supervised learning techniques is that subtle differences between classes, possibly unobservable in a small amount of training data with actual ground truth information (referred henceforth as labeled data), are more likely to be detected and exploited to achieve more reliable classification.

Among the several most commonly used semi-supervised techniques (e.g., self-training, co-training), we experimentally found co-training [1] to be most effective for the IO detection problem (details omitted due to space restrictions). Co-training is a method where two classifiers work in parallel to improve predictions. These classifiers work with different sensor features to gain different perspectives and uncover different patterns. That is, each data point is classified by 2 different classifiers working with different features/attributes and the result with higher confidence is used to retrain and improve both classifiers. The two perspectives underlying the co-training approach based on different feature sets ensure that the training of classifiers is not affected by same biases. The idea behind co-training is shown schematically in Figure 2. See [6, 2, 1] for more details.

Note that supervised learning based classifier approach has the same fundamental limitation as IODetector in that a supervised learning based classifier model trained in one environment may not be accurate in other environments. While collecting labeled data to train in each new environment would make supervised learning approach work but will be impractical. Semi-supervised learning approach essentially overcomes this problem by generating labeled data on the fly without user involvement.

3.1 Data collection

In addition to the features used by IODetector (magnetic variance, cell signal strength, light intensity, proximity sensors and

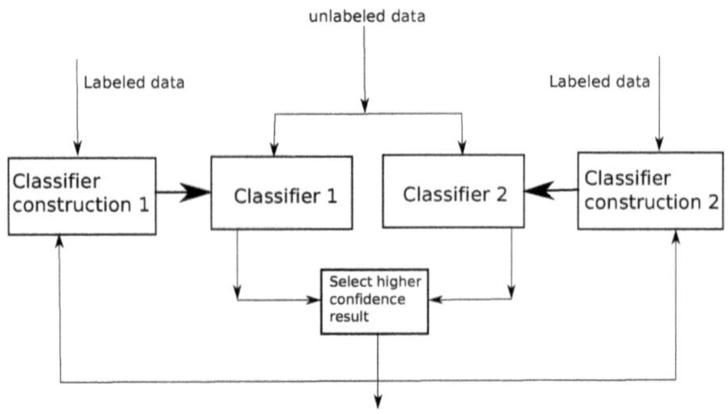

Figure 2: Co-training with 2 classifiers operating with different feature sets. The higher confidence classification for each data is used as the training label to improve classification.

time of day), our method relies on a slightly more expanded set including other light weight features: battery temperature and microphone detected noise amplitude.

To evaluate our semi-supervisied learning (co-training) approach, using a custom Android app, we collected more than 3800 samples of sensor data with a fair distribution between three environments: university campus, city center and residential area. To assess the accuracy of different approaches, the Android app relies on an interface for volunteers who participated in the data collection to manually input (indoor/outdoor) ground-truth information.

3.2 Feature ranking and selection

In building the two classifiers for co-training, we balanced the feature sets in terms of reliability. We ranked the features using different machine learning techniques and then split them into two sets with a fair distribution. Using Naive Bayes analysis of feature importance, we determined the following distribution: Set1: {light intensity, time of the day, proximity value and battery temperature} and Set2: {sound amplitude, cell signal strength, magnetic variance}. Using the SVM Attribute ranking we balanced the two sets into: Set1: {cell signal strength, light intensity, time of day and proximity value} and Set2: {battery temperature, sound amplitude and magnetic variance}. We then evaluated the performance of each of these two feature distributions as part of the classifiers in the co-training approach.

3.3 Evaluation of Co-training

For our co-training method, we chose a small number of labeled instances (300) from one environment (campus) plus 1000 unlabeled instances from the other two environments. For each instance, the system takes the higher confidence classification to be the inferred label for re-training (see Fig. 2). Table 1 presents the accuracy of different configurations of the co-training method with 1200 completely separate instances used for evaluation spread across different environments. The best performance was obtained by a combination of Naive Bayes classifiers using a distribution of features based on the SVM ranking.

In a direct comparison with the previous solutions (IODetector and GPS) and a supervised learning approach (with 300 labeled instances from campus environment for training), our solution using co-training with SVM Attributes distribution has better results by at least 10% (Table 2). These results do not capture other advantages of our approach that include: similar energy consumption as IODetector method; model adaptation without user involvement; and fully implementable on the phone.

Features Distribution	Classifier 1	Classifier 2	Performance (%) Co-training
Naive Bayes based	J48	J48	83.0
	LWL	LWL	78.17
	Naive Bayes	Naive Bayes	91.66
SVM Attribute ranking based	J48	J48	86.67
	LWL	LWL	78.16
	Naive Bayes	Naive Bayes	**93.33**

Table 1: Accuracy with different configurations of co-training method.

Solution	Performance (%)
GPS	75.23
IODetector	35.74
Supervised learning	81.29
Co-training (SVM Attr.)	**93.33**

Table 2: IO detection accuracy for previous solutions (GPS, IODetector), supervised learning on IODetector features and our co-training method.

4. CONCLUSIONS

We have considered the problem of determining whether a user is indoors or outdoors using low power sensors readily available on modern smartphones. We show that existing solutions are too energy hungry or fail to provide accurate results across a range of environments user may typically encounter, due to the use of fixed environment agnostic thresholds in the underlying estimation schemes. To address the fundamental issue of model adaptation on the fly transparent to the user, we employed a novel approach based on semi-supervised learning (specifically, co-training technique). Our adaptive solution not only outperforms existing techniques but also supervised learning based classifier approach. In on-going and future work, we intend to demonstrate the value of our proposed approach in the context of various use cases.

5. ACKNOWLEDGMENTS

We thank Charles Sutton for helpful discussions.

6. REFERENCES

[1] A. Blum and T. Mitchell. Combining Labeled and Unlabeled Data with Co-training. In *Proceedings of the Eleventh Annual Conference on Computational Learning Theory*, COLT' 98, 1998.

[2] O. Chapelle. *Semi-Supervised Learning*. MIT Press, Cambridge, Mass, 2006.

[3] L. Ravindranath, C. Newport, H. Balakrishnan, and S. Madden. Improving Wireless Network Performance Using Sensor Hints. In *Proc. USENIX NSDI*, 2011.

[4] H. Wang, S. Sen, A. Elgohary, M. Farid, M. Youssef, and R. R. Choudhury. UnLoc: No Need to War-Drive: Unsupervised Indoor Localization. In *Proc. MobiSys*, 2012.

[5] P. Zhou, Y. Zheng, Z. Li, M. Li, and G. Shen. IODetector: A Generic Service for Indoor Outdoor Detection. In *Proc. SenSys*, 2012.

[6] X. Zhu. *Semi-Supervised Learning with Graphs*. PhD thesis, Carnegie Mellon University, 2005.

Poster: Styrofoam - A Tightly Packed Coding Scheme for Camera-based Visible Light Communication

David Ramirez*, Robert LiKamWa*, and Jason Holloway*

Department of Electrical and Computer Engineering
Rice University, Houston, TX 77005

dar4@rice.edu, roblkw@rice.edu, jh25@rice.edu

ABSTRACT

Screen-to-camera visible-light communication links are fundamentally limited by inter-symbol interference, in which the camera receives multiple overlapping symbols in a single capture exposure. By determining interference constraints, we are able to decode symbols with multi-bit depth across all three color channels. We present Styrofoam, a coding scheme which optimally satisfies the constraints by inserting blank frames into the transmission pattern. The coding scheme improves upon the state-of-the-art in camera-based visible-light communication by: (1) ensuring a decode with at least half-exposure of colored multi-bit symbols, (2) limiting decode latency to two transmission frames, and (3) transmitting 0.4 bytes per grid block at the slowest camera's frame rate. In doing so, we outperform peer unsynchronized VLC transmission schemes by 2.9x. Our implementation on smartphone displays and cameras achieves 69.1 kbps.

Categories and Subject Descriptors

C.2.1 [**Network Architecture and Design**]: Wireless Communication

General Terms

Algorithms; Design; Theory

Keywords

Visible light communications; camera synchronization; mobile systems

1. INTRODUCTION

Various camera-based visible light communication solutions have encoded light on LED arrays [5] and screen displays [6]. However, in all cases, the lack of synchronization between the screen and camera limits the rate of communication–if the light source transmits faster than the camera's frame rate, the camera will capture multiple code exposures in a single image. Previous works have avoided or mitigated the inter-symbol interference by slowing the frame rate [1], by sacrificing color channels [3], or by inserting additional coding frames [2].

As opposed to avoiding the interference of capturing multiple codes, we design our system, ***Styrofoam***, by characterizing and constraining inter-symbol interference through the introduction of a blank frame. By limiting the duration of the blank frame, we maximize the transmission rate of symbols while guaranteeing the ability to decode multi-bit symbols over a half-exposure. Thus, Styrofoam inserts "air" (blank frames) in the "package" (transmission) to guarantee that it can be safely "unpacked" (decoded).

We show that enabling multi-bit codes far outweighs the cost of introducing a blank frame. Additionally, Styrofoam supports continuous streams; it decodes after receiving two frames, regardless of when the transmission began.

We have implemented and characterized Styrofoam by transmitting a streaming barcode on a 60 fps LCD screen with a 30 fps smartphone camera receiver. On this setup, we achieved a 2.9x faster throughput than other mobile streaming barcodes.

MobiCom'14, September 7-11, 2014, Maui, Hawaii, USA.
ACM 978-1-4503-2783-1/14/09 10.1145/2639108.2642901
http://dx.doi.org/10.1145/2639108.2642901.

2. COMMUNICATION CHANNEL MODEL

In order to faithfully mimic communication scenarios encountered "in the wild", we design a system model for unsynchronized uni-directional communication between a light-emitting transmitter and a camera receiver.

2.1 Screen Transmitter Model

We adopt a transmission scheme similar to other VLC works, namely, streaming a barcode over a grid of blocks hosted by an LED array or display screen updating on a fixed frame rate period. We treat grid blocks as orthogonal channels and model each separately. Each grid block transmits one RGB color per frame period.

Inter-Symbol Interference

As the camera and display are unsynchronized, the receiver's captured grid block r_j can capture multiple transmitted symbols s_k in a single exposure. The symbols are linearly weighted by the time spent in exposure. Thus, we model the received block r_j as a linear combination:

$$r_j = \sum \alpha_{jk} s_k, \qquad (1)$$

where α_{jk} is the proportion of time the kth transmitted symbol is exposed in the jth camera frame.

Timing Blocks

Adjacent to each row of blocks, we use two timing blocks to allow the receiver to directly observe α_{jk} values. We set one timing block to be on during even-indexed frames with the other timing

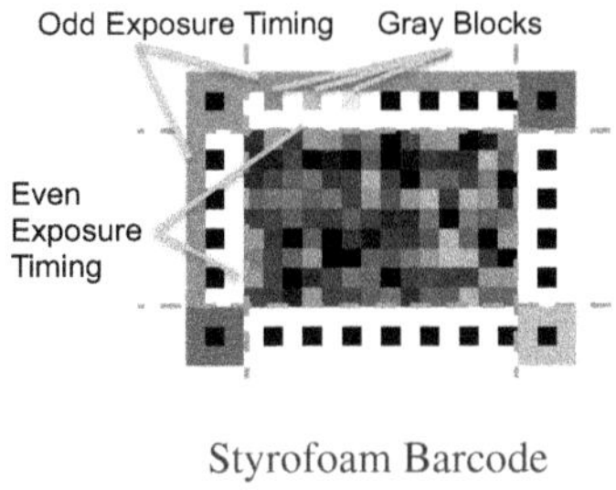

Figure 1: Styrofoam barcodes. Styrofoam slightly adapts the tracking markers used by COBRA, using the first and third rows and columns to denote the per-row symbol exposure times.

block on during odd-indexed frames. Both timing blocks transmit the maximum value of red. The values of the timing blocks, once linearized, are the α_{jk} exposure coefficients.

3. CODING SCHEME

We design the Styrofoam coding scheme to decode symbols in spite of inter-symbol interference by inserting blank frames between symbol transmissions. Introducing these gaps decreases the transmit frame rate, but enables each symbol to carry more depth, ultimately increasing the data rate.

3.1 Constraining Interference

Symbol Visibility

To ensure that all symbols are captured by a frame in the capture stream, each symbol must be displayed for at least one capture period. As the exposure time is always less than the capture separation time, this also ensures that inter-symbol interference is limited to two symbols.

Symbol Resolvability

We define a *pure* capture as having no interference, i.e., only one $\alpha_{jk} \neq 0$: $r_{jk}^{\text{pure}} = \alpha_{jk} s_k$, and a *mixed* capture as having captured a pair of symbols: $r_{jk}^{\text{mix}} = \alpha_{jk} s_k + \alpha_{j(k+1)} s_{(k+1)}$.

Symbols received in pure captures are resolvable by dividing by the exposure coefficient:

$$s_k = \frac{r_{jk}^{\text{pure}}}{\alpha_{jk}}, \quad (2)$$

where α_{jk} is directly observed, as described in Section 2.1.

In a mixed capture, a target symbol in a pair can be resolved as long as the other symbol is resolved. For example, if s_k is the target symbol and $s_{(k+1)}$ was previously resolved, then s_k can be solved by

$$s_k = \frac{r_{jk}^{\text{mix}} - \alpha_{j(k+1)} s_{(k+1)}}{\alpha_{jk}}. \quad (3)$$

Therefore, every target symbol in a mixed capture pair with a resolvable symbol, becomes resolvable.

Symbol Discernability

To decode the value of a target symbol in either a pure or mixed capture, α_{jk} must be sufficiently large to prevent numerical instability from the divide operation. For symmetry, we target that $\alpha_{jk} > 0.5$ for a symbol k to be decodable from capture j. Note that in a mixed capture, the mixed symbol's α_{jk} coefficient is only used to weight the symbol subtraction, and does not have to satisfy the constraint. Therefore, to decode properly, the target symbol must carry at least half of the frame exposure to be resolved.

Symbol Color Constancy

Color cross-talk causes captures with multiple color channels to misrepresent symbol values. Hence, only a single color channel must be exposed in a capture frame. While symbols are limited to single color channels, this additionally implies that decodable mixed captures must contain symbols with matching color channels.

3.2 Scheduling Symbol Transmission

Following the constraints, we design Styrofoam to transmit and decode frames in spite of inter-symbol interference.

Capture Frame Rate vs. Symbol Time

Each symbol must be displayed for the maximum supported capture period, corresponding to the camera with the slowest frame rate. This naturally ensures that each symbol is seen as a target symbol with sufficient exposure in a pure capture or a mixed capture.

While pure captures can be directly decoded, the next section details how to decode mixed captures.

Mixed Capture Decode

Consider the mixed capture case where the target symbol A precedes the mixed symbol B. By the target symbol definition, A was exposed for $\alpha_{jk} \geq 0.5$. The capture period is forced to be less than symbol spacing by fixing the latter, thus the next frame's exposure will begin at least α_{jk} before the transmission of symbol B ends, guaranteeing that $\alpha_{(j+1)(k+1)} \geq \alpha_{jk} \geq 0.5$. Therefore, the mixed symbol B experiences a sufficient exposure as a target symbol in either a pure or mixed capture. Thus, A can be decoded if B can be decoded. We can thus inductively prove that all symbols in a mixed capture chain can eventually be decoded so long as one of the mixed symbols occurs in a pure capture. (The case when the target symbol follows the mixed symbol holds in the reverse direction.) Waiting for a pure capture induces latency before symbols can be decoded. Therefore, to reduce decode latency to N symbols, we transmit a blank frame after every N^{th} symbol. As we are guaranteed to have a target symbol of $\alpha_{jk} \geq 0.5$, the blank frame time simply needs to fill in the maximum possible remainder: half of the symbol displayed time.

Styrofoam Coding Transmission

Combining the design parameters, the (N=2) Styrofoam transmission scheme, shown in Figure 2, is summarized as follows: After transmitting a blank frame, we transmit a symbol s_k over two frames, followed by an s_{k+1}, followed by another blank frame.

As the symbol display time (twice the display frame period) must be greater than any supported capture period, this requires that the display transmit at twice the frame rate of the slowest camera. Thus, on each block, Styrofoam transmits symbols at 0.8 the frame rate of the slowest receiver.

This is a slower symbol rate than related schemes; LightSync [2] transmits 1 symbol per block at the frame rate of the slowest receiver. However, while their system is limited to 1-bit per symbol, our packing scheme provides a guaranteed exposure of each symbol so that color levels can be robustly determined, allowing Styrofoam to transmit multiple bits per block, ultimately delivering a superior transmission rate.

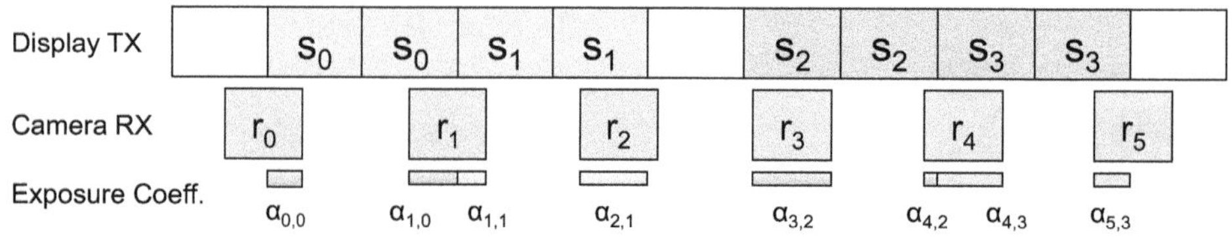

Figure 2: Styrofoam transmission scheme for a single block. Symbols are sent over two display transmitter frames.

3.3 Unpacking Symbols from Camera Frames

Styrofoam unpacks a block's symbols by observing the timing blocks associated with its row. Pure captures will have either the odd or the even exposure timing blocks illuminated. Mixed captures will have both values active.

The unpacking is thus very lightweight, as at most 3 arithmetic operations are required to decode a block. Furthermore, for unresolved mixtures, the unpacking only needs to store a block and its timing values for one frame. This minimizes the memory overhead as well as the latency of the decode. Each symbol is decoded within two transmit frames.

4. EVALUATION AND USE CASES

To characterize the practicality of the coding scheme, we decode streams transmitted and received on commodity smartphones. To receive, we sample camera frames at 30 fps on a Nokia Lumia 1020. To transmit codes, we use a Blackberry Z30, transmitting a 60 fps video. Sending 720 blocks per frame and transmitting 8 bits per 5 transmitter frames yields an effective transmission rate of 69.1 kbps and a decode latency of 30 ms.

We analyze our captured codes offline with MATLAB. We ensured the full range of our transmitter was visible by manually setting ISO and exposure. This setup decodes with 100% accuracy.

On such a system, we can demonstrate two valuable use cases for Styrofoam:

File Transfer
File transfer without pairing allows data transmission between devices with minimal burden. Our demonstration uses Styrofoam to transfer files, such as images captured by the camera, between multiple devices.

Streaming Audio
Audio streaming over VLC allows users to listen privately to provided music or narration on separate devices with no pairing required. Our demo uses a video stream with the audio stream being sent over a Styrofoam channel. This showcases Styrofoam's ability to transmit real-time streams to mobile devices.

5. DISCUSSION

In this work, our contribution is limited to symbol scheduling to recover from interference. Our scheme leaves open avenues of research to enhance Styrofoam's transmission.

Code registration in time and space
For this iteration of Styrofoam, we assume the adoption of previous works' spatial timing blocks and corner markers to register our code. However, we note that the spatial timing reduces a 42x26 grid block by 34% to a final code space of a 36x20 grid of blocks. We will consider improvement by minimizing sacrificed code space in registering codes in time and space.

Color Coding
We plan to characterize a noise model across a range of devices. To optimize the communication scheme, a generalizable investigation should tightly characterize the noise and linearity in the transmission and reception in a multi-color channel.

Real-Time Computation Characterization
We plan to investigate systems issues, including computation and memory complexity of our decode operations, and energy efficiency tradeoffs with regards to the image capture [4]. We speculate that system overhead is low, as the arithmetic recovery operations are simple and unresolved frames only need to be held for one frame.

6. CONCLUSION

We design Styrofoam, a camera-based VLC coding scheme that ensures that symbols can be decoded despite inter-symbol interference due to lack of synchronization. We do this by inserting a short blank frame in our transmission pattern. Our scheme allows for code symbols to be represented by multi-bit R, G, or B values, leading to high code density. This results in a 2.9x faster data transmission rate than peer algorithms, such as LightSync or Unsynchronized 4D Barcodes.

7. REFERENCES

[1] T. Hao, R. Zhou, and G. Xing. Cobra: color barcode streaming for smartphone systems. In *Proc. Mobisys*, pages 85–98. ACM, 2012.

[2] W. Hu, H. Gu, and Q. Pu. Lightsync: unsynchronized visual communication over screen-camera links. In *Proc. Mobicom*, pages 15–26. ACM, 2013.

[3] T. Langlotz and O. Bimber. Unsynchronized 4d barcodes. *Advances in Visual Computing*, pages 363–374, 2007.

[4] R. LiKamWa, B. Priyantha, M. Philipose, L. Zhong, and P. Bahl. Energy characterization and optimization of image sensing toward continuous mobile vision. In *Proc. MobiSys*. ACM, 2013.

[5] D. O'Brien, L. Zeng, H. Le-Minh, G. Faulkner, J. W. Walewski, and S. Randel. Visible light communications: Challenges and possibilities. In *Personal, Indoor and Mobile Radio Communications, 2008. PIMRC 2008. IEEE 19th International Symposium on*, pages 1–5. IEEE, 2008.

[6] S. Perli, N. Ahmed, and D. Katabi. Pixnet: interference-free wireless links using lcd-camera pairs. In *Proc. Mobicom*. ACM, 2010.

Poster: Hearing Your Breathing: Fine-grained Sleep Monitoring Using Smartphones

Yanzhi Ren†, Chen Wang†, Yingying Chen†, Jie Yang‡
†Stevens Institute of Technology, Hoboken, NJ 07030, USA
†{yren2,cwang42,yingying.chen}@stevens.edu
‡Florida State University, Tallahassee, FL 32306, USA
‡jie.yang@cs.fsu.edu

ABSTRACT

Sleep monitoring has drawn increasingly attention as the quality and quantity of the sleep are important for maintaining a person's health and well-being. For example, inadequate and irregular sleep are usually associated with serious health problems such as fatigue, depression and cardiovascular disease. Traditional sleep monitoring systems, such as PSG, involve wearable sensors with professional installations, and thus are limited to clinical usage. Recent work in using smartphone sensors for sleep monitoring can detect several events related to sleep, such as body movement, cough and snore. Such coarse-grained sleep monitoring however is unable to detect the breathing rate which is a vital sign and health indicator. This work presents a fine-grained sleep monitoring system which is capable of detecting the breathing rate by leveraging smartphones. Our system exploits the readily available smartphone earphone that placed close to the user to capture the breath sound reliably. Given the captured acoustic signal, our system performs noise reduction to remove environmental noise and then identifies the breathing rate based on the signal envelope detection. Our experimental evaluation of six subjects over six months time period demonstrates that the breathing rate monitoring is highly accurate and robust under various environments. This strongly indicates the feasibility of using the smartphone and its earphone to perform continuous and noninvasive fine-grained sleep monitoring.

1. INTRODUCTION

There exists a broad array of healthcare related applications that benefit from fine-grained sleep monitoring – an understanding of the sleep quality and quantity as well as the breathing rate during sleep. For example, inadequate and irregular sleep can lead to serious health problems such as fatigue, depression, cardiovascular disease and anxiety [1]. And breathing rate monitoring is critical to detect early signs for several diseases such as diabetes and heart disease [2]. The breathing rate monitoring can also be applied in the sleep apnea diagnosis and treatment for asthma [3]. It is thus important to enable the fine-grained sleep monitoring which can facilitate these healthcare related applications.

MobiCom'14, September 7-11, 2014, Maui, Hawaii, USA.
ACM 978-1-4503-2783-1/14/09.
http://dx.doi.org/10.1145/2639108.2642898 .

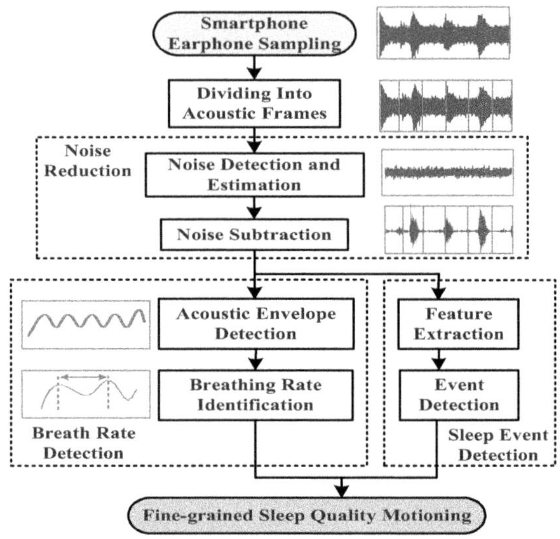

Figure 1: The architecture of our system

The challenge in fine-grained sleep monitoring lies in solutions that can provide breathing rate detection with minimal cost and without requiring invasive diagnostic devices. Traditional sleep monitoring systems, such as Poly-somnography (PSG) [4], are able to provide fine-grained sleep monitoring including breathing rate detection. They however involve wearable sensors and professional installations, and thus are limited to clinical usage. The high complexity and cost prevent these systems from large scale and long term deployment. Some commercial monitoring products (e.g., ZEO [5]) have been designed based on PSG. They are obtrusive and hard to use: the user is required to wear a device during sleep, which may change her daily sleep habits. Several smartphone Apps, such as *Sleep as Android* [6] and *iSleep* [7], can perform noninvasive sleep monitoring by using the smartphone build-in microphone and motion sensors. These apps however only provide coarse-grained monitoring such as the detection of body movement, cough and snore. An iPhone App called Respiratory [8] tries to find persons' respiratory rate by detecting and analyzing the movements of the users's abdomen while they are breathing. However, the phone has to be placed between the user's ribcage and stomach, which is invasive and cannot support long term respiratory rate monitoring.

This work demonstrates that fine-grained non-invasive sleep monitoring with minimal cost is possible (i) using the readily available off-the-shelf smartphone and (ii) the sound captured by smartphone's earphone placed close to the user. Our system explores the breath sound which are generated by the air flow for breathing rate detection. Studies [9] show that the airway flow is correlated with the amplitude of the respiratory sound during normal breathing. It is thus possible to monitor the breathing rate from the breath sound. Several unique challenges however exist when utilizing breath sound for supporting the fine-grained sleep monitoring. First, the sound of user's breathing is usually weak, posing difficulty in capturing the breath sound by using smartphone's build-in microphone. Second, the background noise generated by various sources including the air condition, heater and traffic outside the house significantly affects the recorded breath sound. Third, the acoustic characteristics of breath sound vary dramatically among users, requiring the breathing rate detection method to be adaptive to different users.

To cope with these challenges, we explore a novel point by using the readily available smartphone earphone. The benefit of using earphone is two-fold. First, it is relative easier to place the earphone close to user's nose than that of the smartphone itself for recording the weak breath sound. Second, the earbuds on earphone are essentially microphones. The earbuds thus can be further utilized to improve the sound quality once they are connected together with the input of microphone by using off-the-shelf connecters. Given the recorded acoustic sound, we perform noise estimation and substraction to reduce the impact of background noise. We then exploit the high correlation between a user's breathing cycles to make our breathing rate detection method adaptive to different users. We summarize our main contributions as follows:

- We utilize the smartphone earphone to capture and enhance the breath sound for fine-grained sleep monitoring.
- We perform noise detection and subtraction to reduce the impact of background noise while preserving the features present in the breath sound for breathing rate detection.
- By exploiting the correlation relationship inherent in a user's breathing cycles, our breathing rate detection method is adaptive to different users.
- We evaluate our system with six subjects over six months. The results show that our system is highly accurate and robust in breathing rate detection under various environments.

2. SYSTEM DESIGN

2.1 System Overview

The basic idea of our system is to use smartphone's earphone to capture and enhance breath sound for fine-grained sleep monitoring. As illustrated in Figure 1, the system takes as input time-series acoustic signal captured by the earphone placed close to the user. The breath sound can be further enhanced by using the input from the earbuds after connecting the earbuds with the input of microphone by using off-the-shelf connecters. The acoustic signal is then preprocessed to remove environmental noise via noise detection and subtraction. The next two components of our system are the breathing rate detection and sleep event detection. Our system first distinguishes the event sound from the breath sound. Given the breath sound, we first perform signal envelop detection, based on which the breathing rate can be identified adaptively for different users. Whereas the sleep event detection, such as body movement, cough and snore, can be done by using existing method [7]. Our system then integrates the breathing rate and the sleep events for fine-grained sleep monitoring. This work primarily focuses on the breathing rate detection. We detail each step in the follow.

2.2 Noise Reduction

Most people usually sleep in a relatively quiet environment. However, the background noise generated by various sources including the air condition, heater and traffic outside the house is unavoidable during sleep in some cases. The background noise acoustically added to the breath sound may significantly degrade the performance of sleep monitoring. To build a robust system that can be resistant to different background noises, we first perform noise reduction to reduce the effects of background noise.

2.2.1 *Noise Detection*

Noise reduction aims to clean the recorded acoustic sounds by subtracting the estimated noise components. In our work, we propose to estimate the noise components from time frames that only contain ambient noise (i.e., noise frames). We thus first distinguish the noise frames from the non-noise frames in the recorded acoustic sounds.

Specifically, the collected acoustic signal is first sampled with the frequency of 8 kHz and segmented into frames with $K = 800$ samples each. A bandpass filter is then applied to the raw audio data to remove both high and low frequency sounds that are not related to the breathing events. The lower and upper cutoff frequencies are set as 100 Hz to 1500 Hz. We choose the lower cutoff frequency as 100 Hz because it can remove most of the common electronic noise at lower frequency band. The upper cutoff frequency at 1500 Hz is selected because the most sound generated by breathing events is below 1500 Hz [10].

The key difference between the ambient noise and the breath sound is their stability. This is due to the fact that the ambient noise is relative stable when comparing to the breath sound. We thus can detect frames that only contain ambient noise from a sequence of frames by calculating the variance $v_i = \text{var}(F_i)$ for the i-th frame F_i to capture the stability of the acoustic signal within the frame. However, such variances may vary with different noise profiles. To deal with this, our system further performs the variance normalization to achieve a robust noise detection:

$$\overline{v_i} = \frac{v_i - v_{mean}}{v_{std}} \tag{1}$$

where v_{mean} and v_{std} denote the mean and standard deviation of variance values within an observation window respectively. After normalization, we choose 1 as the threshold to identify the noise frames as follows: if $\overline{v_i} < 1$, frame F_i will be detected as the frame that only contain ambient noise and vice versa.

2.2.2 *Noise Subtraction*

After detecting the noise frames, our system performs noise subtraction after estimating the noise spectral magnitude from the detected frames. Specifically, let $\{\hat{r}(l), 0 \leq l \leq N-1\}$ be a sequence of acoustic samples after filtering and $\{n(l), 0 \leq l \leq N-1\}$ be the noise that has been added to the clean acoustic signal $\{r(l), 0 \leq l \leq N-1\}$. Their relationships thus can be represented as $\{\hat{r}(l) = r(l) + n(l), 0 \leq l \leq N-1\}$. Taking the Fourier transform, we have:

$$\hat{R}(e^{jw}) = R(e^{jw}) + N(e^{jw}) \tag{2}$$

where $\hat{R}(e^{jw})$, $R(e^{jw})$ and $N(e^{jw})$ denote the Fourier transform of sequence $\hat{r}(l)$, $r(l)$ and $n(l)$, respectively. To estimate the frequency spectrum of the breath sound $R(e^{jw})$, we can estimate the noise magnitude spectrum $N(e^{jw})$ and then subtract it from the spectrum of the recorded acoustic data $\hat{R}(e^{jw})$:

$$R(e^{jw}) = [\left|\hat{R}(e^{jw})\right| - E(\left|N(e^{jw})\right|)]e^{j\theta_{\hat{R}(e^{jw})}} \tag{3}$$

where the magnitude of the noise is estimated using the average value $E(\left|N(e^{jw})\right|)$ derived from detected noise frames and the phase is estimated by the phase of $\hat{R}(e^{jw})$. Finally, we can obtain the cleaned acoustic signal $\{r(l), 0 \leq l \leq N-1\}$ after taking the Inverse Fourier transform on $R(e^{jw})$.

2.3 Breathing Rate Detection

After noise reduction, we first extract the envelope of the acoustic signal. We then utilize the strong correlation relationship between breath cycles to search for the time length between the breath cycle pattern to derive the breathing rate.

2.3.1 Envelope Detection

The envelope captures the trend changes of the acoustic signal and thus can be used for the breath cycle detection. Given N acoustic samples have been equally divided into L frames with $K = 800$ samples each: $F_i = \{r(l), (i-1)K \leq l < iK - 1\}, i = 1, ..., L$ with $LK - 1 = N$, we first computes the maximum absolute value of the acoustic samples in each frames as $M_i = \max(|F_i|) = \max\{|r(l)|, (i-1)K \leq l < iK - 1\}$. We then perform the interpolation to make the length of each sequence consistent. The interpolation allows the sequence of maximum absolute values having the same length as the sequence of the input acoustic samples. In particular, we align the extracted sequence $\{M_i, i = 1, ..., L\}$ to the length N by using the cubic spline interpolation. The sequence after interpolation is considered as the detected envelope and can be represented as:

$$\{e(0), ..., e(N-1)\} = Interpolation\{M_1, ..., M_L\} \quad (4)$$

2.3.2 Breathing Rate Identification

The identified envelope $\{e(l), l = 0, ..., N-1\}$ contains the information of the breath cycles. To identify the breathing rate, we utilize the correlation inherent in the user's breath cycles. The correlation among breath cycles allows us to detect a user's breath rate accurately. This is because the time length between the breath cycle patterns is resistant to the acoustic sample distortion caused by irregular breathing. To identify this time length, we examine the similarity between acoustic samples as a function of the time lag between them. The basic idea is that the acoustic samples should be highly correlated when the time lag is equal to the breathing period. Such time lag can be then used to identify the breathing rate.

Note that the period of a periodic signal (i.e., the envelope $\{e(l), l = 0, ..., N-1\}$) is defined as the smallest amount of samples it takes to repeat itself. Thus, it satisfies $e(l) = e(l+T)$ if T is equal to the period. We assume the minimum and maximum interval between the breath cycles under normal conditions have $T_{\min}$ and $T_{\max}$ samples respectively. Given the range of adult's normal breathing rate and the sampling frequency of the microphone, we can determine reasonable values for $T_{\min}$ and $T_{\max}$ as 19200 and 40000 samples, respectively. We then define a function $f(T)$ to measure the similarity between acoustic samples as a function of the time lag T between them:

$$f(T) = \frac{\sum_{l=0}^{N-T_{\max}-1} |e(l) - e(l+T)|}{N - T_{\max}}, T_{\min} \leq T \leq T_{\max} \quad (5)$$

To identify the breathing rate, we search for a set of W local minimums (i.e., $\{\tau_k, 1 \leq k \leq W\}$) from $f(T)$ by varying T from $T_{\min}$ to $T_{\max}$. For each τ_k, it satisfies that $f(\tau_k) < f(T)$ for any $T \in (\tau_k - d, \tau_k + d)$, where d is a pre-defined small distance with $d > 0$. Since the period of a periodic signal is defined as the smallest amount of samples it takes to repeat itself, the first local minimum τ_1 therefore corresponds to the period of envelope $\{e(l), l = 0, ..., N-1\}$. And the breathing rate thus can be identified as $1/\tau_1$.

3. PERFORMANCE EVALUATION

We conduct experiments using Iphone 4 and its earphone with 6 subjects over a period of 6 months to evaluate the effectiveness of our system in breathing rate monitoring. During the experiment, the earphone is placed in two different positions: the participant

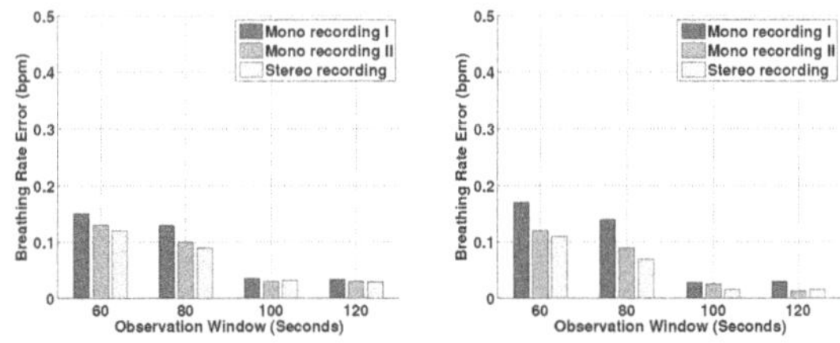

(a) Wearing earphone (b) Besides the pillow

Figure 2: Performance of breathing rate estimation under different length of observation period.

wears the earphone and the participant puts the earphone besides the pillow. For each position, we conduct our experiments under two different environments: the quiet environment and the relatively noisy environment with the air condition on. To obtain the ground truth of the breathing rate, the NEULOG Respiration Monitor Logger Sensor [11] is put inside a monitor belt attached to the user's ribcage. The ground truth of the breathing rate is then calculated based on the air pressure in the monitor belt. We use the breathing rate error, which is defined as the difference between the estimated breathing rate and the actual breathing rate, to evaluate our system.

Figure 2 (a) and (b) present the accuracy of breathing rate estimation with different length of observation window when the earphone is placed in two different positions. We observe that the overall detection accuracy increases as the length of observation window increases. This is because more breath cycles exist in a longer observation window which captures the breathing rate more accurately. We further observe that an observation window of 100 seconds is sufficient for our scheme to achieve a reasonable detection accuracy (i.e., a breathing rate error of less than 0.1 breaths per minute (bpm)). Further, the figure clearly shows that similar detection accuracy is achieved when the smartphone is placed at different positions. Finally, our detection accuracy is within 0.3 bpm even if under noisy environment, indicating our system is robust to ambient noises.

4. REFERENCES

[1] J. M. Parish, "Sleep-related problems in common medical conditions," *Chest Journal*, 2009.

[2] J. E. Shaw, N. M. Punjabi, J. P. Wilding, K. G. M. Alberti, and P. Z. Zimmet, "Sleep-disordered breathing and type 2 diabetes: A report from the international diabetes federation taskforce on epidemiology and prevention," *Diabetes research and clinical practice*, 2008.

[3] P. X. Braun, C. F. Gmachl, and R. A. Dweik, "Bridging the collaborative gap: Realizing the clinical potential of breath analysis for disease diagnosis and monitoringâĂŞtutorial," *IEEE Sensors Journal*, 2012.

[4] K. C. et al, "Practice parameters for the indications for polysomnography and related procedures: an update for 2005," *Sleep*, 2005.

[5] "ZEO." http://www.myzeo.com/sleep/, 2014.

[6] "Sleep as android." https://sites.google.com/site/sleepasandroid/., 2014.

[7] T. Hao, G. Xing, and G. Zhou, "isleep: Unobtrusive sleep quality monitoring using smartphones," in *Proceedings of the 11th ACM Conference on Embedded Networked Sensor Systems*, 2013.

[8] "Respiratory Rate." http://appcrawlr.com/ios/respiratory-rate, 2014.

[9] V. Harper, H. Pasterkamp, H. Kiyokawa, and G. Wodicka, "Modeling and measurement of flow effects on tracheal sounds," *Biomedical Engineering, IEEE Transactions on*, 2003.

[10] N. Gavriely, Y. Palti, and G. Alroy, "Spectral characteristics of normal breath sounds," *J Appl Physiol*, 1981.

[11] "NEULOG Respiration Monitor Logger Sensor." http://www.neulog.com/, 2014.

Programming Software-Defined Wireless Networks

Roberto Riggio, Tinku Rasheed
CREATE-NET, Trento, Italy
first.lastname@create-net.org

Mahesh K. Marina
The University of Edinburgh, UK
mahesh@ed.ac.uk

ABSTRACT

Programming wireless networks requires accounting for multiple complex operations, such as monitoring interference and allocating radio resources. Employing the Software-Defined Networking (SDN) paradigm eases the implementation of such tasks when augmented with suitable high-level programming abstractions. In this work, we present a set of programming abstractions modeling three fundamental aspects of a wireless networks, namely state management, resource provisioning, and network state collection. We also describe our proof-of-concept implementation of the proposed abstractions focusing on WiFi networks and show its use for realizing typical control tasks such as mobility management and traffic engineering as *Network Apps*.

Categories and Subject Descriptors

C.2.3 [**Network Operations**]: Network management

Keywords

WiFi, Programming Abstractions, Network Management

1. INTRODUCTION

Rapid adoption of smartphones and tablets is fuelling the dramatic rise in mobile data traffic, which has led mobile operators to explore coping mechanisms. Mobile data offloading via public WiFi hotspots is one such key approach. Typically, public WiFi networks are managed via a centralized proprietary controller with limited flexibility for operators to tailor the behavior of their networks. Software-Defined Networking (SDN) offers a more open and systematic framework, promising simplified network control and management when enhanced with suitable high-level abstractions while at the same time allowing operators to deploy new services and features as *Network Apps*.

In this work we present three programming abstractions for WiFi networks, especially keeping in mind the emerging need to flexibly manage large number of public WiFi hotspots. They complement the existing programming abstractions for SDN-enabled networks that are aimed at wired networks (e.g., [2, 4, 1]). Between them, the proposed abstractions address the three fundamental elements that compose a WiFi network control loop, namely: collecting the *wireless* network state; implementing control and management tasks; and disseminating the new configuration to the network elements.

MobiCom'14, September 7-11, 2014, Maui, Hawaii, USA.
ACM 978-1-4503-2783-1/14/09.
http://dx.doi.org/10.1145/2639108.2642897 .

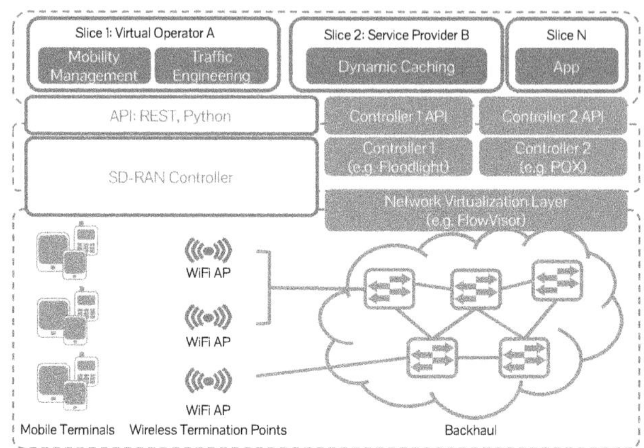

Figure 1: The reference network architecture.

We realize these abstractions via a proof-of-concept implementation that includes a Python–based Software Development Kit (SDK) and Software-Defined RAN (SD–RAN) Controller. This implementation provides a platform to realize features of WiFi–based WLANs such as mobility management and traffic engineering as *Network Apps* running on top of the *SD–RAN Controller*. Moreover, the SDN principles on which the platform is based also allow for advanced network virtualization functionality.

Figure 1 sketches the reference network architecture and introduces the terminology used throughout the paper. We use the term Wireless Termination Points (*WTP*) to refer to the physical devices that form the wireless network and provide wireless clients with connectivity. When WiFi is the only wireless technology involved, *WTP*s basically coincide with WiFi Access Points (APs). The proposed abstractions are exposed from a centralized *SD–RAN Controller*. *Network Apps* runs on top of the *SD–RAN Controller* in their own slice of resources.

2. WIRELESS ABSTRACTIONS

In this section, we will introduce our three key abstractions for WiFi networks, namely: the *Light Virtual Access Point* (*LVAP*); the *Resource Pool*; and the *Interference Map* (see Fig. 2). A *Resource Block* is like in 3GPP mobile networks and represents the minimum chunk of resources that can be assigned to a client, while the *LVAP* represents the state of a client scheduled on a set of *Resource*

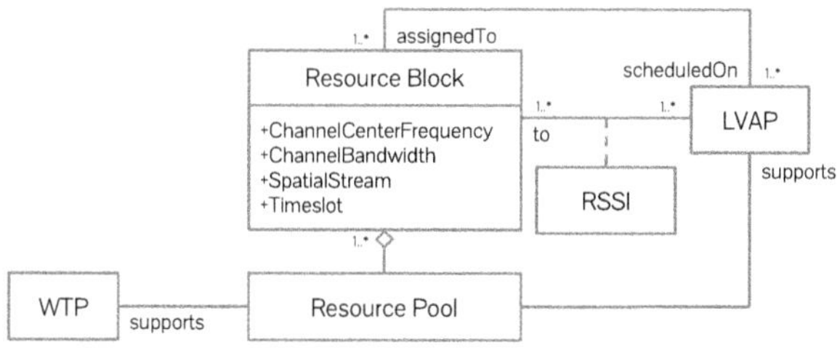

Figure 2: UML class-diagram of the proposed abstractions.

Blocks. Both the *LVAPs* and the *WTPs* support a set of *Resource Blocks*, named *Resource Pool*. A relationship exists between each *LVAP/Resource Block* pair modeling the link quality between the two entities, for example using RSSI; the *Interference Map* abstraction captures this relationship.

2.1 The Light Virtual Access Point

The LVAP abstraction builds on top of [3] which provides a high–level interface through which the state of a wireless client can be manipulated. The implementation of such an interface is required to handle all the technology–dependent details such as association, authentication, and resource scheduling. A wireless client attempting to join the network will trigger the creation of a new *LVAP*. Such *LVAP* is specific to the newly associated client (in a WiFi network the *LVAP* can be thought as a Virtual AP with its own BSSID). As a result each *WTP* will host as many *LVAPs* as the number of clients currently communicating with it. Removing an *LVAP* from a *WTP* and instantiating it on another *WTP* effectively results in a handover.

2.2 The Resource Pool

Programming WiFi networks mandates for a way to expose the programmer with a consistent view of the network resources. The fundamentals of wireless communications basically calls for two main family of strategies to allocate resources in a wireless network: scheduled access and random access. In the former case, resources for a wireless link are allocated in the time, frequency, and space[1] domain. In the latter case, a common random access scheme for medium access is used by all participating wireless clients in order to reduce collisions. WiFi belongs to the latter family and exploits CSMA/CA as random access scheme.

The *Resource Pool* abstraction goes beyond the concept of a cell and exposes the network programmer with the collective resources across time, frequency, and space that are available in the whole network. The minimum allocation unit in the *Resource Pool* is the *Resource Block* and is identified by a channel, a time interval, a spatial stream, and the *WTP* at which it is available. The *Resource Pool* is exposed to the programmer through a set P where each *Resource Block* $b \in P$ is a 3–tuple $\langle f, t, s\rangle$, where f is the channel, t is the time period, and s is the spatial stream. A channel is a 2–tuple $\langle c, b\rangle$ where c and b, respectively, are the center frequency and the bandwidth. For example, the *Resource Pool* made available by an 802.11n AP supporting 2 spatial streams and 40 MHz–wide channels would be represented by the tuple $((36, HT40), \infty, 1)$, $((36, HT40), \infty, 2)$ — ∞ for the time period implies that *Resource Blocks* are allocated for an unspecified period as is common with CSMA/CA based WiFi networks.

These same abstractions can also be used to model the resource requests coming from the clients. This allows expressing resource allocation problems as an intersection between the *Resource Blocks* available in the network and the *Resource Blocks* supported by a client. Information on the link quality experienced by the requesting *LVAP* can be used to further filter the set of candidate *Resource Blocks*, possibly based on application–driven requirements. A non–empty set of *Resource Blocks* so determined suggests a feasible solution for the resource allocation problem, and an optimal choice (based on performance criteria of interest) from this set can then be made. Note that it may not be meaningful to move tasks, such as resource scheduling and rate adaptation, operating at fast timescales to the remote *SD–RAN Controller*; such operations would be physically implemented in a distributed manner within the *WTPs*.

2.3 The Interference Map

As wireless channel and interference characteristics vary over time and space, they need to be taken into account for effective resource allocation. Similarly, application layer requirements also need to be considered. For example, it may make sense for a hotspot operator to optimize system throughput or network utilization whereas in other instances it may be important to ensure allocation of minimum amount of resource for each client. The *Interference Map* abstraction provides network programmers with a full view of the network state in terms of interference and channel quality between *Resource Blocks* and *LVAPs*. The latter essentially consists of a matrix R (typically sparse) where each entry $R(m, l)$ is the channel quality between the *Resource Block* m and the *LVAP* l. In WiFi networks *Interference Map* related information can be obtained via passive measurements on the received traffic.

3. SOFTWARE-DEVELOPMENT KIT

In this section we briefly describe the salient features of our Python–based SDK[2] using some practical examples. The platform supports multiple logical virtual networks each characterized by its own SSID and a set of *WTPs*. *Network App* can be instantiated within one or multiple virtual networks.

Resource Management. The following Python function assigns an *LVAP* to a random *Resource Block* whose RSSI to the *LVAP* is greater than -65 dB:

```
def handover(lvap, wtps):

  # Initialize the Resource Pool
  pool = ResourcePool()

  # Add all available Resource Blocks
  for wtp in wtps.values():
    pool = wtp.supports | pool

  # Select matching Resource Blocks
  matches = pool & lvap.supports

  # Filter matching Resource Blocks by RSSI
  valid = [block for block in matches
              if block.rssi_to[lvap] >= -65]

  # Perform handover
  lvap.assigned_to = valid.pop()
```

The method above accepts two parameters as input: an *LVAP* and a list of *WTPs*. The method initializes the network *Resource Pool* with the *Resource Blocks* available at every *WTP*. Then, an intersection between the network *Resource Pool* and the *LVAP Resource Pool* is computed. The resulting set is then traversed in order

[1]Notice that, for spread spectrum–based technologies, such as UMTS, also the code space shall be considered.

[2]Available at http://empower.create-net.org

to filter–out the *Resource Block* whose RSSI to the *LVAP* is below a certain threshold (-65dB in this case). Finally, one random *Resource Block* matching the above condition is assigned to the *LVAP*. For the sake of simplicity, error handling code has been omitted.

Querying. Packets counters allow programmers to track the traffic exchanged by a certain *LVAP*. For example:

```
s = pkts_count(bins = [500, 1460, 8192],
               lvap = '11:22:33:44:55:66',
               every = 5000)
```

The statement above tracks the packets transmitted and received by a certain *LVAP* and aggregates the information into the specified bins. The counters' current state can be accessed with:

```
>>> s.tx_samples
[60, 10, 0]
```

Meaning that the *LVAP* transmitted 60, 10, and 0 packets smaller or equal to respectively 500, 1460, and 8192 bytes. Similarly, `bytes_count` allows to track the bytes transmitted and received by the *LVAP*.

Interference Tracking. The *Interference Map* allows the developers to meet *LVAP*s' traffic requirements. Moreover, *Network App* can react to changes in the network conditions by setting callbacks that are triggered when the measured RSSI for a given set of *LVAP*s verifies a specified condition. For example:

```
t = rssi(lvaps = '11:22:33:44:55:66'
         relation = 'GT',
         value = -50 )
t.callback = handle_rssi_trigger
```

The callback is triggered the first time the RSSI of the *LVAP* goes above -50 dB at any *WTP* in network. After the trigger has fired the first time and as long as the RSSI remains greater than -50 dB, the callback method is not called again by the same *WTP*, however the same callback can be triggered by multiple *WTP*s. In order to detect RSSI values that are going below the -50 dB threshold another trigger must be created.

4. USE CASE: MOBILITY MANAGEMENT

In this section we sketch basic *Mobility Manager* as a sample *Network App* that makes use of the proposed abstractions. The *Mobility Manager* leverages RSSI tracking to detect when a wireless client's link quality is deteriorating. Moreover, the *Mobility Manager* periodically checks if a better handover opportunity exists. The *Mobility Manager* code is reported below.

```
class MobilityMngr(BPW):

  # Initialize the object
  def __init__(self, pool, period=5):
    BPW.__init__(self, pool, period)
    r = self.rssi(relation='LT',
                  value=-70,
                  lvap="FF:FF:FF:FF:FF:FF")
    r.callback = self.callback

  # Check if a better handover plan
  # can be found
  def loop(self):
    for lvap in self.lvaps().values():
      handover(lvap, self.wtps())

  # Callback on low RSSI
  def callback(self, lvap, wtp):
    handover(lvap, self.wtps())

# Initialize the App
def launch(pool, period=5):
    return MobilityMngr(pool, int(period))
```

A *Network App* in our implementation is essentially a Python module that can be loaded/unloaded at run–time. Each module is required to implement a `launch` method called when the module is initialized. The above *Mobility Manager* implementation consists of a single class implementing three methods: (i) the *constructor* which creates an RSSI trigger matching all *LVAP*s in the network; (ii) *loop*, which periodically checks if an *LVAP* shall be handed–over to another *WTP*; and (iii) *callback* which is invoked when the RSSI is going below a certain threshold in which case the *handover* routine is invoked.

5. CONCLUSIONS

In this work we have proposed a set of high–level programming abstractions for WiFi networks. The proposed primitives allow new features and services to be implemented as software modules hiding away the implementation details of the underlying technology. We also developed a proof-of-concept implementation including an SDK and a *SD–RAN Controller*. As future work we plan extend the proposed abstractions to mobile (LTE/LTE–Advanced) networks.

6. REFERENCES

[1] C. Monsanto, N. Foster, R. Harrison, and D. Walker. A compiler and run-time system for network programming languages. In *Proc. of ACM POPL*, 2012.

[2] C. Monsanto, J. Reich, N. Foster, J. Rexford, and D. Walker. Composing software-defined networks. In *Proc. of USENIX NSDI*, 2013.

[3] L. Suresh, J. Schulz-Zander, R. Merz, A. Feldmann, and T. Vazao. Towards programmable enterprise WLANS with Odin. In *Proc. of ACM HotSDN*, 2012.

[4] A. Voellmy, H. Kim, and N. Feamster. Procera: A language for high-level reactive network control. In *Proc. of ACM HotSDN*, 2012.

ColPhone: A Smartphone is just a piece of the puzzle

Ahmed Salem, Tamer Nadeem
Department of Computer Science
Old Dominion University, VA, USA
{asalem, nadeem}@cs.odu.edu

ABSTRACT

Smartphones have created a strong tie with human beings. It is likely to have plenty of smartphones in the same proximity. However, users are limited with the capabilities of a single device. In this work we propose *ColPhone* a framework that facilitates collaboration between smartdevices in the vicinity to share their resources providing users hardware upgrade for their devices. Further, we implemented an application (3D Story Teller) on top of *ColPhone* , and measured the impact of collaboration on smartphone's power consumption.

Keywords

Smartphone, Collaboration, Android, Bluetooth, WiFi-P2P, Pure Data.

Categories and Subject Descriptors

H.5.3 [**Group and Organization Interfaces**]: Collaborative Computing.

1. INTRODUCTION

Mobile devices yet smartphones have made the break through to human lives. It is very likely to have plenty of smartphones in the same proximity due to their owners motion, or availability of old unused ones with processing, sensing, and storage capabilities. In this work we propose a framework to utilize this frequently occurring scenario.

ColPhone is a framework that facilitates a co-ordinated cooperation between smart devices available in the proximity. It provides smartphone users access to a new set of resources without changing their devices. Smart devices in the proximity can share a portion of their idle resources to be used by others. In return they will receive the same feature upon need, in addition to the results of previous operations (e.g. sensing information) to avoid duplicated processing and power misuse. Further, this new approach opens the horizon for application that was not possible on one device. 3D story teller is an example where a story can be read from multiple device (e.g. one character per device). The devices' location and character distribution among devices can emulate the story as a movie.

MobiCom'14, Sep 07-11 2014, Maui, HI, USA
ACM 978-1-4503-2783-1/14/09.
http://dx.doi.org/10.1145/2639108.2642906 .

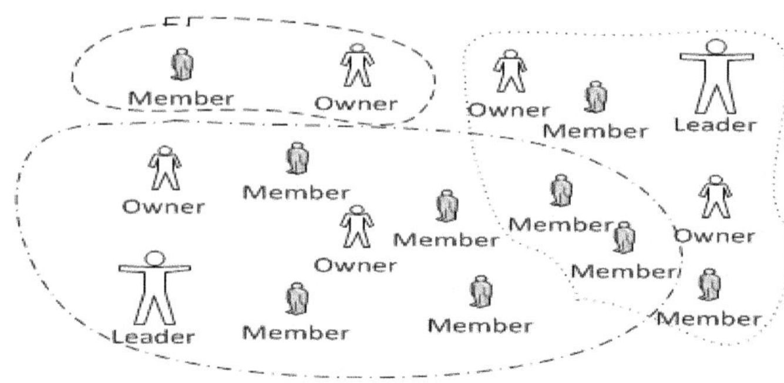

Figure 1: Groups.

2. RELATED WORK

Peer to peer communication have been around for a while. The evolution of smartphones encouraged researchers to consider taking the peer to peer communication to mobile devices. The outcome of that merging came in the form of a typical peer to peer network with all its infrastructure dependency either on WiFi or cellular networks. The difference came in the application level to have Apps run smartphone efficient [4]. Smartphones with all their resources and closeness to users can do better.

Duan et al. proposed a stochastic model to encourage smartphones to collaborate with each other [3]. They divided the smartphone activities into two categories data acquisition and distributed computing. They considered smartphones as a set of resources CPU, memory, storage, battery life, and connectivity. They proposed an analytical model without considering empirical issues

CoMon is a platform used to build cooperation groups of nearby smartphones[5]. The key idea is to pass the sensing information collected by a smartphone to others saving their energy. They took the GPS as a high energy consuming module and compared between constantly reading its values versus getting them from other peers.

RIO is a system proposed to Control the I/O resources of one phone (e.g. Camera, Speaker) through another [2]. They used kernel device files to share readings between 2 Android devices. This approach does not scale as the kernel device files sees all the incoming values from a single device.

3. FRAMEWORK

ColPhone is a role oriented architecture where each smartphone can play one or more roles throughout the execution life-cycle. In this section we will explain the roles used, the features every role has as shown in Fig 2.

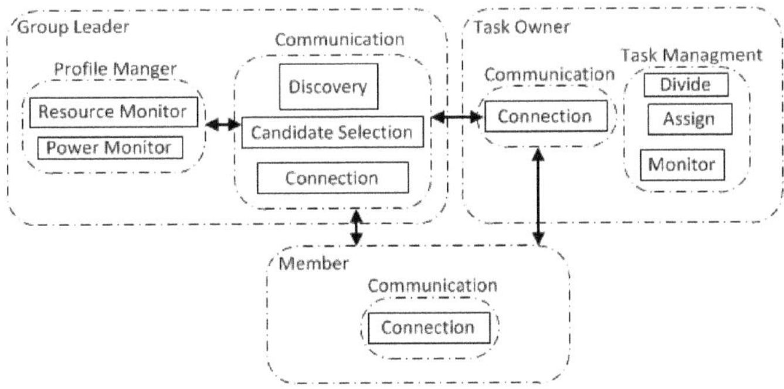

Figure 2: Framework.

3.1 Roles and Players

Roles are functional behaviors that can be played by every smartphone. We define three roles for our scheme as shown in Fig. 1 :

Group Leader: the role responsible for the management and monitoring of task execution. Further, this role is responsible for coordinating between the task owner role players.

Task Owner: the role of the node issuing the task to be performed. This role has four main jobs: First, task breakdown into services that can run on different devices in parallel; Second, request a list of recruited members from the group leader and assign services to them; Third, delegate the execution monitoring to the group leader; Finally, Collect the resulting feedback from members.

Group Member: the role responsible for following the instructions received from the group leader to achieve a collaboration architecture.

Task owner role is introduced to enhance *ColPhone* performance. It is likely for wireless networking protocols to have a group leader that is responsible for managing and controlling members. The infrastructure-less nature of *ColPhone* in addition to the expected multiple service dissemination is likely to decrease the network throughput and consume the smartphone power inefficiently if done through the group leader.

3.2 Functional Modules

ColPhone framework in Fig. 2 has three main functional modules Communication, Profile Management, and Task Management.

The communication module is responsible for finding available smartphones in the proximity through device discovery and candidate selection modules. The *Device Discovery* module senses the medium for available devices. The list of available smartphones are then passed to the *Candidate Selection* module, which sorts them based on their readiness for collaboration. This readiness is categorized in terms of available resources, power levels, and collaboration enrollment. First, the devices that can not provide the requested resources for collaboration are excluded from the list. The remaining smartphones that are currently charging have the highest priority followed by others according to their current power levels. Finally, devices that are currently sharing or have collaboration services to execute are relocated to the end of the list.

The Profile Management module is responsible for providing the *Candidate Selection* with the required in information gathered through it's two sub-modules *Power Monitor*, and *Resource Monitor*. These information is used for sorting of the available smartphones.

The Task Management Module is responsible for splitting the available task into multiple services based on the number of the available smartphones, assigning the services to different smartphone, and monitoring their execution. In case of an execution problem on a smartphone (e.g. it moved out of the communication range), the task manager should assign that service to another smartphone to continue its execution.

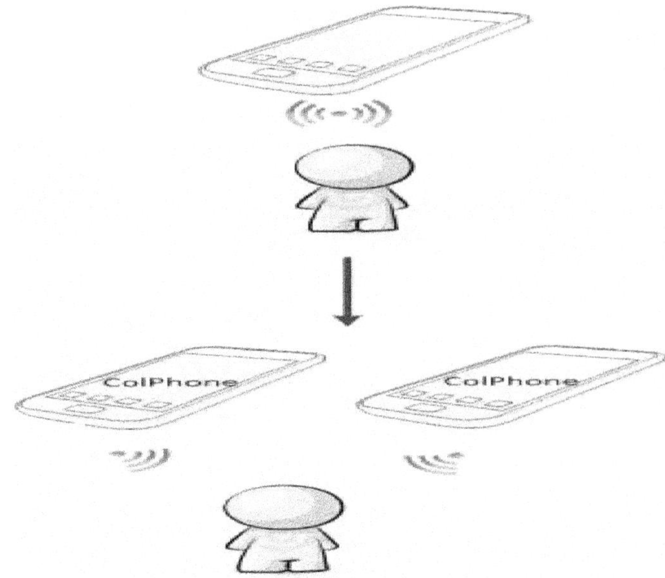

Figure 3: 3D Story Teller

4. 3D STORY TELLER PROTOTYPE

Media applications are one the popular uses of smartphones. 3D Story Teller besides being a normal audio application, it provides the possibility of playing the audio track on multiple devices as illustrated in Fig. 3. The application's idea is based on the fact that people enjoy movies in cinemas more than TVs, because of the difference in sound effects. 3D Story Teller using the features provides by *ColPhone* , splits audio tracks by character to be played on multiple devices. For example, It is now very likely that kids listen to stories through smartphones. 3D Story Teller will enable the sound of each character in the story to come from a different device. We believe that this can provide kids with a more engaging story time.

4.1 Typical Scenario

Upon enabling the collaboration feature, the user plays his audio track as normal from his device. The user's device is now playing the *task owner* role. It then communicates with the *task manager* role to request a list of available smartphones for collaboration specifying the set of requested resources, in this case speakers.

Task manager role being in action uses the features explained before from the *Communication* and *Profile Management* modules to sense the medium and provide the user with a list of devices ready to collaborate.

Once the *task owner* receives the list, it splits the current audio track to N sub-tracks, where N is minimum of characters in the audio track ,and the number available smartphones willing to collaborate. The N sub-tracks are then forwarded to the

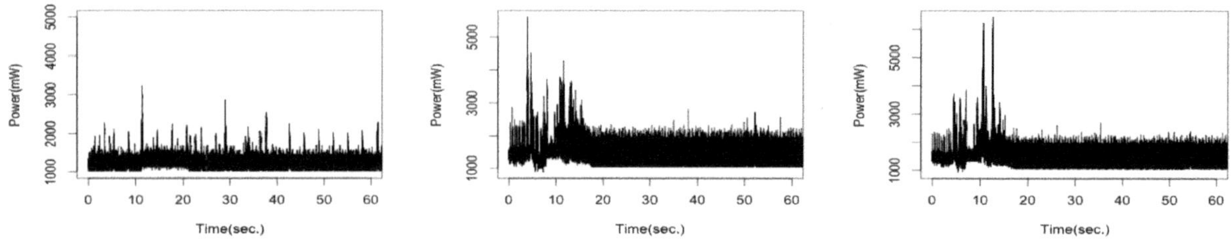

(a) Single Smartphone. (b) Owner. (c) Member.

Figure 4: 3D Story Teller Power Consumption

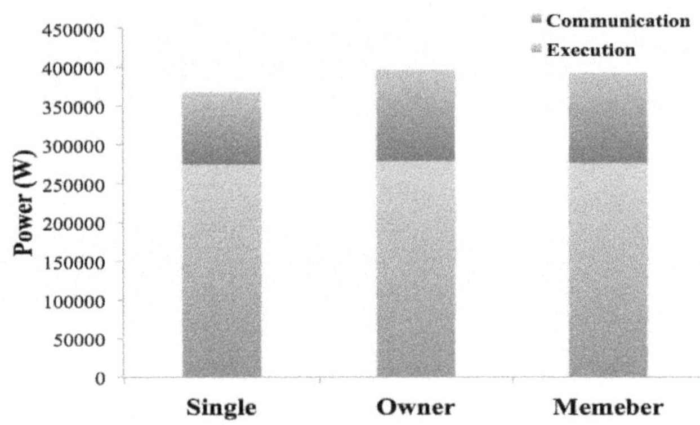

Figure 5: Overall Power Consumption

smartphones, and starts to play. Collaborating smartphones are supposed to keep contact with the *task owner* throughout the execution period. In case of a smartphone quitting the collaboration, the *task owner* is responsible for the track re-assignment.

4.2 Assumptions

1. Proximity is decided by the device's communication range, Wi-Fi P2P in the current version.
2. Communication is established upon user's acceptance.
3. Security, and Privacy are maintained throughout the communication.

4.3 Prototype implementation

We implemented a prototype for the 3D story teller application using Android Samsung Galaxy note N7000 phones to play the leader/owner, and member roles. Further, we generated an audio track of 2 characters, and used Pure Data (PD) to control the tracks through Android APIs [1, 6].

The scenario starts with a smartphone playing the full audio track. Upon the arrival of a collaborator, a version of the file is disseminated to it with the character to play and timing information. The audio then comes out from both phone till one of the phones quit or the audio track is over.

4.4 Performance Measures

The execution of the implemented prototype was monitored using Monsoon power monitor as shown in Fig. 4.

Fig 4 depicts the 3D story teller power consumption in three cases: (a) using a single smartphone, (b, c) shows the owner and member roles respectively when *ColPhone* is used to run the application. Figure 5 shows the overall power required for communication, and audio mode for the three previous cases. Hence, the impact of *ColPhone* on the smartphone power consumption is mild since the communication is likely to happen only at the first contact.

5. CONCLUSION AND FUTURE WORK

In this work, we proposed an initial attempt to build an infrastructureless smartphone collaboration system that we called *ColPhone* . We presented the system design roles and modules. We explained how both roles and modules interact together to achieve a smooth collaboration process. Finally, we implemented a prototype for the 3D story teller application using *ColPhone* , and showed its energy consumption.

Our Future work will include expanding the framework design and implementation to host other applications. In this work we showed an I/O bound application (3D story teller), we further plan to measure *ColPhone* 's performance while hosting other application categories. Further we will be using a hybrid of Bluetooth, and WiFi-P2P for power efficient connection phase, and higher data rate in service dissemination respectively. Our future work will also consider relaxing the current security, and privacy assumptions.

6. REFERENCES

[1] http://puredata.info/.

[2] M. H. Y. Ardalan Amiri Sani, Kevin Boos and L. Zhong. Rio: A system solution for sharing i/o between mobile systems. In *Proc. MobiSys*. ACM, 2014.

[3] L. Duan, T. Kubo, K. Sugiyama, J. Huang, T. Hasegawa, and J. Walrand. Incentive mechanisms for smartphone collaboration in data acquisition and distributed computing. In *INFOCOM, 2012 Proceedings IEEE*, pages 1701–1709. IEEE, 2012.

[4] S. Kosta, V. C. Perta, J. Stefa, P. Hui, and A. Mei. Clone2clone (c2c): Peer-to-peer networking of smartphones on the cloud. In *5th USENIX Workshop on Hot Topics in Cloud Computing (HotCloudâĂŹ13)*, 2013.

[5] Y. Lee, Y. Ju, C. Min, S. Kang, I. Hwang, and J. Song. Comon: cooperative ambience monitoring platform with continuity and benefit awareness. In *Proceedings of the 10th international conference on Mobile systems, applications, and services*, pages 43–56. ACM, 2012.

[6] A. Salem and T. Nadeem. Colphone: A smartphone is just a piece of the puzzle. In *Proceedings of the 2014 ACM conference on Pervasive and ubiquitous computing adjunct publication*. ACM, 2014.

Poster: Come Closer - Proximity-based Authentication for the Internet of Things

Hossein Shafagh
Department of Computer Science
ETH Zurich, Switzerland
shafagh@inf.ethz.ch

Anwar Hithnawi
Department of Computer Science
ETH Zurich, Switzerland
hithnawi@inf.ethz.ch

ABSTRACT

This paper presents a proximity-based authentication approach for the *Internet of Things* (IoT) that works in-band by solely utilizing the wireless communication interface. The novelty of this approach lies in its reliance on ambient radio signals to infer proximity within about one second, and in its ability to expose imposters located several meters away. We identify relevant features sensed from the RF channel to establish a notion of proximity across co-located low-power devices. We introduce our proximity-based authentication protocol and show the feasibility of our approach with an early prototype using off-the-shelf 802.15.4 sensors and an evaluation conducted in a real-world environment.

Categories and Subject Descriptors

C.2.0 [**Computer-Communication Networks**]: General – Security and protection

Keywords

Wireless Communication; Security; Internet of Things

1. INTRODUCTION

With the advent of the IoT, there is a rise in the number of smart devices that are empowered with sensing, actuating and communication capabilities to enhance and create unique forms of interaction with our immediate surroundings. As these devices are integrated in our proximate living space, they deal with sensitive and private data that can be misused to infer information about our daily habits. This consequently raises unique security and privacy challenges that drive the need for security to be an integral part of any IoT system. Due to cost, size and energy efficiency requirements, commodity IoT devices are designed with minimalistic physical interfaces. Among these interfaces, the radio transceiver is the common physical interface, which makes it a natural candidate to be utilized for security services.

MobiCom'14, Sep 07-11 2014, Maui, HI, USA
ACM 978-1-4503-2783-1/14/09.
http://dx.doi.org/10.1145/2639108.2642904.

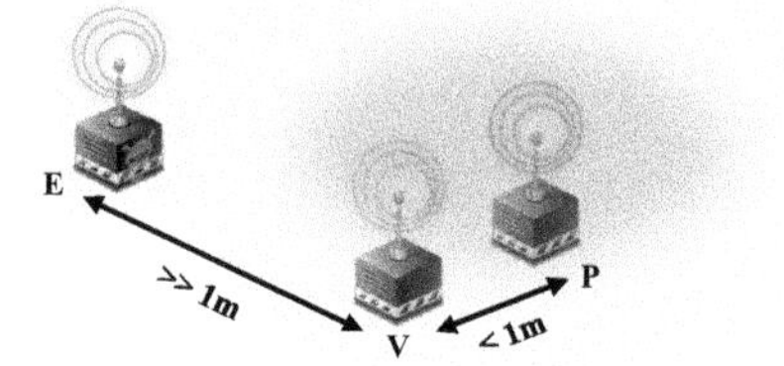

Figure 1: Proximity-based authentication of two co-located devices P and V, in the presence of an adversary E.

The ubiquity of the wireless medium, has given a raise to the number of RF communication technologies and devices being used, particularly in the ISM bands. This implies that there is a form of continuous energy fluctuations in the wireless channel, generated by a diverse set of communication technologies. RF signals constitute a source of electromagnetic energy that radiates in the channel. As the RF signals traverse the medium they undergo many propagation effects that can cause large or small scale energy losses. This energy is absorbed and scattered in different directions as it propagates in the space, thus inducing different levels of observed energy spatially and temporally. At the same time, the perceived RF signals appear to be highly correlated in two co-located points. The correlation drastically decreases as the distance between the two points increases. Quantifying these variations of energy in the channel by sampling the cumulative RF signal strength at a high rate provides us with a unique time-variant metric that we source for our proximity-based authentication approach.

In order to protect the communication of two smart devices, traditionally pre-shared keys are used, and recently *Public-Key Cryptography* (PKC) has been advocated. The former does not scale for the IoT, and the latter is not affordable by highly resource-constrained devices. Specifically, the mere use of PKC-based key agreement protocols, such as *Diffie-Hellman* (DH) without authentication, for instance by means of certificates, leaves the communication vulnerable to man-in-the-middle attacks.

In this work, we propose a proximity-based authentication approach for low-power IoT devices. This approach is based on correlating fine-grained samples of channel information in form of *Energy Levels* (EL). In order to compensate for the narrow-band of low-power transceivers, i.e., 2 MHz, we collect the channel information over several frequencies. In contrast to existing approaches, we do not require the exchange of huge amounts of packets, which increases the energy efficiency of our protocol in favor of less radio pollution. We utilize the broadcast nature of the wireless medium and how electromagnetic signals from uncontrolled transmitters are propagating and affecting the level of energy perceived by nodes. The results of our experiments show the feasibility of our protocol even for underutilized networks.

2. RELATED WORK

The temporal and spatial variations in the radio channel have been exploited by researchers in RF-based localization, secure key extraction, and proximity estimation. In RF-based localization [7, 6], the range between a device and the reference points is estimated by means of RSSI. Afterwards, techniques such as triangulation can be used to estimate the relative location. Key extraction approaches [4, 8, 10] use the reciprocal behavior of communication links to generate a secure key between two end-points. These approaches are complementary to our work, since they aim at securing the communication between two nodes without prior knowledge, whereas we provide proximity-based authentication.

Prominent RF-based proximity estimation approaches are: Amigo [3], Ensemble [2], and ProxiMate [9]. Amigo relies on observing the channel in promiscuous mode for 802.11 frames. The observed packets and their corresponding RSSI readings are fed to a classifier which determines proximity. In order to reach low false positive rates, more than 5 s are needed. Ensemble relies on RSSI readings of packets generated by a network of trusted devices. It requires at least 3 trusted devices in communication range, each sending 40 packets per second for 70 s. ProxiMate relies similar to our approach on ambient RF signal. However, they focus on TV signals and require software-defined radios to extract the required features (amplitude and phase) from the signal.

Proximity estimation can as well be achieved by other means such as *Time-of-Arrival* (TOA). Rasmussen et al. [5] introduce an RF distance bounding technique based on TOA, which requires high processing time in the range of nanoseconds, since an error of 3 ns results into an estimation error of approx. 3 m. They achieve this high precision with a custom designed radio-chip.

In this work, we present a proximity-based authentication, which is based on captured energy level variations. These variations exist due to propagation effects on ambient RF signals from inter/cross-technology devices emitting in the same frequency bands. Considering the resource-constraints of smart devices, we limit the number of packet transmissions to a few packets that are required to indicate the next channel rendez-vous, i.e., frequency, and to achieve loose synchronization for signal acquisition. During the inter-packet times, we collect EL readings. The signal acquisition time is a protocol parameter which is related to the level of experienced entropy.

3. ATTACKER MODEL

In our attacker model, as depicted in Figure 1, we distinguish between passive and active attackers, who are not in the proximity of the genuine device. By design, we are immune against a passive attacker, who eavesdrops on the medium aiming at observing a similar physical channel. This is due to the fact that we rely on the continuous stochastic channel properties that are uncorrelated in the time and spatial domains. An active attacker who makes use of jamming by means of emitting energy with certain patterns, aims at deceiving two not co-located nodes to falsely decide they are

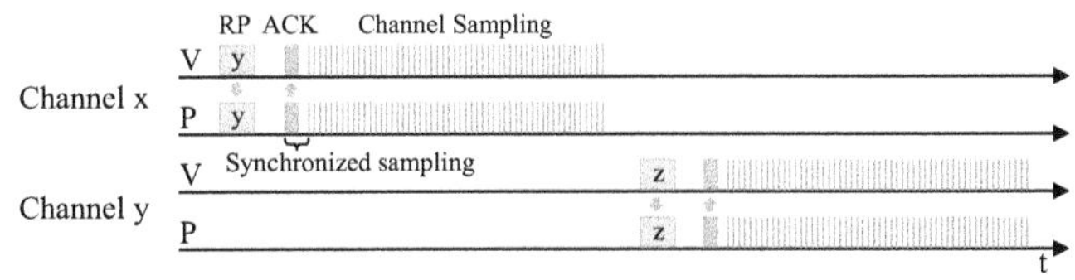

Figure 2: Signal acquisition stage of our protocol for two rounds at channels x and y. The *Rendez-vous Packet* (RP) indicates the next channel for sampling. The ACK is used for a synchronized sampling at a rate of 7.69 kHz, which lasts for 234 ms.

in close range. Due to radio wave characteristics such as fading, reflection, diffraction and scattering, such an attack is complex. Additionally, by taking the level of induced energy which disperses by distance [1] into our algorithm, we make such an attack more difficult. In future work, we quantify the effectiveness of an active attacker.

4. SYSTEM ARCHITECTURE

In this section, we describe our authentication protocol.

Signal acquisition and quantization. *Proofer* (P) initiates the handshake with a request packet. Upon reception of such a packet, *Verifier* (V) sends a *Rendez-vous Packet* (RP) indicating the next communication channel. As the low-power transceivers typically communicate over narrow-band channels, i.e., 2 MHz, certain channels may be exposed to less variations. Hence, in order to increase the chances of capturing enough channel variations, we rely on several channels. Possible rendez-vous channels are the 16 available channels of 802.15.4. To optimize the channel selection, V maintains a profile of good channels that exhibit high variations based on previous observations. After receiving the RP, P sends a MAC-layer *Acknowledgment* (ACK) to V. We use the ACK for a loose synchronization required for an aligned signal acquisition. This is achieved with a sampling routine starting immediately after reception of the ACK. P and V sample the EL at a frequency rate of 7.69 kHZ for the time unit t_{el} (in our experiments t_{el}=234 ms corresponding to 1800 readings). After t_{el}, V sends the next RP on the previously announced rendez-vous channel, where the same procedure of EL sampling repeats. This procedure, as depicted in Figure 2, continues n times, until V requests the proof of proximity from P. Currently, we consider $n \in \{3, 4, 5\}$ which depends on the quality of the signal acquired by V. The end-points divide the $i \in \{1..n\}$ collected signal traces, h_v^i and h_p^i, into $j \in \{1..45\}$ blocks $b_v^{i,j}$, each consisting of 40 channel readings. The block size corresponds to 5.2 ms. This achieves a downsampling from 1800 to 45 values. For each block $b_v^{i,j}$ and respectively $b_p^{i,j}$, we compute the maximum induced power level which we rely on for the correlation algorithm. At the same time, we validate if all blocks $b_d^{i,j}$ from the two devices $d \in \{v, p\}$ have experienced enough entropy, i.e., randomness:

$$R(d,i,j,k) = \begin{cases} 1 & \text{if } b_d^{i,j}[k] > (mean(b_d^{i,j}) + \alpha) \\ 1 & \text{if } b_d^{i,j}[k] < (mean(b_d^{i,j}) - \alpha) \\ 0 & \text{otherwise} \end{cases}$$

$$\forall\, i \in [1..n],\ j \in [1..45],\quad R\_ratio_d^{i,j} = \frac{\sum_{k=1}^{40} R(d,i,j,k)}{40} > 0.1 \tag{1}$$

To this end, we require that in each block at least 10% of the readings deviate by about α=2 dBm from its average readings. At a higher level, we require that again 10% of all

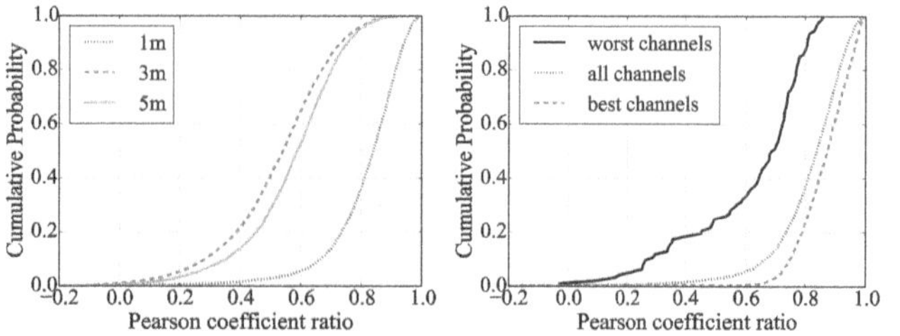

(a) Three Distances (b) Channels at 1 m

Figure 3: CDF of Pearson correlation coefficient computed over 38400 traces, collected with 802.15.4 motes, at several distances, and over all frequencies.

blocks fulfill the entropy condition:

$$\forall\ i \in [1..n], \quad R\_ratio\_total_d^i = \frac{\sum_{j=1}^{45} R\_ratio_d^{i,j}}{45} > 0.1 \qquad (2)$$

Traces not fulfilling this requirement are discarded, due to low entropy. V observes the quality of traces during the handshake and if required increases n, the number of rounds.
Reconciliation. The alignment of traces is achieved by a synchronized sampling. As illustrated in Figure 2, after the ACK transmission, P waits t_s μs, which is the time required for V to receive and process the ACK, and enter the sampling routine. This way, both end-points start to sample the channel at the same time. We decided against exchange of the channel hopping sequence at the beginning of the handshake, to avoid possible inaccuracies due to channel switching and clock drifts. Hence, the channel rendez-vous packets serve as a measure for a synchronized signal acquisition.
Correlation. For each pair of traces h_v^i and h_p^i, we compute the degree of correlation by means of the Pearson correlation coefficient r. We use the induced power levels for the calculation of the Pearson correlation coefficient. If the majority of the traces have a high correlation, then physical proximity can be assumed. We detail our decision for a majority vote in the next section based on our empirical observations.

5. EXPERIMENTS

In order to validate our assumptions about the correlation of channel variations at co-located devices, we perform experiments within our offices using TelosB motes, a low-power sensor node with an 802.15.4 compatible radio transceiver, and a built-in omnidirectional antenna.

We use Contiki OS for our implementation and collect approx. 800 traces in each of the 16 channels. The two nodes are placed in line-of-sight, at distances of 1, 3, and 5 m. Our measurements are conducted mainly at night, and accumulate to more than 38400 traces. We compute the Pearson correlation coefficient averaged over all channels for these distances. As depicted in Figure 3(a), for co-located devices at distance 1 m, 80% of the runs exhibit a correlation coefficient ratio higher than 0.7. For distances 3 and 5 m, only 15% to 20% of the runs have a higher ratio than 0.7. Setting the threshold for proximity to a correlation ratio of 0.7 results into 15% false negatives (rejected co-located nodes) and 15% to 20% false positives (falsely accepted far nodes). With a simple majority vote over at least 3 runs, we reduce the amount of false negatives and false positives. More importantly, the randomness of the channel varies over time and frequency. As depicted in Figure 3(b), the two best channels exhibit high correlation coefficients, whereas the worse two

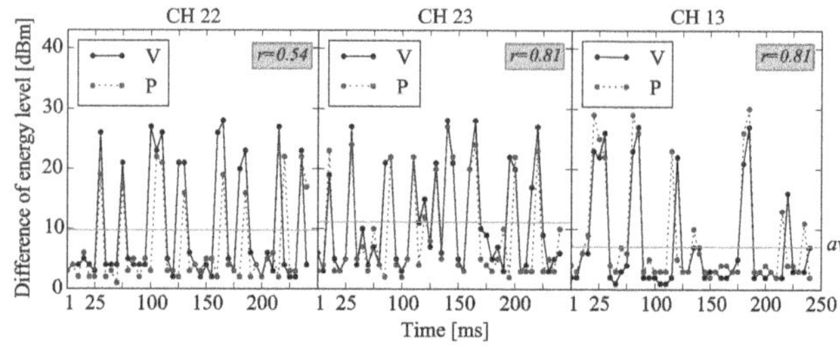

Figure 4: Three selected traces from co-located devices. All traces, experience enough randomness, measured in form of deviations from the average value (depicted as a gray line). Traces from channels 23 and 13 have a good correlation coefficient r.

channels behave similarly to distanced nodes. To explain our majority-vote-based proximity decision, as illustrated in Figure 4, we selected three traces from co-located devices at three different channels. The traces exhibit enough randomness. However, only the middle and right traces show a high correlation coefficient. The first trace has a low correlation coefficient, though we observe a similar trend on the readings. This is due to different energy levels, which implies different distances, explaining the low correlation coefficient.

6. FUTURE WORK

In this paper, we introduced our proximity-based authentication scheme, tailored for resource-constrained devices. We presented the results of our prototype implementation on TelosB motes. Currently, we are improving our correlation algorithm, and extending our implementation. We plan to conduct extensive measurements to assess the impact of cross-technology interference, static environments with low entropy, mobility and human motion on our protocol.

7. REFERENCES

[1] A. Hithnawi et al. Low-Power Wireless Channel Quality Estimation in the Presence of RF Smog. DCOSS'14.

[2] A. Kalamandeen et al. Ensemble: Cooperative Proximity-based Authentication. MobiSys'10.

[3] A. Varshavsky et al. Amigo: Proximity-based Authentication of Mobile Devices. UbiComp'07.

[4] J. Croft et al. Robust Uncorrelated Bit Extraction Methodologies for Wireless Sensors. IPSN'10.

[5] K.B. Rasmussen et al. Realization of RF Distance Bounding. USENIX Security'10.

[6] M. Youssef et al. Challenges: device-free passive localization for wireless environments. Mobicom'07.

[7] N. Patwari et al. Relative Location Estimation in Wireless Sensor Networks. *Transactions on Signal Processing*, 51(8), 2003.

[8] S. Jana et al. On the Effectiveness of Secret Key Extraction from Wireless Signal Strength in Real Environments. MobiCom'09.

[9] S. Mathur et al. ProxiMate: Proximity-based Secure Pairing Using Ambient Wireless Signals. MobiSys'11.

[10] S. Mathur et al. Radio-Telepathy: Extracting a Secret Key from an Unauthenticated Wireless Channel. MobiCom'08.

Poster – Cognitive Networking in a Self-Powered Wireless Sensor Network Testbed

Petros Spachos
Electrical and Computer Engineering
University of Toronto, Canada
petros@ece.utoronto.ca

Dimitrios Hatzinakos
Electrical and Computer Engineering
University of Toronto, Canada
dimitris@comm.utoronto.ca

ABSTRACT

Scalability and sustainability are two fundamental requirements in Wireless Sensor Networks (WSNs). Inch scale sensor nodes can operate unattended for long periods if they have sufficient energy sources. In this work, a Self-Powered Sensor Network (SPSN) testbed is introduced. SPSN is cost-efficient and has large-scale deployability. It combines cognitive networking principles with efficient routing approaches and energy harvesting techniques. SPSN is used for indoor CO_2 monitoring as well as for outdoor gas leak detection. The performance of the system for channel estimation at an outdoor environment is examined. Experimental results show that SPSN can be used for a plethora of other applications as well.

Categories and Subject Descriptors

C.2.1 [**COMPUTER-COMMUNICATION NETWORKS**]: Network Architecture and Design—*Wireless communication*

Keywords

Cognitive radio networks; Testbeds; Self-powered wireless sensor networks; Routing protocols;

1. INTRODUCTION

Characterized as one of the key technologies contributing to the so-called "digital evolution", modern Wireless Sensor Network (WSN) platforms are endowed with the ability to create networked artifacts (human and non-human) to sense their environment, and accordingly adapt their behaviour in beneficial manners. The potential applications are numerous, including effective monitoring and sustainable governance in structural health, disaster relief, transportation, law enforcement, and public safety and security.

A major rationale for these WSN technologies is that they can enable the users to make decisions in a "smarter", more "aware" and "responsive" manner [3]. Indeed, a distributed monitoring capacity gives us a "novel" visualization of our environment that allows more effective planning: the ability to respond in a more timely fashion, and to develop more effective actions to resolve environmental problems. The social and economic implications can be enormous, not only for public but also for private organizations. Evidently, this technological innovation impacts many aspects of human life: health and safety, information and communications, energy and environment, as well as security, to name a few.

However, while there are irrefutable advantages to be reaped with the WSN infrastructures, these strategic values are not without caveats. On the one hand, the larger a sensor network becomes, the smarter and more responsive we become, as our visualization becomes more global and informative. On the other hand, as the size of the network increases, so does the associated complexity and management [2]. To facilitate deployment and acceptance of such networks, the sensor nodes must be inexpensive, non-intrusive, and communicate effectively. Together, these conditions imply two fundamental requirements that influence the operation of the network: scalability and sustainability. Without these two requirements, the operation and impact of the WSN would be questionably limited, if not short-lived.

Motivated by the WSN tremendous potentials, coupled with the technological limitations affecting the current WSN platforms as described above, in this work a Self-Powered Sensor Network (SPSN) testbed is introduced. The SPSN testbed consists of self-powered wireless sensor nodes. The nodes can operate indoor with batteries and outdoor with a solar system [1], depending on the application requirements.

2. SYSTEM FRAMEWORK

In this section, an application scenario is given followed by the system requirements and the system models of the introduced SPSN framework.

2.1 Application scenario

A self-powered WSN monitoring application is considered. The application can be indoor or outdoor. A number of wireless sensor nodes along with a number of simple relay nodes are deployed in the monitoring area. Each node is equipped with a sensor module and a wireless transmission module. The data from the sensor module are passed to the transmission module which forwards all the necessary data to the control room, through the relay nodes. The relay nodes have the same wireless transmission module with the sensor nodes however, they only have communication capabilities. Both the sensor units and the relay nodes are battery powered for indoor applications. For an indoor application, a monitor-

MobiCom'14, September 7-11, 2014, Maui, Hawaii, USA.
ACM 978-1-4503-2783-1/14/09.
http://dx.doi.org/10.1145/2639108.2642909 .

ing system of CO_2 levels in a building is considered. For outdoor systems the units are equipped with solar panels and perform energy scavenging. For an outdoor application a gas leak detection system is studied.

2.2 System requirements

A monitoring system has a number of requirements, depending on the application scenario. Apart from general system requirements, such as the size of the units and the cost per unit, at the network level, the proposed system has the following requirements:

- *Real-time data aggregation.* The packets related to the CO_2 levels or the gas leakage, should be delivered to the destination on time with a minimum delay.
- *Energy efficient sensor units.* The units should operate unattended for long periods of time and hence, the network lifetime is important. An energy conserving routing protocol should be applied.
- *Drop-and-play units.* The units should be able to join or leave the network at any time.
- *Location information.* The location of the even should be included in the packet towards the destination. Location information can be acquired with the use of a number of techniques.
- *Coexistence problem.* The system should have minimum interference with other infrastructures. Especially in the indoor case, the system should be flexible in the spectrum selection and not interfere with other WLANs.

2.3 System Modules

SPSN framework has three important modules: the *sensor units*, the *relay nodes* and the *control room*. In the following, a brief description of each module is given.

- **Sensor unit.** The sensor unit is the monitoring module. It consists of a prototype radio board [4] that has two antennas and performs the spectrum sensing and the routing protocol. Also, it has a sensor node attached. The sensor can monitor the concentration of CO_2 as well as gas leakages, temperature and humidity. The development board (the sensor and the radio), is connected either to a $9V$ battery (indoor) or to a solar system (outdoor), depending on the application. The solar system consists of a photovoltaic solar panel with operating voltage $5V$ and operating current $560mA$. The panel is connected to the rechargeable battery through a charger. The battery is a polymer lithium ion battery of $6600mAh$ and $3.7V$. The sensor unit with the solar system is shown in Fig.1(a) along with the schematic diagram with the connection of the different components in Fig.1(b). For the indoor system, a battery is connected right before the Voltage regulator in Fig.1(b).
- **Relay node.** The relay node has the same radio board with the sensor unit. This module however, does not have a sensor. Hence, the total energy consumption is lower. It performs the main packet forwarding and uses either $2AA$ batteries or a solar system. Periodically, the relay nodes broadcast advertisement packets. In this way, the network maintains location information about the sensor units, through Received Signal Strength Indication (RSSI) values and information about nodes which joined or left the network. The relay node is shown in Fig.2 its specifications are shown in Table 1.

(a) Sensor unit for outdoor applications.

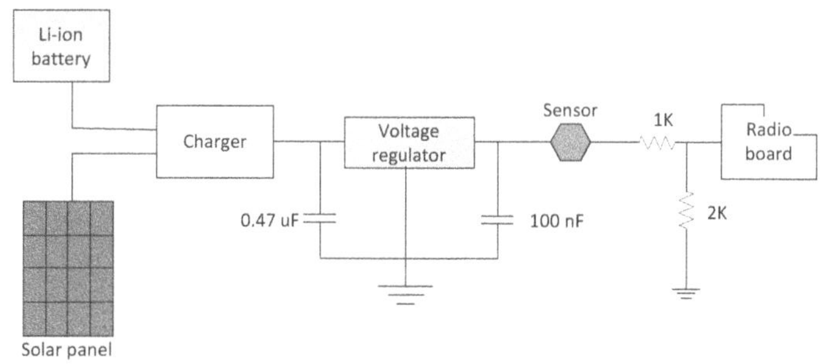

(b) Circuit Schematic.

Figure 1: SPSN can operate both indoor and outdoor. In (a) is an example of an outdoor sensor unit along with its circuit schematic in (b).

- **Control room.** This is a radio board connected to a computer. This radio board is the destination of all the packets. When a packet arrives, the radio decomposes it and forwards the necessary information to the GUI. The GUI displays location and monitoring information regarding the relay nodes and the sensor units in real time. For the location we use the RSSI values of the different packets and a simple triangulation method.

3. EVALUATION

SPSN represents our second generation Cognitive Radio Network (CRN) routing testbed architecture. In particular, SPSN testbed composed of:

- 50 relay nodes and 20 sensor units,
- units and nodes can work outdoor with solar panels or indoor with batteries,

Table 1: Radio board specifications.

Parameter	Unit	Value
Radio range	*meters*	20
Frequency range	*GHz*	2.405-2.483
Bandwidth	*MHz*/channel	5
Receiver sensitivity	*dBm*	-94
Transmitting power	*dBm*	-25
Power Cons. (Sleep)	*uA*	1
Power Cons. (Work)	*mA*	25

Figure 2: Relay nodes.

- remote access to the testbed for centralized control and management,
- open source protocol library for easy deployment and
- enhanced GUI for localization and monitoring applications.

To evaluate the performance of SPSN, outdoor experiments were performed. A channel estimation at an outdoor environment was conducted. Three channels were used for the radio boards. For the experiment 31 relay nodes were used. The nodes were placed in a straight line with 1 m distance between them. Each unit broadcasted packets for 2 $min.$. From the packets the RSSI value [5] was extracted. 4480 values were collected with an average of 154 values in each distance. For the theoretical calculation of RSSI the following formula was used:

$$RSSI(d) = -10 \times n \times log(d) + A \quad (1)$$

where n is the propagation path loss exponent, d is the distance from the sender and A is the received signal strength at one meter of distance.

Table 2 shows the theoretical value, the average RSSI value and the standard deviation (SD) for 10 distances. The results for all the distances can be seen in Fig. 3.

As it can be inferred from the results, the experimental results are close to the theoretical for an outdoor application. Hence, SPSN can provide realistic results for channel estimation at an outdoor environment.

4. CONCLUSIONS AND FUTURE WORKS

In this work, a Self-Powered Sensor Network (SPSN) system is proposed. The main components of the system were described. Also, the performance of the system for a channel estimation at an outdoor environment was examined. The experimental results are promising.

Further study on the performance of SPSN at a complex indoor environment should be conducted. Moreover, the performance of the nodes under a non-line-of-sight model should be examined. Finally, some optimizations on the tool should be made before the SPSN testbed becomes publicly available for research projects.

Table 2: Distance, theoretical and experimental RSSI and SD.

Distance	Theoretical [dBm]	Exp. [dBm]	SD
3 m	-52.88	-50.14	1.32
6 m	-61.01	-56.77	1.48
9 m	-65.76	-62.11	1.53
12 m	-69.13	-67.21	1.02
15 m	-71.75	-69.04	1.62
18 m	-73.89	-72.67	1.32
21 m	-75.69	-72.86	1.13
24 m	-77.26	-74.97	1.41
27 m	-78.64	-76.22	1.09
30 m	-79.88	-77.1	1.02

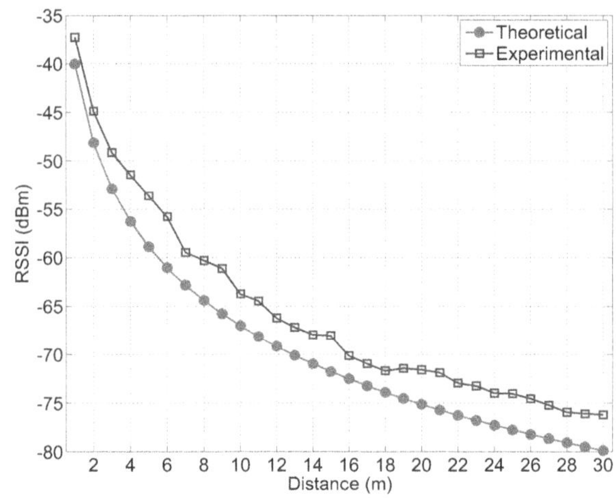

Figure 3: Comparison of theoretical and experimental RSSI.

5. ACKNOWLEDGEMENTS

This work was supported in part by the Natural Sciences and Engineering Research Council of Canada (NSERC), and by the MRI-Ontario under an ORF-RE grant.

6. REFERENCES

[1] C. Alippi and C. Galperti. An adaptive system for optimal solar energy harvesting in wireless sensor network nodes. *IEEE Transactions on Circuits and Systems I: Regular Papers*, 55(6):1742–1750, July 2008.

[2] V. Gungor and G. Hancke. Industrial wireless sensor networks: Challenges, design principles, and technical approaches. *IEEE Transactions on Industrial Electronics*, 56(10):4258–4265, Oct. 2009.

[3] V. Gungor, B. Lu, and G. Hancke. Opportunities and challenges of wireless sensor networks in smart grid. *IEEE Transactions on Industrial Electronics*, 57(10):3557–3564, Oct. 2010.

[4] P. Spachos, L. Song, and D. Hatzinakos. Prototypes of opportunistic wireless sensor networks supporting indoor air quality monitoring. *IEEE Consumer Communications and Networking Conference (CCNC)*, pages 851–852, Jan. 2013.

[5] F. Viani, L. Lizzi, P. Rocca, M. Benedetti, M. Donelli, and A. Massa. Object tracking through rssi measurements in wireless sensor networks. *Electronics Letters*, 44(10):653–654, May 2008.

Poster – SEA-OR: Spectrum and Energy Aware Opportunistic Routing for Self-Powered Wireless Sensor Networks

Petros Spachos
Electrical and Computer Engineering
University of Toronto, Canada
petros@ece.utoronto.ca

Dimitrios Hatzinakos
Electrical and Computer Engineering
University of Toronto, Canada
dimitris@comm.utoronto.ca

ABSTRACT

An appealing solution for unattended surveillance and monitoring applications is Self-powered Wireless Sensor Networks (WSNs). One of the main reasons is that the energy which is derived from power harvesting can significantly extend the network lifetime. Consequently, the network can work unattended for long periods. However, WSNs are characterized by multi-hop lossy links and resource constrained nodes while they have to face the coexistence problem with other applications. Opportunistic Routing (OR) is a routing paradigm to improve network performance in lossy wireless networks. At the same time, Cognitive Radio (CR) technology enables unlicensed operation in licensed bands. In this work, a combination of these two research approaches in a novel routing protocol is presented. A Spectrum and Energy Aware Opportunistic Routing (SEA-OR) protocol is proposed and designed for Self-powered WSNs. Moreover, a prioritization scheme which balances the packet advancement, the residual energy and the link reliability is introduced. Preliminary results show an improvement in network lifetime and delivery ratio. The performance of the introduced protocol is also evaluated in prototypes.

Categories and Subject Descriptors

C.2.1 [**COMPUTER-COMMUNICATION NETWORKS**]: Network Architecture and Design—*Wireless communication*; C.2.2 [**COMPUTER-COMMUNICATION NETWORKS**]: Network Protocols—*Routing protocols*

Keywords

Cognitive radio networks; Cognitive routing protocols; Self-powered wireless sensor networks

1. INTRODUCTION

Wireless Sensor Networks (WSNs) hold great promise as an enabling technology for a variety of applications, including event monitoring and tracking. A principal reason is that low cost inch scale sensors can be designed to work unattended for long periods of time. However, survivability is a looming threat for WSNs and their successful deployment. The network lifetime is solely decided by how the limited energy of each node is utilized. In addition, the devices that use the unlicensed bands increase every day hence, there is an increased demand on efficient spectrum utilization.

Opportunistic Routing (OR) [1] along with cognitive networking principles can alleviate these problems. The dynamic aspect of OR offers a set of candidate paths to the destination while cognitive radio quickly adapts to the dynamic spectrum conditions [3]. Hence, self-powered and cognitive enable WSNs can prolong network lifetime. Moreover, their deployment would have the least impact on the current infrastructures. The protocol that would be applied in these networks should be carefully designed and follow the network restrictions. Self-powered nodes have limited computational and storage capabilities while the spectrum sensing should carefully use the limited energy sources.

In this work, a Spectrum and Energy Aware Opportunistic Routing (SEA-OR) protocol for Self-powered WSNs is introduced. Moreover, a novel metric to prioritize the neighbour nodes is proposed. The new metric balances the packet advancement, the residual energy and the link reliability. SEA-OR achieves to extend network lifetime while it retains a high delivery ratio. The protocol is simulated and compared with Geographic Opportunistic Routing (GeOR) similar to [5]. Finally, SEA-OR has been applied to prototypes at our Self-Powered Sensor Network (SPSN) testbed.

2. SYSTEM ARCHITECTURE

The introduced SEA-OR protocol was developed for our second generation Cognitive Radio Network (CRN) testbed architecture. The protocol was designed for an outdoor monitoring system for gas leak detection. The system has three important components: the **sensor units**, the **relay nodes** and the **control unit**.

Each **sensor unit** has a gas sensor connected with the radio board. The radio board has two antennas to perform the cognitive networking: one for channel sensing and one for packet transmission. The board is connected with a rechargeable battery which draws energy from a solar panel. During the daylight, when the rechargeable battery is fully charged, the board draws energy straight from the solar panel. When there is no sufficient sunlight for the panel, the board draws energy from the battery. The sensor unit

MobiCom'14, September 7-11, 2014, Maui, Hawaii, USA.
ACM 978-1-4503-2783-1/14/09.
http://dx.doi.org/10.1145/2639108.2642914 .

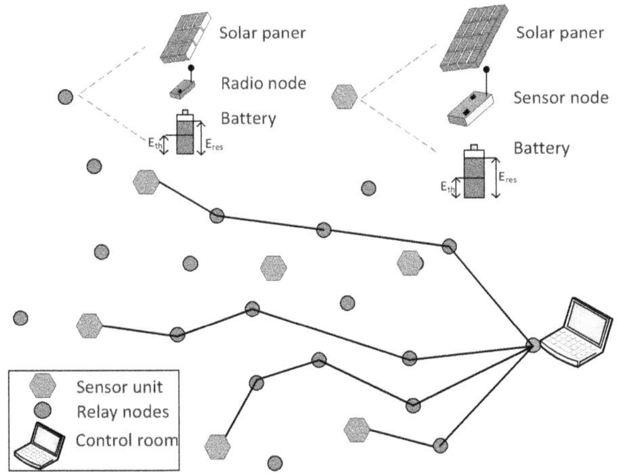

Figure 1: An outdoor gas leak detection system consists of self-powered units. The units have a threshold (E_{th}) in their batteries. If the battery level is below the threshold, they stop participate in any transmission and focus on energy harvesting.

forwards all the crucial information to the relay nodes over wireless communication, following the SEA-OR protocol.

The **relay nodes** have the same radio board with the sensor units. They forward all the packets towards the control room. Since there is no sensor attached to the board, the energy consumption at the relay nodes is significantly smaller in comparison with the energy consumption at the sensor units. Hence, the solar panel and the battery capacity at the relay nodes are smaller.

The **control room** is a radio board connected to a computer. This is the destination of all the packets. The radio board decomposes all the packets and displays the information on the GUI that have been developed.

Figure 1 depicts the outdoor system and its main components. Whenever there is a gas leakage in the monitoring area, the sensor units which are close, transmit packets with information regarding the leakage. The packets reach the control room and the system administrator is notified. A monitoring system like that poses a number of challenges:

Challenge 1: Network lifetime. Take Fig.1 for example. If the sensor units forward all the packets over the same relay nodes, these nodes will run out of energy after a number of transmissions. In this case, there will not be network connectivity which is a great threat for monitoring systems. Even though the nodes are powered with solar panels, they will acquire extra time to recharge their batteries to a level that they can participate in packet transmission again.

Challenge 2: Location information. There are many geographical routing protocols in the literature that can optimize the network performance. Usually, they use the distance between the communicate nodes as prioritization metric. The more accurate this information, the better the performance of the metric. However, in networks with high density and without advanced location estimation technologies, this metric might not be easily used. On the other hand, if advanced location systems are used, the cost and the power consumption per unit will increase.

Challenge 3: Wireless network coexistence. Heterogeneity and coexistence are characteristics of every unlicensed band. As more and more wireless devices use the 2.4 GHz radio spectrum, the coexistence of 2.4 GHz wireless devices which operate at the same place has become a challenging topic. The system should be able to cope with issues such as spectrum availability detection, interference mitigation and spectrum sharing.

Challenge 4: Dynamic changes. The monitoring system is deployed and should work unattended for long periods of time. Hence, it needs mechanisms to adopt successfully to a rapidly changing environment. For instance, the link between nodes might not be available due to obstacles from the environment. The system should be able to deliver the necessary packets to the destination on time.

To cope with these challenges, SEA-OR is proposed.

3. SEA-OR DESIGN

Central to the design of SEA-OR is a novel neighbour prioritization metric for Self-powered WSNs.

SEA-OR Overview. SEA-OR discovers multiple paths towards the destination according to the spectrum dynamics as well as node availability and energy level in the node. The paths are centred around the shortest path. The protocol opportunistically expands or shrinks these paths, based on the spectrum availability and the residual energy of the neighbour nodes. The discovery and coordination of the forwarder set follows the RTS/CTS handshake approach. The transmitter senses for an available channel and broadcasts a RTS packet. SEA-OR opportunistically forwards packets across the links with the highest spectrum availability. The candidate node that replies first with a CTS packet, becomes the next relay node.

The novelty of SEA-OR protocol is on the prioritization mechanism. When a candidate node receives a RTS packet, it waits for a backoff time $T_{backoff}$ before it replies with a CTS packet. This time is designed for self-powered sensor nodes with limited computational capabilities. The nodes are prioritized based on a combination of the channel quality, the distance and the residual energy in the node. The formula to calculate the $T_{backoff}$ is as follows:

$$T_{backoff} = C_1 \times (E_{th} - E_{res}) \times \log(\frac{RSSI(d)}{A})) + SIFS \quad (1)$$

where C_1 is a constant related with the capacity of the battery, E_{th} is the threshold below which a node stops transmitting, E_{res} is the percentage of the residual energy in the node, d is the distance from the sender and A is the RSSI at one meter of distance. The $T_{backoff}$ can be seen in Fig. 1.

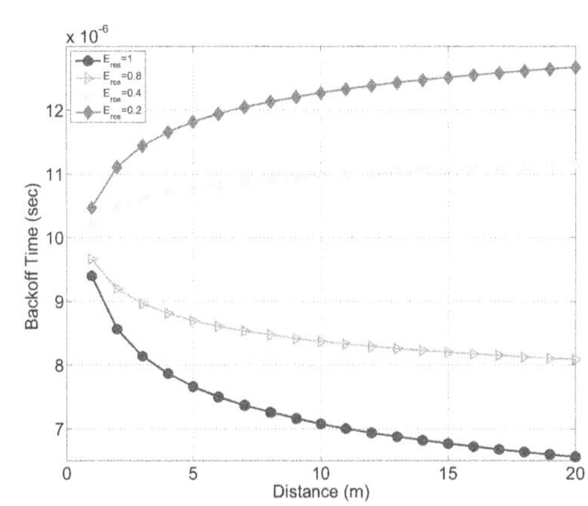

Figure 2: The $T_{backoff}$ for nodes in different distances from the transmitter and for different E_{res}, following Eq.1 for $E_{th} = 0.55$, $C_1 = 10^5$ and A = -40.

From Eq.1, the two important factors are the residual energy and the RSSI. The first can be acquired with a simple circuit on the sensor units and the relay nodes. The RSSI value can be found on every packet captured from the node. Also, it can be used to calculate the distance between nodes but it is not of high accuracy. It is however, accurate enough to prioritize the nodes based on their location and link quality. The constant values for these examples are the values used in our testbed and are related with the prototypes we developed [4]. When the nodes have similar E_{res}, SEA-OR tends to use nodes which are in greater distance and hence, closer to the destination. However, as the E_{res} decreases, the protocol uses nodes that are closer to the transmitter. In this way, the nodes have sufficient time to perform power harvesting and not run out of energy.

SEA-OR addresses the four challenges as mentioned above.

Extend network lifetime. SEA-OR uses the residual energy of the nodes for prioritization of the forwarder set. The nodes participate in packet transmission according to their remaining energy. When the E_{res} is under E_{th}, the node does not participate in any transmission. This mechanism is adopted to avoid nodes from running out of energy.

When a node has low energy, the probability of receiving a packet is low. As the node increases the energy levels through the energy harvesting phase, it increases its probability of becoming a relay node for a packet transmission.

Use of RSSI. In this approach, RSSI is used as an indicator of the relative location of the nodes. SEA-OR uses this information and not the exact location. The indicator is used to find nodes close to the transmitter. Most important for system implementation, RSSI information does not add any extra overhead. RSSI can also be used as link quality indicator. As an example, if the RSSI value is below a threshold, the node knows that the channel is idle.

Opportunistic spectrum access. Before every packet transmission, the sender senses for the best available channel. The packet transmission takes place over the link with the highest spectrum availability at the time of the transmission. This approach also decreases the interference with other devices that use the same band and alleviates the problem of network coexistence.

Opportunistic routing. The SEA-OR protocol discovers paths towards the destination on demand. There is no predefined routing. For every packet transmission, the best available path is selected. This path is base on the network conditions at the transmission time. Any dynamic changes, like node and link availability, will change the best path. SEA-OR adapts to these changes quick and does not require any reconfiguration on the nodes.

4. EVALUATION

A preliminary evaluation of SEA-OR performance was conducted. The sensor nodes are randomly deployed in a $100 \times 100\ m^2$ area using a Poisson distribution with a $\lambda = 0.101$. Every node has on average 8 neighbour nodes and the transmission range of each node is 12 m. The protocol was compared with GeOR.

Ten topologies were evaluated. The number of nodes in each topology varies between 900 to 1100. The distance between the source and the destination was varied between 20 to 200 meters. For each topology the source generated 1000 packets towards the destination. In every topology, 10 different source-destination pairs were selected.

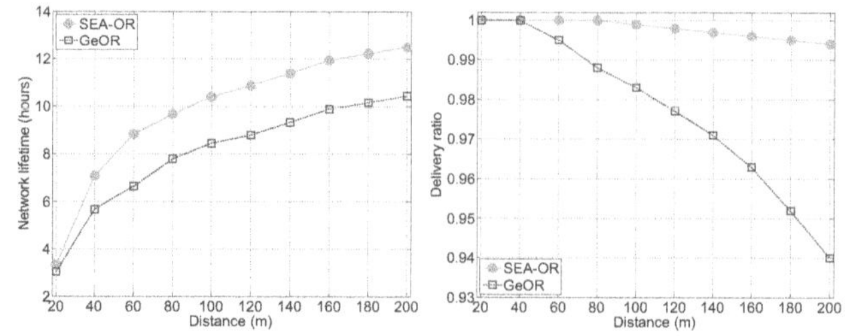

(a) Network lifetime (b) Delivery ratio

Figure 3: Performance comparison between SEA-OR and GeOR in different source-destination distances.

Network lifetime. Network lifetime has plenty of definitions [2], depending on the application. In this work, and for a monitoring application, network lifetime is considered as the time until "connectivity" or "coverage" is lost, i.e. there are no paths between the source and the destination or one of the nodes runs out of energy. The network lifetime of the two protocols is shown in Fig. 3(a).

SEA-OR significantly improves network lifetime over GeOR. As the distance between the source and the destination increases, there are more nodes in the routing path. The spectrum awareness of SEA-OR forwards the packets in shorter time than GeOR. As a consequence, the nodes have to remain active for a shorter time and the energy consumption per node is smaller.

Delivery ratio.SEA-OR improves the delivery ratio of GeOR, as shown in Fig.3(b). The use of RSSI in the prioritization metric, helps SEA-OR decrease collisions and forward the packets over reliable links. Consequently, the number of retransmissions decreases.

5. CONCLUSIONS

In this work SEA-OR is introduced, a Spectrum and Energy Aware Opportunistic Routing protocol for Self-powered WSN. SEA-OR uses a novel prioritization metric to balance residual energy and packet advancement. The protocol was also compared with GeOR. It increases network lifetime while it keeps high delivery ratio. Also, the protocol has been implemented in prototypes in the SPSN testbed. Future work includes comparison of SEA-OR with other approaches over the testbed.

6. REFERENCES

[1] S. Biswas and R. Morris. Exor: Opportunistic multi-hop routing for wireless networks. *SIGCOMM Comput. Commun. Rev.*, 35(4):133–144, Aug. 2005.

[2] I. Dietrich and F. Dressler. On the lifetime of wireless sensor networks. *ACM Trans. Sen. Netw.*, 5(1):5:1–5:39, Feb. 2009.

[3] I. Pefkianakis, S. Wong, and S. Lu. Samer: Spectrum aware mesh routing in cognitive radio networks. In *IEEE Symposium on New Frontiers in Dynamic Spectrum Access Networks, (DySPAN)*, pages 1–5, Oct 2008.

[4] P. Spachos, L. Song, and D. Hatzinakos. Prototypes of opportunistic wireless sensor networks supporting indoor air quality monitoring. *IEEE Consumer Communications and Networking Conference (CCNC)*, pages 851–852, Jan. 2013.

[5] K. Zeng, W. Lou, J. Yang, and D. R. Brown, III. On throughput efficiency of geographic opportunistic routing in multihop wireless networks. *Mob. Netw. Appl.*, 12(5):347–357, Dec. 2007.

Poster: Detecting Client Mobility in WLANs Using PHY Layer Information

Li Sun
University at Buffalo, SUNY
Buffalo, NY 14260
lsun3@buffalo.edu

Souvik Sen
HP Labs
Palo Alto, CA 94304
souvik.sen@hp.com

Dimitrios Koutsonikolas
University at Buffalo, SUNY
Buffalo, NY 14260
dimitrio@buffalo.edu

ABSTRACT

The continuously increasing number of smartphones and tablets allow the users to access Wireless LANs (WLANs) while undergoing different types of mobility, posing new challenges to wireless protocols. Current history-based WLAN protocols do not work well in mobile settings where wireless conditions change rapidly. Thus, today's WLANs need to be able to determine the type of the client's mobility and employ appropriate strategies in order to sustain high performance. While previous work tried to detect mobility using hints from sensors available in mobile devices, in this work, we demonstrate how different mobility modes can be distinguished by using physical layer information – Channel State Information (CSI) and Time-of-Flight (ToF) – available at commodity APs, with no modifications on the client side. Our testbed experiments show that our mobility classification algorithm achieves more than 92% accuracy in a variety of scenarios. In addition, we demonstrate how fine-grained mobility determination can be exploited to greatly improve performance of client roaming and MIMO beamforming.

Categories and Subject Descriptors

C.2.1 [**Network Architecture and Design**]: Wireless communication

Keywords

Wireless; WLAN; Mobility; PHY layer

1. INTRODUCTION

With the proliferation of smartphones, tablets, and the advent of the BYOD phenomenon, mobile devices are soon becoming the preferred medium of Internet access in Wireless LANs (WLANs). Due to their smaller form factor, these truly mobile devices allow the users to access the wireless network while undergoing different forms of mobility. However, client mobility poses difficult problems to the WLAN protocols. In static scenarios, the wireless channel remains stable and hence wireless protocols can refer to the past history, carefully adapting themselves to avoid failures and maximize performance. In contrast, during mobility, wireless conditions may change frequently requiring protocols to be agile and apply different strategies. Designing such strategies is not trivial because they depend on the actual type of mobility demonstrated by the client. E.g., the WLAN should try to roam the client to a better AP only when the client is moving away from her AP and should not consider roaming for the other scenarios because it is unlikely that a better AP will be discovered. Likewise, mechanisms to obtain higher throughput in modern 802.11n/ac WLANs, such as beamforming, rate adaptation, frame aggregation, multiuser-mimo (MU-MIMO), require different optimizations based on the intensity of client mobility – which determines the length of past history that a wireless protocol can refer to.

Today's WLAN protocols are unable to detect client mobility. They generally rely on the past history to generate optimal performance for stationary clients. However, such a general framework is slow to adapt to client mobility. Recent work [1] tried to detect mobility using on-board sensors in a smartphone. Although this technique can broadly classify between stationary and device mobility, it requires changes at both the client and the AP in order to benefit download traffic because client mobility state is unknown to the AP and it also requires the sensors to be always on consuming battery life. Rather than changing the client, which is a more difficult proposition, in this work we demonstrate how different mobility modes can be distinguished by using physical (PHY) layer information available at commodity APs.

MobiCom'14, September 7-11, 2014, Maui, Hawaii, USA.
ACM 978-1-4503-2783-1/14/09.
http://dx.doi.org/10.1145/2639108.2642892.

2. MOBILITY CLASSIFICATION

We identify four broad categories of client mobility. If the client is stationary, it can be in the *static mobility mode* when there are no significant environmental changes affecting the channel between the AP and the client. A static client may also be in the *environmental mobility mode* when the channel changes due to external movements. Of course the client itself may be moving – a mobility mode that we call *device mobility*. The client may experience different speeds under device mobility. We identify two broad and dominant categories of device mobility in WLANs. First, the user may slowly move the device although she is stationary or her movement is confined within a small area, which we define as *micro mobility*. E.g., the user may be attending a VoIP call over WiFi and a little movement of her head may displace her smartphone. On the other hand, the client may change its location as its user walks from one location to another. In such scenarios, we classify the client to be under *macro mobility*.

We use HP MSM 460 APs with Atheros AR9390 chipset and Samsung Galaxy S5 smart phones. We tuned the AP at 5.805GHz us-

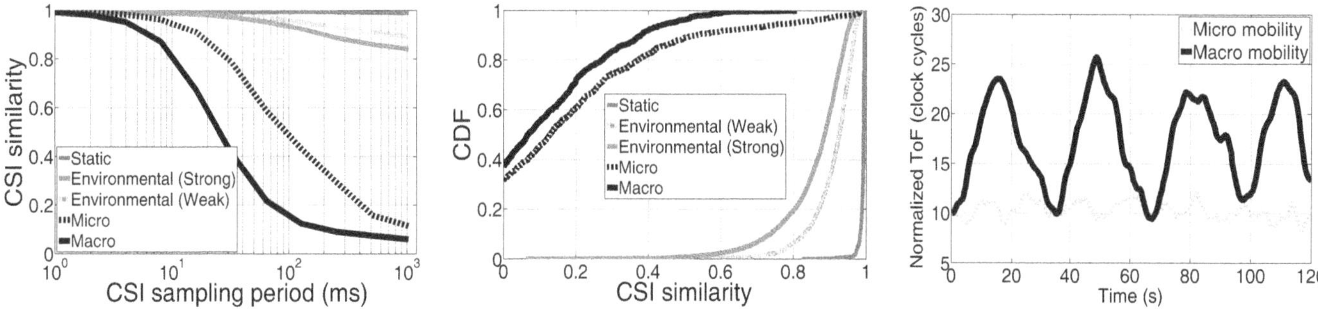

Figure 1: (a) Variation of CSI similarity values over time. (b) CDF of CSI similarity values for various mobility modes. (c) ToF values over time under device mobility. The user walks towards and away from the AP periodically in the macro-mobility scenario.

ing 40MHz channel and 802.11n protocol. We sent regular data packets from the AP and collected CSI, ToF, and Received Signal Strength Indicator (RSSI) information from the acknowledgment (ACK) sent by the client. We ran four different experiments to analyze different classes of mobility. Our goal is to develop simple classification schemes that can distinguish the above four scenarios.

2.1 Classifying Mobility using RSSI

We first explored the possibility of classifying the mobility mode of the client based on the RSSI of the client. In our experiments, we found that RSSI is quite stable in static scenarios in a quiet environment, but it is susceptible to any changes in the environment; often, the RSSI variation under environmental mobility is higher than the observed variation under device mobility. Therefore, we concluded that it is difficult to distinguish between environmental and device mobility solely based on RSSI. In the following, we will show how Channel State Information (CSI) can conclusively classify static, environmental, and device mobility, and how Time-of-Flight (ToF) can distinguish between the two types of device mobility.

2.2 Classifying Mobility using CSI

Any transmitted signal from the client undergoes reflections and arrives along multiple paths (multipath) at the AP. The wireless channel is expected to vary under environmental or device mobility because the fine-grained multipath structure may change. Those fine-grained variations are hard to be captured by RSSI because it aggregates all multipath components as one indicator. However, we found the same variations can be reliably detected by CSI because it captures the multipath characteristics from each subcarrier in the frequency domain. We characterize the *similarity* between two CSI samples by calculating the Pearson correlation coefficient with magnitudes on all subcarriers.

Figure 1(a) shows that the similarity stays close to 1 in the static case because the CSI matches across time on a stable channel. In contrast, the similarity drops sharply under environmental or device mobility. We further found that the similarity drops faster for device mobility than environmental mobility. This is because environmental mobility typically affects only a few multipath components, whereas if the client itself is moving, all multipath components will be affected. Figure 1(b) shows the distribution of similarity of consecutive CSI samples collected at every 0.5 seconds. Clearly, it is easy to find threshold values to distinguish between static, environmental, and device mobility. However, we found it is difficult to distinguish between micro mobility and macro mobility using CSI, even using larger sampling periods.

2.3 Classifying Device Mobility using ToF

To further classify device mobility, we utilize the intuition that the distance between the client and the AP under macro mobility changes more than that under micro mobility. Client's distance can be estimated based on RSSI [2] or CSI [3]. However, it was shown that RSSI and CSI are unreliable [4]. Instead, we utilize ToF [4, 5]. ToF is defined as the round trip propagation time of a signal transmitted between the AP and the client, which is proportional to the distance between them. The Atheros chipset can precisely compute the Time-of-Departure (ToD) of a data packet when it is sent out from the PHY layer. On correct reception of the packet, the client waits for a fixed SIFS duration and starts responding with an ACK. The chipset also reports an estimated Time-of-Arrival (ToA) of the ACK at the AP. The difference between the ToA and ToD contains the ToF between the AP and the client.

Figure 1(c) plots the ToF values over time for two different device mobility scenarios. For the micro mobility scenario, when the user naturally moves the device only within a small area, noisy ToF values can sometimes wrongly indicate changes in distance. However, the change in noisy ToF values in the micro-mobility case is quite random, while for the macro mobility scenario the ToF either steadily increases or decreases. This happens because within a reasonable time interval a walking user may either approach or move away from the AP, without changing her orientation. Therefore, we maintain a moving window of ToF values to detect macro mobility. Only if all the ToF values in the moving window suggest an increasing (moving away) or decreasing (moving towards) trend, we declare that the client is under macro mobility, otherwise the client is under micro mobility.

2.4 Evaluation of Mobility Classification

We implement our mobility detection scheme on the AP. We sample the CSI of the client every $500ms$ from existing data packet transmissions and maintain a moving average of the similarity between consecutive CSI values in 3 seconds. We compare the CSI similarity values with empirically chosen thresholds to distinguish between static, environmental and device mobility. If the CSI similarity indicates device mobility, we further consult ToF values to distinguish between micro and macro mobility (including moving directions). To deal with measurement noise [4], we sample the client's ToF readings every $200ms$ and aggregate them every second using a median filter.

We evaluate our scheme at more than 100 locations for over 24 hours. At each location we subject the client to different forms of mobility. Table 1 presents our overall performance results. We

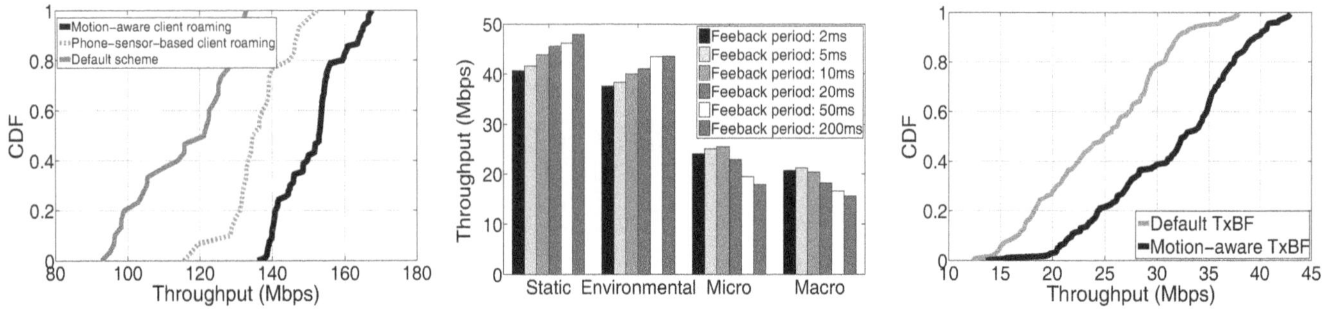

Figure 2: (a) Comparison of controller-based client roaming scheme with existing protocols. (b) Average throughput vs. CSI feedback period in different mobility scenarios with beamforming. (c) CDF of throughput gain for 300 different links subjected to a variety of mobility modes with beamforming.

find that the accuracy of our mobility detection scheme is more than 92% in all scenarios.

Table 1: Evaluation of mobility classification.

Ground truth	Detection result (%)			
	Static	Environmental	Micro	Macro
Static	99.7	0.3	0	0
Environmental	4.55	92.78	2.67	0
Micro-mobility	0	3.58	95.59	0.83
Macro-mobility	0	0	1.7	98.3

3. MOBILITY-AWARE PROTOCOL DESIGN

Client roaming. We first demonstrate how the knowledge of the client's moving direction at the AP can optimize client roaming. By default, a client associates with the AP with the strongest RSSI value and will trigger a handoff only when RSSI falls below a predefined threshold. Such a scheme is agnostic of the user's mobility; a moving client often remains wrongly connected to a far away AP, adversely affecting its own as well as the overall network performance. In [1], the authors proposed to use phone sensors to detect client mobility and request the phone to scan for better APs more aggressively. However, frequent scanning is time consuming and wastes energy and prevents the client from transmitting or receiving data (impacting throughput). To address this issue, rather than designing a scheme that requires changes at the client, we propose a controller-based protocol that roams the client to the appropriate AP whenever necessary.

In our scheme, the current AP of the client continuously determines the client mobility mode and shares it with the controller. If the current AP indicates that the client is moving away from it, the controller instructs the neighboring APs to periodically send NULL data frames to the client and compute the client's distance, RSSI, and heading information to themselves. If the client is moving towards another AP whose signal strength is similar or higher, we add that AP in the candidate set. If the controller finds at least one such better AP, it instructs the current AP to disassociate the client and asks only the APs in the candidate set to respond to the client's probe request. Consequently, the client roams to a better AP, ultimately improving performance. We evaluate our scheme on a 6-AP testbed in a 50x50 meter office by walking along its corridors. Figure 2(a) shows that our proposal performs better than the phone-sensor based scheme and improves median throughput by 31% over the default scheme.

Beamforming. Secondly, we studied how knowledge of client mobility can improve the performance of beamforming. Effective beamforming relies on timely CSI feedback from clients. Infrequent feedback will result in performance loss. However, too frequent feedback will be harmful because packets are transmitted at lower bit-rate in the feedback procedure which consumes more channel time. We use an AP as a client because we found none of the popular phones support explicit beamforming. Figure 2(b) shows that the optimal CSI feedback period decreases as the intensity of mobility increases and the default 200ms only benefits the static scenario. Therefore, we modified the WiFi driver at the AP to vary the feedback period based on the mobility mode of the client – 200ms for static, 50ms for environmental mobility, 10ms for micro-, and 5ms for macro-mobility. We conducted device-mobility experiments on 300 links and compared the performance of the adaptive feedback scheme with the default scheme which uses a statically configured 200ms feedback period. Figure 2(c) shows that our scheme outperforms the default scheme by 33% in the median case.

Client roaming and beamforming are not the only two wireless protocols that can benefit from client mobility. Currently, we are working on exploiting knowledge of client mobility to improve rate adaptation, frame aggregation, and MU-MIMO.

4. REFERENCES

[1] Hari Balakrishnan Lenin Ravindranath, Calvin Newport and Samuel Madden. Improving Wireless Network Performance Using Sensor Hints. In *USENIX NSDI*, 2011.

[2] Krishna Chintalapudi, Anand Padmanabha Iyer, and Venkata N Padmanabhan. Indoor localization without the pain. In *Proceedings of the sixteenth annual international conference on Mobile computing and networking*, pages 173–184. ACM, 2010.

[3] Souvik Sen, Jeongkeun Lee, Kyu-Han Kim, and Paul Congdon. Avoiding multipath to revive inbuilding wifi localization. In *Proceeding of the 11th annual international conference on Mobile systems, applications, and services*, pages 249–262. ACM, 2013.

[4] Alex Mariakakis, Souvik Sen, Jeongkeun Lee, and Kyu-Han Kim. Single access point based indoor localization. In *Proceeding of the 12th annual international conference on Mobile systems, applications, and services.*

[5] Domenico Giustiniano and Stefan Mangold. Caesar: carrier sense-based ranging in off-the-shelf 802.11 wireless lan. In *Proceedings of the Seventh COnference on emerging Networking EXperiments and Technologies*, page 10. ACM, 2011.

Poster–SaveAlert: An Efficient and Scalable Sensor-driven Danger Detection System

Güliz Seray Tuncay, Kirill Varshavskiy, Robin Kravets, Klara Nahrstedt
University of Illinois, at Urbana-Champaign
{tuncay2, varshav2, rhk, klara}@illinois.edu

ABSTRACT

SaveAlert is an adaptive framework for crowd-monitoring and danger-detection using off-the-shelf smartphones and other peripherals such as smartwatches. It is a system that provides users with an increased awareness of their surroundings by detecting and notifying them of impending danger, by relying only on sensor data collected from the users. Our framework's novelty is in how it performs efficient sensor data collection from potentially a large number of people by limiting the disturbance and stress on the existing Wi-Fi and cellular infrastructure. To the best of our knowledge, this is the first crowd-monitoring framework that takes advantage of peer-to-peer connections to perform local aggregation to alleviate the stress on existing infrastructures for better scalability and efficiency.

Categories and Subject Descriptors

C.2.4 [**Distribtued Systems**]: Distributed Applications; C.3 [**Special-Purpose and Application-Based Systems**]: Signal processing systems; H.3.4 [**Systems and Software**]: Distributed systems

Keywords

Crowd Dynamics; Crowd Monitoring; Crowd Sensing; Danger Detection; Safety

1. INTRODUCTION

SaveAlert is a system for monitoring crowds, identifying impending danger and notifying users of this situation. The system is similar to the AmberAlert system [1], which has been implemented in some operating systems to broadcast emergency response; however, SaveAlert goes out of the scope of *only* providing notifications, and it provides a systematic way of detecting hazardous events. To identify the danger, SaveAlert does not require any user intervention and relies only on sensor data collected using the smartphones owned by the people in the crowd.

MobiCom'14 Sep 07-11 2014, Maui, HI, USA.
ACM 978-1-4503-2783-1/14/09.
http://dx.doi.org/10.1145/2639108.2642908 .

SaveAlert is designed to work in scenarios in which there is a high density crowd and participation from a majority of users will put too much stress on the existing WiFi and cellular infrastructure due to the high upload rate required by such applications. In order to reduce the stress, saveAlert adopts the hierarchical CrowdWatch approach proposed in [2]. In this approach, some super nodes called watchers and samplers are dynamically selected to collect sensor data from nearby users via peer to peer data transmission techniques such as Bluetooth and Wi-Fi Direct. These nodes also perform local processing and aggregation on the collected sensor data to optimize the total amount of data uploaded to the cloud for analysis. In this work, we perform simulations to evaluate the performance of this architecture, propose a new technique for super node (leader) selection and finally present our Android implementation of SaveAlert that enables efficient and scalable crowd-monitoring by realizing the CrowdWatch architecture.

2. ARCHITECTURE

SaveAlert adopts the hierarchical architecture proposed in [2]. In this architecture, a 3-level hierarchy is established among the users. At the top of the hierarchy, there are watcher nodes that communicate with the CrowdWatch cloud using WiFi or cellular network connection. The mid-level users are called samplers, that are scattered around a watcher's Wi-Fi region to maximize coverage. These nodes are responsible of collecting data from their low power (LP) radio neighborhood (i.e., Bluetooth) and sending it to the corresponding watcher after aggregating the collected data. The lowest-level users of the system are sensing nodes, that collect sensor data and send it to the sampler node in their LP neighborhood. Figure 1 illustrates the CrowdWatch/SaveAlert architecture.

2.1 Leader selection algorithms

In [2], the author use a contention-based selection technique that requires the users to synchrhonize their clocks to dynamically select leader nodes. Since this is hard to achieve in realistic scenarios, we propose a new and simplified selection technique that does not require any clock synchronization. In this technique, a sensor node broadcasts an leader inquiry message to find out if any leaders exists in its vicinity. if this node does not get a response message within a certain time period, it becomes the leader. Figure 2 illustrates how this leader selection algorithm operates. It is important to note that it does not create any problem for the system when there actually exists a leader

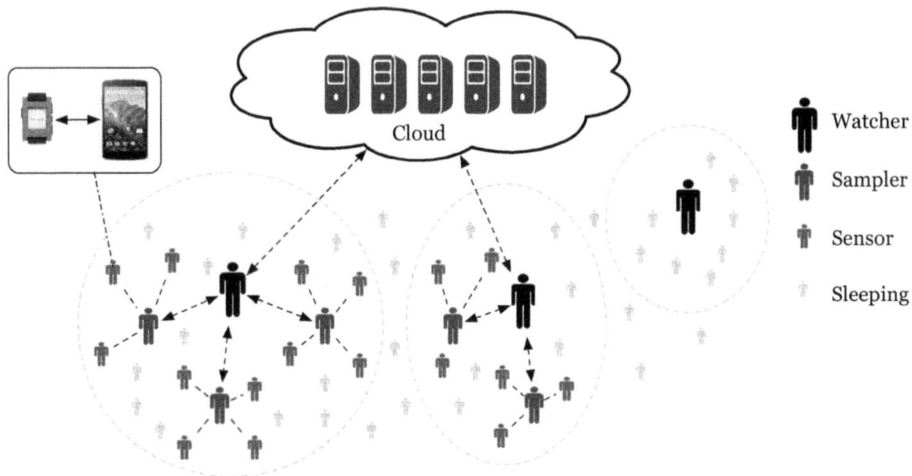

Figure 1: CrowdWatch/SaveAlert architecture.

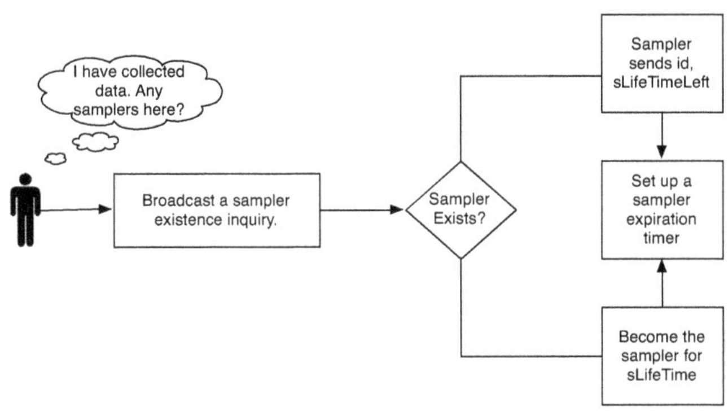

Figure 2: Leader selection algorithm

in the inquirer's vicinity and the leader's response message simply arrives late. The system is expected to still operate correctly even when there are multiple leaders controlling overlapping regions.

3. INITIAL RESULTS

To evaluate the performance of the CrowdWatch architecture, we implemented simulations using the OMNeT++ network simulation framework with a MiXiM plugin that supports dual radios for each node [3]. We compared the performance of the CrowdWatch framework with that of traditional approaches where there is no coordination between the participating nodes and all nodes use the Wi-Fi or the cellular network infrastructure to directly upload sensor data. We simulated an application that tries to estimate the population density in a crowd.

3.1 Accuracy

Figure 3 plots the accuracy of system. It can be seen that the accuracy is low when the number of nodes is small. This is because the probabilistic sensing employed by CrowdWatch results in incomplete coverage of the area when the nodes are too scattered. However, as the number of nodes increase, which is the intended scenario for CrowdWatch, this inefficiency is resolved.

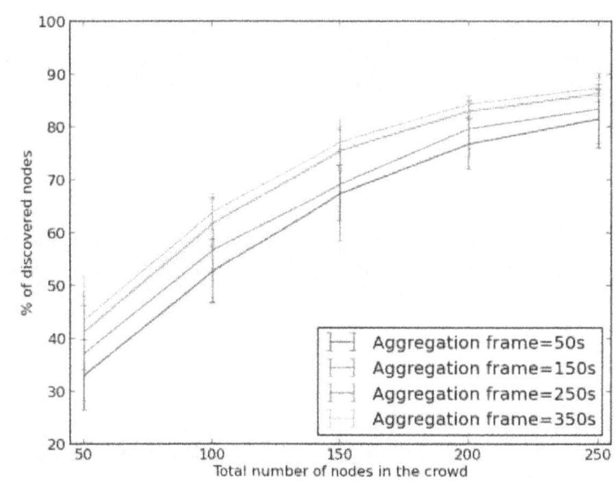

Figure 3: Accuracy of CrowdWatch with different aggregation frames. Aggregation frame indicates how often the cloud aggregates data.

3.2 Total message size received by the cloud

Figure 4 shows the number of messages sent in CrowdWatch versus traditional crowd-sensing systems. Here, we are assuming that the data that is collected by the crowd-sensing application can be perfectly aggregated. As can be seen from the figure, the number of messages sent by the traditional systems is about 10 orders of magnitude larger than that of CrowdWatch and this difference gets even more drastic when the number of nodes in the system increases.

4. IMPLEMENTATION

In [4], we presented an initial implementation of SaveAlert that works on the Android platform. In this implementation, the system detects if the audio-levels go extremely high in some users' vicinity and informs users within a certain radius of the possible danger via their smartphones and other peripherals such as smartwatches. Each node periodically collects audio-levels and pushes updates to the server. If Wi-

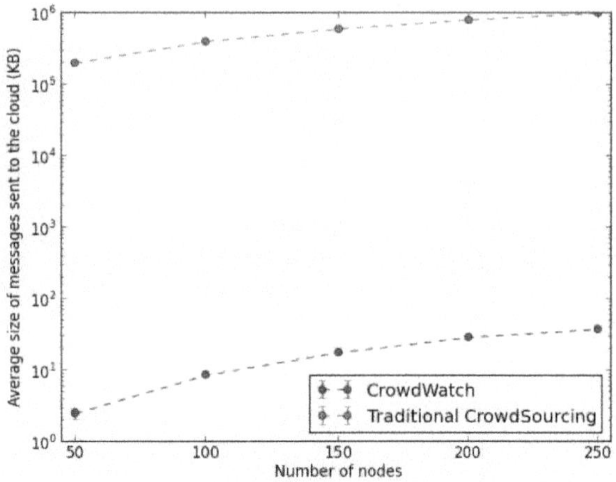

Figure 4: Size of messages sent in CrowdWatch vs traditional systems (log scale)

Fi direct functionality is enabled in the phone, then these updates will go through a watcher node (then to the CrowdWatch cloud) as in the CrowdWatch architecture. The cloud is responsible of analyzing the uploaded sensor data and sending distress signals if the average of last five samples from one device is above a certain threshold that can be configured through the application. Only the users that are within a certain geographical radius (that can be selected in the application) will be notified by the cloud.

5. CONCLUSIONS AND FUTURE WORK

In this paper, we presented our system called SaveAlert, which is intended to provide users with an increased awareness of their surroundings by detecting and notifying them of impending danger. As off-the-shelf smartphones proliferate with continuous advances in their capacity and capabilities, we believe our system will become more prominent in providing awareness and safety to its users.

As future work, we would like to extend our application to different data types such as raw audio, accelerometer, gyroscope and image. This requires us to conduct a thorough analysis on what we can infer from different data types, how we can perform meaningful aggregation on the data and how we can analyze this data (i.e. signal processing techniques). We also would like to deploy our implementation real crowded scenarios to evaluate the performance of the application.

6. REFERENCES

[1] http://www.amberalert.gov/.

[2] Robin Kravets, Hilfi Alkaff, Andrew Campbell, Karrie Karahalios, and Klara Nahrstedt. Crowdwatch: Enabling in-network crowd-sourcing. In *Proceedings of the Second ACM SIGCOMM Workshop on Mobile Cloud Computing*, MCC '13, 2013.

[3] Ólafur Helgason and Sylvia T. Kouyoumdjieva. Enabling multiple controllable radios in omnet++ nodes. In *Proceedings of the 4th International ICST Conference on Simulation Tools and Techniques*, SIMUTools '11, 2011.

[4] Guliz Seray Tuncay, Kirill Varshavskiy, and Robin Kravets. Demo: Savealert: Design for a sensor-driven crowdwatch danger detection system. In *Proceedings of the 12th Annual International Conference on Mobile Systems, Applications, and Services*, MobiSys '14, 2014.

Poster:Doppler Effect based Device-free Moving Object Localization

Kang Zhao,Dingyi Fang,Xiaojiang Chen*,Yuan Zhang,Weike Nie,Tianzhang Xing
Northwest University, Xi'an, China
kang.z.nwu@gmail.com,{dyf,xjchen,zhangyuan,nwk,xtz}@nwu.edu.cn

ABSTRACT

This poster introduces MoveLoc, a system that locates a moving object without carrying any devices from detecting Doppler shifts reflected off the moving object. It works even if the object walking or running in different directions without any training. MoveLoc does not require the user to carry any communication devices, yet its accuracy exceeds current moving object localization systems using Radio Signal Strength(RSS). We implement the system and evaluate the performance on moving person by experiments. Experimental result shows that MoveLoc achieves an average location accuracy of 0.69 meters and reduces the equipment deployment density compared with other known wireless moving object localization approaches using RSS.

Categories and Subject Descriptors

C.2.1 [**Network Architecture and Design**]: [Wireless Communication]

Keywords

Device-free localization;Doppler shifts;Wireless Sensing.

1. INTRODUCTION

Moving object locating is attractive in wireless network nowadays for supporting various applications, e.g., wildlife monitoring, vehicle tracking and patient localization in hospitals. As the security of people, organizations and their properties are increasingly threatened by unauthorized intruders or other aspects of life, there is a growing intelligent security system need to monitor environments well-supported by detecting and locating unknown device-free moving object methods. The commercial equipments including passive infrared and video camera, have a high accuracy, are costly for large scale scenario due to various reasons. Its limitation has spurred interest in developing new

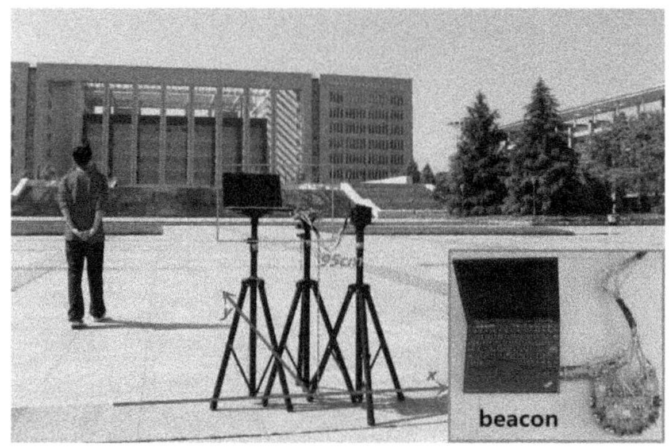

Figure 1: MoveLoc in Localization.

localization device that is more accurately and sparse deployment. A sparse deployment is more scalable and will reduce the costs of equipment and communication, especially in large scale scenario. Some researchers have proposed RASS[5], midpoints and intersection ways[6], which employ RSS fingerprints moving object with a small locating latency. Unfortunately, some methods based on training, which requires dedicated labor efforts to measure the signal parameters at fine grained grid points. Because they are susceptible to intrinsic fluctuations and external disturbances, the signatures have to be re-calibrated periodically to ensure accuracy. Besides, RSS is easily influenced by environmental dynamics leading localization accuracy unstable and even getting worse. Researchers began to explore the potential of using Doppler shifts to detect a moving object with a large speed range from mountains of stationary objects. Current WiSee system[4] is one of these initial systems[1], which provide a proof of new concept. However, their ability at localization is modest: they only detect whether the object is getting closer or further away with respect to the beacon.

This poster presents MoveLoc, a device-free moving object localization system that provides sufficient accuracy in the sparse deployment without requiring neither the object carrying any wireless devices nor any training. MoveLoc is the first Doppler effect based wireless localization system with a large localization speed range. The basic idea of MoveLoc is detecting the Doppler shifts reflected off moving object and mapping from the shifts to the angle of arrival (AoA) using different directional antennas though beacons. Then, taking advantages of multiple AoA information from beacons to realize localization.MoveLoc are able to maintain high accuracy in the sparsely deployed area.

*corresponding author.

MobiCom'14, September 7-11, 2014, Maui, Hawaii, USA.
ACM 978-1-4503-2783-1/14/09.
http://dx.doi.org/10.1145/2639108.2642913 .

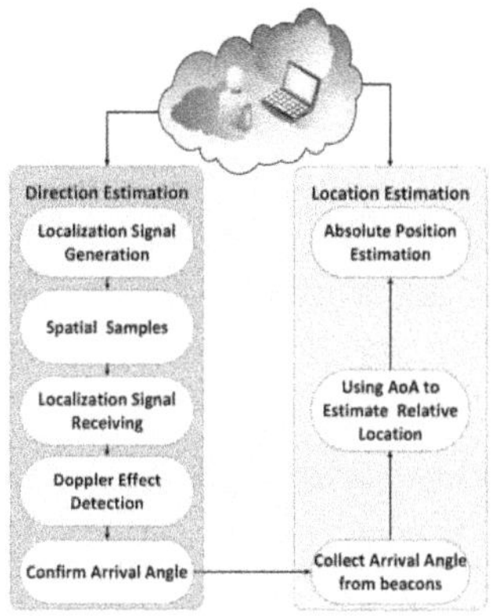

Figure 2: The localization process in MoveLoc.

2. MOVELOC

In this section, we introduce the architecture of the MoveLoc system and its challenges. MoveLoc works in two phases: direction estimation and location estimation(Fig.2). MoveLoc relies on beacons to collect angles and the location of beacons for localization. In the first phase, beacons transmit the generated radio signals and receive them from reflected off the object, and map from the detected Doppler shifts to arrival angle by multiple directional antennas. In the second phase, the user collects the arrival angles from multiple beacons and combines the arrival angles with beacons location to achieve object localization.

To achieve this architecture, we address the following challenges:

(a) How do we extract the small Doppler shifts from object movement of different direction via radio signal? Doppler shift is the observed frequency change as the source of the waves and the receiver moving relative to each other. We can see the detail according to the Doppler shift given by:

$$\Delta f \propto \frac{2v\cos(\theta)}{c} f_0,$$

where c is the speed of light in the medium, f_0 is the transmitter's center frequency, v is the speed of moving object and θ is the angle between signal direction and the direction of moving object.

However, human moving results in a very small Doppler shifts that is difficult to detect from a radio signal. In this aspect, WiSee's approach[4] uses narrowband pulse signal to detect the small Doppler shifts caused by human motion, which has a good performance in Doppler shifts detecting. It is enough for a gesture recognition system that only requires to distinguish Doppler shifts from narrowband signal with obvious threshold. In MoveLoc, however, the direction of object's movement is uncertain, which means the θ is uncertain. Seriously, the Doppler shifts even can't be directly demarcated. As a consequence, it is a goal that detects Doppler shifts from the narrowband signal and noise. For instance, considering an object moves at 1.3m/sec[2] and the θ is 89.2°, which will result in a Doppler shift of about 4 Hertz for a narrowband signal transmitted at 10.5 GHz, which means the resulting Doppler shift is orders of magnitude submerged in noise. Identifying such small Doppler shifts from these transmissions can be a challenge.

MoveLoc presents a design that transforms the received narrowband signal frequency value into a new detecting value which can be easy to detect small Doppler shifts with a threshold value. To achieve this, we design a *Sliding Cumulative Difference Window*(SCDW) for the receiver part in beacon, which can not only detect small Doppler shifts soon but also quickly return to a low level preparing for the next Doppler shifts by considering the characteristics of Doppler shifts by sampling. Specifically, we define three significant steps described above as :1)first we let $\{D_1, ..., D_n\}$ be a sequence of recorded receiving signal frequency by the beacon and estimate the mean value N_{ave} of noise; 2)$Sum_i = Sum_{i-1} + D_i - N_{ave}$, where Sum_i is the metric for adding window and $Sum_0 = 0$; 3)$V_i = |Sum_i - Sum_{i-w}|$, where V_i is the new detecting value after the SCDW and w is the window size. The Fig.3 shows an illustration of Doppler shifts signal detection by using our design system prototype. When an object moves towards the beacon($\theta = 89.2°$), the upper plot shows the observed signal frequency around central frequency along time series, and the lower plot shows the new detecting value after the SCDW of the observed signal frequency. We can easily distinguish between noise and Doppler shifts with a threshold h. In the meanwhile, the new detecting value will back below the threshold in a short time after Doppler shifts to the end.

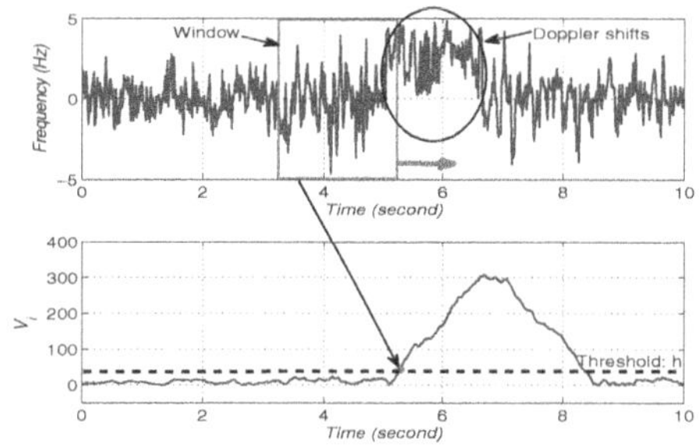

Figure 3: Sliding Cumulative Difference Window.

(b) How does MoveLoc using beacons map from Doppler shifts to arrival Angles? After the Doppler shifts are detected, we need to map from Doppler shifts to AoA via directional antennas. The traditional approach relies on rotating a directional antenna or using a steerable beam directional antenna to realize AoA estimation. However, it is too rigorous to gather reflected signals directions on localization area in real time that the beacon only gets a single radio and one antenna. Such methods can only detect a moving object under some restrictions, which may not always be practical. Besides, there is a simple way using multiple fixed directional antennas oriented along different direction receiving the reflected radios during localization. Unfortunately, it will bring a high requirement in terms of beam width and numbers to directional antennas if we need fine-grained angle information for localization[3]. What's more, some reflection blind spots is inevitable.

In the face of these, we design an *Accumulative Ring Algorithm*(Fig.4) using multiple fixed directional antennas without limitations both in beam width and numbers. We leverage the characteristics that detecting center frequency of directional antennas works with some difference and let the directional antennas exist overlapping coverage. In this algorithm, a grid array is used to represent the maximum direction in which a moving object will likely be. In confirming arrival angle step(Fig.2), the corresponding grids in

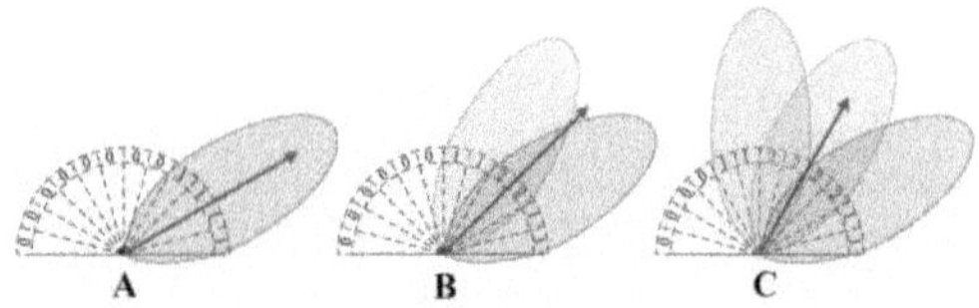

Figure 4: Accumulative Ring Algorithm.

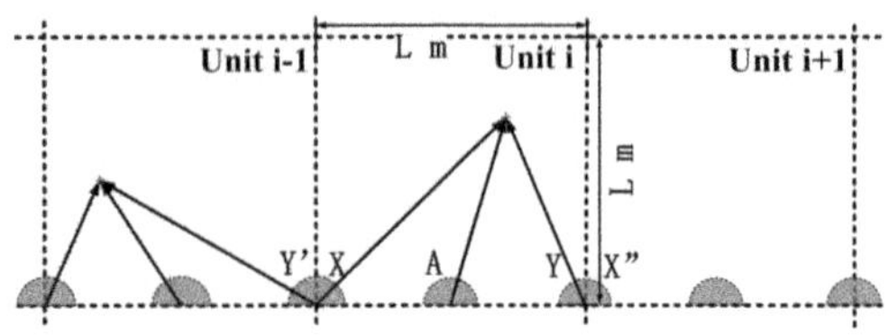

Figure 5: The deployment of MoveLoc.

accumulative ring are incremented if a directional antenna detects Doppler shifts. Once all antennas are computed, the resulting angle information is used to find middle direction in the maximum overlapping grids (e.g. the middle direction of with value 2 in Fig.4).

(c) How does MoveLoc deploy to achieve Localization?

In order to ensure that MoveLoc are able to locate all the moving object, a low-density deployment manner, which can provide angle information converted from Doppler shifts, is needed. We need to divide the whole object area into $N \times N$ unit square, so that the location range of MoveLoc can the unit square and the problem can be simplified as unit localization. Obviously in one unit, the moving object can be located in a simple way that use sine theorem with known both AoA information and the location from 2 beacons. While it is more complicated than the imagination, it should be considered that the Doppler shifts can't be detected when $\theta = 90°$. Hence the deployment is not only we need a sparse deployment to make the system more practical than before but also ensure the accuracy of localization. To address the above issue, we can use vertical property:

Property 1: there is only one straight line perpendicular to the known straight line in a same plane.

Considering the property and the above problems, MoveLoc adopts a 3-beacons deployment in a unit. 3-beacons are the minimum number to get enough AoA information from each localization. As shown in Fig.5, beacon X and beacon Y in unit i is the main locator beacon and beacon A play an assistant role in case either X or Y loses to detect Doppler shifts. This strategy is due to the simulation result, which shows selecting the both sides of the Angle of the beacon from one unit information will achieve a higher localization accuracy when the Angles are acquired. It is need to be mentioned that the deployment manner can improve the utilization rate of beacons too. For instance, the X beacon in unit i plays a Y' beacon role in unit $i-1$ parallel to the Y beacon role in unit i.

3. PRELIMINARY RESULTS

We implement a prototype of the beacon and use it to evaluate the performance of MoveLoc localization system in real world field. Since MoveLoc needs at least three beacons to build localization unit, we put the beacon in X, A, Y (Fig.5) in unit i to collect angles when an object moving at the same position and the same direction, and test the unit area sizes with $4m \times 4m$ square and the beacon distance with 2m. Based on 1023 tested data for 26 tested object positions, we compare the CDF curve of localization errors between the MoveLoc system and previous systems (RASS, Midpoint and Intersection) with a same equipment spacing curve as shown in Fig.6. We can achieve an accuracy of 0.69 meters on average. Compared with both the midpoint and intersection systems, the localization accuracy of MoveLoc is significantly improved, especially when the erroneous tolerance is smaller than 2 meters. Although the RASS system take training measure with a lot of pre-work, MoveLoc still can greatly improve the localization accuracy when the erroneous tolerance is smaller than 1.5 meters.

In addition, we also compare the beacon deployment density with preceding systems in simulation. As Fig.7 shows the rate between MoveLoc and Midpoint (or Intersection) changes with the increasing rows and columns. Obviously, the rate increases from 33.33% to nearly 50% with the key factor column rising. It means MoveLoc system has lower beacon deployment of density especially in the small-scale deployment. Compared with RASS, MoveLoc still has a rate of 97.40%. Thus our MoveLoc system is more desirable for both in sparse deployment and localization accuracy without any pain for training.

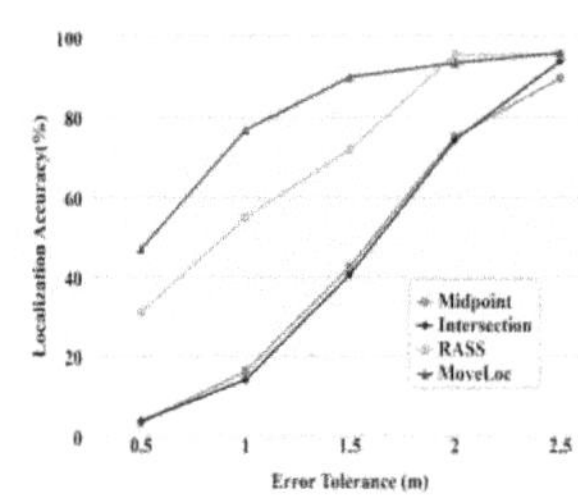

Figure 6: Localization accuracy comparison.

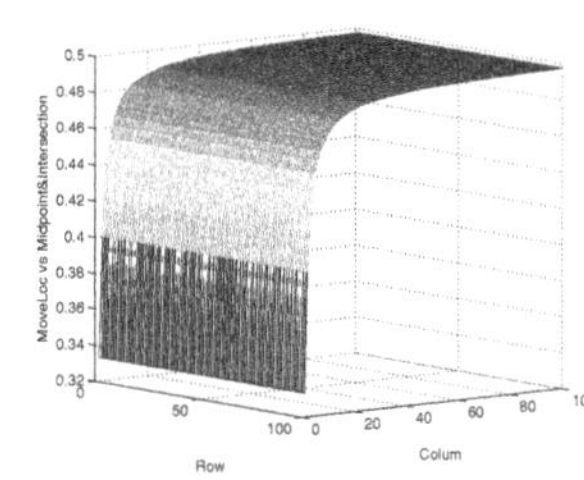

Figure 7: The deployment density in MoveLoc v.s. Midpoint & Intersection.

4. ACKNOWLEDGMENTS

This work was supported by the NSFC(61170218, 61272461, 61373177,61070176,61202198), Project National Key Technology R&D Program 2013BAK01B02, the Key Project of Chinese Ministry of Education 211181.

5. REFERENCES

[1] F. Adib and D. Katabi. See through walls with wifi! In *ACM SIGCOMM*, 2013.

[2] R. Bohannon. Comfortable and maximum walking speed of adults aged 20-79 years: reference values and determinants. *Age and ageing*, 1997.

[3] S. J. Orfanidis. *Electromagnetic waves and antennas*. Rutgers University, 2002.

[4] Q. Pu, S. Gupta, S. Gollakota, and S. Patel. Whole-home gesture recognition using wireless signals. In *ACM MobiCom*, 2013.

[5] D. Zhang, Y. Liu, X. Guo, and N. L. M. Rass: A real-time, accurate, and scalable system for tracking transceiver-free objects. *Parallel and Distributed Systems*, 2013.

[6] D. Zhang, J. Ma, Q. Chen, and N. L. M. An rf-based system for tracking transceiver-free objects. In *PerCom*, 2007.

MobiCom'14 Panel Overview

Applying the Lessons Learnt for Navigating the Future — A Conversation with the Pioneers

Victor Bahl
Moderator
Microsoft Research
bahl@microsoft.com

Panelists

Leonard Kleinrock
UCLA

Randy Katz
UC Berkeley

Imrich Chlamtac
CreateNet

ABSTRACT

The great French writer, historian and philosopher Voltaire once asked, "Is there anyone so wise as to learn by the experience of others?" In celebration of the 20th MobiCom conference, join us for a thought provoking discussion between pioneers of our field on the lessons they have learnt over their illustrious career paths that accelerated the pace of technology adoption and enabled world-wide societal impact. Learn from our heroes as they share with us gems of wisdom on how to choose a great problem, what to avoid and how to be successful as you build your own remarkable careers.

MobiCom'14, September 7-11, 2014, Maui, Hawaii, USA.

http://dx.doi.org/10.1145/2639108.2641728

Luxapose: Indoor Positioning with Mobile Phones and Visible Light

Ye-Sheng Kuo, Pat Pannuto, Ko-Jen Hsiao, and Prabal Dutta
Electrical Engineering and Computer Science Department
University of Michigan
Ann Arbor, MI 48109
{samkuo,ppannuto,coolmark,prabal}@umich.edu

ABSTRACT

We explore the indoor positioning problem with unmodified smartphones and slightly-modified commercial LED luminaires. The luminaires—modified to allow rapid, on-off keying—transmit their identifiers and/or locations encoded in human-imperceptible optical pulses. A camera-equipped smartphone, using just a single image frame capture, can detect the presence of the luminaires in the image, decode their transmitted identifiers and/or locations, and determine the smartphone's location and orientation relative to the luminaires. Continuous image capture and processing enables continuous position updates. The key insights underlying this work are (i) the driver circuits of emerging LED lighting systems can be easily modified to transmit data through on-off keying; (ii) the rolling shutter effect of CMOS imagers can be leveraged to receive many bits of data encoded in the optical transmissions with just a single frame capture, (iii) a camera is intrinsically an angle-of-arrival sensor, so the projection of multiple nearby light sources with known positions onto a camera's image plane can be framed as an instance of a sufficiently-constrained angle-of-arrival localization problem, and (iv) this problem can be solved with optimization techniques. We explore the feasibility of the design through an analytical model, demonstrate the viability of the design through a prototype system, discuss the challenges to a practical deployment including usability and scalability, and demonstrate decimeter-level accuracy in both carefully controlled and more realistic human mobility scenarios.

Categories and Subject Descriptors

B.4.2 [**HARDWARE**]: Input/Output and Data Communications—*Input/Output Devices*; C.3 [**COMPUTER-COMMUNICATION NETWORKS**]: Special-Purpose and Application-Based Systems

General Terms

Design, Experimentation, Measurement, Performance

Keywords

Indoor localization; Mobile phones; Angle-of-arrival; Image processing

MobiCom'14, September 7–11, 2014, Maui, HI, USA.
ACM 978-1-4503-2783-1/14/09.
http://dx.doi.org/10.1145/2639108.2639109

1. INTRODUCTION

Accurate indoor positioning can enable a wide range of location-based services across many sectors. Retailers, supermarkets, and shopping malls, for example, are interested in indoor positioning because it can provide improved navigation which helps avoid unrealized sales when customers cannot find items they seek, and it increases revenues from incremental sales from targeted advertising [11]. Indeed, the desire to deploy indoor location-based services is one reason that the overall demand for mobile indoor positioning in the retail sector is projected to grow to $5 billion by 2018 [7]. However, despite the strong demand forecast, indoor positioning remains a "grand challenge," and no existing system offers accurate location and orientation using unmodified smartphones [13].

WiFi and other RF-based approaches deliver accuracies measured in meters and no orientation information, making them a poor fit for many applications like retail navigation and shelf-level advertising [2, 5, 31]. Visible light-based approaches have shown some promise for indoor positioning, but recent systems offer landmarks with approximate room-level semantic localization [21], depend on custom hardware and received signal strength (RSS) techniques that are difficult to calibrate, or require phone attachments and user-in-the-loop gestures [13]. These limitations make deploying indoor positioning systems in "bring-your-own-device" environments, like retail, difficult. Section 2 discusses these challenges in more detail noting, among other things, that visible light positioning (VLP) systems have demonstrated better performance than RF-based ones.

Motivated by a recent claim that "the most promising method for the new VLP systems is angle of arrival" [1], we propose a new approach to accurate indoor positioning that leverages trends in solid-state lighting, camera-enabled smartphones, and retailer-specific mobile applications. Our design consists of visible light beacons, smartphones, and a cloud/cloudlet server that work together to determine a phone's location and orientation, and support location-based services. Each beacon consists of a programmable oscillator or microcontroller that controls one or more LEDs in a luminaire. A beacon's identity is encoded in the modulation frequency (or Manchester-encoded data stream) and optically broadcast by the luminaire. The smartphone's camera takes pictures periodically and these pictures are processed to determine if they contain any beacons by testing for energy in a target spectrum of the columnar FFT of the image. If beacons are present, the images are decoded to determine the beacon location and identity. Once beacon identities and coordinates are determined, an angle-of-arrival localization algorithm determines the phone's absolute position and orientation in the local coordinate system. Section 3 presents an overview of our proposed approach, including the system components, their interactions, and the data processing pipeline that yields location and orientation from a single image of the lights and access to a lookup table.

Our angle-of-arrival positioning principle assumes that three or more beacons (ideally at least four) with known 3-D coordinates have been detected and located in an image captured by a smartphone. We assume that these landmarks are visible and distinguishable from each other. This is usually the case when the camera is in focus since unoccluded beacons that are separated in space uniquely project onto the camera imager at distinct points. Assuming that the camera geometry is known and the pixels onto which the beacons are projected is determined, we estimate the position and orientation of the smartphone with respect to the beacons' coordinate system through the geometry of similar triangles, using a variation on the well-known bearings-only robot localization and mapping problem [10]. Section 4 describes the details of estimating position and orientation, and dealing with noisy measurements.

So far, we have assumed that our positioning algorithm is given the identities and locations of beacons within an overhead scene image, but we have not discussed how are these extracted from an image of modulated LEDs. Recall that the beacons are modulated with a square wave or transmit Manchester-encoded data (at frequencies above 1 kHz to avoid direct or indirect flicker [26]). When a smartphone passes under a beacon, the beacon's transmissions are projected onto the camera. Although the beacon frequency far exceeds the camera's frame rate, the transmissions are still decodable due to the rolling shutter effect [9]. CMOS imagers that employ a rolling shutter expose one or more columns at once, and scan just one column at a time. When an OOK-modulated light source illuminates the camera, distinct light and dark bands appear in images. The width of the bands depend on the scan time, and crucially, on the frequency of the light. We employ an image processing pipeline, as described in Section 5, to determine the extent of the beacons, estimate their centroids, and extract their embedded frequencies, which yields the inputs needed for positioning.

To evaluate the viability and performance of this approach, we implement the proposed system using both custom and slightly-modified commercial LED luminaires, a Nokia Lumia 1020 smartphone, and an image processing pipeline implemented using OpenCV, as described in Section 6. We deploy our proof-of-concept system in a university lab and find that under controlled settings with the smartphone positioned under the luminaires, we achieve decimeter-level location and roughly 3° orientation error under lights when four or five beacons are visible. With fewer than four visible beacons, or when errors are introduced in the beacon positions, we find that localization errors increase substantially. Fortunately, in realistic usage conditions—a person carrying a smartphone beneath overhead lights—we observe decimeter position and single-digit orientation errors. Although difficult to directly compare different systems, we adopt the parameters proposed by Epsilon [13] and compare the performance of our system to the results reported in prior work in Table 1. These results, and others benchmarking the performance of the VLC channel, are presented in Section 7.

Our proposed system, while promising, also has a number of limitations. It requires a high density of overhead lights with known positions, and nearby beacons to have accurate relative positions. Adequate performance requires high-resolution cameras which have only recently become available on smartphones. We currently upload entire images to the cloud/cloudlet server for processing, which incurs a significant time and energy cost that is difficult to accurately characterize. However, we show simple smartphone-based algorithms that can filter images locally, or crop only the promising parts of an image, reducing transfer costs or even enabling local processing. Section 8 discusses these and other issues, and suggests that it may soon be possible to achieve accurate indoor positioning using unmodified smartphones in realistic retail settings.

Param	EZ	Radar	Horus	Epsilon	Luxapose
Reference	[5]	[2]	[31]	[13]	[this]
Position	2-7 m	3-5 m	~1 m	~0.4 m	~0.1 m
Orientation	n/a	n/a	n/a	n/a	3°
Method	Model	FP	FP	Model	AoA
Database	Yes	Yes	Yes	No	Yes
Overhead	Low	WD	WD	DC	DC

Table 1: Comparison with prior WiFi- and VLC-based localization systems. FP, WD, AoA, and DC are FingerPrinting, War-Driving, Angle-of-Arrival, and Device Configuration, respectively. These are the reported figures from the cited works.

2. RELATED WORK

There are three areas of related work: RF localization, visible light communications, and visible light positioning.

RF-Based Localization. The majority of indoor localization research is RF-based, including WiFi [2,5,15,27], Motes [14], and FM radio [4], although some have explored magnetic fingerprinting as well [6]. All of these approaches achieve meter-level accuracy, and no orientation, often through RF received signal strength from multiple beacons, or with location fingerprinting [4,6,14,29]. Some employ antenna arrays and track RF phase to achieve sub-meter accuracy, but at the cost of substantial hardware modifications [27]. In contrast, we offer decimeter-level accuracy at the 90th-percentile under typical overhead lighting conditions, provide orientation, use camera-based localization, require no hardware modifications on the phone and minor modifications to the lighting infrastructure.

Visible Light Communications. A decade of VLC research primarily has focused on high-speed data transfer using specialized transmitters and receivers that support OOK, QAM, or DMT/OFDM modulation [12], or the recently standardized IEEE 802.15.7 [22]. However, smartphones typically employ CdS photocells with wide dynamic range but insufficient bandwidth for typical VLC [21]. In addition, CdS photocells cannot determine angle-of-arrival, and while smartphone cameras can, they cannot support most VLC techniques due to their limited frame rates. Recent research has shown that by exploiting the rolling shutter effect of CMOS cameras, it is possible to receive OOK data at close range, from a single transmitter, with low background noise [9]. We also use the same effect but operate at 2-3 meter range from typical luminaires, support multiple concurrent transmitters, and operate with ambient lighting levels.

Visible Light-Based Localization. Visible light positioning using one [19,30,32] or more [20,28] image sensors has been studied in simulation. In contrast, we explore the performance of a real system using a CMOS camera present in a commercial smartphone, address many practical concerns like dimming and flicker, and employ robust decoding and localization methods that work in practice. Several visible light positioning systems have been implemented [13,21,24]. ALTAIR uses ceiling-mounted cameras, body-worn IR LED tags, and a server that instructs tags to beacon sequentially, captures images from the cameras, and performs triangulation to estimate position [24]. Epsilon uses LED beacons and a custom light sensor that plugs into a smartphone's audio port, and sometimes requires users to perform gestures [13]. The LEDs transmit data using BFSK and avoid persistent collisions by random channel hopping. The system offers half-meter accuracy. In contrast, we require no custom hardware on the phone, can support a high density of lights without coordination, require no special gestures, provide orientation, and typically offer better performance. Landmarks provides semantic (e.g. room-level) localization using rolling shutter-based VLC [21], but neither accurate position nor orientation, like our system does.

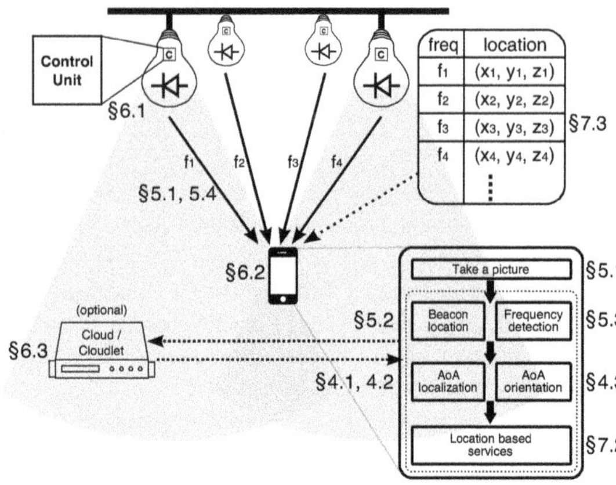

Figure 1: Luxapose indoor positioning system architecture and roadmap to the paper. The system consists of visible light beacons, mobile phones, and a cloud/cloudlet server. Beacons transmit their identities or coordinates using human-imperceptible visible light. A phone receives these transmissions using its camera and recruits a combination of local and cloud resources to determine its precise location and orientation relative to the beacons' coordinate system using an angle-of-arrival localization algorithm, thereby enabling location-based services.

3. SYSTEM OVERVIEW

The Luxapose indoor positioning system consists of visible light beacons, smartphones, and a cloud/cloudlet server, as Figure 1 shows. These elements work together to determine a smartphone's location and orientation, and support location-based services. Each beacon consists of a programmable oscillator or microcontroller that modulates one or more LED lights in a light fixture to broadcast the beacon's identity and/or coordinates. The front-facing camera in a hand-held smartphone takes pictures periodically. These pictures are processed to determine if they contain LED beacons by testing for the presence of certain frequencies. If beacons are likely present, the images are decoded to both determine the beacon locations in the image itself and to also extract data encoded in the beacons' modulated transmissions. A lookup table may be consulted to convert beacon identities into corresponding coordinates if these data are not transmitted. Once beacon identities and coordinates are determined, an angle-of-arrival localization algorithm determines the phone's position and orientation in the venue's coordinate system. This data can then be used for a range of location-based services. Cloud or cloudlet resources may be used to assist with image processing, coordinate lookup, database lookups, indoor navigation, dynamic advertisements, or other services that require distributed resources.

4. POSITIONING PRINCIPLES

Our goal is to estimate the location and orientation of a smartphone assuming that we know bearings to three or more point-sources (interchangeably called *beacons*, *landmarks*, and *transmitters*) with known 3-D coordinates. We assume the landmarks are visible and distinguishable from each other using a smartphone's built-in camera (or *receiver*). The camera is in focus so these point sources uniquely project onto the camera imager at distinct pixel locations. Assuming that the camera geometry (e.g. pixel size, focal length, etc.) is known and the pixels onto which the landmarks are projected can be determined, we seek to estimate the position and orientation of the mobile device with respect to the landmarks' coordinate system. This problem is a variation on the well-known bearings-only robot localization and mapping problem [10].

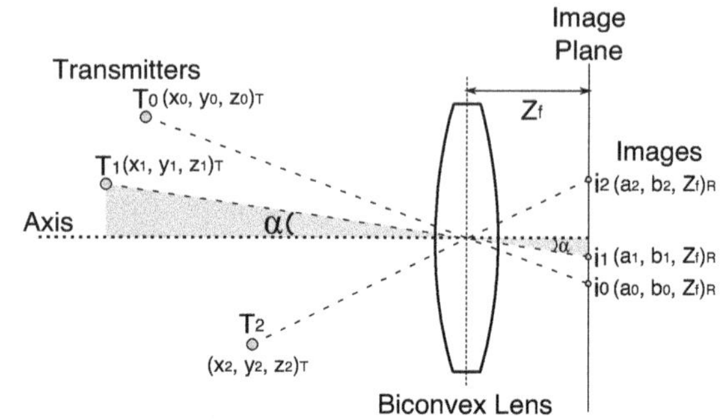

Figure 2: Optical AoA localization. When the scene is in focus, transmitters are distinctly projected onto the image plane. Knowing the transmitters' locations $T_j(x_j, y_j, z_j)_T$ in a global reference frame, and their image $i_j(a_j, b_j, Z_f)_R$ in the receiver's reference frame, allows us to estimate the receiver's global location and orientation.

4.1 Optical Angle-of-Arrival Localization

Luxapose uses optical angle-of-arrival (AoA) localization principles based on an ideal camera with a biconvex lens. An important property of a simple biconvex lens is that a ray of light that passes through the center of the lens is not refracted, as shown in Figure 2. Thus, a transmitter, the center of the lens, and the projection of transmitter onto the camera imager plane form a straight line. Assume that transmitter T_0, with coordinates $(x_0, y_0, z_0)_T$ in the transmitters' global frame of reference, has an image i_0, with coordinates $(a_0, b_0, Z_f)_R$ in the receiver's frame of reference (with the origin located at the center of the lens). T_0's position falls on the line that passes through $(0, 0, 0)_R$ and $(a_0, b_0, Z_f)_R$, where Z_f is the distance from lens to imager in pixels. By the geometry of similar triangles, we can define an unknown scaling factor K_0 for transmitter T_0, and describe T_0's location $(u_0, v_0, w_0)_R$ in the receiver's frame of reference as:

$$u_0 = K_0 \times a_0$$
$$v_0 = K_0 \times b_0$$
$$w_0 = K_0 \times Z_f$$

Our positioning algorithm assumes that transmitter locations are known. This allows us to express the pairwise distance between transmitters in both the transmitters' and receiver's frames of reference. Equating the expressions in the two different domains yields a set of quadratic equations in which the only remaining unknowns are the scaling factors $K_0, K_1, \ldots, K_n$. For example, assume three transmitters T_0, T_1, and T_2 are at locations $(x_0, y_0, z_0)_T$, $(x_1, y_1, z_1)_T$, and $(x_2, y_2, z_2)_T$, respectively. The pairwise distance squared between T_0 and T_1, denoted $d_{0,1}^2$, can be expressed in both domains, and equated as follows:

$$\begin{aligned} d_{0,1}^2 &= (u_0 - u_1)^2 + (v_0 - v_1)^2 + (w_0 - w_1)^2 \\ &= (K_0 a_0 - K_1 a_1)^2 + (K_0 b_0 - K_1 b_1)^2 + Z_f^2 (K_0 - K_1)^2 \\ &= K_0^2 \left|\overrightarrow{Oi_0}\right|^2 + K_1^2 \left|\overrightarrow{Oi_1}\right|^2 - 2K_0 K_1 (\overrightarrow{Oi_0} \cdot \overrightarrow{Oi_1}) \\ &= (x_0 - x_1)^2 + (y_0 - y_1)^2 + (z_0 - z_1)^2, \end{aligned}$$

where $\overrightarrow{Oi_0}$ and $\overrightarrow{Oi_1}$ are the vectors from the center of the lens to image i_0 (a_0, b_0, Z_f) and i_1 (a_1, b_1, Z_f), respectively. The only unknowns are K_0 and K_1. Three transmitters would yield three quadratic equations in three unknown variables, allowing us to find K_0, K_1, and K_2, and compute the transmitters' locations in the receiver's frame of reference.

Figure 3: Receiver orientation. The vectors x', y', and z' are defined as shown in the picture. The projection of the unit vectors $\hat{x}'$, $\hat{y}'$, and $\hat{z}'$ onto the x, y, and z axes in the transmitters' frame of reference give the elements of the rotation matrix $\mathbf{R}$.

4.2 Estimating Receiver Position

In the previous section, we show how the transmitters' locations in the receiver's frame of reference can be calculated. In practice, imperfections in the optics and inaccuracies in estimating the transmitters' image locations make closed-form solutions unrealistic. To address these issues, and to leverage additional transmitters beyond the minimum needed, we frame position estimation as an optimization problem that seeks the minimum mean square error (MMSE) over a set of scaling factors, as follows:

$$\sum_{m=1}^{N-1}\sum_{n=m+1}^{N}\{K_m^2\left|\overrightarrow{Oi_m}\right|^2 + K_n^2\left|\overrightarrow{Oi_n}\right|^2 - 2K_mK_n(\overrightarrow{Oi_m}\cdot\overrightarrow{Oi_n}) - d_{mn}^2\}^2,$$

where N is the number of transmitters projected onto the image, resulting in $\binom{N}{2}$ equations.

Once all the scaling factors are estimated, the transmitters' locations can be determined in the receiver's frame of reference, and the distances between the receiver and transmitters can be calculated. The relationship between two domains can be expressed as follows:

$$\begin{bmatrix} x_0 & x_1 & \dots & x_{N-1} \\ y_0 & y_1 & \dots & y_{N-1} \\ z_0 & y_1 & \dots & z_{N-1} \end{bmatrix} = \mathbf{R} \times \begin{bmatrix} u_0 & u_1 & \dots & u_{N-1} \\ v_0 & v_1 & \dots & v_{N-1} \\ w_0 & w_1 & \dots & w_{N-1} \end{bmatrix} + \mathbf{T},$$

where $\mathbf{R}$ is a 3-by-3 rotation matrix and $\mathbf{T}$ is a 3-by-1 translation matrix.

The elements of $\mathbf{T}$ (T_x, T_y, T_z) represent the receiver's location in the transmitters' frame of reference. We determine the translation matrix based on geometric relationships. Since scaling factors are now known, equivalent distances in both domains allow us to obtain the receiver's location in the transmitters' coordinate system:

$$(T_x - x_m)^2 + (T_y - y_m)^2 + (T_z - z_m)^2 = K_m^2(a_m^2 + b_m^2 + Z_f^2),$$

where (x_m, y_m, z_m) are the coordinates of the m-th transmitter in the transmitters' frame of reference, and (a_m, b_m) is the projection of the m-th transmitter onto the image plane. Finally, we estimate the receiver's location by finding the set (T_x, T_y, T_z) that minimizes:

$$\sum_{m=1}^{N}\{(T_x - x_m)^2 + (T_y - y_m)^2 + (T_z - z_m)^2 - K_m^2(a_m^2 + b_m^2 + Z_f^2)\}^2$$

4.3 Estimating Receiver Orientation

Once the translation matrix $\mathbf{T}$ is known, we can find the rotation matrix $\mathbf{R}$ by individually finding each element in it. The 3-by-3 rotation matrix $\mathbf{R}$ is represented using three column vectors, $\overrightarrow{r_1}$, $\overrightarrow{r_2}$, and $\overrightarrow{r_3}$, as follows:

$$\mathbf{R} = \begin{bmatrix} \overrightarrow{r_1} & \overrightarrow{r_2} & \overrightarrow{r_3} \end{bmatrix},$$

where the column vectors $\overrightarrow{r_1}$, $\overrightarrow{r_2}$ and $\overrightarrow{r_3}$ are the components of the unit vectors $\hat{x}'$, $\hat{y}'$, and $\hat{z}'$, respectively, projected onto the x, y, and z axes in the transmitters' frame of reference. Figure 3 illustrates the relationships between these various vectors. Once the orientation of the receiver is known, determining its bearing requires adjusting for portrait or landscape mode usage, and computing the projection onto the xy-plane.

5. CAMCOM PHOTOGRAMMETRY

Our positioning scheme requires that we identify the points in a camera image, (a_i, b_i, Z_f), onto which each landmark $i \in 1 \dots N$ with known coordinates, (x_i, y_i, z_i), are projected, and map between the two domains. This requires us to: (i) identify landmarks in an image, (ii) label each landmark with an identity, and (iii) map that identity to the landmark's global coordinates. To help with this process, we modify overhead LED luminaires so that they beacon optically—by rapidly switching on and off—in a manner that is imperceptible to humans but detectable by a smartphone camera.

We label each landmark by either modulating the landmark's LED at a fixed frequency or by transmitting Manchester-encoded data in the landmark's transmissions (an approach called camera communications, or *CamCom*, that enables low data rate, unidirectional message broadcasts from LEDs to image sensors), as Section 5.1 describes. We detect the presence and estimate the centroids and extent of landmarks in an image using the image processing pipeline described in Section 5.2. Once the landmarks are found, we determine their identities by decoding data embedded in the image, which either contains an index to, or the actual value of, a landmark's coordinates, as described in Section 5.3. Finally, we estimate the capacity of the CamCom channel we employ in Section 5.4.

5.1 Encoding Data in Landmark Beacons

Our system employs a unidirectional communications channel that uses an LED as a transmitter and a smartphone camera as a receiver. We encode data by modulating signals on the LED transmitter. As our LEDs are used to illuminate the environment, it is important that our system generates neither direct nor indirect flicker (the stroboscopic effect). The Lighting Research Center found that for any duty cycle, a luminaire with a flicker rate over 1 kHz was acceptable to room occupants, who could perceive neither effect [26].

5.1.1 Camera Communications Channel

When capturing an image, most CMOS imagers expose one or more columns of pixels, but read out only one column at a time, sweeping across the image at a fixed *scan rate* to create a *rolling shutter*, as shown in Figure 4a. When a rapidly modulated LED is captured with a CMOS imager, the result is a banding effect in the image in which some columns capture the LED when it is on and others when it is off. This effect is neither visible to the naked eye, nor in a photograph that uses an auto-exposure setting, as shown in Figure 4b. However, the rolling shutter effect is visible when an image is captured using a short exposure time, as seen in Figure 4c.

In the Luxapose design, each LED transmits a single frequency (from roughly 25-30 choices) as Figure 4c shows, allowing different LEDs or LED constellations to be distinctly identified. To expand the capacity of this channel, we also explore Manchester encoded data transmission, which is appealing both for its simplicity and its absence of a DC-component, which supports our data-independent brightness constraint. Figure 4d shows an image captured by an unmodified Lumia 1020 phone 1 m away from a commercial 6 inch can light. Our goal is to illustrate the basic viability of sending information over our VLC channel, but leave to future work the problem of determining the optimal channel coding.

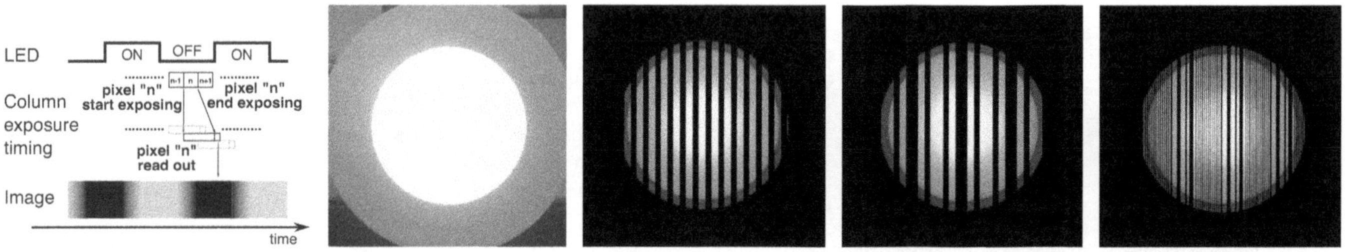

(a) Banding pattern due to the rolling shutter effect of a CMOS camera capturing a rapidly flashing LED. Adjusting the LED frequency or duty cycle changes the width of light and dark bands in the image, allowing frequency to be detected and decoded.

(b) Auto Exposure. Image of an LED modulated at 1 kHz with a 50% duty-cycle taken with the built-in camera app with a default (auto) exposure settings. The modulation is imperceptible.

(c) Pure Tone. Image of an LED modulated at 1 kHz with a 50% duty-cycle taken with a short exposure setting. The modulation is clearly visible as a series of alternating light and dark bands.

(d) Manchester Encoding. Image of an LED modulated at 1 kHz with a 50% duty-cycle transmitting Manchester-encoded data taken with a short exposure setting. Data repeats 0x66.

(e) Hybrid Encoding. Image of an LED alternating between transmitting a 3 kHz Manchester encoded data stream and a 6 kHz pure tone. Data is 4 symbols and the preamble is 2 symbols.

Figure 4: CMOS rolling shutter principles and practice using various encoding schemes. All images are taken by a Lumia 1020 camera of a modified Commercial Electric T66 6 inch (10 cm) ceiling-mounted can LED. The camera is 1 m from the LED and pictures are taken with the back camera. The images shown are a 600 × 600 pixel crop focusing on the transmitter, yielding a transmitter image with about a 450 pixel diameter. The ambient lighting conditions are held constant across all images, demonstrating the importance of exposure control for CamCom.

5.1.2 Camera Control

Cameras export many properties that affect how they capture images. The two most significant for the receiver in our CamCom channel are exposure time and film speed.

Exposure Control. Exposure time determines how long each pixel collects photons. During exposure, a pixel's charge accumulates as light strikes, until the pixel saturates. We seek to maximize the relative amplitude between the on and off bands in the captured image. Figure 5 shows the relative amplitude across a range of exposure values. We find that independent of film speed (ISO setting), the best performance is achieved with the shortest exposure time. The direct ray of light from the transmitter is strong and requires less than an on-period of the transmitted signal to saturate a pixel. For a 1 kHz signal (0.5 ms on, 0.5 ms off), an exposure time of longer than 0.5 ms (1/2000 s) guarantees that each pixel will be at least partially exposed to an on period, which would reduce possible contrast and result in poorer discrimination between light and dark bands.

Film Speed. Film speed (ISO setting) determines the sensitivity or gain of the image sensor. Loosely, it is a measure of how many photons are required to saturate a pixel. A faster film speed (higher ISO) increases the gain of the pixel sense circuitry, causing each pixel to saturate with fewer photons. If the received signal has a low amplitude (far from the transmitter or low transmit power), a faster film speed could help enhance the image contrast and potentially enlarge the decoding area. It also introduces the possibility of amplifying unwanted reflections above the noise floor, however. As Figure 5 shows, a higher film speed increases the importance of a shorter exposure time for high contrast images. We prefer smaller ISO values due to the proximity and brightness of indoor lights.

5.2 Finding Landmarks in an Image

Independent of any modulated data, the first step is to find the centroid and size of each transmitter on the captured image. We present one method in Figures 6a to 6e for identifying disjoint, circular transmitters (e.g. individual light fixtures). We convert the image to grayscale, blur it, and pass it through a binary OTSU filter [18]. We find contours for each blob [25] and then find the minimum enclosing circle (or other shape) for each contour. After finding each of the transmitters, we examine each subregion of the image independently to decode data from each light. We discuss approaches for processing other fixture types, such as Figure 18, in Section 8.

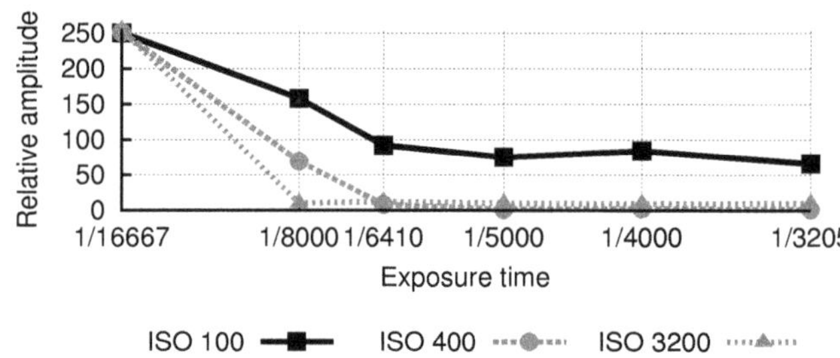

Figure 5: Maximizing SNR, or the ratio between the brightest and darkest pixels in an image. The longer the exposure, the higher the probability that a pixel accumulates charge while another saturates, reducing the resulting contrast between the light and dark bands. As film speed (ISO) increases, a fewer number of photons are required to saturate each pixel. Hence, we minimize the exposure time and film speed to maximize the contrast ratio, improving SNR.

5.3 Decoding Data in Images

Once the centroid and extent of any landmarks are found in an image, the next step is to extract the data encoded in beacon transmissions in these regions using one of four methods.

Decoding Pure Tones – Method One. Our first method of frequency decoding samples the center row of pixels across an image subregion and takes an FFT of that vector. While this approach decodes accurately, we find that it is not very precise, requiring roughly 200 Hz of separation between adjacent frequencies to reliably decode. We find in our evaluation, however, that this approach decodes more quickly and over longer distances than method two, creating a tradeoff space, and potential optimization opportunities.

Decoding Pure Tones – Method Two. Figures 6g to 6j show our second method, an image processing approach. We first apply a vertical blur to the subregion and then use an OTSU filter to get threshold values to pass into the Canny edge detection algorithm [3]. Note the extreme pixelation seen on the edges drawn in Figure 6i; these edges are only 1 pixel wide. The transmitter captured in this subregion has a radius of only 35 pixels. To manage this quantization, we exploit the noisy nature of the detected vertical edge and compute the weighted average of the edge location estimate across each row, yielding a subpixel estimation of the column containing the edge.

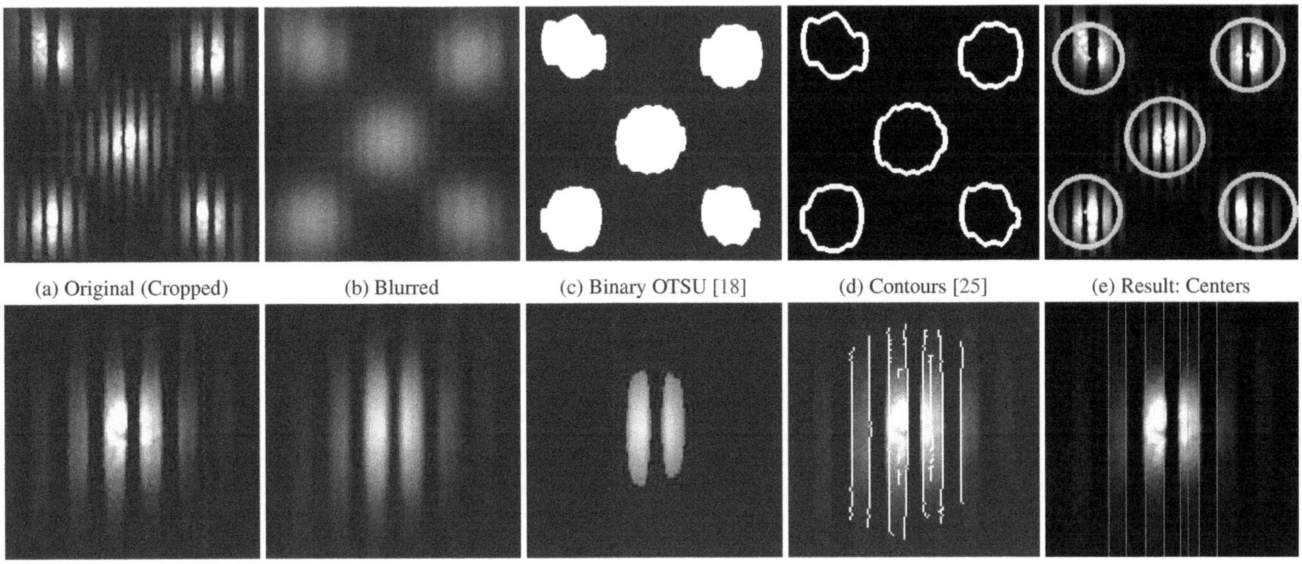

(a) Original (Cropped) (b) Blurred (c) Binary OTSU [18] (d) Contours [25] (e) Result: Centers

(f) Subregion (131×131 px) (g) Vertical Blur (h) ToZero OTSU [18] (i) Canny Edges [3] (j) Result: Frequency

Figure 6: Image processing pipeline. The top row of images illustrate our landmark detection algorithm. The bottom row of images illustrate our image processing pipeline for frequency recovery. These images are edited to move the transmitters closer together for presentation.

Near the transmitter center, erroneous edges are sometimes identified if the intensity of an *on* band changes too quickly. We majority vote across three rows of the subregion (the three rows equally partition the subregion) to decide if each interval is light or dark. If an edge creates two successive light intervals, it is considered an error and removed. Using these precise edge estimates and the known scan rate, we convert the interval distance in pixels to the transmitted frequency with a precision of about 50 Hz., offering roughly 120 channels (6 kHz/50 Hz). In addition to the extra edge detection and removal we also attempt to detect and insert missing edges. We compute the interval values between each pair of edges and look for intervals that are statistical outliers. If the projected frequency from the non-outlying edges divides cleanly into the outlier interval, then we have likely identified a missing edge, and so we add it.

Decoding Manchester Data. To decode Manchester data, we use a more signal processing-oriented approach. Like the FFT for tone, we operate on only the center row of pixels from the subregion. We use a matched filter with a known pattern (a preamble) at different frequencies and search for the maximum correlation. When found, the maximum correlation also reveals the preamble location. The frequency of the matched filter is determined by the number of pixels per symbol. It can be calculated as $\frac{F_s}{2\times n}$, where F_s is the sampling rate of the camera and n is an integer. As the frequency increases, n decreases, and the quantization effect grows. For example, F_s on the Lumia 1020 is 47.54 kHz, so an n value of 5 matches a 4.75 kHz signal. Using the best discrete matched filter, we search for the highest correlation value anywhere along the real pixel x-axis, allowing for a subpixel estimation of symbol location, repeating this process for each symbol.

Decoding Hybrid Transmissions. To balance the reliability of detecting pure tones with the advantages of Manchester encoded data, we explore a hybrid approach, alternating the transmission of a pure tone and Manchester encoded data, as Figure 4e shows. By combining frequency and data transmission, we decouple localization from communication. When a receiver is near a transmitter, it can take advantage of the available data channel, but it can also decode the frequency information of lights that are far away, increasing the probability of a successful localization.

5.4 Estimating Channel Capacity

The size of the transmitter and its distance from the receiver dictate the area that the transmitter projects onto the imager plane. The bandwidth for a specific transmitter is determined by its image length (in pixels) along the CMOS scan direction. Assuming a circular transmitter with diameter A m, its length on the image sensor is $A \times f/h$ pixels, where f is the focal length of the camera and h is the height from the transmitter to the receiver. The field of view (FoV) of a camera can be expressed as $\alpha = 2 \times \arctan(\frac{X}{2\times f})$, where X is the length of the image sensor along the direction of the FoV. Combining these, the length of the projected transmitter can be expressed as $\frac{A\times X}{h\times 2\times \tan(FoV/2)}$.

As an example, in a typical retail setting, A is 0.3~0.5 m and h is 3~5 m. The Glass camera ($X = 2528$ px, 14.7° FoV) has a "bandwidth" of 588~1633 px. The higher-resolution Lumia 1020 camera ($X = 5360$ px, 37.4° FoV) bandwidth is actually lower, 475~1320 px, as the wider FoV maps a much larger scene area to the fixed-size imager as the distance increases. This result shows that increasing resolution alone may not increase effective channel capacity without paying attention to other camera properties.

6. IMPLEMENTATION DETAILS

To evaluate the viability and performance of the Luxapose design, we implement a prototype system using a variety of LED luminaires, an unmodified smartphone, and a Python-based cloudlet (all available at https://github.com/lab11/vlc-localization/).

6.1 LED Landmarks

We construct landmarks by modifying commercial LED luminaires, including can, tube, and task lamps, as shown in Figure 7a, but full-custom designs are also possible. Figure 7b shows the modifications, which include cutting (×) and intercepting a wire, and wiring in a control unit that includes a voltage regulator (VR) and a microcontroller (MCU) or programmable oscillator (OSC) controlling a single FET switch. We implement two control units, as shown in Figure 7c, for low- and high-voltage LED driver circuits, using a voltage-controlled oscillator with 16 frequency settings.

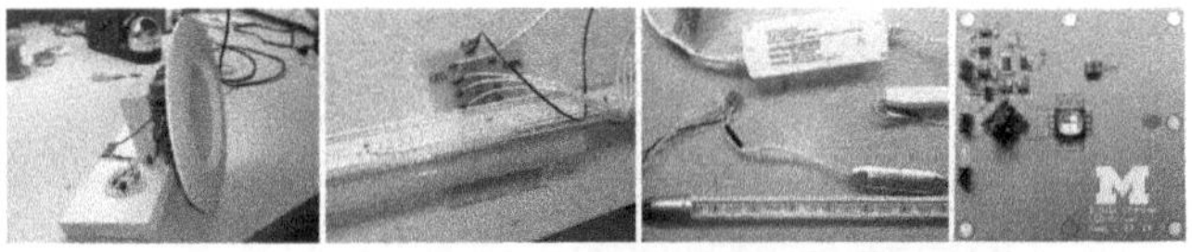

(a) LED landmarks: can, tube, task, and custom beacons.

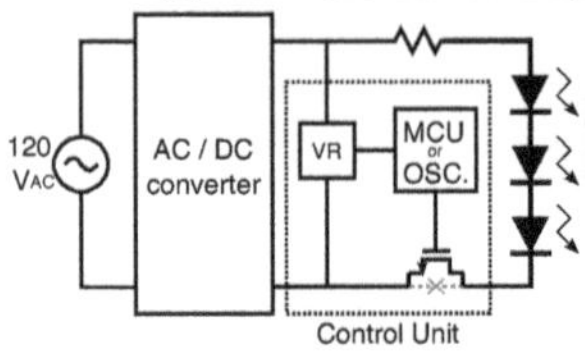

(b) Luminaire modifications.

(c) Programmable control units.

Figure 7: LED landmarks. (a) Commercial and custom LED beacons. (b) A commercial luminaire is modified by inserting a control unit. (c) Two custom control units with 16 programmable tones. The units draw 5 mA and cost ~$3 each in quantities of 1,000, suggesting they could be integrated into commercial luminaires.

6.2 Smartphone Receiver

We use the Nokia Lumia 1020 to implement the Luxapose receiver design. The Lumia's resolution—7712×5360 pixels—is the highest among many popular phones, allowing us the greatest experimental flexibility. The deciding factor, however, is not the hardware capability of the smartphone, but rather its OS support and camera API that expose control of resolution, exposure time, and film speed. Neither Apple's iOS nor Google's Android currently provide the needed camera control, but we believe they are forthcoming. Only Windows Phone 8, which runs on the Lumia, currently provides a rich enough API to perform advanced photography [16].

We modify the Nokia Camera Explorer [17] to build our application. We augment the app to expose the full range of resolution and exposure settings, and we add a streaming picture mode that continuously takes images as fast as the hardware will allow. Finally, we add cloud integration, transferring captured images to our local cloudlet for processing, storage, and visualization without employing any smartphone-based optimizations that would filter images.

We emphasize that the platform support is not a hardware issue but a software issue. Exposure and ISO settings are controlled by OS-managed feedback loops. We are able to coerce these feedback loops by shining a bright light into imagers and removing it at the last moment before capturing an image of our transmitters. Using this technique, we are able to capture images with $1/7519$ s exposure on ISO 68 film using Google Glass and $1/55556$ s exposure and ISO 50 on an iPhone 5; we are able to recover the location information from these coerced-exposure images successfully, but evaluating using this approach is impractical, so we focus our efforts on the Lumia.

Photogrammetry—the discipline of making measurements from photographs—requires camera characterization and calibration. We use the Nokia Pro Camera application included with the Lumia, which allows the user to specify exposure and ISO settings, to capture images for this purpose. Using known phone locations, beacon locations, and beacon frequencies, we measure the distance between the lens and imager, Z_f (1039 pixels, 5620 pixels), and scan rate (30,880 columns/s, 47,540 columns/s), for the front and back cameras, respectively. To estimate the impact of manufacturing tolerances, we measure these parameters across several Lumia 1020s and find only a 0.15% deviation, suggesting that per-unit calibration is not required.

Camera optics can distort a captured image, but most smartphone cameras digitally correct distortions in the camera firmware [23]. To verify the presence and quality of distortion correction in the Lumia, we move an object from the center to the edge of the camera's frame, and find that the Lumia's images show very little distortion, deviating at most 3 pixels from the expected location.

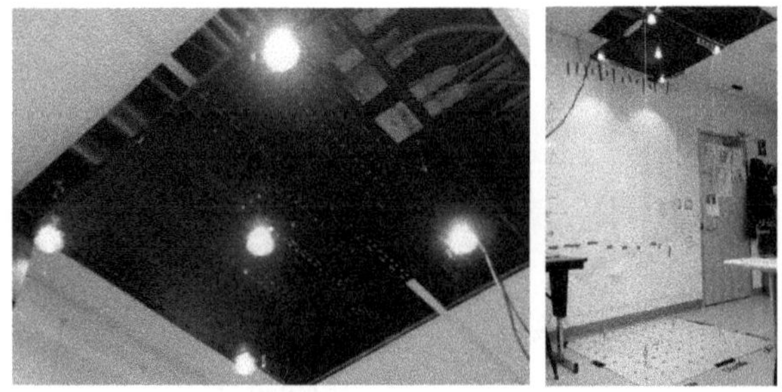

Figure 8: Indoor positioning testbed. Five LED beacons are mounted 246 cm above the ground for experiments. Ground truth is provided by a pegboard on the floor with 2.54 cm location resolution.

The distance, Z_f, between the center of lens and the imager is a very important parameter in AoA localization algorithms. Unfortunately, this parameter is not fixed on the Lumia 1020, which uses a motor to adjust the lens for sharper images. This raises the question of how this impacts localization accuracy. In a simple biconvex lens model, the relationship between s_1 (distance from object to lens), s_2 (from lens to image), and f (focal length) is:

$$\frac{1}{s_1} + \frac{1}{s_2} = \frac{1}{f}$$

where s_2 and Z_f are the same parameter but s_2 is measured in meters whereas Z_f is measured in pixels. s_2 can be rewritten as $\frac{s_1 \times f}{s_1 - f}$. For the Lumia 1020, $f = 7.2$ mm. In the general use case, s_1 is on the order of meters which leads to s_2 values between 7.25 mm ($s_1 = 1$ m) and 7.2 mm ($s_1 = \infty$). This suggests that Z_f should deviate only 0.7% from a 1 m focus to infinity. As lighting fixtures are most likely 2$\sim$5 m above ground, the practical deviation is even smaller, thus we elect to use a fixed Z_f value for localization. We measure Z_f while the camera focuses at 2.45 m across 3 Lumia phones. All Z_f values fall within 0.15% of the average: 5,620 pixels.

While the front camera is more likely to face lights in day-to-day use, we use the back camera for our experiments since it offers higher resolution. Both cameras support the same exposure and ISO ranges, but have different resolutions and scan rates. Scan rate places an upper bound on transmit frequency, but the limited exposure range places a more restrictive bound, making this difference moot. Resolution imposes an actual limit by causing quantization effects to occur at lower frequencies; the maximum frequency decodable by the front camera using edge detection is $\sim$5 kHz, while the back camera can reach $\sim$7 kHz. Given Hendy's Law—the annual doubling of pixels per dollar—we focus our evaluation on the higher-resolution imager, without loss of generality.

6.3 Cloudlet Server

A cloudlet server implements the full image processing pipeline shown in Figure 6 using OpenCV 2.4.8 with Python bindings. On an unburdened MacBook Pro with a 2.7 GHz Core i7, the median processing time for the full 33 MP images captured by the Lumia is about 9 s (taking picture: 4.46 s, upload: 3.41 s, image processing: 0.3 s, estimate location: 0.87 s) without any optimizations. The cloudlet application contains a mapping from transmitter frequency to absolute transmitter position in space. Using this mapping and the information from the image processing, we implement the techniques described in Section 4 using the `leastsq` implementation from SciPy. Our complete cloudlet application is 722 Python SLOC.

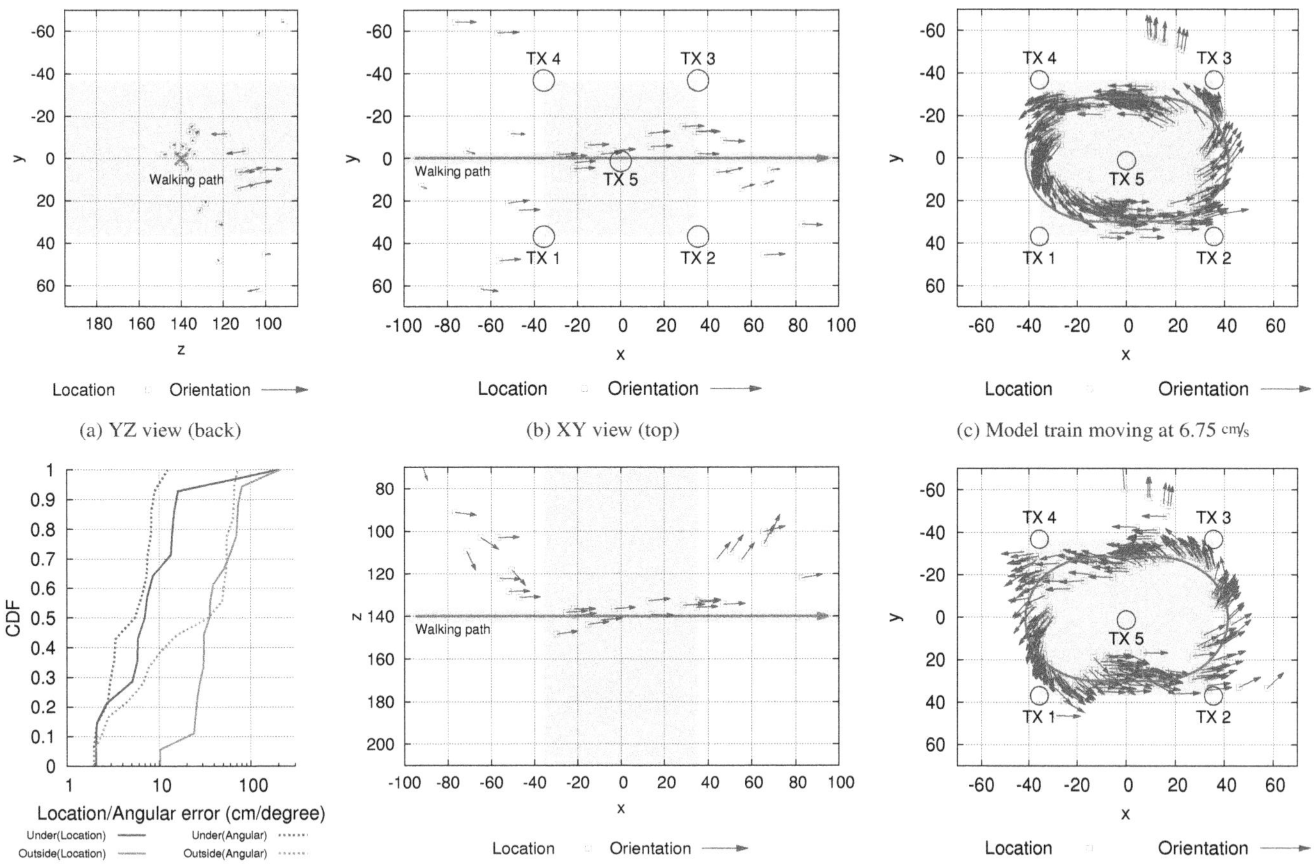

(a) YZ view (back)

(b) XY view (top)

(c) Model train moving at 6.75 cm/s

(d) CDF of location and angular error

(e) XZ view (side)

(f) Model train moving at 13.5 cm/s

Figure 9: Key location and orientation results under realistic usage conditions on our indoor positioning testbed. The shaded areas are directly under the lights. (a), (b), and (e) show Luxapose's estimated location and orientation of a person walking from the back, top, and side views, respectively, while using the system. A subject carrying a phone walks underneath the testbed repeatedly, trying to remain approximately under the center ($x = -100 \ldots 100, y = 0, z = 140$). We measure the walking speed at ~1 m/s. (d) suggests location estimates (solid line) and orientation (dotted line) under the lights (blue), have lower error than outside the lights (red). (c) and (f) show the effect of motion blur. To estimate the impact of motion while capturing images, we place the smartphone on a model train running in an oval at two speeds. While the exact ground truth for each point is unknown, we find the majority of the estimates fall close to the track and point as expected.

7. EVALUATION

In this section, we evaluate position and orientation accuracy in both typical usage conditions and in carefully controlled settings. We also evaluate the visible light communications channel for pure tones, Manchester-encoded data, and a hybrid of the two. Our experiments are carried out on a custom indoor positioning testbed.

7.1 Experimental Methodology

We integrate five LED landmarks, a smartphone, and a cloudlet server into an indoor positioning testbed, as Figure 8 shows. The LED landmarks are mounted on a height-adjustable pegboard and they form a 71.1×73.7 cm rectangle with a center point. A complementary pegboard is affixed to floor and aligned using a laser sight and verified with a plumb-bob, creating a 3D grid with 2.54 cm resolution of known locations for our experimental evaluation. To isolate localization from communications performance, we set the transmitters to emit pure tones in the range of 2 kHz to 4 kHz, with 500 Hz separation, which ensures reliable communications (we also test communications performance separately). Using this testbed, we evaluate indoor positioning accuracy—both location and orientation—for a person, model train, and statically.

7.2 Realistic Positioning Performance

To evaluate the positioning accuracy of the Luxapose system under realistic usage conditions, we perform an experiment in which a person repeatedly walks under the indoor positioning testbed, from left to right at 1 m/s, as shown from the top view of the testbed in Figure 9b and side view in Figure 9e. The CDF of estimated location and orientation errors when the subject is under the landmarks (shaded) or outside the landmarks (unshaded) is shown in Figure 9d. When under the landmarks, our results show a median location error of 7 cm and orientation error of 6°, substantially better than when outside the landmarks, which exhibit substantially higher magnitude (and somewhat symmetric) location and orientation errors.

To evaluate the effect of controlled turning while under the landmarks, we place a phone on a model train running at 6.75 cm/s in an oval, as shown in Figure 9c. Most of the location samples fall on or within 10 cm of the track with the notable exception of when the phone is collinear with three of the transmitters, where the error increases to about 30 cm, though this is an artifact of the localization methodology and not the motion. When the speed of the train is doubled—to 13.5 cm/s—we find a visible increase in location and orientation errors, as shown in Figure 9f.

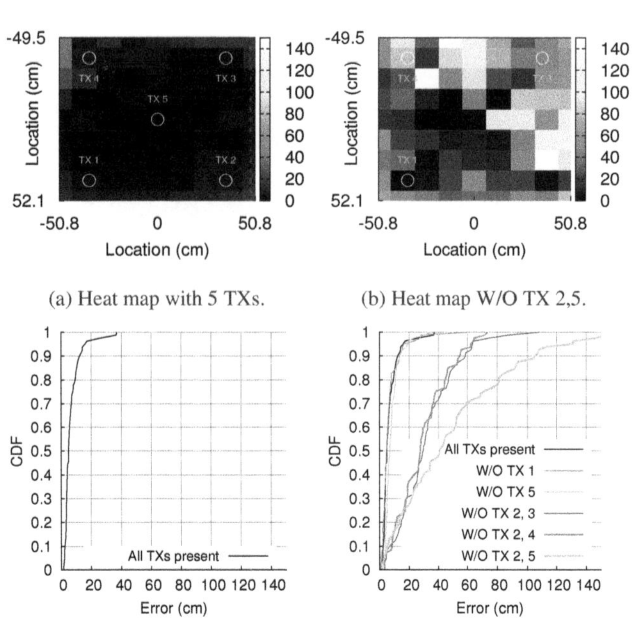

(a) Heat map with 5 TXs.

(b) Heat map W/O TX 2,5.

(c) CDF with all TXs present.

(d) CDFs when TXs removed.

Figure 10: Localization accuracy at a fixed height (246 cm). (a) shows a heat map of error when all 5 transmitters are present in the image, and (c) shows a CDF of the error. (d) explores how the system degrades as transmitters are removed. Removing any one transmitter (corner or center) has minimal impact on location error, still remaining within 10 cm for ~90% of locations. Removing two transmitters (leaving only the minimum number of transmitters) raises error to 20~60 cm when corners are lost and as high as 120 cm when the center and a corner are lost. As shown in the heat map in (b), removing the center and corner generates the greatest errors as it creates sample points with both the largest minimum distance to any transmitter and the largest mean distance to all transmitters.

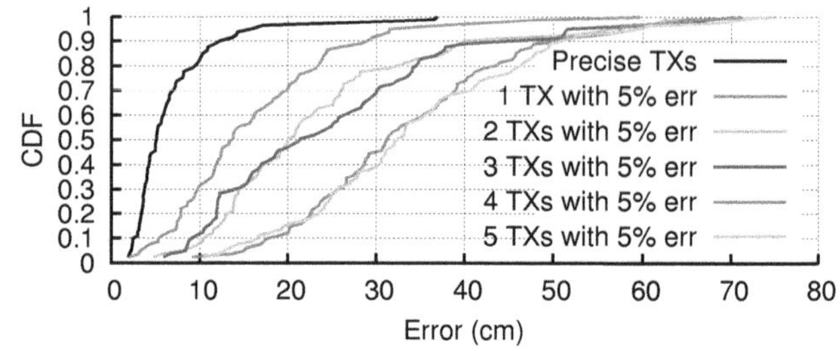

Figure 11: CDF of location error from a 5% error in absolute transmitter location under the same conditions as Figure 10a. This experiment simulates the effect of installation errors.

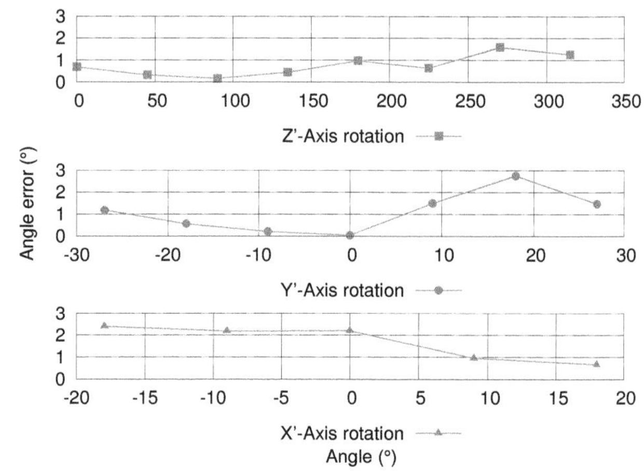

Figure 12: We rotate the mobile phone along axes parallel to the z'-, y'-, and x'-axis. Along the z'-axis, the mobile phone rotates 45° at a time and covers a full circle. Because of FoV constraints, the y'-axis rotation is limited to -27° to 27° and the x'-axis is limited to -18° to 18° with 9° increments. The experiments are conducted at a height of 240 cm. The angle error for all measurements falls within 3°.

7.3 Controlled Positioning Accuracy

To evaluate the limits of positioning accuracy under controlled, static conditions, we take 81 pictures in a grid pattern across 100 × 100 cm area 246 cm below the transmitters and perform localization. When all five transmitters are active, the average position error across all 81 locations is 7 cm, as shown in Figure 10a and Figure 10c. Removing any one transmitter, corner or center, yields very similar results to the five-transmitter case, as seen in the CDF in Figure 10d.

Removing two transmitters can be done in three ways: (i) removing two opposite corners, (ii) removing two transmitters from the same side, and (iii) removing one corner and the center. Performing localization requires three transmitters that form a triangle on the image plane, so (i) is not a viable option. Scenario (iii) introduces the largest error, captured in the heatmap in Figure 10b, with an average error as high as 50 cm in the corner underneath the missing transmitter. In the case of a missing side (ii), the area underneath the missing transmitters has an average error of only 29 cm. Figure 10d summarizes the results of the removing various transmitter subsets.

In our worst case results, on an unmodified smartphone we are able to achieve parity (∼50 cm accuracy) with the results of systems such as Epsilon [13] that require dedicated receiver hardware in addition to the infrastructure costs of a localization system. However, with only one additional transmitter in sight, we are able to achieve an order of magnitude improvement in location accuracy.

Thus far, we have assumed the precise location of each transmitters is known. Figure 11 explores the effect of transmitter installation error on positioning by introducing a 5% error in 1–5 transmitter positions and re-running the experiment from Figure 10a. With 5% error in the origin of all five transmitters, our system has only a 30 cm 50th percentile error, which suggests some tolerance to installation-time measurement and calibration errors.

To evaluate the orientation error from localization, we rotate the phone along the x', y', and z' axes. We compute the estimated rotation using our localization system and compare it to ground truth when the phone is placed 240 cm below the 5 transmitters. Figure 12 shows the orientation accuracy across all 3 rotation axes. The rotation errors fall within 3° in all measurements.

7.4 Frequency-Based Identification

We evaluate two frequency decoders and find that the FFT is more robust, but edge-detection gives better results when it succeeds.

Rx Frequency Error vs Tx Frequency. Figure 13 sweeps the transmit frequency from 1 to 10 kHz in 500 Hz steps and evaluates the ability of both the FFT and edge detector to correctly identify the transmitted frequency. The edge detector with 1/16667 s exposure performs best until 7 kHz when the edges can no longer be detected and it fails completely. The FFT detector cannot detect the frequency as precisely, but can decode a wider range of frequencies.

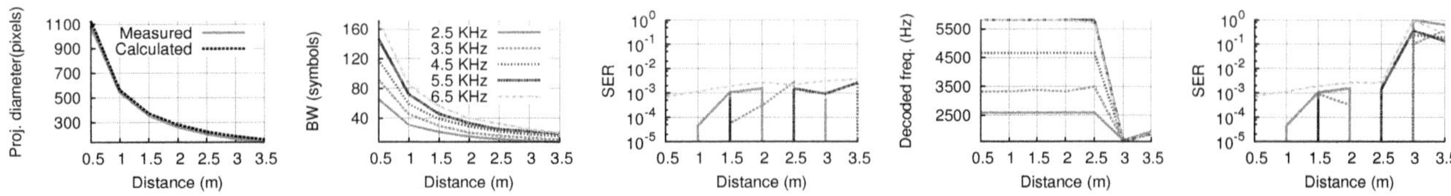

(a) Transmitter length (b) Available bandwidth (c) SER (Known f.) (d) Frequency decoding (e) SER (Unknown f.)

Figure 15: Examining the decodability of Manchester data across various transmit frequencies and distances. Figures (b) through (e) share the same legends. The transmitted frequencies are 2.5 KHz, 3.5 KHz, 4.5 KHz, 5.5 KHz and 6.5 KHz.

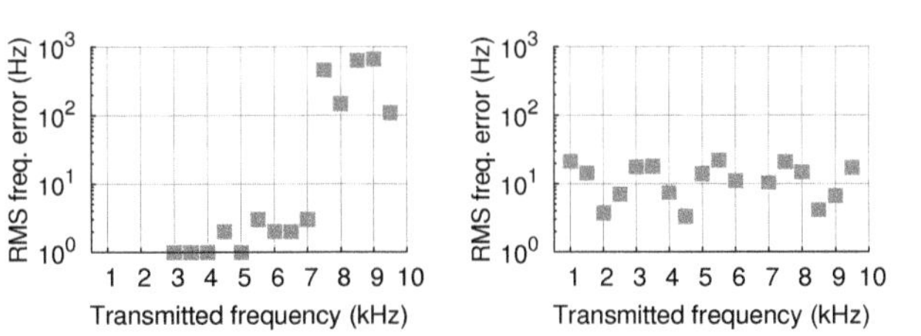

(a) Using edge detection (b) Using FFT

Figure 13: Frequency recovery at 0.2 m, 1/16667 s, ISO 100. The edge detector performs better until ~7 kHz when quantization causes it to fail completely. The FFT method has lower resolution but can decode a wider frequency range.

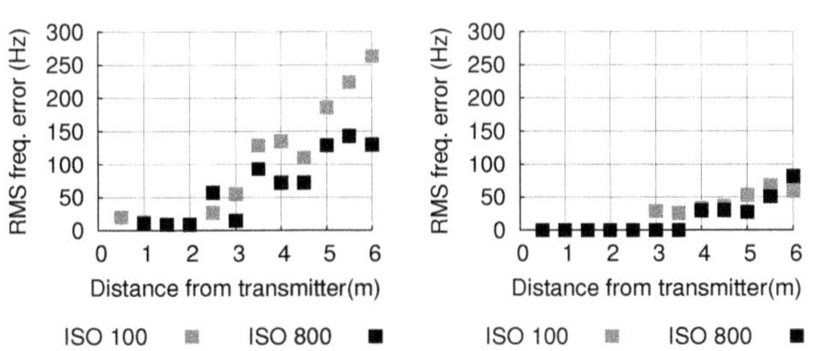

(a) Using edge detection (b) Using FFT

Figure 14: As distance grows, the light intensity and area fall super-linearly. Using a higher ISO amplifies what little light is captured, enhancing frequency recoverability. We transmit a 1 kHz frequency on a commercial LED and find that the decoded frequency error remains under 100 Hz for distances up to 6 m from the transmitter.

Rx Frequency Error vs Tx Distance. As the distance between the transmitter and phone increases, the received energy at each pixel drops due to line of sight path loss [8]. The area of the transmitter projected onto the imager plane also decreases. These factors reduce the ability to decode information. In Figure 14 we use a 10 cm diameter 14 W Commercial Electric can light to explore the impact of distance on our ability to recover frequency, and the effect of varying the ISO to attempt to compensate for the lower received power. As intensity fades, the edge detection cannot reliably detect edges and it fails. The FFT method is more robust to this failure, as it is able to better take advantage of pixels with medium intensity.

The Importance of Frequency Channels. Human constraints and optics constraints limit our bandwidth to 1~7 kHz. With an effective resolution of 200 Hz, the FFT decoder can only identify about 30 channels, and thus can only label 30 unique transmitters. The finer 50 Hz resolution of the edge detector allows for about 120 channels. A typical warehouse-style store, however, can easily have over 1,000 lights. We explore techniques for more efficiently using this limited set of frequency channels in Section 8.

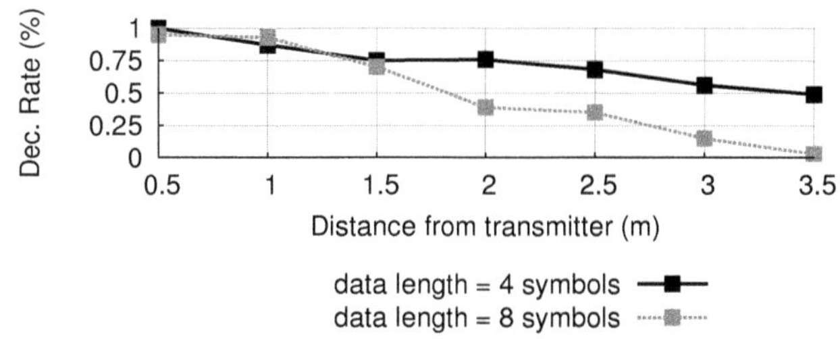

Figure 16: Hybrid decoding is able to better tolerate the frequency quantization ambiguity than pure Manchester. Shorter data has a higher probability of being correctly decoded at long distances.

7.5 Decoding Manchester Data

The relative size of a transmitter in a captured image dominates data decodability. If the physical width of a transmitter is A and the distance from the imager is D, the width of the transmitter on the image is $A/D \times Z_f$ pixels. Figure 15a shows measured width in pixels and theoretical values at different distances. Figure 15b shows the effect on the maximum theoretical bandwidth when using Manchester encoding for various frequencies. Figure 15c finds that if the transmitter frequency is known, the symbol error rate (SER) is $\sim 10^{-3}$. Our sweeping match filter is able to detect frequency until a quantization cutoff, as Figure 15d shows. When the frequency is not known a priori, Figure 15e shows that the SER correlates strongly with the ability to decode frequency.

7.6 Decoding Hybrid Data

Hybrid decoding first decodes the pure tone frequency and then is able to use the known frequency to improve its ability to decode the data. As distance increases, the probability of capturing the data segment in the limited transmitter area falls, thus Figure 16 finds that shorter messages are more robust to large distances.

8. DISCUSSION

In this section, we discuss some limitations of our current system and potential directions for future work.

Deployment Considerations. In real settings, all LED locations must be known, although only the relative distances between closely located LEDs must be known with high accuracy. Although not trivial, it does not seem difficult to ensure that this condition holds. We have deployed a grid of sixteen luminaires in our lab, and we analyze the effect of location errors on localization accuracy in Section 7.3. We note that almost any localization system must know the anchor locations. In a practical setting, this would be done, presumably, with the aid of blueprints and a laser rangefinder.

Usability. Our system targets an active user, so that the front-facing camera naturally observes the ceiling during use. Passive localization (e.g. while the phone is in a pocket) is out of scope.

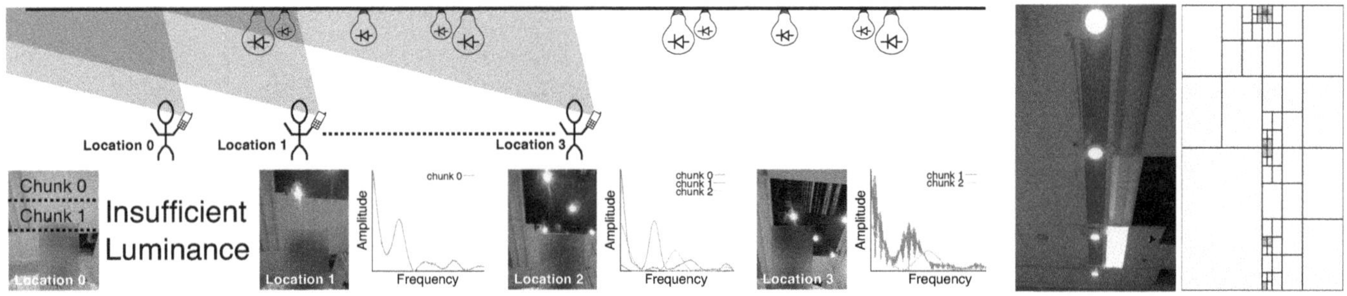

(a) Local Filtering. (b) Normal Exp. (c) Partitioned Img.

Figure 17: (a)Local filtering. In this experiment, we walk under our testbed, capturing images at about 1 fps. We divide each frame into 8 "chunks" and run an FFT along the center row of pixels for each chunk. The FFTs of non-negligible chunks are presented next to each image. At each location, we also capture an image taken with traditional exposure and film speed settings to help visualize the experiment; the FFTs are performed on images captured with 1/16667 s exposure on ISO 100 film. (b)-(c), Recursive Searching. The image is partitioned and each segment is quickly scanned by taking an FFT of the column sum of each segment. Segments with no peaks are discarded and segments with interesting peaks are recursed into until the minimum decodable transmitter size (~60 pixels) is found.

Figure 18: (left) The same LED tube imaged twice at 90° rotations shows how multiple beacons can be supported in a single lamp. (right) A single fixture can support multiple LED drivers (four here). An image capturing only this fixture could be used to localize.

Distance. Distance is the major limitation for our system. Received signal and projected image size are strongly affected by distance. We find that a 60 pixel projection is roughly the lower bound for reliable frequency decoding. However, as camera resolutions increase, our usable distance will improve.

Local Filtering. Not all images capture enough transmitters to successfully localize. It would be desirable to perform some local filtering to discard images that would not be useful for positioning, thus avoiding the cost of transferring undecodable images to the cloud. We explore one such possibility in Figure 17a. The phone selects a sampling of image rows and performs an FFT, searching for the presence of high frequency components. This fast and simple algorithm rejects many images that would not have decoded.

Alternative Image Processing. Building on the local filtering concept, another possible approach for locating transmitters in the captured image, like Figure 17b, may be a divide and conquer technique, as shown in Figure 17c. As this algorithm already partitions the image into bins with FFTs, it is also well suited to solve the problem of separating non-disjoint transmitters. If only the filtered chunks are processed, the processing load is substantially reduced—from 33 MP to 0.42 MP (13 chunks $\times$ (33/1024) MP/chunk), dramatically reducing image transfer time to the cloudlet, and the processing time on the cloudlet. This approach may even allow positioning to occur entirely on the smartphone.

Fixture Flexibility. Our system requires that at least three transmitters are captured and decoded. Many LED fixtures, such as office fluorescent T8 tube replacements, are actually multiple LED transmitters in a single fixture. Figure 18 shows how a single LED tube can transmit multiple beacons (left) and how a fixture with multiple tubes could support the non-collinear transmitter requirement (right). Localizing with this fixture would require improving our image processing, which currently assumes disjoint, circular transmitters.

Interference. Since only the direct line-of-sight path is captured by our short exposure time, there is little danger from interference regardless of transmitter density (for two transmitters' projections to alias, the pixel quantization must be so poor that they are only mapping to a few pixels and are undecodable anyway).

Limited Frequency Channels. Our system has a limited set (up to 120) of frequencies with which to label each transmitter. One method to increase the number of labels would be to have each transmitter alternate between two frequencies ($\binom{120}{2} = 7140$). Reliably and accurately estimating inter-frame motion (e.g. using the accelerometer and gyroscope), however, could prove difficult, making it difficult to match transmitter projections across frames.

A simpler approach that still requires only a single image is to simply re-use labels and leverage transmitter adjacency relationships. As our system captures contiguous images and requires at least three landmarks to localize, the adjacency relationships between lights form another constraint that can uniquely identify transmitters. Actually identifying transmitters with this system is surprisingly simple. For each frequency observed, consider all possible transmitter locations and compute the total inter-transmitter distance. The set of transmitters that minimizes this distance are the actual transmitters. This transmitter labeling technique is the same minimization procedure already used by the processing for AoA estimation.

Dimmable LEDs. Dimming is a requirement in 802.15.7. LEDs can be dimmed by either reducing their current or using PWM. As PWM dimming may affect our transmitted signal, we briefly explore its impact by PWM dimming an LED using a frequency higher than the phone's scan rate (we use 1 MHz, 10% duty cycle). We find that it does not affect our ability to decode data.

Privacy. Our design does not require interaction with the local environment. Luminaires are unidirectional beacons and image capture emits no signals. If needed, the lookup table can be acquired once out of band, and processing could be done either on the phone or a user's private cloud. A user can thus acquire location estimates without sharing any location information with any other entity.

9. CONCLUSIONS

Accurate indoor positioning has been called a "grand challenge" for computing. In this paper, we take a small step toward addressing this challenge by showing how unmodified smartphones and slightly-modified LED lighting can support accurate indoor positioning with higher accuracy than prior work. Our results show that it is possible to achieve decimeter location error and 3° orientation error by simply walking under an overhead LED light while using one's smartphone. When used in typical retail settings with overhead lighting, this allows a user to be accurately localized every few meters, perhaps with dead reckoning filling in the gaps. Although our current approach has many drawbacks, none appear to be fundamental. Having demonstrated the viability of the basic approach, future work could explore the rolling shutter channel, improve channel capacity, increase image processing performance, and reduce positioning error.

10. ACKNOWLEDGMENTS

This work was supported in part by the TerraSwarm Research Center, one of six centers supported by the STARnet phase of the Focus Center Research Program (FCRP), a Semiconductor Research Corporation program sponsored by MARCO and DARPA. This research was conducted with Government support under and awarded by DoD, Air Force Office of Scientific Research, National Defense Science and Engineering Graduate (NDSEG) Fellowship, 32 CFR 168a. This material is based upon work partially supported by the National Science Foundation under grants CNS-0964120, CNS-1111541, and CNS-1350967, and generous gifts from Intel, Qualcomm, and Texas Instruments.

11. REFERENCES

[1] J. Armstrong, Y. A. Sekercioglu, and A. Neild. Visible light positioning: A roadmap for international standardization. *IEEE Communications Magazine*, 51(12), 2013.

[2] P. Bahl and V. N. Padmanabhan. RADAR: An in-building RF-based user location and tracking system. In *Proc. 19th Annual Joint Conference of the IEEE Computer and Communications Societies. (INFOCOM '00)*, volume 2, 2000.

[3] J. Canny. A computational approach to edge detection. *IEEE Transactions on Pattern Analysis and Machine Intelligence*.

[4] Y. Chen, D. Lymberopoulos, J. Liu, and B. Priyantha. FM-based indoor localization. In *Proc. of the 10th International Conference on Mobile Systems, Applications, and Services (MobiSys '12)*, 2012.

[5] K. Chintalapudi, A. Padmanabha Iyer, and V. N. Padmanabhan. Indoor localization without the pain. In *Proc. of the 16th ACM Annual International Conference on Mobile Computing and Networking (MobiCom '10)*, 2010.

[6] J. Chung, M. Donahoe, C. Schmandt, I.-J. Kim, P. Razavai, and M. Wiseman. Indoor location sensing using geo-magnetism. In *Proc. of the 9th International Conference on Mobile Systems, Applications, and Services (MobiSys '11)*, 2011.

[7] P. Connolly and D. Boone. Indoor location in retail: Where is the money? ABI Research Report, 2013.

[8] K. Cui, G. Chen, Z. Xu, and R. D. Roberts. Line-of-sight visible light communication system design and demonstration. *7th IEEE IET International Symposium on Communication Systems Networks and Digital Signal Processing*, 2010.

[9] C. Danakis, M. Afgani, G. Povey, I. Underwood, and H. Haas. Using a CMOS camera sensor for visible light communication. In *IEEE Globecom Workshops*, 2012.

[10] M. C. Dean. *Bearings-Only Localization and Mapping*. PhD thesis, Carnegie Mellon University, 2005.

[11] A. Jovicic, J. Li, and T. Richardson. Visible light communication: Opportunities, challenges and the path to market. *IEEE Communications Magazine*, 51(12), 2013.

[12] T. Komine and M. Nakagawa. Fundamental analysis for visible-light communication system using LED lights. *IEEE Transactions on Consumer Electronics*, 50(1), 2004.

[13] L. Li, P. Hu, C. Peng, G. Shen, and F. Zhao. Epsilon: A visible light based positioning system. In *Proc. of the 11th USENIX Symposium on Networked Systems Design and Implementation (NSDI '14)*, 2014.

[14] K. Lorincz and M. Welsh. Motetrack: A robust, decentralized approach to RF-based location tracking. *Personal Ubiquitous Computing*, 11(6), Aug. 2007.

[15] E. Martin, O. Vinyals, G. Friedland, and R. Bajcsy. Precise indoor localization using smart phones. In *Proc. of the ACM International Conference on Multimedia*, 2010.

[16] Microsoft. PhotoCaptureDevice class. http://msdn.microsoft.com/en-us/library/windowsphone/develop/windows.phone.media.capture.photocapturedevice.

[17] Nokia. Camera explorer. https://github.com/nokia-developer/camera-explorer, 2013.

[18] N. Otsu. A Threshold Selection Method from Gray-level Histograms. *IEEE Transactions on Systems, Man and Cybernetics*, 9(1), 1979.

[19] G. B. Prince and T. D. Little. A two phase hybrid RSS/AoA algorithm for indoor device localization using visible light. In *IEEE Global Communication Conference (GLOBECOM '12)*, 2012.

[20] M. S. Rahman, M. M. Haque, and K.-D. Kim. Indoor positioning by led visible light communication and image sensors. *International Journal of Electrical and Computer Engineering (IJECE)*, 1(2), 2011.

[21] N. Rajagopal, P. Lazik, and A. Rowe. Visual light landmarks for mobile devices. In *Proc. of the 13th ACM/IEEE International Conference on Information Processing in Sensor Networks (IPSN '14)*, 2014.

[22] S. Rajagopal, R. D. Roberts, and S.-K. Lim. IEEE 802.15.7 visible light communication: Modulation schemes and dimming support. *IEEE Communications Magazine*, 50(3), 2012.

[23] A. Richardson, J. Strom, and E. Olson. AprilCal: Assisted and repeatable camera calibration. In *Proc. of International Conference on Intelligent Robots and Systems (IROS '13)*, 2013.

[24] M. Sakata, Y. Yasumuro, M. Imura, Y. Manabe, and K. Chihara. Location system for indoor wearable PC users. In *Workshop on Advanced Computing and Communicating Techniques for Wearable Information Playing*, 2003.

[25] S. Suzuki et al. Topological structural analysis of digitized binary images by border following. *Computer Vision, Graphics, and Image Processing*, 30(1), 1985.

[26] J. Tan and N. Narendran. A driving scheme to reduce AC LED flicker. *Optical Engineering*, 2013.

[27] J. Xiong and K. Jamieson. ArrayTrack: A fine-grained indoor location system. In *Proc. of the 10th USENIX Symposium on Networked Systems Design and Implementation (NSDI '13)*, 2013.

[28] S.-H. Yang, E.-M. Jeong, D.-R. Kim, H.-S. Kim, Y.-H. Son, and S.-K. Han. Indoor three-dimensional location estimation based on LED visible light communication. *Electronics Letters*, 49(1), January 2013.

[29] Z. Yang, C. Wu, and Y. Liu. Locating in fingerprint space: Wireless indoor localization with little human intervention. In *Proc. of the 18th ACM Annual International Conference on Mobile Computing and Networking (MobiCom '12)*, 2012.

[30] M. Yoshino, S. Haruyama, and M. Nakagawa. High-accuracy positioning system using visible LED lights and image sensor. In *IEEE Radio and Wireless Symposium (RWS '08)*, 2008.

[31] M. A. Youssef and A. Agrawala. The Horus WLAN location determination system. In *Proc. of the 3rd International Conference on Mobile Systems, Applications, and Services (MobiSys '05)*, 2005.

[32] Z. Zhou, M. Kavehrad, and P. Deng. Indoor positioning algorithm using light-emitting diode visible light communications. *Optical Engineering*, 51(8), 2012.

Experiencing and Handling the Diversity in Data Density and Environmental Locality in an Indoor Positioning Service

Liqun Li, Guobin Shen, Chunshui Zhao, Thomas Moscibroda,
Jyh-Han Lin, Feng Zhao
Microsoft
{liqul, jackysh, chunzhao, moscitho, jyh-han.lin, zhao}@microsoft.com

ABSTRACT

Diversity in training data density and environment locality is intrinsic in the real-world deployment of indoor localization systems and has a major impact on the performance of existing localization approaches. In this paper, through micro-benchmarks, we find that fingerprint-based approaches are preferable in scenarios where a dense database is available; while model-based approaches are the method of choice in the case of sparse data. It should be noted, however, that practical situations are complex. A single deployment often features both sparse and dense sampled areas. Furthermore, the internal layout affects the propagation of radio signals and exhibits environmental impacts. A certain number of measurement samples may be sufficient for one part of the building, but entirely insufficient for another. Thus, finding the right indoor localization algorithm for a given large-scale deployment is challenging, if not impossible; there is no one-size-fits-all indoor localization approach.

Realizing the fundamental fact that the quality of the location database capturing the actual radio map dictates localization accuracy, in this paper, we propose Modellet, an algorithmic approach that optimally approximates the actual radio map by unifying model-based and fingerprint-based approaches. Modellet represents the radio map using a *fingerprint-cloud* that incorporates both measured real fingerprints and virtual fingerprints, which are computed from models with a local support, based on the key concept of the *supporting set*. We evaluate Modellet with data collected from an office building as well as 13 large-scale deployment venues (shopping malls and airports), located across China, U.S., and Germany. Comparing Modellet with two representative baseline approaches, RADAR and EZPerfect, demonstrates that Modellet effectively adapts to different data densities and environmental conditions, substantially outperforming existing approaches.

Categories and Subject Descriptors

C.2 [**Computer-Communication Networks**]: Miscellaneous

MobiCom'14, September 7-11, 2014, Maui, Hawaii, USA.

ACM 978-1-4503-2783-1/14/09 ...$15.00.
http://dx.doi.org/10.1145/2639108.2639118.

Keywords

Indoor Localization; Fingerprint; Model

1. INTRODUCTION

In recent years, indoor localization has been one of the most deeply and frequently studied problems both in the mobile computing research community, and in industry (over 90 companies now in the indoor localization alliance [3]). WiFi-based indoor localization approaches have been the center of attention, due to their low deployment cost, potential for reasonable accuracy and readiness to be applied to mobile devices. Existing WiFi-based solutions usually fall into one of two categories: fingerprint-based [5,20,40] and model-based approaches [9,11,15,23]. The former fingerprints locations in the area of interest and then searches for the best matching location, while the latter trains a signal propagation model using training/calibration data and then applies trilateration for localization. While these methods have been shown to achieve promising localization accuracy (below 10 meters at 90%tile) under lab conditions, large-scale accurate indoor localization systems have yet to be developed. For example, given real-world fingerprint sampling conditions, the localization accuracy of existing approaches in large venues like shopping malls and airports can still be up to 20∼30m at 90%tile; similar results are reported by Google [2].

One reason for this well-known and frequently-lamented discrepancy is that academic research has so far mostly focused on only one part of the problem: location inference, i.e., resolving the position for a given WiFi signal. However, for any given location inference algorithm, it is how well the location database captures the actual radio map that dictates localization accuracy. Thus, it is crucial to acquire (and maintain) a high-quality database.

In our experience with over 13 large-scale industrial deployments, we have found that the challenges lie in both data density and environmental conditions. It is often difficult, if even possible, to obtain an equally dense set of high-quality samples across an entire building complex. And even if it was possible to get a spatially uniform sample database (in some subareas), the different local environments (room layout, AP deployment, etc) imply that the sampled fingerprints may yield high-accuracy localization in one location, while being entirely insufficient in others. Such reality poses a fundamental challenge to existing WiFi-based indoor localization approaches, partially explaining their inadequate performance in practice. A key insight suggested by this study is that different localization approaches are preferably applied under different conditions (data density, environment); for a given approach, parameters should be fine-tuned for different locations within the same deployment. In other words, there is no one-size-fit-all solution among existing localization algorithms, even for a single deployment. Such a conclusion is also implicitly supported by observations from [6, 12], in which the authors did extensive measurements and experiments in a lab setting.

In this paper, we set out to attack the challenges of nonuniform data density and environmental impact by designing a systematic and unified way to better approximate the actual radio map using whatever data samples are available. We propose *Modellet*, an algorithmic approach that optimally approximates the actual radio map by unifying a model-based and fingerprint-based approach.

Inspired by the practice of visualizing a surface through meshing neighboring vortexes in computer graphics, in Modellet, we try to approximate the possibly irregular radio map by 'meshing' neighboring fingerprints. In particular, Modellet adapts to the specific local data density and environmental conditions by fusing information from both measured fingerprints and signal propagation models, based on the key concepts of the *supporting set*. A supporting set is a set of real fingerprints from which a derived model can best approximate the local radio map. Borrowing from the practice of using point cloud to represent arbitrary object in 3D modelling, we propose a *fingerprint-cloud* notion to approximate the actual radio map, i.e., representing arbitrary shaped radio map from dense fingerprints. A fingerprint-cloud incorporates both real and virtual fingerprints, where virtual fingerprints are spatially uniformly sampled across areas of interest and computed via the signal propagation model obtained from the supporting set.

The combination of fingerprint-cloud and supporting set enables Modellet to always adjust to the locally optimal trade-off between model-based and fingerprint-based approaches, and to optimally fine-tune the algorithm parameters. An effective device gain estimation method is also proposed to address device diversity. As a result, Modellet performs well under real-world noisy and nonuniform datasets, and in different environmental conditions. We are aware that several previous studies have examined localization accuracy against various data densities and environmental conditions, like [5, 6, 12, 17, 26] among others. However, to the best of our knowledge, we are the first to try designing a systematic approach that automatically adapts to data density, which may change as more data flows in.

In summary, we make the following major contributions:

- We establish how different families of localization algorithms perform differently under different data densities and environmental conditions. To the best of our knowledge, this is the first in-depth study in this field.
- We design a unifying localization framework called Modellet, which addresses the challenges of nonuniform data density and environmental impacts from a database construction aspect. Using the concept of fingerprint-cloud and supporting set, Modellet ensures an optimal use of available sample data in the vicinity of the location in question. An effective device gain estimation method is also proposed.
- We conduct extensive experiments based on real data collected from an office building and over 13 large venues, located in China, US, and Germany. Such large-scale evaluations for indoor localization using realistic databases have rarely been published.

The paper is organized as follows: Section 2 describes the motivating observations regarding data density and environmental conditions. We provide the overview of Modellet in Section 3, followed by details on its core concepts in Sections 4 and 5. We further present a way to address the device gain diversity in 6. We evaluate Modellet in Section 7. We discuss practical issues and possible extensions in Section 8 and provide an overview of existing the state-of-the-art indoor localization methods in Section 9. Section 10 concludes this paper.

2. MOTIVATION

2.1 Properties of Real Service Data

We conduct real world deployments of indoor localization services at multiple large shopping malls, airports and enterprise buildings. The large scale real world training data collected during such deployments reveals two features that do not stand out from those collected in a lab environment in early research papers.

Nonuniform Data Density: The data we obtained, through both war-walking and tap-and-point methods of data collection by third-party vendors, are of different density across different subareas of various indoor environments. For example, the pathway areas usually have much denser training data than the inner parts of the shops in a mall. There are many reasons for the surveyor cannot perform long time data collection inside shops without getting consent from the shop owner; it is more challenging to figure out precise positions within shops than on the pathways as the maps contain little information about inner shops; pathways can be surveyed by regular walking while inside shops have to be collected point by point. The situation will not change substantially for crowdsourcing-based data collection (e.g., [22, 31, 33, 38]) as popular places and pathways will always have more chances to be visited and hence enjoy more frequent data collection. In addition, the WiFi infrastructure may be updated with APs removed, relocated or added. Thus, it is unlikely to obtain a location database that has all indoor areas sampled dense enough and up to date.

Environmental Impact: Indoor environments are typically divided into many smaller functional areas such as corridors, rooms and shops, among others. They are usually separated using cement, wood or glass walls that cause different penetrations and reflections of radio signal. Unlike office or campus building environments, shopping malls and airports are usually constructed very differently. Their internal layouts are much less regular and may be arbitrarily divided to meet different functional requirement. In particular, shopping malls and airports often contain large atria. This renders them very challenging environments for indoor positioning. Signals from multiple floors can be heard at locations near the atrium. It is difficult even to locate user's correct floor.

2.2 Impact on Localization

To understand how training data density and environmental conditions may affect localization accuracy, we carry out several microbenchmarks to understand their impact. In our experiments, we consider RADAR [5] and EZPerfect [9, 28], which are representative fingerprint-based and model-based localization approaches, respectively.

- **RADAR** first collects fingerprints from various known locations to build up a fingerprint database. It then determines the position of an incoming fingerprint by comparing it against all fingerprints in the database, and averages the locations of a few fingerprints nearest in signal space.
- **EZPerfect** adopts the log-distance path loss (LDPL) model [28] and trains model parameters from fingerprints with known locations. Model parameters instead of fingerprints are stored in the location database. Trilateration or multilateration is applied to estimate the location for an incoming fingerprint.

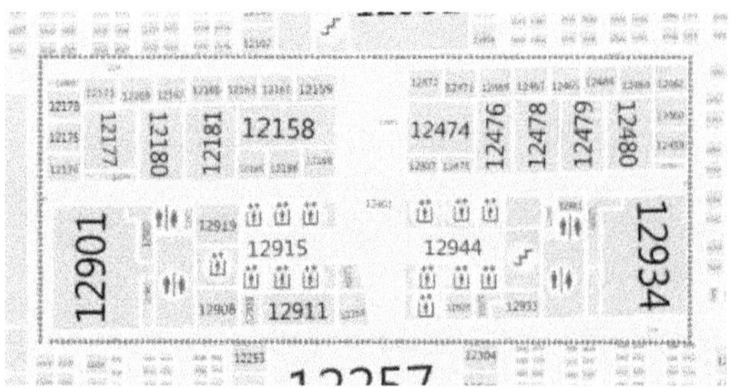

Figure 1: A $75m \times 40m$ office area for data collection. Each red dot represents a sampling location. One fingerprint is collected for each location.

Horus [40], a proven approach that outperforms RADAR, was not considered here. Horus achieves excellent performance by exploring temporal diversity (i.e., repeated sampling at the same location) to iron out random errors in signal readings. However, the data collection time is prohibitive in real world deployment. Even with war-walking based data collection, venues like large shopping malls in our evaluation in Section 7 still require a whole day (around 8 hours) to fill each $10 \times 10m^2$ grid only $20 \sim 30$ fingerprints, far below the number of samples (100) per $1 \sim 2m$ apart adopted in [40].

The data for our benchmarks was densely collected along the corridors in an office building, as shown in Fig. 1. Fingerprints are collected $\sim 0.6m$ apart, producing a total of 329 fingerprints. The high data density allows us to emulate sparser data collection via downsampling. As corridors have much simpler structure than other areas such as inner shops, we expect the findings below would be more severe for other indoor areas.

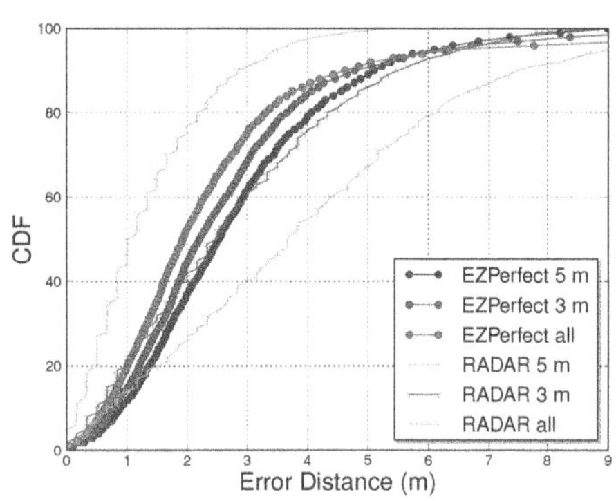

Figure 2: Localization errors at different data densities, for RADAR and EZPerfect. '3m' and '5m' are the grid size for downsampling, and 'all' means using all the data.

Impact of Data Density: We first split the whole dataset into training (80%) and testing (20%) data. Then, we vary the density of the training data by uniform downsampling. Fig. 2 shows the comparisons between RADAR and EZPerfect under various data densities. In the figure, '3m', '5m' and 'all' means retaining one sample every 3 meters, one sample every 5 meters and using all samples, respectively. We can see that EZPerfect outperforms RADAR on downsampled data, while RADAR achieves better accuracy with full data. Thus we make the following observation:

Observation 1: Fingerprint- and model-based approaches are more suitable for different densities. With dense training data, fingerprint-based schemes yields better accuracy; whereas with sparse training data, model-based ones are better.

As indoor location services may obtain new training data over time, e.g., through additional surveys or contributions of real users, the density of training data may vary. The above observation implies that the location service should be able to automatically adapt to and make best use of all available training data. A similar observation is made in [6], where the authors experiment with different number of sniffers (called landmarks) to locate one transmitter and found different sniffer densities favor different localization methods. The difference with our observation lies in that ours is made from varying densities of collected fingerprints.

Impact of Environmental Conditions: To show how the physical layout of indoor environment affects indoor localization, we highlight in Fig. 3 the measured RSSs and the model fitness errors for a randomly picked AP. Here, the fitness error refers to the difference between the measured and model-calculated RSSs. In the left figure, a bubble stands for an observation. The size and color of the bubble represent the magnitude of RSS: the larger and the redder the bubble, the higher the RSS, and vise versa. We can see that the signal attenuates at very different speed along different corridors. For instance, positions A and B are the same distance from the AP, but their RSSs differ by 10dB. In the right figure, bubble size indicates the magnitude of fitness error, and the green or blue color stands for a positive or negative error. From the figures, we make the follow observation:

Observation 2: The internal layout of an environment significantly impacts radio signal propagation. Applying a single omni-model to all observations always yields large fitness errors. Yet nearby positions tend to see a similar fitness error, which indicates the existence of environmental locality.

Note that the environmental impact is orthogonal to the training data density. No matter how dense the data is, the environmental impact persists.

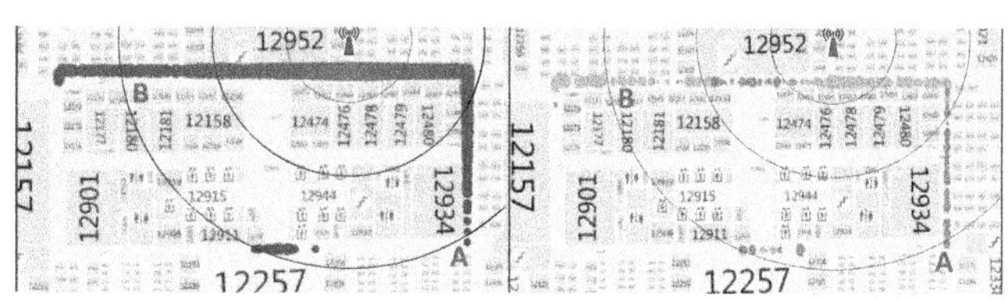

Figure 3: The observed RSSs and model fitness errors of a randomly picked AP along the corridors.

Observation Analysis: The above observations are rooted at the irregularity of a *radio map* – a map of signal strengths at different locations, and the ability to approximate the radio map from training data. The localization process is actually a process to find the best match(es) to a given fingerprint from the radio map and return the position of the best match(es). The better we can approximate the actual radio map, the better the localization accuracy that can be achieved.

When the training data are sparse, the radio map cannot be well approximated with few fingerprints. However, under the assumption of a radio propagation model, the radio map can be better approximated. The model requires only a few samples to train the model parameter. On the contrary, when the training data are dense, distances between fingerprints are close. Thus, direct use of the fingerprints can well approximate the radio map, whereas an oversimplified omni-model will lead to a high fitness error.

The second observation is easy to understand. The walls block or alter the radio signal propagation paths. An overall omni-model must be a compromise between all observations, and nearby positions in the area warded by same walls tend to have a similar model fitness error.

Though our observations are based on two specific localization schemes, i.e., RADAR and EZPerfect, the above analysis can be generalized to the whole class of solutions. Fingerprint based approaches approximate the radio map with nonparametric models. Thus, they essentially require dense data for better approximation, due to lack of knowledge in between measurements. On the other hand, omni-model based solutions use an oversimplified signal propagation model to fit the measurements, leading to underfitting under a dense database.

2.3 Simple Hybrid Does Not Work

The above analysis suggests that a simple hybrid of fingerprint-based and model-based solutions may automatically adapt to various data densities. There may be different hybrid versions. An intuitive method could be to switch between the two approaches depending on data density. i.e., if the data density is higher than the threshold, we use a fingerprint-based approach, otherwise, we choose a model-based approach. However, it is nontrivial, if not impossible, to find this optimal threshold across various areas. Motivated by observation 2, a second approach is to apply a fingerprinting approach in complex areas and apply a model-based approach in large and open areas such as [18,21]. However, they all rely on the assumption of knowing the exact information of the wall (material and thickness) and AP (power and position). Unfortunately, such an assumption is generally unrealistic. A third method is to first apply fingerprinting and obtain a few top candidates with which a model is then trained from the resulting candidates. This approach, however, is dictated by the accuracy of the candidates returned from fingerprinting.

2.4 Challenges Towards Real World Services

Microbenchmarks and analyses reveal that the following challenges and requirements regarding the best use of training data ought to be addressed to provide high accuracy indoor localization services.

- Nonuniform data density. The system should be able to automatically adapt to training data densities, sparse to dense, which may even be altered over time.
- Environmental locality. The system should explore the environmental localities in an autonomous way, without the assumption of any priori knowledge of actual layout.

In addition, the well-known RSS fluctuation problem and device diversity problem (i.e., different devices or the same device at different battery levels may have different receiver gain) have to be tackled as well.

3. MODELLET OVERVIEW

We set out to attack the challenges of nonuniform data density and environmental locality through the design of a systematic and unified way to better approximate the actual radio map. We further handle the device diversity problem through a dedicated device gain estimation process.

3.1 Concepts in Modellet

As a thought process, if we think of the radio map as an unknown, possibly irregular surface, the task of approximating the radio map is then to reconstruct the surface from observations contained in the training fingerprints. Inspired by the practice of visualizing a surface by meshing neighboring vortexes in computer graphics, we may also mesh the neighboring fingerprints to approximate the radio map.

Supporting Set: Directly meshing neighboring fingerprints is improper as it implies a simple linear interpolation for positions in between. The radio map produced in this way would be very noisy due to RSS fluctuations and exhibits of discontinuity across mesh boundaries. To work around this, we incorporate *local models*. The intuition is simple: while one omni-model does not work well for the entire area under the AP's coverage, good local models still exist in smaller subareas. Therefore, if we can properly divide AP's coverage into small zones, we can better approximate the radio map using zonal models.

Clearly, the central task is to identify proper surrounding fingerprints, termed as a *supporting set*, in the proximity of any *location of interest*. The term location of interest, through out this paper, is referred to as the location whereas we predict its received signal strength from surrounding APs. Local models can then be built from the supporting set. Fig. 4 illustrates the supporting set for a location of interest (green circle) for a certain AP. While not showing, we point out that the supporting set for different APs and different interested positions will be different.

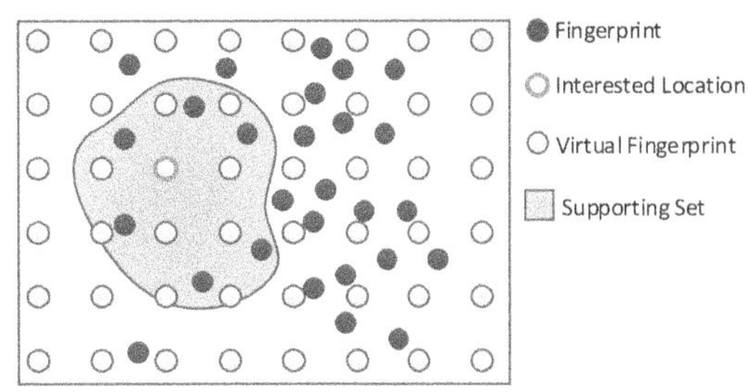

Figure 4: Conceptional illustration of the key concepts in Modellet. The supporting set includes only measured fingerprints (red dots). A virtual fingerprint may be at any position of interest.

The supporting set concept allows us to effectively explore environmental locality. In addition, as the number of parameters of the model is fixed (e.g., four parameters for LDPL model), the size of the supporting set is thus also limited, even though we usually adopt more fingerprints than necessary to iron out RSS fluctuations. This implies that the supporting set, and hence the local models and the resulting approximation to the radio map, is able to adapt to varying training data densities. The denser the training data, the more local (i.e., smaller spatial coverage) the supporting set. We elaborate the decision of supporting set and its adaptation mechanism in Section 4.

Fingerprint Cloud: It is infeasible to represent the radio map directly using supporting sets or corresponding derived local models. For any position of interest, a proper supporting set can be identified and hence a local model can be built for any AP that can be heard at that position. While the models of nearby positions will be the same if their supporting sets are identical, the number of potential supporting sets (hence models) of an AP may still be large. In addition, a real radio map usable for indoor localization consists of the maps of all APs. Due to different AP positions and their intersections with the physical layout, the supporting sets for different APs at the same position of interest are usually different.

To effectively represent the radio map, we propose the *fingerprint-cloud* (FP-Cloud) concept, which is borrowed from the point-cloud used in 3D modeling. Just like point-cloud represents arbitrary shaped 3D models directly with dense sampling points, we capture the irregular radio map using *dense* fingerprints. As the actually collected fingerprints may not be dense enough, we create *virtual fingerprints* (VFPs) at positions that were not sampled, or more specifically at the locations of interest. Fig. 4 shows the FP-Cloud of a subarea where the white circles and red circles indicate the positions of virtual and real fingerprints, respectively.

Like a real fingerprint, a VFP also consists of a list of BSSID and RSS pairs annotated with a given location. The difference is the RSSs in VFP are calculated using the local signal propagation model (detailed in Section 5) whereas they are derived from real fingerprints. Evidently, incorporating both real and virtual fingerprints, FP-Cloud captures information from both real measurements and local signal propagation knowledge.

3.2 Modellet System Overview

The overall system architecture of Modellet is shown in Fig. 5. Similar to other indoor position systems, Modellet also consists of an offline database (FP-Cloud) construction process and an online location inference process. To generate the FP-Cloud, a venue is first surveyed by cite survey specialists or crowdsources to obtain training data. The training data is directly incorporated into the FP-Cloud as raw fingerprints. The positions of virtual fingerprints (VFPs) are then determined as locations of interest. For each location of interest, the supporting set is identified. The VFP is then generated by obtaining and applying the local model from the fingerprints in the supporting set. VFPs are stored in the FP-Cloud.

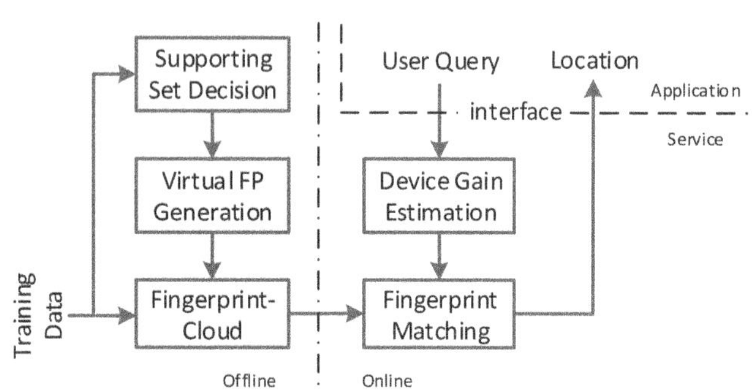

Figure 5: The Modellet system architecture.

In the online phase, upon receiving a query fingerprint, a device gain estimation process is executed. The estimated device gain and the user fingerprint are fed to the fingerprint matching engine, which returns the most likely location for the user query. Note that many location inference algorithms may be applied here. For instance, RADAR finds the K nearest neighbours (KNN) based on the signal strength vector distance, and uses the averaged location. EZPerfect uses trilateration to calculate one location minimizing the aggregated error distances to all APs. Even stochastic methods can be used [20, 40]. In our implementation, we use KNN as RADAR does.

4. SUPPORTING SET

The primary purpose of identifying the supporting set is to obtain a local model to better approximate the local surface of the radio map. A proper supporting set should also adapt to the training data density, and thus should be data-driven. When more data is available, the supporting set should be more concentrated.

4.1 Spatial Kernel Function

Rigid schemes (e.g., always selecting a certain number of fingerprints nearest to the position of interest) should be avoided even though they also adapt to data density. For rigid schemes, if a small number is set, they are not robust to RSS fluctuations; whereas if a large number is set, they may fail to identify a valid supporting set when data is sparse. Also, when the density is high, they may lead to underfitting.

In Modellet, we avoid hard decisions in identifying the supporting set. Instead we allow a large range of fingerprints to contribute but assign higher weights to fingerprints closer to the location of interest through a spatial kernel function.

Consider a set of n observations for a certain BSSID

$$S = \{s_1, s_2, \cdots, s_n\}$$

The goal is to estimate the RSS at a certain location of interest based on S through the local model. Let d_i be the Euclidean distance from the location of interest to the ith observation s_i. We set the weight of s_i as a function of d_i, denoted as $w_i = K(d_i)$ where $K(\cdot)$ is a kernel function which is monotonously decreasing with d_i. We compared various kernel functions such as uniform, tri-cube, and Gaussian, and finally pick the normalized Gaussian for its robustness over signal fluctuations. Our kernel function thus looks like

$$K(d) = e^{(d_{min} - d)/k} \tag{1}$$

where k is called *bandwidth* which controls the impact of locality, and d_{min} is the distance from the location of interest to the closest observation among S. When $k \to \infty$, all measurements are assigned weight 1, which implies no impact from locality. We decrease the value of k to make it more biased for observations in proximity. One special case is that all observations in S are far from the location of interest, leading to small weight for all observations. We carry out normalization ensuring the weight of the observation closest to be 1.

In Modellet, we adopt the widely used log-distance path loss (LDPL) model [9, 15, 23], described as follows:

$$RSS_{x,y} = P_0 - 10\gamma \log d_{x,y} \tag{2}$$
$$d_{x,y} = \sqrt{(x_0 - x)^2 + (y_0 - y)^2}$$

where P_0 and γ are the reference power and path loss constant, respectively. (x_0, y_0) is the 2D location of the AP.

The parameters, namely P_0, γ, x_0, and y_0, are learnt from the observations in the supporting set, as in [9], with the difference being the minimizing of the aggregated *weighted* fitting errors, defined in the following equation:

$$E = \sum_{i \in [1,n]} w_i \cdot |s_i - \hat{s}_i| \tag{3}$$

where $\hat{s}_i$ is the calculated RSS with the the learnt LDPL model. Optimization is conducted using Gradient Descent in our implementation to minimize Eq. (3) in order for a set of parameters for a BSSID.

4.2 Finding The Optimal Kernel Bandwidth

A key parameter of the kernel function is the bandwidth, i.e., k in Eq. (1). As discussed above, a k that is too large eliminates the impact of locality, while one that is too small may cause overfitting to observations. Therefore, the goal of finding the optimal kernel bandwidth is: if one model fits the signal attenuation well, the supporting set should be large (i.e., large k), and vice verse (i.e., small k).

We develop a modified leave one out cross validation (LOOCV) for optimal kernel bandwidth selection. LOOCV is widely used for kernel bandwidth selection, especially with limited training data size. The process is purely driven by data. The conventional LOOCV is more suitable for homogeneous data, whereas a global optimal kernel bandwidth is selected. However, the signal propagation in an indoor environment is actually heterogeneous (hence the locality). Intuitively, for open areas where the signal attenuates smoothly, it is better to use larger bandwidth values for robustness against random signal strength fluctuations. In contrast, small bandwidth values should be used for locations where the signal strength varies more significantly.

Our modified LOOCV searches an optimal kernel bandwidth for each location of interest. There are two phases:

- Given a set of n observations $s_i, i \in [1, n]$, we carry out n rounds. In the ith round, we use s_i for validation and the rest $n-1$ for training. We iterate k_i in a certain range (like $[1, 30]$), and find the one that minimizes the validation error $|s_i - \hat{s}_i|$. After n rounds, we derive a set of optimal kernel bandwidths $k_i, i \in [1, n]$, each corresponding to an observation.

- For each location of interest, we infer its kernel bandwidth based on the kernel bandwidths of nearby observations derived from the previous phase. Specifically, we adopt the mean kernel bandwidth of the top few nearest observations.

An underlying assumption here is that the kernel bandwidths of nearby locations are similar, which is implied by our observations in Section 2.

4.3 Effectiveness Verification

So far, we have discussed how to find an appropriate bandwidth for each location of interest. Figure 6 shows the signal strength heat map estimated for a certain AP using uniform (i.e., global, not using supporting set) and locality-aware LDPL models using supporting set, respectively. For uniform models, we basically set the weight of all observations to 1. We evaluate the localization accuracy of using uniform and locality-aware LDPL models with EZPerfect and RADAR. The results are shown in Fig. 7 and 8. One can see FP-Cloud with uniform models always outperforms EZPerfect and RADAR. By using locality-aware models, the gain further increases. Fig. 9 highlights the gain of using locality-aware models ($2.5m$ at 90%tile) over with uniform models ($3.5m$ at 90%tile), which is significant. Hereafter in our experimentation, Modellet always refers to FP-Cloud with locality-aware models.

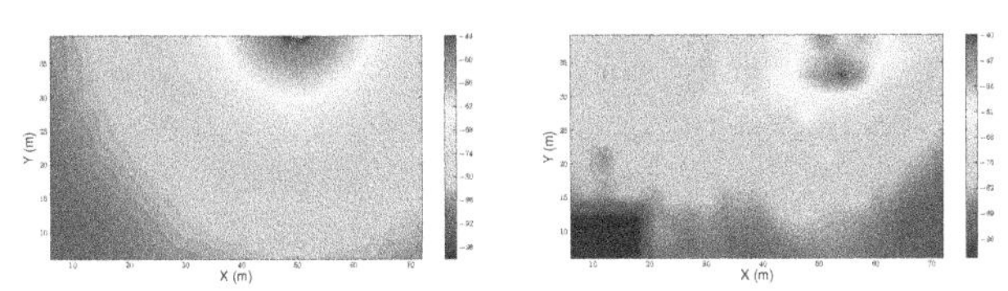

Figure 6: The heat map of signal strengths of the AP calculated with uniform (left) and locality-aware (right) LDPL models.

5. FINGERPRINT CLOUD

In essence, FP-Cloud is to use discrete fingerprint samples to approximate the continuous radio map. Shaped by the actual physical layout, the radio map can be highly irregular. Therefore, a certain density is necessary to ensure approximation accuracy. As the real collected fingerprints may not be dense enough, virtual fingerprints are computed to fill in.

In Modellet, we adopt uniform sampling for simplicity. One example is shown in Fig. 4 where the VFPs distribute uniformly. The only parameter in generating the FP-Cloud is the sampling interval. In general, the VFPs should be as dense as possible to reflect the variation in signal strength. However, due to the possible imperfection of the signal propagation model (i.e., LDPL), the calculated virtual fingerprints have errors. Inserting overly dense virtual fingerprints may incur the side-effect of reduced robustness in searching for multiple nearest neighbours during the fingerprint matching phase. We will evaluate various sampling intervals in Section 7.2.

Through Section 4, we have discussed how to obtain a local model for any specific location of interest. Intuitively, we compute a radio map for each AP as shown in Fig. 6 (right). The final radio map is a union of the radio map of all APs, which is represented with FP-Cloud in Modellet. Having decided the positions of virtual fingerprints, their RSSs are calculated with local signal propagation models in the form of Eq. (2), for any particular VFP. Note that the list of APs in a virtual fingerprint is not necessarily a union of all the APs appearing in the database, but only those seen by the real fingerprints in proximity of the VFP.

6. DEVICE DIVERSITY HANDLING

Two collocated devices may receive significantly different signal strengths from the same AP due to the difference in hardware. Fig. 10 shows the histogram of RSS offsets measured by two collocated phones (HTC Titan and Nokia Lumia 900) at various locations. Specifically, the data is collected in a large shopping mall, where the two devices are put at various locations to measure the RSSs from surrounding APs. Fig. 10 is plotted by grouping the measurements by the two devices at the same location, and calculating the difference of the RSSs for the same BSSID. Fig. 10 is plotted based on data for all BSSIDs. One can see the offset value follows a Gaussian-like distribution centered around $-20dB$.

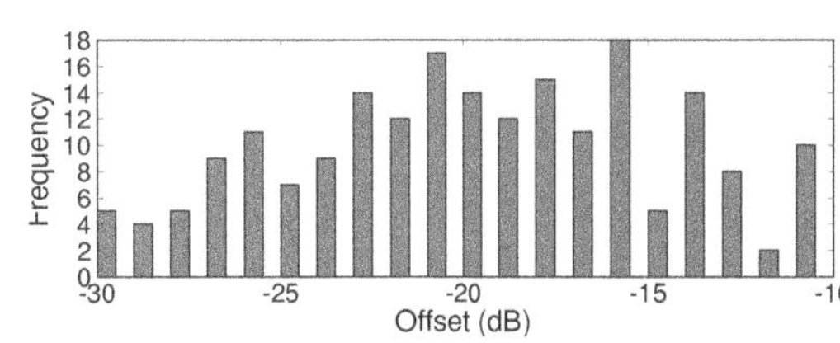

Figure 10: Offset between RSSs measured by two different devices.

Such a large gain offset can lead to bad localization results if the database is constructed with one device and directly used by another [13, 14, 29]. One solution is to measure the hardware gain offset between any pair of devices, which, however, is not scalable [29]. Authors in [13] evaluate existing methods, and concluded that the effectiveness of using RSS differences between observed APs in each fingerprint, instead of the absolute RSSs, which however significantly enlarges the dimension of fingerprints. In Modellet, we employ a light-weighted scheme during fingerprint matching as shown in Fig. 5. The idea is somewhat similar to [14] where Expectation Maximization (EM) is used to jointly estimate the location as well as device power level. However, the system architecture in [14] is different from ours where sniffers are deployed to locate a mobile client.

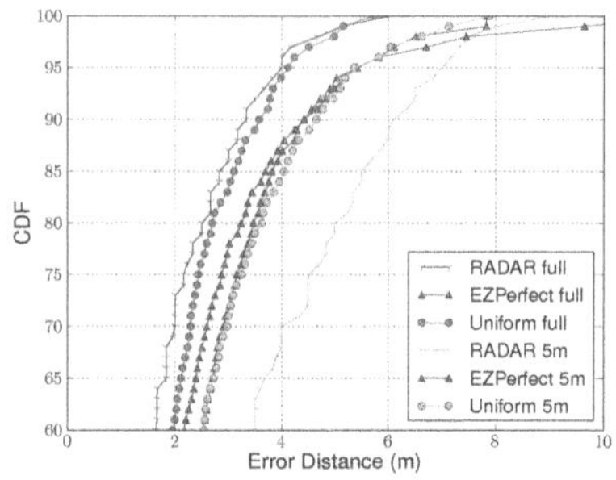

Figure 7: Comparisons of EZPerfect, RADAR, and Uniform.

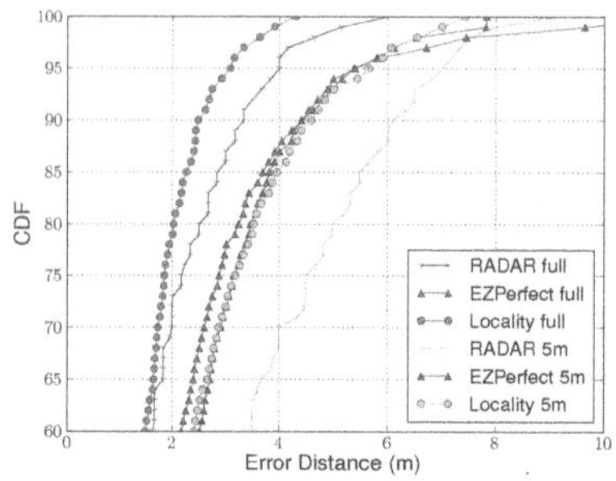

Figure 8: Comparison result of EZPerfect, RADAR, and Locality.

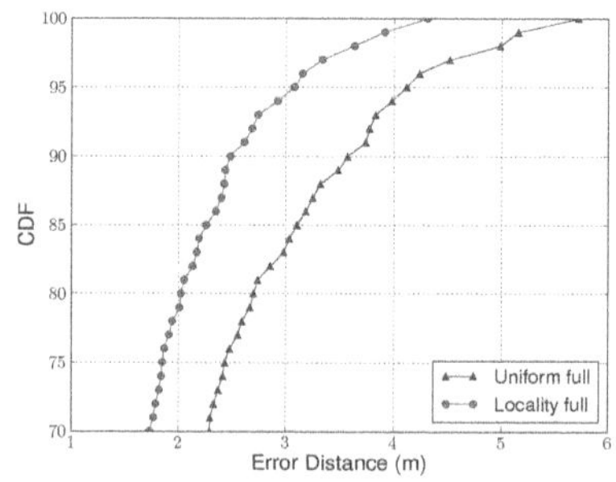

Figure 9: Comparison result of Uniform and Locality with full dataset.

Our scheme is detailed as follows. The conventional way of calculating the signal space distance Δ_{ij} between a pair of fingerprints $f_i = (r_1, r_2, \cdots, r_n)$ and $f_j = (s_1, s_2, \cdots, s_n)$ is

$$\Delta_{ij} = \sum_{k}^{n} |r_k - s_k| \tag{4}$$

We modify the calculation by adding a constant δ, such that $\Delta_{ij} = \sum_{k}^{n} |r_k - s_k + \delta|$. We vary δ in a certain range, and the gain offset o_{ij} between the two devices is estimated in Eq. (5) and the corresponding signal space distance Δ'_{ij} between f_i and f_j is calculated in Eq. (6).

$$o_{ij} = \arg\min_{\delta} \Delta'_{ij} \tag{5}$$

$$\Delta'_{ij} = \sum_{k}^{n} |r_k - s_k + o_{ij}| \tag{6}$$

In the offset estimation above, we simplify the transformation between a pair of devices (A and B) as a constant, i.e., $RSS_A = a \cdot RSS_B + \delta$ where $a = 1$. Actually, the measurement study in [29] found a is close to 1. It is therefore rare that two fingerprints measured at different locations by the same device have a constant offset between the RSSs of each observed AP, given APs deployed in various locations. We evaluate our solution with data collected by the two devices. The result is presented in Section 7.4.

7. EVALUATION

In this section, we evaluate the localization accuracy of Modellet, as well as other representative localization methods, with data collected from real, large scale deployments. We hope to reestablish a sense of achievable indoor localization accuracy using WiFi. Our key insights and understanding are summarized as follows:

- Modellet consistently outperforms the two baselines, RADAR and EZPerfect, in a small-scale office environment as well as large shopping malls and airports. The localization performance in office areas is consistent with what is reported in existing literature, while that in large venues is more contradictory. Possible reasons include uneven and inconsistent (on and off irregularly) AP deployment, with high transmission power (even could be heard several hundred of meters away).

- Generating dense VFPs for the FP-Cloud increases computation cost, but does not imply high localization accuracy. In fact, dense VFPs eliminate the robustness of fingerprint matching by finding the top few nearest neighbors. Thus, there is an optimal density which should be learnt offline.

- Modellet is not restricted to the LDPL model, but also others like the linear model. The LDPL model achieves a higher localization accuracy than the linear model, especially when the database is sparse.

- The device diversity problem significantly affects the localization accuracy. The scheme proposed in Section 6 handles the problem effectively with data collected by two devices from a large shopping mall.

7.1 Experiments Setup

We collect data with a cell phone from an office building in China and 13 large venues including shopping malls and airports (in the U.S. and Germany). The survey plan with a total of 221 fingerprints for the office building is shown in Fig. 11 where each red dot represents one fingerprint. Fig. 12 and Fig. 13 show the survey plan in two shopping malls. In this work, we collect data point by point for each venue. However, Modellet (as described in Section 3-6) is not tied up with any specific data collection approach. Other approaches like war-walking or crowdsourcing are also supported.

Table 1 shows the venue names along with the data coverage area, number of observed BSSIDs, and number of fingerprints. Most of the venues are in the U.S. with Alexa Shopping Mall located in Berlin, Germany. For these large venues, we have denser data coverage (3 $\sim$ 5m each) along the corridors and less for inner shop areas. Typically, for small sized inner shops, we have only one sample there, and a few scattered samples in large shops. The data along the corridors and in inner locations are collected separately. In this dataset, even though only one sample is taken for each location, data collection still consumes several hours for venues in Table 1.

We notice that in office buildings (or on a campus where most APs are deployed by one party), the APs are deployed more regularly to ensure uniform network coverage, whereas the APs in shopping malls or airports are placed less coordinated. Moreover, the APs' coverage in office areas is typically smaller to mitigate interference (e.g., 20 $\sim$ 30m) whereas the APs in those large venues have much larger coverage, some of which can even be heard hundreds of meters away.

7.2 Evaluation on An Office Area

The purpose of the evaluation on a relatively small office area (still over $3000m^2$) is two-fold: first, we want to examine a few settings like the density of the virtual fingerprints, and the usage of an LDPL model instead of a linear model; second, we want to evaluate the performance gain of Modellet against RADAR and

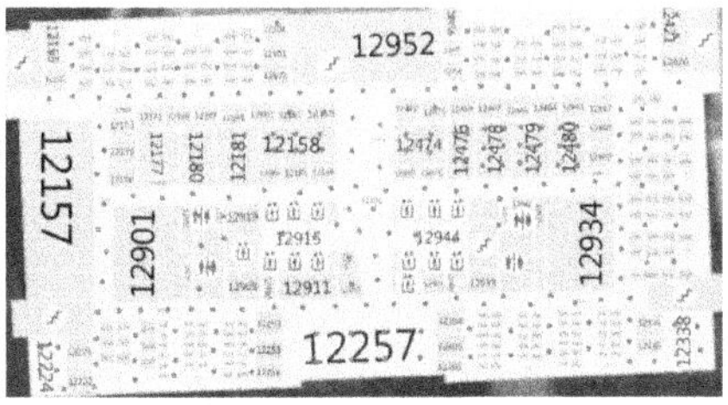

Figure 11: Data collection plan for an office building in Beijing, China.

Figure 12: Data collection plan for the Alexa Shopping Mall in Berlin, German.

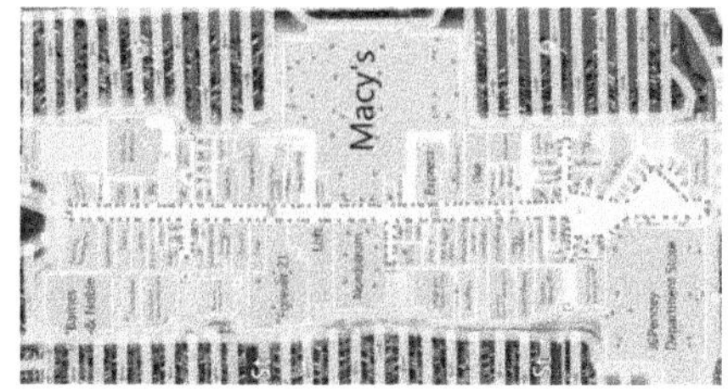

Figure 13: Data collection plan for the North Gate Mall in Seattle, U.S.

Venue Name	Area (m^2)	Bssids	FPs
Bellevue Square Mall	89216	1349	453
Redmond Town Center	29812	232	171
The Bravern	24244	675	148
Alexa Shopping Mall	35472	260	262
Commons At Federal Way	102172	398	329
Crossroads	129449	227	256
Los Angeles Intl Airport	127893	743	287
Marketplace at Factoria	135596	376	292
Northgate Mall	94810	749	403
Pacific Place	8619	258	97
South Hill Mall	237028	506	202
Supermall-Great Northwest	231188	440	632
Tacoma Mall	157491	749	455

Table 1: Basic statistics (spatial coverage, AP number and fingerprints collected) of the 13 venues and the survey data used in our evaluations.

EZPerfect in an office environment, which is the most common environment used by previous works.

Virtual fingerprint density: We vary the FP-Cloud VFP density from one per $1 \times 1m^2$ to one per $10 \times 10m^2$, and use all data from the small office area for experiments. To evaluate localization accuracy, we randomly partition the data into training (80%) and testing (20%). We conduct five batches and obtain the average performance, which is the default setting applied to all experiments hereafter.

We plot the localization error at 90%tile under various densities in Fig. 14. The error is defined as the 2D distance between the localization result and the groundtruth. Interestingly, we see that $5m$ (i.e., one sample per $5 \times 5m^2$) achieves the best accuracy. The reason is when virtual fingerprints becomes too dense, the robustness introduced by finding the top few nearest neighbours (in fingerprint matching in Fig.5) is eliminated. Imagine that, once the virtual fingerprints become extremely dense, the search process implicitly fallbacks to finding the top 1 nearest neighbour. We thus pick one per $5 \times 5m^2$ as our setting hereafter. Though it is hard to claim $5m$ is always the optimal setting, such a density makes adjacent virtual fingerprints differentiate enough from each other.

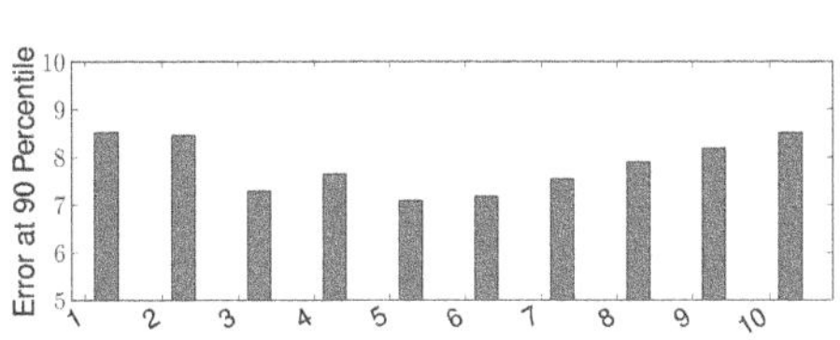

Figure 14: Performance at various VFP densities.

LDPL model vs. Linear model: We choose to use the LDPL model in Modellet. Modellet is actually not limited to the LDPL model. Other models like linear model can also be adopted. For instance, the linear model is defined as

$$RSS_{x,y} = \alpha \cdot x + \beta \cdot y + \gamma \tag{7}$$

where α, β, and γ are three AP dependent unknown parameters which can also be learnt from the calibration data. To implement the linear model, we simply replace the LDPL model with the linear model. Here we compare the localization accuracy of the LDPL model and the linear model at various data densities. For this purpose, after partitioning the whole dataset for training and testing, we do grid-based downsampling to emulate sparser data. Fig. 15 shows the comparison between using LDPL and linear models with full and downsampled datasets (with $10 \times 10m^2$ grid), respectively.

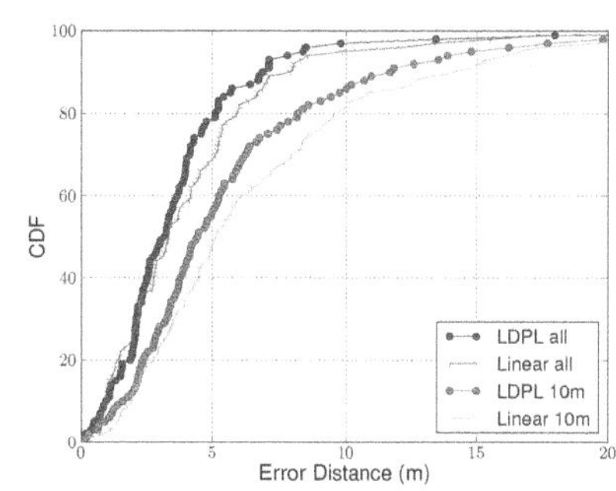

Figure 15: Localization accuracy comparison between LDPL and linear models.

In Fig. 15, one can see that the LDPL model outperforms the linear model at various data densities. The gap between the two gets larger at the sparse dataset. When the data is dense, filling in the blank using the LDPL model or the linear model does not make a significant difference. However, when data gets sparse, the LDPL model fits signal attenuation better than the linear model which assumes signal attenuates linearly.

Comparison Results: We carry out experiments comparing Modellet, RADAR, and EZPerfect in terms of localization accuracy. The result is shown in Fig. 16. One can see that EZPerfect outperforms RADAR on the dataset, which however has a long tail at high percentiles. Modellet achieves the best accuracy compared with RADAR and EZPerfect. The localization accuracy at 90%tile for the three are 6.4m, 8.3m, and 8.6m, respectively. The results presented here, as well as in our microbenchmarks, confirm the correctness of our implementation of RADAR and EZPerfect, as we can achieve reasonably good accuracy (sub 10m at 90%tile) in typical office buildings. The results are *consistent* with those

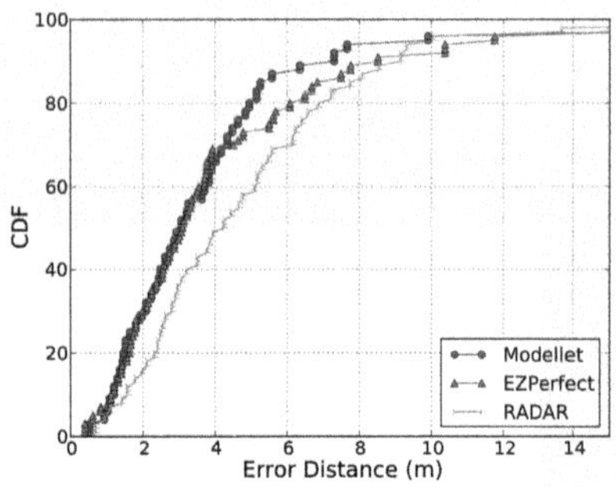

Figure 16: Localization accuracy evaluated based on data from an office building.

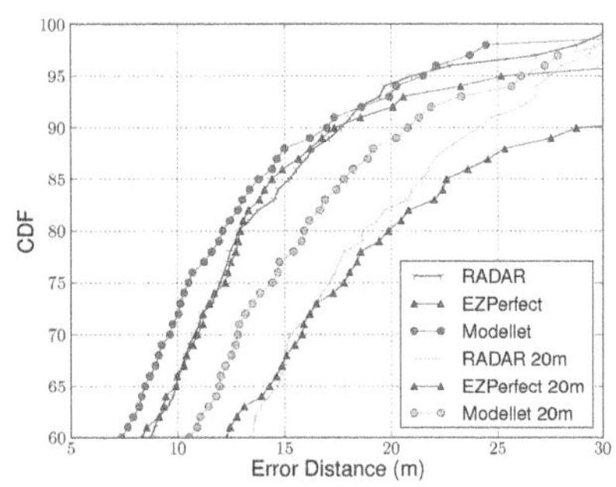

Figure 17: Localization accuracy evaluated based on data from Alexa Shopping Mall.

reported by most existing WiFi signal strength based indoor localization approaches.

7.3 Evaluations on Large Venues

We compare the localization accuracy of RADAR, EZPerfect, and Modellet using data collected from 13 large venues, listed in Table 1. As we have done before, we use the whole dataset as well as downsampled data for evaluation. As the original data is already sparse as shown in Fig. 12 and 13, we use grid size of 20m for downsampling. Before showing statistic result across all venues, we first show comparison result between RADAR, EZPerfect, and Modellet in Fig. 17 and Fig. 18, using data from the two venues shown in Fig. 12 and Fig. 13, respectively.

The first observation is that Modellet outperforms RADAR and EZPerfect at various data densities. The improvements are much larger than what we observed in our microbenchmarks or the small office area, especially when data is sparse. One reason is that the data density as well as environment become more diverse in such scenarios. As Modellet always takes advantage from both fingerprint-based and model-based approaches, the gain is enlarged under such conditions. The second observation is that localization accuracy becomes much worse in large venues than in a small office area. This contradicts with the results reported in existing literature. One important reason is that most existing works evaluate based on a well-maintained dataset collected in a lab area with ideal AP deployment.

Fig. 19 and Fig. 20 show the performance of RADAR, EZPerfect, and Modellet across the 13 venues. The x axis shows the prefixes of venue names. For each approach, we perform RADAR, EZPerfect, and Modellet with full and downsampled datasets, respectively. We show the localization errors at 50%tile and 90%tile in one stacked bar for each approach.

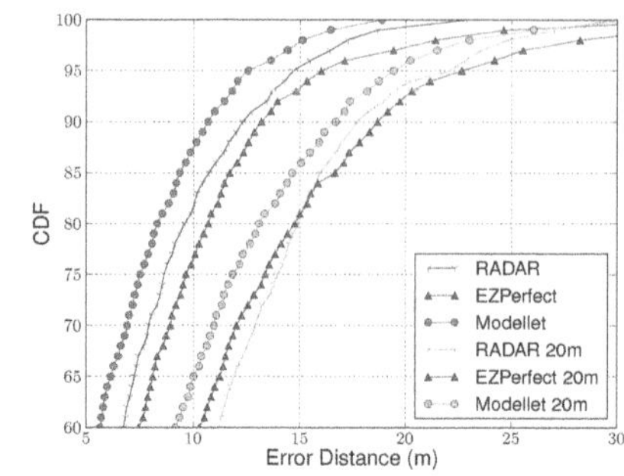

Figure 18: Localization accuracy evaluated based on data from the North Gate Mall.

We can see the localization errors vary significantly in different venues. The venue we show in Fig. 18 achieves the best localization accuracy with error at 90% close to 10m, while others range from 20m to 30m. For most venues, Modellet outperforms both RADAR and EZPerfect, or is as good as the better of the two. We do observe in 3 venues, i.e., South Hill Mall, Supermall, and Bellevue Square Mall, that EZPerfect or RADAR achieves the best (only at 90%tile). However, from Fig. 19, we can see the gaps between Modellet and the better of RADAR and EZPerfect in these 3 venues are small. On average, Modellet reduces errors at 50%tile and 90%tile by 0.77m and 1.14m, respectively, in comparison with the best of RADAR and EZPerfect over the 13 venues. Compared with the worst of the two, the mean reductions are 1.34m and 2.78m, respectively at 50%tile and 90%tile.

In Fig. 19, we can see that RADAR outperforms EZPerfect in 11 venues at 90%tile, and 12 venues at 50%tile. After downsampling the dataset with grid size 20m, we find that RADAR still achieves much better result than EZPerfect in most venues at 90%tile, shown in Fig. 20. However, at 50%tile, EZPerfect yields better result than RADAR in 6 venues, and similar result in another 2 venues. Note that this is partially consistent with our findings in our microbenchmark in Fig. 2 where EZPerfect works consistently better than RADAR when data is sparse. The reason is that when data becomes extremely sparse, the test cases collected in inner stores can cause bad localization due to a lack of appropriate models. In contrast, RADAR always maps the localization results to existing fingerprints, which thus eliminates producing tremendous large errors. Modellet still yields similar comparison results where the gain is larger than in Fig. 19. Modellet achieves the best performance in 12 venues, except for only one, i.e., The Bravern. Modellet reduces the errors at 50%tile and 90%tile by 0.9m and 1.44m, respectively, in comparison with the best in the two baselines, and 1.46m and 4.0m with the worst, respectively.

7.4 Handling Device Diversity Problem

We have discussed handling device diversity problem in Section 6. In our implementation, we set $\delta \in [-20, +20]$ dB. We collect data from a large shopping mall (i.e., the Pacific Place Mall) with two devices (i.e., HTC Titan and Nokia Lumia 900). We compare the localization performance with and without applying our light-weighted scheme handling the device diversity problem. The comparison result is shown in Fig. 21. One can see that as the gain offset between the two devices is as large as $20dB$. , localization result becomes extremely bad without handling the

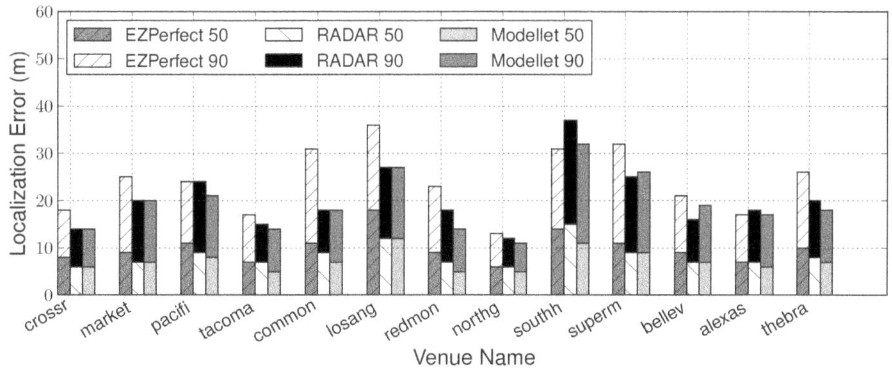

Figure 19: Localization accuracy for the 13 venues with full datasets.

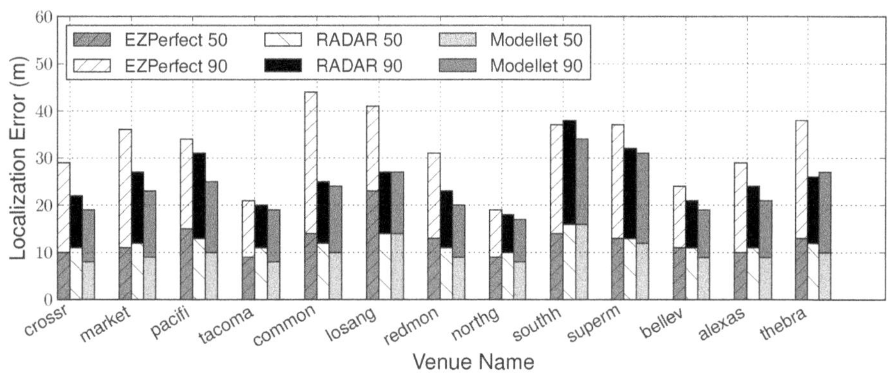

Figure 20: Localization accuracy for the 13 venues downsampled by 20m grid.

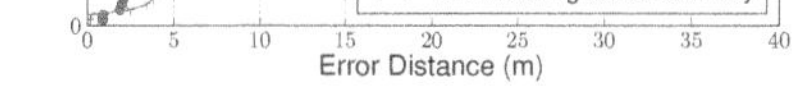

Figure 21: Localization accuracy before and after handling device diversity.

device diversity problem. In comparison, with our scheme, the localization accuracy is greatly and consistently improved by 40%.

8. DISCUSSIONS

Data Acquisition: Site survey needs to be done from time to time to update the database in order for facility changes like removing/replacing old APs and adding new APs. In this work, we assume the hiring of a site survey specialist to profile each venue for bootstrapping. With this method, we ensure a reasonably good initial user experience. Further more, we obtain a database collected by a standard device, which make it easier to deal with the device diversity issue as explained in Section 6. After bootstrapping, we adopt crowdsourcing to update the database. In practice, crowdsourcing can be carried out leveraging people already in the venue of interest. For instance, shop owners have incentive to help data collection in order to provide a better in-store user experience. We thus make the localization database maintainance scalable.

Power Adaptation Reality: Modern APs feature the capability of *adaptive power control*, where an AP automatically changes its power level [1]. If the power changes frequently (e.g., every 10min) in a random fashion, the existing models will be impaired, leading to unpredictable localization result for all WiFi RSS based localization approaches. However, according to [1], the main purpose for power adaptation is to ensure coverage while reducing interference among neighboring APs. Therefore, as long as no neighboring AP fails, the power level for each AP remains stable after convergence. We are also aware that this capability is especially designed for enterprise networks where APs work collaboratively. In large shopping malls or airports, a large fraction of APs are deployed by third party shop owners. The transmit power of these APs are typically stable, which is confirmed with our collected data.

Dealing with Large Errors: For a localization service, large localization errors are harmful to the user experience. In practice, large errors could be caused by various reasons, e.g., a bad WiFi scan during site survey or user query. One opportunity to eliminate large errors is to perform multiple scans at each sampling location either for site survey or user localization. For localization, the result averaged over multiple scans typically outperforms that with a single scan [40]. Another opportunity is to leverage the inertial sensors to continuously track the user, and thus correct big errors with filtering such as [22]. However, one drawback of tracking schemes is the increased battery consumption by sensors.

Adding Map Information: A few studies [17, 21] show the potential of adding map information to improve localization accuracy. While such accurate information is usually missing in reality, Modellet can easily incorporate the map information, if they are indeed available, by lowering the weights of real fingerprints intervened by walls.

Cost of FP-Cloud: The cost we pay is the need to store a large number of virtual fingerprints in the FP-Cloud. It will lead to larger storage and memory consumption, and longer downloading time. As the client can cache the database locally, only incremental cost need to be paid when the database is updated. Moreover, the database can be compressed significantly as a large amount of space is for storing duplicated BSSIDs ($\sim$ 10% of the original size after compression in zip format in our empirical evaluation). Therefore, such extra storage cost is still affordable. Generating FP-Cloud also requires high computation power, especially for large venues. First of all, the complexity is mainly determined by the density of VFP, and thus is controllable. Moreover, the models are trained offline in the cloud which thus is less a concern.

Extension to Multi-story Buildings: Floor detection is a crucial yet non-trivial indoor localization problem, especially in large shopping malls where large open areas exist. Generally, floor detection is a locality decision problem from a 3D perspective. In this paper we do not touch floor detection due to space limits. However, our experiments confirm that Modellet is still very effective for floor detection. It achieves over 95% accuracy on average.

9. RELATED WORK

Early indoor localization projects use dedicated location devices, such as Active Badge [36] and Cricket [30]. Later, significant effort is spent on ubiquitous, less expensive indoor localization services, including infrastructure independent (Geo-magnetic field, IMU sensors, etc.) [10, 22, 31, 34], infrastructure dependent which further consists of leveraging existing infrastructure (WiFi, FM, etc.) [4, 5, 8, 9, 15, 17, 20, 39–41], and those deploying new infrastructure (acoustic, LED, etc.) [16, 25, 27, 28, 37]. In this paper, we focus on WiFi based indoor localization, for its wide availability, no extra deployment cost, reasonable accuracy, and readiness to apply to mobile devices.

Among existing work, tremendous effort has been devoted to investigating better WiFi localization algorithms. Most existing WiFi based approaches can be divided into two categories: *fingerprint-based* and *model-based*.

Fingerprint-based techniques: The category of fingerprint-based approaches is pioneered by RADAR [5], and followed by numerous improvement algorithms [20, 40]. By and large, they can be classified into deterministic approaches (e.g., [5, 7, 12, 19]) or stochastic approaches (e.g., [20, 40]). The former directly calculates the distance between fingerprints and finds the most matched one or multiple fingerprints. The latter computes the likelihood of a query fingerprint against those in the database that also contain statistical information of fingerprints. Interpolation schemes were also proposed to match the query fingerprint to the database including interpolated fingerprints [7, 19]. Recent advancement has shown that sub-meter accuracy can be achieved by exploring physic layer information [32] or ranging between devices in proximity [24, 28]. In general, a high quality database is required to obtain high localization accuracy, as shown by extensive experiments with multiple algorithms [6, 12]. Thus, the major drawback of fingerprint-based approaches is the excessive time and labor it takes to construct the database via site survey. A few recent studies [22, 31, 33, 38] demonstrate the possibility of leveraging crowdsourcing to reduce the burden of site survey. However, designing a sustainable incentive mechanism of crowdsourcing remains a challenge.

Model-based techniques: Schemes in this category use a RF propagation model to derive RSS at various locations. The log-distance path loss (LDPL) model is a widely used model [9, 11, 15, 23]. Typically, a few measurements are required to train the model for each AP. In TIX [15], each AP is assumed to be able to sense APs nearby, and therefore, no extra calibration is required. EZ relieves the assumption, [9] requires only minimum labelled fingerprints along with a large amount of unlabelled fingerprints, and is able to achieve reasonable accuracy. Later in [28], it is shown that, by having data all labelled in EZ, the accuracy can further be improved (this scheme is called EZPerfect). When precise building structure information is known, it is possible to adopt more sophisticated ray-tracing techniques, as shown in ARIADNE [17]. Recently, the authors of [35] have evaluated a few model-based schemes including [11, 15, 23] on a moderate-scaled testbed, and concluded that the achieved accuracy is much worse than reported under realistic conditions.

Summary of differences: So far, most effort has been spent on improving localization accuracy upon a well maintained dataset. Less attention has been paid to intrinsic properties of practically collected location databases, which leads to a mismatch between the reported localization accuracy and reality as implied in [35]. In this paper, we propose Modellet which augments the radio map with virtual fingerprints. Our work differentiates from existing work in several ways. We show that such properties, i.e., data density and environment diversities, significantly impact localization accuracy. We also show that a single approach (fingerprint-based or model-based) or simple hybrid cannot address such issues. Finally, we propose Modellet to adapt between fingerprint-based and model-based approaches, driven by the data density and environment diversities.

10. CONCLUSION AND FUTURE WORK

In this paper, we have identified the data density and environment diversities problems that arise from real-world WiFi-based indoor localization system deployments. We have designed Modellet that attacks the problem by constructing a location database that best approximates the actual radio map based on the new concepts of the supporting set and fingerprint-cloud. We evaluate and compare Modellet and existing representative indoor localization systems, namely RADAR and EZPerfect, with data collected at an office building and 13 large venues. The results confirm the effectiveness of Modellet and also reveal the inadequate performance of existing systems in real-world deployment.

As to future work, we will look into the database maintenance problem, which is critical to provide long running indoor localization services.

11. ACKNOWLEDGMENTS

We appreciate the comments and feedback received from anonymous reviewers and the shepherd to enhance the quality of this paper.

12. REFERENCES

[1] Cisco wireless lan controller configuration guide, release 4.1.

[2] Googlers Talk Indoor Maps For 40 Minutes. http://www.webpronews.com/googlers-talk-\\indoor-maps-for-40-minutes-video-2013-05.

[3] IN-Location Alliance. http://www.in-location-alliance.com/.

[4] M. Azizyan, I. Constandache, and R. Roy Choudhury. Surroundsense: mobile phone localization via ambience fingerprinting. In *Mobicom*, pages 261–272. ACM, 2009.

[5] P. Bahl and V. N. Padmanabhan. Radar: An in-building rf-based user location and tracking system. In *INFOCOM*, volume 2, pages 775–784. Ieee, 2000.

[6] G. Chandrasekaran, M. Ergin, J. Yang, S. Liu, Y. Chen, M. Gruteser, and R. Martin. Empirical evaluation of the limits on localization using signal strength. In *SECON*, pages 1–9, 2009.

[7] M. Y. Chen, T. Sohn, D. Chmelev, D. Haehnel, J. Hightower, J. Hughes, A. LaMarca, F. Potter, I. Smith, and A. Varshavsky. Practical metropolitan-scale positioning for gsm phones. In *UbiComp*, pages 225–242. Springer, 2006.

[8] Y. Chen, D. Lymberopoulos, J. Liu, and B. Priyantha. Fm-based indoor localization. In *Mobisys*, pages 169–182. ACM, 2012.

[9] K. Chintalapudi, A. Padmanabha Iyer, and V. N. Padmanabhan. Indoor localization without the pain. In *Mobicom*, pages 173–184. ACM, 2010.

[10] J. Chung, M. Donahoe, C. Schmandt, I.-J. Kim, P. Razavai, and M. Wiseman. Indoor location sensing using geo-magnetism. *MobiSys*, page 141, 2011.

[11] L. F. M. de Moraes and B. A. A. Nunes. Calibration-free wlan location system based on dynamic mapping of signal strength. In *Proceedings of the 4th ACM international workshop on Mobility management and wireless access*, pages 92–99. ACM, 2006.

[12] E. Elnahrawy, X. Li, and R. Martin. The limits of localization using signal strength: a comparative study. In *SECON*, pages 406–414, 2004.

[13] S.-h. Fang, C.-h. Wang, S.-m. Chiou, and P. Lin. Calibration-free Approaches for Robust Wi-Fi Positioning Against Device Diversity : A Performance Comparison. *VTC Spring*, 2012.

[14] A. Goswami, L. E. Ortiz, and S. R. Das. Wigem: a learning-based approach for indoor localization. In *COnference on emerging Networking EXperiments and Technologies*, page 3. ACM, 2011.

[15] Y. Gwon and R. Jain. Error Characteristics and Calibration-free Techniques for Wireless LAN-based Location Estimation. *MobiWac*, pages 2–9, 2004.

[16] P. Hu, L. Li, C. Peng, G. Shen, and F. Zhao. Pharos : Enable Physical Analytics through Visible Light based Indoor Localization. *HotNets*, 2013.

[17] Y. Ji, S. Biaz, S. Pandey, and P. Agrawal. Ariadne: a dynamic indoor signal map construction and localization system. In *Mobisys*, pages 151–164. ACM, 2006.

[18] N. Kodippili and D. Dias. Integration of fingerprinting and trilateration techniques for improved indoor localization. In *WOCN*, pages 1–6. IEEE, 2010.

[19] P. Krishnan, A. Krishnakumar, W.-H. Ju, C. Mallows, and S. Gamt. A system for lease: Location estimation assisted by stationary emitters for indoor rf wireless networks. In *INFOCOM*, volume 2, pages 1001–1011. IEEE, 2004.

[20] J. Krumm and J. Platt. Minimizing calibration efforts for an indoor 802.11 device location measurement system. *MSR-TR-2003-82*, 2003.

[21] B. Li, A. G. Dempster, C. Rizos, and J. Barnes. Hybrid method for localization using WLAN. *Spatial Sciences Conference*, 2005.

[22] F. Li, C. Zhao, G. Ding, J. Gong, C. Liu, and F. Zhao. A reliable and accurate indoor localization method using phone inertial sensors. In *Ubicomp*, pages 421–430. ACM, 2012.

[23] H. Lim, L.-c. Kung, J. C. Hou, and H. Luo. Zero-Configuration , Robust Indoor Localization : Theory and Experimentation. *INFOCOM*, pages 1–13, 2005.

[24] H. Liu, Y. Gan, J. Yang, S. Sidhom, Y. Wang, Y. Chen, and F. Ye. Push the limit of wifi based localization for smartphones. In *Mobicom*, pages 305–316. ACM, 2012.

[25] K. Liu, X. Liu, and X. Li. Guoguo : Enabling Fine-grained Indoor Localization via Smartphone Categories and Subject Descriptors. *Mobisys*, 2013.

[26] D. Madigan, E. Einahrawy, R. P. Martin, W.-H. Ju, P. Krishnan, and A. Krishnakumar. Bayesian indoor positioning systems. In *INFOCOM 2005*, volume 2, pages 1217–1227. IEEE, 2005.

[27] A. Matic, A. Papliatseyeu, V. Osmani, and O. Mayora-Ibarra. Tuning to your position: Fm radio based indoor localization with spontaneous recalibration. In *PerCom*, pages 153–161. IEEE, 2010.

[28] R. Nandakumar, K. K. Chintalapudi, and V. N. Padmanabhan. Centaur : Locating Devices in an Office Environment. In *Mobicom*, 2012.

[29] J.-g. Park, D. Curtis, and J. Ledlie. Implications of Device Diversity for Organic Localization. *INFOCOM*, pages 3182–3190, 2011.

[30] N. B. Priyantha, A. Chakraborty, and H. Balakrishnan. The cricket location-support system. In *Mobicom*, pages 32–43. ACM, 2000.

[31] A. Rai, K. K. Chintalapudi, V. N. Padmanabhan, and R. Sen. Zee: Zero-effort crowdsourcing for indoor localization. In *Mobicom*, pages 293–304. ACM, 2012.

[32] S. Sen, B. Radunovic, R. R. Choudhury, and T. Minka. You are facing the mona lisa: spot localization using phy layer information. In *Mobisys*, pages 183–196. ACM, 2012.

[33] G. Shen, Z. Chen, P. Zhang, T. Moscibroda, and Y. Zhang. Walkie-Markie : Indoor Pathway Mapping Made Easy. *NSDI*, 2013.

[34] S. P. Tarzia, P. a. Dinda, R. P. Dick, and G. Memik. Indoor localization without infrastructure using the acoustic background spectrum. *MobiSys*, 2011.

[35] D. Turner, S. Savage, and A. C. Snoeren. On the empirical performance of self-calibrating wifi location systems. In *LCN*, pages 76–84. IEEE, 2011.

[36] R. Want, A. Hopper, V. Falcão, and J. Gibbons. The active badge location system. *TOIS*, 10(1):91–102, 1992.

[37] J. Xiong and K. Jamieson. ArrayTrack : A Fine-Grained Indoor Location System. *NSDI*, (279976):71–84, 2013.

[38] Z. Yang, C. Wu, and Y. Liu. Locating in fingerprint space: wireless indoor localization with little human intervention. In *Mobicom*, pages 269–280. ACM, 2012.

[39] S. Yoon, K. Lee, and I. Rhee. Fm-based indoor localization via automatic fingerprint db construction and matching. In *Mobisys*, pages 207–220. ACM, 2013.

[40] M. Youssef and A. Agrawala. The horus wlan location determination system. *Mobisys*, 2005.

[41] M. A. Youssef, A. Agrawala, and A. Udaya Shankar. Wlan location determination via clustering and probability distributions. In *PerCom*, pages 143–150. IEEE, 2003.

Travi-Navi: Self-deployable Indoor Navigation System

Yuanqing Zheng[†,§], Guobin Shen[†], Liqun Li[†], Chunshui Zhao[†], Mo Li[§], Feng Zhao[†]
[†]Microsoft Research, Beijing, China
[§]Nanyang Technological University, Singapore
{yuanqing1, limo}@ntu.edu.sg, {jackysh, liqul, chunzhao, zhao}@microsoft.com

Abstract

We present Travi-Navi – a vision-guided navigation system that enables a self-motivated user to easily bootstrap and deploy indoor navigation services, without comprehensive indoor localization systems or even the availability of floor maps. Travi-Navi records high quality images during the course of a guider's walk on the navigation paths, collects a rich set of sensor readings, and packs them into a navigation trace. The followers track the navigation trace, get prompt visual instructions and image tips, and receive alerts when they deviate from the correct paths. Travi-Navi also finds the most efficient shortcuts whenever possible. We encounter and solve several challenges, including robust tracking, shortcut identification, and high quality image capture while walking. We implement Travi-Navi and conduct extensive experiments. The evaluation results show that Travi-Navi can track and navigate users with timely instructions, typically within a 4-step offset, and detect deviation events within 9 steps.

Categories and Subject Descriptors

H.5.2 [**Information interfaces and presentation**]: User interface – *User-centered design*; C.3.3 [**Special-Purpose and Application-based Systems**]: Real-time and embedded systems

General Terms

Design, Experimentation, Performance

Keywords

Indoor navigation, Image direction, Self-deployable system

1. INTRODUCTION

There are many situations in real life, including business, social, and personal scenarios, where people have a strong need for navigation services. For instance, a shop owner may want to direct customers to his shop. At a social gathering, early arriving guests may want to guide latecomers. People have for a long time resorted to non-technical solutions in these situations. For example, shop owners post flyers with their addresses or briefly describe routes to attract customers, and latecomers can call friends for landmarks. Such approaches, however, have various shortcomings. For instance, customers need to find the addresses and follow a sequence of landmarks, which may not be a trivial task. If the building floorplans are unavailable or hard to read, the trip can be frustrating. Locating floorplans can also be troublesome in gigantic malls. Moreover, customers may take wrong turns when no one is around to guide them. When customers want to visit multiple shops, it is not easy to plan trips and minimize detours.

On the other hand, despite extensive research into indoor localization, the wide deployment of indoor localization and navigation systems have yet to be realized. Prior schemes attempted to build full blown localization systems before publishing location services. For instance, WiFi fingerprinting-based localization systems need to sample signal strengths and construct radio maps in advance [7, 36]. Such approaches require intensive initial efforts to bootstrap localization services. With the lack of pre-deployed comprehensive indoor localization and navigation services, we ask the following question: *Can we enable users to easily bootstrap their own indoor navigation services by themselves without dependency on a pre-deployed localization system or even the availability of floor maps?*

In this paper, we provide an affirmative answer through the systematic design and implementation of Travi-Navi – a vision-guided navigation system that enables a user to easily deploy his own indoor navigation services. Inspired by our own navigation experiences, in Travi-Navi, a guider records landmarks (pathway images, sensor readings, radio signals, etc.) along a path and shares them with followers. Using the guider's directions, our application runs on the follower's mobile device and automatically guides the follower by presenting pathway images and indicating turns, etc. Travi-Navi implicitly leverages the follower's visual recognition capability by providing them pathway images to correct slight direction ambiguity and enhance navigation experiences.

The Travi-Navi design naturally avoids the dependency on any pre-deployed localization services or even the floor maps but faces particular challenges. (1) Pathway images contain rich visual information for followers but rapidly drain the battery power. Images taken during a walk can get blurred due to camera shake. How to control energy usage while at the same time ensuring the image quality remains an important issue to address. (2) As the guider's trace only covers the sampled path while most areas are uncharted, it is very hard to accurately track followers on the guider's trace and generate synchronized directions. Providing correct directions at right time is important as both incorrect and untimely directions may lead to wrong turns. We expect our system to alert users in a timely manner when they veer off the correct path. (3) As users

MobiCom'14, September 07 - 11 2014, Maui, HI, USA.
Copyright 2014 ACM 978-1-4503-2783-1/14/09...$15.00.
http://dx.doi.org/10.1145/2639108.2639124.

may visit multiple destinations, a friendly navigation system is expected to intelligently plan routes. The navigation traces are independently provided by different guiders without coordination, so it is challenging to find efficient shortcuts among the traces. Ideally, our system should be able to guide users along the optimal path among the available traces to the destinations.

Based on prior research efforts, we have devised several sensor fusion techniques to address the above challenges. (1) To ensure high quality navigation images, we predict image quality based on motion hints from step detection, heading direction and rotation measurement. In particular, we infer stable shooting time using accelerometer readings and trigger image capture to ensure image quality and avoid blurred images. (2) To accurately track a follower and generate synchronized directions, we incorporate both magnetic field distortions and WiFi fingerprint sequences to complement IMU (Inertial Measurement Unit) sensor based dead reckoning and thereby accurately project the follower onto the guider's trace. (3) To find shortcuts and plan routes, we detect overlapping segments and crossing points of multiple traces shared by possibly different guiders. In particular, we detect overlapping segments by measuring their similarity of magnetic field signals and WiFi fingerprint sequences. We identify crossing points by exploiting the mutual trends of average gross distances between sequences of WiFi fingerprints: as a user gets closer to a crossing point, we observe a decreasing trend in average gross distance and an increasing trend when the user moves away. Thus, provided multiple navigation traces to multiple destinations, our application can automatically find shortcuts, weave the traces to form a holistic trace, and guide users to destinations with minimum detours.

We consolidate the above techniques and implement Travi-Navi on the Android platform. The sensor data collection, tracking, and navigation instruction generation are performed in real time. We conducted extensive experiments under various conditions (e.g., day and night, work day and weekend) and navigated users using Travi-Navi in both an office building and a large shopping mall. In experiments, Travi-Navi showed promising results with accurate and timely instructions (within a 4m offset) and prompt deviation alerts (within 9m).

The contributions of this work are not limited to the application centric design of Travi-Navi that enables users to easily deploy their own navigation services without pre-deployed localization systems. Rather, we see more potential as an effective crowdsourcing solution to gradually build up general purpose indoor localization systems. Realizing the challenge of constructing massive location database to bootstrap the localization services, many recent schemes have proposed crowdsourcing the data collection [29, 32, 35]. However, it is hard to find a sustainable incentive mechanism and to ensure data quality in these crowdsourcing schemes. Travi-Navi naturally alleviates such challenges, since users of Travi-Navi are self-motivated and traces collected by guiders can be verified by the followers. With enough penetration of such systems, we can aggregate navigation traces and gradually build up comprehensive indoor localization and navigation systems.

2. OVERVIEW

2.1 A usage example

Figure 1 illustrates a usage scenario of Travi-Navi, where a restaurant owner provides a navigation trace to customers.

When the restaurant owner (as a guider) arrives at an entrance of the mall (e.g., entrance C in Figure 1), he turns on Travi-Navi and collects navigation traces. As he holds the mobile phone in an upright position and walks to the restaurant, Travi-Navi captures

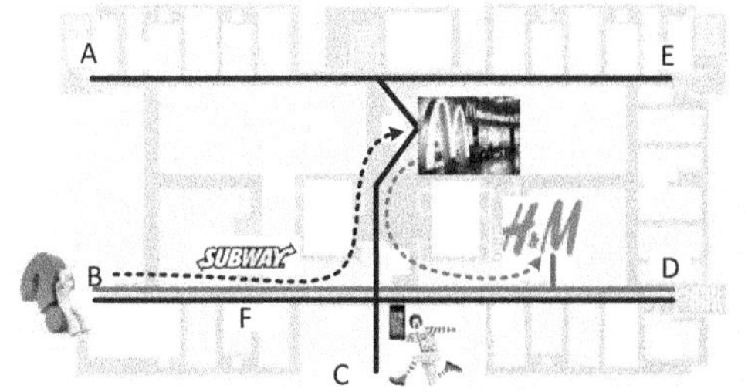

Figure 1: A usage scenario of Travi-Navi. McD collects traces along aisles in blue, and those by H&M are in red. A shortcut (with a red dashed line) between McD and H&M is identified from two guiders' traces.

pathway images and samples WiFi fingerprints and IMU sensors. Travi-Navi automatically processes all sensor data and packs them into a navigation trace. If there are many entrances (e.g., entrances A, B, D, and E), the guider may want to survey multiple paths from each entrance. As it does not need to cover every corner inside the mall, the trace collection load is still light. We note that the primary scenarios of Travi-Navi are planar applications (i.e., navigation on single floors). For shopping malls with multiple floors, the guider may treat lift lobbies and staircases as entrances. We plan to navigate users across multiple floors in our future work.

A customer (as a follower) downloads the traces and navigates to the restaurant. Travi-Navi locks on to the customer at the entrance (i.e., entrance B in Figure 1). As the customer naturally holds his mobile phone in his hand and moves forward, Travi-Navi tracks his progress on the guider's trace by comparing instant sensor readings (IMU sensor and WiFi signals) against the navigation trace. Travi-Navi shows the guider's pathway images and the directions (see UI in Section 4.1). The customer may download multiple traces for different destinations (e.g., the restaurant and the nearby shop in Figure 1). In such a case, Travi-Navi is able to identify a shortcut depicted as a red dashed line.

2.2 Design challenges

Our design avoids dependency on pre-deployed localization services or floorplans. Unlike general-purpose localization schemes, which try to locate users on to the floorplan, our design needs to only track the follower with respect to the guider's pathway and give timely directions. As a result, a guider (e.g., the restaurant owner) can easily survey the possible routes connecting followers to the destination. We see that the route contains necessary information for navigation purposes, and the guider can skip the other areas on the floor.

Such a substantially relaxed requirement for trace collection enables a guider to easily deploy his own navigation service. Yet, it makes locating users on the floorplan very challenging and renders most convention localization schemes infeasible. For instance, WiFi fingerprint based localization schemes cannot accurately locate users, as the WiFi fingerprints only cover a small portion of the whole floor. Thus, given a WiFi fingerprint, localization schemes cannot determine whether it is on the pathway or uncharted areas. Conventional trilateration localization methods cannot be applied to locate users either, since the location of WiFi access points cannot be determined solely based on a route trace. Even with an exhaustive site survey of the whole floor, current localization schemes cannot ensure a high localization accuracy to differentiate pathways (e.g., two close corridors with a distance <5m). Deploying dedicated infrastructure [1, 34] can indeed improve localization accuracy but it incurs a substantial deployment cost. As a result, many basic requirements in navigation become challenging to fulfill with route traces.

Our design explores the possibility of leveraging visual recognition compatibility of the followers to assist navigation. This allows the active involvement of followers rather than to have them passively following directions of mobile devices. Provided pathway images, followers can easily take correct pathways from many nearby pathways, which may not be possible if we resort to localization systems. As guiders capture images while they walk, the images can easily get blurred. One naive approach might be to first capture many frames regardless of image quality and later filter out these blurred ones, which incurs high energy cost in image capture as well as high computational overhead in image processing. To solve this problem, we infer the optimal time to capture the image with accelerometer readings and trigger image capture to ensure image quality.

Our system intelligently identifies shortcuts and plans optimized routes for users visiting multiple destinations. The trip planning would be trivial if the floorplans and accurate localization services are immediately available. However, as navigation traces are independently provided by different guiders without coordination (e.g., the blue trace to the restaurant and the red trace to the nearby shop in Figure 1), we need to design efficient and robust methods to merge the traces so as to find shortcuts. Unlike trip planning on floorplans, our design aims to determine the relative positions between route traces rather than their absolute locations on the floor.

3. Travi-Navi DESIGN

3.1 Functional Architecture

Figure 2 sketches the functional architecture. In the following, we briefly describe the key components.

Motion engine. Travi-Navi builds on prior research into IMU sensor (i.e., accelerometer, gyroscope, and compass) based dead-reckoning. It adopts a simple yet robust step detection method based on the rising edges of filtered accelerometer readings. It detects turns using a virtual bounding pathway that is more robust to sensor noise than inferences from instant heading changes. More importantly, the motion engine also outputs motion hints to assist image capture to reduce power consumption and ensure image quality.

Trace packing. Travi-Navi captures pathway images and samples WiFi and IMU sensors as guiders walk along pathways to destinations. It employs lightweight motion hints to indicate the best time for image capture to reduce power consumption. It automatically packs sensor data into navigation traces, where they are step-indexed by the relative positions to the beginning of the trace. The navigation traces can be shared directly to users or via a cloud server.

Navigation engine. With a guider's navigation trace, the navigation engine processes a user's instant sensor readings and generates navigation instructions. It first locks on users to the trace, typically at the entrances, using WiFi fingerprints. As entrances are typically distant to one another (>20m), Travi-Navi can confidently lock on users. As users walk towards a destination, it incorporates WiFi fingerprints and magnetic field distortions to complement IMU-based dead-reckoning. It accurately tracks users with respect to the guider's trace and generates corresponding position-indexed pathway images and instructions. If users want to visit multiple destinations, it automatically detects shortcuts and plans routes.

Note that the motion engine and the trace packing module are common to both the guider and the follower applications. There is a slight difference in sensor data collection. Guiders need to scan WiFi fingerprints at higher frequencies, whereas followers may scan WiFi less frequently to save energy. The navigation engine is solely used by followers.

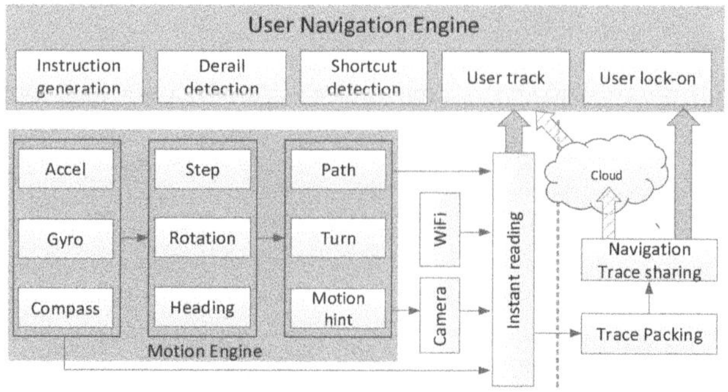

Figure 2: Architecture of the Travi-Navi system. The motion engine is common to both the guider and the follower.

3.2 Vision-guided navigation

Humans have superior visual recognition capability. Provided pathway images, a follower can easily differentiate two pathways that are close to each other and identify the correct one. Our system leverages the wide adoption of cameras on mobile devices to provide intuitive visual directions to followers.

Motion hints for image capture. As images are captured while walking, the pathway images may get blurred due to camera shake. To capture a clear image, one may capture image frames at a high rate and filter out the blurred ones, which involves extensive computations and high power consumption. To solve this problem, we design a simple and effective method to predict image quality before capturing pathway images to reduce power consumption and ensure image quality. The idea is inspired by the observation of the correlation between image quality and different walking phases. Figure 3 shows the consecutive frames taken during one walking step. Due to body vibration and subsequent camera shake, the first few images are blurred, while the last few are sharper. When we examine a sequence of frames taken during several steps, we observe alternating image qualities exhibiting periodic patterns. We aim to capture only sharp pathway images and display them to users.

We quantify image qualities using the detectable image features (such as edges and corners) extracted by computer vision techniques. Intuitively, given the same shooting target, a larger number of detectable features indicate sharper images. For instance, the feature extraction algorithm detects 315 keypoints in the first frame (Figure 3(a)) and 405 keypoints in the last frame (Figure 3(f)), respectively. Figure 4 plots the number of features in each frame against the differential of the accelerometer magnitude. When a user steps down, we observe a spike in the differential of the accelerometer magnitude. In the figure, right after the user steps down, the image qualities drop mainly due to body vibration. Generally, the images taken during the sharp turnings are similarly blurred due to the rotational motion of the camera, though image quality soon recovers after the user finishes a turn.

In Travi-Navi, we predict an optimal time for image capture by exploiting the average-crossing point on the rising edge of accelerometer magnitude. At such instants, mobile devices are generally stabilized during a step. Thus, Travi-Navi can automatically trigger image capture while a guider is walking. In addition, Travi-Navi also measures orientation and rotation changes and avoids capturing images during rapid turns. We note that although the low quality images are not captured, Travi-Navi does record the turns and inform users during navigation. In addition, when the

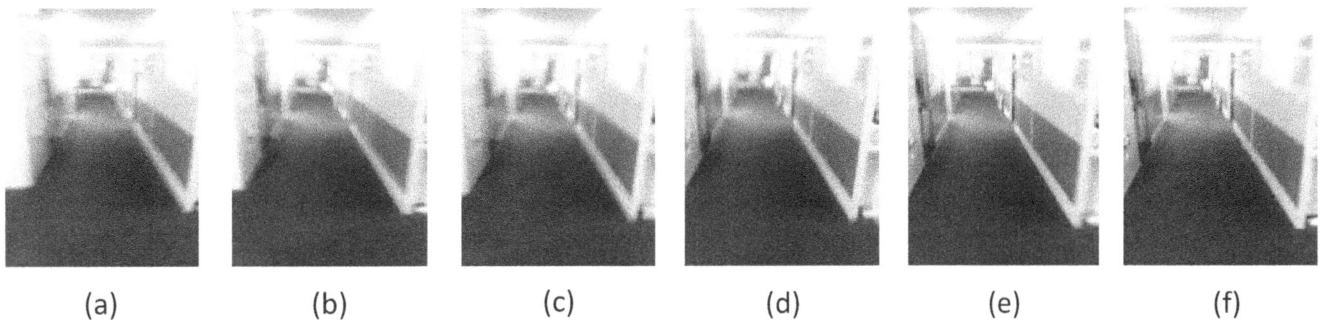

Figure 3: Consecutive frames during one walking step (taken by Samsung Galaxy S2).

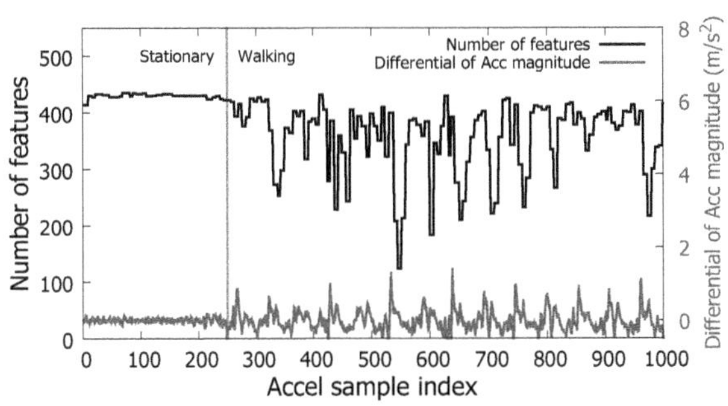

Figure 4: Image quality drops when user steps down.

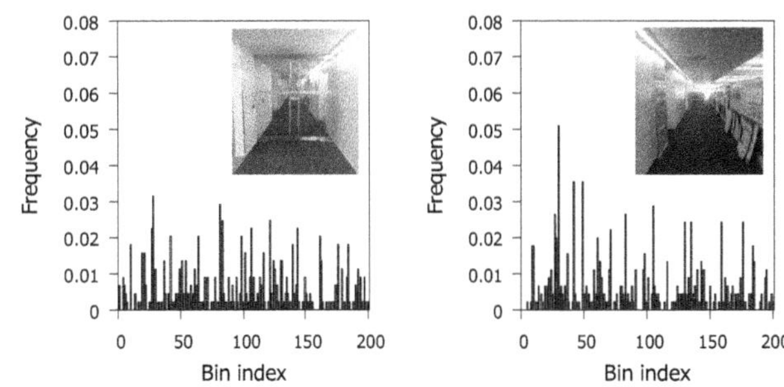

Figure 5: Image feature histogram.

guider finishes turning (normally a 5-step duration) and high image quality is again ensured, Travi-Navi quickly resumes image capture without missing the start of new pathways.

Usage of captured images. The clear images captured in a guider's trace serves two purposes. The primary purpose is navigation guidance, which implicitly exploits a follower's visual recognition capability to help navigation. To this end, pathway images and sensor signals are step-indexed in a guider's trace. Travi-Navi tracks followers with respect to the guider's trail and present proper pathway images to followers during navigation.

Since indoor environments exhibit distinct visual features (e.g., ambient color, geometric shapes, etc) [6], smart mobile devices may infer a follower's position on a guider's trail by comparing an image taken by the follower against the guider's images. Thus, when a follower (e.g., a Google Glass user) can easily take images during a trip, Travi-Navi may also incorporate images into the user tracking process. A mobile phone user is unlikely to take images continuously. However, the user may want to take pictures and retrieve the most similar images from the guider's traces. Then, the user can select and confirm the image of the pathway the user is actually on and start the navigation from there.

Image matching and retrieval. We extract image features of local geometric shapes as well as ambient colors and carry out image matching. Image matching operates in a pipeline. First, discriminative points are extracted for each image, called keypoints [19, 27, 20, 18]. The keypoints in each image can be viewed as visual "words" describing the image [17]. Similar visual "words" are clustered to form a "dictionary". Then, each image is described with a histogram, measuring the frequency of each word in the dictionary. We compute the similarity of two images by comparing their histograms. The histograms of images are represented with fixed-sized vectors whose length equals the dictionary size (i.e. 200) as shown in Figure 5.

To retrieve the most similar images, Travi-Navi incorporates color histograms (describing ambient colors) to extend the keypoint histograms (describing local geometric shapes). As images taken on each pathway capture similar ambiences, Travi-Navi clusters the images taken on the same pathway into one group. Travi-Navi labels image groups with pathway segment IDs and trains the linear support vector machine (SVM) as an image classifier. Travi-Navi also adds image shooting angles inferred from device orientation to image matching. In practice, the pathway images may appear similar and in this case Travi-Navi may fail to differentiate them accurately. Travi-Navi can enrich the diversity by incorporating other sensing modalities such as WiFi and magnetic field measurements.

3.3 Lock-on, tracking and deviation handling

Lock-on at entrances. When a follower enters a mall and starts Travi-Navi, Travi-Navi first needs to lock on to the follower. As the entrances of buildings (e.g., malls) are generally distant (>20m), it is likely to observe distinct WiFi signals at different entrances. Thus, Travi-Navi scans WiFi signals and compares them against the WiFi signals in guider's trace and locks on to the follower at the entrance. For shopping malls with multiple floors, guiders may not collect traces directly from mall entrances. Instead, they may collect the traces from lift lobbies or staircases, i.e., entrances to the floor. Lifts and staircases can be reliably identified using WiFi coverage information and accelerometer readings [32]. We discuss how we lock on to users in uncharted areas in §3.4.

Tracking follower. Travi-Navi adopts the particle filter [25] to track the user's progress on the guider's trails. After locking on the user at an entrance, Travi-Navi generates particles spread around the entrance to approximate the user's location. Each particle represents a possible position of the user and is updated according to IMU sensor based dead-reckoning [11, 16, 25, 32, 33]. Each particle is weighted according to the measurements of multiple sensing modalities. As such, the less likely particles are gradually filtered out and the centroid of the particles approximate the actual position of a follower. We describe the step detection and heading measurement techniques for completeness.

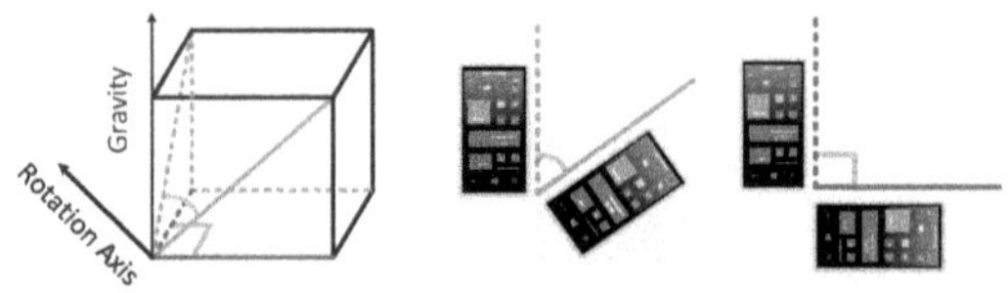

Figure 6: Orientation measurement. Travi-Navi projects the gyroscope measurements to the ground plane.

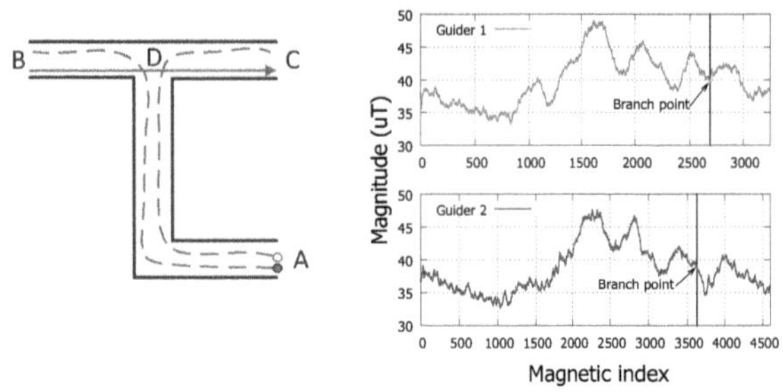

(a) Walking Paths (b) Magnetic Measurements

Figure 7: Two walking paths with overlapping segments and corresponding magnetic field measurements.

Dead-reckoning: Travi-Navi uses the weighted moving average to filter out noise in accelerometer readings. It tracks the average and variance of accelerometer magnitude. Stationary and walking states are differentiated using an empirical threshold on variance. To detect steps, it searches rising edges of accelerometer magnitude. For heading measurement, as users naturally hold mobile phones, the device heading generally aligns with walking directions. However, due to the severe magnetic field distortion inside buildings, the compass does not always point the heading direction [9, 39]. As the gyroscope is immune to magnetic field distortion and can measure rotations by integrating angular velocities, we leverage the gyroscope and fuse it with compass [38]. We have observed that natural holding gestures tend to tilt up phones, which may misalign the device reference frame and the world coordinate system as illustrated in Figure 6.

We have found that when a user holds a phone with a 45° angle to the earth surface and takes a 90° turn, the gyroscope only measures 60° around the rotation axis. We project the rotation measurement to the world coordinate system to measure the actual turning angles leveraging the gravity sensor [21].

To compensate for the differences in step length and heading measurement noise, a zero mean gaussian noise is added to each particle's step length and the measured heading directions in dead-reckoning. If Travi-Navi detects steps, each particle is then updated to a new location. After that, each particle is weighted according to the follower's instant WiFi signal as well as magnetic field readings. Travi-Navi measures the centroid of weighted particles to approximate a follower's position. The weighted particles are resampled after weight normalization. The tracking process is repeated until the user reaches the destination.

Magnetic signal weighting: Next, we describe how Travi-Navi weights each particle according to observed magnetic field readings. Although the magnetic directed dead-reckoning suffers severe errors inside buildings, the magnetic distortions are stable and provide discriminative power [9, 32]. Figure 7 shows the walking paths of two guiders with overlapping pathway segments, and the magnetic field distortions observed on the trails. We see that the magnitude of magnetic field varies along the trails. The patterns of the common segment are very similar, which confirms the stability of the magnetic field [9, 32].

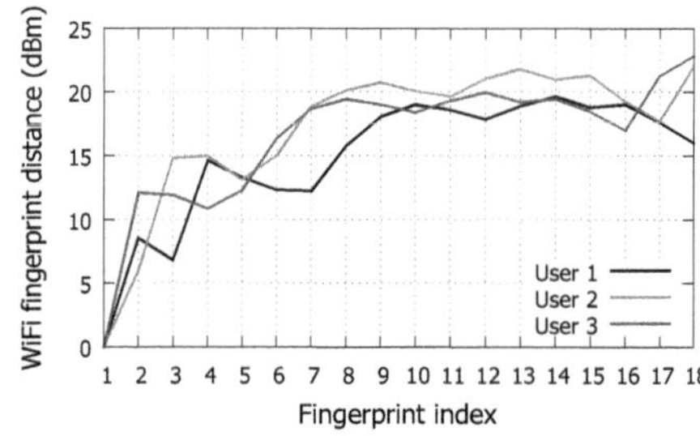

Figure 8: WiFi fingerprints are collected as users walk along a pathway. We see WiFi similarity decreases as the walking distance increases.

Leveraging the distinctive patterns of the magnetic field, Travi-Navi finds the most similar subsequence of magnetic measurements on the guider's trace to track a follower. Travi-Navi uses the dynamic time warping (DTW) algorithm [28] to compare the sequence similarity to compensate for the difference in speeds between the guider and the follower. DTW searches for the best alignment that minimizes the total cost using standard dynamic programming and the cost is defined as the difference of aligned magnetic magnitudes. When particles need to be updated, their weights are set according to their DTW costs via a Gaussian kernel. In particular, for the ith particle, its weight is set as follows:

$$weight_m^i = e^{-\frac{d_i}{k}} \tag{1}$$

where d_i is the DTW cost and k is a tunable parameter.

In our experiments, we observed that the magnetic field readings may exhibit similar patterns on distant pathway segments. A longer walking trail enriches diversity and improves discernibility. As followers are tracked on a step basis, the gain from further increasing the monitoring window (e.g., > 5steps) becomes marginal. We balance the computation overhead and discernibility by setting an empirical 5-step window.

WiFi signal weighting: With WiFi signal strength measurements, Travi-Navi gives greater weights to the more likely particles and iteratively filters out the less probable ones. We denote the user's and the guider's WiFi fingerprints as $F_t^u = (R_1^u, R_2^u, \ldots, R_n^u)$ and $F_t^g = (R_1^g, R_2^g, \ldots, R_n^g)$, where R_i^j is the RSSI of the ith AP observed by j at time t. In practice, we set -99dBm to the RSSI of undetectable APs. The distance between fingerprints F^u and F^g is measured by [35]

$$Dis(F^u, F^g) = \frac{1}{n}\sum_{k=1}^{n} |R_k^u - R_k^g|. \tag{2}$$

Similarly, we measure the geographical distance (i.e., Euclidian distance) of dead-reckoning positions between P^u and P^g by

$$Dis(P^u, P^g) = ||P^u - P^g||. \tag{3}$$

Figure 8 plots the WiFi distance $Dis(F_1, F_t)$ of three different walks along the same pathway. We see that the distances of WiFi fingerprints to the first fingerprint gradually increase as the users walk farther. Due to signal noise, larger distances may not always mean farther locations (e.g., $Dis(F_1, F_4)$ > $Dis(F_1, F_7)$ for user 1). Based on this trend, however, we see that within a small number of steps (e.g., 5 steps) larger distances of WiFi fingerprints generally indicate farther locations on a pathway. In other words, the geographic distance and WiFi signal distance should be *correlated* on a pathway. Based on this observation, Travi-Navi weights the particles with the correlation of the Euclidian distances and the WiFi fingerprint distances. Let $\overrightarrow{D}^i_{\texttt{Euc}} = \{Dis(P^i, P_t^g)\}$ and $\overrightarrow{D}^i_{\texttt{WiFi}} = \{Dis(P^i, P_t^g)\}$, $(1 \le t \le m)$ denote the Euclidian

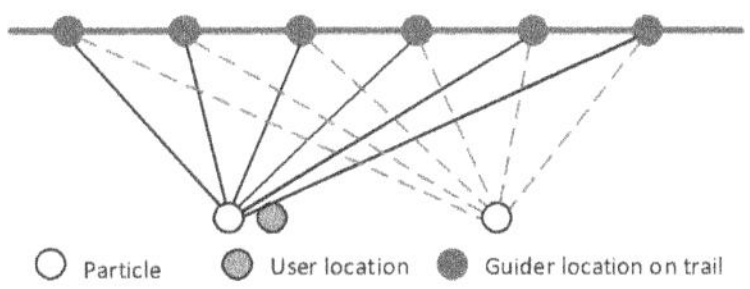

Figure 9: The more probable particle is weighted higher based on the correlation of Euclidean and WiFi distance.

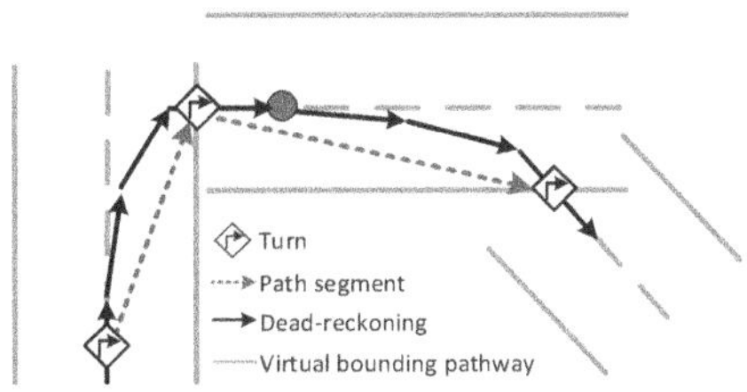

Figure 10: Turn detection. Travi-Navi detects turns if the user walks through the virtual bounding pathways.

distances and WiFi distances from the ith particle to the guider's m dead-reckoning positions and associated WiFi fingerprints, respectively. Then, the ith particle is weighted as follows

$$weight_w^i = \begin{cases} Corr(\overrightarrow{D}_{\mathtt{Euc}}^i, \overrightarrow{D}_{\mathtt{WiFi}}^i) & \text{, if} > 0 \\ 0 & \text{, otherwise} \end{cases} \quad (4)$$

As illustrated in Figure 9, a particle closer to a user's real position would be weighted higher than a distant one, as the distances from the more probable particle would be more correlated to the measured WiFi distances. Note that the use of correlation as a similarity metric naturally incorporates multiple WiFi fingerprints, enhancing robustness against WiFi signal strength fluctuations.

Magnetic and WiFi Fusion: In Travi-Navi, we assign equal weights to magnetic and WiFi signals and multiply the two weights to fuse them as follows

$$weight^i = weight_m^i \cdot weight_w^i$$

We note that one may evaluate the reliability of magnetic and WiFi signals, e.g., by measuring their variation over time, and assign different weights accordingly. Such a weighting strategy may improve the tracking accuracy compared with the current equal weighting method. In practice, the current method provides sufficient tracking accuracy for the purpose of Travi-Navi. To reduce power consumption, a follower may reduce the WiFi sampling rate and accordingly reduce the weight of WiFi measurements. If the WiFi scan is saved, particles are weighted using only magnetic signals. If query pathway images are captured, we may assign higher weights to the retrieved pathway accordingly. It should be noted that the optimal weighting strategy remains as an open question.

Deviation detection and handling. If followers deviate from the correct path, Travi-Navi should be able to detect the deviation events and promptly alert the followers. Additionally, followers may intentionally take short detours to avoid obstacles. We detect deviations using two simple intuitions. First, if there are mismatched turns between a guider's trace and a follower's dead-reckoning, Travi-Navi changes the tracking state to a pre-alert state. Second, if the user indeed deviates, the centroid position of particles will not change much, which is substantially different from normal walking. Thus, we conclude a deviation event when observing mismatched turns and no or slight centroid position changes for a few steps.

Turn detection: Many methods detect turns by measuring instant heading changes during a walk, which often results in false detections due to sensor noise. Based on the observation that the pathways and corridors are generally long, straight and narrow areas, we attempt to confine dead-reckoning trails with virtual bounding pathways, as depicted in Figure 10. In particular, Travi-Navi builds a 4-step wide virtual bounding pathway with the direction of the first two steps (to take into consideration body swing rhythm) [5]. Travi-Navi tests whether a user walks through the virtual bounding pathway after updating the user's position. If the user deviates from the original direction and walks outside the virtual bounding pathway, Travi-Navi detects turns and builds a new virtual bounding pathway with the heading direction of the last two dead-reckoning steps; otherwise Travi-Navi considers the user to be walking without turning. Virtual bounding pathway based detection is more robust to the noise in heading measurements. In wide areas, e.g., parking lots, users tend to take short paths and their dead-reckoning trails can be confined with several concatenated virtual bounding pathways. The pathway images are more helpful in wide open areas, as the users can easily identify the scenes.

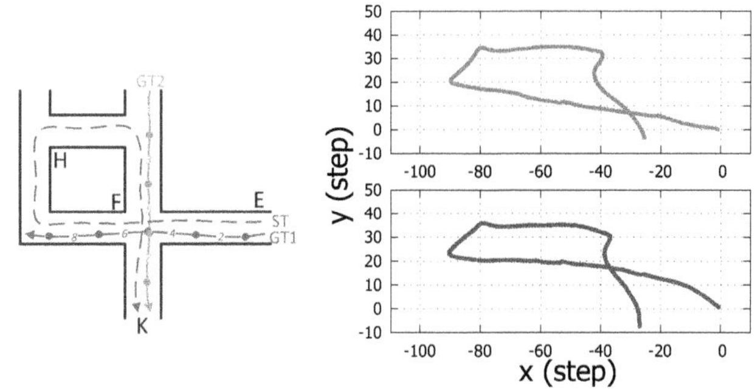

(a) Actual Walking Path (b) DR Captured ST Traces

Figure 11: Traces with crossing shortcuts.

Deviation handling: When Travi-Navi detects a possible deviation event with a detection window of 4 steps, it immediately marks the deviating position and reflects the change in UI by changing the guiding arrow from a solid to dashed lines. It also displays the dead-reckoning trail to inform the user. Followers may intentionally take short detours to avoid obstacles and return to correct routes. If the particles revive in a short amount of time, Travi-Navi resumes user tracking and transits to the navigation state. Travi-Navi confirms a deviation event with a detection window of 6 steps. Once a deviation event is confirmed, it prompts the user and shows instructions to guide the user back to the deviating position. Meanwhile, it also shows the pathway image of the deviating position.

Travi-Navi does not assume the user will truly follow the instructions to walk back. The user may continue the exploration. Travi-Navi tries to relock on to the user by continuing the particle filtering process as the user walks. When the particles reconverge on the guider's trail indicating that the user has returned to the correct path, it prompts the user regarding the successful relock on and continues the navigation.

3.4 Finding shortcuts

A navigation service should be able to find shortcuts and plan trips for users. We identify two situations in which we may find shortcuts for users.

Case 1: Find shortcuts from multiple traces with overlapping segments. Users may want to visit multiple places (e.g., a restaurant after shopping). As illustrated in Figure 7(a), a user wants to visit shops at location B and C starting from entrance A. The user downloads two traces (A-B and A-C), and navigates to B first. Now to visit C, Travi-Navi needs to find the shortcut and navigate the user from B to C directly.

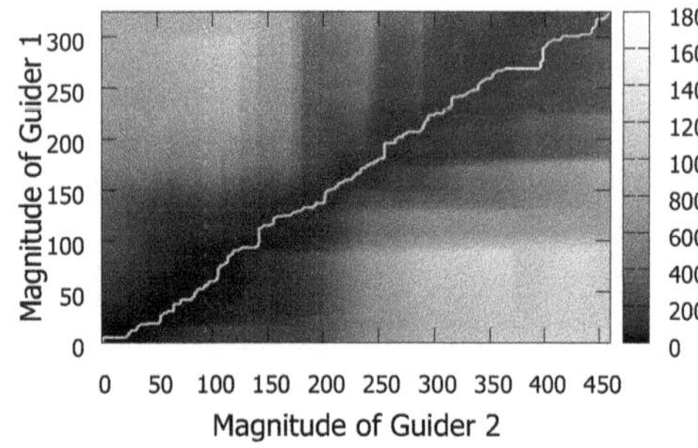

(a) DTW cost matrix.

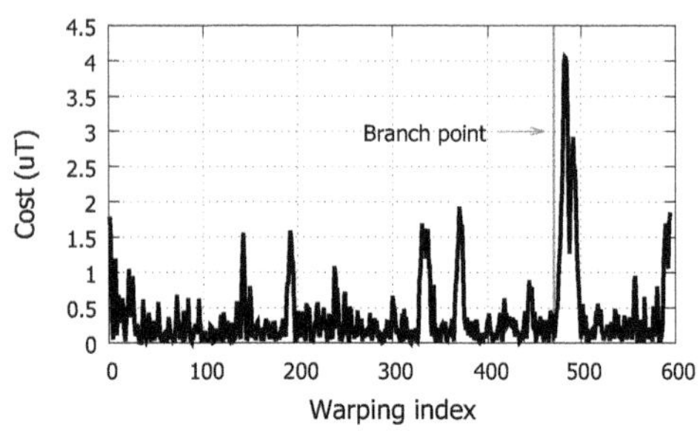

(b) Cost of each warping

Figure 12: Magnetic field readings on common pathways are similar and can be used to detect shortcuts.

Case 2: Find shortcuts from crossing traces. Multiple guiders' trails may only cross each other and lack long overlapping segments. This case is more common for self-helping users such as car finders. Figure 11(a) depicts such cases where GT1 and GT2 are two crossing traces from different guiders, and ST shows a self-helping user trace. In ST, the user visits a shop at H and then another shop at K. To navigate the user back to entrance E, ideally we would guide the user to crossing point F and then to E.

The task of finding shortcuts would become simple if the navigation traces to multiple destinations can be properly merged. The key is to accurately find the overlapping segments (for Case 1) and the crossing points (for Case 2).

Finding overlapping segments. One intuitive approach to merge the guiders' traces is through trace replay – to emulate the navigation process of one guider on another guider's trace. However, this approach does not work well. First, the different signals prior to the overlapping segment (due to the different starting points) will drive divergent particle distribution. It therefore negatively affects the convergence of particles when it comes to the overlapping portion. Consequently, the identified overlaps will be much shorter than the actual overlapping segments. Short overlaps may even be missed. Secondly, the particle filtering, especially before particle convergence, involves relatively high computation. Unlike user tracking, which amortizes the computation over the whole navigation process, Travi-Navi needs to efficiently merge the traces in shortcut detection. Prior methods detect distinguishable signal landmarks inside buildings (e.g., unique WiFi fingerprints, motion patterns) as anchors to correct dead-reckoning drifts and align traces. However, as reported, such landmarks may be few in number and not always detectable [32, 35, 29].

Travi-Navi adopts lightweight trace merging algorithms to efficiently find overlapping segments and reliably merge multiple traces, even if no landmarks can be found. In particular, we design a magnetic signal based detection and WiFi signal based verification process.

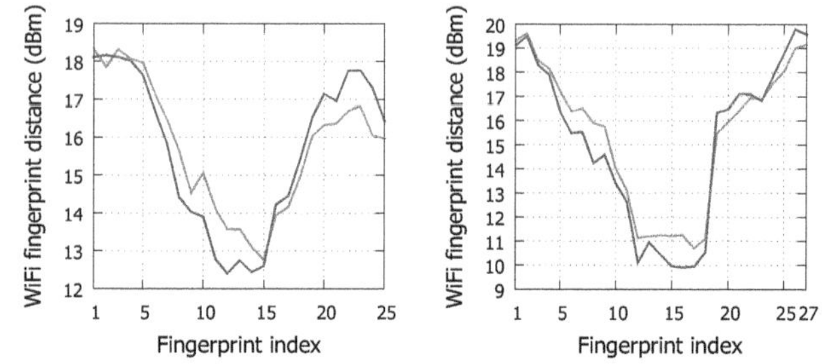

(a) North to South path (b) East to West path

Figure 13: "V"-shaped trend of WiFi fingerprint distances at crossing points.

Magnetic field based detection: As in the tracking case, we also apply Dynamic Time Warping (DTW) [28] to counter for possibly warped magnetic signal sequences, except that here, DTW is applied to the whole sequence. To reduce the computation and memory overhead involved in processing the data sampled at the highest rate, we perform a 10-fold downsampling, i.e., averaging over 10 samples, without affecting the shapes of two magnetic sequence outlines.

Figure 12(a) plots the cost matrix of DTW after the downsampling for matching the two magnetic sequences shown in Figure 7(b). The line in Figure 12(a) highlights the minimum cost warping of the two sequences. In the upper-right corner of the figure, we observe a "⌟"-shaped turn (highlighted in yellow) on the minimum cost line. This is because after the branch point the magnetic fields exhibit distinct patterns and no good matches can be found between the two sequences. Figure 12(b) plots the costs involved in each warping alignment along the minimum cost line. We see that due to the lack of good matches, the costs immediately increase after the branch point. Also, unlike other narrow short spikes due to noise, the tallest spike remains high for a relatively long period. Travi-Navi sets empirical thresholds for the cost and window size to detect the branch point.

WiFi based verification: Travi-Navi performs post verification using *a sequence of* WiFi observations to ensure correct detection of overlapping segments. If DTW indeed finds correct overlapped segments, the WiFi fingerprints observed on one guider's trace would be very similar to those observed on the other.

In Travi-Navi, guiders perform frequent WiFi scans whereas followers may scan less frequently. We compensate for different WiFi scan speeds on different devices by pairing WiFi scans at the closest positions when calculating the average WiFi signal distances. Evidently, the average distance between all WiFi pairs is small for correct alignment. However, if the segments are misaligned, the average distance will be large. The more misaligned, the larger the average distance. Through experiments, we have decided on an empirical threshold (10dBm) to determine a good alignment. Note that, unlike the tracking case where a single WiFi fingerprint is utilized, here we have to rely on *a sequence of* WiFi scans for robustness.

For overlapping segments with opposite directions, Travi-Navi can detect the overlaps by reversing one of the two traces and apply the above detection method.

Finding crossing points. Since the crossing traces only have small overlapping areas, the above overlapping segment detection methods cannot detect crossing points. While the traces contain WiFi fingerprints, they cover only a very small portion of the whole indoor radio environment. We cannot confirm a crossing point by testing if some fingerprints in one trace are localized on another trace with conventional WiFi localization techniques [7]. We note that the small distance in WiFi fingerprints is necessary but not sufficient to identify shortcuts.

Recognizing that closer positions should show more similar WiFi fingerprints as evidenced in Figure 8, and further inspired by [29] in which the trend of AP signal strengths is used to detect WiFi-Marks, we design a crossing point detection method by comparing the trend of *average gross distances* of fingerprints in one trace to the fingerprints in the other. Figure 11 depicts an example of two crossing traces GT1 and GT2. Two guiders sample WiFi fingerprints as they walk along GT1 and GT2, respectively. We calculate the average gross distance – the average of the pair-wise WiFi distances to a window of consecutive fingerprints in the other trace, e.g., the average WiFi distance of one fingerprint on GT1 to those on GT2. Pair-wise WiFi distance is calculated using Eq. 2.

Figure 13 shows the average of gross WiFi distances between WiFi fingerprints in the portions near the crossing point of the two user traces shown in Figure 11(b). We clearly see the "V"-shaped turning of the trend. It is important that such trends should be *mutual*, i.e., the same trend should exist when checking fingerprints on one trace against those on the other, and vice versa. When two paths meet at a "T" crossing point, Travi-Navi cannot identify the shortcut by detecting the mutual decreasing-and-increasing trends in WiFi fingerprint distances. In practice, however, since the two paths are likely to join and form overlapping segments, Travi-Navi can detect such shortcuts leveraging magnetic readings.

Navigation instruction on shortcuts. Once overlapping segments or crossing points among multiple traces are found, we can merge them by grafting one trace to another trace. The only subtlety of navigation on shortcuts is that certain trace segments may need to be played in reverse.

User lock-on from uncharted areas. A follower may not start Travi-Navi at entrances and want to navigate from uncharted areas using a guider's trace. In this case, the follower may first walk around and record a walking trace. Travi-Navi reuses the above shortcut identification modules to detect whether the follower's walking trace has any overlapping segments or crossing points with the guider's trace. Once Travi-Navi confirms that the follower is on the guider's trail, it can lock on the follower and starts navigation.

4. SYSTEM EVALUATION

In this section, we present the evaluation of key functional components of Travi-Navi. We then evaluate Travi-Navi in representative indoor environments for a better understanding of Travi-Navi's effectiveness and limitation.

4.1 Implementation

We implement Travi-Navi on the Android platform (version 4.2.2). The current version of Travi-Navi involves 6k lines of Java implementing all the functional modules of functional architecture (Figure 2). We adopt the OpenCV library (version 2.4.6) written in C to implement the image processing and image matching via JNI. In particular, we adopt the ORB algorithm [27] as it is orders of magnitude faster than SURF and SIFT [19] and can extract image features in real time on mobile devices (e.g., Samsung Galaxy S2 with one dual-core 1.2GHz processor). We adopt the bag-of-visual-words algorithm [17], which uses k-means to cluster image features. For image classification, we adopt the linear SVM with the default optimal parameter setting of OpenCV [4]. The image resolution is set to 320×240 which balances the image quality and the processing overhead. Each image is saved as a JPEG file and the file size is around 20KB. We enable the auto-focus in image capture. Travi-Navi packs the guider and the user functional modules into one application and reuses the common modules. All experimental results were obtained via online processing on mobile devices and visualized offline if not specified otherwise.

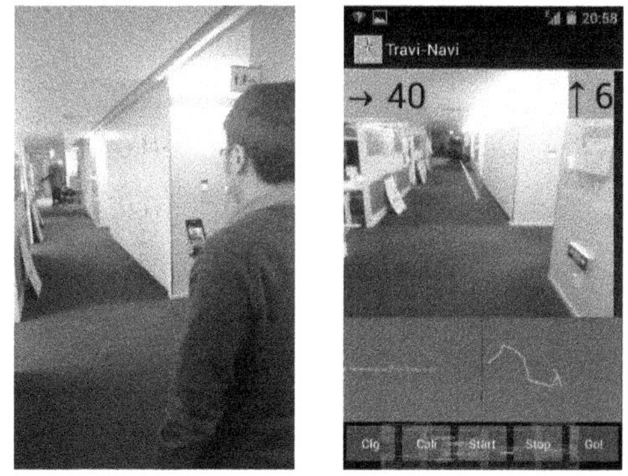

Figure 14: A user trying out Travi-Navi (Left), and the UI snapshot of our Travi-Navi client (Right).

The user interface presents navigation instructions as illustrated in Figure 14. The center of the UI shows guider's pathway image. As the follower moves forward, Travi-Navi tracks the follower and updates the guider's pathway image accordingly. In addition to the pathway image, Travi-Navi also presents the turning instructions (i.e., turn right by 40 degrees at the next turn, presented as $\rightarrow$ 40) and the number of remaining steps to the next turn (i.e., 6 steps, presented as $\uparrow$ 6). In addition, it also measures the instant heading direction (blue arrow) and presents the guider's heading direction on the path (purple arrow).

4.2 Evaluation

We tested Travi-Navi on a variety of Android mobile devices (Samsung Galaxy S2, S4, Note3, HTC Desire, and HTC Droid Incredible 2). Due to limited availability, Travi-Navi has not yet been evaluated on wearable devices such as Google glass.

We conducted experiments on both an office building floor and the first floor of a large shopping mall with a testing area of about 1900m^2 and 4000m^2 during different times of day. The lighting conditions during business hours allow guiders to capture bright pathway images. The guiders record traces with mobile phones held in an upright attitude and capture pathway images using back cameras as they walk to destinations. As the surroundings can be occluded, guiders need to find a less crowded time to capture pathway images. Followers naturally hold mobile phones and follow navigation instructions. For the purpose of this evaluation, Travi-Navi recorded the followers' traces as well. Overall, we collected 12 navigation traces covering all the main pathways of the testing areas' entrances. The total length of navigation traces was about 2.8km. We recruited 4 volunteer followers who walked many times on different routes, with a total walking distance of around 10km in the experiments.

4.2.1 *Motion hints*

Image quality. Images taken by guiders during the walk provide visual guidance to users. Due to camera shack, the images could become blurred. We evaluate whether motion hints could improve the image quality. We use the number of detectable ORB features in images as the quality metric to quantify the image quality. Generally, computer vision techniques can detect more features in sharper images than blurred ones. We also tested other image quality metrics (e.g., the maximum value of Laplacian transformation), which are highly correlated with our metric but more subject to image noise.

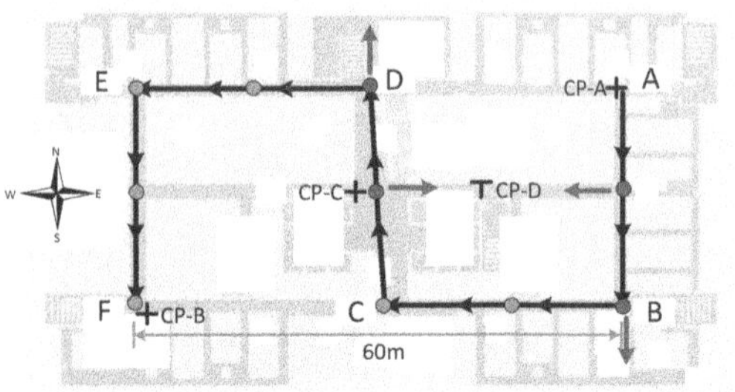

Figure 15: Office building navigation trail.

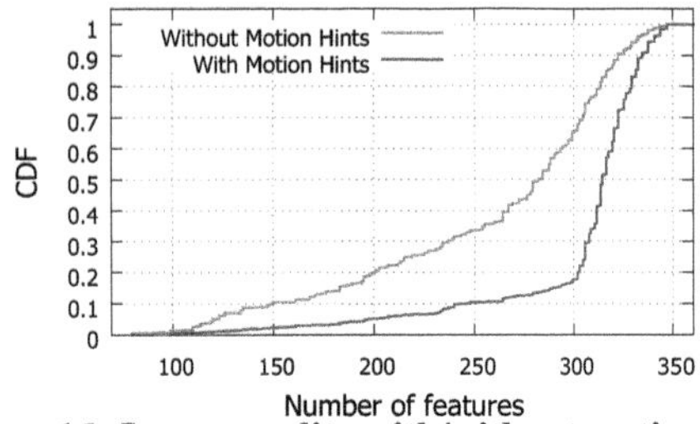

Figure 16: Image quality with/without motion hints.

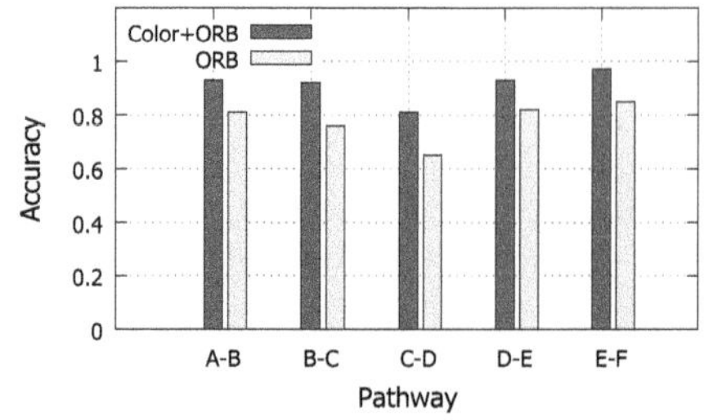

Figure 17: Pathway image retrieval performance.

We walked along the same route and captured images with/without the assistance of motion hints, respectively. We measured the number of features in the images captured during walks inside the office building. Figure 16 plots the CDFs of the number of features with/without the assistance of motion hints. The results show that the motion hints can predict better shooting opportunities and effectively capture sharper pathway images.

Pathway image retrieval. Smart mobile devices may roughly infer a user's location (e.g., pathway-level localization) using image matching techniques. We integrate the local geometric shapes described using ORB features and the ambient color histograms to form image features. We capture images triggered by motion hints at each step on the trail from A $\rightarrow$ B $\rightarrow \cdots \rightarrow$ F in our office building as depicted in Figure 15. We label the images with the pathways (i.e., A $\rightarrow$ B, B $\rightarrow$ C, ..., E $\rightarrow$ F) and train the linear SVM. SVM training takes several seconds on mobile devices (Samsung Galaxy S2) but we note that it only involves a one-time training cost. A guider may train the SVM using a server and share the SVM classifier with users to classify images in real time on mobile phones.

Users take images on pathways and query Travi-Navi for their locations. Before triggering image capture, Travi-Navi consults the shooting angle by looking up the instant device orientation. If the device is facing either the floor or ceiling, Travi-Navi does not perform image capture or matching, and inform the users to adjust the shooting angle. In the experiment, each of the 4 users took 25 pathway images to query locations. In Figure 17, we found that Travi-Navi achieves pathway-level localization with reasonably high accuracy by combining the ORB feature and a color histogram. The accuracy on path C $\rightarrow$ D is lower. Examining the images on the path, we found that the lower accuracy is mainly due to the line of sight blockage. Travi-Navi needs to capture a query image with a substantial portion that has not been occluded to retrieve the correct image in the navigation trace.

4.2.2 User tracking and navigation

User lock-on. Travi-Navi locks on users at entrances by comparing observed WiFi fingerprints against those in navigation traces. We collected WiFi fingerprints at 6 entrances of the shopping mall. The number of observable WiFi APs varied from 6 to 13 at the entrances. The geographic distance between the entrances closest to each other was around 20m. We randomly selected one WiFi fingerprint at each entrance and computed the WiFi distances to the other fingerprints at the same or different entrances. The experiment results are plotted in Figure 18, which shows the maximum WiFi distance to the fingerprints collected at the same entrance and the minimum WiFi distance to fingerprints collected at different entrances. We found that the WiFi fingerprint distances at the same entrance were substantially smaller than to fingerprints at different entrances. This gap allows Travi-Navi to lock on to users at the entrances (separated by >20m) with 100% accuracy. We also tested in our office building at the main entrance and 4 emergency exits on the same floor (separated by >25m) and achieved correct lock-ons as well.

Tracking follower. Travi-Navi tracks a follower's progress on the guider's trace and gives directions. We measured the tracking error to evaluate the promptness of instructions and tested whether Travi-Navi can navigate users to their destinations. A guider collected navigation traces in the office building following the trails plotted in Figure 15. The guider took 202 steps and 2min to walk the trail (A $\rightarrow$ F), with a total length of around 150m. In practice, a guider (e.g., restaurant owner) should take the most convenient path for followers (e.g., customers). To obtain the ground truth, the guider taps the mobile phone to record timestamps when the guider reaches the checkpoints depicted as green and red dots in Figure 15.

Travi-Navi navigated the 4 followers starting from A to F. We note that the followers were not informed of the navigation routes, the final destination, or the checkpoint locations. In the experiments, all the followers successfully reached the destination under the direction of Travi-Navi. During the navigation, Travi-Navi recorded timestamps along with the instructions presented to users. Meanwhile, a shadow person followed behind the volunteers and recorded the timestamps when the volunteers arrived at checkpoints.

We measured the tracking errors by the offset between the instructions presented to followers and the instructions recorded by the guider at each checkpoint. The offset results are shown in Figure 19, in the unit of steps as instructions are updated on a step basis. The experiment results show that Travi-Navi has small tracking errors within 4 steps. We carried out a user study with the 4 users after they reached the destination. According to our user study, user 1 and user 2 specified the direction as "almost synchronized", while user 3 and user 4 experienced slightly delayed and early directions, respectively. As users normally took around 0.6s per step, the time offset of instructions was within 3s for all users.

Deviation detection. Travi-Navi should quickly detect deviation events and notify users. In the experiment of deviation detection, Travi-Navi navigates the 4 volunteering followers from A to F as in the previous user tracking experiment. To measure the effectiveness of deviation detection, we intentionally asked the 4 users to deviate at 4 bifurcating points depicted as red dots and follow the pathways indicated as red arrows in Figure 15. Travi-Navi enters the pre-alert stage with a detection window of 4 steps and confirms a deviation with a detection window of 6 steps. Thus, we set the

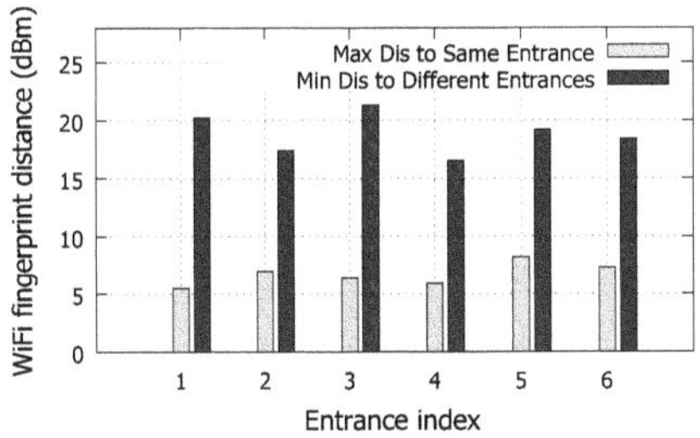

Figure 18: Distances between WiFi fingerprints at 6 entrances.

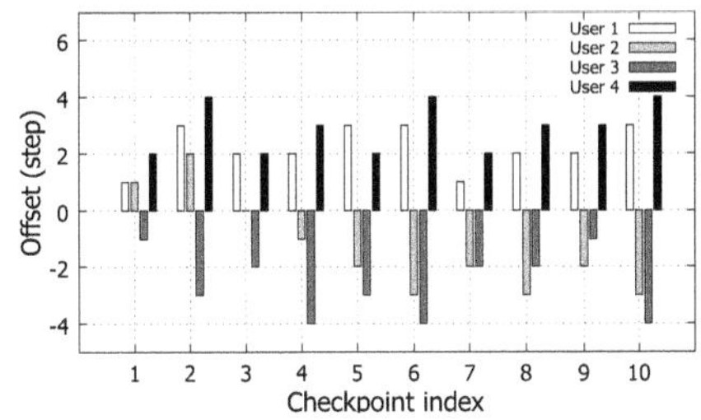

Figure 19: User tracking accuracy for different users at 10 checking points.

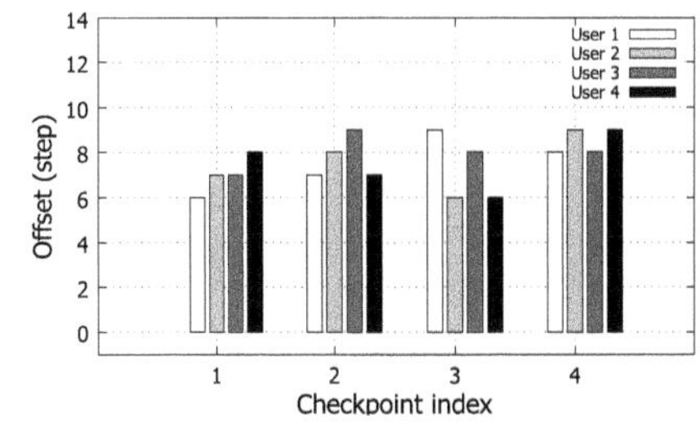

Figure 20: Deviation detection for different users at 4 turns.

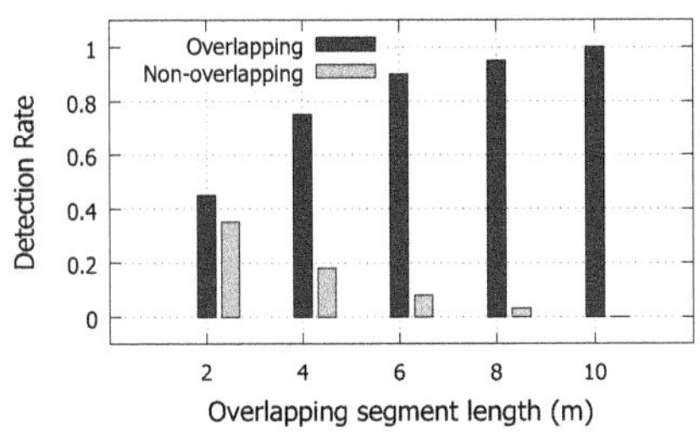

Figure 21: Overlapping segment detection results.

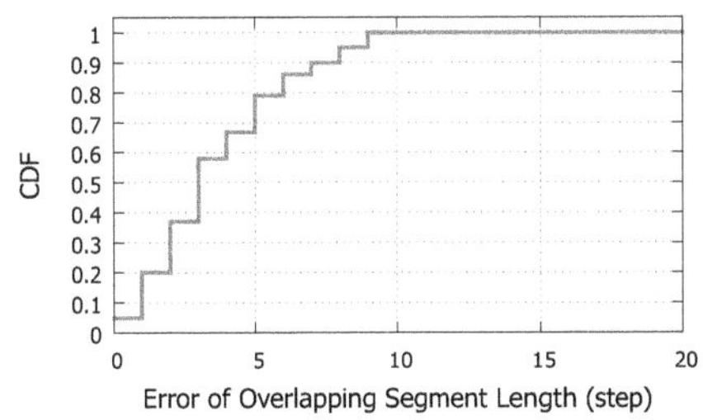

Figure 22: CDF of error of overlapping segment length.

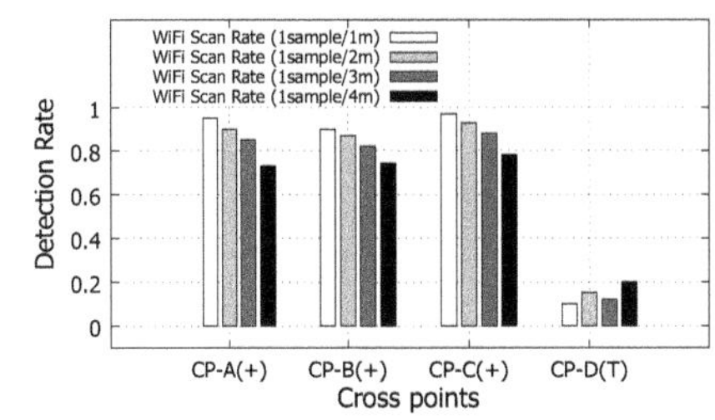

Figure 23: Crossing point detection results.

deviation detection window to be 6 steps. Travi-Navi recorded the instructions (including deviation alerts if any) presented to users.

We present the steps that users took before Travi-Navi alerted the users in Figure 20. We found that Travi-Navi detected the deviation events within 9 steps. We also measured deviation detections that were false positives. We walked along the trail from A to F for 4 rounds (approximately 600m in total) and observed only 3 false alarms. Note that in Travi-Navi, we set a deviation detection threshold of 6 steps. When we decrease the threshold, Travi-Navi triggers more false alarms, while in return being more prompt in detecting deviation events.

4.2.3 *Shortcut identification*

We examine whether Travi-Navi can accurately identify shortcuts among guiders' traces.

Overlapping segments. We collect 100 walking traces with different overlapping segment lengths and conduct shortcut identification. As a user may only want to be navigated to a small number of destinations, Travi-Navi only needs to reliably identify the shortcuts among a dozen traces. We note that two walking trails of opposite directions may also have overlapping segments. To solve this problem, Travi-Navi reverses one of the two traces and identifies overlapping segments with opposite walking directions (§3.4).

Figure 21 plots the success rates with varying overlapping lengths. We found that Travi-Navi achieved a 90% success rate when the overlapping length was around 6m, and detected all overlapping segments when the length was 10m. The success rate decreased as the overlapping length became shorter. We also measured the false detection rates by matching traces with varying lengths against non-overlapping traces. In the figure, shorter traces tend to have higher false detection rates. When the trace length was 6m, the false detection rate decreased to 8% and no false detection was observed when the length reached 10m.

Among the correctly detected overlapping segments, we plot the CDF of differences between the actual overlapping segment length and the detected one in Figure 22. We found that about 50% of detected overlapping segments are within 3 steps and all detection errors are within 9 steps. Considering the corridor widths in practice, such accuracies are sufficient for shortcut detection.

Crossing points. We evaluate Travi-Navi's performance in detecting crossing points with the mutual trends in WiFi fingerprint distance. To conduct the experiment, we scanned WiFis at 3 crossing points (CP-A, CP-B, and CP-C) indicated by "+" in Figure 15. In addition, we also scanned WiFi at a "T"-shaped crossing point (CP-D). To study the detection performance with different WiFi scan frequencies, we first collected one WiFi fingerprint every 1m (i.e., 1sample/1m), and downsampled WiFi fingerprints to emulate lower scanning frequencies. Figure 23 plots the success rates of detecting the crossing points. We found that the detection rates at the "+" crossing points were above 80% with 1 WiFi scan per 3m. Travi-Navi cannot detect "T"-shaped shortcuts, since such a crossing point does not exhibit decreasing-and-increasing trends *mutually* (§3.4). In practice, however, two paths meeting at "T"-shaped crossing points are likely to join and form overlapping segments, and Travi-Navi can reliably detect the overlapping shortcuts leveraging magnetic readings.

4.2.4 *Energy consumption*

As guiders collect navigation traces with IMU, WiFi, and cameras, it incurs relatively high power consumption. We measure the power consumption on various models of mobile phones using the Monsoon power monitor [3]. The power monitor directly supplies power to the phones and accurately tracks the current and voltage. To accurately measure the power consumption of Travi-Navi, we first turn off all background services and applications. The WiFi module was turned on and the screen brightness was set to auto-adjustment mode. All the sensor modules (e.g., IMU and WiFi) were sampled and processed in real time. As we need to wire the phones for measurement, we have to make the phones stationary. We synthetically triggered image capture and updated pathway images in Travi-Navi every 0.6s.

Figure 24 plots the working currents measured on the Samsung Galaxy S2 in different working modes as an example. The current was sampled at 5KHz using the power monitor and averaged over

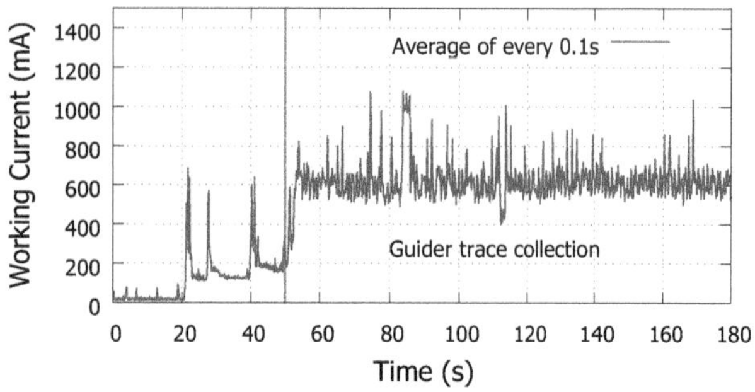

(a) Guider mode.

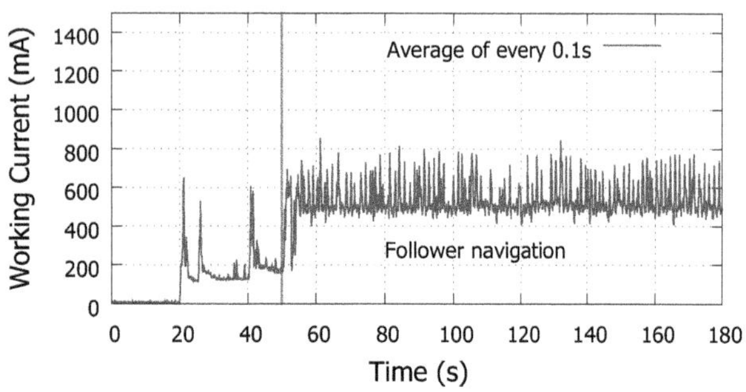

(b) Follower mode.

Figure 24: Power measurement with Samsung Galaxy S2.

every window of 0.1s. In Figure 24(a), the phone was in sleep mode during the period from 0s to 20s. We woke up the phone at around 20s. We then unlocked the phone at around 25s. We launched Travi-Navi at 40s and started the trace collection at 50s. The trace collection finished at 180s. Similarly, Figure 24(b) plots the power measurement when Travi-Navi was working in the follower mode from 50s to 180s. We repeated the experiments 10 times and characterized the power draws in different modes in Table 1. The guider mode of Travi-Navi drew power at around 616.50mA and the expected battery life was 2.92h. The follower mode incurred less power consumption at around 532.20mA and the expected battery life was 3.38h for the SGS2 with an 1800mAh battery.

We measured the expected battery life of the Samsung Galaxy Note3 with a 3200mAh battery and HTC Droid Incredible 2 with a 1450mAh battery. The measurement results are presented in Table 2. Powered by a large battery, the expected life of Note3 was around 4.75h in guider mode, and 5.62h in follower mode, respectively. The expected battery life of HTC Droid Incredible 2 was 3.14h in guider mode and 3.89h in follower mode, respectively. The expected battery life time was shorter for the HTC Droid Incredible 2 compared with Note3, mainly because of its smaller battery.

The current version of Travi-Navi has not yet been extensively optimized for energy efficiency. Travi-Navi may reduce the image sampling rate to save energy and benefit from the energy efficient mobile vision techniques [18]. When magnetic field distortions exhibit sufficient discriminative patterns, Travi-Navi may disable WiFi scans and weight particles solely with magnetic measurements. Travi-Navi can also leverage the adaptive particle filtering techniques (e.g., KLD-sampling [12]) to reduce power consumption. Travi-Navi can benefit from energy efficient co-processor architectures for sensor fusion as well [30].

Table 1: Power consumption measurements on Samsung Galaxy S2 with an 1800mAh battery. We measure the average power, the average current, and the expected battery life.

Mode	Period	Power	Current	Battery Life
Sleep	0s–20s	75.39mW	20.41mA	88.20h
Idle	20s–50s	676.49mW	183.15mA	9.83h
Guider	50s–180s	2276.35mW	616.50mA	2.92h
Follower	50s–180s	1965.13mW	532.20mA	3.38h

Table 2: Expected battery life measurements in different modes on 3 models of mobile phones.

	SGS2	Note3	Incredible2
Battery Capacity	1800mAh	3200mAh	1450mAh
Battery Life (Guider)	2.92h	4.75h	3.14h
Battery Life (Follower)	3.38h	5.62h	3.89h

5. RELATED WORK

Indoor localization is an extensively studied field. Many systems such as Cricket [22] and PinPoint [37] achieve high position accuracy with dedicated hardware deployment. Many methods such as Radar [7] and Horus [36] leverage existing WiFi infrastructure. Some recent works explore the magnetic field for indoor localization [9, 26]. All these methods require labor-intensive site surveys. Participatory systems like PlaceLab [15], ActiveCampus [13], and LiveLabs [2] evaluate localization in the real world. Leveraging rich sensing modalities on smartphones, SurroundSense [6] infers logical surroundings from ambient signatures.

Many crowdsourcing-based indoor localization systems [32, 8, 35, 25, 10, 23] lack incentives to attract enough participation especially when the services cannot provide benefits. Unlike those works, Travi-Navi enables users to easily deploy their own navigation services without comprehensive localization services and thereby directly benefit from service deployment, while the crowdsourcing systems typically require huge number of volunteers who may not directly benefit from participation.

Technique-wise, Travi-Navi draws strength from prior inertial sensor based tracking [16, 35, 25], which typically assumes the availability of floor maps and confine dead-reckoning drifts with map constraints. Instead, Travi-Navi intelligently fuses magnetic and WiFi signals to accurately track a user's progress on a guider's navigation trace. Some works [32, 29] seek to construct indoor maps and bootstrap localization services exploiting walking traces shared by crowds. They identify various landmarks to merge user traces, which is similar to one of the shortcut identification cases in Travi-Navi.

Escort [10] navigates users to their friends inside buildings without relying on accurate localization services. Escort corrects dead-reckoning drifts leveraging crowd encounters and special audio beacons. Riehle *et al.* [26] navigate blind users leveraging magnetic distortions and give audio instructions. Unlike previous methods, Travi-Navi augments indoor navigation with motion vision by providing followers with the guider's pathway images. Travi-Navi attempts to enable a user to easily bootstrap navigation services without infrastructure support. Travi-Navi synthesizes radio and magnetic signals to correct IMU based dead-reckoning drifts and identifies shortcuts.

Recent advances in mobile sensing and computer vision open new research opportunities. OPS [20] locates distant objects by synthesizing GPS localization and images taken from different angles with the Structure from Motion (SfM). TagSense [24] tags images with locations and activities inferred from smartphone sensors. FOCUS [14] indexes crowdsourced videos via content-based clustering with the complementary synergy of SfM and sensor hints. GigaSight [31] proposes a framework for crowdsourcing videos that enables deep content-based search. LiKamWa *et al.* [18] analytically characterize energy consumption of image and video capture and propose quality-energy tradeoff strategies. Travi-Navi augments indoor navigation with mobile vision, and avoids unnecessary power consumption and computation leveraging motion hints inferred from IMU sensors.

6. CONCLUSION

This paper describes our attempts to design, implement, and evaluate Travi-Navi, a vision-guided indoor navigation system. The key idea is to enable self-motivated users to easily deploy indoor navigation services without assuming a comprehensive indoor localization service or even the availability of floor maps. We incorporate magnetic field distortion and WiFi signals in particle filtering to ensure accurate user tracking. We further develop effective methods to detect shortcuts among overlapping and intersecting navigation traces. We devise a method to automatically capture high quality images while walking using motion hints. We implicitly leverage the users' visual recognition capability by providing them pathway images to correct slight direction ambiguity and enhance navigation experiences. Extensive experimental results and feedback from user trials confirm the effectiveness of Travi-Navi. We plan to further optimize Travi-Navi and reduce power consumption in the future.

7. ACKNOWLEDGEMENT

We would like to thank the anonymous shepherd and reviewers for providing constructive feedback and valuable input for improving the quality of this paper. We acknowledge the support of the NTU Nanyang Assistant Professorship (NAP) grant M4080738.020 and Microsoft research grant FY 12-RES-THEME-001.

8. REFERENCES

[1] High Accuracy Indoor Positioning (Nokia BLE). https://research.nokia.com/.

[2] LiveLabs. http://livelabs.smu.edu.sg/.

[3] Monsoon Power Monitor. http://www.msoon.com/LabEquipment/PowerMonitor/.

[4] OpenCV. http://opencv.org/.

[5] G. Ananthanarayanan, M. Haridasan, I. Mohomed, D. Terry, and C. A. Thekkath. StarTrack: A Framework for Enabling Track-based Applications. In *ACM MobiSys*, 2009.

[6] M. Azizyan, I. Constandache, and R. Roy Choudhury. SurroundSense: Mobile Phone Localization via Ambience Fingerprinting. In *ACM MobiCom*, 2009.

[7] P. Bahl and V. N. Padmanabhan. RADAR: An In-Building RF-based User Location and Tracking System. In *IEEE INFOCOM*, 2000.

[8] K. Chintalapudi, A. Padmanabha Iyer, and V. N. Padmanabhan. Indoor Localization Without the Pain. In *ACM MobiCom*, 2010.

[9] J. Chung, M. Donahoe, C. Schmandt, I.-J. Kim, P. Razavai, and M. Wiseman. Indoor Location Sensing Using Geo-magnetism. In *ACM MobiSys*, 2011.

[10] I. Constandache, X. Bao, M. Azizyan, and R. R. Choudhury. Did You See Bob?: Human Localization Using Mobile Phones. In *ACM MobiCom*, 2010.

[11] I. Constandache, R. R. Choudhury, and I. Rhee. Towards Mobile Phone Localization without War-Driving. In *IEEE INFOCOM*, 2010.

[12] D. Fox. KLD-Sampling: Adaptive Particle Filters. In *NIPS*, 2001.

[13] W. G. Griswold, P. Shannahan, S. W. Brown, R. Boyer, M. Ratto, R. B. Shapiro, and T. M. Truong. ActiveCampus - Experiments in Community-Oriented Ubiquitous Computing. *Computer*, 37(10), 2004.

[14] P. Jain, J. Manweiler, A. Acharya, and K. Beaty. FOCUS: Clustering Crowdsourced Videos by Line-of-sight. In *ACM SenSys*, 2013.

[15] A. LaMarca, Y. Chawathe, S. Consolvo, J. Hightower, I. Smith, J. Scott, T. Sohn, J. Howard, J. Hughes, F. Potter, J. Tabert, P. Powledge, G. Borriello, and B. Schilit. Place Lab: Device Positioning Using Radio Beacons in the Wild. In *PERVASIVE*, 2005.

[16] F. Li, C. Zhao, G. Ding, J. Gong, C. Liu, and F. Zhao. A Reliable and Accurate Indoor Localization Method Using Phone Inertial Sensors. In *ACM UbiComp*, 2012.

[17] F.-F. Li and P. Perona. A Bayesian Hierarchical Model for Learning Natural Scene Categories. In *IEEE CVPR*, 2005.

[18] R. LiKamWa, B. Priyantha, M. Philipose, L. Zhong, and P. Bahl. Energy Characterization and Optimization of Image Sensing Toward Continuous Mobile Vision. In *ACM MobiSys*, 2013.

[19] D. G. Lowe. Object Recognition from Local Scale-Invariant Features. In *IEEE ICCV*, 1999.

[20] J. G. Manweiler, P. Jain, and R. Roy Choudhury. Satellites in Our Pockets: An Object Positioning System Using Smartphones. In *ACM MobiSys*, 2012.

[21] P. Mohan, V. N. Padmanabhan, and R. Ramjee. Nericell: Rich Monitoring of Road and Traffic Conditions Using Mobile Smartphones. In *ACM SenSys*, 2008.

[22] N. B. Priyantha, A. Chakraborty, and H. Balakrishnan. The Cricket Location-support System. In *ACM MobiCom*, 2000.

[23] A. Purohit, Z. Sun, S. Pan, and P. Zhang. SugarTrail: Indoor Navigation in Retail Environments without Surveys and Maps. In *IEEE SECON*, 2013.

[24] C. Qin, X. Bao, R. Roy Choudhury, and S. Nelakuditi. TagSense: A Smartphone-based Approach to Automatic Image Tagging. In *ACM MobiSys*, 2011.

[25] A. Rai, K. K. Chintalapudi, V. N. Padmanabhan, and R. Sen. Zee: Zero-effort Crowdsourcing for Indoor Localization. In *ACM MobiCom*, 2012.

[26] T. H. Riehle, S. M. Anderson, P. A. Lichter, N. A. Giudice, S. I. Sheikh, R. J. Knuesel, D. T. Kollmann, and D. S. Hedin. Indoor Magnetic Navigation for the Blind. In *IEEE EMBC*, 2012.

[27] E. Rublee, V. Rabaud, K. Konolige, and G. Bradski. ORB: an efficient alternative to SIFT or SURF. In *IEEE ICCV*, 2011.

[28] S. Salvador and P. Chan. Toward accurate dynamic time warping in linear time and space. *Intelligent Data Analysis*, 11(5):561–580, 2007.

[29] G. Shen, Z. Chen, P. Zheng, T. Moscibroda, and Y. Zhang. Walkie-Markie: Indoor Pathway Mapping Made Easy. In *USENIX NSDI*, 2013.

[30] H. Shen, A. Balasubramanian, E. Yuan, A. LaMarca, and D. Wetherall. Improving Power Effciency using Sensor hubs without Re-coding Mobile Apps. *Technical Report of University of Washington*, 2014.

[31] P. Simoens, Y. Xiao, P. Pillai, Z. Chen, K. Ha, and M. Satyanarayanan. Scalable Crowd-sourcing of Video from Mobile Devices. In *ACM MobiSys*, 2013.

[32] H. Wang, S. Sen, A. Elgohary, M. Farid, M. Youssef, and R. R. Choudhury. No Need to War-drive: Unsupervised Indoor Localization. In *ACM MobiSys*, 2012.

[33] H. Wang, Z. Wang, G. Shen, F. Li, S. Han, and F. Zhao. WheelLoc: Enabling Continuous Location Service on Mobile Phone for Outdoor Scenarios. In *IEEE INFOCOM*, 2013.

[34] R. Want, A. Hopper, V. Falcão, and J. Gibbons. The Active Badge Location System. *ACM Trans. Inf. Syst.*, 10(1):91–102, Jan. 1992.

[35] Z. Yang, C. Wu, and Y. Liu. Locating in Fingerprint Space: Wireless Indoor Localization with Little Human Intervention. In *ACM MobiCom*, 2012.

[36] M. Youssef and A. Agrawala. The Horus WLAN Location Determination System. In *ACM MobiSys*, 2005.

[37] M. Youssef, A. Youssef, C. Rieger, U. Shankar, and A. Agrawala. PinPoint: An Asynchronous Time-Based Location Determination System. In *ACM MobiSys*, 2006.

[38] P. Zhou, M. Li, and G. Shen. Use It Free: Instantly Knowing Your Phone Attitude. In *ACM MobiCom*, 2014.

[39] P. Zhou, Y. Zheng, Z. Li, M. Li, and G. Shen. IODetector: A Generic Service for Indoor Outdoor Detection. In *ACM SenSys*, 2012.

Accurate Indoor Localization With Zero Start-up Cost

Swarun Kumar Stephanie Gil Dina Katabi Daniela Rus
Massachusetts Institute of Technology
{swarun, sgil, dk, rus}@mit.edu

ABSTRACT

Recent years have seen the advent of new RF-localization systems that demonstrate tens of centimeters of accuracy. However, such systems require either deployment of new infrastructure, or extensive fingerprinting of the environment through training or crowdsourcing, impeding their wide-scale adoption.

We present Ubicarse, an accurate indoor localization system for commodity mobile devices, with no specialized infrastructure or fingerprinting. Ubicarse enables handheld devices to emulate large antenna arrays using a new formulation of Synthetic Aperture Radar (SAR). Past work on SAR requires measuring mechanically controlled device movement with millimeter precision, far beyond what commercial accelerometers can provide. In contrast, Ubicarse's core contribution is the ability to perform SAR on handheld devices twisted by their users along unknown paths. Ubicarse is not limited to localizing RF devices; it combines RF localization with stereo-vision algorithms to localize common objects with no RF source attached to them. We implement Ubicarse on a HP SplitX2 tablet and empirically demonstrate a median error of 39 cm in 3-D device localization and 17 cm in object geotagging in complex indoor settings.

Categories and Subject Descriptors C.2.2 [**Computer Systems Organization**]: Computer-Communications Networks

Keywords Wireless; Localization; Wi-Fi; SAR; PHY

1. INTRODUCTION

Recent years have witnessed a major interest in developing accurate RF-based localization systems that enable users to navigate indoor spaces much like what GPS provides for outdoor environments [26, 19, 37]. Many advances have been made, leading to localization solutions that deliver an accuracy of tens of centimeters [37, 15, 33]. Unfortunately, none of these solutions have actually reached today's users. This is because past work that provides accurate RF-localization falls in one of two categories: 1) It either requires the deployment of new infrastructure (specialized access points [15], antenna arrays [37], acoustic beacons [19], etc.), or, 2) it needs exhaustive fingerprinting of the environment to learn the spatial distribution of signal strength, either in a training phase [28, 18] or via crowdsourcing [26, 5] to achieve meter accuracy at best. Ideally, we would like to achieve tens of centimeters accuracy for RF localization of mobile devices, without any fingerprinting or specialized infrastructure.

MobiCom'14, September 7-11, Maui, Hawaii, USA.

ACM 978-1-4503-2783-1/14/09 ...$15.00
http://dx.doi.org/10.1145/2639108.2639142.

Figure 1: Twisting the Mobile Device. The user twists the device about its vertical (z) axis, as shown in the figure on the left. The red circles indicate antenna locations. On the right, we depict the top view of a candidate device trajectory as measured by a Vicon motion capture system.

In principle, if mobile devices can be outfitted with a large antenna array [37, 15], they could accurately identify the spatial direction of incoming RF signals. Thus, they could localize themselves relative to the locations of neighboring Wi-Fi access points without requiring fingerprinting or modified infrastructure. In fact, public databases of access point locations are already available for a large number of buildings [34]. Of course, it is infeasible to mount a large antenna array on a small low-power handheld device. But what if today's mobile devices could somehow emulate the localization capability of a large antenna array?

We present Ubicarse[1], an indoor geo-location system that enables mobile devices to indeed emulate a large antenna array. At first, it might seem that one can use Synthetic Aperture Radar (SAR) to mimic an antenna array on a handheld device. Unfortunately, SAR in its existing form is unsuitable for handheld devices. To understand why this is the case, note that a moving antenna performs SAR by collecting signal snapshots as it moves along its trajectory, and jointly processing these snapshots to emulate a large antenna array traced out by that trajectory. Therefore for SAR to mimic a particular antenna array geometry, it must first know the position of the moving antenna at every point along its trajectory. Satisfying this requirement is relatively easy in radar systems where the speed and trajectory of the antenna movement are finely controlled. Unfortunately, when a user moves her handheld device, neither its speed nor its trajectory can be accurately controlled. To get a feel for the accuracy required, in 802.11a/n, even a small error of 2 cm in the relative position of the moving antenna leads to an error of 60 degrees in identifying the direction of the source.

One might consider using motion sensors (accelerometer, gyroscope, compass) present in most mobile devices to estimate antenna positions as it moves. Unfortunately, since SAR requires sub-centimeter accuracy in the device position along its trajectory, commercial motion sensors are virtually unusable to measure such fine-grained translation [22] and can at best be used to measure orientation from their gyroscopes.[2] Requiring the user to rotate the device

[1]The Spanish word Ubicarse derives from the Latin root *ubi* and signifies to locate or situate oneself with precision.

[2]This is because accelerometers report the net acceleration of the device including gravity, which must be subtracted out and the result integrated twice to obtain translation.

on a perfect arc with zero translation of the device center would preclude measuring this translation but is impractical to enforce.

Ubicarse addresses this challenge by developing a new formulation of SAR that is translation-resilient. Specifically, we allow the user to twist her mobile device about its vertical axis, as shown in Fig. 1. Even if the twisting involves unknown trajectories (that include translation), we can accurately compute SAR knowing only the rotation estimate from the gyroscope. To do so, we exploit the MIMO capability of modern wireless cards. Suppose the mobile device has two antennas. The distance between these antennas is fixed independent of how the user moves her device. Thus, whenever the user translates the device, the relative position vector of both its antennas remains the same. In contrast, as the device rotates, the relative position vector of the antennas, also rotates. Leveraging these observations, we develop a new SAR formulation that operates on *relative* wireless channels to estimate the direction of the access point's signal, purely based on the device's orientation with no information required on its exact position or translation. We analytically demonstrate that Ubicarse's translation-resilience holds under the same assumptions made for standard SAR and antenna arrays, both in single path and in the presence of multipath effects. We also implement the system and demonstrate a localization accuracy of the mobile device within few tens of centimeters, with no specialized infrastructure or fingerprinting.

Ubicarse is not limited to localizing RF devices; it can also localize common objects that have no RF source attached to them. Specifically, we leverage the camera available on most mobile devices to enable a user to learn the location of an object of interest by simply snapping photographs of the object from multiple perspectives. At first, it might seem that this application can be satisfied simply by tagging the object in the photograph with the position of the mobile device, obtained from RF-based localization. Such an approach however would yield poor tagging accuracy, particularly when the user cannot get too close to the object, for e.g., tagging a broken overhead lamp to report it to the facilities department.

To achieve high-precision geotagging, Ubicarse exploits the synergy between its WiFi-based localization capability and stereo vision algorithms used for 3-D reconstruction. Specifically, today's vision algorithms can accurately localize an object with respect to the set of camera coordinates from which the object was imaged [29], but it cannot find the coordinates of the object with respect to a global reference. In contrast, Ubicarse's SAR localization can identify the global positions of the device's camera accurately, but has no information about the object. Therefore, by combining the two methods, we can localize an object to within tens of centimeters in global coordinates – a promising step towards a future where we can tag or search for objects in the physical world using only our mobile devices, much the way we currently search for information on the web.

We implemented Ubicarse on a HP SplitX2 Tablet equipped with Intel 5300 wireless cards and Yei Technology motion sensors. We build on the 802.11 CSI tool [13] to obtain the wireless channels on the tablet. We conducted our experiment in a large university library, with books arranged in multiple shelves and racks that emulate the complex multipath characteristics of large warehouses and departmental stores, where indoor localization has been of particular interest. Our experiments reveal the following:

- **Translation Resilient SAR:** Ubicarse's SAR is resilient to unknown translations. We move the device along complex trajectories including several random walks and curves. We use Ubicarse to localize the direction of access point placed at distances from 2 to 12 m without knowledge of the trajectory of the movement. Our results show a median error in angle of 3.4° across trajectories, demonstrating the translation-resilience of Ubicarse's SAR.
- **Device Localization:** We ask a population of users to twist the tablet to localize themselves relative to the access points in the environment. The results show that Ubicarse localizes the tablet with a median error of 39 cm in full three dimensional space. Thus, Ubicarse achieves its goal of accurate localization without requiring either new infrastructure or signal fingerprinting.
- **Object Localization:** We integrate Ubicarse with the VisualSFM computer vision toolkit [35] and evaluate its object geotagging capability. We use Ubicarse to localize books in the library relative to the access points, by taking a few pictures of them. Our results show a median error of 17 cm in full 3-D space, which, surprisingly, is superior to Ubicarse's device localization. Indeed we show that a joint optimization of Ubicarse and vision has an interesting side-effect: we can significantly refine Ubicarse's device (i.e. camera) location estimates simply by studying the relative camera locations output by vision algorithms, corresponding to pictures snapped from different perspectives. In doing so, we show that Ubicarse's localization accuracy improves to a median of 15 cm from ground truth.

Contributions Ubicarse is an indoor localization system that achieves tens of centimeters of accuracy on commodity mobile devices, with no specialized infrastructure or fingerprinting. Ubicarse achieves this through a novel formulation of Synthetic Aperture Radar that is translation resilient, making it practical to deploy on handheld devices. Further, Ubicarse uses the cameras on mobile devices to help users geo-tag objects around them to within tens of centimeters. We implement Ubicarse on commodity tablets and experimentally validate its accuracy in complex indoor settings.

2. PRIMER ON SYNTHETIC APERTURE RADAR

Synthetic Aperture Radar has been widely used in aircrafts and satellites to map the topography of the Earth's surface [9]. Recent systems [33, 32] have also leveraged SAR for RFID localization.

SAR's primary goal is to allow a single-antenna wireless receiver to isolate and analyze the multiple signal paths emanating from a wireless transmitter. Specifically, it computes a *multipath profile*, which measures the relative signal power received from the transmitting source along different spatial directions (see Fig. 2). To do this, SAR leverages a simple principle: a moving receiver antenna snapshots the wireless signals at different spatial locations. Combined, these channel snapshots mimic a multi-antenna array (Fig. 2). Thus, one can simply apply standard antenna array equations [24] on the signals received at each antenna position to compute the multipath profile. For instance, one can apply equations for a linear antenna array [37] if the receive antenna moves on a line, or a circular antenna array [7], if the receiver rotates about a circle.

To understand SAR more formally, lets examine a special case of SAR for a received single path.[3] We focus on emulation of a circular antenna array, a scenario that is particularly relevant for this paper. Let's suppose the receive antenna rotates about the origin along a circle, taking n snapshots of the wireless channel from a source along a direction α_T as shown in Fig. 2. From basic channel models, we can write the the wireless channel h_i measured by the receiver at the ith snapshot (where $i = 1, \ldots, n$) as the complex number [30]:

$$h_i = \frac{1}{d} e^{\frac{-j2\pi}{\lambda}(d + r\cos(\alpha_T - \phi_i))} \quad (1)$$

Where (r, ϕ_i) is the antenna's polar coordinates at snapshot i (Fig. 2), d is its distance to the source, and λ the signal wavelength.

[3]We explicitly deal with the more general multipath case in §4.2

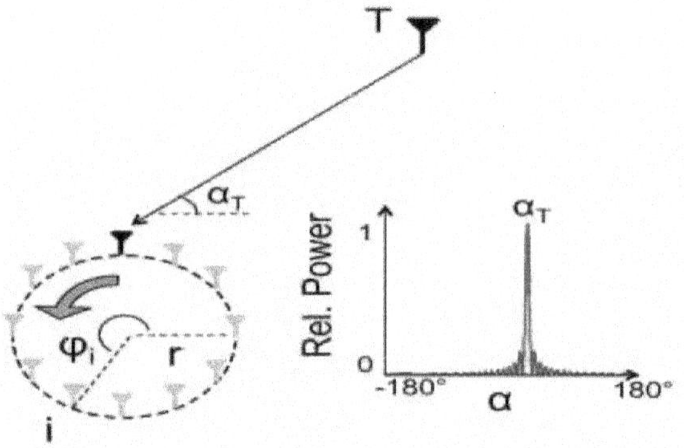

Figure 2: Circular SAR. Depicts a single antenna moving in a circle of radius r to emulate a circular antenna array. Gray antennas depict points where channel snapshots were taken. At snapshot i, the antenna is at an azimuthal angle ϕ_i. The multipath profile for a line-of-sight transmitter T has a sharp peak at the direction of the source α_T.

At this point, SAR computes the relative signal power along each spatial direction to generate a multipath profile. To do this, it needs two inputs: The measured channel snapshots h_i along the antenna trajectory, and the positions (r, ϕ_i) of the antenna along this trajectory. It then finds the relative power $P(\alpha)$ along direction α as:

$$P(\alpha) = \left| \frac{1}{n} \sum_{i=1}^{n} h_i e^{\frac{+j2\pi}{\lambda} rcos(\alpha - \phi_i)} \right|^2 \quad (2)$$

Notice that the above multipath power profile $P(\alpha)$ is maximum precisely if $\alpha = \alpha_T$, i.e. along the true direction of the source. This is because the terms $h_i e^{\frac{+j2\pi}{\lambda} rcos(\alpha - \phi_i)}$ are identical in phase, and therefore add up constructively when $\alpha = \alpha_T$ (see Eqn. 1), and tend to add up destructively as α deviates from α_T. Therefore, the multipath profile can be used to accurately ascertain the physical direction of a transmitter, a property crucial for indoor localization.

SAR makes an important assumption: It assumes accurate knowledge of the position of the device at different points in time relative to some fixed origin in space (e.g. its initial location). Clearly, from Eqn. (2), in order to compute $P(\alpha)$ one must know the polar coordinates (r, ϕ_i) of the antenna positions. To get a feel for the accuracy in position required, in 802.11a/n, even a small error of 2 cm in the relative position of the moving antenna leads to an error of about 3 m in localization, when the transmitting source is 6 m away. The assumption of accurately known antenna trajectories is valid in radar systems where the speed and trajectory of the movement are finely controlled. In the following sections, we describe how this assumption poses an important challenge to our system, where users cannot be expected to move their devices along accurately known trajectories.

3. OVERVIEW OF UBICARSE

Ubicarse enables accurate indoor localization of commercially available mobile devices with no prior infrastructure or fingerprinting. At the heart of Ubicarse's device localization is the ability to perform SAR using today's off-the-shelf Wi-Fi cards and motion sensors (i.e. chips containing accelerometers, magnetometers and gyroscopes). In its traditional form, SAR assumes that channel models have a clear dependence on both the position and orientation of the antennas (see Eqn. (1) and Fig. 2). Therefore computation of an accurate multipath profile requires precise knowledge of how the antennas are located in space. However, users of Ubicarse cannot be expected to move their devices along precise trajectories. Consequently, Ubicarse must rely on the device's motion sensors to infer its position and orientation over time. Unfortunately, applying SAR using commodity motion sensors is challenging for the following reasons: (1) They are virtually unusable to measure device translation at fine granularity [22], as necessitated by SAR; (2) While the orientation they measure is accurate for short time intervals, the accuracy reduces over time due to integration drift [11].

In §4 and §5, we describe how Ubicarse resolves the above challenges to accurately perform SAR even if a user twists her device along unknown trajectories to obtain multipath profiles. In §6, we explain how Ubicarse uses these multipath profiles to accurately localize the mobile device. In §7, we show how Ubicarse integrates with vision algorithms to accurately geotag objects of interest in the environment, enabling a new class of mobile applications.

4. TRANSLATION-RESILIENT SAR

In this section, we describe how Ubicarse performs SAR even if the user moves her device along complex unknown trajectories. Specifically, we address the challenge that commodity motion sensors only provide accurate orientation information and do not provide accurate translation data that is crucial to perform SAR (see §2). Therefore, Ubicarse must perform SAR in a manner resilient to any device translation the user causes as she twists her device, yet correctly obtains the multipath signal profile.

To achieve this goal, Ubicarse leverages the MIMO capability of modern wireless cards. In particular, we consider mobile devices with just two MIMO antennas that measure the wireless channels from any single antenna of a wireless access point. As the user twists her device, the two antennas sample the wireless channel at each point in the device trajectory. The channel snapshots emulate a virtual array of antennas, where the number of virtual antennas depend on the number of channel samples. The main challenge however, is to perform SAR using the channel samples gathered from the two moving physical MIMO antennas, using only the orientation of the device and without its translation information.

Ubicarse's key idea to achieve this is as follows: Instead of performing SAR by plugging in the wireless channels measured at the antennas, Ubicarse feeds into SAR a quantity we call the *relative wireless channel* between the two physical antennas. Unlike channels on individual antennas that depend on the absolute antenna positions, the relative channel only depends on the relative position vector between the two antennas. Recall that the distance between the two antennas on a device is fixed, regardless of how the user moves her device. Thus, whenever the user translates her device, the relative position vector of both its antennas remains the same. In contrast, as the device rotates, the relative position vector of the antennas, also rotates. Hence, by plugging in relative channels into the SAR formulation, Ubicarse obtains multipath profiles with no information on device center translation.

4.1 Description of Translation Resilient SAR

We explain how Ubicarse satisfies two properties: 1) It is translation-resilient; 2) It correctly estimates SAR profiles.

Translation-Independence: We begin by presenting our solution for line-of-sight scenarios (i.e. free-space scenarios), where the signal from the transmitter arrives along one dominant path. For simplicity, we assume that both the transmitter and our device lie on a two-dimensional plane (extension to 3D is described in §4.2). We consider a transmitting source T placed at the origin and a two-antenna receiver device, as shown in Fig. 3. As the user twists the receiving device, it takes n different snapshots at the wireless signals, each at different orientations and positions. The two antennas of the device are separated by a distance of r (typically, 6 to

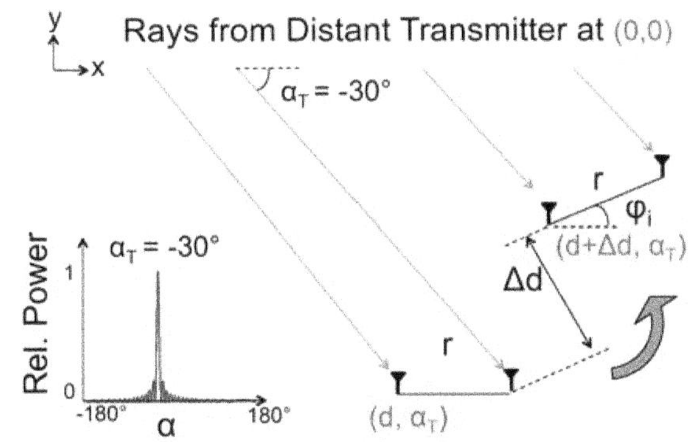

Figure 3: Ubicarse's SAR. Shows polar coordinates (in green) of the device at an offset Δx_i and Δy_i along the x and y-axis and orientation ϕ_i. Note that $\Delta d = \Delta y_i / \sin \alpha_T$. The origin of the system $(0,0)$ is at the transmitter.

20 cm).[4] Denote the initial polar coordinates of the first receive antenna as (d, α_T) relative to the transmitter where d is the distance between the transmitter and receiver. Note here that the main goal of SAR is to estimate α_T which captures the direction of the transmitting source relative to the device.

As the user moves the device, its antenna coordinates at any snapshot i (where $i = 1, \ldots, n$) depend on two quantities: 1) The translation of the device along the x and y axes at the snapshot relative to its initial location denoted by Δx_i and Δy_i. 2) The orientation of the device ϕ_i, relative to the x-axis is shown in Fig. 3. Hence, our goal is to perform SAR purely based on orientation ϕ_i, with no information on translation along the x and y axes: Δx_i, Δy_i.

Though our goal is to perform SAR without knowledge of the translation (Δx_i and Δy_i), clearly if the device is translated by a large distance with respect to the source, the angle of arrival itself (the quantity that we are interested in estimating) will change. Therefore in our system we assume that during SAR computation, the source is at a far distance compared to the movement of the tablet (a standard assumption for SAR and antenna arrays in general [37, 9]). The form of translation independence we seek in the current SAR formulation is robustness to local translations of the device center as the person twists the tablet as shown in Fig. 1. To achieve this goal, we first need to characterize the wireless channel of the source's signal measured at the antennas in each snapshot taken by the receiving device. We can apply simple geometry to write the polar coordinates of the two antennas as: $(d + \frac{\Delta y_i}{\sin \alpha_T}, \alpha_T)$ and $(d + \frac{\Delta y_i}{\sin \alpha_T} + r\cos(\alpha_T - \phi_i), \alpha_T)$ (as shown in Fig. 3) where the polar angle α_T is the same for the two antennas under our far distance assumption. From basic wireless channel models [30], we can write the wireless channels $h_{1,i}$ and $h_{2,i}$ measured at the receive antenna 1 and 2 during its ith snapshot as:

$$h_{1,i} = \frac{1}{d + \frac{\Delta y_i}{\sin \alpha_T}} e^{\frac{-j2\pi}{\lambda}(d + \frac{\Delta y_i}{\sin \alpha_T})} \approx \frac{1}{d} e^{\frac{-j2\pi}{\lambda}(d + \frac{\Delta y_i}{\sin \alpha_T})} \tag{3}$$

$$h_{2,i} = \frac{1}{d + \frac{\Delta y_i}{\sin \alpha_T} + r\cos(\alpha_T - \phi_i)} e^{\frac{-j2\pi}{\lambda}(d + \frac{\Delta y_i}{\sin \alpha_T} + r\cos(\alpha_T - \phi_i))} \tag{4}$$

$$\approx \frac{1}{d} e^{\frac{-j2\pi}{\lambda}(d + \frac{\Delta y_i}{\sin \alpha_T} + r\cos(\alpha_T - \phi_i))} \tag{5}$$

Where λ denotes the wavelength of the wireless signal. Note that the approximations hold assuming $\Delta x_i, \Delta y_i \ll d$, i.e. the source is far relative to the movement of the device, as in standard SAR [9].

[4]Ubicarse assumes that the distance between the two antennas on the device is known. This is typically available from the manufacturer's specification for a given device.

We now define the relative wireless channel at the ith snapshot $\hat{h}_i = h_{2,i} h^*_{1,i}$, where $(.)^*$ denotes the complex conjugate. Intuitively, the relative wireless channel captures the relative phase between channels of the two antennas. Mathematically, the relative channel is given by:

$$\hat{h}_i = h_{2,i} h^*_{1,i} = \frac{1}{d^2} e^{\frac{-j2\pi}{\lambda}(d + \frac{\Delta y_i}{\sin \alpha_T} + r\cos(\alpha_T - \phi_i))} e^{\frac{+j2\pi}{\lambda}(d + \frac{\Delta y_i}{\sin \alpha_T})} \tag{6}$$

$$= \frac{1}{d^2} e^{\frac{-j2\pi}{\lambda} r\cos(\alpha_T - \phi_i)} \tag{7}$$

Interestingly, note that the relative channel is independent of device translation (Δx_i and Δy_i) and is dependent only on the orientation ϕ_i. In fact, we observe that the relative wireless channel $\hat{h}_i$ is identical in form to the wireless channel of a single antenna rotating about a circle of radius r as discussed in Eqn. 1 of §2 (barring a constant factor $\frac{1}{d} e^{\frac{j2\pi d}{\lambda}}$). Intuitively, this stems from the fact that relative to the frame of reference of the first antenna, the second antenna simply appears to move around a circle.

As a result, we can simply "plug-in" the relative channels into standard circular SAR equations (Eqn. 2 from §2) to derive the multi-path profile of the transmitter's signal as follows:

$$P(\alpha) = \left| \frac{1}{n} \sum_{i=1}^{n} \hat{h}_i e^{\frac{+j2\pi}{\lambda} r\cos(\alpha - \phi_i)} \right|^2 \tag{8}$$

Hence, even if the user twists the device in arbitrary ways, causing both rotation and translation to the device, its two antennas never translate relative to each other, and can therefore emulate a circular antenna array.

We make the following important observations on computing the multipath profile as in Eqn. 8 above:

- The complexity of our algorithm is $O(n * \log(m))$ where n is the number of channel snapshots, and m is the desired resolution in angle of arrival. The complexity is logarithmic in m since one can first perform SAR at a low resolution, and repeat SAR iteratively at higher resolutions only at angles of highest power.
- Note that the wireless channels used in the above equations must capture both magnitude and the phase of the received signal. Our implementation therefore uses the channel state information (CSI) measured by a wireless card that are complex numbers, unlike received signal strength (RSS).
- The above solution can be readily extended to OFDM systems (like 802.11n), by averaging the power-profile computed for each OFDM sub-carrier.
- Our system only requires wireless channels measured from a single antenna at the 802.11 access point and two antennas at the client. If channels from more than one antenna on a Wi-Fi access point are available, the power profiles can be measured from each individual antenna, and the results averaged.

Correctness of Multipath Profile: One might wonder if the multipath profiles generated by the above technique are indeed correct. Specifically, do the power profiles indicate a sharp peak at precisely the direction of the source α_T to help localize the source? Indeed, it is easy to observe from Eqn. 7 and 8 that $P(\alpha)$ achieves a maximum value of $1/d^4$, when $\alpha = \alpha_T$, since all components $\hat{h}_i e^{\frac{+j2\pi}{\lambda} r\cos(\alpha - \phi_i)}$ add up constructively in phase, just as in a circular antenna array. As α deviates from α_T, these components gradually begin to add up destructively. Of course, the precise shape of $P(\alpha)$ over α depends on how the user physically re-orients the device, i.e. the distribution of orientations ϕ_i. In fact, one can show that if we expect the user to simply twist the device randomly, so that ϕ_i's

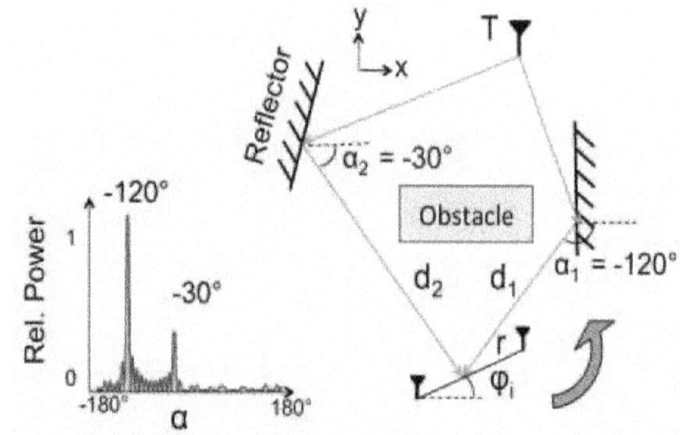

Figure 4: Multipath Scenarios. Depicts the path lengths d_k's and direction of the sources α_k's for a simple multipath scenarios. The corresponding power profile reveals peaks at the desired α_k values.

at least span a semi-circle (i.e. an angle of π)[5], the following lemma holds (Proof in Appendix A):

LEMMA 4.1. *Suppose the orientation $\phi_i \sim \mathcal{U}(\gamma - \pi/2, \gamma + \pi/2)$, at snapshot $i = 1, \ldots, n$ is uniformly distributed for some constant γ, the expected value of the multipath power profile $E[P(\alpha)]$ in line-of-sight, at each $\alpha \in [0, 2\pi]$ over the distribution of $\{\phi_1, \ldots, \phi_n\}$ is given by:*

$$E[P(\alpha)] = \frac{1}{d^4}\left[J_0(\kappa)^2 + \frac{1 - J_0(\kappa)^2}{n}\right] \quad (9)$$

$$\text{Where, } \kappa = \frac{4\pi r \sin\left(\frac{\alpha_T - \alpha}{2}\right)}{\lambda} \quad (10)$$

And $J_0(\kappa)$ is the Bessel-function of the first kind[4]. □

Notice that as the number of snapshots n increases, the first term dominates and the expected power profile resembles a squared Bessel function $J_0(\kappa)^2$. Visually, this function resembles a squared sinc-function with a sharp peak when $\kappa = 0$, i.e. $\alpha = \alpha_T$. Fig. 3 plots the expected profile for a line-of-sight source at $\alpha_T = -30°$. The profile indeed resembles the squared Bessel function with a clear peak at $\alpha = -30°$.

4.2 Extending to Multipath Scenarios

While our discussion so far has considered a source at line-of-sight (i.e. free-space scenarios), in this section, we focus on multipath scenarios (i.e. non-free space scenarios). Specifically, we show that Ubicarse continues to be resilient to translation in these scenarios, while generating correct multipath profiles, indicating the direction of the various paths of the signal.

Assume that the device receives signals from m distinct paths, of length $d_1 \ldots, d_m$, arriving along directions $\alpha_1, \ldots, \alpha_m$, as in Fig. 4. Hence, SAR's goal is to infer the set of signal directions $\alpha_1, \ldots, \alpha_m$ based on the wireless channels and device orientation.

Suppose the device captures n snapshots of the wireless channels as the user twists it. As before, we denote by $(\Delta x_i \text{and} \Delta y_i)$, the translation of the device along the x and y axes and by ϕ_i, the orientation of the device relative to its initial position and orientation during the ith snapshot. We then express the wireless channels on the two receive antennas as:

$$h_{1,i} \approx \sum_{k=1}^{m} \frac{s_k}{d_k} e^{\frac{-j2\pi}{\lambda}(d_k + \frac{\Delta y_i}{\sin\alpha_k})} \quad (11)$$

$$h_{2,i} \approx \sum_{k=1}^{m} \frac{s_k}{d_k} e^{\frac{-j2\pi}{\lambda}(d_k + \frac{\Delta y_i}{\sin\alpha_k} + r\cos(\alpha_k - \phi_i))} \quad (12)$$

Where s_k is a constant complex number that refers to the attenuation and phase shift along signal path k ($k = 1, \ldots, m$) and λ is the wavelength of the signal, as before.

We can then compute the relative wireless channels $\hat{h}_i = h_{2,i}h_{1,i}^*$ that we plan to feed into SAR as:

$$\begin{aligned}\hat{h}_i =& \sum_{k=1}^{m} \frac{s_k}{d} e^{\frac{-j2\pi}{\lambda}(d + \frac{\Delta y_i}{\sin\alpha_k} + r\cos(\alpha_k - \phi_i))} \sum_{k=1}^{m} \frac{s_k}{d} e^{\frac{+j2\pi}{\lambda}(d + \frac{\Delta y_i}{\sin\alpha_k})} \\ =& \sum_{k=1}^{m} \frac{s_k}{d_k} e^{\frac{-j2\pi}{\lambda} r\cos(\alpha_k - \phi_i)} \left[\frac{s_k}{d_k} + \sum_{l \neq k} \frac{s_l}{d_l} e^{\frac{+j2\pi}{\lambda}(\frac{\Delta y_i}{\sin\alpha_l} - \frac{\Delta y_i}{\sin\alpha_k})}\right]\end{aligned} \quad (13)$$

Notice that the first term of the relative channel in Eqn. 13 above is nearly identical to Eqn. 7 in the line-of-sight scenario, and is independent of any translation $\Delta x_i, \Delta y_i$ between channel snapshots. Unfortunately, the second term indeed depends on translation. However, two observations work in our favor: First, if the device's translation remains constant between snapshots, the second term reduces to a constant multiplier, which merely scales the profile. Second, even if the device translation varies between snapshots, any variance (i.e. noise) caused by the second term drops significantly when summing over a large number of snapshots.

Surprisingly, these observations can help us show that by performing SAR over several snapshots, Ubicarse is resilient to device translation in multipath scenarios. Further, this property holds regardless of how the device is actually translated by the user as she twists the device. Of course, we stress that this translation cannot be unbounded, and must be relatively small compared to the distance of the device from the transmitting source, a standard assumption made by SAR and antenna array systems [37, 9]. More formally, for a device that is twisted randomly by the user over an angle of π or more, the following lemma holds (Proof in Appendix B):

LEMMA 4.2. *Suppose the orientation $\phi_i \sim \mathcal{U}(\gamma - \pi/2, \gamma + \pi/2)$, at snapshot $i = 1, \ldots, n$ is uniformly at random for some constant γ, the expected value of the multipath power profile $E[P(\alpha)]$ in multipath scenarios, at each $\alpha \in [0, 2\pi]$ over the distribution of $\{\phi_1, \ldots, \phi_n\}$ is given by:*

$$E[P(\alpha)] = \left(\sum_{k=1}^{m}\left[\frac{s_k^2}{d_k^2} + E_k\right] J_0(\kappa_k)\right)^2 + \frac{1}{n} Var[\hat{h}_i e^{\frac{j2\pi r\cos(\alpha - \phi_i)}{\lambda}}]$$

$$\text{Where, } \kappa = \frac{4\pi r \sin\left(\frac{\alpha_T - \alpha}{2}\right)}{\lambda}, E_k = E\left[\sum_{l \neq k} \frac{s_k s_l}{d_k d_l} e^{\frac{j2\pi\Delta y_i(\frac{1}{\sin\alpha_l} - \frac{1}{\sin\alpha_k})}{\lambda}}\right]$$

And $J_0(\kappa)$ is the Bessel-function of the first kind[4]. □

Over a large number of snapshots n, the expected multipath profile resembles the squared sum of Bessel functions (which resemble sinc functions) with peaks corresponding to the different multipath directions scaled by their relative signal power. In other words, by inspecting the peaks of the profile $P(\alpha)$ one can infer the different multipath directions $\alpha_1, \ldots, \alpha_m$. Fig. 4 plots the profile for a non-line-of-sight source with two paths along $-30°$ and $-120°$. Notice that we indeed observe distinct peaks at each of the two angles, scaled by their relative signal strength.

[5]Our algorithm requires the user to twist the device by an angle of at least π (i.e. a semicircle). We then sample the channels gathered by the device such that the resulting distribution of orientations resembles a uniform distribution over some interval of π.

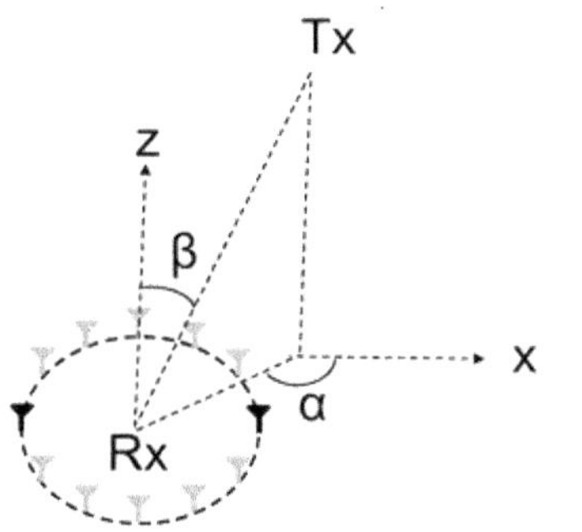

Figure 5: Generalizing to 3-D. Depicts the definition of α and β, respectively the azimuthal and polar angle from which the signal arrives.

4.3 Generalizing to Three Dimensions

Our above solution can be readily generalized to three-dimensions. Such a generalization is particularly important, since it is difficult to restrict users of Ubicarse to perfectly rotate their devices in a two dimensional plane. To better understand our solution, consider a two-antenna receiver device, as before and a signal path arriving from azimuthal angle α and polar angle β, as shown in Fig. 5. Suppose the user twists the device about a given axis.[6] Let ϕ_i be the current azimuthal angle of the second receive antenna relative to the first and θ_i denote the polar angle, during the i snapshot. From basic geometry, we can derive the difference between the path lengths to the two antennas is $r\cos(\alpha - \phi_i)\sin(\beta - \theta_i)$, where r is the separation between the two antennas. As a result, we can derive the power-profile along the direction (α, β) by slightly modifying Eqn. 8 as:

$$P(\alpha, \beta) = \left| \frac{1}{n} \sum_{i=1}^{n} \hat{h}_i e^{\frac{+j2\pi}{\lambda} r\cos(\alpha - \phi_i)\sin(\beta - \theta_i)} \right|^2 \quad (14)$$

Notice that the SAR power profile equation indeed resembles the expression for circular SAR in 3-D [7], as before. Further, note that much like standard circular antenna arrays [7], even if the user rotates the device entirely on a 2-D plane (e.g., the xy-plane), the above expression returns the angle-of-arrival in a 3-D space.

4.4 Robustness to Frequency Offsets

Recall that a wireless receiver (e.g., the user's tablet) experiences a carrier frequency offset (CFO) and sampling frequency offset (SFO) with respect to a wireless transmitter (e.g., an access point) [25]. The CFO and SFO cause an additional phase rotation, independent of the antenna movement, which unless eliminated can accumulate over time, causing errors in the SAR output. Fortunately, since the two antennas on the mobile device experience the same offsets with respect to the source, taking the relative channel eliminates that effect. Consequently, Ubicarse's SAR is robust to frequency offsets as well.

5. ACTIVE DRIFT COMPENSATION

In this section, we address the following challenge: The error in orientation reported by motion sensors accumulates gradually over time, leading to significant errors in SAR. This is because gyroscopes measure angular velocity and any systematic error in this velocity integrates over time and leads to a drift in orientation [11]. However, over time windows of a few seconds, this drift can be approximated as an unknown but linear shift in orientation [23].

[6]In principle, the user can twist the device about any axis, provided the axis of rotation is not parallel to the line joining the two antennas, i.e. so that the relative rotation of the two antennas is non-zero.

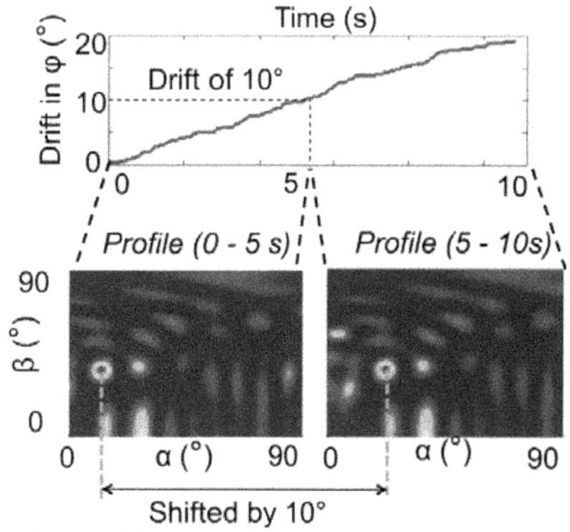

Figure 6: Drift in Orientation. The figure (above) plots the drift error over time for 10 seconds. The accumulated drift is 10° between two $5s$ intervals. The 3-D multipath profiles corresponding to these intervals (below) indicate a shift of precisely 10° (profiles zoom-in over a small range for clarity).

Ubicarse leverages this property to actively estimate and correct for drift in real-time, just as the user twists her device.

Ubicarse resolves orientation drift by making a key observation: A linear drift in orientation leads to a constant shift in SAR multipath profiles generated by Ubicarse. Specifically, suppose we perform SAR over two different time windows to obtain two multipath profiles. Let's say that the gyroscope incurred a drift of δ between these intervals. Recall from Eqn. 8 that any multipath profile $P(\alpha)$ depends on angles of the form $\alpha - \phi_i$, where ϕ_i is the orientation of the device during the ith snapshot. Consequently, if each ϕ_i is shifted by an offset δ between the two time windows, then α is also shifted by the same value δ between them. In other words, any accumulation of drift δ between the two intervals effectively results in a shift of precisely δ between the two multipath profiles. Hence, by estimating the shift δ between the two multipath profiles, we can accurately estimate, and therefore correct for the gyroscope drift between the two intervals.

To illustrate this in an example, Fig. 6 depicts the orientation in drift of 10° between two 5 second intervals during one of our experiments. We observe that the corresponding multipath profiles are also shifted by about 10°. We can then directly estimate and actively correct for this drift in real-time by applying phase correlation [10], a standard technique from computer graphics to estimate shifts between two (noisy) images by calculating their phase difference in the 2-D Fourier domain.

Finally, note that since Ubicarse performs drift correction in real-time, it does not rely on predetermined characteristics of the gyroscope and is thus general to different hardware configurations.

6. ACCURATE DEVICE LOCALIZATION

In this section, describe how Ubicarse leverages SAR multipath profiles to accurately localize the device. Ubicarse first obtains these profiles by asking the user to twist the device about its vertical axis. It then issues beacon frames to multiple neighboring access points, to elicit response frames and estimate channels from these access points. It then simultaneously performs SAR to these access points and obtains multipath profiles. In the absence of multipath, each profile contains a single peak towards the direction of the corresponding access point. Ubicarse can then apply standard triangulation [16] to localize itself relative the access points. In principle,

Ubicarse needs to perform SAR to a minimum of three surrounding access points to localize the device.

Localization under Multipath: In practice, SAR profiles may contain multiple peaks owing to multipath. As a result, there exists an inherent ambiguity in the direction of these access points relative to the device. Ubicarse addresses this challenge using the following two key observations.

First, as noted in [37], the multipath peaks in an antenna-array profile can be differentiated from the direct path peak using the following observation: The direct peak in a profile persists even as the receiving device's position is slightly perturbed, whereas multipath peaks change significantly or disappear altogether (Fig. 9 in [37]). In fact, as Ubicarse explicitly requires a user to twist the device to perform SAR, such perturbations are inherent to our system and this is a fact that we exploit.[7] Therefore, by performing SAR on two different segments of the device's trajectory (emulating two antenna arrays at slightly different locations), one can compare the resulting multipath profiles to eliminate peaks that do not persist between these profiles.

Second, often devices are surrounded by more than three access points. This leads to an over-constrained optimization problem for triangulation, which can be formulated as a least-square fitting problem [16]. Notice that the peaks corresponding to the direct path to each of many different access points agree on a unique location for the device, and therefore lead to a good fit. In contrast, multipath peaks of the access points indicate conflicting locations for the device leading to poor fits. Therefore, by selecting the set of peaks to access points that achieve the best fit in the optimization problem (i.e. agree the most geometrically), Ubicarse can identify the set of direct paths to these access points.

Obtaining Global Device Orientation: One of the key benefits of Ubicarse is the ability to not just find the device's global position, but also its global orientation, relative to the access points' frame of reference. Notice that global orientation is not available from the device's gyroscope, which only measures angular velocity, and therefore can only be used to find relative orientation between two time intervals.[8] The key reason Ubicarse can readily estimate device orientation is that it computes the angle-of-arrival of signals from the access points. In particular, Ubicarse knows the angle of the access point, relative to the axis of its own body . But after performing localization, Ubicarse also knows the direction of this access point relative to the global x-axis. Hence, by simply subtracting the two angles, Ubicarse can compute its orientation ψ relative to the world's x-axis.

7. APPLICATION TO OBJECT GEOTAGGING

In this section, we show how Ubicarse's accurate indoor localization of mobile devices opens the door to a new class of applications: precision geotagging of indoor objects with no RF source attached to them. This would enable users to catalog and share the location of objects of interest they observe around them, i.e., products in a warehouse or artifacts in a museum. To enable this application, we leverage the fact that in addition to Wi-Fi chips and gyroscopes, most wireless devices also have cameras on them. Today, vision toolkits can be applied to overlapping photos taken from these cameras to produce 3D pointclouds, or *relative* 3D positions, for imaged objects [29].

[7]Notably however, the direct path peak does experience a shift due to drift as discussed in §5, although the peak's magnitude remains the same, and its shift is consistent.

[8]While the device's compass can be used to compute global orientation, such compasses are fairly inaccurate [14] and easily misled by any surrounding magnetic fields.

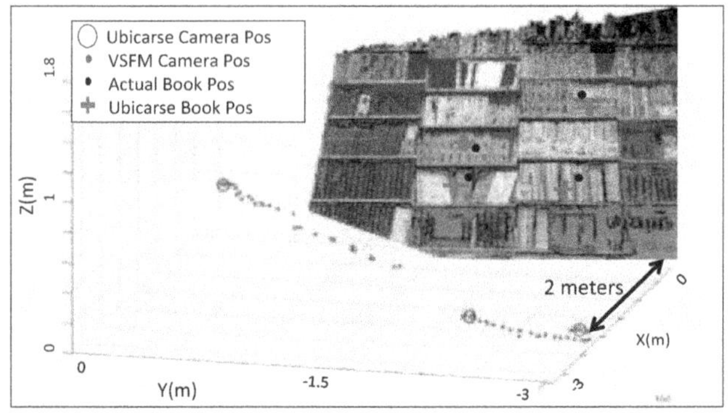

Figure 7: Point cloud of library shelving and VSFM reconstruction with camera positions and anchored camera positions. Anchored camera positions are those camera positions with both Ubicarse localization coordinates in the global frame and relative coordinates in the coordinate frame of the 3D reconstruction. These anchor points are used in Equation (15) to find a suitable transform to a the global frame.

In particular, these vision toolkits use multiple snapshots taken of a single scene from different vantage points in order to reconstruct the 3D positions of objects in the image as a point cloud. While these tools are impressively accurate at inferring relative distances and orientations in the local coordinate frame of the camera, they cannot provide information on the positions of the camera or photographed objects in the *global* frame that a user cares about. For example, a vision-based reconstruction can accurately determine that the biology magazine stack is one foot away from the physics magazine stack, but cannot determine that these magazine stacks are located in shelf-5 of the mezzanine level room in the NY public library. In contrast, Ubicarse's core ability is that it can determine the global position of the device's camera at a given point in time. Hence we can synergize the fine-grained relative distances of object-to-camera computed by the vision toolkit, with the accurate global camera-position provided by Ubicarse. This allows for a joint optimization problem that provides the global position of the objects of interest. Surprisingly, we show that this joint optimization has an interesting side-effect: one can further refine Ubicarse's device localization by using the relative camera positions between the different snapshots, that are output by the vision toolkit. This leads to an integrated system that capitalizes upon the best of both technologies for device and object localization.

Vision Algorithms: To better understand how object localization works, we provide a briefly introduce vision algorithms for 3-D imaging. The goal of these algorithms is to read a set of 2-D images of the object snapped by the device's camera from multiple perspectives to obtain two outputs:

- *3-D reconstruction of the object*: obtained in the frame of reference of the device camera. This reconstruction is a 3-D point cloud (Fig. 7), containing the (x, y, z) coordinates of points on the object's surface in a 3-D frame of reference whose origin is at the camera's initial position and axes along its initial orientation.
- *Relative Camera Positions and Orientation*: of the vantage points where the 2-D images were taken, defined relative to the camera's initial position and orientation.

At a high level, vision algorithms obtain these quantities in three phases: First, they identify salient features [2] (e.g. corners or distinctive textures) in each of the images. Next, these features are used to identify positions of the same object between these images.

Finally, they apply advanced algorithms such as [29], which uses the distance of the same features to the different camera positions from where the images were taken, to infer relative object positions and camera positions.

Accurate Object Localization: Once a 3D pointcloud of the imaged objects is constructed via the vision algorithm, a suitable transformation must be found in order to map the object locations into the (global) reference frame of the environment. To do this, we employ Ubicarse's translation-resilient localization in N different positions and orientations where the snapshots were taken (assuming N is at least three). The N camera positions can now serve as anchor points, points for which we have both global positions $\{x_{g_1}, \ldots, x_{g_N}\}$ provided by Ubicarse, and relative positions, $\{x_{p_1}, \ldots, x_{p_N}\}$ in the coordinate frame of the reconstructed point cloud. A relationship (or transformation) between the two coordinate systems can be found via the following optimization problem that can readily be solved for the unknown transformation (rotation R and translation t) that minimizes the following error in fit (see Algorithm 1):

$$\min_{R,t} \sum_{i=1}^{N} ||x_{g_i} - (Rx_{p_i} + t)||^2 \tag{15}$$

In general the more anchor points you have, the more accurately you can find the transformation. [9] The rotation R and translation t are now the key relationship between the point cloud and global coordinate frames and in particular, it can be applied to any object in the point cloud in order to find the global position of that object.

Refining Device Localization: Finally, we note that the above joint optimization has an interesting side-effect: Ubicarse can leverage the relative camera locations output by vision algorithms to greatly refine its own device localization. Specifically, visual algorithms excel at finding relative camera locations, particularly when they observe a rich set features at pixel resolution. Therefore, by applying the transformation to the camera positions returned by VSFM we now have two sets of position estimates for the camera, both in the global reference frame. In this way, one can accurately compensate for relative errors in Ubicarse's indoor positioning. Indeed, our results in §9.5 show that such an optimization greatly improves median localization accuracy by as much as 86% as compared to just using Ubicarse alone.

Algorithm 1 Object Geo-tagging: Finding the transformation, rotation R and translation t, between local and global coordinates

```
function GETTRANSFORM(X_g, X_p)
    ▷ X_g = {x_g1, ..., x_gN}: Set of N positions in global frame
    ▷ X_p = {x_p1, ..., x_pN}: Set of N positions in local camera frame
    C = Σ_{i=1}^{N} (x_gi − mean(X_g))(x_pi − mean(X_p))*
    ▷ Where (.)*: conjugate transpose, and mean(.): average of elements
    [U, S, V] = svd(C)          ▷ Perform SVD of covariance matrix C
    R = VU*                     ▷ Rotation Matrix
    t = mean(X_p) − R × mean(X_g)   ▷ Translation Vector
    return R, t
end function
```

8. IMPLEMENTATION AND EVALUATION

We implemented Ubicarse on a HP SplitX2 Tablet running Ubuntu Linux equipped with Intel 5300 wireless cards and a Yei Technology motion sensor (i.e. an accelerometer, gyroscope and compass). We build on the 802.11 CSI tool [13] to obtain the wireless channels on the tablet. We implement Ubicarse's translation resilient SAR completely in software (C++ and Matlab). For each experiment, we allow users to twist their devices randomly along its vertical axis, spanning a wide range of orientations. We configure the tablet to transmit beacon packets (10 times per second) to elicit responses from nearby access points and measure their channels.[10] We then combine this with gyroscope readings from the motion sensor to perform SAR *simultaneously* to all access points, as the user twists the device.

[9] In practice, the above optimization also needs to account for camera calibration and scaling, whose details we omit for brevity.

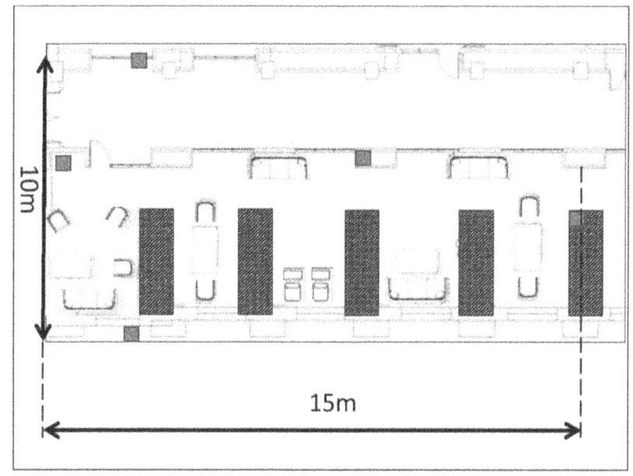

Figure 8: Library floorplan and testbed: APs are red squares; book shelves are shown as hashed rectangles.

We implement Ubicarse's object localization by integrating it with the VisualSFM (VSFM) toolkit [35] for 3-D reconstruction of objects. We use the tablet's built-in 5.7 Megapixel camera to take images of objects of interest.

We conducted our experiment in a university library, with books arranged in multiple shelves and racks that emulate the complex multipath characteristics of large warehouses and departmental stores, where indoor localization has been of particular interest, as shown in Fig. 8. We leverage five unmodified 802.11n access points in and around the library, as shown by red squares in Fig. 8 to perform device localization and vary the tablet's location between several randomly chosen locations. The access points are configured to the 5 GHz Wi-Fi frequency band. We obtain the locations of access points and tablet centers to sub-centimeter accuracy in a global coordinate frame through direct measurements and using architectural drawings of the library. To perform object localization, we capture images from multiple perspectives of different randomly chosen books in the library. We then apply a joint optimization using VSFM's reconstructed 3D point cloud and Ubicarse's device localization to locate the object.

Baseline: We compare Ubicarse against an angle-of-arrival scheme that treats the two antennas on the device as a 2-antenna array. We chose this baseline, since it uses only 2-antennas like our system, does not require specialized infrastructure or additional calibration input unlike other schemes, leading to a fair comparison.

9. RESULTS

We present four categories of results to evaluate Ubicarse: 1) Validating Translation Resilience of Ubicarse's SAR for different trajectories. 2) Computing Angle of Arrival in 3-D space. 3) Localizing devices in 3-D. 4) Geotagging Objects of Interest.

[10] The results in this paper sample the wireless channels for a minimum of 25-30 packets over a semi-circular arc of rotation.

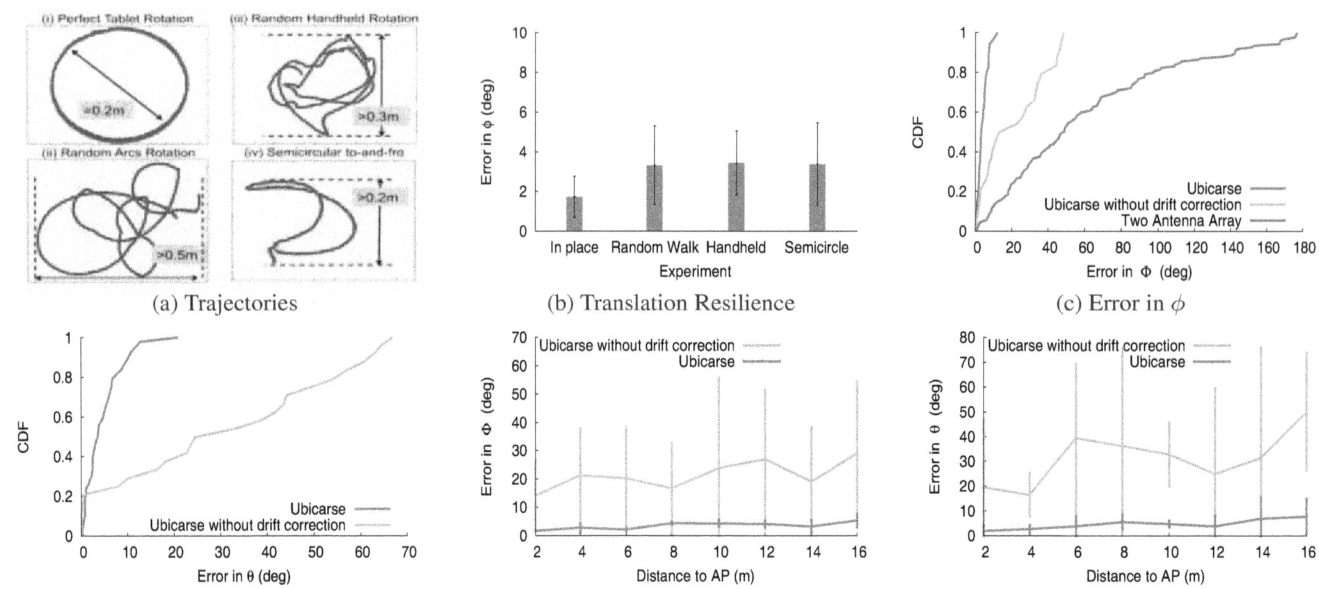

(a) Trajectories
(b) Translation Resilience
(c) Error in ϕ
(d) Error in θ
(e) Error in ϕ vs. distance
(f) Error in θ vs. distance

Figure 9: (a) Plots the different trajectories of antenna centers (b) Translation resilience of SAR: Plots mean and Standard deviation of error in azimuthal angle for different trajectories. (c)-(d) CDF of error in Angle of arrival (ϕ and θ), for Ubicarse, Ubicarse without drift correction and 2-Antenna Array. (e)-(f) Error in azimuthal, polar angle versus distance from the access point.

9.1 Translation Resilient SAR

In this experiment, we demonstrate that Ubicarse's new formulation of SAR is resilient to device translation, as described in §4. Specifically, we consider different device trajectories, including random motion of the antenna's center on the order of half a meter.

Method: We perform our experiments in a mm-precision motion capture room [1] where the mobile device was tagged with infrared markers to accurately track the motion of the antenna centers for the purpose of evaluation. SAR was computed entirely using one YEI technologies gyroscope mounted on the tablet and channel measurements acquired from the Wi-Fi card. A single transmitting source was present and the experiment was conducted at distances of 2m to 12m from the source across multiple line-of-sight locations (we consider non-line-of-sight in §9.2).

We moved the tablet in four different types of trajectories: (1) In-place rotation; (2) 2D random trajectory within 0.5 m diameter; (3) A random handheld 3D twisting motion (i.e. including variations in polar angles) up to 0.3 m in diameter (4) A handheld semi-circular to-and-fro twist. For the first two trajectories, we mount the device on a roomba robot for stable trajectories on a 2-D plane.

Fig. 9(a) demonstrates actual trajectory traces from our experiments where these traces are representative of each of the four classes of trajectories described above.

Results: Our results in Figure 9(b) show a mean error of 3.3° for the random 2-D trajectory, 3.4° even as the center of the antennas is translated randomly by the user in three dimensional space and 3.3° if the user traces a simple semi-circular to-and-fro twist. Our results demonstrate that Ubicarse's translation resilient SAR correctly identifies the angle of arrival for the two cases to within 1.6°, 1.7° and 1.6° respectively on average as compared to the ideal case of rotation in place.

9.2 Angle of Arrival Estimation on a Tablet

We measure the accuracy of angle-of-arrival estimation in both the azimuthal angle (ϕ) and polar angle (θ) obtained over each handheld twist of the device in line-of-sight (LOS) and non-line-of-sight (NLOS) settings.

Method: We conduct our experiment in the university library as in §8. We place the device at different distances from the access points. In NLOS settings, Ubicarse identifies the direct path using the methods in §6. We compare our results against two important benchmarks: 1) A 2-antenna array composed of the two antennas on the device directly, as opposed to performing SAR. 2) Ubicarse without the gyroscope drift compensation presented in §5.

Results: Fig. 9(c)-(d) shows that our method achieves a median of accuracy of 3.2° in the azimuthal orientation of the device and 3.6° in polar angle. We observe that gyroscope drift can cause angle inaccuracies of more than 18° in ϕ (29° in θ) and as large as 48° in ϕ (67° in θ) if left uncompensated. As a result, Ubicarse's drift compensation in §5 plays an important role in achieving high accuracy. Fig. 9(c) also shows that the 2-antenna array has a poor median error of 49° in azimuthal angle owing to the lack of resolution from using only two antennas. Note that Figure 9(d) does not compare with the two antenna benchmark since two antennas alone are insufficient to obtain 3-D information [24].

Fig. 9(e)-(f) depicts the error in ϕ and θ respectively, against the distance of the device to the wireless access point. We observe that the error in these angles increases only marginally across distances ranging from $2m$ to $16m$.

9.3 Tablet Localization

In this experiment, we evaluate Ubicarse's accuracy in device localization in the university library setting.

Method: We gather aggregate results on device localization by in twenty five randomly chosen locations where users twist a Ubicarse enabled tablet in the university library setting. Ubicarse's localization was performed to find relative position of the device with respect to commodity access points whose locations were known with respect to the library floor plan. For device and object localization we present results in the three-dimensional Euclidean space as well as global orientation (in the X-Y plane) as given by the ψ angle

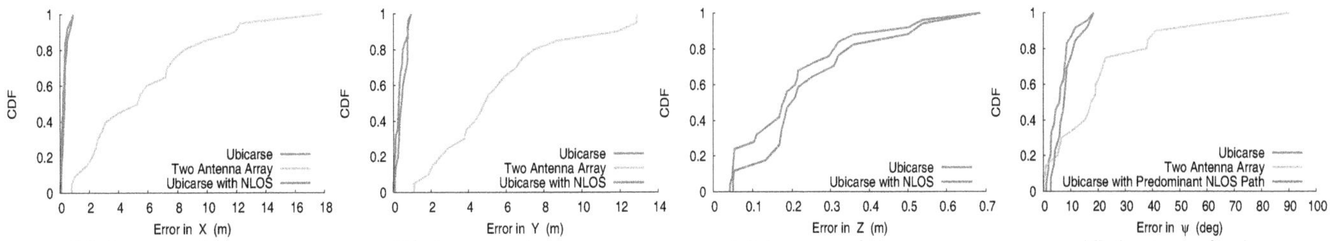

(a) Accuracy in x (b) Accuracy in y (c) Accuracy in z (d) Accuracy in ψ

Figure 10: Tablet Localization: Plots CDF of error in device localization.

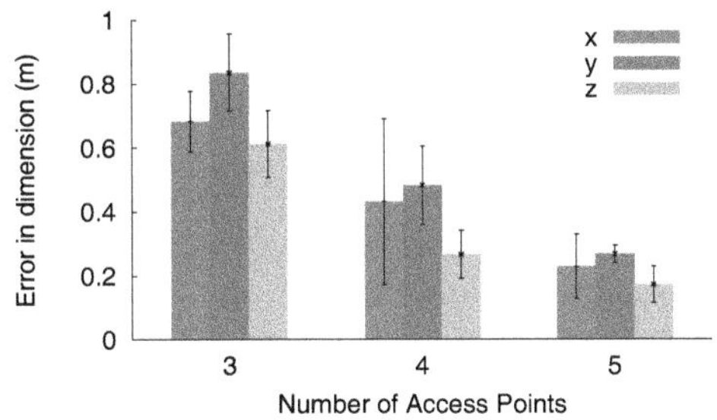

Figure 11: Ubicarse's Device Localization Accuracy measured against the number of wireless access points.

described in §6.[11] These experiments were conducted both in line-of-sight (LOS) and non-line-of-sight (NLOS) settings during peak library hours with pedestrian foot traffic. In particular, we classify locations as non-line-of-sight (NLOS) only when the predominant (highest power) peak in the multipath profile is not the direct path to at least one neighboring AP. Our localization technique explicitly handles multipath as described in section 6.

Results: Our results in Fig. 10 for localization using five surrounding access points demonstrate a median device localization error of 39 cm, where along each dimension we demonstrate a median error of 22 cm in x, 28 cm in y, and 18 cm in z and 6.09° in global device orientation (ψ). Furthermore we show that Ubicarse still performs well in NLOS, incurring a small additional median error of 10 cm in x, 18 cm in y, and 2 cm in z and 7.7° in ψ as compared to the LOS case. Thus, Ubicarse achieves its goal of accurate localization without requiring either new infrastructure or signal fingerprinting.

Fig. 11 plots Ubicarse's error in localization along x, y and z measured against the number of randomly chosen access points used to triangulate the location of the device. We notice that the error in localization reduces with increasing number of surrounding access points. This is because, as described in §6, computing multipath profiles to an increasing number of surrounding access points, can help mitigate ambiguity due to multipath. Further, redundant measurements from over three APs reduces the noise in localization.

9.4 Object Geotagging

In this experiment, we evaluate Ubicarse's object geotagging capabilities (See §7) to localize arbitrarily chosen books on a bookshelf in the library setting.

Method: We conduct our experiments in a library setting with shelving that houses many books, journals, and magazines, a picture of which can be found in Figure 7. This implementation emulates similar applications in a warehouse, department store, or other such settings where a person can catalog objects of interest. In particular we show that there is a distinct advantage to localizing far away objects more accurately than simply using the camera's location as a geotag. We compare the object localization we achieve using Ubicarse plus VSFM against the accuracy of using the camera's location directly as a position tag for the book.

Results: Fig. 12(a)-(c) shows that the method of Ubicarse plus VSFM attains a median error in distance of 17 cm, where along each dimension we find an error of 5 cm in x, 15 cm in y and 4 cm in z for localization accuracy of books on library bookshelves whose distance from the camera varies from 1 to 3 m. Therefore simply using the camera's position as a geotag for the books would result in up to 3 m of inaccuracy.

Surprisingly, a comparison of Figures 12 and 10 reveals that *a greater accuracy in object localization* can be obtained by a combination of Ubicarse with VSFM than using either method standalone. This is because these two methods are highly complimentary and a thoughtful integration unlocks an effective method for localization *refinement* (see §7). We provide further results on this concept in the next section.

9.5 Refined Tablet Localization using Vision

The previous section suggests that a method to achieve a fine-scaled object position fix is to integrate an accurate device localization method, Ubicarse, with visual toolkits like VSFM. In this experiment, we study if this improvement applies both ways, i.e. if device localization can be refined using inputs from vision toolkits.

Method: Our method for refinement of camera positions derives from the discussion in §7. We transform the camera locations discovered by VSFM into the global coordinate system, using Algorithm 1. We then output the transformed camera locations as the result of Ubicarse's localization.

Results: Fig. 12(d) shows that a Ubicarse plus VSFM integration achieves a significant improvement in localization performance with a median of 15 cm error from ground truth. We report a median improvement in localization accuracy of 66 % in X, 16% in Y and 86% in the Z dimension. Therefore, integration of Ubicarse with vision algorithms also serves to improve device localization.

10. RELATED WORK

Related work falls under two broad categories:

Indoor RF Localization: RF localization have had three main approaches for indoor localization: The first require deploying specialized infrastructure to perform accurate indoor localization, e.g. acoustic [21, 19], RFIDs [33, 32], specialized access points [15], and antenna arrays [37]. The second mandates signal fingerprinting [3, 27, 39] either in a training phase or via crowdsourcing [26, 38, 18]. The third advocate modeling the wireless signal instead of

[11] In principle, Ubicarse can be used to find orientations along other planes as well. We omit these results for brevity.

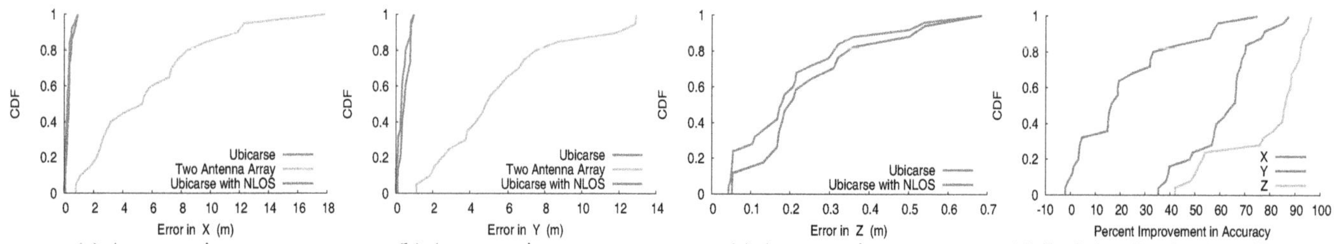

(a) Accuracy in x (b) Accuracy in y (c) Accuracy in z (d) Refining Device Localization

Figure 12: (a)-(c) **Object Localization**: Plots CDF of error in object geotagging. (d) Demonstrates refinement of Device localization using object geo-tagging

measurements [17, 5, 12], but at the expense of accuracy. In contrast to these systems, Ubicarse obviates the need for new infrastructure or fingerprinting to achieve tens of centimeter of accuracy by emulating large antenna arrays using only commodity mobile devices.

Ubicarse builds on past work in Synthetic Aperture Radar (SAR) that leverage precise mechanically controlled antenna movements or advanced motion sensing equipment for radar imaging [9] and RFID localization [33, 32]. Unlike these systems, Ubicarse provides a new formulation of SAR that is translation resilient, making it suitable for mobile devices held by users.

Several RF localization papers use mobile motion sensors as hints for localization, either coupled with Wi-Fi signal strength for fingerprinting [36, 3, 26] or with GPS measurements [6, 31]. Instead, Ubicarse uses the device's gyroscope only to measure its relative orientation to help emulate antenna arrays and achieves significantly improved accuracy.

Object Geo-tagging: There has been much work in computer vision on stereo-imaging and 3D-reconstruction to localize objects relative to known camera locations or to find relative locations of different objects in the same scene [2, 29]. Ubicarse builds on this work, coupled with RF localization, to obtain object locations in the global frame.

Several solutions for indoor device and object localization have been proposed in the literature that use specialized hardware, e.g. depth cameras [20] or odometry/laser-based simultaneous localization and mapping [8], which are unavailable for today's mobile devices, unlike Ubicarse.

11. CONCLUSION AND FUTURE WORK

We presented Ubicarse, an indoor localization system to achieves tens of centimeters of accuracy on commodity mobile devices, without requiring specialized infrastructure or fingerprinting. Ubicarse's provides a new formulation of SAR that allows mobile devices to emulate an antenna array; where this formulation is tolerant to unknown translation of the antenna center of up to half a meter. We implement Ubicarse on a commodity tablet and demonstrate tens of centimeter accuracy in both device localization and object geotagging in complex indoor settings. We believe evaluating our system on a wide-range of mobile devices, particularly smartphones, is an important task for future work.

Acknowledgments: We thank Guy Rosman for his invaluable help in the geo-tagging application. We thank Omid Abari, Fadel Adib, Haitham Hassanieh, Ezz Hamed, Jue Wang, Arthur Berger, Jouya Jadidian, Zack Kabelac, Hariharan Rahul, Lixin Shi, Deepak Vasisht, and our reviewers for their insightful comments. This research is funded by NSF, ONR and the MAST project under ARL Grant W911NF-08-2-0004. We thank members of the MIT Center for Wireless Networks and Mobile Computing: Amazon, Cisco, Google, Intel, Mediatek, Microsoft, ST Microelectronics, and Telefonica for their interest and general support.

12. REFERENCES

[1] VICON T-Series. http://www.vicon.com. VICON.
[2] M. Agrawal and K. Konolige. Real-time localization in outdoor environments using stereo vision and inexpensive gps. ICPR. 2006.
[3] M. Azizyan, I. Constandache, and R. Roy Choudhury. Surroundsense: Mobile phone localization via ambience fingerprinting. MobiCom, 2009.
[4] F. Bowman. *Introduction to Bessel Functions*. Dover Publications, 2012.
[5] K. Chintalapudi, A. Padmanabha Iyer, and V. N. Padmanabhan. Indoor localization without the pain. MobiCom, 2010.
[6] I. Constandache, R. Roy, and C. I. Rhee. Compacc: Using mobile phone compasses and accelerometers for localization. In *In INFOCOM*, 2010.
[7] R. Fenby. Limitations on directional patterns of phase-compensated circular arrays. *REE*, 1965.
[8] B. Ferris et al. WiFi-SLAM using gaussian process latent variable models. IJCAI, 2007.
[9] P. J. Fitch. *Synthetic Aperture Radar*. Springer, 1988.
[10] H. Foroosh, J. Zerubia, and M. Berthod. Extension of phase correlation to subpixel registration. *Image Processing, IEEE Transactions on*, 2002.
[11] J. Georgy et al. Modeling the stochastic drift of a mems-based gyroscope in gyro/odometer/gps integrated navigation. *IEEE ITS*, 2010.
[12] A. Goswami, L. Ortiz, and S. Das. Wigem: A learning-based approach for indoor localization. CoNEXT, 2011.
[13] D. Halperin, W. Hu, A. Sheth, and D. Wetherall. Tool release: Gathering 802.11n traces with channel state information. *ACM SIGCOMM CCR*, 2011.
[14] M. Hölzl, R. Neumeier, and G. Ostermayer. Analysis of compass sensor accuracy on several mobile devices in an industrial environment. In *EUROCAST*. 2013.
[15] K. Joshi, S. Hong, and S. Katti. PinPoint: Localizing Interfering Radios. NSDI, 2013.
[16] Z. Li et al. Robust statistical methods for wireless localization in sensor networks. In *IPSN*, 2005.
[17] H. Lim, L.-C. Kung, J. C. Hou, and H. Luo. Zero-configuration indoor localization over 802.11 wireless infrastructure. *IEEE Wirel. Netw.*, 2010.
[18] H. Liu, Y. Gan, J. Yang, S. Sidhom, Y. Wang, Y. Chen, and F. Ye. Push the limit of WiFi based localization for smartphones. Mobicom, 2012.
[19] K. Liu et al. Guoguo: Enabling fine-grained indoor localization via smartphone. MobiSys, 2013.
[20] Microsoft. Kinect. http://www.kinect.com.
[21] R. Nandakumar et al. Centaur: Locating devices in an office environment. Mobicom, 2012.

[22] M. Niessner, A. Dai, and M. Fisher. Combining Inertial Navigation and ICP for Real-time 3D Surface Reconstruction. Eurographics, 2014.
[23] H. Nyqvist et al. A high-performance tracking system based on camera and IMU. In *FUSION*, 2013.
[24] S. J. Orfanidis. Electromagnetic waves and antennas. http://www.ece.rutgers.edu/ orfanidi/ewa/.
[25] H. Rahul et al. Jmb: Scaling wireless capacity with user demand. In *SIGCOMM*, 2012.
[26] A. Rai, K. K. Chintalapudi, V. N. Padmanabhan, and R. Sen. Zee: Zero-effort crowdsourcing for indoor localization. Mobicom, 2012.
[27] S. Sen, B. Radunovic, R. R. Choudhury, and T. Minka. You are facing the mona lisa: Spot localization using phy layer information. MobiSys, 2012.
[28] S. P. Tarzia, P. A. Dinda, R. P. Dick, and G. Memik. Indoor localization without infrastructure using the acoustic background spectrum. MobiSys, 2011.
[29] B. Triggs et al. Bundle adjustment – a modern synthesis. In *Vision Algorithms Theory/Practice*, 2000.
[30] D. Tse and P. Vishwanath. *Fundamentals of Wireless Communications*. Cambridge University Press, 2005.
[31] H. Wang, S. Sen, A. Elgohary, M. Farid, M. Youssef, and R. R. Choudhury. No need to war-drive: Unsupervised indoor localization. MobiSys, 2012.
[32] J. Wang, F. Adib, R. Knepper, D. Katabi, and D. Rus. RF-compass: Robot object manipulation using rfids. MobiCom, 2013.
[33] J. Wang and D. Katabi. Dude, where's my card?: RFID positioning that works with multipath and non-line of sight. SIGCOMM, 2013.
[34] WiGle. Database. `https://wigle.net`.
[35] C. Wu. VisualSFM : A Visual Structure from Motion System. `http://ccwu.me/vsfm/`.
[36] C. Wu, Z. Yang, Y. Liu, and W. Xi. Wireless indoor localization without site survey. In *INFOCOM*, 2012.
[37] J. Xiong and K. Jamieson. Arraytrack: A fine-grained indoor location system. NSDI, 2013.
[38] Z. Yang, C. Wu, and Y. Liu. Locating in fingerprint space: Wireless indoor localization with little human intervention. Mobicom, 2012.
[39] M. Youssef and A. Agrawala. The Horus WLAN location determination system. MobiSys, 2005.

APPENDIX

A. Proof of Lemma 4.1

In this section, we derive the expected value of SAR multi-path power profiles for line-of-sight scenarios as stated in Lemma 4.1. We consider the scenario in Fig. 3, where a transmitting source T is in line-of-sight relative to a two-antenna receiver device. By substituting the relative wireless channel from Eqn. 7 into the multipath power profile from Eqn. 8, and simplifying terms we get:

$$\hat{h}_i = h_{2,i}h_{1,i}^* = \frac{1}{d^2}e^{\frac{-j2\pi r cos(\alpha_T - \phi_i)}{\lambda}} \tag{16}$$

Thus, the multi-path power profile (See Eqn. 8) is:

$$P(\alpha) = \frac{1}{d^4}\left|\frac{1}{n}\sum_{i=1}^{n} e^{-j\kappa \sin\psi_i}\right|^2 = \frac{1}{d^4}\left|\frac{1}{n}\sum_{i=1}^{n} e_i\right|^2 \tag{17}$$

Where $\kappa = \frac{4\pi r \sin\left(\frac{\alpha_T - \alpha}{2}\right)}{\lambda}$, is independent of device orientation, $\psi_i = \phi_i - \frac{\alpha_T + \alpha}{2}$ and $e_i = e^{-j\kappa \sin\psi_i}$.

At this point, our goal is to evaluate the expected value of $P(\alpha)$ over the device orientation between snapshots. To do this, let us consider the case where the snapshots are taken at random device orientations spanning an angle of π (i.e. a semi-circle) so that $\phi_i \sim \mathcal{U}(\gamma - \pi/2, \gamma + \pi/2)$ is chosen uniformly at random. Since γ depends on ϕ_0, we choose ϕ_0 such that, $\psi_i \sim \mathcal{U}(-\pi/2, \pi/2)$ is also a uniformly distributed random variable. Under these assumptions, let us look at the distribution of the quantity $e_i = e^{-j\kappa sin\psi_i}$. Specifically, the mean and variance of e_i is given by $E[e_i] = \frac{1}{\pi}\int_{-\pi/2}^{\pi/2} e^{-j\kappa sin\psi} d\psi = J_0(\kappa)$ and $\text{Var}[e_i] = E[|e_i|^2] - |E[e_i]|^2 = 1 - J_0(\kappa)^2$ respectively, where $J_0(\cdot)$ is the well-known Bessel-function of the first kind[4].

Next, we look at $\frac{1}{n}\sum_{i=1}^{n} e_i$. Applying central limit theorem for large n, this quantity is normally distributed with mean $J_0(\kappa)$ and variance $\frac{1-J_0(\kappa)^2}{n}$. Specifically, the variance of this distribution:

$$\text{Var}\left[\frac{1}{n}\sum_{i=1}^{n} e_i\right] = E\left[\left|\frac{1}{n}\sum_{i=1}^{n} e_i\right|^2\right] - \left|E\left[\frac{1}{n}\sum_{i=1}^{n} e_i\right]\right|^2$$

$$\frac{1 - J_0(\kappa)^2}{n} = d^4 E[P(\alpha)] - J_0(\kappa)^2$$

$$\tilde{P}(\alpha) = E[P(\alpha)] = \frac{1}{d^4}\left[J_0(\kappa)^2 + \frac{1 - J_0(\kappa)^2}{n}\right]$$

Which desired expected SAR profile, as in Lemma 4.1. □

B. Proof of Lemma 4.2

We derive the expected SAR power profiles in multipath scenarios as in Lemma 4.2. Recall the relative wireless channel between two antennas of the receiver at snapshot i is given by Eqn. 13, such that the multipath profile $P(\alpha)$, depends on the sum of terms of the form $g_i = \hat{h}_i e^{\frac{j2\pi r \cos(\alpha - \phi_i)}{\lambda}}$ (Eqn. 8). Each term is:

$$g_i = \sum_{k=1}^{m} D_k e^{\frac{-j2\pi}{\lambda} r(\cos(\alpha_k - \phi_i) - \cos(\alpha - \phi_i))} = \sum_{k=1}^{m} D_k e^{-j\kappa_k \sin\psi_{i,k}}$$

Where similar to Appendix A, $\kappa_k = \frac{4\pi r \sin\left(\frac{\alpha_k - \alpha}{2}\right)}{\lambda}$ and $D_k = \frac{s_k}{d_k}\left[\frac{s_k}{d_k} + \sum_{l\neq k}\frac{s_l}{d_l} e^{\frac{+j2\pi}{\lambda}\left(\frac{\Delta y_i}{\sin\alpha_l} - \frac{\Delta y_i}{\sin\alpha_k}\right)}\right]$, depend only on translation, while $\psi_{i,k} = \phi_i - \frac{\alpha_k + \alpha}{2}$ depends only on orientation. As a result, D_k and $e^{-j\kappa_k \sin\psi_{i,k}}$ are independent, and we can write: the expectation $E[g_i] = \sum_{k=1}^{m} E[D_k]E[e^{-j\kappa_k \sin\psi_{i,k}}] = \sum_{k=1}^{m}\left[\frac{s_k^2}{d_k^2} + E_k\right] J_0(\kappa_k)$, assuming that ϕ_i's are chosen uniformly at random. Here we denote $E_k = E\left[\sum_{l\neq k}\frac{s_k s_l}{d_k d_l} e^{\frac{j2\pi\Delta y_i\left(\frac{1}{\sin\alpha_l} - \frac{1}{\sin\alpha_k}\right)}{\lambda}}\right]$.

Finally, let us look at the summation $\frac{1}{n}\sum_{i=1}^{n} g_i$. Applying central limit theorem for large n, this quantity is normally distributed with mean $\sum_{k=1}^{m}\left[\frac{s_k^2}{d_k^2} + E_k\right] J_0(\kappa_k)$ and variance $\frac{Var[g_i]}{n}$. Specifically, the variance of this distribution is:

$$\text{Var}\left[\frac{1}{n}\sum_{i=1}^{n} g_i\right] = E\left[\left|\frac{1}{n}\sum_{i=1}^{n} g_i\right|^2\right] - \left|E\left[\frac{1}{n}\sum_{i=1}^{n} g_i\right]\right|^2$$

$$E[P(\alpha)] = \left(\sum_{k=1}^{m}\left[\frac{s_k^2}{d_k^2} + E_k\right] J_0(\kappa_k)\right)^2 + \frac{1}{n}\text{Var}[\hat{h}_i.e^{\frac{j2\pi r \cos(\alpha - \phi_i)}{\lambda}}]$$

Which desired expected SAR profile, as in Lemma 4.2. □

Magnetic MIMO:
How To Charge Your Phone in Your Pocket

Jouya Jadidian Dina Katabi
Massachusetts Institute of Technology
{jouya, dk}@mit.edu

ABSTRACT

This paper bridges wireless communication with wireless power transfer. It shows that mobile phones can be charged remotely, while in the user's pocket by applying the concept of MIMO beamforming. However, unlike MIMO beamforming in communication systems which targets the radiated field, we transfer power by beamforming the non-radiated magnetic field and steering it toward the phone. We design MagMIMO, a new system for wireless charging of cell phones and portable devices. MagMIMO consumes as much power as existing solutions, yet it can charge a phone remotely without being removed from the user's pocket. Furthermore, the phone need not face the charging pad, and can charge independently of its orientation. We have built MagMIMO and demonstrated its ability to charge the iPhone and other smart phones, while in the user's pocket.

Categories and Subject Descriptors C.2.2 [**Computer Systems Organization**]: Computer-Communications Networks

Keywords Wireless Power Transfer, MIMO, Magnetic Resonance, Energy, Beamforming, Mobile and Wearable Devices

1. INTRODUCTION

Wireless power transfer promises to revolutionize mobile computing and enable smart phones and portable devices to be permanently unplugged. Yet, while wireless chargers are now available for many mobile phones, their utility is quite limited. We still need to remember to regularly charge our mobile phones; only instead of inserting the cable every time, we can now put the phone on a charging pad. To many of us, this is not the wireless charging we hoped for. We would like to have our cell phones charged in our pockets, and never again worry about forgetting to charge the phone.

Past work on wireless power transfer, however, cannot deliver this vision. Transfering a significant amount of power wirelessly is typically done via the magnetic field, which is highly directional and its value drops very quickly with distance. As a result, state-of-the-art phone chargers are limited to distances of one or a few centimeters, and require the phone to be perfectly aligned with the charging pad.

Yet, a small increase in the distance and flexibility of wireless charging would translate to a big improvement in the user experience. In particular, many people are office workers who spend multiple hours a day sitting at their desks [9]. It would be highly desirable to have phone chargers that work at distances of about 30 or 40 cm and can charge a phone independently of its orientation. One could then attach a charging pad below the desk and use it to charge the user's phone whenever she is sitting at her desk. With such a setup, many of us would hardly ever need to take a phone out of our pocket to charge it. Achieving this vision however is not easy given the directionality and fast drop in the magnetic field.

This paper delivers a system that can charge a cell phone at distances of about 40 cm, and works independently of how the phone is oriented in the user's pocket. Our approach builds on analogous designs common for wireless data communications. Wireless communications use multi-antenna beamforming to concentrate the energy of a signal in a particular direction in space. As a result, these systems can reach longer distances and change the directionality (i.e., orientation) of their signal to focus it on the receiver. Past work on RF beamforming however operates in the far field, where the separation between transmitter and receiver is significantly larger than the wavelength. Wireless charging however operates in the near field, where it relies on the magnetic field for its power transfer. Our aim is to extend the principles of MIMO beamforming to focus the magnetic field in the spatial direction of the phone we want to charge.

Our design, called MagMIMO, enables wireless charging systems to focus their power transfer and beam it towards the phone, in a manner analogous to beamforming in wireless communications. Specifically, state of the art wireless charging uses a technique called inductive resonance [17]. A source coil in the charging pad is used to generate the magnetic field. The phone is equipped with a receiving coil which may be inside the phone's case or in an attached sleeve. When the magnetic field traverses the phone's coil, it generates a current that charges the battery. These two coils are the transmit and receive antennas of the wireless system. Current systems use a single transmit coil and hence the receiving coil in the phone has to be close and well aligned with the transmit coil in the pad to collect the energy in the magnetic field. In contrast, MagMIMO uses multiple coils on the transmitter side in a manner similar to multi-antenna wireless communication systems. The currents in the various coils are coordinated so that their magnetic fields combine constructively at the phone's coil –i.e., create a beam toward the phone. The resulting beam is spatially steered according to the location of the phone.

As in traditional MIMO beamforming, focusing the magnetic field's beam toward the phone requires the source to know the channels.[1] In communication systems this is addressed either by having the receiver measure the channels and send them back to the source, or by listening to some transmission from the receiver and inferring the reciprocal channels [33]. In MagMIMO, we neither need the receiver to directly send us the channels nor to transmit so that we may listen to the reciprocal channels. Because of the magnetic coupling between the transmitter and receiver, our source can measure the parameters for beamforming simply by measuring the load the receiver's circuit imposes on the transmitter's circuit. This enables the

MobiCom'14, September 7-11, Maui, Hawaii, USA.

ACM 978-1-4503-2783-1/14/09
http://dx.doi.org/10.1145/2639108.2639130 ...$15.00.

[1] Like in RF systems, the channels are complex coefficients that capture how the transmitter's signal is received.

phone to convey the channel information to the power source without extra overhead.

We have built a prototype of MagMIMO and tested it with the iPhone 4s in the aforementioned office set-up. We also compared the prototype against commercial iPhone chargers (i.e., Energizer Qi, Duracell, RAVpower) as well as recent published work (WiTricity 2000M [36], UW prototype [30]). Since these baselines use different input power, we set the combined input power of MagMIMO's source coils to be about the average input power used by the various baselines. Our results show the following:

- MagMIMO can charge the iPhone at distances up to 40 cm, whereas commercial chargers and academic systems are limited to 1 cm and 10 cm, respectively.
- MagMIMO charging time is lower than all baselines for the same distance. The charging time naturally increases for longer distances. For example at distances of 30 cm, MagMIMO charges the iPhone from a dead battery to a full charge within an average of 4 hours and 50 minutes, which is about twice as much as it takes to charge the iPhone 4s when directly plugged to the power source.[2]
- MagMIMO can charge the iPhone at any orientations –i.e., from perfect alignment at 0 degree to an orthogonal alignment at 90 degrees. In contrast, all baselines fail at 10 degrees or lower, except WiTricity 2000M [36] which operates up to 30 degrees.
- In experiments run with a population of users who carried their own smart phones while working at a desk, MagMIMO has succeeded in charging the user's phone independent of whether the user kept the phone in her shirt, pants, or jacket pocket. We have also conducted experiments in which the user placed his or her phone on the desk in a random position, either directly on the surface of the desk, or in a backpack, or on top of other objects (e.g., a book). MagMIMO has succeeded in charging the phone in all of these scenarios. The charging time from a dead battery varied between 2h:53m and 6h:15m, depending on the phone location and the movements of the user.

Contributions: So far, wireless power transfer has been developed in isolation from the vast and powerful literature on wireless communications. By bridging the two research areas, this paper is able to present the first demonstration of wireless charging of a smart phone while in the user's pocket. This performance is enabled by a novel design that focuses the magnetic flux from multiple coils in a steerable beam and points it at the phone, in a manner analogous to multi-antenna beamforming in wireless communications. The design can charge unmodified smart phones at distances up to 40 cm, and works regardless of the phone orientation with respect to the charging pad.

2. RELATED WORK

Wireless power transfer has been successfully adopted in cell phone chargers [7, 36] and electric car chargers [10]. It is also proposed for charging sensors [12, 19, 11], consumer electronics [25, 20], and medical implants [15, 14, 26]. Practical schemes for charging phones and similar consumer devices however are limited to distances of few centimeters and require the receiver coil to be aligned with the charging pad [7, 8, 27, 36, 25]. Examples of wireless power transfer at longer distances either require a large and heavy receiver coil, as in cars [10], or they can only deliver very little power sufficient to light an LED at $\sim$10–200mW [37], but cannot charge a cell phone battery which requires a few Watts [2].

[2]Note that these numbers are for charging the iPhone starting from a dead battery. For this scenario, it took 2 hours and 15 minutes to charge the phone when directly plugged to the power outlet, which is consistent with previously reported measurements [2].

The literature also has examples of systems that use "multi-coils" but none of these technologies shapes the magnetic flux in a steerable beam, analogous to traditional MIMO beamforming. Past work on multi-coil power transfer falls in three categories: Some schemes use multiple transmit coils but at any time, turn only one coil on – typically the coil closest and most aligned with the receiver coil [10, 23]. Other schemes use passive coils that operate as repeaters [26, 34, 35]. A third category uses one transmitter coil but attempts to power multiple devices each with its own receiver coil [18]. MagMIMO is fundamentally different from these approaches because it actively shapes the combined magnetic flux of the coils as a beam, and dynamically steers this beam towards the receiver to maximize power delivery.

A recent startup named Ossia [39, 31] proposed to power phones remotely using a very large array of WiFi MIMO transmitters. In contrast to all of the above work as well as MagMIMO, which deliver power via the magnetic field, WiFi MIMO delivers power using RF radiation. While RF radiation can be used to deliver a small amount of power as in RFIDs, delivering a large amount of power via radiation can cause local heating inside the human body [22]. This is because radiated power at hundreds of MHz–GHz frequencies can easily be absorbed by water that constitutes majority of the human body [38]. Hence, power transfer technologies have so far avoided operating in the radiation mode. Furthermore, given the limited public information about the technology underlying Ossia, it is unclear how efficient their approach is (meaning how long it takes to charge the phone) and whether the technology obeys the FCC regulations. Nevertheless, the technology is useful for environments in which humans are not present, such as automatic wireless battery charging of sensor networks in an industrial environment. While MagMIMO's design is inspired by MIMO RF techniques used in wireless communications, MagMIMO is the first technology that provides beamforming of the magnetic field and develops the underlying mathematical formulation and system architecture.

Finally, in §5.3, we use a form of in-band communication to detect the presence of a chargeable phone and adapt to changes in its load. This design is motivated by past work on wireless power transfer that used in-band communication for device discovery (e.g., [16] and [32]), but differs in the details of our communication protocol.

3. PRIMER

Wireless power transfer systems deliver power via magnetic coupling between the transmitter's and receiver's circuits [20]. As shown in Fig. 1(a), a coil of conductive material, e.g., copper, is connected to an AC power source to generate an oscillating magnetic field. A second conducting coil, brought very close to the first, would experience an oscillating magnetic flux. Variations in the magnetic flux traversing the secondary coil induce an electric current, which may be used to power devices like phones.

To increase efficiency, state of the art wireless chargers add a capacitance to both the transmitter and receiver circuits and make them resonate at the same frequency [20, 25], as illustrated in Fig. 1(b). With magnetic resonance, once the source voltage at the transmitter triggers oscillation, the circuit can keep resonating back and forth without consuming extra energy [21]. Of course in practice some of the energy is dissipated in the intrinsic resistance of the coil, but the overall efficiency of power transfer is significantly higher.

It is important to realize that power transfer depends on the amount of magnetic flux traversing the secondary coil, as shown in Fig. 2. In the case of a single transmitter coil, aligning the receiver coil with the source coil maximizes the magnetic flux through the receiver coil and hence the amount of energy delivered to the phone, as in Fig. 2(a). On the other hand, if the receiver coil is orthogonal to the transmitter

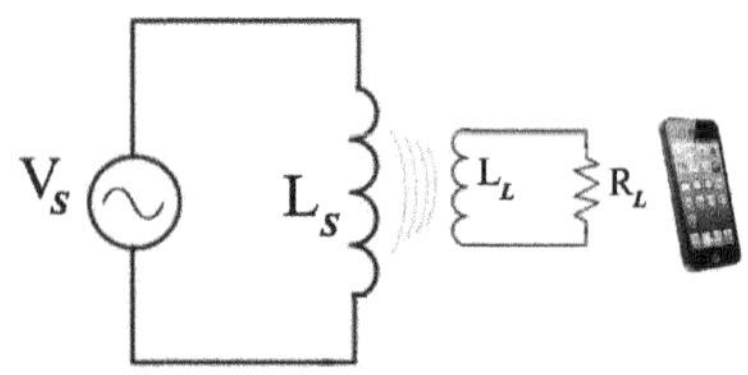

(a) Inductive charging circuit

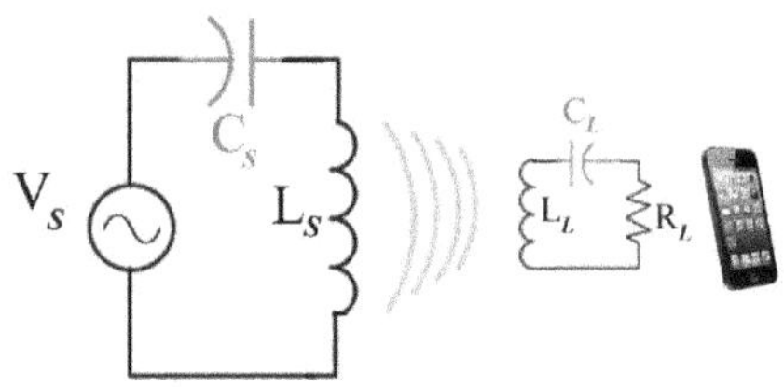

(b) Resonant charging circuit

Figure 1: Illustration of wireless power transfer.

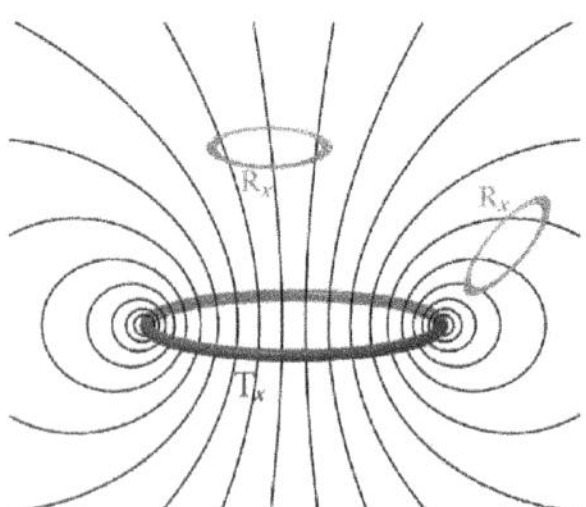

(a) Aligned Tx/Rx coils with maximum flux linkage

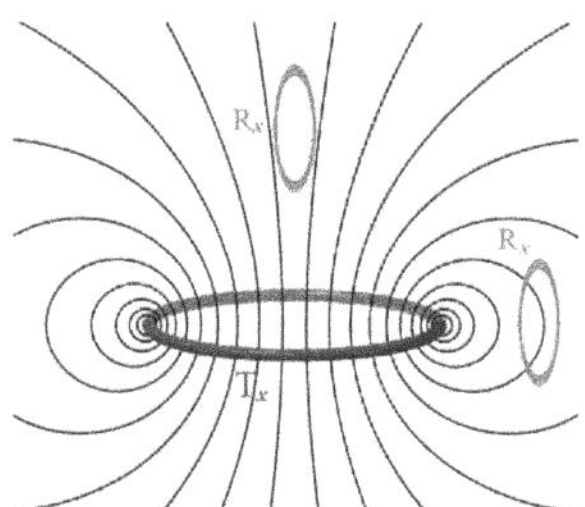

(b) Orthogonal Tx/Rx coils with minimum flux linkage

Figure 2: Magnetic flux through the receiver coil and its impact on power transfer. The power transfer is high in (a) where the Tx-Rx coils are aligned and the magnetic flux through the receiver coil is large, but there is zero power transfer in (b) due to perpendicular transmitting and receiving coils.

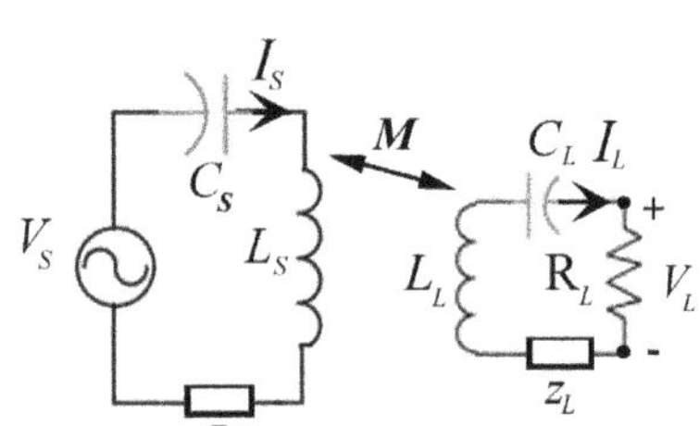

Figure 3: Illustration of a single-Tx-coil power transfer circuit.

coil (on the centerline or on the same plane as the transmitter), no magnetic flux will traverse the receiver coil and hence no energy will be delivered, as in Fig. 2(b).

3.1 Basic Circuit Equations

The above concepts can be mathematically captured via basic circuit equations [38]. Consider the illustration in Fig. 3 which shows the power transmitter and the receiver being magnetically coupled. The term M refers to the mutual inductance between the two circuits, i.e., the amount of magnetic coupling. It depends on the parameters of the two circuits as well as the relative distance and orientation of the coils on both sides. As explained earlier, due to magnetic coupling the transmitter circuit induces a current in the receiver circuit, i.e., it delivers power to the receiver. The resulting receiver current,

Figure 4: 2-D array of Tx coils, installed underneath an office desk surface, delivers power to Rx coil attached to the phone.

I_L, is a direct function of the magnetic coupling, M, the transmitter current I_s, and the circuit parameters and can be computed using basic circuit equations:

$$I_L(R_L + j\omega L_L + \frac{1}{j\omega C_L} + z_L) = j\omega M I_s, \tag{1}$$

where R_L, L_L, C_L,, and z_L are the receiver's resistance, inductance, capacitance, and complex impedance, respectively, and ω is the frequency of the system.

Due to magnetic coupling, not only the transmitter impacts the receiver, but the receiver also impacts the transmitter as follows:

$$V_s = I_s(j\omega L_s + \frac{1}{j\omega C_s} + z_s) - j\omega M I_L, \tag{2}$$

where V_s is the voltage on the transmitter side, I_s is the transmitter current, and L_s, C_s and z_s are the inductance, capacitance and complex impedance of the transmitter circuit.

The above equations are for any frequency ω. However, when the circuit operates at its resonance frequency as they should in a wireless power transfer system, the terms $j\omega L$ and $\frac{1}{j\omega C}$ cancel each other and hence disappear from the above equations.

In the rest of the paper, we use (1) and (2) to derive the magnetic-beamforming relations. As we will see in §5.1, since our design builds a MIMO transmitter, there are multiple transmitter circuits not just one. Hence, the terms MI_s and MI_L in (1) and (2) will be replaced by $\sum M_i I_{si}$ and $\sum M_i I_L$, respectively, where M_i is the mutual inductance between the receiver and the i_{th} source circuit in which current, I_{si}, flows.

4. DESIGN SPECIFICATIONS

MagMIMO is designed to charge phones remotely while a user is setting at her desk, as described in §1. We aim for satisfying distances in the range of ~30 cm to 40 cm, and all possible phone orientations, while keeping the input power on par with present wireless chargers.

The transmitter consists of n similar coils deployed underneath the surface of a typical office desk as shown in Fig. 4. The only assumption we have is that the desk surface is not made of conducting metals. The receiving coil is a small coil that can be incorporated either inside the phone or in its sleeve. There are no assumptions on the charged phones. The system works properly with off the shelf smartphones by feeding the charging power through the USB port.

5. MAGMIMO

MagMIMO performs what we call multi-coil magnetic-beamforming, which is analogous to (but not the same as) multi-antenna beamforming in wireless communications. This design concentrates the magnetic flux along a beam, so that the power transfer can reach further distances. It also steers the resulting

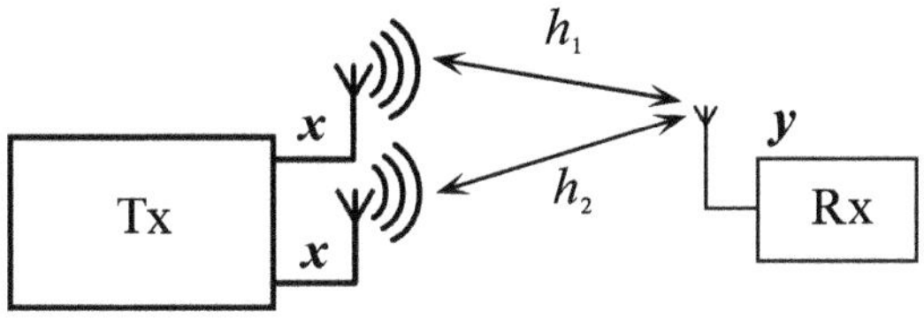

(a) Standard MIMO: $\boldsymbol{y} = (h_1 + h_2)\boldsymbol{x}$

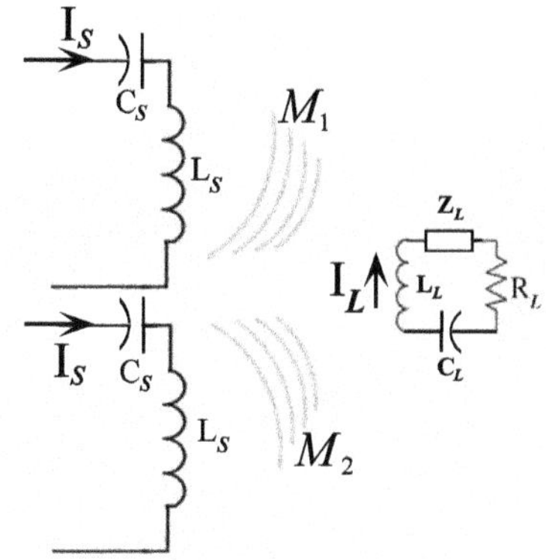

(b) MagMIMO: $\boldsymbol{I}_L = \frac{j\omega}{z_L+R_L}(M_1 + M_2)\boldsymbol{I}_s$

Figure 5: Illustration of the analogies between standard MIMO and MagMIMO: (a) In standard MIMO, the output, $\boldsymbol{y}$, at the receiver antenna, is a linear combination of the input signal $\boldsymbol{x}$, where the combiners are the wireless channels, h_1 and h_2; (b) similarly in MagMIMO, the current induced in the receiver coil, I_L, is a linear combination of the input current I_s, where the combiners are proportional to the mutual inductances between the receiver and each transmitter, M_1 and M_2.

beam and adjusts the direction of the magnetic flux to accommodate the orientation of the receiver coil in the phone.

5.1 Magnetic-Beamforming in MagMIMO

In this section, we explain the analogy between the conventional beamforming in communication systems and MagMIMO's magnetic-beamforming. We then leverage that analogy to derive the rules governing magnetic-beamforming.[3] For clarity, we consider a 2-antenna MIMO transmitter. Generalization to a larger number of antennas is straightforward.

Consider a standard MIMO transmitter with two antennas as shown in Fig. 5(a). Say we want to beamform the signal $\boldsymbol{x}$ to the receiver. From standard MIMO equations [4], [33], we know that the received signal $\boldsymbol{y}$ can be expressed as:

$$\boldsymbol{y} = (h_1 + h_2)\boldsymbol{x}, \tag{3}$$

where h_1 and h_2 are the wireless channels from the two transmitting antennas to the receiving antenna.

We also know that we can maximize the SNR of $\boldsymbol{y}$ at the receiver by beamforming the transmitted signal $\boldsymbol{x}$. This is done by using a beamforming vector (α_1, α_2), and transmitting $\alpha_1\boldsymbol{x}$ on the first antenna, and $\alpha_2\boldsymbol{x}$ on the second antenna. By Maximal-Ratio Combining (MRC), the elements of the beamforming vector should satisfy:

$$\alpha_i = \frac{h_i^*}{\sum_{i=1}^{n} |h_i|^2}, \tag{4}$$

where h_i^* is the complex conjugate of the channel coefficient h_i. Intuitively, the beamforming vectors above ensure that the signal from each antenna is rotated and weighted according to the phase and strength of the channel, such that the signals from all antennas are aligned to maximize the power at the receiver.

Now, consider the power transfer system in Fig. 5(b), where we would like to beam the magnetic field resulting from the two coils on the transmitter to maximize the power transferred to the receiver's coil. Maximizing the power at the receiver means maximizing the current induced in the receiver's coil, I_L. As explained in §3, the transmitter impacts the receiver's current, I_L, via the mutual inductance between the transmitting coils and the receiving coil, as shown in Fig. 5(b). Thus, the mutual inductance plays the role of magnetic channels. Let us refer to the transmitter's current by I_s. Applying basic circuit equations, we can write the current in the receiving coil as a function of the current fed to the transmitting coils. In particular, we can apply (1) while taking into account that we have two transmit coils (instead of just one):

$$I_L(R_L + z_L + j\omega L_L + \frac{1}{j\omega C_L}) = j\omega(M_1 + M_2)I_s, \tag{5}$$

where M_1 and M_2 are the mutual inductances between the receive coil and the two transmit coils; ω is the frequency of AC current at the transmitter; and R_L, z_L, L_L, C_L are the resistance, impedance, inductance, and capacitance on the receiver's side.

The equation above shows that the receiver current, I_L (which is analogous to the received signal $\boldsymbol{y}$ in a MIMO communication system) can be expressed in terms of the source current, I_s (which is analogous to the source symbol $\boldsymbol{x}$ in a communication system). Taking into account that power transfer systems are tuned to the frequency of resonance and hence the terms $\frac{1}{j\omega C_L}$ and $j\omega L_L$ cancel each other out, we can re-write (5) as:

$$I_L = (m_1 + m_2)I_s, \tag{6}$$

where:

$$m_i = \frac{j\omega}{z_L + R_L} M_i. \tag{7}$$

The term m_i is the scaled version of the magnetic inductance between the transmitting coil and receiving coil. We refer to m_i as the magnetic channel between Tx_i and Rx.

Comparing (6) with (3), it is clear that they have the same format. Thus, similar to traditional MIMO beamforming, we can maximize the current induced in the receiver's coil, I_L, by scaling the current flowing in the transmitter's coils I_s with a magnetic-beamforming vector (β_1, β_2), such that:

$$\beta_i = \frac{m_i^*}{\sum_{i=1}^{n} |m_i|^2}, \tag{8}$$

[3]Nonetheless, we note that shaping the non-radiated magnetic field as a beam while analogous to traditional beamforming is also quite different from it and cannot be implemented by simply using traditional beamforming. These are two different phenomena: the former operates over the near-field magnetic flux while the latter operates over the far-field propagating waves. Thus, while the analogy is helpful in understanding and developing the design, MagMIMO requires developing a new mathematical formalization that optimizes power transfer.

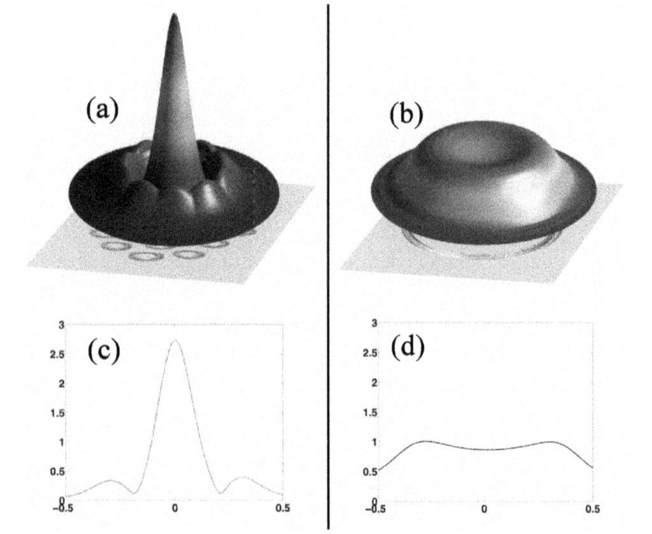

Figure 6: Comparison of the magnetic flux density. The figure plots the magnetic flux in cartesian coordinates resulting from (left): magnetic-beamforming using MagMIMO system and (right): a large single coil. (a) and (b) show the 3–D distribution of the flux density, while (c) and (d) show 2–D planar cuts of quantities shown in (a) and (b), respectively. By comparing left and right panels, it is clear that MagMIMO has effectively focused the filed in the desired direction. The occupied area and the input power is the same for both systems.

where m_i^* is the complex conjugate of the magnetic channel m_i, and $\beta_i I_s$ is the current in the transmitter's i^{th} coil.

We note that maximizing the receiver's current, I_L, naturally translates to magnetic-beamforming the field toward the receiver's coil, in a manner similar to how maximizing the received symbol, $\mathbf{y}$, translates to standard MIMO beamforming. This is because the magnetic field amplitude at the receiver coil is proportional to I_L [38]. The proportionality means that maximizing I_L is identical to maximization of the local magnetic flux magnitude at the receiver coil.[4]

To illustrate this relation, Fig. 6 shows the result of MagMIMO's magnetic-beamforming, as expressed in the above equations, and compares it with an omnidirectional magnetic field resulting from a large single coil. The quantity shown in this figure is the magnitudes of the magnetic flux density normalized by the peak of the large single coil's magnetic flux density. The total occupied area and the input power for the single coil and the multiple Tx coils of MagMIMO are the same. The simulation data shown in Fig. 6 are obtained by using AC/DC module of COMSOL Multiphysics [6], a commercial computation packages commonly used for electromagnetic simulations.

As can be seen in this figure, the concentrated magnetic flux generated by MagMIMO magnetic-beamforming is significantly higher than the single coil's magnetic field despite the fact that they consume the same input power. Therefore, MagMIMO has successfully beamformed the magnetic field. The reason that MagMIMO is able to create a higher magnetic flux maximum with the same power as the single coil is that the field is lower at other points in space except on the center line, which is the direction of the receiver in our simulation. Hence, MagMIMO concentrates the input power in the desired direction. The advantage of MagMIMO magnetic-beamforming is even higher than expressed in Fig. 6, since the power delivered to the receiver is proportional to the *square* of the magnetic flux that traverses the receiver coil [38].

[4]In fact $\mathbf{y}$ in (3) is the voltage of the receiver antenna that is proportional to the electric field of the incident wave at the receiver, in a similar way that I_L is proportional to the magnetic field at the receiver coil.

Also note that the beam is steered as the receiving coil moves or turns, i.e., changes its location or orientation. This is because the mutual inductances, M_i's, change with the receiver's location and orientation, similarly to how channels change when the receiver's location changes in MIMO communication systems. In contrast, existing solutions have no way for steering the magnetic flux towards the phone as it changes location or orientation and hence need the phone to be aligned with the charging pad.

5.2 MagMIMO Protocol

This section describes the procedure that MagMIMO follows to beamform its signal to the receiver, and adapt to receiver's movements by steering the beam as needed. The procedure has three steps: channel estimation, magnetic-beamforming, and automatic beam steering, as detailed below.

1. ***Magnetic Channel Estimation***: In communication systems, a MIMO transmitter needs to learn the channels from itself to the receiver in order to compute the magnetic-beamforming vector. Similarly, a MagMIMO transmitter needs to learn the magnetic channels to the receiver (i.e., the m_i's) to compute its magnetic-beamforming vector.

   In communication systems, the transmitter obtains the channels either by having the receiver measure the channels and send them back to the transmitter, or by listening to some transmission from the receiver and inferring the reciprocal channels [33]. Unlike communication systems, in MagMIMO, we neither need the receiver to directly send the channels to the source nor to transmit so that the source may listen to the reciprocal channels. Because of magnetic coupling between the transmitter and receiver, our transmitter can estimate the channels simply by measuring the load that the receiver imposes on the transmitter circuit. In particular, from §3.1, the impact of the receiver on each of the transmitter's coils can be captured using (2) as:

$$V_{s_i} = I_{s_i}(j\omega L_{s_i} + \frac{1}{j\omega C_{s_i}} + z_{s_i}) - j\omega M_i I_L, \tag{9}$$

   where V_{s_i} and I_{s_i} are the voltage and current of the ith Tx coil. L_{s_i}, C_{s_i} and z_{si} are the inductance, capacitance, and impedance of the ith Tx coil, and M_i is its mutual inductance with the receiver's coil.

   The above equation can be used to measure the magnetic channels from the transmitter to the receiver. Specifically, periodically, we apply a known voltage, V_{s_i}, to the ith Tx coil, and then measure the current I_{s_i} flowing through the coil while keeping the other transmit coils open circuit. Dividing the known voltage by the measured current gives us the total impedance of the Tx coil, $z_i' = \frac{V_{si}}{I_{s_i}}$. Substituting from (9) and given that the system is tuned to the frequency of resonance and hence $\frac{1}{j\omega C_{s_i}}$ and $j\omega L_{s_i}$ cancel out, we have:

$$z_i' = \frac{V_{s_i}}{I_{s_i}} = z_{si} - j\omega M_i \frac{I_L}{I_{si}}. \tag{10}$$

   Since during the channel measurement phase only one Tx coil is active at any time and the other are open circuit, we can use (1) to estimate I_L and substitute it in (10). We can also cancel out $\frac{1}{j\omega C_L}$ and $j\omega L_L$ since the circuit is operating at its resonance frequency, which yield:

$$\omega^2 M_i^2 = (z_i' - z_{s_i})(R_L + z_L), \tag{11}$$

   where z_i' is the measured impedance of Tx$_i$, while other Tx coils are silent, meaning that they are open circuited, and z_{s_i} is the intrinsic impedance of Tx$_i$.[5]

[5]This impedance represents the total impedance of the transmitter coil in the absence of a receiver, which includes the impedance of

Equation (11) allows the wireless power transmitter to compute the absolute value of the mutual inductance between each of its coils and the receiver's coil, i.e., $|M_i|$. This equation however does not provide the sign of M_i. To determine the sign, one should define a positive direction for a reference coil and compute the sign of the M_i's with respect to that reference, which we explain in detail in Appendix §A.

Once the absolute value and sign of M_i are known, they are substitued in Equation (7). As a result, the magnetic channel between the ith transmit coil and the receive coil can be computed as:

$$m_i = j\gamma_i \sqrt{\frac{z_i' - z_{s_i}}{R_L + z_L}}, \tag{12}$$

where γ_i is an indicator variable whose value is $+1$ if the sign of M_i is positive and -1 otherwise.

2. ***Magnetic-Beamforming***: Once the magnetic channels are estimated, the optimum beamforming parameters are immediately derived from (8), and the currents of each transmit coil is set to satisfy: $I_{si} = \beta_i I_s$. Assigning these currents to the Tx coils ensures that the beam is accurately steered toward the receiver coil.[6]

   Therefore, the way we perform the beam steering in MagMIMO is essentially similar to standard MIMO beam steering. The steering is performed automatically based on the data collected from channel estimation, and then depending on each transmitter's channel, the system selects an appropriate feeding scheme (derived from (8) and (13)) for the optimum wireless charging.

3. ***Automatic Beam Steering***: The phone's position and orientation can change during the charging process, causing the magnetic channels between the transmitter and receiver coils to change. Thus, it is essential that steps 1 and 2 are repeated every few seconds so that MagMIMO is able to re-steer its beam to deliver the optimal power every time the user changes the location and/or orientation of the phone.

5.3 Feedback from the Receiver

Up to this point, we have made two key assumptions: 1) the phone is always present within the reach of MagMIMO and 2) the receiver load resistance is constant. These two assumptions are not necessarily true in practice. The phone may be not in range, in which case, MagMIMO should turn off the charging system to save energy. As for the receiver's load, R_L, it is a function of the battery's instantaneous charge level, and continuously increases as the phone's battery fills up [2], as shown in Fig. 7. Hence, the power transmitter needs to learn the current value of R_L to accurately compute the magnetic channels and the beamforming vector.

the DC voltage supply, amplifier and intrinsic resistance of L_{s_i} and C_{s_i}.

[6] In practice, it is more convenient to apply voltages rather than currents –i.e., use a voltage source. Thus, we can easily compute the source voltages that generate the desired currents, I_{si}, using standard circuit equations as:

$$\begin{pmatrix} V_{s1} \\ V_{s2} \\ \vdots \\ V_{sn} \end{pmatrix} = \begin{pmatrix} z_{s1} & j\omega M_{1,2} & \cdots & j\omega M_{1,n} & j\omega M_1 \\ j\omega M_{2,1} & z_{s2} & \cdots & j\omega M_{2,n} & j\omega M_2 \\ \vdots & \vdots & \ddots & \vdots & \vdots \\ j\omega M_{n,1} & j\omega M_{n,2} & \cdots & z_{sn} & j\omega M_n \end{pmatrix} \begin{pmatrix} I_{s_1} \\ I_{s_2} \\ \vdots \\ I_{s_n} \\ -I_L \end{pmatrix} \tag{13}$$

where V_{si}, z_{si}, I_{si} stand for the voltage, internal impedance, and the current of the i_{th} source circuit, and $M_{i,j}$ is the mutual inductance between transmit coils i and j. All of the elements in the right hands side of (13) are either known from the offline tuning of the system or determined after channel estimation and magnetic-beamforming vector calculation. In particular, $I_{si} = \beta_i I_s$ where I_s is the AC current, and $I_L = \sum m_i I_{s_i}$.

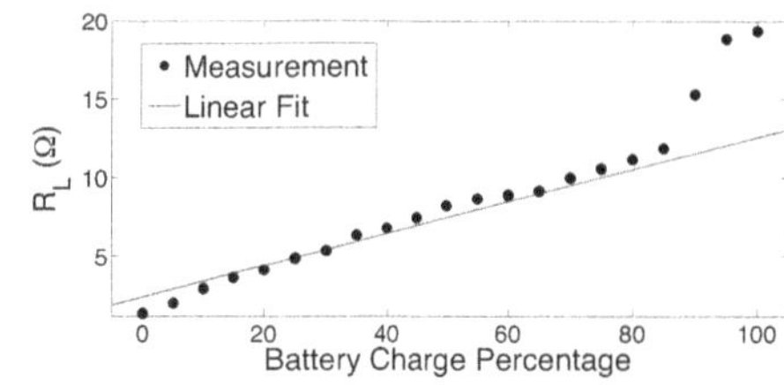

Figure 7: Changes in R_L as the phone charges.

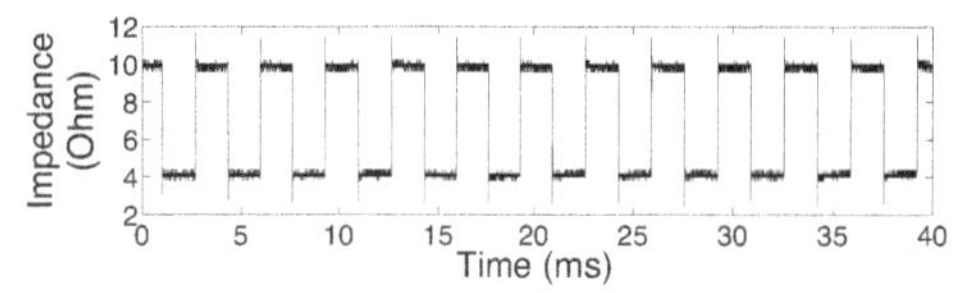

(a) Transmitted feedback signal from Rx coil

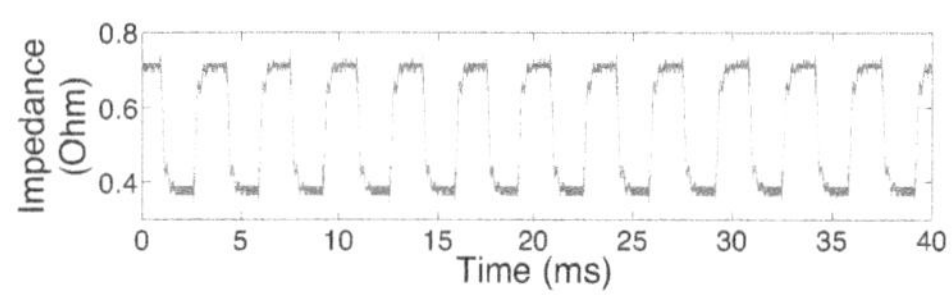

(b) Received feedback signal by Tx coil

Figure 8: Feedback sent from Rx and received by Tx. The width of the pulse encodes the value of R_L and the presence of the pulse train conveys that a phone equiped with a MagMIMO receiver is in reach of the MagMIMO's transmitter.

In this section, we explain how MagMIMO employs feedback communication from the receiver to detect the presence of the phone and the current value of the load resistance. One option for sending this feedback is to use out-of-band communication via some low power radio, e.g., Bluetooth. This solution is undesirable since it needs an additional radio on the charger and may not work if the phone is completely discharged. In MagMIMO, we send the feedback in-band by having the receiver modulate the power transfer signal, in a manner similar to how RFIDs communicate with their reader.

We leverage the coupling between the transmitter and receiver, due to which changes in the impedance of the receiver's circuit translate to proportional changes in the reflected impedance at the transmitter. Thus, in MagMIMO, the receiver measures R_L and communicates its value to the transmitter by turning a switch on and off to change the reflected impedance. The value of R_L is encoded in the width of the pulse. The pulse is repeated multiple times for reliability. Fig. 8 shows the pulses transmitted from the power receiver and how they are received at the power transmitter. The example in the figure is for R_L equal to 8.25 Ω.

On the other side, Tx coil uses the presence of the pulse train as an indication that a phone is within the reach and it needs power. It also finds out the value of R_L by decoding and measuring the pulse width. Note that the Tx can immediately discover the impact of switching the impedance at the receiver due to the coupling between Tx and Rx.

The R_L estimation and in-band communication is repeated every few minutes (every 5 minutes in our prototype). Whenever the value of R_L changes, the channels are updated according to (12).

The above feedback approach is very energy efficient and does not add too much complexity to the system. All of the measurements and modulations on the Rx side are done using the energy harnessed from the transmitter, not the phone's battery. Therefore, MagMIMO works seamlessly even for a completely discharged phone.

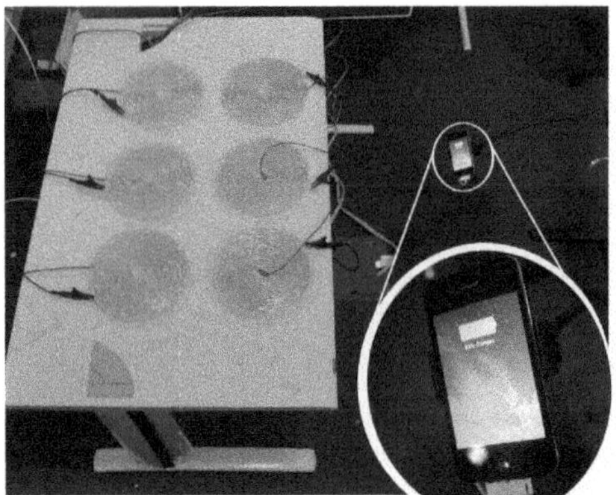

Figure 9: MagMIMO prototype. The figure shows the transmit coils placed on a regular office desk; the receiver coil is attached to back of the phone.

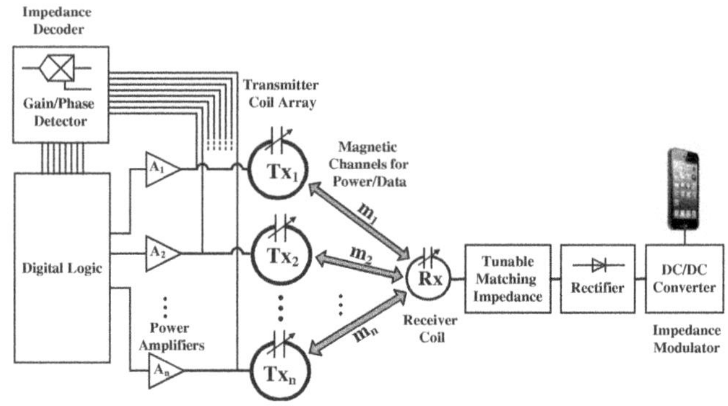

Figure 10: Block diagram of MagMIMO prototype. The magnetic channels, m_1,m_2, ..., m_n, are estimated by measuring the reflected Rx impedance at each Tx coil. The digital logic controls the currents in the Tx coil array. The matching impedance circuit, rectifier and DC/DC converter condition the voltage and current of the load/receiver.

6. PROTOTYPE IMPLEMENTATION

We built a prototype of MagMIMO using off-the-shelf components (Fig. 9). The transmitter can be attached to a regular office desk with metallic, plastic and wood contents. The only restriction of the system is that the desk surface must not be conductive. The receiver circuit has a small coil and can be attached to the back of the phone. It charges unmodified phones via the USB port.

The prototype resonates at a single frequency of 1.0 MHz. The electromagnetic compatibility constraints have been followed so that the MagMIMO prototype is compliant with FCC regulations (both part 15 and part 18). Note, however, that while the prototype operates at this particular frequency, magnetic-beamforming for power transfer is independent of the frequency.[7]

Our implementation, illustrated in Fig. 10, has three components:

1. The transmitter can be powered from a standard 60 Hz power outlet. The transmitter circuit consists of six[8] transmitting coils (Tx_i) resonating with their own serial capacitors. The area of each Tx coil is 0.05 m^2 which is powered by its own tunable power amplifier (A_i). The transmitting coils and power amplifiers are specifically designed and built to have low resistive and switching losses, respectively. The transmitter occupies the total area of 0.38 m^2 on a regular office desk and is fed by 20 W combined input power across all coils.

   The MagMIMO transmitter adjusts both amplitude and phase of the current in each Tx coil in accordance with the description in §5.2. Adjustments of both phase and magnitude are necessary since the magnetic-beamforming vectors are complex numbers (see Equation 8). The amplitude is updated by controlling the voltage at the input of the amplifier and the phase is updated using controllable phase shifters. The details of the circuit are as follows: The phase and amplitude of each coil's voltage are calculated based on equations 8-13 by a microcontroller. The microcontroller then updates the amplitude by changing the magnitude of the DC input of a controllable DC-DC buck converter, and updates the phase using controllable phase-shifter. The resulting voltage controls a DC-AC inverter similar to that in [28] and applies the desired voltage to the respective Tx coil. The combination of these three blocks, "DC-DC converter, Phase shifter, DC-AC inverter," is the block referred to as "amplifier" in Fig. 10 (i.e., A1, A2, ... , A6).

2. The receiver coil is quite small with an area of 0.005m^2 and a thickness of a few millimeters. Hence, it can be easily incorporated into the sleeve of the phone. The receiver's circuit consists of a self-tuning matching circuit, full bridge rectifier and a DC/DC converter attached to the Rx coil resonating with a high Q capacitor. The Rx circuit is connected to the phone's USB port and hence can be incorporated with unmodified phones.

3. The digital logic component periodically estimates the channels between the transmit coils and the receiver by measuring the impedance of each Tx coil with the aid of a gain/phase detector (Fig. 10). In addition, the logic control system is always listening for the feedback signal transmitted from the receiver. After each channel estimation and feedback reception, the logic component controls the currents that feed the Tx coils to beamform the magnetic field and steer it toward the phone. Once the phone is out of reach, i.e., all the channels are weaker than the threshold and the feedback signal is no longer received, the control logic disconnects the input power, and enters the sleep mode. Only feedback detection remains active in this mode to detect a new receiver.

We have used off-the-shelf components to build the prototype. An ordinary AC/DC converter has been used to convert the 60-Hz electricity from the outlet to feed the Class-E single GaN switch power amplifiers [28] which in turn feed the transmitting coils. To build the resonating Tx and Rx coils, we have used general-purpose copper tubings with diameters of 1/8' and 1/16', respectively. We have used ultra low Equivalent Series Resistance (ESR) microwave ceramic capacitors. The detailed specifications of the used components are in the Appendix §B. The entire prototype costs less than $100.

7. EVALUATION

We empirically evaluate MagMIMO and compare its performance with and the performance of state-of-the-art wireless chargers.

7.1 Baselines

We compare the MagMIMO with the following systems:

[7]Generally, frequencies in the range of hundreds of kHz to a few tens of MHz are suitable for wireless charging [5]. For example, Qi, Duracell, and RAVpower operate at a few hundred kHz [7, 27, 8], Witricity operates at 6.78MHz [36], and the UW prototype sweeps the frequencies from 8 to 22 MHz [30, 29].

[8]Magnetic-beamforming can be used with a different number of coils similarly to how traditional beamforming can operate with a different number of antennas. The larger the number of coils the narrower the beam and the better the performance. As we show in the result section, a choice of 6 Tx coils increases the charging range to 40 cm and can support any phone orientation. We also ran experiments with only two coils. Such a system has an approximately 15% higher charging range compared to a single Tx coil and cannot support all phone orientations.

Table 1: Input power for different wireless charging solutions

Technology	Input Power (W)
RAVpower	7.5
Duracell Powermat	18
Energizer Qi	22
Witricity WiT-2000M	24
UW Prototype	30
Large Single Coil	20
Selective Coil-Array	20
MagMIMO	**20**

- Three of the best commercially available wireless chargers: Duracell Powermat [7], Energizer Qi [8], and RAVpower [27].
- Two of the state-of-the-art magnetic resonance prototypes, i.e., WiT-2000M [36] and UW prototype [30]. These two prototypes are not publicly available. Therefore the data for these two cases have been extracted from [36] and [30], respectively.
- A large single transmit coil with a total area equal to the total area of MagMIMO's six Tx coils.
- A selective coil-array, which uses the same six Tx coils used by MagMIMO. However instead of employing the MagMIMO protocol to set the Tx currents in the coils, this system assigns the total input power to the best coil out of the six Tx coils –i.e., the coil that delivers the highest power to the receiver. To identify the best coil for each measured receiver position, we try each coil in a round robin manner, and report the result for the coil that delivers the maximum power at the receiver.

Table 1 lists the input power consumed by each of the compared systems. Since, the compared baselines differ in their input power, we set MagMIMO's total input power to the median of the compared system. Note that MagMIMO input power is lower than Energizer Qi, WiT-2000M, and the UW prototype.

7.2 Testing Environment

The system is shown in Fig. 9. The MagMIMO's coils are placed on the desk only for illustration purposes. In operational mode, Tx coils are placed underneath the surface. We have used a regular iPhone 4s as the testbench cellphone. We have not made any software or hardware modifications on the phone. We simply used its USB port to charge it. The phone and the receiver circuit, attached to its back, have been held with an adjustable plastic arm which easily provides different distances and orientations, as shown in Fig. 9. All tests are run in a standard office environment, while people are working at their desks and naturally moving around.

7.3 Charging as a Function of Distance

We evaluate the ability of MagMIMO to deliver power as the distance between the transmitter and the receiver increases, and compare the performance with the aforementioned baselines. We measure the distance between the receiver and the transmitter as the length of the shortest straight line that connects the Rx coil to the nearest Tx coil. Note that this is a conservative measure of distance (i.e., we underestimate the distance) because it is measured between the nearest parts of the transmitter and receiver as opposed to the centers of the transmitter and the receiver (which are more separated due to the area of coils). In each run, we measure the time it takes the charging system to fully charge the iPhone 4s starting from a dead battery. We repeat the same experiments for MagMIMO, the large single Tx coil, the selective coil array and the commercial chargers. In each run, we move the receiver to a different location in the 3D

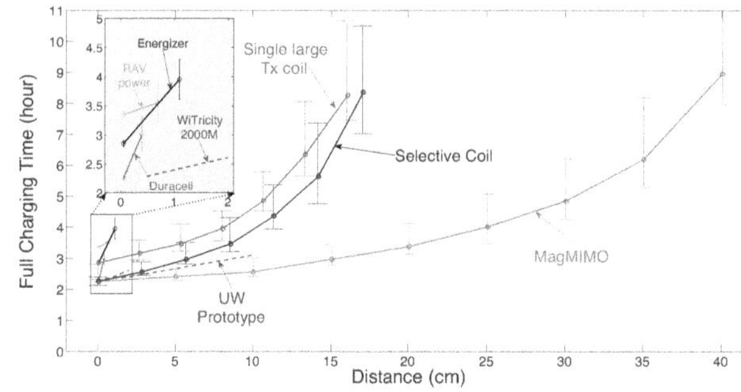

Figure 11: Charging from a dead battery as a function of distance. For each case, the phone has been placed at different distances from the pad to test the time that it takes for the phone to fully charge. All three commercially available wireless chargers simply do not provide any distance beyond 1 cm.

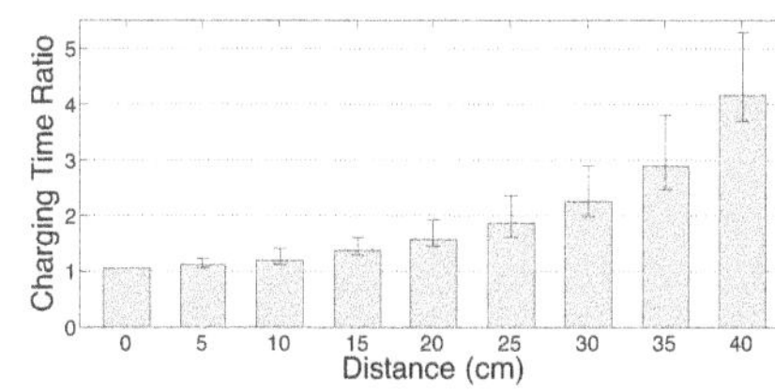

Figure 12: Charging time ratio. MagMIMO wireless charging time divided by wired (plugged-in) charing time.

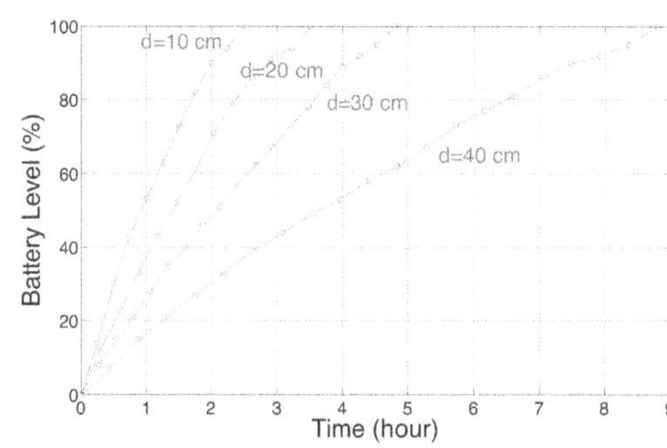

Figure 13: Change in battery level as MagMIMO charges the phone.

space around the transmitter, using the flexible phone holder shown in Fig. 9. We also compare with WiT-2000M [36] and the UW prototype described in [30]. However, since these prototypes are not publicly available, our comparison with these systems is based on the results reported by their designers in [36] and [30], respectively.

Fig. 11 plots, for each system, the charging time starting from a dead battery as a function of the distance between the transmitter and receiver. The error bars show the minimum and 90th percentile of the charging time. The figure reveals the following: First, MagMIMO charging time is smaller than the baselines at any distance for which the baselines are functional. Second, MagMIMO significantly increases the maximum charging distance. MagMIMO maximum charging distance is 40 cm. In comparison, the commercial chargers and WiT 2000M fail to charge the phone at distances of one to two centimeters, whereas the UW prototype, and the single coil, fail at 10 cm and 15 cm respectively. The selective coil-array, which similarly to MagMIMO uses six coils, fails at a distance of 17 cm. This range is significantly lower than that of MagMIMO, which demonstrates the benefits of MagMIMO's magnetic-beamforming over a best coil design. Third, as expected, in all systems, the charging time increases with distance. For example, when the separation between

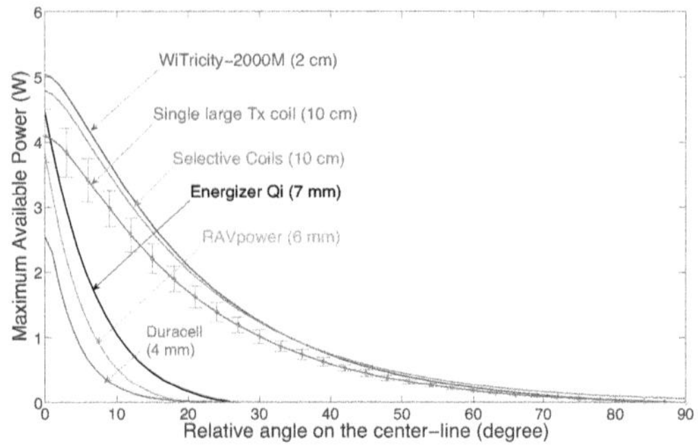

Figure 14: Output power as a function of orientation angle. For the large single Tx coil (at 10 cm) and WiT-2000M (at 2 cm), the maximum available output power from Rx coil significantly drops beyond 30°. The situation is even worse for three of the best commercial wireless chargers (Duracell at 4 mm, RAVpower at 6 mm and Energizer at 7 mm all on the centerlines), as the available power is negligible for angles larger than ~10°.

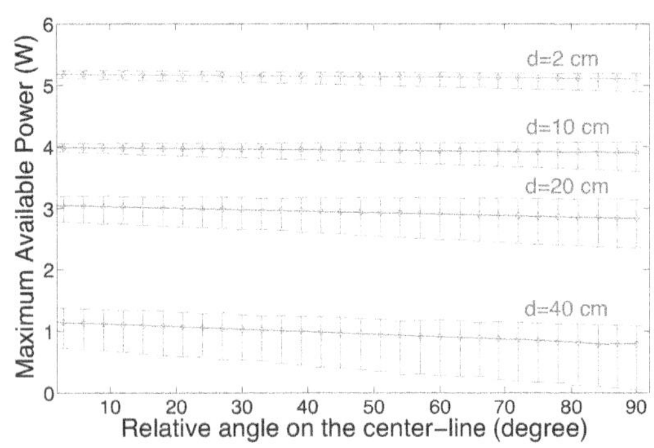

Figure 15: Output power as a function of orientation angle. MagMIMO using collaborative magnetic-beamforming between Tx coils is able to deliver maximum power to the Rx circuit in all situations even if Rx is orthogonal to one of the Tx coils.

the transmitter and receiver is 30 cm, it takes MagMIMO 4 hours and 50 minutes to charge the phone from a dead battery to full charge.

One may also wonder how MagMIMO's charging time compares with charging the phone by plugging it to the power outlet. In our experiments, plugged-in charging takes 2 hours and 15 minutes to charge the iPhone 4s from a dead battery to a full charge. This number is consistent with prior measurements in the literature [2]. Based on these measurements, we plot in Fig. 12 the ratio of MagMIMO's charging time to plugged-in charging, for different distances. The figure shows that up to 10 cm, the time taken by MagMIMO is on par with plugged-in charging. At 25 cm to 30 cm, MagMIMO takes twice as much time to charge the phone in comparison to plugged-in charging. The ratio becomes 3 to 4 times for longer distances.

The above numbers provide an upper bound on the charging time. Most users rarely charge the phone from a completely dead battery. In particular, Fig. 13 shows the charge in the battery as a function of the charging time. This figure enables the reader to estimate how much time it takes to charge the phone between two specific battery levels, for a particular distance. For example, to charge the iPhone's battery from 30% to 80% full, MagMIMO takes about 1.5 hours at 20 cm and 2.5 hours at 30 cm.

7.4 Charging as a Function of Orientation

Next, we evaluate the ability of MagMIMO to charge the phone independent of its orientation with respect to the charging pad, and compare it with the various baselines. We measure the orientation

Table 2: Charging the phone in the user's pocket

Number of users	Range (cm)	Avg. time (h:mm)	Comments
3	10–30	4:30	Working on a laptop
3	15–25	3:50	Reading a book
1	20–40	5:50	Phone in shirt's pocket
2	20–30	5:10	Phone in jacket's pocket
2	20–40	6:15	Moving very often

Table 3: Charging the phone on the desk

Number of users	Avg. time (h:mm)	Comments (Average number of movements)
6	2:53	Phone placed on the desk surface (3)
2	3:40	Phone contained in a purse/bag (9)
3	3:27	Phone placed on another object (7)

of the receiver with respect to the transmitter as the minimum angle between the planes created by the transmitter coil(s) and the receiver coil. We empirically measure the performance as a function of orientation for MagMIMO, the selective coil-array, the large single Tx coil, and the commercial chargers. We also compare with WiT-2000M based on their specification sheet. However, we cannot compare with the UW prototype since [29, 30] do not provide information about how they address orientation for phone charging.[9]

We note that since the compared schemes do not support the same distance, we could not fix one distance and compare all schemes. Thus, for the baselines we plot the performance as a function of orientation, for their operational distances. For MagMIMO, we plot in the performance as a function of orientation, for a variety of distances up to 40 cm.

Figs. 14 and 15 compare the performance dependency of different systems on the relative angle between the receiver coil (Rx) and the transmitter coil(s) (Tx pad). The horizontal axis of this figure shows the relative angle and the vertical axis shows the power delivered to the receiver at that specific relative angle.

The results in Fig. 14 show that, for the baselines, the maximum available power strongly depends on the relative angle between the phone and the charging pad. For the large single Tx coil (at 10 cm), like other single coil technologies, the available power significantly drops beyond 30°. The same is true for the WiT-2000M (at 2 cm), which uses a similar technology. The selective coil-array (at 10 cm) is not any better despite its use of multiple coils. The situation is much worse for three of the best commercial wireless chargers, as the power is negligible for angles larger than ~10°.

In contrast, Fig. 15 shows that MagMIMO is able to deliver a consistent power level to the phone in all situations even if it is orthogonal to the Tx coils. This is due to MagMIMO beam-steering capability which allows it to adapt the direction of the magnetic flux according to the orientation of the phone. Compare MagMIMO's performance with the selective coil-array, which although adapts the choice of coil according to the receiver's position, it does not have a beam-steering capability and as a result it cannot charge the phone as its orientation gets more orthogonal to the charging pad.

7.5 User Experiments

We have performed experiments with a population of users to validate that MagMIMO can indeed charge a user's phone while she is working at her desk. We also validate that MagMIMO works with different smartphone models.

In each experiment, a different user was asked to attach the receiver circuit to his/her own smartphone and keep it in his/her pocket,

[9]The paper shows orientation results only for large receive coils which cannot be attached to a phone.

Table 4: MagMIMO's transfer efficiency at different distances

Distance	0.5 cm	2 cm	5 cm	10 cm	20 cm	30 cm	40 cm
Efficiency	89%	87%	74%	53%	34%	19%	11%

while sitting normally at the desk. The user can keep other objects in the same pocket with the phone, e.g., coins, keys, etc. The phone screen was checked for its battery level every few minutes. The smartphones used herein are Samsung Galaxy SIII, 2×Apple iPhone 4s, 2×Apple iPhone 5s, Samsung Galaxy S III, 2×Samsung Galaxy S4, Samsung Galaxy Note II, Motorola Droid Ultra, and LG Lucid 2. The phones were charged from a dead battery to a full charge.

The results in Table 2 show that MagMIMO always succeeded in charging the user's phone independent of the phone's type and whether the user kept the phone in her shirt, pants, or jacket pocket.

Some users like to keep their phones on the desk to check messages and notifications. Thus, we conducted experiments in which we asked the users to put their phones wherever they want on the desk. The users were allowed to keep the phone in their back-pack or purse, or to put the phone on top of any nonmetallic object instead of directly putting it on the desk surface. The users were also allowed to change the position of their phone any time as they wish. Table 3 shows that MagMIMO succeeded in charging the phone in all of these scenarios with an average charging time between 2h:53m and 3h:40m.

7.6 Power Transfer Efficiency

The transfer "efficiency" is the received power at the Rx coil divided by the total input power at the Tx coils. We measured the efficiency of MagMIMO for varying distances in the range $[0.5\ cm, 40\ cm]$. Table 4 reports MagMIMO's average efficiency as a function of the distance, where the average is taken over different phone orientations. The efficiency of MagMIMO at a close distance is 89%. The efficiency at tens of centimeters may look low, however to the best of our knowledge, our efficiency numbers are the highest for magnetic resonance at such distances with a small receiver coil that fits in the back of a phone. In particular, the Witricity baseline is reported to have a maximum efficiency of 86% for distances less than 2cm [36], which is lower than MagMIMO. [36] does not report the efficiency at distances larger than 2cm. However, since it cannot charge a phone beyond 2cm (while MagMIMO can), one can conclude that the efficiency at such distances is smaller than MagMIMO.

Note that the size of the Rx coil is a determining factor for efficiency, since one can always collect more magnetic flux using a larger Rx coil. Past papers that reports higher efficiency at distance use large Rx coils unsuitable for a phone. For example, [17] achieves higher efficiency but uses a 3-D Rx coil whose diameter is 60 cm and has a depth of 20 cm, making it unsuitable for our application.

7.7 Impact of Charging on Temperature

We have measured the temperature rise on MagMIMO's Tx and Rx coils as well as the commercially available wireless chargers using a temperature gun infrared thermometer [24]. Over a period of seven hours, the maximum temperature rise for MagMIMO is 2°C when the system performs at its maximum power. For the commercially available wireless chargers, however, the temperatures rises to an uncomfortable level. Over seven hours the temperature rises of 23°C, 22°C, and 16°C were measured for Energizer, RAV power and Duracell, respectively. Therefore, MagMIMO's operation over long periods of time results in a temperature rise that is 10× smaller than the baselines over the same period of time.[10]

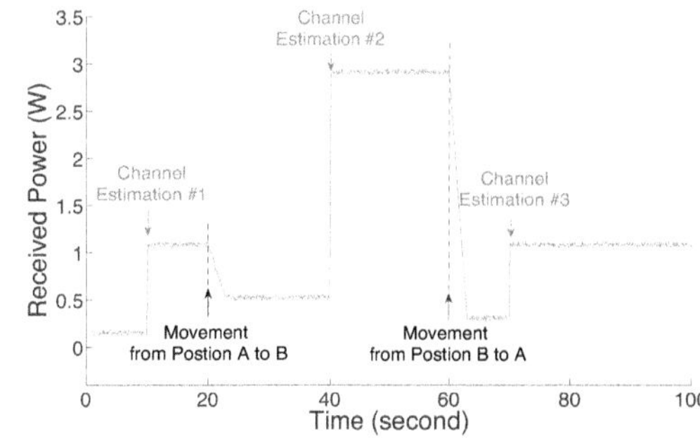

Figure 16: Microbenchmark for channel estimation and magnetic-beamforming performance. A receiver has been moved from position A at t=20s to position B, and then again back to position A at t=60s. MagMIMO performs channel estimation and magnetic-beamforming every 30 seconds starting from t=10s. The figure shows the role of channel estimation and beam steering in adapting to movements.

7.8 Microbenchmark

Next, we focus on the performance of the individual components of MagMIMO and how they contribute toward its effectiveness.

Channel Estimation. To investigate the effectiveness of MagMIMO's channel estimation, we perform a series of experiments, in which the receiver (load) moves during the experiment from one position to another causing a change in the magnetic channels. Fig. 16 illustrates one of these experiments in which the phone is moved from position A (at 38 cm from Tx) to position B (at 22 cm from Tx), and then again from position B back to position A. The figure plots the power delivered to the phone over time. As can be seen in this figure, MagMIMO adapts to changes in the channels; the received power is significantly raised due to magnetic-beamforming at every channel estimation at t=10s, 40s and 70s.

Feedback. To validate the effectiveness of feedback communication in MagMIMO we perform a set of experiments with and without feedback. Figure 17 plots the results of a representative example, where MagMIMO has been powering a load (placed at 30 cm from Tx) that abruptly changes on 5 occasions (C1–C5). In particular, R_L starts from 5Ω, and each time it is increased by 2Ω. The instantaneous received powers of the system with and without feedback communication are plotted against time on top/red and bottom/black profiles, respectively. For both sets of the results in Fig. 17, the channel estimation is enabled and all other parameters of systems are exactly similar.

As can be seen in Fig. 17, the feedback from the receiver helps MagMIMO better estimate the load and hence have more accurate channel estimates. In the absence of such feedback the performance can severely drop due to inaccurate load value, which leads to inaccurate channel estimates.[11]

8. Concluding Remarks

[10]We also note that it is safe to touch the MagMIMO coils even if they are not insulated. We have measured the touching voltage showing that the touch voltage is always under 10 volts, which is way lower than the safety threshold [13].

[11]The reason why the power slightly degrades even in the presence of the feedback is that the impedance matching hardware is optimal only within a certain range. This is a hardware limitation independent of the accuracy of the feedback.

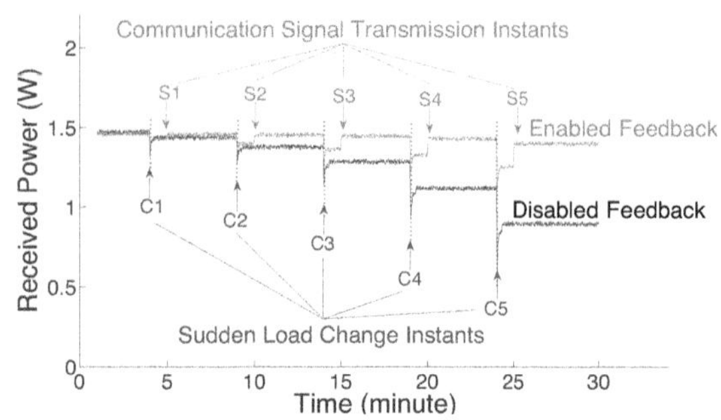

Figure 17: Microbenchmark of feedback communication. The load is made to abruptly change at C1–C5. The figure shows that the feedback transmitted by the receiver at S1–S5 is properly used to update the next beamforming matrix, resulting in a raise in received power level to deal with the change in the load. In contrast, the system with disabled feedback suffers a significant loss whenever the load deviates from the presumed value.

This paper introduces MagMIMO, a system that charges portable devices such as cell phones at distances up to 40 cm and independently of the device's position and orientation, while commercial chargers and academic systems are limited to less than 10 cm. MagMIMO achieves this by adapting the wireless communication concept of MIMO beamforming to concentrate the resonating magnetic field on the receiver device to maximize the power transfer efficiency. Evaluation of MagMIMO's prototype proves that it makes a significant improvement both in the reliability and efficiency of the wireless power transfer. Finally, we note that MagMIMO does not require any modification to the phone and hence can be used with today's phones by incorporating the small receiver coil (and circuit) in a sleeve attached to the phone. In future work, we envision extending MagMIMO to support simultaneous charging of multiple devices, in a manner analogous to the multi-user MIMO technique. We will also consider extensive user studies that explore the typical distance between a working user and her desk, and the impact of MagMIMO's improved range and flexible orientation on the user experience.

Acknowledgments: We thank Omid Abari, Fadel Adib, Arthur Berger, Diego Cifuentes, Ezz Hamed, Haitham Hassanieh, Zack Kabelac, Swarun Kumar, Hariharan Rahul, Lixin Shi, Deepak Vasisht, Jue Wang and our reviewers for their insightful comments. This research is funded by NSF. We thank members of the MIT Center for Wireless Networks and Mobile Computing: Amazon, Cisco, Google, Intel, Mediatek, Microsoft, ST Microelectronics, and Telefonica for their support.

9. REFERENCES

[1] Analog Devices Inc. datasheet for AD8302 LF-2.7 GHz gain and phase detector.
[2] Apple Inc. *Rechargeable Li-based Batteries*, 2013.
[3] Arduino. Uno datasheet. http://arduino.cc/.
[4] D. W. Bliss, K. W. Forsythe, and A. M. Chan. MIMO Wireless Communication. *Lincoln Lab, MIT*, 2005.
[5] F. Carobolante. Wireless power transfer, overcoming the technological hurdles. In *APEC*. IEEE, 2014.
[6] COMSOL Inc. *Reference guide 4.3b*, 2013.
[7] Duracell Corp. *PowerMat Technologies*, 2011.
[8] Energizer. Qi-Enabled 3 Position Inductive Charger.
[9] Ergotron Inc. *To Sit or Stand? Almost 70% of Full Time American Workers Hate Sitting, but They do it all Day Every Day*, 2013.
[10] S. Hasanzadeh, S. Vaez-Zadeh, and A. H. Isfahani. Optimization of a Contactless Power Transfer System for Electric Vehicles. *IEEE Trans. Vehic. Tech.*, 2012.
[11] L. He, Y. Gu, J. Pan, and T. Zhu. On-demand charging in wireless sensor networks: Theories and applications. In *WASA*, 2010.
[12] L. He, Y. Gu, J. Pan, and T. Zhu. On-demand charging in wireless sensor networks: Theories and applications. In *IEEE Conf. on Mobile Ad-Hoc and Sensor Systems*, 2013.
[13] IEC. Standard 60364: Electrical installations for buildings. Part 1: Low-voltage electrical installations.
[14] S. Kelly, P. Doyle, A. Priplata, O. Mendoza, and J. L. Wyatt. Optimal primary coil size for wireless power telemetry to medical implants. In *ISABEL*, 2010.
[15] S. Kim, J. S. Ho, and A. S. Y. Poon. Wireless power transfer to miniature implants: Transmitter optimization. *IEEE Trans. Antennas Propag.*, 2012.
[16] S.-H. Kim, Y.-S. Lim, and S.-J. Lee. Magnetic resonant coupling based wireless power transfer system with in-band communication. *Journal of Semiconductor Technology and Science*, 13(6):562–568, 2013.
[17] A. Kurs, A. Karalis, R. Moffatt, J. D. Joannopoulos, P. Fisher, and M. Soljacic. Wireless power transfer via strongly coupled magnetic resonances. *Science*, 2007.
[18] A. Kurs, R. Moffatt, and M. Soljacic. Simultaneous mid-range power transfer to multiple devices. *Applied Physics Letters*, 96(4):044102, 2010.
[19] K. Li, H. Luan, and C.-C. Shen. Qi-ferry: Energy-constrained wireless charging in wireless sensor networks. In *IEEE Wireless Comm. and Networking Conf.*, 2012.
[20] M. Kesler, Witricity Corp. *Highly Resonant Wireless Power Transfer*, 2013.
[21] H. Mohseni, J. Jadidian, A. A. Shayegani-Akmal, E. Hashemi, A. Naieny, and E. Agheb. In-situ insulation test of 400 kV GIS. *IEEE Transactions on Dielectrics and Electrical Insulation*, 15(5):1449–1455, 2008.
[22] J. Nadakuduti and P. G. L. Lu. Operating frequency selection for loosely coupled wireless power transfer with respect to RF emissions and exposure. *IEEE Wireless Power Transfer Conf.*, 2013.
[23] F. S. A. Note. Low-power wireless charger transmitter design using MC56F8006 DSC.
[24] Omega Inc. Temperature gun infrared thermometers.
[25] Qualcomm. WiPower Technology.
[26] A. K. RamRakhyani and G. Lazzi. Multicoil telemetry system for compensation of coil misalignment effects in implantable systems. *IEEE Antennas and Wireless Propagation Letters*, 11:1675–1678, 2012.
[27] RAV Power. datasheet for Qi-Enabled Charger.
[28] L. Roslaniec and D. J. Perreault. Design of variable-resistance class E inverters for load modulation. *IEEE ECCE*, 2012.
[29] A. P. Sample, D. Meyer, and J. Smith. Analysis, experimental results, range adaptation of magnetically coupled resonators for wireless power transfer. *IEEE Trans. Ind. Electron.*, 2011.
[30] A. P. Sample, B. H. Waters, S. T. Wisdom, and J. R. Smith. Enabling Seamless Wireless Power Delivery in Dynamic Environments. *IEEE Proceedings*, 2013.
[31] TechCrunch. Cota by ossia aims to drive a wireless power revolution and change how we think about charging, 2013.
[32] Texas Instruments. Qi compliant wireless power transmitter manager.
[33] D. Tse and P. Vishwanath. *Fundamentals of Wireless Communications*. Cambridge University Press, 2005.
[34] B. Wang, W. Yerazunis, and K. H. Teo. Wireless power transfer: Metamaterials and array of coupled resonators. *Proceedings of the IEEE*, 101:1359–1368, June 2013.

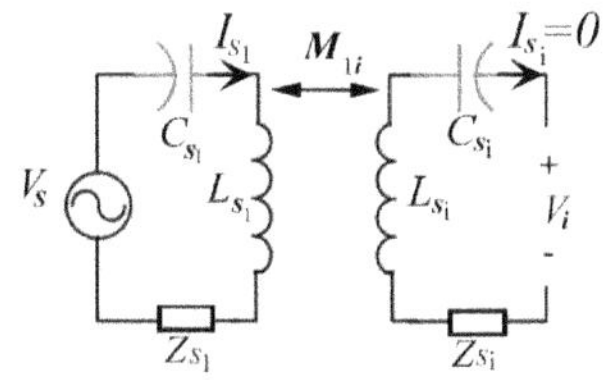

Figure 18: Off-line calibration between Tx coils

[35] H. Wang. Multiple-resonator magnetic resonant coupling wireless power transfer. Master's thesis, University of Pittsburgh, Pittsburgh, PA, Feb. 2012.

[36] Witricity Corp. *Developers Kit for Mobile, data sheet "WiT-2000M"*, 2013.

[37] Witricity Corp. *Prodigy: a hands-on demonstration system*, 2014.

[38] M. Zahn. *Electromagnetic Field Theory: A Problem Solving Approach.* Hillsdale, N.J. : L. Erlbaum Associates, 1990.

[39] H. Zeine. *Patent Application: Wireless Power Transmission System.* US 2012/0193999 A1, 2012.

APPENDIX

A. Computing the Sign of M_i

The signs of the M_i's are defined with respect to some reference Tx coil. Let us pick the first Tx coil as the reference. In this case, M_1 is positive by definition, and we are interested in computing the sign of M_i for the other Tx coils. (Note that we could have defined M_1 to be negative, in which case all M_i's would flip sign, and hence the voltages induced by the Tx coils at the receiver coil will all flip sign, without any change in the power delivered to the receiver).

The computation of the sign of M_i involve two steps:

(a) One-time Calibration Step: The objective of this step is to compute the mutual inductance between Tx_1 (the reference coil) and Tx_i, i.e., M_{1i}. Since this value is independent of the receiver and does not change over time, it can be computed by the manufacturer offline, in the absence of any Rx coil.

To compute M_{1i}, we apply a source voltage V_s on the first Tx coil (the reference), and leave all other Tx coils open-circuit, as shown in Fig. 18. The figure focuses only on the part of the circuit that involves Tx_1 and Tx_i, and ignores the other Tx coils (which is feasible because they are open circuit). Since the circuit operates at its resonance frequency, the terms involving L and C cancel each other. Further, $I_i = 0$ since the Tx_i coil is left open circuit. Using the basic circuit equations (i.e., KVL), we write:

$$V_s = I_{s1} Z_{s1} \quad \text{(applying KVL to Tx}_1\text{)} \tag{14}$$

$$V_i = j\omega M_{1i} I_{s1} \quad \text{(applying KVL to Tx}_i\text{)} \tag{15}$$

The above two equations yield:

$$M_{1i} = \frac{V_i}{V_s} \cdot \frac{Z_{s1}}{j\omega}, \tag{16}$$

where V_s and Z_{s1} are known, ω is the resonance frequency, and V_i is directly measured. Hence, the above equation provides the value of M_{1i}.

(b) Online Step to Compute the Sign of M_i: As stated in §5.2, Equation (11) provides us with the absolute value of M_i for any i, but not its sign. We also know the sign of M_1 is positive. Hence we know M_1 fully. We also know M_{1i} from the initial calibration step. Given this information, we can measure the sign of M_i as follows: In the presence of the receiver, and during the channel estimation procedure, we apply the source voltage on Tx_1 (the reference coil), while leaving all other Tx coils open circuit, as shown in Fig. 19. Applying

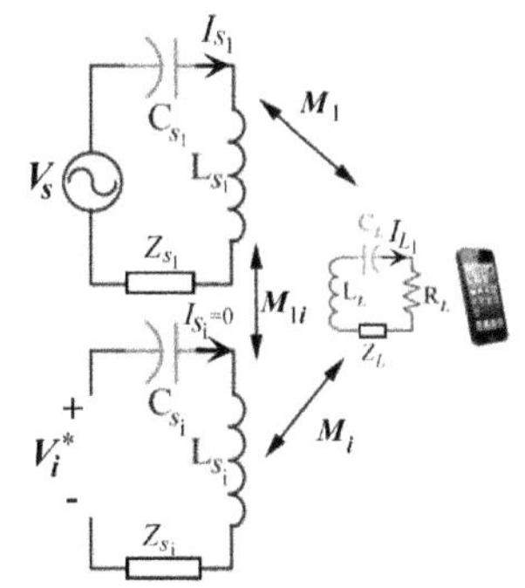

Figure 19: Determining the sign of Tx-Rx mutual inductance

basic circuit equations (i.e., KVL) to the receiver coil yields:

$$j\omega M_1 I_{s1} = I_{L1}(R_L + Z_L) \tag{17}$$

By rearranging the above equation we obtain:

$$I_{L1} = \frac{j\omega M_1 I_{s1}}{R_L + Z_L} \tag{18}$$

Next, we apply KVL to the Tx_i coil, which yields:

$$V_i^* = j\omega M_{1i} I_{s1} + j\omega M_i I_{L1}. \tag{19}$$

We can substitute I_{L1} from (18) in the last equation to obtain:

$$j\omega M_i = \frac{V_i^* - j\omega M_{1i} I_{s1}}{I_{L1}}. \tag{20}$$

In the above equation, all values are known, except for the sign of M_i. Specifically, V_i^* and I_{s1} can be directly measured at the transmitter. M_{1i} is known from the calibration step, and I_{L1} can estimated from (18), where all other values are known. Hence we can determine the sign of M_i as:

$$Sign(M_i) = Sign(\frac{V_i^* - j\omega M_{1i} I_{s1}}{j\omega I_{L1}}). \tag{21}$$

We note two points. First, since mutual inductances are real numbers (no imaginary part), the sign above is well-defined, i.e., the value on the right hand side of the equation inside the sign function is real and has a well-defined sign. Second, the reader may wonder why we do not use Equation (20) to directly determine the magnitude of M_i as well as its sign. The reason is that I_{L1} is typically small and hence sensitive to measurement errors. Since we divide by I_{L1}, the measurement error can be large and hence the exact value of M_i based on the above equation is less accurate than the value based on (11).

B. Off-the-shelf components used in the MagMIMO prototype

We have designed six tunable single switch power amplifiers based on the description of [28]. The power amplifiers are synchronized every 30 seconds by the digital logic through switch drivers [28], when the system estimates each individual channel by shutting down other Tx coils. The digital logic uses an Arduino micro-controller [3]. Six gain/phase detector ICs (AD8302: 2.7 GHz RF/IF [1]) report the voltages, currents and impedances of all coils to the digital logic at any given time. The pulse train on the receiver side is generated by a SiT1534 ultra low power oscillator. Resonance capacitors are ultra low ESR AVX corporation ceramic capacitors (3.6KV 5% NP0 3838), which provide high Q at high voltages, with negligible loss and temperature rise. To build the Tx and Rx coils, we have used generic refrigeration copper tubings.

Itus: An Implicit Authentication Framework for Android

Hassan Khan, Aaron Atwater, and Urs Hengartner
Cheriton School of Computer Science
University of Waterloo
Waterloo, ON Canada
{h37khan,aatwater,urs.hengartner}@uwaterloo.ca

ABSTRACT

Security and usability issues with pass-locks on mobile devices have prompted researchers to develop implicit authentication (IA) schemes, which continuously and transparently authenticate users using behavioural biometrics. Contemporary IA schemes proposed by the research community are challenging to deploy, and there is a need for a framework that supports: different behavioural classifiers, given that different apps have different requirements; app developers using IA without becoming domain experts; and real-time classification on resource-constrained mobile devices. We present Itus, an IA framework for Android that allows the research community to improve IA schemes incrementally, while allowing app developers to adopt these improvements at their own pace.

We describe the Itus framework and how it provides: **ease of use**: Itus allows app developers to use IA by changing as few as two lines of their existing code—on the other hand, Itus provides an oracle capable of making advanced recommendations should developers wish to fine-tune the classifiers; **flexibility**: developers can deploy Itus in an application-specific manner, adapting to their unique needs; **extensibility**: researchers can contribute new behavioural features and classifiers without worrying about deployment particulars; **low performance overhead**: Itus operates with minimal performance overhead, allowing app developers to deploy it without compromising end-user experience. These goals are accomplished with an API allowing individual stakeholders to incrementally improve Itus without re-engineering new systems. We implement Itus in two demo apps and measure its performance impact. To our knowledge, Itus is the first open-source extensible IA framework for Android that can be deployed off-the-shelf.

Categories and Subject Descriptors

D.4.6 [**Security and Protection**]: Authentication

MobiCom'14, September 7-11, 2014, Maui, Hawaii, USA.

ACM 978-1-4503-2783-1/14/09 ...$15.00.
http://dx.doi.org/10.1145/2639108.2639141.

Keywords

Security; Implicit Authentication; Behavioural Biometrics

1. INTRODUCTION

Smartphones contain a wealth of personal data including banking information, contacts, photos, videos, texts and emails. Smartphones that are used as bring your own devices (BYODs) may also contain confidential corporate data. In order to protect confidential data on smartphones from unauthorized access, primary authentication mechanisms (including PINs, pass-locks, draw-a-secret, fingerprint- or facial-recognition systems) are used. Organizations also use mobile device management (MDM) solutions to enforce password policies on BYODs to protect corporate data.

However, a recent survey found that 56% of smartphone owners do not configure PINs or pass-locks on their devices [24]. Since smartphone sessions tend to be short and frequent, all-or-nothing pass-locks reduce usability [4, 19]. While MDM solutions can enforce password policies, they aggravate the usability issues. According to a prediction by Gartner, 20% of enterprise BYOD programs will fail by 2016 due to overly restrictive policies of MDMs [36]. In addition to usability issues, pass-locks have also been subject to operating system flaws [39], smudge attacks [3] and shoulder surfing attacks. The limitedly available fingerprint- and facial-recognition systems have also been shown to be vulnerable to attacks [41].

These limitations have prompted researchers to develop implicit authentication (IA) schemes as a second line of defense to mitigate security and usability issues with explicit authentication mechanisms (such as pass-locks) [9]. IA schemes for smartphones authenticate a user by using distinctive, measurable patterns of device use that are gathered from the device users without requiring deliberate actions [9]. These IA schemes allow enterprises to relax pass-lock policies and complement them with IA. In case an adversary bypasses a pass-lock, IA may be able to detect it and lock the device or alert the user via email. Similarly, smartphone owners who do not wish to use pass-locks due to inconvenience can use IA to get limited protection from unauthorized use. Despite this utility and the reasonable performance of contemporary IA schemes, they are not deployed in practice. The lack of IA adoption is due to the challenges involved in creating an IA framework that is flexible enough to be used by a general audience. To date, there is no publicly available implementation of such a framework addressing these challenges.

Since contemporary IA schemes require the interception of user input events, some researchers have proposed including IA mechanisms at the platform level [14, 23], such that the operating system or app framework is responsible for providing IA to all apps on the system in an app independent manner. However, this approach has its own limitations in terms of flexibility and extensibility. First, different apps have different characteristics and a generic platform-level behaviour-based classifier may not be suitable for different apps. For example, a classifier based on keystroke behaviour may not be suitable while using a banking app where the user interacts through swipes. A classifier that constantly monitors all possible kinds of input would be problematic in terms of performance and battery life. The difference in app characteristics can also severely reduce the accuracy of IA schemes by as much as 20% [11, 22]. Furthermore, IA performed at the platform level would not be able to distinguish which activities within an app require protection by an authentication mechanism [22]. For example, the banking app may have a "locate ATM" feature that anyone using the device would be permitted to use (without the annoyance of triggering an IA rejection). Secondly, platform-level IA mechanisms would need to be managed by the platform developers or some central authority. However, IA is a relatively new area that still experiences radical revisions due to the research findings in such areas as the use of novel sensors or wearable devices for IA [28, 35], and the research findings on the usability and acceptance of IA schemes. The platform developers in this case are more inclined toward accepting mature contributions, which will lock out many developers.

These usability and flexibility limitations can be circumvented by enabling the apps themselves (that require IA) to implicitly authenticate users. By delegating IA to apps, we provide: usability—an app would only require authentication of a user while he is using the app, and since the app is in the foreground, it has access to event data and can launch an activity to lock the functionality in case of misuse—and flexibility: app developers can choose the behavioural classifier that is suitable for their app. However, the app developer requires domain-specific knowledge (e.g., of suitable behavioural classifiers, underlying machine learning algorithms, and their parameterization) and significant effort to provide IA support. An IA library could ease the burden of the app developers by abstracting away most of the details with a convenient API.

The challenges to creating such a framework include making the resulting library easy to use for app developers who are interested in providing IA to their users without the need to become domain experts. On the other hand, it should also be flexible enough to cater for app-specific functionality. Moreover, it must be extensible by the researchers developing novel IA schemes. Finally, it should not have a noticeable impact on performance or battery life to end-users, especially given the computational constraints of smartphones.

We present Itus[1], a framework that separates the domain knowledge of IA from its deployment. Itus has been designed to enable app developers to effortlessly provide IA support in their apps by modifying as few as two lines of code. At the same time, we provide app developers with an oracle that bridges the domain knowledge gap by forming recommendations on optimal sets of behavioural features and classifiers tailored for their particular apps. Itus is designed with extensibility in mind, allowing IA developers to iteratively contribute improvements to the framework. To demonstrate this we port three existing IA schemes to Itus. We demonstrate ease of use by adding Itus to two demo apps and we perform empirical evaluations to demonstrate Itus' low performance overhead. We hope that Itus will enable the research community to collaborate better to further the research in the IA domain.

The main contributions of this paper include:

1. We provide[2] the first IA framework for Android that can be used by app developers with minimal effort. It is implemented as a library at the user level and thus can be used right away without the need to root any devices or be added to the OS, although it could become part of mobile platforms in the future.

2. We provide researchers with an open-source, fully implemented system for rapid prototyping and deployment of new IA schemes. This is exemplified by the fact that we are able to implement three prominent IA schemes [5, 12, 14] using Itus.

3. We provide the Itus Oracle, a tool for app developers to automatically determine appropriate behavioural classifiers, suitable sets of features and optimum operating points of various configuration parameters for their apps. The Oracle also provides a way for us to curate the availability of IA schemes without hindering the ability for other developers and researchers to contribute to Itus.

4. We show that flexible and adaptable IA is possible on smartphones with acceptable performance overhead.

2. MOTIVATION

We consider our audience to be two-fold: the app developers who wish to incorporate IA into their apps, and the IA developers who wish to improve existing IA schemes. In this section, we first discuss some sample apps and the motivations their developers might have for including IA support. We then discuss the community of app developers that Itus targets in § 2.1, and the community of IA developers in § 2.2.

We consider the following apps as potential candidates for using IA:

An Enterprise Email Client: Provides employees access to corporate emails from their mobile devices.

A Web Browser: Provides all the standard web browser features including a password manager.

The email client app gives access to large amounts of sensitive corporate data. If employees were to install the app on their personal devices, the risk of information leakage is significantly increased. Adding IA at the app level allows the employer to ensure only authorized users are accessing sensitive data without disincentivizing users from installing the app on their own devices due to inconvenient security mechanisms. The developers of the browser, on the other hand, might be interested in providing their users the convenience of a password manager with the increased security of IA. The web browser could be used by anyone for non-sensitive sites

[1]Itus, Greek god of protection

[2]`https://crysp.uwaterloo.ca/software/itus/`

(e.g., lending the device to a friend to check the weather). When a site with a stored password is accessed, the password manager might then hand over a password only if IA decides that the user's recent activity pattern is as expected. Otherwise, the password manager will explicitly ask for the user's master password.

2.1 App Developers

Next, we refine our model of the spectrum of involvement by the app developers adding support for IA. In particular, we consider two levels of developer interest in IA frameworks:

Cursory interest: app developers who only want to add support for IA to their apps without tuning its accuracy or providing any application-specific behaviour. There are several types of app developers that may fall into this category. In the most trivial case, an app developer may simply be interested in experimenting with IA and wants to add it to their app without spending significant time on configuration and re-engineering of their app. Or, the app developer may be developing an app that contains such generic tasks that the default behaviour is "good enough" out-of-the-box. For example, consider the email client described above—user typing cadence tends to be unique enough [12] that the default keystroke classifier can easily deal with most usage scenarios of this app.

Significant interest: app developers who wish to fine-tune Itus for accuracy and performance. Such developers might do one or more of the following: restricting calculation of behavioural features to some subset to minimize computational overhead; configuring parameters of machine learning algorithms; experimenting with beta users to determine which configurations work best and retaining the data gathered during this phase for later training. It is important that Itus be able not only to support these developers in their efforts but to facilitate them by providing tools to assist and automate in these scenarios.

2.2 IA Developers

We now discuss the other class of audience— the developers who wish to contribute to Itus' IA schemes. To this end, we consider two representative scenarios.

Consider first those developers who wish to improve existing IA schemes (for example, investigating a novel set of behavioural features or simply tuning parameters). To demonstrate the efficacy of their proposal, they need to develop a prototype and evaluate its performance. Ideally, they should have access to an existing framework, giving them the necessary components to perform tasks common to all IA schemes (e.g., data storage, training, classification) without re-engineering. Itus should allow these developers to rapidly prototype their ideas without having their contributions moderated.

Secondly, consider developers who want to add support for behavioural classification modules that the core Itus framework does not anticipate. Specifically, the framework should allow for new machine learning classification algorithms and new sensor-derived behavioural features to be included alongside the core framework.

Itus should support these stakeholders and provide them with interfaces so that they can use or contribute to the framework as smoothly as possible.

3. DESIGN GOALS

In the previous section we highlighted the two-fold audience we consider while developing the Itus framework: app developers and IA developers. Both groups of developers are important for a successful IA framework to be adopted and remain relevant over time. In this section, we outline our design goals for Itus' framework for IA, and how they support both groups of developers in their efforts to provide usable IA to end users.

Separation of roles: Performing end-user authentication in a secure, usable manner is a challenging task that involves collaboration between IA developers and app developers. Our IA framework should synergize the efforts of different stakeholders to protect user data on mobile devices. In this spirit, we aim to incorporate a clear separation of roles that distinguishes between app developers, who may not be domain experts in the mechanisms underlying the system, from the IA developers or researchers working to improve the system.

Ease of Use: Our framework should not simply permit app developers to provide IA support in their apps, but also provide the app developer with an API to do so with minimal effort. App developers should be rewarded for their extra attention to user security, not punished with a burden of extended development time. Our goal is for Itus to be deployable in a reasonable default configuration with the absolute minimum number of lines of code changed as possible. The API should also allow configuration directives to be provided in as straightforward a manner as possible.

Flexibility: While ease of use is critical for adoption of IA by the broader audience of app developers, it is also important to make considerations for developers who have unique app needs or who wish to fine-tune the accuracy or performance of the IA scheme to their app. For example, for the web browser example discussed in § 2, the developer might be interested in making authentication decisions in a heavily context-aware manner. To this end, he might decide that after users start playing an embedded video, they are likely to hand off the device to another person and thus it would be undesirable for the IA mechanism to interrupt viewing with an explicit authentication prompt. In the case of the enterprise email client, the company's IT department may wish to invest heavily to provide high accuracy to ensure data security. In this case, the app developers should be able to configure Itus with pre-recorded training data or parametrize the classifier to improve its accuracy. We consider design features that allow for such examples of app-specific functionality when providing flexibility to app developers.

Extensibility: Extensibility is a prerequisite design goal of any system that is to be adopted by the community. Individual IA developers should be able to create and evaluate prototypes for various subcomponents of the Itus framework without any dependence on a centralized authority, and they should be able to distribute successful IA schemes independently from the core Itus framework. Ideally, this leads to a situation in which IA developers are able to deploy iterative improvements to the IA schemes while simultaneously allowing app developers to adopt these improvements at their own, perhaps asymmetric, rate. Our framework should allow each of these groups to make contributions without becoming embroiled in the specifics of framework subcomponents unrelated to their particular tasks.

Performance: Finally, performance in terms of computational overhead and power consumption is important to both the app developers and the researchers working on IA. App developers are especially concerned with any performance penalty that is going to be imposed on their apps, as this has a direct effect on their end-users' experience. Therefore, it is important that the framework itself consumes minimal resources so as to allow the behavioural classification subcomponents as much time as possible to perform their tasks before the end user is able to discern any differences.

4. ARCHITECTURE

This section gives an overview of the Itus system architecture. The core architecture of Itus, illustrated in Figure 1, is as follows: app developers extend a customized Android activity called `SecureActivity`, provided by the Itus library. Itus is then able to intercept user interaction events, which are passed through feature extractors called `Measurements` to obtain feature vectors. The Itus Agent gathers these feature vectors and hands them to the classification algorithms for training and classification. In the event a classifier returns a negative result (failed authentication), the Itus Agent then either notifies the parent app of the failure or independently switches the app view to a lock screen. In what follows, we will elaborate on how each of these links in the chain fit into the Itus framework.

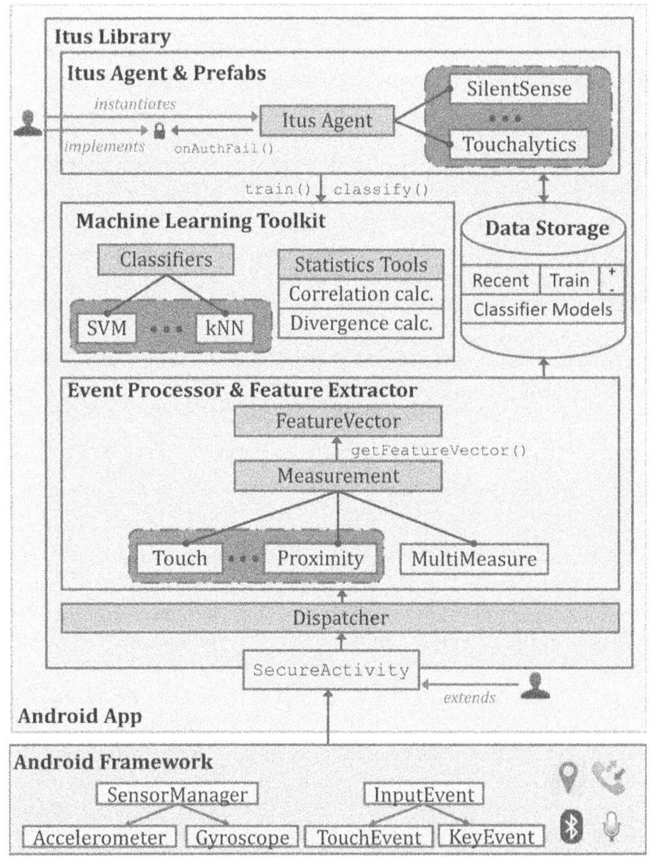

Figure 1: Itus framework architecture. Subclasses that are intended to be contributed by IA developers are in dark blue dotted boxes. The interfaces exposed to app developers are in red font.

4.1 SecureActivity

Interactive Android apps are composed of one or more "activities", which are app components that present the device user with a user interface to the app's functionality. When a developer creates a new Android app, one of the first steps is to create a subclass of Android's `Activity` class. Itus provides its own subclass of `Activity` called `SecureActivity`. To add IA to an app using Itus, a developer simply changes any classes that extend `Activity` to extend `SecureActivity` instead. This provides an incredibly simple way for developers to add Itus to their existing apps, supporting our ease-of-use goal discussed in § 3. It also makes it trivial for developers to partition apps composed of multiple activities into those that require authentication and those that do not (for example, a banking app may not want to authenticate a person when he is locating a nearby ATM); this supports our flexibility goal. This implementation puts our framework in an ideal place to intercept user interaction events with the app in order to then use them as behavioural features for classification.

4.2 Measurement and subclasses

Behavioural biometrics research examines a broad array of sensor values that may be useful for distinguishing between different device users. Examples include touch-screen input [5, 10, 11, 14, 23, 33], keystrokes on a physical or rendered keypad [8, 12, 20, 27, 40], and readings taken from an on-board accelerometer [13, 15]. In the Itus framework, we generalize these widely varying channels to say that behavioural features are generally calculated using some form of *measurements* taken from some on-board sensor. Thus we provide an abstract class in Itus called `Measurement`, subclasses of which are intended to extract measurements from any source accessible within the Android API (or extensions). To further our examples of sensor values, Itus might contain subclasses of `Measurement` called `Touch`, `Keystroke`, and `Movement`, respectively.

`Measurement` objects can register to receive events allowing them to process input data, which are subsequently passed to them via a callback method called `procEvent()`. There are two types of sensor readings: event-driven inputs and continuous readings. Event-driven inputs are intuitive to handle; registered handlers are called to process an event as soon as it occurs. The touch and keystroke examples are cases of event-driven inputs. Continuous readings, in which a sensor provides measurements any time it is polled (e.g., the accelerometer), are more subtle to handle. To deal with these, we create `Periodic` events, which function similarly to clock timer interrupts. `Measurement` objects analyzing continuous feedback sensors are then invoked periodically at parameterizable intervals. Some `Measurements` may provide feature values calculated from an aggregate of sensor readings and not at every regular time interval; for these objects, we allow the event-processing function to simply consume data and indicate that it is not yet ready to provide any feature values.

4.3 Dispatcher

In the last subsection, we said that events are given to various `Measurement` subclasses for feature extraction. In keeping with our performance goals outlined in § 3, it would not be efficient to invoke the procEvent method of every single Measurement for every single event. Instead, we create a Dispatcher class, which is responsible for delegating event processing to any configured Measurement objects. When Itus is configured at run-time to use a given Measurement subclass, an initialisation method is run from within that class. The primary purpose of initialisation method is to register with the Dispatcher and specify which events the Measurement would like to receive. Any events handled by Itus—either intercepted from user input by SecureActivity or generated periodically—are thus given to the Dispatcher, which in turn looks up the event type in a table to see which Measurements have registered for it, optionally adds context information, and passes them the event data via procEvent().

4.4 FeatureVector

As discussed previously, Measurement subclasses are responsible for taking data from events and turning them into useful feature values. When procEvent() is called to deliver event data to a Measurement object, the Measurement object will signal the Dispatcher if it has a new set of feature values ready to be exported. After receiving the signal, the Dispatcher will invoke the getFeatureVector() method of the Measurement subclass to retrieve these values. Specifically, the feature values are stored in a class called FeatureVector. This class is a 2-tuple made up of an array of double values and a boolean representing the class of the feature vector (valid/invalid user).

4.5 DataStorage

A FeatureVector, as obtained above, is processed as follows: if training has already been performed, then we simply classify this most recent sample. If training has yet to be performed, the FeatureVector should be stored until enough data is collected to perform training. In both cases, the Dispatcher will hand the FeatureVector over to a DataStorage object, which will store the FeatureVector in a list (hereafter called a "bin") depending upon the classifier state. In the former case, when training is complete, the FeatureVector will be placed into a bin labeled **bin_recent**, which can have an upper limit imposed on its size; this results in a sliding window, or FIFO queue, in which older data is discarded after consumption by the classification module or upon arrival of newer data. In the latter case, when training is pending, the FeatureVector is placed in the longer-term **bin_training** to be used for training once the bin reaches sufficient size.

The DataStorage object is also used to store classifier models once they have been trained. It has get() and put() methods allowing arbitrary data to be stored, allowing IA developers to use it as a convenient storage mechanism via the app's internal storage.

4.6 Itus Agent

Now that we have discussed the basic modules of our framework, we provide details of how the actual invocation of training and classification are coordinated. These are done by a class called Itus, which we refer to as the 'Itus Agent'. The Itus Agent runs in a separate thread from the main app. It is the main object that an app developer will interact with when they are adding the Itus framework to their app and configuring it. An instance of the Itus Agent class performs the configuration for all subcomponents of the Itus framework, including which Measurement subclasses are used and which classifiers are employed (see § 4.8). The Itus Agent drives the periodic events described in § 4.2, enforces the authentication policy with training/classification and, where necessary, locks the app in the event of a failure to implicitly authenticate.

In more detail, once training has been completed and a classifier has been obtained, the Itus Agent then simply runs it periodically against the recent FeatureVectors stored in **bin_recent**. If a classifier returns a negative result representing an unauthorized user, the Itus Agent reacts by performing its configured (or default) lock-screen action. If training has yet to be completed, the Agent explicitly authenticates the user in order to establish the ground truth for training data.

4.7 Itus Oracle

While we separate the domain knowledge of IA from its deployment by providing app developers with a high-level API to provide IA support in their apps, we understand the importance of correct selection of behavioural classifiers and suitable parametrization of the underlying machine learning algorithms. To bridge the gap between app developers' inexperience with IA schemes and the need for advanced configurations, we provide the Itus Oracle to automatically determine the right classifier and optimal configuration parameters.

To use the Itus Oracle, the app developer deploys Itus in 'configuration mode'. In this mode, Itus collects and logs all feature vectors and gathers other measurements concerning the data collection and performance of the app, such as timestamps, data sources, and processing times. After multiple sessions of beta use in the configuration mode, the developer then connects the device to a development computer and runs the Itus Oracle. The Itus Oracle downloads the logged data from the device and analyzes it. It experiments with various machine learning tools, including any classification algorithms compatible with Itus, and provides suggestions based on its analysis to the app developer. Finally, it repackages the data and configurations as a standalone Itus library that the developers can then import directly to their app. Repackaging also enables the Itus Oracle to bundle only the required Itus Prefabs which reduces the runtime memory footprint of the Itus library. More information about the implementation of the Itus Oracle is provided in § 6.

4.8 Machine Learning Toolkit

The number of viable candidates for machine learning algorithms for classifying behavioural feature sets is continually expanding. This is due not only to the ongoing research in the field but also due to the fact that a classifier may work well in combination with a certain feature set, while other classifiers may perform much better in cases where it is weak. Therefore, it is highly desirable that the Itus framework be able to add support for many classification algorithms without the development overhead of coupling them tightly with the rest of the IA framework.

Itus does this by defining a Classifier interface with two self-documenting methods: train(List<FeatureVector>) and classify(FeatureVector). The classify() method should return **boolean** value **true** for the positive class (authorized user) and **false** for the negative class (unauthorized user). More fine-grained control, such as interacting with confidence values, can be obtained by accessing **Classifier** objects directly. The learned classifier is transparently loaded to and from disk between app launches via the DataStorage object. We initially provide Itus with an implementation of the k-nearest-neighbours (kNN) classifier, and a wrapper that allows the Java version of libSVM (Support Vector Machines) [6] to be used as **Classifiers**.

Finally, the machine learning toolkit also contains statistics tools to measure correlation and divergence between features to determine effectiveness of features of behavioural classifiers. The Itus Oracle uses these tools to generate recommendations on features which should be used for an app.

5. WORKFLOW

In this section we outline the workflow that app developers must follow to provide IA support in their apps using Itus. We also discuss how IA developers can benefit from Itus and in return how they can contribute.

5.1 App Developers

As discussed in § 2.1, we broadly consider two types of app developers: those who want to use IA out-of-the-box, and those who want to tune the accuracy or performance of Itus. For the former type, Itus can be effortlessly imported and used in their apps. The app developer simply (i) identifies activities that should be protected, (ii) extends the activities from Itus' SecureActivity class, and (iii) starts the main thread of an Itus object. Training and classification are performed automatically at this point (see § 6 for details).

On the other hand, if the developer wants to tune the performance or the accuracy of a classifier, he uses the Itus Oracle to determine the best configurations for his app. To this end, the app developer (i) identifies activities that require implicit authentication and extends them from SecureActivity, (ii) starts Itus in configuration mode and gives device(s) to beta users for data collection, (iii) connects the device to the Itus Oracle (on the desktop) so that it can analyze data and generate recommendations, (iv) chooses from the recommended configurations so that the Itus Oracle can repackage the library, and (v) adds the repackaged library to the app and disables configuration mode.

Most classifiers require negative (non-owner) training data in order to provide high accuracy. For this, an app can either use default negative instances included with Itus, or it may package a subset of data collected during configuration mode as negative training data. Since data collected during the configuration mode is labeled against each user, the negative training set of a user is created by excluding his data. We anticipate that after Itus is released in the public domain, it will also benefit from IA datasets that have been made publicly available by the research community [13, 14, 31, 37].

5.2 IA Developers

§ 2.2 presented two types of IA developers we envision contributing to Itus. Itus provides deliberate separation for contributions to the IA mechanism. In § 4.2 we described how new sensor features are added to Itus by extending the Measurement class. Similarly, § 4.8 described how new classification algorithms are added to Itus be extending the **Classifier** class. These subclasses can be contributed to Itus independently by the second group of IA developers discussed in § 2.2.

§ 4.6 explained how app-specific configurations are stored in an **Itus** object. Itus can provide for a variety of default configurations by simply distributing pre-built **Itus** objects. In the Itus framework, we call such objects Prefabs and implement them by deriving subclasses of **Itus**. These subclasses inherit all the functionality of the default Itus Agent, and simply need to add a constructor that performs any configuration directives that would normally be added by the app developer. These Prefabs can be compiled and distributed separately from the Itus framework, allowing the first group of developers discussed in § 2.2 to propose new configurations or even modified behaviour of the Itus Agent without needing their contribution to be accepted upstream by the core Itus framework.

6. IMPLEMENTATION

We implemented the Itus framework in Android Java and the Itus oracle in Python. Itus is currently about 22,000 lines and has been released in open source. Itus is distributed as a standalone library of 773KB and it can be imported and used by any Android project that supports Android version 2.23 and above. This allows Itus to support the majority of the Android devices in use today (98.8% Android devices in-the-wild as of March, 2014 [16]). In this section, we discuss some of the significant implementation decisions of Itus.

Event Interception: The API of Itus has been designed to abstract away the underlying low-level event collection from the app developer. While there exist mobile sensor collection frameworks such as SoundSense [25] and Jigsaw [26], unfortunately these frameworks exist for Nokia and Apple iOS and not for the Android OS. For event handling in Android Activities, Android provides EventListener and EventHandler to the app developers. Every user activity in an app is derived from the Android Activity class and these events are first delivered to Activity.dispatchTouchEvent(). We provide the SecureActivity class, which extends the Activity class and additionally provides constructs to optionally intercept and copy events before delivering them to the users. App developers who want to provide IA support in their apps are expected to extend SecureActivity for transparent event interception.

Data Storage: For permanent storage, Itus uses an app's internal storage. We chose internal storage since: an app's internal storage can only be accessed by the app itself and a malicious app cannot gain access to the training model; and accessing an app's internal storage space does not require any explicit permissions. We require the training model classes be **Serializeable** so they can be written and subsequently read from the permanent storage automatically.

Training Set Size and Retraining: To perform training when the user first interacts with a new app, a sufficient amount of data must be collected. The definition of 'sufficient' here has some room for interpretation, and so we provide two distinct ways for developers to specify the training data threshold: absolutely and empirically. In the absolute case, the developer sets the minimum threshold to some integer value (N), and when **bin_training** receives N samples of FeatureVectors, training is triggered. In the empirical case, the developer specifies some minimum accuracy level to be attained during training before considering training to be complete. Here, the Itus Agent runs training periodically and evaluates accuracy using x-fold cross-validation (where x is another parameter) and stops when it achieves the desired target accuracy. This second method is obviously significantly more performance-heavy than simply training at N instances, so the oracle tool in § 4.7 helps developers determine appropriate values of N.

In order to improve the user experience by reducing false rejects, Itus provides app developers with the option to automatically retrain the classifier to improve its accuracy. To this end, Itus first temporarily stores the `FeatureVectors` that are classified as non-owner's by the behavioural classifier. It then triggers the lockout activity to explicitly authenticate the user. If the user successfully authenticates, Itus uses the misclassified feature vectors to retrain the behaviour-based classifier. While retraining improves the user experience, in addition to training overhead, it requires additional storage space to save misclassified `FeatureVectors`.

Lockout Action: In case of authentication failure, the app developer may launch the device's default authentication mechanism (PINs/pass-locks). However, a large number of device owners do not configure pass-locks on their devices and furthermore, if the attacker has gained access to the device, he has already compromised the primary authentication mechanism. Therefore, to support our off-the-shelf design goal, Itus provides app developers with a default `PasswordConfigure` activity, which is displayed when the app is launched for the first time to configure a password that should be used for explicit authentication in case the IA scheme detects misuse. Itus also provides a `LockoutActivity` to lock the app when misuse is detected. The `LockoutActivity` is also used during the training phase to establish the ground truth during data collection. The `LockoutActivity` overrides the `onBackPressed` method of `Activity` to ignore in-app navigation attempts.

In addition to this, we provide the app developer with a more flexible option to deal with authentication failures. The app developer registers a callback object, implementing our `AuthFailedListenter` interface. This interface specifies a single `onAuthFailed` method, which will be called whenever a classifier fails to implicitly authenticate the user. The app developer is then able to handle authentication failure in any manner desired, supporting our flexibility goal from § 3. For example, a browser might choose to delete the session cookies for any websites the user is currently logged in to.

Managing Timeouts: Itus provides app developers with the ability to pause and resume IA to reduce performance overheads and to save battery life. Itus also provides app developers with the functions to configure timeout intervals so that once a user is successfully authenticated, Itus pauses feature collection and training for the specified interval and resumes its operations when interval times out. App developer can also specify whether they want to reset timeouts and resume IA in case of a screen-off event.

Multi-measurements and Multimodal Classifiers: For advanced IA scenarios, we enable the app developers to use multi-measurements by employing feature samples from different measurement modules. For example, the SilentSense classifier [5] uses events from touch input and data from the motion sensor. Itus provides constructs that can

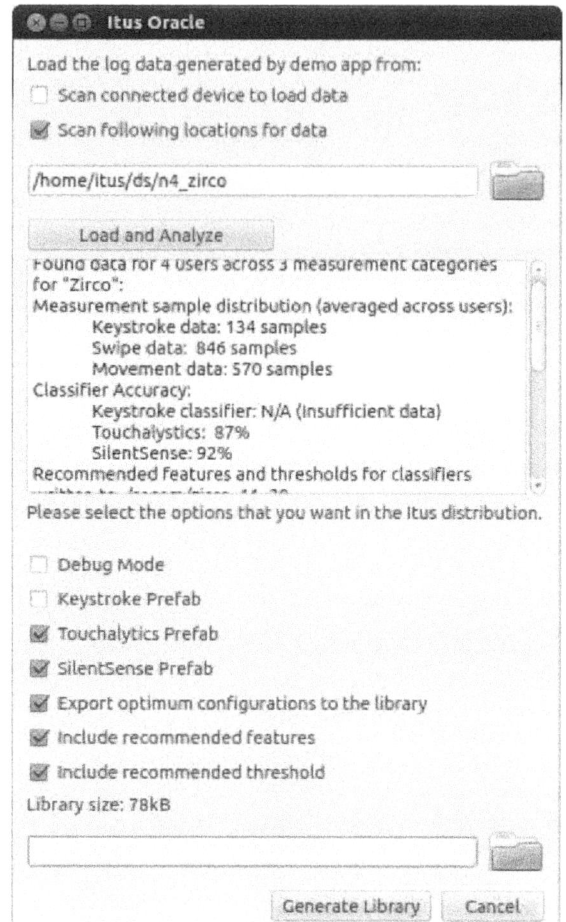

Figure 2: Itus Oracle utility

be used by the app developer to define relationships between measurement data from different sources (`MultiMeasurement` in Figure 1). The app developer simply defines the causal relationship between two events and the resultant `FeatureVector` is automatically generated. Similarly, Itus provides high-level constructs to the app-developer to use multiple behavioural classifiers. These constructs can be used by the developers to combine the authentication score from different behavioural classifiers in a pre-condition or majority score setting. For example, the enterprise email client might use a location-based classifier as a pre-condition to trigger a touch-based classifier.

Itus Oracle: The Itus Oracle identifies suitable classifiers, optimal feature sets, and operating threshold recommendations for the app developer. It determines an appropriate classifier by evaluating the accuracy of Itus Prefabs on the data collected during the configuration mode. This decision also takes into account the availability of data for different Itus Prefabs. The optimal feature set for a particular app is determined by calculating information gain for each feature on collected data. For example, for a navigation app, Itus would automatically detect that the direction of a swipe is not a good feature (due to its high variance on sampled data). Finally, the Itus Oracle provides the app developer with the optimum threshold values by determining the operating point with the highest accuracy.

We provide a screenshot of the Itus oracle in Figure 2. The summary and recommendations generated by the Itus Oracle are shown in the text box. For now, this information (such as confidence intervals and cross-validation results) is simply displayed in raw form to the developer, which may require some statistics knowledge to interpret. In future iterations, we aim to parse these results for more concise recommendations. Based on the recommendations, the Itus Oracle also generates an Itus library that the app developer can readily use in his app.

Prefabs Selection: In the future, we envision using the Oracle as a method of curating the implementations of IA presented to app developers. This will allow us to prevent malicious schemes from entering the ecosystem, such as an IA developer creating a keystroke `Measurement` that also functions as a keylogger. However, as running the Oracle or accepting its recommendations are not necessary steps in order to use Itus, this approach allows for researchers to freely experiment with IA, and for IA developers to distribute standalone extensions to Itus. For now, we want to provide a diverse set of prefabs with Itus to demonstrate its extensibility. To this end, we choose a keystroke classifier [12], a classifier based on touch behaviour (Touchalytics) [14] and a classifier based on the micro-movements of the mobile device caused by touch (SilentSense) [5]. The keystroke classifier and Touchalytics only use user generated events (`KeyEvent` and `TouchEvent`, respectively) while SilentSense uses data that merges user generated events (`TouchEvent`) with periodic events (accelerometer data). Furthermore, the keystroke classifier and Touchalytics use kNN for classification while SilentSense employs SVM for classification.

7. PERFORMANCE EVALUATION

To provide a seamless user experience, it is critical for Itus to have minimum performance overhead. Furthermore, since smartphones are power constrained devices, high battery consumption of Itus may reduce its utility. In this section, we first discuss the experimental setup that we use for performance evaluation and we then provide the results of our evaluation.

7.1 Experimental Setup

Device Selection: For performance evaluations, we use an HTC Nexus 1 and an LG Nexus 4. The HTC Nexus 1 has Android OS v2.23 (`Gingerbread`) on a 1GHz processor with 512MB of RAM. The LG Nexus 4 has Android OS v4.4 (`KitKat`) on a quad-core 1.5 GHz processor with 2GB of RAM. Our selection of these diverse devices supplies an overview of Itus performance on both old and recent hardware.

Performance Metrics For empirical evaluations, we are only interested in the performance of Itus and we do not evaluate the accuracy of the IA schemes employed. We refer interested readers to the original papers [5, 12, 14] for the accuracy evaluations and default parameters used here (such as window sizes and sampling rates). For performance evaluations, we measure the performance overhead in terms of elapsed CPU time and heap size of the app. We also evaluate the battery consumption overhead of Itus. Finally, we evaluate the impact of Itus on user experience by measuring the relative performance overhead of Itus with our demo apps.

```java
public class MainActivity extends SecureActivity
    implements IToolbarsContainer, OnTouchListener,
    IDownloadEventsListener {

    @Override
    public void onCreate(Bundle savedInstanceState) {
        super.onCreate(savedInstanceState);
        INSTANCE = this;
        /*create an Instance of Touchalytics classifier
         * & start the Itus thread*/
        (new Touchalytics()).start();
```

(a) Using a Prefab to provide IA support

```java
    @Override
    public void onCreate(Bundle savedInstanceState) {
        super.onCreate(savedInstanceState);
        INSTANCE = this;

        /*Configure & launch Itus*/
        Itus itus = new Itus(this);
        String [] featureList = {"Start X", "Start Y",
                "Average Velocity", "Interstroke Time"};
        Classifier svm = new SVMClassifier(
            featureList.length, "negative_instances");
        svm.setFeatureScaling(true);

        Measurement touch = new Touch();
        touch.setFeatureList(featureList);
        itus.useMeasurement(touch);
        itus.setTrainingSize(100);
        itus.useClassifier(svm);
        itus.start();
```

(b) Using low-level constructs to provide IA support

Figure 3: Itus' development overhead for Zirco Browser

Demo Apps For demo apps to evaluate for performance purposes, we choose: (i) Zirco Browser[3]: an open-source browser with between 50,000 and 100,000 installs at the Google Play Store; and (ii) TextSecure[4]: a popular open-source encrypted communication app with between 100,000 and 500,000 installs at the Google Play Store. These apps were selected as our demo apps for two reasons: (i) both apps manage private data of the user, and (ii) usage of these apps results in different event types (`TouchEvent` for Zirco and `KeyEvent` for TextSecure), which allows us to test the different classifiers discussed in § 6.

7.2 Evaluation Results

Development Overhead: For a developer who is employing Itus Prefabs, the development overhead is minimal. While quantification of development overhead is a non-trivial task, we herein provide our experience of adding Itus to the demo apps. To avoid any bias due to the absence of a learning curve, we only report development overhead in terms of the number of lines of code added/modified. To provide default IA support in Zirco Browser and TextSecure, in addition to importing the Prefab class, we only modified 2 lines of code. As discussed in § 5, the app developer extends the `SecureActivity` class and launches a suitable Prefab (both operations are highlighted in Figure 3a).

However, if the app developer wants to optimize the classifiers, there would be more development overhead (depending

[3]`https://play.google.com/store/apps/details?id=org.zirco`

[4]`https://play.google.com/store/apps/details?id=org.thoughtcrime.securesms`

		Initialization		Feature Extraction		Training		Classification	
		CPU(ms)	Heap(kB)	CPU(ms)	Heap(kB)	CPU(ms)	Heap(kB)	CPU(ms)	Heap(kB)
N1	Keystroke	21 (2.08)	185(5.6)	<1 (≃0)	<1 (≃0)	<1 (≃0)	<1 (≃0)	0.2 (≃0)	3.1 (0.19)
	Touchalytics	5 (0.27)	17.3 (2.6)	0.27 (≃0)	7.8 (0.03)	65 (2.16)	48.9 (1.4)	1.7 (≃0)	51.3 (1.4)
	SilentSense	1162 (81)	1236 (15)	0.75 (≃0)	14.6 (1.1)	10384 (91)	2472 (18)	0.12 (≃0)	3.7 (0.04)
N4	Keystroke	12 (0.95)	186 (2.3)	<1 (≃0)	<1 (≃0)	<1 (≃0)	<1 (≃0)	0.05 (≃0)	2.9 (0.13)
	Touchalytics	3 (0.27)	16 (0.62)	0.05 (≃0)	11 (0.48)	15 (0.5)	53 (0.74)	1.08 (≃0)	56 (5.11)
	SilentSense	972 (67)	776 (34)	0.55 (≃0)	16.8 (0.4)	5937 (329)	2453 (39)	0.07 (≃0)	4.2 (0.28)

Table 1: Performance evaluation of different configurations of Itus. 95% confidence intervals are provided in parenthesis. N1: Nexus 1 and N4: Nexus 4.

on the type of optimizations). The app developer can use the Itus Oracle to perform optimizations automatically or choose to manually perform optimizations in order to control certain aspects of IA scheme. In Figure 3b, we show one of the possible workflows an app developer might follow to manually employ touch behaviour features for IA using the SVM classifier. The 10 lines of code (Line 132 - 144) in Figure 3b show how the developer: (i) instantiates Itus (Line 132); (ii) defines a list of feature that should be used by the `Measurement` module (Line 133, 139, 140); (iii) configures parameters of the SVM classifier (Line 135 - 137); and (iv) configures Itus to use the `Measurement` and `Classifier` objects, and starts the Itus Agent (Line 141 - 144).

Performance Evaluation of Itus: We instrument Itus to measure its performance overhead in terms of elapsed CPU time and size of heap memory for different runtime configurations. Since the operations of Itus depend on events that cannot be accurately controlled manually, for repeatable experiments we use Monkey scripts [2] to simulate event generation. We repeat each experiment 15 times for three different runtime configurations and report averages in Table 1. Table 1 shows that both the keystroke classifier and Touchalytics require much less CPU time and heap memory. More specifically, the feature extraction and classification operations that are triggered for every input event, take under 1 and under 2 ms for the keystroke and touch classifiers, respectively on the Nexus 4 device. On the other hand, SilentSense—which uses SVM—takes close to 1 and 6 seconds for initialization and training, respectively. The CPU and memory overhead in the initialization process is due to the loading of negative instances from an app's internal storage. However, this overhead is incurred only once; after the creation of the training model, feature extraction and classification takes less than a millisecond for a swipe. The execution results show that both devices are able to extract features, and classify in a reasonable amount of time.

Battery Consumption Overhead of Itus: We use PowerTutor [42] to measure battery consumption overhead by Itus. Micro-level overheads are recorded only during individual user input events and are computed relative to the individual demo apps, while macro-level overheads are recorded across a longer period of usage and computed relative to the device. For reproducible experiments, we do not perform any network operations (i.e., swipes are made on pre-downloaded pages in Zirco and for TextSecure the typed message is not transmitted). Finally, battery consumption overhead results do not include the one-time training cost of Itus prefabs.

	Overhead on the app	Overhead on the device
Keystroke	38.6% (2.8)	1.23% (0.24)
Touchalytics	8.91% (0.64)	3.74% (0.53)
SilentSense	14.2% (0.95)	6.23% (0.89)

Table 2: Battery consumption overhead of Itus Prefabs on demo apps with a Nexus 1 device. Standard deviations are calculated across every hour of testing for each of 12 hours, and are shown in parentheses.

For overhead at the micro-level, we measure the power consumption of the Keystroke prefab by generating 160 keystroke events for classification. Similarly, we generate 40 swipe events for classification by the Touchalytics and SilentSense prefabs. Our empirical evaluation results, provided in the "overhead on the app" column of Table 2. The battery overhead for TextSecure is significantly higher because the battery consumption for normal operation is negligible (unlike Zirco which requires relatively expensive graphic rendering when swiped).

Computation of the macro-level overhead is a non-trivial task due to the large number of variables involved, such as the number of running apps, network connection (3G/WiFi) and the usage of other apps by the device user. To mitigate these variations, we create a simple setup in which Nexus 1 devices are only executing the demo app, the Google Mail app, the Google Talk app and the Launcher app. These devices are also executing the default supporting systems Network Location, User Dictionary, Media Server and the Radio and WiFi subsystems. Monkey scripts [2] were used to generate 40 swipe and 160 keystroke events after every 10 minute interval for 12 hours. Table 2 provides the results for the macro level overhead in the "overhead on the device" column. It can be observed from these results that all Itus Prefabs incur reasonably low overhead (1.23%, 3.74% and 6.23% for Keystroke, Touchalytics and SilentSense prefabs, respectively) even on Android devices with a minimal set of apps running.

Performance Overhead on Demo Apps: In addition to the performance evaluation of standalone Itus, we also measure the performance overhead imposed by Itus on two demo apps. The objective of this evaluation is to show that the relative performance overhead of Itus is negligible enough to not compromise user experience. We instrument and measure elapsed CPU time and heap memory size for the demo apps with and without Itus. The experiment with Zirco was conducted by accessing the BBC and CNN home-

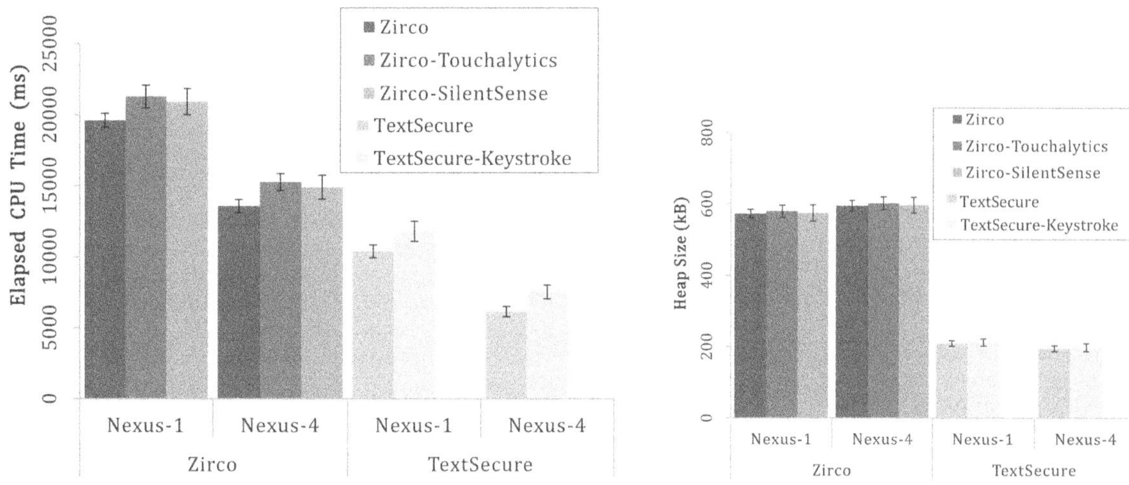

(a) CPU Overhead

(b) Memory Overhead

Figure 4: Itus' CPU and memory overhead for demo apps. Error bars represent 95% confidence intervals.

pages using Zirco and swiping 20 times on each website without any delays. The experiment with the TextSecure app was conducted by composing a text message of 160 characters (network transmission was not included). Figures 4a, 4b show the CPU overhead and memory overhead for demo apps, respectively. It can be observed from Figure 4 that the CPU and memory overhead for Itus is negligible and Itus can be used without compromising user experience.

8. LIMITATIONS

Itus is part of our on-going research work. We have evaluated Itus on a variety of Android devices from different manufacturers and found it to be robust. However, there are a few limitations to deployment on old and low-end Android devices. Processing intensive IA schemes on Android devices with low-end processors might affect user experience. Similarly, for IA schemes that rely on sensor data from different on-board sensors, the accuracy of Itus will be negatively affected on some of the old devices with low sampling rates. However, these are trivial limitations given the high penetration of modern Android devices.

Another limitation of our approach is that each instance of Itus executes in isolation from other instances on the same device. Therefore, every app that uses Itus requires a separate training model and an instance of the Itus library in memory. This requires additional storage and increases apps' memory footprints (although it should be noted that the Itus Oracle can be used to reduce the memory footprint, as discussed in § 4.7). Finally, while independent execution of multiple Itus instances precludes any information sharing across these instances, this is by design to prevent any potential security issues arising from malicious apps.

Itus deployment is of course subject to all the limitations of existing IA mechanisms, including the requirement that it be configured to track representative input data from the current operator of a device. If, for example, an intruder comes across a device resting on a stable surface and protected by the SilentSense prefab, there would be no movement data available to classify him. Furthermore, it may be possible for attackers to use mimicry attacks to defeat IA [30] or to root a device. One of the benefits of providing an extensible IA framework is that Itus can easily incorporate defences against mimicry attacks as soon as they are proposed by security researchers. Attackers rooting a device are hard to defend against in general and not part of our threat model.

9. RELATED WORK

Explicit authentication schemes (such as pass-locks, facial and fingerprint recognition) are only partly related to our work since we understand their importance as a primary defense mechanism. We only advocate application of IA as a second line of defense due to usability [4, 19] and security issues [1, 41, 39] of explicit authentication schemes.

For IA on smartphones, various behaviour-based classifiers have been proposed that employ users' call / text patterns [34], location patterns [38], keystroke patterns [8, 12, 20, 27, 40], proximity to known devices [21, 29], gait patterns [13, 15], and touch screen input behaviour [5, 10, 11, 14, 23, 33]. Furthermore, some approaches have proposed to combine behaviour-based classifiers and contextual information from multiple sources [29, 32, 34] to implicitly authenticate a user. We differ from these prior research efforts in that our work places emphasis on the architecture and deployment aspects of an IA approach, rather than the efficacy of behaviour-based classifiers. In fact, any existing IA scheme can be deployed using our architecture to mitigate the limitations discussed in § 2.

Clarke et al. [7] proposed the design of a framework to support continuous and transparent authentication using facial, voice and keystroke biometrics. Crawford et al. [9] proposed a similar system that supports multimodal combination of these biometrics. However, the focus of their work is to provide design guidelines of such a framework for an IA scheme that operates at the device-level. Contrary to their approach, we propose a framework that enables app developers to integrate continuous authentication in their apps directly. Furthermore, the authors of [7, 9] only provide design guidelines for transparent and continuous authentication systems and stop short of providing an implementation of their design that can be used by device owners. Riva et al. [29] have built a prototype to use face recognition, proximity, phone placement, and voice recognition to progressively authenticate a user. Their prototype on Windows phone reduces the number of required authentications by 42%. While they have a common goal with our work in terms of when to authenticate, their scheme would require kernel-level support to operate and therefore has the limitations discussed in § 1.

There are a few approaches that have a common goal with ours in terms of providing an optimal trade-off between usability and security. For example, Hayashi et al. [19] discuss the inefficiency of the all-or-nothing access model and suggest that a user should be authenticated only when a sensitive app is launched. They also discuss shared access scenarios and propose an activity lock that can be used by a device owner to share specific screens in an app or a group account to share a specific set of apps between multi-user environments. In a related work, [17, 18] use multiple implicit factors (from user context) to determine how to explicitly authenticate a user. However, our work is different from these approaches since in addition to allowing an app developer to selectively invoke an authenticating module based on the type of an app, we delegate IA tasks to an app and not to the device.

10. CONCLUSION

We have proposed Itus, a framework for providing IA support on smartphones, and provided an open-source implementation for Android. Itus separates the domain knowledge of IA from its deployment to bridge the gap between IA research and practice. The architecture of Itus is designed with flexibility in mind for app developers, allowing them choice between modular subcomponents implementing different mechanisms for behavioural feature classification. The Itus framework is easily extensible to allow IA developers to easily provide such subcomponents. Itus also provides application developers with the ability to optionally configure the behaviour of the IA mechanism to their application's needs by using an Oracle program to determine suitable classifiers and configuration parameters. The API of Itus has been designed to trivialize the effort to provide IA in Android apps. Empirical evaluations of Itus in real-world demo apps show that it has minimum overhead. We have made Itus publicly available in open-source for Android and we are currently working on providing support for more IA schemes in Itus. In future work, we will conduct usability studies to determine the efficacy of IA on smartphones for users and the utility of Itus for app developers. We hope that Itus will enable the research community to collaborate better to further research in the IA domain and also to enable the adoption of IA.

11. ACKNOWLEDGMENTS

Thanks to the anonymous reviewers for their valuable comments. We also thank Google and NSERC for their support.

12. REFERENCES

[1] Android Authority. Android jelly bean face unlock liveness check easily hacked with photo editing. `http://www.androidauthority.com/android-jelly-bean-face-unlock-blink-hacking-105556/`, Mar. 2014.

[2] Android Tools. Application exerciser monkey. `http://developer.android.com/tools/help/monkey.html`, Mar. 2014.

[3] A. J. Aviv, K. Gibson, E. Mossop, M. Blaze, and J. M. Smith. Smudge attacks on smartphone touch screens. In *Usenix Workshop on Offensive Technologies*. Usenix, 2010.

[4] N. Ben-Asher, N. Kirschnick, H. Sieger, J. Meyer, A. Ben-Oved, and S. Möller. On the need for different security methods on mobile phones. In *Proceedings of the 13th International Conference on Human Computer Interaction with Mobile Devices and Services*, pages 465–473. ACM, 2011.

[5] C. Bo, L. Zhang, X.-Y. Li, Q. Huang, and Y. Wang. Silentsense: silent user identification via touch and movement behavioral biometrics. In *Proceedings of the 19th Annual International Conference on Mobile Computing & Networking*, pages 187–190. ACM, 2013.

[6] C.-C. Chang and C.-J. Lin. Libsvm: a library for support vector machines. *ACM Transactions on Intelligent Systems and Technology*, 2(3):27, 2011.

[7] N. Clarke, S. Karatzouni, and S. Furnell. Flexible and transparent user authentication for mobile devices. In *Emerging Challenges for Security, Privacy and Trust*, pages 1–12. Springer, 2009.

[8] N. L. Clarke and S. Furnell. Authenticating mobile phone users using keystroke analysis. *International Journal of Information Security*, 6(1):1–14, 2007.

[9] H. Crawford, K. Renaud, and T. Storer. A framework for continuous, transparent mobile device authentication. *Computers & Security*, 39:127–136, 2013.

[10] A. De Luca, A. Hang, F. Brudy, C. Lindner, and H. Hussmann. Touch me once and i know it's you!: implicit authentication based on touch screen patterns. In *Proceedings of the 2012 ACM Annual Conference on Human Factors in Computing Systems*, pages 987–996. ACM, 2012.

[11] T. Feng, J. Yang, Z. Yan, E. M. Tapia, and W. Shi. Tips: Context-aware implicit user identification using touch screen in uncontrolled environments. In *Proceedings of the 15th Workshop on Mobile Computing Systems and Applications*. ACM, 2014.

[12] T. Feng, X. Zhao, B. Carbunar, and W. Shi. Continuous mobile authentication using virtual key typing biometrics. In *12th IEEE International Conference on Trust, Security and Privacy in Computing and Communications*, pages 1547–1552. IEEE, 2013.

[13] J. Frank, S. Mannor, and D. Precup. Activity and gait recognition with time-delay embeddings. In *AAAI Conference on Artificial Intelligence*, 2010.

[14] M. Frank, R. Biedert, E. Ma, I. Martinovic, and D. Song. Touchalytics: On the applicability of touchscreen input as a behavioral biometric for continuous authentication. *IEEE Transactions on Information Forensics and Security*, 8(1):136–148, 2013.

[15] D. Gafurov, K. Helkala, and T. Søndrol. Biometric gait authentication using accelerometer sensor. *Journal of Computers*, 1(7):51–59, 2006.

[16] Google Play. Google play install stats. http://developer.android.com/about/dashboards/index.html, Mar. 2014.

[17] A. Gupta, M. Miettinen, N. Asokan, and M. Nagy. Intuitive security policy configuration in mobile devices using context profiling. In *International Conference on Social Computing, Privacy, Security, Risk and Trust*, pages 471–480. IEEE, 2012.

[18] E. Hayashi, S. Das, S. Amini, J. Hong, and I. Oakley. Casa: context-aware scalable authentication. In *Proceedings of the Ninth Symposium on Usable Privacy and Security*, page 3. ACM, 2013.

[19] E. Hayashi, O. Riva, K. Strauss, A. Brush, and S. Schechter. Goldilocks and the two mobile devices: going beyond all-or-nothing access to a device's applications. In *Proceedings of the Eighth Symposium on Usable Privacy and Security*, page 2. ACM, 2012.

[20] S.-s. Hwang, S. Cho, and S. Park. Keystroke dynamics-based authentication for mobile devices. *Computers & Security*, 28(1):85–93, 2009.

[21] A. Kalamandeen, A. Scannell, E. de Lara, A. Sheth, and A. LaMarca. Ensemble: cooperative proximity-based authentication. In *Proceedings of the 8th International Conference on Mobile Systems, Applications, and Services*, pages 331–344. ACM, 2010.

[22] H. Khan and U. Hengartner. Towards application-centric implicit authentication on smartphones. In *Proceedings of the 15th Workshop on Mobile Computing Systems and Applications*. ACM, 2014.

[23] L. Li, X. Zhao, and G. Xue. Unobservable reauthentication for smart phones. In *Proceedings of the 20th Network and Distributed System Security Symposium*, volume 13, 2013.

[24] Lookout Blog. Sprint and lookout consumer mobile behavior survey. http://blog.lookout.com/blog/2013/10/21/sprint-and-lookout-survey/, Mar. 2014.

[25] H. Lu, W. Pan, N. D. Lane, T. Choudhury, and A. T. Campbell. Soundsense: scalable sound sensing for people-centric applications on mobile phones. In *Proceedings of the 7th International Conference on Mobile Systems, Applications, and Services*, pages 165–178. ACM, 2009.

[26] H. Lu, J. Yang, Z. Liu, N. D. Lane, T. Choudhury, and A. T. Campbell. The jigsaw continuous sensing engine for mobile phone applications. In *Proceedings of the 8th ACM Conference on Embedded Networked Sensor Systems*, pages 71–84. ACM, 2010.

[27] E. Maiorana, P. Campisi, N. González-Carballo, and A. Neri. Keystroke dynamics authentication for mobile phones. In *Proceedings of the 2011 ACM Symposium on Applied Computing*, pages 21–26. ACM, 2011.

[28] S. Mare, A. Molina-Markham, C. Cornelius, R. Peterson, and D. Kotz. Zebra: Zero-effort bilateral recurring authentication. In *IEEE Symposium on Security and Privacy*. IEEE, 2014.

[29] O. Riva, C. Qin, K. Strauss, and D. Lymberopoulos. Progressive authentication: deciding when to authenticate on mobile phones. In *Proceedings of the 21st USENIX Security Symposium*, 2012.

[30] A. Serwadda and V. V. Phoha. When kids' toys breach mobile phone security. In *Proceedings of the 2013 ACM SIGSAC conference on Computer & Communications Security*, pages 599–610. ACM, 2013.

[31] A. Serwadda, V. V. Phoha, and Z. Wang. Which verifiers work?: A benchmark evaluation of touch-based authentication algorithms. In *IEEE Sixth International Conference on Biometrics: Theory, Applications and Systems*, pages 1–8. IEEE, 2013.

[32] A. Shabtai, U. Kanonov, and Y. Elovici. Intrusion detection for mobile devices using the knowledge-based, temporal abstraction method. *Journal of Systems and Software*, 83(8):1524–1537, 2010.

[33] M. Shahzad, A. X. Liu, and A. Samuel. Secure unlocking of mobile touch screen devices by simple gestures: you can see it but you can not do it. In *Proceedings of the 19th Annual International Conference on Mobile Computing & Networking*, pages 39–50. ACM, 2013.

[34] E. Shi, Y. Niu, M. Jakobsson, and R. Chow. Implicit authentication through learning user behavior. In *Information Security*, pages 99–113. Springer, 2011.

[35] B. Shrestha, N. Saxena, H. T. T. Truong, and N. Asokan. Drone to the rescue: Relay-resilient authentication using ambient multi-sensing. In *Proc. Eighteenth International Conference on Financial Cryptography and Data Security*, 2014.

[36] P. Steiner. Going beyond mobile device management. *Computer Fraud & Security*, 2014(4):19–20, 2014.

[37] A. Striegel, S. Liu, L. Meng, C. Poellabauer, D. Hachen, and O. Lizardo. Lessons learned from the netsense smartphone study. *SIGCOMM Computer Communication Review*, 43(4):51–56, Aug. 2013.

[38] A. Studer and A. Perrig. Mobile user location-specific encryption (mule): using your office as your password. In *Proceedings of the Third ACM Conference on Wireless Network Security*, pages 151–162. ACM, 2010.

[39] Threatpost. Lock screen bypass flaw found in samsung androids. http://threatpost.com/lock-screen-bypass-flaw-found-samsung-androids-030413/77580, Mar. 2014.

[40] S. Zahid, M. Shahzad, S. A. Khayam, and M. Farooq. Keystroke-based user identification on smart phones. In *Recent Advances in Intrusion Detection*, pages 224–243. Springer, 2009.

[41] Zdnet. Apple iphone fingerprint reader confirmed as easy to hack. http://www.zdnet.com/apple-iphone-fingerprint-reader-confirmed-as-easy-to-hack-7000021065/, Mar. 2014.

[42] L. Zhang, B. Tiwana, Z. Qian, Z. Wang, R. P. Dick, Z. M. Mao, and L. Yang. Accurate online power estimation and automatic battery behavior based power model generation for smartphones. In *Proceedings of the eighth IEEE/ACM/IFIP International Conference on Hardware/Software Codesign and System Synthesis*, pages 105–114. ACM, 2010.

Caiipa: Automated Large-scale Mobile App Testing through Contextual Fuzzing

Chieh-Jan Mike Liang[‡], Nicholas D. Lane[‡], Niels Brouwers[*], Li Zhang[⋆], Börje F. Karlsson[‡], Hao Liu[†], Yan Liu[◁], Jun Tang[⋈], Xiang Shan[⋈], Ranveer Chandra[‡], Feng Zhao[‡]

[‡]Microsoft Research [*]Delft University of Technology [⋆]University of Science and Technology of China
[†]Tsinghua University [◁]Shanghai Jiao Tong University [⋈]Harbin Institute of Technology

ABSTRACT

Scalable and comprehensive testing of mobile apps is extremely challenging. Every test input needs to be run with a variety of *contexts*, such as: device heterogeneity, wireless network speeds, locations, and unpredictable sensor inputs. The range of values for each context, e.g. location, can be very large. In this paper we present *Caiipa*, a cloud service for testing apps over an expanded mobile context space in a scalable way. It incorporates key techniques to make app testing more tractable, including a context test space prioritizer to quickly discover failure scenarios for each app. We have implemented Caiipa on a cluster of VMs and real devices that can each emulate various combinations of contexts for tablet and phone apps. We evaluate Caiipa by testing 265 commercially available mobile apps based on a comprehensive library of real-world conditions. Our results show that Caiipa leads to improvements of 11.1x and 8.4x in the number of crashes and performance bugs discovered compared to conventional UI-based automation (i.e., monkey-testing).

Categories and Subject Descriptors

H.3.4 [**Systems and Software**]: Performance evaluation

Keywords

Mobile app testing; Contextual Fuzzing

1. INTRODUCTION

The popularity of mobile devices, such as smartphones and tablets, is fueling a thriving global mobile app ecosystem. Hundreds of new apps are released daily, e.g. about 300 new apps appear on Apple's App Store each day [6]. In turn, 750 million Android and iOS apps are downloaded each week from 190 different countries [18]. Each newly released app must cope with an enormous diversity in device- and environment-based operating *contexts*. The app is expected to work across differently sized devices, with multiple form factors and screen sizes, in varied countries, across a multitude of carriers and networking technologies. Developers must test their applications across a full range of mobile operating contexts prior to an app release to ensure a high quality user experience. However, judging from the frequency of app failures and performance problems after release, it still seems a far off goal [31]. This challenge is made worse by low consumer tolerance for buggy apps. In a recent study, only 16% of smartphone users continued to use an app if it crashed twice soon after download [30]. As a result, app attrition is very high – one quarter of all downloaded apps are used just once [30]. Mobile users only provide a brief opportunity for an app to show its worth, and poor performance and crashes are not tolerated.

Today, developers have only a limited set of tools to test their apps under different mobile contexts. Tools for collecting and analyzing data logs from already deployed apps (e.g., [5, 33, 7]) require them to be first released before problems can be corrected. Through limited-scale field tests (e.g., small beta releases or internal dogfooding) log analytics can be applied prior to public release but these tests lack broad coverage. Testers and their local conditions are likely not representative of a public (particularly global) app release. Inducing issues via fault injection could be used to test consequences of specific situations. However, it requires specific tools to be available and expertise in choosing which issues to inject, while also being prone to the creation of inconsistencies [23] (i.e., artificial situations that may not be realistic).

One could use readily available platform simulators ([13, 20]) to test the app under a specific GPS location and network type, such as Wi-Fi. However, in addition to being limited in the contexts they support, these simulators do not provide a way to systematically explore representative combinations of operating contexts under which mobile apps might be used. Knowledge of previous crashes (either from the developer's own experience or from data repositories) could guide the exploration, but those only cover previously observed scenarios and don't map well to performance analysis. Moreover, even if such data is available, one still has the problem of analysing it to identify the specific problematic contexts to use for testing; which has scalability issues if done manually and is noise prone if automatic (e.g., by association rule mining).

To address this challenge, we propose a new approach to mobile app testing named *contextual fuzzing* [10]. This technique incorporates two key advances over existing alternative methods such as simulators that simply round-robin over a limited sets of common conditions. First, apps are exposed

MobiCom'14, September 7-11, 2014, Maui, Hawaii, USA.

ACM 978-1-4503-2783-1/14/09 ...$15.00.
http://dx.doi.org/10.1145/2639108.2639131.

to a large-scale library of diverse contexts synthesized from the actual conditions observed in the wild. Thousands of contexts are considered; for example, the throughput and loss rates observed for Wi-Fi and 3G networks around the world – rather than only testing expected network behavior as quoted on technical specifications. Second, because of the wide-range of potential contexts to which an app can be exposed, a custom app-specific priority order of contexts is determined. Conditions expected to be highly relevant to the tested app are applied first in favor of less relevant ones; for example, an app might be sensitive to poor network connectivity or low memory conditions and so this category of contexts will be prioritized over CPU- or GPS-oriented tests. These two core techniques combine to enable contextual fuzzing to highlight potential problems before an app is even released to the public.

To demonstrate the power of contextual fuzzing, we design and implement *Caiipa*[1] – a prototype cloud service that can automatically probe mobile apps in search of performance issues and crash scenarios caused by certain mobile contexts. Developers are able to test their apps by simply providing an app binary to the Caiipa service. Apps are then monitored while being exercised within a host environment that can be programmatically perturbed to emulate key forms of device and environment context. By systematically perturbing the host environment an unmodified version of the mobile app can be tested for context-related issues. A summary report is then generated detailing the problems observed, the trigger conditions, and how they can be reproduced. Detailing the scenarios in which issues happen is especially important for developers to be able to decide what actions to take.

This paper makes the following contributions:

- We extend *contextual fuzzing* – a new approach for mobile app testing – by introducing techniques for synthesizing a comprehensive library of context stress tests from readily available telemetry data sources. This enables developers to identify context-related performance issues and sources of app crashes prior to releasing their apps (§ 2).
- We develop techniques for the scalable exploration of the mobile context space. Specifically, we propose a learning algorithm that leverages similarities between apps to identify which conditions will impact previously unseen apps using observations from those apps already tested (§ 3).
- We design a cloud service, called Caiipa, to which app developers and testers can submit their apps to identify context-related problems. This service consists of a pool of virtual machines and real hardware devices that support either smartphone or tablet apps, while emulating a variety of complex context combinations (§ 4).

We evaluate Caiipa using a workload of 235 Windows 8 Store apps (for tablets) and 30 Windows Phone 8 apps based on a wide-ranging library of 10,504 real-world contexts. Our experiments show exploring the mobile context space leads to an 11.1x improvement in the number of crashes discovered during testing relative to UI automation based testing. Moreover, we find crashes we discover from automated pre-release testing take at most around 2.6% of the time (for 94.7% of the crashes) compared to waiting for the same bug to appear within a commercially available crash reporting system. Finally, Caiipa is able to identify 8.4x more performance issues compared to standard monkeying.

[1] Caiipa means "island of monkeys" in Tupi-Guarani. We adopt this name because the contextual fuzzing approach provides a diverse environment for conventional UI-testing to be performed.

2. CONTEXTUAL FUZZING IN CAIIPA

Caiipa targets the needs of two types of users:

- **App Developers** who use Caiipa to complement their existing testing procedures by stress-testing code under hard to predict combinations of contexts, e.g. another country, or different phones.
- **App Distributors** who accept apps from developers and offer them to consumers (such as, entities operating marketplaces of apps) – distributors must decide if an app is ready for public release and cope with reviewing thousands of apps per week[2].

Consequently, Caiipa has the following design requirements:

- First, and most importantly, it needs to be *comprehensive*. Since testing all possible contexts, e.g. every possible lat-long location, would take a long time, Caiipa needs to come up with cases that are representative of the real-world, and where apps often fail or misbehave.
- Second, and usually in contradiction to the first requirement, it should be *responsive* and provide quick, timely feedback to users. We strive to provide feedback in the order of minutes, which is very challenging given the number of contexts, and their combinations for which the apps need to be tested. Consequently, Caiipa needs to quickly determine the most relevant test cases to apply to submitted apps.
- Third, it needs to be able to detect unexpected problems, rather than perform spot tests for specific failures (e.g., common bugs that cause many failures but can easily be found by targeted approaches). In order to find these unforeseen issues, the conditions under which they might occur need to be tested for.
- Fourth, it should be *black box*. We cannot always assume access to app source code. Although instrumentation of binaries has been shown to work for some Windows Phone apps [28], even for a given platform there are many types of apps (e.g., managed, HTML, native). Also, we want methods that can generalize to Windows, Android, and iOS devices.

2.1 The Mobile Context Test Space

We believe the following three mobile contexts, and the variations therein, capture most context-related bugs in mobile apps. To the best of our knowledge there are no existing ways to systematically test these context variations.

Wireless Network Conditions. Variation in network conditions leads to different *latency, jitter, loss, throughput and energy consumption*, which in turn impacts the performance of many network-facing apps (e.g., 84% of Android apps in a large-scale survey request networking permissions [37]). These variations could be caused by the operator, signal strength, technology in use (e.g. Wi-Fi vs. LTE), mobile handoffs, vertical handoffs from cellular to Wi-Fi, and the country of operation. For example the RTTs to the same end-host can vary by 200% based on the cellular

[2] 8,500 app are reviewed weekly by the Apple App Store [6].

operator [17], even given identical locations and hardware, the bandwidth speeds between countries frequently can vary between 1 Mbps and 50 Mbps [35], and the signal strength variation changes the energy usage of the mobile device [22].

Device Heterogeneity. Variations in devices require an app to perform across different *chipset, memory, CPU, screen size, resolution, and availability of resources (e.g. NFC, powerful GPU, etc.).* This device heterogeneity is severe. 3,997 different models of Android devices – with more than 250 screen resolution sizes – contributed data to OpenSignal database during a recent six month period [26]. We note that devices in the wild can experience low memory states or patterns of low CPU availability different from developer expectations, e.g. a camera briefly needs more memory, and this can affect user experience on a low-end device.

Sensor Input. Sensors are commonly used by apps, for instance, surveys of Android marketplaces indicate between 22% and 42% of apps localize through GPS or Wi-Fi [34, 37]. These apps need to work across *availability of sensors, their inputs, and variations in sensor readings themselves.* For example, a GPS or compass might not work at a location, such as a shielded indoor building, thereby affecting end user experience. Furthermore, depending on the location or direction, the app response might be different. Apps might sometimes cause these sensors to consume more energy, for example, by polling frequently for a GPS lock when the reception is poor. The sensors also sometimes have jitter in their readings, which an app needs to handle.

2.2 Caiipa Overview

Caiipa is implemented as a cloud service with the components shown in Figure 1. App developers (or distributors) submit binaries of their apps (i.e. an app packages). Caiipa then runs the app under a controlled environment (AppHost) either in an emulator or on real hardware, while simulating various contexts (networks, carriers, locations, etc.) using the Perturbation Layer. It continuously monitors the performance of the app under each context; and PerfAnalyzer outputs a report with all cases where it found the app to have a bug, where a bug can be a crash, a performance anomaly (e.g., CPU), or an unexpected energy drain.

However, as mentioned earlier, running all possible combinations of contexts is not feasible. To address this challenge, we propose two techniques. First, ContextLib uses machine learning techniques to identify representative contexts by (i) determining which combinations of contexts are likely to occur in the real world, and (ii) removing redundant combinations of contexts. This is a preprocessing step, which we run periodically on crowdsourced data as explained in § 4. Second, ContextPrioritizer sorts different context combinations, and runs those with higher likelihood of detecting failures before others. This helps Caiipa to quickly discover the problematic scenarios. AppHost Dispatcher reads the prioritized test cases from ContextPrioritizer and sends each test to the appropriate AppHost.

2.3 Caiipa System Components

As shown in Figure 1, Caiipa consists of five components: (1) ContextLib, (2) ContextPrioritizer, (3) AppHost Dispatcher, (4) AppHost, and (5) PerfAnalyzer.

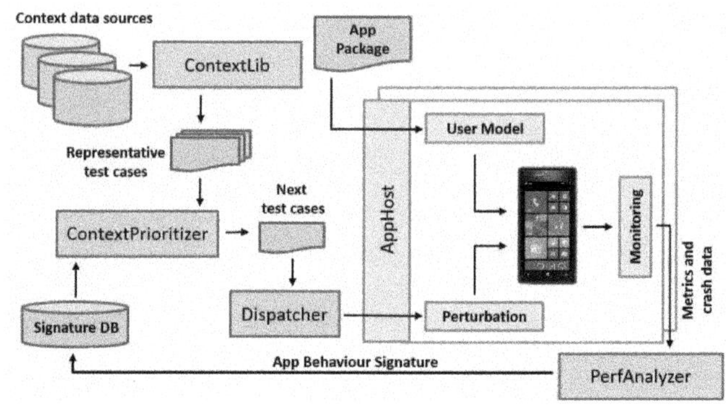

Figure 1: Caiipa system diagram.

ContextLib. ContextLib stores definitions of various mobile context conditions (e.g. loss, delay, jitter at a location) and scenarios (e.g. handoff from Wi-Fi to 3G). ContextLib is populated using datasets collected from real devices (e.g., OpenSignal [25] and WER [7]) in addition to (1) challenging mobile contexts defined by domain experts; and, (2) a small number of test cases designed to target key device categories (see AppHost Dispatcher for more). Because context datasets are typically large-scale (OpenSignal, for instance, contains millions of network observations) and because not every raw context in a dataset will be an effective test condition, ContextLib performs a two-stage test case generation process that first filters redundant contexts that do not significantly impact app behavior (i.e., resource consumption); before then generating test cases not from just individual contexts (e.g., a network condition), but also based on context transitions (e.g., 3G to 4G) and the co-occurrence contexts of different types (e.g., fast network with low memory).

ContextPrioritizer. ContextPrioritizer determines the order in which the contexts from ContextLib should be performed, and communicates this ordering to AppHost Dispatchers. Aggregate app behavior (i.e., crashes and resource use) collected and processed by PerfAnalyzer from AppHosts, is used by ContextPrioritizer to build and maintain app similarity measurements that determine this prioritization. Both prioritization and similarity computation are online processes. As each new set of results is reported by an AppHost, more information is gained about the app being tested, resulting potentially in re-prioritization based on new behavior similarities between apps being discovered. Through prioritization two outcomes occur: (1) redundant or irrelevant contexts are ignored (e.g., an app is discovered to never use the network, so network contexts are not used); and, (2) contexts that negatively impact similar apps are prioritized (e.g., an app that behaves similarly to streaming apps would have network contexts prioritized).

AppHost Dispatcher. Apps run within a controlled environment called AppHost. AppHosts can be instantiated either on a VM or on real hardware. The AppHost Dispatcher makes this decision based on the test case workload generated by ContextPrioritizer. In order to scale testing, most test cases are run on a VM, which AppHost Dispatcher selects from a AppHost pool. However, AppHosts running on real devices are used by Caiipa in two situations. First, in the event the app is native or mixed code and unable to be run on an emulator[3], or when an app uses specific hardware that is difficult to emulate, such as the camera or NFC interface. Second, when ContextPrioritizer selects any of the small number of device-related test cases included in ContextLib (such as the case corresponding to a low-end smartphone that causes testing to be done using a device representative of that category).

AppHost. The AppHost has three main functions:

UI Automation (Monkeying). We use a User Interaction Model (see §4) that generates user events (e.g., touch events, key presses, data input) based on weights (i.e. probability of invocation) assigned to specific UI items. Our technique works on tablets and phones, and is able to execute most of the scenarios for an app. As there is no dependency between our model and other Caiipa components, it can be replaced by a more elaborate one without negative impact. Moreover, we also allow developers to customize its weights.

Simulating Contexts (Perturbation). This component simulates conditions, such as different CPU performance levels, amount of available memory, controlled sensor readings (e.g., GPS reporting a programmatically defined location), and different network parameters to simulate different network interfaces (e.g., Wi-Fi, GPRS, WCDMA), network quality levels, and network transitions (3G to Wi-Fi) or handoffs between cell towers. Each one of these is implemented using various kernel hooks or drivers (4). This layer is extensible and new contexts can be added as required.

Monitoring. During test execution AppHost closely records app behaviour in the form of a log of system-wide and per-app performance counters (e.g., network traffic, disk I/Os, CPU and memory usage) and crash data. To accommodate the variable number of logging sources (e.g., system built-in services and customized loggers), AppHost implements a plug-in architecture where each source is wrapped in a *monitor*. Monitors can either be time-driven (i.e., logging at fixed intervals), or event-driven (i.e., logging as an event of interest occurs, like specific UI events).

PerfAnalyzer. This component identifies crashes, and possible bugs (e.g. battery drain, data usage spikes, long latency) in the large pool of monitoring data generated by AppHosts. To identify failures that do not result in a crash, it uses anomaly detection that assumes norms, based on previous behavior of (1) the target app and (2) an app group that are similar to the target app.

Crashes by themselves provide insufficient data to identify their root cause. Interpretation of them is key to providing actionable feedback to developers. PerfAnalyzer processes crash data across crashes to provide more focused feedback and helps narrow down the possible root cause. Also, if the app developer provides debug symbols, it can find the source code location where specific issues were triggered.

PerfAnalyzer augments the bug data with relevant contextual information to help identify the source of problems. The generated report includes resource consumption changes prior to crash, the set of perturbed conditions, and the click trace of actions taken on the app (along with screenshots), thus documenting its internal computation state and how the app got there; which is missing in regular bug tracking systems or if only limited data from the crash moment is available. The generated aggregate report also allows developers to find commonalities and trends between different crash instances that might not be easily visible.

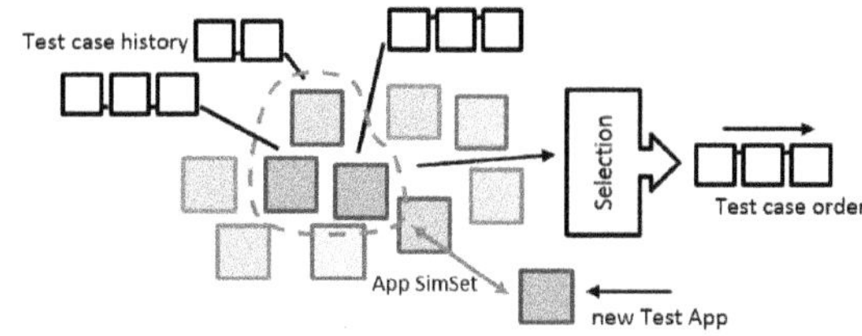

Figure 2: ContextPrioritizer dataflow.

3. PRIORITIZING TEST CASES

ContextLib maintains a test case collection that runs into the thousands. At this scale, the latency and computational overhead of performing the full test suite becomes prohibitive to users. To address this challenge, ContextPrioritizer finds a *unique per-app sequence of test cases* that increases the marginal probability of identifying crashes (and performance issues) for each test case performed. The key benefit is that exercising only a fraction of the entire ContextLib can still discover important context-related crashes and performance bugs. We note that its use is optional, and users can also manually specify the order of test cases.

Overview. Figure 2 presents the dataflow of ContextPrioritizer. Within the overall architecture of Caiipa, the role of ContextPrioritizer is to determine the next batch of test cases (chosen from ContextLib) to be applied to the user-provided test app.

The underlying approach of ContextPrioritizer is to learn from prior experience when prioritizing test cases for a fresh unseen test app. ContextPrioritizer first searches past apps to find a group that should perform similarly to the current test app (referred to as a `AppSimSet`). And then, it examines the test case history of each member of the `AppSimSet`, identifying potentially "problematic" test cases that may result in faults. These problematic test cases are then prioritized ahead of others in an effort to increase the efficiency by which problems in the current app are discovered.

While we informally refer to app(s) in this description (e.g., test app, or apps in a `AppSimSet`), more precisely this term points to an *app package* that includes both (1) a mobile app and (2) an instance of a User Interaction Model (see §4). This pairing is necessary because the code path and resource usage of an app are highly sensitive to the user input. Conceptually, an app package represents a particular usage scenario within an app.

Algorithm 1 details precisely ContextPrioritizer operation. In what follows we explain the key algorithmic phases.

App Similarity Set. In addition to the sheer number of potential test cases, context fuzzing is complicated by the fact that a given app will likely only be sensitive to a fraction of all test cases in ContextLib. However, it is also non-trivial to predict which test cases are important for any particular test app – without first actually trying the combination. For example, an app that sporadically uses the network for checking program updates may be fairly insensitive to many network related test cases; wasting resources on testing this part of the mobile context space. Reasonable heuristics for optimizing the assignment of test apps to test cases – such as, inspecting the API calls made by an app, and linking cer-

[3] This limitation applies only to ARM binaries.

Algorithm 1: ContextPrioritizer

```
Input  : Prioritization Request for App_i
         Len_i: Length of required TestSeq_i
Output: TestSeq_i for App_i
AppSimSet ⟵ {}                       /* compute AppSimSet */
For ∀App_j ∈ AppHist
    ResSimSet ⟵ {}
    For ∀Res_k ∈ ResSet
        If KS.ResTestIsTrue(App_i, App_j,Res_k)
            ResSimSet ⟵ Res_k
        EndIf
    End
    If |ResSimSet| / |ResSet| ≥ KS_thres
        AppSimSet ⟵ App_j
    EndIf
End
ResCrash ⟵ {}                        /* compute ResCrash */
For ∀App_k ∈ AppSimSet
    For ∀Crash_l ∈ AppHist[App_k]
        ResCatSet ⟵ ResCat(Crash_l, CAT_thres)
        For ∀Res_j ∈ ResSet
            If Res_j ∈ ResCatSet
                ResCrash[Res_j] ⟵ Crash_l
            EndIf
        End
    End
End
TestSeq_i ⟵ {}     /* select Test Case Sequence */
While |TestSeq_i| ≤ Len_i
    CrashVote ⟵ {}              /* voting - Tier One */
    For ∀ Res_j ∈ ResCrash
        Temp ⟵ TopN(ResCrash[Res_j],RES_thres)
        CrashVote ⟵ Temp
        ResCrash[Res_j] - Temp
    End
    TestSeq_i ⟵ TopN(CrashVote,1)  /* Tier Two */
End
```

tain contexts (e.g., network-related test cases) to API calls (e.g., network-related APIs) – would have been confused by the prior example.

ContextPrioritizer counters this problem by identifying correlated system resource usage metrics as a deeper means to understand the relationship between two apps. The intuition underpinning this approach is that two apps that have correlated resource usage (such as memory, CPU, network) are likely to have shared sensitivity to similar context-based test cases. For example, in deciding which test cases to first apply to the prior example app (with sporadic network usage), this approach would identify previous test apps that also had sporadic network usage – recognized by similarities in network resource consumption. Then, it prioritizes other test cases over network-related ones, with the insight of the potential network insensitivity.

The building block operation within ContextPrioritizer is a *pairwise similarity comparison* between a new test app, and a previously tested app (called `KS.ResTestIsTrue()` in Algorithm 1). This is done for each system resource metric while both apps were exposed to the same test case (i.e., context). A standard statistical test is performed to understand if the distribution of the time-series data for this particular metric generated by each app is likely drawn from the same underlying population (i.e., the distributions are statistically the same). To do this, we apply the Kolmogorov-Smirnov (K-S) test [4], with an α of 0.05. The outcome of this test is binary, either the distributions are found to be the same or not. We expect other statistical tests (i.e., a K-S alternative) would produce comparable results.

ContextPrioritizer uses the above described pairwise comparison multiple times to construct a unique **AppSimSet** for each new test app. During this process, ContextPrioritizer considers a collection of j resource metrics – called **ResSet** (listed in Table 2). For each resource metric, the pairwise tests are performed between the current test app and all prior test apps (i.e., **AppHist**.) In many cases, ContextPrioritizer is able to compare the same pair of apps and same resource metrics more than once (for example, under different test cases). For the prior test app to be included in **AppSimSet**, it must pass the statistical comparison test a certain percentage of times ($\mathtt{KS}_{thres}$). We empirically set $\mathtt{KS}_{thres} = 65\%$, as it is not too loose to differentiate cases such as image-centric and video-centric news apps, and not too restrictive to result in similar clusters with virtually interchangeable members.

Importantly, no comparison between the current and past test apps can be performed until at least a few test cases are performed. ContextPrioritizer uses a bootstrapping procedure to do this, whereby a small set of test cases are automatically executed before prioritization. We select these test cases experimentally by identifying k test cases with a high initial rate of causing crashes[4]. Bootstrapping is important only briefly as test app data quickly accumulates once Caiipa starts to run.

Test Case History Categorization. As many crashes are caused by abnormal resource usage (e.g., excessive memory), they can be tied to resource metrics. The motivation for categorization of test case history is two-fold. First, it allows non-context related crashes (e.g., division by zero) to be ignored during prioritization. Second, the frequency of crashes fluctuates significantly between resource categories (e.g., network-related crashes are much more common that hardware-related ones). As a result, fair comparisons for later Test Case Sequence selection are only possible *intra*-category instead of inter-category.

The intuition supporting the use of abnormal resource usage to categorize test case history is that a fall or rise in the resource metric consumption immediately prior to a crash is a signal of a likely cause. As we find that most real-world contexts have an immediate impact on app behavior, we compare the resource consumption of the last three user clicks to that of the rest. Typically, the crash is then tied to the resource metrics with the largest gradient (either positive or negative). This procedure is called `ResCat()` in Algorithm 1. Due to potential inaccuracies, during ContextPrioritizer execution the top $\mathtt{CAT}_{thres}$ most likely resource metrics are tied to each crash (by default $\mathtt{CAT}_{thres}$ is set to 3).

Test Case Sequence Selection. ContextPrioritizer uses a two-tiered voting process to arrive at a sequence of test cases ($\mathtt{TestSeq}_i$) to be applied to the test app ($\mathtt{App}_i$). The tiered process ensures no single resource category dominates test case selection.

[4] We set k to 3 and find the best test cases. As test case creation is data-driven, we manually name them: `GPRS*`, `802.11b*`, and `4G*`, for their similarity to conditions for those network types.

Context Dimension	Raw Entries	Description	Source
Network	9,500+	Cellular in Locations Wi-Fi Hotspot Cellular Operators	Open Signal
Platform	220/23 (W8/WP8)	CPU Utilization Ranges Memory Ranges	Watson
Sensor	300	Locations	FourSquare
Others	49	Transitions, Extreme Cases	Hand-picked

Table 1: Context Library.

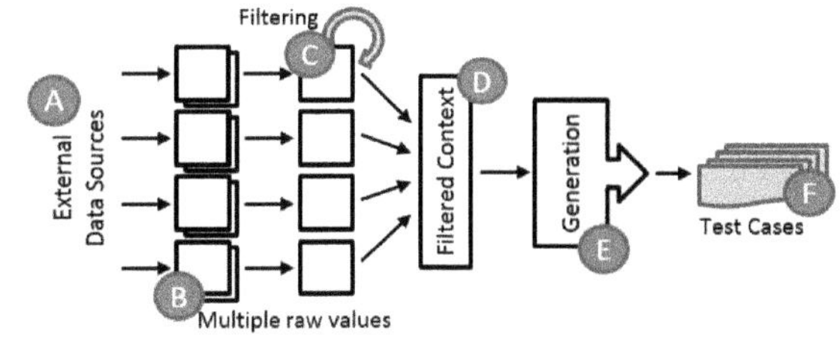

Figure 3: ContextLib dataflow, showing the components and processes: (A) Context Sources; (B) Raw Context; (C) Redundancy Filtering; (D) Filtered Context; (E) Test Case Generation; and, (F) Test Cases.

At each tier the voting setup is the same. Each time a test case results in a crash is treated as a vote, any crash that is categorized as being non-context related is ignored. The order of test cases is determined by the popularity in terms of weighted crashes observed in past test apps contained within `AppSimSet` – in Algorithm 1 this is computed by `TopN()`.

The differences between the two tiers are in the pools of context-related crashes considered. For each past test app, the first tier looks at which test case crashes happened for each resource metric (`ResCrash`). Then, the top $\texttt{RES}_{thres}$ popular test cases is picked for each app, and aggregated at the second tier. A single test case is chosen, but this process is repeated for a test case sequence. We set $\texttt{RES}_{thres}$ to be 10 in our current Caiipa implementation.

4. CAIIPA IMPLEMENTATION

This section presents the implemented testing framework components (see Figure 1). The entire Caiipa prototype consists of ≈ 31k lines of code, broken into: ContextLib 1.9kloc; ContextPrioritizer 2.2kloc; AppHost 20kloc; and PerfAnalyzer 6.8kloc.

ContextLib. Our current library contains 10,504 raw contexts, as summarized in Table 1. The majority of the ContextLib is populated by Open Signal [25] (a global public dataset of crowd-sourced cellular measurements) as an external data source. We limit the number of cities to 400, which include 50 mobile carriers. Additional tests (e.g., memory and CPU) can be sourced from telemetry databases. Finally, a number of hard-coded raw ContextLib records are included for: (1) challenging scenarios that are not available from current context sources – examples include sudden drops in available memory; in addition to (2) a small number of device-specific test cases (e.g., low-end smartphone, ARM-architecture tablet) that correspond to actual devices in our testbed.

Figure 3 illustrates the main components of ContextLib. It pulls raw data from various databases and services (A), such as those listed in Table 1, and populates the raw tables (B). Redundant and duplicate contexts are then suppressed for each context (C), to lead to a filtered set of context instances (D). We then combine different contexts (network, memory, CPU, etc.) (E) that generates the list of test cases (F), which feeds to ContextPrioritizer. The two algorithmic components – (C) Redundancy Filtering and (E) Test Case Generation – shown Figure 3 operate as follows.

Redundancy Filtering. As a first step, we remove duplicate entries from the raw contexts (*rcs*). However, this step by itself is not sufficient. ContextLib also filters *rcs* if apps do not demonstrate large changes in *system resource usage* relative to other contexts. The underlying assumption is that large changes in resources are an indicator that the app is being exercised in significantly different ways by a context[5]. Resource-based filtering is performed separately for each category of context (e.g., network, memory, CPU). The goal is to arrive at $\texttt{f}dom_i$ for each category – a collection of key context conditions (e.g., a problematic or common memory level) within the ith context type (e.g., memory-related context) that often cause apps to behave (i.e., consume resources) differently.

To find $\texttt{f}dom_i$ we begin by using training examples – that is, pairs of *rc* and corresponding normalized resource usage. Training examples are collected in two ways: (1) by periodically testing a representative workload of popular mobile apps; and (2) via the output of app testing from standard Caiipa operation. We perform matrix decomposition on this training data to learn a projection matrix $\texttt{dom.i}_{prj}$ for each context category. This matrix maps contexts (e.g., a change in device memory availability) to a n-dimension resource vector space of app usage parameterized by the same 19 system metrics used by ContextPrioritizer (see Table 2).

Initially each $\texttt{f}dom_i$ contains all *rcs* (i.e., the 10,504 context-only records available from context sources) projected using $\texttt{dom.i}_{prj}$ and so represented as 19-dimension resource usage vectors. Next, dimensionality reduction is performed on each $\texttt{f}dom_i$ using Multi-dimensional Scaling [4] (MDS). This removes irrelevant dimensions for a particular context category (e.g., I/O-related system metrics might only be weakly relevant within a networking-related context category). Finally, to remove *rcs* with correlated system metrics (and thus redundant) we apply a density-based clustering algorithm – DBSCAN [4][6].

Test Case Generation. Filtered contexts are used to form three types of test cases. First, test cases based solely on individual filtered contexts themselves. Second, contexts fused together to form *transition* context test cases within the same domain (e.g., a transition from one memory condition to another). Third, *multi-domain* context test cases made from the combination of contexts that test the co-occurrence of multiple types of context conditions (e.g., simultaneously-occurring specific network and CPU contexts).

Generation of test case types is as follows. First, all filtered contexts are automatically used to generate test cases – a trivial step. Next, candidate *transition* and *multi-domain* test cases are generated. For each filtered domain ($\texttt{f}dom_i$) a companion *transition* domain is created. For example, the network domain is paired with a network-*transitions* domain. Transition domains contain entries capturing all pos-

[5] Under the expectation that the same UI steps are being repeated.

[6] Although we use MDS and DBSCAN, many other dimensionality reduction and density-based clustering techniques are likely to perform equally well.

sible transitions from one context to another, within that domain (i.e., $\texttt{f}dom_i \times \texttt{f}dom_i$). This step is needed because context transitions (such as, switching from Wi-Fi to 3G network connectivity) are common situations for mobile apps to fail. A Cartesian product is then performed across all filtered domains, including the new transition ones ($\texttt{f}dom_1 \times \cdots \texttt{f}dom_n$). This creates candidate test cases that span context domains. However, a side-effect of this process is that new redundant *transition* and *multi-domain* test cases can be introduced. To remove these we perform one final round of redundancy filtering over all test cases; the output of this filtering is the final set of test cases. In the end, the number of test cases (i.e., ContextLib size) is determined by clustering parameters that influence both phases of ContextLib. For DBSCAN and MDS these principally are *dim* and *MinPts* [4] but equivalent parameters exist in alternative clustering algorithms. In our implementation these values are empirically set and default to $\{dim : 5, MinPts : 15\}$.

AppHost Dispatcher. AppHosts run either on VMs or on real devices. VMs are used for the majority of tests for testbed scalability and are maintained as a pool of AppHosts on Microsoft Azure. To support the testing of device-sensitive context, we use four categories of devices in our testbed – two smartphones (Lumia 520 and 1020) and two tablets (Microsoft Surface RT, Samsung 700T1A Slate) – each corresponding to specific device test cases in ContextLib.

AppHost Dispatcher allocates test cases picked by ContextPrioritizer for an app to either the VM pool or specific hardware. Tests are assigned to a device if they require a certain hardware architecture (e.g., requiring ARM to run), or when the app uses certain components flagged as requiring real-hardware. In such cases all tests picked for the app are performed on a real device with the AppHost perturbing, for example, the network or GPS, to examine different contexts. Alternatively, for apps that are otherwise able to be run on an emulator, certain test cases may still be performed on hardware, with the remainder being executed on emulators. This occurs when ContextPrioritizer includes any of the device-specific test cases (e.g., low-end smartphone) in the collection of tests picked for the app.

The Dispatcher manages each AppHost node (both VM- and device-based nodes) via an RPC-like framework.

AppHost. Each AppHost is controlled by the AppHost Dispatcher. AppHosts support both Windows 8 (W8) and Windows Phone 8 (WP8) apps. As shown in Figure 4, an AppHost is comprised of four main components: 1) Controller, 2) UI Automation Service, 3) Perturbation Service, and 4) Data Manager.

The Controller is responsible for orchestrating the other components inside the AppHost. A sub-module of the Controller, called AppHost Daemon, encapsulates the OS-specific coordination of UI automation, context emulation, and app monitoring. When the app under test is a W8 app, the controller and all other modules run on the target OS. This allows W8 apps within AppHost to be exercised (with user input), observed (via monitors and data manager), and for the context to be carefully controlled (via perturbation).

To support WP8 apps, an inner host running the WP8 OS is used. WP8 apps run inside this inner host (a WP8 VM) and are exercised and monitored with phone-specific modules. The W8 Controller and Data Manager still run unchanged. But AppHost sub-modules (e.g., Daemon, the

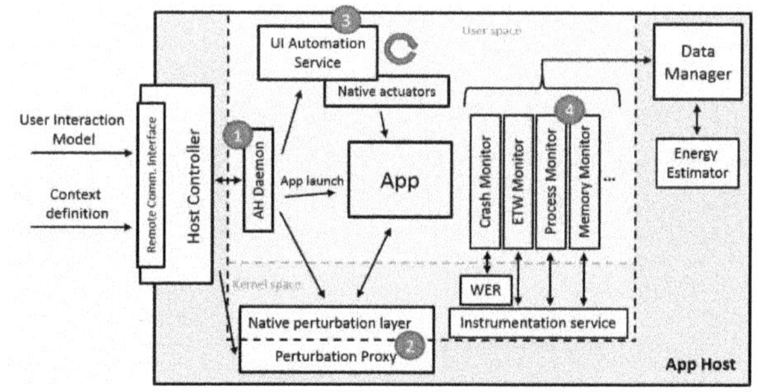

Figure 4: Implementation components of AppHost.

native layer of the Perturbation service) run on the Windows Phone OS. Some perturbation modules (Perturbation Proxy) are reused without change, whereby the outer host OS has its context manipulated which propagates into the inner phone VM.

Monitoring Modules. DataManager instantiates the appropriate monitors to collect data depending on app type and platform. Under W8, two monitors log system-wide and per-app performance counters through WMI. A third monitor collects crash data from the system event log and the local WER system. Finally, a fourth monitor hooks to the Event Tracing for Windows (ETW) service to capture the output of `msWriteProfilerMark` JavaScript method in Internet Explorer; which allows writing debug data from HTML5/JS Windows Store apps. Under WP8, monitors also log crash data and system and app counters, but use OS-specific infrastructure. Finally, under both platforms we enable an energy consumption estimation monitor based on WattsOn [22].

Perturbation Modules. Network perturbation is implemented on top of Network Emulator for Windows Toolkit (NEWT)[7], a kernel-space network driver. NEWT exposes four network properties: download/upload bandwidth, latency, loss rate (and model), and jitter. To which we introduced real-time network property updates to emulate network transitions and cell handoffs.

Modern VM managers expose settings for CPU resource allocation on a per-instance basis. By manipulating these processor settings, we can make use of three distinct CPU availability states: 20%, 50%, and 100%. To control the amount of available memory to apps, we use an internal tool that allows AppHost to change available system memory. Finally, we implemented a virtual GPS driver to feed apps with spoofed coordinates and other GPS responses. Our UDP-controlled virtual GPS driver raises a state-updated event and a data-updated event to trigger the OS location services to refresh the geolocation data.

As noted, the WP8 AppHost can re-use parts of the W8 perturbation layer (like CPU or network throttling), rather than implementing its own.

User Interaction Model. As W8 Store apps and WP8 apps are "page"-based, the app UI is represented as a tree, where nodes represent the pages (or app states), and edges represent the invoke-able UI elements. We provide a stand alone authoring tool allowing a user to assign a weight to each UI element. Higher weights indicate a higher probability of a particular UI element being invoked. However, by default – if the authoring tool is not used – each UI element has

[7] Part of the Microsoft Visual Studio package.

an equal weight. Due to platform differences in UI automation APIs (i.e., W8 vs. WP8) we implement two native UI actuators, each using a OS-specific automation framework.

PerfAnalyzer. To report actionable feedback to developers, PerfAnalyzer focuses on two areas: (1) System resource consumption that is higher than expected under certain contexts (e.g., energy bugs); and, (2) Crashes linked to metadata assisting in root cause analysis.

Performance Outliers. To determine if the target app being tested exhibits abnormal behavior, we first find the set of similar apps over measurements from previous tests (see §3). Then, we perform MeanDIST-based outlier detection [16], and see whether the test app is in the outlier group. Our current implementation assumes 5% of the population are outliers, which can be adjusted by the user. Users can filter and rank outliers within a table view based on: (1) the frequency at which they occur; (2) the magnitude in difference to the comparison *norm*; and (3) a particular metric type.

Crash Analysis. To collect and interpret crash data, Caiipa connects to Microsoft WER (Windows Error Reporting), a service on every Windows system to gather information about crashes for reporting and debugging. WER aggregates error reports likely originating from the same bug by a process of labeling and classifying crash data (see [7] for details). The resulting data is then correlated to changes in resource consumption prior to the crash for reporting.

5. EVALUATION

This section is organized by the following major results: (1) ContextLib is able to effectively balance the trade-off between increasing the rate of discovering app problems (e.g., crashes and freezes) while reducing the number of test cases required; (2) ContextPrioritizer can find up to 47% more crashes than the conventional baselines, with the same amount of time and computing resources; (3) Caiipa increases the number of crashes and performance outliers found over the current practice by a factor of 11× and 8×, respectively; and (4) we share lessons learned to help future mobile app development.

5.1 Methodology

In the proceeding experiments, we use two datasets that are tested using our Caiipa prototype hosted in Azure (see §4), specifically: (1) 235 mobile Windows 8 Store apps that target tablet devices (hereafter W8 apps); (2) 30 Windows Phone 8 apps that target smartphones (hereafter WP8 apps). All apps are free to download from the Microsoft Windows Store and Windows Phone Store, respectively; selected from the list of top-free non-game downloads.

To define our test case workload we first pick three representative cities from different continents with a large number of mobile device users: Seattle, London, and Beijing. Next, we utilize ContextLib to generate a total of 350 test cases. We use the standard context sources part of our current ContextLib implementation listed in Table 1. In addition, we add five hand-coded network profiles not present in the OpenSignal database, namely: `802.11b`, `WCDMA`, and `4G` – as familiar network scenarios developers can use as reference points; and `GPRS out of range` and `GPRS handoff`, as scenarios involving cell tower changes. We limit the potential memory configurations generated by ContextLib to just two to focus more closely on the networking parameter space.

Resource Type	Description
Network	{datagrams/segments} {recieved/sent} per sec
	total TCP {connection/failure/active}
	total TCP {established/reset}
Memory	current amount of % {virtual/physical} memory used
	max amount of % {virtual/physical} memory used
	{current,max} amount of % {paged} memory used
CPU	% {processor/user} time
Disk	bytes {written/read} per sec

Table 2: System resources used in the Caiipa prototype.

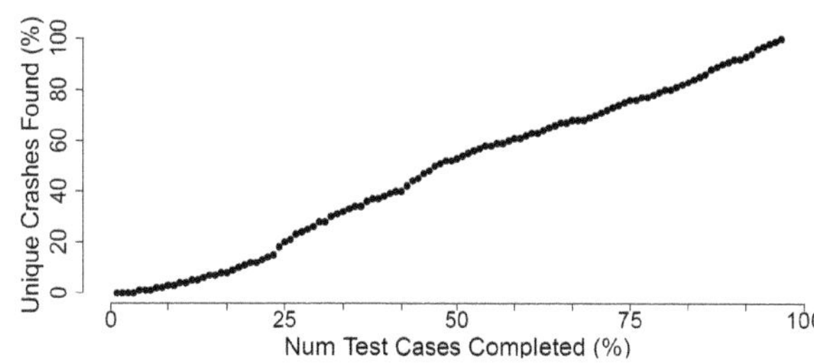

Figure 5: CDF of unique crashes found when incrementally adding test cases from ContextLib.

Finally, we include four device-specific test cases tied to real hardware: two phones (Lumia 520 and 1020) and two tablets (Microsoft Surface RT, Samsung 700T1A), selected as representatives of device classes.

We configure Caiipa to test individual apps three times under each test case, with an individual test session under one test case being five minutes in duration. Table 2 lists the 19 system resource metrics and performance counters logged during our experiments. Finally, we use the term *crash* to represent both app freezes and unexpected app terminations.

5.2 Mobile Context Test Space Exploration

Our first experiments examines two key Caiipa components, namely: ContextLib and ContextPrioritizer.

ContextLib. We begin by examining key questions regarding test cases in our ContextLib design: Is a large-scale ContextLib really necessary, or are many of our tests in ContextLib redundant? And, how effective is ContextLib in capturing the same detected crashes if exhaustively testing a much larger volume of raw context conditions?

To highlight any potentially redundant test cases in ContextLib, we perform an experiment where we test each app (both W8 and WP8) while withholding differing fractions of the 350-tests in the library. If unnecessary test cases are present in ContextLib we should see certain test cases being responsible for a disproportionate amount of the crashes.

Figure 5 compares the fraction of *unique* crashes found by Caiipa against the fraction of ContextLib made available during testing. This figure suggests that each test case observes, in general, new additional unique crashes. This observation justifies that the entire ContextLib we use is necessary for testing. In fact, Figure 5 has a reasonably constant slope, which also implies that all test cases are equally important in testing for app crashes. We find there is no small subset of tests in ContextLib that are significantly more responsible for detecting more crashes than others. Therefore, it is not possible to find a significant fraction of the different types of crashes we find with Caiipa by using only a few common failure-causing contexts.

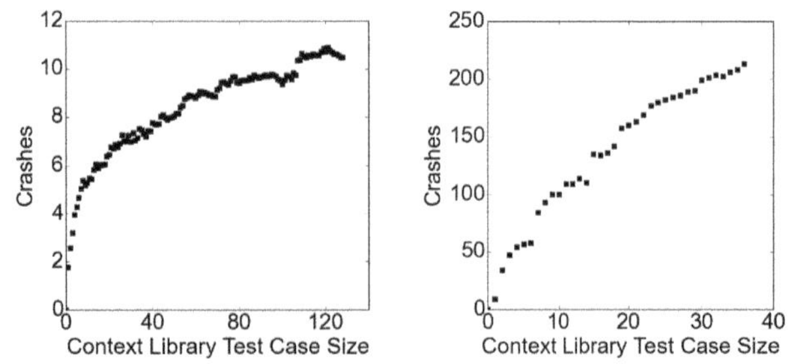

(a) (b)

Figure 6: Context Library filtering performance: a) 500 raw contexts for 4 apps; b) 200 raw contexts for 50 apps.

Next, to further investigate the effectiveness of the ContextLib techniques, we perform the following two experiments. In each experiment, a selection of apps is initially tested under a set of raw contexts taken directly from our context sources (detailed in §4). We then repeat the experiment using a experiment-specific ContextLib of varying size synthesized from the same set of raw contexts (not the full ContextLib used by Caiipa). The objective is to observe how many crashes identified with the full-set of raw contexts later go undetected as the number of test cases in the ContextLib is lowered. If ContextLib techniques are effective, it will be able to maintain reasonably high crash detection rates even when the number of test cases drops dramatically.

Figure 6(a) shows an experiment using four representative W8 apps – one from four distinct app categories. By using fewer apps we are able in this experiment to use a large number of raw context, specifically: 500. Using Caiipa, we test each app under each raw context and on average, each app crashes 16 times. The figure reports the per-app average crash number. It shows that by using ContextLib we are able to find a relatively high fraction of the crashes with the raw contexts even as the number of test cases is lowered. For example, we find on average by using only 60 test cases (only 12% of the original total of 500) we are able to find 50% of all crashes.

Figure 6(b) presents an experiment with the same methodology except for a much larger number of apps. We use 50 of the W8 apps detailed in §5.3, but consequently must lower the number of raw contexts used to only 200. In this figure we report the total number of crashes in this app population. When testing all the raw contexts we find a total of 312 crashes. Again we find ContextLib to be effective in discovering most of these app crashes with significantly fewer than the total raw contexts. As one example, Figure 6(b) shows it is able to find around 60% of all of these crashes using only $\approx$ 35 test cases.

ContextPrioritizer. The evaluation metric is the number of crashes found as **(1)** the time budget varies, and **(2)** the amount of available computing resource varies. We used three comparison baselines. First, *Oracle* has the complete knowledge of the measurements for all apps (including untested ones), and it represents the upper-bound. *Random* is a common approach that randomly picks an untested case to run at each step. Finally, *Vote* does not rely on finding apps with similar behavior, and uses test cases that yield the most crashes in all previously tested apps.

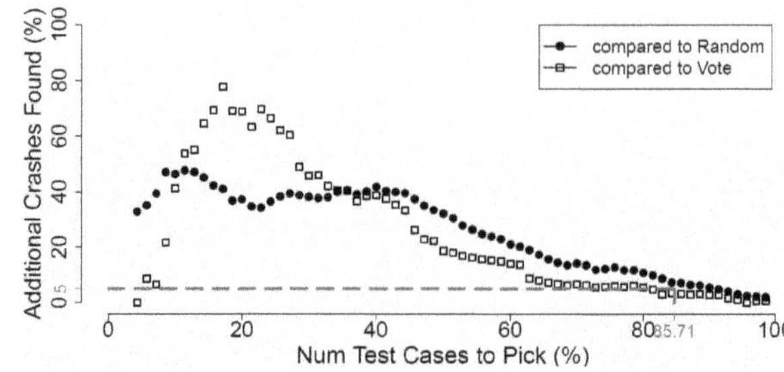

Figure 7: % more crashes that ContextPrioritizer finds given a time budget. 41.1% and 77.6% more crashes than Random and Vote, respectively, within 1-hour. Its gain over baselines falls below 5% only after exploring 85.71% of the entire test space.

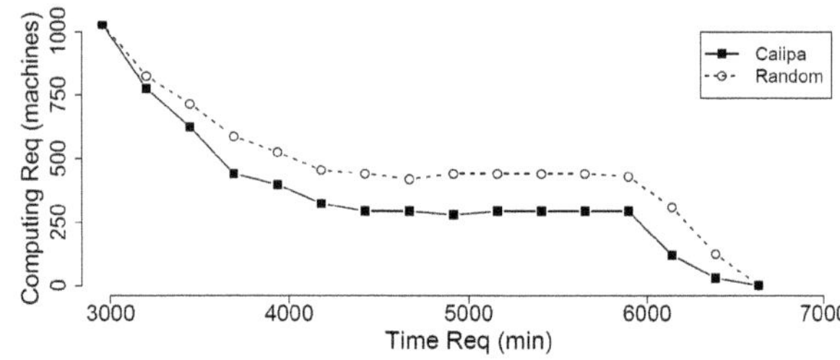

Figure 8: Feasible combinations of time and computing budget to try to find at least 10 crashes in each of the 235 tablet apps. Caiipa uses much less time and computing resources.

Time Budget. We start with the question: given sufficient time to exercise the target app under x test cases, which x cases would reveal the most app crashes. We note that one test case runs for a fixed duration (e.g., five minutes). Figure 7 shows the results with the Windows 8 dataset, and we highlight two observations.

First, Caiipa reports a higher number of crashes than Random and Vote. On average, it can find 30.90% and 28.88% more crashes than Random and Vote, respectively. We note the Caiipa exhibits the most gain when the time budget is relatively limited, or selecting less than 60% of all test cases. In fact, Caiipa can find up to 47.63% and 77.61% more crashes than Vote and Random, respectively. These results demonstrate the gain from our two testing principles: learning from app test history, and considering only apps with similar behavior in resource consumption.

Second, as the time budget increases, testing tools can run through more test cases. This implies that the probability of picking the set of test cases that cause crashes also increases, regardless of the technique used. Therefore, the gain from using different techniques will eventually experience a diminishing return. For example, the dotted lines in Figure 7 show that the gain from ContextPrioritizer falls below 5% when there is enough time budget to explore at least 85.71% of the test space. Assuming 85.71% of our context library of 350 test cases, running five minutes for each test case would take a total of 24.99 hours to complete.

Resource Tradeoff. We note that, since app testing is highly parallelizable, multiple apps can be exercised at the same time on different machines. At the extreme with an infinite amount of computing resources, all prioritization techniques would perform equally well, and the entire dataset can finish in one test-case time. Given this assumption is not practical in the real world, we calculate the speed up that Caiipa offers under various amount of available resources.

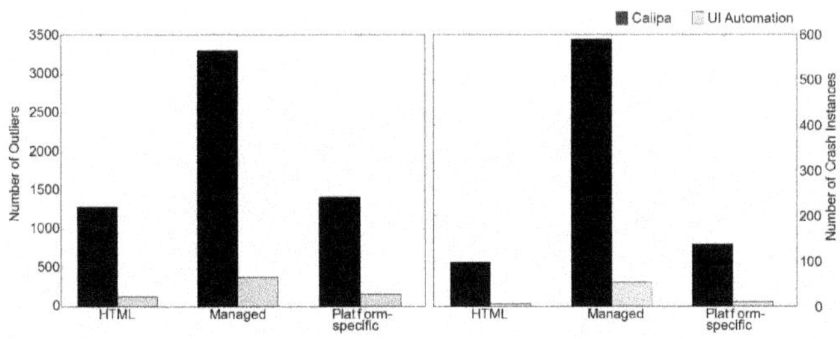

Figure 9: Performance outliers and **unique** crashes by type.

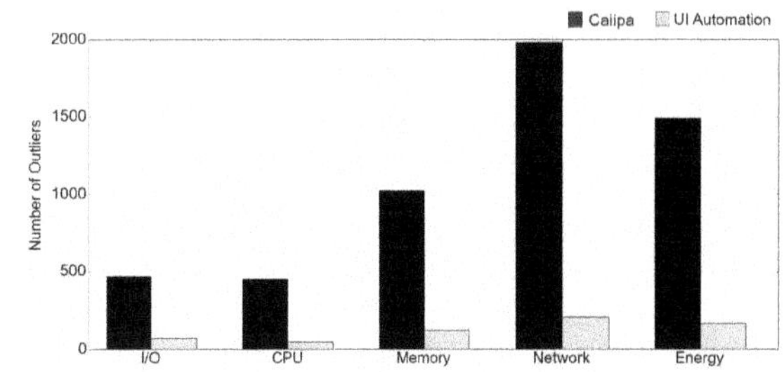

Figure 10: App performance outliers, by resource usage.

Figure 8 illustrates combinations of computing resources and time required to find at least 10 crashes in each of the 235 Windows 8 Store apps. For apps that have less than 10 crashes, we run through all test cases. First, the figure shows increasing the resource in one dimension can lower the requirement on the other. Second, by estimating the information gain of each pending test case, Caiipa can reach the goal faster and with fewer machines. For example, to find **all** crashes as set in our target within a time limit of 4425 minutes, Caiipa needs 294 machines – 33% less than the nearest benchmark. Finally, in this dataset, the break-even point for Random is at the time budget of 6,630 minutes, or $> 90\%$ of the total possible time for testing all combinations of apps and test cases.

5.3 Aggregate App Context Testing

In our next set of experiments, we investigate crashes and performance outliers identified by Caiipa within a set of popular publicly available mobile apps.

Comparison Baseline. We compare Caiipa to a conventional UI automation approach as a comparison baseline. This baseline represents current common practice for testing mobile apps. To implement a UI automation approach we use the default UIM already part of Caiipa (see §4). However, during app testing under the UI automation approach context is not perturbed.

To perform these experiments all steps are repeated twice. Once using Caiipa and then repeated under UI automation. Since the setup is identical for each run of the same app, differences in crashes and performance outliers detected are due to the inclusion of contextual fuzzing by Caiipa.

Summary of Findings. Overall, Caiipa is able to discover significantly more crashes (11.4×) and performance outliers (8.8×) than the baseline solution for W8 apps. And approximately 5.5× more crashes and 9× more outliers for WP8 apps. Furthermore, with Caiipa, 107 out of the 235 W8 apps tested observe at least one crash – in aggregate, Caiipa discovers 661 **unique** crash incidents (from a total of 9,103 crashes) and 4,589 performance outliers. Similarly, 17 of the 30 WP8 apps crash 197 times (26 **unique** crashes) and register 635 performance anomalies. Crash uniqueness is defined by error code and stack trace. This result is somewhat surprising, as these apps are in production and already presumedly went through testing.

Findings by Categories. Figure 9 shows the number of crashes and performance outliers categorized by app source code type: HTML-based, managed code, and apps containing platform-specific code (native or mixed code apps). The observation is that Caiipa is able to identify significantly more potential app problems across categories. For example, in all categories, this difference in the number of outliers found is a factor of approximately 8×.

Figure 10 shows performance outliers broken down by resource type. The figure suggests that both disk activity (i.e., I/O) and CPU appear to have approximately the same number of performance outlier cases. Interestingly, most outliers are network or energy related. From the top energy outliers, we observe that the root cause of high energy consumption correlates with the underlying network condition. Under lossy network conditions, the cause is typically connection resets. Under reasonably good network conditions, the cause is typically the amount of incoming network traffic.

Time to Discovery. In an effort to understand how the time taken for Caiipa to identify crash conditions compares to the analysis of user submitted crash reports we looked into the WER backend database (see 4). We analyzed the internal WER reports for all the crashes Caiipa is able to find during our experiments. Our preliminary analysis of this data compares how long it took for these same crashes to appear in WER database after the app was released.

Overall, for W8 apps, Caiipa takes, on average, only 11.8% (std dev 0.588) of the time needed by WER (2.6% of the time if considering 94.7% of the crash population). Similarly, for WP8 apps this percentage is even lower at 1.3% (std dev 0.025). By closely looking at the data, we see that a few W8 apps quickly crashed in the wild, with crash reports being submitted less than one hour after release, thus reducing the time difference to our proactive approach. We speculate that part of the much better performance in WP8 apps is related to their lower complexity and current lower adoption rates when compared to W8 apps.

5.4 Experiences and Case Studies

Finally, we highlight some identified problem scenarios that mobile app developers might be unfamiliar with, thus illustrating how Caiipa can help prevent ever more common context-related bugs.

Location Bugs. Seemingly every mobile app today uses location information. Unfortunately, this also introduces the opportunity for developer errors – *location bugs.* We now detail one representative location bug, concerning an app released by a US-based magazine publisher. Test results from Caiipa emulating location (i.e., GPS input and network conditions) detected that while the app was robust in US conditions, it was very brittle in other countries. For example, we find the app is 50% more likely to crash under China conditions then US ones.

Network Transitions. Mobile devices experience network transitions frequently throughout the day. For example, handoffs from Wi-Fi to 3G when users leave their home. It is critical apps be robust to such transitions.

During tests, Caiipa uncovered a prototypical example demonstrating these issues in a popular Twitter app. We noticed frequent crashes under certain network conditions. By performing a larger number of test iterations we find that whenever a (simulated) user attempts to tweet during a network handoff from a "fast" (e.g., Wi-Fi) to "slow" (e.g., 2G) network, the app crashes nearly every time. Without the source code, it is hard to know the root cause of the issue. However, it is a clear example of the type of feedback that is possible using Caiipa.

Exception Handlers. During our experiments, we notice a group of music streaming apps which tend to crash with higher frequency on slow and lossy networks. By performing decompiled code analysis [32], we find that the less crash-prone music apps apply a significantly more comprehensive set of exception handlers around network-related system calls. Although not surprising, this highlights how Caiipa is a promising way to compare mobile apps at scale and develop new best practices for the community.

Unintended Outcomes from Sensor Use. Caiipa highlighted an interesting *energy bug* in a location tracking app. The app registers for location updates to be triggered whenever a minimum location displacement occurs. However, we find the app set the threshold to be very tight ($\approx$ 5m accuracy). During testing we perturb the reported accuracy of the location estimate provided to the app (see §4). We find, at typical location accuracy values ($\approx$ 25m), the app requests location estimates at a much higher frequency. As a result, the app consumes energy at much higher rates than expected. This unexpected outcome would be otherwise hard to recognize during non-context based testing.

6. DISCUSSION

We discuss overarching issues related to Caiipa.

Caiipa Software Release. Currently available as a web service in beta trial at Microsoft (Figure 11), the system is already in use by app development teams responsible for 11 apps. The service also allows us to test more effective ways of providing feedback to developers on the detected issues. We are preparing for a wider release in the coming months and targeting additional scenarios, such as developers who must test for compatibility issues against multiple platforms.

Hardware vs Emulators. Currently Caiipa makes limited use of the support for physical devices (i.e. to run platform-specific code and as individual test cases). A better analysis of the tradeoffs between emulation and real devices is ongoing as well as tracking of hardware-specific metrics (e.g. GPU usage, device temperature) and usage of chipset features (e.g. co- and multi-processor).

Context Emulation. While emulating mobile context can be seen as a form of bug inducement, it presents a number of advantages over other such approaches. For example, by exploring context Caiipa can detect unforeseen situations. Other intrusive approaches like fault injection lose these benefits. They must rely on historical data on past issues, which limits their scope to previously detected problems. Furthermore, this data needs to be processed either manually (which does not scale) or automatically (which is

Figure 11: Caiipa beta web service.

error prone) to identify the root cause issues to be injected in the target system. Special care needs to be paid to this analysis as they can cause faults not possible during actual usage, or detect bugs not representative of real workloads.

Context Emulation Limitations. Caiipa currently exposes only coarse-grained hardware parameters (i.e., CPU clock speed and available memory). Although it can accommodate real devices in the test client pool to achieve hardware coverage, Caiipa lacks support for low-level hardware modelling, such as Wi-Fi energy states. We leave the support for an expanded perturbation layer as future work.

Real-World Mobile Context Collection. While our system utilizes real-world data to emulate mobile contexts, we recognize that some datasets are difficult to collect. For example, an extensive, easily generalized, database regarding users app interaction is not yet available. Of special interest for connected apps, carrier-specific characteristics (e.g. blocking of ports or protocols, DNS solving, routing) can be a source of problems. Collecting and representing this information as part of context present many challenges. We will explore additional context sources in future work.

Testing Limitations. Many apps suffer from issues that are not directly related to crashes nor performance, such as layout issues, language errors, or usability problems. While Caiipa can detect app hangs or excessive battery drain issues, it does not address the category of content-related visual problems. Games also present challenges for automated testing, from precision of UI interactions (e.g. gestures) to gameplay constraints (e.g. only pressing jump when approaching an enemy), and they are out of scope for Caiipa.

Applicability to Other Platforms. While our prototype runs on Windows-based OSs, the core design also works on other platforms (e.g., iOS). Recently, we completed a preliminary Android prototype that is functionally equivalent to the original Window-centric implementation detailed in this paper. This prototype has yet to be evaluated, but we expect similar findings for Android-based apps as we report for Windows apps. Because of its design, such as our black-box app assumption and replaceable UI automation, Caiipa is much easier to port to alternative platforms.

7. RELATED WORK

We propose new methods for using context during mobile app testing. Our results complement existing techniques, including static analysis and fault injection.

Mobile App Testing. There are many commercial telemetry solutions for mobile devices [5, 33, 7]. Carat [24] focuses on energy bugs by periodically uploading coarse-grained battery and system status. AppInsight [28] adds visibility into the critical paths of asynchronous mobile apps. Unlike Caiipa, these are post-release solutions.

Many proactive testing tools are also available. However, most tools cover only a small subset of mobile contexts. For example, specialized tools [13] and libraries [21] exist for UI automation testing. Also, there is considerable work into generating UI input for testing of a specific goal (e.g., code coverage) [36, 14, 3, 1, 27]. Additional proactive testing tools emulate a limited set of predefined network conditions. This emulation is controlled either manually [13, 20] or via scripts [19]. In contrast to Caiipa, these tools do not allow fine-grained control over network parameters, nor accurate emulation of contexts such as network handoffs.

VanarSena [29] is a related effort that employs a greybox testing approach, leveraging instrumentation, to find bugs. It focuses on increased monkey UI testing efficiency (using a proposed *hit testing* approach along with instrumentation) and conventional fault injection of common crash inducing conditions (e.g., unhandled HTTP error codes). Unlike Caiipa, [29] can not test app performance (such as energy bugs) and is unable to test unmanaged code due to its dependence on instrumentation. We envision combining Caiipa and VanarSena into a seamless testing service that leverages the strengths of both systems [9].

State Space Exploration. The software testing community has proposed techniques to efficiently explore program state space, which mostly rely on hints extracted from source code or app test history. Whitebox fuzzing is one technique that requires source code. For example, SAGE [11] tests for security bugs by generating test cases from code analysis. [2] explores code paths within mobile apps and reduces path explosion by merging redundant paths. Model checking is another popular technique, where the idea is to build models of the app based on specs or code [15].

Finally, [12] proposes a test prioritization scheme using inter-app similarity between code statement execution patterns. However, as Caiipa does not require source code it is more broadly applicable. Directed testing (e.g. [8]), is a type of technique using a feedback-loop but for the same app. Caiipa uses similar methods, but across apps.

8. CONCLUSION

This paper presents Caiipa, a testing framework that applies the *contextual fuzzing* approach to test mobile apps over an expanded mobile context space in a scalable way. Our results show Caiipa can find many more bugs and performance issues than existing tools that consider none or a subset of the mobile context. Additionally, by linking context parameters to the detected issues, Caiipa provides additional information for developers to understand the causes of bugs and better prioritize their correction.

9. REFERENCES

[1] D. Amalfitano, et al. Using GUI Ripping for Automated Testing of Android Applications. In ASE 2012.

[2] S. Anand, M. Naik, H. Yang, and M. Harrold. Automated Concolic Testing of Smartphone Apps. In FSE 2012.

[3] T. Azim et al. Targeted and Depth-first Exploration for Systematic Testing of Android Apps. In OOPSLA 2013.

[4] C. M. Bishop. Pattern Recognition and Machine Learning (Information Science and Statistics). Springer, August 2006.

[5] Crashlytics. `http://www.crashlytics.com`.

[6] Fortune. `http://fortune.com/2009/08/22/40-staffers-2-reviews-8500-iphone-apps-per-week/`.

[7] K. Glerum et al. Debugging in the (Very) Large: Ten Years of Implementation and Experience. In SOSP 2009.

[8] P. Godefroid, N. Klarlund, and K. Sen. Dart: Directed Automated Random Testing. In PLDI 2005.

[9] R. Chandra et al. Towards Scalable Automated Mobile App Testing. Technical Report MSR-TR-2014-44, 2014.

[10] C. Liang et al. Contextual Fuzzing: Automated Mobile App Testing Under Dynamic Device and Environment Conditions. Technical Report MSR-TR-2013-100, 2013.

[11] P. Godefroid et al. Sage: Whitebox Fuzzing for Security Testing. Communications of the ACM, 55(3):40–44, 2012.

[12] A. Gonzalez-Sanchez, et al. Prioritizing Tests for Fault Localization through Ambiguity Group Reduction. In Proceedings of the IEEE/ACM ASE 2011.

[13] Google. UI/Application Exerciser Monkey. `http://developer.android.com/tools/help/monkey.html`.

[14] F. Gross, G. Fraser, and A. Zeller. Search-based System Testing: High Coverage, No False Alarms. In ISSTA 2012.

[15] H. Guo, et al. Practical Software Model Checking Via Dynamic Interface Reduction. In SOSP 2011.

[16] V. Hautamaki, I. Karkkainen, and P. Franti. Outlier Detection Using k-nearest Neighbour Graph. In ICPR 2004.

[17] J. Huang, et al. Uncovering Cellular Network Characteristics: Performance, Infrastructure, and Policies. Technical Report MSU-CSE-00-2, 2013.

[18] Flurry. `http://www.flurry.com/bid/91911/Electric-Technology-Apps-and-The-New-Global-Village`.

[19] B. Jiang, et al. Mobiletest: A Tool Supporting Automatic Black Box Test for Software on Smart Mobile Devices. In Proceedings of AST 2007.

[20] Simulation Dashboard for Windows Phone. `http://msdn.microsoft.com/library/windowsphone/develop/jj206953`.

[21] UI Automation Verify. `http://msdn.microsoft.com/en-us/library/windows/desktop/hh920986`.

[22] R. Mittal, et al. Empowering Developers to Estimate App Energy Consumption. In Mobicom 2012.

[23] R. Natella et al. On Fault Representativeness of Software Fault Injection. IEEE Trans. on Software Eng., 39(1), 2013.

[24] A. J. Oliner, et al. Carat: Collaborative Energy Diagnosis for Mobile Devices. In SenSys 2013.

[25] Open Signal. `http://opensignal.com`.

[26] Open Signal. Signal Reports. `http://opensignal.com/reports/fragmentation.php`.

[27] V. Rastogi et al. Appsplayground: Automatic Security Analysis of Smartphone Applications. In CODASPY 2013.

[28] L. Ravindranath, et al. AppInsight: Mobile App Performance Monitoring in the Wild. In OSDI 2012.

[29] L. Ravindranath, et. al. Automatic and Scalable Fault Detection for Mobile Applications. In MobiSys 2014.

[30] Techcrunch. `http://techcrunch.com/users-have-low-tolerance-for-buggy-apps-only-16-will-try-a-failing-app-more-than-twice`.

[31] Crittercism. `http://pages.crittercism.com/rs/crittercism/images/crittercism-mobile-benchmarks.pdf`.

[32] Telerik. JustDecompile. `http://www.telerik.com`.

[33] TestFlight. `http://testflightapp.com/`.

[34] Bit9. `https://www.bit9.com/download/reports/Pausing-Google-Play-October2012.pdf`.

[35] A. I. Wasserman. Software Engineering Issues for Mobile Application Development. In FSE - FoSER workshop, 2010.

[36] L. Yan and H. Yin. DroidScope: Seamlessly Reconstructing the OS and Dalvik Semantic Views for Dynamic Android Malware Analysis. In USENIX Security Symposium, 2012.

[37] T. Boksasp, et al. Android Apps and Permissions: Security and Privacy Risks. NTNU Trondheim TR, June 2012.

Rethink Energy Accounting with Cooperative Game Theory

Mian Dong
Rice University
dongmian@gmail.com

Tian Lan
George Washington University
tlan@gwu.edu

Lin Zhong
Rice University
lzhong@rice.edu

ABSTRACT

Energy accounting determines how much a software principal contributes to the total system energy consumption. It is the foundation for evaluating software and for operating system based energy management. While various energy accounting policies have been tried, there is no known way to evaluate them directly simply because it is hard to track all hardware usage by software in a heterogeneous multicore system like modern smartphones and tablets.

In this work, we argue that energy accounting should be formulated as a cooperative game and that the Shapley value provides the ultimate ground truth for energy accounting policies. We reveal the important flaws of existing energy accounting policies based on the Shapley value theory and provide Shapley value-based energy accounting, a practical approximation of the Shapley value, for battery-powered mobile systems. We evaluate this approximation against existing energy accounting policies in two ways: (*i*) how well they identify the top energy consuming applications, and (*ii*) how effective they are in system energy management. Using a prototype based on Texas Instruments Pandaboard and smartphone workload, we experimentally demonstrate existing energy accounting policies can deviate by 400% in attributing energy consumption to running applications and can be up to 25% less effective in system energy management when compared to Shapley value-based energy accounting.

Categories and Subject Descriptors

D.4.1 [**Operating Systems**]: Process Management

Keywords

Energy accounting; Energy management; Mobile systems

1. INTRODUCTION

The ability to account system resource usage by software is key to the design and operation of computers. While modern computers can account CPU and memory usage by software easily, they can not yet do so for energy, an increasingly important system resource due to electricity and thermal concerns. We use *software principals* to denote the software entities to which energy consumption has to be attributed. Examples of software principal include applications, processes, threads, and tasks. Given the system energy consumption E and the set of software principals $\mathbb{N} = \{1,2,\ldots,n\}$ that are active during time interval T, *energy accounting* determines the energy contribution of each software principal in $\mathbb{N}$. Energy accounting is the foundation for evaluating software by their energy use, e.g., [23, 19], and for operating system (OS) based energy management that schedules processes for tradeoffs between system energy consumption and process utility, e.g., [32, 25].

Energy accounting is a long-standing hard problem for multiprocessing systems in which multiple software principals can be active at the same time. In the past decade, many energy accounting policies have been tried for various applications as exemplified recently by [33, 23, 19, 31], including the "Battery" feature in Android. However, there is no known *ground truth* against which a policy could be evaluated. The fundamental reason is that it is practically infeasible to track how software uses each hardware component in a heterogeneous multicore system like modern mobile devices. Usually, only the total system energy consumption can be measured, and the usage of only a few hardware components, e.g., CPU and memory, can be attributed to a software principal.

In this work, we explore cooperative game theory for energy accounting, reveal the important flaws of existing policies, and suggest a novel policy that does not have these flaws. Our key insight is that *energy accounting can be formulated as a cooperative game theory problem*: when multiple players participate in a game and the game produces a surplus, how should that surplus be divided among the players? Note that "cooperative" implies that the players can influence each other via both collaboration and competition. In energy accounting, the game is the system during time interval T, players software principals, and energy consumption the surplus. We show that the Shapley value [27], a single value solution to this problem, provides the theoretical ground truth for energy accounting. We show how existing accounting policies violate the four self-evident properties that uniquely define the Shapley value.

We further provide a practical approximation of the Shapley value, called *Shapley value-based energy accounting*, for battery-powered mobile devices. It is infeasible to obtain the exact Shapley value in practice because calculating it requires the system energy consumption for all possible combinations of software principals under question, i.e., $E(\mathbb{S})\ \forall\ \mathbb{S} \subseteq \mathbb{N}$. Our Shapley value-based energy accounting acquires system energy consumption *in situ* for very short time intervals, down to 10 ms, uses heuristics to estimate $E(\mathbb{S})$ for unobserved $\mathbb{S}$, and extend the Shapley value theory to work with partially defined cooperative games and non-deterministic energy consumption $E(\mathbb{S})$. We report a prototype implementation

MobiCom'14, September 7-11, 2014, Maui, Hawaii, USA.

http://dx.doi.org/10.1145/2639108.2639128.

based on Google Android, Texas Instruments PandaBoard ES with OMAP4460, and MAXIM DS2756 battery fuel gauge.

Using this prototype, we experimentally demonstrate how erroneous existing energy accounting policies can be (up to 400%), how little difference in energy management can they make, and that Shapley value-based energy accounting outperforms other energy accounting policies in energy management by up to 25%. Our results also show that sophisticated energy accounting policies used in recent work are not better than very simple ones as long as they guarantee that energy contributions from all software principals add up to the total system energy consumption. Our results mandate a rethinking of energy accounting and its application in energy management. Not only can existing energy accounting policies be off-the-mark by a large degree (now we know why many Android users feel the "Battery" feature is inaccurate), but also existing budget-based energy management may be unnecessarily complicated yet underperforming. While our prototype and evaluation are based on battery-powered mobile systems, we believe most of our results are directly applicable to other computer systems as long as fairly high-frequency system energy measurements are available.

In summary, we make the following contributions to energy accounting in both theory and practice.

- We show that energy accounting should be formulated as a cooperative game and that the Shapley value provides the theoretical ground truth. We reveal how existing accounting policies fail the axiomatic properties required by this ground truth.
- We provide Shapley value-based energy accounting, a practical approximation of the Shapley value, for battery-powered mobile devices. Using a prototype realization, we demonstrate our approximation is superior to existing energy accounting policies experimentally.

The rest of this paper is organized as follows. Section 2 provides necessary background and introduces existing energy accounting policies. Section 3 presents the Shapley value as ground truth for energy accounting. Section 4 describes key techniques to acquire system energy consumption in short time intervals *in situ* in order to realize Shapley value-based energy accounting. Section 5 and Section 6 present system implementation and evaluation, respectively. Section 7 surveys related work. Section 8 discusses how this work can be extended and concludes the paper.

2. BACKGROUND

We first provide some background to the problem and describe existing energy accounting policies.

2.1 Problem Definition and Notations

Energy accounting determines how much a software principal contributes to the system energy consumption. Let T denote the time during which the system energy consumption E must be attributed; $\mathbb{N} = \{1,2,\ldots,n\}$ denote the software principals that are active during this time. An energy accounting policy determines the contribution ϕ_i by process $i \in \mathbb{N}$ to the system energy consumption E. Mathematically a policy is a family of mapping $\{\phi_i(E(\mathbb{N})), \forall i \in \mathbb{N}\}$ from total energy consumption $E(\mathbb{N})$ to per-software principal energy consumptions ϕ_i.

A self-evident property that an energy accounting policy must have is: $\sum_i \phi_i = E(\mathbb{N})$. That is, the sum of energy contributions by all software principals must be the same as the total system energy consumption. We call this property *Efficiency* according to [27].

Table 1 summarizes the main notations used in this paper.

Table 1: Notations

Symbol	Description
T	Time in which system energy consumption is under question
$\mathbb{N}$	A set of n software principals that are active during T
m	Max number of concurrent software principals allowed
$\mathbb{S}$	A subset of $\mathbb{N}$; a *coalition* of software principals
$E(\mathbb{S})$	System energy consumption in T if only $\mathbb{S}$ are active
ϕ_i	Contribution by software principal i to $E(\mathbb{N})$
σ	System state that is out of the control of the processes
$E(\mathbb{S},\sigma)$	System energy consumption when $\mathbb{S}$ are active with state σ

2.2 Existing Energy Accounting Policies

We next discuss the major types of energy accounting policies reported in the literature.

Policy I: $\phi_i = E(\mathbb{N})/|\mathbb{N}|$. This policy states that the energy contributed by software principal i is equal to the total energy consumption divided by the number of software principals. That is, each software principal gets an equal share of the total energy consumption.

Policy II: $\phi_i = E(\{i\})$. This policy states that the energy contributed by software principal i is the same as its stand-alone energy consumption $E(\{i\})$ when only software principal i is running in the system. WattsOn [19] utilizes such policy to obtain the energy consumption of each mobile application to enable third-party app developers to improve energy efficiency of their products.

Policy III: $\phi_i = E(\mathbb{N}) - E(\mathbb{N} \setminus \{i\})$. This policy states that the energy contributed by software principal i is equal to its marginal energy contribution, which is the difference between system energy consumption when software principal i is running and when it is not running, while all other conditions remain unchanged [34].

Policy IV: The energy contributed by software principal i is equal to the sum of system energy consumption over all scheduling intervals when software principal i is scheduled in CPU. PowerScope [12] used this policy to account energy consumption of each program running in a system. Obviously, this approach will work only if one software principal can be running at the same time.

Policy V: This sophisticated policy relies on a system energy model $E = f(x_1, x_2, \ldots, x_p)$ where $x_k, k = 1,2,\ldots p$, are predictors that can be obtained in software such as CPU and memory usage. The policy figures out how much software principal i contributes to each of the predictors, $x_{k,i}$ and determines the energy contribution by i by plugging $x_{k,i}$ back into f, i.e., $\phi_i = f(x_{1,i}, x_{2,i}, \ldots, x_{k,i}, \ldots, x_{p,i})$. To have the Efficiency property described above, however, f must be a linear function, i.e., $E = \beta_0 + \sum_{k=1}^{p} \beta_k \cdot x_k$ and there must be a heuristic to split the constant β_0 among the software principals. Variants of Policy V have been used by Android [1], PowerTutor [2] and AppScope [31] for smartphones, by ECOSysem [32] for laptops, by Joulemeter [14] and Power Container [28] for servers, and by Quanto [13] for sensor networks. Policy V, however, is fundamentally limited because how it determines the energy contribution by a software principal depends on how it estimates the system energy consumption. In particular, the estimation can only consider resource usage that can be attributed to individual software principals; and the estimation must employ a linear model. These two limitations can be very problematic for modern mobile systems where many hardware components including some major energy consumers are invisible to the OS [20], e.g., system bus and graphics, and others whose usage cannot be easily attributed to a software principal, e.g., GPS and display. Moreover, it has been shown that linear models are inadequate for estimating system energy consumption [17, 8]. As a result, Policy V can not only significantly underestimate the energy contribution by a software principal but also fail to attribute a significant portion of system energy consumption to running software principals. Due to the lack of ground truth for energy accounting, the problems of Policy V have never been quantified.

In the rest of the paper, we will reveal the fundamental flaws of these energy accounting policies analytically (Section 3.3) and quantitatively (Section 6.3).

3. SHAPLEY VALUE AS GROUND TRUTH

We now introduce the Shapley value as the ground truth for energy accounting. We will discuss how the theory can be applied to energy accounting and demonstrate how existing energy accounting policies lack one or more of the four properties that uniquely define the Shapley value. In Section 4 and Section 5, we will discuss how to address system challenges of realizing Shapley value-based energy accounting and provide a practical, approximate implementation, respectively.

3.1 Shapley Value

We observe a problem similar to energy accounting has been extensively studied in cooperative game theory: how to determine the contribution of each individual player in a game with multiple players? Consider a cooperative game where a set of n players, $\mathbb{N} = \{1,\ldots,n\}$, collectively generate a grand surplus $v(\mathbb{N})$. The set of players, $\mathbb{N}$, is also called the *grand coalition*. Plainly speaking, "cooperative" here refers to the fact the players are not playing in isolation: they can influence each other via both collaboration and competition. Let $v: 2^n \rightarrow \mathbb{R}$ be a *characteristic function* that describes the payoff $v(\mathbb{S})$ a subset of players $\mathbb{S} \subseteq \mathbb{N}$ can gain by playing the same game. A powerful result proven by Shapley in 1953 [27] defines the Shapley value $\phi_i(v)$ for $i = 1,\ldots,n$ as the *unique* way to distribute the grand surplus $v(\mathbb{N})$ among the n players that satisfies four simple axioms:

Efficiency: The sum of share of all players is the grand surplus, i.e. $\sum_i \phi_i(v) = v(\mathbb{N})$. This is the Efficiency property mentioned in Section 2.2.

Symmetry: Symmetric players receive equal shares, i.e., if $v(\mathbb{S} \cup \{i\}) = v(\mathbb{S} \cup \{j\})\ \forall \mathbb{S} \subseteq (\mathbb{N} \setminus \{i,j\}))$, then $\phi_i(v) = \phi_j(v)$. That is, if replacing player i with player j in any coalition does not change the game surplus and vice versa, the shares of the two players should be identical.

Null Player: Player i receives zero share if he does not change the payoff in any coalition $\mathbb{S}$, i.e., if $v(\mathbb{S} \cup \{i\}) = v(\mathbb{S})\ \forall \mathbb{S} \subseteq \mathbb{N}$, then $\phi_i(v) = 0$. That is, if adding a player to any coalition does not change the game surplus, the player should receive zero.

Additivity: The share to player i in a sum of two games is the sum of the allocations to the player in each individual game, i.e., $\phi_i(v) + \phi_i(w) = \phi_i(v+w)$, $\forall i$. That is, if we view two games as a single game, the share a player receives from the combined game should be the same as the sum of what he would receive from each of the two original games.

The Shapley value is the unique distribution function that satisfies the above four axioms:

$$\phi_i(v) = \sum_{\mathbb{S} \subseteq \mathbb{N} \setminus \{i\}} \frac{v(\mathbb{S} \cup \{i\}) - v(\mathbb{S})}{(|\mathbb{N}| - |\mathbb{S}|)\binom{|\mathbb{N}|}{|\mathbb{S}|}}, \qquad (1)$$

where $|\mathbb{S}|$ is the cardinality of $\mathbb{S}$, i.e., the number of members of $\mathbb{S}$; similarly, $|\mathbb{N}|$ is the number of members of $\mathbb{N}$, or n; $\binom{|\mathbb{N}|}{|\mathbb{S}|}$ is $|\mathbb{N}|$-choose-$|\mathbb{S}|$. The Shapley value captures the *average marginal contribution* of player i, averaging over all the different sequences according to which the grand coalition ($\mathbb{N}$) could be built up from the empty coalition. It has been widely applied for solving benefit/cost sharing problems in diverse fields, including computer science, e.g., [18, 11]. To calculate the Shapley value $\phi_i(v)$, one need not only the grand surplus when all n players play, $v(\mathbb{N})$, but also the surplus when any subset of the n players play, or $v(\mathbb{S})$ for all $\mathbb{S} \subseteq \mathbb{N}$.

3.2 Ground Truth for Energy Accounting

We argue the Shapley value provides a natural and intuitive ground truth for energy accounting. We treat the time interval T in which the system under question consumes energy as the cooperative game; the software principals active in the same time interval $\mathbb{N}$ the players; and total system energy consumption, $E(\mathbb{N})$, the grand surplus to distribute. Thus, the energy contribution ϕ_i by software principal i is given by the Shapley value $\phi_i(v)$ of the game with $v(\mathbb{S}) = E(\mathbb{S})$ $\forall \mathbb{S} \subseteq \mathbb{N}$ in Equation (1). Note that to calculate the Shapley value, one must know the system energy consumption in the same time interval T if only a subset of $\mathbb{N}$ are active during T for all possible subsets, i.e., $E(\mathbb{S})\ \forall \mathbb{S} \subseteq \mathbb{N}$. This poses a significant challenge to the practical use of the Shapley value as the ground truth for energy accounting. In Section 4, we will present techniques that partially overcome this challenge to provide a practical approximation of the ground truth.

Since the Shapley value is uniquely defined by the four axioms, we show that these four axioms are self-evident and logical for energy accounting. *(i) Efficiency* requires the sum of the energy contributions by all software principals be equal to the total system energy consumption. In other words, an energy accounting policy must be able to apportion energy consumption among software principals without any residual left. This is the same Efficiency property discussed in Section 2.2. *(ii) Symmetry* requires two software principals to be assigned the same energy contribution if replacing one with the other under any circumstances does not change the system energy consumption. *(iii) Null Player* requires that if adding a software principal under any circumstances does not change the system energy consumption, the energy contribution by this software principal should be zero. Finally, *(iv) Additivity* says that if we break T into multiple time intervals and apply the same accounting policy to them, the energy attributed to a software principal in T should be equal to the sum of energy attributed to it in these shorter time intervals under the same energy accounting policy.

It is important to note that these four axioms are the properties for energy accounting policies; they are not assumptions made for the computer or its software. The Shapley value is the only possible policy that has all four properties and should be considered as the ground truth for energy accounting.

3.3 Existing Policies Against the Shapley Value

While it is infeasible to obtain the Shapley value in practice, we can reveal the flaws of the five types of existing policies against the four axioms that uniquely define the Shapley value. Table 2 summarizes how they violate the four axioms. In Section 6, we will offer quantitative evidence regarding their flaws.

Policy I violates *Null Player* because a software principal always gets positive energy contribution according to it.

Policy II violates *Efficiency*. For example, consider a system with two software principals. According to Policy II, energy contributed by software principal 1, or software principal 2, is equal to its stand-alone energy consumption $E(\{1\})$, or $E(\{2\})$, respectively. However, to satisfy *Efficiency* requires $\phi_1 + \phi_2 = E(\{1\}) +$

Table 2: How existing energy accounting policies violate the axioms that define the Shapley value

Policies	Efficiency	Symmetry	Null Player	Additivity
I			×	
II	×		×	
III	×			×
IV		×	×	
V	×	×	×	

$E(\{2\}) = E(\{1,2\})$. Unfortunately, the last equality does not hold in many cases, e.g., when software principals 1 and 2 share some system resources, one usually observes $E(\{1\})+E(\{2\}) > E(\{1,2\})$.

Policy III violates *Efficiency*. Using the same example above, Policy III requires $\phi_1 = E(\{1,2\}) - E(\{2\})$ and $\phi_2 = E(\{1,2\}) - E(\{1\})$. Thus, the sum of shares is $\phi_1 + \phi_2 = 2E(\{1,2\}) - E(\{1\}) - E(\{2\})$. Again, $E(\{1\}) + E(\{2\}) = E(\{1,2\})$ is necessary for *Efficiency* to hold. The LEA^{2}P platform [26] utilizes an improved Policy III that normalizes all the $\phi_i = E(\mathbb{N}) - E(\mathbb{N} \setminus \{i\})$ to enforce *Efficiency*. However, the normalization will lead to violation of *Additivity* because different normalization factors may be used in different time intervals.

Policy IV does not work for multiprocessing systems. To extend Policy IV for multiprocessing systems, one can attribute energy consumption to software principals based on their CPU usage, as in [3]. Such extension, however, violates *Null Player* because a software principal always has positive CPU usage and thus positive energy contribution according to the policy. It further violates *Symmetry* due to its heavy dependency on timing of energy consumption. For instance, the same software principal may be charged different energy bills when it consumes energy through asynchronous I/O operations and suffers random delays, as mentioned by [32].

Policy V violates the *Efficiency*, *Symmetry*, and *Null Player*. First, the inaccuracy in its energy model as highlighted in Section 2.2 may lead to violation of *Efficiency*. Second, there may exist software principals that make use of different hardware components, but make the same energy contributions in all coalitions. These software principals are indistinguishable with respect to their energy behaviors and therefore should be charged equal energy bills according to *Symmetry*. However, if they make different contributions to the predictors in the used energy model, Policy V would dictate that these software principals make different energy contributions and thus would violate *Symmetry*. Finally, a software principal always gets positive energy contribution because it requires CPU time and system resources so that it always makes positive contributions to the predictors of the energy model.

4. SHAPLEY VALUE-BASED ENERGY ACCOUNTING

While we argue that the Shapley value should be considered as the ground truth for energy accounting, this ground truth is practically impossible to obtain via measurement. The key problem is to obtain $E(\mathbb{S})$ for all $\mathbb{S} \subseteq \mathbb{N}$, which poses three system challenges. (*i*) First, there are 2^n subsets for n software principals. One must obtain $E(\mathbb{S})$ for all the 2^n different coalitions, which can be practically infeasible. (*ii*) Second, $E(\mathbb{S})$ depends on not only which software principals are running, but also the dynamics of software execution such as the CPU time of each software principal and the execution order. Therefore, $E(\mathbb{S})$ is not a fixed number but a random variable. The variance of $E(\mathbb{S})$ introduces uncertainty in energy accounting by the Shapley value. (*iii*) Finally, $E(\mathbb{S})$ is further affected by the hardware state in a mobile system such as CPU frequency, LCD brightness, and WiFi active/idle mode. This will introduce even more variance in $E(\mathbb{S})$.

In this section, we present techniques to partially overcome the above challenges so that we can implement an energy accounting policy that is based on the Shapley value yet practical. We call this policy *Shapley value-based energy accounting*. This policy is not the same as the Shapley value but rather an approximate, in the sense that the input for the Shapley value calculations, $E(\mathbb{S})$, are estimated using practical methods.

4.1 Key Ideas

We tackle the first two challenges by using very short time intervals, i.e.,10 ms, as the game. In a shorter time interval, fewer software principals can run and the software execution dynamics has less impact on energy consumption. On the other hand, measuring or estimating the system energy consumption E for them will be less accurate and less efficient. Our experience with our prototype reported later has led us to believe 10 ms strives a good balance between these two aspects. By monitoring the system energy consumption *in situ* for an extended period of time, one can potentially acquire $E(\mathbb{S})$ for many different $\mathbb{S}$. Modern mobile systems already have a battery interface that measures system energy consumption at a modest rate [8]. Using this interface, it has been shown that system energy consumption for 10 ms time intervals can be estimated *in situ* with about 80% accuracy [8]. In Section 5.1, we present an enhanced battery interface that is able to measure system energy consumption of 10 ms time intervals with an accuracy over 95%.

We address the third challenge by incorporating hardware states as a condition into $E(\mathbb{S})$. Let σ denote current hardware state. We can estimate system energy consumption for a coalition $\mathbb{S}$ given the hardware state σ, denoted by $E(\mathbb{S},\sigma)$. As a result, one can apply the Shapley value separately to time intervals with a given hardware state. However, such an approach will further increase the number of $E(\mathbb{S},\sigma)$. As a result, there will be $E(\mathbb{S},\sigma)$ for numerous $\mathbb{S}$ and σ that are not observed by measurement. Therefore, we employ two solutions to estimate unknown $E(\mathbb{S},\sigma)$ from measured $E(\mathbb{S},\sigma)$ in historical data.This is the focus of Section 4.2. Finally, we extend Shapley value-based energy accounting to deal with non-deterministic factors in system energy consumption in Section 4.3.

4.2 Partially Defined Shapley Value

When $E(\mathbb{S},\sigma)$ is not observed for some $\mathbb{S}$ or σ, the classic Shapley value cannot be applied directly to determine per-software principal contribution. In such a cooperative game with unknown coalition values, the Shapley value is "partially" defined [30]. We now describe our techniques to determine the partially-defined Shapley value for per-software principal energy accounting. All the $E(\mathbb{S},\sigma)$ can be represented in a two-dimension matrix, with only a part of the all the elements can be obtained by measurement. As shown in Figure 1, we use *recursive definition* to fill all the columns, and *linear estimation* to fill all the rows. Finally, we use *M-games* to reduce the number of rows needed.

4.2.1 Recursive Definition

We first present a method to recursively define the Shapley value for all partially defined games. The key idea is to approximate $E(\mathbb{S})$ for unobserved $\mathbb{S}$ by the energy costs allocated to members of $\mathbb{S}$, which are presumably solvable by the Shapley value. We introduce the following extension of a partially defined game E to a fully defined one:

$$\hat{E}(\mathbb{S}) = \begin{cases} E(\mathbb{S}) & \text{if } \mathbb{S} \text{ is known} \\ \sum_{i\in\mathbb{S}} \phi_i(\hat{E}) & \text{otherwise} \end{cases} \quad (2)$$

Here $\phi_i(\hat{E})$ is the Shapley value of the fully defined game $\hat{E}$, corresponding to energy cost attributed to software principal i. By extending E to $\hat{E}$, we are assuming that the energy cost of an unknown coalition $\mathbb{S}$ is approximately the sum of the energy cost of members of the coalition $\mathbb{S}$. To complete the definition, $\phi_i(\hat{E})$ is the standard Shapley value for $\hat{E}$ as defined by Equation (1).

We note that the definition above is recursive since $\hat{E}$ and $\phi_i(\hat{E})$ are defined by each other. Therefore, we use an iterative algorithm to compute the Shapley value $\phi_i(\hat{E})$. At each iteration, we compute $\phi_i(\hat{E})$ for the fully defined game $\hat{E}$, and whenever the computation needs to probe an unknown coalition $\mathbb{S}$, then $\hat{E}(\mathbb{S})$ is calculated using the Shapley value $\phi_i(\hat{E})$ obtained in previous iteration.

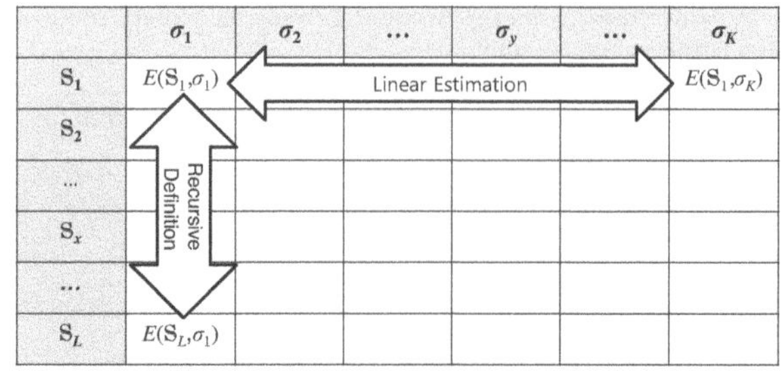

Figure 1: Estimation from partial information. Columns are filled by recursive definition and rows are filled by linear estimation.

4.2.2 *Linear Estimation*

We further utilize a linear model to estimate energy costs of unobserved coalitions for different $E(\mathbb{S}, \sigma_y)$ with the same coalition $\mathbb{S}$ but different power states σ_y, $y = 1, 2, \ldots, K$. Suppose that an unknown energy cost $E(\mathbb{S}_x, \sigma_y)$ of coalition $\mathbb{S}_x$ needs to be estimated for the set of resulting feasible coalitions to form a desired structure. We can employ the least-square method to find a linear substitute for σ_y based on the energy costs of other coalition in the same states, e.g., $E(\mathbb{S}_l, \sigma_y)$, $l \in 1, 2, \ldots, L$ and $E(\mathbb{S}_l, \sigma_k)$, $k = 1, 2, \ldots, K$, $k \neq y$. More precisely, we derive $K+1$ parameters $\theta_0, \theta_1, \ldots, \theta_K$ by solving the following optimization problem:

$$\text{minimize} \quad \sum_{l:l \neq x} \|E(\mathbb{S}_l, \sigma_y) - \sum_{k=1;k\neq y}^{K} \theta_k \times E(S_l, \sigma_k)\|$$

Then we can calculate $E(\mathbb{S}_x, \sigma_y)$ by

$$E(\mathbb{S}_x, \sigma_y) = \sum_{k=1;k\neq y}^{K} \theta_k \times E(\mathbb{S}_x, \sigma_k). \tag{3}$$

4.2.3 *M-games*

We consider a symmetric, partially-defined game where the number of software principals in the coalition, or $|\mathbb{S}|$, solely determines whether $E(\mathbb{S})$ is known. For example, if any set of up to m concurrent software principals have been measured for their energy consumption, we can use the measurements to find energy consumption for all coalitions $\mathbb{S}$ satisfying $|\mathbb{S}| \leq m$, while coalition of size greater than m are treated as unknown. Let M be a set of known coalition sizes. An M-game is defined through energy costs $E(\mathbb{S})$ for coalitions whose sizes are in M, i.e., $|\mathbb{S}| \in M$. Notice that we assume that the energy cost of the grand coalition $\mathbb{N}$ is always known. It is easy to see that an M-game becomes a fully-defined cooperative game if M contains all possible coalition sizes.

A reduced Shapley value is defined on M-games [30] and it satisfies the axioms of additivity, efficiency, dummy-player and symmetry. For an M-game, the energy contribution of software principal i is given by

$$\phi_i = \frac{1}{n} \sum_{m \in M} \left[\frac{\sum_{|\mathbb{S}|=m, i \in \mathbb{S}} E(\mathbb{S})}{\binom{n-1}{m-1}} - \frac{\sum_{|\mathbb{R}|=m, i \notin \mathbb{R}} E(\mathbb{R})}{\binom{n-1}{m}} \right] \tag{4}$$

This formula can be interpreted as the average, over all known coalition sizes, of the differences between the coalitions $\mathbb{S}$ containing software principal i and that coalitions $\mathbb{R}$ not containing software principal i. If all coalitions are known, then the average is taken among all coalition sizes and reduces to the classic Shapley value defined in (1).

4.3 Dealing with Non-deterministic $E(\mathbb{S})$

So far we have attributed a single value of energy consumption to a software principal given the hardware states. However, the energy contribution by a software principal may vary due to many factors other beyond the hardware states considered. For example, the transmission power of the 3G/4G radio interface highly depends on volatile cellular signal strength and thus results in non-deterministic energy consumption. Uncertainty also arises from CPU scheduling and memory management. As a result, $E(\mathbb{S})$ should be treated as a non-deterministic variable, instead of single value. To take non-deterministic $E(\mathbb{S})$ into account, we extend our Shapley value-based energy accounting framework by treating $E(\mathbb{S})$ as a random variable and leverage all the theory work on random Shapley value that require the distribution. The only thing that requires modification in our system is the Shapley value calculation, while the statistics of $E(\mathbb{S})$, e.g., mean and variance can be obtained from the history.

For each coalition $\mathbb{S}$, we regard its energy consumption $E(\mathbb{S})$ as a random variable, whose distribution can be measured from the history. For random $E(\mathbb{S})$, we still use the Shapley value defined in (1) in Section 3 to calculate per-software principal energy $\vec{\phi}_i(E)$ for $i = 1, \ldots, N$, which now becomes a random variable. It is easy to see that the distribution of $\vec{\phi}_i(E)$ can be obtained by a convolution of the PDFs of energy consumption variables $E(\mathbb{S})$. In this section, we are mostly interested in the mean and variance of $\vec{\phi}_i(E)$, which indicate the average per-software principal energy consumption and how far it is spread out. Let $\mu[X]$ be the expectation of a random variable X and Var the variance. Using (1), we can derive the mean of per-software principal energy

$$\mu[\phi_i(v)] = \sum_{\mathbb{S} \subseteq \mathbb{N} \setminus \{i\}} \frac{\mu[E(\mathbb{S} \cup \{i\})] - \mu[E(\mathbb{S})]}{(|\mathbb{N}| - |\mathbb{S}|)\binom{|\mathbb{N}|}{|\mathbb{S}|}}, \tag{5}$$

and the variance of per-software principal energy

$$\text{Var}[\phi_i(v)] = \sum_{\mathbb{S} \subseteq \mathbb{N} \setminus \{i\}} \frac{\text{Var}[E(\mathbb{S} \cup \{i\})] + \text{Var}[E(\mathbb{S})]}{\left\{(|\mathbb{N}| - |\mathbb{S}|)\binom{|\mathbb{N}|}{|\mathbb{S}|}\right\}^2}, \tag{6}$$

A small variance indicates that the per-software principal energy tends to be very close to the mean and hence to be less volatile, while a high variance indicates that the per-software principal energy is very spread out from the mean and has large volatility.

4.4 What is Approximated?

It is important to note that when the measurement and estimation of $E(\mathbb{S})$ and $E(\mathbb{S}, \sigma)$ are accurate, the above heuristics will lead to the exact Shapley value. Unfortunately there is inaccuracy in both the *in situ* measurement and the heuristics-based estimation of unknown $E(\mathbb{S}, \sigma)$. As a result, our design approximates the payoffs of the game, essentially approximating the game itself. The approximation of provided by our Shapley value-based energy accounting is indeed the actual Shapley value of the approximate game.

Figure 2: Prototype: a TI PandaBoard ES and a MAXIM DS2756 battery fuel gauge evaluation module.

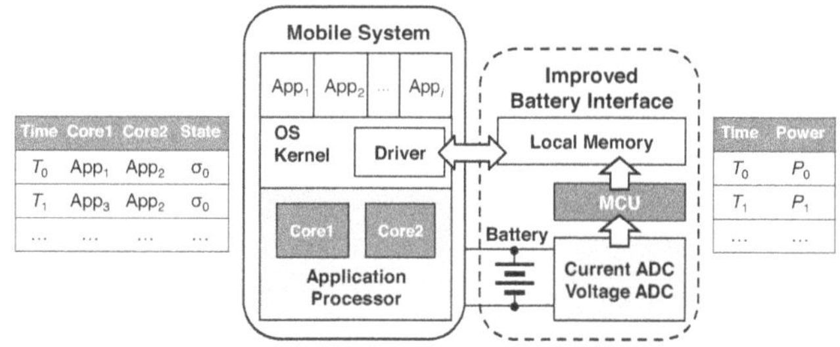

Figure 3: Architecture of the *in situ* high-speed, high-accuracy energy measurement solution: The battery interface measures energy periodically and stores the measurement data with timestamps in its local memory; the mobile system also maintains a timestamped data structure of application combination executed in the OS kernel, utilizes a driver to read the energy measurement data structure from the local memory in the battery interface, and combines the two data structures to get all the $E(\mathbb{S})$.

5. IMPLEMENTATION

We have implemented a prototype of Shapley value-based energy accounting described in Section 4. The prototype includes a Texas Instruments (TI) PandaBoard ES [4] and a MAXIM DS2756 battery fuel gauge evaluation module (EVM) [5], as shown in Figure 2. The PandaBoard ES serves as a mobile system and is powered by an external battery pack. It comes with Android 4.04 and a TI OMAP4460 application processor, similar to that used by the Galaxy Nexus smartphone and RIM Playbook. The DS2756 EVM serves as an enhanced battery interface and measures the energy consumption by the Pandaboard ES from the external battery pack at 200 Hz. The measurement data is transferred from DS2756 EVM to the PandaBoard ES through GPIO using the 1-wire communication protocol.

The prototype uses *application* as software principal. We chose application instead of OS process because end users often care about the energy contribution by application, not by process, and because there are much fewer applications than processes. According to a recent study [29], the top ten most frequently used applications account for the total usage time by as much as 90%. Therefore, the prototype only considers the top ten applications for each user and treat other applications as a single software principal "other". It also combines all the Android system activities as a single software principal to be consistent with Android's Battery feature. As a result, the prototype accounts energy for up to 12 software principals.

We next elaborate the implementations of the enhanced battery interface and the software.

5.1 *In Situ* Measurement of $E(\mathbb{S})$

As explained in Section 4, the key to Shapley value-based energy accounting is to efficiently obtain the system energy consumption for very short time intervals, i.e., 10 ms. While prior work has demonstrated reasonably accurate estimation for 10 ms intervals using battery interfaces in commodity mobile devices [8], our prototype employ an enhanced battery interface that achieves even higher accuracy, i.e., over 95%. It does so with an ultra low-power system-on-a-chip consisting of a 16-bit microcontroller (MCU), 32 KB on-chip memory and two 14-bit analog-to-digital converters (ADCs) that comes with the DS2756 EVM, overall with a few hundred μW of active power consumption. Prior to prototyping, we performed extensive analysis to determine the measurement requirement: 8-bit ADC at 200 Hz as summarized in Section 5.1.1.

Our implementation includes both software in the mobile system and an enhanced battery interface as illustrated by Figure 3. The MCU in the enhanced battery interface periodically measures the voltage of and the discharge current from the battery using two 14-bit ADCs, calculates the energy consumption, and writes it to the local memory along with a timestamp. The battery interface driver running in the mobile system reads the local memory in the battery interface via a serial bus in the standard smart battery interface upon a request from the mobile OS. The driver also keeps a timestamped record for the Android UID of applications that are running in each OS scheduling period as well as the hardware state of the system. Then the mobile OS combines the timestamped energy data from the battery interface and the local timestamped UID data to obtain the system energy consumption for each scheduling period.

It is critical to synchronize the UID data collected by the battery interface driver in the mobile system and the energy data collected by the battery interface. The UID data collected by the driver is timestamped with a timer based on a high accuracy clock. The energy data, however, is timestamped by the timer based on a local low-accuracy clock of the MCU, usually implemented using an LC oscillator to achieve power efficiency. Inaccuracy in the energy data timestamp will lead to that the energy data misalign with the UID data. To tackle this challenge, the prototype employs two techniques. First, the driver periodically writes the OS timestamp to a specific memory location in the battery interface and the latter utilizes this timestamp to correct its own timer. Then, the data transfer delay between the mobile system and the battery interface is further accounted with a simple calibration procedure.

5.1.1 *Measurement Requirement*

The key component of the enhanced battery interface in Figure 3 is the ADC. The most important properties of an ADC are *sampling rate* and *resolution*. Insufficient sampling rate or resolution will cause error in energy measurement while excessive high sampling rate or resolution will lead to energy waste.

In order to determine the sufficient sampling rate and resolution, we characterize the power consumption traces of three commercial smartphones (Samsung Galaxy S, S II, and S III), and ten popular applications as shown in Table 3. We employ one external power supply for constant 4.2 V input and measure the current drawn. We employ a high-speed Oscilloscope to collect the ground truth power traces, using 500 KHz sampling rate, for each of the device and application.

Sampling Rate: By examining the spectrum of the power traces, we are able to identify 200 Hz as sufficient to include 99% of power density in spectrum for all the applications. As an example, Figure 4 (left) shows the power spectrum of Galaxy S III running the Phone application. We can see most of energy locates in the low-frequency range, while the high-frequency spectrum is flat. As shown in the black curve in the figure, 200 Hz sampling rate includes over 99% of the signal energy. The power traces of other

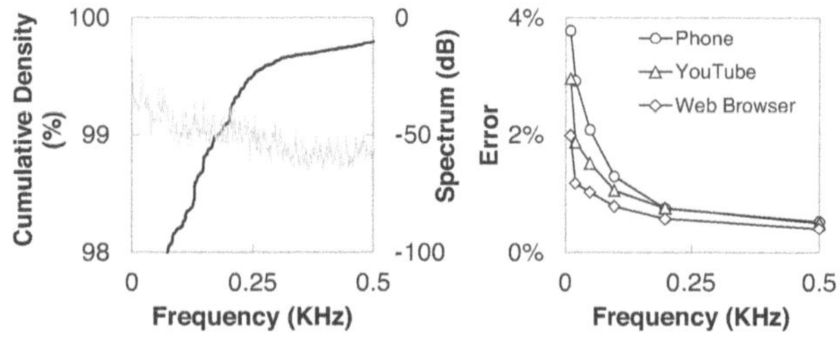

Figure 4: Smartphone workload power characterization for sampling rate: 200 Hz sampling rate is able to cover 99% of the signal information of the power trace (left); 200 Hz sampling rate introduces 1% error in energy measurement of each 10 ms (right).

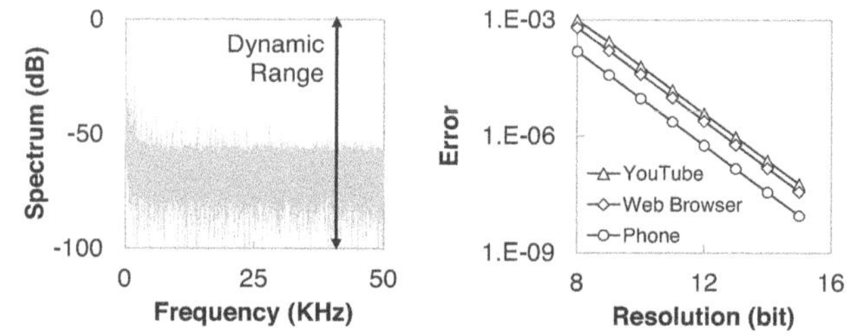

Figure 5: Smartphone workload power characterization for resolution: dynamic range of power trace is around 100 dB and requires a 16-bit ADC for faithful measurement (left); using a 8-bit ADC introduces 0.1% error in energy measurement of each 10 ms (right).

Table 3: Sufficient sampling rate for applications to have 99% of the signal energy of the power consumption trace (Unit: Hz)

Application	Galaxy S	Galaxy S II	Galaxy S III
Phone	197	185	200
SMS	97.1	88.5	93.3
Web Browser	102	105	95.4
Facebook	107	95.5	102
Google Hangout	87.2	85.3	80.8
YouTube	97.4	91.6	102
CamCorder	18.9	24.1	15.1
GPS Navigation	32.5	46.1	30.7
Quake III	67.2	85.6	90.8
Angry Bird	28.4	45.5	57.2

applications show similar characteristics (See Table 3). We next use the 500 KHz data traces as the ground truth and investigate the average error in each 10 ms introduced by using a sampling rate less than 500 KHz. Figure 4 (right) shows the three applications with the highest errors. As shown in the figure, a 200 Hz sampling rate introduces less than 1% error for 10 ms intervals. Therefore, we conclude that 200 Hz sampling rate is sufficient for all the characterized applications on all the smartphones in our experiment.

Resolution: Resolution of an ADC is determined by the dynamic range of the input signal. We characterize the dynamic range by reducing quantization noise below the background noise. As shown in Figure 5 (left), background noise is around -100 dB in normalized spectrum; this implies the effective number of bit (*ENOB*) should be 16 or more because $SNR = 1.76 + 6.02 \times ENOB$. Thus, a 16-bit ADC is sufficient to record transient power trace. We also study how much error will be introduced by using an ADC of lower resolution. As shown in Figure 5 (right), the quantization error introduced by using a 8-bit ADC only introduces 0.1% error in the system energy measurement for each 10 ms.

To summarize, an 8-bit ADC with 200 Hz sampling rate is sufficient for the system energy measurement for 10 ms time intervals needed by Shapley valued-based energy accounting. Thanks to fast development in low-power CMOS technology, a 15-bit audio ADC, with sampling rate higher than 20 KHz, only consumes less than 200 μW [24]. The power consumption of a 8-bit ADC with 200 Hz sampling rate should be negligible.

5.2 Software

Our prototype includes two software modules: one energy measurement module running in the enhanced battery interface and one energy accounting module running in the mobile system. The energy measurement module provides timestamped 200 Hz energy measurement data. The energy accounting module collects $E(\mathbb{S}, \sigma)$, estimates the missing $E(\mathbb{S}, \sigma)$, and calculates energy contribution by each application using Shapley value-based energy accounting.

The energy measurement module is a stand-alone process running in the battery interface's MCU, developed in C language with about 830 lines of code. We use software interrupts to realize the 200 Hz energy measurement. After synchronization described above, the MCU acquires the Android OS timestamp from the mobile system, updates its local timer, and uses this local timer to trigger interrupts to get ADC readings of voltage and current measurement and calculate the energy consumption accordingly.

The energy accounting module in the mobile system includes two sub-modules: $E(\mathbb{S}, \sigma)$ collection and Shapley value calculation. The $E(\mathbb{S}, \sigma)$ collection sub-module includes two parts, i.e., a kernel modification to align timestamp and energy measurement and a user-space thread to collect data. We modify the Android kernel to include the timestamped data structure (See Figure 3) in the kernel space. Upon process context switch, the OS updates the data structure by appending a new entry to it. This data structure is exposed to the user-space thread in the /sys virtual file system. The $E(\mathbb{S}, \sigma)$ collection sub-module is developed on the top of the Android 4.04 code base with 17 files change and totally 2700 lines of code modification.

The Shapley value calculation sub-module is a user-space application. It periodically reads the timestamped data structure from the virtual file system before the data structure overflows and stores the measurement data in the SD card. When the measurement data in the SD card accumulates to a threshold, the user-space thread launches a routine to estimate unknown $E(\mathbb{S}, \sigma)$ from historical measurement data, as illustrated in Figure 1. In our current implementation, we set the threshold as 100 MB, approximately the data of one day.

6. EVALUATION

Using the prototype described in Section 5, we next report a two-part evaluation of energy accounting policies. First, we evaluate how well our Shapley value-based energy accounting approximates the Shapley value and outperforms existing accounting policies in three aspects: (*i*) the accuracy of $E(\mathbb{S})$ estimation; (*ii*) the capability to identify "top energy consumer"; and (*iii*) the application in energy management. Second, we evaluate energy accounting results from existing policies and those from Shapley value-based energy accounting and demonstrate how different they can be.

6.1 Experimental Setup

In our experiment, we employ four benchmarks: (*i*) *Download*: Network intensive process that downloads a large file using HTTP protocol via WiFi. (*ii*) *Web*: Android built-in web browser application to visit web pages as recorded in a URL list via WiFi. Each

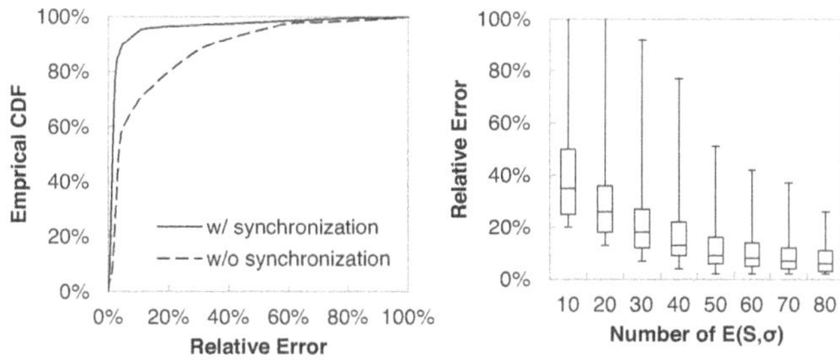

Figure 6: Error in obtaining $E(\mathbb{S},\sigma)$: Over 90% of energy measurement by the battery interface are with error less than 5% and synchronization does improve accuracy (left); estimation has a median error of 10% using one third of total $E(\mathbb{S},\sigma)$ (right).

webpage is loaded and shown for thirty seconds before next one is loaded. *(iii) Video*: Video player based on ffmpeg. *(iv) Game*: Quake 3, an open source 3D video game, played with the included demo scripts.

Out of the four benchmarks, Video, Web and Game cannot run at the same time because they must be executed in the foreground to present content on the screen. Therefore, we further define three scenarios that represent three typical use cases with multiple applications concurrently running:

- Scenario 1: Web + Download + Android.
- Scenario 2: Video + Download + Android.
- Scenario 3: Game + Download + Android.

We leverage the LiveLab mobile usage traces [29] to complement the above benchmarks. The LiveLab usage traces record daily mobile app and web usage for 34 iPhone 3GS users from six to twelve months and are available from [6]. The URL list used in Web includes top twenty most visited websites from the LiveLab traces. For each website, we randomly selected ten pages from the database for the URL list.

6.2 Shapley Value-based Energy Accounting

As described in Section 3, the Shapley value should be the ground truth for energy accounting in theory. In practice, however, it is infeasible for one to obtain the "true" Shapley value. Therefore, we choose to use three following *indirect* ways to evaluate how our Shapley value-based energy accounting approximates the Shapley value and outperforms other accounting policies. First, we evaluate how accurate the $E(\mathbb{S})$ can be estimated by our implementation. Second, we evaluate how much better our implementation, compared to existing policies, can identify the "top energy consumer" or the app that contributes most to the total system energy consumption. Third, we evaluate how much better our implementation can help energy management in enhancing utility value compared to existing policies.

6.2.1 *Accuracy of $E(\mathbb{S})$ estimation*

We first evaluate the accuracy of energy measurement by the prototype by comparing the measurement results against readings by a high-end oscilloscope. As shown in Figure 6 (left), over 90% of measurement are with error less than 5%. This is significantly better than the accuracy achieved using existing battery interface as reported in [8]. Figure 6 (left) also illustrates the importance of synchronization. As shown in the figure, 90% of measurement are with error less than 30% without synchronization.

We then evaluate the accuracy of energy estimation from partial data. The prototype support 12 states in total, i.e., four states for

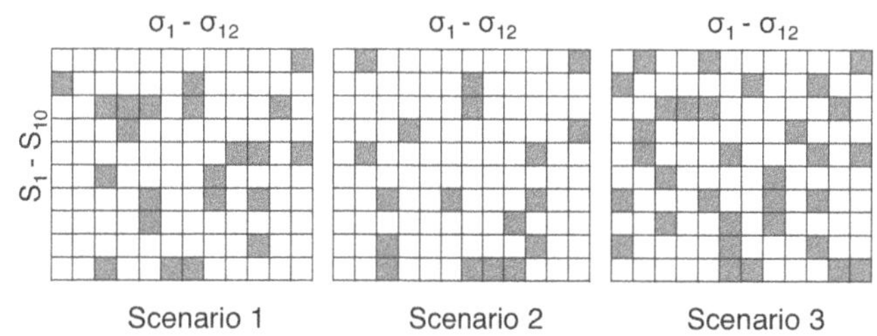

Figure 7: Footprint of all the missing $E(\mathbb{S},\sigma)$ (grey cells) and obtained $E(\mathbb{S},\sigma)$ from measurement (white cells) in all three scenarios.

CPU and three states for WiFi. There are 10 application combinations for each of the three scenarios included in our experiment. Therefore, thee are 120 $E(\mathbb{S},\sigma)$ for each scenarios. In our experiment, we run each scenarios for a sufficient long period and finally obtain 97, 102, and 86 $E(\mathbb{S},\sigma)$, respectively. The footprint of the missing $E(\mathbb{S},\sigma)$ and obtained $E(\mathbb{S},\sigma)$ from measurement are illustrated in Figure 7. Each of the 10 by 12 matrix represents a scenario where each row represents each application combination $\mathbb{S}$ and each column represents each states σ. A grey cell means the corresponding $E(\mathbb{S},\sigma)$ is missing while a white cell means the corresponding $E(\mathbb{S},\sigma)$ is obtained from measurement. We treat these obtained $E(\mathbb{S},\sigma)$ (white cells) as ground truth and randomly choose part of these $E(\mathbb{S},\sigma)$ to estimate the remaining part. Figure 6 (right) shows the results. As shown in the figure, our estimation algorithms can achieve a median error of 10% only using one third, or 40 out of 120, of the total number of $E(\mathbb{S},\sigma)$.

6.2.2 *Identify Top Energy Consumer*

We next evaluate how well energy accounting policies can identify the mobile application that contributes most to the system energy consumption in a day of use, or *top energy consumer*. In particular, we compare our implementation of Shapley value-based energy accounting against Policy V, the most widely used policy by many systems including Android. Our methodology is to replay real-world mobile application usage traces on our prototype with reduced fidelity.

We use the LiveLab mobile usage traces for replay. Because the LiveLab traces are collected from iPhone and have up to hundreds of iOS foreground applications, all without user input, we have to reduce them in the following ways in order to replay them on our Android prototype. First, we reduce the foreground applications to only five software principals: Web, Video, Game, Mail, and Music. We categorize all the apps from the LiveLab traces into one of these five software principals. For example, we treat all game apps as Game; all email and instant messenger apps as Mail; and all web browsing and social networking apps as Web. We ignore applications that do not belong to any of the five types, such as Map, Alarm and Calculator. To replay Web, Video, and Game, we invoke the Web, Video, and Game Android benchmarks described in Section 6.1, respectively. We invoke the Android native email client to send a precomposed email and receive in order to replay Mail and invoke ffmpeg to play an MP3 file to replay Music. Second, we use the Download benchmark described in Section 6.1 to mimic background services in Android such as data sync of social networking apps. In our experiment, we make Download start every fifteen minutes and run for one minute. These reductions lead to replay traces with only six software principals, i.e., Web, Video, Game, Mail, Music and Download.

We also make the following changes to our prototype described in Section 5 for replay. First, we change the power supply from the

Table 4: Top energy consumers identified by Shapley value-based accounting (*Shapley*) and Policy V when they disagree for 19 out of the 50 days of LiveLab data tested

#	User	Shapley	Policy V	#	User	Shapley	Policy V
1	A	Game	Download	11	B	Video	Mail
2	A	Game	Download	12	B	Music	Download
3	A	Game	Download	13	C	Web	Download
4	A	Game	Download	14	C	Web	Download
5	A	Game	Mail	15	C	Music	Download
6	A	Game	Mail	16	C	Music	Mail
7	A	Game	Mail	17	D	Game	Mail
8	B	Game	Download	18	D	Music	Download
9	B	Game	Download	19	E	Mail	Web
10	B	Video	Download				

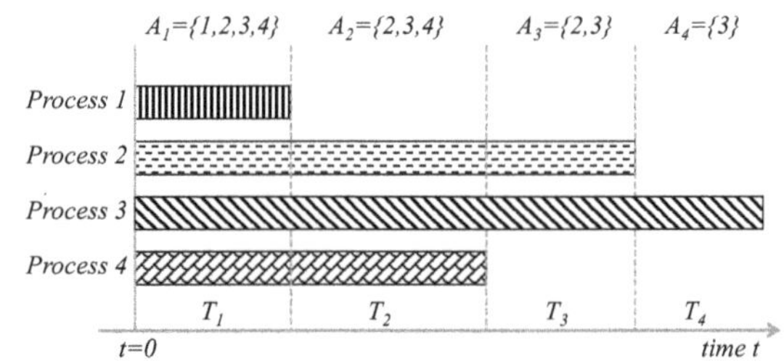

Figure 8: Illustration of four processes and their executions under budget-based energy management (BEM).

external battery pack to a USB cable connected to a PC to support sufficient long time for our experiment. As a result, the enhanced battery interface measures the voltage (around 5V) and the current in the USB cable and calculates the power consumption. Second, we deploy an Android ADB based testing framework in the PC to automatically launch and terminate applications in the PandaBaord through the USB cable. By feeding the usage trace to the testing framework, we are able to replay the reduced LiveLab usage traces on our prototype.

We randomly select five out of the 34 users in the LiveLab trace database and label them as User A to User E. We then randomly choose ten days of usage traces for each user to produce 50 days of usage traces. We evaluate the energy accounting policies by how well they identify the top energy consumer for each of the 50 days of usage when the traces are replaced in the prototype as described above. Out of the 50 days, Policy V and Shapley value-based energy accounting disagree on the top energy consumer for 19 days as summarized by Table 4.

We then replay the traces of the 19 days two more times but in each time we exclude the top energy consumer reported by Policy V and Shapley value-based accounting, respectively. We find that, for all 19 cases, the energy consumption excluding top energy consumers identified by Shapley value-based energy accounting is lower than its Policy V counterpart. This finding indicates Shapley value-based energy accounting identifies an application that contributes more energy than that identified by Policy V does. As shown in Table 4, many disagreements are due to Policy V underestimating the energy contribution of GPU, e.g., in the case of a heavy mobile gamer like User A. We also observe that Policy V tends to overestimate network related applications such as Download and Mail. The reason is that the network interface wakeup and timeout to enter the sleep state consumes a significant amount of energy; when the network interface is already active, the additional energy consumed by the a short period of data traffic is relatively small. Policy V, however, only estimates energy consumption base on the amount of data traffic, which easily leads to false accounting results. This also confirms the observations by [22].

6.2.3 Application in Energy Management

Energy accounting is the foundation to OS-based energy management that seeks to control the energy use by processes and schedule their execution to maximize aggregate system utility under energy constraints. Various energy accounting policies have been tried [12, 32, 14, 28, 25, 15]. We now evaluate energy accounting policies in the context of energy management, in particular, the popular budget-driven energy management (BEM) [32, 25, 15]. We show that existing accounting policies achieve 5% to 25% less utility compared to our Shapley value-based energy accounting.

In BEM, each process receives an independent energy budget and disburses it according to the energy accounting policy. The use of per-process budget not only enables a single energy source to be shared by applications in a fair and simple fashion, but also offers composability among processes. For instance, in a smartphone, an energy budget can be reserved for phone calls to guarantee certain talk time. Each process is assigned a utility function $U_i(t_i)$, which measures the utility of process i receiving run time t_i. $U_i(t_i)$ is assumed to be monotonically increasing and concave [7]. The goal of BEM is to allocate per-process budgets $B_1,\dots,B_n$ among n processes, in order to maximize aggregate utility $\sum_{i=1}^{n} U_i(t_i)$ under total energy available. We next present the problem formulation.

Process Run Time: We consider n independent processes, denoted by $\mathbb{N} = \{1,2,\dots,n\}$. Under BEM, each process is scheduled to run until its energy budget reaches zero. To determine process run time, we suppose that processes deplete their energy budgets in the following order: $\pi(1),\pi(2),\dots,\pi(n)$, where $\pi(k)$ be the kth process that runs out of energy budget (If multiple processes reach zero budget simultaneously, then their ordering can be arbitrary). Then, the execution of all n processes can be divided into n epochs, $T_1,T_2,\dots,T_n$, where each epoch T_k represents the time interval between successive energy depletion of processes $\pi(k-1)$ and $\pi(k)$. It is easy to verify that the sequence of active processes $\mathbb{A}_k = \{\pi(k),\pi(k+1),\dots,\pi(n)\}$ within each epoch T_k form a contraction with $\mathbb{A}_{k+1} \subseteq \mathbb{A}_k$ for $k = 1,\dots,n$.

Figure. 8 illustrates our model for $n = 4$ processes. Given process $\pi(1) = \{1\}$ is the first to run out of budget, epoch T_1 consists of 4 active processes $\mathbb{A}_1 = \{1,2,3,4\}$, while epoch T_2 consists of 3 active processes $\mathbb{A}_2 = \{2,3,4\}$. Similarly, $\pi(2) = \{4\}$ and $\pi(3) = \{2\}$ means that epoch T_3 contains 2 active processes $\mathbb{A}_3 = \{2,3\}$ and epoch T_4 contains a single process $\mathbb{A}_4 = \{3\}$. Using these notations, we can describe process execution under BEM by n distinct epochs. The total run time received by process i is given by $t_i = \sum_{k=1}^{\pi^{-1}(i)} T_k$ where process i depletes its budget at the end of $\pi^{-1}(i)$-th epoch, and the summation is over all epochs where i is active. We refer to t_i as the run time assigned to process i.

Energy Constraints: BEM relies on energy accounting to split total energy consumption among individual processes. Let $\phi_i(E(\mathbb{S}))$ denote the energy consumption attributed to process i according to the energy accounting policy during a scheduling unit in which $\mathbb{S}$ are scheduled to run and $i \in \mathbb{S}$. After this scheduling period, $\phi_i(E(\mathbb{S}))$ will be deducted from process i's energy budget B_i. When a process runs out of budget, it will not be scheduled any more. Using our notations above, total energy attributed to each process i is the sum of individual energy bill $\phi_i(E(\mathbb{A}_k))$ over all epochs $k = 1,\dots,\pi^{-1}(i)$ where process i is active. It implies that

$$\sum_{k=1}^{\pi^{-1}(i)} \phi_i(E(\mathbb{A}_k)) \cdot T_k = B_i. \tag{7}$$

Further, the total system energy consumption must be bounded by the battery capacity, C, i.e., $\sum_{i=1}^{n} B_i \le C$.

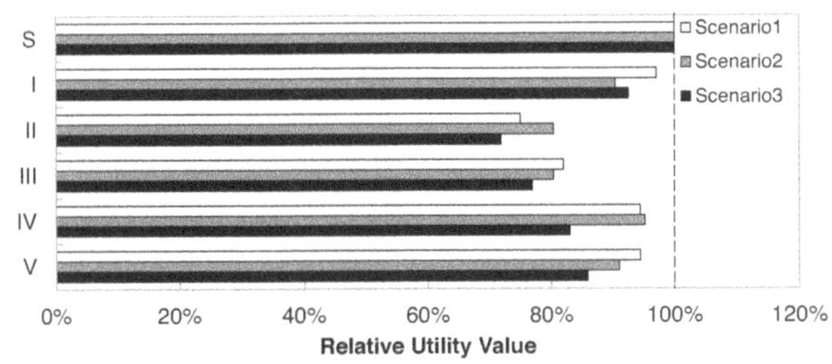

Figure 9: Optimal utility values achieved by BEM with various energy accounting policies. All numbers are normalized by that achieved by Shapley value-based accounting (S).

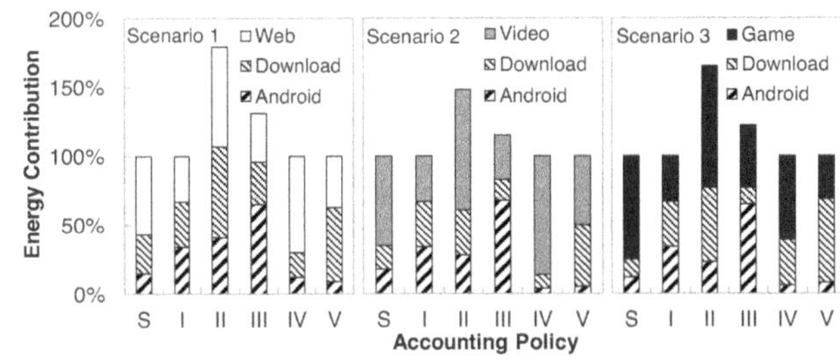

Figure 10: Energy accounting results for Shapley value-based accounting (S) and Policy I-V. The energy consumption (Y axis) is normalized by the total system energy consumption.

Utility Optimization: Each process is assigned a utility function $U_i(t_i)$, which measures the utility of process i receiving run time t_i. We make the common assumption that $U_i(t_i)$ is assumed to be monotonically increasing and concave [7].

The goal of BEM is to allocate per-process budgets $B_1, \ldots, B_n$ among n processes, in order to maximize aggregate utility $\sum_{i=1}^{n} U_i(t_i)$ under energy capacity C. More precisely, we formulate it as the following utility optimization:

Problem BEM :

$$\text{maximize} \quad \sum_{i=1}^{n} U_i(t_i) \tag{8}$$

$$\text{subject to} \quad t_i = \sum_{k=1}^{\pi^{-1}(i)} T_k, \ \forall i, \tag{9}$$

$$\sum_{k=1}^{\pi^{-1}(i)} \phi_i(E(\mathbb{A}_k)) \cdot T_k = B_i \ \forall i \tag{10}$$

$$\sum_{i=1}^{n} B_i \leq C \tag{11}$$

$$\text{variables} \quad \pi, B_i, T_k. \tag{12}$$

Notice that the optimization is a joint maximization over per-process budgets B_i, epoch length T_k, and process ordering π, which are not independent. It is easy to see that Problem BEM is non-convex due to arbitrary process ordering π.

We implement BEM with various energy accounting policies on top of Android's own kernel scheduler. Our implementations uses *application* instead of process as the schedule entity for the same reason described in Section 5.1 To solve the BEM optimization problem, we uses the GNU Scientific Library to implement the standard Newton Method [7]. The BEM optimization is triggered when a new application is launched or every 100 seconds, depending on which comes first. The BEM optimization can take as long as several milliseconds in our experiment, which is comparable to the length of process scheduling period itself.

Our results show that Shapley value-based energy accounting is superior compared to other accounting policies, achieving the highest optimal utility value in BEM. In our experiment, we combine BEM with energy accounting based on each of Policy I to V and Shapley value-based accounting, as shown in Figure 9. To guarantee fairness, we set the utility function as the total execution time of the two applications in three scenarios using the proportional fairness utility function, the weights for the foreground application and background application is 80% and 20%, respectively. Figure 9 shows the corresponding optimal utility values of the optimization for the six combinations. Among all the combinations, Shapley value-based energy accounting (S) has the highest utility value and we make it as the baseline to normalize the utility values of other combinations. As shown in the figure, all other energy accounting policies achieve 5% to 25% less utility value than Shapley value-based energy accounting. In particular, Policy II and Policy III have the least utility values because they violate Axiom of Efficiency. This is because, when Efficiency does not hold, the energy budget of an application can either be depleted earlier than expected or be left unfinished in the end. In both cases, the total energy will not be used efficiently, eventually leading to reduced utility value.

Moreover, we observe that Policy V, the most sophisticated policy used in recent work, is no better than much simpler Policy I and Policy IV in energy management. This suggests that existing budget-based energy management solutions may be unnecessarily complicated. This result is unsurprising because Policy I, IV, and V are all applying a linear function to divide the total energy consumption to multiple components, each component for an application. The only difference is the coefficients in the linear function. By solving the BEM optimization, one can always find the optimal budget for the linear function as long as the Efficiency property holds. In Chapter 3 of [9], a formal proof of this property is provided.

6.3 Evaluating Existing Policies

The previous evaluation experiments demonstrate our implementation performs well as an approximation of the Shapley value. We next evaluate the five types of energy accounting policies described in Section 2.2 by comparing their results against those from our approximation of the Shapley value. The implementations of Policy I to IV are straightforward. We implement Policy V using the system energy model from the open source project PowerTutor [2], which is very similar to Android's own. We update the coefficients of the model following the procedures described in [33] based on offline power benchmarking and linear regression using the benchmark data. The accuracy of the updated model is higher than 90% for one reading per second.

Figure 10 presents the accounting results for the three scenarios. The Y axis is normalized by the total system energy consumption. If a policy meets the Axiom of Efficiency, the stacked energy contribution should be exactly 100%.

All the five types of energy accounting policies can deviate from our approximation of the Shapley value significantly. Policy II and Policy III obviously violate the Axiom of Efficiency, corroborating our analysis summarized in Table 2. Policy IV is inaccurate because it only considers the usage of CPU. Therefore, Policy IV tends to overestimate for applications that require high CPU activities such as Video in Scenario 2. Policy V is inaccurate because its energy model does not account the usage of GPU. This is obvious in Scenario 3 where Game extensively uses GPU and Policy V significantly underestimate its energy use. As a result, Policy V overestimates the energy contribution of Download by four times.

7. OTHER RELATED WORK

In Section 2.2, we already discussed representative work in energy accounting and evaluated their policies throughout the paper. We next discuss related work in the applications of energy accounting, i.e., energy management and software evaluation, where Shapley value-based energy accounting can be readily applied. Due to the space limit, we mainly discuss related work in mobile systems.

Energy Management: ECOSystem [32] presents "currentcy", an abstraction of energy and incorporates it into energy management. Energy consumption by each hardware component is modeled as charge in "currentcy" that attributed to each running process. This is exactly the BEM approach as described in 6.2.3. Like ECOSystem, Cinder [25] also utilize BEM, but advances ECOSystem by providing more sophisticated mechanisms for processes to delegate. Both energy management solutions employ a version of Policy V that uses a software-based energy model. Therefore, their performance is limited by the drawbacks of Policy V as discussed in Section 3.3 and experimentally demonstrated in Section 6.3.

Evaluating Software for Energy Efficiency: Energy accounting is also popularly used for evaluating software. Existing work often employs various forms of Policy V for this purpose. Pathak et al [23] developed a framework based on their FSM model [22]. Such framework logs the traces of system calls by each application and performs an offline analysis that assigns energy contribution to each application based on the FSM model and the system call traces. To solve the same problem, Carat [21] resorts to crowdsouring. Carat samples the battery level of an iPhone periodically and what applications are actively running in each sample period. After collecting sufficient data from many users, Carat can identify energy-hungry applications. There is also work that addresses energy issues of smartphones without direct information of energy consumption. For example, eDoctor [16] is able to identify abnormal battery drain issues on smartphones by capturing the execution-phase time-varying behavior of each application.

8. CONCLUDING REMARKS

In this paper we answer an important and long-standing question about energy accounting with theory, practical approximation, and experimental evaluation: how to evaluate an energy accounting policy? Our answer is: the Shapley value should serve as the ground truth for energy accounting. We analytically show how existing energy accounting policies violate the four self-evident axioms that define the Shapley value. More importantly, we also show that an approximation of the Shapley value can be practically realized with *in situ* high-rate energy measurement. Using a mobile system development board, we realize this approximation, called Shapley value-based energy accounting, and show existing energy accounting policies deviate significantly from it. Our results are fundamental to evaluating energy accounting policies that have been widely used in software evaluation and energy management.

Shaley value-based accounting vs. Policy V

It is important to reflect on why our Shapley valued-based energy accounting actually works better than other energy accounting policies. While the limitations of Policies I to IV are obvious, Policy V warrants more discussion. Policy V takes a *spatial* view of energy consumption. That is, it views energy consumption as resulting from a collection of energy-consuming hardware resources. Therefore, it reduces energy accounting to (*i*) resource usage accounting that relates resource usage to software principals and (*ii*) energy modeling that relates energy consumption to resource usage. To improve the accuracy of this approach, one has to improve resource usage accounting, especially the "spatial" resolution of resource usage accounting. While the usage of many hardware resources can be easily attributed to software principals in modern computers, e.g., CPU, memory and network interface, that of many others cannot. This is particularly true for the system-on-chips used in mobile systems that often integrate a large number of specialized hardware modules not visible to the OS. To account the usage of these modules requires per-module hardware support like that exploited by iCount [10]. That is, hardware modification to improve the "spatial" resolution of resource usage accounting is likely to be distributed, making it costly. More importantly, without better resource usage accounting, one cannot improve Policy V with more energy measurement data.

In contrast, Shapley value-based energy accounting takes a *temporal* view of energy consumption. That is, it views energy consumption as resulting from a collection of time intervals, or games. It reduces energy accounting to (*i*) measuring the system energy consumption and (*ii*) knowing which software principals are active in each time interval. The challenge to this approach, as highlighted at the beginning of Section 4, lies in that one has to obtain the energy consumption of time intervals in which all possible coalitions of software principals under question are active. That is, we need $E(\mathbb{S})\ \forall\ \mathbb{S} \subseteq \mathbb{N}$. Shapley value-based energy accounting addresses this by *in situ* energy measurement of very short time intervals and by using heuristics to estimate the energy consumption ($E(\mathbb{S})$) for unobserved coalitions ($\mathbb{S}$). To improve it, one needs (*i*) more accurate, higher rate energy measurement and (*ii*) more measurements so that more coalitions ($\mathbb{S}$) are observed. In contrast to how Policy V has to be improved, the required hardware modification is localized, i.e., only the battery interface, and more measurements will help. Therefore, we believe our Shapley value-based energy accounting not only is better than versions of Policy V in use today but also has a brighter prospect in practice moving forward.

Shortcomings aside, Policy V does have practical values, especially in evaluating and optimizing software for energy efficiency. It can be very good at identifying top energy consumers or energy-draining misbehaviors that consume energy via the hardware resources accounted by the policy, e.g., CPU, memory and data traffic. Because it relates system energy consumption to resource usage, it can offer insight into how software is draining energy and provide guideline for software optimization. In contrast, Shapley value-based energy accounting does not provide such insight at all.

Potential improvements

Again, the key to Shapley value-based energy accounting is to obtain $E(\mathbb{S})\ \forall\ \mathbb{S} \subseteq \mathbb{N}$. While we provide a suite of techniques to acquire and estimate $E(\mathbb{S})$ in Section 4, our solutions can be further improved in three important ways.

Using better resource usage accounting: Policy V can be improved with better resource usage accounting as discussed above. Improved resource usage accounting can equally improve Shapley value-based energy accounting: instead of using Shapley value-based energy accounting for the whole system energy consumption, one can now use it only for the portion of system energy consumption that cannot be attributed to accounted resource usage.

Using the crowd: In Section 4, we presented a few heuristics to obtain $E(\mathbb{S})$ for $\mathbb{S} \subseteq \mathbb{N}$ that are not observed in the system under question. As a model of smartphone is usually used by hundreds of thousands of users, the users of the same model can help each other by contributing their own observations of $E(\mathbb{S})$. Each observation includes the energy consumption, unique identities of the running software principals ($\mathbb{S}$), device model, hardware state (σ). The observations made by one device can be compacted and uploaded to a central server occasionally, e.g., when connected via WiFi and wall-powered. Similarly, a device can look up the same server for observations for the same model that are unavailable locally.

Our work can also be extended to further attribute the energy use by the OS to processes. Our current implementation treats the OS as a separate principal and allocates its own share of energy use. The OS, however, can perform a service on behalf of a process, e.g., sending a packet out through TCP/IP. Therefore, it is reasonable to attribute the energy use by such services to the process being served. Our implementation can be easily modified for this purpose because a modern OS like Linux keeps track of the processes that it is serving. Our implementation will be able to calculate the energy use by the OS when serving a process; the only modification is to attribute this energy use to the process, instead of the OS itself.

Acknowledgements

This work was supported in part by NSF Grants CNS #1065506 and CNS #1218041. The authors thank the anonymous reviewers, especially the paper shepherd, for their useful feedbacks that help improve the final version of the paper. .

9. REFERENCES

[1] `http://source.android.com/`.

[2] `http://powertutor.org/`.

[3] `http://www.dianxinos.com/`.

[4] `http://pandaboard.org/content/pandaboard-es`.

[5] `http://www.maximintegrated.com/en/products/power/DS2756EVKIT.html`.

[6] `http://livelab.recg.rice.edu/`.

[7] S. Boyd and L. Vandenberghe. *Convex Optimization*. Cambridge University Press, 2004.

[8] M. Dong and L. Zhong. Self-constructive high-rate system energy modeling for battery-powered mobile systems. In *Proc. ACM MobiSys*, 2011.

[9] Mian Dong. *Energy accounting and optimization for mobile systems*. PhD thesis, Rice University, 2013.

[10] P. Dutta, M. Feldmeier, J. Paradiso, and D. Culler. Energy metering for free: Augmenting switching regulators for real-time monitoring. In *Proc. IEEE. IPSN*, 2008.

[11] J. Feigenbaum, C. H. Papadimitriou, and S. Shenker. Sharing the cost of multicast transmissions. *Journal of Computer and System Sciences*, 63(1), 2001.

[12] J. Flinn and M. Satyanarayanan. PowerScope: A tool for profiling the energy usage of mobile applications. In *Proc. IEEE WMCSA*, 1999.

[13] R. Fonseca, P. Dutta, P. Levis, and I. Stoica. Quanto: Tracking energy in networked embedded systems. In *Proc. USENIX OSDI*, 2008.

[14] A. Kansal, F. Zhao, J. Liu, N. Kothari, and A.A. Bhattacharya. Virtual machine power metering and provisioning. In *Proc. ACM Symp. Cloud Computing*, 2010.

[15] H. Lim, A. Kansal, and J. Liu. Power budgeting for virtualized data centers. In *2011 USENIX Annual Technical Conf.*, 2011.

[16] X. Ma, P. Huang, X. Jin, P. Wang, S. Park, D. Shen, Y. Zhou, L. K. Saul, and G. M. Voelker. eDoctor: Automatically diagnosing abnormal battery drain issues on smartphones. In *Proc. USENIX NSDI*, 2013.

[17] J.C. McCullough, Y. Agarwal, J. Chandrashekar, S. Kuppuswamy, A.C. Snoeren, and R.K. Gupta. Evaluating the effectiveness of model-based power characterization. In *USENIX Annual Technical Conf.*, 2011.

[18] V. Misra, S. Ioannidis, A. Chaintreau, and L. Massoulié. Incentivizing peer-assisted services: a fluid Shapley value approach. In *ACM SIGMETRICS Performance Evaluation Review*, 2010.

[19] R. Mittal, A. Kansal, and R. Chandra. Empowering developers to estimate app energy consumption. In *Proc. ACM MobiCom*, 2012.

[20] R. Muralidhar, H. Seshadri, K. Paul, and S. Karumuri. Linux-based ultra mobile PCs. In *Proc. Linux Symposium*, 2007.

[21] A. J. Oliner, A. P. Iyer, I. Stoica, E. Lagerspetz, and S. Tarkoma. Carat: Collaborative energy diagnosis for mobile devices. In *Proc. ACM SenSys*, 2013.

[22] A. Pathak, Y. C. Hu, M. Zhang, P. Bahl, and Y. M. Wang. Fine-grained power modeling for smartphones using system call tracing. In *Proc. ACM EuroSys*, 2011.

[23] A. Pathak, Y.C. Hu, and M. Zhang. Where is the energy spent inside my app?: fine grained energy accounting on smartphones with Eprof. In *Proc. ACM EuroSys*, 2012.

[24] A. Pena-Perez, E. Bonizzoni, and F. Maloberti. A 84dB SNDR 100kHz bandwidth low-power single op-amp third-order $\Delta\Sigma$ modulator consuming 140μW. In *Proc. IEEE ISSCC*, 2011.

[25] A. Roy, S.M. Rumble, R. Stutsman, P. Levis, D. Mazieres, and N. Zeldovich. Energy management in mobile devices with the Cinder operating system. In *Proc. ACM EuroSys*, 2011.

[26] S. Ryffel. LEA^{2}P: the linux energy attribution and accounting platform. Master's thesis, Swiss Federal Institute of Technology (ETH), Zurich, Switzerland, 2009.

[27] Lloyd Shapley. A value for n-person games. In H.W. Kuhn and A.W. Tucker, editors, *Contributions to the Theory of Games, volume II*, pages 307–317. Princeton University Press, 1953.

[28] K. Shen, A. Shriraman, S. Dwarkadas, X. Zhang, and Z. Chen. Power containers: An OS facility for fine-grained power and energy management on multicore servers. In *Proc. ACM ASPLOS*, 2013.

[29] C. Shepard, A. Rahmati, C. Tossell, L. Zhong, and P. Kortum. Livelab: measuring wireless networks and smartphone users in the field. *ACM SIGMETRICS Performance Evaluation Review*, 38(3), 2010.

[30] S.J. Willson. A Value for Partially Defined Cooperative Games. *International Journal on Game Theory*, 21:371–384, 1993.

[31] C. Yoon, D. Kim, W. Jung, C. Kang, and H. Cha. AppScope: Application energy metering framework for android smartphone using kernel activity monitoring. In *USENIX Annual Technical Conf.*, 2012.

[32] H. Zeng, C.S. Ellis, A.R. Lebeck, and A. Vahdat. ECOSystem: Managing energy as a first class operating system resource. In *Proc. ACM ASPLOS*, 2002.

[33] L. Zhang, B. Tiwana, Z. Qian, Z. Wang, R.P. Dick, Z.M. Mao, and L. Yang. Accurate online power estimation and automatic battery behavior based power model generation for smartphones. In *Proc. IEEE/ACM/IFIP CODES+ISSS*, 2010.

[34] L. Zhong and N.K. Jha. Graphical user interface energy characterization for handheld computers. In *Proc. ACM CASES*, 2003.

BYOzzzz: Focusing on the Unsolved Challenges of Mobility, an Industry Perspective

Kit Colbert
VMware, Inc.
Palo Alto, CA, USA

ABSTRACT

The next frontier of mobility – from behavioral analysis for the app ecosystem to geolocation on steroids – presents challenges as tough as the opportunities are expansive. What is the TCP/IP of the Internet of Things era? And who will build it? Hyper-aware smartphones that know you're in the snack aisle are great for retailers, but who's addressing the security implications? The industry is charting its strategic course, but there is an exciting opportunity for researchers and academia to provide the coordinates towards the solutions to mobility's hardest problems.

In this keynote, Kit Colbert, Chief Technology Officer for End-User Computing at VMware, will discuss the unsolved challenges in mobility, and the possibilities that will be unlocked when the industry and academia partner on finding the answers.

Author Keywords

Mobility; applications; software; smartphones; security

ACM Classification Keywords

Software – General

BIO

Kit Colbert, the CTO of End-User Computing at VMware, is driving technical strategy and advanced development of innovative solutions for VMware's desktop, social, and mobility products. A 10-year veteran at VMware, Kit previously held roles as the Chief Architect and Principal Engineer for Horizon Workspace and as the lead Management Architect for the vCenter Operations Suite. At the start of his career, he was the technical lead behind the creation, development, and delivery of the vMotion and Storage vMotion features in vSphere.

Kit holds a ScB in Computer Science from Brown University and is a recognized thought-leader on End-User Computing and Cloud Management trends. He speaks regularly at industry conferences, on the main stage at VMworld, and is the desktop and mobility voice for the VMware Office of the CTO blog.

MobiCom'14, September 7-11, 2014, Maui, Hawaii, USA.
ACM 978-1-4503-2783-1/14/09.
http://dx.doi.org/10.1145/2639108.2639418

Robust Network Compressive Sensing

Yi-Chao Chen, Lili Qiu, Yin Zhang
The University of Texas at Austin
{yichao,lili,yzhang}@cs.utexas.edu

Guangtao Xue, Zhenxian Hu
Shanghai Jiao Tong University
{gt_xue,huzhenxian}@sjtu.edu.cn

ABSTRACT

Networks are constantly generating an enormous amount of rich diverse information. Such information creates exciting opportunities for network analytics. However, a major challenge to enable effective network analytics is the presence of *missing data*, *measurement errors*, and *anomalies*. Despite significant work in network analytics, fundamental issues remain: (i) the existing works do not explicitly account for anomalies or measurement noise, and incur serious performance degradation under significant noise or anomalies, and (ii) they assume network matrices have low-rank structure, which may not hold in reality.

To address these issues, in this paper we develop *LENS decomposition*, a novel technique to accurately decompose a network matrix into a low-rank matrix, a sparse anomaly matrix, an error matrix, and a small noise matrix. LENS has the following nice properties: (i) it is general: it can effectively support matrices with or without anomalies, and having low-rank or not, (ii) its parameters are self tuned so that it can adapt to different types of data, (iii) it is accurate by incorporating domain knowledge, such as temporal locality, spatial locality, and initial estimate (*e.g.*, obtained from models), (iv) it is versatile and can support many applications including missing value interpolation, prediction, and anomaly detection. We apply LENS to a wide range of network matrices from 3G, WiFi, mesh, sensor networks, and the Internet. Our results show that LENS significantly out-performs state-of-the-art compressive sensing schemes.

Categories and Subject Descriptors

C.2.3 [**Computer-Communication Networks**]: Network Operations – Network monitoring

General Terms

Algorithms, Measurement, Performance

Keywords

Compressive Sensing; Traffic Matrix; Anomaly Detection

MobiCom'14, September 7-11, 2014, Maui, Hawaii, USA.

http://dx.doi.org/10.1145/2639108.2639129.

1. INTRODUCTION

Motivation: Wireless networks are constantly generating an enormous amount of rich and diverse information. Such information creates exciting opportunities for network analytics. Network analytics can provide deep insights into the complex interactions among network entities, and has a wide range of applications in wireless networks across all protocol layers. Example applications include spectrum sensing, channel estimation, channel feedback compression, multi-access channel design, data aggregation, network coding, wireless video coding, anomaly detection, and localization.

Challenges: A major challenge to enable effective network analytics is the presence of *missing data*, *measurement errors*, and *anomalies*. Failures in measurement systems and network losses can lead to missing data. On the other hand, many network tasks require complete data to operate properly. For example, traffic engineering requires knowing the complete traffic matrix between all source and destination pairs in order to properly provision traffic and avoid congestion. Wireless rate adaptation needs SNR information across all OFDM subcarriers in order to compute effective SNR [16]. Channel selection requires knowledge of received signal strength (RSS) information across all channels in order to select the best channel. Moreover, anomalies and erroneous data are common in real-world network data. It is challenging to distinguish genuine network structure and behavior of interest from anomalies and measurement imperfections in a robust and accurate fashion.

There are numerous approaches to interpolate missing data. They all exploit certain structure in the data. Many studies assume that network matrices (*e.g.*, traffic matrices, delay matrices, RSS matrices) exhibit low-rank structure (*i.e.*, the matrix can be well approximated by the product of two factor matrices with few columns). Accurate extraction of such sparse or low-rank structure is crucial for a variety of network analysis tasks. For example, traffic matrix estimation method *tomo-gravity* [47, 48, 49]) achieves high accuracy by exploiting the fact that traffic matrices can be well approximated using the gravity model, which is a rank-1 matrix. The low-rank nature of Internet delay matrix is essential to the effectiveness of network coordinate systems [34, 30]. The presence of sparse or low-rank structure is also a key assumption behind compressive sensing [8, 14, 7, 37, 38, 50]. For example, Zhang *et al.* develop a novel *spatio-temporal compressive sensing* framework that leverages the spatio-temporal characteristics of real-world traffic matrices and their sparse or low-rank structure.

The immense complexity and heterogeneity of these datasets imply that many assumptions and operational conditions required by existing compressive sensing techniques may not hold [50]. In particular, our analysis show that many real network matrices are not low rank. Violation of low rank assumption significantly reduces the effectiveness of existing compressive sensing approaches.

Another key limitation of existing work is that they do not explicitly account for anomalies or measurement noise. Real-world network datasets often contain a plethora of (i) errors (*e.g.*, missing or erroneous measurements), (ii) noise (introduced by either Mother Nature or measurement procedure itself), and (iii) anomalies (caused by network events such as flash crowds, failures, attacks, *etc.*). The performance of existing approaches seriously degrades under significant noise or anomalies. It remains a fundamental challenge to develop new techniques that can accurately distinguish genuine structure and behavior of interest from errors, noise, and anomalies common in real-world network data.

Our approach: In this paper, we first develop ***LENS decomposition***, a novel technique to accurately decompose network data represented in the form of a matrix into a low-rank matrix, a sparse anomaly matrix, an error term, and a small noise matrix. This decomposition naturally reflects the inherent structures of real-world data and is more general than existing compressive sensing techniques by removing the low-rank assumption and explicitly supporting anomalies. We further generalize the problem to incorporate domain knowledge, such as temporal stability, spatial locality, and/or initial estimation (*e.g.*, obtained from a model). We formulate this problem as a convex optimization problem, and develop an Alternating Direction Method (ADM) to efficiently solve it.

Our approach has several nice properties: (i) it supports a wide range of matrices: with or without anomalies, and with or without low-rank structure, (ii) its parameters are either exactly computed or self tuned, (iii) it can incorporate domain knowledge, and (iv) it supports various network applications, such as missing value interpolation, prediction, and anomaly detection.

We evaluate LENS using a wide range of network matrices, including traffic matrices from 3G, WiFi, and the Internet, channel state information (CSI) matrices, RSSI matrices in WiFi and sensor networks, and expected transmission time (ETT) traces from UCSB Meshnet. Our results show that it significantly out-performs state-of-the-art compressive sensing methods including Sparsity Regularized Matrix Factorization (SRMF) under anomalies [50].

2. ANALYSIS OF NETWORK MATRICES

Network	Date	Duration	Resolution	Size
3G traffic	Nov. 2010	1 day	10 min.	472×144
WiFi traffic	Jan. 2013	1 day	10 min.	50×118
Abilene traffic [2]	Apr. 2003	1 week	10 min.	121×1008
GÉANT traffic [42]	Apr. 2005	1 week	15 min.	529×672
1 channel CSI	Feb. 2009	15 min.	1 frame	90×9000
multi. channels CSI	Feb. 2014	15 min.	1 frame	270×5000
Cister RSSI [35]	Nov. 2010	4 hours	1 frame	16×10000
CU RSSI [6]	Aug. 2007	500 frames	1 frame	895×500
UMich RSS [43]	April 2006	30 min.	1 frame	182×3127
UCSB Meshnet [41]	April. 2006	3 days	1 min.	425×1527

Table 1: Datasets under study.

2.1 Datasets

Table 1 lists the network matrices used for our study. We obtained 3G traces from 472 base stations in a downtown area of a major city in China during Oct. 2010. We generate traffic matrices by computing the aggregated traffic every 10 minutes. $M(i,t)$ represents the total traffic volume to and from base station i during time interval t, where t is a 10-minute interval.

We also got WiFi traffic from a large university in China, and generated traffic matrices based on the traffic collected at the 50 most loaded access points (APs) on Jan. 4, 2013. $M(i,t)$ denotes the total traffic to/from AP i during the t-th 10-minute time interval.

In addition to wireless traffic matrices, we also use traffic matrices from Abilene (Internet2) [2] and GÉANT [42], which are standard traffic matrices used in several previous studies (*e.g.*, [22, 24, 46, 50]) and useful for comparison. Abilene traces report total end-to-end traffic between all pairs in a 11-node network every 10 minutes. GÉANT traces report total traffic between all pairs in a 23-node network every 15 minutes.

For diversity, in addition to traffic matrices, we also obtain signal strength and expected transmission time (ETT). We use the following SNR and RSS matrices: (a) our 1 channel CSI traces, (b) our multi-channel CSI traces, (c) Cister RSSI traces, (d) CU RSSI traces, and (e) UMich RSS. We collected (a) by having a moving desktop transmit back-to-back to another desktop and letting the receiving desktop record the SNR across all OFDM subcarriers over 15 minutes using the Intel Wi-Fi Link 5300 (iwl5300) adapter. The modified driver [20] reports the channel matrices for 30 subcarrier groups in a 20MHz channel, which is about one group for every two subcarriers according to the standard [3]. The sender sends 1000-byte frames using MCS 0 at a transmission power of 15 dBm. Since MCS0 has 1 stream and the receiver has 3 antennas, the NIC reports CSI as a 90×1 matrix for each frame. We collect (b) on channels 36, 40, 44, 48, 149, 153, 157, 161, and 165 at 5GHz. The transmitter starts from channel 36, and sends 10 packets before switching to the next channel. The receiver synchronizes with the transmitter and also cycle through the 9 channels, which yields 270×1 matrix for each frame. In addition, we use Cister RSSI traces [35], CU RSSI traces [6], and UMich RSS traces [43], all of which are publicly available at CRAWDAD [12]. $M(f,i)$ in Cister traces denotes RSSI on IEEE 802.15.4 channel f in the i-th frame, $M(l,i)$ in CU traces denotes RSSI of the i-th frame at location l, and $M(s,i)$ in UMich-RSS trace denotes the RSS measurement received by the s-th sensor pair in the i-th packet. We also use ETT traces from UCSB Meshnet [41], which contains the ETT of every links in a 20-node mesh network. We generate the ETT matrix $M(l,t)$, where $M(l,t)$ denotes the ETT of the link l during the t-th 10-second window.

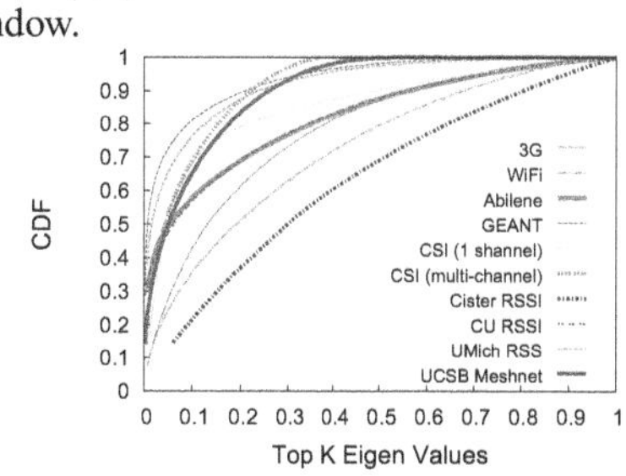

Figure 1: CDF of energy that are contained in the top K singular values of the original matrices.

2.2 Analysis

Rank analysis: For each network matrix, we mean center each row (*i.e.*, subtract from each row its mean value). We then apply singular value decomposition (SVD) to examine if the mean-centered matrix has a good low-rank approximation. The metric we use is the fraction of total variance captured by the top K singular values, *i.e.*, $\left(\sum_{i=1}^{K} s_i^2\right) / \left(\sum_i s_i^2\right)$, where s_i is the i-th largest singular value and $\left(\sum_i s_i^2\right)$ gives the total variance of the mean-centered coordinate matrix. Note that $1 - \left(\sum_{i=1}^{K} s_i^2\right) / \left(\sum_i s_i^2\right)$ is the relative approximation error of the best rank-K approximation with respect to the squared Frobenius norm.

Figure 1 plots the fraction of total variance captured by the top K singular values for different traces. As it shows, from low to high, UCSB Meshnet, GÉANT, multi-channel CSI, UMich RSS, RON, 1-channel CSI, CU RSSI, Abilene, WiFi, 3G, and Cister RSSI matrices take 7.5%, 20.8%, 22.0%, 23.9%, 47.2%, 48.9%,

55.8%, 57.0%, 58.0%, 68.1%, and 81.0% singular values to capture 90% variance, respectively. Therefore, only UCSB Meshnet, GÉANT, multi-channel CSI, and UMich RSS are close to low rank.

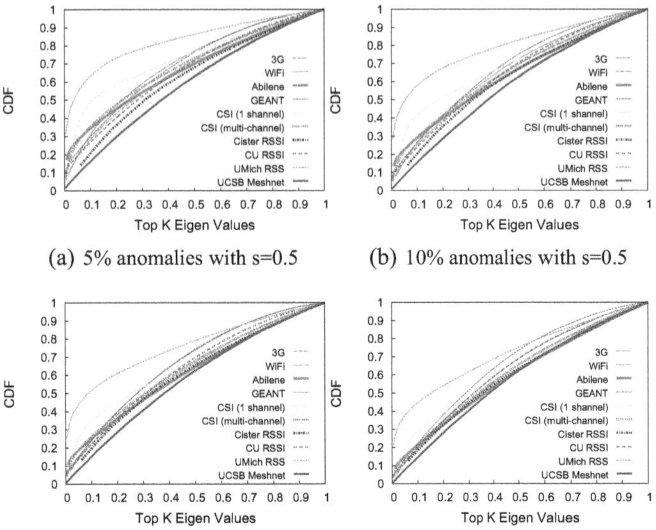

(a) 5% anomalies with s=0.5 (b) 10% anomalies with s=0.5

(c) 5% anomalies with s=1 (d) 10% anomalies with s=1

Figure 2: CDF of energy that are contained in the top K singular values under anomalies in traffic matrices.

Next we inject anomalies to see how it affects the results. We inject anomalies to a portion of the entries in the original matrices. Following the standard anomaly injection method used in existing work [22, 18, 31], we first use exponential weighted moving average (EWMA) to predict the future entries based on their past values (*i.e.*, $y = \alpha x + (1-\alpha)y$, where $\alpha = 0.8$ in our evaluation) and use the maximum difference between the actual and predicted value as the anomaly size to be injected. We vary the fraction of entries to inject anomalies from 5% to 10%, and also scale the anomaly size by s, which is 0.5 or 1. As shown in Figure 2, when we inject more anomalies or larger anomalies, more singular values are required in order to capture the variance of the matrices. This trend is consistent across all traces. For example, as shown in Figure 2(a)-(b), when we inject 5% and 10% anomalies with s=0.5, it takes 60.9% and 67.6% singular values to capture 90% variance in UMich Meshnet, 71.0% and 75.8% in WiFi trace, and 75.7% and 80.0% in 1-channel CSI trace. As shown in Figure 2(c)-(d), when we inject 5% and 10% anomalies with s=1, the corresponding numbers are 72.5% and 76.9% in UMich Meshnet, 72.0% and 78.3% in WiFi trace, and 81.7% and 84.1% in 1-channel CSI trace. The other matrices exhibit the same trend.

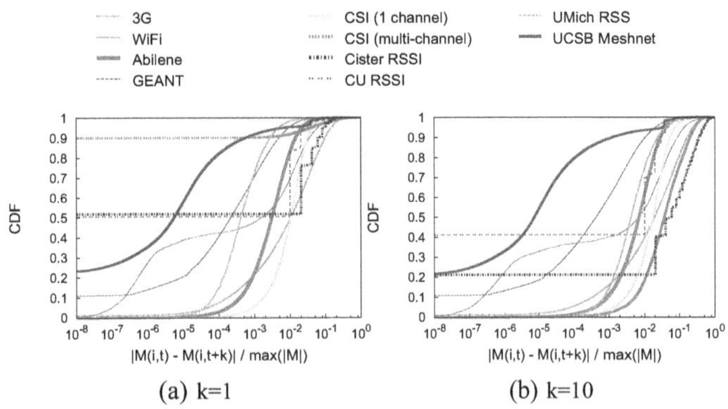

(a) k=1 (b) k=10

Figure 3: CDF of normalized difference between i-th and i+k-th time slot.

Temporal stability: Figure 3 plots the CDF of normalized temporal variation (*i.e.*, $\frac{x(i)-x(i-t)}{max(x(i))}$) across different traces. As it shows, different traces exhibit varying degrees of temporal stability. For example, 3G and Cister RSSI have high variation: the two adjacent entries differ by 6.1%-9.8% in 90% cases, and 10 time-slot apart entries differ by 16.7%-36.2% in 90%. In comparison, UMich Meshnet and GÉANT have low variation, where the adjacent entries differ by 0.3%-0.5% in 90% cases and 10 time-slot apart entries differ by 1.0%-2.4% in 90%. The other traces are in between.

Summary: The major findings from the above analysis include: (i) Not all real network matrices are low rank. (ii) Adding anomalies further increases the rank. (iii) Temporal stability varies substantially across different traces. These findings motivate us to develop a general compressive sensing framework to support diverse matrices that may not be low rank, exhibit different degrees of temporal stability, and may even contain anomalies.

3. LENS DECOMPOSITION

In this section, we first present LENS decomposition framework. Next we develop an alternating direction method for solving the decomposition problem. Then we describe how to set the parameters.

3.1 LENS Decomposition Framework

Overview: There are many factors that contribute to real network matrices, including measurement errors, anomalies and inherent noise. To capture this insight, we decompose the original matrix into a Low-rank component, an Error component, a Noise component, and a Sparse anomaly component (hence the acronym LENS decomposition). This is motivated by the following observations:

- Low-rank component: Network matrices often exhibit significant redundancy. A concrete form of redundancy is that the network matrix of interest can be well approximated by low-rank matrices. For example, TM estimation makes use of the gravity model [47], which is essentially a rank-1 approximation to matrices. [36] uses low-rank matrices for localization.
- Sparse component: Anomalies are common in large network dataset. Anomalies may arise from a number of factors. For example, traffic anomalies may be caused by problems ranging from security threats (*e.g.*, Distributed Denial of Service (DDoS) attacks and network worms) to unusual traffic events (*e.g.*, flash crowds), to vendor implementation bugs, and to network misconfigurations. Such anomalies are typically not known a priori and are sparse [11, 25].
Note that there can be systematic effects that are only sparse after some transformation (*e.g.*, wavelet transform). For example, a major level shift may result in persistent changes in the original data (and is thus not sparse). But after wavelet transform (or simple temporal differencing), it becomes sparse.
- Error and artifacts: The measurement and data collection procedure may also introduce artifacts. For example, a SNMP traffic counter may wrap around, resulting in negative measurements. One can always try his best to apply domain knowledge to filter out obvious errors and artifacts (*e.g.*, missing data or negative traffic measurements). However, in general it is difficult to filter out all such artifacts. The advantage of considering both anomalies and errors jointly is that the parts that cannot be filtered can get absorbed by the sparse components.
- Noise. Noise is universal, making clean mathematical models "approximate" in practice. For example, real-world network

matrices are typically only approximately low-rank as opposed to exactly low-rank.

Therefore a natural approach is to consider the original dataset as a mixture of all these effects. It is useful if one can decompose the original matrix into individual components, each component capturing one major effect.

Basic formulation: The basic LENS decomposition decomposes an original $m \times n$ data matrix D into a low-rank matrix X, a sparse anomaly matrix Y, a noise matrix Z, and an error matrix W. This is achieved by solving the following *convex* optimization problem:

$$\begin{aligned} \text{minimize:} \quad & \alpha\|X\|_* + \beta\|Y\|_1 + \frac{1}{2\sigma}\|Z\|_F^2, \\ \text{subject to:} \quad & X + Y + Z + W = D, \\ & E. * W = W. \end{aligned} \tag{1}$$

where X is a low-rank component, Y is a sparse anomaly component, Z is a dense noise term, and E is a binary error indicator matrix such that $E[i,j] = 1$ if and only if entry $D[i,j]$ is erroneous or missing, and W is an arbitrary error component with $W[i,j] \neq 0$ only when $E[i,j] = 1$ (thus $E. * W = W$, where $.*$ is an element-wise multiplication operator). Since W fully captures the erroneous or missing values, we can set $D[i,j] = 0$ whenever $E[i,j] = 1$ without loss of generality. The constraint enforces D to be the sum of X, Y, and Z when D is neither missing nor has errors (since $E[i,j]. * W[i,j] = 0$ in this case), while imposing no constraint when D is missing or has error (since $E[i,j]. * W[i,j] = W[i,j]$ allows $W[i,j]$ to take an arbitrary value to satisfy $X + Y + Z + W = D$).

The optimization objective has the following three components:

- $\|X\|_*$ is the nuclear norm [38, 37] of matrix X, which penalizes against high rank of X and can be computed as the total sum of X's singular values.
- $\|Y\|_1$ is the ℓ_1-norm of Y, which penalizes against lack of sparsity in Y and can be computed as $\|Y\|_1 = \sum_{i,j} |Y[i,j]|$.
- $\|Z\|_F^2$ is the squared Frobenius norm of matrix Z, which penalizes against large entries in the noise matrix Z and can be computed as $\|Z\|_F^2 = \sum_{i,j} Z[i,j]^2$.

The weights α, β and $\frac{1}{2\sigma}$ balance the conflicting goals to simultaneously minimize $\|X\|_*$, $\|Y\|_1$ and $\|Z\|_F^2$. We describe how to choose these weights in Section 3.3.

Generalized formulation: Below we generalize both the constraints and the optimization objective of the basic formulation in Eq. (1) to accommodate rich requirements in the analysis of real-world network matrices.

First, the matrix of interest may not always be directly observable, but its linear transform can be observed though subject to missing data, measurement errors, and anomalies. For example, end-to-end traffic matrices X are often not directly observed, and what can be observed are link load D. X and D follow $AX = D$, where A is a binary routing matrix: $A(i,j) = 1$ if link i is used to route traffic for the j-th end-to-end flow, and $A(i,j) = 0$ otherwise. We generalize the constraints in Eq. (1) to cope with such measurement requirements:

$$AX + BY + CZ + W = D \tag{2}$$

Here A may capture tomographic constraints that linearly relate direct and indirect measurements (*e.g.*, A is a routing matrix in the traffic matrices). B may represent an over-complete anomaly profile matrix. If we do not know which matrix entries may have anomalies, we can simply set B to the identity matrix I. It is also possible to set $B = A$ if we are interested in capturing anomalies in X. Without prior knowledge, we set C to be the identity matrix.

Prior research on network inference and compressive sensing highlights the importance of incorporating domain knowledge about the structure of the underlying data. To capture domain knowledge, we introduce one or more penalty terms into the optimization objective: $\sum_{k=1}^{K} \|P_k X Q_k^T - R_k\|_F^2$, where K is the number of penalty terms. We also introduce a weight γ to capture our confidence in such knowledge.

Examples of domain knowledge include temporal stability constraints, spatial locality constraints, and initial estimation of X (*e.g.*, [47] derives initial traffic matrices using the gravity model [21]). Temporal and spatial locality are common in network data [32, 44, 15]. Such domain knowledge is especially helpfulwhen there are many missing entries, making the problem severely under-constrained.

Consider a few simple cases. First, when $k = 1$, P_1 is an identity matrix I, R_1 is a zero vector, we can set $Q_1 = Toeplitz(0, 1, -1)$, which denotes the Toeplitz matrix with central diagonal given by ones, the first upper diagonal given by negative one, *i.e.*,

$$Q = \begin{bmatrix} 1 & -1 & 0 & 0 & \dots \\ 0 & 1 & -1 & 0 & \ddots \\ 0 & 0 & 1 & -1 & \ddots \\ \vdots & \ddots & \ddots & \ddots & \ddots \end{bmatrix}. \tag{3}$$

Q^T denotes the transpose of matrix Q. $P_1 X Q_1^T$ captures the differences between two temporally adjacent elements in X. Minimizing $\|P_1 X Q_1^T - R_1\|_F^2 = \|P_1 X Q_1^T\|_F^2$ reflects the goal of making X temporally stable. For simplicity, this is what we use for our evaluation. In general, one can use similar constraints to capture other temporal locality patterns during different periods (*e.g.*, seasonal patterns or diurnal patterns).

Next we consider the spatial locality, which is represented by P. If $k = 1$, $R_1 = 0$, Q_1 is an identity matrix I, we can set P_1 to reflect the spatial locality. For example, if two adjacent elements in the matrix have similar values, we can set $P = Toeplitz(0, 1, -1)$. Similarly, if different parts of the matrix have different spatial locality patterns, we can use different P's to capture these spatial locality patterns. For simplicity, our evaluation considers only temporal stability, which is well known to exist in different networks. We plan to incorporate spatial locality in the future.

Finally, if we have good initial estimate of X_{init} (*e.g.*, [47] uses the gravity model to derive the initial TM), we can leverage this domain knowledge by minimizing $\|X - X_{init}\|$ (*i.e.*, $R_1 = X_{init}$). This term can be further combined with spatial and/or temporal locality to produce richer constraints.

Putting everything together, the general formulation is:

$$\begin{aligned} \text{minimize:} \quad & \alpha\|X\|_* + \beta\|Y\|_1 + \frac{1}{2\sigma}\|Z\|_F^2 + \\ & \frac{\gamma}{2\sigma}\sum_{k=1}^{K} \|P_k X Q_k^T - R_k\|_F^2, \\ \text{subject to:} \quad & AX + BY + CZ + W = D \\ & E. * W = W. \end{aligned} \tag{4}$$

Note that our formulation is more general than recent research on compressive sensing (*e.g.*, [50, 9, 38, 37]), which do not consider anomalies, have simpler constraints (*e.g.*, there is no A, B, or C), and have less general objectives.

3.2 Optimization Algorithm

The generality of the formulation in Eq. (4) makes it challenging to optimize. We are not aware of any existing work on compressive sensing that can cope with such a general formulation. Below we first reformulate Eq. (4) to make it easier to solve. We then consider the augmented Lagrangian function of the reformulated problem and develop an Alternating Direction Method to solve it.

Reformulation for optimization: Note that X and Y appear in multiple locations in the objective function and constraints in the optimization problem 4. This coupling makes optimization difficult. To reduce coupling, we introduce a set of auxiliary variables $X_0, X_1, \cdots, X_K$ and Y_0 and reformulate the problem as follows:

$$\begin{aligned}\text{minimize:} \quad & \alpha\|X\|_* + \beta\|Y\|_1 + \frac{1}{2\sigma}\|Z\|_F^2 \\ & + \frac{\gamma}{2\sigma}\sum_{k=1}^{K}\|P_k X_k Q_k^T - R_k\|_F^2, \\ \text{subject to:} \quad & AX_0 + BY_0 + CZ + W = D, \\ & E.*W = W, \\ & X_k - X = 0 \quad (\forall k = 0, \cdots, K), \\ & Y_0 - Y = 0. \end{aligned} \tag{5}$$

where Y_0 and $X_k (0 \le k \le K)$ are auxiliary variables. Note that formulations Eq. (5) and Eq. (4) are equivalent.

Alternating Direction Method for solving (5)**:** We apply an Alternating Direction Method (ADM) [4] to solve the convex optimization problem in (5). Specifically, we consider the augmented Lagrangian function:

$$\begin{aligned} & \mathcal{L}(X, \{X_k\}, Y, Y_0, Z, W, M, \{M_k\}, N, \mu) \\ \triangleq \quad & \alpha\|X\|_* + \beta\|Y\|_1 + \frac{1}{2\sigma}\|Z\|_F^2 \\ & + \frac{\gamma}{2\sigma}\sum_{k=1}^{K}\|P_k X_k Q_k^T - R_k\|_F^2 \\ & + \langle M, D - AX_0 - BY_0 - CZ - W\rangle && (6) \\ & + \sum_{k=0}^{K}\langle M_k, X_k - X\rangle && (7) \\ & + \langle N, Y_0 - Y\rangle && (8) \\ & + \frac{\mu}{2}\cdot\|D - AX_0 - BY_0 - CZ - W\|_F^2 && (9) \\ & + \frac{\mu}{2}\cdot\sum_{k=0}^{K}\|X_k - X\|_F^2 && (10) \\ & + \frac{\mu}{2}\cdot\|Y_0 - Y\|_F^2 && (11) \end{aligned}$$

where M, $\{M_k\}$, N are the Lagrangian multipliers [1] for the equality constraints in Eq. (5), and $\langle U, V\rangle \triangleq \sum_{i,j}(U[i,j]\cdot V[i,j])$ for two matrices U and V (of the same size). Essentially, the augmented Lagrangian function includes the original objective, three Lagrange multiplier terms (6)–(8), and three penalty terms converted from the equality constraints (9)–(11). Lagrange multipliers are commonly used to convert an optimization problem with equality constraints into an unconstrained one. Specifically, for any optimal solution that minimizes the (augmented) Lagrangian function, the partial derivatives with respect to the Lagrange multipliers must be 0. Hence the original equality constraints will be satisfied. The penalty terms enforce the constraints to be satisfied. The benefit of including Lagrange multiplier terms in addition to the penalty terms is that μ no longer needs to iteratively increase to ∞ to solve the original constrained problem, thereby avoiding ill-conditioning [4]. Note that we do not include terms corresponding to constraint $E.*W = W$ in the augmented Lagrangian function, because it is straightforward to enforce this constraint during each iteration of the Alternating Direction Method without the need for introducing additional Lagrange multipliers.

The ADM algorithm progresses in an iterative fashion. During each iteration, we alternate among the optimization of the augmented Lagrangian function by varying each one of X, $\{X_k\}$, Y, Y_0, Z, W, M, $\{M_k\}$, N while fixing the other variables. Introducing auxiliary variables $\{X_k\}$ and Y_0 makes it possible to obtain a close-form solution for each optimization step. Following ADM, we increase μ by a constant factor $\rho \ge 1$ during each iteration. When involving only two components, ADM is guaranteed to converge quickly. In our general formulation, convergence is no longer guaranteed, though empirically we observe quick convergence in all our experiments (*e.g.*, as shown in Section 4). We plan to apply techniques in [13] to ensure guaranteed convergence in future work. We further improve efficiency by replacing exact optimization with approximate optimization during each iteration. Appendix A gives a detailed description on the steps during each iteration.

Improving efficiency through approximate SVD: The most time-consuming operation during each iteration of the Alternating Direction Method is performing the singular value decomposition. In our implementation, we add an additional constraint on the rank of matrix X: $rank(X) \le r$, where r is a user-specified parameter that represents an estimated upper bound on the true rank of X. We then explicitly maintain the SVD of X and update it approximately during each iteration through the help of rank-revealing QR factorization of matrices that have only r columns (which are much smaller than the original matrices used in SVD). We omit the details of approximate SVD in the interest of space.

3.3 Setting Parameters

Setting α, β and σ: A major advantage of our LENS decomposition is that a good choice of the parameters α and β can be analytically determined without requiring any manual tuning. Specifically, let σ_D be the standard deviation of measurement noise in data matrix D (excluding the effect of low-rank, sparse, and error terms). For now, we assume that σ_D is known, and we will describe how to determine σ_D later in this section. Moreover, we first ignore the domain knowledge term and will adaptively set γ for the domain knowledge term based on the given α and β.

Let density $\eta(D) = 1 - \frac{\sum_{i,j} E[i,j]}{m \times n}$ be the fraction of entries in D that are neither missing nor erroneous, where the size of D is $m \times n$ and the size of Y is $m_Y \times n_Y$. $E[i,j]$ can be estimated based on domain knowledge. For example, we set $E[i,j] = 1$ if the corresponding entry takes a value outside its normal range (*e.g.*, a negative traffic counter) or measurement software reports an error on the entry. Moreover, our evaluation shows that LENS is robust against estimation error in $\eta(D)$.

We propose to set:

$$\alpha = (\sqrt{m_X} + \sqrt{n_X})\cdot\sqrt{\eta(D)} \tag{12}$$

$$\beta = \sqrt{2\cdot\log(m_Y \cdot n_Y)} \tag{13}$$

$$\sigma = \theta\cdot\sigma_D \tag{14}$$

where (m_X, n_X) is the size of X, (m_Y, n_Y) is the size of Y. θ is a user-specified control parameter that limits the contamination of the dense measurement noise σ_D when computing X and Y. In all our experiments, we set $\theta = 10$, though it is also possible to choose θ adaptively, just like how we choose γ as described later in this section.

Below we provide some intuition behind the above choices of α and β using the basic formulation in Eq. (1). The basic strategy is to consider all variables except one are fixed. Our evaluation shows that these choices work well in practice.

Intuition behind the choice of α: Consider the special case when all variables except that X are already given and stay fixed. Then we just need to solve:

$$\min_X \quad \alpha \cdot \|X\|_* + \frac{1}{2\sigma} \cdot \|D - X - Y - W\|_F^2 \tag{15}$$

since $Z = D - X - Y - W$. We can prove the optimal X in Eq. (15) can be obtained by performing soft-thresholding (a.k.a., shrinkage) on the singular values of $D - Y - W$. That is,

$$\begin{aligned} X_{\text{opt}} &= \mathsf{SVSoftThresh}(D - Y - W,\ \alpha \cdot \sigma) \\ &\triangleq U * \mathsf{SoftThresh}(S,\ \alpha \cdot \sigma) * V^T, \end{aligned} \tag{16}$$

where $[U, S, V] = \mathsf{svd}(D - Y - W)$ is the singular value decomposition of $(D - Y - W)$ (thus $D - Y - W = USV^T$), and $\mathsf{SoftThresh}(S,\ \alpha\sigma) = \mathsf{sign}(S). * \max\{0,\ \mathsf{abs}(S) - \alpha\sigma\}$ ($\mathsf{sign}(S) = S./\mathsf{abs}(S)$). Intuitively, soft-thresholding eliminates the contamination on the singular values of X due to the dense measurement noise σ_D.

From asymptotic random matrix theory [33], for a random matrix with entries drawn *i.i.d.* from a Gaussian distribution with probability $\eta(D)$, its norm (*i.e.*, the largest singular value) is bounded by $O((\sqrt{m} + \sqrt{n}) \cdot \sqrt{\eta(D)} \cdot \sigma_D)$ with a high probability. So a good heuristic is to set the soft threshold to:

$$\alpha \cdot \sigma = (\sqrt{m} + \sqrt{n}) \cdot \sqrt{\eta(D)} \cdot \sigma_D \cdot \theta,$$

where θ is a control parameter that captures the desired separation from the influence of dense measurement noise σ_D. Therefore, we simply set $\alpha = (\sqrt{m} + \sqrt{n}) \cdot \sqrt{\eta(D)}$ and $\sigma = \theta \cdot \sigma_D$.

Intuition behind the choice of β: Now suppose X is given and we need to solve:

$$\min_Y \quad \beta \|Y\|_1 + \frac{1}{2\sigma} \cdot \|D - X - Y - W\|_F^2 \tag{17}$$

We can prove that the optimal Y for (17) can be obtained by performing soft-thresholding (a.k.a., shrinkage) on the entries of $D - X - W$. Specifically, we have:

$$Y_{\text{opt}} = \mathsf{SoftThresh}(D - X - W,\ \beta \cdot \sigma), \tag{18}$$

where soft-thresholding eliminates the contamination on entries of Y due to the dense measurement noise.

In the context of standard compressive sensing setting:

$$\min_y \quad \beta * \sigma_d \cdot \|y\|_1 + \frac{1}{2} \cdot \|y - d\|_2^2,$$

where y is a vector of length n_y, and σ_d is the standard deviation of the vector of observables d. As justified in Basis Pursuit De-Noising (BPDN) [10], a penalty term $\beta = \sqrt{2 \cdot \log(n_y)}$ should be used, where n_y is the number of elements in Y. Similarly, in our context, a good heuristic is to set the soft threshold to:

$$\beta \cdot \sigma = \sqrt{2 \cdot \log(m_Y \cdot n_Y)} \cdot \sigma_D \cdot \theta.$$

So we simply set $\beta = \sqrt{2 \cdot \log(m_Y \cdot n_Y)}$ and $\sigma = \theta \cdot \sigma_D$.

Estimating σ_D: When σ_D is not known in advance, we simply estimate it from entries of $D - AX_0 - BY_0 - W$ during each iteration in the Alternating Direction Method (see Appendix A). Specifically, let $J = D - AX_0 - BY_0 - W$, we estimate σ_D as the standard deviation of $\{J[i,j] \mid E[i,j] = 0\}$. It is also possible to use a more robust estimator (*e.g.*, the mean absolute value), which gives similar performance in our experiments.

Searching for γ: γ reflects the importance of domain knowledge terms. It is challenging to find an appropriate γ, since its value depends on how valuable are the domain knowledge versus the information from the measurement data. Therefore instead of using a fixed value, we automatically learn γ without user feedback or ground-truth of the real missing entries as follows. Given the incomplete data matrix D, we further drop additional entries of D and apply our algorithm under several γ values, and quantify the error of fitting the entries that were present in D but dropped intentionally during the search (so we know their true values). We adopt the value of γ that gives the lowest fitting error on these entries as the final γ and apply it to our final matrix interpolation, which only has the real missing elements.

Supporting the general formulation: In the general formulation in Eq. (4), we first ensure that matrices A, B, C are properly scaled such that each column of A, B, C has unit length (i.e. the square sum of all elements in a column is equal to 1). We also automatically scale P_k, Q_k, R_k such that each row of P_k and Q_k has unit length. We then use the same choice of α, β, σ, and γ as in the basic formulation.

4. EVALUATION

4.1 Evaluation Methodology

Performance metrics: We quantify the performance in terms of estimation error of the missing entries and anomaly detection accuracy. We drop data from existing network matrices and compare our estimation with the ground truth. We use Normalized Mean Absolute Error (NMAE) to quantify the estimation error. NMAE is defined as follow:

$$NMAE = \frac{\sum_{i,j:M(i,j)=0} |X(i,j) - \hat{X}(i,j)|}{\sum_{i,j:M(i,j)=0} |X(i,j)|}, \tag{19}$$

where X and $\hat{X}$ are the original and estimated matrices, respectively. We only measure errors on the missing entries. For each setting, we conduct 10 random runs, which drop random set of data, and report an average of these 10 runs.

We quantify the anomaly detection accuracy using *F1-score* [45], which is the harmonic mean of precision and recall: *F1-score* $= \frac{2}{1/precision + 1/recall}$, where precision is the fraction of anomalies found by anomaly detection schemes that are indeed real anomalies we injected and recall is the fraction of real anomalies that are correctly identified by anomaly detection schemes. The higher F1-score, the better. F1-score of 1 is perfect. We report an average of 10 random runs.

Anomaly generation: As mentioned in Section 2.2, we find the maximum difference between the original trace and the EWMA prediction, and then inject the anomaly of this size to the trace. We vary the anomaly size using different scaling factors s and the fraction of anomalies to understand their impacts.

Different dropping modes: As in [50], we drop data in the following ways: (i) PureRandLoss: elements in a matrix are dropped independently with a random loss rate; (ii) xxTimeRandLoss: xx% of columns in a matrix are selected and the elements in these selected columns are dropped with a probability p to emulate random losses during certain times (*e.g.*, disk becomes full); (iii) xxElemRandLoss: xx% of rows in a matrix are selected and the elements in these selected rows are dropped with a probability p to emulate certain nodes lose data (*e.g.*, due to battery drain); (iv) xxElemSyncLoss: the intersection of xx% of rows and p% of columns in a matrix are dropped to emulate a group of nodes experience the same loss events at the same time; (v) RowRandLoss: drop random rows to emulate node failures, and (vi) ColRandLoss: drop random columns for completeness. We use PureRandLoss as the default, and further use other loss models to understand impacts of different loss models. We feed the matrices after dropping as the input to LENS, and use LENS to fill in the missing entries.

Schemes evaluated: We compare the following schemes:

- Base: It approximates the original matrix as a rank-2 approximation matrix $X_{base} = \overline{X} + X_{row}1^T + 1X_{col}^T$, where 1 is a column vector consisting of all ones and X_{row} and X_{col} are computed using a regularized least square according to [50].
- SVD Base: As shown in [50], SVD Base, which applies SVD to $X - X_{base}$, out-performs SVD applied directly to X. We observe similar results, so below we only include SVD Base.
- SVD Base + KNN: We obtain the result from SVD Base and then apply K nearest neighbors (KNN) to perform local interpolation to leverage the local structure.
- SRMF: Sparsity Regularized Matrix Factorization (SRMF) leverages both low-rank and spatio-temporal characteristics [50].
- SRMF+KNN: It combines SRMF results with local interpolation via KNN [50].
- LENS: We use the output from the LEN decomposition as described in Section 3.

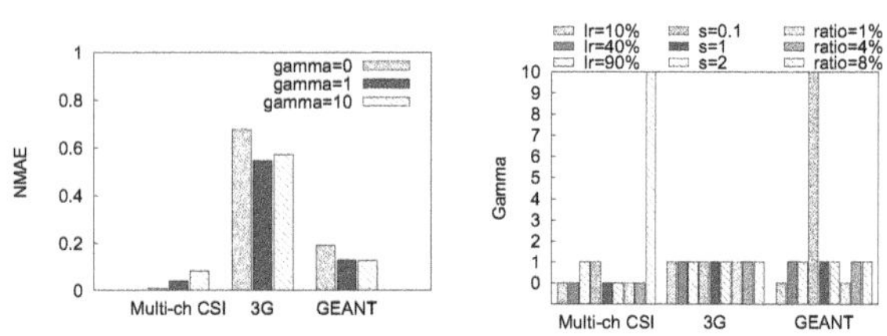

(a) NMAE of different γ (b) γ under different conditions

Figure 4: (a) NMAE of different γ: learned γ is 0 for multi-channel CSI, 1 for 3G, and 10 for GÉANT under no anomalies. (b) The learned γ under loss rates = 10%, 40%, 90%; anomaly size $s = 0.1, 1, 2$; ratio of anomalies = 1%, 4%, 8%.

4.2 Performance Results

Self learned γ: LENS supports many types of domain knowledge as described in Sec. 3.1. Our evaluation only considered temporal stability for simplicity and γ reflects its importance. To illustrate the benefit of self learning, Figure 4 (a) shows the performance under different γ values and different traces. Figure 4 (b) shows the best γ under different traces, loss rates, anomaly sizes, and ratio of anomalies. There does not exist a single γ that works well for all traces or conditions. Self tuning allows us to automatically select the best γ for these traces and achieves low NMAE in all cases.

Varying dropping rates: We first compare different schemes in terms of interpolation accuracy measured using NMAE. Figure 5 shows the interpolation error as we randomly inject anomalies to 5% elements with $s = 1$. For clarity of the graphs, we cap the y-axis so that we can focus on the most interesting parts of the graphs. We observe that LENS consistently out-performs the other schemes. In terms of NMAE, LENS < SRMF + KNN < SRMF < SVD Base + KNN < SVD Base. LENS reduces NMAE by 35.5% over SRMF, 27.8% over SRMF+KNN, 59.8% over SVD Base, and 44.9% over SVD Base + KNN on average. Moreover, the error is low for high-rank matrices. For example, the highest rank matrices in our datasets are 1-channel CSI, CU RSSI, Abilene, WiFi, 3G, and Cister RSSI matrices. Their corresponding NMAE are 0.05, 0.05, 0.3, 0.69, 0.74, 0.1, respectively. Most of them have low errors except WiFi and 3G. The error does not monotonically increase with the loss rate because an increasing loss rate reduces the number of anomalies, which may help reduce the error.

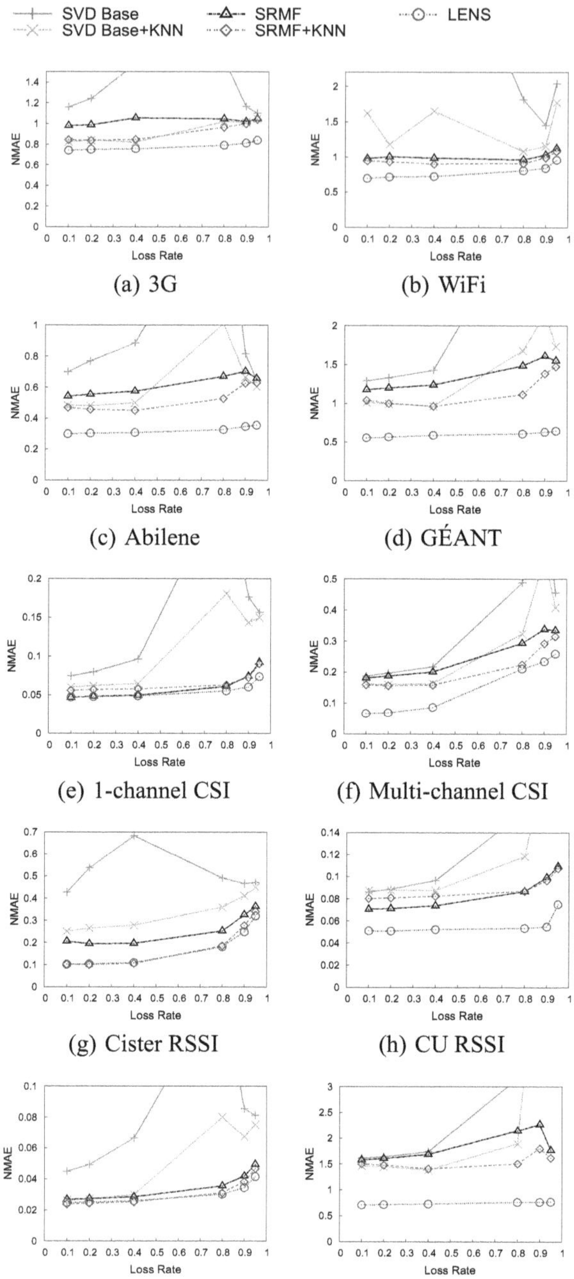

(a) 3G (b) WiFi (c) Abilene (d) GÉANT (e) 1-channel CSI (f) Multi-channel CSI (g) Cister RSSI (h) CU RSSI (i) UMich RSS (j) UCSB Meshnet

Figure 5: Interpolation performance under varying data loss rates under 5% anomalies and $s = 1$.

Figure 6 summarizes the results under varying data loss rates and no anomaly. In most traces, LENS performs comparably to SRMF+KNN, the best known algorithm under no anomaly. In UCSB Meshnet, LENS already out-performs SRMF+KNN even without injecting additional anomalies. This is likely because the trace has more anomalies before our anomaly injection. In UCSB

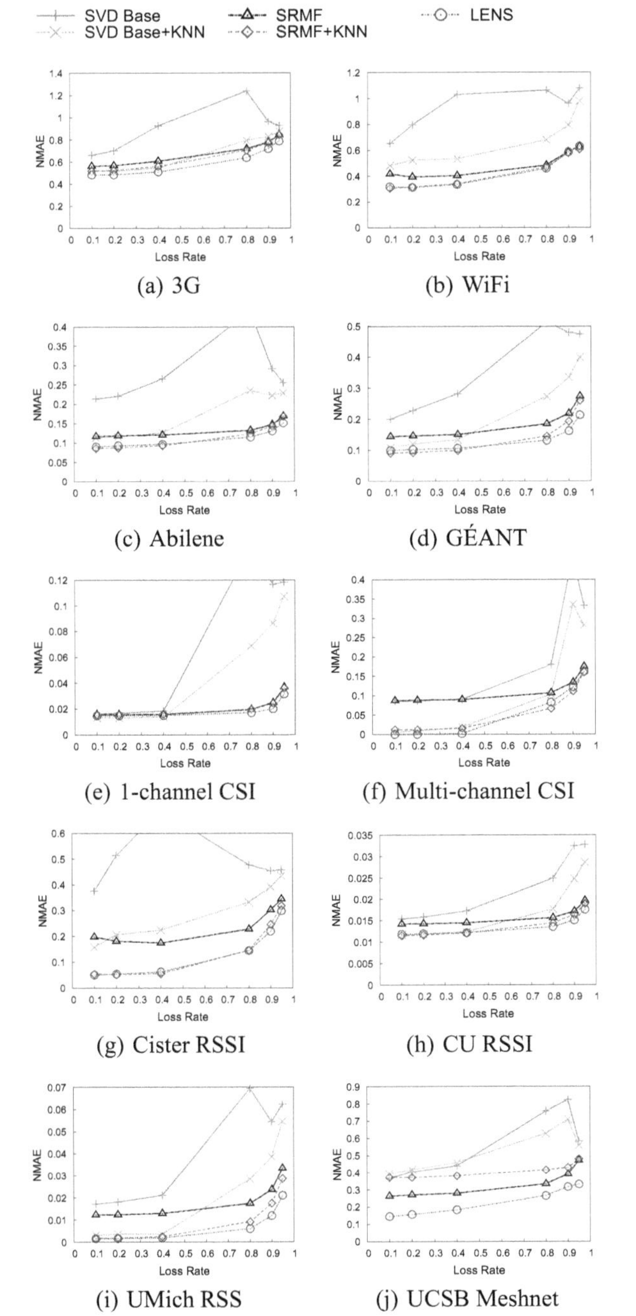

Figure 6: Interpolation performance under varying data loss rates and no anomaly.

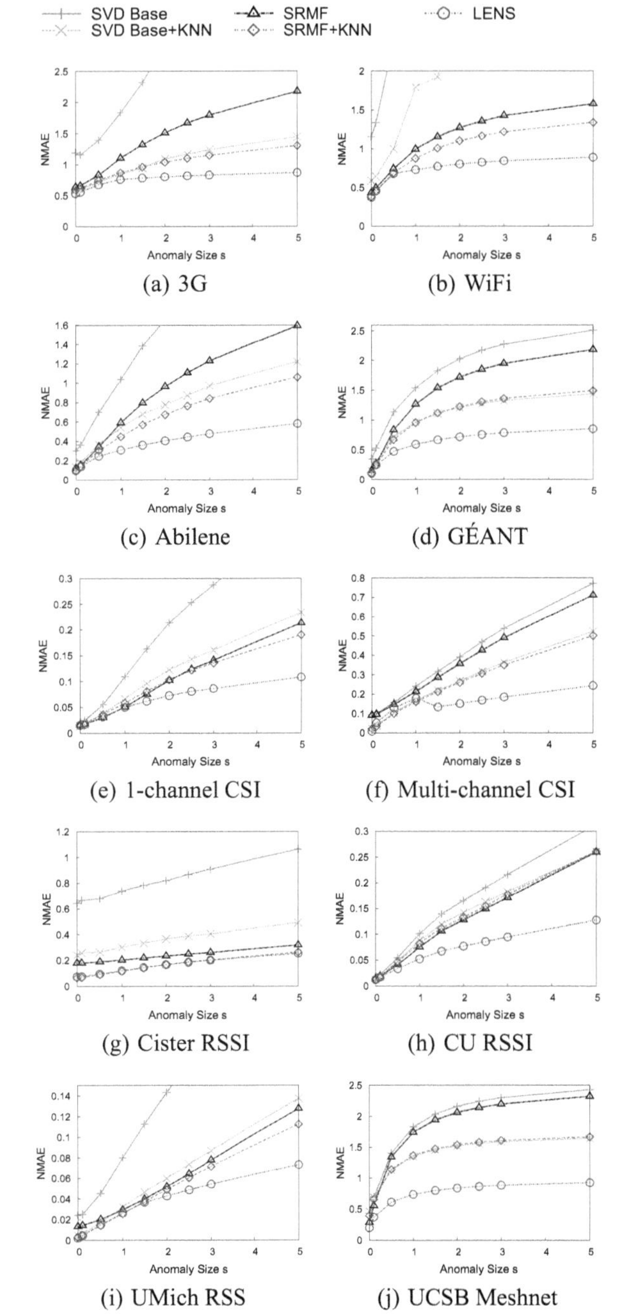

Figure 7: Impact of anomaly sizes when ratio of anomalies = 5% and loss rate = 50%.

Meshnet trace, 3.2% of EWMA prediction errors are larger than 5 times standard deviation from mean, whereas the corresponding numbers in other traces are 1.2%-2.4%. 3G trace has the second largest number of EWMA prediction error where we can also see LENS shows 7.7% improvement over SRMF+KNN.

Varying anomaly sizes: Figure 7 shows the interpolation performance as we vary the anomaly size s. LENS significantly outperforms all the other schemes. Its benefit increases with the anomaly size. For example, when $s = 1$, the NMAE of LENS is 33.7% lower than SRMF, 20.2% lower than SRMF+KNN, 61.8% lower than SVD Base, and 34.8% lower than SVD Base+KNN. The corresponding numbers under $s = 2$ are 44.9%, 31.9%, 69.8%, and 45.8%, respectively. Moreover, as we would expect, NMAE of all schemes tends to increase with the anomaly size in all traces, though the NMAE of LENS increases more slowly than the other schemes, since LENS explicitly separates anomalies before data interpolation. These results highlight the importance of anomaly detection in interpolation.

Varying the number of anomalies: Figure 8 shows the interpolation performance as we vary the number of anomalies. As before, LENS out-performs SRMF and SVD based schemes. The improvement ranges between 25.3-59.7% with 8% anomalies and 30.1-54.5% with 16% anomalies. In addition, the NMAE increases with the number of anomalies. Among different schemes, the rate of increase is slowest in LENS due to its explicit anomaly detection and removal.

Varying noise sizes: Figure 9 shows the interpolation performance as we vary the noise sizes. We inject noise to all the elements in the original matrices. The size of the noise follows normal distribution with mean 0 and standard deviation σ where σ is varied from 1%

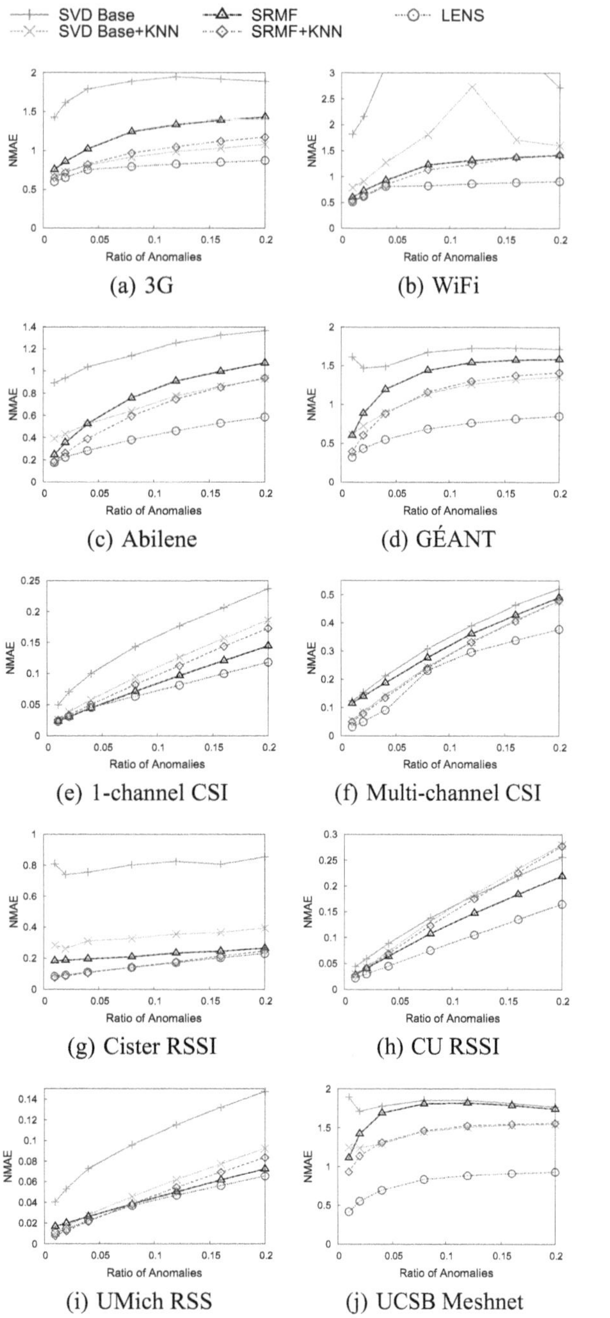

Figure 8: Impact of number of anomalies when the loss rate = 50% and $s = 1$.

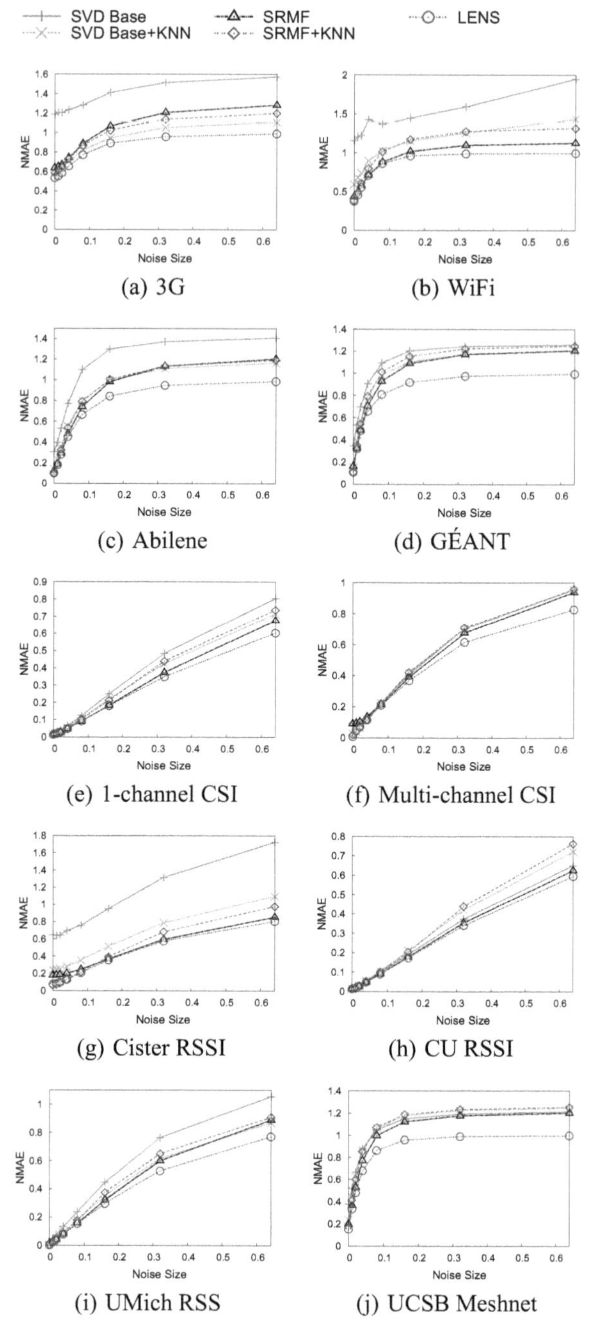

Figure 9: Impact of noise sizes when the loss rate = 50% and no anomaly.

to 64% of the maximal value in the matrix. As before, LENS out-performs the other schemes.

Different dropping modes: Next we compare the interpolation accuracy under different dropping modes. In the interest of brevity, Figure 10 shows interpolation error for UCSB Meshnet traces. NMAE is similar for the other traces. As we can see, LENS yields lowest NMAE under all dropping modes. It out-performs SRMF-based schemes by 52.9%, and out-perform SVD-based schemes by 60.0%.

Prediction: Prediction is different from general interpolation because consecutive columns are missing. SVD is not applicable in this context. KNN does not work well either since temporally or spatially near neighbors have missing values. Figure 11 shows the prediction error as we vary the prediction length (*i.e.*, prediction length l means that the first $1 - l$ columns are used to predict the remaining l columns). We include Base in the figure since [50] shows Base is effective in prediction. LENS out-performs SRMF, which out-performs Base.

Figure 12 further compares Base, SRMF, and LENS as we vary anomaly size. LENS continues to out-perform SRMF and Base. On average, it improves SRMF by 17.7%, and improves Base by 30.4%. Figure 13 shows the performance as we vary the number of anomalies. LENS continues to perform the best, out-performing SRMF by 29.6% and Base by 34.6%.

Anomaly detection: We further compare the accuracy of anomaly detection as we inject anomalies to 5% elements with $s = 1$. SRMF detects anomalies based on the difference between the actual and estimated values, and consider the entry has an anomaly if its difference is larger than a threshold. LENS considers all entries whose Y values are larger than a threshold as anomalies. Following [50], for each of the schemes, we choose a threshold to achieve

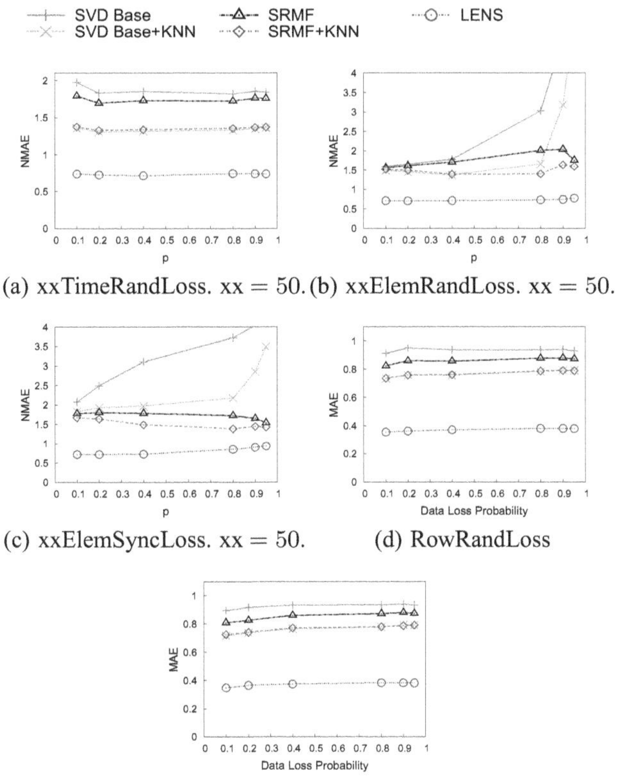

(a) xxTimeRandLoss. xx = 50. (b) xxElemRandLoss. xx = 50.

(c) xxElemSyncLoss. xx = 50. (d) RowRandLoss

(e) ColRandLoss

Figure 10: UCSB Meshnet: interpolation performance under various dropping models and 5% anomalies. xx and p in (a)-(c) are defined in Section 4.1

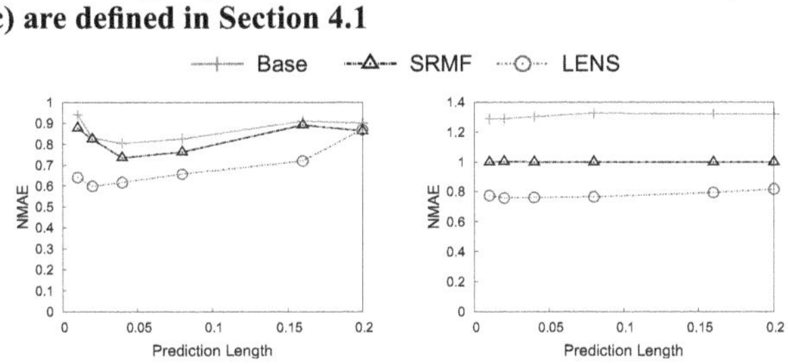

(a) WiFi (b) UCSB Meshnet

Figure 11: Prediction performance under 5% anomalies

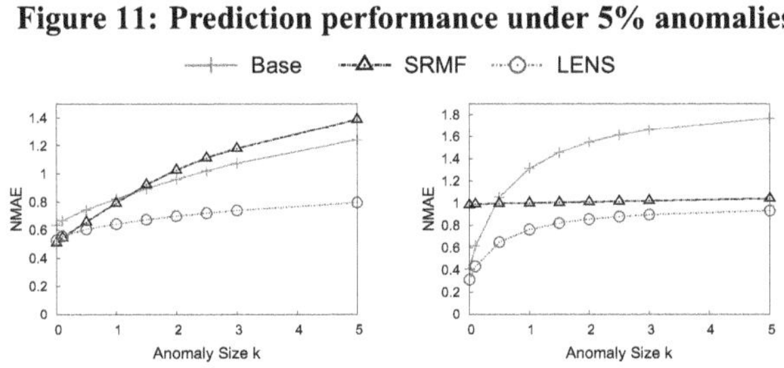

(a) WiFi (b) UCSB Meshnet

Figure 12: Prediction performance with various anomaly sizes, 5% anomalies, and 10% prediction length.

the false alarm probability within 10^{-5}. As shown in Figure 14, LENS consistently out-performs SRMF+KNN. In 3G and Cister RSSI traces, its F1-score is 17.6% higher than that of SRMF+KNN. This shows that LENS is effective in anomaly detection.

Computational time: Figure 15 compares the computation time of LENS and SRMF when both use 500 iterations. As we can see, LENS has much smaller computation time due to local optimiza-

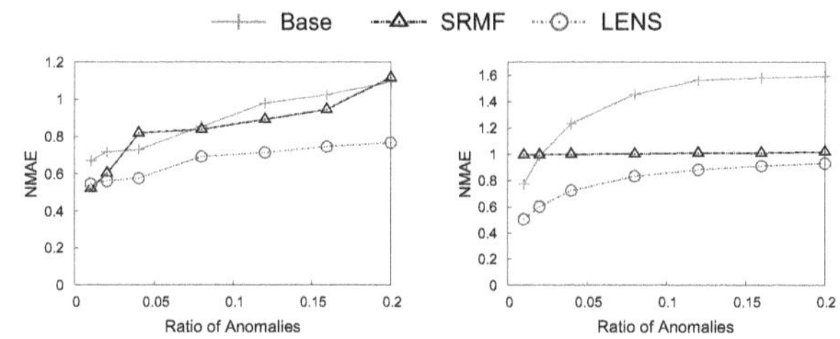

(a) WiFi (b) UCSB Meshnet

Figure 13: Prediction performance with various number of anomalies when the prediction length = 10%

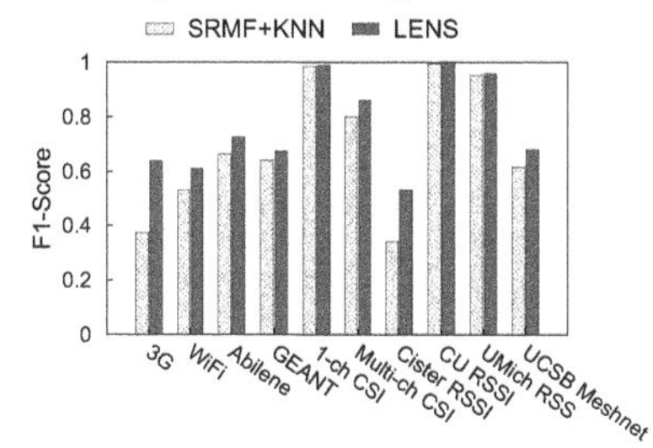

Figure 14: Anomaly detection performance as we inject anomalies to 5% elements with $s = 1$.

tion in ADM. This makes it feasible to perform efficient search over different parameters. Figure 16 further shows that LENS converges within 200-250 iterations.

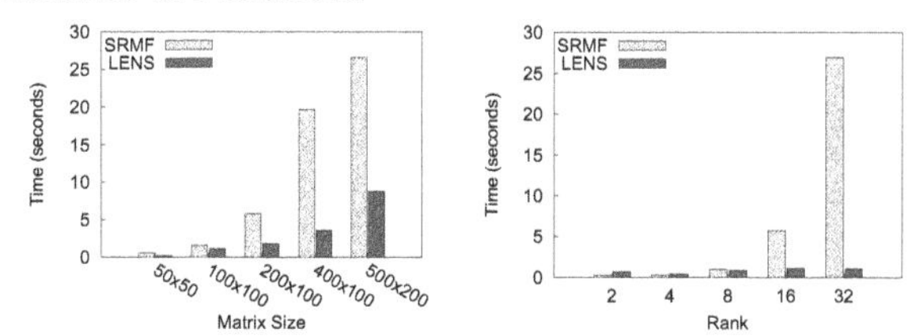

(a) vary matrix sizes (rank=10) (b) vary ranks (100 × 100 matrices)

Figure 15: Computation time

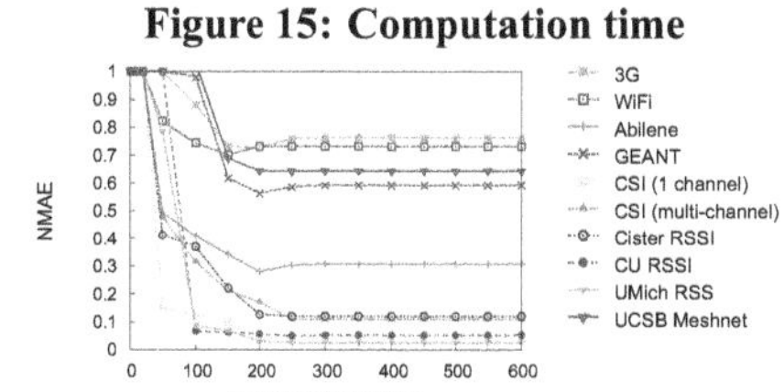

Figure 16: The interpolation performance of LENS under various number of iterations when the loss rate = 50% and $s = 1$.

5. RELATED WORK

Compressive sensing: LENS belongs to the realm of *compressive sensing*, a generic methodology for extracting and exploiting the presence of certain types of structure and redundancy in data from many real-world systems. Compressive sensing has recently attracted considerable attentions from statistics, approximation theory, information theory, and signal processing [8, 14, 7, 37, 38, 50] and is rapidly becoming a vibrant research area of its own.

Most existing compressive sensing works assume that the matrices satisfy low-rank property. However, this assumption may not hold in as we show in Section 2. Violation of such assumption significantly limits the accuracy of these techniques.

Significant work has been done for solving under-determined linear inverse problems. Missing value interpolation, prediction, and network tomography can be cast into the same formulation. As described in [48], many solutions solve the regularized least-squares problem: $\min_{\mathbf{x}} \|\mathbf{y} - A\mathbf{x}\|_2^2 + \lambda^2 J(\mathbf{x})$, where $\|\cdot\|_2$ denotes the L_2 norm, λ is a regularization parameter, and $J(\mathbf{x})$ is a penalization functional. In L_2 norm minimization, which is a widely used solution to linear inference problem, $J(\mathbf{x}) = \|\mathbf{x}\|_2^2$. In L_1 norm minimization, another commonly used scheme, $J(\mathbf{x}) = \|\mathbf{x}\|_1$ (*i.e.*, the L_1 norm of $\mathbf{x}$). Other regularization terms include $\|X\|_*$, the nuclear norm of matrix X, and spatio-temporal terms $\|SX\|_F^2$ and $\|XT^T\|_F^2$ in [50]. Unique advantages of LENS formulation include (i) its general formulation to account for a low-rank component, a sparse anomaly component, a dense but small noise term, and domain knowledge, (ii) its effective optimization algorithm to solve the general decomposition problem, and (iii) a data-driven procedure to learn the parameters. Its formulation is more general than existing work (*e.g.*, [50]) in that [50] requires the original matrix to be well approximated by the product of two low-rank matrices, whereas LENS relaxes this constraint and allows the delta between the original matrix and sparse anomaly matrix to be approximated by the product of two low-rank matrices. Moreover, LENS allows a linear coefficient in each of the decomposed terms and supports general forms of domain knowledge.

Anomaly detection: Anomaly detection has been extensively studied. PCA (*e.g.*, [19, 22, 23]) has been widely used for anomaly detection. PCA has several well known limitations: it is sensitive to how many principal components are used [39] and vulnerable to data poisoning [40]. Barford et al. [5] uses wavelets to decompose an original signal into low-, mid-, and high-frequency components and use the high-frequency components for anomaly detection. [46] presents a framework that incorporates a variety of anomaly detectors. [50] uses SRMF for anomaly detection based on the difference between estimated and actual matrix values. [26] proposes a multi-scale robust subspace algorithm to identify changes in performance. NICE [29] uses statistical correlation to detect chronic network problems. Mercury [28] detects persistent behavior changes using the time-alignment for distributed triggers. [27] combines different anomaly detection methods, such as EWMA, FFT, Holt-Winters, and Wavelets to boost the performance. [17] uses both customer call dataset and network crash log in IPTV to detect anomalies. It first finds heavy hitters where there might be anomalies with high probability and then use EWMA to detect anomalies. We complement the above work by developing a general framework that explicitly accounts for anomalies during missing value interpolation to avoid contamination.

6. CONCLUSION

This paper presents *LENS decomposition* to decompose a network matrix into a low-rank matrix, a sparse anomaly matrix, an error matrix, and a dense but small noise matrix. Our evaluation shows that it can effectively perform missing value interpolation, prediction, and anomaly detection and out-perform state-of-the-art approaches. As part of our future work, we plan to apply our framework to network tomography (*e.g.*, traffic matrix estimation based on link loads and link performance estimation based on end-to-end performance). As part of our future work, we plan to apply LENS to enable several important wireless applications, including spectrum sensing, channel estimation, and localization.

Acknowledgements

This work is supported in part by NSF Grants CCF-1117009, CNS-1343383, NSFC 61170237, and Singapore NRF CREATE E2S2.

7. REFERENCES

[1] Lagrange multiplier. `http://en.wikipedia.org/wiki/Lagrange_multiplier`.

[2] The Abilene Observatory Data Collections. `http://abilene.internet2.edu/observatory/data-collections.html`.

[3] LAN/MAN Standards Commmittee of the IEEE Computer Society. Part 11: Wireless LAN Medium Access Control and Physical Layer (PHY) Specifications . *IEEE Standard 802.11*, 2009. `http://standards.ieee.org/getieee802/download/802.11n-2009.pdf`.

[4] Augmented lagrangian method. `http://en.wikipedia.org/wiki/Augmented_Lagrangian_method`.

[5] P. Barford, J. Kline, D. Plonka, and A. Ron. A signal analysis of network traffic anomalies. In *Proc. of IMW*, 2002.

[6] K. Bauer, D. McCoy, D. Grunwald, and D. C. Sicker. CRAWDAD data set CU/RSSI (v. 2009-06-15). http://crawdad.cs.dartmouth.edu/cu/rssi/, May 2009.

[7] E. Candes and B. Recht. Exact matrix completion via convex optimization.

[8] E. Candes and T. Tao. Near optimal signal recovery from random projections: Universal encoding strategies? *IEEE Trans. on Information Theory*, 52(12):5406–5425, 2006.

[9] E. J. Candes, X. Li, Y. Ma, and J. Wright. Robust principal component analysis?, 2009. Manuscript. Available from `http://www-stat.stanford.edu/~candes/papers/RobustPCA.pdf`.

[10] S. S. Chen, D. L. Donoho, Michael, and A. Saunders. Atomic decomposition by basis pursuit. *SIAM Journal on Scientific Computing*, 20:33–61, 1998.

[11] G. Cheng, H. Chen, D. Cheng, Z. Zhang, and J. Lan. Anomaly detections in internet traffic using empirical measures. *International Journal of Innovative Technology and Exploring Engineering*, Feb. 2013.

[12] Crawdad. `http://crawdad.cs.dartmouth.edu`.

[13] W. Deng, M.-J. Lai, Z. Peng, and W. Yin. Parallel multi-block ADMM with o(1/k) convergence. *UCLA CAM 13-64*, 2014.

[14] D. Donoho. Compressed sensing. *IEEE Trans. on Information Theory*, 52(4):1289–1306, 2006.

[15] B. George, S. Kim, and S. Shekhar. Spatio-temporal network databases and routing algorithms: A summary of results. In *Proceedings of the 10th International Conference on Advances in Spatial and Temporal Databases*, SSTD'07, pages 460–477, Berlin, Heidelberg, 2007. Springer-Verlag.

[16] D. Halperin, W. Hu, A. Sheth, and D. Wetherall. Predictable 802.11 packet delivery from wireless channel measurements. In *Proc. of SIGCOMM*, 2010.

[17] C.-Y. Hong, M. Caesar, N. Duffield, and J. Wang. Tiresias: Online anomaly detection for hierarchical operational network data. In *Proc. of ICDCS*, 2012.

[18] L. Huang, X. Nguyen, M. Garofalakis, and J. M. Hellerstein. Communication-efficient online detection of network-wide anomalies. In *Proc. of IEEE INFOCOM*, 2007.

[19] Y. Huang, N. Feamster, A. Lakhina, and J. J. Xu. Diagnosing network disruptions with network-wide analysis. In *Proc. of ACM SIGMETRICS*, 2007.

[20] 802.11n channel measurement tool. `http://ils.intel-research.net/projects/80211n-channel-measurement-tool`.

[21] J. Kowalski and B. Warfield. Modeling traffic demand between nodes in a telecommunications network. In *Proc. of ATNAC*, 1995.

[22] A. Lakhina, M. Crovella, and C. Diot. Diagnosing network-wide traffic anomalies. In *Proc. of ACM SIGCOMM*, 2004.

[23] A. Lakhina, M. Crovella, and C. Diot. Mining anomalies using traffic feature distributions. In *Proc. of ACM SIGCOMM*, 2005.

[24] A. Lakhina, K. Papagiannaki, M. Crovella, C. Diot, E. D. Kolaczyk, and N. Taft. Structural analysis of network traffic flows. In *Proc. of ACM SIGMETRICS*, 2004.

[25] L. F. Lu, Z.-H. Huang, M. A. Ambusaidi, and K.-X. Gou. A large-scale network data analysis via sparse and low rank reconstruction. *Discrete Dynamics in Nature and Society*, Feb. 2013.

[26] A. Mahimkar, Z. Ge, J. Wang, J. Yates, Y. Zhang, J. Emmons, B. Huntley, and M. Stockert. Rapid detection of maintenance induced changes in service performance. In *Proc. of ACM CoNEXT*, 2011.

[27] A. Mahimkar, A. Lall, J. Wang, J. Xu, J. Yates, and Q. Zhao. Anomaly detection in large operational networks. In *Proc. of ICDCS*, 2011.

[28] A. Mahimkar, H. H. Song, Z. Ge, A. Shaikh, J.Wang, J. Yates, Y. Zhang, and J. Emmons. Detecting the performance impact of upgrades in large operational networks. In *Proc. of ACM SIGCOMM*, 2010.

[29] A. Mahimkar, J. Yates, Y. Zhang, A. Shaikh, J. Wang, Z. Ge, and C. T. Ee. Troubleshooting chronic conditions in large IP networks. In *Proc. of ACM CoNEXT*, 2008.

[30] Y. Mao and L. K. Saul. Modeling distances in large-scale networks by matrix factorization. In *Proc. of IMC*, New York, NY, USA, 2004.

[31] S. Nagaraja, V. Jalaparti, M. Caesar, and N. Borisov. P3ca: Private anomaly detection across ISP networks. In *Proc. of PETS*, volume 6794. Springer, 2011.

[32] A. Navaz, S.Gopalakrishnan, and R.Meena. Anomaly detections in internet traffic using empirical measures. *International Journal of Innovative Technology and Exploring Engineering*, Feb. 2013.

[33] D. Needell. Non-asymptotic theory of random matrices. Lecture 6: Norm of a random matrix, 2007. Stanford Math 280 Lecture Notes. Available at `http://www-stat.stanford.edu/~dneedell/lecs/lec6.pdf`.

[34] T. E. Ng and H. Zhang. Predicting internet network distance with coordinate-based appoaches. In *Proc. of INFOCOMM*, 2002.

[35] C. Noda, S. Prabh, M. Alves, T. Voigt, and C. A. Boano. CRAWDAD data set Cister/RSSI (v. 2012-05-17). http://crawdad.cs.dartmouth.edu/cister/rssi/, 2005.

[36] S. Rallapalli, L. Qiu, Y. Zhang, and Y.-C. Chen. Exploiting temporal stability and low-rank structure for localization in mobile networks. In *Proc. of ACM MobiCom*, 2010.

[37] B. Recht, M. Fazel, and P. A. Parrilo. Guaranteed minimum rank solutions to linear matrix equations via nuclear norm minimization. preprint.

[38] B. Recht, W. Xu, and B. Hassibi. Necessary and sufficient condtions for success of the nuclear norm heuristic for rank minimization. In *47th IEEE Conference on Decision and Control*, December 2008.
[39] H. Ringberg, A. Soule, J. Rexford, and C. Diot. Sensitivity of PCA for traffic anomaly detection. In *Proc. of ACM SIGMETRICS*, 2007.
[40] B. I. Rubinstein, B. Nelson, L. Huang, A. D. Joseph, S. h. Lau, S. Rao, N. Taft, and J. D. Tygar. Antidote: understanding and defending against poisoning of anomaly detectors. In *Proc. of ACM IMC*, 2009.
[41] UCSB meshnet. `http://www.crawdad.org/ucsb/meshnet/`.
[42] S. Uhlig, B. Quoitin, S. Balon, and J. Lepropre. Providing public intradomain traffic matrices to the research community. *ACM SIGCOMM Computer Communication Review*, 36(1):83–86, January 2006.
[43] Umich RSS. `http://crawdad.cs.dartmouth.edu/umich/rss/`.
[44] M. Wang, A. Ailamaki, and C. Faloutsos. Capturing the spatio-temporal behavior of real traffic data. *Perform. Eval.*, 49(1-4):147–163, Sept. 2002.
[45] Wikipedia. F1 score. http://en.wikipedia.org/wiki/F1_score.
[46] Y. Zhang, Z. Ge, A. Greenberg, and M. Roughan. Network anomography. In *Proc. of ACM IMC*, 2005.
[47] Y. Zhang, M. Roughan, N. Duffield, and A. Greenberg. Fast accurate computation of large-scale IP traffic matrices from link loads. In *Proceedings of ACM SIGMETRICS*, June 2003.
[48] Y. Zhang, M. Roughan, C. Lund, and D. Donoho. An information-theoretic approach to traffic matrix estimation. In *Proc. of ACM SIGCOMM*, Aug. 2003.
[49] Y. Zhang, M. Roughan, C. Lund, and D. Donoho. Estimating point-to-point and point-to-multipoint traffic matrices: An information-theoretic approach. *ACM/IEEE Transactions on Networking*, 13(5):947–960, Oct. 2005.
[50] Y. Zhang, M. Roughan, W. Willinger, and L. Qiu. Spatio-temporal compressive sensing and Internet traffic matrices. In *Proceedings of ACM SIGCOMM*, 2009.

APPENDIX

A. DETAILS OF THE ALTERNATING DIRECTION METHOD

Each iteration of the Alternating Direction Method involves the following steps:

1. Find X to minimize the augmented Lagrangian function $\mathcal{L}(X, \{X_k\}, Y, Y_0, Z, W, M, \{M_k\}, N, \mu)$ with other variables fixed. Removing the fixed terms, the objective is:
$$\text{minimize: } \alpha\|X\|_* + \frac{\mu}{2}\sum_{k=0}^{K}\|X_k + M_k/\mu - X\|_F^2.$$
Let $J = \frac{1}{K+1}\sum_{k=0}^{K}(X_k + M_k/\mu)$, and $t = \frac{\alpha/\mu}{K+1}$. We can simplify the objective to the following:
$$\text{minimize: } t\|X\|_* + 1/2\|X - J\|_F^2.$$
According to matrix completion literature, this is a standard nuclear norm minimization problem and can be solved by applying soft thresholding on the singular values of J. Specifically, we have:
$$X = \mathsf{SVSoftThresh}(J, t).$$
For a given J and t, let $J = USV^T$ be the singular value decomposition of J. We have: $\mathsf{SVSoftThresh}(J, t) \triangleq U\mathsf{SoftThresh}(S, t)V^T$, where
$$\mathsf{SoftThresh}(S[i, j], t) \triangleq \mathsf{sign}(S[i, j])\max(0, |S[i, j]| - t).$$
2. Find X_k to minimize $\mathcal{L}(X, \{X_k\}, Y, Y_0, Z, W, M, \{M_k\}, N, \mu)$ with other variables fixed ($k = 1, 2, ..., K$). This gives:
$$\text{minimize: } \frac{\gamma}{2\sigma}\|P_k X_k Q_k^T - R_k\|_F^2 + \frac{\mu}{2}\|X_k + M_k/\mu - X\|_F^2.$$
This is a least square problem with respect to X_k. The optimal solution can be obtained by forcing the gradient of the objective to be zero. That is,
$$\frac{\gamma}{\sigma}P_k^T(P_k X_k Q_k^T - R_k)Q_k^T + \mu(X_k + M_k/\mu - X) = 0. \quad (20)$$
Let $J = X - M_k/\mu$, and $R = P_k^T R_k Q_k + \frac{\mu\sigma}{\gamma}J$. Eq. (20) simplifies to
$$P_k^T P_k X_k Q_k^T Q_k + \frac{\mu\sigma}{\gamma}X_k = R. \quad (21)$$
Perform eigendecomposition on $P_k^T P_k$ and $Q_k^T Q_k$ and let $USU^T = P_k^T P_k$; $VTV^T = Q_k^T Q_k$, where U and V are orthogonal matrices, S and T are diagonal matrices. We have: $S(U^T X_k V)T + \frac{\mu\sigma}{\gamma}(U^T X_k V) = U^T RV$. Through a change of variable, let $H = U^T X_k V$, Eq. (21) becomes:
$$SHT + \frac{\mu\sigma}{\gamma}H = U^T RV. \quad (22)$$
Let $\mathbf{s} = diag(S)$, $\mathbf{t} = diag(T)$ be the diagonal vector of S and T, respectively. Eq. (22) is equivalent to $(\mathbf{st}^T + \frac{\mu\sigma}{\gamma}). * H = U^T RV$. Since U and V are orthogonal matrices, we can easily find X_k from H as $X_k = UHV^T$. So we have: $H = (U^T RV)./(\mathbf{st}^T + \frac{\mu\sigma}{\gamma})$, where $./$ is an operator for element-wise division. Thus,
$$X_k = UHV^T = U\left((U^T RV)./(\mathbf{st}^T + \frac{\mu\sigma}{\gamma})\right)V^T.$$
3. Find X_0 to minimize $\mathcal{L}(X, \{X_k\}, Y, Y_0, Z, W, M, \{M_k\}, N, \mu)$ with other variables fixed ($k = 1, 2, ..., K$). This gives:
$$\begin{aligned}\text{minimize:}\quad & \langle M, D - AX_0 - BY_0 - CZ - W\rangle \\ & + \langle M_0, X_0 - X\rangle \\ & + \mu/2\|D - AX_0 - BY_0 - CZ - W\|_F^2 \\ & + \mu/2\|X_0 - X\|_F^2\end{aligned}$$
That is,
$$\begin{aligned}\text{minimize:}\quad & \|X_0 - X + M_0/\mu\|_F^2 \\ & + \|D - BY_0 - CZ - W + M/\mu - AX_0\|_F^2\end{aligned}$$
Let $J_0 = X - M_0/\mu$ and $J = D - BY_0 - CZ - W + M/\mu$. It becomes:
$$\text{minimize:} \|X_0 - J_0\|_F^2 + \|AX_0 - J\|_F^2$$
Letting the gradient be zero leads to: $X_0 - J_0 + A^T(AX_0 - J) = 0$. Therefore, $X_0 = \text{inv}(A^T A + I)(A^T J + J_0)$.
4. Find Y to minimize $\mathcal{L}(X, \{X_k\}, Y, Y_0, Z, W, M, \{M_k\}, N, \mu)$ with other variables fixed. This gives:
$$\text{minimize:} \beta\|Y\|_1 + \langle N, Y_0 - Y\rangle + \mu/2\|Y_0 - Y\|_F^2$$
That is:
$$\text{minimize:} \beta/\mu\|Y\|_1 + 1/2\|Y_0 + N/\mu - Y\|_F^2.$$
Let $J = Y_0 + N/\mu$. $t = \beta/\mu$. It becomes: $t\|Y\|_1 + 1/2\|J - Y\|_F^2$. This can be easily solved as $Y = \mathsf{SoftThresh}(J, t)$. To see why, the problem can be solved for each element of Y separately. So we just need to find $Y[i, j]$ that minimizes: $t|Y[i, j]| + 1/2(J[i, j] - Y[i, j])^2$.
5. Find Y_0 to minimize $\mathcal{L}(X, \{X_k\}, Y, Y_0, Z, W, M, \{M_k\}, N, \mu)$ with other variables fixed. This gives:
$$\begin{aligned}\text{minimize:}\quad & \langle M, D - AX_0 - BY_0 - CZ - W\rangle \\ & + \langle N, Y_0 - Y\rangle \\ & + \mu/2\|D - AX_0 - BY_0 - CZ - W\|_F^2 \\ & + \mu/2\|Y_0 - Y\|_F^2\end{aligned}$$
Let $J_0 = Y - N/\mu$, $J = D - AX_0 - CZ - W + M/\mu$. It becomes minimize: $\|Y_0 - J_0\|_F^2 + \|BY_0 - J\|_F^2$ Letting the gradient = 0, we obtain: $Y_0 - J_0 + B^T(BY_0 - J) = 0$. So $Y_0 = \text{inv}(B^T B + I)(B^T J + J_0)$.
6. Find Z to minimize $\mathcal{L}(X, \{X_k\}, Y, Y_0, Z, W, M, \{M_k\}, N, \mu)$ with other variables fixed. This gives:
$$\begin{aligned}\text{minimize:}\quad & \frac{1}{2\sigma}\|Z\|_F^2 + \langle M, D - AX_0 - BY_0 - CZ - W\rangle \\ & + \frac{\mu}{2}\|D - AX_0 - BY_0 - CZ - W\|_F^2.\end{aligned}$$
Let $J = D - AX_0 - BY_0 - W + M/\mu$, it becomes:
$$\frac{1}{2\mu\sigma}\|Z\|_F^2 + \frac{1}{2}\|CZ - J\|_F^2.$$
Letting the gradient = 0 yields: $Z = \text{inv}(\frac{1}{\mu\sigma}I + C^T C)(C^T J)$.
7. Find W to minimize $\mathcal{L}(X, \{X_k\}, Y, Y_0, Z, W, M, \{M_k\}, N, \mu)$ with other variables fixed. This gives:
$$\begin{aligned}\text{minimize:}\quad & \langle M, D - AX_0 - BY_0 - CZ - W\rangle \\ & + \mu/2\|D - AX_0 - BY_0 - CZ - W\|_F^2.\end{aligned}$$
That is:
$$\text{minimize: } \|D - AX_0 - BY_0 - CZ - W + M/\mu\|_F^2$$
So $W = E. * (D - AX_0 - BY_0 - CZ + M/\mu)$ (recall that $W = E. * W$).
8. Update estimate for σ_D as follows. Let $J = D - AX_0 - BY_0 - W$. We then compute σ_D as the standard deviation of $J[E = 0]$ and update $\sigma = \theta\sigma_D$. In our implementation, we fix $\theta = 10$.
9. Update estimates for the Lagrangian multipliers M, M_k and N according to: $M = M + \mu \cdot (D - AX_0 - BY_0 - CZ - W)$, $M_k = M_k + \mu \cdot (X_k - X)$ $(k = 0, \cdots, K)$, $N = N + \mu \cdot (Y_0 - Y)$.
10. Update $\mu = \mu \cdot \rho$. In our implementation, initially $\mu = 1.01$ and $\rho = 1.01$. Every 100 iterations, we multiply ρ by 1.05.

EkhoNet: High Speed Ultra Low-power Backscatter for Next Generation Sensors

Pengyu Zhang, Pan Hu, Vijay Pasikanti, Deepak Ganesan
School of Computer Science
University of Massachusetts, Amherst, MA 01003
{pyzhang, panhu, vijaykp, dganesan}@cs.umass.edu

ABSTRACT

This paper argues for a clean-slate redesign of wireless sensor systems to take advantage of the extremely low power consumption of backscatter communication and emerging ultra-low power sensor modalities. We make the case that existing sensing architectures incur substantial overhead for a variety of computational blocks between the sensor and RF front end — while these overheads were negligible on platforms where communication was expensive, they become the bottleneck on backscatter-based systems and increase power consumption while limiting throughput. We present a radically new design that is minimalist, yet efficient, and designed to operate end-to-end at tens of μWs while enabling high-data rate backscatter at rates upwards of many hundreds of Kbps. In addition, we demonstrate a complex reader-driven MAC layer that jointly considers energy, channel conditions, data utility, and platform constraints to enable network-wide throughput optimizations. We instantiate this architecture on a custom FPGA-based platform connected to microphones, and show that the platform consumes 73× lower power and has 12.5× higher throughput than existing backscatter-based sensing platforms.

Categories and Subject Descriptors

C.2.1 [**Computer-Communication Networks**]: Network Architecture and Design

Keywords

Architecture, Backscatter, Sensor, Wireless

1. INTRODUCTION

A fundamental assumption that has driven the design of sensor networks for decades is that communication is the most power-hungry component of an individual sensor system. The power consumption gap between communication and other modules has driven a plethora of design choices in sensor networks, primarily by encouraging designers to reduce data at the source, thereby minimizing the amount of data that needs to be communicated.

MobiCom'14, September 7-11, 2014, Maui, Hawaii, USA.
Copyright 2014 ACM 978-1-4503-2783-1/14/09 ...$15.00.
http://dx.doi.org/10.1145/2639108.2639138.

Table 1: Power consumption of accelerometer, audio, ecg, and image sensors.

	Accel [1]	Audio [2]	ECG [3]	Camera [14]
Power	6μW	15.3μW	60μW	0.7μW

We argue that this assumption does not hold when it comes to passive radios such as backscatter. Backscatter requires extraordinarily simple circuitry since the carrier wave is generated by a reader, and a sensor only needs to modulate the signal to transmit information, thereby eschewing power-hungry components of a typical active radio. The simplicity and inherent efficiency of backscatter means that the energy gap between communication and other components of a system has narrowed dramatically.

These observations have profound implications on the design of next-generation wireless sensing systems that operate using backscatter. The primary implication is that the bottleneck in terms of power consumption has shifted away from communication to computation and sensing. But sensing is often not the bottleneck as well — the past decade has seen dramatic reductions in the power consumption of sensors such as microphones, cameras, ECG, accelerometers, and others, many of which consume only μWs of power while sampling at high rates (Table 1). Thus, both backscatter communication and a variety of low-power sensors can operate at μWs of power, and the key question becomes one of optimizing the rest of the system to match these numbers. This requires that we re-think every component between the sensor and RF interface — data acquisition, data processing, buffering, packetizing, MAC, and many others now become the bottleneck for achieving ultra-low power operation.

In this paper, we overturn the design principle governing wireless sensor design from one that is focused on minimizing communication to one focused on optimizing the computational elements between the sensor and RF interface. But optimizing computation is easier said than done, and requires an understanding of every module of the sensing platform, in-depth analysis of how to eliminate overhead from these modules, and design of a modified architecture to support an optimized design.

But our efforts to optimize computation raises an unexpected problem. If we do nothing to reduce data at the source, we need the bandwidth to be able to transfer raw data from the sensor to infrastructure. While backscatter communication is efficient in terms of power, throughputs achieved by practical backscatter-based systems have been abysmal. Despite several efforts at improving throughputs of backscatter [13, 27, 8, 22, 12], the best case throughput is still only around 20 kbps even when only a single node is present, and drops dramatically to barely hundreds of bits/second when there are multiple devices sharing the network. These numbers are not encouraging — for example, a microphone sampled at 8-44 KHz requires transmit rates upwards of 704 kbps, a far cry from the throughput that backscatter platforms are able to support today.

This leads us to the central question that we address in this paper: *how can we design a backscatter-based wireless sensor system that achieves whole-system power consumption of μWs, while simultaneously increasing data rates to support raw data transfer from sensors at several hundreds of kilobits/second.* Our goal is aggressive — as a point of comparison, an existing backscatter-based sensor, the UMass Moo (or the UW WISP) consumes about 2mW of power while transmitting at a few kilobits/second when there are multiple devices present. Thus, we seek to drop the system-wide power consumption by more than two orders of magnitude while simultaneously enabling two orders of magnitude increase in the data rates.

Our contributions are two-fold. First, we present a novel backscatter-based sensor platform, Ekho, that achieves our design goal to optimize power by eliminating computational overhead from the sensor to RF pipeline. We start with a deep dive at what computational modules are present between the sensor and RF interface on a typical low-power sensor platform, and measure their power consumption, before launching into a minimalist design that is optimized for power. Our second contribution is a network stack, EkhoNet, that is designed to be minimalist and enable bandwidth scale up to support data rates of hundreds of Kbps while supporting tens of nodes. While each Ekho node is minimalist, our MAC layer leverages resources at the reader to enable utility-energy and channel-aware optimization of bit rates and slot sizes across nodes.

Our results on a USRP reader and Ekho nodes show that:

- For operating an accelerometer at 400Hz, Ekho consumes 35μW of power, 7.6× lower than the 266μW of the Moo and 3.3× lower than the 118μW of WISP5.0. For operating an audio sensor at 44kHz, Ekho consumes 37μW of power, 76× lower than the Moo and 13.5× lower than the WISP5.0.
- We show that EkhoNet can scale to a network of several high bandwidth sensors. When a network of ten Ekho nodes equipped with microphones transmit simultaneously to a reader, we achieve a throughput of 780 kbps as a result of interleaving the data streams at the MAC layer. We also use an energy-utility-channel aware scheduler, and show that over 50% of the audio sensors achieve a median MOS score larger than 2, significantly higher than a baseline scheme that assigns sampling rates evenly across all nodes.

2. CASE FOR Ekho

In this section, we make the case that backscatter communication is extremely cheap and overturns the widely held premise that communication is more expensive than computation. We focus on the tradeoff between computation and communication since many commonly used sensors are already extremely efficient in terms of power. We begin with a discussion of why backscatter is efficient.

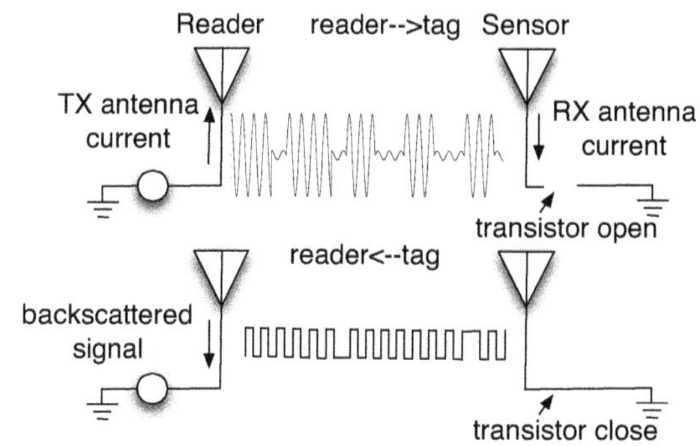

Figure 1: Backscatter communication basics.

2.1 Backscatter radio RF front end

Backscatter radios are designed to enable ultra low power wireless communication. As shown in Figure 1, a reader provides a carrier wave, which can be modulated with information to enable ultra low power wireless communication. While the carrier wave can also be rectified by a sensor for energy harvesting, our focus in this paper is on backscatter as a low-power radio, whether energy is obtained via harvesting or a battery, hence we focus on the communication rather than harvesting aspects of backscatter.

To transmit data, a sensor toggles the state of a transistor to detune its antenna and reflect the carrier wave back to the reader with its own information bits. Because the sensor does not actively generate RF signal as active radio systems, the power consumption of the backscatter radio is very low. In addition, the on-off transition overhead of backscatter radios is very short because backscatter radios do not have to warm up the RF analog circuits for data transmission unlike active radio systems. As a result, there is little overhead incurred while transmitting via backscatter, even when transmitting at a high rate. For example, one key component of the backscatter analog RF front end of the WISP [6] is a MOSFET transistor (BF1212WR). Its power consumption follows the equation of CV^2F where C is the capacitance of the transistor, V is the digital drain-source voltage, and F is the frequency of operating the transistor. When this transistor is toggled at a slow rate of 10Hz, it consumes 55pW of power, and even when toggled at a high rate of 1MHz, it only consumes 5.5μW of power. Thus, backscatter radios consume of the order of μWs of power, even for high rate data transfer.

2.2 Why compute if its cheaper to transmit?

The power consumption of backscatter radio has surprising implications on sensor system design, and challenges long-held views about communication vs computation tradeoffs in these systems.

Computation vs Communication: A common assumption in designing sensor systems has been that computation is significantly cheaper than communication, often by many orders of magnitude. This view has shaped a plethora of efforts for in-network processing, signal compression, subsampling, and other such approaches to reduce data at the source prior to communication. Indeed, this tradeoff has been reinforced by performance/power trends over the past decade — power consumption of embedded processors have

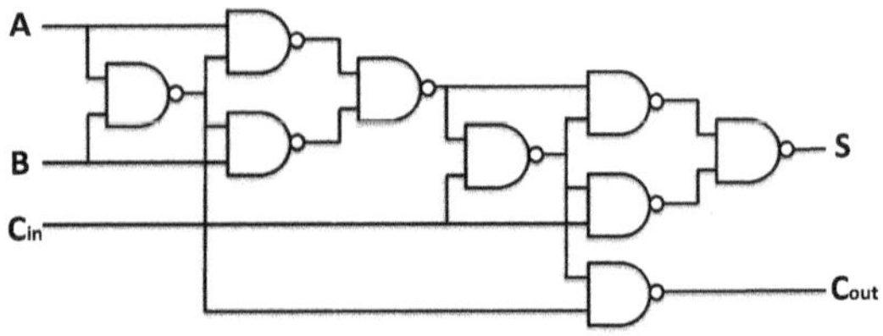

(a) 1 bit adder circuits for computation.

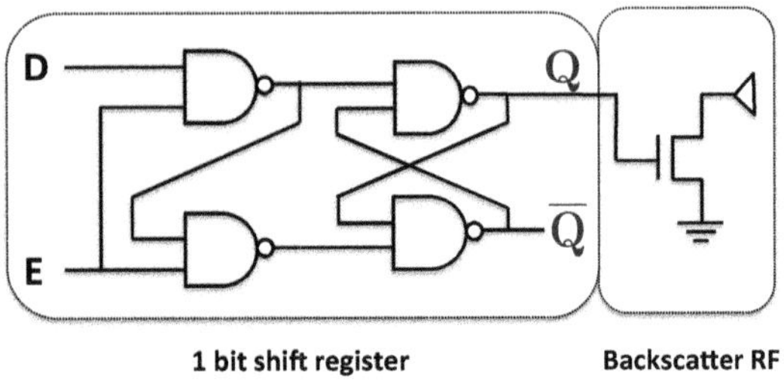

(b) 1 bit shift register controls a backscatter transistor.

Figure 2: 1 bit adder and 1 bit shift register circuit.

dropped dramatically, while power reduction in active radios has been relatively slower.

However, backscatter communication challenges this long-held view. Backscatter is inherently extraordinarily efficient since the carrier wave is generated by the reader, and the tag only backscatters the signal without any additional amplification. Thus, each bit of backscatter is extremely simple, and only requires a handful of gates (Figure 2). This implies that for computation to be cheaper energy-wise, the computational operations on each bit would have to use fewer gates than that required to communicate the bit. This is often a tall order due to the simplicity of backscatter.

Consider, for example, a simple aggregation operation that sums ten sensor readings before transmitting the aggregate value over the radio. On traditional sensor platforms, such data reduction would have direct and significant power benefits since communication dominates power, and our aggregation scheme cuts this cost by a factor of ten. The same operation on a backscatter-based platform has dubious benefits. Figure 2 shows that the number of NAND gates required for summing two bits is roughly nine (thirty six transistors), but only four NAND gates (sixteen transistors) and an additional transistor for backscattering the signal are needed to transmit the same data via the shift-register controlled backscatter RF! As power consumption is proportional to number of transistors, a nine gate adder consumes 2.1× more power than the shift-register controlled backscatter RF.

It is necessary to add a few caveats to our simplified comparison of computation and communication. The clock rates of communication subsystems are limited by signal to noise ratio considerations, whereas the clock rates of processors can be higher, and thereby reduce power. In addition, low-power processors use many tricks to reduce power consumption including optimized signal processing circuits, different power domains, extremely tight duty-cycling, and so on. Despite these optimizations, the cards are stacked against computation. Backscatter is so incredibly simple in terms of circuitry that even matching the efficiency of backscatter becomes a challenging architectural design problem.

Thus, the crux of our argument is the following: *backscatter drives down the optimal cross-over point between computation vs communication, such that communication of raw data may be preferable to computation in a wider spectrum of real-world scenarios.*

Implications on architecture design: This observation has an immediate implication on the architecture of a backscatter-based sensor platform. Traditional sensing platforms add a lot of computational modules between the sensor and the radio for sensor data acquisition, processing, filtering, buffering, etc. The contribution of these components to overall power consumption of an active radio-based sensor system is minimal and can largely be ignored. However, on backscatter-based platforms, these components become the bottleneck.

This raises an intriguing question — with the power consumption of backscatter being so low, would it in fact be more efficient to eliminate all of these modules en-bloc, and just connect the sensor directly to the radio? In other words, would it be better to just stream every bit of data that is sensed directly through the radio?

We take a measurement-driven approach towards answering these questions. First, we look at the computational blocks between sensing and the RF interface on existing backscatter-based sensing platforms to understand how much power they consume, as well as why they suffer in terms of throughput. Second, we build on our empirical study and design a radically new backscatter-based sensor platform that addresses these limitations.

3. INVESTIGATING EXISTING WIRELESS SENSING ARCHITECTURES

In this section, we investigate why current backscatter-based platforms are unable to achieve end-to-end power consumption of μWs for high-rate sensing and transfer. We also investigate why they are unable to achieve high-data rate communication, particularly while operating at low power. To empirically understand these factors, we look at the UMass Moo/UW WISP class platforms that are equipped with sensors, a low-power MCU (MSP 430 family) and a backscatter radio.

3.1 Poor energy efficiency

We start with a break down of the power consumed by three key computational modules on a UMass Moo (Figure 3): 1) the sensor data acquisition subsystem which handles the protocols for operating sensors, 2) the data handling subsystem on a micro-controller where sensor data is stored, processed (if needed), formatted into packet, and sent to the network stack, and 3) the network stack implemented in a combination of hardware and software.

3.1.1 Sensor data acquisition

Sensor data acquisition is a relatively simple operation — some sensors have an on-board ADC, hence data acquisition is via a protocol such as SPI or I2C, whereas other sensors just provide an analog signal which is digitized using the micro-controller's ADC. Despite its simplicity, even these operations are not as cheap as one might expect. For example, sampling an accelerometer via the SPI bus would require

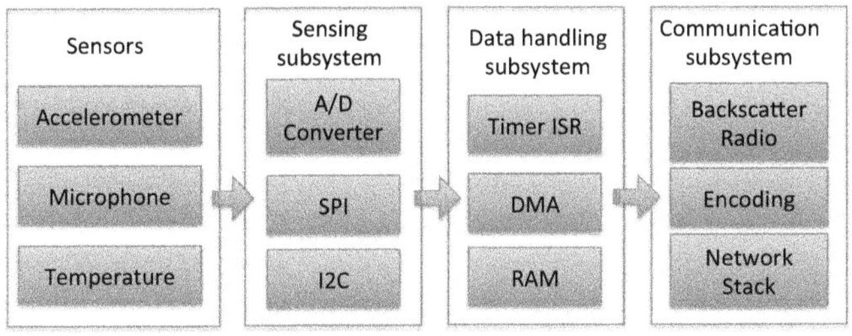

Figure 3: Computational blocks on existing backscatter-based sensors.

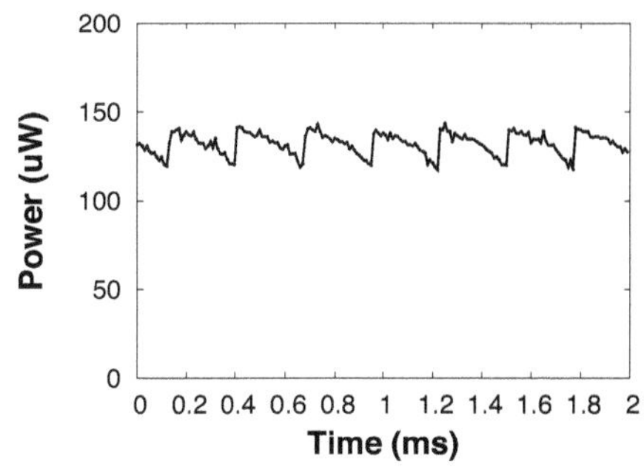

Figure 4: Power consumed for handling timer interrupts at 4kHz. The MCU is unable to switch to sleep mode due to frequent interrupts.

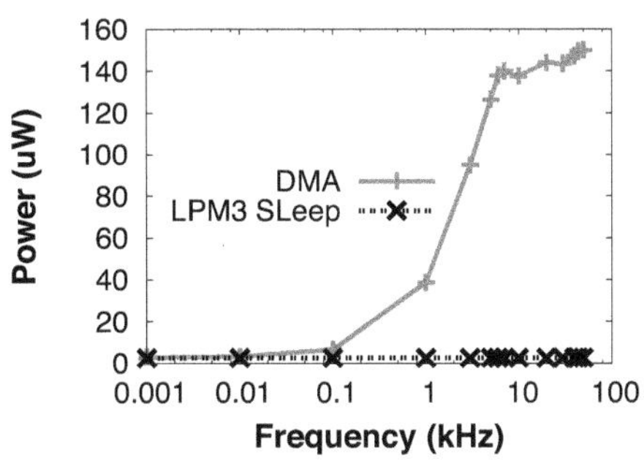

Figure 5: The power consumption of DMA transfer at different frequencies.

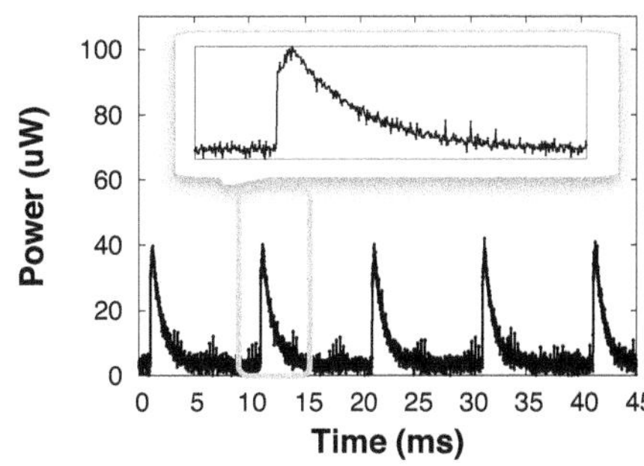

Figure 6: Power consumption of DMA transfer at 100Hz. DMA is slow to return to sleep mode.

periodic wakeup of the MCU to fill the SPI buffer, sending the read command and read address to the sensor, as well as providing the clock for the SPI bus. The overall result is that the MCU is active for about 40% of the time when acquiring data from an accelerometer sampling at 400 Hz. This acquisition operation, in itself, consumes 84μW of power, 14$\times$ higher than the accelerometer (6μW). The cost of acquiring audio data is equally high — when sampling an audio sensor (ADMP803) at 44KHz, acquisition consumes 492μW of power, 14.5$\times$ higher than the audio sensor (34μW).

3.1.2 Data handling subsystem

The data handling subsystem is the block that processes the acquired sensor data, formats and packetizes it, and sends it to the network stack. To minimize this overhead, sensor systems typically operate in a duty-cycled mode where the MCU is turned on for a minimal amount of time needed to handle the data, before switching back into sleep mode to conserve energy.

However, this optimization is no longer effective when this subsystem handles high-rate sensors. Figure 4 shows the power consumption for executing the timer interrupt service routine to handle each acquired audio sample. At high rate, the MCU is rarely able to switch completely back into the ultra-low power sleep mode due to frequent interrupts. Thus, the overall power consumption of the data handling module is roughly the ballpark of active mode power consumption of the MCU (a few mW), which is several orders of magnitude higher than the power consumed by the sensor.

One method to reduce power of the data handling subsystem is to use Direct Memory Access (DMA), which allows transfer of data from the sensor to memory without waking up the MCU. This raises the possibility that waking up the MCU can, perhaps, be avoided altogether if the data is transferred directly from the sensor to the network queue without any processing.

Surprisingly, DMA does not reduce power consumption. Figure 5 shows empirically measured power consumption for DMA transfer on an MSP 430, which moves the sensor data from a sensor to a local memory at different frequencies. We observe that while DMA is efficient at low rates (e..g below 100Hz), it has high power consumption at high transfer rates — for example, DMA transfer consumes 149.2 μW of power at 44 kHz, 60$\times$ higher than the 2.5 μW of LPM3 sleep mode of the MCU. This is surprising since one would expect that the MCU is in sleep mode while DMA operates.

The culprit for high power consumption of DMA turns out to be its tail energy consumption. Figure 6 shows the power consumption of repeated DMA transfer at 100 Hz. This experiment is done with an MSP 430 set to LPM3 sleep mode and a timer that periodically triggers DMA transfer. When a DMA transfer is initiated, its power consumption increases to 40μW within 10us, and starts decreasing once the DMA transfer is done. However, the power consumption decays at a relatively slow rate compared to the sharp increase, resulting in a long tail of roughly 3.5ms. When the DMA transfer frequency is high, such as 5kHz shown in Figure 5, the long tail leads to high power consumption. While we are not certain about the cause of this behavior, one hypothesis is that the system waits for more data before it times out and switches to a lower power mode. This behavior is common in many power savings circuits, for example, in smartphone radios [7, 17], and is typically done to amortize the cost of waking up and shutting down a hardware subsystem.

3.1.3 Communication subsystem

The final computational component of a sensor platform is the communication stack, which includes the PHY, MAC and upper layers. While the RF interface of backscatter is extremely low-power, the other layers add more overhead. For example, on the UW WISP or UMass Moo platforms, the backscatter radio is controlled by a hardware timer which needs to be configured and handled in software. In addition, the EPC Gen 2 network stack on these devices is implemented in software, and results in substantial overhead since the MCU needs to handle protocol messages. In fact, the MCU needs to be on for 67% of the time for processing network stack messages at the software layer while only 7% of the time is used for data transmission. As a consequence, the software on UMass Moo platform consumes 2mW of power, which is three orders of magnitude higher than the power consumption of a low-power sensor.

As with the data handling subsystem, the software overhead of the network stack can be reduced by using hardware peripherals to control the radio. One commonly available hardware peripheral on MCUs is the Universal Asynchronous Receiver and Transmitter (UART). This is particularly useful for a backscatter radio since UART generates an ASK signal, which can be directly transmitted via backscatter (which uses OOK). At the first glance, the UART peripheral has the potential to dramatically reduce the cost of running the network stack because it can operate when the MCU stays in deep sleep mode. However, its buffer needs to be filled with sensor data, which in turn needs to be done with either DMA or software, both of which are expensive energy-wise. As a result, even the UART-driven backscatter radio consumes roughly 2mW.

3.2 Poor transmission efficiency

The second key drawback of existing backscatter-based sensors is the abysmal throughputs that they achieve. For example, even though there have been many efforts to improve backscatter throughput, the ceiling is still less than 20kbps for a single node [13, 27, 8, 22], and drops to hundreds of bits/second in a network with multiple devices. Clearly, this is far below what is needed for streaming raw sensor data from high-rate sensors.

One factor that limits the throughput is the poor efficiency in clock utilization. For example, the UMass Moo and WISP take 48 clock ticks to send a single bit of data, which causes a 48× reduction of the maximum possible throughput that is achievable with the system clock. We find three reasons for this inefficiency. First, both transmission and reception logic is implemented in software which, naturally, is inefficient in the use of the clock. Although the transmission and reception code on the Moo and WISP platforms are optimized in assembly instructions, one bit transmission and reception still has substantial overhead. Second, EPC Gen 2 PHY-layer encoding further reduces the clock utilization efficiency. To minimize the DC components during data transmission, each bit is encoded into a sequence of pulses using Miller encoding. For example, the Miller-4 encoding

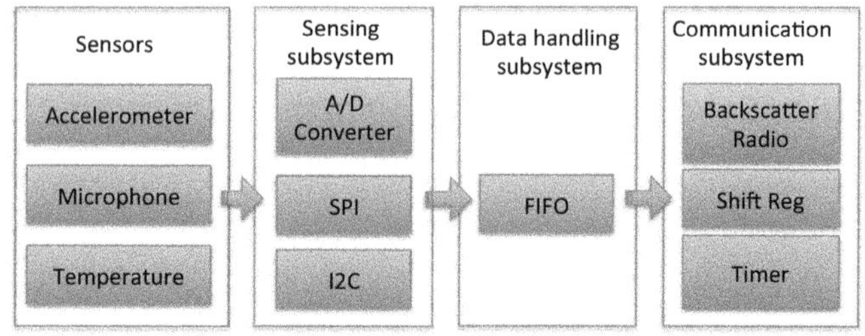

Figure 7: The key components of Ekho.

used by Moo and WISP platforms uses eight pulses to encode one bit of data, resulting in further drop of throughput by a factor of eight. Third, the EPC Gen 2 MAC layer is extremely inefficient for high bandwidth data transfer. While this is a point that has been made many times before [13, 27, 8, 22], an efficient alternative that achieves high throughput using backscatter is lacking.

3.3 Summary

Thus, the limitations of the computational blocks on existing backscatter-based sensor platforms lead us to the following observation. The primary culprit in terms of power is the MCU's active mode power consumption, and the fact that many operations (sensor acquisition, data handling, communication) require execution of instructions on the MCU. Surprisingly, optimizing the system by leveraging hardware peripherals such as DMA and UART do not solve the problem, particularly at high data rates due to tail power consumption, and coupling between different components of the sensing to communication pipeline. In terms of throughput, the primary issues stem from inefficient utilization of the clock due to a combination of software overheads, encoding overheads, and an inefficient MAC layer standard. In conjunction, these limitations call for a *clean-slate re-design of a backscatter-based sensor platform* from the ground up for extremely low power consumption and high data rates.

4. THE Ekho PLATFORM

Our solution is Ekho, a backscatter-based sensor platform that is optimized for ultra low power operation and high-speed streaming from sensors. We outline the platform architecture followed by the MAC layer.

4.1 Eliminating computational blocks

At the platform level, the design of Ekho is minimalist. We simply remove as many computational blocks between the sensor and RF analog front end as possible in favor of communicating raw data. Figure 7 shows the key components in Ekho.

Ekho reduces the overhead of data acquisition from the sensor by implementing the SPI and ADC sampling logic on a small CPLD (FPGA). Implementing these blocks in hardware means that we can make them as fast as needed without incurring the software overhead of waking up a microcontroller.

Ekho substantially reduces the overhead of handling sensor data by a minimalist approach that uses a FIFO buffer between the sensors with RF analog front end. The FIFO buffer is the minimum element that is needed between sensing subsystem and communication subsystem to deal with

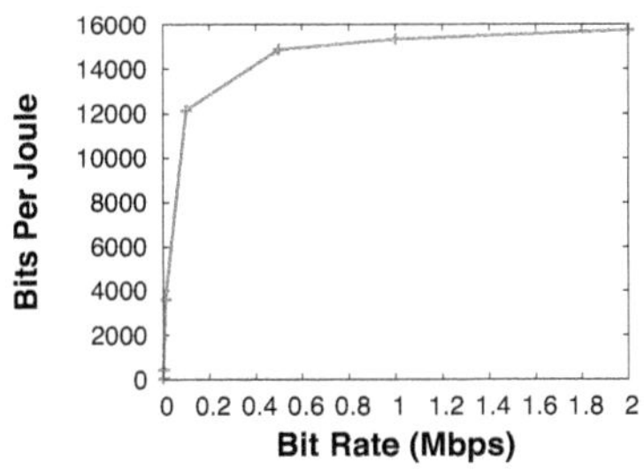

Figure 8: Efficiency of backscatter radio (in bits/joule).

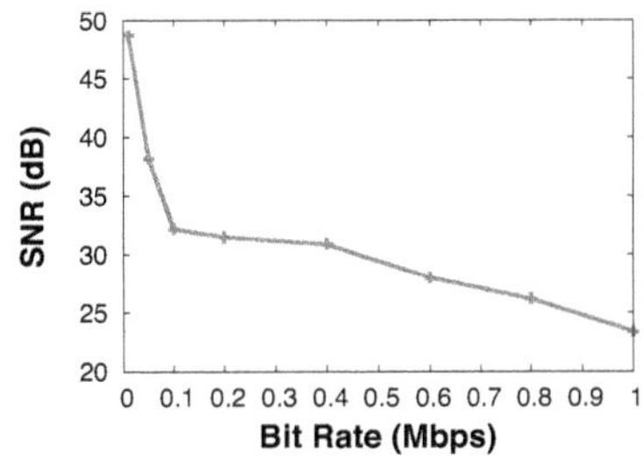

Figure 9: SNR at different bit rates when device is placed 1m from a reader.

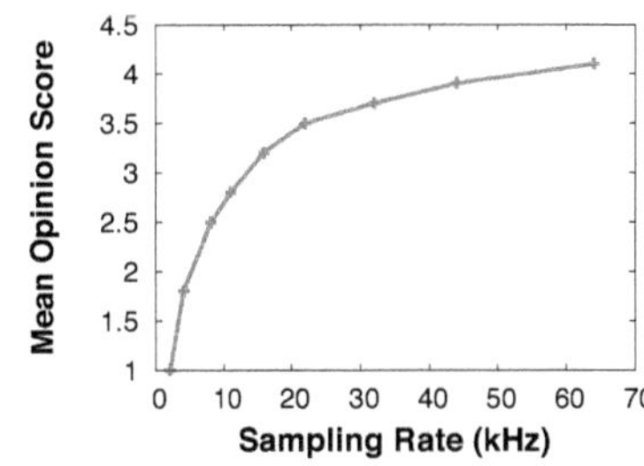

Figure 10: Mean Opinion Score (MOS) at different sampling rates for a microphone.

short delays in transmitting the data over the backscatter link, for example, due to intermittent scheduling of a device. In this manner, Ekho eliminates software and tail energy overhead that was observed on existing backscatter-based platforms.

The final computational component of the pipeline is the communication subsystem. Unlike EPC Gen 2 that is designed for a broad range of RFID tags, Ekho is designed solely for streaming sensor data from nodes to a reader. A protocol designed solely for streaming data from sensors can be quite simple. The reader informs each node of a timer value that specifies the period with which to transfer data in its FIFO buffer, and a rate that determines how fast to transfer the data. The only hardware component required for this protocol to work is a timer and shift register. Once the timer fires, a shift register converts the input sensor data to an ASK signal that is used to modulate backscatter radios.

In the current instantiation of Ekho, we do not perform any encoding of data. While the need for encoding to deal with harsh wireless conditions and interference is well-known, it also makes the hardware more complex, and consequently more power hungry. For example, the default configuration on the UMass Moo/UW WISP platforms is Miller-4 encoding incurs overhead of several hundreds of gates. Thus, while encoding may be useful in some cases, we do not employ it in Ekho.

4.2 The EkhoNet MAC layer

We now turn to the second part of our performance puzzle — achieving high throughputs that are upwards of many hundreds of kilobits/second across different nodes in the network. A high speed MAC is important for supporting an architecture where raw data transfer is the norm rather than the exception.

MAC layer designs are very well understood, particularly in cases such as ours where a central controller performs TDMA-like scheduling of sensor nodes. However, the key point in our design is two-fold: a) even though the sensor node is designed to be extremely simple, the decision making logic can be placed at the reader, thereby enabling surprisingly complex scheduling mechanisms across a network of extremely simple sensor nodes, and b) our MAC is holistic in that it takes into account utility of data, channel-awareness, energy consumption, as well as other hardware considerations, in-order to maximize throughput.

4.2.1 MAC Design Considerations

At the heart of EkhoNet is the logic that is used to determine when each node should transfer, and what rate they should transfer. Before we answer this question, we need to understand several characteristics of Ekho including: a) how do MAC-layer parameters impact the energy-efficiency of the platform? b) what are the signal-to-noise ratios at which data transmitted by Ekho can be successfully decoded? c) what criteria should we use to decide what sampling rate to use when sufficient bandwidth is not available? and d) what are the implications of platform considerations such as clock drift and buffer size? We now empirical examine these considerations in greater detail, and discuss the implications on selection of MAC layer parameters.

Bits/Joule: The first question we ask is how energy-efficiency of data transfer depends on the bit rate. Figure 8 shows the efficiency of a shift register controlled backscatter radio across different bit rates. At low rates, there is a steep increase in efficiency as bit rate increases due to the fact that constant power consumption by the system is amortized over more bits being transferred. However, improvements in efficiency diminish once the bit rate increases beyond 1Mbps since the relationship between power and frequency of the shift register is roughly linear, hence there are not much improvements possible. The power curve suggests that, from energy perspective, we should choose the fastest bit rate possible for data transmission.

Signal to Noise Ratio: While faster bit rates are preferable due to higher energy efficiency of transfer, SNR degrades as bit rate increases. Figure 9 shows the SNR when we deploy a transmitter 1 meter from the reader and change its transmission bit rate. As bit rate increases, the SNR decreases steadily as one would expect. When the SNR is lower than 10dB, decoding becomes difficult on our software-defined radio based reader platform, which gives us an upper bound on the fastest bit rate that can be supported by the system without losing bits.

Utility of data: Since EkhoNet is designed for high-rate sensors, one question that needs to be addressed is how to decide on appropriate sampling rates when the overall data rates at full sampling rates exceed capacity. On our existing system, we are limited to 1Mbps aggregate transfer rate across all nodes since the SDR-based reader is only able to support 8M samples per second due to the limitations of the realtime signal processing logic. This means that we can easily reach the SDR limit when we operate a network of sensors. For example, a network of five audio sensors sampling at 44 KHz, and transmitting raw data generates an aggregate bandwidth of 3.5Mbps, well above what can be supported by EkhoNet.

Our solution is to take into consideration the utility of data generated by the different sensor nodes. Figure 10 shows an example of one utility function, Mean Opinion Score (MOS), which is a commonly used metric for characterizing the quality of transmitted audio [5]. The MOS score can be used to guide decisions regarding which node is allocated bandwidth.

Clock drift: Another consideration in determining slot sizes is clock drift. For example, in our implementation of Ekho, we use a crystal oscillator driven system clock that can drift at upwards of 50 ppm. If two nodes transferred at 1 Mbps, then they would drift by 1200 clock cycles each minute. The reader can handle clock drift in two ways. First, when assigning slots, it can allocate guard bands in each slot to allow for some drift. However, guard bands should be kept to a minimum to reduce bandwidth wastage. Second, the reader has the luxury of observing how the gap between slots varies as nodes transfer, and can detect when collision occurs by looking at the constellation plot of the signal [22]. Thus, when the reader suspects that slots have bled into each other, it can send a reset pulse that informs all nodes to reset their timers. Note that this is possible for backscatter because reader messages are broadcast and received by all nodes. A reset pulse is simply implemented by shutting off the carrier for a short, pre-defined duration, which is detected by each node. While reset pulses can be short, it should be used infrequently since there can be robustness issues if a node does not receive the pulse. This can result in further collisions resulting in more reset pulses until the network synchronizes.

Buffer size: One additional constraint introduced by the Ekho hardware platform is that the FIFO buffer size on the device is limited, hence if the slot sizes are too long, samples will be lost since the buffer will overflow.

4.2.2 Channel-Utility-Energy aware Rate Selection

Given the above constraints, the overall problem that the reader faces can be described as follows: select the optimal bit rate and slot size such that aggregate utility of received data is maximized and aggregate energy consumption minimized, subject to constraints on the buffer sizes, SNR, and guard bands. We formalize this problem below.

We assume that the following parameters are given:

- The minimum SNR, 10 dB in our system, at which the reader can decode bits with low bit-error rate.
- The maximum achievable bit-rate r_i that is higher than the minimum SNR.
- The maximum sampling rate of each node $s_{max}(i)$.
- The size of each sample in bits, b, bits/sample.
- The fraction of each slot that should be a guard band δ.

Given these values, we need to choose the sampling rates for each sensor s_i, and the fraction of time allocated to each node t_i by taking into account the following objective:

- $\sum_{i=1}^{n} U(\mathbf{s})$ which is a measure of the aggregate utility obtained from all sensor data received from the nodes.

The constraints are the following:

- $\sum_i t_i \leq 1$, i.e the fraction of time allotted to nodes sum up to at most one (less than one if the network is operating below its limit).
- $s_i \leq s_{max}(i)$, which restricts the sampling rate for a sensor to be below the maximum.
- $(1-\delta)t_i r_i = b\, s_i$, which ensures that the production of data from the sensor, and transmission of data from the radio are matched i.e. the node can transmit what is being sensed. The term $(1-\delta)$ is present since there's a guard band for each slot.

The overall optimization is shown below (in vector form for compactness). Here, $\mathbf{s}$ and $\mathbf{t}$ are the vectors of sampling rates and the fraction of time allocated to each node, which need to be determined, and $\mathbf{r}$ is the vector of bit rates chosen for each node based on SNR. The symbol $\preceq$ stands for element-wise inequality (i.e. one for each node).

$$\begin{aligned} \underset{\mathbf{s},\mathbf{t}}{\text{maximize}} \quad & \mathbf{1}^{\mathbf{T}} U(\mathbf{s}) \\ \text{subject to} \quad & \mathbf{t}^{\mathbf{T}}\mathbf{1} \leq 1 \\ & \mathbf{s} \preceq s_{max}\mathbf{1} \\ & (1-\delta)\text{diag}(\mathbf{t})\mathbf{r} = b\,\mathbf{s} \end{aligned}$$

Typically, the utility function is concave, for example in the case of MOS score (Figure 10). Hence, the objective is to maximize the sum of concave utility functions, and the constraints are linear, hence the optimization can be solved by standard convex optimization methods. Note that the optimization returns the fraction of time for each node — this can be converted to an actual slot size by scaling by an appropriate period such that each node is capable of buffering the data in its local FIFO buffer.

5. IMPLEMENTATION

Figure 11 shows the prototype of Ekho, which implements all the design elements described in section 4. The current prototype measures 1.8 by 2.4 inches, but we believe future revisions can shrink this even further. We now briefly describe the key sub-components used in the prototype.

5.1 Hardware

The first key hardware element is an ultra low power FPGA (Igloo Nano AGLN250) that manages the various sub-components of the Ekho platform. Most key components of the Ekho architecture, including the sensing, data handling, and communication subsystems, are implemented within the FPGA. The particular FPGA was chosen because it has low static current consumption and has a 32k bits (2KB) RAM, which also determines the maximum size of our FIFO buffer.

The next key design element is the backscatter circuit that can operate at high speed. As the device toggles the state of a transistor that connects to the antenna, an OOK signal that carries modulated information is generated. However, on existing backscatter platforms, the static current of the transistor is provided by the harvested RF energy, which might vary across time. The varying RF power affects the amount current that is provided to the transistor and leads to unstable edges of the generated OOK signal. Therefore, decoding becomes challenging when the data rate is high.

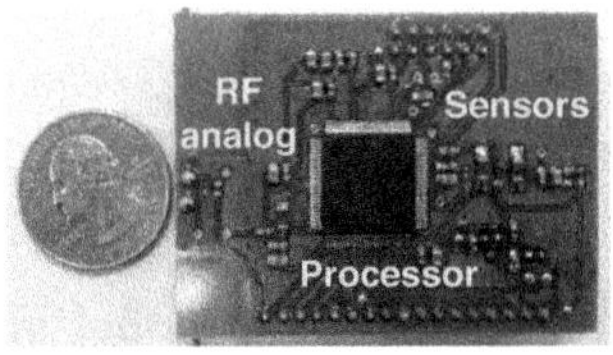

Figure 11: Ekho is implemented as a low-profile printed circuit board with small form factor.

Our backscatter circuit directly provide a small bias current to the transistor and retains a sharp edge for the generated OOK signal.

A critical element of our hardware design is the clock system which drives the FPGA logic. The core of our clock system is a 1MHz ultra low power crystal oscillator that directly feeds into the FPGA. The 1MHz clock is divided to drive different components of the architecture because sensing, data handling, and communication subsystems operate at different speeds. Our clock system is different from the Moo and WISP platforms, where a digital generated clock (DCO) is used. Although the DCO can also be divided for driving different components, it couples the operational modes of the system and its clock speed, as a result of which the high speed clock is only available when the system operates as a whole in a high power mode.

5.2 Software defined backscatter reader

We used the USRP N210 mother board and the SBX RF daughterboard to build our software defined backscatter reader for receiving high speed backscatter signals from Ekho. We construct a signal processing pipeline that is able to track the amplitude of the carrier wave that is used as the reference for decoding the OOK signal generated by Ekho. Our decoding is different from Moo and WISP platforms where Miller-4 encoding is used on top of the OOK signal and a decoding template can be used for correlating the received signal and output a bit when the template matches the received signal. In Ekho, the data is sent directly via OOK and encoding is not used. Therefore, we need to track the amplitude of carrier wave to determine whether the received signal is a high or low pulse.

5.3 MAC layer protocol

Figure 12 shows the timing diagram of the Ekho MAC layer. The first stage is to inventory the nodes in the network, and obtain information about their SNR and other sensor-related information. This phase executes very similar to an EPC Gen 2 singulation phase, where nodes can select a slot to transfer in, and send a short sequence of bits with the appropriate information. After the singulation phase, the reader executes the optimization algorithm described in §4 and determines the time period and bit rate for each sensor, which is then relayed to the sensor. The reader initiates the singulation phase under several circumstances: a) when significant changes are observed in SNR, which might signify changes in position or orientation, and b) when collisions are detected, which might signify that a new node is attempting to join the network.

Once the reader informs each sensor of its bit rate and period, it initializes slots by sending a synchronization signal during which it shuts down the carrier for a short 10 μs

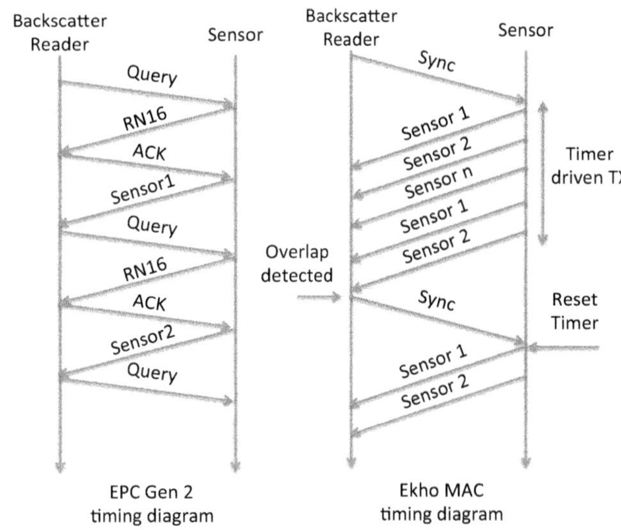

Figure 12: Timeline of Ekho MAC.

window. This pulse informs all nodes simultaneously that they should start their timers, thereby initiating the TDMA schedule. The length of the sync message needs to be chosen small enough to amortize overhead, but large enough to be detectable at the sensor, hence our choice of 10μs.

When the reader detects that data transmitted during adjacent slots are overlapping into each other (due to clock drift), it re-issues a synchronization pulse to restart the timers on all nodes. Overlap between sensors can be detected by looking at the constellation map of the received signal — if two clusters are present, it indicates that a collision-free signal is received and if more clusters are present, it indicates that a collided signal is observed [22]. If multiple synchronization pulses fail to eliminate collisions, the reader switches back into inventory mode.

6. EVALUATION

We now evaluate the overall performance of EkhoNet including 1) demonstrating the power benefit of the Ekho architecture, 2) benchmarking the performance of the EkhoNet MAC, and 3) evaluating EkhoNet's ability to support high-rate streams from many sensors while operating at extremely low power consumption.

6.1 Experimental setup

We deploy 10 Ekho nodes 1 feet to 9 feet from a backscatter reader. Our experiments do not cover distances larger than 9 feet because of the poor signal quality beyond 9 feet. This is a result of the 100mW maximum power issued by the SBX RF daughterboard, which is 10× smaller than commercial RFID readers.

To understand the power benefits of Ekho, we compare against the UMass Moo (equivalent of Intel WISP 4.0) and the WISP5.0 platforms. Since the WISP5.0 platform is not currently available, we evaluate its power consumption with a prototype that uses the same MCU (MSP430FR5969). Since the MCU is the main power hog in the system, this provides a good proxy for measuring power consumption.

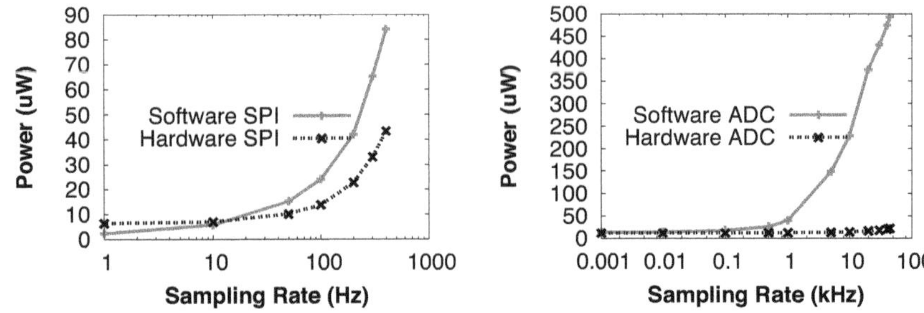

(a) Accelerometer.

(b) Microphone.

Figure 13: Power reduction for sensing subsystem: a) sampling an accelerometer, b) sampling a microphone.

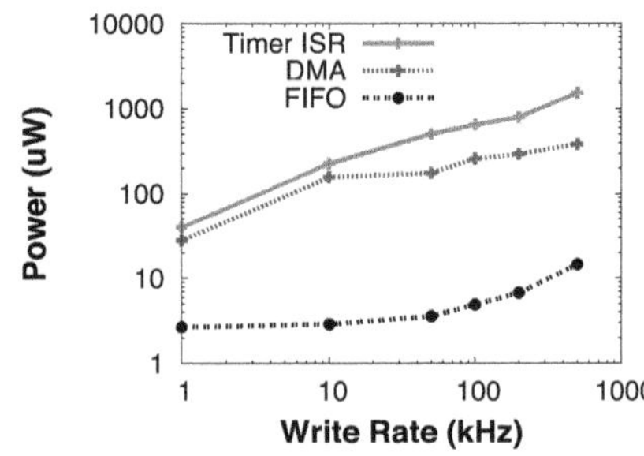

Figure 14: Power reduction for data transfer to network queue.

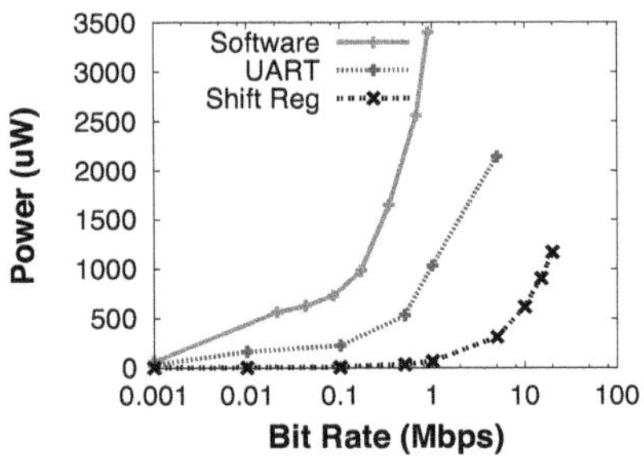

Figure 15: The power consumption of operating a backscatter radio.

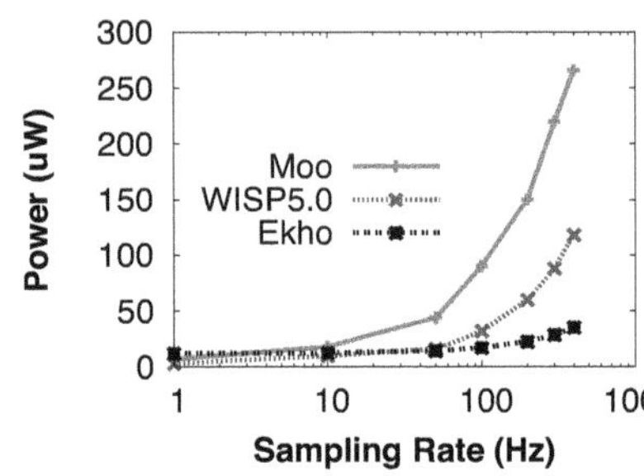

Figure 16: Whole-system power consumption for operating an accelerometer sensor.

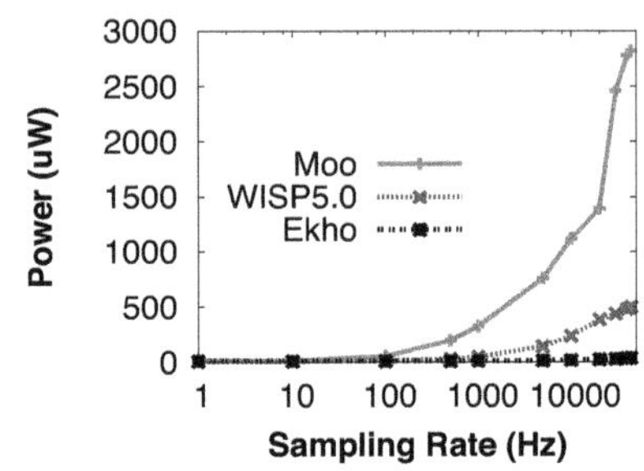

Figure 17: Whole-system power consumption for operating an audio sensor.

6.2 Ekho power benchmarks

We begin our evaluation by validating the claim that the power optimizations on Ekho can substantially reduce the overheads incurred by existing platforms. We follow the organization in §4, and show benchmarks for each module — sensor data acquisition, sensor data handling, and network stack.

Figure 13 measure the power of the sensing subsystem when Ekho interacts with two types of sensors — an accelerometer with on-board ADC that connects to the MCU via a SPI interface, and an audio sensor where the MCU's ADC is used to sample the sensor. We compare Ekho versus a WISP/Mote-class sensor device (i.e. a device where the sensor connects to an MCU that acquires data). In both cases, we can see that Ekho reduces power consumption substantially — for sampling the accelerometer, Ekho reduces power by 1.5× at 400Hz by eliminating the overhead of software-controlled SPI, and for sampling the audio sensor, Ekho reduces power by 22× by trimming the overhead of running the software-controlled ADC at 44kHz.

Figure 14 measures the power consumption of the data handling subsystem of Ekho, which is composed by a 2kB FIFO buffer for connecting sensors to the RF analog front end. The 2kB FIFO buffer only consumes 26.5μW of power when data is written into the FIFO at 500kHz, 14.4× lower than the 384μW consumed by DMA driven data migration and 92× lower than the 1.5mW consumed by timer driven data migration.

Figure 15 shows the power consumption of the communication subsystem which is composed of a shift register and backscatter radio. At 1Mbps, Ekho's communication subsystem consumes only 77μW of power, 13.4× lower than a UART controlled backscatter radio implemented on the WISP and 44× lower than a software controlled backscatter radio implemented on the WISP. For software and UART controlled backscatter radios, we do not measure power at bit rates higher than 6Mbps because the maximum clock on rate on WISP platform is 24MHz, which limits the maximum achievable bit rate.

6.3 Whole-system power consumption

Having looked at power benchmarks for individual components of Ekho, we turn to a whole-system power measurement from sensing to transmission. We look at the overall power consumed by Ekho when operating the same two sensors as earlier — accelerometer and microphone.

We start with a measurement of Ekho with an accelerometer. The sensor has a built-in ADC and talks via SPI to the sensor platform. Figure 16 shows that at 1Hz, the power consumption of Ekho is higher than Moo and WISP5.0 platforms. This is because the static current consumption of the FPGA at the core of Ekho is 8.9μA, much higher than the 0.1μA static current draw of Moo and WISP5.0. However, when the frequency of operating the accelerometer increases, the power consumed by Moo and WISP5.0 platforms increases significantly while the Ekho system still consumes only tens of μW. At 400Hz, the Ekho system consumes 35μW of power, 7.6× lower than the 266μW of Moo and 3.3× lower than the 118μW of WISP5.0.

We now turn to power measurements when Ekho is connected to a microphone. An external ADC is used to sample the audio sensor, and send a digital signal to the core plat-

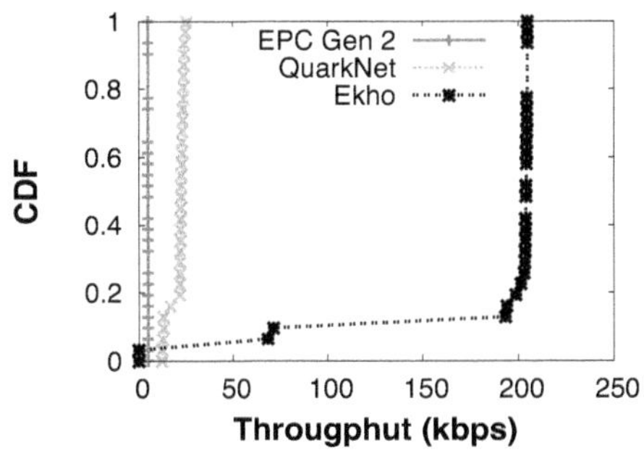

Figure 18: Comparing throughputs of EPC Gen 2, QuarkNet on Moo vs Ekho across 30 locations.

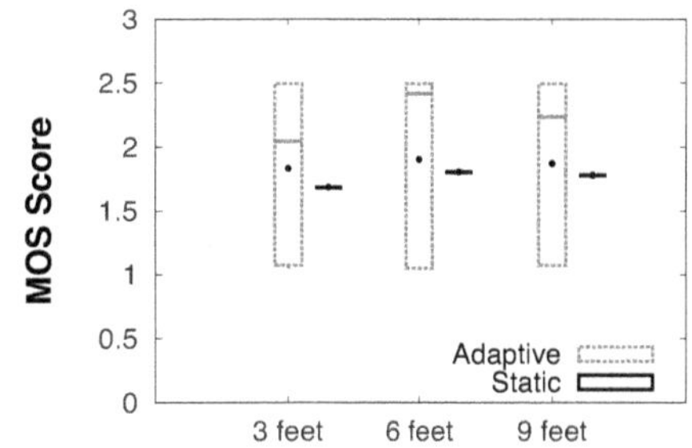

Figure 19: Boxplot of the MOS scores for 10 Ekho nodes with microphones at 3 locations (3 ft, 6 ft, 9 ft).

form (Moo, WISP5.0, or Ekho). Figure 17 shows the power consumption of the three platforms. At 44kHz, the Ekho system only consumes 37μW of power, 76$\times$ lower than the Moo and 13.5$\times$ lower than the WISP5.0.

In conclusion, Ekho is particularly efficient when using higher rate sensors that sample at frequencies of hundreds of Hz. A crucial observation is that even when the sensing rate increases by two orders of magnitude from the accelerometer at 400Hz to the microphone at 44kHz, the overall power consumption remains almost the same. This shows that Ekho scales up very well as sampling rate increases. In addition, Ekho is able to operate with sensors that use SPI or provide an analog signal while retaining high efficiency.

6.4 Evaluating EkhoNet's throughput

Having discussed the power benefits of Ekho, we now turn to look at the performance of Ekho's transfer rate.

We start with the throughput achieved by a single node. Since the Moo and WISP platforms currently support only a 256Kbps baud rate, we fix Ekho's clock to operate at the same rate. We then compare Ekho's throughput against the Moo executing EPC Gen 2 [24], and QuarkNet [25]. Figure 18 shows the cumulative throughput across 30 locations. The 30 locations are chosen randomly between 1 feet to 9 feet from a backscatter reader.

There are two key observations. First, we see that the throughput achieved by Ekho is 45$\times$ higher than Gen 2 and 8$\times$ higher than QuarkNet on the Moo. EPC Gen 2 suffers greatly due to protocol overhead, and therefore achieves abysmal overall throughput. Although QuarkNet is a highly optimized system that is designed for micro powered sensors, its throughput is limited by the fact that the PHY layer (encoding, etc) is implemented in software on Moo, which reduces throughput. Second, we see that there are a few locations where our design decision to eschew encoding hurts us. At those locations, the received signal can still be decoded by EPC Gen 2 and QuarkNet because of the SNR benefit of Miller-4 encoding. However, it can be seen that this is a small fraction of the overall range of the reader. (Note that if encoding is essential, it is possible to add this module to Ekho at the cost of some additional power consumption and reduced throughput.)

We now turn to the throughput achieved by a network of nodes, and evaluate the benefits of our energy and utility function aware bit rate selection algorithm. We deploy 10 Ekho nodes with microphones at three locations (3 feet, 6 feet, and 9 feet from a backscatter reader). The maximum sampling rate of each audio sensor is 44kHz and each sample data is 16 bits. As a result, an audio sensor can generate up to 706k bits data per second. In contrast, the overall network transmission capacity of EkhoNet is 1Mbps in our current instantiation since each device is equipped with a 1Mbps clock. Thus, 10 audio sensors in front a backscatter reader can saturate the 1Mbps network easily, which means that adapting the bit rate as well as the sampling rate of each sensor is necessary.

When channel is saturated, the selection of bit rate is intuitive because maximum bit rate which meets the lowest SNR decoding threshold (10dB) should be used. The selection of sampling rate follows the energy-utility joint optimization we formulated in §4.

Figure 19 shows the MOS score obtained by 10 audio sensors at 3 locations. Our optimization framework attempts to allocate bandwidth such that sensors with higher SNR can get the bandwidth they need for achieving higher MOS scores. As a baseline, we compare against a scheme that allocates bandwidth equally across all sensors. The median and mean MOS scores achieved by EkhoNet is higher than the baseline scheme — 50% of the nodes have MOS scores higher than two, which is acceptable audio quality, whereas the uniform allocation scheme has MOS scores of about 1.7, which means poor audio quality. A breakdown across nodes shows that our algorithm assigns higher sampling rate to sensor 1 to 5 because they have higher SNR. While other application-specific utility functions are possible, these results demonstrate that despite the simplicity of Ekho platforms, the EkhoNet MAC can be more complex and optimize network-wide throughput, energy and utility.

7. RELATED WORK

Backscatter communication: There has been much recent emphasis on backscatter communication. Some efforts have explored bandwidth limitations of backscatter communication in terms of throughput including Flit [13], Buzz [22], and Blink [27]. While there are interesting ideas underlying each of these, the overall throughput achieved by EkhoNet is orders of magnitude higher than the above systems as a result of a clean-slate design. Other efforts have focused on using harvested power in an efficient manner including QuarkNet [25][26] and Dewdrop [8] — these approaches are complementary to EkhoNet and can be used in conjunction with the ideas in this paper.

In addition to the above, there have been many interesting ideas on using backscatter for real-world applications. Ambient Backscatter [20] uses the backscatter of FM signals for short-range communication between tags to enable credit-card transactions. AllSee [18] explores the backscattered signal for gesture recognition. These ideas can potentially benefit from an Ekho-like platform that is designed to reduce power consumption while increasing bandwidth.

Much literature has explored the design of MAC layer protocols for RFIDs, and several of these approaches specifically address data collection from RFID-scale sensors [9, 13, 22, 25]. Viewed in isolation, our MAC layer protocol is simplistic since its merely a stripped down version of TDMA, hence it relates to most of the above protocols. However, our work should be viewed not just as a MAC layer, but a system-wide re-design to strip computational overhead from backscatter-based sensors, and thereby achieve higher efficiency.

Optimized sensing platforms: There have been many highly optimized sensor hardware designs proposed over the past decade. At a high level, these can be separated into two classes — optimized hardware platforms designed for specific applications, and optimized hardware platforms that are intended as a building block for research and applications. One example in the former class is the NeuralWISP [16], a wireless neural interface that operates on harvested RF energy. Some examples in the latter class are the Michigan M^3 [19], an impressive mm^3 sensor that operates at low power, and the Epic Mote [11], which is a modular mote-class platform for enabling low-power wireless sensor network applications.

EkhoNet differs from these efforts in that it is designed for raw data transfer from high-rate sensors at extremely low power levels. Thus, it is a general-purpose platform for sensors similar to the second class of devices, but focused on backscatter and high-rate sensors. As a result, the underlying design principles and optimizations are completely different from those that drive the other class of platforms.

8. DISCUSSION

While Ekho provides substantial performance benefits over the state-of-art in backscatter-based sensor platforms, there are several questions that we have not completely addressed in our evaluation. We discuss these in this section.

FPGA v.s. MCU: One of the design choices in Ekho is the use of an FPGA rather than MCU — this choice greatly reduces the computational and data migration overheads between the sensor and radio, but in the process, it sacrifices ease of programmability. While FPGA programming has become easier in recent years due to improved IDEs and GUI interfaces [4], it requires familiarity with logic design at the circuits level. MCUs, on the other hand, are much more natural to program using commonly used high-level languages such as C, which is one of the reasons for its wide use on sensor platforms.

We believe that the greater difficulty in programming FPGAs is not as much of an issue for Ekho as for other platforms. Wireless sensors are designed to be intelligent, autonomous nodes that can adapt to dynamics in energy levels, channel conditions, routing changes, and others. In contrast, Ekho is designed to be a "dumb" peripheral for a powerful reader that simply forwards the raw sensor data over a backscatter link. Much of the decision-making logic that is traditionally implemented on the sensor side are performed at the reader. Thus, Ekho can be viewed as just another sensor, with an interface that allows the reader to set sampling rates and bit rates (as shown in §4).

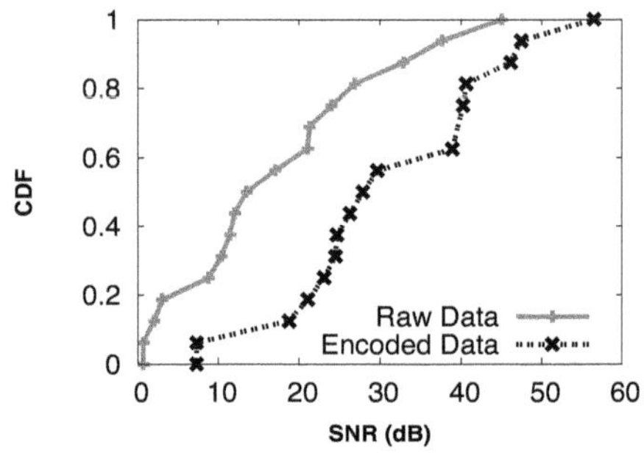

Figure 20: SNR of transmitting encoded data and raw data across 20 locations.

Power benefits: The results presented in this paper compare Ekho against existing backscatter-based sensing platforms such as the WISP, but one question is whether we would have significant power benefits if we compared against an FPGA implementation of the WISP. Our evaluation did not address this question since re-implementing the entire sensing, computation, and communication pipeline of the WISP on an FPGA is a substantial effort, but we provide a qualitative comparison.

Existing research work [21] on RFIDs suggests that an EPC Gen 2 tag implemented on FPGA usually consumes 5K to 10K logic gates. Clearly, an EPC Gen 2 tag does not perform any operation related to sensing. Therefore, sensor sampling, data migration, buffering, and other tasks would incur additional overhead. For example, Touhafi and Glesner et al [10, 15] investigate an FPGA (Spartan3-2000) based sensing platform which consumes 1200K gates, several orders of magnitude higher than an EPC Gen 2 tag. Our Ekho implementation consumes only 6K gates, which is comparable to an EPC Gen 2 tag and significantly less than what we would expect with an FPGA version of the WISP. Since the power consumption of an FPGA depends on the number of gates used, Ekho should still be significantly more efficient.

Encoding: Another design decision that needs more discussion is that Ekho eschews encoding in an effort to be minimalist. Unsurprisingly, this can be problematic in scenarios where the wireless channel is noisy. Figure 20 shows a simple experiment where we place a tag at 20 locations between 1–9 ft in front of a reader, and look at the SNR with EPC Gen 2's Miller-4 encoding, and without encoding. The decoding threshold for our backscatter reader is 10dBm, so any signal lower than this threshold cannot be decoded correctly. As expected, there is about a 10dB difference between encoded and uncoded signal. The SNR is higher than 10dB in 80% of the locations for uncoded data, and higher than 10dB in about 90% of the locations after encoding. This comes at a high cost, however, since the node consumes 8× more power for achieving the same bit rate.

Thus, our point is simply that encoding is yet another computation block on a backscatter-based sensor platform. While the power consumption of techniques like encoding are insignificant in most radios, the pros and cons deserve to be examined more carefully for ultra-low power platforms such as Ekho.

Applications: Finally, this paper does not focus on applications of Ekho, but we view our work as an enabler for a variety of applications. While the idea of backscatter-based sensing is not new [23], many existing efforts are about networking simple, low rate sensors (e.g. temperature, pressure, etc). But the need for backscatter in such scenarios is debatable — active-radio based wireless sensors operate for years on coin cells at low sensing and communication rates. But rich sensors such as microphones and cameras operate primarily in a tethered manner since data rates are far too high for continuous communication. Our work seeks to bridge the gap, and enable camera networks or microphone networks to stream data continuously in an untethered manner. The benefits of streaming raw sensor data to internet-connected infrastructure is immense since one can use vast amount of computational resources to jointly process the data streams and enable smart applications. A simple example would be continuous speaker recognition and transcription of meeting notes by deploying a tethered reader and dozens of untethered Ekho nodes at different locations in a conference room.

9. CONCLUSION

In this paper, we present a powerful backscatter wireless sensing architecture, Ekho, that can sample sensors at tens of kHz and transmit data wirelessly at several hundreds of kbps, while only consuming tens of μWatts of power. The key observation in Ekho is that backscatter wireless communication is energy-wise much cheaper than computation. Therefore, by eliminating the overheads of sensing subsystem, data handling subsystem, and communication subsystems, we enable the whole sensing-communication pipeline to operate at extremely low power. Over the Ekho platform, we design a MAC layer that allocates bit-rates across nodes while taking into account energy-efficiency, utility of data, and a variety of platform-level considerations. We believe that EkhoNet can enable new explorations in backscatter-based sensing systems, and enable new applications that use ultra-low power high-rate sensors.

Acknowledgements

We thank the anonymous reviewers for their insightful comments. This research was partially funded by NSF grants CNS-1218586, CNS-1217606, and CNS-1239341.

10. REFERENCES

[1] Analog devices adxl362 accelerometer sensor. http://www.analog.com/static/imported-files/data_sheets/ADXL362.pdf.

[2] Analog devices mems microphone admp803. http://www.analog.com/static/imported-files/data_sheets/ADMP803.pdf.

[3] The cbvs ecg-on-chip. http://www.clearbridgevitalsigns.com/chip.html.

[4] Libero ide. http://www.microsemi.com/products/fpga-soc/design-resources/design-software/libero-ide.

[5] Mean opinion score. http://en.wikipedia.org/wiki/Mean_opinion_score.

[6] WISP: Wireless Identification and Sensing Platform. http://seattle.intel-research.net/wisp/.

[7] N. Balasubramanian, A. Balasubramanian, and A. Venkataramani. Energy consumption in mobile phones: a measurement study and implications for network applications. In *ACM SIGCOMM IMC 2009.*

[8] M. Buettner, B. Greenstein, and D. Wetherall. Dewdrop: an energy-aware runtime for computational rfid. In *USENIX NSDI 2011.*

[9] M. Buettner and D. Wetherall. A software radio-based uhf rfid reader for phy/mac experimentation. In *RFID (RFID), 2011 IEEE International Conference on*, pages 134–141. IEEE, 2011.

[10] A. De la Piedra, A. Braeken, and A. Touhafi. Sensor systems based on fpgas and their applications: a survey. *Sensors*, 12(9):12235–12264, 2012.

[11] P. Dutta and D. Culler. Epic: An open mote platform for application-driven design. In *IEEE IPSN 2008.*

[12] J. Gummeson, S. S. Clark, K. Fu, and D. Ganesan. On the limits of effective hybrid micro-energy harvesting on mobile crfid sensors. In *ACM MobiSys 2010.*

[13] J. Gummeson, P. Zhang, and D. Ganesan. Flit: a bulk transmission protocol for rfid-scale sensors. In *ACM MobiSys 2012.*

[14] S. Hanson, Z. Foo, D. Blaauw, and D. Sylvester. A 0.5 v sub-microwatt cmos image sensor with pulse-width modulation read-out. In *JSSCC 2010.*

[15] H. Hinkelmann, A. Reinhardt, S. Varyani, and M. Glesner. A reconfigurable prototyping platform for smart sensor networks. In *Programmable Logic, 2008 4th Southern Conference on*, pages 125–130. IEEE, 2008.

[16] J. Holleman, D. Yeager, R. Prasad, J. R. Smith, and B. Otis. Neuralwisp: An energy-harvesting wireless neural interface with 1-m range. In *BioCAS'08*, pages 37–40. IEEE, 2008.

[17] J. Huang, F. Qian, A. Gerber, Z. M. Mao, S. Sen, and O. Spatscheck. A close examination of performance and power characteristics of 4g lte networks. In *ACM MobiSys 2012.*

[18] B. Kellogg, V. Talla, and S. Gollakota. Bringing gesture recognition to all devices. In *USENIX NSDI 2014.*

[19] Y. Lee, G. Kim, S. Bang, Y. Kim, I. Lee, P. Dutta, D. Sylvester, and D. Blaauw. A modular $1mm^3$ die-stacked sensing platform with optical communication and multi-modal energy harvesting. In *ISSCC 2012.*

[20] V. Liu, A. Parks, V. Talla, S. Gollakota, D. Wetherall, and J. R. Smith. Ambient backscatter: wireless communication out of thin air. In *ACM SIGCOMM 2013.*

[21] P. Peris-Lopez, J. C. Hernandez-Castro, J. M. Estevez-Tapiador, and A. Ribagorda. LamedÑa prng for epc class-1 generation-2 rfid specification. *Computer Standards & Interfaces*, 31(1):88–97, 2009.

[22] J. Wang, H. Hassanieh, D. Katabi, and P. Indyk. Efficient and reliable low-power backscatter networks. In *ACM SIGCOMM 2012.*

[23] D. J. Yeager, P. S. Powledge, R. Prasad, D. Wetherall, and J. R. Smith. Wirelessly-charged uhf tags for sensor data collection. In *RFID, 2008 IEEE International Conference on*, pages 320–327. IEEE, 2008.

[24] H. Zhang, J. Gummeson, B. Ransford, and K. Fu. Moo: A batteryless computational rfid and sensing platform. Technical report, Tech. Rep. UM-CS-2011-020, 2011.

[25] P. Zhang and D. Ganesan. Enabling bit-by-bit backscatter communication in severe energy harvesting environments. In *NSDI 2014.*

[26] P. Zhang, D. Ganesan, and B. Lu. Quarkos: Pushing the operating limits of micro-powered sensors. In *Proceedings of the 14th USENIX conference on Hot Topics in Operating Systems*, pages 7–7. USENIX Association, 2013.

[27] P. Zhang, J. Gummeson, and D. Ganesan. Blink: a high throughput link layer for backscatter communication. In *ACM MobiSys 2012.*

A Case for Enhancing Dual Radio Repeater Performance Through Striping, Aggregation, and Channel Sharing*

Sayandeep Sen
IBM Research, India
sayandes@in.ibm.com

Michael Griepentrog
Cisco Meraki, USA
mgriepen@cisco.com

Jongwon Yoon
Univ. of Wisconsin-Madison, USA
yoonj@cs.wisc.edu

Suman Banerjee
Univ. of Wisconsin-Madison, USA
suman@cs.wisc.edu

ABSTRACT

The work in this paper is a systematic research and engineering effort in exploring the design space of multi-interface wireless repeater systems. We present the design, implementation and evaluation of a wireless repeater system, *Multifacet*, which opportunistically utilizes multiple interfaces to enhance capacity. The system is designed to be transparent to application endpoints and does not need any end application modifications for adoption. *Multifacet* incorporates several techniques to achieve efficient bandwidth utilization across multiple interfaces – (a) coordinated channel sharing, (b) a simplified backpressure based striping technique, (c) a single link abstraction, and (d) the ability to seamlessly migrate a client to the optimal channel. *Multifacet* is implemented on off-the-shelf dual band wireless repeater and demonstrates high speeds (337 Mbps) operation. On average, *Multifacet* performs 50% better than traditional AP/repeater setups, and in the best case, more than 2× better.

Categories and Subject Descriptors

C.2.1 [**Computer Communication Networks**]: Network Architecture and Design – Wireless Communication

Keywords

Wireless repeater; Dual radio AP; Implementation

1. INTRODUCTION

There is a growing demand for high bandwidth wireless delivery mechanisms in varied home settings. For example, cable and satellite providers offer products which stream content from their *single* set-top box to multiple TVs customer's home over wireless. The gaming vendors are selling hardware with the ability to stream games from gamer's desktops to their living room (Steam Big Picture, NVIDIA Project SHIELD). To meet the increased demands for higher bandwidth, wireless equipment vendors and research community are continually striving to come up with new standards (802.11n, 802.11ac/ad etc.), which promise throughput in ranging from hundreds of Mbps to a few Gbps. Unfortunately, the predominantly harsh operating environment with high interference and sometimes non line-of-sight to the client implies that newer solutions that increase the raw data rates do not always deliver commensurate increase in client throughput.

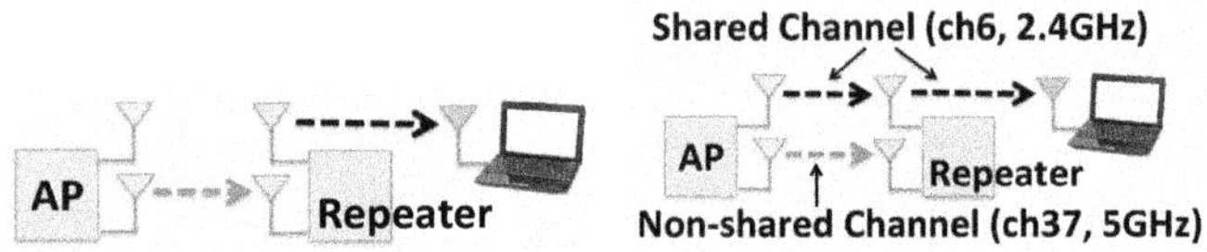

(a) Traditional repeater (b) *Multifacet* repeater

Figure 1: Logical architecture of repeater.

Wireless range extenders, also referred to as repeaters [1,2,4,6], are the de facto solution to improve the performance of clients which experience bad connectivity from the Access Point (AP) either due to large distance of separation or excessive interference on the wireless channels and when bringing the AP close to the client or vice versa is not possible. A repeater enhances performance by dividing a single poor quality path into two improved segments by rebroadcasting signals from a given AP to devices that would normally be out of the AP's range or is not able to achieve a given user's performance constraints. Figure 1(a) shows the most flexible and sophisticated repeater system which features two wireless interfaces. Evidently this mode of operation achieves higher throughputs than a far away client directly attempting to connect to the AP. The dual-interface repeater serves the client through one of the radios (say, operating in the 2.4 GHz band) and the repeater, in turn, connects to the AP through its other radio (operating in the 5 GHz band). In fact dual-interface repeaters, together with dual-interface APs provide the maximum performance in terms of range, throughput, and overall experience, according to the vendors.

In this paper, we show that in certain settings dual-interface AP and repeater systems can deliver even higher throughput to their clients by making software-only modifications. The insight is to opportunistically utilize both the radios of the AP to send data to the repeater as shown in Figure 1(b). We design and implement *Multifacet* (or Multi interface Transport) based on the above insight to enhance client performance. As AP-repeater link shares the channel with repeater-client link, *Multifacet* can provide gains

*S. Sen and M. Griepentrog were graduate students at the University of Wisconsin-Madison during the course of this work.

MobiCom'14, September 7-11, 2014, Maui, Hawaii, USA.

http://dx.doi.org/10.1145/2639108.2639133.

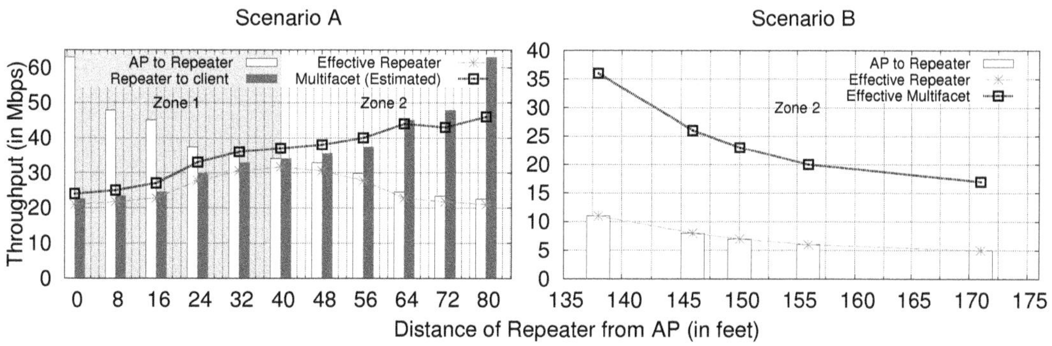

Figure 2: The performance benchmark of dual-interface repeater system and our formulation-based estimates of *Multifacet*. In the experiments the AP–repeater link was operating over a 20 MHz channel in 5GHz band and the repeater–client link was sharing a 20 MHz channel in 2.4 GHz band with the AP–repeater link (Figure 1(b)). We omit the repeater–client throughputs for Scenario B for clarity, which were always significantly high in this scenario.

only for certain channel configurations. Further, even in favorable conditions it is not straightforward to realize the throughput gains at client as one of the AP-repeater link shares the channel with repeater-client link.

How *Multifacet* differs from other general solutions of multi-hop multi-radio systems: Our repeater setup can be considered as a simpler version of a multi-hop multi-radio wireless mesh network. In particular, *Multifacet* just has two hops – one hop has two parallel links, while the other has a single link. While significant research exists in efficient wireless mesh network design, e.g., in channel assignment, routing strategies, load balancing of flows, and more [16–19, 21], such solutions are not pertinent to our problem. This is because of the fact that prior solutions *work on flows and do not address the problem of splitting individual flows across multiple interfaces*. A key uniqueness of *Multifacet* from prior mesh networking literature, thus, comes from its focus on efficiently splitting a flow over multiple interfaces at high data rates under varying channel conditions. Similarly, prior work has addressed the issue of using multiple parallel WiFi links simultaneously at full capacity (Glia [31]), it does not support partitioning of a single flow across these multiple interfaces. Hence, approaches such as Glia alone, are not suited to support high bandwidth media flows in high interference scenarios. The unique aspects of *Multifacet* is the set of algorithmic optimizations (a simplified back pressure technique, synchronous channel migration on demand, and soft reliability), and implementation-based refinements that present a single link abstraction to unchanged flow endpoints.

Key contributions: *Multifacet* is a systematic research and engineering effort to significantly enhance the performance and achievable throughputs when using repeaters in the most challenging wireless home environments. We make the following contributions:

- Show how the performance of dual-radio repeaters can be enhanced by leveraging multiple interfaces (§ 2).
- Design and implement *Multifacet* – a dual interface repeater system to opportunistically use multiple interfaces on a desktop platform and Netgear WNDR3800 (§3 and § 4).
- Show that *Multifacet* is within 15% of the theoretical optimal 90% of the time (§ 5.1). Demonstrate that our system works at high speeds (achieving 337 Mbps for TCP, § 5.4).

2. *MULTIFACET* IN A NUTSHELL

Multifacet is stylized for repeaters with the central goal of opportunistically leveraging the excess capacity of downstream channel. We explain the benefits that *Multifacet* can provide next.

When does *Multifacet* help? To answer the question, we first study how repeater performance varies (Figure 1(a)) in realistic settings while varying conditions. Specifically, we measure TCP throughput delivered by repeater systems using off-the-shelf dual-interface AP (WNDR4500), repeater (WN2500RP), and a client laptop, all operating over 802.11n channels in Figure 2. In Scenario (A), the separation between the AP and the client in a home environment (across multiple rooms and walls) is set to 80 feet, and the repeater is placed at different locations in between. It can be seen that the AP–repeater and the repeater–client links, each operating with different radios and different channels, individually get between 20 Mbps and 60 Mbps in different deployments of the repeater. The effective end-to-end throughput marked as effective repeater in Figure 2 is the minimum of the two hops and is limited to 20–30 Mbps. The problem of reduced throughput exacerbates with higher separation between the AP and the client. Scenario (B) shows an even greater separation between the two (up to 170 feet) leading to poorer performance, and the maximum end-to-end throughput using a dual-interface repeater is down to about 5 Mbps.

Now striping traffic as advocated by *Multifacet* will be helpful when the repeater-client link has higher capacity than AP-repeater link as the extra capacity of repeater-client link can then be shared with AP-repeater link. As an example, consider the link capacities at 64 feet from AP in Figure 2. The throughput between the repeater-client is around 45 Mbps and for the AP-repeater links is 20 Mbps. Assuming similar data rates for both AP-repeater and repeater-client links would imply that $\sim$25 Mbps of capacity of shared channel is wasted. A part of this capacity can easily taken by AP-repeater link by operating on the channel. This wasted capacity is precisely what *Multifacet* intends to use for sending more traffic from AP to repeater by contending on the shared channel, in turn increasing throughput delivered to clients.

Note that the careful placement of repeater at a location does not completely obviate the problem of traffic scheduling. This is due to the time varying nature of wireless interference in dense urban home settings, which causes variability in channel conditions at different times of day. This apart, the client is expected to be mobile within the confines of his home, which might frequently change the optimal repeater placement.

How much gains can *Multifacet* provide? We present a numerical analysis to characterize the expected performance improvement due to *Multifacet*. We assume that perfect prediction and scheduling of traffic is possible to balance throughputs along upstream (AP–repeater) and downstream (repeater–client). Let D_S denote the single hop throughput of the downstream link in isolation between the repeater and the client. Similarly, U_S and U_{NS} denote the throughput of the two upstream links (each in isolation) between the AP and repeater. S corresponds to the link operating on the same channel as the downstream link, and NS corresponds to the link that is on the non-shared channel. The estimation of expected performance improvement is based on two observations: (i) For *Multifacet* to provide benefits, D_S has to be greater than U_{NS}. This is true for all experiments marked Zone 2 in Figure 2, and (ii) a queue build up in repeater–client radio would imply that the repeater is getting more packets from AP than it can send to the client. This is suboptimal[1] as it would simply lead to accumulation of packets at repeater without enough time to send them to client. Hence, *the fraction of the shared channel assigned to AP–repeater link should not cause queue build up in repeater–client radio.*

Now, let us focus on a single unit of time. For this time unit, assume that a flow's traffic is split at the AP to send U_{NS} data units over the non-shared channel and an additional K data units on the shared uplink channel to the repeater. This implies, the AP would occupy the shared channel for $\frac{K}{U_S}$ time units. To avoid buildup of packets in repeater, the repeater would need to transmit the entire $U_{NS} + K$ to the client within its time of operation on the shared channel. To do so, the repeater-client link should be active for $\frac{U_{NS}+K}{D_S}$ time units over the shared channel. Hence in steady state to avoid queue build up, the following invariant would be satisfied for a single time unit:

$$\frac{K}{U_S} + \frac{U_{NS} + K}{D_S} = 1 \quad (1)$$

The above equation states that the fraction of time occupied by AP-repeater link and repeater–client link on the shared channel should add up to 1. Rewriting,

$$K = \left(1 - \frac{U_{NS}}{D_S}\right) / \left(\frac{1}{U_S} + \frac{1}{D_S}\right) \quad (2)$$

and the total end-to-end throughput is $U_{NS} + K$.

In Figure 2 we also show the total end-to-end throughput of *Multifacet* that is estimated by the above formulation based on the measured values of U_{NS}, U_S, and D_S. We can see that under different scenarios (Zone 2), the total throughput due to *Multifacet* can be *more than double that of a standard and unchanged repeater implementation.* For example, in Scenario A at a separation of 80 feet, *Multifacet* in theory can provide up to 48 Mbps throughput 2.4× higher than standard repeater implementation (20 Mbps).

One observation is that *Multifacet* will not be useful in many scenarios where $U_{NS} > D_S$, as is true for all cases in Zone 1. However, there are sufficient other scenarios (Zone 2) where even the high-end and highly capable WiFi systems (our AP, repeater and client laptop use 2×2 MIMO and 802.11n), the end-to-end realized throughputs are as low as a few Mbps. In our experience these challenging scenarios, indeed, occur in large homes and spaces with thicker walls and greater degree of interference. In fact, this is why repeaters (including dual-interface versions) are being sold by all leading vendors in the marketplace. By allowing the overall system to be able to more than double the throughput using *Multifacet* can make a significant difference in the type of high-bandwidth applications that will be feasible under these circumstances.

What is hard about *Multifacet*? The basic concept of *Multifacet* is fairly simple – allow an individual flow to be striped across two WiFi paths between an AP and a repeater and aggregate the flow before forwarding it to the client. To ensure that wide deployment, *Multifacet* does not require any changes to applications and endpoints making the deployment possible by simply installing new software in the AP and the repeaters. This is achieved by providing a single link abstraction to ongoing flows even though internally, the packets are striped and aggregated across two interfaces.

[1] In present context *optimal* throughput is defined as the maximum throughput that can be delivered to a client under the constraints of underlying link layer technology.

The biggest challenge of the system is in its careful design of algorithms that (i) scales to very high 802.11n speeds (∼100 Mbps), (ii) reacts efficiently to changing channel conditions, and (iii) in its implementation in the specific AP and repeater form factors. With two parallel links operating at these speeds, and occasionally experiencing channel fluctuations, a small mistake in deciding how much traffic to send in each path can cause hundreds of packet reorders, and losses. The performance penalty is particularly high for TCP flows which react badly to bursty reorder and packet losses. Thus, our algorithms for striping traffic need to be *simple* and *nimble* so that they can efficiently react to even small changes to channel conditions across two parallel paths.

Further, given that one channel is shared between one of the upstream links and the downstream link, it is critical to design efficient control loop to coordinate between traffic forwarding decisions between these two links. The importance of efficient coordination becomes apparent by realizing that in its absence the upstream link can potentially dominate the downstream link on the shared channel. This will in turn lead to significant degradation in performance as repeater will keep getting more packets to deliver but would not get access to the channel to deliver it. To this end, we implement a light weight distributed control loop – a simplified back pressure technique – that monitors the available capacity of these links in making striping and traffic forwarding decisions.

In addition to the challenges of traffic striping, the availability of two parallel links in the upstream path presents us an interesting opportunity. If the non-shared link experiences poor performance, it might be more beneficial to switch the operating channel of this link to a better and non-congested one. We therefore designed mechanisms to opportunistically switch the non-shared link to different channels. We do not consider switching the shared channel as the only link between the client and repeater operates on it and switching channel can severely impact any active flows to the client.

3. *MULTIFACET* DESIGN

We describe the techniques used in *Multifacet* to address the challenges highlighted in previous section.

3.1 Simplified backpressure based striping

The goal of the striping algorithm is to ensure optimal utilization of the capacity of the constituent links under all channel conditions. This implies that the striping algorithm should be able to *quickly shift traffic load* from one interface to another if the channel conditions worsen.

The striping algorithm works in two phases: the bootstrap and the steady state. In the bootstrap state, the *Multifacet* AP assigns a fixed number (*Device_threshold*) of packets to all interfaces in a round-robin manner. The intention is to gauge the capacity of the constituent links by monitoring the performance of delivering the initial set of packets. Once, *Device_threshold* number of packets have been striped through all interfaces, the striping algorithm enters the steady state. In steady state, more packets would be scheduled only after feedback of success/failure is received from the underlying device. The above behavior ensures that *we only schedule packets the link can support*. Furthermore, we ensure that *each link always have some backlogged packets to transmit, or we would lose out on available transmission opportunities.* The faster link will send feedback more frequently and subsequently have more traf-

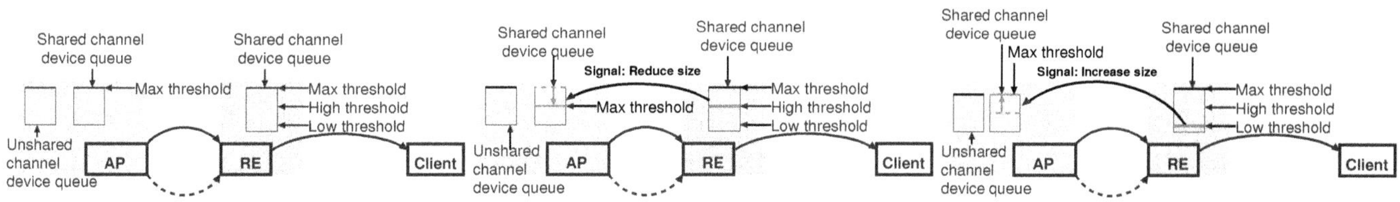

(a) *Multifacet* logical design (b) Restrict traffic (c) Increase traffic

Figure 3: Co-ordinated transmission throttling for the shared channel shown for downlink transmission of packets. (a) Shows the logical architecture of the system wherein repeater periodically monitors the number of unsent packets at the repeater destined for the client. (b) The unsent packet queue grows beyond its maximum threshold, triggering a reduction in packets sent from AP over the shared channel. (c) The queue of unsent packets is below minimum threshold and AP can potentially send more packets to the repeater over the shared channel.

fic scheduled to it, while the link with lesser capacity would send feedback at slower pace, and thus would get less packets.

While in steady state, if the bandwidth demanded by the applications is well below the capacity of the underlying links, the *Multifacet* AP switches back to striping the packets in a round-robin fashion across the constituent links. The above state is indicated by a very small number of packets on *all* client interfaces for which no feedback has been received from the underlying device.

3.2 Co-ordinated transmission throttling for congestion control

The goal of transmission throttling logic is to ensure that the uplink (AP–repeater) over shared channel occupies only the extra bandwidth after all downlink (repeater–client) traffic is sent. Figure 3(a) shows the logical setup for efficiently utilizing the spare capacity of the shared channel. The transmission throttling logic bootstraps from a state where *Multifacet* is operating like a traditional repeater, i.e., the AP is not sending any traffic over the shared channel. In steady state the system tries to incrementally probe the shared channel for extra bandwidth between the AP and repeater. The repeater continuously monitors the number of unsent packets destined to the client. The event of unsent packets count growing beyond a (user specified) threshold signifies that the AP traffic has exceeded its allowable bandwidth, thus taking away capacity from the repeater–client link. In this case the repeater module sends a congestion initiation signal to the AP module as shown in Figure 3(b). The transmission throttling module at AP reacts to the congestion message by reducing the *Device_threshold* parameter for the wireless interface operating on the shared channel. Reducing this parameter automatically reduces the number of packets scheduled by the backpressure packet striping algorithm. This in turn provides a larger share of the shared channel to the repeater.

Analogously, a lower than threshold number of unsent packets at the repeater signifies that the spare capacity is present on the shared channel. In this case, repeater signals the AP to increase the volume of traffic on the shared channel. The AP accordingly increases the percentage of traffic scheduled by increasing the *Device_threshold* for the wireless interface operating on the shared channel as shown in Figure 3(c). The repeater sends a status quo signal to the AP if the number of unsent packets stays between the lower and upper thresholds. We use a MIMD algorithm to adjust the *Device_threshold* at the AP.

Correctness of behavior: Note that the behavior of transmission throttling logic would be incorrect when the repeater-client link has enough traffic to saturate the shared channel on its own, however the AP-repeater link is still allowed to operate on the shared channel. From previous discussion (Figure 2), we know that repeater operates in two zones. We explain why our transmission throttling logic would behave correctly and choke AP–repeater link in both the zones. In zone 1, $D_S \leq U_{NS}$. Hence, $D_S \leq U_S + U_{NS}$ which implies that a queue of unsent packets would build up in repeater. The accumulated traffic will eventually cross the allowable threshold leading in repeater leading to choking of AP–repeater link (Figure 3(b)). In zone 2, assume that the AP–repeater link achieves K' throughput. Now, based on Equation 1, the repeater–client link can only support $K + U_{NS}$ data units per second. Whereas it is receiving $K' + U_{NS}$ data units per second and $K' > K$. Hence, $K' - K$ ($[K' + U_{NS}]$ - $[K + U_{NS}]$) amount of traffic will accumulate in repeater–client queue every second. Eventually, the queue size will cross the allowable threshold leading to reduction of AP–repeater traffic over shared channel.

3.3 A single link abstraction

We hide the underlying multiple parallel wireless links and present the abstraction of a single virtual link. This implies that packets of a single flow need to be delivered in order across the virtual link, analogous to sending packets across a single physical wireless link. To maintain single link abstraction we handle re-orders for the case when packets of a single flow is striped across two or more links. Note that any packets lost due to wireless error will be retransmitted by the source the resulting end-to-end re-orders, of course, do not need to be handled by our system.

Comparison to multi-path TCP: An alternative to our single link abstraction is to utilize a generalized multi-path transport protocol, e.g., MPTCP [29, 34, 39] depicted in Figure 4(a). It requires deployment at the two endpoints, and an ability in software to stripe packets across the different WiFi interfaces. The other alternative is the *Multifacet* (Figure 4(b)) that requires no endpoint changes but implements various algorithmic techniques that are deployed on two ends of the special wireless link. It is intuitive that the MPTCP approach (implemented at the transport layer) is efficient for general scenarios the multiple alternate Internet paths diverge and merge at arbitrary points in the Internet, but the *Multifacet* approach (implemented at the network layer) is more suitable for the specific scenario at hand. There are three advantages of *Multifacet* over the MPTCP. First, *Multifacet* works with unchanged endpoints and can be deployed in a transparent manner. Second, *Multifacet* exploits custom knowledge of WiFi properties to combine various data striping choices with selection of link parameters (PHY rates, re-transmission, etc.) to achieve higher throughputs than a WiFi-unaware MPTCP. Third, an end-to-end packet striping and adaptation mechanism of MPTCP operates at a control loop latency of 50-100 ms (typical Internet path latencies), while in *Multifacet*, the same mechanism operates at a control loop latency of 1-2 ms or less (typical single-hop WiFi latencies). All of these combined, leads to significant performance advantages as demonstrated in § 5.2.

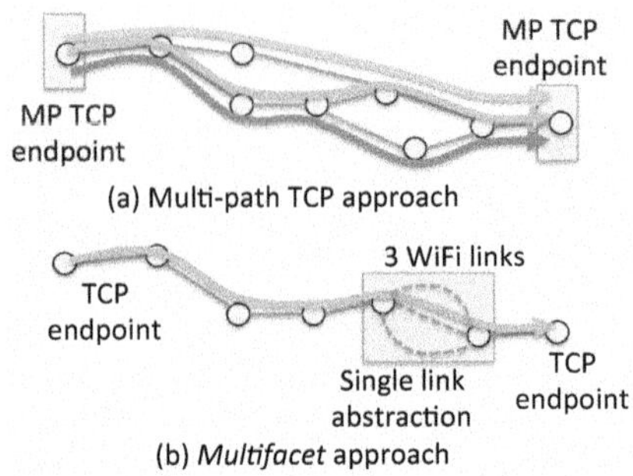

Figure 4: MPTCP is a generalized multi-path transport solution while *Multifacet* is customized to a single wireless hop with multiple parallel WiFi paths.

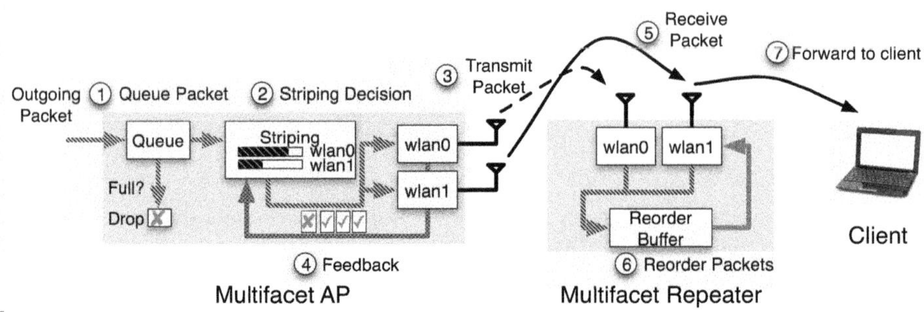

Figure 5: Flow of packet inside *Multifacet* system.

The performance inefficiency of MPTCP is due to the well known phenomenon of *self-interference* between two links operating over the shared channel. Self-interference causes the transmitter on upstream (downstream) link backing off after carrier sensing the transmissions of the downstream (upstream) on the same channel. In fact, it is to avoid this very problem the AP–repeater and repeater--client links are operated on different channels in state-of-art repeater systems. MPTCP suffers from the self-interference problem when operating on the two paths over the shared channel. As a result, MPTCP is incapable of saturating the links and resulting in low performance. In contrast, *Multifacet* actively prioritizes the operation of the repeater-client link over the AP-repeater link due to reasons explained in Section 1. This results in optimal avoidance of self-interference leading to high performance (evaluation in § 5.2).

3.4 Synchronous channel migration

To ensure higher capacity in undesirable circumstances, *Multifacet* triggers channel migration on a non-shared channel, especially when the quality of the non-shared channel between AP–repeater underperforms (below a threshold). During the channel migration process, the *Multifacet* AP first stops sending packets on the non-shared channel and sends a channel switch announcement (CSA) in its beacon frames. Once both the AP and repeater have migrated, the *Multifacet* AP carries out a bandwidth test similar to the one proposed in [28] for a duration of 20 milliseconds. If the achievable throughput is higher than what was previously observed, the channel migration process stops. Otherwise, we revert back to the original channel. We call this the *Adequate* scheme and contrast it with a *Best* scheme where the channel search explores all possible channels and picks the one that maximizes throughput (evaluation in §5.4).

Finally, note that we do not try to migrate the shared channel as a design choice. This is because of the fact that the only link between the client and repeater is operational on the shared channel, and hence the shared channel cannot be seamlessly changed without disrupting the flow to the client.

4. IMPLEMENTATION ASPECTS

Multifacet is implemented by augmenting various software components of both AP and repeater wireless network stack on a Linux 3.2.0 kernel. Specifically, we have modified the Linux *bridge*, *bonding*, ath9k, Linux mac80211 drivers and Hostapd AP daemon. It does not require any modifications at the client. For experimentation we used Atheros AR9220 and AR9380 chipset based 802.11a/b/g/n capable network interfaces for our system. The flow of packet (AP–repeater–client) is depicted in Figure 5. We describe the implementation details next.

Simplified backpressure based striping: Scheduling is performed within the bridge driver. Incoming packets are first enqueued in a small buffer, which we have added to handle fluctuations in link capacity (step 1 in Figure 5). We replace the forwarding logic of the bridge with our backpressure algorithm described in § 3.1 (step 2). If the scheduler can not find an available interface (where the number of unacknowledged packets is less than *Device_threshold*), no packets are sent. When an interface is available, we dequeue a packet from buffer, add an IP option (which contains a sequence number and the interface the packet was sent on) to the packet and send it on the appropriate interface (step 3). Once a packet succeeds or fails, the ath9k driver sends feedback to the bridge driver, which is then incorporated into striping algorithm. If the buffer is not empty, additional packets are sent to the interfaces until *Device_threshold* is reached or the buffer is emptied.

Single link abstraction: The Linux bridge driver is used to implement the *Multifacet* AP interface. The WiFi NICs are in AP mode with distinct SSIDs and are ports of the bridge interface. Being ports of a bridge implies that all repeater/client traffic passes through the bridge code, where our code resides. To achieve the facade of a single interface at the repeater, we enslave the constituent wireless interfaces under a bond interface. The repeater interfaces associate with a specific AP interface based on the SSID. We add an IP option header at the AP to allow us to re-order packets at the repeater as well as to notify our striping algorithm of the (un)successful delivery of a packet.

Packet reordering: For re-order management, we have modified the bridge driver to assign a 32-bit sequence number to each packet which is stored as an IP option and implemented a circular re-order buffer. We also include an interface identifier to help lower layers provide feedback for our striping algorithm. As shown in Figure 5 (step 6), all packets arriving on different interfaces are placed in our re-order buffer. The AP assigned sequence number is used for re-ordering. In our implementation, the re-order buffer stores up to thousands of packets, but no longer than 10 milliseconds, for any missing prior packets. Typically most packets need to wait a few hundred microseconds to be correctly ordered when they arrive across different links.

Controlled sharing of channel: The spectrum is shared between the AP and repeater by monitoring queue build-up at the repeater for packets destined to a client. We modify the wireless stack on the repeater to periodically send control packets to the AP to indicate the presence of congestion, which is determined if the queue size passes a certain threshold. These control packets indicate to the AP

Evaluation scenarios	Section / Figure	Experiment variation / Results
vs. Traditional repeater	§5.1, Fig.6(b)	Uncontrolled: Avg. 35% TCP throughput gain, Max. 2.5×
	§5.1, Fig.7	Controlled: Avg. 70% TCP/UDP throughput gain, 8.7 dB PSNR gain
vs. MPTCP	§5.2, Fig.8	Varying path delay: 19% throughput gain (Max. 2×)
vs. Overhearing mesh	§5.3, Fig.9	110% throughput gain
Design choices of *Multifacet*	§5.4, Fig.12	Coordinated transmission throttling: *Multifacet* reacts within 200msec
	§5.4, Fig.13	Reorder buffer: 27% throughput gain with reorder buffer
	§5.4, Tab.5	Packet buffering: Avg. 10% TCP throughput gain, Max. 30%
vs. 802.11n	§5.5, Fig.16(b)	High interference: 6× throughput gain

Table 1: Summary of the key evaluation scenarios and results described in § 5.

to maintain, increase, or decrease the amount of traffic it should send. The transmission throttling is based on MIMD logic.

Synchronous channel migration: We modify Hostapd to insert channel switch announcements (CSAs) in beacon frames and mac80211 driver to send a specific (user-defined) number of beacons with CSA announcements to ensure successful reception of notification. A CSA notifies associated stations that the AP is switching to a different channel at a predefined time (in beacon interval). The modified mac80211 driver decrements the time until channel switch in each successive beacon. After sending the last beacon the Hostapd driver performs the channel switch.

Porting to WNDR 3800: Our initial prototype was built on a six core 2.6 GHz desktop with 8 GB RAM. When porting to our target platform, Netgear's WNDR 3800 (single core, 680 MHz, 128 MB RAM) experienced a 30% performance drop. To ensure optimal performance, we reduced the replaced mutex protected shared data structures with atomic variables in the packet striping and reordering logic resulting in a ~10% improvement in performance. We also replaced workqueue based scheduling mechanism with the simpler and faster *tasklet* data structure leading to performance improvements in tens of Mbps. Finally, our initial port executed the entire *Multifacet* decision logic on a per packet basis leading to severe inefficiency on a single core system due to non-preemptible nature of most operations (e.g., mac80211, ath9k drivers stalling for updating information for every packet). Rewriting the code to operate on batch of packets led to amortizing of the stalling penalty leading to ~15% performance improvement.

5. EVALUATION

We benchmark the end-to-end performance of *Multifacet* by comparing to that of *Traditional repeater* – a baseline system where only a single link exists between AP–repeater and repeater-client as depicted in Figure 1(a); and *Multifacet*-naive – a simple strawman solution using round-robin discipline for striping across the two interfaces connecting repeater and AP without co-ordinated transmission throttling; under various controlled and uncontrolled settings (§ 5.1). All the repeater tests were conducted using our WNDR3800 based implementation for *Multifacet*. For *Traditional repeater* we used a vanilla OpenWrt image. In § 5.2 we compare the performance of *Multifacet* with *MPTCP*, an end-to-end multipath transport protocol using the modified kernel available at [5]. We have used the *coupled* congestion control algorithm for MPTCP experiments. We have used HighSpeed TCP congestion control algorithm for the results reported in the paper. We have observed similar results when operating TCP with BIC, CUBIC, TCP New Reno congestion control algorithms as well. Results omitted for the sake of brevity. We benchmark the advantages of *Multifacet* over overhearing based mesh routing in § 5.3. We micro-benchmark the efficacy of design choices made in *Multifacet* in § 5.4. Specifically, to understand the benefits of various design choices for link aggregation we conduct experiments with clients connected to the repeater via Ethernet and hence, data destined for the client traverses only a single hop (over two wireless interfaces) from AP to repeater. We use a desktop based setup to stress test the efficiency of various system components with high-bandwidth flows (we use $3X3$ MIMO in desktops comparing to $2X2$ MIMO in WNDR3800). Finally, we highlight connecting to repeater via Ethernet as an interesting design choice for implementing high bandwidth wireless solutions, when a single high speed (802.11n) link is unable to meet such demands (§ 5.5). We summarize the results in Table 1.

Traffic/media sources and metrics: Experiments were conducted in both the 2.4 GHz and the 5 GHz band with 40 MHz channel (unless stated otherwise), with the former being more interference-prone than the latter. We use *aggregate end-to-end* TCP throughput as our primary metric. In addition, we have experimented with end-to-end UDP throughput, HTTP-based dynamic streaming and RTP/UDP-based streaming to characterize performance enhancements offered by *Multifacet* to media applications. For the RTP/UDP-based video experiments, we used the Evalvid mp4trace streaming server [8] to send Ducks video clip [12] of 10 seconds duration encoded at an average bitrate of 20 Mbps (with maximum 40 Mbps). We report *Peak Signal to Noise Ratio (PSNR)*, a measure of perceptual quality of video as our primary metric. For TCP and UDP experiments, each result is the average of 20 iterations of 10 second runs. In different experiments, the traffic traversed some Internet path segment (varying between 0 ms and 100 ms) before it reached the wireless links. The additional delay of the wired segment was controlled using the NetEm tool [11]. The delay was introduced at the traffic source (Iperf or video server) machine and was kept constant for a given experiment (i.e., no variability was introduced).

Testbed: The experiments were conducted in a floor of a University building with around thirty five APs unregulated APs active across all the channels with five or more APs active on the channels on which we were conducting our experiments. Figure 6(a) shows the plan of the testbed and various locations used for different experiments. The presence of many unregulated access points gave us the confidence that our experimental results will be replicable over a large gamut of real world settings.

5.1 Overall Performance

In uncontrolled settings: We randomly select 30 location pairs for the AP, repeater, client and a pair of interfering nodes from the set of locations in Figure 6(a). For each location we compare TCP throughput for *Multifacet*, *Multifacet*-naive normalized to the performance of Traditional repeater and present results in Figure 6(b). *Multifacet* performance is 35% higher than Traditional repeater in 50% of the cases. For about 8% of the cases, the performance of *Multifacet* is same as Traditional repeater. These settings correspond to Zone 1 described in Figure 2. We also find that *Multifacet* performs about 2.5× better than Traditional repeater in the best case and the specific experiment setting corresponds to Zone 2, as it

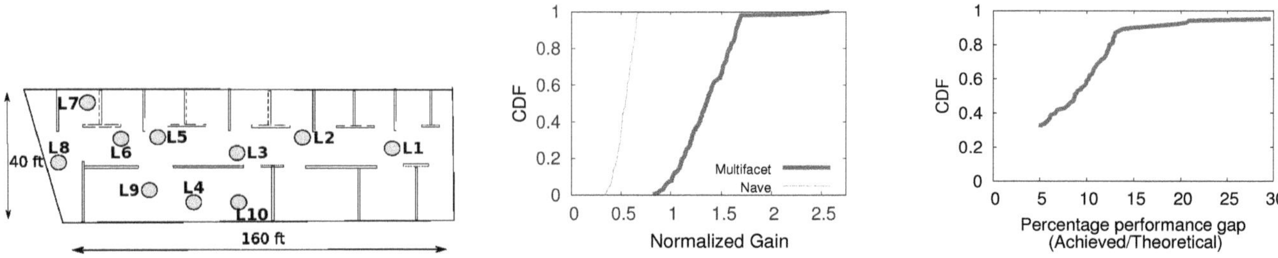

(a) AP, repeater, client and interferer locations (b) TCP gain (c) Comparison to theoretical opt.

Figure 6: (a) Deployment. (b) *Multifacet* improves on average 35% throughput gain over Traditional repeater (max. 2.5×). (c) *Multifacet* performance is within 15% of the theoretical performance 90% of time. The theoretical performance improvement is calculated using Equation 2

	Bottleneck (channel)	AP	Rpt	Client	Interferer	Placement mapping (Figure 2)
$\mathcal{C}1$	repeater–client (shared)	L1	L2	L5	L6–L8	Scenario A (zone 1)
$\mathcal{C}2$	AP–repeater (shared)	L9	L6	L5	L4–L10	Scenario A (zone 2, till 64 meter in Figure 2)
$\mathcal{C}3$	AP–repeater (non-shared)	L9	L6	L5	L4–L10	Scenario B

Table 2: Three bottleneck scenarios used for controlled experiments in § 5.1. The equivalent scenario in Figure 2 is also mentioned.

allows *Multifacet* to utilize shared channel capacity. These settings correspond to the cases when the capacity of the AP–repeater link is much higher on the shared channel than on the non-shared channel. This result makes sense as the Traditional repeater only utilizes the non-shared channel for uplink, whereas *Multifacet* is able to utilize an higher capacity shared channel in addition to the non-shared channel for uplink. However, *Multifacet*-naive performs worse than Traditional repeater as round-robin scheduling of packets over two interfaces leads to unconstrained transmission by AP–repeater on the shared link with repeater-client link. This in turn reduces the capacity of repeater-client below that of Traditional repeater.

We benchmark the degree of inefficiency of *Multifacet* compared to the optimal bandwidth calculated using Equation (1,2). In Figure 6(c), we find that for 90% of the time *Multifacet* is within 15% of theoretically optimal performance. The inefficiency is due to the backpressure algorithm which operates in a conservative manner. We also notice that in the worst case *Multifacet* performance is 30% lower than theoretically optimal value. This was due to operation on a very weak repeater-client link and in the presence of an uncontrolled interferer which led to multiple triggering of congestion signals leading to TCP throughput drops.

In controlled settings: The performance improvements of *Multifacet* system over Traditional repeater depends on the relative capacity of the three links that it uses. To characterize this dependency of *Multifacet* performance, we create following three cases (Table 2) where the bottleneck link varies: ($\mathcal{C}1$) repeater-client link is bottleneck due to presence of a competing link close to client, ($\mathcal{C}2$) AP–repeater shared channel is the bottleneck due to presence of competing link near AP, and ($\mathcal{C}3$) AP–repeater non-shared channel is the bottleneck due to presence of a competing link on the same channel near repeater. We also mention the matching placement of AP, repeater and client scenarios (from Figure 2 in § 2) alongside each case. The capacity of the non-bottlenecked links were similar and we deterministically varied the capacity of bottlenecked link between 10–50% of the non-bottlenecked links by controlling the capacity of the competing link. The Traditional repeater system uses non-shared channel between the AP and repeater, and the shared channel between the repeater and client. For $\mathcal{C}1$ and $\mathcal{C}2$ we ensured the competing link had low power to not disrupt communication for the other link operating on the same channel.

We measure the end-to-end TCP/UDP throughput and calculate PSNR of RTP video stream under the three cases and present them in Figure 7. Normalized throughput gain is calculated as the throughput ratio of *Multifacet* to Traditional repeater. In $\mathcal{C}1$, repeater–client link is the bottleneck. This makes efficient utilization of spare capacity of shared channel futile. Hence, the performance of *Multifacet* is similar to that of Traditional repeater as the co-ordinated transmission throttling ensures that the AP does not stripe packets on shared link. In contrast, for $\mathcal{C}2$ and $\mathcal{C}3$, repeater–client link is not the bottleneck and hence *Multifacet* can start utilizing the spare shared channel capacity leading to client throughput improvement over Traditional repeater. $\mathcal{C}3$ is the most favorable condition for our system as Traditional repeater is bottlenecked by the AP–repeater link, whereas due to presence of spare capacity in the shared channel *Multifacet* delivers 70% higher throughput to the client (Figure 7(a)). In $\mathcal{C}2$, the expected gains are lower since the AP–repeater link over shared channel can only send minimal extra traffic, however *Multifacet* still provides 20% better throughput in this case.

We also present the normalized UDP throughput gain of *Multifacet* over Traditional repeater in Figure 7(b). Similarly, *Multifacet* improves the throughput significantly (at most 78%) when utilizing the additional link ($\mathcal{C}3$). Figure 7(c) shows that *Multifacet* provides an additional 8.7dB improvement in PSNR comparing to that of Traditional repeater in $\mathcal{C}2$. In all the experiments, *Multifacet*-naive performance is worse than Traditional repeater as the round-robin scheduling at AP stripes a high number of packets on the shared channel without any feedback about the congestion caused to the repeater–client link. This leads to packets being delivered on the non-shared AP–repeater link that cannot be delivered to the client. In contrast, *Multifacet*'s co-ordinated channel access logic desists the AP from sending traffic on the shared channel when enough capacity does not exist.

Multiple clients: We have experimented with four clients and presented the aggregate throughput received by the clients in Table 3. As shown, increasing the number of clients leads to a proportional drop in individual client throughput, while the aggregate throughput remains similar. We did not observe starvation at a specific client. This is expected as the co-ordinated transmission throttling algorithm ensures that the access to shared channel is given to the AP-client links and only when spare capacity is available, the AP-Repeater link is allowed to operate on the shared channel.

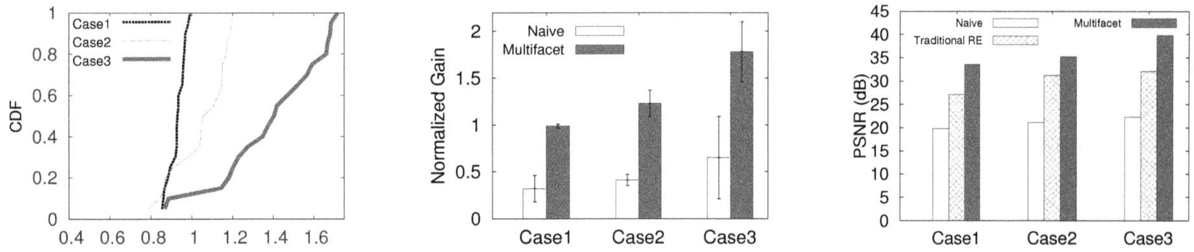

(a) Normalized TCP gain (b) Normalized UDP gain (c) PSNR

Figure 7: (a) and (b) *Multifacet* provides significant TCP/UDP throughput gains (up to 1.7×) in case of $C2$ and $C3$. (c) *Multifacet* provides good/excellent (MOS) video quality independent of channel conditions. (PSNR of ≥37 is excellent, 31-37 is good, 25-31 is fair, 20-25 is poor and ≤20 is bad Mean Opinion Score (MOS) [32].)

No. of Clients	*Multifacet* Aggr. (Avg.) TCP throughput	Trad. repeater Aggr. (Avg.) TCP throughput (Mbps)
1	31.2 (31.2)	19.1 (19.1)
2	30.5 (15.25)	19.8 (9.9)
3	31.1 (10.36)	18.2 (6.1)
4	30.8 (7.7)	19.2 (4.8)

Table 3: Aggregate and per client average (in brackets) TCP throughput performance of multiple clients when connected to *Multifacet* and Traditional repeater systems.

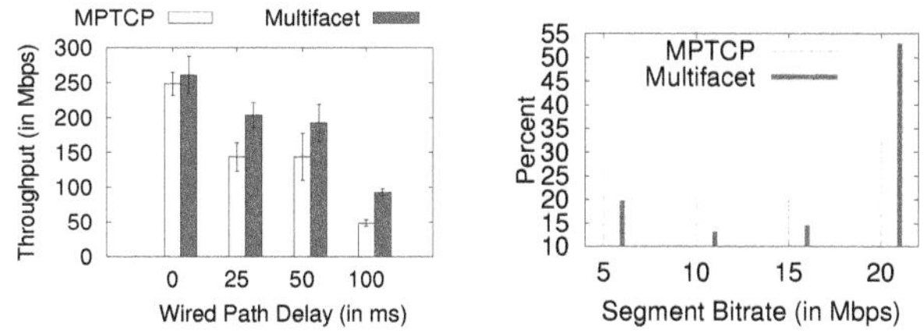

(a) Comparing MPTCP to *Multifacet* while varying delays (b) Comparison of the proportion of video segment bitrates

Figure 8: (a) *Multifacet* provides 2× throughput than MPTCP in case of 100 ms delay. (b) *Multifacet* clients fetch more segments at the highest bitrate.

5.2 Comparison with MPTCP

Varying path delay: We compare *Multifacet* and MPTCP's performance, with varying path latency between the source and destination, using the delay setting option of NetEm [11] tool (note that we did not introduce any variability in the delay). Figure 8(a) shows the performance of the two alternatives: (i) MPTCP which treats the two links as two separate paths and implements its congestion control algorithm by deciding how much traffic to send on each, and (ii) *Multifacet* which abstracts this into a single wireless link and uses the HighSpeed TCP congestion control algorithm. In the best case (no additional delay), MPTCP has 16% lower throughput.

MPTCP suffers from *self-interference* problem between two links operating over shared channel as we describe in § 3.3 and hence MPTCP is incapable of saturating the links leading to low performance. In contrast, *Multifacet* actively prioritizes the operation of the repeater-client link over the AP-repeater link resulting in optimal avoidance of self-interference leading to high performance. The performance gap increases with increasing wired path latency, with MPTCP's throughput at 100 ms path delay is about 50% of *Multifacet*. This is expected since *Multifacet*'s backpressure based flow management is closer to the wireless interfaces and hence, more responsive to small variations across two links. In contrast, MPTCP can only react in an end-to-end manner.

HTTP dynamic streaming: Next we compare the performance of *Multifacet* and MPTCP when a client is watching a 20 Mbps video. We encode 30 second segments of a 5 minute clip of Bluray quality (1080p) to create 5, 10, 15, and 20 Mbps video sources. The client fetches different video segments at the bitrate it believes the network has capacity for. Figure 8(b) shows the distribution of segments fetched by client for both *Multifacet* and MPTCP. We observed that 53% of segments fetched by *Multifacet* were 20 Mbps, versus 33% for MPTCP. Overall, the *Multifacet* clients enjoy higher video quality for longer durations than MPTCP clients.

5.3 Mesh routing with overhearing

Overhearing based mesh routing schemes [16, 22] improve performance over traditional mesh by allowing downstream nodes to overhear transmissions from upstream nodes. Overhearing also mandates that overhearing nodes operate on the same frequency as the upstream transmitter. In contrast, *Multifacet* operates the links over independent channels. To compare the performance of overhearing based schemes, we operate our repeater setup with both links on same channel. We calculate the throughput achieved when the client is directly associated with the AP. We assume 100% overhearing and consider the sum of throughput of repeater (over one channel) and the throughput between AP and client as the maximum potential improvements due to repeater with overhearing. Figure 9 shows the throughput attained by *Multifacet*, repeater with one channel and repeater with overhearing. As can be seen from the plot, overhearing improved performance by 21% over a simple repeater. The gains of overhearing are lower as AP is far apart from client which is typical setting for repeater. However, *Multifacet* outperforms repeater with overhearing by ∼110% as the penalty of operating on a single channel over two hops (more than halving of bandwidth) is far higher than the gains of overhearing.

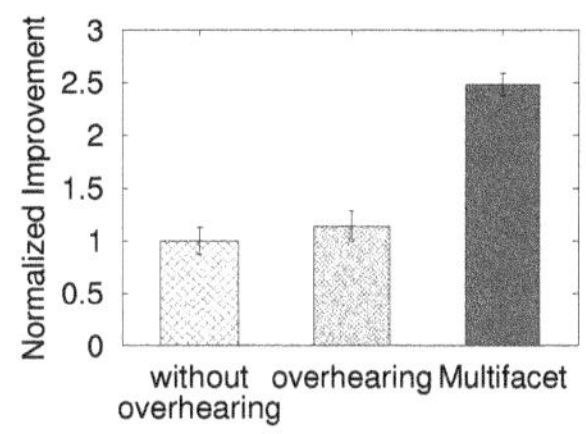

Figure 9: Overhearing provides 20% improvement, while *Multifacet* performs ∼110% better than an overhearing repeater

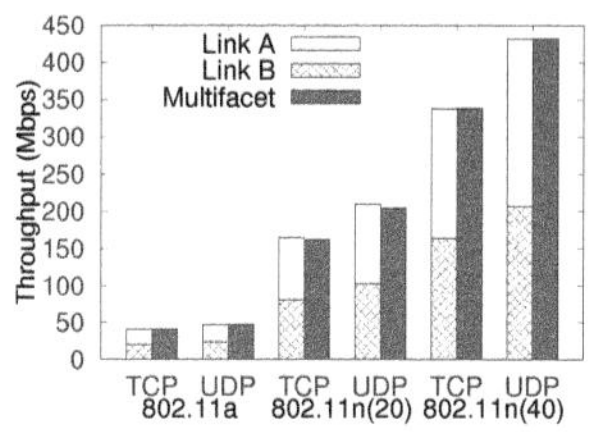

Figure 10: *Multifacet* is able to aggregate almost all available capacity of the two links across multiple technologies and at various speeds of operation.

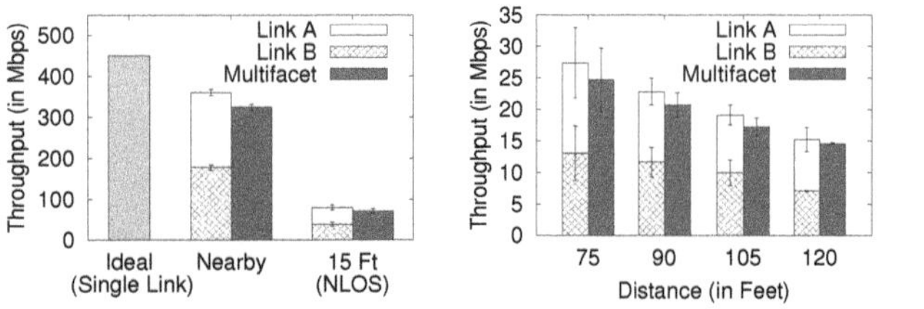

Figure 11: Comparing *Multifacet* with a single 802.11n link. The real applicability of *Multifacet* occurs at a NLOS separation of 70 feet or more.

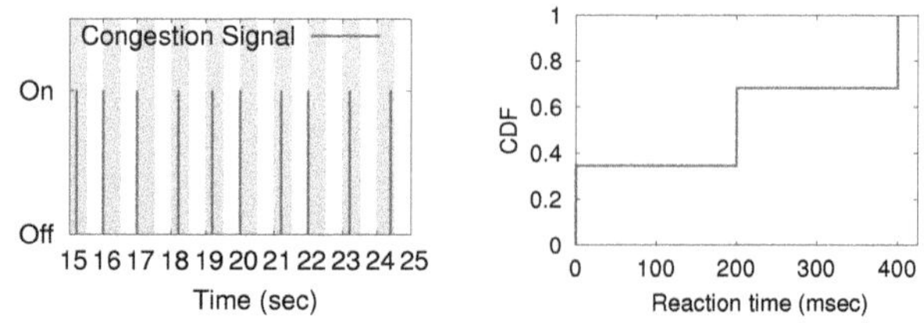

(a) Congestion control pattern (b) CDF of reaction time

Figure 12: (a) *Multifacet* quickly reacts to interference. (b) Reaction time is less than 200 msec in 70% of cases.

5.4 Micro Benchmarks

We study the contribution of specific design features of *Multifacet* to overall performance.

Ability to aggregate bandwidth over single wireless hop at highest speeds: We run the experiments in the desktop setup with WiFi NICs (3×3 MIMO) which offers higher speeds than WNDR3800 with (2×2 MIMO). In Figure 10, we present the throughput obtained using *Multifacet* with two WiFi links when compared to a single WiFi link of the same type. The plot shows both UDP and TCP throughputs when using (i) 802.11a links only, (ii) 802.11n links using 20 MHz channels, and (iii) 802.11n links with 40 MHz channels. We also show the throughput of each individual link when operating in isolation. These experiments were conducted in interference-free channels (achieved using RF cables). Hence, it captures the best case throughputs observed for each scenario. *Multifacet* using dual 3×3 MIMO interfaces is able to provide 337 Mbps TCP throughput and 431 Mbps for UDP. More importantly, in all cases, *Multifacet* is able to provide the sum of each link's bandwidth, and even for TCP throughputs with congestion control mechanisms. The ability to deliver capacity equal to the sum of the bandwidth of constituent links also implies that the additional queuing and buffering latencies of *Multifacet* system are negligible.

The above results calibrate *Multifacet* performance at the highest throughput cases. For more practical settings, we next evaluate *Multifacet* over-the-air in an uncontrolled (but relatively clean, 5 GHz) environment, where the (non line-of-sight) distance between the client–AP pair was varied. Figure 11 shows that the throughput of *Multifacet* was always within 10% of the aggregate bandwidth of individual links. This figure also brings out one of the key motivations for multi-interface systems. While a single 802.11n link achieves 180 Mbps throughput when minimally separated, it drops to 43 Mbps at a mere non line-of-sight separation of 15 feet, and to about 7-8 Mbps at a separation of 120 feet. In the presence of additional interference, these throughputs drop even further. *It is in these type of scenarios that Multifacet, with its ability to aggregate throughput, has practical use cases in indoor environments.*

Co-ordinated transmission throttling: To evaluate how quickly *Multifacet* adapts to the channel capacity, we project an interference every one sec during 200 sec experiment. The interference traffic at 30 Mbps was sent between two laptops placed near the client laptop with 500 msec ON and 500 msec OFF periods on the shared channel. The interference was sent at a low enough power to ensure no disruption to AP-repeater link over the shared channel. In the ON period, the queue of unsent packets destined for client starts to build up at repeater. We characterize the reaction time of transmission throttling algorithm after introducing the interference.

Figure 12(a) highlights one particular example of time series when the interference is injected and the congestion algorithm is triggered. We have observed similar pattern (quick start of transmission throttling) in the number of experiments and present some part of it for the sake of brevity. We also present the CDF of response time of *Multifacet* in Figure 12(b) as showing almost 70% of response time is less than 200 msec (especially, 35% cases react promptly as soon as the interference is injected) and transmission throttling algorithm is triggered within 400 msec in all cases. This shows the efficacy of our congestion detection and scheduling accordingly. The quick response ensures that *Multifacet* AP-repeater link utilizes the shared channel only when spare capacity is available and backs-off quickly when spare capacity decreases. The reaction time can be further reduced by increasing the frequency of congestion feedback however at the cost of added traffic overhead and more importantly due to increased possibility of reaction to transient channel variations. Based on empirical experimentation we find that 200 msec provides optimal transmission throttling.

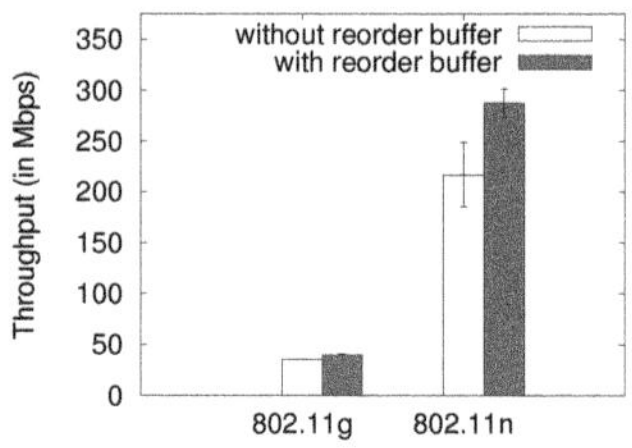

Figure 13: Throughput drops drastically when we do not have a reorder buffer to ensure TCP packets are not delivered out of sequence. The throughput drop is around 5 Mbps (10%) in 802.11a/g mode and 60 Mbps (25%) in 802.11n mode.

Benefits of reorder buffer: We evaluate the utility of a reorder buffer by comparing the performance of *Multifacet* system with and without one. For our experiments we have used a reorder buffer size of 2048 packets, which we have empirically found to work well for links operating in both 802.11a/g and 802.11n mode. In Figure 13, we find that in absence of a reorder buffer the TCP throughput degrades by 5 Mbps for the *Multifacet* system with links operating in 802.11a/g mode while it degrades by 60 Mbps with 802.11n links. The performance penalty is due to the triggering of TCP's retransmission and transmission throttling mechanism in presence of re-orderings in the received data.

Backpressure based striping algorithm: We evaluate the reaction times of the striping algorithm as a function of capacity changes in one of its constituent links. To characterize how quickly the backpressure based data striping algorithm can shift traffic load when one of its links becomes bad, we carry out an experiment, in which we introduce interference in the two channels of operation in an alternating on/off fashion. This interference is in the form of a traffic flow of 20 Mbps during the on duration that last 20 sec at a time. We measure the output from each link through these periods of interference. In our backpressure based system (Figure 14(a)), the output of the interfered link goes down, and causing a shift of the corresponding traffic into the other link. For instance, in time durations 45-65 sec, Link A sheds its load to Link B *immediately* which

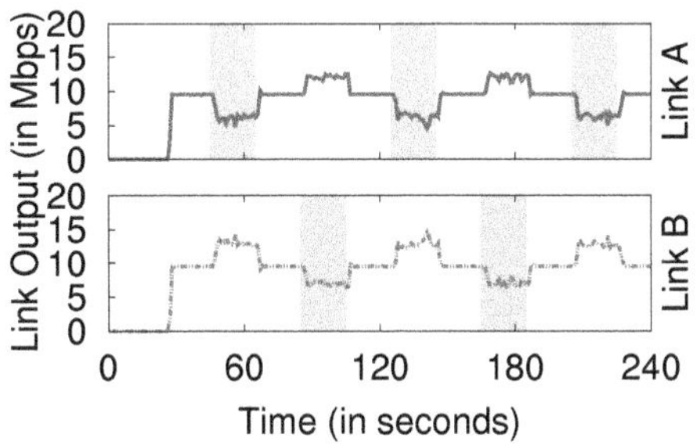

(a) Backpressure

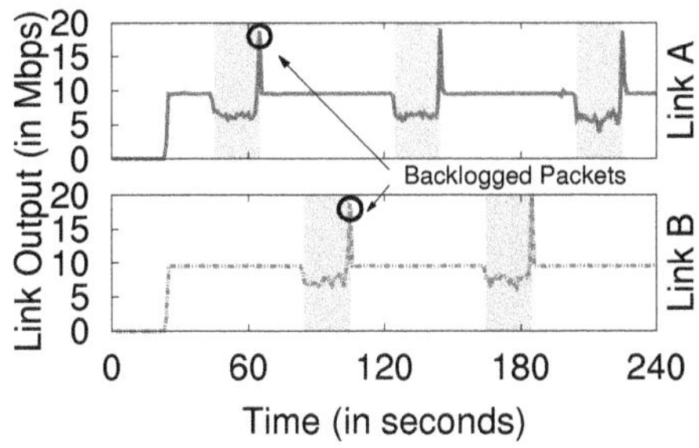

(b) Round-Robin

Figure 14: (a) The proportion of packets shift over time in the presence of other stations. (b) The Round-Robin scheme does not compensate for the reduced capacity by scheduling the backlog on the other interface.

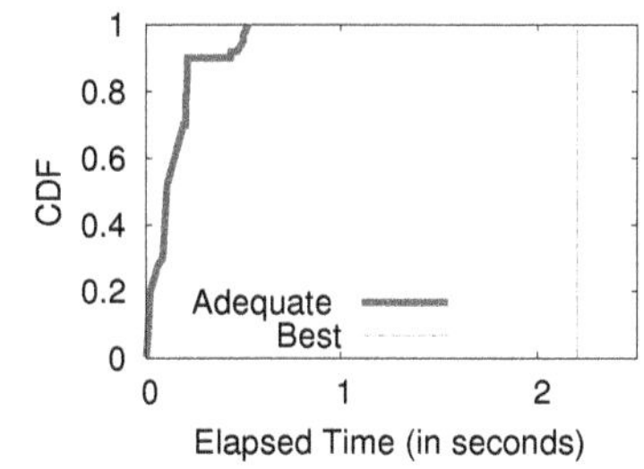

Figure 15: CDF of time duration required by the channel selection algorithms to converge on next channel.

Multi-radio mesh routing	*Multifacet*
1.62	2.15

Table 4: Table comparing performance of a multi-radio joint routing (adapted from ROMA [18]) and channel assignment algorithm with *Multifacet* packet striping. The values are normalized to that of a traditional repeater.

Buffering	TCP Throughput 802.11a/g (Mbps)	TCP Throughput 802.11n (Mbps)
Without	37.21 (1.82)	81.64 (3.34)
With	41.54 (0.29)	89.53 (0.26)

Table 5: Adding a packet buffer in *Multifacet* AP leads to several Mbps of throughput improvements.

proportionally increases. In contrast, in a round-robin based system (Figure 14(b)), no such load shifting would happen, and the interfered link would eventually release its backlogged packets in one burst (around 65 sec), leading to overall poor end-to-end behavior.

Comparison with multi-radio mesh routing: Traditional multi-hop, multi-radio mesh routing and channel assignment algorithms operate at flow level. In other words, they do not stripe packets from individual flows across multiple interfaces. Hence, such algorithms will just offer performance equal to that offered by a traditional repeater system. To highlight the relative benefits of our packet backpressure based packet striping and co-ordinated transmission throttling algorithm, we implement the routing logic of one such routing algorithm ROMA [18] as our packet striping decision logic[2]. Table 4, shows that *Multifacet* offers a 115% performance enhancement over traditional repeater system, compared to 62% gains offered by the routing logic of ROMA. The reason for ROMA's bad performance is that the routing logic explicitly tries to minimize the interference for the repeaterclient link on the shared channel[3]. Thus it is very conservative usage of the shared link. In contrast, *Multifacet* due its tight control loop can aggressively utilized the shared link while leading to a higher performance.

Packet buffering at *Multifacet* AP: To understand the benefits of the small packet buffer at the *Multifacet* AP, we determine the achievable TCP/UDP throughput with and without the packet buffering. We used a packet buffer of 200 packets for experiments and present the results in Table 5. As we can see, installing a packet buffer in the *Multifacet* AP increases TCP throughput by 10% when operating in 802.11a/g and 802.11n mode. The above results validate our decision of placing a small buffer in *Multifacet* AP. Note that above reported experiments were done in normal channel conditions without any external interference. We have found that the gains due to packet buffering goes up to 30% when the link conditions are more variable due to greater channel contention from other sources. The result is in agreement with our intuition that a packet buffer allows us to leverage bursty channel conditions by letting us send packets when the conditions are favorable.

Synchronous channel migration: We now illustrate the advantages of the *Adequate* channel selection algorithm over the more exhaustive but slower *Best* scheme, as described in § 3.4. In our system we limit the maximum number of channels that the AP needs to probe to 10. To trigger a channel switch, we degrade the quality of an operational channel quality by introducing interference. In both approaches, the AP uses a CSA with 2 beacon intervals, and hence the channel switch happens 200 msec after the CSA is triggered by the AP. Since the throughput measurement carried out by the sender takes about 20 msec for each channel, the total time to migrate to the next channel and measure its performance takes about 0.22 sec. Figure 15 shows that in 86% of the cases, *Adequate* needs to probe just 3 channels (i.e., 0.66 sec) to identify a channel that is sufficient to support the offered load. As we probe at most ten channels, the *Best* scheme needs around 2.2 sec to probe all channels and identify the best switch candidate.

5.5 Does 802.11n and other high speed technologies obviate *Multifacet*?

One could, perhaps, argue that the existing 802.11n standard with a maximum PHY data rate of 450 Mbps (for a 3×3 MIMO system) is adequate for all media delivery needs, and hence eliminates the need for a multi-radio solution. Our experiments reveal that under good channel conditions and minimal signal attenuation, a single 802.11n link can achieve throughputs in the 60-210 Mbps range. In this performance range, the client connected via *Multifacet* would achieve an even better throughput. However, at these speeds, the single 802.11n solution is more than adequate for all practical HD media applications, including the scenario where we attempt to stream a Blu-ray player to a nearby television set.

While the use of these high speed technologies advance the throughputs at the high end, when the signal attenuates across one or more walls in an indoor environment, or if there is sufficient interference in the channel, the actual throughputs of 802.11n can degrade sharply *to below 20 Mbps, and sometimes even below 5 Mbps.* It is in these lower throughput ranges that a throughput aggregation

[2]To maintain fairness, we implement packet reordering logic for ROMA as well.

[3]Minimizing intra-path interference is the desired behavior of ROMA. When we let ROMA reduce interference over AP-repeater link its performance is worse

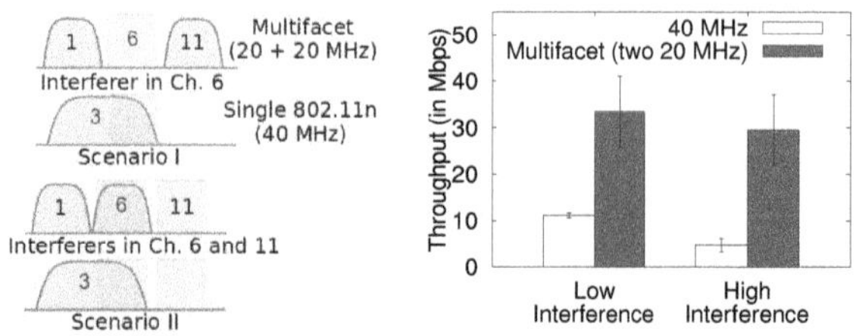

(a) Interference scenarios (b) Throughput gain of *Multifacet*

Figure 16: (a) A single 40 MHz 802.11n link (using 3×3 MIMO) performs far worse than a *Multifacet* system configured to use a total of 40 MHz of spectrum, using AP-repeater links operating on two 20 MHz channels on the 2.4 GHz band. (b) Experiment corresponding to interference Scenario II shown in (a).

system such as *Multifacet* becomes necessary and useful. A dual radio AP-repeater link can easily achieve double the throughput in these scenarios as it uses twice the spectrum (of a single WiFi link).

This gain is, however, not simply because of a wider spectrum occupancy of AP-repeater link. The flexibility provided by the multiplicity of wireless interfaces is a significant contributor to performance gain. If we limit the dual radio AP-repeater link to a total of 40 MHz (each WiFi interface uses a 20 MHz channel) and compare it with a single 40 MHz 802.11n link, in certain cases, we still observe performance advantages of our solution. For instance, in Scenario I shown in Figure 16(a), there is interference in channel 6 of the 2.4 GHz band (say, due to an independent AP). A single 40 MHz 802.11n link operating in this part of spectrum would experience significant interference from this source, while the proposed solution would be able to easily avoid this interferer. Even in Scenario II shown, where both solutions experience interference in at least 20 MHz of their operating spectrum, the overall impact of interference is far less for dual link AP-repeater link.

Figure 16(b) shows the significant advantages of the multi-interface approach to flexible channel bonding (operating at the MAC layer) compared to the PHY layer bonding approach. The figure shows results from experiments conducted in the 2.4 GHz band in corresponding to Scenario II of Figure 16(a). In this case, there are two other interferers occupying channels 6 and 11 and the AP-repeater picks channels 1 and 6 for operation. In contrast, the 802.11n 40 MHz system (operating with same amount of spectrum) picks channel 3. When the interferers emit a low volume of interfering traffic, *Multifacet* AP-repeater link aggregation achieves *more than double the throughput while occupying the same amount of spectrum.* When the interferers emit a higher volume of interference, *the gains are more than 6×*.

6. RELATED WORK

Multi-interface networking: Networking over multiple wired interfaces has been used in context of bandwidth aggregation, load-balancing and multi-homing. For example, researchers [26, 27, 38] presented mechanisms to bundle multiple, highly predictable, wired ATM links to construct a high bandwidth link. In contrast, in *Multifacet*, the WiFi links have significant variability and unpredictable changes in channel conditions and our solution is stylized to the various properties of two hop wireless networks.

Multipath TCP [29] and SCTP [37] are transport layer protocols designed to send a single flow over multiple paths. These schemes need modifications to end host systems and applications to handle packet re-ordering and related issues. In contrast, *Multifacet* is a custom dual interface repeater which does no need application of system modifications at end host modifications. Authors in [25, 33] study end-to-end flow striping techniques, however, our flow striping is not end-to-end but restricted to a single hop.

Akin to MPTCP, mHTTP [23] utilizes simultaneous multi paths over a network which only requires application layer supports and modifications on socket interface. In contrast, *Multifacet* is implemented on MAC and network layers for efficiently operating multiple links while maintaining transparency.

Multi-interface links: Glia [31] is a system, similar to *Multifacet* to an extent as they explore the use of parallel WiFi links simultaneously for high throughput. However, it differs in the core challenge being addressed by *Multifacet* – Glia does not stripe packets of a single (TCP or UDP) flow over different WiFi links and instead focuses on the aggregate throughputs of a large number of flows partitioned across different links. FatVAP [28] is a system to opportunistically aggregate bandwidth from multiple WiFi APs using a single client WiFi radio interface. Again, in contrast to *Multifacet*, the FatVAP system does not stripe packets from a single flow over these different APs. Finally, the MAR system [35] explores bandwidth aggregation over multiple low bandwidth 2.5G links for vehicular applications. In their experiments, the system limits each flow to a single 2.5G network only. In contrast, we explore the challenges of striping a single flow over two high-speed WiFi links.

Multi-hop wireless communication: Authors in [13–21] have proposed channel assignment, routing, network coding etc. for improving the performance of mesh networks. Researcher in [24, 30, 36] have presented resource reuse and rate allocation algorithms to exploit spectral efficiency in mesh networks. We note that *Multifacet*'s gains are independent of rate adaptation algorithm used in constituent links. This is due to the fact that *Multifacet* deals with efficient scheduling of traffic over the links operating between AP-Repeater-Client. In contrast, a rate adaptation algorithm will be concerned with identifying the best modulation and coding scheme (MCS) for a given channel condition and not with when and how many packets to send on a given link. The key idea in such prior works is to optimally leverage multi-radio capability for improving throughputs across such networks. Our two-hop configuration of *Multifacet* is a special case of the multi-hop multi-radio mesh network, where there are two parallel links in the upstream hop and a single link in the downstream hop. Additionally, once a channel is assigned to the downstream hop (to the client), it cannot be easily changed or else this can be disruptive to the client when a high bandwidth flow is active. In our design of *Multifacet*, we focus primarily on techniques to opportunistically use the excess bandwidth of upstream links to enhance performance. Such prior works *operate at a flow level and do not address the problem of splitting individual flows across multiple interfaces*. The key uniqueness of *Multifacet* from prior mesh networking literature, thus, comes from its focus on efficiently splitting a flow over multiple interfaces at high data rates under varying channel conditions. Hence, this paper is quite complementary to the general body of work in the context of multi-radio multi-hop wireless mesh networks.

Wireless range extenders: There are several commercial dual band range extenders [2–4], in addition to traditional routers [1,6], which aim to provide extended wireless coverage both indoors and outdoors. In spite of having multiple radios, these products simply rebroadcast traffic from the AP based on a static configuration. *Multifacet* improves upon this by intelligently scheduling packets sent to the repeater while providing a single link abstraction. Range extenders [9, 10], which operate both links on a single channel are inferior in performance to dual band wireless range extenders and have been superseded by dual band devices.

Future MIMO based systems: MIMO based technologies such as directional MIMO antennas [7] have been used in outdoor settings to increase the range and capacity of wireless systems. Versions of such techniques customized to operate in indoor settings can provide an alternative solution for extending wireless coverage. Thus, obviating the need for repeater altogether. The main difference of *Multifacet* from such systems is that we make software only modifications on COTS repeater to enhance performance of state-of-art repeater systems, whereas, MIMO systems will necessitate hardware changes.

7. CONCLUSIONS

Wireless repeater devices are a special case of two hop wireless mesh setups and are extensively used in various settings to enhance the quality of wireless access for clients. Repeater products are available today from all leading vendors (Netgear, Linksys, Belkin, DLink, Apple, etc.), and especially dual-interface repeaters are top selling products. In this work, we present the design, implementation and evaluation of *Multifacet* – a software solution for dual-interface repeaters for providing increased bandwidth capacity to clients. *Multifacet* needs only software modifications to work on off-the-shelf dual band wireless APs and repeater. We demonstrate its superiority over conventional approaches through experimentation in varied wireless environments. Video demonstration of the performance of *Multifacet* can be found at `http://youtu.be/0W1Mj1T6MkY`

Acknowledgements

We thank Michael Bower for his help in conducting repeater experiments. We are grateful to the anonymous reviewers whose comments helped bring the paper to its final form. All authors are supported in part by the US National Science Foundation through awards CNS-1040648, CNS-0916955, CNS-0855201, CNS-0747177, CNS-1064944, CNS-1059306, CNS-1345293, CNS-1343363, and CNS-1258290.

8. REFERENCES

[1] Apple AirPort Express, http://www.apple.com/airportexpress

[2] Cisco range extender, http://www.pcmag.com/article2/0,2817,2399489,00.asp

[3] Belkin range extender, http://www.belkin.com/us/F9K1106-Belkin/p/P-F9K1106

[4] Netgear range extender, http://netgear.com/home/products/wireless-range-extenders/WN2500RP.aspx

[5] MultiPath TCP - Linux Kernel implementation, http://mptcp.info.ucl.ac.be

[6] OpenWrt, http://www.openwrt.org

[7] Directional outdoor MIMO, http://www.fortinet.com/products/fortiap/outdoor-MIMO-antennas.html

[8] EvalVid - A Video Quality Evaluation Tool-set, www.tkn.tu-berlin.de/research/evalvid/

[9] Linksys RE1000, http://support.linksys.com/en-us/support/rangeexpanders/RE1000

[10] Netgear WN2000RPT, http://www.netgear.com/home/products/wireless-range-extenders/wn2000rpt.aspx

[11] Network Emulation, http://www.linuxfoundation.org/collaborate/workgroups/networking/netem

[12] Xiph.Org–Test Media page, http://media.xiph.org/video/derf

[13] S. Biswas and R. Morris, "ExOR: Opportunistic Multi-hop Routing for Wireless Networks", *ACM Sigcomm*, 2005.

[14] K. Chebrolu, B. Raman and S. Sen, "Long-Distance 802.11b Links: Performance Measurements and Experience", *ACM MobiCom*, 2006.

[15] J. Camp, J. Robinson, C. Steger and E. Knightly, "Measurement driven Deployment of a Two-tier Urban Mesh Access Network", *ACM MobiSys*. 2006.

[16] S. Chachulski, M. Jennings, S. Katti and D. Katabi, "Trading Structure for Randomness in Wireless Opportunistic Routing", *ACM Sigcomm*, 2007.

[17] B. Ko, V. Misra, J. Padhye and D. Rubenstein, "Distributed Channel Assignment in Multi-Radio 802.11 Mesh networks", *WCNC*, 2007.

[18] A. Dhananjay, H. Zhang, J. Li and L. Subramanian, "Practical, Distributed Channel Assignment and Routing in Dual-radio Mesh Networks", *ACM Sigcomm*, 2009.

[19] A. Raniwala and T. Chiueh, "Architecture and Algorithms for an IEEE 802.11-based Multi-Radio Wireless Mesh Networks", *IEEE Infocom*, 2005.

[20] K. Ramachandran, I. Sheriff, E. Belding and K. Almeroth, "A Multi-Radio 802.11 Mesh Network Architecture", *ACM Mobile Networks and Applications*, 13(1):132-146, 2008.

[21] R. Draves, J. Padhye and B. Zill, "Routing in Multi-Radio, Multi-Hop Wireless Mesh Networks", *ACM MobiCom*, 2004.

[22] E. Rozner, J. Seshadri, Y. Mehta and L. Qiu, "SOAR: Simple Opportunistic Adaptive Routing Protocol for Wireless Mesh Networks", *IEEE Transactions on Mobile Computing*, 2009.

[23] J. Kim, R. Khalili, A. Feldmann, Y-C. Chen and D. Towsley, "Multi-Source Multi Path HTTP (mHTTP): A Proposal", *arXiv*, 2013.

[24] L-W. Chen, Y-C. Tseng, Y-C. Wang, D-W. Wang and J-J. Wu, "Exploiting Spectral Reuse in Routing, Resource Allocation, and Scheduling for IEEE 802.16 Mesh Networks", *IEEE Transactions on Vehicular Technology*, 58(1), 2009.

[25] K. Chebrolu, B. Raman and R. Ramesh, "A Network Layer Approach to Enable TCP over Multiple Interfaces", *ACM Wireless Networking*, 11(5):637-650, 2005.

[26] J. Duncanson, "Inverse Multiplexing", *IEEE Communications Magazine*, 1994.

[27] P. Fredette, "The Past, Present, and Future of Inverse Multiplexing", *IEEE Communications Magazine*, 1994.

[28] S. Kandula, K. C-J. Lin, T. Badirkhanli and D. Katabi, "FatVAP: Aggregating AP Backhaul Capacity to Maximize Throughput", *ACM NSDI*, 2008.

[29] H. Han, S. Shakkottai, C. Hollot, R. Srikant and D. Towsley, "Multi-path TCP: A Joint Congestion Control and Routing Scheme to Exploit Path Diversity on the Internet", *IEEE/ACM Transactions on Networking*, 14(6):1260-1271, 2006.

[30] J. Tang, G. Xue and W. Zhang, "Cross-layer Optimization for End-to-End Rate Allocation in Multi-Radio Wireless Mesh Networks", *Wireless Networks*, 15(1), pp 53-64, 2009.

[31] S. Kakumanu and R. Sivakumar, "Glia: A Practical Solution for Effective High Datarate Wifi-Arrays", *ACM MobiCom*, 2009.

[32] Z. Orlov, "Network-Driven Adaptive Video Streaming in Wireless Environments", *IEEE PIMRC*, 2008.

[33] D. S. Phatak and T. Goff, "A Novel Mechanism for Data Streaming Across Multiple IP Links for Improving Throughput and Reliability in Mobile Environments", *IEEE Infocom*, 2002.

[34] C. Raiciu, S. Barre, C. Pluntke, A. Greenhalgh, D. Wischik and M. Handley, "Improving Datacenter Performance and Robustness with Multipath TCP", *ACM Sigcomm*, 2011.

[35] P. Rodriguez, I. Pratt, J. Chesterfield, R. Chakravorty and S. Banjeree, "MAR: A Commuter Router Infrastructure for the Mobile Internet", *ACM Mobisys*, 2004.

[36] S. Kompella, S. Mao, Y. T. Hou and H. D. Sherali, "On Path Selection and Rate Allocation for Video in Wireless Mesh Networks", *IEEE/ACM Transactions on Networking*, 17(1):212-224, 2009.

[37] R. Stewart, "Stream Control Transmission Protocol", *RFC 4960, IETF*, 2007.

[38] C. B. S. Traw and J. M. Smith, "Striping within the Network Subsystem", *IEEE Network*, 9(4):22-32, 1995.

[39] D. Wischik, C. Raiciu, A. Greenhalgh and M. Handley, "Design, Implementation and Evaluation of Congestion Control for Multipath TCP", *ACM NSDI*, 2011.

Cutting the Cord: a Robust Wireless Facilities Network for Data Centers

Yibo Zhu, Xia Zhou[§], Zengbin Zhang, Lin Zhou, Amin Vahdat[†], Ben Y. Zhao and Haitao Zheng
University of California, Santa Barbara [§]Dartmouth College [†]University of California, San Diego & Google
{yibo,zengbin,linzhou,ravenben,htzheng}@cs.ucsb.edu, xia@cs.dartmouth.edu, vahdat@cs.ucsd.edu

ABSTRACT

Today's network control and management traffic are limited by their reliance on existing data networks. Fate sharing in this context is highly undesirable, since control traffic has very different availability and traffic delivery requirements. In this paper, we explore the feasibility of building a dedicated wireless *facilities network* for data centers. We propose *Angora*, a low-latency facilities network using low-cost, 60GHz beamforming radios that provides robust paths decoupled from the wired network, and flexibility to adapt to workloads and network dynamics. We describe our solutions to address challenges in link coordination, link interference and network failures. Our testbed measurements and simulation results show that Angora enables large number of low-latency control paths to run concurrently, while providing low latency end-to-end message delivery with high tolerance for radio and rack failures.

Categories and Subject Descriptors

C.2.1 [**Network Architecture and Design**]: Wireless communication

Keywords

Data centers, 60 GHz wireless, wireless beamforming

1. INTRODUCTION

With the recent rapid growth in data center networks, come dramatic increases in management complexity. Yet despite advances in Software Defined Networks (SDNs) [11, 15] and network/traffic engineering design [7, 10, 12], little has changed in how data centers deliver control traffic.

We believe the time is right to introduce the *facilities network* as a core tool for managing data center networks. The facilities network is orthogonal to the data plane, and is responsible for multiple critical jobs. For example,

- *Control Plane* – Data center networks require an orthogonal network to support network control protocols. With the arrival of SDNs, a variety of protocols will traverse the control plane between network control servers [28] and hardware switches. For example, the control plane can install forwarding table updates or reset hardware in response to switch failures in the data plane [40].
- *Facility Bring up and Installation* – Hardware devices do not arrive with appropriate operating system images, device configurations, or security keys. These images must be installed on the data center floor. While the process is automated, it cannot rely on a data plane network to communicate with switches/servers, because much of the data plane could be inoperative.

MobiCom'14, September 7-11, 2014, Maui, Hawaii, USA.
Copyright 2014 ACM 978-1-4503-2783-1/14/09 ...$15.00.
http://dx.doi.org/10.1145/2639108.2639140.

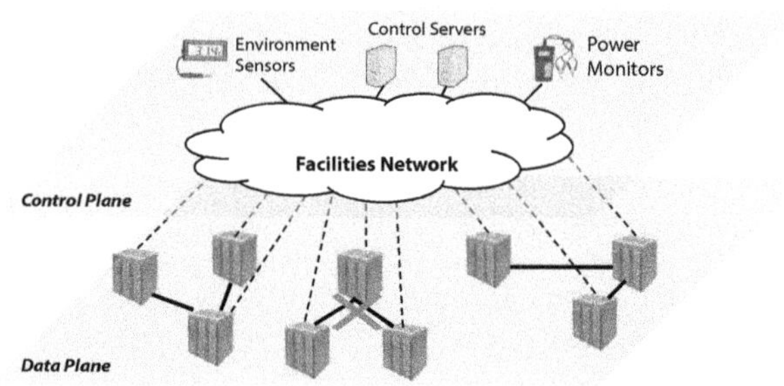

Figure 1: A facilities network providing robust delivery of control traffic in a data center.

Compared to traditional data plane networks, the facilities network has very different requirements. First, it requires substantially lower bandwidth, *e.g.* hundreds of Mbps rather than 40Gbps [7, 10, 12], and its bandwidth demands grow at much slower rates than those of the data plane. Second, control traffic has much tighter constraints on packet delivery latency. Even "moderate" delivery delays to route updates or policy changes can have a dramatic impact on overall network performance [12, 32, 33].

Third and most importantly, the facilities network requires significantly higher availability and long-term survivability than the data plane. Hence, it cannot share fate with the data plane network, and must be isolated from faults and outages in the data plane. For example, it must remain available during constant physical upgrades to the data center. In a facility with 10's–100's of MW of infrastructure, substantial portions of the building are always undergoing upgrades that may tear out entire rows of cable trays. The facilities network should remain available for the lifetime of the building, *e.g.*, 10–20 years, rather than the lifetime of a cluster, *e.g.*, 3–5 years. While brief outages in data plane networks are acceptable, the underlying facilities network must fail last and fail least, because it is the basis for recovering from data plane failures and monitoring critical hardware. This rules out in-band solutions such as VLANs [5].

We show an example of a facilities network in Figure 1, where an orthogonal facilities network provides control servers with access to sensors at data center racks, environmental sensors, and power junctions. Even as the data network experiences failures from hardware faults or planned maintenance, the facilities network remains available.

Design Space. Given its substantially lower bandwidth and higher availability requirements, one approach to building a facilities network is simply to use a second, smaller instance of the data plane network. However, this faces a number of practical challenges. First, a data plane network is built for speed. 40Gb/s ports are likely overkill for a facilities network. The size and reach of the network would also dramatically increase hardware costs. Second, data plane networks are wired networks. Whenever a new switch, power unit, A/C unit or battery is added, it must be connected via cables. Planning the necessary cable tray infrastructure to connect arbitrary points in the network is a costly logistical challenge [2, 38].

Third, cables in the facilities network would likely be copper (for cost, reach, and compatibility with older devices), and typically cannot coexist with optics in the same cable tray because of interference and weight issues [31]. Further, copper cables are 10x the bulk of optical fiber [23]. So while the facilities network has fewer ports, the bulk of the control cable infrastructure may actually exceed the data plane.

Finally, fault isolation is a challenge. It is difficult to build a wired control infrastructure that is orthogonal to and independent of a data plane, because the data plane undergoes physical upgrades on a regular basis. Upgrading power and cooling units is a common operation in the maintenance of a data center building. The simplest and fastest way[1] is to cordon off an area and "bulldoze" equipment. But if a wired control infrastructure shares physical facilities, *e.g.* cable trays, with the data plane, they will suffer the same outage patterns. Trying to isolate and preserve a "bisection" of copper cables for the wired facilities network in practice is difficult or intractable.

A Wireless Facilities Network. These issues motivate us to explore the design and architecture of a wireless facilities network *physically decoupled from the data plane*. We consider both wireless networks on commodity WiFi, and networks built using recent advances on 60GHz 3D beamforming links [44]. Our experiments confirm that contention-based access produces large, unpredictable packet delivery delays in WiFi networks, far outside the acceptable range for a facilities network. Instead, we consider using directional wireless links in the unlicensed 60GHz band. These links are highly directional, provide high data rates, and attenuate quickly with distance [20, 44]. This limits interference footprint and allows multiple wireless links to transmit simultaneously.

Two challenges follow from the choice of directional wireless links. First, based on significantly better throughput and interference characteristics, directional links would be implemented using horn antennas over phased antenna arrays. However, the benefits come at the cost of slow tuning delays from the physical tuning mechanism. This significantly limits the ability of the facilities network to support low-delay communication between racks and control servers. Second, even with much smaller interference footprints, directional links can still experience interference and associated delays in a high density setting.

In this paper, we describe the design of *Angora*, a facilities network that employs a structured 60GHz wireless overlay to support low delay, robust, any-to-any communication. We summarize the key contributions of our work below.

[1]Upgrade speed translates directly to dollars; consider the depreciation cost of leaving 10MW of servers idle for four weeks.

- First, we propose a fixed structured network design for Angora based on Kautz graphs, which addresses the issue of directional link coordination and antenna tuning delays. This provides any-to-any communication with bounded delays, and eliminates link coordination except when significant numbers of racks fail or move their positions.
- Second, we use location-aware ID assignment to manage physical positioning of wireless links and reduce interference between nearby directional flows. This improves Angora's ability to support parallel wireless links.
- Third, we modify the Kautz graph to support arbitrary network sizes, and design routing algorithms that leverage redundant paths for fault recovery.
- Finally, we evaluate Angora using both simulations and experimental measurements on a 60GHz testbed. We find that Angora paths work well in practice: the 3D beamforming links are very stable over time, and offer throughput and latency comparable to wired networks. Angora's structured network topology creates large angular separation between nearby links, effectively minimizing interference and producing low, predictable end-to-end message latency. Simulations show that Angora can provide high levels of flow concurrency and low-latency packet delivery, and is highly robust against node and link failures.

Network management is an important challenge for data centers growing in both size and complexity. Our work provides a first step towards a robust facilities network capable of delivering control traffic with low latency, even during periods of disruption that could hinder or disrupt portions of the data network. As network managers gain experience deploying and operating facilities networks, we expect their requirements to continue to adapt to an evolving set of monitoring and management applications.

2. REQUIREMENTS AND DESIGN SPACE

We now describe the requirements for facilities networks, and explore the design space and basic challenges. We assume standard wired connectivity from servers to Top of Rack (ToR) switches, and focus on building a facilities network at the rack level.

2.1 Requirements

A viable design for a data center facilities network must satisfy three key requirements.

Reliability. The facilities network must be reliable under equipment failures and upgrades, and support a range of management applications [7, 28, 37]. Upon single component (*e.g.* radio, rack) failures or the removal of an entire row of racks for upgrades, it must continue to route traffic around failures with minimal delays.

It must also support management applications running on either a single controller [7] or a cluster of controllers [28, 37]. Because controllers can run on any racks, the facilities network must adapt to different controller configuration and placement. This argues for support of *any-to-any* rack communication.

Bounded Delay. An effective facilities network must deliver control traffic within bounded time [28]. For example, flow control mechanisms such as Hedera [7] require the controller to pull a large volume ($\approx$ 1.3MByte) of flow statistics from each switch within hundreds of ms [12]. Similarly, a common SDN paradigm [11] involves punting the first packet of flows to a central controller to install specific per-flow hardware rules.

Scalability. The implementation of the facilities network must scale to large data centers. In particular, protocols for the facilities network must incur minimal overhead and scale gracefully to a large number of flows.

2.2 Candidate Wireless Solutions

With these requirements in mind, we consider potential wireless technologies for the facilities network.

WiFi. WiFi is the obvious choice given its cost and availability. The problem, however, is its large interference footprint. In densely packed data centers, WiFi MIMO or channel allocation techniques can only mitigate interference to a limited degree. Thus flows will contend for medium access, resulting in large, unpredictable contention latencies. For example, with only 10 competing flows, it takes up to $2s$ to download a 2MB message using 802.11n [1]. We further confirm this by performing latency experiments where racks upload messages to a central controller using off-the-shelf 802.11n and 802.11ac equipment[2]. As expected, upload latency per message grows with the number of competing flows, and varies significantly across flows. 20 1.3MB 802.11n flows can take anywhere from $539ms$ to $3.6s$ to complete, with an average of $2.5s$.

While recent advances in multi-user MIMO/interference alignment allow multiple flows to run simultaneously, they require significant coordination among transmitters, which can translate into unpredictable MAC latencies. Clearly, it would be difficult for a WiFi-based network to meet the bounded latency requirements in dense data center environments.

Another concern regarding WiFi is the danger of information leakage and electromagnetic attacks. In particular, attackers can also use high-power radiation devices to produce heavy interference and disrupt an entire facilities network.

60GHz. Recent studies have proposed the use of 60GHz links in data centers [20, 35, 44]. 60GHz technology operates on a band of 7GHz unlicensed spectrum, with multi-Gbps data rates at a range of 100+m [44]. 60GHz has several features that enable it to provide wired-like connectivity.

- *Stability*: Placed on the top of server racks of 7-9 feet in height, 60GHz static links are *highly stable* in the data center scenario. Their transmissions follow the free-space propagation model without multipath fading [20, 44]. We also confirmed this by testing two different off-the-shelf 60GHz radios over 3 weeks (see §5.1). The standard deviation of link throughput is less than 0.5% of the average throughput.
- *Small interference footprint*: 60GHz links are directional and experience fast link attenuation. In particular, we leverage recent work on 3D beamforming [44], which reflects 60GHz beams off the ceiling[3], bypassing obstacles in the 2D plane and further reducing the interference footprint.
- *Security*: 60GHz signals are directional and cannot penetrate walls or large obstacles, thus are generally immune to eavesdropping and electromagnetic attacks in data centers.
- *Availability*: Recent low-cost silicon implementations make 60GHz radios affordable. While high-end 60GHz radios offer 1Gbps at 100+m [44], the WiloCity chipset costs only $37.5, and already offers 1Gbps at 20m using a basic 2x8 antenna array. Its range can be extended using narrow-beam antennas [20]. Since typical med-sized data centers (*e.g.* 320 racks) require a 40-50m range, 60GHz and WiFi hardware costs and energy consumptions are comparable.

Given these considerations, we rule out WiFi as the core transmission technology, and instead consider potential facilities network designs using 60GHz beamforming links.

One may consider a hybrid wired-wireless solution that places 60GHz radios on the ceilings (as access points) and 60GHz radios on top of the racks (as stations), forming LoS links between the APs and stations. We can connect these 60GHz APs via a wired backbone (on the ceiling). While feasible, this solution faces the same fault tolerance problem, *i.e.* the "bulldoze" problem stated in the introduction. It also requires additional cabling and switches to connect the 60GHz APs on the ceiling. Therefore, in this paper we focus on designing a completely wireless solution using 60GHz 3D beamforming, which does not require any wired backbone.

2.3 Key Design Challenges

While 60GHz links seem promising as a link layer primitive for a facilities network, there are a number of challenges to address in any practical system.

Challenge 1: Coordination of Directional Links. The first problem is link coordination. 60GHz radios are highly directional, and thus must align their antennas before communication. Current 60GHz data center designs set up links dynamically [20, 44], requiring an extra "coordination" signaling path and a central scheduler to coordinate end-points. This brings considerable latency and complexity when deploying and managing the facilities network.

Challenge 2: Limited Number of Radios. Fixed surface area on server racks limits the number of radios placed atop each rack. For example, today's standard rack is 4ftx2ft and a 60GHz radio is 1ftx1ft [44], so at most 8 radios can sit atop each rack. Because 60GHz links are highly directional, each rack can only communicate with a small, constant number of peers in parallel. This limited "node degree" makes it hard for a rack to reach any other rack with bounded delay.

Challenge 3: Link Interference. 60GHz links produce small interference footprints, which are further reduced using 3D reflection. However, two links still interfere if their destinations are close and their arrival angles are similar. Such interference makes it hard to guarantee bounded delay.

3. ANGORA 60GHZ OVERLAY

To address the above challenges, we introduce *Angora*, a wireless facilities network formed by connecting server racks with static 60GHz 3D beamforming links. Angora is a *schedule-free wireless overlay*, built using 60GHz radios with fixed antenna directions, inter-connecting all racks using a small *constant* number of hops (see Figure 2(a)).

This facilities network design provides three key benefits.

- Antenna directions are pre-tuned and fixed for a given topology[4], and no antenna alignment/rotation is necessary regardless of changing traffic patterns. This eliminates the need for link coordination and associated delays, while simplifying bootstrapping and fault detection/recovery.
- A well-designed overlay guarantees short paths between any two racks, with a maximum diameter that scales logarithmically with the number of racks. Thus, latency between two racks is both small and predictable.
- The overlay supports any model of control traffic. A single network can support arbitrary control traffic patterns, including one-to-one, one-to-many and many-to-many.

[2]802.11ac: Netgear 6300 AP with 6200 adapters; 802.11n: D-Link DIR-825 AP with laptops using BCM4322/4331 chipsets.

[3]3D beamforming requires clearance above racks, which is already in place based on images of some of Google's data centers [3].

[4]Physical rack placements in data centers rarely change, except during upgrades or repairs. Thus it is feasible to fix antenna directions for a given overlay topology while applying fault recovery (see §4.3) to handle unexpected interruptions.

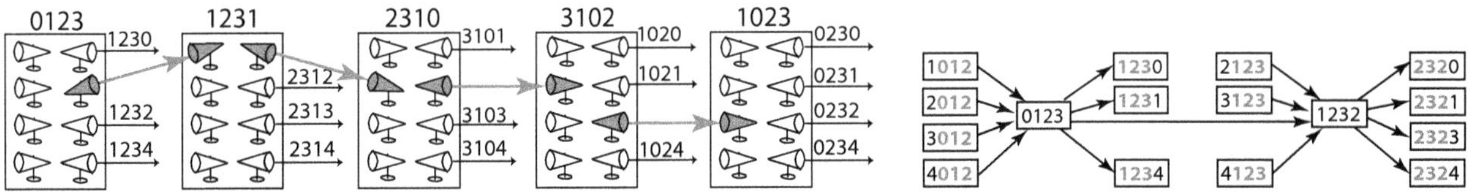

(a) The Angora overlay built from 3D beamforming links: an example path

(b) Kautz Overlay

Figure 2: High-level view of the Angora wireless facilities network. (a) An example path from one ToR switch (rack ID 0123) to a controller hosted in the rack of ID 1023. Each rack has 8 radios (connected by a small switch), 4 for incoming and 4 for outgoing links. Radios used by this Angora path are in green, and each green arrow represents a 3D beamforming link. (b) Two nodes in a Kautz graph (d=4,k=4). Each node points to 4 nodes whose $(k-1)$-digit prefix matches its own $(k-1)$-digit suffix.

The key to attaining these properties is the structure of the overlay network. We considered two approaches, an unstructured approach, *i.e.* a random topology, and a structured approach, *i.e.* using a compact routing graph.

A Randomized (Unstructured) Approach. Wireless radios give us the flexibility to set up or reconfigure wireless links between any two racks as necessary. In a simple, *randomized* approach to network construction, links are created by connecting pairs of randomly chosen nodes (racks) with available ports. Prior work in wired data center networks shows that a randomized graph topology can provide flexibility and short paths [36].

In our context, a randomized graph topology offers several potential benefits. First is simplicity. Implementing randomized link creation is straightforward and potentially more robust against implementation errors. Second, randomized topologies should offer short paths in practice [36]. Finally, they should provide built-in path redundancy, potentially offering high availability and robustness to random failures.

The tradeoff, is unpredictability. While random graphs provide good properties for *most* paths, there will always be a non-insignificant tail in any probabilistic distribution, *i.e.* some portion of all paths will experience undesirable properties such as longer paths or high link interference. These performance artifacts will have an outsized impact on overall performance, as end-to-end performance is usually determined by the weakest link [14].

A Structured Approach. The alternative is to impose structure on the overlay in return for stronger performance guarantees and more predictability. A naive approach is to organize all links into a single tree rooted at some network controller. This, however, makes a strong assumption that traffic patterns (and controller locations) are static, and more importantly, known to the system *a priori*. It also limits bisection bandwidth and utility of parallel flows.

Instead, we turn our attention to Kautz graphs [26], a structured graph topology that guarantees paths between all node pairs are bounded. We chose it over other well-known structures such as de Bruijn graphs [13] because of four reasons. *First*, for a network of size N, Kautz graph guarantees the path between any two nodes has at most $\log_d(\frac{d}{d+1} \cdot N)$ hops, thus strictly bounding latency between any two racks. Such guarantee on all node pairs also eliminates the need for knowing traffic patterns and controller locations a priori. *Second*, Kautz graphs require only constant degree per node, which address our constraint of limited radios per rack. Specifically, each node/rack has d incoming and d outgoing edges, which translates into $2d$ radios placed atop each rack. *Third*, relative to de Bruijn (and other graphs), Kautz graphs distribute flows more evenly through the network, and guarantee a smaller network diameter[5]. *Finally*, routing on a Kautz topology is simple and uses digit-shifting, which is easily implemented in today's switches using prefix-matching.

We now briefly describe the Kautz topology to provide context for Angora. In a Kautz (d, k) graph with N nodes (racks), each node's out-degree d and the graph diameter k satisfy the equation $N = d^k + d^{k-1}$. Each node's ID has k digits with base $d+1$. We represent a nodeID by $x_0 x_1..x_{k-1}$, where $x_i \neq x_{i+1}, x_i \in [0, d]$, and $0 \leq i < k$. A node n_i keeps pointers to d nodes whose first $k-1$ digits match n_i's last $k-1$ digits (shown in Figure 2(b)). Routing proceeds by choosing the successor who will match the destination ID with one more digit, left-shifting the node ID by one digit at each hop. For example, the route from 0123 to 4321 would proceed as 0123→1234→2343→3432→4321. Thus at most k hops connect any two nodes. For a network of 320 racks, each with 8 radios, any rack can reach another within 4 hops.

Summary. Given the above discussion, we choose the Kautz topology over a probabilistic, randomized network topology to satisfy the deterministic performance properties desired in a data center context. Our choice echoes designs made years ago in the peer-to-peer networking space, where structured overlays with bounded performance guarantees were chosen over random topologies [16]. A structured network is also easier to bootstrap. Each node's nodeID can be statically mapped to an unique IP address using a carefully chosen hash function. We will also show in §4 that the organized structure of Kautz graphs enables further reduction of wireless interference in data centers by optimizing node ID assignment.

4. ANGORA DESIGN

Angora's basic design addresses two fundamental challenges facing the facilities network: pre-tuned antenna directions remove the need of link coordination, while constant-degree overlay supports any traffic pattern using a fixed set of radios. When implementing Kautz graphs using wireless links, however, we identified a new set of practical challenges: 1) handling the correlation between link interference and ID assignment, 2) developing Kautz graph algorithms to support incomplete graphs, and 3) providing robustness against node and link failures. We now describe our solutions to these three key challenges.

4.1 Interference-Aware ID Assignment

Our first challenge is to assign logical node IDs in a Kautz graph to physical racks in the data center[6]. This assignment determines link placement and thus network interference conditions. Even with 3D beamforming 60GHz links, interference is a serious problem in dense data centers. A suboptimal link placement can de-

[5]For a fixed degree d and node count $N = d^k + d^{k-1}$, the Kautz graph has the smallest diameter of any possible directed graph.

[6]Given the small surface space atop each rack, we found the mapping of radios to links at each node has minimum impact on overlay performance. We thus applied a random mapping uniformly to all the nodes. This differs from [44] which requires antenna rotation.

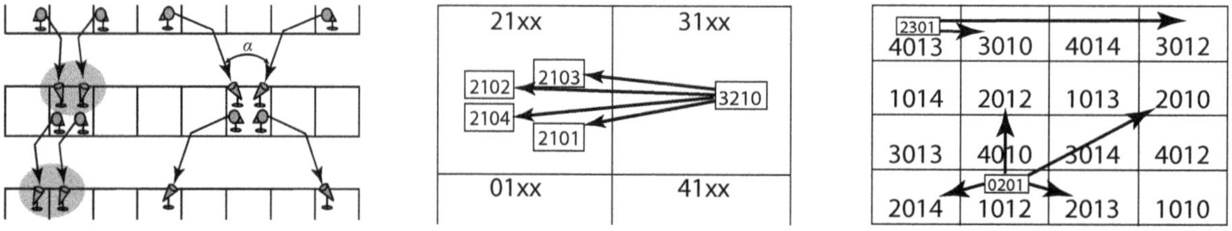

(a) Link interference (b) Hierarchical ID Assignment (c) Hybrid ID Assignment

Figure 3: (a) Using 3D beamforming, nearly parallel links targeting the same region can interfere with each other, but increasing the 3D angular separation α between links reduces interference. (b) Hierarchical ID assignment increases angular separation from many nodes to a single target, but links from a single source to nearby destinations can still interfere. (c) The proposed Hybrid ID assignment interleaves nodes by prefix and suffix, increasing angular separation and minimizing interference for links. For both (b) and (c), each directed link represents a ceiling-reflected beamforming link toward the destination, as illustrated in (a).

grade link concurrency, reducing the number of simultaneous transmissions possible.

Intuition says that 60GHz links targeting nearby destinations will experience stronger interference, but interference can be effectively reduced by increasing 3D angular separation between two links, *i.e.* α in Figure 3(a). We test this property using two types of off-the-shelf 60GHz radios. Results confirm the correlation with 3D angular separation, and found that in general, 10-12° of angular separation is sufficient to nullify link interference (see §5.1). Motivated by this intuition, we seek to identify node ID assignments that can maximize 3D angular separations between links.

Naive Solutions. Our search started from a few intuitive solutions, *i.e. sequential*, where we assign IDs to racks in row or column order, *Hilbert*, where we assign IDs by ordering the racks using a space-filling Hilbert Curve [22], and *random* ID assignment. We run simulations to test these schemes in terms of path concurrency under various traffic patterns. Results show that both sequential and Hilbert produced significant interference and reduced concurrency, allowing at most 15-20% of links to be simultaneously active. This is because in a Kautz link, the source and destination IDs match in all but 1 digit, *e.g.* 0123 points to 1230, 1231, 1232 and 1234 (Figure 2(b)). Thus, for both sequential and Hilbert assignments a sizable number of link pairs will experience significant interference. Random assignment performs better, but is unpredictable, and a small portion of assignments always experienced poor concurrency.

Hierarchical Scheme. Instead, we propose a "hierarchical" scheme where we divide the data center into d regions. For every group of d nodes whose IDs differ only on the first digit, *e.g.* $0xyz$, $2xyz$, $3xyz$, and $4xyz$, we assign them into each of the d different regions (Figure 3(b)). This maximizes angular separation for *incoming links* to a single rack/node, since the previous hop for each node comes from a different region. Experiments confirmed that this gets near-perfect concurrency for all-to-one traffic workloads but does not address interference between links coming from the same rack, *i.e.* one-to-many workloads. As shown in Figure 3(b), the 4 outgoing links from 3210 arrive at closely located racks and interfere with each other.

Hybrid Scheme. A better "hybrid" assignment can maximize angular separation between pairs of incoming links and also between pairs of outgoing links of each rack. For clarity, we use *middle-digits* to refer to all digits of a nodeID except the first and last digits. To achieve maximum angular separation, we partition the network layout into d^2 regions. d^2 nodes share each unique string of middle-digits. For example, in a Kautz (4,4) graph, there are 16 nodes with ID that matches $x01y$, where $x \in \{1,2,3,4\}$, and $y \in \{0,2,3,4\}$. We distribute them into the d^2 different regions such that IDs that differ only in the first or the last digit will be maximally separated in physical space.

The layout shown in Figure 3(c) is for node degree $d = 4$. Consider rack 0201; its outgoing links point to 2010, 2012, 2013 and 2014, which are well-separated from each other. Also consider rack 2301's two outgoing links pointing to 3010 and 3012. The two links might appear to be in parallel, yet they are well-separated in the 3D beamforming context.

LEMMA 1. *The hybrid ID assignment scheme achieves the optimal angular separation between pairs of incoming (and outgoing) links on each rack.*

The proof is in the Appendix. We also show that in a typical rectangular data center layout, the above angular separation is at least 14°. This means that with today's off-the-shelf radios, the hybrid ID assignment eliminates interference between incoming (and outgoing) links on each rack.

Optimal ID Assignment & Channel Allocation. Ultimately, we seek to minimize interference among all links in the network. However, doing so is challenging - finding the optimal ID assignment is NP-hard (proof omitted due to space limits). Fortunately, Angora can leverage channel allocation to reduce interference across potentially interfering links. In this paper, we apply a simple greedy channel assignment because it already leads to reasonable performance under heavy traffic (see §6). We leave optimization of ID assignment and channel allocation to future work.

4.2 Handling Arbitrarily Sized Networks

Our next challenge comes from the fact that Kautz graph algorithms do not currently address *incomplete* graphs, *i.e.* networks whose size does not match a complete Kautz graph where $N = d^k + d^{k-1}$. Prior algorithms for routing in incomplete Kautz graphs [18, 19] are unusable because they require node in-degrees (thus the number of radios per rack) to grow arbitrarily. De Bruijn graphs face the same problem. Thus we need a solution that makes it easy to incrementally grow the Kautz graph, *i.e.* add racks to grow from a Kautz (d, k) network to a Kautz $(d, k+1)$ network, all while maintaining the Kautz properties (bounded degree per node and bounded hops between any pair of nodes).

Growing a Kautz Graph. Our solution works by allowing nodes with different length nodeIDs to coexist in the same network. We start with a complete Kautz (d, k) network of $d^k + d^{k-1}$ nodes, where each nodeID has k digits. We add new nodes to the network by assigning nodeIDs of length $k+1$, and inserting them into the middle of existing links. We show an example in Figure 4, where we add new nodes to a Kautz (4,4) graph to become an incomplete

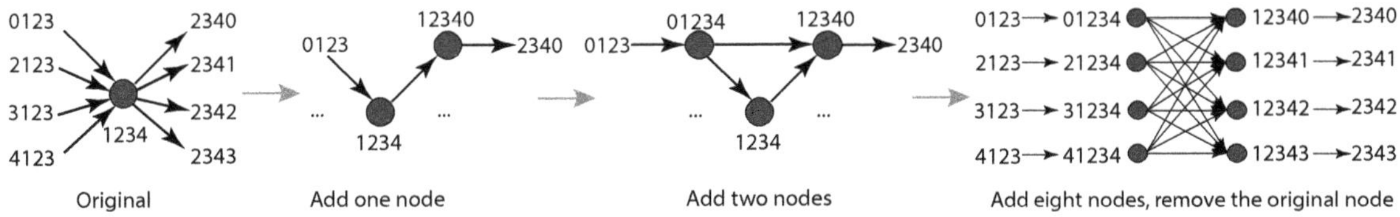

Figure 4: Add seven nodes to existing graph by replacing Node 1234 with eight new nodes 01234, 21234, 31234, 41234, 12340, 12341, 12342, 12343. The eight new nodes together perform the same functionality as Node 1234 from outside's view.

Kautz (4,5). To add a new node n_i, we first randomly choose a 4-digits node n_O, *e.g. 1234*, from Kautz (4,4). Then we assign a 5-digit nodeID to new node n_i, and insert it into one of links adjacent to n_O. If the link routes to n_O, we set n_i's ID by adding 1 digit prefix to n_O; otherwise we add 1 digit suffix.

When adding another node n_j, we repeat the process on another link adjacent to n_O. After inserting n_j, we also check if there are other existing 5 digit nodes it should link to based on the Kautz (4,5) protocol. In Figure 4, adding new node 01234 requires creating an additional link to node 12340. New nodes are added sequentially until all incoming and outgoing links to n_O have new nodes attached, except 1. When this happens, the original n_O node modifies its nodeID to 5 digits, and attaches itself to the last link. In our example, 1234 becomes 12343 after 7 new nodes have been inserted into all but 1 of its adjacent links.

This process is repeated at every node in the original Kautz (d, k) network, gradually replacing each original node with $2d$ new nodes with $k + 1$ digit nodeIDs. At this point, the entire network will be a complete Kautz $(d, k + 1)$ graph. During this process, the network is an *incomplete* Kautz $(d, k + 1)$ graph and all properties of the Kautz graph hold: a) each node has at most d incoming and d outgoing links; b) maximum hop count of an incomplete Kautz $(d, k + 1)$ is $3k/2$.

Serialization. Our algorithm requires new node additions to be serialized across the network. In other words, nodes are added sequentially, not in parallel. This is to avoid corner cases in the network topology, where an older node n_O with k digits might be disconnected from one of its newly neighbors with $k + 1$ digits, yet remain the destination of another node. By serializing node additions, we guarantee a consistent view of whether n_O exists or has been renamed. This constraint is reasonable in data center, since it involves the manual addition of a rack by an administrator/operator.

Finally, the ID assignment for incomplete Kautz graphs is very similar to that of complete graphs. We leave the details for brevity.

4.3 Fault Detection and Recovery

Availability and robustness to faults are key properties of a facilities network. The network should be available despite individual component failures (*i.e.* radios, rack switches), external interruptions (*i.e.* link disruption or blockage), and even when significant portions of the data plane are down for maintenance or upgrades. Here we describe fault-detection and recovery algorithms to deal with link, node and correlated failures.

We define three types of faults as follows:

- *Link Failures*: a 60GHz 3D beamforming link can fail due to radio hardware failure, wireless interference, radio misalignment, or external blockage.
- *Node Failures*: a node can be shut down by sudden rack power loss, or rack switch failure.
- *Correlated Failures*: a cluster of spatially correlated nodes, *e.g.* an entire row of racks, can fail concurrently due to planned maintenance or network upgrades.

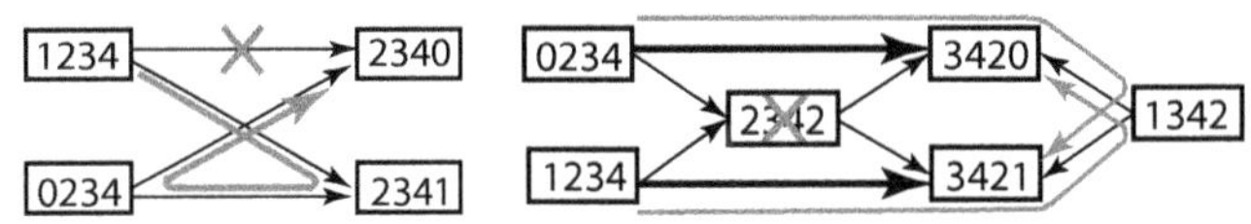

(a) Link failure (b) Node failure

Figure 5: Fault-tolerant routing with 4 radios per rack. (a) A failed link can be recovered by a detour with 2 extra hops. (b) A rack failure requires antenna rotation to build new link (bold lines), and can be recovered by either 1 hop or a 3-hop detour.

Fault Detection. Fault recovery requires timely fault detection. It is particularly important for a transmitter to identify the true cause of the error, *i.e.* whether it is a node failure or a link failure, since fault recovery mechanisms for each are quite different. This detection is also non-trivial, since link failures and node failures result in the same outcome from the transmitter's point of view: losses of all link layer beacons and ACKs. For link failures, we focus on "long-term" wireless transmission failure, and rely on 802.11's DCF mechanism to address temporary failures due to interference.

We use explicit feedback to distinguish between different failures. If a receiver rack n (in link $m \Rightarrow n$) detects an abnormality, *e.g.* radio interface is down or no beacons received for some period, n sends a feedback packet to the transmitter m using standard Kautz routing. Kautz routing guarantees that the paths $m \Rightarrow n$ and $n \Rightarrow m$ are always disjoint, and the feedback packet will avoid the problematic radio. If m is up, receiving a feedback packet means its link to n has failed, and it triggers the link failure handling mechanism. Otherwise, if m detects a down interface and no feedback packets are received after some suitable period, then the transmitter can assume that the rack is down, and it needs to trigger a node-failure recovery mechanism.

Handling Link Failures. If a single link $m \Rightarrow n$ fails, we recover by forwarding traffic to n around the faulty link. Although Kautz graphs have good redundancy, the deterministic digit-shifting routing provides no redundancy. Thus we route forward using another outgoing link from m to another neighbor n'. By definition, n' differs from n in only the last digit. Therefore there must a forward link to n' from m', where m' is some node that differs from m in only the last digit. We can route in reverse on this link (from n' back to m'), then forward from m' to n, effectively using a 3 hop detour to circumvent the failure. We show a simple example of this using a base-4 overlay in Figure 5(a), where the red detour $(1234 \rightarrow 2341 \rightarrow 0234 \rightarrow 2340)$ replaces a single failed link $1234 \rightarrow 2340$.

Handling Node Failures. A ToR switch failure or rack power failure represents a node failure in the Kautz graph. When a node n fails, all of its incoming and outgoing radio links also fail. Recovery requires repairing all links that route through the failed node, and involves retuning radios pointing to the failed node to new receivers.

For a Kautz network with degree d, we must ensure that each of the d links routing through the failed node n_f can reach their destinations. The high level intuition is that we pair up n_f's d incoming link radios with the destination radios of its d outgoing links. These radios pair up to form new links that bypass the failed n_f. We show an example in Figure 5(b), where node 2342 failed, and two of its incoming links from 0234 and 1234 are redirected to two of its outgoing neighbors. Since the new links cannot reach all of 2342's outgoing neighbors, it reaches the missing neighbors via one hop redirection, *e.g.* 0234 → 3420 → 1342 → 3421. While we only showed half of 2342's incoming links, the other links extrapolate in the same manner. Although we only show redirection from each incoming link to one outgoing neighbor, the link also reroutes to the two unpictured outgoing neighbors the same way, *i.e.* 0234 reroutes to 3422 and 3423. This allows us to maintain full connectivity.

When a node n_f fails, it creates a "hole" in the routing mesh that flows route around. Any flow not targeting n_f as its destination maintains its connectivity. However, routing around the hole introduces overhead. Therefore, we assume that if and when new nodes are added, they should first be assigned nodeIDs that allow them to fill existing holes in the network. Doing so restores the links before the failure, and eliminates the redirection required for fault recovery.

Handling Correlated Node Failures. Our hybrid assignment provides good robustness towards correlated node failures, by spatially spreading out nodes with closeby IDs. That is, nodes serving as detours in case one of them fails are guaranteed to be well-separated in the data center layout. This provides hard guarantee that detour paths remain available and maintain network connectivity after up to 55% correlated node failures (see results in §6).

Complexity. Our proposed fault handling mechanisms are low in computation complexity. Handling node failures require retuning antenna orientation, which introduces a small overhead when using horn antennas. As antenna arrays are becoming more sophisticated and available, we can remove this overhead by replacing horn antennas with antenna arrays that use instantaneous electronic beam switching. Overall, since the proposed mechanisms are of low complexity, Angora is easy to troubleshoot and repair.

Adding Redundancy. In our current design of Angora, the fault handling algorithms already provide very high reliability (see results in §6). To further enhance reliability, the data center administrators can add redundant links in Angora to improve its fault tolerance just like those proposed for wired networks, at the cost of increased infrastructure spending.

5. TESTBED EXPERIMENTS

Using off-the-shelf 60GHz radios, we implemented a "proof-of-concept" prototype of Angora. We use it to evaluate the suitability of 60GHz and our Angora design. We also validate 60GHz propagation/interference models, which we use to drive network simulations in §6. For all experiments, we used a metal reflector at a ceiling height of 4m.

Our experiments used two different 60GHz radios:

WiloCity radios. Our primary testbed consists of six pairs of Dell 6430u laptops and D5000 docks (Figure 6). Each has a WiloCity 60GHz radio chipset with a 2x8 antenna array, operating according to the IEEE 802.11ad standard for 60GHz. We found the low-cost 2x8 array creates a wide beam (nearly 40° in width), and compensated this by attaching a metal box to each device, emulating a horn antenna of 10° beamwidth. Our experiments confirm that this modification does not affect link throughput/latency.

HXI radios. Our second testbed includes a single pair of HXI Gigalink 6451 radios, the same hardware as two prior works [20, 44]. Each radio operates on a proprietary (non-802.11ad) configuration, has a horn antenna of 10° 3dB beamwidth and runs on a fixed 1.25Gbps rate.

5.1 Is 60GHz Suitable for Facilities Networks?

We set up 3D beamforming links to mimic data center transmissions in the presence of human movement, temperature variations and structural vibrations. By examining 60GHz link-level performance, we confirm its suitability as an alternative to wired links in a facilities network.

Range. Our measurements show that the HXI radio has a range of 42m at 0dBm transmit power and 144m at 10dBm power, sufficient for today's medium data centers (40mx50m, 320 racks, 12800 servers). The WiloCity radio has a shorter range of 22m, because its 2x8 antenna array's gain is at least 12 dB[7] lower than the horn antenna. It can support today's small data centers (20mx20m, 80 racks, 3200 servers).

Throughput & Latency. The WiloCity radio uses 802.11ad rate adaptation and its link rate (reported by the driver) decreases gracefully with the link distance from 3.85Gbps (at <1m) to 770Mbps (at 22m). The iperf TCP throughput is capped to 1Gbps, due to the laptop's 1Gbps Ethernet interface. The HXI link achieves a fixed 800Mbps TCP rate. For both radios, ping latency is less than 1ms.

Link Stability. We repeat iperf experiments once per second, and record link TCP throughput continuously for 3 weeks. Figure 7 shows the CDF of per-second throughput for both radios, indicating that both radio links are stable over time. This confirms the feasibility of using 60GHz links to build reliable, high-performance connections.

Interference vs. Angular Separation. We build two directional links using WiloCity hardware, and examine their link throughputs as we vary the 3D angular separation between them. Experimentation with multiple link configurations seen in medium-sized data centers [44] all led to the same conclusion. Figure 8 shows the normalized throughput degradation for two configurations, where the links are 8.4m or 12.5m long. 3D angular separation of <6° produces 30-70% throughput loss, which disappears completely once the angular separation reaches 12°. Finally, we obtained a similar result from HXI radios where 10° separation is sufficient.

5.2 Angora Microbenchmarks

Using the WiloCity testbed, we build Angora overlay paths to study path-level TCP performance. We focus on impact of path length and self-interference on each path, and interference between multiple paths. For evaluation, we use both iperf and a TCP file transfer program to emulate management tasks in data centers, *e.g.* controller pushing a 10KB update to a rack switch, or pulling a 1.3MB status update from a rack. To build multi-hop paths, we "bridge" the wired NIC and the 60GHz NIC on Dell laptops. Such "software" switching is CPU-bound and reduces TCP rate from the baseline 1Gbps down to 660Mbps.

Single-Path Performance. Most Angora paths are multi-hop, so a common concern is self-interference across hops. With 3D beamforming, this only occurs when receivers of two hops are closeby (on the same or neighboring racks), and their 3D angular separation is small. Here each link is bi-directional – reverse link carries TCP and MAC acks.

[7] In theory, such 12dB loss translates into 4x range reduction.

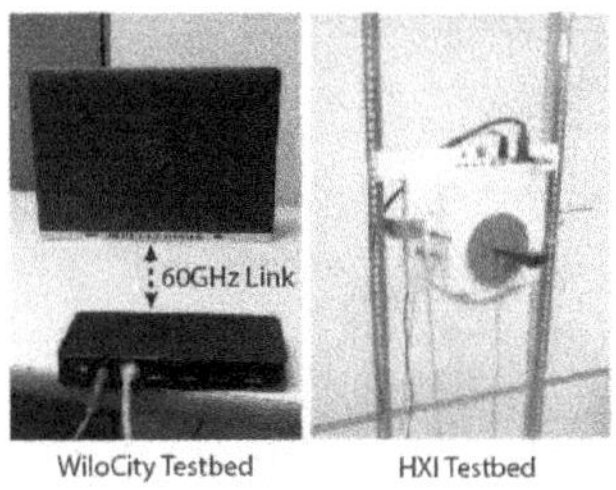

Figure 6: The two 60GHz radios.

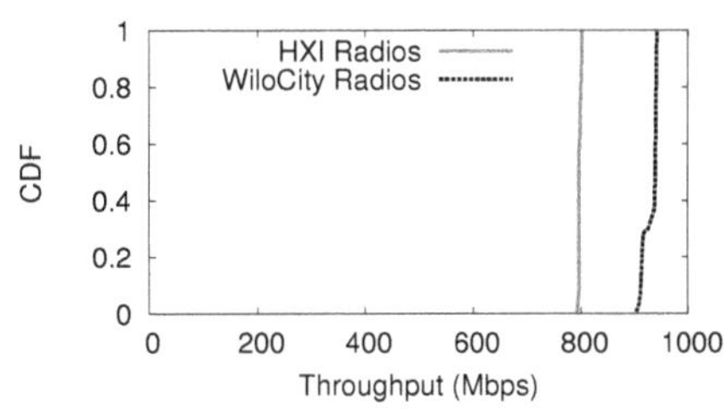

Figure 7: CDF of per-second TCP throughput of 60GHz links over 1 month.

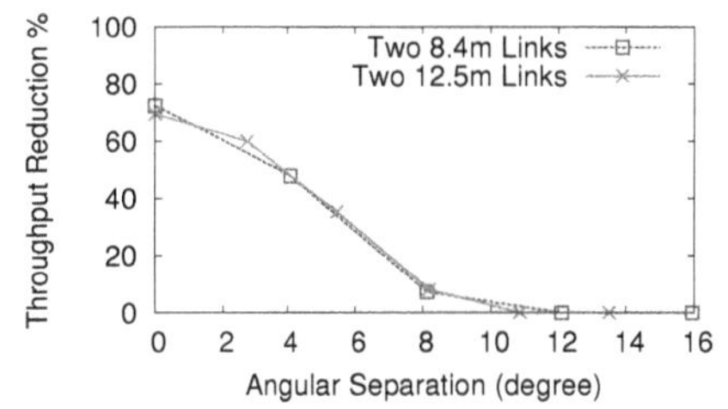

Figure 8: Link throughput degradation vs. the angular separation between two links.

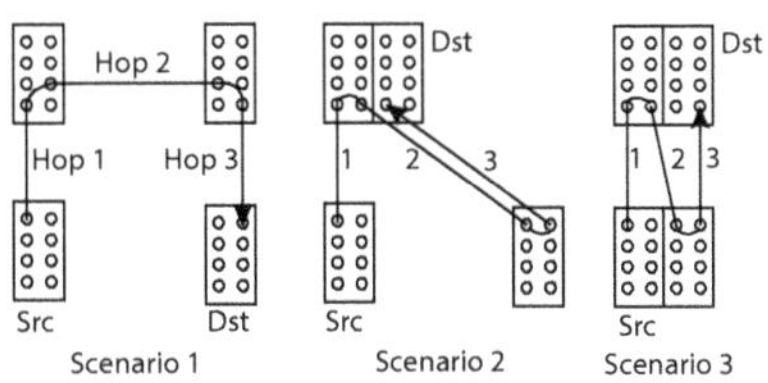

(a) 3-hop overlay paths with different interference scenarios

Scenario	# of channels	TCP Thpt	10KB Msg. Latency	1.3MB Msg. Latency
1	1	654Mbps	3.1ms	30.8ms
2	1	173Mbps	4.8ms	84.9ms
	2	663Mbps	3.2ms	30.7ms
3	1	118Mbps	9.7ms	168.7ms
	2	413Mbps	4.6ms	48.3ms

(b) End-to-end results of 3 scenarios in (a)

Path Length	TCP Thpt	10KB Latency	1.3MB Latency
1 hop w/o bridging	940Mbps	1.3ms	19.0ms
1 hop	665Mbps	1.7ms	25.4ms
2 hops	662Mbps	2.5ms	30.5ms
3 hops	654Mbps	3.1ms	31.0ms
4 hops	665Mbps	3.5ms	35.9ms

(c) End-to-end results vs. path length

Figure 9: Angora single path performance. (a)(b) 3 single-path scenarios and their end-to-end performance. Self-interference exists but can be effectively suppressed via channel allocation. (c) Single path message delay scales gracefully with path length.

Figure 9 shows three 3-hop paths (no hops interfere, hop 2 and 3 interfere, hop 1, 2, 3 all interfere) and their end-to-end results from our testbed measurements. Specifically, when all hops use a single channel, path #2's self-interference reduces its throughput by 76% and increases message latency by 54%-175%. But with two channels, path #2 becomes interference-free, and path #3's loss reduces to only 30%.

Clearly the impact of self-interference is evident but can be effectively suppressed via channel allocation. This is only an issue when the path length exceeds the channel count (3 in 802.11ad) and when the channel assignment does not "spread" the channels evenly across hops. However, this happens rarely. For a medium-sized data center (320 racks), simulations show that when using random channel allocation only 0.72% of all paths experience self-interference using Kautz graphs (2.2% using a Random topology).

Next, we measure for each single path the impact of path length on end-to-end performance. Our experiments do not consider self-interference, since they appear in less than 1% of all paths. Figure 9(c) lists the throughput and average latency for 10KB or 1.3MB messages, and for reference the results for 1 hop paths without software bridging. For all these cases, the standard deviation of message latency is less than 10% of the average. These results show that the 660Mbps throughput cap from the software bridge also increases per-hop latency. Even so, Angora paths have small message latency: 3.5ms for 10KB messages, 35ms for 1.3MB messages. Message latency scales gracefully with path length.

Cross-Path Interference. Next we examine how interference affects concurrent paths. While Angora (Kautz+hybrid ID) nullifies interference among links on the same rack, a small number of disjoint but closeby paths can still interfere when running concurrently. Figure 10 shows a representative 2-path example extracted from Kautz and Random topologies assuming all links use the same channel. We implemented and evaluated these paths using our testbed. For Kautz, each path obtains 259Mbps TCP throughput (3.9ms latency for 10KB messages, 48.9ms for 1.3MB), while for Random, it reduces to 129Mbps (5.3ms latency for 10KB, 81.6ms for 1.3MB). This shows that cross-path interference does exist under heavy traffic and can lead to latency tails. However, its impact can be effectively reduced using channel allocation (based on our large-scale results in §6).

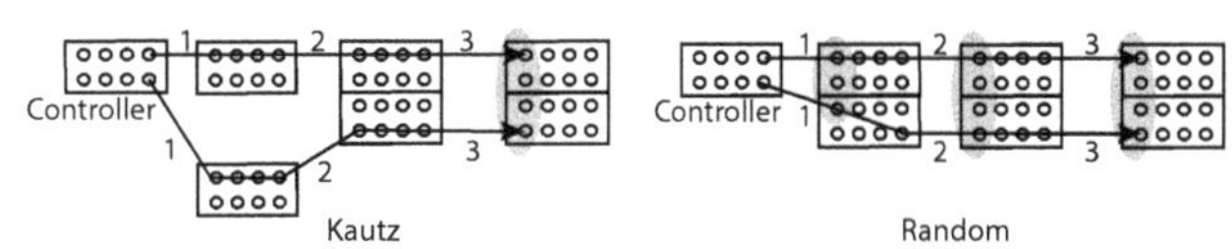

Figure 10: Examples on cross-path interference. Kautz guarantees that there is no cross-path interference within 2 hops from the controller. Random may have cross-path interference at any hop.

Note that Kautz graphs experience much less cross-path interference (thus much smaller latency tails) than Random topologies. This is because hybrid ID assignment ensures that links affected by cross-path interference are at least 2 hops away from any controller[8], putting a hard limit on the interference. For Random, interference can occur at any hop around a controller (see Figure 10), and affect other paths/flows sharing these links. The result is longer latency tails, later also seen from our large-scale simulations in §6.

6. LARGE-SCALE EVALUATION

We perform detailed NS3 simulations to evaluate Angora at larger scales, focusing on its ability to deliver control messages with bounded latency and robustness against failures. We seek to understand how the topology choice (*i.e.* Kautz vs. Random) and hardware choice (*i.e.* horn antennas vs. antenna arrays) affect its performance.

Simulation Setup. We implement Angora in NS3, adapting the 60GHz flyways code [20] to include 3D beamforming radios (half-duplex), 802.11ad MAC (backoff and ACKs), overlay routing, and TCP. TCP ACKs are sent via the overlay path back to the source. We use existing data center designs [44]: each rack hosts 8 radios,

[8]As shown in Figure 10, with Kautz/hybrid ID assignment, the first hop destinations from each controller are well-separated, preventing cross-path interference within 2 hops from the controller.

Path Length	Overlay w/ 320 racks			Overlay w/ 1280 racks		
	Kautz	DeBruijn	Random	Kautz	DeBruijn	Random
< 4	26.0%	16.2%	23.5%	6.6%	4.2%	6.4%
4	74.0%	63.8%	42.8%	19.6%	11.6%	17.1%
5	0%	19.9%	32.3%	73.8%	63.4%	42.4%
6	0%	0.1%	1.4%	0%	20.6%	32.8%
>6	0%	0%	0%	0%	0.2%	1.3%

(a) Network sizes 320 and 1280 (complete Kautz graphs)

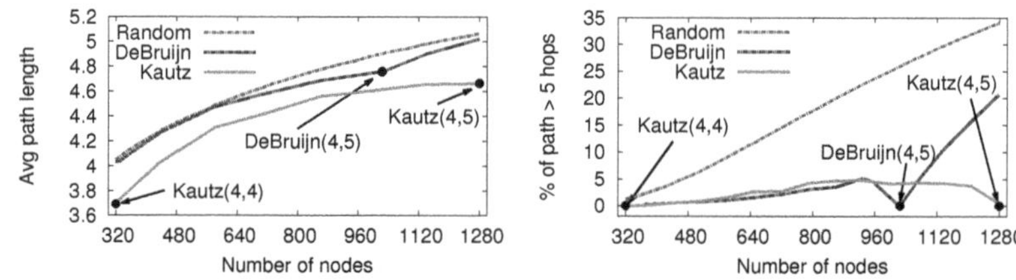

(b) Arbitrary network sizes

(c) Arbitrary network sizes

Figure 11: Angora's path length. (a) The path length distribution for data centers with 320 and 1280 racks. (b-c) Average path length and percentage of path lengths exceeding 5 hops for data centers of various sizes, representing *incomplete* Kautz graphs. The structured overlays (Kautz and DeBruijn) outperform the unstructured overlay (Random).

connected via a standard switch (6.4MB queue). Radio processing and switching delays are 10ns [6]) and 500ns [9]. We use a reflector at 4m height.

We configure the NS3 physical layer with the free-space propagation model, validated by our testbed experiments and prior work [20, 44]. Our simulations consider both horn antennas and antenna arrays By default, each radio is equipped with a standard horn antenna with 10° 3dB beamwidth. We derive detailed radiation patterns of the horn antennas according to the Kelleher's universal horn pattern [27]. We also verify that the Kelleher's model matches well with the horn antennas (10° 3dB beamwidth) used in our experiments, as well as that used in [20]. For antenna arrays, we calculate their radiation patterns following the standard rectangular array definitions from [21]. We set the maximum transmit power (10dBm) and rate table based on the 802.11ad specification [4]. Since the 802.11ad standard defines 3 orthogonal channels (2.16GHz each), we apply a simple greedy algorithm to preselect a channel for each link, prioritizing links directly connected to rack(s) housing controllers. We leave optimization of channel assignment to future work.

We consider data center layouts used by prior works [20, 44]: racks are grouped into 5×5 clusters; each cluster is a row of 10 racks with no inter-spacing; aisles separating the clusters are 3m (between columns) and 2.4m (between rows). We test data centers of size 320 racks to 1280 racks.

6.1 Path Length

We consider three overlay topologies: Kautz, de Bruijn and Random. For Random, we run 10000 rounds to obtain statistically significant results. Figure 11(a) lists the path length distribution for data centers of 320 and 1280 racks. For Kautz, they both lead to a complete graph, *i.e.* *Kautz* (4,4) and *Kautz* (4,5), respectively. As expected, the Kautz topology provides strict bounds on path length (4 and 5 respectively). In contrast, Random topologies have a longer tail: in 33% of cases, it leads to 1 more hop, and in 1.3% of the cases it leads to 2 more hops. This is consistent with prior work on randomized networks [36].

We also consider data centers of size between 320 and 1280, representing incomplete Kautz graphs and de Bruijn graphs. Figure 11(b)-(c) plot the average path length and the tail (the percentage of paths with more than 5 hops). In both cases, Kautz outperforms: its average path length grows gracefully with network size, and the ratio of long paths (>5 hops) is within 5%. These results validate our choice of Kautz graphs as the network topology, and the efficacy of our algorithms to support incomplete graphs.

6.2 Path Concurrency

To evaluate Angora's ability to support parallel flows, we randomly select M racks to communicate with one or multiple controllers. For each M, we run 2000 rounds with random rack and controller locations, and compute path concurrency as the portion of all paths able to run concurrently[9]. We experimented with three different traffic patterns: multiple racks to controller(s), controller(s) to multiple racks, and a random mix of the first two. Since they lead to similar conclusions, we only show the random mix results, which consistently have the lowest path concurrency of the three.

# of Flows	Overlay w/ 320 racks			Overlay w/ 480 racks		
	Kautz (hybrid ID)	Kautz (random ID)	Random	Kautz (hybrid ID)	Kautz (random ID)	Random
40	93%	90%	82%	88%	83%	77%
80	93%	89%	78%	84%	81%	75%
160	93%	88%	76%	81%	78%	71%

Table 1: The bottom 2% path concurrency, a single controller.

Topology choice	320 racks, 80 flows w/ varying # of controllers				
	1	2	4	6	8
Kautz (hybrid ID)	93%	88%	88%	85%	81%
Kautz (random ID)	89%	80%	80%	79%	79%
Random	78%	76%	68%	65%	60%

Table 2: The bottom 2% path concurrency, 1-8 controllers.

Table 1 lists the bottom 2%-percentile path concurrency (across 2000 rounds) when a single controller is present, for data centers of size 320 racks (a complete Kautz graph) and 480 racks (an incomplete Kautz graph). Our key observations are as follows. When using horn antennas, both Kautz and Random graphs maintain high path concurrency (>70%) for the two data center sizes, even when 160 flows compete. Kautz shows a sizable advantage over Random, which can be attributed to two factors: reduced path length (thus less interference) and hybrid ID assignment that effectively scatters the directional links. Our hypothesis is confirmed by results of "Kautz with random IDs" in Table 1.

We obtain the same conclusion from results with multiple controllers (Table 2). Because distributing flows across multiple controllers creates more traffic hotspots and active wireless links, path concurrency decreases with more controllers. While the impact is significant for Random topologies (60% for 8 controllers), Kautz gracefully degrades from 93% for 1 controller to 81% for 8 controllers, again benefitting from a more controlled network structure.

6.3 Path Latency

Next we study a more practical question: *Can Angora provide reliable communication with bounded latency, even when multiple racks communicate with controller(s) in parallel?* For this we examine end-to-end latency of TCP traffic in a medium-sized data

[9]Multiple paths run *concurrently* if each link's SINR can support its target rate. The target rate is the aggregated flow rate of all the flows that share the link in absence of any interference.

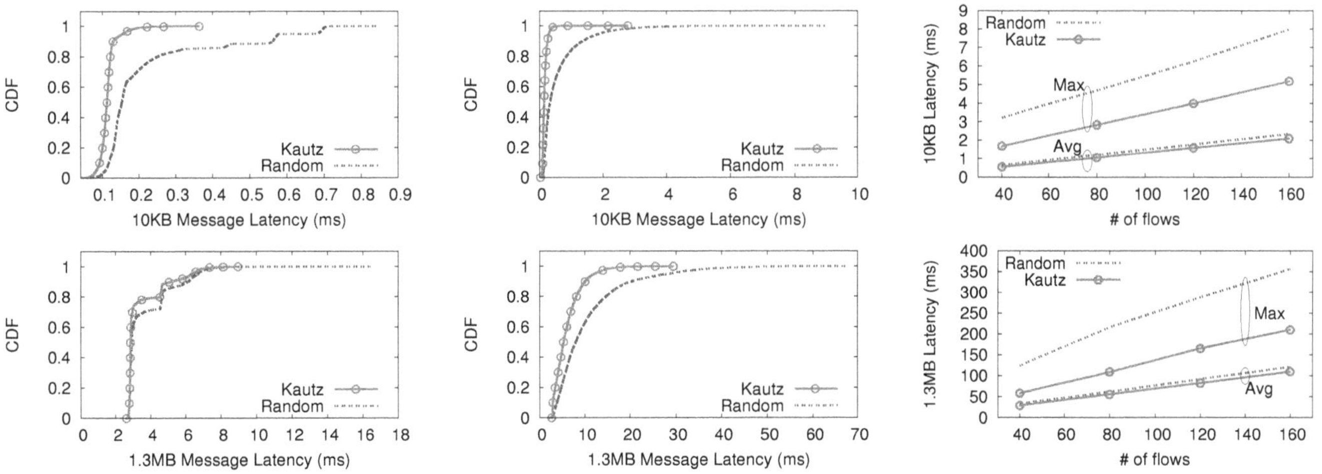

(a) 10KB and 1.3MB single flows (b) 10KB and 1.3MB bursty flows (c) 10KB and 1.3MB synchronized flows

Figure 12: Angora's end-to-end TCP delay performance when carrying 10KB (top) and 1.3MB (bottom) messages. (a) CDF of single flow latency. (b) CDF of per-message latency of the two bursty flows. (c) The maximum and average per-message latency of multiple synchronized flows.

center (320 racks). In the absence of real control traffic traces, we consider three traffic patterns: single-flow, bursty multi-flow, and synchronized multi-flow.

Single-flow. At any given time, only a single rack communicates with the controller. We consider messages of size 10KB (*e.g.* SDN flow setup), 1.3MB (*e.g.* flow table and statistics [7, 12]) and 10MB (*e.g.* VM images).

Figure 12(a) shows the statistical distribution of per-message latency across all combination of rack and controller locations. We omit the 10MB figure due to space limit. We note that end-to-end latency is very low. For Kautz, maximum delay is bounded by 0.45ms for 10KB, 9ms for 1.3MB and 65ms for 10MB messages[10]. 90% of its flows experience delay less than 0.2ms, 5ms and 52ms respectively. We note there is a delay tail, because a small number of flows still experiences self-interference, which triggers MAC backoffs and occasional retransmissions. Kautz's more uniform results are due to a combination of shorter path lengths and stronger interference suppression.

Bursty Multi-flow. We consider two bursty scenarios where all racks send messages to a single controller over a period of 10 seconds. The first assumes each rack sends 10KB messages with an exponential distributed inter-arrival time of mean 15ms. The second increases message size to 1.3MB but reduces the mean of inter-arrival time to 500ms. We repeat each experiment for 100 rounds and randomize controller locations. Figure 12(b) shows that per-message latency is small for both Kautz and Random topologies, <9ms for 10KB messages and <70ms for 1.3MB. As before, the key difference between the two topologies is reduced variability (shorter tail, 3ms/30ms) for Kautz.

Synchronized Multi-flow. Multiple racks send or receive a single control message from controllers, and all flows start at the *same* time, creating heavy competition. Figure 12(c) shows latency of 10KB and 1.3MB messages with 40 to 160 flows. Even with 160 parallel flows, both Kautz and Random are able to offer good average latency results. Kautz again outperforms Random, with maximum delays as low as 50% of Random.

[10]The latency is lower than the WiloCity testbed result (§5.2) because we remove the bridging artifact and use a horn antenna.

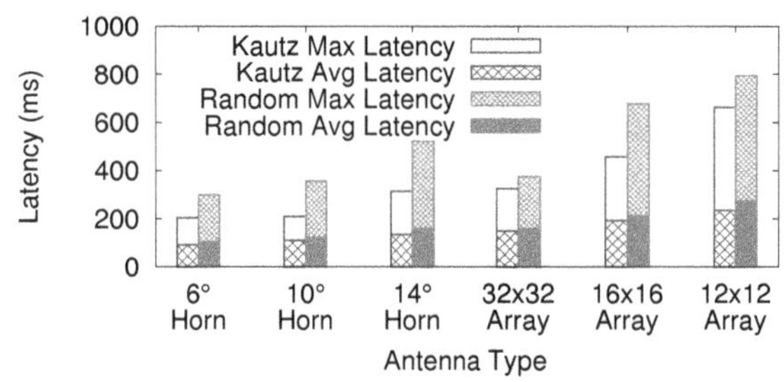

Figure 13: Impact of antenna choice: maximal and average per-message latency, 160 synchronized flows, 1.3MB messages.

Impact of Radio Hardware. To understand the impact of radio choice, we compare latency performance when using six different 60GHz antennas: horn antennas with 6°, 10° and 14° beamwidth which are typical commercial configurations, and antenna arrays of 32x32, 16x16 and 12x12 in size which have been prototyped [8, 30]. We repeat the above latency experiments and results of different traffic types lead to similar conclusions. We only show the result of 160 synchronized flows with 1.3MB messages, which represent the heaviest traffic load and flow competition.

Figure 13 shows the maximal and average per-message latency for Kautz and Random topologies. We make two key observations. *First*, antenna arrays lead to higher latency than horn antennas even though their main beam is narrower, *i.e.* 3.2°, 6.3°, and 8.5° respectively. This is because their side-beam emissions create extra interference that is harder to "suppress" via topology design. One can reduce side-beams by increasing antenna elements, *i.e.* from 12x12 to 32x32, at a higher cost. Another potential solution is to use interference nulling [29] to proactively cancel observed interference, which is an interesting open research direction.

Second, across all antenna configurations, Kautz consistently outperforms Random. As a result, a facilities network with Kautz/hybrid ID can meet the same latency requirements using cheaper hardware. For example, to pull 1.3MB route table within 500ms [12, 33], 16x16 arrays or 14° horn antennas should suffice for Kautz graphs, while Random requires 32x32 arrays or 10° horn antennas.

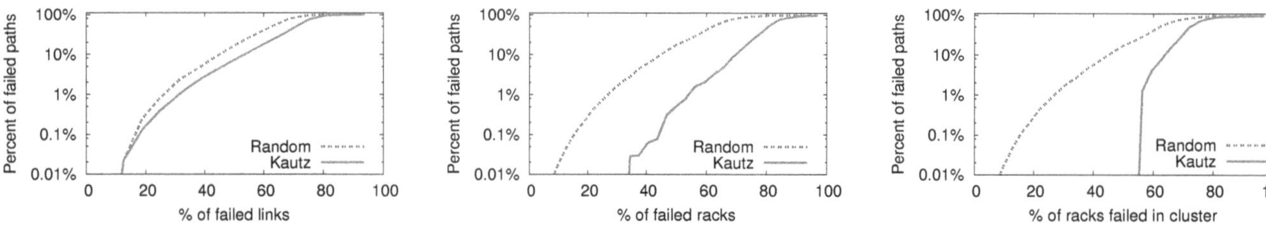

(a) Link failure (b) Node failure (c) Correlated node failure

Figure 14: Percentage of failed paths in Angora under different types of failures, using both Kautz and Random overlays.

Failure Percentage	5%	10%	15%	20%	25%
Rack Failure	2.0%	3.2%	4.2%	5.2%	6.3%
Link Failure	5.7%	11.2%	17.1%	23.5%	30.0%

Table 3: Average path length increases slightly during failures.

6.4 Fault Tolerance

We now evaluate Angora's robustness against failures. We create random failures by randomly disabling links and racks, and correlated failures by randomly removing consecutive rows of racks. We repeat each experiment with 1000 rounds, and examine how failures affect path connectivity. For Kautz, we apply recovery schemes described in §4.3. For Random, the fault recovery is done by re-identifying the shortest path in the current directed graph via global search. Figure 14 compares the percentage of failed paths under different failures. We see Angora is highly robust against all three types of failures. Using the Kautz overlay maintains 99% path availability for individual or correlated rack failure rates up to 50%, and for link failure rates up to 30%.

We also make two key observations. *First*, comparing the two graph structures, Kautz provides higher availability, especially for node failures. In particular, Kautz maintains perfect availability under correlated failures even when half of all racks are unavailable. This is because Kautz's hybrid ID assignment "spreads" out overlay links widely across racks, thus a path is unlikely to be colocated with its backup. *Second*, while Random leads to similar performance across all three types of failures, Kautz is more robust against node failures than link failures. The reason is that Kautz realigns radios to handle node failures, but not for link failures. We do not propose using radio realignment to recover from link failures, because searching for available radios to realign is a nontrivial task that may introduce considerable latency.

Latency Impact. Finally, we find that the latency cost of recovering from single link and rack faults is bounded (at most the latency of a 3-hop detour). Simulations show that average path length increases gracefully as the percentage of failure increases, as shown in Table 3. For example, The average path length only increases by 8% when 25% of all nodes fail, and 30% when 25% of links fail. Latency of detoured paths grow linearly with their path length, while existing flows in the neighborhood experience little impact.

7. RELATED WORK

Data Center Networking. Existing works focus on improving data plane performance, either by scheduling flows more efficiently (*e.g.* [7]) or by proposing new architectures (*e.g.* [9, 17, 36, 43]). In contrast, our work is to build a facilities network, a second network that differs significantly from the data plane in both characteristics and requirements.

60GHz in Data Centers. Recent works have utilized 60GHz links to augment data plane's bandwidth [20, 24, 25, 34, 41, 44]. Their key objective is to improve data plane bandwidth and address traffic hotspots. The 60GHz links are set up on-demand, thus requiring link coordination, antenna rotation, and/or centralized scheduling that introduce additional delay. Such extra delay makes these designs unsuitable for our targeted facilities network, which is highly delay sensitive but requires substantially lower bandwidth than the data plane. In contrast, the focus of Angora is to deliver management traffic via the facilities network with small bounded delay and high robustness. To this end, our solution, while supporting any-to-any rack communication, removes the need for link coordination/scheduling and antenna rotation that lead to considerable complexity and latency (up to 1s) in existing designs [44].

Another 60GHz in data centers proposal is to completely replace wired networks [35, 39] by 60GHz links. Unlike [35, 39] that require specialized server design and rack hardware, our design supports today's standard data center equipment.

SDN Control Plane. Active research has focused on SDN control plane designs, from operating systems to scalable designs [12, 28, 37, 42]. The reliable delivery of control traffic, however, has been often taken granted. Yet recent measurements show that control traffic delivery significantly affects network performance [12]. Our facilities network fills in this gap by delivering SDN control traffic and a wide variety of management traffic reliably in real-time.

8. CONCLUSION

We consider the problem of building an orthogonal facilities network as a core tool for managing data center networks. Our solution is Angora, a Kautz network built on 60GHz 3D beamforming links. Angora uses a small number of radios per rack to connect any pair of racks with a robust, latency-bounded path. We address multiple challenges including wireless interference, robustness to route and radio failures, and evaluate Angora using both experimental measurements and simulations. We believe that Angora is the first step towards the development of a robust and practical data center facilities network.

9. ACKNOWLEDGMENTS

The authors thank the anonymous reviewers for their feedback. This work is supported in part by by NSF grant CNS-1317153 and research gifts from Google and Cisco.

10. REFERENCES

[1] 802.11n: The end of ethernet? http://www.arubanetworks.com/pdf/technology/whitepapers/wp_Burton_End_of_Ethernet.pdf.

[2] Creating the data center of tomorrow. http://csmedia.corning.com/CableSystems/%5CResource_Documents%5Carticles_rl%5CLAN-1225-EN.pdf.

[3] Google data center images. http://www.google.com/about/datacenters/gallery/#/all.

[4] IEEE P802.11ad/D0.1: Enhancements for very high throughput in the 60 GHz band. TGad D0.1, May 2010.

[5] IEEE802.1Q - Virtual LANs. http://www.ieee802.org/1/pages/802.1Q.html.
[6] LightPointe Aire X-Stream 60GHz 1.25Gbps Wireless Bridges. http://www.lightpointe.com.
[7] Al-Fares, M., Radhakrishnan, S., Raghavan, B., Huang, N., and Vahdat, A. Hedera: dynamic flow scheduling for data center networks. In *NSDI* (2010).
[8] Al Henawy, M., and Schneider, M. Planar antenna arrays at 60GHz realized on a new thermoplastic polymer substrate. In *EuCAP* (2010).
[9] Alizadeh, M., Kabbani, A., Edsall, T., Prabhakar, B., Vahdat, A., and Yasuda, M. Less is more: Trading a little bandwidth for ultra-low latency in the data center. In *NSDI* (2012).
[10] Benson, T., Anand, A., Akella, A., and Zhang, M. Microte: fine grained traffic engineering for data centers. In *CoNEXT* (2011).
[11] Casado, M., Freedman, M. J., Pettit, J., Luo, J., McKeown, N., and Shenker, S. Ethane: taking control of the enterprise. In *SIGCOMM* (2007).
[12] Curtis, A. R., Mogul, J. C., Tourrilhes, J., Yalagandula, P., Sharma, P., and Banerjee, S. DevoFlow: Scaling flow management for high-performance networks. In *SIGCOMM* (2011).
[13] de Bruijn, N. G. A combinatorial problem. In *Koninkli- jke Nederlandse Akademie van Wetenschappen* (1946), vol. 49.
[14] Dean, J., and Ghemawat, S. MapReduce: simplified data processing on large clusters. *Commun. ACM* (Jan. 2008), 107–113.
[15] Greenberg, A., Hjalmtysson, G., Maltz, D. A., Myers, A., Rexford, J., Xie, G., Yan, H., Zhan, J., and Zhang, H. A clean slate 4D approach to network control and management. *CCR 35*, 5 (2005).
[16] Gummadi, K., Gummadi, R., Gribble, S., Ratnasamy, S., Shenker, S., and Stoica, I. The impact of DHT routing geometry on resilience and proximity. In *Proc. of SIGCOMM* (2003).
[17] Guo, C., Lu, G., Li, D., Wu, H., Zhang, X., Shi, Y., Tian, C., Zhang, Y., and Lu, S. BCube: a high performance, server-centric network architecture for modular data centers. In *SIGCOMM* (2009).
[18] Guo, D., Liu, Y., and Li, X. BAKE: A balanced Kautz tree structure for peer-to-peer networks. In *INFOCOM* (2008).
[19] Guo, D., Wu, J., Chen, H., and Luo, X. Moore: An extendable peer-to-peer network based on incomplete Kautz digraph with constant degree. In *INFOCOM* (2007).
[20] Halperin, D., Kandula, S., Padhye, J., Bahl, P., and Wetherall, D. Augmenting data center networks with multi-gigabit wireless links. In *SIGCOMM* (2011).
[21] Hansen, R. C. *Phased array antennas*, 2nd ed. John Wiley & Sons, 2009.
[22] Hilbert, D. Ueber die stetige Abbildung einer Line auf ein Flächenstück. *Mathematische Annalen 38*, 3 (1891), 459–460.
[23] Hoss, R., and Lacy, E. *Fiber optics*. Prentice Hall, 1993.
[24] Katayama, Y., Takano, K., Kohda, Y., Ohba, N., and Nakano, D. Wireless data center networking with steered-beam mmwave links. In *WCNC* (2011).
[25] Katayama, Y., Yamane, T., Kohda, Y., Takano, K., Nakano, D., and Ohba, N. Mimo link design strategy for wireless data center applications. In *WCNC* (2012).
[26] Kautz, W. Bounds on directed (*d*, *k*) graphs. *Theory of cellular logic networks and machines, AFCRL-68-0668 Final report* (1968).
[27] Kelleher, K. *The Microwave Engineers' Handbook and Buyers' Guide*, 5th ed. New York: Horizon Press, 1964.
[28] Koponen, T., Casado, M., Gude, N., Stribling, J., Poutievski, L., Zhu, M., Ramanathan, R., Iwata, Y., Inoue, H., Hama, T., and Shenker, S. Onix: a distributed control platform for large-scale production networks. In *OSDI* (2010).
[29] Nikolaidis, G., Zhushi, A., Jamieson, K., and Karp, B. Cone of silence: adaptively nulling interferers in wireless networks. *SIGCOMM CCR* (2010).
[30] Nishi, S., and Tokuda, K. Development of mm-wave video transmission system-development of antenna. In *APMC* (2001).
[31] Pearson, E. R. *Professional Fiber Optic Installation: The Essentials For Success*. Pearson Technologies Incorporated, 2011.
[32] Phemius, K., and Thales, M. B. Openflow: Why latency does matter. In *IFIP/IEEE IM* (2013).
[33] Raiciu, C., Barre, S., Pluntke, C., Greenhalgh, A., Wischik, D., and Handley, M. Improving datacenter performance and robustness with multipath TCP. In *SIGCOMM* (2011).
[34] Ranachandran, K., Kokku, R., Mahindra, R., and Rangarajan, S. 60GHz data-center networking: wireless => worryless? *NEC Technical Report* (2008).
[35] Shin, J.-Y., Sirer, E. G., Weatherspoon, H., and Kirovski, D. On the feasibility of completely wireless data centers. In *ANCS* (2012).
[36] Singla, A., Hong, C.-Y., Popa, L., and Godfrey, P. B. Jellyfish: Networking data centers randomly. In *NSDI* (2012).
[37] Tootoonchian, A., and Ganjali, Y. HyperFlow: a distributed control plane for OpenFlow. In *INM/WREN* (2010).
[38] Vahdat, A., Al-Fares, M., Farrington, N., Mysore, R. N., Porter, G., and Radhakrishnan, S. Scale-out networking in the data center. *Micro, IEEE 30*, 4 (2010), 29–41.
[39] Vardhan, H., Ryu, S.-R., Banerjee, B., and Prakash, R. 60ghz wireless links in data center networks. *Computer Networks 58* (January 2014), 192–205.
[40] Wu, X., Turner, D., Chen, C.-C., Maltz, D., Yang, X., Yuan, L., and Zhang, M. NetPilot: automating datacenter network failure mitigation. In *SIGCOMM* (2012).
[41] Yamane, T., and Katayama, Y. An effective initialization of interference cancellation algorithms for distributed mimo systems in wireless datacenters. In *GLOBECOM* (2012).
[42] Yu, M., Rexford, J., Freedman, M. J., and Wang, J. Scalable flow-based networking with DIFANE. In *SIGCOMM* (2010).
[43] Zats, D., Das, T., Mohan, P., Borthakur, D., and Katz, R. DeTail: reducing the flow completion time tail in datacenter networks. In *SIGCOMM* (2012).
[44] Zhou, X., Zhang, Z., Zhu, Y., Li, Y., Kumar, S., Vahdat, A., Zhao, B. Y., and Zheng, H. Mirror mirror on the ceiling: Flexible wireless links for data centers. In *SIGCOMM* (2012).

APPENDIX

The hybrid ID assignment maximizes angular separation between pairs of outgoing links and between pairs of incoming links on each rack.

Proof. We provide a sketch of the proof due to space limitations. The proof consists of three steps. *First*, using geometry, we prove that for 3D beamforming, maximizing angular separation of a rack's outgoing (incoming) links is equivalent to maximizing the physical distance between their receivers (transmitters). For Kautz graphs, these are "sibling" racks whose IDs have the same middle-digits, but different first/last digit. Furthermore, it is easy to show that maximizing the physical distance between siblings is achieved by properly placing each group of d^2 racks sharing the same middle-digits into d^2 distinct regions.

Second, assuming the data center layout is a rectangle of size $L \times H$ ($L \leq H$), we prove that for $d = 4$, for any ID assignment, the minimum physical distance between any two siblings is upper-bounded by $L/2$. This is because each rack has $2d - 2$ (6 when $d = 4$) siblings that need to be separated. Consider the rack placed in the middle of the rectangle. There is not enough space to separate its incoming (outgoing) siblings by $L/2$. The same proof applies to $d = 3, 5, 6$ although the upper-bound may vary.

Finally, we prove that for $d = 4$, the hybrid ID assignment proposed in Section 4 achieves the optimal value of $L/2$ in terms of the minimum sibling separation. Similarly, for $d = 3, 5, 6$, we also found the corresponding hybrid ID assignments which achieve their corresponding upper-bounds. This concludes our proof. □

We now show that with the hybrid ID assignment, the angular separation between any two links $\geq 14°$ in a typical rectangular data center layout.

Using the rack size and spacing described in [20, 44], a data center containing 320 racks (8 rows, 40 racks per row) is 30m×24m large. Assuming the ceiling is 4m high from the top of racks, it is easy to verify that the minimum angular separation in the whole data center is 14.6°. Furthermore, as long as the layout size and ceiling height scale proportionally, this minimum angular separation value will not change. For a fixed ceiling height, the larger the layout, the larger the angular separation. This means that the hybrid ID assignment scales well to larger data centers with a guarantee of $14° +$ angular separation.

We Can Hear You with Wi-Fi!

Guanhua Wang†, Yongpan Zou†, Zimu Zhou†, Kaishun Wu‡§, Lionel M. Ni†‡
† Department of Computer Science and Engineering
‡ Guangzhou HKUST Fok Ying Tung Research Institute
Hong Kong University of Science and Technology
§ College of Computer Science and Software Engineering, Shenzhen University
{gwangab, yzouad, zzhouad, kwinson, ni}@cse.ust.hk

ABSTRACT

Recent literature advances Wi-Fi signals to "see" people's motions and locations. This paper asks the following question: Can Wi-Fi "hear" our talks? We present WiHear, which enables Wi-Fi signals to "hear" our talks without deploying any devices. To achieve this, WiHear needs to detect and analyze fine-grained radio reflections from mouth movements. WiHear solves this micro-movement detection problem by introducing *Mouth Motion Profile* that leverages partial multipath effects and wavelet packet transformation. Since Wi-Fi signals do not require line-of-sight, WiHear can "hear" people talks within the radio range. Further, WiHear can simultaneously "hear" multiple people's talks leveraging MIMO technology. We implement WiHear on both USRP N210 platform and commercial Wi-Fi infrastructure. Results show that within our pre-defined vocabulary, WiHear can achieve detection accuracy of 91% on average for single individual speaking no more than 6 words and up to 74% for no more than 3 people talking simultaneously. Moreover, the detection accuracy can be further improved by deploying multiple receivers from different angles.

Categories and Subject Descriptors

C.2.1 [**Network Architecture and Design**]: Network communications

Keywords

Wi-Fi Radar; Micro-motion Detection; Moving Pattern Recognition; Interference Cancelation

1. INTRODUCTION

Recent research has pushed the limit of ISM (Industrial Scientific and Medical) band radiometric detection to a new level, including motion detection [9], gesture recognition [32], localization [8], and even classification [12]. We can now detect motions through-wall and recognize human gestures, or even detect and locate tumors inside human bodies [12]. By detecting and analyzing signal reflection, they enable Wi-Fi to "SEE" target objects.

Can we use Wi-Fi signals to "HEAR" talks? It is commonsensical to give a negative answer. For many years, the ability of hearing people talks can only be achieved by deploying acoustic sensors closely around the target individuals. It costs a lot and has a limited sensing and communication range. Further, it has detection delay because the sensor must first record the sound and process it, then transmit it to the receiver. In addition, it cannot be decoded when the surrounding is too noisy.

This paper presents WiHear (Wi-Fi Hearing), which explores the potential of using Wi-Fi signals to HEAR people talk and transmit the talking information to the detector at the same time. This may have many potential applications: 1) WiHear introduces a new way to hear people talks without deploying any acoustic sensors. Further, it still works well even when the surrounding is noisy. 2) WiHear will bring a new interactive interface between human and devices, which enables devices to sense and recognize more complicated human behaviors (e.g. mood) with negligible cost. WiHear makes devices "smarter". 3) WiHear can help millions of disabled people to conduct simple commands to devices with only mouth motions instead of complicated and inconvenient body movements.

How can we manage Wi-Fi hearing? It sounds impossible at first glance, as Wi-Fi signals cannot detect or memorize any sound. The key insight is similar to radar systems. WiHear locates the mouth of an individual, and then recognizes his words by monitoring the signal reflections from his mouth. By recognizing mouth moving patterns, WiHear can extract talking information the same way as lip reading. Thus, WiHear introduces a micro-motion detection scheme that most of previous literature can not achieve. And this minor movement detection can also achieve the ability like leap motion [1]. The closest works are WiSee [32] and WiVi [9], which can only detect more notable motions such as moving arms or legs using doppler shifts or ISAR (inverse synthetic aperture radar) techniques.

To transform the above high-level idea into a practical system, we need to address the following challenges:

(1) How to detect and extract tiny signal reflections from the mouth only? Movements of surrounding people, and other facial movement (e.g. wink) from the target user may affect radio reflections more significantly than mouth movements do. It is challenging to cancel these interferences from the received signals while retaining the information from the tiny mouth motions.

MobiCom'14, September 7-11, 2014, Maui, Hawaii, USA.

ACM 978-1-4503-2783-1/14/09 ...$15.00.
http://dx.doi.org/10.1145/2639108.2639112.

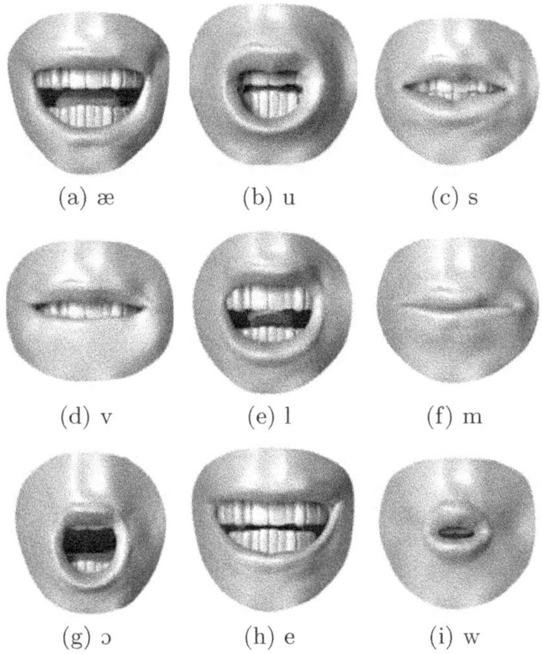

Figure 1: Illustration of vowels and consonants [31] that WiHear can detect and recognize, ©Gary C. Martin.

To address this issue, WiHear first leverages MIMO beamforming to focus on the target's mouth to reduce irrelevant multipath effects introduced by omnidirectional antennas. Such avoidance of irrelevant multipath will enhance WiHear's detection accuracy, since the impact from other people's movements will not dominate when the radio beam is located on the target individual. Further, since for a specific user, the frequency and pattern of wink is relatively stable, WiHear exploits interference cancelation to remove the periodic fluctuation caused by wink.

(2) How to analyze the tiny radio reflections without any change on current Wi-Fi signals? Recent advances harness customized modulation like Frequency-Modulated Carrier Waves (FMCW) [8]. Others like [15] use ultra wide-band and large antenna array to achieve precise motion tracking. Moreover, since mouth motions induce negligible doppler shifts, approaches like WiSee [32] are inapplicable.

WiHear can be easily implemented on commercial Wi-Fi devices. We introduce *mouth motion profiles*, which *partially* leverage multipath effects caused by mouth movements. Traditional wireless motion detection focuses on movements of arms or body, which can be simplified as a rigid body. Therefore they remove all the multipath effects. However, mouth movement is a non-rigid motion process. That is, when pronouncing a word, different parts of the mouth (e.g. jaws and tongue) have different moving speeds and directions. We thus cannot regard the mouth movements as a whole. Instead, we need to leverage multipath to capture the movements of different parts of the mouth.

In addition, since naturally only one individual is talking during a conversation, the above difficulties only focus on single individual speaking. How to recognize multiple individuals' talking simultaneously is another big challenge. The reason for this extension is that, in public areas like airports or bus stations, multiple talks happen simultaneously. WiHear enables hear multiple individuals' simultaneously talks using MIMO technology. We let the senders form multiple radio beams to locate on different targets. Thus, we can regard the target group of people as the senders of the reflection signals from their mouths. By implementing a receiver with multiple antennas and enabling MIMO technology, it can decode multiple senders' talks simultaneously.

Summary of results: We implemented WiHear in both USRP N210 [6] and commercial Wi-Fi products. Fig.1 depicts some syllables (vowels and consonants) that WiHear can recognize [1]. Overall, WiHear can recognize 14 different syllables, 33 trained and tested words. Further, WiHear can correct recognition errors by leveraging related context information. In our experiments, we collect training and testing samples at roughly the same location with the same link pairs. All the experiments are per-person trained and tested. For single user cases, WiHear can achieve an average detection accuracy of 91% to correctly recognize sentences made up of no more than 6 words, and it works in both line-of-sight (LOS) and non-line-of-sight (NLOS) scenarios. With the help of MIMO technology, WiHear can differentiate up to 3 individuals' simultaneously talking with accuracy up to 74%. For through-wall detection of single user, the accuracy is up to 26% with one link pair, and 32% with 3 receivers from different angles. In addition, based on our experimental results, the detection accuracy can be further improved by deploying multiple receivers from different angles.

Contributions: We summarize the main contributions of WiHear as follows:

- WiHear exploits the radiometric characteristics of mouth movements to analyze micro-motion in a non-invasive and device-free manner. To the best of our knowledge, this is the first effort using Wi-Fi signals to hear people talk via PHY layer CSI (Channel State Information) on off-the-shelf WLAN infrastructure.
- WiHear achieves lip reading and speech recognition in LOS, NLOS and through-wall scenarios.
- WiHear introduces *mouth motion profile* using partial multipath effect and discrete wavelet packet transformation to achieve lip reading with Wi-Fi.
- We simultaneously differentiate multiple individuals' talks using MIMO technology.

In the rest of this paper, we first summarize related work in Section 2, followed by an overview in Section 3. Section 4 and 5 detail the system design. Section 6 extends WiHear to recognize multiple talks. We present the implementation and performance evaluation in Section 7, discuss the limitations in Section 8, and conclude in Section 9.

2. RELATED WORK

The design of WiHear is closely related to the following two categories of research.

Vision/Sensor based Motion Sensing. The flourish of smart devices has spurred an urge for new human-device interaction interfaces. Vision and sensors are among prevalent ways to detect and recognize motions.

[1]Jaws and tongue movement based lip reading can only recognize 30%∼40% of the whole vocabulary of English [19]

Popular vision-based approaches include Xbox Kinect [2] and Leap Motion [1], which use RGB hybrid cameras and depth sensing for gesture recognition. Yet they are limited to the field of view and are sensitive to lighting conditions. Thermal imaging [29] acts as an enhancement in dim lighting conditions and non-line-of-sight scenarios at the cost of extra infrastructure. Vision has also been employed for lip reading. [21] and [20] present a combination of acoustic speech and mouth movement image to achieve higher accuracy of automatic speech recognition in noisy environment. [28] presents a vision-based lip reading system and compares viewing a person's facial motion from profile and front view.

Another thread exploits various wearable sensors or handhold devices. Skinput [24] uses acoustic sensors to detect on-body tapping locations. Agrawal et al. [10] enable writing in the air by holding a smartphone with embedded sensors. TEXIVE [13] leverages smartphone sensors to detect driving and texting simultaneously.

WiHear is motivated by these precise motion detection systems, yet aims to harness the ubiquitously deployed WiFi infrastructure, and works non-intrusively (without on-body sensors) and through-wall.

Wireless-based Motion Detection and Tracking. WiHear builds upon recent research that leverages radio reflections from human bodies to detect, track, and recognize motions [35]. WiVi [9] initializes through-wall motion imaging using MIMO nulling [30]. WiTrack [8] implemented an FMCW (Frequency Modulated Carrier Wave) 3D motion tracking system at the granularity of 10cm. WiSee [32] recognizes gestures via Doppler shifts. AllSee [27] achieves low-power gesture recognition on customized RFID tags.

Device-free human localization systems locate a person by analyzing his impact on wireless signals received by pre-deployed monitors, while the person carries no wireless enabled devices [42]. The underlying wireless infrastructure varies, including RFID [43], Wi-Fi [42], ZigBee [39], and the signal metrics range from coarse signal strength [42] [39] to finer-grained PHY layer features [40][41].

Adopting a similar principle, WiHear extracts and interprets reflected signals, yet differs in that WiHear targets at finer-grained motions from lips and tongue. Since the micro motions of the mouth produce negligible Doppler shifts and amplitude fluctuations, WiHear exploits beamforming techniques and wavelet analysis to focus on and zoom in the characteristics of mouth motions only. Also, WiHear is tailored for off-the-shelf WLAN infrastructure and is compatible with the current Wi-Fi standards. We envision WiHear as an initial step towards centimetre-order motion detection (e.g. finger tapping) and higher-level human perception (e.g. inferring mood from speech pacing).

3. WIHEAR OVERVIEW

WiHear is a wireless system that enables commercial Wi-Fi devices to hear people talks using OFDM (Orthogonal Frequency Division Multiplexing) Wi-Fi devices. Fig.2 illustrates the framework of WiHear. It consists of a transmitter and a receiver for single user lip reading. The transmitter can be configured with either two (or more) omnidirectional antennas on current mobile devices or one directional antenna (easily changeable) on current APs (access points). The receiver only needs one antenna to capture radio reflections. WiHear can be extended to multiple APs or mobile devices to support multiple simultaneous users.

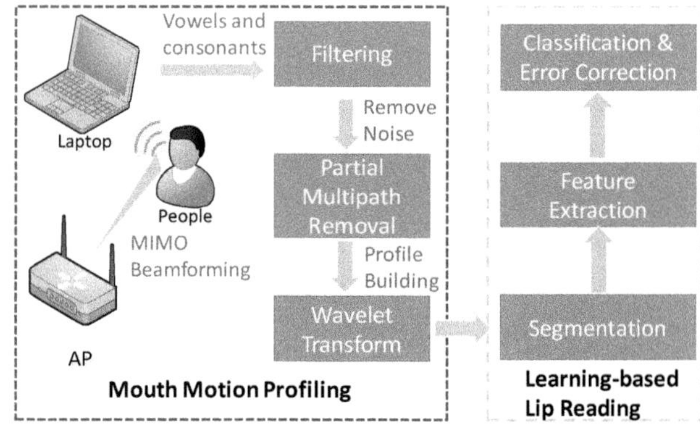

Figure 2: Framework of WiHear.

WiHear transmitter sends Wi-Fi signals towards the mouth of a user using beamforming. WiHear receiver extracts and analyzes reflections from mouth motions. It interprets mouth motions in two steps:

1. **Wavelet-based Mouth Motion Profiling.** WiHear sanitizes received signals by filtering out-band interference and partially eliminating multipath. It then constructs mouth motion profiles via discrete wavelet packet decomposition.

2. **Learning-based Lip Reading.** Once WiHear extracts mouth motion profiles, it applies machine learning to recognize pronunciations, and translates them via classification and context-based error correction.

At the current stage, WiHear can only detect and recognize human talks if the user performs no other movements during speaking. We envision the combination of device-free localization [40] and WiHear may achieve continuous Wi-Fi hearing for mobile users. For irrelevant human interference or ISM band interference, WiHear can tolerant irrelevant human motions 3m away from the link pair without dramatic performance degradation.

4. MOUTH MOTION PROFILING

The first step of WiHear is to construct *Mouth Motion Profile* from received signals.

4.1 Locating on Mouth

Due to the small size of the mouth and the weak extent of its movements, it is crucial to concentrate maximum signal power towards the direction of the mouth. In WiHear, we exploit MIMO beamforming techniques to locate and focus on the mouth, thus both introducing less irrelevant multipath propagation and magnifying signal changes induced by mouth motions [16]. We assume the target user does not move when he speaks.

The locating process works in two steps:

1) The transmitter sweeps its beam for multiple rounds while the user repeats a predefined gesture (e.g. pronouncing [æ] once per second). The beam sweeping is achieved via a simple rotator made by stepper motors similar in [44]. We adjust the beam directions in both azimuth and elevation as in [45]. Meanwhile, the receiver searches for the time when the gesture pattern is most notable during each round of sweeping. With trained samples (e.g. waveform of [æ]

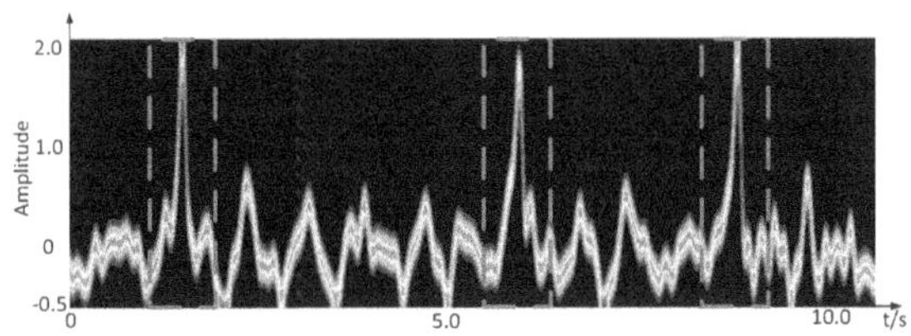

Figure 3: The impact of wink (as denoted in the dashed red box).

for the target user), the receiver can compare the collected signals with trained samples. And it chooses the time stamp in which the collected signals share highest similarity with trained samples.

2) The receiver sends the selected time stamp back to the transmitter and the transmitter then adjusts and fixes its beam accordingly. After each round of sweeping, the transmitter will get the time stamp feedback to adjust the emitted angle of the radio beam. The receiver may also further feedback to the transmitter during the analyzing process to refine the direction of the beam.

Based on our experimental results, the whole locating process usually costs around 5-7 seconds, which is acceptable in real-world implementation. And we define correctly locating as the mouth is within the beam's coverage. For single user scenarios, we tested 20 times with 3 times failure, and thus the accuracy is around 85%. For multiple user scenarios, we define the correct locating as all users' mouths are within the radio beams. We tested with 3 people for 10 times with 2 times failure, and thus the accuracy is around 80%.

4.2 Filtering Out-Band Interference

As the speed of human speaking is low, signal changes caused by mouth motion in the temporal domain are often within 2-5 Hz [38]. Therefore, we apply band-pass filtering on the received samples to eliminate out-band interference.

In WiHear, considering the trade-off between computational complexity and functionality, we adopt a 3-order Butterworth IIR band-pass filter [17], of which the frequency response is defined by equation 1. Butterworth filter is designed to have maximum flat frequency response in the pass band and roll off towards zero in the stop band, which ensures the fidelity of signals in target frequency range while removing out-band noises greatly. The gain of an n-order Butterworth filter is:

$$G^2(w) = |H(jw)|^2 = \frac{G_0^2}{1 + (\frac{w}{w_c})^{2n}} \quad (1)$$

where $G(w)$ is the gain of Butterworth filter; w represents the angular frequency; w_c is the cutoff frequency; n is the order of filter, in our case, n=3; G_0 is the DC gain.

Specifically, since normal speaking frequency is 150-300 syllables/minute [38], we set the cutoff frequency to be (60/60-300/60) Hz to cancel the DC component (corresponding to static reflections) and high frequency interference. In practice, as the radio beam may not be narrow enough, a common low-frequency interference is caused by winking. As shown in Fig.3, however, the frequency of winking is smaller than 1 Hz (0.25 Hz on average). Thus, most of reflections from winking are also eliminated by filtering.

4.3 Partial Multipath Removal

Unlike previous work (e.g. [8]), where multipath reflections are eliminated thoroughly, WiHear performs *partial* multipath removal. The rationale is that mouth motions are non-rigid compared with arm or leg movements. It is common for the tongue, lips, and jaws to move in different patterns and deform in shape sometimes. Consequently, a group of multipath reflections with similar delays may all convey information about the movements of different parts of the mouth. Therefore, we need to remove reflections with long delays (often due to reflections from surroundings), and retain those within a delay threshold (corresponding to non-rigid movements of the mouth).

WiHear exploits CSI of commercial OFDM based Wi-Fi devices to conduct partial multipath removal. CSI represents a sampled version of the channel frequency response at the granularity of subcarrier. An IFFT (Inverse Fast Fourier Transformation) is first operated on the collected CSI to approximate the power delay profile in the time domain [36]. We then empirically remove multipath components with delay over 500 ns [25], and convert the remaining power delay profile back to the frequency domain CSI via an FFT (Fast Fourier Transformation). Since for typical indoor channel, the maximum excess delay is usually less than 500 ns [25], we set it as the initial value. The maximum excess delay of power delay profile is defined to be the temporal extent of the multipath that above a particular threshold. The delay threshold is empirically selected and adjusted based on the training and classification process (Section 5). More precisely, if we cannot get well-trained waveform (i.e. easy to be classified as a group) of one specific word/syllable, we empirically adjust the multipath threshold value.

4.4 Mouth Motion Profile Construction

After filtering and partial multipath removal, we obtain a sequence of cleaned CSI. Each CSI represents the phases and amplitudes on a group of 30 OFDM subcarriers. To reduce computational complexity with keeping the temporal-spectral characteristics, we explore to select a single representative value for each time slot.

We apply identical and synchronous sliding windows on all subcarriers and compute a coefficient C for each of them in each time slot. The coefficient C is defined as the peak to peak value on each subcarrier within a sliding window. Since we have filtered the high frequency components, there would be little dramatic fluctuation caused by interference or noise [17]. Thus the peak-to-peak value can represent human talking behaviors. We also compute another metric, the mean of signal strength in each time slot for each subcarrier. The mean values of all subcarriers facilitate us to pick the several subcarriers (in our case, we choose ten such subcarriers) which represent the most centralized ones, by analyzing the distribution of mean values in each time slot. Among the chosen subcarriers, based on C calculated within each time slot, we pick the waveform of the subcarrier which has the maximum coefficient C. By sliding the window on each subcarrier synchronously, we can pick a series of waveform segments from different subcarriers and assemble them into a single one by arranging them one by one. We define the assembled CSIs as a *Mouth Motion Profile*.

Some may argue that this peak-to-peak value may be dominated by environment changes. However, note that the frequency of Wi-Fi signals is much higher than that of human mouth movement. We have filtered the high frequency components, and the sliding window we use is 200 ms (we can change the duration of sliding window according to different people's speaking patterns). These two reasons may ensure that, for most scenarios, our peak-to-peak value is dominated by mouth movements. Further, we use all the 30 subcarrier information to remove irrelevant multipath and keep partial multipath in Section 4.3. Thus we do not waste any information collected from PHY layer.

4.5 Discrete Wavelet Packet Decomposition

WiHear performs discrete wavelet packet decomposition on the obtained *Mouth Motion Profiles* as input for the learning based lip reading.

The advantages of wavelet analysis are two-folds: 1) It facilitates signal analysis on both time and frequency domain. This attribute can be leveraged in WiHear for analysing the motion of different parts on mouth (e.g. jaws and tongue) in varied frequency domains. It is because each part of mouth moves at different pace. It can also help WiHear locate the time periods for different parts of mouth motion when one specific pronouncing happens. 2) It achieves fine-grained multi-scale analysis. In WiHear, the motion of mouth when pronouncing some syllables shares a lot in common (e.g. [e],[i]), which makes them difficult to be distinguished. By applying discrete wavelet packet transform to the original signals, we can figure out the tiny difference which is beneficial for our classification process.

Discrete wavelet packet decomposition is based on the well-known discrete wavelet transform (DWT), where a discrete signal $f[n]$ is approximated by a combination of expansion functions (the basis).

$$f[n] = \frac{1}{\sqrt{M}} \sum_{k} W_{\phi}[j_0, k]\phi_{j_0,k}[n] + \frac{1}{\sqrt{M}} \sum_{j=j_0}^{\infty} \sum_{k} W_{\psi}[j, k]\psi_{j,k}[n] \quad (2)$$

where $f[n]$ represents the original discrete signal, which is defined in $[0, M-1]$, including totally M points. $\phi_{j_0,k}[n]$ and $\psi_{j,k}[n]$ are both discrete functions defined in $[0, M-1]$, called wavelet basis. Usually, the basis sets $\phi_{j_0,k}[n]_{k\in Z}$ and $\psi_{j,k}[n]_{(j,k)\in Z^2, j\geq j_0}$ are chosen to be orthogonal to each other in order for the convenience of obtaining the wavelet coefficients in the decomposition process, which means:

$$< \phi_{j_0,k}[n], \psi_{j,m}[n] >= \delta_{j_0,j}\delta_{k,m} \quad (3)$$

In discrete wavelet decomposition, during the decomposition procedure, the initial step splits the original signal into two parts, approximation coefficients (i.e. $W_{\phi}[j_0, k]$) and detail coefficients (i.e. $W_{\psi}[j, k]$). After that, the following steps consist of recursively decomposing the approximation coefficients and detail coefficients into two new parts, respectively, using the same strategy as in initial step. This offers the richest analysis: the complete binary tree in the decomposition producer is produced as shown in Fig.4:

The wavelet packet coefficients in each level can be computed using the following equations as:

$$W_{\phi}[j_0, k] = \frac{1}{\sqrt{M}} \sum_{n} f[n]\phi_{j_0,k}[n] \quad (4)$$

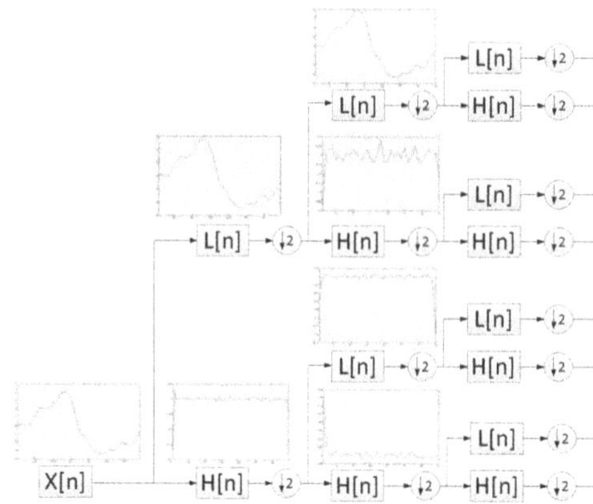

Figure 4: Discrete wavelet packet transformation.

$$W_{\psi}[j, k] = \frac{1}{\sqrt{M}} \sum_{n} f[n]\psi_{j,k}[n], \quad j \geq j_0 \quad (5)$$

where $W_{\phi}[j_0, k]$ refers to the approximation coefficients while $W_{\psi}[j, k]$ represents the detailed coefficients respectively.

The efficacy of wavelet transform relies on choosing proper wavelet basis. One approach that aims at maximizing the discriminating ability of the discrete wavelet packet decomposition is applied, in which a class separability function is adopted [33]. We applied this method for all possible wavelets in the following families: Daubechies, Coiflets, Symlets, and got their class separability respectively. Based on their classification performance, a Symlet wavelet filter of order 4 is selected.

5. LIP READING

The next step of WiHear is to recognize and translate the extracted signal features into words. To this end, WiHear detects the changes of pronouncing adjacent vowels and consonants by machine learning, and maps the patterns to words using automatic speech recognition. That is, WiHear builds a wireless-based provocation dictionary for automatic speech recognition system [18]. To make WiHear an automatic and real-time system, we need to address the following issues: segmentation, feature extraction and classification.

5.1 Segmentation

The segmentation process includes inner word segmentation and inter word segmentation.

For inner word segmentation, each word is divided into multiple phonetic events [26]. And WiHear then uses the training samples of pronouncing each syllable (e.g. sibilants and plosive sounds) to match the parts of the word and then using the syllables' combination to recognize the word.

For inter word segmentation, since there is usually a short interval (e.g. 300 ms) between pronouncing two successive words, WiHear detects the silent interval to separate words apart. Specifically, we first compute the finite difference (i.e., sample-to-sample difference) of the signal we obtained, which is referred as S_{dif}. Next we apply a sliding window to S_{dif} signal. Within each time slot, we compute the absolute mean value of signals in that window to determine whether this window is active or not, w.r.t, by comparing with a dynamically computed threshold, we can determine whether the user is speaking within time period that the sliding win-

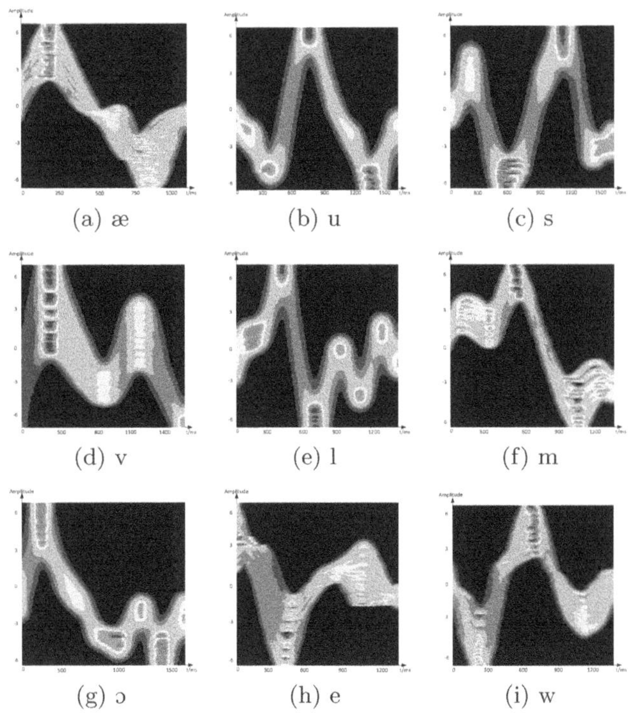

(a) æ (b) u (c) s

(d) v (e) l (f) m

(g) ɔ (h) e (i) w

Figure 5: Extracted features of pronouncing different vowels and consonants.

dow covers. In our experiments, the threshold is set to be 0.75 times the standard deviation of the differential signal across the whole process of pronouncing a certain word. This metric identifies the time slot when signal changes rapidly, indicating the process of pronouncing a word.

5.2 Feature Extraction

After signal segmentation, we can obtain wavelet profiles for different pronunciations, each with 16 4th-order sub-waveforms from high frequency to low frequency components. We then apply a Multi-Cluster/Class Feature Selection (MCFS) scheme [22] to extract representative features from wavelet profiles to reduce the quantity of sub-waveforms. MCFS produces an optimal feature subset by considering possible correlations between different features, which better conforms to the dataset. Fig.5 shows the features selected by MCFS w.r.t. the mouth motion reflections in Fig.1, which differ in each pronunciation.

5.3 Classification

For a specific individual, his speed and rhythm of speaking each word share similar patterns. We can thus directly compare the similarity of the current signals and previously sampled ones by generalized least squares [14].

For scenarios where the user speaks at different speeds, we can use dynamic time warping (DTW) [37] to classify the same word spoken at different speeds into the same group. DTW overcomes the local or global time series' shifts in time domain. It calculates intuitive distance between two time series waveforms. For more information, we recommend [34] which describes it in detail. Further, for people that share similar speaking patterns, we can also use DTW to enable word recognition with only 1 training individual.

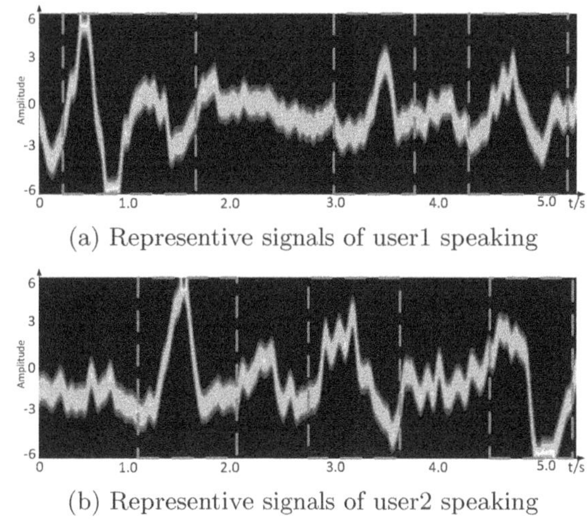

(a) Representive signals of user1 speaking

(b) Representive signals of user2 speaking

Figure 6: Feature extraction of multiple human talks with ZigZag decoding on a single Rx antenna.

5.4 Context-based Error Correction

So far we only explore direct word recognition with mouth motions. However, since the pronunciations spoken are correlated, we can leverage context-aware approaches widely used in automatic speech recognition [11] to improve recognition accuracy. As a toy example, when WiHear detects "you" and "ride", if the next word is "horse", WiHear can automatically distinguish and recognize "horse" instead of "house". Thus we can easily reduce the mistakes in recognizing words with similar mouth motion pattern, and further improve recognition accuracy. Therefore, after applying machine learning for classification of signal reflections and mapping to their corresponding mouth motions, we use context-based error correction to further enhance our lip reading recognition.

6. EXTENDING TO MULTIPLE TARGETS

For one conversation, it is common that only one person is talking at one time. Therefore it seems sufficient for WiHear to track one individual each time. To support debate and discussion, however, WiHear needs to be extended to track multiple talks simultaneously.

A natural approach is to leverage MIMO techniques. As shown in previous work [32], we can use spatial diversity to recognize multiple talks (often from different directions) at the receiver with multiple antennas. Here we also assume that people stay still while talking. To simultaneously track multiple users, we can first let each of them perform a unique pre-defined gesture (e.g. Person A repeatedly speaks [æ], Person B repeatedly speaks [h], etc.). Then we try to locate radio beams on them. The detailed beam locating process is illustrated in Section 4.1. After locating, WiHear's multi-antenna receiver can detect their talks simultaneously by leveraging spatial diversity in MIMO system.

However, due to additional power consumption of multiple RF links [27] and physical sizes of multiple antennas, we explore an alternative approach called *ZigZag cancelation* to support multiple talks with only one receiving antenna. The key insight is that, for most of the circumstances, multiple people do not begin pronouncing each word exactly at the

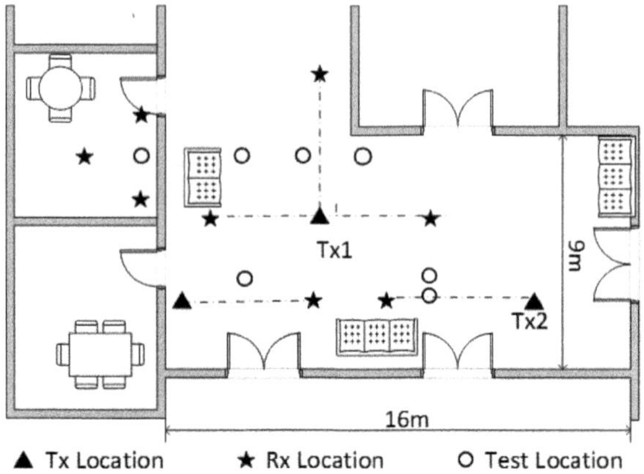

Figure 7: Floor plan of the testing environment.

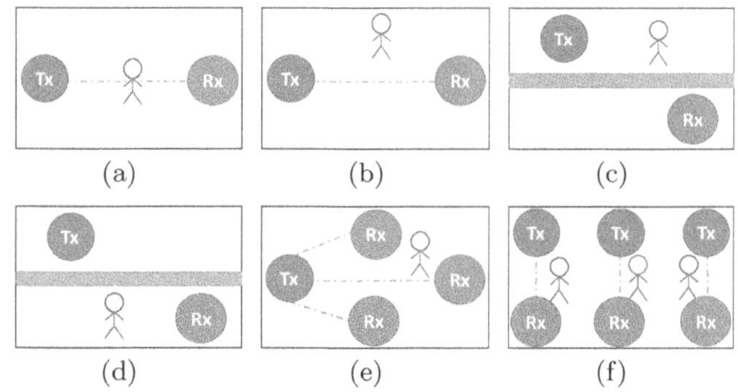

Figure 8: Experimental scenarios layouts. (a) line-of-sight; (b) non-line-of-sight; (c) through wall Tx side; (d) through wall Rx side; (e) multiple Rx; (f) multiple link pairs.

same time. Therefore we can use *ZigZag cancelation*. After we recognize the first word of a user, we can predictably recognize the word he would like to say. Then in the middle of the first person speaking the first word, the second person speaks his first word. We can rely on the previous part of the first person part of first word, and use this information to predict the following part of his first word, and we can cancel the following part of first person speaking the first word and recognize the second person speaking. And we repeat the process back and forth. Thus we can achieve multiple hearing without deploying additional devices.

Fig.6(a) and Fig.6(b) depict the speaking of two users, respectively. After segmentation and classification, we can see each word as encompassed in the dashed red box. As is shown, three words from user1 have different starting and ending time compared with those of user2. Take the first word of the two users as an example, we can first recognize the beginning part of user1 speaking word1, and then use the predicted ending part of user1's word1 to cancel in the combined signals of user1 and user2's word1. Thus we use one antenna to simultaneously decode two users' words.

7. IMPLEMENTATION AND EVALUATION

We implement WiHear on both commercial Wi-Fi infrastructure and USRP N210 [6] and evaluate its performance in typical indoor scenarios.

7.1 Hardware Testbed

We use a TP-LINK TL-WDR4300 wireless router as the transmitter, and a 3.20GHz Intel(R) Pentium 4 CPU 2GB RAM desktop equipped with Intel 5300 NIC (Network Interface Controller) as the receiver. The transmitter possesses directional antennas TL-ANT2406A and operates in IEEE 802.11n AP mode at 2.4GHz. The receiver has 3 working antennas and the firmware is modified as in [23] to report CSI to upper layers.

During the measurement campaign, the receiver continuously pings packets from the AP at the rate of 100 packets per second and we collect CSIs for 1 minute during each measurement. The collected CSIs are then stored and processed at the receiver.

For USRP implementation, we use GNURadio software platform [3], and implement WiHear into a 2×2 MU-MIMO system with 4 USRP N210 [6] boards and XCVR2450 daughterboards, which operate in the 2.4GHz range. We use IEEE 802.11 OFDM standard [7], which has 64 sub-carriers (48 for data). We connect USRP N210 nodes via Gigabit Ethernet to our laboratory PCs, which are all equipped with a qual-core 3.2GHz processor, 3.3GB memory and running Ubuntu 10.04 with GNURadio software platform [3]. Since USRP N210 boards cannot support multiple daughter boards, we combine two USRP N210 nodes with an external clock [5] to build a two-antenna MIMO node. We use the other two USRP N210 nodes as clients.

7.2 Experimental Scenarios

We conduct the measurement campaign in a typical office environment and run our experiments with 4 people (1 female and 3 males). We conduct measurements in a relatively open lobby area covering $9m \times 16m$ as Fig.7. To evaluate WiHear's ability to achieve LOS, NLOS and through-wall speech recognition, we extensively evaluate WiHear's performance in the following 6 scenarios (shown in Fig.8).

- **Line of sight.** The target person is on the line of sight range between the transmitter and the receiver.
- **None line of sight.** The target person is not on the line of sight places, but within the radio range between the transmitter and the receiver.
- **Through wall Tx side.** The receiver and the transmitter are separated by a wall (roughly 6 inches). The target person is on the same side as the transmitter.
- **Through wall Rx side.** The receiver and the transmitter are separated by a wall (roughly 6 inches). The target person is on the same side as the receiver.
- **Multiple Rx.** One transmitter and multiple receivers are on the same side of a wall. The target person is within the range of these devices.
- **Multiple link pairs.** Multiple link pairs work simultaneously on multiple individuals.

Due to the high detection complexity of analyzing mouth motions, for practical issues, the following experiments are per-person trained and tested. Further, we tested two different types of directional antennas, namely, TL-ANT2406A

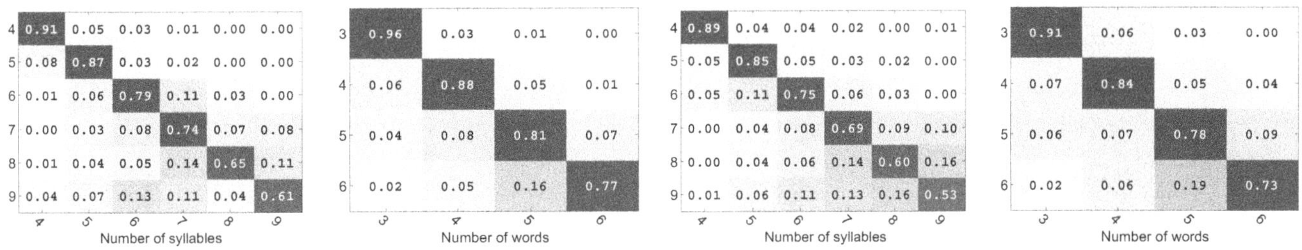

(a) (b) (c) (d)

Figure 9: Automatic segmentation accuracy for (a) inner-word segmentation on commercial devices; (b) inter-word segmentation on commercial devices; (c) inner-word segmentation on USRP; (d) inter-word segmentation on USRP.

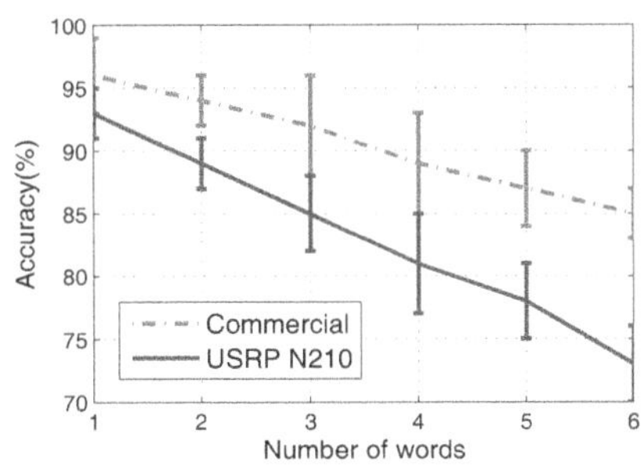

Figure 10: Classification performance.

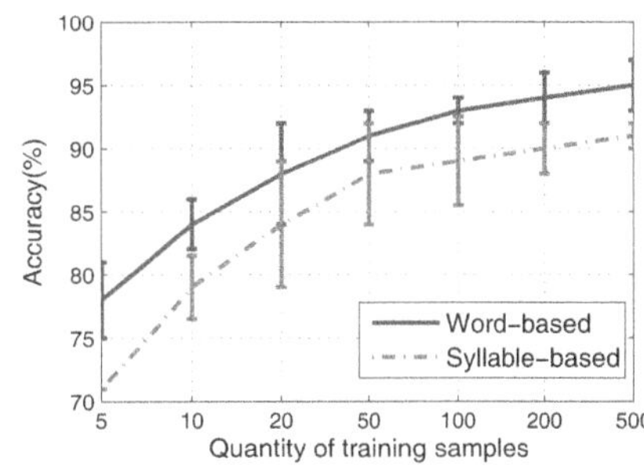

Figure 11: Training overhead.

and TENDA-D2407. With roughly the same location of users and link pairs, we found that WiHear does not need training per commercial Wi-Fi device. However, for devices that have huge differences like USRPs and commercial Wi-Fi devices, we recommend per device training and testing.

7.3 Lip Reading Vocabulary

As previously mentioned, lip reading can only recognize a subset of vocabulary [19]. WiHear can correctly classify and recognize following syllables (vowels and consonants) and words.

Syllables: [æ], [e], [i], [u], [s], [l], [m], [h], [v], [ɔ], [w], [b], [j], [ʃ].

Words: see, good, how, are, you, fine, look, open, is, the, door, thank, boy, any, show, dog, bird, cat, zoo, yes, meet, some, watch, horse, sing, play, dance, lady, ride, today, like, he, she.

We note that it is unlikely any words or syllables can be recognized by WiHear. However, we believe the vocabulary of the above words and syllables are sufficient for simple commands and conversations. To further improve the recognition accuracy and extend the vocabulary, one can leverage techniques like Hidden Markov Models and Linear Predictive Coding [14], which is beyond the scope of this paper.

7.4 Automatic Segmentation Accuracy

We mainly focus on two aspects of segmentation accuracy in LOS and NLOS scenarios like Fig.8(a) and Fig.8(b): inter word and inner word. Our tests consist of speaking sentences with varied quantity of words ranging from 3 to 6. For inner word segmentation, due to its higher complexity, we try to speak 4-9 syllables in one sentence. We test on both USRP N210 and commercial Wi-Fi devices. Based on our experimental results, we found that the performance for LOS (i.e. Fig.8(a)) and NLOS (i.e. Fig.8(b)) achieve similar accuracy. Given this, we average both LOS and NLOS performance as the final results. And Section 7.5, 7.6, 7.7 follow the same rule.

Fig.9 shows the inner-word and inter-word segmentation accuracy. The correct rate of inter-word segmentation is higher than that of inner-word segmentation. The main reason is that for inner-word segmentation, we directly use the waveform of each vowel or consonant to match the test waveform. Since different segmentation will lead to different combinations of vowels and consonants, even some of the combinations do not exist. In contrast, inter-word segmentation is relatively easy since it has a silent interval between two adjacent words.

When comparing between commercial devices and USRPs, we find the overall segmentation performance of commercial devices is a little better than USRPs. The key reason may be the number of antennas on the receiver. The receiver NIC card of commercial devices has 3 antennas whereas MIMO-based USRP N210 receiver only has two receiving antennas. Thus the commercial receiver may have richer information and spacial diversity than USRP N210's receiver.

7.5 Classification Accuracy

Fig.10 depicts the recognition accuracy on both USRP N210s and commercial Wi-Fi infrastructure in LOS (i.e. Fig.8(a)) and NLOS (i.e. Fig.8(b)). We also average the performance of LOS and NLOS for each kind devices. All the correctly segmented words are used for classification. We define the correct detection as correctly recognizing the

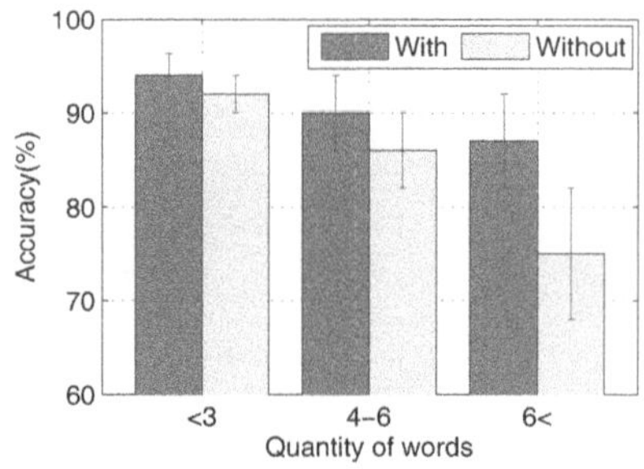

Figure 12: With/without context-based error correction.

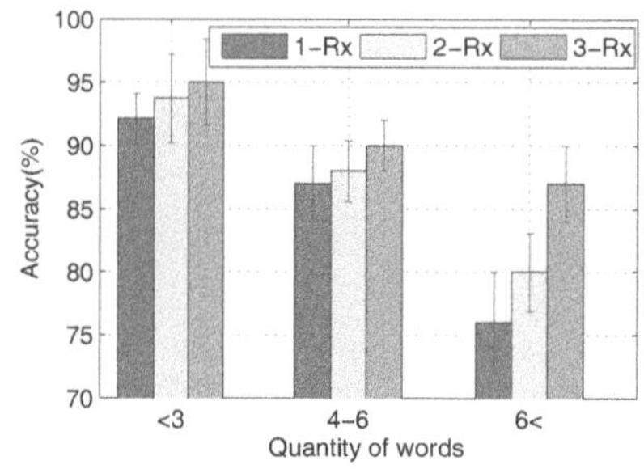

Figure 13: Performance with Multiple Rx.

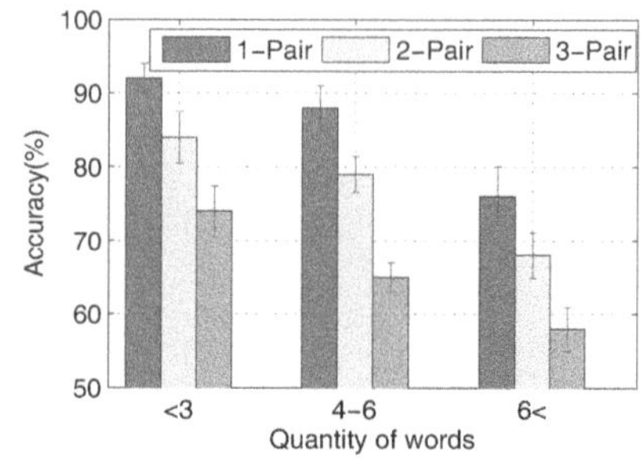

Figure 14: Performance of multiple users with multiple link pairs.

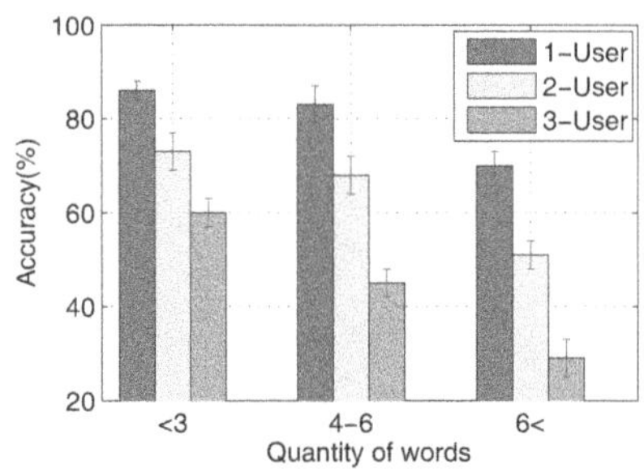

Figure 15: Performance of zigzag decoding for multiple users.

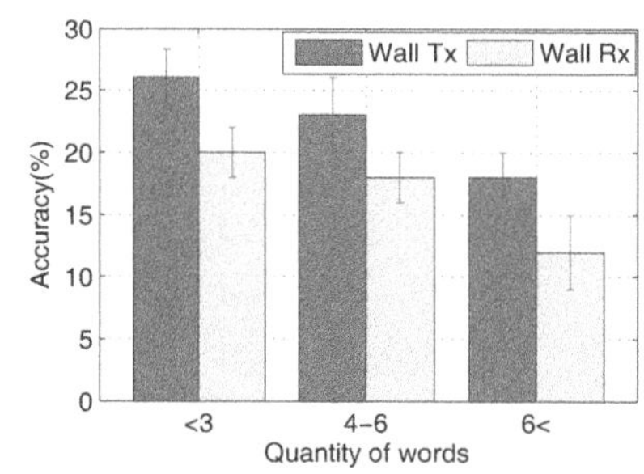

Figure 16: Performance of two through wall scenarios.

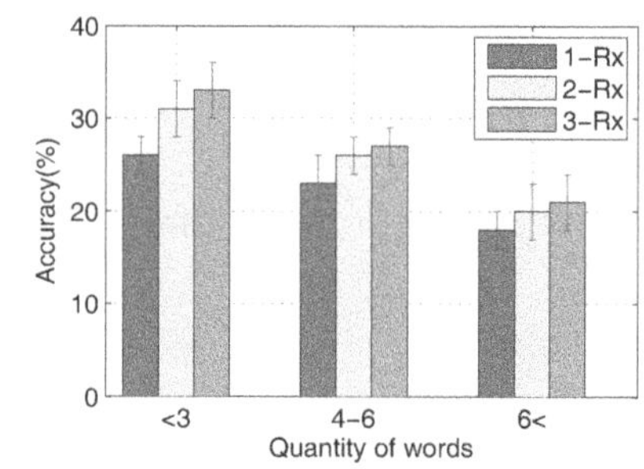

Figure 17: Performance of through wall with multiple Rx.

whole sentence and we do not use context-based error correction here. As is shown in Fig.10, the accuracy performance of commercial Wi-Fi infrastructure system achieves 91% on average with no more than 6-word sentences. In addition, with multiple receivers deployed, WiHear can achieve 91% on average with fewer than 10-word sentences, which is further discussed in Section 7.8.

Results show that the accuracy of commercial Wi-Fi infrastructure with directional antenna is much higher than that of USRP devices. The overall USRP accuracy performance for 6-word sentences is around 82%. The key reasons are two-folds: 1) the USRP N210 uses omni-directional antennas which may introduce more irrelevant multipath. 2) the receiver of commercial Wi-Fi product has one more antenna, which gives one more dimension of spacial diversity.

Since overall commercial Wi-Fi devices perform better than USRP N210, we mainly focus on commercial Wi-Fi devices in the following evaluations.

7.6 Training Overhead

WiHear requires a training process before recognizing human talks. We evaluate the training process in LOS and NLOS scenarios in Fig.8(a) and Fig.8(b), and then average the performance. Fig.11 shows the training overhead of WiHear. For each word or syllable, we present the quantity of training set and its corresponding recognition accuracy. As a whole, we can see that for each word or syllable, the accuracy of word-based is higher than syllable-based scheme. Given this result, empirically we choose the quantity of training sample ranging from 50 to 100, which has good recognition accuracy with acceptable training overhead.

However, the training overhead of word-based scheme is much larger than syllable-based one. Note that the amount of syllables in a language is limited, but the quantity of words is huge. We should make a trade off between syllable-based recognition and word-based recognition.

7.7 Impact of Context-based Error Correction

We evaluate the importance of context-based error correction in LOS and NLOS scenarios as in Fig.8(a), Fig.8(b), and then average the performance. We compare WiHear's recognition accuracy with and without context-based error correction. We divide the quantity of words into 3 groups, namely fewer than 3 words (i.e. <3), 4 to 6 words (i.e. 4-6), more than 6 words but fewer than 10 words (i.e. 6<). By testing different quantity of words in each group, we average the performance as the group's recognition accuracy. The following sections follow the same rule.

As shown in Fig.12, without context-based error correction, the performance drops dramatically. Especially in the scenario of more than 6 words, context-based error correction achieves 13% performance gain than without it. This is because the longer the sentence, the more context information can be exploited for error correction.

Even with context-based error correction, the detection accuracy still tends to drop for longer sentences. The main problem is segmentation. For syllable-based technique, it is obviously hard to segment the waveforms. For word-based technique, even though a short interval often exists between two successive words, the magnitudes of waveforms during these silent intervals are not strictly 0. Thus some of them may be regarded as part of the waveforms of some words. This may cause wrong segmentation of the words and decrease the detection accuracy. Thus the detection accuracy is dependent on the number of words. The performance in the following parts suffers from the same issue.

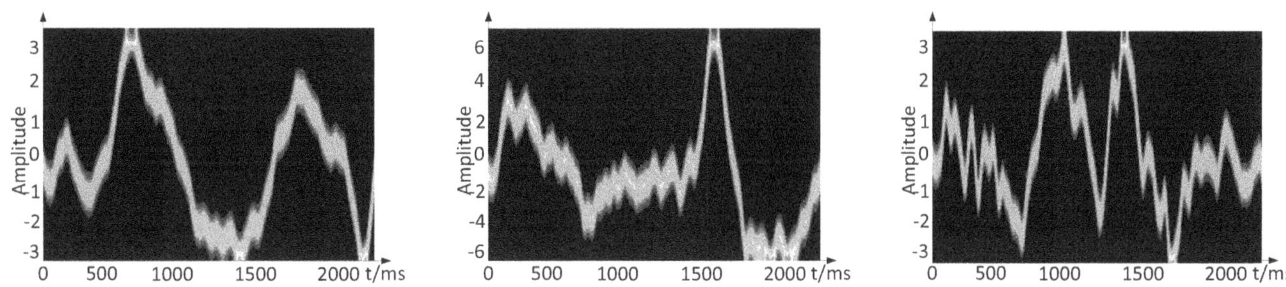

(a) GOOD 0° (b) GOOD 90° (c) GOOD 180°

Figure 18: Example of different views for pronouncing words.

7.8 Performance with Multiple Receivers

Here we analyze radiometric impacts of human talks from different perspectives (i.e. scenarios like Fig.8(e)). Specifically, to enhance recognition accuracy, we collect CSI from different receivers in multiple angle of views.

Based on our experiments, even though each NIC receiver has 3 antennas, the spatial diversity is not significant enough. In other words, the mouth motion's impacts on different links in one NIC are quite similar. This may be because the antennas are closely placed to each other. Thus we propose to use multiple receivers for better spatial diversity. As shown in Fig.18, the same person pronouncing the word "GOOD" has different radiometric impacts on the received signals from different perspectives (from the angles of 0°, 90° and 180°).

With WiHear receiving signals in different perspectives, we can build up *Mouth Motion Profile* with these dimensions of different receivers. Thus it will enhance the performance and improve recognition accuracy. As depicted in Fig.13, with multiple (3 in our case) dimensional training data, WiHear can achieve 87% accuracy even when the user speaks more than 6 words. It ensures the overall accuracy to be 91% in all three words' group scenarios. Given this, if it is needed for high accuracy of Wi-Fi hearing, we recommend to deploy more receivers from different views.

7.9 Performance for Multiple Targets

Here we present WiHear's performance for multiple targets. We use 2 and 3 pairs of transceivers to simultaneously target on 2 and 3 individuals, respectively (i.e. scenarios like Fig.8(f)). As shown in Fig.14, compared with a single target, the overall performance decreases with the number of targets increasing. Further, the performance drops dramatically when each user speaks more than 6 words. However, the overall performance is acceptable. The highest accuracy of 3 users' simultaneously talking less than 3 words is 74%. The worst situation can achieve nearly 60% accuracy with 3 users speaking more than 6 words at the same time.

For *ZigZag cancelation* decoding, since NIC card [23] has 3 antennas, we enable only one antenna for our measurement. As depicted in Fig.15, the performance drops more severely than that of multiple link pairs. The worst case (i.e. 3 users, 6<words) only achieves less than 30% recognition accuracy. Thus we recommend to use *ZigZag cancelation* scheme with no more than 2 users who speak fewer than 6 words. Otherwise, we increase link pairs to ensure the overall performance.

7.10 Through Wall Performance

We tested two through wall scenarios, target on the Tx side (Fig.8(c)) and on the Rx side (Fig.8(d)). As shown in Fig.16, although recognition accuracy is pretty low (around 18% on average), compared with the probability of random guess (i.e. 1/33=3%), the recognition accuracy is acceptable. Performance with target on the Tx side is better.

We believe by implementing interference nulling as in [9] can improve the performance, which unfortunately cannot be achieved with commercial Wi-Fi products. However, an alternative approach is to leverage spatial diversity with multiple receivers. As shown in Fig.17, with 2 and 3 receivers, we can analyze signals from different perspectives with the target on the Tx side. Especially with 3 receivers, the maximum accuracy gain is 7%. With trained samples from different views, multiple receivers can enhance through wall performance.

7.11 Resistance to Environmental Dynamics

We evaluate the influence of other ISM-band interference and irrelevant human movements on the detection accuracy of WiHear. We test these two kinds of interference in both LOS and NLOS scenarios as depicted in Fig.8(a) and Fig.8(b). The resistance results of these two scenarios also share high similarity. Thus here we depict environmental effects on NLOS scenarios in Fig.19.

As shown in Fig.19, one user repeatedly speaks a 4-word sentence. For each of the following 3 cases, we collect the radio sequences of speaking the repeated 4-word sentence for 30 times and draw the combined waveform in Fig.19. For the first case, we remain the surroundings stable. With pre-trained waveform of each word that the user speaks, as shown in Fig.19(a), we can easily recognize 4 words that user speaks. For the second case, we let three men randomly stroll in the room but always keep 3 m away from the WiHear's link pair. As shown in Fig.19(b), the words can still be correctly detected even though the waveform is loose compared with that in Fig.19(a). This loose character may be the effect of irrelevant human motions. For the third case, we use a mobile phone to communicate with an AP (e.g. surfing online) and keep them 3 m away from WiHear's link pair. As shown in Fig.19(c), the generated waveform fluctuates a little compared with that in Fig.19(a). This fluctuation may be the effect of ISM band interference.

Based on above results, we can conclude that WiHear can be resistant to ISM band interference and irrelevant human motions 3m away without significant recognition performance degradation.

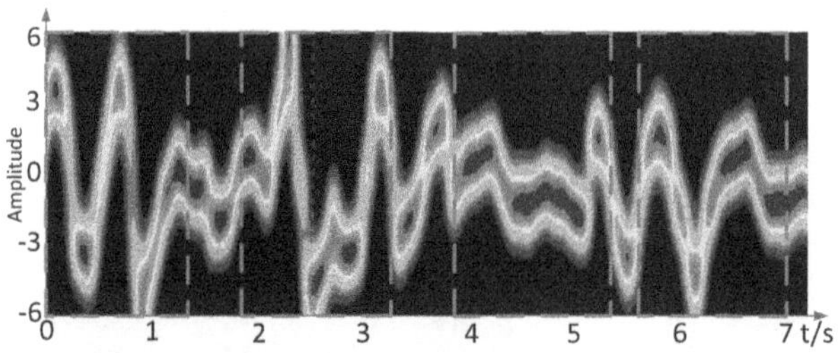

(a) Waveform of a 4-word sentence without interference of ISM band signals or irrelevant human motions

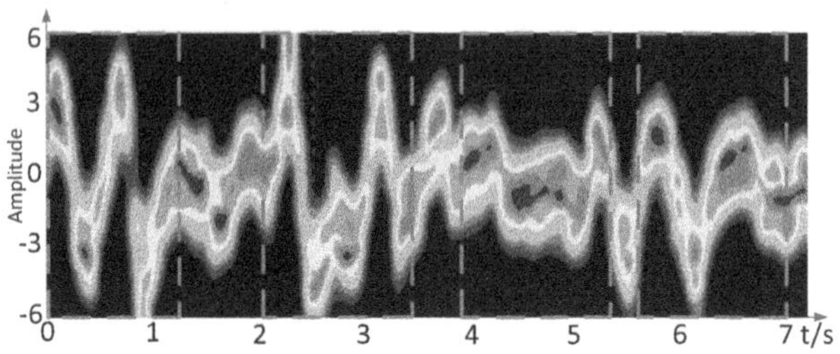

(b) Impact of irrelevant human movements interference

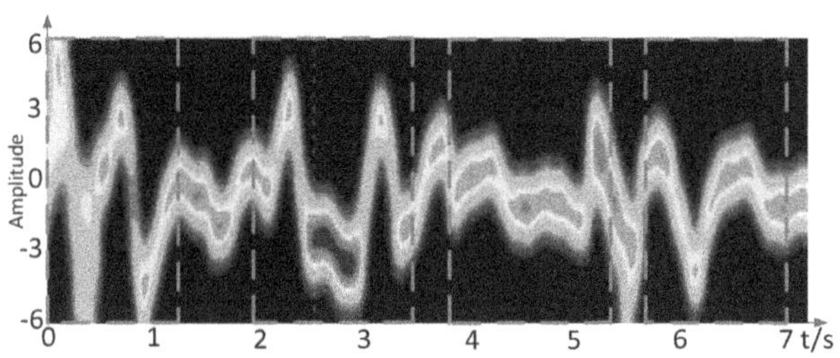

(c) Impact of ISM band interference

Figure 19: Illustration of WiHear's resistance to environmental dynamics.

8. DISCUSSION

So far we assume people do not move when they speak. It is possible that a person talks while walking. We believe the combination of device-free localization techniques [40] and WiHear would enable real-time tracking and continuous hearing. We leave it as a future direction.

Generally, people share similar mouth movements when pronouncing the same syllables or words. Given this, we may achieve Wi-Fi hearing via DTW (details in Section 5.3) with training data from one person, and testing on another individual. We leave it as part of the future work.

Due to the longer distance between the target person and the directional antenna, the larger noise and interference occurs. For long range Wi-Fi hearing, we recommend grid parabolic antennas like TL-ANT2424B [4] to accurately locate the target for better performance.

To support real-time processing, we can only use CSI on one subchannel to reduce the computational complexity. Since we found the radiometric impact of mouth motions is similar across subchannels, we may safely select one representative subchannel without sacrificing much performance. However, the full potential of the whole CSI information is still under-explored.

We can extend WiHear to detect other micro motions, e.g. finger motions, like the vision-based device Leap Motion [1]. By deploying multiple link pairs from different angles, we can detect simple finger motions such as which one or multiple fingers are moving ups and downs.

9. CONCLUDING REMARKS

This paper presents WiHear, a novel system that enables Wi-Fi signals to hear talks. WiHear is compatible with existing Wi-Fi standards and can be extended easily to commercial Wi-Fi products. To achieve lip reading, WiHear introduces a novel system for sensing and recognizing micro-motions (e.g. mouth movements). WiHear consists of two key components, *mouth motion profile* for extracting features, and learning-based signal analysis for lip reading. Further, *Mouth motion profile* is the first effort that leverage *partial* multipath effects to get the whole mouth motions' impacts on radio. Extensive experiments demonstrate that WiHear can achieve recognition accuracy of 91% for single user speaking no more than 6 words and up to 74% for hearing no more than 3 users simultaneously.

WiHear may have many application scenarios. Since Wi-Fi signals do not require LOS, even though experimental results are not promising, we believe WiHear has the potential to "hear" people talks through walls and doors within the radio range. In addition, WiHear can "understand" people talking, which can get more complicated information from talks than gesture-based interfaces like Xbox Kinect [2] (e.g. mood). Further, WiHear can also help disabled people to conduct simple commands to devices with mouth movements instead of inconvenient body gestures. We can also extend WiHear for motion detection on hands. Since WiHear can be easily extended into commercial products, we envision it as a practical solution for Wi-Fi hearing in real-world deployment.

Acknowledgment

This research is supported in part by Program for New Century Excellent Talents in University (NCET-13-0908), Guangdong Natural Science Funds for Distinguished Young Scholar (No.S20120011468), New Star of Pearl River on Science and Technology of Guangzhou (No.2012J2200081), Hong Kong RGC Grant 16207714, China NSFC Grant 61202454.

10. REFERENCES

[1] Leap Motion, `https://www.leapmotion.com/`.
[2] Xbox Kinect, `http://www.xbox.com/en-US/kinect`.
[3] GNU software defined radio, `http://www.gnu.org/software/gnuradio`.
[4] TP-LINK 2.4GHz 24dBi Grid Parabolic Antenna, `http://www.tp-link.com/en/products/details/?categoryid=2474&model=TL-ANT2424B#over`.
[5] *Oscilloquartz SA, OSA 5200B GPS Clock.* `http://www.oscilloquartz.com`.
[6] *Universal Software Radio Peripheral.* Ettus Research LLC, `http://www.ettus.com`.
[7] *Wireless LAN Medium Access Control (MAC) and Physical Layer (PHY) Specifications.* IEEE Std 802.11, 2012.
[8] F. Adib, Z. Kabelac, D. Katabi, and R. C. Miller. 3d tracking via body radio reflections. In *USENIX NSDI*, 2014.

[9] F. Adib and D. Katabi. See through walls with wi-fi! In *ACM SIGCOMM*, 2013.

[10] S. Agrawal, I. Constandache, S. Gaonkar, R. R. Choudhury, K. Cave, and F. DeRuyter. Using mobile phones to write in air. In *ACM MobiSys*, 2011.

[11] M. Aynehband, A. M. Rahmani, and S. Setayeshi. Coast: Context-aware pervasive speech recognition system. In *IEEE International Symposium on Wireless and Pervasive Computing*, 2011.

[12] D. Bharadia, K. R. Joshi, and S. Katti. Full duplex backscatter. In *ACM HotNets*, 2013.

[13] C. Bo, X. Jian, X.-Y. Li, X. Mao, Y. Wang, and F. Li. You're Driving and Texting: Detecting Drivers Using Personal Smart Phones by Leveraging Inertial Sensors. In *ACM MobiCom*, 2013.

[14] J. Bradbury. Linear predictive coding. *Mc G. Hill.*

[15] G. L. Charvat, L. C. Kempel, E. J. Rothwell, C. M. Coleman, and E. L. Mokole. A through-dielectric radar imaging system. *IEEE Transactions on Antennas and Propagation*, 58(8), 2010.

[16] L. J. Chu. Physical limitations of omni-directional antennas. *Journal of Applied Physics*, 1948.

[17] G. Cohn, D. Morris, S. N. Patel, and D. S. Tan. Humantenna: Using the body as an antenna for real-time whole-body interaction. In *ACM SIGCHI*, 2012.

[18] M. Cooke, P. Green, L. Josifovski, and A. Vizinho. Robust automatic speech recognition with missing and unreliable acoustic data. *Speech Communication*, 2001.

[19] B. Dodd and R. Campbell. *Hearing by eye: The psychology of lip-reading.* Lawrence Erlbaum Associates, 1987.

[20] P. Duchnowski, M. Hunke, D. Busching, U. Meier, and A. Waibel. Toward movement-invariant automatic lip-reading and speech recognition. In *Proceedings of 1995 International Conference on Acoustics, Speech, and Signal Processing*, 1995.

[21] P. Duchnowski, U. Meier, and A. Waibel. See me, hear me: Integrating automatic speech recognition and lip-reading. In *Proc. Int. Conf. Spoken Lang. Process*, 1994.

[22] I. A. Gheyas and L. S. Smith. Feature Subset Selection in Large Dimensionality Domains. *Pattern Recognition*, 2010.

[23] D. Halperin, W. Hu, A. Shethy, and D. Wetherall. Predictable 802.11 packet delivery from wireless channel measurements. In *ACM SIGCOMM*, 2010.

[24] C. Harrison, D. Tan, and D. Morris. Skinput: Appropriating the body as an input surface. In *ACM SIGCHI*, 2010.

[25] Y. Jin, W. S. Soh, and W. C. Wong. Indoor localization with channel impulse response based fingerprint and nonparametric regression. *IEEE Transactions on Wireless Communications*, 9(3), 2010.

[26] H. Junker, P. Lukowicz, and G. Troster. On the automatic segmentation of speech signals. In *Proceedings of IEEE International Conference on Acoustics, Speech, and Signal Processing*, 1987.

[27] B. Kellogg, V. Talla, and S. Gollakota. Bringing gesture recognition to all devices. In *USENIX NSDI*, 2014.

[28] K. Kumar, T. Chen, and R. M. Sternl. Profile view lip reading. In *Proceedings of 2007 International Conference on Acoustics, Speech, and Signal Processing*, 2007.

[29] E. Larson, G. Cohn, S. Gupta, X. Ren, B. Harrison, D. Fox, and S. N. Patel. Heatwave: Thermal imaging for surface user interaction. In *ACM SIGCHI*, 2011.

[30] K. C.-J. Lin, S. Gollakota, and D. Katabi. Random access heterogeneous mimo networks. In *ACM SIGCOMM*, 2011.

[31] G. C. Martin. Preston blair phoneme series. `http://www.garycmartin.com/mouth_shapes.html`.

[32] Q. Pu, S. Gupta, S. Gollakota, and S. Patel. Whole-home gesture recognition using wireless signals. In *ACM MobiCom*, 2013.

[33] N. Saito and R. Coifman. Local discriminant bases and their applications. *Journal of Mathematical Imaging and Vision*, 5(4):337–358, 1995.

[34] S. Salvador and P. Chan. Toward accurate dynamic time warping in linear time and space. *Intell. Data Anal.*, 11(5), Oct. 2007.

[35] M. Scholz, S. Sigg, H. R. Schmidtke, and M. Beigl. Challenges for device-free radio-based activity recognition. In *Workshop on Context Systems, Design, Evaluation and Optimisation*, 2011.

[36] S. Sen, J. Lee, K.-H. Kim, and P. Congdon. Avoiding multipath to revive inbuilding wifi localization. In *ACM MobiSys*, 2013.

[37] J. Wang and D. Katabi. Dude, where's my card? rfid positioning that works with multipath and non-line of sight. In *ACM SIGCOMM*, 2013.

[38] J. R. Williams. Guidelines for the use of multimedia in instruction. In *Proceedings of the Human Factors and Ergonomics Society 42nd Annual Meeting*, 1998.

[39] J. Wilson and N. Patwari. Radio Tomographic Imaging with Wireless Networks. *IEEE Transactions on Mobile Computing*, 9(5):621–632, 2010.

[40] J. Xiao, K. Wu, Y. Yi, L. Wang, and L. Ni. Pilot: Passive Device-free Indoor Localization Using Channel State Information. In *IEEE ICDCS*, 2013.

[41] Z. Yang, Z. Zhou, and Y. Liu. From RSSI to CSI: Indoor Localization via Channel Response. *ACM Computing Surveys*, 46(2):25:1–25:32, 2013.

[42] M. Youssef, M. Mah, and A. Agrawala. Challenges: Device-free Passive Localization for Wireless Environments. In *ACM MobiCom*, 2007.

[43] D. Zhang, J. Zhou, M. Guo, J. Cao, and T. Li. TASA: Tag-Free Activity Sensing Using RFID Tag Arrays. *IEEE Transactions on Parallel and Distributed Systems*, 22(4):558–570, 2011.

[44] W. Zhang, X. Zhou, L. Yang, Z. Zhang, B. Y. Zhao, and H. Zheng. 3D Beamforming for Wireless Data Centers. In *ACM Hotnets*, 2011.

[45] X. Zhou, Z. Zhang, Y. Zhu, Y. Li, S. Kumar, A. Vahdat, B. Y. Zhao, and H. Zheng. Mirror Mirror on the Ceiling: Flexible Wireless Links for Data Centers. In *ACM SIGCOMM*, 2012.

Use It Free: Instantly Knowing Your Phone Attitude

Pengfei Zhou, Mo Li
Nanyang Technological University, Singapore
{pfzhou, limo}@ntu.edu.sg

Guobin Shen
Microsoft Research, China
jackysh@microsoft.com

ABSTRACT

The phone attitude is an essential input to many smartphone applications, which has been known very difficult to accurately estimate especially over long time. Based on in-depth understanding of the nature of the MEMS gyroscope and other IMU sensors commonly equipped on smartphones, we propose A^3 – an accurate and automatic attitude detector for commodity smartphones. A^3 primarily leverages the gyroscope, but intelligently incorporates the accelerometer and magnetometer to select the best sensing capabilities and derive the most accurate attitude estimation. Extensive experimental evaluation on various types of Android smartphones confirms the outstanding performance of A^3. Compared with other existing solutions, A^3 provides $3\times$ improvement on the accuracy of attitude estimation.

Categories and Subject Descriptors

C.4 [**Performance of Systems**]: Modeling techniques, Performance attributes; C.5.3 [**Computer System Implementation**]: Portable devices

Keywords

Mobile Phone Attitude, Gyroscope, IMU Sensors, Attitude Calibration

1. INTRODUCTION

The phone attitude gives the 3D orientation of the phone with respect to the earth coordinate system. It is an essential input to many phone applications including mobile gaming, 3D photography [12, 18], gesture and activity recognition [17, 20], dead reckoning based localization and navigation [11, 24, 25, 26], etc. Since the first integration into smartphones in 2010, the MEMS gyroscope, capable of measuring the 3 dimensional angular velocities, has been exploited to estimate phone attitude by continuously integrating the angular velocities. However, unlike those high precision gyroscopes used in nautical, aviation and robotic navigation systems, the MEMS gyroscope has been widely blamed for its poor accuracy.

The problem becomes particularly challenging in practice as people may take their phones in arbitrary ways, hold in different body positions such as in hands, pockets, or bags, and make complicated motion styles. Figure 1 shows the phone attitude estimation results of a popular Android app[1] using the gyroscope. Figure 1(a) depicts the initial attitude estimation and Figure 1(b) depicts the estimation for the same phone attitude after 1 minute random motion. Obviously, there is a significant difference in the two attitude estimates, which corresponds to the phone attitude tracking error. Some recent research works exploited the gyroscope for heading direction estimation. Their reports also confirmed the severity of gyroscope drifts in minute level runs even when the mobile phone is held relatively still to the user [19, 22, 24]. Although there have been many efforts made to address a similar problem (rigid body orientation) in robotics domain [14, 15, 8, 16], our study reveals that directly adopting those approaches cannot provide satisfactory performance, mainly due to the lack of fundamental understanding of the MEMS gyroscope and other IMU (Inertial Measurement Unit) sensors on smartphones. As a concrete example, current Android API directly borrows existing Kalman-based sensor fusion techniques to estimate the phone attitude and suffers significant performance degradation in many conditions.

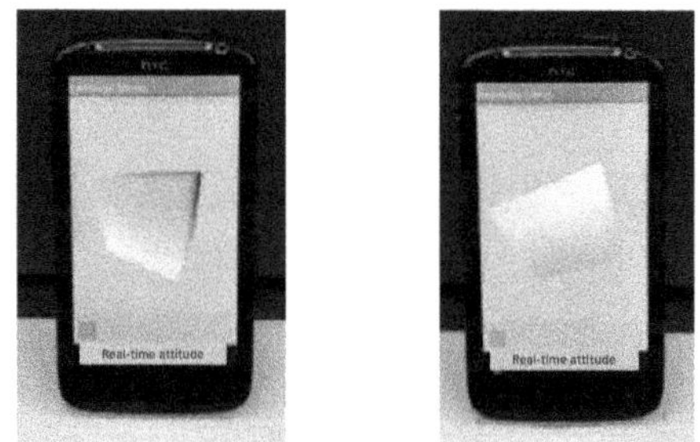

(a) Initial attitude estimation. (b) Attitude estimation after 1 minute.

Figure 1: Phone attitude tracking error of a popular smartphone app.

In this paper, we conduct detailed experimental study to understand the fundamental performance of the MEMS gyroscope. We follow the device specification and conduct controlled experiments to investigate how different environmental factors impact on the gyroscope performance and how the best accuracy can be achieved in an appropriate condition range. We also characterize the nature of two other IMU sensors on smartphones, the accelerometer and compass, to understand their performance in different conditions. Based on such comprehensive understanding, we propose to estimate the phone attitude primarily based on the 3-axis angular ve-

[1] The app is called "Android Sensor Box" available at Google Play with about 1,000,000 downloads.

MobiCom'14, September 7-11, 2014, Maui, Hawaii, USA.

http://dx.doi.org/10.1145/2639108.2639110.

locities obtained from the gyroscope, but also incorporate the compass and the accelerometer for opportunistic calibration. The three types of IMU sensors are of different natures and their accuracy varies in different condition ranges. In particular, the gyroscope provides a cumulative estimation of the attitude through continuous integration on angular velocities that is accurate in general but suffers from error accumulation. On the other hand, the compass sensor and accelerometer provide instant attitude estimation without cumulative errors but the accuracy is highly instant environment and motion dependent. We develop a practical approach that calibrates the cumulative gyroscope estimation when we have higher confidence in compass and accelerometer readings. In practical usage, it is non-trivial to identify "good" calibration opportunities. Intuitively, the compass sensor outputs accurate geomagnetic north when the phone is outdoor and the gravity direction can be accurately extracted from accelerometer when the phone is static. Such opportunities, however, would be too few in practice to provide timely calibration. In this work we propose an "opportunistic calibration" technique that looks at the concordance of the three types of sensors in estimating short period attitude changes. High consistency indicates high instant confidence of the compass and gravity outputs and thus a positive calibration opportunity. Sufficient calibration opportunities can be identified using this approach.

We incorporate the proposed design and techniques and develop A^3, an Accurate and Automatic Attitude detector for smartphones. A prototype system is implemented and comprehensively tested with three types of Android smartphones, including HTC Sensation, Samsung i9100, and LG Google Nexus 4. We evaluate the performance of A^3 across various scenarios and in multiple popular apps, and compare A^3 with other possible competitors. The experiment results demonstrate that A^3 provides $3\times$ improvement over alternative solutions. Higher performance gain can be achieved the user motion is intense (e.g., running). Meanwhile, the power consumption of A^3 is measured moderate and acceptable for long runs on commodity smartphones.

The contribution of this work includes (1) detailed studies to understand the basic performance of smartphone IMU sensors and their sensitivity to environments; (2) based on such understanding, a novel and practical smartphone attitude estimation method which intelligently exploits the sensing redundancy of the gyroscope, compass and accelerometer; and (3) a prototype system of A^3 on Android platform which outperforms existing competitors in various environments and conditions. To our knowledge, A^3 significantly pushes forward the state-of-the-art of phone attitude estimation. A^3 makes it practically feasible to instantly obtain the phone attitude in free motion and for long runs.

The rest of the paper is organized as follows. §2 presents the background and motivation of our problem. §3 describes the principle of MEMS gyroscopes in attitude tracking and characterizes its performance. §4 studies the compass sensor and accelerometer, and describes how they can be leveraged to calibrate gyroscopes. §5 describes the opportunistic calibration technique and presents the final A^3 system design. §6 presents the experimental evaluation results. §7 discusses the related works and §8 concludes this paper.

2. BACKGROUND AND MOTIVATION

Instantly knowing the phone attitude is essential to many applications. For example, the phone attitude can be treated as a key user input for enhanced entertainment in many gesture-based mobile phone games. In 3D photography, the instant phone attitude information helps to retrieve accurate depth information from the pictures taken. In recent dead reckoning based localization and navigation studies, tracking the phone attitude yields the heading of people movement for trajectory mapping.

App	Type	Time	Error
3D camera (Android)	3D photography	4mins	40°
Seene (iPhone)	3D photography	3mins	25°
Sensor Box (Android)	mobile app	3 mins	65°
Jenga (Android)	game	6 mins	35°
Jenga (iPhone)	game	5 mins	30°
Showdown (iPhone)	game	10 mins	38°

Table 1: The attitude estimation error measured from popular apps.

The gyroscopes have been playing a critical role in estimating phone attitude since the first integration to smartphones in 2010[2]. Recent use experience, however, suggests that poor accuracy can be achieved for long period of tracking. Table 1 lists the measured errors of some popular apps from Google Play and Apple Store. The apps typically bear $25°{\sim}65°$ errors within less than 10 minutes, which significantly impair the use experience. For example, the 3D photography apps like the "3D Camera" for Android and "Seene" for iPhone track the phone attitude when users take multiple pictures and then combine different pictures into one based on the estimated phone attitude. The big attitude estimation error can result in obvious distortion of the final generated picture. In the "Jenga" game, the phone attitude is tracked and taken as input. The user can change the perspective of view to fully inspect a 3D Jenga tower by rotating the phone. The large cumulative tracking errors require frequent reset of the phone attitude from the user. In dead reckoning based localization, accurately detecting the user heading is important but remains unsolved. As the user walks, the localization error due to the heading error is rapidly accumulated, which is up to 20m within 10 mins according to recent studies [22, 24].

One cause of such errors is the limited precision of the state-of-the-art MEMS gyroscope. Compared with high precision gyroscopes like the Fiber Optic Gyroscope (FOG) that can achieve stability down to $10^{-4\circ}/h$, the MEMS gyroscope is manufactured with low cost based on the Coriolis Vibrating Gyroscope (CVG) principle. In CVG, as the plane of oscillation is rotated, the response detected by the transducer is due to the Coriolis term in its equations of motion. CVG translates the response into the instant 3-axis angular velocities of the phone and continues integration has to be performed on the output to obtain angular increments over the previous attitude. Instantly detecting the absolute attitude thus relies on precise tracking of phone attitude changes, which is known of substantial cumulative errors.

Although no much progress has been made for improving the attitude detection accuracy in the field of mobile phone study, many efforts have been made in robotics domain to address a similar problem, i.e., estimating rigid body orientation. Recent studies in robotics [14, 8, 16, 15] explore the capabilities of magnetometers and accelerometers in orientation estimation, and integrate with the gyroscopes to improve the accuracy. The devised MARG (Magnetic, Angular Rate, and Gravity) orientation for robotic systems performs sensor fusion with input from all three types of sensors to derive the final estimation. Detailed review of related works will be given in Section 7. The performance and characteristics of the sensors used in robotic systems are different from those used on smartphones. For example, compared with the MEMS gyroscope on smartphones, the mechanical and START [1, 8, 21] gyroscopes

[2]iPhone 4 was the first smartphone model that integrates the 3-axis gyroscope. Gyroscopes were later widely integrated in other Android and Windows Phone devices.

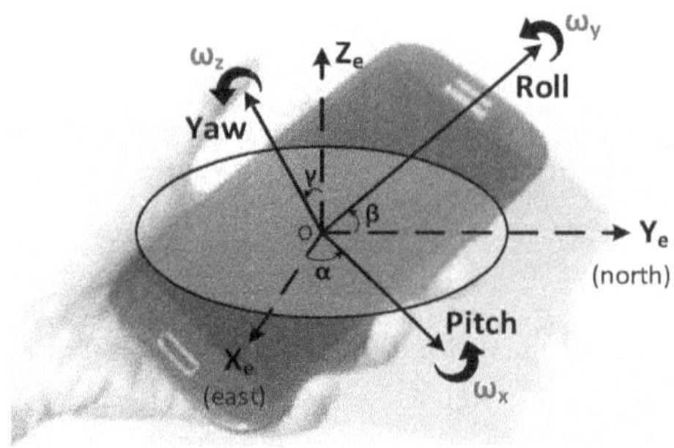

Figure 2: The output of the MEMS gyroscope is 3 angular velocities around the *Roll*, *Yaw*, and *Pitch* axis in the phone body-frame.

used in robotic systems are based on different physical rationales, and usually have higher accuracy but different frequency responses to motions. No existing studies, however, have quantitatively understood the nature of smartphone MEMS sensors and their performance in different condition ranges. As a result, straightforward sensor fusion, e.g., Kalman-based approaches [14, 8, 16] with unsorted sensor input, cannot guarantee high accuracy. Besides, the motion patterns and usage environments of robotic systems are also very different with those of smartphones. To our knowledge, simply migrating the approaches for robotic systems to smartphone platforms results in suboptimal performance. For example, the Android API `getRotationMatrixFromVector()` directly adopts existing Kalman-based sensor fusion algorithms to calculate the phone attitude. As the experimental evaluation reveals, the estimation error of Android API may reach 40° or higher in many cases.

In this paper, we comprehensively characterize the nature of the MEMS gyroscopes on modern smartphones, and derive optimized settings and techniques to improve the gyroscope performance in practical working conditions. We then incorporate the compass and accelerometer. While the gyroscope detects 3-axis angular velocities, being able to remove 3 degrees of freedom, the compass measures the geomagnetic north and the 3-axis accelerometer can derive the gravity direction from the 3 axis linear acceleration, providing the capability of removing another 3 degrees of freedom. We thus develop an intelligent calibration approach which selects the best 3 degrees of freedom to determine the phone attitude based on quantitative error estimation of the three different IMU sensors under different condition ranges. Our approach roots in the comprehensive understanding of smartphone IMU sensors and thus fundamentally outperforms existing competing solutions.

3. UNDERSTANDING MEMS GYROSCOPE

The MEMS gyroscope used in smartphones detects the 3-axis angular velocities of the phone. To derive the instant phone attitude, we need to perform continuous integration on the angular velocities.

3.1 Angular Velocity Integration

We deal with two coordinate systems in deriving the phone attitude. One is the earth coordinate system (we call "geo-frame" in this paper) and the other is the smartphone body coordinate system (we call "body-frame" in this paper). The goal is to get the phone attitude in the geo-frame, i.e., to calculate the relative difference between the body-frame and geo-frame. Figure 2 depicts the output of the MEMS gyroscope, which is real-time angular velocities (ω_x, ω_y, and ω_z) around the *Roll*, *Yaw*, and *Pitch* axis in the smartphone body-frame. X_e (pointing to the Earth east), Y_e (pointing to the earth north) and Z_e (parallel with the gravity) are the three reference axes in the geo-frame. With continuous integration, the phone attitude can be calculated and represented as the relative difference of the two coordinate systems, which can be described by a rotation matrix, or the angles between the three supporting axes in the two frames, i.e., α, β, and γ (shown in Figure 2).

The MEMS gyroscope has been widely blamed for its poor performance and rapid error cumulation. In this study, however, we find many existing works did not make full efforts to comprehensively understand the MEMS gyroscope working rationale and performance characteristics, leading to suboptimal or inappropriate use of them. For example, the following presents a segment of the code for integrating the 3-axis angular velocities provided in "Android Developers" site [2].

```
//Axis of the rotation sample
float axisX = event.values[0];
float axisY = event.values[1];
float axisZ = event.values[2];
// Calculate the angular speed of the sample
float omegaMagnitude = sqrt(axisX*axisX +
    axisY*axisY + axisZ*axisZ);
// Normalization
...
// Integrate around this axis with the angular
    speed by the timestep into a quaternion
float thetaOverTwo = omegaMagnitude * dT / 2.0f;
float sinThetaOverTwo = sin(thetaOverTwo);
float cosThetaOverTwo = cos(thetaOverTwo);
deltaRotationVector[0] = sinThetaOverTwo * axisX;
...
```

According to Euler's rotation theorem, any rigid body rotation can be represented by a single rotation about some rotation axes. The above code assumes a fixed rotation axis[3] in the body-frame at any particular integration interval, and calculate `omegaMagnitude` as the resultant rotation velocity of the phone. In practice, as the phone rotates, the rotation axis of the phone keeps changing in the body-frame and estimating rotation axis in the geo-frame using the resultant velocity in the body-frame is inappropriate. Such a method results in significant error accumulation, especially when the sampling rate cannot keep up with the shift of phone rotation (which unfortunately is true in most cases as the sampling rate is usually capped at around 600Hz for the MEMS gyroscope). Above code logics have been practiced in the current Android OS, i.e., `handleGyro()` [3] in operating the gyroscope output to derive the attitude for its API. The method calculates the rotation axis in the geo-frame based on the phone angular velocity measured in the body-frame.

In this paper we apply the Euler Axis/Angle method to do the integration and tackle the problem from the perspective of the geo-frame, which is fixed during the phone motion. The method finds an equation for the rotation speed in the geo-frame based on differential. As the equation is directly constructed in the geo-frame, there is no need to make assumption on fixed rotation axis. During the integration, the total phone motion time is divided into multiple time slots and the phone rotation is a sequential combination of the rotation within each slot. The mathematical illustration of the method is detailed in Appendix §A.

[3]The rotation of a three-dimensional object is always around an imaginary line which is called the rotation axis which may keep changing during the rotation. The rotation axis may not pass through the object's body.

3.2 Practical Settings and Techniques

Sensor specifications and configuration. The ADIS1626x series of MEMS gyroscopes are widely used in many smartphone models like HTC Sensation series smartphones. Some other gyroscope models like the AGD1 2022 FP6AQ MEMS gyroscope (used in iPhone) has similar performance. In this paper, we primarily study the ADIS1626x series and the performance of other models can be inferred. For a typical MEMS gyroscope, there are multiple sensor dynamic range r selections (e.g., $\pm320°$/sec, $\pm160°$/sec and $\pm80°$/sec for ADIS1626x series) and sensor bandwidth b selections (e.g., 50Hz and 330Hz for ADIS1626x series). The sensor bandwidth sets a cut-off frequency in responding to phone motions. A higher bandwidth setting can measure higher frequency motion and vibration. Table 2 depicts a part of the data sheet of the ADIS1626x series gyroscope. For different selections of the sensor dynamic range and bandwidth, the output noise is different. As shown in Table 2, the output noise under the setting "$r = \pm80°$/sec, $b = 50$Hz" is 0.1°/sec. The noise level increases when larger dynamic range or higher sensor bandwidth is selected. Due to the high degree of phone motion, "$r = \pm320°$/sec, $b = 330$Hz" is the default setting for most smartphones. According to the data sheet, the temperature and linear acceleration affect the output noise of the gyroscope as well, which we will later investigate for practical understanding.

Practical settings and techniques. According to the default setting in smartphones ($r = \pm320°$/sec and $b = 330$Hz) and the Nyquist theorem, we set the sensor sampling rate to be 660Hz. Typically the MEMS gyroscope cannot support higher sampling rate due to hardware limitations. Determining the window size T_w for integrating the angular velocities needs careful consideration. Generally small T_w provides finer granularity in performing the integration but too small T_w leads to aggressive computation which is not necessary if the phone motion is low and may exceed the processing capacity of the phone. On the other hand, as long as T_w is set fixed, no matter how small it is there are always chances that the angular velocities suddenly change within the window, leading to inaccurate integration. In this paper, we apply adaptive integration interval for performing angular velocity integration. We use the Euler Axis/Angle method introduced in §3.1 to integrate the measured angular velocity for each individual interval when the angular velocities do not change (or the change is sufficiently small). Typically, the interval width is about 5ms$\sim$50ms, which depends on the specific phone motion. In our implementation with Android smartphones, the callback function `onSensorChanged()` in `SensorEventListener` is used to determine whether the angular velocities change and thus the current integration interval. The angular velocity samples are continuously monitored and reported only when the sensor readings change.

Performance. We experiment with the phone model Samsung Galaxy S2 i9100 to examine the proposed method and techniques in phone attitude estimation. In the experiment, we initialize the phone with a preset attitude. We hold the phone in hands and take 1 minute and 5 minute walks in the lab, respectively, after which we put the phone back to its original position and attitude, and measure the estimation error. We take 20 runs for each test, and compare the errors of our method and the method with the Android implementation shown in §3.1. The attitude estimation error is a rotation matrix describing the difference between the ground truth and the estimated result. To visualize the error, we plot the biggest angle error from the 3 axes. This gauge is used throughout the paper to describe the attitude estimation error. Figure 3 compares the errors of both methods. For the 1 minute walks, the 90th percentile and medium errors of our method are 7° and 3°, respectively. For the Android method, the 90th percentile and medium errors, however, are much higher, 27.5° and 19.8°, respectively. For the 5 minute walks, the 90th percentile and medium errors of our method are 31.2° and 22.3°, respectively, and those of the Android method are up to 103° and 79°, respectively. From the experiment results, we see that the MEMS gyroscope is able to provide significantly improved quality of attitude tracking with the Euler Axis/Angle method and our optimization techniques.

Parameter	Sensor Settings/Conditions	Typ	Unit
Output noise	$r = \pm320°$/sec, $b = 330$Hz	0.9	°/sec (rms)
	$r = \pm320°$/sec, $b = 50$Hz	0.4	°/sec (rms)
	$r = \pm160°$/sec, $b = 50$Hz	0.2	°/sec (rms)
	$r = \pm80°$/sec, $b = 50$Hz	0.1	°/sec (rms)
Temperature coefficient	ADIS 1626x	0.005	°/sec/°C
Linear acceleration	Any axis	0.2	°/sec/g

Table 2: The key specifications of the ADIS1626x series of MEMS gyroscopes. The "Typ" column gives the typical output noise for a certain setting. r is the sensor dynamic range and b is the sensor bandwidth (also called "cut-off frequency").

3.3 Performance Characterization

We further do controlled experiments to understand the MEMS gyroscope performance in different condition ranges of different environmental factors.

Temperature. The temperature for the best MEMS gyroscope performance is 25°C. For MEMS gyroscopes in smartphones, however, the temperature compensation has already been done in the sensor chip with an embedded temperature sensor. The calibration temperature range is -40°C$\sim$+85°C with a single temperature point calibration. As suggested in Table 2, the temperature coefficient is merely 0.005°/sec/°C. In order to better understand the impact of temperature, we vary the environment temperature from -20°C to +45°C and study the sensor performance. According to the experiment result, the estimation error caused by the temperature variation lies within a very small range (<0.002°/sec/°C) and is negligible. Thus different from other possible working scenarios, the temperature is not a main influencing factor for MEMS gyroscopes in smartphone applications.

Time. According to the rationale of MEMS gyroscopes in deriving the phone attitude, the tracking error accumulates when angular velocity integration is performed. We perform a set of experiments to understand how the time impacts on the error accumulation. We initialize the phone in a preset attitude, and then use the phone in random ways (e.g., playing phone games, walking with the phone in the pocket). After time t, we put the phone back to the original attitude. We repeat the experiment 20$\sim$30 times for t = 10s, 1 minute, 5 minutes and 10 minutes, respectively. Figure 4 plots the statistical results about the tracking errors. We see that the tracking error for 10s period is very small. The 90th percentile error is only 3.8°. The tracking error grows up as the time increases. When t = 1 minute, the 90th percentile and medium errors are 13.9° and 5.9°, respectively. When t = 5 minutes, the 90th percentile and medium tracking errors grow up to 38.7° and 29.4°, respectively. After 10 minutes, the medium tracking error becomes 39.2° and the minimum tracking error is bigger than 21° that is unacceptable in practical usage. The experiment results demonstrate that the attitude tracking error is generally accurate for short time (e.g., less than 1 minute) but may accumulate substantially with time.

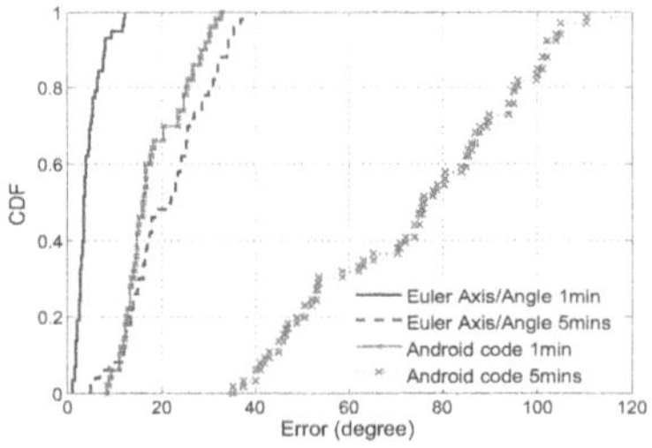

Figure 3: Phone attitude estimation results of different methods.

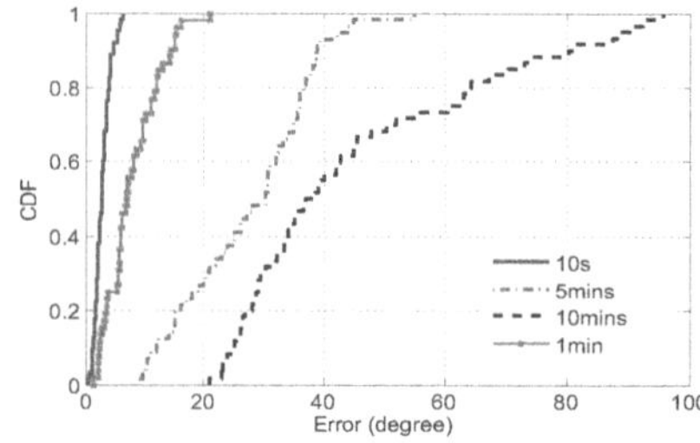

Figure 4: MEMS gyroscope error for different tracking time.

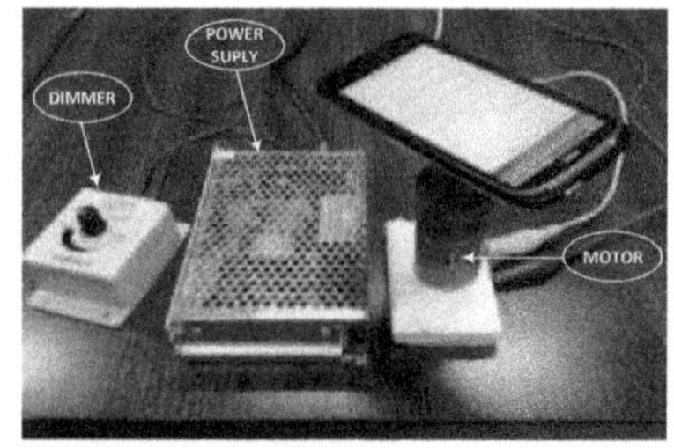

Figure 5: Gyroscope measurement devices.

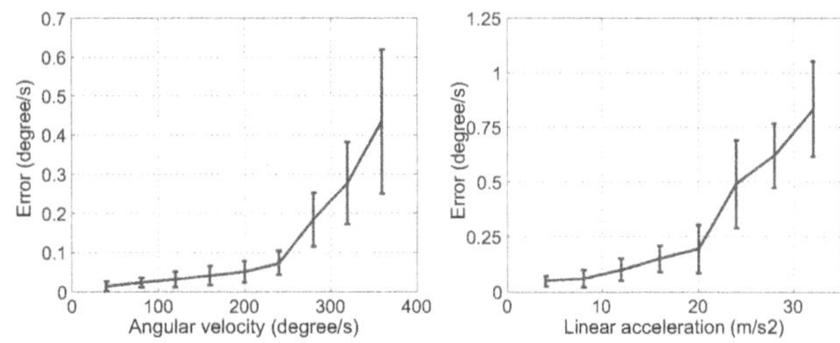

(a) Error v.s. angular velocity. (b) Error v.s. linear acceleration.

Figure 6: Impact of (a) angular velocity and (b) linear acceleration on the MEMS gyroscope performance.

Motion. The smartphone motion is typically a combination of rotational and translational motion. Thus we investigate two motion factors, i.e., the angular velocity ω and linear acceleration a. Although the translational motion does not change the phone attitude, it may influence gyroscope performance. Table 2 suggests that the sensor output error caused by linear acceleration is $0.2°$/sec/g, but the linear acceleration range, within which the gyroscope can work comfortably, is unclear. Meanwhile, what is the impact of the angular velocity within and out of the dynamic range ($\pm 320°$/sec) needs further study.

To investigate the impact of angular velocity, we put the phone on a rotation plate, the rotation velocity of which is controlled by an adjustable motor (shown in Figure 5). The motor is controlled through a sliding rheostat by adjusting the input voltage. We test different velocities and for each velocity setting, we rotate the phone 30 rounds and repeat the experiment for 10 times. To investigate the impact of linear acceleration, we put the phone in a sloping track and force it to speed. We intentionally control the slope and thrust force to provide different linear accelerations. The actual runtime acceleration is measured by the accelerometer.

Figure 6(a) and (b) plot the tracking error under different settings, which is the accumulated error in degree per second. Figure 6(a) shows that although the dynamic range of angular velocity is $\pm 320°$/sec, when $\omega < 240°$/sec, the error cumulation is small, stable, and roughly proportional to the angular velocity, usually smaller than $0.08°$/sec. When $\omega > 240°$/sec, the rate jumps up significantly. It could be as big as $0.2°$/sec for $\omega = 280°$/sec and $0.4°$/sec for $\omega = 360°$/sec, respectively. Meanwhile, the error exhibits significant variation and becomes hard to predict. Figure 6(b) shows the error cumulation caused by the linear acceleration is relatively higher. When $a < 2g$, the error cumulation rate is relatively stable, roughly proportional to the instant acceleration and usually smaller than $0.2°$/sec. When $a > 2g$, the output error quickly rises and becomes uncontrolled. It can be as high as $0.5°$/sec for $a = 2.4g$ and $0.75°$/sec for $a = 3.2g$, respectively.

We see that for both motion factors, the gyroscope tracking error is relatively small, stable and controlled for a certain safe range, e.g., $\omega < 240°$/sec and $a < 2g$. When those "out-of-range motions" occur, the error rapidly goes up and becomes unbounded to predict. Such out-of-range smartphone motions are common in daily smartphone usage such as strong swings when playing mobile games, vibration and rotation in the pocket during running, etc. It significantly pollutes the consequent attitude estimation result as the phone attitude is calculated with continuous integration.

Based on the experiments, the MEMS gyroscope performance can be summarized as follows:

- The attitude tracking error accumulates as the time increases. If the phone motion is within the safe range and sensor bandwidth, the gyroscope tracking result is accurate in a short time period.
- The attitude tracking error is highly related to the phone motions, i.e., the angular velocity and linear acceleration. The high out-of-range motion significantly pollutes the consequent attitude tracking result.

4. INSTANT ATTITUDE DETECTION

The basic MEMS gyroscope performance cannot provide continuous high accuracy attitude detection due to the error cumulation and out-of-range phone motions. In this section, we describe how we incorporate the independent measurements from the compass and accelerometer to assist the gyroscope in tracking the phone attitude.

4.1 Compass and Accelerometer

Compass. The compass measures the geomagnetic north from the detected geo-magnetic field. The accuracy, however, is unstable, especially indoors where steel structures and electrical appliances may significantly distort the geo-magnetic field. Recent studies report reasonably high compass accuracy for outdoor usage but complicated performance for indoor usage [11, 27]. Figure 7 plots the estimated earth north using the compass indoors and outdoors. In the experiment, we keep the phone attitude unchanged and move around indoors and outdoors. The compass earth north estimation is recorded and then compared to the ground truth to calculate the error. For most of the time, we see accurate outdoor compass output, i.e., $< 5°$ error. The indoor compass output is much more complicated that it could be more than $50°$ off the ground truth (from the 30th to 60th second) or as low as a few degree error (from the start to 10th second) at particular moments. Generally, the outdoor compass output is of reasonable quality and much more reliable than the indoor output. The indoor output accuracy varies significantly depending on the instant ambient environment.

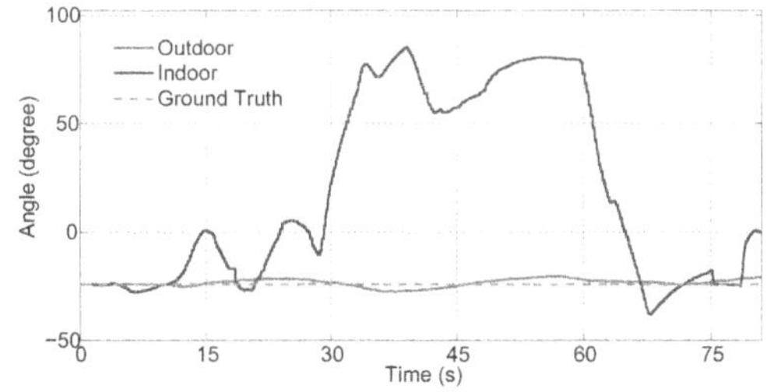

Figure 7: Indoor and outdoor compass performance.

Accelerometer. Most smartphone platforms provide the API of retrieving gravity (e.g., `Sensor.TYPE_GRAVITY` in Android and `GLGravity` in Apple iOS) from the accelerometer readings. With the help of the powerful Butterworth filter [9], the acceleration caused by phone motion can be filtered out and the frequency components of gravity can be extracted, i.e., the direction of Y_e in the smartphone body-frame. We denote the components of gravity along the X, Y and Z axis to be (g_x, g_y, g_z), where $\sqrt{g_x^2 + g_y^2 + g_z^2} = g$. The filter cut-off frequency is normalized to 1 radian/sec and the frequency response (gain) is

$$G(\omega_0) = \sqrt{\frac{1}{1 + {\omega_0}^{2n}}}, \qquad (1)$$

where ω_0 is the angular frequency and n is the number of poles in the filter. The smartphone motion is typically composed of the rotational and translational parts, both of which may cause acceleration variation along the 3 axes. According to the Butterworth filter rationale, if the noise frequency is higher than its cut-off frequency, the high frequency signal caused by the translational motion can be filtered out. The noise caused by the phone rotation, however, cannot be fully filtered out if the rotation frequency is high. The frequency response (gain) $G(\omega_0)$ of Butterworth filter becomes small when ω_0 gets big. Generally the gravity can be accurately extracted when the phone rotation is slight and no constant linear acceleration is imposed. A specific example is when the phone is put static.

Attitude from compass and gravity. As depicted in Figure 8, given the direction of gravity on the phone body-frame, the phone attitude is constrained on a conical surface in the geo-frame. On the other hand, the compass outputs the angle δ between Y' and Y_e axis (pointing to the earth north) in the geo-frame, where Y' is the projection of Y axis of the body-frame on the X_e-Y_e plane of the geo-frame. Considering the angle δ between Y' and Y_e, we can thus uniquely fix the phone attitude on the conical surface. This provides us an alternative of removing 3 degrees of freedom to determine the phone attitude if we have accurate compass and gravity output. The detailed construction of the rotation matrix for the phone attitude is provided in Appendix §B.

Compared with gyroscope. The attitude estimation from the compass and accelerometer is independent and of different nature compared with the result from the gyroscope. The compass and accelerometer give instant status estimation which is unrelated to any previous estimations, while the gyroscope gives a cumulative estimation of the attitude through continuous integration on angular velocities. Figure 9 compares the attitude estimation from the gyroscope and that from the compass and accelerometer during an 8 minute walk. We see a clear difference in the natures of their estimations. In most of the time, the gyroscope produces small estimation errors which, however, accumulate with time. A few sudden jumps of the error (e.g., in the 5th minute, probably due to out-of-range phone motion) significantly contribute to the final cumulative error. On the other hand, the compass and accelerometer perform in very different ways. They have the opportunity to produce a few very good estimations but many bad ones as well. The estimation errors depend on instant phone statuses and do not accumulate. Such different natures in their performance provide us the opportunity to complement the gyroscope estimation with calibration from the compass and accelerometer at "good" moments.

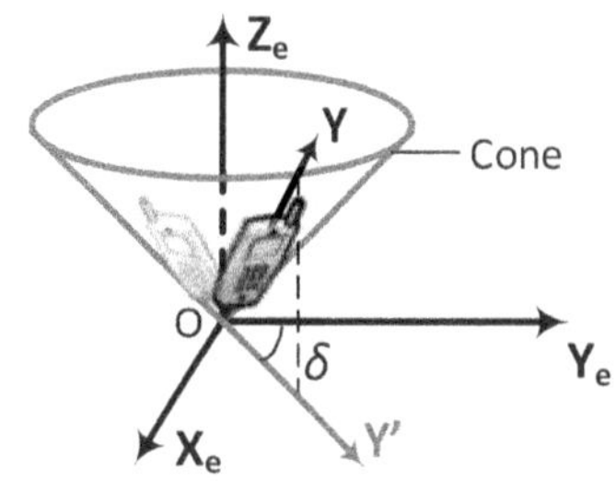

Figure 8: Attitude from the compass and gravity.

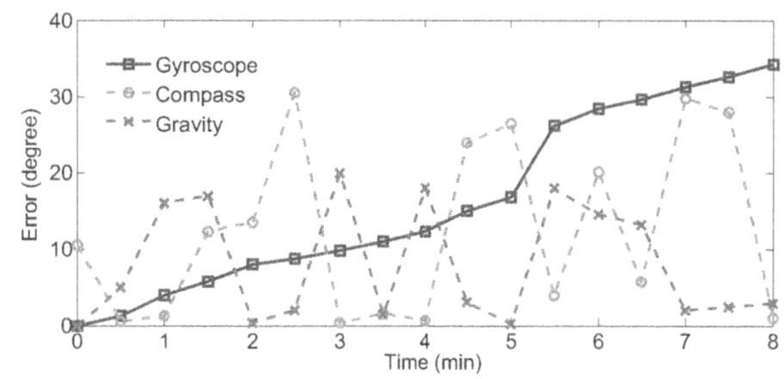

Figure 9: The performance of gyroscope, compass and accelerometer in an instant trajectory.

4.2 Putting It All Together

We incorporate the three IMU sensors and propose A[3], an accurate and automatic attitude detector to continuously estimate the phone attitude. Figure 10 illustrates the A[3] system architecture. There are two major components: gyroscope tracking and calibration. As depicted in Figure 10 (left), A[3] tracks the phone attitude using the gyroscope. The angular velocities are adaptively integrated to calculate the phone attitude (the rotation matrix $\mathbf{R}$). The tracking error E_g of the gyroscope is carefully estimated based on the real time monitoring of the phone motion. As summarized in §3.3, the MEMS gyroscope error is mostly related to the two motion parameters, i.e., the angular velocity ω and linear acceleration a. In this paper, we assume the impact from the two parameters is independent, i.e., the phone's rotational and translational motion independently affects the measurement of Coriolis vibration. For each integration interval i, the accumulated error e_i is thus measured as

$$e_i = f_\omega(\omega_i)\Delta t_i + f_a(a_i)\Delta t_i,$$

where f_ω is a functional relationship between the angular velocity ω_i and the error, and f_a is a functional relationship between the linear acceleration a_i and the error. Δt_i is the length of the tracking interval. The gyroscope tracking error at time t_x is accumulated as

$$E_g(t_x) = \sum_{t=t_0}^{t_x} e_i = \sum_{t=t_0}^{t_x} [f_\omega(\omega_i)\Delta t_i + f_a(a_i)\Delta t_i], \qquad (2)$$

where t_0 is the start point of current tracking. f_ω and f_a can be determined according to the experimental understanding from Figure 6. When the angular velocity $\omega < 240°$/sec, the estimation error follows a Gaussian distribution with limited variation. The

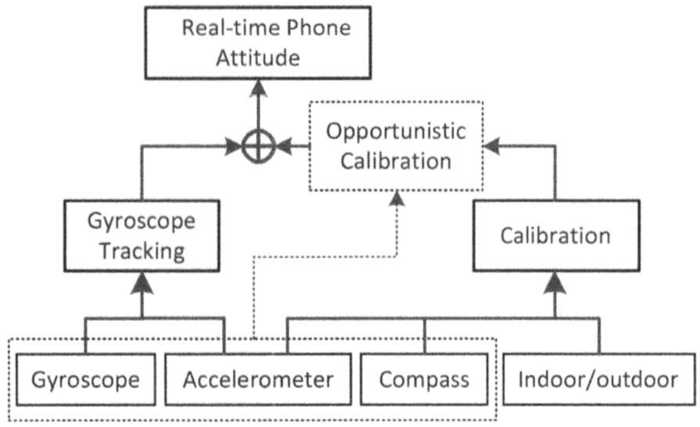

Figure 10: A^3 architecture.

mean linearly increases as ω increases towards 240°/sec. When $\omega > 240°$/sec, the error rises much higher with intensified variation, being hard to predict. Thus in A^3 system, we set f_ω linear for the safe range when $\omega < 240°$/sec and unbounded when $\omega > 240°$/sec:

$$f_\omega(\omega) = \begin{cases} 0.0003\omega, & \text{if } \omega < 240°/\text{sec} \\ unbounded, & \text{if } \omega \geq 240°/\text{sec}. \end{cases}$$

The impact of the linear acceleration a is similar with the angular velocity , with $a < 2g$ a safe range where the error linearly increases with a and $a > 2g$ of unbounded error:

$$f_a(a) = \begin{cases} 0.001a, & \text{if } a < 2g \\ unbounded, & \text{if } a \geq 2g. \end{cases}$$

Above error estimation is based our experimental understanding of ADIS1626x series gyroscope which is the most widely adopted MEMS gyroscope. Other gyroscopes can be parameterized slightly differently, but in the same essence when experimental results are available. As depicted in Figure 10 (right), A^3 automatically detects good calibration opportunities when the compass output and the extracted gravity direction are accurate.

According to our understanding on the compass rationale, the indoor/outdoor information can be effectively used to indicate the compass accuracy. We use a simplified version of IODetector [27] to perform indoor/outdoor detection with the light sensor and cellular module on smartphones. The compass output is considered accurate only when strict outdoor context is detected. For the gravity output to be accurate, we set a rigorous condition on the instant angular velocity, i.e., $\omega < 15°$/sec. When both the compass and gravity outputs are obtained in valid conditions, we confirm a calibration opportunity. The phone attitude derived from the compass and gravity calibrates what obtained from gyroscope tracking if its estimated tracking error $E_g > 5°$. The consequent gyroscope tracking is then carried on the calibrated attitude basis to produce real time phone attitude.

5. OPPORTUNISTIC CALIBRATION

The proposed calibration method sets rigorous conditions in qualifying the calibration opportunities so the accuracy is guaranteed. In practice, the rigorous conditions result in too few opportunities to timely calibrate gyroscope drifts, e.g., no calibration indoors or when the phone motion is intense. Those cases, however, are common for most attitude based applications, e.g., playing games with intense phone motion, indoor localization, etc.

Simply lowering the condition requirements, on the other hand, may harm the calibration quality and thus the accuracy of attitude estimation. In this section, we introduce an opportunistic calibration technique to identify more "good" opportunities. The basic idea is that we leverage the gyroscope estimation to capture phone attitude dynamics. As our experiments reveal in §3.3, the gyroscope can provide very accurate attitude tracking in short time periods (e.g., within 10s). Although the instant attitude estimation of gyroscope may not be accurate due to base errors from previous states, the estimated attitude change is accurate for most of the time (when phone motion is within the safe range of the gyroscope), which sets a very good reference. We compare with the attitude change derived from the compass and gravity, and if both estimations derive the same change of phone attitude we believe the compass and gravity make an accurate attitude estimation. As the output of the compass and gravity is the instant attitude estimation, which is independent of previous states of the phone, we can then use it to reset the current attitude estimation and continue the gyroscope estimation from the new attitude base.

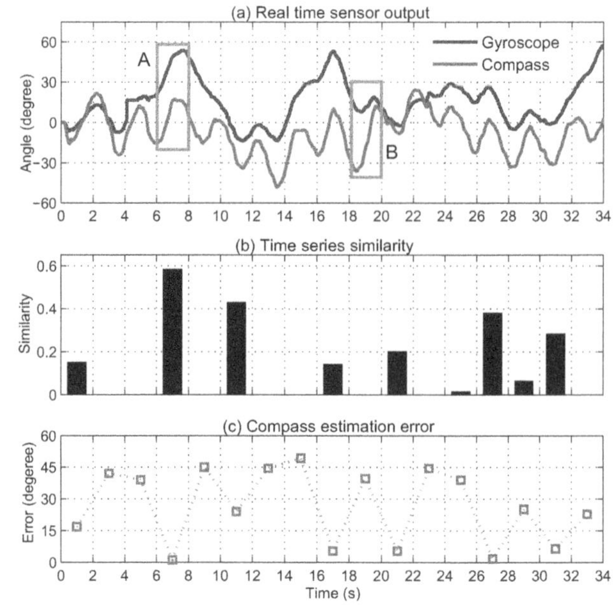

Figure 11: The time series similarity of compass and gyroscope sensor output, and the related compass error.

We denote C as the compass output of the earth north, G as the gravity direction extracted from the accelerometer, and S as the attitude estimation from the gyroscope. We compare the time series similarity of the changes of C and S as well as G and S in the period. If the changes of C and G are "parallel" with S, we can validate their instant accuracy. We examine how C and G are "parallel" instead of "correlated" with S to validate their quality because it indicates a stronger degree of synchronization between two time series signals. For each detection window d, suppose the compass output is $C = \{c_1, c_2, \cdots, c_n\}$ and the corresponding earth north direction extracted from the gyroscope estimation is $S_c = \{s_{c1}, s_{c2}, \cdots, s_{cn}\}$. We calculate their time series similarity p as

$$p = \frac{1}{2^{Var(S_c - C)}}, \tag{3}$$

where $Var(S_c - C)$ is the variance of their difference. $p = 1$ indicates the highest parallel degree. A bigger p indicates a higher similarity between the two.

Figure 11 depicts the results of the gyroscope and compass output on earth north for a half minute walk in an indoor office. We set the similarity detection window of 2 second width. Due to the exponential property of Equation (3), we see that for most of the time

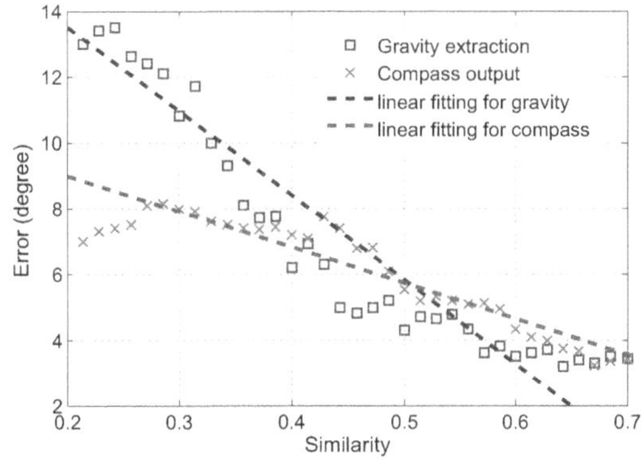

Figure 12: The calibration error for different similarities.

the similarity $p \approx 0$ and only when the compass output changes in a very similar trend with the gyroscope output, $p > 0.2$. For example, in the detection window A in Figure 11(a) and (b), the compass output is almost parallel to the gyroscope output with $p = 0.6$. On the contrary, in the detection window B, although the two outputs are highly correlated with each other, their time series similarity is smaller than 0.02 and not parallel.

Figure 11(c) summarizes the compass output error measured in the experiment trace. We see that a big p generally corresponds to a small output error of the compass (e.g., the 6th$\sim$8th second and 26th$\sim$28th second). This may not always be true, e.g., at the window of 10th$\sim$12th second, the compass output error reaches almost $29°$ although the similarity p is as high as 0.5, because the phone motion at that moment exceeds the safe range of the gyroscope. In order to guarantee the quality of the calibration, we set the requirement of $\omega < 240°$/sec and $a < 2g$. so the gyroscope estimation is guaranteed a truthful reference. We look after the gravity estimation from the accelerometer in a similar procedure. We test the similarity of G and S with Equation (3) but project to the gravity direction. We denote p_c as the similarity of C and S, and p_g as the similarity of G and S for each detection window of 2 seconds. We confirm the detection of a calibration opportunity if both p_c and $p_g > 0.2$.

For the valid calibration opportunities, we estimate the error of the instant phone attitude derived from the compass and accelerometer. We primarily look at the values of p_c and p_g, as they indicate how well the instant attitude estimation conforms to the truthful reference. In order to figure out the error of each calibration opportunity according to the similarity, we experiment with 3 types of smartphones across various conditions to learn their relationship. We experiment with various phone usage patterns such as walking, running, and playing phone games, etc. We collect the sensor data in 21 indoor and 9 outdoor sites, respectively. For each site, we repeat the experiment around 10 times. Figure 12 plots our statistical average of measurement results. For both the gravity and compass output, the error decreases as expected when the similarity increases. Linear fittings well approximate such relationships. We see that the gravity extraction error is bigger than the compass error when similarity $p < 0.5$ and smaller when $p > 0.5$. The error of their combination is influenced by both compass estimation and gravity extraction. Thus we estimate the error of compass E_1 and error of gravity E_2 through linear fitting separately.

$$E_1 = -32.14p_c + 19.93,\ E_2 = -12.86p_g + 11.57.$$

The error of their combination E_c is estimated as $E_c = \max\{E_1, E_2\}$, where E_c fits to the bigger error of the two. An opportunistic calibration is qualified if $E_c < E_g$. Algorithm 1 presents the high-level pseudo code of A3 opportunistic calibration algorithm.

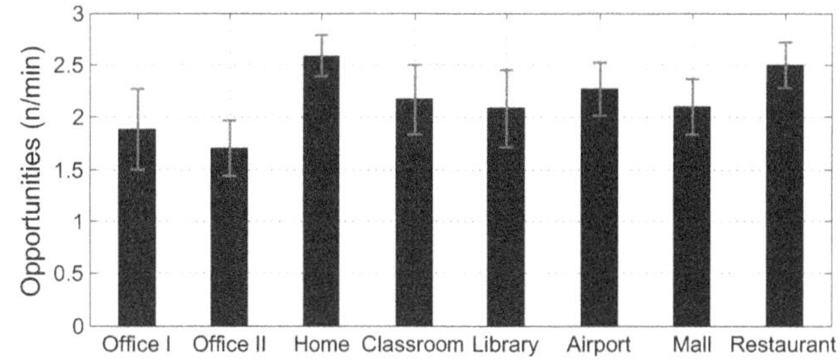

Figure 13: The number of calibration opportunities detected at different places.

Algorithm 1 A^3 Opportunistic Calibration Algorithm

Input:
Rotation matrix R_g from the gyroscope and R_c from the combination of gravity and compass;
Estimation error of the gyroscope E_g and error of the combination of gravity and compass E_c;
Similarity parameter p_c and p_g;
Output:
Final rotation matrix R.

```
if p_c > 0.2 and p_g > 0.2 then
    if E_c < E_g then
        R ← R_c
        R_g ← R_c
    else
        R ← R_g
else
    R ← R_g
```

Opportunistic calibration provides a much broader range of calibration opportunities, not necessarily constrained in modest usage and outdoors. We do extensive experiments to examine different indoor places when walking with the phone free in the pocket. Figure 13 plots the number of qualified calibration opportunities detected per minute. There are in average 2 opportunities detected per minute with the highest at home (2.6) and the lowest in office II (1.7). Such opportunities are abundant for timely gyroscope calibration, considering the less than $5°$ attitude tracking error per minute.

The final A^3 system employs the opportunistic calibration (dashed part in Figure 10) which overrides the opportunity detection method in §4.2.

6. EVALUATION

We implement A^3 on the Android platform and experiment with three different phone models and under different conditions. We first present the experiment devices and settings in §6.1. We demonstrate detailed system performance of a typical experiment trial and report statistical performance for different scenarios in §6.2. We study heading estimation as a particular application of A^3 and compare the performance with existing techniques in §6.3. We compare A^3 performance with several popular smartphone apps and games in §6.4. We investigate the power consumption of A^3 in §6.5. The following details the experiment methodology and the evaluation results.

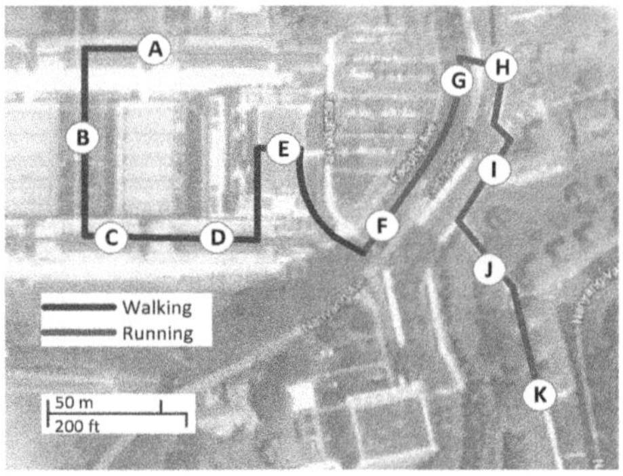

Figure 14: An instant experimental trace in our campus.

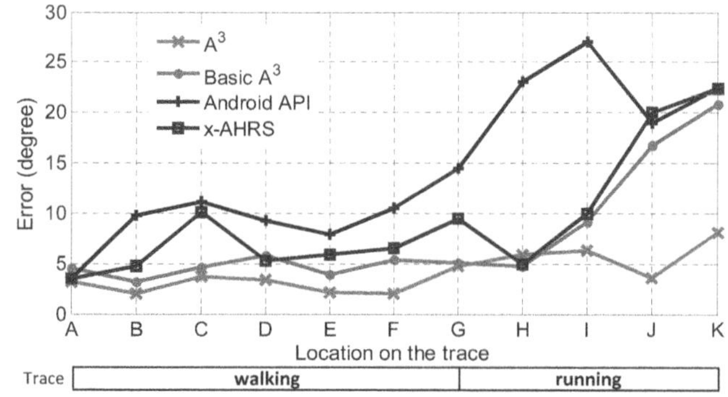

Figure 15: Attitude estimation error of different methods along the experimental trace.

6.1 Experiment Devices and Settings

Smartphones. We implement A^3 on Android 4.2 platform and experiment with three different types of smartphones including HTC Sensation XE, Samsung Galaxy S2 i9100, and LG Google Nexus 4, all of which are equipped with MEMS gyroscopes, accelerometers and magnetism sensors, etc. Their RAM and CPU capacity can easily support the computation of A^3. As A^3 is independent of platforms, we believe it can be easily implanted to other OS platforms or phone models such as Windows Phone and Apple iOS based smartphones.

Experiment settings. We primarily evaluate the attitude estimation performance in three different scenarios, including walking with the phone in hand, walking with the phone free in the pocket and running with the phone in hand. We experiment at different sites including the office, home, the airport, the shopping mall, laboratory, etc. The error is evaluated as the biggest angle error among the three axes, the same as in previous sections.

Comparison. We conduct comparative experiment to investigate the performance of following approaches:

- **A^3**: The complete implementation of A^3 system.
- **Basic A^3**: Basic A^3 implementation as introduced in 4.2 where the opportunistic calibration is not incorporated.
- **Android API**: The Android API `getRotationMatrixFromVector()` practices the Kalman-based orientation estimation algorithms [14, 8, 16] which perform unsorted sensor fusion. As a system API, it has been invoked in many apps for various applications like indoor localization, navigation and human activity recognition. We do not try to optimize its parameters for being not able to locate any available documents on optimizing the Android API.
- **x-AHRS**: The x-AHRS algorithm [15] is one of the latest orientation estimation algorithms which produces AHRS (Attitude Heading Reference Systems) input for robotic systems and wearable systems. It has been integrated and made commercially available in the x-IMU sensor boards [4]. To our knowledge, x-AHRS produces the best reported attitude estimation till now.

6.2 Performance in Different Conditions

We conduct a number of experiment trials with different use conditions. Figure 14 depicts one trace. The total length of the trace is approximately 700 meters. We experiment with different activities during the trial including walking (from A to G) and running (from G to K). We cannot track the continuous estimation error on the trace because obtaining the continuous ground truth of the phone attitude is not possible. Thus for each intermediate segment, we report the system error at individual testing spots (A-K), where the phone attitude ground truth is manually collected. We perform 5 different attitude estimation methods simultaneously in the trial and summarize their tracking errors in Figure 15.

According to the results in Figure 15, A^3 outperforms all other methods during the entire trace except for point H, where "basic A^3" and "x-AHRS" perform slightly better. This could be due to some suboptimal calibration conducted in A^3. Nevertheless, no apparent performance degrade of A^3 is observed during the entire trial. For all the methods, they perform better for walking segments and worse for running segments. This is because the phone motion when we are walking is much smoother and of lower motion frequency than the running scenario. Thus usually the phone motion is within the gyroscope sensor dynamic range. The Android API produces worst results in all of the four methods across the entire trace. Its attitude estimation error on the walking trace is bounded within 15° but significantly jumps up to 27° on the running segments. The estimation results from the "x-AHRS" algorithm are relatively smooth. The estimation error on the entire walking trace is smaller than 10° and smaller than 5° at A, B and H. However, on the running trace, as the phone motion is of high frequency, x-AHRS cannot optimally fuse the sensor outputs and the error is as high as 20°. Its performance is comparable with "basic A^3" at D and H, but worse than "basic A^3" at other locations. The "basic A^3" performs the closest to A^3, outperforming other approaches at most of the time, which demonstrates the performance gain from the careful gyroscope operation and quality calibration with the compass and accelerometer. The performance gap between "basic A^3" and A^3 tells the gain of opportunistic calibration technique.

For statistical comparison we perform experiments in three scenarios, namely walking with the phone in hand, walking with the phone in pocket, and running with the phone in hand. We examine the attitude tracking error in 20 minute usage. We perform about 40 runs for each scenario. All the 4 methods are performed simultaneously during the each run. The statistical results are displayed in Figure 16~18. Figure 16 presents the CDF of the estimation errors during walking with the phone in hand. The median estimation errors of Android API, "x-AHRS", "basic A^3" and A^3 are approximately 17.4°, 11°, 9.5° and 4.2°, respectively. Their 90th percentile errors are 37.1°, 25.3°, 17.9° and 8.3°, respectively. The Android API produces the worst result in such a scenario. Figure 17 presents the CDF of the estimation errors during walking with the phone in pockets. The mobile phone has a higher freedom in the pocket and results in degraded performance for all methods. The median estimation errors of the 4 methods are approximately 28.6°, 20.5°, 16.5° and 7°, respectively. The 90th percentile errors are 53.5°, 32.6°, 21.4° and 11.5°, respectively. Figure 18 the CDF

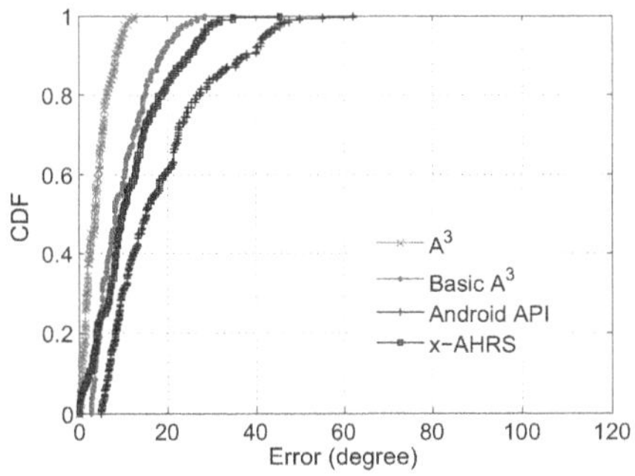

Figure 16: Walking with the phone in hand.

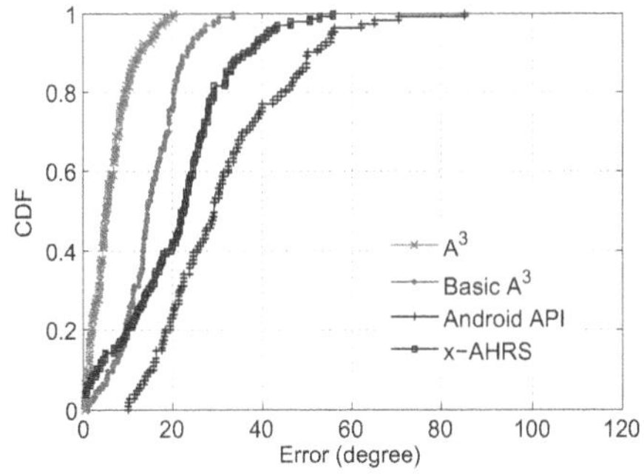

Figure 17: Walking with the phone in the pocket.

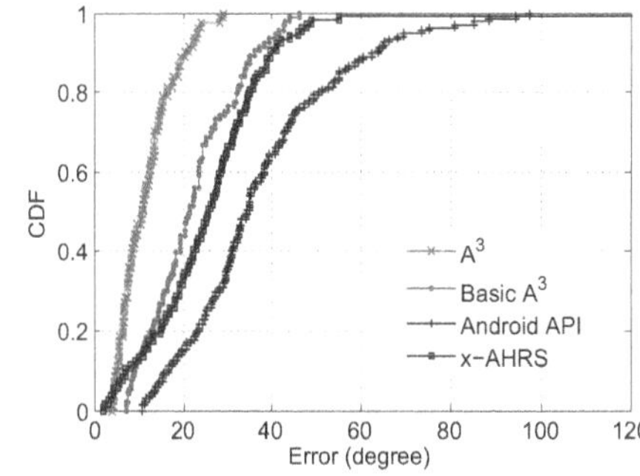

Figure 18: Running with the phone in hand.

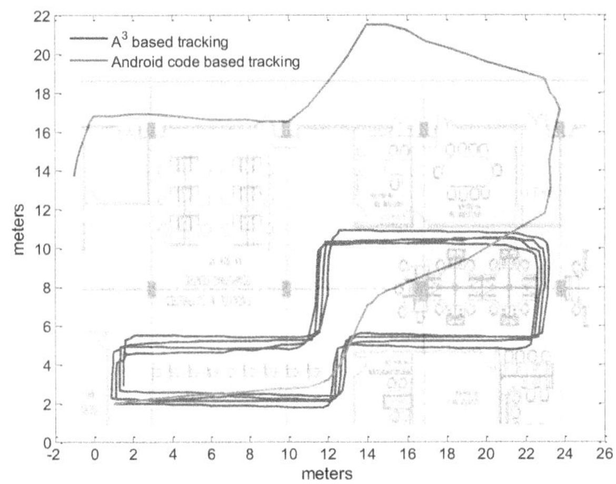

Figure 19: Dead-reckoning based tracking result using A^3 and the Android code shown in §3.1 for heading estimation, respectively.

of the estimation errors during running with the phone in hand. The median estimation errors are approximately 35°, 23.4°, 20.3° and 9.7°, respectively. The 90th percentile errors are 60.6°, 40.5°, 37.4° and 18.5°, respectively. We see that A^3 consistently outperforms the rest in all scenarios. Higher gain can be obtained when more motion freedom of the phone is allowed. Even without opportunistic calibration, the "basic A^3" still slightly outperforms the others in statistics for most of the time. The results demonstrate how the understanding of the IMU sensors and the comprehensive use of them help to provide huge performance gain.

6.3 Application in Heading Estimation

The detected phone attitude can be directly used to estimate the user heading in dead-reckoning. In this section, we conduct a case study to examine how A^3 can be applied to achieve accurate heading estimation. The same as existing works in heading estimation, we assume that the phone is held in hand with the *Roll* axis of the phone pointing to the user heading direction (as a matter of fact, while the phone is held relatively still to the human body we can always transform the phone attitude to extract the heading direction).

We implement a dead-reckoning based tracking approach based on step counting [10, 24], but apply A^3 to estimate the user heading. As Figure 19 depicts, we experiment with such an approach on a 58m circular path in the lab. Heading estimation is very accurate. As a result, after 7 minute walking on the path for 4 rounds, the tracking error is merely 1.3m. We see from Figure 19 that the error is mainly due to the shift from inaccurate distance estimation in steps, not the heading estimation. As a comparison, we also record the result of using the Android code shown in §3.1 for heading estimation. As Figure 19 depicts, the estimated trajectory deviates from the actual path and the error rapidly propagates. After walking for only 1 round, the tracking error accumulates to 13.2m. We see that the error mainly comes from the heading deviation during the turns. We could not directly compare A^3 with some existing dead-reckoning approaches [10, 24] as the source code was not available to us, but according to the publicly reported results, A^3 is highly likely to outperform them.

App	Type	Time	App Error	A^3 Error
Sensor Box	Sensor app	1 min	40°	3.5°
		5 mins	50°	5°
		10 mins	75°	6.4°
Show Down	Game	1 min	9°	5°
		5 mins	30°	7°
		10 mins	35°	6°
Gyroscope Rotate	Sensor app	1 min	10°	5°
		5 mins	28°	8°
		10 mins	45°	4.5°

Table 3: Comparison of A^3 with phone apps/games.

6.4 Comparison with Popular Apps

Many smartphone apps and games detect and take the phone attitude change as input. We also examine the performance of A^3 in comparison with those of several popular apps and games from Google Play, including "Android Sensor Box", "Show Down", and "Gyroscope Rotate". All 3 apps use gyroscope to track the phone attitude dynamics. We test the performance of the three apps in 1 minute, 5 minutes and 10 minutes scale, respectively. For each app, we initialize the phone with a preset attitude and then use it in random ways, after which we put the phone back to the initial attitude. For each app, we let A^3 simultaneously run at the background and compare the attitude tracking accuracy of A^3 with those of the apps. We repeat each experiment for 10 runs and calculate the average estimation error, which is summarized in Table 3.

We see substantially gained performance over all the 3 apps, particularly when the phone is played for a longer time. After 1 minute usage, the attitude estimation error of all the apps vary from 9° to 40°. The error grows up to 28°~50° after 5 minute usage and 35°~75° after 10 minute usage. On the contrary, the error of A^3 slight increases with time and maintains within 8°. As we do not have access to the source codes of those apps, we do not have precise knowledge on their approaches in attitude tracking. We speculate that none of them make careful efforts in using the gyroscope, nor incorporate any calibration techniques, as their attitude tracking errors apparently accumulate fast. It seems that they did not even invoke the Android API but only used the direct output from the gyroscope.

6.5 Power Consumption

We measure the power consumption of A^3 on Samsung Galaxy S2 i9100 mobile phone. We measure the average working current of A^3 using Monsoon power monitor. The phone's battery capacity is 6.11Wh (1650mAh). We measure the power consumption of the mobile phone under 6 different use cases, i.e., screen off, screen on, sampling sensors only, basic A^3, A^3 and the use of Android API. Figure 20 plots how the working current changes when different operations are performed. The plotted working current is a moving average value of every 0.1 second.

The working current is close to 0 initially when the phone screen is off, and jumps to around 155mA when the screen is on. In order to test the algorithms on the same baseline, we turn off the phone screen from the 100th second and run the algorithms at the background. From the 100th second, the phone starts continuously sampling the sensor readings but does not perform any computation. The sampling rates of different sensors are set to be the same with those of A^3. The average working current is about 80mA. We let the phone run different attitude tracking algorithms from the 130th second. We see comparable overall working current for all three approaches. The basic A^3 algorithm is performed from the 130th to 220th second. The working current increases a little to about 90mA. From the 220th second, A^3 algorithm is running and the average current is about 95mA and that of running Android API is similar. Although different algorithms perform differently in estimating the phone attitude, their power consumption is comparable and slightly higher than "sampling sensors only". According to the result, the data processing of all the algorithms similarly contributes extra amount of around 5$\sim$15mA current. The power consumption of the three algorithms is moderate and acceptable for long runs on commodity smartphones.

7. RELATED WORK

Orientation and attitude estimation. The most related work in the literature is the estimation of the IMU or MARG orientation for wearable systems and robotic systems. Kalman filter was widely used in those works to fuse different sensor inputs. Barshan *et al.* [8] propose to estimate the orientation of the robots for mobile robotics applications using inertial sensor models and an extended Kalman filter. Marins *et al.* [16] present an extended Kalman filter for real-time estimation of rigid body orientation using MARG sensors. Different robotic applications may have different requirements, which ask for specific algorithm and system design. Kong *et al.* [13] present an algorithm for inertial navigation system using a generic error propagation model. Lee *et al.* [14] propose a sensor fusion technique of sensors (gyro and tilt) to measure the balancing angle of the inverted pendulum robot system. Most recently, Madgwick *et al.* [15] develop an orientation estimation algorithm for the x-IMU sensor board [4]. A quaternion representation of orientation is used to describe the coupled nature of orientation in 3 dimensions and fuse the sensor inputs. Those approaches exploit the sensing redundancy of different sensors in attitude detection. Without fundamental understanding of smartphone MEMS sensors and their performance variations with environment dynamics, those approaches cannot make appropriate error control in sensor fusion, and thus cannot provide satisfactory performance when applied to smartphones. Simple parameter optimization on Kalman-based approaches will not address the problem because it is based on the frequency responses of different sensors not the quality of raw sensor readings. The error of raw sensor readings is environment dependent that frequency response cannot fully capture.

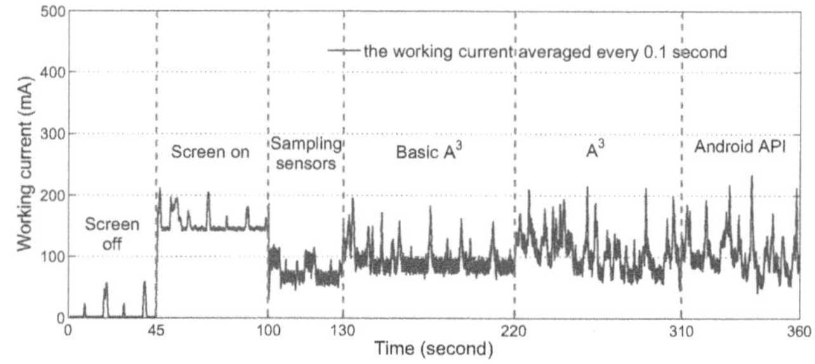

Figure 20: Energy consumption measurement of different algorithms.

Heading estimation. There have been many research works on user heading estimation for indoor localization, navigation and tracking, etc. Walkie-Markie [22] uses the gyroscope to estimate the user heading for indoor pathway mapping. UnLoc [24] makes use of the gyroscope and compass for accurate user heading estimation in dead-reckoning based indoor localization. Headio [23] aggregates the ceiling images of an indoor environment, and by using computer vision-based pattern detection techniques to provide directional references. Afzal *et al.* [7] propose to identify the magnetic field measurements for estimating user heading. As we show in §6.3, the phone attitude output of A^3 can be used to produce the heading estimation with higher accuracy. Besides, A^3 solely utilizes the IMU sensors on the phone and is thus orthogonal to some of above techniques.

Attitude based applications. A^3 benefits a broad range of other applications such as image stabilization [12], 3D photography [18, 5], and phone apps, etc. Karpenko *et al.* [12] perform video stabilization and rolling shutter correction based on real-time attitude estimation using the gyroscope. Oth *et al.* [18] develop a calibration procedure to determine the rolling shutter line delay using the gyroscope. Snapily3D [5] enables 3D camera on smartphone to store images with different aspect ratios, which relies on the gyroscope to estimate the phone attitude. Phone attitude information is vital to a great number of phone apps and games. Significantly improved attitude estimation with A^3 essentially benefit those applications.

8. CONCLUSION

This paper presents A^3 for accurate phone attitude detection. With careful and intelligent use of the gyroscope and other IMU sensors, A^3 makes it possible to estimate the mobile phone attitude in free motion. The experiment results demonstrate A^3 provides far better tracking accuracy than other possible competitors and maintains the high accuracy during long runs. One future work is to explore how well the attitude tracking result can be applied to support other novel applications like localization, tracking, mobile gaming, etc.

9. ACKNOWLEDGEMENTS

We would like to thank the anonymous reviewers for their constructive insights and valuable comments for improving the quality of the paper. We acknowledge the support from Singapore MOE AcRF Tier 2 grant MOE2012-T2-1-070 and NTU Nanyang Assistant Professorship (NAP) grant M4080738.020.

10. REFERENCES

[1] Solid State Angular Rate Gyro. `http://www.watson-gyro.com/products/rate-gyro-ARS-spec.html`.

[2] Andriod Developer Sensor Event. `http://developer.android.com/reference/android/hardware/SensorEvent.html`.

[3] Android sensor sevice source code. `https://android.googlesource.com/platform/frameworks/native/+/master/services/sensorservice/`.

[4] x-IMU sensor board. `http://www.x-io.co.uk/products/x-imu/`.

[5] Snapily 3D. `http://www.snapily3d.com/`.

[6] Gimbal Lock. `http://www.chrobotics.com/library/understanding-quaternions`.

[7] M. Afzal, V. Renaudin, and G. Lachapelle. Magnetic field based heading estimation for pedestrian navigation environments. In *Proceedings of IPIN 2011*, pages 1–10, 2011.

[8] B. Barshan and H. Durrant-Whyte. Inertial navigation systems for mobile robots. *IEEE Transactions on Robotics and Automation*, 11(3):328–342, 1995.

[9] S. Butterworth. On the theory of filter amplifiers. *Wireless Engineer*, 7(6):536–541, 1930.

[10] I. Constandache, X. Bao, M. Azizyan, and R. R. Choudhury. Did you see bob?: Human localization using mobile phones. In *Proceedings of ACM MobiCom 2010*, pages 149–160, 2010.

[11] I. Constandache, R. Choudhury, and I. Rhee. Towards mobile phone localization without war-driving. In *Proceedings of IEEE INFOCOM 2010*, pages 1–9, 2010.

[12] A. Karpenko, D. Jacobs, J. Baek, and M. Levoy. Digital video stabilization and rolling shutter correction using gyroscopes. Technical Report CSTR 2011-03, Stanford University, 2011.

[13] X. Kong. Ins algorithm using quaternion model for low cost imu. *Robotics and Autonomous Systems*, 46(4):221 – 246, 2004.

[14] H.-J. Lee and S. Jung. Gyro sensor drift compensation by kalman filter to control a mobile inverted pendulum robot system. In *Proceedings of IEEE ICIT 2009*, pages 1–6, 2009.

[15] S. Madgwick, A. J. L. Harrison, and R. Vaidyanathan. Estimation of imu and marg orientation using a gradient descent algorithm. In *Proceedings of IEEE ICORR 2011*, pages 1–7, 2011.

[16] J. Marins, X. Yun, E. Bachmann, R. Mcghee, and M. Zyda. An extended kalman filter for quaternion-based orientation estimation using marg sensors. In *Proceedings of IEEE/RSJ IROS 2001*, volume 4, pages 2003–2011, 2001.

[17] E. Miluzzo, A. Varshavsky, S. Balakrishnan, and R. R. Choudhury. Tapprints: your finger taps have fingerprints. In *Proceedings of ACM MobiSys 2012*, pages 323–336, 2012.

[18] L. Oth, P. Furgale, L. Kneip, and R. Siegwart. Rolling shutter camera calibration. In *Proceedings of IEEE CVPR*, pages 1360–1367, 2013.

[19] A. Rai, K. K. Chintalapudi, V. N. Padmanabhan, and R. Sen. Zee: zero-effort crowdsourcing for indoor localization. In *Proceedings of ACM Mobicom 2012*, pages 293–304, 2012.

[20] M. Shahzad, A. X. Liu, and A. Samuel. Secure unlocking of mobile touch screen devices by simple gestures: You can see it but you can not do it. In *Proceedings of ACM MobiCom 2013*, pages 39–50, 2013.

[21] T. Shelley and J. Barrett. Vibrating gyro to keep cars on route. *Eureka on Campus, Eng. Materials and Design*, 4:17, 1992.

[22] G. Shen, Z. Chen, P. Zhang, T. Moscibroda, and Y. Zhang. Walkie-markie: Indoor pathway mapping made easy. In *Proceedings of USENIX NSDI 2013*, pages 85–98, 2013.

[23] Z. Sun, S. Pan, Y.-C. Su, and P. Zhang. Headio: Zero-configured heading acquisition for indoor mobile devices through multimodal context sensing. In *Proceedings of ACM UbiComp 2013*, pages 33–42, 2013.

[24] H. Wang, S. Sen, A. Elgohary, M. Farid, M. Youssef, and R. R. Choudhury. No need to war-drive: unsupervised indoor localization. In *Proceedings of ACM MobiSys 2012*, pages 197–210, 2012.

[25] Z. Yang, C. Wu, and Y. Liu. Locating in fingerprint space: Wireless indoor localization with little human intervention. In *Proceedings of ACM Mobicom 2012*, pages 269–280, 2012.

[26] Y. Zheng, G. Shen, L. Li, C. Zhao, M. Li, and F. Zhao. Travi-navi: Self-deployable indoor navigation system. In *Proceedings of ACM MobiCom 2014*, 2014.

[27] P. Zhou, Y. Zheng, Z. Li, M. Li, and G. Shen. Iodetector: a generic service for indoor outdoor detection. In *Proceedings of ACM SenSys 2012*, pages 361–362, 2012.

APPENDIX

A. EULER AXIS/ANGLE METHOD

We use a rotation matrix $\mathbf{R}$ given in terms of a unit vector $\mathbf{e}$ along the rotation axis (called "Euler axis" in Euler's rotation theorem), and the angle θ to describe the rotation of the phone. According to the Rodrigues' rotation formula,

$$\mathbf{R} = \mathbf{I}cos\theta + \mathbf{e}(\mathbf{e} \cdot \mathbf{I})(1 - cos\theta) + (\mathbf{e} \times \mathbf{I})sin\theta, \tag{4}$$

where $\mathbf{I}$ is $\begin{pmatrix} 1 & 0 & 0 \\ 0 & 1 & 0 \\ 0 & 0 & 1 \end{pmatrix}$ in the geo-frame. The body-frame rotates about $\mathbf{e}$ at the speed of $\frac{d\mathbf{R}(t)}{dt} = \dot{\theta}\mathbf{e}$ in the geo-frame. The rotation speed also can be represented as $\mathbf{R}(t)\Omega(t)$, where $\Omega(t) = \{\omega_x, \omega_y, \omega_z\}$ and $\mathbf{R}(t)$ is the time-varying rotation matrix. Thus we have

$$\frac{d\mathbf{R}(t)}{dt} = \mathbf{R}(t)\Omega(t). \tag{5}$$

There are two possible solutions to calculate $\mathbf{R}(t)$, the Euler Angles and the Euler Axis/Angle. In practice, when the smartphone rotates 90°, using the Euler Angle suffers from a singularity which results in the Gimbal Lock problem [6] and significantly pollutes the calculation result. In this paper, we use the Euler Axis/Angle. We define a unit vector $\mathbf{q} = \{\bar{q}^T, q_4\}^T$, where $q_4 = cos\frac{\theta}{2}$, $\bar{q} = \{q_1, q_2, q_3\}^T = sin\frac{\theta}{2}\mathbf{e}$, and $|\bar{q}|^2 + q_4^2 = 1$. According to the rotation process, the rotation matrix $\mathbf{R}$ can be calculated as

$$\mathbf{R} = \begin{bmatrix} q_1^2-q_2^2-q_3^2+q_4^2 & 2(q_1q_2-q_4q_3) & 2(q_1q_3+q_4q_2) \\ 2(q_1q_2+q_4q_3) & -q_1^2+q_2^2-q_3^2+q_4^2 & 2(q_2q_3-q_4q_1) \\ 2(q_3q_1-q_4q_2) & 2(q_3q_2+q_4q_1) & 2q_1^2-q_2^2+q_3^2+q_4^2 \end{bmatrix}.$$

With Equation (4) and (5), we finally have

$$\frac{d\mathbf{q}(t)}{dt} = \frac{1}{2} \begin{bmatrix} q_4(t) & -q_3(t) & q_2(t) \\ q_3(t) & q_4(t) & -q_1(t) \\ -q_2(t) & q_1(t) & q_4(t) \\ -q_1(t) & -q_2(t) & -q_3(t) \end{bmatrix} \begin{bmatrix} \omega_x(t) \\ \omega_y(t) \\ \omega_z(t) \end{bmatrix}. \tag{6}$$

With this non-singularity differential equation, we can produce successive rotations if the initial state $\mathbf{q}(0)$ and the real-time angular velocities $\Omega(t)$ during the rotation are available. In our system implementation, we use the fourth-order Runge-Kutta method to solve Equation (6).

B. ATTITUDE FROM COMPASS AND GRAVITY

The phone attitude in the geo-frame using compass and gravity is represented by the rotation matrix $\mathbf{R}$:

$$\mathbf{R} = \begin{bmatrix} \frac{b^2-ccos\delta}{acos\delta-bsin\delta}\sqrt{K} & sin\delta & a \\ \frac{ac}{acos\delta-ab}\sqrt{K} & cos\delta & b \\ \sqrt{K} & b & c \end{bmatrix}, \tag{7}$$

where $a = \frac{-g_x}{g}$, $b = \frac{-g_y}{g}$, $c = \frac{-g_z}{g}$ and $g = \sqrt{g_x^2 + g_y^2 + g_z^2}$.

$$K = \frac{((acos\delta - ab)(acos\delta - bsin\delta))^2}{a^2(acos\delta - bsin\delta)^2} + ((b^2-ccos\delta)(acos\delta-ab))^2 + ((acos\delta - ab)(acos\delta - bsin\delta))^2. \tag{8}$$

E-eyes: Device-free Location-oriented Activity Identification Using Fine-grained WiFi Signatures

Yan Wang†, Jian Liu†, Yingying Chen†, Marco Gruteser*, Jie Yang‡, Hongbo Liu§
†Stevens Institute of Technology, Hoboken, NJ 07030, USA
*Rutgers University, North Brunswick, NJ 08902, USA
‡Florida State University, Tallahassee, FL 32306, USA
§Indiana University-Purdue University Indianapolis, Indianapolis, IN 46202, USA
†{ywang48, jliu28, yingying.chen}@stevens.edu, *gruteser@winlab.rutgers.edu,
‡jie.yang@cs.fsu.edu, §hl45@iupui.edu

ABSTRACT

Activity monitoring in home environments has become increasingly important and has the potential to support a broad array of applications including elder care, well-being management, and latchkey child safety. Traditional approaches involve wearable sensors and specialized hardware installations. This paper presents device-free location-oriented activity identification at home through the use of existing WiFi access points and WiFi devices (e.g., desktops, thermostats, refrigerators, smartTVs, laptops). Our low-cost system takes advantage of the ever more complex web of WiFi links between such devices and the increasingly fine-grained channel state information that can be extracted from such links. It examines channel features and can uniquely identify both in-place activities and walking movements across a home by comparing them against signal profiles. Signal profiles construction can be semi-supervised and the profiles can be adaptively updated to accommodate the movement of the mobile devices and day-to-day signal calibration. Our experimental evaluation in two apartments of different size demonstrates that our approach can achieve over 96% average true positive rate and less than 1% average false positive rate to distinguish a set of in-place and walking activities with only a single WiFi access point. Our prototype also shows that our system can work with wider signal band (802.11ac) with even higher accuracy.

Categories and Subject Descriptors

H.4 [**Information Systems Applications**]: Miscellaneous

Keywords

Channel State Information (CSI); WiFi; Activity Recognition; Device-Free; Location-Oriented;

1. INTRODUCTION

There exists a broad range of applications that benefit from higher-level contextual information—an understanding of activities that persons are engaged in, not just their position inside a coordinate system. For example, activity recognition is the essential part of a trend towards the quantified self. By tracking a sequence of meaningful activities and generating statistics for a person, it is possible to monitor well-being and suggest behavioral changes that improve health. Such activity tracking is arguably even more compelling for children and the elderly. In aging-in-place settings, it can be helpful to understand whether established routines are still followed since the absence of usual activities can be an important indicator for detecting falls and other situations of need.

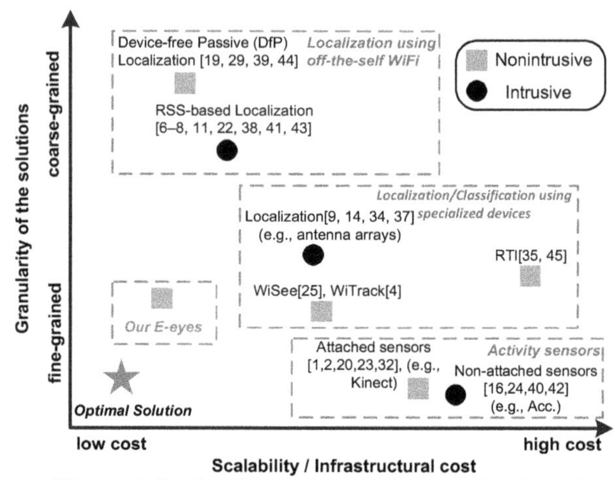

Figure 1: Design Space: comparing to related work.

Existing solutions. The challenge in activity recognition for these applications lies in finding solutions that can provide sufficiently accurate tracking and recognition with minimal infrastructure requirements and without the need to carry a dedicated device. As illustrated in Figure 1, existing activity recognition solutions [1, 2, 15, 16, 20, 23, 24, 32, 40, 42] primarily rely on dedicated sensors that are worn by the tracking subjects or cameras, motion sensors and other special sensors that are installed in the environment [1, 20, 32]. These solutions require either significant infrastructure installation or diligent usage of the wearable device. More generally, some activities that are tied to particular places can also be inferred from location systems [7, 44], either device-based or device-free, but these system cannot distinguish multiple activities that occur in the same place. Device-free systems do not require persons to carry any devices, but they require a dense placement of tens of sensors to create a mesh of wireless links inside the area of interest. Perhaps most related to our work is the effort to use detailed physical layer measurements such as Doppler shifts from one single wireless monitor to detect people's movement, location, and even gestures. The granularity of the monitoring ranges from coarser movements (such as Wi-Vi [5]) to fine-grained gestures (such as WiSee [25] and WiTrack [4]). However, these systems all have been prototyped with USRP software radios and require a specialized receiver that extracts carrier wave features that are not

MobiCom'14, September 7-11, 2014, Maui, Hawaii, USA.
Copyright 2014 ACM 978-1-4503-2783-1/14/09 ...$15.00.
http://dx.doi.org/10.1145/2639108.2639143.

reported in current WiFi systems. In addition, activity identification differs from gesture recognition in that the system needs to identify a more loosely defined series of motions over a period of time rather than a single well-defined body movement. For example, an activity such as cooking includes several movements to fetch, prepare, and mix ingredients that are not always exactly the same and do not necessarily occur in the same sequence, making it difficult to detect with gesture recognition techniques that are designed for precise single motions such as a punch.

Approach. This paper explores a novel point in the design space and demonstrates that device-free location-oriented activity recognition is possible (i) using the existing channel state information provided by IEEE 802.11n devices and (ii) using relatively few wireless links, such as those to existing in-home WiFi devices. The system exploits the trend to wider bandwidths (e.g., 802.11ac), and in particular, the more fine-grained channel state information that is being tracked in MIMO communications. Whereas traditional received signal strength (RSS) measurements are a single quantity per packet that represents signal-to-interference-plus-noise ratio (SINR) over the channel bandwidth, channel state information contains amplitude and phase measurements separately for each OFDM subcarrier. Due to the slight frequency delta, separate subcarriers experience different multipath fading. While such effects are often averaged out, when looking at a single average RSS measurement, the individual subcarrier measurements are more likely to change when small movements have altered the multipath environment. This essentially means that our system will not just detect obstructions on the direct path but can also take advantage of the rich web of reflected rays to cover a space. This makes it possible to operate with a single access point and a small set of stationary WiFi devices, which likely already exist or will exist soon in many buildings.

Moreover, many of the important daily activities that the device-free, location-oriented activity identification system (dubbed E-eyes) is designed to identify are linked to a few specific locations in the home, for example, cooking is usually limited to the kitchen and brushing teeth is limited to sinks. We seek therefore to identify activities from CSI signal measurement by comparing them to location-activity profiles. We also seek to distinguish two activities that occur in the same location, meaning that multiple location-oriented activity profiles can have the same location. We refer to this approach as location-oriented activity identification or as location-activity profiles, because the profiles are affected by both the activities that people perform and the location people are in. While traditional activity identification is more location independent [16, 42], our approach prioritizes device-free operation and detection of more loosely-defined daily activities involving a series of motions as opposed to gestures or basic sitting, walking, running classification. Our system can also be extended to recognize the same activity occurring in different locations by constructing multiple location-activity profiles for the same activity.

More specifically, our system first obtains wireless signals from off-the-shelf WiFi devices (e.g., Intel WiFi Link 5300 NICs) and classifies the wireless signals as belonging to an in-place or a walking activity. We refer these two types of activities as loosely-defined because they may involve non-repetitive body movements and the sequences of body movements involved may not remain the same across repetition. Examples of loosely-defined activities include cooking dinner in front of the stove, eating dinner at the dining table, exercising on a treadmill, or working at a desk. Walking activities involve movements between rooms or across a larger room. The system then applies novel matching algorithms to compare the amplitude measurements against known profiles that identify the activity. If known profiles do not exist or change afterwards, it can also apply semi-supervised learning strategies to establish or adaptively update profiles. Our system is device-free because it relies only on the existing WiFi environment (e.g., smart appliances connecting to a WiFi AP) and the person who performs the activities does not have to carry any device. This approach allows reusing the existing WiFi AP deployment in homes for location-oriented activity recognition, without the need for additional stationary infrastructure or wearable sensors. The contributions of our work are summarized as follows:

- We show that the channel state information (CSI) from off-the-shelf 802.11n devices can be utilized to identify and distinguish in-place activities inside a home with a much smaller set of transmitting devices than in previous device-free localization solutions.
- We develop a monitoring framework that can run on a single WiFi AP with its connected devices and use the associated profile matching algorithms to compare amplitude profiles against those from known activities.
- We explore dynamic profile construction. The profile can be adaptively updated to accommodate the movement or replacement of wireless devices (e.g., laptop or smartphone) and the day-to-day profile calibration.
- We conduct extensive experiments in two different-sized apartments over a 4-month time period to demonstrate that a single AP with 3 connected devices can accurately distinguish 8 walking activities between rooms (20 rounds each), 9 daily activities (50 rounds each), and over more than 100 rounds of other activities with an average detection rate of over 96% and an average false positive rate less than 1%. With only one device, the detection rate can still achieve around 92% with a similar false positive rate.
- We show through experiments how the trend to wider channels (e.g., 802.11ac) will further enhance recognition since it allows measurements over many additional subcarriers.

Limitations. Our system has the following limitations: first, our system E-eyes is mainly designed for and tested with a single occupant at home, which is an important scenario, such as in an aging-in-place environment. It may be extended to multiple persons, however this would require a much larger set of profiles covering different combinations of activities. Second, E-eyes was tested without pets or other movements at home. While the effect of small pets is probably negligible, larger pets may pose additional signal processing challenges. Third, E-eyes relies on a relatively stable environment (e.g., no furniture movement). While it could detect such environment changes, each would trigger an activity profile updating procedure, which may require user input.

The rest of the paper is organized as follows. In Section 2, we place our work in the context of related research. The background, challenges, and system overview of E-eyes are provided in Section 3. In Section 4, we present the proposed activity recognition schemes. We then describe the implementation of E-eyes in Section 5. In Section 6, we perform extensive evaluation of our system in real environments with two apartments. The related issues of E-eyes are discussed in Section 7. Finally, we conclude our work in Section 8.

2. RELATED WORK

There has been active work in using dedicated sensors for activity recognition [1, 2, 15, 16, 20, 23, 24, 32, 40, 42]. Sensors can be either attached to a person's body [16], or placed on target objects with which people interact [15]. For example, an accelerometer

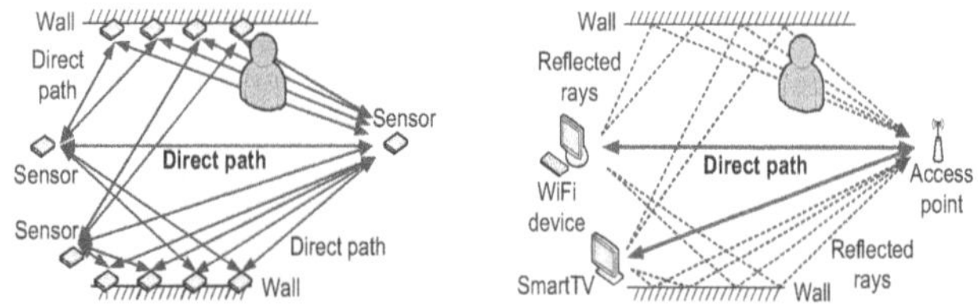

(a) Existing work: link-centric using RSS (b) Illustration of reflected rays

Figure 2: CSI takes the advantage of multipath effects and captures the detailed changes on different subcarriers.

is attached on human body to detect falls in Philips Lifeline [24], whereas a motion sensor is attached to a door to detect movement in GrandCare [32]. Another wearable sensor is the acoustic sensor used in BodyScop for classifying activities, such as eating and coughing [42]. Vision based systems [1, 20], such as Leap [2] and Kinect [23], can be used to track user movements and gestures. These dedicated sensors can achieve fine-grained activity recognition. However, they need the installation and maintenance of dedicated sensors which usually entail high costs and are thus not scalable.

Another body of related work is indoor localization systems which can be extended to activity recognition [6–9, 11, 14, 17, 21, 22, 30, 34, 37, 38, 41, 43]. These systems localize a wireless emitter using Received Signal Strength (RSS) [6–8, 11, 17, 22, 38, 41, 43], OFDM channel state information [30], antenna arrays [14, 37], RFID tags [34], rotating anchors [9], or visible LED lights [21]. These systems provide various accuracy ranging from several meters (e.g., RSS-based) to sub-meter but require people to carry a wireless emitter. This can be intrusive and poses the problem of people, especially the elderly with age-related memory loss, forgetting to carry such a device. Furthermore, they need the support of wireless infrastructure, either lightweight devices such as re-use multiple access points if available [7, 11, 22] or costly specialized devices, such as antenna arrays [14, 37]. The infrastructural cost of these systems thus prevents their large scale deployment.

The radio tomography imaging (RTI) [35, 45] and device-free passive (DfP) localization [19, 29, 39, 44], like our system, do not require a device be attached to or carried by the user. The state of art RTI requires tens or hundreds of wireless sensors to achieve sub-meter accuracy, while DfP localization [19, 29] with four WiFi APs has an accuracy of several meters. Several works [13, 31] propose to distinguish some basic activities such as walking, crawling, standing and lying based on RSS using a set of receivers or USRP SDR devices. These systems are either impractical for roaming deployment or not accurate enough for fine-grained activity recognition.

Recent work in using a single wireless monitor to detect human movement or location [4, 5, 25] can be used for activity recognition as well. The granularity of the activity can be inferred from these systems is either modest (such as Wi-Vi [5]) or fine-grained (such as WiSee [25] and WiTrack [4]). However, these systems all require a specialized WiFi monitor (e.g., USRP) for extracting the carrier wave. In contrast, we use an off-the-shelf WiFi device for activity recognition. Our method can provide fine-grained activity recognition by re-using existing home WiFi network and thus has much higher scalability for wide deployment. Furthermore, different from WiSee that focuses on recognizing well-defined, quick gestures, our work aims to discriminate loosely defined daily activities that involve a series of body movements over a certain period of time. In recognizing such loosely defined daily activities, we find that channel characteristics, such as the statistical distribution and time series, are more suitable for distinguishing between activities lasting a certain period of time than quick gestures.

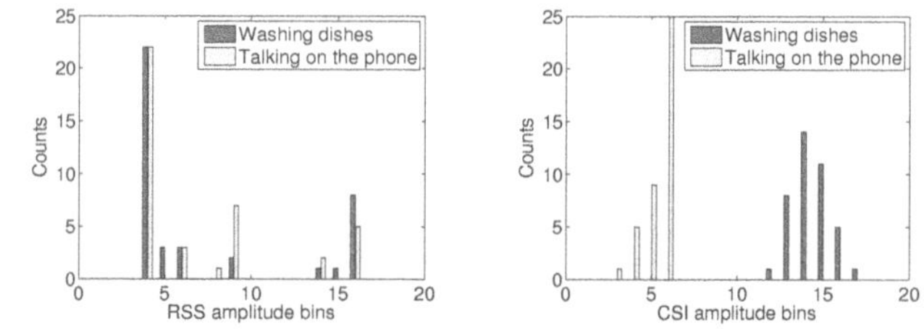

(a) RSS distribution (b) CSI distribution

Figure 3: Histograms of RSS amplitude and CSI amplitude of a particular subcarrier for two different in-place activities at the same position: washing dishes and talking on the phone nearby the sink.

3. DESIGN OF E-EYES

To build a low-cost solution leveraging WiFi signatures in a home environment, we devise an approach that senses and identifies fine-grained WiFi signal changes when an activity is performed. In this section, we discuss the intuition, challenges and overview of our system design.

3.1 Intuition

This work seeks to exploit two trends. First, WiFi usage has expanded from providing laptop Internet connectivity to connecting smart devices such as TVs, game consoles, surveillance cameras, refrigerators, and loudspeakers to home networks and the Internet. This provides a larger number of WiFi links inside homes, some of which use constant beaconing. Second, WiFi radios provide more fine-grained channel measurements over wider bandwidths. With 802.11n MIMO systems, it became necessary for radios to track more fine-grained channel state information. On it's standard 20MHz channel, 802.11n radios measure amplitude and phase for each of the 52 orthogonal frequency-division multiplexing (OFDM) subcarriers. With 40MHz channels, measurements are available for 128 subcarriers. The emerging IEEE 802.11ac standard supports even wider bandwidths. These measurements essentially allow estimating the channel frequency response. In contrast, the traditional received signal strength (RSS) was only a single value per packet, typically a SINR reading averaged over the entire channel bandwidth.

Measuring the channel frequency response has important implications for detecting and differentiating minute movements. Inside buildings, signal propagation is dominated by multipath, that is the received signal amplitude (or strength) is the combined amplitude of signals arriving over many different paths (scattered from and reflected off different objects). Since the individual signals can constructively or deconstructively, combine based on their individual phase shifts, this effect can lead to large differences in the combined amplitude, which is commonly known as small-scale fading. A small change in frequency, however, can have a large effect on the combined signal. The amount of frequency change for a signal amplitude to become uncorrelated with its previous value is also known as the coherence bandwidth and can be estimated as $B_c = \frac{1}{D}$ where D is the delay spread of the arriving multipath signals. Interestingly, the width of an OFDM subcarrier is chosen to match this coherence bandwidth to simplify receiver design. This means that amplitude measurements on each subcarrier will provide many uncorrelated combinations of the received multipath components, which increases the likelihood that some are affected by a small movement. A single RSS measurement over the signal bandwidth, in comparison, averages out many of these detailed small scale fading effects.

Figure 3 shows a motivational experiment where two different activities were conducted in the same location: talking on the phone

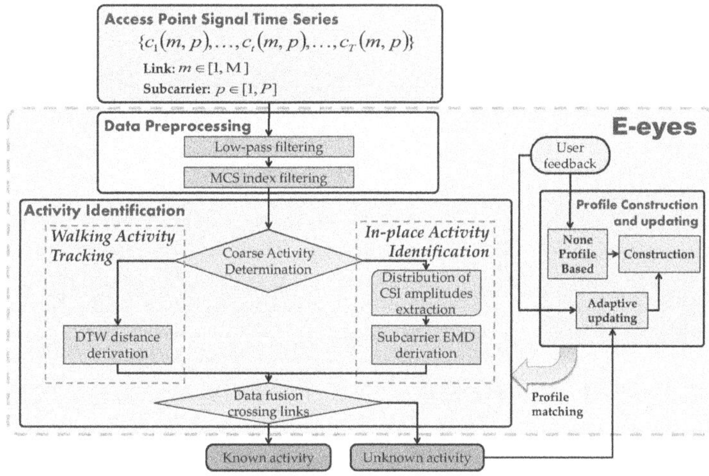

Figure 4: System flow of activity recognition using CSI.

and washing dishes. The histograms of RSS readings collected for both of these activities show relatively little difference. The histograms of CSI amplitudes (quantized to 20 bins) for a specific subcarrier, however, show very distinct distributions that can clearly distinguish these different movements in the same location. The insight is that since an activity involves a series of body movements during a certain period of time, the distribution of CSI amplitudes is a desirable channel statistic that can capture unique characteristics of activities in both time and frequency domains.

With more WiFi devices in homes and the ability to measure small changes in multipath rays, our intuition suggests that it might be possible to track activities and movements around a home with only this existing infrastructure. Device-free localization and activity recognition requires that at least one measurable RF rays travels through any location of interest, because the presence or movement of a human body at this position would only alter the propagation of these rays. Earlier device free localization system have therefore blanketed spaces with tens of transceivers to create a fine mesh of measurable direct links. As illustrated in Figure 2(a) and (b), such a measurable mesh can now also be created by all the multipath rays from only a handful of WiFi devices instead of requiring many additional devices.

3.2 Challenges

Realizing such a system that seeks to recognize activities at an access point using CSI measurements from only a small number of WiFi links raises a number of challenges:

Profile Uniqueness and Robustness. CSI measurements can be affected by signal interferences, user movements, and changing environments. To identify activities, the system has to match signatures or features of activities to measurements in a way that is robust to noisy signal readings collected from WiFi devices in real-world environments yet are still sufficiently unique to map to a specific activity.

Algorithm Generality. Distinguishing different activities needs different information of activities. For example, one activity might involve walking from one room to another (which generates a time series of CSI measurements without an obvious pattern), whereas another activity (e.g., washing dishes in the kitchen) is only performed at one location with repetitive gestures (which results in CSI measurements with repetitive patterns). These different types of activities will lead to very different signal characteristics, and our algorithm should be general enough to profile and identify them.

Profile Generation. After system installation or after significant changes to the environment, appropriate profiles for activities may not exist. The system should be able to assist with profile generation, to reduce the effort of this process.

3.3 System Overview

The basic idea of our system is to match CSI patterns against activity profiles. As illustrated in Figure 4, the system takes as input time-series amplitude measurements, which can be collected at a single access point with off-the-shelf hardware (e.g., Intel 5300 NIC). The amplitude measurements are available for each subcarrier on a link and are collected over several links to rarely moved devices (such as home entertainment devices or appliances). We discuss later on how the system might be extended to also take advantage of mobile devices when they do not move. The system can take advantage of CSI measurements from existing traffic across these links, or if insufficient network traffic is available, the system might also generate periodic traffic for measurement purposes. This data is then preprocessed to remove outliers via a low-pass filter and to filter out artifacts introduces by rate adaptation, where the radios switch to different modulation and coding schemes.

The core of our system, E-eyes, are the *Activity Identification* and the *Profile Construction and Updating*. Activity identification encompasses two different activity matching approaches to address the generality challenge. The system distinguishes between walking activities and in-place activities. In general, a walking activity causes significant pattern changes of the CSI amplitude over time, since it involves significant body movements and location changes. An in-place activity (such as watching TV on a sofa) only involves relative smaller body movements and will not cause significant amplitude changes but present certain repetitive patterns. It thus first applies a moving variance thresholding technique to discriminate the two types of activities. The cumulative moving variance across all subcarriers can be expected to be greater for walking activities than in-place activities. Moreover, our system leverages the moving variance to segment the long-term CSI trace. Since the trace often contains multiple different activities over time, moving variance is used to determine the start and end of individual activities.

Next, our system identifies activities by calculating the similarity between such a CSI segment and the pre-constructed activity profiles. Based on the characteristics of walking and in-place activities, we develop two separate similarity metrics and classifiers. For walking activities, we use the *Multiple-Dimensional Dynamic Time Warping (MD-DTW)* technique, which can align a trace with larger CSI changes to the profile while correcting for differences in speed. For in-place activities, we base the comparison on CSI distributions (i.e., histograms) rather than the exact time series to

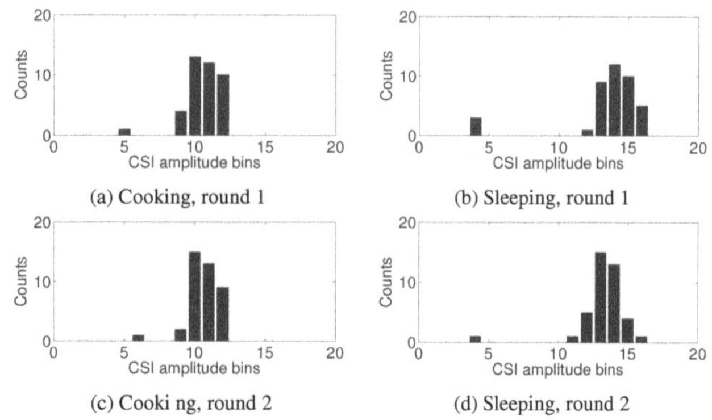

(a) Cooking, round 1 (b) Sleeping, round 1

(c) Cooki ng, round 2 (d) Sleeping, round 2

Figure 5: Histogram of CSI amplitudes on a particular subcarrier for cooking and sleeping.

achieve higher robustness to the repetitive but often more random patterns generated by such activities. We use the *Earth Mover Distance (EMD)* to quantify the similarity of two distributions.

To construct activity profiles, our system can utilize a semisupervised approach. It starts with continuous monitoring of a home environment and applies a clustering-based method to identify multiple similar instances of an activity without a matching profile (referred to *non-profile based*). Users can then label the resulting clusters to create known activity profiles. Furthermore, this technique can be used to detect and update activity profiles after significant changes in the environment (e.g., the media console WiFi device has been moved from one side of the room to the other side or the furnishings have been significantly altered). Users can provide feedback and trigger a profile update (after such environmental changes) by using the Non-profiling Clustering (Section 5.2).

4. ACTIVITY IDENTIFICATION

In this section, we first describe *Coarse Activity Determination*. We then present *In-place Activity Identification* and *Walking Activity Tracking* components in our system. And we also discuss how our system can benefit from wider signal bandwidths using 802.11ac.

4.1 Coarse Activity Determination

Since various activities cause different degrees of signal changes, we apply the *moving variance* on top of the CSI measurements to capture this difference and determine the category of the activity. In particular, a large moving variance indicates the presence of a walking activity whereas a small moving variance represents the presence of an in-place activity or no activity at all. The detailed steps are presented as follows:

Step 1. We denote the CSI samples of P subcarriers as $C = \{C(1), \ldots, C(p), \ldots, C(P)\}$, where $C(p) = [c_1(p), \ldots, c_T(p)]'$ represents T CSI amplitudes on the pth subcarrier. We further denote the moving variances of the P subcarriers as $V = \{V(1), \ldots, V(p), \ldots, V(P)\}$, where $V(p) = [v_1(p), \ldots, v_T(p)]$ are the moving variances derived from $C(P)$. Our system can then calculate the *cumulative moving variance* of CSI samples crossing P subcarriers as $\mathcal{V} = \sum_{p=1}^{P} V(p)$.

Step 2. The next step is to examine the cumulative moving variances to determine whether the collected CSI samples contain a walking activity or an in-place/no activity. If the maximum cumulative moving variance $\max(\mathcal{V})$ is larger than the threshold τ_v, the CSI samples are determined to contain a walking activity, otherwise they contain an in-place/no activity. We empirically determine the threshold through 40 rounds of different walking activities and in-place activities in apartment environments. A threshold, $\tau_v = 20$, is found to be able to distinguish over 98% of walking and in-place activities in our experiments.

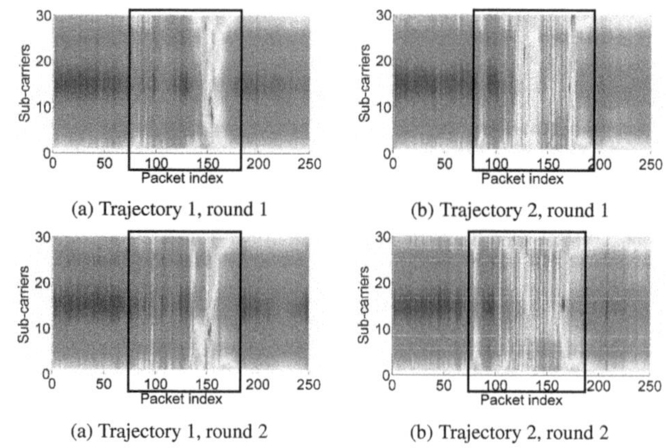

(a) Trajectory 1, round 1 (b) Trajectory 2, round 1

(a) Trajectory 1, round 2 (b) Trajectory 2, round 2

Figure 6: Similar CSI time series pattern for same walking trajectory.

Compared with recognizing gestures, people's daily in-place activities do not have such strictly pre-defined patterns but result in a relatively stable distribution of CSI amplitude due to the presence of the human body and loosely defined body motions. In E-eyes, segmentation is first performed in the task of Coarse Activity Determination by examining the CSI variance in the collected trace. Note that Coarse Activity Determination can be also used to identify the starting and ending of both walking activities and in-place activities, since walking activities often separate in-place activities. If the segmented CSI trace belongs to an in-place activity, we will further use the EMD technique [28] to compare the distribution of CSI amplitudes in a sliding time window with in-place activity profiles (Section 4.2) to identify different activities within this trace. If the segmented CSI trace is recognized as a walking activity, we will further identify the walking trajectory or the passing of doorways (Section 4.3).

4.2 In-place Activity Identification

4.2.1 *Characteristics*

We find that an in-place activity results in a relatively stable distribution of CSI amplitude due to the presence of the human body and (possibly) repetitive body movement over time. Furthermore, different in-place activities cause different distributions of CSI amplitude as the location and/or the repetitive body movement patterns and the posture of the human body are different for different in-place activities. We illustrate the similarity of the CSI amplitude distribution for the same activity, and the difference of the CSI amplitude distribution for two different in-place activities (i.e., cooking in a kitchen and sleeping on a bed) at a particular subcarrier (subcarrier 12) in Figure 5. We observe that the CSI amplitude distributions are similar for the same activity at different rounds, but distinctive for different activities. This important observation inspires us to exploit the distribution of CSI amplitude to distinguish different in-place activities and shows that a particular in-place activity can be identified by comparing against known profiles.

4.2.2 *In-place Activity Classifier*

Based on the characteristics of the in-place activities, we employ the earth mover's distance (EMD) [28] technique, which is a well-known approach for evaluating the similarity between two probability distributions. The EMD calculates the minimal cost to transform one distribution into the other. Our classifier seeks to compare the distribution of the testing CSI measurements to those of the known in-place activity profiles by using the EMD metric. CSI measurements being tested are identified to contain a known activity when the resulted minimal cost (i.e., minimal EMD distance) is small enough.

Specifically, at run time, our system first identifies the testing CSI measurements as a *candidate* of a particular known in-place activity if the EMD distance from the candidate to the known in-place activity is the minimum among the EMD distances to all known activities stored in the CSI profiles. Then our system further confirms the candidate known in-place activity by comparing the resulted minimal EMD distance to a threshold, which can be empirically determined in the profile construction. The candidate known in-place activity is confirmed if the minimal EMD distance is less than the threshold, otherwise, it will be identified as an unknown activity. An alternate way to determine whether the testing CSI measurements correspond to a known activity or not is to use an outlier detection method, such as the median absolute deviation (MAD) [27], to examine whether the resultant minimum EMD distance is within a range. To determine the range, an EMD distance pool containing the minimal EMD distances of previous successfully identified activities is needed in the profiles. We note that our system can also recognize the same in-place activities occurring in different locations by comparing the testing CSI measurements to a set of CSI profiles constructed when the same activities occur in different locations. In this case, the profile for an activity is a set of CSI profiles instead of a single CSI profile, and the testing CSI measurements are determined to contain the activity if it has the minimum EMD distance to any of the CSI profiles belonging to the activity profile.

4.3 Walking Activity Tracking

4.3.1 Characteristics

We find that the CSI collected from walking activities is changing constantly over time due to body movement and change of locations. In particular, Figure 6 presents CSI amplitude of each subcarrier versus the packet index (i.e., time series) for two different walking paths in two experimental runs. We observe that the CSI measurements exhibit similar changing patterns for the same trajectory in different rounds, whereas the changes of CSI measurements over time are different for different trajectories. This observation indicates that the CSI pattern is dominated by the unique path of each walking activity.

Furthermore, since there are always in-place activities before and after a walking activity, ideally we can identify the walking activity by identifying the in-place activities at both ends. However, the starting and ending points of the walking activity can be anywhere inside the space. It is possible that the two endpoints are not that meaningful and thus no such in-place activity profiles are constructed. To tackle this problem, we propose to further build the CSI measurement profile when the person passes through doorways. Since, in general, a person must pass through a door way when walking from one room to another, they can be utilized to facilitate walking activity tracking. By identifying the doorway the person moves through, our system can determine a walking activity in high level without requiring extensive profiling of paths that have less meaningful starting and ending locations.

4.3.2 Walking Activity Discrimination

Walking Path Discrimination. Since people may walk at different speeds for the same trajectory, we propose using Dynamic Time Warping (DTW) [26] to align the testing CSI measurements to those of known activities in the profile. We then identify the activity contained inside the testing CSI measurements based on the similarity measures using DTW. DTW stretches and compresses required parts to allow a proper comparison between two data sequences. This is useful to match CSI samples from different walking speeds in real-world scenarios. In our system, CSI measurements are in a format that reports the channel metrics for multiple subcarrier groups (e.g., 30 subcarriers). To perform multi-dimensional sequence alignment, our system employs Multi-Dimensional Dynamic Time Warping (MD-DTW) [33], in which the vector norm is utilized to calculate the distance matrix according to:

$$d(c_i, c_j') = \sum_{p=1}^{P} (c_i(p) - c_j'(p))^2, \qquad (1)$$

where $C = c_1, c_2, ..., c_T$ and C'=$c_1', c_2', ..., c_T'$ are two CSI sequences for walking path discrimination, and where P is the number of dimensions of the sequence data (with P=30 for CSI sample). A least cost path is found through this matrix and the MD-DTW distance is the sum of matrix elements along the path.

During activity identification, our system distinguishes each walking activity by calculating the MD-DTW distance between the testing CSI measurements and all the known walking activities in CSI profiles. Our system stores the segment of CSI measurements of known activities in profiles. If the MD-DTW distance is less than a threshold (i.e., considering it as a known activity), we then regard the corresponding CSI measurements labeled in the CSI profiles with the minimum distance as the activity identified for the testing measurements.

Doorway Discrimination. Doorway discrimination is used to handle the case where the testing CSI measurements are unknown after attempting to match them with the profile database. We seek to identify which doorway the person passes through and the corresponding walking activity can then be recognized in a high-level. This strategy makes our system more robust and handles the case when people are moving freely. The possible activities are strongly tied to which doorway the person passes by. For example, passing through kitchen doorway in the noon time is very likely followed by cooking or eating.

In particular, our system also collects CSI for profiling when people pass through doorways during walking activity profile construction (i.e., constructing doorway profiles). It then compares the testing CSI measurements using a sliding window approach to that of the doorway profiles. The EMD distance used in in-place activity recognition is applied for such comparison. Therefore, distinguishing between passing different doorways is transformed into an in-place activities identification. To show the feasibility of this strategy, we test 20 rounds each for 8 walking trajectories (refer to Figure 7) in two different-size apartments. Table 1 shows the doorway detection ratio (DR) of each trajectory corresponding to the doorway passed. Our approach achieves an average detection accuracy of over 96.25%, which is sufficient as a supplementary to walking trajectory discrimination.

4.4 Extension to Wider-band WiFi Signals

The direction of WiFi protocol development moves towards extending the channel capacity and data transmission rate. A very efficient way to achieve the extension is to use wider-band channels, for example 802.11n protocol has the option to use 40MHz channels to increase the data rate from 54Mbits/s to 150Mbits/s per spatial stream. Similarly, the next generation WiFi protocol 802.11ac would support 80MHz and 160MHz channels with the data rate up to 867Mbits/s per spatial stream. The increasing trend of the channel bandwidth also brings us more available subcarriers in each channel (i.e., 114 subcarriers for a 40MHz channel,

Table 1: Doorway Detection Accuracy.

1-BR Apt.	Bedroom↔Kitchen	Kitchen↔Bathroom
DR	1	0.975
2-BR Apt.	Outside↔Bedroom1	Bedroom2↔Bathroom
DR	1	0.875

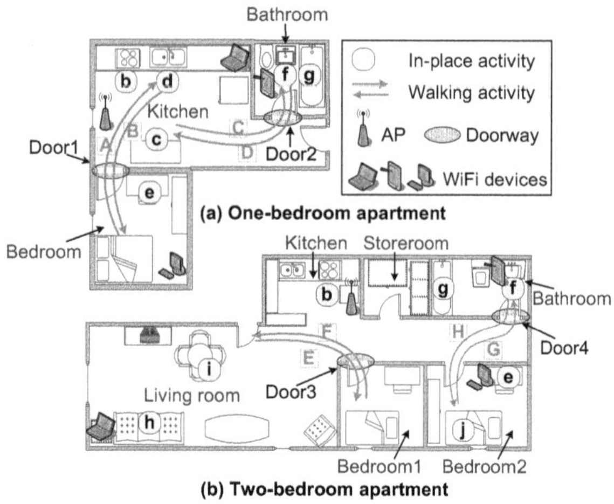

Figure 7: Experimental setups and the illustration of activities in two different-size apartments: (a) one-bedroom apartment and (b) two-bedroom apartment.

242 subcarriers for a 80MHz channel), which suggests that using wider-band signals could potentially increase the performance of activity recognition using CSI measurements since more subcarriers available in CSI would increase the chance to capture the detailed small-scale fading effects caused by small activities. In this direction, we seek to extend E-eyes to use a wider-band signal providing CSI measurements with more subcarrier information which is expected to help improve the activity recognition accuracy especially for in-place activities. We utilize two 40MHz channel in 802.11n to emulate an 80MHz channel in 802.11ac in our experiments.

5. IMPLEMENTATION

5.1 Activity Profile Construction

In our system, we collect the CSI measurements of typical activities for profile construction. In particular, we use the distribution of CSI amplitude to profile in-place activities and the sequence of CSI amplitude for walking activities. If multiple WiFi devices are available, the profile is constructed by using each WiFi device. Additionally, we build a profile for "empty room" (i.e., no one inside the room), which is a special case of an in-place activity. When constructing profiles, it is possible the profile of an activity from a particular WiFi device is similar to the profile of "empty room" when the activity is very far away from that device.

5.2 Non-profiling Clustering

After profile construction, the activity profiles may still change due to many factors. For example, the activity profiles may change over time due to the involved WiFi device being moved to another location, e.g., the desktop being moved from one room to another. Furthermore, the activity profiles may also get affected by day-to-day environmental changes. Therefore, our system E-eyes requires a method that can adaptively update activity profiles. We propose a process called *non-profiling clustering*, in which E-eyes first utilizes a semi-supervised approach to cluster the daily activities from the collected CSI measurements, and then label each activity to produce CSI profiles. After clustering, the CSI measurements from the same type of activities are clustered together. Once significant changes of profiles are detected, E-eyes utilizes users' feedback (i.e., user labels each new cluster returned by non-profile clustering) to perform adaptive profile updating. The non-profiling clustering is also utilized to construct CSI profiles when our system starts without any CSI profile.

We next illustrate this strategy by applying clustering to profile in-place activities. Assume we have R sets of CSI samples from K different unknown activity instances, where each CSI sample set $C^r, 1 \leq r \leq R$, corresponds to one particular activity instance with a certain number of CSI samples. Here we exploit the K-Means clustering technique to discriminate different activity instances based on the EMD between CSI samples.

In order to utilize EMD for clustering, we first calculate the EMD between any particular CSI sample set C^r and all the sample sets (including C^r itself). We then obtain R EMD vectors of length R, i.e., $E^r = \left[E(C^r, C^1), \cdots, E(C^r, C^R)\right]$. Next, the K-means algorithm searches for K appropriate clusters, i.e., $S = s_1, \cdots, s_K$, satisfying the following equation:

$$\arg\min_{S} \sum_{k=1}^{K} \sum_{E^r \in s_k} |E^r - \mu_k|^2, \tag{2}$$

where μ_k is the mean value of the EMD vectors in s_k. Equation 2 searches for K appropriate clusters S that minimizes the variances of the CSI vectors C^r in each cluster.

Table 2 shows the results of clustering based on 400 CSI sample sets involving 8 activity instances, where each set contains 40 CSI samples. Most of the activities can be differentiated from each other with the detection ratio as high as over 84% and an acceptable false positive rate, except the two activities of brushing and bathing in the bathroom due to the small differences in their corresponding CSI patterns, which cannot be differentiated by clustering.

With the relationship between the activity instances and the clusters S, the CSI sample sets correctly classified are used to create new activity profiles. Furthermore, if the profile for a particular activity instance already exists, the system adaptively determines whether to update the activity profile through the comparison with the new profile.

5.3 Data Calibration

Data calibration is used to improve the reliability of the CSI by mitigating the noise presented in the collected CSI samples. The noise sources could be the complicated indoor propagation, the WiFi devices' inner noise (e.g., vibration or ring of devices), and etc.

5.3.1 Low-pass Filtering

Low-pass filtering aims to remove high frequency noise which is unlikely to be caused by human activities as human activities usually have a low frequency range. To remove high frequency noises, we adopt the dynamic exponential smoothing filter (DESF) [10], since it is an exponential smoother that changes its smoothing factor dynamically according to previous samples. The DESF can remove high frequency noise and preserve the features affected by human activities in the CSI measurements.

5.3.2 Modulation and Coding Scheme Index Filtering

Besides the effects from human activities, we find that the modulation and coding scheme (MCS) index, which occasionally changes due to the unstable wireless channel in our experiments, could also influence the amplitude of CSI. To get the changing CSI patterns only affected by human activities, we need to remove the CSI mea-

Table 2: Results of activity identification using clustering without profiles.

Test	empty s_1	cook. s_2	eat. s_3	wash. s_4	study. s_5	brush. s_6	bath. s_7	other s_8
DR	1	0.98	0.88	0.84	0.92	0.66	0.46	0.94
FPR	0.06	0	0.15	0.09	0	0.45	0.43	0.10

Actual Activity Performed

1-bedroom apt.	a	b	c	d	e	f	g	unknown
a: empty	1	0	0	0	0	0	0	0
b: cooking	0	1	0	0	0	0	0	0
c: eating	0	0	1	0	0	0	0	0
d: washing dishes	0	0	0.16	0.84	0	0	0	0
e: studying	0	0	0	0	1	0	0	0
f: brushing	0	0	0.06	0	0	0.94	0	0
g: bathing	0	0	0.02	0	0	0	0.98	0
o: others	0	0	0	0	0	0	0	1

Identified In-place Activity

(a) 1-bedroom apartment

Actual Activity Performed

2-bedroom apt.	a	b	f	g	h	i	j	unknown
a: empty	1	0	0	0	0	0	0	0
b: cooking	0	1	0	0	0	0	0	0
f: brushing	0	0	1	0	0	0	0	0
g: bathing	0	0	0	0.96	0	0	0	0.04
h: watching TV	0	0	0	0	1	0	0	0
i: gaming	0	0	0	0	0	1	0	0
j: sleeping	0	0	0	0	0	0	0.88	0.12
o: others	0	0	0	0	0	0	0.05	0.95

Identified In-place Activity

(b) 2-bedroom apartment

Figure 8: Confusion matrix of in-place activity identification in two different apartments.

surements affected by a different MCS index (indicates different channel condition) for a pure reflection metric of human activities.

Specifically, MCS index is a specification of the high-throughput (HT) physical layer (PHY) parameter in 802.11n standard [3]. It contains the information of the modulation order (e.g., BPSK, QPSK, 16-QAM, 64-QAM), the forward error correction (FEC) coding rate, etc. for transmitting a packet. Each 802.11n packet header contains a 16-bit MCS index, which can be extracted together with the CSI sample of each packet. In particular, we find that CSI measurements with the MCS index greater than 263 [1] can make CSI measurements relatively stable in empty rooms even though it changes in such a range. Therefore, we filter out the CSI measurements with MCS value less than 263 and keep the rest of them for activity identification.

5.4 Data Fusion Crossing Multiple Links

WiFi usage has expanded from providing Internet access to connecting in-home smart devices such as TVs, refrigerators, and loudspeakers. This provides a number of WiFi links to capture an activity simultaneously inside home. Our system E-eyes thus can exploit a number of WiFi links to improve the activity recognition accuracy based on the basic schemes shown in Section 4.

Assume we have L WiFi devices collecting CSI measurements independently and each device has J activity profiles denoted as $\{a_1^l, \ldots, a_j^l, \ldots, a_J^l\}, l = 1, \ldots, L$. The final activity recognition result is the jth activity (profile) that minimizes the weighted summation of the similarities between the collected CSI measurements and the profiles on each WiFi device, i.e.,

$$a_j^* = \arg\min_j \sum_{l=1}^{L} [w_j^l(a_0^l, a_j^l) \times D_j^l], \quad (3)$$

where D_j^l is the EMD or DTW distance (Section 4.2.1 and 4.3) between the CSI measurements and the jth activity profile on the lth WiFi device; $w_j^l(a_0^l, a_j^l)$ is the normalized weight dominated by the significance of the jth activity on the lth WiFi device, which is defined as follows:

$$w_j^l(a_0^l, a_j^l) = \frac{1 - \mathcal{X}(a_0^l, a_j^l)}{\sum_{l=1}^{L} [1 - \mathcal{X}(a_0^l, a_j^l)]}, \quad (4)$$

where a_0^l denotes the profile for empty room on the lth WiFi device, and $\mathcal{X}(a_0^l, a_j^l)$ is the cross correlation between the profile of the empty room and the jth activity on the lth WiFi device. To reduce the computational complexity, only the CSI measurements having significant difference from the empty room profile will be included in the above calculation.

6. EVALUATION

In this section, we present the performance of our E-eyes system using commercial off-the-shelf WiFi devices in two apartments of different sizes.

6.1 Experimental Setup

6.1.1 Devices and Network

We conduct experiments in an 802.11n WiFi network with three off-the-shelf WiFi devices (i.e., two Lenovo T500 laptops and one Lenovo T61 laptop) connected to a single commercial wireless access point (i.e., Linksys $E2500$) in two apartments. The laptops run Ubuntu 10.04 LTS with the 2.6.36 kernel and are equipped with Intel WiFi Link 5300 cards for measuring CSI [12]. While CSI information is only publicly exposed by modified drivers for several chipsets, e.g., Intel WiFi Link 5300 and Atheros AR9390, it is internally tracked by 802.11 MIMO implementations and we expect more chipsets will expose such information in the near future. The packet transmission rate is set to $20pkts/s$. How the rate of packet transmission affects the performance will be discussed in Section 6.2.6. For each packet, we extract CSI for 30 subcarrier groups, which are evenly distributed in the 56 subcarriers of a $20MHz$ channel [3].

6.1.2 Apartments and Activities

We conduct experiments in two apartments of different sizes to test the generality of our system. The experimental setups in these two apartments are shown in Figure 7. The smaller one (i.e., one bedroom apartment) has the size of about 23ft × 20ft with one bedroom, one kitchen and one bathroom, whereas the larger one (i.e., two bedroom apartment) is about 24ft × 36ft with two bed rooms, one storeroom, one kitchen, one living room, and one bathroom. It is commonly accepted that the presence of manifold WiFi devices in home environments is highly possible in the near future. To name a few existing applications: smartTVs in living rooms, thermostats in bedrooms, smart-refrigerators in kitchens, and waterproof wireless speakers in bathrooms. In our experiments, one AP and three WiFi devices are placed at each apartment for daily activity monitoring.

A total of 9 typical daily in-place activities and 8 walking activities (passing through 4 door-ways) with different walking speeds are performed by 4 male adults in both apartments. These activities are listed in Table 3, and are shown in Figure 7. The yellow circles show the in-place activities, whereas the red/blue lines represent the paths of the walking activities. Due to different conditions in the two apartments (e.g., having a TV in the living room or not), we have chosen slightly different yet still typical in-place activities to perform in the two apartments. Note that we find it is typical for in-place activities to occur at dedicated locations in home environments, for example activities in a kitchen usually just occur in front of the sink or stove, beside the refrigerator, or at the dining table, whereas activities in a living room usually occur on the couch. In our experiments, the profiles were generated in one day and testing data was collected over different days. Over the days, one chair was moved to a different room, coffee makers were moved around

[1]The MCS index of 263 corresponds to $20MHz$ bandwidth channel, 802.11a/g/n mixed network, single spatial stream with transmission rate 60Mbps

Actual Activity Performed

1-bedroom apt.	A	B	C	D	unknown	**Door**	Door1	Door2	None
A	1	0	0	0	0	Door1	1	0	0
B	0	1	0	0	0				
C	0	0	0.95	0.05	0	Door2	0	0.975	0.025
D	0	0	0	1	0				
O	0	0	0.1	0	0.9	None	0	0	1

Identified Walking Activity & Doorway

(a) 1-bedroom apartment

Actual Activity Performed

2-bedroom apt.	E	F	G	H	unknown	**Door**	Door3	Door4	None
E	1	0	0	0	0	Door3	1	0	0
F	0.15	0.85	0	0	0				
G	0	0	0.9	0.1	0	Door4	0	0.875	0.125
H	0	0	0	1	0				
O	0.05	0	0	0	0.95	None	0	0	1

Identified Walking Activity & Doorway

(b) 2-bedroom apartment

Figure 9: Confusion matrix of walking activity identification in two different apartments.

in the kitchen and items on tables, such as bowls and bottles, were moved, as usually occurs in daily life. Moreover, we build the profile for the empty room when there is no one at home (i.e., *Empty apartment (a)*). To test the ability of our system on differentiating diverse in-place activities that occur in the same place, we experiment with 4 in-place activities in the one-bedroom apartment: *sleeping on the bed, sitting on the bed, talking besides the sink, and washing dishes near the sink.* Furthermore, the experimenter conducts several in-place and walking activities which are not profiled (i.e., *Other activities (o)*). They are used to evaluate the robustness of our system for recognizing unknown or random activities.

6.1.3 Metrics

We use the following metrics to evaluate the performance of our system.

Confusion Matrix. Each row represents the actual activity performed by the user and each column shows the activity it was classified as by our system. Each cell in the matrix corresponds to the fraction of activity in the row that was classified as the activity in the column.

True Positive Rate (TPR). TPR for an activity A is defined as the proportion of the instances that are correctly recognized as the activity A among actual A performed.

False Positive Rate (FPR). FPR for an activity A is defined as the percentage of the instances that are incorrectly recognized as A among all testing instances other than A.

6.2 Evaluation in Real Apartments

6.2.1 Activity Identification with Multiple WiFi Devices

Figure 8 plots the confusion matrix for the in-place activities recognition in two apartments with three WiFi devices. In the one-bedroom apartment, 7 different in-place activities (see Figure 8(a)) were performed (50 rounds for each). Another 100 rounds of different unknown in-place activities (i.e., $others$) are preformed to evaluate E-eyes's ability of detecting unknown activities. Similarly, in the two-bedroom apartment, 7 different in-place activities as shown in Figure 8(b) (each one has 50 rounds) and 100 rounds of unknown activities are performed. For the one-bedroom apartment, the average accuracy of identifying in-place activities is 97% with a standard deviation of 5.66% whereas in the two-bedroom apartment, the average accuracy of identifying in-place activities is 97.38% with a standard deviation of 4.31%.

Figure 9 plots the confusion matrix for the walking activities identification and doorway passing detection in two apartments. As shown in Figure 7, 4 trajectories for each apartment are performed, and 20 rounds for each trajectory. Similar to that of the in-place activity experiment, we performed 20 rounds of aimless walking activities (i.e., walking in the apartment but no passing through predefined doorways) in each apartment as *others*. For the one-bedroom apartment, the average accuracy is 97% when identifying these 4 walking activities. E-eyes can also achieve high accuracy of detecting doorway passing with an average accuracy of 99.17%. For the two-bedroom apartment, the average accuracy of identifying walking activities is 94%, and the passing doorway can be detected with an accuracy of 95.83%. The above results show that our E-eyes can distinguish a set of in-place activities and walking activities with high accuracy by using only a single WiFi access point in two apartments of different size. Our system E-eyes can thus have potential to support lots of emerging applications such as elder care, well-being management, and latchkey child safety.

6.2.2 Robustness Validation

We next evaluate the robustness of E-eyes by studying the false positive rates (FPRs) of identifying different activities in two apartments. Figure 10 (b) and (d) show that overall E-eyes has very low false positive rates for identifying different activities in two apartments – an average FPR of about 0.6%. The walking activities have higher FPRs which are around 0.8% for both apartments. This is primarily because it is hard to follow exactly the same trajectory every time, and people's body movements maybe different from time to time when walking, such as the sequences of waving arms and alternating two legs. We also observe that the FPRs for identifying all activities are ranging from 0% to 2.5% in both apartments with an average TPR as high as 97% as shown in Figure 10 (a) and (c). The results indicate that E-eyes is robust in identifying both in-place and walking activities in two apartments of different sizes.

6.2.3 Activity Identification with Single WiFi Device

To further show the capability of E-eyes in activity recognition with limited WiFi devices at home, we experiment with only one WiFi device connecting with one single AP. This is a challenging scenario as with only one AP and one WiFi device, the signal affected by the human body may become very weak after going through several walls. We place the WiFi device at one of the previous locations to sense the activities in both apartments. The results are shown in Figure 10. We find that E-eyes is capable of identifying activities accurately when placing a single AP at an appreciate location. In particular, Figure 10 (a) and (b) show that the TPRs of identifying both in-place and walking activities are in general over 90% with FPRs less than 5% in the one-bedroom apartment.

In the two-bedroom apartment, most in-place activities have TPRs over 90% and FPRs less than 2%, except the activity *sleeping*. This is because sleeping involves little body movements and lying on the bed, thus having less effects on altering multipath environments. In addition, Figure 10 (c) and (d) show that the TPRs for walking activities G and H are 0 because they do not generate large moving variances and are classified as *empty room* in the pre-constructed profiles. This is because with the WiFi device and the AP separated by several walls, the conducted activities that are far away from either the WiFi device or the AP will have little effect on altering the multipath environment. Besides G and H, the other two walking activities E and F still have TPRs over 90% with FPRs less than 3%.

6.2.4 Distinguishing Activities in the Same Location

Given that some activities take place at the same location but with different human postures or body movements (e.g., sleeping/sitting on the bed), we experiment with such in-place activities to evalu-

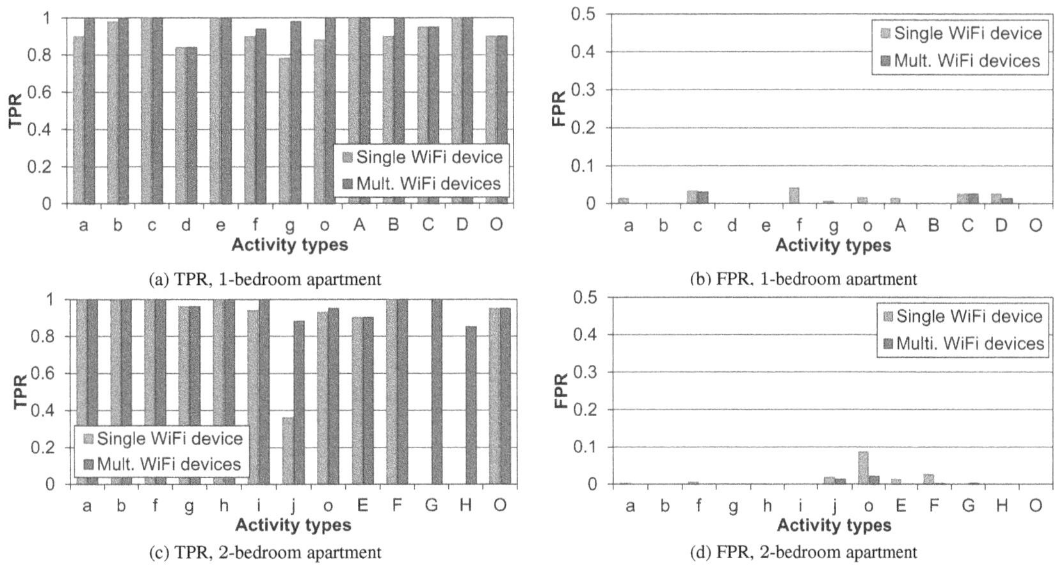

(a) TPR, 1-bedroom apartment

(b) FPR, 1-bedroom apartment

(c) TPR, 2-bedroom apartment

(d) FPR, 2-bedroom apartment

Figure 10: True positive rate and false positive rate, in-place and walking activity recognition in two different apartments.

ate how well E-eyes can distinguish such activities that occur in the same location. We use different numbers of EMD bins to test the impact on the resolution of identifying activities occurring in the same location. Intuitively, a larger number of EMD bins can provide more detailed distribution information. We add two more activities that occur in the same locations as two of the previously considered activities. We therefore experiment with 4 in-place activities in the one-bedroom apartment: sleeping on the *bed*, sitting on the *bed*, receiving calls nearby the *sink* and washing dishes nearby the *sink*. The system compares the measure in-place activity data against 12 profiles (the 10 from Table 3 and the two additional ones). We use the worst TPR (minimum TPR of all activity identification) and the worst FPR (maximum FPR of all activity identification), to evaluate the worst-case performance with different numbers of EMD bins. Figure 11 shows the results of identifying different activities in the same location. We find that the system can achieve high accuracy (over 97%) if the number of EMD bins is greater than 8 when different activities took place at the same locations.

6.2.5 *Activity Recognition Using Wider-band Signals*

Next we study the feasibility of extending E-eyes to work with wider-bandwidth channel of 802.11ac. The bandwidth of a 802.11ac channel is 4 times wider than that of 802.11n. The number of available subcarriers thus increases from 56 in 802.11n to 242 in 802.11ac. Larger numbers of subcarriers provided by 802.11ac therefore have potential to capture in-place activities more accurately and reliably. Since 802.11ac shares the same 5GHz band with 802.11n, we use multiple 802.11n channels to emulate the 802.11ac channel for CSI extraction as no handy tool is available to collect CSI from 802.11ac.

In particular, we use two laptops respectively communicating with two access points to collect CSI measurement from two 802.11n channels (40MHZ) simultaneously at the 5GHz band. The CSI measurements are off-line synchronized and cascaded in frequency domain to emulate the CSI measurements from a 802.11ac channel (80MHz). In order to make sure the two 802.11n channels share the same multipath effect, we use two external antennas for the laptops and place them next to each other. The distance between two antennas is about 2 cm, which is smaller than the half wavelength of the 5GHz WiFi signal (i.e., about 2.8cm). Similarly, we take the internal antennas of the access points out and bind them together with the distance much less than the half wavelength of the 5GHz WiFi signal. We experiment with 7 in-place activities in the two-bedroom apartment with the laptops in the living room and the access points in the kitchen as shown in Figure 7.

Figure 12 presents the performance comparison of E-eyes with the 802.11n and the emulated 802.11ac channel at 5GHz band. We find that E-eyes results in higher accuracy under the emulated 802.11ac than 802.11n, which demonstrates the feasibility of improving the recognition accuracy by utilizing wider-bandwidth of 802.11ac. The TPRs for all in-place activities are over 99%. With such high TPRs, the FPRs are still lower than 1% even for two close proximity activities *f: brushing teeth* and *g: taking a bathing*. Furthermore, comparing to the performance of the same setup using 802.11n with one WiFi device, we find that using the 802.11ac channel has about 4% improvement in the worst TPRs (i.e., increases from 94% to 98% for the activity *i: playing video game*). And the worst FPR drops to 0.67% under 802.11ac from 8.5% under 802.11n for *unknown* activities. This indicates that the wider channels (e.g., 802.11ac) can improve the recognition accuracy since it allows measurements over many additional subcarriers.

6.2.6 *Impact of Traffic Transmission Rate*

Since CSI is measured from each of the received packets, the higher packet transmission rate (PTR) results in larger sizes of CSI measurements for characterizing an activity. We thus study the impact of PTR on the performance of E-eyes. In particular, PTR is changed from $5pkts/s$ to $20pkts/s$ with a fixed step of $5pkts/s$. As the commercial access points send beacon signals at $10beacons/s$ to broadcast their SSID and the connection information, the range

Table 3: Codes for in-place and walking activity profiles.

Code	In-place activity	Code	Walking activity
a	Empty apartment	A	Bedroom→Kitchen
b	Cooking	B	Kitchen→Bedroom
c	Eating	C	Kitchen→Bathroom
d	Washing dishes	D	Bathroom→Kitchen
e	Studying at a table	E	Outside→Bedroom1
f	Brushing teeth	F	Bedroom1→Outside
g	Taking a bath	G	Bedroom2→Bathroom
h	Watching TV on a sofa	H	Bathroom→Bedroom2
i	Playing video games	O	Other wandering paths
j	Sleeping on a bed		
o	Other activities		

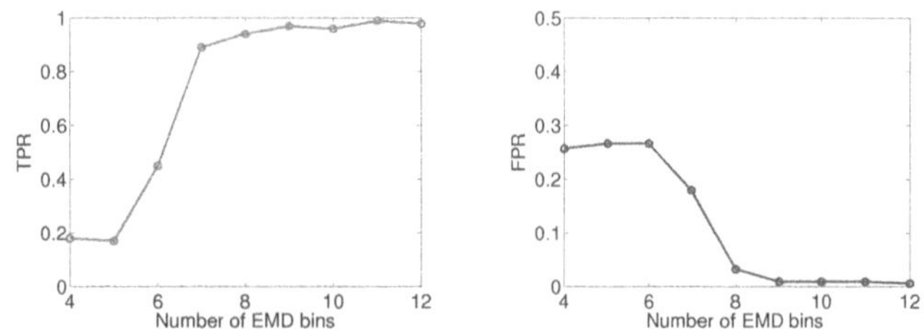

(a) (b)

Figure 11: True positive rate and false positive rate, in worst-case with different numbers of EMD bins.

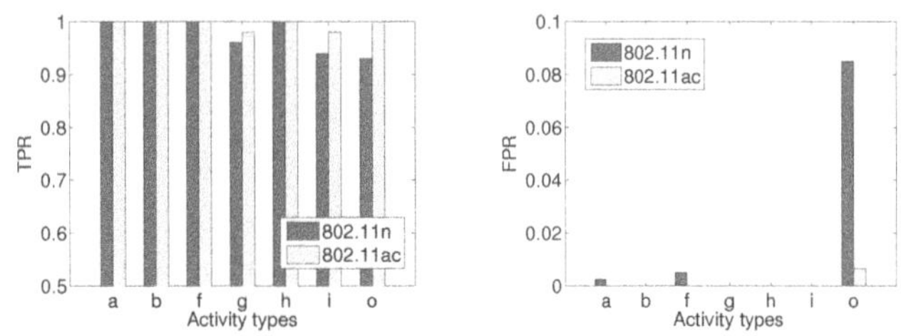

(a) True positive rate (b) False positive rate

Figure 12: True positive rate and false positive rate of activity recognition using 802.11n or emulated 802.11ac channel.

of our PTR is thus reasonable and includes the normal transmission rate that is considered to be energy-efficient ($10 pkts/s$). Figure 13 shows the average TPRs and FPRs over all activities with different transmission rates. The increasing and decreasing trends in TPRs and FPRs respectively demonstrate that higher PTR would help to distinguish different activities. We can see that when the PTR is above 10 pkts/s, the average TPRs and FPRs are respectively over 92% and less than 2%, and the improvement of the increased packet rate is less obvious. The results demonstrate that E-eyes is capable of working with very low PTR, such as the default beacon packet rate in WiFi.

7. DISCUSSION

Presence of Multiple Persons or Pets. The current system is designed for and tested with only a single occupant. We believe that this is an important use case, particularly in an aging-in-place setting, which aims to ensure that a single person can live in his/her home and community safely and independently regardless of age and ability level. Since the temporary presence of additional people in the home can alter signatures, one improvement might be to simply detect this case using existing methods (e.g., [36]) and to suspend operation during this time. It may also be possible to switch to a different set of profiles for multiple persons. The number of profiles needed with multiple persons would increase exponentially, however. A more promising approach therefore would be to find techniques that can isolate concurrent activities in separate spaces from each other and match them against profiles separately. This would involve separating effects detected on different links and we leave this for future work. In addition, pets in the home may also change the environment dynamically. However, such cases only happen when the pet is large and moving around frequently, thus additional signal processing will be required to remove the interference in CSI and we will consider it in future work.

Mobile Devices and Environment Changes. E-eyes relies on stationary WiFi enabled devices, such as refrigerators, smartTVs, mounted cameras, or desktop computers. If a device is moved, our system could detect such changes by detecting many profile deviations across one link or by using other movement detection techniques (e.g., [18]) and then trigger an activity profile updating. In some cases this would require user effort. If the number of available links is large enough, however, the system might still be able to match activities using the remaining links and can automatically update the profile for the changed link. Smaller environment changes might be handled in a similar manner.

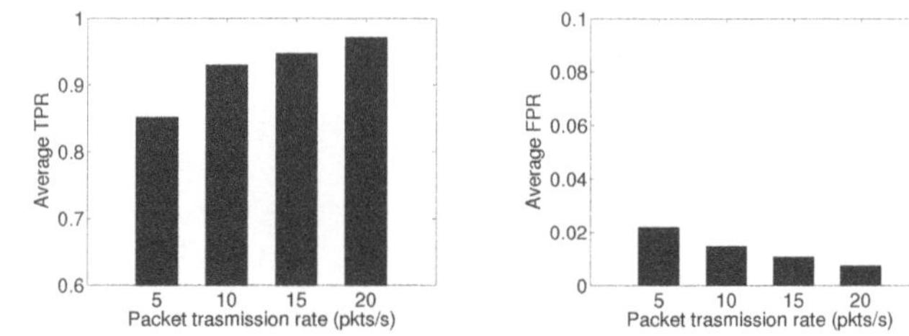

(a) Average true positive rate (b) Average false positive rate

Figure 13: True positive rate and false positive rate of E-eyes with different PTR.

Constant Traffic Requirement. The system has been evaluated with periodic traffic at various rates. When some links are in use, the system could take measurements from existing traffic and downsample to match the expected periodicity. When links are not in use, an AP-based solution could create dummy traffic on links (e.g., TCP SYNs) which invokes a response from the device. Since our system works at rates that are often used in many beaconing applications, such overhead appears manageable.

Activities in the Same Location. This work has exploited that many activities that are meaningful for home monitoring are linked to a few specific locations in the home, such as sinks, kitchens, couches, or desks. This has allowed us to create a limited set of profiles, which combine both location information and activity information. It is an open question to what extent a profile could be used to detect the same activity in a different location, although it is possible to create additional profiles for different locations as long as the number of activities and locations remains manageable. We also have only begun to explore to what extent it is possible to distinguish between different activities in the same location. While our results are promising, it would be useful to explore the limits of this technique by considering a larger number of different activities in the same location and the dependency of the results on the amount of change in the propagation environment.

8. CONCLUSION

Understanding in-home activities that persons are engaged in would facilitate a broad range of applications including wellbeing monitoring and health management. However, providing accurate activity recognition without dedicated wearable or in-building devices is challenging. We exploit the prevalence of WiFi infrastructure and design a system called E-eyes to perform device-free location-oriented activity identification by utilizing the fine-grained channel state information (CSI) available in the existing WiFi protocol (i.e., 802.11n). We find that CSI can capture the unique patterns of small-scale fading caused by different human activities at a subcarrier level, which is not available in the traditional received signal strength (RSS) extracted at the per packet level. Our system benefits from the observation that many important in-home activities occur in one or a few dedicated locations and that it is therefore often sufficient to collect a small number of profiles for these activities in each of these locations. An experiment with two pairs of activities that occur in the same location, however, also showed strong potential for the technique to identify a set of activities that occur in the same place. E-eyes applies matching algorithms to compare the CSI measurements against known profiles to identify the activity. Extensive experiments in two different-sized apartments demonstrate that E-eyes is effective in distinguishing a number of daily activities, and that it can achieve a detection rate as high as 92% with a single AP and only one WiFi device. In addition, we also show how trends to wider-bandwidth channels (e.g., 802.11ac) will enhance activity recognition performance further.

9. ACKNOWLEDGEMENT

This work is supported in part by the National Science Foundation Grants CNS1217387, CNS 0845896 and IIS-1211079.

10. REFERENCES

[1] Familylink. http://www.familylink.net/.

[2] Leap motion. https://www.leapmotion.com.

[3] IEEE Std. 802.11n-2009: Enhancements for higher throughput, 2009. Available at http://www.ieee802.org.

[4] F. Adib, Z. Kabelac, D. Katabi, and R. C. Miller. 3d tracking via body radio reflections. In *Usenix NSDI*, 2014.

[5] F. Adib and D. Katabi. See through walls with wifi! In *ACM SIGCOMM*, 2013.

[6] M. Azizyan, I. Constandache, and R. Roy Choudhury. Surroundsense: mobile phone localization via ambience fingerprinting. In *ACM MobiCom*, 2009.

[7] P. Bahl and V. N. Padmanabhan. Radar: An in-building rf-based user location and tracking system. In *INFOCOM*, 2000.

[8] N. Banerjee and et al. Virtual compass: relative positioning to sense mobile social interactions. In *Pervasive computing*, pages 1–21. 2010.

[9] H.-l. Chang and et al. Spinning beacons for precise indoor localization. In *ACM SenSys*, 2008.

[10] E. S. Gardner. Exponential smoothing: The state of the art. *Journal of forecasting*, 4(1):1–28, 1985.

[11] A. Goswami and et al. Wigem: a learning-based approach for indoor localization. In *ACM CoNEXT*, 2011.

[12] D. Halperin and et al. Tool release: Gathering 802.11n traces with channel state information. *ACM SIGCOMM CCR*, 2011.

[13] J. Hong and T. Ohtsuki. Ambient intelligence sensing using array sensor: Device-free radio based approach. In *CoSDEO workshop*, 2013.

[14] K. Joshi, S. Hong, and S. Katti. Pinpoint: Localizing interfering radios. In *Usenix NSDI*, 2013.

[15] V. Kasteren and et. al". An activity monitoring system for elderly care using generative and discriminative models. *Personal and ubiquitous computing*, 14(6):489–498, 2010.

[16] M. Keally and et al. Pbn: towards practical activity recognition using smartphone-based body sensor networks. In *ACM SenSys*, 2011.

[17] K. Kleisouris, Y. Chen, J. Yang, and R. P. Martin. Empirical evaluation of wireless localization when using multiple antennas. *IEEE TPDS*, 21(11):1595–1610, 2010.

[18] K. Kleisouris, B. Firner, R. Howard, Y. Zhang, and R. P. Martin. Detecting intra-room mobility with signal strength descriptors. In *ACM MobiHoc*, 2010.

[19] A. E. Kosba, A. Saeed, and M. Youssef. Rasid: A robust wlan device-free passive motion detection system. In *PerCom*, 2012.

[20] J. Lei, X. Ren, and D. Fox. Fine-grained kitchen activity recognition using rgb-d. In *ACM UbiComp*, 2012.

[21] L. Li, P. Hu, C. Peng, J. Shen, and F. Zhao. Epsilon: A visible light based positioning system. In *Usenix NSDI*, 2014.

[22] H. Liu, Y. Gan, J. Yang, S. Sidhom, Y. Wang, Y. Chen, and F. Ye. Push the limit of wifi based localization for smartphones. In *ACM MobiCom*, 2012.

[23] Microsoft. X-box kinect. http://www.xbox.com.

[24] Philips. Philips lifeline. http://www.lifelinesys.com/content/.

[25] Q. Pu and et al. Whole-home gesture recognition using wireless signals. In *ACM MobCom*, 2013.

[26] L. R. Rabiner and B.-H. Juang. *Fundamentals of speech recognition*, volume 14. PTR Prentice Hall Englewood Cliffs, 1993.

[27] P. J. Rousseeuw and A. M. Leroy. *Robust regression and outlier detection*, volume 589. John Wiley & Sons, 2005.

[28] Y. Rubner and S. U. C. S. Dept. *Perceptual metrics for image database navigation*. Number 1621 in Report STAN-CS-TR. Stanford University, 1999.

[29] M. Seifeldin and et al. Nuzzer: A large-scale device-free passive localization system for wireless environments. *IEEE Transactions on Mobile Computing*, 12(7):1321–1334, 2013.

[30] S. Sen and et al. Spot localization using phy layer information. In *ACM MobiSys*, 2012.

[31] S. Sigg, S. Shi, and Y. Ji. Rf-based device-free recognition of simultaneously conducted activities. In *CoSDEO workshop*, 2013.

[32] A. Technology. Grandcare systems. http://www.grandcare.com/.

[33] G. Ten Holt, M. Reinders, and E. Hendriks. Multi-dimensional dynamic time warping for gesture recognition. In *the conference of the Advanced School for Computing and Imaging*, 2007.

[34] J. Wang and D. Katabi. Dude, where's my card?: Rfid positioning that works with multipath and nols. In *SIGCOMM*, 2013.

[35] J. Wilson and N. Patwari. Radio tomographic imaging with wireless networks. *IEEE Trans. on Mobile Computing*, 9(5), 2010.

[36] W. Xi and et al. Electronic frog eye: Counting crowd using wifi. In *INFOCOM*, 2014.

[37] J. Xiong and K. Jamieson. Arraytrack: a fine-grained indoor location system. In *Usenix NSDI*, 2013.

[38] J. Yang and Y. Chen. Indoor localization using improved rss-based lateration methods. In *IEEE GLOBECOM 2009*, 2009.

[39] J. Yang, Y. Ge, H. Xiong, Y. Chen, and H. Liu. Performing joint learning for passive intrusion detection in pervasive wireless environments. In *IEEE INFOCOM*, 2010.

[40] J. Yang, J. Lee, and J. Choi. Activity recognition based on rfid object usage for smart mobile devices. *Journal of Computer Science and Technology*, 26(2):239–246, 2011.

[41] S. Yang, P. Dessai, M. Verma, and M. Gerla. Freeloc: Calibration-free crowdsourced indoor localization. In *IEEE INFOCOM*, 2013.

[42] K. Yatani and K. N. Truong. Bodyscope: a wearable acoustic sensor for activity recognition. In *ACM UbiComp*, 2012.

[43] M. Youssef and A. Agrawala. The horus wlan location determination system. In *ACM MobiSys*, 2005.

[44] M. Youssef, M. Mah, and A. Agrawala. Challenges: device-free passive localization for wireless environments. In *MobiCom*, 2007.

[45] Y. Zhao and et al. Radio tomographic imaging and tracking of stationary and moving people via kernel distance. In *IEEE IPSN*, 2013.

Author Index

www.ingramcontent.com/pod-product-compliance
Ingram Content Group UK Ltd.
Pitfield, Milton Keynes, MK11 3LW, UK
UKHW051418290926
15471UKWH00009B/1663

9 781450 333634